D0029346

Thailand

Joe Cummings
Becca Blond, Morgan Konn, Matt Warren, China Williams

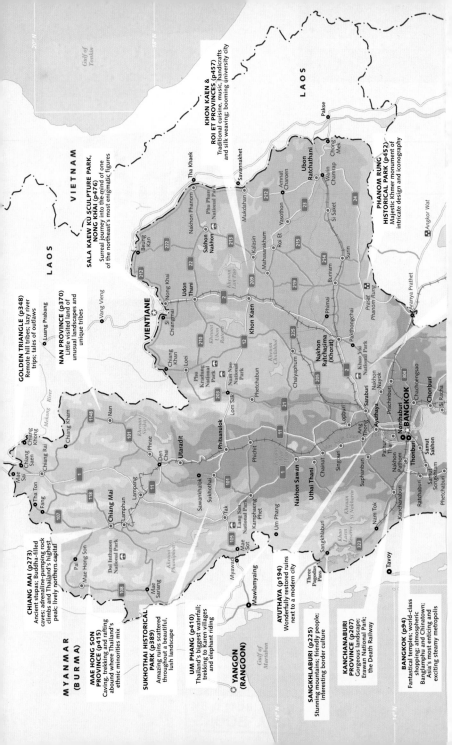

CHIANG MAI (p273)
Ancient stupas; Buddha-filled caves; adrenaline-pumping rock climbs and Thailand's highest peak; lively northern capital

MAE HONG SON PROVINCE (p415)
Caving, trekking and rafting abound where Thailand's ethnic minorities mix

SUKHOTHAI HISTORICAL PARK (p389)
Amazing ruins scattered throughout a beautiful, lush landscape

UM PHANG (p410)
Thailand's biggest waterfall; trekking to Karen villages and elephant riding

AYUTHAYA (p194)
Wonderfully restored ruins next to a modern city

SANGKHLABURI (p225)
Stunning mountains; friendly people; interesting border culture

KANCHANABURI PROVINCE (p207)
Gorgeous landscape; Erawan National Park; the Death Railway

BANGKOK (p94)
Fantastical temples; world-class shopping; atmospheric Banglamphu and Chinatown; Asia's most enticing and exciting steamy metropolis

GOLDEN TRIANGLE (p348)
Remote hill tribes; lazy river trips; tales of outlaws

NAN PROVINCE (p370)
Little visited land of unusual landscapes and unique tribes

SALA KAEW KU SCULPTURE PARK, NONG KHAI (p476)
Surreal journey into the mind of one of the northeast's most enigmatic figures

KHON KAEN & ROI ET PROVINCES (p457)
Traditional cuisine, music, handicrafts and silk weaving; booming university city

PHANOM RUNG HISTORICAL PARK (p452)
Majestic Khmer monument of intricate design and iconography

MYANMAR (BURMA)

LAOS

VIETNAM

Gulf of Tonkin

Gulf of Martaban

YANGON (RANGOON)

VIENTIANE

BANGKOK

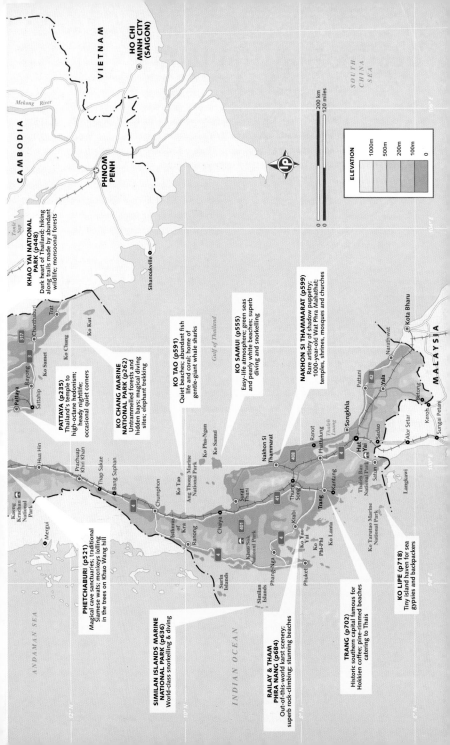

CAMBODIA

VIETNAM

Mekong River

HO CHI MINH CITY (SAIGON)

PHNOM PENH

Sihanoukville

Tonle Sap

KHAO YAI NATIONAL PARK (p448)
Dark heart of Thailand; hiking along trails made by abundant wildlife; monsoonal forests

SOUTH CHINA SEA

Chanthaburi

Trat

Ko Kut

Ko Chang

Rayong

Pattaya

Sattahip

Ko Samet

PATTAYA (p235)
Thailand's temple to high-octane hedonism; heady nightlife; occasional quiet corners

KO CHANG MARINE NATIONAL PARK (p262)
Untrammelled forests and hidden bays; magical diving sites; elephant trekking

Gulf of Thailand

KO TAO (p591)
Quiet beaches; abundant fish life and coral; home of gentle-giant whale sharks

KO SAMUI (p555)
Easy-life atmosphere; green seas and pearly white beaches; superb diving and snorkelling

NAKHON SI THAMMARAT (p599)
Rare artistry of shadow puppetry; 1000-year-old Wat Phra Mahathat; temples, shrines, mosques and churches

Kota Bharu

Narathiwat

Pattani

Yala

Betong

Keroh

Alor Setar

Sungai Petani

Songkhla

Hat Yai

Sadao

MALAYSIA

Phatthalung

Ranot

Thale Noi

Thale Luang

Nakhon Si Thammarat

Surat Thani

Chumphon

Ko Pha-Ngan

Ko Samui

Ko Tao

Ang Thong Marine National Park

Thung Song

Kantang

Trang

Krabi

Ko Yao

Ko Phi-Phi

Ko Lanta

Phang-Nga

Phuket

Khao Sok National Park

Ranong

Chaiya

Isthmus of Kra

Bang Saphan

Thap Sakae

Prachuap Khiri Khan

Hua Hin

Kaeng Krachan National Park

Mergui

Surin Islands

Similan Islands

PHETCHABURI (p521)
Magical cave sanctuaries; traditional Siamese wats; monkeys lolling in the trees on Khao Wang hill

ANDAMAN SEA

SIMILAN ISLANDS MARINE NATIONAL PARK (p636)
World-class snorkelling & diving

INDIAN OCEAN

RAILAY & THAM PHRA NANG (p684)
Out-of-this-world karst scenery; superb rock-climbing; stunning beaches

TRANG (p702)
Historic southern capital famous for Hokkien coffee; pine-rimmed beaches catering to Thais

Thale Ban National Park

Ko Tarutao Marine National Park

Satun

Langkawi

KO LIPE (p718)
Tiny island haven for sea gypsies and backpackers

ELEVATION

1000m
500m
200m
100m
0

200 km
120 miles

Destination Thailand

Forget about the sloganeering 'Land of Smiles'; welcome to the Kingdom of Pleasant Contradictions. Roosters vie with *túk-túk* for bandwidth in the sonic spectrum and traffic halts for elephants rather than for people. The Thais – yes, smiling all the while – dine out five or six times a day yet manage to stay sleek and slender.

Lose yourself in the cool mist of a mountain-top trail trod by post–Stone Age cultures, or in the smoky haze swirling around the world's tallest hotel. Assess the latest Stock Exchange of Thailand reports while sipping Thai-grown *arabica*, roasted in French copper on the café premises, or peruse tall palms angling over pearlescent sand while standing chest-deep in the Andaman Sea.

Follow your eyes, but trust your heart. If you spend some time delving beneath the modern veneer of Bangkok and the provincial capitals, you'll find a world so infused with Buddhism and spirit worship that few would dare choosing a marriage date without consulting a monk or astrologer. Check out the latest Thai pop music craze, and chances are you'll find more than a trace of *lûuk thûng* or *măw lam* woven into the rhythm.

This thick maze of ambiguities and incongruities continues to lure more visitors than any other country in Southeast Asia, along with Thailand's virtually irresistible combination of natural beauty, historic temples, renowned hospitality and robust cuisine. From the stupa-studded mountains of Mae Hong Son to the evergreen limestone islands of the Gulf of Thailand, from the throbbing dance clubs of Bangkok to tranquil villages moored along the Mekong River, this country offers something for every predilection.

JEFF CANTARUTTI

People

Get to know the hospitable Thai people

DALLAS STRIBLEY

ULRIKE WELSCH

DALLAS STRIBLEY

Trust your friendly *túk-túk* driver

Visit Hmong villages (p316) in northern
Chiang Mai Province

Celebrate the start of rice planting at the Royal Ploughing Ceremony (p122), Sanam Luang, Bangkok

JOE CUMMINGS

Bangkok

CHRIS MELLOR

Sellers juggle for space at Damnoen Saduak floating market (p188)

OTHER HIGHLIGHTS

- Hunt for bargains at Chatuchak Weekend Market, a small village of unfiltered commerce (p177)
- Catch the cool river breezes from the back of the Chao Phraya Rivers Express (p183)
- Discover Bangkok's growing contemporary art scene (p129)

RYAN FOX

Marvel at the gilded Buddha images at Wat Pho (p102)

Take to the river to admire the glory of Wat Arun (p103) at sunset

JOHN ELK III

Succumb to the aroma of barbecued fish at Bangkok's lively street markets (p156)

Sit ringside at a *muay thai* match, Lumphini Boxing Stadium (p173)

An intricately decorated guardian deity protects the Emerald Buddha at Wat Phra Kaew (p100)

Islands & Beaches

Island hop between Thailand's beaches by passenger ferry

BRETT SHEARER

Come face to face with the Western skunk anemonefish in the waters off Ko Similan (p639)

MARK STRICKLAND

OTHER HIGHLIGHTS

- Drift towards the Andaman archipelago of the Surin Islands for a quiet, seaside environment away from the modern world (p636)
- Escape the big-city lights with a quick getaway to the upper gulf beaches of Cha-am (p524) and Hua Hin (p527)
- Glide over the submerged pinnacles of Hin Daeng and Hin Muang, off Ko Lanta (p697)

Find your own deserted stretch of sand at Ko Nang Yuan (p592), near Ko Tao, Surat Thani Province

CHERYL CONLON

GLENN BEANLAND

Remember the day's diving and anticipate tomorrow's kayaking in the calm waters around Ao Nang (p679), Krabi Province

EDWARD AM SNIJDERS

Get the adrenaline rushing by parasailing off Patong beach (p660), Phuket

Tread the boards to the low-key sands of Ao Cho (p252), Ko Samet

FRANK CARTER

National Parks & Sanctuaries

DENNIS JONES

Spot crab-eating macaque in the wildlife-laden Khao Sam Roi Yot National Park (p534), Prachuap Khiri Khan Province

Dive amid the technicolour coral trees and multi-hued fish in Similan Islands Marine National Park (p639)

MARK STRICKLAND

OTHER HIGHLIGHTS

- Hike through the evergreen monsoon forest of the popular Phu Kradung National Park, Loei Province (p488)
- Savour the breathtaking views from the top of Thailand's highest peak, Doi Inthanon (p321), Chiang Mai Province
- Find pure solitude in the rolling sandstone hills of Nam Nao National Park (p494), Loei Province

Be enchanted by the magical waterfalls, rivulets and pools in Than Bokkharani National Park (p688), Krabi Province

NICHOLAS REUS

FRANK CARTER

Lumber through the bamboo forests around Um Phang (p410), Tak Province

Charter a long-tail boat to explore the isolated and pristine Ko Tarutao Marine National Park, Satun Province (p715)

KRAIG LIEB

HERMANN MOLL

Catch the early morning mist over lakes in Khao Sok National Park (p553), Surat Thani Province

Historical Temple Architecture

TOM COCKREM

Admire the fine craftsmanship of the treasures at Ayuthaya Historical Park (p195)

OTHER HIGHLIGHTS

- Explore the smaller historic sites related to Khmer and Mon cultures at Lopburi (p204) and Chiang Mai (p288)
- Step back in time to the once powerful Srivijaya kingdom at Borom That Chaiya (p552), Surat Thani Province
- Visit Wat Phra Mahathat (p601), Nakhon Si Thammarat, the most sacred Buddhist temple in southern Thailand

A solitary monk meditates at Wat Si Chum (p390), Sukhothai Historical Park

TOM COCKREM

Delve into the worship of Hindu deities through detail on the stone reliefs at Phanom Rung Historical Park (p452), Buriram Province

ANDERS BLOMQVIST

Contents

Lonely Planet books provide independent advice. Lonely Planet does not accept advertising in guidebooks, nor do we accept payment in exchange for listing or endorsing any place or business. Lonely Planet writers do not accept discounts or payments in exchange for positive coverage of any sort.

หนังสือ Lonely Planet ให้คำแนะนำโดย เป็นอิสระโดยจะ ไม่รับโฆษณา หรือการจ่ายเงิน สินบนใดๆ เพื่อให้มีรายชื่อ ของสถานที่หรือ ธุรกิจปรากฏใน คู่มือเล่มนี้ นักเขียนของ ง Lonely Planet จะไม่มีส่วนลด หรือการจ่าย สินบนใดๆ เพื่อเขียนข้อมูล ในทางบวก

Regional Map Contents

Northern Chiang Mai p317

Southern Chiang Mai p319

Northern Thailand p331

Northeastern Thailand p436

Central Thailand p193

Bangkok pp104–21

Southeastern Thailand pp230–1

Upper Southern Gulf p520

Lower Southern Gulf p545

Andaman Coast p628

The Authors

JOE CUMMINGS
Coordinating Author, Chiang Mai & Andaman Coast Update

Born in New Orleans, Joe developed an attraction to seedy, tropical ports at a young age. An interest in Buddhism and Southeast Asian politics led him to Bangkok, where he took up residence in an old wooden house on a canal and begin exploring the provinces in his spare time. He later delved more deeply into the country as Lonely Planet's *Thailand* and *Bangkok* author through the 1980s, '90s and '00s. When he's not testing mattresses and slurping *tôm yam kûng* for Lonely Planet, Joe dabbles in Thai and foreign film production as a location consultant, script reader/translator and occasional actor.

The Coordinating Author's Favourite Trip

I enjoy a 'north-by-northeast' circuit that begins with a drive from Chiang Mai (p276) over the rolling hills of Phrae and into peaceful Nan Province. In Nan I might look for old Thai Lü–style temples in the capital (p373) and in Pua district further north, then stop for a couple of nights of fresh mountain air in Doi Phu Kha National Park (p378).

Coming down the eastern slopes, I point the hood ornament towards Loei, using the back roads via Nakhon Thai rather than busy Hwy 12. After a brief stop in Dan Sai (p489) I'll head to Chiang Khan (p492) and follow the Mekong River around the northeastern perimeter of Thailand. At Khong Jiam (p513), where the Mekong veers off into Laos and Cambodia, I'll pause for a night's stay and a meal at my favourite restaurant (Hat Mae Mun) before starting the return trip.

Doi Phu Kha National Park
Chiang Mai ○ ○ Nan & Pua
Phrae○ ○Chiang Khan
Nakhon Thai○○Dan Sai
Khong Jiam○

BECCA BLOND
Upper Southern Gulf, Lower Southern Gulf & Andaman Coast

Becca first became enthralled with Thailand when she visited the country on a round-the-world trip a few years back. A self-described beach bum, she jumped at the opportunity to explore the country (especially its beaches) in more depth – even if that meant travelling during the monsoon season and seeing more rain than sun. When she's not on the road for Lonely Planet, Becca resides in Boulder, Colorado (where there's plenty of sunshine), and spends her days playing in the mountains and dreaming about the ocean.

MORGAN KONN
Central Thailand & Northern Thailand

When Morgan set out on her first world tour, she had no idea she'd never leave the first destination. She started in Thailand, and stayed in Thailand. Month after month she kept planning to leave, but didn't. Seven years and four continents later, Morgan is still convinced that Thailand is one of the world's best travel destinations. She just can't seem to get enough of the food, people and landscape. In fact, when she's not out travelling she spends Sunday mornings at the Thai cultural centre in her home town of Berkeley, California. In addition to writing guidebooks, Morgan fancies herself as a visual artist and suspects she'll eventually settle down.

MATT WARREN   Southeastern Thailand & Northeastern Thailand
A native of southwestern England, Matt first travelled to Thailand after finishing school as a fresh-faced teenager and has been travelling back and forth between the UK and Southeast Asia every year since. Now based in London, he pays his way as a reporter for a number of national newspapers, heading off into Asia whenever Lonely Planet, or the news, calls him that way. Matt has contributed to numerous Lonely Planet titles including *Southeast Asia on a Shoestring* and *Indonesia*.

CHINA WILLIAMS   Bangkok
Thailand doesn't know it, but China Williams is a kindred citizen. She adopted the country while teaching English in Surin, the northeast's elephant capital. Officially, she is a full-blooded American, having grown up in South Carolina and migrated from one coast to another. She is now temporarily stationed in the vacationlands of Maine with her husband, Matt, and is furiously packing for an upcoming move to San Francisco.

CONTRIBUTING AUTHORS

Dr Trish Batchelor wrote the Health chapter. She is a general practitioner and travel-medicine specialist who works at the Ciwec Clinic in Kathmandu, Nepal. She is also a medical advisor to the Travel Doctor New Zealand clinics. Trish teaches travel medicine through the University of Otago, and is interested in underwater and high-altitude medicine, and in the impact of tourism on host countries. She has travelled extensively through Southeast and east Asia, and particularly loves high-altitude trekking in the Himalayas.

LONELY PLANET AUTHORS

Why is our travel information the best in the world? It's simple: our authors are independent, dedicated travellers. They don't research using just the Internet or phone, and they don't take freebies in exchange for positive coverage. They travel widely, to all the popular spots and off the beaten track. They personally visit thousands of hotels, restaurants, cafés, bars, galleries, palaces, museums and more – and they take pride in getting all the details right, and telling it how it is. For more, see the authors section on www.lonelyplanet.com.

Getting Started

Most people find travel in Thailand to be relatively easy and economical. Of course a little preparation will go a long way towards making your trip even more hassle-free and fun.

WHEN TO GO

The best time to visit most of Thailand is between November and February, primarily because during these months it rains the least and is not too hot. This is also Thailand's main season for both national and regional festivals.

If you plan to focus on the mountains of the northern provinces, the hot season (March to May) and early rainy season – say June to July – is not bad either, as temperatures are moderate at higher elevations. Haze from the burning-off of agricultural fields during these months, however, do obscure visibility in the north. Northeastern and central Thailand, on the other hand, are best avoided during the March to May hot season, when temperatures may break into the plus 40°C during the day and aren't much lower at night. Because temperatures are more even year-round in the south (being closer to the equator), the beaches and islands of southern Thailand are a good choice for respite when the rest of Thailand is miserably hot.

See Climate Charts (p726) for more information.

Road travel in remote rural areas may be difficult during the southwestern monsoon from July to October, when roads may be inundated or washed out for days at a time. Elsewhere the rains seldom interfere with travel.

Thailand's peak tourist season runs from November to late March, with secondary peak months in July and August. If your main objective is to avoid crowds and to take advantage of discounted rooms and low-season rates, you should consider travelling during the least crowded months (typically April, May, June, September and October),

COSTS & MONEY

Thailand is an inexpensive country to visit by almost any standards. Those on a budget should be able to get by on 300B to 500B per day outside Bangkok, covering basic food, guesthouse accommodation,

---

DON'T LEAVE HOME WITHOUT...

Pack light wash-and-wear clothes, plus a sweater/pullover or light jacket for chilly evenings and mornings in northern Thailand during the height of the cool season (December and January). Slip-on shoes or sandals are highly recommended – they are cool to wear and easy to remove before entering a Thai home or temple.

You can buy toothpaste, soap and most other toiletries cheaply almost anywhere in Thailand. Most Thai women don't use tampons, so they can be difficult to find outside of a few expat-oriented shops in Bangkok. If you're coming for a relatively short interval, it's best to bring your own. Sanitary napkins are widely available from minimarts and supermarkets throughout Thailand. See p763 for a list of recommended medical items.

Don't forget to bring a small torch (flashlight) – power blackouts are not uncommon in rural Thailand, even in Chiang Mai.

Be sure to check government travel advisories for Thailand before you leave. See p728 for general security issues.

TOP TENS

Must-see Films

If you're interested in Thai cinema's 'new wave', these are the best rides so far in descending order of excellence. See p80 for more detail.

- *Mon Rak Transistor* (2001)
- *Nang Nak* (1998)
- *Mekhong Full Moon Party* (2002)
- *Satree Lex (Iron Ladies)* (2000)
- *6ixty-nin9* (1999)
- *Fun Bar Karaoke* (1997)
- *Ong Bak* (2004)
- *Blissfully Yours* (2002)
- *Child of the North-East* (1983)
- *Tropical Malady* (2004)

Festivals & Events

Virtually every week of the calendar a new festival opens somewhere in Thailand. Here's our pick of the ones worth seeking out. See p733 for more information on Thai festivals.

- **January** That Phanom Festival, That Phanom (p499)
- **February** Phra Nakhon Khiri Diamond Festival, Phetchaburi (p523)
- **Late March/early April** Prasat Hin Khao Phanom Rung Festival, Buriram (p452)
- **April** Songkran, Chiang Mai (p293)
- **May/June** Phi Ta Khon Festival, Dan Sai, Loei (p490)
- **May/June** Rocket Festival, northeastern Thailand
- **Mid- to late July** Khao Phansa (Candle Festival), Ubon Ratchathani (p508)
- **Late September to early October** Vegetarian Festival, Phuket (p649)
- **November** Loi Krathong, Sukhothai (p391)
- **November** Surin Annual Elephant Roundup, Surin (p514)

National Parks & Wildlife Sanctuaries

Thailand has over a hundred national parks and wildlife sanctuaries, and you could spend a lifetime exploring them all. To help prioritise your choices, we have provided our list of favourites:

- Khao Sok National Park, Surat Thani (p553)
- Um Phang Wildlife Sanctuary, Tak/Kanchanaburi (p410)
- Kaeng Krachan National Park, Phetchaburi (p523)
- Khao Yai National Park, Nakhon Ratchasima (p448)
- Doi Inthanon National Park, Chiang Mai (p321)
- Doi Phu Kha National Park, Nan (p378)
- Nam Nao National Park, Loei (p494)
- Thaleh Ban National Park, Satun (p719)
- Khao Sam Roi Yot National Park, Prachuap Khiri Khan (p534)
- Thung Salaeng Luang National Park, Phetchabun/Phitsanulok (p388)

nonalcoholic beverages and local transport, but not film, souvenirs, tours, long-distance transport or vehicle hire. Travellers with more money to spend will find that for around 600B to 1000B per day, life can be quite comfortable.

In Bangkok there's almost no limit to the amount you *could* spend, but if you avoid the tourist ghettos and ride the public bus system you can get by on slightly more than you would spend in the provinces. Spending 1000B or more per day for accommodation, you'll be able to enjoy air-con, hot water, TV and operator-assisted telephone in the provinces, while in Bangkok and larger cities 1500B to 2000B per day brings with it all the modern amenities – IDD phone, 24-hour hot water and air-con, carpeting, swimming pool, fitness centre and all-night room service. Of course you can spend even more if you stay in the best rooms in the best hotels and eat at the most expensive restaurants in town.

TRAVEL LITERATURE

Canadian poet Karen Connelly realistically yet poetically chronicles a year of small town living in northern Thailand, in *The Dream of a Thousand Lives: A Sojourn in Thailand* (2001).

Thailand Confidential (2005), by ex-Rolling Stone correspondent Jerry Hopkins, weaves a loving exposé of everything expats and visitors love about Thailand and much they don't, and thus makes an excellent read for newcomers.

Charles Nicholls, Pico Iyer, Robert Anson Hall and several other well-known and not-so-well-known authors have contributed modern travel essays to *Travelers' Tales Thailand: True Stories*, recently updated in 2002. Savvy travel tips are sprinkled throughout.

A more serious collection of literature is available in *Traveller's Literary Companion: Southeast Asia* (1999), edited by Alastair Dingwall. The Thailand chapter is packed with excerpts from various works by Thai and foreign authors.

Anna Leonowens' *The English Governess at the Siamese Court* (1870) contained liberally embellished descriptions of Siamese life that were later transformed into three Hollywood movies and a Broadway musical.

INTERNET RESOURCES

Lonely Planet (www.lonelyplanet.com) Country-specific information as well as reader information exchange on the Thorn Tree forum.

Thai Students Online (www.thaistudents.com) Sriwittayapaknam School in Samut Prakan maintains the country's largest and most informative noncommercial website on virtually all aspects of Thai life and culture.

Thailand Daily (www.thailanddaily.com) Part of World News Network, offering a thorough digest of Thailand-related news in English.

ThaiVisa.com (www.thaivisa.com) Aside from the site's extensive, impartial info on visas for Thailand, you'll find plenty of travel-related material, news alerts and a helpful forum for both visitors and expats.

Tourism Authority of Thailand (www.tat.or.th) Contains a province guide, up-to-date press releases, tourism statistics, TAT contact information and planning hints.

HOW MUCH?

1st-class bus Bangkok to Surat Thani 380B

Beach bungalow on Ko Pha-Ngan 150-300B

One-day Thai cooking course, Chiang Mai 800B

National park admission 200B

Dinner for two at a midrange restaurant 300B

Itineraries

CLASSIC ROUTES

SOUTHERN SOJOURN
Two Weeks or More / Surat Thani to Satun

Explore the dockside markets of **Surat Thani** (p547) and the famed forest temple of **Wat Suan Mokkhaphalaram** (p552) in nearby Chaiya to start off. If you have time, make a side trip west to **Khao Sok National Park** (p553), one of Thailand's most important refuges for tigers and rainforest.

Further down the Thai-Malay Peninsula, **Nakhon Si Thammarat** (p600), former capital of ancient Tambralinga, is worth a visit for its historic wat, mosques, national museum and fine southern Thai cuisine. Two off-the-beaten-track side excursions to consider are beach-tripping at **Hat Sichon** (p600) and the mountain hike in **Khao Luang National Park** (p605).

From Nakhon Si Thammarat head to **Songkhla** (p606) for stellar seafood and Thai-style beachcombing. Dash across the peninsula to **Trang** (p702) to savour the capital's laid-back ambience and near-deserted beaches at nearby **Hat Jao Mai** (p708) and **Ko Kradan** (p709). From Trang it's a short hop to the Thai Muslim-majority provincial capital of **Satun** (p710), where you can find boats out to the stunning Andaman archipelago protected by **Ko Tarutao Marine National Park** (p715). If you're heading southward to Malaysia, Satun is also a convenient exit point from Thailand.

Train from Bangkok to Chaiya and Surat Thani. Bus to Nakhon Si Thammarat, then local bus to Khao Luang or Hat Sichon. From Nakhon Si Thammarat, bus to Songkhla, Trang and Satun, then boat to Ko Tarutao Marine National Park.

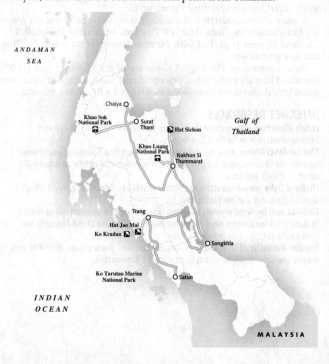

NORTHERN LOOP   Two Weeks / Phitsanulok to Chiang Rai

Start in **Phitsanulok** (p380), where the night market is as much a source of entertainment as it is a place to eat, and the Phra Jinnarat Buddha ranks second only to Bangkok's Emerald Buddha in sanctity. At the next stop, **Sukhothai** (p388), the birthplace of Thai culture, you'll need at least two full days to enjoy all of the historical park and other local attractions. Don't miss neighbouring **Si Satchanalai–Chaliang Historical Park** (p394), a more low-profile version of Sukhothai, with elephants.

From Sukhothai continue north to **Chiang Mai** (p276) to pick up road rags at the night bazaar and grind the *faràng* food you won't find elsewhere in the north. Zig southwest to **Doi Inthanon National Park** (p321) for green, misty highs, then zag west to **Mae Sariang** (p415) and north to **Mae Hong Son** (p419) to view how Shan, hill-tribe and Thai cultures mix in the Salween River valleys.

Next up is **Pai** (p429), a small Shan-Yunnanese crossroads that is quickly becoming northern Thailand's trekking centre, as well as the live-music capital of the north. From Pai head to **Chiang Dao** (p324) for a spooky cave walk or hike through the jungle, then on to **Tha Ton** (p326) to catch a **boat ride** (p329) down the Mae Kok to **Chiang Rai** (p339), stopping off at hill-tribe villages along the way if you have time. From Chiang Rai it's an easy half-day trip back to Chiang Mai.

Phitsanulok to Sukhothai by local bus, then bus to Si Satchanalai–Chaliang Historical Park. Train or direct bus from Phitsanulok to Chiang Mai. For Doi Inthanon bus first to Chom Thong, then *săwngthăew* from Doi Inthanon to Chiang Mai. Mae Sariang to Mae Hong Son, Pai and Tha Ton via local bus, then boat to Chiang Rai and bus back to Chiang Mai.

GRAND CIRCUIT   One Month / Bangkok to Bangkok

If you've got a month to 'do' Thailand, spend a few days in **Bangkok** (p94; or leave it till last) then take a slow ride north with one- or two-night stopovers in **Lopburi** (p202) and **Sukhothai** (p388) to take in the historic temple architecture. From Sukhothai continue to **Chiang Mai** (p276), cultural capital of the north, for several days of old city walks, *khâo sawy* (northern Thai–style curry noodles) and rock-climbing at nearby **Tham Meuang On** (p290). While in the north, consider a side trip into the slower-paced hinterlands; we recommend either Mae Hong Son Province or Tak Province.

From Chiang Mai backtrack to the former royal capital of **Ayuthaya** (p194), where you can mosey through yet another historical park and find convenient travel connections to Isan (northeastern Thailand).

Begin your Isan peregrination in **Phimai** (p444), a charming, smaller town with of one of Thailand's most impressive Khmer-style, Angkor-period temple complexes. From nearby **Khorat** (p438), launch further northeast to **Khon Kaen** (p457) to view its superior national museum collection, nosh on the best Isan food in the region and listen to live *măw lam* (Isan folk-pop). From Khon Kaen you can head north to **Nong Khai** (p475) and a road circuit along the Mekong River to **Ubon Ratchathani** (p505) or, if you've had enough of Isan, make a beeline for the Gulf coast of southeastern Thailand.

Slide down the Thai–Malay Peninsula to spend the last week of your trip kicking back on Thailand's famous islands. From November to May (when there's no southwest monsoon), choose the Andaman Sea side – **Khao Lak** (p637), **Phuket** (p644) or **Krabi** (p673) – or the Gulf side – **Ko Samui** (p555) or **Ko Pha-Ngan** (p576) – the rest of the year (stick to the west coasts of the islands during the northeast monsoon, November to February).

Train from Bangkok to Chiang Mai, stopping in Lopburi and Sukhothai. Bus from Chiang Mai to Ayuthaya, then another bus on to Phimai. From Phimai to Khon Kaen, then Trat and back to Bangkok via bus. Take the train to Surat Thani, jumping-off point for the Ko Samui archipelago, or fly direct to Ko Samui or Phuket.

ROADS LESS TRAVELLED

MISTY MOUNTAIN HOP   Three Weeks / Mae Sot to Wawi

At **Mae Sot** (p404), a town perched on the Thai–Myanmar border, and as much Karen-Burmese as it is Thai, you can visit the border market or day-trip to Myawadi, across Mae Nam Moei in Myanmar.

Take the high and winding 'Death Highway' south to **Um Phang** (p410), a district famous for its pristine waterfalls (including Thailand's largest, **Nam Tok Thilawsu**; p411), white-water rapids, working elephants and trekking possibilities, yet little visited by foreigners. If you have the time and stamina, consider hiking south to **Letongkhu** (p412), centre of a Karen priest cult.

Return to Mae Sot and grab a *săwngthăew* going north to **Mae Sariang** (p415) and continue through the Mae Hong Son Province loop on to Tha Ton as described in the Northern Loop itinerary (p23). Instead of taking the boat to Chiang Rai, however, get a ride up to the Yunnanese mountain settlement of **Mae Salong** (p348). From Mae Salong you can follow a network of roads high along narrow mountain ridges all the way to **Doi Tung** (p355), one of the major centres for opium poppy growing in decades past.

From Doi Tung loop back around, via **Chiang Rai** (p339) to **Wawi** (p329), an intriguing area where hill-tribe and Yunnanese populations grow some of the best tea in the country.

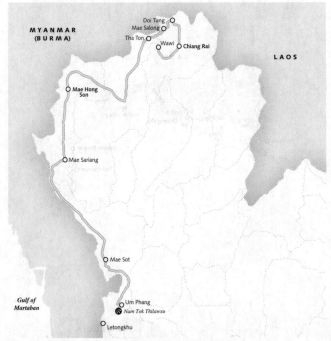

Best done by rented car, jeep or motorcycle; or else bus from Tak to Mae Sot, then *săwngthăew* to Um Phang and Mae Sariang, then bus again to Mae Hong Son and Pai. Bus to Tha Ton, *săwngthăew* to Mae Salong and Doi Tung, bus to Chiang Rai and *săwngthăew* to Wawi.

ISAN SPECIAL
Two Weeks / Dan Sai to That Phanom

This route brings you to some of the lesser known areas of northeastern Thailand (Isan), along with a leisurely sojourn along the Mekong River. Start in the agricultural centre of **Dan Sai** (p489), Loei Province, with a look at **Phra That Si Songrak** (p489), a striking stupa that was built by devout Lao and Thai Buddhists centuries ago, or better yet visit during the **Phi Ta Khon festival** (p734) usually held in June. Take in a possible side trip from Dan Sai to see the Lao–Thai border trade at nearby Na Haew.

From Dan Sai continue northeast to **Chiang Khan** (p492), a mellow cotton-growing district of wooden architecture overlooking the Mekong River. Follow the Mekong downriver from Chiang Khan to **Sangkhom** (p483), where little-visited waterfalls are close at hand, and to **Si Chiangmai** (p483), a sleepy town opposite Vientiane, Laos, where spring-roll wrappers are made.

After Si Chiangmai continue eastward towards Nong Khai, with a stop-off at **Wat Phra That Bang Phuan** (p482), an old and highly revered Lao temple, if you're inclined. In **Nong Khai** (p475), Thailand's main overland/over-river gateway to Laos, you'll have a chance to sample delicious Lao and Vietnamese cuisine, visit a bizarre Hindu-Buddhist **sculpture garden** (p476) and browse the bustling **Tha Sadet market** (p481).

Following the Mekong east – and, as it curves to the southeast – you can take advantage of a side trip to **Wat Phu Thok** (p484), a meditation wat atop a lofty sandstone outcrop, or speed along to the riverside towns of **Nakhon Phanom** (p495) and **That Phanom** (p497). In both of these towns you can still see a few vestiges of Lao-French–style architecture, and in That Phanom the very famous Lao stupa for which the town is named.

Bus from Loei to Dan Sai, then back to Loei for buses or *săwngthăew* onward to Chiang Khan, Sangkhom, Si Chiangmai and Nong Khai. *Săwngthăew* from Beung Kan to Wat Phu Tok. Bus to Nakhon Phanom and That Phanom.

ANDAMAN HIDEAWAYS   Three Weeks / Ranong to Ko Tarutao

Ready to escape Thailand's mass-market beaches and have more of the sand to yourself? Start at the far north of the Andaman Sea side of the Thai–Malay Peninsula, where the dozens of islands off the coast of **Ranong Province** (p629) have yet to be invaded by chain resorts and group tours. The tail end of Myanmar's mysterious Mergui Archipelago, you'll find plenty of long, undisturbed beaches, natural island forest and traditional fishing villages.

Only a few of the islands in the north Andaman offer any visitor facilities. **Ko Chang** (p634) and **Ko Phayam** (p635) will delight those looking for the hippie-style bungalow life now missing from Ko Samui and Phuket.

Moving further south, stop off at **Khao Lak/Laem Ru National Park** (p638), where whale-sized boulders decorate a turquoise bay. Among Khao Lak's advantages are its proximity to the uninhabited islands of **Similan Islands Marine National Park** (p639) as well as the nearby inland Khao Lak/Laem Ru National Park. Although the tsunami forced resorts right on the beach to close, many on higher ground are operating at full capacity

Your beach odyssey continues at the next Andaman stop, **Ko Yao Noi** (p672), a small island off the coast of Phuket with sleepy, Muslim farming villages, white-sand beaches and good snorkelling.

Finish off with a visit to Ko Tarutao archipelago, which encompasses both the karst islands protected by **Ko Tarutao Marine National Park** (p715) and those such as **Ko Adang** (p717) and **Ko Rawi** (p717). On **Ko Lipe** (p718), an island in the Tarutao archipelago (but not part of the national park), you can visit a Moken (sea gypsy) colony, enjoy excellent diving and plan overnight camping trips to neighbouring islets.

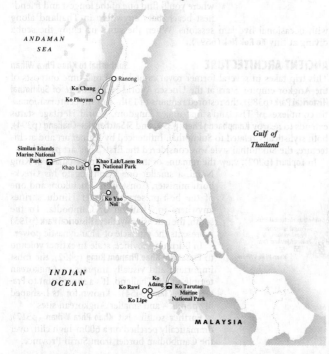

Plane or bus to Ranong, then *sǎwngthǎew* to Saphan Pla for the boat onward to Ko Chang and Ko Phayam. Reach Ko Yao by boat from Phuket, and Ko Tarutao by boat from Pak Bara. There are daily boats between Ko Lipe and Ko Tarutao.

TAILORED TRIPS

BEACH BLANKET BABYLON   Ko Samet to Ko Lanta

Here's a trip for coasties who need sports gear and nightlife to go with sand and sea. Start with **Ko Samet** (p249), where you can windsurf at Ao Hin Kok by day and share 'buckets of joy' (Sang Som whisky served in an ice bucket with Coke, soda, Red Bull and multiple straws) with fellow beachgoers at night.

Cruise south along the Gulf of Thailand to **Ko Tao** (p591), the northern-most inhabited island in the Samui archipelago and one of the best places to

go scuba diving (or to learn how to dive if you've never been). Join the foreign dive community for sunset drinks at rustic local bars.

Hit the next island south, **Ko Pha-Ngan** (p576) for the monthly **Full Moon Party** (p581) on Hat Rin, then recuperate with long swims at peaceful **Hat Khuat** (p584) for a few days. Hop to **Ko Samui** (p555) next. Stay at friendly, inexpensive **Hat Mae Nam** (p563), dine on fresh seafood at depend-able restaurants in **Hat Bo Phut** (p572) and end the night partying at the discos in **Hat Chaweng** (p574) and bodysurfing in the moonlight.

Shoot across the Thai–Malay Peninsula and down the Andaman coast to **Ko Lanta** (p695), where you'll find one of the longest and friend-liest beach bars anywhere in Thailand along with occasional live jam sessions. When the sun's up enjoy the scuba diving at tiny **Ko Rok Nok** (p697).

ANCIENT ARCHITECTURE   Sukhothai to Khao Phra Wihan

This trip takes in several former royal capitals and one-time outposts of the Angkor empire. Start at the Unesco World Heritage site of **Sukhothai Historical Park** (p389), the restored remains of 13th- to 14th-century monas-tic complexes of Thailand's first major kingdom. World Heritage status extends to nearby **Kamphaeng Phet** (p399) and **Si Satchanalai–Chaliang** (p394), both stylistically related to Sukhothai. Influenced by Khmer art and archi-tecture, the Sukhothai style was considered the first 'Thai' art period.

In **Lopburi** (p202), view the remains of the extraordinary palace of King Narai, a smaller one belonging to his Greek-born minister, Constantine Phaulkon, and one of the best-preserved Khmer Hindu shrines anywhere in Thailand or Cambodia. To the south, the extensive **Ayuthaya Historical Park** (p195) represents the pinnacle of Thai dynastic power.

In Buriram Province, scale an extinct volcano to **Prasat Hin Khao Phanom Rung** (p452), the most important and visually impressive Angkorean temple site in Thailand. It's a short jaunt to **Pra-sat Meuang Tam** (p454) – known for its L-shaped lily ponds – and smaller Angkorean sites.

Further south visit **Khao Phra Wihan** (p517), dramatically perched on a 600m-high cliff, over the Cambodian border from Surin Province.

CULINARY PILGRIMAGE

Foodies from all over the world flock to Thailand seeking out the original and authentic flavours of Thai cuisine. While you could easily spend a lifetime exploring the *kŭaytĭaw* (noodles), *kaeng* (curries) and *yam* (spicy salads) lore, this two-week romp can serve as a good introduction.

Bangkok (p155), the epicentre of Thai cuisine, is the place for central Thai curries, *yam* and *tôm yam* (spicy lemongrass-based soup). You'll also find the best Thai-Chinese offerings here in (no surprise) **Chinatown** (p159).

Kaeng mét má-mûang (cashew curry) is the dish to try in **Phuket** (p651) and **Ranong** (p632), where cashews are grown. Hit **Trang** (p704) in southern Thailand to stain your shirt with the best *khànŏm jiin náam yaa* (thin rice noodles with fish curry), washed down with *ko-píi* (Hokkien-style brewed coffee). Further south in **Satun** (p713), irresistible Malay dishes such as *rotii kaeng* (flatbread or 'roti' with curry dip) and *mátàbà* (stuffed *rotii*) are plentiful. Anywhere along the coasts of the Thai–Malay Peninsula you'll find seafood most other countries can only dream about.

Northeastern Thailand will thrill travellers who are hooked on the Isan trio of *kài yâang* (grilled marinated chicken), *khâo nĭaw* (sticky rice) and *sôm-tam* (spicy green papaya salad). For the best head to **Khon Kaen** (p461) or **Udon Thani** (p470). Try **Nong Khai** (p480) for *kaeng lao* (Lao-style bamboo-shoot soup) and **Ubon Ratchathani** (p509) for succulent *lâap pèt* (spicy minced duck salad). The *khâo sawy* (curried noodles) is as addictive to noodle lovers as the *náam phrík nùm* (green chilli dip) is to chilli-heads in both **Chiang Mai** (p300) and **Chiang Rai** (p345).

THAILAND FOR KIDS   Bangkok to Hua Hin

This circuit is designed to offer children plenty to see and do without any marathon travel distances. Bangkok, itself as hyperactive as any preteen, has enough attractions for nearly a week. If animals amuse then centrally located **Dusit Zoo** (p139) is a sure bet, as are the cobra-milking antics at **Queen Saovabha Memorial Institute** (p130).

On the outskirts of Bangkok you'll find croc shows and elephant 'roundups' at **Samphran Elephant Ground & Zoo** (p140) and **Safari World** (p140), said to be the largest open-air zoo in the world. Culture and history bundled into a walkable, climbable form is available at the scale replicas of Thailand's most famous ruins sites at **Muang Boran** (p191) in nearby Samut Prakan.

A train excursion to Kanchanaburi and then across the famous **'Bridge Over the River Kwai'** (p209) will excite all but the most jaded kids. Outside of town take the tykes along the scenic, safe trails following the seven-tiered waterfall at **Erawan National Park** (p219) or climb the hilltop ridge leading to the colourful temples of **Wat Tham Seua** and **Wat Tham Khao Noi** (p223).

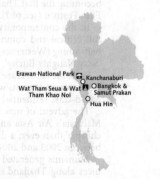

End the trip with a relaxing stay at the beachside resort of **Hua Hin** (p527), whose advantages include relatively calm waters, plenty of restaurant variety and pony rides on the beach.

Snapshot

Thailand continues to weather the seas of change, both global and regional, without losing its soul. The economy seems to have fully recovered from the 1997 to 1998 Asian Financial Crisis, tourism is booming and the nation has topped Southeast Asia's growth scores for the last two years.

FAST FACTS

Area: 514,000 sq km

Border Countries: Cambodia, Laos, Malaysia, Myanmar (Burma)

Population: 64,800,000

Literacy: 92.6%

Religion: 95% Buddhist

GDP per capita (purchasing power parity): US$7400

Inflation: 1.8%

Original name: Siam

Number of tigers left in Thailand today: around 2000

Coastline: 3219km

The success of Bangkok's Skytrain has been a boon to residents and visitors alike, and the opening of the Metro subway in late 2004 has further boosted city spirits. Meanwhile Thailand's 'second city' (in spirit if not in population figures), Chiang Mai, is busy making plans for similar mass transit as well as expanded expressway links.

The avian flu epidemic that began in China in 2003 and threatened lives in Thailand well into 2004 appears to have been contained (see p43). More challenging has been the continuing disquiet in three of Thailand's southern provinces, Yala, Pattani and Narathiwat, where Muslim nationalists have not taken kindly to PM Thaksin Shinawatra's strong-arm tactics (see p44).

Thailand's puritanical, growth-oriented Thai Rak Thai (TRT; Thais Love Thais) party remains in power and poised to tackle another four-year term. In an effort to keep the populace in a more 'productive' mode, the Thaksin administration has begun enforcing 1am closing times for most bars, discos and other entertainment venues around the country (see p43). In a country long accustomed to all-night revelry, the move has occasioned a loss of employment for an estimated 100,000 Thais.

Nevertheless, TRT's liberal dispersion of funds to village development programmes, along with a loosening of credit restrictions for consumers at large, have endeared many ordinary Thais to the party. Meanwhile Thai academics and intellectuals have stepped up their public derision of the government for its human rights record and overly loose credit policies, forecasting another crash predicated on non-performing loans.

Near the forefront of Thai news these days is the 364-km Trans-Thai Malaysia gas pipeline, destined to carry gas from the Gulf of Thailand to northern Malaysia. Protests in the south, however, threaten to derail the project before even the first pipe has been laid.

Thailand's New Wave cinema, which began with the modest success of Thai-directed films on the international festival circuit, has gathered steam, with Apichatpong Weerasethakul's *Tropical Malady (Sut Pralat)* becoming the first Thai film ever to earn a Jury Prize at the 2004 Cannes Film Festival (see p82).

In the contemporary music scene, the rock group Silly Fools rose to full critical and commercial success, while *lûuk khrêung* – half-Thai, half-*faràng* (Westerner) – Tata Young had an international hit single with 'Sexy Naughty Bitchy'.

Spas, the latest craze in tourism, are mushrooming all over the country, from simple day spas with inexpensive massage and herbal treatments to world-class residential retreat facilities.

The advent of new budget airlines in the region, most prominently Malaysia's Air Asia and Thailand's Nok Air, has made domestic flying cheaper than ever; a direct result was a 20% increase in tourist arrivals between 2003 and 2004.

Tsunamis generated by an Indian Ocean earthquake struck six provinces along Thailand's Andaman coast in December 2004, resulting in

5000 confirmed deaths and 3000 missing. Roughly half of the victims were Thai citizens and the other half tourists. None of the islands and beaches in the Gulf of Thailand was affected at all, and even much of the Andaman shoreline received little or no damage.

Local communities, with the help of world relief organisations and hundreds of international volunteers, have done an impressive job of reconstruction and relief in the affected Andaman areas. Tourism along most of the coast has returned to normal capacity in terms of infrastructure. Unfortunately for those making a livelihood from Andaman tourism, the average number of visitors has dropped considerably, even though there is currently no reason to avoid the area.

History

PREHISTORY

Modern linguistic theory and archaeological evidence suggest that the first true agriculturists in the world, perhaps also the first metal workers, spoke an early form of Thai and lived in what we know today as Thailand. The Mekong River valley and Khorat Plateau in particular were inhabited as far back as 10,000 years ago, and rice was grown in the Ban Chiang and Ban Prasat areas of northeastern Thailand as early as 4000 BC (China, by contrast, was growing and consuming millet at the time). The Ban Chiang culture began bronze metallurgy before 3000 BC; the Middle East's Bronze Age arrived around 2800 BC, China's a thousand years later. Ban Chiang bronze works were stronger than their Mesopotamian or Chinese counterparts, mainly due to Ban Chiang's access to the abundant tin resources of the Thai-Malay Peninsula.

Given the nomadic nature of the early Thais, the exact origins of the Thai – or the broader Austro-Thai – culture continues to be a matter of academic debate. While most scholars favour a region vaguely stretching from Guangxi in southern China to Dien Bien Phu in northern Vietnam, a more radical theory says the Thais descended from an ocean-based civilisation in the western Pacific. The former supposition rests on linguistic theory, particularly the mapping of tones from dialect to dialect, thus establishing migrational directionality. The oceanic proponents trace the development of symbols and myths in Thai art and culture to arrive at their conclusions.

Naga: Cultural Origins in Siam & the West Pacific by Sumet Jumsai (1997) is an inspired piece of speculative theory on the supposed oceanic origins of Thai people and culture, with nods to the late R Buckminster Fuller.

THAI MIGRATION

This vast, non-unified zone of Austro-Thai influence spread all over Southeast Asia at various times, including as far away as the islands of Indonesia and Southwest China. In Thailand, these Austro-Thai groups belonged to the Thai-Kadai and Mon-Khmer language families.

The Thai-Kadai is the most significant ethno-linguistic group in all of Southeast Asia, with 72 million speakers extending from the Brahmaputra River in India's Assam state to the Gulf of Tonkin and China's Hainan Island. To the north, there are Thai-Kadai speakers well into the Chinese provinces of Yunnan and Guangxi, and to the south they are found as far as the northern Malaysian state of Kedah. In Thailand and Laos they are the majority populations, and in China, Vietnam and Myanmar (Burma) they are the largest minorities. The predominant Thai half of the Thai-Kadai group includes the Ahom (Assam), the Siamese (Thailand), the Black Thai or Thai Dam (Laos and Vietnam), the Thai Yai or Shan (Myanmar and Thailand), the Thai Neua (Laos, Thailand and China), the Thai Lü (Laos, Thailand and China) and the Yuan (Laos and Thailand). The less numerous Kadai groups (under a million) include such comparatively obscure languages in southern China as Kelao, Lati, Laha, Laqua and Li.

A linguistic map of southern China, northeastern India and Southeast Asia clearly shows that the preferred zones of occupation by the Thai

Check out www.museum.upenn.edu/new/research/Exp_Rese_Disc/Asia/banchiang/banchiang.shtml if you're interested in Thailand's earliest civilisation.

4000–3000 BC	6th–10 centuries
Northeastern Thailand pioneers rice cultivation and bronze metallurgy	Theravada Buddhism establishes itself among Mon communities in central Thailand

peoples have been river valleys, from the Red (Hong) River in the south of China and Vietnam to the Brahmaputra River in Assam, India. At one time there were two terminals for movement into what is now Thailand. The 'northern terminal' was in the Yuan Jiang and other river areas in China's modern-day Yunnan and Guangxi provinces, and the 'southern terminal' along central Thailand's Mae Nam Chao Phraya (Chao Phraya River). The human populations remain quite concentrated in these areas today, while areas between the two were merely intermediate relay points and have always been less populated.

The Mekong River valley between Thailand and Laos was one such intermediate zone, as were river valleys along the Nan, Ping, Kok, Yom and Wang rivers in northern Thailand, plus various river areas in Laos and also in the Shan State of Myanmar. As far as historians have been able to piece together from scant linguistic and anthropological evidence, significant numbers of Austro-Thai peoples in southern China or northern Vietnam probably began migrating southward and westward in small groups as early as the 8th century AD – most certainly by the 10th century.

These migrant Thais established local polities along traditional social schemata according to *meuang* (roughly 'principality' or 'city-state'), under the rule of chieftains or sovereigns called *jâo meuang*. Each *meuang* was based in a river valley or section of a valley. Some *meuang* were loosely collected under one *jâo meuang* or an alliance of several.

Wherever Thais met indigenous populations of Tibeto-Burmans and Mon-Khmers in the move south and westward (into what is now Myanmar, Thailand and Laos), they were somehow able to displace, assimilate or co-opt them without force. The most probable explanation for this relatively smooth assimilation is that there were already Thai peoples indigenous to the area.

The Legend of Suriyothai (2002), a Francis Ford Coppola re-edit of the royally financed, four-hour original (*Suriyothai*), recounts a famous 1548 battle between Bago (part of Burma) and Siam.

EARLY KINGDOMS

With no written records or chronologies it is difficult to say with certainty what kind of cultures existed among the *meuang* of Thailand before the middle of the first millennium AD. However, by the 6th century an important network of agricultural communities was thriving as far south as modern-day Pattani and Yala, and as far north and northeast as Lamphun and Muang Fa Daet (near Khon Kaen).

Theravada Buddhism was flourishing and may have entered the region during India's Ashoka period, in the 3rd or 2nd century BC, when Indian missionaries are said to have been sent to a land called Suvannabhumi (Land of Gold). Suvannabhumi most likely corresponds to a remarkably fertile area stretching from southern Myanmar, across central Thailand, to eastern Cambodia. Two different cities in Thailand's central river basin have long been called Suphanburi (City of Gold) and U Thong (Cradle of Gold).

www.thaiworldview .com/art_hist.htm has thumbnail histories of the various Thai royal capitals.

Dvaravati

This collection of *meuang* was given the Sanskrit name Dvaravati (Place of Gates), the city of Krishna in the Indian epic poem *Mahabharata*. The French art historian Georges Coedès discovered the name on some coins that were excavated in the Nakhon Pathom area, which seems to have

8th–10th centuries	9th–13th centuries
Thai-Kadai peoples from northern Vietnam and southern China begin migrating into the Mekong River valley	Angkor influence extends across central Thailand, leaving magnificent stone temples in its wake

http://sunsite.au.ac.th
/thailand/thai_his offers
a succinct history of
Thailand, maintained by
Assumption University of
Thailand.

been the centre of Dvaravati culture. The Dvaravati period lasted until the 11th or 12th century AD and produced many works of art, including Buddha images (showing Indian Gupta influence), stucco reliefs on temple walls and in caves, architecture, exquisite terracotta heads, votive tablets and various sculptures.

Dvaravati may have been a cultural relay point for the Funan and Chenla cultures of ancient Laos and Cambodia to the northeast and east. The Chinese, through the travels of the famous pilgrim Xuan Zang, knew the area as Tuoluobodi, between Sriksetra (Myanmar) and Isanapura (Laos-Cambodia).

The main ethnicity of the Dvaravati peoples was Mon, whose culture quickly declined in the 11th century under the political domination of the invading Khmers, who made their headquarters in Lopburi. A Mon kingdom – Hariphunchai – in today's Lamphun Province, held out until the late 12th or early 13th century, when it was annexed by northern Thais.

Khmer Influence

The Khmer conquests from the 7th to 11th centuries introduced Khmer art, language and religion as cultural influences. Some of the Sanskrit terms in the Mon-Thai vocabulary entered the language during the Khmer period between the 11th and 13th centuries. Monuments from this period located in Kanchanaburi, Lopburi and many northeastern towns were constructed in the Khmer style and are comparable to architecture in Angkor.

Elements of Brahmanism, Theravada Buddhism and Mahayana Buddhism were intermixed as Lopburi became a religious centre, and some elements of each Buddhist school – along with Brahmanism – remain in Thai religious and court ceremonies today.

Other Kingdoms

While all this was taking place, a Thai state called Nan Chao (AD 650–1250) was flourishing in what later became Yunnan and Sichuan in China. Nan Chao maintained close relations with imperial China and the two neighbours enjoyed much cultural exchange. Although Thais from Nan Chao and other Thai settlements had long been migrating southward, settling in and around what is today Laos and northern Thailand, this migration increased when the Mongols, under Kublai Khan, conquered Nan Chao in 1253.

Meanwhile a number of Thais became mercenaries for the Khmer armies in the early 12th century, as depicted on the walls of Angkor Wat. The Khmers called the Thais 'Syam', and this was how the Thai kingdom eventually came to be called Syam, or Sayam. In Myanmar and northwestern Thailand the pronunciation of Syam became 'Shan'. The English trader James Lancaster penned the first known English transliteration of the name as 'Siam' in 1592.

Meanwhile southern Thailand – the upper Malay Peninsula – was under the control of the Srivijaya empire, the headquarters of which may have been located in Palembang, Sumatra, between the 8th and 13th centuries. The regional centre for Srivijaya was Chaiya, near modern Surat Thani. Remains of Srivijaya art can still be seen in Chaiya and its environs.

1238	14th–15th centuries
Several Thai principalities resist Khmer suzerainty and unite to form Sukhothai, considered to be the first Thai kingdom	Ayuthaya annexes Sukhothai, then vanquishes the neighbouring Angkor empire and becomes one of the wealthiest cities in the world

Sukhothai & Lan Na Thai Periods

Several Thai principalities in the Mekong River valley united in the 13th and 14th centuries, when Thai princes wrested the lower north from the Khmers – whose Angkor government was declining fast – to create Sukhothai (Rising of Happiness). They later took Hariphunchai from the Mon to form Lan Na Thai (Million Thai Rice Fields).

In 1238 the Sukhothai kingdom declared its independence under King Si Intharathit and quickly expanded its sphere of influence, taking advantage not only of the declining Khmer power but the weakening Srivijaya domain in the south. Sukhothai is considered by the Thais to be the first true Thai kingdom. It was annexed by Ayuthaya in 1376, by which time a national identity of sorts had been forged.

Under King Ramkhamhaeng, the Sukhothai kingdom extended from Nakhon Si Thammarat in the south to the upper Mekong River valley (Laos), and to Bago (Myanmar). For a short time (1448–86) the Sukhothai capital was moved to Phitsanulok.

Ramkhamhaeng also supported Phaya Mengrai of Chiang Mai, and Phaya Ngam Meuang of Phayao, two northern Thai *jâo meuang*, in the 1296 founding of Lan Na Thai, nowadays often known simply as 'Lanna'. Lanna extended across northern Thailand to include the *meuang* of Wiang Chan along the middle reaches of the Mekong River. In the 14th century, Wiang Chan was taken from Lanna by Chao Fa Ngum of Luang Prabang, who made it part of his Lan Xang (Million Elephants) kingdom. Wiang Chan later flourished as an independent kingdom for a short time during the mid-16th century and eventually became the capital of Laos in its royal, French (during which it got its more popular international spelling 'Vientiane') and now socialist incarnations. After a period of dynastic decline, Lanna fell to the Burmese in 1558.

Ayuthaya Period

The Thai kings of Ayuthaya grew very powerful in the 14th and 15th centuries, taking over U Thong and Lopburi, former Khmer strongholds, and moving east in their conquests until Angkor was defeated in 1431. Even though the Khmers were their adversaries in battle, the Ayuthaya

---

FISH IN THE WATER, RICE IN THE FIELDS

Many Thais today have a sentimental, romantic view of the Sukhothai period, seeing it as a 'golden age' of Thai politics, religion and culture – an egalitarian, noble period when all the people had enough to eat and the kingdom was unconquerable. Among other accomplishments, the third Sukhothai king, Ramkhamhaeng, encouraged the use of a fledgling Thai writing system, which became the basis for modern Thai; he also codified the Thai form of Theravada Buddhism, as borrowed from the Sinhalese.

A famous passage from Sukhothai's Ramkhamhaeng inscription reads:

This land of Sukhothai is thriving. There is fish in the water and rice in the fields…The King has hung a bell in the opening of the gate over there; if any commoner has a grievance which sickens his belly and grips his heart, he goes and strikes the bell; King Ramkhamhaeng questions the man, examines the case and decides it justly for him.

Bang Rajan (2000), by Thanit Jitnukul, is a cine-epic of a doomed Thai rebellion against 18th-century Burmese rule, with John Ford/ Akira Kurosawa style battle scenes.

kings adopted large portions of Khmer court customs and language. One result of this acculturation was that the Thai monarch gained more absolute authority during the Ayuthaya period and assumed the title *devaraja* (god-king; *thewárâat* in Thai) as opposed to the *dhammaraja* (dharma-king; *thammárâat*) title used in Sukhothai.

Ayuthaya was one of the greatest and wealthiest cities in Asia, a thriving seaport envied not only by the Burmese but by the Europeans, who were in great awe of it. It has been said that London, at the time, was a mere village in comparison. The kingdom sustained an unbroken 400-year monarchical succession through 34 reigns, from King U Thong (r 1350–69) to King Ekathat (r 1758–67).

By the early 16th century Ayuthaya was receiving European visitors and a Portuguese embassy was established in 1511. The Portuguese were followed by the Dutch in 1605, the English in 1612, the Danes in 1621 and the French in 1662. In the mid-16th century Ayuthaya and the independent kingdom of Lanna came under the control of the Burmese, but the Thais regained rule of both by the end of the century. In 1690 Londoner Engelbert Campfer proclaimed, 'Among the Asian nations, the Kingdom of Siam is the greatest. The magnificence of the Ayuthaya Court is incomparable'.

Companion novels *The Falcon of Siam* (1988) and *The Falcon Takes Wing* (1991), by Axel Aylwen, capture the feel and historical detail of 17th-century Siam through the escapades of historical figure Constantine Phaulkon.

The Burmese invaded Ayuthaya again in 1765 and the capital fell after two years of fighting. This time the invaders destroyed everything sacred to the Thais, including manuscripts, temples and religious sculpture. But the Burmese were unable to maintain a foothold in the kingdom, and Phraya Taksin, a half-Chinese, half-Thai general, made himself king in 1769, ruling from the new capital of Thonburi on the banks of the Mae Nam Chao Phraya, opposite Bangkok. The Thais regained control of the country and further united the provinces to the north with central Siam.

Taksin eventually came to regard himself as the next Buddha; his ministers, who did not approve of his religious fantasies, deposed and then executed him.

THE SOLIDIFICATION OF BANGKOK POWER
Founding of the Chakri Dynasty

One of Taksin's key generals, Chao Phraya Chakri, came to power and was crowned in 1782 as Phra Yot Fa. He moved the royal capital across the river to Bangkok and ruled as the first king of the Chakri dynasty. In 1809 his son, Loet La, took the throne and reigned until 1824. Both monarchs assumed the task of restoring the culture, which had been severely damaged by the Burmese decades earlier.

THE FALCON OF SIAM

An exceptional episode unfolded in Ayuthaya when Constantine Phaulkon, a Greek, became a high official in Siam under King Narai, from 1675 to 1688. Wisely courting royal favour by fending off would-be colonisation by the Dutch and the English, he nevertheless allowed the French to station 600 soldiers in the kingdom. Eventually the Thais, fearing a takeover, expelled the French and executed Phaulkon. Siam sealed itself off from the West for 150 years following this experience with the *faràng* (a foreigner of European descent or Westerner; from *faràngsèt*, meaning 'French').

1765	1769
Ayuthaya's wealth attracts the attention of the Burmese, whose siege reduces the city to a devastated shell	Phaya Taksin rallies the Thai forces and drives out the Burmese, appointing himself king at the new capital of Thonburi

The third Chakri king, Phra Nang Klao (r 1824–51), went beyond reviving tradition and developed trade with China, while increasing domestic agricultural production. He also established a new royal title system, posthumously conferring 'Rama I' and 'Rama II' upon his two predecessors and taking the title 'Rama III' for himself. During Nang Klao's reign, American missionary James Low brought the first printing press to Siam and produced the country's first printed document in Thai script. Missionary Dan Bradley published the first Thai newspaper, the monthly *Bangkok Recorder*, from 1844 to 1845.

Rama IV & Reform

Commonly known as King Mongkut (Phra Chom Klao to the Thais), Rama IV was a colourful and innovative Chakri king. He originally missed out on the throne in deference to his half-brother, Rama III, and lived as a Buddhist monk for 27 years. During his long monastic term he became adept in Sanskrit, Pali, Latin and English, studied Western sciences and adopted the strict discipline of local Mon monks. He kept an eye on the outside world and, when he took the throne in 1851, immediately courted diplomatic relations with a few European nations, taking care to evade colonisation.

In addition, he attempted to demythologise Thai religion by aligning Buddhist cosmology with modern science, and founded the Thammayut monastic sect, based on the strict discipline he had followed as a monk.

King Mongkut loosened Thai trade restrictions and many Western powers signed trade agreements with the monarch. He also sponsored Siam's second printing press and instituted educational reforms, developing a school system along European lines. Although the king courted the West, he did so with caution and warned his subjects, 'Whatever they have invented or done which we should know of and do, we can imitate and learn from them, but do not wholeheartedly believe in them.' Mongkut was the first monarch to show his face to Thai commoners in public.

Rama V & Modernisation

Mongkut's son King Chulalongkorn (known to the Thais as Rama V or Chula Chom Klao; r 1868–1910) continued his father's tradition of reform, especially in the legal and administrative realms. Educated by European tutors, Rama V abolished prostration before the king as well as slavery and corvée (state labour). Siam further benefited from relations with European nations and the USA: railways were built, a civil service was established and the legal code restructured. Although Siam still managed to avoid European colonisation, the king was compelled to concede territory to French Indochina (Laos in 1893 and Cambodia in 1907) and British Burma (three Malayan states in 1909) during his reign.

Rama V's son, King Vajiravudh (Mongkut Klao or Rama VI; r 1910–25), was educated in Britain and during his reign he introduced educational reforms including compulsory education. He further 'Westernised' the nation by conforming the Thai calendar to Western models. His reign was clouded by a top-down push for Thai nationalism that resulted in strong anti-Chinese sentiment.

Si Phaendin: Four Reigns (1981), by Kukrit Pramoj, novelises Thai court life and social change from the late 19th century to the Japanese bombing raids of the 1940s and is the most widely read historical novel ever published in Thailand.

1782	1851
King Taksin becomes deranged; Chao Phraya Chakri takes over as king, moving the capital across Mae Nam Chao Phraya to Bangkok	King Mongkut (Rama V) ascends the Chakra throne, instituting a period of reform and opening diplomatic relations with Europe

Thailand: A Short History (1982), by David Wyatt, offers a succinct overview from the early Thai era through to the 1980s.

Before Vajiravudh's reign, Thai parents gave each of their children a single, original name, with no surname to identify family origins. In 1909 a royal decree required the adoption of Thai surnames for all Thai citizens – a move designed to parallel the European system of family surnames and to weed out Chinese names.

In 1912 a group of Thai military officers unsuccessfully attempted to overthrow the monarchy, the first in a series of coup attempts that have plagued Thai history. As a show of support for the Allies in WWI, Vajiravudh sent 1300 Thai troops to France in 1918.

REVOLUTION & MILITARISATION

While Vajiravudh's brother, King Prajadhipok (Pokklao or Rama VII; r 1925–35) ruled, a group of Thai students living in Paris became so enamoured of democratic ideology that in 1932 they mounted a successful coup d'état against absolute monarchy in Siam. This bloodless revolution led to the development of a constitutional monarchy along British lines, with a mixed military-civilian group in power (see the box opposite).

A royalist revolt in 1933 sought to reinstate absolute monarchy, but it failed and left Prajadhipok isolated from the royalist revolutionaries and the constitution-minded ministers. One of the king's last official acts was to outlaw polygamy in 1934, leaving behind the cultural underpinnings that now support Thai prostitution.

In 1935 the king abdicated without naming a successor and retired to Britain. The cabinet promoted his nephew, 10-year-old Ananda Mahidol, to the throne as Rama VIII, although Ananda didn't return from school in Switzerland until 1945. Phibul Songkhram, a key military leader in the 1932 coup, maintained an effective position of power from 1938 until the end of WWII.

Under the influence of Phibul's government, the country's English name was officially changed in 1939 from Siam to Thailand (*pràthêt thai* in Thai). Pràthêt is from the Sanskrit *pradesha* (country). 'Thai' is considered to have the connotation of 'free', although in actual usage it refers to the Thai, Tai or T'ai peoples, who are found as far east as Tonkin, as far west as Assam, as far north as southern China, and as far south as northern Malaysia.

Ananda Mahidol came back to Thailand in 1945 but was shot dead in his bedroom under mysterious circumstances in 1946. Although there was apparently no physical evidence to suggest assassination, three of Ananda's attendants were arrested two years after his death and executed in 1954. No public charges were ever filed, and the consensus among historians today is that the attendants were 'sacrificed' to settle a karmic debt for allowing the king to die during their watch. His brother, Bhumibol Adulyadej, succeeded him as Rama IX. Nowadays no-one ever speaks or writes publicly about Ananda's death – whether it was a simple gun accident or a regicidal plot remains unclear.

WWII & Post-War Periods

During the Japanese invasion of Southeast Asia in 1941, the Phibul government sided with Japan and Phibul declared war on the USA and Britain in 1942. But Seni Pramoj, the Thai ambassador in Washington,

1902	1932
Siam annexes Yala, Pattani and Narathiwat from the former sultanate of Pattani	Following a bloodless coup, Rama VII presides over a change from absolute monarchy to a constitutional monarchy

CAFÉ-BREWED COUP

As Bangkok prospered in the early 20th century, many wealthy merchant families sent their children to study abroad in Europe. Students of humbler socio-economic status who excelled in school had access to government scholarships for overseas study as well. In 1924 a handful of Thai students in Paris formed the Promoters of Political Change, a group that met in Paris cafés to discuss ideas for a future Siamese government patterned after democratic Western models.

After completing studies in Paris and returning to Bangkok, three of the 'Promoters' – attorney Pridi Phanomyong and military officers Phibul Songkhram and Prayoon Phamonmontri – organised an underground 'People's Party' dedicated to the overthrow of the Siamese system of government. The People's Party found a willing moral accomplice in Rama VII, and a bloodless revolution in 1932 transformed Thailand from an absolute monarchy into a constitutional one.

refused to deliver the declaration. Phibul resigned in 1944 under pressure from the Thai underground resistance (known as Thai Seri), and after V-J Day in 1945, Seni became premier. Seni changed the English name of the country back to 'Siam' but kept 'Prathet Thai' as the official Thai name.

In 1946 Seni was unseated in a general election and a democratic civilian group took power under Pridi Phanomyong, a law professor who had been instrumental in the 1932 revolution. Pridi's civilian government survived long enough to create the 1946 Constitution of the Thai Kingdom, only to be overthrown by Phibul, then a field marshal, in 1947.

Using the death of Prajadhipok as a pretext, Phibul suspended the constitution and reinstated 'Thailand' as the country's official English name in 1949. Phibul's government took an extreme anticommunist stance, refused to recognise the newly declared People's Republic of China and became a loyal supporter of French and US foreign policy in Southeast Asia. Pridi, meanwhile, took up exile in China.

In 1951 power was wrested from Phibul by General Sarit Thanarat, who continued the tradition of military dictatorship. However, Phibul retained the actual title of premier until 1957 when Sarit finally had him exiled. Elections that same year forced Sarit to resign and go abroad for 'medical treatment'; he returned in 1958 to launch another coup. This time he abolished the constitution, dissolved the parliament and banned all political parties, maintaining effective power until he died of cirrhosis in 1963.

From 1964 to 1973 the Thai nation was ruled by the army officers Thanom Kittikachorn and Praphat Charusathien. During this time Thailand allowed the USA to establish several military bases within its borders in support of the US campaign in Vietnam.

Reacting to the political repression, 10,000 Thai students publicly demanded a real constitution in June 1973. On 14 October of the same year the military brutally suppressed a large demonstration at Thammasat University in Bangkok, but King Bhumibol and General Krit Sivara, who sympathised with the students, refused to support further bloodshed, forcing Thanom and Praphat to leave Thailand. Oxford-educated Kukrit Pramoj took charge of a 14-party coalition government and steered a leftist agenda past a conservative parliament.

Despite many minor errors in his novel *The Revolutionary King* (2001), William Stevenson is successful in conveying why King Rama IX of Thailand prevailed against nearly overwhelming odds to become the most beloved king in Thai history.

1934	1939
Polygamy, a Thai tradition, is outlawed	Siam changes its name to 'Thailand'

Among Kukrit's lasting achievements were a national minimum wage, the repeal of anticommunist laws and the ejection of US military forces from Thailand.

Polarisation

Kukrit's elected constitutional government ruled until 6 October 1976, when students demonstrated again, this time protesting against Thanom's return to Thailand as a monk. Thammasat University again became a battlefield as border-patrol police and right-wing paramilitary civilian groups assaulted a group of 2000 students holding a sit-in. It is estimated that hundreds of students were killed and injured in the fracas, and more than a thousand were arrested. Using public disorder as an excuse, the military stepped in and installed a new right-wing government with Thanin Kraivichien as premier.

This bloody incident disillusioned many Thai students and older intellectuals not directly involved with the demonstrations. Numerous idealists 'dropped out' of Thai society and joined the People's Liberation Army of Thailand (PLAT), a group of armed communist insurgents based in the hills who had been active since the 1930s.

In October 1977 the military replaced Thanin with the more moderate General Kriangsak Chomanand in an effort to conciliate antigovernment factions. When this failed, the military-backed position changed hands again in 1980, leaving Prem Tinsulanonda at the helm. By this time PLAT had peaked with around 10,000 members. A 1981 coup attempt by the 'Young Turks' (a group of army officers who had graduated together from the Chulachomklao Royal Military Academy and styled themselves after a 1908 military movement at the heart of the Ottoman Empire) failed when Prem fled Bangkok for Khorat in the company of the royal family.

Stabilisation

Prem served as prime minister until 1988 and is credited with the political and economic stabilisation of Thailand in the post–Vietnam War years (only one coup attempt in the 1980s!). The major success of the Prem years was a complete dismantling of the Communist Party of Thailand (CPT) and PLAT through an effective combination of amnesty programmes (which brought the students back from the forests) and military action. His administration is also considered to have been responsible for a gradual democratisation of Thailand that culminated in the 1988 election of his successor, retired general and businessman Chatichai Choonhavan. Prem continues to serve as a privy councillor and is an elder statesman (ràtthàbùrùt) of the country.

It may be difficult for later arrivals to Thailand to appreciate the political distance Thailand covered in the 1980s. Under Prem, for example, a long-standing 1am curfew in Bangkok was lifted, and dissenting opinions were heard again in public.

Ever since 1932, every leading political figure in Thailand has needed the support of the Thai military to survive. Considering Thailand's geographic position during the Cold War years, it's not difficult to understand their influence. But as the threat of communist takeover (either

The Moonhunter (2001; directed by Bhandit Rittakol) is a dramatisation of events following the 14 October 1973, when a government massacre sent student demonstrators into the hills to join the communists.

1946	1941–45
Rama VIII dies and the present king, Rama IX, succeeds; Thailand's first democratically elected government comes to power	Japanese forces occupy parts of Thailand until they're defeated at the close of WWII

from within or from nearby Indochinese states) diminished, the military gradually began loosening its hold on national politics.

Under Chatichai, Thailand enjoyed a brief period of unprecedented popular participation in government. Around 60% of Chatichai's cabinet members were former business executives rather than the ex-military officers in the previous cabinet. Thailand entered a new era in which the country's double-digit economic boom ran concurrently with democratisation. Critics praised the political maturation of Thailand, even if they also grumbled that corruption seemed as rife as it ever was. By the end of the 1980s, however, certain high-ranking military officers had become increasingly dissatisfied, complaining that Thailand was being run by a plutocracy.

THE STRUGGLE FOR DEMOCRACY
February 1991 Coup & its Aftermath

On 23 February 1991 the military overthrew the Chatichai administration in a bloodless coup *(pàtìwát)* and handed power to the newly formed National Peace-Keeping Council (NPKC), headed by General Suchinda Kraprayoon. Although it was Thailand's 19th attempted coup and one of 10 successful coups since 1932, it was only the second coup to overthrow a democratically elected civilian government. The NPKC abolished the 1978 constitution and dissolved the parliament, charging Chatichai's civilian government with corruption and vote-buying. Rights of public assembly were curtailed but the press was only closed down for one day.

Following the coup, the NPKC appointed a handpicked civilian prime minister, Anand Panyarachun, former ambassador to the USA, Germany, Canada and the UN, to dispel public fears that the junta was planning a return to 100% military rule. Anand claimed to be his own man, but like his predecessors – elected or not – he was allowed the freedom to make his own decisions only insofar as they didn't affect the military. In spite of obvious constraints, many observers felt Anand's temporary premiership and cabinet were the best Thailand has ever had, either before or since.

In December 1991, Thailand's national assembly passed a new constitution that guaranteed a NPKC-biased parliament – 270 appointed senators in the upper house stacked against 360 elected representatives. Under this constitution, regardless of who was chosen as the next prime minister or which political parties filled the lower house, the government would remain largely in the hands of the military.

A general election in March 1992 ushered in a five-party coalition government with Narong Wongwan, whose Samakkhitham (Justice Unity) Party received the most votes, as premier. But amid US allegations that Narong was involved in Thailand's drug trade, the military exercised its constitutional prerogative and replaced Narong with (surprise, surprise) General Suchinda in April 1992.

In May 1992, several huge demonstrations demanding Suchinda's resignation – led by the charismatic Bangkok governor, Chamlong Srimuang – rocked Bangkok and larger provincial capitals. Chamlong won the 1992 Magsaysay Award (a humanitarian service award issued by a foundation in the Philippines) for his role in galvanising the public to reject Suchinda. After street confrontations between the protesters and

The semi-academic chronicle *The Balancing Act: A History of Modern Thailand* (1991), by Joseph Wright Jnr, starts with the 1932 revolution and ends with the February 1991 coup.

1973	1976
Thai students, workers and farmers unite to repel military dictatorship and install a democratic government	Protestors slaughtered at Thammasat University; students flee to the mountains and join the PLAT; martial law is instituted in Bangkok

the military near Bangkok's Democracy Monument resulted in nearly 50 deaths and hundreds of injuries, Suchinda resigned, having been premier for less than six weeks. Anand Panyarachun was reinstated as interim premier, winning praise for his fair and efficient administration.

Musical Chairs & a New Constitution

The September 1992 elections squeezed in veteran Democrat Party leader Chuan Leekpai, who helmed a four-party coalition government. A food vendor's son and native of Trang Province instead of a general, tycoon or academic, the new premier didn't fit the usual mould. Although well regarded for his honesty and high morals, Chuan accomplished little in the areas of concern to the majority of Thais, most pointedly Bangkok traffic, national infrastructure and the undemocratic NPKC constitution.

After Chuan was unseated in a vote of no confidence, a new general election ushered in a seven-party coalition led by the Chart Thai (Thai Nationality) Party. At the helm was billionaire Banharn Silapa-archa, whom the press called a 'walking ATM'; they immediately attacked his tendency to appoint from a reservoir of rural politicians known to favour big business over social welfare. In September 1996 the Banharn government collapsed amid a spate of corruption scandals and a crisis of confidence.

The November 1996 national election, marked by electoral violence and accusations of vote buying, saw the former deputy prime minister and army commander Chavalit Yongchaiyudh, of the New Aspiration Party, secure premiership with a dubious mix of coalition partners.

In July 1997, following several months of warning signs that almost everyone in Thailand and in the international community chose to ignore, the Thai currency fell into a deflationary tailspin and the national economy crashed and screeched to a virtual halt.

Two months later the Thai parliament voted in a new constitution that guaranteed, at least on paper, more human and civil rights than had hitherto been codified in Thailand. As the first national charter to be prepared under civilian auspices, the 'people's constitution' fostered great hope in a population emotionally battered by the ongoing economic crisis.

Hope faded as Chavalit, living up to everyone's low expectations, failed to deal effectively with the economy and was forced to resign in November 1997. An election brought Chuan Leekpai back into office, where he did a reasonably decent job as an international public-relations man for the crisis.

A Fledgling Democracy

In January 2001, billionaire and former police colonel Thaksin Shinawatra was named prime minister after winning a landslide victory in compulsory nation-wide elections – the first in Thailand to be held under strict guidelines established by the 1997 constitution. Thaksin's party, Thai Rak Thai (Thais Love Thais; TRT), espouses a populist platform at perceivable odds with the man's enormous wealth and influence. Thaksin owns the country's only private radio station and his family owns Thailand's largest telecommunications company, which has lucrative coverage not only throughout Thailand but contracts with the governments of

Get hold of *Thailand's Boom and Bust* (1998), by Pasuk Phongpaichit and Chris Baker, for an expert analysis of the '80s and '90s boom, and consequent crash in 1997.

1982	1991–92
A general amnesty reduces the ranks of the armed insurgency to a handful; the communist movement is vanquished; martial law ends	A military coup lands General Suchinda in power and when protestors are shot, King Rama IX intervenes and democracy is restored

India and Myanmar as well. He has publicly stated his party's ambition to stay in office for four consecutive terms, or 16 years.

Meanwhile many Thai citizens, fed up with the government's slowness to right perceived wrongs in the countryside, continue to plague the administration with regular large-scale demonstrations. Most demonstrations plead for government relief from hardships caused by the shrinking economy, while some demand that the government dismantle World Bank or Asian Development projects, such as the Kheuan Pak Mun (Pak Mun Dam), that have been established without their consent. The government has promised land reform to help farmers, but these issues continue to smoulder, leaving observers to wonder if Thailand isn't heading for a period of unrest similar to that seen in the 1970s.

The Thaksin administration's main reaction so far has been to reject all criticism from within and outside Thailand as 'un-Thai'. In 2002 two *Far Eastern Economic Review* correspondents were nearly ejected from Thailand for reporting on business connections between Thaksin and the Crown Prince. Although in the end they were allowed to remain in the kingdom, the censorious action shocked many observers for whom Thailand was Southeast Asia's greatest bastion of press freedom.

In 2003 Thaksin announced a 'war on drugs' that would free the country of illicit drug use within 90 days. Lists of drug dealers and users were compiled in every province and the police were given arrest quotas to fulfil or else lose their jobs. Within two months over 2000 Thais on the government blacklist had been killed. The Thaksin administration denied accusations by the UN, the US State Department, Amnesty International and Thailand's own human rights commission that the deaths were extrajudicial killings by Thai police. Independent observers claim that the 'war on drugs' has succeeded in increased prices but not reduced drug use.

In the south during 2001–02, a decades-old Muslim nationalist movement, perhaps responding to the Thaksin administration's strengthening culture of authoritarianism, began reheating. Sporadic attacks on police stations, schools, military installations and other government institutions, resulted in a string of Thai deaths. Although targets were usually government officials or civil servants, Buddhist monks and a few Thai civilians also became victims.

In early 2004 three further crises in public confidence shook the nation. First avian influenza turned up in Thailand's bird and poultry population, and when it became known that the administration had been aware about the infections since November 2003, both the EU and Japan banned all imports of Thai chicken. Avian flu claimed the lives of eight Thais – all of whom were infected while handling live poultry – before the crisis was under control. Although there was no evidence to suggest that eating cooked chicken placed people at risk, most markets and restaurants were forced to quit selling chicken altogether. By mid-2004 the epidemic had cost the Thai economy 19 billion baht.

Just as the bird flu disaster seemed to be dissipating, the Interior Ministry announced that as of 1 March 2004 all entertainment establishments in Thailand would be required to close at midnight. Public reaction against this decision was so strong (mafia figures who controlled parts of Bangkok reportedly announced a billion-baht price on the prime

Visit www.globalsecurity.org/military/world/war/thailand2.htm for a history of Muslim nationalism in Thailand, from 1959 to the present.

minister's head) that the government back-pedalled, allowing nightspots to stay open till 1am, regardless of zoning.

Immediately on the heels of the uproar over new closing hours, police gunned down 112 machete-wielding Muslim militants – most of them teenagers – inside an historic mosque in Pattani. Then in October 2004 police broke up a large demonstration in southern Thailand, and while they were transporting around 1300 arrestees in overcrowded trucks, at least 78 died of suffocation or from being crushed under the weight of other arrestees.

On 26 December 2004, a magnitude 9.3 earthquake – the second-largest quake in recorded history – erupted on the floor of the Indian Ocean off the northwest coast of Sumatra. The resulting series of tsunamis claimed nearly 300,000 lives in countries along the Indian Ocean rim, and caused untold property damage. Along Thailand's Andaman coast the waves struck six provinces, reaching as high as 10m in the worst-hit areas.

Thailand's tsunami toll reached 5000 confirmed dead, with 3000 still missing at the time of writing. Beaches and islands in the Gulf of Thailand were unaffected. Relief and reconstruction efforts in Khao Lak, Ko Phi-Phi and Phuket have moved quickly and aggressively to restore normal living conditions in the most heavily damaged areas. Meanwhile tourism along the Andaman coast has slumped since the tsunami, while the Gulf side has experienced a resulting boom in visitor numbers.

Prime Minister Thaksin's speedy handling of the tsunami disaster, along with yet more promises of rural development, brought the TRT a landslide victory in the general election of February 2005. Meanwhile echoes of the bird flu, drug-war deaths, early bar closing policy and 'disquiet in the South' crises continue to haunt the administration. The Democrat opposition, on the other hand, has yet to put forth a positive platform that will prevent Thaksin and TRT from fulfilling their boast to remain in power for another 16 years.

The government's brutal suppression of Muslim nationalists in the south results in escalating violence in Yala, Pattani and Narathiwat

26 December 04

Devastating tsunami hits Thailand's Andaman Coast, killing 5000 and temporarily paralysing tourist and fishing industries

Food & Drink

Night market food stall,
Bangkok
JERRY ALEXANDER

Standing at the crossroads of numerous ancient and culturally continuous traditions dominated by India, China and Asian Oceania, Thailand has adapted cooking techniques and ingredients from all three of these major spheres of influence as well as the culinary kits carried by passing traders and empire-builders from the Middle East and southern Europe. Today's Thai cooks concoct a seemingly endless variety of dishes, whether from 300-year-old court recipes, the latest in Euro-Thai fusion or simple dishes guided by seasonal and regional necessity.

You will quickly discover that eating is one of life's great pleasures in Thailand. The average Thai takes time out to eat, not three times per day, but four or five. Sitting down at a roadside *rót khěn* (vendor cart) after an evening of cinema or nightclubbing, a Thai may barely have finished one steaming bowl of noodles before ordering a second round, just to revel in the experience a little longer.

Varieties of Thai rice
on sale
JERRY ALEXANDER

STAPLES & SPECIALITIES
Rice
Thailand has led the world in rice exports since the 1960s, and the quality of Thai rice, according to many discerning Asians, is considered the best in the world. Thailand's *khâo hǎwm málí* (jasmine rice) is so coveted that there is a steady underground business in smuggling bags of the fragrant grain to neighbouring countries.

Rice is so central to Thai food culture that the most common term for 'eat' is *kin khâo* (literally, 'consume rice') and one of the most common greetings is *'Kin khâo láew rěu yang?'* (Have you consumed rice yet?). All the dishes eaten with rice – whether curries, stirfries or soups – are simply classified as *kàp khâo* (with rice). Only two dishes using rice as a principal ingredient are common in Thailand, *khâo phàt* (fried rice) and *khâo mòk kài* (chicken biryani), neither of which is native to Thailand.

Bangkok's Khao San Rd
is a noodle-lover's
paradise

JULIET COOMBE

Noodles

You'll find four basic kinds of noodle in Thailand. Hardly surprising, given the Thai fixation on rice, is the overwhelming popularity of *kǔay-tǐaw,* made from pure rice flour mixed with water to form a paste which is then steamed to form wide, flat sheets. These are then folded and sliced into noodles of varying sizes.

The king of Thai noodledom, *kǔaytǐaw* comes as part of many dishes. The simplest, *kǔaytǐaw náam,* is noodles served in a bowl of plain chicken or beef stock along with bits of meat and pickled cabbage, with *phàk chii* (coriander leaf) as garnish. *Kǔaytǐaw phàt* involves the quick stirfrying of the noodles in a wok with sliced meat, *phàk kha-náa* (Chinese kale), soy sauce and various seasonings. Chilli-heads must give *kǔaytǐaw phàt khîi mao* (drunkard's fried noodles) a try. A favourite lunch or late-night snack, this spicy stirfry consists of wide rice noodles, fresh basil leaves, chicken or pork, seasonings and a healthy dose of fresh sliced chillies.

The most well-known *kǔaytǐaw* dish among foreigners is *kǔaytǐaw phàt thai* (*phàt thai* for short), a plate of thin rice noodles stirfried with dried or fresh shrimp, bean sprouts, fried tofu, egg and seasonings. On the edge of the plate the cook usually places little piles of ground peanuts and ground dried chilli, along with lime halves and a few stalks of spring onion, for self-seasoning.

Another kind of noodle, *khànǒm jiin,* is produced by pushing rice-flour paste through a sieve into boiling water, much the way Italian-style pasta is made. *Khànǒm jiin* is eaten doused with various curries.

The third genre of noodle, *bà-mìi,* is made from wheat flour and sometimes egg. It's yellowish in colour and round in shape, like yellow spaghetti. *Bà-mìi* is sold only in fresh bundles, and unlike both *kǔaytǐaw* and *khànǒm jiin,* it must be cooked immediately before serving.

Finally there's *wún-sên,* an almost clear noodle made from mung-bean starch and water. *Wún-sên* (literally, 'jelly thread') is used for only three dishes in Thailand: *yam wún-sên,* a hot and tangy salad made with lime juice, fresh sliced *phrík khîi nǔu* (mouse-dropping peppers), mushrooms, dried or fresh shrimp, ground pork and various seasonings; *wún-sên òp puu,* bean thread noodles baked in a lidded clay pot with crab and seasonings; and *kaeng jèut,* a bland, Chinese-influenced soup with ground pork, soft tofu and a few vegetables.

Preparing *kǔaytǐaw* for
the masses

JERRY ALEXANDER

Curries

In Thai, *kaeng* (it rhymes with the English 'gang') is often translated as 'curry' but actually describes any dish with a lot of liquid and can thus refer to soups (such as *kaeng jèut*) as well as the classic chilli-based curries such as *kaeng phèt* (spicy *kaeng*) for which Thai cuisine is famous. All chilli-based *kaeng* start as fresh – not powdered – ingredients that are smashed, pounded and ground in a stone mortar and pestle to form a thick, aromatic and extremely pungent paste. Typical ingredients include dried chilli, galangal (also known as Thai ginger), lemongrass, kaffir lime (peel, leaves or both), shallots, garlic, shrimp paste and salt. Green curries will add coriander seeds and a touch of cumin.

During cooking, most *kaeng* are blended in a heated pan with coconut cream, to which the chef adds the rest of the ingredients along with coconut milk to thin and flavour the *kaeng*. Some recipes omit coconut milk entirely to produce a particularly fiery *kaeng* known as *kaeng pàa* (forest curry).

Hot & Tangy Salads

Standing right alongside *kaeng* in terms of Thai-ness is the ubiquitous *yam*, a hot and tangy salad containing a blast of lime, chilli, fresh herbs and a choice of seafood, roast vegetables, noodles or meats. Thais prize *yam* dishes so much that they are often eaten on their own, without rice, before the meal has begun. On Thai menus, the *yam* section will often be the longest. The usual English menu translation is either 'Thai-style salad' or 'hot and sour salad'.

Lime juice provides the tang, while fresh chillies produce the heat. Other ingredients vary, but plenty of leafy vegetables and herbs are usually present, including lettuce (often lining the dish) and mint leaves. Lemongrass, shallots, kaffir lime leaves and Chinese celery may also come into play. Most *yam* are served at room temperature or just slightly warmed by any cooked ingredients.

Yam are the spiciest of all the Thai dishes, and *yam phrík chíi fáa* (spur chilli *yam*) is the hottest. A good *yam* dish to start sampling these dishes if you're not so chilli-tolerant is *yam wún-sên,* bean-thread noodles tossed with shrimp, ground pork, coriander leaf, lime juice and fresh sliced chillies.

Chillies at Pak Khlong Market, Bangkok

RICHARD I'ANSON

Ingredients for a Thai curry

JERRY ALEXANDER

Bounty from the Gulf of Thailand, Hua Hin

CHRIS MELLOR

Stirfries & Deep-Fries

The simplest dishes in the Thai culinary repertoire are stirfries (*phàt*), brought to Thailand by the Chinese, famous for being able to stirfry a whole banquet in a single wok. Despite stirfry's Chinese origins, *phàt* dishes are never served here with soy sauce as a condiment except in Chinese restaurants. Instead they come with *phrík náam plaa* (fish sauce with sliced chillies) on the side.

The list of Thai dishes that you can *phàt* (stirfry) is seemingly endless. Many are better classified as Chinese, such as *néua phàt náam-man hăwy* (beef in oyster sauce). Some are clearly Thai-Chinese hybrids, such as *kài phàt phrík khǐng*, in which chicken is stirfried with ginger, garlic and chillies – ingredients shared by both traditions – but seasoned with fish sauce. Also leaning towards the Thai side – if only because cashews are native to Thailand but not to China – is *kài phàt mét mámûang hǐmáphaan* (sliced chicken stirfried in dried chillies and cashews), a favourite with *faràng* tourists.

Thâwt (deep-frying in oil) is generally reserved for snacks like *klûay thâwt* (fried bananas) or *pàw-pía* (egg rolls). One exception is *plaa thâwt* (fried fish), which is the most common way you'll find any fish prepared. A very few dishes require ingredients to be dipped in batter and then deep-fried, such as *kài thâwt* (fried chicken) and *kûng chúp pâeng thâwt* (batter-fried shrimp).

Soups

Thai soups fall into two broad categories, *tôm yam* and *kaeng jèut*, that are worlds apart in terms of seasonings. *Tôm yam* is almost always made with seafood, though chicken may also be used. It's often translated on English menus as 'hot and sour Thai soup', although this often misleads non-Thais to relate the dish to Chinese hot-and-sour soup, which is thinner

A northern Thai village speciality, *yam phàk kum* contains galangal, lemongrass, dried chilli, Thai eggplant and pickled *phàk kum*, a local herb

JERRY ALEXANDER

in texture, milder and includes vinegar. *Tôm yam* is meant to be eaten with rice, not alone. The first swallow often leaves the uninitiated gasping for breath.

Lemongrass, kaffir lime peel and lime juice give *tôm yam* its characteristic tang. Fuelling the fire beneath *tôm yam*'s often velvety surface are fresh *phrík khîi núu* and sometimes a half-teaspoonful of *náam phrík phǎo* (a paste of dried chillies roasted with *kà-pì;* shrimp paste). Many cooks add galangal for extra fragrance. Coriander leaf garnish adds to both appearance and fragrance.

Kaeng jèut (bland soup) in contrast is a soothing broth seasoned with little more than soya or fish sauce and black pepper. Although the number of variations on *kaeng jèut* are seemingly endless, common ingredients include *wún-sên* (mung-bean starch noodles), *tâo hûu* (tofu), *hǔa chai tháo* (Chinese radish) and *mǔu sàp* (ground pork).

Fruit

Thais consume fruit at every opportunity. Common fruits that are in season all year include *máphráo* (coconut), *faràng* (guava), *khànǔn* (jackfruit), *mákhǎam* (tamarind), *sôm khǐaw-wǎan* (mandarin orange), *sôm oh* (pomelo), *málákaw* (papaya), *taeng moh* (watermelon) and *sàppàrót* (pineapple). All are most commonly eaten fresh, and sometimes dipped in a mixture of salt, sugar and ground chilli.

No discussion of Thai fruit is complete without a mention of *thúrian* (durian), dubbed the king of fruits by most Southeast Asians yet despised by many foreigners. A member of the aptly named *Bombacaceae* family, this heavy, spiked orb resembles an ancient piece of medieval weaponry. Inside the thick-shell lie five sections of plump, buttery and pungent flesh. The durian's ammonia-like aroma is so strong that many hotels in Thailand, as well as Thai Airways International, ban the fruit from their premises.

Durian, a taste experience

JULIET COOMBE

Guarding the watermelons

JERRY ALEXANDER

Sweets for sale at
Banglamphu Market,
Bangkok

RICHARD I'ANSON

Sweets

English-language Thai menus often print a section called 'Desserts', even though the concept doesn't exist in Thai cuisine, nor is there a translation for the word. The closest equivalent, *khǎwng wǎan,* simply means 'sweet stuff' and refers to all foods whose primary flavour characteristic is sweetness. Sweets mostly work their way into the daily Thai diet in the form of between-meal snacks, hence you won't find *khǎwng wǎan* in a traditional Thai restaurant at all. Instead they're prepared and sold by market or street vendors.

Ingredients for many Thai sweets include grated coconut, coconut milk, rice flour, cooked sticky rice, tapioca, mung-bean starch, boiled taro and fruits. For added texture and crunch, some may also contain fresh corn kernels, sugar-palm kernels, lotus seeds, cooked black beans and chopped water chestnuts. Egg yolks are a popular ingredient for *khǎwng wǎan* – including the ubiquitous *fǎwy thawng* (literally, 'golden threads') – probably influenced by Portuguese desserts and pastries introduced during the early Ayuthaya era.

Thai sweets similar to the European concept of 'sweet pastry' are called *khànǒm.* Here again the kitchen-astute Portuguese were influential. Probably the most popular *khànǒm* are bite-size items wrapped in banana or pandan leaves, especially *khâo tôm kà-thí* and *khâo tôm mát.* Both consist of sticky rice grains steamed with *kà-thí* (coconut milk) inside a banana-leaf wrapper to form a solid almost taffy-like mass.

Fruit vendor's stall,
Bangkok

JOHN HAY

TRAVEL YOUR TASTEBUDS

Every tourist eats the stirfries, the grilled chicken, the mild *phánaeng* curry, but if you want to say you *really* ate Thai, then you must dabble in at least a few of the following.

- **kaeng phèt kài nàw mái** – chicken and bamboo-shoot curry, a working-class mainstay at *ráan khâo kaeng* (rice-and-curry shops)

- **kǔaytǐaw plaa** – rice noodles with fish balls (boiled ground-fish balls)

- **tôm yam pó tàek** – when you tire of *tôm yam kûng,* try *pó tàek* – 'broken fish trap' – a similar broth with the addition of basil and assorted seafood

- **mîang kham** – tiny chunks of lime, ginger and shallot, toasted grated coconut, roasted peanuts, fresh sliced chillies and dried shrimp, all wrapped up in a wild-tea leaf with sweet-sour tamarind sauce. One bite, and it shouts 'Thailand'.

- **náam phrík plaa thuu** – chilli dip made with shrimp paste and served with steamed mackerel and parboiled vegetables – one of the main Thai staples but one that few foreigners dare try

- **plaa dàet diaw** – 'once-sunned fish', a whole fish split down the middle, sun-dried for half a day, then deep-fried and served with a mango-peanut sauce

- **sǎngkhayǎa fák thawng** – creamy egg-and-palm-sugar custard baked inside a Thai pumpkin

- **yam hǔa plii** – spicy banana-flower salad

Only If You Dare:

- **yam phrík chíi fáa** – hot and tangy salad centred on fresh *phrík chíi fáa* (very spicy 'sky-pointing' chillies)

DRINKS
Coffee & Tea

Thais are big coffee drinkers, and good-quality *arabica* and *robusta* are cultivated in hilly areas of northern and southern Thailand. The traditional filtering system is nothing more than a narrow cloth bag attached to a steel handle. The bag is filled with ground coffee, and hot water poured through producing *kaafae thŭng* (bag coffee) or *kaafae boh-raan* (traditional coffee). The usual *kaafae thŭng* is served in a glass, mixed with sugar and sweetened with condensed milk – if you don't want either, be sure to specify *kaafae dam* (black coffee) followed with *mâi sài náam taan* (without sugar).

Black tea, both local and imported, is available at the same places that serve real coffee. *Chaa thai* derives its characteristic orange-red colour from ground tamarind seed added after curing. *Chaa ráwn* (hot tea) will almost always be with condensed milk and sugar, so specify if you want black tea. Chinese-style tea is *náam chaa*. *Chaa yen* is a tall glass of Thai iced tea with sugar and condensed milk. Without milk, and sometimes with a slice of lime, ask for *chaa dam yan sài má-nao* (chilled black tea).

Fruit Drinks & Soft Drinks

The all-purpose term for fruit juice is *náam* (water/juice) *phŏn-lá-mái* (fruit). When a blender or extractor is used, you've got *náam khán* (squeezed juice), hence *náam sàppàrót khán* is fresh-squeezed pineapple juice. *Náam âwy* (sugar cane juice) is a Thai favourite and a very refreshing accompaniment to *kaeng* dishes. A similar juice from the sugar palm, *náam taan sòt,* is also very good and both are full of vitamins and minerals. Mixed fruit blended with ice is *náam pon* (literally, 'mixed juice') as in *náam málákaw pon,* a papaya shake.

Beer

Advertised with such slogans as *pràthêht rao, bia rao* (Our Land, Our Beer), the Singha label is considered the quintessential 'Thai' beer by *faràng* and locals alike. Pronounced *sĭng* (not 'sing-ha'), it claims about half the domestic market, and has an alcohol content of 6%. Singha is sold in bottles and cans, and is also available on tap as *bia sòt* (draught beer) in many Bangkok pubs and restaurants.

Beer Chang, matches the hoppy taste of Singha but pumps the alcohol content up to 7%. It is significantly cheaper than Singha, offering more bang per baht. Singha's cheaper brand, Leo, costs only slightly more than Beer Chang but is similarly high in alcohol. You'll find other, even cheaper, Thai beers in supermarkets, but rarely in restaurants.

Dutch-licensed but Thailand-brewed Heineken and Singapore's Tiger brand are also popular selections.

Rice Whisky

Rice whisky is a favourite of the working class in Bangkok since it's more affordable than beer. Most rice whiskies are mixed with distilled sugarcane spirits and thus have a sharp, sweet taste not unlike rum, with an alcohol content of 35%. The most famous brand, Mekong (pronounced *mâe khŏng*), costs around 120B for a large bottle *(klom)* or 60B for the flask-sized bottle *(baen)*. More popular nowadays is the slightly more expensive Sang Som.

More-expensive Thai whiskies produced from barley and appealing to the can't-afford-Johnnie-Walker-yet set include Blue Eagle, 100 Pipers and Spey Royal, each with 40% alcohol content. These come in shiny boxes, much like the expensive imported whiskies they're imitating.

Singha beer was first brewed to an original recipe in 1934

JERRY ALEXANDER

Fresh fruit-juice stall on Th Phra Athit, Bangkok

RICHARD I'ANSON

Grilled mackerel

PETER HINES

WHERE TO EAT & DRINK

All restaurants, large and small, are referred to by the single Thai term *ráan aahǎan* (literally 'food shop'). Most consist of a garage-like space in a *hâwng tǎew* (row house), with a simple collection of utilitarian tables and chairs lined up along the walls. Decoration may be limited to a few Singha or Sang Som posters, or something more incongruous such as a faded picture of the Swiss Alps. Fluorescent lighting – cheap and cool – is the norm. Such restaurants typically specialise in a single cuisine, whether local or regional.

The more generic *ráan aahǎan taam sàng* (food-to-order shop) can often be recognised by one or more tall refrigerated cabinets with clear glass windows at the front of the shop. These will be filled with many of the raw ingredients – Chinese kale, tomatoes, chopped pork, fresh or dried fish, noodles, eggplant, spring onions – for a standard repertoire of Thai and Chinese dishes. As the name of the eatery implies, the cooks attempt to prepare any dish you can name, including any kind of rice or noodle dish as well as more complex multidish meals. Most of the standard Thai dishes are available, including those in the *tôm yam, yam* and *phàt* categories.

More upmarket restaurants – offering printed menus with English – are usually only found in provincial capitals or tourist resorts. Average Thais prefer to order their favourite dishes without referring to a menu at all, so these more-expensive restaurants only cater to an upper-class clientele with more international tastes. It is in such restaurants that you will find air-conditioning, tablecloths and individual soup bowls.

Night Markets

Dried fish at a night market in Bangkok

JERRY ALEXANDER

One of the simplest and most pleasurable venues for dining out in Thailand is the night market, which can vary from a small cluster of metal tables and chairs alongside the road to more elaborate affairs that take up

whole city blocks. What they all have in common are a conglomeration of *rót khĕn* (vendor carts) whose owners have decided that a particular intersection or unused urban lot makes an ideal location to set up their mobile kitchens.

There are two types, firstly the *tàlàat yen* (evening market), which sets up just before sunset and stays open till around 9pm or 10pm – possibly later in large cities. The second is the *tàlàat tôh rûng* (open-until-dawn market), which begins doing business around 11pm and keeps going until sunrise. Typical places to look for them include in front of day markets, next to bus or train stations and at busy intersections.

VEGETARIANS & VEGANS

The number of vegetarian restaurants in Thailand is increasing, thanks largely to Bangkok's ex-Governor, Chamlong Srimuang, whose strict vegetarianism inspired a nonprofit chain of *ráan aahăan mangsàwírát* (vegetarian restaurants) in Bangkok and several provincial capitals. The food at these restaurants is usually served buffet-style and is very inexpensive. Dishes are almost always 100% vegan, that is no meat, poultry, fish, dairy or egg products.

Cooking *phàk bûng fai daeng* (red fire-water spinach)

JOE CUMMINGS

Chinese restaurants are also a good bet since many Chinese Buddhists eat vegetarian food during Buddhist festivals. Other easy, though less common, venues for vegetarian meals include Indian restaurants, which usually feature a vegetarian section on the menu.

The phrase 'I'm vegetarian' in Thai is *phŏm kin jeh* (for men) or *dì-chăn kin jeh* (for women). Loosely translated this means 'I eat only vegetarian food', which includes no eggs and no dairy products – in other words, total vegan.

HABITS & CUSTOMS

Thais extend a hand towards a bowl of noodles, a plate of rice or a banana leaf–wrapped snack with amazing frequency. There are no 'typical' times for meals, though the customary noon to 1pm lunch break tends to cluster diners in local restaurants at that hour.

Outdoor diners on Tha Chang, Ratanakosin, Bangkok

RICHARD I'ANSON

Coconut sweets, Th
Chakrawat in Bangkok's
Chinatown

RICHARD I'ANSON

Ready-to-use ingredients,
Tha Chang, Ratanakosin,
Bangkok

RICHARD I'ANSON

Nor are certain genres of food restricted to certain times of day. Practically anything can be eaten first thing in the morning, whether it's sweet, salty or chilli-ridden. *Khâo kaeng* (curry over rice) is a very popular morning meal, as are *khâo mǔu daeng* (red pork over rice) and *khâo man kài* (sliced steamed chicken cooked in chicken broth and garlic and served over rice).

Thais tend to avoid eating alone. Dining with others is always preferred from the Thai perspective because it means everyone has a chance to sample several dishes. A single diner usually sticks to one-plate dishes such as fried rice or curry over rice.

Originally Thai food was eaten with the fingers, and it still is in northern and northeastern Thailand, and for certain foods such as *khâo niaw* (sticky rice). In the early 1900s, restaurateurs began setting their tables with fork and spoon to affect a 'royal' setting, and it wasn't long before fork-and-spoon dining became the norm in Bangkok and later throughout the kingdom.

To most Thais, pushing a fork into one's mouth is almost as uncouth as putting a knife in the mouth in Western countries. Thais use forks instead to steer food onto the spoon.

Tà-kìap (chopsticks) are reserved for dining in Chinese restaurants or for eating Chinese noodle dishes, so don't ask for them in a Thai restaurant. Noodle soups are eaten with a spoon in the left hand (for spooning up the broth) and chopsticks in the right.

Whether at home or in a restaurant, Thai meals are always served 'family-style', that is from common serving platters. Traditionally, the party orders one of each kind of dish, perhaps a curry, a fish, a stirfry, a *yam*, a vegetable dish and a soup, taking care to balance cool and hot, sour and sweet, salty and plain. One dish is generally large enough for two people. One or two extras may be ordered for a large party.

When serving yourself from a common platter, put no more than one spoonful onto your plate at a time. It's customary at the start of a shared meal to eat a spoonful of plain rice first – a gesture that recognises rice as the most important part of the meal. Sometimes serving spoons are provided. If not, you simply dig in with your own spoon.

For the most part, *tôm yam* and other soups aren't served in individual bowls except in tourist restaurants or in more elegant restaurants. You serve yourself from the common bowl, spooning broth and ingredients over your rice or into your own spoon.

Don't pick up a serving plate to serve yourself. Proper Thai food etiquette means leaving the plate on the tabletop and reaching over to it with your spoon, even if it means stretching your arm across the table. If you can't reach the platter at all, it's best to hand your plate to someone near the serving platter, who can then place some food on your plate. Most Thais will do this automatically if they notice you're out of platter range.

Always leave some food on the serving platters as well as on your plate. To clean your plate and leave nothing on the serving platters says to your hosts 'you didn't feed me enough'. This is why Thais tend to over-order at social occasions – the more food is left, the more generous the host appears.

COOKING COURSES
See p726 for information on studying the art of Thai cuisine.

EAT YOUR WORDS
While some restaurants in Thailand may have English-language menus, most will not. So you'll need to have some stock phrases on hand to tell *phàt thai* from *khâo phàt*. For pronunciation guidelines see p772.

Useful Phrases
EATING OUT

I'd like...	*khǎw...*
Not too spicy please.	*khǎw mâi phèt mâak*
glass	*kâew*
cup	*thûay*
fork	*sâwm*
spoon	*cháwn*
plate	*jaan plào*
napkin	*kràdàat chét pàak*
Thank you, that was delicious.	*khàwp khun mâak, aràwy mâak*
Bring the bill, please.	*khǎw bin*

VEGETARIAN & SPECIAL MEALS

Does this dish have meat?	*aahǎan jaan níi sài néua sàt mǎi*
I'm allergic to...	*phǒm/di-chǎn pháe...*
I don't eat...	*phǒm/di-chǎn kin... mâi dâi*
meat	*néua sàt*
chicken	*kài*
fish	*plaa*
seafood	*aahǎan tháleh*
pork	*mǔu*
Please don't use fish sauce.	*karúnaa mâi sài náam plaa*
Please don't use MSG.	*karúnaa mâi sài phǒng chuu-rót*
Don't add salt.	*mâi sài kleua*

Rambutan, the red hairy-skinned, lycheelike fruit

JULIET COOMBE

Food Glossary
Staples

ah-hǎan thá-leh	อาหารทะเล	seafood
jóhk	โจ๊ก	thick rice soup or congee
kài	ไก่	chicken
khài	ไข่	egg
khànǒm	ขนม	Thai sweets
khâo jâo	ข้าวเจ้า	white rice
khâo klâwng	ข้าวกล้อง	brown rice
khâo phàt	ข้าวผัด	fried rice
khâo plào	ข้าวเปล่า	plain rice
khâo	ข้าว	rice
kǔaytǐaw	ก๋วยเตี๋ยว	rice noodles
kûng	กุ้ง	variety of shrimp, prawn and lobster
mǔu	หมู	pork
néua	เนื้อ	beef, meat
pèt yâang	เป็ดย่าง	roast duck
pèt	เป็ด	duck
plaa mèuk	ปลาหมึก	squid; cuttlefish (generic)
plaa	ปลา	fish
puu	ปู	crab
thâwt man plaa	ทอดมันปลา	fried fish cake

Corn on the cob from an outdoor grill

JERRY ALEXANDER

Vegetables

hèt	เห็ด	mushrooms
mákhěua	มะเขือ	eggplant/aubergine
mákhěua-thêht	มะเขือเทศ	tomatoes
man faràng	มันฝรั่ง	potatoes
phàk	ผัก	vegetables

tâo-hûu	เต้าหู้	tofu
thùa ngâwk	ถั่วงอก	mung bean sprouts
thùa pòn	ถั่วป่น	ground peanuts
thùa thâwt	ถั่วทอด	fried peanuts

Condiments

khǐng	ขิง	ginger, as known in the West
kleua	เกลือ	salt
náam jîm	น้ำจิ้ม	dipping sauces
náam plaa	น้ำปลา	fish sauce
náam sii-íw	น้ำซีอิ๊ว	soy sauce
náam sôm sǎai chuu	น้ำส้มสายชู	vinegar
náamtaan	น้ำตาล	sugar
phàk chii	ผักชี	coriander leaf
phǒng chuu rót	ผงชูรส	monosodium glutamate
phrík	พริก	chilli
sàránàe	สะระแหน่	mint
thùa fàk yao	ถั่วฝักยาว	long bean, yard bean, green bean
thùa lěuang	ถั่วเหลือง	soybean

Fruit

phǒn-lá-mái	ผลไม้	fruit
faràng	ฝรั่ง	guava
klûay	กล้วย	banana
mákhǎam	มะขาม	tamarind
málákaw	มะละกอ	papaya
mámûang	มะม่วง	mango
mánao	มะนาว	lime
mang-khút	มังคุด	mangosteen
máphráo	มะพร้าว	coconut
ngáw	เงาะ	rambutan
taeng moh	แตงโม	watermelon

Peanuts on sale in Chiang Mai

JERRY ALEXANDER

Roadside vegetable stall

JERRY ALEXANDER

Drinks

bia	เบียร์	beer
chaa jiin	ชาจีน	Chinese tea
chaa	ชา	tea
kaafae	กาแฟ	coffee
khrêuang dèum	เครื่องดื่ม	beverages
náam âwy	น้ำอ้อย	raw, lumpy cane sugar/sugar cane juice
náam dèum	น้ำดื่ม	drinking water
náam khǎeng	น้ำแข็ง	ice
náam sôm	น้ำส้ม	orange juice
náam tâo-hûu	น้ำเต้าหู้	soy milk
náam	น้ำ	water or juice
nom jèut	นมจืด	milk

Methods of Preparation

đip	ดิบ	raw
nêung	นึ่ง	steamed
phǎo	เผา	grilled (chillies, vegetables, fish & shrimp only)
phàt	ผัด	stirfried
tôm	ต้ม	boiled
thâwt	ทอด	deep fried
yâang	ย่าง	grilled

The Culture

THE NATIONAL PSYCHE
Traditional Culture

Thais don't have a word that corresponds with the English term 'culture'. The nearest equivalent, *wáthánátham*, emphasises fine arts and ceremonies. Ask Thais to define their culture and they'll often talk about architecture, food, dance and festivals. Religion – a big Western influence on culture is considered more or less separate from *wáthánátham*.

When outsiders speak of 'Thai culture' they're referring to behavioural modes rooted in the history of Tai migration throughout Southeast Asia, with commonalities shared by the Lao people of neighbouring Laos, the Shan of northeastern Myanmar (Burma) and the numerous tribal Tais found in isolated pockets from Dien Bien Phu (Vietnam), all the way to Assam (India). These modes are most prevalent in Thailand, the largest of the Tai homelands.

The most 'modernised' of the existing Tai societies, the cultural underpinnings are evident in virtually every facet of life. 'Westernised' aspects (eg the wearing of trousers instead of a *phâakhamáa* (sarong), the presence of automobiles, cinemas and 7-Eleven stores) show how Thailand has adopted and adapted elements from other cultures. Nevertheless there are certain aspects of Thai society that virtually everyone recognises as 'Thai'.

SÀNÙK

The Thai word *sànùk* means 'fun' and anything worth doing – even work – should have an element of *sànùk*, otherwise it automatically becomes drudgery. This doesn't mean Thais don't want to work, just that they approach tasks with a sense of playfulness. Nothing condemns an activity more than *mâi sànùk* – 'not fun'. While you're in Thailand, sit down beside a rice field and watch workers planting, transplanting or harvesting rice. That it's back-breaking labour is obvious, but there's generally lots of *sànùk* – flirtation between the sexes, singing, trading insults and cracking jokes. The famous Thai smile comes partially out of this desire to make *sànùk*.

SAVING FACE

Thais believe strongly in the concept of saving face, ie avoiding confrontation and endeavouring not to embarrass yourself or other people (except when it's *sànùk* to do so). The ideal face-saver doesn't bring up negative topics in conversation, and when they notice stress in another's life, they usually won't say anything unless that person asks for help. Laughing at minor accidents – such as when someone trips and falls down – may seem callous but it's really just an attempt to save face on behalf of the person undergoing the mishap. This is another source of the Thai smile – it's the best possible face for almost any situation.

Talking loudly is perceived as rude by cultured Thais, whatever the situation. When encounters take a turn for the worse, try to refrain from getting angry – it won't help matters, since losing your temper means a loss of face for everyone present.

STATUS & OBLIGATION

All relationships in traditional Thai society – and those in the modern Thai milieu as well – are governed by connections between *phûu yài*

The Vanishing Face of Thailand: Folk Arts and Folk Culture (1997) is an anthology of journalist Suthon Sukphisit's series of articles for the *Bangkok Post*, focusing on disappearing local craftsmanship and traditions.

Letters from Thailand (1969), by Botan and translated by Susan Fulop Kepner, provides penetrating insights into Thai ways through letters from a Chinese immigrant to his family in China.

Mekhong Full Moon Party (2002; Jira Malikul) is an entertaining film that burrows deep into the Thai cultural psyche, using the legend of Nong Khai's famous *naga* lights (see p478) as a springboard for juxtaposing folk beliefs, modern science and Thai Buddhism in a rural Isan community.

('big person' or senior) and *phûu náwy* ('little person' or junior). *Phûu náwy* defer to *phûu yài* following simple lines of social rank defined by age, wealth, status and personal and political power. Some examples of 'automatic' *phûu yài* status include adults (versus children), bosses (versus employees), elder classmates (versus younger classmates), elder siblings (versus younger siblings), teachers (versus pupils), members of the military (versus civilians), Thais (versus non-Thais) and so on.

Although this tendency towards social ranking is to some degree shared by many societies around the world, the Thai twist lies in the set of mutual obligations linking *phûu yài* to *phûu náwy*. *Phûu náwy* are supposed to show a degree of obedience and respect (together these concepts are covered by the single Thai term *kreng jai*) towards *phûu yài*, but in return *phûu yài* are obligated to care for or 'sponsor' the *phûu náwy* they have frequent contact with. In such relationships *phûu náwy* can, for example, ask *phûu yài* for favours involving money or job access. *Phûu yài* reaffirm their rank by granting requests when possible; to refuse would be to risk a loss of face and status.

Age is a large determinant where other factors are absent or weak. In such cases the terms *phîi* (elder sibling) and *náwng* (younger sibling) apply more than *phûu yài* and *phûu náwy*, although the intertwined obligations remain the same. Even people unrelated by blood quickly establish who's *phîi* and who's *náwng*. This is why one of the first questions Thais ask new acquaintances is 'How old are you?'.

When dining, touring or entertaining, the *phûu yài* always picks up the tab; if a group is involved, the person with the most social rank pays the bill for everyone, even if it empties his or her wallet. For a *phûu náwy* to try and pay would risk loss of face.

Money plays a large role in defining *phûu yài* status in most situations. A person who turned out to be successful in his or her post-school career would never think of allowing an ex-classmate of lesser success (even if they were once on an equal social footing) to pay the bill. Likewise a young, successful executive will pay an older person's way in spite of the age difference.

The novel *Patpong Sisters: An American Woman's View of the Bangkok Sex World* (1994), by Cleo Odzer, about an anthropologist conducting research on Thai women working in the Patpong red-light district, comes to the unique conclusion that prostitution is empowering work for women who grow up in Thailand with few other employment possibilities.

The implication is that whatever wealth you come into is to be shared, at least partially, with those less fortunate. This doesn't apply to strangers – but always comes into play with friends and relatives.

LIFESTYLE

Tune in to any Thai TV channel around 8pm and let soap opera plots draw a rough outline of the Thai story. Most series are set in the capital and although they are hardly realistic – the men are always handsome, the women beautiful, their automobiles are spotless – the plotlines are propped up by Thai realities. A young Thai Isan girl from the northeastern countryside takes a cleaning job in a wealthy Bangkok household, and the resulting weekly culture clashes keep Thai viewers glued to the screen. In another a college student argues with his father, a *khâa râatchákaan* (government civil servant), over whether he should spend a Saturday afternoon at a fashionable shopping area notorious for tattoo parlours, punk hair salons and the abundance of unaccompanied girls in revealing spaghetti-strap tops.

Individual lifestyles vary tremendously according to family background and income. If you could sneak a peek at what Thais eat for breakfast, you'd have a fighting chance at guessing both. *Khâo tôm phúi*, an array of small dishes of dried fish, peanuts and pickled vegetables eaten with hot rice soup, indicates probable Chinese ancestry. Add a plate of pricey sweet cured sausage and they're middle-class Chinese Thai. Spot a bowl of steaming *kaeng khîaw-wǎan* (sweet-green curry) or *kaeng phèt* (Thai red curry) over rice and it's likely your diner comes from mostly Thai genes, and prefers a basic, economic diet. The same Thai choosing ham, eggs and toast, chased with espresso, has money and has probably travelled abroad. Meanwhile a *thai pàk tâi* in southern Thailand might be digging into *khâo yam*, a spicy salad of rice, shaved lemongrass, toasted coconut and tamarind sauce.

Walk the streets early in the morning, and you'll catch the flash of shaved heads bobbing above bright ochre robes, as monks engage in *bindabàat*, the daily house-to-house alms food-gathering. Thai men are expected to shave their heads and don monastic robes at least once in their lives. Some enter the monkhood twice, first as 10-vow novices in their pre-teen years and again as fully ordained, 227-vow monks after the age of 20.

Green-hued onion domes looming over lower rooftops belong to mosques and mark the neighbourhood as Muslim, while brightly painted and ornately carved cement spires indicate a Hindu temple. A handful of steepled Christian churches, including a few historic ones, have taken root over the centuries in Chanthaburi and other places near the borders of former French Indochina – Cambodia and Laos – as well as in Bangkok. In urban centres, large round doorways topped with heavily inscribed Chinese characters and flanked by red paper lanterns mark the location of *sǎan jâo*, Chinese temples dedicated to the worship of Buddhist, Taoist and Confucian deities.

Thai royal ceremonies remain almost exclusively the domain of one of the most ancient religious traditions still functioning in the kingdom, Brahmanism. White-robed, topknotted priests of Indian descent keep alive an arcane collection of rituals that, it is believed, must be performed regularly to sustain the three pillars of Thai nationhood, namely sovereignty, religion and the monarchy. Such rituals are performed regularly at a complex of shrines near Wat Suthat in Bangkok.

Animism predated the arrival of all other religions in Thailand and still plays an important role in the everyday life of most residents who believe that *phrá phuum* (guardian spirits) inhabit rivers, canals, trees and other natural features. The Thais build shrines to house the displaced spirits. These dollhouse-like structures perch on wood or cement pillars next to their homes and receive daily offerings of rice, fruit, flowers and water. Peek inside the smaller, more modest spirit homes and you'll typically see a collection of ceramic or plastic figurines representing the property's guardian spirits.

Larger, more-elaborate spirit shrines stand alongside hotels and office buildings and may contain bronze images of Brahma or Shiva. Day and night you'll see Thais kneeling before such shrines to offer flowers, incense and candles, and to pray for favours from these Indian 'spirit kings' (see p68).

One in 10 citizens lives and works in Bangkok and some 60% of the country's wealth is concentrated here. The legal minimum daily wage in Bangkok and the adjacent provinces of Samut Prakan, Samut Sakhon, Pathum Thani, Nonthaburi and Nakhon Pathom amounted to 170B (US$4.50) in 2004, roughly 35B higher than the rest of Thailand.

A typical civil servant at an entry-level government job earns around 7000B per month, but with promotions and extra job training may earn up to 15,000B. In the private sector an office worker starts at about the same level but will receive quicker pay raises.

Child of the North-East (Luk Isan) (1983; Wichit Khunawut) follows the ups and downs of a farming family living in drought-ridden Isan; it became one of the first films to offer urban Thais an understanding of the hardships endured in the country.

www.cs.ait.ac.th/wutt /wutt.html for background on Thailand's royals.

In rural areas, female members of a family typically inherit the land and throughout Thailand women tend to control the family finances. Women constitute 55% of all enrolments in secondary and tertiary schools and about half of the workforce, outranking many countries in both categories. In economics, academia and health services, women hold most of the administrative positions – 80% of all Thai dentists are female.

So much for the good news. Although women generally fare well in education, the labour force and in rural land inheritance, their cultural

---

RESPONSIBLE TRAVEL

Thais are tolerant of most kinds of behaviour as long as it doesn't insult the two sacred cows of monarchy and religion. For information on how to behave when visiting hill tribes in Thailand, see p427.

Monarchy

Avoid disparaging remarks about anyone in the royal family. The monarchy is held in considerable respect in Thailand and visitors should also be respectful. The penalty for lese-majesty is seven years' imprisonment.

Although it's OK to criticise the Thai government and Thai culture openly, it's considered a grave insult to Thai nationhood, and to the monarchy, not to stand when you hear the national or royal anthems. Radio and TV stations in Thailand broadcast the national anthem daily at 8am and 6pm; in towns and villages this can be heard over public loudspeakers in the streets. The Thais stop whatever they're doing to stand during the anthem (except in Bangkok, where nobody can hear anything above the street noise) and visitors are expected to do likewise. The royal anthem is played just before films are shown in public cinemas; again, the audience always stands until it's over.

Temple Etiquette

Correct behaviour in temples entails several considerations, the most important of which is to dress neatly and to take your shoes off when you enter any building that contains a Buddha image. Buddha images are sacred objects, so don't pose in front of them for pictures and definitely do not clamber upon them.

Shorts or sleeveless shirts are considered improper dress for both men and women when visiting temples. Thai citizens wearing either would be turned away by monastic authorities, but except for the most sacred temples in the country (eg Wat Phra Kaew in Bangkok and Wat Phra That Doi Suthep near Chiang Mai), Thais are often too polite to refuse entry to improperly clad foreigners. Some wat will offer trousers or long sarongs for rent so that tourists dressed in shorts may enter the compound.

Monks are not supposed to touch or be touched by women. If a woman wants to hand something to a monk, the object should be placed within reach of the monk or on the monk's 'receiving cloth', not handed directly to him. When sitting in a religious edifice, keep your feet pointed away from any Buddha images. The usual way to do this is to sit in the 'mermaid' pose in which your legs are folded to the side, with the feet pointing backwards.

Since most temples are maintained from the donations received, when you visit a temple please remember to make a contribution.

Social Gestures & Attitudes

Thee traditional greeting is with a prayer-like palms-together gesture known as a wâi. If someone wâi-s you, you should wâi back (unless wâi-ed by a child or serviceperson). Most urban Thais are familiar with the international-style handshake and will offer the same to a foreigner, although a wâi is always appreciated.

standing is less than that of men. An oft-repeated Thai saying reminds us that men form the front legs of the elephant, women the hind legs (at least they're pulling equal weight). Parts of some Buddhist temples may be off-limits to women, and when hanging laundry, the custom is always to place female underwear lower than men's!

Thailand's commercial sex industry actually caters far more to the local market (about 95%) than to foreign visitors. The infamous red-light districts that have perpetually captivated Western media attention are limited to a few areas of Bangkok, Pattaya and Phuket.

Thais are often addressed by their first name with the honorific *Khun* or other title preceding it. Other formal terms of address include *naai* (Mr) and *naang* (Miss or Mrs). Friends often use nicknames or kinship terms like *phîi* (elder sibling), *náwng* (younger sibling), *mâe* (mother) or *lung* (uncle), depending on the age difference.

A smile and a cheery *sàwàt-dii khráp/khâ* (the all-purpose Thai greeting) goes a long way towards calming the initial trepidation that locals may feel upon seeing a foreigner, whether in the city or the countryside.

Books and other written materials are given a special status over other secular objects. Hence you shouldn't slide books or documents across a table or counter-top, and never place them on the floor – use a chair if table space isn't available.

Feet & Head

The feet are the lowest part of the body (spiritually as well as physically) so don't point your feet at people or point at things with your feet. Don't prop your feet on chairs or tables while sitting. Never touch any part of someone else's body with your foot.

In the same context, the head is regarded as the highest part of the body, so don't touch Thais on the head (or ruffle their hair). If you touch someone's head accidentally, offer an immediate apology or you'll be perceived as very rude.

Don't sit on pillows meant as headrests, as this represents a variant of the taboo against head-touching.

Never step over someone, even on a crowded 3rd-class train where people are sitting or lying on the floor. Instead squeeze around them or ask them to move.

In rural areas and at temple fairs food is often eaten while seated on the floor; stepping over the food is a sure way to embarrass and offend your Thai hosts.

Shoes

These should not be worn inside Thai people's homes, nor in some guesthouses and shops. If you see a pile of shoes at or near the entrance, you should remove your shoes before entry. Several Thais have confided in us that they can't believe how oblivious some foreigners seem to be of this simple and obvious custom. To them wearing shoes indoors is disgusting and the behaviour of those who ignore the custom is nothing short of boorish.

Dress

Shorts (except knee-length walking shorts), sleeveless shirts, tank tops (singlets) and other beach-style attire are not appropriate dress for anything other than on the beach or at sporting events. Sandals or slip-on shoes are OK for almost any but the most formal occasions.

Thais would never dream of going abroad and wearing dirty clothes, so they are often shocked to see Westerners travelling around in clothes that apparently haven't been washed in weeks. If you keep up with your laundry, you'll receive much better treatment wherever you go.

Bathing nude at beaches in Thailand is illegal. Topless bathing for females is frowned upon in most places except on heavily-touristed islands such as Phuket, Samui and Samet. According to Thailand's National Parks Act, any woman who goes topless on a National Park beach (eg Ko Chang, Ko Phi-Phi, Ko Samet) is breaking the law.

Tolerance towards sex extends to homosexuality, and Thailand has a relatively open and liberal attitude towards gay orientations compared to most other nations.

POPULATION

Estimated at 65 million the population of Thailand is currently growing at just under 1% per annum, because of a vigorous nationwide family-planning campaign.

Over one-third of all Thais live in urban areas. Bangkok is by far the largest city with around six million people in the city proper, or eight million including the adjacent provinces.

Fun Bar Karaoke (1997) – this cinematic satire of Bangkok life received critical acclaim for its realistic depiction of modern urban living mixed with sage humour.

Ranking the nation's other cities by population depends on whether you look at the rather limited municipal districts *(thêtsàbaan)* or more realistic metropolitan districts *(meuang)*. Using the *meuang* measure, after Bangkok, the five most-populated cities in descending order (not counting the densely populated 'suburb' provinces of Samut Prakan and Nonthaburi, which rank second and third if considered separately from Bangkok) are: Udon Thani (population 244,000), Chonburi (221,000), Nakhon Ratchasima (210,000), Chiang Mai (196,000) and Hat Yai (191,000). Most other towns have populations below 100,000.

On the 2002 UN Human Development Index, Thailand received an overall ranking of 76, falling in the upper half of the UN-designated 'medium human development' range. The average life expectancy is 70 years, the highest in mainland Southeast Asia. It has a relatively youthful population; only about 12% are older than 50 years and 6% are aged over 65.

The Thai Majority

Some 75% of citizens are ethnic Thais, who can be divided into four groups: Central Thais, or Siamese, of the Chao Phraya Delta (the most densely populated region of the country); Thai Lao of northeastern Thailand; Thai Pak Tai of southern Thailand; and northern Thais. Each group speaks its own dialect and to a certain extent practises customs unique to its region. Politically and economically the Central Thais are the dominant group, although they barely outnumber the Thai Lao.

Small minority groups who speak Thai dialects include the Lao Song (Phetchaburi and Ratchaburi); the Phuan (Chaiyaphum, Phetchaburi, Prachinburi); the Phu Thai (Sakon Nakhon, Nakhon Phanom, Mukdahan); the Shan (Mae Hong Son), the Thai Khorat or Suay (Khorat); the Thai Lü (Nan, Chiang Rai); the Thai-Malay (Satun, Trang, Krabi) and the Yaw (Nakhon Phanom, Sakon Nakhon).

The Chinese

People of Chinese ancestry – second- or third-generation Hakka, Chao Zhou, Hainanese or Cantonese – make up 11% of the population. In northern Thailand there is also a substantial number of Hui-Chinese Muslims who emigrated from Yunnan in the late 19th century to avoid religious and ethnic persecution during the Qing dynasty.

Ethnic Chinese in Thailand probably enjoy better relations with the majority of the population than they do in any other country in Southeast Asia – although there was a brief spell of anti-Chinese sentiment during the reign of Rama VI (1910–25; see p37). Wealthy Chinese also introduced their daughters to the royal court as consorts, developing royal connections and adding a Chinese bloodline that extends to the current king.

Other Minorities

The second-largest ethnic minority are the Malays (3.5%), most of whom reside in the provinces of Songkhla, Yala, Pattani, Satun and Narathiwat. The remaining 10.5% of the population is divided among smaller non-Thai-speaking groups like the Vietnamese, Khmer, Mon, Semang (Sakai), Moken (*chao leh* sea gypsies), Htin, Mabri, Khamu and a variety of hill tribes.

A small number of Europeans and other non-Asians reside in Bangkok and the provinces.

Hill Tribes

Ethnic minorities in the mountainous regions of northern Thailand are often called 'hill tribes', or in Thai vernacular, *chao khǎo* (mountain people). Each hill tribe has its own language, customs, mode of dress and spiritual beliefs.

Most are of seminomadic origin, having from Tibet, Myanmar, China and Laos during the past 200 years or so. They are 'fourth world' people in that they belong neither to the main aligned powers nor to the developing nations. Rather, they have crossed and continue to cross national borders, often fleeing oppression by other cultures, without regard for recent nationhood.

Language and culture constitute the borders of their world. Some groups are caught between the 6th and 21st centuries, while others are gradually being assimilated into modern life. Many tribes people are also moving into lowland areas as montane lands become deforested by both traditional swidden (slash-and-burn) cultivation and illegal logging.

The Tribal Research Institute in Chiang Mai recognises 10 different hill tribes but there may be up to 20. The institute estimates the total hill-tribe population to be around 550,000.

The tribes most likely to be encountered by visitors fall into three main linguistic groups: the Tibeto-Burman (Lisu, Lahu, Akha), the Karenic (Karen, Kayah) and the Austro-Thai (Hmong, Mien). Within each group there may also be several subgroups, eg Blue Hmong, White Hmong; these names usually refer to predominant elements of clothing, that vary between the subgroups.

Hill tribes tend to have among the lowest standards of living. Although it's tempting to correlate this with traditional lifestyles, their situation is compounded, in most cases, by a lack of Thai citizenship. Without the latter, they don't have the right to own land or even to receive the minimum wage, plus they may be denied access to health care and schooling. In the last couple of decades, efforts to integrate hill tribes into Thai society via free education and the issuing of Thai identity cards may have improved the lot of a minority of tribes people. Of course the irony is that further Thai assimilation will threaten their cultural identities.

The Shan (Thai Yai, meaning 'large Thai') are not included in the following descriptions as they are not a hill-tribe group per se – they have permanent habitations and speak a language similar to Thai. The Shan are considered by Thai scholars to have been the original inhabitants of the area. Nevertheless, Shan villages are often common stops on hill-tribe treks.

The following comments on dress refer mostly to the females as hill-tribe men tend to dress like rural Thais. The population figures are taken from the most recent estimates.

www.hilltribe.org teaches you about the hill tribes of northern Thailand, and how to behave yourself in hill-tribe villages.

AKHA (I-KAW)

Pop: 48,500
Origin: Tibet
Present locations: Thailand, Laos, Myanmar, Yunnan
Economy: rice, corn, opium
Belief system: animism, with an emphasis on ancestor worship
Cultural characteristics: Headdress of beads, feathers and dangling silver ornaments. Villages are along mountain ridges or on steep slopes 1000m to 1400m in altitude. The well-known Akha Swing Ceremony takes place from mid-August to mid-September, between planting and harvest. The Akha are among the poorest of Thailand's ethnic minorities and tend to resist assimilation into the Thai mainstream. Like the Lahu, they often cultivate opium for their own use.

www.faqs.org/faqs
/thai/culture is the
newsgroup's informative
digest on Thai culture.

Akha houses are constructed of wood and bamboo, usually atop short wooden stilts and roofed with thick grass. At the entrance of every traditional Akha village stands a simple wooden gateway consisting of two vertical struts joined by a lintel. Akha shamans affix various charms made from bamboo strips to the gateway to prevent malevolent spirits from entering. Standing next to the gateway are crude wooden figures of a man and a woman, each bearing exaggerated sexual organs, in the belief that human sexuality is abhorrent to the spirit world.

LAHU (MUSOE)

Pop: 73,200
Origin: Tibet
Present locations: south China, Thailand, Myanmar
Economy: rice, corn, opium
Belief system: theistic animism (supreme deity is Geusha); some groups are Christian
Cultural characteristics: Black-and-red jackets with narrow skirts for women, bright green or blue-green baggy trousers for men. The Lahu tend to live at about 1000m altitude. There are five main groups – Red Lahu, Black Lahu, White Lahu, Yellow Lahu and Lahu Sheleh. Known to be excellent hunters, the Thai term for this tribe, *musoe,* is derived from a Burmese word meaning 'hunter'.

Houses are built of wood, bamboo and grass, and usually stand on short wooden posts. Intricately woven Lahu shoulder bags *(yâam)* are prized by collectors. Lahu food is probably the spiciest of all the cuisines.

LISU (LISAW)

Pop: 28,000
Origin: Tibet
Present locations: Thailand, Yunnan
Economy: rice, corn, opium, livestock
Belief system: animism with ancestor worship and spirit possession
Cultural characteristics: The women wear long multicoloured tunics over trousers and sometimes black turbans with tassels. Men wear baggy green or blue pants pegged in at the ankles. Premarital sex is said to be common (although some observers dispute this), along with freedom in choosing marital partners. Patrilineal clans have pan-tribal jurisdiction, which makes the Lisu unique among hill-tribe groups (most of which have power centred with either a shaman or a village headman). Lisu villages are usually in the mountains at about 1000m. Homes are built on the ground, and consist mostly of bamboo and grass. Older homes – today quite rare – may be made from mud brick or mud-and-bamboo thatch.

MIEN (YAO)
Pop: 40,300
Origin: central China
Present locations: Thailand, south China, Laos, Myanmar, Vietnam
Economy: rice, corn, opium
Belief system: animism with ancestor worship and Taoism
Cultural characteristics: Women wear trousers and black jackets with intricately embroidered patches and red fur-like collars, along with large dark blue or black turbans. The Mien are heavily influenced by Chinese traditions and they use Chinese characters to write their language. They settle near mountain springs at between 1000m and 1200m. Kinship is patrilineal and marriage is polygamous. They are highly skilled at crafts such as embroidery and silversmithing. Houses are built of wood or bamboo thatch, at ground level.

HMONG (MONG OR MAEW)
Pop: 124,000
Origin: south China
Present locations: south China, Thailand, Laos, Vietnam
Economy: rice, corn, opium
Belief system: animism
Cultural characteristics: Tribespeople wear simple black jackets and indigo or black baggy trousers (White Hmong) with striped borders or indigo skirts (Blue Hmong) and silver jewellery. Sashes may be worn around the waist, and embroidered aprons draped front and back. Most women wear their hair in a large bun. They usually live on mountain peaks or plateaus above 1000m. Houses, made of wood or thatch, sit on the ground. Kinship is patrilineal and polygamy is permitted. The Hmong are Thailand's second-largest hill-tribe group and are especially numerous in Chiang Mai Province.

KAREN (YANG OR KARIANG)
Pop: 322,000
Origin: Myanmar
Present locations: Thailand, Myanmar
Economy: rice, vegetables, livestock
Belief system: animism, Buddhism, Christianity, depending on the group
Cultural characteristics: Thickly woven V-neck tunics of various colours (unmarried women wear white). Kinship is matrilineal and marriage is monogamous. They tend to live in lowland valleys and practise crop rotation rather than swidden agriculture. Karen homes are built on low stilts or posts, with the roofs swooping quite low. There are four distinct Karen groups – the Skaw (White) Karen, Pwo Karen, Pa-O (Black) Karen and Kayah (Red) Karen. These groups number about half of all hill-tribe people.

EDUCATION
At 92.6%, Thailand's literacy rate is one of the highest in Southeast Asia. Free public schooling is compulsory for nine years. Although high value is placed on education as a way to achieve material success, at most levels the system itself tends to favour rote learning over independent thinking.

Thailand's public school system is organised around six years at the primary (*pràthŏm*) level, beginning at the age of six, followed by either three or six years of secondary (*mátháyom*) education. The three-year

Check out www.thailand
life.com – created by a
Thai student and now
one of the most comprehensive online collections
of Thai cultural vignettes.

course is for those planning to follow school with three to five years of trade school (wí-chaa-chîip), while the six-year course (mátháyom) is for students planning to continue at the tertiary (ùdom) level ie university. Less than nine years of formal education is the national norm.

Private and international schools for the foreign and local elite are found in Bangkok and Chiang Mai, and in the other large provincial cities. The country boasts over 30 public and five private universities, as well as numerous trade schools and technical colleges.

A teaching certificate may be obtained after attending a two-year, post-secondary programme at one of the many teachers' colleges. Two of Thailand's universities, Thammasat and Chulalongkorn, are considered to be among the top 50 in Asia.

SPORT
Muay Thai (Thai Boxing)

Almost anything goes in this martial sport, both in the ring and in the stands. If you don't mind the violence (in the ring), a Thai boxing match is worth attending for the pure spectacle – the wild musical accompaniment, the ceremonial beginning of each match and the frenzied betting throughout the stadium.

All surfaces of the body are considered fair targets and any part of the body, except the head, may be used to strike an opponent. Common blows include high kicks to the neck, elbow thrusts to the face and head, knee hooks to the ribs and low crescent kicks to the calf. Punching is considered the weakest of all blows and kicking merely a way to 'soften up' one's opponent; knee and elbow strikes are decisive in most matches.

A ram muay (boxing dance) precedes every match. This ceremony usually lasts about five minutes and expresses obeisance to the fighter's guru (khruu), as well as to the guardian spirit of Thai boxing. The complex series of gestures and movements is performed to the ringside musical accompaniment of Thai oboe (pìi) and percussion.

Fighters wear sacred headbands and armbands into the ring for good luck and divine protection. The headband is removed after the ram muay, but the armband, which contains a small Buddha image, is worn throughout the match.

With around 60,000 full-time boxers in Thailand, matches are staged at provincial rings and temple fairs all over the country. The most competitive are fought at two Bangkok stadiums, Ratchadamnoen and Lumphini.

For more on muay thai courses, see p727.

Kràbìi-Kràbawng

Another traditional martial art still practised in Thailand is kràbìi-kràbawng. It focuses on hand-held weapons, in particular the kràbìi (sword), phlawng (quarter-staff), ngáo (halberd), dàap sǎwng meu (a pair of swords held in each hand) and mái sun-sàwk (a pair of clubs). Although for most Thais kràbìi-kràbawng is a ritual artefact to be displayed during festivals or at tourist venues, the art is still solemnly taught according to a 400-year-old tradition handed down from Ayuthaya's Wat Phutthaisawan. The king's elite bodyguards are trained in kràbìi-kràbawng; many Thai cultural observers perceive it as a 'purer' tradition than muay thai.

Modern kràbìi-kràbawng matches are held within a marked circle, beginning with a wâi khruu ceremony and accompanied throughout by a musical ensemble. Thai-boxing techniques and judo-like throws are employed in conjunction with weapons techniques. Although sharpened

www.muaythai.com is one of the most comprehensive websites on traditional Thai kickboxing.

Ong Bak: Muay Thai Warrior (2003; Prachya Pinkaew) is a film that hearkens back to early Jackie Chan. A sacred Buddha is stolen from a Thai village, and one of the villagers uses his incredible muay thai skills to retrieve the image from Mafioso in Bangkok.

SIAMESE FOOTBALL

Football (soccer) is very popular throughout Thailand as both a spectator and participatory sport. In 2004 Prime Minister Thaksin Shinawatra tried to buy a majority share in Liverpool Football Club, but public aversion to the idea persuaded him not to follow through on the purchase.

---

weapons are used, the contestants refrain from striking their opponents – the winner is decided on the basis of stamina and the technical skill displayed.

Tàkrâw

Sometimes called Siamese football in old English texts, *tàkrâw* refers to games in which a woven rattan ball about 12cm in diameter is kicked around. The rattan (or sometimes plastic) ball itself is called a *lûuk tàkrâw*. Popular in several neighbouring countries, *tàkrâw* was introduced to the Southeast Asian Games by Thailand, and international championships tend to alternate between the Thais and Malaysians. The traditional way to play *tàkrâw* in Thailand is for players to stand in a circle (the size depending on the number of players) and simply try to keep the ball airborne by kicking it soccer-style. Points are scored for style, difficulty and variety of kicking manoeuvres.

A popular variation on *tàkrâw* – and the one used in intramural or international competitions – is played like volleyball, with a net, but with only the feet and head permitted to touch the ball. It's amazing to see the players perform aerial pirouettes, spiking the ball over the net with their feet. Another variation has players kicking the ball into a hoop 4.5m above the ground – basketball with feet, and no backboard!

MEDIA

Thailand's 1997 constitution guarantees freedom of the press, although the Royal Police Department reserves the power to suspend publishing licences for national security reasons. Newspaper editors nevertheless exercise self-censorship in certain realms, particularly with regard to the monarchy.

Thai press freedom reached its high watermark in the mid-1990s, while Chuan Leekpai's Democrat Party was in power. After the 1997 economic downturn and the ascension of Thaksin Shinawatra's Thai Rak Thai (TRT) Party, Thailand's media have found themselves increasingly subject to interference by political and financial interests.

Before the 2001 general election, Shin Corp, a telecommunications conglomerate owned by PM Thaksin's family, bought a controlling interest in iTV, Thailand's only independent TV station. Shortly thereafter the new board sacked 23 iTV journalists who complained that the station was presenting biased coverage of the election to favour Thaksin and TRT. Almost overnight, the station transformed from an independent, in-depth news channel to an entertainment channel with flimsy, pro-Thaksin news coverage.

The country's international reputation for press freedom took another serious dent in 2002 when two Western journalists were nearly expelled for reporting on a public address presented by the Thai king on his birthday, a portion of which was highly critical of PM Thaksin. In 2004 Veera Prateepchaikul, editor-in-chief of the *Bangkok Post*, lost his job due to direct pressure from board members with ties to Thaksin and TRT. Allegedly the latter were upset with *Post* criticism of the way in which the PM handled the 2003–04 bird flu crisis.

www.thaiworldview.com/culture/htm is a useful website with photos covering everything from housing to Thai TV and cinema.

Observers agree that Thai press freedom has reached it lowest ebb since the 1970s era of Thai military dictatorship, and will probably remain there as long as TRT are in power.

RELIGION
Buddhism

Approximately 95% of Thai are Theravada Buddhists. Scholars sometimes refer to the religion as Lankavamsa (Sinhalese lineage) Buddhism because this form of Buddhism came from Sri Lanka during the Sukhothai period. Prior to the arrival of Sinhalese monks in the 13th century, an Indian form of Theravada existed at the kingdom of Dvaravati (6th to 10th centuries), while Mahayana Buddhism of the Tantric variety was known in pockets of the northeast under Khmer control in the 10th and 11th centuries. One of the most complete selections of material on Theravada Buddhism available on the Web can be found at www.accesstoinsight.org.

Since the Sukhothai period (13th to 15th centuries), Thailand alone has maintained an unbroken canonical tradition and 'pure' ordination lineage. Ironically, when the ordination lineage in Sri Lanka broke down during the 18th century under Dutch persecution, it was Thailand that restored the *sangha* (Buddhist monastic community) there.

Theravada doctrine stresses the three principal aspects of existence: *dukkha* (stress, unsatisfactoriness, disease), *anicca* (impermanence, transience of all things) and *anatta* (insubstantiality or nonessentiality of reality – no permanent 'soul'). These three concepts, when 'discovered' by Siddhartha Gautama in the 6th century BC, were in direct contrast to the Hindu belief in an eternal, blissful self *(paramatman)*. Hence Buddhism was originally a 'heresy' against India's Brahmanic religion. Gautama, an Indian prince-turned-ascetic, subjected himself to many years of severe austerity before he realised that this was not the way to reach the end of suffering. He became known as Buddha, 'the enlightened' or 'the awakened' and as Gautama Buddha spoke of four noble truths that had the power to liberate any human being who could realise them.

The ultimate end of Theravada Buddhism is *nibbana* ('nirvana' in Sanskrit), which literally means the 'blowing out' or extinction of all grasping and thus of all suffering *(dukkha)*. Effectively, it is also an end to the cycle of rebirths (both moment-to-moment and life-to-life) that is existence.

In reality, most Thai Buddhists aim for rebirth in a 'better' existence rather than the supramundane goal of *nibbana*. By feeding monks, giving donations to temples and performing regular worship at the local wat they hope to improve their lot, acquiring enough merit (*puñña* in Pali; *bun* in Thai) to prevent or at least reduce their number of rebirths. The concept of rebirth is almost universally accepted in Thailand, even by non-Buddhists, and the Buddhist theory of karma is well expressed in the Thai proverb *tham dii, dâi dii; tham chûa, dâi chûa* (good actions bring good results; bad actions bring bad results).

All the Tiratana (Triple Gems) revered by Thai Buddhists – the Buddha, the Dhamma (the teachings) and the Sangha (the Buddhist community) – are quite visible in Thailand. The Buddha, in his myriad sculptural forms, is found on a high shelf in the lowliest roadside restaurants as well as in the lounges of expensive Bangkok hotels. The Dhamma is chanted morning and evening in every wat and taught to every Thai citizen in primary school. The Sangha is seen everywhere in the presence of orange-robed monks, especially in the early morning hours when they perform their alms rounds, in what has almost become a travel-guide cliché in motion.

Being Dharma: The Essence of the Buddha's Teachings (2001), by Ajahn Chah, is an inspiring and informative collection of talks on Buddhist practice given by the late Thai forest monk Ajahn Chan.

Thai Buddhist nun, Chatsumarn Kabilsingh, writes about what it means to be Thai, female and Buddhist in *Thai Women in Buddhism* (1991).

Thai Buddhism has no particular 'Sabbath' or day of the week when Thais are supposed to make temple visits. Instead, Thai Buddhists visit the wat whenever they feel like it, most often on *wan phrá* (excellent days), which occur every 7th or 8th day depending on phases of the moon. On such visits typical activities include: the traditional offering of lotus buds, incense and candles at various altars and bone reliquaries around the wat compound; the offering of food to the temple *sangha* (monks, nuns and lay residents – monks always eat first); meditating (individually or in groups); listening to monks chanting *suttas* or Buddhist discourse; and attending a *thêt* or Dhamma talk by the abbot or some other respected teacher.

What the Buddha Never Taught (1993), by Timothy Ward, is an amusing account of the author's sojourn at an international Buddhist monastery near Ubon Ratchathani.

MONKS & NUNS

Socially, every Thai male is expected to become a monk (*bhikkhu* in Pali; *phrá* or *phrá phíksù* in Thai) for a short period in his life, optimally between the time he finishes school and the time he starts a career or marries. Men or boys under 20 years of age may enter the *sangha* as novices (*samanera* in Pali; *naen* in Thai) – this is not unusual since a family earns great merit when one of its sons 'takes robe and bowl'. Traditionally, the length of time spent in the wat is three months, during the Buddhist lent *(phansăa)*, which begins in July and coincides with the rainy season. However, nowadays men may spend as little as a week to accrue merit as monks. There are about 32,000 monasteries in Thailand and 460,000 monks; many of these monks are ordained for a lifetime.

Monks who live in the city usually emphasise study of the Buddhist scriptures, while those living in the forest tend to emphasise meditation.

At one time India had a separate Buddhist monastic lineage for females. The fully ordained nuns were called *bhikkhuni* and observed more vows than monks did – 311 precepts as opposed to the 227 followed by monks. The *bhikkhuni sangha* travelled from its birthplace in India to Sri Lanka around two centuries after the Buddha's lifetime, taken there by the daughter of King Ashoka, Sanghamitta Theri. However, the tradition died out there following the Hindu Chola invasion in the 13th century. Monks from Siam later travelled to Sri Lanka to restore the male *sangha*, but because there were no ordained *bhikkhuni* in Thailand at the time, Sri Lanka's *bhikkhuni sangha* wasn't restored until very recently.

In Thailand, the modern equivalent is the *mâe chii* (mother priest) – women who live the monastic life as *atthasila* (eight-precept) nuns. They are largely outnumbered by male monastics (by 46 to one). Thai nuns shave their heads, wear white robes and take vows in an ordination procedure similar to that of the monks. Generally speaking, *mâe chii* nunhood in Thailand isn't considered as 'prestigious' as monkhood.

Visit www.thaifolk.com/Doc/culture2_e.htm for details on Thai festivals, folk rituals and common Buddhist ceremonies.

THAILAND'S FIRST FEMALE ORDINATION

In February 2002 Mae Chee Varangghana Vanavichayen underwent a *samanera* (novice Buddhist nun) ordination at Wat Songthamkalayanee in Nakhon Pathom. The ordination was conducted in the Sinhalese style by eight *bhikkhuni* hailing from Sri Lanka, Indonesia and Taiwan. Four years earlier, two Thai women had been ordained in Sri Lanka but this was the first female ordination ever to take place on Thai soil. The tradition was revived in Sri Lanka via ordination from Mahayana Buddhist nuns.

Thailand's clerical leaders publicly criticised the ordination as contrary to tradition, but did nothing to obstruct the ceremony or annul the ordination afterwards, leading many to believe that the hierarchy views the new lineage as inevitable.

OK Baytong (2003; Nonzee Nimibutr) is set in the Thai-Malaysian border town of Betong, Yala, and follows a man who leaves the Buddhist monkhood to care for his niece after his sister dies; it's full of insights into southern Thai ways of life and the Thai Muslim nationalist movement.

The average Thai Buddhist makes a great show of offering new robes and household items to the monks at the local wat but pays much less attention to the nuns. This is mainly due to the fact that nuns generally don't perform ceremonies on behalf of lay people, so there is often less incentive for people to make offerings to them. Furthermore, many Thais equate the number of precepts observed with the total merit achieved; hence nunhood is seen as less 'meritorious' than monkhood because *mâe chii* keep only eight precepts.

A recent movement to ordain *bhikkhuni* in Sri Lanka, however, has provided new opportunities, and in 2002 a Thai woman was fully ordained in Thailand (see the boxed text, p69) for the first time.

FURTHER INFORMATION

Wat Bowonniwet A Buddhist bookshop across the street from the north entrance to this temple (p124) in Bangkok sells a variety of English-language books on Buddhism.

World Fellowship of Buddhists (☎ 0 2661 1284-90; www.wfb-hq.org; 616 Soi 24, Th Sukhumvit, Bangkok). Senior *faràng* (Westerner) monks hold English-language Dhamma/meditation classes here on the first Sunday of each month from noon to 6pm.

Other Religions

A small percentage of Thais, and most of the Malays in the south (which amounts to about 4% of the total population), are followers of Islam. Half a per cent of the population – primarily missionised hill tribes and Vietnamese immigrants – profess Christian beliefs, while the remaining half per cent are Confucianists, Taoists, Mahayana Buddhists and Hindus. Mosques (in the south) and Chinese temples are common enough that you will probably come across some while travelling throughout Thailand. Before entering any temple, sanctuary or mosque you must always remove your shoes, and in a mosque your head must be covered.

Arts

At the crossroads of mainland Southeast Asia, Thailand's art scene has been influenced by many sources. As well as the arts of such native groups as the Mon and the Khmer, these include the great artistic traditions of nearby India and China, not to mention the subtle renderings of Indo- and Sino-influenced art in neighbouring countries such as Cambodia and Myanmar. During the 19th and 20th centuries Thailand also received a steady colonial and postcolonial cultural influx from Europe. In the more tightly connected modern world of aero- and cyberspace, there are influences from just about every corner of the globe.

ARCHITECTURE
Traditional Architecture

Home and temple architecture traditionally followed relatively strict rules of design that dictated proportion, placement, materials and ornamentation. With the modernisation of Thailand in the 19th and 20th centuries, stylistic codification gave way first to European functionalism, and then to stylistic innovation in more recent times.

The traditional Thai residential architecture consists either of single-room wooden houses raised on stilts or more elaborate structures of interlocking rooms with both indoor and shaded outdoor spaces, all supported at least 2m above the ground on stilts. Since originally all Thai settlements were founded along river or canal banks, the use of stilts protected the house and its inhabitants from flooding during the annual monsoon. Even in areas where flooding wasn't common, the Thais continued to raise their houses on stilts until relatively recently, using the space beneath the house as a cooking area, for tethering animals, or for parking their bicycles and motor vehicles. Teak has always been the material of choice for wooden structures, although with the shortage of teak in Thailand these days, few houses less than 50 years old are constructed of teak.

Rooflines in central, northern and southern Thailand are steeply pitched and often decorated at the corners or along the gables with motifs related to the *naga*, a mythical sea serpent long believed to be a spiritual protector of Thai-speaking cultures throughout Asia. In southern Thailand, bamboo and palm thatch have always been more common building materials than wood, and even today these renewable plant sources remain important construction elements.

In urban areas of the south you'll also see thick-walled structures of stuccoed brick – architecture that was introduced by Chinese, Portuguese, French and British settlements along the Malay Peninsula. In Thailand's four southernmost provinces, it's not unusual to come upon houses of entirely Malay design in which high masonry pediments or foundations, rather than wood stilts, lift the living areas well above the ground. Roofs of tile or thatch tend to be less steeply pitched, and hipped gables – almost entirely absent in traditional Thai architecture further north – are common in these Malay-influenced buildings.

Temple Architecture

Technically speaking, a wat (from the Pali-Sanskrit *avasa* dwelling for pupils and ascetics) is a Buddhist compound where men or women can be ordained as monks or nuns. Almost every village in Thailand has at

Classic Thai: Architecture, Design and Interiors (2002), by Chamsai Jotisalikorn, Virginia di Crocco, and Alexander Hay-Whitton, is an elegant coffee-table book that combines the photography of Luca Invernizzi Tettoni with essays by several leading experts on Thai architecture and design.

For highlights of Thai Buddhist architecture around the country, visit www.orientalarchitecture.com/directory.htm.

The coffee-table perennial *Thai Style* (1989), by William Warren and Gretchen Liu, is bolstered by the excellent photography of Luca Invernizzi Tettoni and will appeal to those with a general interest in Thai residential design, both interior and exterior.

least one wat, while in towns and cities they're quite numerous. Without an ordination area (designated by *sěmaa* stone markers), a monastic centre where monks or nuns reside is simply a *sǎmnák sǒng* (monastic residence). The latter are often established as meditation retreat facilities in forest areas, sometimes in conjunction with larger *wát pàa* (forest monasteries).

The typical wat compound in Thailand will contain at the very least an *uposatha* (*bòt* in central Thai, *sǐm* in northern and northeastern Thai), a consecrated chapel where monastic ordinations are held, and a *vihara* (*wíhǎan* in Thai), where important Buddha images are housed. Classic Thai *vihara* and *uposatha* architecture usually involves a steeply pitched roof system tiled in green, gold and red, and often constructed in tiered series of three levels, representing the triple gems of Buddhism: the Buddha, the Dhamma and the Sangha. Partial fourth and fifth tiers may also be included to shade porticoes at the front, rear or sides of the building. The front of the *wíhǎan bòt*, at a minimum, will feature an open veranda; often the veranda will extend around the entire perimeter of the building.

Another classic component of temple architecture throughout the country is the presence of one or more stupa (*jehdii* in Thai, from the Pali *cetiya*), a solid cone-shaped monument that pays tribute to the enduring stability of Buddhism. Stupas come in myriad styles, from simple inverted bowl-shaped designs imported from Sri Lanka to the more elaborate multi-sided stupas of northern Thailand, heir to the great Thai-Lao kingdoms of Lan Na and Lan Xang. Many stupas are believed to contain 'relics' (pieces of bone) belonging to the historical Buddha. In northern and northeastern Thailand such stupas are known as *thâat*.

Other structures typically found in wat compounds include one or more *sǎalaa* (open-sided shelters for community meetings and Dhamma lectures); a number of *kùtì* (monastic quarters); a *hǎw trai* (Tripitaka library where Buddhist scriptures are stored); a *hǎw klawng* (drum tower), sometimes with a *hǎw rákhang* (bell tower); various stupas (the smaller squarish stupas are *thâat kràdùuk* bone reliquaries, where the ashes of deceased worshippers are interred); plus various ancillary buildings – such as schools or clinics – that differ from wat to wat according to local community needs.

Contemporary Architecture

Thais began mixing traditional Thai with European forms in the late 19th and early 20th centuries, as exemplified by Bangkok's Vimanmek

---

HISTORICAL PARKS

The Fine Arts Department, under the Ministry of Education, has developed key archaeological sites into well-cared-for historical parks (*ùtháyaan pràwàttisàat*): Ayuthaya (p195) in Ayuthaya Province; Kamphaeng Phet (p399) in Kamphaeng Phet Province; Meuang Singh (p221) in Kanchanaburi Province; Prasat Hin Khao Phanom Rung (p452) in Buriram Province; Phra Nakhon Khiri (p521) in Phetchaburi Province; Prasat Phimai (p444) in Nakhon Ratchasima Province; Si Thep in Phetchabun Province; and Sukhothai (p389); Si Satchanalai–Chaliang (p394) in Sukhothai Province; Phu Phra Bat in Udon Thani Province; and Sri Thep in Phetchabun Province. Wiang Kum Kam (p288) near Chiang Mai was the area's earliest historical settlement.

These parks are administered by the Fine Arts Department to guard against theft and vandalism. Unesco has declared the ruins at Ayuthaya, Kamphaeng Phet, Si Satchanalai–Chaliang and Sukhothai as World Heritage sites, which makes them eligible for UN funds and/or expertise in future restoration projects.

ARCHITECTURAL ETHICS

Thailand has done a fine job of preserving historic religious architecture, from venerable old stupas to ancient temple compounds. In fact, the Department of Fine Arts enforces various legislation that makes it a crime to destroy or modify such monuments and even structures found on private lands are protected.

On the other hand, Thailand has less to be proud of in terms of preserving secular civil architecture such as old government offices and shophouses. Some of Bangkok's Ratanakosin and Asian Deco buildings have been preserved, as have a string of Sino-Portuguese residences and shophouses in Phuket, but typically only because the owners of these buildings took the initiative to do so. Thailand has no legislation in place to protect historic buildings or neighbourhoods.

Worse yet is the plight of vernacular regional architecture such as the wooden Shan-style shophouses of Mae Hong Son and Pai or the Lanna teak houses of Phrae, Lampang and Chiang Mai. These are fast disappearing, often to be replaced by plain cement structures of no historic or artistic value.

Other countries, such as Mexico, have regulations that allow the registration of historic homes, and whole neighbourhoods can be designated as national monuments. In neighbouring Laos, Unesco has helped to preserve the charming Lao-French architecture of Luang Prabang by designating the city as a World Heritage site.

If Thailand doesn't take steps soon to preserve historic secular architecture, its towns and cities are in danger of losing much of their visual charm.

Teak Mansion (p125), the Author's Wing of the Oriental Hotel (p151), the Chakri Mahaprasat (p102) next to Wat Phra Kaew, the Thai-Chinese Chamber of Commerce on Th Sathon Tai and any number of older residences and shophouses in Bangkok or provincial capitals throughout Thailand. This style of architecture is usually referred to as 'old Bangkok' or 'Ratanakosin'.

During the 1920s and '30s a simple Thai Deco style emerged, blending European Art Deco with functionalist restraint. Bangkok possesses the richest trove of Art Deco in Southeast Asia, surpassing even former colonial capitals such as Hanoi, Jakarta, Kuala Lumpur and Singapore.

Buildings of mixed heritage in the north and northeast exhibit French and English influences, while those in the south typically show Portuguese influence. Shophouses (*hâwng thăew*) throughout the country, whether 100 years or 100 days old, share the basic Chinese shophouse design, where the ground floor is reserved for trading purposes while the upper floors contain offices or residences.

In the 1960s and '70s, the trend in modern Thai architecture, inspired by the European Bauhaus movement, moved towards a boring functionalism – the average building looked like a giant egg carton turned on its side. The Thai aesthetic, so vibrant in the pre-WWII era, almost entirely disappeared in this characterless style of architecture.

When Thai architects finally began experimenting again during the building boom of the mid-1980s, the result was hi-tech designs such as ML Sumet Jumsai's famous robot-shaped Bank of Asia on Th Sathon Tai in Bangkok. The 'Robot Building' represents one of the last examples of architectural modernism in Bangkok, a trend which had all but concluded by the mid 1980s.

In the late '80s and early '90s, a handful of rebellious architects began incorporating traditional Thai motifs – mixed with updated Western classics – in the design of new buildings. Rangsan Torsuwan, a graduate of Massachusetts Institute of Technology (MIT), introduced the neoclassic (or neo-Thai) style; the best example is the new Grand Hyatt

The New Thai House (2003), by Robert Powell, is a photographic survey and analysis of 20 custom-designed Thai homes built within the last two decades, all projects that have helped define trends in modern Thai residential architecture.

Erawan (p149) in Bangkok. Another architect using traditional Thai architecture in modern functions is Pinyo Suwankiri, who has designed a number of Bangkok's government buildings.

SCULPTURE, PAINTING & OTHER VISUAL ARTS

Delicate clay and terracotta engravings found on cave walls and on votive tablets date as far back as the 6th century in Thailand, although if you count the bronze culture of Ban Chiang, sculptural endeavours began at least 4000 years ago.

Historically the most commonly sculpted materials have been wood, stone, ivory, clay and metal. Depending on the material used, artisans employ a variety of techniques (including carving, modelling, construction and casting) to achieve their designs.

Thailand's most famous sculptural output has been its bronze Buddha images, coveted the world over for their originality and grace. Nowadays historic bronzes have all but disappeared from the art market in Thailand. Most are zealously protected by temples, museums or private collectors.

Modern sculpture can be split into two camps, one imitating Western or Japanese trends, and the other reviving Thai themes but interpreting them in new ways. An example of the latter came along when artist Sakarin Kreu-On fashioned a huge, hollow Buddha head from a mixture of clay, mud, papier-mâché, glue and turmeric. Entitled *Phawang Si Leuang* (Yellow Trance), the work was displayed lying on its side, nearly filling a small room, during a successful world tour.

As with sculpture, Thai painting traditions were mostly confined to religious art, in which the application of natural pigments to temple walls became the favoured medium. Always instructional in intent, such painted images ranged from the depiction of the *Jataka* (stories of the Buddha's past lives) and scenes from the Indian Hindu epic *Ramayana*, to elaborate scenes detailing daily life in Thailand.

Lacking the durability of other art forms, pre-20th century religious painting is limited to very few surviving examples. The earliest surviving temple examples are found at Ayuthaya's Wat Ratburana (1424; p197), Wat Chong Nonsi in Bangkok (1657–1707; p131) and Phetchaburi's Wat Yai Suwannaram (late 17th century).

Nineteenth-century religious painting has fared better. Ratanakosin-style temple art is in fact more highly esteemed for painting than for sculpture or architecture. Typical temple murals feature rich colours and lively detail. Some of the finest are found in Wihan Buddhaisawan Chapel (p122) in Bangkok and at Wat Suwannaram (p133) in Thonburi.

However the study and application of mural painting techniques have been kept very much alive. Modern mural projects are undertaken somewhere within the country, practically every day of the year, often using improved techniques and paints that promise to hold fast much longer than the temple murals of old.

Temple murals have regained the interest of a privileged few who receive handsome sums for painting the interior walls of well-endowed ordination halls. Chakrabhand Pasayakrit's postmodern murals at Wat Tritosathep Mahawarawihan in Banglamphu, Bangkok, only half completed, are being hailed as a masterwork of Thai Buddhist art of any era.

One of the most important modern movements in Thai art has been an updating of Buddhist themes, begun in the 1970s with painters Pichai Nirand, Thawan Duchanee and Prateung Emjaroen. The movement has grown stronger since their early efforts combined modern Western

A good precis of traditional Thai sculpture up to modern times can be found at http://sunsite.au.ac.th/thailand/Thai_Arts/sculp.html.

See the website www1.thaimain.org/en/intro/craft.html for a concise summary of craft techniques used for classical Thai art.

THAILAND'S FATHER OF MODERN ART

The beginnings of Thailand's modern art movement can be attributed to Italian artist Corrado Feroci, who was first invited to Thailand by Rama VI in 1924. Feroci's design of Bangkok's Democracy Monument was inspired by Italy's fascist art movement of the 1930s. He also created the bronze statue of Rama I that stands at the entry to Memorial Bridge, and several monuments around the city. Feroci founded the country's first fine arts institute in 1933, a school that eventually developed into Silpakorn University, Thailand's premier training ground for artists. In gratitude, the Thai government made Feroci a Thai citizen, with the Thai name Silpa Bhirasri.

schemata with Thai motifs, moving from painting into sculpture and then into mixed media. Currently the most important artists working in this neo-Thai, neo-Buddhist school include Surasit Saokong, Songdej Thipthong, Monchai Kaosamang, Tawatchai Somkong and Montien Boonma. All are frequently exhibited and collected outside of Thailand.

Secular sculpture and painting in Bangkok have enjoyed more limited international success, with impressionism-inspired Jitr (Prakit) Buabusaya and Sriwan Janehuttakarnkit among the very few to have attained this vaunted status. On Thailand's more limited art stage, famous names currently include artists of the 'Fireball' school such as Vasan Sitthiket and Manit Sirwanichpoom, who specialise in politically-motivated, mixed-media art installations. These artists delight in breaking Thai social codes and means of expression. Even when their purported message is Thai nationalism and self-sufficiency, they are sometimes considered in some art quarters to be 'anti-Thai'.

In Manit's infamous 'Pink Man On Tour' series of art events, he dressed artist Sompong Thawee in pink from head to toe and had him parade with a shopping cart through popular tourist sites to protest the selling of Thai culture. Less famous are Manit's evocative black-and-white photographic pieces denouncing capitalism and consumerism, typically identified as unwelcome Western imports. A typical Vasan work dangles cardboard silhouettes from thick steel ropes, accompanied by the title 'Committing Suicide Culture: the only way for Thai farmers to escape debt.'

Thaweesak Srithongdee, one of several newer Thai artists who manage to skirt both the neo-Buddhist and Fireball movements, paints flamboyantly iconic human figures with bulging body parts. Sculptor Manop Suwanpinta similarly moulds the human anatomy into fantastic shapes that often intersect with technological features, such as hinged faces that open to reveal inanimate content.

For an excellent reference on the top Thai contemporary artists, galleries and collections, visit www.rama9art.org /artisan/bangkok /main.html.

Flavours – Thai Contemporary Art (2003), by Steven Pettifor, focuses on the work of some of Thailand's most prominent contemporary artists.

MUSIC

Throughout Thailand you'll find a diversity of musical genres and styles, from the serene court music that accompanies classical dance-drama to the chest-thumping house music played at dance clubs. Virtually every musical movement heard and seen in the West has been turned upside down by its Thai version.

Traditional Music

Classical central-Thai music *(phleng thai doem)* features a dazzling array of textures and subtleties, hair-raising tempos and pastoral melodies. The classical orchestra is called the *pìi-phâat* and can include as few as five players or more than 20. Among the more common instruments is the *pìi*, a woodwind instrument that has a reed mouthpiece; it is heard

The Traditional Music of Thailand (1976) is based on author David Morton's 1964 PhD dissertation; it is the most complete survey of traditional Thai music in the English language.

prominently at Thai-boxing matches. The four-stringed *phin,* plucked like a guitar, lends subtle counterpoint, while the *ránâat èhk,* a bamboo-keyed percussion instrument resembling the xylophone, carries the main melodies. The slender saw, a bowed instrument with a coconut-shell soundbox, provides soaring embellishments, as does the *khlùi* (wooden Thai flute).

One of the more attention-drawing *pìi-phâat* instruments, the *kháwng wong yài* consists of tuned gongs arranged in a semicircle and played in simple rhythmic lines to provide a song's underlying fabric. Several types of drums, some played with the hands, some with sticks, carry the beat, often through several tempo changes in a single song. The most important is the *tà-phon* (*thon*), a double-headed hand-drum that sets the tempo for the entire ensemble. Prior to a performance, the players offer incense and flowers to the *tà-phon* considered to be the 'conductor' of the music's spiritual content.

The standard Thai scale divides the eight-note octave into seven full-tone intervals, with no semitones. Thai scales were first transcribed by the Thai-German composer Peter Feit (Thai name: Phra Chen Duriyanga), who also composed Thailand's national anthem in 1932.

The *pìi-phâat* ensemble was originally developed to accompany classical dance-drama and shadow theatre, but can be heard these days in straightforward performances at temple fairs and concerts.

Thai Pop

The Overture (2004), by Ittisoontorn Vichailak, is a melodrama inspired by the life of composer Luang Pradit Phairao. In 19th-century Thailand, a *ranâat èhk* artist rises in the royal court to defend Thai classical music traditions against the strengthening influx of European music.

Popular Thai music has borrowed much from Western music, particularly in instrumentation, but still retains a distinct flavour of its own. The best-selling of all modern musical genres in Thailand remains *lûuk thûng.* Literally 'children of the fields', *lûuk thûng* dates back to the 1940s and is analogous to country-and-western music in the USA, and it's a genre that tends to appeal most to working class Thais. Subject matter almost always cleaves to tales of lost love, tragic early death and the dire circumstances of farmers who work day in and day out and at the end of the year still owe money to the bank.

There are two basic *lûuk thûng* styles: the original Suphanburi style, with lyrics in Standard Thai; and an Ubon style sung in Isan dialect. Thailand's most famous *lûuk thûng* singer, Pumpuang Duangjan, rated a royally-sponsored cremation when she died in 1992 and a major shrine at Suphanburi's Wat Thapkradan receives a steady stream of worshippers.

Chai Muang Sing and Siriporn Amphaipong have been the most beloved *lûuk thûng* superstars for several years. Other big *lûuk thûng* names include ex-soap opera star Got Chakraband, and Monsit Kham-soi, whose trademark silky – almost sleazy – vocal style has proved enormously popular.

Another genre more firmly rooted in northeastern Thailand, and nearly as popular in Bangkok, is *măw lam.* Based on the songs played on the Lao-Isan *khaen* (a wind instrument devised of a double row of bamboo-like reeds fitted into a hardwood soundbox), *măw lam* has a simple but very insistent bass beat topped by plaintive vocal melodies. If *lûuk thûng* is Thailand's country-and-western, then *măw lam* is the blues.

Jintara Poonlap and Chalermphol Malaikham are the current reigning queen and king of *măw lam.* These singers and others also perform *lûuk thûng prá-yúk,* a blend of *lûuk thûng* and *măw lam* that is emerging as *măw lam* loses its 'country bumpkin' image. Purists, however, eschew the latter in favour of rootsier, funkier *măw lam* artists such as Rumpan Saosanon. Sommainoi Duangcharoen goes in a completely different direction, mixing a bit of jazz and even rap into his *mǎw lam*. Tune into Bangkok radio station Luk Thung FM (FM95.0) for large doses of both *lûuk thûng* and *mǎw lam*.

The 1970s ushered in a new style inspired by the politically conscious folk rock of the USA and Europe, which the Thais dubbed *phleng phêua chii-wít* (music for life). Most identified with the Thai band Caravan – who still perform regularly – this style remains the most major musical shift in Thailand since *lûuk thûng* arose in the 1940s. Songs of this nature have political and environmental topics rather than the usual love themes. During the authoritarian dictatorships of the '70s many of Caravan's songs were officially banned. Another durable example of this style, Carabao, took *phleng phêua chii-wít*, fused it with *lûuk thûng*, rock and heavy metal, and spawned a whole generation of imitators as well as a chain of barn-like performance venues seating a thousand or more.

A good precis of traditional Thai music in contemporary society can be found at http://sunsite.au.ac.th/thailand/Thai_Arts/music.html.

Thailand also has a thriving teen-pop industry – sometimes referred to as T-Pop – centred on artists who have been chosen for their good looks, and then mated with syrupy song arrangements. Currently singers who are *lûuk khrêung* – half-Thai, half-*faràng* (Westerner) – and sport English names are particularly popular, eg Tata Young, Nicole Theriault, Peter Corp and Thongchai 'Bird' Macintyre. Teen girl pop singers Palmy or Mint play much the same roles in Bangkok as Britney Spears and Christina Aguilera play in the West, while D2B holds up the boy-band end of the market.

Among the disc-buying public, karaoke CDs and VCDs comprise a huge share of the market. Many major Thai artists – even alt rock groups – release VCDs specially formatted for karaoke-style sing-alongs, complete with song lyric subtitles.

Thai Alt/Indie

The 1990s saw a reaction to the packaging concept as an alternative pop scene – known as *klawng sěhrii* (free drum) or *phleng tâi din* (underground music) in Thailand – grew in Bangkok. Hip-hop/ska artist Joey Boy not only explored new musical frontiers but released lyrics that the Department of Culture banned.

Modern Dog, a Brit-pop inspired band of four Chulalongkorn University graduates, is generally credited with bringing independent Thai music into the mainstream, and its success prompted an explosion of similar bands and indie recording labels.

www.ethaicd.com has the best online selection of Thai CDs, VCDs and DVDs.

Crowd-pleasers Loso (from 'low society') updated Carabao's affinity for Thai folk melodies and rhythms with indie guitar rock. The Thai music industry has responded with a rash of similar Thai headbangers designed to fill stadiums and outsell the indies. One of the most successful of the latter is Silly Fools, who lace classic Thai rock anthems with electronica. Major alternative acts in Thailand include the aforementioned Modern Dog, its Britpop-inspired rivals Pru and Day Tripper, punk metal Ebola and electronica/underground Futon. Made up of British, Thai and Japanese band members, Futon's remake of Iggy Pop's proto-punk classic 'I Wanna Be Your Dog' hit big in Thailand, and its album *Don't Mind the Botox* has been internationally distributed.

For the latest indie Thai, tune into Fat Radio, FM104.5.

Jazz & World Music Influences

Yet another inspiring movement in modern Thai music has been the fusion of international jazz with Thai classical and folk motifs. Fong Nam, a Thai orchestra led by American composer Bruce Gaston, performs an inspiring blend of Western and Thai classical motifs that have become

RECOMMENDED THAI POP CDS

- Bakery Music: *Lust For Live* – collection of live alt rock performances by Modern Dog, Chou Chou, Yokee Playboy, POP and Rudklao Amraticha
- Banyen Raggan: *Khaw Du Jai Kawn* – a good introduction to *măw lam*
- Blackhead: *Handmade* – straight-ahead Thai grunge rock
- Carabao: *Made in Thailand* – Carabao's most classic and internationally popular album
- Caravan: *Khon Kap Khwai* – The album that kicked off the *phleng phêua chii-wít* movement.
- Fong Nam: *The Nang Hong Suite* – brilliant Thai funeral music, but think New Orleans second-line cheer, rather than dirge
- Joey Boy: *Joey Boy's Anthology* – thirteen Thai ska/hip-hop tracks from Joey Boy's seven years with Bakery Music
- Loso: *The Best of Loso* – Thai anthems of teen angst
- Modern Dog: *Modern Dog* – The Dog's debut album is still its best.
- Pumpuang Duangjan: *Best* – compilation of the late *lûuk thûng* diva's most famous tunes

a favourite choice for movie soundtracks, TV commercials and tourism promotion. However, a live Fong Nam performance is not to be missed.

Another leading exponent of this genre is the composer and instrumentalist Tewan Sapsanyakorn (also known as Tong Tewan), who plays soprano and alto sax, violin and *khlùi* (wooden Thai flute) with equal virtuosity. Tewan's compositions are often based on Thai melodies, but the improvisations and rhythms are drawn from such diverse jazz sources such as Sonny Rollins and Jean-Luc Ponty.

Fat Radio 104.5, Bangkok's main alternative pop station, has its own website at www.thisis click.com/1045main.php with streaming audio.

THEATRE & DANCE

Traditional Thai theatre consists of six dramatic forms: *khŏhn* (formal masked dance-drama depicting scenes from the *Ramakian* – the Thai version of India's *Ramayana* – originally performed only for the royal court); *lákhon* (a general term covering several types of dance-drama, usually for non-royal occasions, as well as Western theatre); *lí-keh* (likay; a partly improvised, often bawdy folk play featuring dancing, comedy, melodrama and music); *mánohraa* (the southern Thai equivalent of *lí-keh*, but based on a 2000-year-old Indian story); *năng* (shadow plays limited to southern Thailand); *lákhon lék* or *hùn lŭang* (puppet theatre); and *lákhon phûut* (contemporary spoken theatre).

Khŏhn

In all *khŏhn* performances, four types of characters are represented – male humans, female humans, monkeys and demons. Monkey and demon figures are always masked with the elaborate head coverings often seen in tourist promo material. Behind the masks and make-up, all actors are male. Traditional *khŏhn* is a very expensive production – Ravana's retinue alone (Ravana is the *Ramakian*'s principal villain) consists of over 100 demons, each with a distinctive mask.

Perhaps because it was once limited to royal venues and hence never gained a popular following, the *khŏhn* or *Ramakian* dance-drama tradition nearly died out in Thailand. Bangkok's National Theatre (p172) was once the only place where *khŏhn* was regularly performed for the public; the renovated Chalermkrung Royal Theatre (p172) now hosts occasional *khŏhn* performances enhanced by laser graphics and hi-tech audio.

Scenes performed in traditional *khŏhn* (and *lákhon* performances; see below) come from the 'epic journey' tale of the *Ramayana,* with parallels in the Greek *Odyssey* and the myth of Jason and the Argonauts. The central story revolves around Prince Rama's search for his beloved Princess Sita, who has been abducted by the evil 10-headed demon Ravana and taken to the island of Lanka. Rama is assisted in his search and in the final battle against Ravana by a host of mythical half-animal, half-human characters including the monkey-god Hanuman.

Lákhon

The more formal *lákhon nai* (inner *lákhon,* performed inside the palace) was originally performed for lower nobility by all-female ensembles. Today it's a dying art, even more so than royal *khŏhn.* In addition to scenes from the *Ramakian, lákhon nai* performances may include traditional Thai folk tales; whatever the story, text is always sung. *Lákhon nâwk* (outer *lákhon,* performed outside the palace) deals exclusively with folk tales and features a mix of sung and spoken text, sometimes with improvisation. Both male and female performers are permitted. Like *khŏhn* and *lákhon nai,* performances are becoming increasingly rare.

Much more common these days is the less refined *lákhon chaatrii,* a fast-paced, costumed dance-drama usually performed at upcountry temple festivals or at shrines (commissioned by a shrine devotee whose wish was granted by the shrine deity). *Chaatrii* stories have been influenced by the older *mánohraa* theatre of southern Thailand.

A variation on *chaatrii* that has evolved specifically for shrine worship, *lákhon kâe bon* involves an ensemble of around 20 members, including musicians. At an important shrine like Bangkok's Lak Meuang, four different *kâe bon* troupes may alternate performances, each for a week at a time, as each performance lasts from 9am till 3pm and there is usually a long list of worshippers waiting to hire them.

Lí-Keh

In outlying working-class neighbourhoods in Bangkok you may be lucky enough to come across the gaudy, raucous *lí-keh.* This theatrical art form is thought to have descended from drama-rituals brought to southern Thailand by Arab and Malay traders. The first native public performance in central Thailand came about when a group of Thai Muslims staged a *lí-keh* for Rama V in Bangkok during the funeral commemoration of Queen Sunantha. *Lí-keh* grew very popular under Rama VI, peaked in the early 20th century and has been fading slowly since the 1960s.

Most often performed at Buddhist festivals by troupes of travelling performers, *lí-keh* presents a colourful mixture of folk and classical music, outrageous costumes, melodrama, slapstick comedy, sexual innuendo and up-to-date commentary on Thai politics and society. Foreigners – even those who speak fluent Thai – are often left behind by the highly idiomatic, culture-specific language and gestures. For true *lí-keh* aficionados, the coming of a renowned troupe is a bigger occasion than the release of a new *Matrix* sequel at the local cinema.

Marionettes

Lákhon lék (little theatre), also known as *hùn lŭang* (royal puppets), like *khŏhn,* was once reserved for court performances. Metre-high marionettes made of *khòi* paper and wire, wearing elaborate costumes modelled on those of the *khŏhn,* are used to convey similar themes, music and dance movements.

Sounding the Center: History and Aesthetics in Thai Buddhist Performance (1986), by Deborah Wong, is an interesting analysis of the way ritual is integrated into Thai music and dance.

Two to three puppetmasters are required to manipulate each *hùn lŭang* – including arms, legs, hands, even fingers and eyes – by means of wires attached to long poles. Stories are drawn from Thai folk tales, particularly *Phra Aphaimani*, and occasionally from the *Ramakian*. The *hùn lŭang* puppets themselves are highly collectable; the Bangkok National Museum has only one example in its collection. A smaller, 30cm court version called *hùn lék* (little puppets) are occasionally used in live performances; only one puppeteer is required for each marionette in *hùn lék*.

www.mirrorartgroup
.org is the website of
an NGO in Chiang Rai
province dedicated to
hill-tribe arts.

Another Thai puppet theatre, *hùn kràbàwk* (cylinder puppets) is based on popular Hainanese puppet shows. It uses 30cm hand puppets that are carved from wood, and they are viewed from the waist up. The best place to see *lákhon lék* is at the Natayasala (Joe Louis Puppet Theater; p172) in Bangkok.

Năng

Shadow-puppet theatre – in which two-dimensional figures are manipulated between a cloth screen and a light source at night-time performances – has been a Southeast Asian tradition for perhaps five centuries. Originally brought to the Malay Peninsula by Middle Eastern traders, the technique eventually spread to all parts of mainland and peninsular Southeast Asia; in Thailand it is mostly found in the south. As in Malaysia and Indonesia, shadow puppets in Thailand are carved from dried buffalo or cow hides (*năng* in Thai).

Two distinct shadow-play traditions survive in Thailand. The most common, *năng tàlung*, is named after Phattalung Province, where it developed around Malay models. Like their Malay-Indonesian counterparts, Thai shadow puppets represent an array of characters from classical and folk drama, principally the *Ramakian* and *Phra Aphaimani* in Thailand. A single puppetmaster manipulates the cut-outs, which are bound to the ends of buffalo-horn handles. *Năng tàlung* is still occasionally seen at temple festivals in the south, mostly in Songkhla and Nakhon Si Thammarat Provinces. Performances are also held periodically for tour groups or visiting dignitaries from Bangkok.

The second tradition, *năng yài* (big hide), uses much larger cut-outs, each bound to two wooden poles held by a puppetmaster; several masters may participate in a single performance. *Năng yài* is rarely performed nowadays because of the lack of trained *năng* masters and the expense of the shadow puppets. Most *năng yài* that are made today are sold to interior designers or tourists; a well-crafted hide puppet may cost as much as 5000B.

In addition to the occasional performance in Nakhon Si Thammasat or Bangkok, *năng yài* can be seen at Wat Khanon in Amphoe Photharam, Ratchaburi Province, where *năng yài* master Khru Chalat is passing the art along to younger men. There's usually a performance at the wat from 10am to 11am Saturday.

Contemporary Theatre

Lákhon phûut ('speaking theatre', or live contemporary theatre as it's known in the West) is enjoyed by a small, mainly elite audience in Bangkok. Virtually the entire scene, such as it is, centres around Patravadi Theatre (p172).

CINEMA

Bangkok Film launched Thailand's movie-making industry with the first Thai-directed silent movie, *Chok Sorng Chan*, in 1927. Silent films proved to be more popular than talkies right into the 1960s, and as late as 1969 Thai studios were still producing them from 16mm stock.

The arrival of 35mm movies in Thailand around the same time brought a proliferation of modern cinema halls and a surge in movie-making. Many Thais consider the '60s to be a golden age of Thai cinema. Over half of the approximately 75 films produced annually during this period starred the much-admired onscreen duo of actors Mit Chaibancha and Petchara Chaowaraj.

Thai film production in the '70s and early '80s was mostly limited to inexpensive action or romance stories. Among notable exceptions, 1983's *Child of the North-East (Luk Isan)*, based on a Thai novel of the same name, followed the ups and downs of a farming family living in drought-ridden Isan. *Luk Isan* became one of the first popular films to offer urban Thais an understanding of the hardships endured by many northeasterners. The Thai movie industry almost died during the '80s and early '90s, swamped by Hollywood extravaganzas and the boom era's taste for anything imported.

While the 1997 to 1998 Southeast Asian economic crisis threatened to further bludgeon the ailing industry, a lack of larger budgets, coupled with the need to compete with foreign films, brought about a new emphasis on quality rather than quantity. The current era boasts a new generation of seriously good Thai directors, several of whom studied film abroad during Thailand's '80s and early '90s boom period.

> The award-winning *Mon Rak Transistor* (2001), by Pen-Ek Ratanaruang, is the best of several Thai films that dramatise the *lûuk thûng* music scene.

Recent directorial efforts have been so encouraging that Thai and foreign critics alike speak of a current Thai 'new wave'. The current crop of directors favour gritty realism, artistic innovation and a strengthened Thai identity. Pen-Ek Ratanaruang's *Fun Bar Karaoke*, a 1997 satire of Bangkok life in which the main characters are an ageing Thai playboy and his daughter, received critical acclaim for its true-to-life depiction of modern urban living blended with sage humour. The film played well to international audiences but achieved only limited box-office success at home.

A harbinger of things to come for the Thai film industry arrived with Nonzee Nimibutr's 1998 release of *Nang Nak*, an exquisite re-telling of a famous Thai spirit tale that had seen no fewer than 20 previous cinematic renderings. *Nang Nak* not only featured excellent acting and period detailing, but managed to transform Nak into a sympathetic character rather than a horrific ghost. The film became the largest-grossing film in Thai history, out-earning even *Titanic*, and earned awards for best director, best art director and best sound at the 1999 Asia-Pacific Film Festival.

Hot on the heels of *Nang Nak's* success came the 2000 film *Satree Lex (Iron Ladies)*, which humorously dramatised the real-life exploits of a Lampang volleyball team made up almost entirely of transvestites and transsexuals. At home, this Yongyoot Thongkongtoon–directed film became Thai cinema's second-largest grossing effort to date, and was the first Thai film ever to play the art house cinemas of Europe and America on general release.

The next Thai film to garner international attention was 2000's *Suriyothai*, an historic epic directed by Prince Chatri Chalerm Yukol. Forty months and US$20 million in the making, the three-hour film lavishly narrates a well-known episode in Thai history in which an Ayuthaya queen sacrifices herself at the 1548 Battle of Hanthawaddy to save her king's life. Although rich in costumes and locations, it flopped overseas and was widely criticised for being ponderous and overly long. Legendary American producer-director Francis Ford Coppola re-edited the film to create a shorter, more internationally palatable version (*Legend of Suriyothai*), albeit one of limited appeal nonetheless.

For indications that Thailand's role in world cinema will continue to expand, one need look no further than Pen-Ek's acclaimed *Mon Rak Transistor* (2001) broke ground by seizing a thoroughly Thai movie theme – the tragic-comic odyssey of a young villager who tries to crack the big time *lûuk thûng* music scene in Bangkok – and upgrading production values to the highest international standards.

One of Thai cinema's proudest moments arrived when Cannes 2002 chose *Blissfully Yours (Sut Sanaeha)* for the coveted Un Certain Regard (Of Special Consideration) screening, an event that showcases notable work by new directors. Helmed by Apichatpong Weerasethakul, the film dramatises a budding romance between a Thai woman and an illegal Burmese immigrant.

Another favourite on the 2002 festival circuit, and a blockbuster in Thailand as well, Jira Malikul's *Mekhong Full Moon Party (15 Kham Deuan 11)*, juxtaposes folk beliefs about mysterious 'dragon lights' emanating from Mekong River with the scepticism of Bangkok scientists and news media, as well as with Thai Buddhism. It's also the first Thai feature film where most of the script is written in the Isan dialect, necessitating standard Thai subtitles.

Another watershed occurred when the 2004 Cannes Film Festival awarded Apichatpong's dream-like *Tropical Malady (Sut Pralat)* the Jury Prize. None of Apichatpong's films have generated much interest in Thailand, however, where they are seen as too Western in tone. Better received, box office-wise, both in Thailand and abroad, was director's Prachya Pinkaew's *Ong Bak* (2004), widely hailed as one of the finest 'old-school' martial arts films of all time.

The Arts of Thailand (1999), by Steven Van Beek, is a thorough account of artistic movements in Thailand from the Bronze Age to the Ratanakosin era.

LITERATURE

The written word has a long history in Thailand, dating back to the 11th or 12th century when the first Thai script was fashioned from an older Mon alphabet. The first known work of literature to be written in Thai is thought to have been composed by Sukhothai's Phaya Lithai in 1345. This was *Traiphum Phra Ruang,* a treatise that described the three realms of existence according to a Hindu-Buddhist cosmology. According to contemporary scholars, this work and its symbolism was, and continues to be, of considerable influence on Thailand's artistic and cultural universe.

Classical

The 30,000-line *Phra Aphaimani*, composed by poet Sunthorn Phu in the late 18th century, is Thailand's most famous classical literary work. Like many of its epic predecessors around the world, it tells the story of an exiled prince who must complete an odyssey of love and war before returning to his kingdom in victory.

But of all classical Thai literature, *Ramakian* is the most pervasive and influential in Thai culture. The Indian source, *Ramayana,* came to Thailand with the Khmers 900 years ago, first appearing as stone reliefs on Prasat Hin Phimai and other Angkor temples in the northeast. Eventually, however, the Thais developed their own version of the epic, which was first written down during the reign of Rama I. This version contained 60,000 stanzas and was a quarter longer than the Sanskrit original.

Although the main theme remains the same, the Thais embroidered the *Ramayana* by providing much more biographical detail on arch-villain Ravana (Dasakantha, called Thotsakan, or '10-necked' in the *Ramakian*) and his wife Montho. Hanuman, the monkey-god, differs substantially in the Thai version, in his flirtatious nature (in the Hindu version he follows a strict vow of chastity). One of the classic *Ramakian* reliefs at Bangkok's Wat Pho depicts Hanuman clasping a maiden's bared breast as if it were an apple.

Also passed on from Indian tradition are the many *Jataka* life stories of the Buddha (*chaa-dòk* in Thai). Of the 547 *jataka* tales in the Pali *Tipitaka* (Buddhist canon), each one chronicling a different past life, most appear in Thailand almost word-for-word as they were first written down in Sri Lanka.

A group of 50 'extra' stories, based on Thai folk tales of the time, were added by Pali scholars in Chiang Mai 300 to 400 years ago. The most popular *Jataka* in Thailand is one of the Pali originals known as the *Mahajati* or *Mahavessantara*, the story of the Buddha's penultimate life. Interior murals in the ordination chapels of Thai wat typically depict this *Jataka* and nine others: Temiya, Mahajanaka, Suvannasama, Nemiraja, Mahosatha, Bhuridatta, Candakumara, Narada and Vidhura.

Origins of Thai Art (2004), by Elizabeth Gosling, is a well-researched and authoritative text that recognises that the arts of Thailand bring together cultures both Tai and pre-Tai, while dismantling the notion that there is a single Tai culture.

Poetry

During the Ayuthaya period, Thailand developed a classical poetic tradition based on five types of verse – *chǎn*, *kàap*, *khlong*, *klawn* and *râi*. Each of these forms uses a set of complex, strict rules to regulate metre, rhyming patterns and number of syllables. Although all of these poetic systems use the Thai language, *chǎn* and *kàap* are derived from Sanskrit verse forms from India, while *khlong*, *klawn* and *rai* are native forms. The Indian forms have all but disappeared from 21st-century use.

During the political upheavals that characterised the 1970s, several Thai newspaper editors, most notably Kukrit Pramoj, composed lightly disguised political commentary in *klawn* verse. Modern Thai poets seldom use the classical forms, preferring to compose in blank verse or with song-style rhyming.

Contemporary

The first Thai-language novel appeared only around 70 years ago, in direct imitation of Western models. Thus far, no more than 10 have been translated into English. Considered the first Thai novel of substance, *The Circus of Life* (Thai 1929; English 1994) by Arkartdamkeung Rapheephat follows a young, upper-class Thai as he travels to London, Paris, the USA and China in the 1920s. The novel's existentialist tone created quite a stir in Thailand when released and became an instant bestseller. The fact that the author, himself a Thai prince, took his own life at the age of 26 has added to the mystique surrounding this work.

The late Kukrit Pramoj, former ambassador and Thai prime minister, novelized Bangkok court life from the late 19th century through the 1940s in *Four Reigns* (Thai 1935; English 1981), the longest novel ever published in Thai. *The Story of Jan Darra* (Thai 1966; English 1994), by journalist and short-story writer Utsana Phleungtham, traces the sexual obsessions of a Thai aristocrat as they are passed on to his son. Director/producer Nonzee Nimibutr turned the remarkable novel into a rather melodramatic film, *Nang Nak* (p81). Praphatsorn Seiwikun's well-tuned, rapid-paced *Time in a Bottle* (Thai 1984; English 1996) turned the life dilemmas of a fictional middle-class Bangkok family into a bestseller.

Jack Reynolds' 1950s *A Woman of Bangkok* (originally published as *A Sort of Beauty* in 1956, and republished under the new name shortly thereafter), a well-written and poignant story of a young Englishman's descent into the world of Thai brothels, remains the best novel yet published with this theme. Expat writer Christopher G Moore covers the Thai underworld in his 1990s novels *A Killing Smile, Spirit House, A Bewitching Smile* and a raft of others, with an anchor firmly hooked into the go-go bar scene.

The Lioness in Bloom is an eye-opening collection of 11 short stories written by or about Thai women and translated by Susan Fulop Kepner.

For a look at rural life in Thailand, the books of Pira Sudham are unparalleled. Sudham was born into a poor family in northeastern Thailand and has written *The Force of Karma, Monsoon Country, People of Esarn* and his latest, *Shadowed Country*. These books are not translations – Sudham writes in English in order to reach a worldwide audience.

Thai wunderkind SP Somtow has written and published more titles in English than any other Thai writer. Born in Bangkok, educated at Eton and Cambridge, and now a commuter between two 'cities of angels' – Los Angeles and Bangkok – Somtow's prodigious output includes a string of well-reviewed science fiction/fantasy/horror stories, including *Moon Dance, Darker Angels* and *The Vampire's Beautiful Daughter*. The most accessible Somtow novel, and the one most evocative of Thai culture, is *Jasmine Nights* (1995). Following a 12-year-old Thai boy's friendship with an African-American boy near Bangkok in the 1960s, this semi-autobiographical work blends Thai, Greek and African myth, American Civil War lore and a dollop of magic realism into a seamless whole.

Environment

THE LAND

Thailand covers 514,000 sq km, making it slightly smaller than the US state of Texas, or about the size of France. Its shape on the map has been likened to the head of an elephant, with its trunk extending down the Malay peninsula. The centre of Thailand, Bangkok, sits at about 14° north latitude – level with Madras, Manila, Guatemala and Khartoum.

The country's longest north–south distance is about 1860km, but its shape makes distances in any other direction 1000km or less. Because the north–south reach spans roughly 16 latitudinal degrees, Thailand has perhaps the most diverse climate in Southeast Asia. Twenty-three of its 76 provinces enjoy direct access to the sea and its potential for trade and seafaring livelihoods.

The topography varies from high mountains in the north (the south-ernmost extreme of ranges tumbling down from the Tibet Plateau) to limestone-encrusted tropical islands in the south that are part of the Malay Archipelago.

The rivers and tributaries of northern and central Thailand drain into the Gulf of Thailand via the Chao Phraya Delta near Bangkok; Mae Nam Mun and other northeastern waterways exit into the South China Sea via the Mekong River.

These broad geographic characteristics divide the country into four main zones. The fertile central region is dominated by Mae Nam Chao Phraya. The northeast, the kingdom's poorest region (thanks to 'thin' soil plus occasional droughts and floods), is a plateau rising some 300m above the central plain. Northern Thailand is a region of mountains and fertile valleys, and the southern peninsula extends to the Malaysian border and is predominantly rainforest.

Extending from the east coast of the Malay peninsula to Vietnam, the Sunda Shelf separates the Gulf of Thailand from the South China Sea. On the opposite side of the peninsula, the Andaman Sea encompasses the Indian Ocean east of India's Andaman and Nicobar Islands. Thailand's Andaman Sea and Gulf of Thailand coastlines form 2710km of beaches, hard shores and wetlands. Hundreds of oceanic and continental islands lie offshore on both sides.

See South East Asia Rivers Network (Searin) at www.searin.org/indexE .htm for issues relating to riverine ecosystems.

WILDLIFE

Unique in the region because its north–south axis extends some 1800km from mainland to peninsular Southeast Asia, Thailand provides potential habitats for an astounding variety of flora and fauna.

Animals

Variation in the animal kingdom follows geographic and climatic differences. The indigenous fauna of Thailand's northern half is mostly of Indochinese (mainland Southeast Asia) origin while that of the south is generally Sundaic (ie typical of peninsular Malaysia, Sumatra, Borneo and Java). The invisible dividing line between the two zoogeographical zones runs across the Isthmus of Kra, about halfway down the southern peninsula. The large overlap area between zoogeographical and vegetative zones – from around Prachuap Khiri Khan on the southern peninsula to Uthai Thani in the lower north – means that much of Thailand is a potential habitat for plants and animals from both zones.

The Mammals of Thailand (1988), by Boonsong Lekagul and Jeffrey McNeely, remains the classic on Thai wildlife in spite of a few out-of-date references.

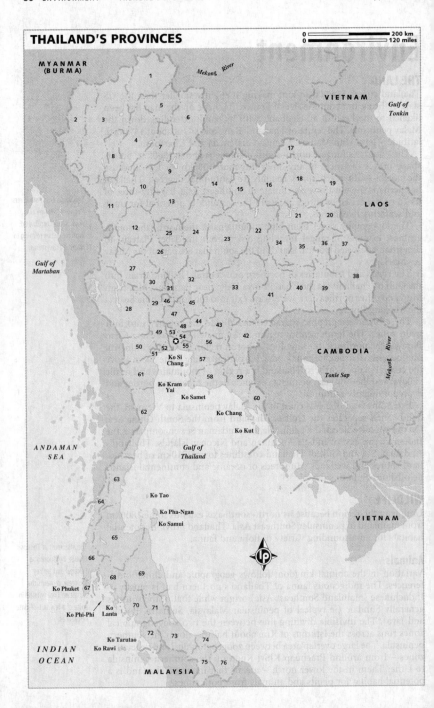

1	Chiang Rai	27	Uthai Thani	53	Nonthaburi
2	Mae Hong Son	28	Kanchanaburi	54	Bangkok
3	Chiang Mai	29	Suphanburi	55	Samut Prakan
4	Lampang	30	Chai Nat	56	Chachoengsao
5	Phayao	31	Singburi	57	Chonburi
6	Nan	32	Lopburi	58	Rayong
7	Phrae	33	Nakhon Ratchasima	59	Chanthaburi
8	Lamphun	34	Mahasarakham	60	Trat
9	Utaradit	35	Roi Et	61	Phetchaburi
10	Sukhothai	36	Yasothon		(Phetburi)
11	Tak	37	Amnat Charoen	62	Prachuap Khiri Khan
12	Kamphaeng Phet	38	Ubon Ratchathani	63	Chumphon
13	Phitsanulok	39	Si Saket	64	Ranong
14	Loei	40	Surin	65	Surat Thani
15	Nong Bualamphu	41	Buriram	66	Phang-Nga
16	Udon Thani	42	Sa Kaew	67	Phuket
17	Nong Khai	43	Prachinburi	68	Krabi
18	Sakon Nakhon	44	Nakhon Nayok	69	Nakhon Si
19	Nakhon Phanom	45	Saraburi		Thammarat
20	Mukdahan	46	Ang Thong	70	Trang
21	Kalasin	47	Ayuthaya	71	Phattalung
22	Khon Kaen	48	Pathum Thani	72	Satun
23	Chaiyaphum	49	Nakhon Pathom	73	Songkhla
24	Phetchabun	50	Ratchaburi	74	Pattani
25	Phichit	51	Samut Songkhram	75	Yala
26	Nakhon Sawan	52	Samut Sakhon	76	Narathiwat

Thailand is particularly rich in birdlife, with over 1000 recorded resident and migrating species – approximately 10% of the world's bird species. Insect species number some 6000, and the country's marine environment counts tens of thousands of species.

Indigenous mammals, mostly found in dwindling numbers within the country's national parks or wildlife sanctuaries, include tigers, leopards, elephants, Asiatic black bears, Malayan sun bears, pangolin, gaur (Indian bison), banteng (wild cattle), serow (an Asiatic goat-antelope), sambar deer, barking deer, mouse deer, gibbons, macaques, tapir, dolphins and dugongs (sea cows). Around 40 of Thailand's 300 mammal species, including clouded leopard, Malayan tapir, tiger, Irrawaddy dolphin, goral, jungle cat, dusky langur and pileated gibbon, are on the International Union for Conservation of Nature (IUCN) list of endangered species.

Around 200 to 300 wild tigers are thought to be hanging on in Khao Yai, Kaeng Krachan, Huay Kha Khaeng/Thung Yai Naresuan, Nam Nao, Thap Lan, Mae Wong and Khao Sok National Parks. Although tiger hunting and trapping is illegal, poachers continue to kill the cats for the lucrative overseas Chinese pharmaceutical market; among the Chinese, the ingestion of tiger penis and bone is thought to have curative effects.

Species of herpetofauna in Thailand number around 313 reptiles and 107amphibians. These include four sea turtle species, along with numerous snake varieties of which six are venomous: the common cobra (six subspecies), king cobra (hamadryad), banded krait (three species), green viper, Malayan viper and Russell's pit viper. Although the relatively rare king cobra can reach up to 6m in length, the nation's largest snake is the reticulated python, which can reach a whopping 10m. The country's many lizard species include two commonly seen in homes and older hotels or guesthouses – túk-kae (a large gecko) and jîng-jòk (a smaller house lizard) – as well as larger species such as the black jungle monitor.

Bird lovers should seek out the Guide to the Birds of Thailand (1991), by Boonsong Lekagul and Phillip Round, for a comprehensive descriptions of Thailand's numerous avian species.

The Wild Animal Rescue Foundation of Thailand (WAR; www.warthai .org) is dedicated to the welfare and preservation of native species.

Plants

As in the rest of tropical Asia, most indigenous vegetation in Thailand is associated with two basic types of tropical forest: monsoon forest (with a distinct dry season of three months or more) and rainforest (where rain falls more than nine months per year). Forest cover varies by region from

The Elephant Keeper (1987; directed by Prince Chatrichalerm Yukol) – when an honest forestry chief tries to protect the wilderness from illegal logging powered by wealth and corruption, he is assisted by a courageous mahout and his faithful elephant.

a high of 43% in the north to a low of 12% in the northeast. The most heavily forested province is Chiang Mai, followed by Kanchanaburi.

Monsoon forests amount to about a quarter of all natural forest cover in the country. They're marked by deciduous tree varieties, which shed their leaves during the dry season to conserve water. About half of all Thailand's forest cover consists of rainforests, all of it in southern Thailand, while a few zones support a mix of monsoon forest and rainforest vegetation. The remaining quarter of the country's forest cover consists of freshwater swamp forests in the delta regions; forested crags amid the karst topography of both the north and south; mangroves in the south; and pine forests at higher altitudes in the north.

The country's most famous flora includes an incredible array of fruit trees, bamboo (more species than any other country outside China), tropical hardwoods and over 27,000 flowering species, including Thailand's national floral symbol, the orchid.

NATIONAL PARKS, RESERVES & WILDLIFE SANCTUARIES

A system of wildlife sanctuaries was first provided for in the Wild Animals Reservation and Protection Act of 1960, followed by the National Parks Act of 1961, which established the kingdom's national park programme, with the setting up of Khao Yai National Park. Today the kingdom boasts 112 national parks, plus over a thousand 'nonhunting areas', wildlife sanctuaries, forest reserves, botanical gardens and arboretums; see the table opposite for the country's top protected areas. Nineteen of the national parks are marine parks that protect coastal, insular and open-sea areas. Altogether these cover more than 13% of the country's

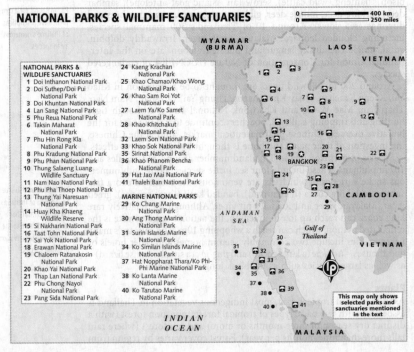

NATIONAL PARKS & WILDLIFE SANCTUARIES

NATIONAL PARKS & WILDLIFE SANCTUARIES
1 Doi Inthanon National Park
2 Doi Suthep/Doi Pui National Park
3 Doi Khuntan National Park
4 Lan Sang National Park
5 Phu Reua National Park
6 Taksin Maharat National Park
7 Phu Hin Rong Kla National Park
8 Phu Kradung National Park
9 Phu Phan National Park
10 Thung Salaeng Luang Wildlife Sanctuary
11 Nam Nao National Park
12 Phu Pha Thoep National Park
13 Thung Yai Naresuan National Park
14 Huay Kha Khaeng Wildlife Reserve
15 Si Nakharin National Park
16 Taat Tohn National Park
17 Sai Yok National Park
18 Erawan National Park
19 Chaloem Ratanakosin National Park
20 Khao Yai National Park
21 Thap Lan National Park
22 Phu Chong Nayoi National Park
23 Pang Sida National Park

24 Kaeng Krachan National Park
25 Khao Chamao/Khao Wong National Park
26 Khao Sam Roi Yot National Park
27 Laem Ya/Ko Samet National Park
28 Khao Khitchakut National Park
32 Laem Son National Park
33 Khao Sok National Park
35 Sirinat National Park
36 Khao Phanom Bencha National Park
39 Hat Jao Mai National Park
41 Thaleh Ban National Park

MARINE NATIONAL PARKS
29 Ko Chang Marine National Park
30 Ang Thong Marine National Park
31 Surin Islands Marine National Park
34 Ko Similan Islands Marine National Park
37 Hat Nopphrat Thara/Ko Phi-Phi Marine National Park
38 Ko Lanta Marine National Park
40 Ko Tarutao Marine National Park

This map only shows selected parks and sanctuaries mentioned in the text

Park	Features	Activities	Best Time to Visit	Page
Doi Inthanon	granitic mountains, birdlife, serow, Siamese hare, gibbon	hiking, birding, hill-tribe trekking	Nov-May	p321
Doi Phu Kha	mountains, caves, karst formations, waterfalls	hiking, hill-tribe trekking	Nov-May	p378
Thung Salaeng Luang	mountains, monsoon forest, wild boar, elephant, clouded monitor, red jungle fowl	hiking, rafting, caving	Nov-May	p388
Khao Lak/Laem Ru	mountains, beaches, rainforest, serow, tapir, sea eagle, hornbill, orchid	birding, hiking, swimming, snorkelling	Jan-May	p638
Khao Luang	mountains, rainforest, sambar, clouded leopard, serow, macaque, tiger, hornbill	hiking, camping, birding	Dec-May	p605
Khao Phanom Bencha	mountains, rainforest, wild pig, serow, langur, gibbon, hornbill	hiking, birding	Jan-May	p687
Khao Sam Roi Yot	mangroves, serow, Irrawaddy dolphins	hiking, camping	Jun-Feb	p534
Khao Sok	pristine rainforest, tigers, *Rafflesia*	hiking, boating	Feb-May	p553
Khao Yai	monsoon forest, elephant, gaur, deer, gibbon	hiking, camping, wildlife watching	Nov-Feb, Jun-Oct	p448
Ko Lanta	islands, rainforest, mangrove, tropical fish, dugong, Brahminy Kite, water monitor	hiking, snorkelling, diving	Nov-May	p697
Ko Chang	mountainous islands, coral, tropical fish	hiking, snorkelling, diving	Jan-May	p262
Similan Islands	granitic islands, coral, tropical fish	snorkelling, diving	Nov-May	p639
Ko Tarutao	karst, islands, coral, tropical fish, fishing cat, monitor lizard	hiking, snorkelling, fishing (Ko Lipe only)	Nov-May	p715
Nam Nao	mountains, monsoon forest, Asiatic black bear, leopard, gaur, orchids	hiking, camping	Jan-May	p494
Phu Kradung	mountains, elephants, Asia jackals, barking deer, gibbon	hiking	Jan-May	p488
Thaleh Ban	karst, rainforest, tapir, serow, hornbill, flying gecko	hiking, camping	Dec-May	p719
Than Bokkharani	karst, rainforest, mangrove, Brahminy kite, Bengal monitor, civet, gibbon, langur	hiking, swimming	Dec-May	p688
Um Phang Wildlife Sanctuary	monsoon forest, caves, rapids, waterfalls	hiking, elephant trekking, white-water rafting	Nov-May	p410

land and sea area, which means Thailand has one of the highest percentages of protected areas of any nation in the world.

The majority of the parks, reserves and sanctuaries are well maintained by the **Royal Forest Department** (RFD; www.forest.go.th/default_e.asp), but a few, notably Hat Noppharat Thara/Ko Phi-Phi Marine National Park, have allowed rampant tourism to threaten the natural environment. Poaching, illegal logging and shifting cultivation have also taken their toll on protected lands, but over the last decade or so the government has been cracking down on these issues with some success.

Marine national parks along the Andaman coast experienced varying amounts of damage from the December 2004 tsunami. Roughly 5% of the coral in reef systems associated with these parks are estimated to have been heavily damaged by the waves or by debris brought by the waves. None of the damage was extensive enough to interfere with park activities in the long run, and all of the parks are open as usual.

Researched and written by James David Fahn, environmental editor for the *Nation*, an English-language Bangkok daily, *A Land on Fire: The Environmental Consequences of the Southeast Asian Boom* (2003) is a study of the precarious state of Southeast Asia's environment, focusing mainly on Thailand.

ENVIRONMENTAL ISSUES
Forests & Wildlife

Thailand, typical of countries with high population densities, has put enormous pressure on its ecosystems. Logging and agriculture have reduced natural forest cover from around 70% (50 years ago) to a current estimate of 29%, according to the World Resources Institute. This percentage is on par with the global average but above average for Asia.

The loss of forest has been accompanied by dwindling wildlife resources. Species that are notably extinct in Thailand include the kouprey (a type of wild cattle), Schomburgk's deer and the Javan rhino, but innumerable smaller species have also fallen by the wayside.

In response to environmental degradation, the Thai government has created a large number of protected parks, reserves and sanctuaries since the 1970s, and has enacted legislation to protect specific plant and animal species. The government hopes to raise the total forest cover to 40% by the middle of this century. The latest World Conservation Monitoring Centre report from the UN Environment Programme (UNEP) confirms that Thailand has designated protected status for more forest cover than any other nation in South or Southeast Asia, both proportionately (30%) and in square kilometres (51,300 sq km).

In 1989 all logging was banned in Thailand following a disaster the year before in which hundreds of tonnes of cut timber washed down deforested slopes in Surat Thani Province, burying a number of villages and killing more than 100 people. It is now illegal to sell timber felled in the country, and all imported timber is theoretically accounted for before going on the market.

Thailand is a signatory to the UN Convention on International Trade in Endangered Species (Cites), and although Thailand has a better record than most of its neighbours, corruption hinders government attempts to shelter 'exotic' species from the illicit global wildlife trade. A crackdown on restaurants serving 'jungle food' (aahǎan pàa) – exotic and often endangered wildlife species like barking deer, bear, pangolin, civet and gaur – has been fairly successful.

In any case wildlife experts agree that the greatest danger faced by Thai fauna is neither hunting nor the illegal wildlife trade but rather habitat loss – as is true worldwide. If the forests, mangroves, marshes and grasslands are protected, they will in turn protect the animals.

The RFD is under constant pressure to take immediate action in the areas where preservation laws have gone unenforced, especially coastal zones where illegal tourist accommodation has flourished. Slowness to respond in the cases of Ko Phi-Phi and Ko Samet suggests vested interests area involved.

Forestry department efforts are also hampered by a lack of personnel and funds. The average ranger is paid less than 140B per day – some aren't paid at all but receive food and lodging – to take on armed poachers backed by the rich and powerful Chinese godfathers who control illicit timber and wildlife businesses.

Marine resources are also threatened by a lack of long-range conservation goals. The upper portion of the Gulf of Thailand, between Rayong and Prachuap Khiri Khan, was once one of the most fertile marine areas in the world. Now there is a significant lack of marine life due to overfishing. Experts say it's not too late to rehabilitate the upper gulf by reducing pollution and the number of trawlers, and by restricting commercial fishing to certain zones. An effective ban on the harvest of mackerel *(plaa thuu)* in the spawning stages has brought stocks of this fish back from the brink of total depletion.

Pollution

Urban air quality is one of the nation's most significant environmental issues, particularly in Bangkok and adjacent provinces. At least a million Bangkok inhabitants suffer from respiratory problems or allergies triggered by air pollution. However, according to a December 2002 World Bank report, air quality in Thailand has improved substantially over the past decade. Bangkok air is now rated of higher quality than that of Beijing, Jakarta, New Delhi and Manila. Third-party reports also claim that lead, dust and carbon monoxide levels in Thailand's urban centres had decreased to an acceptable level, due to the government's emphasis

SEUB NAKASATHIEN

One of the Thai environmental movement's biggest heroes to date is a man who spent much of his adult life trying to protect the kingdom's forests.

After graduating from Kasetsart University with two degrees in forestry, Seub Nakasathien began working for the Wildlife Conservation Division of the Royal Forest Department (RFD) in the mid 1970s. Stationed at a small wildlife sanctuary in Chonburi Province, Seub made his first encounters with poachers, and earned the respect of both his peers and criminals with his straightforward and fair treatment.

After completing a master's degree in environmental conservation overseas, Seub returned to Thailand and was promoted to the chief management position at Huay Kha Khaeng Wildlife Sanctuary in 1989. Here he once again came into contact with poachers as well as illegal loggers, and once again his efforts met with measured success.

When the RFD granted a logging concession to a plywood company in some areas of Huay Kha Khaeng, Seub found himself in combat with the RFD itself. Frustrated with the way the department paid lip service towards conservation while collecting large sums of money from logging contracts, Seub appealed to Unesco to designate the Thung Yai/Huay Kha Khaeng Wildlife Sanctuary a World Heritage site.

In September 1990 Seub donated his research gear to a wildlife centre, built a shrine dedicated to the spirits of park rangers who had given their lives to protect Huay Kha Khaeng and apparently committed suicide. Although the circumstances surrounding his death are unclear, Seub's commitment to Thailand's wildlife and ecology has become an inspiration for the environmental movement in Thailand and beyond.

For more information about Seub's life and legacy, and about a charitable fund created in his name, see www.seub.or.th in Thai.

on phasing out leaded petrol, improving diesel quality and using cleaner technologies designed to lessen air pollution.

Thailand's efforts to convert vehicle owners from leaded to unleaded petrol over the last 15 years resulted in a 20-fold decrease in ambient lead levels between 1991 and 2001. As of 2004 new emission standards require lower sulphur contents in petrol and diesel. The expansion of mass transit networks in the capital, beginning with the BTS Skytrain and MRTA subway, also promise to improve air quality in the capital, and Chiang Mai will soon follow suit with its own electric railway.

Greenpeace's online Southeast Asia headquarters at www.greenpeace southeastasia.org carries regular Thailand-related reports.

Air pollution isn't entirely confined to urban areas. During the annual dry season, November to April, the burning of agricultural fields as well as household rubbish and leaves poses a significant problem in terms of adding fine particulate matter (PM) to the air. Some communities, such as Chiang Mai municipality, have enacted bans on all open burning, although enforcement has thus far been anything but thorough.

Excessive levels of sulphur dioxide in the Mae Moh Valley, where residents report a higher-than-average number of deaths from heart failure and chronic respiratory problems, have been traced to over a dozen coal-fired facilities at the Mae Moh power plant complex. Thailand's government-operated Electricity Generating Authority (EGAT) has responded to complaints by installing sulphur scrubbers to reduce emissions. The Thai government has warned polluting industries that if they fail to meet environmental regulations they will face closure.

Water pollution varies according to region but is, as would be expected, most acute in the Bangkok metropolitan area because of the relatively high concentration of factories, particularly east of the city. Chemical run-off from agribusiness, coastal shrimp farming and untreated sewage also pollutes groundwater and coastal areas. Offshore oil and gas exploration in the Gulf of Thailand has also increased marine pollution.

The Bangkok Metropolitan Administration (BMA) is developing a system of sewage-treatment plants in the Chao Phraya Delta area with the intention of halting all large-scale dumping of sewage into Gulf waters, but similar action needs to be taken along the entire eastern seaboard, which has become Thailand's industrial centre.

Thailand's 1991 Environmental Protection Act in 1992, along with the 1997 'people's constitution' (see p42) requires that public hearings be held before the government embarks on development projects with potential environmental impact. Weak enforcement and noncompliance continue to thwart the intent of such legislation. Environmental nongovernmental organisations (NGOs) are increasingly filling the gap between legislation and compliance, but the country still has a long way to go to balance the needs of economic growth with those of resource sustainability.

Tourism & the Environment

Conscious that the country's natural beauty is a major tourist attraction for both residents and foreigners, and that tourism is one of Thailand's major revenue earners, the government has stepped up efforts to protect wilderness areas and to add more acreage to the park system. In Khao Yai National Park, for example, all hotel and golf-course facilities were removed a few years ago in order to reduce human influence on the park environment. As a result of government and private sector pressure on the fishing industry, coral dynamiting has been all but eliminated in the Similan and Surin Islands, to preserve these areas for tourist visitation.

However, tourism has also made negative contributions. Eager to make fistfuls of cash, hotel developers and tour operators have rushed to provide ecologically inappropriate services for visitors in sensitive areas. Ko Phi-Phi and Ko Samet are two national park islands notorious for over-development and public land encroachment.

What can the average visitor to Thailand do to minimise the impact of tourism on the environment? We recommend the following:

- Don't buy coral or sea shells – it's illegal in Thailand to buy or sell either.
- Avoid all restaurants serving 'exotic' wildlife species.
- When using hired boats near coral reefs, insist that boat operators not lower their anchor onto coral formations.
- Refrain from purchasing or accepting drinking water offered in plastic bottles wherever possible. When there's a choice, request glass water bottles, which are recyclable in Thailand. The deposit is refundable when you return the bottle to any vendor who sells drinking water in glass bottles.
- In outdoor areas where rubbish has accumulated, consider organising an impromptu clean-up crew to collect plastic, Styrofoam and other nonbiodegradables for delivery to a regular rubbish pick-up point.
- Volunteer to collect (and later dispose of) rubbish when trekking or boating.

An increasing number of guesthouses now offer drinking water from large, reusable plastic water containers, so that visitors may fill up their own canteens or water bottles.

Thais sensitive to Western paternalism are quick to point out that on a global scale the so-called 'developed' countries contribute far more environmental damage than does Thailand. For example, per capita greenhouse emissions for Thailand on average create less than one tenth of the amounts contributed by Australia, Canada and the USA.

> The Thailand Environ-
> ment Institute (www
> .tei.or.th/main.htm) is
> a non-profit research
> institute devoted to
> sustainable human
> development.

By expressing your desire to use environmentally friendly materials – and by taking direct action to avoid the use and indiscriminate disposal of plastic – you can provide an example of environmental consciousness not only for the Thais but for other international visitors.

Visitors may want to consider filing letters of complaint regarding any questionable environmental practices with the Tourism Authority of Thailand, Wildlife Fund Thailand and the RFD at the following ad-dresses. Markets selling endangered species should also be duly noted – consider enclosing photos to support your complaints.

Asian Society for Environmental Protection (CDG-Seapo; ☎ 0 2524 5363; web.ait.ac.th /~tony/asep/index.php; Asian Institute of Technology, Bangkok 10501)

Forest Protection Office (☎ 0 2579 3004, 0 2579 5266; wildlife_protection@forest.go.th; Royal Forest Department, 61 Th Phahonyothin, Bangkhen, Bangkok 10900)

Network for Environmentally & Socially Sustainable Tourism Thailand (NESSThai; beartai@bkk.loxinfo.co.th; PO Box 48, Krabi)

Office of the National Environment Board (☎ 0 2279 7190; 60/1 Soi Phibun Watthana 7, Th Rama VI, Bangkok 10400)

Project for Ecological Recovery (☎ 0 2681 0718; 409 TVS Bldg, 4th fl, Soi Rohitsuk, Th Prachabamphen, Bangkok 1031)

Tourism Authority of Thailand (TAT; ☎ 0 2250 5500; www.tat.or.th; 1600 Th Phetburi Tat Mai, Ratchathewi, Bangkok 10400)

Wild Animal Rescue Foundation of Thailand (WAR; ☎ 0 2712 9515; www.warthai.org; 65/1 Soi 55, Th Sukhumvit 55, Bangkok 10110)

World Wide Fund Thailand (WWFT; ☎ 0 2524 6128; www.wwfthai.ait.ac.th; WWF Program Office, Asian Institute of Technology, PO Box 4, Klong Luang, Pathum Thani 12120)

BANGKOK

Bangkok

In this steamy, sprawling mess you'll find an intensely devout city famous for debauchery, a traditional village encased in a concrete jungle and a chaotic but orchestrated universe of speeding bodies. How does this swiftly tilting megalopolis juggle the ancient and the modern, the manic and the relaxed? With Thailand's graceful appreciation of contradictions, of course.

Everyone will tell you that Bangkok isn't the 'real' Thailand and to shuffle through as quickly as possible. If you listen to the naysayers and nervously huddle on Th Khao San until a cramped minivan whisks you to the islands, you're flirting with the 'village syndrome', a romantic notion that developing countries sacrifice their integrity by modernising or adopting outside influences (even though the perceived indigenous culture is a product of historical hybridisation). In fact, nowhere else is Thailand's *khwaam pen thai* ('Thai-ness') more apparent than against the ultramodern backdrop of skyscraper canyons, screaming traffic and excessive commercialisation. Right there beside the 21st-century façade are spirit shrines receiving daily devotions, pushcart vendors more adored than white-tablecloth restaurants and daily encounters with the strange, revolting and beguiling. Within all the neon and air-con is yet another aspect of the resilient Thai spirit.

HIGHLIGHTS

- Making a pilgrimage to the sacred temples of **Wat Phra Kaew** (p100) and **Wat Pho** (p102)
- Catching the cool river breezes from the back of the **Chao Phraya River Express** (p133) at sunset
- Getting completely lost in **Chinatown**'s crowded sois and markets (p126)
- Cheering along with the betting crowd at a **muay thai** (boxing) match (p173)
- Spending a day shopping with the hip Thai teens in **MBK** (p174) or **Siam Square** (p175), or with the filthy rich at the **Emporium** (p175)
- Enjoying VIP luxury at Bangkok's ultra-modern **movie theatres** (p171)

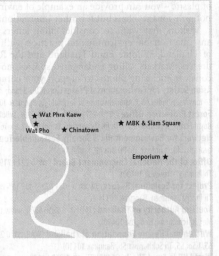

★ Wat Phra Kaew
★
Wat Pho ★ Chinatown

★ MBK & Siam Square

Emporium ★

| ■ TOTAL AREA: 1568 SQ KM | ■ POPULATION: APPROX 7.5 MILLION | ■ ELEVATION: 12M (39FT) |

HISTORY

Both the centre of government and culture today, Bangkok was a historical miracle during a time of turmoil following the Burmese invasion. Following the fall of Ayuthaya in 1767, the kingdom fractured into competing city-states. Of the rival factions, General Taksin emerged as a decisive and charismatic unifier who established his base in Thonburi, on the western bank of Mae Nam Chao Phraya (Chao Phraya River), a convenient location for sea trade from the Gulf of Thailand. Taksin proved more of a military strategist than a popular ruler and was deposed by another important military general, Chao Phraya Chakri, who moved the capital across the river in 1782 to a more defensible location in anticipation of a Burmese attack. The succession of his son in 1809 established the present-day dynasty and Chao Phraya Chakri is referred to as Rama I.

Court officials envisioned the new capital as a resurrected Ayuthaya, complete with an island district (Ko Ratanakosin) carved out of the swampland and cradling the royal court (the Grand Palace) and a temple to the auspicious Emerald Buddha (Wat Phra Kaew). A thick wall encircled the emerging city, filled with stilt and floating houses ideally adapted to seasonal flooding.

Modernity came to the capital in the late 19th century as European aesthetics and technologies filtered east. During the reigns of Rama IV (King Mongkut) and Rama V (King Chulalongkorn), Bangkok received its first paved road (Th Charoen Krung) and a new royal district (Dusit) styled after European palaces.

Bangkok was a gangly town when soldiers from the American war in Vietnam came to rest and relax in the city's go-go bars and brothels. It wasn't until the boom years of the 1980s and 1990s that Bangkok exploded into a full-fledged metropolis crowded with hulking skyscrapers and an endless spill of concrete gobbling up rice paddies and green space. The city's extravagant tastes have been tamed by the 1997 economic meltdown and in an effort to address its legendary traffic, Bangkok now boasts an elevated light-rail system (Skytrain) and an underground subway (Metro).

ORIENTATION

Occupying the east side of Mae Nam Chao Phraya, Bangkok proper can be divided in two by the main north–south railway terminating at Hualamphong train station.

The portion between the serpentine river and the railway is old Bangkok, a district of holy temples, crowded markets and family-owned shophouses. Swarming either side of the train station is the dense neighbourhood of Chinatown, a frenzy of red, gold and neon. Chinatown's chaos is subdued by Ko Ratanakosin, the former royal palace district and Bangkok's most spectacular tourist attraction. Heading north up the river is charming Banglamphu and the famous tourist strip of Khao San Rd (Th Khao San). Crowning the old city is Dusit, a planned homage to the great European capitals, and the easy-going neighbourhood of Thewet.

East of the railway is new Bangkok – an equally repulsive and charming replication of a sci-fi megalopolis. Siam Square is a universe of boxy shopping centres that attracts fashion-savvy Thai teenagers and oil-fortune

---

CITY OF ANGELS

Krungthep mahanakhon amonratanakosin mahintara ayuthaya mahadilok popnopparat ratchathani burirom udomratchaniwet mahasathan amonpiman avatansathit sakkathattiya witsanukamprasit

A real tongue-twister, Bangkok's official name was conveniently truncated to Krung Thep (City of Angels) for everyday usage, although the breathtaking 43 syllables were transformed into a hypnotic pop tune by Asanee-Wasan in 1989 and its recitation by memory is always a winning bar game. The bombastic title translates roughly as 'Great City of Angels, Repository of Divine Gems, Great Land Unconquerable, Grand and Prominent Realm, Royal and Delightful Capital City Full of Nine Noble Gems, Highest Royal Dwelling and Grand Palace, Divine Shelter and Living Place of Reincarnated Spirits'.

But why does the rest of the world call it 'Bangkok'? Turns out the royal capital was founded on a little village named Bang Makok (Place of Olive Plums) and stubborn foreign traders never bothered to adjust their appellation.

princesses on shopping vacations. Thanon Sukhumvit runs a deliberate course from the geographic city centre to the Gulf of Thailand with limb-like tributaries reaching into corporate expatriate cocoons and the bar-girl scene at Soi Cowboy and Nana Entertainment Plaza. Bangkok's financial district centres along Th Silom, which cuts an incision from the river to Lumphini Park. Intersecting Th Silom near the river, Th Charoen Krung was Bangkok's first paved road and once the artery for the city's original mercantile pursuits of shipping; the narrow sois branch off through the old *faràng* quarters littered with decaying Victorian monuments, churches and the famous Oriental Hotel. True to the city's resistance to efficiency, there are two main embassy districts: Th Withayu (Wireless Rd) and Th Sathon.

On the opposite (west) side of the river is Thonburi, which was Thailand's capital for 15 years, before Bangkok was founded. *Fàng thon* (Thonburi Bank), as it's often called by Thais, seems more akin to the provincial capitals than Bangkok's glittering high-rises.

Bangkok Addresses

Any city as large and unplanned as Bangkok can be tough to get around. Street names are often unpronounceable to begin with, compounded by the inconsistency of Romanised spellings and a mystifying array of winding streets that never lead where a map dares to propose.

Building numbers are equally confounding; the string of numbers divided by slashes and dashes (ie 48/3–5 Soi 1, Th Sukhumvit) indicate lot disbursements rather than

---

STREET ALIASES

As there is no standardisation for transliterating Thai into the Roman alphabet, Bangkok's streets operate under many aliases. Here are some common variants:

- Rajadamri, Ratchadamri, often abbreviated as Rat'damri

- Phetburi, Phetchaburi, and the eastern extension becomes Phetburi Tat Mai (often appearing as its English translation: New Phetburi)

- Phra Ram (I–VI) or Rama (I–VI)

---

sequential geography. The number before the slash refers to the original lot number; the numbers following the slash indicate buildings (or entrances to buildings) constructed within that lot. The pre-slash numbers appear in the order in which they were added to city plans, while the post-slash numbers are arbitrarily assigned by developers. As a result, you'll find the numbers along a given street don't always run consecutively.

The Thai word *thànŏn* (Th) means road, street or avenue. Hence Ratchadamnoen Rd (sometimes called Ratchadamnoen Ave) is always Th Ratchadamnoen in Thai.

A soi is a small street or lane that runs off a larger street. So, the address referred to as 48/3–5 Soi 1, Th Sukhumvit, will be located off Th Sukhumvit on Soi 1. Alternative ways of writing the same address include 48/3–5 Th Sukhumvit Soi 1, or even just 48/3–5 Sukhumvit 1. Some Bangkok sois have become so large that they can be referred to both as *thànŏn* and soi, eg Soi Sarasin/Th Sarasin and Soi Asoke/Th Asoke. Smaller than a soi is a *tràwk* (usually spelt *trok*) or alley.

Maps

A map is an essential for finding your way around Bangkok. Apart from Lonely Planet's *Bangkok* city map, the *Tour 'n' Guide Map to Bangkok Thailand* is the best resource for using the city's extensive bus system. But at the time of writing, the map hadn't been regularly updated and didn't indicate the prefix addition of '50' to all air-con bus routes.

The long-running and oft-imitated *Nancy Chandler's Map of Bangkok* is a schematic guide to the city, with listings of out-of-the-way places, beloved restaurants and relating colourful anecdotes about neighbourhoods and markets. It is an entertaining visual guide but it is not recommendable as your primary navigator.

If travelling to districts outside central Bangkok, invest in *Bangkok & Vicinity A to Z Atlas*, which covers the expressways and surrounding suburbs.

INFORMATION
Bookshops

Aporia Books (Map pp110-11; ☎ 0 2629 2919; 131 Th Tanao; bus 511, 56, river ferry Tha Phra Athit) New and used English, French and German titles.

Asia Books Sukhumvit (Map pp112-13; ☎ 0 2252 7277; Soi 15, 221 Th Sukhumvit; Skytrain Asoke); Central World

BANGKOK IN...

One Day
Make an early morning visit to **Wat Phra Kaew** and the **Grand Palace** (p100), quirky **Wat Pho** (p102) and the crowded **Amulet Market** (p103). Charter a long-tail boat through Thonburi's **canals** (p133) and to **Wat Arun** (p103).

For dinner, head to **Ton Pho** (p157), **MBK Food Centre** (p157) or **Harmonique** (p161). Then go-go to **Patpong**'s red-light district (p171).

Three Days
Do as the Thais do – go **shopping** (p173). Zip to and fro aboard the ultramodern **Skytrain** (p184). Glimpse into old-style Bangkok with a trip to **Jim Thompson's House** (p127). And wrap up the daylight hours with a traditional **Thai massage** (p132).

For dinner, head to **Vientiane Kitchen** (p163) or **Hua Lamphong Food Station** (p164). See how the moneyed Thais live at **Q Bar** (p170) or **Diplomat Bar** (p168).

One Week
Now that you're accustomed to the noise, pollution and traffic, you are ready for **Chinatown** (p126) and its congested markets. On the weekend, take the Skytrain to **Chatuchak Weekend Market** (p177) for intensive souvenir and bizarre sights hunting. For a little R&R, take a river ferry to **Ko Kret** (p131), a car-less island north of central Bangkok.

Plaza (Map pp118-19; 3rd fl, Central World Plaza, cnr Th Ploenchit & Th Ratchadamri; Skytrain Chitlom); Siam Discovery Centre (Map pp118-19; 4th fl, Siam Discovery Center, Th Phra Ram I; Skytrain Siam); Thaniya Plaza (Map pp114-16; 3rd fl, Thaniya Plaza, Th Silom; Skytrain Sala Daeng); Emporium (Map pp112-13; 3rd fl, Emporium, Th Sukhumvit; Skytrain Phrom Phong) One of the best English-language bookshop chains.
Dasa Book Café (Map pp112-13; ☎ 0 2661 2993; 710/4 Th Sukhumvit, btwn Soi 26 & 28; Skytrain Phrom Phong) Book recycler of many languages.
Elite Used Books (Map pp112-13; 593/5 Th Sukhumvit near Soi 33/1; Skytrain Phrom Phong) Used titles in English, Chinese, French, German and Swedish.
Kinokuniya (Map pp112-13; ☎ 0 2664 8554; 3rd fl, Emporium, Th Sukhumvit; Skytrain Phrom Phong) Multi-language selections, magazines, children's books.
Rim Khob Fah Bookstore (Map pp110-11; ☎ 0 2622 3510; 78/1 Th Ratchadamnoen, Democracy Monument; ⏰ 8.30am-7pm; bus 511, 512, khlong taxi to Tha Phan Fah) Small selection of Department of Fine Arts booklets on culture and history.
Shaman Books (Map pp110-11; ☎ 0 2629 0418; 71 Th Khao San; ⏰ 8am-11pm; bus 511, 56, river ferry Tha Phra Athit) Large selection of used fiction, guidebooks and Aseana.
Suksit Siam (off Map pp110-11; ☎ 0 2222 5698; 113-115 Th Fuang Nakhon, south of Mae Thorani Shrine; ⏰ 9am-4pm Mon-Fri, 9am-3pm Sat; bus 507, 508) Alternative views on Thai and international politics, especially works by outspoken social critic Sulak Sivaraksa and the progressive Santi Pracha Dhamma Institute.

Cultural Centres
Various Thai and foreign associations organise cultural events, film festivals and lectures for fraternising with compatriots or internationally versed Thais.
Alliance Française (Map p117; ☎ 0 2670 4200; www.alliance-francaise.or.th; 29 Th Sathon Tai; bus 17, 22, 62)
American University Alumni (AUA; Map pp118-19; ☎ 0 2252 8170; www.auathailand.org; 179 Th Ratchadamri; Skytrain Ratchadamri)
British Council (Map pp118-19; ☎ 0 2652 5480; www.britishcouncil.or.th; 254 Soi Chulalongkorn 64, Siam Square, Th Phra Ram I; Skytrain Siam)
Foreign Correspondents Club of Thailand (FCCT; Map pp118-19; ☎ 0 2652 0580; www.fccthai.com; Penthouse, Maneeya Center, 518/5 Th Ploenchit; Skytrain Chitlom)
Goethe Institut (Thai-German Cultural Centre; Map p117; ☎ 0 2287 0942; www.goethe.de; 18/1 Soi Goethe, btwn Th Sathon Tai & Soi Ngam Duphli; subway Lumphini)
Japan Foundation (Map pp112-13; ☎ 0 2260 8560; 159 Soi Asoke, Serm-mit Tower, Th Sukhumvit; bus 136, 206)
Thailand Cultural Centre (TCC; Map pp104-5; ☎ 0 2245 7742; www.thaiculturalcenter.com; Th Ratchadaphisek; subway Thailand Cultural Centre) See p173.

Emergency
Tourist Assistance Centre (☎ 0 2281 1348; ⏰ 8am-midnight) A division of Tourism Authority of Thailand (TAT) dealing specifically with tourist safety. English speakers available.
Tourist police (☎ 1155; ⏰ 24hr) An English-speaking unit investigates criminal activity involving tourists, including

> **GUIDEBOOKS**
>
> Lonely Planet's *Bangkok* is ideal for those spending a month or more in the capital city. For weekenders, pick up a copy of Lonely Planet's *Best of Bangkok*.

gem scams; they can also act as a bilingual liaison with the regular police.

If you can speak Thai, or can find someone to call on your behalf, contact the city's main emergency facilities at the following numbers.

Ambulance ☎ 1554/1646
Fire ☎ 199
Police/Emergency ☎ 191

Internet Access

There is no shortage of Internet cafés in Bangkok competing against each other to offer the cheapest and fastest connection. The newest terminal on the block is usually that month's best find. Rates vary depending on the concentration and affluence of Net-heads – Banglamphu is infinitely cheaper than Sukhumvit or Silom with rates as low as 1B per minute. The shopping centres in Siam Square typically have competitively priced access.

Internet Resources

2Bangkok (www.2Bangkok.com) Obsessed with charting construction and infrastructure projects, including translations from Thai newspapers.

Asia-Hotels (www.asia-hotels.com) Handy rundown on hotels, their amenities and comments from former guests.

Bangkok Recorder (www.bangkokrecorder.com) Online city magazine covering music trends, nightlife (curfew crackdowns) and other vexing capital questions.

Bangkok Thailand Today (www.bangkok.thailandtoday .com) Solid tips on shopping, nightlife, dining and sightseeing, with an emphasis on the river and Ko Ratanakosin.

Khao San Road (www.khaosanroad.com) News, reviews and profiles of Bangkok's famous tourist ghetto.

Libraries

Besides offering an abundance of reading material, Bangkok's libraries make a peaceful escape from the heat and noise.

National Library (Map pp106-7; ☎ 0 2281 5212; Th Samsen; admission free; ◷ 9am-7.30pm; river ferry Tha Thewet) Magazines, foreign-language titles on Thailand and recordings by the King.

British Club's Neilson Hays Library & Rotunda Gallery (Map pp114-16; ☎ 0 2233 1731; 195 Th Surawong; day use 50B, annual 1400B; ◷ 9.30am-4pm Tue-Sun; Skytrain Chong Nonsi) The oldest English-language library in Thailand with over 20,000 volumes, including children's books and titles on Thailand.

Siam Society (Map pp112-13; ☎ 0 2661 6470; 131 Soi Asoke, Th Sukhumvit; ◷ 9.30am-7.30pm; Skytrain Asoke, subway Sukhumvit) Royal patronage society with a public-access library on academic subjects.

Media

Bangkok Metro Glossy monthly magazine targeted at the city's sophisticates.

Bangkok Post No-nonsense English-language daily with Friday and weekend supplements covering city day- and night-life.

Farang An irreverent monthly magazine following the tears and fears of the backpacker and expat community.

Gavroche French-language magazine with news and views.

Nation Evening edition daily with more style and flair than the *Bangkok Post*.

Medical Services

Thanks to its high standard of hospital care, Bangkok is fast becoming a destination for medical tourists shopping for more affordable dental check-ups, elective surgery and cosmetic procedures. Pharmacists (chemists) throughout the city can diagnose and treat most minor ailments (Bangkok belly, sinus and skin infections etc). Contact **Rutnin Eye Hospital** (Map pp112-13; ☎ 0 2258 0442; 80/1 Soi Asoke) for urgent eye care.

The following hospitals offer 24-hour service and most have English-speaking staff.

Bangkok Adventist (Mission) Hospital (Map pp106-7; ☎ 0 2282 1100; 430 Th Phitsanulok; bus 16, 23, 99)

Bangkok Christian Hospital (Map pp114-16; ☎ 0 2634 0560; 124 Th Silom; Skytrain Sala Daeng)

BNH (Map pp114-16; ☎ 0 2632 0540-87; 9 Th Convent, off Th Silom; Skytrain Sala Daeng)

Bumrungrad Hospital (Map pp112-13; ☎ 0 2253 0250; 33 Soi 3, Th Sukhumvit; Skytrain Ploenchit & Nana) Considered the five-star facility with US accreditation.

Phayathai Hospital 1 (Map pp106-7; ☎ 0 2245 2620; 364/1 Th Sri Ayuthaya; bus 503)

Samitivej Hospital (off Map pp112-13; ☎ 0 2392 0011-9; 133 Soi 49, Th Sukhumvit)

St Louis Hospital (Map pp114-16; ☎ 0 2675 9300; 215 Th Sathon Tai; Skytrain Surasak)

Money

Regular bank hours in Bangkok are 10am to 4pm, and ATMs are common in all areas of the city. Many Thai banks have currency-exchange offices, open from 8.30am to 8pm (some even later). Go to 7-Eleven shops or other reputable places to break 1000B bills; don't expect a vendor or taxi to able to make change on a bill 500B or larger.

Post

Main post office (Map pp114-16; ☎ 0 2233 1050; Th Charoen Krung; ⏰ 8am-8pm Mon-Fri, 8am-1pm Sat & Sun; river express Tha Si Phraya) Services include poste restante (1B) and packaging (⏰ 8.30am-4.30pm Mon-Fri, 8.30am-noon Sat), within the main building. Do not send money or valuables via regular mail. Branch post offices throughout the city also offer poste restante and parcel services.

Telephone & Fax

Bangkok's former area code (☎ 02) has now been incorporated into all telephone numbers dialled locally or from outside the city. Public phones for both domestic and international calls are well distributed throughout the city but are tricky finding one that is quiet enough to have a conversation. Try the shopping centres for air-con and noiseless comfort.

Communications Authority of Thailand (CAT; Map pp114-16; ☎ 0 2573 0099; Th Charoen Krung; ⏰ 24hr; river ferry Tha Si Phraya) Next door to the main post office; offers Home Country Direct service, fax transmittal and phonecard services.

Telephone Organization of Thailand (TOT; Map pp118-19; ☎ 0 2251 1111; Th Ploenchit; Skytrain Chit-lom) Long-distance calling services and an English version of Bangkok's *Yellow Pages*.

Tourist Information

Official tourist offices distribute maps, brochures and advice on sights and activities. Don't confuse these free services with the licensed travel agents who book tours and transportation on a commission basis. Often, travel agencies incorporate elements of the official national tourism name ('TAT' or Tourism Authority of Thailand) into their own to encourage business.

Bangkok Tourist Division (Map pp110-11; ☎ 0 2225 7612-5; www.bangkoktourist.com; 17/1 Th Phra Athit; ⏰ 9am-7pm; river ferry Tha Phra Athit) City-specific tourism department; yellow information booths staffed by student volunteers are located throughout the city.

TAT main office (Map pp106-7; ☎ 0 2250 5500; www.tourismthailand.org; 4th fl, 1606 Th Phetburi Tat Mai; ⏰ 8.30am-4.30pm; Skytrain Asoke) City and country travel information.

TAT airport information desk (Map pp104-5; arrival hall, Terminals 1 & 2, Bangkok International Airport; ⏰ 8am-midnight) Accommodation and transportation information.

Tourist Police/Tourist Assistance Centre (Map pp110-11; ☎ 1155; Th Ratchadamnoen Nok; ⏰ 24hr; bus 503, 509, 73, 201) Near the boxing stadium. Handles matters involving theft and crimes against tourists

Travel Agencies

Bangkok is packed with travel agencies where you can book bus and air tickets. Some are reliable and offer unbelievably low prices, while others are fly-by-night scams issuing bogus tickets with no recourse for the offended traveller. Ask for recommendations from fellow travellers before making a major purchase from a travel agent. The following are some long-running agencies:

Diethelm Travel (Map p117; ☎ 0 2255 9150; www.diethelm-travel.com; 140/1 Th Withayu, Kian Gwan Bldg, 14th fl; bus 13, 17, 62)

STA Travel (Map pp114-16; ☎ 0 2236 0262; www.statravel.com; 14th fl, Wall Street Tower, 33/70 Th Surawong; Skytrain Sala Daeng) Maintains reliable offices that specialise in discounted yet flexible air tickets.

Vieng Travel (Map pp110-11; ☎ 0 2280 3537; www.viengtravel.com; Trang Hotel, 99/8 Th Wisut Kasat; bus 49)

DANGERS & ANNOYANCES

You are more likely to be charmed than coerced out of your money in Bangkok. Practised con artists capitalise on Thailand's famous friendliness and a revolving door of fresh, trusting tourists.

Bangkok's most heavily touristed areas – Wat Phra Kaew, Jim Thompson's House, Th Khao San – are favourite hunting grounds for expert cons. The most typical scenario involves a well-dressed, professional-acting person who appears to come to your aid when an attraction is 'closed' for the day. They will then graciously arrange a 10B *túk-túk* (motorised pedicab) ride to an undiscovered wat, which is usually a thin guise for taking you and your wallet for the proverbial 'ride'. Don't believe anyone on the street who tells you that a popular attraction is closed for a holiday; check for yourself. And don't engage in any sort of purchase – gems, tailors or jewellery – to which you've been referred by a helpful stranger.

PRELUDES TO A RIP-OFF

In an ongoing crusade to outsmart Bangkok's crafty scam artists, here is a handy primer for recognising them before they spot you.

▪ Remember your mother's advice: don't talk to strangers. In this self-absorbed city, the only people interested in chatting you up are usually interested in your wallet, not cultural exchange. You should be doubly suspicious if they look sweet and innocent; if they were really sincere, they would be too polite to approach you.

▪ If you ignore your mother's advice and talk to said stranger, your suspicion-meter should register wildly if the stranger says (a) that wherever you're going is closed, (b) that he or she knows someone who is studying/working in your home country, or (c) there is a great one-day sale on jewellery, gems or silk.

▪ A túk-túk driver offers a sightseeing tour for 20B. Do the maths: petrol and time will get paid by you thanks to a commission from whatever tailor or furniture store the driver 'happens' to know about.

▪ A metered taxi quotes a price for your destination. Any quoted price is usually three times higher than using the meter. Most in-town destinations are around 50B to 80B.

More obvious are the túk-túk drivers who are out to make a commission by dragging you to a local silk, tailor or jewellery shop, even though you've requested an entirely different destination. Even if you're in the market for a tailor, avoid the hidden commissions by patronising businesses who don't engage in this practice.

Then there is the long-running and quite infamous gem scam, in which you act as an agent for selling bulk quantities of gems in your home country. It is only after you cough up the quoted wholesale price of the gems, will you discover that your unexpected windfall consists only of a collection worthless pieces of glass.

Uncharacteristically aggressive robberies have been perpetrated by groups of kàthoey (lady-boys), typically around the lower Sukhumvit bar area. Lone, and generally drunk, foreign men have reportedly been approached by a solo kàthoey ('Hello, where you go, handsome?') who then creates a diversion while a partner swipes the victim's wallet.

Even though Thai children are taught to toss their garbage out of windows, foreigners should avoid following suit. This includes cigarette butts as well. An underpaid police officer will be more than happy to enforce the law (however broadly interpreted) on a foreigner who might possibly have the 1000B fine that the average Thai most certainly doesn't.

The tourist police can be quite effective in dealing with some of the 'unethical' business practices and crime. But there is little the tourist police can do if you think you've been overcharged for gems (or any other purchase).

See p728 for more information on safe travel and scams.

SIGHTS
Ko Ratanakosin
เกาะรัตนโกสินทร์   **Map p120**

Ko Ratanakosin is the ancient royal district housing Bangkok's most famous and stunning attractions. These sights are within walking distance of each other and best visited early in the morning before the day comes to a boil. Ignore the touts who will try to steer you to other minor temples or gem shops.

Directly across the river is Thonburi, which served a brief tenure as the Thai capital after the fall of Ayuthaya. Today the area along the river is easily accessed from cross-river ferries and there are museums and temples that are historical complements to those on the Bangkok side.

WAT PHRA KAEW & GRAND PALACE
วัดพระแก้ว/พระบรมมหาราชวัง

Also known as the Temple of the Emerald Buddha, **Wat Phra Kaew** (☎ 0 2623 5500; admission to temple & palace complex 200B, 2hr guided tours 100B; ☸ 8.30am-3.30pm; bus 508, 512, river ferry Tha Chang) is an architectural wonder of gleaming jehdii (stupas) seemingly buoyed above the ground, with polished orange-and-green roof tiles piercing the humid sky, mosaic-encrusted pillars and rich marble pediments. The highly stylised ornamentation is a shrine to the Emerald Buddha, and the temple complex adjoins the former residence of the monarch, the Grand Palace.

This ground was consecrated in 1782, the first year of Bangkok rule, and today is a pilgrimage destination for devout Buddhists and nationalists. The 94.5-hectare grounds encompass more than 100 buildings that represent 200 years of royal history and architectural experimentation. Most of the architecture, royal or sacred, can be classified as Ratanakosin (or old-Bangkok style).

Housed in a fantastically decorated *bòt* and guarded by pairs of mythical giants (*yaksha*), the **Emerald Buddha** is the temple's primary attraction. It sits atop an elevated altar, barely visible amid the gilded decorations. The diminutive figure is always cloaked in royal robes, one for each season (hot, cool and rainy). In a solemn ceremony, the king himself changes the garments at the beginning of each season.

Extensive **murals of the Ramakian** (the Thai version of the Indian epic *Ramayana*) line the inside walls of the compound. Originally painted during the reign of Rama I (1782–1809) and continually restored, the murals illustrate the epic in its entirety, beginning at the north gate and moving clockwise around the compound.

Except for an anteroom here and there, the buildings of the **Grand Palace** (Phra Borom Maharatchawong) are now put to use by the king only for certain ceremonial

occasions such as Coronation Day; the king's current residence is **Chitlada Palace** in the northern part of the city. The exteriors of the four buildings are worth a swift perusal for their royal bombast. The intrigue and rituals that occurred within the walls of this once cloistered community are relatively silent to the modern visitor. A fictionalised version is told in the trilogy *Four Reigns*, by Kukrit Pramoj.

Borombhiman Hall (eastern end), a French-inspired structure that served as a residence for Rama VI, is occasionally used to house visiting foreign dignitaries. In April 1981 General San Chitpatima used it as headquarters for an attempted coup. The building to the west is **Amarindra Hall**, originally a hall of justice but used today for coronation ceremonies.

TRAVELS OF THE EMERALD BUDDHA

The Emerald Buddha (Phra Kaew Morakot) holds a prominent position in Thai Buddhism not just because of its size (a mere 75cm) or its original material (probably jasper quartz or nephrite jade rather than emerald). In fact, the Emerald Buddha was just another ordinary image, with no illustrious pedigree, until its monumental 'coming out' in 15th-century Chiang Rai. During a fall, the image revealed its luminescent interior which was then covered with plaster and gold leaf (a common practice to safeguard valuable Buddhas from being stolen). After a few successful stints in various temples throughout northern Thailand, Laotian invaders stole the image in the mid-16th century.

The Emerald Buddha achieved another promotion in the cult of Buddha images some 200 years later when Thailand's King Taksin waged war against Laos, retrieving the image and mounting it in Thonburi. Later, when the capital moved to Bangkok and the crown was moved to General Chakri, the Emerald Buddha was honoured with one of the country's most magnificent monuments (Wat Phra Kaew).

The largest of the palace buildings is the **Chakri Mahaprasat**, the Grand Palace Hall. Built in 1882 by British architects using Thai labour, the exterior shows a peculiar blend of Italian Renaissance and traditional Thai architecture. This is a style often referred to as *faràng sài chá-daa* (Westerner in a Thai crown) because each wing is topped by a *mondòp* – a heavily ornamented spire representing a Thai adaptation of the Hindu *mandapa* (shrine). The tallest of the *mondòp*, in the centre, contains the ashes of Chakri kings; the flanking *mondòp* enshrine the ashes of Chakri princes. Thai kings traditionally housed their huge harems in the inner palace area, which was guarded by combat-trained female sentries.

Last, from east to west, is the Ratanakosin-style Dusit Hall, which initially served as a venue for royal audiences and later as a royal funerary hall.

The admission charge for the complex includes entrance to the Royal Thai Decorations & Coins Pavilion (located on the same grounds) and to Dusit Park (p125), which includes Vimanmek teak mansion and Abhisek Dusit Throne Hall.

WAT PHO
วัดโพธิ์(วัดพระเชตุพน)

The modest hero of Bangkok's holy temples, **Wat Pho** (Wat Phra Chetuphon; ☎ 0 2221 9911; Th Samanchai; admission 20B, guided tours 100-300B; ☯ 8am-5pm; bus 508, 512; river express Tha Tien) features a host of superlatives: the largest reclining Buddha and the largest collection of Buddha images in Thailand, and the country's earliest centre for public education.

Almost too big for its shelter, the tremendous **reclining Buddha**, 46m long and 15m high, illustrates the passing of the Buddha into nirvana (ie the Buddha's death). The figure is modelled out of plaster, around a brick core and finished in gold leaf. Mother-of-pearl inlay ornaments the eyes and feet, the latter displaying 108 different auspicious *láksànà* (characteristics of a Buddha).

The **Buddha images** on display in the other four *wíhǎan* are worth a nod. Particularly beautiful are the Phra Chinnarat and Phra Chinnachai Buddhas, both from Sukhothai, in the west and south chapels. The galleries extending between the four chapels feature no less than 394 gilded Buddha

images, many of which display Ayuthaya or Sukhothai features. The remains of Rama I are interred in the base of the presiding Buddha image in the *bòt*.

A small collection of tiled stupas commemorates the first three of the Chakri kings (Rama III has two stupas) and there are 91 smaller stupas. Note the square bell shape with distinct corners, a signature of Ratanakosin style.

Wat Pho is also the national headquarters for the teaching and preservation of traditional Thai medicine, including Thai massage, a mandate legislated by Rama III when the tradition was in danger of extinction. The famous massage school is now located outside the temple area (p132), but stone inscriptions showing yoga and massage techniques still remain in the temple grounds serving their original purpose as visual aids.

The rambling grounds of Wat Pho, which stretch along both sides of Th Chetuphon, also contain an old Tripitaka (Buddhist scriptures) library, a sermon hall and a school building for classes in Abhidhamma (Buddhist philosophy).

WAT MAHATHAT
วัดมหาธาตุ

Sightseeing is not the reason to wander through the whitewashed gates of **Wat Mahathat** (☎ 0 2221 5999; 3 Th Maharat; ☯ 9am-5pm; bus 506, 512, 53, river ferry Tha Chang or Tha Maharat). But prospective students of Buddhist meditation will find a warm reception from the English-speaking director of the temple's **International Buddhist Meditation Centre** (which is located in Section 5), where classes in sitting and walking meditation are held three times daily.

Founded in the 1700s, Wat Mahathat is the national centre for the Mahanikai monastic sect and headquarters for the renowned Maha Chulalongkorn Rajavidyalaya, one of Bangkok's two Buddhist universities. Religious scholarship is extended to visiting foreigners with twice-monthly lectures in English on different aspects of dhamma. Stop by Section 5 for lecture topics and room assignment.

Accommodation is also available on the temple grounds to male and female meditation trainees provided they follow the temple's strict regulations.

AMULET MARKET
ตลาดพระเครื่องวัดมหาธาตุ

Just outside the theological solitude of Wat Mahathat is a more vibrant application of Thailand's diverse spirituality. A **tàlàat phrá khrêuang** (holy amulet market; Th Maharat; 9am-5pm) claims coveted sidewalk space and rabbit-warren sois near Tha Phra Chan, displaying a wide variety of small talismans carefully scrutinised by collectors. Monks, taxi drivers and people in dangerous professions are the most common customers well-versed in the different powers of the images. Also along this strip are handsome shop houses overflowing with family-run herbal-medicine and traditional massage shops. In the cool season, vendors sell aromatic herbal soups that ward off colds and sinus infections.

WAT ARUN
วัดอรุณฯ

Striking **Wat Arun** (0 2466 3167; Th Arun Amarin, Thonburi; admission 20B; 9am-5pm; cross-river ferry from Tha Tien) commands a martial pose as the third point in the holy triumvirate (along with Wat Phra Kaew and Wat Pho) of Bangkok's early history. After the fall of Ayuthaya, King Taksin ceremoniously clinched control here on the site of a local shrine (formerly known as Wat Jaeng) and established a royal palace and temple, housing the Emerald Buddha. The temple was renamed after the Indian god of dawn (Aruna) and in honour of the literal and symbolic founding of a new Ayuthaya.

It wasn't until the capital and the Emerald Buddha were moved to Bangkok that Wat Arun received its most prominent characteristic: the 82m-high *prang* (Khmer-style tower). The tower was begun during the first half of the 19th century by Rama II and later completed by Rama III because the porous mud was an inferior base for the engineering technology at the time. Not apparent from a distance are the ornate floral mosaics made from broken, multihued Chinese porcelain, a common temple ornamentation in the early Ratanakosin period, when Chinese ships calling at the port of Bangkok used tonnes of old porcelain as ballast.

Also worth an inspection is the interior of the *bòt*. The main Buddha image is said to have been designed by Rama II himself.

The murals date from the reign of Rama V; particularly impressive is one that depicts Prince Siddhartha encountering examples of birth, old age, sickness and death outside his palace walls, an experience that led him to abandon the worldly life. The ashes of Rama II are interred in the base of the presiding Buddha image.

Between the *prang* and the ferry pier is a huge sacred banyan tree tied with multicoloured cloth. Scattered around the periphery are simple wooden cut-outs of Thai dancers luring visitors to snap a picture. A fairly innocuous scam is at work here: after the camera has clicked, a hawker emerges to collect a fee of 40B, although no charge is posted in front of the figures.

LAK MEUANG (CITY PILLAR)
ศาลหลักเมือง

Serving as the spiritual keystone of Bangkok, **Lak Meuang** (cnr Th Ratchadamnoen Nai & Th Lak Meuang; admission free; 8:30am-5:30pm; bus 506, 507, river ferry Tha Chang) is a phallic-shaped wooden pillar erected by Rama I during the founding of the new capital city in 1782. Today the structure shimmers with gold leaf and is housed in a white cruciform sanctuary. Part of an animistic tradition, the pillar embodies the city's guardian spirit ('Phra Sayam Thewathirat') and also lends a practical purpose as a marker of the town's crossroads and measuring point for distances between towns.

The taller of the two pillars, which was carved from *chaiyá-préuk* (tree of victory, or laburnum wood), was cut down in effigy following the Burmese sacking of Ayuthaya during 1767. Through a series of Buddhist-animist rituals, it is believed that the felling of the tree empowered the Thais to defeat the Burmese in a series of battles. Thus it was considered an especially talismanic choice to mark the founding of the new royal capital. Two metres of the pillar's 4.7m total length are buried in the ground.

If you happen to wander through and hear the whine of traditional instruments, investigate the source as a commissioned dance (*lákhon kâe bon*) may be in progress. Brilliantly costumed dancers measure out subtle movements as thanks to the guardian spirit for granting a worshipper's wish.

(Continued on page 122)

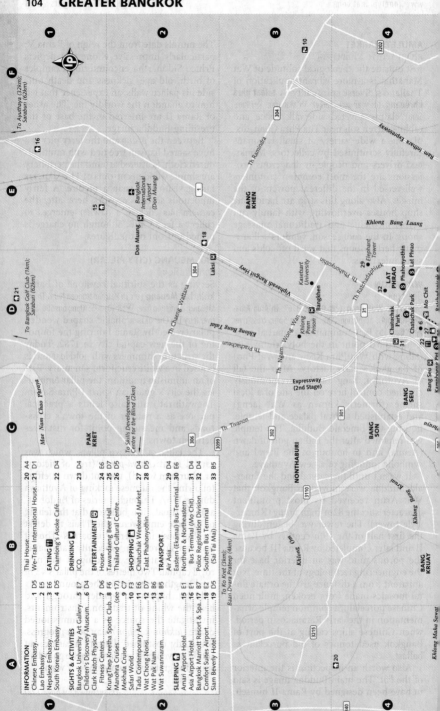

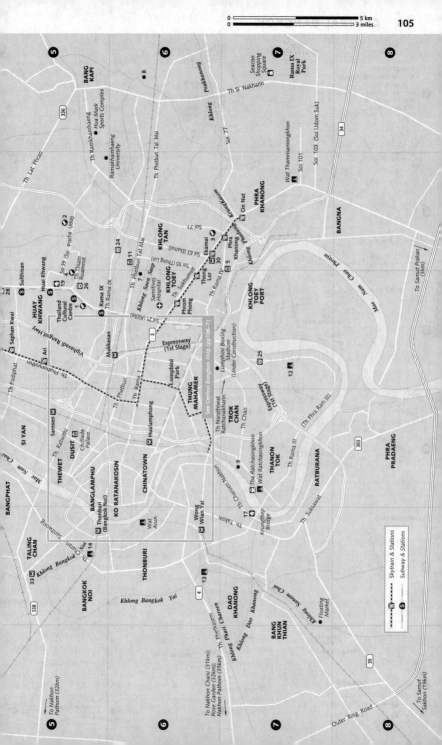

0 — 5 km
0 — 3 miles

BANG KAPI

Seacon Shopping Square

Rama IX Royal Park

Th Sí Nakharin

Prakhanong

Khlong

Soi 77

Hua Mark Sports Complex

Th Ramkhamhaeng

Th Lat Phrao

336

Th Phetburi Tat Mai

Ramkhamhaeng University

Wat Thammamongkhon

Soi 101

Soi 103 (Soi Udom Suk)

BANGNA

34

Soi 71

On Nut

PHRA KHANONG

2 (Soi Pracha Uthit)

Soi 39 (Soi Pracha Uthit)

24

11

Th Thiam Ruammit

19

Sulthisan

28

Huai Khwang

HUAY KHWANG

Th Phibun-thin

Th Ratchadaphisek

Th Phetburi Tat Mai

7

Samitivej Hospital

Soi Soong Lor

KHLONG TAN

Ekamai

3

Soi 63 (Ekamai)

Soi 55 (Thong Lor)

30

Phra Khanong

5

KHLONG TOEY

Khlong

KHLONG TOEY PORT

Mae Nam Chao Phraya

To Samut Prakan (3km)

Th Sukhumvit

Thong Lor

Phrom Phong

Th Rama IV

26

Rama IX

Th Rama IX

Thailand Cultural Centre

Soi 21 (Asoke)

Makkasan

Expressway (1st Stage)

3

Th Ratchadamri

Lumphini Boxing Stadium (Under Construction)

25

12

Phetburi

Th Phetburi

Th Rama I

Th Phahonyothin

Viphavadi Rangsit Hwy

Samsen

Saphan Khwai

Ari

SI YAN

Th Padiphat

Th Phahonyothin

DUSIT

Chitlada Palace

Th Ratwithi

THEWET

BANGLAMPHU

Th Samsen

Lumphini Park

THUNG MAHAMEK

See Central Bangkok Map (pp106-7)

Th Naratthiwat Ratchanakharin

TROK CHAN

Th Chan

Expressway (1st Stage)

(Th Phra Ram III)

303

PHRA PRADAENG

Hualamphong

CHINATOWN

KO RATANAKOSIN

Th Charoen Nakhon

9

Tha Ratchasingkhon

Wat Ratchasingkhon

THANON TOK

Th Rama III

RATBURANA

Thonburi (Bangkok Noi)

BANGLAMPHU

Th Nakhon Chaisi

THONBURI

Wat Arun

Wong Wian Yai

17

Krungthep Bridge

Th Sukhawat

BANGKOK NOI

33

Khlong Bangkok Noi

14

Th Charoen

Khlong Bangkok Yai

TALING CHAN

338

Mae Nam Chao Phraya

To Nakhon Pathom (32km)

To Nakhon Chaisi (31km);
Rose Garden (32km);
Nakhon Pathom (35km)

Th Phetkasem

Th Phasi Charoen

DAO KHANONG

13

4

Khlong Dao Khanong

BANG KHUN THIAN

Khlong Sanam Chai

Floating Market

Krungthep Bridge

Th Taksin

35

Outer Ring Road

To Samut Sakhon (19km)

	Skytrain & Stations
S	Subway & Stations

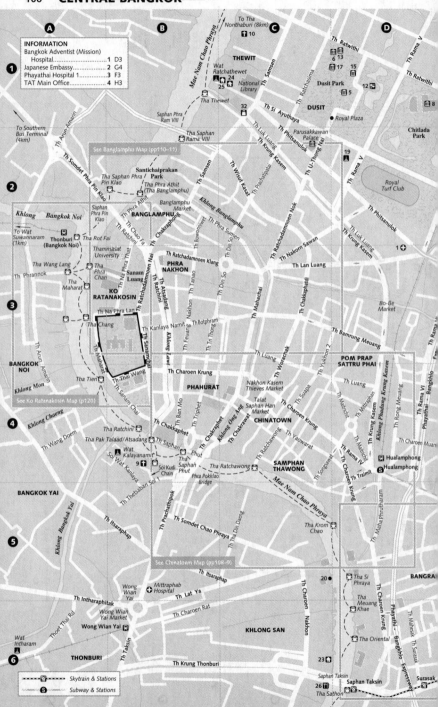

INFORMATION

Bangkok Adventist (Mission)	
Hospital.....................................1	D3
Japanese Embassy.........................2	G4
Phayathai Hospital 1......................3	F3
TAT Main Office...........................4	H3

To Tha Nonthaburi (8km)

THEWIT

Th Ratwithi

Th Ratwithi

DUSIT

Dusit Park

Royal Plaza

Parusakkawan Palace

Chitlada Park

Royal Turf Club

Bo-Be Market

POM PRAP SATTRU PHAI

Wat Ratchathewet

National Library

Tha Thewet

Saphan Phra Ram VIII

Tha Saphan Rama VIII

See Banglamphu Map (pp110–11)

Santichaiprakan Park

Tha Saphan Phra Pin Klao

Tha Phra Athit (Tha Banglamphu)

BANGLAMPHU

Banglamphu Market

Khlong Banglamphu

Khlong Bangkok Noi

To Wat Suwannaram (1km)

Thonburi (Bangkok Noi)

Thammasat University

Tha Wang Lang

Th Phrannok

Tha Phra Chan

Tha Maharaj

KO RATANAKOSIN

PHRA NAKHON

Tha Chang

Saphan Phra Pin Klao

BANGKOK NOI

Tha Tien

See Ko Ratanakosin Map (p120)

Khlong Mon

Th Arun Amarin

BANGKOK YAI

Tha Ratchini

Tha Pak Talaad/Atsadang

Wat Kalayanamit

Soi Wat Kanlaya

Soi Kudi Chin

PHAHURAT

CHINATOWN

Nakhon Kasem Thieves Market

Talat Saphan Han Market

Tha Ratchawong

SAMPHAN THAWONG

Phra Pokklao Bridge

Tha Saphan Phut

Hualamphong

Hualamphong

See Chinatown Map (pp108–9)

Khlong Chaeng

Th Wang Doem

Tha Ratchini

Th Itsaraphap

Th Somdet Chao Phraya

Mae Nam Chao Phraya

Tha Krom Chao

Tha Si Phraya

Tha Meuang Khae

BANGRA

Th Inttharaphitak

Wong Wian Yai

Mittraphab Hospital

Th Lat Ya

Wong Wian Yai Market

Wong Wian Yai

KHLONG SAN

Tha Oriental

Wat Intharam

THONBURI

Th Taksin

Th Krung Thonburi

Saphan Taksin

Saphan Taksin

Tha Sathon

Surasak

Skytrain & Stations

Subway & Stations

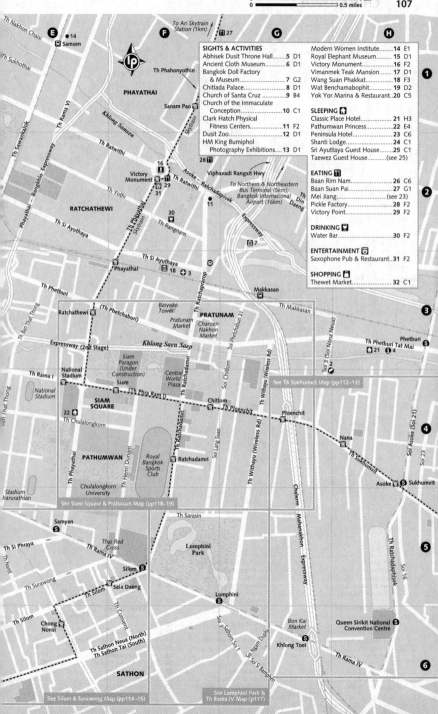

SIGHTS & ACTIVITIES

Abhisek Dusit Throne Hall........5 D1
Ancient Cloth Museum............6 D1
Bangkok Doll Factory
  & Museum......................7 G2
Chitlada Palace...................8 D1
Church of Santa Cruz...........9 B4
Church of the Immaculate
  Conception....................10 C1
Clark Hatch Physical
  Fitness Centers...............11 F2
Dusit Zoo.......................12 D1
HM King Bumiphol
  Photography Exhibitions....13 D1
Modern Women Institute........14 E1
Royal Elephant Museum........15 D1
Victory Monument................16 F2
Vimanmek Teak Mansion........17 D1
Wang Suan Phakkat.............18 F3
Wat Benchamabophit...........19 D2
Yok Yor Marina & Restaurant..20 C5

SLEEPING 🛌

Classic Place Hotel.............21 H3
Pathumwan Princess............22 E4
Peninsula Hotel..................23 C6
Shanti Lodge....................24 C1
Sri Ayuttaya Guest House......25 C1
Taewez Guest House..........(see 25)

EATING 🍴

Baan Rim Nam..................26 C6
Baan Suan Pai..................27 G1
Mei Jiang.....................(see 23)
Pickle Factory..................28 F2
Victory Point...................29 F2

DRINKING 🍷

Water Bar.......................30 F2

ENTERTAINMENT 🎭

Saxophone Pub & Restaurant..31 F2

SHOPPING 🛍

Thewet Market...................32 C1

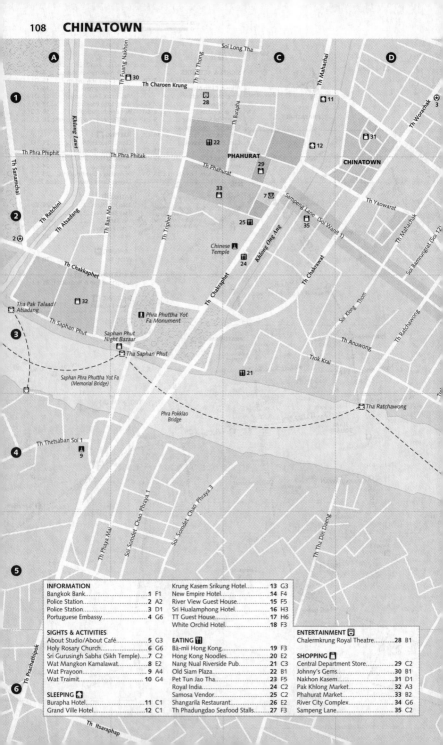

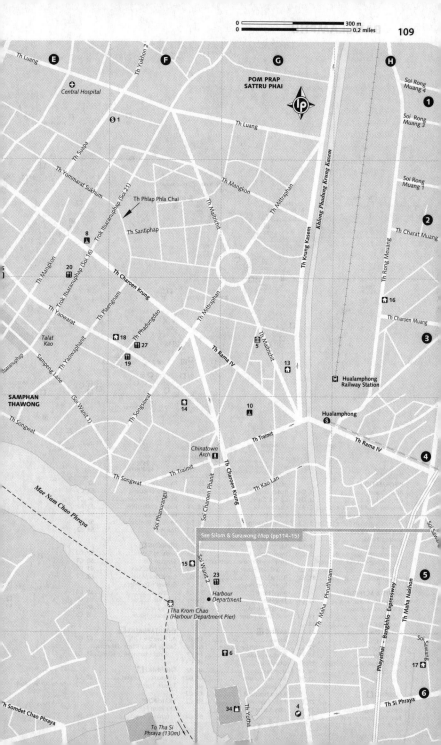

A **B** **C** **D**

To Tha Saphan
Rama VIII (150m)

Th Wisut Kasat

Sol 5

1

23

Sol 3

37

Wat
Samphraya

Th Samsen

57

Wat Sangwet

2

52   36

Sol 1

41

Sol 6

59

Santichaiprakan
Park   Phra Sumen Fort

56

Tha Saphan Phra
Pin Klao

Tha Phra Athit
(Tha Banglamphu)

49   50

70

Th Phra Athit

67

Sol 2

48   35

8

Th Somdet Phra Pin Klao

58

See Ko Ratanakosin Map (p120)

62

Khlong Banglamphu

Saphan
Phra Pin
Klao

34

Sol
Chana
Songkhram

46

69

Th Phra Athit

55

25

33

66   60

Th Krai Si

Th Tani

Th Tanao

17

BANGLAMPHU

Wat
Chana
Songkhram

3

22

Sol Rongmai

28

Th Chao Fa

9

Th Chakraphong

40

Th Rambutri

Th Ratchini

Th Na Phra That

13

45

5

63   53

24

54

31

7

32   44   14   65

61   Th Khao San

29   26

27   30

1

51

Mosque

To Tha Rot
Fai (150m)

Soi Damnoen Klang Neua

Th Tanao

Sanam
Luang

To Mae Thorani
Shrine (40m);
Suksit Siam (750m)

Th Ratchini

38

Th Ratchadamnoen Klang

PHRA
NAKHON

Wat
Mahanophara

Th Mahanot

64

Th Botphram

To Phai Thong (50m);
Suksit Siam (50m)

Trok Fung Tong

Th Tri Thong

INFORMATION	
Aporia Books	1 D4
Bangkok Bank	2 D1
Bangkok Tourist Division	3 A3
Banglamphu Post Office	4 D3
Chana Songkhram Police Station	5 C3
Rim Khob Fah Bookstore	6 E4
Shaman Books	7 C3
Siam Commercial Bank	8 D2
Tourist Information Booth	9 C3
Tourist Police/Tourist Assistance Centre	10 C3
Vieng Travel	11 E2

SIGHTS & ACTIVITIES	
Democracy Monument	12 E4
Jitti's Gym Thai Boxing & Homestay	13 D3
Kraichitti Gallery	14 C3
Monk's Bowl Village	15 F6
Sao Ching-Cha	16 E6
Wat Bowonniwet	17 D3
Wat Intharawihan	18 E1
Wat Rajanadda	19 F5
Wat Saket	20 G5
Wat Suthat	21 E6

SLEEPING	
Baan Sabai	22 B3
Bamboo Guest House	23 C1
Barn Thai Guest House	24 C3

Bella Bella House	25 B3
Buddy Lodge	26 D3
Central Guest House	27 C3
Chai's House	28 B3
Classic Inn	29 D3
Donna Guesthouse	30 D4
Kawin Place	31 C3
Khao San Palace Hotel	32 C3
Mango Lagoon Place	33 B3
New Siam GH	34 B2
New World House Apartments & Guest House	35 D2
Rajata Hotel	36 D2
River Guest House	37 C1
Royal Hotel	38 C4
Thai Hotel	39 F1
Viengtai Hotel	40 D3
Villa Guest House	41 D2

EATING	
Arawy	42 E5
Baan Phanfah Restaurant	43 F4
Chabad House	44 C3
Chochana	45 C3
Hemlock	46 B2
Isan Restaurants	47 G2
Jeh Hoy	48 D2
Khrua Nopparat	49 C2
Kuay Tiaw Mae	50 C2
May Kaidee's & Vegetarian Restaurants	51 D4

Phon Sawan	52 D2
Prakorb's House	53 C3
Ranee Guesthouse	54 C3
Ricky's Coffeeshop	55 B3
Roti-Mataba	56 C2
Somsong Photchana	57 C1
Ton Pho	58 B2

DRINKING	
Baghdad Café	59 D2
Bangkok Bar	60 C3
Center Khao San	61 C3
Dong Dea Moon	62 C2
Gulliver's Traveller's Tavern	63 C3
Lulla Bar	64 D5
Molly Bar	65 C3
Sawasdee House	66 C3

ENTERTAINMENT	
Ad Here the 13th	67 D2
Sanam Muay Ratchadamnoen (Ratchadamnoen Stadium)	68 G3

SHOPPING	
Banglamphu Market	69 C2
Taekee Taekon	70 C2

TRANSPORT	
Tha Phan Fah (Khlong Taxis)	71 F5

0   300 m
0   0.2 miles

E 18

F 39

G Th Phitsanulok

Parusakkawan Palace

H

Th Likhit

To Wat Benchamabophit (300m)

Th Krung Kasem

Th Luk Luang

Khlong Phadung Kasem

Th U-Thong Nai

Wat Mai Amaratarot

Th Wisut Kasat

• 11

Th Prachatipatai

Government House •

Th Luk Luang

Th Nakorn Pathom

Th Rama V

Wat Trithotsathep

Th Krung Kasem

🍴 47

📷 68

Trok Bahn Lo

Th Phaniang

⚬ 10

Th Phra Sumen

Th Ratchadamnoen Nok

Th Din So

Th Nakorn Sawan

Th Phaniang

Wat Sunthon

🍴 43

Th Lan Luang

🛏 12

• 6

🛏 19

Th Damrong Rak

Th Chakaphatdi

📮 71

Khlong Saen Saeb

Th Damrong Rak

🛏 2

Golden Mount

🛏 20

Soi 2

Wat Thepthidaram

Th Din So

Th Boriphat

Soi Maen Si

Soi Maan

Soi Samranat

• 16

Th Bamrung Meuang

21

Th Burapha

Th Siri Phong

Th Mahachai

Soi Ban Baht

15 •

Soi Ban Baht

Th Worachak

Devi Mandir

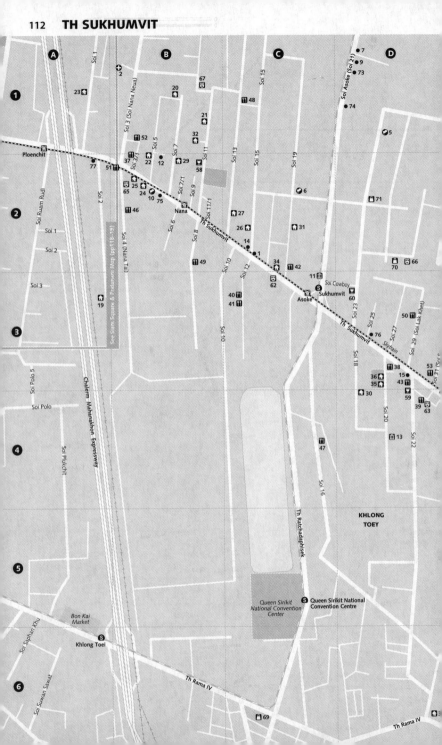

0 — 300 m
0 — 0.2 miles

Th New Pretburi

INFORMATION
Asia Books	1 C2
Asia Books	(see 68)
Bumrungrad Hospital	2 B1
Dasa Book Café	3 F4
Elite Used Books	4 E4
Indian Embassy	5 D1
Israeli Embassy	6 C2
Japan Foundation	7 D1
Kinokuniya	(see 68)
Philippine Embassy	8 F5
Rutnin Eye Hospital	9 D1
Siam Society	(see 11)
Swedish Embassy	10 B2

SIGHTS & ACTIVITIES
Ban Kamthieng	11 C3
Buathip Thai Massage	12 B2
Fitness First	(see 24)
Gallery F-Stop	13 D4
Marble House	14 C2
Phunnee Foot Massage	15 D3
Santisuk Tennis Courts	16 E3
UFM Food Centre	17 E2
World Fellowship of Buddhists	18 E4

SLEEPING
Atlanta	19 A3
Bel-Aire Princess	20 B1
Federal Hotel	21 B1
Fortuna Hotel	22 B2
Golden Palace Hotel	23 A1
Landmark Bangkok	24 A2
Majestic Suites	25 B2
Manhattan	26 C2
Miami Hotel	27 C2
Novotel Lotus Bangkok	28 E3
Park Hotel	29 B2
Rembrandt Hotel	30 D4
Sam's Lodge	31 C2
Suk 11	32 B1
The Davis	33 D6
Westin Grande Sukhumvit	34 C2
Windsor Hotel	35 D3
Windsor Suites Hotel	36 D3

EATING
Al Hussain	37 B2
Atlanta Coffeeshop	(see 19)
Bei Otto	38 D3
Bourbon St Bar & Restaurant	39 D4
Cabbages & Condoms	40 C3
Crepes & Co	41 C3
Dosa King	42 C2
Govinda	43 C3
Greyhound Café	(see 68)
Hong Ahan 55	44 G5
Hua Lamphong Food Station	45 F6
Jool's Bar & Restaurant	46 B2
Kuppa	47 C4
La Piola	48 C1
Le Banyan	49 B2
Maha Naga	50 D3
Marriott Cafe	51 B2
Nasir al-Masri Restaurant & Shishah	52 B1
Pizzeria Bella Napoli	53 D3
Soi 38 Night Market	54 G6
Tamarind Café	(see 13)
Vega Café	55 E3
Vientiane Kitchen	56 G5
Youzen Restaurant	(see 36)

DRINKING
Bull's Head & Angus Steakhouse	57 E4
Cheap Charlie's	58 B2
Jool's	(see 46)
Larry's Dive Center Bar & Grill	59 D4
Ship Inn	60 D3
Suan Ahahn Pa Loet Rot	61 E4

ENTERTAINMENT
Casanova	(see 65)
Living Room	62 C3
Mambo Cabaret	63 D4
Mystique	64 D2
Nana Entertainment Plaza	65 B2
Narcissus	66 D2
Q Bar	67 B1
SF Cinema	(see 68)

SHOPPING
Emporium Shopping Centre	68 E4
Greyhound	(see 68)
Khlong Toey Market	69 C6
Nandakwang	70 D2
Rasi Sayam	71 D2

TRANSPORT
Eastern Bus Terminal (Ekamai)	72 H6
Lufthansa Airlines	73 D1
Myanmar Airways International	74 D1
Nok Air	75 E3
Scandinavian Airlines	76 D3
Vietnam Airlines	77 A2

To Samitivej Hospital (50m)

Prommit Hospital

Benjasiri Park

Phrom Phong

Soi 33 (Daeng Udom)

Soi 37 (Soi Phromchai)

Soi 32/1

Soi 39 (Phrompong)

Soi 24
Soi 26
Soi 28
Soi 30
Soi 32
Soi 34
Soi 26

Soi 41
Soi 43
Soi 45
Soi 49
Soi 51
Soi 53
Soi 36
Soi 38

Soi Thong Lor 3
Soi Thong Lor 1
Thong Lor

Soi 55
Soi 57
Soi 59
Soi 61
Soi 63 (Soi Ekamai)

Sukhumvit Soi 63 (Soi Ekamai)
Soi 2

Ekamai

A ··· **B** ··· **C** ··· **D**

1

Soi Charoen Phanit

Th Charoen Krung

Th Maha Phuthaaram

Soi Phra Nakharet

2

Th Si Phraya

Soi Kaeo Fa

Th Naret

See Chinatown Map (pp108–9)

Royal
Orchid
Sheraton **23**

79

BANGRAK

76

Soi Santi Phap

3

Tha Si Phraya

Soi 30

Soi 43

Soi Phuttha Osot

6

46

7 9

Soi 32

Th Charoen Krung

Th Surawong

Soi 26

Soi 22

Soi 20 (Soi Pradit)

45

52

Soi 18

38

Soi 34

Soi 13 (Trok Vaithi)

4

Tha Meuang Khae

8

Soi 36

Haroon
Mosque

15

39

Mahesak
Hospital

Soi 24

49

Soi 38 (Soi Oriental)

27

Soi 40

Soi 34

Th Mahesak

Soi 30

Soi 32

Soi 28

29

18

Phayathai–Bangkok Expressway

Soi 15

Th Pan

62

Th Silom

72

Soi 17

Th Pramuan

69

19
Silom Galleria

Tha Oriental

44

Soi 42

Th Surasak

Soi Silom 19

Th Pan

48

Wat Suan Phlu

5

Soi Wat Suan Phlu

28

34

66

Soi Si Wiang

Saphan
Taksin

Th Charoen Krung

Th Chazat Wiang

Surasak

6

Saphan Taksin

35

Tha Sathon (Central Pier)

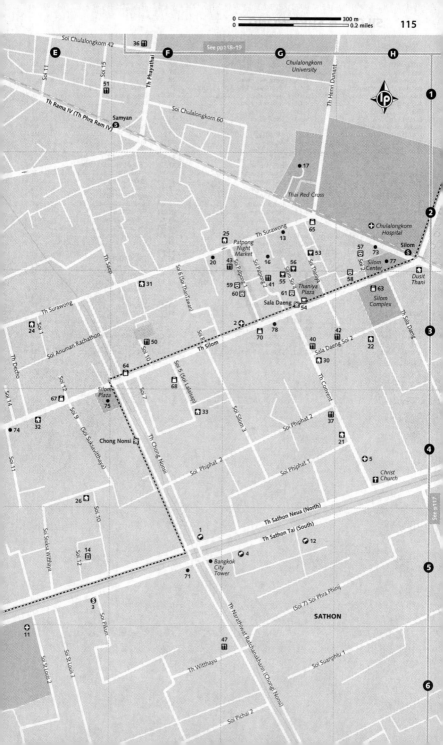

0   300 m
0   0.2 miles

See pp118–19

E   Soi Chulalongkorn 42   36   **F**   **G**   **H**

Soi 11   Soi 15   Th Phayathai   Chulalongkorn University   1

51

Th Rama IV (Th Phra Ram IV)

Samyan **S**   Soi Chulalongkorn 60

17   2

Thai Red Cross

Chulalongkorn Hospital

25   Th Surawong   65   57 73   Silom **S**

Patpong Night Market   13   Silom Center   77   Dusit Thani

20   43   16   56   53

Th Saep   59   55   58   63

31   60   41   61   Thaniya Plaza   Silom Complex

Sala Daeng   54

Th Surawong   2   70 78   42   Th Sala Daeng

Soi 1   24   Soi Anuman Rachathon   50   40   30   22 3

Soi 6 (Soi Thaniawan)   Sala Daeng Soi 2

64   Th Silom   Soi 5 (Soi Lalaisap)   68

Th Decho   67   Silom Plaza   Th Convent   37

Soi 12   Soi 9 (Soi Suksavithaya)   75   33   Soi Phiphat 2   21   4

74   32   Chong Nonsi   Soi Silom 3   5

Soi 14   Soi 11   Soi 7   Soi Phiphat 2   Soi Phiphat 1   Christ Church

26   Th Sathon Neua (North)

14   Th Sathon Tai (South)   12

Soi Seuksa Witthaya   Soi 10   1   4

Soi 12   71   Bangkok City Tower   SATHON

S   3   (Soi 7) Soi Phra Phinij

11   Th Narathiwat Ratchanakharin (Chong Nonsi)   Soi Suanphlu 1

Soi St Louis 2   47   Th Witthayu   6

Soi St Louis 3   Soi Pichai 2

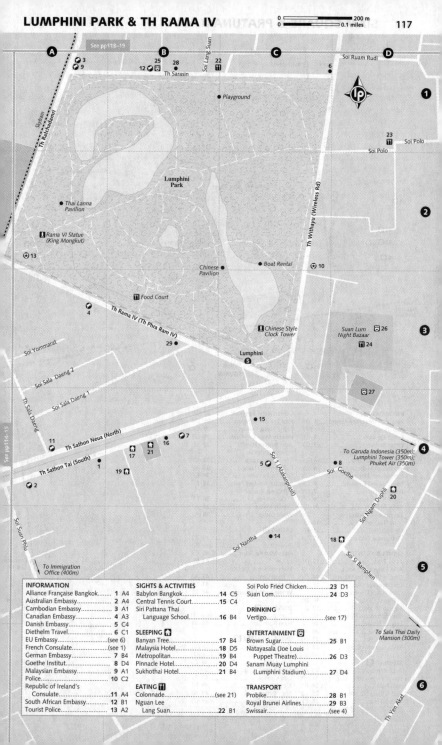

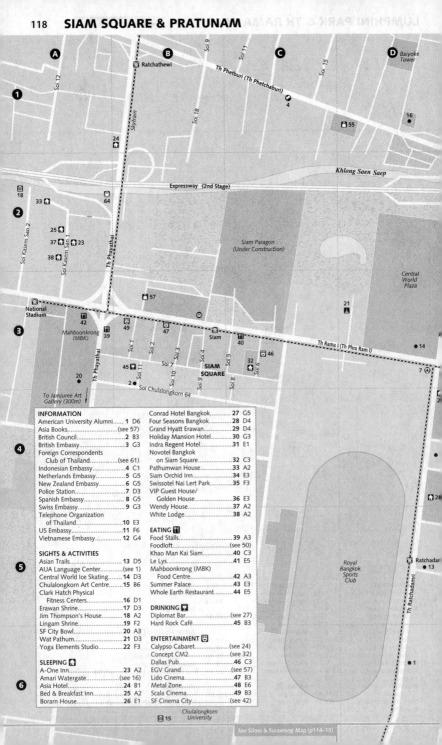

INFORMATION

American University Alumni	**1** D6
Asia Books	(see 57)
British Council	**2** B3
British Embassy	**3** G3
Foreign Correspondents Club of Thailand	(see 61)
Indonesian Embassy	**4** C1
Netherlands Embassy	**5** G5
New Zealand Embassy	**6** G5
Police Station	**7** D3
Spanish Embassy	**8** G5
Swiss Embassy	**9** G3
Telephone Organization of Thailand	**10** E3
US Embassy	**11** F6
Vietnamese Embassy	**12** G4

SIGHTS & ACTIVITIES

Asian Trails	**13** D5
AUA Language Center	(see 1)
Central World Ice Skating	**14** D3
Chulalongkorn Art Centre	**15** B6
Clark Hatch Physical Fitness Centers	**16** D1
Erawan Shrine	**17** D3
Jim Thompson's House	**18** A2
Lingam Shrine	**19** F2
SF City Bowl	**20** A3
Wat Pathum	**21** D3
Yoga Elements Studio	**22** F3

SLEEPING

A-One Inn	**23** A2
Amari Watergate	(see 16)
Asia Hotel	**24** B1
Bed & Breakfast Inn	**25** A2
Borarn House	**26** E1
Conrad Hotel Bangkok	**27** G5
Four Seasons Bangkok	**28** D4
Grand Hyatt Erawan	**29** D4
Holiday Mansion Hotel	**30** G3
Indra Regent Hotel	**31** E1
Novotel Bangkok on Siam Square	**32** C3
Pathumwan House	**33** A2
Siam Orchid Inn	**34** E3
Swissotel Nai Lert Park	**35** F3
VIP Guest House/ Golden House	**36** E3
Wendy House	**37** A2
White Lodge	**38** A2

EATING 🍴

Food Stalls	**39** A3
Foodloft	(see 50)
Khao Man Kai Siam	**40** C3
Le Lys	**41** E5
Mahboonkrong (MBK) Food Centre	**42** A3
Summer Palace	**43** E3
Whole Earth Restaurant	**44** E5

DRINKING 🍸

Diplomat Bar	(see 27)
Hard Rock Café	**45** B3

ENTERTAINMENT 🎭

Calypso Cabaret	(see 24)
Concept CM2	(see 32)
Dallas Pub	**46** C3
EGV Grand	(see 57)
Lido Cinema	**47** B3
Metal Zone	**48** E6
Scala Cinema	**49** B3
SF Cinema City	(see 42)

0 —— 300 m
0 —— 0.2 miles

PRATUNAM

Soi Wattanawong

Th Makkasan

Th Ratchaprarop

Soi Wattanasin

Charoen
Nakhon
Market

Soi Phetchaburi 31

Soi Phetburi 35

Chalem Mahanakhon Expressway

26

Th Phetburi

63

Soi 32

Khlong Saen Saep

Soi Chitlom

19

35

Soi Somkhit

Th Withayu Neua (Wireless Rd Nth)

65

53

See Th Sukhumvit Map (pp112-13)

Soi 1

54

Gaysorn

34

52 President
Tower

9

43

10

36

22

50

Erawan Bangkok
Boutique Mall
Under Construction)

61
Maneeya
Centre
Chitlom

60

Th Ploenchit

30

3

Skytrain

Ploenchit

59

4

Mahatlek Luang 1

Soi Lang Suan

12

ni Mahatlek Luang 2

Sub-Soi 3

41

5

Soi Tonson

Th Withayu (Wireless Rd)

27

Mahatlek Luang 3

44

6

8

11

48

58

See Lumphini Park & Th Rama IV Map (p117)

SHOPPING
Alta Moda..........................(see 14)
Central Department Store....**50** F3
Fly Now.............................**51** D3
Gaysorn Plaza....................**52** E3
Jaspal...............................(see 57)
Mae Fah Luang..................(see 57)
Nagi Arts..........................**53** G2
Narayana Phand.................**54** E3
Pantip Plaza......................**55** D1
Pratunam Market................**56** E1
Siam Center & Siam
  Discovery Center..............**57** B3
Sunny Camera....................(see 42)
Triphum............................(see 51)

TRANSPORT
Air New Zealand.................**58** F6
Avis..................................**59** G4
Cathay Pacific Airways........**60** F4
China Airlines....................(see 62)
Gulf Air............................**61** E3
KLM-Royal Dutch Airlines....(see 62)
Malaysia Airlines................(see 60)
Northwest Airlines..............**62** D4
Tha Pratunam (Khlong Taxis)..**63** E2
Tha Ratchathewi
  (Khlong Taxis).................**64** A2
Tha Withayu (Khlong Taxis)..**65** G2
United Airlines...................(see 58)

OTHER
Sindhorn Building...............(see 58)

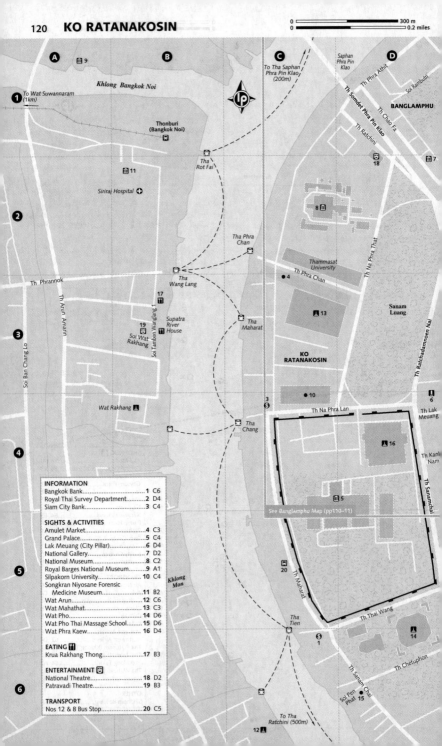

0   300 m
0   0.2 miles

Khlong Bangkok Noi

A 🏛 9   **B**   **C** To Tha Saphan
Phra Pin Klao
(200m)   Saphan
Phra Pin
Klao   **D**

1 To Wat Suwannaram
(1km)

Thonburi
(Bangkok Noi) 🚉

BANGLAMPHU

Th Phra Athit
Soi Rambutri
Th Chao Fa
Th Somdet Phra Pin Klao
Th Ratchini

Tha
Rot Fai

🏛 18   🏛 7

🏛 11

Siriraj Hospital ✚

2   8 🏛

Tha Phra
Chan

Thammasat
University
Th Phra Chan

Th Na Phra That

**Sanam
Luang**

Th Phrannok

Tha
Wang Lang   ● 4

🚉 13

Th Arun Amarin

17 🏛

3   19 🚉
Soi Wat
Rakhang   Supatra
River
House   Tha
Maharat

**KO
RATANAKOSIN**

Soi Ban Chang Lo

Soi Lamton Wang Lang

● 10

Th Ratchadamnoen Nai

4   Wat Rakhang 🛕

3 Ⓢ   Th Na Phra Lan

Lak
Meuang
6 🏛

Tha
Chang   🛕 16

Th Lak
Meuang

Th Kanlaya
Nam

Th Sanamchai

See Banglamphu Map (pp110–11)

🏛 5

5   Khlong
Mon

20 🚉
Th Maharat

INFORMATION
Bangkok Bank.....................................**1** C6
Royal Thai Survey Department..........**2** D4
Siam City Bank...................................**3** C4

SIGHTS & ACTIVITIES
Amulet Market...................................**4** C3
Grand Palace......................................**5** C4
Lak Meuang (City Pillar).....................**6** D4
National Gallery..................................**7** D2
National Museum...............................**8** C2
Royal Barges National Museum.........**9** A1
Silpakorn University............................**10** C4
Songkran Niyosane Forensic
  Medicine Museum...........................**11** B2
Wat Arun..**12** C6
Wat Mahathat....................................**13** C3
Wat Pho...**14** D6
Wat Pho Thai Massage School...........**15** D6
Wat Phra Kaew..................................**16** D4

EATING 🍴
Krua Rakhang Thong...........................**17** B3

ENTERTAINMENT 🎭
National Theatre................................**18** D2
Patravadi Theatre..............................**19** B3

TRANSPORT
Nos 12 & 8 Bus Stop..........................**20** C5

Tha
Tien

Th Thai Wang

🛕 14

Th Chetuphon

Ⓢ 1

Th Sanam Chai
Soi Pen
Phat 15 ●

6   To Tha
Ratchini (500m)

12 🛕

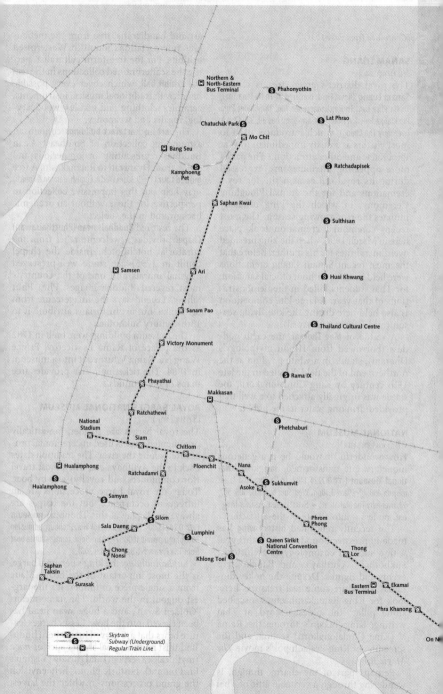

Northern & North-Eastern Bus Terminal

Phahonyothin

Lat Phrao

Chatuchak Park

Mo Chit

Bang Seu

Ratchadapisek

Kamphoeng Pet

Saphan Kwai

Sulthisan

Samsen

Ari

Huai Khwang

Sanam Pao

Thailand Cultural Centre

Victory Monument

Phayathai

Rama IX

Makkasan

Ratchathewi

National Stadium

Phetchaburi

Siam

Chitlom

Hualamphong

Ploenchit

Ratchadamri

Nana

Hualamphong

Asoke

Sukhumvit

Samyan

Silom

Phrom Phong

Sala Daeng

Lumphini

Chong Nonsi

Queen Sirikit National Convention Centre

Thong Lor

Khlong Toei

Saphan Taksin

Surasak

Eastern Bus Terminal

Ekamai

Phra Khanong

On N

Skytrain
Subway (Underground)
Regular Train Line

BANGKOK

(Continued from page 103)

SANAM LUANG
สนามหลวง

The royal district's green area is scruffy **Sanam Luang** (Royal Field; bordered by Th Na Phra That, Th Na Phra Lan, Th Ratchadamnoen Nai, Th Somdet Phra Pin Klao; admission free; ⏰ 5am-8pm; bus 30, 32, 47, 53, river ferry Tha Chang), which introduces itself to most visitors as a dusty impediment to Wat Phra Kaew and other attractions. The park's more appealing attributes are expressed during its royal duties as a site for royal cremations and for the annual Ploughing Ceremony, in which the king officially initiates the rice-growing season. The most recent ceremonial cremation took place here in March 1996, when the king presided over funeral rites for his mother. Before that the most recent Sanam Luang cremations were held in 1976, without official sanction, for Thai students killed in the demonstrations of that year. A large kite competition is also held here during the kite-flying season (mid-February to April).

A statue of **Mae Thorani**, the earth goddess (borrowed from Hindu mythology's Dharani), stands in a white pavilion at the northern end of the field. Erected in the late 19th century by King Chulalongkorn, the statue was originally attached to a well that provided drinking water to the public.

NATIONAL MUSEUM
พิพิธภัณฑสถานแห่งชาติ

How wonderful it would be if a generous monetary gift transformed Bangkok's **National Museum** (☎ 0 2224 1402; Th Na Phra That 1; admission 40B; ⏰ 9am-3.30pm Wed-Sun; bus 503, 506, 507, 53, river ferry Tha Mahathat) – Southeast Asia's largest, no less – into a state-of-the-art facility.

The recently renovated **history wing** has made impressive bounds towards this goal with a succinct chronology of prehistoric, Sukhothai-, Ayuthaya- and Bangkok-era events and figures. Despite the hokey dioramas, there are some real treasures here: look for King Ramakamhaeng's inscribed stone pillar, the oldest record of Thai writing; King Taksin's throne; the Rama V (King Chulalongkorn) section; and the screening of King Prajadhipok's movie *The Magic Ring*.

Perhaps part of the charm, though, is wandering through a veritable attic of Thai art and handicrafts, free from the meticulous interpretations found in Westernised exhibits. For the free-form culturalist, peruse the scatterbrained collections in the **central exhibit hall**, which cover every possible handicraft: traditional musical instruments, ceramics, clothing and textiles, woodcarving, regalia and weaponry.

The **art** and **artefact buildings** contain an astounding collection of Southeast Asian Buddhas representing major periods and styles, from Dvaravati to Ratanakosin. A free **guided tour** (⏰ 9.30am Wed in English, German & French) may help put this impressive collection in perspective for those without an academic background in the subject.

The restored **Buddhaisawan (Phutthaisawan) Chapel** provides a welcome relief from the curatorial hotchpotch. Inside the chapel (built in 1795) are some well-preserved original murals and one of the country's most revered Buddha images, Phra Phut Sihing. Legend says the image came from Sri Lanka, but art historians attribute it to 13th-century Sukhothai.

The museum buildings were built in 1782 as the palace of Rama I's viceroy, Prince Wang Na. Rama V turned it into a museum in 1884. The ticketing office provides free maps of the grounds.

ROYAL BARGES NATIONAL MUSEUM
เรือพระที่นั่ง

The royal barges are slender, fantastically ornamented vessels used in ceremonial processions along the river. The tradition dates back to the Ayuthaya era, when most travel (for commoners and royalty) was by boat. Today the royal barge processions are an infrequent occurrence, but the barges are always on display at this Thonburi **museum** (☎ 0 2424 0004; Khlong Bangkok Noi, Thonburi; admission 30B, photo permit 100B; ⏰ 9am-5pm; tourist shuttle boat from Tha Phra Athit/Banglamphu 20B).

Suphannahong, the king's personal barge, is the most important of the boats. Made from a single piece of timber, it's the largest dugout in the world. The name means 'Golden Swan', and a huge swan head has been carved into the bow. Lesser barges feature bows that are carved into other Hindu-Buddhist mythological shapes such as *naga* (mythical sea serpent) and *garuda* (Vishnu's bird mount). Historic photos help envision the grand processions in which the largest of the barges would require a rowing crew of 50 men, plus seven umbrella bearers, two helmsmen and two navigators, as well as a flagman, rhythm-keeper and chanter.

The easiest way to get to the museum is by the tourist boat from Tha Phra Athit (20B). You can also walk from the Bangkok Noi train station (accessible by ferrying to Tha Rot Fai) up and over the canal via the elevated highway, but the walk is unpleasant and you'll encounter uninvited guides who will charge for their service. The museum is also a stop on long-tail boat trips through Thonburi's canals.

NATIONAL GALLERY
หอศิลปแห่งชาติ
The humble **National Gallery** (☎ 0 2282 8525, 0 2281 2224; Th Chao Fa; admission 30B; ۞ 9am-4pm Wed-Sun; river ferry Tha Phra Athit) belies the country's impressive tradition of fine arts. Among the non-air-conditioned rooms in an early Ratanakosin-era building are works of traditional and contemporary art, mostly by artists who receive government support. The general consensus is that it's not Thailand's best – in fact, some of the art renegades criticise it as a 'dead zone' – but the gallery is worth a visit if you need an escape from the crowds.

SILPAKORN UNIVERSITY
มหาวิทยาลัยศิลปากร
Thailand's first **art university** (☎ 0 2225 4350; Th Na Phra Lan; ۞ 8am-7pm Mon-Fri, 8am-4pm Sat, Sun; bus 503, 506, 508, 12, 44, river ferry Tha Chang), opposite the Grand Palace, originally trained civil servants in traditional painting techniques. It then led the nation's transition into European and contemporary art, thanks to the contributions of Professor Silpa Bhirasri (Corrado Feroci), an Italian artist who designed the Democracy Monument (right). A student and faculty art gallery is open to the public.

Banglamphu   Map pp110–11
บางลำพู
Swarmed by low-slung shop houses and residential sois, Banglamphu is Bangkok's most charming neighbourhood with easy access to the river and lots of opportunities for unfettered wandering. It is also home to Th Khao San, a decompression zone for backpackers transiting in and out of the country.

Khao San's long tourist-trapping tentacles – Internet cafés, Western-style restaurants, silver shops, beer stalls – sprawl throughout neighbouring streets but quickly disappear as you move away from the river. In the Thai parts of the area there is lots of work-day street life – safari-uniformed civil servants and lottery-ticket dealers with their wooden portfolio boxes. Bus is the primary public transportation option for inland destinations. The water taxi along Khlong Saen Saeb is another convenient option for hopping over to Siam Square or Sukhumvit.

DEMOCRACY MONUMENT
อนุสาวรีย์ประชาธิปไตย
One of the first striking landmarks you'll notice on your way into Banglamphu is this large, Art Deco **monument** (Th Ratchadamnoen Klang, Th Din So; river ferry Tha Phra Athit, bus 511, 512, 44) of four stylised angel wings arranged in the traffic circle. It was erected in 1932 to commemorate Thailand's momentous transformation from absolute to constitutional monarchy. Italian artist Corrado Feroci designed the monument and buried 75 cannon balls in its base to signify the year BE 2475 (AD 1932). Before immigrating to Thailand to become the nation's 'father of modern art', Feroci designed monuments for Italian dictator Benito Mussolini. In recent years 'The Demo' has become a favourite spot for public demonstrations, most notably during the antimilitary, pro-democratic protests of 1992.

WAT SAKET & GOLDEN MOUNT
วัดสระเกศ
Even if you're wat-ed out, you should break your Beer Chang routine with a brisk walk to **Wat Saket** (☎ 0 2223 4561; btwn Th Worachak & Th Boriphat; admission to Golden Mount 10B; ۞ 8am-5pm; bus 508, 511, khlong taxi to Tha Phan Fah). Like all worthy summits, the temple's Golden Mount (Phu Khao Thong), which is visible from Th Ratchadamnoen and situated on the western side of the grounds, plays a good game of optical illusion, appearing closer than its real location. Serpentine steps wind through an artificial hill shaded by gnarled trees, some of which are signed in English, and past graves and pictures of ghostly looking residents.

This artificial hill was created when a large stupa, under construction by Rama

III, collapsed because the soft soil beneath would not support it. The resulting mud-and-brick hill was left to sprout weeds until Rama IV built a small stupa on its crest. Rama V (King Chulalongkorn) later added to the structure and housed a Buddha relic from India (given to him by the British government) in the stupa. The concrete walls were added during WWII to prevent the hill from eroding. Every year in November there is a big festival on the grounds of Wat Saket, which includes a candle-lit procession up the Golden Mount.

At the peak, you'll find a breezy 360-degree view of Bangkok's most photogenic side and a 10B admission fee.

WAT RAJANADDA
วัดราชนัดดา

Across Th Mahachai from Wat Saket, **Wat Rajanadda** (Ratchanatda; ☎ 0 2224 8807; cnr Th Ratchadamnoen Klang & Th Mahachai; ✆ 9am-5pm; bus 505, 56, khlong taxi to Tha Phan Fah) dates from the mid-19th century. It was built under Rama III and is an unusual specimen, possibly influenced by Burmese models. The wat has a well-known market selling Buddhist amulets or magic charms (phrá phim) in all sizes, shapes and styles. The amulets not only feature images of the Buddha, but also famous Thai monks and Indian deities. Full Buddha images are also for sale. Wat Rajanadda is an expensive place to purchase a charm, but a good place to look.

MONK'S BOWL VILLAGE
บ้านบาตร

Just when you start to lament the adverse effects of tourism, pay a visit to this **handicraft village** (☎ 0 2223 7970; Soi Ban Baht, Th Bamrung Meuang; ✆ 10am-8pm; bus 508, khlong taxi to Tha Pan Fah), within walking distance of Th Khao San. This is the only surviving village established by Rama I to make the rounded bowls (bàat) that the monks carry to receive food alms from faithful Buddhists every morning. Today, the average monk relies on a bowl mass-produced in China, but the traditional technique survives in Ban Baht (Monk's Bowl Village) thanks to patronage by tourists.

About half a dozen families still hammer the bowls together from eight separate pieces of steel representing, they say, the eight spokes of the Wheel of Dharma (which symbolise Buddhism's Eightfold Path). The joints are fused in a wood fire with bits of copper, and the bowl is polished and coated with several layers of black lacquer. A typical output is one bowl per day. If you purchase a bowl (starting at 600B), the craftsperson will show you the equipment and process used. To find the village from Tha Pan Fah (khlong taxi pier), head south along Th Boriphat, past Th Bamrung Meuang, then turn left into Soi Ban Baht.

WAT SUTHAT & SAO CHING-CHA
วัดสุทัศน์/เสาชิงช้า

Brahmanism predated the arrival of Buddhism in Thailand and its rituals were integrated into the dominant religion. This **temple** (☎ 0 2224 9845; Th Bamrung Meuang; admission 20B; ✆ 8.30am-9pm; bus 508, khlong taxi to Tha Phan Fah) is the headquarters of the Brahman priests who perform the Royal Ploughing Ceremony in May. Begun by Rama I and completed in later reigns, Wat Suthat boasts a wíhǎan with gilded bronze Buddha images (including Phra Si Sakayamuni, one of the largest surviving Sukhothai bronzes) and colourful, but decaying, jataka murals. The wat also holds the rank of Rachavoramahavihan, the highest royal-temple grade; and the ashes of Rama VIII (Ananda Mahidol, the current king's deceased older brother) are contained in the base of the main Buddha image in the wíhǎan.

Suthat's priests also perform rites at two nearby Hindu shrines: Thewa Sathaan (Deva Sathan), which contains images of Shiva and Ganesh; and the smaller Saan Jao Phitsanu (Vishnu Shrine), dedicated to Vishnu.

The spindly red arch in the front of the temple is **Sao Ching-Cha** (Giant Swing), which formerly hosted a spectacular Brahman festival in honour of Shiva. Participants would swing in ever-higher arcs in an effort to reach a bag of gold suspended from a 15m bamboo pole. Many died trying and the ritual was discontinued during the reign of Rama VII. Stroll along Th Bamrung Meuang past the nearby religious-paraphernalia shops filled with huge Buddhas, monk robes and other devotional items.

WAT BOWONNIWET
วัดบวรนิเวศ

Bangkok's second Buddhist university, Mahamakut University, is housed at **Wat Bowon-**

niwet (Wat Bovornives or Wat Bowon; cnr Th Phra Sumen & Th Tanao; ☼ 8am-5:30pm; bus 15, 53, river ferry Tha Phra Athit) and is the national headquarters for the Thammayut monastic sect. King Mongkut, founder of this minority sect, began a royal tradition by residing here as a monk – in fact he was the abbot of Wat Bowon for several years. King Bhumibol and Crown Prince Vaj-iralongkorn, as well as several other males in the royal family, have been temporarily ordained as monks. India, Nepal and Sri Lanka all send selected monks to study here. The temple was founded in 1826, when it was known as Wat Mai. Because of its royal status, visitors should be particularly care-ful to dress properly for admittance to this wat – no shorts or sleeveless shirts.

WAT INTHARAWIHAN
วัดอินทรวิหาร

Marked by its gigantic, modern 32m stand-ing Buddha, **Wat Intharawihan** (☎ 0 2628 5550; Th Wisut Kasat; ☼ 8am-5pm; bus 30, 53, 49) borders Th Wisut Kasat at the northern edge of Banglamphu. Check out the hollowed-out, air-con stupa with a lifelike image of Luang Phaw Toh, a famous monk.

Dusit   Map pp106–7
In the name of modernity, Rama V (King Chulalongkorn) moved the royal seat to this planned district complete with the wide avenues and the measured elegance of such European capitals as Paris and London. If you're suffering from Bangkok-overload, Dusit's quiet poise will be a welcome relief. Sights are spread out and don't make rec-ommendable strolls; rely on public buses or taxis.

DUSIT PARK
สวนดุสิต

Dainty **Dusit Park** (☎ 0 2628 6300; bounded by Th Ratwithi, Th U-Thong & Th Ratchasima; adult/child 100/50B, admission free with Grand Palace ticket; ☼ 9.30am-4pm; bus 510, 70) is the girl-next-door of Bangkok's attractions – photogenic and relaxed. In addition to its architecture and gardens, this is a convenient place to see perform-ances of traditional Thai dancing (10.30am and 2pm). Dusit Park's attractions include Vimanmek Teak Mansion, Abhisek Dusit Throne Hall, Royal Elephant Museum, HM King Bumiphol Photography Exhibitions and Ancient Cloth Museum. Admission to the park allows entry to all sights within the complex.

Following Rama V's European tour, he returned home with visions of European castles swimming in his head and set about transforming these styles into a uniquely Thai expression. The royal palace, throne hall and minor palaces for extended family were all moved here from Ko Ratanakosin, the ancient royal court. Today the current King has yet another home (Chitlada Pal-ace) and this complex now contains a house museum and other cultural collections.

Because this is royal property, visitors should wear long pants (no capri pants) or long skirts and shirts with sleeves.

Vimanmek Teak Mansion
พระที่นั่งวิมานเมฆ

Originally constructed on Ko Si Chang in 1868 and moved to the present site in 1910, this beautiful L-shaped, three-storey man-sion contains 81 rooms, halls and ante-rooms, and is said to be the world's largest golden teak building. The staircases, oc-tagonal rooms and lattice work are nothing short of magnificent, but in spite of this, the mansion retains a surprisingly serene and intimate atmosphere.

Vimanmek was the first permanent build-ing on the Dusit Palace grounds. It served as Rama V's residence in the early 1900s. The interior of the mansion contains various personal effects of the king, and a treasure trove of early Ratanakosin art objects and antiques.

Compulsory English-language tours last an hour. Don't expect to learn a lot on the tours as the guide's English is quite la-boured and tours tend to overlap with one another.

Abhisek Dusit Throne Hall
พระที่นั่งอภิเศกดุสิต

Originally built as a throne hall for Rama V in 1904, the smaller Abhisek Dusit Throne Hall is typical of the finer architecture of the era. Victorian-influenced gingerbread architecture and Moorish porticoes blend to create a striking and distinctly Thai ex-terior. The hall houses an excellent display of regional handiwork crafted by members of the Promotion of Supplementary Oc-cupations & Related Techniques (Support) foundation, an organisation sponsored by

Queen Sirikit. Among the exhibits are cotton and silk, *málaeng tháp* (collages made from metallic, multicoloured beetle wings), damascene and nielloware, and basketry.

Royal Elephant Museum
พิพิธภัณฑ์ช้างต้น

Near the Th U-Thong entrance, two large stables that once housed three white elephants – animals whose auspicious albinism automatically made them crown property – are now a museum. One of the structures contains artefacts and photos outlining the importance of elephants in Thai history and explaining their various rankings according to physical characteristics. The second stable holds a sculptural representation of a living royal white elephant (now kept at the Chitlada Palace, home to the current Thai king). Draped in royal vestments, the statue is more or less treated as a shrine by the visiting Thai public.

HM King Bumiphol Photography Exhibitions

Near the Th Ratwithi entrance, two residence halls display a collection of photographs and paintings by the present monarch. Among the many loving photos of his wife and children are also historic pictures of the king playing clarinet with Benny Goodman and Louis Armstrong in 1960.

Ancient Cloth Museum

Nearby is a beautiful collection of traditional silks and cottons that make up the royal cloth collection.

WAT BENCHAMABOPHIT
วัดเบญจมบพิตร (วัดเบญจฯ)

Made of white Carrara marble, **Wat Ben** (Marble Temple; cnr Th Si Ayuthaya & Th Phra Ram V; admission 20B; ⏰ 8am-5.30pm; bus 503, 72) was built in the late 19th century under Rama V (King Chulalongkorn). The large cruciform *bòt* is a prime example of modern Thai wat architecture. The base of the central Buddha image, a copy of Phitsanulok's Phra Phuttha Chinnarat, contains the ashes of Rama V. The courtyard behind the *bòt* exhibits 53 Buddha images (33 originals and 20 copies) representing famous figures and styles from all over Thailand and other Buddhist countries.

RAMA V CULT

A bronze figure of a military-garbed leader may seem like an unlikely shrine, but Bangkokians are flexible in their expression of religious devotion. Most importantly, the figure is no forgotten general – this is Rama V (King Chulalongkorn; 1868–1910), who is widely credited for steering the country into the modern age and for preserving Thailand's independence from European colonialism. He is also considered a champion of the common person for his abolition of slavery and corvée (the requirement that every citizen be available for state labour when called). His accomplishments are so revered, especially by the middle class, that his statue attracts worshippers who make offerings of candles, flowers (predominantly pink roses), incense and bottles of whisky, and is the site of a huge celebration during the anniversary of the monarch's death.

Chinatown
Map pp108–9
เยาวราช (สำเพ็ง)

Bangkok's Chinatown (called 'Yaowarat' after its main thoroughfare, Th Yaowarat) comprises a confusing and crowded array of commerce that is antithetically organised into predictable guild-like districts – rubber bath plug stores in one block, bulk plastic bags in another, hand-made signs, hand guns and even used vinyl LP records. The district was born in 1782 when Bangkok's Chinese population, many of them labourers who came to build the new capital, were moved here from today's Ko Ratanakosin by the royal government.

The neighbourhood's energy is exhausting and exhilarating. There are endless pedestrian wanderings, especially in the tiny sois along the river, but getting in and out of Chinatown is snagged by continuous traffic. The river express connects the neighbourhood to Ko Ratanakosin, Banglamphu and Silom, but slow-moving buses are needed for inland Siam Square and Sukhumvit.

WAT MANGKON KAMALAWAT
วัดมังกรกมลาวาส

Explore the labyrinthine passageways of this busy Chinese-style **temple** (Neng Noi Yee; Th Charoen Krung, east of Th Ratchawong; ⏰ 9am-6pm;

bus 501, 507, 73, river ferry Tha Ratchawong) to find Buddhist, Taoist and Confucian shrines. During the annual Vegetarian Festival, religious and culinary activities are centred here. But almost any time of day or night, this temple is packed with worshippers lighting incense, filling the ever-burning altar lamps with oil and making offerings to their ancestors. The Thai name means Dragon Lotus Temple.

HUALAMPHONG STATION
สถานีรถไฟหัวลำโพง

At the southeastern edge of Chinatown, the **main train station** (Th Phra Ram IV; subway Hualamphong, bus 501, 507, 53, 73) was built by Dutch architects and engineers just before WWI and is one of the city's earliest and best examples of Thai Art Deco. Its vaulted iron roof and neoclassical portico demonstrate engineering that was state of the art in its time, while the patterned, two-toned skylights exemplify pure de Stijl-style, Dutch modernism.

PHAHURAT
พาหุรัด

At the western edge of Chinatown is a small but thriving Indian district, generally called **Phahurat** (around intersection of Th Phahurat & Th Chakraphet). Here, dozens of Indian-owned shops sell all kinds of fabric and clothes. Behind the more obvious shopfronts along these streets, in the bowels of the blocks, is **Phahurat Market** (Th Phahurat & Th Chakraphet; bus 73, river ferry Tha Saphan Phut), an endless bazaar selling flamboyant Bollywood fabric and other necessities.

THE DRAGON'S UNDERBELLY

The favourite plot line of action movies, Chinatown's 1882 census documented 245 opium dens, 154 pawnshops, 69 gambling establishments and 26 brothels. The pawnshops, along with myriad gold shops, still remain popular businesses in Chinatown, while the other three vices have gone underground. Brothels continue to exist under the guise of 'tea halls' (rohng chaa), backstreet heroin dealers have replaced the opium dens and the illicit card games convene in the private upstairs rooms of certain restaurants.

In an alley off Th Chakraphet, is **Sri Gurusingh Sabha** (Sikh Temple; Th Phahurat; ☉ 9am-5pm; bus 53, 73; river ferry Tha Saphan Phut). Basically it's a large hall, reminiscent of a mosque interior, devoted to the worship of the *Guru Granth Sahib*, the 16th-century Sikh holy book, which is itself considered to be a 'living' guru and the last of the religion's 10 great teachers. Reportedly the temple is the second-largest Sikh temple outside India. Visitors are welcome, but they must remove their shoes. If you arrive on a Sikh festival day you can partake of the *langar* (communal Sikh meal served in the temple).

WAT TRAIMIT
วัดไตรมิตร

The attraction at **Wat Traimit** (Temple of the Golden Buddha; ☎ 0 2623 1226; cnr Th Yaowarat & Th Charoen Krung; admission 20B; ☉ 9am-5pm; subway Hualamphong, bus 53) is, undoubtedly, the impressive 3m-tall, 5.5-tonne, solid-gold Buddha image, which gleams like no other gold artefact we've ever seen. Sculpted in the graceful Sukhothai style, the image was 'discovered' some 40 years ago beneath a stucco or plaster exterior, when it fell from a crane while being moved to a new building within the temple compound. It has been theorised that the covering was added to protect it from marauding hordes, either during the late Sukhothai period or later in the Ayuthaya period when the city was under siege by the Burmese. The temple itself is said to date from the early 13th century.

Siam Square & Pratunam   Map pp118–19

Boxy shopping centres dominate the landscape of Siam Square's teeming commercial zone. Back behind the modern façade is the former lifeblood of the neighbourhood: soot-coloured Khlong Saen Saeb, lined with rickety wooden shacks, drying laundries and the more residential area of Pratunam. Skytrain and the *khlong* taxis provide easy access to most attractions here.

JIM THOMPSON'S HOUSE
บ้านจิมทอมป์สัน

A pretty place to pass some time, **Jim Thompson's House** (☎ 0 2216 7368, 0 2215 0122; Soi Kasem San 2, Th Phra Ram I; adult/child 100/50B; ☉ 9am-5pm, compulsory tours (English & French) every 10min; Skytrain National Stadium, bus 508, 73, khlong taxi to Ratchathewi) is also a museum-quality preservation of

WILDLIFE SPOTTING IN BANGKOK

This concrete jungle has a diverse range of urban 'wildlife', a different breed from that inhabiting the Thai jungles. Here is a guide for spotting these critters in their natural settings:

Ronald McBoyfriend – Characteristics: older *faràng* man with dyed reddish hair. Habitat: Nana entertainment complex or compatriot bar. This ancient species usually has a serious Thai girlfriend or wife. The faux red hair is a sure sign that he was ordered to cover up his grey hair for a trip to meet the parents in the provinces.

Faràng khîi nók – Characteristics: dreadlocks, fishermen's pants and serious body odour. Habitat: Th Khao San. Literally 'bird-shit foreigner', referring to the species' extreme stinginess, this subset of the broader *faràng* family is constantly bragging about their haggling prowess.

Khan thawng – Characteristics: solo embittered *faràng* women working in Bangkok. Habitat: barstools in Silom Soi 4. Literally 'golden bowl', the Thai word for spinster also describes these specimens who spend their spare time complaining about the dysfunctional *faràng* men who are only interested in dating Thai women.

Dèk Hi-So – Characteristics: Bilingual Thais or *lûuk khrêung* (half Thai-*faràng*) with VIP credit cards. Habitat: Kuppa, Emporium Shopping Centre or a chauffeured car. Bangkok's equivalent of the Paris Hilton crowd, these high-society socialites have strapping trust funds and bling-bling tastes.

Khunyïng – Characteristics: Imelda Marcos helmet hairdos, jewel-toned Thai silks, thick pancake makeup. Habitat: Emporium Shopping Centre, official ceremonies, heading an entourage of merit-makers. 'Khunyïng' is a royal title earned through marriage to a high official or through individual merit. Not all women who adopt the uniform have the title; these wannabes are called 'Khunnai'.

Thai residential architecture and Southeast Asian art. Another hook is the home's former owner, Jim Thompson, a compelling character who created an international appetite for Thai silk.

Born in Delaware in 1906, Thompson was a New York architect who briefly served in the Office of Strategic Services (forerunner of the CIA) in Thailand during WWII. Following the war he found New York too tame and so returned to Bangkok. Thai silk caught his connoisseur's eye; he sent samples to fashion houses in Milan, London and Paris, gradually building a steady worldwide clientele.

A tireless promoter of traditional Thai arts and culture, Thompson collected parts of various derelict Thai homes in central Thailand and had them reassembled in the current location in 1959. One striking departure from tradition is the way each wall has its exterior side facing the house's interior, thus exposing the wall's bracing system. His small but splendid Asian art collection and his personal belongings are also on display in the main house.

Thompson's story doesn't end with his informal reign as best-adapted foreigner. While out for an afternoon walk in the Cameron Highlands of western Malaysia in 1967, Thompson mysteriously disappeared. That same year his sister was murdered in the USA, fuelling various conspiracy theories to explain the disappearance. Was it communist spies? Business rivals? Or a man-eating tiger? The most recent theory – for which there is apparently some hard evidence – has it that the silk magnate was accidentally run over by a Malaysian truck driver who hid his remains. *Jim Thompson The Unsolved Mystery*, by William Warren, is an excellent book on Thompson, his career, residence and subsequent intriguing disappearance.

ERAWAN SHRINE
ศาลพระพรหม

A seamless merging of commerce and religion occurs at all hours of the day at this bustling **shrine** (San Phra Phrom; cnr Th Ratchadamri & Th Ploenchit; admission free; ☯ 8am-7pm; Skytrain Chitlom, bus 501, 508, 511, 513, khlong taxi to Tha Pratunam).

Claiming a spare corner of the Grand Hyatt Erawan hotel, the four-headed deity Brahma (Phra Phrom in Thai) represents the Hindu god of creation and was originally built to ward off bad luck during the construction of the first Erawan Hotel (now torn down to make way for the current structure). Apparently the developers of the original Erawan (named after Airvata, Indra's three-headed elephant mount) first erected a typical Thai spirit house but decided to replace it with the more impressive Brahman shrine after several serious mishaps delayed the hotel construction. The shrine was later adopted by the lay community as it gained a reputation for granting wishes. Worshippers who have a wish granted may return to the shrine to commission the musicians and dancers, who are always on hand for an impromptu performance.

Silom & Around

Forming the artery of Bangkok's financial district, Th Silom has only a few daytime tourist attractions scattered among its corporate hotels, office towers and wining-and-dining restaurants. As Th Silom approaches Th Charoen Krung, the area becomes spiced with the sights and smells of its Indian and Muslim residents. The sliver of land that buffers Th Charoen Krung from the river was the international mercantile district during Bangkok's shipping heyday. Crumbling Victorian buildings and luxury hotels now occupy this neighbourhood of tributary sois.

MODERN ART GALLERIES

The contemporary art scene in Bangkok is growing faster than the city limits with a diversity of visual voices and venues. Thanks to creative entrepreneurs, nonreligious art was finally given display space in unlikely places – restaurants and pubs outside the watchful eye of the dominating aesthetic. The success of art in a social context prompted an emergence of commercial galleries cultivating a market for art buyers as well as art appreciators. While the galleries below have daily opening hours, a visit during an exhibition opening is an interesting social convergence of arty types, social climbers and freebie moochers. Pick up a copy of the free *Art Connection* brochure for a map and listing of galleries, and refer to *Bangkok Metro* magazine for a calendar of exhibition openings.

About Studio/About Café (Map pp108-9; ☎ 0 2623 3927; 418 Th Maitrichit; subway Hualamphong) Cutting-edge Thai artists, working in alternative and experimental media; phone for hours.

Bangkok University Art Gallery (Map pp104-5; ☎ 0 2350 3500; 3rd fl, Bldg 9, Kluay Nam Thai Campus, Th Phra Ram IV; 9am-5pm) This is considered to be one of the most avant-garde of Bangkok's art universities.

Chulalongkorn Art Centre (Map pp118-19; ☎ 0 2218 2964; 7th fl, Library Bldg, Chulalongkorn University, Th Phayathai; 8am-7pm Mon-Fri, 8am-4pm Sat) Major names in the modern art scene, as well as international artists.

Gallery F-Stop (Map pp112-13; ☎ 0 2663 7421; Tamarind Café, 27 Soi 20, Th Sukhumvit; 11am-11pm; Skytrain Asoke) Restaurant-gallery for photography with approachable exhibits.

H Gallery (Map pp114-16; ☎ 0 1310 4428; 201 Soi 12, Th Sathon beside Bangkok Bible College; noon-6pm Wed-Sat; Skytrain Chong Nonsi) Leading commercial gallery for emerging Thai abstract painters.

Jamjuree Art Gallery (off Map pp118-19; ☎ 0 2218 3645; Jamjuree Bldg, Chulalongkorn University, Th Phayathai; 10am-7pm Mon-Fri, noon-4pm Sat & Sun; Skytrain Siam bus 501, 502) Modern spiritual themes and brilliantly coloured abstracts from emerging student artists.

Kraichitti Gallery (Map pp110-11; ☎ 0 1623 8284; Sunset Street Complex, Th Khao San; 3-11pm; bus 511, 53, river ferry Tha Phra Athit) An ambitious intersection of photography and entertainment in an elegant 100-year-old home smack dab on Th Khao San.

Tadu Contemporary Art (Map pp104-5; ☎ 0 2645 2473; 7th fl, Barcelona Motors Bldg, 99/2 Th Tiamruammit; 10am-6pm Mon-Sat; subway Thailand Cultural Centre) Major centre for art, culture and conversation.

Tang Gallery (Map pp114-16; ☎ 0 2630 1114; basement fl, Silom Galleria, 91 9/1 Th Silom; 11am-7pm Tue-Sat, noon-6pm Sun; Skytrain Chong Nonsi) Chinese modern artists.

Thavibu Gallery (Map pp114-16; ☎ 0 2266 5454; 3rd fl, Silom Galleria, 91 9/1 Th Silom; 11am-7pm Tue-Sat, noon-6pm Sun; Skytrain Chong Nonsi) Artists from Cambodia, Thailand and Burma.

Silom's most famous attraction is Patpong, a raunchy circus of go-go bars and an oddly complementary market of pirated goods. Traffic is notorious in this part of town, but the Skytrain, subway and river express provide some transport relief.

SRI MARIAMMAN TEMPLE
วัดพระศรีมหาอุมาเทวี(วัดแขกสีลม)

As flourishing as it is flamboyant, this **Hindu temple** (Wat Phra Si Maha Umathewi; Map pp114-16; ☎ 0 2238 4007; cnr Th Silom & Th Pan; 6am-8pm; bus 502, 504, 505, 15) visually pounces off the block. Built in the 1860s by Tamil immigrants in the centre of a still thriving ethnic enclave, the main temple is a stacked façade of intertwined, full-colour Hindu deities, topped by a gold-plated copper dome. In the centre of the main shrine is Jao Mae Maha Umathewi (Uma Devi, also known as Shakti, Shiva's consort); her son Phra Khanthakuman (Subramaniam) is on the right; on the left is her other son, elephant-headed Phra Phikkhanet (Ganesh). Along the left interior wall sit rows of Shiva, Vishnu and other Hindu deities, as well as a few Buddhas, so that just about any non-Muslim, non-Judaeo–Christian Asian can worship here – Thai and Chinese devotees come to pray and offer bright-yellow marigold garlands alongside the Indian residents.

Thais call this temple Wat Khaek – *khàek* is a colloquial expression for people of Indian descent. The literal translation is 'guest', an obvious euphemism for a group of people you don't particularly want as permanent residents; hence most Indians living permanently in Thailand don't appreciate the term.

LUMPHINI PARK
สวนลุมพินี

Named after the Buddha's place of birth in Nepal, **Lumphini Park** (Map p117; Th Phra Ram IV, btwn Th Withayu & Th Ratchadamri; admission free; 5am-8pm; Skytrain Sala Daeng, subway Lumphini, bus 504, 505, 507) is the best way to escape Bangkok without leaving town. Shady paths, a large artificial lake and swept lawns temporarily blot out the roaring traffic and hulking concrete towers.

One of the best times to visit the park is before 7am when the air is fresh (well, relatively so for Bangkok) and legions of

Chinese are practising *taijiquan* (t'ai chi). Also in the morning, vendors set up tables to dispense fresh snake blood and bile, considered health tonics.

Boats can be rented at the lake and a weight-lifting area in one section becomes a miniature muscle beach on weekends. Other facilities include a snack bar, an asphalt jogging track, several areas with tables and benches for picnics, and a couple of tables where women serve Chinese tea. The park reawakens with the evening's cooler temperatures – aerobics classes collectively sweat to a techno soundtrack.

In the kite-flying season (mid-February to April), Lumphini becomes a favoured flight zone; kites *(wâo)* can be purchased in the park during these months.

QUEEN SAOVABHA MEMORIAL INSTITUTE (SNAKE FARM)
สถานเสาวภา

Snake farms tend to gravitate towards carnival-esque rather than humanitarian, except at this **Red Cross research institute** (Map pp114-16; ☎ 0 2252 0161; cnr Th Phra Ram IV & Th Henri Dunant; admission 70B; 8.30am-4.30pm Mon-Fri, 8.30am-noon Sat & Sun; Skytrain Sala Daeng, subway Samyan). Representatives of all the venomous snakes – common cobra, king cobra, banded krait, Malayan pit viper, green pit viper and Russell's viper – are used to prepare antivenin, which is distributed throughout the country. Founded in 1923, the snake farm was only the second of its kind in the world (the first was in Brazil).

Tourists are welcome to view the **milkings** (11am & 2.30pm Mon-Fri, 11am Sat & Sun) and **feedings** (2.30pm Mon-Fri) or to stroll the small garden where the snakes are kept in escape-proof cages. The snakes tend to be camera-shy during nonperformance times.

A booklet entitled *Guide to Healthy Living in Thailand*, published jointly by the Thai Red Cross and the US embassy, is available at the institute.

Sukhumvit
Map pp112–13

Executive-strength expat neighbourhoods branch off marathon-running Th Sukhumvit. More time will be spent here eating, drinking and perhaps sleeping (as there is a high concentration of midrange hotels here) than sightseeing. The Skytrain is the primary public transportation option.

BAN KAMTHIENG
บ้านคำเที่ยง

An engaging **house museum** (☎ 0 2661 6470; Siam Society, 131 Soi 21/Asoke, Th Sukhumvit; adult/child 100/50B; ◷ 9am-5pm Mon-Sat; Skytrain Asoke), Ban Kamthieng transports visitors to a northern Thai village complete with informative displays of daily rituals, folk beliefs and everyday household chores, all within the setting of a traditional-style wooden house. This museum is operated by and shares space with the Siam Society, the publisher of the renowned *Journal of the Siam Society* and a valiant preserver of traditional Thai culture. A reference library is open to visitors and contains titles on anything you'd want to know about Thailand (outside the political sphere, since the society is sponsored by the royal family).

Greater Bangkok
WANG SUAN PHAKKAT
วังสวนผักกาด

An overlooked treasure, **Lettuce Farm Palace** (Map pp106-7; ☎ 0 2245 4934; Th Sri Ayuthaya, near Th Ratchaprarop; admission 100B; ◷ 9am-4pm; Skytrain Phayathai, bus 504, 63) is a collection of five traditional wooden Thai houses that was once the residence of Princess Chumbon of Nakhon Sawan and before that a lettuce farm – thus the name. Within the stilt buildings are displays of art, antiques and furnishings, and the landscaped grounds are a peaceful oasis complete with ducks and swans, and a semi-enclosed garden.

The diminutive **Lacquer Pavilion**, at the back of the complex, dates from the Ayuthaya period and features gold-leaf *jataka* (stories of the Buddha's past lives) and *Ramayana* murals, as well as scenes from daily Ayuthaya life. The building originally sat in a monastery compound on Mae Nam Chao Phraya, just south of Ayuthaya. Larger residential structures at the front of the complex contain displays of Khmer-style Hindu and Buddhist art, Ban Chiang ceramics and a very interesting collection of historic Buddhas, including a beautiful late U Thong-style image.

RAMA IX ROYAL PARK
สวนหลวง ร.9

Opened during 1987 to commemorate the 60th birthday of King Bhumibol, Bangkok's newest **green area** (Suan Luang; Map pp104-5; Th Sukhumvit Km 103; admission 10B; ◷ 6am-6pm) covers 81 hectares and includes a water park and botanic gardens. Since its opening, the latter has developed into a significant horticultural research centre. Take bus 2, 23 or 25 from On Nut Skytrain station to Soi Udom Suk (Soi 103), off Th Sukhumvit in Phra Khanong district, then a green minibus to the park. Alternatively, you can take air-con bus 145 from Chatuchak Weekend Market, getting off at the first intersection after the two large shopping malls, Seacon Square and Seri Centre. Turn left and catch either an orange minibus or *săwngthăew* for the remaining 10-minute ride.

WAT CHONG NONSI
วัดช่องนนทรีย์

Close to the Bangkok side of the river, this **temple** (Map pp104-5; Th Nonsi, off Th Phra Ram III; ◷ 8:30am-6pm) contains some notable *jataka* murals painted between 1657 and 1707. It is the only surviving Ayuthaya-era temple in which both the murals and architecture are of the same period with no renovations. As a single, 'pure' architectural and painting unit, it's considered quite important for the study of late Ayuthaya art.

KO KRET
เกาะเกร็ด

Soothe your nerves with a half-day getaway to this car-free **island** (off Map pp104–5) in the middle of Mae Nam Chao Phraya, at Bangkok's northern edge. It is home to one of Thailand's oldest settlements of Mon people, who were the dominant culture in central Thailand between the 6th and 10th centuries AD. The Mon are also skilled potters, and Ko Kret continues the culture's ancient tradition of hand-thrown earthenware. Along the narrow footpaths that circumnavigate the island are small pottery shops behind which the potters work in open-air studios with relaxed precision. Beside the long-tail boat pier, a Mon Buddhist temple called **Wat Paramai Yikawat**, also known simply as 'Wat Mon', contains a Mon-style marble Buddha. A leisurely stroll around the island provides a fascinating contrast to the Big Mango's streetlife – Ko Kret's rush hour may consist of two motorcycles, and the counterparts to those fierce soi dogs are now lazy creatures too content to scratch themselves.

THE CATHOLIC SIDE OF THE CITY OF ANGELS

During the international sea trade between the East and West, many European nations established corporate and diplomatic headquarters in the tidal flats of Mae Nam Chao Phraya. The most influential, but least visible today, are the Portuguese, credited for building several stately Catholic churches in Bangkok that are now filled with parishioners from the former French colonies of Indochina.

In the Talat Noi district and dating from 1787, **Holy Rosary Church** (Map pp108-9; ☎ 0 2266 4849; 1318 Th Yotha, near River City; ☽ mass Mon-Sat 6am, Sun 6.15am, 8am & 10am; river ferry Tha Si Phraya) is known in Thai as Wat Kalawan, from the Portuguese 'Calvario'. French inscriptions beneath the Stations of the Cross were added in the late 19th century when the church was rebuilt by Vietnamese and Cambodian Catholics. This old church has a splendid set of Romanesque stained-glass windows, gilded ceilings and a Christ statue that is carried through the streets during Easter celebrations.

Church of the Immaculate Conception (Map pp106-7; ☎ 0 2243 2617; extn 167 Soi 11, Th Samsen; ☽ variable; river ferry Tha Thewet) dates back to 1674, but the present building claims an 1837 reconstruction and a Cambodian parish. One of the original church buildings survives and is now used as a museum housing holy relics.

Church of Santa Cruz (Map pp106-7; ☎ 0 2466 0347; Soi Kudi Jiin, Thonburi; ☽ 5:30-8:30am & 6-8pm; cross-river ferry from Tha Pak Talaad/Atsadang) occupies the former Portuguese district, a land grant from King Taksin in appreciation of loyalty after the fall of Ayuthaya.

Current transport options from Bangkok include hiring a long-tail boat from the Nonthaburi Pier (accessible via river express boat heading north); rates start at 600B for two hours. Another longer, but shoestringy, option is to take the river express to Nonthaburi; transfer to a Laem Thong-bound boat and alight at Tha Pak Kret; transfer to a cross-river ferry to Ko Kret – *voila*!

You can also join the Sunday tours operated by **Chao Phraya River Express** (Map p134; ☎ 0 2623 6001; fax 0 2225 3002; adult/child 300/250B; ☽ 9am-3.30pm), which depart from Tha Maharat and include stops at dessert-making villages and a floating market.

ACTIVITIES
Traditional Massage
Bangkokians regard traditional massage as a vital part of preventative health care and frequent massage parlours more regularly than gyms. You'll have no trouble finding a massage shop (rather they'll find you), but after a few visits to the backpacker hangars, packed full of groaning customers, you may want a more focused, professional experience. A good sign is a small shop off the main path, but don't be deterred by a petite masseuse – many of them have vice-grip strength.

The primary training ground for the masseuses that deploy across the country is **Wat**

Pho Thai Massage School (Map p120; ☎ 0 2221 3686; Soi Penphat, Th Sanam Chai; massage 250-470B; ☽ 8am-5pm; bus 501, 507, 508, river express Tha Tien).

Don't worry that **Marble House** (2hr traditional massage 400B; ☽ 10am-midnight; Silom Map pp114-16; ☎ 0 2235 3529; 37/18-19 Soi Surawong Plaza, Th Surawong; Skytrain Sala Daeng; Sukhumvit Map pp112-13; ☎ 0 2651 0905, 3rd fl, Ruamchit Plaza, 199 Th Sukhumvit at Soi 15) is in the middle of the sleazy Thaniya scene. The work of its traditional masseurs doesn't reflect the neighbouring 'friendly' services. The air-conditioned teak rooms make massages even more restorative.

Other tried-and-true practitioners, including blind masseurs, can be found at **Buathip Thai Massage** (Map pp112-13; ☎ 0 2251 2627; 4/13 Soi 5, Th Sukhumvit; 1hr Thai traditional massage 270B, foot massage 250B; ☽ 10am-midnight; Skytrain Nana), which is on a small subsoi behind the Amari Boulevard Hotel.

Phunnee Foot Massage (Map pp112-13; ☎ 0 2250 2699; 12/3 Soi 22, Th Sukhumvit; 1hr foot massage 250B; ☽ 10am-10pm; Skytrain Phrom Phong) is a local chain well-known for expert foot massages, but don't expect much from the décor.

Skills Development Centre for the Blind (sŭun pháthánaa sàmàtthàphâap khon taa bàwt; off Map pp104-5; ☎ 0 2583 7327; Pak Kret, north of central Bangkok; 1½hr with/without air-con 140/100B) is a government outreach programme that trains the blind in Thai massage, creating what many people consider to be expert masseuses because of the blind's sensitive sense of touch. While a massage might be memorable, getting here is the primary adventure. Take the Chao Phraya river ferry north to Nonthaburi, where you will connect to a Laem Thong boat (5.45am to 5.45pm) to Tha Pak Kret. From the pier, hire a motorcycle taxi to take you to the Skills Development Centre (10B one way). You'll need a little Thai to pull this off, but Pak Kret villagers are pretty easy-going and willing to listen to foreigners massacre their language.

River & Canal Trips

In 1855 British envoy Sir John Bowring wrote: 'The highways of Bangkok are not streets or roads but the river and the canals. Boats are the universal means of conveyance and communication'. Glimpses of the watery ways of the 'Venice of the East' are still evident even though the wheeled motor vehicle has long since become Bangkok's conveyance of choice. A vast network of canals and river tributaries surrounding Bangkok (Map p134) still carries a motley fleet of watercraft, from paddled canoes to rice barges. In these areas many homes, trading houses and temples remain oriented towards life on the water and provide a fascinating glimpse into the past, when Thais still considered themselves *jâo náam* (water lords). See p141 for organised trips along the river and to Ayuthaya.

MAE NAM CHAO PHRAYA

An exploration of the King of Rivers is a journey through Thailand's watery heart. Hulking barges transport sand from the silting mouth to points upriver, or long-tail boats ricochet from one bank to another kicking up the muddy water into a boil. At each pier, the boat hands plead to the crowd to keep a 'cool heart' *(jai yen)* and allow the gap between dock and boat to subside before disembarking or boarding. The cool breezes and reddish glow of sunset will surely woo reluctant Bangkok-philes.

The **Chao Phraya River Express** (☎ 0 2623 6001; fax 0 2225 3002; tickets 10-15B) is a modest commuter service that ferries locals and tourists up and down the river. The terminus for most northbound boats is Tha Nonthaburi and for most southbound boats is Tha Sathon (also called Central Pier), near the Saphan Taksin Skytrain station. By catching

a boat with a green flag (from a green-flag serviced pier), you can go as far north as Pak Kret or as far south as Wat Ratchasingkhon (around 25B). Standard boats run about every 15 minutes throughout the day, and express boats run during morning and evening rush hours. See p183 for more information about boat travel.

Mit Chao Paya (☎ 0 2225 6179; Tha Chang) arranges long-tail boat tours along the river to sights such as the Royal Barges National Museum, Wat Phra Kaew and Grand Palace, and Wat Arun at most river piers, especially Tha Chang. It usually costs 400B for one hour, excluding admission and various mooring fees. These sights, however, are easily accessible via public transport.

If interested in tracing the path that most early visitors took to the capital city, you can hire long-tail boats from any pier to travel south to the Gulf of Thailand, 30km downriver, passing **Khlong Toey** (off Map p134), Bangkok's deep-water port, along the way. The town of Samut Prakan (p191) stands sentry at the river's mouth.

KHLONG BANGKOK NOI

Dive into the heart of the old agricultural community of **Khlong Bangkok Noi**, just across the river in Thonburi. The further up the *khlong* you go, the better the scenery, with teak houses on stilts, old temples and plenty of greenery. Stop off at **Wat Suwannaram** (Map pp104-5; ☎ 0 2434 7790; 33 Soi 32, Th Charoen Sanitwong; ☉ 5am-9pm; Tha Wat Suwan) to view 19th-century *jataka* murals painted by two of

---

FLOWERING TROUBLE

Forming floating carpets where birds alight and garbage collects, water hyacinths are the femme fatale of river environments. This invasive species was imported to Thailand by Rama V's (King Chulalongkorn) wife after a visit to Indonesia. The plant was originally intended as a decorative flower for the palace ponds but soon escaped to the river frontier, where it clogs waterways and spreads into virgin territory. One promising industry for this aquatic weed is to dry the stalks and weave them into furniture and rugs, which are sold in furniture stores and shopping centres throughout the city.

CHAO PHRAYA RIVER EXPRESS & THONBURI CANALS

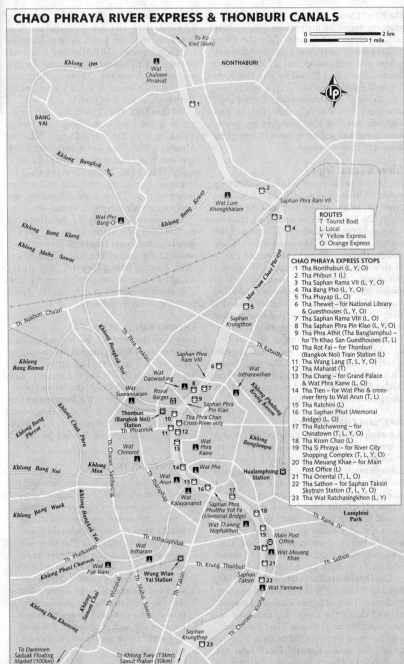

ROUTES
T Tourist Boat
L Local
Y Yellow Express
O Orange Express

CHAO PHRAYA EXPRESS STOPS
1 Tha Nonthaburi (L, Y, O)
2 Tha Phibun 1 (L)
3 Tha Saphan Rama VII (L, Y, O)
4 Tha Bang Pho (L, Y, O)
5 Tha Phayap (L, O)
6 Tha Thewet – for National Library & Guesthouses (L, Y, O)
7 Tha Saphan Rama VIII (L, O)
8 Tha Saphan Phra Pin Klao (L, Y, O)
9 Tha Phra Athit (Tha Banglamphu) – for Th Khao San Guesthouses (T, L)
10 Tha Rot Fai – for Thonburi (Bangkok Noi) Train Station (L)
11 Tha Wang Lang (T, L, Y, O)
12 Tha Maharat (T)
13 Tha Chang – for Grand Palace & Wat Phra Kaew (L, O)
14 Tha Tien – for Wat Pho & cross-river ferry to Wat Arun (T, L)
15 Tha Ratchini (L)
16 Tha Saphan Phut (Memorial Bridge) (L, O)
17 Tha Ratchawong – for Chinatown (T, L, Y, O)
18 Tha Krom Chao (L)
19 Tha Si Phraya – for River City Shopping Complex (T, L, Y, O)
20 Tha Meuang Khae – for Main Post Office (L)
21 Tha Oriental (T, L, O)
22 Tha Sathon – for Saphan Taksin Skytrain Station (T, L, Y, O)
23 Tha Wat Ratchasingkhon (L, Y)

RIVER SURGERY

Mae Nam Chao Phraya experiences a diurnal tide that is felt as far as 180km upriver, a penomenon that enabled ocean-going sailing ships to trade with Ayuthaya. One tricky bend in the river, from the present-day sights of Wat Arun to Thammasat University, required the digging of a shortcut to aid nonmotorised vessels. The original course of the river has been linguistically demoted to Khlong Bangkok Noi, which is not a canal at all.

early Bangkok's foremost religious muralists. Art historians consider these the best surviving temple paintings in Bangkok.

Long-tail public boats (one way 30B; 🕑 8am-3pm Mon-Fri, every 2½hr) leave from Tha Chang and travel via Khlong Bangkok Noi to Bang Yai, dropping off residents along the way. Sightseers are discouraged from using this boat during commuting hours.

OTHER THONBURI CANALS

Using hired long-tail boats, you can explore **Khlong Bangkok Yai**, which passes Wat Intharam, where a stupa contains the ashes of Thonburi's King Taksin, who was assassinated in 1782. Fine gold-and-black lacquerwork adorning the main *bòt* doors depicts the mythical *naariiphŏn* tree, which bears fruit that's shaped like beautiful maidens. Durian plantations line picturesque **Khlong Om**, which loops back to the river from the northern stretch of Khlong Bangkok Noi. **Khlong Mon**, between Bangkok Noi and Bangkok Yai, offers more typical canal scenery, including orchid farms.

The usual cost of hiring a long-tail boat to explore these canals is around 600B for one hour and 800B to 900B for two hours. Shop around at the different piers for a competitive price and clarify that the quote is for the duration of the trip, regardless of number of people. Make sure the price is agreed upon before climbing aboard – you can't bargain very well in the middle of the river!

Tha Chang usually has the largest selection of boats, but most piers offer boat hire. Don't forget to check in at less popular piers, such as Tha Ratchawong, if other operators are too aggressive. Avoid touts who

offer to 'arrange' a tour for you, in exchange for a commission from the boat driver.

Sports Facilities

If you're dedicated to the cause of athletics in this energy-sucking climate, you need access to an air-conditioned facility. Most membership gyms, residential condos and top-end hotels have fitness centres, squash and tennis courts, and some have swimming pools. There are also informal groups that play football, badminton and cricket, as well as **hash house harrier groups** (www.bangkok hhh.com). And once the tropical acclimatisation is complete, join the morning and evening joggers at the local parks.

Golf courses are typically located outside of central Bangkok, but are of international standards; test out your nine iron at **Bangkok Golf Club** (off Map pp104-5; ☎ 0 2501 2828; www.golf .th.com; 99 Th Tivanon) or **KrungThep Kreetha Sports Club** (Map pp104-5; ☎ 0 2379 3716; www.thailandgolf paradise.com; Th Krungthep Kreetha).

Swimming pools are usually open to the public for a day-use fee plus an annual membership fee. The most affordable and centrally located is the 50m pool at the **National Stadium** (Map pp106-7; ☎ 0 2215 1535; Th Phra Ram I; 🕑 hrs vary; day use 30B, annual membership 300B), although the lanes are often taken for swimming lessons. Nearby, **Pathumwan Princess Hotel** (Map pp106-7; day use 450B, annual membership 22,000B) has a 25m lap pool perched on a lush rooftop, and a sports facility.

All-purpose gyms include the **British Club** (Map pp114-16; ☎ 0 2234 0247; www.britishclubbang kok.org; 189 Th Surawong; fitness centre 🕑 6am-9pm), which is open to citizens of Australia, Canada, New Zealand and the UK, or to other nationals through a waiting list. Among the sports facilities are a pool, golf driving range, and squash and tennis courts.

MEMBERS ONLY

Bangkok's bluebloods and accomplished nouveau riche enjoy the status, privilege and..., oh yeah, sports facilities at the exclusive **Royal Bangkok Sports Club** (RBSC; Map pp106-7; ☎ 0 2251 0181-86; btwn Th Henri Dunant & Th Ratchadamri). Commoners among us can gain a glimpse of greener pastures during public horse-racing events held twice a month.

Clark Hatch Physical Fitness Centers (www.clark hatchthailand.com; Amari Atrium Hotel Map pp104-5; ☎ 0 2718 2000; 4th fl; 1880 Th Phetburi Tat Mai; subway Phetburi; Century Park Map pp106-7; ☎ 0 2246 7800; 5th fl, Th Ratchaprarop; Skytrain Victory Monument; Amari Watergate Hotel Map pp118-19; ☎ 0 2653 9000; 8th fl; khlong taxi Tha Pratunam) is a top-class operation whose locations all have weight machines, aerobics classes, pool, sauna and massage. Annual membership fees start at 19,000B.

Fitness First (Map pp112-13; ☎ 0 2237 0777; Landmark Bangkok, 138 Th Sukhumvit, btwn Soi 4 & 6) is the city's largest in-hotel health club with all the bells and whistles.

Yoga Elements Studio (Map pp118-19; ☎ 0 2655 5671; www.yogaelements.com; 23rd fl, Soi Chitlom, 29 Vanissa Bldg) teaches classes in Vinyasa and Ashtanga yoga and offers attractive introductory rates.

There are public tennis courts at **Central Tennis Court** (Map pp114-16; ☎ 0 2213 1909; 13/1 Soi Atakanprasit, Th Sathon Tai) and **Santisuk Tennis Courts** (Map pp112-13; ☎ 0 2391 1830; Soi 33, Th Sukhumvit).

WALKING TOUR

WALK FACTS

Start Tha Chang
Finish Thammasat University
Distance 2.1km
Duration 1-2 hours

Ko Ratanakosin

On this action-packed walking tour, you can efficiently tick off Bangkok's 'must-sees' in just one morning. Thankfully, the city's highlights reside in compact Ko Ratanakosin, the former royal district filled with gleaming temples and bustling markets. It is best to start early before the heat and the hordes have descended. Remember to dress modestly (long pants and skirts, shirts with sleeves and closed-toed shoes) in order to gain entry to the temples. Also ignore any strangers who approach you offering advice on sightseeing or jewellery, gem and tailor shops.

Start at **Tha Chang (1)** and follow Th Na Phra Lan east to the third gate into the **Wat Phra Kaew & Grand Palace (2**; p100). The Grand Palace has been supplanted by Chitlada Palace as the primary residence of the royal family, but it is still used for ceremonial occasions. Wat Phra Kaew is a gleaming

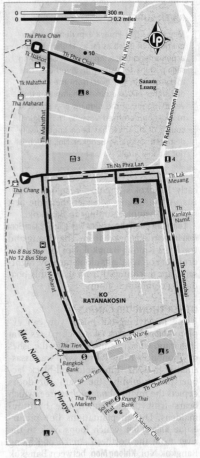

example of Bangkok temple architecture at its most baroque.

A quick diversion across the street from the temple will lead to **Silpakorn University (3**; Th Na Phra Lan), Thailand's premier fine-arts university. Originally founded as the School of Fine Arts, by Italian artist Corrado Feroci, the university campus includes part of an old palace built for Rama I.

Backtrack east and cross Th Sanamchai to the home of Bangkok's city spirit, **Lak Meuang (4**; p103), which is generally alive with the spectacle of devotion – including burning joss sticks and traditional dancers. Go south down Th Sanamchai for 500m, and turn right onto Th Chetuphon, where you'll enter **Wat Pho (5**; p102), home to the

BANGKOK

giant reclining Buddha and lots of quiet nooks and crannies.

If your feet are aching, head towards **Wat Pho's massage school** (6; p132), south of Tha Tien. Take Th Mahathat north to Th Thai Wang and turn left to catch the cross-river ferry to Khmer-influenced **Wat Arun** (7; p103).

Back in Bangkok, head up Th Maharat and stop for a spot of lunch from one of the open-air restaurants or stalls along the way. North of Th Na Phra Lan, Th Maharat becomes an informal healing centre of herbal apothecaries and sidewalk amulet sellers, respectively catering to the health of one's body and spirit. On your right is **Wat Maha-that** (8; p102), one of Thailand's respected Buddhist universities and headquarters of its largest Buddhist sect. Take a left into the narrow alley immediately after Trok Maha-that to discover the cramped **amulet market** (9; p103), where religious amulets (*phrá khrêuang*) representing various Hindu and Buddhist deities are sold. Follow the alley all the way towards the river to appreciate how extensive the amulet trade is.

If you've worked up yet another appetite, hop over to the next alley, Trok Nakhon, to a dim alternate world of food vendors, some of whom sport a river view. The graduation-gown stalls and swarm of white-and-black uniforms is an obvious clue that you are approaching **Thammasat University** (10; Th Phra Chan), known for its law and polit-ical science departments. The campus was also the site of the bloody October 1976 pro-democracy demonstrations, when hundreds of Thai students were killed or wounded by the military.

If you've made it this far, feel free to call it a day. Hang a left on Th Phra Chan towards Sanam Luang to return home by bus (air-con bus 506, 507, 509, 511, 512; or ordinary bus 39, 44, 47). Alternatively you could take a cross-river ferry from Tha Phra Chan to Tha Wang Lang, where you can pick up Chao Phraya express boats in either direction.

COURSES

For the curious types, there are loads of courses either designed for or adapted to fit foreigners who want to know more about any aspect of Thailand, from cooking to meditation.

Cooking

One of the best ways to crack Thailand's lengthy menu is to take a cooking course. Bangkok has several different courses aimed at backpackers, expat housewives, and wan-nabe master chefs.

Blue Elephant Thai Cooking School (Map pp114-16; ☎ 0 2673 9353; www.blueelephant.com; Thai Chine Bldg, 233 Th Sathon Tai; Skytrain Surasak) provides a basic introduction (2800B) to Thai tech-niques and ingredients; morning and after-noon classes are held daily. The morning session includes a trip to the market.

The **Modern Women Institute** (Map pp106-7; ☎ 0 2279 2831; 45/6-7 Th Setsiri) offers a multiday course (7000B) led by a TV and radio per-sonality and will provide all the basics for making curries, noodles and desserts.

Oriental Hotel Cooking School (Map pp114-16; ☎ 0 2659 9000; Oriental Hotel, Soi 38/Soi Oriental, Th Charoen Krung) features a plush six-day course (US$120) including demonstrations, lec-tures and hands-on work under the direc-tion of well-known chefs. Recipes mix old traditions with new techniques and guid-ance is given for how to order from a Thai menu.

Thai House (Map pp104-5; ☎ 0 2903 9611; www .thaihouse.co.th; Bang Yai, Nonthaburi) is held in a homey traditional teak house about 40 minutes north of Bangkok by boat. You can choose between one- to three-day pro-grammes (3550B to 16,650B), which include preparing Thai standards (*tôm yum, phàt thai* and various curries). There are also cooking and lodging packages available.

UFM Food Centre (Map pp112-13; ☎ 0 2259 0620-33; 593/41 Soi 33, Th Sukhumvit) is the most serious and thorough cooking school in Thailand, with a multilayered curriculum designed to turn a novice into an expert. Most classes are offered in Thai and you will need at least four people for an English-language class.

Meditation Courses

Although at times Bangkok may seem like the most un-Buddhist place on earth, there are several places where foreigners can learn about Theravada Buddhist meditation.

For more information about meditation centres or teachers with English skills in Bangkok and beyond, contact the **Inter-national Buddhist Meditation Centre** (☎ 0 2623 5881), which is affiliated with Wat Mahat-hat (p138) or the **World Fellowship of Buddhists**

(WFB; Map pp112-13; ☎ 0 2661 1284; www.wfb-hq.org; Soi 24, Th Sukhumvit, beside Benjasiri Park), which sells a guide to mediation centres. Also visit the online guide to Thai meditation centres at www.dhammathai.org for instructions on applications, size of monastery and proficiency of English.

See the Culture chapter for background information on Buddhism (p68) and temple etiquette (p60).

Wat Mahathat (see p102; ☎ 0 2222 6011) provides daily meditation instruction based on the Mahasi Sayadaw system of developing the *satipatthana* (foundations of mindfulness). Phra Suphe speaks flawless English, and there are often Western monks or long-term residents available to interpret. The International Buddhist Meditation Centre hosts twice-monthly lectures on various aspects of Buddhism.

Wat Pak Nam (Map pp104-5; ☎ 0 2467 0811; Th Thoet Thai, Phasi Charoen, Thonburi), where hundreds of monks and nuns reside during the Buddhist Lent *(phansǎa)*, has hosted many foreigners (especially Japanese) over the years. The meditation teacher speaks some English and there are usually people around who can interpret. The emphasis is on developing concentration through *nimitta* (acquired mental images) in order to attain *jhana* (state of 'absorption'). To get there take bus No 504, 509 or 103. The wat can also be reached by chartered long-tail boat.

The World Fellowship of Buddhists also hosts meditation classes from 2pm to 6pm on the first Sunday of every month, led by English-speaking monks from Wat Pa Nanachat, Ubon Ratchathani.

Baan Dvara Prateep (off Map pp104-5; ☎ 0 1845 5445; www.baandvaraprateep.com; 53/3 Mu 5, Ko Kret) is a perfect solution for the moderately mindful. This meditation and cultural retreat is more relaxed than the strict temple environment. Meditation classes focus on relieving stress and achieving peace and culture classes connect visitors to Thai handicrafts.

Other centres:

Sorn-Thawee Meditation Centre (☎ 0 3854 1405; Bangkla, Chachoengsao 24110)

Wat Asokaram (☎ 0 2395 0003; Soi Udumchai, Bang Na-Trat Highway, Samut Prakan)

Muay Thai (Thai Boxing)

The following camps provide instruction in English and accept men and women. Food and accommodation are usually provided at *muay thai* camps for an extra charge. The website www.muaythai.com contains loads of information on training camps.

Fairtex Muay Thai (☎ 0 2757 5148; www.fairtexbkk .com; 99/5 Mu 3, Soi Buthamanuson, Th Thaeparak, Bangpli, Samut Prakan; tuition per day US$15) is a popular, long-running camp south of Bangkok.

Jitti's Gym Thai Boxing & Homestay (Sor Vorapin; Map pp110-11; ☎ 0 2282 3551; 13 Soi Krasab, Th Chakraphong; tuition per month 10,000B), in west Banglamphu, specialises in training foreign students of both genders.

Muay Thai Institute (Map p186; ☎ 0 2992 0096; www.muaythai-institute.net; Rangsit Muay Thai Stadium, 336/932 Th Prachatipat, Pathum Thani; tuition per course US$160), north of Bangkok International Airport, is associated with the respected World Muay Thai Council. The institute offers a fundamental course (consisting of three levels of expertise), which can be completed in 120 days, as well as courses for instructors, referees and judges.

Thai Language & Culture Studies

Several schools in Bangkok offer courses in Thai language.

AUA Language Center (Map pp118-19; ☎ 0 2252 8170; www.auathai.com; 179 Th Ratchadamri; Skytrain Ratchadamri; tuition per hr 92B) is run by the American University Alumni (AUA) and is one of the largest English-language teaching institutes in the world. *Paw hòk* (6th-grade primary-school level, essential for working in the public school system) courses are available.

Chulalongkorn University's Intensive Thai Office (Map pp118-19; ☎ 0 2218 4899; www.arts.chula.ac.th; Faculty of Arts, Chulalongkorn University, Th Phayathai; Skytrain Siam) offers a 100-hour programme consisting of three basic, three intermediate and three advanced courses, each lasting five weeks (25,000B). The university's Faculty of Arts also offers a two-year Masters of Arts degree in Thai Studies Section (tuition US$1490). Participants have the opportunity to study and analyse a considerable body of knowledge under the supervision of recognised Thai experts in the field. The language of instruction is English.

Chulalongkorn University's Continuing Education Center (☎ 0 2218 3908; www.cec.chula.ac.th; 5th fl, Vidhyabhathan Bldg, 12 Soi Chulalongkorn, Chulalongkorn University; Skytrain Siam) offers a two-week intensive Thai studies course called Perspectives on Thailand (US$950). The 60-hour programme includes classes in Thai culture, economics, history, politics, religion, art, geography, language, trade and current events. Classes are offered once a year in July only. Students who have taken the course say they have found the quality of instruction excellent.

Siri Pattana Thai Language School (Map p117; ☎ 0 2286 1936; YWCA, 13 Th Sathon Tai) offers Thai language lessons as well as preparation for the *paw hòk* exam.

Union Language School (Map pp114-16; ☎ 0 2233 4482; union_lang@yahoo.com; Christ Church Thailand Bldg, 109 Th Surawong) is generally recognised as having the best and most rigorous course (many missionaries study here). Union employs a balance of structure-oriented and communication-oriented methodologies in 80-hour, four-week modules. Private tuition is also available.

Thai Massage Courses

Wat Pho Thai Massage School (Map p120; ☎ 0 2221 3686; watpottm@netscape.net; 392/25-28 Soi Phenphat 1, Th Maharat; ⏰ 9am-7pm; river ferry Tha Tien) offers two 30-hour courses – one on general Thai massage, the other on massage therapy. Tuition is 7000B. Shorter classes include a 15-hour foot massage course and an infant and child massage course; each costs 3600B. For those so inclined there are also longer one- to three-year programmes that combine Thai herbal medicine with massage for a full curriculum in Thai traditional medicine. Some knowledge of Thai will ease the communication barrier in all of these courses. The school is outside the temple compound in a nicely restored old Bangkok shophouse.

BANGKOK FOR CHILDREN

Want to ingratiate yourself into Thai culture? Bring your children along as passports. The family is so revered in Thailand that even the most aloof taxi driver will warm to a fat *faràng* baby. Blonde-headed children will get even more attention, and all ages will be showered with affection and treats.

Bangkok Doll Factory & Museum (Map pp106-7; ☎ 0 2245 3008; 85 Soi Ratchataphan/Soi Mo Leng; admission free; ⏰ 8am-5pm Mon-Sat) houses a colourful selection of traditional Thai dolls, both new and antique. This museum is really hard to find: approach via Th Si Ayuthaya head-

ing east. Cross under the expressway past the intersection with Th Ratchaprarop and take the soi to the right of the post office. Follow this windy street until you start seeing signs.

Need to beat the heat? Try pretending you're much closer to the Arctic circle at the indoor **Central World Ice Skating** (Map pp118-19; 7th fl, Central World Plaza, cnr Th Phra Ram I & Th Ratchadamri; admission 150B; ⏰ 10am-8.30pm Mon-Fri, 10am-2.45pm Sat & 3.30-8.30pm Sat & Sun; Skytrain Chitlom, khlong taxi to Tha Pratunam).

Learning is disguised as fun at the hands-on **Children's Discovery Museum** (Map pp104-5; ☎ 0 2615 7333; Chatuchak Park, Th Kamphaeng Phet 4, opposite Chatuchak Weekend Market; adult/child 70/50B; ⏰ 9am-5pm Tue-Fri, 10am-6pm Sat & Sun; Skytrain Mo Chit, subway Chatuchak Park). Most activities are geared to early-elementary-aged children. There is also a toddler-aged playground at the back of the main building.

The collection of animals at Bangkok's 19-hectare **Dusit Zoo** (Map pp106-7; ☎ 02 281 2000; Th Phra Ram V, btwn Th Ratwithi & Th Sri Ayuthaya; adult/child 50/30B; ⏰ 9am-5pm; bus 510, 18; river ferry Tha Thewet) includes more than 300 mammals, 200 reptiles and 800 birds, including relatively rare indigenous species such as banteng, gaur, serow and some rhinoceros. The facilities are a bit tired, but if nothing else, the zoo is a nice place to get away from the noise of the city and observe how Thai people amuse themselves – mainly by eating. The shady grounds feature trees labelled in English, Thai and Latin, plus a lake in the centre with paddle boats for hire. There's also a small children's playground.

For kite-flying (in season), playgrounds and lots of room to stretch legs and lungs, **Lumphini Park** (p130) is a trusty ally in the cool hours of the morning and evening.

Come for a milking and see the lethal snakes become reluctant altruists at the antivenin-producing **Queen Saovabha Memorial Institute** (p130).

SF City Bowl (Map pp118-19; ☎ 0 2611 7171; 7th fl, Mahboonkrong, cnr Th Phra Ram I & Th Phayathai; admission 70-90B; ⏰ 10am-1am; Skytrain National Stadium) occupies many a Thai teenagers' spare time and baht. It's like stepping into a psychedelic video game.

Join the novice monks and other children as they sprinkle tiny pellets of fish food (which are sold on the pier) into the river at **Tha Thewet** (Thewet Pier; Map pp106-7; Th Samsen;

THEME & AMUSEMENT PARKS

Just outside Bangkok are a host of artificial tourist attractions that provide either the see-the-whole-country-in-an-hour theme or the standard Western-style amusement park. It's often worth booking tickets through travel agencies, if their packages include round-trip transport.

Rose Garden Country Resort (Map p186; ☎ 0 3432 2588-93; www.rose-garden.com; Nakhon Pathom; ⏰ 8am-5.30pm), 32km west of Bangkok, is a resort encompassed by a faux Thai cultural village with demos of handicrafts, dancing, traditional ceremonies and martial arts. The 24-hectare garden area boasts 20,000 rose bushes and there is a golf course.

Samphran Elephant Ground & Zoo (Map p186; ☎ 0 2284 1873; Nakhon Pathom; adult/child 250/150B; ⏰ 8am-5.30pm), 33km west of Bangkok, is where you can see elephant 'roundups' and crocodile shows. There are a number of other animals in zoo-like conditions. Crocodile wrestling, elephant and magic shows are held in the afternoon.

Safari World (Map pp104-5; ☎ 0 2914 4100; www.safariworld.com; 99 Th Ramindra 1, Minburi; adult/child 780/570B; ⏰ 9am-5pm), 45km east of Bangkok, is a 69-hectare wildlife park said to be the largest 'open zoo' in the world. It's divided into two portions, the drive-through Safari Park and the walk-through Marine Park. The 5km Safari Park drive (in air-con coaches or your own vehicle) visits eight habitats with an assortment of giraffes, lions, zebras, rhinos, monkeys, elephants, orang-utans, and other African and Asian animals. A Panda House displays rare white pandas, and the Marine Park focuses on trained dolphin performances. By public transport, catch a 26 bus from the Victory Monument to Minburi, then a sǎwngthǎew to the park. A taxi costs about 300B and can be arranged at most hotels.

But if you've got a budding crocodile hunter, consider a quick safari to the **Crocodile Park** (p191), south of Bangkok.

⏰ 7am-7pm), transforming the muddy veneer into a brisk boil of flapping bodies.

Near the old Portuguese quarter in Thonburi, **Wat Prayoon** (Map pp108-9; 24 Th Prachadhipok cnr Thetsaban Soi 1, beside Memorial Bridge; admission free; ⏰ 8am-6pm; cross-river ferry from Tha Pak Talaad/Atsadang) is an artificial hill cluttered with miniature shrines and a winding path encircling a turtle pond. Vendors sell cut fruit for feeding to the resident turtles.

BIZARRE BANGKOK

If you've joined the routine of the lotus-eaters and have stopped noticing the taxi-cab shrines, the groundskeepers sweeping the lawns, the children bathing in the filthy canals, or mangy soi dogs wearing T-shirts, then you need to wake up and smell the fish sauce. Or spend the day experiencing Bangkok's freakier side.

Kàthoey Cabaret

Thailand's second class of women (kàthoey transvestites and transgenders) push gender-bending to gender-illusion, in turn fooling many unsuspecting foreign visitors. While night stalkers will no doubt encounter lady-boys at go-go bars, the more straight-laced visitor can witness the magic of sequinned

costumes, big hair, and natural hour-glass figures at the city's kàthoey cabarets. **Calypso Cabaret** (Map pp118-19; ☎ 0 2261 6355, 0 2216 8937; Asia Hotel, 296 Th Phayathai; tickets 800B; ⏰ showtimes 8.15pm & 9.45pm) and **Mambo Cabaret** (Map pp112-13; ☎ 0 2662 0441; Washington Theatre, Th Sukhumvit, btwn Soi 22 & 24; tickets 600B; ⏰ showtimes 8.30pm & 10pm) host choreographed stage shows of Broadway high kicks and lip-synched pop tunes.

House of Gems

The friendly proprietor of this novelty **archaeology store** (Map pp114-16; ☎ 0 2234 6730; 1218 Th Charoen Krung, near Th Surawong; ⏰ 10am-6pm Mon-Sat; bus 75, 115, 116, river ferry Tha Oriental) knows why you've come even before the door shuts behind you. 'You want to see poopy?' he giggles and slides open a plexiglass display case filled with prehistoric dinosaur droppings. Next you get to handle the 'gems' and see the differences between the post-digestion favours of carnivores versus herbivores. If this is our legacy, we're going veggie. A little scientific, a little adolescent, the store also sells sharks' teeth and trilobite fossils.

Lingam Shrine at Nai Lert Park

Clusters of carved stone and wooden phalli surround a spirit house and shrine (Saan Jao

Mae Thap Thim; Map pp118-19; Nai Lert Park Hotel, Th Withayu; Skytrain Ploenchit, khlong taxi Tha Withayu) built by millionaire businessman Nai Loet to honour Jao Mae Thap Thim, a female deity thought to reside in the old banyan tree on the site. Someone who made an offering shortly thereafter had a baby, and the shrine has received a steady stream of worshippers – mostly young women seeking fertility – ever since. To get here if facing the entrance of the Raffles hotel follow the small concrete pathway to the right which winds down into the bowels of the building beside the car park. The shrine will be at the end of the building next to the *khlong*.

Songkran Niyosane Forensic Medicine Museum

Holy gun-shot wound, Batman, this grisly **museum** (Map p120; ☎ 02 419 7000; 2nd fl, Forensic Pathology Bldg, Siriraj Hospital, Th Phrannok, Thonburi; admission 40B; ☽ 8.30am-4.30pm Mon-Fri; river ferry Tha Rot Fai) will efficiently separate the aspiring doctors from the reluctant patients. One of seven medical museums on the hospital premises, this one's claim to fame is the leathery cadaver of Si Ouey, an infamous Thai serial killer, and other appendages and remnants of famous murders, including the bloodied T-shirt from a victim who was

---

WHERE YOU GO?

Getting around Bangkok has always been a challenge, even way back in the 18th century as canals were ceding to roads and human-drawn rickshaws (*rót chék*) were the era's taxis. During the early 20th century, the rickshaw gave way to the squeaky three-wheeled pedicab (*săamláw*), which benefited from Bangkok's flat terrain. At certain arched bridges, however, the incline was too steep and passengers would have to walk across themselves. Once cars and trucks dominated the roadways, the *săamláw* was replaced by its motorised counterpart: the three-wheeled, onomatopoeic *túk-túk*. These wily go-carts fly around corners, kicking up a cloud of blue smoke and coughing like asthmatic power saws. Even though most short-term visitors will get ripped-off by unscrupulous *túk-túk* drivers, few can resist the call 'Hey you, where you go?'

---

stabbed to death with a dildo, an instrument that usually brings pleasure.

From Tha Rot Fai, follow the road to the second entrance into the Siriraj Hospital campus. The museum building will be on your left.

TOURS
Dinner Cruises

A dozen or more companies in Bangkok run regular dinner cruises along Mae Nam Chao Phraya. It's a fine way to dine outdoors when the weather is hot – away from city traffic, cooled by a river breeze and amid the twinkling city lights – although the food is usually mediocre. Several of the dinner boats cruise under the well-lit Saphan Phra Ram IX, the longest singlespan cable-suspension bridge in the world. The less expensive, more casual boats allow you to order as little or as much as you want from moderately priced menus with a modest per person surcharge.

Yok Yor Marina & Restaurant (Map pp106-7; ☎ 0 2281-6972; www.yokyor.co.th; 885 Soi Somdet Chao Phraya 17, Thonburi; adult/child 70/35B plus meal costs; ☽ 8-10pm) is a favourite among Thai friends celebrating birthdays and joining in choruses of 'Happy Bert-day'.

Manohra (Map pp104-5; ☎ 0 2476 0022; www.manohracruises.com; Bangkok Marriott Resort & Spa, Thonburi) is a converted teak rice barge that offers a **dinner cruise** (adult/child 1400/700B plus tax, service & drinks; ☽ 7.30-10pm). If you're commitment shy, try the sunset **cocktail cruise** (640B plus tax & service; ☽ departs 6pm), which includes one drink and a light snack. A free river taxi operates between Tha Sathon (near Saphan Taksin Skytrain station) for the 15-minute trip to Manohra's pier at Bangkok Marriott Resort & Spa.

Bang Pa-In & Ayuthaya Cruises

All-day or overnight trips take a northern course from Bangkok to the ruins of the former royal capital of Ayuthaya (p195) and/or to the nearby summer palace of Bang Pa-In. To ruin-weary travellers, the river journey might broaden the historical centre's appeal.

Chao Phraya River Express Boat (☎ 0 2623 6001; fax 0 2225 3002; adult/child round trip 390/300B; ☽ 7.30am-6pm Sun) does a reasonably priced tour to Bang Pa-In, Bang Sai and Wat Phailom on Sunday only. The tour price does not include lunch or admission fees, and the boat departs from Tha Maharat (Map p120).

For a real indulgence, climb aboard the **Mekhala** (Map pp104-5; ☎ 0 2256 7168; www.mekhala cruise.com; Menam Riverside Hotel; s/d round trip US$285/235) or the **Manohra 2** (Map pp104-5; ☎ 0 2476 0022; www.manohracruises.com; Bangkok Marriott Resort & Spa, Thonburi; s/d round trip US$735/975), which are both restored, teak rice barges decorated with antiques and Persian carpets. These beauties are the nautical equivalent of the *Eastern & Oriental Express* train with sleeping cabins. The *Mekhala* trip is a two-day, one-night excursion to Ayuthaya. In the evening the boats anchor at a wat, where a candle-lit dinner is served. The next morning passengers offer food to the monks from the wat, and then the barge moves on to Bang Pa-In.

Bicycle Tours

Several tour companies organise half-day cycling tours of Bangkok's countryside (it does really exist). All equipment and transportation is provided. Contact **ABC Amazing Bangkok Cyclists** (☎ 0 2712 9301; www.realasia .net; tours from 1000B; ☺ 10am-6pm) or **SpiceRoads** (☎ 0 2712 5305; http://spiceroads.com; tours from 2500B; ☺ 7am-5pm).

FESTIVALS & EVENTS

In addition to the national (usually religious) holidays, there's always something going on in Bangkok. Check the TAT website (www.tourismthailand.org) or the Bangkok Tourist Bureau (http://bangkoktourist.bma .go.th) for exact dates. The hotels and cultural centres also host various international festivals.

January
Bangkok International Film Festival (mid-January; www.bangkokfilm.org) Home-grown talent and overseas indies arrive on the silver screens. If you haven't heard, Bangkok is fast becoming a movie hybrid between Bollywood and Hong Kong.

The River of Kings (mid-January to mid-February; www.theriverofkingsbangkok.com) Spectacular sound-and-light show over 12 consecutive nights alongside Mae Nam Chao Phraya at Tha Ratchaworadit (between Tha Tien and Tha Chang). With the illuminated Grand Palace and Wat Phra Kaew in the background, a combination of Thai dance, music and animation make for an intensely visual experience.

February/March
Chinese New Year Thai-Chinese celebrate the lunar New Year, with a week of house-cleaning, lion dances and fireworks. Most festivities centre around Chinatown.

March
Kite-Flying Season During the windy season, colourful kites battle it out over the skies of Sanam Luang and Lumphini Park.

April
Songkhran (mid-April) The celebration of the Thai New Year has morphed into a water war with high-powered water guns and water balloons being launched at suspecting and unsuspecting participants.

May
Royal Ploughing Ceremony (dates vary) His Majesty the King commences rice-planting season with a royal-religious ceremony at Sanam Luang.

Miss Jumbo Queen Contest (early May) With fat-trends creeping across the globe, Thailand hosts a beauty pageant for extralarge (over 80kg) women who display the grace of an elephant at Nakhon Pathom's Samphran Elephant Park.

August
Queen's Birthday (August 12) The queen's birthday is recognised as Mother's Day throughout the country. In Bangkok, festivities centre around Th Ratchadamnoen and the Grand Palace.

September
International Festival of Music & Dance (mid-September to early October) An extravaganza of arts and culture is sponsored by the Thailand Cultural Centre (www.thaiculturalcenter.com).

September/October
Vegetarian Festival (dates vary) A 10-day Chinese-Buddhist festival wheels out streetside vendors serving meatless meals announced with yellow banners. The greatest concentration of vendors is found in Chinatown.

October/November
King Chulalongkorn Day (October 23) Rama V is honoured on the anniversary of his death at his revered Royal Plaza statue in Dusit (Map pp106–7). Crowds of devotees come to make merit of incense and flower garlands.

November
Loi Kràthong (early November) A beautiful festival where, on the night of the full moon, small lotus-shaped boats made of banana leaf and containing a lit candle are set adrift on the river.

GAY & LESBIAN BANGKOK

With out-and-open nightspots and annual pride events, Bangkok's homosexual community enjoys an unprecedented amount of tolerance considering the region. But discretion is still the rule and the expectation from a mainstream society who is willing to turn a blind eye as long as the closet door is closed.

Utopia (www.utopia-asia.com) is an online resource for the Southeast Asian gay community listing entertainment venues, news and views and providing travel services. **Dreaded Ned** (www.dreadedned.com) also does a rundown on gay nightlife in Bangkok and Pattaya. **Lesla** (www.lesla.com) is a Thai-English portal for Bangkok's lesbian (*tom-dees* in Thai) community.

Tucked into two dead-end sois (Soi 2 and 4), Silom's strip of gay clubs and bars is Bangkok's pink triangle where cruising limits reach highway speeds. The crowd is a mix of money-boys (male prostitutes) and shopping Westerners, along with Thai guppies (gay professionals) and even some voyeuristic straight couples. Many of the trendy restaurants and bars, like **Eat Me** (p162) or the **Diplomat Bar** (p168), also serve as gathering places for Bangkok's young and spendy gays. Other local scenes centre around Th Ramkamhaeng and Saphan Kwai, both north of the city. The *tom-dee* crowd hangs out at **Hemlock** (p157) and other art bars along Th Phra Athit or at gay and straight venues throughout town.

DJ Station (Map pp114-16; ☎ 0 2266 4029; 8/6-8 Soi 2, Th Silom; cover 300B; Skytrain Sala Daeng) Muscleboys and flamboyant characters shake it to hard house at this long-standing dance club.

Balcony (Map pp114-16; ☎ 0 2235 5891; 8/6-8 Soi 4, Th Silom; Skytrain Sala Daeng) On the warm-up, people-watching soi, this is a classic good-times bar for ogling and angling.

Freeman (Map pp114-16; ☎ 02 632 8032; small soi btwn Soi 2 and Soi Thaniya, Th Silom; Skytrain Sala Daeng) Reputedly the best cabaret in town, Freeman's midnight shows are a little raunchier than the typical tourist-oriented *kàthoey* shows.

ICQ (Map pp104-5; ☎ 0 2272 4775 Th Kamphaengphet, Chatuchak; Skytrain Mo Chit, subway Chatuchak) A local favourite for loud and lushy behaviour among the well-dressed trendies.

Telephone (Map pp114-16; ☎ 0 2234 3279; 114/11-13 Soi 4, Th Silom; Skytrain Sala Daeng) Nothing beats a good gimmick and this low-key bar has old-fashioned telephones at every table so you can ring your good-looking neighbour.

Vega Café (Map pp112-13; ☎ 0 2258 8273; 32/1 Soi 39, Th Sukhumvit; Skytrain Phrom Phong) Casual, lesbian-owned restaurant-pub pours such powerful cocktails that the cliquish tables of friends can no longer resist the urge to kick up their heels.

Coffee Society (Map pp114-16; ☎ 0 2235 9784; 18 Th Silom; ⏰ 8am-4am Mon-Sat, 10am-4am Sun; Skytrain Sala Daeng) The pink triangle's default community centre hosts art displays, informal conferences and a little caffeine-laced cruising.

Babylon Bangkok (Map p117; ☎ 0 2213 2108; 50 Soi Atakanprasit, Th Sathon Tai; ⏰ 5am-11pm; subway Lumphini) Ranked as one of the top 10 gay men's saunas in the world, Babylon Bangkok includes a bar, roof garden, gym, massage room, steam and dry saunas, and spa baths. The spacious, well-hidden complex also has accommodation.

Fat Festival (early November) Sponsored by FAT 104.5FM radio, Bangkok's indie-est indie bands gather for an annual mosh.

Asiatopia (mid-November) Performance artists from across Southeast Asia converge on Bangkok's public spaces and theatres.

Bangkok Pride (mid November; www.utopia-asia.com) A weeklong festival of parades, parties and awards is organised by the city's gay businesses and organisations.

December

King's Birthday (December 5) Locals celebrate their monarch's birthday with lots of parades, home shrines, fireworks.

SLEEPING

Accommodation in Bangkok ranges from the ultra-luxurious to bargain-hunters' gems. Probably the best variety and quality of budget places to stay of any Asian capital is one of the reasons why it's such a popular destination for roving world travellers. Because of the wide distribution of places, you might first narrow your choices by neighbourhood.

For close to two decades, Banglamphu and its tourist ghetto of Th Khao San have reigned as the most likely crash-pad for a recent Bangkok arrival. Fast becoming a rival, Chinatown is less touristy and is stealing many of the independent-minded travellers from Banglamphu; it is also conveniently close to Hualamphong train station for inconvenient departure or arrival times. Both neighbourhoods offer a variety of affordable options and are less urbanised than other areas, meaning that the mangy dogs far outnumber the skyscrapers.

The Siam Square area is centrally located between old and new Bangkok and is on both Skytrain lines. High-rise numbers and low-rise guesthouses offer the greatest variety of budget and luxury levels within striking distance to shopping centre nirvana.

Th Sukhumvit and Th Silom are major business areas with corporate hotel chains and package-tour specials. The Sukhumvit area tends to attract sex tourists visiting the nearby go-go bars.

Thanks to the new subway, the old travellers' centre around Soi Ngam Duphli off Th Phra Ram IV may see renewed interest from visitors tied to the convention centre or overflow from Th Silom. In the meantime, the area holds fast to a Vietnam-era seediness.

Banglamphu
Map pp110–11

Banglamphu, the neighbourhood that includes the backpacker street of Th Khao San, is a well-padded landing zone for jet-lagged travellers. As a rule you can arrive anytime at night and find a place to crash. And services abound: you can't swing a túk-túk driver without hitting an inexpensive Internet shop, Beer Chang stall or pad Thai vendor.

If you're hanging out in the low-end of the budget range, just show up and start hunting as most cheapies don't take reservations. Many of the 150B specials are on or just off Th Khao San and are virtually indistinguishable from each other – small dirty rooms with toilet and shower down the hall. If you don't plan on stumbling home in the wee hours, look for a room on one of the quieter alleys off Th Khao San or Th Tanao.

More and more, the neighbourhood is gravitating towards the multistorey, upper-budget phenomenon with in-room décor (truly a revolution compared to the former flophouse aesthetic of dried projectile vomit) and comfort (air-con, sturdier beds, private bathrooms). New hotels are always

---

WHAT TO EXPECT IN BANGKOK

In this book, we list high-season rack rates. For midrange and top-end hotels, search online booking agencies (such as www.asiatravel.com) or individual hotel websites for promotional rates.

- Budget (100B to 600B) – Don't expect much in the low end of this price range. From 100B to 300B, you'll get rooms with thin partitions, fan and a shared bathroom (no hot water). Once you step up to the 400B range, you should start to expect air-con, private bathroom with hot-water shower and walls thick enough to block out noise.

- Midrange (600 to 3000B) – The biggest mixed bag of all, the midrange level starts out with the high-quality guesthouses (offering the best value), then moves into a grey area of mediocrity. Above 1000B, the hotels have all the appearance of a hotel back home – a bell-boy, uniformed desk clerks, and a well polished lobby – but without the predictability. Most rooms boast TV (with international channels), refrigerator, minibar, phone and a desk (Internet access is not always available). But there are always quirks. Some hotels have recently remodelled rooms that are bright and cheery, while others are worn and tired. Same goes for bathrooms. Swimming pools and complimentary breakfasts are noted in the review. In the low season (March to November), you may be able to get a low-occupancy discount. Some hotels also charge a 7% tax.

- Top end (over 3000B) – These hotels will maintain international standards and have at least one pool either tropically landscaped or with city views, fitness and business centres and sometimes a spa. Rooms typically have data ports, IDD international phones, international cable channels, minibar, safety-deposit boxes etc. Rates usually include breakfast. Special perks are listed in the individual reviews. The hotels in this category will add a 10% service charge plus 7% tax to hotel bills.

opening up, accompanied by attractive promotional rates.

Beware of the lobby make-over trend, in which a hotel splashes new paint and fancy uniforms on its staff but ignores a similar treatment to the threadbare rooms. Always ask to look at a room before committing.

Most of the year, it pays to visit several guesthouses before making a decision, but in the high season (December to February), take the first vacant bed you come across. The best time of day to find a vacancy is around check-out time, 10am or 11am.

BUDGET

Bella Bella House (☎ 0 2629 3090; 74 Soi Rambutri, Th Chakraphong; s 170B, d 300-500B; bus 506, 53, river ferry Tha Phra Athit; ✖) Just past Soi Chana Songkhram, Bella Bella has great views into the tiled roofs of the neighbouring temple. Rooms are spartan and clean with rickety beds, but the bathrooms are new and shiny. Singles have shared bathrooms. As with most guesthouses, the desk staff tends to be the usual cast of grumpy teenagers.

Donna Guesthouse (☎ 0 2281 9374; subsoi off Soi Damnoen Klang, Th Ratchadamnoen; d 200-300B; bus 506, 53, river ferry Tha Phra Athit; ✖) Dear Donna, we are so happy to have found you. The sign pointing down a little subsoi was followed on a whim, and tucked back in there was a clean and quiet nest with big twin beds, new comforters and big shared bathrooms.

Mango Lagoon Place (☎ 0 2281 4783; Soi Rambutri, Th Chakraphong; d 600-800B; bus 506, 53, river ferry Tha Phra Athit; ✖) Sunny, lemon-yellow complex has an outdoor sitting area and café. The rooms look surprisingly like real hotel rooms: thick beds, wall-to-wall carpet (a bad idea in the tropics), big TVs, and art on the wall. Better get here before this pristine specimen turns into an old hag with too much use. Bathrooms are shared.

New Siam GH (☎ 0 2282 4554; www.newsiam.net; 21 Soi Chana Songkhram, Th Phra Athit; s 190B, d 250-500B; river ferry Tha Phra Athit, bus 506, 53; ✖ ✦) Long-running New Siam is a smart spot to park your grungy backpack. It passed the schoolmarm's cleanliness inspection (shower curtains are mould free). Singles share bathrooms, while some doubles have private facilities. There are also small, self-accessible lockers for safe keeping of valuables.

Kawin Place (☎ 0 2281 7511; 86 Th Khao San; s 250B, d 350-550B; bus 506, 53, river ferry Tha Phra Athit; ✖)

LATE-NIGHT TOUCHDOWN

A lot of nail-biting anxiety is expended on the international flights arriving in Bangkok around midnight. Will there be taxis into town, will there be available rooms, will my family ever hear from me again? Soothe those nagging voices with the knowledge that most international flights arrive late and that Bangkok is an accommodating place. Yes, there are taxis and even an airport bus service (see p181). And if you haven't made hotel reservations, go straight to Th Khao San, which stays up late, is full of hotels and guesthouses, and sees a near continuous supply of 'fresh-off-the-birds' just like you. But do keep in mind that jet lag, noise and lack of cleanliness may all hinder a restful night if you opt for a budget cheapie. On the other hand, Th Khao San has plenty of watering holes to smooth the path to slumberland.

Every visit, this place has a different name, but the chain-smoking, front-desk clerk remains and so do the reliable budget boxes. A new building has been recently acquired, sporting well-polished wooden floors and gleaming bathrooms. The more expensive doubles have private bathrooms. The older wing has shared squat toilets.

Barn Thai Guest House (☎ 0 2281 9041; Trok Mayom; s/d 300/400B; bus 506, 53, river ferry Tha Phra Athit) Converted wooden house in a tiny alley off Trok Mayom, is a good option for quiet solo travellers. The kindly grandmother keeps the place neat and clean and locks the front gate at midnight (no exceptions). Singles share bathrooms.

Chai's House (☎ 0 2281 4901; 49/4-8 Soi Rongmai; s/d 150/250B; bus 506, 53, river ferry Tha Phra Athit) Take a right off the soi running beside Baan Sabai and you'll reach this family-run guesthouse with all shared bathrooms. It's a quiet and secure spot that enforces a 1am curfew.

Central Guest House (☎ 0 7265 5893; Trok Bowonrangsi, Th Tanao; s/d 120/160B; bus 506, 53, river ferry Tha Phra Athit) These rough-and-tumble ovens, with shared bathrooms, are reminiscent of Khao San's 'frontier' days of all-night carousing and meagre budgets. The experience here might be akin to crashing in your art-school buddies' spare room. To get here, make a right at the small tree shrine.

Villa Guest House (☎ 0 2281 7009; 230 Soi 1, Th Samsen; s/d 250/500B; bus 506, 53, 30, river ferry Tha Phra Athit & Tha Saphan Ram VIII) Just over the *khlong* is a great residential neighbourhood of bicycle-riding children and chatting housewives. This old teak house occupies a womb-like garden amidst the village noises of crowing roosters and the smells of mesquite cooking fires. With only 10 fan rooms (all with shared bathrooms), Villa is often full and recommends making reservations.

River Guest House (☎ 0 2280 0876; 18/1 Soi 3/Soi Wat Samphraya, Th Samsen; d 150-170B; bus 506, 53, 30, river ferry Tha Phra Athit & Tha Saphan Ram VIII) Deep into a serpentine soi, River Guest House has a friendly and relaxed mood with a popular common area for tale-swapping. The rooms share bathrooms and are nothing special.

Rajata Hotel (☎ 0 2281 8977; 46 Soi 6, Th Samsen; s/d 360/480B; bus 506, 53, 30, river ferry Tha Phra Athit & Tha Saphan Ram VIII; 🖳) The best of the soi 'no-tell' motels, Rajata is an odd mix of hourly visitors who need lots of privacy (note the interior car park) and backpackers who are amused by the postcard fodder.

Also recommended:

Baan Sabai (☎ 0 2629 1599; 12 Soi Rongmai, off Soi Rambutri; s 190B, d 300-600B; bus 506, 53, river ferry Tha Phra Athit; 🖳) Singles share bathrooms.

Bamboo Guest House (☎ 0 2282 3412; Soi 3, Th Samsen; s/d/f 150/120/330B; bus 506, 53, 30, river ferry Tha Phra Athit, Tha Saphan Ram VIII) Shared bathrooms.

Classic Inn (☎ 0 2281 7129; 259 Th Khao San; d 250-450B; bus 506, 53, river ferry Tha Phra Athit; 🖳) Both shared and private facilities.

Khao San Palace Hotel (Khao San Palace Inn; ☎ 0 2282 0578; 139 Th Khao San; d 300-450B; bus 506, 53, river ferry Tha Phra Athit; 🖳)

MIDRANGE

Buddy Lodge (☎ 0 2629 4477; www.buddylodge.com; 265 Th Khao San; d 2000-2500B; bus 506, 53, river ferry Tha Phra Athit; 🖳 🖳) Splashy boutique hotel has proved to the sceptics that Th Khao San-ers are maturing into bigger spenders. Creating the mood of a breezy tropical manor house, the rooms are outfitted with traditional Thai designs, terracotta tiled floors and simple wood-panelled walls. And then at your doorstep is the continuous freak show of Th Khao San.

Viengtai Hotel (☎ 280 5434; www.viengtai.co.th; 42 Th Rambutri; d 1600-2000B; bus 506, 53, ferry Tha Phra Athit; 🖳 🖳) Before Th Khao San was 'discovered', this was an ordinary Chinese-style hotel in a quiet neighbourhood. Over the years the Viengtai has continually renovated its rooms so that it now reigns as a solid and comfortable choice for visiting families, sunburned island hoppers, and recent arrivals. Make advance bookings for cheaper rates.

New World House Apartments & Guest House (☎ 0 2281 5596; http://new-world-lodge-hotel.th66.com; Soi 2, Th Samsen; d with/without breakfast from 1200/900B; bus 506, 53, 30, river ferry Tha Phra Athit & Tha Saphan Ram VIII; 🖳) It is surprising to find such a big hotel in a residential neighbourhood; in fact it is easy to walk right by it and never notice. You'll be glad you did, if you score a room on the 4th or 5th floor, which have recently been renovated and boast terraces overlooking Khlong Banglamphu.

Royal Hotel (☎ 0 2222 9111-26, fax 0 2224 2083; cnr Th Ratchadamnoen Klang & Th Atsadang; d incl breakfast 1600B; bus 511, river ferry Tha Phra Athit; 🖳 🖳) Hotel version of the coiffed Thai matrons, the Royal bears the distinction of being the third-oldest hotel in Bangkok. It must have something going for it, since it was full (with no rooms to view) on three separate visits. It is just a short – yet treacherous, traffic-filled – walk from the Ko Ratanakosin sites. The 24-hour coffee shop is a favourite local rendezvous. Most taxi drivers know this hotel as the 'Ratanakosin' (as the Thai sign on top of the building reads), not as the Royal.

Thewet

Map pp106–7

Thewet, the district north of Banglamphu near the National Library, is another travellers' enclave, especially for families and the over-30 crowd. It is a lovely leafy area, but during the rainy season it is prone to flooding.

Sri Ayuttaya Guest House (☎ 0 2282 5942; Soi Thewet, Th Si Ayuthaya; d 300-450B; bus 503, 30, river ferry Tha Thewet; 🖳) Decidedly the best of the brood, Sri Ayuttaya has romantic rooms with pretty hardwood floors, exposed brick and other stylish touches.

Shanti Lodge (☎ 0 2281 2497; 37 Soi Thewet, Th Si Ayuthaya; d 300-450B; bus 503, 30, river ferry Tha Thewet; 🖳) The omphalos of the street's family-owned (all the same family) guesthouses, Shanti waxes and wanes in popularity. Thin bamboo walls don't do a good job of blocking out the neighbours, but some travellers swoon over the Zen-like atmosphere.

SMOKING IN THE CAPITAL

Bangkok has ignited a better deterrent to smoking than city-wide bans. The answer – asphyxiating air pollution. Only smokers with Olympic prowess can power through the smoker's cough brought on by a day's sightseeing tour. If you accept the challenge, then be aware of the following smoking restrictions.

Most budget guesthouses discourage smoking in the rooms as a fire-prevention measure, midrange hotels could not care less where you light up, and top-enders provide nonsmoking and smoking rooms upon request.

Air-conditioned restaurants do not permit smoking, but air-conditioned bars do despite an unenforced city ban. Don't smoke in the Skytrain or subway stations. And don't throw your butts on the ground – the police love to pop foreigners for a hefty littering fine.

Taewez Guest House (☎ 0 2280 8856; 23/12 Soi Thewet, Th Si Ayuthaya; s/d 150/350B; bus 503, 30, river ferry Tha Thewet; ⚙) At the end of the block, Taewez's no-frills concrete rooms vary greatly in quality, but the spot ranks high with travellers because of the buddy-movie mood that flourishes in the common spaces. Singles share a bathroom.

Thai Hotel (Map pp110-11; ☎ 0 2629 2100; fax 0 2280 1299; 78 Th Prachatipatai; s/d 950/1250B; bus 12, 56; ⚙ 🍴) A popular business option, Thai Hotel has modern standards and a reserved atmosphere. A complimentary shuttle bus delivers guests to area attractions. Next door, a little open-air Chinese coffee shop makes the best *kaafae yen* (iced Thai coffee) in the city.

Chinatown   Map pp108–9

Crowded and chaotic, Chinatown is the traditional host of mainland Chinese tourists and Indian import-exporters. Lately, Western backpackers can slip into the neighbourhood with little fanfare – a distinctly anonymous experience from the usual walking-ATM treatment you'll get elsewhere. The hotels in the heart of Chinatown are high-rise numbers with basic midrange amenities and relatively easy-going rates; accommodation around the Hualam-

phong area can provide simple shelter before making a Bangkok escape.

This area is central but difficult to get in and out of (unless travelling by boat) because of a steady supply of traffic.

TT Guest House (☎ 0 2236 2946; fax 0 2236 3054; 516-518 Soi Sawang, Th Maha Nakhon; d 250-280B) In a locals-only neighbourhood, this family-run guesthouse is an easy walk to the train station. Step through the gate into a shaded courtyard perfect for sipping the coffee and a newspaper. The rooms, which share bathrooms, are clean with a few touches to stave off blandness. To get here, follow Th Maha Nakhon underneath the expressway, turn left onto Soi Sawang and follow it all the way to the end of the block of shophouses past the machine shops and deep-fry woks.

Sri Hualamphong Hotel (☎ 0 2214 2610; 445 Th Rong Muang; d 200B) Along the eastern side of Hualamphong train station, this old Chinese-style shop has a grand ornamented staircase, a proprietor with character and simple padlocked partitions. Bathrooms are shared.

Burapha Hotel (☎ 0 2221 3545-9, fax 0 2226 1723; cnr Th Mahachai & Th Charoen Krung; d 550-650B; bus 501, 507, 73, river ferry Tha Saphan Phut; ⚙) On the edge of Chinatown, Burapha has simple rooms claimed primarily by solo import-exporters hitting the wholesale shops on Sampeng Lane (Soi Wanit; p177). Interestingly, the hotel segregates by floor the Western, Chinese and Indian guests.

Krung Kasem Srikung Hotel (☎ 0 2225 0132; fax 0 2225 4705; 1860 Th Krung Kasem; d 550-600B; subway Hualamphong, bus 25, 35, 53; ⚙) West of the train station, this high-rise offers more security and comfort than other budget options nearby. The exterior rooms are super noisy, looking out on the constant stream of traffic.

New Empire Hotel (☎ 0 2234 6990-6, fax 0 2234 6997; 572 Th Yaowarat; d 600-800B; bus 73, river ferry Tha Ratchawong; ⚙) A short walk from Wat Traimit (p127), New Empire delivers with its 'deluxe' rooms. If you're wondering what a third-world boarding house looks like, check out the floor for standard rooms, which serve mainly as a dorm for Chinese-Thai labourers from the southern provinces. Rooms with exterior windows are a bit noisy, but it's in a great location.

River View Guest House (☎ 0 2234 5429; fax 0 2237 5428; 768 Soi Phanurangsi, Th Songwat; d 700-800B; river ferry Tha Si Phraya; ☒) It is a real shame when a quirky place like this raises its rates but not its cleanliness standards. The pluses include a great hidden location amid machine shops and stream-like soi, just north of River City Complex, and a river-view restaurant on the top floor. But the rooms aren't on speaking terms with mops or brooms. If you want to see for yourself, you'll need these directions: heading north from Th Si Phraya along Charoen Krung, take a left into Th Songwat (before the Chinatown Arch), then the second left onto Soi Phanurangsi. You'll start to see signs at this point and the road will become barely passable in a car.

Also recommended:

Grand Ville Hotel (☎ 0 2225 0050; 930 Th Mahachai; s/d from 1700/1900; bus 501, 507, 73, river ferry Tha Saphan Phut; ☒ ☒)

White Orchid Hotel (☎ 0 2226 0026; fax 0 2255 6403; 409-421 Th Yaowarat; d 1200-1700B; ☒)

Siam Square & Pratunam   Map pp118–19

The Siam Square and Pratunam area is centrally located on both Skytrain lines and smack dab in the middle of the city's shopping orgy. Walkways from the Skytrain stations to the shopping malls deliver fragile passengers directly into air-con comfort without having to sully themselves with a trip to ground level. The area is also perfect for those who have been away from civilisation for a while and are starved for bookshops, cinemas and Western fast food (psst, we won't tell anyone). The only drawback is that nightlife is nonexistent, but you're a short cab ride to nightspots in Silom or Sukhumvit.

In the shadow of MBK (p174), a low-key backpacker community bunks down on Soi Kasem San 1, intermixed with a local community of lunching shop girls and commuting office workers. The foreign crowd is an early-to-bed, early-to-rise troupe dedicated to do-it-yourself itineraries. Taxi drivers have a terrible time understanding us foreigners when we pronounce this street. To bridge the language barrier, try telling them that Soi Kasem San 1 is across from the National Stadium (*trong khâam sanǎam kii-laa hàeng châat*).

BUDGET

Wendy House (☎ 0 2216 2436; fax 0 2216 8053; Soi Kasem San 1, Th Phra Ram I; d from 500B; Skytrain National Stadium, khlong taxi Tha Ratchathewi; ☒) Wendy House is as professional as they come with a sweet-as-sugar desk staff and a genuine Thai-style concern for the guests. Although the rooms are on the small side, they are crisp and clean with cheery paint jobs. If you're a light sleeper, ask for a room away from the metal stairwell.

A-One Inn (☎ 0 2215 3029; www.aoneinn.com; 25/13-15 Soi Kasem San 1; d from 500B; Skytrain National Stadium, khlong taxi Tha Ratchathewi; ☒) Quietly watched over by a dog named Robin Hood and a soap-opera addicted staff, A-One sees a lot of return business and is usually so full that only the room off the lobby Internet room is available. The upstairs rooms are better value.

White Lodge (☎ 0 2216 8867; fax 0 2216 8228; 36/8 Soi Kasem San 1, Th Phra Ram I; d from 400B; Skytrain National Stadium, khlong taxi Tha Ratchathewi; ☒) Another Soi Kasem San denizen, White Lodge has a smoking patio for charting the day's events as well as clean if somewhat small rooms.

Bed & Breakfast Inn (☎ 0 2215 3004; Soi Kasem San 1, Th Phra Ram I; s/d 400/500B; Skytrain National Stadium, khlong taxi Tha Ratchathewi; ☒) This maze-like guesthouse includes breakfast in its rates and standard, unremarkable rooms.

MIDRANGE

Asia Hotel (☎ 0 2215 0808; www.asiahotel.co.th; 296 Th Phayathai; d from 2000B; Skytrain Ratchathewi, khlong taxi Tha Ratchathewi; ☒ ☒) A favourite with ageing backpackers with fatter wallets and creakier joints, this huge place has a good location and large rooms with generous-sized bathrooms. A walkway from the Skytrain is another plus, sparing visitors the barrage of 'whereyougos' from the taxis and *túk-túk* that park outside.

Holiday Mansion Hotel (☎ 0 2255 0099; fax 0 2253 0130; 53 Th Withayu; d incl breakfast from 2000B; Skytrain Ploenchit; ☒ ☒) A solid midrange option, the Mansion is a poster-child of provincial sophistication. There is a pleasant interior courtyard pool, marble lobby and a dusty grandfather clock (the standard uniform for hotels of this calibre). The generous-sized rooms are decorated in electric blue but are entering the sunset years of their career. There is no difference between the deluxe and grand deluxe rooms, so don't go for the up-sale. The whole package becomes utterly charming when good promotions give your credit card a holiday.

Pathumwan House (☎ 0 2612 3580; fax 0 2216 0180; 22 Soi Kasem San 1, Th Phra Ram I; d per day 1000-1400B, per month 24,000-40,000B; Skytrain National Stadium, khlong taxi Tha Ratchatewi; ✕) Not to be confused with Pathumwan Princess (p150), this long-term hotel does a brisk overflow business of one-nighters when the guesthouses down the road are full. With spacious rooms, wet bar and TV, this is a good option for independent-minded first-timers who will be fighting off jet lag. It is tucked back into the crook of the soi and decorated by a collection of singing caged birds.

Borarn House (☎ 0 2253 2252; www.borarnhouse .com; 487/48 Soi Wattanasin, Th Ratchaprarop; s/d incl breakfast 850/950B; bus 511, 512; ✕) The rooms here are nothing special, particularly the bathrooms. But the surrounding area is quite a treat – buried deep inside Pratunam. To get here, pick up the soi directly across from the Indra Regent Hotel and follow it past open-air views of daily life along the ever-narrowing street. The hotel courtyard is guarded by six huskies sweating under their thick fur coats.

Siam Orchid Inn (☎ 0 2255 3140; siam_orchidinn@ hotmail.com; Th Ratchadamri; d incl breakfast 1100-1200B; Skytrain Chitlom; ✕) Tucked back behind the hulking shopping centres is this petite inn filled with Thai reproduction antiques. By cutting a few corners staying here, you'll have more baht to burn shopping nearby.

VIP Guest House/Golden House (☎ 0 2252 9535; fax 0 2252 9538; 1025/5-9 Th Ploenchit; d incl breakfast 2000B; Skytrain Chitlom; ✕) Shiny lobby of this small inn leads to rooms with mammoth-sized beds and parquet floors. Bathrooms, however, don't have tubs, only showers. VIP is down a little alley near TOT, at the corner of King's Antiques.

Indra Regent Hotel (☎ 0 2208 0022-33; www.indra hotel.com; 120/126 Th Ratchaprarop, d from 2600B; Skytrain Chitlom, khlong taxi Tha Pratunam; ✕ ☱) This soot-stained box doesn't look like much from the outside, but the interior has been refreshingly remodelled delivering one of the better values in this price range. Junior suites are touted as the best buys.

TOP END

Conrad Hotel Bangkok (☎ 0 2690 9999; www.conrad hotels.com; 87 Th Withayu; d from US$170; Skytrain Ploen-chit; ✕ ☱) For the 30-something jet-setters, Bangkok's legendary luxury hotels are as musty as Grandma's attic. Only the Conrad delivers enough nouveau style and attitude for this media-weened and media-gleaned universe. The rooms are exquisitely decorated with Thai silks and rich earth tones, and the bathrooms transform washing into spa-ing with deep soak tubs and overhead 'rain' showerheads. According to embittered guests, the hotel flunks out on service. No matter, all the somebodies drown their cares in bottles of bubbly at the in-hotel Diplomat Bar and Club 87 (p168).

Grand Hyatt Erawan (☎ 0 2254 1234; www.bang kok.hyatt.com; cnr Th Ratchadamri & Th Ploenchit; d from US$280; Skytrain Chitlom; ✕ ☱) Just an elevated walkway from the *haute couture* Gaysorn Plaza, the Erawan is one of Bangkok's best regarded neoclassics. The soaring jungle atrium provides instant urban escape and the mezzanine level displays a small selection of the hotel's contemporary Thai art collection. Rooms are sleek and modern with fully functional European-style tubs and tall shower heads. Rooms at the rear of the hotel overlook the prestigious Royal Bangkok Sports Club racetrack.

Four Seasons Bangkok (☎ 0 2250 1000; www .fourseasons.com; 155 Th Ratchadamri; d from US$190; Sky-train Chitlom; ✕ ☱) Bangkok's well-regarded Regent Hotel has been adopted by the Four Seasons chain. This is classic Thai architecture with a spectacular traditional mural descending a grand staircase and neck-craning artwork on the ceiling. Still boasting a formidable reputation in the business realm, the Four Seasons has an efficient 24-hour business centre. It should be noted, though, that standard rooms are situated around a non-air-conditioned courtyard.

Swissotel Nai Lert Park (☎ 0 2253 0123; www.swiss otel.com; 2 Th Withayu; d from US$200; ✕ ☱) For-merly an outpost of the Hilton chain, this highly ranked hotel has changed hands (and names) to the Raffles International group. What does remain is the exquisite garden with a private jogging track and a tropically landscaped pool providing an instant elixir to jet lag.

Novotel Bangkok on Siam Square (☎ 0 2255 6888; www.accorhotels-asia.com; Soi 6, Siam Square; d from 3000B; Skytrain Siam; ✕ ☱) For business or leisure, Novotel Siam is conveniently located near public transport and shopping. Rooms are spitting images of corporate class back home, but the deluxe are better suited for business purposes.

Amari Watergate (☎ 0 2653 9000; www.amari .com; 847 Th Phetburi; s/d from US$180/200; Skytrain Chitlom, khlong taxi Tha Pratunam; ✄ ✦) This 34-storey hotel is right in the centre of Bangkok's Pratunam district and its crowded street market, near Th Ratchaprarop intersection. The large rooms receive a stylish blending of Thai and European details, and the large fitness centre keeps off those extra pounds graciously added by too many Thai sweets. The 8th-storey pool catches breezes and views unimaginable from street level.

Pathumwan Princess (Map pp106-7; ☎ 0 2216 3700; www.pprincess.com; s from 4600, d from 5200B, ste 9000B; Skytrain Siam; ✄ ✦) Families rave about this corporate hotel because it is connected to MBK shopping centre and the Skytrain. The lobby is a subdued echo chamber of clean lines and modern design. The deluxe rooms have a work desk and huge bathrooms with separate shower and tub, and the suites boast two TVs and fabulous views (your choice between pool or city views). The sky-high swimming pool is another plus.

Silom

Map pp114–16

This business district has the city's greatest concentration of luxury hotels – all boasting coveted riverfront property. Moving east, hotels range from economy class to affluent business and not a single budget option. Traffic can be thick in these parts.

MIDRANGE

Niagara Hotel (☎ 0 2233 5783; 26 Soi 9/Suksavitthaya, Th Silom; d 680B; Skytrain Chong Nonsi; ✄) From the outside Niagara looks like just another crummy no-tell motel, but inside is one of the best bargains in Silom. The rooms are immaculate. A fresh coat of paint brings cheer to the institutional setting and the rock-hard bed is graced with a plush comforter. A dubious perk is the three channels of 24-hour pornography on the TV.

Bangkok Christian Guest House (☎ 0 2233 6303; www.bcgh.org; 123 Sala Daeng Soi 2, Th Convent; d 1100-1500B; Skytrain Sala Daeng; ✄) Puritan austerity reigns at this recently refurbished boarding house originally serving Protestant missionaries after WWII. Today all are welcome – as long as you aren't accompanied by durian or alcohol. A 2nd-floor children's play area and lots of tourist information are also available.

TAXI TO NOWHERE

In most large cities, the taxi drivers are usually seasoned navigators familiar with every out-of-the-way neighbourhood. This is not the case in Bangkok where many a displaced farmer finds himself ploughing the city streets in a metered cab after a failed rice crop. Further complicating matters is the language barrier: most street names are multisyllabic requiring acrobatic tone variations that if mispronounced will induce confused head-scratching. Even borrowed words from English have their own peculiar Thai pronunciation. To ensure that you'll be able to return home, grab your hotel's business card, which will have directions in Thai.

Anna's Café & Bed (☎ 0 2632-1323; 44/16 Th Convent; d/f 850/950B; Skytrain Sala Daeng; ✄) If you need to budget in this pricey part of town, Anna's is often described as a boutique B&B but is really a guesthouse in all of its basic glory. The rooms are plain and simple, private rooms have en suite bathrooms and the only family room sleeps four. The attached café serves European and Thai cuisine.

Intown Residence (☎ 0 2639 0960; fax 0 2236 6886; 1086/6 Th Charoen Krung, btwn Th Si Phraya & Soi 30; d 600-700B; river ferry Tha Si Phraya; ✄) Once you dive into the neighbourhood's sois, the Intown's merits become stronger. This is a Muslim, mainly Indian, neighbourhood providing a subtle twist on Bangkok's diversity index. Intown's rooms are unremarkable but the desk staff are friendly and helpful.

Silom Village Inn (☎ 0 2635 6810; silom-village-inn@ thai.com; 286 Th Silom; d from 1800B; river ferry Tha Oriental; ✄) Forming a little miniresort, Silom Village is a convenient option for souvenir shopping at the attached Silom Village Trade Centre and catching a dinner-dance show at the open-air restaurant. Rooms are tidy but pick up too much street noise in the front.

Swiss Lodge (☎ 0 2233 5345; www.swisslodge.com; 3 Th Convent; d incl breakfast 2880-4000B; Skytrain Sala Daeng; ✄ ✦) The small inn with big-guy muscles, the Swiss Lodge prides itself on its personal touches – handwritten welcome notes to return guests, predawn breakfasts for early-morning departures. Jump in and out of the thick of things with its central location and soundproofed rooms, which are a tad tight. It's also green; rooftop panels help supply 90% of the hotel's hot-water needs.

La Résidence Hotel (☎ 0 2233 3301, fax 0 2237 9322; 173/8-9 Th Surawong; d 1000-1500B, ste 2700B; Skytrain Chong Nonsi; ✷) La Résidence is a hip boutique inn with playfully and individually decorated rooms. A standard room is very small and fittingly decorated like a child's bedroom. The next size up is more mature and voluptuous with blood-red walls and modern Thai motifs.

Montien Hotel (☎ 0 2233 7060; www.montien .com; 54 Th Surawong; d from 2500B; Skytrain Sala Daeng; ✷ ✷) The old guard of Thai high-end, Montien receives patronage from the diplomatic corps. From the rooms on the south wing, you can get a view of blazing Patpong. This is not the height of fashion or luxury, but the desk staff are kind and the costumed door attendants man their posts with precision.

Tarntawan Place (☎ 0 2238 2620; www.tarntawan .com; 119/5-10 Th Surawong; d 2150-3000B; Skytrain Sala Daeng; ✷) A decent midrange choice right in the heart of Patpong, this place has a good business centre with free email and local calls and 24-hour breakfast.

Also recommended:

Trinity Silom Hotel (☎ 0 2231 5333; fax 0 2231 5417; 150 Soi 5, Th Silom; d incl breakfast 1450-2500B; Skytrain Chong Nonsi; ✷ ✷) Rumour has it that the executive suites are a bargain.

Tower Inn (☎ 0 2237 8300-4; www.towerinnbangkok .com; 533 Th Silom; d 2000B; Skytrain Chong Nonsi; ✷ ✷) Request a recently renovated room.

TOP END

Peninsula Hotel (Map pp106-7; ☎ 0 2861 2888; www .peninsula.com; 333 Th Charoen Nakhon, Thonburi; d from US$260; private pier near Tha Oriental; ✷ ✷) Across the river in Thonburi, the Peninsula Hotel is one of the highest-ranking luxury hotels in the world. The lobby feels like an Asian interpretation of a mausoleum – polished marble with squat, squared hallways, a hushed sense of privilege and pedigree. Being on the Thonburi side of the river, rooms have breathtaking views of Bangkok's high-rises. A complimentary ferry service shuttles guests

---

AUTHOR'S CHOICE

Oriental Hotel (Map pp114-16; ☎ 0 2237 8282; www.mandarinoriental.com; 48 Soi Oriental/Soi 38, Th Charoen Krung; d US$300; river ferry Tha Oriental; ✷ ✷) What started out as a roughshod boarding house for European seafarers in the late 19th century, was transformed into an aristocratic magnet by Hans Niels Anderson, the founder of the formidable East Asiatic Company (which operated between Bangkok and Copenhagen). He hired an Italian designer to build the Author's Wing, which was the city's most elaborate secular building; all other grand architecture at the time was commissioned by the king.

With a dramatic setting beside Mae Nam Chao Phraya, the famous guests cemented the hotel's reputation. A Polish-born sailor named Joseph Conrad, stayed here in between nautical jobs in 1888. W Somerset Maugham stumbled into the hotel with an advanced case of malaria contracted during his overland journey from Burma. In his feverish state, he heard the German manager arguing with the doctor about how a death in the hotel would hurt business. Maugham's recovery and completion of *Gentleman in the Parlour: A Record of a Journey from Rangoon to Haiphong* contributed long-lasting literary appeal to the hotel. Other notable guests have included Noël Coward, Graham Greene, John le Carré, James Michener, Gore Vidal and Barbara Cartland. Some modern-day writers even claim that a stay in the Oriental will overcome writers block.

It is consistently rated as one of the best hotels in the world. Once you've stayed here the staff will remember your name, what you like to eat for breakfast, even what type of flowers you'd prefer in your room. For the full bygone immersion, stay in one of the original Garden Wing rooms rather than the newer tower.

Even if you haven't graduated to luxury class, you can still soak up the ambience. Stop by for a cocktail at the Bamboo bar or to toast the 'swift river' as Noël Coward did from the riverside terrace. For tea-totallers, an afternoon brew is served in the historic Author's Lounge, filled with black-and-white photographs of Rama V. To ensure the aristocratic leanings in a less formal age, the hotel enforces a dress code (no shorts, sleeveless shirts or sandals allowed).

to and from Bangkok. The Peninsula is also known for its affiliated golf course.

Shangri-La Hotel (☎ 0 2236 7777; www.shangri-la .com; 89 Soi Wat Suan Phlu, Th Charoen Krung; d US$200; Skytrain Saphan Taksin, river ferry Tha Sathon; ⊠ ⊠) Another riverside hotel, the Shangri-La strives for a New Asia aesthetic with tasteful, unimposing décor. This is dressed-down luxury, where service and comfort outpaces formality and where families won't feel like bulls in a china shop. The riverside rooms have balconies lined with magenta bougainvilleas.

Soi Ngam Duphli & Thanon Sathon
Map p117

If you were hitting the Asian hippie trail back in the 1970s, you would have laid your love beads at a guesthouse in this area off Th Phra Ram IV, near Lumphini Park. Some shoestringers still filter into this traffic-clogged area to get business done at the nearby embassies or to trade the post-beach scene on Khao San with a 'busted-flat-in-Bangkok' seediness. Corporate types may start to eye this area now that the Lumphini subway stop has made it more accessible to the convention centre.

In a hive-like colony along Th Sathon are several top-end hotels that counterbalance Soi Ngam Duphli's proletariat aesthetic. The hotels are stylish examples of luxury, but the location is severed from the Skytrain by a shadeless and traffic-clogged mega-road.

BUDGET & MIDRANGE
Sala Thai Daily Mansion (☎ 0 2287 1436; 15 Soi Si Bamphen, off Soi Ngam Duphli; d 200-350B; subway Lumphini, bus 507, 74, 109,116) At the end of a narrow cul-de-sac southeast of Lumphini Park, this small family-run guesthouse is more akin to the lodging options in the provinces than the anonymous hotels typically found in Bangkok. All rooms are standard issue – four walls, bed and a light with shared bathroom. To get here, take a left off Soi Ngam Duphli at the 7-Eleven, then take the second left and the first right.

Malaysia Hotel (☎ 0 2286 3582; fax 0 2287 1457; 54 Soi Ngam Duphli, Th Phra Ram IV; s 600-660B, d 700-760B; subway Lumphini, bus 507, 74, 109, 116; ⊠ ⊠) The Malaysia was once Bangkok's most famous budget lodge and even gave shelter to Maureen and Tony Wheeler on their maiden shoestring trip through Southeast Asia. Nowadays it is an HQ for gay sex tourists,

but the well-maintained rooms and trim prices makes it a good spot for those who can overlook or even be amused by the raging hormone scene.

Pinnacle Hotel (☎ 0 2287 01110; www.pinnacle hotels.com; 17 Soi Ngam Duphli, Th Phra Ram IV; d incl breakfast 2000-2500B; subway Lumphini, bus Nos 507, 74, 109 & 116; ⊠ ⊠) A surprisingly nice hotel for the area with a gracious lobby and rooms with clean bathrooms. There's also a fitness centre with sauna, steam room and outdoor rooftop Jacuzzi.

TOP END
Banyan Tree (☎ 0 2679 1200; www.banyantree.com; 21/100 Th Sathon Tai; d US$180; Skytrain Sala Daeng; ⊠ ⊠) Wrapping guests in a calm cocoon of woodland colours and lemongrass fragrance, the Banyan Tree melts away the troubles of battling the 'Kok. Suites are magnificent with separate work and sleep areas, two TVs, and deep soak tubs. Don't miss the award-winning spa or the rooftop bar.

Sukhothai Hotel (☎ 0 2344 8888; www.sukhothai .com; 13/3 Th Sathon Tai; d from US$280; ⊠ ⊠) Stylishly unique, the Sukhothai mines the temple monuments of its namesake, Thailand's ancient capital, for design inspiration. White colonnaded antechambers look out at exterior pool shrines with floating stupas or serene Buddha figures. The rooms are exquisitely decorated and have hardwood floors and war room–sized bathrooms.

Metropolitan (☎ 0 2625 3333; www.metropolitan .como.bz; 27 Th Sathon Tai, d from US$240; ⊠ ⊠) Bangkok goes ga-ga for the new kid in town and the name-droppers have been seeding this London-based boutique in fertile ground. Past the techno-pulsed lobby, though, you can glimpse a PR-campaign in full tilt. The City rooms do little to hide their cramped dormitory past (this is the old YMCA building) replete with minimalist-cum-torturous couches. At least the bathroom is big enough for rock-star primping. Guests are granted honorary entrance to the exclusive members-only bar.

Sukhumvit
Map pp112–13

Staying in this area puts you in the newest part of Bangkok. Thanon Sukhumvit can clearly be divided into two personalities. West of Soi Asoke (Soi 21) is the sex-tourist sector ruled by girlie bars, charged hormones and the quintessential Nana couple

Fabric stall outside Wat Arun (p103), Bangkok

Intricate roof tiles around the central courtyard of Wat Benchamabophit (p126), Bangkok

Monk, Grand Palace entrance, Wat Phra Kaew (p100), Bangkok

Silhouette of Wat Phra Kaew (p100), Bangkok

Traditional Thai dancer, Vimanmek Teak Mansion (p125), Bangkok

Inside Shanghai Tang designer boutique, Emporium Shopping Centre (p175), Th Sukhumvit, Bangkok

Amulet stall outside Wat Mahathat (p102), Bangkok

Chakri Mahaprasat (p102), Grand Palace, Bangkok

(see overweight, older *faràng* man with a young, beautiful Thai girl). The age-old phenomenon of sex and love for money is on full display here and is either heaven on earth or evil incarnate. If you're not wowed or amused by it, stay elsewhere. East of Soi Asoke, every imaginable nationality calls Bangkok home, forming a motley, yet well-paid, expat community.

Because visitors with larger budgets stay in Sukhumvit, tourist services are more expensive here than in Banglamphu. Although traffic is horrendous because of the one-way streets, the Skytrain has opened up vast frontiers from the start of Th Sukhumvit at Th Ploenchit to well beyond the Eastern bus terminal.

BUDGET

The Atlanta (☎ 0 2252 1650, 0 2252 6069; fax 0 2656 8123; 78 Soi 2, Th Sukhumvit; d 485-665B; Skytrain Ploenchit; ✿ ☎) You half expect Humphrey Bogart to trot down the stairs in this perfectly preserved, mid-20th-century lobby. For budget digs, the Atlanta delivers a lot of style: old-fashioned letter-writing desks (remember, before Internet) and a jungle-landscaped swimming pool. Another plus is that the Atlanta is also the only hotel in the area that openly forbids sex tourists. The run-down rooms could use renovation.

Suk 11 (☎ 0 2253 5927; www.suk11.com; dm 250B, s/d 450/500B; Skytrain Nana; ✿) A garden village has been re-created amid Sukhumvit's traffic at this budget-friendly spot. Mood music along with toast-and-jam breakfasts are enjoyed in the shady common space. Advance reservations required.

MIDRANGE

Federal Hotel (☎ 02 253 0175; federalhotel@hotmail .com; 27 Soi 11, Th Sukhumvit; d from 900B; Skytrain Nana; ✿ ☎) Since its freewheelin' days as an R&R stop for American GIs, the Federal has gone upmarket, sort of, and now enjoys the affectionate nickname of 'Club Fed' from its sexpat fans. The upstairs rooms are comfortably decorated with rattan furniture and generous beds. The ground-level rooms, however, should be avoided as these occasionally flood in the rainy season. The real draw is the frangipani-lined pool and time-warped American-style coffee shop.

Sam's Lodge (☎ 0 2253 2993; www.samslodge .com; 28-28/1 Soi 19, Th Sukhumvit; d 700-900B; Skytrain

Asoke; ✿) Above Ambassador & Smart Fashion tailor shop, this guesthouse is shiny and new with touches of Japanese minimalism and a cosy roof terrace. All rooms share bathrooms (a missing component judging by the price) and some don't have windows. According to the desk clerk, the place also discourages prostitutes and bad manners.

Golden Palace Hotel (☎ 0 2252 5115; fax 0 2254 1538; 15 Soi 1, Th Sukhumvit; s/d 750/850B; Skytrain Ploenchit; ✿ ☎) A contender in the featherweight division of midrange, Golden Palace is an institutional vision in aquamarine. The rooms are a decent size, but have torture-chamber stiff beds and weary bathrooms. Don't fear, you can always wash away extra grime in the sunny swimming pool.

Fortuna Hotel (☎ 0 2251 5121; fax 0 2253 6282; 19 Soi 5; s/d 1200/1500B; Skytrain Nana; ✿ ☎) Near Little Arabia, this is a friendly midsized hotel popular with Japanese businesspeople. Rooms have a surprising amount of personality and the omnipresent girlie-bar scene isn't as obvious within this high-rise cocoon.

Majestic Suites (☎ 0 2656 8220; www.majestic suites.com; 110-110/1 Th Sukhumvit, btwn Soi 4 & 6; s/d 1160/1500B; Skytrain Nana; ✿) Small and friendly, Majestic has hermetically sealed rooms that deliver privacy and quiet even with screaming Sukhumvit right outside. Front rooms even have a bird's-eye view of the street's traffic-snarled grandeur. The petite among us will find the rooms cosy, while others may argue for the term 'cramped'.

Miami Hotel (☎ 0 2253 0369; miamihtl@asiaaccess .net.th; 2 Soi 13, Th Sukhumvit; s/d 650/700B; Skytrain Nana; ✿ ☎) Bearing the mark of the GI days in more ways than its name, the Miami has a strange down-and-out charm. The *kàthoey* desk clerk, poolside lounge lizards and lumpy beds have all the makings of a greenhorn-does-Bangkok novel.

Bel-Aire Princess (☎ 0 2253 4300; bela@dusit.com; 16 Soi 5, Th Sukhumvit; d incl breakfast from 2000B; Skytrain Nana; ✿ ☎) Talk about schizophrenic, this hotel is all dolled-up with a stylish lobby but then drops the act with its war-weary elevator and hallway. Just as you've abandoned hope, the rooms redeem themselves with new bathroom facilities and only slightly unsightly beds. Unique to this price range, the room scent is the smell of clean rather than cover-up air freshener.

Manhattan (☎ 0 2255 0166; www.hotelmanhattan .com; 13 Soi 15, Th Sukhumvit; s/d incl breakfast 1400/1600B;

Skytrain Asoke; ✗ ➜) Discerning visitors will find that the Manhattan is a reliable middle-of-the-road option. The rooms are a good size and as sterile as those at American chain hotels.

Park Hotel (☎ 0 2255 4300; www.parkhotelbkk .com; Soi 7, Th Sukhumvit; s/d 2000/2400B; Skytrain Nana; ✗ ➜) Go strolling for a deep discount to make the Park Hotel more of a walk in the park. The rooms are decently sized, but the beds are as lumpy as Thanksgiving's mashed potatoes. The hotel is beer-belly deep in the girlie bar scene.

Windsor Hotel (☎ 0 2258 0160; fax 0 2258 1491; 8-10 Soi 20, Th Sukhumvit; s/d incl breakfast 2000/2400B; ✗) Tour groups and corporate travellers claim the bulk of rooms at this no-nonsense hotel and recommend the Minister-level rooms.

TOP END

The Davis (☎ 0 2260 8000; www.davisbangkok.net; Soi 24, Th Sukhumvit; d from US$100; ✗ ➜) Closer to Th Rama IV entrance to the soi, the Davis is a peach of a place with cool sophistication and rooms decorated like a Raj's palace, a Kyoto hermitage or a Burmese plantation. Freshen up in the big marble bathrooms after a dreamy slumber in the fluffy beds. Straight from the pages of *Architectural Digest*, the detached Thai villas are polished to a burnished golden wood with deep sleigh beds and big sunny windows arranged around a private lap pool and garden.

Landmark Bangkok (☎ 0 2254 0404; www.landmark bangkok.com; 138 Th Sukhumvit, btwn Soi 4 & 6; d from US$170; Skytrain Nana; ✗ ➜) This business behemoth is diversifying to tourist families these days. But the rooms still boast all the amenities, like green marble bathrooms and separate shower and tub. The smallest in the catalogue, though, isn't big enough for enthusiastic gesticulating. If you're below floor 20 request a room at the rear for a better view.

Novotel Lotus Bangkok (☎ 02 261 0111; www .novotellotus.com; 1 Soi 33, Th Sukhumvit; d from 4800B; Skytrain Phrom Phong; ✗ ➜) Accor's second Bangkok branch is a well-designed modern creation with a soothing lotus pond in the centre of the lobby. Rooms are plush and private. There are also exquisite suites on a semiprivate floor with a terrace.

Rembrandt Hotel (☎ 0 2261 7100; www.rembrandt bkk.com; 19 Soi 18, Th Sukhumvit; d from US$125; ste from US$250; Skytrain Asoke; ✗ ➜) Rembrandt is

an executive strength hotel with tastefully decorated rooms and is within easy striking distance to the convention centre.

Westin Grande Sukhumvit (☎ 02 651 1000; www .westin.com/bangkok; 259 Th Sukhumvit at Soi 19; US$95-110; Skytrain Asoke; ✗ ➜) Modern monstrosity has been fully renovated to shed its old image as the Grand Pacific. The superficial make-over in the lobby has even penetrated the rooms, which now boast the trademarked 'Heavenly' beds, as soft and cosy as an eternal reward should be. Bathrooms have separate tub and shower with a shower head that is *faràng*-sized.

Windsor Suites Hotel (☎ 0 2262 1234; www.wind sorsuiteshotel.com; s/d incl breakfast from 6000B/6500B; ✗ ➜) Affiliated with the midrange Windsor Hotel, this place features spacious suites each with two TVs should you find Bangkok horribly boring.

Greater Bangkok

Thai House (Map pp104-5; ☎ 0 2903 9611; www.thai house.co.th; 32/4 Mu, Bang Yai, Nonthaburi; d from 1200B) North of central Bangkok in Nonthaburi (about 40 minutes away by Chao Phraya River Express) is this traditional Thai home surrounded by fruit trees that has been converted into a guesthouse. Contact the proprietors for transportation details. The guesthouse also conducts cooking courses open to guests and nonguests (see p137).

Classic Place Hotel (Map pp106-7; ☎ 0 2255 4444-9; www.classicplace.co.th; 1596 Th Phetburi Tat Mai; d 1700B; ✗ ➜) With the opening of the subway, this hotel has been brought closer into central Bangkok's grasp, plus airport getaways are quick and easy. Rooms are straightforward and underwent a modest make-over less than a year ago. Deluxe level is worth the step up.

Siam Beverly Hotel (Map pp104-5; ☎ 0 2275 4397; fax 0 2290 0170; 188 Th Ratchadaphisek; d incl breakfast from 1800B; subway Huai Khwang; ✗ ➜) Siam Beverly is relatively affordable with adequately sized rooms and tolerable bathrooms. It's not spectacular but the service is friendly and the rooms have all the amenities.

Bangkok Marriott Resort & Spa (Map pp104-5; ☎ 0 2476 0022; www.marriott.com; 257/1-3 Th Charoen Nakhon, Thonburi; d from US$200; private river ferry; ✗ ➜) Outside the central area, but along the river, the Marriott is a place where you can get away from it all – home, hassles and even Bangkok. A serene atmosphere is created by the expansive and airy lobby, and the amenities (swimming pool, gardens and tennis courts) deter visitors from staging exploratory missions into Bangkok. Reviews are mixed about the quality of the service.

Airport Area   Map pp104–5
Need a place to catch a few zzzs before catching a flight? All of these options are close to Bangkok International Airport (Don Muang) and charge significantly more than what a hotel room in town would cost. Unless you've missed a flight or have a short layover, overnighting in central Bangkok with an early morning departure is still a feasible option. The new Suvarnabhumi airport in eastern Bangkok is expected to open in the summer of 2006, but no details for airport accommodation were available at the time of writing.

Amari Airport Hotel (☎ 0 2566 1020; www.amari .com/airport; d from US$190; ✖ ⌨) Connected to the airport by an air-conditioned walkway, this is obviously the closest hotel to Bangkok International Airport (Don Muang), giving it little incentive to stay competitive. Readers complain that service and quality have deteriorated over the years. Amari also offers 'ministay' rates for layovers of up to three hours.

Asia Airport Hotel (☎ 0 2992 6999; www.asiahotel .co.th; d from 2000B; ✖) Ten minutes north of the airport at the Km 28 marker. Rooms are comfortable and clean, if a little outdated, and a shuttle service to the airport is provided.

Comfort Suites Airport (☎ 0 2552 8921-9; www .pinnaclehotels.com/comfort; 88/117 Viphavadi Rangsit Hwy; r 2500-2600B; ✖) One of the airport area's better values. It is about five minutes away and there is a free airport shuttle.

We-Train International House (☎ 0 2967 8550-4; www.we-train.co.th; 501/1 Mu 3, Th Dechatungkha, Sikan, Don Muang; dm 200B, r 740B; ✖ ⌨) Operated by a nonprofit women's group with proceeds going to fund emergency shelters for abused women and children. The hotel has an airport pick-up service and there's a helpful map and directions on the hotel's website.

EATING
No matter where you go in Bangkok, food is always there. There is so much variety just at street level that days can go by without stepping inside a restaurant. Enacting the modern equivalent of hunter-gatherers, many visitors skip from stall to stall sampling *kŭaytĭaw* (noodles), plates of *râat khâo* (rice with curry poured over it) or *mùat phàt* (stirfries) for 25B to 40B.

When the need comes for a restaurant, Bangkok's best are the décor-less mom-and-pop shops that concentrate only on the food; most of these restaurants hover around 50B to 100B for a main dish. As the prices increase, so does the ambience – more servers, traditional Thai antiques, white tablecloths or ultramodern outfits. Be careful treading in these waters as dining in Bangkok's fashionable or touristy restaurants is sometimes more for show than for the cuisine.

While Thai food may be sufficiently exotic, Bangkok offers an international menu prepared by its many immigrant communities. Chinatown is naturally a good area for Chinese food. In a corner of Chinatown, known as Phahurat, and around Th Silom, Indian residents keep themselves and the culinary traveller well fed in small closet-sized restaurants. In the crowded bazaar-like area of Little Arabia, just off Th Sukhumvit, there is Middle Eastern cuisine. All of Europe and America have their culinary embassies that prepare the tastes of home in the *haute* fashion for power players or as pub grub to cure homesickness.

Banglamphu   Map pp110–11
This area near the river is one of the best for cheap Thai eats. Open-air restaurants

---

USING THE RIGHT TOOL FOR THE JOB

If you're not offered chopsticks, don't ask for them. Thais only use chopsticks to eat noodle soups or other inherited dishes from China. For dishes served over rice, like curries and stirfries, the locals use a fork and spoon. These Western utensils were adopted during the reign of Rama V (King Chulalongkorn), but the conventions for using a fork and spoon were abandoned by the ever resourceful Thais. To better capture the wily grains of rice or heavily sauced dishes, Thais use a fork (much like we use a knife) to push food on to the spoon, which then enters the mouth. From the Thai standpoint, sticking a fork in the mouth is not only rude but strange.

and street vendors claim the majority of grazing options. Because of the backpacker presence, Western and vegetarian food are well represented. Duck into the maze of sois for more authentic streetside eating than what you'll find along Th Khao San.

THAI

Roti-Mataba (cnr Th Phra Athit & Th Phra Sumen; dishes 50–80B; ☻ breakfast, lunch & dinner Tue-Sun; river ferry Tha Phra Athit) A Bangkok legend, Roti-Mataba does a whirlwind business of delicious *kaeng mátsàmàn* (Thai Muslim curry) served with

---

STREET EATS

Surely you've heard the rumours about what food in Bangkok is safe to eat, right? Let's see, how does it go: avoid ground meat, crushed ice, something borrowed, something blue – no that's not quite it. Just to be on the safe side, take that mental list and toss it in the first stinky *khlong*. By and large, most street food is not only hygienic but delicious. Granted you'll get Bangkok belly, which is often a personal intolerance to chillies or Beer Chang, rather than a tainted plate of *khâo phàt* (fried rice). At least with the street vendors you can see all the action, whereas you don't know the state of affairs in the supposedly 'safe' guesthouse kitchen.

If you're thoroughly convinced that streetside eating is a healthy pursuit, here is a profile of each neighbourhood's general grazing options.

Banglamphu   Map pp110–11

As you'll quickly discover, Th Khao San is great for late-night snacking: fresh fruit, spring rolls, shwarma sandwiches, and stand-and-gulp *phàt thai*. Near the 7-11 on Th Rambutri, post-imbibing Thais fend off a hangover with a bowl of *jóhk* (rice porridge), which is also a good antidote to Bangkok belly. Soi Rambutri does a brisk business of grilled fish, chicken and cold beer. Nighttime stalls on Th Samsen, between Soi 2 and 8, serve *sôm-tam* (spicy green papaya salad), *kŭaytĭaw*, and *râat nâa* (noodles with gravy).

A few Muslim vendors occupy Trok Surat, between the shoe stores on the western side of Th Chakraphong between Th Tani and Th Rambutri. The noodle vendor down this soi does semi-vegetarian noodles with fluffy cubes of tofu and seafood.

Siam Square   Map pp118–19

If you're staying on or nearby Soi Kasem San 1, you don't have to suck motorcycle fumes crossing Th Phra Ram I and Th Phayathai to find something to eat. A row of vendors on the soi cater mainly to lunching Thais but have mastered international sign-language.

Just to the right of Siam Square's Scala cinema, plunge into the alley that curves behind the Th Phayathai shops to find a row of cheap food stalls (closed weekends). If approaching this alley from Th Phayathai, look for the sign that reads 'food centre'. Behind the Sindhorn Building on Th Withayu, a village of umbrella-shaded vendors cater to lunch-time crowds.

At night a noodle vendor serving handmade noodles and wontons sets up at the base of the National Stadium Skytrain station, near the entrance to Soi Kasem San 1.

Silom   Map pp114–16

Just off Th Silom at Soi Pradit (Soi 20), a market assembles in front of the Masjid Mirasuddeen mosque every day. Daytime vendors sell fresh fruit, takeaway meals and spicy *khànǒm jiin* (stark, white-rice noodles served with curry sauce). There are also a few duck noodle vendors (just look for signs with a duck). **Talat ITF** (Soi 10) has a string of food stalls purveying pots of curry and miles of noodles. **Lunch stalls** can also be found on Soi Sala Daeng 2 and on Soi 7. A mid-day vendor ekes out a small business selling *khâo mòk kài* (chicken biryani) in front of the Irish X-Change.

Sukhumvit   Map pp112–13

Soi 38 Night Market (Soi 38, Th Sukhumvit; dishes 30–50B; ☻ 8am-3am) offers gourmet night-noshing and stays open late for the bleary-eyed clubbers. Try a busy bowl of *kŭaytĭaw* Hong Kong or Chinese-style spring rolls.

rotii (fried flatbread), and chicken or vegetable *mátàbà* (a stuffed *rotii*). Directly opposite Phra Sumen Fort, the cramped shop has
an upstairs air-con dining area and outdoor
tables barely big enough for its loyal fans.

   Ton Pho (☎ 0 2280 0452; Th Phra Athit; dishes 60-
100B; ☺ lunch & dinner; river ferry Tha Phra Athit) Right
beside Tha Phra Athit (Tha Banglamphu) is
a converted floating dock that does all the
staples with the expertise of a Thai grandmother. Do the litmus test here: the lack of
décor inversely matches the strength of the
food.

   Khrua Nopparat (Th Phra Athit; dishes 60-100B;
☺ lunch & dinner; river ferry Tha Phra Athit) With as
much charm as a school cafeteria, the Nopparat's Kitchen devotes all of its resources
to the menu. The dishes are a little small,
so don't shy away from the Thai tradition
of over-ordering. Winners include the deep-
fried shrimp or *phàt phak kha-náa* (stirfried
Chinese greens).

   Hemlock (☎ 0 2282 7507; 56 Th Phra Athit; dishes
80-200B; ☺ dinner; river ferry Tha Phra Athit) Living-
room-sized restaurants line Th Phra Athit
and form a social gathering point for
Banglamphu's Thai bohemians (writers,
artists and intellectuals). This cosy gem has
an eclectic menu inspired by ancient literary works; try the flavourful *mîang kham*
(tea leaves wrapped with ginger, shallots,
peanuts, lime and coconut flakes) or *náam
phrík khàa* (spicy dipping sauce served with
vegetables and herbs), both items that don't
usually pop up on menus. Upstairs is an art
exhibit and performance space for considering the ongoing dialogue between traditional Thailand and modernisation.

   Arawy (Alloy; 152 Th Din So; dishes 35B; ☺ breakfast
& lunch; bus 10, 19, 42, khlong taxi to Tha Phan Fah) Opposite the Municipal Hall and a few doors
down from a 7-Eleven store, this matron
of meatless is one of the best Thai vegetarian restaurants in the city. A selection
of prepared dishes makes it user-friendly,
and the cook brings out the flavour of the
veggies without the tasteless oil spill. The
green curry is a real zinger. The restaurant
was inspired by the strict vegetarianism of
Chamlong Srimuang, the ex-governor of
Bangkok.

   Ranee Guesthouse (77 Trok Mayom; dishes 70-120B;
☺ breakfast, lunch & dinner; bus 506, 56, river ferry Tha
Phra Athit) Quantity-loving vegetarians will
appreciate this guesthouse kitchen, which

AUTHOR'S CHOICE

Mahboonkrong (MBK) Food Centre (Map
pp118-19; 4th fl MBK, cnr Th Phayathai & Th Phra
Ram I; dishes 30B; Skytrain National Stadium)
Sounds ridiculous to recommend eating at
a shopping mall in such a culinary capital,
but Bangkok's mall food courts are the indoor versions (smog and humidity free) of
the outdoor markets. See the modern world
isn't so bad. Plus all the streetside meals
are accompanied here with English translations. Consider this a food boot-camp –
after a few sessions here, you'll be equipped
for outdoor reconnaissance. In order to play
the food-court game, you have to buy coupons from the ticket desk and then cash in
whatever you don't spend.

serves large portions of vegetable-adoring
dishes. Stirfries are cooked to perfection
and can be enjoyed in a quiet garden
courtyard where the owner's children play
pretend dinner party. Specify if you want
brown rice.

   May Kaidee's (sub-soi off Soi Damnoen Klang; dishes
20-50B; ☺ lunch & dinner; bus 506, 56, river ferry Tha
Phra Athit) For an all-veggie menu at meatless
prices, follow Th Khao San to Th Tanao and
jog right to the small soi beside the Burger
King (yup, Khao San has gone corporate)
and then another left to a string of vegetarian shops near Srinthip Guest House.

   Kuay Tiaw Mae (Th Phra Athit; dishes 30-50B; ☺ lunch
& dinner; river ferry Tha Phra Athit) Two doors down
from Roti-Mataba (opposite), this might be
the most stylish *kŭaytĭaw* (rice noodles)
shop in the universe, with wooden benches
and deliberate art hanging on the walls. The
kŭaytĭaw tôm yam (rice noodles in a spicy
lemongrass broth) with pork or tofu keeps
noodle fans reverently bowed.

   Somsong Photchana (☎ 0 2282-0972; soi beside
Phra Sumen Fort, near Wat Sangwet; dishes 20B; ☺ lunch;
river ferry Tha Phra Athit) You usually have to beat
a trail up to Sukhothai to get a bowl of the
town's unique interpretation of *kŭaytĭaw
Sukhothai* (noodle soup with green beans).
Luckily this regional twist has come to
Bangkok in the form of an unpretentious
neighbourhood noodle shop. If you're new
to the noodle game, this one is a winner
because the broth is so tasty that you don't
need to add seasoning.

Phon Sawan (80 Th Samsen; dishes 35B; ✆ lunch & dinner; bus 506, 53, river ferry Tha Phra Athit) Directly across from the Bangkok Bank, this simple shop feeds Banglamphu expats tofu-based Thai-Chinese dishes, served on a bed of hearty *khâo klâwng* (brown rice). Once you pass Soi 4 on Th Samsen, keep an eye out for a handwritten 'Vegetarian Food' sign inside the simple shopfront.

Phai Thong (off Map pp110-11; Th Fueang Nakhon; dishes 70-120B; ✆ 11am-2pm & 5-10pm Sun-Fri, 5-10pm Sat; river ferry Tha Tien & Tha Chang) Across from the Ministry of Interior, this Thai-Chinese restaurant does a creative twist on *kǔaytǐaw lort puu* (rolled sheets of rice noodle stuffed with crabmeat), spicy *nǎem thâwt* (fried pork sausage), boneless *hàw mòk plaa* (fish and herbs in a coconut cream curry sauce) and the silent hero *phàt phàk Yeepun* (a tender squash-like vine stirfried in oyster sauce). Go with a big group so that you can justify filling the table with colourful dishes.

Jeh Hoy (cnr Th Samsen & Soi 2; dishes 50-100B; ✆ dinner; bus 506, 53, river ferry Tha Phra Athit) If it is feeding time, this open-air restaurant has the best ad campaign around – an ice tray loaded down with seafood and the hypnotic manoeuvrings of the wok cook. Try the Hokkien special *puu phàt phǒng kàrii*

(crab stirfried with curry powder and egg). If it is too busy, skip down the soi to other similar outfits.

Baan Phanfah Restaurant (✆ 0 2281 6237; 591 Th Phra Sumen; dishes 80-120B; ✆ lunch & dinner; bus 511, 512, khlong taxi to Tha Phan Fah) All dressed up and nowhere but the tourist ghetto to go? Break away from the banana-pancake nation to this nearby restaurant-gallery. Spot-on Thai cuisine is perfectly mastered within a gracious Sino-Portuguese mansion on Khlong Banglamphu. Choose your perch from the outdoor courtyard serenaded by lounge music or within the crisp white walls adorned with modern art.

INTERNATIONAL

Ricky's Coffeeshop (22 Th Phra Athit; dishes 80-150B; ✆ 9am-9pm; river ferry Tha Phra Athit) Why Thais prefer the Wonder variety of bread is a great mystery. But you can gnaw your way to carbo bliss with Ricky's crusty baguettes. Now, they aren't as good as Indochina's, but with the addition of blue-veined Danish cheese, oil and vinegar, they certainly satisfy the palate.

Chochana (Shoshana; unnamed soi off Th Chakraphong; dishes 100-150B; ✆ 11am-11pm; bus 506, 56, river ferry Tha Phra Athit) One of Khao San's longest-running Israeli restaurants, tucked away

---

VEGETARIAN

Although most Thais regard vegetarianism as antithetical to good sense, there are several strong currents of meatless philosophies represented in Bangkok's restaurant scene.

Banglamphu has the greatest concentration of vegetarian-friendly restaurants thanks to the nonmeat-eating *faràng*; these are typically low-scale stirfry shops that do something akin to what your hippie roommates have brewing in their kitchens. A few standouts include **May Kaidee's** (p157), **Ranee Guesthouse** (p157), and **Phon Sawan** (above).

An indigenous vegetarian movement can be found in the food centres operated by the Santi Asoke community. Likened to the Amish of the USA, Santi Asoke is an ascetic Buddhist sect that practises self-sufficiency through agriculture and strict vegetarian diets based on religious teachings. The food centres are operated in conjunction with Bangkok's former governor Chamlong Srimuang, who popularised both the sect and vegetarianism during his corruption-reducing tenure in the 1980s and 90s. **Baan Suan Pai** (p165), **Chamlong's Asoke Café** (p166) and **Arawy** (p157) are all affiliated centres.

Indian, Chinese and Muslim restaurants are also veggie-friendly. **Dosa King** (p164) and **Yogi** (p162) are both solely vegetarian. During the vegetarian festival in October, the whole city goes mad for tofu, and stalls and restaurants indicate their nonmeat menu with yellow banners; Chinatown has the highest concentration of stalls.

A more modern trend in vegetarianism is the health-conscious gourmet treatment that is well-established overseas. Stylish spots, such as **Govinda** (p165) and **Tamarind Café** (p165), deliver date settings for vegetarian epicures, tired of suffering with the meatless after-thoughts on most menus.

in an almost secret alley beside the petrol station, Chochana serves gut-filling falafel-and-hummus plates, but don't overlook the tasty *baba ghanoush* and *hazilim*.

Chabad House (Th Rambutri; dishes 100-200B; lunch & dinner Sun-Fri; bus 506, 56, river ferry Tha Phra Athit) One plus to sharing the beaten path with Israeli travellers is the opportunity to sample the Mediterranean's comfort food. This well-scrubbed café serves Israeli-style kosher food in a relatively sedate atmosphere (no one is arguing about the bill, that is, not usually).

Prakorb's House (0 2281 1345; 52 Th Khao San; dishes 50-100B; breakfast, lunch & dinner; bus 506, 56, river ferry Tha Phra Athit) Good old Prakorb's does exceptionally good guesthouse fare. A huge menu covers all Southeast Asia's interpretations of Western breakfasts, but the real winner is the chewy cup of hot coffee.

Chinatown & Phahurat   Map pp108–9

When you mention Chinatown, Bangkokians begin dreaming of noodles, usually prepared by street vendors lining Th Yaowarat after dark. During the annual Vegetarian Festival (which is in September/October and centred around Wat Mangkon Kamalawat on Th Charoen Krung), the neighbourhood explodes with street stalls and vendors.

On the western rind of the neighbourhood is the Indian fabric district of Phahurat, filled with small restaurants and stalls tucked into the soi off Th Chakraphet. The soi next to the old ATM building, near the sari centre, shelters a popular samosa push-cart vendor.

Hong Kong Noodles (136 Trok Itsaranuphap, Th Charoen Krung; dishes 30B; lunch & dinner; bus 507, 53, 73, river ferry Tha Ratchawong) Deep in the heart of a fresh-meat market, this busy shop does a bustling trade in steaming bowls of roast duck noodles. Next door is its sister restaurant **Hong Kong Tim Sum**, for takeaway dim sum and steamed pork buns.

Bà-mìi Hong Kong (cnr Th Yaowarat & Soi Yaowiphanit; dishes 50B; dinner; river ferry Tha Ratchawong, bus 507, 53, 73) Look for a big red sign with Chinese characters near the gold shop and you will have found a noodle adventure. This street stall serves egg noodles (*bà-mìi*) and shrimp-stuffed wontons (*kíaw*) with capitalistic variety. Customers tick off their choices on an order sheet (all in Thai); but don't fret about being illiterate, here is a guide.

CHINATOWN STREET EATS

Even if you've mastered the street stalls in other parts of town, little of that savvy can be translated into the variations that appear in the night markets in Chinatown. Here is a quick introduction to the street vendors and the dishes worth noting. Once you've met and befriended these dishes, you'll spot them in other neighbourhoods too.

- **kŭay jáp** – This steamy soup consists of tubular noodles, pork offal and *mŭu krăwp* in a broth spiced with star anise. Try it at the vendor who sets up in the lobby of the 3rd-rate movie theatre at 404 Th Yaowarat.

- **hăwy jaw** and **hae kĕun** – Usually sold together, these blistered sausages are wrapped in tofu and stuffed with either crab (*hăwy jaw*; whitish in colour and formed into segments) or shrimp (*hae kĕun*; orange-coloured tubes).

- **hăwy thâwt** – Fried mussels in batter are prepared in wide flat-bottomed skillets; a well-known vendor sets up near the Th Phadungdao and Th Yaowarat intersection.

- **herbal drinks** – Huge ice coolers spill over with small plastic bottles of oddly coloured liquid all along Th Yaowarat. In keeping with the Chinese observances of food as medicine, these drinks are made from various herbal teas for their health benefits. The yellow ones are chrysanthemum; brown, lotus root (*náam râak bua*); and the green, a kind of water plant (*náam bai bua bòk*).

The left-hand column reads from top to bottom: *bà-mìi hâeng* (egg noodles without broth), *bà-mìi náam* (egg noodles in broth), *kíaw hâeng* (wontons without broth), *kíaw náam* (wontons in broth), *bà-mìi kíaw hâeng* (egg noodles and wontons together without broth), *bà-mìi kíaw náam* (egg noodles and wontons in broth).

Now the top row from left to right, reads: *mŭu daeng* (red pork), *puu* (crab), and *puu mŭu daeng* (red pork and crab together). So now that you've cracked the script, you write the number of bowls under each corresponding square. After trying all the combos, we prefer *bà-mìi hâeng puu mǔu daeng* (one down and three across).

Th Phadungdao Seafood Stalls (cnr Th Phadungdao & Th Yaowarat; dishes 150-250B; 6-10pm; river ferry Tha Ratchawong, bus 507, 53, 73) After sunset, this street sprouts outdoor barbecues, iced seafood trays and sidewalk seating. Servers dash every which way, cars plough through narrow openings, and before you know it you're tearing into a plate of grilled prawns like a starved alley cat.

Shangarila Restaurant (0 2235 7493; 206 Th Yaowarat; dishes 200-500B; lunch & dinner; bus 507, 53, 73, river ferry Tha Ratchawong) Near the corner of Th Ratchawong, this venerable old gal stays in the restaurant race with a family-buffet favourite of Peking duck and a wide selection of dim sum.

Royal India (0 2221 6565; 392/1 Th Chakraphet; dishes under 80B; lunch & dinner; bus 508, 507, 25, river ferry Tha Saphan Phut) Over in Phahurat, the Indian fabric district, Royal India is a long-running favourite because of its North Indian cuisine, heavily influenced by Moghul or Persian flavours and spices. Follow the signs off Th Chakraphet into a concrete alley.

Old Siam Plaza (Ground fl, Old Siam Plaza, cnr Th Phahurat & Th Triphet; dishes 50-100B; lunch; bus 508, 507 & 25, river ferry Tha Saphan Phut) The Thai version of Willy Wonka's factory occupies the ground floor of this shopping centre. Seemingly savoury ingredients, such as beans, corn and rice, are turned into syrupy sweet desserts right before your eyes. Such transformations include *lûuk chúp* (miniature fruits made of beans), *tàkôh* (coconut pudding in banana leaves) and *khànǒm bêuang* (taco-shaped pancakes filled with shredded coconut and golden threads of sweetened egg yolks).

Pet Tun Jao Tha (Harbour Department Stewed Duck; 0 233 2541; 945 Soi Wanit 2; dishes 40B; lunch & dinner; river ferry Tha Si Phraya) A few doors down from the Harbour Department building, this famous noodle shop is frequently crowned as an 'undiscovered' gem by the foreign press. While the shop is hard to find, the culinary excellence of the house speciality, *kǔaytǐaw* served with stewed or roasted duck or goose, is debateable.

Siam Square & Pratunam   Map pp118–19

When in Shop-landia, you must pay homage to the mall food courts, which are a subset of the market-vendor cult. You'll also find every imaginable Western and Japanese fast-food chains, including a *wai*-ing Ronald McDonald. For finer dining, a culinary row has sprouted on Soi Lang Suan, off Th Ploenchit near Chitlom Skytrain station, with a variety of international and Thai dinner options.

THAI

Le Lys (0 2652 2401; 75 sub-Soi 3, Soi Lang Suan; dishes 80-200B; lunch & dinner; Skytrain Chitlom) A soothing respite from Bangkok's traffic and the pressures of formality, Le Lys is tucked into a breezy colonial house and garden. Superb Thai dishes, such as *kaeng phèt mǔu yâang bai chà-om* (roast pork curry with acacia leaves), are easily plucked from a menu accompanied by appetising photos. Some diners snack and drink in between sets of *la pétanque* (French lawn bowling) in the restaurant's backyard.

Khao Man Kai Siam (Siam Chicken; 280 Th Phra Ram I; dishes 35-50B; lunch & dinner; Skytrain Siam) If your germ phobia prevents you from gorging on the street, then head to this sterile air-con spot for a streetside speciality: *khâo man kài* (boiled chicken over rice with a lemon-grass broth served on the side). Despite the antiseptic setting, it still maintains the traditional calling card – dangling chicken carcasses in front of the kitchen.

Whole Earth Restaurant (0 2252 5574; 93/3 Soi Lang Suan; dishes 100-200B; lunch & dinner) Family-friendly restaurant will put your vegetarian conscience and your belly at ease, but your taste buds might feel left out. The Thai dishes are all extremely fresh but lacking in flair, an obvious shortcoming considering the fetching prices.

INTERNATIONAL

Foodloft (0 2655 7777; 7th fl, Central Chitlom, Th Ploenchit; dishes 100-300B; lunch & dinner; Skytrain Chitlom) It is hard to improve on Foodloft's enthusiastic slogan: 'New, trendy, upmarket, international dining concept'. Wow, what a mouthful, and all under one roof? Indeed the standard cafeteria formula has been transformed into a stylish eatery with a drinkable city view. Almost every ethnic cuisine is represented and some claim the thin-crust pizzas are the city's best (although, in the spirit of a pizza democracy, we disagree).

BREAKFAST OF CHAMPIONS

What's for breakfast in the City of Angels? Well, judging by the platoon of *túk-túk* drivers parked outside your hotel, Thailand's morning main-stay is an M150 energy drink and a cigarette. Too nutritious, you say? In addition to the name-only guesthouse pancakes, the Western breakfast tradition is charmingly pantomimed at the **Atlanta Coffeeshop** (p163) and the coffee shop of the **Federal Hotel** (p153), both more appealing for their flashback in time than for mastery in the kitchen. Expats who have forgotten what a toaster looks like go to **Bourbon St Bar & Restaurant** (p165). Yuppy Thais who claim international upbringings prefer the gourmet chic of **Kuppa** (p165). And anyone who has the Gaul to do so, savour the savoury and sweet crepes at **Crepes & Co** (p164).

Hard Rock Café (☎ 0 2254 0830; Soi 11, Siam Square; dishes 150-300B; ✆ lunch & dinner; Skytrain Siam) The Bangkok branch (p168) of the London anchor serves a gringo-proud plate of nachos and other American-style pub grub, easily washed down with the evening's two-for-one beer specials. Look for the *túk-túk* captioned 'God is my co-pilot' coming out of the building's façade.

Silom   Map pp114–16
At lunchtime the financial district goes into a feeding frenzy at the shanty villages of street vendors or the buffets at the English-Irish pubs. Dinner offerings include more gourmet attire with a handful of elegant restaurants preparing international fusion and royal Thai cuisine. Simple, family-run Indian restaurants proliferate towards the western end of Th Silom and Th Surawong.

THAI
Chulalongkorn University Canteen (Soi Chulalongkorn 42, Th Phayathai, Chulalongkorn Campus; dishes 20B; ✆ lunch; subway Samyan) You might be the only one here not in uniform, but who could say no to an innocent noodle craving? The university's canteen does a delicious sesame seed–encrusted *kài thâwt* (fried chicken) that is served solo or atop a steaming bowl of noodles. You can also get the noodles spiked with a lip-tingling *tâm yam* broth. A little

Thai is needed to order, but no conversation is required to gulp it down beside the uni students copying each others' homework.

Talat Sam Yan (Chulalongkorn Soi 6, near cnr of Th Phayathai & Th Rama IV; dishes 50B; ✆ lunch & dinner) This two-storey pavilion has a busy fresh food market on the 1st floor with a lunch and dinner emporium on the 2nd floor. During lunch, the meals are a curious Thai adaptation of the Western heart-attack special: slabs of meat are slathered in sweet and spicy sauces and then wrapped in processed cheese.

Ban Chiang (☎ 0 2236 7045; 14 Soi Si Wiang, Th Surasak; dishes 90-150B; ✆ lunch & dinner; Skytrain Surasak) A barely tamed garden girthed by a wooden fence marks the entrance to Ban Chiang, which delivers a homage to the fiery cuisine of the northeast. Occupying a restored wooden house with simple décor, this restaurant is a favourite of undiscerning tour groups and sometimes tip-toes too close to mediocre (avoid the *tôm yam kûng*). Luckily the *yam plaa duk foo* (salad of fried shredded catfish) swoops in to rescue any sagging opinions.

Harmonique (☎ 0 2237 8175; Soi 34, Th Charoen Krung; dishes 60-150B; ✆ lunch & dinner Mon-Sat) Earning more points in ambience than cuisine, Harmonique is a rambling oasis with seating in the banyan tree–filled courtyard and converted wooden shophouse. With twinkling fairy lights and marble-topped tables, you might not notice (or be troubled by) the shortcomings of the bland dishes.

Blue Elephant (☎ 0 2673 9352; 233 Th Sathon Tai; dishes 200-500B; ✆ lunch & dinner; Skytrain Surasak) Set in a refurbished Sino-Thai colonial building with service fit for royalty, the Blue Elephant balances the once-secret recipes of the monarchy with international fusion. The salmon *lâap* (salad with mint leaves) is an ingenious exchange of flavours and *phàk bûng fai daeng* (stirfried water greens) is spiked with the smoky flavour of mesquite, but the Muslim *(mátsàmàn)* lamb curry is too sweet.

Sara-Jane's (☎ 0 2676 3338; 55/21 Th Narathiwat Ratchanakharin; dishes 90-200B; ✆ lunch & dinner) One of Bangkok's most famous *faràng* (who is married to a Thai) has built a small food empire from the marriage of Isan and Italian food. There is another branch in Siam Square, but this location puts more passion into the otherwise incongruous food traditions.

BANGKOK

INDIAN & MUSLIM

Sallim Restaurant (☎ 0 2237 1060, Soi 32, Th Charoen Krung; dishes 50-70B; ☺ lunch & dinner; river ferry Tha Meuang Khae) Open-air restaurant could easily win the dubious and challenging award for the dirtiest restaurant in Thailand, but the food is fabulous. Don't even bother looking at the English menu, which in no way corresponds to the daily offerings. Instead leap into one of the southern Thai-Muslim curries – *kaeng kài* (chicken), *néua* (beef) or *plaa* (fish) – served along with your choice of rice or *rotii* (two loaves should be enough). The restaurant is the last option along the right-hand block.

Yogi (Soi Phuttha Osot, Th Mahesak; dishes 70-100B; ☺ lunch & dinner Mon-Sat; river ferry Tha Oriental) Practically sawed in half by the nearby expressway, this New York City–sized restaurant whips up all-vegetarian South Indian meals in an even smaller kitchen. Wash up before digging in at the outdoor sink.

Muslim Restaurant (1356 Th Charoen Krung; dishes under 40B; ☺ lunch & dinner; river ferry Tha Oriental) Near the intersection of Th Silom, this bare-bones place has been feeding various Lonely Planet authors for over 20 years. The faded walls and stainless steel tables don't make for the best décor, but an assortment of curries and *rotii* are displayed in a clean glass case for easy pointing and eye-catching allure.

Indian Hut (☎ 0 2635 7876; Th Surawong; dishes 90-250B; ☺ lunch & dinner; river ferry Tha Oriental) Opposite the Manohra Hotel, Indian Hut proudly displays a slightly altered Pizza Hut logo (so much for pesky copyright laws) and specialises in Nawabi (Lucknow) cuisine for a well-scrubbed business set. The vegetarian samosa, fresh prawns cooked with ginger and homemade *paneer* are all must nibbles.

Naaz (Soi 43/Soi Saphan Yao, Th Charoen Krung; dishes 50-70B; ☺ lunch & dinner; river ferry Tha Oriental) Pronounced 'Naat' in Thai, this neighbourhood corner is often cited as having the richest *khâo mòk kài* (chicken biryani) in the city. The milk tea is also very good, and so is the house dessert, *firni*, a Middle Eastern pudding spiced with coconut, almonds, cardamom and saffron. Approach Naaz via Th Charoen Krung.

INTERNATIONAL

Mizu's Kitchen (☎ 0 2233 6447; Soi Patpong 1, Th Silom; dishes 80-150B; ☺ noon-1am; Skytrain Sala Daeng, subway Silom) Holding fast to the styles of Bangkok's

AUTHOR'S CHOICE

Eat Me Restaurant (☎ 0 2238 0931; Soi Phiphat 2, off Th Convent; dishes 150-400B; ☺ dinner; Skytrain Sala Daeng, subway Silom) One of the city's most successful fusion restaurants, Eat Me excels in creativity with a luscious tuna tartare, glass-noodle spring rolls and five-lettuce salad. The waitstaff are well-versed in the expectations of foreign patrons and the chic décor is accented by rotating exhibits of modern Thai artists.

R&R days – trattoria-style chequered tablecloths, faded posters of calendar girls and a Patpong address – Mizu's does Japanese versions of Western food (such as macaroni and cheese), as well as steak and vegetable hot plates. It's hard to differentiate between the dishes – they're all warm and salty and a perfect companion for a slurred-speech night.

Le Bouchon (☎ 0 2234 9109; 37/17 Soi Patpong 2, Th Silom; dishes 150-300B; ☺ lunch & dinner Mon-Sat, dinner Sun; Skytrain Sala Daeng, subway Silom) Between two of Patpong's most famous strip bars is this respectable French bistro that specialises in the wholesome cuisine of Provence. To really do one night in Bangkok, suck down a cereal-bowl's worth of *crème brûlée* and then go catch a Patpong ping-pong show.

Irish Xchange (☎ 0 2266 7160; 1-4 Sivadon Bldg, Th Convent; dishes 150-300B; ☺ lunch & dinner; Skytrain Sala Daeng, subway Silom) To brush up on your knife-wielding skills, stop in for meat pies and pork chops, just a few of the dairy-eaters favourites, at this Irish-style pub. Check out the daily lunch specials to ease the budget burden.

Angelini (☎ 0 2236 7777; Shangri-La Hotel, 89 Soi Wat Suan Phlu; dishes 500B; ☺ lunch & dinner; river ferry Tha Oriental) The Shangri-La's beloved Italian restaurant, Angelini manages to be simultaneously grand and relaxed with *haute cuisine* and an intimate setting overlooking the river. Too bad there is no buffet to ease the bill blow.

Sirocco (☎ 0 2624 9555; 63rd fl, State Tower, 1055 Th Silom; dishes 500-1000B; ☺ dinner; river ferry Tha Oriental) More interesting as a trivia tidbit than as an affordable dinner option, the Bangkok elite prefer their meals sky high. Fine views and fine prices have an intoxicating effect, especially on wooing couples (so we are told). Grilled Australian tenderloin and the dessert buffet stand out amid an otherwise mediocre melange.

Lumphini

Map p117

Soi Polo Fried Chicken (☎ 02 655 8489; 137/1-2 Soi Polo, Th Withayu; dishes 160B; ☺ lunch & dinner; Skytrain Ploenchit, subway Lumphini) Golden and crispy on the outside, moist and meaty inside and sprinkled with fried garlic bits – it is easy to see why this is considered the best *kài thâwt* (fried chicken) in town. One half-order will generously feed two, but don't forget about ordering sticky rice for the spicy dipping sauces.

Suan Lom (Th Withayu & Th Phra Ram IV; dishes 100-150B; ☺ dinner; subway Lumphini) Thailand's version of a German beer garden, Bangkok's government-funded night bazaar has several football fields worth of outdoor tables arranged around stage shows of super loud Thai pop performances. Hardly the stuff of postcards, this gaudy, electrified production is more Thai than the floating markets. The main pursuit here is drinking, but rarely is liquid sustenance separated from solid. Litter your table with all the Thai classics, brought to you by a wafer-thin girl who will unintentionally call all the women in the party 'sir'.

Nguan Lee Lang Suan (☎ 0 22500936; Central Bangkok map; cnr Soi Lang Suan & Th Sarasin; dishes 150-250B; ☺ dinner; Skytrain Chitlom) Hardly more than a mess hall, this sweaty open-air place specialises in Chinese-style seafood and *kài lâo daeng* (chicken steamed in Chinese herbs).

Sukhumvit

Map pp112–13

This avenue, stretching east all the way to the city limits, is the communal dining room of most of Bangkok's expat communities, from Italian to Arabic. While a recent arrival might not be craving the tastes of home, many of these satellite stations are good observation points on the city's many microcosms. Sukhumvit's restaurants also provide an interesting looking-glass through which to view a universal occurrence – locals embracing 'exotic' cuisines.

THAI

Atlanta Coffeeshop (☎ 0 2252 6069; Atlanta Hotel, 78 Soi 2, Th Sukhumvit; dishes 50-120B; ☺ breakfast, lunch & dinner; Skytrain Ploenchit) Impeccably preserving

the era of pill-box hats and white gloves, the Atlanta is the most grounded fashion idol in Bangkok. The subdued diner features a heavily annotated menu (itself a crash course in Thai cuisine), scratchy recordings of Thai, classical and jazz (including an hour of King Bhumibol's compositions beginning at noon). Vegetarian, standard Thai and Western breakfasts are all exemplary selections.

Hong Ahan 55 (☎ 0 2391 2021; 1087-1091 Th Sukhumvit; dishes 80-120B; ☺ dinner; Skytrain Thong Lor) Naked little storefront is too busy whipping up such crowd pleasers as saffron-spiked *puu phàt phǒng kàrìi* (crab curry), than primping in design couture.

Vientiane Kitchen (☎ 0 2258 6171; 8 Soi 36, Th Sukhumvit; dishes 120-200B; ☺ lunch & dinner; Skytrain Thong Lor) Easier to find than Hua Lamphong, Vientiane Kitchen is a cultural display for the reluctant tourist. In a big barn-like structure, *mǎw lam* bands play all the rollicking tunes of the Isan countryside while the fiery *tôm yum goong*, *lâap mǔu* (minced pork salad),

---

WHAT'S FOR DINNER?

Do too many dining choices cripple you with indecision? We've taken the liberty here of providing a cross-section of Bangkok's culinary landscape.

- **Best Thai Restaurants:** Vientiane Kitchen (above), Ban Chiang (p161), Hemlock (p157), Ton Pho (p157), Soi Polo Fried Chicken (left)

- **Best Date Restaurants:** Le Lys (p160), Baan Phanfah Restaurant (p158), Sirocco (opposite), Maha Naga (p164)

- **Best Snapshots of Bangkok's Expat & Immigrant Communities:** Nasir al-Masri Restaurant & Shishah (p164), Dosa King (p164), Le Bouchon (opposite), La Piola (p164)

- **Best Places for Style & Substance:** Eat Me Restaurant (opposite), Crepes & Co (p164)

- **Best Restaurants to Brag about in Backpacker Circles:** Chochana (p158), Pickle Factory (p165), Th Phadungdao Seafood Stalls (p159), Mizu's Kitchen (p162), hotel buffets (p166), Victory Point (p165)

kài yâang (grilled marinated chicken) will give you a bee-stung pout without collagen injections.

Maha Naga (☎ 0 2662-3060; Soi 29, Th Sukhumvit; dishes 300-700B; ☺ 11:30am-2:30pm & 5pm-1am; Skytrain Phrom Phong) Although the children of Thai and Western parents are usually destined for pop-stardom in Bangkok, the same can not be said for fusion restaurants. One notable exception is upmarket Maha Naga, named after the mythical sea serpent. A constant interplay between the two traditions' kitchen cabinets and cooking pots have created such interesting combinations as deep-fried prawn rolls served with plum sauce and crispy vermicelli, scallops in Thai-style gravy and pork chops topped with *sôm-tam* (spicy green papaya salad).

Hua Lamphong Food Station (☎ 0 2661 3538; 92/1 Soi 34, Th Sukhumvit; dishes 150-330B; ☺ dinner; Skytrain Thong Lor) Although it is nowhere near Bangkok's main train station despite the name, reaching this restaurant is like a journey to the provinces. Decorated with country Thai furnishings, it serves delicious Isan and northern-Thai food, and has traditional music nightly from 8pm to 10pm. From Th Sukhumvit, take a motorcycle taxi to the restaurant, which is too hard to find on foot.

Cabbages & Condoms (☎ 0 2229 4611; Soi 12, Th Sukhumvit; dishes 150-200B; ☺ lunch & dinner; Skytrain Asoke) If you haven't cottoned on to the rustic aspects of Thai food, then Cabbages & Condoms is a perfect 'wading' pool. Familiar ingredients appear in dishes like *yam wun sên* (mung bean noodle salad). Plus this isn't just another tourist venture, all proceeds go towards sex-education and AIDS-prevention programmes in Thailand through the Population and Community Development Association (PDA), headquartered next door. A reminder of its community outreach appears in the form of a packaged condom, a clever alternative to the traditional after-dinner mint.

INDIAN & MUSLIM

Al Hussain (75/7 Soi 3/1; dishes 100-200B; ☺ lunch & dinner; Skytrain Nana) Just off Th Sukhumvit near Soi 3 (Soi Nana Neua), there is a winding maze of cramped sublanes known as Little Arabia, where the number of Middle Eastern and African residents make Thais seem like foreigners. At the crossroads is this open-air café displaying an irresistible steam table of vegetarian and meat curries, along with *dahl* (curried lentils), *aloo gobi* (spicy potatoes and cauliflower), *naan* (bread) and rice. There is also air-con dining.

Nasir al-Masri Restaurant & Shishah (☎ 0 2253 5582; 4/6 Soi 3/1, Th Sukhumvit; dishes 80-120B; ☺ breakfast, lunch & dinner; Skytrain Nana) Can't miss this blinding silver temple to Egyptian food. The fruity perfume from the nearby *shishah* smokers scents the predinner atmosphere, until the sensory banquet arrives. Worth crowding the table is the sesame-freckled flatbread, creamy hummus and flawlessly fried falafels. Open until 4am.

Dosa King (☎ 02 6511651; 265/1 Soi 19, Th Sukhumvit; ☺ lunch & dinner; Skytrain Asoke) Nosh alongside the sari-wrapped mamas or clubbing teenagers at this Punjabi vegetarian favourite. The regional speciality, *dosa* (a thin, stuffed crepe), adorn most tables like ancient parchment scrolls. (If you don't know, you eat these with your hands, using the wrapper as a spoon.)

INTERNATIONAL

Crepes & Co (☎ 0 2653 3990; 18/1 Soi 12, Th Sukhumvit; dishes 140-280B, ☺ breakfast, lunch & dinner; Skytrain Asoke) Cottage oasis creates delicate, platter-sized crepes stuffed with smoky bacon and woodsy mushrooms, as well as mud-thick coffee. Whirlwind tours of Morocco and the Mediterranean are also found on the menu. Servers, striped in the colours of the French flag, sail these piping hot dishes to the garden-view tables.

La Piola (☎ 0 2253 8295; 32 Soi 13, Th Sukhumvit; set menu 1000B; ☺ dinner Tue-Sat; Skytrain Nana) A basement full of good times and good food is La Piola's main course. There's no menu, just enjoy whatever three-course extravaganza Mama has put together – antipasto, three pasta mains, and dessert. Meanwhile owner Pietro personally greets all the tables and suave cousin Pino serenades the crowd with Frank Sinatra tunes.

Pizzeria Bella Napoli (☎ 02 259 0405; 3/3 Soi 31, Th Sukhumvit; dishes 200-500B; ☺ dinner Mon-Fri, lunch Sat & Sun; Skytrain Phrom Phong) In Bangkok's Little Italy, an eclectic and boisterous crowd gulps down glasses of blood-red wine and gooey and Bangkok's best, garlicky wood-fired pizzas in this Neapolitan outpost. Prepare to be jealous when the table next to you orders the prosciutto-bridge pizza.

Jool's Bar & Restaurant (☎ 0 2252 6413; Soi 4/Soi Nana Tai; dishes 150-280B; ☺ lunch & dinner; Skytrain Nana) Just past Nana Entertainment Plaza, Jool's is the neighbourhood watering hole for veteran sexpats. But all types stumble through the door for the generous portions of English-style roasts and pies (some of the best in town), served with a side order of men acting like boys.

Tamarind Café (☎ 0 2663 7421; 27 Soi 20, Th Sukhumvit; dishes 200-250B; ☺ lunch & dinner; Skytrain Asoke) Pacific Rim cuisine goes vegetarian at this sleek eatery. Imaginative fresh juice concoctions will stave off a cold or transport you to a long-forgotten beach vacation. Main dishes fuse together Asia's heavyweight cuisines with a California sensibility for freshness and flavour. Tamarind shares space with Gallery F-Stop (p129), which hosts rotating photography exhibits.

Kuppa (☎ 0 2663 0495; 39 Soi 16, Th Sukhumvit; dishes 200-400B; ☺ breakfast, lunch & dinner; Skytrain Asoke) Sleek reflecting pools and modern rattan furniture attract a fashionable bunch for fashionably late brunch. Real salads (no iceberg here) and US grain-fed beef are some of the menu standouts.

Greyhound Cafe (☎ 02 664 8663; 2nd fl, Emporium, btwn Soi 22 & 24, Th Sukhumvit; dishes 100-250B; ☺ lunch & dinner; Skytrain Phrom Phong) Oh the follies of fashion; this trendy café continues the lifestyle branding efforts of Thailand's hottest design label, Greyhound. Although everyone knows fashion types don't eat, the point is to be seen (notice how the tables lining the main thoroughfare are always full.) And how about the food? Like the clientele, the hybrid menu on offer here emphasises updated Thai cuisine after a sojourn in southern Europe.

Govinda (☎ 0 2663 4970; 22 Soi, Th Sukhumvit; mains 150-300B; ☺ dinner; Skytrain Phrom Phong) Regarded as one of Bangkok's best veggie restaurants, this place cooks up splendid Italian food based on soya and unusual vegetables. The restaurant is near the mouth of the soi in the shopping complex before Larry's Dive Shop.

Le Banyan (☎ 0 2253 5556; 59 Soi 8, Th Sukhumvit; dishes 390-450B; ☺ dinner Mon-Sat; Skytrain Nana) In a charming Ratanakosin-style house surrounded by a lush garden, this is one of the top French restaurants in the city and probably the best that isn't associated with a luxury hotel. The French-managed kitchen

covers the territory from *ragout d'escargot* (snail stew) to *maigret de canard avec foie gras* (duck breast with duck liver). It has a superb wine list. The restaurant is further down the lane than you would expect; keep an eye out for the artistically trimmed bamboo hedge.

Bei Otto (☎ 0 2262 0892; 1 Soi 20, Th Sukhumvit; dishes 250-500B; ☺ lunch & dinner; Skytrain Asoke) When you get a hankering for pork knuckles, German-style sausages and freshly baked bread, come along to this informal Bavarian embassy. An attached beer cellar pours draughts of imported pilsners and bottles of chewy wheat beer.

Bourbon St Bar & Restaurant (☎ 0 2259 0328; Soi 22; dishes 150-300B; ☺ breakfast, lunch & dinner; Skytrain Asoke & Phrom Phong) Near Mambo Cabaret, this New Orleans-style restaurant fills an empty niche in Bangkok's expat kitchen. Americans gush over the hardy breakfasts (toast, done the right way, and eggs Benedict) and Mexican concoctions with spot-on salsa, while US virgins are still trying to solve the riddle of chicken-fried steak.

Greater Bangkok

Pickle Factory (Map pp106-7; ☎ 0 2246 3036, 55 Soi 21, Th Ratwithi; dishes 150-200B; ☺ dinner; Skytrain Victory Monument) Occupying a 1970s-vintage Thai house, the Pickle Factory creates a dinner party mood with indoor sofa-seating and outdoor tables around a pool – in short, the perfect place to kick back for an evening with friends. The menu includes creatively topped pizzas, such as Chiang Mai sausage and holy basil paste with wing beans. Take a taxi as the footpath-less sois and threat of soi dogs are formidable guardians.

Victory Point (Map pp106-7; Th Phayathai & Th Ratwithi; dishes 25-30B; ☺ dinner; Skytrain Victory Monument) Lining the busy roundabout is a squat village of concrete stalls lit in neon under the collective title 'Victory Point'. Near the fairy lights is a beer-and-food garden centred around a pop-stage show. Order a pitcher and a few plates of the zesty Thai classics for a thoroughly satisfying meal. Above ground, the real drama unfolds as university students cruise the elevated walkways. Bad boys show off their break-dancing moves or their disaffected Sid Vicious sneers to groups of giggling girls.

Baan Suan Pai (Bamboo Garden House; Map pp106-7; ☎ 0 2615 2454; Th Phahonyothin; dishes 25B; ☺ lunch

& dinner; Skytrain Ari) Just past the petrol station before Soi 4, this vegetarian food centre offers a garden's bounty of diversity. Right by the door, buy coupons from the woman at the desk. The coupons are printed with Thai numbers only, but the denominations are colour-coded as follows: green, 5B; purple, 10B; blue, 20B; red, 25B. Most plates offer the choice of three stirfries, but there's also sushi and noodles. Everything is strictly vegetarian here, even lacking the ubiquitous fish sauce. Don't miss the handmade ice cream of such exotic flavours as passionfruit, lemongrass and lotus root.

Chamlong's Asoke Café (Map pp104-5; ☎ 0 2272 4282; 580-592 Th Phahon Yothin; Chatuchak; dishes 20-30B; ☯ lunch Sat & Sun) Operated by the Asoke Foundation, the vegetarian restaurant near the Chatuchak Weekend Market is one of Bangkok's oldest. It is tough to find though: take the footbridge across Th Kamphaeng Phet, away from the market, and towards the southern end of Th Phahonyothin. Take the first right onto a through street, and walk past nightclubs and bars into the car park (the parking attendants might even ask for your keys so they can fetch your car). Head to your right, and you'll see a new block of buildings selling bulk food stuff; you're getting closer because these are organic wholesalers (smell that 'health-food store' scent?). The restaurant is at the end of this strip. Like Baan Suan Pai, you buy tickets at the front desk. An adjacent store sells organic products produced by the self-sufficient Asoke communities.

River Restaurants

River restaurants come in numerous shapes and prices, but all share the cool evening breezes and incredible views. Because the river is the primary draw, the food typically runs a distant second. To counterbalance this trend, come for a few appetisers and a drink and leave the feasting to the eyes. See p141 for dinner cruises that ply the river.

Nang Nual Riverside Pub (Map pp108-9; ☎ 0 2223 7686; Trok Krai, Th Mahachak; dishes 90-170B; ☯ dinner) Not far from Tha Ratchawong, this outdoor deck is a drinking and snacking spot where groups of friends gather around whisky sets and plates of *kàp klâem* (drinking food), such as spicy salads and *kài sǎam yàang* (peanuts mixed with fresh chillies and chunks of ginger, lime and shallot). If you

hit this spot at the right time, the bar's blaring pop music will be competing for valuable air space with the Muslim call to prayer from the mosque across the river.

Baan Rim Nam (Map pp106-7; ☎ 0 2860 4500; 723 Th Charoen Nakhon; dishes 200-300B; ☯ lunch & dinner) Across the river in Thonburi, you can dine amid the bright lights of the Shangri-La and Oriental Hotels. Take a cross-river ferry (2B), from the end of the lane in front of the Shangri-La Hotel, to the wooden pier on the Thonburi shore. Wind through the narrow lanes until you come to a main road (Th Charoen Nakhon), then turn left. Near a large shopping centre, follow the signs for the restaurant. The ferry operates until around 2am.

Krua Rakhang Thong (Map p120; ☎ 0 2848 9597; Soi Wang Lang, Thonburi; dishes 80-150B; ☯ lunch & dinner) Breezy converted house boasts the famous dual-temple view (Wat Arun and Wat Phra Kaew) from its 2nd-floor dining terrace. Stick to a few fried appetisers to avoid disappointment. The restaurant is a lovely walk from Tha Wang Lang (reached from the Bangkok side by a cross-river ferry at Tha Chang); from the pier turn left at the first through street past the market crowded with veggie sellers and vendors glued to the same TV soap operas. The Roman-script sign at the entrance reads 'River View'.

Hotel Buffets

Before Bangkok really grew into its urban skin, the luxury hotels provided the city with the most elaborate and sophisticated dining. But now as independent restaurants push Bangkok into culinary frontiers, the hotel restaurants have assumed a more traditional role of catering to out-of-town guests, business meetings and as status symbols.

One area where the hotel restaurants still excel is the buffet (lunch, dinner and Sunday brunch). The huge spread offers a one-stop introduction to Thai food, a raw bar, continental specialities, or a dim sum exploration. Lunch usually runs from 11.30am to 2pm, and dinner from 5pm to 10pm. Reservations are recommended, and business casual (long sleeves, closed-toe shoes) will probably suffice, at least for daytime dining. Most luxury hotels have magnificent buffets, but here are a few standouts.

The Colonnade (Map p117; ☎ 0 2287 0222, 1st fl, Sukhothai Hotel, 13/3 Th Sathon; set price 1200-1500B)

Nonguests should find an excuse to visit the Sukhothai Hotel to relish the elegant combination of ancient and modern architecture. One splurge-worthy possibility is the cultishly popular Sunday brunch with free-flowing champagne, made-to-order lobster bisque, caviar, imported cheeses, foie gras. A jazz trio supplies background music.

Marriott Cafe (Map pp112-13; ☎ 0 2656 7700; JW Marriott Hotel, 4 Th Sukhumvit at Soi 4) An American-style abundance lines the buffet tables with fresh oysters, seafood, pastas and Japanese food.

Summer Palace (Map pp118-19; ☎ 0 2656 0444; InterContinental Bangkok, 973 Th Ploenchit; set lunch for 2 people 760B) Boasting a Hong Kong chef, this hotel restaurant does an authentic dim sum lunch that includes such delicacies as steamed snowfish dumplings and steamed rice noodles accompanied by soup, two entrees and a dessert.

Jade Garden (Map pp114-16; ☎ 0 2233 7060; Montien Hotel, 54 Th Surawong; buffet 700-800B) The hotel dim sum here is as good as luxury names, but at less than one-third of the price. Although not quite as fancy in presentation, the food is nonetheless impressive.

Lord Jim's (Map pp114-16; ☎ 0 2659 9000; Oriental Hotel; Soi Oriental/Soi 38, Th Charoen Krung; buffet 1000B) Named after Joseph Conrad's novel set in Bangkok, Lord Jim's is designed to imitate the interior of a 19th-century Asian steamer, with a view of the river and a menu focusing on seafood.

Mei Jiang (Map pp106-7; ☎ 0 2861 2888; Peninsula Hotel, Thonburi; dim sum 65-220B, set lunch 720B) Classy dim sum is nibbled from a riverfront perch at the top-notch Peninsula Hotel. The crab dumplings can be paired with set lunches, including crispy barbecued suckling pig and other Chinese treatments.

Youzen Restaurant (Map pp112-13; ☎ 0 2262 1234; Windsor Suites Hotel, Soi 20, Th Sukhumvit; lunch buffet 300B) Killer Japanese lunch buffet caters to all of your raw cravings without netting your wallet.

DRINKING

Where can you get a drink in this town? Just about anywhere will water your gullet. Banglamphu has an artsy vibe in an otherwise status-conscious city. Funky apartment-sized bars cater to the city's literary cliques around Th Phra Athit. Connoisseurs of drunken abandon prefer the

---

SOBERING NEWS

What used to be a modern-day Sodom with all-night, anything-goes carousing has been efficiently transformed into a sanitised Singapore by Prime Minister Thaksin's new social order. Unbribable police officers enforce 1am closing time for bars and 2am for dance clubs, clubbers are often nabbed for on-the-spot drug testing, and even the sex shows have been cleaned up. Dance clubs will even turn away the elderly if they don't have ID to prove their age. But thanks to the city's entrepreneurial spirit, holes in the curfew laws are discovered more quickly than a breached dam. After closing time, the party moves out to the street where beer gets sold out of quickly removable coolers or at night markets serving food.

UN-style freak show on Th Khao San. Thanon Silom and Sukhumvit represent the stock-and-trade of Bangkok bars: English-Irish–style pubs and yuppie bars.

Banglamphu   Map pp110–11
TH KHAO SAN
The tourist strip of Th Khao San is one big, mutliculti party with every imaginable outlet for swilling and socialising. Shirtless Euros, draped around the closest stable body, guzzle big Beer Chang. Mixed Thai-*faràng* couples sip sweet cocktails at bars converted from VW buses. Thai teenagers flex their rebellious streak by getting fake dreadlocks. Even moneyed Thais have joined the street parade at chic wine-sipping bars. Grab a front-row view at one of Th Khao San's street-facing bars, like **Center Khao San** or retreat into air-con comfort at **Gulliver's Traveller's Tavern**.

TH RAMBUTRI & SOI RAMBUTRI
Just a drunken stumble from techno-charged Th Khao San, these sister streets separated by Th Chakraphong offer a more mellow scene for audible conversation at open-air lounges such as **Molly Bar** or **Dong Dea Moon**. This is also where you'll find barely legal Thai clubs, like **Bangkok Bar**, for guzzling pop music and cocktails.

TH PHRA ATHIT
A charming stretch of wooden shophouses has been converted into stylish bars and

cafés, popular among Thai university students and arty types. Exuding a bohemian confidence, these bars usually host a solo singer and a weeping guitar while patrons share plates of food or plough through bottles of whisky. Pick whichever one has the best music and convivial crowd.

Lulla Bar (☎ 0 2622 2585; Th Mahanot) Feel like doing some urban Indiana-Jonesin'? The off-campus hang-out of a rotating cast of Silpakorn students has been transformed into a makeshift bar. Hardly anybody who isn't a friend bothers to cross the threshold, making the odd foreigner who finds the place a barfly conquistador. The food is fantastic, the beers are cold, and the soundtrack skips through such classics as the Beatles and the Cure.

Baghdad Café (Soi 2, Th Samsen) Just over the Khlong Banglamphu is this sardine-tight *shishah* bar for puffing pungent fruit tobacco on Arabic water pipes and chatting with your neighbours about distant lands. A divergence from the Arabic tradition is that alcohol is sold right alongside.

Siam Square & Pratunam   Map pp118–19

Diplomat Bar (☎ 0 2690 9999; Conrad Hotel, 87 Th Withayu) Moguls, models and media types toast their good fortune of being 'fabulous' at Bangkok's latest incarnation of conspicuous consumption. The bubbly and the grapey spirits are raised in grand toasts while the diva-led lounge band serenades. Those who are unbeaten by bottle's end, traipse over to Club 87, the hotel's dance club, to seal the deal on the night's bed warmer.

Hard Rock Café (☎ 0 2254 0830; Soi 11, Siam Square) Add this to your international checklist, Bangkok's outpost of the London chain has a guitar-shaped bar and features the full range of cocktails and a small assortment of local and imported beers. The crowd is an ever-changing assortment of Thais, expats and tourists. From 10pm onwards there's also live music.

Silom & Lumphini

Barbican Bar (Map pp114–16; ☎ 0 2234 3590; 9 Soi Thaniya, Th Silom) Surrounded by massage parlours with teenage prom queens cat-calling at Japanese businessmen, this is a straight-laced yuppie bar where office crews come for happy-hour drinks and stay until closing time.

Vertigo (Map p117; ☎ 0 2679 1200; Banyan Tree Hotel, 21/100 Th Sathon Tai) Sky-high, open-air bar will literally take your breath away. From ground level, the elevator delivers you to the 59th floor where you weave your way through dimly lit hallways, *wai*-ing attendants, and narrow sets of stairs to the roar of Bangkok traffic far below. Come at sunset and grab a coveted seat to the right of the bar for more impressive views.

O'Reilly's Irish Pub (Map pp114–16; ☎ 0 2632 7515; 62/1-2 Th Silom) At the entrance to Thaniya Plaza (corner of Th Silom and Soi Thaniya), O'Reilly's needs to be on everyone's map for its wallet-friendly, happy-hour specials and proximity as a warm-up spot to Silom's dance clubs (see p170).

Sukhumvit   Map pp112–13

Cheap Charlie's (Soi 11, Th Sukhumvit; ☾ closed Sunday) Claiming the noble honour of serving the cheapest beer on the block, this wooden stall festooned with junk-yard decorations is a favourite happy-hour spot for the neighbourhood's wage-slave *faràng*. Turn sharp left, before the Federal Hotel, at the 'Sabai Sabai Massage' sign to join the collective milling and swilling.

Jool's (☎ 0 2252 6413; Soi 4, Th Sukhumvit) A few doors down from the Nana Entertainment Plaza, Jool's is a sinking ship of a dive bar navigating through bleary blathermouths and the district's commercial 'friendliness'. Bum pinches over the bar, racy jokes and the drunkest of the lot sitting at the helm, the horseshoe-shaped bar encourages entertaining exhibitionism and spinning of tall tales. With a ring of the captain's bell, indicating a free round, the mood shifts to a good-times drinking club.

Bull's Head & Angus Steakhouse (☎ 0 2261 0665; Soi 33/1, Th Sukhumvit) A beautiful galleried bar, the Bull's Head is well suited to imagining foggy London nights with a chill-defeating pint of Guinness or Kilkenny. Quiz nights, toss-the-boss happy hours and plenty of other creative drinking specials dominate the weekly schedule.

Ship Inn (9/1 Soi 23; ☾ 9am-midnight) Situated just around the corner from the Soi Cowboy, stepping inside delivers you into the cocoon of a quiet drinking crowd. The bar is as well stocked as a ship captain's quarters and it is a well-established stop on the darts circuit.

Suan Ahahn Pa Loet Rot (☎ 0 2258 5070; Soi 33/1) A little piece of the provinces has been cultivated amid Bangkok's concrete embrace. On its patio, shaded by the hair-like tendrils of an ancient banyan tree, displaced Thais share whisky sets and tasty snacking dishes.

Larry's Dive Center, Bar & Grill (☎ 0 2663 4563; Soi 22; dishes 95-175B) In a bright-yellow, two-storey building, Larry's serves Key West ambience with Canadian humour. Before you dismiss this as an oxymoron, stop in for the weekly drink specials or signature drink, the little-known Bloody Caesar (vodka and Clamato juice) – a post-op version of the Bloody Mary. There's an attached dive shop, should you get the urge to go snorkelling in a nearby canal.

Central Bangkok　　　　　　Map pp106–7
Water Bar (☎ 0 2642 7699; 107/3-4 Th Rangnam) Every new arrival should learn the whisky-set routine, a drinking tradition more at home at Thai family gatherings than in flash hotels. At this misnomered bar, just a short walk from Victory Monument, the Sang Som set (Thai whisky with Coke, soda and ice) still reigns as the tipple of choice. The attentive waitress will keep your glass filled to the right proportions (two fingers whisky, a splash of coke, the rest soda) after which you should offer up a toast and drain the night away.

ENTERTAINMENT
Bangkok's entertainment scene goes well beyond its naughty nightlife image, a hangover from the days when the City of Angels was an R&R stop for GIs serving in Vietnam in the 1960s and early '70s. Today, Bangkok boasts a heady assortment of nightlife, from yuppie lounges to unplugged jam bars. Like any big city, Bangkok loves the next, big thing: brew pubs, salsa clubs and hip hop bars all enjoy a short-lived firework display.

Even if you're usually in bed by 9pm, Bangkok still offers interesting postdinner diversions from flash cinemas to traditional cultural performances.

Live Music
Brown Sugar (Map p117; ☎ 0 2250 1825; 231/20 Th Sarasin, opposite Lumphini Park) Crescent City would be proud of this cluttered jazz space of odd angles and smoking chops. Brown

---

> **KEEPING UP WITH THE NIGHTCRAWLERS**
>
> Want to know what's hot and what's not? To keep up with the quick-change, late-night scene, check the entertainment listings in the *Bangkok Metro* or *Farang* magazines. The best source for the line-up at the city's live music clubs is the website www.bangkokgigguide.com.

Sugar whips up inspired performances that lean towards be-bop and brass. On Sunday nights, the high-powered musicians touring the luxury hotels come here to jam.

Saxophone Pub & Restaurant (Map pp106-7; ☎ 0 2246 5472; 3/8 Th Phayathai) A Bangkok institution, Saxophone is reminiscent of a German beer cellar with brilliant acoustics and up-close views of the nightly bands. Reggae, rhythm and blues, jazz and rock will bridge any troubling language barriers. From the Skytrain station's elevated walkway, descend the stairs near Victory Point.

Ad Here the 13th (Map pp110-11; 13 Th Samsen) Beside Khlong Banglamphu, Ad Here is everything a neighbourhood joint should be – lots of regulars, cold beer and heart-warming tunes delivered by a masterful house band starting at 10pm. The band does a version of 'Me and Bobby McGee' that will make you swear Janis Joplin has been reincarnated. Everyone knows each other, so don't be shy about mingling.

Living Room (Map pp112-13; ☎ 0 2653 0333; Sheraton Grande Sukhumvit, 250 Th Sukhumvit, btwn Soi 12 & 14) With studio-style perfection, the well-scrubbed jazz bands of international calibre put a sizzle into the men's club aesthetic of this hotel bar. Order yourself a Johnny on the rocks and pretend you're a 1st-class internationalist.

Radio City (Map pp114-16; ☎ 0 2266 4567; Soi Patpong 1) Wet your whistle and shake your tail-feathers after going hoarse from bargaining at the Patpong night market at this long-time favourite. Grab a drink on the patio to watch the haggling up close or duck inside for cover renditions of three decades of rock-&-roll hits. The masters of ceremonies include a Thai Elvis and a Tom Jones impersonator. Come late with a sufficient amount of social lubrication to enjoy the vacation-land cheesiness of the place.

AUTHOR'S CHOICE

Dallas Pub (Map pp118-19; ☎ 0 2255 3276; 412/1 Siam Square, Soi 6) Siam Square closes down quickly at night, making this Thai-country bar a handy asset. Just across the street from the Novotel hotel, this local's spot is filled with a rustic wooden interior, buffalo horns and American Wild West paraphernalia – the aesthetic of the songs-for-life genre, a musical protest movement from the 1980s. Come before 9pm for the acoustic bands whose soulful ballads coax crowd singalongs, eyes closed tight in solidarity. Follow the alley to the narrow stairs to reach the bar.

Bamboo Bar (Map pp114-16; ☎ 0 2236 0400; Oriental Hotel, Soi 38/Oriental, Th Charoen Krung) The Oriental's Bamboo Bar is famous for its live lounge jazz, which holds court inside a colonial-era cabin of lazy fans, broad-leafed palms and rattan decor.

Tawandaeng Beer Hall (Map pp104-5; ☎ 0 2678 1114; 462/61 Th Narathiwat Ratchanakharin cnr Th Phra Ram III) So you've had it with English pubs, yuppies and hotel bars and want something more local. You'll find half of Bangkok in this huge, village-sized brewhouse sipping German-style microbrews and singing with stage pop shows. Between sets, choruses of 'Happy Birthday' erupt from overcrowded tables. Another draw is the Wednesday night performance by Fong Nam, a fusion band of Western and Thai classical music.

Metal Zone (Map pp118-19; ☎ 0 2255 1913; Soi Lang Suan) Heavy metal rocks on at this homage to the hair-throwing and lip-jutting glam-damnery. Along with the dungeons-and-dragons décor a regular line-up of bands authentically does everything from thrash to Gothic to speed metal, Ozzy squeal to Axel rasp, even a few convoluted Helmet tunes. The volume level is perfect – loud enough for chest compression, but not so loud as to extract blood from the ears.

Dance Clubs

High-powered cocktails and spike heels populate the internationally bred dance and lounge clubs in the City of Angels. The fickle beautiful people are constantly on the move leaving behind the stylish carcasses to tourists and working girls.

Bangkok's discos burn strong and bright on certain weekends or during hot 'theme' nights, but then fall into comatosed slumbers on the off nights. Watch the city magazines for a visit from a foreign DJ, the latest music craze or the newest player on the scene. Cover charges for clubs and discos range from 500B to 600B and usually include a drink. Don't even think about showing up before 11pm.

Lucifer (Map pp114-16; ☎ 02 234 6902; 2nd fl above Radio City, Soi Patpong 1, Th Silom) The keystone of Bangkok's dance halls, the Lord of the Underworld has chosen a consistently tripped-out techno-rave soundtrack. The modest cover charge also ensures that warm bodies pack the floor when other clubs are empty.

Mystique (Map pp112-13; ☎ 0 2662 2374; 71/8 Soi 31, Th Sukhumvit) Perfect for the commitment shy, this new dance darling mixes and matches from fresh-faced hip-hop on the 1st floor to the milder-mannered electronica scene on the 2nd floor. Or escape it all in the chill-out patio with flickering candles and Latin-tribal beats. Go straight through the first intersection of Soi 31 and turn left at the yellow car-park sign.

Tapas (Map pp114-16; Soi 4, Th Silom) The ambassador of Soi 4's dead-end cruise, Tapas is a rendezvous point for the paired and the pair-able. In its Moroccan-inspired spaces, small samplers fit every taste: from the outdoor people-watching tables to the upstairs dance floor of soulful sounds and sweaty bodies. There are lots of corners encouraging cosy behaviour.

Q Bar (Map pp112-13; ☎ 0 2252 3274; Soi 11, Th Sukhumvit) Much debate rages over Bangkok's reigning 'it' bar. New York–style industrial chic is merged with groovy beats and competent cocktails (including absinthe and 40 kinds of Vodka), but dissenters charge that the beautiful crowd has migrated elsewhere. For the nobodies though, there is room for their own dance moves, some of which are straight off a Nana stage. To find it, take Soi 11 all the way to the end and hang a left.

Narcissus (Map pp112-13; ☎ 0 2258 2549; 112 Soi 23, Th Sukhumvit) A gaudy Roman-style temple to techno and trance, self-obsessed Narcissus throws the spotlight on international top-shelf DJs. Come with your dancing clothes and a fistful of cash when the big names are spinning.

Concept CM2 (Map pp118-19; ☎ 0 2255 6888; basement, Novotel Bangkok Hotel, Soi 6, Siam Square) An unabashed hotel disco, CM2 is an odd mix of seedy, touristy, and silly rolled into one.

Go-Go Bars

'We don't come to Thailand for the ruins', was an overheard insult delivered by a veteran sex tourist to an unsuspecting backpacker. He was right, many male visitors come only for the women or, in some cases, the men. The shopping venues for potential partners occupy a whole subset of Bangkok's nightlife, from massage parlours and go-go clubs to pick-up bars. There are thousands of books written on Bangkok's sexy underbelly, but Stickman's Guide to Bangkok (www.stickmanbangkok.com) offers a palatable perspective on the give-and-take of 'doing' Bangkok.

Patpong (Map pp114-16; Soi Patpong 1 & 2, Th Silom) Bangkok's most famous red-light district has calmed down a lot over the years and now draws more sightseers than flesh-seekers. The open-air tourist market on Patpong 1 has drawn much of the attention away from erotica. There are still a handful of go-go bars, mainly concentrated on Soi Patpong 2, that have morphed into circus displays of 'fuckey' and ping-pong shows for tourists and couples. Avoid bars touting 'free' sex shows as there are usually hidden charges, and when you try to ditch the outrageous bill the doors are suddenly blocked by muscled bouncers.

The gay men's equivalents can be found on nearby Soi Thaniya and Soi Anuman Ratchathon. Along with male go-go dancers and 'bar boys', several bars feature live sex shows, which are generally much better choreographed than the hetero equivalents on Patpong.

Soi Cowboy (Map pp112-13; btwn Soi 21 & Soi 23, Th Sukhumvit) A single lane strip of 25 to 30 bars claims direct lineage to the post-Vietnam War '70s, when a black American ex-GI nicknamed 'Cowboy' was among the first to open a self-named go-go bar off Th Sukhumvit. A real flesh trade functions amid the flashing neon that goes something like this: boy meets girl, boy pays to temporarily liberate girl from bar for playtime at hotel, the new couple may profess love if the price is right. For a fly-on-the-wall perspective, stop in at the nearby Internet cafés to see

groups of bar girls writing love-letter emails to their new sugar daddies; the well-worn piece of paper in front of them is something of a 'master' love letter.

Nana Entertainment Plaza (Map pp112-13; Soi 4/ Soi Nana Tai, Th Sukhumvit) This three-storey complex forms a nucleus of strip clubs that comes complete with its own guesthouses, used almost exclusively by female bar workers for illicit assignations. The 'female' staff at **Casanova** consists entirely of Thai transvestites and transsexuals – this is a favourite stop for foreigners visiting Bangkok for sex reassignment surgery.

Cinemas

Get out of the smog and heat at one of the city's hi-tech cinemas. For the royal treatment, opt for the VIP tickets (500B), with reclining seats, table service and spotless bathrooms – you'll deserve this before the cattle car–class flight back home. Regular seats cost 100B to 150B. All movies screened in Thai cinemas are preceded by the Thai royal anthem and everyone is expected to stand respectfully for its duration.

All of Hollywood's big releases plus a steady diet of locally bred comedies hit Bangkok's cinemas in a timely fashion. The foreign films are often altered before distribution by Thailand's film censors; usually this involves obscuring nude sequences, although gun fights are sometimes edited

---

CELLULOID REVOLUTION

The Land of Smiles used to be the Land of Sappy Movies until a new breed of film-makers started bringing visual storytelling to the silver screen. Spotlighted at the annual Bangkok International Film Festival (p142) and at art houses such as Scala, Lido and House, locally made movies have cultivated a devoted fan base of bohemians and intellectuals, both domestic and international, although commercial success still eludes the artier flicks. Keep an eye out for new releases from the reigning Midas of Thai cinema, Nonzee Nimibutr; the MTV-fueled Danny and Oxide Pang brothers; and past Cannes winners Pen-Ek Ratanaruang and Apichatpong Weerasethakul. For a historical snapshot of Thai cinema, see p80.

out too. Film buffs may prefer the weekly or twice-weekly offerings at Bangkok's foreign cultural clubs and centres. For contact details, see p97).

At the following cinemas, English movies are shown with subtitles rather than being dubbed in Thai.

EGV Grand (Map pp118-19; ☎ 0 2812 9999; Siam Discovery Center, Th Phra Ram; Skytrain Siam)

House (Map pp104-5; UMG Bldg, RCA, Th Phra Ram IX; subway Rama IX)

Lido Cinema (Map pp118-19; ☎ 0 2252 6498; Siam Square, Th Phra Ram I; Skytrain Siam)

SF Cinema City (Map pp118-19; ☎ 0 2611 6444; 7th fl, Mahboonkrong, cnr Th Phra Ram I & Th Phayathai; Skytrain National Stadium)

SF Cinema (Map pp112-13; ☎ 0 2260 9333; 6th fl, Emporium, Th Sukhumvit, btwn Soi 22 & 24; Skytrain Phrom Phong)

Scala Cinema (Map pp118-19; ☎ 0 2251 2861; Siam Square, Soi 1, Th Phra Ram I; Skytrain Siam)

Traditional Arts Performances

As Thailand's cultural repository, Bangkok offers an array of dance and theatre performances. For more information about these ancient arts, see p75 and p78. Dusit Park (p125) also hosts daily classical dance performance in between tours of the teak mansion.

Chalermkrung Royal Theatre (Map pp108-9; Sala Chaloem Krung; ☎ 0 2222 0434; cnr Th Charoen Krung & Th Triphet; bus 507, 508) In a Thai Art Deco building found at the edge of the Chinatown-Phahurat district, this theatre provides a striking venue for *khŏhn* (masked dance-drama based on stories from the *Rama-kian*). When it opened in 1933, the royally funded Chalermkrung was the largest and most modern theatre in Asia, with state-of-the-art film projection technology and the first chilled-water air-con system in the region. Prince Samaichaloem, a former student of the École des Beaux-Arts in Paris, designed the hexagonal building. A 1993 renovation brought the historic monument into the technological age with computer-generated laser graphics.

Khŏhn performances last about two hours plus intermission. Other Thai performing-arts and film festivals may also be scheduled at the theatre. Check the local newspapers for current performance schedules.

The theatre requests that patrons dress respectfully, which means no shorts, tank tops or sandals. Bring along a wrap or long-sleeved shirt in case the air-con is running full blast.

Natayasala (Joe Louis Puppet Theater) (Map p117; ☎ 0 2252 9683, www.joelouis-theater.com; Suan Lum Night Bazaar, cnr Th Phra Ram IV & Th Withayu; tickets 600B; ☼ show 7.30pm) The ancient art of Thai puppetry was heroically rescued by Sakorn Yangkhiawsod, more popularly known as Joe Louis, in 1985. Today his children carry on the tradition of re-enacting the *Ramakian* by using these knee-high puppets requiring three puppeteers to strike human-like poses. In 2004 Princess Galyani Vadhana gave the theatre its new name, Natayasala. Suan Lum Night Bazaar may close in the near future, and if that happens, Natayasala will have to move elsewhere. See p176 for more details.

National Theatre (Map p120; ☎ 0 2224 0171; Th Chao Fa; admission 20-200B) Near Saphan Phra Pin Klao, the National Theatre holds Thailand's most traditional *lákhon* and *khŏhn* performances. The theatre has regular monthly performances; stop by the Bangkok Tourist Division (p99) for a monthly calendar. A highly contentious redevelopment plan has proposed demolition and relocation of this theatre in order to create a riverside promenade. Stay tuned to the local papers or www.2bangkok.com for current updates.

Patravadi Theatre (Map p120; ☎ 0 2412 7287; www .patravaditheatre.com; 69/1 Soi Wat Rakhang; tickets 300-500B; ☼ performances vary) Next to the Supatra River House in Thonburi, this open-air theatre is Bangkok's leading promoter of avant-garde dance and drama. Led by Patravadi

---

SHRINE DANCING

Stumbling across the minor-chord cacophony of a commissioned shrine dance (*lákhon kâe bon*) can be an unexpected visual and cultural treat and a release from the ever-present self-consciousness of being a tourist. At **Lak Meuang** (p103) and **Erawan Shrine** (p128) worshippers whose wishes have been granted hire dance troupes in gratitude. Although many of the dance movements are the same as those seen in *lákhon*, these relatively crude performances are specially choreographed for ritual purposes, and don't represent true classical dance forms. But it is colourful – the dancers wear full costume and are accompanied by live music.

Mejudhon, who is a famous Thai actress, the troupe's performances blend traditional Thai arts and folk tales with modern choreography, music and costumes. There are also Friday and Saturday Thai classical dance classes open to the public. A free river shuttle picks up patrons at Tha Mahathat, near Silpakorn University; reservations for performances are recommended.

Sala Rim Nam (Map pp114-16; ☎ 0 2437 2918, 0 2437 3080; Oriental Hotel, Soi Oriental/Soi 38, Th Charoen Krung; tickets 1700B; ⏰ 7-10pm) The Oriental Hotel's affiliated dinner theatre is a Thai-pavilion decked out in teak, marble and bronze. Readers rave about the hour-long classical dance performance, but give the food a mediocre rating, a common trait of many dinner-theatres; reservations are recommended.

Thailand Cultural Centre (Map pp104-5; ☎ 0 2247 0028; www.thaiculturalcenter.com; Th Ratchadaphisek btwn Th Thiam Ruammit & Th Din Daeng; subway Thailand Cultural Centre) Occasionally, classical dance performances are held at this venue featuring a concert hall, art gallery and outdoor studios. Regional Thai concerts, featuring *lûuk thûng* (Thai country music) and Khorat Song from the town of Khorat, cycle through the calendar. International dance and theatre groups are also profiled, especially during the International Festival of Dance & Music (p142).

Thai Boxing (Muay Thai)

The best of the best fight at Bangkok's two boxing stadiums: **Lumphini Stadium** (Sanam Muay Lumphini; Map p117; Th Phra Ram IV; subway Lumphini) and **Ratchadamnoen Stadium** (Sanam Muay Ratchadamnoen; Map pp110-11; Th Ratchadamnoen Nok; bus 503, 509, 70). Tickets at both stadiums cost 500B for 3rd-class; 800B, 2nd class; and 1500B, ringside. Be forewarned that these admission prices are more than double what Thais pay, and the inflated price offers no special service or seating. In fact, at Ratchadamnoen Stadium, foreigners are sometimes corralled into an area with an obstructed view. As long as you are mentally prepared for the financial jabs from the promoters, then you'll be better prepared to enjoy the real fight. Lumphini is likely to close at the end of 2005 (along with the Night Bazaar; see p176), and activities will move to a new stadium under construction on Th Nang Linji (Map pp104-5).

Ringside puts you right up on the central action but amid a fairly subdued crowd where gambling is prohibited. Second-class seats are filled with backpackers and numbers runners who take the bets from the crowd. Like being in the pit of a stock exchange, hand signals fly between the 2nd- and 3rd-class areas communicating bets and odds. The 3rd-class area is the rowdiest section. Fenced off from the rest of the stadium, most of the die-hard fans follow the match (or their bets) too closely to sit down. If you're lukewarm on watching two men punch and kick each other, then 3rd-class offers the diversion of the crowd.

Fights are held throughout the week alternating between the two stadiums. Ratchadamnoen hosts the matches on Monday, Wednesday and Thursday at 6pm and on Sunday at 5pm. Lumphini hosts matches on Tuesday, Friday and Saturday at 6pm. Aficionados say the best-matched bouts are reserved for Tuesday nights at Lumphini and Thursday nights at Ratchadamnoen. There are a total of eight to 10 fights of five rounds a piece. The stadiums don't usually fill up until the main events, which usually start around 8pm or 9pm.

There are English-speaking 'staff' outside the stadium who will practically tackle you upon arrival. Although there have been a few reports of scamming, most of these assistants help steer visitors to the foreigner ticket windows and hand out a fight roster; they can also be helpful in telling you which fights are the best match-ups. (Some say that welterweights, between 135 and 147 pounds, are the best). To keep everyone honest, though, remember to purchase tickets from the ticket window not from a person outside the stadium.

As a prematch warm-up, catch a plate of *kài yâang* (grilled chicken) and other northeastern dishes from the restaurants surrounding the Ratchadamnoen Stadium.

SHOPPING

Regular visitors to Asia know that, in many ways, Bangkok beats Hong Kong and Singapore for good deals on handicrafts, textiles and designer knock-offs. And for the shopping addicts, Thailand's well-honed sense of fun is elevated to elation in the shopping malls and markets where bargaining is all smiles and compliments.

The difficulty is finding your way around since the city's intense urban tangle makes orientation sometimes difficult. A good shopping companion is *Nancy Chandler's Map of Bangkok,* with annotations on all sorts of small and out-of-the-way shopping venues and markets *(tàlàat).*

Antiques

Real Thai antiques are rare and costly. Most Bangkok antique shops keep a few authentic pieces for collectors, along with lots of pseudo-antiques or traditionally crafted items that look like antiques. The majority of shop operators are quite candid about what's really old and what isn't.

Nagi Arts (Map pp118-19; ☎ 0 2253 2826; 27/4 Th Withayu Neua; khlong taxi to Tha Withayu, Skytrain Chitlom, bus 62, 76) Once occupying the grounds of the preservationist Siam Society, Nagi has moved to a larger facility directly across the street from Raffles Nai Lert Park hotel. But the collection is just as eclectic as before – ancient textiles, old texts and Asian journals, and regional Buddhas.

River City Complex (Map pp108-9; Th Yotha, off Th Charoen Krung; ☾ many stores close Sun; river ferry Tha Si Phraya) Near the Royal Orchid Sheraton Hotel, this multistorey shopping centre is an all-in-one stop for old-world Asiana. Several high-quality art and antique shops occupy the 3rd and 4th floors. **Acala** is a gallery of unusual Tibetan and Chinese artefacts. **Old Maps & Prints** offers one of the best selections of one-of-a-kind, rare maps and illustrations, with a focus on Asia. Although the quality is high, the prices are too, as many wealthy tourists filter in and out.

Triphum (Map pp118-19; ☎ 0 2656 1795; 3rd fl, Gaysorn Plaza; Th Ploenchit; Skytrain Chitlom) Southeast Asian art and antiques avaiable here achieve at-home museum worthiness. Savour the detail of the mother-of-pearl inlaid cabinets and lacquerware scripture texts.

Department Stores & Shopping Centres

Bangkok may be crowded and polluted, but its department stores are modern oases of order. By no accident, the Skytrain stations often have shaded walkways delivering passengers directly into nearby stores without ever having to set foot on ground level.

One pesky tradition is that shop assistants follow you around the store from rack to rack like the lonely new girl at school. This is the definition of Thai 'service' rather than an indication that they've sniffed you out as a shoplifter. Be sure you're satisfied with an item as returns are an unimported phenomenon.

Central Department Store (Map pp118-19; flagship store ☎ 0 2233 6930-9; 1027 Th Ploenchit; Skytrain Chitlom) Generally regarded as the all-round best for quality and selection, Central has 13 branches in Bangkok in addition to this chi-chi flagship. Assume the self-assured, slightly bored air of a telecom princess before being bludgeoned at the rack for being a large (when in the 'real' world you are petite). And if you're curious about local hooks, look for Thai designers, like Tube, and the Thai cosmetic brand Erb.

Siam Center & Siam Discovery Center (Map pp118-19; cnr Th Phra Ram I & Th Phayathai; Skytrain National Stadium & Siam) These linked sister centres feel almost monastic in their hushed hallways compared to frenetic MBK, just across the street. Siam Discovery Center excels in home décor with the whole 3rd floor devoted to Asian-minimalist styles and jewel-toned fabrics. Attached Siam Center, Thailand's first shopping centre built in 1976, hardly shows its age thanks to such age-defying stores as must-have basics for the slaves to Thai name brands. Set to open in 2005, the affiliated Siam Paragon, being constructed on the once lush gardens of the Siam Intercontinental, plans to duplicate the upmarket collection of the Emporium.

Mahboonkrong (MBK; Map pp118-19; ☎ 0 2217 9111; cnr Th Phra Ram I & Th Phayathai; Skytrain National Stadium) Capturing the spirit of Thailand's outdoor markets into comfy air-con, MBK is a Bangkok teen's home away from home. On any given weekend, half the city can be found here combing through an inexhaustible range of small stalls and shops or shuffling (sometimes tentatively) up and down the escalators. This is the cheapest place to buy contact lenses, mobile (cell) phones and accessories, and name-brand knock-offs. The Travel Mart on the 3rd floor stocks a reasonable supply of travel gear and camping equipment – not the highest quality but useful in a pinch.

Siam Square (Map pp118-19; btwn Th Phra Ram I & Th Phayathai) This low-slung commercial universe is a network of some 12 sois lined with trendy teenage shops, many of which are the first ventures of young designers. For the fully endowed Westerner, the fashions here won't cover their left foot, but the fast-food options will soothe homesickness. The varying weekend product promotions are always an entertaining pit of model girls and breakdancers.

Gaysorn Plaza (Map pp118-19; cnr Th Ploenchit & Th Ratchadamri; Skytrain Chitlom) A *haute couture* catwalk, Gaysorn's spiralling staircases and all-white halls preserve all of fashion's beloved designers under museum-curatorship style. Thai fashion leaders, like Fly Now (2nd floor), have also sewn themselves into this international collage. The top floor is an irresistible stroll through chic and antique home décor.

Emporium Shopping Centre (Map pp112-13; 622 Th Sukhumvit, cnr Soi 24; Skytrain Phrom Phong) You might not have access to the beautiful people's nightlife scene, but you can observe their spending rituals at this temple to red hot and classic cool. Robust expat salaries and trust funds dwindle amid Prada, Miu Miu, Chanel and Thai brands such as Greyhound and Propaganda.

Pantip Plaza (Map pp118-19; ☎ 0 2656 5030; 604 Th Phetchaburi; Skytrain Ratchathewi) North of Siam Square, this is the best place to buy computer equipment and digital cameras. It has five storeys of computer stores ranging from legit to flea market, covering genuine and openly pirated software, peripherals and hardware.

Fashion & Textiles

The market on Khao San carries all the 'going native' clothes needed for the backpacker uniform, a look that may rival denim jeans in longevity. For a little fashion exploration, take a peek into the trends and tastes of the elite and stylish at these equally native designers.

Mae Fah Luang (Map pp118-19; ☎ 0 2658 0424; www.doitung.org; 4th fl, Siam Discovery Center, cnr Th Phayathai & Th Phra Ram; Skytrain Siam) For a royally funded project, Mae Fah Luang ventures into impressive fashionable realms with its feminine cotton suits and skirts. The hand-

made cotton and linen come from villages formerly involved with poppy production.

Fly Now (Map pp118-19; ☎ 0 2656 1359; 2nd fl, Gaysorn Plaza, cnr Th Ploenchit & Th Ratchadamri; Skytrain Chitlom) With the rise of such designers as Chamnan Phakdeesuk, Bangkok is hoping to position itself as a regional couture closet. The flattering lines of Khun Chamnan's designs have made it all the way to London's Fashion Week runways and back.

Jaspal (Map pp118-19; ☎ 0 2658 1000-19; Siam Discovery Center, cnr Th Phayathai & Th Phra Ram I; Skytrain Siam) Cute snappy basics boldly tattooed with this home-grown label pop up on all the Siam Square prince and princesses and even on regional MTV hosts. Don't be surprised if you see misspelled rip-offs in the markets. There are also branches at the Emporium (Map pp112–13) and Central World Plaza (Map pp118–19).

Greyhound (Map pp112-13; ☎ 0 2260 7121; www.greyhound.co.th; 2nd fl, Emporium, Th Sukhumvit, btwn Soi 22 & 24; ⏰ 10.30am-10pm; Skytrain Phrom Phong) Streetwear for people who have drivers and dual citizenship, Greyhound is a local lifestyle brand that includes the posey Greyhound Cafe (p165). There are also branches in the Siam Center (Map pp118–19) and in Central Chitlom.

Alta Moda (Map pp118-19; ☎ 0 2255 9533; 1st fl, Central World Plaza, cnr Th Phra Ram I & Th Ratchadamri; Skytrain Chitlom, khlong taxi to Tha Pratunam) If you've taken the leap into the tailoring realm, peruse the silk, cotton and linen options from international fashion houses.

Jim Thompson (Map pp114-16; ☎ 0 2632 8100; www.jimthompson.com; 9 Th Surawong; ⏰ 9am-9pm; Skytrain Sala Daeng & Silom) The company credited with creating an international market for Thai silk is now solidly positioned with the tastes of the middle-aged mamas. Bolts of fabric, silk scarves and neckties, table accessories are all of the highest quality. Beware of touts hanging around this store trying to divert customers to another shop that pays commissions. The branch on the 4th floor of the Emporium (Map pp112–13) carries younger designs.

Handicrafts

The tourist markets have tonnes of factory-made pieces that will pop up all along the tourist route. The shopping centres sell a little better quality at proportionally higher prices, but the independent shops sell the best quality all round.

Silom Village Trade Centre (Map pp114-16; Soi 24; Th Silom) Behind the Silom Village Inn, this arcade full of compact shops sells souvenir-quality reproductions, including teak carvings, textiles, *khon* masks and ceramics. The pace is relaxed and rarely crowded.

Narayana Phand (Map pp118-19; ☎ 0 2252 4670; Th Ratchadamri; Skytrain Chitlom, khlong taxi to Tha Pratunam) A bit on the touristy side, this huge warehouse is a government-run enterprise funnelling run-of-the-mill knick-knacks to the masses. No haggling is necessary at this place.

Maison des Arts (Map pp114-16; ☎ 0 2233 6297; 1334 Th Charoen Krung; ☻ 11am-6pm Mon-Sat; Skytrain Saphan Taksin, bus 75, 115, 116, river ferry Tha Oriental) For the recently hitched couple still struggling to populate their new nest, these hand-hammered, stainless steel flatware pieces might be what the registry was lacking. The bold style dates back to a 15th-century tradition, and the staff apply no pressure to the indecisive shoppers.

Suan Lum Night Bazaar (Map p117; cnr Th Withayu & Th Phra Ram IV; ☻ 6pm-midnight; subway Lumphini, bus 13, 17, 76, 106) This government-backed bonanza is a tour group–friendly night market selling modern Thai souvenirs and handicrafts that rank a notch above the street-stall varieties. Somehow bargaining is almost nonexistent. The Night Bazaar, as well as the neighbouring Lumphini Boxing Stadium, stands on a valuable piece of land belonging to the Crown Property Bureau (CPB), which is currently seeking business partners who can pay higher rents. Once a new deal is agreed upon, the Night Bazaar will close down, which will most likely be by the end of 2005.

Rasi Sayam (Map pp112-13; ☎ 0 2258 4195; 32 Soi 23, Th Sukhumvit; ☻ 9am-5.30pm Mon-Sat; Skytrain Asoke) In a shady wooden house, Rasi Sayam sells charming wall hangings, *benjarong* (Thai ceramics), basketry and pottery that are made specifically for this shop by handicraft villages.

Nandakwang (Map pp112-13; ☎ 0 2258 1962; 108/3 Soi 23, Th Sukhumvit; Skytrain Nana) A branch of a factory shop from northern Thailand, Nandakwang specialises in high-quality woven cotton handbags, totes and table linens. There are also some precious stuffed animals. To get there, take the first street on the right as you head north up Soi 23. There is also another branch in Siam Discovery Center (Map pp118–19).

Taekee Taekon (Map pp110-11; ☎ 0 2629 1473; 118 Th Phra Athit; ☻ 10am-5pm Mon-Sat; river ferry Tha Phra Athit) Representing Thailand's main silk-producing regions, this charming store has a beautiful selection of table runners and wall hangings. You'll also find small examples of celadon and blue-and-white china.

Gems & Jewellery

Recommending specific shops is tricky, since one coloured stone looks as good as another to the average eye – the risk of a rip-off is much greater than for most other shopping items. Be sceptical of recommendations from *túk-túk* drivers, hotel staff, strangers on the street and even from fellow travellers (who might be in denial about being ripped off). One shop that's been a long-time favourite with Bangkok's expats for service and value in set jewellery is **Johnny's Gems** (Map pp108-9; ☎ 0 2224 4065; 199 Th Fuang Nakhon), off Th Charoen Krung.

THE WAR ON THE GEM SCAM

We're begging you, if you aren't a gem trader then don't buy unset stones in Thailand – period. Countless tourists are sucked into the prolific and well-rehearsed gem scam in which they are taken to a store by a helpful stranger and are tricked into buying bulk gems that can supposedly be resold in their home country for 100% profit. The expert con artists (part of a well organised cartel) seem trustworthy and convince tourists that they need a citizen of the country to circumvent tricky customs regulations. Guess what, the gem world doesn't work like that, and what most tourists end up with are worthless pieces of glass. By the time you sort all this out, the store has closed, changed names and the police do little to help. Want to know more or want to report a scam? Visit www.2Bangkok.com and navigate to the 'Gem Scam' page for five years' worth of tracking the phenomenon or go to Thai Gems Scam Group (www.geocities.com/thaigemscamgroup) for photos of touts who troll the temples for victims.

Markets

Quintessential Thailand and all its do-it-yourself entrepreneurial spirit can be found among the city's markets, occupying unused alleys or treacherous sidewalks. Most vendors are women who raise their children alongside a stall packed with an odd assortment of plastic toys, household goods and polyester clothes in Asian sizes mixed with knock-off designer watches and bags. Even more interesting are the food markets where Thais forage for brightly coloured tapioca desserts, spicy curries and fruit that look like medieval torture devices.

ALL-PURPOSE MARKETS

Chatuchak Weekend Market (Talat Nat Jatujak; Map pp104–5; 8am-6pm Sat & Sun; Skytrain Mo Chit, subway Chatuchak Park) This is it, the big one you've heard about. The behemoth of Thai markets where everything imaginable is for sale – from handmade silks from the provinces, extra-small fashion for the art-school fashionistas, fighting cocks and fighting fish, fluffy puppies and every imaginable souvenir. Although variety is its claim to fame, the markets speciality is clothing. Don't forget to try out your bargaining skills.

Plan to spend a full day, as there's plenty to see, do and buy. But come early to beat the crowds and the heat. If everything starts to inexplicably suck, then you are suffering from dehydration and need a pit-stop at one of the many food stalls. There is an information centre (which hands out maps) and a bank with ATMs and foreign-exchange booths at the Chatuchak Park offices, near the northern end of the market's Soi 1, Soi 2 and Soi 3. Schematic maps and toilets are conveniently located throughout the market.

There are a few vendors out on weekday mornings and a daily vegetable, plant and flower market opposite the market's southern side. One section of the latter, known as the Aw Taw Kaw Market, sells organically grown fruit and vegetables and is a good spot for tasty duck curry.

Sampeng Lane (Map pp108–9; Soi Wanit 1, Chinatown; river ferry Tha Ratchawong) Wholesale market runs roughly parallel to Th Yaowarat, bisecting the two districts of Chinatown and Phahurat. Pick up the narrow artery from Th Ratchawong and follow it through its many manifestations – handbags, house-

wares, hair decorations, stickers, Japanese animation gear, plastic beeping keychains. As the lane cuts across into Phahurat, fabric shops, many operated by Indian (mostly Sikh) merchants, start to dominate. Unless you're shopping for a grassroots import-export group, Sampeng is more for entertainment than for purchases.

Nakhon Kasem (Map pp108–9; Th Yaowarat & Th Chakrawat; river ferry Tha Saphan Phut) Also known as the Thieves Market because this area used to specialise in stolen goods, Nakhon Kasem has gone legit with industrial-sized cooking equipment, spare electronic parts, and other bits you didn't even know could be resold. For the budding entrepreneur, all the portable street stall gear for frying bananas, making *phàt thai* or grinding coconuts are sold here.

Phahurat Market (Map pp108–9; Th Phahurat & Th Triphet, across from Old Siam Plaza; river ferry Tha Saphan Phut) The Indian fabric district prefers boisterous colours, faux fur, neon sparkles and everything you'll need for a Halloween costume or a traditional Thai dance drama. Deeper into the market are cute clothes for kids and good deals on traditional Thai textiles.

Pratunam Market (Map pp118–19; cnr Th Phetburi & Th Ratchaprarop; 8am-6pm; khlong taxi to Tha Pratunam) Considered the in-town version of Chatuchak, Pratunam is a tight warren of stalls trickling deep into the block. Cheap clothes, luggage, bulk toiletries, market-lady sarongs and souvenirs are just a few options.

Banglamphu Market (Map pp110–11; Th Chakkraphong, Th Tanao & Th Tani; 9am-6pm; river ferry Tha Phra Athit) Spread out over several blocks, the Banglamphu market attracts a no-nonsense crew of street vendors selling snacks, handbags, brassieres, pyjamas, household items and night-blooming jasmine flower buds (*phuang malai*). You may never come here on purpose, but passing through invariably leads to a purchase.

Soi Lalaisap (Map pp114–16; Soi 5, Th Silom; open 8am-6pm; Skytrain Chong Nonsi) The 'money-melting' street has a number of vendors selling all sorts of cheap clothing, watches and homewares during the day. Regular perusers say that imperfections from name-brand factories often appear in the stacks.

Khlong Toey Market (Map pp112–13; cnr Th Phra Ram IV & Th Narong) Beside Bangkok's port, this market is the cheapest all-purpose choice proffering regional food stuff, fresh meat and kitchen supplies.

FLOWER MARKETS

Pak Khlong Market (Map pp108-9; Th Chakkaphet & Th Atsadang; ⊙ 8am-6pm; river ferry Tha Saphan Phut) Near the river and the mouth of Khlong Lawt, Pak Khlong is the city's largest wholesale flower source. The colourful displays of baby roses and delicate orchids are endless and so inexpensive that even a cement-cell dweller on Th Khao San could afford a bouquet. Pak Khlong is also a big market for vegetables and will soon be renovated to be Bangkok's latest tourist attraction. If the controversial plans are carried out, the area will be developed into a tourist park complete with floating market and green space.

Thewet Market (Map pp106-7; Th Krung Kasem, off Th Samsen) You'll find a good selection of tropical flowers and plants available at this low-key market creating a temporary garden near Tha Thewet.

Talat Phahonyothin (Map pp104-5; Phahonyothin Market; Th Kampaengphet; Skytrain Mo Chit, Subway Chatuchak Park) The city's largest plant market is opposite the southern side of Chatuchak Market.

TOURIST MARKETS

The souvenir sellers have an amazing knack for sniffing out what new arrivals want to haul back home – perennial favourites include raunchy T-shirts, Thai axe pillows, bootleg CDs and synthetic sarongs. Not all tourist markets are created equally: porn is hard to come by on Th Khao San, but plentiful on Th Sukhumvit; and hemp clothing is noticeably absent from Patpong.

Th Sukhumvit Market (Map pp112-13; Th Sukhumvit btwn Soi 2 & 12, 3 & 15; ⊙ 11am-10.30pm; Skytrain Nana) Knock-offs bags and watches, stacks of skin-flick DVDs, Chinese throwing stars, penis lighters and other questionable gifts for your high-school aged brother predominate at this market peddling to package and sex tourists.

Th Khao San Market (Map pp110-11; Th Khao San, ⊙ 11am-11pm; river ferry Tha Phra Athit) The main guesthouse strip in Banglamphu is a day and night shopping bazaar for the serious baht-pinchers. Cheap T-shirts, bootleg CDs, wooden elephants, hemp clothing, Thai axe pillows (a traditional Thai wedge-shaped pillow), fisherman pants, and other

goods that make backpackers go ga-ga. Ask around to find out which of the vendors sell the best-quality CDs, many skip so bad that they aren't worthy of a second career as a coaster.

Patpong Night Market (Map pp114-16; Patpong Soi 1 & 2, Th Silom; ⊙ 6pm-midnight; Skytrain Sala Daeng) Drawing more crowds than the ping-pong shows, this market continues the street's illicit leanings with a deluge of pirated goods. Bargain with intensity as first-quoted prices tend to be astronomically high.

Photography Supplies & Processing

If you haven't joined the digital revolution, Bangkok still has a wide selection of slide and print film. **Central Department Store** (Map pp118-19; Th Ploenchit) also has a good camera department with some surprisingly reasonable prices.

Foto Hobby (Map pp114-16; ☎ 0 2231 3232; 3rd fl, Silom Complex, Th Silom) Operated by an award-winning Thai photographer, this pro-shop sells Canon EOS and other equipment.

Image Quality Lab (IQ Lab; Map pp114-16; ☎ 0 2266 4080; 160/5 ITF Bldg, Th Silom) In Silom, follow the car park into the ITF building to reach a small island of shops. Quick, professional-quality processing of most film types is available at these outlets.

Niks/Nava Import Export (Map pp114-16; ☎ 0 2233 2288; 166 Th Silom; ⊙ 11am-4pm Mon-Fri; Skytrain Chong Nonsi) On the northwestern corner of Soi 12, Niks sells all types of professional equipment, and services for Nikon, Mamiya and Rollei.

Sunny Camera Charoen Krung (Map pp114-16; ☎ 0 2235 2123, 0 2233 8378; 1267/1 Th Charoen Krung); Silom (Map pp114-16; ☎ 0 2236 8627, 144/23 Th Silom); MBK (Map pp118-19; ☎ 0 2217 9293, 3rd fl, MBK). For a wide range of camera models and brands, this multibranch dealer is worth a look.

Tailors

Tailors are as prolific as massage parlours in Bangkok and so are the scams. Workmanship ranges from shoddy to excellent, so it pays to ask around before committing yourself. And don't be fooled by the cut-rate specials, such as four shirts, two suits, a kimono and a safari suit (!) all in one package – you'll be disappointed by the quality. Avoid any tailor shop suggested by a stranger you meet on the street or by a túk-túk driver, as these usually pay high

---

YOU CLEAN UP GOOD

Thanks to the diplomatic corps in Bangkok, the old-world tradition of custom tailoring is alive and well and affordable for the proletariat among us. In order to get the best deal, you need to enter the negotiations as an informed participant. Here is a quick primer on the basics, giving you a spring board for gathering more sartorial expertise.

Material

You want a material light enough to drape but not too light that it will wrinkle. Worsted wool from Italy or England is usually the best candidate. Squeeze the fabric and then release it to see if it snaps back into shape without wrinkling. A suit made from a quality fabric should achieve a pressed look after a day's hanging.

Style

Determine what the primary function of your suit will be – work, evening or formal. This will determine the suit's silhouette. For a classic business suit, the jacket is typically cut with natural, sloping shoulders and tapered at the waist. Jackets with double vents or side vents, favouring the Saville Row aesthetic, are considered the best compromise between form and function. Pleated trousers (with two pleats on either side of the zipper) are often prescribed for conservative longevity. Cuffs help the pleats hang straight.

Fittings

Bring a dress shirt and dress shoes for fittings. For the jacket, the collar shouldn't creep up or flap away from your neck and 2cm (¾in) of the shirt collar should stand above the jacket. The jacket should lie flat across the shoulders without puckering. A smooth unbroken line should follow the shoulder all along the sleeve.

For the trousers, make sure the pleats aren't opening while standing. The front crease should intersect the middle of the kneecap and finish in the middle of the shoe. The bottom of the trouser should end on the top of the shoe, covering the socks while walking.

For striped patterns, make sure stripes line up at the seams.

---

commissions, thus driving the cost of the work far beyond its normal value.

Selecting a tailor is a courtship that takes time to develop and is built on communication and respect. Before you engage a tailor on a big custom job, assess their workmanship by looking at works in progress or commissioning them to copy a small item of clothing. 'Designer' shirts can be knocked off for not much more than a tenth of the designer price. Wear the piece for awhile to make sure it can withstand wear and tear before returning with business.

Once you find a tailor you trust, the next hurdle is selecting quality fabric. Be especially wary of 100% cotton claims, which are usually a blend of cotton and a synthetic. More than a few tailors will actually try to pass off full polyester or synthetics as cotton. Good-quality silk, on the other hand, is plentiful. Be suspicious of fake Italian and English wools as well; inspect the border of the fabric for any misspellings (usually a

sign of an inferior fabric being passed off as an import). If the tailoring shop doesn't offer fabrics to your liking, you can supply your own material from another source.

Shirts and trousers can be turned around in 48 hours or less with only one fitting. But no matter what a tailor may tell you, it takes more than one or two fittings to create a good suit, and most reputable tailors will ask for two to five sittings.

A sturdy custom-made suit of a quality wool should cost US$250. Tailor-made silk shirts should cost no more than US$15 to US$25.

GETTING THERE & AWAY
Air

Bangkok is a major centre for international flights throughout Asia (see p744 for details about services to and from the city from abroad). Be warned that many travel agencies in Bangkok, especially on Th Khao San, are more crooked than a mountain pass.

Bangkok International Airport (Map p104-5; Don Muang; general inquiries ☎ 0 2535 1111; departures ☎ 0 2535 1254, 0 2535 1386; arrivals ☎ 0 2535 1301, 0 2535 1149; www.airportthai.co.th) is 25km north of the city and receives all international and domestic flights until the opening of the new Suvarnabhumi airport. The future of Don Muang after the opening is unclear. Some proponents want it to continue as a domestic and cargo airport, while others want to retire it from commercial service.

Suvarnabhumi International Airport (Map p186; ☎ 0 2723 0000; www.bangkokairport.org) is under construction at Nong Ngu Hao (Cobra Lake), 25km east of Bangkok, and is scheduled to open some time in 2006 or later, much later, says everyone but the prime minister. Once the new airport is up to full capacity, it will be the largest airport in Asia and able to handle Airbus A380s (555-seaters).

AIRLINES

Thailand's national carrier, **Thai Airways International** (THAI; Map p114-16; reservations ☎ 0 2280 0060, ☎ 0 2232 8000; Empire Bldg, 485 Th Silom) operates many domestic air routes from Bangkok.

The airline budget bug has taken a hold in Asia. No-frills airlines, offering cheaper and more flexible fares than traditional airlines, link Bangkok with regional capitals or major cities within Thailand. Costs are kept low by cutting out complimentary beverage and food service, and most have open seating plans. In the case of Orient Thai, you can even save money by just showing up at the airport to buy a ticket rather than advance booking. The following budget airlines have offices in Bangkok.

Air Asia (Map p104-5; ☎ 0 2515 9999; www.airasia.com; 18th fl, Block B, Elephant Tower, Th Ratchadaphisek)

Bangkok Airways (Map pp104-5; ☎ 0 2265 5678, 0 2265 5555; www.bangkokair.com; 99 Mu 14, Th Viphavadi Rangsit) At the airport.

Dragon Air (Map p114-16; ☎ 0 2266 2651-4; www.dragonair.com; 15th fl, Unit B, Silom Complex, 191 Th Silom)

Nok Air (Map pp112-13; ☎ 1318; www.nokair.co.th; 11th fl, Pacific Place, 140 Th Sukhumvit)

Orient Thai (Map pp114-16; ☎ 0 2267 2999; www.orient-thai.com; 17th fl, Jewellery Center, 138/70 Th Naret)

Phuket Air (off Map p117; ☎ 0 2679 8999; www.phuketairlines.com; 34th B fl, Lumphini Tower, 1168/71 Th Rama IV)

Bus

Bangkok is the centre for bus services that fan out all over the kingdom.

BUS STATIONS

There are three main public bus terminals. Allow an hour to reach all terminals from central Bangkok.

Northern & Northeastern bus terminal (Map pp104-5; for northern routes ☎ 0 2936 3659-60; for northeastern routes ☎ 0 2936 2852, 0 2936 2841-8; Th Kamphaeng Phet) is just north of Chatuchak Park. It's also commonly called Moh Chit station (sàthǎanii mǎw chít). Buses depart from here for northern and northeastern destinations such as Chiang Mai and Nakhon Ratchasima (Khorat), as well as Ayuthaya and Lopburi. Buses to Aranya Prathet also leave from here, not from the Eastern bus terminal as you might expect. To reach the bus station, take Skytrain to Mo Chit and transfer onto city bus 512 and 523, 3, 49 or 77.

Eastern bus terminal (Map pp104-5; ☎ 0 2391 2504; Soi 40/Soi Ekamai, Th Sukhumvit) is the departure point for buses to Pattaya, Rayong, Chanthaburi and other points east. Most people call it Ekamai station (sàthǎanii èkkà mai). The Skytrain stops at its own Ekamai station in front of Soi 40.

Southern bus terminal (Map pp104-5; ☎ 0 2434 7192; Hwy 338/Th Nakhon Chaisi & Th Phra Pinkao, Thonburi) handles buses south to Phuket, Surat Thani and closer centres to the west like Nakhon Pathom and Kanchanaburi. This station known as Sai Tai Mai (sàthǎanii sàai tâai mài) is in Thonburi. To reach the station, take bus 503, 507, 509, 511, 30, 124 or 127. There are plans are to move the terminal further out of town to the Buddhamonthon Soi 3 area, but at the time of research, nothing had transpired.

BUS COMPANIES & SAFETY

The most reputable bus companies depart from the public bus terminals. Private buses and minivans that pick up customers from tourist centres such as Th Khao San experience a higher incidence of reported theft, lateness and unreliability. On these tourist-oriented services, the alleged VIP bus turns out to be a cramped minibus that arrives four hours late. Readers have also consistently reported having their stowed bags rifled through or even being gassed and having valuables stolen directly from their person.

When travelling on all night buses take care of your belongings. Keep all valuables on your person, not stored in your luggage.

For details on bus fares to/from other towns and cities in Thailand, the relevant destination chapters.

Train

Bangkok is the terminus for the main rail services to the south, north, northeast and east. There are two principal train stations.

Hualamphong station (Map pp108-9; general information ☎ 1690, advance booking ☎ 0 2220 4444; Th Phra Ram IV) handles services to the north, northeast and south. Smiling 'information' staff will try to direct all arrivals to a TAT-licensed travel agency in the mezzanine level who will arrange transportation on a commission basis. To skip the charge, make all arrangements on the ground floor at ticketing windows. To get to the station from Sukhumvit take the subway to the Hualamphong stop. From western points (Banglamphu, Thewet) take bus 53.

Thonburi station (Map p120; Bangkok Noi) handles services to Nakhon Pathom, Kanchanaburi and Nam Tok. The station can be reached by river ferry to Tha Rot Fai.

GETTING AROUND

The main obstacle to getting around Bangkok is the traffic, which introduces a 45-minute delay to any daytime outings. This means advance planning is a must when you are attending scheduled events or arranging appointments.

If you can travel by river, canal or Skytrain from one point to another (ie avoid the roads), it's always the best choice.

To/From the Airport

Depending on the traffic, expect an hour's transit time between central Bangkok and the airport. A free shuttle bus runs between the international and domestic terminal.

BANGKOK INTERNATIONAL AIRPORT (DON MUANG)

Airport Bus

A private bus service operates three different routes into Bangkok from the airport. Tickets cost 100B per person, and buses run every 30 minutes from 6am to 12.30am. A

map showing the designated stops is available at the airport; the buses on each route make approximately six stops in each direction. If you're travelling solo, this service is cheaper than a taxi, but if there is more than one person in your party, a taxi is more cost effective.

From the international terminal, follow the signs for ground transportation. The Airport Bus counter is to the left of the taxi desk directly beside the terminal.

- A-1 runs into the Silom business district via Pratunam and Th Ratchadamri, stopping at big hotels like the Century, Grand Hyatt Erawan, Regent Bangkok and Dusit Thani.
- A-2 runs to Banglamphu via Th Phayathai, Th Lan Luang, Th Ratchadamnoen Klang, Th Tanao, Th Phra Athit and then Sanam Luang; this is the best route for the Victory Monument, Democracy Monument or Banglamphu/Th Khao San areas. In Banglamphu, it stops on Th Phra Athit near Soi Chana Songkhram.
- A-3 runs to Th Sukhumvit, including Ekamai station (for buses east to Pattaya and Trat) and Soi 55 (Soi Thong Lor). Hotel stops include the Sheraton and the Westin Grande.

Public Bus

Commuter public buses travel from the airport to Bangkok. These are the cheapest options, but take the longest and aren't recommendable for first-time arrivals as it is difficult to identify your stop if you're unfamiliar with the city. Buses stop on the highway in front of the airport.

There are two non-air-con bus routes and four air-con routes; take note, however, that the non-air-con buses no longer accept passengers carrying luggage. The trip into central Bangkok on an airport bus will cost 18B (air-con bus) or 4B to 5.50B (ordinary bus).

- Air-con bus 29 runs 24 hours a day and is best suited for destinations in Siam Square and the Hualamphong area. After entering the city via Th Phahonyothin, (which turns into Th Phayathai), the bus passes Th Phetburi (get off to change buses for Banglamphu), then Th Phra Ram I at Siam Square and Mahboonkrong shopping centre (for buses out to Th Sukhumvit, or to walk to Soi Kasem San 1). It finally turns right on Th Phra

Ram IV to go to the Hualamphong district (where the main train station is located). You'll want to go the opposite way on Th Phra Ram IV for the Soi Ngam Duphli lodging area.

- Air-con bus 513 operates from 4.30am to 9pm. This bus best serves destinations in the Th Sukhumvit area. Leaving the airport, the bus travels Th Phahonyothin (like 29), turning left at Victory Monument to Th Ratchaprarop, then south to Th Ploenchit, where it travels east along Th Sukhumvit all the way to Bang Na.

- Air-con bus 504 operates from 4.10am to 8.30pm and is best suited for destinations in the Silom area. It begins with a route parallel to that of bus 29 bus – down Th Viphavadi Rangsit to Th Ratchaprarop and Th Ratchadamri (Pratunam district), crossing Th Phetburi, Th Phra Ram I, Th Ploenchit and Th Phra Ram IV, then down Th Silom and left on Th Charoen Krung to Thonburi.

- Air-con bus 510 goes from the airport to the Southern bus terminal in Thonburi and operates from 4.10am to 9.30pm.

- Ordinary bus 59 (no luggage permitted) operates 24 hours. It zigzags through to Banglamphu (the Democracy Monument area) from the airport, a trip that can take up to 1¾ hours or more in traffic.

Taxi

After a long flight, you owe it to yourself to take a taxi from the airport. Taxis provide door-to-door service from the airport to your hotel. Most reliable for first-time visitors are the metered taxis; from the arrivals hall in the airport, follow the signs to the metered-taxi desk, which is right outside the international terminal. Metered cabs should cost 200B to 300B depending on the destination, plus 50B airport surcharge and tolls (40B to 80B).

Nonmetered taxis will approach you in the arrival hall or in the metered-taxi line. In the past, these gypsy cabs were pretty ruthless in overcharging or even robbing customers. Touts from the old taxi mafia that used to prowl the arrival area are still around and may approach you with fares of around 200B. Their taxis have white-and-black plates and are not licensed to carry passengers, hence you have less legal recourse in the event of an incident than if you take a licensed taxi (yellow-and-black plates).

The occasional metered-taxi driver will refuse to use his meter and quote a flat rate of 300B to 400B; however, this is rarer than it used to be. Passengers now receive a bilingual Taxi-Meter Information sheet, issued by the Department of Land Transport, which indicates the name of the driver, the taxi licence number, the date and the time. A phone number for registering complaints against the driver is listed on this sheet, if you should have a problem. The passenger – *not* the driver – is supposed to keep this sheet. The driver may want to glance at the sheet to read your destination, but you should receive it back immediately.

Metered taxis, flagged down on the highway in front of the airport (turn left from the arrival hall), are even cheaper since they don't have to pay the 50B airport surcharge. When the queue at the public-taxi desk is particularly long, it's sometimes faster to go upstairs or walk out to the highway and flag one down.

Train

You can also get into Bangkok from the airport by train; this is recommendable for middle-of-the-day arrivals and departures. Inside Terminal 1 follow the signs for trains to Bangkok; you'll cross the highway via the pedestrian bridge, which leads to Don Muang train station. Buy tickets from the booth on the airport side of the tracks. The fare from Don Muang to Bangkok is 5B to 21B, depending on the type of train (ordinary, rapid, express).

Trains heading into Bangkok run half-hourly from 2am to 6.30am. There is a 2½-hour gap until the next train at 9am and then a succession of hourly departures until 8.45pm. It takes 45 minutes to one hour to reach Hualamphong, the main station in central Bangkok.

In the opposite direction trains depart almost hourly between 6.00am and noon. Services resume at 2pm until 11pm.

Bus 53 runs from Hualamphong station to Banglamphu. The bus stop is next to the station beside a gang of motorcycle and *túk-túk* drivers who would gladly accept your business.

Some travellers disembark from the airport and catch trains from Don Muang train station to Ayuthaya, Sukhothai, Khorat or other points in the north or northeast, thus avoiding Bangkok altogether.

SUVARNABHUMI INTERNATIONAL AIRPORT
At the time of writing, the new international airport had not yet opened nor had any transport links, so information is subject to change. According to plans, the airport will be accessible by five highway links, and transit time to central Bangkok is estimated to be 35 to 45 minutes. Metered taxi fares should be equal to those from Don Muang, approximately 200B to 300B, since each is relatively equidistant from central Bangkok. Public-bus or airport-bus information was not available at the time of research.

Slotted for completion in 2006–07, the Airport Train Link will provide express service from the airport to central Bangkok at Phayathai (corner of Th Phayathai and Phra Ram VI, with access to the Phayathai Skytrain station). According to initial planning, the express train service will run every 15 minutes, take about 15 minutes to reach the airport and cost 150B to 200B. The line will also be used for commuter services – which will run every 30 minutes, take about 30 minutes, and the fare is based on distance. The commuter trains will stop at eight stations between the airport and the central terminus; these include Ratchaprarop (Th Ratchaprarop near Th Sri Ayuthaya) and Makkasan (near Th Phetburi and Th Ratchadaphisek with access to Phetburi subway station), and other suburban stops.

Boat
Once the city's dominant form of transport, public boats still survive along the mighty Mae Nam Chao Phraya and on a few interior *khlong*.

Chao Phraya River Express (☎ 0 2617 7340; www .chaophrayaboat.co.th) is one of Bangkok's most scenic transport options. It runs commuter ferries along the river from Wat Ratchasingkhon, in south-central Bangkok, northwards to Nonthaburi. The river express overlaps with the Skytrain at Tha Sathon-Saphan Taksin Station. See the map, p134 for routes and piers.

The company operates four boat lines: two express lines (indicated by yellow or orange flags), the local line (without a flag) and the tourist line. Express boats stop at certain piers during morning and evening commute periods (usually 6am to 9am and 3pm to 7pm) and cost 10B to 25B, depending on the destination.

Local boats stop at all piers from 6am to 7.30pm, and cost 6B to 10B. The tourist boat operates from 9:30am to 4pm from Tha Sathon to 10 major sightseeing piers (including Tha Chang, Tha Phra Athit, among others); tickets, regardless of destination, are 15B. Hold on to your ticket as proof of purchase (an occasional formality).

There are also flat-bottomed cross-river ferries that connect Thonburi and Bangkok. These piers are usually next door to the river express piers and cost 2B per crossing.

Khlong Taxis, operated by the Bangkok Metropolitan Authority, traverse two lengthy and useful canal routes: Khlong Saen Saep (Banglamphu to Bang Kapi) and Khlong Phasi Charoen in Thonburi (Kaset Bang Khae port to Saphan Phra Ram I). Although the *khlong* taxis are much faster than buses, the canals are seriously polluted and passengers typically hold newspapers over their clothes and faces to prevent being splashed by the blackened water. Obviously, this is not the best choice of transport if you're dressed for a formal occasion.

For Bangkok-based visitors, the Khlong Saen Saep canal service is the quickest option for travelling from Siam Square or Pratunam to Banglamphu. The piers include Tha Withayu (Map pp118–19; near Raffles Nai Lert), Tha Pratunam (Map pp118–19; near Pratunam market), Tha Ratchathewi (Map pp118–19; near Asia Hotel), Tha Phan Fah (Map pp110–11; near Wat Saket). Fares cost 5B to 8B and service runs from 6am to 7pm. It is also useful for points in outer Sukhumvit and Bang Kapi that aren't conveniently reached via Skytrain. A trip from Banglamphu to Ramkhamhaeng University area costs 10B and takes only 40 minutes. (Alternatively, a bus would take at least an hour under Bangkok's normal traffic conditions.).

Bus
Buses are the best option in Chinatown, Banglamphu, Thewet and Dusit, and other areas not well-serviced by Skytrain. The buses are also a lot cheaper than the newer

public transport options, but are also subject to the hassles of traffic. The city's public-bus system, which is operated by Bangkok Metropolitan Transit Authority (BMTA). Fares are as follows:

- Cream-and-blue air-con buses cost 8B for the first 8km, and increase by 2B increments up to 20B to 24B, depending on the distance travelled. Orange Euro 2 air-con buses are 12B for any distance, while white-and-pink air-con buses cost 25B to 30B. The air-con buses are not only cooler (temperature-wise), but are usually less crowded during nonrush hours.
- Ordinary (fan) white-and-blue buses cost 5B for any journey under 10km, red buses cost 4B and green buses, 3.50B. Smaller 'baht buses' plying the lanes are painted red and maroon, and cost 2B each.

Most of the bus lines run between 5am and 11pm, except for the all-night, cream-and-red ordinary buses, which run from 10pm to 5am on some routes and cost 5B. Buddhist monks and novices travel free.

One air-con service that's never overcrowded is the pink-and-white Microbus; it stops taking passengers once every seat is filled. The fare is a flat rate of 20B – you deposit the money in a box at the front of the bus (exact change only). A couple of useful Microbus lines include the No 6, which starts on Th Si Phraya (near the River City shopping complex) and proceeds to the Siam Square area, then out to Th Sukhumvit; and the No 8, which runs between the Victory Monument area and Banglamphu district.

SAFETY
Be careful with your belongings while travelling on Bangkok buses. The place you are most likely to be 'touched' is on the crowded ordinary buses. Razor artists abound, particularly on buses in the Hualamphong station area. These dexterous thieves specialise in slashing your backpack, shoulder bag or even your trouser pockets with a sharp razor and slipping your valuables out unnoticed. Hold your bag in front of you and stay alert.

Car & Motorcycle
For short-term visitors, you will find parking and driving a car in Bangkok more

trouble than it is worth. Even long-term expats typically opt for a chauffeured car rather than battling the Buddhist approach to driving. If you need private transport, consider hiring a car and driver through your hotel or hire a taxi driver that you find trustworthy.

If you're not dissuaded, cars and motorcycles can be rented throughout town, including such international chains as **Avis** (Map pp118-19; ☎ 0 2255 5300; 2/12 Th Withayu) and **Budget** (☎ 0 2552 8921; Bangkok International Airport). There are more rental agencies along Th Withayu and Th Phetburi Tat Mai. Some also rent motorcycles. Rates start at around 1480B per day or 9300B per week, excluding insurance. An International Driving Permit and passport are required for all rentals.

For long cross-country trips, you might consider buying a new or used motorcycle and reselling it when you leave. See p756 for more details on road rules.

Motorcycle Taxi
At the mouth of the soi, motorcycle taxis camp out to deliver passengers the last few kilometres home; a soi trip is usually 10B. Motorcycle taxis can also be hired for longer journeys as a nick-in-time antidote to gridlock; fares in these instances are about the same as *túk-túk*, except during heavy traffic, when they may cost a bit more.

Riding on the back of a speeding motorcycle taxi is a close approximation to an extreme sport. Keep your legs tucked in – the drivers are used to carrying passengers with shorter legs than those of the average Westerner and they pass perilously close to other vehicles while weaving in and out of traffic. Women wearing skirts should sit sidesaddle and gather any extra cloth to avoid it catching in the wheel or drive chain.

Skytrain
The most comfortable option for travelling in 'new' Bangkok (Silom, Sukhumvit and Siam Square), the Skytrain is an elevated rail network that sails over the city's notorious traffic jams. Thais refer to it as *rót fai fáa* (sky train). So far two lines have been built by the **Bangkok Mass Transit System Skytrain** (BTS; ☎ 0 2617 7300; www.bts.co.th) – Sukhumvit and Silom lines.

The Sukhumvit Line terminates in the north of the city at the Mo Chit station,

Face of Buddha statue, Wat Pho (p102), Bangkok

Monks in front of the Golden Mount, Wat Saket (p123), Bangkok

Skytrain (p184) track over Th Sukhumvit, Bangkok

Outdoor dining, Chinatown (p159),
Bangkok

Chao Phraya River Express boat (p183) on Mae
Nam Chao Phraya, Bangkok

Damnoen Saduak floating market (p188), southwest of Bangkok

next to Chatuchak Park, and follows Th Phayathai south to Siam interchange station at Th Rama I and then swings east along Th Phloenchit and Th Sukhumvit to terminate at the On Nut station, near Soi 81, Th Sukhumvit. There are plans in hand to extend this line 9km southeast to Samut Prakan.

The Silom line runs from the National Stadium station, near Siam Square, and soon after makes an abrupt turn to the southwest, continuing above Th Ratchadamri, down Th Silom to Th Narathiwat Ratchanakharin, then out Th Sathon until it terminates next to the foot of Saphan Taksin on the banks of Mae Nam Chao Phraya. There are plans to extend this line a further 2km over the river into Thonburi and possibly as far as Wong Wian Yai train station.

Although the Skytrain has yet to make a sizable dent in Bangkok traffic, many affluent commuters have switched from the crowded air-con buses of BMTA to the Skytrain. Another advantage of the Skytrain is that it offers a pleasant semi-bird's-eye view of the city, allowing glimpses of greenery and historic architecture not visible at street level.

TRAVELLING ON THE SKYTRAIN

Trains run frequently from 6am to midnight along both the lines. Fares vary from 10B to 40B, depending on your destination. Ticket machines at each station accept 5B and 10B coins only, but change is available from the information booths. The staffed booths are also where you would buy value-stored tickets. Brochures available at the information booths detail the various commuter and tourist passes.

Once through the ticket gates, follow the signs for the desired line and terminus. You can change between the two lines at the double-height Siam station (also known as 'Central Station'), in front of Siam Square and Siam Center. Free maps of the system are available at all Skytrain station ticket booths. All trains are air-conditioned, often heavily so.

Subway

The first line of Bangkok's subway opened in 2004 and is operated by the **Metropolitan Rapid Transit Authority** (MRTA; www.mrta.co.th). Thais call the subway *rót fai tâi din* or 'Metro'.

The line connects the train station of Bang Sue with Chatuchak (with access to the Mo Chit Skytrain station), Thailand Cultural Centre, Sukhumvit (with access to Asoke Skytrain station), Queen Sirikit Convention Centre, Lumphini Park, Silom (with access to Sala Daeng Skytrain station) and terminates at Hualamphong.

Trains operate 5am to midnight and cost 14B to 36B, depending on distance. Future extensions will connect Hualamphong to Chinatown and Thonburi.

One main advantage to the subway is that it has made the train stations (Hualamphong and Bang Sue) more accessible from eastern city points.

Taxi

Metered taxis *(tháeksii miitôe)* were introduced in Bangkok in 1993 and have signs on top reading 'Taxi Meter'. Fares for the metered taxis are always lower than those for nonmetered. Metered taxis charge 35B at flag fall for the first 2km, then 4.50B for the next 10km, 5B for 13km to 20km, and 5.50B for any distance over 20km, but only when the taxi travels at 6km/h or more; at speeds under 6km/h, a surcharge of 1.25B per minute kicks in. Freeway tolls – 30B to 40B depending where you start – must be paid by the passenger.

A 24-hour **phone-a-taxi** (☎ 0 2377 1771, 0 2319 9911) is available for an extra 20B.

Taxis are usually plentiful except during peak commute hours or when bars are closing (1am to 2am).

Taxis that hang around tourist centres typically refuse to use the meter and will quote an exorbitantly high rate instead. You are more likely to find an honest cabbie if you walk out to a main thoroughfare.

Fares to most places within central Bangkok cost 60B to 80B, and you should add 10B or 20B if it's during peak hour or after midnight. You can flag down a cab on the street for trips to the airport.

You can hire a taxi all day for around 1000B or 1500B, depending on how much driving is involved.

Túk-Túk

In heavy traffic, *túk-túk* are usually faster than taxis since they're able to weave between cars and trucks. On the down side, they have no air-con, so you have to breathe all that lead-soaked air (at its thickest in the middle of Bangkok's wide avenues) and deal with dodgy drivers.

The typical *túk-túk* fare nowadays offers no savings over a metered taxi – around 40B for a short hop (eg Siam Square to Soi 2 Sukhumvit).

Túk-túk drivers tend to speak less English than taxi drivers, so many new arrivals have a hard time communicating their destinations. Túk-túk drivers are also famous for deliberately taking customers to the wrong destination to collect commissions from certain restaurants, gem shops or silk shops. Beware of *túk-túk* drivers who offer to take you on a sightseeing tour for 10B or 20B – it's a touting scheme designed to pressure you into purchasing overpriced goods.

AROUND BANGKOK

If you're itching to get out of the capital city, but don't have a lot of time, consider a day trip to some of the neighbouring towns.

At Bangkok's doorstep are all of Thailand's provincial charms – you don't have to go far to find ancient religious monuments, floating markets, architectural treasures, and laid-back fishing villages.

WAT PHAILOM
วัดไผ่ล้อม

North of Bangkok in Pathum Thani Province, this old, wooden Mon **wat** (Amphoe Sam Kok; ☺ 6am-6pm) is noted for the tens of thousands of open-billed storks (*Anastomus oscitans*) that nest in bamboo groves opposite it, from December to June. Donations are appreciated. Temple architecture buffs will note the Ayuthaya-style *bòt*, backed by a Mon stupa.

The temple is 51km from the centre of Bangkok. Take a Pathum Thani–bound bus (16B) from Bangkok's Northern bus terminal and cross the river by ferry to the wat grounds. Bus 33 from Sanam Luang goes all the way to Phailom and back. The Chao Phraya River Express tours that go to Bang Pa-In each Sunday also stop at Wat Phailom (see p141).

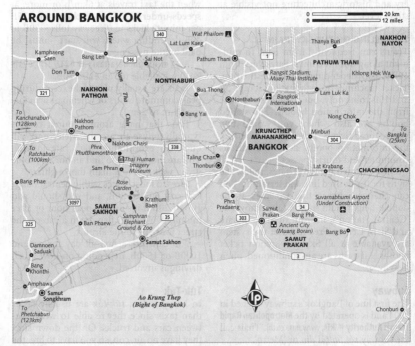

NAKHON PATHOM
นครปฐม

pop 120,657

Nakhon Pathom is a typical provincial Thai city whose visible link to its claim as the country's oldest is the Phra Pathom Chedi. The town also proudly wears its first-born status within its name, which derives from the Pali 'Nagara Pathama' meaning 'First City'. At one time Nakhon Pathom functioned as the centre of the Dvaravati kingdom, a loose collection of Mon city states that flourished between the 6th and 11th centuries AD in Mae Nam Chao Phraya valley. Some historians speculate that the area may have been inhabited before India's Asokan period (3rd century BC), as there is a theory that Buddhist missionaries from India visited Nakhon Pathom at that time.

Sights
In the centre of town, **Phra Pathom Chedi**, rising to 127m, is the tallest Buddhist monument in the world. The original stupa, which is buried within the massive orange-glazed dome, was erected in the early 6th century by Theravada Buddhists of Dvaravati (possibly at the same time as Myanmar's famous Shwedagon stupa), but in the early 11th century the Khmer king, Suriyavarman I of Angkor, conquered the city and built a Brahman *prang* over the sanctuary. The Burmese of Bagan, under King Anawrahta, sacked the city in 1057 and the *prang* lay in ruins until King Mongkut had it restored in 1860. There is even a Chinese temple attached to the outer walls of the stupa, next to which outdoor *lí-keh* (Thai folk dance-drama) is sometimes performed.

On the eastern side of the monument, in the *bòt*, is a Dvaravati-style Buddha seated in a European pose similar to the one in Wat Phra Meru in Ayuthaya. It may, in fact, have come from there.

The wat surrounding the stupa enjoys the kingdom's highest temple rank, Ratchavoramahavihan; it's one of only six temples so honoured in Thailand. King Rama VI's ashes are interred in the base of the Sukhothai-era Phra Ruang Rochanarit, a large standing Buddha image in the wat's northern *wíhǎan*. Also of interest are the many examples of Chinese sculpture carved from a greenish stone that came to Thailand as ballast in the bottom of 19th-century Chi-

nese junks. Opposite the *bòt* is a **museum** (admission 20B; 🕑 9am-4pm Wed-Sun), which contains some interesting Dvaravati sculpture.

Southeast of the city stands **Phra Phutthamonthon**, a Sukhothai-style standing Buddha. At 40.7m, it is reportedly the world's tallest, and it's surrounded by a 400-hectare landscaped park that contains sculptures representing the major stages in the Buddha's life (eg a 6m-high Dharma wheel, carved from a single slab of granite). The Buddha statue was designed by Corrado Feroci. All Bangkok–Nakhon Pathom buses pass the access road to the park; from there you can walk, hitch or flag a *sǎwngthǎew* into the park itself. From Nakhon Pathom you can also take a white-and-purple Salaya bus; the stop is on Th Tesa across from the post office.

Thai Human Imagery Museum (☎ 0 3433 2607; foreigners/Thais 200/50B; 🕑 9am-5.30pm Mon-Fri, 8.30am-6pm Sat & Sun), outside of town at the Km 31 marker on Th Pinklao–Nakhon Chaisi (the highway to Bangkok), contains an exhibition of lifelike resin sculptures. A group of Thai artists reportedly spent 10 years studying their subjects and creating the figures, which fall into four categories: famous Buddhist monks of Thailand, former kings of the Chakri dynasty, Thai lifestyles and chess playing. The museum is near Phra Phutthamonthon park, and an inexpensive motorcycle taxi can deliver you between the two places.

Eating
Nakhon Pathom has an excellent **market** along the road between the train station and Phra Pathom Chedi; its *khâo lǎam* (sticky rice and coconut steamed in a length of bamboo) is reputed to be the best in Thailand. There are many good, inexpensive food vendors and restaurants in this area.

An old standby on Th Thesa, east of the stupa, is the inexpensive Chinese **Tang Ha-Seng** (no Roman-script sign); there are two branches, one at No 71/2-3 and another at No 59/1-2.

Ratchaphreuk (no Roman-script sign; Th Ratchadamnoen), near Soi 5 directly west of Phra Pathom Chedi, offers a pleasant Thai *sǎalaa* setting. If you catch this place on a slow day, your only dining companions will be members of Kiss, the Beatles and other rock-star posters adorning the walls.

Getting There & Away

Nakhon Pathom is 56km west of Bangkok.

Air-con bus 997 and 83 leave from the Southern bus terminal (in Thonburi) for Nakhon Pathom (35B, one hour, frequent departures). To return to Bangkok, catch one of the idling buses on Th Phayaphan, a block from the train station. Buses to Damnoen Saduak floating market (bus 78) and to Phetchaburi (bus 73) leave from the same stop, departing about every 30 minutes.

You can also wave down Samut Sakhon-bound buses (402, 25B) at this stop.

Ordinary trains (3rd class) leave Thonburi (Bangkok Noi) station for Nakhon Pathom at 7.45am and 1.50pm (14B, approximately 1¼ hours) en route to Kanchanaburi and Nam Tok. The return train leaves Nakhon Pathom at 8.55am and 4.20pm. There are more frequent trains to and from Bangkok's Hualamphong station (31B to 60B, two hours) throughout the day.

DAMNOEN SADUAK FLOATING MARKET

ตลาดน้ำดำเนินสะดวก

Wooden canoes laden with multicoloured fruits and vegetables, paddled by Thai women wearing indigo-hued clothes and wide-brimmed straw hats – this quintessential picture of Thailand might have wooed you to this country, but this image is over 20 years old and is more a piece of history than a current snapshot. An updated version would show rows and rows of souvenir stands lining the canals, and boatloads of tourists glued to their cameras. The floating fruit vendors are still there, but the piles of exotic colours have diminished to a few lacklustre, overpriced bunches of bananas.

So should you scratch the famous floating market (tàlàat náam) off your list? Not so fast – despite its decay, the floating market can still be fun, if you regard it as a souvenir market instead of a slice of Thai culture.

The best advice is to arrive in Damnoen Saduak the night before, stay at the conveniently located Noknoi Hotel (right) and get up around 7am or 8am to see the market. By 9am the package tours from Bangkok arrive, draining what little authenticity is left.

You can hire a boat from any pier that lines Th Sukhaphiban 1, which is the land route to the floating market area. The going rate is 150B to 200B per person per hour.

Beyond the market, the residential canals are quite peaceful and can be explored by hiring a boat for a longer duration. South of the floating market are several small family businesses that welcome tourists; these include a Thai candy maker, a pomelo farm and a knife crafter. Damnoen Saduak's enthusiastic tourist office can arrange transport to these attractions for a two- to three-hour tour (around 500B for the boat). The tourist office can also arrange homestays and canal trips.

Sleeping

Noknoi (Little Bird; ☎ 0 3225 4382; d 180-320B; 🔀) About a 15-minute walk from the floating market, the Noknoi is clean and quiet.

Ban Sukchoke Resort (☎ 0 3225 4301; d 800-1400B) Comfortable bungalows set over the canal. There is also a small house that sleeps 10 people. Ban Sukchoke is 1.5km northwest of Damnoen Saduak's market area.

Getting There & Away

Damnoen Saduak is 104km southwest of Bangkok between Nakhon Pathom and Samut Songkhram. Air-con bus 78 and 996 go direct from Bangkok's Southern bus terminal to Damnoen Saduak (65B, two hours, every 20 minutes from 6.30am to 9pm).

Most buses will drop you off at a pier along Khlong Hia Kui or Khlong Damnoen Saduak where you can hire a boat directly to the floating market. The regular bus stop is in town just across the bridge. A yellow săwngthăew (5B) does a frequent loop between the floating market and the bus stop in town.

SAMUT SAKHON

สมุทรสาคร

pop 68,398

Samut Sakhon is popularly known as Mahachai because it straddles the confluence of Mae Nam Tha Chin and Khlong Mahachai. Just a few kilometres from the Gulf of Thailand, this busy port features a lively market area and a pleasant breezy park around the crumbling walls of **Wichian Chodok Fort** (Hwy 35). A few rusty cannon pointing towards the river testify to the fort's original purpose of guarding the mouth of Mae Nam Tha Chin from foreign invaders. Before the arrival of European traders in the 17th century, the town was known as Tha Jin (Chinese pier) because of the large number of Chinese junks that called here.

A few kilometres west of Samut Sakhon, along Hwy 35, is the Ayuthaya-period **Wat Yai Chom Prasat**, which is known for the finely carved wooden doors on its *bòt*. You can easily identify the wat by the tall Buddha figure standing at the front. To get here from Samut Sakhon, take an orange westbound bus (10B) heading towards Samut Songkhram from the bus station; the wat is only a 10-minute ride from the edge of town.

Getting There & Away

Samut Sakhon is located 28km southwest of Bangkok.

Air-con bus 976 (25B, 1½ hours) from the Southern bus terminal in Thonburi leaves for Samut Sakhon throughout the day. Buses also run between Samut Sakhon and Samut Songkhram (15/22B ordinary/air-con, one hour).

Samut Sakhon is nearly midway along the 3rd-class, short-line 'Mahachai' train route that runs between Thonburi's Wong Wian Yai station (see the box below). The fare costs 10B and there are roughly hourly departures and returns from 5.30am to 7pm.

SAMUT SONGKHRAM
สมุทรสงคราม
pop 34,949
Commonly known as 'Mae Klong', this provincial capital lies along a sharp bend in Mae Nam Mae Klong and just a few kilometres from the Gulf of Thailand. Due to the flat topography and abundant water sources, the area surrounding the city is well suited for the steady irrigation needed to grow guavas, lychees and grapes. Along the highway from Thonburi, visitors will pass a string of artificial sea lakes used in the production of salt. A profusion of coconut palms makes the area look unusually lush, considering its proximity to Bangkok.

Samut Songkhram is a fairly modern city with a large market area between the

MAHACHAI SHORTLINE
Sometimes it is all about the journey, rather than the destination. This is certainly the case for taking the Mahachai Shortline to the string gulf-side towns southwest of Bangkok. The adventure begins when you take a stab into Thonburi looking for the **Wong Wian Yai train station** (Map pp106-7; Th Taksin; bus 37). Just past the traffic circle is a fairly ordinary food market, which camouflages the unceremonious end of this commuter line.

Only 15 minutes out of the station and the city density yields to palm trees, small rice fields and marshes filled with giant elephant ears and canna lilies. There's lots of peaking into homes and shops where locals go to pick up odds and ends or a shot of rice whisky for the morning commute.

The wilderness and backwater farms evaporate quickly as you enter Mahachai. This is the end of the first segment, so work your way along the road that runs parallel to the train tracks through a dense market of fishermen boots and trays of tentacled seafood to the harbour pier. The harbour is clogged with water hyacinth, which forms floating islands for fish-hunting cranes and bug-chasing birds. Just beyond are the big wooden fishing boats, pregnant with the day's catch and draped like a veiled widow with fishing nets. Boarding the ferry, you have to jockey for space with the motorcycles that cross back and forth, driven by school teachers and errand-running housewives.

Once on the other side, take a right at the first intersection, follow it all the way through the temple and past the drying fish racks to the train tracks and turn right to reach the station. This is Ban Laem, from which trains continue on to Mae Klong (Samut Songkhram) at 7.30am, 10.10am, 1.30pm and 4.40pm.

Ban Laem is a sleepy little station that keeps up a convincing charade that no one has ever come or gone from here. Along the route to Mae Klong, the wilderness is so dense that it seems the surrounding greenery might gobble up the train tracks, so that the middle of nowhere stays that way. You'll be surprised once you reach the bustling city of Samut Songkhram with this back-door entrance.

train and bus stations. The sizable **Wat Phet Samut Worawihan**, in the centre of town near the train station and river, contains a renowned Buddha image called Luang Phaw Wat Ban Laem.

At the mouth of Mae Nam Mae Klong, not far from town, is the province's most famous tourist attraction, a bank of fossilised shells known as **Don Hoi Lot**. The type of shells embedded in the bank come from clams with a tube-like shell *(hăwy làwt)*. The shell bank is best seen late in the dry season (typically April and May) when the river has receded to its lowest level. To get to Don Hoi Lot you can hop on a blue *săwngthăew* (10B, 15 minutes) in front of Somdet Phra Phuttalertla Hospital at the intersection of Th Prasitwatthana and Th Thamnimit. Or you can charter a boat from Tha Talat Mae Klong, a scenic journey that takes about 45 minutes.

Wat Satthatham, 500m along the road to Don Hoi Lot, is notable for its *bòt* constructed of golden teak and decorated with 60 million baht worth of mother-of-pearl inlay. The inlay covers the temple's interior and depicts scenes from *jataka* murals above the windows and the *Ramakian* (the Thai version of the Indian classic, *Ramayana*) below.

Ban Benjarong (☎ 0 3475 1322; ◷ 8am-10.30pm) is a small factory in a modern house that produces top-quality *benjarong*, the traditional five-coloured Thai ceramics. Here you can watch craftsmen painting the intricate arabesques and ornate floral patterns for which *benjarong* is known. This isn't the glossy stuff you see at Chatuchak Market in Bangkok, but the real thing; prices start at about 1000B. Another local attraction is the **Orchid Farm**, which is 4km north of Samut Songkhram on the road to Damnoen Saduak. Despite its commercial and tourism functions, it is really quite impressive for the colour of its orchids. Ban Benjarong and the orchid farm can both be reached via the Samut Songkhram–Damnoen Saduak bus.

King Buddhalertla Naphalai Memorial Park (◷ park 9am-6pm, museum 9am-4pm Wed-Sun; museum admission 10B) is dedicated to King Rama II, who was a native of Amphoe Amphawa. The museum is housed in traditional central-Thai houses set on two hectares and contains a library of rare Thai books, antiques

---

HOMESTAYS

To get a better glimpse of the traditions of Samut Songkhram's water-borne culture, sign up for the homestays organised by **Baan Song Thai Plai Pong Pang** (☎ 0 3475 7333) in Amphoe Amphawa. For a day or two you can join the daily routine of one of the district's residents. You sleep on the floor under a mosquito net, make morning offerings to the monks, walk the narrow plank pathways crisscrossing the canals or tour around by hired long-tail boat. On certain lunar days, a floating market is held. From Samut Songkhram take a blue local bus (10B) to Amphawa and a motorcycle taxi to Baan Khok Ket. Accommodation is 350B per night and 500B for long-tail–boat hire.

---

from early-19th-century Siam and an exhibition of dolls depicting four of Rama II's theatrical works (*Inao, Mani Phichai*, a version of the *Ramakian* and *Sang Thong*). Behind the houses is a lush botanic garden and beyond that, a drama school. To get to the park take an Amphawa-bound blue bus (10B) to Talat Nam Amphawa, then walk over the bridge and follow the road that goes through the gardens of Wat Amphawan Chetiyaram.

Getting There & Away

Samut Songkhram is Thailand's smallest province and is 74km southwest of Bangkok. Buses from Bangkok's Southern bus terminal to Damnoen Saduak also stop in Samut Songkhram (40B, 1½ hours) near the train station and down the street from the Siam Commercial Bank. There are also many daily buses to Samut Sakhon (15/25B ordinary/air-con, one hour). Taxis and local buses park at the intersection of Th Ratchayat Raksa and Th Prasitphatthana.

Samut Songkhram is the southernmost terminus of the Mahachai Shortline. There are four departures to Samut Songkhram (10B; one hour; 7.30am 10.10am, 1.30pm, 4.40pm) and four return trips (6.20am, 9am, 11.30am, 3.30pm). See the boxed text (p189) for more information. The train station is located on Th Kasem Sukhum where it terminates at Th Prasitphatthana, near the river.

SAMUT PRAKAN

สมุทรปราการ

pop 378,694

At the mouth of Mae Nam Chao Phraya, where it empties into the Gulf of Thailand, Samut Prakan (sometimes referred to as Meuang Pak Nam) smells fishier than the ocean. Most residents' lives revolve around fishing, even if they are landlubbers. Motorcycle taxi drivers mend fishing nets while waiting for a fare; vendors shoo flies from crates of iced ocean dwellers.

The city's name means 'Ocean Wall', a reference to **Phra Chula Jawm Klao Fort**, built around 1893, 7km south of the provincial hall.

Ancient City

เมืองโบราณ

Billed as the largest open-air museum in the world, **Muang Boran** (☎ 0 2323 9253; www .ancientcity.com; adult/child 100/50B; ☽ 8am-5pm) covers more than 80 hectares of peaceful countryside littered with 109 scaled-down facsimiles of many of the kingdom's most famous monuments. The grounds have been shaped to replicate Thailand's general geographical outline, with the monuments placed accordingly.

Visions of Las Vegas and its corny replicas of world treasures may spring to mind, but the Ancient City is architecturally sophisticated – a preservation site for classical buildings and art forms. It's also a good place for undistracted bicycle rides (50B rental), as it is usually quiet and never crowded.

The Ancient City is 33km from Bangkok along the Old Sukhumvit Hwy, outside central Samut Prakan. From Samut Prakan take a green minibus No 36 (6B), which passes the entrance to the Ancient City. Nervous types should sit on the left-hand side of the bus to watch for the 'Muang Boran' sign. To return to town, cross the main highway and catch a white No 36 *săwngthăew* (5B), which

can also drop you off at the road leading to the Crocodile Farm.

Samut Prakan Crocodile Farm & Zoo

ฟาร์มจระเข้สมุทรปราการ

Claiming to be the world's largest, **Samut Prakan Crocodile Farm & Zoo** (☎ 0 2387 0020; www .paknam.com; adult/child 300/200B; ☽ 7am-6pm) holds on to 60,000 crocs, including the largest known Siamese crocodile, a boy named Yai who's 6m long and weighs 1114kg. The zoo also boasts elephants, monkeys and snakes and trained-animal shows – including croc wrestling.

Items made from crocodile hide that are certified by the Convention on International Trade in Endangered Species (Cites) – belts, handbags, shoes – are available from the farm's gift shop.

From central Samut Prakan, you can get to the crocodile farm by taking the blue No S61 *săwngthăew*; this will go directly to the gate. If you are coming from the Ancient City, catch a white No 36 *săwngthăew* (5B) to the farm's access road and then a motorcycle taxi (10B) to the entrance.

Getting There & Away

Ordinary bus 25 (3.50B) and air-con bus 507, 508 and 511 (16B) ply regular routes between central Bangkok and Pak Nam (central Samut Prakan). The trip can take up to two hours, depending on traffic. If the traffic is horrendous, consider catching the Skytrain's Sukhumvit line to On Nut station and then catching the aforementioned buses on the road heading out of Bangkok.

The bus station is on Th Srisamut in front of the harbour and the market. Make a note of where the Bangkok bus drops you off because Samut Prakan has very few street signs in Roman script. *Săwngthăew* and minibuses to the town's attractions are usually parked nearby; see those sections for specific transportation details.

Central Thailand

Packed with history and stunning scenery, Central Thailand is becoming increasingly popular among travellers. Home to some of the most friendly and easygoing people, this central heartland within train-shot of Bangkok offers travellers an heavy dose of culture and adventure.

Nearly everyone makes a stop in Ayuthaya to see some of Thailand's most impressive ruins and most follow it up with a quick peek at Lopburi, the town with the monkeys. But not everyone makes it out to Kanchanaburi, home to a powerful piece of WWII history and some of Thailand's most impressive natural attractions. Don't miss the unforgettable, picture-perfect waterfalls in this province – they're even easy to visit via public transport.

For those who want to get off the beaten path and see a slice of Myanmar (Burma), the deceptively quiet border town of Sangkhlaburi is just a few hours by road from Kanchanaburi. It's a low-key cultural melting pot that is becoming increasingly geared for tourism.

HIGHLIGHTS

- Visiting the ancient ruins of **Ayuthaya** (p195), Unesco World Heritage Site and former capital of Siam

- Reflecting on the historical attractions of Kanchanaburi including the infamous **Death Railway** (p209) and **cemeteries** (p211) memorialising those fallen during WWII

- Indulging in the natural beauty of the waterfalls of **Erawan** (p219) and **Sai Yok** (p220) National Parks near Kanchanaburi

- Teasing the local monkey gangs while marvelling at the ancient stone temples in the long-inhabited city of **Lopburi** (p202)

- Getting a taste of Myanmar (Burma) and shop for bargains at **Three Pagodas Pass** (p227) near Sangkhlaburi

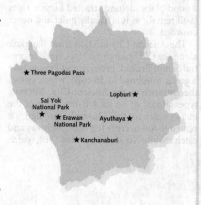

★ Three Pagodas Pass

Sai Yok
National Park
★

★ Erawan
National Park

Lopburi ★

Ayuthaya ★

★ Kanchanaburi

History

Crumbling remnants of Thailand's history dot this region. In the long-settled and relatively rural provinces of Ayuthaya and Lopburi are some of Thailand's most impressive Buddhist and Hindu ruins, some of which date back to when all of central Thailand was a far-flung outpost of the Angkorian Empire of the ancient Khmer.

Lopburi is considered to be one of Thailand's oldest cities, dating from the Dvaravati period (6th to 11th centuries) when the Khmer reign expanded to include much of present-day Thailand. Many of the *prang* (stupa) of Lopburi's disappearing wats are architecturally related to the primary Khmer post in present-day Cambodia. Lopburi resisted pressure from Sukhothai but was eventually absorbed into the Ayuhaya kingdom during the 14th century. The remains of King Narai's palace in the old city is a symbol of its political pinnacle of the 17th century. Amazingly, modern Lopburi has mushroomed up against the remains of the historic old city, making it quite a unique sight.

Slightly younger Ayuthaya was founded in 1350 and was an important trade centre from the 14th to 18th centuries. Foreign populations became notable in the 16th century and the city became a political powerhouse until 1767 when the Burmese sacked the place. The opulence and diversity of the old city is still evident in the remnants of the palaces and temples, which are now a Unesco World Heritage site.

But this central part of Thailand is also home to a history that is much closer to today. Kanchanaburi Province is home to the infamous Death Railway of WWII, the project that brought thousands of POWs to their deaths and never did become fully functional.

Climate

It can dump rain in Sangkhlaburi for days while Kanchanaburi only sees sun; though they look close together on the map, they are divided by mountains and altitude. It can be significantly cooler in Sangkhlaburi than other parts of this region. Ayuthaya and Lopburi sit in a wide open plain that

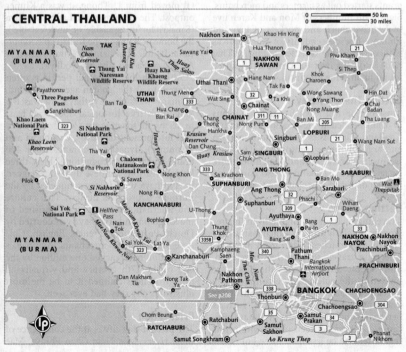

CENTRAL THAILAND

receives similar amounts of rain and heat as Bangkok.

National Parks

Kanchanaburi is a wild and mountainous province that once acted as a natural barrier to Myanmar (Burma) to the west. The province is best known for the infamous Death Railway, but it is also home to some of Thailand's most spectacular and pristine national parks. Erawan and Sai Yok national parks are easy to reach and home to some of Thailand's most stunning waterfalls and wildlife. Lesser visited, and more difficult to reach Si Nakharin, Chaloem Ratanakosin and Khao Laem national parks are worth the effort for those seeking solitude.

Language

The people of central Thailand share a common dialect that is considered 'standard' Thai simply because Bangkok, the seat of power, happens to be in the region. High concentrations of Chinese are found in the cities of the central provinces since this is where a large number of Chinese immigrants started out as farmers and merchants. Significant numbers of Mon and Karen live in Kanchanaburi, and pockets of Lao and Phuan – the descendents of war captives who were forcibly resettled following Thai raids into Laos over the centuries – can be found in all three provinces.

Getting There & Away

Most people will leave Bangkok on a bus or train headed to destinations in central Thailand. The bus is faster, more modern and arguably more comfortable. The train is slower, more scenic and sometimes more social. Central Thailand is also connected to the north and northeast via train.

Getting Around

Travelling by train is a highlight in this region, particularly around Kanchanaburi but also on the stretches to and from Bangkok. The train travels through less-developed, more scenic areas whereas the buses are limited to the quicker more commercially developed roads. Sometimes the bus is the only option between two places, such as between Kanchanaburi and Ayuthaya. Because distances between places within this region tend to be less than three hours, ordinary class buses and trains are usually sufficient.

AYUTHAYA PROVINCE

AYUTHAYA

พระนครศรีอยุธยา

pop 81,400

Whether you came to Thailand to see ruins or not, Ayuthaya is not to be missed. The proximity to Bangkok (86km), number of attractions and amount of interpretive information make it an easy place to absorb some Thai history. The ruins of the ancient capital are not as close together as those in Lopburi, or as atmospheric as those of Sukhothai, but they are equally impressive. If you have time, spend a couple days here. And if you like street food, don't miss the markets and do sample the many regional snacks and desserts.

History

Ayuthaya was the Siamese royal capital from 1350 to 1767. Before 1350, when the capital moved from U Thong, it was a Khmer outpost. The city was named after Ayodhya (Sanskrit for 'unassailable' or 'undefeatable'), the home of Rama in the Indian epic *Ramayana*. Its full Thai name is Phra Nakhon Si Ayuthaya (Sacred City of Ayodhya).

Although the Sukhothai period is often referred to as the 'golden age' of Thailand, in many ways the Ayuthaya era was the kingdom's true historical apex – at least in terms of sovereignty (which extended well into present-day Laos, Cambodia and Myanmar), dynastic endurance (over 400 years) and world recognition. Thirty-three kings of various Siamese dynasties reigned in Ayuthaya until it was conquered by the Burmese. During its heyday, Thai culture and international commerce flourished in the kingdom and Ayuthaya was courted by Dutch, Portuguese, French, English, Chinese and Japanese merchants. Ayuthaya's population had reached one million by the end of the 17th century and virtually all foreign visitors claimed it to be the most illustrious city they had ever seen.

Orientation

The present-day city is at the confluence of three rivers: Mae Nam Chao Phraya, Mae

Nam Pa Sak and the smaller Mae Nam Lopburi. A wide canal links them, encircling the town. Long-tail boats can be rented from the boat landing across from Chan Kasem Palace for a tour around the river; several of the old wat (temple) ruins (Wat Phanan Choeng, Wat Phutthaisawan, Wat Kasatthirat and Wat Chai Wattanaram) may be glimpsed from the canal, along with picturesque views of river life.

There is a small travellers' ghetto concentrated on Soi 1, Th Naresuan, just north of the bus terminal.

Information

EMERGENCY
Tourist Police (☎ 0 3524 1446, emergency ☎ 1155; Th Si Sanphet)

INTERNET ACCESS
Some guesthouses offer Internet services starting at a steep 60B per hour. The ever-changing Internet shops clustered on and around Soi 1, Th Naresuan offer better deals at 20B per hour with a 10B minimum.

MEDICAL SERVICES
Ayuthaya hospital (☎ 0 3524 1446; Th U Thong at Th Si Sanphet) Has an emergency centre and several English-speaking doctors.

MONEY
ATMs are abundant in the city, especially along Th Naresuan near the Amporn Shopping Centre.
Bank of Ayuthaya (Th U Thong nr Th Naresuan)
Kasikorn Bank (Th Naresuan)
Siam City Bank (Th U Thong)
Siam Commercial Bank (Th Naresuan)

POST
Main post office (Th U Thong; ☻ 8.30am-4.30pm Mon-Fri, 9am-noon Sat) Has an international telephone service (☻ 8am-8pm) upstairs. There's also a small branch post office in the TAT office.

TOURIST INFORMATION
Tourist Authority of Thailand (TAT; ☎ 0 3524 6076, 0 3524 1672; 108/22 Th Si Sanphet; ☻ 8am-4.30pm) Has officially take over the municipal building at the end of Th Rotchana. The free interactive display upstairs offers a comprehensive introduction to the history of Ayuthaya. Be careful not to mistake the older, smaller office up the street with this more detailed resource.

Dangers & Annoyances
If you're on a bike, motorised or otherwise, watch out for unpredictable traffic, uneven roads and bag-snatchers. Daypacks in unprotected front baskets are easy to grab at traffic stop lights.

Also, be wary of the local dog packs. They won't take notice of you unless you cross into their territory which will trigger a shrill chorus of barking, exposed fangs and even biting.

Sights
AYUTHAYA HISTORICAL PARK
อุทยานประวัติศาสตร์พระนครศรีอยุธยา

A Unesco World Heritage site, Ayuthaya's historic temples are scattered throughout this once magnificent city and along the encircling rivers. Several of the more central ruins – Wat Phra Si Sanphet, Wat Mongkhon Bophit, Wat Na Phra Meru, Wat Thammikarat, Wat Ratburana and Wat Phra Mahathat – can be visited on foot, but avoid the hottest part of the day (11am to 4pm). Or you can get to more temples and ruins by renting a bicycle (see p201). If you want to see everything, you could hire a bicycle for the central temples and charter a long-tail boat to see the outlying ruins along the river (see p201). Admission costs and opening hours are listed where applicable.

Wat Phra Si Sanphet
วัดพระศรีสรรเพชญ์

Once the largest **temple** (admission 30B; ☻ 9am-6pm) in Ayuthaya, this wat is now known for the line of three impressive *chedi* (stupas). They are prime examples of the quintessential Ayuthaya style, which has been identified with Thai art more than any other single style in its time. Royal temples/palaces for several Ayuthaya kings utilised this design. Built in the 14th century, the compound once contained a 16m-high standing Buddha covered with 250kg of gold, which was melted down by the Burmese conquerors.

Wat Mongkhon Bophit
วัดมงคลบพิตร

This **monastery** (☻ 8.30am-4.30pm Mon-Fri, to 5.30pm Sat & Sun), near Wat Phra Si Sanphet, contains one of Thailand's largest Buddha images, a 15th-century bronze casting. The present *wíhǎan* (Buddhist image sanctuary) dates from 1956.

CENTRAL THAILAND

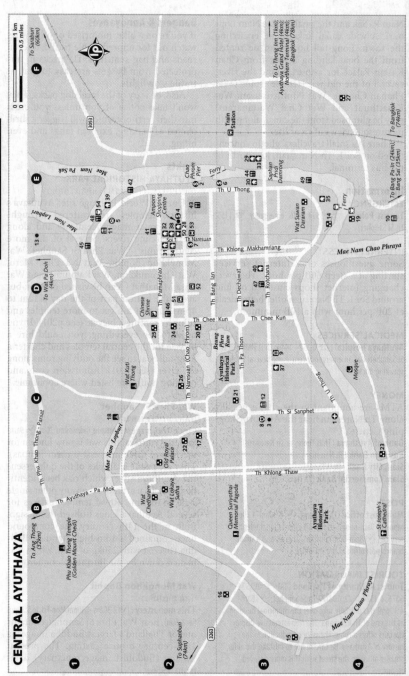

CENTRAL AYUTHAYA

Wat Phra Mahathat
วัดพระมหาธาตุ

One of Ayuthaya's most photographed sites is on the grounds of this **temple** (admission 30B; ☺8am-6pm). Built during the reign of King Ramesuan in the 14th century, it is home to the Buddha head embedded in twisted tree roots. Despite extensive damage – not much was left standing after the Burmese hordes had finished – the Khmer-style tower is still impressive: it was one of the first built in the capital.

Wat Ratburana
วัดราชบูรณะ

The Ayuthaya period murals in the *chedi* of this **monastery** (Ratcha-burana; admission 30B; ☺8am-6pm) are in better shape than those across the road at Wat Phra Mahathat.

Wat Thammikarat
วัดธรรมิกราช

To the east of the royal palace grounds, inside the river loop, Wat Thammikarat features overgrown *chedi* ruins and lion sculptures.

Wat Phanan Choeng
วัดพนัญเชิง

On weekends Buddhist pilgrims from Bangkok come to this **temple** (admission 20B; ☺8am-5pm) to perform an impressive ritual. They purchase lengthy strips of saffron-coloured cloth and drape it over the shoulder of a 19m-high sitting Buddha image in the main *wíhǎan*. The image is named after Sam Po, a Chinese explorer who visited Ayuthaya in

1407, and is highly revered by Thai-Chinese. The wat was built in the early 13th century, before Ayuthaya became a Siamese capital, so it's possibly Khmer.

The easiest way to get to Wat Phanan Choeng is by ferry from the pier near Phom Phet Fortress. You can take a bicycle with you on the boat (2B).

Wat Na Phra Meru (Phra Mehn)
วัดหน้าพระเมรุ

This **temple** (admission 20B; ☺8am-5pm Mon-Fri, to 5.30pm Sat & Sun) is notable because it escaped destruction from Burmese attack in 1767. The main *bòt* (central sanctuary) was built in 1546 and contains an amazing carved wooden ceiling and a splendid Ayuthaya-era crowned sitting Buddha, 6m high. Inside a smaller *wíhǎan* behind the *bòt* is a greenstone Buddha from Sri Lanka in a European pose (sitting in a chair); it's said to be 1300 years old. The walls of the *wíhǎan* show traces of 18th- or 19th-century murals.

Also noteworthy are the fortress-like walls and pillars of the main *bòt*. During the Burmese invasion, Myanmar's Chao Along Phaya chose this site from which to fire a cannon at the palace; the cannon exploded and the king was fatally injured, thus ending the sacking of Ayuthaya. It has required restoration over the years, so it is not in its original form.

Wat Yai Chai Mongkhon
วัดใหญ่ชัยมงคล

Wat Yai (admission 20B; ☺8am-5pm), as the locals call it, is southeast of the town proper, but

CENTRAL THAILAND

RUIN THE DARK

If you think the remains of an ancient era are amazing by day, you should see them at night. Some of Ayuthaya's most impressive ruins take on an even more impressive other-worldliness after dark when they are dramatically illuminated. The grounds are not open, but it is still worth it to walk by or enjoy dinner at a nearby restaurant. Wat Ratburana, Wat Chai Wattanaram, Wat Phra Ram and Wat Mahathat are all lit up from 7pm to 9pm.

can be reached by *túk-túk* (motorised *săam-láw*, or three-wheeled pedicab) for 30B. It's a quiet old place that was once a famous meditation wat, built by King U Thong in 1357. The compound contains a very large *chedi* from which the wat takes its popular name (*yài* means 'big'), and a large reclining Buddha. There are monks and a community of Buddhist nuns residing here.

OTHER TEMPLES

Just north of Wat Ratburana, to the west of a colourful Chinese shrine, are the smaller ruins of **Wat Suwannawat**. The 400-year-old brick remains of eight *chedi*, a *bòt* and a *wíhăan* are arranged in a circle – a typical early Ayuthaya layout.

The ruined Ayuthaya-style tower and *chedi* of **Wat Chai Wattanaram** (admission 30B; 8am-6pm), on the western bank of Mae Nam Chao Phraya southwest of the city centre, have been restored. These ruins can be reached by boat or by bicycle via a nearby bridge. If you go by road, you'll pass **Wat Kasatthirat** on the way.

A short boat ride north along Mae Nam Lopburi will bring you to modern **Wat Pa Doh**. In front of the *bòt* a unique Sukhothai-style walking Buddha image strides over a narrow arch, symbolising the crossing from *samsara* to nirvana.

NATIONAL MUSEUMS

The building that houses the **Chantharakasem National Museum** (Chan Kasem Palace or Phra Ratchawong Chan Kasem; Th U Thong; admission 30B; 9am-4pm Wed-Sun) is a museum in itself. King Rama IV had this palace rebuilt and established as a museum in 1936. It's design is based on the palace built for King Naresuan by

his father in 1577. Both its pleasant grounds and collection of gold treasures from Wat Phra Mahathat and Wat Ratburana make it a worthwhile stop.

The less charming but larger **Chao Sam Phraya National Museum** (admission 30B; 9am-4pm Wed-Sun) is worth a peak for those with an interest in Thai Buddhist sculpture, particularly of the Ayuthaya style. Don't miss the traditional teak house on the western edge of the property. A selection of books on Thai art and archaeology is on sale at the ticket kiosk.

AYUTHAYA HISTORICAL STUDY CENTRE
ศูนย์ศึกษาประวัติศาสตร์อยุธยา

The US$6.8-million **Ayuthaya Historical Study Centre** (0 3524 5124; Th Rotchana; combined admission adult/student 100/50B; 9am-4.30pm Mon-Fri, to 5pm Sat & Sun), funded by the Japanese government, is the most modern and impressive museum in town. It's filled with awesome models including one of Wat Phra Si Sanphet. Its hi-tech exhibit area in the main building covers five aspects of Ayuthaya's history: city development, port, administration, lifestyles and traditions. The **annexe**, which stands in what was the Japanese quarter, contains an exhibit on foreign relations with Ayuthaya. Dedicate a couple of hours to fully appreciate what is here.

ELEPHANT KRAAL
เพนียดคล้องช้าง

This *kraal* is the only restored version of the wooden stockades once used for the annual roundup of wild elephants that is open to the public. A huge fence of teak logs planted at 45-degree angles kept the elephants in; the king had a special raised pavilion from which to observe the thrilling event. It's about 4km from the centre of town so you can either ride a bicycle here or hire a *túk-túk* (50B).

Tours

BOAT TOURS

Informal boat tours (250B per hour for up to 10 people) can be arranged at the pier near the night market. The Krungsri River Hotel (opposite) offers more luxurious options.

NIGHT TOURS

Several guesthouses offer night tours of the ruins (100B per person). These tours can be cancelled at the last minute if not enough people sign up.

Festivals & Events

The **Loi Krathong festival** at nearby Bang Pa-In (p201) is considered one of the more traditional versions in central Thailand (no firecrackers allowed).

Sleeping

The following prices are typical rack-rates. Some top-end places offer huge discounts (up to 50%) during the low season (April to November). Few budget or midrange places offer discounts.

BUDGET

Most of Ayuthaya's budget options are clustered around the mini-backpacker ghetto of Soi 1, Th Naresuan. In addition to being approached by commission-hungry sǎam-láw (three-wheeled pedicab) and túk-túk drivers, you may be approached by owners of new guesthouses. If you're in no hurry, new places are worth a look since they tend to be the cleanest, cheapest deals in town.

Note that several serious complaints have been made about service and tours at Ayuthaya Guest House.

Baan Lotus Guest House (☎ 0 3525 1988; 20 Th Pamaphrao; r 300B; ✗) Hands-down this is the best value for those not seeking out a party atmosphere. Everything from the hostesses to the linen is nicer at this beautifully restored teak home. Get a room overlooking the lotus-covered pond and let the frogs and birds drown out the distant traffic. A restaurant and a few air-conditioned rooms may be finished by the time you get here.

Baan Khun Phra (☎ 0 3524 1978; 48/2 Th U Thong; dm/s/d 150/250/350B) Occasionally called Ayuthaya Youth Hostel, this rambling 80-year-old teak house is the most atmospheric place in town. Rooms are tastefully decorated with the friendly owner's antique collection. Ask for a room near the river, as street traffic can be more than annoying.

PU Guest House (☎ 0 3525 1213; 20/1 Soi Thaw Kaw Saw; s/d/tr from 180/250/300B; ✗ 🖳) Just off the main drag, this clean and friendly place offers a low-key social atmosphere and comfortable rooms. Those with air-con, TV and mini-bar are particularly good value.

Tony's Place (☎ 0 3525 2578; 12/18 Soi 1, Th Naresuan; r 160-450B; ✗) It's the party atmosphere

(there's a popular bar with pool table downstairs) that keeps this place packed. The cheerful staff make everyone feel welcome. Rooms are reasonable, if a bit shabby, and shared toilets can get overused. The restaurant here is worth a visit.

Chantana Guest House (☎ 0 3532 3200; 12/22 Soi 1, Th Naresuan; r 250-240B; ✗) Shiny, modern, no-frills rooms and sweet staff make Chantana a safe choice. The 2nd-storey rooms with balconies are far better than those downstairs without windows.

Other recommendations:

Sherwood Guest House (☎ 0 6514 9510; 21/25 Th Dechawat; r from 250B; ✗ 🖳 🖭) Ordinary rooms with shared bathroom.

PS Guest House (☎ 0 6334 7207; Th Pamaphrao; s/d 100/150B) Sparse, basic rooms in a teak house.

U-Thong Hotel (☎ 0 3525 1136; Th U Thong; s/d from 300/370B) Adequate, worn and near the night market.

MIDRANGE

The following midrange places offer rooms with fridge and TV.

Wieng Fa Hotel (☎ 0 3524 3252; 1/8 Th Rotchana; r 400-500B; ✗) Helpful, professional and cosy, this is a good choice for families that don't need a swimming pool. Rooms are spacious but worn. All-you-can-drink coffee is available for 20B. English is spoken.

Suan Luang Hotel (Royal Garden; 96 Th Rotchana; ☎ 0 3524 5537; r 500-600B; ✗) Slightly institutional, this five-storey hotel has unimaginative rooms and professional staff that speak little English. The six- and twelve-bed rooms are good for large groups.

Ayothaya Riverside Hotel (☎ 0 3523 4873; fax 0 35 24 4139; 91 Th Rotchana; s/d incl breakfast from 900/1200B) A cut below the top-end, the Riverside has been recently renamed and is slowly being renovated. Its major boast is an interesting floating restaurant on a converted rice barge.

TOP END

River View Place Hotel (☎ 0 3524 1444; 35/5 Th U Thong; r from 2800B; ✗ ✗ 🖳 🖭) Classiest of the centrally located top-end options. Rooms and bathrooms are luxuriously spacious and most have stunning river views from small balconies. Booking through an agent, online or otherwise, brings rates down by 50%.

Krungsri River Hotel (☎ 0 3524 4333; www.krungsri river.com; 27/2 Th Rotchana; s/d 1800/2000, ste 6000-15,000B; ✗ 🖭) Nine-storey hotel is one of Ayuthaya's flashiest digs. Facilities include three restaurants, a karaoke bar, fitness centre, spa, gift shop, bowling alley and snooker club. It also offers several river cruise options.

Ayothaya Hotel (☎ 0 3523 2855; fax 0 3525 1018; 12 Soi 2, Th Thetsaban; r 1200-3500B; ✗ 🔀 🖳 🗩) Although it's a bit dated, the Ayothaya offers a comfortable escape from the hot, busy streets of the city. With a doorman, professional English-speaking staff, spacious modern rooms and a central location, it's popular with Thais and foreigners alike.

U-Thong Inn (☎ 0 3524 2236; www.uthonginn.com; 210 Th Rotchana; r 1900B, ste 2850-23,550B; ✗ 🔀 🖳 🗩) Complete with a conference centre, this newly renovated and expanded hotel offers everything an executive would need in a hotel. Facilities include a spa and fitness centre. The old wing is mostly standard rooms while the new wing is all suites, many with separate sitting areas. Discounts of up to 50% are given in the low season. It's not very convenient for exploring the town without wheels.

Ayuthaya Grand Hotel (☎ 0 3533 5483; fax 0 3533 5492; 55/5 Th Rotchana; r 1300-1850B; ✗ 🔀 🗩) Although it offers all the modern conveniences, the Ayuthaya Grand is east of the centre and inconvenient unless you have a car. It's a bit more dated than other top-end options, but it's a step up from midrange.

Eating
RESTAURANTS
Malakor (Th Chee Kun; Thai dishes 50-100B; ✆ 9.30am-midnight) This charming, two-storey wooden house has an incredible view of Wat Ratburana, which is most stunning after dark when it's all lit up. It serves a range of un-Westernised Thai dishes, and a good selection of jitter-inducing coffees.

Moradok-Thai (☎ 0 3532 3422; Th Rotchana; dishes 80-150B; ✆ 10am-midnight) Popular with Thai tourists, this cosy restaurant boasts an extensive menu, including some nice wines. It's also a good place to soak up the air-con after touring the ruins.

Chainam (☎ 0 3525 2013; 36/2 Th U Thong; dishes 35-80B) Pleasantly situated overlooking the river, Chainam has long attracted foreigners with its extensive bilingual menu. The Western breakfast is a highlight, but it mostly serves Thai dishes.

29 Steak (Th Pamaphrao; dishes 35-90B; ✆ 3.30pm-11pm) Yep, the focus here is steak. But there are plenty of Western-style salads and other veggie options, plus many Thai favourites. It's popular with a casual local crowd.

Tony's Place (dishes 40-90B) The restaurant at Tony's (p199) is the best of the guesthouse eateries and prepares a few very savoury curries.

There are several floating restaurants on Mae Nam Pa Sak, three on either side of Saphan Pridi Damrong (Pridi Damrong Bridge) on the west bank, and one on the east bank north of the bridge. **Phae Krung Kao** (dishes 60-150B; ✆ 10am-2am), on the southern side of the bridge on the west bank, has the best reputation. **Baan Khun Phra** (☎ 0 3524 1978; 48/2 Th U Thong; 40-80B), on the river behind the guesthouse of the same name, serves quite good food, including a few Western options, and has the most intimate atmosphere of the riverside places.

SELF-CATERING
Whatever you do in Ayuthaya, make at least one trip to the Hua Raw Night Market or the Night Market. Even if you don't want to eat a meal here, at least sample the variety of sweets and fruits. The stalls at the Chao Phrom Market offer a good variety of Thai-Chinese and Muslim dishes during the day.

Drinking
Keep your ears open for the newest spots in town. The following are the most reliable.

Moon Café (Soi 1, Th Naresuan; snack foods 15-50B; ✆ 3pm-midnight) Low-lit and eclectically decorated, this intimate spot is a good place to mingle with locals and fellow travellers.

Tony's Place The pool table is the focus of this sometimes-rowdy and always-popular watering hole (see p199).

Getting There & Away
BOAT
There are no scheduled or chartered boat services that operate between Bangkok and Ayuthaya.

Several hotels in Bangkok operate luxury cruises to Bang Pa-In with side trips by bus to Ayuthaya for around 1600B to 1900B per person, including a lavish lunch. Longer two-day trips in converted rice barges start at 6200B. See p142 for details.

BUS
Ayuthaya has two bus terminals. The buses from the south, west and east stop at the

main bus terminal (Th Naresuan). Long-distance northern buses stop at the Northern terminal, 5km east of the centre.

Frequent buses run between the main terminal and the airport (39B, 1½ hours) and Bangkok's Northern and Northeastern terminals (41B, two hours) from 5am to 7pm. Air-con buses leave from a couple of blocks east of the main bus terminal. They run along the same route every 20 minutes between 5.40am and 7.20pm (64B, two hours). Minivans to Bangkok (45B, two hours) leave from Th Bang Ian, east of the main bus terminal, every 20 minutes between 5am and 5pm. They drop passengers at Bangkok's Victory Monument.

Several guesthouses have started offering an overpriced (250B) mini-bus service to Kanchanaburi. Alternatively, hourly buses to Suphanburi (40B, 1½ hours) will connect you to buses to Kanchanaburi (39B, 1½ hours) without having to go into Bangkok.

Buses to Lopburi (40B, two hours) leave frequently from the main terminal.

Oversized *săwngthăew* (pick-up trucks used as buses or taxis; also written as *songthaew*) to/from Bang Pa-In (13B, one hour) leave often from the main bus terminal.

TRAIN
The trains to Ayuthaya leave Hualamphong station in Bangkok (3rd class 15B, 1½ hours) almost hourly from 6am to 10pm. Train schedules are available from the information booth at Hualamphong station.

From Ayuthaya's train station, the quickest way to reach the old city is to walk west to the river, where you can take a short ferry ride across (2B).

Upon arrival at Bangkok International Airport, savvy repeat visitors to Thailand sometimes choose to board a northbound train direct to Ayuthaya rather than head south into the Bangkok maelstrom. This only works if you arrive by air during the day or early evening, as the last train to Ayuthaya leaves Bangkok's Hualamphong train station at 10pm. There are frequent 3rd-class trains throughout the day between Don Muang station (opposite the Bangkok International Airport) and Ayuthaya.

Getting Around
Săamlăw and shared *túk-túk* ply the main city roads from 5B to 10B per person, depending on distance. A *túk-túk* from the train station to any point in old Ayuthaya should cost around 30B; on the island itself figure no more than 20B per trip.

For touring the ruins, the most economical and ecological option is to rent a bicycle from one of the guesthouses (30B to 50B per day). You can hire a *săamlăw* or *túk-túk* by the hour or by the day to explore the ruins, but the prices are quite high by Thai standards (200B per hour for anything with a motor in it, 500B all day when things are slow). Many drivers ask upwards of 700B for a day's worth of sightseeing – it would be much less expensive simply to catch separate rides from site to site.

It's also interesting to hire a boat from Chan Kasem Palace to do a semicircular tour of the island and see some of the less accessible ruins. A long-tail boat that will take up to eight people can be hired for 500B for a two- to three-hour trip with stops at Wat Phutthaisawan, Wat Phanan Choeng and Wat Chai Wattanaram.

AROUND AYUTHAYA
Bang Pa-In
บางปะอิน
Twenty kilometres south of Ayuthaya is Bang Pa-In, which is a curious collection of **palace buildings** (admission 100B; ⏰ 8am-3.45pm) in a wide variety of architectural styles. It's a pleasant escape from the bustle of Bangkok or Ayuthaya and an interesting look at the tastes and lifestyle of Thai Royalty, but it's not a must-see.

Highlights of Bang Pa-In are the **Thai pavilion**, the Chinese-style **Wehat Chamrun Palace** and the **Withun Thatsana** building, which looks like a lighthouse with balconies. The rest of the buildings are memorials and colonial-style royal residences. The gardens include an interesting topiary garden where the bushes have been trimmed into the shape of a small herd of elephants.

Wat Niwet Thamaprawat, across the river and south from the palace grounds, is an unusual wat that looks much more like a miniature Gothic Christian church than anything from Thailand. Like Bang Pa-In, it was built by Rama V (Chulalongkorn). You get to the wat by crossing the river in a small trolley-like cable car. The crossing is free.

During November, the **Loi Krathong festival** (p734) is celebrated here in traditional style.

Bang Pa-In can be reached by minibus – it's really a large *săwngthăew* – (13B, one hour), which departs from the edge of Ayuthaya's Chao Phrom Market on Th Naresuan. From Bangkok there are buses every half-hour from the Northern and Northeastern bus terminal (ordinary 29B, air-con 44B; one hour). The train service from Bangkok (3rd class 12B, one hour) is much less frequent.

The **Chao Phraya River Express Boat** (☎ 0 2623 6001) does a tour every Sunday from Tha Maharat in Bangkok. The tour leaves Bangkok at 8am and returns around 6pm, making stops at Bang Pa-In and Bang Sai Royal Folk Arts & Crafts Centre. The fare of 350B per person does not include lunch or the entrance fee to the Bang Pa-In complex (100B) or the Bang Sai Royal Folk Arts & Crafts Centre (100B). For details on more expensive river cruises to Bang Pa-In, which include tours of old Ayuthaya, see p141.

Bang Sai Royal Folk Arts & Crafts Centre
ศูนย์ศิลปาชีพบางไทร

This 115-hectare **craft centre** (☎ 0 3536 6092; admission 100B; ☺ 9am-5pm Mon-Fri, to 6pm Sat & Sun), in Beung Yai, Amphoe Bang Sai, is an important training centre for artisans. Under the auspices of Queen Sirikit's Promotion of Supplementary Occupations & Related Techniques (Support) Foundation, handicraft experts teach craft techniques to novices while at the same time demonstrating them for visitors. The centre has craft demonstrations daily except Monday; call for more information.

LOPBURI PROVINCE

LOPBURI
ลพบุรี

pop 57,600

Inhabited since at least the Dvaravati period (6th to 11th centuries AD), Lopburi is brimming with ruins and statuary that span a remarkable 12 centuries. The Lopburi National Museum houses an incredible collection of Dvaravati artefacts and visitors are consistently impressed by the juxtaposition of ancient brick ruins and not-so-ancient shop houses. But it's the resident troop of mischievous monkeys that really keep the curious coming to Lopburi.

Most of Lopburi's highlights can be seen and appreciated in one or two days en route between Ayuthaya and Phitsanulok (Northern Thailand). The town's stock of sleeping options is notably limited, but adequate for a night or two.

History

During the Dvaravati period between the 6th and 11th centuries AD, Lopburi was called Lavo. In the 10th century when the Angkor empire was extended to include Lavo, the Prang Khaek (Shiva Shrine), San Phra Kan (Kala Shrine) and Prang Sam Yot (Three Spired Shrine) were built, as well as the impressive tower at Wat Phra Si Ratana Mahathat.

Power over Lopburi was wrested from the Khmers in the 13th century as the Sukhothai kingdom to the north grew stronger, but the Khmer cultural influence remained to some extent throughout the Ayuthaya period. King Narai fortified Lopburi in the mid-17th century to serve as a second capital when the kingdom of Ayuthaya was threatened by a Dutch naval blockade. His palace in Lopburi was built in 1665 and he died there in 1688.

Orientation

Lopburi is distinctly split with a new 1940s section about 2km east of the old town. The new town is centred around two large roundabouts, and is of little interest except as a place to crash or catch the bus. All the historical sites in the old town can be visited by foot and are convenient to the train station.

Information

Communications Authority of Thailand (CAT; Th Phra Narai Maharat; ☺ 8am-6pm) Next to the post office, between the new and old city. Has a Home Country Direct phone.

Hospital (☎ 0 3641 1250)

Police (☎ 0 3641 1013; Th Na Phra Kan)

TAT (☎ 0 3642 2768-9; Th Phraya Kamjat) Has helpful maps and brochures. Sometimes staff will let you stow your pack in the office.

Sights

PHRA NARAI RATCHANIWET
พระนารายณ์ราชนิเวศน์

Start your tour of Lopburi at **King Narai's Palace** (☺ 7am-5.30pm). After King Narai's death

CENTRAL THAILAND

LOPBURI

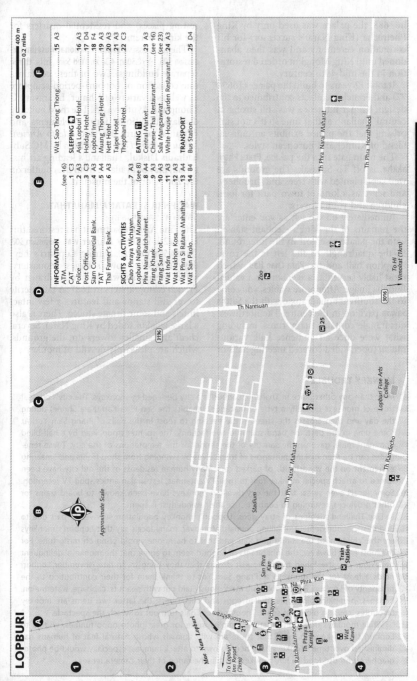

| 0 | 400 m |
| 0 | 0.2 miles |

INFORMATION
ATM..(see 16) C3
CAT..1 C3
Police...2 A3
Post Office...................................3 C3
Siam Commercial Bank..................4 A3
TAT...5 A4
Thai Farmer's Bank........................6 A3

SIGHTS & ACTIVITIES
Chao Phraya Wichayen....................7 A3
Lopburi National Museum...........(see 8)
Phra Narai Ratchaniwet..................8 A4
Prang Khaek...................................9 A3
Prang Sam Yot.............................10 A3
Wat Indra....................................11 A3
Wat Nakhon Kosa.......................12 A3
Wat Phra Si Ratana Mahathat......13 A4
Wat San Paolo.............................14 B4

Wat Sao Thong Thong..................15 A3

SLEEPING
Asia Lopburi Hotel.......................16 A3
Holiday Hotel...............................17 D4
Lopburi Inn..................................18 F4
Muang Thong Hotel.....................19 A3
Nett Hotel....................................20 A3
Taipei Hotel.................................21 A3
Thepthani Hotel...........................22 C3

EATING
Central Market.............................23 A3
Chinese-Thai Restaurant...........(see 16)
Sala Mangsawirat.....................(see 23)
White House Garden Restaurant...24 A3

TRANSPORT
Bus Station..................................25 D4

Approximate Scale

To Lopburi
Inn Resort
(2km)

Mae Nam Lopburi

To Lopburi Inn Resort (2km)

Th Surasongkhram

San Phra
Kan

Th Wichayen

Th Na Phra Kan

Th Ratchadamnoen

Th Phraya Kamjat

Wat Kawit

Th Sorasak

Train Station

Th Ramdecho

Th Naresuan

Zoo

Stadium

Lopburi Fine Arts
College

Th Phra Narai Maharat

Th Phra Narai Maharat

Th Phra Horathibodi

To HI
Vimolrat (1km)

3016

3196

in 1688, the palace was used only by King Phetracha (King Narai's successor) for his coronation ceremony and was then abandoned until King Mongkut ordered restoration in the mid-19th century.

It took 12 years to build the palace (1665–77) and French architects contributed to the design. Khmer influence was still strong in central Thailand at that time so it's not surprising that the palace exhibits an unusual blend of Khmer and European styles.

The main gate into the palace, **Pratu Phayakkha**, is off Th Sorasak. The grounds are well kept, planted with trees and shrubbery, and serve as a kind of town park for local children and young lovers.

Immediately on the left as you enter are the remains of the king's elephant stables, with the palace reservoir in the foreground. In the quadrangle to the left is the royal reception hall and the **Phra Chao Hao**, which most likely served as a *wíhãan* for a valued Buddha image. After more stables, you come to the southwest quadrangle with the **Suttha Sawan** pavilion in the centre. The northwest quadrangle contains many ruins, including what were once an audience hall, various *sãalaa* (open-sided covered meeting halls or

resting places) and residential quarters for the king's harem.

The impressive **Lopburi National Museum** (admission 30B; 8.30am-4.30pm Wed-Sun) fills three separate buildings. Two of these contain a fine collection of Lopburi-period sculpture as well as a variety of Khmer, Dvaravati, U Thong and Ayuthaya art. The third building displays traditional farm implements and dioramas of farm life. *A Guide to Ancient Monuments in Lopburi*, written by MC Subhadradis Diskul, Thailand's leading art historian, may be available from the counter on the 2nd floor of the museum.

WAT PHRA SI RATANA MAHATHAT
วัดพระศรีรัตนมหาธาตุ

The Fine Arts Department has restored this large 12th-century Khmer **wat** (admission 30B; 7am-5pm Wed-Sun). During Lopburi's heyday, it was the town's largest monastery, a fact clearly shown on a map drawn by French cartographers in 1687. A tall laterite tower still stands and features a few intact lintels and some ornate stucco. There is also a large *wíhãan* added by King Narai. Several *chedi* and smaller towers dot the grounds, which are pleasantly devoid of monkeys.

MONKEY TROUBLE

More than any other place in Thailand, Lopburi is a city besieged by monkeys. The city's original troop of monkeys (actually a type of macaque) inhabits the San Phra Kan (Kala Shrine) during the day and then crosses the street in the evening to roost in the halls of Prang Sam Yot. At some time in the past, the band split into two factions. The splinter troop, lead by a half-blind dominant male, gave up the sanctity of the shrine for the temptations of the city. These renegades can be seen making nuisances of themselves by swinging from shop fronts and smearing excrement on the windshields of parked cars. Many human residents of the old city have been forced to attach special monkey foils to their TV antennas, lest simian antics spoil TV reception. Some locals even swear that the city-dwelling monkeys have been known to board trains for other provinces, returning to Lopburi once their wanderlust is spent.

Like Thailand's legions of stray dogs, Lopburi's monkey population survives in part due to Buddhist discouragement of killing animals. Moreover, many locals say that Lopburi's monkeys are the 'children' of the Hindu god Kala and that to harm one would bring on misfortune. For the most part, however, the inhabitants of Lopburi seem to agree that the monkeys' delinquent behaviour is outweighed by the tourist dollars that they bring in. In late November Lopburi holds a feast for the monkeys at Prang Sam Yot to thank them for their contribution to the prosperity of Lopburi. Buffet tables are meticulously laid out with peanuts, cabbage, watermelon, bananas, pumpkin, pineapple, boiled eggs and cucumbers; the latter two items are monkey favourites, causing plenty of spats. Thousands of Thais turn out to watch the spectacle.

While monkeys frolicking on stone temples make for great photo opportunities, visitors to Lopburi should keep in mind that these are wild animals whose natural fear of humans has diminished over time. Monkeys have been known to attack humans, especially would-be photographers who use food to lure monkeys within the range of their camera lenses.

OTHER TEMPLES

Built by the Khmers in the 12th century, **Wat Nakhon Kosa** may originally have been a Hindu shrine. The U Thong and Lopburi images found at the temple and in the Lopburi National Museum are thought to have been added later. There's not much left of this wat, but the foliage growing on the brick ruins is an interesting sight. However, half-hearted attempts to restore it with modern materials and motifs detract from the overall effect. A notably larger base below the monument was uncovered several years ago.

A partial brick and stucco tower is all that's left of **Wat San Paolo**, a Jesuit church founded by the Portuguese during King Narai's reign. A contingent of a dozen French priests came to run the church in 1687. An octagonal, three-storey celestial observatory was also erected here, though it is unclear under whose direction it was built.

Northwest of the palace centre, this **Wat Sao Thong Thong** is in pretty poor shape. The *wíhǎan* and large seated Buddha are from the Ayuthaya period; King Narai restored the *wíhǎan* (changing its windows to an incongruous but intriguing Gothic style) so it could be used as a Christian chapel. Niches along the inside walls contain Lopburi-style Buddhas with *naga* (serpent) protectors.

Practically nothing is known about the history of **Wat Indra** (Th Ratchadamnoen), which is now merely a sizable brick foundation.

PRANG KHAEK
ปรางค์แขก

Situated on a triangular slice of land bordered by Th Wichayen to the north, Prang Khaek features towers with Khmer-style brickwork. The structure is thought to have originally been a temple to the Hindu god Shiva and dates back to the 11th century.

CHAO PHRAYA WICHAYEN
บ้านวิชาเยนทร์

King Narai built this Thai-European **palace** (admission 30B) as a residence for foreign ambassadors, of whom the Greek Constantine Phaulkon was the most famous. Phaulkon became one of King Narai's advisers and was eventually a royal minister. In 1688, as Narai lay dying, Phaulkon was assassinated by Luang Sorasak, who wanted power for himself. The palace is across the street and northeast of Wat Sao Thong Thong.

PRANG SAM YOT
ปรางค์สามยอด

Opposite San Phra Kan, this **shrine** (admission 30B; ☺ 8am-6pm) represents classic Khmer-Lopburi style and is another Hindu-turned-Buddhist temple. Originally, the three towers symbolised the Hindu Trimurti of Shiva, Vishnu and Brahma. Now two of them contain ruined Lopburi-style Buddha images. Some Khmer lintels can still be made out, and some appear unfinished.

A rather uninteresting U Thong-Ayuthaya imitation Buddha image sits in the brick sanctuary in front of the linked towers. At the back are a couple of crudely restored images, probably once Lopburi style. The grounds allotted to Prang Sam Yot are quite small and virtually surrounded by modern buildings. The best view of the monument would probably be from one of the upper floors of the Muang Thong Hotel (p206). The monument is lit up at night and constantly crawling with monkeys.

Festivals & Events

In mid-February the Phra Narai Ratchaniwet is the focus of the three-day **King Narai Festival**, which includes *lákhon ling* (traditional drama performed by monkeys) and the exhibit and sale of local, woven textiles.

Sleeping

Most travellers choose to stay in the old city, but the more modern hotels in the new city are better value if you can afford the extra baht. Some of the midrange hotels here are an exceptional deal.

BUDGET

Lopburi's budget hotels are quite adequate, if cheap, basic and worn. Beware: many have deceptively well-restored lobbies.

HI Vimolrat (Lopburi Youth Hostel; ☎ 0 3661 3731; www.tyha.org/LopburiYH.html; 5/19 Mu 3, Th Naresuan; dm/d/q 120/320/350B; ☒) Inconveniently located southeast of the city, this hostel is a good place to meet young Thais and other travellers. It's fairly new so rooms are cleaner and more pleasantly decorated than the local competition. The train station, Phra Narai Ratchaniwet and Prang Sam Yot ruins are all just a 60B *túk-túk* ride away.

Asia Lopburi Hotel (☎ 0 3661 8894; cnr Th Sorasak & Th Phraya Kamjat; s/d from 200/240B; ☒) All rooms are not maintained equally here; some have new paint while others desperately need a coat. Look at more than one before settling in and be sure to ask for a room away from the street.

Nett Hotel (☎ 0 3641 1738; 17/1-2 Th Ratchadamnoen; r from 160B; 🔀) Clean and friendly option is a bit sleepy and some rooms are depressingly dark and cramped.

Other recommendations:

Taipei Hotel (☎ 0 3641 1524; 24/6-7 Th Surasongkhram; r from 140B; 🔀) Decent but dark rooms, welcoming staff.

Muang Thong Hotel (☎ 0 3641 1036; 1/1-11 Th Prang Sam Yot; r 140B) Great location, dumpy rooms.

MIDRANGE & TOP END

Thepthani Hotel (☎ 0 3641 1029; Th Phra Narai Maharat; r 400B; 🔀) Located half-way between old and new Lopburi, Thepthani is the best midrange value. Rooms are spacious with spotless linens, cable TV and central hot water. Blue buses between old and new town will drop you here for 3B.

Lopburi Inn (☎ 0 3641 2300; fax 0 3641 1917; 28/8 Th Phra Narai Maharat; r incl breakfast 500-1200B; 🔀) The Lopburi Inn features very nice rooms with all the amenities.

Lopburi Inn Resort (☎ 0 3642 0777; 144 Tambon Tha Sala; s/d/ste 1200/1300/1700B; 🔀 🛋) You may need a sense of humour to appreciate the extensive monkey theme at this resort. It may not be sophisticated or contemporary, but it is the nicest place in town, with everything you'd expect including a fitness centre.

Holiday Hotel (☎ 0 3641 1343; Soi Suriyothai 2, Th Phra Narai Maharat; r from 400B; 🔀) Popular with middle-class Thais.

Eating

There are a few good restaurants in the old town. Some of the street food, especially the bite-sized snacks available near the market, are a real treat. Restaurants on the side streets of Th Ratchadamnoen and Th Phraya Kamjat also offer good value, while some of the cheap curry vendors down the alleys and along the smaller streets in old Lopburi are a real treat.

White House Garden Restaurant (Th Phraya Kamjat; dishes 60-120B; 🕙 10am-4pm) Across the street from the TAT office, this pleasant little spot offers a range of Thai-Chinese specialties. Generous portions and high-quality vegetarian dishes keep travellers happy.

Chinese-Thai Restaurant (Th Sorasak; dishes 20-60B) Next to the Asia Lopburi Hotel, this restaurant offers simple, decent food at reasonable prices.

Sala Mangsawirat (Vegetarian Pavilion, Central Market; dishes 15-30B; 🕙 9am-2pm) In the heart of the market, this is an inexpensive – but not especially appetising – Thai veggie place.

Central Market (off Th Ratchadamnoen & Th Surasongkhram) Just north of the palace, this market is a great place to pick up *kài thâwt* or *kài yâang* (fried or roast chicken) with sticky rice; *hàw mòk* (soufflé-like fish and coconut curry steamed in banana leaves); *klûay khàek* (Indian-style fried bananas); and a wide selection of fruit, satays, *khâo krìap* (crispy rice cakes), *thâwt man plaa* (fried fish cakes) and other delights.

In the evenings there is also a **night market** (Th Na Phra Kan).

Getting There & Away

BUS

Buses to Lopburi leave Ayuthaya (40B, 1½ hours) every 10 minutes. From Bangkok, buses leave about every 20 minutes (from 5.30am to 8.30pm) from the Northern and Northeastern bus terminal (62B ordinary, 85B for air-con, three hours).

Lopburi can also be reached from the west via Kanchanaburi or Suphanburi. Take a local orange bus (no air-con) from Kanchanaburi, take a local orange bus to Suphanburi (38B, 2½ hours); there's beautiful scenery all the way. From the Suphanburi bus terminal you can also catch a direct bus to Lopburi (40B, three hours).

If you happen to miss the direct bus, you can also hopscotch to Lopburi by catching a bus first to Singburi or Ang Thong, across the river from Lopburi. The scenery is even better between Suphanburi and Singburi (2½ hours) – you'll pass many old, traditional Thai wooden houses (late Ayuthaya style), countless rice paddies and small wat of all descriptions. Finally, at the Singburi bus station, catch one of the frequent buses to Lopburi (45 minutes). The Singburi bus makes a stop in front of Prang Sam Yot in old Lopburi – if you get off here, you won't have to backtrack from the new city. An alternative to the Suphanburi to Singburi route is to take a bus to Ang Thong and then a share taxi or bus to Lopburi. This is a little faster but not quite as scenic.

Lopburi can be reached from the north-east via Khorat (Nakhon Ratchasima) on air-con buses for 85B.

TRAIN
Ordinary, 3rd-class only trains depart from Bangkok's Hualamphong station for northern parts at 7.05am, 8.35am, 11.15am, 1pm, 2.10pm and 8.10pm (28B, three hours). Rapid trains leave Bangkok at 7.45am, 3pm, 6.10pm, 8pm and 10pm (2½ hours). Express trains (No 9, 11 and 13) stop in Lopburi, leaving Bangkok at 8.25am, 5.20pm and 7.25pm (2½ hours). Excluding rapid or express surcharges, 1st- and 2nd-class fares are 64B and 123B respectively. These trains stop in Ayuthaya (13B in 3rd class, one hour).

The only way to continue on to Phitsanulok from Lopburi is via train (1st/2nd/3rd class 40/96/200B, five to seven hours). There are several morning trains, but only a 2pm and 5.24pm train in the afternoon.

Getting Around
Săwngthăew run along Th Wichayen and Th Phra Narai Maharat between the old and new towns for 5B per passenger; there is also a system of city buses (5B). *Săamláw* will go anywhere in the old town for 30B.

KANCHANABURI PROVINCE

Rugged frontier province is home to some of Thailand's largest waterfalls and most extensive wildlife sanctuaries. Its mountains form a natural boundary with Myanmar, discouraging major population growth and preserving a wilder way of life. These mountains also provide a slightly cooler climate than Bangkok, especially in the evenings. But it's not nature or border culture that attracts tourists to Kanchanaburi. Most come to see the 'Bridge on the River Kwai'.

KANCHANABURI
กาญจนบุรี
pop 61,800
Kanchanaburi is 130km west of Bangkok in the slightly elevated valley of Mae Nam Mae Klong amid hills and sugar-cane plantations. Meuang Kanz, Kan'buri, or just Kan (as the locals call it) receives many visitors, both Western and Asian. Visitors of all stripes will find Kanchanaburi a pleasant town with plenty to do and a convenient springboard for treks into the province's lush forests.

Mae Nam Mae Klong is a focus for much weekend and holiday activity among the Thais – it's a popular destination for students from Bangkok. A number of floating discos – party boats that go up and down the river – host nightly music and revelry that reverberates off the river and gives riverside accommodation an acoustic pummelling. If you don't like noise, consider staying further off the river.

You may notice the fish-shaped street signs in Meuang Kan – they represent *plaa yîisók,* the most common food fish in Mae Nam Mae Klong and its tributaries.

History
Kanchanaburi was originally established by Rama I as a first line of defence against the Burmese, who might use the old invasion route through the Three Pagodas Pass on the Thailand–Myanmar border. Today it remains a popular smuggling route into Myanmar.

During WWII the Japanese used Allied prisoners of war (POWs) to build the infamous Death Railway along this same invasion route, from Mae Nam Khwae Noi to the pass. Thousands of prisoners died as a result of brutal treatment by their captors, their experiences chronicled by Pierre Boulle in his book *The Bridge on the River Kwai* and popularised by the movie of the same name. The bridge is still there (still in use, in fact) and so are the graves of the Allied soldiers.

Orientation
The traveller scene is concentrated around Th Mae Nam Khwae, outside of the city centre towards the Death Railway Bridge, but near the train station. The bus terminal is in the small city centre which can be managed on foot. But you'll want a bicycle or *săamláw* to get from town to Th Mae Nam Khwae or to the bridge and many of the in-town sights.

Information
EMERGENCY
Tourist Police (☎ 0 3451 2668) There are several locations around town.

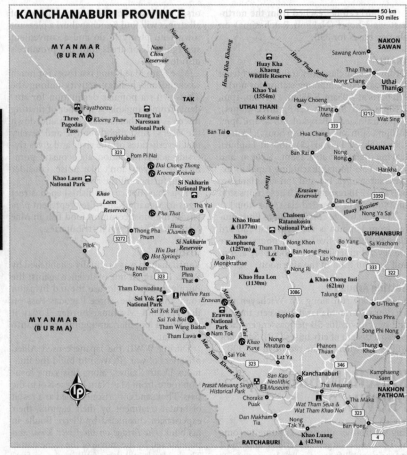

KANCHANABURI PROVINCE

0 ——————— 50 km
0 ——————— 30 miles

MYANMAR (BURMA)

Nam Khlong

Nam Chou Reservoir

Payathonzu

Three Pagodas Pass

Kloeng Thaw

Thung Yai Naresuan National Park

Sangkhlaburi

Pom Pi Nai

323

Dai Chong Thong

Kroeng Krawia

Khao Laem National Park

Khao Laem Reservoir

Pha That

Si Nakharin National Park

Tha Yai

Thong Pha Phum

Huay Khamin

Si Nakharin Reservoir

Hin Dat Hot Springs

3272

Pilok

Phu Nam Ron

323

Tham Daowadung

Tham Phra That

MYANMAR (BURMA)

Sai Yok National Park

Hellfire Pass

Sai Yok Yai

Sai Yok Noi

Tham Wang Badan

Tham Lawa

Erawan

Erawan National Park

Nam Tok

Prasat Meuang Singh Historical Park

Chorake Puak

Dan Makham Tia

Ban Mongkrathae

Khao Kamphaeng (1257m)

Tham Than Lot

Khao Huat (1177m)

Khao Hua Lon (1130m)

3086

Nong Khon

Nong Ri

Khao Pang

Sai Yok

323

Lat Ya

Nong Khratum

Ban Kao Neolithic Museum

Wat Tham Seua & Wat Tham Khao Noi

Nong Tak Ya

Khao Luang (423m)

RATCHABURI

Huay Taphoen

Chaloem Ratanakosin National Park

Krasiaw Reservoir

Dan Chang

3350

Huay Krasiaw

Nong Ya Sai

Ban Nong Preu

Lao Khwan

SUPHANBURI

333

Bo Yang

Sa Krachom

Khao Chong Insi (621m)

Talung

322

U-Thong

Khao Phra

Song Phi Nong

Phanom Thuan

Tha Meuang

346

Kanchanaburi

Kamphaeng Saen

NAKHON PATHOM

Tha Maka

323

Ban Pong

4

Huay Kha Khaeng

Huay Kha Khaeng Wildlife Reserve

Khao Yai (1554m)

TAK

UTHAI THANI

Huay Choeng

Kok Kwai

Ban Tai

Hua Chang

Ban Rai

Nong Rong

NAKON SAWAN

Sawang Arom

Thap Than

Nong Chang

Uthai Thani

Thung Men

3213

Wat Sing

CHAINAT

Hankha

Bophloi

Mae Nam Khwae Yai

Mae Nam Khwae Noi

INTERNET ACCESS
Internet cafés change names and locations often, but there are always several connections available along Th Mae Nam Khwae, and one or two on Th Rong Hip Oi. Prices vary from 20B per hour to 60B per hour, so it's best to shop around. Some guesthouses have a computer for guests.

INTERNET RESOURCES
General tourist information is available online at www.kanchanaburi-info.com.

LAUNDRY
Guesthouses and places along Th Mae Nam Khwae will do laundry for about 15B per kilo. Get off the main drag for better deals.

Nat & Dear Laundry (☎ 0 9678 8829; Th Chaokunen; per kilo 5B)
Nok Laundry (☎ 0 1990 5789; Th Chaokunen; per kilo 5B)

MEDICAL SERVICES
Thanakarn Hospital (☎ 0 3462 2358; Th Saengchuto) Near the junction of Th Chukkadon, this hospital is best equipped for foreign visitors.

MONEY
Several major Thai banks can be found around Th Saengchuto near the market and bus terminal. Most offer foreign-exchange services and ATMs. Both the following services have a money-changing service, which is useful on weekends and holidays.

AS Mixed Travel (☎ 0 3451 2017; 52 Soi Rong Hip Oi; Apple's Guesthouse)
Punnee Cafe & Bar (☎ 0 3451 3503; Th Ban Neua)

POST
Main post office (Th Saengchuto; ☼ 8.30am-4.30pm Mon-Fri, 9am-2pm Sat) Around the corner from the CAT office.

TELEPHONE
CAT (☼ 7am-10pm) This office has an international telephone service. There are also numerous private shops along Th Mae Nam Khwae offering long-distance calls.

TOURIST INFORMATION
TAT (☎ 0 3451 1200, 0 1239 0767; Th Saengchuto) Hands out free maps of the town and province. It also has comprehensive information on accommodation, activities and transportation.

Sights
THAILAND–BURMA RAILWAY CENTRE
ศูนย์รถไฟไทย–พม่า
This well-designed, contemporary **museum** (☎ 0 3451 0067; www.tbrconline.com; 73 Th Jaokannun; admission 60B; ☼ 9am-5pm) is the best place to start

your exploration of the Kanchanaburi area. Opened in March 2003, the museum aims to offer a non-partisan explanation of the Thailand–Burma railway, why it was built, why people died building it and what has happened since the end of the war. Each of the eight galleries is packed with interesting facts presented in a dynamic way. For instance, the first gallery has a life-size wooden bridge model that was built exactly the same way as the original bridge. Perhaps the most emotive exhibit is the 'rice wagon' boxcar that is the same size as those that were used to transport prisoners from Singapore and Malaysia to Thailand. Visitors can stand inside the boxcar and imagine what it was like to be packed inside it with a dozen other prisoners for days on end. The models of the landscape and faithful reproductions of Japanese designs show why building the railway was such a treacherous challenge.

DEATH RAILWAY BRIDGE
สะพานข้ามแม่น้ำแคว
This little railroad bridge probably would not attract any visitors if it were not for its

---

WHY BRIDGE THE RIVER KWAI?

The dramatic story behind the so-called 'Bridge on the River Kwai', or Saphan Mae Nam Khwae, is an unforgettable tale. The materials for the bridge were brought from Java by the Imperial Japanese Army during its 1942–43 occupation of Thailand. In 1945 the bridge was bombed several times and was only rebuilt after the war – the curved portions of the bridge are original. The first version of the bridge, completed in February 1943, was all wood. In April of the same year a second bridge of steel was constructed.

It is estimated that 16,000 prisoners of war (POWs) died while building the Death Railway to Myanmar (Burma), of which the bridge was only a small part. The strategic objective of the railway was to secure an alternative supply route for the Japanese conquest of Myanmar and other Asian countries to the west. Construction of the railway began on 16 September 1942 at existing stations in Thanbyuzayat, Myanmar and Nong Pladuk, Thailand. Japanese engineers at the time estimated that it would take five years to link Thailand and Myanmar by rail, but the Japanese army forced the POWs to complete the 415km, 1m-gauge railway (of which roughly two-thirds ran through Thailand) in 16 months. Much of the railway was built in difficult terrain that required high bridges and deep mountain cuttings. The rails were finally joined 37km south of Three Pagodas Pass; a Japanese brothel train inaugurated the line. The Death Railway Bridge was in use for 20 months before the Allies bombed it in 1945. Only one POW is known to have escaped, a Briton who took refuge among pro-British Karen guerrillas.

Although the number of POWs who died during the Japanese occupation is horrifying, the figures for the labourers, many from Thailand, Myanmar, Malaysia and Indonesia, are even worse. It is thought that 90,000 to 100,000 labourers died in the area.

Today little remains of the original railway as the rails were torn up by Thailand following WWII. Many of these rails were used to build the primitive sun shelters found at rural railway stations – look closely and you may notice these at some of the smaller railway stations in Thailand's northeast.

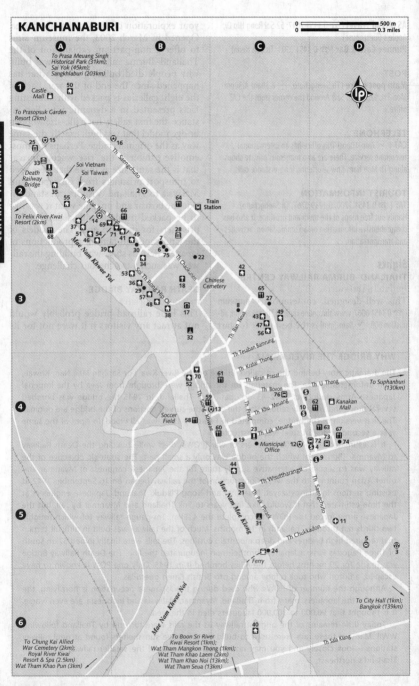

KANCHANABURI

0 — 500 m
0 — 0.3 miles

CENTRAL THAILAND

A

To Prasa Meuang Singh
Historical Park (31km);
Sai Yok (45km);
Sangkhlaburi (203km)

Castle
Mall

1

50

To Prasopsuk Garden
Resort (2km)

25
15
33
20

Soi Vietnam
Soi Taiwan

Death
Railway
Bridge

35
55

26

2

To Felix River Kwai
Resort (2km)

68

37
14
51
54
46
71
41
39

66

45
30

34

B

Th Saengchuto

16

2

Th Mae Nam Khwae

Mae Nam Khwae Yai

53
36
29
57
48
38

Soi Th Rong Hip O

3

7
6
75

Th Chukkunen

22

18

17

32

64

Train
Station

28

C

42

65
27

8

43
47
56

49

Chinese
Cemetery

Th Ban Neua

Th Tesaban Bamrung

Th Kratai Thong

Th Hiran Prasat

D

To Suphanburi
(130km)

70
52

61

4

Soccer
Field

59
13
58
60

Th Song Kwae

44
21

5

19

Municipal
Office

23

Th Prasat

Th Khu Meuang

Th Lak Meuang

12

Th Bovon
76

Th U Thong

Th Wisuttharangsi

Th Pak Phraek

31

Mae Nam Mae Klong

Th Chukkadon

Ferry

Mae Nam Khwae Noi

1
10

62
63

Kanakan
Mall

67
74

72
73

9

Th Saengchuto

11

5
3

To City Hall (1km);
Bangkok (139km)

6

To Chung Kai Allied
War Cemetery (2km);
Royal River Kwai
Resort & Spa (2.5km);
Wat Tham Khao Pun (3km)

24

40

To Boon Sri River
Kwai Resort (1km);
Wat Tham Mangkon Thong (1km);
Wat Tham Khao Laem (2km);
Wat Tham Khao Noi (13km);
Wat Tham Seua (13km)

Th Sala Klang

INFORMATION				
Bangkok Bank	**1** C4	Test of Thai	**27** C3	Sugar Cane Guest House II	**55** A2
Border Patrol Police	**2** B2	Thailand-Burma Railway Centre	**28** B2	VL Guest House	**56** C3
CAT	**3** D5	Toi's Tours	**29** B3	VN Guest House	**57** B3
Kasikornbank	**4** D4	Toi's Tours	**30** B3		
Main Post Office	**5** D5	Wat Chaichumphon	**31** C5	EATING	
Nat & Dear Laundry	**6** B3	Wat Neua	**32** B3	Apple's Restaurant	(see 34)
Nok Laundry	**7** B2	WWII Museum	**33** A2	Floating Restaurants	**58** B4
Punnee Cafe & Bar	**8** C3			Food Vendors	**59** B4
TAT	**9** D4	SLEEPING		Jukkru	**60** C4
Thai Military Bank	**10** C4	Apple's Guesthouse	**34** B3	Market	**61** C4
Thanakam Thospital	**11** D5	Bamboo House	**35** A2	Market	**62** D4
Tourist Police	**12** C4	Ban Vimol	**36** B3	Market	**63** D4
Tourist Police	**13** C4	Blue Star Guest House	**37** A2	Night Market	**64** B2
Tourist Police	**14** A2	J Guest House	**38** B3	Sabai-jit Restaurant	**65** C3
Tourist Police	**15** A2	Jolly Frog	**39** B3	Schluck Restaurant	**66** B2
Tourist Police	**16** B2	Kasem Island Resort	**40** C6	Srifa Bakery	**67** D4
		Little Creek Hideaway Main Office	**41** B2	Sutjai	**68** A2
SIGHTS & ACTIVITIES		Luxury Hotel	**42** C3		
AS Mixed Travel	(see 34)	MK Hotel	**43** C3	DRINKING	
Chinese Temple	**17** B3	Nita Raft House	**44** C5	Beer Barrel Bar	**69** A2
Church	**18** B3	Ploy Guesthouse	**45** B2	Discovery	**70** B4
City Gate	**19** C4	Pong Phen Guesthouse	**46** A2	No Name Bar	**71** B2
Japanese War Memorial	**20** A2	Prasopsuk Hotel	**47** C3		
Jeath War Museum	**21** C5	River Guest House	**48** B3	TRANSPORT	
Kanchanaburi Allied War Cemetery	**22** B3	River Kwai Hotel	**49** C3	Air-Con Buses	
Lak Meuang Shrine	**23** C4	RS Hotel	**50** A1	to Bangkok	**72** D4
Long-Tail Boats	**24** C5	Sam's House	**51** A2	Bus Station	**73** D4
Railway Museum	**25** A2	Sam's Place	**52** B4	Minibus to Sangklhaburi	**74** D4
Safarine	**26** A2	Sam's River Raft Guest House	**53** B3	NB Motorcycle	**75** B3
		Sugar Cane Guest House I	**54** A2	Taxi Stand	**76** C4

unbelievable history. The bridge serves different purposes for different visitors. For some, it is a doorway to their lost memories and lost lives. For most visitors it is a symbol of the ills of war, a reminder of how inhumane humans can be during war. If you don't already know about the history of the bridge, be sure to visit the Thailand–Burma Railway Centre (p209) before visiting the bridge itself.

Train enthusiasts should not miss the old locomotives used during WWII that are parked on display near the bridge. During the last week of November and first week of December there is a nightly sound-and-light show at the bridge, commemorating the Allied attack on the Death Railway in 1945. It's a big scene, with the sounds of bombers and explosions, fantastic bursts of light, and more. The town gets a lot of Thai tourists during this week, so book early if you want to witness this spectacle.

The bridge spans Mae Nam Khwae Yai, a tributary (Khwae Yai literally translates as 'large tributary') of Mae Nam Mae Klong, which is 2.5km from Kanchanaburi's Lak Meuang shrine (làk meuang, town pillar/phallus). The most enjoyable way to get to the bridge from town is to rent a bicycle or motorcycle (50B to 150B per day). The cheapest way is via train (2B), but the easiest way is to catch a northbound săwngthăew (10B) along Th Saengchuto.

ALLIED WAR CEMETERIES
สุสานทหารสงครามโลกครั้งที่2

There are two cemeteries containing the remains of Allied POWs who died in captivity during WWII: the **Kanchanaburi Allied War Cemetery** and the **Chung Kai Allied War Cemetery**. The first is just off Th Saengchuto. The second is across Mae Nam Mae Klong in the west of town and a few kilometres down Mae Nam Khwae Noi (Little Tributary River).

Within walking distance of the train station and the guesthouses near Th Mae Nam Khwae, the Kanchanaburi Allied War Cemetery is usually a cool spot on a hot Kanchanaburi day. It's well cared for with green lawns and healthy flowers. From Th Saengchuto, hop a northbound orange săamláw (No 2) – the fare is 5B. Jump off at the English sign in front of the cemetery on the left, or ask to be let off at the sù-săan (cemetery). Just before the cemetery on the same side of the road there is a very colourful **Chinese cemetery** with burial mounds and inscribed tombstones.

The easiest way to get to the Chung Kai Allied War Cemetery is to rent a bicycle or motorcycle and ride there yourself. Cross the Saphan Wat Neua and then another smaller bridge just past the football field before continuing southwest about 3km. Follow the curving road through a wooded area until you reach the cemetery on your left. Like the more visited cemetery north of town, the Chung Kai burial plaques carry names, military insignia and short epitaphs for Dutch, British, French and Australian soldiers. This cemetery sees fewer tourists than the Kanchanaburi Allied War Cemetery but is just as well kept.

About 1km southwest of the Chung Kai cemetery is a dirt path that leads to **Wat Tham Khao Pun**, one of Kanchanaburi's many cave temples. This wat became notorious in late 1995 when a drug-addicted monk living at the wat murdered a British tourist and disposed of her corpse in a nearby sinkhole. The monk was defrocked and sentenced to death (commuted to life imprisonment without parole by the king in 1996). During WWII the cave complex was used by the Japanese to store weapons and equipment, and some of the smaller chambers are said to have been used to imprison and torture POWs. Despite the gruesome history, the caves are filled with images of the Buddha, Hindu deities and Thai kings, and attract a trickle of pilgrims from around Thailand. The cave complex is fairly extensive and more interesting than similar caves at Wat Tham Seua.

JEATH WAR MUSEUM
พิพิธภัณฑ์สงคราม

This worn but heart-felt **museum** (Th Wisuttharangsi; admission 30B; ☻ 8.30am-6pm), next to Wat Chaichumphon (Wat Tai), is worth visiting just to sit on the cool banks of Mae Nam Mae Klong. Phra Maha Tomson Tongproh, a Thai monk who devotes much energy to promoting the museum, speaks some English and can answer questions about the exhibits, as well as supply information about what to see around Kanchanaburi and how best to get there. The museum is a replica of the bamboo-*atap* huts used to house Allied POWs during the occupation. The long huts contain various photographs taken during the war, drawings and paintings by POWs, maps, weapons and other war memorabilia. The acronym Jeath represents the meeting of Japan, England, Australia/America, Thailand and Holland at Kanchanaburi during WWII.

The war museum is at the west end of Th Wisuttharangsi (Visutrangsi), not far from the TAT office. The common Thai name for this museum is *phíphíttháphan sŏngkhraam wát tâi*.

LAK MEUANG (CITY PILLAR)
ศาลหลักเมือง

Like many older Thai cities, Kanchanaburi has a *làk meuang* enclosed in a shrine at what was originally the town centre. The shrine is located on Th Lak Meuang, which intersects with Th Saengchuto two blocks north of the TAT office.

The bulbous-tipped pillar is covered with gold leaf and is much worshipped. Unlike Bangkok's Lak Meuang you can get as close to this pillar as you like – there's no curtain.

Within sight of the pillar, towards the river, stands Kanchanaburi's original **city gate**.

Activities
COOKING COURSES
If you are thinking about taking a cooking course in Thailand, consider doing it here. **Test of Thai** (Th Saengchuto) is run by the lovely duo who also run Apple's Guesthouse (p214). Their highly recommended full-day Thai cooking courses (900B per person) are held in this specially designed kitchen. Everyone raves about the morning trip to the market and the humorous instructor. But the best part is that you pick which dishes you want to make from the menu for Apple's restaurant. Apple's special curry paste is available for sale at Test of Thai along with a small selection of local OTOP (One Tambon One Product) handicrafts. To reserve an apron, contact Apple or Noi at their Guest House.

TREKKING
The 'treks' offered by agencies and guesthouses of Kanchanaburi are lightweight. Most agencies have decided to focus on one-day tours, of which the 4km walk to the top of Erawan Falls (p219) is the most serious. These tours are, however, the easiest way to see the best the area has to offer.

Most of the tours visit a mixture of the major nearby attractions. Any combination of Hellfire Pass, hot springs, caves, waterfalls, kayaking, elephant riding and train riding is possible. Typical prices vary from 500B to 800B per person per day depending on the activities. Elephant riding is the big-money option. Overnight treks are also offered and include a visit to a Karen village in addition to an elephant ride and a short river journey on a bamboo raft.

Be careful when choosing a trek as many companies will cancel at the last minute if not enough people sign up. New companies pop up every season, so ask around for recommendations. The following agencies are reputable and long-running.

AS Mixed Travel (☎ 0 3451 2017; www.applenoi -kanchanaburi.com; Apple's Guesthouse) A locally owned, reliable and well-organised company that runs the highest-quality tours. In the high season it also offers one- and two-day cycling trips and three-day combo cycling/trekking programmes.

Toi's Tours (☎ 0 3451 4209; 45/3 Th Rong Hip Oi) If you need a French-speaking guide, is a good option. There is a second office on Th Tha Makam.

KAYAKING

Whether or not you're an experienced paddler, river kayaking is a great way to explore Kanchanaburi. The French-managed **Safarine** (☎ 0 3462 4140; www.safarine.com; 4 Th Taiwan; ☺ closed Sun) is a complete tour company that specialises in river-based trips. It will design custom tours for groups of two to 80 people for two hours to two days. Trips cost between 300B for a couple of hours to 1000B for a full day. The guides speak English, French, Thai and Chinese and trips include all necessary equipment and insurance. You can also rent kayaks and canoes without guides.

Quirky Kanchanaburi
WWII MUSEUM
พิพิธภัณฑ์สงครามโลกครั้งที่2

Despite what the sign says in front, this **Art Gallery & War Museum** (admission 30B; ☺ 9am-6pm), unlike the Jeath Museum, is a monument to kitsch. This garish museum, just south of the Death Railway Bridge, looks like a Chinese temple on the outside and has a random, almost ridiculous, collection of stuff inside. While entertaining, it's not an essential stop.

The larger, more lavish of the two buildings has nothing to do with WWII and little to do with art, unless you include the brash murals throughout. The bottom floor contains Burmese-style alabaster Buddhas and a *phrá khrêuang* (sacred amulets) display. Upper floors exhibit Thai weaponry from the Ayuthaya period, ceramics and brightly painted portraits of all the kings in Thai history. On the 5th and uppermost floor – above the royal portraits (flirting with lese-

majesty) – is the history of the Chinese family who built the museum, complete with a huge portrait of the family's original patriarch in China.

A smaller building opposite holds WWII relics, including photos and sketches made during the POW period and a display of Japanese and Allied weapons. Along the front of this building stand life-size sculptures of historical figures associated with the war, including Churchill, MacArthur, Hitler, Einstein, de Gaulle and Hirohito. The English captions are sometimes unintentionally amusing or disturbing – a reference to the atomic bomb dropped on Hiroshima, for example, reads 'Almost the entire city was destroyed in a jiffy'. Even more odd is a diorama of the famous bridge being bombed. During the war, the Japanese forced POWs to stand on the bridge in an unsuccessful attempt to deter allied bombing, and this is depicted in the diorama with life-size, papier-mâché POWs, emaciated and dressed in loincloths (a few of which are askew, revealing some anatomically bizarre details). More light-hearted is the collection of Miss Thailand clothing on the 2nd floor.

WAT THAM MANGKON THONG
วัดถ้ำมังกรทอง

The 'Cave Temple of the Golden Dragon' has long been an attraction because of the 'floating nun' – a *mâe chii* (Thai Buddhist nun) who meditated while floating on her back in a pool of water. The original nun passed away, but a disciple continues the tradition – sort of. The current floating nun does not meditate but instead she strikes Buddha-like poses based upon traditional *mudra* (ritual hand movements). Chinese and Korean tour groups come in droves to see the spectacle that takes place in a tank surrounded by bleachers and a high wall – a mini-colosseum especially built for the purpose. If you come here alone, please note that the nun doesn't float for less than 200B. If you show up when a group is there, it's worth 10B just to watch the Asian tourists' reactions to the floating nun's poses. With each new pose there's a frenzy of camera flashes. Most tour groups hit this temple in the evening around 5pm.

A long, steep series of steps with dragon-sculpted handrails leads on up the craggy mountainside behind the main *bòt* to a complex of limestone caves. Follow the string of light bulbs through the front cave and you'll come out above the wat with a view of the valley and mountains. One section of the cave requires crawling or duck-walking, so wear appropriate clothing and shoes – the cave floor can be slippery.

Another cave wat called **Wat Tham Khao Laem** is off this same road about 1km to 2km from Wat Tham Mangkon Thong towards the pier. It can be seen on a limestone outcrop back from the road some 500m or so. The cave is less impressive than the one at Wat Tham Mangkon Thong, but there are some interesting old temple buildings on the grounds.

Getting There & Away

You'll need a bicycle or motorcycle to get out here. Heading southeast down Th Saengchuto from the TAT office, turn right on Th Sala Klang (opposite the City Hall). Cross the bridge (locally called Saphan Sala Klang) and continue for another kilometre. The road can be dusty in the dry season but at least it's flat.

Tours

BOAT TRIPS

Several small-time enterprises offer raft trips up and down Mae Nam Mae Klong and its various tributaries. The typical raft is a large affair with a two-storey shelter that will carry 15 to 20 people. The average rental cost per raft is 1500B for half a day and 3500B for an overnight trip, divided among as many people as you can shoehorn on the boat. Such a trip would include stops at Hat Tha Aw (Tha Aw Beach), Wat Tham Mangkon Thong, Wat Tham Khao Pun and the Chung Kai Allied War Cemetery, plus all meals and one night's accommodation on the raft. Alcoholic beverages are usually extra. Bargaining can be fruitful as there are said to be over 500 rafts available in the city.

Inquire at any guesthouse or the TAT office about raft trips.

LONG-TAIL BOATS

One way to see the same river sights at a lower cost is to hire a long-tail boat instead of a raft. Long-tail boats cost around 500B per hour and can take up to six passengers.

> **SLEEP TIGHT, DON'T LET THE KARAOKE BITE**
>
> Before deciding that sleeping right on the river is the way to go, consider the following factors. Most of the riverfront accommodation comprises basic shacks that sit on steel pontoons and lack proper screens to keep mosquitos out. Only those with air-conditioning are mosquito-tight. What's worse is that some guesthouses still pump river water into the bathrooms which usually means the waste water and sewage are dumped directly into the river. While a few guesthouses have successfully hidden their elicit plumbing from guests, others leave their set-up in plain view. If in doubt, fill the bathroom sink with water. It will be readily apparent if the water came from the river or not. Also note that on weekends and holidays boisterous floating disco traffic can go on all night. Some of the rafts even have karaoke and the echoing sound of a tone-deaf performer can irritate the heaviest of sleepers. All that said, the river is nearly silent during the week and there are some very romantic riverside options.

For 1000B a group could take a two-hour long-tail boat trip to visit the Jeath War Museum, Wat Tham Khao Pun, Chung Kai Allied War Cemetery and the Death Railway Bridge. Boats can be hired from the boat pier off Th Chukkadon or at the Jeath War Museum.

Sleeping

Kanchanaburi has an increasing number of places to stay. Many budget guesthouses are adding rooms with air-con and hot water showers, so they can straddle the distance between budget and midrange.

Săamláw drivers get a 50B to 100B kickback for each foreign traveller they bring to certain guesthouses (on top of what they charge you for the ride), so don't believe everything they say with regard to 'full', 'dirty' or 'closed' – see for yourself. Some guesthouses will provide free transport from the bus or train station if you call.

BUDGET

Apple's Guesthouse (☎ 0 3451 2017; www.applenoi -kanchanaburi.com; 52 Soi Th Rong Hip Oi; s/d 200/250B)

Superfriendly, ultraclean and extra-relaxed, Apple's has been the focus of many letters home. It's a homey place with comfortable outdoor seating areas for socialising and well-screened, well-ventilated rooms for sound sleeping. The on-site restaurant and one-day Thai cooking courses (see p212) both get rave reviews.

Blue Star Guest House (☎ 0 3451 2161; 241 Th Mae Nam Khwae; r 150-600B; ✵) Budget rooms here are ordinary, but the more expensive A-frame bungalows overlooking the river are extraordinary. They are creatively constructed with naturally twisted wood, reminiscent of a fantasy tree house. Don't believe anyone who tells you this place is closed or full; the helpful owner doesn't pay commissions. There is also a pleasant, open-air restaurant on the premises.

Jolly Frog (☎ 0 3451 4579; 28 Soi China; s/d/q from 70/150/400B; ✵) With a range of cheap rooms and a killer riverside lawn (fabulous for tanning), the Jolly Frog has long been the happening spot for backpackers. Beware the gauntlet of fly-by-night businesses (trekking, massage and tattooing) that have sprouted up around the entrance.

Pong Phen Guesthouse (PP Guest house; ☎ 0 3451 2981; www.pongphen.com; 5 Soi Banglated, Th Tha Makam; r from 230-280B; ✵) New collection of modern rooms with glistening tile floors, spacious patios and a lush garden has quickly become a favourite. There are some cheaper rooms with shared bathroom, while the more expensive rooms have hot showers.

Sugar Cane Guest House (☎ 0 3462 4520; 22 Soi Pakistan, Th Mae Nam Khwae; s/d from 150/250B; ✵) Sugar Cane has nice river-raft rooms that share a wide veranda. The riverside restaurant serves tasty meals and management is friendly and helpful.

Sugar Cane Guest House II (7 Soi Cambodia; r from 200B) Closer to the bridge and quite pleasant.

Little Creek Hideaway Valley (☎ 0 3451 0127; www .littlecreekhideawayvalley.com; camping 80B, r 270-300B) If you see no reason to be in town, this amazing getaway has a curious collection of African-style bungalows, a fabulous swimming pool, thumping dance club and delicious wood-fired pizzas. It's about 4km from town, but provides frequent scheduled pick-ups from the bus station, the train station and its offices on Th Mae Nam Khwae.

VL Guest House (☎ 0 3451 3546; Th Saengchuto; r from 200B; ✵) Rooms inside this hotel-like building all have televisions and are good value if you don't mind being away from other guesthouses. Rooms in the back are significantly quieter.

Nita Raft House (☎ 0 3451 4521; 27/1 Th Pak Phraek; s 80B, d 120-180B) If you want a cheap but well-run option away from the backpacker action, Nita's is a good choice during the week. On weekends, it's in the middle of the docking area for the floating discos. Some doubles have showers.

VN Guest House (☎ 0 3451 4082; vnguesthouse@ yahoo.com; 44 Soi Th Rong Hip Oi 2; s/d from 60/80B; ✵) VN has small, basic raft rooms. The chilled-out staff will you pick you up from the bus station.

MK Hotel (☎ 0 3462 1143-4; Th Saengchuto; r 300-600B; ✵) Straddling the line between budget and midrange, MK comes complete with its own karaoke bar. Each of the 52 rooms has two beds. Pay 100B more for TV or a hot-water shower.

The following three places are owned by the same family and all have on-site restaurants and a range of rooms.

Sam's River Raft Guest House (☎ 0 3462 4231; 48/1 Th Rong Hip Oi 2; www.samsguesthouse.com; s/d from 80/120B; ✵) The rooms on the raft here are a good option if you want to sleep on the water. The cement-row 'bungalows' are dark, basic and crowded – but, hey, they're cheap. The elevated bamboo bungalows are well-ventilated and share a funky bathroom.

Sam's House (☎ 0 3451 5956; www.samsguesthouse .com; Th Mae Nam Khwae; d 150-350B, with air-con 300-450B; ✵) The cheapies here are a tiny step up from a cement cell, but the bamboo bungalows are nice. The two-room suite sleeps four and is a great spot for a family.

Sam's Place (☎ 0 3451 3971; www.samsguesthouse .com; 7/3 Th Song Khwae; s/d 150B, with air-con 350B; ✵) Within earshot of the floating discos and karaoke restaurants, this is the original, most rugged, of Sam's places.

Other recommendations:

Bamboo House (☎ 0 3462 4470; 3-5 Soi Vietnam, Th Mae Nam Khwae; r 200-500B; ✵) Serene, well-kept and close to Death Railway, but far from in-town action.

Prasopsuk Hotel (☎ 0 3451 1777; Th Saengchuto; r from 200B; ✵) OK value motel-style hotel with rooms opening onto a parking lot.

River Guest House (☎ 0 3451 2491; 42 Soi Rong Hip Oi 2, Th Mae Nam Khwae; r from 150B; ✵ ▢) Bare-bone rooms. Check air-con before settling in.

J Guest House (☎ 0 3462 0307; Th Rong Hip Oi; s/d 100/120B) Cosy, basic, windowless rafts in a lotus-filled lagoon. Beware the mosquitos.

MIDRANGE

Many midrange places offer discounts during the low season (April to November). Call ahead or check with TAT (p209) to find out just how low the prices are before checking in. Most rooms in midrange accommodation are air conditioned.

Kasem Island Resort (☎ 0 3451 3359, in Bangkok ☎ 0 2255 3604; r from 750B; ☒ ☒) On an island in the middle of Mae Nam Mae Klong, about 200m from the end of Th Chukkadon, lie the tastefully designed, thatched cottages and house rafts of Kasem Island Resort. They are cool, clean and quiet; the swimming pool and outdoor bar and restaurant are perfect for kicking back. The resort has an office and parking lot near Th Chukkadon, where you can arrange for a free shuttle boat to the island; shuttle service stops at 10pm.

Ploy Guesthouse (☎ 0 3451 5804; www.ploygh .com; 79/2 Th Mae Nam Kwai; r 650-850B; ☒) With gracious staff and remarkable rooms, Ploy Guesthouse is excellent value for the aesthete. It doesn't look like very much from the outside, but the contemporary, Siam-style rooms elegantly mix classic and modern design elements. The downstairs rooms have open-air showers that look onto a small, tropical garden. Don't miss the view from the elevated restaurant/bar. Discounts are available through their website.

Luxury Hotel (☎ 0 3451 1168; 284/1-5 Th Saengchuto; s/d from 350/450B; ☒) Close to the cemetery, this single-storey, motel-like place offers all the modern conveniences, including satellite TV. The professional staff are pleasant and rooms are spacious, but the place isn't exactly luxurious.

Boon Sri River Kwai Resort (☎ 0 3451 5143; r 400-800B; ☒) Big Western-style hotel on the river offers everything a local player would want in a vacation. It does have a roughness about it, but it's still a good deal if you want to get away from other travellers. It's opposite the Wat Tham Mangkon Thong south of town.

Prasopsuk Garden Resort (☎ 0 3451 3215; 6/1 Mu 8, Th Pattana; r 1000-1200B; ☒ ☒) Equipped with a karaoke bar, Prasopsuk can get noisy on the weekends. The clientele is mostly Thais, many of whom arrive in dark-windowed

luxury cars ready for a little hedonism. The grounds are pleasant and quiet during the week but, situated to the northwest out past the Death Railway, it's not convenient to town or sightseeing without a car.

Ban Vimol (☎ 0 3451 4831; 48/5 Soi Th Rong Hip Oi 2; r 600B; ☒) Almost-charming, bamboo rooms on the river with air-con and hot showers are a good deal. But the grounds and the cheaper non-air rooms (150B) are pretty run down.

RS Hotel (☎ 0 3462 5128; 264 Th Saengchuto; r 700-2400B; ☒ ☒) With all the added comforts you'd expect from a hotel that caters to tour groups, the RS is a reasonable if uninteresting choice.

TOP END

Although the following places fall into the top-end category, they do vary in quality. They all offer the expected amenities, such as air conditioning and swimming pool, but some offer quite a bit more.

Felix River Kwai Resort (☎ 0 3451 5061, www.felix hotels.com/riverkwai; s/d/ste 2000/2200/3500B; ☒ ☒ ☒) West of town, this resort's beautifully landscaped grounds house a golf course, tennis courts and two pools. There is also a full-service fitness centre with sauna at this luxurious place on the western bank of the river. Rooms are spacious with hardwood floors and IDD phones, cable TV and minifridge. Two-room suites are enormous.

Royal River Kwai Resort & Spa (☎ 0 3465 3297; 88 Kanchanaburi-Saiyok Rd; d/ste 1400/2900B; ☒ ☒ ☒) Stylishly Zen, the rooms could be featured in an interior-design magazine. The riverside, wood-decked pool is the real highlight (available to non-guests for 200B). The location is inconvenient if you're without motorised wheels.

River Kwai Hotel (☎ 0 3451 3348; www.riverkwai .co.th; 284/3-16 Th Saengchuto; r incl breakfast from 1400B; ☒ ☒) One of Kanchanaburi's flashier digs, with a disco and bar out the front of the hotel. The uniform-clad staff are extra helpful. Rooms are modern and spacious but lack character. Rooms all have a mini-fridge and cable TV. If you are seeking a Western atmosphere, this is a good option. Discounts are readily available.

Eating

Kanchanaburi is a festive, prosperous town and people seem to eat out a lot. Thanon Saengchuto near the River Kwai Hotel is

Thailand's longest wooden bridge links Sangkhlaburi to the Mon village of Wang Kha (p225), Kanchanaburi

BILL WASSMAN

ANDERS BLOMQVIST

Chedi of Wat Phra Si Sanphet (p195), Ayuthaya Historical Park

Hands and feet of the Buddha, Wat Na Phra Mehn, Ayuthaya Historical Park (p197)

FRANK CARTER

JULIET COOMBE

Prang Sam Yot (p205), Lopburi

Elephant riding, Kanchanaburi Province (p212)

MICK ELMORE

Bridge on the River Kwai (p209), Kanchanaburi

DENNIS J

packed with inexpensive restaurants catering mostly to a local clientele. As elsewhere in Thailand, the best places are generally the most crowded. There are many good Chinese, Thai and Isan-style places where Th U Thong crosses Th Saengchuto. Alternatively, an ever-changing assortment of tourist-driven restaurants line Th Mae Nam Khwae near the guesthouses. Don't miss the night market where local snacks are the highlight.

Apple's Restaurant (Apple's Guesthouse; Th Mae Nam Khwae; dishes 40-80B) Unlike most guesthouses, this restaurant is worth visiting even if you are not staying here. You can taste Apple's culinary passion and creativity in every bite. The *kaeng mátsàmàn* (Muslim-style curry) and the banana pancake – perhaps the best in Thailand – are the notorious favourites. Ask about seasonal specials, such as banana blossom fondue.

Schluck Restaurant (Th Mae Nam Khwae; dishes 80-140B; ☻ 6pm-2am; ✖) If you're after steak and other Western specialities, this cool, low-lit, late-night spot is the best bet in town. Hours are notably shorter in the low season (April to November).

Sutjai (dishes 40-150B) A garden-style place on the western bank of the river next to the one-lane bridge. It has a bilingual menu, but little English is spoken. It's a little out of the way, but better than the other riverside restaurants in town.

Jukkru (no Roman-script sign; dishes 40-120B) This restaurant is the best on the row opposite the floating restaurants – look for the blue tables and chairs.

Sabai-jit Restaurant (Th Saengchuto; dishes 40-80B) Just north of the River Kwai Hotel, this boisterous place has more than good prices on beer and Mekong whisky. The food is consistently good and the atmosphere is quite lively. Come here with a group if you can. Not everything is listed on the English menu, so if you see something that you'd like to try, just point.

Punnee Cafe & Bar (☎ 0 3451 3503; Th Ban Neua; dishes 40-80B) Long-running place is better for information than food (see Money, p208). The ex-pat owner knows just about everything about the area, but only the Western breakfast is worth eating here. There are also used paperback books for sale or trade.

Srifa Bakery (east of the bus station) Srifa handles most of the pastry and bread business

in town. On the west side of the bus station, it's a modern place that has everything from Singapore-style curry puffs to French-style pastries.

There are several large floating restaurants down on the river. The food quality varies but it's hard not to enjoy the atmosphere. Most of them cater to Thais out for a night of drinking and snacking, so if you go, don't expect Western food or large portions.

Good, cheap eating places can be found in the markets at Th Prasit and between Th U Thong and Th Lak Meuang, east of Th Saengchuto. In the evenings, a sizable **night market** (Th Saengchuto) convenes near the Th Lak Meuang intersection.

There are also **food vendors** (Th Song Khwae) on both sides of the road, along the river near the modern tourist police office, where you can buy inexpensive takeaways and picnic on mats along the riverbank.

Drinking

A crop of bars, complete with videos, pool tables and prostitutes, have sprouted up along Th Mae Nam Khwae. Many of the establishments seem to be run by Westerners so they may not survive the government's ongoing crackdown.

Beer Barrel Bar (Th Mae Nam Khwae) Under a marvellous banyan tree, this outdoor beer garden is a social highlight in Kanchanaburi. Just follow the blaring music to the wooden barrel sign. If the mosquitos are out, they'll be in full force here.

No Name Bar (Th Mae Nam Khwae) With a range of Western snacks in big portions and satellite TV for football games and BBC, this place sees a steady stream of tourists.

Discovery (Th Song Khwae) This is the only non-karaoke disco in town. It fills to the gills on weekends. Don't let the lack of *faràng* discourage you from dancing the night away here. This is a great place to meet locals.

Getting There & Away
BUS

Ordinary buses depart from Bangkok for Kanchanaburi from the Southern Bus Terminal every 15 minutes between 4am and 6.30pm (48B, three hours). Buses back to Bangkok leave Kanchanaburi between the same hours. Air-con (2nd class) buses cost 62B and leave at similar intervals.

First-class air-con buses leave Bangkok's Southern Bus Terminal every 15 minutes from 5am to 7pm (79B). Air-con buses only take about two hours to reach Bangkok. The first bus out is at 4am; the last one to Bangkok leaves at 7pm.

Buses to Kanchanaburi leave frequently throughout the day from nearby Nakhon Pathom (28B, 1½ hours). For travellers heading to the south, Nakhon Pathom makes a good connecting point – this way you avoid having to go back to Bangkok. Other frequent direct bus services are available to/from Ratchaburi (461, 36B, 2½ hours), Sangkhlaburi (8203, 84B, five hours) and Suphanburi (411, 35B, 2½ to three hours), where you can easily connect to Ayuthaya.

SHARE TAXI & MINIVAN

Many complaints have been made about the minibus services organised by guesthouses. They take passengers to Ayuthaya (250B per person, 2½ hours) and to Bangkok (150B per person, 2½ hours) but are notorious for speeding and packing passengers in like sardines; ride at your own risk.

Air-con minibuses also run to Sangkhlaburi (118B, four hours) from an office east of the bus terminal.

TRAIN

Ordinary trains leave Bangkok's Thonburi (Bangkok Noi) station at 7.35am and 1.45pm for Kanchanaburi. Only 3rd-class seats are available (25B). Trains return to Bangkok (Thonburi station) from Kanchanaburi at 7.26am and 2.50pm, arriving at 10.25am and 5.40pm. Ordinary train tickets to Kanchanaburi can be reserved on the day of departure only.

Officially these trains leave from the Thonburi station on the western bank of Mae Nam Chao Phraya. In actuality, the trains leave from a temporary station about 1km away, but the government runs a free săwngthăew from the old station to the temporary one. Tickets are still purchased at the old station. Whether or not this situation is temporary is unclear. Travelling by train is slower than going by bus, but the scenery is stunning. Sadly, passenger use on this line has dropped off dramatically over the past few years, and as usage drops, so too does reliability. Late arrivals are common.

Three trains daily depart from Kanchanaburi station for the Death Railway Bridge. The same trains go on to the end of the line at Nam Tok (17B, two hours), which is near Nam Tok Sai Yok (Sai Yok Falls; p220). The trains depart from the bridge at 6.11am and 10.51am, and 4.37pm. The first train doesn't run on weekends and holidays. Nam Tok is 8km from Nam Tok Khao Pang and 18km from Hellfire Pass and the Mae Nam Khwae village. Returning from Nam Tok, there are trains at 5.25am and 1pm and 3.15pm.

Tourist Trains

The SRT operates a special **tourist train** (☎ 0 3456 1052, Bangkok ☎ 0 2223 7010) on weekends and holidays that leaves around 6.30am and returns at 8.30pm. The return fare is 200B for an air-con seat, 100B for fan. The day trip includes a stop in Nakhon Pathom to see Phra Pathom Chedi (p187), a visit to the Death Railway Bridge (p209), a minibus to Prasat Meuang Singh Historical Park (p221) for a short tour, a walk along an elevated 'Death Railway' bridge (no longer in use), a three-hour stop at the river for lunch and a bat cave visit, before returning to Bangkok with a one-hour stopover at one of the war cemeteries. This itinerary does change so call first and buy tickets at least one day in advance.

On weekends and holidays a **steam train** runs between Kanchanaburi and Wang Pho (10.25am departure, 2pm return, with a 90-minute stopover at the waterfall) for 100B one way, 150B return. These tickets should be booked in advance, although it's worth trying on the day even if you're told it's full. The SRT changes the tour itinerary and price from time to time.

Getting Around

Unless you are in the mood to be thoroughly fleeced, don't even consider letting a săamláw driver show you around – the asking price for an hour-long tour is 500B. The town is not large, so getting around on foot or bicycle is easy. A săamláw or motorcycle taxi from the bus or train stations to the river area and most guesthouses should cost around 20B to 30B. Săwngthăew run up and down Th Saengchuto and Th Pak Phraek for 5B to 10B per passenger depending on distance.

Motorcycles can be rented at some guest-houses, or at one of the many shops along Th Mae Nam Khwae. These places tend to come and go though, and it's difficult to recommend one. One that is reliable is **NB Motorcycle** (☎ 0 3451 1087; Th Chaokunen; ⏱ 7.30am-7pm), which rents 100/125cc motorcycles for 150/200B per day.

If possible, it's best to rent a bicycle from the place where you're staying. Prices range from 50B to 100B per day, with some real beaters available for 30B per day.

You can take the train from the Kanchanaburi station out to the Death Railway Bridge, a three-minute ride (2B). There are three trains per day at 6.11am (No 485), 10.51am (No 257) and 4.37pm (No 259). These same trains continue on to Nam Tok.

The river ferry that crosses Mae Nam Mae Klong costs 5B per person. Sometimes there's an extra few baht charge for bikes (motor or push) taken on the ferry, although usually it's included in the 5B fare.

AROUND KANCHANABURI

To the north and west of Kanchanaburi, heading towards Three Pagodas Pass, is some of Thailand's most beautiful scenery. Many guesthouses and tour agencies in the provincial capital can arrange day trips to the surrounding region. However, most of the attractions can be reached by motorcycle or bus (see opposite).

Kanchanaburi Province has seven major waterfalls *(nam tok)*, all northwest of Kanchanaburi. They are Erawan, Trai Trang, Khao Pang, Sai Yok, Pha That and Huay Khamin. Of these, the three most worth visiting – if you're looking for grandeur and swimming potential – are Erawan, Sai Yok and Huay Khamin. Erawan is the easiest to get to from Kanchanaburi, while Sai Yok and Huay Khamin are best visited only if you are able to spend the night near the falls.

Erawan National Park

อุทยานแห่งชาติเอราวัณ

This 550-sq-km **park** (☎ 0 3457 4222; admission per person 200B; ⏱ 8am-4pm) is the most visited national park in Thailand and one of the most beautiful.

The seven-tiered waterfalls, which feed into Mae Nam Khwae Yai, are what most people come here to see. From the visitors centre, the top pool is 2km (the first level is

reached 700m from the visitors centre). The trail can be steep, slippery and non-existent from place to place, so wear good walking shoes or sneakers. Also bring a bathing suit as several of the pools beneath the waterfalls are great for swimming. The uppermost fall is said to resemble Airvata (Erawan in Thai), the three-headed elephant of Hindu mythology.

The waterfalls here, as elsewhere in Kanchanaburi, are best visited during the rainy season or in the first two months of the cool season, when the pools are full and the waterfalls most impressive. The peak crowds arrive at Erawan in mid-April around the time of the Songkran Festival (when there's not much water; see p733); weekends can also be crowded.

Two limestone caves in the park worth visiting are **Tham Phra That** (12km northwest of the visitors centre via a rough road) and **Tham Wang Badan** (54km west). Thung Na Dam appears 28km before Erawan. Bicycles are available for rent (20B per day) near the entrance.

Official park **bungalows** (☎ 0 3457 4222, in Bangkok ☎ 0 2562 0760; bungalows 800-1500B) sleep between two and 50 people. The park staff can also make arrangements for you to sleep in unofficial housing from 50B to 100B per person, or you can pitch a tent for 5B.

Riverside **Erawan Resort Guest House** (☎ 0 1907 8210; 140 Mu 4; r 200-2000B; ⏱), off the highway before the park entrance, has small, solid bungalows with attached bathroom.

Pha Daeng Resort (☎ 0 3451 3909; r 500-2700B; ⏱), further towards Kanchanaburi along the same road as Erawan Resort, near the Km 46 marker, has a variety of air-con rooms and bungalows.

There are food stalls near the park entrance and at the bus station, outside the park. To cut down on rubbish, food is not allowed beyond the second level of the falls.

GETTING THERE & AWAY

Buses run from Kanchanaburi to Erawan (26B, 1½ hours) every 50 minutes from 8am to 4pm. The bus will drop you off right at the entrance. Ask for *rót thammádaa pai náam tók eh-raawan* (ordinary bus going to Nam Tok Erawan). If you just want to visit the park for the day, take the first bus, so you have enough time to appreciate Erawan

CENTRAL THAILAND

and catch the last bus back to Kanchanaburi at 4pm.

Hellfire Pass
ช่องเขาขาด

The Australian-Thai Chamber of Commerce completed the Hellfire Pass Memorial project (www.dva.gov.au/commem/oawg/thailand.htm) in 1998. The purpose of the project is to honour the Allied POWs and Asian conscripts who died while constructing some of the most difficult stretches of the Burma-Thailand Death Railway, 80km northwest of Kanchanaburi. 'Hellfire Pass' was the name the POWs gave to the largest of a 1000m series of mountain cuttings through soil and solid rock, which were accomplished with minimal equipment (3.5kg hammers, picks, shovels, steel tap drills, cane baskets for removing dirt and rock, and dynamite for blasting).

The original crew of 400 Australian POWs was later augmented with 600 additional Australian and British prisoners, who worked around the clock in 16- to 18-hour shifts for 12 weeks. The prisoners called it Hellfire Pass because of the way the largest cutting at Konyu looked at night by torch light. By the time the cuttings were finished 70% of the POW crew had died and were buried in the nearby Konyu Cemetery.

The memorial consists of a marked trail that follows the railway remains through the 110m Konyu cutting, then winds up and around the pass and continues through the jungle as far as Compressor cutting (about a three-hour walk). At the far end of Konyu cutting is a memorial plaque fastened to solid stone, commemorating the deaths of the Allied prisoners. There are actually seven cuttings spread over 3.5km – four smaller cuttings and three larger ones. The website provides a map of the walking trail.

There is also a cleared path to the **Hin Tok trestle bridge,** northwest of the Konyu cutting. This bridge was called the 'Pack of Cards' by the prisoners because it collapsed three times during construction. Eventually some of the track may be restored to exhibit rolling stock from the WWII era. A **museum** at the Hellfire Pass trailhead contains artefacts from the era and a short documentary film featuring reminiscences of survivors, which is screened continuously. In lieu of admission, donations are greatly appreciated.

GETTING THERE & AWAY
Access to Hellfire Pass is via the Royal Thai Army (RTA) farm on Rte 323, between Kanchanaburi and Thong Pha Phum. Proceeding northwest along Rte 323, the farm is 80km from Kanchanaburi, 18km from the Nam Tok train terminus. The entrance to the memorial is well marked.

Buses for Thong Pha Phum leave Kanchanaburi every half hour from 8am to 4.30pm. The fare to Hellfire Pass is 27B and the trip takes about 1½ hours. Tell the driver *châwng khǎo kháat* (Hellfire Pass).

The museum is a short walk from the road. From there, follow the ramp from its entrance down to the trailhead. A fork in the trail gives hikers the option of taking a 500m trail through a bamboo forest or down a concrete stairway directly to the railway. If you can spare the time (about one hour), taking the 'bamboo trail' is more rewarding as it affords an initial view of the cutting from a lookout point above it. From Konyu cutting, follow the railway south to the concrete stairway that leads back up to the museum, or continue along the railway in a northwesterly direction through four cuttings and over six trestle bridges. This latter hike is only recommended if you arrive early and are up to walking for a few hours.

Sai Yok National Park
อุทยานแห่งชาติไทรโยค

About 100km northwest of Kanchanaburi, scenic Nam Tok Sai Yok Yai and Nam Tok Sai Yok Noi are part of 500-sq-km **Sai Yok National Park** (admission per person 200B). It was at Sai Yok National Park that the famous Russian-roulette scenes in the 1978 movie *The Deer Hunter* were filmed. In addition to the park's waterfalls, other attractions include the limestone caves Tham Sai Yok, Tham Kaew and Tham Phra, the remains of a Death Railway bridge and Japanese cooking stoves (actually little more than piles of brick), and a network of clear streams that bubble up from springs in the park. There are established footpaths and trails between the falls, caves, railway bridge and a bat cave where people come to watch clouds of bats stream out at dusk.

Nam Tok Sai Yok Noi is higher than Nam Tok Sai Yok Yai, but the volume of falling water is greater at the latter. Sai Yok Yai

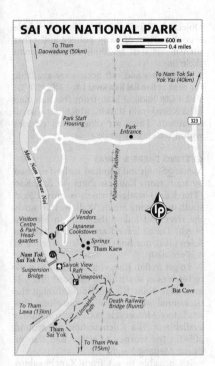

SAI YOK NATIONAL PARK

Yok National Park; they sleep up to six. **Saiyok View Raft** (☎ 0 3451 4194; r 500B), on the river near the suspension bridge, rents out tidy rooms on floating rafts with private bathroom. For an extra 100B you get breakfast and dinner; for an extra 200B you get all meals included. There are a couple of other **raft houses** (r 400-600B) along the river in the park.

There is a row of permanent food stalls next to the parking lot near the visitors centre.

GETTING THERE & AWAY

If you are going to the park specifically to see the waterfalls, be sure to tell the driver whether you're going to Sai Yok Yai or Sai Yok Noi, as the falls are some 40km apart. The falls can be reached via a bus bound for Thong Pha Phum or Sangkhlaburi. The buses to Sai Yok Yai (38B, two hours) leave Kanchanaburi's bus terminal every 30 minutes between 6am and 6.30pm, but the last bus back to Kanchanaburi passes at about 4.30pm. The trip to Sai Yok Noi takes just over an hour (25B) with the last bus back to Kanchanaburi passing at 5pm. You can also get to Sai Yok Noi by taking the train to Nam Tok and then hiring a *săwngthăew* for half a day to take you to Sai Yok Noi and back to the Nam Tok station. This should cost no more than 400B, but the isolation of this end-of-the-line train station has made some *săwngthăew* drivers greedy.

Prasat Meuang Singh Historical Park

อุทยานประวัติศาสตร์ปราสาทเมืองสิงห์

Approximately 43km west of Kanchanaburi are the remains of a key 13th-century Khmer outpost of the Angkor empire called **Meuang Singh** (☎ 0 3459 1122; admission 40B; ☼ 8am-5pm). Located on a bend in Mae Nam Khwae Noi, the recently restored city ruins cover 73.6 hectares and were declared a historical park under the administration of the Fine Arts Department in 1987. Originally this location may have been chosen by the Khmers as a relay point for trade along Mae Nam Khwae Noi.

All the Meuang Singh shrines are constructed of laterite bricks and are situated in a huge grassy compound surrounded by layers of laterite ramparts. Sections of the ramparts show seven additional layers of earthen walls, suggesting cosmological

is more set up for visitors and hence gets busloads of Thai tourists. Sai Yok Noi is more relaxing.

The eight-room **Tham Daowadung**, one of Thailand's prettiest limestone caves, is further north in the park while **Tham Lawa** is in the park's far southwestern corner; both are best visited by taking boat trips to an access point along Mae Nam Khwae Noi, then hiking in. **Hin Dat Hot Springs** (admission 5B) is 40 minutes north of Tham Daowadung by boat. The *bàw náam ráwn* (hot springs) have been upgraded recently and now have changing rooms and bathrooms. The hot springs are no longer looked after by the monks at the nearby Buddhist monastery, so women are now welcome.

Notable wildlife in the park includes Kitti's hog-nosed bats (the world's smallest mammal), regal crabs, barking deer, blue pittas, wreathed hornbills, gibbons, Malayan porcupines, slow loris and serow. There are also wild elephants that occasionally cross over from Myanmar.

Forestry department **bungalows** (☎ 0 2579 5734; bungalows 800-2100B) are available at Sai

symbolism in the city plan. Evidence of a sophisticated water system has also been discovered amid the ramparts and moats.

The town encompasses four groups of ruins, although only two groups have been excavated and are visible. In the centre of the complex is the principal shrine, **Prasat Meuang Singh**, which faces east (towards Angkor). Walls surrounding the shrine have gates in each of the cardinal directions. A reproduction of a sculpture of Avalokitesvara stands on the inside of the northern wall and establishes Meuang Singh as a Mahayana Buddhist centre. The original is in the National Museum in Bangkok. Inside the main *prang* is a reproduction of a sculpture of Prajnaparamita, another Mahayana Buddhist deity.

To the northeast of the main *prasat* are the remains of a smaller **shrine** whose original contents and purpose are unknown. Near the main entrance to the complex at the north gate is a small **museum** which contains various sculptures of Mahayana Buddhist deities and stucco decorations, most of which are reproductions.

Clear evidence that this area was inhabited before the arrival of the Khmers can be seen in another small **museum** to the south of the complex next to the river. The roof shelters two human skeletons arranged in a prehistoric burial site and a detailed explanation of the findings, which include an ornate bronze spoon. A more complete exhibit of local Neolithic remains is at the Ban Kao Neolithic Museum. Prasat Meuang Singh and Ban Kao are reached by the same train service, see right.

Ban Kao Neolithic Museum

พิพิธภัณฑ์บ้านเก่ายุคหิน

During the construction of the Death Railway along Mae Nam Khwae Noi, a Dutch POW named Van Heekeren uncovered Neolithic remains in the village of Ban Kao (Old Town), about 7km southeast of Meuang Singh. After WWII, a Thai–Danish team retraced Van Heekeren's discovery, concluding that Ban Kao is a major Neolithic burial site. Archaeological evidence suggests it may have been inhabited 10,000 years ago.

A small but well-designed **museum** (admission 40B; ☺ 8am-4.30pm Wed-Sun), displaying 3000- to 4000-year-old artefacts from the excavation of Ban Kao has been established near the site.

Objects are labelled in English and include a good variety of early pottery and other utensils, as well as 2000-year-old human skeletons.

Bungalows and raft houses are available for rent at **Ban Rai Rim Kwai** (☎ 0 3465 4077; 333 Mu 2; r 1200-2400B), 3.5km from the Ban Kao (Tha Kilen) train station, which has a small restaurant. There are other small eateries within walking distance.

GETTING THERE & AWAY

Meuang Singh and Ban Kao are best reached by train from Kanchanaburi via Ban Kao (Tha Kilen) station, which is only 1.5km south of Meuang Singh. Walk west towards the river and follow the signs to Meuang Singh. Trains leave Kanchanaburi for Tha Kilen (10B, one hour) at 6.07am, 11am and 4.37pm daily.

To get to Ban Kao, you may have to walk or hitch 6km south along the road that follows Mae Nam Khwae Noi, although the occasional *săwngthăew* passes along this road, too. Motorcycle taxis are sometimes available at Tha Kilen station for around 30B for the journey to either Ban Kao or Prasat Meuang Singh.

It's possible to get from Kanchanaburi to Meuang Singh and back in one day by catching the first train there and the last one back.

If you have your own transport, Ban Kao and/or Meuang Singh would make convenient rest stops on the way to Hellfire Pass or Sangkhlaburi.

Coming from the Erawan National Park area, there's no need to backtrack all the way to Kanchanaburi before heading north on Rte 323. A paved road heads west from Rte 3199 at the Km 25 marker, then proceeds 16km to meet Rte 323 between the Km 37 and 38 markers – thus cutting half a day's travel from the old loop. This winding, scenic, lightly trafficked short cut is tremendous for cycling.

Si Nakharin National Park

อุทยานแห่งชาติเขื่อนศรีนครินทร์

Part of the little-visited Si Nakharin National Park, **Huay Khamin** (Turmeric Stream) has what are probably Kanchanaburi Province's most powerful waterfalls. The pools under the waterfalls are large and deep and this is an excellent place for swimming. Explorations further afield in the park can be rewarding for self-contained campers. Elephants and other wildlife are not uncommon.

GETTING THERE & AWAY

Getting to Huay Khamin can be difficult. The 45km road from the Erawan falls is in bad condition and takes at least two hours by motorcycle or rugged 4WD (you must bring your own transport). The falls can also be reached by a similarly rugged – and much longer – dirt road from Rte 323 north of Thong Pha Phum.

An alternative is to charter a boat from Tha Reua Khun Phaen, a pier on the southeastern shore of Kheuan Si Nakharin (Si Nakharin Reservoir) in the village of Ban Mongkrathae. The price varies – according to your bargaining skills and the mood of the boat pilots – from 1200B to 3500B; this need not be as expensive as it sounds if you bring a group (boats can hold up to 20 people). A good price for a long-tail boat with five to 10 people would be 1500B return. If you can afford it, the floating option is much better than going overland.

Wat Tham Seua & Wat Tham Khao Noi

วัดถ้ำเสือ/วัดถ้ำเขาน้อย

These large, hilltop **monasteries** about 15km southeast of Kanchanaburi are important local pilgrimage spots, especially for Chinese Buddhists. Wat Tham Khao Noi (Little Hill Cave Monastery) is a Chinese temple monastery similar in size and style to Penang's Kek Lok Si. Adjacent is the half-Thai, half-Chinese–style Wat Tham Seua (Tiger Cave Monastery). Both are built on a ridge over a series of small caves. Wat Tham Khao Noi is not much of a climb, since it's on the side of the slope. Seeing Wat Tham Seua means climbing either a steep set of *naga* stairs or a meandering set of steps past the cave entrance.

A climb to the top is rewarded with views of Mae Nam Khwae on one side and rice fields on the other. Wat Tham Seua features a huge sitting Buddha facing the river, with a conveyor belt that carries money offerings to a huge alms bowl in the image's lap. The easier set of steps to the right of the temple's *naga* stairs leads to a cave and passes an aviary with peacocks and other exotic birds. The cave contains the usual assortment of Buddha images.

GETTING THERE & AWAY

By public transport, you can take a bus (5B) to Tha Meuang (12km southeast of Kanchanaburi), then a motorcycle taxi (30B) from near Tha Meuang Hospital directly to the temples.

If you're on a motorbike or bicycle, take the right fork of the highway when you reach Tha Meuang, turn right past the hospital onto a road along the canal and then across the Kheuan Meuang (City Dam). Wat Tham Seua and Wat Khao Noi is a further 4km. Once you cross the dam, turn right down the other side of the river and follow this road for 1.4km, then turn left towards the pagodas, which can be seen easily from here. The network of roads leading to the base of the hill offers several route possibilities – just keep an eye on the pagodas and you'll be able to make the appropriate turns.

By bicycle, you can avoid taking the highway by using back roads along the river. Follow Th Pak Phraek in Kanchanaburi southeast and cross the bridge towards Wat Tham Mangkon Thong, then turn left on the other side and follow the gravel road parallel to the river. Eventually (after about 14km) you'll see the Kheuan Meuang up ahead – at this point you should start looking for the hill-top pagodas on your right. This makes a good day trip by bicycle – the road is flat all the way and avoids the high-speed traffic on the highway. You can break your journey at Ban Tham, a village along the way with its own minor cave wat.

Chaloem Ratanakosin National Park (Tham Than Lot)

อุทยานแห่งชาติเฉลิมรัตนโกสินทร์(ถ้ำธารลอด)

This 59-sq-km **national park** (Tham Than Lot; admission 200B), 97km north of Kanchanaburi, is of interest to spelunkers because of two caves, Tham Than Lot Yai and Tham Than Lot Noi, and to naturalists for its waterfalls and natural forests. Three waterfalls – Trai Trang, Than Ngun and Than Thong – are within easy hiking distance of the bungalows and camp ground. **Bungalows** (Bangkok ☎ 0 2579 5734; bungalows 500-1000B) sleep 10 to 12 people or pitch your own tent for 5B per person. Parts of the park are believed to have been an ancient battleground and some locals think it's haunted. **Tham Phra That**, just off the road near the entrance to the park, is 300m long, with waterfalls.

Buses from Kanchanaburi to Ban Nong Preu (28B, two to three hours) leave every 20 minutes between 6.15am and 6.30pm. Once in Ban Nong Preu, you can catch a săwngthăew or minivan to the park. Most visitors arrive by car, jeep or motorcycle.

KANCHANABURI TO THREE PAGODAS PASS

Three Pagodas Pass (Phrá Jedii Săam Ong) was one of the terminals of the Death Railway (p209) in WWII, and for centuries has been a major relay point for Thai–Burmese trade. Until 1989, when the Myanmar government took control of the Myanmar side of the border from insurgent armies, it was a place that the TAT and the Thai government would rather you'd forget about (much like Mae Salong in the north some years ago), but since then it's been promoted as a tourist destination. There's really not much to see at the pass – the attraction lies in the journey itself and the impressive scenery along the way.

It's an all-day journey and will require you to spend at least one night in Sangkhlaburi, which is an interesting off-the-track destination in itself. The distance between Kanchanaburi and Sangkhlaburi alone is about 200km, so if you take a motorcycle it is imperative that you fill up before you leave Kanchanaburi and stop for petrol again in Thong Pha Phum, the last town before Sangkhlaburi. By bicycle this would be a very challenging route, but it has been done.

The roads from Thong Pha Phum to Sangkhlaburi and from Sangkhlaburi to Three Pagodas Pass are now all paved. The best time to go is in the cooler months of January and February. During the rainy season nearly the whole of Amphoe Sangkhlaburi is under water, making travel difficult.

The road between Kanchanaburi and Thong Pha Phum passes through mostly flat terrain interrupted by the odd limestone outcrop. This is sugar-cane country, and if you're travelling by bicycle or motorcycle during harvest you'll have to contend with huge cane trucks, which strew pieces of cane and dust in their wake – take extra care. Cassava is also cultivated but the cassava trucks aren't such a nuisance.

The road between Thong Pha Phum and Sangkhlaburi is one of the most beautiful

in Thailand. It winds through mountains of limestone and along the huge Khao Laem Dam, a hydroelectric dam near Thong Pha Phum. North of Thong Pha Phum is a major teak reforestation project. In spite of the fact that the road surface is in good condition during the dry season, steep grades and sharp curves make this a fairly dangerous journey, especially the last 25km or so before Sangkhlaburi.

Thong Pha Phum
ทองผาภูมิ

Surrounded by scenic karst topography, the area around the small town of Thong Pha Phum is becoming an increasingly popular destination for Thai tourists. Many of its inhabitants – mainly Mon or Burmese – originally congregated here to work on the construction of the Kheuan Khao Laem. Today, the dam is a major draw and has its own visitor's centre.

The town of Thong Pha Phum isn't much, with all of its businesses (including one ATM) along one street. Mae Nam Khwae Noi runs along the east side of town and there are some interesting **walks** and **day trips** in the area. You can, for example, ford the river over a footbridge close to town to climb a prominent limestone cliff topped by a wat.

Further afield are **Nam Tok Dai Chong Thong** (35km north via Rte 323), **Nam Tok Kroeng Krawia** (32km north), **Nam Tok Pha That** (30km south at the Km 105 marker) and **Hin Dat Hot Springs** (32km south at the Km 106 marker). All are accessible from the highway.

All of the places to stay here cater to Thai tourists. On the southern side of the town's main street and off the highway, **Som Jainuk Bungalow** (☎ 0 3459 9067; 29/10 Mu 1; r from 120B; 🕸) has basic, clean rooms around a shaded courtyard. The newer, all air-con building has larger, more comfortable rooms with hot-water showers. The same owner has raft rooms on the lake for 500B to 3000B.

So Boonyong Bungalows (☎ 0 3459 9441; 27 Mu 1; r from 120B; 🕸) has ordinary rooms, but tends to be quieter because it's bit further off the street.

Ban Chaidaen Phuphaphum Hotel (☎ 0 3459 9035; r 700-1200B; 🕸), out on the highway, has more upmarket rooms with satellite TV, fridge and other amenities.

Green World Hot Spring Resort & Golf Club (☎ 0 3459 9210, in Bangkok ☎ 0 2539 4613; r 800-

1100B; 🔀), 33km south of town near the Km 108 marker, is a huge resort with posh rooms and a golf course that is open to the public. Green fees are 300B during the week and 500B on the weekends. The hot spring and cool pool are also open to the public for 100B.

Just beyond the dam, west of town, are several rustic lakeside resorts with thatched bungalows and raft houses in the 500B to 2000B range. Most visitors are Thais in big groups (college students are the main clientele here) and the rooms are typically huge and devoid of furniture so that up to twenty can share sleeping quarters. If business is slow you may be able to have a big room to yourself for 200B to 300B.

In typical Mon style, several shops and vendors along the main street proffer curry in long rows of pots; instead of two or three curry choices more typical of Thai vendors, the Mon vendors lay out eight or more – all delicious. The best variety is at a shop called **Roi Maw** (Hundred Pots); a branch of the same shop can be found in a relatively new shophouse on the highway just south of town.

A small **night market** convenes near the centre of town each evening with the usual rice and noodle dishes.

Saep-i-li, a riverside restaurant near the highway bridge, serves good Isan food but it's more set up for drinking and snacking.

GETTING THERE & AWAY
Ordinary buses (8203) depart from the Kanchanaburi bus station for Thong Pha Phum every half-hour between 6am and 6.30pm (54B, three hours). Air-con buses and minivans to Sangkhlaburi also stop in Thong Pha Phum for about half the regular fare from Kanchanaburi to Sangkhlaburi (see p227).

Sangkhlaburi
อำเภอสังขละบุรี
pop 10,300
This small but important Kanchanaburi outpost is inhabited by a mixture of Burmese, Karen, Mon and Thai people, but mostly Karen and Mon. You'll find very little English spoken out this way – in fact, you may hear as much Burmese, Karen and Mon as Thai. There is also a small and relatively unknown population of Lao here.

It offers visitors a chance to get a taste of Myanmar without having to go there.

Sangkhlaburi sits at the edge of the huge Kheuan Khao Laem and was created after the dam flooded out an older village near the confluence of the three rivers that now feed the reservoir. There's not much to do in town except explore the small **markets** for Burmese handicrafts such as checked cotton blankets, *longyi* (Burmese sarongs) and cheroots. The town comes alive on **Mon National Day**, celebrated during the last week of July.

The distance between Kanchanaburi and Sangkhlaburi is about 230km. From Thong Pha Phum to Sangkhlaburi it's 74km.

INFORMATION
For foreign-exchange services head to Siam Commercial Bank (ATM), in the city centre near the market, and Phornphalin Hotel. Internet has arrived and although the exact location is always changing, it's typically within eye-shot of the market. There is an international phone in front of the post office. Immigration is around the corner from the Phornphalin Hotel, and should be visited before going to the border.

SIGHTS & ACTIVITIES
Wang Kha
Thailand's longest wooden bridge crosses a section of the lake near town to a friendly **Mon settlement** (Wang Kha) of traditional Mon-style wooden homes connected by dirt paths. A market in the village purveys goods smuggled from Myanmar, China and India; there are also a few food vendors with pots of rich Mon curry. On weekends **cockfights** are held around the village – to find one just listen for the enthusiastic cheers of the spectators. The village can be reached in five or 10 minutes by boat, or by walking or cycling over the bridge. It's a wonderful place to spend an afternoon, taking in sights (sarong-clad villagers etc) that are typical of Myanmar but very uncommon in Thailand.

Wat Wang Wiwekaram
วัดวังวิเวการาม
Also known as Wat Mon because most of the monks here are Mon, this monastery is about 3km north of the town on the edge of the reservoir. A tall and revered *chedi*,

Chedi Luang Phaw Uttama, is the centre-piece of the wat. Constructed in the style of the Mahabodhi *chedi* in Bodhgaya, India, the *chedi* is topped by 400B (about 6kg) of gold. A disintegrating *chedi* is located about 50m south of the tall one and is 300 to 400 years old. From the edge of the monastery grounds is a view of the tremendous lake and the three rivers that feed into it.

A new section of the Mon temple built across the road features a flashy, multi-roofed *wíhǎan* with stainless-steel-plated pillars, heavy carved wooden doors and marble banisters. It's surrounded by a carp-filled moat. Local rumour has it that it was built from profits made selling weapons and other supplies to the Mon and Karen armies; the wildest stories even claim that a huge weapons cache is stashed beneath the *wíhǎan*. A more likely source of sup-port for the wat was the black-market tax collected by the Mon rebel soldiers on all goods smuggled through their territory.

A Burmese **handicrafts market** convenes at the wat daily from mid-morning until sunset. The selection of wares is as good if not better than what's on offer at Three Pagodas Pass.

Kheuan Khao Laem
เขื่อนเขาแหลม

This huge lake was formed when a dam was constructed across Mae Nam Khwae Noi near Thong Pha Phum in 1983. The lake submerged an entire village at the conflu-ence of the Khwae Noi, Ranti and Sangkha-lia Rivers. The spires of the village's **Wat Sam Prasop** (Three Junction Temple) can be seen protruding from the lake in the dry season.

Canoes can be rented for exploring the lake, or for longer trips you can hire a long-tail boat and pilot. **Lake boating** is a tranquil pastime, best early in the morning with mist and bird life; early evening is also good for bird-watching. At one time a sprawling Mon refugee camp was accessible from the lake, but it was recently moved inland. The district's Mon refugee camps are off limits to visitors. Access is limited to those with a permit proving their official humanitarian purpose.

A branch meditation centre of the Sunya-taram Forest Monastery in Kanchanaburi is found on the lake's **Ko Kaew Sunyataram** (Sunyataram Jewel Isle). Permission to visit

must be obtained from Sunyataram Forest Monastery, 42km before Sangkhlaburi.

P Guest House (below) can arrange bam-boo-raft or long-tail **boat trips** on the lake (one of the most popular is a journey by raft along Mae Nam Sangkhalia), **elephant riding** and **jungle trekking** for 850B per person per day.

Day trips to nearby waterfalls are also a possibility. The rates depend on how many people are on the trip, but they tend to be very reasonable.

SLEEPING

P Guest House (☎ 0 3459 5061; www.pguesthouse .com; 8/1 Mu 1; s/d from 150/200B; 🏠) The well-kept bungalows here are worth the walk (about 1.2km from the bus stop). All of the charming, spacious, stone bungalows have verandas along a slope overlooking the lake. Cheaper rooms share a remarkably clean bathroom. P does packages (850B) that in-clude rafting on the lake and elephant rid-ing, as well as a room for one night. It also rents canoes and kayaks (100B per hour) and motorcycles (200B per day).

Ponnatee Resort (☎ 0 3459 5134; 84 Mu 1; r 800-1200B; 🏠) Trickling down the hillside over-looking the lake, this maze-like hotel has modern but drab rooms, some with stun-ning views. It has long been popular with French travellers. The restaurant is worth visiting for its gorgeous setting and its speciality, Chinese-style BBQ (250B) that could feed a group of four.

Burmese Inn (☎ 0 3459 5146; www.sangkhlaburi .com; 52/3 Mu 3; r from 120-400B; 🏠) The garden is lovingly cared for and the view over the wooden bridge to the Mon village is more than picturesque. The cheaper rooms in the wooden row houses are very basic, with Thai-style (very hard) mattresses and holes in the floor (annoying during mosquito sea-son). More expensive rooms are in cement bungalows, some with private balconies and TVs. The Austrian owner is extremely knowledgable about the area.

Phornphalin Hotel (☎ 0 3459 5039; s/d from 200/350B; 🏠) Phorn's rooms range from de-cent to gross. Upstairs, non-carpeted rooms with windows are best.

A handful of 'resorts' along the shore of the lake are more oriented towards Thai tourists than Westerners and come and go with each season.

EATING

Don't leave town without trying the local Burmese curry. There are a couple of places around the market that serve a delicious assortment of curries (15B).

Burmese Inn (dishes 30-60B) The restaurant here is known for its Burmese curry, but also does other Thai dishes quite well.

P Guest House (☎ 0 3459 5061; www.pguesthouse .com; 8/1 Mu 1; dishes 30-60B) Serves Western and Thai food. There's also a decent restaurant downstairs at **Phornphalin Hotel** that features an extensive English menu.

Rung Arun Restaurant (dishes 30B-80B) Opposite the Phornphalin, this restaurant also serves good Thai-Chinese food.

Baan Unrak Bakery (☎ 0 3459 5428; www.geocities .com/baanunrak; snacks 10-30B) For banana bread, chocolate cake and coffee, come to Baan, which raises money to support the nearby centre for abandoned children and destitute mothers. Sometimes it also makes home-made pizza. It's on the road that runs between Burmese Inn and P Guest House.

SHOPPING

Visitors interested in acquiring some Karen weaving should check out the small selection at the Baan Unrak Bakery. If you like what you see, ask about visiting the bigger store at the Baan Unrak Centre.

GETTING THERE & AWAY

Ordinary bus 8203 leaves the Kanchanaburi bus station for Sangkhlaburi (90B) at 6am, 8.40am, 10.20am and noon, and takes five to six hours, depending on how many mishaps occur on the Thong Pha Phum to Sangkhlaburi road. An air-con bus (151B) leaves at 9am and 1.30pm and takes four hours.

A minivan service from Kanchanaburi to Sangkhlaburi via Thong Pha Phum (118B, three hours) leaves six times daily, from 7.30am to 4.30pm. From Sangkhlaburi the vans depart from near the market seven times daily between 6.30am and 3.30pm. From either end it's usually best to reserve your seat a day in advance.

If you go by motorcycle or car you can count on about four hours to cover the 217km from Kanchanaburi to Sangkhlaburi, including three or four short rest stops. Alternatively, you can make it an all-day trip and stop off in Ban Kao, Meuang Singh and Hellfire Pass. Be warned, however, that this is not a trip for the inexperienced motorcyclist. The section of the road from Thong Pha Phum to Sangkhlaburi (74km) requires sharp reflexes and previous experience on mountain roads. This is also not a motorcycle trip to do alone as stretches of the highway are practically deserted – it's tough to get help if you need it and easy to attract the attention of would-be bandits.

Three Pagodas Pass (Payathonzu)

ด่านเจดีย์สามองค์

The pagodas themselves are rather small, but it is the remote nature of this former black-market outpost that draws a trickle of visitors. Control of the Myanmar side of the border once vacillated between the Karen National Union and the Mon Liberation Front, since Three Pagodas (Chedi Sam Ong) was one of several 'toll gates' along the Thailand–Myanmar border where insurgent armies collected a 5% tax on all merchandise that crossed the border. These ethnic groups used the funds to finance armed resistance against the Myanmar government. Now the border crossing and the town on the Myanmar side, Payathonzu, are controlled by the Myanmar government, although much of the long border between the two countries is not under government control.

The Karen people conduct a huge multi-million-dollar business in illegal mining and logging, the products of which are smuggled into Thailand by the truckload. Pressure for control of these border points has increased since the Thai government enacted a ban on all logging in Thailand in 1989, which has of course led to an increase in teak smuggling.

In late 1988 heavy fighting broke out between the Karen and the Mon for control of the 'toll gate' here. Since this is the only geographical location for hundreds of kilometres in either direction where a border crossing is convenient, this is where the Mon army (which has traditionally controlled this area) had customarily collected the 5% tax on smuggling. The Karen insurgents do the same at other points northwards along the Thailand–Myanmar border. Myanmar government pressure on the Karen further north led to a conflict between the Karen and the Mon over Three Pagodas trade and the village on the Myanmar side was virtually burnt to the ground.

The Myanmar government wrested control of the town in 1989 from both the Karen and Mon and has been firmly established there ever since. It renamed the town Payathonzu (Three Pagodas) and filled it with shops catering to an odd mix of troops and tourists.

If you are interested in crossing the border here, visit the immigration office in Sangkhlaburi to check the status beforehand. At the time of research the border was open daily from 6am to 6pm (but immigration doesn't open until 8am), the cost to cross was US$10 or 450B and all paperwork was handled at the border.

Depending on the political situation, foreigners are sometimes allowed to cross the border here for day trips, but you must complete the necessary paperwork in Sangkhlaburi before coming to the border. Apply for your border pass by visiting the Sangkhlaburi immigration office (around the corner from the Phornphalin Hotel) and providing two passport-sized photos and one copy each of the photo and visa pages of your passport. Once your pass is in order, proceed to the border and pay US$10 on the Myanmar side. Unlike the border crossing at Mae Sai in Chiang Rai, this crossing is not an 'official' crossing, and your passport isn't actually stamped, so don't bother coming up here to get some more Thai visa time on your passport.

A true frontier town, Payathonzu has around a half-dozen Burmese **teahouses** (a couple of them with *nam-bya* – the Burmese equivalent to Indian naan bread), one **cinema**, several mercantile **shops** with Burmese *longyi* (sarongs), cheroots, jade and clothes, and a few general souvenir shops with Mon-Karen-Burmese handicrafts. It is necessary to bargain; traders speak some English and also some Thai. In general the goods are well priced.

A Buddhist temple, **Wat Suwankhiri**, can be seen on a bluff near the town.

A Myanmar military checkpoint at the edge of town usually bars all visitors from leaving the town limits.

Three Pagodas Pass hosts a large **Songkran Festival** during April, which is complete with cockfights, hemp-fisted, Thai–Burmese kick-boxing, and Karen, Thai, Burmese and Mon folk dancing.

GETTING THERE & AWAY
The 19km-paved road to Three Pagodas Pass begins 4km before you reach Sangkhlaburi off Rte 323. At this intersection there is a Thai police checkpoint where you may have to stop for minor interrogation, depending on recent events in the Three Pagodas Pass area. Along the way you'll pass a couple of villages inhabited by Mon or Karen people.

If you don't have wheels, *săwngthăew* to Three Pagodas Pass (30B, 40 minutes) leave about every hour between 6am and 6.40pm from a lot near Sangkhlaburi's central market. The last *săwngthăew* back to Sangkhlaburi leaves Three Pagodas Pass at around 5pm or 6pm.

The border is only a short walk from the *săwngthăew* stop in Three Pagodas Pass.

KHAO LAEM NATIONAL PARK & AROUND
อุทยานแห่งชาติทุ่งใหญ่นเรศวร/
อุทยานแห่งชาติเขาแหลม

Approximately 34km south of Sangkhlaburi between the Km 39 and 40 markers, you'll find a turn-off on the east side of the highway for the 3200-sq-km **Khao Laem National Park** (admission 200B), Thailand's largest protected land parcel. This rough dirt road leads to **Nam Tok Takien Thong**, where pools are suitable for swimming nearly year-round. There are at least two other tracks off the highway into the sanctuary, but to find anything of interest you really should go with a guide – check with the Burmese Inn or P Guest House in Sangkhlaburi (p226).

Tham Sukho is a large limestone cave shrine just off the highway at the Km 42 marker.

Nearby, **Thung Yai Naresuan Nature Reserve** is one of the last natural habitats in Thailand for the tiger, whose total numbers nationwide are estimated to be less than 500, perhaps no more than 250.

Southeastern Thailand

Part paradise, part pandemonium, Southeastern Thailand offers hedonism and hush in equal measure. Revealing peaceful postcard vistas before hollering in your ear with a megaphone, it isn't always an easy cocktail to swallow. Although the region remains an incongruous mix of the overdeveloped and the untouched, most visitors find their niche somewhere along the line.

At one end of the spectrum, Pattaya is a concrete testament to Thailand's boom-time tourist economy. Here, glossy high-rise hotels house the armies of tourists that flock to the coast for a high-octane diet of sun, sand and, more controversially, sex. At the other extreme, sections of the Ko Chang archipelago are as quiet and untouched as they ever were. Tracts of virgin rainforest survive on Ko Chang itself, and, while developers are fast gobbling up the island's northernmost beaches, others remain blissfully unspoilt.

Most of the province, however, lies somewhere between Jekyll and Hyde, and Ko Samet is a case in point. The northern end of the island is a jumble of beach bars, tourist tat and deck chairs – its southern reaches are largely untouched, offering a scattering of isolated guesthouses and a clutch of unspoilt empty bays. Get tired of one extreme, and you need only trudge a few hundred metres to sample the antidote.

While the coast dominates this region, Southeastern Thailand is more than just the sum of its beaches. The quiet backstreets of Trat lure many travellers from the tourist trail, and the throbbing gem markets of Chanthaburi are as colourful as the precious stones themselves. Add a diversion to some of the country's smallest national parks (including Khao Khitchakut and Khao Chamao/Khao Wong), and you really will have sampled four seasons in one day.

SOUTHEASTERN THAILAND

HIGHLIGHTS

- Catching a transvestite cabaret show before burning the midnight oil in **Pattaya** (p235), Thailand's temple to high-octane hedonism
- Kicking back with a book on the pristine beaches of **Ko Samet's** (p249) southeastern coast
- Clambering onto the back of an elephant, and vanishing in the untramelled forests of **Ko Chang** (p262)
- Soaking up local living with a stint in one of **Trat's** (p259) romantic wooden guesthouses
- Wandering through Chanthaburi's bustling **gem markets** (p256), before taking the slow road to Cambodia's back door at **Hat Lek** (p261)

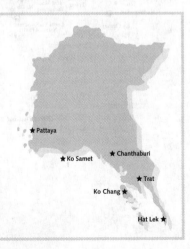

★ Pattaya

★ Chanthaburi

★ Ko Samet

★ Trat

Ko Chang ★

Hat Lek ★

SOUTHEASTERN THAILAND

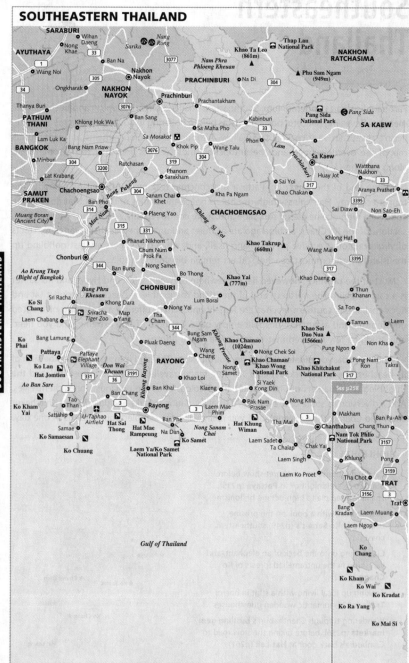

See p258

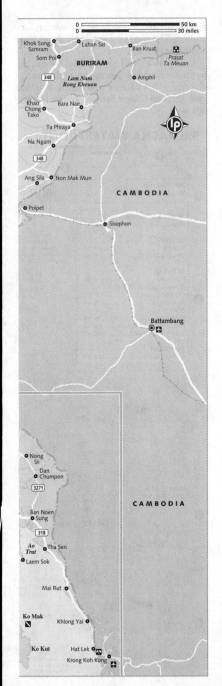

Climate

Southeast Thailand generally experiences a three-season, monsoonal climate, with a relatively cool dry season from November to December, followed by a hot dry season that stretches from January to May, and then a hot rainy season in the period from June to October. If you are here during the wet season, Ko Samet stays unusually dry and is the region's most 'monsoon-proof' island.

National Parks

The islands of Ko Samet (p249) and Ko Chang (p262) both fall within national parks (the Laem Ya/Ko Samet National Park and Ko Chang Marine National Park respectively) and are the region's biggest draw cards outside Pattaya. Ko Chang in particular is covered in dense, unspoilt forest and offers plenty of scope for those wanting to make a beeline 'back to nature'.

Khao Chamao/Khao Wong (p248), Khao Khitchakut (p258) and Nam Tok Phlio (p258) National Parks all hold fewer surprises, but are nevertheless worth a visit if you fancy a quick break from the coastal hubbub.

Getting There & Away

For the majority of travellers, a trip into, and then through, southeastern Thailand is a slow eastward progression from Bangkok to Hat Lek on the Cambodian border. Regular air-con buses link the capital with all the major towns, but for those who'd rather arrive fully fired, there are also flights from Phuket and Ko Samui to Pattaya, and from Bangkok to Trat. A less convenient, once-daily train service also links Bangkok with Pattaya.

If you are coming from northeast Thailand, regular air-con bus services travel to Rayong and Pattaya from both Khorat and Ubon Ratchathani.

Getting Around

On the whole, getting around southeastern Thailand is no problem, with good bus links between all the chief attractions. During the day, hourly ferries run to the region's islands throughout the year, although services to the outlying islands of the Ko Chang archipelago are almost nonexistent during the low, wet season.

SOUTHEASTERN THAILAND

CHONBURI PROVINCE

SRI RACHA

ศรีราชา

pop 145,000

The once quiet fishing port of Sri Racha has spread its wings in recent years and new developments have brought the requisite, metropolitan whirlwind of coughing traffic, billboards and gridlock to much of the town. The waterfront, at the heart of old Sri Racha, retains at least some of its one-time mystique. Along this stretch of water, rickety wooden pontoons, supporting hotels, restaurants and markets jut out into the sea and colourful timber boats buzz in and out of harbour. Much of the history has crumbled away, but Sri Racha remains a distinctly Thai town, where the gaudy, touristy trappings of nearby Pattaya have yet to find a foothold.

Thai food aficionados will also be pleased to hear that Sri Racha is home to the famous spicy sauce *náam phrík sǐi raachaa* – slather it on your seafood here.

Information

Krung Thai Bank (cnr Th Surasakdi 1 & Th Jermjompol; 8.30am-4.30pm Mon-Fri) Has an ATM and change facilities.

Post office (Th Jermjompol; 8.30am-4.30pm Mon-Fri, until noon Sat) A few blocks north of the Krung Thai Bank.

Sights

On the upside, **Sriracha Tiger Zoo** (0 3829 6571; www.tigerzoo.com; adult/child 300/150B; 8am-6pm) boasts more than 200 Bengal tigers, as well as a world-famous tiger-breeding facility and 100,000 crocodiles. On the downside, those keen to witness tigers in their natural habitat may be disappointed to see some of the cats jumping through fiery hoops as part of the zoo's programme of circus shows.

The complex is very popular with Asian package tourists, but if you catch it during a quieter moment, the zoo remains one of the easiest places in Thailand to get up close and personal (try and ignore the bars) with Thailand's grandest felines.

The circus shows – also with crocodile-wrestling and chimpanzee events – occur throughout the day and cost 30/20B extra

per adult/child – telephone for more information. The zoo is off Rte 3241, about 9km southeast of town.

On **Ko Loi**, a small rocky island connected to the mainland by a long jetty at the northern end of Sri Racha's waterfront, you can visit the **Thai-Chinese Buddhist temple** (daylight hours).

SRI RACHA WATERFRONT

0 — 200 m
0 — 0.1 miles

INFORMATION
Krung Thai Bank......................1 B4
Post Office.............................2 B3

SIGHTS & ACTIVITIES
Thai-Chinese Buddhist Temple ..3 A3

SLEEPING
Samchai.................................4 A4
Siriwatana Hotel.....................5 A4

EATING
Hua Hat................................6 B4
Italian Restaurant Il Giardino
  Italiano...............................7 B3
Jarin....................................8 A4
Market..................................9 B5
Picha Bakery........................10 B4
Pop....................................11 B3
Seaside Restaurant...............12 A5

TRANSPORT
Ordinary Bus Stop.................13 B3
Sǎwngthǎew to Naklua..........14 B5

To Air-Con Bus Stop (1km); Laemthong Hotel (1km); City Hotel (1km); Bangkok (102km)

Th Surasak

Ko Loi 3

Park 2

Jermjompol Soi 1

7

11 13

Th Sri Racha Nakorn 3

Ao Krung Thep (Bight of Bangkok)

5

10

Soi 10

Th Surasakdi 1

6 1

8

Pier

Soi 14

To Ko Si Chang (13km)

Soi 16

Th Jermjompol

12

Soi 18

Th Surasakdisanguan

9

Clock Tower

14

Municipal Office

To Sriracha Tiger Zoo (9km); Naklua (27km); Pattaya (31km)

Sleeping

Sri Racha is more of a transit point than an overnight stop. The most authentic – albeit basic – places to stay, however, are the rambling wooden hotels built on piers over the waterfront. Those after a few more creature comforts will have to stay further out.

Siriwatana Hotel (☎ 0 3831 1037; 35 Th Jermjompol; s/d 160/200B) Hovering over the water on timber stilts, this cheerful place boasts creaky wooden architecture, seaside sounds and a flick of rustic old Siam charm. The rooms – and especially the bathrooms – are basic, but the price is right. Try not to spend too long looking down through the floorboards into the sea though, as all sorts of junk gets washed in on the tide.

Samchai (☎ 0 3831 1800; Soi 10; s & d 380-400B; 🅿) A little further south, this seaside place brings air-con into the equation and offers a greater choice of rooms. The welcomes are a little colder though and the few concessions to midrange comfort come at the expense of some of Siriwatana's more chaotic charm. The air-con rooms are reasonable though, and it also has cheaper rooms with fan (260B).

City Hotel (☎ 0 3832 2700; www.citysriracha.com; 6/126 Th Sukhumvit; r 1376B; 🅿 🖥) The escalator which runs from the street to this hotel's 2nd-floor reception is hardly a stairway to heaven, but the air-con is cranked up good and high, the marble surfaces sparkle and the receptionists can grin with the best of them. The atmosphere is a little sterile, but the rooms are capacious and, if you can cope with the humidity, you can also pump some iron in the gym.

Laemthong Hotel (☎ 0 3832 2888; fax 0 3832 2888; 139-2/1 Th Sukhumvit; r 974B; 🅿 🖥) This 20-storey outfit peddles itself as an 'exclusive place for executives'. The sparse lobby, complete with deafeningly loud TV, lacks some of the promised glamour, but the midrange rooms are clean and perfectly passable.

Eating

Seafood is Sri Racha's culinary trump card and the **market**, near the clock tower at the southern end of town, is the cheapest, most colourful place for a snack. In the evenings the market offers everything from noodles to fresh fish.

Seaside Restaurant (Soi 18; dishes 60-200B; 🕙 10am-10pm) The weather has taken its toll on this simple wooden place at the end of the pier, but the bilingual seafood menu remains a big hit with important-looking, local government types. The views here are as good as anything the promenade has to offer and the sound of the sea gently lapping against the foundations, adds some audio to the maritime vista.

Picha Bakery (☎ 0 3832 4796; cnr Th Jermjompol & Th Surasakdi 1; snacks 15-30B; 🕙 8am-10pm) At the other end of the spectrum, this little bakery is an oasis of air-con and pathological cleanliness. Stop here for decent coffee and passable pastries.

Jarin (no English sign; ☎ 0 3831 1968; Soi 14; dishes 50-80B; 🕙 10am-8pm) Bare-bones, seafront place has very good one-plate seafood dishes, especially *khâo hàw mòk thá-leh* (steamed seafood curry with rice). It's a good spot to linger if you're waiting for a boat to Ko Si Chang.

Italian Restaurant Il Giardino Italiano (19/40 Th Jermjompol; dishes 60-200B; 🕙 5-10pm) A strange melange of Thai and Italian decorative influences, this little eatery nevertheless boasts the requisite check tablecloths and gigantic pepper grinders. It also has a good crack at whipping up some authentic, Mediterranean dishes.

Other recommendations:

Pop (Th Jermjompol; dishes 50-200B; 🕙 5-11pm) Waterfront beer, snacks and satellite sports fixtures.

Hua Hat (Th Jermjompol 102; dishes 50-180B; 🕙 11am-9pm) Authentic Chinese eats.

Getting There & Away

Buses to Sri Racha depart from Bangkok's Eastern bus station every 30 minutes from 5.30am to 7pm (ordinary 54B, air-con 94B; 1¾ hours). Ordinary direct buses stop near the pier for Ko Si Chang, but through buses and air-con buses stop on Th Sukhumvit (Hwy 3), near the Laemthong Hotel, from where there are *túk-túk* to the pier (30B).

White *sǎwngthǎew* (small pick-up truck) to Naklua (north Pattaya) leave from near the clock tower in Sri Racha frequently throughout the day (17B, 30 minutes). Once you're in Naklua you can easily catch another *sǎwngthǎew* on to central Pattaya. Local buses (25B, 30 minutes) also run to Pattaya from near the Laemthong Hotel on Th Sukhumvit.

Boat services to Ko Si Chang leave from Soi 14 (see p235).

Getting Around

You can get just about anywhere in town via motorcycle taxi or *túk-túk* for 25B to 40B.

KO SI CHANG

เกาะสีชัง

pop 4100

Barely more than a flake of green in the big blue Bight of Bangkok, and conspicuously lacking in pristine beaches, Ko Si Chang may seem like an unlikely footfall on the Thai tourist trail. Although this little island does lack the whizz-bang appeal of Ko Samet and Ko Chang, its quiet hills, peppered with places of historical interest, make for a nifty retreat from the capital.

There's not much in the way of beach life, but visitors are scarce during the week and standing on the cliffs by Sri Phitsanu Bungalow, or visiting the limestone caves at the heart of the Tham Yai Phrik Vipassana Monastery, you may feel like you have the place all to yourself. Like most of the islands in this area, Ko Si Chang does get busy during weekends.

Orientation & Information

The island's one small settlement faces the mainland and is the terminus for the Sri Racha ferry. A bumpy road network links the village with all the other sights.

Kasikornbank (99/12 Th Atsadang; ☉ 8.30am-3.30pm Mon-Fri) Has an ATM and currency-exchange facilities.

Tourist Services Centre (☎ 0 3821 6201; Th Atsadang; ☉ 9am-4.30pm Mon-Fri) Opposite the Sichang Palace Hotel; offers limited tourist information. It's on the main road to the right as you walk up from the pier.

Sights & Activities

The Buddhist **Tham Yai Phrik Vipassana Monastery** (☎ 0 3821 6104; ☉ daylight hours) is built around a number of meditation caves running into the island's central limestone ridge and offers fine views from its hilltop stupa. Monks and *mâe chii* (nuns) from across the country come to take advantage of the cave's peaceful environment, and foreigners wishing to sample monastic life are also welcomed. Those wishing to study at the monastery can do so free of charge (just phone ahead to make sure there is space and bring your passport), but you'll be expected to follow the monastery's strict code of conduct. Whether you visit for only an hour, or stay an entire month, leave an appropriate donation (roughly equivalent to basic food and lodging if staying a few days) with the monk or nun who shows you around.

Decent beaches really are at a premium on the island, but there are a handful passable swimming spots. Secluded **Hat Tham** (also called Hat Sai) can be reached by following a branch of the ring road to the back of the island. During low tide there's a strip of sand here. A partially submerged cave can be visited at the eastern end of the little bay.

At the western end of the island (about 2km from the pier), you can visit **Hat Tha Wang Palace** (Th Chakra Pong; admission free; ☉ 9am-5pm). The carefully managed lawns are a prime picnic spot for visiting Bangkok types, who share the gardens with the island's foraging white squirrels. The palace was once used by Rama V (Chulalongkorn) over the summer months, but was abandoned when the French briefly occupied the island in 1893. The main throne hall – a magnificent golden teak structure called Vimanmek – was moved to Bangkok in 1910. The Fine Arts Department has since restored the remaining palace buildings, which were named after the king's consorts, Pongsri, Wattana and Apirom, and there are a few historical exhibits to peruse.

On the crest of the hill, overlooking Hat Tha Wang, is a large white *chedi* (stupa) that holds **Wat Atsadangnimit** (☉ daylight hours), a small, consecrated chamber where Rama V used to meditate. The unique Buddha image inside was fashioned more than 50 years ago by a local monk. Nearby you'll come to a stone outcrop wrapped in holy cloth. The locals call it 'Bell Rock' because it rings like a bell when struck.

Not far from Wat Atsadangnimit is a large limestone cave called **Tham Saowapha** (admission free; ☉ daylight hours), which appears to plunge deep into the island. If you have a torch, it's worth poking your nose into.

The most imposing and idiosyncratic sight on the island is the ornate **San Jao Phaw Khao Yai Chinese Temple** (☉ daylight hours). During Chinese New Year in February, the island is overrun with Chinese visitors from the mainland. This is one of Thailand's most interesting Chinese temples, with shrine caves, multiple levels and a good view of the ocean. It is at the eastern edge of the town, high on a hill overlooking the sea.

Sleeping

Sichang Palace (☎ 0 3821 6276; fax 0 3821 6030; Th Atsadang 81; r 810B; 🔀) Calling it a 'palace' may be setting the bar a little high, but this three-storey place in the heart of the main town has plenty of ostentatious trimmings, including boat-shaped chandeliers and a brace of welcoming carved wooden statues at the door. Spotless and comfortable, it also has the best rooms on the island. You'll pay an extra 200B for a sea view and 190B for breakfast.

Sri Phitsanu Bungalow (☎ 0 3821 6034; 38/3 Mu 2 Th Devavongse; r 500B) Location is all at this quiet little outfit. Perched on the cliffs, with its rooms and one- (800B) and two-bed (1500B) bungalows on the tip of the precipice facing the sea, Sri Phitsanu has the prettiest ocean views on the island. Weeds are now beginning to push through the concrete and the rooms no longer look their best, but this place remains a good bet for a well-priced bed. To get there, take the first right past the Tiewpai Park Resort, then follow the road past the Tham Yai Phrik Vipassana Monastery – a *sǎamláw* will cost you 30B from the ferry terminal.

Sichang View Resort (☎ 0 3821 6210; r 800B; 🔀) Near the Chinese temple, with decent sunset views, this has a restaurant, gardens and some fancy 'deluxe' rooms with hot water and cable TV (1400B).

Other recommendations:

Benz Bungalow (☎ 0 3821 6091; Th Makhaam Thaew; r 600B; 🔀) With clean if slightly scruffy rooms near the gate of Hat Tha Wang.

Home & Sea (☎ 0 3821 6237; Th Makhaam Thaew; r 600B; 🔀) Offers basic rooms with TV and fridge or bizarre, five-sleeper boats (1000B) for that Noah's Ark ambience. It's next to Benz, on the ferry terminal side.

Eating

The town has several small restaurants, but don't expect fireworks. Most of the hotels have decent eateries.

Pan & David Restaurant (☎ 0 3821 6629; 167 Mu 3 Th Makhaam Thaew; mains 60-160B; 🕙 10am-10pm) Right next to Home & Sea, on the road to Hat Tha Wang, this colourful and upbeat alfresco diner offers plenty of sea air and a whole load of scrumptious Thai, veggie and Western fare.

Getting There & Away

Boats to Ko Si Chang leave hourly from the pier in Sri Racha at the end of Soi 14, Th Jermjompol. The fare is 30B each way; the first boat leaves at about 6am and the last at 7pm. The last boat back to Sri Racha from Si Chang is at 6pm. For more information, you can contact the **Sangprateep Boat Service** (☎ 0 3831 3687; 🕙 7am-7pm), one of the ferry operators, at its office on the pier in Sri Racha.

Getting Around

For such a small island, Ko Si Chang has some of the biggest motorcycle taxis you are likely to see.

They will take you anywhere on the island for 20B to 30B or give you a complete tour of the island for 150B per hour. Asking prices tend to be outrageous, so haggle hard.

PATTAYA

พัทยา

pop 80,000

A throbbing monument to holiday hedonism, Pattaya whips up a seedy, summer cocktail enjoyed by more than a million visitors per year. More Costa del Bangkok than authentic Thailand, it is a garish, gaudy mix many may prefer to avoid. Those after temples, open spaces and history should give Pattaya an extremely wide berth, but the city moves to the kind of unashamedly decadent rhythm some may find irresistible.

Cutting a crescent around Pattaya Bay, the city's main beach is a peninsula of basting suntanned flesh, souvenir stalls and sand castles. Skyscrapers cast their long shadows across the yellow sand as revving motorcycles and jet skis provide the soundtrack. The coconut scent of suntan oil hangs in the air, and a knot of high-rise hotels, dive shops, and golf courses cater to the legions of package tourists who march off the charter flights every season.

But Pattaya is a late riser and the city really comes to life after dark, when the go-go bars glow red and thunderous basslines call night owls to happy hour at a menagerie of dance clubs. Sex tourists appear to run the streets during the graveyard shift but, whatever your tastes, you will doubtless find something here to keep the midnight oil burning.

Even rowdy Pattaya, however, has some quieter corners. South of Pattaya proper, Hat Jomtien caters to a calmer crowd, while the city's offshore wrecks and reefs offer some of the most accessible diving in the

SOUTHEASTERN THAILAND

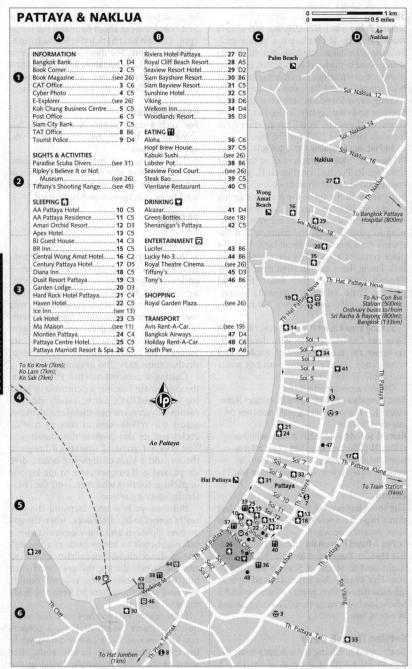

PATTAYA & NAKLUA

0 — 1 km
0 — 0.5 miles

INFORMATION
Bangkok Bank......................**1** D4
Book Corner.........................**2** C5
Book Magazine..................(see 26)
CAT Office...........................**3** C6
Cyber Photo........................**4** C5
E-Explorer.........................(see 26)
Koh Chang Business Centre...**5** C5
Post Office..........................**6** C5
Siam City Bank....................**7** C5
TAT Office..........................**8** B6
Tourist Police.....................**9** D4

SIGHTS & ACTIVITIES
Paradise Scuba Divers........(see 31)
Ripley's Believe it or Not
  Museum..........................(see 26)
Tiffany's Shooting Range.....(see 45)

SLEEPING
AA Pattaya Hotel................**10** C5
AA Pattaya Residence.........**11** C5
Amari Orchid Resort...........**12** D3
Apex Hotel.........................**13** C5
BJ Guest House...................**14** C5
BR Inn...............................**15** C5
Central Wong Amat Hotel....**16** C2
Century Pattaya Hotel.........**17** D5
Diana Inn..........................**18** C5
Dusit Resort Pattaya...........**19** C3
Garden Lodge....................**20** D3
Hard Rock Hotel Pattaya.....**21** C4
Haven Hotel.......................**22** C5
Ice Inn..............................(see 13)
Lek Hotel...........................**23** C5
Ma Maison.........................(see 11)
Montien Pattaya.................**24** C4
Pattaya Centre Hotel...........**25** C5
Pattaya Marriott Resort & Spa.**26** C5

Riviera Hotel Pattaya..........**27** D2
Royal Cliff Beach Resort......**28** A5
Seaview Resort Hotel..........**29** D2
Siam Bayshore Resort.........**30** B6
Siam Bayview Resort...........**31** C5
Sunshine Hotel...................**32** C5
Viking...............................**33** D6
Welkom Inn.......................**34** D4
Woodlands Resort..............**35** D3

EATING
Aloha...............................**36** C6
Hopf Brew House................**37** C5
Kabuki Sushi.....................(see 26)
Lobster Pot........................**38** B6
Seaview Food Court...........(see 26)
Steak Bao..........................**39** C5
Vientiane Restaurant..........**40** C5

DRINKING
Alcazar.............................**41** D4
Green Bottles....................(see 18)
Shenanigan's Pattaya.........**42** C5

ENTERTAINMENT
Lucifer.............................**43** B6
Lucky No 3........................**44** B6
Royal Theatre Cinema........(see 26)
Tiffany's...........................**45** D3
Tony's..............................**46** B6

SHOPPING
Royal Garden Plaza...........(see 26)

TRANSPORT
Avis Rent-A-Car.................(see 19)
Bangkok Airways...............**47** D4
Holiday Rent-A-Car...........**48** C5
South Pier........................**49** A6

To Ko Krok (7km);
Ko Larn (7km);
Ko Sak (7km)

Ao Naklua

Palm Beach

Soi Naklua 12

Soi Naklua 14

Naklua

Soi Naklua 16

Th Naklua

27

To Bangkok Pattaya
Hospital (800m)

16

29

Soi Naklua 18

Wong
Amat
Beach

20

35

Th Hat Pattaya Neua

19

12   45

To Air-Con Bus
Station (500m);
Ordinary buses to/from
Sri Racha & Rayong (800m);
Bangkok (133km)

14

Soi 1

Soi 2

34

Soi 3

Soi 4

41

Soi 5

Th Pattaya 3

Soi 6

1

9

Ao Pattaya

21

24

47

17

Th Pattaya Klang

To Train Station
(1km)

31

Soi 8   Soi 7

Soi 9

32

Pattaya

Soi 10

7

Hat Pattaya

39 25

10

15 Soi 11

11

Soi 12

13

37

5

22 23

18

6   2

4

26

40

42

36

48

Th Hat Pattaya & Post Office

Th Bua Khao

44

49

43 38

Soi 2

46

Soi 3

30

Th Cliff

Th Pattaya 3

Soi Viking

3

Th Pattaya Tai

8

To Hat Jomtien
(1km)

Th Phra Tamnak

33

Bangkok area. A little chunk of Florida laid out along the Gulf of Thailand, Pattaya lacks subtlety in the manner of a TV soap opera, but it can become dangerously addictive to those who choose to watch.

History

US GIs provided the kick-start that began Pattaya's dramatic transformation from quiet fishing village into throbbing tourist mecca when they began yomping down to the coast in search of fun and frolics from their base in Nakhon Ratchasima. That was 1959. By the time of the Vietnam War, the flow had become a flood as troops on leave arrived to soak up Pattaya's lucrative cocktail of sun, sand and sex. Package – and sex – tourists followed, and southeastern Thailand's golden goose soon grew fat on the seemingly bottomless pot of dollars pouring into the local economy. With little sign of a slowdown in sight, Pattaya's continued growth seems set to continue.

Orientation

Curving around Ao Pattaya (Pattaya Bay), Hat Pattaya (Pattaya Beach) is the city's showcase stretch of sand. Thanon Hat Pattaya runs along the beach and is lined with hotels, shopping centres and, towards the north, go-go bars. At the southern end of Th Hat Pattaya, Walking St is a semipedestrianised area chock-a-block with restaurants and nightclubs. The alleyways running between Th Hat Pattaya and Th Pattaya 2 each have their own character: Soi 13 is filled with pleasant, midrange hotels, while Soi 3 is at the heart of the city's gay area, dubbed 'Boy's Town'.

Naklua, to the north, and Hat Jomtien, to the south, also have their own beaches and tend to cater to a quieter, more family-oriented crowd. Pattaya's sexier side is less on show.

MAPS

The *Explore Pattaya* magazine, available free from the tourist office, includes one of the best maps of the town.

Information

BOOKSHOPS

Book Corner (Map p236; Soi Post Office; 🕑 10am-10pm) For a decent selection of English-language fiction and travel guides.

WHAT'S IN A NAME?

Given Pattaya's international appeal, some of the streets are known by both their Thai and English names. We have stuck with the Thai names, although some city maps use the English equivalent. Examples of the Thai street names, with the English equivalent in brackets include: Th Hat Pattaya (Beach Rd), Th Hat Jomtien (Jomtien Beach Rd), Th Hat Pattaya Neua (North Pattaya Rd), Th Pattaya Klang (Central Pattaya Rd) and Th Pattaya Tai (South Pattaya Rd). To further confuse matters, while all maps (including ours) agree that the two alleys south of Soi 13 are called Soi Yamato and Soi Post Office, they are respectively labelled Soi 13/1 and Soi 13/2 on street signs.

Book Magazine (Map p236; 1st fl, Royal Garden Plaza, Th Pattaya 2; 🕑 11am-11pm) For English-language newspapers and magazines.

EMERGENCY

Tourist Police (Map p236; 🕾 1155; tourist@police.go.th; Th Pattaya 2)

INTERNET ACCESS

There are Internet cafés across town.
E-Explorer (Map p236; 🕾 0 3871 0238; Shop B-8, 1st fl, Royal Garden Plaza, Th Pattaya 2; per min 2B; 🕑 11am-11pm) Serves great coffee.
Koh Chang Business Centre (Map p236; 🕾 0 3871 0145; Soi post office; per min 1B; 🕑 9am-midnight)

MEDICAL SERVICES

Bangkok Pattaya Hospital (off Map p236; 🕾 0 3842 7777; www.pbh.co.th; 301 Mu 6, Th Sukhumvit, Naklua; 🕑 24hr) For 1st-class health care.

MONEY

There are banks with ATMs and currency exchange facilities across Pattaya.
Bangkok Bank (Map p236; cnr Th Pattaya 2; 🕑 9.30am-7pm Mon-Fri)
Siam City Bank (Map p236; Th Pattaya 2; 🕑 9am-4.30pm Mon-Fri) Has a Western Union money transfer facility and **late night exchange window** (🕑 9am-8pm).

NEWSPAPERS & MAGAZINES

Explore Pattaya, a free fortnightly magazine distributed around town, contains information on events and attractions as well as hotel and restaurant listings. *What's On*

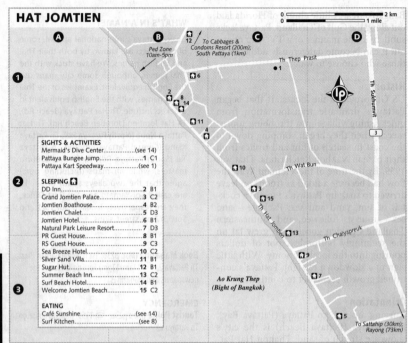

HAT JOMTIEN

SIGHTS & ACTIVITIES	
Mermaid's Dive Center..................(see 14)	
Pattaya Bungee Jump..........................1	C1
Pattaya Kart Speedway.....................(see 1)	

SLEEPING	
DD Inn...2	B1
Grand Jomtien Palace.........................3	C2
Jomtien Boathouse..............................4	B2
Jomtien Chalet....................................5	D3
Jomtien Hotel.....................................6	B1
Natural Park Leisure Resort................7	D3
PR Guest House...................................8	B1
RS Guest House...................................9	C3
Sea Breeze Hotel..............................10	C2
Silver Sand Villa...............................11	B1
Sugar Hut...12	B1
Summer Beach Inn............................13	C2
Surf Beach Hotel...............................14	B1
Welcome Jomtien Beach....................15	C2

EATING	
Café Sunshine................................(see 14)	
Surf Kitchen...................................(see 8)	

Labels on map: Ped Zone 10am–5pm; To Cabbages & Condoms Resort (200m); South Pattaya (1km); Th Thep Prasit; Th Sukhumvit; Th Wat Bun; Th Hat Jomtien; Th Chaiyapruek; Ao Krung Thep (Bight of Bangkok); To Sattahip (30km); Rayong (73km)

Pattaya is a similar monthly publication. *Pattaya Mail* (www.pattayamail.com), a weekly newspaper, makes for some absorbing reading as Pattaya's famed social ills are well covered – much of the mayhem you'll read about here never makes it into the Bangkok papers. Not surprisingly given Pattaya's popularity with German-speakers there is also a weekly German-language newspaper, *Pattaya Blatt* (www.pattayablatt.com).

POST
Post office (Map p236; Soi 13/2; ☑ 8.30am-4.30pm Mon-Fri, 9am-noon Sat)

TELEPHONE
Communications Authority of Thailand (CAT; Map p236; cnr Th Pattaya Tai & Th Pattaya 3; ☑ 8.30am-4.30pm Mon-Fri, 9am-noon Sat) Southeast of central Pattaya.
Cyber Photo (Map p236; ☎ 0 3841 1508; Th Pattaya 2; ☑ 10.30am-midnight) You can make international calls and get your photos developed at the same time.

TOURIST INFORMATION
Tourism Authority of Thailand (TAT; Map p236; ☎ 0 3842 8750; tatchon@tat.or.th; 609 Mu 10, Th Pra

Tamnak; ☑ 8.30am-4.30pm) At the northwestern edge of Rama IX Park. There are plenty of brochures and staff are reasonably helpful. Pick up a copy of *Pattaya Info* (www .pattayainfo.com), which includes a useful map and eating, drinking and sleeping listings.

TRAVEL AGENCIES
You won't have to walk far to find a travel agency selling trips across Thailand.
Koh Chang Business Centre (Map p236; ☎ 0 3871 0145; Soi Post Office; ☑ 9am-midnight) Specialises in trips to Ko Chang and Ko Samet.

Dangers & Annoyances
It is worth remembering that sex tourism is a booming industry in Pattaya and that large sections of the city are chock full of go-go bars and strip clubs. This seedier side of Pattaya is hard to avoid, especially at night, and if you are travelling with young children prepare yourself for some awkward questions.

Sights & Activities
BEACHES
Hat Pattaya is the city's showcase stretch of sand, sporting legions of sunbathers, hordes

of souvenir sellers and, just offshore, swarms of buzzing jet skis and speedboats. The sand is reasonably clean here, the water is generally calm and there's enough razzmatazz to keep even the most reluctant beachcomber entertained for some time: think Florida in southeast Asia.

Hat Jomtien (Jawmthian), about 1km south of Pattaya, stretches for a sweeping 6km and is considerably quieter than its northern neighbour. You're relatively removed from Pattaya's sex scene at this beach, but some stretches of the promenade are looking a little washed out.

Hat Naklua, a smaller beach north of Pattaya, is also quiet and fairly tastefully developed. Jomtien and Naklua are the places where families tend to stay, as Pattaya and south Pattaya are pretty much given over to single male tourists or couples on package tours.

The islands of **Ko Larn**, **Ko Krok** and **Ko Sak** are around 7km offshore and have some popular beaches – especially **Hat Ta Waen** on Ko Larn. Boats leave Pattaya's **South Pier** (Map p236) every two hours between 8am and 4.30pm (20B). The last boat back from Ko Larn is at 5pm.

WATER SPORTS

Pattaya is the most convenient diving location to Bangkok, although it can't really compete with Thailand's showcase sites. In recent years the fish population has dwindled considerably and visibility is often poor due to heavy boat traffic. Nearby Ko Larn, Ko Sak and Ko Krok are fine for beginners, but accomplished divers may prefer the 'outer islands' of Ko Man Wichai and Ko Rin, which have more visibility. In most places you can expect 3m to 9m of visibility under good conditions, or in more remote sites 5m to 12m. Further southeast, the shipwrecks of *Petchburi Bremen* and *Hardeep* off Sattahip and Samae have created artificial reefs and are interesting dive sites. In mid-2004, the Thai navy scuttled HMS *Khram* in 30m of water off Ko Phi. Many operators now offer excursions there and it promises to become one of the area's better dive destinations.

Diving costs are quite reasonable: a two-dive excursion averages between 1900B and 2900B for boat, equipment, underwater guide and lunch. Snorkellers may join day trips for 500B to 800B. For shipwrecks, the price goes up to 3000B to 3500B (depending

---

RESPONSIBLE DIVING

Please consider the following tips when diving and help preserve the ecology and beauty of Thailand's reefs:

- Never use anchors on the reef, and take care not to ground boats on coral.

- Avoid touching or standing on living marine organisms or dragging equipment across the reef. Polyps can be damaged by even the gentlest contact. If you must hold on to the reef, only touch exposed rock or dead coral.

- Be conscious of your fins. Even without contact, the surge from fin strokes near the reef can damage delicate organisms. Take care not to kick up clouds of sand, which can smother organisms.

- Practise and maintain proper buoyancy control. Major damage can be done by divers descending too fast and colliding with the reef.

- Take great care in underwater caves. Spend as little time within them as possible as your air bubbles may be caught within the roof and thereby leave organisms high and dry. Take turns to inspect the interior of a small cave.

- Resist the temptation to collect or buy corals or shells or to loot marine archaeological sites (mainly shipwrecks).

- Ensure that you take home all your rubbish and any litter you may find as well. Plastics in particular are a serious threat to marine life.

- Do not feed fish.

- Minimise your disturbance of marine animals. *Never* ride on the backs of turtles.

on the season), and for an overnight trip with five to seven dives, expect to pay up to 6000B per person. Full National Association of Underwater Instructors (NAUI) or Professional Association of Dive Instructors (PADI) Open Water certification courses, which take three to four days, cost 9000B to 12,000B for all instruction and equipment.

Some shops do half-day group trips to nearby islands for as little as 500B per person, and to islands a bit further out for 650B; these prices include lunch, beverages and transport, but not equipment rental beyond mask, fins and snorkel.

Average equipment-rental rates per day are: mask, fins and snorkel 200B to 250B; regulator 300B to 400B; buoyancy compensation device 250B to 400B; weight belt 150B; tank 150B; wetsuit 300B; or full scuba outfit 1500B. Airfills typically cost 100B to 150B. To protect themselves from steep baht fluctuations, some dive operators quote only in US dollars.

Some of the dozens of operators in town:

Aquanauts Diving (☎ 0 3842 9117; Th Hat Pattaya)

Dave's Diver Den (☎ 0 3842 0411; fax 0 3836 0095; 190/11 Mu 9, Th Pattaya Klang)

Mermaid's Dive Center (Map p238; ☎ 0 3823 2219; www.mermaiddive.com; Soi White House, Hat Jomtien)

Paradise Scuba Divers (Map p236; ☎ 0 3871 0567; Siam Bayview Resort)

Pattaya and Jomtien have some of the best water-sports facilities in Thailand. Water-skiing costs around 1000B per hour; parasailing 200B to 300B a shot (about 10 to 15 minutes); and windsurfing 500B an hour. Game fishing is also a possibility; the rental rates for boats, fishing guides and tackle are quite reasonable. Hat Jomtien is the best spot for windsurfing, not least because you are a little less likely to run into parasailors or jet skiers.

OTHER SIGHTS & ACTIVITIES

Parents and fans of all things quirky can head to **Ripley's Believe It or Not Museum** (Map p236; ☎ 0 3871 0294; 2nd fl; Royal Garden Plaza, Th Pattaya 2; adult/child 370/270B; ✆ 11am-11pm), which puts a Disneyesque spin on the world's oddities. Just look for the plane sticking out of the front of the shopping mall.

Next stop for speed freaks should be the **Pattaya Kart Speedway** (Map p238; ☎ 0 3842 2004; 248/2 Th Thep Prasit Soi 9; ✆ 9am-6pm), where you can race go-karts around an impressive 1km loop. There's also a beginner's track and an off-road circuit. Prices start at 250B for ten minutes in a 10HP kart.

Just outside the city, **Pattaya Elephant Village** (Map pp230-1; ☎ 0 3824 9818; www.elephant-village-pattaya.com; ✆ according to show & trek times) is a nonprofit sanctuary for former working elephants. As well as a daily 1½-hour Elephant Show (450B), which begins at 2.30pm and demonstrates various training techniques, the sanctuary also offers one- (450B) and 3½-hour (1500B) elephant treks. Short treks begin at 9am, 10.30am, 12.30pm and 4pm, while the longer treks start at 10.30am and 4pm – you are advised to book ahead. The village is 7km off the Sukhumvit Rd: take a left turn at the Km 144.5 sign towards Siam Country Club, then turn right at the intersection 4km down the road.

There are dozens of other activities on offer in Pattaya, including shooting at **Tiffany's Shooting Range** (Map p236; ☎ 0 3842 9642; Ground fl, Tiffany's, Th Pattaya 2; 200B plus ammunition costs; ✆ 9am-10pm), a 56m bungee jump at **Pattaya Bungee Jump** (Map p238; ☎ 0 3830 0608; www.paintballpark-pattaya.com; 248/10 Mu 12, Th Thep Prasit; first jump/repeat jump 850/400B; ✆ 9am-6pm) and golf. Golf packages at all of the area's major courses can be booked via telephone through **ECT Golf Organization** (☎ 0 3830 0927; www.pattayagolfpackage.com). Packages start at 1650B per person and run Monday to Thursday.

Sleeping

BUDGET

The number of places to stay in Naklua, Pattaya and Hat Jomtien is mind-boggling – there are close to 200 hotels, guesthouses and bungalows. Because of low occupancy rates, some hotels offer special deals, especially midweek; bargaining for a room may also net a lower rate. On weekends and holidays, the cheaper rooms tend to book out.

North Pattaya and Naklua are quieter if you want to avoid the full-on nightlife of south Pattaya. Hat Jomtien is also calmer, but it can suffer from a slightly dreary, off-season feel.

An average hotel room costs 450B to 2000B, and for guesthouses the prices range from around 300B to 750B. Many places charge per room, rather than offering single and double prices.

Pattaya

The cheapest guesthouses are in south Pattaya, along Th Pattaya 2, the street parallel to Th Hat Pattaya. Most are clustered near Soi 6, 10, 11 and 12. Overall, however, you get much better value for money by splashing out a little more on one of the midrange places.

Ice Inn (Map p236; ☎ 0 3872 0671; ice-inn@yahoo .com; 528/2-3 Th Pattaya 2; r 250-550B; ❂ 💻) Still sporting the gloss of a relatively new facelift, this snug little number above an Internet café and art shop is welcoming ('we take care of you' it promises), pathologically spotless and excellent value.

Apex Hotel (Map p236; ☎ 0 3842 9233; www.apex hotelpattaya.com; 216/2 Th Pattaya 2; r 500B; ❂ 🅿) It's hardly at the apex of Pattaya's hotel scene and things are looking a bit crumbly these days, but the 'marble' and 'carpet' rooms do come with TV and fridge. The 'marble' rooms face the back and are the quietest after dark.

BR Inn (Map p236; ☎ 0 3842 6449; 224/26 Mu 10, Soi 12; r 400B; ❂) Homely, family-run place is basic, but good value if you're on a budget. Don't expect much in the way of fireworks, but smiles come as standard.

Viking (Map p236; ☎ 0 3842 3164; fax 0 3842 5964; 43/5 Mu 10, Soi Viking; r 400B; ❂ 🅿) Situated in south Pattaya, this reasonably friendly spot offers a welcome dose of calm and none of the latter-day Scandinavian hell-raising hinted at in the name. The rooms are basic, but perfectly comfortable for this price range.

BJ Guest House (Map p236; ☎ 0 3842 1147; 463 Mu 9; r 450B; ❂) It doesn't provide much to write home about, but BJ only claims to offer three storeys of well-appointed, cheap rooms by the beach – and in that it comes up trumps.

Hat Jomtien

RS Guest House (Map p238; ☎ 0 3823 1867; Th Hat Jomtien; r 350-400B; ❂) Cleanest villa on a slightly scruffy stretch of beach near Th Chaiya-preuk, RS is one of the cheapest places to stay. The whole place is a little underlit, but the small rooms are fine for a night's shut-eye.

PR Guest House (Map p238; ☎ 0 3823 3404; fax 0 3823 3405; 144/12-14 Soi Jomtien 4; r 500B; ❂) Functional rather than thrilling, this family-run, unassuming place is basic and a little bland, but

the rooms are passable and the owners are friendly. It's just off Th Hat Jomtien, turn off at the 7-Eleven store.

Surf Beach Hotel (Map p238; ☎ 0 3823 1025-6; 75/1 Th Hat Jomtien; r 550B; ❂) Passable spot has a slightly frumpy, off-season air about it, but the rooms are comfortable and the staff manage to pull at least a little charm out of the bag. A view of the ocean will cost you an extra 100B.

DD Inn (Map p238; ☎ 0 3823 2995; 410/50 Th Hat Jomtien; r 550B; ❂) At the northern end of Hat Jomtien beach, this so-so backup option has decent rooms, but at the expense of anything approximating atmosphere. Get out on the town though, and you won't give a monkey's.

Jomtien Hotel (Map p238; ☎ 0 3825 1606; fax 0 3825 1097; 403/74 Mu 12, Th Hat Jomtien; r 300-450B; ❂) Bottom-end tourist hotel lacks a beachfront location, but prices do seem to have been lowered accordingly. The paint's a bit flaky and no-one's been changing the light bulbs for a while; as well as the standard air-con rooms, it also has some scruffy fan options.

MIDRANGE

Pattaya has an excellent range of midrange hotels with stiff competition keeping standards high and prices (relatively) low. Hotels do tend to age fast in Pattaya however, so it's worth keeping an eye out for the latest openings.

Pattaya

Ma Maison (Map p236; ☎ 0 3842 9318; fax 0 3842 6060; Soi 13; r 800B; ❂ 🅿) Offering a little more Continental appeal, this French-oriented place makes a few concessions to Gallic nostalgia, with a reasonably authentic French menu, chalet-style accommodation and a decent range of French tipples from the bar. Popular (book ahead), idiosyncratic and good value, it even has a *piscine* (pool).

Haven Hotel (Map p236; ☎ 0 3871 0988; www.the haven-hotel.com; 185 Soi 13; r 950B; ❂ 🅿) Just across the road from Ma Maison, this chic midranger has a handful of cosy rooms, which are packed full of mod cons including TV, stereo and a fridge full of beer. The pool is never more than a few steps away and there's plenty of hush for those wanting to escape the Pattaya hubbub.

Diana Inn (Map p236; ☎ 0 3842 9675; www.diana pattaya.co.th; 216/6-20 Th Pattaya 2; r 750B; ❂ 🅿)

Pleasant outfit sells itself as 'nice and clean' and more or less lives up to its promise. The surroundings can become raucous during the graveyard shift, but the rooms are comfortable, there's plenty of foliage in the lobby area and the Green Bottles pub downstairs offers a welcome oasis for insomniacs.

Lek Hotel (Map p236; ☎ 0 3842 5552; lek_hotel@ hotmail.com; 284/5 Th Pattaya 2; r 750-1000B; ﹡) Plenty of sparkling marble gives this 'executive' midranger a glossier feel. Lots of late-night hubbub drifts up into the rooms at the front of the building though.

AA Pattaya Residence (Map p236; ☎ 0 3842 3403; aaresidence@yahoo.com; 109/20 10 Soi 13; r 1110B; ﹡) Some swanky, central rooms are available at this shiny new place just up from Ma Maison. Standards are high and the rooms are among the best in this category, but the prices are a little high for what's on offer. Big discounts are sometimes available though, and if you can get them to go as low as 800B, this represents a very good deal.

AA Pattaya Hotel (Map p236; ☎ 0 3842 8656; aahotel@yahoo.com; Soi 13; r 750B; ﹡ ﹡) Just a skip from the beach, this clean, unpretentious spot offers midrange comforts at borderline budget prices.

Welkom Inn (Map p236; ☎ 0 3842 2589; fax 0 3836 1193; 103/1 Mu 9, Soi 3, Th Hat Pattaya; r 750B; ﹡ ▢ ﹡) Attracting a largely German crowd, this reliable place has a brace of eateries, a spacious pool and plenty of life. On the downside, it's a little worn and things can get noisy once the beer starts to flow.

Century Pattaya Hotel (Map p236; ☎ 0 3842 7800; www.sawadee.com/pattaya/century; 129/16 Th Pattaya Klang; r incl breakfast 942B; ✗ ﹡ ▢ ﹡) Hovering on the cusp of the top end, this reliable favourite has the dimensions of a package hotel, and most of the amenities to boot. In general, however, the place is a little charmless.

Sunshine Hotel (Map p236; ☎ 0 3842 9247; fax 0 3842 1302; 217/1 Soi 8; r 700-900B; ﹡ ﹡) Tucked away in Pattaya, Sunshine lacks…well… sunshine, but all the rooms come with air-con, TV and fridge. Rooms in the newer building are more expensive, but the rooms in the original building are just as comfortable. The hotel also has a restaurant that stays open until midnight.

Naklua

Riviera Hotel Pattaya (Map p236; ☎ 0 3822 5230; fax 0 3822 5764; 157/1 Soi Wat Pa Samphan, Th Naklua;

r 600B; ﹡ ﹡) Cosy and quiet, this attractive cheapie has some snug, good-value rooms and plenty of atmosphere for the money at least.

Garden Lodge (Map p236; Th Naklua; ☎ 0 3842 9109; fax 0 3842 1221; r 750B; ﹡) Another great option for those wanting to escape the push and shove of central Pattaya, this pleasant outfit features air-con rooms, plus a clean pool and good service. It is built around a circular drive just off Th Naklua.

Seaview Resort Hotel (Map p236; ☎ 0 3842 4825; Soi Naklua 18; r incl breakfast 750B; ﹡) On a quiet lane off Th Naklua, this is an L-shaped four-storey hotel with snug rooms.

Hat Jomtien

Peaceful Hat Jomtien has mostly midrange condotel places with prices ranging from 500B to 1100B.

Jomtien Boathouse (Map p238; ☎ 0 3875 6143; www.jomtien-boathouse.com; 380/5-6 Th Hat Jomtien; r 850; ﹡) Doting on its nautical theme, this sparkling new outfit has snug, simple rooms, a cosy pub with a terrace for sundowners and fresh varnish smells in the air. An excellent bet.

Grand Jomtien Palace (Map p238; ☎ 0 3823 1405; www.grandjomtienpalace.com; 356 Th Hat Jomtien; r 1099B; ﹡ ﹡) About the fanciest – if not the most charming – option on Hat Jomtien itself, this multistorey bigwig draws crowds of package tourists with its high standards and reasonable price tag. It's a little dowdy if you look too closely, but excellent value overall.

Welcome Jomtien Beach (Map p238; ☎ 0 3823 2701; www.welcome.co.th; 427 Mu 12 Th Hat Jomtien; r incl breakfast 1080B; ﹡ ﹡) Near Grand Jomtien, this oversized place has an extremely grand atrium, but an apparent dearth of character. A few more lights would cheer things up, but the tariff is attractive and you won't go far wrong with the comfy rooms.

Summer Beach Inn (Map p238; ☎ 0 3823 1777; fax 0 3823 1778; Th Hat Jomtien; r 700B; ﹡) Tucked back slightly from the road, the lobby of this five-storey hotel is filled with quirky, seaside bric-a-brac. The comfortable rooms are a little more down-to-earth though, and come with satellite TV.

Other recommendations:

Jomtien Chalet (Map p238; ☎ 0 3823 1205-8; 57/1 Mu 1, Th Hat Jomtien; r 1200B; ﹡) Slightly down-trodden – and overpriced – place with small bungalows and rooms in an old railway carriage.

Sea Breeze Hotel (Map p238; ☎ 0 3823 1056-8; fax 0 3823 1059; Th Hat Jomtien; r 1000B; 🏊) A pleasant, well-run place with TV and fridge in every room.
Silver Sand Villa (Map p238; ☎ 0 3823 1289; fax 0 3823 2498; r 800-1000B; 🏊) Set back from the main drag, with spacious double rooms in either the old or slightly better new wings.
Summer Beach Inn (Map p238; ☎ 0 3823 1777; fax 0 3823 1778; Th Hat Jomtien; r 700B; 🏊) A friendly, five-storey, good-value place with fairly new rooms that all include satellite TV and fridge.

TOP END

Pattaya is really a resort for package tourists and convention goers, so there are plenty of options in this more expensive price range. All the following hotels have air-con rooms and swimming pools (unless otherwise noted). Many of the top-end hotels have reduced rates on standard singles and doubles, so it's worth asking if anything cheaper is available when requesting a rate quote. Rooms are also often cheaper when booked through a Bangkok travel agency, or via the Internet.

Pattaya

Dusit Resort Pattaya (Map p236; ☎ 0 3842 5611; www.dusit.com; 240/2 Th Hat Pattaya Neua; r 6239B; 🏊 🏊 💻 🍴) Chic comes standard at this aristocrat of Pattaya hotels. It has oodles of class, top-notch service and the air of a luxury big-hitter. For those into the facility statistics, the Dusit boasts 500 rooms, two pools, tennis and squash courts, a health centre, a semiprivate beachfront and exceptional dim sum in the rooftop restaurant. A sea view will cost you 7062B, although discounts of up to 20% are readily offered during the low season.

Amari Orchid Resort (Map p236; ☎ 0 3842 8161; www.amari.com/orchid; Th Hat Pattaya Neua; s/d incl breakfast 3137/3378B; 🏊 🏊 💻 🍴) Jostling with the Dusit for the top slot at the north end of Hat Pattaya, this is another opulent option – but comes in at nearly half the price. Its 234 rooms are set on four lush hectares containing an Olympic-sized swimming pool, two tennis courts, children's playground, minigolf, garden chess and one of the best Italian restaurants in Pattaya.

Pattaya Marriott Resort & Spa (Map p236; ☎ 0 3841 2120; www.marriotthotels.com; 218/2-4 Mu 10, Th Hat Pattaya; r incl breakfast US$104; 🏊 🏊 💻 🍴) Undisputed king of the hill in the central swathe of Pattaya, this king-sized outfit has lashings of class, an army of sycophantic staff, some sympathetically traditional features and all the usual five-star amenities. Conveniently, it also towers over the city's biggest, air-con shopping mall.

Royal Cliff Beach Resort (Map p236; ☎ 0 3825 0421-30; www.royalcliff.com; Th Cliff; r 6877-14,831B; 🏊 🏊 💻 🍴) Classiest number in the south, the Royal Cliff pretty much sits at the end of its own peninsula. One section of the hotel caters for package tours, while a second dazzlingly swish wing offers superlative standards.

Hard Rock Hotel Pattaya (Map p236; ☎ 0 3842 8759; www.hardrockhotels.net; Th Hat Pattaya; r incl breakfast 3000B; 🏊 🏊 💻 🍴) Dripping with rock memorabilia, this 'cool' outfit has celebrity-themed rooms and the type of lively staff that can muster a dozen renditions of 'Have a Nice Day' per hour and still look like they mean it. The décor has a done-on-the-cheap air about it though, and the prevailing Club 18–30 ambience is a little too tacky to be A-list rock and roll.

Montien Pattaya (Map p236; ☎ 0 3842 8155-6; www.montien.com; Th Hat Pattaya; r 4708B; 🏊 🏊 💻 🍴) Long-established place gets lots of German package tourists, but the walk-in rates are rather high for the quality on offer. If everything else is full though, you could do a lot worse than a bed here.

Moving downmarket slightly, the following places offer all the usual facilities, served up with a little less gloss. They cater primarily to groups of package tourists.

Pattaya Centre Hotel (Map p236; ☎ 0 3842 5877; fax 0 3842 0491; Soi 12, Th Hat Pattaya; r incl breakfast 1566B; 🏊 🍴) Wear and tear is the biggest problem here, although the legions of package tourists in the lobby don't seem too bothered. Glamorous it is not, but if you're after reliable, upmarket standards at a reasonable price, this might just be your place.

Siam Bayview Resort (Map p236; ☎ 0 3842 3871; www.siamhotels.com; 310/2 Th Hat Pattaya; r incl breakfast 2472B; 🏊 🏊 🍴) Right in the heart of central Pattaya, this reliable outfit is well placed and will never be far away when you decide to finally call it a night. It also has two swimming pools.

Siam Bayshore Resort (Map p236; ☎ 0 3842 8678-81; www.siamhotels.com; Th Pattaya Tai; r incl breakfast 3095B; 🏊 🏊 💻 🍴) Cut from the same cloth as the Siam Bayview, this labyrinthine place, set on south Pattaya's quieter edge, offers slightly higher standards at a slightly higher price. Discounts of up to 30% are available during the low season and it is only a short stroll from bustling Walking St.

Cabbages & Condoms Resort (Map p238; ☎ 0 3825 0035; www.cabbagesandcondoms.co.th; Th Phra Tamnak Soi 4; r/ste 1483/10,358B 🔀 🔀 🖾) As with the C&C restaurants around Thailand, this resort puts all its profits towards HIV/AIDS education and prevention. It's the brainchild of Thai MP Mechai Viravaidya (you'll sometimes see him staying here) and the quality and standard of service are high. The resort has its own stretch of beach, and there are plenty of different rooms.

Naklua

Central Wong Amat Hotel (Map p236; ☎ 0 3842 6990; fax 0 3842 8599; 277-8 Mu 5, Th Naklua; r 3310B; 🔀 🔀 🖾 🖾) On Hat Naklua, this is one for those eager to retreat into some peace and quiet come nightfall. The hotel grounds are expansive and all the usual amenities come as standard.

Woodlands Resort (Map p236; ☎ 0 3842 1707; www .woodland-resort.com; 164/1 Th Naklua; r incl breakfast 1800B; 🔀 🔀 🖾) Slightly more personal and family-oriented, this is a good bet for those with kids in tow; it has a children's pool, playground and baby-sitting services.

Hat Jomtien

Sugar Hut (Map p238; ☎ 0 3825 1686; www.sugar-hut .com; 391/18 Th Pattaya Tai; r incl breakfast 8430B; 🔀 🔀 🖾) Slightly eccentric, charismatic spot takes a step back towards nature, with expansive, leafy grounds filled with rabbits and peacocks, some beautifully designed, traditional-style bungalows and plenty of elegant charm. It's a fair hike from the beach, on the road connecting Pattaya and Hat Jomtien, but this is one of the city's great escapes. Discounts of up to 50% are available off season.

Natural Park Leisure Resort (Map p238; ☎ 0 3823 1561; www.naturalparkresort.com; 412 Th Hat Jomtien; r incl breakfast 1400B; 🔀 🖾) Low-riser is looking ever so slightly jaded these days, but it has oodles more charm than most of the bigger resorts on this stretch and makes a few concessions to traditional, rustic design.

Eating

Fast food and seafood rule the culinary roost on the busy streets of Pattaya. Bustling burger bars stoke the ovens of the recovering party crowd, while the city's best seafood eateries cook up the latest catch for those after something a little more 'authentic'. But Pattaya is a big city, and just about any craving – and appetite – is catered for somewhere along the way.

Lobster Pot (Map p236; ☎ 0 3842 6083; 228 Walking St; dishes 80-300B; 🕑 noon-1am) With a cornucopia of seafood oddities on ice out front, this is the place to pig out on Thailand's manifold *fruits de mer*. Seaside views provide the backdrop, while the crowds provide the references – appetites ahoy!

Aloha (Map p236; ☎ 0 3872 3175; Th Pattaya 2; dishes 180-400B; 🕑 11am-11pm) Oozing eccentric Polynesian character, you enter this place through a Flintstones-style, concrete cave entrance. Don't be too alarmed though, the seafood-oriented menu draws its influences from the four corners of the globe and boasts plenty to get hungry stomachs growling. You can also wash your meal down with one of its speciality cocktails – we recommend a Suffering Bastard, or a Tongan Punch (yep, the painful kind).

Vientiane Restaurant (Map p236; ☎ 0 3841 1298; 485/18 Th Pattaya 2; dishes 70-300B; 🕑 11.30am-midnight) For something a little more…well… authentic, this highly recommended outfit gathers up all the flavours of the orient and brings them together under one tiled roof. An illustrated menu shows you everything on offer from gargantuan dressed lobsters to unidentifiable, but undoubtedly exciting, Chinese dishes.

Hopf Brew House (Map p236; ☎ 0 3871 0650; Th Hat Pattaya 219; 🕑 3pm-1am Sun-Fri, 4pm-2am Sat) As much a restaurant as a pub (opposite), this top-notch watering hole whips up an array of scrumptious, northern European bar food, from sizzling schnitzels to the type of pizzas Rome was built for.

Steak Bao (Map p236; ☎ 0 3871 0870; Th Hat Pattaya 481; dishes 60-260B; 🕑 9am-midnight) Slap bang on the seafront, this airy diner has sports on the TV, good times on the agenda and everything from frog's legs to Pad Thai on the menu. Come in for breakfast, lunch or dinner.

Surf Kitchen (Map p238; ☎ 0 3823 1710; Th Hat Jomtien; dishes 60-250B; 🕑 7am-midnight) Cooking up some of Hat Jomtien's best eats, this alfresco spot offers a taste of everything from Hungarian to Hawaiian – you can peruse plastic models of its specialities out front first. It has a happy hour from 3pm to 7pm and there's some inside seating for when the monsoon tips its load.

Café Sunshine (Map p238; Th Hat Jomtien; dishes 40-200B; 8am-midnight) Leafy spot hardly whips up *haute cuisine*, but local and international dishes more than fill a hole and there's a lively, welcoming atmosphere.

The central shopping mall, **Royal Garden Plaza** (Map p236; Th Pattaya 2; 11am-11pm) features all the usual fast food chains, plus the cheap and cheerful **Seaview Food Court** (Map p236; dishes 25-70B; 11am-11pm) located on the 2nd floor. For something a little more upmarket, try the top-notch sushi at **Kabuki Sushi** (Map p236; 0 3842 5009; shop B-39, 1st fl; dishes 200-700B), on the next floor down.

Drinking

Leafy many drinking haunts double as go-go bars, nightclubs and cabaret venues (see below), there are plenty of places around where you can simply go and grab a good, old-fashioned tipple.

Hopf Brew House (Map p236; 0 3871 0650; Th Hat Pattaya 219; 3pm-1am Sun-Fri, 4pm-2am Sat;) With lashings of Germanic beer hall charm, this upmarket pub promises everything from drooping foam-soaked moustaches to oompah bands and creaking wooden furniture. The beer is brewed on the premises and releases a little more atmosphere with every glass that's emptied. Expect to pay a European-size bar tab and wear smart casual to get past the bouncers.

Shenanigan's Pattaya (Map p236; 0 3871 0641; Th Pattaya 2; 9am-2am;) The Irish tricolour flies proud over this Celtic outfit. It's chock-a-block with all the usual pseudo-Irish bric-a-brac, there's rivers of Guinness on tap and, come nightfall, good *craic* comes as standard.

Green Bottles (Map p236; 0 3842 9675; 216/6-20 Th Pattaya 2; 11am-2am;) There's not a whole lot of history in Pattaya, but the fact that this cosy pub celebrates its c 1988 origins suggests it's one of the city's more 'traditional' offerings. Snug and dark, it's the ideal spot for a dose of the hair of the dog.

Entertainment

Merry-making in Pattaya, aside from the professional sex scene, means everything from hanging out in a video bar to dancing

all night at one of the discos in south Pattaya. The best place to start is Th Hat Pattaya. At its southern end, this main drag becomes 'Walking St' a self-styled, semipedestrianised 'International Meeting Zone', with bars and clubs to satisfy every proclivity. Nearby, 'Pattaya Land' encompasses Soi 1, 2 and 3 and is one of the most concentrated bar areas. The many gay bars on Soi 3 are announced by a sign reading 'Boy's Town'.

CLUBS & CABARETS

Tony's (Map p236; 0 3842 5795; www.tonydisco.com; 139/15 Walking St; admission free; 8.30pm-2.30am) Big bouncing nightlife supernova has it all, offering everything from a deafeningly loud, neon-lit disco, to pool tables and a 99B buffet dinner. If you've had a few too many, you can even go two rounds with its in-house Thai boxer – and pay for the privilege (200B).

Lucifer (Map p236; 0 3871 0216; Walking St; admission free; 10pm-2.30am;) Rather more upmarket, this compact club is awash with devilishly plush trimmings, with windows looking out towards the sea. Live bands play the evening away and seating is at tables and in cosy booths. Out front, under the extravagant neon awnings, there's also a small **bar** (from 6pm) for those who prefer to start a little earlier.

Tiffany's (Map p236; 0 3842 1700; www.tiffany-show.co.th; 464 Mu 9, Th Pattaya 2; show 600B; from 6pm;) Pattaya has a thing for transvestite cabaret shows. Ablaze with high camp colour and jiggery-pokery, Tiffany's shows are staged nightly at 6pm, 7.30pm and 9pm.

Alcazar (Map p236; 0 3841 0225; 78/14 Th Pattaya 2; 600B; from 6.30pm;) is even more glamorous and has daily shows at 6.30pm, 8pm, 9.30pm and 11pm (Saturday only).

Lucky No 3 (Map p236; Th Hat Pattaya; admission free; 6pm-2am) Just before the beginning of Walking St, this no-frills girlie bar packs out with the early evening crowd, who flock here for drinks promotions, action in the Thai boxing ring and a bit of slap and tickle. It's not one for the faint-hearted.

CINEMAS

Royal Theatre Cinema (Map p236; 0 3842 8057; shop C30, 2nd fl, Royal Garden Plaza; 80B) If you'd rather escape the hubbub in a darkened room, you can catch the latest Hollywood releases here.

PATTAYA VICE

Pattaya's notoriety for sex tourism revolves around a huge collection of discos, outdoor bars and transvestite cabarets comprising Pattaya's red-light district at the southern end of the beach. That part of south Pattaya known as 'the village' attracts a large number of prostitutes, including *kàthoey* (transvestites), who pose as female hookers and ply their trade among the droves of *faràng* (Western) sex tourists. There is also a prominent gay sex-for-sale scene in Pattaya. White prostitutes from as far away as Romania and Russia (favourites with male Asian sex tourists) and black male prostitutes from Nigeria (primarily servicing female sex tourists from Japan) can all be had in Pattaya. Talk about one-stop shopping! Of course, prostitution is just as illegal here as elsewhere in the country – which is to say, enforcement of the laws against it is cyclic at best.

Local authorities and travel agents have been trying to improve Pattaya's image for years, usually with media blitzes and glossy brochures. Of late, the strict enforcing of a 2am closing time for all entertainment venues has put a dent in the sex industry.

Shopping

Thanon Hat Pattaya is lined with stalls selling everything from pirate DVDs and CDs to T-shirts and jewellery. For more serious shopping, head to the **Royal Garden Plaza** (Map p236; Th Pattaya 2; � 11am-11pm).

Getting There & Away

AIR

Bangkok Airways (Map p236; ☎ 0 3841 2382; www .bangkokair.com; 75/8 Mu 9, Th Pattaya 2; ☉ 8.30am-4.30pm Mon-Fri, until noon Sat) links **U-Taphao airfield** (☎ 0 3824 5599; about 30km south of Pattaya) with Ko Samui (one way/return 2640/5280B; daily) and Phuket (one way/return 3405/6910B; daily). While the quoted standard rates are high, promotional return fares for both of the destinations go as low as 3350B – book ahead.

BUS

Air-con buses from **Bangkok's Eastern bus terminal** (☎ 0 2274 4484) leave every 30 minutes from 4.30am to 7.30pm (94B, 2½ hours).

They also run from the Northern bus station for the same fare.

In Pattaya, the **air-con bus station** (Map p236; Th Hat Pattaya Neua) is near the intersection with Th Sukhumvit. Air-con buses run every half hour from here to Bangkok's Eastern bus station (94B, 2½ hours) between 5.30am and 9pm, and to Bangkok's Northern bus station (94B, 2½ hours), for connections to Chiang Mai, between 5.30am and 7.30pm.

Several hotels and travel agencies run minibuses to addresses within Bangkok, or east to Ko Samet and Ko Chang – the fares start at about 150B. Try **Koh Chang Business Centre** (Map p236; ☎ 0 3871 0145; Soi post pffice; ☉ 9am-midnight), or ask at your hotel.

From Sri Racha, you can grab a public bus on Th Sukhumvit to Pattaya (25B, 30 minutes) – in Pattaya, they stop near the corner of Th Sukhumvit and Th Pattaya Neua. From here, you can also flag down buses to Rayong (ordinary/air-con 50/80B; 1½ hours).

From the air-con bus station, there are also regular services between Pattaya and several northeastern towns, including Nakhon Ratchasima (ordinary/air-con 210/160B; four hours).

TRAIN

One train per day travels between Pattaya and Bangkok's Hualamphong station (48B; 3¾ hours). It leaves Bangkok at 6.55am and returns from Pattaya at 2.50pm. Schedules for this service are subject to change, so check times at **Pattaya train station** (Map p236; ☎ 0 3842 9285) before travelling.

Getting Around

CAR & MOTORCYCLE

Avis Rent-A-Car (Map p236; ☎ 0 3836 1628, 0 3842 8755; www.avisthailand.com; Th Hat Pattaya Neua; ☉ 9am-5pm) has offices at the Dusit Resort Pattaya and the Hard Rock Hotel, and is by far the most expensive option. Of course, if something goes wrong you don't have to worry about any hassles (like a formerly unseen disclaimer popping up in your insurance policy). Avis also offers a pick-up and drop-off service at your hotel.

Holiday Rent-A-Car (Map p236; ☎ 0 3842 6203; www.pattayacar-rent.com; Th Pattaya 2; ☉ 9am-5pm) is a cheaper local option and also offers full insurance. Prices for a 1500cc Toyota Soluna start at 1300B per day (1551B with full insurance). Big discounts are offered for week- and month-long rentals.

If you trawl the streets, local travel agents offer Suzuki jeeps for as little as 800B per day, but expect to pay through the nose if you have an accident.

Motorcycles cost 150B to 200B per day for a 100cc machine; a 125cc to 150cc will cost 300B, and you'll even see a few 750cc to 1000cc machines for hire for 500B to 1000B. There are motorcycle hire places along Th Hat Pattaya and Th Pattaya 2. Pattaya is a good place to purchase a used motorcycle – check the rental shops.

SĂWNGTHĂEW

Locally known as 'baht buses', *săwngthăew* cruise Th Hat Pattaya and Th Pattaya 2 frequently – just hop on and when you get out pay 10B anywhere between Naklua and south Pattaya, or 20B as far as Jomtien. Price lists posted in the back of the vehicles state the maximum amount drivers can charge for any given journey.

Many readers have complained about having taken the 10B *săwngthăew* with local passengers and then having been charged a higher 'charter' price of 20B to 50B. Make sure that you establish the correct fare in advance.

You can charter these vehicles for around 150B per hour.

RAYONG PROVINCE

PATTAYA TO KO SAMET

From Pattaya, most tourists hotfoot it down the coast to the relative calm of Ko Samet. The little port of Ban Phe is the jumping-off point for this island, but a brief stop in the commercial centre of Rayong is usually on the cards for a change of buses and a spot of lunch. If you're Samet-bound, it doesn't make much sense to hang around the mainland beaches, but there are a few other strips of sand and small islands in the vicinity.

For information about travelling to and from Rayong and Ban Phe, see p254.

Rayong

ระยอง

pop 47,000

The provincial capital of Rayong is not a tourist destination, nor does it pretend to

be. That said, this smoggy strip of banks, markets and shops is a major transport interchange and you are likely to have to switch buses here if you are en route to Ko Samet. If you do arrive too late to make the onward connections for the island ferry, there are a few reasonable places to bed down for the night.

INFORMATION

TAT (☎ 0 3865 5420; kaminry@hotmail.com; 153/4 Th Sukhumvit; ⏱ 8.30am-4.30pm) Has a tourist information office, with maps and fairly up-to-date lists of accommodation and sights in Rayong and Chanthaburi Provinces.
Thai Bank (Th Sukhumvit 144/53-55; ⏱ 9am-3.30pm Mon-Fri) One of several banks along Rayong's main drag, Th Sukhumvit, that have exchange services and ATMs.

SLEEPING & EATING

Star Hotel Rayong (☎ 0 3861 4901; www.starhotel .th.com; 109 Th Rayong Trade Center; r incl breakfast 1500B; ⧉ ⧉) Rayong's swankiest offering caters to visiting business honchos and offers the usual four-star amenities in one big glassy package. To get there from the bus station, walk away from Th Sukhumvit, take a left at the top of the square and the hotel will come into view on your right.

Rayong President Hotel (☎ 0 3861 1307; Th Sukhumvit; r incl breakfast 600B; ⧉) There's not much 'presidential' about this unassuming place, but it offers decent, midrange rooms. The hotel is located down a small side street, so it's quiet at night. From the bus station, cross to the other side of Th Sukhumvit, turn right and after about three minutes' walk you'll see a sign pointing down a side street to the hotel.

For cheap food, check out the **market** near the Thetsabanteung cinema, or the string of **restaurants** and **noodle shops** that strecthes along Th Taksin Maharat, just south of Wat Lum Mahachaichumphon.

Ban Phe

บ้านเพ

The little port of Ban Phe is only on the map thanks to its role as a launch pad for nearby Ko Samet. However, the busy seafood markets on the promenade near the ferry terminal are worth poking your nose into if you have an hour or so to kill.

You can check email, or make an international phone call at **Tan Tan Café** (☎ 0 1925 6713; Soi 2; per min 1B; ⏱ 7.30am-7pm), down a lane opposite the ferry terminal. There's an ATM outside the 7-Eleven store, directly across from the ferry terminal.

SLEEPING & EATING

There are several hotels in Ban Phe near the central market and within walking distance of the pier.

Hotel Diamond (☎ 0 3865 1826; fax 0 3865 1757; 286/12 Mu 2; r 350-500B; ⚡) Turn left out of the ferry terminal, walk 150m down the main road and you will come to this reasonable little hotel. Making yourself understood in English is a team effort, but the simple rooms are fine for a night's shuteye.

Pines Beach Hotel (☎ 0 3865 1636; fax 0 3865 2103; 38/6 Mu 1, Phe-Klaeng-Krum; r 690-990B; ⚡ ⚡) Ban Phe's showcase resort is looking more than a tad flaky – and empty. If you want all the creature comforts you can get your hands on though, this is the place to come. It's 1km east down the main road – turn right out of the ferry terminal.

Stone Monkey (☎ 0 3865 3671; 281/93 Soi 2; dishes 40-150B; ⏱7am-7pm) Breakfasts, pizzas and Thai dishes top the menu at this jazzy little café. It's down an alley opposite the ferry terminal.

Around Rayong & Ban Phe
KHAO CHAMAO/KHAO WONG NATIONAL PARK
อุทยานแห่งชาติเขาชะเมา-เขาวง
Although less than 85 sq km, **Khao Chamao/ Khao Wong National Park** (☎ 0 3889 4378; reserve@ dnp.go.th; 200B; ⏱ 8.30am-4.30pm) – which actually overlaps into Chanthaburi Province – is famous for limestone mountains, high cliffs, caves, dense forest and waterfalls. According to park officials, the park is home to populations of tigers, wild elephants and bears. It is inland from Ban Phe, about 17km north of the Km 274 marker off Hwy 3 – to get to the park, take a *săwngthăew* from Ban Phe to the Km 274 marker for 30B, and another *săwngthăew* (10B) to the park.

You can stay here in a **camp site** (about 10B plus per person 50B) or rent a **bungalow** (sleeps 2; r 800B) – reserve accommodation on the email address above or ☎ 0 2562 0760.

ISLANDS & BEACHES
Ko Man Klang and **Ko Man Nok**, along with **Ko Man Nai** to their immediate west, are part of Laem Ya/Ko Samet National Park. This official designation has not kept away all development, only moderated it. Ko Man Nai is home to the **Turtle Conservation Centre** (☎ 0 3861 6096; ⏱9am-4pm), which is a breeding place for endangered sea turtles and has a small visitors centre that describes their life cycle. It is most easily visited on a tour arranged by one of the following accommodation options, or on a boat tour from Ko Samet (see p251).

A small island near Rayong is **Ko Saket**, which is just a 20-minute boat ride from the beach of Hat Sai Thong (turn south off Hwy 3 at the Km 208 marker).

Suan Son (Pine Park), 5km further down the highway from Ban Phe, is a popular place for Thai picnickers and has white-sand beaches as well.

Suan Wang Kaew is 11km east of Ban Phe and has more beaches and **Ko Thalu**, across from Suan Wang Kaew, is said to be a good diving area. Other resort areas along the Rayong coast include **Laem Mae Phim** and **Hat Sai Thong**. **Hat Mae Rampeung**, a 10km strip of sand between Ban Taphong and Ban Kon Ao (11km east of Rayong), is also part of Laem Ya/Ko Samet National Park.

SLEEPING
Ko Man Klang and Ko Man Nok offer upmarket accommodation packages that include boat transport from the nearest pier along with all meals. These can only be arranged by phone in advance through Bangkok reservation numbers.

Ko Nok Island Resort (Bangkok office ☎ 0 2860 3025-6; fax 0 2860 3028; s/d 2500/5000B; ⚡) Situated on Ko Man Nok, this classy resort has a one-night, two-day package. The island is 15km off Pak Nam Prasae (53km east of Ban Phe).

Raya Island Resort (Bangkok office ☎ 0 2316 6717; s/d 1400/2800B; ⚡ ⚡) Comfortable place has 15 bungalows and plenty of hush. Prices include boat transport and full board. It is eight kilometres off Laem Mae Phim (27km east of Ban Phe), on Ko Man Klang

GETTING THERE & AWAY
Public transport to the pier departure points for the two small islands off Rayong can be arranged in Ban Phe. On weekends and holidays there may be share taxis (*săwngthăew*) out to the piers; otherwise you'll have to charter a vehicle from the

Traditional Thai massage, Hat Sai Khao (p266),
Ko Chang

MARTIN LLADÓ

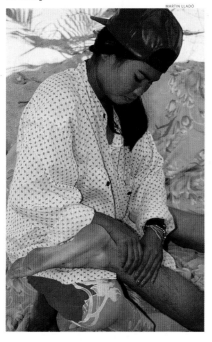

CRAIG PERSHOUSE

Palm tree–lined Hat Kaibae (p267),
Ko Chang

Beach on Ko Kham, Ko Chang Marine National Park (p262)

WOODS WHEATCROFT

Outdoor restaurant, Ko Samet (p253)

Ko Mak (p265), Ko Chang Marine National Park

Supply and tourist boat serving Ko Chang (p270)

market for 60B to 100B one way – be sure to make a pick-up arrangement for your return.

KO SAMET

เกาะเสม็ด

Ko Samet is a bit of a mixed bag. On the one hand, its proximity to Bangkok has made it a popular weekend escape for young Thais keen to frolic in the sunshine before Monday morning rolls round once again. As a result, the northern end of the island, around the main beach of Hat Sai Kaew, has become a scruffy jumble of baking bodies, beach bars, volleyball nets and dripping ice creams. Here, zinc cream, Speedos and a sun visor are *de rigueur*.

But that is not the whole story: as you head south through Ao Hin Khok (the de facto backpackers' ghetto), towards Ao Thian and distant Ao Wai, Ko Samet's eastern shore gets steadily quieter. Scattered along these more southerly sections are some pretty bays and more than a handful of pristine, soda-white beaches. In short, if you're prepared to make the journey, there are still a few pockets of paradise to be found among the developments. Perennially dry, with a relatively monsoon-proof climate, you even have a better than average chance of getting a week of blue skies.

Despite being under the protection of the National Parks Division – as part of the Laem Ya/Ko Samet National Park – areas of Ko Samet are literally buckling under the weight of exploitative development projects. Investors' cash still speaks louder than the law along some stretches of the coastline, but other parts of the island seem set to retain their looks for a few years yet.

History

Ko Samet won a permanent place in Thai literature when classical Thai poet Sunthorn Phu set part of his epic *Phra Aphaimani* on its shores. The story follows the travails of a prince exiled to an undersea kingdom ruled by a lovesick female giant. A mermaid aids the prince in his escape to Ko Samet, where he defeats the giant by playing a magic flute. Formerly Ko Kaew Phitsadan or 'Vast Jewel Isle' – a reference to the abundant white sand – this island became known as Ko Samet or 'Cajeput Isle' after the cajeput tree that grows in abundance here and is

very highly valued as firewood throughout Southeast Asia. Locally, the *samet* tree has also been used in boat building.

Orientation

Ko Samet is a T-shaped island. Most of the beaches, and developments, are located on the island's eastern shore – there are only a handful of upmarket hotels on the west coast, clustered around pretty Ao Prao bay. Na Dan, the island's biggest village and the terminus for the Ban Phe ferry is on the north coast, facing the mainland. A dusty, potholed road runs north–south from Na Dan to Ao Kiu Na Nok and east–west from Ao Hin Khok to Ao Prao.

Information

Ko Samet is a national park and the entrance fee (adult/child 200/100B) is collected at a small parks office between Na Dan and Hat Sai Kaew – retain your ticket for inspection. There is another office on Ao Wong Doan.

On the main road between Na Dan and Hat Sai Kaew, you will also find the **police station** (☎ 1155), the **Health Centre** (☎ 0 3864 4123; ☉ 8.30am-8pm Mon-Fri, to 4.30pm Sat & Sun) and the island's only **ATM**, which is attached to the 7-Eleven store by the main parks office.

Opposite the ferry terminal, **Nah Daan Center** (☎ 0 3864 4115; ☉ 8.30am-5pm Mon-Fri, until noon Sat) is a travel agent offering transport and accommodation bookings.

There are number of **Internet cafés** near the parks office, or you can check your email at **Naga's Bungalows** (☎ 0 3864 4035; Ao Hin Khok; per min 2B; ☉ 8am-11pm), which also doubles as a **post office**.

Dangers & Annoyances

Ko Samet has been highly malarial in the past and, while the health centre now claims to have the problem under control, the island is infested with mosquitoes – cover up and use appropriate prophylactics (see p766).

It should also be pointed out that Ko Samet has what is probably Thailand's largest and most loathsome collection of stray dogs, many of them with advanced cases of mange. The crusty curs can be especially disturbing during meal times when they park themselves nearby and stare longingly at your food.

Troops of masseurs patrol the island's northern beaches and can get bothersome

KO SAMET

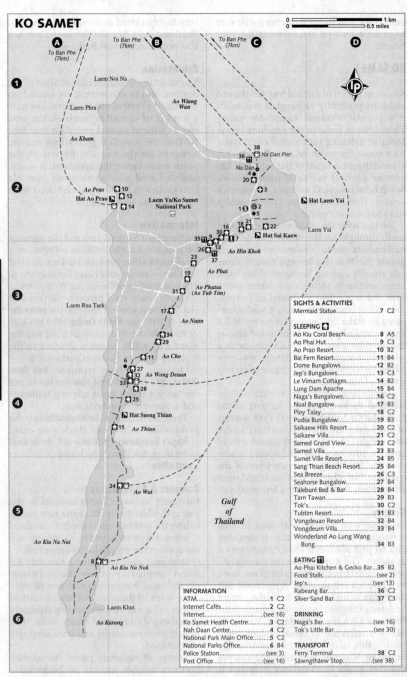

| 0 | 1 km |
| 0 | 0.5 miles |

SOUTHEASTERN THAILAND

SIGHTS & ACTIVITIES
Mermaid Statue......................**7** C2

SLEEPING
Ao Kiu Coral Beach..................**8** A5
Ao Phai Hut.............................**9** C3
Ao Prao Resort........................**10** B2
Bai Fern Resort.......................**11** B4
Dome Bungalows.....................**12** B3
Jep's Bungalows......................**13** C3
Le Vimarn Cottages.................**14** B2
Lung Dam Apache....................**15** B4
Naga's Bungalows....................**16** C2
Nual Bungalow........................**17** B3
Ploy Talay...............................**18** C2
Pudsa Bungalow......................**19** B3
Saikaew Hills Resort................**20** C2
Saikaew Villa...........................**21** C2
Samed Grand View..................**22** C2
Samed Villa.............................**23** B3
Samet Ville Resort...................**24** B5
Sang Thian Beach Resort.........**25** B4
Sea Breeze.............................**26** C3
Seahorse Bungalow.................**27** B4
Taleburé Bed & Bar.................**28** B4
Tarn Tawan.............................**29** B3
Tok's......................................**30** C2
Tubtim Resort.........................**31** B3
Vongdeuan Resort...................**32** B4
Vongdeurn Villa......................**33** B4
Wonderland Ao Lung Wang
    Bung.................................**34** B3

EATING
Ao Phai Kitchen & Gecko Bar...**35** B2
Food Stalls............................(see 2)
Jep's.....................................(see 13)
Rabeang Bar...........................**36** C2
Silver Sand Bar.......................**37** C3

DRINKING
Naga's Bar.............................(see 16)
Tok's Little Bar.......................(see 30)

TRANSPORT
Ferry Terminal........................**38** C2
Sǎwngthǎew Stop...................(see 38)

INFORMATION
ATM.......................................**1** C2
Internet Cafés.........................**2** C2
Internet................................(see 16)
Ko Samet Health Centre..........**3** C2
Nah Daan Center.....................**4** C2
National Park Main Office........**5** C2
National Parks Office...............**6** B4
Police Station........................(see 3)
Post Office...........................(see 16)

if business is slow. The further south you head, the less you will be disturbed.

Activities & Tours

Jimmy's Tours (☎ 0 9832 1627) runs a variety of tours around Ko Samet and the neighbouring islands. A six-hour boat tour (10am to 4pm) of the neighbouring islets, including the Turtle Conservation Centre (p248) on Ko Man Nai costs 700B per person (with a minimum group size of 10 people), while a one-hour quad-bike trip around the island costs 1200B per person. Tours can be booked direct through Jimmy's or via most hotels.

Ploy Scuba Diving (☎ 0 3864 4212; www.ployscuba .com; ☺ 9am-5pm) runs dive trips to a number of sites around the island.

Sleeping

Ko Samet is becoming increasingly popular and prices are creeping up accordingly. Apart from the glitzier resorts on Ao Prao (which charge up to 16,050B for a suite), most places on the east coast charge from 200B for a simple bamboo hut, to 1200B for a stylish air-con bungalow.

We quote standard weekday rates, which *may* (it's all about supply and demand) as much as double in price during weekends and holidays. If you do turn up at the weekend, make sure you ask for the reduced weekly rate come the Monday – this reduction is often conveniently forgotten.

We include telephone numbers (very few have websites or fax numbers) for all the resorts with phones, but reservations aren't always taken, or honoured – most places work on a first-come-first-served system. There are also offices – and plenty of touts – offering reservations in Ban Phe, but prices tend to be inflated.

Every bungalow operation on the island has at least one restaurant and most have running water and electricity. Some places only have electricity at night.

EAST COAST

The two most developed (overdeveloped) beaches are Hat Sai Kaew and Ao Wong Deuan. All of the other spots are still relatively peaceful.

Hat Sai Kaew

Known as 'Diamond Sand', this is the island's biggest beach; it is also the busiest. The sand

here is white and relatively clean, but the sea is lined with hotels, bars and restaurants and those after peace and quiet may find the relentless hubbub a bit off-putting. Accommodation is solid here, but it does lack character and can be a bit dreary.

Samed Grand View (☎ 0 3864 4220; www.grand viewthai.com; r 600-1800B; ⊠) Still awash with the flush of youth, this glossy new opening offers a little more sparkle than its neighbours and has a grand stretch of sand out front. Expect a surfeit of garden ornaments, and some good, comfortable rooms.

Saikaew Villa (☎ 0 3864 4144; r 300-1000B; ⊠) Big, brash and a hit with package tourists, this complex of bungalows offers predictable, homogenous comfort in holiday-camp surrounds.

Ploy Talay (☎ 0 3864 4212; r 300-700B; ⊠) This is another Hat Sai Kaew staple and has a slightly gloomy restaurant out front.

Ao Hin Khok

At the south end of Hat Sai Kaew, statues of the prince and the mermaid from Sunthorn Phu's epic (see p249) gaze lovingly into each other's eyes. This marks the beginning of Ao Hin Khok, a pretty stretch of sand, lined with trees and boulders. With some of the cheapest accommodation on the island, as well as some of its liveliest bars, this area has become something of a backpackers' favourite – and with good reason.

Jep's Bungalows (☎ 0 3864 4112; www.jepbunga low.com; r 400B) Tumbling down the hillside, Jep's eponymous bungalows are reached via a steep wooden walkway through the trees behind the reception area. The wooden huts are basic, but there's a shady, romantic restaurant on the beach out front and video shows come nightfall. If you take the bungalows at the far end of the property, prices may go as low as 200B.

Naga's Bungalows (☎ 0 3864 4035; r 400B; ☐) Encircled by a perimeter of bizarre, concrete creatures, Naga's is one of the island's original hideaways. Fresh paint remains something of a stranger to these walls, but the punters still come and there's a pleasant, lively atmosphere. It also has cheaper rooms with shared bathroom (200B).

Tok's (☎ 0 3864 4072; r 400B) Tok's offers more of the same. The further back from the beach you go, the bigger the discount you'll get – try and get it down to 200B.

Ao Phai

Around the next headland is another shallow bay with a nice wide beach, although it can get fairly crowded.

Samed Villa (☎ 0 3864 4094; www.samedvilla.com; r 500-1400B; 🔀) Fairy lights and water features announce that this swoosh midranger rules the Ao Phai roost. It's a fair way from the noisy razzmatazz of the northern end of the beach, the bungalows are cosy and they haven't skimped on the trimmings.

Ao Phai Hut (☎ 0 3864 4075; s 300-800B; d 400-1200B; 🔀) Romance flourishes here at night, when candlelit tables are laid out on the beach. Otherwise, there's a decent steakhouse and the type of bungalows you wouldn't be ashamed to put your granny in.

Sea Breeze (☎ 0 3864 4124; r 700B; 🔀) The bungalows are all a bit on top of each other here, but it remains popular and basic fan rooms, with shared bathroom, can be had for as little as 150B.

Ao Phutsa

Pudsa Bungalow (r 500B) Better bungalows are close to the water, but have a look inside before agreeing to stay there as some are grungier than others.

Tubtim Resort (r 500-1000B) At the southern end of the beach, this has so-so bungalows on a hillside.

Ao Nuan

If you blink, you'll miss this beach, which is one of the more secluded places to stay without having to go to the far south of the island.

Nual Bungalow (r 300B) A flick of the wilderness creeps into this no-frills place. Some rooms are a bit rickety, but silence seekers are will have a field day. It's a five-minute walk over the headland from Ao Phutsa.

Ao Cho

A five-minute walk across the next headland from Ao Nuan, Ao Cho (Chaw), like the island's dogs, is a tad mangy. It's far quieter than Ao Wong Deuan to its south, but it looks like this scruffy little beach has fallen right out of vogue.

Tarn Tawan (☎ 0 3864 4070; islandtour1999@hotmail .com; s/d 300/400B) Built out of corrugated iron and wicker, Tarn Tawan has passable rooms and a decent restaurant. The patchy lawns could do with some TLC, though.

Wonderland Ao Lung Wang Bung (r 400B) Looks like weather and time have given this place a two-on-one battering. Tiny, dingy doubles go as low as 150B, but standards are decidedly so-so for somewhere with such an ostentatious name.

Ao Wong Deuan

Jet-skis and speedboats have crept into this once-quiet bay. Despite the crowds, it's still a pleasant spot and the midrange accommodation options are all pretty slick. Direct ferries (60B each way) run from here to Ban Phe at 8.30am, midday and 4pm, and back at 9.30am, 1.30pm and 5pm. Services increase at the weekend.

Vongdeuan Resort (☎ 0 3865 1777; fax 0 3865 1819; r 700-1000B; 🔀) Right in the heart of the action, this tiptop place sits right on the beach and offers a spread of snug bungalows.

Vongduern Villa (☎ 0 3865 2300; fax 0 3865 1741; r 700-1000B; 🔀) With more floaty white décor than your average R&B pop video, the bungalows here offer some pleasant views and a pocketful of romance.

Taleburé Bed & Bar (☎ 0 1862 9402; r 1500B; 🔀) At the southern end of the bay, this pleasant spot makes a few concessions to cutting-edge design, but falls rather short of the bullseye. The attractive garden setting earns a gold star, but the bungalows are simply too patchy to be as 'bling' as the owners would have you believe.

Other recommendations:

Bai Fern Resort (☎ 0 3865 1527; r 450-500B; 🔀)
A quiet spot at the northern end of the beach.

Seahorse Bungalow (☎ 0 3865 3740; r 400-700; 🔀)
A labyrinthine resort.

Ao Thian

From this point south things start to get much quieter. Better known by its English name, Candlelight Beach, Ao Thian is very scenic, with stretches of sand and rocky outcrops – the builders are moving in, though.

Sang Thian Beach Resort (☎ 0 3865 3210; r 400-1200B; 🔀) With a higher 'Have a Nice Day!' count than pretty much anywhere else on the island, this relatively new opening takes top marks for friendliness and a good score for its bungalows, which come well equipped and pathologically clean. There's a little bar/eatery on the lovely beach below.

Lung Dam Apache (r 500B) At the southern end of the bay, this has rustic bungalows with veranda and attached bathroom. During the high season the restaurant sets up on the beach for drinks under the stars. A long-running favourite with repeat visitors to the island.

Other Bays

The southern reaches of the island are still practically untouched, with only a couple of hotels spread over as many kilometres of coastline. Lovely Ao Wai is about 1km from Ao Thian, but can be reached from Ban Phe by chartered speedboat.

Samet Ville Resort (☎ 0 3865 1682; www.sametvilleresort.com; r 900-1300B; 🐾) With its isolated location and limited number of guests, this place has something of the Lost City about it – even the staff can be hard to find. On the downside, it looks like the resort is fighting a losing battle with the surrounding foliage, while the unparalleled peace and quiet is a major bonus.

A 20-minute walk over the rocky shore from Ao Wai, Ao Kiu Na Nok also had only one place to stay at the time of writing.

Ao Kiu Coral Beach (r 700B) Bits of this increasingly rickety place look less than stable. That said, the beach here is gorgeous, the welcomes are warm and the atmosphere is fabulously laid-back. Another plus is that it's a mere five-minute walk to the western side of the island and a view of the sunset.

WEST COAST

The playground of Ko Samet's posher set, little Ao Prao gets fabulous sunsets – it's one of the few west-facing beaches – and offers a clutch of chic hotels. Speedboat transfers to all of these hotels from the mainland are included in the price.

Le Vimarn Cottages (☎ 0 2438 9771; www.aopraoresort.com; r 6955B; 🐾 🖳) Ko Samet's flagship resort is a heady blend of traditional and modern, with beautifully elegant, Thai-style decorative trimmings as well as plenty of 21st-century creature comforts. It offers everything from scuba diving to windsurfing, there's the on-site **Dhivarin Spa** (☎ 0 3864 4104) and if you're really looking for a treat, settle for one of its opulent suites (16,050B including a welcome fruit basket).

Ao Prao Resort (☎ 0 2438 9771; www.aopraoresort.com; r 4325B; 🐾) At the other end of the beach, the same chain's slightly less opulent outfit offers bountiful comforts for a little less

cash. Lush tropical gardens keep the world of work at bay.

Dome Bungalows (☎ 0 2938 1811; www.limacoco.com; r 2500B; 🐾) Despite being the cheapest option on the beach, the bungalows here are still a little overpriced for what's on offer. All the rooms come with TV and fridge and there's a good restaurant out front.

There is a daily boat between Ban Phe and Ao Prao for 80B per person.

NA DAN

If you are inclined to stay in Na Dan – which is extremely unlikely – try the following:

Saikaew Hills Resort (☎ 0 3864 4234; r 250-400B; 🐾) Central motel-style place, just up from the ferry terminal, is clean and welcoming, but why stay in a town when the beach is only a skip away?

Eating & Drinking

Eating and drinking are pretty much one and the same on Ko Samet. Many of the 'restaurants' host happy hours, while all but a handful of the 'bars' offer evening fish fries on top of their standard bar snack menus. To make things even easier, many of these eatery-cum-watering-holes are attached to hotels, meaning you never have to stumble far from your bed to get a good feed and an ice-cold beer.

Needless to say, nowhere on Ko Samet looks set to scoop a Michelin star in the foreseeable future, but the standard traveller's staples are widely available and reasonably cheap – look out for the nightly barbecues, particularly along Ao Hin Khok and Ao Phai. Drinking-wise, a number of places offer nightly 'toss-a-coin' promotions – they are well advertised. If you're lucky, a fortuitous string of heads or tails (you decide) will see you drinking at half price for a good chunk of the evening.

Most of the choice is on Hat Sai Kaew, Ao Hin Khok and Ao Phai, but hotels on the remote stretches will also make sure you don't go hungry.

Jep's (☎ 0 3864 4112; Ao Hin Khok; dishes 40-150B; 🕑 8am-11pm) With tables tipping down a scenic stretch of sand and with a clutch of pine trees providing the daytime shade, this is one of the island's better eateries. Videos play all night in the roofed section, the menu spans occident and orient, and the fact that there seem to be as many uniformed waiters as punters, means that the service is slick and swift.

Silver Sand Bar (☎ 0 6530 2417; Ao Phai; ☼ 1pm-2am) As the clock ticks down towards the witching hour, the island's night owls congregate here to knock back the cocktails and bump and grind to cheesy dance music. So close to the sea you can almost smell the salt, it is often the island's busiest nightspot and a small hotdog stand caters to those with the munchies.

Ao Prao Resort (☎ 0 2438 9771; Ao Prao; dishes 50-300B; ☼ 9am-11pm) One of the few restaurants with sunset views, this semi-stylish haunt promises romantic, candlelit evenings and a more upmarket menu. The setting is fab, but the quality of the food doesn't quite warrant the inflated price tag.

Ao Phai Kitchen & Gecko Bar (Ao Phai; dishes 40-120B; ☼ 8am-2am) Running on the back of its four staple ingredients – pool, video nights, beer and passable food – this popular place serves a reasonable array of western and Thai fare late into the night. Food of the barbecue is a little more expensive, but well worth the extra.

Tok's Little Bar (☎ 0 3864 4072; Ao Hin Khok; dishes 40-120B; ☼ 1pm-2am) There's not a whole lot to this sticks-and-straw beach bar, but the staff, who double as all-round entertainers, play the music loud, put on fire shows and flirt with the girls. It gets busiest at 'toss-a-coin' time (9.30pm) and it hosts some excellent barbecues at the weekend.

Naga's Bar (☎ 0 3864 4035; Ao Hin Khok; dishes 40-120B; ☼ 1pm-2am) This is more of the same next door to Tok's.

Rabeang Bar (Na Dan; dishes 30-100B; ☼ 8am-2am) Right by the ferry terminal, with a terrace over the water, this is a pleasant spot for a wee snack if you're waiting for the boat back to the mainland.

For seriously cheap, colourful eats, check out the **food stalls** which set up in the late afternoon on the road between Na Dan and Hat Sai Kaew.

Getting There & Away
BOAT
To Ko Samet
The cheapest way to get to Ko Samet is on one of the passenger ferries that depart throughout the day from Ban Phe's Saphan Nuan Tip pier – opposite the 7-Eleven, where the buses and *sǎwngthǎew* stop. Fer-

ries (one way/return 50/100B, 40 minutes) depart hourly for Na Dan (on the northern tip of the island) from 7am to 5pm and tickets can be bought from a small **Tourist Information Center** (☎ 0 3889 6155; ☼ 7am-5pm) on the pier itself. From Ban Phe, three scheduled ferries (9.30am, 1.30pm, 5pm) also make the run to Ao Wong Deuan (one way/return 60/120B, one hour). Occasionally, ferries also run to Ao Wai and some of the other beaches, but schedules have been sporadic of late, so it's best not to rely on them.

The touts tend to congregate around the ferry terminal and numerous travellers have complained about them selling ferry tickets at inflated prices as well as hassling them into prebooking accommodation on the island. The best advice is to ignore them and to go straight to the ticket office.

Alternatively, you can charter a speedboat to any of the island's beaches. They are quite expensive (1000B to Na Dan or 1200B to Ao Wai), but they take up to 10 passengers for this price, making it an attractive alternative if you are travelling in a group. You can charter speedboats at the pier – the Tourist Information Center has a full price list.

From Ko Samet
Ferries (one way/return 50/100B) return to Ban Phe from the pier in Na Dan hourly from 7am to 5pm – buy your ticket at the pier. There are also three scheduled ferries per day from Ao Wong Deuan (one way/return 60/120B; 8.30am, midday, 4pm). Ferries also run from a number of the other beaches, but schedules are unreliable so ask your hotel for the latest details.

If you want to get off the island in a hurry, you can also charter a speedboat. You can book these at most hotels, or call **Jimmy's Tours** (☎ 0 9832 1627). Prices start at 1000B from Na Dan and 1200B from Ao Wai.

BUS
A short walk down Bangkok's Th Khao San will lead you past no end of signs advertising transport to Ko Samet. The minibuses are rarely what they are cracked up to be in the adverts, but prices start at 250B and the services, which take 2½ hours, do remove the hassle of getting to the capital's distant Eastern bus terminal. If you're coming from

Pattaya, similar services (150B, 1¼ hours) are offered by agencies such as **Koh Chang Business Centre** (Map p236; ☎ 0 3871 0145; Soi 13/2, Pattaya; ⏰ 9am-midnight).

For those who want the flexibility and economy of arranging their own travel, the way to go is to take an air-con bus from Bangkok's Eastern bus terminal to Rayong (124B, 2½ hours, hourly) and then a *săwng-thăew* to Ban Phe (20B, 25 minutes) – these leave as soon as they are full. There are also buses without air-con going direct to Ban Phe (80B, four hours, four daily) from Bangkok. Both buses from Bangkok, and *săwngthăew* from Rayong stop in front of Ban Phe's ferry terminal.

Buses also go to Chanthaburi from Rayong (55B, 2½ hours, five daily). To get one of these, you need to catch a *túk-túk* (20B) to the bus stop on Th Sukhumvit (Hwy 3).

Minibuses from Ban Phe to Bangkok's Th Khao San and Pattaya can be arranged through several of the guesthouses on Ko Samet, or through travel agencies in Ban Phe near the 7-Eleven opposite the ferry terminal. Minibuses to Bangkok leave twice every day (250B, 2½ hours). Minibuses to Pattaya leave five times daily (150B, 1¼ hours).

Getting Around

If you take the boat from Ban Phe to Na Dan, you can easily walk the distance to Hat Sai Kaew, Ao Hin Khok or Ao Phai. A checkpoint on the road to Hat Sai Kaew collects the 200B national park entrance fee. If you're travelling further down the island, or have a lot of luggage, you can take a *săwngthăew*. At least one of these meets every ferry and they run down to the bottom of the island.

Set fares for transport around the island from Na Dan are posted on a tree in front of the pier. If they can be filled, you won't have much trouble paying the standard fares (10B to Hat Sai Kaew, 20B to Ao Phai, 30B to Ao Prao and 40B to Ao Thian and Ao Wai). If they can't, you may have to charter the whole vehicle (100B to Hat Sai Kaew, 150B to Ao Phai, 200B to Ao Prao, 300B to Ao Thian and 400B to Ao Wai).

There is a bumpy road from Na Dan all the way to the southern tip of the island, and a few cross-island trails as well. Near Sea Breeze bungalows in Ao Phai, the main

road south turns inland and heads down the middle of the island. A little further along the road is where the cross-island road to Ao Prao on the west coast starts. Motorcycles are a useful way of getting around and can be rented in Na Dan, or from a number of bungalow operations on Hat Sai Kaew, Ao Phai and Ao Prao. Figure on about 300B for 24 hours.

CHANTHABURI PROVINCE

CHANTHABURI

จันทบุรี
pop 90,000

The so-called City of the Moon is proof positive that all that glitters is not gold. Here, gemstones do the sparkling and the glimmer goes right the way into the traders' pockets. A centre for the buying and selling of sapphires and rubies from across Southeast Asia, Chanthaburi is primarily a bustling commercial centre. But the city, with its large Vietnamese population, is steeped in its own history, and quiet alleyways, French-style cathedral (the largest in Thailand) and Chinese temples provide a welcome antidote to the push and shove of its more mercantile face.

History

The city's Vietnamese community began arriving in the 19th century, when Christian refugees flocked to the city to escape religious and political persecution in what was then Cochin China (southern Vietnam). A second wave followed in the 1920s and 1940s, fleeing French rule, and a third arrived after the 1975 communist takeover of southern Vietnam. From 1893 to 1905, while negotiating with the Siamese over the borders for Laos and Cambodia, the French occupied Chanthaburi, stamping their own identity on the town as well.

Orientation

Th Si Chan, which runs parallel to the river, is the city's commercial heart and Chanthaburi's famed gem shops can be found on and around this thoroughfare. The bus station and large King Taksin Park are about 800m west of this street.

SOUTHEASTERN THAILAND

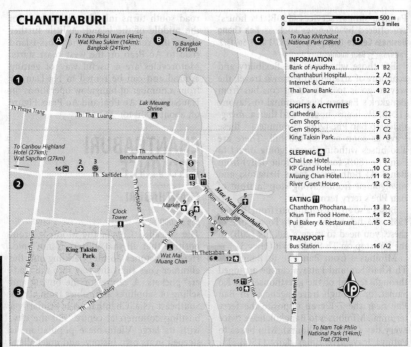

CHANTHABURI

0 — 500 m
0 — 0.3 miles

INFORMATION
Bank of Ayudhya.........................1 B2
Chanthaburi Hospital...................2 A2
Internet & Game..........................3 B2
Thai Danu Bank............................4 B2

SIGHTS & ACTIVITIES
Cathedral.....................................5 C2
Gem Shops..................................6 C3
Gem Shops..................................7 C2
King Taksin Park..........................8 A3

SLEEPING
Chai Lee Hotel.............................9 B2
KP Grand Hotel..........................10 C3
Muang Chan Hotel.....................11 B2
River Guest House.......................12 C3

EATING
Chanthorn Phochana...................13 B2
Khun Tim Food Home..................14 B2
Pui Bakery & Restaurant..............15 C3

TRANSPORT
Bus Station.................................16 A2

Information

Given the amount of money changing hands here, banks with change facilities and ATMs can be found across town

Bank of Ayudhya (Th Khwang; 8.30am-3.30pm Mon-Fri)

Chanthaburi Hospital (0 3932 1378; Th Saritidet; 6am-9pm)

Internet & Game (0 3932 1430; Th Saritidet; per hr 20B; 10am-10pm)

Thai Danu Bank (Th Si Chan; 8.30am-3.30pm Mon-Fri)

Sights & Activities

Peering through thick magnifying glasses and peddling their wares from roadside stalls along Th Si Chan and Th Thetsaban 4, the city's **gem dealers** are Chanthaburi's living, breathing highlight. Streets surrounding their shops and stalls are chock-a-block with all the banter and intrigue of the hard sell, and you can spend hours watching buyers and sellers haggle until they are blue in the face. Unless you really know what you are doing, though, this is strictly a spectator sport. Great deals can be clinched by the

savvy, but amateurs are likely to go home with empty pockets and a bagful of worthless rocks. Plenty of glossy, air-con gem shops in the same area offer pricier, but less risky deals.

The Vietnamese and French have also left an indelible stamp on the face of Chanthaburi. Creaking **shop houses** run alongside the river on Th Rim Nam and garish **Chinese temples** appear to fill every available space. The French-style **cathedral** (daylight hours), across a footbridge from Th Rim Nam, is the architectural highlight. A small missionary chapel was built on this site in 1711, but after undergoing four reconstructions between 1712 and 1906 (the last was carried out by the French) the structure has expanded into the largest building of its kind in Thailand.

King Taksin Park (24hr) is the town's main oasis and is filled with picnicking families and, judging by some of the expressions on show, a few of those who have lost out on the gem market. Whatever your motives, it's a pleasant spot for a quiet, ponderous stroll.

A few kilometres north of town off Rte 3249 is **Khao Phloi Waen** (Sapphire-Ring Mountain; admission free; ☾ daylight hours), which is only 150m high but features a Sri Lankan-style *chedi* on top, built during the reign of Rama IV. Tunnels dug into the side of the hill were once gem-mining shafts.

Wat Khao Sukim (☾ daylight hours) doubles as a local meditation centre and is 16km north of Chanthaburi off Rte 3322. The **museum** (donation appreciated; ☾ daylight hours) on the *wat* (temple) grounds contains all manner of valuables donated to the temple, such as jade carvings, ceramics and antique furniture, as well as resin figures of some of Thailand's most revered monks.

Festivals

During the first week of June every year there is a **gem festival** and Chanthaburi can get very crowded.

Sleeping

Accommodation can get very busy – you are advised to book ahead.

River Guest House (☎ 0 3932 8211; theriver _chant@hotmail.com; Th Si Chan 3/5-8; r 150-350B; ☒ ☐) Perched right on the riverbank, this shiny new opening has a terrace café overlooking the water and modest, well-priced rooms. Sadly, the main road overlooks the hotel, but with fan rooms from 150B, you'd have to do mighty well on the gem market to find better value in Chanthaburi.

KP Grand Hotel (☎ 0 3932 3201-13, kpgrand@yahoo .com; 35/200-201 Th Trirat; r incl breakfast 1200B; ☒ ☐) Just across the river, this is the favoured stomping ground of visiting gem dealers. Unlike the contents of its guests' suitcases, the hotel itself is starting to lose its sparkle, but all the usual four-star amenities are on offer, including the requisite but less welcome muzak.

Caribou Highland Hotel (☎ /fax 0 3932 3431; Th Chawan Uthit; r 1400B incl breakfast; ☒ ☐) Slightly more salubrious still, this glitzy place offers some of the best accommodation in town – large air-con rooms with TV, IDD phone and fridge (room rates are often discounted to 900B including breakfast).

Muang Chan Hotel (☎ 0 3932 1073; fax 0 3932 7244; Th Si Chan 257-259; r 230-350B; ☒) Friendly staff give this humble, central place a lift. The rooms are plain and a little dowdy, but at least they're clean.

Chai Lee Hotel (☎ 0 3931 3767; Th Khwang; s 170-300B, d 210-330B; ☒) Downtown haunt has a whiff of skid row about it, with a rather bizarre reception in an underground car park. It's perennially popular though, and the rooms are fine.

Eating

To try those famous Chanthaburi noodles, *kŭaytĭaw sên jan*, head for the Chinese-Vietnamese part of town along Mae Nam Chanthaburi and you'll see variations on the basic rice noodle theme, including delicious crab with fried noodles. You'll also find a smorgasbord of food stalls around the gem stalls – dealing makes you hungry, don't you know?

Chanthorn Phochana (☎ 0 3931 2339; Th Benchamarachutit 102/5-8; dishes 35-150B; ☾ 11am-10pm) Fragrant smells and smiling faces say it all at this popular Thai/Chinese place. A dazzling array of dishes pack out the menu, and more than make up for the frumpy décor.

Pui Bakery & Restaurant (☎ 0 3934 0437; Th Trirat 35/130-131; dishes 80-270B; ☾ 8am-10pm) Largely catering to the expat crowd, this little café/diner cranks the air-con to the max, keeps Heinz ketchup on the tables and offers everything from *phàt thai* to ostrich steak.

Khun Tim Food Home (Th Rim Nam; dishes 30-100B; ☾ 11am-10pm) Photogenic rickety restaurant is housed in an old wooden house on the river. The Thai-language menu is limited, but the food is authentically tasty. It's down a little alley, just south of the Th Saritidet intersection.

Getting There & Away

Buses operate between Chanthaburi and Bangkok's Eastern bus terminal (air-con/ normal 148/100B, 4½ hours) every half hour throughout the day – less frequently at night. Buses also travel to Rayong (normal 55B, 2½ hours, five daily) and Trat (air-con/ normal 58/30B, 1½ hours, hourly).

If you have your own set of wheels, take Rte 317 north to Sa Kaew, then along Hwy 33 west to Kabinburi and Rte 304 north to Khorat. From Sa Kaew you can also head eastwards and reach Aranya Prathet on the Thailand–Cambodia border after just 46km. From this border crossing you can take a share taxi from Poipet on the Cambodian side of the border to Siem Reap (near Angkor Wat).

AROUND CHANTHABURI

Two small national parks are within an hour's drive of Chanthaburi. Both are malarial, so take the usual precautions.

Khao Khitchakut National Park (☎ 0 3945 2074; reserve@dnp.go.th; 200B; ⏰ 8.30am-4.30pm) is about 28km northeast of town off Rte 3249 and is known for Nam Tok Krathing waterfall. It's one of Thailand's smallest national parks (59 sq km) although the unprotected forest surrounding the park is much larger and is said to harbour herds of wild elephants. There's a series of trails to the falls nearest the park headquarters, but visitors are discouraged from going deeper into the forest without being accompanied by a ranger as a guide.

You can stay here in a **camp site** (about 10B plus 50B per person) or rent a **bungalow** (sleeps 2; r 800B). Reserve accommodation by email at the address above or ☎ 0 2562 0760.

To get to Khao Khitchakut by public transport, take a *săwngthăew* from the northern side of the market in Chanthaburi (25B, 45 minutes). The *săwngthăew* stops 1.5km from the park headquarters on Rte 3249, from which point you'll have to walk.

Nam Tok Phlio National Park (☎ 0 3943 4528; reserve@dnp.go.th; admission 200B; ⏰ 8.30am-4.30pm), off Hwy 3, is only 14km to the southeast of Chanthaburi and features plentiful waterfalls, Phra Nang Ruar Lom stupa (c 1876) and the Along Khon *chedi* (c 1881).

You can stay here in a **camp site** (about 10B plus 50B per person), or rent a **bungalow** (sleeps 6; r 1800B). Reserve accommodation on the email address above or ☎ 0 2562 0760.

To get to the park, catch a *săwngthăew* from the northern side of the market in Chanthaburi to the park entrance (20B, 30 minutes).

TRAT PROVINCE

Trat Province is Thailand's back door into Cambodia and gem trading is a favoured method of putting rice on the table – unsurprisingly, *tàlàat phloi* (gem markets) abound. A sad by-product of this gem mining, however, has been the destruction of vast tracts of land – the topsoil is stripped away, leaving hectares of red-orange mud.

But there's plenty more of note to keep your camera busy. Ko Chang boasts a string

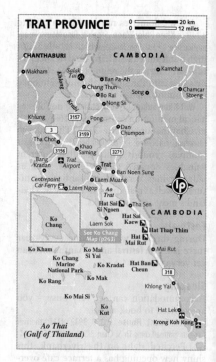

TRAT PROVINCE

of top-notch beaches and plenty more can be found along the sliver of land that runs down along the coast bordering Cambodia – of these, **Hat Sai Si Ngoen**, **Hat Sai Kaew**, **Hat Thap Thim** and **Hat Ban Cheun** are all worth a peep.

At the Km 70 marker, off Rte 318, is **Jut Chom Wiw** (Lookout Point), where you can get a panorama of the surrounding area, including Cambodia. Trat Province's southeasternmost point is at **Hat Lek**, which is also a jumping-off point for trips along the Cambodian coast.

TRAT

ตราด

pop 21,000

At first glance, Trat's provincial capital offers little more than traffic noise and heat. Beneath the busy face of things, however, is evidence of a quieter, older way of life, lived out among the back alleys and wooden shop houses of its higgledy-piggledy thoroughfares. Although many visitors get to see little more of Trat than the inside of its bus station, those who stray off the main drag often find themselves staying longer than they planned.

Orientation & Information

Bangkok Trat Hospital (☎ 0 3953 2735; Th Sukhumvit; ☻24hr) Best bet for treatment; 400m north of the centre.

Koh Chang New Travel Agency (☎ 0 3953 1135; Th Sukhumvit; ☻8am-5pm) Can help with plane and bus tickets.

Krung Thai Bank (Th Sukhumvit; ☻8.30am-4.30pm Mon-Fri) One of plenty of banks in Trat. Has an ATM and currency-exchange facilities.

Tle & Tin Internet (☎ 0 3952 4567; per min 1B; ☻10am-10pm) Check your emails here.

Tratosphere Books (Rimklong Soi 23; ☻8am-10pm) Has second-hand English-language titles

Sights

Wat Plai Khlong (Wat Bupharam; ☻9am-5pm) offers a quiet – during the week – retreat from the heave-ho of central Trat. Several of the wooden buildings date to the late Ayuthaya period, including the *wíhăan* (large hall), bell tower and *kùtì* (monk's quarters). The *wíhăan* contains a variety of sacred relics and Buddha images dating from the Ayuthaya period and earlier. It is 2km west of the centre.

Trat has more than its fair share of **markets** – have a wander through the day market beneath the municipal shopping centre off Th Sukhumvit; the old day market off Th Tat Mai; and the day market next to the air-con bus office. The latter becomes a night market in the evening.

Trat is famous for *náam-man lěuang* (yellow oil), a herb-infused liquid touted as a remedy for everything from arthritis to stomach upsets. It's produced by a resident, Mae Ang-Ki (Somthawin Pasananon), using a secret pharmaceutical recipe that has been handed down through her Chinese-Thai family for generations. The Thais say that if you leave Trat without a couple of bottles of Mae Ang-Ki's yellow oil, then you really haven't been to Trat. This stuff really works! Put a couple of drops on your palms, rub them together and take a good whiff: it's quite a rush! It's also great for aches and pains, and is available at all the pharmacies in town for 80B.

Sleeping

Trat has a great selection of cheap hotels, housed in traditional wooden buildings on and around Th Thana Charoen. In fact, there's a dearth of pricier places and it's almost impossible to pay more, even if you want to.

Pop Guest House (☎ 0 3951 2392; popson1958@ hotmail.com; Th Thana Charoen 1/1; r 200B; 🖳) Staying at this cosy place is just like visiting your mum – the owner will pamper you silly. There is a huge selection of tidy rooms – including cheap doubles with shared bathrooms (100B) and one glossy air-con room (400B) – a little eatery serving scrumptious snacks and, for homesick football aficionados, a Manchester United banner hanging over the reception desk.

SOUTHEASTERN THAILAND

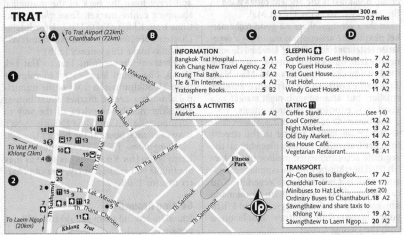

TRAT

0   300 m
0   0.2 miles

INFORMATION	
Bangkok Trat Hospital	1 A1
Koh Chang New Travel Agency	2 A2
Krung Thai Bank	3 A2
Tle & Tin Internet	4 A2
Tratosphere Books	5 B2

SIGHTS & ACTIVITIES	
Market	6 A2

SLEEPING 🏠	
Garden Home Guest House	7 A2
Pop Guest House	8 A2
Trat Guest House	9 A2
Trat Hotel	10 A2
Windy Guest House	11 A2

EATING 🍴	
Coffee Stand	(see 14)
Cool Corner	12 A2
Night Market	13 A2
Old Day Market	14 A2
Sea House Café	15 A2
Vegetarian Restaurant	16 A1

TRANSPORT	
Air-Con Buses to Bangkok	17 A2
Cherdchai Tour	(see 17)
Minibuses to Hat Lek	(see 20)
Ordinary Buses to Chanthaburi	18 A2
Săwngthăew and share taxis to Khlong Yai	19 A2
Săwngthăew to Laem Ngop	20 A2

Trat Guest House (☎ 0 3951 1152; Soi Khunpoka Lakmuang 4; r 80B) All creaking wood and blooming flower baskets, this pretty place looks like it has been lifted straight off the lid of a chocolate box. Rooms are modest, but comfortable and share a bathroom. It is down a little alleyway between Pop Guest House and Cool Corner.

Windy Guest House (☎ 0 3952 4419; Th Thana Charoen; s/d 80/100B; 🖳) This wooden outfit tinkers on the edge of the canal and offers soothing, lapping water noises and a very warm welcome. The rooms are typically basic with shared bathrooms.

Garden Home Guest House (☎ 0 3952 1018; Th Sukhumvit; r 100B) Wind your way through the owner's cactus collection and the wooden reception area and you'll find a couple of basic rooms in a friendly, local home. You can catch up on all the latest news from the gossiping grannies out front. Bathrooms are shared.

Trat Hotel (☎ 0 3951 1091; fax 0 3951 2233; Th Sukhumvit; r 220-370; 🕃) This slightly dowdy place offers a few more creature comforts – like a lift. For 130B extra, you can even get hot water.

Eating

With all the markets in Trat, you're hardly ever more than 50m from something good to eat. The **indoor market** beneath the shopping centre has a food section, with cheap noodle and rice dishes from early morning to early evening. Another good spot for a cheap breakfast is the ancient **coffee stand** in the old day market on Th Tat Mai.

In the evenings, there's a good **night market** next to the air-con bus station – a **vegetarian restaurant** (dishes 20B; 🕑 6am-2am) down a nearby lane offers a few pots of tasty veggie food at knockdown prices. On Mae Nam Trat, in the northern part of town, is another smaller, but atmospheric **night market** – a good choice for long, leisurely meals.

Cool Corner (☎ 0 6156 4129; Th Thana Charoen; dishes 40-150B; 🕑 7am-10pm) Catering to the street's traveller fraternity, this airy place has all the requisite accoutrements: mellow tunes, lavish fried breakfasts, English-language magazines and, last but not least, Vegemite. You can drink shakes, pig out on homemade sausages and excellent veggie fare and flick your cigarette into ashtrays emblazoned with the George Cross.

Sea House Café (Th Sukhumvit; dishes 40-120B; 🕑 8.30am-1am) Dangling shells and pot plants provide the décor, real coffee adds the perks and decent Thai and international food tops the menu at this cheerful little diner. You can even surf the Internet (1B per minute).

Getting There & Away
BANGKOK

Bangkok Airways (☎ 0 3952 5767; Trat Airport; www .bangkokair.com) flies twice daily between Trat and Bangkok (one way/return 1500/3000B). Book tickets at its Trat airport office, or through a travel agent – see p259.

Cherdchai Tour (☎ 0 3951 1062; Th Sukhumvit; 🕑 7am-11pm) air-con buses for Bangkok's Eastern bus terminal (189B, 5½ hours) leave from outside the office hourly between 7am and 4pm and at 6pm and 11pm.

For Trat, air-con buses (189B, 5½ hours) and ordinary buses (119B, eight hours) leave from Bangkok's Eastern bus terminal hourly from 7am to 5pm.

CHANTHABURI

Cherdchai Tour's air-con Bangkok services also stop in Chanthaburi (58B, 1¼ hours). Ordinary buses between Chanthaburi and Trat (30B, 1½ hours) leave hourly from 6am to 5.30pm from a stop opposite Cherdchai Tour on Th Sukhumvit.

KHLONG YAI, HAT LEK & LAEM NGOP

Săwngthăew and share taxis go to Khlong Yai (ordinary/chartered 35/400B, 45 minutes) and leave from the back of the municipal shopping centre market. *Săwngthăew* continue from Khlong Yai to Hat Lek (ordinary/ chartered 30/200B, 20 minutes); motorcycle taxis also make this journey (50B).

Direct minibuses from Trat to Hat Lek (100B, one hour) leave every 45 minutes from Th Sukhumvit in front of the municipal shopping centre market. Guesthouses also offer minibus services all the way to Sihanoukville in Cambodia (500B) – you'll have to change buses at the border though.

Săwngthăew (20B, 25 minutes) go to Laem Ngop (for Ko Chang) as soon as they are full. If you are in a hurry, you can charter one for 150B.

Getting Around

Săamláw around town should cost 10B per person.

AROUND TRAT
Beaches
The sliver of Trat Province that extends southeast along the Cambodian border is fringed by several Gulf of Thailand beaches. **Hat Sai Si Ngoen** (Silver Sand Beach) lies just north of the Km 41 marker off Hwy 3. Nearby, at the Km 42 marker, is **Hat Sai Kaew** (Crystal Sand Beach) and at the Km 48 marker, **Hat Thap Thim** (also known as Hat Lan); they're OK to walk along the water's edge or picnic in the shade of casuarina and eucalyptus trees. The only place for accommodation here is the **Sun Sapha Kachat Thai** (Thai Red Cross; ☎ 0 3950 1015; r 700B), which has comfortable bungalows with all the usual amenities, as well as a restaurant.

The only other beach with accommodation is **Hat Ban Cheun**, a very long stretch of clean sand near the Km 63 marker. The 6km road that leads to the beach passes a defunct Cambodian refugee camp. There are the usual casuarina and eucalyptus trees, a small **restaurant** and basic **bungalows** (200B) set on swampy land behind the beach. Travellers have reported that the friendly family that manages the operation is quite accommodating.

Laem Ngop
แหลมงอบ
Laem Ngop is the jumping-off point for Ko Chang (see p270). **TAT** (☎ 0 3959 7255; 100 Mu 1, Th Trat-Laem Ngop; ◷ 8.30am-4.30pm) has an information office where you can swat up on Ko Chang info. A little further north, there is an **immigration office** (☎ 0 3959 7261; Th Trat-Laem Ngop; ◷ 8.30am-4.30pm Mon-Fri), where you can apply for visa extensions.

Between the two, **Kasikornbank** (Th Trat-Laem Ngop; ◷ 8.30am-3.30pm Mon-Fri) has an exchange counter.

SLEEPING & EATING
There's usually no reason to stay here – there are regular boats to Ko Chang during the day and Trat is only 20km away. If you do get stuck, however, there are a couple of good accommodation choices.

Chut Kaew Guest House (☎ 0 3959 7088; s/d 80/160B) A five-minute walk from the harbour on the right side of the road, this has clean(ish) rooms with bamboo-thatch walls and shared bathrooms. Food and laundry services are also available.

Laem Ngop Inn (☎ 0 3959 7044; s/d 450/600B; ⚟) Swankier place brings air-con into the equation, but if you'd rather sweat it out, cheaper fan bungalows (300B) are also available. It is further up the road than Chut Kaew and down a side lane.

Near the pier in Laem Ngop are several rustic seafood **eateries** with views of the sea and islands.

GETTING THERE & AWAY
Share taxis to Laem Ngop (shared/chartered 20/150B, 20 minutes) leave Trat from a stand on Th Sukhumvit next to the municipal shopping centre market. They depart regularly throughout the day, but after dark you will have to charter. Travel agents on Th Laem Ngop and on Ko Chang arrange daily minibuses to Th Khao San in Bangkok (350B, five to six hours).

Khlong Yai
คลองใหญ่
There's not a whole lot to Khlong Yai but for a cluster of old wooden buildings west of the highway surrounded by the town's more modern concrete face. Town life focuses on the large, central market.

Suksamlan Hotel (☎ 0 3958 1109; s/d 300/350B; ⚟) is an old-fashioned Thai Chinese–style place offering reasonable rooms on a street between the market and the highway. It also has spartan fan rooms (150B). **Bang In Villa** (☎ 0 3958 1401; r 150-300B; ⚟) is a little more contemporary than Suksamlan, and a little less charming, putting its guests to bed in comfortable bungalows. It's a little out of town, off Hwy 3.

See opposite for information about public transport to Khlong Yai.

HAT LEK TO CAMBODIA
The small Thai border outpost of **Hat Lek** is the southernmost part on the Trat mainland. There's not much here apart from a small market just before the border crossing itself.

Motorcycle and automobile taxis are available from Hat Lek across the border into Cambodia for 30B and 50B. There is accommodation on the island of Koh Kong in Cambodia, but little to keep you there. If you plan to continue further, you can embark on a four-hour boat ride (US$15) to Sihanoukville. There is only one boat per day to Sihanoukville and it leaves at 8am, so if you don't get across the border early you'll have to spend a night on Koh Kong. Basically, if you want to get from Trat to Sihanoukville in one day on the boat, you should be on the 6am minibus to Hat Lek and at the border with passport in hand as soon as it opens at 7am. From Koh Kong, there are also minibuses that go to Sihanoukville (550B) and Phnom Penh (650B); both leave at 9am. This border crossing closes at 8pm.

Cambodian tourist visas (1200B) are usually available at the border (bring a passport photo), but you should check with the Cambodian embassy in Bangkok before heading out there. If you are going into Cambodia for a day trip, you might need to have a valid Thai visa to return to Thailand. Nowadays Thailand grants most nationalities a one-month visa on arrival. If your nationality is not on the instant-visa list, you will find yourself stuck in Cambodia.

See p260 for transport information to Hat Lek.

KO CHANG MARINE NATIONAL PARK & AROUND

อุทยานแห่งชาติเกาะช้าง

Misty peaks and knotted forest, silent beaches and empty spaces: welcome to Ko Chang, Thailand's second-largest island and the pride of the northern coast. At the heart of the Ko Chang Marine National Park, and cloaked in one of Southeast Asia's best-preserved rainforests, Ko Chang's interior is an Edenic wilderness as chock-a-block with snakes and exotic fruit as the biblical garden itself. Beaches stretch the length of the west coast and hidden bays and coves provide refuge for wannabe Crusoes.

The government's plans to transform the island into a playground for hotshots and big spenders are slowly coming into effect, and sections of Ko Chang's west coast are gradually becoming as raucous and developed as the surrounding rainforest is quiet and untouched. A new road, slicing a path through a swathe of virgin forest en route to Hat Yao, is just the latest stage of Ko Chang's steady evolution.

Resorts may be popping up at a breakneck rate, but an eerie stillness hangs over much of Ko Chang and its wildlife – including stump-tailed macaques, small Indian civets,

monitor lizards and reticulated pythons – continue to thrive in the quieter corners of the island. Get off the road and you enter a whole new world.

Despite an upmarket shift, the island's backpacking scene also continues to flourish. The result is an excellent spread of accommodation, with something to suit every budget and taste. Live it up with a cold one on Hat Sai Khao at night, and vanish into the wilderness come dawn.

Ko Chang is also surrounded by a clutch of smaller islands. After a spell on the big island, side trips to Ko Kut, Ko Mak, Ko Kham, Ko Wai and Ko Lao Ya are well worth the journey.

Orientation & Information

The **national park** (☎ 0 3953 8100; 200B; reserve@dnp .go.th; ☷ 8am-5pm) is divided into four units, with offices at Ban Khlong Son, Tha Than Mayom, just west of Nam Tok Khlong Plu and Ban Salak Phet. All offer roughly the equivalent information, but the Tha Than Mayom visitors centre features informative displays on park flora and fauna.

Entry fees (200B) are collected at any one of the four park offices. Be sure to keep your receipt as rangers may demand payment from visitors who don't have one.

Ferries from the mainland dock at the northern end of the island, and all but a handful of the hotels and restaurants are on the west coast, where most of the beaches are. Hat Sai Khao (White Sands Beach) is the busiest development, while distant Hat Yao (Long Beach), at the southeastern end of the island, is the quietest stretch of sand – and so far without a hotel. A paved road now goes *most* of the way around the island, but at time of writing you still could not drive between Ban Bang Bao and Salak Phet.

EMERGENCY

The local **police headquarters** (☎ 0 3958 6191) is in Ban Dan Mai.

COVER UP ON KO CHANG

Nudity and topless sunbathing are forbidden by law in Ko Chang Marine National Park; this includes all beaches on Ko Chang, Ko Kut, Ko Mak, Ko Kradat etc.

INTERNET ACCESS

Internet access is relatively easy to find all the way down the west coast.

Earthlink (Hat Sai Khao; per min 2B; ⏲ 10.30am-11pm) For cool coffees at the northern end of Hat Sai Khao.

Friends Net (☎ 0 9832 4850; White Sands Plaza, Hat Sai Khao; per min 2B; ⏲ 9am-10pm) Halfway along Hat Sai Khao, in the White Sands Plaza shopping centre.

MEDICAL SERVICES

Ko Chang Hospital (☎ 0 3952 1657; Ban Dan Mai) Near the police headquarters.

Ko Chang International Clinic (☎ 0 3955 1151; Hat Sai Khao) For English-speaking doctors and international-standard medical attention on Hat Sai Khao.

MONEY

There are plenty of banks with ATMs and change facilities along Hat Sai Khao. **Siam Commercial Bank** (Hat Sai Khao; ⏲ 8.30am-3.30pm) also has an exchange window, which stays open until 8pm.

POST

There is a small **post office** (⏲ 9am-4.30pm Mon-Fri) near the ferry terminal at Ban Khlong Son.

TOURIST OFFICES

The nearest tourist office is in Laem Ngop (p261). The free magazine *Koh Chang, Trat & The Eastern Islands* comes out quarterly, is widely available on the island and is

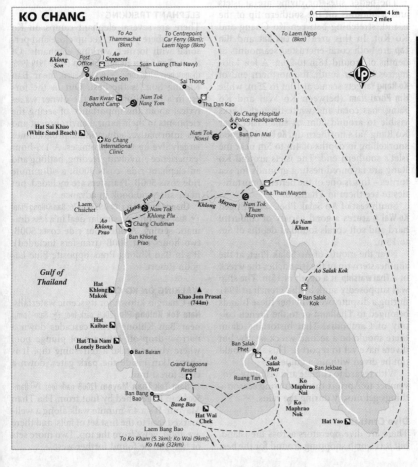

KO CHANG

0   4 km
0   2 miles

To Ao Thammachat (8km)
To Centrepoint Car Ferry (8km); Laem Ngop (8km)
To Laem Ngop (8km)

Ao Khlong Son
Post Office
Ao Sapparot
Suan Luang (Thai Navy)
Ban Khlong Son
Sai Thong

Ban Kwan Elephant Camp
Nam Tok Nang Yom
Tha Dan Kao

Ko Chang Hospital & Police Headquarters

Hat Sai Khao (White Sand Beach)
Ko Chang International Clinic
Nam Tok Nonsi
Ban Dan Mai

Laem Chaichet
Khlong Prao
Nam Tok Khlong Plu
Chang Chutiman
Khlong   Mayom
Nam Tok Than Mayom
Tha Than Mayom

Ao Khlong Prao
Ban Khlong Prao

Ao Nam Khun

Gulf of Thailand
Hat Khlong Makok
Khao Jom Prasat (744m)

Ao Salak Kok
Ban Salak Kok

Hat Kaibae
Hat Tha Nam (Lonely Beach)
Ban Bairan

Ban Salak Phet
Ao Salak Phet
Ban Jekbae

Grand Lagoona Resort
Ruang Tan
Ko Maphrao Nai

Ban Bang Bao
Ao Bang Bao
Ko Maphrao Nok

Hat Wai Chek
Hat Yao

Laem Bang Bao
To Ko Kham (5.3km); Ko Wai (9km); Ko Mak (32km)

SOUTHEASTERN THAILAND

packed with useful listings and tips. You can also check its website www.whitesands thailand.com. Another useful website, with accommodation and entertainment listings, is www.kochangisland.com.

Sights & Activities

DIVING & SNORKELLING

Ko Chang doesn't offer the best diving in the country, but the island still has more than enough to keep passionate bubble-blowers blowing. There's plenty of columnar and stagshorn coral, reef life includes blue-tipped rays, moray eels, batfish, trigger fish and white-tip reef sharks and, if you're lucky, you may just catch a passing whale shark.

The better sites for diving are at islets and seamounts off the southern tip of the island, stretching between Ko Chang and Ko Kut. In this area **Hin Luk Bat** and **Hin Lap** are both coral-encrusted seamounts at depths of around 18m to 20m. A few kilometres further south, the northern end of **Ko Rang Yai** gets scenic at 10m to 25m, while **Hin Phrai Nam** (between Ko Wai and Ko Rang) has coral and white-tip reef sharks visible to around 20m. A small islet near Ko Rang Yai's northern tip, **Ko Kra**, has good snorkelling in depths of 4m to 5m near the islet's southern end. The islets around Ko Rang are favoured nesting grounds for sea turtles – this is one of the better opportunities to see them in Thailand.

Southwest of Ao Salak Phet, reef-fringed **Ko Wai** features a good variety of colourful hard and soft corals found at depths of 6m to 15m.

Near the mouth of Ao Salak Phet, at the southeastern tip of the island, lies the wreck of a **Thai warship** at a depth of 15m. The ship was supposedly sunk by the French in 1941 during a dispute over whether these islands belonged to Thailand or to the French colony of Cambodia. Thai historians claim there should be a second wreck nearby but divers have yet to report it. This site should not be dived without a guide.

With regard to climate and visibility, November to April is the best diving season – things get murky during the rains.

Dive Centres

There are dive operators across the island, but it is worth shopping around for the best

prices. In general, full PADI Open Water certification comes in at around 11,000B, with most shops charging 2,200B for a two-dive package including equipment hire and lunch. Some shops close down, or reduce their services, during the monsoon (June to September).

Recommended operators:

Eco Divers (☎ 0 3955 1037) On the road down to Tree House at Hat Tha Nam (Lonely Beach).

OK Diving (☎ 0 9936 7080; ok.diving@chaiyo.com) At the northern end of Hat Sai Khao.

Ploy Scuba Diving (☎ 0 6143 9318; www.ployscuba .com) With shops on the pier in Ban Bang Bao and by the 7-Eleven on Hat Sai Khao.

SeaHorse Divecenter (☎ 0 1996 7147; www.ede .ch/seahorse) Located at Kaibae Hut resort at Hat Kaibae.

ELEPHANT TREKKING

There are several elephant camps on Ko Chang where you can get up close and personal with former working elephants. Of these, **Ban Kwan Elephant Camp** (☎ 0 1919 3995; changtone@yahoo.com; ☺ 8.30am-5pm), near Ban Khlong Son, is the best. Out in the forest in a beautiful setting the owner waxes lyrical about the importance of seeing the elephants in their natural environment and his informative, educational programmes largely live up to his promises. A 1½-hour 'experience', involving feeding, bathing and an elephant ride, costs 900B; a 40-minute ride costs 500B. Transfers are included, but make sure you book in advance.

Chang Chutiman (☎ 0 9939 6676; Ban Khlong Prao; ☺ 8am-4pm) offers a similar deal in a less dramatic setting. A one-hour ride costs 500B; two hours cost 900B (transfers included). It's in Ban Khlong Prao, opposite Blue Lagoon Resort.

WALKING ON KO CHANG

Ko Chang is known for its scenic waterfalls. **Nam Tok Khlong Plu** (200B park fee; ☺ 8am-5pm), near Ban Khlong Prao, cascades down a narrow drop-off into a cool plunge pool where you can take a refreshing dip. It is about 1km inside the park gates, down a clear forest trail.

Nam Tok Than Mayom (200B park fee; ☺ 8am-5pm) can be reached by foot from Tha Than Mayom. It's a 45-minute walk along a well-marked trail to the first set of falls, and there are good views from the top. Two more sets of falls can be found further west.

As both Nam Tok Khlong Plu and Nam Tok Than Mayom are inside the boundaries of the National Park, you will have to pay the 200B park entry fee.

If you're looking for more of a grunt, just head for the interior – the steep, forested hills will have you sweating in no time. A footpath connects Ban Khlong Prao on the west coast, with Khlong Mayom on the east, but this all-day cross-island route shouldn't be undertaken without a local guide as the jungle is quite dense.

Don't try Ban Bang Bao to Ao Salak Phet unless you're an experienced tropical hiker with moderate orienteering skills – there are a lot of hills and many interconnecting trails. If you don't get lost, this hike will take four to six hours. Should you decide to attempt it, carry enough food and water for an overnight stay, just in case.

If you do get lost on a trek, climb the nearest hill and try to locate the sea or a stream to get a bearing on where you are. Following any stream will usually take you either to a village or to the sea. Then you can either follow the coast or ask directions.

At the southeastern end of Ao Bang Bao, around a headland that leads to Ao Salak Phet, is a beautiful and secluded beach, **Hat Wai Chek**. A road now also runs right past **Hat Yao**, so you can drive down to this quiet stretch of sand and stroll along the coast.

COOKERY

The **Koh Chang Thai Cookery School** (☎ 0 1940 0649; Ban Khlong Prao), at the Blue Lagoon resort in Ban Khlong Prao, offers fun cookery courses for those wanting to take home an aptitude for Thai kitchen tinkering. Half-day courses cost 600B and you can expect to learn three recipes per visit. Book ahead.

OTHER ACTIVITIES

Some of the guesthouses at Hat Sai Khao and Hat Kaibae rent out kayaks, sailboards, boogie boards, masks and snorkels. Mountain bikes can be rented for 150B per day at several places on the island, most of which are at Hat Sai Khao and Hat Kaibae.

SURROUNDING ISLANDS

Other major islands in the park include Ko Kut and Ko Mak. On **Ko Kut** you'll find beaches mostly along the western side, at Hat Tapho, Hat Khlong Chao and Hat Khlong

Yai Ki. The water off some of these beaches is the most amazing shade of turquoise. A dirt road runs between Ban Khlong Hin Dam, the island's main village on the west coast, and Ao Salat, along the northeastern shore. Other villages on the island include Ban Ta Poi, Bang Ao Salat, Ban Laem Kluai, Bang Khlong Prao and Ban Lak Uan. Nam Tok Tan Sanuk and Khlong Chao offer inland water diversions. The nearby small islands of **Ko Rang** and **Ko Rayang** have good coral in spots. Ko Kut can be reached from Khlong Yai on the mainland or from Ko Mak.

Ko Mak, the smallest of the three main islands, has a scenic beach along the northwest bay. Monsoon forest covers 30% of the island while coconut plantations take up another 60%. A few tractors and jeeps travel along the single paved road that leads from the pier to the main village. It is possible to rent motorcycles and organise diving trips from the resorts on the island.

Ko Wai has some of the best coral and is excellent for snorkelling and diving. There is also a handful of bungalow operations. **Ko Kham** is also recommended for underwater explorations; accommodation is available. **Ko Lao Ya** has natural attributes similar to those at Ko Wai, with one rather expensive place to stay. The tiny **Ko Rang** archipelago, southwest of Ko Chang, is a primary nesting ground for the endangered hawksbill sea turtle.

Sleeping

KO CHANG

Most of Ko Chang's beaches are on the west coast, and it is here that you will find the majority of the places to stay. Growing investment in the island and government plans to transform Ko Chang into an upmarket resort have spawned a starburst of midrange and top-end resorts, but there are plenty of backpacker-style haunts to choose from as well. In fact, whether you want to bed down in a basic bamboo hut, or a plush air-con honeymoon suite, Ko Chang will have something to tickle your fancy.

Prices fluctuate according to season on Ko Chang and the *low* season rates (available June to October) quoted here can increase by up to 50% during busy, peak season (November to May) weekends. When things are quiet, and you're staying for more than a couple of days, discounts are often available, but it is worth remembering that some of the more remote options may well shut down when business is slow.

Ban Khlong Son

At the northern tip of the island is the largest village, Ban Khlong Son, which has a network of piers at the mouth of the *khlawng* (canal; also spelled *khlong*), a wat, a school, several noodle shops and a health clinic.

Aiyapura Resort (☎ 0 3955 5111; www.aiyapura .com; r 2000B; ✖ 🍴 🖳 🛜) Proof positive that Ko Chang is now catering to Thai bigwigs and a glamour foreign set, this is a blueprint for the island's more upmarket offerings. Top-notch rooms and spacious bungalows (7000B) are in a landscaped coconut grove and there's a colossal seaside pool for swimmers who'd rather not get salt in their eyes. Cut off from the busy beach-front strip of Hat Sai Khao, this is a good spot for those after plenty of hush and long, lazy cocktail hours. It's down a little road, just south of Ban Khlong Son.

Hat Sai Khao & Hat Kai Mook

Hat Sai Khao starts just south of here and is the island's most popular beach strip, with a cluster of resorts, restaurants and bars taking centre stage along a sweep of so-so, white(ish) sand. It isn't the most romantic of settings, but there's plenty of life and a good spread of eating and sleeping options. The low season (June to October) prices quoted here increase by as much as 50% during peak periods. The following hotels run from north to south along the beach.

Boo's Independant Bungalows (☎ 0 7136 0876; boo_independant@yahoo.ge; Hat Sai Khao; r 150B) A staunch contender for the island's quirkiest accommodation plaudit, Boo's takes inspiration from the *Robinson Crusoe* school of architecture, and succeeds in making a hotel out of a mountain of driftwood. Those after creature comforts may find the flotsam-chic styling a little hard to swallow, but this ramshackle outfit has character aplenty. It is at the northern end of the beach, away from the road.

Star Beach Bungalows (☎ 0 1940 2195; Hat Sai Khao; r 150-200B) With a labyrinth of rickety wooden bungalows stacked up against a cliff face, Star Beach takes the hallucinogenic whizz-bang out of the Boo's Bungalows formula, offering the same rickety rooms but with a little less psychedelica.

KC Grande Resort (☎ 0 3955 1199; Hat Sai Khao; r 200-2500B; 🛜) At the north end of the road through Hat Sai Khao, this popular mid-ranger is slowly scaling the price ladder – the 'Grande' was added just recently – with a wide range of bungalows in a leafy garden. There are cheap bamboo huts (although these are scheduled for demolition), slightly overpriced 'standard' cabins right on the beach and some considerably more opulent 'superior' bungalows a little further back.

Tonsai (☎ 0 9895 7229; Hat Sai Khao; r 350B) Across the road from the beach, these pleasant little bungalows are tucked away behind a giant banyan tree. You can eat and drink to your heart's content in the tree-house restaurant or simply soak up the peace and quiet in the pretty garden.

Cookies Hotel (☎ /fax 0 3955 1056; Hat Sai Khao; r 800B; 🛜) This homogenous, motel-style development offers predictable standards – including muzak – and pleasant, spotless rooms. The related **Cookies Bungalows** (☎ as above; r 400B) resort, across the road on the beach, offers fan rooms. All prices skyrocket when rooms fill up during high season.

Logan's Place (☎ 0 6149 8523; www.logansthailand .com; Hat Sai Khao; r 1600B; 🛜) Efficient service and oh-so-Scandinavian Ikea styling come as standard at this Swedish-run outfit. Fresh paint smells still drift down the corridors and there's a spick-and-span expat-style eatery downstairs.

Tantawan (☎ 0 3955 1168; Hat Sai Khao; r 300B) Slightly garish, red-brick bungalows are more inner-city Manchester than beachside Thailand, but there's a good backpacker vibe in the seaside eatery and the staff don't charge extra for a smile. You will pay 50B more if you want to open your door on to the beach though.

Bamboo Hotel (☎ 0 1945 4106; Hat Sai Khao; r 200-800B; 🛜) Labyrinthine place offers a smorgasbord of accommodation options, from humble bamboo affairs with shared bathroom to decent air-con cottages. A slightly irritating holiday-camp ambience prevails though, and some of the décor – the blue roofs are unlikely to kick-start a fad – is decidedly dodgy.

Apple Bungalows (☎ 0 3955 1228; Hat Sai Khao; r 300-700B; 🛜) Another resort with one foot on the quality escalator, Apple now has a clutch of smartish air-con bungalows to complement its selection of the older, fan-cooled huts.

Koh Chang Kacha Resort (☎ 0 3955 1223; www .kohchangkacha.com; Hat Sai Khao; r 400-1000B; 🔀) Offering something with a little more sparkle, this tidy little resort offers stylish rooms in a wood-and-brick block overlooking the sea.

Plaloma Cliff Resort (☎ 0 3955 1119; fax 0 3955 1118; Hat Sai Khao; r 1500B; 🔀 🖳) At the southern end of Hat Sai Khao, this sprawling mid-ranger is away from the fray and offers comfortable bungalows, decent facilities, some faux Thai styling and a bit much concrete.

Saffron on the Sea (☎ 0 3955 1253; Hat Kai Mook; r 500-800B; 🔀) Pitching for that cottage feel, this isolated little resort has immaculate if plain rooms in a spread of thatched cottages and eccentric round towers. There's considerably more sea than beach out front, but the attached eatery boasts pleasant ocean views.

Ao Khlong Prao

About 4km south of Hat Sai Khao is Ao Khlong Prao (Coconut Bay), which incorporates the village of Ban Khlong Prao. The following hotels run from north to south.

Boutique Resort & Spa (☎ 0 3955 1050; boutique _resort@hotmail.com; Ao Khlong Prao; r 1000B; 🔀) It's a bit of an ugly duckling from the road, but the entrance opens up into a pleasant little Shangri-la, with a spread of authentically decorated wooden bungalows built around a series of decorative pools. Soak up the bubbles in the Jacuzzi, or treat yourself to a massage at the spa (400B per hour).

Coconut Beach Resort (☎ 0 3955 1272; www.web seiten.thai.li/coconut; Ao Khlong Prao; r 600-2500B; 🔀) This old-timer is a bit of a mishmash these days, with a collection of old fan and air-con bungalows by the sea and a newly constructed and exotic überblock of upmarket rooms hogging the limelight out back.

Ko Chang Resort & Spa (in Bangkok ☎ 0 2277 5256; www.kohchangresortandspa.com; Ao Khlong Prao; r 2500B; 🔀 🖳) Ignore the baroque menagerie of decorative concrete animals and this swanky place offers a well-priced upmarket experience, with plentiful mod cons and perennially high standards. Two-night packages start at 3970B, including meals and transfers from Bangkok.

KP Huts (☎ 0 1782 0180; Ao Khlong Prao; r 200B) At the other end of the spectrum, this no-frills spot has simple bamboo huts, scat-tered through a quiet coconut grove. The bathrooms are shared. Canoes are available for hire and the only rule (in English) is 'no fireworks!'

Blue Lagoon Resort (☎ 0 1940 0649; Ao Khlong Prao; r 350B) There are more basic bungalows at this lagoon-side resort. The main reason to come here, however, is to attend the excellent cookery course (p265).

Hat Kaibae

South of the lagoon is Hat Kaibae. As at Hat Sai Khao, new developments are sprouting up at a fair whack and prices are moving upwards accordingly. On the upside, there are a growing number of places to choose from. The following hotels run from north to south.

Chang Park Resort (☎ 0 6330 7663; www.chang parkresort.com; Hat Kaibae; r 2500-800B; 🔀 🖳) Bringing some bling to the beach, this place has ritzy rooms and bungalows, a spa and sweeping gardens cut through with water features. The parades of white concrete elephants might take the 'Chang' theme a little far though.

Relax Centre (☎ 0 1854 1000; Hat Kaibae; r 300B; 🖳) Across the road from the beach, this pleasant outfit offers some decent cement bungalows and a scattering of bamboo huts with shared bathroom (100B). The huts are only available from October to May.

Lee's Bungalows (Hat Kaibae; r 100-400B) A little further south, this spartan spot goes back to basics, offering no-frills thatched huts with shared and private facilities in rustic surrounds. Thankfully (for some), it still makes a few concessions to the modern world and its 'real coffee' can kick-start even the most committed deadhead.

KB Bungalows (☎ 0 1862 8103; Hat Kaibae; r 1200B; 🔀) Garden ornaments make this place a little cluttered, but the comfy bungalows are spacious and the setting is pleasant. There are a lot of coconut trees though – watch your head! Cheaper fan bungalows come in at 500B.

Sea View Resort (☎ 0 3952 9022; www.seaviewkoh chang.com; Hat Kaibae; r 2000B; 🔀 🖳) The atmosphere's a little thin, but a big beach, a spa, a pool and a fleet of little golf buggies for ferrying you around scoop this upmarket place a few gold stars. If you happen to be travelling with your extended family, it also has enormous 'superior' villas (6500B).

SOUTHEASTERN THAILAND

Hat Tha Nam

South from Hat Kaibae is Hat Tha Nam – otherwise known as Lonely Beach. While it's becoming less and less lonely with each season, there are some long-running favourites here. The following resorts are open year-round, but many Hat Tha Nam resorts close their doors during the low season.

Tree House Lodge (☎ 0 1847 8215; Hat Tha Nam; r 100B) Drop your watch in the sea, this oh-so-Bohemian backpacker hangout doesn't 'do' time. The cute Noddy-does-the-Orient bungalows, with shared bathrooms, back on to a wooden chill-out space, where wannabe hippies strum endless Led Zeppelin riffs from a canopy of hammocks. Friendly and fun, this is one of Ko Chang's little gems. It's down a bumpy track opposite Boogie Boogie Oodie.

Maggie's Bungalows (Hat Tha Nam; r 100B) A little closer to the main road, this quiet spot with the same facilities is a good bet if Tree House Lodge is full.

Bai Lan Resort (☎ 0 9938 7237; Hat Tha Nam; r 400B) Sturdy sandals are required for walks along the rocky beach, but the bamboo bungalows, tumbling down a lush green hill, are pleasant and there's a little eatery with great views up by the road.

South Coast

The south coast tends to get pretty quiet during low season, but the little fishing village of Bang Bao, largely built along a rickety wooden pier, makes an interesting base for those wanting a more authentic Ko Chang experience.

Ko Chang Hill Resort (☎ 0 1762 2621; Ban Bang Bao; r 500B; 🟦) Just north of Ban Bang Bao, this soporific resort has some tidy modern bungalows in quiet grounds overlooking the village.

Paradise Bang Bao (☎ 0 9934 8044; Ban Bang Bao; r 100B) Teetering over the water on Bang Bao's wooden pier, this cuter-than-cute shoebox spot boasts some of the island's smallest rooms that share bathrooms. Don't be put off though, it makes a nice break from the Hat Sai Khao mainstream.

Grand Lagoona Resort (Bangkok ☎ 0 2618 7400; www.grandlagoona.com; Ao Bang Bao; r 4500-12,000B; 🟦 🟦 🟦) Further east and surrounded by it's own minikingdom, this opulent place sports a private beach, a seven-deck floating hotel and activities galore. The atmosphere

can be a little snooty (you have to pay 100B just to get inside), but there are plenty of rooms to choose from (including swoosh suites) and standards are superlative.

East Coast

The east coast of the island is practically devoid of hotels – and beaches – but there are a few decent options in the extreme southwest, around Ao Salak Phet.

Ploy Talay (Bangkok office ☎ 0 2539 2120; www .kohchangploytalay.com; r 300-1000B; 🟦) It's a long way from the hubbub, but there isn't much of a beach here – you have to paddle out to a nearby islet in a complimentary kayak. The air-con rooms are comfortable, if a little overpriced.

Judo Resort (☎ 0 9925 4122; r 1000B; 🟦) Brand new air-con rooms will suit those after creature comforts, while very basic tents (100B), on raised platforms, cater to the budget crowd. Kayaks for the requisite paddle out to the beach are also available.

A new road now runs from just south of Judo Resort to Long Beach. Still the quietest stretch of sand on the island, Long Beach remains almost completely undeveloped, although this now looks set to change. It's our bet that a clutch of new openings will appear during the life of this book, so keep your eyes peeled.

OTHER ISLANDS

Ko Kut, Ko Mak, Ko Kradat, Ko Kham and Ko Wai are quieter and more secluded than Ko Chang; however, transport can be a little tricky – although from December to April there are daily boats – you can't just pick up and walk down the beach to another bungalow if you don't like the one you've landed at. Except at the package places, room rates overall are less expensive than on Ko Chang.

From May to November, it's a good idea to call in advance to make sure boat transportation is available. Many hotels close down from June to September.

Ko Kut

As on Ko Chang, the best beaches are found along the west coast, particularly at Hat Tapho. It is possible to visit the island on your own, but you will find it next to impossible to get accommodation without being on a package tour. These typically last two nights and three days and include accommodation, all meals, trips to waterfalls and snorkelling. You could always try getting a room as a walk-in, but the resorts are really not equipped to handle individual travellers. If you can get them to agree to take you, you'll end up paying through the nose. The clientele is almost all Thai.

The prices listed for the following upmarket bungalow operations are per person rates for a basic two-night and three-day package in a standard room, including meals, transfers and park fees – book via the individual telephone numbers. Packages are also advertised, and can be booked online at www.koh-chang.com.

Ko Kut Cabana (☎ 0 3952 2955; Hat Tapho; r 4000B; ⊠) Swank bungalows on the busy (for Ko Kut) west coast.

Kut Island Resort (Bangkok office ☎ 0 2374 3004; Ao Yai Kerd; r 4350B; ⊠) With wood-finished cottages on the east coast.

Peter Pan Resort (Bangkok office ☎ 0 2966 1800; Ao Yai Kee; r 4800B; ⊠) With more upmarket, traditionally styled bungalows on the west coast, just south of Hat Tapho.

Ko Mak

Like Ko Kut, many 'resorts' on Ko Mak are set up for package tourists, or are upgrading their facilities to allow them to do so. It is difficult to get accommodation at these places without being on a package tour. These typically last two nights and three days and include accommodation, all meals, trips to waterfalls and snorkelling. As with Ko Kut, you could always try getting a room as a walk-in, but the bigger resorts really aren't equipped to handle individual travellers, and you'll end up paying three times as much as if you'd booked a package. The clientele is almost all Thai, many of whom come for deep-sea fishing trips that can be booked here as well.

The saving grace is that there are still a few non-resorts that rent rooms the old fashioned way, with no strings attached. The following take walk-in guests on a nightly basis.

Ko Mak Coco-Cape (Bangkok office ☎ 0 2711 2058; r 2900B; ⊠) This plleasant outfit offers pernight pricing in a wide range of accommodation options, from basic fan rooms with shared bathroom (500B), through air-con rooms with private bathroom (2900B), to

classy suites with a Jacuzzi on a private boat (4300B).

Ko Mak Resort (Bangkok office ☎ 0 2319 6714-5; r 700B) On the western bay, amid a coconut and rubber plantation, this friendly place has bungalows with fan and bathroom. You pay according to the position of the bungalow, so expect rates to go as high as 2500B if you want to be right on the beach.

TK Huts (☎ 0 3952 1631; r 350B) Rather more spartan in design, this friendly outfit has basic huts with shared bathroom (200B) and bungalows with fan and private bathroom (350B). The best rooms are near the beach.

Call ahead, as some of these places close during the rainy season.

Ko Kradat

Ko Kradat Resort (Bangkok office ☎ 0 2368 2675; r 1900B; ⊠) This reasonably plush resort has pleasant bungalows but normally only takes guests on a package basis.

Ko Kham

Ko Kham Resort (r 200-700B) Midranger offers bamboo huts and more upmarket bungalows. During the November-to-May high season you can get a boat here from Tha Laem Ngop.

Ko Wai

Ko Wai Paradise (r 200-1200B) Welcoming spot has simple wooden bungalows on the beach and a couple of larger bungalows with two rooms behind the restaurant.

Eating

Most of Ko Chang's accommodation outfits have attached restaurants and, if you are staying on one of the island's more isolated beaches, eating in your hotel will likely be your best option.

At the northern end of the island, Hat Sai Khao has the highest concentration of eateries.

Oodie's Place (Hat Sai Khao; mains 60-260B; ⊙ noon-1am) The simple bamboo surroundings of this lively spot belie some seriously scrumptious French fare, including French onion soup and a mean Chateaubriand. Videos are shown in the early evening and live bands shake the stage from 10pm. There's also a good selection of Asian dishes, including excellent Korean barbecues. It's at the northern end of Hat Sai Khao, across the road from the beach.

Tonsai (☎ 0 9895 7229; Hat Sai Khao; mains 40-150B; ☽ noon-midnight) For those who prefer to eat among the branches of an ancient Banyan, this little eatery serves up simple Thai and Western grub in a wooden tree house. Seating is on scatter cushions and the ambience is distinctly Bohemian.

Cookies Restaurant (☎ 0 3955 1056; Hat Sai Khao; mains 50-200B; ☽ 6am-midnight) Throbs from dawn until…well…midnight, whipping up a massive variety of dishes from around the globe and serving them on a wooden terrace overlooking the sea. If it's all about bums on seats, this place wins hands down.

Invita (☎ 0 3955 1326; Hat Sai Khao; mains 60-250B; ☽ 11am-11pm) Bring out your giant pepper grinders, this air-con Italian offers wood-fired pizza good enough to get even Mamma heading east. If you'd rather eat on the beach, they also deliver to the Hat Sai Khao area.

There is another concentration of decent eateries – this time specialising in seafood – along the pier in Ban Bang Bao.

Chow Lay Seafood (Ban Bang Bao; mains 90-200B; ☽ noon-10pm) The tanks of live crab and fish out front say it all: pick what you want, watch it cooked and then wash it down with a drink and sleepy views across the ocean.

Ruan Thai (☎ 0 1489 5081; Ban Bang Bao; mains 90-190B; ☽ noon-10pm) Giant, juicy prawns top the billing in this rustic place. The restaurant's manifesto waxes lyrical about great ingredients cooked simply and the cooking proves its point.

The Bay (☎ 0 1773 4860; Ban Bang Bao; mains 60-200B; ☽ 11am-11pm) Rather hipper than the Bang Bao regulars, this Western-oriented place plays VH1 on the TV, whips up a great selection of juices and shakes and focuses on fresh, fragrant Thai cooking.

Getting There & Away
KO CHANG

Laem Ngop is the main jumping-off point for Ko Chang and the neighbouring islands. Regular *sǎwngthǎew* (20B, 20 minutes) link the port – and nearby piers – with Trat.

A number of ferries make the crossing to Ko Chang from the Laem Ngop area. From the main pier in Laem Ngop itself, **passenger ferries** (one way 50B, one hour) leave for Tha Dan Kao hourly (every two hours June to September) between 9am and 5pm.

The **Centrepoint Car Ferry** (☎ 0 3953 8196) departs hourly between 6am and 6pm from a pier two kilometres west of Laem Ngop and also sails for Tha Dan Kao. One-way tickets for passengers/cars cost 30/80B (prices sometimes increase during the high season) and the crossing takes about 45 minutes. A regular, wooden **backpacker ferry** also sails from here (one way 30B, one hour) during daylight hours and leaves when it's full.

Ko Chang Car Ferry (☎ 0 3952 8288) runs hourly from 7am until 6pm between Ao Thammachat (another 4km west of Centrepoint) and Ao Sapparot. Tickets cost the same as the Centrepoint ferry.

Sǎwngthǎew meet passengers from the ferries and shuttle them to the island's various beaches – or to Trat if you are travelling the other way.

KO MAK & KO KHAM

From November to May, a daily **ferry** (180B, three hours) to Ko Mak, via the nearby Ko Kham, leaves from the pier in Laem Ngop at 3pm, with an additional service departing at 8.30am on Friday, Saturday and Monday. The daily service returns from Ko Mak at 8am, while the additional service returns to Laem Ngop on Friday, Sunday and Thursday at 2pm. During the rainy season, services are slashed and may be cancelled altogether during poor weather.

From October to May, you can also reach Ko Mak and Ko Kham from Ban Bang Bao on Ko Chang. **Island Hopper** (☎ 0 1865 0610) ferries leave from the Bang Bao pier at 9am daily, returning from Ko Mak at 2pm. They cost 300B one way and take two hours.

If you reserve a package at one of the island's bigger resorts, transport from Laem Ngop will be included.

KO KUT

Ko Kut can be something of a headache to get to, although sporadic services do link the island with Laem Ngop and Ban Bang Bao. Rather than risk being stranded, it is always safer to check the latest schedules for Ko Kut with the **TAT office** (☎ 0 3959 7255; 100 Mu 1, Th Trat-Laem Ngop; ☽ 8.30am-4.30pm) in Laem Ngop.

KO WAI

From November to May, a boat leaves Laem Ngop for Ko Wai daily at 3pm (130B, 2½ hours). It returns the next day at approximately 8am. The Island Hopper service from Ban Bang Bao (see opposite) also stops at Ko Wai (200B, 45 minutes).

Getting Around

BOAT

Charter trips to nearby islands average 500B to 800B for a half-day, or 1000B to 2000B all day, depending on the boat and distances covered. Ensure that the charter includes everything and that there are no 'hidden expenses'. At the southern end of the island, you can charter a long-tail boat or fishing boat between Hat Kaibae and Bang Bao for 1000B, or around 150B per person if shared by a boatful of passengers.

MOTORCYCLE

Bungalow operators along the west coast charge as little as 140B per day for a motorcycle during the low season; expect to pay 300B from November to May. Ko Chang's winding roads claim several tourists a year though – take special care!

SĀWNGTHĀEW

The *sǎwngthǎew* meeting the boats at Tha Dan Kao and Ao Sapparot charge 30B per person to Hat Sai Khao, Hat Kaibae and Ban Khlong Prao on the west coast. Between Tha Dan Kao and Ban Salak Phet, the local price is only 30B per person, although tourists may be charged more.

PRACHINBURI & SA KAEW PROVINCES

The largely rural provinces of Prachinburi and Sa Kaew are peppered with many small Dvaravati and Khmer ruins. The latter province's name means 'Jewel Pool', a reference to various Mon-Khmer reservoirs in the area. Little more than loose collections of laterite blocks, most will be of little interest to the casual visitor. The provincial capitals and larger towns lie next to the banks of Mae Nam Prachin – now paralleled by the eastern railway line and Hwy 33 – in the midst of a rice-growing region crossed by canals. The eastern districts of Prachinburi, centred around Amphoe Sa Kaew, attained separate provincial status in January 1994.

NATIONAL PARKS

To the north of Prachinburi, Rte 3077 leads to Khao Yai National Park (p448). North and northeast of Kabinburi, the length of the southern escarpment of the Khorat Plateau, are the contiguous Thap Lan and Pang Sida National Parks.

At 2235 sq km, the **Thap Lan National Park** (☎ 0 3721 9408; reserve@dnp.go.th; 200B; ⊗ 8am-5pm) is Thailand's second-largest national park and, in celebration of Queen Sirikit's 72nd birthday, is now part of her Dong Phayayen Khao Yai Forest Complex. Well known as a habitat for the abundant *tôn laan* (talipot palm), which was once used for Buddhist manuscripts, the park is also home to elephants, tigers, gaur, sambar, barking deer, palm civets, hornbills and gibbons. It is also hoped that the kouprey, a very rare species of primitive cattle, still lives here, although it has been more than 30 years since the last official sighting. Although illegal logging has taken its toll on the park in recent years, restorative tree-planting programmes have finally started to redress the imbalance.

Facilities in the park are minimal; anyone wanting to explore the interior should contact the rangers at **park headquarters** (☎ 0 3721 9408) in Thap Lan village. The rangers can arrange for a tour of the park and provide camping permits (50B per person). There are three six-bed bungalows (1800B) – book through the email address above.

There is no public transport to the park entrance, which is around 32km north of Kabinburi via Rte 304 (the road to Nakhon Ratchasima).

Approximately 30km southeast of Thap Lan close to Sa Kaew, **Pang Sida National Park** (☎ 0 3724 6100; reserve@dnp.co.th; 200B; ⊗ 8am-5pm) is smaller but hillier than Thap Lan. Streams that flow through the park form several scenic waterfalls, including **Nam Tok Pang Sida** and **Nam Tok Na Pha Yai** near the park headquarters, and the more difficult to reach **Suan Man Suan Thong** and **Nam Tok Daeng Makha**.

SA MORAKOT & SA KAEW

สระมรกต/สระแก้ว

Southeast of Prachinburi provincial capital via Rtes 319 and 3070, in the village of Ban Sa Khoi (between Khok Pip and Sa Maha Pho on Rte 3070), is the Angkor-period **Sa Morakot** (admission free; ⊗ daylight hours). Thai for 'Emerald Pool', this was an important Khmer reservoir during the reign of Angkor's Jayavarman VII. Original laterite-block sluices next to the dam, along with assorted *sěmaa* (boundary stones), *naga* sculptures, pedestals and a sandstone lingam, can still be seen here.

Water from this reservoir is considered sacred and has been used in Thai coronation ceremonies.

Sa Kaew (Jewel Pool; admission free; ☼ daylight hours), another historic reservoir site, is just south of Khok Pip off Rte 3070. This one features a Dvaravati-period laterite quarry with some surviving bas-relief on the walls.

There are a number of other Dvaravati and Angkor laterite foundations in the area.

ARANYA PRATHET
อรัญประเทศ

pop 57,000

The border town of Aranya Prathet (aka Aran) has long been a magnet for refugees fleeing the more turbulent chapters of Cambodia's roller-coaster 20th century, with displaced Cambodians flooding into the area following both the Khmer Rouge takeover of 1975 and the subsequent Vietnamese invasion of 1979. Even as late as 1998, random skirmishes between Khmer Rouge guerrillas and the Phnom Penh government continued to send Cambodian citizens scurrying over the border. With the Khmer Rouge gone, the area is now considered safe and the border between Aranya Prathet and the Cambodian town of Poipet is fully open to all visitors. A Cambodian visa on arrival (US$20 plus one passport photo) is usually available at the border between 7am and 5pm, but you should check with the Cambodian embassy in Bangkok before heading out there. Some tourists have complained about border officials demanding bribes – most will back down if you question them politely.

A crackdown on gambling in Phnom Penh has caused a glut of casinos to be built in Poipet. Most cater to Thais from Bangkok, but former Khmer Rouge bigwigs have also been known to enjoy a flutter. The staggering contrast between the visiting high rollers and the dirt-poor locals has created sights that are not easily forgotten.

Parts of this area are still heavily mined – do not stray from marked roads and paths.

Sights

The large market of **Talat Rong Kleua**, at the northern edge of town, attracts a rag-tag crowd of Cambodians who sell gems, textiles, basketry, brass and other handicrafts to the Thais. It's a fascinating spot to visit just to observe the steady stream of Cambodians crossing the border with huge hand-pulled carts piled high with market goods. Rickety rickshaws made of wood and bicycle tyres transport up to six passengers at a time between the market and the border crossing. There are several simple restaurants serving Thai food in the market.

Sleeping

Aran Mermed Hotel (☎ 0 3722 3655; fax 0 3722 3665; 33 Th Tanawithi; r/ste 1200/2500B; ⌘) If you've just broken the bank in Poipet, this is where you'll stay on your way back through Thailand. It's not the flashest of places, but it's the best you'll get out here, with large air-con rooms and decent facilities.

Aran Garden 2 (☎ 0 3723 1070; fax 0 3723 1905; 110 Th Rat Uthit; r 200-400B; ⌘) If the gambling gods haven't smiled on you, this is a decent budget bet, with comfy fan rooms and slightly more salubrious air-con offerings.

There are plenty of **food stalls** around Talat Rong Kleua.

Getting There & Away

Ordinary buses from Bangkok's Northern and Northeastern bus station to Aranya Prathet (112B, five hours) leave on an hourly basis from 5.30am to 4.30pm; air-con buses (200B; 4¼ hours) leave hourly from 5.30am to 10.30am and from noon to 5pm.

If you are using your own vehicle you can also reach Aranya Prathet travelling from Chanthaburi Province to the south via Rte 317, or from Buriram Province to the north via Rte 3068.

BORDER CROSSING (CAMBODIA)

A *túk-túk* from Aranya Prathet to the border crossing costs 50B.

From Poipet on the Cambodian side you can take a pick-up truck to Siem Reap, for Angkor Wat, or to Sisophon. From Sisophon you can ride another pick-up to Battambang, and from there it's possible to catch a train all the way to Phnom Penh. See Lonely Planet's *Cambodia* guidebook for more information.

Chiang Mai Province

Chiang Mai straddles the most important historical crossroads of northern Southeast Asia, a fertile region of mountains, valleys and rivers where peoples from China, Laos, Myanmar (Burma) and Thailand have long traded goods and ideas in a fusion of cultures. This blend has been further enlivened by the presence of tribal societies – such as the Hmong-Mien, Thai Lü and Phuan – whose ethnic heritage knows no fixed political boundaries.

In past centuries Chiang Mai served as an entrepôt for flourishing caravan trade in opium, silks and timber. Today it remains northern Thailand's principal hub for tourism, education, agriculture and cross-border commerce between Thailand, Laos and Myanmar.

Outside of the provincial capital, Chiang Mai Province boasts more natural forest cover than any other province in the north. Cycling, hiking, bird-watching and river rafting attract those interested in northern Thailand's natural surrounds, while visitors keen on learning more about the region's ethnic minorities can visit semiremote villages on mountain slopes.

The three highest mountain peaks in Thailand are all found in Chiang Mai Province: Doi Inthanon (2595m), Doi Phahom Pok (2285m) and Doi Chiang Dao (2195m).

HIGHLIGHTS

- Tasting serenity in the brick-lined meditation tunnels of **Wat U Mong** (p287)
- Scaling the limestone cliffs of **Crazy Horse Buttress** (p290), Tham Meuang On
- Hiking the forest trails of Thailand's highest peak, **Doi Inthanon** (p321)
- Visiting the **Chiang Mai Night Bazaar** (p285) and surveying the ultimate souvenir stand
- Enjoying a **traditional Thai massage** (p290) or enrolling in a course to become a thumb master yourself

CHIANG MAI PROVINCE

Climate

Chiang Mai Province has much the same climate as adjacent provinces in the north. Most visitors will find the weather is most enjoyable from November through mid-February, when temperatures are mild and rain is scarce.

During the cool season (December to February), temperatures can warrant a jacket or pullover at night, particularly at higher elevations.

From February until the monsoon season begins in June, a thick haze often forms over the city, a combination of dust and smoke from the burning off of rice fields near the city. The hot season (March to May) can be brutal in Chiang Mai, although temperatures don't burst the thermometer as much as they do in Lampang or in northeastern Thailand. You'll find some relief from heat (and to a lesser extent, the smoke) at the cooler elevations of Chiang Dao and Doi Inthanon, or anywhere else where you can get above the Mae Ping plains.

The annual monsoons are generally lighter in Chiang Mai than in central or southern Thailand, lasting from June to October in Chiang Mai, rarely into November. Chiang Mai city can flood when rains are unusually heavy.

Language

Around 80% of the people living in Chiang Mai Province are native to the area, belonging to an ethnic group once known as Yuan or Yün, or less frequently Phayap. Nowadays many Chiang Mai residents consider these to be pejorative names and they prefer the term *khon meuang* (people of the Tai principality).

Most non-hill-tribe people speak Northern Thai as their first language. Northern Thai – or *kham meuang* (speech of the Tai principality) – is very similar to Standard Thai, as spoken in Central Thailand, and with a mutual intelligibility rated at greater than 70%.

Standard Thai is taught in local schools and is the official language of all government agencies. Thus most educated Chiang Mai residents can speak Standard Thai, and will usually do so automatically with anyone from outside the region.

Northern Thai has its own script, based on a half-millennium-old Mon script that

was originally used only for Buddhist scripture. The script became so popular during the Lanna period that it was exported for use by the Thai Lü in China, the Khün in the eastern Shan State and other Thai-Kadai–speaking groups living between Lanna and China. Although few northerners nowadays can read the Northern Thai script – often referred to as 'Lanna script' – it is occasionally used in signage to add a Northern Thai cultural flavour. The script is especially common for use on signs at the entrance gates of Chiang Mai monasteries, although the name of the wat (temple) will also be written in Thai (and occasionally Roman) script.

Very few outsiders bother to learn Northern Thai, since Standard Thai is so widely spoken. Unless you have a very keen interest in learning the Northern dialect, it's best to stick to Standard Thai, as many Northerners seem to take offence when outsiders try speaking *kham meuang* to them. This attitude dates back to a time, perhaps no more than 25 or 30 years ago, when Central Thais considered Northerners to be very backward, and thus made fun of their language.

The Language chapter (p771) covers only the Standard Thai dialect. If you're interested in learning *kham meuang,* the only generally available book is *Lanna Language* by Kobkan Thangpijaigul. All materials are written out in Lanna script, International Phonetic Alphabet (IPA), English translation and Thai translation. It's mostly intended for people who are already fluent, or very familiar with, Central Thai. An optional 90-minute cassette tape is also available to go with the text.

Getting There & Away

Chiang Mai International Airport fields dozens of daily flights from Bangkok, as well as less frequent flights from Phuket and various other cities in Thailand. There are also international connections with cities in Myanmar, China and Laos.

Chiang Mai serves the main road transport hub for all of northern Thailand, with virtually every town and village linked to the city by bus or *săwngthăew* (small pickup truck with benches in the back). Most buses to other provinces in the north (as well as elsewhere in Thailand) arrive at and depart from the Chiang Mai Arcade (New) bus terminal.

CARAVANS OF NORTHERN THAILAND

Dating from at least the 15th century, Chinese-Muslim caravans from Yunnan Province (China) used Chiang Mai as a 'back-door' entry and exit for commodities transported between China and the Indian Ocean port of Mawlamyaing (Moulmein) in Myanmar (Burma) for international seagoing trade.

British merchant Ralph Fitch, the first person to leave an English-language chronicle of Southeast Asian travel, wrote of his 1583 to 1591 journey through Thailand: 'To the town of Jamahey (Chiang Mai) come many merchants out of China, and bring a great store of Muske, Gold, Silver, and many other things of China worke.'

The principal means of transport for the Yunnanese caravaneers were ponies and mules, beasts of burden that were in contrast with the Southeast Asian preference for oxen, water buffalo and elephants. The Chinese Muslims who dominated the caravan traffic owed their preferred mode of conveyance, as well as their religious orientation, to mass conversions effected during the Mongol invasions of Yunnan in the 13th century. The equestrian nature of the caravans led the Thais to call the Yunnanese *jiin haw* (galloping Chinese).

Three main routes emanated from the predominantly Thai Xishuangbanna (Sipsongpanna) region in southern Yunnan into northern Thailand, and onward to the Gulf of Martaban via Mawlamyaing. The western route proceeded southwest from Simao to Chiang Rung (now known as Jinghong), then went on through Chiang Tung (Kengtung) to Fang or Chiang Rai.

The middle route went south to Mengla near the border of China and Laos, crossed Laos via Luang Nam Tha, and entered Thailand at Chiang Khong (which was an independent principality at the time) on the Mekong River. At this point the middle route merged with the western route at Chiang Rai Province, and formed a single route through Chiang Mai to Mae Sariang, a line that continued along the Salawin River to Mawlamyaing in present-day Myanmar.

The third route went from Simao to Phongsali in northern Laos then via Luang Prabang (Laos), crossing the Mekong River to Nan and Phrae before curving northwestward via Lampang and Lamphun to Chiang Mai.

Principal southward exports along these routes included silk, opium, tea, dried fruit, lacquerware, musk, ponies and mules, while northward the caravans brought gold, copper, cotton, edible birds' nests, betel nut, tobacco and ivory. By the end of the 19th century many artisans from China, northern Burma and Laos had settled in the area to produce crafts for the steady flow of regional trade. The city's original transhipment point for such trade movements was a market district known as Ban Haw, a stone's throw from today's Night Bazaar in Chiang Mai.

CARAVAN ROUTES

The State Railway of Thailand's northern line terminates in Chiang Mai, and many travellers arrive by overnight train from Bangkok.

Getting Around

Buses and *săwngthăew* run frequently to towns and villages around Chiang Mai Province from Chiang Mai's Chang Pheuak bus terminal. Cars, 4WD vehicles, pick-up trucks and motorcycles are easily rented in Chiang Mai for excursions around the province.

CHIANG MAI

เชียงใหม่

pop 170,300

One of the many questions Thais may ask a foreigner visiting Thailand is 'Have you been to Chiang Mai yet?', underscoring the feeling that Chiang Mai is a keystone of any journey to Thailand. Along with Sukhothai further south, it was the first Southeast Asian state to make the historic transition from domination by Mon and Khmer cultures to a new era ruled by Thais. Although Thais idealise their beloved northern capital as a quaint, moated and walled city surrounded by mountains with legendary, mystical attributes, the truth is Chiang Mai has all but left that image behind to become a modern, cosmopolitan city exhibiting many of the hallmarks of contemporary world culture and technology.

More than 700km northwest of Bangkok, Chiang Mai has in excess of 300 temples (121 within the *thêtsàbaan* or municipal limits) – almost as many as are in Bangkok – a circumstance that makes the old city centre visually striking. Auspicious Doi Suthep rises 1676m above the city to the west, providing an ever-present reminder that this fast-developing centre is mountain-bound.

Many visitors stay in Chiang Mai longer than planned because of the high quality and low price of accommodation, food and shopping; the cool nights (compared with central Thailand); the international feel of the city; and the friendliness of the people. With the increasing number of cultural and spiritual learning experiences available to visitors in Chiang Mai these days – Thai language, Thai massage, Thai cooking, yoga and Vipassana

(insight meditation) – Chiang Mai has become much more than just a quick stop on the northern Thailand tourist circuit.

Conservation measures include a ban on high-rise construction within 93m of a temple, Mae Nam Ping (Ping River) and city walls/moats, thereby protecting about 87% of all land within municipal limits. Designed to halt any future condo developments along Mae Nam Ping in order to preserve the city's skyline, this law has for the most part been very effective. Corruption prevents full implementation, however, and every few years a huge multistorey building opens within illegal proximity of the river, the city moat or a historic temple.

On the brighter side, Chiang Mai has the most comprehensive municipal recycling programme in the country; there are recycling bins on roadsides around the town that accept glass, plastic and paper.

The best time of year to visit Chiang Mai is between July and March, when the weather is relatively pleasant, the air is clearest and the surrounding hills are green. From April to June it is hot and dry, and a haze tends to collect in the air over the surrounding valley. September is the rainiest month, although even then there are clear days.

HISTORY

Thai king Phaya Mengrai (also spelt Mangrai), originally from the Mekong riverside principality of Ngoen Yang (which is present-day Chiang Saen), established Nopburi Si Nakhon Ping Chiang Mai in 1296 after conquering the Mon kingdom of Hariphunchai (modern Lamphun). Traces of the original 1296 earthen ramparts can still be seen today along Th Kamphaeng Din in Chiang Mai.

Later, in an alliance with Sukhothai in the 14th and 15th centuries, Chiang Mai (New Walled City) became a part of the larger kingdom of Lan Na Thai (Million Thai Rice Fields), which extended as far south as Kamphaeng Phet and as far north as Luang Prabang in Laos. During this period Chiang Mai became an important religious and cultural centre – the eighth world synod of Theravada Buddhism was held here in 1477.

The Burmese capture of the city in 1556 was the second time the Burmese had control of Chiang Mai Province. Before Phaya Mengrai's reign, King Anawrahta of Pagan (present-day Bagan) had ruled Chiang Mai Province in the 11th century. This time around, the Burmese ruled Chiang Mai for more than 200 years.

In 1775 Chiang Mai was recaptured by the Thais under Phaya Taksin, who appointed Chao Kavila, a *jâo meuang* (chieftain) from nearby Lampang principality, as viceroy of northern Thailand. In 1800 Kavila built the monumental brick walls around the inner city, and expanded the city in southerly and easterly directions, establishing a river port at the end of what is today Th Tha Phae (*thâa phae* means 'raft pier').

Under Kavila, Chiang Mai became an important regional trade centre. Many of the later Shan- and Burmese-style temples seen around the city were built by wealthy teak merchants who emigrated from Burma during the late 19th century. Not all the Shan residents were merchants, however. In 1902 several hundred labourers, most of them Shan, protested against the practice of corvée (involuntary service to the state) by refusing to construct roads or otherwise follow government orders. The ensuing skirmishes between corvée labourers and Chiang Mai troops – dubbed the Shan Rebellion by historians – didn't resolve the issue until the custom was discontinued in 1924.

The completion of the northern railway to Chiang Mai in 1921 finally linked the north with central Thailand. In 1927 King Rama VII and Queen Rambaibani rode into the city at the head of an 84-elephant caravan, becoming the first central Thai monarchs to visit the north, and in 1933 Chiang Mai officially became a province of Siam.

Long before tourists began visiting the region, Chiang Mai was an important centre for handcrafted pottery, umbrellas, weaving, silverwork and woodcarving. By the mid-1960s tourism had replaced commercial trade as Chiang Mai's number one source of outside revenue.

After Chiang Mai born-and-raised politician Thaksin Shinawatra became Thailand's prime minister in 2001, the city found itself the focus of a Thaksin-initiated development drive. The premier has vowed to make Chiang Mai one of the nation's primary centres of information technology, expand the airport, build more superhighways and double the size and wealth of the city within five years. Many local residents have reacted

with dismay to these proclamations, and have organised a vocal movement to counter runaway growth and preserve quality of life. Whether the slow-growth proponents will win the battle remains to be seen.

Meanwhile, the number of air-passenger arrivals into Chiang Mai has more than doubled since Thaksin took office, and a slough of new five-star hotels is under construction in and around the city.

ORIENTATION

The old city of Chiang Mai is a neat square bounded by moats and partial walls. Thanon Moon Muang, along the eastern moat, is the centre for cheap accommodation and eateries. Thanon Tha Phae runs east from the middle of this side and crosses Mae Nam Ping, changing into Th Charoen Muang.

The train station and the main post office are further down Th Charoen Muang, a fair distance from the city centre. There are two intercity bus terminals in Chiang Mai, one near Pratu Chang Pheuak (White Elephant Gate; Map pp282–4) and a larger one called Chiang Mai Arcade (Map pp278–80).

Several of Chiang Mai's important temples are within the moat area, but there are others to the north and west. Doi Suthep rises up to the west of the city and its temples give you a fine view over the city.

Maps

Navigating around Chiang Mai is pretty simple, although a copy of Nancy Chandler's *Map of Chiang Mai*, available in bookshops, is a worthwhile 150B investment. It shows the main points of interest, shopping venues and oddities that you would be most unlikely to stumble upon by yourself. *Groovy Map Chiang Mai Map'n'Guide*, also in bookshops, adds Thai script and more nightspots.

The Tourism Authority of Thailand (TAT) puts out a sketchy city map that is free and available from the TAT office on Th Chiang Mai–Lamphun. Several other ad-laden giveaway maps are also available in tourist shops and restaurants.

INFORMATION
Bookshops

Backstreet Bookshop (Map pp282–4; 7/8 Th Chang Moi Kao) Selection of used paperbacks in English, French and German, as well as hardcovers.

CHIANG MAI

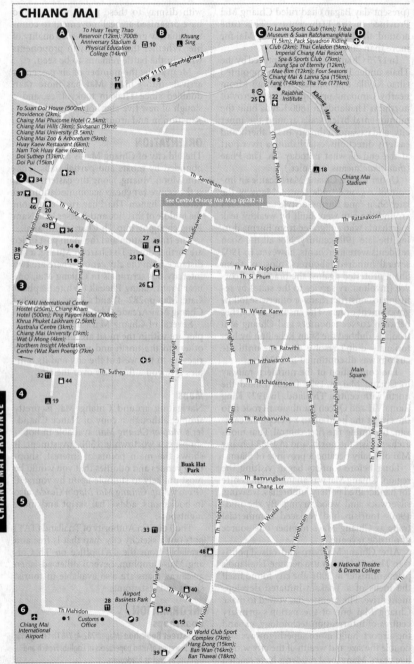

CHIANG MAI PROVINCE

To Huay Teung Thao Reservoir (12km); 700th Anniversary Stadium & Physical Education College (14km)

Khuang Sing

To Lanna Sports Club (1km); Tribal Museum & Suan Ratchamangkhala (1.5km); Pack Squadron Riding Club (2km); Thai Celadon (5km); Imperial Chiang Mai Resort, Spa & Sports Club (7km); Jirung Spa of Eternity (12km); Mae Rim (12km); Four Seasons Chiang Mai & Lanna Spa (15km); Fang (148km); Tha Ton (171km)

Hwy 11 (Th Superhighway)

To Suan Dol House (500m); Providence (2km); Chaing Mai Phucome Hotel (2.5km); Chiang Mai Hills (3km); Sudsanan (3km); Chiang Mai University (3.5km); Chiang Mai Zoo & Arboretum (5km); Huay Kaew Restaurant (6km); Nam Tok Huay Kaew (6km); Doi Suthep (13km); Doi Pui (15km)

Rajabhat Institute

Chiang Mai Stadium

Th Santitham

Th Chang Pheuak

See Central Chiang Mai Map (pp282–3)

Th Huay Kaew

Th Nimmanhaemin

Soi 1

Soi 9

Th Srimankhalajan

To CMU International Center Hostel (250m); Chiang Kham Hotel (500m); Ping Payom Hotel (700m); Khrua Phuket Laikhram (2.5km); Australia Centre (3km); Chiang Mai University (3km); Wat U Mong (4km); Northern Insight Meditation Centre (Wat Ram Poeng) (7km)

Th Hussdisawee

Th Ratanakosin

Th Sanan Kla

Th Mani Nopharat

Th Si Phum

Th Wiang Kaew

Th Chaiyaphum

Th Bunreuangrit

Th Arak

Th Singharat

Th Ratwithi

Th Inthawarorot

Th Ratchadamnoen

Th Phra Pokklao

Th Ratchaphakhinai

Main Square

Th Suthep

Th Samlan

Th Ratchamankha

Th Moon Muang

Th Kotchasan

Buak Hat Park

Th Bamrungburi

Th Chang Lor

Th Thiphanet

Th Wualai

Th Nontharam

Th Bunreuangrit

Th Sumwong

National Theatre & Drama College

Chiang Mai International Airport

Th Mahidon

Customs Office

Airport Business Park

Th Om Muang

Th Hai Ya

Th Wualai

To World Club Sport Complex (7km); Hang Dong (15km); Ban Wan (16km); Ban Thawai (18km)

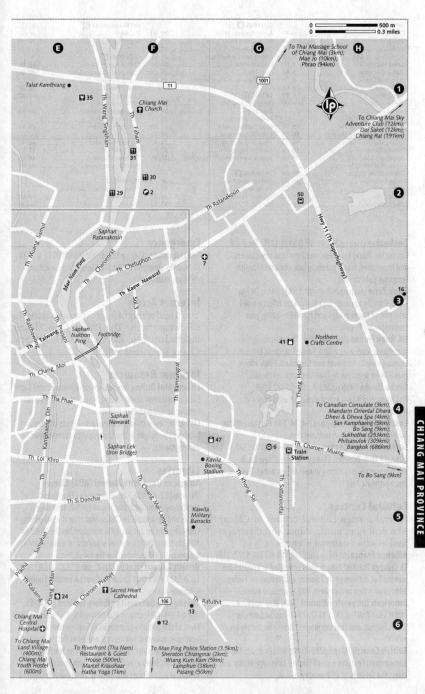

Bookazine (Map pp282-4; ☎ 0 5328 1370; Ground fl, Chiang Inn Plaza) European and American newspapers and magazines, travel guides, maps and other English-language publications.

Book Zone (Map pp282-4; ☎ 0 5325 2418; Th Tha Phae) Directly opposite Wat Mahawan; offers a good selection of travel guides and travel literature, plus contemporary fiction.

DK Book House (Map pp282-4; Th Kotchasan) Warehouse-like store with a limited range of English-language books on travel and Southeast Asian affairs, plus a large selection of Thai-language textbooks.

Gecko Books (Map pp282-4; ☎ 0 5387 4066; Th Chiang Moi Kao) Largest choice of used books in the city.

Lost Book Shop (Map pp282-4; 34/3 Th Ratchamankha) Small used bookshop, good selection.

Suriwong Book Centre (Map pp282-4; ☎ 0 5328 1052; 54 Th Si Donchai) Chiang Mai's best new book selection, especially strong in non-fiction about Thailand and Southeast Asia.

Cultural Centres

Several foreign cultural centres in Chiang Mai host film, music, dance and theatre, as well as other cultural events.

Alliance Française (Map pp282-4; ☎ 0 5327 5277; 138 Th Charoen Prathet) French films (subtitled in English) are screened at 4.30pm every Tuesday and at 8pm on Friday; admission is free to members, 30B to general public.

American University Alumni (AUA; Map pp282-4; ☎ 0 5327 8407, 0 5321 1377; 73 Th Ratchadamnoen) Offers English and Thai language courses (for details see p291).

British Council (Map pp282-4; ☎ 0 5324 2103; 198 Th Bamrungrat) Features a small English-language library and offers the services of an honorary consul.

Emergency

Tourist police (Map pp282-4; ☎ 0 5324 8130, 0 5324 8974, 24hr emergency 1155; Th Chiang Mai-Lamphun; ⏱ 6am-midnight)

Internet Access

You'll find plenty of Internet centres along the following streets: Tha Phae, Moon Muang, Ratchadamnoen, Ratchadamri, Huay Kaew, Chang Khlan and Suthep.

Internet Resources

Chiang Mai Online (www.chiangmai-online.com) Some basic information about Chiang Mai, along with comprehensive accommodation listings.

City Life (www.chiangmainews.com) Posts articles on local events, culture and art, along with current news developments.

Libraries

American University Alumni (AUA) Library (Map pp282-4; 24 Th Ratchadamnoen) The second most comprehensive collection of English-language books and periodicals in Chiang Mai after the university. Entry requires an annual 400B membership fee (100B for AUA students, 200B for other students) or a one-month temporary 150B membership fee for visitors.

British Council (Map pp282-4; ☎ 0 5324 2103; fax 0 5324 4781; 198 Th Bamrungrat) A smaller English-language library.

Chiang Mai University Library (off Map pp278-80; ☎ 0 5394 4531; Chiang Mai University, Th Huay Kaew) Most of the 200,000-plus books in English here are academic-oriented, but there is plenty of fiction and lighter reading as well. Visitors are welcome. The Northern Thai Information Service, on the library's 4th floor, archives historical publications and other printed material related

Silk-weaving loom, Chiang Mai (p311)

Elephant, Chiang Mai Province (p318)

Hill tribe woman and child, Chiang Mai (p289)

Young monks collecting alms, Chiang Mai (p285)

Traditional handicrafts (p307), Chiang Mai

TOM COCKREM

Ornate door at Wat Phra That Doi Suthep (p316), just outside Chiang Mai

GEOFF STRINGER

Young monk reading, Chiang Mai (p285)

BILL WA

to northern Thailand's 17 provinces and their culturally similar neighbours: the Shan State in Myanmar, Yunnan Province in southwest China and northern Laos. Artefacts on display include 500-year-old Thai Buddhist palm-leaf manuscripts.

Media

Chiangmai Mail Weekly newspaper; good source of local news.

City Life Oriented as much towards residents as tourists, with articles on local culture and politics, as well as listings of local events.

Medical Services

At most hospitals in Chiang Mai, many of the doctors speak English.

Chiang Mai Ram Hospital (Map pp282-4; ☎ 0 5322 4861; Th Bunreuangrit) The most modern hospital in town, with higher-than-average prices.

Chip Aun Thong Dispensary (Map pp282-4; ☎ 0 5323 4187; 48-52 Th Chang Moi) Traditional Chinese medicine, Chinese doctor on staff.

Lanna Hospital (Map pp278-80; ☎ 0 5335 7234; Th Superhighway) One of the better hospitals in town, less expensive than Chiang Mai Ram.

Maharaj Hospital (Map pp278-80; ☎ 0 5322 1310; Faculty of Medicine, Th Suthep)

Malaria Centre (Map pp282-4; ☎ 0 5322 1529; 18 Th Bunreuangrit) Does blood checks for malaria at no charge.

McCormick Hospital (Map pp278-80; ☎ 0 5326 2200; Th Kaew Nawarat) Former missionary hospital, good for minor treatment, and inexpensive.

Mungkala (Map pp282-4; ☎ 0 5327 8494, 0 5320 8431; mungkala@cm.ksc.co.th; 21-25 Th Ratchamankha) Traditional Chinese clinic offering acupuncture, massage and herbal therapy.

Money

All major Thai banks have several branches throughout Chiang Mai, many of them along Th Tha Phae; most are open 8.30am to 3.30pm. In the well-touristed areas – for example, the Chiang Mai Night Bazaar, Th Tha Phae and Th Moon Muang – you'll find ATMs and bank-operated foreign-exchange booths open as late as 8pm.

SK Moneychanger (Map pp282-4; ☎ 0 5327 1864; 73/8 Th Charoen Prathet; ⏱ 8am-6pm Mon-Sat) Private agency specialising in cash exchanges in several currencies (travellers cheques are also accepted) – usually at better rates than the banks.

Western Union (Map pp278-80; ☎ 0 5322 4979; Central department store, Kad Suan Kaew Shopping Centre, Th Huay Kaew) Also at any post office; send or receive money by wire.

Post

Mail Boxes Etc (MBE; Map pp282-4; ☎ 0 5381 8433; Th Chang Khlan) Conveniently located on the same street as the Chiang Mai Night Bazaar, MBE offers the usual private mail services, including rental boxes, mailing supplies, packing services, stationery and a courier service.

Main post office (Map pp278-80; ☎ 0 5324 1070; Th Charoen Muang) Other useful branch post offices are at Th Singarat/Samlan, Th Mahidon at Chiang Mai International Airport, Th Charoen Prathet, Th Phra Pokklao, Th Chotana and Chiang Mai University.

Telephone

Many Internet cafés are able to arrange inexpensive Internet phone hook-ups.

Communcations Authority of Thailand (CAT; Map pp278-80; ☎ 0 5324 1070; Th Charoen Muang; ⏱ 7am-10pm) Behind the main post office.

Home Country Direct Phones Chiang Inn Plaza (Map pp278-80; 100/1 Th Chang Khlan); Chiang Mai International Airport (Map pp278-80); Main post office (Map pp278-80; Th Charoen Muang); Thai Airways International (THAI; Map pp282-4; 240 Th Phra Pokklao); TAT (Map pp282-4; Th Chiang Mai-Lamphun) Easy one-button connection to foreign operators in a number of countries around the world.

Tourist Information

TAT (Map pp282-4; ☎ 0 5324 8604; Th Chiang Mai-Lamphun; ⏱ 8am-4.30pm) Friendly English-speaking staff can answer questions, and there are racks filled with free maps and brochures.

DANGERS & ANNOYANCES

Upon arrival in Chiang Mai by bus or train, most waiting *săwngthăew* and *túk-túk* (motorised pedicab) drivers will try to get you to a particular hotel or guesthouse so that they can collect a commission. Since the better guesthouses refuse to pay any commissions, this means if you follow the driver's lead you may end up at a place with less appealing conditions or an out-of-the-way location. A handful of guesthouses now maintain their own free shuttle services from the train station. At any rate if you call a guesthouse from the bus or train station, staff will be delighted to arrange a ride to avoid paying such exorbitant commissions.

Beware bus or minivan services from Th Khao San in Bangkok, which often advertise a free night's accommodation in Chiang Mai if you buy a Bangkok–Chiang Mai ticket. What usually happens on arrival is that the 'free' guesthouse demands you sign up for one of the hill treks immediately; if

CENTRAL CHIANG MAI

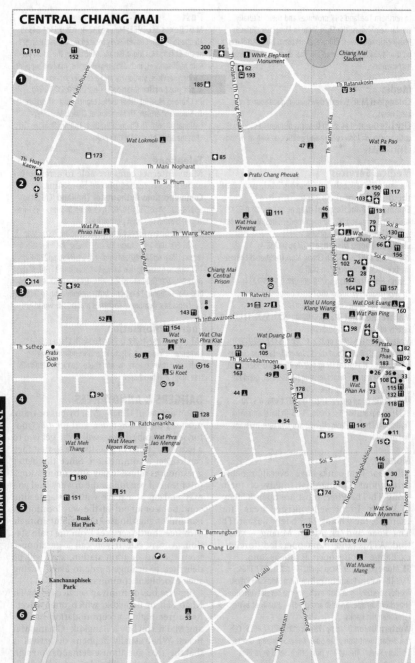

CHIANG MAI PROVINCE

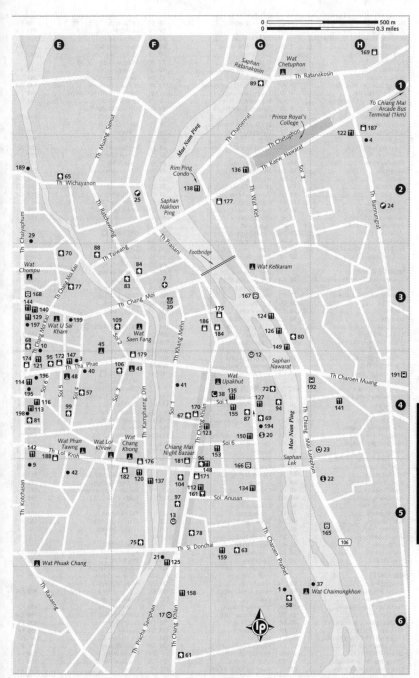

CHIANG MAI PROVINCE

you don't, the guesthouse is suddenly 'full'. Sometimes they levy a charge for electricity or hot water. The better guesthouses don't play this game. Theft is more of a risk on the Th Khao San buses than on legitimate buses that leave from Bangkok's Moh Chit terminal.

Many less expensive guesthouses in Chiang Mai will evict guests who don't engage trekking or tour services through the guesthouse, or who don't eat meals regularly at the guesthouse. We've tried to avoid listing guesthouses where this practice is known to happen, but if in doubt, be sure to ask before checking in whether it's OK to take a room only.

SIGHTS
Chiang Mai Night Bazaar
เชียงใหม่ไนท์บาซาร์
Arguably Chiang Mai's biggest tourist attraction, the **Chiang Mai Night Bazaar** (Map pp282-4; Th Chang Khlan btwn Th Tha Phae & Th Si Donchai; 5pm-11pm), is the modern legacy of the original Yunnanese trading caravans that stopped here along the ancient trade route between Simao (in China) and Mawlamyaing (on Myanmar's Gulf of Martaban coast). Today the market sprawls along Th Chang Khlan between Th Tha Phae and Th Si Donchai every night of the year, rain or dry, holiday or no.

For full details, see p309.

Wat Chiang Man
วัดเชียงมั่น
A stone slab inscription, engraved in 1581 and erected at **Wat Chiang Man** (Map pp282-4; 0 5337 5368; Th Ratchaphakhinai), bears the earliest known reference to the city's 1296 founding. It is thus thought to be the oldest wat in the city, and founded by Phaya Mengrai. The wat features typical northern Thai temple architecture, with massive teak columns inside the *bòt* (central sanctuary; *sǐm* in Northern Thai).

Two important Buddha images are kept in a glass cabinet inside the smaller sanctuary, to the right of the *sǐm*. The Phra Sila, a marble bas-relief Buddha that stands 20cm to 30cm high, is supposed to have come from Sri Lanka or India 2500 years ago, but since no Buddha images were produced anywhere before around 2000 years ago, then it must have arrived later. The well-known

Phra Satang Man, a crystal seated Buddha image, was shuttled back and forth between Thailand and Laos like the Emerald Buddha. It's thought to have come from Lavo (Lopburi) 1800 years ago and stands just 10cm high.

Red-and-gold stencilled murals on the walls of the *sǐm*, which were completed in 1996 to celebrate the 700th anniversary of the founding of the city, depict scenes from the life of Chiang Mai's founding father, Phaya Mengrai.

The chapel housing the venerated images is open between 9am and 5pm. Wat Chiang Man is off Th Ratchaphakhinai in the northeastern corner of the old city.

Wat Phra Singh
วัดพระสิงห์
Chiang Mai's most visited Buddhist temple, **Wat Phra Singh** (Map pp282-4; 0 5381 4164; Th Singarat) owes its fame to the fact that it houses the city's most revered Buddha image, Phra Singh (Lion Buddha). Started by King Pa Yo in 1345, the *wíhǎan* (large hall in a Thai temple) that houses the Phra Singh image was completed between 1385 and 1400. Architecturally it's a perfect example of the classic northern Thai or Lanna style followed during this period from Chiang Mai to Luang Prabang. The Phra Singh Buddha supposedly comes from Sri Lanka, but it is not particularly Sinhalese in style. As it is identical to two images in Nakhon Si Thammarat and Bangkok, and has quite a travel history (Sukhothai, Ayuthaya, Chiang Rai, Luang Prabang – the usual itinerary for a travelling Buddha image, involving much royal trickery), no-one really knows which image is the real one, nor can anyone document its place of origin. The *sǐm* was finished in about 1600.

Wat Phra Singh's main stupa displays classic Lanna style with its octagonal base. Wihan Lai Kham, a small chapel next to the stupa, features sumptuous *laai kham* (gold pattern) stencilling on its interior back wall. The *wíhǎan* is also well known for the narrative mural paintings which run along its main walls and date back to c 1870. The scene on the south wall depicts the popular northern Thai story of a divine golden swan, Phra Suwannahong.

Paintings on the north wall, executed by an ethnic Chinese thought to have trained in Bangkok, display a much higher level of skill. A small figure above one of the windows is thought to be a self-portrait of the artist.

Wat Prasat
วัดปราสาท

Opposite the north side of Wat Phra Singh stands **Wat Prasat** (Map pp282-4; ☎ 0 5381 0188; Th Inthawarorot), one of the oldest unreconstructed temple structures in Chiang Mai. Its multi-tiered roofs and wood-and-plaster walls are characteristic of traditional Lanna-style architecture. Inside, at the far end of the *wíhăan,* some striking *laai kham* designs decorate the walls. Unlike most northern Thai *laai kham,* which tend to be purely decorative or iconic, the gold-stencilled patterns at Wat Prasat narrate episodes from the Buddha's last life.

On the south wall a painting depicts a smiling Buddha passing into *parinibbana* (the entry into *nibbhana* at death, after having reached enlightenment), his disciples grieving around him. On the opposite wall, Prince Siddhartha renounces the world by cutting off his long tresses, while in an adjacent scene he achieves enlightenment under the Bodhi tree. These murals are thought to have been executed around 1900.

Wat Chedi Luang
วัดเจดีย์หลวง

This **temple complex** (Map pp282-4; ☎ 0 5327 8595; main entrance Th Phra Pokklao) encloses a very large and venerable Lanna-style stupa dating from 1441. Now in partial ruins, stories say it was damaged by either a 16th-century earthquake or the cannon fire of King Taksin in 1775 during the recapture of Chiang Mai from the Burmese.

The Phra Kaew ('Emerald' Buddha), now held in Bangkok's Wat Phra Kaew, sat in the eastern niche here in 1475. Today there is a jade replica of the original Phra Kaew sitting in its place, financed by the Thai king and carved in 1995 to celebrate the 600th anniversary of the stupa (according to some reckonings), and the 700th anniversary of the city.

A restoration of the great stupa of the wat, financed by Unesco and the Japanese government, stopped short of creating a new spire, since no-one knows for sure how the original superstructure looked. New Buddha images have been placed in three of the four directional niches.

New porticoes and *naga* (mythical serpent) guardians for the stupa lack the finesse of the originals. On the southern side of the monument, six elephant sculptures in the pediment can be seen. Five are cement restorations; only the one on the far right – without ears and trunk – is original brick and stucco.

The *làk meuang* (guardian deity post) for the city can be seen in a small building to the left of the compound's main entrance.

Wat Jet Yot
วัดเจ็ดยอด

Out of town on the northern highway loop near the National Museum, **Wat Jet Yot** (Map pp278-80; ☎ 0 5321 9483; Hwy 11/Superhighway) was built in the mid-15th century to host the eighth World Buddhist Council in 1477. Based on the design of the Mahabodhi Temple in Bodhgaya, India, the proportions for the Chiang Mai version are quite different from the Indian original; it was probably modelled from a small votive tablet depicting the Mahabodhi in distorted perspective. The seven spires (*jèt yâwt*) represent the seven weeks Buddha was supposed to have spent in Bodhgaya after his enlightenment.

Some of the original stucco relief, depicting Bodhisattva (Buddhist saints, usually associated with Mahayana Buddhism) remains on the outer walls of the old *wíhăan.* There's an adjacent stupa of undetermined age and a very glossy *wíhăan.* The entire area is surrounded by well-kept lawns. It's a pleasant, relaxing temple to visit.

Wat Jet Yot is a bit too far from the city centre to reach on foot; by bicycle it's easy or you can take a red *săwngthăew.*

Wat Phan Tao
วัดพันเถา

Diagonally adjacent to Wat Chedi Luang, **Wat Phan Tao** (Map pp282-4; ☎ 0 5381 4689; Th Phra Pokklao) contains a large, old teak *wíhăan* that is one of the unsung treasures of Chiang Mai. Constructed of moulded wooden teak panels fitted together and supported by 28 gargantuan teak pillars, the *wíhăan* features *naga* bargeboards inset with coloured mirror mosaic. On display inside are old temple bells, some ceramics, a few old northern-style gilded wooden Buddhas and antique cabinets stacked with old palm-leaf manuscripts. Also in the compound are some old monastic quarters.

There's a wall dividing Wat Phan Tao from Wat Chedi Luang, but you can walk through small gates from one to the other.

Wat U Mong
วัดอุโมงค์

This **forest wat** (off Map pp278-80; ☎ 0 5327 3990; Soi Wat U Mong) was first used during Phaya Mengrai's rule in the 14th century. Bricklined tunnels through a large, flat-topped hill were allegedly fashioned around 1380 for the clairvoyant monk Thera Jan. The monastery was abandoned at a later date and wasn't reactivated until a local Thai prince sponsored a restoration in the late 1940s. The since-deceased Ajahn Buddhadasa, a well-known monk and teacher at southern Thailand's Wat Suanmok, sent a number of monks to re-establish a monastic community at U Mong in the 1960s.

One building contains modern artwork by various monks who have resided at U Mong, including several foreigners. A marvellously grisly image of the fasting Buddha – ribs, veins and all – can be seen in the grounds on top of the tunnel hill, along with a very large and highly venerated stupa. Also on the grounds is a small artificial lake, surrounded by *kùtì* (monastic cottages).

A small library/museum with English-language books on Buddhism can be found on the premises. Resident foreign monks give talks in English on Sunday afternoon at 3pm by the lake.

To get to Wat U Mong, travel west on Th Suthep for about 2km and take the signed left; then follow the signs for another kilometre to Wat U Mong.

Note that there is another temple named Wat U Mong in Chiang Mai, a smaller urban version found in the old city. To make sure a *săwngthăew* or *túk-túk* driver understands you want the original, ask for 'Wat U Mong Thera Jan'.

Wat Suan Dok
วัดสวนดอก

Phaya Keu Na, the sixth Lanna king, built this **temple** (Map pp278-80; ☎ 0 5321 8967; Th Suthep) in a forest grove in 1373 as a place where the visiting Phra Sumana Thera, who was a

teaching monk from Sukhothai, could spend the rains retreat. The large, open *wíhăan* was rebuilt in 1932. The *bòt* contains a 500-year-old bronze Buddha image and vivid *jataka* (Buddha's past-life stories) murals. Amulets and Buddhist literature printed in English and Thai can be purchased inexpensively in the *wíhăan*.

On the grounds stands a group of striking whitewashed Lanna stupas, framed by Doi Suthep when viewed from the east. The large central stupa contains a Buddha relic that, according to legend, miraculously duplicated itself in the 14th century. The duplicate relic was mounted on the back of a white elephant (commemorated by Chiang Mai's Pratu Chang Pheuak), which was allowed to wander until it 'chose' a site on which a wat could be built to enshrine it. The elephant stopped and died at a spot on Doi Suthep, 13 km west of Chiang Mai, where Chiang Mai residents built **Wat Phra That Doi Suthep**.

Today Wat Suan Dok is home to a large population of resident monks and novices, many of them students at the monastery's Mahachulalongkorn Buddhist University. See p293 for details on how visitors may interact with monastic students at Wat Suan Dok.

Wat Ku Tao
วัดกู่เต้า

North of the moat, near Chiang Mai Stadium, **Wat Ku Tao** (Map pp278-80; ☎ 0 5321 1842) dates from 1613 and has a unique stupa that looks like a pile of diminishing spheres, a Thai Lü design common in Yunnan, China. The stupa is said to contain the ashes of Tharawadi Min, a son of the Burmese king Bayinnaung, ruler of Lanna from 1578 to 1607.

Wat Chiang Yeun
วัดเชียงยืน

Another unique local temple is the 16th-century **Wat Chiang Yeun** (Map pp282-4; Th Mani Nopharat) outside the northeastern corner of the old city, east of Pratu Chang Pheuak. Besides the large northern-style stupa here, the main attraction is an old Burmese colonial-style gate and pavilion on the eastern side of the school grounds attached to the wat.

Catering to Shan and Burmese temple-goers, a few shops and street vendors in the vicinity of Wat Chiang Yeun sell Burmese-style pickled tea (*mîang* in Thai) and Shan-style noodles.

Wat Chetawan, Wat Mahawan & Wat Bupparam
วัดเชตวัน/วัดมหาวัน/วัดบุปผาราม

These three wats along Th Tha Phae feature highly ornate *wíhǎan* and stupas designed by Shan or Burmese artisans. Financed by Burmese teak merchants who immigrated to Chiang Mai a century or more ago, evidence of Shan/Burmese influence is easily seen in the abundant peacock symbol (a solar symbol common in Burmese and Shan temple architecture) and the Mandalay-style standing Buddhas found in wall niches. At **Wat Mahawan** (Map pp282–4; ☎ 0 5384 0189; Th Tha Phae) and **Bupparam** (Map pp282–4; ☎ 0 5327 6771; Th Tha Phae), no two guardian deity sculptures are alike; the whimsical forms include monkeys or dogs playing with lions and various mythical creatures. Wat Bupparam contains a charming little *bòt* constructed of teak and decorated in pure Lanna style.

Wat Sisuphan
วัดศรีสุพรรณ

This **wat** (Map pp282–4; ☎ 0 5320 0332; Th Wualai) south of the moat was founded in 1502, but little remains of the original structures except for some teak pillars and roof beams in the *wíhǎan*. The murals inside show an interesting mix of Taoist, Zen and Theravada Buddhist elements. Wat Sisuphan is one of the few wats in Chiang Mai where you can see the Poy Luang (also known as Poy Sang Long) Festival, a Shan-style group ordination of young boys as Buddhist novices, in late March.

Wat Phuak Hong
วัดพวกหงส์

Located behind Buak Hat Park (Suan Buak Hat; Map pp282–4), this **wat** (☎ 0 5327 8864; Th Samlan) contains the locally revered Chedi Si Pheuak. The stupa is more than 100 years old and features the 'stacked spheres' style seen only here and at Wat Ku Tao, and most likely influenced by Thai Lü stupas in China's Xishuangbanna district, Yunnan.

Mosques and Hindu & Sikh Temples
Of the 12 mosques in Chiang Mai, the oldest and most interesting is **Matsayit Chiang Mai** (Chiang Mai Mosque; Map pp282–4; Soi 1, Th Charoen Prathet), sometimes called Ban Haw Mosque, between Th Chang Khlan and Th Charoen Prathet, not far from the Chiang Mai Night Bazaar. Founded by *jiin haw* more than 100 years ago, it still primarily caters to this unique ethnic group; you'll hear Yunnanese spoken as often as Thai within the compound. Along this soi (lane) are several Yunnanese Muslim restaurants that serve *khâo sawy kài* (curried chicken and noodles) as a speciality.

The most colourful of Chiang Mai's two Hindu temples is the brightly painted, traditional shrine room (*mandir*) and the tower (*sikhara*) of **Devi Mandir Chiang Mai** (Map pp282–4; Th Ratanakosin), opposite Chiang Mai Stadium. **Namdhari Sikh Temple** (Map pp282–4; Th Ratchawong), between Th Chang Moi and Th Tha Phae, is the place of worship for the Namdhari sect of Sikhism.

Wiang Kum Kam
เวียงกุมกาม

These **excavated ruins** (off Map pp278–80; admission 30B; 8.30am-5pm) are tucked away near the banks of Mae Nam Ping, 5km south of the city via Hwy 106 (also known as Th Chiang Mai–Lamphun). The earliest historical settlement in the Chiang Mai area, it was established by the Mon in the 11th or 12th century as a satellite town for the Hariphunchai kingdom. The city was abandoned in the early 18th century due to massive flooding, and visible architectural remains are few – only the four-sided Mon-style stupa of Wat Chedi Si Liam and the layered brick pediments of Wat Kan Thom (the Mon name; in Thai the temple was known as Wat Chang Kham) are left. Chedi Si Liam is said to have been inspired by the similar stupa at Wat Kukut in Lamphun.

Over 1300 inscribed stone slabs, bricks, bells and stupas have been excavated at the site. So far, the most important archaeological discovery has been a four-piece inscribed stone slab, now on display in the Chiang Mai National Museum. The early-11th-century inscriptions on this slab indicate that the Thai script predates King Ramkhamhaeng's famous Sukhothai inscription (introduced in 1293) by 100 or more years.

An ideal way to reach Wiang Kum Kam is to hire a bicycle; follow Th Chiang Mai–Lamphun southeast for approximately 3km and look for a sign to the ruins on the right. From this junction it's another 2km to the ruins. You could also hire a *túk-túk* or red *sǎwngthǎew* to take you there for around 80B (one way).

Once you've finished looking around you can walk back to Th Chiang Mai–Lamphun and catch a *sǎwngthǎew* or a blue Chiang Mai–Lamphun bus back into the city.

Chiang Mai National Museum
พิพิธภัณฑสถานแห่งชาติเชียงใหม่

Established in 1954 with a lone curator overseeing a small collection of Lanna Buddhas and potsherd (fragments of pottery), **Chiang Mai National Museum** (Map pp278-80; ☎ 0 5322 1308, 0 5340 8568; admission 30B; ⏳ 9am-4pm Wed-Sun) has grown to having a full-time staff of 20 cataloguing and caring for up to a million artefacts. These items are shared among four important national museums in Chiang Mai, Lamphun, Chiang Saen and Nan, all under the auspices of the Chiang Mai National Museum. The museum displays a very good selection of Buddha images in all styles, including a huge bronze Buddha downstairs. Pottery is also displayed downstairs, while upstairs there are household and agricultural tools, along with historic weaponry.

The museum is close to Wat Jet Yot on Hwy 11 (also known as 'the Superhighway'), which curves around the city.

Tribal Museum
พิพิธภัณฑ์ชาวเขา

Originally founded in 1965 on the ground floor of the Tribal Research Institute on Chiang Mai University campus, this **museum** (off Map pp278-80; ☎ 0 5321 0872; admission free; ⏳ 9am-4pm Mon-Fri, closed public hols, slide & video shows 10am-2pm) moved to its new location overlooking a lake in Suan Ratchamangkhala on the northern outskirts of the city in 1997. The octagonal facility houses a large collection of handicrafts, costumes, jewellery, ornaments, household utensils, agricultural tools, musical instruments and ceremonial paraphernalia, along with various informative displays concerning the cultural features and backgrounds of each of the major hill tribes in Thailand. There is also an exhibition on activities carried out by the Thai royal family on behalf of the hill tribes, as well as various bits of research and development sponsored

by various governmental and nongovernmental agencies.

Chiang Mai Arts & Cultural Centre
หอศิลปวัฒนธรรมเชียงใหม่

Chiang Mai's former Provincial Hall, originally built in 1924 and a masterpiece of post-colonial Thai architecture has been converted into a cultural space with interactive exhibits, music, historical displays and more. The **museum** (Map pp282-4; ☎ 0 5321 7793; Th Phra Pokklao; admission 90B; ⏳ 8.30am-5.30pm Tue-Sun) was awarded a Royal Society of Siamese Architects award in 1999 for its faithful architectural restoration.

Anusawari Sam Kasat (Three Kings Monument)
อนุสาวรีย์สามกษัตริย์

These **three bronze sculptures** (Map pp282-4; Th Phra Pokklao) portray men standing in 14th-century royal costume. They represent Phaya Ngam Meuang, Phaya Mengrai and Phaya Khun Ramkhamhaeng, the three northern Thai-Lao kings most associated with Lanna history. The statuary has become a shrine to local residents, who regularly leave their offerings of flowers, incense and candles at the bronze feet in return for hoped-for blessings from the powerful spirits of the three kings.

Suan Buak Hat (Buak Hat Park)
สวนบวกหาด

This well-maintained public **park** (Map pp282-4; ⏳ 8am-5pm), wedged into the southwestern corner of the old city quadrangle, is Chiang Mai's miniature counterpart to Bangkok's Lumphini Park, with pleasant expanses of grass, fountains and palms; many people jog in this area.

Chiang Mai Zoo & Arboretum
สวนสัตว์/แหล่งเพาะพันธุ์ไม้ป่าเขตร้อนเชียงใหม่

Out towards Doi Suthep, 6km northwest of the Chiang Mai city centre, are the shady, nicely landscaped and hilly **Chiang Mai Zoo & Arboretum** (off Map pp278-80; ☎ 0 5335 8116, 0 5322 2479; adult/child 30/5B, motorcycle/bicycle 10B, car/truck 30B; ⏳ 8am-5pm). Except for the name of each species, most signs are in Thai only. More than 5000 birds (150 species) fly about the zoo's **Nakhon Ping Birdwatching Park**. A few snack vendors scattered around the park offer simple rice and noodle dishes. The quiet, lush arboretum is a favourite local jogging spot.

Chiang Mai University (CMU)

มหาวิทยาลัยเชียงใหม่

The city's principal public **university** (off Map pp278-80; ☎ 0 5384 4821; Th Huay Kaew) was established in 1964, becoming the first Thai university to be established outside Bangkok. Today the 3490-acre university boasts more than 18,000 students and 2000 lecturers divided among 107 departments.

Although scholastically CMU doesn't compare overall to such notable Bangkok universities as Silpakorn, Chulalongkorn or Thammasat, the CMU has earned special respect for its faculties of engineering and medical technology.

The main campus lies 2km west of the city centre in a 716-acre wedge of land between Th Suthep and Th Huay Kaew; there are entrances to the campus along both roadways. Students live in more than 20 dormitories on campus as well as in off-campus housing. The abundant green areas between the faculty buildings and student residences, along with the tree-shaded, tranquil **Ang Kaew** reservoir, are pleasant places for strolling. For more vigorous movement, the campus offers a **fitness park** and **sports track**, both open to the public at no charge, as a well as a public **swimming pool** with a small usage fee.

Other facilities on the main campus include restaurants, banks, a post office, an art gallery, bookshop and grocery store.

ACTIVITIES

Rock Climbing

Rock-climbing instruction is offered by **Chiang Mai Rock Climbing Adventures** (Map pp282-4; ☎ 0 6911 1470; www.thailandclimbing.com; 55/3 Th Ratchaphakhinai; day trips per person 1500-200B; multiday intensives 5500-9500B). It features trips to a set of limestone cliffs, known as **Crazy Horse Buttress**, behind Tham Meuang On about 20km east of Chiang Mai. Rates include two guides trained in first aid and CPR, transport, food, drinking water, equipment rental, insurance and T-shirt. The office located on Th Ratchaphakhinai has gear sales and rental, and a bouldering wall for practice sessions.

At 15m high and 16m wide, the **Peak Rock-Climbing Plaza** (Map pp282-4; ☎ 0 5382 0777; 28/2 Th Chang Khlan; per hr from 150B; ☽ 5pm-midnight) has one of the largest rock-climbing walls in Southeast Asia. Nonclimbers can watch the action from several adjacent bars and restaurants. Rates include equipment rental.

Massage & Day Spas

All of the places that teach massage (see p292) offer massage services as well, usually for 150B to 200B per hour. There are also dozens of *nûat phǎen boraan* (traditional massage) centres all around the city, often doing massage for as little as 100B per hour, but most people find that the massage schools give the best service. Some of the top hotels have excellent spas, though rates for massage will cost at least 10 times more than traditional massage services in the city. Recommended massage centres include the following:

Bor Nguen (Map pp282-4; ☎ 0 5320 6432; 9 Soi 2, Th Moon Muang) Excellent inexpensive foot and body massage, with or without oil, plus sauna and body scrub available.

Chiang Mai Oasis Spa (Map pp278-80; ☎ 0 5322 7494, 0 9851 3158; 102 Th Sirimangkhalajan) Well-managed day spa with very reasonable prices.

Dheva Spa (off Map pp278-80; ☎ 0 5388 8888; Dhara Dhevi Chiang Mai, 51/4 Th Chiang Mai-San Kamphaeng) Chiang Mai's newest and grandest spa (3100 sq m) is part of the huge new Mandarin Oriental Dhara Dhevi resort complex, east of the city. Expect premium prices and premium service.

Jirung Spa of Eternity (off Map pp278-80; ☎ 0 5386 1611; www.spaofeternity.com; 99 Mu 7, Rim Tai, Mae Rim) A medium-priced, high-quality spa about 20 minutes' drive north of Chiang Mai in Mae Rim.

Lanna Spa (off Map pp278-80; ☎ 0 5329 8181; Four Seasons Chiang Mai, Th Mae Rim-Samoeng Kao) High-end spa at the Four Seasons resort in Mae Rim. Very pricey.

Let's Relax Chiangmai Pavilion (Map pp282-4; ☎ 0 5381 8498; 2nd fl, 145/27 Th Chang Khlan); Chiang Inn Plaza (Map pp282-4; ☎ 0 5381 8198) Offers massages that are generally of superior quality, and are performed in a very clean and professional atmosphere. In addition to full-body massage, half-hour back and shoulder massage, arm massage and foot massage are available. Inexpensive.

Thai Boxing

Lanna Muay Thai Boxing Camp (Kiatbusaba; off Map pp278-80; ☎ 0 5389 2102; www.lannamuaythai.com; 64/1 Soi Chiang Khian; fees per day/month 250/7000B; simple camp accommodation per month 3000B) offers authentic *muay thai* (Thai boxing) instruction to foreigners as well as Thais. Several

Lanna students have won stadium bouts, including the famous transvestite boxer Parinya Kiatbusaba. According to the director, 'Foreign boxers are much sought after and we offer match-ups with local boxers at all levels of competition'.

Flying

Chiang Mai Sky Adventure Club (off Map pp278-80; ☎ 0 5386 8460, 0 1993 6861; flying@cmnet.co.th; 143 Mu 6, Tambon Choeng Doi, Amphoe Doi Saket; per person 1200B) offers 15-minute flights over the Doi Saket area, including transport from your hotel to the airfield.

Oriental Balloon Flights (☎ 0 5339 8609; per person US$190) arranges one-hour, early morning hot-air balloon cruises over the Chiang Mai countryside. The rate includes transport to/from your hotel or guesthouse, plus a champagne breakfast.

Cycling

Chiang Mai Bicycle Club (☎ 0 5394 3018) organises a trip almost every Sunday, leaving between 7am and 7.30am from the square in front of Pratu Tha Phae (Map pp282-4). These trips typically take routes outside of town.

Horse Riding

Pack Squadron Riding Club (off Map pp278-80; ☎ 0 5329 7478; member per hr 100B, nonmember accompanied by member per hr 200B, nonmember per hr 300B, membership fee per yr 1500B, riding lessons ☺ 5-6pm), with a stable of over 35 horses (many of them thoroughbreds), is a Thai army-sponsored club offering two-hour rides from 8am every Sunday. It's 2km north of the Superhighway off the road to Mae Rim.

Informal Northern Thai Group

The 20-year-old **Informal Northern Thai Group** (INTG; Map pp278-80; 138 Th Charoen Prathet; admission 20B; ☺ 7.30pm every 2nd Tue) meets at the Alliance Française. The usual evening format involves a lecture from a resident or visiting academic on some aspect of Thailand or Southeast Asia, followed by questions and answers and an informal drink afterwards at a local bar or restaurant.

Swimming

Landlocked Chiang Mai can get very hot, particularly from March to July. Fortunately, local opportunities for a refreshing swim abound.

Chiang Mai has several swimming pools open to the public. Typical fees are 30B to 100B per day (public pools are cheaper than hotel or private pools), while annual memberships start at around 300B. Some recommended public pools are listed below:

Amari Rincome Hotel (Map pp278-80; ☎ 0 5389 4884; Th Huay Kaew at Th Nimanhemin)

Awana Sleep & Swim Guesthouse (Map pp282-4; ☎ 0 5341 90057; Soi 1, Th Ratchadamnoen)

Chiang Mai University (off Map pp278-80; ☎ 0 5322 1699; Faculty of Education, Th Huay Kaew)

Maharaj Hospital (Map pp278-80; ☎ 0 5322 1310; Faculty of Medicine, Th Suthep)

Physical Education College (off Map pp278-80; ☎ 0 5321 0825; 700th Anniversary Stadium)

Top North Guest House (Map pp282-4; ☎ 0 5327 8900; 15 Soi 2, Th Moon Muang)

World Club Sport Complex (off Map pp278-80; ☎ 0 5343 1501; 178/832 Mu 7, Nong Khwai, Th Hang Dong)

Tennis

Anantasiri Tennis Courts (Map pp278-80; ☎ 0 5322 2210; off Hwy 11), opposite Chiang Mai National Museum, is the best public tennis facility in Chiang Mai. The eight courts are lit at night, and you can hire a 'knocker' (tennis opponent) for a reasonable hourly fee in addition to the regular court fee.

Other recommended tennis courts available in Chiang Mai:

Amari Rincome Hotel (Map pp278-80; ☎ 0 5322 1130, 0 5322 1044; Th Huay Kaew)

Chiang Mai Land Village (off Map pp278-80; ☎ 0 5327 2821; Th Chiang Mai Land) South of the city.

Gymkhana Club (Map pp278-80; ☎ 0 5324 1035; Th Ratuthit)

Lanna Sports Club (off Map pp278-80; ☎ 0 5322 1911; Th Chotana) North of the city.

COURSES
Language & Culture

American University Alumni (AUA; Map pp282-4; ☎ 0 5327 8407, 0 5321 1377; aualanna@loxinfo.co.th; 73 Th Ratchadamnoen; 30hr course 2700B, 60hr course 3500B) The basic AUA Thai course consists of three levels with 60 hours of instructions. There are also 30-hour courses in 'small talk', reading and writing, and northern Thai. More expensive private tutoring is also available.

Australia Centre (off Map pp278-80; ☎ 0 5381 0552; fax 0 5381 0554; Soi 5, Th Suthep, behind Chiang Mai University) Offers a 30-hour course in 'survival Thai' over a two-week period.

Chiang Mai Thai Language Center (Map pp282-4; ☎ 0 5327 7810; cmat@loxinfo.co.th; 131 Th Ratchadamnoen; 30hr course 2200B) Thai language courses for beginners to advanced learners.

Payap University (Map pp282-80; ☎ 0 5330 4805 ext 250-1; intpros@payap.ac.th; Th Kaew Nawarat; 60hr course 6000B, 120hr course 12,000B) Intensive 60- and 120-hour Thai language courses at beginner, intermediate and advanced levels. These focus on conversational skills, as well as elementary reading and writing, and Thai culture. Payap also offers a Thai Studies Certificate Program, which involves two semesters of classroom lectures and field trips.

Thai Cooking

Courses in Thai cuisine are another staple of Chiang Mai's vacation learning scene. Nowadays at least a dozen independent schools, as well as virtually every guesthouse in Chiang Mai, offer cooking classes from 700B to 900B a day.

Classes typically include an introduction to Thailand's herbs and spices, a local market tour, cooking instructions and a recipe booklet. Of course, you get to eat the delicious Thai food as well – everything from Chiang Mai–style chicken curry to steamed banana cake.

We've received good reports about the following courses:

Baan Thai (Map pp282-4; ☎ 0 5335 7339; info@cookinthai.com; 11 Soi 5, Th Ratchadamnoen)

Chiang Mai Thai Cookery School (Map pp282-4; ☎ 0 5320 6388; www.thaicookeryschool.com; 1-3 Th Moon Muang)

Gap's Thai Culinary Art School (Map pp282-4; ☎ 0 5327 8140; gap_house@hotmail.com; Gap's House, 3 Soi 4, Th Ratchadamnoen)

Kao Hom (off Map pp278-80; ☎ 0 5386 2967; www.kaohom.com; 180/1 Th Chiang Mai–Mae Rim) On the way to Mae Rim.

Siam Thai Cookery School (Map pp282-4; ☎ 0 5327 1169; siam-kitchen@bangkok.com; 5/2 Soi 1, Th Loi Kroh)

Traditional Massage

More visitors learn to pummel bodies the Thai way in Chiang Mai than anywhere else in Thailand. Tuition starts at around 3500B for 10 days. The following places are recommended for their massage classes:

Ban Nit (Map pp282-4; Soi 2, Th Chaiyaphum) A unique, one-on-one course available from Khun Nit, an older woman who is a specialist in deep-tissue, nerve and herbal massages. Length of study and payment for Nit's

tutelage is up to the individual – according to what you can afford. Most students live in and eat meals with Nit and her family.

Lek Chaiya (Map pp282-4; ☎ 0 5327 8325; www.nervetouch.com; 25 Th Ratchadamnoen; 5-day course 4000B) Khun Lek, a Thai woman who has been massaging and teaching for more than 40 years, specialises in *jàp sên* (similar to acupressure) and the use of medicinal herbs.

Old Medicine Hospital (OMH; Map pp278-80; ☎ 0 5327 5085; 78/1 Soi Siwaka Komarat, Th Wualai) The OMH curriculum is very traditional, with a northern-Thai slant (the Thai name for the institute actually means Northern Traditional Healing Hospital). There are two courses a month year-round, except for the first two weeks of April. Classes tend to be large during the months of December to February, small the rest of the year.

Thai Massage School of Chiang Mai (TMC; off Map pp278-80; ☎ 0 5385 4330; www.tmcschool.com; Th Chiang Mai-Mae Jo) Although it's northeast of town, and is Chiang Mai's most expensive massage school, TMC has a solid, government-licensed massage curriculum, including an intensive teacher training.

Buddhist Meditation

Northern Insight Meditation Centre, Wat

Ram Poeng (off Map pp278-80; ☎ 0 5327 8620; watrampoeng@hotmail.com; admission free) The 10- to 26-day individual intensive courses in Vipassana are taught by a Thai monk or nun, with Western students or bilingual Thais acting as interpreters. The formal name for Wat Ram Poeng is Wat Tapotaram. To get there by public transport, take a *săwngthăew* west on Th Suthep to Ton Phayom Market. From here take a *săwngthăew* south along Th Khan Khlong Chonlaprathan about 1km and get off when you see the signed wat entrance on the right. Or charter a *săwngthăew* or *túk-túk* all the way.

Wat Suan Dok (Map pp278-80; ☎ 0 5327 3149, 0 5327 3105, 0 5327 3120; Th Suthep; admission free) A relatively new programme here offers an English-language introduction to Buddhist meditation that runs from Sunday afternoon to Monday morning, with an overnight stay at the monastery.

Yoga

Marcel Kraushaar Hatha Yoga (off Map pp278-80; ☎ 0 5327 1555; marcelandyoga@hotmail.com; 129/79 Chiang Mai Villa 1)

Yoga Studio (Map pp282-4; ☎ 0 7891 4883; www.yoga-chiangmai.com; 90/1 Th Ratchamankha)

Jewellery-Making

Nova Artlab (Map pp282-4; ☎ 0 5327 3058; nova@thaiway.com; 16/1 Soi 4, Th Tha Phae) Teaches the fundamentals of jewellery craft in workshops lasting from one day to a month.

Indian Cooking

Indian Restaurant Vegetarian Food (Map pp282-4; ☎ 0 5322 3396; Soi 9, Th Moon Muang) Offers inexpensive cooking lessons; see p302.

QUIRKY CHIANG MAI
Museum of World Insects

พิพิธภัณฑ์แมลงโลก

If the idea of face-to-face encounters with prehistoric flying superinsect, giant scarab or long-tailed scorpion excites, then visit this private **museum** (Map pp278-80; ☎ 0 5321 1891; Soi 13, Th Sirimangkhalajan; admission 200B; ☺ 9am-5pm). Aside from perusing a detailed, well-labelled collection of preserved insects, you'll learn about the habits and habitats of Thailand's 422 mosquito species – 18 of which were named by the owner, renowned entomologist Manop Rattanarithikul.

Foreign Cemetery

สุสานต่างชาติ

For spooky atmosphere, head out to this **historic cemetery** (Map pp278-80; Th Chiang Mai-Lamphun) near the Gymkhana Club. Century-old headstones bearing American, English and European names mark the remains of traders, missionaries, failed entrepreneurs and numerous other expats who have died in Chiang Mai. A bronze statue of Queen Victoria, imported from Calcutta, India, during the Raj era, stands sentinel.

Monk Chat

มราวาสสนทนาวัดสวนดอก

A room at **Wat Suan Dok** (Map pp278-80; ☎ 0 5327 3149, 0 5327 3105, 0 5327 3120; Th Suthep; admission free; ☺ 5pm-7pm Mon, Wed & Fri) is set aside for foreigners to meet and chat with resident monks and novices. It is an chance for the monastic students to practise their English and for foreigners to learn about Buddhism and Thai life. To find the room, enter the wat from the main entrance and walk straight past the large *wíhăan* to a smaller building 100m or so into the temple grounds. Turn right at this smaller temple, and watch for the 'Monk Chat' signs. The monastery asks that visitors dress modestly – covered shoulders, no shorts or short skirts – and that women visitors take care not to make physical contact with the monks.

TOURS
River Cruises

From a small pier on Mae Nam Ping behind Wat Chaimongkhon, **Mae Ping River Cruises** (Map pp282-4; ☎ 0 5327 4822; Th Charoen Prathet; per person 300B) offers two-hour daytime cruises in roofed boats that stop at a small fruit farm, about 40 minutes away, where free samples and a beverage are provided. Tours run any time between 8.30am and 5pm. The Thai dinner cruise offers a set menu (400B; alcoholic drinks cost extra) and goes from 7.15pm to 9.30pm.

The Riverside Bar & Restaurant also has dinner cruises; see p305.

FESTIVALS & EVENTS

During the week-long **Winter Fair** (*thêtsàkaan ngaan reuduu năo*) in late December and early January, the area around Pratu Tha Phae assumes a country-fair atmosphere, with an abundance of rustic booths purveying northern Thai culinary delicacies, handicrafts, local designer clothing and just about anything else that can be traded.

Perhaps Chiang Mai's most colourful festival is the **Flower Festival** (*thêtsàkaan mái dàwk mái pràdàp*), also called the Flower Carnival, held annually in February (dates vary from year to year). Events occur over a three-day period and include displays of flower arrangements, a parade of floats decorated with hundreds of thousands of flowers, folk music, cultural performances and the Queen of the Flower Festival contest. Most activities are centred at Buak Hat Park near the southwestern corner of the city moat. People from all over the country turn out for this occasion, so book early if you want a room in town.

In mid-April the **Songkran Water Festival** is celebrated with an enthusiasm bordering on pure pandemonium. Thousands of revellers line up along all sides of the moat, and temporary pumps are installed so that water can be sucked from the moats and sprayed with liberal abandon. It is virtually impossible to stay dry during the five days of this festival.

In May the **Intakin Festival** (*ngaan tham bun săo inthákin*), held at Wat Chedi Luang and centred around the city *làk meuang*, propitiates the city's guardian deity to ensure that the annual monsoon will arrive on time. Also in May – when the mango crop is ripe – a **Mango Fair** (thêtsàkaan mámûang) is celebrated in Buak Hat Park, with lots of mango eating and the coronation of the Mango Queen.

During the festival of **Loi Krathong**, usually celebrated in late October or early November, Chiang Mai's river banks are alive with people floating the small lotus-shaped boats that mark this occasion. In Chiang Mai this festival is also known as Yi Peng, and some khon meuang (people of northern Thailand) celebrate by launching cylindrical-shaped hot-air balloons, lighting up the night skies with hundreds of pinpoints of light.

SLEEPING
Budget

Inexpensive guesthouses are clustered in several areas, primarily along the streets and lanes off Th Moon Muang and along several lanes running south off Th Tha Phae. You'll also find a few along Th Charoen Prathet, parallel to and west of Mae Nam Ping; and along Th Charoenrat east of Mae Nam Ping.

There are basically two kinds of budget guesthouse accommodation – old family homes converted into guest rooms (these usually have the best atmosphere although the least privacy) and hotel- or apartment-style places with rows of cell-like rooms. In both, the furnishings are basic – a bed and a few sticks of furniture. You can assume that rooms under 150B won't have a private bathroom but will probably have a fan.

The cheaper guesthouses make most of their money from food service and hill-tribe trekking rather than from room charges, hence you may be pressured to eat and to sign up for a trek. Places that charge 200B or more usually don't hassle guests in this way.

Many of the guesthouses can arrange bicycle and motorcycle rental. If you phone a guesthouse, most will collect you from the train or bus terminal for free if they have a room (this saves them having to pay a commission to a driver).

INNER MOAT AREA

Golden Fern Guest House (Map pp282-4; ☎ 0 5327 8423; www.goldenfern.com; 20 Soi 8, Th Phra Pokklao; r 250-400B; 🔀) The Golden Fern is a well-run, clean faràng-managed 30-room guesthouse

in a converted apartment building, and it is often full.

Blue Diamond (Map pp282-4; ☎ 0 5321 7120; bluediamondcm@hotmail.com; 35/1 Soi 7, Th Moon Muang; r 100-150B) Well-kept rooms, a good location, and a pleasant café with above-average guesthouse fare draws a steady clientele.

Smile House (Map pp282-4; ☎ 0 5320 8661; smile 208@loxinfo.co.th; 5 Soi 2, Th Ratchamankha; r 300-450B; 🔀) Smile House offers rooms in an old Thai house surrounded by a row of newer rooms. The charming outdoor eating area attached to the renovated house is a plus. The guesthouse rents motorcycles and bicycles, and also offers other travel services. This house once served as the 'safe house' of infamous Shan-Chinese opium warlord Khun Sa whenever he came to Chiang Mai.

Jonadda Guest House (Map pp282-4; ☎ 0 5322 7281; jonadda@hotmail.com; 23/1 Soi 2, Th Ratwithi; r 200-300B) This newer place run by an Aussie-Thai couple has spotless rooms and a pleasant attached café, and it's very convenient to the pub crawl area off Th Ratwithi.

Awana Sleep & Swim Guesthouse (Map pp282-4; ☎ 0 5341 9005; info@awanasleep.com; Soi 1, Th Ratchadamnoen; r 300-600B; 🔀 🏊) This relatively new spot behind the Montri Hotel upgrades the usual apartment-court ambience with the addition of a swimming pool.

RCN Court (Map pp282-4; ☎ 0 5341 8280-2, 0 5322 4619; fax 0 5321 1969; 35 Soi 7, Th Moon Muang; r 350-600B; 🔀) Although the building exterior isn't as pleasing as that of Safe House Court, it's very clean, friendly, and offers fax and laundering services. Monthly rates are available.

Eagle House 2 (Map pp282-4; ☎ 0 5321 0620; www .eaglehouse.com; 26 Soi 2, Th Ratwithi; dm 60B, r 180-360B; 🔀) This three-storey, modern building has basic rooms but a pleasant garden sitting area. It's fairly quiet except when the bars around Th Ratwithi get going from 9pm to midnight.

Supreme House (Map pp282-4; ☎ 0 5322 2480; fax 0 5321 8545; 44/1 Soi 9, Th Moon Muang; r 100-250B) This nondescript three-storey, hotel-like building has a loyal repeat clientele, partly due to the well-stocked paperback library on the bottom floor, and partly due to the fact that the management doesn't sell treks.

Lamchang House (Map pp282-4; ☎ 0 5321 0586, 0 5321 1435; Soi 7, Th Moon Muang; r 160B) Run by a Thai family, this wooden Thai-style house offers a small garden restaurant. Popular with Israelis.

Gap's House (Map pp282-4; ☎ 0 5327 8140; info@gaps-house.com; 3 Soi 4, Th Ratchadamnoen; r 350-750B; 🔀) Behind the AUA, Gap's has wooden or brick houses built around a quiet garden that's filled with antiques. Famous for its nightly vegetarian buffet, Gap's also offers a Thai cooking course (p292).

Anodard Hotel (Map pp282-4; ☎ 0 5327 0755; fax 0 5327 0759; 57-59 Th Ratchamankha; r 450B; 🔀 🖳) An older hotel in the inner-city area, the Anodard has well-kept rooms in a building that would have been called 'modern' 30 years ago, with a restaurant and nightclub on the premises.

Top North Guest House (Map pp282-4; ☎ 0 5327 8900; fax 0 5327 8485; 15 Soi 2, Th Moon Muang; r 300-600B; 🔀 🖳) Top North is a popular, efficiently run place with a swimming pool and travel agency.

Sumit Hotel (Map pp282-4; ☎ 0 5321 1033; ☎ / fax 0 5321 4014; 198 Th Ratchaphakhinai; r 200-300B; 🔀) On a relatively quiet section of Th Ratchaphakhinai, inside the old city, the Sumit offers clean, large rooms in the classic Thai-Chinese style. You can choose a room with one big bed or two twin beds for the same rate. All have a private bathroom; the more expensive air-con rooms have hot water. This is very good value for anyone avoiding the guesthouse scene, and possibly the best hotel deal in the old city.

Safe House Court (Map pp282-4; ☎ 0 5341 8955; 178 Th Ratchaphakhinai; r 350-400B; 🔀) This budget choice features very clean rooms with an apartment court feel, all with phone, fridge, toilet and hot-water shower, plus daily maid service. Monthly rates are available.

Roong Ruang Hotel (Roong Raeng; Map pp282-4; ☎ 0 5323 4746; fax 0 5325 2409; 398 Th Tha Phae; r 300-600B; 🔀) With a prime location near Pratu Tha Phae, on the eastern side of the city moat, all rooms face an inner courtyard with pleasant sitting areas out the front. The more expensive rooms have air-con. This is a good place to stay for the Flower Festival in February as the Saturday parade passes right by the entrance, but for the same reason it's probably not the best choice for the raucous Songkran and Loi Krathong festivals. There's another entrance on Th Chang Moi Kao.

CM Apartments (Map pp282-4; ☎ 0 5322 2100; 7 Soi 7, Th Moon Muang; r 250-450B) A favourite with young Thai boarders, CM is convenient to Talat Somphet (Somphet Market; see p305) and the western moat area.

Rendezvous Guest House (Map pp282-4; ☎ 0 5321 3763; fax 0 5341 9009; 3/1 Soi 5, Th Ratchadamnoen; r 180-300B; 🔀) This is a slightly faded three-storey guesthouse where all rooms have hot water, TV, phone and fridge.

Chiang Mai White House (Map pp282-4; ☎ 0 5335 7130; whitehouse@ezebox.com; 12 Soi 5, Th Ratchadamnoen; r 250-350B; 🔀) This guesthouse features clean, quiet rooms with cable TV in air-con rooms.

PRATU THA PHAE TO THE RIVER

Daret's House (Map pp282-4; ☎ 0 5323 5440; 4/5 Th Chai-yaphum; r 80-120B) A long-time backpackers' fave with stacks of basic, well-worn rooms. The large sidewalk café at the front is popular.

Happy House (Map pp282-4; ☎ 0 5325 2619; fax 0 5325 1871; 11/1 Th Chang Moi Kao; r 100-280B; 🔀) Around the corner from Daret's, on narrow Th Chang Moi Kao, Happy House is similar-looking but quieter and slightly better tended.

Eagle House 1 (Map pp282-4; ☎ 0 5323 5387; fax 0 5321 6368; Soi 3, Th Chang Moi Kao; r 100-150B) The simple rooms could use more maintenance according to several readers. French, German, English and Spanish are spoken.

Sarah Guest House (Map pp282-4; ☎ 0 5320 8271; info@sarahguesthouse.com; 20 Soi 4, Th Tha Phae; r 240-400B; 🔀) Older Thai house with a nice garden setting, an on-the-premises cooking school and trekking services.

Baan Jongcome (Map pp282-4; ☎ 0 5327 4823; 47 Soi 4, Th Tha Phae; r 350-450B; 🔀) A little more upmarket than other places on Soi 4, this place features comfortable rooms in a three-storey building.

Veerachai Court (Map pp282-4; ☎ 0 5325 1047; fax 0 5325 2402; 19 Soi 2, Th Tha Phae; r 400B; 🔀) Two buildings – a nine-storey building on the eastern side of the lane and a four-storey one on the western side – provide clean, quiet, but smallish rooms with TV. Monthly rates are available.

Le Pont (Map pp282-4; ☎ 0 5324 1661, 0 5324 1712; fax 0 5324 7000; 14 Th Charoenrat; r 450-600B; 🔀) Near Saphan Nawarat, opposite the Riverside Bar & Restaurant, Le Pont looks impressive, with its office, sitting area and restaurant housed in a 120-year-old teak residence. Rates for air-con guest rooms in an adjacent modern wing are reduced for stays of a week or more. The only drawback is that you can hear the live music from the Riverside until the bands shut down around 1am.

Little Home Guest House (Map pp282-4; ☎ 0 5320 6939; littleh@loxinfo.co.th; 1/1 Soi 3, Th Kotchasan; r 300-450B; ✸) Not far from the moat and DK Book House, Little Home offers large, clean, comfortable rooms in a modern Thai-style building. The upstairs rooms have private balconies.

New Mitrapap Hotel (Map pp282-4; ☎ 0 5323 5436; fax 0 5325 1260; 94-98 Th Ratchawong; r 340-450B; ✸) This is a classic Thai-Chinese spot on Chiang Mai's small Chinatown, between the east moat and Mae Nam Ping. The air-con rooms are a better deal than those with fan. It's close to several inexpensive Chinese restaurants, as well as the Talat Warorot (Warorot Market; p308).

Pun Pun Guest House (Map pp282-4; ☎ 0 5324 3362; punpun@armms.com; 321 Th Charoenrat; r 175-300B) American-owned, with tidy bungalows, or rooms in a quaint two-storey wooden Thai-style house. Assets include a fully stocked bar, snooker table and riverfront promenade.

Prince Hotel (Map pp282-4; ☎ 0 5325 2025; fax 0 5325 1144; 3 Th Taiwang; r 450-600B ✸ ✺) This is a Thai classic with good – if time-worn – rooms, plus a restaurant and a popular coffee shop.

TH CHANG KHLAN

Chiang Mai Youth Hostel (off Map pp278-80; ☎ 0 5327 6737; www.chiangmaiyha.org; 29 Th Papao, off Th Chang Khlan; r 150-300B; ✸) Chiang Mai Youth Hostel offers pleasant, simple rooms in a relatively quiet location. For Hostelling International members only, but a temporary membership valid for one night costs 50B. Call for free pick-up.

Riverfront Guest House (Tha Nam; off Map pp278-80; ☎ 0 5327 5125; thanam@chmail.loxinfo.co.th; 43/3 Th Chang Khlan; r 400B; ✸) Attached to the Riverfront Restaurant, this guesthouse along the west bank of Mae Nam Ping offers rooms in a classic Thai-style teak house that's more than 100 years old.

PRATU CHANG PHEUAK AREA

The following hotels are close to the Chang Pheuak bus terminal (for Chiang Dao, Fang and Tha Ton).

Chawala Hotel (Map pp278-80; ☎ 0 5321 4939, 0 5321 4453; 129 Th Chotana; r 150-300B; ✸) Basic rooms, popular with upcountry Thais.

Chiang Mai Phu Viang Hotel (☎ 0 5322 1632; 5-9 Soi 4, Th Chotana; r 200-320B; ✸) Small but clean rooms at the lower end of the rates, while for a bit more money there are spacious

rooms with better facilities. A restaurant and coffee shop are on the premises.

Midrange

In this range you can expect daily room cleaning, the option of air-con (some places have rooms with fan also) and – in hotels – TV and telephone. If there is anything that marks a guesthouse, it's the absence of these latter appliances.

Baan Kaew Guest House (Map pp282-4; ☎ 0 5327 1606; fax 0 5327 3436; 142 Th Charoen Prathet; r 650B; ✸) Opposite Wat Chaimongkhon and two doors south of the Alliance Française, Baan Kaew is set far back off the road, so it's very quiet. Well-maintained rooms boast cross-ventilation, fridge and outdoor sitting areas. Meals are available in a small outdoor dining area.

YMCA International Hotel (Map pp282-4; ☎ 0 5322 1819, 0 5322 2366; fax 0 5321 5523; 11 Th Mengrairasmi; r 600B; ✸ ▢) This is tucked away in a quiet spot outside the northwestern corner of the moat. Facilities at the hotel include a travel agency, handicraft centre and cafeteria.

Montri Hotel (Map pp282-4; ☎ 0 5321 1069/70; fax 0 5321 7416; 2-6 Th Ratchadamnoen; r 575-750B; ✸) A five-storey hotel on the busy corner of Th Moon Muang and Th Ratchadamnoen. Rates include tax, service and breakfast. Street-facing rooms are bombarded with noise from Th Moon Muang, which reflects off Tha Phae wall.

Lai-Thai Guesthouse (Map pp282-4; ☎ 0 5327 1725; www.laithai.com; 111/4-5 Th Kotchasan; r 660B; ✸ ✺) Lots of northern Thai décor affixed to what is otherwise just another three-storey hotel court. Rooms come with cable TV and minibar.

Galare Guest House (Map pp282-4; ☎ 0 5381 8887; www.galare.com; 7/1 Soi 2, Th Charoen Prathet; r 920B; ✸) A well-managed guesthouse with spacious rooms, the Galare is popular with repeat visitors for its Mae Nam Ping location and proximity to both the Chiang Mai Night Bazaar and Mae Ping post office. The traffic over nearby Saphan Nawarat can be a bit noisy. Discounts are readily available in low season.

Chiang Mai SP Hotel (Map pp282-4; ☎ 0 5321 4522; fax 0 5322 3042; 7/1 Soi 7, Th Moon Muang; r 850-950B; ✸) Once a monthly rental only, the SP has been renovated and now charges by the night. It's convenient to Talat Somphet (see p305) and the western moat area.

Buarawong Residence (Map pp282-4; ☎ 0 5327 3283; fax 0 5382 0602; 129/9 Th Rajang; r incl breakfast 590-790B; ✸ ☒) One of the more reasonably priced high-rises near the Night Bazaar.

River View Lodge (Map pp282-4; ☎ 0 5327 1110; fax 0 5327 9019; 25 Soi 2, Th Charoen Prathet; r 1450-2000B; ✸ ☒) The River View Lodge offers 36 well-appointed rooms in a two-storey, L-shaped building on spacious, landscaped grounds. Discounts may be available from May to August. The friendly owner has a small collection of classic cars on display in the parking lot.

Pornping Tower Hotel (Map pp282-4; ☎ 0 5327 0099; www.pornpingtower.com; 46-48 Th Charoen Prathet; r 1000-1500B; ✸) This large, 324-room high-rise looming over the back of the Chiang Mai Night Bazaar has comfortable rooms that list for 1766B but at the time of writing were going for rates given here. From the ambience of the reception area, one might expect to pay much more. The Pornping is most famous for Bubbles, still the most popular disco in town, but there are also two restaurants (one of them open 24 hours), a lobby bar, karaoke lounge, live music club, fitness centre and massage service.

Royal Lanna (Map pp282-4; ☎ 0 5381 8773; fax 0 5381 8776; 119 Th Loi Kroh; r incl breakfast 1050B; ✸ ☒) The Royal Lanna towers over the Chiang Mai Night Bazaar, with good views of the city on one side and Doi Suthep on the other. Rooms come with TV and fridge. Monthly rates are available.

Tapae Place Hotel (Map pp282-4; ☎ 0 5327 0159, 0 5328 1842; fax 0 5327 1982; 2 Soi 3, Th Tha Phae; r 550-1000B; ✸) Rooms in this large, modern, L-shaped building are a bit worn. The hotel's main drawcard is that it's only a few steps away from the banks, shops and restaurants of Th Tha Phae.

BP Chiang Mai City Hotel (Map pp282-4; ☎ 0 5327 0710; www.bpchiangmai.com; 154 Th Ratchamankha; r incl breakfast 1200B; ✸ ☒) Formerly the Felix City Inn, this friendly and efficient hotel offers 134 comfortable rooms.

Red Hibiscus Guesthouse (Map pp282-4; ☎ 0 5321 7631; www.redhibiscus.com; 1 Soi 2, Th Arak; r 750B, mini-ste 1500B; ✸) Looking like a cross between a hotel and a modern Thai home, this 10-room, three-storey guesthouse has helpful English-speaking staff who can arrange everything from car rentals to flight reservations.

Suan Doi House (off Map pp278-80; ☎ 0 5322 1869; www.suandoihouse.com; 38/3 Th Huay Kaew; r 950-1400B;

☒) Very clean and well run, this is a favourite with those visiting nearby CMU. It's set back off Th Huay Kaew, so is relatively quiet, and there's a good Vietnamese restaurant on the premises. Discounts are available in the off-season.

Lotus Pang Suan Kaew Hotel (PSK; Map pp278-80; ☎ 0 5322 4444; www.lotuspangsuankaew.com; 99/4 Th Huay Kaew; r 1000-1400B; ✸ ☒) Tucked away behind Kad Suan Kaew shopping centre, the rambling, 420-room PSK has extensive facilities, including a beer garden, three restaurants, coffee shop, lobby bar, snooker hall, fitness centre, massage centre, nightclub, tennis and squash courts, swimming pool and, of course, sheltered access to the shopping centre.

Sri Tokyo Hotel (Map pp282-4; ☎ 0 5321 3899; fax 0 5321 1102; 6 Th Bunreuangrit; r 590-690B; ✸) Next door to Chiang Mai Ram Hospital and conveniently close to Kad Suan Kaew shopping centre; street noise can be a problem in the front rooms.

Chiang Mai Phucome Hotel (off Map pp278-80; ☎ 0 5321 1026; fax 0 5321 6422; 21 Th Huay Kaew; 900-1100B; ✸) Once the best hotel in the city, the Phucome is nowadays very middle-of-the-road but a fair deal for a room with all amenities. West of the city, the hotel remains a favourite with many visiting Thais and features a restaurant, coffee shop and massage centre.

Chiangmai President Hotel (Map pp282-4; ☎ 0 5325 1025; fax 0 5325 1032; 226 Th Wichayanon; r 850-1200B; ✸ ☒) One of the oldest 'modern' hotels in the city, the President is very popular with Thai business travellers and is the closest hotel in the city to the US consulate. The hotel's dark coffee shop is legendary.

Suriwongse Hotel (Map pp282-4; ☎ 0 5327 0051, in Bangkok ☎ 0 2541 5275; suriwongse_htl_cnx@hotmail.com; Th Loi Kroh; r incl breakfast 1250-1450B; ✸ ☒) This hotel is close to the Night Bazaar, and has large rooms (rates include tax and service), a coffee shop, restaurant, and a massage centre.

Chiang Mai Hills (off Map pp278-80; ☎ 0 5321 0030; fax 0 5321 0035; 18 Th Huay Kaew; r 1500B; ✸ ☒) In the Th Huay Kaew business district, west of the city, and convenient to shopping, rates for these 249 well-appointed rooms include breakfast. Fitness and sauna facilities are available.

Ping Payom Hotel (off Map pp278-80; ☎ 0 5327 7497; fax 0 5327 8803; 99/41 Th Suthep; r 800B; ✸) One of the few hotels near CMU – and right around the corner from Talat Ton Phayom – the Ping Payom sees very few foreign guests but is a decent enough place to spend a night or two. Facilities include a karaoke bar and massage parlour.

Chiang Kham Hotel (off Map pp278-80; ☎ 0 5328 1016; fax 0 5327 8809; 7/35 Th Suthep; r 600-800B; ✕) With a predominantly Thai clientele, the Chiang Kham offers basic rooms similar to those at the Ping Payom.

New Asia Hotel (Map pp282-4; ☎ 0 5325 2426; fax 0 5325 2427; 55 Th Ratchawong; r 580-1000B; ✕) This very Chinese hotel in Chiang Mai's bustling Chinatown has a restaurant and coffee shop.

Top North Hotel (Map pp282-4; ☎ 0 5327 9623; topnorthhotel@hotmail.com; 41 Th Moon Muang; r 600-800B; ✕ ☒) High-rise very close to Pratu Tha Phae, but set far enough off Moon Muang that it's quiet. Good-size rooms have TV and fridge.

Providence (off Map pp278-80; ☎ 0 5389 3123; fax 0 5322 1750; 99/9 Th Huay Kaew; r 700-900B; ✕) Further out on Huay Kaew, the Providence features a restaurant, coffee shop and lobby bar.

Diamond Riverside (Map pp282-4; ☎ 0 5327 0080-5; fax 0 5327 1482; 33/10 Th Charoen Prathet; r 1150-1400B; ✕ ☒) A favourite with visiting Thai government employees, the Diamond Riverside has a prime location on the banks of Mae Ping, and has a coffee shop, restaurant and massage centre. Rooms in the old streetside wing are less expensive – and less comfortable – than those in the new wing.

Northern Inn (Map pp282-4; ☎ 0 5321 0002; fax 0 5321 5828; 234/18 Th Mani Nopharat; r 500B; ✕) Close to Pratu Chang Pheuak and the Chang Pheuak bus terminal, midbudget package tourists use this hotel extensively.

Iyara Hotel (Map pp278-80; ☎ 0 5322 2245, 0 5321 4227; fax 0 5321 4401; 126 Th Chotana; r 500-700B; ✕) Several long blocks north of Pratu Chang Pheuak and opposite the teachers college, Rajabhat Institute, the Iyara is popular with Thai business travellers and Rajabhat visitors. A restaurant and coffee shop are on the premises.

CHIANG MAI UNIVERSITY (CMU)

Uniserv Hostel (off Map pp278-80; ☎ 0 5322 4672; fax 0 5321 6244; Chiang Mai University; r 400-750B; ✕) On CMU campus, close to the Th Huay Kaew side, Uniserv is a large hotel-like structure with clean rooms, good service and a very good Thai restaurant out the back. You don't have to be a student to stay here.

CMU International Center Hostel (off Map pp278-80; ☎ 0 5394 2881; www.ic.cmu.ac.th; Th Nimanhemin; r 650-750B; ✕ 🖳) Housed in CMU's busy International Center, this cosy hostel offers 88 rooms, all with TV and fridge. Downstairs there's a Doi Wawi café and Lemongrass restaurant (room rates include breakfast, and monthly rates are available).

Top End

In general, hotel rates for luxury hotels are lower in Chiang Mai than in Bangkok. You can expect to pay anywhere from 1500B to 8000B for large, well-maintained rooms with air-con, TV and International Direct Dial (IDD) telephone in hotels with a restaurant (usually more than one), swimming pool and fitness centre. Booking through a travel agency or via the Internet almost always means lower rates, or try asking for a hotel's 'corporate' discount.

In 2004 and 2005 the city saw a sudden boom in the simultaneous construction of several five-star properties. In addition to those listed below, hammers and drills are busy assembling Chiang Mai branches of Singapore's Shangri-La, Phuket's Chedi, Conrad Bangkok and Bangkok's Banyan Tree.

IN TOWN

Ratchamankha (Map pp282-4; ☎ 0 5390 4111; www .rachamankha.com; 6 Th Ratchamankha; r 6500-8500B; ✕ ☒) Walking into this architect-owned hotel, tucked into a soi behind Wat Phra Singh and currently all the rage among visiting glitterati, is like walking into the compound of a 16th-century Lanna temple built for royalty. In addition to its 24 tastefully decorated, supremely serene guest rooms, the Ratchamankha boasts a gourmet dining room (see p300) and an art gallery filled with high-end silverwork, lacquerware, hill-tribe jewellery, Buddha images and ceramics unearthed while the hotel was under construction.

D2hotel (Map pp282-4; ☎ 0 5328 1033; www.d2 hotels.com; 100-101 Th Chang Khlan; r 3000-6000B; ✕ ☒ 🖳 ☒) Chiang Mai's ultimate flashpacker digs, it's oriented towards hipper upscale visitors, both Thai and foreign, and filled with stylish lighting and furniture, plus high-speed Internet. Facilities include two restaurants, a bar, fitness centre, business club lounge and spa.

Tamarind Village (Map pp282-4; ☎ 0 5341 8898; www.tamarindvillage.com; 50/1 Th Ratchadamnoen; r 4000-6000B; ⊠ ⊠ ⊠) A fusion of Thai and Mediterranean architectural styles, this quiet spread with 40 rooms on the grounds of an old tamarind orchard features a pool, bar, modest restaurant, and, like its more upscale sister the Ratchamankha, easy access to old city sights.

Karinthip Ville (Map pp282-4; ☎ 0 5323 5414; www.karinthipville.com; 50/2 Th Chang Moi Kao; r 2000-3600B; ⊠ ⊠) This new spot is tucked away in a quiet soi off Th Chang Moi, opposite Wat Chomphu, and has nicely landscaped grounds. The rooms are all the same size, the different rates reflecting the value of the furnishings only.

Chiang Mai Plaza Hotel (Map pp282-4; ☎ 0 5327 0036; fax 0 5327 2230; 92 Th Si Donchai; r 2925B; ⊠ ⊠ ⊠) This large but friendly hotel not far from the Chiang Mai Night Bazaar boasts a spacious lobby with live northern-Thai music in the evenings, a lobby bar, restaurant, wood-panelled sauna, fitness centre and a well-kept pool area with shade pavilions. Nonsmoking rooms are available, which is unusual for a place charging less than 3000B.

Sheraton Chiangmai (off Map pp278-80; ☎ 0 5327 5300; www.sheraton-chiangmai.com; 318/1 Th Chiang Mai-Lamphun; r 6000B; ⊠ ⊠ ⊠ ⊠) Across Saphan Mangrai on the east bank of Mae Nam Ping, the Sheraton's capacious rooms are popular with Western business travellers. Facilities include three restaurants, a coffee shop, fitness centre, swimming pool, sauna and beauty salon.

Amari Rincome Hotel (Map pp278-80; ☎ 0 5322 1130, 0 5322 1044; www.amari.com; 1 Th Nimanhemin; r 4000-6000B; ⊠ ⊠ ⊠ ⊠) Very reliable business hotel. Amenities include a well-received Italian restaurant, coffee shop, lobby bar, conference facilities, tennis court and swimming pool.

Imperial Mae Ping Hotel (Map pp282-4; ☎ 0 5328 3900; www.imperialhotels.com; 153 Th Si Donchai; r 2120-5000B; ⊠ ⊠) This is a sprawling hotel near the Chiang Mai Night Bazaar and with well-outfitted standard rooms. A coffee shop, three restaurants and pool are on the premises. Touring Thai bands play the ballroom on occasion.

Chiang Mai Orchid Hotel (Map pp278-80; ☎ 0 5322 2091; www.chiangmaiorchid.com; 100 Th Huay Kaew; r 2500B; ⊠ ⊠ ⊠ ⊠) A 266-room hotel next to Kad Suan Kaew shopping centre, the Chiang Mai Orchid is oriented towards business travellers and upscale package tourists, and offers a fitness centre, business centre, pool, beauty salon and bookshop.

Novotel Chiang Mai (Map pp282-4; ☎ 0 5322 5500; www.accorhotels-asia.com; 183 Th Chang Pheuak; r 1500B; ⊠ ⊠ ⊠) Although the location off a very busy street north of Pratu Chang Pheuak is less than ideal, the Novotel is a bargain considering the spacious modern rooms. Two restaurants and a bar fill out the premises, and Rim Ping, the city's best supermarket, is close by.

Royal Princess (Map pp282-4; ☎ 0 5328 1033; rpc@dusit.com; 112 Th Chang Khlan; r 1900-2250B; ⊠ ⊠) In the middle of the Chiang Mai Night Bazaar, facilities at this hotel include international, Chinese and Japanese restaurants and a lobby bar. This hotel is mainly used by package tourists.

Empress Hotel (Map pp278-80; ☎ 0 5327 0240; reservations@empresshotels.com; 199 Th Chang Khlan; r 1900-2500B; ⊠ ⊠ ⊠ ⊠) Near Chiang Mai Central Hospital, the Empress caters to a mostly Asian clientele. The hotel facilities include a restaurant, coffee shop, fitness centre and disco.

Amity Green Hills (Map pp278-80; ☎ 0 5322 0100; amity@loxinfo.co.th; 24 Th Chiang Mai-Lampang; r 2600-2900B; ⊠ ⊠ ⊠ ⊠) A short distance northeast off Th Huay Kaew, on Hwy 11 (the 'Super-highway'), facilities at Amity Green Hills include a restaurant, coffee shop, lobby bar, business centre, conference room and fitness room. The location is less than ideal for walking to restaurants or attractions.

OUT OF TOWN

North of the city in the Mae Rim/Mae Sa area are a few plush countryside resorts. Most of these establishments have free shuttle vans to/from the city.

Mandarin Oriental Dhara Dhevi (off Map pp278-80; ☎ 0 5388 8888; www.mandarinoriental.com; 51/4 Th Chiang Mai-San Kamphaeng; r US$485-1200; ⊠ ⊠ ⊠ ⊠) Almost a kingdom unto itself, the new Dhara Dhevi, 5km east of the city, has taken 52 partially wooded acres just east of the city limits and filled them with architecture inspired by Greater Lanna (including neighbouring Shan State, northern Laos and Sipsongpanna/Xishuangbanna in southern China) at its 15th- to 17th-century peak. The 310-sq-metre spa is the largest in northern Thailand. The resort opened in December 2004 with 64 units, with another 78 to be completed in 2005.

Four Seasons Chiang Mai (off Map pp278-80; ☎ 0 5329 8181; www.fourseasons.com; Th Mae Rim-Samoeng Kao; r US$400; ✗ ✗ ☐ ☑) Located north of the city, this is one of Chiang Mai's premier resorts, featuring 64 vaulted pavilion suites (each around 75 sq metres), plus two- and three-bedroom residences spread amid eight hectares of landscaped gardens and rice terraces worked by water buffalo. On the premises are a state-of-the-art, semi-outdoor cooking school, two full-service restaurants, a bar, a health club, two swimming pools and two illuminated tennis courts. The resort's 900-sq-metre Lanna Spa has earned much acclaim. Rates, quoted in dollars only, don't include tax and service.

Jirung Spa of Eternity (off Map pp278-80; ☎ 0 5386 1611; www.spaofeternity.com; 99 Mu 7, Rim Tai, Mae Rim; r 3600B; ✗ ✗ ☐ ☑) Near the Four Seasons, this spa-centred resort offers comfortable 70- to 140-sq-metre suites. In addition to various spa treatments, Jirung hosts regular yoga and meditation sessions.

Imperial Chiang Mai Resort, Spa & Sports Club (off Map pp278-80; ☎ 0 5329 8326; www.imperialhotels .com; 284 Mu 3, Don Kaew, Th Chiang Mai-Fang; r US$46-52; ✗ ☐ ☑) Seven kilometres from town in Amphoe Mae Rim, this sprawling, 113-sq-km resort boats 45 rooms and three two-storey luxury suites. Living up to its name, the resort boasts air-con squash courts, a badminton hall, six hard- and clay-surface tennis courts, fitness centre, sauna, gymnasium, two swimming pools and a polo club (under renovation at the time of writing). You have to pay extra for the badminton, squash and tennis facilities but everything else is free for guests. Rates, quoted in dollars only, don't include tax and service.

EATING

You won't lack for variety in Chiang Mai as the city has arguably the best assortment of restaurants of any city in Thailand outside of Bangkok. Chiang Mai's guesthouses serve a typical menu of Western food along with a few pseudo-Thai dishes. If you're interested in authentic Thai cuisine, you'll do well to leave the guesthouse behind for the most part.

Thai

Ratchamankha (Map pp282-4; ☎ 0 5390 4111; 6 Th Ratchamankha; dishes 120-320B) Tucked away in the sumptuous grounds of the boutique hotel of the same name (see p298), behind Wat Phra Singh, one dines at the Ratchamankha to enjoy the antique-laden atmosphere as much as the food. And of course to be able to say that you have eaten here. The menu is Thai-centred, with hints of Vietnam, Japan and Europe floating at the periphery. While waiting for a table, have a drink at the bar, which has lithographs by Henry Moore, Robert Motherwell, and other early-20th-century artists.

Heuan Phen (Map pp282-4; ☎ 0 5327 7103; 112 Th Ratchamankha; dishes 40-120B; ☽ 8.30am-3pm & 5-10pm) Classy and highly regarded for its northern- Thai food. Among the house specialities are *khànŏm jiin náam ngíaw* (thin rice noodles with a peanut and pork-blood sauce), *khâo sawy* (egg noodles in a curried broth), *lâap khûa* (northern-style minced-meat salad), *náam phrík nùm* (a chilli dip made with roasted peppers), *kaeng hang-leh* (very rich Burmese-style pork curry), *kaeng awm, kaeng khae,* and other *aahăan phéun meuang* (local food). Daytime meals are served in a large dining room out the front, while evening meals are served in an atmospheric antique-decorated house at the back.

Heuan Sunthari (no Roman-script sign; Map pp278-80; ☎ 0 5325 2445; 46/2 Th Wang Singkham; dishes 40-100B; ☽ 10am-11pm) Rustic dining areas built on several levels open onto the west bank of the river. The owner – the famous northern Thai singer Soontaree Vechanont – performs at the restaurant on weekends, and other local musicians during the week. The menu is a pleasant blend of northern, northeastern and central Thai specialities.

Si Phen Restaurant (Map pp282-4; ☎ 0 5331 5328; 103 Th Inthawarorot; dishes 30-75B; ☽ 9am-5pm) This inexpensive stopover near Wat Phra Singh specialises in both northern- and northeastern-style dishes. The kitchen prepares some of the best *sôm-tam* (spicy papaya salad) in the city, including a variation made with pomelo fruit. The *kài yâang khâo nĭaw* combo (grilled chicken and sticky rice) – another Isan favourite – is also very good, as is the *khâo sawy* (chicken in a curried broth with noodles) and *khànŏm jiin* (Chinese noodles) with either *náam yaa* (fish sauce) or *náam ngíaw* (sweet, spicy sauce) – always incredible.

Khrua Phuket Laikhram (no Roman-script sign; off Map pp278-80; ☎ 0 5327 8909; 1/10 Th Suthep; dishes 40-100B; ⏰ 8.30am-2pm & 4-8.30pm, closed 12th, 13th, 27th & 28th of every month) This small family-run restaurant near Chiang Mai University is worth hunting down for its delicious, cheap, authentic home-style southern and central Thai cooking. If there are no tables available downstairs, try the upstairs dining room. Along with the pans of curries displayed out the front, house specialities include *yâwt máphráo phàt phèt kûng* (spicy stir-fried shrimp with coconut shoots), *khâo phàt pó tàek* (fried rice with seafood and kaffir lime) and *khâo yam* (a delicious southern Thai-style rice salad). There are no English menus, and all signs are in Thai.

Huay Kaew Restaurant (Heuan Huay Kaew; off Map pp278-80; Th Huay Kaew) This atmospheric collection of rustic wooden pavilions overlooking Nam Tok Huay Kaew on the road up Doi Suthep is the perfect place to take a long, comfortable afternoon meal. The menu is mostly northern and northeastern Thai.

Aroon (Rai) Restaurant (Map pp282-4; ☎ 0 5327 6947; 45 Th Kotchasan; dishes 40-80B; ⏰ 8am-10pm) One of Chiang Mai's oldest and best-known restaurants gets a bad rap from local expat residents who mistakenly assume it's not authentic simply because so many tourists eat here. In fact Aroon has a strong local Thai following who know what to order. House strengths are northern Thai dishes. Look for Chiang Mai specialities such as *kaeng hang-leh*, *kaeng awm* and *kaeng khae*. The latter two dishes are more like stews than curries, and rely on local roots and herbs for their distinctive, bitter-hot flavours. Downstairs you'll find more exotic dishes in trays near the cashier, including bamboo grubs and other forest goodies. The spacious open-air dining area upstairs is favoured by night-time clientele, and in hot weather it's cooler than downstairs.

Dalaabaa Bar & Restaurant (Map pp282-4; ☎ 0 5324 2491; 113 Th Bamrungrat; dishes 80-180B; ⏰ closed Sun) This trendy eatery, with subdued lighting washing over orange and red silks, brings a Bangkok-style sophistication to Chiang Mai dining with a clever Thai fusion menu.

Le Grand Lanna (off Map pp278-80; ☎ 0 5385 0111; www.legrandlanna.com; Mandarin Oriental Dhara Dhevi Hotel, 51/4 Th Chiang Mai-San Kamphaeng; dishes 120-240B)

Part of the Mandarin Oriental Dhara Dhevi complex, Le Grand Lanna actually predated the resort with a 4000-sq-m complex of restored wooden northern Thai buildings filled with antique furniture, high-end art and handicrafts. The cuisine can be wonderful, especially the upmarket versions of northern-Thai specialities.

Ratana's Kitchen (Map pp282-4; ☎ 0 5387 4173; 320-322 Th Tha Phae; dishes 60-80B; ⏰ 9am-11pm) An air-con spot that's owned by an English-Thai couple, Ratana's is situated in a prime Th Tha Phae location near Book Zone. The inexpensive menu offers Thai dishes from several regions, as well as a few *faràng* items. If you're driving, you can usually park in the compound of the adjacent Wat Chetawan.

Chinese

Mitmai Restaurant (Map pp282-4; ☎ 0 5327 5033; 42/2 Th Ratchamankha; dishes 40-80B; ⏰ 9am-9pm) A clean, simple and spacious Yunnanese place specialising in delicious vegetable soups made with pumpkin, taro, snowpeas. mushrooms or other vegetables. Try the *tôm sôm plaa yâwt máphráo* (hot-and-sour fish soup with coconut shoots). The bilingual menu also includes *yam* (tangy, Thai-style salad) made with Chinese vegetables, as well as Yunnanese steamed ham, Chinese medicine chicken and many vegetarian dishes. No MSG is used in the cooking.

Jok Somphet (Map pp282-4; cnr Th Ratchaphakhinai & Th Si Phum; dishes 20-30B; ⏰ 6am-11pm) Facing the northern moat, Jok Somphet is popular for its namesake *jóhk*. The friendly proprietors also make decent *khâo sawy kài* and other noodles – *bà-mìi* (wheat noodles), *kǔaytǐaw* (rice noodles) – with chicken, beef or pork.

China Palace (off Map pp278-80; ☎ 0 5327 5300; Sheraton Chiangmai, 318/1 Th Chiang Mai-Lamphun; dishes 80-220B) The best place to splurge on Chinese food is this plush spot at the Sheraton that specialises in excellent Cantonese cuisine.

Chiang Mai's small **Chinatown** (Map pp282-4; Th Ratchawong) is in an area centred around this street, north of Th Chang Moi. Here you'll find a whole string of inexpensive Chinese rice and noodle shops, most of them offering variations on Tae Jiu (Chao Zhou) and Yunnanese cooking.

Noodles

Khâo sawy – a Shan-Yunnanese concoction of chicken (or, less commonly, beef), spicy curried broth and flat, squiggly, wheat noodles – is one of the most characteristic Chiang Mai noodle dishes. It's served with small saucers of shallot wedges, sweet-spicy pickled cabbage and a thick red chilli sauce.

The oldest area for *khâo sawy* is Ban Haw, the *jiin haw* area around the Matsayit Chiang Mai on Soi 1, Th Charoen Prathet, around the corner from the Diamond Riverside Hotel and Galare Guest House and not far from the Chiang Mai Night Bazaar – in fact, this is where the *jiin haw* caravans of yore used to tie up.

Khao Soi Lam Duan (Map pp278–80; Th Faham; dishes 25–50B) This place serves large bowls of beef, pork or chicken *khâo sawy*. Also on the menu are *kao-lǎo* (soup without noodles), *mǔu sà-té* (grilled spiced pork on bamboo skewers), *khâo sawy* with beef or pork instead of chicken, *khànǒm rang phêung* (literally, beehive pastry, a coconut-flavoured waffle), Mekong rice whisky and beer. Two more very good *khâo sawy* places along this same stretch are **Khao Soi Samoe Jai** (Map pp278–80; Th Faham) and **Khao Soi Ban Faham** (Map pp278–80; Th Faham).

Khao Soi Prince (Map pp282–4; Th Kaew Nawarat; dishes 20–35B; ☉ 9am-3pm) Near Prince Royal's College, this is regarded by many locals as their favourite spot for authentic *khâo sawy*. The *khâo mòk kài* (Thai-style chicken biryani) is also well worth trying here.

Just Khao Soy (Map pp282–4; ☎ 0 5381 8641; 108/2 Th Charoen Prathet; dishes 70–100B) Lives up to its name by serving nothing but the local speciality. This is the grand, gourmet version, served on a wooden artist's palette with several condiments, including coconut milk to thicken the broth at will – and at four times the price of Ban Haw's *khâo sawy*. Two different noodle shapes are offered, Chiang Mai style and Mae Salong style.

Rot Sawoei (Map pp282–4; Th Arak; dishes 25–35B) Around the corner from Buak Hat Park, this unassuming open-air spot is famous for its delectable *kǔaytǐaw kài tǔn yaa jiin* (rice noodles with Chinese herb-steamed chicken) that practically melts off the bone. A normal bowl costs 25B, while a *phísèht* (special) order with extra chicken costs 35B.

Kuaytiaw Kai Tun Coke (Map pp282–4; Th Kamphaeng Din; dishes 40B) A small food stall directly opposite the main entrance to the Imperial Mae Ping Hotel prepares a simpler version

of *kǔaytǐaw kài tǔn yaa jiin* but substitutes Coca-Cola for the Chinese herbs. Here the chicken is marinated in cola and spices overnight before then being steamed and served with rice noodles. It's actually quite good and has become famous as far away as Bangkok.

Rot Neung (no Roman-script sign; Map pp282–4; Th Charoen Prathet; dishes 30B; ☉ 9am-9pm) Opposite the Diamond Riverside Hotel, Rot Neung serves some of the best *kǔaytǐaw lûuk chín plaa* (rice noodle soup with fish balls, strips of fishcake and fish wonton) in Chiang Mai. If you thought you didn't like fish balls – ground fish rolled into balls – give them a second try here, as Rot Neung makes them fresh and sells them to many other stands in town.

Yunnanese-run **Khao Soi Feuang Fah** (no Roman-script sign; Map pp282–4; Soi 1, Th Charoen Prathet; dishes 20–40B; ☉ 5am-5pm) and **Khao Soi Islam** (no Roman-script sign; Map pp282–4; Soi 1, Th Charoen Prathet; dishes 20–40B; ☉ 5am-5pm), near Matsayit Chiang Mai, serve *khâo sawy* as well as Muslim curries, *khànǒm jiin* (choice of two sauces: *náam yaa* or *náam ngíaw*), and *khâo mòk kài* (the Thai-Muslim version of chicken biryani). Khao Soi Islam also serves *khâo mòk pháe* (goat biryani).

Indian, Muslim & Israeli

Along Soi 1, Th Charoen Prathet, between Th Chang Khlan and Th Charoen Prathet and near Matsayit Chiang Mai, are a number of simple restaurants and alley vendors selling inexpensive but tasty Thai Muslim curries and *khâo sawy*. *Néua òp hǎwm* ('fragrant' Yunnanese Muslim-style dried beef), a speciality of Chiang Mai, is also sold along the lane. A food vendor, also on this lane, does delicious *rotii* (Indian flat bread) as well as chicken martabak (*mátàbà kài*; *rotii* stuffed with chicken).

Sophia (Map pp282–4; dishes 20–40B; ☉ 8am-7pm Sat-Thu) On the opposite side of the lane from Khao Soi Islam and Khao Soi Feuang Fah (see above), Sophia serves good curries and *khâo mòk kài*.

Indian Restaurant Vegetarian Food (Map pp282–4; ☎ 0 5322 3396; Soi 9, Th Moon Muang; dishes 20–60B; ☉ 8am-11pm) A very friendly, family-owned place that serves cheap and adequate vegetarian thalis as well as individual Indian dishes. The owners also offer Indian cooking lessons.

Shere Shiraz (Map pp282-4; ☎ 0 5327 6132; Soi 6, Th Charoen Prathet; dishes 50-100B) Serves mostly north-Indian food, with a few south-Indian dishes. The extensive menu includes many vegetarian dishes.

Arabia (Map pp282-4; ☎ 0 5381 8850; Anusan Night Market; dishes 30-80B) This small restaurant does north-Indian-Pakistani-Arab–style cuisine very well, perhaps better than any of the others in terms of the freshness of the flavours. Don't let the fact that it's often empty or nearly so throw you off the trail; it has a steady and discerning, if small, clientele.

Jerusalem Falafel (Map pp282-4; ☎ 0 5327 0208; 35/3 Th Moon Muang; dishes 40-80B; ☻ 9am-11pm Sat-Thu) Serves a selection of falafels, shashlik, hummus, and other Israeli specialities, as well as Thai and vegetarian food, baguettes, pizza, soups, salads, gelato, and delicious homemade cakes and pies.

Sa-Nga Choeng Doi (no Roman-script sign; Map pp282-4; Th Charoensuk; dishes 25-40B; ☻ 8am-4pm) This long-running favourite makes the best *khâo mòk kài* and *mátàbà* in town; if you happen to be near the YMCA in Amphoe Santitham, it's a five-minute walk away. The homemade, unsweetened yogurt here is also highly recommended.

Italian

Da Stefano (Map pp282-4; ☎ 0 5387 4189; 2/1-2 Th Chang Moi Kao; dishes 60-120B) An intimate, well-decorated, air-con place, Da Stefano focuses on fresh Italian cuisine, with one of the better wine lists in town.

Giorgio Italian Restaurant (Map pp282-4; ☎ 0 5381 8236; 2/6 Th Prachasamphan; dishes 100-200B) Chiang Mai's most ambitious, and some say the best, Italian eatery features a full range of pasta, some of it homemade. The salads are particularly good, while the décor is classy and retro.

Pum Pui Italian Restaurant (Map pp282-4; ☎ 0 5327 8209; 24 Soi 2, Th Moon Muang; dishes 60-120B; ☻ 11am-11pm) This casual garden-style spot near Top North Guest House features a low-key garden setting and moderate prices; the menu includes olive paté and other antipasto, along with salads, several vegetarian selections, ice cream, breakfast, Italian wines and espressos. The complimentary Italian breads served at the beginning of all meals are excellent.

La Gondola (Map pp282-4; ☎ 0 5330 6483; dishes 60-120B) This branch of Da Stefano, behind Rim Ping Condo on Mae Nam Ping, offers a similar menu to Pum Pui with atmospheric, under-the-stars seating on a grassy area by the river.

La Villa Pizzeria (Map pp282-4; ☎ 0 5327 7403; 145 Th Ratchadamnoen; dishes 50-120B) Set in and around a large, old Thai house, La Villa serves pizza baked in a wood-fired oven, and the rest of the Italian food on the menu is tops.

M Cuisine (off Map pp278-80; Th Suthep; dishes 40-100B) Charming trattoria-style outdoor spot near Chiang Mai University, and the least expensive Italian eatery in the city. Some of the dishes, such as the spicy clam spaghetti (a steal at 60B, complete with garlic bread and salad), are clearly oriented towards the Thai palate – and taste all the better for it. To find this place, look for the very narrow soi running south off Th Suthep just east of Soi Wat U Mong. A sign at the mouth of the soi reads 'Pizza Steak' (but stick with the bargain pasta here and avoid both the pizza and the steak).

International

Art Café (Map pp282-4; ☎ /fax 0 5320 6365; cnr Th Tha Phae & Th Kotchasan; dishes 50-110B; ☻ 10am-10pm) Facing Pratu Tha Phae, this very popular air-con rendezvous prepares a combination of vegetarian and nonvegetarian Italian, as well as Thai, Mexican and American food, including pizza, sandwiches, pasta, enchiladas, tacos, salads, ice cream, pies, tiramisu, shakes, fruit juices and coffees. This restaurant is 100% smoke-free.

Home Restaurant (Map pp282-4; ☎ 0 6184 6618; 36 Th Chaiyaphum; dishes 40-120B; ☻ 9am-11pm) Good-value Thai, northern Thai and vegetarian fare is on offer here, plus sandwiches, cakes and pies. The food is served in a quiet, laid-back open-air dining area behind an older wooden Thai house.

House (Map pp282-4; ☎ 0 5341 9011; 199 Th Moon Muang; dishes 80-180B, set menu 990B; ☻ 6pm-11pm) This ambitious restaurant occupies a mid-20th-century house that once belonged to an exiled Burmese prince. The menu successfully fuses Thai and European elements, complemented by an excellent wine list and attentive service. The separate wine and tapas bar is a good choice for lighter fare.

Libernard Café (Map pp282-4; ☎ 0 5323 4877; 295-299 Th Chang Moi; dishes 40-80B; ☻ 7.30am-5pm) Libernard serves fresh Arabica coffee grown in Thailand and roasted daily on the premises.

The array of pancakes and other breakfast specialities also deserve acclaim, and Thai food is available as well. If you're looking for Thai coffee to take home, this is the place to buy it, either ground or whole-bean.

Love at First Bite (Map pp282-4; ☎ 0 5324 2731; 28 Soi 1, Th Chiang Mai-Lamphun; pastries 40-60B; ☺ 10.30am-6pm) Yes it's almost too good to be true, that the glass-fronted refrigerators stocked with all manner of cheesecakes, layer cakes, pies, blintzes and more could taste as delicious as they look. But they do. There are a few tables where you can sit and drink coffee or tea while sampling the fruits of the Thai owners' 27-year sojourn in the USA.

UN Irish Pub (Map pp282-4; ☎ 0 5321 4554; 24/1 Th Ratwithi; dishes 50-100B; ☺ 9am-midnight) This 'pub' offers baked goods, good coffee, muesli, yogurt, sandwiches, pasta, pizza, vegetarian dishes, baked potatoes, ice cream, some Thai food, beer on tap, and fruit and vegetable juices. The homey indoor section is decorated with Irish kitsch and there's pleasant garden seating out the back.

Bake & Bite (Map pp282-4; ☎ 0 5328 5185; 6 Soi 1, Th Kotchasan; dishes 30-100B; ☺ 7am-6pm Sun-Fri, to 3pm Sat) This tiny place, wedged behind Suriwongse Plaza, prepares some delicious European- and American-style pastries, pies and sandwiches on your choice of several breads.

Mike's Burgers (Map pp282-4; cnr Th Chaiyaphum & Th Chang Moi; dishes 70-80B; ☺ 6pm-3am) Grab a stool for a dose of après-clubbing hand-made burgers and chili fries.

Chiangmai Saloon (Map pp282-4; ☎ 0 6161 0690; 80/1 Th Loi Kroh; dishes 60-150B) Ignore the ersatz Wild West décor, and head straight for the best steaks and Tex-Mex in town. Best bar T-shirt, too.

Upper Crust Café (Map pp282-4; ☎ 0 5381 8183; Chiang Inn Plaza, Th Chang Khlan; dishes 40-80B; ☺ 10am-11pm) Good pastries (especially the mango cheesecake), light Mexican dishes and sandwiches, coupled with fast service.

Mango Tree Café (Map pp282-4; ☎ 0 5320 8292; 8/2-3 Th Loi Kroh; dishes 50-100B; ☺ 7.30am-11pm) Set amid a strip of downmarket hostess bars at the west end of Th Loi Kroh, Mango Tree nonetheless prevails with good *faràng* and Thai fare. Live music most nights.

Amazing Sandwich Phra Pokklao (Map pp282-4; 252/3 Th Phra Pokklao; ☎ 0 5321 8846; dishes 60-90B); Huay Kaew Map pp278-80; 20/2 Th Huay Kaew; ☎ 0 5340 4174; dishes 60-90B) Three doors north of the Thai Air-

ways International office, this small air-con place specialises in fresh baguettes with your choice of a dozen fillings, as well as lasagne, vegetable pie and quiche.

Chez John (Map pp278-80; ☎ 0 5320 1551; 18/1 Th Mahidon; dishes 80-160B) Near the airport and opposite the customs office, Chez John prepares moderately priced French cuisine as well as having a large selection of wines.

Popular among German expatriates and visitors are the **Bierstube** (Map pp282-4; ☎ 0 5327 8869; 33/6 Th Moon Muang; dishes 50-100B; ☺ 7.30am-11pm), near Pratu Tha Phae, and **Haus München** (Map pp282-4; ☎ 0 5327 4027; 115/3 Th Loi Kroh; dishes 40-100B), east of Chiangmai Pavilion. Next to Haus München are three more European eateries, all in a row along Th Loi Kroh: **Red Lion English Pub & Restaurant** (Map pp282-4; Th Loi Kroh), **German Hofbräuhaus** (Map pp282-4; Th Loi Kroh) and **Café Benelux** (Map pp282-4; Th Loi Kroh), each serving the type of cuisine their names imply. **Grillstation** (Map pp282-4; ☎ 0 5381 8355; 23/8 Th Charoen Prathet; dishes 50-120B) also features a German-oriented menu specialising in excellent grilled meats and sausages.

The main fast-food district in Chiang Mai runs along Th Chang Khlan, in the Chiang Mai Night Bazaar area (Map pp282-4). This strip features the usual Western fast-food outlets, most of which are clustered within the Chiang Inn Plaza. Similar franchise-style places can be found in the Kad Suan Kaew shopping centre (Map pp278-80) Th Huay Kaew and at Central Airport Plaza (Map pp278-80) near the airport.

Vegetarian

Chiang Mai is blessed with more than 25 vegetarian restaurants, most of them very inexpensive. All of the Indian restaurants mentioned earlier in this section feature short vegetarian sections in their menus.

AUM Vegetarian Food (Map pp282-4; ☎ 0 5327 8315; 65 Th Moon Muang; dishes 30-70B; ☺ 8am-9pm) Near Pratu Tha Phae, AUM has long been popular with travellers because of its easy location. The all-veggie menu features a varied list of traditional Thai and Chinese dishes, including northern and northeastern Thai dishes, prepared without meat or eggs. There is an upstairs eating area with cushions on the floor and low tables.

Mangsawirat Kangreuanjam (Map pp282-4; Soi 1, Th Inthawarorot; dishes 10-20B; ☺ 8am-early afternoon) Look for the difficult-to-see English sign that reads 'Vegetarian Food', and a cluster of stainless steel pots. The cooks put out 15 to 20 pots of fresh, 100% Thai vegetarian dishes daily. The dishes feature lots of bean curd, squash, peas, pineapple, sprouts and potato, and the desserts are good.

Biaporn (Map pp282-4; Soi 1, Th Si Phum; dishes 20-30B; ◷ 10am-3pm) Within the old city quadrangle, just north of SK Guest House, this is another very inexpensive Thai vegetarian place, but with a more limited selection of dishes.

Vegetarian Centre of Chiang Mai (Map pp278-80; ☎ 0 5327 1262; 14 Th Om Muang; dishes 10-15B; ◷ 6am-2pm Sun-Thu) Sponsored by the Asoke Foundation, an ascetically minded Buddhist movement, the long-running Vegetarian Centre serves extremely inexpensive but very good cafeteria-style veg – you push a tray along a rack and point out what you want. A small health-food section to one side of the restaurant offers dried gluten, nuts, beans, herbs, vegetarian chilli sauces, natural beauty products, herbal medicines and Dharma books (mostly in Thai).

Suandok Vegetarian (Map pp278-80; Th Suthep; dishes 10-20B; ◷ 7am-2pm) This tiny stall just west of the entrance to Wat Suan Dok offers a simple array of inexpensive, wholesome Thai vegetarian dishes and brown rice.

Whole Earth Restaurant (Map pp282-4; ☎ 0 5328 2463; 88 Th Si Donchai; dishes 90-200B) The food here is Thai and Indian (both vegetarian and nonvegetarian) and the atmosphere is suitably mellow, as are the toned-down flavours.

Vihara Liangsan (Map pp282-4; ☎ 0 5381 8094; 199/23 Th Chang Khlan; lunch from 25B; ◷ 9am-2pm) This hard-to-find spot is down a narrow lane off Th Chang Khlan, about 500m south of the Night Bazaar area. You serve yourself from a long buffet table (the food is a mix of Chinese and Thai vegetarian, with lots of tofu and gluten), then place your plate – including rice – on a scale and pay by weight. It's best to get here between 11am and 1pm as the food sometimes runs out. If you telephone in advance, however, you can arrange for later meal service, including in the evenings when it's usually closed.

On the River

Riverside Bar & Restaurant (Map pp282-4; ☎ 0 5324 3239; Th Charoenrat; dishes 60-120B; ◷ 10am-1am) This rambling set of older wooden buildings, 200m north of Saphan Nawarat, has been the most consistently popular riverside place for over 20 years. The food – Thai, Western and vegetarian – is always good, and it's as popular with Thais as with *faràng*. The atmosphere is convivial and there's live music nightly. Another plus is that you can choose from indoor and outdoor dining areas. There's also an 8pm dinner cruise – you can board the boat any time after 7.30pm.

Good View (Map pp282-4; ☎ 0 5324 1866; 13 Th Charoenrat; dishes 60-120B) Next door to the Riverside, Good View offers more open-air areas and is more popular with Thais than *faràng*. The huge menu covers everything Thai. There's live music here also.

Gallery (Map pp282-4; ☎ 0 5324 8601; 25-29 Th Charoenrat; dishes 60-120B) This is a more elegant eatery in a converted 100-year-old teak Chinese shophouse that's half art gallery, half restaurant. The quality of the food and service goes up and down, but the setting remains the primary attraction.

Riverfront Restaurant (Tha Nam; off Map pp278-80; ☎ 0 5327 5125; 43/3 Th Chang Khlan; dishes 50-100B) Along the western bank of Mae Nam Ping, this restaurant is housed in an old, northern Thai–style building. The Riverfront is pretty reliable for northern, northeastern and central Thai cuisine. A northern-Thai folk ensemble performs in the evenings.

See p300 for a description of Heuan Sunthari, on the west bank of the river.

Food Centres

Galare Food Centre (Map pp282-4; Th Chang Khlan) This big indoor/outdoor cluster of permanent vendors, opposite the main Chiangmai Night Bazaar building, is good; free Thai classical dancing is featured nightly.

At the **Kad Suan Kaew Shopping Centre** (Map pp278-80; Th Huay Kaew) and **Central Airport Plaza** (Map pp278-80; Th Mahidon), food centres gather vendors selling all kinds of Thai and Chinese dishes at reasonable prices.

Night Markets

Chiang Mai is full of interesting day and night markets stocked with very inexpensive and very tasty foods.

Talat Somphet (Somphet Market; Map pp282-4; Th Moon Muang; ◷ 6am-6pm) North of the Th Ratwithi intersection, this market sells cheap takeaway curries, *yam*, *làap* (spicy minced-meat salad), *thâwt man* (fried fish cakes), sweets and seafood.

Chiang Mai Night Market (Map pp282-4; Th Bamrungburi; 6pm-5am) Another good hunting ground is this very large and popular night market near Pratu Chiang Mai. People tend to take their time here, making an evening of eating and drinking – there's no hustle to vacate tables for more customers.

Talat Warorot (Map pp278-80; cnr Th Chang Moi & Th Praisani; 6am-5pm) In the upstairs section are a number of basic stalls for *khâo tôm* (rice soup), *khâo man kài* (chicken rice), *khâo mǔu daeng* ('red' pork with rice), *jóhk* and *khâo sawy*, with tables overlooking the market floor. It's not the best cooking in Chiang Mai by a long shot, but it's cheap. A set of vendors on the ground floor specialise in inexpensive noodles – this area is particularly popular.

Anusan Night Market (Map pp282-4; btwn Th Chang Khlan & Th Charoen Prathet; 6pm-midnight) Near Chiang Mai Night Bazaar, this market attracts both tourists and Thais. If you wander over here, look for the stalls that are crowded – they're usually the best. All these places have English menus. The large *khâo tôm* place near the market entrance, Uan Heh-Hah, still packs in the customers; the most popular dish is the *khâo tôm plaa* (fish and rice soup), but other specialities worth trying include curried fish balls and curry-fried crab.

Talat San Pa Khoi (San Pa Khoi Market; Map pp278-80; off Th Charoen Muang) Has a better selection and lower prices than Anusan. A curry stand here is probably the only place in Chiang Mai where you can find fresh Thai curries past 11pm. It stays open until around 5am and is very popular with late-night partiers.

DRINKING

Drunken Flower (Mao Dokmai; Map pp278-80; 0 5321 2081; 295/1 Soi 1, Th Nimanhemin) This is a cosy indoor/outdoor bar and restaurant with a mixed Thai and expat crowd, especially local NGO staffers. There's plenty to nosh on while drinking. Most weekends locals perform live folk music.

Sudsanan (off Map pp278-80; Th Khan Khlong Chonlaprathan) Sudsanan (pronounced sùt sa-naen; Isan slang for 'most fun'), a rustic bamboo-and-wood shelter just off the canal road is the number-one hangout for local Thai poets, writers, would-be intellectuals and *phleng phêua chii-wít* (Thai folk) musicians.

Foreigners are welcome, and there's excellent live music nightly.

Writer's Club & Wine Bar (Map pp282-4; 141/3 Th Ratchadamnoen) Run by an ex-foreign correspondent, this simple shopfront bar attracts a steady stream of expats and tourists, including a few resident writers.

Drunk Studio (Map pp278-80; 0 9997 7037; 32/3 Th Atsadathon) This unique spot near Talat Kamthiang (Kamthiang Market), decorated in a deliberately nonchic way with junked auto and bus parts, is Chiang Mai's unofficial headquarters for live alternative music. Thai bands play grunge, hardcore, nu-metal, *phêua chíiwít* (Thai 'songs for life') and other styles nightly.

O'Malley's Irish Pub (Map pp282-4; 0 5327 1921; Anusan Night Market) Guinness on tap in an appropriately woody décor.

Darling Wine Pub (Map pp278-80; 0 5322 7427; 49/21 Th Huay Kaew) Darling serves fine wines by the glass or bottle in a sophisticated but relaxed atmosphere.

The Pub (off Map pp278-80; 0 5321 1550; 189 Th Huay Kaew) In an old Tudor-style cottage set well off the road, this venerable Chiang Mai institution semisuccessfully calls up the atmosphere of an English country pub. The Friday evening happy hour is popular.

UN Irish Pub (Map pp282-4; 0 5321 4554; 24/1 Th Ratwithi) There's nothing particularly Irish here other than some kitsch on the walls, and the beers are all Thai-brewed, but it's quiet and the comfortable upstairs area is suitable for solo reading or writing. On some evenings there's live music upstairs, and during Tuesday's open mic session, everyone is welcome to sing or play an instrument. Football (soccer) matches are regularly shown on satellite TV as well. The pub also offers a wide variety of food (see p304).

Pinte Blues Pub (Map pp282-4; 33/6 Th Moon Muang) This place deserves some sort of award for staying in business so long (more than 20 years) while serving only espresso and beer, and for sticking to a single music format the whole time. Huge collection of blues CDs and tapes.

Sax Music Pub (Map pp282-4; 0 6916 6807; Th Moon Muang) Not far from Pinte Blues Pub, Sax plays a wide variety of CDs, from jazz to hip-hop, in a narrow downstairs area. An upstairs 'studio' hosts live jam sessions on Wednesday and Saturday.

Kafé (Map pp282-4; Th Moon Muang, btwn Soi 5 & Soi 6) The daily happy hour here is popular among both expats and Thais.

Yoy Pocket (Map pp282-4; Th Ratwithi) This is a funky spot reminiscent of some of the homier café-pubs along Th Phra Athit in Bangkok.

Behind the building that houses the Yoy Pocket is a cluster of rustic outdoor bars catering to backpackers and expats. The first one to open in this area, and still the largest, **Rasta Café** plays recorded reggae, dub, African and Latin music, and is quite popular in the high season. In the same area, similarly rustic **Heaven Beach** and **Life House** often feature live local bands.

ENTERTAINMENT

Live Music

Riverside Bar & Restaurant (Map pp282-4; ☎ 0 5324 3239; 9-11 Th Charoenrat; ☺ until 2am or 3am) On Mae Nam Ping, this is one of the longest-running live music venues in Chiang Mai. Two cover bands play at either end of the rambling wooden building nightly. It's usually packed with both foreigners and Thais on weekends, so arrive early to get a table on the veranda overlooking the river. There are two indoor bars, both full of regulars, with separate bands. The food here is also good (see p305).

Good View (Map pp282-4; ☎ 0 5324 1866; 13 Th Charoenrat) Next door to Riverside, Good View changes bands more frequently and is quite popular. It also has a restaurant (see p305).

Le Brasserie (Map pp282-4; ☎ 0 5324 1665; 37 Th Charoenrat) A block or so north of Good View, this has become a favourite late-night spot (11.15pm to 1am) to listen to a talented Thai guitarist named Took play energetic versions of Hendrix, Cream, Dylan, Marley, the Allmans, and other 1960s and 1970s classics. A couple of other local bands warm up the house before Took comes on, often to a packed house. Food service is available inside the bar or out the back by the river.

Warm-Up (Map pp278-80; ☎ 0 9993 2963; Th Nimanhemin) The Warm-Up occasionally hosts nationally known Thai bands. On other nights local bands play Thai pop and reggae. This place is packed with students from Ratchamangkala Institute of Technology.

Guitar Man (Map pp282-4; ☎ 0 5381 8110, 68/5-6 Th Loi Kroh) Guitar Man offers a small café-like setting, with live music nightly.

Discos

At the following three listings, the crowd tends to be very young.

Gi Gi's (Map pp282-4; ☎ 0 5330 2340-1; Th Chiang Mai-Lamphun) East of Mae Nam Ping, Gi Gi's is one of the most popular nonhotel discos.

Discovery (Map pp278-80; Ground fl, Kad Suan Kaew Shopping Centre) Also a very popular nonhotel disco.

Nice Illusion (Map pp282-4; Th Chaiyaphum) Near the moat, Nice Illusion gets so crowded on some nights there's barely room to move.

Warm-Up (Map pp278-80; ☎ 0 9993 2963; Th Nimanhemin) Has a separate section for dancing to recorded music that is as popular as its live music room (see left).

Some of the larger hotels have discos with hi-tech recorded music and cover charges of 100B to 300B. The most active hotel discos in town are **Stardust** (off Map pp278-80; Sheraton Chiangmai), **Crystal Cave** (Map pp278-80; Empress Hotel) and the always-popular **Bubbles** (Map pp282-4; Porping Tower Hotel). Bubbles (also known as Space Bubble) has the most regular local clientele.

Cinemas

Major Cineplex (Map pp278-80; ☎ 0 5328 3939; Central Airport Plaza, 2 Th Mahidon; 80-100B) This theatre complex boasts a state-of-the-art sound system and the option of 'honeymoon seats', pairs of seats without a middle armrest for romantic couples. Along with the latest Thai films, first-run foreign films with English soundtracks are shown.

Chiang Mai University (off Map pp278-80) Every Sunday at 3pm there are showings of different foreign films – usually art films of the Bergman and Buñuel variety – at the main auditorium of the Art & Culture Center. Admission is free.

Two other cinemas showing first-run foreign as well as Thai films are the Vista cinemas at **Kad Suan Kaew shopping centre** (Map pp278-80; Th Huay Kaew) and **Vista 12 Huay Kaew** (Map pp278-80; Th Huay Kaew).

SHOPPING

As Chiang Mai is Thailand's main handicraft centre, it's ringed by small cottage factories and workshops where you can watch craftspeople at work. In general, however, merchandise you see at factories outside the city will cost more than it would in Chiang Mai unless you're buying in bulk.

CHIANG MAI PROVINCE

Hundreds of shops all over Chiang Mai sell hill-tribe and northern-Thai craftwork, but a lot of the selection is commercial and touristy junk churned out for the undiscerning. The nonprofit outlets often have the best quality and, although the prices are sometimes a bit higher than at the Chiang Mai Night Bazaar, a higher percentage of your money goes directly to the hill-tribe artisans.

Antiques

Chiang Mai Night Bazaar (Map pp282-4; Th Chang Khlan) Around the bazaar is probably the best place to look for 'copy' antiques. Inside the Nakorn Ping Night Bazaar building, towards the back on the 2nd floor, are a few small shops with real antiques.

Lost Heavens (Map pp282-4; Chiang Mai Night Bazaar Bldg ☎ 0 5327 8185; Stall 2, 2nd fl, Th Chang Khlan; 234 Th Tha Phae ☎ 0 5325 1557) Among the best of the Night Bazaar's antique shops, Lost Heavens specializes in Mien tribal artefacts. It's in

the 'antiques corner' towards the back left of the Night Bazaar building. The second store is opposite Wat Bupparam.

Under the Bo (Map pp282-4; ☎ 0 5381 8831; Stall 22-23, Chiang Mai Night Bazaar) Carries many unique pieces, in the form of furniture, antique bronze and wood figures, old doors, woodcarvings and weaving from Africa, South Asia and Southeast Asia. It isn't cheap, but many of the items are one-of-a-kind. It has another shop out on the road to Hang Dong, about 5km southwest of Th Mahidon.

Many antique shops can be found along Th Tha Phae and along Th Loi Kroh. Burmese antiques are becoming more common than Thai, as most of the Thai stuff has been bought by collectors, and you can get some great buys on antique Burmese furniture from the British colonial period.

Hang Dong, 25km south of Chiang Mai, is even better for antique furniture of all kinds; see p320 for details.

MARKETS

Talat Warorot (Map pp282-4; off Th Chang Moi; ☽ 5am-6pm) Locally called *kàat lŭang* (northern Thai for 'great market'), this is the oldest and most famous market in Chiang Mai. Although the huge enclosure is quite dilapidated (ignore the scary-looking escalators, which haven't functioned for years), it's an especially good market for fabrics and cooking implements, along with inexpensive cosmetics, clothing, handicrafts and prepared foods (especially northern Thai foods). Across the street from Talat Warorot stands the very similar Talat Lamyai, which has the same daily opening hours.

Chiang Mai Night Market (Talat Pratu Chiang Mai; Map pp282-4; Th Bamrungburi) Near Pratu Chiang Mai, this fresh-food market is particularly busy with locals shopping for takeaway Thai and northern Thai food. The indoor area is open from 4am until around noon, while outside vendors continue to sell until nightfall. A night food market then sets up across the street next to the moat and stays open past midnight.

Chiang Mai Plant Market (Talat Dok Mai Chiang Mai; Map pp278-80; ☽ around 9am-sunset) Just south of Talat Thiphanet, this is the perfect place to pick up some greenery to feather your Chiang Mai nest if you're settling in long term.

Flower Market (Map pp282-4; Th Praisani; ☽ daily) Locally called *tàlàat dàwk mái*, this is a quick stop for flowers only, and especially fresh *phuang má-lai* (jasmine garlands), is this nameless market near Talat Warorot.

Talat Thanin (Map pp282-4; off Th Chotana; ☽ 5am-early evening) North of Pratu Chang Pheuak, this clean and well-run market is the best spot for prepared foods.

Talat Ton Phayom (off Map pp278-80; Th Suthep) Across from Chiang Mai University, this market features all manner of fresh produce and cooked foods. Because CMU students make up a good portion of the clientele, prices tend to be low. Talat Ton Phayom is slated to be demolished to make room for an expanded road system in the next year or two.

Talat San Pa Khoi (Map pp278-80; off Th Charoen Muang) and **Talat Thiphanet** (Map pp278-80; Th Thipanet) are large municipal markets that offer all manner of goods and see few tourists. San Pa Khoi opens around 4am and does a brisk trade until around 10am, then slows until an hour before nightfall.

CHIANG MAI PROVINCE

Ceramics

Thai Celadon (off Map pp278-80; ☎ 0 5321 3541, 0 5321 3245; 112 Th Chotana) About 6km north of Chiang Mai, Celadon turns out ceramics modelled on the Sawankhalok pottery that used to be made hundreds of years ago at Sukhothai and exported all over the region. With their deep, crackle-glaze finish, some of the ceramic pieces are very beautiful and the prices are often lower than in Bangkok.

Mengrai Kilns (Map pp282-4; ☎ 0 5327 2063; 79/2 Th Arak) In the southwestern corner of the inner moat area near Buak Hat Park, Mengrai Kilns is reliable.

Other ceramic stores can be found close to the Old Chiang Mai Cultural Centre.

Chiang Mai Night Bazaar

The mother of all Chiang Mai tourist shopping, Chiang Mai Night Bazaar (Map pp282-4) refers to a multiblock area that stretches along Th Chang Khlan from Th Tha Phae to Th Si Donchai. Made up of several different roofed areas, ordinary glass-fronted shops and dozens of street vendors, the market offers a huge variety of Thai and northern Thai goods, as well as designer goods (both fake and licensed, so look carefully) at very low prices – if you bargain well. Many importers buy here because the prices are so good, especially when buying in large quantities.

Good buys include Phrae-style *sêua mâw hâwm* (blue cotton farmer's shirt), northern- and northeastern-Thai hand-woven fabrics, *yâam* (shoulder bags), hill-tribe crafts (many tribespeople set up their own stalls here; the Akha wander around on foot), opium scales, hats, silver jewellery, lacquerware, woodcarvings, iron and bronze Buddhas, as well as many other items.

If you need any new travelling clothes, a light cotton dress, trousers or *yâam* can be bought for 2000B or less, and *sêua mâw hâwm* cost 90B to 120B, depending on size. Spices – everything from a *tôm yam* (soup made with lemongrass, chilli, lime and usually seafood) herbal mix to pure saffron – are available from several vendors. Cashew nuts, roasted or raw, are often less expensive here than in southern Thailand where they're grown.

Chiangmai Night Bazaar Building (Th Chang Khlan) holds a couple of dozen permanent shops selling antiques, handicrafts, rattan and hardwood furniture, textiles, jewellery, pottery, basketry, silverwork, woodcarving and other items of local manufacture. Prices can be very good if you bargain hard. **Chiang Mai** (2nd fl, Chiangmai Night Bazaar Bldg), one of our favourite shops here, carries a selection of well-made cotton T-shirts silk-screened with more than 30 different old Chiang Mai designs, along with equally well-designed silver-and-bead jewellery and a changing selection of interesting accessories.

Except in the few shops with fixed prices (like the aforementioned Chiang Mai), you must bargain patiently but mercilessly. The fact that there are so many different stalls selling the same merchandise means that competition effectively keeps prices low, if you haggle. Look over the whole bazaar before you begin buying. If you're not in the mood or don't have the money to buy, it's still worth a stroll, unless you don't like crowds – most nights it's elbow to elbow.

Several restaurants and many food trolleys feed the hungry masses. Down Soi Anusan at the southern end of Th Chang Khlan, the **Anusan Night Market** (Map pp282-4; Soi Anusan, Th Chang Khlan) has lots of good Thai and Chinese food at night, and in the early morning (from 5am to 9am) you'll find fresh produce and noodle vendors.

Clothing

All sorts of shirts, blouses and dresses, plain and embroidered, are available at very low prices, but make sure that you check on the quality carefully. The Chiang Mai Night Bazaar and shops along Th Tha Phae and Th Loi Kroh have good selections.

Lanes off the north side Th Tha Phae, near Talat Warorot, boast dozens of shops signed in Thai only that offer excellent deals on readymade Thai cotton and silk clothing, both traditional and modern.

One shop selling good ready-made clothing made from northern-Thai textiles is **Sri Sanpanmai** (☎ 0 5389 4372; G-59 Kad Suan Kaew, Th Huay Kaew) inside Kad Suan Kaew (see p311).

TAILORS

There are a number of tailor shops off Th Kotchasan near Aroon (Rai) Restaurant, including **Florida**, **Chao Khun**, **Chaiyo** and **Progress**. Another strip of tailors, catering mostly to tourists, can be found along Th Chang Khlan in the Chiang Mai Night Bazaar area. Prices are reasonable, and often cheaper than in Bangkok.

City Silk (Map pp282-4; ☎ 0 5323 4388; 336 Th Tha Phae) More or less opposite Wat Mahawan, City Silk specialises in silk tailoring for women. English is spoken here, and service is friendly and professional. Ask to see some finished work before choosing a shop.

Contemporary Art

Outside of Bangkok, Chiang Mai is Thailand's leading art centre and dozens of small galleries offer fine Thai contemporary art in the city. Among the better ones are:

Aka Wilai (Map pp282-4; ☎ 0 5330 6521; www .akawalai.com; 35 Th Ratanakosin)

Galerie Panisa (Map pp282-4; ☎ 0 5320 2779; 189 Th Mahidon)

Gongdee Gallery (Map pp278-80; ☎ 0 5322 5032; www.gongdee.com; Soi 1, Th Nimanhemin)

HQ Gallery (Map pp282-4; ☎ 0 5381 4717; www .hqartgallery.com; 3/31 Th Samlan)

La Luna Gallery (Map pp282-4; ☎ 0 5330 6678; www .lalunagallery.com; 190 Th Charoenrat)

Essential Oils & Spa Products

Several shops around town specialise in extracting oils from local herbs such as lemongrass and Thai bergamot to create essential oils, massage oil, herbal cosmetics and natural toiletries. One of the better shops, with the most complete stock, is **Laan Pai Lin** (Map pp278-80; ☎ 0 5322 2036; Nantawan Arcade, 6/12 Th Nimanhemin).

Lacquerware

Decorated plates, containers, utensils and other items are made by building up layers of lacquer over a wooden or woven bamboo base. Burmese lacquerware, smuggled into the north, can often be seen, especially at Mae Sai, the northernmost point of Thailand. There are several lacquerware factories in San Kamphaeng, southeast of Chiang Mai.

Local Handicrafts

Sunday Walking Street (Map pp282-4; Th Ratchadamnoen; ⏲ 2pm-10pm Sun) Stretching along a few blocks at the eastern end of Th Ratchadamnoen, this is a better-than-average collection of handicrafts vendors. While the market is being held, only pedestrians are permitted in the area. Even if you don't plan on shopping, a stroll along the Sunday Walking Street can be enjoyable as it's the one time of the week when the old city is relatively quiet.

Thai Tribal Crafts (Map pp282-4; ☎ 0 5324 1043; 208 Th Bamrungrat) Near the McCormick Hospital, this place is run by two church groups on a nonprofit basis and has a good selection of quality handicrafts.

Hill-Tribe Products Promotion Centre (Map pp278-80; ☎ 0 5327 7743; 21/17 Th Suthep) This royally sponsored project is near Wat Suan Dok; all the profits from sales go to hill-tribe welfare programmes.

The YMCA International Hotel also operates a nonprofit handicrafts centre. The two commercial markets with the widest selections of northern-Thai folk crafts are Talat Warorot (see p308), at the eastern end of the road, and the Chiang Mai Night Bazaar (p285) for separate entries on each of these markets.

Musical Instruments

Perhaps because northern Thailand is one of Asia's major locales for both wild and cultivated bamboo, Chiang Mai has attracted interest in the crafting of 'saxophones' from bamboo (although the first such instruments seem to have taken shape some 40 years ago in Jamaica). Actually a hybrid between the saxophone and the recorder (sax shape and sax reed, recorder fingering), the instruments come in several keys. For each saxophone the bamboo must be carefully selected, cut into short rings, which are roasted over a fire to temper them, and then fitted and glued into the familiar curved shape. The sonic characteristics of the bamboo perfectly compliment the traditional cane sax reed to produce a very mellow, slightly raspy sound.

Two Chiang Mai residents make these delightful little instruments, which produce amazing volume considering their relatively small size. **Joy of Sax** (☎ 0 9261 3321) sells bamboo saxes through **Lost Heavens** (Map pp282-4; ☎ 0 5325 1557; 234 Th Tha Phae), which is opposite Wat Bupparam. You can also contact the Joy of Sax workshop directly. **Elephant Lightfoot** (Map pp282-4; ☎ 0 5387 9191; 4/1 Th Chaiyaphum) has a shopfront near Pratu Tha Phae and makes F, G, B-flat and E-flat models. **Lanna Music** (Map pp282-4; ☎ 0 5327 4144; 148/1 Th Phra Pokklao) Sells and repairs northern-Thai musical instruments.

Rattan

Hangdong Rattan (Map pp282-4; ☎ 0 5320 8167; 54-55 Th Loi Kroh) For higher-quality furniture and accessories made from this jungle vine, check out, in addition to the many items on display, this place takes custom orders.

Two cheaper rattan shops can be found along the northern side of Th Chang Moi Kao, two blocks east of the moat. This is the place to buy chairs, small tables, chaise longues, planters, floor screens, settees, bookshelves and other everyday household items.

Shopping Centres & Department Stores

Chiang Mai more than 15 shopping complexes with department stores. **Central Airport Plaza** (Map pp278-80; Th Mahidon), centred around a branch of Bangkok's Central Department Store, is the best, with **Kad Suan Kaew Shopping Centre** (Map pp278-80; Th Huay Kaew) a close second. There are several upmarket shops in both complexes. **Computer Plaza** (Map pp282-4; Th Mani Nopharat) and **Pantip Plaza** (Map pp282-4; Th Chang Khlan) are the places to go for computer supplies.

Silverwork

Sipsong Panna (Map pp278-80; ☎ 0 5321 6096; Nantawan Arcade, 6/19 Th Nimanhemin) Opposite the Amari Rincome Hotel, Sipsong Panna is a more upmarket place for jewellery collected in Thailand, Laos, Myanmar and southwestern China. Hill-tribe jewellery, which is heavy, chunky stuff, is very nice.

Thai Khün silversmiths from Kengtung in Myanmar's Shan State migrated to Chiang Mai a century or two ago and established several silverwork shops just south of the Pratu Chiang Mai city gate. Today you can visit the workshops of their descendents along Th Wualai.

Textiles

Very attractive lengths of material can be made into all sorts of things. Thai silk, with its lush colours and pleasantly rough texture, is a particularly good bargain and is usually cheaper here than in Bangkok. Talat Warorot is one of the best and least expensive places to look for fabrics, but take care, as many items said to be silk are actually polyester.

Studio Naenna (off Map pp278-80; ☎ /fax 0 5322 6042; 138/8 Soi Chang Khian, Th Huay Kaew) Operated by Patricia Cheeseman, an expert on Thai-Lao textiles who has written extensively on the subject.

The Loom (Map pp282-4; ☎ /fax 0 5327 8892; Chiang Inn Plaza, 100/1 Th Chang Khlan) Carries very fine fabrics from northern and northeastern Thailand, Laos and Cambodia.

Duangjitt House (Map pp278-80; ☎ 0 5324 2291, 0 5324 3546) This is another good source of textiles. It's on a lane off Th Thung Hotel opposite the Northern Crafts Centre building – call for an appointment.

Several individual shops in town focus on the high-quality traditional (sometimes antique) Thai and Lao fabrics, sold by the metre or made into original-design clothes. A list of the best places in town would have to include **Sbun-Nga** (Map pp278-80; ☎ 0 5322 2261; Nantawan Arcade; Th Nimanhemin) and **Nandakwang** (Map pp278-80; ☎ 0 5320 0655; Nantawan Arcade, Th Nimanhemin), both near the Amari Rincome.

You'll also find several shops selling antique Thai and Lao textiles on Th Loi Kroh. These include **Woven Dreams** (Map pp282-4; ☎ 0 5327 2569; 30/1 Th Loi Kroh) and **Success Silk Shop** (Map pp282-4; ☎ 0 5320 8853; 56 Th Loi Kroh), which both feature Thai silk ready-made and made-to-order clothes using fabrics from Thailand, Laos and Cambodia. Many are patched together from old hand-woven textiles and made into dresses, skirts, shirts and jackets. They also offer silk scarves, woven hats and *yâam* – all more or less sized for *faràng*.

If you want to see where and how the cloth is made, go to the nearby town of San Kamphaeng for Thai silk, or to Pasang, south of Lamphun, for cotton.

Umbrellas

At Bo Sang, the 'umbrella village', 9km ease of Chiang Mai, you will find hand-painted paper umbrellas of all kinds, from simple traditional brown ones to giant rainbow-hued parasols. See p318 for more details about the village.

Woodcarving

Many types of carvings are available, including countless elephants. Teak salad bowls are good and very cheap. Many shops along Th Tha Phae and near the Chiang Mai Night Bazaar stock wood crafts, or you can go to the source – Hang Dong and Ban Thawai.

GETTING THERE & AWAY

Air

INTERNATIONAL

Regularly scheduled international flights fly into **Chiang Mai International Airport** (Map pp278–80; ☎ 0 5327 0222) from the following cities:

Kunming (THAI; ☎ 0 5321 1021)
Singapore (Silk Air; ☎ 0 5327 6459)
Taipei (Mandarin Airlines; ☎ 0 5320 1268)
Vientiane, Luang Prabang (Lao Aviation; ☎ 0 5322 3401)
Yangon, Mandalay (Air Mandalay; ☎ 0 5381 8049)

DOMESTIC

Until recently your domestic airline choices for reaching Chiang Mai were limited, but since 2003 Thailand has been going through a period of air route deregulation which has resulted in several low-fare, no-frills airline start-ups. Fares are now very much in flux, ranging from special advance purchase fares of as low as 598B one way from Bangkok aboard Nok Air to as high as 2200B for the same sector on THAI (or more in business class).

The **Thai Airways International** (THAI; Map pp278–80; ☎ 0 5321 1044-7; 240 Th Phra Pokklao) office is located in the Airport Business Park. The airline operates eight one-hour flights between Bangkok and Chiang Mai daily (plus additional flights on certain days of the week). The unrestricted fare is 2200B one way in economy class, less expensive with advance booking. THAI also flies between Chiang Mai and Mae Hong Son (970B) and Phuket (4640B).

Bangkok Airways (Map pp278–80; ☎ 0 5321 0043-4; Chiang Mai International Airport) has daily flights to/from Bangkok (via Sukhothai; 2180B) and Sukhothai (850B).

Relative newcomers, all located at Chiang Mai International Airport (Map pp278–80), are: **Nok Air** (☎ 1318), **Air Asia** (☎ 0 2515 9999) and **Orient Thai** (☎ 0 5392 2159). They all fly between Bangkok and Chiang Mai for around 1500B normal fare, occasionally as low as 598B. Nok Air, a subsidiary of THAI, has the most frequent daily departures.

Bus

Departing from Bangkok's newer Northern and Northeastern bus terminal (also known as Moh Chit) there is just one ordinary 3rd-class bus each day to Chiang Mai (215B, 12 hours) leaving around 3pm. There are 12

2nd-class air-con buses a day (322B, 10 to 11 hours), but note that the air-con doesn't always work.

More comfortable 1st-class air-con buses with toilets and 32 seats leave every half hour 6.45am to 9pm (470B, 10 hours). The government VIP buses, with 24 seats that recline a bit more than the seats in 1st-class air, have about six departures each day, from either Bangkok or Chiang Mai, between 7pm and 9pm plus one in the morning around 9am (625B, 10 hours).

Ten or more private tour companies run air-con buses between Bangkok and Chiang Mai, departing from various points throughout both cities. Return tickets are always somewhat cheaper than one-way tickets. The fares cost 300B to 400B, depending on the bus. The government buses from the Northern and Northeastern bus terminal in Bangkok are generally more reliable and on schedule than the private ones booked in Banglamphu and other tourist-oriented places.

Travel agencies in Bangkok are notorious for promising services they can't deliver, such as reclining seats or air-con that works. Several Th Khao San agencies offer bus tickets to Chiang Mai for as little as 250B, including a night's free stay at a guesthouse in Chiang Mai. Sometimes this works out well, but the buses can be substandard and the 'free' guesthouse may charge you 40B to 50B for electricity or hot water, or apply heavy pressure for you to sign up for one of its treks before you can get a room. Besides, riding in a bus or minivan stuffed full of foreigners and their bulky backpacks is not the most cultural experience.

Several readers have complained that they purchased tickets for large air-con or even VIP buses from Th Khao San and at the last minute were shunted into cramped minivans. We recommend avoiding these buses altogether; use public buses from Bangkok's Northern and Northeastern bus terminal instead.

Government buses between Chiang Mai and other northern towns depart frequently throughout the day (at least hourly), except for the Mae Sai, Khon Kaen, Udon, Ubon and Khorat buses, which have only morning and evening departures. (See the table, opposite, for fares and destinations for government buses.)

Scaling the cliff at Tham Meuang On (p290), outside Chiang Mai

JOE CUMMINGS

Chiang Mai Night Bazaar (p309)

JERRY ALEXANDER

Young Lisu girls from Chiang Dao (p324), Chiang Mai Province

JERRY ALEXANDER

Stucco relief statues, Wat Jet Yot (p286), Chiang Mai

DENNIS JOHNSON

Paving workers, Chiang Mai (p276)

BECCA POSTERINO

Buddha images at Wat Phra That Doi Suthep (p316), just outside Chiang Mai

GLENN BEA

BUS DESTINATIONS FROM CHIANG MAI

Destination	Fare (B)	Duration (hr)
Chiang Dao*	29	1½
Chiang Khong	121	6½
air-con	169	6
1st class air-con	218	6
Chiang Rai	77	4
air-con	98	3
1st class	139	3
VIP	216	3
Chiang Saen	95	4
1st class air-con	171	3½
Chom Thong*	23	2
Fang*	60	3
van	100	3
Hang Dong*	10	½
Khon Kaen (via Tak)	243	12
air-con	340	12
1st class air-con	437	12
Khon Kaen (via Utaradit)	219	11
air-con	340	11
1st class air-con	394	11
Khorat	243	12
1st class air-con	437	12
VIP	510	12
Lampang	25	2
air-con	52	2
1st class air-con	70	2
Lamphun	12	1
Mae Hong Son		
(via Mae Sariang)	143	8
air-con	257	8
via Pai	100	7
air-con	130	7

Destination	Fare (B)	Duration (hr)
Mae Sai	95	5
air-con	108	5
1st class air-con	171	5
VIP	266	5
Mae Sariang	78	4-5
1st class air-con	140	4-5
Mae Sot	134	6½
1st class air-con	241	6½
Nan	128	6
air-con	179	6
1st class air-con	230	6
Pai	60	4
air-con	80	4
Phayao	67	3
air-con	94	2½
1st class air-con	121	2½
Phrae	79	4
air-con	111	3½
1st class air-con	142	3½
Phitsanulok	132-140	5-6
air-con	184-196	5½
Sukhothai	122	6
air-con	171	5
Tha Ton*	70	4
Udon Thani	228	12
air-con	319	12
1st class air-con	410	12

* Leaves from Chang Pheuak bus terminal. All other buses leave from the Chiang Mai Arcade bus terminal (also called New Terminal) off Th Kaew Nawarat.

For buses to destinations within Chiang Mai Province use the **Chang Pheuak bus terminal** (Map pp282-4; ☎ 0 5321 1586; Th Chotana), while for buses outside the province use the **Chiang Mai Arcade bus terminal** (Map pp278-80; ☎ 0 5324 2664), also called New Terminal. From the town centre, a *túk-túk* or chartered *sǎwngthǎew* to the Chiang Mai Arcade terminal should cost 40B to 50B; to the Chang Pheuak terminal you should be able to get a *sǎwngthǎew* at the normal 10B per person rate.

Train

Chiang Mai–bound rapid trains leave Bangkok's **Hualamphong station** (☎ 0 2220 4334, 0 2220 1690) daily at 3pm (air-con 2nd and 3rd class)

and 10pm (non-air-con 2nd-class sleeper and 3rd class), arriving at 5.35am and 1.05pm respectively. Express diesel railcars depart at 8.25am and 7.25pm (air-con 2nd-class only) and arrive at 8pm and 7.40am.

Special express trains depart daily at 6pm (air-con 1st- and 2nd-class sleeper and non-air-con 2nd-class sleeper) and 7.40pm (air-con 1st- and 2nd-class only), arriving in Chiang Mai at 8am and 9.05am.

The basic 2nd-class one-way fare is 281B, plus either the special express (80B), express (60B) or rapid (40B) surcharges. Add 100B for an upper berth and 150B for a lower berth in a non-air-con 2nd-class rapid train (130B and 200B respectively on the special express). For air-con 2nd-class rapid trains,

CHIANG MAI PROVINCE

add 220/270B for upper/lower sleepers (250/320B on special express trains). For example, if you take a non-air-con 2nd-class upper berth on a rapid train, your total fare will be 461B (321B plus 100B plus 40B). Tickets for the 'express diesel railcar' (Nos 9 and 11) cost the same as air-con 2nd-class seats on an express.

The basic 1st-class fare is 593B; berths are 520B per person and are available on the special express and rapid trains only.

Berths on sleepers to Chiang Mai are increasingly hard to reserve without booking well in advance; tour groups sometimes book entire cars. The return trip from Chiang Mai to Bangkok doesn't seem to be as difficult, except during the Songkran (mid-April) and Chinese New Year (late February to early March) holiday periods.

Chiang Mai's neat and tidy **train station** (Map pp278-80; ☎ 0 5324 5363; Th Charoen Muang) has an ATM and two advance booking offices, one at the regular ticket windows outdoors (open 5am to 9pm), the other in a more comfortable air-con office (open 6am to 8pm). The booking office has a computerised reservation system through which you can book train seats for anywhere in Thailand up to 60 days in advance. There is also a left-luggage facility that is open 4.50am to 8.45pm. The cost is 10B per piece for the first five days and 15B per piece thereafter, with a 20-day maximum.

GETTING AROUND
To/From the Airport
There is only one licensed airport taxi service, charging 100B for comfortable sedan cars that can take up to four or five people and their luggage. Pick up a ticket at the taxi kiosk just outside the baggage-claim area, then present your ticket to the taxi drivers outside by the main arrival area exit. The airport is only 2km to 3km from the city centre.

You can charter a túk-túk or red săwng-thăew from the centre of Chiang Mai to the airport for 50B or 60B.

Bicycle
Cycling is a good way to get around Chiang Mai if you don't mind a little traffic and, at the denser intersections, vehicular fumes. The city is small enough so that everywhere is accessible by bicycle, including Chiang

Mai University, Wat U Mong, Wat Suan Dok and the Chiang Mai National Museum on the outskirts of town.

Basic Chinese- or Thai-manufactured bicycles can be rented for around 30B to 50B a day from several of the guesthouses or from various places along the east moat:

Bike & Bite (Map pp282-4; ☎ 0 5341 8534; 23/1 Th Si Phum) This is a combination Thai restaurant and mountain-bike rental/tour company.

Contact Travel (Map pp282-4; ☎ 0 5327 7178; www .activethailand.com; 73/7 Th Charoen Prathet) This outfit rents rugged 21-speed mountain bikes for 200B a day. It also operates cycling tours around the province.

Song Bicycle (☎ 0 5321 3404; 3/4-6 Th Si Phum)

Velocity (Map pp282-4; ☎ 0 5341 0665; 177 Th Chang Pheuak) Velocity rents mountain and racing bikes, offers guided tours and carries all kinds of cycling accessories.

If you have your own bicycle with you, and need repairs or hard-to-find parts, your best bet is Canadian-owned **Top Gear Bike Shop** (Map pp282-4; ☎ 0 5323 3450; topgearbike@hotmail .com; 173 Th Chang Moi), near Soi 2.

Bus
Chiang Mai has just one city bus line of limited use. Known as the 'pink bus' among foreigners, it runs from a housing estate on Th Chiang Mai–Hang Dong, south of the city a few kilometres, to the centre of the old city and back, via Central Airport Plaza (but not the airport itself). The fare is 10B and the bus operates 5.30am to 10pm.

Most Chiang Mai residents take săwng-thăew and many also own their own bicycles or motorcycles.

Car & Motorcycle
Cars, 4WDs and minivans are readily available at several locations throughout the city. Be sure that the vehicle you rent has insurance (liability) coverage – ask to see the documents and carry a photocopy with you while driving.

Two of the best agencies in town for service and price are **North Wheels** (Map pp282-4; ☎ 0 5397 4478; www.northwheels.com; 70/4-8 Th Chai-yaphum) near Talat Somphet, and **Journey** (Map pp282-4; ☎ 0 5320 8787; www.journeycnx.com; 283 Th Tha Phae), near Pratu Tha Phae. Both offer hotel pick-up and delivery as well as 24-hour emergency road service, along with insurance. Sample rentals at North Wheels include Nissan Sunny for 1000B for 24

MASS TRANSIT FOR CHIANG MAI?

Ever since Chiang Mai's original four-line city bus system was closed down in 1997, both residents and visitors have lamented the lack of regular public transport in the city. In the meantime private vehicle use has grown tremendously, with concomitant traffic jams and noxious auto emissions.

After years of rumour, the municipal government in 2004 finally hired Chiang Mai University to carry out a feasibility study for Chiang Mai mass transit, to be funded in part at the national level. The main objective will be to establish a light electric rail system, supplemented by air-conditioned buses and private metered taxis.

The biggest roadblock standing in the way of the plan is the powerful red *săwngthăew* mafia, who have bribed, cajoled and physically threatened all newcomers who have tried to provide other forms of local transport. As is obvious to everyone who lives in Chiang Mai, the over-abundant *săwngthăew* tend to exacerbate, rather than relieve, local traffic congestion.

The study will finish within 10 months, and construction on the rail system is supposed to begin within two years.

hours and Toyota 4WD pick-ups for 1500B a day (2000B a day with a driver). Journey rents Suzuki Caribians for only 700B per day. At both companies discounted weekly and monthly rates are available.

It's very important to choose a car-rental agency carefully, by reputation rather than what's on paper. Also realise that whatever happens, you're still responsible for personal injury and medical payments of anyone injured in connection with a traffic accident.

Other prominent rental agencies include the following:

Avis Royal Princess Hotel (Map pp282-4; ☎ 0 5328 1033; 122 Th Chang Khlan); Chiang Mai International Airport (Map pp278-80; ☎ 0 5320 1798-9)
Budget (Map pp278-80; ☎ 0 5320 2871; Chiang Mai International Airport)
National Car Rental (Map pp278-80; ☎ 0 5321 0118; Amari Rincome Hotel)

If you are planning to hire a motorcycle, Honda Dream 100cc step-throughs can be rented for 100B to 200B a day, depending

on the season, the condition of the motorcycle and length of rental. Prices are very competitive in Chiang Mai because there's a real glut of motorcycles. For two people, it's cheaper to rent a small motorcycle for the day to visit Doi Suthep than to go up and back in a *săwngthăew*. Occasionally you'll see slightly larger 125cc to 150cc Hondas or Yamahas for rent for 200B to 250B a day.

The availability of motorcycles bigger than 150cc varies from year to year but you can usually find 250cc Japanese off-road motorcycles (500B, 350B low season) or 600cc motorcycles (800B to 900B) at agencies specialising in larger motorcycles.

Motorcycle-rental places come and go with the seasons. Many of them are lined up along the eastern side of the moat on Th Moon Muang, Th Chaiyaphum and Th Kotchasan. Among the more established and more reliable are the following:

C&P Bike Service (☎ 0 5327 1161; 51 Th Kotchasan)
Dang Bike Hire (Map pp282-4; ☎ 0 5327 1524; 23 Th Kotchasan)
Goodwill Motorcycle Hire (☎ 0 5325 1186; 26/1 Soi 2, Th Chang Moi)
Lek Big Bike (☎ 0 5325 1840; 74/2 Th Chaiyaphum)
Mr Mechanic (Map pp282-4; ☎ 0 5321 4708; 4 Soi 5, Th Moon Muang)
Pop Rent-A-Car (Map pp282-4; ☎ 0 5327 6014; near Soi 2, Th Kotchasan)

These agencies offer motorcycle insurance for around 50B a day, not a bad investment considering you could face a 25,000B to 60,000B liability if your bike is stolen. Most policies have a high deductible (excess), so in cases of theft you're usually responsible for a third to half of the motorcycle's value – even with insurance. More casual rental places that specialise in quick, easy and cheap rentals of 100cc bikes can be found along Th Moon Muang.

Several car-rental places also rent motorcycles. An excellent website on motorcycle touring and rental in northern Thailand is the **Golden Triangle Rider** (www.gt-rider.com).

Metered Taxi

In 2004 a company dared to begin operating a small fleet of metered, air-con taxis in Chiang Mai. Fares start at 30B for the first 2km, plus 4B for each additional kilometre. Most trips in the city limits will cost 50B or less. Since there are so few operating at this point, the only way to be assured of engaging their services is to call **Taxi Meter** (☎ 0 9261 4209).

Săwngthăew, Túk-Túk & Săamláw

Hordes of red *săwngthăew* ply the streets of Chiang Mai looking for passengers. Flag one down, state your destination and if it is going that way you can ride for 10B. It's best to board one that already has passengers if you're worried about getting overcharged. Some drivers try to charge lone passengers (both Thais and *faràng*) 20B instead of the usual 10B. If you're the only passenger and you're going to an out-of-the-way place, that may be reasonable, but if you're going, say, from Pratu Tha Phae to Talat Waro-rot – a relatively short and well-travelled distance – you shouldn't have to pay more than the normal 10B fare. You can charter (*mǎo*) a *săwngthăew* anywhere in the city for 60B or less.

Túk-túk work only on a charter or taxi basis, at 30B for short trips and 40B to 60B for longer ones. After midnight in enter-tainment areas such as along Th Charoen-rat near the Riverside and the Brasserie, or down towards Gi Gi's, most *túk-túk* charge a flat 50B for any trip back across the river.

Chiang Mai still has loads of *săamláw* (pedicabs, also spelt 'samlor'), especially in the old city around Talat Warorot. *Săamláw* cost around 20B to 30B for most trips.

AROUND CHIANG MAI

Chiang Mai is ringed with interesting attrac-tions within a half day's travel of the city. Among the highlights are two small but significant museums in Mae Rim, sacred Doi Suthep and surrounding Doi Suthep and Doi Pui National Parks, the traditional Northern Thai villages and natural environ-ment of Doi Inthanon, the historic Lanna-style temples of Lamphun Lampang and trekking around Chiang Dao and Tha Ton.

DOI SUTHEP

ดอยสุเทพ

Sixteen kilometres northwest of Chiang Mai is Doi Suthep (1676m), a peak named after the hermit Sudeva, who lived on the mountain's slopes for many years. Near its summit is **Wat Phra That Doi Suthep**; first es-

tablished in 1383 under King Keu Naone, it is one of the north's most sacred temples. A staircase of 300 steps leads to the wat at the end of the winding road up the mountain. You also have the option of riding a tram from the parking lot to the wat grounds for 20B.

At the top, weather permitting, there are some fine views of Chiang Mai. Inside the cloister is an exquisite Lanna-style, copper-plated stupa topped by a five-tiered gold umbrella – one of the holiest stupas in Thai-land. Within the monastery compound, the **International Buddhism Center** (IBC; ☎ 0 5329 5012; www.chedi5000.com; admission free, donations appreciated) offers a daily teaching program on Bud-dhism, meditation and chanting, along with longer residential retreats, plus language instruction in Pali and Thai for Buddhism.

About 4km beyond Wat Phra That Doi Suthep is **Phra Tamnak Phu Phing**, a winter pal-ace for the royal family with **palace gardens** (admission free; ☯ 8.30am-12.30pm & 1-4pm Sat, Sun & holidays). The road that passes the palace splits off to the left, stopping at the peak of Doi Pui. From there, a dirt road proceeds for a couple of kilometres to a nearby Hmong hill-tribe village. If you won't have a chance to visit remote villages, it's worth visiting this one, even though it is well touristed. You can buy Hmong handicrafts here and see traditional homes and costumes, al-though these are mostly posed situations.

If you're cycling or driving to the sum-mit, you can stop off along the way at the waterfalls, **Nam Tok Monthathon** (admission 200B; ☯ 8am-sunset), 2.5km off the paved road to Doi Suthep. The trail is well marked; if you're interested in checking the falls out, have the *săwngthăew* driver drop you off on the way up the mountain. Pools beneath the falls hold water year-round, although swimming is best during or just after the annual monsoon. The falls can be a little crowded on weekends. The 200B fee allows you to visit other waterfalls on the road to Suthep.

DOI PUI NATIONAL PARK

อุทยานแห่งชาติดอยปุย

Most visitors do a quick tour of the temple, the Hmong village and perhaps the win-ter palace grounds, altogether missing the surrounding park. This 261-sq-km **reserve** (adult/child under 14 yrs 200/100B; ☯ 8am-sunset) is

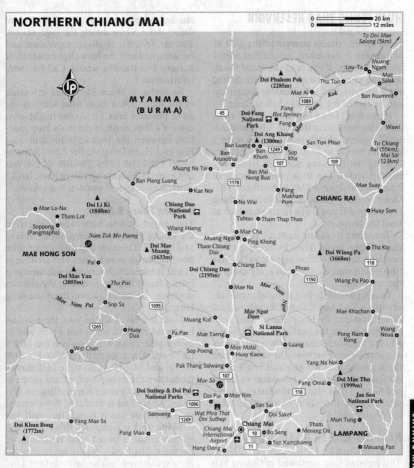

NORTHERN CHIANG MAI

home to more than 300 bird species and nearly 2000 species of ferns and flowering plants. Because of its proximity to urban Chiang Mai, development of the park has become a very sensitive issue. The western side of the park has been severely disturbed by poachers and land encroachers, including around 500 hill-tribe families.

There are extensive hiking trails in the park, including one that climbs 1685m Doi Pui; the summit is a favourite picnic spot. Other trails pass Hmong villages that rarely get foreign visitors. Bungalow and dormitory accommodation is available near the park headquarters (past the temple car park on the right). Depending on who's on duty at the park headquarters, there are also maps available here. Mountain bikers will find lots of fat-tyre fun.

A 4km trail also leads to the scenic and more isolated Nam Tok Sai Yai (Sai Yai waterfalls), and connects with a trail that leads to Nam Tok Monthathon.

Getting There & Away

Săwngthăew to Doi Suthep leave Chiang Mai throughout the day from the western end of Th Huay Kaew in front of Chiang Mai University. Doi Suthep *săwngthăew* fares are 40B up and 30B back per person. *Săwngthăew* depart from Pratu Chang Pheuak and the Chiang Mai Zoo. To Phra Tamnak Phu Phing and Doi Pui add 20B in each direction.

CHIANG MAI PROVINCE

HUAY TEUNG THAO RESERVOIR

อ่างเก็บน้ำห้วยตึงเฒ่า

Head for this sizable **reservoir** (off Map pp278-80; admission free; ☼ 8am-sunset), about 12km north-west of the city, if you're in the mood for an all-day swim and picnic, especially during the hotter months. Windsurfing equipment can be rented for around 150B an hour.

If you don't bring your own, food is available from vendors at the lake, who maintain small bamboo-thatch huts over the water's edge for people to sit in. The local speciality is *kûng tên* (dancing shrimp), freshwater shrimp served live in a piquant sauce of lime juice and *phrík lâap* (a Northern Thai blend of spicy herbs and chillies). Fishing is permitted if you'd like to try your luck at hooking lunch.

Travelling by car or motorcycle you can reach Huay Teung Thao by driving 10km north on Rte 107 (follow signs towards Mae Rim), then west 2km past an army camp to the reservoir.

Cyclists would do best to pedal to the reservoir via Th Khan Khlong Chonlaprathan. Head west on Th Huay Kaew, then turn right just before the canal. Follow Th Khan Khlong Chonlaprathan north until it ends at a smaller road between the reservoir and the highway; turn left here and you'll reach the lake after another kilometre or so of pedalling. From the northwestern corner of the moat, the 12km bicycle ride takes about an hour.

NAM TOK MAE SA & SAMOENG

น้ำตกแม่สา/สะเมิง

This forested loop northwest of Chiang Mai via Mae Rim and/or Hang Dong makes a good day or overnight trip. Although dotted with tourist developments – resorts, orchid farms, butterfly parks, elephant camps, snake farms, botanic gardens, antique and handicraft shops – the Rte 1096/1269 loop through the Mae Sa Valley is very scenic in spots. **Nam Tok Mae Sa** is only 6km from the Mae Rim turn-off from Rte 107, which in turn is 12km north of Chiang Mai. Further along the loop are several Hmong villages.

There are at least four places along the loop that call themselves elephant 'camp', 'farm' or 'village'. Best of the bunch is the **Maesa Elephant Camp** (☎ 0 5320 6247; www.elephant camps.com; elephant show 80B, elephant ride per person 300B), near Nam Tok Mae Sa, which features one-hour elephant shows at 8am and 9.40am daily, plus 1.30pm during the high season. You can feed the elephants sugar cane and bananas, and visit the baby elephants in their nursery and training school. Call for more information.

Samoeng, at the westernmost extension of the loop (35km from Mae Rim), is the most peaceful area for an overnight stay, since it's 5km north of the main loop junction between the highways to/from Mae Rim and Hang Dong via Rte 1269. **Samoeng Resort** (☎ 0 5348 7072; r 750-6500B; ☒), about 1.5km outside Samoeng village itself, has 15 quiet, well-designed wooden bungalows.

Getting There & Away

You can get a *săwngthăew* to Samoeng from the Chang Pheuak bus terminal in Chiang Mai for 40B. There are two daily departures, one that leaves around 9am and another at 11am. It takes 2¾ hours to reach Samoeng from Chiang Mai. In Samoeng the vehicles stop near the market, across from Samoeng Hospital.

Since it's paved all the way, the winding loop road makes a good ride by bicycle or motorcycle. From Samoeng you can take a northwest detour along Rte 1265 to Rte 1095 for Pai and Mae Hong Son; the 148km road (about two thirds unpaved, a third paved so far) breaks north at the Karen village of Wat Chan, where fuel is available. Government road crews are slowly paving this road, but until the work is completed this is the longest stretch of unpaved road remaining in northern Thailand – highly recommended for experienced off-highway bikers (and only in the dry season). The road passes by a few Hmong and Karen villages.

BO SANG & SAN KAMPHAENG

ปอสร้าง/สันกำแพง

Bo Sang (also often spelt 'Baw Sang' or 'Bor Sang'), 9km east of Chiang Mai on Rte 1006, is usually called the Umbrella Village because of its many umbrella manufacturers. Almost the entire village consists of craft shops selling painted umbrellas, fans, silverware, straw handiwork, bamboo and teak, statuary, china, celadon and lacquerware, along with tacky Chiang Mai and northern-Thai souvenirs and some quality items.

The larger shops can arrange overseas shipping at reasonable rates. As at Chiang

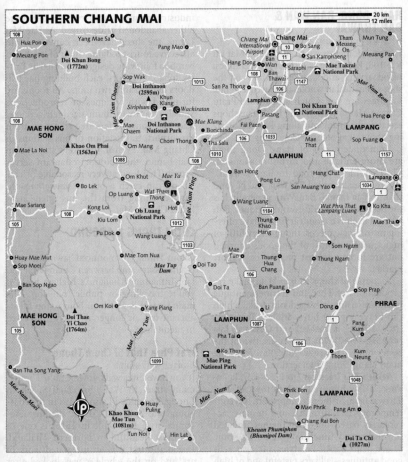

SOUTHERN CHIANG MAI

Mai Night Bazaar, discounts are offered for bulk purchases here. Some of the places will also pack and post parasols, apparently quite reliably.

In late January the **Bo Sang Umbrella Festival** (*thêtsàkaan rôm*) features a colourful umbrella procession during the day and a night-time lantern procession. Although it sounds touristy, this festival is actually a very Thai affair; a highlight is the many northern-Thai music ensembles that perform in shopfronts along Bo Sang's main street.

Four or 5km further down Rte 1006 is San Kamphaeng, which flourishes on **cotton and silk weaving**. Shops offering finished products line the main street, although the actual weaving is done in small factories

down side streets. There are some good deals to be had here, especially in silk. For cotton, you'd probably do better in Pasang, a lesser-known village near Lamphun, although you may see shirt styles here not available in Pasang.

Getting There & Away

Buses to Bo Sang and San Kamphaeng leave Chiang Mai frequently during the day from the northern side of Th Charoen Muang, east of Mae Nam Ping. The bus stop is towards the train station and across from Talat San Pa Khoi. The fare is 6B to Bo Sang and 8B to San Kamphaeng. White *sǎwngthǎew* leave from Chang Pheuak bus terminal and make the trip to either destination for 6B.

HANG DONG, BAN WAN & BAN THAWAI
หางดง/บ้านวัน/บ้านถวาย

Fifteen kilometres south of Chiang Mai on Rte 108, **Hang Dong** is famous for ceramics, woodcarving and antiques. Many of the shops here deal in wholesale as well as retail, so prices are low. Catch a bus from Pratu Chiang Mai to Hang Dong (8B). The shops are actually strung out along Rte 108, starting about 2km before Hang Dong.

Immediately east of Hang Dong there are more antique and furniture shops on Th Thakhilek (the road to Ban Thawai), an area usually called **Ban Wan**, and beyond that, in **Ban Thawai**. Ban Wan generally has the best-quality furniture and antiques. Ban Thawai itself is a woodcarving village offering mostly new pieces, though very little of high quality as most of the goods churned out are for the tourist or overseas export market.

A couple of shops in Ban Wan make reproductions of Thai and Burmese antique furniture using salvaged old teak, which can be very good buys. **Srithong Thoprasert** (☎ 0 5343 3112; Th Thakhilek) and **Crossroads Asia** (☎ 0 5343 4650; 214/7 Th Thakhilek) are two of the better ones. They're about 500m from the main Hang Dong intersection.

Nakee's Asia Treasures (☎ 0 5344 1357; Th Thakhilek), a few hundred metres towards Ban Thawai from Srithong Thoprasert, has contemporary Thai furniture and designer accessories based on older themes updated for form and function (including some fusion with Santa Fe styles). It also sells good antiques – all very tasteful and of high quality.

SAN PA THONG
สันป่าตอง

Further south down Rte 108, this overgrown village is home to a huge and lively weekly **water buffalo and cattle market** (5.30am-10am Sat). In addition to livestock, the market purveys used motorcycles and bicycles at prices that beat Chiang Mai's. If you want breakfast, there are also plenty of food vendors.

In San Pa Thong, **Kao Mai Lanna Resort Hotel** (☎ 0 5383 4470; www.kaomailanna.com; Km 29, Th Chiang Mai-Hot; r 1500-2000B; 🐶) is almost reason enough to travel this far. As southern China supplanted northern Thailand as a major source of tobacco for the world cigarette industry, many tobacco-curing sheds were either abandoned or destroyed. At Kao Mai Lanna, the sheds have been converted into attractive tourist lodging. Built of brick and bamboo following designs imported by British tobacco brokers, each building has two floors divided into two units. All rooms are furnished with antiques or reproductions and also feature medium-sized refrigerators. Kao Mai Lanna offers free transport from the airport, train station or bus stations in Chiang Mai. Even if you don't stay at Kao Mai Lanna, the outdoor restaurant serves superb Thai food at very reasonable prices.

You can catch a bus or *săwngthăew* to San Pa Thong from the bus queue near Pratu Chiang Mai.

CHOM THONG & AROUND
จอมทอง

Chom Thong (pronounced 'jawm thawng') is a necessary stop between Chiang Mai and Doi Inthanon, Thailand's highest peak, if you're travelling by public transport. The main temple is worth an hour's stop for its ancient *bòt*, or longer if you're interested in meditation.

Wat Phra That Si Chom Thong
วัดพระธาตุศรีจอมทอง

If you have time, walk down Chom Thong's main street to Wat Phra That Si Chom Thong. The gilded Lanna stupa in the compound was built in 1451 and the Burmese-Lanna–style *bòt*, built in 1516, is one of the most beautiful in northern Thailand. Inside and out it is an integrated work of art, and on the whole is well looked after by the local Thais. Fine woodcarving can be seen along the eaves of the roof and inside on the ceiling, which is supported by massive teak columns. The impressive altar is designed like a small *praasàat* (enclosed shrine), in typical Lanna style, and is said to contain a relic from the right side of the Buddha's skull.

Nearby is a glass case containing ancient Thai weaponry. Behind the *praasàat* altar is a room containing religious antiques.

Vegetarian Restaurant (Watjanee; dishes 25B; ⏰ 8am-4pm), just a few doors up from the wat compound, offers simple one-plate rice and noodle dishes that substitute meat with tofu and gluten. Look for the yellow pennants out the front.

MEDITATION RETREATS

Under the direction of Ajahn Thong, formerly of Wat Ram Poeng in Chiang Mai, meditation retreats in the style of the late Mahasi Sayadaw are held regularly at a lay centre in back of **Wat Phra That Si Chom Thong** (☎ 0 5382 6869). Meditation students are asked to stay a minimum of two weeks; the optimum course lasts 21 days. Students dress in white, and stay in a group of *kùtì* (meditation huts) at the back of the wat. The schedule is very rigorous.

Some students continue their individual practice at a forest monastery in Amphoe Chom Thong known as Wat Tham Thong, 5km before the town of Hot (south of Chom Thong) off Rte 108. The abbot at the latter monastery, Ajahn Chuchin Vimaro, teaches the same style of Vipassana.

Doi Inthanon National Park

อุทยานแห่งชาติดอยอินทนนท์

Thailand's highest peak, Doi Inthanon (often abbreviated as Doi In; 2590m) has three impressive waterfalls cascading down its slopes. Starting from the bottom these are **Nam Tok Mae Klang** (admission 200B; ☺ 8am-sunset), **Nam Tok Wachiratan** and **Nam Tok Siriphum**. The first two have picnic areas and food vendors. Nam Tok Mae Klang is the largest and the easiest to get to; you must stop here to get a bus to the top of Doi Inthanon. Nam Tok Mae Klang can be climbed nearly to the top, as there is a footbridge leading to rock formations over which the water cascades. Nam Tok Wachiratan is also very pleasant and less crowded.

The views from Doi Inthanon are best in the cool dry season from November to February. You can expect the air to be quite chilly towards the top, so take a jacket or sweater. For most of the year a mist, formed by the condensation of warm humid air below, hangs around the highest peak. Along the 47km road to the top are many terraced rice fields, tremendous valleys and a few small hill-tribe villages. The mountain slopes are home to around 4000 Hmong and Karen tribespeople.

The entire mountain is a national park (482 sq km), despite agriculture and human habitation. One of the top destinations in Southeast Asia for naturalists and bird-watchers, the mist-shrouded upper slopes produce abundant orchids, lichens, mosses and epiphytes, while supporting nearly 400 bird varieties, more than any other habitat in Thailand. The mountain is also one of the last habitats of the Asiatic black bear, along with the Assamese macaque, Phayre's leaf-monkey and a selection of other rare and not-so-rare monkeys and gibbons, as well as the more common Indian civet, barking deer and giant flying squirrel – around 75 mammalian species in all.

Most of the park's bird species are found between 1500m and 2000m; the best bird-watching season is from February to April, and the best spots are the *beung* (bogs) near the top.

Phra Mahathat Naphamethanidon, a stupa built by the Royal Thai Air Force to commemorate the king's 60th birthday in 1989, is off the highway between the Km 41 and 42 markers, about 4km before reaching the summit of Doi Inthanon. In the base of the octagonal stupa is a hall containing a stone Buddha image.

The 200B entry fee collected for Nam Tok Mae Klang near the foot of the mountain is good for all stops on the Doi Inthanon circuit; be sure to keep your receipt.

Park Bungalows (☎ 0 5331 1608; tents 40B, r 800-1000B), 31km north of Chom Thong, can be reserved at the park headquarters in Chom Thong. Blanket hire is 10B.

In Chom Thong, inquire at Wat Phra That Si Chom Thong for a place to sleep.

Getting There & Away

Buses to Chom Thong leave regularly from just inside Pratu Chiang Mai at the south moat as well as from the Chang Pheuak bus terminal in Chiang Mai. Some buses go directly to Nam Tok Mae Klang and some go only as far as Hot, although the latter will let you off in Chom Thong. The fare to Chom Thong, 58km from Chiang Mai, is 23B.

From Chom Thong there are regular *săwngthăew* (15B) to Mae Klang, about 8km north. *Săwngthăew* from Mae Klang to Doi Inthanon (per person 30B) leave almost hourly until late afternoon. Most of the passengers are locals who get off at various points along the road, thus allowing a few stationary views of the valleys below.

For another 15B you can go south from Chom Thong to Hot, where you can get buses west on to Mae Sariang or Mae Hong Son. However, if you've been to Doi Inthanon and the waterfalls, you probably won't have time to make it all the way to Mae Sariang or Mae Hong Son in one day, so you may want to stay overnight in the park or in Chom Thong.

LAMPHUN

ลำพูน

pop 15,200

This quiet town, capital of the province of the same name, lies southeast of Chiang Mai on the banks of Nam Mae Kuang.

Best visited as a day trip from Chiang Mai, Lamphun was, along with Pasang, the centre of a small Hariphunchai principality (AD 750–1281) originally ruled by the semilegendary Mon queen, Chama Thewi. Long after its Mon progenitor and predecessor Dvaravati was vanquished by the Khmer, Hariphunchai succeeded in remaining independent of both the Thais and the Khmer.

During the second week of August, Lamphun hosts the annual **Lam Yai Festival**, which features floats made of fruit and, of course, a Miss Lam Yai contest.

Sights

There are many more nearby temples than that two described here. Although none enjoys the fame of Wat Phra That Hariphunchai and Wat Chama Thewi, many of them are quite old and atmospheric.

WAT PHRA THAT HARIPHUNCHAI

วัดพระธาตุหริภุญชัย

Thais consider the tallest stupas at this wat to be one of the eight holiest stupa in Thailand. Built on the site of Queen Chama Thewi's palace in 1044 (1108 or 1157 according to some datings), this temple lay derelict for many years until Khruba Siwichai, one of northern Thailand's most famous monks, made renovations in the 1930s. It boasts some interesting post-Dvaravati architecture, a couple of fine Buddha images and two old stupas of the original Hariphunchai style. The tallest stupa, Chedi Suwan, dates from 1418, is 46m high and is surmounted by a nine-tiered gold umbrella weighing 6.5kg.

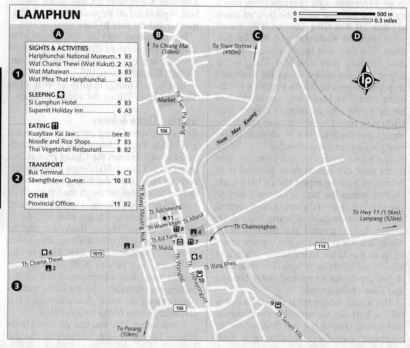

LAMPHUN

| SIGHTS & ACTIVITIES | |
| Hariphunchai National Museum..**1** B3 |
| Wat Chama Thewi (Wat Kukut)..**2** A3 |
| Wat Mahawan..........................**3** B3 |
| Wat Phra That Hariphunchai......**4** B2 |

| SLEEPING 🏠 | |
| Si Lamphun Hotel.....................**5** B3 |
| Supamit Holiday Inn.................**6** A3 |

| EATING 🍴 | |
| Kuaytiaw Kai Jaw....................(see 8) |
| Noodle and Rice Shops.............**7** B3 |
| Thai Vegetarian Restaurant........**8** B2 |

| TRANSPORT | |
| Bus Terminal...........................**9** C3 |
| Săwngthăew Queue................**10** B3 |

| OTHER | |
| Provincial Offices.....................**11** B3 |

To Chiang Mai (38km)

To Train Station (450m)

Market

Th San Pa Yang

106

Nam Mae Kuang

Th Rawp Meuang Nok

Th Ratchawong

Th Waem Kham Th Attarot

Th Rot Kaew

Th Mukda

Th Chaimongkon

Th Wangai

Th Inthayongyot

Th Wang Khwa

Th Sanam Kila

To Hwy 11 (1.5km); Lampang (52km)

114

1015

Th Chama Thewi

To Pasang (10km)

0 — 500 m
0 — 0.3 miles

WAT CHAMA THEWI
วัดจามเทวี

A more unusual Hariphunchai stupa can be seen at Wat Chama Thewi (popularly called Wat Kukut), which is said to have been erected in the 8th or 9th century as a Dvaravati monument. It was later rebuilt by the Hariphunchai Mon in 1218. As it has been restored many times since then, it's now a mixture of several schools of architecture. The stepped profile bears a remarkable resemblance to the 12th-century Satmahal Prasada at Polonnaruwa in Sri Lanka.

Each side of the stupa – known as Chedi Suwan Chang Kot – has five rows of three Buddha figures, diminishing in size on each higher level. The standing Buddhas are in Dvaravati style, although made recently.

HARIPHUNCHAI NATIONAL MUSEUM
พิพิธภัณฑสถานแห่งชาติลำพูน

Across the street from Wat Phra That Hariphunchai, Lamphun's **Hariphunchai National Museum** (☎ 0 5351 1186; fax 0 5353 0536; Th Inthayongyot; admission 30B; ☒ 9am-4pm Wed-Sun) has a small collection of artefacts from the Dvaravati, Hariphunchai and Lanna kingdoms. Some signs are in English, there's a small bookshop and it's a cool escape from the heat.

Sleeping & Eating

Supamit Holiday Inn (☎ 0 5353 4865; fax 0 5353 4355; Th Chama Thewi; s/d 250-400B; ☒) Although it bears no relation to the international hotel chain, this is a solid choice, with helpful staff and 50 clean rooms. An open-air restaurant on the 5th floor serves good fare. It's across from Wat Chama Thewi.

Si Lamphun Hotel (no Roman-script sign; ☎ 0 5351 1176; Soi 5, Th Inthayongyot; s/d 100/200B) This place was undergoing a complete facelift when we visited. When it re-opens prices are likely to increase, but it's the easiest accommodation to find because it's on the main thoroughfare.

Noodle and rice shops (Th Inthayongyot) There is a string of decent food shops south of Wat Phra That.

Thai vegetarian restaurant (Th Wangsai; dishes 15-30B; ☒ 7am-7pm Mon-Sat) One block off the main road, this restaurant serves delicious meatless curries and stirfried vegetables; dishes include rice. Look for the yellow pennant out front.

Kuaytiaw Kai Jaw (Th Wangsai; dishes 15B) Near the Thai vegetarian restaurant, Kuaytiaw Kai Jaw specialises in the unusual combination of rice noodles with a sausage made from chicken, carrots and seaweed. It tastes better than it sounds.

Getting There & Away

Blue *săwngthăew* to Lamphun from Chiang Mai leave at 30-minute intervals throughout the day from Th Chiang Mai–Lamphun near the southern side of Saphan Nawarat. In the reverse direction, *săwngthăew* leave Lamphun from the queue near the intersection of Th Inthayongyot and Th Wang Khwa. The 26km ride (14B, one hour) is along a beautiful country road, parts of which are bordered by tall dipterocarp trees.

Ordinary buses to Chiang Mai (12B) leave from the **bus terminal** (Th Sanam Kila), and in the reverse direction, from Chang Pheuak bus terminal or along Th Chiang Mai–Lamphun in Chiang Mai.

PASANG
ปาซาง

Not to be confused with Bo Sang, the umbrella village, Pasang is known for its cotton weaving. It's not really a shopping destination, but more of a place to see how the weaving is done. The selection of cotton products are limited mostly to floor coverings, tablecloths and other useful household items.

Wat Chang Khao Noi Neua, off Rte 106 towards the southern end of town, features an impressive gilded Lanna-style stupa. Near the wat is a cotton-products store called **Wimon** (no Roman-script sign), where you can watch people weaving on looms in the front of the shop. You'll also find a few **shops** near the main market in town, opposite Wat Pasang Ngam. A few vendors in the **market** also sell blankets, tablecloths, *phâakhamáa* (cotton wraparounds), shirts and other woven-cotton products.

A *săwngthăew* will take you from Lamphun to Pasang for 10B. If you're heading south to Tak Province under your own power, traffic is generally lighter along Rte 106 to Thoen than on Hwy 11 to Lampang; a winding 10km section of the road north of Thoen is particularly scenic. Both highways intersect Hwy 1 south, which leads directly to Tak's capital.

WAT PHRA PHUTTHABAHT TAHK PHAH
วัดพระพุทธบาทตากผ้า

Regionally famous, this wat belonging to the popular Mahanikai sect is a shrine to one of the north's most renowned monks, Luang Pu Phromma. It's about 9km south of Pasang or 20km south of Lamphun off Rte 106 in the Tambol Ma-Kok (follow Rte 1133 1km east). It contains a lifelike resin figure of the deceased monk sitting in meditation.

One of his disciples, Ajahn Thirawattho, teaches meditation to a large contingent of monks who are housed in *kùtì* (a monk's hut or living quarters) of laterite brick. Behind the spacious grounds are a park and a steep hill mounted by a stupa. The wat is named after an unremarkable Buddha footprint (*phrá phútthábàat*) shrine in the middle of the lower temple grounds and another spot where Buddha supposedly dried his robes (*tàak phâa*).

A *săwngthăew* from Lamphun to the wat costs 20B.

DOI KHUN TAN NATIONAL PARK
อุทยานแห่งชาติดอยขุนตาล

This **park** (☎ 0 5351 9216-7; admission 200B) receives around 10,000 visitors a year, making it one of northern Thailand's least visited. It's unique in that the main access is from the Khun Tan train station (1½ hours, five daily trains from Chiang Mai). Once at the Khun Tan station, cross the tracks and follow a steep, marked path 1.3km to park headquarters. By car take the Chiang Mai–Lampang highway to the Mae Tha turn-off, then follow signs along a steep unpaved road for 18km.

The 255-sq-km park ranges in elevation from 350m at the bamboo forest lowlands to 1363m at the pine-studded summit of Doi Khun Tan. Wildflowers, including orchids, ginger and lilies, are abundant. In addition to a well-marked trail covering the mountain's four peaks, there's also a trail to **Nam Tok Tat Moei** (7km round trip). Thailand's longest train tunnel (1352m), which opened in 1921 after six years of manual labour by thousands of Lao workers (several of whom are said to have been killed by tigers), intersects the mountain slope.

Bungalows (☎ 0 2562 0760; bungalows 1800-4800B) for six to 48 people are available near the park headquarters. Or you can pitch your own tent for 10B; food is available at a small shop near the park headquarters. The park is very popular on cool season weekends.

NORTH TO THA TON

MAE TAENG & CHIANG DAO
แม่แตง/เชียงดาว

The mountainous area around Mae Taeng – especially southwest of the junction of Rtes 107 and 1095 – has become a major trekking area because of the variety of Lisu, Lahu, Karen and Hmong villages in the region. Rafting along Mae Taeng is so popular these days that there's a permanent rafting centre. **Maetaman Rafting & Elephant Camp** (☎ 0 5329 7060, 0 5329 7283; fax 0 5329 7283; 535 Rim Tai, Mae Rim) is west of Rte 107 in Mae Rim.

The **Elephant Training Centre Chiang Dao** (Km 56, Rte 107; performances 60B), off Rte 107 between Mae Taeng and Chiang Dao, is one of several training centres in the area that puts on elephant shows (at 9am and 10am daily) for tourists. If you haven't seen the one in Lampang Province (in Thung Kwian), this is a reasonable alternative.

From the main four-way junction at Chiang Dao, those with their own wheels – preferably a mountain bike, motorcycle or truck – can head east to visit Lahu, Lisu and Akha villages within a 15km ride. Roughly 13.5km east from Rte 107 is the Lisu village of **Lisu Huay Ko**, where rustic accommodation is available.

Tham Chiang Dao
ถ้ำเชียงดาว

The main attraction along the way to Fang and Tha Ton is this **cave complex** (admission 10B), which is 5km west of Rte 107 and 72km north of Chiang Mai.

The complex is said to extend some 10km to 14km into Doi Chiang Dao (2285m); the interconnected caverns that are open to the public include Tham Mah (7365m long), Tham Kaew (477m), Tham Phra Non (360m), Tham Seua Dao (540m) and Tham Nam (660m).

Both Tham Phra Non and Tham Seua Dao contain religious statuary and are electrically illuminated (and thus easily explored on one's own), while Tham Mah, Tham Kaew and Tham Nam have no light fixtures. A guide with a pressurised gas lantern can be hired for 100B between up to eight people.

The interior cave formations are quite spectacular in places – more than 100 of them are named.

Local legend says this cave complex was the home of a *reusii* (hermit) for a thousand years. As the legend goes, the sage was on such intimate terms with the deity world that he convinced some *thewádaa* (the Buddhist equivalent of angels) to create seven magic wonders inside the caverns: a stream flowing from the pedestal of a solid-gold Buddha; a storehouse of divine textiles; a mystical lake; a city of *naga* (mythical serpents); a sacred immortal elephant; and the hermit's tomb. No, you won't find any of the seven wonders; the locals say these are much deeper inside the mountain, beyond the last of the illuminated caverns.

The locals also say that anyone who attempts to remove a piece of rock from the cave will forever lose their way in the cave's eerie passages.

There is a wat complex outside the cavern and a collection of vendors selling roots, herbs and snacks (mostly noodles).

The surrounding area is quite scenic and largely unspoiled. From the summit of **Doi Chiang Dao** (also called Doi Luang; 2195m), allegedly Thailand's highest limestone mountain, there are spectacular views. Beyond Tham Chiang Dao along the same rural road is a smaller sacred cave retreat complex called **Samnak Song Tham Pha Plong** (Tham Pha Plong Monastic Centre), where Buddhist monks sometimes meditate. A long, steep stairway leads to a large stupa beautifully framed by forest and limestone cliffs.

Sleeping & Eating

Over the last five years or so, Chiang Dao has enjoyed a surge in popularity among visitors who have discovered there's more to the area than just Tham Chiang Dao.

Malee's Nature Lovers Bungalows (☎ 0 1961 8387; r 100-300B) The pioneer of eco-friendly tourism in the area, Malee's is about 1.3km past the entrance to Tham Chiang Dao (heading towards the mountains). Follow the left fork where the road splits 1km past the cave entrance, and you'll find Malee's on the right, about 100m off the road. Friendly and knowledgeable Thai owner Malee has dorm beds and six thatch-and-brick bungalows with private bathroom. Malee can arrange trekking, rafting and bird-watching trips in

the area. If you'd rather hike on your own, maps are available showing hiking routes to the top of Doi Chiang Dao and through the nearby Chiang Dao National Park.

Chiang Dao Nest (☎ 0 6017 1985; nest.chiangdao .com; bungalows 495B) Another 200m or so beyond Malee's, the setting for the six simple bungalows here delivers excellent forest and mountain views. The owners, an Englishman and his Thai wife, can arrange similar trekking and bird-watching assistance as at Malee's. Even if you don't stay here, pop over for a meal in the gourmet **restaurant** (✐ 8am-10pm), which turns out amazingly good European fare (not as surprising when you find out the Thai owner once worked as a chef in London).

Chiang Dao Nest 2 (☎ 0 6017 1985; bungalows 395B) A slightly newer branch, with the same owners as Chiang Dao Nest, this is a cluster of five bungalows about 600m past the cave turn-off on the left side of the road. The restaurant at Chiang Dao Nest 2 focuses on Thai cuisine.

Chiang Dao Lodge (☎ 0 5345 6041; chiangdaolo dge@yahoo.co.uk; Ban Ba Bong, Mae Na, Chiang Dao; r 400B; 🖳) Another Englishman's hideaway in the mountains, overlooking a stream and rice fields. If you're coming from Chiang Mai, turn left off Rte 107 at the sign 'Chiang Dao Lodge', about 4km before reaching Chiang Dao town. Follow the road for about 3km until it becomes a dirt track. Chiang Dao Lodge is situated a short distance down this track on the right.

Baan Krating Chiang Dao (☎ 0 1952 0067; chiang dao@baankrating.com; Km 63, Rte 107; r 2000-2800B) Ten well-appointed wooden villas stand alongside a stream, vegetable gardens and fruit orchards. It's 9km before the town of Chiang Dao, on Rte 107, coming from Chiang Mai.

Chiang Dao Inn Hotel (☎ 0 5345 5134; fax 0 5345 5132; 20 Mu 6, Rte 107; r 600-650B) If you need to stay in the middle of town, this Thai business hotel (an older wooden wing, plus a modern L-shaped wing) is the most comfortable choice.

Pieng Dao Hotel (☎ 0 5323 2434; Ban Chiang Dao, Rte 107; r 120-200B) This is the least expensive choice in town, and one of the few old wooden hotels still operating in the north; the rooms here are basic to say the least.

You can stock up on basic food needs at the daily **fresh market** off the main street through Chiang Dao.

CHIANG MAI PROVINCE

Getting There & Away

Buses to Chiang Dao from Chiang Mai's Chang Pheuak terminal depart every 30 minutes between 5.30am and 5.30pm (29B, 1½ hours). From town you can easily charter *sǎwngthǎew* to Malee's and Chiang Dao Nest; if staying at Baan Krating, ask the bus driver to let you off at Km 63 along Hwy 107.

DOI ANG KHANG
ดอยอ่างขาง

About 20km before Fang is the turn-off for Rte 1249 to Doi Ang Khang, Thailand's 'Little Switzerland'. Twenty-five kilometres from the highway, this 1300m peak has a cool climate year-round and supports the cultivation of flowers, fruits and vegetables that are usually found only in more temperate climates.

A few hill-tribe villages (Lahu, Lisu and Hmong) can be visited on the slopes. You can pick up a free map of the area at the main military checkpoint on Rte 1249, the shortest road up the mountain's eastern slopes. Some interesting do-it-yourself treks can be made in the area.

Nineteen kilometres before the turn-off to Doi Ang Khang, you can make a 12km detour west off Rte 107 onto a dirt road to visit Ban Mai Nong Bua, another Kuomintang (KMT) village with an atmosphere like that of Ban Luang.

A more scenic route is the 'back road' to Doi Ang Khang via Rte 1178, which winds along a ridge to the mountain's western slopes. Along this route, Ban Arunothai was until recently visited regularly by United Wa State Army soldiers who were moving *yaa bâa* (crude amphetamine pills) from across the border in Myanmar to the Thai market. On the 'back road' (Rte 1178) up to Doi Ang Khang, the village of Ban Luang is another interesting stopover for an antique Yunnanese atmosphere. In the vicinity you'll see plenty of ponies and mules still used to transport local goods.

Near the summit of Doi Ang Khang and the Yunnanese village of Ban Khum, there are several places to stay. Most are relatively modest A-frame bungalows positioned along a hillside, such as **Lung Kiat Chok Chai** (r 100-300B) and **Suwannaphum** (r 100-300B), each with basic rooms with shared shower and toilet for the cheaper ones, or with private facilities if you pay more. **Naha Guest House** (☎ 0 5345 0008; Ban Khum, Tambon Mae Ngan, Fang; per person 100B) has large multiperson bungalows with shared hot-water shower and toilet.

Angkhang Nature Resort (☎ 0 5345 0110; ang khang@amari.com; 1/1 Mu 5, Ban Khum, Tambon Mae Ngan, Fang; r 2500-3500B; ☐ ☒), part of the Amari Hotel Group, is an unexpectedly plush hotel featuring large, tastefully designed bungalows spread over a slope. The huge, attractive lobby boasts stone fireplaces at either end for use in the cool season. There is a good, if pricey, restaurant on the premises.

At the base of the slope studded with the cheaper bungalows are a couple of open-air restaurants serving a variety of dishes with an emphasis on Thai and Yunnanese Muslim cuisine.

If you like the Yunnanese village of Ban Luang enough to spend the night, **Ang Khang Remember Resort** (r 200B) and **Ban Luang Resort** (r 150-250B) are at the edge of town, about 4km before Doi Ang Khang. Whether you stay or not, stop off for a delicious bowl of *khâo sawy* at **Ali Restaurant** (dishes 20-25B; ☒ 8am-8pm), next to the village mosque. *Khâo sawy* here, as elsewhere in the northern mountains of Chiang Mai, is served in a clear broth – rather than with coconut milk – in the original Yunnanese manner, along with a plate of fresh pickled cabbage (rather than the cured pickled kind one normally sees in Chiang Mai). The Chinese buns and *phàt yâwt thùa lanthao* (stirfried snowpea shoots) are also very tasty here.

FANG & THA TON
ฝาง/ท่าตอน

North from Chiang Mai along Rte 107, the city of Fang was originally founded by Phaya Mengrai in the 13th century, although as a human settlement and trading centre for *jiin haw* caravans, the locale dates back at least 1000 years. More recently the surrounding district has become a conduit for *yaa bâa* manufactured by the Wa in Myanmar.

Although Fang may not look particularly inviting at first pass, the town's quiet backstreets are lined with some interesting little shops in wooden buildings. The Shan/Burmese–style Wat Jong Paen (near the New Wiang Kaew Hotel) has a very impressive stacked-roof *wíhǎan*.

There are Mien and Karen villages nearby that you can visit on your own, but for most people Fang is just a road marker on the way to Tha Ton. Most visitors also prefer Tha Ton's more rural setting to stay overnight. It's only half an hour or so by *săwngthăew* to the river from Fang or vice versa.

Two banks along the main street in Fang offer currency exchange.

About 10km west of Fang at Ban Meuang Chom, near the agricultural station, is a system of hot springs which are part of Doi Fang National Park. Just ask for the *bàw náam ráwn* (*baw náam háwn* in northern Thai). On weekends there are frequent *săwngthăew* carrying Thai picnickers from Fang to the hot springs.

Tha Ton is little more than a *săwngthăew* stand and a collection of river boats, restaurants, souvenir shops and tourist accommodation along a pretty bend in Mae Nam Kok. As a tourist destination, the main focus is the river dock, launching point for Mae Nam Kok trips to Chiang Rai, with treks to the many hill-tribe settlements in the region a distant second place.

There is a **tourist police office** (8.30am-4.30pm) near the bridge.

For something to do, climb the hill to **Wat Tha Ton** and the **Chinese shrine** for good views of the surrounding area. A large temple bell, which sounds every morning at 4am (wake-up call for monks) and again at 6am (alms-round call), can be heard throughout the valley surrounding Tha Ton. The monks also teach **Vipassana meditation** (6-8pm) in English nightly.

Trekking & Rafting

There are some pleasant walks along Mae Nam Kok. Within 20km of Fang and Tha Ton you can visit local villages inhabited by Palaung (a Karennic tribe that arrived from Myanmar around 16 years ago), Black Lahu, Akha and Yunnanese on foot, mountain bike or motorcycle.

Treks and rafting trips can be arranged through any local guesthouse or hotel in Tha Ton. Typical trips aboard bamboo houserafts with pilot and cook for three days cost 2400B per person (minimum four people), including all meals, lodging and rafting.

On the first day you'll visit several villages near the river and spend the night in a Lisu village; on the second day rafters visit hot springs and more villages, and then spend the night on the raft; and on the third day you dock in Chiang Rai.

You could get a small group of travellers together and arrange your own houseraft with a guide and cook for a two- or three-day journey down river, stopping off in villages of your choice along the way. A house-raft generally costs 600B per person per day, including simple meals, and takes up to six people – so figure on 1800B for a three-day trip. Police regulations require that an experienced boat navigator accompany each raft – the river has lots of tricky spots and there have been some mishaps.

As an alternative to the bamboo raft trips, **Lost Valley Adventure** (in Chiang Rai ☎ 0 5375 2252; www.lostvalleyadventure.com; 2 days & 1 night 1800B) offers trips aboard inflatable rubber rafts.

Near the pier (Tha Ton) you can rent inflatable kayaks to do your own paddling in the area. Upstream a few kilometres the river crosses into Myanmar. See p329 for details on organised river trips to Chiang Rai.

Sleeping & Eating

FANG

New Wiang Kaew Hotel (☎ 0 5245 1046; 22 Th Sai Rattabat; r 150-180B) Behind the Fang Hotel, off the main street, this is an OK choice with basic rooms, some with hot water.

Ueng Khum Hotel (UK Hotel; ☎ 0 5345 1268; 227 Th Tha Phae; r 150-350B;) Around the corner from New Wiang Kaew, this hotel has bungalow-style accommodation around a courtyard.

Parichat Restaurant (Th Rop Wiang; dishes 25-45B; 8am-8pm) Near the highway market, Parichat serves Yunnanese specialities such as *khâo sawy, man-thoh* (*mantou* in Mandarin; steamed buns) and *khâo mòk kài*, plus *kŭaytĭaw* (rice noodles), *khâo phàt* (fried rice) and other standards.

Further down Th Rop Wiang in Fang is a row of cheap Isan restaurants and *lâo dawng* (herbal liquor) bars.

THA TON

The best places to stay in Tha Ton tend to be on the opposite side of the river from the riverboat dock.

Garden Home (☎ 0 5337 3015; r 200-800B) A tranquil place along the river in Tha Ton, about 150m from the bridge, with thatched-roof bungalows spaced well apart among lots of litchi trees and bougainvillea. There are also a few stone bungalows, and three larger, more luxurious bungalows on the river with small verandas, and a TV and fridge. From the bridge, turn left at the Thaton River View Hotel sign to find it.

Baan Suan Riverside Resort (☎ 0 5337 3214; fax 0 5337 3215; r incl breakfast 300-1000B; ❄) Has small cement air-con bungalows with terraces back from the river; fan rooms in a cement building, also back off the river; and a couple of large air-con wooden bungalows with terraces right on the river. The grounds are beautifully landscaped, and an attached restaurant overlooks the river.

Thaton River View Hotel (☎ 0 5337 3173; fax 0 5345 9288; Tha Ton; r incl breakfast 1000-1400B; ❄) Further upstream along the river, this quiet resort hotel has 33 rooms facing the river and joined by wooden walkways. The hotel's restaurant is the best in the area.

Thaton Chalet (☎ 0 5337 3155-7; fax 0 5337 3158; 1000-2000B; ❄) A four-storey hotel next to the bridge, with stone façade. All rooms have carpet and TV. The hotel features a pleasant beer garden right on the river, as well as an indoor restaurant.

Chan Kasem (☎ 0 5345 9313; r 90-300B) The nearest to the riverboat pier, Chan Kasem boasts a dining area on the river and a variety of simple rooms with shared bathroom in the older wooden section, plus nicer ones in a brick bungalow.

Naam Waan Guest House (Th Tha Phae; r 150B) In back of Chan Kasem, this is a friendly place with 10 tidy rooms, and appears to receive the most positive feedback from travellers.

Thip's Travellers House (Chao Phae; ☎ /fax 0 5349 5312; 1/7 Th Tha Phae; r 100-140B) This old standby is convenient to the bus stop from Fang: it's near the bridge where the road from Fang meets the river. Rooms are thin-walled and facilities basic, but there's a nice little café out the front.

Apple Guest House (r 300-400B) Opposite the boat landing in a bulky two-storey building; there's an upmarket restaurant on the ground floor and spacious light-filled rooms above.

Maekok River Village Resort (☎ 0 5345 9355; www.track-of-the-tiger.com; r 2625-5250B) Further downstream along the river, this sprawling affair offers four-bed rooms as well as two-bed poolside rooms. On the grounds are a pool and restaurant. A variety of activities including massage, cooking classes, trekking, rafting, mountain biking and caving can be arranged through the resort. It's popular with tour groups.

Asa's Guest Home (Lou-Ta; per person 200B) About 15km northeast of Tha Ton, in Lou-Ta, the nearest Lisu village. Situated near the top of the village, with a bit of a view, Asa's offers four clean, basic bamboo-walled rooms in a bamboo-thatch house. Rates include two meals. The friendly family here can arrange various one- and two-day jungle trips in the area, including visits to Karen, Lahu, Lisu, Akha, Mien and Shan villages. To get to Asa's Guest Home take a yellow *săwngthăew* from Tha Ton for 15B (or motorcycle taxi for 30B) and ask to get off in Lou-Ta.

Several little noodle stands can be found in the vicinity of the bus queue, and there are a few rustic food stalls near the pier and near the bridge. **Racha Roti** (Th Phae) in front of Thip's Travellers House features 16 flavours of *rotii*. A local culinary speciality is *lûu*, a northern-Thai salad made with pig's blood.

Getting There & Away
BUS & SĂWNGTHĂEW

Buses to Fang (60B, 3½ hours) leave from the Chang Pheuak bus terminal in Chiang Mai every 30 minutes between 5.30am and 5.30pm. Air-con minivans make the trip to Fang (100B, 3½ hours) every 30 minutes between 7.30am and 4.30pm, leaving from behind the Chang Pheuak bus terminal on the corner of Soi Sanam Kila.

From Fang it's about 23km to Tha Ton. A *săwngthăew* does the 40-minute trip for 12B; the larger orange buses from Fang leave less frequently and cost 12B. Buses leave from near the market, or you can wait in front of the Fang Hotel for a bus or *săwngthăew*. Both operate from 5.30am to 5pm only.

Buses to Mae Sai cost 38B from Tha Ton, 45B from Fang.

The river isn't the only way to get to points north of Tha Ton. Yellow *săwngthăew* leave from the northern side of the river in Tha Ton to Mae Salong in Chiang Rai Province every 30 minutes or so between 7am and 3pm (50B, 2½ hours). You can charter an entire *săwngthăew* for 450B one way, 650B return. Hold on tight – the road is steep and winding.

If you're heading west to Mae Hong Son Province, it's not necessary to dip all the way south to Chiang Mai before continuing on. At Ban Mae Malai, the junction of Rte 107 (the Chiang Mai–Fang highway) and Rte 1095, you can pick up a bus to Pai for 45B; if you're coming from Pai, be sure to get off at this junction to catch a bus north to Fang.

MOTORCYCLE
Motorcycle trekkers can also travel between Tha Ton and Doi Mae Salong, 48km northeast over a fully paved but sometimes treacherous mountain road. There are a couple of Lisu and Akha villages on the way. The 27km or so between Doi Mae Salong and the village of Muang Ngam are very steep and winding – take care, especially in the rainy season. When conditions are good, the trip can be done in 1½ hours.

You can take a motorcycle on most boats to Chiang Rai for an extra charge.

RIVER TRIP TO CHIANG RAI
From Tha Ton you can make a half-day long-tail boat trip to Chiang Rai down Mae Nam Kok. The regular passenger boat takes up to 12 passengers, leaves at 12.30pm and costs 250B per person. You can also charter a boat all the way for 1700B, which among six people works out to be about 33B more per person but gives you more room to move. A boat can be chartered any time between 7am and 3pm. The trip is a bit of a tourist trap these days as the passengers are all tourists (what local will pay 250B to take the boat when they can catch a bus to Chiang Rai for less than 40B?), and the villages along the way sell cola and souvenirs – but it's still fun. The best time to go is at the end of the rainy season in November when the river level is high.

The travel time down river depends on river conditions and the skill of the pilot, taking anywhere from three to five hours. You could actually make the boat trip in a day from Chiang Mai, catching a bus back from Chiang Rai as soon as you arrive, but it's better to stay in Fang or Tha Ton, take the boat trip, then stay in Chiang Rai or Chiang Saen before travelling on. You may sometimes have to get off and walk and push the boat if it gets stuck on sand bars.

Some travellers take the boat to Chiang Rai in two or three stages, stopping first in **Mae Salak**, a large Lahu village that is about a third of the distance, or **Ban Ruammit**, a Karen village about two-thirds of the way down. Both villages are well touristed these days (charter boat tours stop for photos and elephant rides), but from here you can trek

to other Shan, Thai and hill-tribe villages, or do longer treks south of Mae Salak to **Wawi**, a large multiethnic community of *jiin haw*, Lahu, Lisu, Akha, Shan, Karen, Mien and Thai peoples. The Wawi area has dozens of hill-tribe villages of various ethnicities, including the largest Akha community in Thailand (Saen Charoen) and the oldest Lisu settlement (Doi Chang).

Another alternative is to trek south from Mae Salak all the way to the town of **Mae Suay**, where you can catch a bus on to Chiang Rai or back to Chiang Mai. You might also try getting off the boat at one of the smaller villages (see the boat fares table following). Another alternative is to make the trip (much more slowly) upriver from Chiang Rai – this is possible despite the rapids.

Near Ban Ruammit on the opposite river bank (50B, 1½ hours by boat from Chiang Rai) are some very pretty **hot springs**. Don't even think about entering the water – it's scalding. From here you can hike about an hour to **Akha Hill House** (☎ 0 5374 5140; r 40-200B), wholly owned and managed by Akha tribespeople. This rustic guesthouse is in a beautiful setting overlooking a mountain valley; a waterfall and several other villages (Akha, Mien, Lisu, Karen and Lahu) are within walking distance. The guesthouse can organise overnight trips into the forest with guides who build banana-palm huts and cook meals using sections of bamboo. It can also be reached by road from Chiang Rai, 26km away. Call for free pick-up (once daily between 4pm and 4.30pm).

Several of the guesthouses in Tha Ton organise raft trips down the river – see p327.

A boat leaves once daily from **Tha Ton public pier** (☎ 0 5345 9427) at 12.30pm. The table below shows boat fares from Tha Ton.

Destination	Fare (B)
Ban Mai	75
Mae Salak	80
Pha Tai	90
Jakheu	100
Kok Noi	110
Pha Kwang	120
Pha Khiaw	170
Hat Wua Dam	180
Pong Man Ron	200
Ban Ruammit	200
Chiang Rai	250

Northern Thailand

The first true Thai kingdoms arose in northern Thailand, endowing this region with a wide range of traditional culture and architecture, such as the country's most beautiful Thai temple ruins. It's also the home of Thailand's hill tribes, whose cultures are dissolving rapidly in the face of the country's modernisation and foreign tourism. Despite this, the scenic beauty of the north has been fairly well preserved – the region boasts more natural forest cover than any other – and a distinct northern Thai culture thrives.

Northern Thais are very proud of their local customs, considering northern ways to be part of Thailand's 'original' tradition and culture. Look for symbols frequently displayed by northern Thais to express cultural solidarity – clay water jars placed in front of homes, *kàlae* (carved wooden 'X' motifs) that decorate house gables, Shan or hill tribe–style shoulder bags and the ubiquitous *sêua mâw hâwm* (indigo-dyed rice-farmer's shirt) worn on Friday at many banks, universities and other institutions throughout the north.

HIGHLIGHTS

- Exploring the awesome ruins of Thailand's 'golden age' at **Sukhothai** and **Si Satchanalai–Chaliang Historical Parks** (p389 and p394).

- Visiting **Um Phang** (p410), where the end of the road leads to Thailand's biggest, most beautiful waterfall

- Getting off the beaten path in **Nan** (p373), where unique tribes, landscapes and traditions abound

- Tasting a little of Myanmar in **Myawadi** (p409), across the river from Mae Sot

- Spelunking, trekking and rafting through the dense forests of **Mae Hong Son Province** (p415)

★ Mae Hong Son Province

★ Nan

★ Si Satchanalai–Chaliang Historical Park

★ Sukhothai Historical Park

★ Myawadi

★ Um Phang

NORTHERN THAILAND

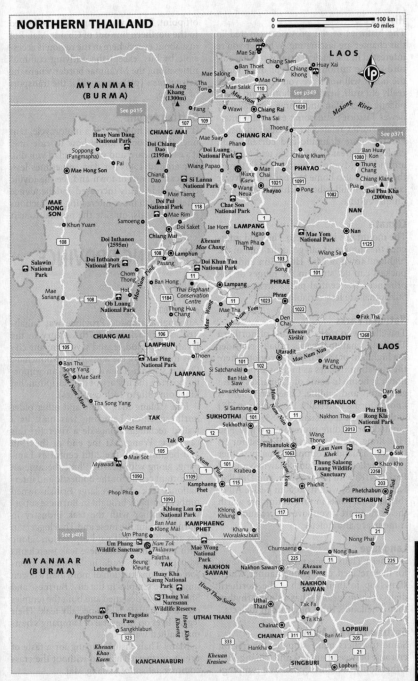

0   100 km
0   60 miles

LAOS

MYANMAR (BURMA)

See p415

Tachileik
Mae Sai
Ban Thoet Thai   Chiang Saen   Chiang Khong   Huay Xai
Mae Salong
Mae Chan
110
See p349

Mekong River

Doi Ang Khang (1300m)
Tha Ton
Fang
Wawi   Chiang Rai   1020
107   109   1   Tha Sai

CHIANG MAI
Mae Suay   **CHIANG RAI**
Doi Chiang Dao (2195m)   Phan
Doi Luang National Park   Chun
Wiang Papao   Mae Chai   **PHAYAO**
Chiang Dao   Wang Kaew   1021   Phayao   1091
Si Lanna National Park   Wang Neua   Pong   1082
Mae Taeng   Chae Son National Park

See p371

Chiang Kham   1080   Ban Huay Kon
Thung Chang
Chiang Klang
Pua   Doi Phu Kha (2000m)

MAE HONG SON
Huay Nam Dang National Park
Soppong (Pangmapha)
Pai
Mae Hong Son

118
Doi Pui National Park
Mae Rim
Samoeng
Doi Saket
Chiang Mai
Jae Hom

NAN
Mae Yom National Park
Nan
1125
Wiang Sa

108
Khun Yuam

Doi Inthanon (2595m)
Doi Inthanon National Park
Lamphun
LAMPANG
Ngao
Kheuan Mae Chang
Tham Pha Thai
103
Song
101

Salawin National Park

Mae Sariang

Chom Thong
Hot
Pasang
Ban Hong
108
108
11
1184
Thai Elephant Conservation Centre
Lampang
11
Mae Tha
1023
PHRAE
Phrae
1022
Fak Tha

Ob Luang National Park
Thung Hua Chang
Den Chai
Kheuan Sirikit
UTARADIT
1268
LAOS

Mae Nam Ping

Mae Wang

Mae Nam Yom

CHIANG MAI
106
LAMPHUN
1
Thoen
101
102
Utaradit
Wang Pa Chun

Ban Tha Song Yang
Mae Ping National Park
Mae Sarit
LAMPANG
Si Satchanalai
Ban Hat Siaw
Sawankhalok
Dan Sai

Mae Nam Meri
Tha Song Yang

TAK
Mae Ramat
Si Samrong
SUKHOTHAI
101
Sukhothai
12
PHITSANULOK
Nakhon Thai
Phu Hin Rong Kla National Park
2013
Lom Sak

Mae Sot
Myawadi
105
Tak
12
Wang Thong
1063
Phitsanulok
12
Khao Kho
2258

1090
1109
Krabeu
101
115
Kamphaeng Phet
Lam Nam Khek
Thung Salaeng Luang Wildlife Sanctuary
Phichit
203
Phetchabun
PHETCHABUN

Phop Phra
1090
Khlong Lan National Park
Ban Mae Klong Mai
Khlong Khlung
KAMPHAENG PHET
Khanu Woralaksabun
PHICHIT
117
113
21

See p401
Um Phang
Um Phang Wildlife Sanctuary
Nam Tok Thilawsu
Palatha
TAK
Mae Wong National Park
Chumsaeng
Nong Bua
11
225

Letongkhu
Beung Kleung
Huay Kha Kaeng National Park
NAKHON SAWAN
Nakhon Sawan
Kheuan Mae Wong
225

MYANMAR (BURMA)
Payathonzu
Thung Yai Naresuan Wildlife Reserve
Three Pagodas Pass
Sangkhlaburi
323
UTHAI THANI
Uthai Thani
NAKHON SAWAN
1
Tak Fa
Ta Khli

Kheuan Khao Kaem
KANCHANABURI
Kheuan Krasiaw
333
Chainat
CHAINAT
311
11
Ban Mi
LOPBURI
205
21

Hankha
SINGBURI
1
Lopburi

Huay Thap Salao

Huay Kha Khaeng

NORTHERN THAILAND

History

The histories of the provinces covered in this chapter are fascinating. Whether you're interested in the ancient origins of Thai culture or the curious stories of drug lords, the north will not leave you bored. For the really old stuff, head to Sukhothai and Kamphaeng Phet. Nan and Phrae have slightly newer histories and some especially interesting stories related to the teak industry. For the more dramatic and current stuff, explore the areas like Mae Sai and Mae Sot around the Myanmar border. Don't forget, the north is also home to Thailand's diverse collection of hill tribes, each with their own unique culture.

Climate

The mountains in northern Thailand influence the climate. It can get quite cold in the highland town of Mae Hong Son and rain pockets can get stuck in the ranges of Tak province. The central-plains areas around Sukhothai are less variable.

National Parks

Travellers who make it to one of northern Thailand's national parks usually consider it a highlight of their trip. In a region where the elevation reaches as high as 2000m, the north is home to some of Thailand's rarest geography and wildlife. Chae Son (p338) is known for its waterfalls. Doi Luang (p337) and Thung Salaeng Luang (p388) were designated for wildlife protection. While Phu Hin Rong Kla (p386) is of interest for its ties to Thailand's communist party. Other parks in the north include Salawin National Park (p418) with its lazy river, and Doi Phu Kha (see p378) with its 2000m peaks. All of the national parks in this section are worth the extra effort if you love nature and want some peace and quiet.

Language

Northern Thais (khon meuang) are known for their relaxed, easy-going manner, which shows up in their speech – the northern dialect (kham meuang) has a slower rhythm than Thailand's three other main dialects.

Getting There & Away

Some travellers make stops in this region en route between Bangkok and Chiang Mai. Others only use Chiang Mai as a jumping-off point. Either way, train access is limited to the northern line out of Chiang Mai. But just about everywhere in the region is accessible by bus, except the outlying communities along the Myanmar border where the săwngthăew (pick-up truck) is the transport of choice.

Getting Around

If you know how to ride a motorcycle, rent one. If you don't know how to ride one, it's easy to learn and you'll be glad you did. For around 150B per day, sometimes less, you can get out of town and see the idyllic countryside. This increased independence often leads to more interesting interactions with the locals, outside the normal tourist circuit.

LAMPANG PROVINCE

LAMPANG

ลำปาง
pop 50,700

Although Lampang Province was inhabited as far back as the 7th century in the Dvaravati period, legend says Lampang city was founded by the son of Hariphunchai's Queen Chama Thewi, playing an important part in the history of the Hariphunchai kingdom (8th to 13th centuries).

Like Chiang Mai, Phrae and other older northern cities, Lampang was built as a walled rectangle alongside a river (in this case Mae Wang). At the end of the 19th and beginning of the 20th centuries Lampang, along with nearby Phrae, became an important centre for the domestic and international teak trade. A large British-owned timber company brought in Burmese supervisors familiar with the teak industry in Burma to train Burmese and Thai loggers in the area. These well-paid supervisors, along with independent Burmese teak merchants who plied their trade in Lampang, sponsored the construction of more than a dozen impressive temples in the city. Burmese and Shan artisans designed and built the temples out of local materials, especially teak. Their legacy lives on in several of Lampang's best-maintained wats.

Many Thais visit Lampang for a taste of urban northern Thailand without the crass commercialism of Chiang Mai.

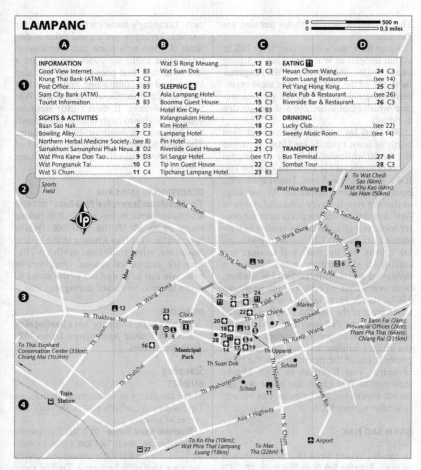

LAMPANG

INFORMATION
Good View Internet...................**1** B3
Krung Thai Bank (ATM)..............**2** C3
Post Office.................................**3** B3
Siam City Bank (ATM)................**4** C3
Tourist Information....................**5** B3

SIGHTS & ACTIVITIES
Baan Sao Nak...........................**6** D3
Bowling Alley...........................**7** C3
Northern Herbal Medicine Society..(see 8)
Samakhom Samunphrai Phak Neua..**8** D2
Wat Phra Kaew Don Tao.............**9** C3
Wat Pongsanuk Tai....................**10** C3
Wat Si Chum............................**11** C4

Wat Si Rong Meuang..................**12** B3
Wat Suan Dok...........................**13** B3

SLEEPING 🛏
Asia Lampang Hotel...................**14** C3
Boonma Guest House.................**15** C3
Hotel Kim City..........................**16** B3
Kelangnakorn Hotel...................**17** C3
Kim Hotel.................................**18** C3
Lampang Hotel..........................**19** C3
Pin Hotel..................................**20** C3
Riverside Guest House................**21** C3
Sri Sangar Hotel.....................(see 17)
Tip Inn Guest House...................**22** B3
Tipchang Lampang Hotel............**23** B3

EATING 🍴
Heuan Chom Wang.....................**24** C3
Koom Luang Restaurant............(see 14)
Pet Yang Hong Kong..................**25** C3
Relax Pub & Restaurant...........(see 26)
Riverside Bar & Restaurant........**26** C3

DRINKING
Lucky Club.............................(see 22)
Sweety Music Room.................(see 14)

TRANSPORT
Bus Terminal............................**27** B4
Sombat Tour.............................**28** C3

Information

There are many banks with ATMs along Th Boonyawat, especially near Wat Suan Dok.

Good View Internet (☎ 0 5423 1171; Th Thakhrao Noi; per hr 20B; ⏱ 8am-10pm)

Post office (Th Thakhrao Noi) Near the tourist information office.

Tourist information office (☎ 0 5421 9300; Th Thakhrao Noi) Locally run, with a decent map of the area and details about local sights.

Sights & Activities

WAT PHRA KAEW DON TAO
วัดพระแก้วดอนเต้า

This wat, on the northern side of the Mae Wang, housed the Emerald Buddha (now in Bangkok's Wat Phra Kaew, see p100)

from 1436 to 1468. The main stupa shows Hariphunchai influence, while the adjacent *mondòp* (a square, spire-topped shrine room) was built in 1909. The *mondòp*, decorated with glass mosaic in typical Burmese style, contains a Mandalay-style Buddha image. A display of Lanna artefacts (mostly religious paraphernalia and woodwork) can be viewed in the wat's **Lanna Museum** (admission by donation).

OTHER TEMPLES

Two wats built in the late 19th century by Burmese artisans are **Wat Si Rong Meuang** and **Wat Si Chum**. Both have temple buildings constructed in the Burmese 'layered' style, with tin roofs gabled by intricate woodcarvings.

The current abbots of these temples are Burmese.

Apart from the *wíhǎan* (any large hall in a Thai temple) at Wat Phra That Lampang Luang (p336), the *mondòp* at **Wat Pongsanuk Tai** is one of the few remaining local examples of original Lanna-style temple architecture, which emphasised open-sided wooden buildings.

Wat Chedi Sao (☎ 0 5432 0233), about 6km north of town towards Jae Hom, is named for the 20 whitewashed Lanna-style stupas on its grounds (*sao* is northern Thai for 20). It's a well-endowed wat, landscaped with bougainvillea and casuarina. At one edge of the wat stands a very colourful statue of Avalokiteshvara, while a pavilion in the centre features a gilded Buddha similar in style to the Phra Phutha Chinnarat in Phitsanulok (p380). But the wat's real treasure is a solid-gold, 15th-century seated Buddha on display in a glassed-in **pavilion** (☺ 8am-5pm), built over a square pond. The image weighs 1507g, stands 38cm tall and is said to contain a piece of the Buddha's skull in its head and an ancient Pali-inscribed golden palm leaf in its chest; precious stones decorate the image's hairline and robe. A farmer reportedly found the figure next to the ruins of nearby Wat Khu Kao in 1983. Monks stationed at Wat Chedi Sao make and sell herbal medicines; the popular *yaa màwng* is similar to tiger balm.

BAAN SAO NAK
บ้านเสานัก

In the old Wiang Neua (north city) section of town, **Baan Sao Nak** (Many Pillars House; ☎ 0 5422 7653; admission 30B; ☺ 10am-5pm) was built in 1895 in the traditional Lanna style. A huge teak house supported by 116 square teak pillars, it was once owned by a local *khunying* (a title equivalent to 'Lady' in England); it now serves as a local museum. The entire house is furnished with Burmese and Thai antiques; three rooms display antique silverwork, lacquerware, bronzeware, ceramics and other northern-Thai crafts. The area beneath the house is often used for ceremonial dinners.

HORSE CARTS

Lampang is known throughout Thailand as Meuang Rot Mah (Horse Cart City) because it's the only town in Thailand where **horse carts** are still used as public transport. These days, Lampang's horse carts are mainly for tourists. Trying to get a good price is difficult. A 15-minute horse-cart tour around town costs 150B; for 200B you can get a half-hour tour that goes along beside Mae Wang, and for 300B a one-hour tour that stops at Wat Phra Kaew Don Tao and Wat Si Rong Meuang. If there's little business you may be able to negotiate the price down to 120B per half-hour or 200B per hour. The main horse-cart stands are in front of the old provincial office and the Tipchang Lampang.

TRADITIONAL MASSAGE

The **Samakhom Samunphrai Phak Neua** (☎ 0 6586 0711; Northern Herbal Medicine Society; 149 Th Pratuma; massage per 30min/hr 100/150B, sauna 100B; ☺ 8am-8pm), next to Wat Hua Khuang in the Wiang Neua area, offers traditional northern-Thai massage and herbal saunas. Once you've paid, you can go in and out of the sauna as many times as you want during one visit.

BOWLING

Yep, that's right, Lampang has a **bowling alley** (basement, Th Thipawan shopping centre; 3 games 100B; ☺ 10.30am-11.30pm).

Sleeping
BUDGET

There are plenty of economical choices on Th Boonyawat, which passes through the centre of town.

Riverside Guest House (☎ 0 5422 7005; riverside family@yahoo.com; 286 Th Talat Kao; r 350B, ste 600B; ⊠) For the aesthetically concerned, this is *the* place to stay in Lampang. Tucked away near the river, the tasteful rooms in this upgraded old teak building are surrounded by equally stylish landscaping. Some rooms are a bit cramped, but you can stretch out in the pleasant outdoor areas. The guesthouse offers basic breakfast, fax service, international calls, motorcycle rental, laundry service and sightseeing tours. Italian, French, English and Thai are spoken.

Asia Lampang Hotel (☎ 0 5422 7844; www.asia lampang.com; 229 Th Boonyawat; r 380B, ste 420-550B; ⊠) All of the wood-accented rooms in this long-running place are a good value, especially the large, suite-style rooms on the 5th floor. The pleasant street-level Koom Luang restaurant (opposite) and basement nightclub, Sweety Music Room (opposite), attract a mature crowd. Rooms have hot-water showers and TVs.

Boonma Guest House (☎ 0 5432 2653; 256 Th Talat Kao; r 250B) This family-run place features a couple of spacious cement rooms behind a gorgeous teak home. It lacks a comfortable place to hang out, but it's still good value.

Lampang Hotel (☎ 0 5422 7311; 696 Th Suan Dok; r from 180B; 🕃) More expensive rooms have televisions at this ordinary, clean place. It's quite popular with younger Thais on the weekends.

Kim Hotel (☎ 0 5421 7721; fax 0 5422 6929; 168 Th Boonyawat; r 340B; 🕃) Approaching midrange status in amenities, this three-storey hotel has clean, comfortable rooms with hot water and TV.

Kelangnakorn Hotel (☎ 0 5421 6137; Th Boon-yawat; r from 260B; 🕃) Popular with travelling salesmen, this hotel has modernish rooms with worn wooden furniture, cable TV and a friendly reception.

Other recommendations:

Sri Sangar Hotel (Si Sa-Nga; ☎ 0 5421 7070; 213-215 Th Boonyawat; s/d 100/180B) Older but chummy. Basic, cheap rooms.

Tip Inn Guest House (☎ 0 5422 1821; 143 Th Talat Kao; r 160-260B; 🕃) Adequate, but crammed rooms.

MIDRANGE & TOP END

Rooms in the following hotels all have hot-water showers and in-room TVs.

Pin Hotel (☎ 0 5422 1509; www.travelideas.net; 8 Th Suan Dok; r from 450, ste 850B; 🕃) The Pin feels like a modern American chain hotel, like a Hyatt or Marriott, only it's smaller and more intimate. The service is professional, the lobby has comfortable, well-lit sitting areas and rooms are uniform but spacious, with two double beds, satellite TV and a small fridge. There is a decent restaurant and room service. It caters largely to international travellers and would easily cost double in Chiang Mai.

Tipchang Lampang Hotel (☎ 0 5422 6501; fax 0 5422 5362; 54/22 Th Thakhrao Noi; r incl breakfast 600-900B; 🕃 🕃) This disco-era, supersized hotel with tennis courts, cocktail lounge and sup-per club sounds more luxurious than it feels. The reception is professional and it's popu-lar with upper-middle-class Thais.

Hotel Kim City (☎ 0 5431 0238; fax 0 5422 6635; 274/1 Th Chatchai; r 500-900B) Another big, modern place, this sits a bit outside the city centre and is an adequate choice only if you have your own wheels.

Eating

Lampang has a good selection of restaur-ants. It's not ultradiverse like Chiang Mai, but the quality is pretty high. Several of the more expensive hotels have restaurants with a nice atmosphere and above-average food.

Riverside Bar & Restaurant (☎ 0 5422 1861; 328 Th Thip Chang; dishes 45-190B; 🕃 11am-midnight) This rambling old teak structure on the river is definitely the most popular place in town. There's live music, a full bar and an enor-mous menu of vegetarian, northern-Thai and Western dishes. The homemade gelato and pizza nights are favourites (gelato only available on pizza nights!). Prices are rea-sonable and service is excellent.

Koom Luang Restaurant (☎ 0 5422 7844; www .asialampang.com; 229 Th Boonyawat; dishes 50-100B; 🕃 6.30am-midnight; 🕃) Choose between air-con or street-fresh seating at this northern Lanna–style restaurant. The Thai and Chi-nese dishes are far more authentic than the European.

Relax Pub & Restaurant (Th Thip Chang; dishes 50-150B; 🕃 6pm-midnight) Just west of the River-side, Relax is a little more punk-rock with neon lights, industrial architecture and more amplified music. The food's good and the scene is more energetic than the Riverside.

Pet Yang Hong Kong (Th Boonyawat; dishes 25-40B; 🕃 8am-6pm) This is the best spot for roast duck with rice (or noodles). It's opposite Kim Hotel, near several other rice and noo-dle joints.

Heuan Chom Wang (☎ 0 5422 2845; 276 Th Talat Kao; dishes 40-100B; 🕃 11am-11pm) This roman-tic, open-air place fronting the river occu-pies a beautiful old teak building down an alley off Th Talat Kao. The menu is strictly non-Westernised northern- and central-Thai fare. Service is attentive but English is limited.

Drinking

In addition to the Riverside Bar and Relax Pub (above), Lampang has a couple of other nightspots.

Lucky Club (Th Talat Kao; drinks 15-50B; 🕃 6pm-midnight) Boasting 'happiness you can touch', this low-lit, almost chic spot is a hip place to enjoy a drink if you prefer downtempo to live rock 'n' roll.

Sweety Music Room (229 Th Boonyawat; 🕃 7pm-1am) Down the stairs from the Koom Luang

Restaurant, this retro nightspot plays a good range of Western favourites until 11.30pm, when the mood gets romantic. Dance jams turn on at 12.30am. The room's always dark, the booths are spacious and the house band is lively, but not all that good.

Getting There & Away
AIR
Daily flights between Lampang and Bangkok (2015B) are offered by **PB Air** (☎ 0 5422 6238, Bangkok ☎ 0 2261 0220; www.pbair.com; Lampang Airport).

BUS
From Chiang Mai, buses to Lampang (25B, 50B to 65B with air-con, two hours) leave from the Chiang Mai Arcade terminal about every half-hour during the day and also from next to Saphan Nawarat in the direction of Lamphun. Bus services also depart Lamphun (29B).

Air-con buses go to Lampang from Phitsanulok's main bus terminal (140B via the new route, four hours; 145B via the old route, five hours). To/from Bangkok each way there are ordinary buses (176B, 7½ hours, four per day), also 2nd-class air-con buses (246B, three per day), 1st-class buses (389B, six per day) and one 24-seat VIP bus (550B, daily). The bus terminal in Lampang is some way out of town – 10B by shared *sǎwngthǎew*.

To book an air-con bus from Lampang to Bangkok or Chiang Mai head to **Sombat Tour** (☎ 0 5432 3361; Th Boonyawat).

TRAIN
Trains run between Chiang Mai and Lampang (2nd/3rd class 37/15B, two hours).

AROUND LAMPANG
Sights & Activities
WAT PHRA THAT LAMPANG LUANG
วัดพระธาตุลำปางหลวง
Arguably the most beautiful wooden Lanna temple found in northern Thailand, Wat Phra That Lampang is centred on the open-sided **Wihan Luang** and is one attraction not to be missed. Believed to have been built in 1476, the impressive *wíhǎan* features a triple-tiered wooden roof supported by teak pillars and is considered to be the oldest existing wooden building in Thailand. A huge, gilded *mondòp* in the back of the

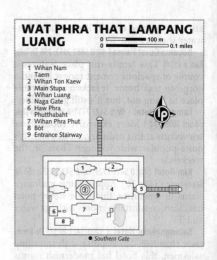

WAT PHRA THAT LAMPANG LUANG

0 ———— 100 m
0 ———— 0.1 miles

1 Wihan Nam Taem
2 Wihan Ton Kaew
3 Main Stupa
4 Wihan Luang
5 Naga Gate
6 Haw Phra Phutthabaht
7 Wihan Phra Phut
8 Bòt
9 Entrance Stairway

● Southern Gate

wíhǎan contains a Buddha image cast in 1563. The faithful leave small gold-coloured Buddha figures close to the *mondòp* and hang Thai Lü weavings behind it.

Early 19th-century **jataka murals** (stories of the Buddha's previous lives) are painted on wooden panels around the inside upper perimeter of the *wíhǎan*. The tall **Lanna-style stupa** behind the *wíhǎan*, raised in 1449 and restored in 1496, measures 24m at its base and is 45m high. The small and simple **Wihan Ton Kaew**, to the north of the main *wíhǎan*, was built in 1476. The oldest structure in the compound is the smaller 13th-century **Wihan Phra Phut** to the south of the main stupa; the *wíhǎan* to the north of the stupa, **Wihan Nam Taem**, was built in the early 16th century and, amazingly, still contains traces of the original murals.

The **Haw Phra Phutthabaht**, a small white building behind the stupa, has been turned into a male-only camera obscura. When you enter and shut the door an image of the stupa is projected, via a small hole in the door, onto a white sheet that is hanging on the wall. Trust us, ladies: you're not missing much.

The lintel over the entrance to the compound features an impressive dragon relief – once common in northern Thai temples but rarely seen these days. This gate supposedly dates to the 15th century.

In the arboretum outside the southern gate of the wat, there are now three worthwhile **museums**. One displays mostly festival paraphernalia, plus some Buddha figures. Another, called 'House of the Emerald Buddha', contains a miscellany of coins, banknotes, Buddha figures, silver betel-nut cases, lacquerware and other ethnographic artefacts, along with three small, heavily gold-leafed Buddhas placed on an altar behind an enormous repoussé silver bowl. The third, a fine small museum, features shelves of Buddha figures, lacquered boxes, manuscripts and ceramics, all well labelled in Thai and English.

Wat Phra That Lampang Luang is 18km southwest of Lampang in Ko Kha. To get there by public transport from Lampang, flag an eastbound *săwngthăew* on Th Rawp Wiang. A chartered motorcycle taxi from the Ko Kha *săwngthăew* station to the temple costs 20B to 30B.

If you're driving or cycling from Lampang, head south on the Asia 1 Hwy and take the Ko Kha exit, then follow the road over a bridge and bear right. Follow the signs and continue for 2km over another bridge until you see the temple on the left. If you're coming from Chiang Mai via Hwy 11, turn south onto Rte 1034 18km northwest of Lampang at the Km 13 marker – this route is a 50km shortcut to Ko Kha that avoids much of Lampang.

THAI ELEPHANT CONSERVATION CENTER
ศูนย์อนุรักษ์ช้างไทย

In Amphoe Hang Chat northwest of Lampang, outside Thung Kwian between Km 28 and 29, this unique **facility** (☎ 0 5422 8035, 0 5422 9042; www.changthai.com; admission 50B; public shows 10am & 11am daily, 1.30pm Fri, Sat & holidays Jun-Feb) promotes the role of the Asian elephant in ecotourism and provides free medical treatment and care for sick elephants from all over Thailand.

In addition to the standard tourist show, the 122-hectare centre offers exhibits on the history and culture of elephants as well as elephant rides (8am to 3.30pm, 200/400/800B for 15/30/60 minutes) through the surrounding forest. At 9.45am (and at 1.15pm on weekends) the elephants do bathing performances in the river. The show generally includes a musical ensemble of elephants playing over-sized musical instruments, including drums, to create a sort of chaotic trance music.

Decorative paper made from elephant dung is available as a souvenir along with paintings by elephants at the gift shop. Visitors are invited to see the papermaking facilities; just follow the signs.

The camp is 33km from town and can be reached by Chiang Mai–bound bus or *săwngthăew* from Lampang's main bus terminal. Let the driver know where you are headed and get off at the Km 37 marker. The centre is 1.5km from the highway. Alternatively, you can hire a blue *săwngthăew* for 350B to 500B at the bus terminal.

Mahout Training

The Conservation Center has special **programmes** (1-/3-day course 1500B/4000B, per day for 10+ days incl training, lodging & food 1500B) for those interested in learning the skills of the *khwaan cháang* or mahout (elephant caretaker). If you want a quick taste of the mahout's life, you can sign on for a one-day course and learn a few simple commands for leading an elephant, experiment with dung paper, ride an elephant in the jungle and take a tour of the elephant hospital.

A more involved three-day, two-night homestay programme includes all meals, a night's lodging in a well-equipped, wood and bamboo bungalow and another night at a jungle camp, plus a general introduction to elephant care and training. Those with a higher level of commitment can choose longer programmes of 10 days, a month, or longer.

OTHER ATTRACTIONS

North and east of Lampang are the cotton-weaving villages of **Jae Hom** and **Mae Tha**. You can wander around and find looms in action; there are also plenty of shops along the main roads.

Tham Pha Thai (Pha Thai Cave) is 66km north of Lampang, between Lampang and Chiang Rai about 500m off Hwy 1. Besides the usual cave formations (stalagmites and stalactites), Tham Pha Thai has a large Buddha image.

The province is well endowed with waterfalls. Three are found within Amphoe Wang Neua, roughly 120km north of the provincial capital: **Wang Kaew**, **Wang Thong** and **Than Thong** (Jampa Thong). Wang Kaew is the largest, with 110 tiers. Near the summit is a Mien hill-tribe village. This area became part of the 1172-sq-km **Doi Luang National Park** in 1990; animals protected by the park

ELEPHANTS IN THAILAND

The elephant is one of the most powerful symbols in Thai culture and until 1917 a white elephant appeared on the Thai national flag. Historically Thais have worked side-by-side with elephants on farms and in the jungle and elephants were the superweapons of Southeast Asian armies before the advent of tanks and big guns. Today elephants are still revered in Thai society and are a strong drawcard for Western tourists.

Currently, experts estimate there are now fewer than 3000 wild elephants in Thailand, more than India but fewer than Myanmar. There are fewer than 2300 domesticated elephants. The numbers of both wild and domestic animals are steadily dwindling. Around 1900 it was estimated that there were at least 100,000 elephants working in Thailand; by 1952 the number had dropped to 13,397. Today, Tak Province has the highest number of elephants and is one of only three provinces (the other two are Mae Hong Son and Surin) where the elephant population has actually increased over the last couple of decades.

Elephant mothers carry their calves for 22 months. Once they are born, working elephants enjoy a three- to five-year childhood before they begin training. The training, which is under the guidance of their mahouts, takes five years. They learn to push, carry and stack logs, as well as bathing and walking in procession.

Working elephants have a career of about 50 years; so when young they are trained by two mahouts, one older and one younger – sometimes a father-and-son team – who can see the animal through its lifetime. Thai law requires that elephants be retired and released into the wild at age 61. They often live for 80 years or more.

As a mode of jungle transport, the elephant beats any other animal or machine for moving through a forest with minimum damage – its large, soft feet distribute the animal's weight without crushing the ground. Interestingly, an adult elephant can run at speeds of up to 23km/h but puts less weight on the ground per square centimetre than a deer!

In 1989 logging was banned in Thailand, resulting in decreased demand for trained elephants. Some owners, however, continue to work their elephants in the illegal logging industry along the Thai–Myanmar border. Sadly, some animals are pumped full of amphetamines so they can work day and night.

The plight of these unemployed creatures is becoming an issue of national concern. Many domesticated elephants are increasingly neglected, mistreated or abandoned by owners who often cannot afford to care for them. Meanwhile, destruction of forests and ivory-trade poaching are placing the wild-elephant population in increasing jeopardy. The Asian elephant is now officially classified as an endangered species.

Rising numbers of unemployed elephants also means unemployed mahouts; many mahouts have begun migrating with their elephants to large Thai cities, even Bangkok. They earn money simply by walking the animal through the streets and selling bananas and sugarcane to people to feed the elephants. In these urban environments, the elephants often suffer; in 1998 an elephant died in Bangkok after getting one of its legs caught in a sewer culvert.

Elephant conservation experts are urging tourists *not* to feed elephants in the cities. A better way to make contact with these beautiful animals is at the Thai Elephant Conservation Center (TECC) in Lampang Province (p337) or at other bona fide conservation facilities. 'The only viable alternative for Asian elephants today is tourism,' says Richard Lair, a long-time consultant to the TECC.

For more information about the state of elephants in Thailand check on the TECC website (www.changthai.com).

include serow, barking deer, pangolin and the pig-tailed macaque.

In Amphoe Meuang Pan, about halfway between Wang Neua and Lampang, is another waterfall, **Nam Tok Jae Sawn**, part of the 593-sq-km **Chae Son National Park** (☎ 0 5422 9000; Tambon Jae Son, Amphoe Muang Ban, Lampang; admission 200B). Elevations in the park reach above 2000m. Jae Sawn has six drops, each with its own pool; close to the falls are nine hot springs. Small huts house circular baths, recessed into the floor and lined with clay tiles, that are continuously filled with water direct from the spring. For 20B you can take a 20-minute soak, preceded and followed by an invigorating cold-water shower.

Camping is permitted in both Chae Son and Doi Luang National Parks. Chae Son has a **visitors centre**, 12 **bungalows** for hire and a **restaurant**, but food must be ordered in advance of your visit. Several privately run **food/snack stalls** provide sustenance as well. For further information, contact the **Royal Forest Department** (☎ 0 2579 7223, 0 2579 5734; Th Phahonyothin, Chatuchak, Bangkok) of the Natural Resources Conservation Office.

CHIANG RAI PROVINCE

Chiang Rai, the northernmost province in Thailand, is one of the country's most rural areas. Half of its northern border, separating the province and nation from Laos, is formed by the Mekong River. Mountains form the other half, cleaving Myanmar from Thailand, with the junction of Nam Ruak (Ruak River) and Mekong River at Thailand's peak. The fertile Mekong flood plains to the east support most of the agriculture in the province; to the west the land is too mountainous for most crops. One crop that thrives on steep mountain slopes is opium, and until recently Chiang Rai was the centre for most of the opium in Thailand.

Crop substitution and other development projects sponsored by the late Princess Mother (the king's mother), along with accelerated law enforcement, have pushed much of the opium trade over the border into Myanmar and Laos. While there are undoubtedly still pockets of the trade here and there, even a few poppy patches, Chiang Rai's Golden Triangle fame is now mostly relegated to history books and museums.

CHIANG RAI

เชียงราย
pop 73,300

Phaya Mengrai founded Chiang Rai in 1262 as part of the Lao-Thai Lanna kingdom and it didn't become a Siamese territory till 1786, then a province in 1910. Lots of wealthy Thais began moving to Chiang Rai in the 1980s, and in the early 1990s the

area saw a development boom as local entrepreneurs speculated on the city's future. Things have calmed down a bit and a few guesthouses have closed, although having an airport has increased its potential as a major tourist destination.

About 180km from Chiang Mai, the city northern Thais know as 'Siang Hai' has been marketed in tourist literature as 'the gateway to the Golden Triangle'. Thais often tout Chiang Rai as an alternative to Chiang Mai, although it's not nearly as colourful and there's less to do in town. On the other hand it's a little more laid-back, and anyone interested in trekking will find they can reach village areas quicker than from Chiang Mai.

Information

Chiang Rai is well supplied with banks, especially along Th Thanalai and Th Utarakit. Internet access is readily available around town and costs 40B per hour. It's especially abundant around the Wang Come Hotel.

Bangkok Bank (Th Thanalai) Has an ATM, as do several other banks in town.

Communications Authority of Thailand office (CAT; cnr Th Ratchadat Damrong & Th Ngam Meuang; ◷ 7am-11pm Mon-Fri) Offers international telephone, Internet and fax services.

Gare Garon (869/18 Th Phahonyothin; ◷ 10am-10pm) Stocks the only second-hand English books in town; also sells coffee, tea and some handicrafts.

Main post office (Th Utarakit; ◷ 8.30am-4.30pm Mon-Fri; 9am-noon Sat, Sun & holidays) South of Wat Phra Singh.

Overbrooke Hospital (☎ 0 5371 1366; Th Singkhlai) A modern hospital that treats foreigners.

Tourism Authority of Thailand office (TAT; ☎ 0 5374 4674, 0 5371 1433; tatcei@loxinfo.co.th; Th Singkhlai; ◷ 8.30am-4.30pm) Reasonably helpful – distributes useful brochures and can recommend accommodation.

Sights
WAT PHRA KAEW

วัดพระแก้ว

Originally called Wat Pa Yia (Bamboo Forest Monastery) in local dialect, this is the city's most revered Buddhist temple. Legend says that in 1434 lightning struck the temple's octagonal stupa, which fell apart to reveal the Phra Kaew Morakot or Emerald Buddha (actually made of jade). After a long journey that included a long stopover

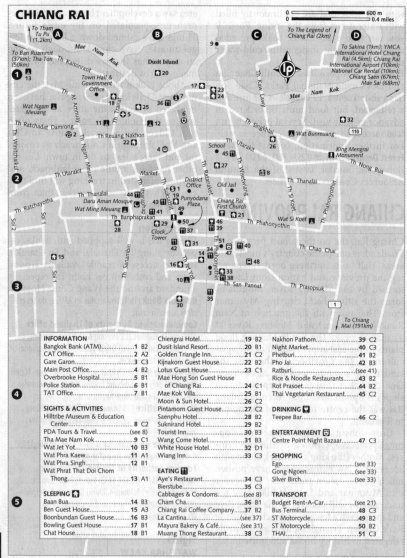

CHIANG RAI

INFORMATION		
Bangkok Bank (ATM).................**1**	B2	
CAT Office....................................**2**	A2	
Gare Garon..................................**3**	C3	
Main Post Office..........................**4**	B2	
Overbrooke Hospital....................**5**	B1	
Police Station...............................**6**	B1	
TAT Office....................................**7**	B1	

SIGHTS & ACTIVITIES		
Hilltribe Museum & Education		
Center.......................................**8**	C2	
PDA Tours & Travel..............(see 8)		
Tha Mae Nam Kok.......................**9**	C1	
Wat Jet Yot...............................**10**	B3	
Wat Phra Kaew...........................**11**	A1	
Wat Phra Singh...........................**12**	B1	
Wat Phrat That Doi Chom		
Thong......................................**13**	A1	

SLEEPING		
Baan Bua....................................**14**	B3	
Ben Guest House.........................**15**	A3	
Boonbundan Guest House............**16**	B3	
Bowling Guest House...................**17**	B1	
Chat House.................................**18**	B1	

Chiengrai Hotel...........................**19**	B2	
Dusit Island Resort......................**20**	B1	
Golden Triangle Inn....................**21**	C2	
Kijnakorn Guest House.................**22**	B2	
Lotus Guest House.......................**23**	C1	
Mae Hong Son Guest House		
of Chiang Rai...........................**24**	C1	
Mae Kok Villa.............................**25**	B1	
Moon & Sun Hotel......................**26**	C2	
Pintamorn Guest House...............**27**	C2	
Saenphu Hotel............................**28**	C2	
Suknirand Hotel..........................**29**	B2	
Tourist Inn..................................**30**	B3	
Wang Come Hotel.......................**31**	B3	
White House Hotel......................**32**	D1	
Wiang Inn..................................**33**	C3	

EATING		
Aye's Restaurant........................**34**	C3	
Bierstube...................................**35**	C3	
Cabbages & Condoms............(see 8)		
Cham Cha...................................**36**	B1	
Chiang Rai Coffee Company........**37**	B2	
La Cantina...........................(see 37)		
Mayura Bakery & Café...........(see 31)		
Muang Thong Restaurant...........**38**	C3	

Nakhon Pathom..........................**39**	C2	
Night Market..............................**40**	C3	
Phetburi.....................................**41**	B2	
Pho Jai......................................**42**	B3	
Ratburi...............................(see 41)		
Rice & Noodle Restaurants.........**43**	C2	
Rot Prasoet................................**44**	B2	
Thai Vegetarian Restaurant........**45**	C2	

DRINKING		
Teepee Bar.................................**46**	C2	

ENTERTAINMENT		
Centre Point Night Bazaar..........**47**	C3	

SHOPPING		
Ego......................................(see 33)		
Gong Ngoen........................(see 33)		
Silver Birch.........................(see 33)		

TRANSPORT		
Budget Rent-A-Car...............(see 21)		
Bus Terminal..............................**48**	C3	
ST Motorcycle............................**49**	B2	
ST Motorcycle............................**50**	B2	
THAI..**51**	C3	

in Vientiane, Laos, this national talisman is now ensconced in the temple of the same name in Bangkok (p101).

In 1990, Chiang Rai commissioned a Chinese artist to sculpt a new image from Canadian jade. Named the Phra Yok Chiang Rai (Chiang Rai Jade Buddha), it was intentionally a very close but not exact replica of the Phra Kaew Morakot in Bangkok, with dimensions of 48.3cm across the base and 65.9cm in height, just 0.1cm shorter than the original. The image is housed in the impressive Haw Phra Kaew, which sits towards the back of the wat compound.

The main *wíhǎan* is a medium-sized, well-preserved wooden structure with unique carved doors. The stupa behind it dates to the late 14th century and is typical Lanna style.

WAT JET YOT
วัดเจ็ดยอด

The namesake for this wat is a seven-spired stupa similar to the stupa in Chiang Mai's Wat Jet Yot, but without stucco ornamentation. Of more aesthetic interest is the wooden ceiling of the front veranda of the main *wíhǎan*, which features a unique Thai astrological fresco.

WAT PHRA SINGH
วัดพระสิงห์

Housing yet another copy of a famous Buddha image, this temple was built in the late 14th century during the reign of Chiang Rai's King Mahaphrom. A sister temple to Chiang Mai's Wat Phra Singh, its original buildings are typical northern Thai–style wood structures with low, sweeping roofs. The impressive dragon-carved gate looks to be of Thai Lü design. The main *wíhǎan* houses a copy of Chiang Mai's Phra Singh Buddha.

WAT PHRA THAT DOI CHOM THONG
วัดพระธาตุดอยจอมทอง

This hilltop wat northwest of Wat Phra Kaew has partial views of the river and gets an occasional river breeze. The Lanna-style stupa here was supposedly built in 940, impossible since Lanna hadn't yet been founded! Most likely it dates to the 14th to 16th centuries, and may cover an earlier Mon stupa inside. King Mengrai, Chiang Rai's founder, first surveyed the site for the city from this peak.

HILLTRIBE MUSEUM & EDUCATION CENTER
พิพิธภัณฑ์และศูนย์การศึกษาชาวเขา

This **museum and handicrafts centre** (☎ 0 5374 0088; www.pda.or.th/chiangrai; 620/1 Th Thanalai; admission 50B; ☺ 9am-6pm Mon-Fri, 10am-6pm Sat & Sun) is a good place to visit before undertaking any hill-tribe trek. The museum and gift shop are on the 3rd floor. Exhibits include typical clothing for six major tribes, folk implements and other anthropological objects. The centre, run by the nonprofit Population & Community Development Association (PDA), also offers a 25-minute slide show on

Thailand's hill tribes with narration in English, French, German, Japanese and Thai. The PDA runs highly recommended treks (below). If you've already been to the Tribal Research Institute at Chiang Mai University, there's little reason to visit this one.

A branch of Bangkok's **Cabbages & Condoms restaurant** is on the premises (p346).

THAM TU PU
ถ้ำตูปู

If you follow Th Winitchaikul across the bridge to the northern side of Mae Nam Kok, you'll come to a turn-off for Tham Tu Pu, 800m from the river. Follow the road 1km, then follow a dirt path 200m to the base of a limestone cliff where the **Tham Tu Pu Meditation Centre** (Samnak Vipassana Tham Tu Pu) sits. Here, you'll find a steep set of stairs leading up to one of the main chambers.

Trekking

More than 20 travel agencies, guesthouses and hotels offer trekking trips, typically in the Doi Tung, Doi Mae Salong and Chiang Khong areas. Many of the local travel agencies merely act as brokers for guides associated with one of the local guesthouses, so it may be cheaper to book directly through a guesthouse. As elsewhere in northern Thailand, you're more assured of a quality experience if you use a TAT-licensed guide.

Trek pricing depends on the number of days and the number of participants and type of activities. Rates range from 800B per person per day in a group of six or more, to 2000B per person per day for two people.

The following agencies in Chiang Rai operate treks and cultural tours where profits from the treks go directly to community-development projects:

Dapa Tours (☎ 0 5371 1354, 0 1764 5221; info@dapa tours.com; 115 Mu 2) Run by Akha, specialises in tours to Akha areas.

Natural Focus (☎ 0 5371 5696; www.naturalfocus ecotour.com; 129/1 Mu 4, Th Pa-Ngiw, Soi 4, Rop Wiang) Specialises in nature tours.

PDA Tours & Travel (☎ 0 5374 0088; 620/1 Th Thanalai, Hilltribe Museum & Education Center; 620/1 Th Thanalai) Culturally sensitive tours led by PDA-trained hill-tribe members.

From Tha Mae Nam Kok (Kok River Pier), boats can take you upriver as far as Tha Ton (see p347). An hour's boat ride east from

NORTHERN THAILAND

TREKKING IN NORTHERN THAILAND

Thousands of visitors trek into the hills of northern Thailand each year. Most come away with a sense of adventure, but some are disillusioned by the experience. The most important ingredient in a good trek is having a good leader-organiser, followed by a good group of trekkers. Some travellers finish a tour complaining more about the other trekkers than about the itinerary, food or trek leader.

Before Trekking

Hill-tribe trekking isn't for everyone. First, you must be physically fit enough to withstand extended uphill and downhill walking, exposure to the elements and spotty food. Second, many people feel awkward walking through hill-tribe villages and playing the role of voyeur.

In cities and villages elsewhere in Thailand, Thais and other lowland groups are quite used to foreign faces and foreign ways (from TV if nothing else). But in the hills of northern Thailand the tribes lead largely insular lives. Therefore, hill-tribe tourism has pronounced effects, both positive and negative. On the positive side, travellers have a chance to see how traditional, subsistence-oriented societies function. Also, since the Thai government is sensitive about the image of their minority groups, tourism may actually have forced it to review and sometimes improve its policies towards hill tribes. On the negative side, trekkers introduce many cultural items and ideas from the outside world that may erode tribal customs to varying degrees.

If you have any qualms about interrupting the traditional patterns of life in hill-tribe areas, you probably shouldn't go trekking. If you do go, keep in mind that anyone who promises you an authentic experience is probably exaggerating at the very least, or at the worst contributing to the decline of hill-tribe culture by leading travellers into untouristed areas.

Choosing a Company

Many trekking guides are freelance and float from company to company, so there's no way to predict which companies are going to give the best service. Many guesthouses that advertise their own trekking companies actually act as commission-charging brokers for off-site operations. The Tourism Authority of Thailand (TAT) office in Chiang Mai (p281) maintains a list of licensed agencies and is making efforts to regulate trekking companies. The TAT recommends that you trek only with members of the Professional Guide Association of Chiang Mai or the Jungle Tour Club of northern Thailand. Still, with more than 200 companies, it's very difficult to guarantee any kind of control. Ultimately the best way to shop for a trek is to talk to travellers who have just returned from one.

In short, if you decide to do a trek, choose your operator carefully, try to meet the others in the group (suggest a meeting), and find out exactly what the tour includes and does not include; there are additional expenses. In the cool season, make sure sleeping bags are provided, as the thin woollen blankets available in most villages are not sufficient for the average visitor. If everything works out, even an organised tour can be worthwhile. Here's a useful check list of questions:

- How many people will there be in the group? (Six to 10 is a good maximum range.)
- Can the organiser guarantee that no other tourists will visit the same village on the same day, especially overnight?
- Can the guide speak the language of each village to be visited? (This is not always necessary, as many villagers can speak Thai nowadays.)
- Exactly when does the tour begin and end? (Some three-day treks turn out to be less than 48 hours in length.)
- Does the tour company provide transport before and after the trek or is it by public bus (which may mean long waits)?

In general, the trekking business has become more conscious of the need to tread carefully in hill-tribe villages than in previous decades. Most companies now tend to limit the number of visits to a particular area and are careful not to overlap areas used by other companies. Everyone benefits from this consciousness: the hill tribes are less impacted by trekkers, the trekkers have a better experience and the trekking industry is more sustainable.

You might find that places other than Chiang Mai or Chiang Rai offer better and less expensive tours from more remote and less-trekked areas. Also, they are generally smaller, friendlier operations and the trekkers are usually a more determined bunch since they're not looking for an easy and quick in-and-out trek. You can easily arrange treks out of Mae Hong Son, Pai, Mae Sai and Tha Ton. If you have a little time to seek out the right people, you can also join organised treks from Mae Sariang, Khun Yuam, Soppong (near Pai), Mae Sot, Um Phang and various out-of-the-way guesthouses elsewhere in the north.

The downside, of course, is that companies outside Chiang Mai are generally subject to even less regulation than those in Chiang Mai, and there are fewer guarantees with regard to terms and conditions.

Costs

Organised treks out of Chiang Mai average around 2100B for a three-day, two-night trek, to 7000B for a deluxe seven-day, six-night trek, including transport, guide, accommodation, three meals per day, sleeping bags, water bottles and rafting and/or elephant riding. Not included are beverages other than drinking water or tea, lunch on the first and last days and personal porters. Rates vary, so it pays to shop around – although these days so many companies are competing for your business that rates have remained pretty stable for the last few years. Elephant rides actually become boring and uncomfortable after an hour or two. Some companies now offer quickie day treks or one-night, two-day programmes. Don't choose a trek by price alone. It's better to talk to other travellers in town who have been on treks.

Seasons

The best time to trek is November to February, when the weather is refreshing, there's little or no rain and wildflowers are in bloom. Between March and May the hills are dry and the weather is quite hot. The second-best time is early in the rainy season, between June and July, before the dirt roads become too saturated.

Independent Trekking

You might consider striking out on your own in a small group of two to five people. Gather as much information as you can about the area you'd like to trek in from the Tribal Museum in Chiang Mai (p289). Browsing the displays will help you identify different tribes, and the inscriptions offer cultural information. Don't bother staff with questions about trekking as this is not their area of expertise.

Be prepared for language difficulties. Few people will know any English. Usually someone in a village will know some Thai, so a Thai phrasebook can be helpful. Lonely Planet publishes a *Hill Tribes Phrasebook* with phrase sections for each of the six major hill-tribe languages.

As in Himalayan trekking in Nepal and India, many people now do short treks on their own, staying in villages along the way. It's not necessary to bring a lot of food or gear, just money for food that can be bought en route at small Thai towns and occasionally in the hill-tribe settlements. (Obviously, be sure to take plenty of water and some high-energy snacks.) However, the TAT strongly discourages trekking on your own because of the safety risk. Check with the police when you arrive in a new district so they can tell you if an area is considered safe or not. A lone trekker is an easy target for bandits.

Safety

Thai police mount regular hill-country patrols and we haven't heard of any trekking groups being robbed for several years now. Still you shouldn't take anything along on a trek that you can't afford to lose. If you leave your valuables with a guesthouse, make sure you obtain a fully itemised receipt before departing on a trek.

Chiang Rai is **Ban Ruammit**, which is a fair-sized Karen village. From here you can trek on your own to Lahu, Mien, Akha and Lisu villages – all of them within a day's walk. Inexpensive room and board (50B per person, meals 25B to 40B) are available in many villages in the river area. Another popular area for do-it-yourself trekkers is **Wawi** (p329), south of the river town of Mae Salak near the end of the river route.

Sleeping

Chiang Rai may have a lot of accommodation to chose from, but most is pretty mediocre and showing its age. However, prices are lower for comparable comfort in other big towns.

BUDGET

Many of Chiang Rai's budget options are downright worn. But every place has some rooms that are better than others, so if you can, check out more than one room before unpacking.

Baan Bua (☎ 0 5371 8880; baanbua@yahoo.com; 879/2 Th Jet Yot; s/d from 180/200B; 🕸) This place can be full any time of the year. It's in a quiet location off Th Jet Yot, and offers 10 large, spotless rooms with hot showers, all in a cement row house with a garden out the front. The well-designed rooms feature screen doors on either side to allow for insect-free cross-ventilation.

Ben Guest House (☎ 0 5371 6775; 351/10 Soi 4 Th Sankhong Noi; r 100-500B; 🕸) This ambitious, friendly, well-maintained place is a good choice for those who don't mind being out of walking distance from the centre. Rooms in a northern Thai–style building made of salvaged teak are much more basic and darker than the newer rooms with bathroom in a brick building. Treks with licensed guides and motorcycle and 4WD rentals can be arranged.

Chat House (☎ 0 5371 1481; chathouse32@hotmail .com; 3/2 Soi Saengkaew, Th Trairat; dm/s/d without bathroom 60/140/150B, s/d from 180/200B; 🕸) On a residential street, with a pleasant garden, Chat has small but good-value, clean rooms in an old Thai house. There are bikes and motorcycles for rent, and 4WD and car rentals as well as guided treks can be arranged. It's a friendly, well-organised, personable place.

Tourist Inn (☎ 0 5371 4682; 1004/4-6 Th Jet Yot; r 150-350B; 🕸 🖳) This place has fairly clean, large rooms and fresh-baked goods downstairs. The cheaper rooms are in the old house. Car and motorcycle rentals can be arranged and the proprietors speak English, Thai and Japanese.

Lotus Guest House (☎ 0 6917 9872; Soi Nang Ing, Th Singkhlai; s/d/q 80/150/300B) Under new management, this place has been cleaned up. Large, well-kept rooms in row houses surround a grassy courtyard. It's popular with Japanese backpackers.

Kijnakorn Guest House (☎ 0 5374 4150-1; 24 Th Reuang Nakhon; r 300-500B; 🕸) More like a hotel than guesthouse, all rooms in this four-storey cement building come with TV, fridge and phone as well as hot-water showers. It's reasonably clean, family-run and appropriately priced, but not very atmospheric.

Suknirand Hotel (☎ 0 5371 1055; fax 0 5371 3701; 424/1 Th Banphaprakan; r from 300B; 🕸) Conveniently located between the clock tower and Wat Ming Meuang, this good-value hotel has plain but clean, updated rooms and is popular with groups of Thai students.

Boonbundan Guest House (☎ 0 5371 7040; fax 0 5371 2914; 1005/13 Th Jet Yot; s/d from 140/150B; 🕸) Contained in a walled compound, this once-popular collection of rooms has something to suit every budget. Some rooms are dingy, others feel like a time capsule; all could use a fresh coat of paint.

Pintamorn Guest House (☎ 0 5371 4161/5427; fax 0 5371 3317; 509/1 Th Ratanaket; s/d/tr from 150/180/250B; 🕸) Guest approval is written on the walls in the dust-covered reception area of this old-timer. The rambling building contains a selection of rooms, all worn, but not devoid of character.

Bowling Guest House (☎ 0 5371 2704; 399 Soi Nang Ing, Th Singkhlai; s/d 80/100B) Rooms are so small here that your fan will likely occupy the bottom third of your bed. But it's clean, family-run and inexpensive.

White House Hotel (☎ 0 5371 3427; rattawitt_mae dan_7@hotmail.com; 789/7 Th Phahonyothin; s/d/tr from 250/350/450B; 🕸 🖳) Popular with Thai families, this decent hotel features 30 large rooms. Rooms with satellite TV are available. The swimming pool is a plus, but the location, away from the centre of town, isn't.

YMCA International Hotel Chiang Rai (☎ 0 5371 3785; ymcawf@loxinfo.co.th; 70 Th Phahonyothin; dm/s/d 90/300/400B; 🕸 🕸 🖳) Although it's institutional, the rooms here are good value for those with their own transport. It's out of town on the highway to Mae Sai. The staff is very helpful and additional facilities include a restaurant, convention room, day-care centre, a small swimming pool, Thai massage and herbal sauna.

Other recommendations:

Chiengrai Hotel (Chiang Rai; ☎ 0 5371 1266; 519 Th Suksathit; s/d from 180/250B; ⛝) An older, well-run place.

Mae Kok Villa (☎ 0 5371 1786; 445 Th Singkhlai; dm/s/d from 80/120/150B) Housed in a former missionary school. Adequate but worn out.

Mae Hong Son Guest House of Chiang Rai (☎ 0 5371 5367; 126 Th Singkhlai; s/d from 80/100B) Almost clean, definitely worn, but friendly.

MIDRANGE

Chiang Rai's midrange has a couple of excellent values.

Golden Triangle Inn (☎ 0 5371 1339/6996; fax 0 5371 3963; 590/2 Th Phahonyothin; r 650-800B; ⛝) This place is more like a home than a hotel. It has 39 tasteful rooms with tile or wood floors and attractive décor. Some rooms have bathtubs, but no rooms have TVs. The landscaped grounds include a café, a Japanese-Thai garden, a Budget car-rental office and an efficient travel agency. It's a popular place, so book in advance.

Moon & Sun Hotel (☎ 0 5371 9279; 632 Th Singhakhai; r/ste 400/800B; ⛝) Bright, new and sparkling clean, this little hotel offers the best-value rooms in town with all the mod cons such as in-room refrigerators, TVs and telephones. Suites have a separate, spacious sitting area and standard rooms have a small desk and built in closet. Staff members speak limited English.

Saenphu Hotel (☎ 0 5371 7300; fax 0 5371 7309; 389 Th Banphaprakan; r from 500B; ⛝) The Saenphu may appear dead from the street, but it's very much happening on the inside and the fully amenitised rooms are a bargain. The hotel's basement nightclub, the Disko Bar, has live music and is a popular local rendezvous spot.

TOP END

Legend of Chiang Rai (☎ 0 5391 0400; www.theleg end-chiangrai.com; 124/15 Kohloy; r 4000-11,000B; ⛝ ⛝ ⛝) All the details have been carefully thought out at this elegant, stylish, and beautifully designed boutique hotel. The spacious bungalows exemplify a fine mixture of contemporary rustic Thai architec-

ture. Each has a pleasant outdoor sitting area, frosted glass for increased privacy and a cool, outdoor-like bathroom with an over-sized shower. The riverside infinity pool is the icing on the comfort-filled cake.

Wiang Inn (☎ 0 5371 1533, Bangkok 0 2513 9804/5; www.wianginn.com; 893 Th Phahonyothin; s/d/ste from 1400/1600/4000B; ⛝ ⛝ ⛝) This full-sized hotel offers all the service and comfort you expect from a business-class hotel. It's popular with upper-class Thais, both families and businessmen as well as international travellers. It has a pleasant, nonsmoking lobby and live lounge music in the restaurant.

Dusit Island Resort (☎ 0 5371 5777-9, Bangkok ☎ 0 2636 3333; chiangrai@dusit.com; r from 3600B; ⛝ ⛝ ⛝) Perched on its own island in Mae Nam Kok (you can't miss its stacked white façade if you arrive in Chiang Rai by boat), this island resort could be just about anywhere in the world. The location insulates guests from the rigours of laid-back Chiang Rai. Facilities include Chinese and European restaurants, a coffee shop, pub and everything else you would expect from a five-star resort.

Wang Come Hotel (☎ 0 5371 1800; fax 0 5371 2973, Bangkok ☎ 0 2252 7750; 869/90 Th Premawiphat; r 1400-1600B, ste 2000-8000B; ⛝ ⛝) The Wang Come is conveniently located, but lacks charm. Rooms are bland and a little rough around the edges, but staff members are polite and there's a banquet room, disco, coffee shop, two restaurants and a nightclub.

Eating

THAI

You'll find plenty of restaurants in the city centre, especially along Th Banphaprakan and Th Thanalai.

Aye's Restaurant (☎ 0 5372 2535; 479 Th Phahonyothin; dishes 75-125B; ⛄ 8am-11pm) Looking for atmosphere and an unbeatable selection of food? This friendly, pleasantly decorated spot draws a big crowd nightly. Everything from the steak schnitzl to the northern Thai curries is tasty and well presented. But the most impressive part of the menu is the wine list.

Muang Thong Restaurant (☎ 0 5371 1162; Th Phahonyothin; dishes 60-100B; ⛄ 24hr) You can't miss the sidewalk side platters of Thai and Chinese dishes here. It's packed nightly. One of the house specialities is *kaeng pàa phèt*, a delicious duck curry.

Sakina (Th Phahonyothin; dishes 15-25B; 8am-5pm Sun-Thu, to noon Fri) On the highway to Mae Sai north of town, Sakina serves an impressive range of Thai Muslim fare. The *kaeng masala kài* (chicken masala curry) is especially good, along with *mátàbà* (*rotii* – Indian flat bread – stuffed with a spicy mix of potatoes and chicken or beef) and *khâo sawy* (egg noodles in a curried broth).

Cabbages & Condoms (☎ 0 5374 0784; 620/1 Th Thanalai; dishes 35-200B; 8am-midnight) On the first floor of the Hilltribe Museum & Education Center, this hip spot serves lots of cocktails and northern-Thai food in a casual indoor-outdoor eating area. Profits from the restaurant are used by the PDA for HIV/AIDS education with the intention of making condoms as easy to find as cabbages.

Rot Prasoet (English sign reads 'Muslim food'; Th Itsaraphap; dishes 25-50B; 7am-8pm) This Thai-Muslim restaurant next to the mosque on Th Itsaraphap dishes up delicious Thai Muslim favourites, including *khâo mòk kài*, a Thai version of chicken biryani. The set lunch is popular.

Nakhon Pathom (no Roman-script sign; Th Phahonyothin; dishes 40-100B; 8am-3pm) Another local restaurant named after a central-Thailand city, Nakhon Pathom is very popular for inexpensive *khâo man kài* (chicken rice) and *kŭaytǐaw pèt yâang* (roast duck with rice noodles).

Cham Cha (Th Singkhlai; dishes 35-90B; 7am-4pm Mon-Sat) This casual little hole-in-the-wall is good for breakfast or lunch. It has all the usual Thai and Chinese standards, along with a few Isan dishes that are not on the English menu, such as *lâap* (spicy minced-meat salad) and *sôm-tam* (spicy green papaya salad), plus ice cream.

Thai vegetarian restaurant (100/2 Th Utarakit; dishes 10-30B; 7am-2pm) A small, pleasant, family-run restaurant located opposite the Chiang Rai Condotel, off Th Utarakit on Th Wisetwiang.

Pho Jai (Th Jet Yot; dishes 20-30B; 8am-3pm) Directly behind the Wang Come Hotel is a very good *khâo sawy* place.

Mayura Bakery & Cafe (Wang Come Hotel; dishes 80-200B; 10am-1am) Resembling an American chain restaurant, this place attached to the Wang Come Hotel sells baked goods and has a selection of Thai and Western dishes.

Along Th Banphaprakan, Phetburi and Ratburi **restaurants** have stacks of platters heaped with cheap, decent central-Thai and Chinese food. The Phetburi has a particularly good selection of Thai curries. Near the bus terminal are the usual **food stalls**; the **night market** (next to the station and Rama I cinema) is also good. There's a string of inexpensive **rice and noodle restaurants** near the Chiengrai Hotel along Th Jet Yot (between Th Thanalai and the clock tower).

INTERNATIONAL

Chiang Rai Coffee Company (Th Jet Yot nr Th Banphaprakan; dishes 30-85B; set meals 85-120B; 7am-10pm) Start your day with a stiff cup of coffee and a filling breakfast. The menu includes real veggie options such as tofu scramble, but will also satisfy those pork-chop-and-potato cravings. It's also a good place to catch up on international TV news or read an English-language newspaper.

La Cantina (Th Wat Jet Yot; dishes 45-100B; 8am-10pm) A variety of Italian dishes and a fun atmosphere ensure that hungry travellers are wooed by the Cantina.

Bierstube (☎ 0 5371 4195; Th Phahonyothin; dishes 40-120B; 9am-11pm) This intimate, open-air restaurant/bar has been recommended for German food.

Drinking & Entertainment

Chiang Rai is pretty quiet at night. A string of bars along Th Wat Jet Yot captures most of the expat business. The go-go bar centre is at Punyodana (formerly Sapkaset Plaza), an L-shaped lane between Th Banphaprakan and Th Suksathit.

Teepee Bar (Th Phahonyothin) A hang-out for backpackers and Thai hippies and a good place to exchange information.

Centre Point Night Bazaar (off Th Phahonyothin) Free northern-Thai music and dance performances are given nightly on a stage here.

Shopping

Prices for antiques and silverwork are sometimes lower in Chiang Rai than in Chiang Mai. Several shops worth checking for handicrafts, silver and antiques can be found along Th Phahonyothin, including the following:

Chiangrai Handicrafts Center (237 Th Phahonyothin)

Ego (869/81 Th Premawiphak) Carries upmarket items such as antique textiles.

Gong Ngoen (873/5 Th Phahonyothin)
Silver Birch (891 Th Phahonyothin)

It's cheaper to buy direct from the craft vendors who set up on the sidewalk in front of the northern entrance to the bus station nightly. Adjacent to the bus station is a tourist-oriented night market that resembles Chiang Mai's but on a much smaller scale.

Getting There & Away

AIR
Chiang Rai International Airport (☎ 0 5379 3555) is 10km north of the city. The terminal has several snack vendors, a Thai Airways–owned restaurant, some souvenir shops, a Chinese tea shop, a money exchange, a post office (open between 7am and 7pm) and rental-car booths.

Air Asia (☎ 0 5379 3545, Bangkok 0 2515 9999; www.airasia.com; Chiang Rai International Airport) operates flights between Bangkok and Chiang Rai (promos from 999B, daily).

Daily flights from Bangkok (2540B, 1¼ hours) are also available via **THAI** (☎ 0 5371 1179; 870 Th Phahonyothin).

Taxis run into town from the airport cost 150B. Out to the airport you can get a *túk-túk* for 80B to 100B.

BOAT
Another way to reach Chiang Rai is via boat along Mae Nam Kok from Tha Ton (for details see p329).

For boats heading upriver, go to the pier in the northwest corner of town. Boats embark daily at 10.30am. Regular long boats from Chiang Rai stop at the following villages (times are approximate for ideal river conditions).

Destination	Fare (B)	Duration (hr)
Ban Ruammit	50	1
Hat Yao	100	2¼
Kok Noi	150	3
Mae Salak	170	4
Pha Khwang	130	2½
Pong Nam Rawn	60	1½
Tha Ton	250	5

You can charter a boat to Ban Ruammit for 650B or all the way to Tha Ton for 1600B. Call **Chiang Rai Boat Tour** (☎ 0 5375 0009) for further information.

BUS
There are two routes to Chiang Rai from Chiang Mai: an old and a new. The old route (*săi kào*) heads south from Chiang Mai to Lampang before heading north through Ngao, Phayao and Mae Chai to Chiang Rai. If you want to stop at these cities, this is the bus to catch, but the trip will take up to seven hours. In Chiang Mai the bus leaves from Th Chiang Mai–Lamphun, near Saphan Nawarat; the fare is 83B (ordinary bus only).

The new route (*săi mài*) heads northeast from Chiang Mai along Rte 118, stopping in Doi Saket and Wiang Papao, and takes about four hours. The fare is 77B ordinary, 98B 2nd-class air-con or 139B for 1st-class air-con. New-route 'green buses' (*rót meh khĭaw*) leave from Chiang Mai's Arcade bus terminal. Chiang Mai to Chiang Rai buses are sometimes stopped by police for drug searches.

The city's **bus terminal** (Th Prasopsuk) is several blocks south of Th Phahonyothin.

Check the table (p385) for information about fares and duration of journeys to bus destinations from Chiang Rai.

Getting Around
A *săamláw* (three-wheeled pedicab) ride anywhere in central Chiang Rai should cost 20B to 30B. *Túk-túk* charge twice that. A city *săwngthăew* system (10B fare) circulates along the main city streets; there are also route *túk-túk* that charge 15B to 20B.

Bicycles and motorcycles can be hired at **ST Motorcycle** (per day bicycles 60-100B, motorcycles older Honda Dreams/newer/250cc Yamaha TTR 150/200/500B; ◷ 8am-6pm; Th Banphaprakan ☎ 0 9537 7088; Th Banphaprakan; Th Wat Jet Yot ☎ 0 5375 2526; Th Wat Jet Yot), which has two locations and takes good care of its bicycles. Many guesthouses also rent motorcycles.

Several small agencies near Wang Come Hotel rent out cars (around 1200B a day), vans (1300B to 1500B) and Suzuki Caribian 4WDs (800B).

The following companies charge a little more than the local offices:
Avis Rent-A-Car (☎ 0 5379 3827; Chiang Rai International Airport)
Budget Rent-A-Car (☎ 0 5374 0442-3; 590 Th Phahonyothin) At Golden Triangle Inn.
National Car Rental (☎ 0 5379 3683; Chiang Rai International Airport)

BUS DESTINATIONS FROM CHIANG RAI

Destination	Fare (B)	Duration (hr)	Destination	Fare (B)	Duration (hr)
Bangkok			Mae Sai		
air-con	370	10	ordinary	25	1½
1st class	452	10	air-con	37	1½
VIP	700	10	Mae Sot		
Ban Huay Khrai			ordinary	200	7½
(for Doi Tung)			air-con	360	7½
ordinary	18	1	Mae Suay		
Basang			ordinary	21	1¼
ordinary	14	¾	air-con	34	1
Chiang Khong			1st class	40	1¼
ordinary	42	2½	Nan		
Chiang Saen			ordinary	95	6
ordinary	25	1½	Phayao		
Fang			ordinary	35	1¾
ordinary	49	2½	air-con	45	1¾
Khon Kaen			1st class	55	1¾
ordinary	239	13	Phitsanulok		
air-con	335	13	ordinary	153	6
1st class	430	13	air-con	214	5
Khorat			VIP	292	5
ordinary	262	14	Phrae		
air-con	472	13	ordinary	118	4
VIP	550	13	air-con	130	4
Lampang			1st class	225	4
ordinary	35	5½	Tak		
air-con	55	5	ordinary	165	6½
1st class	81	5	air-con	297	6½

MAE SALONG (SANTIKHIRI)
แม่สลอง(สันติคีรี)
pop 10,000

Aside from Bangkok's Amphoe Yaowarat, Mae Salong is Thailand's most China-like community. It's nothing like brash Hong Kong or Taipei: the atmosphere here is reminiscent of a small Chinese mountain village. The combination of pack horses, hill tribes (Akha, Lisu, Mien, Hmong) and southern Chinese–style houses conjures up images of a small town or village in southern China's Yunnan Province.

Mae Salong was originally settled by the 93rd Regiment of the Kuomintang (KMT), which fled to Myanmar from China after the 1949 Chinese revolution. After futile intermittent rearguard action against the Chinese communists, the renegades were forced to flee Myanmar in 1961 when the Yangon government decided it wouldn't allow the KMT to remain legally in northern Myanmar. Crossing into northern Thailand with their pony caravans, the ex-soldiers and their families settled into mountain villages and re-created a society like the one they left behind in Yunnan.

After the Thai government granted the KMT refugee status in the 1960s, efforts were made to incorporate the Yunnanese KMT and their families into the Thai nation. Until the late 1980s they didn't have much success. Many ex-KMT persisted in involving themselves in the Golden Triangle opium trade in a three-way partnership with opium warlord Khun Sa and the Shan United Army (SUA). Because of the rough, mountainous terrain and lack of sealed roads, the outside world was rather cut off from the goings-on in Mae Salong, so the Yunnanese were able to ignore attempts by the Thai authorities to suppress opium activity and tame the region.

Infamous Khun Sa made his home in nearby Ban Hin Taek (now Ban Thoet Thai;

p351) until the early 1980s when he was finally routed by the Thai military. Khun Sa's retreat to Myanmar seemed to signal a change in local attitudes and the Thai government finally began making progress in its pacification of Mae Salong and the surrounding area.

In a further effort to separate the area from its old image as an opium fiefdom, the Thai government officially changed the name of the village from Mae Salong to Santikhiri (Hill of Peace). Until the 1980s packhorses were used to move goods up the mountain to Mae Salong, but today the 36km road from Basang (near Mae Chan) is paved and well travelled. The Yunnanese immigrants' equestrian history, alien to the Thais, has led the latter to refer to them as *jiin haw* (galloping Chinese).

In spite of the ongoing 'Thai-isation' of Mae Salong, the town is unlike any other in Thailand. It's not unusual for hotels and restaurants in Mae Salong to boast satellite reception of three TV channels from China and three from Hong Kong. Although the Yunnanese dialect of Chinese remains the lingua franca, the new generation of young people looks more to Bangkok than Taipei for its social and cultural inspirations. Many have left for greater educational and career opportunities.

One of the most important government programmes is the crop-substitution plan to encourage hill tribes to cultivate tea, coffee, corn and fruit trees. This seems to be quite successful, as there are plenty of these products for sale in the town markets, and tea and corn are abundant in the surrounding fields. There's a tea factory in town where you can taste the fragrant Mae Salong teas (originally from Taiwan). The local illicit corn whisky is much in demand – perhaps an all-too-obvious substitution for the poppy. Another local speciality is Chinese herbs, particularly *yaa dawng*, a kind that is mixed with liquor. Thai and Chinese tourists who come to Mae Salong frequently take back a bag or two of assorted Chinese herbs.

The weather is always a bit cooler on the peak of Doi Mae Salong than on the plains below. During the cooler and dry months,

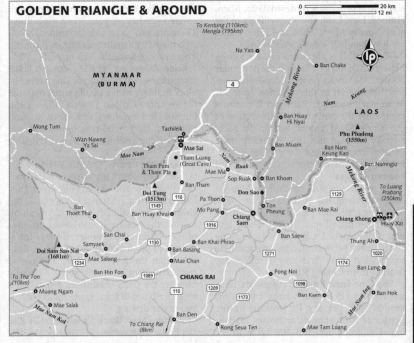

GOLDEN TRIANGLE & AROUND

November to February, nights can actually get cold – be sure to bring sweaters and socks for visits at this time of year.

Minivans full of Thai day-trippers begin arriving in Mae Salong around 10am and leave by 4pm. If you can stay overnight you'll pretty much have the place to yourself in the mornings and evenings.

Information

There is an ATM at the Thai Military Bank opposite Khumnaiphol Resort.

An informal tourism information office, just beyond Mae Salong Villa (right) on the opposite (cliff side) of the road, distributes maps and information about an agrotourism programme to get travellers to visit different tea plantations and factories.

An interesting **morning market** convenes from 5am to 7am (5am to 6am is the peak time) at the T-intersection near Shin Sane Guest House. The market attracts town residents and many tribespeople from the surrounding districts.

Trekking

Shin Sane Guest House has a wall map showing approximate routes to Akha, Mien, Hmong, Lisu, Lahu and Shan villages in the area. Nearby Mien, Akha and Lisu villages are less than half a day's walk away.

The best hikes are north of Mae Salong between Ban Thoet Thai and the Myanmar border. Ask about political conditions before heading off in this direction (towards Myanmar), however. Shan and Wa armies competing for control over this section of the Thailand–Myanmar border do occasionally clash in the area. A steady trade in amphetamines and, to a lesser extent, heroin, flows across the border via several conduit villages.

It's possible to walk south from Mae Salong to Chiang Rai in three or four days, following trails that pass through fairly remote hill-tribe villages. There are also several easily reached hill-tribe villages along the highway between Ban Basang and Mae Salong, but these days they're full of day tourists from Chiang Rai.

Shin Sane Guest House arranges six-hour horseback treks to four nearby villages for around 400B per day. It's possible to hire ponies as pack animals or horses for riding. You could also trek the 12km to the

Lahu village of **Ja-Ju** on your own. A basic **guesthouse** there offers rooms and two meals a day for 50B per person.

Akha Mae Salong Guest House (opposite) also runs treks and can arrange half-day horse-riding tours (400B).

Sleeping

Since the road from Mae Salong to Tha Ton opened, fewer visitors are opting to stay overnight in Mae Salong. The resulting surplus of accommodation often makes prices negotiable, except at holidays when they tend to increase.

Mae Salong Villa (☎ 0 5376 5114/9; fax 0 5376 5039; 5 Mu 1; r 600-1200B) Stunning views are the highlight of this well-maintained collection of clean, bungalow-style rooms in a garden setting with nice terraces. It's better value than the Mae Salong Resort. The onsite Chinese restaurant has views of the mountains and the food is quite good. High-quality tea, grown on the proprietor's tea estate, is for sale.

Khumnaiphol Resort (☎ 0 5376 5001/3; fax 0 5376 5004; 58 Mu 1; r/bungalows 800/1200B) On the road to Tha Ton, 1km south of town near the afternoon market, excellent, new bungalows with covered porches are perched on the hillside. There are also some older, cramped, hotel-style rooms with mattresses that are distinctly Thai in softness (or the lack thereof).

Golden Dragon Inn (☎ 0 5376 5009; 13/1 Th Mae Salong; bungalows/r 300/500B) Occupying a cement-block building with a small garden opposite the mosque, Golden Dragon offers clean but simple bungalows with balconies and somewhat stark hotel-type rooms with hot showers. The newer rooms have two double beds.

Mae Salong Resort (☎ 0 5376 5014; fax 0 5376 5135; Mu 1; r 300-1000B) This 59-room place has a variety of so-so rooms and bungalows (they look good from a distance but are none too clean – beware mouldy carpet). An exhibit hall on the quiet but overgrown grounds of the old military complex displays interesting old photographs, captioned in English, from the KMT era. The Yunnanese restaurant here is worthwhile – especially tasty are the fresh-mushroom dishes. It's a long climb uphill from town, inadvisable if you're not driving.

Shin Sane Guest House (Sin Sae; ☎ 0 5376 5026; 32/3 Th Mae Salong; s/d from 50/100B, bungalow 300B)

Mae Salong's original hotel is a wood affair with a bit of atmosphere. Trekking details are available, including a good trekking map. There is also a little eating area and a place for doing laundry. Calls to prayer from a mosque behind the guesthouse will bring you closer to Allah bright and early in the morning.

Akha Mae Salong Guest House (☎ 0 5376 5103; Th Mae Salong; dm/s/d 50/100/150B) Next door to Shin Sane, this guesthouse occupies a rambling building and is run by a friendly, non-English-speaking Akha family. Handicrafts are made and sold in the reception area. Trekking can be arranged.

Eating

Pàa-thâwng-kŏh (Chinese doughnut) and hot soybean milk at the morning market are an inspiring way to start the day. Don't miss the many street noodle vendors who sell *khànŏm jiin náam ngíaw,* a delicious Yunnanese rice-noodle concoction topped with a spicy pork sauce – Mae Salong's most famous local dish and a gourmet bargain at 15B per bowl.

Around town you'll find a variety of places serving simple Chinese snacks such as fluffy *mantou* (plain steamed Chinese buns) and *saalaapao* (pork-stuffed Chinese buns) served with delicious pickled vegetables. Many of the Chinese in Mae Salong are Muslims so you'll find Muslim Chinese restaurants serving *khâo sawy.*

In town, several teahouses sell locally grown teas and offer complimentary tastings in very traditional, elaborate procedures involving the pouring of tea from a tall, narrow cup into a round cup, said to enhance the tea's fragrance.

Salema Restaurant (Th Mae Salong; dishes 40-100B) Halfway between the Shin Sane Guest House and the day market, Salema serves tasty Yunnanese dishes using locally grown shiitake mushrooms at moderate prices.

Mae Salong Villa (5 Mu 1; dishes 80-150B) Of the hotel restaurants, this is the best. Try the local speciality of black chicken steamed in Chinese medicinal herbs.

Getting There & Away

Mae Salong is accessible via two routes. The original road, Rte 1130, winds west from Ban Basang. Newer Rte 1234 approaches from the south, allowing easier access to Chi-ang Mai. The older route is definitely more spectacular.

To get to Mae Salong by bus, take Mae Sai bus from Chiang Rai to Ban Basang (15B, 1½ hours, every 15 minutes between 6am and 4pm). From Ban Basang, *săwngthăew* head up the mountain to Mae Salong (per person 50B, one hour). It's a little cheaper on the way down from Mae Salong. *Săwngthăew* stop running at around 5pm but you can charter a *săwngthăew* in either direction for about 300B.

You can also reach Mae Salong by road from Tha Ton. See p328 for details.

BAN THOET THAI
บ้านเทิดไทย

Those with an interest in Khun Sa history (see p348) can make a side trip to this Yunnanese-Shan village, 12km off the road between Ban Basang and Mae Salong.

Today many of Ban Thoet Thai's 3000 residents – a mix of Shan, Yunnanese, Akha, Lisu and Hmong – claim to have fond memories of the man once hunted, but never captured, by heroin-consuming countries. The warlord's former camp headquarters, a simple collection of wood and brick buildings on a hillside overlooking the village, has been turned into a free rustic **museum**. There are no set opening hours, and admission is free so you simply have to turn up and ask one of the caretakers to open the exhibition room for you.

Inside, the walls are hung with maps of the Shan States and Mong Tai (the name the Shan use for the independent nation they hope to establish in the future) homelands, a photograph of the former Kengtung (East Shan State) palace and a few political posters. It's not much considering Khun Sa's six years (1976–82) in the area, and of course there is no mention of opium.

A busy **morning market**, part of which was once used to store the Shan United Army arsenal, trades in products from Thailand, Myanmar and China. Khun Sa was also responsible for the construction of **Wat Phra That Ka Kham**, a Shan-style monastery near his former camp.

In case you find yourself stuck in Ban Thoet Thai overnight, **Gredpetch Guest House** (☎ 0 1961 6961; bungalows 300-500B) has reasonable accommodation in sturdy bungalows around a stark garden next to a stream.

NORTHERN THAILAND

MAE SAI
แม่สาย
pop 25,800

Thailand's northernmost town, Mae Sai can be used as a starting point for exploring the Golden Triangle, Doi Tung and Mae Salong. It's also a good spot to observe border life, as Mae Sai is one of the few official overland crossings between Myanmar and Thailand. Don't come expecting bags of atmosphere; the town is little more than a modern trading post.

Foreigners are permitted to cross the border to Tachileik (the town opposite Mae Sai, spelt Thakhilek by the Thais) and continue as far as Kengtung, 163km from Thailand and 100km short of China. Hope-

fully, within a few years, the road should be open all the way to the Chinese border – the town already seems to be preparing for Thailand–China traffic. It's possible to take a boat to China from Chiang Saen (see p359). In spite of the opening, Thai tourists are much more commonly seen in Mae Sai than *faràng* (Westerners).

In February 2001, Burmese forces, apparently in pursuit of Shan State Army rebels, shelled and fired on parts of Mae Sai, invoking retaliatory shelling from the Thai army. During the fighting the whole of Mae Sai was evacuated and the border area was subsequently closed for a time. The crossing closed again between May and October 2002 following a political spat between the

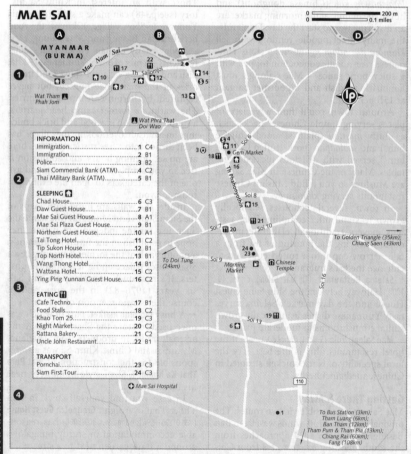

MAE SAI

MYANMAR (BURMA)

Mae Nam Sai

Wat Tham Phah Jom

Wat Phra That Doi Wao

INFORMATION
Immigration..........................1 C4
Immigration..........................2 B1
Police..................................3 B2
Siam Commercial Bank (ATM)....4 C2
Thai Military Bank (ATM)..........5 B1

SLEEPING
Chad House..........................6 C3
Daw Guest House...................7 B1
Mae Sai Guest House...............8 A1
Mae Sai Plaza Guest House........9 B1
Northern Guest House.............10 A1
Tai Tong Hotel......................11 C2
Tip Sukon House....................12 B1
Top North Hotel....................13 B1
Wang Thong Hotel.................14 B1
Wattana Hotel......................15 C2
Ying Ping Yunnan Guest House...16 C2

EATING
Cafe Techno........................17 B1
Food Stalls..........................18 C2
Khao Tom 25.......................19 C3
Night Market.......................20 C2
Rattana Bakery.....................21 C2
Uncle John Restaurant.............22 B1

TRANSPORT
Pornchai.............................23 C3
Siam First Tour.....................24 C3

Gem Market

Th Phaholyothin

To Golden Triangle (35km); Chiang Saen (43km)

To Doi Tung (24km)

Morning Market

Chinese Temple

Mae Sai Hospital

To Bus Station (3km); Tham Luang (6km); Ban Tham (12km); Tham Pum & Tham Pla (13km); Chiang Rai (60km); Fang (108km)

0   200 m
0   0.1 miles

Thai and Myanmar governments. As of this writing it's open again, but it's always a good idea to check the current situation before travelling to Mae Sai.

Information

There's an Internet service (40B per hour) available near the border near the entrance to the Wang Thong Hotel. **Immigration** (☎ 0 373 1008; ☒ 8am-5pm) is at the border.

Sights

Take the steps up the hill near the border to **Wat Phra That Doi Wao**, west of the main street, for superb views over Mae Sai and Myanmar. This wat was reportedly constructed in memory of a couple of thousand Burmese soldiers who died fighting the KMT here in 1965 (you'll hear differing stories around town, including a version wherein the KMT are the heroes).

There are also some interesting **trails** in the cliffs and hills overlooking Mae Sai Guest House and the river.

A persistent rumour says there's a gated cave tunnel that crosses to Myanmar beneath Mae Nam Sai; the entrance is supposedly hidden in the grounds of **Wat Tham Phah Jom**. If it's there, it must be off-limits: Mae Sai Guest House guests are treated to a constant parade of Burmese guys striping off their *longyi* (sarongs) and wading up to their necks across the river.

Sleeping

BUDGET

Mae Sai Guest House (☎ 0 5373 2021; 688 Th Wiengpangkam; bungalows s 100-150B, d 200-500B) This is a pleasant collection of cute, well-maintained bungalows, run by friendly and enthusiastic staff, making it the best budget option. The porches actually extend out the water and cross ventilation is excellent in the riverfront rooms. The charming open-air, riverside restaurant serves good Thai and Western dishes and is a relaxing place to read, socialise or just ponder the distance between Myanmar and Thailand. The staff can also arrange treks. It's about 150m beyond what seems like the end of Th Sailomjoi. It's possible to drive the narrow, one-lane stretch, but move slowly.

Chad House (☎ 0 5373 2054; fax 0 5364 2496; 52/1 Th Phahonyothin; dm/s/d 50/100/150B, bungalows 150B) In a residential neighbourhood near the

bus terminal, this guesthouse is kind of like a homestay. The English-speaking Thai-Shan owners are friendly and helpful and the food is good. Simple rooms have shared hot-water shower facilities. There are a couple of bungalows with private cold-water bathrooms.

Northern Guest House (☎ 0 5373 1537; 402 Th Tham Pha Jum; r 80-350B; ☒) On the banks of Nam Ruak this collection of bunking options has something for every budget traveller. Chose from rustic huts to modern air-con rooms in a two-storey cement building. There's also a nicely landscaped sitting area along the river. The onsite **restaurant** (☒ 7am-midnight) offers room service.

Ying Ping Yunnan Guest House (☎ 0 5364 0507; Soi 6, Th Phahonyothin; r 300B) Above the fancy, bustling and authentic Ying Ping Yunnan Chinese restaurant are 12 very clean and simple rooms with TV, phone and hot-water shower. Little English is spoken but the rooms are a good value.

Top North Hotel (☎ 0 5373 1955; fax 0 5373 2331; 306 Th Phahonyothin; r 300-550B; ☒) A five-minute walk to the bridge to Myanmar, this older, full-size hotel has comfy rooms and friendly staff – and a very auspicious red theme going on.

Tip Sukon House (☎ 0 5364 2816, 0 1883 7318; 734 Th Sailomjoi; r 200-400B; ☒) This newish place has spacious, clean rooms with abused furniture. For those seeking air-con and a hot shower, it's a good deal. Upper-level rooms are significantly nicer than the fan-cooled rooms on the lower levels.

Mae Sai Plaza Guest House (☎ 0 5373 2230; Th Sailomjoi; r 80-120B) You can't miss this rambling, crumbling, 71-room place blanketing the southern hillside along Th Sailomjoi. Unfortunately, the great river views are overshadowed by a general lack of upkeep. If you stay here, pay close attention to how to find your way in and out, and pray that your hut hangs on just one more night.

Other recommendations:

Daw Guest House (☎ 0 5364 0476; 9 Th Sailomjoi; s/d 160/200B) Five tidy, large rooms with hot-water showers.

Wattana Hotel (☎ 0 5373 1002; Th Phahonyothin; r from 200B; ☒) Outdated but well kept.

MIDRANGE

Tai Tong Hotel (Thai Thong; ☎ 0 5373 1975; fax 0 5364 0988; 6 Th Phahonyothin; r 300-900B; ☒) The Tai Tong is a businessman's hotel. Standard rooms do not have TVs but are a good size, with classic older furniture. Suites are larger and have all the midrange amenities. It's possible to get breakfast included in the rate.

Wang Thong Hotel (☎ 0 5373 3388-95; fax 0 5373 3399; 299 Th Phahonyothin; s/d 950/1000B; ste 1500B; 🅿 🅰) For all the amenities of a business-friendly, international-class hotel in a convenient location, look no further than this nine-storey hotel just off Th Phahonyothin. Spacious rooms come with all the amenities and larger double-room suites are also available. Rates do not include tax and service. In addition to the pool there is a pub, disco and a popular restaurant. Off-street parking is guarded.

Eating

Many food stalls offering everything from *khâo sawy* to custard set up at night on the footpaths along Th Phahonyothin. The night market is rather small but the Chinese vendors do good *kǔaytǐaw phàt sii-íu* (rice noodles stir-fried in soy sauce) and other noodle dishes. You can also get fresh *pàa-thâwng-kǒh* and hot soy milk. Across from the district office is a vegetarian restaurant – the sign simply reads 'vegetarian food'.

Uncle John Restaurant (Th Sailomjoi; dishes 50-190B; ☯ 7am-midnight) The barbecue grill, fresh seafood and meats on ice out the front are eye-catchers. Western-sized steaks are the speciality. A range of cocktails is served and the pool table attracts some regular characters. It's a casual setting and tables are limited.

Cafe Techno (Th Sailomjoi; pizzas 100-150B) The choices are limited at this 1st-floor pizza joint. Toppings are limited and there is little else to choose from besides pizza and basic breakfast.

Rattana Bakery (☎ 0 5373 1230; 18 Th Phaho-nyothin; dishes 10-35B; ☯ 8am-5pm) Head here for baked snacks, but don't expect a full meal.

Khao Tom 25 (Th Phahonyothin; dishes 20-45B; ☯ noon-4am) Near Chad House, this is your best bet for late-night eats.

Shopping

Burmese lacquerware, gems, jade and other goods from Laos and Myanmar are sold in shops along the main street. Many Burmese come over during the day from Tachileik

to work or do business, hurrying back by sunset. Gem dealers from as far away as Chanthaburi frequent the gem market that is opposite the police station.

Getting There & Away

Mae Sai's government **bus station** (☎ 0 5364 437) is 2km to the south of the immigration office, a 5B shared *sǎwngthǎew* ride from the city centre. Buses to Mae Sai leave frequently from Chiang Rai (ordinary/air-con 20B/37B, 1½ hours). To/from Chiang Saen by bus costs 20B via Mae Chan. See p360 for different routes between Mae Sai and Chiang Saen.

To/from Chiang Mai there are ordinary (95B, three departures daily) or air-con (2nd/1st class 108/171B, seven daily) buses; this trip takes four to five hours.

There are 1st-class buses going to Mae Sot (394B, 11½ hours, one daily) and Nakhon Ratchasima (Khorat, 505B, 15 hours, four daily).

There are also direct buses to Mae Sai from Fang (45B, two hours) and Tha Ton (36B, 1½ hours) via the Th Tha Ton–Mae Chan. Other destinations include Doi Tung (40B, 1½ hours), Mae Chan (14B, 30 minutes), Mae Salong (60B, 2½ hours) and Sop Ruak (34B, one hour).

You'll find blue *sǎwngthǎew* that leave Mae Sai for Chiang Saen daily for 40B.

BANGKOK

Second-class air-con government buses run to Bangkok (374B, 13 hours, depart 5.20pm and 5.45pm). VIP buses (685B, depart 7am, 5.30pm and 5.45pm) and 1st-class air-con buses (481B, 12 hours, several times daily) and are also available.

Siam First Tour (☎ 0 5364 0123) runs a 1st-class air-con bus from Mae Sai to Bangkok (481B, at 5pm and 5.30pm) and VIP buses to Bangkok (561B, leaving at 6.30pm, 7pm and 7.10pm).

Getting Around

Sǎwngthǎew around town are 5B shared. *Túk-túk* cost 20B to 30B and the motorcycle taxis 10B to 20B. Honda Dreams can be rented between Siam First Tour and the Shell petrol station at **Pornchai** (☎ 0 5373 1136; 4/7 Th Phahonyothin) for 150B a day. **Thong Motorbike**, across from Tip Sukon House, also rents motorcycles at similar rates.

AROUND MAE SAI
Tham Luang
ถ้ำหลวง

About 6km south of Mae Sai off Rte 110, this large cave extends into the hills for at least a couple of kilometres, possibly more. The first cavern is huge, and a narrow passage at the back leads to a series of other chambers and side tunnels of varying sizes. The first kilometre is fairly easy going, but after that you have to do some climbing over piles of rocks to get further in. At this point the roof formations become more fantastic and tiny crystals make them change colour according to the angle of the light. For 30B you can borrow a gas lantern from the caretakers in front of the cave or you can take someone along as a guide (for which there's no fixed fee; just give them whatever you feel they deserve). Apparently, guides sometimes have better things to do during the week.

Tham Pum & Tham Pla
ถ้ำปุ่ม/ถ้ำปลา

Only 13km south of Mae Sai, just off Rte 110 at Ban Tham, these two caves have freshwater lakes inside. Bring a torch to explore the caves, as there are no lights. Another attraction here is the unique cake-like stupa in front of the cave entrance. It's a very large, multitiered structure stylistically different from any other in Thailand.

Doi Tung
ดอยตุง

About halfway between Mae Chan and Mae Sai on Rte 110 is the turn-off west for **Doi Tung**. The name means 'Flag Peak', from the northern Thai word for flag (tung). King Achutarat of Chiang Saen ordered a giant flag to be flown from the peak to mark the spot where two stupas were constructed in AD 911; the stupas are still there, a pilgrimage site for Thai, Shan and Chinese Buddhists.

But the main attraction at Doi Tung is getting there. The 'easy' way is via Rte 1149, which is mostly paved to the peak of Doi Tung. But it's winding, steep and narrow, so if you're driving or riding a motorcycle, take it slowly.

Along the way are Shan, Akha and Musoe (Lahu) villages. Travelling after 4pm – when traffic thins out – is not advisable except along the main routes. It is not safe to trek in this area without a Thai or hill-tribe guide, simply because you could be mistaken for a United States Drug Enforcement Agency agent (by the drug traders) or drug dealer (by the Thai army rangers who patrol the area). You may hear gunfire from time to time, which might indicate that the rangers are in pursuit of the Mong Thai Army (MTA) or Karen rebels or any others who have been caught between the two hostile governments.

On the theory that local hill tribes would be so honoured by a royal presence that they will stop cultivating opium, the late Princess Mother (the king's mother) built the **Doi Tung Royal Villa** (☎ 0 5376 7011; www.doi tung.org; admission 70B; ⏰ 6.30am-5pm), a summer palace, on the slopes of Doi Tung near Pa Kluay Reservoir that is now open to the public as a museum. The rest of the property, including the **Mae Fah Luang Garden** and **Mae Fah Luang Arboretum** (admission 80B; ⏰ 7am-5pm), is also open to the public. There is also a top-end hotel (see p356), a classy **restaurant**, coffee **kiosk** and a Doi Tung **craft shop** up here. This place is popular with bus tour groups.

Another royal project nearby, **Doi Tung Zoo** (admission free; ⏰ 8am-6pm) covers an open space of over 32 hectares. The zoo was first established as a wildlife breeding and animal conservation station, to help reintroduce many species to a reforested Doi Tung. These include Siamese fireback pheasants, peacocks, bears, sambar deer, barking deer and hog deer.

At the peak, 1800m above sea level, **Wat Phra That Doi Tung** is built around the twin Lanna-style stupa. The stupas were renovated by famous Chiang Mai monk Khruba Siwichai early in the 20th century.

Pilgrims bang on the usual row of temple bells to gain merit. Although the wat isn't that impressive, the high, forested setting will make the trip worthwhile. From the walled edge of the temple you can get an aerial view of the snaky road you've just climbed.

A walking path next to the wat leads to a spring and there are other short walking trails in the vicinity.

A bit below the peak is the smaller **Wat Noi Doi Tung**, where food and beverages are available from vendors.

SLEEPING & EATING

If you want to spend the night, **Doi Tung Lodge** (☎ 0 5376 7003; www.doitung.org; Doi Tung Development Project, Mae Fah Luang District; r incl full breakfast per person per 1/2/3 nights 2500/3750/4950B; ✴) is an elegant, boutique mountain lodge with 47 deluxe rooms. A semi-outdoor **restaurant** (⏱ 7am-9pm; dishes 80-200B) offers excellent meals made with local produce, including lots of fresh mushrooms.

GETTING THERE & AWAY

Buses to the turn-off for Doi Tung are 15B from either Mae Chan or Mae Sai. From Ban Huay Khrai, at the turn-off, *săwngthăew* run to Ban Pakha (30B, 30 minutes), or all the way to Doi Tung (60B, one hour).

Road conditions to Doi Tung vary from year to year depending on the state of repair; during the bad spells, the section above Baa Pakha can be quite a challenge to negotiate, whether you're in a truck, 4WD or riding a motorcycle.

You can also travel by motorcycle between Doi Tung and Mae Sai along an even more challenging, 16km, unevenly sealed road that starts in the Akha village of Ban Phame, 8km south of Mae Sai (4km south along Rte 110, then 4km west), and joins the main road about two-thirds of the way up Doi Tung – about 11km from the latter. You can also pick up this road by following the dirt road that starts in front of Mae Sai's Wat Phra That Doi Wao. West of Ban Phame the road has lots of tight curves, mud, rocks, precipitous drops, passing trucks and occasional road-repair equipment – figure on at least an hour by motorcycle or 4WD from Mae Sai.

Although now paved, this is a route for experienced bikers only. The road also runs high in the mountains along the Myanmar border and should not be travelled alone or after 4pm. Ask first in Mae Sai about border conditions. If you want to do a full loop from Mae Sai, ride/drive via Rte 110 south of Mae Sai, then Rte 1149 up to Doi Tung. Once you've had a look around the summit, return to Mae Sai via the Ban Bang Phame aforementioned roads; this means you'll be travelling downhill much of the way.

Cross-Border Trips to Tachileik & Beyond

Foreigners are ordinarily permitted to cross the bridge over Nam Ruak into Tachileik.

On occasion the border may close temporarily for security reasons, so be prepared for possible disappointment if the political situation between Thailand and Myanmar deteriorates again.

For the moment you can enter Myanmar at Tachileik and travel to **Kengtung** or **Mengla** for two weeks upon payment of a US$10 fee and the provision of three passport photos. Your two-week tourist visa can be extended for another two weeks at the immigration office in Kengtung.

If you only want to cross the border into Tachileik for the day, the cost is US$5 or 250B. There is no FEC exchange requirement for day trips. Besides shopping for Shan handicrafts (about the same price as on the Thai side, and everyone accepts baht) and eating some Shan/Burmese food, there's little to do in Tachileik. Around 4000 people cross the bridge to Tachileik daily, most of them Thais shopping for dried mushrooms, herbal medicines, swords and daggers, deer antlers, X-rated DVDs and other cheap and bootlegged imports from China that could get you loads of attention back home from customs. Be wary of cheap cartons of Marlboros and other Western-brand cigarettes, as many are filled with Burmese cigarettes instead of the real thing. Also Thai police have been known to fine travellers in possession of these cigarettes.

Three-night, four-day excursions to the town of Kengtung (called Chiang Tung by the Thais and usually spelt Kyinetong by the Burmese), 163km north, may be arranged on your own as described earlier.

Kengtung is a sleepy but historic capital for the Shan State's Khün culture – the Khün speak a northern Thai language related to Shan and Thai Lü and use a writing script similar to the ancient Lanna script. It's a bit over halfway between the Thai and Chinese borders – eventually the road will be open all the way to China but for now Kengtung is the limit. Built around a small lake and dotted with ageing **Buddhist temples** and crumbling British **colonial architecture**, it's a much more scenic town than Tachileik, and one of the most interesting towns in Myanmar's entire Shan State. About 70% of all foreign visitors are Thais seeking a glimpse of ancient Lanna. Few Westerners are seen in town save for contract employees working for the UN Drug Control Project (UNDCP).

Harry's Guest House & Trekking (☎ 0 1012 1418; 132 Mai Yang Lan; r per person US$5) in Kengtung rents basic rooms in a large house. Harry is an English-speaking Kengtung native who spent many years as a trekking guide in Chiang Mai. **Noi Yee Hotel** (r per person US$8-15), near the centre of town, has large multibed rooms.

For a complete description of Kengtung and the surrounding area, see Lonely Planet's *Myanmar (Burma)* guidebook.

BEYOND KENGTUNG

Eighty-five kilometres north of Kengtung is the Sino–Burmese border district of Mengla (or Mong La as it is sometimes spelt). Although Mengla is mainly a Thai Lü district, in a deal worked out with the Myanmar military it's currently controlled by ethnic Wa, who once fought against Yangon troops but who now enjoy peaceful relations with Yangon (in return for a sizable share in the Wa's thriving amphetamine and opium trade, it's suspected).

A **Drug Free Museum** contains an exhibit on how to refine heroin from opium. The district receives lots of Chinese tourists, who come to peruse Mengla's well-known **wildlife market** and to gamble in the district's several casinos. The largest and plushest, the **Myanmar Royal Casino**, is an Australian–Chinese joint venture. There are also plenty of karaoke bars, discos and other staples of modern Chinese entertainment life. The main currency used in town is the Chinese yuan.

In order to proceed on to Mengla from Kengtung, you must first register at the Kengtung immigration office. The staff at Harry's Guest House (above) can help you accomplish this.

The obvious question is, can you cross the border from Mengla into Daluo, China? The simple answer is, we haven't tried, and we don't know anyone who has.

GETTING THERE & AWAY

The cheapest form of transport to Kengtung are the *săwngthăew* that leave each morning from Tachileik, but reports say Myanmar authorities aren't allowing foreigners to board these. Give it a try anyway, as this sort of situation tends to change. You can rent 4WDs on either side of the border, but Thai vehicles with a capacity of five or fewer passengers are charged a flat

US$50 entry fee, US$100 for vehicles with a capacity of over five. Burmese vehicle hire is more expensive and requires the use of a driver. Whatever the form of transport, count on at least six to 10 gruelling hours (depending on road conditions) to cover the 163km stretch between the border and Kengtung.

The road trip allows glimpses of Shan, Akha, Wa and Lahu villages along the way.

CHIANG SAEN

เชียงแสน

pop 55,000

A sleepy crossroads town on the banks of the Mekong River, Chiang Saen was once the site of an important northern Thai kingdom. Scattered throughout the town today are the ruins of the 14th-century Chiang Saen kingdom – surviving architecture includes several stupas, Buddha images, *wíhăan* pillars and earthen city ramparts. A few of the old monuments still standing predate Chiang Saen by a couple of hundred years; legend says this pre–Chiang Saen kingdom was called Yonok. Formerly loosely affiliated with various northern Thai kingdoms, as well as 18th-century Myanmar, Chiang Saen didn't really become a Siamese possession until the 1880s.

Yunnanese trade routes extended from Simao, Yunnan, through Laos to Chiang Saen and then on to Mawlamyine in Burma, via Chiang Rai, Chiang Mai and Mae Sariang. A less-used route proceeded through Utaradit, Phayao and Phrae.

Nowadays huge river barges from China moor at Chiang Saen, carrying fruit, engine parts and all manner of other imports, keeping the old China–Siam trade route open. Despite this trade, and despite commercialisation of the nearby Golden Triangle, the town hasn't changed too much over the last decade. Practically everything in Chiang Saen closes down by 9pm.

Chiang Saen is an official border crossing for Thai and Lao citizens travelling by ferry to and from the Lao People's Democratic Republic town of Ton Pheung on the opposite side of the river.

Information

Chiang Saen's immigration office has two branches: the main office on the southwest corner of the town's main intersection, and

CHIANG SAEN

INFORMATION
Immigration Office.................1 C2
Main Immigration Office.........2 B2
Police..................................3 B2
Siam Commercial Bank (ATM)..4 B2
Visitors Centre......................5 B2

SIGHTS & ACTIVITIES
Chiang Saen National Museum..6 B2
Wat Chedi Luang...................7 B2
Wat Chom Chang...................8 A1
Wat Pa Sak..........................9 A2
Wat Phakhaopan...................10 B2
Wat Phra That Chom Kitti......11 A1

SLEEPING
Chiang Saen Guest House.......12 C2
Chiang Saen River Hill Hotel...13 B3
Gin's Guest House..................14 C1
JS Guest House.....................15 B2

TRANSPORT
Bus Terminal........................16 B2
Speedboat Landing................17 C2

a smaller one next to the Mekong River pier (for crossings to Ton Pheung).

Siam Commercial Bank (Th Phahonyothin) On the main street leading from the highway to the Mekong River; has an ATM and currency exchange.

Visitors centre (Th Phahonyothin; ⏱ 8.30am-4.30pm Mon-Sat) Has a good relief display showing the major ruin sites as well as photos of various stupas before, during and after restoration.

Sights & Activities

Near the town entrance, the small **Chiang Saen National Museum** (☎ 0 5377 7102; 702 Th Phahonyothin; admission 30B; ⏱ 9am-4pm Wed-Sun) displays arte-facts from the Lanna period and prehistoric stone tools from the area, as well as hill-tribe crafts, dress and musical instruments.

Behind the museum to the east are the ruins of **Wat Chedi Luang**, which features an 18m octagonal stupa in the classic Chiang Saen or Lanna style. Archaeologists argue about its exact construction date but agree it dates to some time between the 12th and 14th centuries.

About 200m from the Pratu Chiang Saen (the historic main gateway to the town's

western flank) are the remains of **Wat Pa Sak**, where the ruins of seven monuments are visible in a **historical park** (admission 20B). The main mid-14th-century stupa combines ele-ments of the Hariphunchai and Sukhothai styles with a possible Bagan influence.

About 2.5km north of Wat Pa Sak on a hilltop are the remains of **Wat Phra That Chom Kitti** and **Wat Chom Chang**. The round stupa of Wat Phra That Chom Kitti is thought to have been constructed before the founding of the kingdom. The smaller stupa below it belonged to Wat Chom Chang. There's nothing much to see at these stupas, but there's a good view of Chiang Saen and the river.

Inside the grounds of **Wat Phakhaopan**, a living wat near the river, stands a magnifi-cent Lanna-period stupa. The large, square base contains walking Lanna-style Buddhas in niches on all four sides. The Buddha fac-ing east is sculpted in the so-called 'calling for rain' *mudra* (pose), with both hands held pointing down at the image's sides – a pose common in Laos but not so common in Thailand.

MEKONG RIVER TRIPS

Boats from China, Laos and Myanmar can be seen unloading their cargoes in the mornings at a boat landing near the customs station stand on the Chiang Saen waterfront.

Six-passenger speedboats jet to Sop Ruak (per boat one way/return 400/700B, 30 minutes), or all the way to Chiang Khong (one way/return 1500/1800B, 1½ to two hours). A fast boat to Chiang Khong (one way/return 2000/2500B) runs for up to 10 people.

Speedboats to Luang Prabang from here are 1490B, the slow boat is 990B.

The most exciting new river trip from Chiang Saen is definitely the three-day, two-night excursion to China (2700B per person). The trip goes through Myanmar and Laos but passengers stay on the boat. You must already have your visa for China (1100B) from Chiang Mai or Bangkok if you intend on travelling through China. The people at Gin's Guest House (below) can book your spot on one of these boats and help you get a visa. It takes at least four workdays to get the visa.

Sleeping

Gin's Guest House (☎ 0 5365 0847/1023; 71 Mu 8; bungalows 200-250B, r 300-700B) On the northern side of town (about 1.5km north of the bus terminal), this pleasant, secluded, affable place has a variety of possibilities (all with attached bathroom) and a variety of prices. Rooms are tasteful but simple and the upstairs veranda is a good place from which to watch the Mekong flow by. Mountain bike and motorcycle rentals are available. Gin also puts together custom tours with car, driver and guide according to the interests of guests. This is also the place to organise boat trips to China.

Chiang Saen River Hill Hotel (☎ 0 5365 0826, Bangkok ☎ 0 2748 9046-8; fax 0 5365 0830, Bangkok 0 2748 9048; 714 Mu 3 Tambon Wiang; r incl breakfast 1000B) This clean, four-storey hotel features good service and some nice northern-Thai furnishing touches. All the rooms have a fridge, TV and phone, along with a floor sitting area furnished with Thai axe pillows, a Thai umbrella and a small rattan table. Ask about off-season discounts.

JS Guest House (☎ 0 5365 1115; 192 Mu 2; dm/r 60/150B) JS offers tidy, simple rooms in a long concrete building with shared bathroom,

plus a few new rooms with private hot-water showers. All rooms are a bit stark, but at these prices, a very good deal. Vegetarian Thai meals and bicycle rentals can also be arranged.

Chiang Saen Guest House (☎ 0 5365 0196; s/d 70/100B, bungalows 250B) This long-running place has a few new good-value rooms with TV and hot-water shower. The older rooms are faded, but reasonable. It's on the road to Sop Ruak, opposite the river.

Eating

Cheap noodle and rice dishes are available at food stalls in and near the market on the river road and along the main road through town from the highway, near the bus stop. A small night market sets up each evening at the latter location and stays open till around midnight.

During the dry months, riverside vendors sell sticky rice, green papaya salad, grilled chicken, dried squid and other fun foods for people to eat while sitting on grass mats along the river bank in front of Chiang Saen Guest House – a very pleasant way to spend an evening. Local specialities include fish or chicken barbecued inside thick joints of bamboo, eaten with sticky rice and *sôm-tam*.

Chom Khong (dishes 35-100B; ⏰ 11am-11pm) Two kilometres south of town via Rte 1129 and back from the river, Chom Khong is a very nice spot amid fruit gardens.

Song Fang Khong (dishes 35-100B; ⏰ 11am-11pm) and **Rim Khong** (dishes 35-100B; ⏰ 11am-11pm) are two *sŭan aahăan* (food garden–style) riverside restaurants in Sop Ruak, off the river road from Chiang Saen. Both offer extensive menus of Thai, Chinese and Isan food. Bring your Thai-language skills.

Getting There & Away

There are frequent buses between Chiang Rai and Chiang Saen (25B, 40 minutes to 1½ hours).

Be sure to ask for the new route (*săi mài*) via Chiang Rai from Chiang Mai (ordinary/air-con 95/171B, five hours). The old route (*săi kào*) meanders through Lamphun, Lampang, Ngao, Phayao and Phan; a trip that takes between seven and nine hours. Alternatively, you can take a bus first to Chiang Rai then change to a Chiang Saen bus (about 4½ hours).

There is also regular bus service from Mae Sai (30B, one hour) and Chiang Khong (50B, two hours).

If you're driving from Mae Sai to Chiang Saen there's a choice of two scenic paved roads (one from the centre of Mae Sai and one near the town entrance), or a wider, busier paved road via Rte 110 to Mae Chan and then Rte 1016 to Chiang Saen.

The roads out of Mae Sai are considerably more direct but there are several forks where you have to make educated guesses on which way to go (signs are occasional). The two roads join not far from the Golden Triangle village of Mae Ma, where you have a choice of going east through Sop Ruak or south through Pa Thon. The eastern route is more scenic.

LAOS

Although boats do travel from here to Laos, the closest crossing open to foreigners is in Chiang Khong (see p364).

Getting Around

A good way to see the Chiang Saen–Mae Sai area is on two wheels. Mountain bikes (per day 50B) and motorcycles (per day 200B) can be rented at Gin's Guest House, while JS Guest House rents out regular bicycles for 40B.

If you are heading southwards to Chiang Khong, Rte 1129 along the river is the road to take.

Săwngthăew travel to Sop Ruak (10B), Mae Sai (30B) and Chiang Khong (50B).

AROUND CHIANG SAEN

Sop Ruak

สบรวก

The borders of Myanmar, Thailand and Laos meet 9km north of Chiang Saen at Sop Ruak, the official 'centre' of the Golden Triangle, at the confluence of Nam Ruak and the Mekong River.

In historical terms, 'Golden Triangle' actually refers to a much larger geographic area, stretching thousands of square kilometres into Myanmar, Laos and Thailand, within which the opium trade is prevalent. Nevertheless hoteliers and tour operators have been quick to cash in on the name by referring to the tiny village of Sop Ruak as 'the Golden Triangle', conjuring up images of illicit adventure even though the adven-

ture quotient here is close to zero. In northern Thai this village is pronounced 'Sop Huak'; many out-of-town Thais don't know either Thai name and simply call it 'Sam Liam Thong Kham' (*săam lìam thawng kham;* Thai for 'Golden Triangle').

Tourists have replaced opium as the local source of gold. Sop Ruak has in fact become something of a tourist trap, with souvenir stalls, restaurants, a massage place and bus loads of package-tour visitors during the day. In the evenings things are quieter.

SIGHTS & ACTIVITIES

The **House of Opium** (admission 20B; ☺ 7am-5pm), a small museum with historical displays pertaining to opium culture, is worth a peek. Exhibits include all the various implements used in the planting, harvest, use and trade of the *Papaver somniferum* resin, including pipes, weights, scales and so on, plus photos and maps. Most labels are in Thai only. The museum is at Km 30, at the southeastern end of Sop Ruak.

The huge pier-attached **Thai–Lao–Chinese–Myanmar Department Store** shopping centre complex has been under construction for several years. The pier is meant to serve passenger-boat traffic between Sop Ruak and China – once the red tape has cleared and such a service becomes established. Eventually three-day cruises to China (15,000B) are expected to be run from here by a company called **Star Cruisers**.

On the Burmese side of the river junction stands the **Paradise Resort's Golden Triangle**, a huge hotel and casino financed by Thai and Japanese business partners who have leased nearly 480 hectares from the Myanmar government. Only two currencies – baht and dollars – are accepted at the hotel and casino.

Ten kilometres north of Chiang Saen on a plot of around 40 hectares opposite the Anantara Resort & Spa, the Mah Fah Luang Foundation has established a 5600-sq-metre **Opium Exhibition Hall** (☎ 0 5378 4444; www.goldentrianglepark.com; Mu 1m Baan Sobruak; admission 300B; ☺ 10am-3.30pm). Opened in 2003, the goal of this impressive facility is to become the world's leading exhibit and research facility for the study of the history of opiate use around the world.

For **Mekong River Cruises** (40min cruise per person/ boat maximum 5 people 300B/500B, longer trips per person return 1800B), local long-tail boat or speedboat trips can be arranged through several local agents. The typical trip involves a circuit around a large island and upriver for a view of the Burmese casino hotel. Longer trips head downriver as far as Chiang Khong. There's a fee of 250B to go onto the casino island for the day (they'll stamp you in and out at the same time), or 500B if you stay overnight.

On longer trips you can stop off at a Lao village on the large river island of **Don Sao**, roughly halfway between Sop Ruak and Chiang Saen. The Lao immigration booth here is happy to allow day visitors onto the island without a Lao visa. A 20B arrival tax is collected from each visitor. There's not a lot to see, but there's an official post office where you can mail letters or postcards with a Laos PDR postmark, a few shops selling T-shirts and Lao handicrafts, and the **Sala Beer Lao**, where you can quaff Lao beer and munch on Lao snacks.

SLEEPING & EATING

Most budget travellers now stay in Chiang Saen. Virtually all the former budget places in Sop Ruak have given way to souvenir stalls and larger tourist hotels.

Anantara Golden Triangle Resort & Spa (☎ 0 5378 4084; www.anantara.com; r/ste 8333/21,393B; 🔊) Recently featured in *Architectural Digest*, Anantara sits on a secluded hillside off the road between Sop Ruak and Mae Sai, directly opposite the Opium Exhibition Hall (opposite). Designed by Thai architect ML Tridhosyuth Devakul, the 90-room complex combines classic northern-Thai design motifs with recycled teak floors with stylish modern touches such as Jim Thompson fabrics and cathedral ceilings. To fit in with the naughty Golden Triangle image, abstract poppy-motif inlays festoon the bottom of the shallow reflecting pool. The windows off the dining area of the restaurant **Dahlia** frame a distant, misty view of Laos and Myanmar. An infinity Jacuzzi, squash and tennis courts, gym, sauna, good library, medical clinic and new spa round out the luxury amenities. Special attractions include the King's Cup Elephant Polo Tournament and mahout-training packages.

Greater Mekong Lodge (☎ 0 5378 4450; www.doi tung.org; s/d 1600/1800B; ✖ 🔊) This hotel is part of the Doi Tung Hall of Opium project. Its spacious, modern bungalows are perched on the slope of a hill overlooking the museum. Views are 1st class and so is the buffet lunch (100B).

Imperial Golden Triangle Resort (☎ 0 5378 4001/5, Bangkok ☎ 0 2653 2201; www.imperialhotels .com; 222 Ban Sop Ruak; r from 2500B; 🔊) Another 1st-class option, this is closer to the cluster of tourist services.

Of the several tourist-oriented restaurants overlooking the Mekong River in Sop Ruak, the best is **Sriwan**, opposite the Imperial Golden Triangle Resort.

GETTING THERE & AWAY

From Chiang Saen to Sop Ruak, a *săwng-thăew* or share taxi costs 10B; these leave every 20 minutes or so throughout the day. It's an easy bicycle ride from Chiang Saen to Sop Ruak.

CHIANG KHONG

เชียงของ

pop 9000

At one time Chiang Khong was part of a small river-bank *meuang* (city-state) called Juon, founded in AD 701 by King Mahathai. Over the centuries Juon paid tribute to Chiang Rai, then Chiang Saen and finally Nan before being occupied by the Siamese in the 1880s. The territory of Chiang Khong extended all the way to Yunnan Province in China until the French turned much of the Mekong River's northern bank into French Indochina in 1893.

More remote yet more lively than Chiang Saen, Chiang Khong is an important market town for local hill tribes and for trade with northern Laos. Nearby are several villages inhabited by Mien and White Hmong. Among the latter are contingents who fled Laos during the 1975 communist takeover and who are rumoured to be involved in an organised resistance movement against the current Lao government.

Huay Xai, opposite Chiang Khong on the Lao side of the river, is a legal point of entry for Laos. Anyone with a valid visa for Laos may cross by ferry. From Huay Xai it's 250km to Luang Nam Tha, a short distance from Boten, a legal border crossing to and from China – see p364 for more information.

Trade between Thailand and China via Chiang Khong is steady. Thai goods going

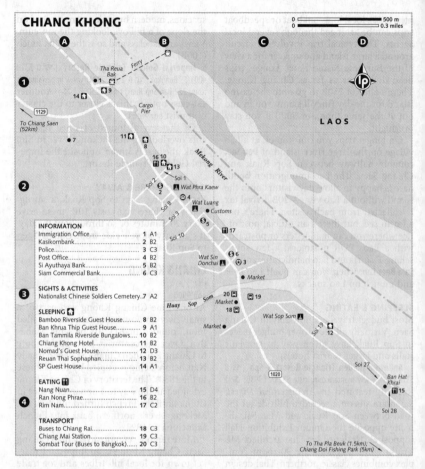

CHIANG KHONG

0 — 500 m
0 — 0.3 miles

LAOS

north include dried and processed food and beverages, cosmetics, machinery, spare parts and agro-industrial supplies.

Information

Si Ayuthaya, **Kasikornbank** and **Siam Commercial Bank** have branches in town with ATMs and foreign-exchange services.

Sights

The current town of Chiang Khong has several northern Thai–style wats of minor interest. **Wat Luang**, on the main road, was once one of the most important temples in Chiang Rai Province and features a stupa dating from the 13th century, which was restored in 1881.

On a hill overlooking the town and the river is a **Nationalist Chinese Soldiers Cemetery**, where more than 200 KMT soldiers are buried. The grave mounds are angled on the hill so that they face China. A shrine containing old photos of KMT soldiers-in-arms stands at the top of the hill.

The village of **Ban Hat Khrai**, about 1km south of Chiang Khong, is famous as being one of the few places where *plaa bèuk* (giant Mekong catfish) are still occasionally caught (see the boxed text, opposite). During the *plaa bèuk* season, mid-April to May, you can watch the small fishing boats coming and going from **Tha Pla Beuk**, about 2km south of Chiang Khong on the Mekong; the turn-off is near Km 137.

Sleeping

Bamboo Riverside Guest House (☎ 0 5379 1621/ 1629; sweepatts@hotmail.com; 71 Mu 1 Hua Wiang; dm 70B, r 150-250B) The chilled-out, bohemian atmosphere at this guesthouse is the direct result of the unusual owner. He's got eclectic taste in music and food and appreciates high-quality and challenging conversations. There are bamboo-thatched dorm rooms as well as private rooms, all of which have an attached hot shower. The restaurant, perched on a deck with views of Laos, serves good Mexican food, carrot cake, bruschetta and coffee.

Ban Tammila Riverside Bungalows (☎ 0 5379 1234; baantammila@hotmail.com; 113 Mu 8; bungalows from 250B, s/d 250/350B) Ban Tammila receives a lot of repeat business. The setting is pleasant and relaxing, rooms are simple but well cared for and the hosts are particularly amiable. Don't miss the small gallery near the entrance. If you're touring by bicycle, or

interested in doing a short bike trip around the area, this would be a good accommodation choice. There's also a very pleasant sitting-dining area by the river.

Reuan Thai Sophaphan (☎ 0 5379 1023; p_dura sawang@hotmail.com; 8 Th Sai Klang; r 350-600B) This guesthouse in a nicely designed multifloor wooden building is more upmarket than its neighbours. Rooms are spacious, simply but carefully decorated and come with two twin beds in order to accommodate groups. There are several places to sit and watch the river roll by. Breakfast is included but it's just a disappointing selection of white bread and instant coffee.

Nomad's Guest House (☎ 0 5365 5537; cresta@ nomadsguesthouse.com; 153/4 Mu 3, Baan Sop Som; s/d from 150/200B) Good rooms, good views, good food and a great philosophy – travel hard, rest easy – are the backbone to this excellent new comer. It's not as convenient as other places in town.

PLAA BÈUK

The Mekong River stretch that passes Chiang Khong is an important fishing ground for the *plaa bèuk* (giant Mekong catfish, *Pangasianodon gigas* to ichthyologists), probably the largest freshwater fish in the world. A *plaa bèuk* takes at least six and possibly 12 years (no-one's really sure) to reach full size, when it will measure 2m to 3m in length and weigh up to 300kg. Locals say these fish swim all the way from Qinghai Province (where the Mekong originates) in northern China. In Thailand and Laos its meaty but mild-tasting flesh is revered as a delicacy.

These fish are taken only between mid-April and May when the river depth is just 3m to 4m and the fish are swimming upriver to spawn in Erhai Lake, Yunnan Province, China. Before netting them, Thai and Lao fishermen hold a special annual ceremony to propitiate Chao Mae Pla Beuk, a female deity thought to preside over the giant catfish. Among the rituals comprising the ceremony are chicken sacrifices performed aboard the fishing boats. After the ceremony is completed, fishing teams draw lots to see who casts the first net, and then take turns casting.

Only a few catfish are captured in a typical season, and the catfish hunters' guild is limited to natives of Ban Hat Khrai. Fishermen sell the meat on the spot for up to 500B or more per kilo (a single fish can bring 100,000B in Bangkok); most of it ends up in Bangkok, since local restaurants in Huay Xai and Chiang Khong can't afford such prices. During harvest season, dishes made with giant catfish may be sold in a makeshift restaurant near the fishermen's landing in Ban Hat Khrai.

Although the *plaa bèuk* is on the Convention on International Trade in Endangered Species (Cites) list of endangered species, there is some debate as to just how endangered it is. Because of the danger of extinction, Thailand's Inland Fisheries Department has been taking protective measures since 1983, including a breed-and-release programme. Every time a female is caught, it's kept alive until a male is netted, then the eggs are removed (by massaging the female's ovaries) and put into a pan; the male is then milked for sperm and the eggs are fertilised in the pan. As a result, well over a million *plaa bèuk* have been released into the Mekong since 1983. Of course, not all of the released fish survive to adulthood. Reservoirs elsewhere in Thailand have had moderate success breeding this fish, however.

At the moment the greatest threat to the catfish's survival is the blasting of Mekong River rapids in China, which is robbing the fish of important breeding grounds.

Ban Khrua Thip Guest House (☎ 0 5363 5859; bungalows 250B) This collection of basic, sturdy, sparsely decorated bungalows near the pier fills up mostly because of location. Each hut has an attached hot-water shower, and towels, toilet paper and soap are supplied.

Chiang Khong Hotel (☎ 0 5379 1182; 68/1 Th Sai Klang; r 200-300B; 🏠) Not as stylish or popular with travellers as other places, this long-running hotel offers good value, well-kept, motel-style rooms with hot-water shower and small TV.

SP Guest House (☎ 0 5379 1767; spguesthouse@hotmail.com; row house r 80-150B, thatched bungalows 120B) The popular SP is a quiet place well off the road on a wooded hillside. Rates for rooms in the row house vary depending on the number of beds and whether or not there's an en suite bathroom. A van shuttle runs to Chiang Mai leaving at noon (220B; five hours).

Eating

There are rice and noodle shops along the main street; none of them are particularly good.

Ran Nong Phrae (dishes 30-80B; 🕙 11am-9pm) On the main street, just northwest of the Ban Tammila Riverside Bungalows, this place serves good *khâo sawy*, Western breakfasts, *kŭaytĭaw* and food made to order.

Rim Nam (dishes 30-80B; 🕙 11am-9pm) On a narrow road down beside the river, is this simple indoor-outdoor restaurant that overlooks the Mekong. The bilingual menu is much shorter than the Thai menu; *yam* (spicy salads) are the house specialities, but the kitchen can whip up almost anything.

Nang Nuan (dishes 80-150B; 🕙 9am-midnight) There's no smoking allowed in this pleasant, open-air eating place overlooking the Mekong. Nang Nuan specialises in fresh river fish, including *plaa bèuk*.

Bamboo Riverside Guest House (☎ 0 5379 1621/1629; 71 Mu 1 Hua Wiang; dishes 40-90B) Has good Thai and *faràng* food, as well as a few Mexican dishes. It's worth seeking out for a meal or dessert even if you're not staying there.

Chiang Doi Fishing Park (☎ 0 5370 1701; Km 5, Rte 1020, Tambon Tha Sai; dishes 40-90B; 🕙 10am-11pm) A good place to stop if you're travelling by road along Rte 1020 from Chiang Rai. The fare at this unassuming roadside place is excellent. You don't have to angle for your own meal from the adjacent lake, though some people try.

Nomad's Guest House (☎ 0 5365 5537; 153/4 Mu 3, Baan Sop Som) Serves excellent pizzas, calzones, salads and Thai dishes, as well as delightful banana cinnamon pancakes.

Getting There & Away

From Chiang Saen, graded and paved 52km-long Rte 1129 is the quickest way to arrive from the west. A second 65km road curving along the river has also been paved and provides a slower but less trafficked alternative. With mountains in the distance and the Mekong River to one side, this road passes through picturesque villages and tobacco and rice fields before joining Rte 1129 just outside Chiang Khong.

Buses depart hourly Chiang Khong and Chiang Rai (42B, 2½ hours) from around 4am to 5pm; the same to/from Chiang Saen. Buses from Chiang Rai and beyond use roads from the south (primarily Rte 1020) to reach Chiang Khong.

Daily buses going to Bangkok (ordinary/air-con/VIP 382/491/573B, nine hours) leave in the evening.

Boats taking up to 10 passengers can be chartered up the Mekong River from Chiang Khong to Chiang Saen for 1800B. Boat crews can be contacted near the customs pier behind Wat Luang, or further north at the pier for ferries to Laos.

BORDER CROSSING (LAOS)

Ferries to Huay Xai, Laos (30B one way), leave frequently between 8am and 5.30pm from Tha Reua Bak, a pier at the northern end of Chiang Khong. A new pier was recently built about 100m southeast of the Tha Reua Bak, but is used for cargo only.

Foreigners can now purchase a 15-day visa for Laos upon arrival in Huay Xai for 1500B or US$30. There is an extra US$1 charge on the weekends. Be sure to get an exit stamp from Thai officials before heading to Laos. Travellers who forget to do this find themselves in uncomfortable situations later on.

Once on the Lao side you can continue on by road to Luang Nam Tha and Udomxai or by boat down the Mekong River to Luang Prabang and Vientiane. **Lao Aviation** (☎ 211026) flies from Huay Xai to Vientiane three times a week.

NORTHERN THAILAND TO YUNNAN, CHINA

It's possible to travel from Thailand to China's Yunnan Province by road via Laos, a land route that ties together the Golden Triangle and Yunnan's Xishuangbanna district (called Sipsongpanna in Thailand) in southwest China. The Thais, Shan and Lao all consider Xishuangbanna to be a cultural homeland.

One can now cross into Laos from Thailand via at least six legal border crossings. Once in Laos, head to Luang Nam Tha or Udomxai, then proceed north to the Lao village of Boten on the Chinese border, close to the Xishuangbanna town of Mengla (Mong La). From Mengla, an existing road leads to Jinghong. To reach Luang Nam Tha from northern Thailand you may cross by ferry from Chiang Khong on the Thai side to Huay Xai on the Lao side. This crossing is fully operational; foreigners may enter Laos here with the proper visa. The Boten crossing is legal for all nationalities.

Another way to reach Boten is via Pakbeng in Laos' Udomxai Province. Pakbeng is midway along the Mekong River route between Huay Xai and Luang Prabang; from Pakbeng a Chinese-built road system continues all the way to Boten. To facilitate trade and travel between China and Thailand, the Chinese have offered to build a new road directly south to the Thai border (Nan Province) from the river bank opposite Pakbeng. For now, Thai authorities are not too happy about this proposed road extension, which is seen as a push towards an 'invasion' of Thailand. During the years of Thai communist insurgency, Communist Party of Thailand cadres used the Pakbeng road to reach Kunming, China, for training in revolutionary tactics.

In the long term, the Mekong River route is also promising. Chinese barges weighing up to 100 tonnes now ply the Mekong eight months a year; from the Chinese border to Chiang Khong, Thailand, the trip takes about five days. During the drier months, however, river transport north of Luang Prabang is hampered by rocks and shallows. Blasting and dredging could make way for boats of up to 500 tonnes to travel year-round, but could have devastating effects on the watercourse and lands downstream.

PHRAE PROVINCE

Phrae Province is probably most famous for the distinctive *sêua mâw hâwm*, the indigo-dyed cotton farmer's shirt seen all over Thailand. 'Made in Phrae' has always been a sign of distinction for these staples of rural Thai life, and since the student–worker–farmer political solidarity of the 1970s, even Thai university professors like to wear them. The cloth is made in Ban Thung Hong outside the town of Phrae.

The annual Rocket Festival kicks off the rice-growing season in May. In Phrae, the biggest celebrations take place in Amphoe Long and Amphoe Sung Men. Look for launching towers in the middle of rice fields for the exact location.

Amphoe Sung Men is also known for **Talat Hua Dong**, a market specialising in carved teak wood. Phrae has long been an important teak centre. Along Rte 101 between Phrae and Nan you'll see a steady blur of teak forests (they are the thickest around the Km 25 marker). Since the 1989 national ban on logging, these forests are all protected by law. Most of the provincial teak business now involves recycled timber from old houses. Specially licensed cuts taken from fallen teak wood may also be used for decorative carvings or furniture (but not in house construction).

The province of Phrae and its neighbouring province of Nan are often overlooked by tourists and travellers alike because of their remoteness from Chiang Mai, but from Den Chai – on the train route north – they're easily reached by bus on Rte 101.

PHRAE
แพร่
pop 21,200

Like Chiang Mai and Lampang, Phrae has an old city partially surrounded by a moat beside a river (here, Mae Nam Yom). Unlike Chiang Mai, Phrae's old city still has lots of quiet lanes and old teak houses – if you're a fan of traditional Thai teak architecture, you'll find more of it here than in any other city of similar size anywhere in Thailand. The local temple architecture has

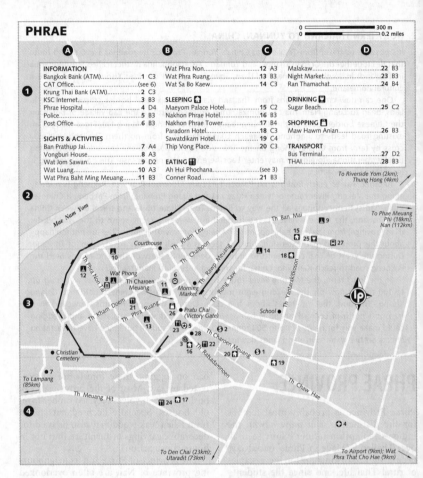

PHRAE

INFORMATION		
Bangkok Bank (ATM)	**1**	C3
CAT Office	(see 6)	
Krung Thai Bank (ATM)	**2**	C3
KSC Internet	**3**	B3
Phrae Hospital	**4**	D4
Police	**5**	B3
Post Office	**6**	B3

SIGHTS & ACTIVITIES		
Ban Prathup Jai	**7**	A4
Vongburi House	**8**	A3
Wat Jom Sawan	**9**	D2
Wat Luang	**10**	A3
Wat Phra Baht Ming Meuang	**11**	B3

Wat Phra Non	**12**	A3
Wat Phra Ruang	**13**	B3
Wat Sa Bo Kaew	**14**	C3

SLEEPING		
Maeyom Palace Hotel	**15**	C2
Nakhon Phrae Hotel	**16**	B3
Nakhon Phrae Tower	**17**	B4
Paradorn Hotel	**18**	B3
Sawatdikarn Hotel	**19**	C4
Thip Vong Place	**20**	C3

EATING		
Ah Hui Phochana	(see 3)	
Conner Road	**21**	B3

Malakaw	**22**	B3
Night Market	**23**	B3
Ran Thamachat	**24**	B4

DRINKING		
Sugar Beach	**25**	C2

SHOPPING		
Maw Hawm Anian	**26**	B3

TRANSPORT		
Bus Terminal	**27**	D2
THAI	**28**	B3

successfully resisted central-Thai influence over the centuries as well. It's a bit unusual: you'll find a mix of Burmese, northern-Thai (Nan and Lanna) and Lao styles.

Southeast of the old city, the newer, more modern Phrae looks like any other medium-sized town in Thailand.

Information

Bangkok Bank (Th Charoen Meuang; 8.30am-3.30pm Mon-Fri) Foreign-exchange service and ATM.

CAT office (Th Charoen Meuang; 8am-8pm) Attached to the main post office. Long-distance calls can be made and you can use a T-card to access the Internet.

Krung Thai Bank (Th Charoen Meuang; 8.30am-3.30pm Mon-Fri) Foreign-exchange service and ATM.

KSC Internet Service Centre (Th Ratsadamnoen; per 30min 20B; 8am-8pm) Catch up on your email.

Phrae Hospital (0 5452 2444) Just east of Th Chaw Hae, southwest of town.

Post office (Th Charoen Meuang; 8.30am-4.30pm Mon-Fri, 9am-noon Sat) Close to the centre of the old city near the traffic circle.

Sights & Activities

WAT LUANG
วัดหลวง

This is the oldest wat in Phrae, probably dating from the founding of the city in the 12th or 13th century. **Phra That Luang Chang Kham**, the large octagonal Lanna-style stupa, sits on a square base with elephants supporting it on all four sides, surrounded by *kùtì* (meditation huts) and coconut palms. As is sometimes seen in Phrae and Nan, the stupa is swathed in Thai Lü fabric.

The veranda of the main *wíhǎan* is in the classic Luang Prabang–Lan Xang style but has unfortunately been bricked in with laterite. Opposite the front of the *wíhǎan* is **Pratu Khong**, part of the city's original entrance gate. No longer used as a gate, it now contains a statue of Chao Pu, an early Lanna ruler. The image is sacred to local residents, who leave offerings of fruit, flowers, candles and incense.

Also on the temple grounds is a **museum** displaying temple antiques, ceramics and religious art dating from the Lanna, Nan, Bago and Mon periods. A 16th-century, Phrae-made sitting Buddha on the 2nd floor is particularly exquisite. There are also some 19th-century photos with English labels on display, including some gruesome shots of a beheading. The museum is usually open weekends only, but the monks will sometimes open it on weekdays on request.

WAT PHRA NON
วัดพระนอน

Southwest a few hundred metres from Wat Luang is a 300-year-old wat named after its highly revered reclining Buddha image *(phrá nawn)*. The *bòt* (central sanctuary) was built around 200 years ago and has an impressive roof with a separate, two-tiered portico and gilded, carved, wooden façade with Ramayana scenes. The *wíhǎan* behind the *bòt* contains the Buddha image, swathed in Thai Lü cloth with bead and foil decoration.

WAT JOM SAWAN
วัดจอมสวรรค์

Outside the old city on Th Ban Mai, this temple was built by local Shan in the late 19th and early 20th centuries, and shows Shan and Burmese influence throughout. The well-preserved wooden *wíhǎan* and *bòt* have high, tiered, tower-like roofs like those in Mandalay. A large copper-crowned stupa has lost most of its stucco to reveal the artful brickwork beneath. A prized possession in the main *wíhǎan* is a Tripitaka section of 16 ivory 'pages' engraved in Burmese.

OTHER TEMPLES
Across from the post office within the old city, **Wat Phra Baht Ming Meuang** houses a

Buddhist school, an old stupa, an unusual, octagonal drum tower made entirely of teak and the highly revered Phra Kosai, which closely resembles the Phra Chinnarat in Phitsanulok. Just outside the northeastern corner of the moat, **Wat Sa Bo Kaew** is a Shan-Burmese-style temple similar to Wat Jom Sawan. **Wat Phra Ruang**, inside the old city, is typical of Phrae's many old city wats, with a Nan-style, cruciform-plan *bòt*, a Lao-style *wíhǎan* and a Lanna stupa. Perhaps this unique mix is actually a coherent design of local (Nan-Phrae) provenance that has yet to be identified.

VONGBURI HOUSE
บ้านวงศ์บุรี

This private **museum** (☎ 0 5462 0153; Th Phra Non Tai; admission 20B; ◷ 8am-5pm) in the two-storey teak house of the last prince of Phrae, is rather worn but still interesting. It was constructed between 1897 and 1907 for Luang Phong-phibun and his wife Chao Sunantha, who once held a profitable teak concession in the city. Elaborate carvings on gables, eaves, balconies and above doors and windows are in good condition. Inside, many of the house's 20 rooms display late-19th-century teak antiques, documents (including early-20th-century slave concessions), photos and other artefacts from the bygone teak-dynasty era. Most are labelled in English as well as Thai.

BAN PRATHUP JAI
บ้านประทับใจ

On the outskirts of the town is **Ban Prathup Jai** (Impressive House; ☎ 0 5451 1008; admission 20B; ◷ 8am-5pm), also called Ban Sao Roi Ton (Hundred Pillar–Filled House), a large northern Thai-style teak house that was built using more than 130 teak logs, each over 300 years old. Opened in 1985, the house took four years to build, using timber taken from nine old rural houses. The interior pillars are ornately carved. It's also filled with souvenir vendors and is rather tackily decorated, so don't take the moniker 'impressive' too seriously.

Sleeping
BUDGET
Several inexpensive hotels can be found along Th Charoen Meuang.

Thip Vong Place (☎ 0 5452 1985; 346/2 Th Chaloen Mueng; r from 280B; ❄) This small hotel offers more than you'd expect in this price range.

MABRI HILL TRIBE

Along the border of Phrae and Nan Provinces live the remaining members of the Mabri (sometimes spelt Mrabri or Mlabri) hill tribe, whom the Thais call *phii tawng lĕuang* (spirits of the yellow leaves). The most nomadic of all the tribes in Thailand, the Mabri customarily move on when the leaves of their temporary huts turn yellow, hence their Thai name. Now, however, their numbers have been greatly reduced (possibly to as few as 150) and experts suspect that few of the Mabri still migrate in the traditional way.

Traditionally the Mabri are strict hunter-gatherers, but many now work as field labourers for Thais or other hill-tribe groups, such as the Hmong, in exchange for pigs and cloth. Little is known about the tribe's belief system, but it's said that the Mabri believe they are not entitled to cultivate the land for themselves. A Mabri woman typically changes partners every five or six years, taking any children from the previous union with her. The Mabris' knowledge of medicinal plants is said to be enormous, encompassing the effective use of herbs for fertility and contraception, and for the treatment of snake or centipede poisoning. When a member of the tribe dies, the body is put in a treetop to be eaten by birds.

In Phrae Province there is a small settlement of around 40 Mabri living in Amphoe Rong Kwang (northeast of the provincial capital, near Phae Meuang Phi) under the protection (some suggest control) of American missionary Eugene Long, who calls himself 'Boonyuen Suksaneh'. The Mabris' village 'Ban Boonyuen' is a classic scenario right out of Peter Mathiessen's *At Play in the Fields of the Lord*. Ban Boonyuen can only be reached on foot or by elephant; the nearest village, which is linked by road, is about 12km away.

Several Mabri families have reportedly abandoned Ban Boonyuen and are now living in Hmong villages in Phrae and Nan. The remaining 100 or so Mabri live across the provincial border in Nan.

The Thai government runs a 'Pre-Agricultural Development of Mabri Society Project' in both provinces to ease the Mabri into modern rural society without an accompanying loss of culture.

According to project leaders, the effort is necessary to protect the Mabri from becoming a slave society within northern Thailand's increasingly capitalist rural economy. Because of their antimaterialist beliefs, the Mabri perform menial labour for the Hmong and other hill tribes for little or no compensation.

All rooms have cable TV, newish furniture and hot-water shower, but lack a window to the outside. For comfort, this is the best choice at this price.

Nakhon Phrae Hotel (☎ 0 5451 1122; fax 0 5452 1937; 29 Th Ratsadamnoen; r 200-560B) A two-minute walk from the old city, this hotel's two wings are on opposite sides of the street. Rooms are large and local tourist information is available in the lobbies of both wings.

Paradorn Hotel (Pharadon; ☎ 0 5451 1177; 177 Th Yantarakitkoson; r from 290B; 🔀) There's an overwhelmingly dated, institutional feel here, but friendly staff. Be sure to avoid the windowless rooms.

Sawatdikarn Hotel (☎ 0 5451 1032; 76-78 Th Yantarakitkoson; r from 100B) This is a reasonable choice for baht-pinching travellers.

MIDRANGE & TOP END

Maeyom Palace Hotel (☎ 0 5452 1028/38; fax 0 5452 2904; 181/6 Th Yantarakitkoson; s/d 1200/1400B; 🔀

🖳 🔊) Opposite the bus terminal, Phrae's top end option has all the modern amenities: carpeted rooms have TV, phone and fridge, and there's a restaurant and lounge. The full-size hotel also provides free transport to and from the airport. Discounts of up to 30% are typical in the low season.

Nakhon Phrae Tower (☎ 0 5452 1321; fax 0 5452 1937; 3 Th Meuang Hit; r from 800B; 🔀) Not as luxurious as the Maeyom Palace, but certainly nicer than other places in town, the Nakhon caters to itinerant government officials. The buffet breakfast (100B) is popular with policemen, and good value if you're hungry. Discounts are available in the low season.

Eating

A very good night market convenes just outside the Pratu Chai intersection every evening. Several food vendors also set up nightly in the lane opposite the Sawatdikarn

Hotel. There's another night market a block or two behind the Paradorn Hotel on weekday evenings only. On Th Ratsadamnoen, near the Nakhon Phrae Hotel and Busarakham Hotel, are several eating options.

Malakaw (Th Ratsadamnoen; meals 40-80B; ⏲ 3.30pm-midnight) This rustic hole-in-the-wall with its rough-cut tables and chairs is a popular place with socialising locals. The ceiling is low and so are the lights, but the menu features fresh, seasonal goodies.

Ah Hui Phochana (no Roman-script sign; Th Ratsadamnoen; dishes 30-120B; ⏲ 5pm-midnight) Next to the Nakhon Phrae Hotel, this Chinese coffee shop offers strong java and various noodle and rice dishes in the evening.

Conner Road (The Orchid; Th Kham Doem; dishes 40-90B; ⏲ 10am-11pm) This indoor-outdoor place, two blocks southwest of the traffic circle in the old city, is decorated with lots of wood and old movie photos. It serves good rice and noodle dishes as well as Thai food. The indoor section is air-con. An English menu is available and there's live music in the evenings.

Ran Thamachat (no Roman-script sign; Th Saisibut; dishes 15-40B; ⏲ 7am-7pm) This is a reliable Thai vegetarian place.

Drinking & Entertainment

Sugar Beach, one of the more salubrious local nightspots, is a large, open-air pavilion near the bus terminal. It's basically just a bar-restaurant but on some nights there's live music.

Riverside Yom, a cluster of pavilions fashioned from grass thatch and pine, fronts the river and features live bluegrass and *phleng phêua chii-wít* (Thai folk) music nightly. It's about 2km northeast of the city centre amid a maze of roads, and thus quite difficult to find; it's best to take a *săamláw* or *săwngthăew*.

Shopping

A good place to buy *mâw hâwm* in Phrae is **Maw Hawm Anian** (no Roman-script sign; 36 Th Chareon Muang), a shop about 60m from the southeastern gate (Pratu Chai) into the old city.

Getting There & Away

AIR

Thai Airways International flies into Phrae each day from Bangkok (2300B, 1½ hours). There is a free shuttle service to the airport

THAI office (☎ 0 5451 1123; 42-44 Th Ratsadamnoen), near the Nakhon Phrae Hotel.

BUS

Most of the buses that depart from Bangkok's Northern and Northeastern bus terminal (ordinary/air-con/VIP 177/319/495B) leave in the evening; there's one ordinary bus that leaves in the morning. The same is true in the reverse direction.

From Chiang Mai's Arcade bus terminal, ordinary buses leave daily at 6.30am and 9am (79B, four hours). Air-con buses leave from the same terminal several times every day between 8am and 10pm (111B; 1st class 142B).

From Chiang Rai, bus services take about four hours to reach Phrae (ordinary/2nd-class air-con/1st-class air-con 79/118/155B).

Buses leave for Den Chai hourly (20B, 30 minutes), where you can catch the northern train line. There are also frequent buses to Nan (47B, two hours).

TRAIN

Tickets to Den Chai station from Bangkok cost 90B for 3rd class, 207B for 2nd class and 431B for 1st class, plus supplementary charges. Trains that arrive at a decent hour are the No 101 rapid (2nd and 3rd class only, departs Bangkok at 6.40am and arrives in Den Chai at 4.03pm), the No 205 ordinary (3rd class only, leaves at 7.05am and arrives at 6.15pm), the No 9 express diesel (2nd class only, leaves at 8.25am and arrives at 3.32pm) and the No 109 rapid (2nd and 3rd class, departs at 10pm and arrives at 8.07am). On the latter service you can get a 2nd-class sleeper.

Blue *săwngthăew* and red buses leave the Den Chai station frequently for the 23km jaunt to Phrae (20B). You can catch them anywhere along the southern end of Th Yantarakitkoson.

Getting Around

A *săamláw* anywhere in the old town costs 20B to 30B; further afield to somewhere like Ban Prathup Jai it can cost up to 40B. Motorcycle taxis are available at the bus terminal; a trip from here to, say, Pratu Chai should cost around 20B.

Shared *săwngthăew* ply a few of the roads (mainly Th Yantarakitkoson) and cost 5B to 10B depending on the distance.

AROUND PHRAE
Wat Phra That Cho Hae
วัดพระธาตุช่อแฮ

On a hill about 9km southeast of town off Rte 1022, this wat is famous for its 33m-high gilded stupa. Cho Hae is the name of the cloth that worshippers wrap around the stupa – it's a type of satin thought to have originated in Xishuangbanna (Sipsongpanna, literally 12,000 Rice Fields, in northern Thai), China. Like Chiang Mai's Wat Doi Suthep, this is an important pilgrimage site for Thais living in the north. The **Phra Jao Than Jai** Buddha image here, which is similar in appearance to Phra Chinnarat in Phitsanulok, is reputed to impart fertility to women who make offerings to it.

The *bòt* has a gilded wooden ceiling, rococo pillars and walls with lotus-bud mosaics. Tiered *naga* (mythical serpent-like being with magical powers) stairs lead to the temple compound; the hilltop is surrounded by a protected forest of mature teak trees.

Săwngthăew between the city and Phra That Cho Hae (12B) are frequent.

Phae Meuang Phi
แพะเมืองผี

The name Phae Meuang Phi means 'Ghost-Land', a reference to this strange geological phenomenon approximately 18km northeast of Phrae off Rte 101. Erosion has created bizarre pillars of soil and rock that look like giant fungi. The area has been made a provincial park; a few walking trails and viewpoints are recent additions. There are picnic pavilions in the park and food vendors selling *kài yâang* (grilled, spiced chicken), *sôm-tam* and sticky rice near the entrance – you may need a drink after wandering around the baked surfaces between the eroded pillars.

Getting to Phae Meuang Phi by public transport entails a bus ride 9km towards Nan, getting off at the signposted turn-off for Phae Meuang Phi, and then catching a *săwngthăew* another 6km to a second right-hand turn-off to the park. From this point you must walk or hitch about 2.5km to reach the entrance. Alternatively, charter a *săwngthăew* for around 200B. *Săwngthăew* drivers seem to hang out at the front of the school.

NAN PROVINCE

Formerly a government-designated 'remote province', Nan before the early 1980s was so choked with bandits and People's Liberation Army of Thailand (PLAT) insurgents that travellers were discouraged from visiting.

With the successes of the Thai army and a more stable political machine in Bangkok during the last two decades, Nan has opened up considerably. The roads that link the provincial capital with the nearby provinces of Chiang Rai, Phrae and Utaradit pass through exquisite scenery of rich river valleys and rice fields. Like Loei in the northeast, this is a province to be explored for its natural beauty and its likeable people.

Nan remains a largely rural province with not a factory or condo in sight. Most of the inhabitants are agriculturally employed, growing sticky rice, beans, corn, tobacco and vegetables in the fertile river plains. Nan is also famous for two fruits: *fai jiin* (a Chinese version of Thailand's indigenous *máfai* – fruit – and *sôm sĭi thawng* – golden-skinned oranges). The latter are Nan's most famous export, commanding high prices in Bangkok and Malaysia. Apparently the cooler winter weather in Nan turns the skin orange (lowland Thai oranges are mostly green) and imparts a unique, sweet-tart flavour. Amphoe Thung Chang supposedly grows the best *sôm sĭi thawng* in the province. Nan is also famous for its *phrík yài hâeng* (long, hot chillies) similar to those grown in China's Sichuan Province. During the hot season, you'll see heaps of these chillies drying by the roadside.

Geography

Nan shares a 227km border with Laos. Only 25% of the land is arable (and only half of that actively cultivated), as most of the province is covered by heavily forested mountains; **Doi Phu Kha**, at 2000m, is the highest peak. Half the forests in the province are virgin upland monsoon forest. Most of the province's population of 364,000 live in the Mae Nam Nan Valley, which is a bowl-shaped depression ringed by mountains on all sides.

The major river systems in the province include the Nan, Wa, Samun, Haeng, Lae

NAN PROVINCE

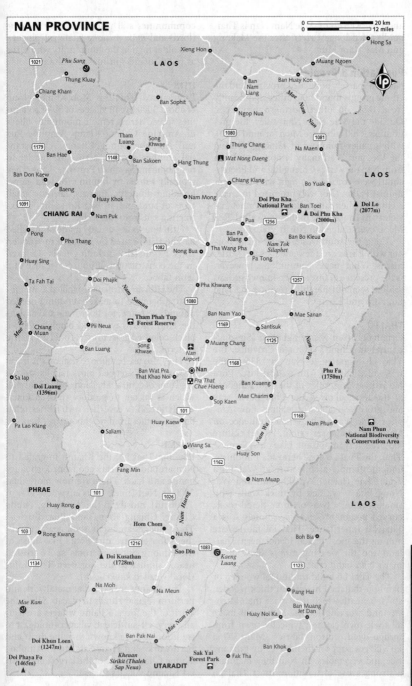

0 — 20 km
0 — 12 miles

LAOS

Hong Sa

1021

Phu Sang

Thung Kluay

Xieng Hon

Muang Ngoen

Ban Huay Kon

Chiang Kham

Ban Sophit

Ban Nam Liang

Ngop Nua

1080

Thung Chang

Mae Nam Nan

1081

Na Maen

Tham Luang

Song Khwae

1179

Ban Hae

1148

Ban Sakoen

Hang Thung

Wat Nong Daeng

Chiang Klang

LAOS

Ban Don Kaew

Baeng

Huay Khok

Nam Mong

Bo Yuak

1091

CHIANG RAI

Nam Puk

Doi Phu Kha National Park

Ban Toei

Doi Lo (2077m)

Pua

1256

Doi Phu Kha (2000m)

Pong

Pha Thang

Ban Pa Klang

Nam Tok Silaphet

Ban Bo Kleua

Huay Sing

1082

Nong Bua

Tha Wang Pha

Pa Tong

Ta Fah Tai

Doi Phajik

Pha Khwang

1257

Lak Lai

Nam Samun

1080

Ban Nam Yao

Mae Sanan

Tham Phah Tup Forest Reserve

1169

Santisuk

Chiang Muan

Pii Neua

Song Khwae

Muang Chang

1125

Nam Wa

Ban Luang

Nan Airport

1168

Phu Fa (1750m)

Sa lap

Ban Wat Pra That Khao Noi

Nan

Ban Kuaeng

Doi Luang (1396m)

Pra That Chae Haeng

Mae Charim

Pa Lao Klang

Sop Kaen

101

Nam Phun

Huay Kaew

1168

Nam Phun National Biodiversity & Conservation Area

Saliam

Wiang Sa

Huay Son

Nam Wa

Fang Min

1162

PHRAE

101

Nam Muap

Huay Rong

1026

LAOS

103

Rong Kwang

Hom Chom

Na Noi

Nam Haeng

Boh Bia

1134

1216

Sao Din

1083

Kaeng Luang

1123

Doi Kusathan (1728m)

Na Moh

Na Meun

Pang Hai

Mae Kam

Ban Muang Jet Dan

Huay Noi Ka

Doi Khun Loen (1247m)

Ban Pak Nai

Mae Nam Nan

Doi Phaya Fo (1465m)

Kheuan Sirikit (Thaleh Sap Neua)

UTARADIT

Sak Yai Forest Park

Fak Tha

Ban Khok

and Pua. At 627km, Mae Nam Nan is Thailand's third-longest river after the Mekong and Mae Nam Mun.

Population & People

Nan is a sparsely populated province and the ethnic groups found here differ significantly from those in other northern provinces. Outside the Mae Nam Nan valley, the predominant hill tribes are Mien (around 8000), with smaller numbers of Hmong. During the Vietnam War, many Hmong and Mien from Nan (as well as Chiang Rai and Phetchabun) were recruited to fight with the communist Pathet Lao, who promised to create a Hmong-Mien king following a Pathet Lao victory in Laos. Some of these so-called 'Red Meos' even trained in North Vietnam.

Along the southwestern provincial border with Phrae are a few small Mabri settlements. What makes Nan unique, however, is the presence of three lesser-known groups seldom seen outside this province: the Thai Lü, Htin and Khamu.

THAI LÜ

Originally from Xishuangbanna (Sipsongpanna) in China's Yunnan Province, the Thai Lü migrated to Nan in 1836 in the wake of a conflict with a local lord. Phra Jao Atityawong, ruler of the Nan kingdom at the time, allowed the Thai Lü to stay and grow vegetables in what is now Amphoe Tha Wang Pha. Their influence on Nan (and to a lesser extent, Phrae) culture has been very important. Like most Siamese Thai, the Thai Lü are Theravada Buddhists, and the temple architecture at Wat Phra That Chae Haeng, Wat Phumin and Wat Nong Bua – typified by thick walls with small windows, two- or three-tiered roofs, curved pediments and *naga* lintels – is a Thai Lü inheritance. Thai Lü fabrics are among the most prized in northern Thailand and the weaving motifs show up in many Nan handicrafts.

The Thai Lü build traditional wooden or bamboo-thatched houses on thick wooden stilts, beneath which they place their kitchens and weaving looms. Many still make all their own clothes, typically sewn from indigo-dyed, cotton fabrics. Many Thai Lü villages support themselves by growing rice and vegetables. In Nan they maintain a strong sense of tradition; most Thai Lü communities still recognise a *jâo meuang* (lord) and *măw meuang* (state astrologer), two older men in the community who serve as political and spiritual consultants.

HTIN

Pronounced 'Tin', this Mon-Khmer group of about 3000 live in villages of 50 or so families spread across remote mountain valleys of Amphoe Chiang Klang, Amphoe Pua and Amphoe Thung Chang. A substantial number also live across the border in neighbouring Sayaburi Province, Laos. They typically subsist by hunting for wild game, breeding domestic animals, farming small plots of land and, in Ban Bo Kleua, by extracting salt from salt wells.

Htin houses are usually made of thatched bamboo and raised on bamboo or wooden stilts. No metal – including nails – is used in the construction of houses because of a Htin taboo.

The Htin are particularly skilled at manipulating bamboo to make everything needed around the house; for floor mats and baskets the Htin interweave pared bamboo with a black-coloured grass to create bold geometric patterns.

They also use bamboo to fashion a musical instrument of stepped pipes (similar to the *angklung* of central Thailand and Indonesia), which is shaken to produce musical tones. The Htin don't weave their own fabrics, often buying clothes from neighbouring Mien.

KHAMU

Like the Thai Lü, the Khamu migrated to Nan around 150 years ago from Xishuangbanna and Laos. There are now more than 5000 in Nan (more than anywhere else in Thailand), mostly in the Wiang Sa, Thung Chang, Chiang Klang and Pua districts. Their villages are established near streams; their houses have dirt floors like those of the Hmong but their roofs sport crossed beams similar to the northern-Thai *kàlae* (locally called *kapkri-aak*).

The Khamu are skilled at metalwork and perform regular rituals to placate Salok, the spirit of the forge. Khamu villages are usually very self-sufficient; villagers hold fast to tradition and are known to value thrift and hard work. Ban Huay Sataeng in Amphoe Thung Chang is one of the largest and easiest Khamu villages to visit.

NAN
น่าน
pop 24,300

Just over 668km from Bangkok, little-known Nan is steeped in history. For centuries it was an isolated, independent kingdom with few ties to the outside world. Ample evidence of prehistoric habitation exists, but it wasn't until several small *meuang* consolidated to form Nanthaburi on Mae Nam Nan in the mid-14th century – concurrent with the founding of Luang Prabang and the Lan Xang (Million Elephants) kingdom in Laos – that the city became a power to contend with. Associated with the powerful Sukhothai kingdom, the *meuang* took the title Waranakhon and played a significant role in the development of early Thai nationalism.

Towards the end of the 14th century Nan became one of the nine northern Thai–Lao principalities that comprised Lan Na Thai (now known simply as Lanna) and the city-state flourished throughout the 15th century under the name Chiang Klang (Middle City), a reference to its position approximately midway between Chiang Mai (New City) and Chiang Thong (Golden City, which is today's Luang Prabang).

The Burmese took control of the kingdom in 1558 and transferred many of the inhabitants to Burma as slaves; the city was all but abandoned until western Thailand was wrested from the Burmese in 1786. The local dynasty then regained local sovereignty and it remained semi-autonomous until 1931 when Nan finally accepted full Bangkok sponsorship.

Parts of the old city wall and several early wat dating from the Lanna period can be seen in present-day Nan. Meuang Nan's wats are distinctive: some temple structures show Lanna influence, while others belong to the Thai Lü legacy brought from Xishuangbanna, the Thai Lü's historical homeland.

Information

Internet services are available around town for 40B per hour.

Bangkok Bank (Th Sumonthewarat) Near the Nan Fah and Dhevaraj hotels. Operates foreign-exchange services and ATMs.

CAT office (Main post office, Th Mahawong; 7am-10pm) Has a Home Country Direct Phone.

Kasikornbank (Th Sumonthewarat) As Bangkok Bank.

Main post office (Th Mahawong; 8.30am-4.30pm Mon-Fri, 9am-noon Sat, Sun & holidays) In the centre of town.

Provincial office (Th Suriyaphong; 9am-4.30pm Mon-Fri, to noon Sat) Has a friendly tourist centre, although not much English is spoken. Maps are sometimes available.

Tourist information centre (8am-5pm) New centre, complete with coffee shop. Opposite Wat Phumin.

Sights
NAN NATIONAL MUSEUM
พิพิธภัณฑ์สถานแห่งชาติน่าน

Housed in the 1903-vintage palace of Nan's last two feudal lords (Phra Jao Suriyapongpalidet and Jao Mahaphrom Surathada), this **museum** (0 5477 2777, 0 5471 0561; Th Pha Kong; admission 30B; 9am-4pm Mon-Sat) first opened its doors in 1973. Relatively recent renovations have made it one of Thailand's most up-to-date provincial museums and, unlike most, this one also has English labels for many items on display.

The ground floor is divided into six exhibition rooms with ethnological exhibits covering the various ethnic groups found in the province, including the northern Thais, Thai Lü, Htin, Khamu, Mabri, Hmong and Mien. Among the items on display are silverwork, textiles, folk utensils and tribal costumes. On the 2nd floor are exhibits on Nan history, archaeology, local architecture, royal regalia, weapons, ceramics and religious art.

The museum's collection of Buddha images includes some rare Lanna styles as well as the floppy-eared local styles. Usually made from wood, these standing images are in the 'calling for rain' posture (with hands at the sides, pointing down) and they show a marked Luang Prabang influence. The astute museum curators posit a Nan style of art in Buddhist sculpture; some examples on display seem very imitative of other Thai styles, while others are quite distinctive, with the ears curving outwards.

Also on display on the 2nd floor is a rare 'black' (actually reddish-brown) elephant tusk said to have been presented to a Nan lord over 300 years ago by the Khün ruler of Chiang Tung (Kengtung). Held aloft by a wooden *garuda* (mythical bird) sculpture, the tusk measures 97cm long and 47cm in circumference.

NAN

0 ────── 400 m
0 ────── 0.2 miles

A   **B**   **C**   **D**

INFORMATION
Bangkok Bank (ATM)	1 C5
CAT office	(see 2)
Kasikorn Bank (ATM)	(see 1)
Main Post Office	2 B5
Police Station	3 B5
Provincial Office	4 B5
Tourist Information Centre	5 B6

SIGHTS & ACTIVITIES
Fhu Travel	6 B5
Nan National Museum	7 B5
Wat Hua Khuang	8 B5
Wat Phra That Chang Kham	9 B5
Wat Phumin	10 B6
Wat Suan Tan	11 B4

SLEEPING
Amazing Guest House	12 D3
Dhevaraj Hotel	13 B5
Doi Phukha Guest House	14 C3
Fahthanin Hotel	15 A4
Nan Fah Hotel	16 C5
Nan Guest House	17 A5
SP Guest House	18 D4

EATING
Da Dario	19 D3
Dhevee Coffee Shop	(see 13)
Jaan Duan	20 C4
Miw Miw	21 C5
Suan Isan	22 B5
Tanaya Kitchen	23 B4
Yota Vegetarian Restaurant	24 B5

SHOPPING
Hattasin	25 C4

TRANSPORT
Baw Khaw Saw Bus Station	26 A6
Choet Chai Tour	27 C4
Oversea Shop	28 B5
P Bike	29 C4
Sombat Tour	30 C4
Sǎwngthǎew to Mae Charim, Wiang Sa & Na Noi	31 C5
Sǎwngthǎew to Tha Wang Pha & Pua	32 B4

Airport

To Pua (50km);
Chiang Rai (192km)

Th Worawichai

Th Mahayot

Th Rat Amnuay

19 🍴
12 🏠

Sports
Field

Wat
Aranyawat
14 🏠

Soi Aranyawat

Soi 2

Sports
Field

Th Premprida

Nan
Technical
School

11 🏯

Th Suan Tan

Th Mahayot

Municipal
Market

Th Anantaworarittidet

Th Pha Kong

Wat Hua
Wiangtai 🏯
27 🚌

25 🏠

Nara
Department
Store

29

15 🏠

Sukasem
Hotel

32 🚌

23 🍴

30 🚌

18 🏠

Th Sumonthewarat

Th Khao Luang

22 🍴
24 🍴

Th Mahawong

20 🍴

21 🍴
1 🏧
16

13 🍴

31

28 ⊗

2 ⊗

Morning
Market

17 🏠

8 🏯

Th Mahaphrom

Th Jettabut

Ratchaphatsadu
Market

6

7 🏛

9 🏯

4

City
Hall

3 ⊗

Th Suriyaphong

Mae Nam Nan

10 🏯

🏧 5

To Phayao (177km)
(Route 1091)

26 🚌

Th Rop Meuang

To Phrae (112km);
Den Chai (135km)
(Route 101)

To Wat Phra That
Chae Haeng (2km)

A building adjacent to the museum sells a few books on Thai art and archaeology.

WAT PHUMIN
วัดภูมินทร์

Nan's most famous temple is celebrated for its cruciform *bòt* that was constructed in 1596 and restored during the reign of Chao Anantavorapitthidet (1867–74). Murals on the walls depicting the *Khatta Kumara* and *Nimi Jatakas* were executed during the restoration by Thai Lü artists; the *bòt* exterior exemplifies the work of Thai Lü architects as well. The murals have historic as well as aesthetic value since they incorporate scenes of local life from the era in which they were painted.

The ornate altar sitting in the centre of the *bòt* has four sides with four Sukhothai-style sitting Buddhas in *maan wíchai* ('victory over Mara' – with one hand touching the ground) posture, facing in each direction.

WAT PHRA THAT CHAE HAENG
วัดพระธาตุแช่แห้ง

Two kilometres past the bridge that spans Mae Nam Nan, heading southeast out of town, this temple dating from 1355 is the most sacred wat in Nan Province. It's set in a square, walled enclosure on top of a hill with a view of Nan and the valley. The Thai Lü–influenced *bòt* features a triple-tiered roof with carved wooden eaves and dragon reliefs over the doors. A gilded Lanna-style stupa sits on a large square base next to the *bòt* with sides 22.5m long; the entire stupa is 55.5m high.

WAT PHRA THAT CHANG KHAM
วัดพระธาตุช้างค้ำ

This is the second-most important **temple** (Th Pha Kong) in the city after Wat Phra That Chae Haeng; the founding date is unknown. The main *wíhǎan*, reconstructed in 1458, has a huge seated Buddha image and faint murals in the process of being painstakingly uncovered. (Sometime in the mid-20th century an abbot reportedly ordered the murals to be whitewashed because he thought they were distracting worshippers from concentrating on his sermons!)

Also in the *wíhǎan* is a set of Lanna-period scrolls inscribed (in Lanna script) not only with the usual Buddhist scriptures but with the history, law and astrology of the time. A *thammâat* (a '*dhamma* seat' used by monks when teaching) sits to one side.

The magnificent stupa behind the *wíhǎan* dates to the 14th century, probably around the same time the temple was founded. It features elephant supports similar to those seen in Sukhothai and Si Satchanalai.

Next to the stupa is a small, undistinguished *bòt* from the same era. Wat Chang Kham's current abbot tells an interesting story involving the *bòt* and a Buddha image that was once kept inside. According to the venerable abbot, in 1955 art historian AB Griswold offered to purchase the 145cm-tall Buddha inside the small *bòt*. The image appeared to be a crude Sukhothai-style walking Buddha moulded of plaster. After agreeing to pay the abbot 25,000B for the image, Griswold began removing the image from the *bòt* – but as he did it fell and the plaster around the statue broke away to reveal an original Sukhothai Buddha of pure gold underneath. Needless to say, the abbot made Griswold give it back, much to the latter's chagrin. The image is now kept behind a glass partition, along with other valuable Buddhist images from the area, in the abbot's *kùtì*. Did Griswold suspect what lay beneath the plaster? The abbot refuses to say.

Wat Phra That Chang Kham is also distinguished by having the largest *hǎw trai* (Tripitaka library) in Thailand. It's as big as or bigger than the average *wíhǎan*, but now lies empty.

The wat is located across from the Nan National Museum.

WAT HUA KHUANG
วัดหัวข่วง

Largely ignored by art historians, this small wat diagonally opposite Wat Phra That Chang Kham features a distinctive Lanna/Lan Xang–style stupa with four Buddha niches, a wooden *hǎw trai* – now used as a *kùtì* – and a noteworthy *bòt* with a Luang Prabang–style carved wooden veranda.

Inside are a carved wooden ceiling and a huge *naga* altar. The temple's founding date is unknown, but stylistic cues suggest this may be one of the city's oldest wats.

WAT SUAN TAN
วัดสวนตาล

Reportedly established in 1456, **Wat Suan Tan** (Palm Grove Monastery; Th Suan Tan) features an interesting 15th-century stupa (40m high) that combines *prang* (Hindu/Khmer-style stupas) and lotus-bud motifs of obvious Sukhothai influence. The heavily restored *wíhǎan* contains an early Sukhothai-style bronze sitting Buddha.

Activities

Nan has nothing like the organised trekking industry found in Chiang Rai and Chiang Mai, but there is one company that leads two- or three-day excursions into the mountains. **Fhu Travel Service** (☎ 0 5471 0636, 0 1287 7209; www.fhutravel.com; 453/4 Th Sumonthewarat; per person (2-person minimum) 'soft' trek 1 day 700-1200B, 2 day & 1 night 1200-2000B, 3 day & 2 nights 1500-2700B) offers treks to Mabri, Hmong, Mien, Thai Lü and Htin villages. The operators have been leading tours for 17 years, and are professional, honest and reliable.

The trekking fees include transport, meals, accommodation, sleeping bag and guide services and prices vary depending on the number of participants.

Fhu also runs boat trips on Mae Nam Nan in December and January when the water level is high enough. White-water rubber-rafting trips on Nam Wa in Mae Charim are offered all year. The prices run from 1300B per person (for trips of seven to eight people) to 2500B per person (for trips of two people). This price includes transport, guide, lunch and safety equipment. Three-day rubber-rafting trips are 3000B to 6000B per person, depending on the number of people. Elephant tours are also available. Tours of the city and surrounding area cost 500B for up to five people. Fhu is also starting to run kayaking trips.

Sleeping

BUDGET

Nan Guest House (☎ 0 5477 1849; 57/16 Th Mahaphrom; s/d from 100/150B) Well maintained and well situated, this guesthouse is the best deal in town. It can be hard to get service, and you should not count on eating meals here despite the readily available menus. But for a clean, comfortable place to sleep, it's an excellent choice. It also organises tours and rents out mountain bikes for 30B per day.

SP Guest House (☎ 0 5477 489; r from 300B; 🐱) Relatively new, very friendly and spotless, this guesthouse is excellent value. It's just off Th Khao Luang beyond the bus stop –

look for the signs. Rooms are spacious and come with TV.

Nan Fah Hotel (☎ 0 5471 0284; 438-440 Th Sumonthewarat; s/d from 380/450B; 🐱) This all-wooden hotel feels like a rooming house, with neat rooms that appear to have gone unchanged for years. They are big enough and very tidy but a little stark. They all come with TV, fridge and hot-water showers. The hallway is a bit of an echo chamber though, and you're sure to hear all of your neighbour's movements. There's a basic restaurant and travel agency on the first floor.

Amazing Guest House (☎ 0 5471 0893; 23/7 Th Rat Amnuay; s/d 100/160B) In a tidy, two-storey house on a quiet lane off Th Rat Amnuay, this intimate place is a bit like staying with your long-lost Thai grandparents. The hosts are sweet, but may be too personable for some. All rooms have wooden floors, clean beds and hot shared showers. Discounts are negotiable for long-term stays.

Doi Phukha Guest House (☎ 0 5475 1517; 94/5 Soi 1 Th Arayawarat; s/d from 70/120B) This rambling old house, in a residential neighbourhood, offers basic sleep space with shared squalid toilets. It's fairly quiet and the management can be helpful.

MIDRANGE

Dhevaraj Hotel (Thewarat; ☎ 0 5471 0094; fax 0 5471 1365; 466 Th Sumonthewarat; s/d from 320/400B; 🐱 🖳) This four-storey hotel, built around a tiled courtyard with a fountain, benefits from a recent interior facelift. It's not quite fancy, but it's the nicest place in Nan. The bottom-end rooms are basic and worn, but rooms with air-con have been tastefully upgraded and are a good deal. Additional onsite conveniences include a restaurant, karaoke and fitness centre.

Fahthanin Hotel (☎ 0 5475 7321-4; 303 Th Anantaworarittidet; r incl breakfast from 700B; 🐱) Seven stories tall, modern but tattered, this hotel is a good deal during the low season when rates hover around 500B. Some rooms have excellent views, but corners have been cut and details have been overlooked. Rooms all have TV, hot shower and minifridge. Slightly larger versions have bathtubs.

Eating

Da Dario (☎ 0 5475 0258; 37/4 Th Rat Amnuay; dishes 60-100B; 🕒 3-10pm Tue-Sat, 11am-10pm Sat & Sun) Next to the Amazing Guest House, this Italian-Thai

ANDERS BLOMQVIST

Seated Buddha statue, Wat Phra Si Ratana Mahathat (p380), Si Satchanalai–Chaliang Historical Park, Sukhothai

Washing day, Sukhothai (p388)

RICHARD I'ANSON

An offering in the hand of a Buddha, Sukhothai Historical Park (p389)

PATRICK HORTON

ANDERS BLOMQVIST

Buddha at Wat Mahathat (p390),
Sukhothai Historical Park

Gold Buddhist celebratory umbrella, Poi Sang Long
festival (p422), Mae Hong Son

JULIET COOMBE

Novice monks, Wat Phra That Doi Kong Mu (p420), Mae Hong Son

ALAIN E

restaurant makes delicious pizza, schnitzel, minestrone and other Western treats. Prices are reasonable, service is excellent, atmosphere is homey and the food attracts a cadre of regulars.

Yota Vegetarian Restaurant (Th Mahawong; dishes 10-30B; ☺ 7am-3pm) Run by the friendliest lady in town who will not let you leave hungry, this is perhaps the best deal in Nan. She's popular and once the food is gone after lunch, that's it for the day.

Tanaya Kitchen (☎ 0 5471 0930; 75/23-24 Th Anantaworarittidet; dishes 30-60B; ☺ 7am-9.30pm) Neat and tidy, with a creative selection of dishes made without MSG, and a variety of vegetarian (and nonvegetarian) options, Tanaya is a good choice for any diet. It caters to a mostly tourist clientele.

Dhevee Coffee Shop (☎ 0 5471 0094; Dhevaraj Hotel, 466 Th Sumonthewarat; dishes 40-120B; ☺ 6am-2am) Modest, clean and reliable, Dhevaraj Hotel's restaurant does good buffets and is open when many other places are closed.

Miw Miw (no Roman-script sign; 347/3 Th Sumonthewarat; dishes 20-50B; ☺ 8am-10pm) Opposite Kasikornbank, this place has good *jók* (broken-rice congee), noodles, real coffee and it is popular in the afternoon for ice-cold *chaa yen* (Thai iced tea).

Suan Isan (☎ 0 5477 2913; Th Sumonthewarat; dishes 30-90B; ☺ 11am-11pm) For Isan food, turn left at the lane next to Rung Thip Sawoei and follow it 200m to this semi-outdoor spot.

Jaan Duan (no Roman-script sign; dishes 20-60B) Opposite the Nara department store, this features ice cream, coffee and curries over rice. It's open morning and evening.

Shopping

Good buys include local textiles, especially the Thai Lü weaving styles from Xishuangbanna. Typical Thai Lü fabrics feature red and black designs on white cotton in floral, geometric and animal designs; indigo and red on white is also common. A favourite is the *lai náam lăi* (flowing-water design) that shows stepped patterns representing streams, rivers and waterfalls.

Local Hmong appliqué and Mien embroidery are of excellent quality. Htin grass-and-bamboo baskets and mats are worth a look, too.

There are several small, artisan-operated shops along Th Sumonthewarat and along Th Mahawong and Th Anantaworarittidet.

Hattasin (☎ 0 5474 1366; 50/10 Th Norkham) A small shop that sells crafts made as part of the Thai Payap Development Association project to improve the standard of living among Nan's ethnic minority groups. The handiwork offered here is among the highest quality available, often including intricate, time-consuming designs. All proceeds go directly to the participating villages – even the administrative staff members are trained village representatives.

Getting There & Away

AIR

PB Air (www.pbair.com; Nan Airport) has also started to run flights from Bangkok (2200B, four flights weekly).

BUS

Baw Khaw Saw (government) buses travel from Chiang Mai, Chiang Rai and Phrae to Nan. The fare from Chiang Mai's Arcade terminal is ordinary bus/air-con/1st class air-con/VIP 117/179/230/328B, six to seven hours. From Chiang Rai there's one daily bus at 9.30am (No 611, 110B) that takes six to seven gruelling hours via treacherous mountain roads – get a window seat as there's usually lots of motion sickness. Buses from Phrae to Nan leave frequently, cost 44B (air-con 62B, two to 2½ hours).

From Nan all but the privately run buses leave from the main terminal at the southwestern edge of town.

Regular government-run air-con buses to Bangkok cost 300B (daily at 8am, 8.30am and 7pm), 1st-class air-con is 387B (daily at 8am and 7pm) and 24-seat VIP buses are 600B (daily at 7pm). The journey takes 10 to 13 hours.

Private 1st-class and VIP Bangkok buses leave from offices located along the eastern end of Th Anantaworarittidet, not far from the Baw Khaw Saw terminal. **Sombat Tour** runs a VIP bus to Bangkok for as low as 390B – check the number of seats before booking. **Choet Chai Tour** offers 1st-class air-con buses (387B, VIP 600B) to Bangkok. Most of these private buses depart between 7pm and 9pm.

SĂWNGTHĂEW

Pick-ups to districts in the northern part of the province (Tha Wang Pha, Pua, Phah Tup) leave from the petrol station opposite

Sukasem Hotel on Th Anantaworarittidet. Southbound *sǎwngthǎew* (for Mae Charim, Wiang Sa, Na Noi) depart from the car park opposite Ratchaphatsadu Market on Th Jettabut.

TRAIN

The northern railway makes a stop in Den Chai, a 46B, three-hour bus ride from Nan.

A Bangkok-bound Sprinter leaves Den Chai at 12.25pm and arrives in Bangkok at 8.10pm. There are also a couple of evening rapid-train departures each day; to be sure of meeting any of these trains, take an early afternoon (1pm or 2pm) Den Chai–bound bus from Nan Baw Khaw Saw bus terminal.

Trains bound for Chiang Mai depart Den Chai at 8.07am (rapid), 10.55am (ordinary) and 3.32pm (express), arriving at Chiang Mai at 12.55pm, 4.10pm and 8pm respectively. The 2nd- and 3rd-class fares to/from Chiang Mai are 74/31B, plus the rapid/express surcharges.

See p369 for more Den Chai train details.

Getting Around

Oversea Shop (☎ 0 5471 0258; 488 Th Sumonthewarat; bicycles/motorcycles per day 50/150B) rents out better bicycles and motorcycles than other places in town. It can also handle repairs.

P Bike (no Roman-script sign; ☎ 0 5477 2680; 331-3 Th Sumonthewarat; Honda Dreams incl helmet & 3rd-party insurance per day 150B), opposite Wat Hua Wiangtai, rents out Honda Dreams and bicycles (per day 20B), and also does repair work.

Sǎamláw around town cost 20B to 30B. Green *sǎwngthǎew* circulating around the city centre charge 5B to 10B per person depending on distance.

AROUND NAN
Doi Phu Kha National Park

อุทยานแห่งชาติดอยภูคา

This **national park** (admission 200B) is centred on 2000m-high Doi Phu Kha in Amphoe Pua and Amphoe Bo Kleua in northeastern Nan (about 75km from Nan). There are several Htin, Mien, Hmong and Thai Lü **villages** in the park and vicinity, as well as a couple of **caves** and **waterfalls** and endless opportunities for forest **walks**. The park is often cold in the cool season and especially wet in the wet season.

The park offers 14 **bungalows** (for 2-7 people 300-2500B). You must bring food and drink-

ing water in from town, as the park office no longer offers food service.

Bamboo Hut (103 Mu 10, Tambon Phu Kha, Amphoe Pua, Nan 55120; r 100B) in Ban Toei, a Lawa-Thai village near the summit at the edge of the park, is a much better choice than the park bungalows. Bamboo Hut offers five clean, well-spaced bamboo-thatch huts with shared bathroom and stupendous mountain and valley views. It leads guests on one- to three-day treks (500B per day, including all meals). Treks visit local waterfalls, limestone caves (Tham Lawng is the biggest cave – about a one-day walk from the guesthouse) and hilltribe villages. This area can get quite cool in the winter months – evening temperatures of 5°C to 10°C are not uncommon – so dress accordingly.

To reach the national park by public transport you must first take a bus or *sǎwngthǎew* north of Nan to Pua (25B), and then pick up one of the infrequent *sǎwngthǎew* to the park headquarters or Bamboo Hut (30B). The one that goes from Nan to Pua leaves about 6am, the one from Pua to Ban Toei at about 7am.

Ban Bo Kleua is a Htin village southeast of the park where the main occupation is the extraction of salt from local salt wells. It's easy to find the main community salt well, more or less in the centre of the village. Many small shops and vendor stands sell the local salt in 2kg bags for 20B; it's delicious stuff. Route 1256 meets Rte 1081 near Ban Bo Kleua; Rte 1081 can be followed south back to Nan (107km) via a network of unpaved roads.

Nong Bua

หนองบัว

This neat and tidy Thai Lü village near the town of Tha Wang Pha, approximately 30km north of Nan, is famous for Lü-style **Wat Nong Bua**. Featuring a typical two-tiered roof and carved wooden portico, the *bòt* design is simple yet striking – note the carved *naga* heads at the roof corners. Inside the *bòt* are some noteworthy but faded *jataka* murals; the building is often locked when religious services aren't in progress, but there's usually someone around to unlock the door. Be sure to leave at the altar a donation for temple upkeep and for its restoration.

You can also see Thai Lü weavers at work in the village. The home of **Khun Janthasom**

Phrompanya, a few blocks behind the wat, serves as a local weaving centre – check there for the locations of looms or to look at fabrics for purchase. Large *yâam* (hilltribe–style shoulder bags) are available for just 50B, while nicely woven neck scarves cost more. There are also several weaving houses just behind the wat.

GETTING THERE & AWAY
Săwngthăew to Tha Wang Pha (15B) leave from opposite Nan's Sukasem Hotel. Get off at Samyaek Longbom, a three-way intersection before Tha Wang Pha, and walk west to a bridge over Mae Nam Nan, then left at the dead end on the other side of the bridge to Wat Nong Bua. It's 3.1km from the highway to the wat.

If you're coming from Nan via your own transport on Rte 1080, you'll cross a stream called Lam Nam Yang just past the village of Ban Fai Mun but before Tha Wang Pha. Take the first left off Rte 1080 and follow it to a dead end; turn right and then left over a bridge across Mae Nam Nan and walk until you reach another dead end, then left 2km until you can see Wat Nong Bua on the right.

Tham Phah Tup Forest Reserve
ถ้ำผาตูบ
This limestone cave complex is about 10km north of Nan and is part of a relatively new wildlife reserve. Some 17 **caves** have been counted, of which nine are easily located by means of established (but unmarked) trails.

From Nan, you can catch a *săwngthăew* bound for Pua or Thung Chang; it will stop at the turn-off to the caves for 10B. The vehicles leave from the petrol station opposite the Sukasem Hotel.

Sao Din
เสาดิน
Literally 'Earth Pillars', Sao Din is an erosional phenomenon similar to that found in Phae Meuang Phi in Phrae Province – tall columns of earth protruding from a barren depression. The area covers nearly 3.2 hectares off Rte 1026 in Amphoe Na Noi, about 60km south of Nan.

Sao Din is best visited by bike or motorbike since it's time consuming to reach by public transport. If you don't have your own wheels, take a *săwngthăew* to Na Noi from the southbound *săwngthăew* station opposite Ratchaphatsadu Market in Nan. From Na Noi you must get yet another *săwngthăew* bound for Fak Tha or Ban Khok, getting off at the entrance to Sao Din after 5km or so. From here you'll have to walk or hitch 4km to Sao Din itself. There are also occasional direct *săwngthăew* from Na Noi.

Northwest of Sao Din, off Rte 1216, is a set of earth pillars called **Hom Chom**.

Other Attractions
There are a couple of interesting destinations in and around the Thai Lü village of **Pua**, roughly 50km north of Nan. In Pua itself you can check out another famous Thai Lü temple, **Wat Ton Laeng**, which is admired for its classic three-tiered roof. **Nam Tok Silaphet** (Silaphet Waterfall) is southeast of Pua just off the road between Pua and Ban Nam Yao. The water falls in a wide swath over a cliff and is best seen at the end of the monsoon season in November. On the way to the falls and west of the road is the Mien village of **Ban Pa Klang**, worth a visit to see silversmiths at work. This village supplies many silver shops in Chiang Mai and Bangkok. Other silverwork Mien villages can be found on Rte 101 between Nan and Phrae.

In the northwest of the province, off Rte 1148 and north of the village of Ban Sakoen, is a huge, 200m-wide cave called **Tham Luang**. The path to the cave is not signposted, but if you ask at the police checkpoint in Ban Sakoen you should be able to get directions or you might even find a guide.

To the south about 100km, **Thaleh Sap Neua** (Northern Lake) formed by Kheuan Sirikit is an important freshwater fishery for Nan, as well as a recreational attraction for Nan residents. **Ban Pak Nai** on its northwestern shore is the main fishing village. Just before Mae Nam Nan feeds into the lake at its extreme northern end, there is a set of river rapids called **Kaeng Luang**.

Every Saturday morning from around 5am to 11am there's a lively Lao-Thai **market** in Thung Chang.

Border Crossing (Laos)
Ban Huay Kon (140km north of Nan) in Amphoe Thung Chang may some day be

open to foreigners. For now it's for Thais and Lao only.

This crossing is just 152km to Luang Prabang or about 300km to the Chinese border at Boten, Laos. From the Lao side of the border crossing, a dirt road leads north-northeast about 45km to the banks of the Mekong River in Laos' Udomxai Province. From here you can either take a boat downriver to Luang Prabang or cross the river and pick up Rte 2 to Muang Xai, the provincial capital. From Muang Xai it's only a couple of hours to the international border with China's Yunnan Province.

PHITSANULOK PROVINCE

PHITSANULOK

พิษณุโลก

pop 100,300

Under the reign of Ayuthaya King Borom Trailokanat (1448–88), Phitsanulok served as the capital of Thailand for 25 years. Because the town straddles Mae Nam Nan near a junction with Mae Nam Khwae Noi, it's sometimes referred to as Song Khwae (Two Tributaries), and it's the only city in Thailand where it's legal to reside on a houseboat within municipal boundaries. No new houseboats are permitted; however, so it's likely that they will gradually disappear.

This vibrant city makes an excellent base from which to explore the lower north. As well as the temples of Wat Phra Si Ratana Mahathat and Wat Chulamani, you can explore the attractions of historical Sukhothai, Kamphaeng Phet and Si Satchanalai, as well as the national parks and wildlife sanctuaries of Thung Salaeng Luang and Phu Hin Rong Kla, the former strategic headquarters of the Communist Party of Thailand (CPT). All of these places are within 150km of Phitsanulok.

The name Phitsanulok is often abbreviated as 'Philok'.

Information

Shops offering Internet access dot the streets around the railway station, near the Topland Hotel and on the western bank of the river near Saphan Ekathotsarot. Prices range

from 15B per hour for slow connections to 60B per hour for the slightly faster connections. Several banks in town offer foreign-exchange services and ATMs. There's also an ATM inside the Wat Phra Si Ratana Mahathat compound.

Bangkok Bank (35 Th Naresuan; ⊗ to 8pm) An after-hours exchange window.

CAT office (Th Phuttha Bucha; ⊗ 7am-11pm) At the post office. Offers phone and Internet services.

Left-luggage storage (train station; per day 10B; ⊗ 7am-10pm)

Main post office (Th Phuttha Bucha; ⊗ 8.30am-4.30pm Mon-Fri, 9am-noon Sat & Sun)

TAT office (☎ 0 5525 2742-3; tatphlok@tat.or.th; 209/7-8 Th Borom Trailokanat; ⊗ 8.30am-4.30pm) Off Th Borom Trailokanat, with knowledgable, helpful staff (some of TAT's best) who hand out free maps of the town and a walking-tour sheet. They also run a sightseeing tram and have up-to-date information about where to rent a motorcycle. This is the official information office for Sukhothai and Phetchabun Provinces as well. If you plan to do the trip from Phitsanulok to Lom Sak, ask for the map of Hwy 12 that marks several waterfalls and resorts along the way.

Sights

WAT PHRA SI RATANA MAHATHAT

วัดพระศรีรัตนมหาธาต

The full name of this temple is Wat Phra Si Ratana Mahathat, but the locals call it Wat Phra Si or Wat Yai. The wat stands near the east end of the bridge over Mae Nam Nan (on the right as you're heading out of Phitsanulok towards Sukhothai). The main *wíhǎn* contains the Chinnarat Buddha (Phra Phuttha Chinnarat), one of Thailand's most revered and copied images. This famous bronze image is probably second in importance only to the Emerald Buddha in Bangkok's Wat Phra Kaew. In terms of total annual donations collected (around 12 million baht a year), Wat Yai follows Wat Sothon in Chachoengsao, east of Bangkok.

The image was cast in the late Sukhothai style, but what makes it strikingly unique is the flame-like halo around the head and torso that turns up at the bottom to become dragon-serpent heads on either side of the image. The head of this Buddha is a little wider than standard Sukhothai, giving the statue a very solid feel.

The story goes that construction of this wat was commissioned under the reign of King Li Thai in 1357. When it was completed, King Li Thai wanted it to contain

PHITSANULOK

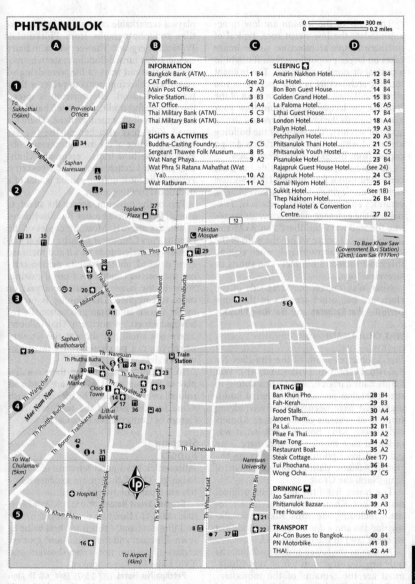

0   300 m
0   0.2 miles

INFORMATION
Bangkok Bank (ATM).............................**1** B4
CAT office.......................................(see 2)
Main Post Office..............................**2** A3
Police Station..................................**3** B3
TAT Office.......................................**4** A4
Thai Military Bank (ATM).................**5** C3
Thai Military Bank (ATM).................**6** B4

SIGHTS & ACTIVITIES
Buddha-Casting Foundry..................**7** C5
Sergeant Thawee Folk Museum.......**8** B5
Wat Nang Phaya..............................**9** A2
Wat Phra Si Ratana Mahathat (Wat
   Yai)..**10** A2
Wat Ratburan..................................**11** A2

SLEEPING 🏠
Amarin Nakhon Hotel.....................**12** B4
Asia Hotel......................................**13** B4
Bon Bon Guest House......................**14** B4
Golden Grand Hotel........................**15** B3
La Paloma Hotel..............................**16** A5
Lithai Guest House..........................**17** B4
London Hotel..................................**18** A4
Pailyn Hotel....................................**19** A3
Petchpailyn Hotel............................**20** A3
Phitsanulok Thani Hotel...................**21** C5
Phitsanulok Youth Hostel.................**22** C5
Pisanuloke Hotel.............................**23** B4
Rajapruk Guest House Hotel..........(see 24)
Rajapruk Hotel................................**24** C3
Samai Niyom Hotel..........................**25** B4
Sukkit Hotel..................................(see 18)
Thep Nakhorn Hotel.........................**26** B4
Topland Hotel & Convention
   Centre.......................................**27** B2

EATING 🍴
Ban Khun Pho.................................**28** B4
Fah-Kerah.......................................**29** B3
Food Stalls......................................**30** A4
Jaroen Tham....................................**31** A4
Pa Lai..**32** B1
Phae Fa Thai...................................**33** A2
Phae Tong.......................................**34** A2
Restaurant Boat..............................**35** A2
Steak Cottage...............................(see 17)
Tui Phochana..................................**36** B4
Wong Ocha.....................................**37** C5

DRINKING 🍸
Jao Samran.....................................**38** A3
Phitsanulok Bazaar..........................**39** A3
Tree House....................................(see 21)

TRANSPORT
Air-Con Buses to Bangkok..............**40** B4
PN Motorbike..................................**41** B3
THAI...**42** A4

To Sukhothai (56km)

Provincial Offices

Saphan Naresuan

Topland Plaza

Pakistan Mosque

To Baw Khaw Saw (Government Bus Station) (2km); Lom Sak (117km)

Saphan Ekathotsarot

Train Station

Night Market

Clock Tower

Lithai Building

Mae Nam Nan

To Wat Chulamani (5km)

Th Ramesuan

Naresuan University

Hospital

To Airport (4km)

three high-quality bronze images, so he sent for well-known sculptors from Si Satchanalai, Chiang Saen and Hariphunchai (Lamphun), as well as five Brahman priests. The first two castings worked well, but the third required three attempts before it was decreed the best of all. Legend has it that a white-robed sage appeared from nowhere to assist in the final casting, then disappeared. This last image was named the Chinnarat (Victorious King) Buddha and it became the centrepiece in the *wíhǎan*. The other two images, Phra Chinnasi and Phra Si Satsada, were later moved to the royal temple of Wat Bowonniwet in Bangkok. Only the Chinnarat image has the flame-dragon halo.

The walls of the *wíhǎan* are low to accommodate the low-swept roof, typical of northern temple architecture, so the image takes on larger proportions than it might in a central or northeastern wat. The brilliant interior architecture is such that when you sit on the Italian marble floor in front of the Buddha, the lacquered columns draw your vision towards the image and evoke a strong sense of serenity. The doors of the building are inlaid with mother-of-pearl in a design copied from Bangkok's Wat Phra Kaew.

Another sanctuary to one side has been converted into a free **museum** (❤ 9am-5.30pm Wed-Sun), displaying antique Buddha images, ceramics and other historic artefacts. *Túk-túk* line the entrance street, souvenir stands line the walkways and there's an ATM and notable tourist police within the walls of the complex. Dress appropriately when visiting this most sacred of temples – no shorts or sleeveless tops.

Near Wat Yai, on the same side of the river, are two other temples of the same period – **Wat Ratburan** and **Wat Nang Phaya**.

WAT CHULAMANI
วัดจุฬามณี

Five kilometres south of the city (bus No 5 down Th Borom Trailokanat, 4B), Wat Chulamani harbours some ruins dating to the Sukhothai period. The original buildings must have been impressive, judging from what remains of the ornate Khmer-style tower. King Borom Trailokanat was ordained as a monk here and there is an old Thai inscription to that effect on the ruined *wíhǎan*, dating from the reign of King Narai the Great.

The tower has little left of its original height, but Khmer-style door lintels remain, including one with a Sukhothai walking Buddha and a *dhammacakka* (Buddhist wheel of law) in the background.

As well as the tower and the *wíhǎan*, the only original structures left at Wat Chulamani are the remains of the monastery walls. Still, there is a peaceful, neglected atmosphere about the place.

SERGEANT MAJOR THAWEE FOLK MUSEUM & BUDDHA-CASTING FOUNDRY
พิพิธภัณฑ์พื้นบ้านนายทวี/โรงหล่อพระ

The **Sergeant Major Thawee Folk Museum** (26/43 Th Wisut Kasat; bus 8; ❤ 8.30am-4.30pm Tue-Sun) dis-

plays a remarkable collection of tools, textiles and photographs from Phitsanulok Province. Sergeant Thawee was a military cartographer turned Buddha caster who recognised that old ways of life were dying so he started collecting items to preserve their place in Thailand. The museum is spread throughout five traditional-style Thai buildings with well-groomed gardens. There's a small, kids' play area behind the two far buildings. Some of the more impressive objects are the bird traps, ceremonial clothing, ancient kitchen utensils and basketry. Perhaps the most unique exhibit is that of a traditional birthing room.

Part of the museum, across the street, is a small **factory** where bronze Buddha images of all sizes are cast. Most are copies of the famous Phra Chinnarat Buddha at Wat Yai. Visitors are welcome to watch and there are even detailed photo exhibits demonstrating the lost-wax method of metal casting. Some of the larger images take a year or more to complete. The foundry is owned by Dr Thawi, an artisan and nationally renowned expert on northern-Thai folklore. There is a small gift shop at the foundry where you can purchase bronze images of various sizes.

In addition to the foundry, there is a display of fighting cocks, which are bred and sold all over Thailand. The official English name for this part of the facility is 'The Centre of Conservative Folk Cock'!

Sleeping
BUDGET

Phitsanulok has a good selection of budget lodgings. The slightly more expensive hotels are a particularly good deal.

Bon Bon Guest House (☎ 0 5521 9058; Th Phayalithai; r 300B; ✖) Don't be discouraged by the building out front – this is the best value in town. It's quiet and the brand-new, spotless rooms all feature hot-water showers and TVs. Little English is spoken.

Petchpailyn Hotel (☎ 0 5525 8844; 4/8 Th Athitaywong; r from 300B; ✖) The spacious rooms with modern, comfortable beds have hot water and cable TV, making it a great deal. A Chinese-style buffet breakfast is included in the rates. Rooms towards the back are considerably quieter.

Lithai Guest House (☎ 0 5521 9626; fax 0 5521 9627; Th Phayalithai; r 220-360B; ✖) Some 60 clean, quiet rooms with plenty of light are strung out over three floors, giving more the feel of an apartment complex than a guesthouse. Prices vary based on amenities like hot water, TV, air-con and fridge. The rooms on the 4th floor with wooden floors and shared bathrooms (200B) are the best deal. Discounts are available for extended stays.

Phitsanulok Youth Hostel (☎ 0 5524 2060; phit sanulok@tyha.org; 38 Th Sanam Bin; dm/s/d/tr/q 120/200/ 300/450/600B; 🏠) This youth hostel is a decent choice during the high season when backpackers fill the place. The rooms feature salvaged teak furniture, but lack windows or any hope of a cross breeze. Some of the rooms with 'private bath' actually feature a middle-of-the-room toilet without walls. From the train station you can reach the hostel by *săamláw* (20B to 30B) or on city bus No 12. From the airport take a *túk-túk* (30B) or a No 12 bus that goes by the hostel (on the right). From the bus terminal, take a *săamláw* (30B) or a No 1 city bus (get off at Th Ramesuan and walk the last 300m).

Pisanuloke Hotel (☎ 0 5524 7555/7999; Th Ekath otsarot; r 180-350B; 🏠) This classic hotel in an old, two-storey building is conveniently located adjacent to the station; all rooms have cold-water facilities. There's a *khâo kaeng* (rice-and-curry) vendor downstairs in the lobby, and plenty of places to eat nearby.

Asia Hotel (☎ 0 5525 8378; fax 0 5523 0419; Th Ekathotsarot; s/d from 200/250B) Be sure to get a room at the back of this four-storey hotel. Rooms, with hot water and TV, are a notable step-up from the Pisanuloke.

London Hotel (☎ 0 5522 5145; 21-22 Soi 1, Th Phut tha Bucha; r 100-150B) Friendly and somewhat spruced-up, this old, wooden, Thai-Chinese hotel is as close to an early-20th-century rooming house as you'll find.

Rajapruk Guest House Hotel (☎ 0 5525 9203; 99/9 Th Phra Ong Dam; r from 280B; 🏠 🛒) Slightly overpriced and very worn, this guesthouse is located behind the more upmarket Rajapruk Hotel. All rooms have hot-water showers. Guests may use the Rajapruk Hotel swimming pool.

Other recommendations:

Sukkit Hotel (☎ 0 5525 8876; 20/1-2 Th Saireuthai; r 150B) Strictly basic and dark. Less noisy than hotels closer to the train station.

Samai Niyom Hotel (☎ 0 5525 8575, 0 5524 7528; 175 Th Ekathotsarot; s/d 280/380B; 🏠) Faded three-storey hotel with ordinary rooms.

MIDRANGE

Phitsanulok's midrange isn't stylish but most places are well cared for. All rooms have hot-water shower, TV and air-con.

Golden Grand Hotel (☎ 0 5521 0234; 66 Th Tham mabucha; s/d 650/850B; ✖ 🏠) If you're longing for a solid, midrange hotel that meets Western standards, this new addition is the place. All of the rooms are spacious, well maintained, brightly decorated and feature a private balcony. The only major drawback is the proximity to the railway tracks.

La Paloma Hotel (☎ 0 5521 7930; fax 0 5521 7935; 103/8 Th Sithamatraipidok; s/d from 980B; ✖ 🏠 🛒) Less convenient than the competition, La Paloma is the grandest in its category. It's six stories with 249 huge, modern, flowery rooms. There's a 24-hour café and the staff will arrange daycare for children with advance notice.

Thep Nakhorn Hotel (☎ 0 5524 4070; fax 0 5524 4075; 43/1 Th Sithamatraipidok; r/ste incl US breakfast for 2 500/1500B; 🏠) This six-storey hotel offers quiet, spacious rooms and suites.

Rajapruk Hotel (☎ 0 5525 8477; fax 0 5525 1395; 99/9 Th Phra Ong Dam; r incl breakfast 550-800B; 🏠 🛒) Although this once-was-grand hotel feels slightly abandoned and is inconvenient, the carpeted, modern rooms are a good value.

Amarin Nakhon Hotel (☎ 0 5521 9069; fax 0 5521 9500; 3/1 Th Chao Phraya Phitsanulok; r from 480B; 🏠) Centrally located with huge rooms and modern amenities, the Amarin used to be more flashy, but is still a good choice. Higher rates include breakfast.

TOP END

Discounts at Phitsanulok's top-end hotels are usually available online and through travel agents. Prices below are for walk-in guests.

Topland Hotel & Convention Centre (☎ 0 5524 7800; www.toplandhotel.com; cnr Th Singhawat & Th Ekathot sarot; s/d from 1800/2000B; ✖ 🏠 🛒) The luxurious Topland is the top of the top end, with a beauty salon, café, snooker club, fitness centre, several restaurants and other facilities. The room rates are great value compared with Bangkok or Chiang Mai prices for similar quality. Free airport transfer is available.

Phitsanulok Thani Hotel (☎ 0 5521 1065; fax 0 5521 1071, in Bangkok ☎ 0 2314 3168; Th Sanam Bin; s/d/ste 1100/1200/2000B; ✖ 🏠 🖥) Part of the Dusit chain, this hotel offers all the basics, plus a few extras. It's tastefully decorated, with a happening disco, a formal restaurant and chill lounge. Rates for suites include breakfast for two.

Pailyn Hotel (☎ 0 5525 2411; 38 Th Borom Trailokanat; s/d/ste incl breakfast 1100/1200/2000B; ✗ ⊠) The Pailyn is a full-sized, nearly luxurious hotel. The lobby is grander than the rooms, but staff members are professional and helpful. There are several restaurants and lounges downstairs.

Eating

Phitsanulok takes its cuisine seriously. In addition to one of the most formal and active night markets, there's a solid collection of high-quality restaurants.

DOWNTOWN

Tui Phochana (Th Phayalithai; dishes 20-45B; ☯ 8am-7pm) East of the Lithai Building, this inexpensive restaurant serves good Thai food and fabulous *yam khànǔn* (curried jackfruit) at the beginning of the cool season. The rest of the curries are outstanding year-round. There are plenty of other cheap Thai restaurants nearby – follow the lunchtime crowds.

Ban Khun Pho (Th Chao Phraya; dishes 45-90B; ☯ 11am-11pm) Opposite the Amarin Nakhon Hotel, this clean, new place is decorated with antiques. On the menu are Thai, Japanese and Western selections. Lunch specials are available from 11am to 2pm.

Steak Cottage (dishes 40-120B; ☯ 7am-2pm & 5-9pm Mon-Sat) In the Lithai Building complex, this eatery does not cater to vegetarians. Along with the namesake steak, it serves other high-quality European and Thai dishes.

Jaroen Tham (Th Sithamatraipidok; dishes 13B; ☯ 8am-noon) A basic, appetising vegetarian spot around the corner from TAT.

There are several Thai-Muslim cafés near the mosque on Th Phra Ong Dam. **Fah-Kerah** (786 Th Phra Ong Dam; dishes 5-20B; ☯ 6am-2pm) is a popular one, where thick *rotii* is served up with *kaeng mátsàmàn* (Muslim curry), fresh yogurt is made daily and the set plate (*rotii kaeng*) is a steal at 20B.

Near the Phitsanulok Youth Hostel are some small **noodle and rice shops**. Around the corner, **Wong Ocha** (no Roman-script sign; Th Sanam Bin; dishes 15-30B; ☯ 8am-10pm) is a permanent stall dishing delicious *kài yâang, khâo nǐaw* (sticky rice) and *yam phàk kràchèt* (water mimosa salad).

Market-style **food stalls** (dishes 20B) cluster just west of the London Hotel near the cinema.

For snacks and self-catering, there's a huge supermarket in the basement of the Topland Shopping Plaza.

La Paloma hotel (p383) has a 24-hour café.

ON THE RIVER

Night market (dishes 40-80B; ☯ 5pm-3am) Several street vendors specialise in *phàk bûng lawy fáa* (literally, floating-in-the-sky morning glory vine), which usually translates as 'flying vegetable'. Originated in Chonburi, this food fad has somehow taken root in Phitsanulok. The dish isn't especially tasty – basically water spinach stir-fried with garlic in soya-bean sauce – but the preparation is a performance: the cook fires up a batch of *phàk bûng* in the wok and then flings it through the air to a waiting server who catches it on a plate. Some of the places are so performance-oriented that the server climbs to the top of a van to catch the flying vegetable! If you're lucky, you'll be here when a tour group is trying to catch the flying vegetables, but is actually dropping *phàk bûng* all over the place.

Pa Lai (no Roman-script sign; Th Phuttha Bucha; dishes 20-30B; ☯ 10am-4pm) Opposite the river, north of Wat Phra Si Ratana Mahathat, this super popular open-air restaurant serves *kǔaytǐaw hâwy khàa* (literally, legs-hanging rice noodles). The name comes from the way customers sit on a bench facing the river, with their legs dangling below. There are several copycats nearby.

Floating restaurants light up Mae Nam Nan at night. Good choices include **Phae Fa Thai** (Th Wangchan; dishes 30-80B; ☯ 11am-11pm) and **Phae Tong** (Th Wangchan; dishes 40-80B; ☯ 11am-11pm). South of the main string of floating restaurants is a pier where you can board a **restaurant boat** (boarding fee 20-40B; meals 80-130B) that cruises Mae Nam Nan nightly. You pay a small fee to board the boat and then order from a menu as you please – there's no minimum charge.

Drinking & Entertainment

The most happening nightspot in town is the **Phitsanulok Bazaar** (Th Naresuan), where several pubs and dance clubs are clustered in a mall-like arrangement. Some places definitely emanate a 'girlie-bar' air, but it's still a fun place to make the rounds. It doesn't get started until after 9pm.

Along Th Borom Trailokanat near the Pailyn Hotel is a string of popular, rockin' Thai pubs.

Jao Samran (Th Borom Trailokanat) Features live Thai-folk and pop with food service after 6pm and music after 8pm.

Tree House (Th Sanam Bin) This semi-outdoor establishment at Phitsanulok Thani Hotel features live bands playing Thai and *faràng* covers.

Getting There & Away

AIR

THAI (☎ 0 5525 8020; 209/26-28 Th Borom Trailokanat) operates daily connections (55 minutes) to Phitsanulok from Bangkok (1380B). A free THAI van service shuttles between Phitsanulok airport and Tak a few times daily.

BUS

Transport options out of Phitsanulok are good, as it's a junction for bus routes both north and northeast. Bangkok is six hours away by bus and Chiang Mai 5½ hours. Buses leave Bangkok's Northern and Northeastern bus station for Phitsanulok several times each day (ordinary/2nd class air-con/

1st class air-con 125/185/218B). Phitsanulok Yan Yon Tour and Win Tour both run VIP buses to/from Bangkok for 250B.

Buses to destinations in other northern and northeastern provinces leave several times daily from the Baw Khaw Saw (government bus station) just outside town on Hwy 12, except for the air-con buses that may depart only once or twice a day.

If you arrive in Phitsanulok by rail or air, take a city bus No 1 to the air-con bus station in the centre, or to the Baw Khaw Saw (government bus) station, for buses out of town.

TRAIN

Two ordinary trains (69B, 3rd class only, nine hours) leave Bangkok for Phitsanulok at 7.05am (Ayuthaya at 9.04am) and 8.35am (Ayuthaya 10.26am). For most people this is a more economical and convenient way to reach Phitsanulok from Bangkok than via bus, since you don't have to go out to Bangkok's Northern and Northeastern bus station.

Rapid trains (2nd class/3rd class 159/69B) depart from Bangkok six times each day at 6.40am, 3.15pm, 6.10pm, 8pm and 10pm (seven hours). The surcharge for the rapid service is 40B. There are also three air-con,

BUS DESTINATIONS FROM PHITSANULOK

Destination	Fare (B)	Duration (hr)
Chiang Mai (via Uttaradit)		
ordinary	120	5
air-con	196	5
Chiang Mai (via Tak)		
ordinary	140	6
air-con	196	6
VIP	216	6
Chiang Rai		
ordinary	153	6
air-con	214	5
VIP	250	5
Kamphaeng Phet*		
ordinary	43	3
air-con	60	2
Khon Kaen		
ordinary	130	5
air-con	153	5
1st class, air-con	203	5
Mae Sot		
air-con minivan	122	5

Destination	Fare (B)	Duration (hr)
Nakhon Ratchasima (Khorat)		
ordinary	148	6
air-con	247	6
VIP	288	6
Nan		
ordinary	112	9
air-con	148	8
Sukhothai**		
ordinary	23	1
air-con	32	1
Tak*		
ordinary	57	3
air-con	71	3
Udon Thani		
ordinary	122	7
air-con	220	7

*Buses to Kamphaeng Phet & Tak leave every hour.
**Buses to Sukhothai leave every half-hour.

NORTHERN THAILAND

2nd-class, express-diesel trains (or 'Sprinter' Nos 3, 5 and 7), at 9.30am, 4pm and 11.10pm daily, which are about an hour quicker than the rapid service.

First class is available on the 3pm rapid train (2nd and 3rd class is also available) and 6pm special express train (2nd class is also available). The basic 1st-class (324B) and 2nd-class (159B) fares do not including the rapid and special express surcharges of 40B and 80B, plus any berth arrangements. There's also a regular train service to Chiang Mai (3rd/2nd/1st class 52/122/269B, five hours); to Lopburi (41/95/201B, nine hours); and to Ayuthaya (54/124/258B, 10 hours).

If you're continuing straight to Sukhothai from Phitsanulok, a *túk-túk* ride from the train station to the bus station 4km away costs 30B to 40B. From there you can catch a bus to Sukhothai, or you can hop on a Sukhothai-bound bus opposite the Topland Hotel on Th Singhawat; a *túk-túk* to Th Singhawat costs 20B from the train station.

Getting Around

Săamláw rides within the town centre should cost 20B to 30B per person. Ordinary city buses cost 4B and there are 13 routes, making it easy to get just about anywhere by bus. A couple of the lines also feature air-con coaches for 6B. The station for city buses is near the train station, off Th Ekathotsarot.

Run by the TAT, the Phitsanulok Tour Tramway (PTT) is one way to see all the sights in one day. The tram leaves from Wat Yai at 9am, costs 20B and stops at 15 sights before returning to Wat Yai at 3pm.

Motorcycles can be rented at **PN Motorbike** (☎ 0 5524 2424; Th Borom Trailokanat; 125cc motorbike per day 200B).

Phitsanulok's airport is just outside town. *Săwngthăew* leave the airport for town every 20 minutes (10B); otherwise, you can catch the No 4 city bus (4B). The big hotels in town run free buses from the airport, and THAI has a door-to-door van service (30B per person).

Rental-car agencies at the airport charge from 1200B per day.

PHU HIN RONG KLA NATIONAL PARK

อุทยานแห่งชาติภูหินร่องกล้า

Between 1967 and 1982, the mountain that is known as Phu Hin Rong Kla served as the strategic headquarters for the Communist

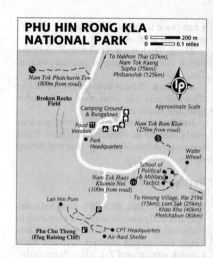

PHU HIN RONG KLA NATIONAL PARK

Party of Thailand (CPT) and its tactical arm, the People's Liberation Army of Thailand (PLAT). The remote, easily defended summit was perfect for an insurgent army. Another benefit was that the headquarters was only 50km from the Lao border, so lines of retreat were well guarded after 1975 when Laos fell to the Pathet Lao. China's Yunnan Province is only 300km away and it was here that CPT cadres received their training in revolutionary tactics. (This was until the 1979 split between the Chinese and Vietnamese communists, when the CPT sided with Vietnam.)

For nearly 20 years the area around Phu Hin Rong Kla served as a battlefield for Thai troops and the communists. In 1972 the Thai government launched a major offensive against the PLAT in an unsuccessful attempt to rout them from the mountain. The CPT camp at Phu Hin Rong Kla became especially active after the Thai military killed hundreds of students in Bangkok during the October 1976 student-worker uprising. Many students subsequently fled here to join the CPT, setting up a hospital and a school of political and military tactics. By 1978 the PLAT ranks here had swelled to 4000. In 1980 and 1981 the Thai armed forces tried again and were able to recapture some parts of CPT territory. But the decisive blow to the CPT came in 1982, when the government declared an amnesty for all the students who had joined the communists after 1976. The departure of most of the students broke the spine of the movement, which had by this time become dependent on their membership. A final military push in late 1982 effected the surrender of the PLAT, and Phu Hin Rong Kla was declared a national park in 1984.

Orientation & Information

The **park** (admission 200B) covers about 307 sq km of rugged mountains and forest. The elevation at park headquarters is about 1000m, so the area is refreshingly cool even in the hot season. Attractions on the main road through the park include the remains of the CPT stronghold – a rustic meeting hall, the school of political and military tactics – and the CPT administration building. Across the road from the school is a water wheel designed by exiled engineering students.

Sights & Activities

A trail leads to **Pha Chu Thong** (Flag Raising Cliff, sometimes called Red Flag Cliff), where the communists would raise the red flag to announce a military victory. Also in this area are an **air-raid shelter**, a **lookout** and the remains of the main **CPT headquarters** – the most inaccessible point in the territory before a road was constructed by the Thai government. The buildings in the park are made out of wood and bamboo and have no plumbing or electricity – a testament to how primitive the living conditions were.

There is a small **museum** at the park headquarters that displays relics from CPT days, including weapons and medical instruments. At the end of the road into the park is a small **White Hmong village**. When the CPT was here, the Hmong were its ally. Now the Hmong are undergoing 'cultural assimilation' at the hands of the Thai government.

If you're not interested in the history of Phu Hin Rong Kla, there are **waterfalls, hiking trails** and **scenic views**, as well as some interesting rock formations – jutting boulders called **Lan Hin Pum**, and an area of deep rocky crevices where PLAT troops would hide during air raids, called **Lan Hin Taek**.

Phu Hin Rong Kla can become quite crowded on weekends and holidays; schedule a more peaceful visit for midweek.

Sleeping & Eating

Thailand's Royal Forest Department rents **bungalows** (☎ 0 5523 3527, Bangkok ☎ 0 2561 4292; bungalows 300-2400B) for two to eight people, in three different zones of the park. You can also pitch a tent for 10B a night or sleep in park tents for 40B per person (no bedding is provided, except blankets for 20B a night). If you want to build a fire, you can buy chopped wood for 150B a night. **Golden House Tour Company** (☎ 0 5525 9973, 0 5538 9002; 55/37 Th Trailokanat) in Phitsanulok can help book accommodations.

Near the camping ground and bungalows are some food vendors. The best are **Duang Jai Cafeteria** – try its famous carrot *sôm-tam* – and **Rang Thong**.

Getting There & Away

The park headquarters is about 125km from Phitsanulok. To get here, first take an early bus to Nakhon Thai (30B, two hours, hourly from 6am to 6pm). From there you can catch a *săwngthăew* to the park (25B, three times daily from 7.30am to 4.30pm).

A small group can charter a pick-up and driver in Nakhon Thai for 600B to 800B for the day. Golden House Tour Company (above) charges 1200B for car and driver; petrol is extra. This is a delightful trip if you're on a motorcycle since there's not much traffic along the way, but a strong engine is necessary to conquer the hills to Phu Hin Rong Kla.

PHITSANULOK TO LOM SAK

Hwy 12 between Phitsanulok and Lom Sak (the scenic 'gateway' to northeastern Thailand) parallels the scenic, rapids-studded Lam Nam Khek. Along the way are several **resorts** and **waterfalls**. As in Phu Hin Rong Kla, the sites here tend to be more popular on weekends and holidays.

Any of the resorts along Hwy 12 can organise **white-water rafting** trips on the Lam Nam Khek along the section with the most rapids, which corresponds more or less with the length of Hwy 12 between Km 45 and 52.

The Phitsanulok TAT office (see p380) distributes a sketch map of attractions along this 130km stretch of road, which marks the resorts and three waterfalls. You may want to bypass the first two waterfalls, **Nam Tok Sakhunothayan** (at the Km 33 marker) and **Kaeng Song** (at the Km 45 marker), which are on the way to Phu Hin Rong Kla and therefore get overwhelmed with visitors. The third, **Kaeng Sopha** at the Km 72 marker, is a larger area of small falls and rapids where you can walk from rock formation to rock formation – there are more or fewer rocks depending on the rains. **Food vendors** provide inexpensive *sôm-tam* and *kài yâang*.

Further east along the road is the 1262-sq-km **Thung Salaeng Luang National Park** (the entrance is at the Km 80 marker), one of Thailand's largest and most important wildlife sanctuaries. Thung Salaeng Luang encompasses vast meadows and dipterocarp forests, and once was home to the PLAT. Among bird-watchers it's known as a habitat for the colourful Siamese fireback pheasant.

If you have your own wheels, you can turn south at the Km 100 marker onto Rte 2196 and head for **Khao Kho** (Khao Khaw), another mountain lair used by the CPT during the 1970s. About 1.5km from the summit of Khao Kho, you must turn onto the very steep Rte 2323. At the summit, 30km from the highway, stands a tall **obelisk** erected in memory of the Thai soldiers killed during the suppression of the communist insurgency. The monument is surrounded by an attractive garden. Gun emplacements and sandbagged lookout posts perched on the summit have been left intact as historical reminders. On a clear day, the 360-degree view from the summit is wonderful.

If you've made the side trip to Khao Kho you can choose either to return to the Phitsanulok–Lom Sak highway, or take Rte 2258, off Rte 2196, until it terminates at Rte 203. On Rte 203 you can continue north to Lom Sak or south to Phetchabun. On Rte 2258, about 4km from Rte 2196, you'll pass **Khao Kho Palace**. One of the smaller royal palaces in Thailand, it's a fairly uninteresting, modern set of structures but has quite a nice rose garden. If you've come all the way to Khao Kho you may as well take a look.

Sleeping & Eating

There are several resorts just off Hwy 12 west of the Rte 2013 junction for Nakhon Thai. **Rainforest Resort** (☎ 0 5529 3085; rnforest@loxinfo.co.th; Km 44; cottages 1000-1800B, 7-person cottage 2400B; ❄) is the best of the lot. Spacious, tastefully designed cottages spread over a hillside facing Mae Nam Khek accommodate up to four people. An indoor-outdoor restaurant serves locally grown coffee and good Thai food. Other resorts in the area, **Wang Nam**

Yen (Hwy 12, Km 46) and **Thanthong** (Hwy 12, Km 46), are similarly priced. **SP Huts** (☎ 0 5529 3402; fax 0 5529 3405; Hwy 12, Km 53; r from 500B) is a bit cheaper.

Getting There & Away

Buses between Phitsanulok and Lom Sak cost 55B each way, so any stop along the way will cost less. During daylight hours it's easy to flag down another bus to continue your journey, but after 4pm it gets a little chancy.

SUKHOTHAI PROVINCE

SUKHOTHAI

สุโขทัย

pop 39,800

As Thailand's first capital, Sukhothai (Rising of Happiness) flourished from the mid-13th century to the late 14th century. The Sukhothai kingdom is viewed as the 'golden age' of Thai civilisation – the religious art and architecture of the era are considered to be the most classic of Thai styles.

The new town of Sukhothai is almost 450km from Bangkok and is undistinguished except for its good municipal market in the town centre. The *meuang kào* (old city) of Sukhothai features around 45 sq km of ruins (which have been made into a historical park) making an overnight stay in New Sukhothai worthwhile, although you can make a day trip to the old city ruins from Phitsanulok.

History

Sukhothai was the first capital of Siam. Established in the 13th century, Sukhothai's dynasty lasted 200 years and had nine kings. The most famous was King Ramkhamhaeng, who reigned from 1275–1317, is credited with developing the first Thai script – his inscriptions are considered the first Thai literature. He also expanded the kingdom to include almost all of present-day Thailand. But a few kings later in 1438, Sukhothai was absorbed by Ayuthaya. See Sukhothai Historical Park for more information (opposite).

Information

There are banks with ATMs scattered all around the central part of New Sukhothai, plus one in Old Sukhothai.

Internet is easy to find in New Sukhothai. Most places cater to computer-game champs,

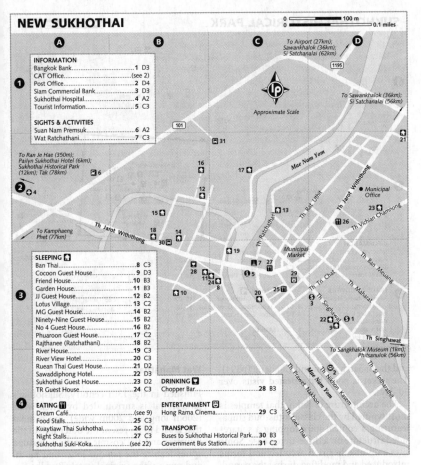

NEW SUKHOTHAI

---

but the connections (40B per hour) are pretty quick. Some guesthouses also offer Internet.

CAT office (Th Nikhon Kasem; ☼ 7am-10pm) Offers international phone services; attached to post office.

Post office (Th Nikhon Kasem; ☼ 8.30am-noon Mon-Fri, 1-4.30pm Sat & Sun, 9am-noon holidays)

Tourist information office (Th Prawet Nakhon; ☼ 9am-5pm Mon-Fri) An unofficial office opposite Wat Ratchathani; hours and information are inconsistent.

Tourist police (Map p390; Sukhothai Historical Park) Opposite the Ramkhamhaeng National Museum.

Sights
SUKHOTHAI HISTORICAL PARK
อุทยานประวัติศาสตร์สุโขทัย

The **Sukhothai ruins** (admission 30-150B, plus bicycles/motorcycles/cars 10/20/50B; ☼ 6am-6pm) are one of Thailand's most impressive World Heritage sites. The park includes remains of 21 historical sites and four large ponds within the old walls, with an additional 70 sites within a 5km radius. The original capital of the first Thai kingdom was surrounded by three concentric ramparts and two moats bridged by four gateways.

The ruins are divided into five zones – central, north, south, east and west – each of which has a 30B admission fee, except for the central section, which costs 40B. For a reasonable 150B you can buy a single ticket (from the kiosk at the entrance to the park) that allows entry to all the Sukhothai sites, plus Sawanworanayok Museum (p396), Ramkhamhaeng National Museum (p390)

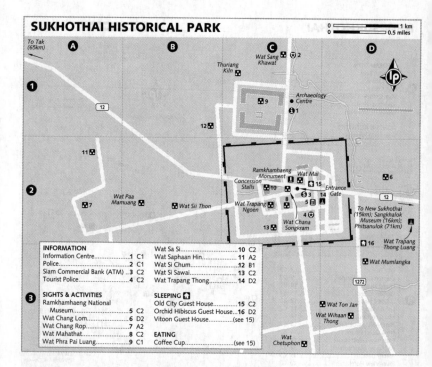

SUKHOTHAI HISTORICAL PARK

INFORMATION		
Information Centre.................1	C1	
Police.................................2	C1	
Siam Commercial Bank (ATM) ..3	C2	
Tourist Police.....................4	C2	

SIGHTS & ACTIVITIES	
Ramkhamhaeng National	
Museum.........................5	C2
Wat Chang Lom...............6	D2
Wat Chang Rop...............7	A2
Wat Mahathat.................8	C2
Wat Phra Pai Luang..........9	C1

Wat Sa Si.......................10	C2
Wat Saphaan Hin............11	A2
Wat Si Chum...................12	B1
Wat Si Sawai..................13	C2
Wat Trapang Thong..........14	D2

SLEEPING	
Old City Guest House........15	A2
Orchid Hibiscus Guest House..16	D2
Vitoon Guest House..........(see 15)	

EATING	
Coffee Cup....................(see 15)	

and the Si Satchanalai and Chaliang (p394). The ticket is good for repeated visits over 30 days.

The architecture of Sukhothai temples is most typified by the classic lotus-bud stupa, featuring a conical spire topping a square-sided structure on a three-tiered base. Some sites exhibit other rich architectural forms introduced and modified during the period, such as bell-shaped Sinhalese and double-tiered Srivijaya stupas. Some of the most impressive ruins are outside the city walls, so a bicycle or motorcycle is essential to fully appreciate everything.

See p394 for details on the best way to tour the park.

Ramkhamhaeng National Museum

พิพิธภัณฑ์สถานแห่งชาติรามคำแหง

A good starting point for exploring the park ruins is **Ramkhamhaeng National Museum** (☎ 0 5561 2167; admission 30B; ⏰ 9am-4pm). A replica of the famous Ramkhamhaeng inscription (see Wiang Kum Kam p288) is kept here among an impressive collection of Sukhothai artefacts.

Wat Mahathat

วัดมหาธาตุ

Finished in the 13th century, Sukhothai's largest wat is surrounded by brick walls (206m long and 200m wide) and a moat that is said to represent the outer wall of the universe and the cosmic ocean. The stupa spires feature the famous lotus-bud motif, and some of the original stately Buddha figures still sit among the ruined columns of the old *wíhǎan*. There are 198 stupas within the monastery walls – a lot to explore in what many consider was the spiritual and administrative centre of the old capital.

Wat Si Chum

วัดศรีชุม

This wat is northwest of the old city and contains an impressive, much-photographed *mondòp* (small square, spired building) with a 15m, brick-and-stucco seated Buddha. Archaeologists theorise that this image is the 'Phra Atchana' mentioned in the famous Ramkhamhaeng inscription. A passage in the *mondòp* wall that leads to the top has been blocked so that it's no longer possible to view the *jataka* inscriptions that line the tunnel ceiling.

Wat Saphan Hin
วัดสะพานหิน

Four kilometres to the west of the old city walls in the west zone, Wat Saphan Hin is on the crest of a hill that rises about 200m above the plain. The name of the wat, which means 'stone bridge', is a reference to the slate path and staircase that leads up to the temple, which are still in place. The site gives a good view of the Sukhothai ruins to the southeast and the mountains to the north and south.

All that remains of the original temple are a few stupas and the ruined *wíhǎan*, consisting of two rows of laterite columns flanking a 12.5m-high standing Buddha image on a brick terrace.

Wat Si Sawai
วัดศรีสวาย

Just south of Wat Mahathat, this shrine (dating from the 12th and 13th centuries) features three Khmer-style towers and a picturesque moat. It was originally built by the Khmers as a Hindu temple.

Wat Sa Si
วัดสระศรี

Also known as 'Sacred Pond Monastery', Wat Sa Si sits on an island west of the bronze monument of King Ramkhamhaeng (the third Sukhothai king). It's a simple, classic Sukhothai-style wat containing a large Buddha, one stupa and the columns of the ruined *wíhǎan*.

Wat Trapang Thong
วัดตระพังทอง

Next to the museum, this small, still inhabited wat with its fine stucco reliefs is reached by a footbridge across the large lotus-filled pond that surrounds it. This reservoir, the original site of Thailand's **Loi Krathong Festival**, supplies the Sukhothai community with most of its water.

Wat Phra Phai Luang
วัดพระพายหลวง

Outside the city walls in the northern zone, this somewhat isolated wat features three 12th-century Khmer-style towers, bigger than those at Wat Si Sawai. This may have

been the centre of Sukhothai when it was ruled by the Khmers of Angkor prior to the 13th century.

Wat Chang Lom
วัดช้างล้อม

Off Hwy 12 in the east zone, Wat Chang Lom (Elephant Circled Monastery) is about 1km east of the main park entrance. A large bell-shaped stupa is supported by 36 elephants sculpted into its base.

Wat Chang Rop
วัดช้างรอบ

On another hill west of the city, just south of Wat Saphan Hin, this wat features an elephant-base stupa, similar to that at Wat Chang Lom.

SANGKHALOK MUSEUM
พิพิธภัณฑ์สังคโลก

If you love ancient, rustically decorated pottery, you might enjoy this **museum** (☎ 0 5561 4333; 203/2 Mu 3 Th Muangkao; admission 100B; ☺ 8am-5pm). It displays an impressive collection of original 700-year-old Thai pottery found in the area, plus some pieces traded from Vietnam, Burma and China. The second floor features some impressive examples of nonutilitarian pottery made as art.

Activities
BICYCLE TOURS
Belgian cycling enthusiast Ronnie of Ban Thai (p392) takes small (four or less) groups on sunset **bicycle tours** (per person 120B). Daily tours leave from Ban Thai around 4pm and include stops at lesser-seen wats and villages. Ronnie can design longer, personalised tours as well.

SWIMMING
Suan Nam Premsuk (admission 40B; ☺ 7am-9pm), at Km 4 marker on Rte 101, is a modest sports complex with a clean swimming pool, tennis courts and ping-pong table. The admission includes use of all the facilities. Look for a couple of tall brick pillars supporting a blue-and-white sign. It can get crowded on the weekends.

Festivals
The **Loi Krathong** festival in November is celebrated for five days in historical Sukhothai. In addition to the magical floating lights,

there are fireworks, folk-dance performances and a light-and-sound production.

Sleeping

Although many places are moving upmarket with their accommodation, Sukhothai
is still dominated by budget options. Most
places are in New Sukhothai.

BUDGET

More and more budget options pop-up in
Sukhothai each year so the competition is
stiff. The local taxi mafia has its hooks in
the guesthouse proprietors, so expect lots
of 'free' advice from the săamláw drivers.
Many guesthouses offer free pick-up from
the bus terminal. Many also rent bicycles
and motorcycles.

Ban Thai (☎ 0 5561 0163; guesthouse_banthai@
yahoo.com; Th Prawet Nakhon; r 120-150B, bungalows
200-250B; ✜) This ultrafriendly place is the
closest you'll come to feeling like you are
staying with a family. Rooms are in excellent shape and the shared bathrooms sparkle. The rustic bungalows have private bath
and sit around an intimate garden. Ban
Thai is a great resource for local information and is a good choice for those travelling with young children. The restaurant is
also good.

Friend House (☎ 0 5561 0172; 52/7 Th Lor Thai;
r 300-550B; ✜) A couple of blocks from the
main road, this quiet cluster of modern
bungalows is good value. The manicured
garden is decorated with cartoonish statues,
the staff is friendly and the rooms are enormous. The whole place feels more professional than similarly priced competition.

TR Guest House (☎ 0 5561 1663; tr_guesthouse@
thaimail.com; 27/5 Th Prawet Nakhon; r 150-300B) The
ultrahelpful owner and his accommodating
staff make this a good choice. The stark
rooms are characterless but spotless and
staff members offer laundry service and
motorcycle rental.

Garden House (☎ 0 5561 1395; toonosman@yahoo
.com; 11/1 Th Prawet Nakhon; r 120B, bungalows 250-350B;
✜) This popular place has several well-kept
rooms (without private bathroom) in a two-
storey house and a series of simple bungalows, all with small porches. The youthful
staff members are extrasocial and the restaurant screens blockbuster movies nightly.

JJ Guest House (jjguesthouse@hotmail.com; Soi Khlong
Mae Ramphan; s/d from 200/250B; ✜) The modern,

sizable cement-and-wood bungalows here
have a Western feel. The staff is friendly and
multilingual (English, French, Dutch and
Thai). The restaurant is known for its fresh
baguettes and croissants.

Sukhothai Guest House (☎ 0 5561 0453; www
.sukhothaiguesthouse.com; 68 Th Vichien Chamnong;
r 300-450B; ✜ ▯) This long-running guesthouse has 12 well-maintained bungalows
packed into a shaded garden. The owners
are friendly and have made a conscientious
effort to provide every service a traveller
would need. Some rooms are a bit cluttered,
but most have a teak-post terrace.

Phuaroon Guest House (☎ 0 5562 0911; phuaroon
_st@hotmail.com; 81/6 Th Khuhasuwan; r 250-500B; ✜)
Arranged around a lawn, Phuaroon's mod-
ern bungalows are spotless, comfortable and
cool. It's near the bus station but a bit far
from town.

River House (☎ 0 5562 2039; riverhouse_7@hotmail
.com; 7 Soi Watkuhasuwan; r 150-250B) Operated by a
young Thai-French couple, with tidy rooms
in an old teak house overlooking the river.

Other recommendations:

No 4 Guest House (☎ 0 5561 0165; 140/4 Soi Khlong
Mae Ramphan, Th Jarot Withithong; bungalows s/d
150/180B) Rustic, bamboo-thatch bungalows. Pleasant
restaurant with tasty food.

Ninety-Nine Guest House (☎ 0 5561 1315, 0 1972
9308; 234/6 Soi Panitsan; dm/s/d 80/120/150B) Clean,
two-storey teak house surrounded by gardens. Run by
a welcoming couple.

Sawaddiphong Hotel (☎ 0 5561 1567; 56/2-5 Th
Singhawat; r 350B; ✜) Clean bed, modern bathrooms
and cable TV.

MG Guest House (☎ 0 5562 0707; nr Th Jarot Withithong; r 300-450B; ✜) American West–style log cabins.
Modern, clean and good value.

The following places are across from the
historical park:

Old City Guest House (☎ 0 5569 7515; 28/7 Mu 3;
r 100-500B; ✜) With a remarkable range of
rooms around a beautiful teak house, Old
City Guest House is an excellent choice if
you want to stay close to the historic park.
Rooms with air-con are modern, big and
good for families. Unfortunately there isn't
a garden area for relaxing.

Vitoon Guest House (☎ 0 5569 7045; 49 Mu 3;
r 250-500B; ✜) Rooms at Vitoon are large and
comfortable but slightly overpriced. The
guest house also rents bicycles and has a
small gift shop.

MIDRANGE

All of the midrange options have air-con and hot-water showers. A number of the following options also offer budget-priced options.

Lotus Village (☎ 0 5562 1484; www.lotus-village .com; 170 Th Ratchathani; r from 600B; ✖) Set in spacious, manicured grounds is a collection of Thai-style houses. The modern rooms are tastefully decorated and are big enough to host a yoga class. Discounts are offered for online reservations. Cheaper older houses on stilts are a haven for mosquitoes in the wet season.

Orchid Hibiscus Guest House (☎ 0 5563 3284; orchid_hibiscus_guest_house@hotmail.com; 407/2 Rte 1272; r 800B, house 1200B; ✖ ✖) If want a place to relax for a couple days in a rural setting, head to Orchid Hibiscus. It's only 1km from the historical park, but is surrounded by open space. The eight charming rooms with four-poster beds are furnished with antique reproductions. There is also a private house that sleeps four and would suit a family well. The manicured grounds have a pool and Jacuzzi. The guesthouse is on Rte 1272 about 600m off Hwy 12 – the turn-off is between Km markers 48 and 49.

Ruean Thai Guest House (☎ 0 5561 2444; 181/20 Soi Pracha Ruammit, Th Jarot Withithong; r 250-800B; ste 2000-3000B; ✖ ✖) In a residential neighbourhood, this guesthouse is rapidly resembling a hotel. The rooms in the original teak house are charming, but the midrange rooms in the cramped cement building are impersonal. New rooms around a swimming pool, accented with recycled teak, promise to be more spacious. Call for free pick-up from the bus station.

Cocoon Guest House (☎ 0 5561 2081; fax 0 5562 2157; 86/1 Th Singhawat; r from 450B; ✖) The four stylish and well-decorated rooms here have architectural features from old Thai houses and are accented with local crafts and antiques. The guesthouse is located behind the Dream Cafe. Bathrooms have an out-doorsy feel.

River View Hotel (☎ 0 5561 1656; fax 0 5561 3373; 38 Th Nikhon Kasem; r 350-800B; ✖) Overlooking the Mae Nam Yom, this hotel remains a favourite among the small traders for its clean, air-con rooms and professional service (such as same-day laundry). The sign says there is a large 'sing-song' coffee shop downstairs.

Rajthanee (Ratchathani; ☎ 0 5561 1031; fax 0 5561 2583; 229 Th Jarot Withithong; r from 300B; ✖) Once the top hotel in town, the Rajthanee has seen better days.

TOP END

Pailyn Sukhothai Hotel (☎ 0 5563 3336, in Bangkok ☎ 0 2215 7110; fax 0 5561 3317, in Bangkok ☎ 0 2215 5640; r from 1200B; ✖ ✖ ✖ ✖) On the road between the old and new cities of Sukhothai, this huge hotel caters mostly to tour groups. It has a disco, health centre and several restaurants, making it a good choice for those seeking a full-sized, full-service, top-end hotel.

Eating

Don't miss New Sukhothai's night stalls. Most are accustomed to accommodating foreigners and even have bilingual, written menus. Intrepid gastronomes can even sample fried bugs and larvae.

Dream Café (☎ 0 5561 2081; Th Singhawat; dishes 60-120B; ✖ 10am-10pm) This romantic, eclectic café is a gem. Decorated with 19th-century Thai antiques, it serves a fabulous selection of desserts, and a variety of pasta and sandwiches. Despite catering primarily to tourists, the food is good and the staff is attentive.

Coffee Cup (Mu 3, Old Sukhothai; dishes 30-120) If you're staying in the old city or are an early riser, come here for breakfast; the coffee is strong and the bread is fresh. They also serve a variety of snacks and a whopping good hamburger. Internet service is 60B per hour.

Sukhothai Suki-Koka (Th Singhawat; dishes 30-90B; ✖ 10am-11pm) Specialising in Thai-style suki-yaki, this bright, homey place is popular for lunch. It serves plenty of Thai dishes but also does sandwiches and pasta.

Ran Je Hae (Th Jarot Withithong; dishes 25-30B; ✖ 10am-9pm) About 350m west of Rte 101, Ran Je Hae specialises in Sukhothai-style *kŭaytiaw* – pork, coriander, green onions, pickled cabbage, pork skins, peanuts, chilli and green beans are added to the basic *kŭaytiaw* recipe.

Kuaytiaw Thai Sukhothai (Th Jarot Withithong; dishes 20-30B; ✖ 9am-8pm) Another good spot to try Sukhothai-style *kŭaytiaw*, about 20m south of the turn-off for Ruean Thai Guest House. The restaurant is in a nice wooden building with a fountain fashioned from ceramic pots out front.

Drinking

Chopper Bar (Th Prawet Nakhon) Travellers and
locals congregate from dusk till hangover
for food, drinks, live music and flirtation
at this place, spitting distance from the little
guesthouse ghetto.

Getting There & Away

AIR

The so-called 'Sukhothai' airport is 27km
from town off Rte 1195, about 11km from
Sawankhalok. It's privately owned by Bangkok Airways and, like its Ko Samui counterpart, is a beautifully designed small airport
using tropical architecture to best advantage.
Bangkok Airways (☎ 0 5563 3266/7, airport ☎ 0 5561
2448; www.bangkokair.com) operates a daily flight
from Bangkok (1800B, 70 minutes). Bangkok Airways charges 90B to transport passengers between the airport and Sukhothai.

Bangkok Airways also flies daily from
Chiang Mai to Sukhothai (850B). Fares for
children are half the adult price. Bangkok
Airways also wings it daily to Luang Prabang (4000B) in Laos.

BUS

Sukhothai is easily reached from Phitsanulok, Tak or Kamphaeng Phet. Buses to/from
Phitsanulok (ordinary/air-con 24/33B, one
hour), leave every half hour or so. Buses to
Tak (ordinary/air-con 31/43B, 1½ hours) and
Kamphaeng (ordinary/air-con 31/43B, 1½
hours) are less frequent, more like hourly.

Departures to Bangkok (ordinary/air-con/
1st class 142/199/256B, six to seven hours)
leave half-hourly from 7am to 11pm.

Buses to and from Chiang Mai (ordinary/
air-con/1st class 122/171/220B, 5½ hours)
via Tak are frequent from 7pm to 2am.

Four air-con buses leave daily for Chiang
Rai (190B, nine hours). The 9am one is a
good choice for Sawankhalok. Otherwise
buses to Sawankhalok (16B, 45 minutes) and
Si Satchanalai (ordinary/air-con 27/38B, one
hour) leave every hour from around 6am
to 6pm.

Other destinations include Khon Kaen
(ordinary/air-con 131/183B, seven hours),
Phrae (air-con 92B, three hours, four times
daily), Lampang (ordinary/air-con 91/127B,
four hours), Nan (104/146B, five hours) and
Si Satchanalai (27/38B, one hour). There are
also nine 12-seat minivans to Mae Sot (100B,
three hours) between 8.30am and 5.30pm.

Getting Around

A ride by *sǎamláw* around New Sukhothai
should cost 20B to 30B. *Sǎwngthǎew* run
frequently from 6.30am to 6pm between
New Sukhothai and Sukhothai Historical
Park (10B, 30 minutes), leaving from Th
Jarot Withithong near Mae Nam Yom. The
sign is on the north side of the street, but
sǎwngthǎew actually leave from the south
side.

The best way to get around the historical
park is by bicycle, which can be rented at
shops outside the park entrance for 20B per
day, or at any guesthouse in New Sukhothai.
Don't rent the first beater bikes you see at
the bus stop in the old city as the better
bikes tend to be found at shops around the
corner, closer to the park entrance.

The park operates a tram service through
the old city for 20B per person.

Transport from the bus terminal into
town in a chartered vehicle costs 30B, or 6B
per person in a shared *sǎwngthǎew*. Unfortunately, drivers often ask for 60B for a charter
or even try to ask 40B for a shared ride after
you've arrived. In the latter case, just give
them the 6B and walk away.

AROUND SUKHOTHAI
Si Satchanalai–Chaliang Historical Park

อุทยานประวัติศาสตร์ศรีสัชนาลัย/ชะเลียง

If you have the time, don't skip this portion
of the Sukhothai World Heritage site. Bring
your imagination and sense of adventure
and you're sure to love this more rustic
collection of truly impressive ruins.

Set among the hills, the 13th- to 15th-
century ruins in the old cities of Si Satchanalai and Chaliang, about 50km north
of Sukhothai, are in the same basic style
as those in the Sukhothai Historical Park,
but the setting is more peaceful and almost
seems untouched. Some people prefer the
atmosphere here over that of Sukhothai.
The **park** (admission 40B, plus per car 50B; ☼ 8.30am-
5pm) covers roughly 720 hectares and is surrounded by a 12m-wide moat. Chaliang,
1km southeast, is an older city site (dating
to the 11th century), though its two temples
date to the 14th century. Those listed below
represent only the more distinctive of the
numerous Si Satchanalai ruins.

An **information centre** (☼ 8.30am-5pm) at the
park distributes free park maps and has a

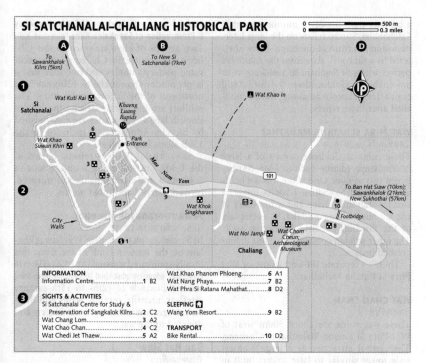

SI SATCHANALAI–CHALIANG HISTORICAL PARK

INFORMATION	Wat Khao Phanom Phloeng...............**6** A1
Information Centre...........................**1** B2	Wat Nang Phaya...............................**7** B2
	Wat Phra Si Ratana Mahathat..........**8** D2
SIGHTS & ACTIVITIES	
Si Satchanalai Centre for Study &	**SLEEPING**
Preservation of Sangkalok Kilns.....**2** C2	Wang Yom Resort.............................**9** B2
Wat Chang Lom................................**3** A2	
Wat Chao Chan................................**4** C2	**TRANSPORT**
Wat Chedi Jet Thaew........................**5** A2	Bike Rental.....................................**10** D2

small exhibit outlining the history and major attractions. There are bicycles to rent (20B) near the entrance gate to the park that are slightly better than those rented where the bus stops on the main road. It also rents sleeping bags (20B) and tents (80B) if you want to spend the night right at the entrance to the park.

The nearby town of Sawankhalok (p397) is the main supply centre for the area.

WAT CHANG LOM
วัดช้างล้อม

This fine temple, marking the centre of the old city of Si Satchanalai, has elephants surrounding a bell-shaped stupa but is somewhat better preserved than its counterpart in Sukhothai. An inscription says the temple was built by King Ramkhamhaeng between 1285 and 1291.

WAT KHAO PHANOM PHLOENG
วัดเขาพนมเพลิง

On the hill overlooking Wat Chang Lom to the right are the remains of Wat Khao Phanom Phloeng, including a stupa, a large

seated Buddha and stone columns that once supported the roof of the *wíhǎan*. From this hill you can make out the general design of the once-great city. The slightly higher hill west of Phanom Phloeng is capped by a large Sukhothai-style stupa – all that remains of Wat Khao Suwan Khiri.

WAT CHEDI JET THAEW
วัดเจดีย์เจ็ดแถว

Next to Wat Chang Lom, these ruins contain seven rows of stupas, the largest of which is a copy of one at Wat Mahathat in Sukhothai. An interesting brick-and-plaster *wíhǎan* features barred windows designed to look like lathed wood (an ancient Indian technique used all over Southeast Asia). A *prasat* (small ornate building with a cruciform ground plan and needle-like spire) and stupa are stacked on the roof.

WAT NANG PHAYA
วัดนางพญา

South of Wat Chang Lom and Wat Chedi Jet Thaew, this stupa is Sinhalese in style and was built in the 15th or 16th century,

NORTHERN THAILAND

a bit later than the other monuments at Si Satchanalai. Stucco reliefs on the large later-ite *wíhăan* in front of the stupa – now shel-tered by a tin roof – date from the Ayuthaya period when Si Satchanalai was known as Sawankhalok. Goldsmiths in the district still craft a design known as *naang pháyaa*, mod-elled after these reliefs.

WAT PHRA SI RATANA MAHATHAT
วัดพระศรีรัตนมหาธาตุ

These ruins at Chaliang consist of a large laterite stupa (dating back to 1448–88) be-tween two *wíhăan*. One of the *wíhăan* holds a large seated Sukhothai Buddha image, a smaller standing image and a bas-relief of the famous walking Buddha, so exemplary of the flowing, boneless Sukhothai style. The other *wíhăan* contains some less distin-guished images.

There's a separate 10B admission for Wat Phra Si Ratana Mahathat.

WAT CHAO CHAN
วัดเจ้าจันทร์

These wat ruins are about 500m west of Wat Phra Si Ratana Mahathat in Chaliang. The central attraction is a large Khmer-style tower similar to later towers built in Lopburi and probably constructed during the reign of Khmer King Jayavarman VII (1181–1217). The tower has been restored and is in fairly good shape. The roofless *wíhăan* on the right contains the laterite outlines of a large standing Buddha that has all but melted away from exposure and weathering.

Sawankhalok Kilns
เตาเผาสังคโลก

The Sukhothai–Si Satchanalai area was once famous for its beautiful pottery, much of which was exported to countries through-out Asia. In China – the biggest importer of Thai pottery during the Sukhothai and Ayuthaya periods – the pieces came to be called 'Sangkalok', a mispronunciation of Sawankhalok. Particularly fine specimens of this pottery can be seen in the national museums of Jakarta and Pontianak in Indonesia.

At one time, more than 200 huge pottery kilns lined the banks of Mae Nam Yom in the area around Si Satchanalai. Several have been carefully excavated and can be viewed at the **Si Satchanalai Centre for Study & Preservation of Sangkalok Kilns** (admission 30B). Two groups of kilns are open to the pub-lic: a kiln centre in Chaliang with exca-vated pottery samples and one kiln; and a larger outdoor Sawankhalok Kilns site 5km northwest of the Si Satchanalai ruins. The exhibits are interesting despite the lack of English labels. These sites are easily visited by bicycle. Admission is included in the 150B all-inclusive ticket.

Sawankhalok pottery rejects, buried in the fields, are still being found. Shops in Sukhothai and Sawankhalok sell misfired, broken, warped and fused pieces.

Sawanworanayok Museum
พิพิธภัณฑ์สวรรค์วรนายก

In Sawankhalok town, near Wat Sawankha-lam on the western bank of the river, this locally sponsored **museum** (☎ 0 5561 4333; 69 Th Phracharat; admission adult/child 100/50B; ☺ 8am-5pm) holds thousands of 12th- to 15th-century artefacts, utensils, ceramic wares and Bud-dha images unearthed by local villagers and donated to the wat.

Ban Hat Siaw
บ้านหาดเสี้ยว

This colourful village southeast of Si Sat-chanalai is home to the Thai Phuan (also known as Lao Phuan), a Tai tribal group that immigrated from the Xieng Khuang Province in Laos about 100 years ago when the Annamese and Chinese were in north-eastern Laos.

The local Thai Phuan are famous for **hand-woven textiles**, particularly the *phâa sîn tiin jòk* (brocade-bordered skirts), which have patterns of horizontal stripes bordered by thickly patterned brocade. The men's *phâa khăo-măa* (short sarong) from Hat Siaw, typically in dark plaids, are also highly regarded.

Practically every stilt house within the village has a loom underneath it; cloth can be purchased at the source or from shops in Sawankhalok. Vintage Hat Siaw textiles, ranging from 80 to 200 years old, can be seen at the Village Old Clothes Museum in central Si Satchanalai.

Another Thai Phuan custom is the use of **elephant-back** processions in local monas-tic ordinations; these usually take place in early April.

Sleeping & Eating

SI SATCHANALAI–CHALIANG HISTORICAL PARK

Wang Yom Resort (Sunanthana; ☎ 0 5563 1380; bungalows from 600B; ✗) This collection of rustic, worn bungalows in a mature garden lies just outside the Si Satchanalai–Chaliang Historical Park, 400m before the southeastern corner of the old city. Service lacks enthusiasm but the large **restaurant** (dishes 50-120B) is reportedly very good. Food and drink are also available at a coffee shop in the historical park until 6pm.

SAWANKHALOK

This charming town about 20km south of the historical park, has a couple of overnight options.

Saengsin Hotel (☎ 0 5564 1818; fax 0 5564 1828; 2 Th Thetsaban Damri 3; s/d from 150/210B; ✗) This hotel is about 1km south of the train station on the main street that runs through Sawankhalok. It has clean, comfortable rooms and a **coffee shop**.

A couple of other options also line the main drag.

This isn't a big town for eating; most food places sell noodles and *khâo man kài* and not much else.

Kung Nam (dishes 40-70B; ✆ 10am-11pm) A Thai and Chinese garden restaurant on the outskirts of Sawankhalok towards Sukhothai, and probably the best spot to chow down in Sawankhalok.

Ko Heng (☎ 0 5564 1616; 144/1 Th Na Meuang; dishes 40-90B; ✆ 10am-3pm) An old riverside Chinese restaurant that's well past its prime. The Hakka-style *kài òp* (baked chicken), however, is still excellent and sells out fast.

Sawankhalok's **night market** assembles along its main streets.

Getting There & Away

BUS

Si Satchanalai–Chaliang Historical Park is off Rte 101 between Sawankhalok and new Si Satchanalai. From New Sukhothai, take a Si Satchanalai bus (ordinary/air-con 25/38B, two hours) and ask to get off at *'meuang kào'* (old city). Alternatively, catch the 9am bus to Chiang Rai, which costs the same but makes fewer stops.

There are two places along the left side of the highway where you can get off the bus and reach the ruins in the park; both involve crossing Mae Nam Yom. The first leads to a footbridge over Mae Nam Yom to Wat Phra Si Ratana Mahathat at Chaliang; the second crossing is about 2km further northwest just past two hills and leads directly into the Si Satchanalai ruins.

TRAIN

Sawankhalok's original train station is one of the main local sights. King Rama VI had a 60km railway spur built from Ban Dara (a small town on the main northern trunk) to Sawankhalok just so that he could visit the ruins.

Amazingly, there's a daily special express (No 7) from Bangkok to Sawankhalok (474B, eight hours), which leaves the capital at 9.30am. Promptly upon arrival, it heads right back to Bangkok, arriving in the city at 11.55pm. It's a 'Sprinter', which means 2nd class air-con, no sleepers, and the fare includes dinner and breakfast. In the reverse direction, train No 4 leaves Sawankhalok for Bangkok at 7am. You can also hop this train to Phitsanulok (33B).

One local train daily, No 405, originating from Taphan Hin (which is 73km north of Nakhon Sawan) also serves Sawankhalok. The train departs Phitsanulok at noon and arrives in Sawankhalok at 2.45pm (3rd class 21B).

Getting Around

You can rent **bicycles** (20B per day) from a shop at the gateway to Wat Phra Si Ratana Mahathat in Si Satchanalai–Chaliang Historical Park.

KAMPHAENG PHET PROVINCE

KAMPHAENG PHET

กำแพงเพชร

pop 27,500

Formerly known as Chakangrao or Nakhon Chum, Kamphaeng Phet (Diamond Wall) was once an important front line of defence for the Sukhothai kingdom but it is now mostly known for producing the tastiest *klûay khài* ('egg banana', a delicious kind of small banana) in Thailand. It's quite a nice place to spend a day or two wandering around the ruins and experiencing a small

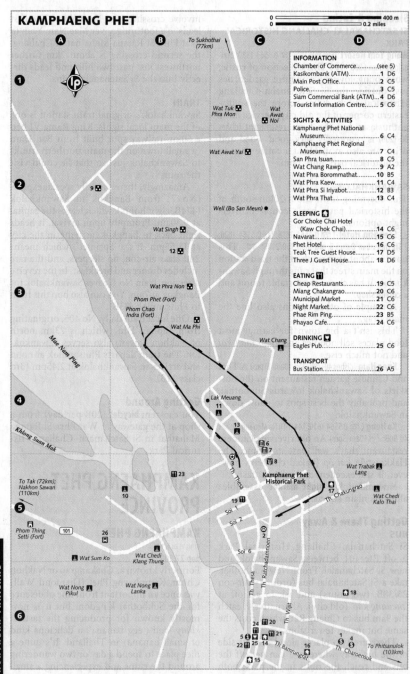

KAMPHAENG PHET

0 — 400 m
0 — 0.2 miles

To Sukhothai
(77km)

INFORMATION
Chamber of Commerce.............(see 5)
Kasikornbank (ATM)......................1 D6
Main Post Office..........................2 C5
Police...3 C5
Siam Commercial Bank (ATM)....4 D6
Tourist Information Centre...........5 C6

SIGHTS & ACTIVITIES
Kamphaeng Phet National
  Museum...................................6 C4
Kamphaeng Phet Regional
  Museum...................................7 C4
San Phra Isuan...........................8 C5
Wat Chang Rawp........................9 A2
Wat Phra Borommathat.............10 B5
Wat Phra Kaew.........................11 C4
Wat Phra Si Iriyabot..................12 B3
Wat Phra That...........................13 C4

SLEEPING
Gor Choke Chai Hotel
  (Kaw Chok Chai).....................14 C6
Navarat....................................15 C6
Phet Hotel................................16 C6
Teak Tree Guest House..............17 D5
Three J Guest House..................18 D6

EATING
Cheap Restaurants....................19 C5
Miang Chakangrao....................20 C6
Municipal Market......................21 C6
Night Market............................22 C6
Phae Rim Ping..........................23 B5
Phayao Cafe.............................24 C6

DRINKING
Eagles Pub...............................25 C6

TRANSPORT
Bus Station..............................26 A5

Wat Tuk
Phra Mon

Wat
Awat
Noi

Wat Awat Yai

Well (Bo San Meun)

Wat Singh

Wat Phra Non

Phom Phet (Fort)

Phom Chao
Indra (Fort)

Wat Ma Phi

Wat Chang

Mae Nam Ping

Khlong Suan Mak

To Tak (72km);
Nakhon Sawan
(110km)

Phom Thing
Setti (Fort)

101

Wat Sum Ko

Wat Chedi
Klang Thung

Wat Nong
Pikul

Wat Nong
Lanka

Lak Meuang

Kamphaeng Phet
Historical Park

Wat Trabak
Lang

Th Chakungrao

Wat Chedi
Kalo Thai

Th Thesa

Soi 1

Soi 2

Soi 6

Th Ratchadamnoen

Th Thesa

Th Wijit

Th Bamrungrat

Th Charoensuk

To Phitsanulok
(103km)

NORTHERN THAILAND

northern provincial capital that receives few tourists.

Information

The privately sponsored **tourist information centre** (Th Thesa; closed Sun) – the sign actually reads 'Chamber of Commerce' – can answer general queries about lodging and restaurants, and has a good map of the town.

Most of the major banks also have branches with ATMs along the main streets near the river and on Th Charoensuk.

The **main post office** (Th Thesa) is just south of the old city. The **police** (☎ 0 5571 1199) await if something goes wrong.

Sights

OLD CITY

เมืองเก่า

Declared a Unesco World Heritage site in 1991, the **Kamphaeng Phet Historical Park** (☎ 0 5571 1921; admission 40B; ☉ 8am-5pm) encloses the old city site where you'll find **Wat Phra Kaew**, which used to be adjacent to the royal palace (now in ruins). It's not nearly as well restored as Sukhothai, but it's smaller, more intimate and less visited. Weather-corroded Buddha statues have assumed slender, porous forms that remind some visitors of Alberto Giacometti (a Swiss sculptor and painter) sculptures. About 100m southeast of Wat Phra Kaew is **Wat Phra That**, distinguished by a large round-based stupa surrounded by columns. This park is popular with joggers and walkers.

KAMPHAENG PHET NATIONAL MUSEUM

พิพิธภัณฑสถานแห่งชาติกำแพงเพชร

The nearby **national museum** (☎ 0 5571 1570; admission 30B; ☉ 9am-noon & 1-4pm Wed-Sun) has the usual survey of Thai art periods downstairs. Upstairs there is a collection of artefacts from the Kamphaeng Phet area, including terracotta ornamentation from ruined temples and Buddha images in both the Sukhothai and Ayuthaya styles.

KAMPHAENG PHET REGIONAL MUSEUM

พิพิธภัณฑ์เฉลิมพระเกียรติกำแพงเพชร

The **regional museum** (☎ 0 5572 2341; admission 10B; ☉ 9am-4pm) is a series of central, Thai-style wooden structures on stilts set among nicely landscaped grounds. There are three main buildings in the museum: one focuses on history and prehistory; one features displays about geography and materials used in local architecture; and the third houses an ethnological museum featuring encased displays of miniature doll-like figures representing various tribes. Push-button recordings in English and Thai explain the displays.

WAT PHRA BOROMMATHAT

วัดพระบรมธาตุ

Across Mae Nam Ping are more neglected ruins in an area that was settled long before Kamphaeng Phet's heyday, although visible remains are postclassical Sukhothai. Wat Phra Borommathat has a few small stupas and one large stupa of the late Sukhothai period that is now crowned with a Burmese-style umbrella added early in the 20th century.

SAN PHRA ISUAN

ศาลพระอิศวร

Near the Kamphaeng Phet Chaloem Phrakiat Museum, the San Phra Isuan (Shiva Shrine) has a sandstone base upon which is a Khmer-style bronze sculpture of Shiva (Isvara). This image is actually a replica: the original is in the Kamphaeng Phet National Museum.

OTHER TEMPLES

Northeast of the old city walls, **Wat Phra Si Iriyabot** has the shattered remains of standing, sitting, walking and reclining Buddha images all sculpted in the classic Sukhothai style. Northwest of here, **Wat Chang Rawp** (Elephant-Encircled Temple) is just that – a temple with an elephant-buttressed wall. Several other temple ruins – most of them little more than flat brick foundations, with the occasional weatherworn Buddha image – can be found in the same general vicinity.

Sleeping

Three J Guest House (☎ 0 5571 3129; threejguest@ hotmail.com; 79 Th Rachavitee; r 200-400B; ☒) This pleasant new collection of unique bungalows has a most hospitable host, Mr Charin, who will gladly pick you up from the bus terminal. Each of the bungalows is unique and the cheapest ones share a clean bathroom. Bicycles and motorcycles are available for rent.

    Teak Tree Guest House (☎ 0 1675 6471; Soi 1 Th Chakungrao; s/d 170/250B) Open only in the high season, this tidy wooden house on stilts offers three rooms with shared hot-water bathroom. The guesthouse is only 10 minutes' walk from the historical park and has bicycles for rent (30B per day).

Gor Choke Chai (Kaw Chok Chai; ☎ 0 5571 1247; Th Charoensuk; r from 300B; ⊠) This is a bustling but friendly place in the centre of the new town not far from the municipal market. It's the best-value hotel in town.

Phet Hotel (☎ 0 5571 2810-5; fax 0 5571 2816; 189 Th Bamrungrat; r 500-750B; ⊠) Popular with middle-class Thais, this comfortable hotel features spacious, well-maintained, modern rooms near the municipal market. Look for the sign on the top of the building. The street-side sign is only in Thai script.

Navarat (Nawarat; ☎ 0 5571 1211; 2 Soi Prapan; r/ste 600/950; ⊠) Set off the road, this five-storey hotel may lack style, but its carpeted rooms are clean and comfortable. There is a coffee shop downstairs and staff members speak some English.

Eating

A small night market sets up every evening in front of the provincial offices near the old city walls and there are also some cheap restaurants near the roundabout.

Miang Chakangrao (☎ 0 5571 1124; 273 Th Ratchadamnoen) Sells local sweets and snacks, particularly the shop's namesake, a fermented tea salad eaten with peanut-rice brittle.

Inexpensive food stalls can be found in a larger **municipal market** (cnr Th Wijit & Th Banthoengjit). Along Th Thesa across from Sirijit Park by the river are several family-friendly, air-con restaurants. **Phayao Cafe** (dishes 40B-100B; ⊠ 10am-midnight) may look closed with its heavily tinted windows, but inside you'll find a casual, family-friendly atmosphere and great ice cream.

There are also a few floating restaurants on the river, including **Phae Rim Ping** (☎ 0 5571 2767; dishes 40-100B; ⊠ 11am-midnight).

Drinking

There are a number of discos with karaoke around Phet Hotel. Some of them feature live music on the weekends.

Eagles Pub (Th Bamrungrat; ⊠ 8pm-1am) A pub with a Western-theme that serves a lot of whisky and a mixture of Thai and Western food (dishes 40B to 100B). Sometimes they have live music.

Getting There & Away

The bus terminal was under construction at the time of writing, so there should be a full-service station with an information desk by the time you get here. Regular buses to/from Bangkok (ordinary/air-con/VIP 125/165/212B, five hours) leave throughout the day. Most visitors arrive from Sukhothai (45B, 1½ hours), Phitsanulok (ordinary/air-con 43/58B, two hours) or Tak (35B, 1½ hours). The government-bus station is across the river from town.

Getting Around

The least expensive way to get from the bus station into town is to hop a shared *săwngthăew* (5B per person) to the roundabout across the river. From there take a *săamláw* anywhere in town for 20B.

TAK PROVINCE

Tak is a wild and mountainous province. Its proximity to Myanmar has resulted in a complex history and unique cultural mix.

In the 1970s the mountains of western Tak were a hotbed of communist guerrilla activity. Since the 1980s the former leader of the local CPT movement has been involved in resort-hotel development and Tak is very much open to outsiders, but the area still has an untamed feeling about it. This province boasts Thailand's largest population of domesticated elephants, which are still commonly used by Karen villagers in western Tak for transport and agricultural tasks.

Western Tak has always presented a distinct contrast with other parts of Thailand because of strong Karen and Burmese cultural influences. The Thailand–Myanmar border districts of Mae Ramat, Tha Song Yang and Mae Sot are dotted with refugee camps, an outcome of the firefights between the Karen National Union (KNU) and the Myanmar government, which is driving Karen civilians across the border. In January 2004 there were an estimated 150,000 unregistered migrant workers from Burma in Tak province alone.

The main source of income for people living on both sides of the border is legal and illegal international trade. The main smuggling gateways on the Thailand side are Tha

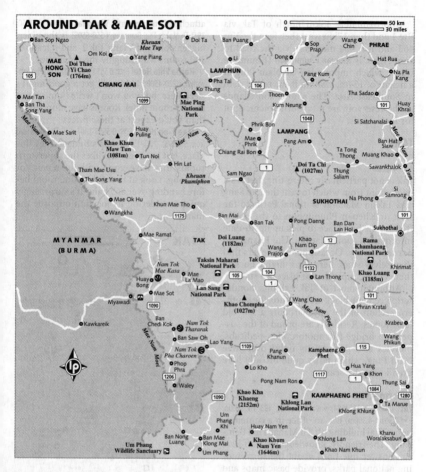

AROUND TAK & MAE SOT

Song Yang, Mae Sarit, Mae Tan, Wangkha, Mae Sot and Waley. One important contraband product is teak, cut by the Karen or the Karenni (Kayah) and then brought into Thailand from Myanmar on large tractor-trailers at night. As much as 200,000B in bribes per truckload is distributed among local Thai authorities who conveniently look the other way. None of the trade is legal since the Thai government cut off all timber deals with the Burmese military in 1997.

The majority of Tak Province is forested and mountainous and is an excellent destination for those wanting to trek. Organised trekking occurs, some further north out of Chiang Mai, most of it locally organised. There are Hmong, Musoe (Lahu), Lisu and White and Red Karen settlements throughout the west and north.

In Ban Tak, 25km upstream along Mae Nam Tak from Tak, you can visit **Wat Phra Borommathat**, the original site of a Thai stupa that, according to legend, was constructed during the reign of King Ramkhamhaeng (1275–1317) to celebrate his elephant-back victory over King Sam Chon, ruler of an independent kingdom once based at or near Mae Sot. The wat's main feature is a large, slender, gilded stupa in the Shan style surrounded by numerous smaller but similar stupas. Many Thais flock to the temple each week in the belief that the stupa can somehow reveal to them the winning lottery numbers for the week.

Approximately 45km north of Tak via Rte 1 and then 17km west (between the Km 463 and Km 464 markers), via the road to Sam Ngao, is **Kheuan Phumiphon** (Bhumibol Dam), which impounds Mae Nam Ping at a height of 154m, making it the tallest dam in Southeast Asia. The shores and islands of the reservoir are a favourite picnic spot for local Thais.

TAK

ตาก

pop 49,200

Tak is not particularly interesting, but it's a good point from which to visit the Lan Sang and Taksin Maharat National Parks to the west or Kheuan Phumiphon to the north. It's also the best place to pick up up-to-date information about Mae Sot, Um Phang and border activity. Occasionally travellers find themselves stuck here for a night. Luckily there are a couple decent places to stay.

Although most of Tak exhibits nondescript, cement-block architecture, the southern section of the city harbours a few old teak homes. Residents are proud of the suspension bridge (for motorcycles, pedicabs, bicycles and pedestrians only) over Mae Nam Ping, which flows quite broadly here even in the dry season.

Information

TAT (☎ 0 5551 3584; www.tak.go.th; 193 Th Taksin; ⏱ 8.30am-4.30pm) has an office in a contemporary Thai building off Th Mahat Thai Bamrung. The friendly, knowledgable staff here can answer questions about the surrounding national parks, provide basic maps and also tell you about organised activities such as rafting and trekking.

Several banks have branches along Th Mahat Thai Bamrung and Th Taksin, all of them with ATMs.

Sleeping & Eating

Few people pause to spend the night in Tak, but if you do you'll find most of the town's hotels on Th Taksin or Th Mahat Thai Bamrung in the town centre.

Viang Tak 2 (☎ 0 5555 1207; 236 Th Chumphon; r/ste 650/950B; 🗙 🖭 🖭) Those who are seeking a little comfort and some professional service should head here. This eight-storey hotel's amenities also include a coffee shop with an excellent river view, karaoke bar and an attached Internet café. **Viang Tak** (☎ 0 5551 1950; 25/3 Th Mahat Thai Bamrung; r 550-650B) is the older, bigger sibling of Viang Tak 2, and it features 100 rooms with roughly the same rates.

Racha Villa Hotel (☎ 0 5551 2360; 307/1 Th Phahonyothin; r 220-450B; 🗙) You'll get a good night's sleep here, but you won't write home about this 58-room hotel. Rooms have more extras than you'd expect at these prices.

Mae Ping Hotel (☎ 0 5551 1807; 619 Th Taksin; s/d from 50/80B; 🗙) Everyone's budget likes this place, but not everyone likes the superworn rooms that have gone without repair for too long. Look at more than one room before handing over any baht. It's surprisingly quiet considering its location opposite the market.

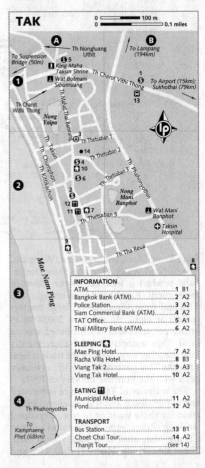

INFORMATION	
ATM	1 B1
Bangkok Bank (ATM)	2 A2
Police Station	3 A2
Siam Commercial Bank (ATM)	4 A2
TAT Office	5 A1
Thai Military Bank (ATM)	6 A2

SLEEPING 🛏	
Mae Ping Hotel	7 A2
Racha Villa Hotel	8 B3
Viang Tak 2	9 A3
Viang Tak Hotel	10 A2

EATING 🍴	
Municipal Market	11 A2
Pond	12 A2

TRANSPORT	
Bus Station	13 B1
Choet Chai Tour	14 A2
Thanjit Tour	(see 14)

You can buy food at the **municipal market** (Th Taksin; dishes 10-30B; ☺ 6am-6pm). **Pond** (Th Taksin; dishes 15-30B; ☺ 8am-3pm) is a simple place near the market specialising in Thai curries.

Getting There & Away

Tak airport, 15km out of town towards Sukhothai on Hwy 12, wasn't operating at last look; the nearest functioning airports are in Phitsanulok and Mae Sot. Thai Airways International provides a shuttle van a few times a day between Phitsanulok airport and the Viang Tak 2 Hotel in Tak.

Tak's **bus station** (Th Charot Vithi Thong) is just outside town. A *túk-túk* will take you to the town centre for around 20B, but it's also possible to walk if you packed light. Frequent buses travel between Tak and Sukhothai (ordinary/air-con 31/43B, 1½ hours).

There is also regular service to Lampang (ordinary/air-con 103/185B, three hours), Chiang Mai (ordinary/air-con 134/241B, four hours), Chiang Rai (ordinary/air-con 200/369B, seven hours) and also to Mae Sai (ordinary/air-con 219/394B, nine hours).

Ordinary government buses depart for Bangkok three times daily (136B, 10 hours), while a 2nd-class air-con bus leaves once a day (177B, eight hours). There are four daily 1st-class air-con departures from Tak to Bangkok and one 10pm departure in the reverse direction (245B, six hours). **Thanjit Tour** and **Choet Chai Tour**, next door, offer 1st-class air-con buses with similar departures and fares.

Air-con buses to Mae Sot (50B) leave at 2pm, 4pm and 5pm. Minivans to Mae Sot leave more frequently (44B, 1½ hours).

AROUND TAK
Taksin Maharat & Lan Sang National Parks
อุทยานแห่งชาติตากสินมหาราช

These small **national parks** (admission 200B) receive a steady trickle of visitors on weekends and holidays, but they are almost empty during the week. Taksin Maharat (established in 1981) covers 149 sq km; the entrance is 2km from the Km 26 marker on Rte 105/Asia Rte 1 (the so-called Pan-Asian Hwy, which would link Istanbul and Singapore if all the intervening countries allowed land crossings) to Mae Sot.

The park's most outstanding features are the 30m, nine-tiered **Nam Tok Mae Ya Pa** and

a record-holding *tàbàak,* a dipterocarp that is 50m tall and 16m in circumference. Birdwatching is said to be particularly good here; known resident and migratory species include the tiger shrike, forest wagtail and Chinese pond heron.

Nineteen kilometres from Tak, Lan Sang National Park preserves 104 sq km surrounding an area of rugged, 1000m-high granite peaks – part of the Tenasserim Range. A network of trails leads to several **waterfalls**, including the park's 40m-high namesake.

The best way to reach the parks is via private car, but the bus to Mae Sot will drop you on the road where you can easily walk to the park entrance. By car take Rte 1103 3km south off Rte 105.

SLEEPING

Lan Sang National Park rents rustic **bungalows** (☎ 0 5551 9278; bungalows 600-4000B) that can accommodate two to 36 people. Two-person **tents** (30B) are also available. Taksin Maharat National Park offers utilitarian **rooms** (☎ 0 5551 1429; r 1000-2400B) that sleep between four and 15 people. Taksin Maharat also has a **camping ground** (tent sites 10B). **Food service** can be arranged in both parks.

Kheuan Phumiphon
เขื่อนภูมิพล

This huge reservoir is a favourite canoeing, swimming, fishing and picnicking destination for Tak residents. The Electrical Generating Authority of Thailand (EGAT) maintains several **bungalows** and **longhouses** (Bangkok ☎ 0 2436 3179; Ban Phak Rap Rong Kheuan Phumiphon ☎ 0 5554 9509; multibed units 400-1000B). On weekends there is bus service from the Tak bus terminal (50B).

Doi Muser Hilltribe Cultural Center
ศูนย์พัฒนาและสงเคราะห์ชาวเขาดอยมูเซอ

At the top of the mountain before you descend into Mae Sot is this small **research and cultural centre** (☎ 0 5551 2131; Km 28 Th Tak-Mae Sot; bungalows 150-500B) where you can visit for the day, or spend the night. Here they grow and sell crops such as tea, coffee, fruits and flowers. Call ahead to find out about seeing a cultural performance. The temperature can go as low as 4°C in the winter. During November and December, *bua tong* flowers (a kind of wild sunflower) blossom around the centre. Information is available from TAT in Tak (p402).

MAE SOT
แม่สอด

Mae Sot is a Burmese–Chinese–Karen–Thai trading outpost that has become a small but simmering tourist destination. Black-market trade between Myanmar and Thailand is the primary source of local revenue, with most transactions taking place in the districts of Mae Ramat, Tha Song Yang, Phop Phra and Um Phang. Mae Sot has also become the most important jade and gem centre along the border, with most of the trade controlled by Chinese and Indian immigrants from Myanmar.

Walking down the streets of Mae Sot, you'll see an interesting ethnic mixture – Burmese men in their *longyi* (sarongs), Hmong and Karen women in traditional hill-tribe dress, bearded Indo-Burmese men and Thai army rangers. Shop signs along the streets are in Thai, Burmese and Chinese. Most of the temple architecture in Mae Sot is Burmese. The town's Burmese population is largely Muslim, while those living outside town are Buddhist, and the Karen are mostly Christian.

The large **municipal market** in Mae Sot, behind the Siam Hotel, sells some interesting stuff, including Burmese clothing, cheap cigarettes, roses, Indian food, sturdy Burmese blankets and velvet thong slippers from Mandalay.

Border skirmishes between Myanmar's central government and the weakening Karen and Kayah ethnic insurgencies can break out at any time, sending thousands of refugees – and the occasional mortar rocket – across the Thai–Myanmar border, elements that add to the area's perceived instability.

The Thai–Myanmar Friendship Bridge links Mae Sot with Myawadi and the highway west to Mawlamyine (Moulmein) and Yangon.

Information

The **tourist police** (☎ 0 5553 3523, 0 5553 4341; Th Asia) have an office one block east of the bus terminal.

Krung Thai Bank, Bank of Ayutthaya and **Siam Commercial Bank** all have ATMs and are conveniently located in the centre of town.

Internet access is available at **Southeast Asia Tours** (Th Intharakhiri; per hr 25B). It also has an international phone service.

DK Book House (Th Intharakhiri), attached to the DK Mae Sot Square Hotel, carries some English-language titles and some good maps of the area, including the Thai military-surveyed topographic map (1:250,000) of the border area entitled *Moulmein*. It covers as far north as Mae Ramat, to the south almost to Um Phang, west to Mawlamyine and only about 50km east of Mae Sot.

Sights & Activities

See p409 for information about visiting Myawadi in Myanmar.

BAN MAE TAO
บ้านแม่เต่า

Wat Wattanaram (Phattanaram) is a Burmese temple at Ban Mae Tao, 3km west of Mae Sot on the road to the Thailand–Myanmar border. Most associate this wat with its huge, modern Burmese-style reclining Buddha. In the main *wíhǎan* on the 2nd floor is a collection of Burmese musical instruments, including tuned drums and gongs.

HERBAL SAUNA

Wat Mani has separate herbal **sauna** (admission 20B; ☉ 3-7pm) facilities for men and women. The sauna volunteers also sell monk-made herbal medicines. The sauna is towards the back of the monastery grounds, past the monks' *kùtì*.

WAT PHRA THAT DOI DIN KIU (JI)
วัดพระธาตุดอยดินกิ๋ว(จิ)

Wat Phra That Doi Din Kiu (Ji) is a forest temple 11km northwest of Mae Sot on a 300m-high hill overlooking Mae Nam Moei and Myanmar. It's a bit difficult for some to find and during Myanmar's dry-season offensives against the KNU, this area is sometimes considered unsafe and the road to the temple is occasionally blocked by Thai rangers. Ask in town about the current situation before heading up the road.

The highlight of this wat is a small stupa mounted on what looks like a boulder that has been balanced on the edge of a cliff. It's reminiscent of the Kyaiktiyo Pagoda in Myanmar.

If you're on a motorcycle, or have a car, take Hwy 105 to Wat Thani Wattharam,

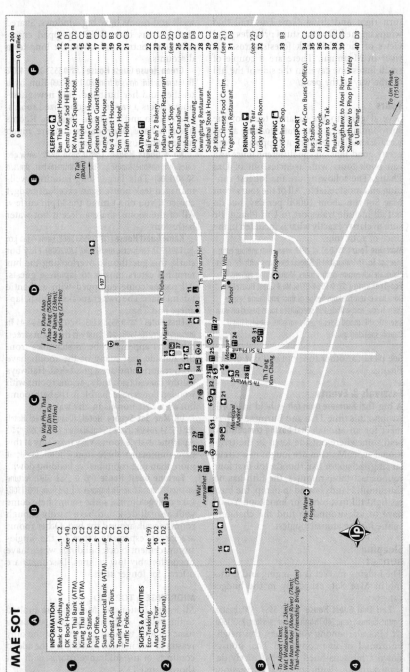

MAE SOT

0 _____ 200 m
0 _____ 0.1 miles

INFORMATION
Bank of Ayuthaya (ATM)..................1 C2
DK Book House...........................(see 14)
Krung Thai Bank (ATM)....................2 C3
Krung Thai Bank (ATM)....................3 C2
Police Station............................4 D2
Post Office..............................5 D2
Siam Commercial Bank (ATM)..............6 C2
Southeast Asia Tours.....................7 C2
Tourist Police...........................8 D1
Traffic Police...........................9 C3

SIGHTS & ACTIVITIES
Eco-Trekking.............................(see 19)
Max One Tour............................10 D2
Wat Mani (Sauna).......................11 D2

SLEEPING 🛏
Ban Thai Guest House....................12 A3
Central Mae Sod Hill Hotel...............13 D1
DK Mae Sot Square Hotel................14 D2
First Hotel.............................15 C2
Fortune Guest House....................16 B3
Green House Guest House................17 C2
Kame Guest House.......................18 C2
No 4 Guest House.......................19 B3
Pom Thep Hotel........................20 C3
Siam Hotel.............................21 C3

EATING 🍴
Bai Fern...............................22 C2
Fah Fah 2 Bakery.......................23 C2
Indian-Burmese Restaurant..............24 D3
KCB Snack Shop........................25 C2
Khrua Canadian.........................26 B2
Krabawng Jaw..........................27 D3
Kuaytiaw Meuang.......................28 C3
Kwangtung Restaurant..................29 C2
Salakthai Steak House..................30 B2
SP Kitchen.............................(see 21)
Thai-Chinese Food Centre..............31 D3
Vegetarian Restaurant..................31 D3

DRINKING 🍸
Crocodile Tear.........................(see 22)
Lucky Music Room.......................32 C2

SHOPPING 🛍
Borderline Shop........................33 B3

TRANSPORT
Bangkok Air-Con Buses (Office)..........34 C2
Bus Station...........................35 C3
Jit Motorcyle..........................36 C3
Minivans to Tak........................37 D2
Phuket Air............................38 C2
Sawngthaew to Moei River..............39 C3
Sawngthaew to Phop Phra, Waley
 & Um Phang...........................40 D3

To Tak (80km)

To Um Phang (151km)

To Khao Mao
Khao Kaeo (500m);
Doi Din Kiu
(ii) (11km)

To Khao Mao
Khao Fang (500m);
Mae Ramat (33km);
Mae Sariang (221km)

To Airport (1km);
Wat Wattanaram (1.2km);
Mae Nam Moei (Moei River) (7km);
Thai-Myanmar Friendship Bridge (7km)

NORTHERN THAILAND

turn right and drive 3km. The trail that winds up the hill to the stupa provides good views of the thick teak forests across the river in Myanmar. There are a couple of small limestone caves in the side of the hill on the way to the peak.

Tours

Several guesthouses arrange tours of the surrounding area. The staff working at the Krua Canadian restaurant (opposite) keep pretty good tabs on the different tours and can book tours with agencies out of Um Phang. The following are the longest running and most reliable. All of the tours from Mae Sot run about 1000B per day, but do not all include transport to Um Phang. Be sure to clarify exactly what is included in the price of your tour.

Max One Tour (☎ 0 5554 2942; www.maxonetour.com; Mae Sot Sq, Th Intharakhiri) Biggest company with the most elaborate adventure-centric tours. Many rafting options.

Eco-Trekking (☎ 0 5554 4976; No 4 Guest House) Mr Oom has extensive knowledge of flora and fauna (especially birds) and will design specialised tours based on your interests. His mood is reportedly variable. He also has a Danish-speaking guide.

See p413 for other tour options out of Um Phang.

Festivals & Events

A big **Thai-Burmese gem fair** is held in April. Around this time Thai and Burmese boxers meet for an annual **Thai-boxing competition**, held somewhere outside town in the traditional style. Matches are fought in a circular ring and go for five rounds; the first four rounds last three minutes, the fifth has no time limit. Hands bound in hemp, the boxers fight till first blood or knockout. You'll have to ask around to find the changing venue for the annual slugfest.

Sleeping

BUDGET

The lodging market is changing and growing in Mae Sot, especially in the budget category.

Ban Thai Guest House (☎ 0 5553 1590; banthai_mth@hotmail.com; 740 Th Intharakhiri; s/d from 250/350B; ✷) Popular among volunteers, this neighbourhood of five converted Thai houses down a hibiscus-lined alley has nicely designed rooms. Bathrooms have riverstone

walls and rooms have big windows. Shared sitting areas have DVD-equipped entertainment centres. Ask about the long-term discounts.

Green House Guest House (☎ 0 5553 3207; 406/8 Th Intarahakhiri; dm/s/d from 80/150/200B) Run by a teacher and her husband, this new guesthouse offers a variety of good-sized rooms, lots of info and a central location. Rooms upstairs have floorboards and are much nicer than those downstairs.

No 4 Guest House (☎ 0 5554 4976; www.geocities.com/no4guesthouse/; 736 Th Intharakhiri; dm/s/d 50/80/100B) This large, long-running, well-managed teak house is an excellent budget choice if you don't mind the 11pm curfew. All of the rooms share a decent hot-water bathroom.

Kame Guest House (☎ 0 5553 5868; kame@dna-j.co.jp; 119/22 Th Chidwana; dm/s/d 80/120/200B) Tidy but stark, this guesthouse overlooking the bus terminal caters mostly to Japanese guests. All rooms come equipped with authentic tatami mats. The owner speaks English, Japanese and Thai.

First Hotel (☎ 0 5553 1233; fax 0 5553 1340; 44 Th Intharakhiri; r 270-450B; ✷) Just off the main street, this hotel appears to be in shambles from the outside, but many of the rooms have been restored and are a good deal. Hallways feature carved teak and spacious rooms with wooden floors have marble in the bathrooms but aren't glamorous in any way.

DK Mae Sot Square Hotel (Duang Kamol Hotel; ☎ 0 5554 2648/9; 298/2 Th Intharakhiri; r 250-400B; ✷) Apartment-style rooms vary in quality at this bare, minimalist, three-storey hotel. Look at more than one room before bedding down.

Fortune Guest House (☎ 0 5553 6392; fortune-maesot@hotmail.com; Th Intharakhiri; s/d from 100/150B) Like college dorms, some rooms here come with a small desk and have hardly enough room to walk around the bed. Other rooms are larger, especially those in the single-storey, cement-block buildings which have uncomfortably low ceilings. Discounts are offered for longer stays.

MIDRANGE & TOP END

Midrange options in Mae Sot are limited to the hotels, which all have cheaper, more basic options without air-con. But the only reason to stay in these hotels is for the added comforts of the midrange rooms with hot showers and TVs.

Porn Thep Hotel (☎ 0 5553 2590; 25/4 Th Si Wiang; r 250-700B; 🗙) Relatively clean and efficiently run, the deluxe rooms in the rear wing are the best deal here. Parking is secure, but note the proximity to the mosque. Rates are sometimes discounted during the rainy season.

Siam Hotel (☎ 0 5553 1376; fax 0 5553 1974; 185 Th Prasat Withi; s/d from 200/250B; 🗙) Although it's basically a truckers' and gem traders' haunt, local rumour has it that Myanmar intelligence agents frequent the Siam. It also sees a fare number of families and has comfortable, if stark, rooms.

Central Mae Sod Hill Hotel (☎ 0 5553 2601-8, Bangkok ☎ 0 2541 1234; cmhadm@cscoms.com; 100 Th Asia; r/ste incl breakfast 900/1200B; 🗙 🗙) This resort is on the highway to Tak, about 1km outside the town centre. Rooms have all you could ask for, and with the tennis courts, a good restaurant, a disco and a cocktail lounge, you hardly need to leave the place.

Eating

Mae Sot is a culinary crossroad with plenty of veggie-friendly options.

RESTAURANTS

Bai Fern (☎ 0 5553 3343; Th Intharakhiri; dishes 40-100B; 🕙 7.30am-10pm) The cosy, wood-furnished Bai Fern has a pleasant atmosphere and is popular all day long. Many come here for the lettuce-packed salads and the Burmese curries, but the coffee and cocktails are excellent as well. Peruse the *Bangkok Post* or the *Nation* while you wait.

Khao Mao Khao Fang (☎ 0 5553 3607; 382 Mu 5, Mae Pa; dishes 40-70B; 🕙 10am-10pm) North of town between the Km 1 and Km 2 markers on the road to Mae Ramat, this is the place for a romantic evening out. A Thai botanist designed this open-air restaurant to make it feel as if you're dining in the forest, with lots of common and not-so-common live plants from around northern Thailand. The Thai cuisine is equally inventive, with such specialities as *yam hèt khon* (a spicy salad made with forest mushrooms only available in September and October) and *mǔu khâo mâo* (a salad of home-cured sausage, peanuts, rice shoots, lettuce, ginger, lime and chilli).

Salakthai Steak House (☎ 0 5553 1016; Th Intharakhiri; dishes 40-150B) Both the indoor air-con seating area and tastefully decorated garden

area offer the nicest eating environment in town. Not everything on the menu is available during the low season and the place can be empty during the week, but it's still a fine choice.

SP Kitchen (Th Asia; dishes 30-80B) Featuring the best Italian food in the province, SP is quite popular with local volunteers. It lacks atmosphere, but the authentic lasagne and raviolis make up for that.

Kwangtung Restaurant (no Roman-script sign; dishes 30-90B; 🕙 10am-10pm) Specialising in Cantonese cooking, this is the best Chinese restaurant in town. None of the signs are in English, but you'll know it when you see (and smell) it.

Khrua Canadian (☎ 0 5553 4659; 3 Th Sri Panit; dishes 30-80B; 🕙 7am-10.30pm) The coffee is strong, the servings are large, the menu is varied, the prices are reasonable and local information is abundant here. It's also the best place to catch up on international news.

QUICK EATS

Indian-Burmese restaurant (Tea Shop; dishes 10-30B; 🕙 8am-8pm) Don't miss the excellent *rotii kaeng*, fresh milk, curries and *khâo sawy* served by this little spot opposite the mosque (the sign reads 'Tea Shop'). Similar places nearby are hit-or-miss.

Vegetarian restaurant (dishes 10-20B; 🕙 7am-7pm) This female-run veggie restaurant is very popular with lunching locals and only serves food until it's gone (which can be as early as 3pm). It's next to the Um Phang *sǎwngthǎew* stop.

Fah Fah 2 Bakery (☎ 0 5553 2569; 417/6-7 Th Tang Kim Chiang; 🕙 7.30am-9pm) Something like an American diner in both style and product, the specialties here are ice cream and French fries. The international breakfasts also receive high marks.

Thai-Chinese food centre (dishes 20-40B; 🕙 8am-4pm) Gem traders frequent vendors serving noodles and curry in a covered open-air space in front of the Siam Hotel.

KCB Snack Shop (Th Intharakhiri; dishes 35-75B; 🕙 8am-9pm) A friendly place a bit further to the west past Soi Ruam Jai.

For cheap Thai takeaway, try the rambling market behind the Siam Hotel.

A favourite local snack is *krabawng jaw* (Burmese for 'fried crispy'), a sort of vegetable tempura. The best place to eat it's at the small vendor stand west of Bai Fern Guest

House on Th Intharakhiri. There's no sign – look for a bubbling wok in front of a two-storey house. They fire up the oil around 5pm and keep cooking until 7pm, or until they've run out of ingredients.

Another local food speciality is *kŭaytĭaw meuang*, a rich bowl of rice noodles covered with sliced pork, greens, peanuts, chilli and green beans – very similar to *kŭaytĭaw sùkhŏthai*. Look for rice-noodle vendors along Th Prasat Withi; the best place is the vendor on the western side of Soi Sapphakan, running north off Th Prasat Withi.

Drinking & Entertainment

Mae Sot has an active nightlife, especially on the weekends.

Crocodile Tear (Th Intharakhiri) Features an extensive selection of mixed drinks, live music and many drunken travellers.

Lucky Music Room (Th Prasat Withi) For more local flavour, you can dance yourself silly at Lucky Music Room, which gets going around 10.30pm and sometimes charges a cover (20B).

Shopping

Many of the Karen refugees make beautiful crafts that they sell to support themselves.

Borderline Shop (☎ 0 5553 1016; 674/14 Th Intharakhiri) has some of the highest-quality items and also features a gallery with nontextile arts for sale.

Getting There & Away

AIR

From Bangkok, **Phuket Air** (☎ 0 5553 1440; www .phuketairlines.com; Mae Sot Airport) flies to Mae Sot (one-way/return 1910/3830B) daily. It also flies to Chiang Mai (1500B) on Monday, Wednesday, Friday and Sunday.

BUS & SĂWNGTHĂEW

If you're heading anywhere other than Bangkok, go to Tak (minivan/air-con bus 44/50B, 1½ hours) where you can easily connect with buses headed to Lampang, Chiang Mai, Chiang Rai and Mae Sai. Buses and minivans leave for Tak hourly. Minivans leave from an office opposite Kame Guest House. Buses leave from a dusty lot off Th Chidwana – also known as the bus station.

Ordinary buses between Bangkok and Mae Sot (172B, 10 hours) depart three times each evening in both directions. First-class air-con buses run between Bangkok and Mae Sot six times daily (310B, nine hours); 2nd-class air-con buses (241B, nine hours) have similar departures. VIP buses (24 seats) to/from Bangkok leave four times daily (480B, eight hours). These buses all leave from the dusty lot off Th Chidwana. Thanjit Tour (Th Intharakhiri) offers 32-seat VIP buses to Bangkok for only 350B, departing at 10pm.

Orange *săwngthăew* serving the northern destinations of Mae Sarit (60B, 2½ hours), Tha Song Yang (50B, 1½ hours) and Mae Sariang (160B, six hours) leave hourly between 6am and noon from the lot opposite Kame Guest House, which the minivans to and from Tak use.

Blue *săwngthăew* to Um Phang (100B, four hours) leave hourly between 7am and 3pm from an office off the southern end of Th Sri Phanit.

Getting Around

Most of Mae Sot can be seen on foot. Regular *săwngthăew* serve surrounding communities including Moei (10B).

Jit Motorcycle (Th Prasat Withi; motorcycles per day 160B) rents out motorcycles. Make sure you test-ride a bike before renting. Cars and vans can be rented for around 1200B a day; ask at any hotel or Bai Fern Restaurant (p407).

Motorcycle taxis and *săamláw* charge 20B for trips around town.

AROUND MAE SOT
Karen & Burmese Refugee Camps

ค่ายผู้อพยพชาวกะเหรี่ยงและพม่า

Several refugee camps have been set up along the eastern bank of Mae Nam Moei in either direction from Mae Sot. Most of the refugees in these camps are Karen fleeing battles between Burmese and KNU troops across the border. The camps have been around for over a decade but the Thai government has generally kept their existence quiet, fearing the build-up of a huge refugee 'industry' such as the one that developed around the Indo-Chinese camps in eastern Thailand in the 1970s.

Although many Thai and foreign volunteers have come to the refugees' aid, the camps are very much in need of outside assistance. Tourists, both Thai and foreign, are no longer permitted to visit the camps,

Detail of Lisu tribal dress, Mae Hong Son (p419)

TOM COCKREM

JOE CUMMINGS

Novice monk, Nan Province (p370)

Natural-fibre carry basket of the Mabri (yellow-leaf) people (p368), Nan Province

JULIET COOMBE

RICHARD I'ANSON

White Karen weaver, Mae Hong Son (p419)

Nam Tok Thilawsu (p411), Um Phang, Tak Province

JOE CUMMINGS

Girls in traditional dress celebrating Loi Krathong (p391), a full moon festival held in November, Sukhothai Historical Park

JOE CU

although if you meet a camp volunteer in Mae Sot you might be able to visit by invitation. Donations of clothes and medicines (to be administered by qualified doctors and nurses) may be offered to the camps via No 4 Guest House in Mae Sot (p406).

Waley

บ้านวะเลย์

Thirty-six kilometres from Mae Sot, Rte 1206 splits southwest off Rte 1090 at Ban Saw Oh and terminates 25km south at the border town of Waley, an important smuggling point.

The Burmese side was once one of two main gateways to Kawthoolei, the Karen nation, but in 1989 the Yangon government ousted the KNU. Until the Thai government cut off all timber trade with Myanmar's military government, teak was the main border trade. Nowadays there's a brisk trade in teak furniture instead.

One can visit hill-tribe villages near **Ban Chedi Kok**, or the **William E Deters Foundation for Gibbon Sanctuary & Wildlife Conservation Project** (www.highland-farm.org; Km 42.8, Rte 1090) near Phop Phra. The latter is a private facility that cares for gibbons and other animals that have been rescued from captivity. It is possible to volunteer and live at the sanctuary, but there is a three-day minimum at a charge of US$20 per person per day, or US$600 per month. The fee includes a very nice room and three meals per day.

GETTING THERE & AWAY

Săwngthăew to Phop Phra (35B) and Waley (40B) depart from Mae Sot every half-hour between 6am and 6pm from the same place as the *săwngthăew* to Um Phang. If you go by motorcycle or car, follow Rte 1090 southeast towards Um Phang and after 36km take Rte 1206 southwest. From this junction it's 25km to Waley; the last 10km of the road are unpaved. Your passport may be checked at a police outpost before Waley.

Border Market & Myawadi

ตลาดริมเมย/เมียวาดี

Experience a slice of Myanmar, or just go for the sake of an instant 30-day visa, by crossing the Mae Nam Moei to Myawadi. Immigration procedures are taken care of at the **Thai immigration booth** (8.30am-4.30pm) at

the bridge, although if you have any problems there's another immigration office in the nearby Mae Moei Shopping Bazaar. It takes around 15 minutes to finish all the paperwork to leave Thailand officially, and then you're free to walk across the arched bridge.

At the other end of the bridge is a rustic **Myanmar immigration booth**, where you'll fill out permits for a one-day stay, pay a fee of US$10 or 500B and leave your passports as a deposit. Then you're free to wander around Myawadi as long as you're back at the bridge by 4.30pm to pick up your passport and check out with immigration.

There is a market about 100m from the river on the Thai side that legally sells Burmese goods – dried fish and shrimp, dried bamboo shoots, mung beans, peanuts, woven-straw products, teak carvings, thick cotton blankets, lacquerware, tapestries, wooden furniture, jade and gems. However, it's not one of the more exciting markets in Thailand, and the Mae Sot market is much more lively. You can also buy black-market *kyat* (Burmese currency) here at favourable rates.

MYAWADI

เมียวาดี

Myawadi is a fairly typical Burmese town with a number of monasteries, schools, shops and so on. The most important temple is **Shwe Muay Wan**, a traditional bell-shaped stupa gilded with many kilos of gold and topped by more than 1600 precious and semiprecious gems. Surrounding the main stupa are 28 smaller stupas, and these in turn are encircled by 12 larger ones. Colourful shrines to Mahamuni Buddha, Shin Upagot and other Buddhist deities follow the typical Mon and central-Burmese style, with lots of mirrored mosaics.

Another noted Buddhist temple is **Myi-kyaungon**, called Wat Don Jarakhe in Thai and named for its crocodile-shaped sanctuary. A hollow stupa at Myikyaungon contains four marble Mandalay-style Buddhas around a central pillar, while niches in the surrounding wall are filled with Buddhas in other styles, including several bronze Sukhothai-style Buddhas. Myawadi's 1000-year-old earthen city walls, probably erected by the area's original Mon inhabitants, can be seen along the southern side of town.

It might sound like Myawadi isn't all that different than Thailand – temples, stupas and Buddhas – but as soon as you step off the bridge, you'll note the differences. As self-proclaimed guides and energetic *săamláw* drivers gather around lone travellers in hopes of a few extra baht you'll feel just how different life is on this side of the river. Few motorised vehicles travel the barely paved main avenue and just about every woman has something large balanced on her head. Because of long-time commercial, social and religious links between Mae Sot and Myawadi, many local residents can speak some Thai.

The **Myawaddy Riverside Club**, a casino on the river about 1km north of town, serves a mostly Thai clientele.

MYAWADI TO MAWLAMYAING (MYANMAR)

Although this route presents an exciting prospect for future overland travel, at the moment foreigners can go no further than Myawadi. Theoretically one could get a bus in Myawadi to Mawlamyaing via Kawkareik. The Myawadi–Kawkareik stretch can be dicey when fighting between Yangon and KNU troops is in progress, while the Kawkareik–Mawlamyaing stretch is generally safe although the road itself is quite rough. Each leg takes at least two hours. Alternately, one could reach Mawlamyaing by getting off the bus in Kyondo and boarding a boat along the Gyaing River. It's conceivable that this road will open to foreigners within the next couple of years.

GETTING THERE & AWAY

Săwngthăew frequently go to the border (10B), 6km west of Mae Sot: ask for Rim Moei (Edge of the Moei). The last *săwngthăew* going back to Mae Sot leaves Rim Moei at 5pm.

UM PHANG & AROUND

อุ้มผาง

Route 1090 goes south from Mae Sot to Um Phang, 150km away. This stretch of road used to be called the 'Death Highway' because of the guerrilla activity in the area that hindered highway development. Those days ended in the 1980s, but lives are still lost because of brake failure or treacherous turns on this steep, winding road through incredible mountain scenery.

Along the way – short hikes off the highway – are two waterfalls, **Nam Tok Thararak** (26km from Mae Sot) and **Nam Tok Pha Charoen** (41km). Nam Tok Thararak streams over limestone cliffs and calcified rocks with a rough texture that makes climbing the falls easy. It's been made into a park of sorts, with benches right in the stream at the base of the falls for cooling off and a couple of outhouse toilets nearby; on weekends food vendors set up here.

The eucalyptus-lined dirt road leaves the highway between the Km 24 and Km 25 markers. A side road at the Km 48 marker leads to a group of government-sponsored hill-tribe villages (Karen, Lisu, Hmong, Mien, Lahu). Just beyond Ban Rom Klao 4 – roughly midway between Mae Sot and Um Phang – is a very large Karen and Burmese refugee camp (called Um Piam) and several Hmong villages.

Sitting at the junction of Mae Nam Klong and Huay Um Phang, Um Phang is an overgrown village populated mostly by Karen. Many Karen villages in this area are very traditional, and elephants are used as much as oxen for farmwork. *Yaeng* (elephant saddles) and other tack used for elephant wrangling are a common sight on the verandas of Karen houses outside of town. You'll also see plenty of **elephants** in other Karen villages throughout the district. The name for the district comes from the Karen word *umpha*, a type of bamboo container in which travelling Karen carried their documents to show to Thai border authorities.

An interesting hike can be done that follows the footpaths northeast of the village through rice fields and along Huay Um Phang to a few smaller Karen villages. At the border where Amphoe Um Phang meets Myanmar, near the Thai-Karen villages of Ban Nong Luang and Ban Huay, is a Karen **refugee village** inhabited by more than 500 Karen who originally hailed from Htikabler village on the other side of border.

South of Um Phang, towards Sangkhlaburi in Kanchanaburi Province, **Um Phang Wildlife Sanctuary** (declared a Unesco World Heritage site in 1999) links with the Thung Yai Naresuan and Huay Kha Kaeng Reserves as well as Khlong Lan and Mae Wong National Parks to form Thailand's largest wildlife corridor and one of the largest intact natural forests in Southeast Asia.

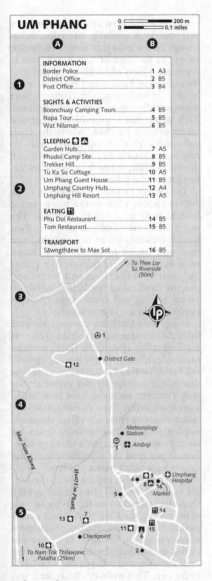

UM PHANG

0 — 200 m
0 — 0.1 miles

Ⓐ   Ⓑ

INFORMATION
Border Police...................................1 A3
District Office...................................2 B5
Post Office.......................................3 B4

SIGHTS & ACTIVITIES
Boonchuay Camping Tours.................4 B5
Napa Tour.......................................5 B5
Wat Nilaman...................................6 B5

SLEEPING 🏠 ⛺
Garden Huts....................................7 A5
Phudoi Camp Site............................8 B5
Trekker Hill....................................9 B5
Tu Ka Su Cottage...........................10 A5
Um Phang Guest House....................11 B5
Umphang Country Huts...................12 A4
Umphang Hill Resort.......................13 A5

EATING 🍴
Phu Doi Restaurant.........................14 B5
Tom Restaurant..............................15 B5

TRANSPORT
Săwngthăew to Mae Sot.................16 B5

To Thee Lor
Su Riverside
(50m)

❸

🛈 1

● District Gate

🏠 12

❹

Meteorology
● Station
✉ 🛬 Airstrip
3

🏠 9 ✚ Umphang
4 ● 🏠 16 Hospital
8 🏠
5 ● Market

🍴 14
7
13 🏠 🏠
11 🏠 🍴 15
● Checkpoint 6

10 🏠
To Nam Tok Thilawjaw; 2 ●
Palatha (25km)

Mae Nam Klong
Huay Um Phang

Information
There is no bank in Um Phang and businesses are not equipped to deal with credit cards, so bring all the cash you'll need with you. There's a **post office**, which has a couple of long-distance phones. The Um Phang Hill Resort (p413) has a slow **Internet** connection for 40B per hour that nonguests can use.

Places in town near Wat Nilawan offer the same connection for 20B per hour.

Sights & Activities
NAM TOK THILAWSU
น้ำตกทีลอซู

In Amphoe Um Phang you can arrange trips down Mae Nam Mae Klong to Nam Tok Thilawsu and Karen villages – inquire at any guesthouse. Typical three-day excursions include a raft journey along the river from Um Phang to the falls, then a two-day trek from the falls through the Karen villages of **Khotha** and **Palatha**, where a 4WD picks up trekkers and returns them to Um Phang (25km from Palatha by road).

Some people prefer to spend two days on the river; the first night at a cave or hot springs along the river before Thilawsu and a second night at the falls. On the third day you can cross the river by elephant to one of the aforementioned villages to be met by a truck and returned to Um Phang. Or you can continue south along the road to Palatha 20km further to the Hmong village of **Kangae Khi**. On the way back to Um Phang from Palatha you can stop off at **Nam Tok Thilawjaw**, which tumbles over a fern-covered cliff.

The scenery along the river is stunning, especially after the rainy season (November and December) when the 200m to 400m limestone cliffs are streaming with water and Nam Tok Thilawsu is at its best. This waterfall is Thailand's largest, measuring an estimated 400m high and up to 300m wide during the rainy season. There's a shallow cave behind the falls and several levels of pools suitable for swimming. Thais consider Nam Tok Thilawsu to be the most beautiful waterfall in the country; it's now part of Um Phang Wildlife Sanctuary.

You can **camp** at the Um Phang Wildlife Sanctuary headquarters near the falls any time of year. Between December and May there are also rooms available for 100B per person, but you must bring your own food. The 1.5km trail between the Sanctuary headquarters and the falls has been transformed into a self-guided nature tour with the addition of well-conceived educational plaques. Surrounding the falls on both sides of the river are Thailand's thickest stands of natural forest, and the hiking in the vicinity of Nam Tok Thilawsu can be superb. The forest here is said to contain more than

NORTHERN THAILAND

1300 varieties of palm; giant bamboo and strangler figs are commonplace, and the orchid tree *(Bauhinia variegata)* can even be seen along the road to Palatha.

Between 1 December and 1 June you can also drive to the falls over a rough 47km road from Um Phang, suitable for 4WD or a skilled dirt-bike rider only. Or follow the main paved road south of Um Phang to Km 19; the walk to the falls is a stiff four hours from here via **Mo Phado** village. A *săwngthăew* goes to the Km 19 marker from Um Phang once daily; ask for *kii-loh sìp kâo* and expect to pay 15B to 20B per person.

RAFTING

Um Phang Khi is a 'new' area for rafting, northeast of Um Phang. Officially there are 47 (some rafting companies claim 67) sets of rapids rated at class III and class IV during the height of the rainy season. The rafting season for Um Phang Khi is short – August to October only – as other times of year the water level isn't high enough. Rafting trips arranged in Um Phang typically cost 2500B for a two-night, three-day programme, or 3000B if booked in Mae Sot. See Tours, opposite for more information.

LETONGKHU TO SANGKHLABURI
เลตองคุ/อำเภอสังขละบุรี

From Ban Mae Khlong Mai, just a few kilometres north of Um Phang via the highway to Mae Sot, a graded dirt road (Rte 1167) heads southwest along the border to **Beung Kleung** (sometimes spelt Peung Kleung), a Karen, Burmese, Indo-Burmese, Talaku and Thai trading village where buffalo carts are more common than motorcycles. The picturesque setting among spiky peaks and cliffs is worth the trip even if you go no further. Impressive **Nam Tok Ekaratcha** is an hour's walk away. *Săwngthăew* from Um Phang usually make a trip to Beung Kleung once a day, and it's possible to stay at the village clinic or in a private home for a donation of 100B per person. On the way you can stop off at the small, traditional Karen village of **Ban Thiphochi**.

Four hours' walk from here along a rough track (passable by 4WD in the dry season), near the Myanmar border on the banks of Mae Nam Suriya next to Sam Rom mountain, is the culturally singular, 109-house village of **Letongkhu** (Leh Tawng Khu).

According to what little anthropological information is available, the villagers, although for the most part Karen in language, belong to the Lagu or Talaku sect, said to represent a form of Buddhism mixed with shamanism and animism. Letongkhu is one of only six such villages in Thailand; there are reportedly around 30 more in Myanmar. Each village has a spiritual and temporal leader called a *pu chaik* (whom the Thais call *reusĭi* – 'rishi' or 'sage') who wears his hair long – usually tied in a topknot – and dresses in white, yellow or brown robes, depending on the subsect.

The current *pu chaik* at Letongkhu is the 10th in a line of 'white-thread' priests dating back to their residence in Myanmar. The sage's many male disciples also wear their hair in topknots (often tied in cloth) and may wear similar robes. All *reusĭi* abstain from alcohol and are celibate. The priests live apart from the village in a temple and practise traditional medicine based on herbal healing and ritual magic. Antique elephant tusks are kept as talismans.

Evangelistic Christian missionaries have infiltrated the area and have tried to convert the Talaku, thus making the Talaku sensitive to outside visitation. Before heading out here call **Ban Lae Tongku** (☎ 0 5556 1008) to make sure this unique community will welcome your visit. Travellers are said to have been turned away upon arrival. If you do visit Letongkhu, take care not to enter any village structures without permission or invitation. Likewise, do not take photographs without permission. If you treat the villagers with respect then you shouldn't have a problem.

You should also inquire about the border status at the TAT office in Tak (p402). Opposite Letongkhu on the Myanmar side of the border, the KNU has set up its latest tactical headquarters. Yangon government offensives against the KNU can break out in this area during the dry months of the year, but when this is happening or is likely to happen, Thai military checkpoints will turn all trekkers back.

Sangkhlaburi (p225) is 90km or a four- to five-day trek from Beung Kleung. On the way (11km from Beung Kleung), about 250m off the road, is the extensive cave system of **Tham Takube**. From Ban Mae Chan, 35km along the same route, there's a dirt road branching out across the border to a

KNU-controlled village. The route to Sangkhlaburi has several branches; the main route crosses over the border into Myanmar for some distance before crossing back into Thailand. There has been discussion of cutting a newer, more direct road between Um Phang and Sangkhlaburi.

Because of the overall sensitive nature of this border area, and the very real potential for becoming lost, ill or injured, a guide is highly recommended for any sojourn south of Um Phang. You may be able to arrange a guide for this route in either Um Phang or Beung Kleung. Umphang Hill Resort in Um Phang (right) can also arrange a trek but you need to give a couple of weeks' notice. The best time of year to do the trek is October to January.

Tours

Several of the guesthouses in Um Phang can arrange trekking and rafting trips in the area. The typical three-night, four-day trip costs about 4500B per person (four or more people). The price includes rafting, an elephant ride, food and a guide service.

Longer treks of up to 12 days may also be possible, and there are day trips to Nam Tok Thilawsu as well. It is worth checking to see what kind of rafts are used; most places have switched to rubber as bamboo rafts can break up in the rough rapids. Choose rubber, unless you are really looking for adventure – such as walking to your camp site rather than rafting there.

Within Um Phang, **Tu Ka Su Cottage** (p414) and **Umphang Hill Resort** (right) have the best equipment and trip designs. Both offer basic three- to six-day rafting and hiking trips to Nam Tok Thilawsu and beyond, including one itinerary that takes rafters through 11 different sets of rapids on Mae Nam Mae Klong. Longer or shorter trips may also be arranged and elephant riding instead of walking is always an option.

Boonchuay Camping Tours (☎ 0 5556 1020; 360 Mu 1) Focus is camping and communing with nature.

Napa Tour (☎ 0 5556 1287; napatour_2@yahoo.com; 115 Mu 1) The most accommodating to vegetarian diets. Good English is spoken and staff members knowledgeable and environmentally conscious.

Umphang Hill Resort (right) Associated with Max One Tour in Mae Sot (p406). It's not necessarily the best, but is the longest-running company in Um Phang. Its emphasis is on leading big groups of foreigners who book ahead of time.

Sleeping

Accommodation in Um Phang is plentiful, but since the majority of visitors to the area are Thai, room rates tend to be a little higher than normal and all of the beds are rock-hard. Most places cater to large groups so their rooms are designed for four or more people. Singles or couples may be able to negotiate lower rates, especially in the wet season.

BUDGET

Phudoi Camp Site (☎ 0 5556 1049, in Bangkok ☎ 0 1886 8783; www.phudoi.com; tent sites 100B, r 400B) Primarily catering to its prebooked tour clients, Phudoi has bungalows set on a well-landscaped hillside near the village centre. The new log cabin–style bungalows are spacious and have verandas. There's also a tent camping area and a restaurant.

Garden Huts (Boonyaporn Guest House; ☎ 0 5556 1093, in Bangkok ☎ 0 1642 7594; www.boonyaporn.com; 8/1 Mu 6; r 300-700B) Operated by a sweet older couple, this collection of bungalows of varying degrees of comfort and size fronts the river. It features pleasant sitting areas and a well-cared-for garden. The strong, Thai-grown coffee is a perky bonus.

Trekker Hill (☎ 0 5556 1090; r 250B) Catering to Danish tour groups, this rustic collection of huts on a steep hillside has views of the valley and Um Phang. The restaurant serves three meals a day and has satellite TV.

Umphang Hill Resort (☎ 0 5556 1063; Mae Sot ☎ 0 5553 1409; www.umphanghill.com; per person 100-200B, bungalows 500-2000B; 🐾) Don't bother staying here unless you're with a large group or are part of one of their tours. The oversize bungalows are designed to sleep six to 20 people and are in grave need of TLC. Bathrooms are infested with mosquitoes, TVs don't work and rooms are not well cleaned between groups, especially in the low season. However, it does run the most tours and have the largest number of English-speaking guides in town. It's across Huay Um Phang to the west of the village centre.

Um Phang Guest House (☎ 0 5556 1073; r 200B, cottages 300B) Near Wat Nilawan, this place is owned by the local *kamnan* (precinct officer). It has motel-like rooms that sleep up to three, and nicer wood-and-brick cottages with hot water that sleep up to four. There's a large outdoor restaurant in an open area near the cottages.

MIDRANGE & TOP END

Midrange options in Um Phang don't have all the bells and whistles of comparably priced places in other areas. They are notably more comfortable and well kept than their cheaper neighbours, though, and take good advantage of the natural scenery in Um Phang.

Tu Ka Su Cottage (Kin Ka Tu; ☎ 0 5556 1295, 0 1825 8238; r 600-1200B, tent sites 50B) West of Huay Um Phang, this is the cleanest and best-run accommodation in Um Phang. The attractive collection of brick-and-stone, multiroom cottages is surrounded by flower and exotic-fruit gardens. The largest bungalows sleep 10, but it's possible to rent half of one of the smaller two-room cottages for between 600B and 750B. There is also a pleasant lawn for camping and the management will even rent you a tent for 150B. All of the bathrooms, including those built for campers, have hot-water showers with an outdoor feel. Tu Ka Su also runs good local trekking-rafting trips, but it only has one English-speaking guide.

Umphang Country Huts (☎ 0 5556 1079; r 400-700B) Off the highway 1.5km before Um Phang, these huts enjoy a nice hilly setting. Rooms in a wood-and-thatch, two-storey building facing Huay Mae Klong share a common veranda. A downstairs room has a bathroom, while a larger upstairs room sleeps four. There are larger, more atmospheric rooms in another two-storey building with private verandas.

Thee Lor Su Riverside (☎ 0 5556 1010; bungalows 600-1200B) The first place you come to as you enter Um Phang coming from Mae Sot. It's about 300m off the road, with small wooden A-frame bungalows facing a stream. It's a bit overpriced even for this market, but a decent option if everything else is full.

Eating

Um Phang has three or four simple noodle and rice shops, plus a morning market and a small sundries shop.

Phu Doi Restaurant (☎ 0 5556 1159; dishes 20-40B; ☺ 8am-10pm) On the main street into town, this has very good food, especially the phá-naeng (mild curry) dishes, but there are also rice dishes, noodles, tôm yam (hot and sour Thai soup) and cold beer. Phu Doi has a bilingual menu and is often the only place open past 9pm.

There is a short string of noodle shops along the main road. **Tom Restaurant** (dishes 20-40B; ☺ 6am-8pm) also does rice dishes.

Getting There & Away

There are sǎwngthǎew to Um Phang from Mae Sot (100B, five hours, 165km) departing several times a day between 7am and 3pm. Sǎwngthǎew usually stop for lunch at windy **Ban Rom Klao 4** on the way.

If you decide to try to ride a motorcycle from Mae Sot, be sure it's one with a strong engine as the road has lots of fairly steep grades. Total drive time is around four hours. The only petrol pump along the way is in Ban Rom Klao 4, 80km from Mae Sot, so you may want to carry 3L or 4L of extra fuel.

MAE SOT TO MAE SARIANG
แม่สอด/แม่สะเรียง

Route 105 runs north along the Myanmar border from Mae Sot all the way to Mae Sariang (226km) in Mae Hong Son Province. The windy, paved road passes through the small communities of **Mae Ramat**, **Mae Sarit**, **Ban Tha Song Yang** and **Ban Sop Ngao** (Mae Ngao). The thick forest in these parts still has a few stands of teak and the Karen villages continue to use the occasional work elephant. Be prepared to show your passport to Thai border patrol often.

If you have your own transport, be sure to stop and check out these friendly, low-key, rarely visited communities. Don't miss **Wat Don Kaew** in Mae Ramat. It's behind the district office and houses a large Mandalay-style marble Buddha. Other attractions on the way to Mae Sariang include **Nam Tok Mae Kasa**, between the Km 13 and Km 14 markers, and extensive limestone caverns at **Tham Mae Usu**, at Km 94 near Ban Tha Song Yang. From the highway it's a 2km walk to Tham Mae Usu; note that in the rainy season, when the river running through the cave seals off the mouth, it's closed.

Instead of doing the Myanmar border run in one go, some people opt to spend the night in Mae Sarit (118km from Mae Sot), then head to Ban Tha Song Yang for an early breakfast in the market before hopping a morning sǎwngthǎew from Ban Tha Song Yang to Mae Sariang. Hourly sǎwngthǎew to Mae Sarit (60B, four hours) leave from Mae Sot between 6am and noon (the same *sǎwngthǎew* continue on to Mae Sariang). Frequent *sǎwngthǎew* connect Mae Sarit to Ban Tha Song Yang (20B, 30 minutes) where morning and midday *sǎwngthǎew* head to Mae Sariang (55B, three hours). If you miss the morning *sǎwngthǎew* from Mae Sarit to Mae Sariang, you can usually arrange to charter a truck for 180B to 220B.

If you decide not to stay overnight in Mae Sarit, just stay on the *sǎwngthǎew* and eventually you'll land in Mae Sariang (160B, 6½ hours) with an exhausted bum. These orange *sǎwngthǎew* leave from Mae Sot's dusty lot north of the police station.

Sleeping & Eating

Mae Salid Guest House (Mae Sarit; s/d 80/100B) is related to Umphang Hill Resort and offers six very basic rooms with private toilet and shared shower. It's east of the main intersection in Mae Sarit.

There is a basic **guesthouse** (s/d 80/100B) in Ban Tha Song Yang near the *sǎwngthǎew* stop on Rte 105. Just follow the signs. If it doesn't suit your fancy, you might be able to arrange a place to stay by inquiring at the main market.

Krua Ban Tai (☎ 0 1887 1102; Th Si Wattana, Ban Tha Sang Yang; dishes 20-50B; ⏱ 8am-9pm) This is a two-storey wooden restaurant in the centre of Ban Tha Song Yang, around the corner from the main market. The creative menu includes good *yam wún sên* (spicy noodle salad) made with freshwater shrimp, and *khâo phàt phánaeng* (curried fried rice).

MAE HONG SON PROVINCE

Thailand's most northwestern province is a crossroads for ethnic minorities (mostly Karen, with some Hmong, Lisu and Lahu), Shan (known locally as Thai Yai) and Burmese immigrants. Reportedly 75% of the province consists of mountains and forest.

As the province is so far from the influence of sea winds and is thickly forested and mountainous, the temperature seldom rises above 40°C, while in January the temperature can drop to 2°C. The air is often misty with ground fog in the winter and smoke from slash-and-burn agriculture in the hot season.

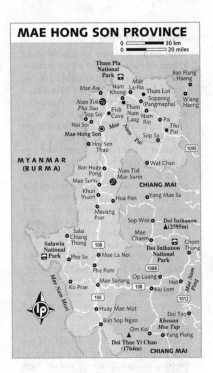

Mae Hong Son Province has undergone a tourist miniboom over the past decade, with many resorts opening in the area around the capital. However, few visitors seem to leave the beaten Mae Hong Son–Soppong–Pai track.

MAE SARIANG

แม่สะเรียง

pop 7800

Many of the hill-tribe settlements in Mae Hong Son Province are concentrated in the districts and towns of Khun Yuam, Mae La Noi and Mae Sariang, which are good departure points for treks to Hmong, Karen and Shan villages. Of these three small towns, Mae Sariang is the largest and offers the most facilities for use as a base camp.

Although there is not much to see in Mae Sariang, it's a pleasant riverside town with a small travel scene. Two Burmese-Shan temples, **Wat Jong Sung** (Uthayarom) and **Wat Si Bunruang**, just off Mae Sariang's main street (not far from the Mae Sariang bus station), are definitely worth a visit if you have time. Built in 1896, Wat Jong Sung is

OPIUM & TREKKING

Some guides are very strict now about forbidding the smoking of opium on treks. This seems to be a good idea, since one problem trekking companies have had in the past is dealing with opium-addicted guides! Volunteers who work in tribal areas also say opium smoking sets a bad example for young people in the villages.

Opium is traditionally a condoned vice of the elderly, yet an increasing number of young people in the villages are now taking opium, heroin and amphetamines. This is possibly due in part to the influence of young trekkers who may smoke once and a few weeks later be hundreds of kilometres away while the villagers continue to face the temptation every day.

Addiction has negative effects for the village as well as the individual's health, including a reduced male labour force and corresponding increase in women's workloads (most addicts are men) and reduced overall agricultural production. Also, an increase in the number of villagers injecting heroin (needles are often shared) has led to skyrocketing rates of HIV infection in hill-tribe villages. Given the already high incidence of HIV infection among northern-Thai prostitutes, some welfare groups say that entire tribal communities will be wiped out unless the rate of infection can be stopped.

the more interesting of the two temples and has slender, Shan-style stupa and wooden monastic buildings.

Information

Mae Sariang has a couple of banks with ATMs and an **immigration office** (☎ 0 5368 1339) that will extend your visa by a couple days if you're in a pinch and on your way to the border.

Activities

TREKKING

Little-known Mae Sariang offers amazing trekking, both scenic and cultural. Because the area around Mae Sariang is far from the popular jumping-off grounds of Mae Hong Son, Chiang Mai or Chiang Rai, you're less likely to see other trekking groups and

the communities you visit are going to be less 'prepared' for you. There is one reputable trekking guide who is from one of the surrounding hill tribes and knows the mountains like a guide should. He calls himself Salawin Tours and can be contacted through any guesthouse, but likes to hang out in the dining area of the Riverside Guest House.

Sleeping

The cheapest rooms in Mae Sariang share a bathroom.

BUDGET

North West Guest House (☎ 0 5368 1956; fax 0 5368 1353; Th Laeng Phanit; s 120B, d 150-200B) The rooms in this large wooden house are simple (think mattress on the floor) but get natural light and are good-sized. Shared hot-water showers are spotless and brand new. The restaurant downstairs serves up excellent meals (often coming from the kitchen at the River House Hotel). Staff members here are chatty, curious and friendly. Rooms vary in size and there are only eight of them, so get here early.

Riverside Guest House (☎ 0 5368 1188; Th Laeng Phanit; s/d from 100/180B; 🔀) This ever-changing guesthouse keeps growing and improving. As the owner keeps adding private bathrooms, TVs and other furniture, the rooms are shrinking and becoming cluttered. The shared bathrooms need a face-lift and a deep de-mosquito treatment. But the views are stunning and the staff, well informed and helpful. There is a mediocre restaurant and a fabulous rooftop patio. The local trekking guide, Salawin Tours, hangs out here.

Kamolsorn Hotel (☎ 0 5368 1204; Th Mae Sariang; r from 350B; 🔀) This multistorey hotel has ordinary but spacious rooms. Limited English is spoken, but the place is friendly, tidy and a fair deal.

Mitaree Hotel (☎ 0 5368 1110; Th Mae Sariang; s/d from 120/200B; 🔀) Mitaree is Mae Sariang's oldest hostelry. It has rooms in the old wooden wing (called the Mitaree Guest House) or rooms with hot-water shower in the new wing. The older wing is popular with Thai truckers.

Mitaree Hotel (New Mitaree; ☎ 0 5368 1109; 24 Th Wiang Mai; s/d from 120/150B, cottages 600-1200B; 🔀) Near the post office, this is another Mitaree Hotel run by the same family. The newer,

MAE SARIANG

INFORMATION
Krung Thai Bank (ATM)............1	B2
Police.....................................2	B2
Post Office.............................3	C2

SIGHTS & ACTIVITIES
Salawin Tours....................(see 10)	

SLEEPING
Kamolsorn Hotel.....................4	B2
Mitaree Hotel..........................5	B2
Mitaree Hotel (New Mitaree)......6	D2
North West Guest House...........7	B1
River House Hotel....................8	B1
River House Resort..................9	B1
Riverside Guest House.............10	B1
See View Guest House.............11	A3

EATING
Inthira Restaurant..................12	B2
Kai Yang Rai Khwan................13	A2
Renu Restaurant....................14	B2
River House Hotel Restaurant..(see 8)	

TRANSPORT
Bus Station..........................15	B1

wooden 'resort' cottages at the back have sitting areas in front, air-con and TV.

See View Guest House (☎ 0 5368 1556; r 200-400B; bungalows 300B) Across the river, the See View offers spacious, very worn, motel-like rooms and overpriced, rustic bungalows. Its open-air Old House restaurant sometimes features live Thai country music during high season – a plus or minus depending on your sleeping schedule. Its tours have disappointed several readers.

MIDRANGE & TOP END

River House Hotel (☎ 0 5362 1201; riverhouse@hotmail .com; 77 Th Laeng Phanit; r from 500B; ❄) The combo of nostalgia-inducing teak and contemporary décor makes this riverside hotel the best spot for design-conscious travellers. Riverview rooms with air-con have private verandas, but are a bit tight on space. Some rooms lack proper ventilation, but all rooms are a big step up from the competition.

River House Resort (☎ 0 5368 3066; www.river househotels.com; Th Laeng Phanit; s/d/ste 1250/1400/ 2000B; ❄) Painted Mediterranean pink, this new hotel has a hint of colonial charm, but authenticity is lacking in the details. The rooms are spacious and tastefully decorated and those on the first floor open onto the river. The place lacks resort facilities such as a pool, but it's still the nicest place in town.

Eating

River House Hotel (☎ 0 5362 1201; riverhouse@hotmail .com; 77 Th Laeng Phanit; dishes 40-160B) For a romantic meal overlooking the wandering river, this is the place. It's rustic with antiqued tables and no white linens, but is pleasantly lit and there is plenty of room between the tables. The food is tasty, especially anything including fresh river fish.

Inthira Restaurant (☎ 0 4368 1529; Th Wiang Mai; dishes 40-80B; ✹ 10am-10pm) This is the town's most popular restaurant for a good reason. Its casual setting with some creative décor is a mere side note to the extensive and tasty menu. Several of the standard Thai and Chinese dishes are available in veggie versions.

Renu Restaurant (☎ 0 5368 1171; Th Wiang Mai; dishes 30-70B; ✹ 10am-11pm) Decorated with pics

NORTHERN THAILAND

of King Bhumibol playing saxophone, this local spot has a more basic menu than the Inthira. The veggie options are limited to fried rice, but adventurous eaters might enjoy the 'nut-hatch curry'.

Kai Yang Rai Khwan (dishes 10-50B; ☼ 10am-5pm) A great spot for Isan-style grilled chicken, sticky rice and *sôm-tam*, at the foot of the bridge crossing towards See View Guest House.

Riverside Guest House (☎ 0 5368 1188; Th Laeng Phanit) Serves relatively inexpensive Thai and *faràng* dishes in pleasant dining areas overlooking the river.

Getting There & Around

Ordinary buses to Mae Sariang leave Chiang Mai's Arcade terminal at 8am, 1.30pm, 3pm and 8pm (70B, four hours). First-class air-con buses depart at 6.30am, 11am and 9pm (140B, four hours). Buses also regularly connect Mae Sariang to Khun Yuam to Mae Hong Song (ordinary/air-con 70/135B, four hours); with a stop midway in Khun Yuam (50B, two hours).

There's one bus daily between Mae Sot and Mae Sariang (160B, six hours). *Sǎwngthǎew* leave for Mae Sot between 6.30am and noon (160B, six hours) but only leave when full. See the Mae Sot to Mae Sariang section (p414) for more details about the *sǎwngthǎew* trip.

Destinations anywhere in town are 10B by motorcycle taxi.

AROUND MAE SARIANG

One trekking option out of Mae Sariang is a boat trip on Mae Nam Salawin, with stops in Karen villages and Mae Sam Laep. From Mae Sam Laep the boat may head upriver to **Salawin National Park**, a 722-sq-km protected area established in 1994. It takes about half an hour to reach the park headquarters from Mae Sam Laep. There are no lodgings, but in the dry season you can pitch a tent for free on a white-sand beach, called Hat Thaen Kaew, along the river in front of the park offices. There are good views of the river and Myanmar from the park headquarters. The park is heavily forested in teak, Asian redwood and cherrywood.

About 36km southeast of Mae Sariang at Ban Mae Waen is **Pan House** (r per person 50B), where a guide named T Weerapan (Mr Pan) leads local treks. Ban Mae Waen itself is a mixed Thai/Karen village in the middle of a Karen district. To get there, take a Chiang Mai–bound bus east on Rte 108 and get out at the Km 68 marker. Ban Mae Waen is a 5km walk south along a mountain ridge and (during the rainy season) across a couple of streams. If you're driving, 4WD is necessary if the road is wet.

Khun Yuam
ขุนยวม

About half way between Mae Sariang and Mae Hong Son, where all northbound buses make their halfway stop, is the quiet mountain town of Khun Yuam. This little-visited town is a nice break from more 'experienced' destinations nearby. There are a couple of places to stay and a few notable sights.

About 5km to the west of Khun Yuam, the atmospheric **Wat To Phae** sits alongside a country stream and boasts a Mon-style stupa, antique wooden monks' residences and an immaculate Burmese-style *wíhǎan*. Inside the latter, take a look at the large, 150-year-old Burmese *kalaga* (embroidered and sequined tapestry) that's kept behind curtains to one side of the main altar. The tapestry depicts a scene from the *Vessantara Jataka* and local devotees believe one accrues merit simply by viewing it.

On the slopes of Doi Mae U Khaw are Ban Mae U Khaw (25km from Khun Yuam via upgraded Rte 1263), a Hmong village, and the 250m Nam Tok Mae Surin (50km northeast of Khun Yuam), reportedly Thailand's highest cataract. The area blooms with scenic *bua thawng* ('golden lotus', more like a sunflower than a lotus) during November; this is also the best time to view the waterfall at its best.

SLEEPING & EATING

Ban Farang (☎ 0 5362 2056/85; 499 Th Ratburana; dm/r 50/200B, bungalows 250-350B) This clean and friendly place off the main road towards the north end of town (look for the signs near the bus stop) has dorm beds, rooms in a row house with private facilities and newer bungalows. It's spiffier than the hotel in town.

Mit Khun Yuam Hotel (☎ 0 5369 1057; 61 Th Chiang Mai-Mae Hong Son; s/d from 150B, tr from 300B; 🚗) On the main road through the town centre, this old wooden hotel is quite adequate for a short stay.

Rustic **accommodation** is available at the Hmong village of Mae U Khaw, between Khun Yuam and Nam Tok Mae Surin.

In Khun Yuam you'll find a collection of modest **rice and noodle shops** along the east side, or Rte 108, towards the southern end of town. Most of these close by 5pm or 6pm. Ban Farang and Mit Khun Yuam Hotel can also arrange meals.

MAE HONG SON
แม่ฮ่องสอน
pop 8300

Surrounded by mountains and punctuated by small but picturesque Nong Jong Kham (Jong Kham Lake), this provincial capital is still relatively peaceful despite the intrusion of daily flights from Chiang Mai. Mae Hong Son has become part of northern Thailand's standard tourist circuit, with plenty of guesthouses, hotels and resorts in the area, many of them catering to Thais. However, much of the capital's prosperity is due to its supply of rice and consumer goods to the drug lords across the border. The town's population is predominantly Shan. Several Karen and Shan villages in the vicinity can be visited as day trips, and further afield are Lisu, Lahu and Musoe villages.

Mae Hong Son is best visited between November and March when the town is at its most beautiful. During the rainy season (June to October) travel in the province can be difficult because there are few paved

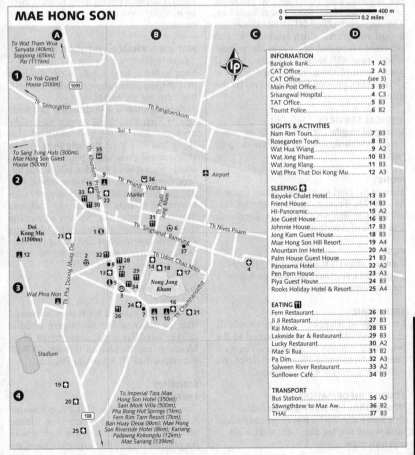

MAE HONG SON

0 — 400 m
0 — 0.2 miles

INFORMATION
Bangkok Bank..........................1 A2
CAT Office...............................2 A3
CAT Office...........................(see 3)
Main Post Office.....................3 B3
Srisangwal Hospital.................4 C3
TAT Office...............................5 B3
Tourist Police.........................6 B2

SIGHTS & ACTIVITIES
Nam Rim Tours.......................7 B3
Rosegarden Tours....................8 B3
Wat Hua Wiang.......................9 A2
Wat Jong Kham.....................10 B3
Wat Jong Klang.....................11 B3
Wat Phra That Doi Kong Mu..12 A3

SLEEPING
Baiyoke Chalet Hotel.............13 B3
Friend House........................14 B3
HI-Panoramic........................15 A2
Joe Guest House....................16 B3
Johnnie House......................17 B3
Jong Kam Guest House...........18 B3
Mae Hong Son Hill Resort.....19 A4
Mountain Inn Hotel...............20 A4
Palm House Guest House........21 B3
Panorama Hotel....................22 A2
Pen Porn House.....................23 A3
Piya Guest House...................24 B3
Rooks Holiday Hotel & Resort..25 A4

EATING
Fern Restaurant.....................26 B3
Ji Ji Restaurant......................27 B3
Kai Mook..............................28 B3
Lakeside Bar & Restaurant......29 B3
Lucky Restaurant...................30 A2
Mae Si Bua...........................31 B2
Pa Dim.................................32 A3
Salween River Restaurant.......33 A2
Sunflower Café......................34 B3

TRANSPORT
Bus Station...........................35 A2
Săwngthăew to Mae Aw.........36 B2
THAI....................................37 B3

To Wat Tham Wua Sunyata (40km); Soppong (65km); Pai (111km)

To Yok Guest House (200m)
1095
Th Sirimongkhon
Th Pangloenikom
Soi 1
Th Phanit
Wattana Market
Th Khunlum Praphat
Th Pradit Jong Kham
Airport
To Sang Tong Huts (300m); Mae Hong Son Guest House (500m)
Th Singhanat Bamrung
Th Nives Pisarn
Doi Kong Mu ▲(1500m)
Th Pha Doong Muay Do
Th Udon Chao Nites
Nong Jong Kham
Th Chamnansathit
Wat Phra Non
Nong Jong Kham
Stadium

To Imperial Tara Mae Hong Son Hotel (350m); Sam Mork Villa (500m); Pha Bong Hot Springs (1km); Fern Rim Tam Resort (7km); Ban Huay Deua (8km); Mae Hong Son Riverside Hotel (8km); Kariang Padawng Kekongdu (12km); Mae Sariang (139km)
108

NORTHERN THAILAND

roads. During the hot season, the Mae Pai valley fills with smoke from slash-and-burn agriculture. The only problem with going in the cool season is that the nights are downright cold – you'll need at least one thick sweater and a good pair of socks for mornings and evenings and a sleeping bag or several blankets.

Information

EMERGENCY

Tourist Police (☎ 0 5361 1812; Th Singhanat Bamrung; 🕙 8.30am-4.30pm) Report mishaps or file complaints about guesthouses and trek operators here.

INTERNET ACCESS

Where there are travellers, there's Internet. But like many places around Thailand, many of Mae Hong Son's places don't last. The non–post office **CAT** (Th Udom Chow) has T-card computers which work out to 10B per hour. Mum-and-pop places charge anywhere from 40B to 60B per hour. Several places around town, including Sunflower Café (p424), provide Internet access by the minute.

MEDICAL SERVICES

Srisangwal Hospital (☎ 0 5361 1378; Th Singhanat Bamrung) A full-service facility that includes an emergency room.

MONEY

Most of the banks on Th Khunlum Praphat have ATMs. Foreign-exchange services are available at Bangkok Bank, Kasikornbank and Bank of Ayudhya.

POST

Main post office (Th Khunlum Praphat; 🕙 8.30am-4.30pm Mon-Fri, closed holidays) Towards the southern end of Th Khunlum Praphat.

TELEPHONE

International telephone service is available at the CAT office, which is attached to the post office – hours are the same. There's a Lenso International Phonecard telephone outside the entrance to the post office.

TOURIST INFORMATION

TAT office (☎ 0 5362 3016; Th Khumlum Praphat; 🕙 8.30am-4.30pm Mon-Fri) In an old two-storey wooden building opposite the post office. Tourist brochures and maps can be picked up here.

Sights

WAT PHRA THAT DOI KONG MU

วัดพระธาตุดอยกองมู

Climb the hill west of town, Doi Kong Mu (1500m), to visit this Shan-built wat, also known as Wat Phai Doi. The view of the sea of fog that collects in the valley each morning is impressive; at other times of the day you get a view of the town. Two Shan stupas, erected in 1860 and 1874, enshrine the ashes of monks from Myanmar's Shan State. Around the back of the wat you can see a tall, slender, standing Buddha and catch views west of the ridge.

A good time to visit the wat is at the end of the annual rains retreat, usually late October depending on the lunar calendar, when it fills with townspeople making merit by bringing food to feed a large number of monks.

WAT JONG KHAM & WAT JONG KLANG

วัดจองคำ/วัดจองกลาง

Next to Nong Jong Kham in the southern part of town are a couple of mildly interesting Burmese-style wats.

Wat Jong Kham was built nearly 200 years ago by Thai Yai (Shan) people, who make up about half of the population of Mae Hong Son Province. **Wat Jong Klang** houses 100-year-old glass *jataka* paintings and has small rooms full of wooden reliefs and figures depicting the *Vessantara Jataka* (the popular *jataka* in which the Bodhisattva develops the Perfection of Giving) – all very Burmese in style. The *wíhǎan* containing these is open 8am to 6pm daily. Wat Jong Klang has several areas that women are forbidden to enter – not unusual for Burmese-Shan Buddhist temples.

WAT HUA WIANG

วัดหัวเวียง

Although its wooden *bòt* is in an advanced state of decay, a famous bronze Buddha in the Mandalay style, called Chao Phlalakhaeng, can be seen in this **wat** (Th Phanit Wattana), east of Th Khunlum Praphat.

Activities

TREKKING

The area around Mae Hong Son towards Soppong is also used by tours from Chiang Mai, which means that in the high season it's possible to see other groups of travellers while trekking through the seemingly pristine jungle. Trekking trips can be arranged at several guesthouses and travel agencies. Rates for most treks are about 600B to 700B per person per day (if there are four or more people), with three to five days the normal duration. Popular routes include the Mae Pai Valley, Amphoe Khun Yuam and north of Soppong. A straightforward six-day trek from east of Mae Hong Son to near Soppong

costs 600B per person per day. As with trekking elsewhere in the north, be sure to clarify when a trek starts and stops or you may not get your money's worth. Nearby Karen villages can be visited without a guide by walking two hours outside of town – several guesthouses in town can provide a map.

The guides at the Sunflower Café (p424) have received excellent reviews. Other recommendations for tours:

'LONG-NECKED' PADAUNG VILLAGES

Some come to Mae Hong Son with the intent to visit one of the nearby Padaung refugee villages where 'long-neck' women live. The women wear a continuous coil around their necks, and sometimes their limbs, that can weigh up to 22kg (but 5kg is most common) and stand as tall as 30cm. The neck coils depress the collarbone and rib cage, which makes their necks look unnaturally stretched. A common myth claims if the coils are removed, the women's necks will fall over from atrophy and the women will suffocate. The women attach and remove the coils at will with no such problems. In fact, there is no evidence that this deformation impairs their health at all.

Nobody knows for sure how the coil custom got started. One theory is that it was meant to make the women unattractive to men from other tribes. Another story says it was so tigers wouldn't carry the women off by their throats. The Padaung claim their ancestors were the offspring of a liaison between the wind and a beautiful female dragon, and that the coil-wearing custom pays tribute to their dragon progenitor. This custom was dying out, but money from tourism has reinvigorated it.

The business of the long-neck as a tourist attraction is largely controlled by the Karenni National Progressive Party (KNPP), a Kayah (Karenni) insurgent group whose reported objective is to establish an independent Kayah state in eastern Myanmar. The Padaung are an ethnolinguistic subgroup of the Kayah.

The biggest Padaung village is Nai Soi (also known as Nupa Ah), 35km northwest of Mae Hong Son. It receives an average of 1200 tourists annually and collects an entry fee (250B per person) the bulk of which is believed to go to the KNPP. The 'long-neck' women receive a small portion of the money collected, but make most of their money selling handicrafts (some say as much as 3000B per month). Typically, a visit consists of extended photography sessions of the coil-adorned women posing, or standing with visitors. The women tell reporters they aren't bothered by the photography, which they consider to be part of their livelihood. As Nai Soi's Ma Nang was quoted in the *Bangkok Post*, 'We had nothing in Myanmar. I had to work relentlessly in the rice fields. We miss our homes, but we don't want to go back.' These people are usually in Thailand by choice, having fled a potentially worse fate in Myanmar amid ethnic war.

Opinions are sharply divided as to the ethics of 'consuming' the Padaung as a tourist attraction. On the surface, viewing the Padaung seems like crass exploitation, but those who have taken the time to learn more about their lives continue to point out that this gives them an opportunity to make a living under current social conditions in Myanmar and Thailand. Thai authorities view Nai Soi as a self-sustaining refugee camp. For visitors the current set-up beats paying a trek operator for the privilege of photographing tribal people when the latter receive nothing.

If you want to see any of the Padaung settlements, any travel agency in Mae Hong Son can arrange a tour for about 700B. You can choose among Hoy Sen Thao (11km southwest of Mae Hong Son, 20 minutes by boat from the nearby Ban Huay Deua landing), Nai Soi (35km northwest) and Huay Ma Khen Som (about 7km before Mae Aw). A couple of hundred metres beyond Nai Soi is a large Kayah refugee settlement, also controlled by the KNPP.

At the entrance to the village your name, passport number and country of residence will be noted on a payment receipt issued by the 'Karenni Culture Department'.

Nam Rim Tours (☎ 0 5361 3925; Th Khunlum Praphat) Funny, professional and knowledgeable. Popular with French travellers but does not speak French.

Rosegarden Tours (☎ 0 5361 1577; www.rosegarden -tours.com; 86/4 Th Khunlum Praphut) English- and French-speaking guides.

RAFTING

Raft trips on the nearby Mae Pai are gaining popularity, and the same guesthouses and trekking agencies that organise treks from Mae Hong Son can arrange the river trips. The most common type of trip sets off from Tha Mae Pai (Pai River Pier) in **Ban Huay Deua**, 8km southwest of Mae Hong Son, for a day-long upriver journey of 5km. From the same pier, down-river trips to the 'long-neck' village of **Kariang Padawng Kekongdu** (Hoy Sen Thao) on the Thailand–Myanmar border are also possible.

Another popular rafting route runs between **Sop Soi** (10km northwest of town) and the village of **Soppong** to the west (not to be confused with the larger Shan trading village of the same name to the east). These day trips typically cost 600B to 800B for six people if arranged in Ban Huay Deua, or 800B to 1200B per person if done through a Mae Hong Son agency. Tha Ban Huay Deua (Ban Huay Deua pier) is to the left of the entrance to the Mae Hong Son Riverside Hotel (see opposite).

The Mae Pai raft trips can be good fun if the raft holds up – it's not uncommon for rafts to fall apart or sink. The Myanmar trip, which attracts travellers who want to see the Padaung or 'long-necked' people (see the boxed text, p421), is a bit of a rip-off and, to some, exploitative – a four-hour trip through unspectacular scenery to see a few Padaung people who have fled to Mae Hong Son to escape an ethnic war in Myanmar. The admission (250B per person) into the town is not included in the price of the rafting trip. When there is fighting between Shan armies and Yangon troops in the area this trip may not be possible.

Festivals & Events

Poi Sang Long Festival (March) Wat Jong Klang and Wat Jong Kham are the focal point of the festival, when young Shan boys are ordained as novice monks in the ceremony known as *bùat lûuk kâew*. Like elsewhere in Thailand, the ordinands are carried on the shoulders of friends or relatives and paraded around the wat under festive parasols, but in the Shan custom the boys are dressed in ornate costumes (rather than simple white robes) and wear flower headdresses and facial make-up. Sometimes they ride on ponies.

Jong Para Festival (October) Another important local event, held towards the end of the Buddhist Rains Retreat – three days before the full moon of the 11th lunar month, so it varies from year to year. The festival begins with local Shan bringing offerings to monks in the temples in a procession marked by the carrying of models of castles on poles. An important part of the festival is the folk theatre and dance, which is performed on the wat grounds, some of it unique to northwest Thailand.

Loi Krathong (November) During this national holiday – usually celebrated by floating *kràthong* (small lotus floats) on the nearest pond, lake or river – Mae Hong Son residents launch balloons called *kràthong sàwǎn* (heaven *kràthong*) from Doi Kong Mu.

Sleeping

BUDGET

New budget options keep springing up in Mae Hong Son. Often the newest places are the best deal, because they're clean and competitively priced. The cheapest rooms share a bathroom, and few places here offer air-con.

Palm House Guest House (☎ 0 5361 4022; 22/1 Th Chamnansthit; r from 250B; ⊠) Family-run but a bit sterile, Palm House offers good value, spacious modern rooms with high-quality hot showers. The second-storey common area affords excellent views of the lake and is a good place to meet travellers. The building is all cement and seems to amplify sound.

Friend House (☎ 0 5362 0119; fax 0 5362 0060; Th Pradit Jong Kham; s/d/d 100/250/400B) Well run, superclean and ultrapopular, Friend's large clean rooms are in a teak house. Upstairs rooms have a view of the lake. Shared hot-water showers are well maintained and there is laundry service on site.

Jong Kam Guest House (☎ 0 5361 1150; Th Pradit Jong Kham; s/d from 80B/100B) The rooms here aren't spankin' new, but they are spankin' clean. The basic A-frame bungalows are all cement with thatched roofs. The property overlooks the lake from the north and the owners are quite friendly and can help you arrange tours and motorcycle rentals.

HI-Panoramic (☎ 0 5361 1757; www.tyha.org/HI -panorama.html; 54/1 Th Khunlum Praphat; r 300B) This new, 20-room hostel has simple, spotless rooms in an elevated, Thai-style house. It has a laundry service and can help you arrange tours and activities. Instead of a garden, it has a parking lot.

Johnnie House (Th Pradit Jong Kham; s/d from 80/100B) The new rooms with private hot-water showers are an excellent deal here. They are spacious with tile floors and plenty of natural light. The shared toilets and showers could use some fixing.

Yok Guest House (☎ 0 5361 1532; 14 Th Sirimongkhon; r 250-400B; ☒ ☒) Small, very quiet and family-run, the nine super-clean rooms here are good value, even though they are a ways from town. There are also a couple of rooms without carpet for 200B.

Mae Hong Son Guest House (☎ 0 5361 2510; 295 Th Makasanti; r 150B, bungalows 350-500B) This secluded guesthouse is both inconvenient and a bit overpriced. The rooms are worn, cramped and dark, and the bungalows lack character, but are reasonably clean. The owner is very friendly, helpful and knowledgable, but the restaurant provides spotty service. It's on the northwest outskirts of town (about 700m west of Th Khunlum Praphat); just follow the signs.

Other recommendations:

Joe Guest House (☎ 0 5361 2417; r with/without bathroom 250/100B) Second-storey rooms are best. Some rooms sleep up to four. Near Wat Jong Kham.

Pen Porn House (☎ 0 5361 1577; www.rosegarden -tours.com/penporn.html; 16/1 Th Wat Muay To; d/q 250/400B) Dark but spacious rooms.

Other less-convenient places can be found around Mae Hong Son – the touts will find you at the bus station.

MIDRANGE
Most midrange options come with air conditioning and private bathroom. The only exception is the huts at Sang Tong.

Sang Tong Huts (☎ 0 5362 0680; www.sangtonghuts .com; bungalows without bath 200-350B, bungalows 500-1500B) Tucked on a hillside on the edge of town, this eclectic collection of unique huts is a fabulous place to stay. The bungalows are well maintained but rustic, lacking window screens or air-con. But they truly provide a sense of being in nature and have been carefully decorated. Do not miss out on the set, communal, five-course dinner – it's excellent. Call ahead or reserve online – this place is popular.

Piya Guest House (☎ 0 5361 1260; 1/1 Th Khunlum Praphat; bungalows 600B; ☒) The quiet garden,

pleasant lake view and good-sized rooms tend to attract a more mature crowd, and is a good choice for families. The cement bungalows have wooden floors, TV and hot showers, but are a bit weathered.

Mae Hong Son Hill Resort (☎ 0 5361 2475; 106/2 Th Khunlum Praphat; bungalows from 400B; ☒) Although it doesn't look like much at first, this quiet spot offers 22 well-kept bungalows, each with a private veranda. It's a friendly, family-run place with all the amenities stuffed into the smallish rooms.

Panorama Hotel (☎ 0 5361 1757; www.panor ama.8m.com; 51 Th Khunlum Praphat; r 600-800B; ☒) The dark, wood-panelled rooms here feel a little more like a lounge than a hotel room, but are still a reasonable deal. Breakfast is available in the lobby for 50B. Rooms on the street have strange enclosed balconies.

Baiyoke Chalet Hotel (☎ 0 5361 1536; fax 0 5361 1533; 90 Th Khunlum Praphat; r 600-1200B; ☒) Rooms here have a few charming details, and are big and modern. It is popular with European tour groups and the restaurant/lounge downstairs can get quite loud, so request a room away from the street, or on an upper level. Low-season rates are 25% less, and breakfast is included.

Mae Hong Son Riverside Hotel (☎ 0 5361 1504, 0 5361 1406; www.mhsriverside.com; Mu 3, Ban Huay Toe, Tambon Pha Bong; s/d 1300/1500B; ☒ ☒) All of the rooms at this modern hotel in the countryside come with a view. Its close proximity to the river keeps it popular with tour groups.

TOP END
Southwest of town a few kilometres towards Ban Huay Deua and Ban Tha Pong Daeng on the river are several 'resorts', which in the Thai sense of the term means any hotel near a rural or semirural area. Many are quite luxurious, service-oriented hotels with pleasantly groomed grounds. Discounts up to 40% are common in the low season, and online discounts can be found any time of year. Prices listed below are for high-season walk-ins.

Fern Rim Tarn Resort (☎ 0 5361 1374; www.fern resort.info; 64 Mu Bo, Tambon Pha Bong; standard/deluxe/ ste 1500/1800/2500B; ☒ ☒ ☒) As long as you don't need a TV, you will love the Fern Rim Tarn. This ecofriendly resort features tasteful Shan-style wooden bungalows, some overlooking rice paddies and others tucked around a lush garden. Nearby trails lead into the adjacent national park. Community-based tours are available and trekking can easily be arranged. Free pick-up is available from the airport and bus terminal. Regular shuttles run to/from town stopping at the Fern Restaurant (below). Low-season discounts are available. To drive here, take Rte 108 7km south of town, turn at the sign and follow the winding road 2km.

Imperial Tara Mae Hong Son Hotel (☎ 0 5361 1021-4; www.imperialhotels.com/taramaehongson; 149 Mu 8; s/d/ste 2448/2880/3600B; ✗ ✗ ✗) Rooms in this upmarket, 104-room hotel all have wood floors and tasteful, contemporary Thai décor. Facilities include a sauna and fitness centre.

Mountain Inn Hotel (☎ 0 5361 8023; 112 Th Khunlum Praphat; standard/deluxe/ste incl breakfast 1000/2000/4000B; ✗) Located in town, the Mountain Inn has clean, medium-sized, rooms with a few decorative highlights around a garden-filled courtyard.

Rooks Holiday Hotel & Resort (☎ 0 5361 2324; rooksgroup@hotmail.com; 114/5-7 Th Khunlum Praphat; r & bungalows 2200-2800B; ✗ 🖵 ✗) Popular with tour groups and families, this hotel can get a lively, even crowded feel. Facilities include tennis courts, disco, snooker club, bakery, coffee shop and restaurant.

Eating

Although Mae Hong Son isn't known for culinary delights, there are plenty of places to fill your belly with curry or fresh-baked bread.

Salween River Restaurant (☎ 0 5361 2050; Th Singhanat Bamrung; dishes 35-80B; ✆ 7am-1am) In addition to being *the* place in town to catch a football match and the local hang-out for volunteers, this place serves excellent hill-tribe coffee, delicate chocolate croissants and local-style Shan specialties. Try the *kài òp* (baked Shan chicken casserole). The owners are very friendly and are a good source of information. The menu also has lots of Western and vegetarian options.

Fern Restaurant (Th Khunlum Praphat; dishes 40-100B; ✆ 10.30am-midnight) The Fern is an upmarket, but casual, option. Service is professional, portions are big and the food is good. Enjoy a bottle of whisky with friends, French wine with your sweetheart or just come for the ice cream. There is live lounge music some nights.

Ji Ji Restaurant (Th Khunlum Praphat; dishes 25-80B; ✆ 7am-7pm) You'll be amazed by the ambitious menu here. With pages of Thai dishes, and many unusual Western specialties like moussaka, shepherd's pie and lasagne, you might find it tough to choose. If you're indecisive, try the delicious spicy-eggplant salad.

Sunflower Café (☎ 0 5362 0549; Th Udom Chaonithet; dishes 40-100B; ✆ 7.30am-9pm) Start your day with an oversized cup of coffee and some fresh-baked bread, or swing by in the afternoon for a light meal of pumpkin soup or stuffed tomatoes, or just wait until dinner and munch on a full-sized homemade pizza.

Pa Dim (Th Khunlum Praphat; dishes 20-40B; ✆ 8am-8pm) Everyone loves this place for its extensive variety of well-priced options and its killer fresh lassi.

Lakeside Bar & Restaurant (Th Pradit Jong Kham; buffet 59B; 10.30am-midnight) The Lakeside is for those who appreciate all-you-can-eat dining, live music and a social atmosphere. This is a good choice for groups and for people looking for a little socialising. It's popular with Thai families for dinner, but after about 10pm it's a place for drinking.

Lucky Restaurant (Th Singhanat Bamrung; dishes 40-100B; ✆ 8am-9pm) Popular with travellers, this place cooks up a lot of savoury meat dishes but has limited offerings for vegetarians. Drinks seem to be the focus and service is an afterthought. But it's a pleasant place to linger over a meal with friends.

Kai Mook (Khai Muk; ☎ 0 5361 2092; 23 Th Udom Chaonithet; dishes 40-100B; ✆ 10am-2pm & 5pm-midnight) This open-air restaurant just off the main street is one of the better Thai-Chinese restaurants in town. Some complain that the portions are small, but it remains popular with both Thais and Westerners for house specialities such as *pèt yâang náam phêung* (roast duck with honey gravy), *plaa châwn sâi ùa* (serpent-headed fish with northern-Thai sausage) and *yam bai kùt* (yam with fern leaves).

Mae Si Bua (Thai Yai Food; Th Singhanat Bamrung; dishes 15-35B; ✆ 10am-6pm) Offers delicious Shan and northern-Thai food.

Getting There & Away

AIR

Thai Airways International has flights to Mae Hong Son from Chiang Mai three times daily (765B, 35 minutes). For many people, the time saved flying to Mae Hong Son versus bus travel is worth the extra baht. Mae Hong Son has a **THAI office** (☎ 0 5361 1297/1194; 71 Th Singhanat Bamrung; ◷ 8am-5pm Mon-Fri).

BUS

From Chiang Mai there are two bus routes to Mae Hong Son: the 270km northern route through Pai (ordinary/air-con 105/147B, seven to eight hours) and the 368km southern route through Mae Sariang (ordinary/air-con 145/261B, eight to nine hours). The fare to Mae Sariang is (ordinary/air-con 78/140B). Two minivans also run to Chiang Mai via Pai (200B, seven hours) at 8am and 9am.

Although it may be longer, the southern route through Mae Sariang is much more comfortable because the bus stops every two hours for a 10- to 15-minute break and larger buses – with large seats – are used. Buses to Mae Hong Son via Mae Sariang leave Chiang Mai's Arcade bus station five times daily between 6.30am and 9pm. In the reverse direction, ordinary buses leave Mae Hong Son for Chiang Mai at 8am, 9am and 8pm; air-con buses depart at 6am, 10.30am and 9pm.

The Pai bus leaves the Chiang Mai Arcade station four times a day at 7am, 9am and 10.30am and 12.30pm. In the opposite direction, buses leave Mae Hong Son at 7am, 8.30am, 10.30am, 12.30pm and 4pm. The 4pm bus only goes as far as Pai. An air-con minivan (Pai 100B, Chiang Mai 200B) departs from Mae Hong Son at 8am.

Ordinary buses to Pai (53B, three hours) also stop in Soppong (35B, 1½ hours), and buses to Mae Sariang stop in Khun Yuam (35B, 1½ hours).

The northern route through Pai, originally built by the Japanese in WWII, is very winding and offers spectacular views from time to time. Because the buses used on this road are smaller, they're usually more crowded and the younger passengers tend to get motion sickness.

Getting Around

It's pretty easy to walk around most of Mae Hong Son. Motorcycle taxis within town cost 20B; to Doi Kong Mu it's 30B one way or 50B return. Motorcycle drivers will also take passengers further afield but fares out of town are expensive. There are now a few *túk-túk* in town, charging 20B to 30B per trip.

Motorcycles are readily available for rent (150B per day) around town. The **Avis Rent-A-Car** (☎ 0 5362 0457-8) office is located at the Mae Hong Son airport. Rates start around 1200B per day.

AROUND MAE HONG SON
Pha Bong Hot Springs
ป่อน้ำร้อนผาป่อง

Eleven kilometres south of the capital at the Km 256 marker on Rte 108, this public park with **hot springs** (◷ 8am-sunset; private bath/bathing room 50/400B) covers 12 sq km. These waters are soakable; you can take a private bath or rent a room. The springs can be reached on any southbound bus.

Mae Aw & Around
แม่ออ

Another day trip from the provincial capital is to Mae Aw, 22km north of Mae Hong Son on a mountain peak at the Myanmar border. Mae Aw is a Chinese KMT settlement, one of the last true KMT outposts in Thailand. There's no feeling of 'wow an exciting place filled with old renegade fighters', just a quiet place with people who basically ignore you, but the scenery is stunning.

The town sits on the edge of a large reservoir and the faces and signs are very Chinese. Occasionally there is fighting along the border between the KMT and the Mong Tai Army, formerly led by the infamous opium warlord Khun Sa but now operating as four splinter units under separate leaderships. When this happens, public transport is usually suspended and you shouldn't go without a guide. The modern Thai name for Mae Aw is Ban Rak Thai (Thai-Loving Village).

Accommodation in some thatched huts is available at **Roun Thai Guest House** (per person/with 2 meals 50/150B) in the Chinese/Hmong village of **Na Pa Paek**, 7.3km southwest of Mae Aw. Two small teashops set up for tourists serve tea, cola and snacks of dubious sterility. You can also purchase a cool souvenir here – a section of bamboo filled with tea labelled 'special blend tea, made by KMT' in English, Thai and Chinese. The better of the two is **Mr Huang Yuan Tea & Restaurant**.

From Na Pa Paek a rough dirt road leads southwest to the Hmong village of Ma Khua

Som (3.5km) and the KMT village of Pang Ung La (6km) on the Myanmar border. Pang Ung La also has a guesthouse.

Very irregular *sǎwngthǎew* go back and forth from Mae Hong Son, but it's so unpredictable that you're better off getting a group of people together and chartering a *sǎwngthǎew*. It will cost you 600B to 1300B (depending on whether the drivers have any paid cargo). This option lets you stop and see the sights along the way. Check Th Phanit Wattana near the municipal market in Mae Hong Son at around 9am to see if there are any *sǎwngthǎew* going. Otherwise any tour agency will send you with a driver and room for four for 1200B.

The trip takes two hours and passes Shan, Karen and Hmong villages, the Pang Tong Summer Palace and waterfalls.

If you have your own transport, please note that the last 7km to Mae Aw past Na Pa Paek can be very troublesome in the wet season.

THAM PLA NATIONAL PARK
อุทยานแห่งชาติถ้ำปลา

A trip to Mae Aw could be combined with a visit to **Tham Pla National Park** (admission 20B) centred on the animistic Tham Pla or **Fish Cave**, a water-filled cavern where hundreds of soro brook carp thrive. These fish grow up to 1m in length and are found only in the provinces of Mae Hong Son, Ranong, Chiang Mai, Rayong, Chanthaburi and Kanchanaburi. The fish eat vegetables and insects, although the locals believe them to be vegetarian and feed them only fruit and vegetables (which can be purchased at the park entrance).

A path leads from the park entrance to a suspension bridge that crosses a stream and continues to the cave. You can see the fish through a 2-sq-metre rock hole at the base of an outer wall of the cave. A **statue** of a Hindu rishi called Nara, said to protect the holy fish from danger, stands nearby. It's a bit anticlimactic, but the park grounds are a bucolic, shady place to hang out; picnic tables are available.

The TAT office in Mae Hong Son has some information about the park. The park is 17km northeast of Mae Hong Son on the northern side of Hwy 1095. October to February is good for star-watching and from November to May is bird-watching

season. Buses to Pai pass by, but renting a motorcycle is the best way to get here.

Mae La-Na
แม่ละนา

Between Mae Hong Son and Pai, Rte 1095 winds through an area of forests, mountains, streams, Shan and hill-tribe villages and limestone caves. Some of Mae Hong Son's most beautiful scenery is within a day's walk of the Shan village of Mae La-Na (6km north of Rte 1095 via a half-sealed road), where you can stay overnight. From here you can trek to several nearby Red and Black Lahu villages and to a few caves within a 4km to 8km radius.

It's possible to walk a 20km half-loop all the way from Mae La-Na to Tham Lot and Soppong, staying overnight in Red Lahu villages along the way. Ask for a sketch map at Top Hill (opposite). Experienced riders can do this route on a sturdy dirt bike – but not alone or during the rainy season.

Local guides will lead visitors to nearby caves. Tham Mae La-Na, 4km from the village, is the largest and most famous – it's threaded by a 12km length of river – and a journey to the cave and through it costs 600B. Tham Pakarang (Coral Cave), Tham Phet (Diamond Cave), Tham Khao Taek (Broken Rice Cave) and Tham Khai Muk (Pearl Cave) all feature good wall formations and cost 200B each for guides. Rates are posted at a small *sǎalaa* near a noodle stand and petrol barrel pumps in the centre of the village; this is also where you may contact the guides during the day. If no-one's at the *sǎalaa* (open-sided, covered meeting hall or resting place) when you go there, just mention *thâm* (cave) to someone at the petrol pumps. Some of the caves may not be accessible during the rainy season.

Even if you don't fancy trekking or caving, Mae La-Na can be a peaceful and mildly interesting cul-de-sac for a short stay. Beyond the Shan-style Wat Mae La-Na, a school, some houses and the previously 'downtown' area around the noodle shops and petrol pumps, there's little to see, but the surrounding mountain scenery is quite pleasing.

The Mae La-Na junction is 51.3km from Mae Hong Son, 13.3km from Soppong and 70.5km from Pai. Twelve kilometres west

---

VISITING VILLAGES

When visiting hill-tribe villages, try to find out what the local customs and taboos are, either by asking someone or by taking the time to observe local behaviour. Here are several other guidelines for minimising the impact you can have on local communities:

- Always ask for permission before taking photos of tribespeople and/or their dwellings. You can ask through your guide or by using sign language. Because of traditional belief systems, many individuals and even whole tribes may object strongly to being photographed.

- Show respect for religious symbols and rituals. Don't touch totems at village entrances or any other object of obvious symbolic value without asking permission. Unless you're asked to participate, keep your distance from ceremonies.

- Exercise restraint in giving things to tribespeople or bartering with them. If you want to give something to the people you encounter on a trek, the best thing is to make a donation to the village school or other community fund. Your guide can help arrange this. While it's an easy way to get a smile – giving sweets to children contributes to tooth decay – remember they probably don't have toothbrushes and toothpaste like you do.

- Set a good example to hill-tribe youngsters by not smoking opium or using other drugs.

- Don't litter while trekking or staying in villages.

- You might also want to check the 'Guidelines for Visitors to Northern Thailand's Mountain Peoples' at www.lanna.com/html/tourists.html.

---

of the three-way junction is a short turn-off for Wat Tham Wua Sunyata, a peaceful forest monastery. The village is 6km north of the junction. Infrequent *săwngthăew* from the highway to the village cost 20B per person – mornings are your best bet.

SLEEPING & EATING

The Mae La-Na community has established a **homestay programme** (per person per night 100B); inquire near the *săalaa*. On a hill overlooking the village, **Top Hill** (per person 50B) is run by the village headman and offers OK bungalow accommodation with shared facilities.

About 12km north of Mae La-Na in the Black Lahu village of Ban Huay Hea (close to the Myanmar border) is the **Lahu Guest House** (per person r 50B), run by a village teacher who speaks English. Lodging is simple and the money goes to a community fund.

About 15km before Mae La-Na in Ban Nam Khong is a dirt road leading 1.4km to **Wilderness Lodge** (dm/bungalow 50/250B). This is a pleasant place overlooking a river valley and is popular for extended stays, but is often closed during the wet season.

Tham Lot
ถ้ำลอด

About 8km north of Soppong is Tham Lot (pronounced *thâm lâwt* and also known as

thâm náam lâwt), a large limestone cave with a wide stream running through it. Along with Tham Nam Lang further west, it's one of the longest known caves in mainland Southeast Asia (although some as yet unexplored caves in southern Thailand may be even longer). It's possible to hike all the way through the cave (approximately 2000m) by following the stream, although it requires some wading back and forth. Apart from the main chamber, there are also three side chambers that can be reached by ladders – it takes two to three hours to explore the whole thing. Where the stream flows out of the cave, thousands of bats and swifts leave the cave at dusk.

At the **park entrance** (8am-5.30pm) you must hire a gas lantern and guide for 100B (one guide can lead up to four people) to take you through the caverns; they no longer permit visitors to tour the caves alone. The guide fee includes visits to the first and third caverns; to visit the second cavern you must cross the stream. Raft men waiting inside the cave charge 10B per person per crossing; in the dry season you may be able to wade across. For 100B you can stay on the raft through the third cavern. If you decide to book a Tham Lot day tour from Mae Hong Son, ask if the tour cost includes guide, lamp and raft fees.

SLEEPING & EATING

Cave Lodge (☎ 0 5361 7203; www.cavelodge.com; dm 60B, bungalows 120-250B, bungalows with bath from 350B) This popular, long-running place is a good choice whether you want to get out and explore, or just laze around and relax. The setting is beautiful and options for adventure abound. Chose from kayaking trips and guided or unguided treks to hill-tribe villages. All the activities are very reasonably priced.

A row of **outdoor restaurants** (dishes 15-35B; ✆ 9am-6pm) outside the park entrance offers simple Thai fare.

Soppong

สบปอง

Soppong is a small but relatively prosperous market village a couple of hours northwest of Pai and about 70km from Mae Hong Son. Since the paving of Rte 1095, Soppong and Tham Lot have become popular destinations for minivan tours from Mae Hong Son and Chiang Mai.

Although for many years this town was known only as Soppong, lately the Thai government has been calling it 'Pangmapha', since the Pangmapha District Office is now located here. The two names seem to be used interchangeably.

Close to Soppong are several Shan, Lisu, Karen and Lahu **villages** that can easily be visited on foot. Inquire at the Jungle Guest House or Cave Lodge in Soppong for reliable information. It's important to ask about the current situation, as the Myanmar border area is somewhat sensitive due to the opium trade and smuggling.

The rough back road between Soppong and Mae La-Na is popular with mountain bikers and off-highway motorcyclists.

If you're here on Tuesday, check out the **market**.

SLEEPING & EATING

Soppong has developed into an important stopping spot for both day and overnight package tours.

Soppong River Inn (☎ 0 5361 7107; www.soppong .com; r 500-700B) The four stylish rooms at this inn are a hybrid of American Southwestern, Thai and Balinese designs, It's the most comfortable choice in the area, with open-air showers, a colourful garden and wonderful riverside sitting areas about 500m

past the market on the road to Mae Hong Son. Some rooms are less than spacious.

Little Eden Guest House (☎ 0 5361 7054; www.little eden-guesthouse.com; r 450-1200B; ⬛ 🖳 ▣) The nine A-frame bungalows around a pleasant, grass-decked pool are well kept but nothing fancy. There are a couple of new, larger, upgraded VIP rooms that make this the best choice for families. The helpful, and very professional, owner speaks Thai, English, Danish and German and can organise all sorts of activities in the area. It's about 300m from the market on the main road towards Pai.

Lemon Hill Guest House (☎ 0 5361 7039; r 200-500B) Near the bus stop, this collection of bougainvillea-strewn huts facing the Nam Lan offers a decent choice. Cheaper rooms are notably more basic than the more expensive, private, hot-water-shower huts with seating areas and river view.

Charming Home (s/d 120/150B) On the opposite side of the road from Lemon Hill, a narrow track leads a kilometre or so (the last half is accessible by foot or bicycle only) to a footbridge over a stream, where you'll come to two well-designed, well-spaced huts with private bathroom sitting on a breezy hillside backed by primary forest. There are many birds in this area and you can easily hike to Lisu and Lahu villages nearby.

Jungle Guest House (☎ 0 5361 7099; s/d from 100/ 120B) About 1km west on the road towards Mae Hong Son, this friendly guesthouse has a few spacious, solid bungalows. The relatively new restaurant overlooking the river serves better fare than most of the other nearby guesthouses.

A short distance out of town towards Mae Hong Son, at Km 143, the open-air **Bean Cafe** (dishes 20-45B; ✆ 8am-6pm) serves good fresh coffee and snacks.

Coffin Caves

ถ้ำผีแมน

A 900-sq-km area of Pangmapha and adjacent districts may contain more caves than any other region in the world. More than 30 of these limestone caverns are known to contain very old wooden coffins carved from solid tree logs. Up to 6m long, the coffins are typically suspended on wooden scaffolds inside the caves and bound with ceremonial tassels (very few of which have been found intact). The coffins – which number in the dozens – are of unknown age and origin, but Thai anthropologists have classified them into at least 14 different design schemes. Pottery remains associated with the sites have also been found.

The local Thais know these burial caves as *thâm phǐi* (spirit caves), or *thâm phǐi maen* (coffin caves). The eight coffin caves that scientists are investigating at the moment are off-limits to the public, but you may be able to find guides in Amphoe Pangmapha willing to tour others. **Tham Nam Lang**, 30km northwest of Soppong near **Ban Nam Khong**, is almost 9km long and said to be one of the largest caves in the world in terms of volume.

Ban Nam Rin
บ้านน้ำริน

At this Lisu village 10km south of Soppong towards Pai, you can stay at **Lisu Lodge** (Chiang Mai ☎ 0 5328 1789; www.lisulodge.com; lodging/ ecotour/trekking packages per person from 1960B). Be sure to book ahead, as the Lisu Lodge does not accept walk-ins.

Getting There & Around
Pai to Mae Hong Son buses stop in Soppong and there are two or three each day in either direction. From Mae Hong Son to Soppong, buses cost ordinary/air-con 35/46B (2½ hours). The trip between Pai and Soppong costs 30/35B (1½ to two hours).

Motorcycle taxis stationed at the bus stop in Soppong will take passengers to Tham Lot or the Cave Lodge for 50B per person; private pick-up trucks will take you and up to five other people for 200B.

PAI
ปาย

pop 3000

Pai (pronounced like the English word 'bye', *not* 'pie') is something of a travellers mecca. It isn't a wat-filled town emanating Thainess. Instead it's a little corner of the world that happens to be in Thailand that seems to attract artists, musicians and foodies. It's got a live-music scene you won't find anywhere else, and some affordable modern art and a delicious range of international culinary treats. Oh, and it's in the middle of a gorgeous green valley with hot springs, rice fields and a lovely lazy river. However, its popularity does surpass its capacity and

the town can feel completely overrun by foreigners in the high season.

Most of the town's population are Shan and Thai, but there's also a small but visible Muslim Chinese population. Attracted by easy living and the small live-music scene, Pai nowadays also features a sizable collection of long-term visitors – mostly *faràng* and Japanese – who use the town as a place to chill out between excursions elsewhere in Asia.

Information
Several places around town offer Internet services and they all charge around 40B per hour.

The **Krung Thai Bank** (Th Rangsiyanon) has an ATM and foreign-exchange service.

Sights & Activities
TREKKING & RAFTING
All the guesthouses in town can provide information on local trekking and a few do guided treks for as little as 600B per day if there are no rafts or elephants involved. Among the more established local agencies are **Back Trax** (☎ 0 5369 9739; Th Chaisongkhram), **Duang Trekking** (at Duang Guest House; p432) and **Northern Green** (☎ 0 5369 9385; Th Chaisongkhram), all with prominent streetside offices, in the centre of town.

Thai Adventure Rafting (TAR; ☎ 0 5369 9111; www.activethailand.com; Th Rangsiyanon) leads excellent two-day, white-water, Mae Pai rafting trips in sturdy rubber rafts from Pai to Mae Hong Son for 2000B per person including food, rafting equipment, camping gear, dry bags and insurance. On the way rafters visit a waterfall, a fossil reef and hot springs; one night is spent at the company's permanent riverside camp. The main rafting season runs from July to December; after that the trips aren't usually offered. Thai Adventure Rafting also has offices in Chiang Mai.

Pai Adventure (☎ 0 5369 9385; cnr Th Rangsiyanon & Th Ratchadamnoen) is another outfit that has been recommended.

ELEPHANT RIDING
Thom's Pai Elephant Camp Tours (☎ 0 5369 9286; www.geocities.com/pai_tours/; Th Rangsiyanon; 1/3hr rides per person 300/550B) offers jungle rides year-round from Thom's camp southeast of Pai near the hot springs. You can choose between riding bareback or in a seat and some

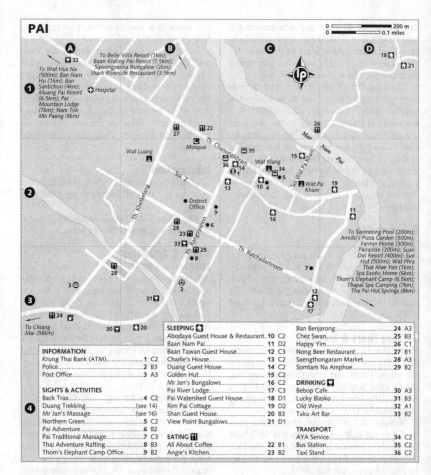

PAI

To Wat Hua Na (500m); Ban Nam Hu (1km); Ban Santichon (4km); Muang Pai Resort (6.5km); Pai Mountain Lodge (7km); Nam Tok Mo Paeng (8km)

To Belle Villa Resort (1km); Baan Krating Pai Resort (1.5km); Sipsongpanna Bungalow (2km); Shark Riverside Restaurant (3.5km)

Hospital

Wat Luang

Th Khetkelang

Mosque

Th Chaisongkhram

Wat Klang

Wat Pa Kham

Soi 2

District Office

Th Rangsiyanon

Th Ratchadamnoen

To Chiang Mai (98km)

To Swimming Pool (200m); Amido's Pizza Garden (300m); Farmer Home (300m); Pairadise (300m); Suan Doi Resort (400m); Sun Hut (500m); Wat Phra That Mae Yen (1km); Spa Exotic Home (6km); Thom's Elephant Camp (6.5km); Thapai Spa Camping (7km); Tha Pai Hot Springs (8km)

INFORMATION
Krung Thai Bank (ATM)....................1 C2
Police...2 B3
Post Office..3 A3

SIGHTS & ACTIVITIES
Back Trax...4 C2
Duang Trekking..........................(see 14)
Mr Jan's Massage.......................(see 16)
Northern Green.................................5 C2
Pai Adventure...................................6 B2
Pai Traditional Massage....................7 C3
Thai Adventure Rafting.....................8 B3
Thom's Elephant Camp Office...........9 B2

SLEEPING
Abodaya Guest House & Restaurant..10 C2
Baan Nam Pai..................................11 D2
Baan Tawan Guest House.................12 C3
Charlie's House.................................13 C2
Duang Guest House.........................14 C2
Golden Hut......................................15 C2
Mr Jan's Bungalows.........................16 C2
Pai River Lodge................................17 C3
Pai Watershed Guest House.............18 D1
Rim Pai Cottage...............................19 D2
Shan Guest House............................20 B3
View Point Bungalows......................21 D1

EATING
All About Coffee..............................22 B1
Angie's Kitchen...............................23 B2

Ban Benjarong.................................24 A3
Chez Swan.......................................25 B3
Happy Yim.......................................26 C1
Nong Beer Restaurant......................27 B1
Saengthongaram Market.................28 A3
Somtam Na Amphoe........................29 B2

DRINKING
Bebop Cafe.....................................30 A3
Lucky Blasko....................................31 B3
Old West..32 A1
Taku Art Bar....................................33 B2

TRANSPORT
AYA Service......................................34 C2
Bus Station......................................35 C2
Taxi Stand..36 C2

rides include swimming with the elephants – a barrel of laughs on a bouncing elephant in the river. Rides include a soak in the hot spring–fed tubs afterwards. Thom's can also arrange a variety of trips including bamboo or rubber rafting, hill-tribe village stays or any combination of the aforementioned for about 1000B per person per day.

BAN SANTICHON
บ้านสันติชน

Northwest of town, a Shan village, a Lahu village, a Lisu village, a KMT village called **Ban Santichon** (San Ti Chuen in Yunnanese) and **Nam Tok Mo Paeng** can all be visited on foot. The Shan, Lisu and KMT villages lie within 4km of Pai, while the Lahu village is near Nam Tok Mo Paeng, which is another 4km further from town (8km total).

You can cut the hike in half by taking a Mae Hong Son–bound bus north about 5km and getting off at a signpost for the falls; from the highway it's only 4km (about 2km beyond the Pai Mountain Lodge). A couple of pools at the base of the falls are suitable for swimming – best just after the rainy season, October to early December.

THA PAI HOT SPRINGS
บ่อน้ำร้อนท่าปาย

Across Mae Nam Pai and 8km southeast of town via a paved road is **Tha Pai Hot Springs** (admission free; soaking 50B), a well-kept local park 1km from the road. A scenic stream flows through the park; the stream mixes with the hot springs in places to make pleasant bathing areas. There are also small public bathing houses into which hot spring water is piped.

WAT PHRA THAT MAE YEN
วัดพระธาตุแม่เย็น

This temple sits atop a hill and has good views overlooking the valley. Walk 1km east from the main intersection in town, across a stream and through a village, to get to the stairs (a decent climb – 353 steps) that lead to the top. Or take the 400m sealed road that follows a different route to the top.

TRADITIONAL MASSAGE & HERBAL SAUNA

Pai Traditional Massage (☎ 0 5369 9121; pttm2001@hotmail.com; Th Sukhapiban 1; massage 1/1½/2hr 150/230/300B, sauna per visit 60B, 3-day massage course around 2000B; ⏱ 4.30am-8.30pm Mon-Fri, 8.30am-8.30pm Sat & Sun) has very good northern-Thai massage, as well as a sauna where you can steam yourself in *sàmǔn phrai* (medicinal herbs). The couple that do the massages are graduates of Chiang Mai's Old Medicine Hospital. Massage and sauna services are available on weekends.

For those into the rougher stuff, another place in town called **Mr Jan's Massage** (Soi Wanchaloem 18; per hr 150B) employs a harder Shan-Burmese massage technique.

SWIMMING

Pool (admission child/adult 20/50B; ⏱ 10.30am-8.30pm) Need to cool off and chill out? Sun yourself on the deck, sip a drink and take a dip at this happening swimming pool. It's not Olympic size, but it's sufficient to escape the heat.

Sleeping

There's lots of accommodation choice in Pai. If you're coming to enjoy the quiet, idyllic countryside, or plan on staying for a while, head out of the town to one of the 'off-map' spots. Budget places are the staple, but more places are moving into the midrange, and the top end has arrived.

BUDGET

Raised bamboo huts is the most sought-after budget accommodation in Pai. But cement bungalows with private bathrooms and no charm are becoming increasingly popular. Long-term discounts are negotiable, especially in the low season.

In Town

Baan Nam Pai (☎ 0 1830 1161; baannampai@hotmail.com; 88 Mu 3, Wiang Tai; bungalows 120-200B) Well kept, friendly and often overlooked, this intimate, well-shaded place is right in town, but feels like the other side of the river. Prices vary with size and the most expensive places are romantic, with natural details such as twisted vines around the windows.

Baan Tawan Guest House (☎ 0 5369 8116/7; www.baantawaninpai.com; 114 mu 4, Wiang Tai; bungalows 200-300B) The older, more charming, more expensive, riverside, two-storey bungalows made with salvaged teak are the reason to stay here. The newer, cement rooms hardly compare, but will do in a pinch. It's quite a social place with plenty of balcony hammocks and a riverside lawn. Motorcycles and inner tubes (for floating down the river) are available for rent.

Pai River Lodge (☎ 0 1439 4490; r 100-200B) Simple huts, arranged in a large circle with a dining and lounge area on stilts in the middle. There are older A-frame huts and a couple of slightly larger, nicer ones. Because of its quiet, scenic location it's often full. Rates may be higher in peak season. Pai River Lodge is towards the river from town, near Baan Tawan Guest House.

Golden Hut (☎ 0 5369 9949; dm/d 50/100B, r 300-500B) Popular for its laid-back atmosphere, garden setting, proximity to town and river, and solid range of accommodation options, Golden Hut is a good place to make friends. The simple thatched huts on stilts along the river, dorm beds and double rooms in a large bamboo-thatch building are all well maintained. There is a restaurant on site.

Mr Jan's Bungalows (☎ 0 5369 9554; Soi Wanchaloem 18; s/d from 50/100B) Mr Jan keeps improving his place with new, modern, shiny-tiled bungalows around a herb garden with fruit trees. There are still a few old-style bamboo huts. All guests have access to facilities where you can bathe with heated, herb-infused water. Massages and herbal saunas are available on site.

Abodaya Guest House & Restaurant (☎ 0 5369 9041; Th Chaisongkhram; r 350B) The new rooms at this guesthouse are behind the restaurant of the same name. Modern, clean, cement rooms have TV but are all pretty dark. It lacks a garden and any notable charm, so the only reason to be here is proximity to town and the bus terminal.

Shan Guest House (☎ 0 5369 9162; r 100-300B) If you want to be close to Pai's nightlife, this well-run and well-worn spot on the southern edge of town off Th Rangsiyanon is a decent option. A rickety dining and lounging pavilion sits on stilts in the middle of a big pond. Long-term discounts are available.

Duang Guest House (☎ 0 5369 9101; fax 0 5369 9581; Th Chaisongkhram; s/d from 70/130B) This rambling complex of two-storey houses and row house is a reasonable choice if you want to be right in town.

Charlie's House (☎ 0 5369 9039; Th Rangsiyanon; s/d from 60/100B) Range of options here. Clean, secure and often full.

Out of Town

There are plenty of basic, baht-saving bamboo huts on the northwest bank of the river. Just cross the bamboo slat bridge near Golden Hut and start wandering. Also southeast of town are a number of places to stay along the road that leads to the hot springs, not very far from Wat Phra That Mae Yen. Most offer simple thatched-roof huts for 50B to 100B.

Sipsongpanna Bungalow & Artist Homestay (☎ 0 5369 8259; sipsongpanna33@hotmail.com; 60 Mu 5, Ban Juang, Wiang Neua; bungalows 250-500B) These seven charming, wooden, riverside bungalows are covered with deft touches. The light, airy décor and separate toilet/shower facilities add to the uniqueness of this place. There are sitting areas sprinkled throughout the grounds and a vegetarian café and art studio. Thai vegetarian-cooking lessons are available. This place is a couple of kilometres from town.

Sun Hut (☎ 0 5369 9730, 0 1960 6519; 28/1 Ban Mae Yen; s/d from 200/250B) This eclectic collection of zodiac-inspired bungalows is one of the more unique and calming places in the area. Bungalows and huts are nicely spaced apart and more expensive bungalows have porches and lots of charm. The turn-off for Sun Hut comes after a bridge over a stream, about 200m before the entrance to Wat Phra That Mae Yen.

Suan Doi Resort (Mu 1, Ban Mae Yen; bungalows from 150B) Just beyond Pairadise towards Wiang Neua, is this collection of wooden A-frame bungalows in a lush, wooded streamside setting. The bungalows are well kept and those without bathrooms have an outdoor sink on a private porch.

Farmer Home (☎ 0 5369 9378, 0 9953 3361; 79 Mu 1, Ban Mae Yen; bungalows 120-500B) Friendly, peaceful and soon to have a swimming pool, Farmer Home is another good place with a variety of accommodation, from crumbling itty-bitty huts to modern, two-storey houses. In the future, air-conditioned bungalows will line the pool. It's about 600m east of the river on a hillock, just past the pool (p431).

Pai Watershed Guest House (1 Mu 1, Ban Mae Yen; s/d 100/150B) About half a kilometre beyond the bamboo bridge, where the trail begins to climb up to a ridge, is Pai Watershed. You'll find good views of the valley, plus quiet surroundings, which attracts many long-term guests.

View Point Bungalows (Wiang Tai; s/d 100/150B) As the name implies, View Point affords good views of town and terraced rice fields. It's near Pai Watershed.

MIDRANGE

Pairadise (☎ 0 9838 7521; www.pairadise.com; 98 Mu 1, Ban Mae Yen; bungalows 450-650B) With a combination of fine bedding and simple décor atop the ridge, Pairadise features a row of nicely designed, spacious bungalows with private hot-water shower. Out front there's a spring-fed pond that's surrounded by gardens and is suitable for swimming.

Rim Pai Cottage (☎ 0 5369 9133, 0 5323 5931; Th Chaisongkhram; r & bungalows 500-800B; 🏊) Rim Pai is charming and older, and like a small village from another time period. Close to the river, it has clean, quiet A-frames with bathroom, electricity and mosquito nets; there are also overpriced rooms in a row house. One large bungalow is available by the river. Rates include breakfast, but it's a bit overpriced and there are some deferred maintenance issues.

Spa Exotic Home (☎ 0 1917 9351, 0 5369 8088; 86 Mu 2, Ban Mae Hi; bungalows 800-1100B) All of the unique, earthy, bungalows here sit around a beautifully landscaped garden and have a private tub for enjoying the onsite mineral water. Service is conscientious and the overall atmosphere is relaxing. Discounts are available from May to August. The restaurant serves good Thai and Western food.

Thapai Spa Camping (in Chiang Mai ☎ 0 5369 3267; kworathep@thaispa.com; Ban Mae Hi; cottages 600-2500B; 🏊) Near Spa Exotic Home, this more manicured place offers 15 wood-and-stone cottages with natural, hot, mineral-water showers. Rooms sleep up to four in two double beds and the more expensive cottages have great porches that overlook the river. There are also outdoor hot-water pools for guests and nonguests (50B per person per day). Full spa services are available on site.

Pai Mountain Lodge (☎ 0 5369 9068; Ban Mo Paeng; bungalows 500-1000B; ☒) Well-maintained, spacious A-frames with hot-water showers and stone fireplaces sleep four and are good value, 7km northwest of Pai near Nam Tok Mo Paeng and several hill-tribe villages. In town you can book a room or arrange transport at 89 Th Chaisongkhram, near Northern Green Tours (p429).

Muang Pai Resort (☎ 0 5327 0906; muangpai-resort .infothai.com; 94 Mu 4, Baan Mor Paeng; bungalows from 1000B; ☒ ☒) Muang Pai is known for its swimming pool, which is cleaner, bigger and quite a bit more pleasant than any other pool in town. The bungalows and garden are so crisp they almost feel plastic. This is a good option for a family with transport.

TOP END

Baan Krating Pai Resort (☎ 0 5369 8255, Bangkok 0 27180854; www.baankrating.com/pai; 119 Th Wiang Nua; r/ste 3000/3800B; ☒) If your dream Thai vacation included ultrasoft sheets, gorgeous rice-paddy and mountain views, and well-designed modern nature-influenced bungalows, Baan Krating might do the trick. In addition to in-room quality, the restaurant serves homegrown jasmine rice and vegetables and will prepare a special meal with ingredients you bring back from the in-town market. The onsite pub features live music, and cooking classes are also available.

Belle Villa Resort (☎ 0 5369 8226-7; www.bellevilla resort.com; 118 Th Wiang Nua; bungalows 2300-2900B; deluxe 4000B; ☒ ☒ ☒) These tasteful bungalows have the right look, but some details have been overlooked. Rooms have terry-cloth bathrobes and DVD players and the wooden deck around the pool is gorgeous.

Eating

IN TOWN

Pai's range of eating options reflects the diversity of international residents and visitors, but there are also a healthy selection of well-priced Thai places.

Amido's Pizza Garden (no phone, no address; dishes 60-140B) Recently hailed as the best pizza in Thailand (even better than Bella Napoli in

Bangkok), this open-air restaurant is not to be missed. It also features a variety of pasta dishes, and daily specials, including delicious beef Bourguignon, are sure to impress even the pickiest gastronome. With advance notice Amido can barbecue a goat and make couscous with all the trimmings or whip up an incredible paella. It's about 300m east of the permanent bridge over Mae Nam Pai, near the school on Th Ratchadamnoen.

Nong Beer Restaurant (☎ 0 5369 9103; Th Chaisongkhram; dishes 20-70B; ☒ 8am-10pm) The service lacks enthusiasm, but the oldest eatery in town remains one of the most reliable with a good range of inexpensive Thai and Chinese standards, as well as *khâo sawy*. Unfortunately, as Pai's traffic increases, the open-air seating here becomes less enjoyable.

Somtam Na Amphoe (dishes 20-30B; ☒ 8am-5pm) This very popular, family-run local spot opposite the District Office makes Pai's best *sôm-tam*, as well as other *tam* (pounded) salad-like dishes using green beans, cucumber and other veggies, along with fresh charcoal-grilled chicken. Servings are big, fresh and a darn good deal.

Happy Yim (☎ 0 1303 0922; 15 Soi Wat Pa Kham; dishes 65-120B) Munch down on some tasty Tex-Mex – made with imported cheese – while listening to live music at this new eatery and nightspot. To complement the popular fajitas, *tostadas* (crisp-fried, thin tortilla) and *quesadillas* (tortilla with cheese), pitchers of margaritas cost 99B before 9pm.

Edible Jazz (Soi Wat Pa Kham; dishes 30-75B; ☒ 2-11pm) The cushions-on-the-floor atmosphere make this a good choice for a leisurely late-night pasta, sandwiches or Mexican. Jazz CDs play in the background and occasionally the Thai owner plays improvisational acoustic guitar. Full cocktail and espresso menu.

All About Coffee (☎ 0 5369 9429; Th Chaisongkhram; dishes 35-65B; ☒ 8.30am-6pm) This stylish little bohemian place ain't cheap, but it serves the best French toast and eye-opening coffee drinks in town. Instead of pop music, expect American ragtime, jazz or blues. Sandwiches are made with homemade bread.

Chez Swan (☎ 0 5369 9111; Th Rangsiyanon; dishes 50-170B; ☒ 8am-11pm) Chez Swan is not for penny-pinchers; it's for those with a hankering for French bistro–style food – including cheeses, quiches and simple steak and potatoes. The wine selection is also pretty good, and the atmosphere is romantic.

NORTHERN THAILAND

Ban Benjarong (Th Rangsiyanon; dishes 40-100B; 11am-10pm) Boasting 'No MSG', this partially open-air restaurant has a good range of Thai dishes and ice cream. It's less of a beer garden than its neighbours. Get a table with views of rice paddies out back.

Angie's Kitchen (0 5369 9093; Th Rangsiyanon; dishes 30-60B; 7.30am-10pm; closed Sun after noon) The 50B set meals are the best deal. The menu includes the typical Thai and Western dishes. It's a nice place to read the paper and catch up on world events over breakfast.

During the day, there's takeaway food at **Saengthongaram Market** (Th Khetkelang).

OUT OF TOWN

Shark Riverside Restaurant (dishes 45-80B; 10am-10pm; closed low season) Located 3.5km from town, this place is said to serve the best Wiener schnitzel this side of Mae Khong. Without wheels, getting to here is a journey, but it's possible to make a day of it by swimming in the river, or renting a boat and fishing in the river after or before your meal. There's a free shuttle back to town and the musical selection is largely jazz.

Drinking & Entertainment

Pai boasts a small but happening live-music scene.

Bebop Cafe (Th Rangsiyanon) Looking like a Shan-Yunnanese shophouse on the outside, and decorated with Asian hippie gear inside. The house band and occasional visiting bands play blues, R&B and rock nightly (from about 9.30pm).

Happy Yim (0 1303 0922; 15 Th Chiang Mai–Mae Hong Son) Partially owned by 'smooth jazz' guitarist Eric Dibbern, this has live music in the evenings and open-mic nights on Wednesday and Sunday.

Lucky Blasko (Th Rangsiyanon) Folk-oriented most nights; open-mic night on Thursday.

Taku Art Bar (Th Rangsiyanon) Partially owned by a well-known Thai artist, Taku is the main centre for visiting Thai hipsters. Bartender Nong has a knack for spinning the right CD at the right moment. Excellent bar snacks.

Old West (0 5369 9174; Th Chaisongkhram) A rustic cowboy-décor bar in front of Mountain Blue Guest Cottages, Old West hosts a variety of local and Chiang Mai bands on weekends. The Thai owner established the original Old West in Bangkok over 15 years ago and has since decamped to Pai.

Krating Club (Baan Krating Pai Resort; 0 5369 8255; www.baankrating.com/pai; 119 Th Wiang Nua) This club brings a touch of Bangkok disco culture to Pai with its industrial décor and high-tech sound system. Live bands sometimes play earlier, after which the house DJ takes over. Local and visiting Westerners appear to prefer the more rustic drinking holes in town, so most of Krating Club's clientele is Thai.

Getting There & Away

Buses (ordinary/air-con 60/84B) leave Chiang Mai's Arcade station at 8.30am, 11am, noon, 2pm and 4pm daily. It's only 134km but the trip takes about three hours due to the steep winding road. From Mae Hong Son there are also five buses a day with the same departure times as from Chiang Mai. This winding 111km stretch takes three to four hours (ordinary/air-con 53B/74B). Buses depart from Pai for Chiang Mai and Mae Hong Son at 7am, 9am, 10.30am, 12.30pm, 2pm and 4pm. Buses from Pai to Soppong cost 30B ordinary, 35B for air-con.

AYA Service runs air-con minibuses to Tha Thom (300B), Chiang Mai (350B), Mae Sai (one way/return 400/500B). They don't run everyday, but depend on demand.

Getting Around

Most of Pai is accessible on foot. For local excursions you can rent bicycles or motorcycles at several locations around town. A place next door to Duang Guest House rents out bicycles for 50B per day (80B for newer bikes). Motorcycles can be rented at **AYA Service** (0 5369 9940; Th Chaisongkhram; bikes per 24 hr 100cc/larger 150/200B).

Motorcycle taxis wait at the taxi stand at the bus stop. Fares are 25B to Ban Nam Hu and Ban Wiang Neua, 35B to Nam Hu Lisaw and Nam Hu Jin, and 45B to Tha Pai.

AROUND PAI

Pai can be used as a base for excursions to hill-tribe villages, such as Ban Santichon (p430). Further afield, the area northeast of Pai has so far been little explored. A network of unpaved roads – some are little more than footpaths – skirts a mountain ridge and the Mae Taeng valley all the way to the Myanmar border near **Wiang Haeng** and **Ban Piang Haeng**, passing several villages along the way. Near Ban Piang Haeng is a Shan **temple** built by Khun Sa, the opium warlord.

Northeastern Thailand

For many tourists, the northeast is Thailand's forgotten backyard, the giant, mysterious space that slides past the window on the bus trip to Laos. But while tourism has left an indelible flip-flop print on many parts of Thailand, this colossal corner of the country continues to live life on its own terms: slowly, steadily and with a profound respect for both heritage and history. Yep, you can admire the glittering tip of the Thai iceberg on the beaches of Ko Samui and Phuket, but it is here, where English is rarely spoken and the tourist trail is at its bumpiest, that you will experience one of the country's most fascinating and idiosyncratic alter egos.

By Thai standards, Isan (or *isǎan*), the collective name for the 19 provinces that make up the northeast, is no guidebook covergirl. At first glance, its cities are predominantly functional and the countryside – dazzlingly green as it is – surrounding the beeline Hwy 2 route between Bangkok and Laos is largely flat and agricultural.

But like the mysterious *naga* fireballs which float up out of the Mekong River near Nong Khai each year, Isan saves its finest surprises for those with the patience to come looking for them. From its fabulously evocative Khmer temple complexes and undiscovered national parks, to its sleepy villages and explosive festivals, the northeast will take time and patience to visit, and a lifetime to forget.

HIGHLIGHTS

- Soaking up Isan's Angkor-era stone age while wandering through the restored temple complexes of **Phanom Rung** (p452), **Phimai** (p444) and **Prasat Khao Phra Wihan National Park** (p517)

- Taking time out from the fast lane with a night in the soporific riverside village of **Chiang Khan** (p492)

- Journeying into the mind of one of the northeast's most enigmatic figures, with a trip to Nong Khai's **Sala Kaew Ku sculpture park** (p476)

- Diving off the beaten track and into the deep end of Isan's vibrant culture at Dan Sai's **Phi Ta Khon Festival** (p490)

- Heading into the dark heart of Thailand with a hike through the forests of the **Khao Yai National Park** (p448)

★ Chiang Khan   ★ Sala Kaew Ku Sculpture Park
★ Dan Sai

★ Phimai

Khao Yai ★ National Park   Phanom Rung ★
★ Prasat Khao Phra Wihan National Park

History

The social history of this enigmatic region stretches back at least 4000 years, to the hazy days when the ancient Ban Chiang culture started tilling the region's fields with bronze tools.

Thais employ the term *ìsǎan* to classify the region (*phâak ìsǎan*), the people (*khon ìsǎan*) and the food (*aahǎan ìsǎan*) of northeastern Thailand. The name comes from Isana, the Sanskrit name for the early Mon-Khmer kingdom that flourished in what is now northeastern Thailand and Cambodia. After the 9th century, however, the Angkor empire held sway over these parts and erected many of the fabulous temple complexes that pepper the region today.

Until the arrival of Europeans, Isan remained largely autonomous from the early Thai kingdoms. But as the French staked out the borders of colonial Laos, so Thailand was forced to define its own northeastern boundaries. Slowly, but surely, Isan would fall under the mantle of the broader Thailand.

Long Thailand's poorest area, the northeast soon became a hotbed of communist activity. Ho Chi Minh spent 1928 to 1929 proselytizing in the area and in the 1940s a number of Indochinese Communist Party leaders fled to Isan from Laos and helped bolster Thailand's Communist Party. From the 1960s, until an amnesty in 1982, guerrilla activity was rife in Isan, especially in the

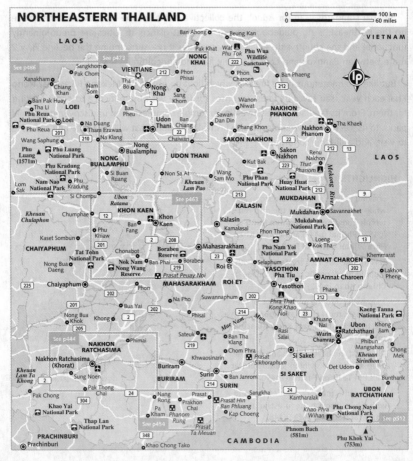

provinces of Buriram, Loei, Ubon Ratchathani, Nakhon Phanom and Sakon Nakhon. But growing urbanisation drew many peasants to the cities and the various insurgencies quickly evaporated in the glare of Thailand's boom years.

Not everyone has benefited though, and Isan's rural areas still have the lowest per-capita income of the country's four major regions.

Climate

Northeast Thailand generally experiences a three-season, monsoonal climate, with a relatively cool dry season from November to late February, followed by a hot dry season from March to May, and then a hot rainy season from June to October. Loei province experiences the most extreme climactic conditions, with both the hottest temperatures and the coldest – it is one of the few places in Thailand where temperatures dip below zero.

National Parks

Northeastern Thailand has an amazing 23 national parks and 21 forest parks, ranging from some of the world's most famous (Khao Yai National Park), to some of the country's least-visited (Tat Ton National Park). Thailand's oldest national park, Khao Yai (p448), is also its most impressive, providing the backdrop for much of the action in Hollywood blockbuster *The Beach* and comprising the largest intact monsoon forest in mainland Asia.

Other highlights include: Phu Kradung (p488) for its great views and high-altitude hiking; Nam Nao (p494) for its dense forest and unspoilt landscapes; Khao Phra Wihan (p517), which offers access to the Khmer temple of the same name; and Phu Wiang (p464), a must for dinosaur-lovers.

Information on all of the region's parks and an online booking service can be found online at www.dnp.go.th/parkreserve.

Language & Culture

Isan language and culture are melting pots of Lao and Khmer influences. The Khmers left behind Angkor Wat–like monuments near Surin, Khorat, Buriram and other northeastern towns, while there are many Lao-style temples – most notably Wat Phra That Phanom – along the Mekong River.

Many of the people living in this area speak Lao and in fact there are more people of Lao heritage in northeastern Thailand than in all of Laos.

Isan cooking is famous for its pungency. Well-known dishes include *kài yâang* (grilled spiced chicken) and *sôm-tam* (spicy salad made with grated papaya, lime juice, garlic, fish sauce and fresh chillies). On a quirkier note, the area is also known for its grilled insects.

The region's music is born out of a distinctive folk tradition and uses instruments such as the *khaen,* a reed instrument with two long rows of bamboo pipes strung together; the *ponglang,* which is like a xylophone and made of short wooden logs; and the *phin,* a type of small three-stringed lute played with a large plectrum. The most popular song form is the *lûuk thûng* (literally 'children of the fields'), which is far more rhythmic than the classical styles of central Thailand.

The best silk in Thailand is said to come from the northeast, particularly Khorat, Khon Kaen and Roi Et. Cotton fabrics from Loei, Nong Khai and Nakhon Phanom are highly regarded, especially those woven using *mát-mìi* methods (in which cotton threads are tie-dyed before weaving, similar to Indonesian *ikat).*

Getting There & Away

The main train and bus lines in the northeast are between Bangkok and Nong Khai, and between Bangkok and Ubon Ratchathani. The northeastern region can also be reached from northern Thailand by bus or from Phitsanulok, with Khon Kaen as the gateway. Many of the major centres are also connected to Bangkok by air. Given the large distances, it is well worth considering a flight to Nong Khai, before using buses and trains to wend your way back south.

Getting Around

If you have time on your side, travelling in the northeast is rarely a problem: most of the towns are linked by bus, or train, and *sǎwngthǎew* (pick-up trucks) services go on to many, but not all, of the smaller villages and temple complexes. If you are short on time, however, remember that distances are large in this part of Thailand and buses are often slow. Consequently, if time is of the essence and you plan to visit the region's more remote sites, a hire car will save a great many headaches.

At time of writing, there were no direct flights *between* destinations in the northeast – they all travel via Bangkok.

NAKHON RATCHASIMA PROVINCE

Silk and stone are the cornerstones of the Nakhon Ratchasima tourist industry and it is well worth dipping an inquisitive toe into both facets of the region's heritage.

First up, history aficionados should soak up the stone remains of the region's Angkor-period heyday. Khmer temples dating from this time still pepper the province and while many have been reduced to amorphic piles of rubble, the restored complexes of Prasat Phimai and Prasat Phanomwan provide an evocative glimpse of times past.

If you're a fashion fetishist, on the other hand, you should explore the region's silk-weaving industry. Still something of a cottage enterprise, Thai silk weaving has its spiritual home in the village of Pak Thong Chai, 30km southwest of the provincial capital of Nakhon Ratchasima (more commonly known as Khorat). Some of the country's best silk cloth comes out of this little town.

And if none of that floats your boat, there's always Khao Yai, Thailand's oldest national park and the jungle backdrop for much of Danny Boyle's movie adaptation of *The Beach*. If it's wilderness you're looking for, you can't help but find it there.

NAKHON RATCHASIMA (KHORAT)

นครราชสีมา(โคราช)

pop 215,000

Khorat doesn't wear its heart on its sleeve. Touch down in the brash gateway to the northeast and only those sporting a hefty set of rose-tinted specs will be reaching for their camera as they step off the bus. A bumper dose of urban hubbub reflects the city's growing affluence and, at first glance, Khorat's one-time historic charm has been all but smothered under a duvet of homogenous development.

Khorat is instead a city you grow to know. Distinctly Isan, with a strong sense of re-

gional identity, this busy centre is at its best, and most idiosyncratic, in its quieter corners, where Thai life, largely untouched by the country's booming tourist industry, goes on in its own uncompromising way.

Despite the historic moat, which surrounds the centre, and the sections of surviving city wall, Khorat is no Chiang Mai. But if you're after a glimpse of a workaday Thai city, where tour buses and souvenir sellers are still something of an enigma, this might just be your ticket.

History

Khorat was once the capital of Lao Klang, covering present-day Khorat, Chaiyaphum and Buriram Provinces. Up until the mid-Ayuthaya era it was actually two towns, Sema and Khorakpura, which merged under the reign of King Narai.

One of seven air bases in Thailand used by the US armed forces to launch air strikes on Laos and Vietnam in the 1960s and '70s was just outside Khorat. A few retired GIs still live in the area with their Thai families and there seem to be more army surplus stores here than anywhere else in Thailand.

Orientation

Central Khorat is contained within a road loop formed on the west and north by the Friendship Hwy (Hwy 2), also known as Th Mittaphap; and connecting routes to the east and south. A historic moat further subdivides the city in two, with the more densely developed half to the east of the Thao Suranari Memorial and a slightly more low-key section to the west, around the train station and bus terminal 1.

Information

INTERNET ACCESS

T-Net (☎ 0 4434 1111; 1st fl, The Mall, Th Mittaphap; per hr 20B; ☉ 10am-10pm)

LAUNDRY

Mr Clean (107 Th Wacharasarit; ☉ 8am-8pm) For cheap, same-day laundry services.

MEDICAL & EMERGENCY

Ratchasima Hospital (☎ 0 4426 2000; Th Mittaphap) For quality medical care.

Tourist Police (☎ 1155; Th Chang Pheuak) Opposite bus terminal 2, north of the city centre.

MONEY

There are banks across town. The following have ATM and exchange facilities:

Bangkok Bank (Th Chumphon; ⏰ 8.30am-3.30pm Mon-Fri)

Bank of Asia (cnr Th Chumphon & Th Jomsurangyat; ⏰ 8.30am-3.30pm Mon-Fri) With Western Union money-transfer facilities.

POST

Post office (Th Jomsurangyat; ⏰ 8am-5pm Mon-Fri, to noon Sat)

TOURIST INFORMATION

Tourism Authority of Thailand (TAT; ☎ 0 4421 3666; www.tourismthailand.org; 2102-2104 Th Mittaphap; ⏰ 8.30am-4.30pm) Has information about Khorat as well as the surrounding region, including Buriram, Surin and Chaiyaphum.

Sights

MAHA WIRAWONG NATIONAL MUSEUM

พิพิธภัณฑสถานแห่งชาติมหาวีรวงศ์

The dust is beginning to settle on some of the exhibits in this **museum** (☎ 0 4424 2958; Th Ratchadamnoen; admission 10B; ⏰ 9am-4pm Wed-Sun), but the interesting collection of Khmer and Ayuthaya-period artefacts includes stone and bronze Buddhas, woodcarvings from an ancient temple and various domestic utensils. Chances are you'll also have the place to yourself. It is a little hidden away, in the grounds of Wat Sutchinda.

THAO SURANARI MEMORIAL

อนุสาวรีย์ท้าวสุรนารี

Thao Suranari is something of a Wonder-woman in these parts. As the wife of the city's assistant governor, she rose to notoriety in 1826, during the reign of Rama III, when she led a ragtag army of locals to victory against the ravaging Vientiane forces of Chao Anu-wong. Some scholars have suggested that the legend was concocted to instil a sense of Thai-ness in the ethnic-Lao people of the province, but locals still flock to her **memorial** (Th Ratchadamnoen; admission free; ⏰ 24hr) in adoring droves. If you're in any doubt about how highly esteemed Thao Suranari is here, just take a moment to look through the hundreds of unique offerings that have been piled up at the base of the monument by supplicants eager for her spiritual protection.

In the evenings you can see performances of *phleng khorâat*, the traditional

Khorat folk song, on a stage near the shrine. It's usually performed by groups of four singers hired by people whose supplications to Thao Suranari have been honoured. To show gratitude to the spirit, they pay for the performance. More than 100 groups are available for hire, usually for 400B to 500B per half-hour performance.

A festival to mark her victory is held annually between late March and early April (see below).

There's not a whole lot left of the memorial, but a small section of the **city wall**, including the old **Chumphon Gate**, can be seen in a fenced off enclosure nearby.

OTHER SIGHTS

Several of the city's wats are worth a visit. **Wat Phra Narai Maharat** (Th Prajak; ⏰ daylight hours) is of interest for two main reasons: it has a Khmer sandstone sculpture of Phra Narai (Narayana or Vishnu), and it also houses Khorat's *làk meuang* (city pillar).

Wat Pa Salawan (Th Suranari; ⏰ daylight hours) is a Thammayut 'forest monastery' and was once surrounded by jungle. It has since been engulfed by the city, but the temple remains a fairly quiet escape from the urban push and shove. The late abbot, Luang Phaw Phut, was quite well known as a meditation teacher and has developed a strong lay following in the area. A few relics belonging to the legendary Ajahn Man are on display in the main *wíhǎan* (hall), a large but simple wooden affair. A cemetery on the grounds has a couple of markers with photos of US veterans who lived out their later years in Khorat. Wat Pa Salawan is in the southwestern sector of the city behind the train station.

Festivals & Events

Khorat explodes into life during the **Thao Suranari Festival**, when city dwellers – in addition to legions of villagers from the surrounding area – come together to celebrate Thao Suranari's victory over the Lao (see left). It's held annually from 23 March to 3 April and features parades, theatre and folk song.

Sleeping

BUDGET

Khorat has plenty of budget hotels, but few cater to the Western backpacker scene. Getting a room in some of the following places will require a few words of Thai, or a whole lot of miming.

Doctor's House (☎ 0 4425 5846; 78 Soi 4, Th Seup Siri; r 180B) One of the few cheapies where guests bearing rucksacks are the norm, this cosy place is more of a homestay than a hotel, with five spacious rooms (with shared bathroom) in a local villa. The owner is full of cheer and his slightly draconian house rules (the gate is locked at 10pm) ensure that there's plenty of peace and quiet.

Chophaya Inn (☎ 0 4424 3825; www.hotelchopha yainnkorat.com; 62/1 Th Jomsurangyat; r 450B; 🖂) This recently renovated spot rises above the jailhouse vibes endemic in many of Khorat's cheaper options. It offers cleanliness, comfort and a little atmosphere for a very rea-

sonable price. It could do with turning on a few more lights though.

Srivijaya Hotel (☎ 0 4424 2194; fax 0 4426 7254; 9-11 Th Buarone; s/d 350/400B; 🖂) Offering a little more gloss and a tad less charm, this pleasant hotel adds a veneer of business-hotel class to the budget-category choices. Comfy rooms promise you a good night's sleep and for 50B extra you can get a TV, carpet and a fridge.

Tokyo Hotel (☎ 0 4424 2788; fax 0 4425 2335; 329-333 Th Suranari; r 250-350B; 🖂) A lick of paint, a brace of ornamental gold lions and some new signs out front have revamped this old school contender. It's a little less fresh on the inside, but the rooms are clean and the price is right.

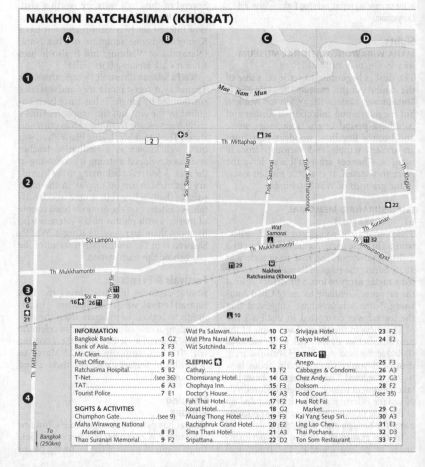

NAKHON RATCHASIMA (KHORAT)

Fah Thai Hotel (☎ 0 4426 7390; fax 0 4425 2797; 35-39 Th Phoklang; r 350B; ✗) This Thai-Chinese outfit is another decent bet, although the dreary corridors are a little reminiscent of an asylum. The rooms are big enough to swing a brace of cats in and the place is generally tidy.

Cathay (☎ 0 4425 2067; 3692/5-6 Th Ratchadamnoen; s/d 200/400B) You won't find much English spoken here, but the spartan rooms just about make it onto the pass list and its location is reasonably convenient for the bus terminals.

Muang Thong Hotel (☎ 0 4424 2090; 46 Th Chumphon; r 120-220B) Offering a little taste of old Khorat, this shaky wooden place is starting to fall apart at the seams. Some people may

find it a little too ramshackle for comfort – especially when it starts vibrating to the karaoke tracks floating in from next door – but a night spent here is certainly an 'experience'. Some facilities are shared.

MIDRANGE

Korat Hotel (☎ 0 4425 7057; korathotel@hotmail.com; 191 Th Atsadang; r 570B; ✗) Set back from the road – a big plus in the noise stakes – this pleasant midranger offers plenty of spotless marble surfaces, comfy rooms and cheery welcomes. And if you can't sleep, you can always go for a late-night Chang at the attached Arthur Bar.

Rachaphruk Grand Hotel (☎ 0 4426 1222; www .rachaphruk.com; 311 Th Mittaphap; r 1100B; ✗ ▣ ⌨)

DRINKING 🖸
Korat Texas 2003.................... **34** E3

ENTERTAINMENT
Klang Cinema............................(see 35)

SHOPPING 🛍
Klang Plaza 2.......................... **35** F3
Mall... **36** C2
Th Manat Night Bazaar........... **37** G3

TRANSPORT
Bus Terminal 1....................... **38** E2
Bus Terminal 2....................... **39** E1
THAI.. **40** E2

'Grand' might be laying it on a little thick, but this slightly dowdy four-star affair is a decent bet if you fancy a few more business-style comforts. Everyone seems to be after the same thing though, and it can get very busy in the lobby.

Sripatana (☎ 0 4425 1652; www.sripatana.com; 346 Th Suranari; r 560B; ✂ 🖳 🖭) So here's the proof that '70s styling made it to Thailand, and stayed way beyond it's welcome. Yep, it's not the hippest of hotels, but the big rooms come at an attractive price.

Chomsurang Hotel (☎ 0 4425 7088; www.chomsur ang.com; 2701/2 Th Mahat Thai; r 800B; ✂ 🖭) A solitary bulb illuminates a solitary receptionist at this slightly gloomy, multistorey offering. The rooms are pretty good though and there are a few midrange facilities – such as a small pool – for creature comfort seekers.

TOP END

Sima Thani Hotel (☎ 0 4421 3100; fax 0 4421 3121; 2112/2 Th Mittaphap; r 1200B; ✂ 🖳 🖭) Standards have slipped since it was sold off by the Sheraton chain, but this remains about the swankiest bet in town. There's a little peeling paint on show, but glass-sided elevators slide up through the central atrium, there's a gym and pool and the staff are sharp and well turned out. Better 'deluxe' rooms – often all that is left if you arrive on spec – cost 1600B.

Royal Princess Khorat (☎ 0 4425 6629; fax 0 4425 6601; 1137 Th Suranari; r 1200B; ✂ 🖳 🖭) On the northeastern outskirts of the city, the Royal Princess was opened by Thailand's Dusit Group, perhaps in an effort not to be out-done by Sima Thani. Starting rates are for standard rooms, and include an excellent breakfast buffet featuring Chinese, Thai and Western food. All rooms have a fridge, bath and satellite TV. Amenities include a lobby bar, restaurant, large pool and business centre.

Eating

Eating on the hoof is best done at one of the city's early evening markets, where Isan specialities can be sampled en masse – keep your eyes peeled for deep-fried insects.

Ton Som Restaurant (☎ 0 4425 2275; Th Wacha-rasarit; mains 60-150B; ✆ 10am-10pm) An odd blend of Thai and Western influences, this top-notch eatery whips up some excellent local specialities and serves them among the Harley Davidson memorabilia. A few *faràng* dishes – presumably catering to ageing US veterans – are also available.

Cabbages & Condoms (☎ 0 4425 8100; 86/1 Th Seup Siri; mains 60-120B; ✆ 10am-10pm) It's in a rather strange location – unless you are staying at Doctor's House – but this regular favourite offers a leafy terrace, plenty of newspaper clippings celebrating its food, a wine list (something of a rarity in this part of Thailand) and tablecloths (another oddity). Food spans the East–West divide, and standards – and prices – are relatively high. Like the original outfit in Bangkok, this is a nonprofit operation sponsored by the Population & Community Development Association.

Chez Andy (☎ 0 4428 9556; Th Manat; mains 80-250B; ✆ 11am-11pm Mon-Sat) Khorat's archetypal expat haunt, this Swiss-managed place – appropriately housed in a red-and-white villa – promises plump steaks, gut-busting grills and staff so attentive they appear to pop out of the woodwork like so many Swiss clock cuckoos.

Thai Pochana (☎ 0 4424 9840; 142 Th Jomsurang-yat; mains 30-120B; ✆ 7am-2am) Taking a step back towards old Khorat, this atmospheric local haunt serves delicious Thai fare in simple, carved wood surrounds. The long-opening hours are an added bonus.

Ling Lao Cheu (no Roman-script sign; ☎ 0 4426 0311; mains 30-100B; ✆ 10am-9.30pm) Point to your favourite fish at this friendly Thai-Chinese spot and it will be out of the tank and into a sizzling wok before you can say 'John Dory'. The Thai menu – no English – has pictures for easy ordering and includes a fantastic array of regional and Chinese favourites. It is down an unnamed street running parallel to Th Jomsurangyat – just look for the bright yellow shop front.

Kai Yang Seup Siri (no Roman-script sign; Th Seup Siri; mains 30-40B; ✆ 10.30am-4pm) Near Doctor's House, this spartan spot has some of the best *kài yâang* and *sôm-tam* in town. There are two Isan places next door to each other here – look for the one with chickens on the grill out the front. Food is usually sold out by 3pm or 4pm.

A line of excellent Isan pavement restaurants can be found along Th Seup Siri. Places come and go, so just wander around until somewhere tickles your fancy. As well as for shopping, **Hua Rot Fai Market** (Th Mukkhamontri) near the Khorat train station is a great place to eat after sundown, as is the **Th Manat night bazaar** (Th Manat); both are at their best from 6pm to 10pm. Cheap and easy eats can also be had at the food court on the 7th floor of **Klang Plaza 2** (Th Jomsurangyat; mains 20-40B; ☽ 10am-9pm).

Other recommendations:

Anego (☎ 0 4426 0530; 62/1 Th Jomsurangyat; dishes 80-250B; ☽ 11am-10pm) For authentic Japanese sushi and noodle dishes.

Doksom (☎ 0 4425 2020; Th Chumphon; ice cream 20-40B; ☽ 9am-6pm) For restorative ice creams.

Drinking

Korat Texas 2003 (☎ 0 4425 6785; 174 Th Jomsurangyat; ☽ 5pm-2am) This alfresco drinking haunt is chock-a-block with lone star state bric-a-brac and sissy (well, real Texans wouldn't approve) flower boxes. You can pull up a bench cut from a log, tap along to the live music (from 10pm) and knock back the beers until the wee small hours.

Entertainment

After listening to the singers at the Thao Suranari Memorial (p439), you can catch a movie at the **Klang Cinema** (☎ 0 4425 9268; Top fl, Klang Plaza, Th Jomsurangyat; movie 60B; ☽ 10am-9pm).

Touristy cultural shows are also hosted by the Sima Thani Hotel (opposite); telephone ahead for the latest programmes.

Shopping

Thanon Manat night bazaar (Th Manat) features cheap clothes, flowers, sunglasses, watches, fruit and food vendors – nothing spectacular, but it's a fine place to spend time.

Of Khorat's malls, the **Mall** (Th Mittaphap; ☽ 10am-10pm) is the largest, glossiest and busiest. **Klang Plaza 2** (Th Jomsurangyat; ☽ 10am-9pm) also offers scores of shops purveying everything from videos to homewares.

As well as its seemingly endless array of army surplus stores, Khorat has many shops that specialise in silk. The highest concentration is along Th Ratchadamnoen, near the Thao Suranari Memorial.

Getting There & Away

AIR

Air Asia (☎ 0 2515 9999; www.airasia.com) flies between Bangkok and Khorat on Wednesday, Friday and Sunday. Flights depart Bangkok at 3.55pm, return at 4.50pm and take about 40 minutes. One-way fares start at 600B –

book early for the cheapest fares. Air Asia is an Internet-based airline, so book online or through the call centre number above.

There is a **Thai Airways International office** (THAI; ☎ 0 4425 2114; www.thaiairways.com; 40-44 Th Suranari; ☽ 8.30am-4.30pm Mon-Fri) in the centre of town, but the airline had suspended flights out of Khorat at the time of writing.

BUS

Buses leave the Northern bus terminal in Bangkok (ordinary/air-con 96/157B, four hours, hourly) from 5am to 7pm.

There are two main bus terminals in Khorat. **Bus terminal 1** (☎ 0 4426 8899; off Th Burin) in the city centre, near the intersection of the Th Mittaphap loop and the highway north to Nong Khai, is principally for destinations within the province. Many of these buses also stop at bus terminal 2 on their way out of town.

BUSES & FARES TO/FROM KHORAT		
Destination	**Fare (B)**	**Duration (hr)**
Chiang Mai		
air-con	437	12
VIP	510	10
Loei		
air-con	220	6
Nakhon Phanom		
air-con	250	7
Nong Khai		
ordinary	110	6
air-con	220	5½
Pattaya		
air-con	210	4
Rayong		
air-con	215	4
Roi Et		
air-con	140	3
Sakon Nakhon		
ordinary	111	6½
air-con	240	6
Ubon		
ordinary	149	6
air-con	260	5
Udon		
ordinary	95	5
air-con	206	4½
Yasothon		
ordinary	80	4
air-con	140	3

Buses to points outside Khorat Province leave from **bus terminal 2** (☎ 0 4425 6006), off the highway to Nong Khai, north of the city centre.

TRAIN

Express trains leave for Bangkok at 10.24am and 6.50pm and take 4½ hours. Normal trains (six hours) leave at 8.22am, 1.10pm, 3.45pm, 8.36pm and 11.28pm. From Bangkok they depart at 5.45am (express), 6.40am, 9.10am, 11.05am (express), 11.45am, 9pm, 9.50pm and 11.40pm. The 1st-class fare (express train only) is 245B, 2nd class is 110B and 3rd class is 50B.

There are also five ordinary trains (2nd/3rd class 213/138B, 6½ hours) plus one express service (1st class 333B, four hours) daily to/from Ubon Ratchathani.

You can contact Khorat's train station on ☎ 0 4424 2044.

Getting Around

Túk-túk cost 60B to most places around the town (30B for a short hop). Motorcycle taxis cost about the same.

AROUND NAKHON RATCHASIMA
Phimai
พิมาย

Blink and you might miss the innocuous little town of Phimai, but at its heart stands one of Northeastern Thailand's finest surviving Khmer temple complexes. Reminiscent of Cambodia's Angkor Wat, which was built

a century later, Prasat Phimai once stood on an important trade route linking the Khmer capital of Angkor with the northern reaches of the realm. Peppered with ruins and surrounded by ragged sections of the ancient town wall, modern-day Phimai still offers a little taste of this historic heyday. There is almost nothing to do here once you have wandered through the ruins – which are far less significant than those at Angkor Wat – but if you prefer the quiet life, this sleepy town makes a pleasant base from which to explore the wider region.

INFORMATION

Kasikornbank (Th Chomsudasadet; ⏰ 8.30am-3.30pm) Near the Prasat Phimai National Historical Park entrance; has ATM and exchange facilities.

Thai Military Bank (Th Anantajinda; ⏰ 8.30am-3.30pm) Near the Prasat Phimai National Historical Park entrance; has ATM and exchange facilities.

Tourist police (☎ 0 4434 1777, emergency ☎ 1155; Th Anantajinda) Also has an office by the park gates.

SIGHTS
Prasat Phimai National Historical Park
อุทยานประวัติศาสตร์พิมาย

What **Prasat Phimai** (☎ 0 4447 1568; Th Anantajinda; admission 40B; ⏰ 7.30am-6pm) lacks in size, it more than makes up for in looks. Started by Khmer King Jayavarman V during the late 10th century and finished by King Suriyavarman I (r AD 1002–49) in the early 11th century, this Hindu-Mahayana Buddhist

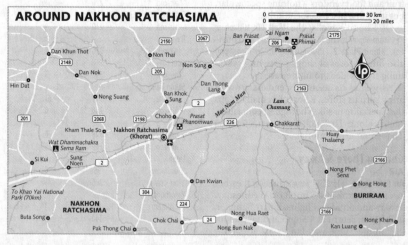

AROUND NAKHON RATCHASIMA

0 —— 30 km
0 —— 20 miles

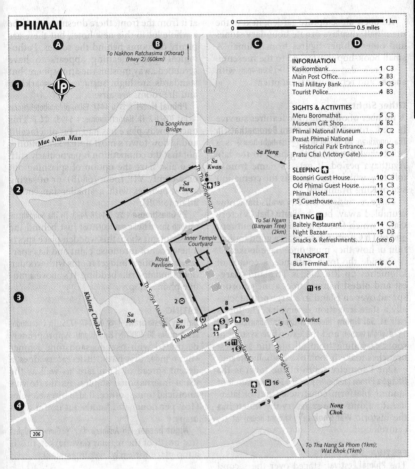

PHIMAI

0 ——————— 1 km
0 ——————— 0.5 miles

INFORMATION
Kasikornbank................................1 C3
Main Post Office.........................2 B3
Thai Military Bank......................3 C3
Tourist Police.............................4 B3

SIGHTS & ACTIVITIES
Meru Boromathat.......................5 C3
Museum Gift Shop......................6 B2
Phimai National Museum............7 C2
Prasat Phimai National
   Historical Park Entrance..........8 C3
Pratu Chai (Victory Gate)...........9 C4

SLEEPING
Boonsiri Guest House.................10 C3
Old Phimai Guest House............11 C3
Phimai Hotel.............................12 C4
PS Guesthouse..........................13 C2

EATING
Baiteiy Restaurant.....................14 C3
Night Bazaar.............................15 D3
Snacks & Refreshments...........(see 6)

TRANSPORT
Bus Terminal.............................16 C4

To Nakhon Ratchasima (Khorat)
(Hwy 2) (60km)

Mae Nam Mun

Tha Songkhram Bridge

Sa Kwan

Sa Plung

Sa Pleng

Inner Temple Courtyard

Royal Pavilions

Khlong Chakrai

Th Suriya Assadong

Sa Bot

Sa Keo

Th Anantajinda

Chomsudasadet

To Sai Ngam (Banyan Tree) (2km)

Market

Th Songkhran

Nong Chok

To Tha Nang Sa Phom (1km);
Wat Khok (1km)

206

---

temple projects a majesty that transcends its size. Although predating Angkor Wat by a hundred years or so, Prasat Phimai nevertheless shares a number of design features with its more famous cousin, not least the roof of its 28m-tall main shrine. It may well be wishful thinking, but the tourist brochures even claim that it might have been the model for Angkor Wat.

Unlike so many of northeastern Thailand's Khmer temples, Prasat Phimai has been elegantly reconstructed by the Fine Arts Department and while it certainly isn't the grandest monument on the circuit, it is one of the most complete. Come here during the week, and you may even get it to yourself.

At the weekend, volunteer guides from **Phimai Witthaya School** (☎ 0 4447 1105) offer free tours.

Phimai National Museum
พิพิธภัณฑสถานแห่งชาติพิมาย
Situated on the banks of Sa Kwan, a 12th-century Khmer reservoir, this **museum** (☎ 0 4447 1167; Th Tha Songkhran; ☉ 9am-4pm) houses a fine collection of Khmer sculptures from Phimai, Phanom Rung and Phanomwan, as well as ceramics from nearby Ban Prasat.

The museum's most prized possession, a stone sculpture of Angkor King Jayavarman VII, comes from Prasat Phimai National Historical Park and looks very much like a sitting Buddha.

An open-air sculpture garden, next to the main hall, displays ornate boundary stones and other Khmer figures from Phimai. A small bookshop is attached to the museum.

There's also a **gift shop** (✿ 9am-4pm) with snacks and refreshments on offer.

Other Sights

A number of other historic features survive in and around Phimai. **Meru Boromathat** (Th Tha Songkhran; admission free; ✿ daylight hours) is a brick *chedi* (stupa) dating back to the late Ayuthaya period. It gets its name from a folk tale, which refers to it as the cremation site of King Bramathat.

Large sections of the city walls have now crumbled away, but the **Pratu Chai** (Victory Gate), which faces Phimai at the southern end of Th Chomsudasadet, is a good indication of how they must once have looked.

Outside the town entrance, a couple of kilometres up Rte 206, is Thailand's largest and oldest banyan tree, a megaflorum spread over an island in a large pond (actually a state irrigation reservoir). The locals call it **Sai Ngam** (Beautiful Banyan; admission free; ✿ daylight hours), and the extensive system of roots cascading from all but the smallest branches make it look like a small forest.

One kilometre south of the town is **Tha Nang Sa Phom** (admission free; ✿ 24hr), an ancient landing platform constructed out of laterite. It adjoins a large reservoir, which has the historic **Wat Khok** (✿ daylight hours) at its centre.

FESTIVALS & EVENTS

The **Phimai Festival**, staged over the second weekend of November, celebrates the town's history and features cultural performances, light shows and dragon boat races. For more information and tickets for the various performances, contact **TAT** (☎ 0 4421 3666; tatsima@tat.or.th; 2102-2104 Th Mittaphap; ✿ 8.30am-4.30pm) in Khorat.

SLEEPING

Old Phimai Guest House (☎ 0 4447 1918; Th Chomsudasadet; dm 80B, r 140-350B; 🍴 🖥) This homey place is a little scruffy, but the backpacker vibe prevails and there's a welcoming atmosphere. It is located down a small alley off Th Chomsudasadet.

Boonsiri Guest House (☎ 0 4447 1159; 228 Th Chomsudasadet; dm 150B, r 350-550B; 🍴) Looking

at it from the front, there doesn't seem to be a whole lot to this new hotel, but there are plenty of rooms behind the scenes. Pathological spring-cleaning appears to have scrubbed away most of the atmosphere, but standards are high, surfaces are sparkling and the rooms are airy.

Phimai Hotel (☎ 0 4447 1306; phimaihotel@korat .in.th; 305/1-2 Th Haruethairome; r 540B; 🍴) This once dowdy place has had a bit of a facelift and is now town's most upmarket option – not that the competition is particularly stiff. You also have the option of splashing out on a comfy VIP room (680B), or of saving a few pennies with a smaller fan-cooled affair (390B).

PS Guesthouse (☎ 0 4428 7490; Th Tha Songkhran; s/d with shared bathroom 100/200B) Just behind the museum gift shop, this wooden place sports a new coat of turquoise paint and has spartan, but spotless budget rooms with wooden floors and no-frills bedding. It's above a mobile phone shop.

EATING

Baiteiy Restaurant (☎ 0 4447 1725; Th Chomsudasadet; mains 30-40B; ✿ 8am-10pm) Appropriately decorated with pseudo-sandstone Khmer engravings, this basic little eatery does a decent spread of Thai fare, as well as the usual international staples. As the town's unofficial tourist office, it also hires bicycles (15B per hour) and hands out useful town maps.

Night bazaar (Th Anantajinda; ✿ 6pm-midnight) Just north of the regular day market, this is a top place for early evening snacks.

GETTING THERE & AWAY

Buses for Phimai leave every half-hour during the day from Khorat's bus terminal 1 (35B, 1¼ hours). The bus terminal in Phimai is around the corner from the Phimai Hotel. The last Phimai bus leaves Khorat's bus terminal 1 at about 10pm; from Phimai the last bus is at 6pm.

GETTING AROUND

Phimai is small enough to walk around. *Săamláw* (three-wheeled pedicab) trips in town cost 20B. If you would like to see more of the town and environs (eg Sai Ngam), you can rent bicycles from Old Phimai Guest House or Baiteiy Restaurant for 15B per hour or 50B per day.

Prasat Phanomwan
ปราสาทพนมวัน

Compared with those at Prasat Phimai, the Khmer ruins of **Prasat Phanomwan** (admission free; ⊙ 24hr) are rather tumbledown. Reconstruction has done something to restore old glories, but the complex lacks the distinctive *prang* (Khmer-style tower) that make so many Khmer temples photogenic and it's harder to get a feel for its original layout. If you are nearby, however, Prasat Phanomwan is certainly worth a quick diversion.

Although the structure is thought to have been originally a shrine to the Hindu god Shiva, images of Buddha that have probably been enshrined here since at least the early Ayuthaya period are still in place and remain the objects of veneration. Until the restoration began, the ruins were actually part of a Buddhist monastery and monks were in charge of maintaining the site.

Although admission was free at the time of writing, a 30B levy (and opening times) is to be introduced.

There are direct buses from Khorat's bus terminal 1 between 7am and 5.30pm (24B, 25 minutes).

Pak Thong Chai
ปักธงชัย

Pak Thong Chai village is one of Thailand's most famous **silk-weaving** centres. Several varieties and qualities of silk are available, and most weavers sell directly to the public, although prices are not necessarily lower than in Khorat or Bangkok. There are around 70 silk factories in the district and plenty of shops – try **Si Chan** (☎ 0 4444 1036; 122-4 Th Siphonrat) or **Thai Hatthaphan** (☎ 0 4444 1518; 194/1 Mu 16, Th Supsiri).

Amarin (☎ 0 4444 1480; 160/2 Th Khorat-Kabin Buri; s/d 250/300B; ⊠), in the village, and the far glitzier **Rooks Khorat Country Club** (☎ 0 1955 2566; r 2400B; ⊠), near the Km 22 marker on Th Khorat–Kabin Buri, offer accommodation.

Pak Thong Chai is 32km south of Khorat on Rte 304. Buses to the village (26B, 40 minutes) leave bus terminal 1 in Khorat every 30 minutes. The last service leaves Khorat at 6pm; from Pak Thong Chai it's 5pm.

Dan Kwian
ด่านเกวียน

Travellers interested in **Thai ceramics** might want to pay a visit to Dan Kwian, which is only 15km southeast of Khorat. This village has been producing pottery for hundreds of years; originally it was a bullock-cart stop for traders on their way to markets in old Khorat (*dàan kwian* means 'bullock-cart checkpoint'). Dan Kwian pottery is famous for its rough texture and rust-like hue – only kaolin sourced from this district produces such results.

Several more-or-less permanent shops line the highway. Prices are very good – many exporters shop for Thai pottery here. It's not all pottery though – clay is shaped and fired into all kinds of art objects, from jewellery to wind chimes. There are also a couple of workshops that produce interesting reproductions of the ancient Khmer sandstone sculpture found at Prasat Phimai and other local sites. There's also a display of old bullock carts from around the country.

To get here from Khorat, hop on a *sǎwngthǎew* from the south or east city gates (12B, 20 minutes).

Sandstone Reclining Buddha Image
พระพุทธไสยาสน์หินทราย

Housed inside **Wat Dhammachakra Sema Ram** in Khorat's Amphoe Sung Noen, this is Thailand's oldest **reclining Buddha** (⊙ daylight hours). Thought to date back to the 8th century, the Dvaravati-style image is unique in that it hasn't been covered with a layer of stucco and a coat of whitewash – it actually looks as old as it is purported to be. The crude but appealing image is protected from the elements by a huge roof, and an altar has been built before it. On display at the wat is a stone rendition of the Buddhist Wheel of Law, also found on the site, which is thought to predate the reclining Buddha image.

Visiting Wat Dhammachakra Sema Ram, 36km southwest of Khorat, is best done as a day trip from there. Sung Noen (25B, 40 minutes) is on the railway line to Bangkok (although only local trains stop here). It can also be reached by any Bangkok-bound, non-air-con bus from Khorat, though the trip may take as long as an hour (40B). From the Sung Noen train station you'll have to hire a *túk-túk* or motorcycle taxi for the final 5km to the wat. Expect to pay about 200B for the return trip, and to wait around an hour or so.

Ban Prasat

บ้านปราสาท

About three thousand years ago, a primitive agricultural/ceramic culture put down roots at Bat Prasat, near the banks of Mae Nam Than Prasat. They survived here for nearly 500 years, planting rice, domesticating animals, fashioning coloured pottery, weaving cloth and, in later years, forging tools out of bronze.

The secrets of this early civilisation were finally revealed during extensive archaeological digs, finally completed in 1991. Many of the **excavation pits** (donations appreciated; ☻ daylight hours) are now on display throughout the village. A small **museum** (☎ 0 4437 7075; donations appreciated; ☻ 8am-5pm) houses the better discoveries, including skeletons and a decent collection of ceramics.

Other layers uncovered during the excavations indicate that the site was later taken over by a pre–Dvaravati Mon city, followed by a 10th-century settlement, which left behind a small brick sanctuary known locally as **Ku Than Prasat** (admission free; ☻ daylight hours). This structure shows both Dvaravati and Khmer characteristics, and may have been a cultural transition point between Mon kingdoms to the west and the Khmer principalities to the east.

Many of the houses in Ban Prasat village are now part of a **cultural homestay programme**, which allows villagers to put up visitors in their homes. The cost is 400B per person per night and includes two meals. Reservations should be made at least one week in advance through the TAT office in Khorat or by calling the village headman, Mr Thiam Laongklang (☎ 0 4436 7075).

GETTING THERE & AWAY

Ban Prasat is 45km northeast of Khorat, off Hwy 2 between Non Sung and Phimai. Some ordinary buses between Phimai and Khorat stop in Ban Prasat (20B, 40 minutes). In Ban Prasat a motorcycle taxi can take you to all three excavation sites, including waiting time of about 15 minutes at each site, for about 100B.

KHAO YAI NATIONAL PARK

อุทยานแห่งชาติเขาใหญ่

Up there on the podium with some of world's greatest national parks, **Khao Yai** (☎ 0 3731 9002; reserve@dnp.go.th; admission 200B; ☻ 8am-

6pm) is Thailand's oldest and most-visited reserve and, covering 2165 sq km, incorporates one of the largest intact monsoon forests remaining in mainland Asia. It has even carved a niche for itself in Hollywood, with its Nam Tok Haew Suwat (waterfall) scooping a starring role in the Danny Boyle film *The Beach*.

Some 200 to 300 wild elephants tramp the park's boundaries; other mammals recorded include sambar deer, barking deer, gaur, wild pig, Malayan sun bear, Asiatic black bear, tiger, leopard, serow, and various gibbons and macaques. In general these animals are most easily spotted during the rainy season from June to October, although most visitors come during the November to February cool season, when the climate is most suited to trekking. Khao Yai also has Thailand's largest population of hornbills, including the great hornbill (*nók kòk* or *nók kaahang* in Thai), king of the bird kingdom, as well as the wreathed hornbill (*nók ngaa cháang;* literally 'elephant-tusk bird'), Indian pied hornbill (*nók khàek*) and rhinoceros hornbill *(nók râet)*. Hornbills breed from January to May, and this is the best time to see them. They also feed on figs, so ficus trees are good places to find them. Caves in the park are home to rare wrinkle-lipped bats and Himalayan ribbed bats.

Rising to 1351m, with the summit of Khao Rom, the park's terrain covers five vegetation zones: evergreen rainforest (100m to 400m); semi-evergreen rainforest (400m to 900m); mixed deciduous forest (northern slopes at 400m to 600m); hill evergreen forest (over 1000m); savannah and secondary-growth forest in areas where agriculture and logging occurred before it was protected.

The park has plenty of hiking trails, many of them formed by the movement of wildlife, but it's all too easy to get lost on the longer tracks – hiring a guide is recommended. Rangers may be able to act as guides for 200B per day. If you do plan to go walking, it is a good idea to take along boots as leeches can be a problem – mosquito repellent also helps keep them away. There are also three wildlife-watching towers in the park.

Colour topographical maps of the park are usually available to buy at the **visitors centre** (☻ 8.30am-4.30pm).

Many of the guesthouses in and around the nearby town of Pak Chong offer tours

of the park. Packages lasting 1½ days start at 1000B, including accommodation, food, a guide and transfers.

Sleeping & Eating

The park offers a huge range of accommodation inside the reserve, from **camping sites** (per person 30B) and basic two-sleeper **bungalows** (r 800B), to rather swankier six-bed **villas** (3500B) with air-con and fridge. Accommodation should be booked through the **reservations office** (☎ 0 2562 0760; reserve@dnp.go.th).

There are also dozens of places to stay in and around the nearby town of Pak Chong.

Palm Garden Lodge (☎ 0 9989 4470; www.palgalo .com; r 400-650B; ☒) This welcoming place allows a little piece of the park to creep into its pleasant grounds, with lush gardens and rustic-style décor. The lodge is 7km south of the park's southern gate, near Ban Kon Khuang on Hwy 33. Tours of the park can be arranged.

Juldis Khao Yai Resort (☎ 0 2556 0251; fax 0 2256 0257; 54 Mu 4, Km 17, Th Thanarat; r 1750B; ☒) This plush place is one of the Khao Yai area originals and offers resort-style standards, pleasant gardens and airy rooms. It is on the road between Pak Chong and the park.

Green Leaf Guest House (☎ 0 4436 5024; r 200B) This old favourite is 7.5km out of town (just beyond the International School) on the way to Khao Yai. Friendly, polished and cosy it serves good food, and has been praised for its informative tours, including bird-watching and night-time 'spot-light' tours to look for nocturnal animals.

Khao Yai Garden Lodge (☎ 0 4436 5178; www.khao yai-garden-lodge.de; r 900B; ☒) Some 7km outside Pak Chong, en route to the park, this expat-run outfit is big with the German set and has a reasonable programme of tours as well as some snug rooms. Fan rooms cost 500B.

Other recommendations:

Pak Chong Highland Country Club (☎ 0 4431 3877; fax 0 4431 3878; 156 Th Pak Chong-Lamsomphung; dm 500B, r 1200B, ste 3000B; ☒) With a wide range of rooms.

Pakchong Landmark (☎ 0 4428 0047; fax 0 4428 0054; 151/1 Th Mittaphap; r 1200B; ☒)

A **night market** (⏰ 5-11pm), near the main highway intersection in Pak Chong, purveys a wide range of Thai and Chinese food.

There are also five **restaurants** in Khao Yai National Park: at the visitors centre, the Orchid Campsite, the Lam Takhong Camp-site, Nam Tok Haew Suwat and Nam Tok Haew Narok.

Getting There & Away

From Bangkok, take a bus (ordinary/air-con 90/150B, three hours, every 30 minutes from 5am to 10pm) from the Northern bus terminal to Pak Chong. You can also get to Pak Chong by train from Bangkok, but it is much slower than the bus.

From Khorat, take a Bangkok-bound bus and get off in Pak Chong (ordinary/air-con 28/65B, one hour).

You can also reach Pak Chong from Ayuthaya (3rd/2nd class 26/58B, 2½ hours) and Khorat (3rd/2nd class 20/50B, 1½ hours) on ordinary trains, which run the route about eight times daily.

From Pak Chong you can catch a *săwng-thăew* to the park's gates for 10B from in front of the 7-Eleven store.

BURIRAM PROVINCE

Touch down in the little provincial capital of Buriram and you might wonder what all the fuss is about. Despite being at the heart of one of Thailand's larger provinces, Buriram itself is little more than a patchwork of roads and a handful of shops. The best advice is to leave the city behind and make a beeline into the countryside, where you will find a landscape chock-a-block with history and peppered with ruins – a massive 143 of them.

The crowning glory is Phanom Rung, a beautifully restored Khmer temple complex straddling the summit of an extinct volcano. One of the most spectacular Angkor monuments in Thailand, Phanom Rung is worth the journey and should impress even those suffering from acute temple overload. For those with an insatiable appetite for ruins, Buriram also offers a smorgasbord of lesser-known ruins, including Prasat Meuang Tam, Ku Rasi, Prasat Ban Khok Ngiu, Prasat Nong Hong, Prasat Ban Thai Charoen, Prasat Nong Kong, Prang Ku Samathom, Prang Ku Khao Plaibat, Prang Ku Suwan Taeng and Prang Ku Khao Kadong. Many are little more than piles of laterite, but the locals are justifiably proud of them – using some as backdrops for Buddhist festivals – and together they create a picture of the crucial role this region once played in the Khmer empire.

BURIRAM
บุรีรัมย์

pop 30,000

The forgettable capital of Buriram is a possible base for exploring the region's temples, but the accommodation scene is poor and there's very little to keep you occupied. Surin (see p516), or the little town of Nang Rong (right), which is closer to Phanom Rung, both offer better sleeping options.

Information

Bangkok Bank (cnr Th Sunthonthep & Th Thani; 8.30am-3.30pm) Has ATM and exchange facilities.

Buriram Comnet (0 4461 2789; 8-10 Th Nivas; per hr 20B; 8am-10pm) Check your email at this place near the train station.

Post office (Th Isan; 8.30am-4.30pm Mon-Fri) South of the centre, near the market.

Sleeping

BURIRAM

Buriram's choice of accommodation is pretty bleak.

Thai Hotel (0 4461 1112; fax 0 6441 2461; 38/1 Th Romburi; r 220-320B;) Seemingly built as a case

study for the crazy school of architecture, this otherwise pleasant little place has decent rooms and a brace of decorative wooden elephants to greet you at the door.

Grand Hotel (no Roman-script sign; 0 4461 1179; 139 Th Nivas; r 210-350B;) There's nothing grand about it – well, that is apart from the shade of turquoise it has been daubed – but this so-so place near the train station has passable rooms and plenty of them. There's no English sign, so just keep an eye out for the colour.

Siriporn Hotel (0 4460 1102; fax 0 4460 1103; 1/141 Th Bulamduan; r 350B;) This prissy pink place is spotlessly clean and extremely neat. It isn't overtly apparent, but you do get the feeling that it may also cater to male clientele of the short-term variety. It is about 1km west down Th Thani, out near the bus station.

NANG RONG

You can also stay closer to Phanom Rung by spending the night at this tiny town off the highway.

Honey Inn (0 4462 2825; http://honeyinn.com; 8/1 Soi Si Kun; d 150-200B) This welcoming home-

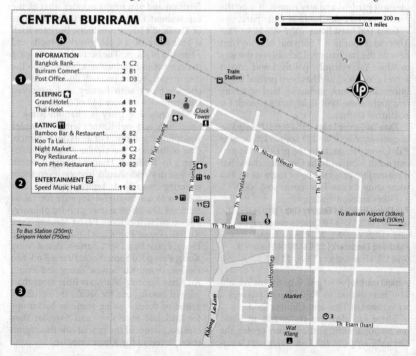

CENTRAL BURIRAM

0 _____ 200 m
0 _____ 0.1 miles

INFORMATION	
Bangkok Bank	1 C2
Buriram Comnet	2 B1
Post Office	3 D3

SLEEPING	
Grand Hotel	4 B1
Thai Hotel	5 B2

EATING	
Bamboo Bar & Restaurant	6 B2
Koo Ta Lai	7 B1
Night Market	8 C2
Ploy Restaurant	9 B2
Porn Phen Restaurant	10 B2

ENTERTAINMENT	
Speed Music Hall	11 B2

Train Station

Clock Tower

Th Plai Meuang

Th Romburi

Th Nivas (Niwat)

Th Samatakan

Th Lak Meuang

Th Thani

Th Sunthonthep

Th Esarn (Isan)

Market

Wat Klang

Khlong La-Lom

To Bus Station (250m);
Siriporn Hotel (750m)

To Buriram Airport (30km);
Sateuk (30km)

stay is run by a knowledgeable, English-speaking teacher and falls into the cosy, slightly tumbledown category of sleeping options, some with shared facilities. To find it, walk 100m from the bus stop to the main road, turn east and go 100m past a petrol station on the left, then turn left just before the hospital and it's about 150m further on the right (past a reservoir). Or take a *săamláw* for 30B. Good food is also available and motorcycles can be rented for 250B per day – very handy for visiting Phanom Rung and Meuang Tam.

PHANOM RUNG & BAN TA PEK

At the time of writing, **camping sites** (per person 40B) and basic **bungalows** (r 600B) were available at the Phanom Rung Historical Park. However, it wasn't certain whether this would continue; check availability on ☎ 0 4463 1746 before you turn up.

  Phanom Rung Resort (☎ 0 4463 1231; 83 Mu 1 Tambon Ta Pek; r 800B; ❷) One kilometre from Phanom Rung, in the nearby village of Ban Ta Pek, this resort-style place has so-so rooms and a handy location.

Eating

In Buriram, at the Th Samatakan and Th Thani intersection, there is a large **night market** (❹ 5-10pm).

  Koo Ta Lai (no Roman-script sign; ☎ 0 4461 2089; 136-138 Th Nivas; mains 30-100B; ❹ 5pm-midnight) Just down from the train station, this Chinese-style place has plenty of fresh fish on display out front and cauldrons of oddities to pick from inside. It's basic but tasty.

  Bamboo Bar & Restaurant (☎ 0 4462 5577; 14/13 Th Romburi; mains 30-100B; ❹ 7am-midnight) With a dart board, satellite TV and an entire wall made out of Heineken and Chang cans, this is the home-from-home of Buriram's expat set. It has a lively atmosphere once the drinking starts, and the menu includes some OK Thai dishes, as well as Western staples from chicken Kiev to Sunday roasts.

  Ploy Restaurant (no Roman-script sign; ☎ 0 4461 3747; Th Romburi; dishes 60-80B; ❹ noon-10pm) Just south of the Thai Hotel, this no-frills eatery whips up some very good Thai food and Western breakfasts with real coffee. Parched vinophiles may also delight in the (limited) wine list.

  Porn Phen Restaurant (no Roman-script sign; ☎ 0 4461 1553; Th Romburi; dishes 30-50B; ❹ noon-10pm)

Near Ploy, this is good for basic Thai food and Isan dishes.

  There are also a few basic eateries at the Phanom Rung Historical Park.

Entertainment

Speed Music Hall (☎ 0 4461 4124; Th Romburi; ❹ 6pm-1am) Speed is indeed the theme at this tub-thumping music club. A silver spaceship hangs in front of a hastily daubed Mars-scape out front and neon lights flicker in the darkness within. It is hidden behind a bizarre 'Neo-Classical' (quotes essential) building just off Th Romburi.

Getting There & Away

AIR

Phuket Air (☎ 0 4462 5066) has a ticket office at the airport and flies once daily to/from Bangkok (one way 1455B).

BUS

Ordinary buses between Khorat and Buriram leave every 20 minutes between 4.30am and 8pm (60B, 2¼ hours). From Surin, ordinary buses head for Buriram at a similar frequency (30B, one hour).

  From Bangkok's Northern bus terminal there are seven air-con services (220B, 5½ hours), and ordinary buses (140B, six hours) also.

TRAIN

Buriram is on the Bangkok–Ubon Ratchathani line. Eight direct trains travel daily between Buriram and Bangkok, with the fastest services leaving Bangkok at 5.45am and 11.05am and departing Buriram for Bangkok at 8.38am and 5.19pm – these take six hours. The slower trains take between seven and eight hours. Trains going in both directions also stop at Khorat (3rd/2nd class 20/40B), which is two hours from Buriram. Fares to Bangkok vary depending on the standard of the trains, but fares start at 70B for 3rd class and 175B for 2nd class and go as high as 565B for an air-con sleeper cabin on one of the overnight services.

  Trains to/from Bangkok start at, or continue on to, Ubon Ratchathani. The fastest train to Ubon departs Buriram at 11.43am and takes 2½ hours. The slower services take about four hours. The quickest train from Ubon is the 2.50pm, which also takes

2½ hours to reach Buriram. Fares to Ubon are 50B for 3rd class, 130B for 2nd class and up to 491B for an air-con sleeper.

You can get up-to-date train information from **Buriram station** (☎ 0 4461 1202).

Getting Around

Săamláw and *túk-túk* going from the Buriram train station charge 20B to the town centre and 40B to the airport.

PRASAT HIN KHAO PHANOM RUNG HISTORICAL PARK

อุทยานประวัติศาสตร์เขาพนมรุ้ง

If there is a knock-me-dead location to be found in this part of Buriram, **Phanom Rung** (☎ 0 4463 1746; admission 40B; ❂ 6am-6pm) has it. Crowning the summit of a spent volcano, 1320 feet above sea level, the sanctuary sits a good 70 storeys above the flat paddy fields below. To the southeast you can clearly see Cambodia's Dongrek mountains and it's in this direction that the capital of the Angkor empire once lay. The Phanom Rung temple complex is the largest and best restored of all the Khmer monuments in Thailand (it took 17 years to complete the restoration) and, although it's not the easiest place to reach, it more than rewards those that make the effort.

Around the time of the nationwide Songkran Festival in April, the local people have their own special celebration, the **Prasat Hin Khao Phanom Rung Festival**, which commemorates the restoration of Phanom Rung. During the morning there is a procession up Khao Phanom Rung, and at nighttime sound-and-light shows and dance-dramas are performed in the temple complex. Staged on the full-moon day for the best solar alignment, the rising sun shines through all 15 of the sanctuary doorways on the morning of the festival. For more information and exact dates of the celebrations each year, get in contact with the **TAT** (☎ 0 4421 3666; tatsima@ at.or.th; 2102-2104 Th Mittaphap; ❂ 8.30am-4.30pm) in Khorat.

Phanom Rung is Khmer for 'Big Hill', but the Thais have added their own word for hill (*khăo*) to the name as well as the word for stone (*hĭn*) to describe the *prasat* (a small ornate building with a cruciform ground plan and a needle-like spire). Its full name is Prasat Hin Khao Phanom Rung.

The Phanom Rung temple was erected between the 10th and 13th centuries, the bulk of it during the reign of King Suriyavarman II (r AD 1113–50), which by all accounts was the apex of Angkor architecture. The complex faces east, towards the original Angkor capital. Of the three other great Khmer monuments of Southeast Asia, Cambodia's Angkor Wat faces west, its Prasat Khao Wihan faces north and Thailand's Prasat Phimai faces southeast. Nobody knows for sure whether these orientations have any special significance, especially as most smaller Khmer monuments in Thailand face east (towards the dawn – typical of Hindu temple orientation).

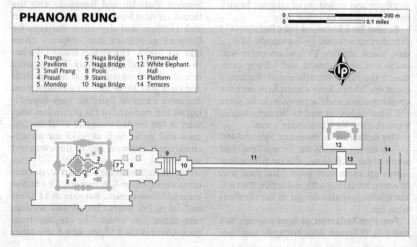

PHANOM RUNG

0 — 200 m
0 — 0.1 miles

1 Prangs
2 Pavilions
3 Small Prang
4 Prasat
5 Mondóp
6 Naga Bridge
7 Naga Bridge
8 Pools
9 Stairs
10 Naga Bridge
11 Promenade
12 White Elephant Hall
13 Platform
14 Terraces

English-speaking guides offer their services at the complex – fees are negotiable. Downhill a bit from the main sanctuary is a visitors centre that houses a scale model of the area as well as some artefacts found at the site.

Design

One of the most remarkable design aspects of Phanom Rung is the promenade leading to the main gate. This is the best surviving example in Thailand. It begins on a slope 400m east of the main tower, with three earthen terraces. Next comes a cruciform base for what may have been a wooden pavilion. To the right of this is a stone hall known locally as the Rohng Cháng Phèuak (White Elephant Hall). On the northern side of this hall are two pools that were probably once used for ritual ablutions before entering the temple complex. Flower garlands to be used as offerings in the temple may also have been handed out here. After you step down from the pavilion area, you'll come to a 160m avenue paved with laterite and sandstone blocks, and flanked by sandstone pillars with lotus-bud tops, said to be early Angkor style (AD 1100–80). The avenue ends at the first and largest of three *naga* (mythical serpent-like creature) bridges.

These *naga* bridges are the only ones that have survived in Thailand. The first is flanked by 16 five-headed *naga* in the classic Angkor style – in fact, these figures are identical to those found at Angkor Wat. After passing this bridge and climbing the stairway you come to the magnificent east gallery leading into the main sanctuary. The central *prasat* has a gallery on each of its four sides and the entrance to each gallery is itself a smaller version of the main tower. The galleries have curvilinear roofs and false-balustrade windows. Once inside the temple walls, have a look at each of the galleries and the *gopura* (entrance pavilion), paying particular attention to the lintels over the porticoes. The craftsmanship at Phanom Rung represents the pinnacle of Khmer artistic achievement, on par with the reliefs at Angkor Wat in Cambodia.

Sculpture

The Phanom Rung complex was originally constructed as a Hindu monument and exhibits iconography related to the worship of Vishnu and Shiva. Excellent sculptures of both Vaishnava and Shaiva deities can be seen in the lintels or pediments over the doorways to the central monuments and in various other key points on the sanctuary exterior.

On the east portico of the *mondòp* (square, spired building) is found a Nataraja (Dancing Shiva), which is late Baphuan or early Angkor style, while on the south entrance are the remains of Shiva and Uma riding their bull mount, Nandi. The central cell of the *prasat* contains a Shivalingam (phallus image).

Several sculpted images of Vishnu and his incarnations, Rama and Krishna, decorate various other lintels and cornices. Probably the most beautiful is the Phra Narai lintel, a relief depicting a reclining Vishnu (Narayana) in the Hindu creation myth. Growing from his navel is a lotus that branches into several blossoms, on one of which sits the creator god Brahma. On either side of Vishnu are heads of Kala, the god of time and death. He is asleep on the milky sea of eternity, here represented by a *naga*. This lintel sits above the eastern gate (the main entrance) beneath the Shiva Nataraja relief.

Getting There & Away

Phanom Rung can be approached from Khorat, Buriram or Surin. From Khorat, take a Surin-bound bus and get off at Ban Ta-Ko (ordinary/air-con 35/60B, 1¼ hours), which is about 14 km past Nang Rong; Ban Ta-Ko is well marked as the turn-off for Phanom Rung.

Once in Ban Ta-Ko there are a number of options. At the Ban Ta-Ko intersection you can either catch a *săwngthăew* (Saturday to Sun only) that's going as far as the foot of Phanom Rung (20B, 20 minutes), or one headed south to Lahan Sai. If you take a Lahan Sai truck, get off at the Ban Ta Pek intersection (you'll see signs pointing the way to Phanom Rung to the east) – it will cost 10B. From Ban Ta Pek, you will then have to hire a motorcycle taxi the rest of the way to Phanom Rung (100B return).

If you don't have the patience to wait for a *săwngthăew*, take a motorcycle taxi from Ban Ta-Ko all the way to Phanom Rung (200B return); for an extra 50B the drivers will add Prasat Meuang Tam (see following).

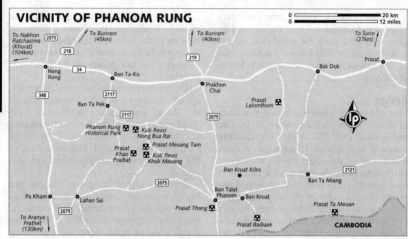

VICINITY OF PHANOM RUNG

These rates include waiting times while you tour the ruins.

It's easier to get to Phamon Rung from Buriram. From here, Chanthaburi-bound buses stop at Ban Ta Pek (ordinary 30B, one hour); you can then continue as above.

From Nang Rong, catch a *săwngthăew* to Ban Ta-Ko (10B, 15 minutes) and go from there. Alternatively, hire a motorbike from Honey Inn (250B per day) and drive yourself.

From Surin, take a Khorat-bound bus and get off at Ban Ta-Ko (ordinary/air-con 35/60B, 1¼ hours), then follow the directions as above.

If you decide to rent a motorbike to visit these sites, pay close attention to the surface of the roads. Southern Isan has some colossal potholes and plenty of roaming cows.

PRASAT MEUANG TAM & OTHER RUINS

In the little village of Khok Meuang, the restored Khmer temple of **Prasat Meuang Tam** (☎ 0 1730 5811; 30B; ☼ 6am-6pm) is an ideal bolt-on to any visit to Phanom Rung, which is only 8km to the northwest. Dating back to the late 10th century and sponsored by King Jayavarman V, this is probably Isan's third most interesting temple complex – after Phanom Rung and Phimai – in terms of size, atmosphere and the quality of restoration work. The whole complex is surrounded by laterite walls, within which are four lotus-filled reservoirs, each guarded by whimsical five-headed *naga*. Sandstone galleries and *gopura,* the latter exquisitely carved, surround five brick *prang*. The towers themselves, being brick, are not nearly as tall or as imposing as the sandstone *prang* at Phanom Rung, but the plan is based on the same design as that of Angkor Wat: the five peaks of Mt Meru, the mythical abode of the Hindu gods. A lintel on one of the towers, depicting Shiva and his consort Uma riding the sacred bull Nandi, suggests that the temple was once a shrine to Shiva. A Shivalingam was also found in the central tower. A small **information centre** (☼ 6am-6pm), across the road from the temple, sells tickets and has some related exhibits in English.

There are plenty more, less impressive ruins in the area – at time of writing, all of the following sites were free and open during daylight hours. East of Phanom Rung are the small Khmer ruins of **Kuti Reusi Nong Bua Rai** and **Prasat Khao Praibat**. Further east of these is **Prasat Lalomthom**. South of Prasat Meuang Tam is **Kuti Reusi Khok Meuang**. From here you can continue southeast to **Prasat Thong** and **Prasat Baibaek**. All of these sites have been restored or stabilised to some degree by the Fine Arts Department and are marked by signs along the highways. Continue via Ban Kruat and Ban Ta Miang (along Rte 2075 and Rte 2121) to **Prasat Ta Meuan** (p515), a secluded Khmer ruins complex on the Thai–Cambodian border. From Ba Ta Miang you can then proceed north to Surin town or continue east along the border to Si Saket and Ubon Ratchathani Provinces.

Getting There & Away

By far the easiest way to visit these ruins is to hire a car or motorbike in Surin or Khorat and to drive yourself – it's simply not worth trying to reach them on public transport. Alternatively, you can contact the guide Khun Pirom of Pirom's House (Sleeping p516) in Surin, who offers highly recommended bespoke tours of the area.

CHAIYAPHUM PROVINCE

Travelling through Chaiyaphum Province, you're almost as likely to run into a tiger as a tourist – and this is not a province with a lot of tigers. Despite its position at the heart of the country, it is a remote, largely unvisited region and remains something of a mystery, even to Thais. Famous for its flowers – and not a whole lot else – Chaiyaphum doesn't offer the traveller much more than a sense of straying off the beaten track, but it's worth a peep if you are into peace and quiet and a more detailed look at Thailand's silk industry.

The several Khmer shrine ruins in the province – none of which are major sites – indicate that the territory was an Angkor,

and later Lopburi, satellite during the 10th and 11th centuries.

CHAIYAPHUM & AROUND

ชัยภูมิ

pop 55,500

Chaiyaphum is a bit of a nowhere town and is a base for visiting the surrounding attractions rather than a destination in itself. In brief, silk lovers should head west to the village of Ban Khwao, history aficionados should make for the Angkor-era tower of Prang Ku and the outdoorsy should visit the relatively unknown Tat Ton National Park. After that, Chaiyaphum is merely a place to bed down for the night.

History

In the late 18th century a Lao court official brought 200 Lao from Vientiane to settle this area, which had been abandoned by the Khmers some 500 years earlier. The community paid tribute to Vientiane but also cultivated relations with Bangkok and Champasak. When Prince Anou (from Vientiane) declared war on Siam in the early 19th century, the Lao ruler of Chaiyaphum, Jao Phraya Lae, wisely switched allegiance to Bangkok, knowing that Anou's armies didn't stand a chance against the more powerful Siamese. Although Jao Phraya Lae lost his life in battle in 1806, the Siamese sacked Vientiane in 1828 and ruled most of western Laos until the coming of the French near the end of the 19th century. Today a

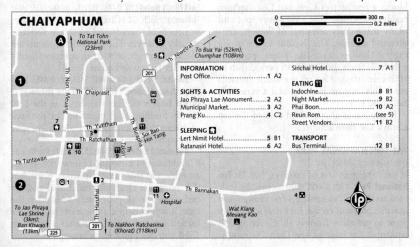

CHAIYAPHUM

INFORMATION	
Post Office	1 A2

SIGHTS & ACTIVITIES	
Jao Phraya Lae Monument	2 A2
Municipal Market	3 A2
Prang Ku	4 C2

SLEEPING	
Lert Nimit Hotel	5 B1
Ratanasiri Hotel	6 A2

Sirichai Hotel..............................7 A1

EATING	
Indochine	8 B1
Night Market	9 B2
Phai Boon	10 A2
Reun Rom	(see 5)
Street Vendors	11 B2

TRANSPORT	
Bus Terminal	12 B1

To Tat Tohn National Park (23km)

Th Niwetrat

To Bua Yai (52km); Chumphae (108km)

Th Non Meuang

201

Th Chaiprasit

12

Th Yutitham

Th Burapha

Th Takun

Soi Ban Hin Tang

Th Ratchathan

Th Tantawan

225

To Jao Phraya Lae Shrine (3km); Ban Khwao (13km)

201

Th Haruthai

To Nakhon Ratchasima (Khorat) (118km)

Th Bannakan

Hospital

Wat Klang Meuang Kao

0   300 m
0   0.2 miles

statue of Jao Phraya Lae (renamed Phraya Phakdi Chumphon by the Thais) stands in a prominent spot in central Chaiyaphum on Th Bannakan.

Information

Post office (Th Bannakan; ☉ 8.30am-4.30pm Mon-Fri) Near the corner of Th Non Meuang.

Sights

BAN KHWAO
บ้านเขว้า

One highlight of a visit into this region is a wander through the silk village of **Ban Khwao** (13km southwest of town on Hwy 225). Silk can also be purchased at Chaiyaphum shops or in the municipal market in the centre of town. Buses to Ban Khwao leave from the bus terminal every 20 minutes between 6am and 6pm (10B, 20 minutes). If you've never observed the silk process – from the cultivation of mulberry trees and propagation of silkworms to the dyeing and weaving of silk thread – you're in for an interesting day.

PRANG KU
ปรางค์กู่

This hollow Khmer **prang** (☉ daylight hours) was constructed during the reign of the final Angkor king, Jayavarman VII (AD 1181–1219), as a place of worship at a 'healing station' on the Angkor temple route between the Angkor capital in Cambodia and Prasat Singh in Kanchanaburi Province. It's not much to look at, just a pile of laterite blocks a few metres high, but Chaiyaphum residents consider this a very holy spot and many make daily offerings of flowers, candles and incense. The Buddha figure inside the *ku* (hollow, cave-like stupa) purportedly hails from the Dvaravati period (6th to 10th centuries). Also on the small grounds are a Shivalingam pedestal and a venerable tamarind tree.

Prang Ku is about 800m east of the Jao Phraya Lae monument.

TAT TON NATIONAL PARK
อุทยานแห่งชาติตาดโตน

It isn't the grandest of reserves, but **Tat Ton National Park** (☎ 0 4481 0020; reserve@dnp.go.th; admission 200B; ☉ 7am-5pm) gets few visitors and makes a pleasant escape for those who really want to get away from it all. Covering 218 sq km at the edge of the Laen Da moun-

tain range, Tat Ton is best known for its photogenic waterfalls: **Tat Ton**, **Tat Klang** and **Pha Phiang**. Nam Tok Tat Ton Falls are the largest, reaching a width of 50m during the May-to-October monsoon. Most of the vegetation in the park is dry dipterocarp forest. The park's animal inhabitants are unlikely to thrill big game seekers, but populations of barking deer, wild pig, mongoose and Siamese hare are relatively commonplace.

The park has **camping sites** (per person 30B) and 10 **bungalows** (for 4 people from 1200B); phone the **reservations office** (☎ 0 2562 0760) to make a booking.

It's best to have your own vehicle to find the park since there's no regular public transport from Chaiyaphum. Alternatively, you can get a *săwngthăew* from Chaiyaphum as far as Ban Khwao (10B, 25 minutes), then hire a *săwngthăew* on to the park for about 100B one way. If you do have your own wheels, the park is 23km northwest of Chaiyaphum via Rte 2051.

Festivals & Events

Chaiyaphum residents celebrate a week-long **festival** in Jao Phraya Lae's honour each year in mid-January. Activities focus on his statue and on a **shrine** erected on the spot where he was killed by Vientiane troops in 1806 – at the base of a tamarind tree about 3km southwest of town off the road to Ban Khwao (Hwy 225).

Sleeping

Lert Nimit Hotel (☎ 0 4481 1522; fax 0 4482 2335; 1/447 Th Niwetrat; r 650B; 🗙) Chaiyaphum doesn't cater to droves of tourists and so this is about as swanky as it gets. The tidy air-con rooms are pleasant enough, or you can opt for a slightly dowdier fan-cooled affair (250B).

Sirichai Hotel (☎ 0 4481 1461; fax 0 4481 2299; 565/1 Th Non Meuang; r 600B; 🗙) This three-star outfit boasts similar standards as the Lert Nimit. Smiling staff make up for the lack of atmosphere and there are also cheaper fan rooms (200B).

Ratanasiri Hotel (☎ 0 4482 1258; cnr Th Non Meuang & Th Ratchathan; r 150-350B; 🗙) Fireworks are not an option at this rather ordinary place, but the rooms are clean and functional and the beds won't break your back. As is often the case, it would help if a few more lights were turned on, but with fan rooms starting at 150B you can't go too far wrong.

Eating

Phai Boon (Th Ratchathan; mains 30-50B; ⏱ 10am-10pm)
Next to the Ratanasiri Hotel, this no-frills
little diner serves the usual Thai and Chinese
standards to a reasonably regular stream of
loyal locals.

Indochine (Th Burapha; mains 50-100B; ⏱ 10am-
10pm) Isan and Vietnamese dishes tip the
billing at this popular place. It's hard to in-
ject much glamour into a sparse room filled
with plastic chairs, but the food certainly
gets the tastebuds buzzing.

Reun Rom (Th Niwetrat; dishes 40-100B; ⏱ 10am-
midnight) Round the back of the Lert Nimit
Hotel, this serves good Thai and Western
food, and is open right the way through to
the witching hour.

Excellent *kài yâang* is the speciality of a
cluster of **street vendors** (Th Bannakan) in front
of the hospital (food is served only during
the day). Chaiyaphum also has a busy **night
market** (⏱ 5-10pm) off Th Taksin.

Getting There & Away

Chaiyaphum can be reached by ordinary bus
(40B, two hours, six daily) from Khon Kaen
and Khorat.

Buses from Bangkok's Northern bus terminal cost 200B for air-con (five hours, 18
daily), and 105B for ordinary (six hours,
every half-hour from 6am to 9pm).

Getting Around

A *túk-túk* should cost no more than 25B for
any destination in town.

KHON KAEN & ROI ET PROVINCES

Farming and textiles still dominate life in
the largely rural provinces of Khon Kaen
and Roi Et, but the area lies at the heart of
Isan and is an excellent place to dip a toe
into the region's culture. On the flipside,
things are booming in Khon Kaen itself and
the city makes for a lively stopover if you
fancy a quick slug of metropolitan living.

KHON KAEN

ขอนแก่น

pop 145,300

On the face of it at least, Khon Kaen is
the darling of Isan's economic boomtime.

The skyline is on the rise, neon illuminates
the night and a bumper crop of bars and
restaurants entertain an expanding middle
class. As the site of the northeast's largest university and an important hub for all
things commercial and financial, the city is
youthful, educated and on the move.

Of course, not everyone will feel the urge
to celebrate in Khon Kaen's downtown clubs.
With a sterile concrete veneer blanketing
most of the centre, this big city has inherited
little of Isan's idiosyncratic appeal. Wandering through traffic, with office blocks above,
it sometimes takes the elephants, trudging
down the busy downtown streets, to remind
you that you are in Thailand at all.

But with fine eateries, swanky hotel rooms
and plenty of places to wear holes in your
dancing shoes, Khon Kaen is the ideal spot
to decompress after humping it through the
northeast's quieter corners.

History

The city gets its name from Phra That Kham
Kaen, a revered *chedi* at Wat Chetiyaphum
in the village of Ban Kham in Amphoe Nam
Phong, 32km to the northeast. Legend says
that early in the last millennium a *thâat* (four-
sided, curvilinear reliquary stupa) was built
over a tamarind tree stump that miraculously
came to life after a contingent of monks carrying Buddha relics to Phra That Phanom (in
today's Nakhon Phanom Province) camped
here overnight. There was no room at That
Phanom for more relics, so the monks returned to this spot and enshrined the relics in
the new That Kham Kaen (Tamarind Heartwood Reliquary). A town developed nearby,
but was abandoned several times until 1789
when a Suwannaphum ruler founded a city at
the current site, which he named Kham Kaen
after the *chedi*. Over the years the name has
changed to Khon Kaen (Heartwood Log).

Information

INTERNET ACCESS

There are dozens of Internet cafés in town,
but many give priority to school children
playing computer games.

Internet (Th Si Chan; per hr 15B; ⏱ 10am-midnight)
Near the Sofitel, this is a good bet.

LAUNDRY

Laundry Quick (☎ 0 4322 8260; Th Si Chan; ⏱ 8am-
9pm) Down an alley by Oasis Plaza.

KHON KAEN

0		1 km
0		0.5 miles

INFORMATION
Air Booking & Travel Centre......1 C3
Internet................................2 C3
Khon Kaen Ram Hospital..........3 B3
Lao Consulate........................4 D2
Laundry Quick.....................(see 33)
Main Post Office.....................5 C3
Siam Commercial Bank.............6 C3
TAT......................................7 C2
Tourist Police.......................(see 7)
Vietnamese Consulate..............8 D3

SIGHTS & ACTIVITIES
Khon Kaen National Museum....9 D2
Wat That..............................10 D4

SLEEPING
Chaipat Hotel.......................11 C3
Charoen Thani Princess...........12 D3
Deema Hotel.........................13 D3
First Choice..........................14 C3
Hotel Sofitel.........................15 C3
Kaen Inn..............................16 C3
Khon Kaen Hotel...................17 C3
Kosa Hotel...........................18 C3
Phu Inn...............................19 C3
Roma Hotel..........................20 C3
Rossukond Hotel...................21 C2
Saen Sumran Hotel................22 C3
Sawasdee Hotel....................23 C3
Si Monkon...........................24 C3

EATING
Big C Department Store...........25 B4
Bualuang Restaurant..............26 D4
D-Day Café........................(see 19)
Em Oht................................27 C3
Food Stalls...........................28 C3
Heuan Laaw.........................29 C3
Hong Kong House..................30 C4
Night Market........................31 C3
Pizza & Bake........................32 C3

SHOPPING
Khon Kaen Otop Centre..........33 C3
Klum Phrae Phan...................34 D3
Laem Laplae.........................35 C3
PK Prathamakhan
  Local Goods Center..............36 C4

TRANSPORT
Air-Con Bus Depot.................37 C3
Ordinary Bus Terminal............38 C2
THAI..................................(see 15)

To Khon Kaen University (4km); Udon Thani (111km)

Th Lang Sunratchakan

Beung Thung Sang

Provincial Hall

Th Sun Ratchakan

Ratchadanuson Park

To Airport (2km); Phitsanulok (295km)

To Kalasin (74km)

Th Prachasamoson

Th Meuang

Th Na Meuang

Th Theparak

Th Phimphaseut

Th Mittaphap

Th Lang Meuang

Th Chatapadung

Th Ammat

Wat Si Chan

Th Si Chan

Th Klang Meuang

Th Chetakhon

Th Robmuang

Th Chuanchun

Oasis Plaza

Train Station

Th Reun Rom

To Chonabot (57km)

To Wat Nong Wang Muang (1km)

Th Kasikon Samran

To Prasat Peuay Noi (66km)

Beung Kaen Nakhon

MEDICAL & EMERGENCY

Khon Kaen Ram Hospital (☎ 0 4333 3900; Th Si Chan) For specialist and emergency care.

Tourist Police (☎ 0 4323 6937, emergency ☎ 1155; Th Prachasamoson) Next door to TAT.

MONEY

There are banks with exchange and ATM facilities at numerous locations across Khon Kaen.

Siam Commercial Bank (cnr Th Si Chan & Th Lang Meuang; ⊙ 8.30am-3.30pm Mon-Fri) One of several banks in this area.

POST

Main post office (cnr Th Si Chan & Th Klang Meuang; ⊙ 8.30am-4.30pm Mon-Fri, 9am-noon Sat)

TOURIST INFORMATION

TAT (☎ 0 4324 4498; www.tourismthailand.org; 15/5 Th Prachasamoson; ⊙ 8.30am-4.30pm) Distributes maps of the city, and can answer general queries on Khon Kaen and the surrounding provinces.

TRAVEL AGENCIES

Air Booking & Travel Centre (☎ 0 4324 4482; 403 Th Si Chan; ⊙ 8.30am-6pm Mon-Sat) Books flights and other travel arrangements.

Sights

Food, drink and a decent bed are the main attractions of Khon Kaen, but the **Khon Kaen National Museum** (☎ 0 4324 2129; Th Lang Sunratch-akan; admission 30B; ⊙ 9am-4pm Wed-Sun) has an interesting collection of artefacts from prehistoric times to the present, including an almost intact Dvaravati votive tablet from near Kalasin, Ban Chiang utensils and items from the Sukhothai and Ayuthaya periods.

On a quirkier note, the region is also relatively famous for its dinosaur fossils (see Phu Wiang National Park, p464), prompting some city businesses to place large **plastic dinosaurs** outside their doors.

Beung Kaen Nakhon (Kaen Nakhon Pond), a 100-hectare lake lined with eateries, walkways and young couples, attracts picnickers and early-evening smoochers to its banks. At the northern end of the lake is **Wat That** (☾ daylight hours), with elongated spires typical of this area, and **Wat Nong Wang Muang** (☾ daylight hours), which features a nine-tier *chedi*, sits at the southern end.

Festivals & Events

The **Silk Fair** and the **Phuk Siaw Festival** are held simultaneously over 12 days from late November to early December. Centred on Ratchadanuson Park and the field in front of the Provincial Hall (Sala Klang), the fes-

tival celebrates the planting of the mulberry tree, a necessary step in the production of silk. Another aspect of the festival is *phùuk sìaw* (friend-bonding), a reference to the *bai sìi* (sacred thread) ceremony in which sacred threads are tied around one's wrists for spiritual protection. The ritual also implies a renewal of the bonds of friendship and reaffirmation of local tradition. Other activities include parades, Isan music, folk dancing, and the preparation and sharing of Isan food.

The **Flowers & Khaen Music Festival** takes place during Songkran, the Thai lunar New Year in mid-April. Along with the customary ritual bathing of important Buddha images at local temples, festival activities in Khon Kaen include parades of floats bedecked with flowers and plenty of Isan music.

Sleeping

BUDGET

Saen Sumran Hotel (☎ 0 4323 9611; 55-59 Th Klang Meuang; s/d 150/250B) The most charismatic of

---

BAI SĪI CEREMONY

Northeastern Thais commonly participate in *bai sĩi* (sacred thread) ceremonies on auspicious occasions such as birthdays, farewells and times of serious illness, and during certain festivals such as Khon Kaen's annual *phùuk sìaw* (friend-bonding) festival. In the *bai sĩi* ceremony, the 32 guardian spirits known as *khwǎn* are bound to the guest of honour by white strings tied around the wrists. Each of the 32 *khwǎn* are thought to be guardians over different organs or functions in a person's body.

Khwǎn occasionally wander away from their owner, which isn't considered much of a problem except when that person is about to embark on a new project or on a journey away from home, or when they're very ill. At these times it's best to perform the *bai sĩi* to ensure that all the *khwǎn* are present and attached to the person's body. A *mǎw phawn* (wish doctor) – usually an elder who has spent some time as a monk – presides over the ritual. Those participating sit on mats around a tiered vase-like centrepiece *(phakhuan)*, which is decorated with flowers, folded banana leaves and branches with white cotton strings hanging down; pastries, eggs, bananas, liquor and money are placed around the base as offerings to the spirits in attendance.

After a few words of greeting, the *mǎw phawn* chants in a mixture of Isan and Pali to convey blessings on the honoured guest, while all in attendance place their hands in a prayer-like, palms-together pose. For part of the chanting segment, everyone leans forward to touch the base of the *phakhuan;* if there are too many participants for everyone to reach the base, it's permissible to touch the elbow of someone who can reach it, thus forming a human chain.

Once the *mǎw phawn* has finished chanting, each person attending takes two of the white strings from the *phakhuan* and ties one around each wrist of the honoured guest, while whispering a short, well-wishing recitation. When all have performed this action, the guest is left with a stack of strings looped around each wrist. Small cups of rice liquor are passed around, sometimes followed by an impromptu *ram wong* (circle dance). For the intended effect, the strings must be kept around the wrists for a minimum of three full days. Some Isan people believe the strings should be allowed to fall off naturally rather than cut off – this can take weeks.

Khon Kaen's cheapies has a wooden front and lashings of once-upon-a-time character. The rooms are a little shaky, but paintings and incongruous Christmas decorations provide the colour downstairs, and if you're spotting the city's plastic dinosaur population, you'll find a T-Rex shackled to the pavement next door.

Si Monkon (☎ 0 4323 7939; 61-67 Th Klang Meuang; r 120-300B; 🗙) This wooden place also has a certain tumbledown charm, but you'll have to be a sound sleeper – the walls are thin. For bargain hunters – with even better earplugs – it also has cheaper fan rooms.

First Choice (☎ 0 4333 3352; 18/8 Th Phimphaseut; r 150-200B; 🗙) This little café is the city's first proto (it's not quite there yet) backpacker hostel, with no-frills rooms up the stairs and a traveller-friendly eatery, serving the usual selection of shakes and snacks, downstairs. Bathrooms are shared.

Roma Hotel (☎ 0 4333 4444; fax 0 4324 2458; 50/2 Th Klang Meuang; r 230-400B; 🗙) Sporting a clutch of eccentric decorative features, including a colossal chandelier and a mural of an idealised Scottish Highland scene, the otherwise barren lobby of this large budget offering might leave you feeling a little cold. The rooms, however, are good value, spotless and comfy.

Deema Hotel (☎ 0 4332 1562; fax 0 4332 1561; 133 Th Chetakhon; r 320B; 🗙) Fronted by a large car park and a tiny pool filled with Koi carp, this homogenous place is functional and a little frumpy. The rooms are quite good value though.

MIDRANGE

Khon Kaen excels in this category, with a fine selection of accommodation within the 450B to 1000B range.

Rossukond Hotel (☎ 0 4323 8576; fax 0 4323 8579; 1/11 Th Klang Meuang; r 550B; 🗙) With wood-panelled walls and womb-red décor, the lobby of this excellent midranger has more character than most of the other options combined. The rooms are spacious and relatively fresh on the décor front and if you're a stickler for detail, there's a 'hygienic' paper cover on every toilet seat.

Khon Kaen Hotel (☎ 0 4333 3222; fax 0 4324 2458; 43/2 Th Phimphaseut; r 600B; 🗙) This seven-storey place also bags a few points for atmosphere, with a pleasant maroon paint job downstairs and the odd nod to traditional décor

throughout. The hotel remains functional rather than fabulous, but the rooms promise a good night's sleep and come with fridge and private balcony.

Sawasdee Hotel (☎ 0 4322 1600; fax 0 4332 0345; 177-179 Th Na Meuang; s 400-890B, d 500-1000B; 🗙) Looking a little like a prefab (and flattened out) Coliseum, this one-time cheapie has now gone a bit more upmarket, with faux leather chairs and plastic flowers in the lobby, and pleasant new rooms above – be warned, some of the rooms are a bit heavy-handed with the pink paint. There are cheaper, older rooms still on offer.

Phu Inn (☎ 0 4324 3174; fax 0 4324 3176; s/d 400/ 500B; 🗙) Benefiting from recent renovations, this Chinese-oriented place by the night market features friendly staff, simple, spotless rooms and some very slow lifts. The beds are good value and discounts are sometimes given.

Kaen Inn (☎ 0 4324 5420; kaeninnhotel@yahoo .com; 56 Th Klang Meuang; s/d 580/660B; 🗙) Long since toppled from the top slot, town's one-time top-ender is now looking rather sorry for itself. Prices have plummeted accordingly however, and if you can stomach the Muzak, artificial flowers and neon lighting, the rooms are a bit of a giveaway.

Chaipat Hotel (☎ 0 4333 3055; fax 0 4323 6860; 106/3 Soi Na Meuang; r 480B; 🗙) Housed in a plain white tower just off Th Na Meuang, this reasonable place features smiley staff, marble floors and, if the brochure is to be believed, a uniformed lady clutching a cocktail in every room. If you fancy a little more class, you can also splash out on a better VIP room (600B).

TOP END

Hotel Sofitel (☎ 0 4332 2155; www.sofitel.com; 9/9 Prachasumran; r 2500B; 🗙 🗙 🖵 🗙) Up with the northeast's best hotels, this International-standard, Accor-run place has plenty of razzle-dazzle, big well-equipped rooms, a gym, and an underground entertainment complex where it even brews its own beer. Promotional rates go as low as 1950B, so check for deals.

Kosa Hotel (☎ 0 4332 0320; kosa@thailand.com; 250-253 Th Si Chan; s/d 1140/1260B; 🗙 🗙 🗙) A little less glitzy than the Sofitel, this is nevertheless a good top-end choice and offers excellent facilities and slick service in the heart of the city's nightlife district.

Charoen Thani Princess (☎ 0 4322 0400; www.royal princess.com; 260 Th Si Chan; r 1200B; ✗ ✗ ☒ ☐ ☒) This towering business hotel draws big crowds and appeals primarily to the conference set. Rooms are plush but a little old-fashioned and the lobby features plenty of model dinosaurs. The karaoke bar is a big draw for local suits.

Eating

Khon Kaen has a fabulous array of restaurants and is the place to satisfy every conceivable craving before heading back out into the countryside.

Heuan Lao (no Roman-script sign; ☎ 0 4324 7202; 39 Th Phimphaseut; mains 40-140B; ⏱ 11am-midnight) In an old-world wooden villa, this atmospheric place is awash with antique bric-a-brac and serves scrumptious Thai and Isan dishes. There's a leafy garden for airy eating out front and lashings of character throughout.

Bualuang Restaurant (☎ 0 4322 2504; Th Rop Buengkaen Nakhon; mains 60-200B; ⏱ 10am-11pm) Ask a local out for dinner and they will probably want to go here. Right on the banks of Beung Kaen Nakhon, it serves up a great spread of Thai and local speciality dishes in a largely alfresco setting.

Em Oht (no Roman-script sign; ☎ 0 4324 1382; 71/22 Th Klang Meuang; mains 30-50B; ⏱ 11am-11pm) This no-frills local haunt lacks a little in décor, but serves up a mean selection of local speciality dishes, including some fabulous Isan sausages, which are strung up for all to see at the front of the restaurant.

Pizza & Bake (☎ 0 4323 8883; Th Klang Meuang; dishes 60-100B; ⏱ 7.30am-11pm) Pizza tops the billing at this Western-style diner and while it's not quite tasty enough to get Mamma running for the plane, it's sure good enough for seconds. It also does some great pick-me-up coffees and a reasonable range of other Thai and Western eats.

D-Day Café (☎ 0 4324 4522; Th Lang Meuang; mains 50-150B; ⏱ 10am-11pm) With sport on the TV, a little leafy terrace out front and salads, sarnies and 'canapés' on the menu, this contemporary eatery caters to young Thais after a taste of the occident.

Hong Kong House (☎ 0 9712 5500; Th Reun Rom; mains 30-100B; ⏱ 11am-9pm) Spotless and minimalist in design, this no-frills Chinese restaurant produces all the old favourites at breakneck speed. And if you want to stay in your hotel room, they also deliver.

First Choice (☎ 0 4333 3352; 18/8 Th Phimphaseut; mains 30-100B; ⏱ 9am-11pm) This traveller-style eatery/hostel has some tasty breakfasts, a reasonable range of vegetarian food and the usual spread of Thai dishes. Eat inside or on a little terrace surrounded by pot plants.

Big C Department Store (☎ 0 4332 5500; Th Mittaphap; mains 20-50B; ⏱ 9am-9pm; ☒) Out on the ring road, this giant department store has a cheap and cheerful food court on the ground floor.

The bustling **night market** (Th Lang Meuang; ⏱ sunset-11pm), between Th Klang Meuang and Th Na Meuang next to the air-con bus terminal, is the life and soul of the budget eating scene, with plenty of excellent food stalls.

In the late afternoon, dozens of **food stalls** (Th Klang Meuang) also open up between Th Si Chan and Th Ammat. Catering to children coming out of the nearby school, they are a great place to sample Isan cuisine's answer to Western junk food.

Shopping

Khon Kaen is a great place to buy handcrafted Isan goods such as silk and cotton fabrics (you can get *mát-mìi* cotton and silk), silver and basketry. A speciality of the northeast is the *mǎwn khwǎan* (literally 'axe pillow'), a stiff triangle-shaped pillow used as an elbow support while sitting on the floor. The most practical way to acquire axe pillows while on the road is to buy them unstuffed (*mâi sài nûn*; literally 'no kapok inserted') – the covers are easily carried and you can stuff them when you get home.

PK Prathamakhan Local Goods Center (☎ 0 4322 4080; 79/2-3 Th Reun Rom; ⏱ 9am-8pm Mon-Sat) This slightly touristy outlet specialises in textiles and handicrafts and is a good one-stop shop if you don't have the time or inclination to spend the day trawling through the smaller stores.

Klum Phrae Phan (☎ 0 4333 7216; 131/193 Th Chatapadung; ⏱ 9am-6pm Mon-Sat) Klum Phrae Phan is run by the Handicraft Centre for Northeastern Women's Development and offers an excellent range of Isan crafts.

Khon Kaen Otop Centre (☎ 0 4332 0320; Oasis Plaza, 250/1 Th Si Chan; ⏱ 9am-6pm Mon-Sat) This large store is most convenient to the top-end hotels, but is predictably touristy as well.

Laem Laplae (no Roman-script sign; ☎ 0 4323 6537; Th Klang Meuang; ⏱ 8.30am-5pm Mon-Sat) You can follow the fabulous aromas to this old-school Isan food store, which sells everything from dried fish to fat, flavoursome sausages. There's no English sign, so look out for the bright yellow and red shop front.

Several shops selling local preserved foods can be found along Th Klang Meuang between Th Prachasamoson and Th Si Chan. The emphasis in these shops is *năem* (a kind of sausage made of raw pickled pork) and other types of sausage or processed meats, such as *sâi kràwk*, *mŭu yaw*, *kun siang mŭu* and *kun siang kài*.

Getting There & Away

AIR

THAI (☎ 0 4322 7701; www.thaiairways.com; Hotel Sofitel, 9/9 Prachasamran; ☺ 8am-9pm Mon-Fri) operates three services daily between Bangkok and Khon Kaen (one way 1205B, 55 minutes).

Air Asia (☎ 0 2515 9999; www.airasia.com) flies daily to/from Bangkok with one-way fares starting as low as 600B. You have to book online or via the above number.

The **airport** (☎ 0 4323 6523, 0 4323 8835) is a few kilometres west of the city centre off Hwy 12.

BUS

Ordinary buses arrive at and depart from a **bus terminal** (☎ 0 4323 7472) on Th Prachasamoson, while air-con buses use a **depot** (☎ 0 4323 9910) near the night market off Th Klang Meuang.

Air-con buses (259B, 6½ hours) leave to/from Bangkok's Northern bus terminal every 30 minutes from 7am to 11pm.

Other air-con destinations from Khon Kaen include: Chiang Mai (394B, 12 hours, 8pm and 9pm only), Chiang Rai (430B, 14 hours, 6pm only), Nakhon Phanom (175B, five hours, four daily), Udon Thani (110B, 2½ hours, hourly), Nong Khai (140B, four hours, six daily), Leoi (131B, 3½ hours, two daily), Roi Et (60B, 1½ hours, hourly) and Rayong (342B, 12 hours, six night buses).

There are regular ordinary buses from Khon Kaen to Khorat (70B, three hours) and Roi Et (40B, two hours).

TRAIN

Trains leave from Bangkok's Hualamphong station for Khon Kaen at 8.20am, 8pm and 8.45pm, arriving eight hours later. Bangkok-bound trains leave Khon Kaen at 9.43am,

8.13pm and 9.23pm. The fares to Bangkok are 157/309/978B for a 3rd-class/2nd-class/1st-class sleeper.

You can get information from the Khon Kaen **train station** (☎ 0 4322 1112).

Getting Around

A regular, colour-coded *săwngthăew* system plies the central city for 10B per person. If you want to charter a vehicle, you usually have to pay a *săwngthăew* or *túk-túk* driver 40B to 60B.

AROUND KHON KAEN
Chonabot
ชนบท

This small town located southeast of the provincial capital of Khon Kaen is famous for *mát-mìi* cotton and silk. *Mát-mìi* is a method of tie-dyeing the fabric threads before weaving and is similar to Indonesian *ikat*. The easiest place to see the fabrics is at **Sala Mai Thai** (Thai Silk Pavilion; ☎ 0 4328 6160; donations appreciated; ☺ 9am-5pm), on the campus of Khon Kaen Industrial & Community Education College (Withayalai Kan Achip Khon Kaen). This resource centre for the local silk industry contains a well-organised exhibit of looms, artefacts and fabrics, including the world's priciest *mát-mìi* silk. There are a couple of traditional northeastern wooden houses next to the exhibition hall. The campus is 1km west of Chonabot on Rte 229, near the Km 12 marker.

Textiles can be purchased directly from silk-weaving houses in Chonabot – look for the tell-tale looms beneath the wooden homes. Even if you're not interested in buying, it's worth wandering around to look at the amazing variety of simple wooden contraptions devised to spin, tie, weave and dry silk.

The more reputable weaving households include those belonging to Khun Suwan, Khun Songkhram, Khun Chin and Khun Thongsuk. Very little English is spoken in Chonabot so it helps considerably if you bring someone along who can speak Thai.

GETTING THERE & AWAY

Săwngthăew to Chonabot depart from the ordinary bus terminal in Khon Kaen hourly between 5.30am and 5.30pm (20B, 45 minutes); the last one back from Chonabot leaves the market around 3.30pm.

AROUND KHON KAEN

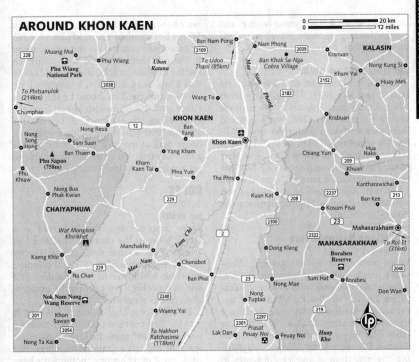

Prasat Peuay Noi
ปราสาทเปือยน้อย

Also known as Ku Peuay Noi, and locally as That Ku Thong, the 12th-century Khmer temple **Prasat Peuay Noi** (admission 30B; ☺ 8.30am-4.30pm) was recently restored at the Khon Kaen government's expense. About the size of Buriram's Prasat Meuang Tam, the east-facing monument comprises a large central sandstone sanctuary surmounted by a partially collapsed *prang* and surrounded by laterite walls with two major gates. The site is rich in sculpted lintels; the restored pediments of sandstone are intricately carved.

GETTING THERE & AWAY
If you have your own wheels, head 44km south from Khon Kaen on Hwy 2 to Ban Phai, then east on Hwy 23 (signposted to Borabeu) for 11km to the turn-off to Rte 2297. Follow Rte 2297 for 24km southeast through a scenic tableau of rice fields to the town of Peuay Noi. The ruins are at the western end of town.

By public transport from Khon Kaen, catch a bus (35B, one hour) or train (25B, one hour) to Ban Phai, then a *săwngthăew* to Peuay Noi (15B, 30 minutes). Start early in the morning if you plan to do this in one day; the last *săwngthăew* back to Ban Phai from Peuay Noi leaves around 3pm. Hitching may be possible.

Ban Khok Sa-Nga Cobra Village
โครงการอนุรักษ์งูจงอาง

The self-styled 'King Cobra Village' of **Ban Khok Sa-Nga** (☎ 0 4324 4498; donations appreciated; ☺ daylight hours) has a thing about snakes. Committed to protecting Thailand's endangered king cobra (*nguu jong aang* in Thai), the locals rear hundreds of the reptiles, which can be seen in cages throughout the village.

This strange custom goes back to the days when the villagers here grew herbs to trade in the region's markets. One herb farmer, Phu Yai Ken Yongla, had the idea of putting on snake shows to attract customers to the village and the art of breeding and training snakes has been nurtured ever since. For a donation, staff at two venues, **Wat Si Thamma** and the **Snake Farm**, will put on shows which feature 'snake boxing' and cobras 'dancing' to music. Shows are staged during daylight hours.

GETTING THERE & AWAY

The village is northeast of Khon Kaen via Hwy 2 and Rte 2039. By bus, leave from Khon Kaen's bus terminal to the turn-off to Ban Khok Sa-Nga (20B, one hour) and then walk or take a motorbike taxi (25B) for the remaining 1.5km to the village. If you're driving from Khon Kaen, just after passing through Ban Nam Phong take the turn-off marked 'Kranuan', near the Km 33 marker. Along the way to Kranuan you should begin seeing English signs for the 'King Cobra Club'.

Phu Wiang National Park

อุทยานแห่งชาติภูเวียง

When uranium miners discovered a dinosaur's patella bone in this region in 1976, palaeontologists were soon to follow, excavating the top of Phu Pratutima and unearthing a fossilised 15m-long herbivore named *Phuwianggosaurus Sirindhornae* (after Her Royal Majesty, Princess Sirindhorn). Dinosaur fever followed (explaining the epidemic of model dinosaurs in Khon Kaen), more remains were uncovered and the **Phu Wiang National Park** (☎ 0 4324 9052; reserve@dnp.go.th; admission 200B; ☺ 8.30am-4.30pm), northwest of Khon Kaen, was born. The park includes a small **museum** (admission free; ☺ 8.30am-4.30pm), with life-size models of the dinosaur species that have since been found in the area, and a 'Dinosaur Trail', which can be followed between the now-enclosed excavation sites. There are also small dinosaur tracks in solid stone (68 have been found), as well as fossils of baby dinosaurs, crocodiles and shells. As the sites are quite spread out, it is best to see the park by car – tours are sometimes available if you call the park in advance.

The park has **camping sites** (per person 30B) and two **bungalows** (r 1200B). You can reserve accommodation via the **reservation hotline** (☎ 0 2562 0760).

GETTING THERE & AWAY

The entrance to the park is about 78km west of the provincial capital. Buses leave from Khon Kaen's ordinary bus terminal to Phu Wiang town (30B, 1½ hours) every

hour between 6am and 6pm. From the Phu Wiang bus terminal you must hire a *túk-túk* or motorbike taxi for the remaining 19km to the park entrance (one way 100B). To see the dinosaur tracks, it's about 12km to Ban Khok Sung, and then a 5km climb up a trail to the site. You should be able to hire either a *túk-túk* or motorbike taxi from the Phu Wiang bus station to either site for around 200B return, including a couple of hours' wait at the park. If you only pay for a one-way trip you'll risk not being able to get a ride back to Phu Wiang.

ROI ET

ร้อยเอ็ด

pop 36,000

Three centuries ago, Roi Et served as a buffer between the clashing Thai and Lao armies. Back at that time, it had 11 city gates, one for each of its 11 vassal colonies; its name, which means 'one hundred and one' is probably a typically macho exaggeration of this number.

Roi Et's long history hasn't followed it into the 21st century; orderly and modern, you can almost smell the drying paint on some of the city's grander buildings. But while most of its historic monuments have vanished into foggy memory, Roi Et retains a charm and sense of identity all its own. With the large Beung Phlan Chai artificial lake at its hub, this is a city that places leisure at the head of the to-do list, moving to a slightly slower urban beat and giving centre stage – on an island in the middle of the lake – to a walking Buddha who looks like he's out for an early evening stroll.

Roi Et Province is known for the crafting of the quintessential Isan musical instrument, the *khaen,* a kind of panpipe made of the *mái kuu* reed and wood. The best *khaen* are reputedly made in the village of Si Kaew, 15km northwest of Roi Et. It takes about three days to make one *khaen,* depending on its size. The straight, sturdy reeds, which resemble bamboo, are cut and bound together in pairs of six, eight or nine. The sound box that fits in the middle is made of *tôn pràduu,* a hardwood that's resistant to moisture.

Information

Main post office (Th Suriyadet Bamrung; ☺ 9am-4.30pm Mon-Fri, to noon Sat)

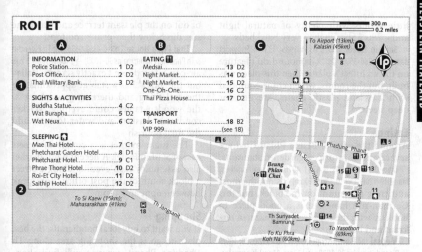

ROI ET

INFORMATION	
Police Station	1 D2
Post Office	2 D2
Thai Military Bank	3 D2

SIGHTS & ACTIVITIES	
Buddha Statue	4 C2
Wat Burapha	5 D2
Wat Neua	6 C2

SLEEPING	
Mae Thai Hotel	7 C1
Phetcharat Garden Hotel	8 D1
Phetcharat Hotel	9 C1
Phrae Thong Hotel	10 D2
Roi-Et City Hotel	11 D2
Saithip Hotel	12 D2

EATING	
Medsai	13 D2
Night Market	14 D2
Night Market	15 D2
One-Oh-One	16 C2
Thai Pizza House	17 D2

TRANSPORT	
Bus Terminal	18 B2
VIP 999	(see 18)

Police station (☎ 1155; Th Suriyadet Bamrung)
Thai Military Bank (cnr Th Ploenchit & Th Sukkasem; ◷ 8.30am-3.30pm) Has an ATM and exchange facilities.

Sights

Wat Neua (Th Phadung Phanit; ◷ daylight hours), in the northern quarter of town, is worth seeing for its 1200-year-old *chedi* from the Dvaravati period, Phra Satup Jedi. This *chedi* has an unusual four-cornered bell-shaped form that is rare in Thailand. Around the *bòt* are a few old Dvaravati *sěmaa* (ordination-precinct marker stones) and to one side of the wat is an inscribed pillar, erected by the Khmers when they controlled this area during the 11th and 12th centuries.

The tall, standing Buddha that towers above Roi Et's minimal skyline is the Phra Phuttha-Ratana-Mongkon-Mahamuni (Phra Sung Yai for short) at **Wat Burapha** (Th Phadung Phanit; ◷ daylight hours). Despite being of little artistic significance, it's hard to ignore. From the ground to the tip of the *ùtsànít* (flame-shaped head ornament) it's 67.8m high. You can climb a staircase through a building that supports the figure to about as high as the Buddha's knees and get a view of the town.

Paths criss-cross the lake of **Beung Phlan Chai** and attract the usual crowd of doting couples, joggers and picnickers. The **walking Buddha** is on an island in the centre.

Sleeping

Phetcharat Garden Hotel (☎ /fax 0 4351 9000; r 580B; ⊠) Some genuinely chic styling earns this

attractive place a few gold stars. The lobby showcases serene East-meets-West décor, with wooden shutters and spinning fans, and the immaculate staff are tirelessly attentive. The standard rooms don't really capture the atmosphere, but the pricier VIP rooms (from 1740B) are the best in town. It's on an unnamed street parallel to Th Haisok – don't confuse this with the nearby Phetcharat Hotel.

Roi-Et City Hotel (☎ 0 4352 0387; fax 0 4352 0401; 78 Th Ploenchit; s/d 1600/1800; ⊠) Catering to the itinerant business set, this swanky number has all the usual executive facilities, but only limited atmosphere. Rooms are sometimes discounted as low as single/doubles 880/990B, making them very good value.

Phetcharat Hotel (☎ 0 4351 1235; Th Haisok; r 350B; ⊠) This large outfit on the main road north is a little dowdy and rooms at the front suffer from persistent traffic noise. Take one of the comfortable rooms at the back, however, and your baht will be money well spent.

Mae Thai Hotel (☎ 0 4351 1036-8; fax 0 4351 2277; 99 Th Haisok; r 420B; ⊠) This old-school giant is a little flaky these days, but the better VIP rooms (750B), which have a bathtub, are comfortable and reasonably well equipped. With a lively karaoke bar downstairs, you don't even need to do your singing in the shower.

Phrae Thong Hotel (☎ 0 4351 1127; 45-47 Th Ploenchit; r 130-220B; ⊠) Insomniacs will bemoan the noise drifting up from the road, but this tidy no-frills spot has some good-value, little rooms with plenty of natural light and – less appealingly – very hard beds.

Saithip Hotel (☎ 0 4351 1985; 133 Th Suriyadet Bamrung; r 260-350B; 🛂) Glamour didn't feature on the architect's plans when this place was built, but the rooms, which come equipped with TVs and plastic chairs, are fine for deep sleepers.

Eating

Around the edge of Beung Phlan Chai are several medium-priced garden restaurants.

One-Oh-One (☎ 0 4351 4070; Th Sunthornthep; mains 40-120B; 🕙 10.30am-10pm) It's not the most authentic restaurant on the block, but this German-run hang-out is a good place to hook up with the expat set over pizza, sauerkraut and beer.

Medsai (no Roman-script sign; ☎ 0 4352 0338; 160/9 Th Ploenchit; mains 30-100B; 🕙 11am-11pm) Karaoke, Chang and some decent Thai cooking (no English menu) conspire to make this place a big hit with the local crowd. Sit indoors or out on the pleasant terrace and watch the sun dip below the…erm…rooftops.

Thai Pizza House (☎ 0 4352 0616; cnr Th Ploenchit & Th Phadung Phanit; mains 30-100B; 🕙 10am-9pm) This air-con eatery doesn't exactly scream 'Italia', but the 'pizza' has a stab at approximating the real thing and there's a good buzz at the wooden tables come evening. Wicker condiment baskets and water features add the final flourish.

The night market is a couple of streets east of Saithip Hotel. A decent night market also assembles each evening along a street a block south of the post office. Both peak between 6pm and 10pm.

Shopping

If you want to buy local handicrafts, the best place to go is the shopping area along Th Phadung Phanit, where you'll find shops selling *măwn khwăan*, *phâa mát-mìi* (thick cotton or silk fabric woven from tie-dyed threads), traditional musical instruments,

---

MĂW LAM & THE KHAEN

Among villages in Isan, the up-tempo Lao-Thai musical tradition of *măw lam* – roughly 'master of verse' – rules. Performances always feature a witty, topical combination of singing and improvised or recited speech that ranges across themes as diverse as politics and sex. Very colloquial, even bawdy language is employed; this is one art form that has always bypassed government censors and provides an important outlet for grass-roots expression. *Măw lam* is most commonly performed at temple fairs and local festivals native to Isan, such as Dan Sai's Phi Ta Khon.

There are four basic types of *măw lam*. The first, *măw lam lǔang* (great *măw lam*), involves an ensemble of performers in costume on stage. *Măw lam khûu* (couple *măw lam*) features a man and woman who engage in flirtation and verbal repartee. *Măw lam jòt* (duelling *măw lam*) has two performers of the same gender who 'duel' by answering questions or finishing an incomplete story issued as a challenge. Finally, *măw lam diaw* (solo *măw lam*) involves only one performer.

The backbone of *măw lam* is the *khaen*, a wind instrument consisting of a double row of bamboo-like reeds fitted into a hardwood soundbox with beeswax. The rows can be as few as four or as many as eight courses (for a total of 16 pipes), and the instrument can vary in length from around 80cm to 2m. Around the turn of the 20th century there were also nine-course *khaen*, but these have all but disappeared. Melodies are almost always pentatonic; ie they feature five-note scales. The *khaen* player blows (as with a harmonica, sound is produced whether the breath is moving in or out of the instrument) into the soundbox while covering or uncovering small holes in the reeds that determine the pitch for each. An adept player can produce a churning, calliope-like music that inspires dancing. The most popular folk dance is the *ram wong* (*lam wong* in Isan), the 'circle dance', in which couples dance circles around one another until there are three circles in all: a circle danced by the individual, the circle danced by the couple and one danced by the whole crowd.

Traditionally the *khaen* was accompanied by the *saw* (a bowed string instrument), although the plucked *phin* is much more common today. In modern *măw lam*, the *khaen* and *phin* are electrically amplified, and electric bass and drums are added to the ensemble to produce a sound enjoyed by Isan people young and old.

sticky-rice baskets and assorted Buddhist paraphernalia.

Getting There & Away

PB Air (☎ 0 4351 8572) flies to/from Bangkok once daily (except Sunday, one way 1800B). There is a ticket office at the airport, which is 13km north of the centre.

From Roi Et's **bus terminal** (☎ 0 4352 5098; Th Jangsanit), frequent buses head to Khon Kaen (ordinary/air-con 40/60B, 1½ hours) and Ubon Ratchathani (ordinary/air-con 65B/120B, three hours).

Thirteen air-con buses a day link Roi Et with Bangkok's Northern bus terminal (280B, seven hours) between 6pm and 10.45pm. **VIP 999** (☎ 0 4351 1466) run one daily VIP bus to Bangkok (455B, seven hours), which leaves Roi Et at 9pm – the office is on the first floor of the bus terminal.

Ordinary-bus destinations include Surin (50B, two hours) and Yasothon (25B, one hour).

Getting Around

It costs 20B to take a *sǎamláw* around Roi Et. To take a *túk-túk,* you'll be paying 20B to 30B.

AROUND ROI ET
Ku Phra Koh Na
กู่พระะโกณา

Around 60km southeast of Roi Et town, near the town of Suwannaphum, are the ruins of **Ku Phra Koh Na** (admission free; ☿ daylight hours), an 11th-century Khmer shrine. The monument comprises three brick *prang* facing east from a sandstone pediment, surrounded by a sandstone-slab wall with four gates. The middle *prang* was replastered in 1928 and Buddha niches were added. A Buddha footprint shrine, added to the front of this *prang,* is adorned with the Khmer monument's original Baphuon-style *naga* sculptures.

The two other *prang* have been restored but retain their original forms. The northern *prang* has a Narai (Vishnu) lintel over one door and a *Ramayana* relief on the inside gable. Watch out for monkeys looking for something to eat.

GETTING THERE & AWAY

Suwannaphum can be reached by frequent buses (25B, one hour) and *sǎwngthǎew* (15B,

one hour) from Roi Et along Rte 215. From Suwannaphum it's another 6km south via Rte 214 to Ku Phra Koh Na (10B, 15 minutes); any Surin-bound bus can stop at Ban Ku, which is at the T-intersection with Rte 2086 east to Phon Sai. The ruins are in a wat compound known locally as Wat Ku.

UDON THANI PROVINCE

UDON THANI
อุดรธานี
pop 227,200

Udon Thani boomed on the back of the Vietnam War, exploding into life as US air bases opened nearby. These days, with the bases closed, it feels a little like the city is still searching for something to fill the vacuum.

As a major transport hub, Udon remains an agricultural market centre for much of the region, but lacks both the urban chutzpah of Khon Kaen and the touristy appeal of Nong Khai. But while nearby Nong Khai is better set up for tourists and is equally convenient for visiting surrounding attractions, Udon Thani gets few visitors and is an alternative, if slightly less romantic, look at Isan life. Despite being right on the highway, a day in Udon Thani is a day spent with one foot off the beaten track.

Information
INTERNET ACCESS
T&A Net Corner (☎ 0 4232 9123; 124/8-9 Th Sri Suk; per hr 20B; ☿ 11am-10pm)

MEDICAL & EMERGENCY
Aek Udon International Hospital (☎ 0 4234 2555; www.aekudon.com; 555/5 Th Pho Si) The best medical facility in the upper Northeastern region.
Tourist police (☎ 0 4224 0616, emergency ☎ 1155; Th Thesa) Next to the TAT office.

MONEY
There are banks with ATMs and exchange facilities across town.
Siam City Bank (Th Pho Si; ☿ 8.30am-3.30pm)
Siam Commercial Bank (Th Pho Si; ☿ 8.30am-4.30pm)

POST
Main post office (Th Wattananuwong; ☿ 8.30am-4.30pm Mon-Fri, 9am-noon Sat, Sun & holidays)

CENTRAL UDON THANI

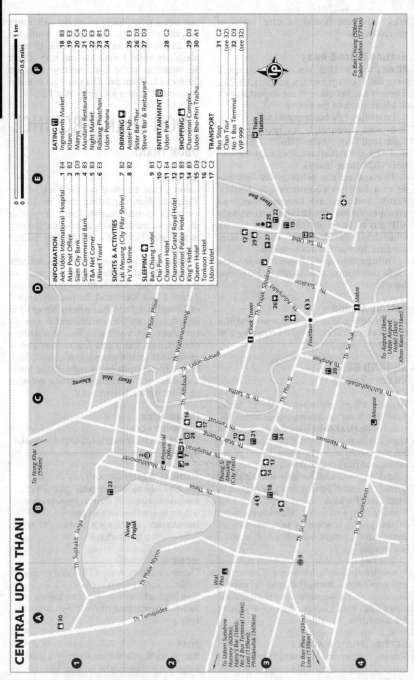

INFORMATION
Aek Udon International Hospital......1	E4
Main Post Office..........................2	B2
Siam City Bank............................3	D3
Siam Commercial Bank..................4	B3
T&A Net Corner............................5	B3
Ultinet Travel.............................6	E3

SIGHTS & ACTIVITIES
Lak Meuang (City Pillar Shrine)........7	B2
Pu Ya Shrine...............................8	B2

SLEEPING
Ban Chiang Hotel.........................9	B3
Chai Porn.................................10	C3
Charoen Hotel............................11	E4
Charoensri Grand Royal Hotel........12	E3
Charoensri Palace Hotel................13	B3
King's Hotel..............................14	B3
Queen Hotel.............................15	D3
Tonkoon Hotel...........................16	C2
Udon Hotel...............................17	C2

EATING
Ingredients Market......................18	B3
Kitaro....................................19	E3
Maeya...................................20	C4
Mandarin Restaurant....................21	C3
Night Market..............................22	E3
Rabiang Phatchani.......................23	B1
Udon Poshana...........................24	C3

DRINKING
Aussie Pub................................25	E3
Sister Bar–The...........................26	D3
Steve's Bar & Restaurant...............27	D3

ENTERTAINMENT
Udon Park................................28	C2

SHOPPING
Charoensri Complex.....................29	D3
Udon Bho-Phin Tracha..................30	A1

TRANSPORT
Bus Stop.................................31	C2
Chan Tour...............................32	D3
No 1 Bus Terminal....................(see 32)
VIP 999.................................(see 32)

www.lonelyplanet.com · UDON THANI PROVINCE •• Udon Thani   469

NORTHEASTERN THAILAND

TOURIST INFORMATION

TAT (☎ 0 4232 5406; www.tourismthailand.org; Th Thesa; ☻ 8.30am-4.30pm) Has information on Udon, Loei and Nong Khai Provinces.

TRAVEL AGENCIES

Ultinet Travel (☎ 0 4234 4041; prachuarb@yahoo.com; Th Sai Uthit; ☻ 8.30am-4.30pm Mon-Sat) For plane tickets and car rental.

Sights

UDORN SUNSHINE NURSERY

อุดรซันชายน์เนอสรี

Ever seen a plant dance? If not, this is the place to do it. Originally earning notoriety for its production of 100% natural orchid perfumes, the **Udorn Sunshine Nursery** (☎ 0 4224 2475; 127 Th Udorn-Nong Samrong; admission 40B; ☻ 7am-6.30pm), just west of town, has since developed a hybrid of *Codariocalyx Motorius Ohashi Leguminosae*, which curiously 'dances' to music. The mature gyrant (despite the way it has been described in the Thai press, it is not an orchid) has long oval leaves, plus smaller ones of similar shape. If you sing or talk to the plant in a high, gentle voice (saxophone or violin works even better), the smaller leaves will begin making subtle back-and-forth motions; sometimes quick, sometimes slow. This is no hype; we've seen it for ourselves – although it was rather sluggish on our last visit.

The nursery is open to the public and the owner, who speaks English, will happily show you around for a donation of 40B. The plants are most active from November to February – the cool season – and between 7am and 10am or 4.30pm and 6pm. The plants are not for sale, and the owner is careful to remove all flowers from plants on public display so that no-one can pilfer them and grow their own. You can, however, buy 'Miss Udon Sunshine', a rare orchid bred for fragrance (and the first ever to be made into a perfume).

To get here, follow signs to Ban Nong Samrong off Hwy 2024, then after 200m, follow the sign reading 'Udon Sunshine'. A *túk-túk* from Udon's city centre would cost about 60B each way.

OTHER SIGHTS

In the northeastern corner of the Thung Si Meuang (City Field) is the **Lak Meuang** (City Pillar Shrine; Th Athibadi; admission free; ☻ 24hr), where

the city's guardian deity is thought to reside. Encrusted with gold leaf and surrounded by offerings of flowers, candles and incense, the pillar shrine sits next to a smaller shrine that contains Phra Phuttha Pho Thong, a Buddha stele of undetermined age. Nearby is the huge and garish **Pu Ya Shrine** (admission free; Th Mukkhamontri; ☻ 24hr), a recently built Chinese shrine that attests to the wealth of the local Thai-Chinese merchant class. Take photos of it now before the vivid colours start to fade.

To get away from the busy central area, walk around **Nong Prajak**, a reservoir and park in the northwestern part of town. This is a favourite area for locals to go jogging, to picnic, and to meet and socialise.

Sleeping

BUDGET

Udon Thani's budget hotels are a rather motley bunch, but there are a few passable options. Nearby Nong Khai has a much better spread of sleeping options.

King's Hotel (☎ 0 4222 1634; Th Pho Si; r 190-200B; ☒) The entrance, reached through a subterranean car park, isn't the most promising of starts, but this Vietnam War–era place (formerly called the Victory Hotel) is cheap and cheerful, if a little worn.

Chai Porn (☎ 0 4222 1913; 209-211 Th Mak Khaeng; s/d 220/320B; ☒) This welcoming place has cheerful staff and while the rooms won't scoop any glamour accolades, they're fine for a night's sleep. On the downside, it looks like there's only one 40W bulb illuminating the whole of the ground floor. There's a 70B discount for rooms with a fan.

Charoensri Palace Hotel (☎ 0 4224 2611; fax 0 4224 2612; 60 Th Pho Si; r 340B; ☒) The gloss has peeled away from this city centre giant, but a few welcome trimmings remain: a lift, English-speaking staff and a ban on firearms among them. Rooms are big and comfortable and for 380B you can have yourself a carpet and fridge too.

Queen Hotel (☎ 0 4222 1451; 6-8 Th Udon-dutsadi; r 180-240B; ☒) Located in a busy market area, this spartan bolthole has 22 simple rooms.

MIDRANGE & TOP END

Charoensri Grand Royal Hotel (☎ 0 4234 3555; fax 0 4334 3550; Charoensri Complex; s/d 1400/1600B; ☒ ☐) At the hub of Udon's main shopping and nightlife district, this is town's glossiest top-ender. The rooms are spacious and immaculate and the service is swift.

Ban Chiang Hotel (☎ 0 4232 7911; www.banchiang hotel.com; 5 Th Mukkhamontri; r 1200B; ✦) The city's second grandest affair can still offer a fair amount of glitter, with the usual business-hotel facilities plus a few concessions to contemporary style. Its attached conference facilities attract plenty of corporate shenanigans and the well-equipped rooms are excellent value if you can negotiate a discount (as low as rooms from 900B).

Charoen Hotel (☎ 0 4224 8155; charoenhotel@hot mail.com; 549-559 Th Pho Si; r 800B; ✦) Occupying the next rung down the glamour ladder, this large business hotel is showing a little age, but offers plenty of trimmings, including a pool.

Tonkoon Hotel (☎ 0 4232 6336; fax 0 4232 6349; 50/1 Th Mak Khaeng; r 700B; ✦) More accurately the 'Tonkon Hotel' – one 'o' of the name has dropped off – this spotless midranger has both the coldest air-con and the largest portrait of the Thai Queen in town. Shiny marble floors, comfy rooms with fridge and TV, and friendly staff come as standard.

Udon Hotel (☎ 0 4224 8160; fax 0 4224 2782; 81-89 Th Mak Khaeng; r 400-550B; ✦) This tidy midranger has had a relatively recent upgrade and offers functional air-con rooms and breakfast. The cheaper rooms are in a 1960s-era building.

Udon Airport Hotel (☎ /fax 0 4234 6223; 14 Mu 1, Th Udon-Nongbualamphu; r 500B; ✦) This pleasant spot is a fair yomp from the centre – it's 3km outside of town, near the airport on Rte 210 – but all rooms feature air-con, fridge, cable TV, IDD phone and breakfast. Other amenities include a restaurant, beer garden and free transport to/from the airport.

Eating

There's a bit of everything to be enjoyed in Udon's eateries.

Udon Poshana (no Roman-script sign; ☎ 0 4222 1756; 244/5 Th Pho Si; mains 30-80B; ✦ 8am-6.30pm) Forty years of serving excellent Chinese food is paying dividends at this atmospheric spot. The chef will talk you (in Thai) through his dishes, which feature all sorts of exotic ingredients, or just point to one of the hanging geese and have it diced and sliced onto fluffy rice.

Maeya (no Roman-script sign; ☎ 0 4222 3889; 78/81 Th Ratchaphatsadu; mains 40-120B; ✦ 10am-10pm)

One part Thai restaurant and three parts English tearoom, this two-storey place has waiters dressed in black tie and a menu stretching from cakes and ice creams to oriental mains.

Mandarin Restaurant (☎ 0 4222 2391; Th Mak Khaeng; mains 30-80B; ✦ 10am-11pm) Ice-cold air-con restores flailing appetites at this pleasant diner. It serves an eclectic mix of Western and Asian dishes, from cream cakes and sandwiches, to Chinese specialities featuring giant crayfish plucked straight from the tank. Whatever you order, the waitresses giggle relentlessly.

Rabiang Phatchani (Th Suphakit Janya; mains 30-80B; ✦ 11am-10pm) Right on the banks of the Nong Prajak reservoir, this Thai-style place whips up a fabulous array of local dishes in no-frills surrounds. Aim to get here for sundown when the (limited) views are at their best.

Kitaro (☎ 0 4224 3094; Charoensri Complex Sq; mains 40-140B; ✦ 11am-2.30pm & 4.30-10pm Mon-Fri, 11am-10pm Sat & Sun) This cheap and cheerful Japanese outfit has plenty of fresh, wasabi-sharp seafood dishes for those facing stirfry overload.

For interest's sake, a stroll through the **ingredients market** (Th Mukkhamontri) is a worthwhile experience. Here, you can buy anything from raw pigs' heads to little bowls of live shrimp meant for slurping down just as they come. Better for cooked food is the **night market** (Th Prajak Silpakorn), just east of the Charoensri Complex.

There are also dozens of bars and eateries in and around **Charoensri Complex** (Th Sai Uthit).

Drinking

Many of the American GIs have left, but the few expats that remain make their presence felt on the city's eating and drinking scene.

Harry's Bar (☎ 0 4234 8837; 19/4 Banliam Bypass; mains 40-200B; ✦ 11am-11pm; ✦) Burgers, beer, darts and just a little bit of *Cheers*-style bar-fly bonhomie make this one of the better expat boltholes.

Steve's Bar & Restaurant (☎ 0 4224 4523; 234/5 Th Prajak Silpakorn; mains 40-150B; ✦ 11am-11pm; ✦) Big crowds gather here for the big Sunday roasts, which are traditionally devoured in front of English Premiership football (shown on an impressive 50-inch screen).

Sister Bar-Ther (☎ 0 4224 4721; Th Adunyadet; ✦ 11am-midnight) This fashionable spot attracts a smattering of Udon's beautiful set, who sit around the dark-wood tables sipping cocktails and posh coffees. Lounge music plays on the decks, football is screened on the TV and the company is friendly and chatty.

Aussie Pub (☎ 0 6108 6359; 67-70 Charoensri Complex Sq; ☺ 11am-midnight) It's not really the hippest spot on the circuit, but this Aussie-style (read: outback) place has a pool table and cold beer.

Entertainment

Udon Park (☎ 0 4232 4755; 36 Th Mak Khaeng) Traditional Isan song and dance is performed nightly at this beer garden across from the Tonkoon Hotel. Prices for meals are moderate (80B to 160B).

Shopping

Udon's main shopping district is centred on Th Pho Si, between the fountain circle and Th Mak Khaeng.

Charoensri Complex (☺ 10am-10pm) This relatively new complex off Th Prajak Silpakorn is one of the largest shopping centres in Isan, with 22,000 sq metres of retail space filled with standard Thai department stores, a huge supermarket, a flock of designer clothing boutiques, several restaurants and coffee shops, and the attached Charoensri Grand Royal Hotel (p469).

Udon Bho-Phin Tracha (☎ 0 4224 5618; Th Tumajaidee; ☺ 9am-6pm Mon-Sat) This large store sells a good selection of silk, handicrafts and traditional artworks.

Getting There & Away

AIR

THAI (www.thaiairways.com) and **Nok Air** (www.nok air.co.th) fly thrice daily to/from Bangkok – tickets can be booked at **Ultinet Travel** (p469). One-way fares start at 1850B for THAI and 740B for Nok Air.

Air Asia (☎ 0 2515 9999; www.airasia.com) flies twice daily to/from Bangkok. Tickets must be booked by telephone, or via the website.

BUS

There are buses leaving Bangkok's Northern bus terminal for Udon hourly throughout the day (air-con/VIP 251/500B, nine to 10 hours) from 5am until 11am.

In Udon, the main **No 1 bus terminal** is off Th Sai Uthit near the Charoen Hotel in the southeastern portion of town. Air-con buses

from here go mostly to points south and east of Udon, including Khorat (142B, 4½ hours, hourly), Sakon Nakhon (120B, 3½ hours, five daily), Khon Kaen (110B, 2½ hours, hourly) and Bangkok (251B, 10 hours, hourly).

There are also a number of private companies with offices at this terminal running buses to Bangkok and Vientiane. **Chan Tour** (☎ 0 4234 3403) operates hourly air-con buses to Bangkok's Northern bus terminal (322B, 9½ hours) most of the day and night. **VIP 999** (☎ 0 4222 1489; No 1 bus terminal) operates a VIP bus to the Northern bus terminal in Bangkok (500B, nine hours) at 8pm and direct air-con buses to Vientiane (80B, two hours) at 7am, 9.30am, 3pm and 5pm.

The **No 2 bus terminal** is on the western outskirts of the city next to the highway, and has buses to destinations including Loei (ordinary/air-con 60/110B, 3½ hours, five daily) and Nong Khai (ordinary 40B, one hour, hourly).

TRAIN

The 8pm (No 77) train is the quickest service from Bangkok, arriving at Udon's train station, east of the centre, at 3.36am the next day; it then continues on to Nong Khai where it terminates at 6am. Slower trains also leave Bangkok on the Nong Khai line at 8.20am and 8.45pm, arriving in Udon at 5.50pm and 8.09am. The 1st-class fare is 459B, 2nd class is 220B and 3rd class is 95B, plus applicable charges for sleeper and express service.

In the reverse direction, trains leave Udon Thani for Bangkok at 8.16am, 6.40pm and 8.03pm, arriving between eight and nine hours later.

Getting Around

You can get anywhere around town by *túk-túk* for between 30B and 60B. *Săamláw* rates should be about the same.

Ultinet Travel (p469) is an agent for Budget car rental, although prices (figure on 1400B per day self-drive) are quite high by Thai standards. Should you want to hire a car with driver, a cheaper alternative is to negotiate for one of the taxis waiting at the **bus stop** (Th Phanphrao) at the northeastern corner of Thung Si Meuang. Figure on no more than 1000B per day for one of these, including the services of a driver, who will be happy to go anywhere in the province, and as far out of the province as Nong Khai or Khon Kaen.

AROUND UDON THANI PROVINCE
Ban Chiang
บ้านเชียง

This town, 50km east of Udon Thani, was once the hub of the ancient Ban Chiang civilisation and archaeological digs here have uncovered a treasure trove of artefacts dating as far back as 7500 years. As well as the original excavation pit of an ancient Ban Chiang burial ground at **Wat Pho Si Nai** (admission 30B; � 8.30am-4.30pm), the nearby **Ban Chiang National Museum** (admission 30B; � 8.30am-4.30pm) is chock-a-block with Ban Chiang exhibits and offers a wonderful insight into the region's distant past. The excavation pit displays 52 human skeletons, in whole or in part, along with lots of pottery. This is worth a trip if you're at all interested in the prehistoric Ban Chiang culture. The well-conceived museum exhibits pottery from all Ban Chiang periods, plus myriad bronze objects recovered from the Pho Si Nai excavation, including spearheads, sickles, axe heads, fish hooks, chisels, arrowheads, bells, rings and bangles.

The Ban Chiang culture, an agricultural society that once thrived in northeastern Thailand, is known for its early bronze metallurgy and clay pottery, especially pots and vases with distinctive burnt-ochre swirl designs, most of which were associated with burial sites. Seven layers of civilisation have been excavated; the famous swirl-design pottery comes from the third and fourth layers. The area was declared a Unesco World Heritage site in 1992.

The locals attempt to sell Ban Chiang artefacts, real and fake, but neither type is allowed out of the country, so don't buy them. Some of the local handicrafts, such as thick hand-woven cotton fabric, are good buys; more than 50 local families are involved in the spinning and weaving of such textiles, along with ceramics and basket-weaving. The other main local livelihoods are rice cultivation, fishing and hunting.

SLEEPING & EATING
Lakeside Sunrise Guest House (☎ 0 4220 8167; s/d 150/200B) Within easy striking distance of the museum, this small, nicely landscaped place is the village's best bet for a budget. Clean, shared facilities are downstairs, while the upper floor boasts a spacious wooden veranda overlooking the lake.

Gecko Villa (www.pansea.com/gecko; r 3600B; ☒ ☒) A little further afield, and surrounded by acres of lush gardens, this glitzy place has some superbly swanky villas and a setting to die for. While you are here, you can take part in cooking classes, or even help to bring in the harvest. No-one seems keen to hand out a phone number – book via the email address – but staff will happily collect you from Udon Thani or whisk you down to Ban Chiang.

There are several simple **restaurants** across from the national museum entrance.

GETTING THERE & AWAY
Săwngthăew run regularly from Udon Thani to Ban Chiang from late morning until about 3.45pm (25B, 40 minutes). In the reverse direction they're frequent from around 6.30am until 10.30am. Catch them from in front of the museum.

Alternatively, take a bus bound for Sakon Nakhon or Nakhon Pathom and get off at the Ban Pulu (30B, 45 minutes) turn-off, a 10-minute *săamláw* ride from Ban Chiang. Buses leave in either direction several times a day, but the last leaves Ban Chiang in the late afternoon.

Phu Phrabat Historical Park
อุทยานประวัติศาสตร์ภูพระบาท
Steeped in local legend and peppered with bizarre rock formations daubed with ancient cave paintings, **Phu Phrabat Historical Park** (☎ 0 4291 0107; admission 30B; � 8.30am-4.30pm), 42km northwest of Udon Thani, is one of the region's highlights, offering great views from the crags of the Phu Phrabat escarpment, plenty of mythical intrigue and an interesting insight into the area's prehistoric heritage.

The formations are a collection of balanced rocks, spires and whale-sized boulders, with several shrines and three wats built in and around them. A well-marked trail meandering through the park takes around two hours to negotiate at a normal walking pace. Some of the trees are labelled with their Latin names, and a climb beyond the rock formations to the edge of the escarpment ends with fine views of the mountains of Laos to the north.

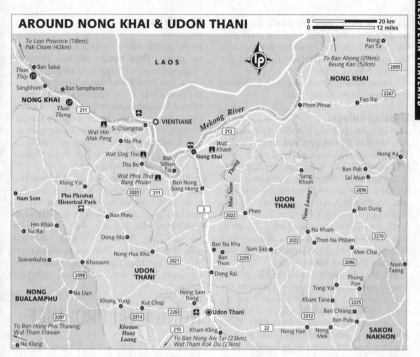

AROUND NONG KHAI & UDON THANI

At the entrance to the area is the largest temple in the historical park, **Wat Phra That Phra Phutthabaht Bua Bok**, with its namesake Lao-style *chedi*. Prehistoric paintings in several grottoes feature wild animals, humans and cryptic symbols. To the southeast of the main wat are the caves of **Tham Lai Meu** and **Tham Non Sao Eh**, and to the west are **Tham Khon** and **Tham Wua Daeng**. These are really more like grottoes or rocky overhangs than caves. There are also some small but sophisticated rock carvings of Buddha images dating back to when the Mon and, later, Khmer ruled this area. For Isan residents, this is an important place of pilgrimage. For visitors, the side-by-side progression from rock art to Buddhist stupa represents a localised evolution of thought and aesthetics.

Most of the bizarre rock formations to be found here are featured in an enchanting local legend about a king (Phaya Kong Phan), his stunningly beautiful daughter (Nang Usua), a hermit (the Rishi Chantra), and a love-struck prince from another kingdom (Tao Baros). The most striking rock formation, a mushroom-shaped out-

crop with a shrine built into it, is said to be the tower where the beautiful princess was forced to live by her overprotective father. Many of these rock formations are signposted with names in Thai and English alluding to the legend, but, unless you're familiar with it, they'll make little sense to you. If you're staying at the Mut Mee Guest House in Nong Khai (p479), ask Julian, the owner, to tell you the story before you go.

The park has three new **bungalows** (☎ 0 4291 0107; per person 400B) if you want to spend some time here, but they're really more geared for visiting groups of Thai students.

GETTING THERE & AWAY
The park is 42km northwest of Udon Thani and 70km southwest of Nong Khai, near the small town of Ban Pheu and can be visited as a long day trip from either Udon or Nong Khai. From Udon it's a 25B bus ride to Ban Pheu; it's 30B from Nong Khai (aim to catch the 7.15am bus from Nong Khai's main bus terminal). From Ban Pheu, take a *săwngthăew* for 15B to the village at the base of the hill and then a motorcycle

taxi to the park itself. You could also charter a motorbike in the Ban Pheu market to take you all the way. If you're using public transport you should plan on leaving the park by 2.30pm.

Easiest of all is to visit the park by rented motorbike from Nong Khai.

Weaving Villages

Two villages renowned for *khít*-pattern fabrics are **Ban Na Kha** and **Ban Thon**, around 16km north of Udon via Hwy 2 on the way to Nong Khai. *Khít* is a geometric, diamond-grid minimal weft brocade commonly used for the centre square of *măwn khwăan* fabrics or other decorative items. Ban Na Kha is just east of Hwy 2, while Ban Thon is 2km further east along a laterite road. Shops in Ban Na Kha that are used to dealing with foreigners include **Songsi Isan Handicraft** (184/1 Mu 1) and **Chanruan Nakha** (92 Mu 1).

Ban Nong Aw Tai, in Amphoe Nong Wua Saw, about 40km southwest of Udon via Rte 210, produces high-quality silk. In this same district is **Wat Tham Kok Du**, a famous meditation wat presided over by abbot Phra Ajahn Kham Fong, whose simple, direct style of teaching has attracted a large number of lay students. Nong Wua Saw is actually part of Nong Bualamphu Province.

Both villages are fairly awkward to reach on public transport, although buses on the Udon Thani to Nong Khai run can drop you near Ban Na Kha, which is just off Hwy 2. See p471 for details of these buses.

Tham Erawan
ถ้ำเอราวัณ

High up the side of a beautiful limestone mountain, **Tham Erawan** (donations appreciated; ☺ daylight hours) is a large cave shrine, featuring a vast seated Buddha. Gazing out over the plains below, the Buddha is visible from several kilometres away and can be reached by a winding staircase of some 700 steps. There's not much to admire in the cave itself, but the views are photogenic and it's a good place to stretch your legs if you happen to be travelling along Rte 210.

The cave is at the back of **Wat Tham Erawan** (☺ daylight hours), which is 2km north of a turn-off between the Km 31 and Km 32 markers on Rte 210. It's near the village of Ban Hong Phu Thawng, west of the town of Na Klang. There is a smaller cave wat near this turn-off – keep going north until you can see the larger, higher cave in the distance. You'll need your own transport to get here.

NONG KHAI PROVINCE

Nong Khai Province, ccupying a narrow, 300km-long sweep along the banks of the Mekong, is a beautiful, intriguing region, with fine views over the river into Laos and a clutch of pretty riverside villages. The capital, Nong Khai, where the Friendship Bridge crosses over into Laos, is one of northeastern Thailand's most popular tourist destin-

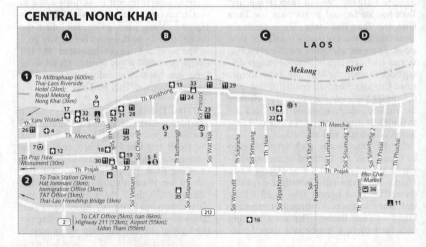

CENTRAL NONG KHAI

ations and features the surreal Sala Kaew Ku sculpture park, a must-see on any jaunt through the region.

NONG KHAI
หนองคาย

pop 61,500

Crammed between nations, Nong Khai is both a historic and physical bridgehead between Thailand and Laos. Spread out along the leafy banks of the Mekong River, the city was once part of the Vientiane kingdom and is now, appropriately, the point at which Hwy 2 finally makes the jump across the border via the Friendship Bridge into Laos.

Lady Luck certainly smiles on the location. As a major staging post on the tourist trail north, Nong Khai benefits from a steady stream of travellers and a clutch of excellent places to stay and eat have sprung up to accommodate them. But Nong Khai's popularity as a stopover is about more than just its proximity to Laos. Seduced by its dreamy river views, sluggish pace of life and surrounding attractions, many who mean to stay an hour, end up bedding down for a week.

Developers have stuck their concrete boots into some of the city's prettier historic districts, but compared to Udon Thani and Khon Kaen further south, Nong Khai has managed to keep at least one of its feet firmly rooted in the past. Cut through with a sprinkling of French colonial villas and a starburst of wats, time, like the Mekong, appears to flow a little more slowly here.

History

Nong Khai once fell within the boundaries of the Vientiane (Wiang Chan) kingdom, which itself vacillated between independence and tribute to either Lan Xang (1353–1694) or to Siam (late 18th century until 1893). In 1827 Rama III gave a Thai lord, Thao Suwothamma, the rights to establish Meuang Nong Khai at the present city site. In 1891, under Rama V, Nong Khai became the capital of *monthon* Lao Phuan, an early Isan satellite state that included what are now Udon, Loei, Khon Kaen, Sakon Nakhon, Nakhon Phanom and Nong Khai Provinces, as well as Vientiane.

The area came under several attacks by *jiin haw* (Yunnanese) marauders in the late 19th century. The 1886-vintage Prap Haw Monument (*pràap haw* means 'defeat of the Haw') in front of the former Provincial Office (now used as a community college) commemorates Thai-Lao victories over Haw invasions in 1874, 1885 and 1886.

When western Laos was partitioned off from Thailand by the French in 1893, the *monthon* capital was moved to Udon, leaving Nong Khai to fade into a provincial backwater.

The opening of the Thai–Lao Friendship Bridge on 8 April 1994 marked the beginning of a new era of development for Nong Khai as a regional trade and transport centre

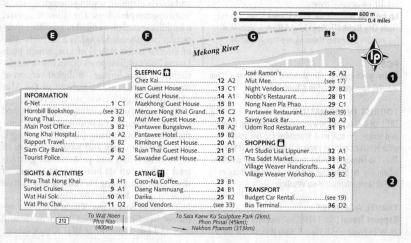

INFORMATION	
6-Net **1** C1	
Hornbill Bookshop..............(see 32)	
Krung Thai..............................**2** B2	
Main Post Office....................**3** B2	
Nong Khai Hospital................**4** A2	
Rapport Travel.......................**5** B2	
Siam City Bank......................**6** B2	
Tourist Police........................**7** A2	
SIGHTS & ACTIVITIES	
Phra That Nong Khai..............**8** H1	
Sunset Cruises.......................**9** A1	
Wat Hai Sok.........................**10** A1	
Wat Pho Chai.......................**11** D2	

SLEEPING 🏠	
Chez Kai..............................**12** A2	
Isan Guest House.................**13** C1	
KC Guest House....................**14** A1	
Maekhong Guest House........**15** B1	
Mercure Nong Khai Grand....**16** C2	
Mut Mee Guest House..........**17** A1	
Pantawee Bungalows...........**18** A2	
Pantawee Hotel....................**19** B2	
Rimkhong Guest House.........**20** A1	
Ruan Thai Guest House.........**21** B1	
Sawasdee Guest House.........**22** C1	
EATING 🍴	
Coco-Na Coffee....................**23** B1	
Daeng Namnuang.................**24** B1	
Darika..................................**25** B2	
Food Vendors.....................(see 33)	

José Ramon's........................**26** A2	
Mut Mee...........................(see 17)	
Night Vendors......................**27** B2	
Nobbi's Restaurant...............**28** B1	
Nong Naen Pla Phao.............**29** C1	
Pantawee Restaurant.........(see 19)	
Savoy Snack Bar...................**30** A2	
Udom Rod Restaurant...........**31** B1	
SHOPPING 🛍	
Art Studio Lisa Lippuner.........**32** A1	
Tha Sadet Market..................**33** B1	
Village Weaver Handicrafts.....**34** B2	
Village Weaver Workshop.......**35** B2	
TRANSPORT	
Budget Car Rental.............(see 19)	
Bus Terminal........................**36** D2	

Mekong River

0   600 m
0   0.4 miles

212

To Wat Noen Phra Nao (400m)

To Sala Kaew Ku Sculpture Park (2km);
Phon Phisai (45km);
Nakhon Phanom (313km)

and the skyline has been creeping slowly upwards ever since.

Orientation & Information

Nong Khai follows the curve of the Mekong River. The Friendship Bridge, which crosses into Laos, is about 3km west of the centre of town and most of the hotels and restaurants are along, or just off, the three parallel streets of Th Rimkhong, Th Meechai and Th Prajak.

BOOKSHOPS

Hornbill Bookshop (☎ 0 4246 0272; Th Kaew Worawut; ✆ 10am-7pm) For new and used English-language books.

IMMIGRATION OFFICES

Immigration Office (☎ 0 4241 2089; ✆ 8.30am-4.30pm Mon-Fri) On the highway bypass that leads to the Friendship Bridge; offers Thai visa extensions.

INTERNET ACCESS

6-Net (Th Rimkhong; per min 15B; ✆ 9am-11pm)
Hornbill Bookshop (☎ 0 4246 0272; Th Kaew Worawut; per min 20B; ✆ 10am-7pm)

MEDICAL & EMERGENCY

Nong Khai Hospital (☎ 1669; Th Meechai) For all medical emergencies.
Tourist police (☎ 0 4224 0616, emergency ☎ 1155; Th Meechai)

MONEY

There are banks with ATM and exchange facilities across town.
Krung Thai (Th Meechai; ✆ 8.30am-4.30pm Mon-Fri)
Siam City Bank (Th Prajak; ✆ 8.30am-3.30pm Mon-Fri) Includes a Western Union money-transfer facility.

POST

Main post office (Th Meechai; ✆ 8.30am-4.30pm Mon-Fri, 9am-noon Sat, Sun & holidays)

TOURIST INFORMATION

TAT (☎ 0 4246 7164; www.tourismthailand.org; Friendship Bridge; ✆ 8.30am-4.30pm Mon-Fri) This small office is tucked away in a row of shop houses next to the Thai–Lao Friendship Bridge checkpoint. The staff distribute information on Nong Khai and surrounding provinces, as well as some information on Vientiane.

TRAVEL AGENCIES

Rapport Travel (☎ 0 4246 0567; rapport@udon.ksc .co.th; Th Prajak; ✆ 8.30am-5.30pm Mon-Sat) For plane

tickets and buses to Udon Thani airport; see p481 for further details.

Sights & Activities

SALA KAEW KU SCULPTURE PARK
ศาลาแก้วกู่

Nong Khai's most enigmatic attraction, **Sala Kaew sculpture park** (Pavilion of Kaew Ku; ☎ 0 1369 5744; admission 10B; ✆ 7.30am-5.30pm) is a surreal, sculptural journey into the mind of a mystic shaman. Built over a period of 20 years by Luang Poo Boun Leua Sourirat, who died in 1996, the park features a weird and wonderful array of gigantic sculptures, ablaze with Hindu-Buddhist imagery.

As his own story goes, Luang Poo, a Lao national, tumbled into a hole as a child, where he met an ascetic named Kaewkoo. Kaewkoo introduced him to the manifold mysteries of the underworld and set him on course to become a Brahmanic yogi-priest-shaman. Shaking up his own unique blend of Hindu and Buddhist philosophy, mythology and icononography, Luang Poo developed a large following in northeastern Thailand, where he had moved following the 1975 communist takeover in Laos.

The park is a real smorgasbord of bizarre cement statues of Shiva, Vishnu, Buddha, and every other Hindu and Buddhist deity imaginable, as well as numerous secular figures, all supposedly cast by unskilled artists under Luang Pu's direction. Some of the sculptures are quite amusing – if you're travelling with kids they'll enjoy the serene and stately elephant wading though a pack of anthropomorphic dogs. The tallest sculpture, a Buddha seated on a coiled *naga* with a spectacular multiheaded hood, is 25m high. Also of interest is the Wheel of Life, which boils Luang Poo's philosophies down into a single, slightly baffling image – a digital version of this is available on the website of the Mut Mee Guest House (www.mutmee.com).

The main shrine building is full of framed pictures of Hindu and Buddhist deities, temple donors, and Luang Pu at various ages, plus smaller bronze and wooden figures of every description and provenance, guaranteed to throw an art historian into a state of disorientation. Luang Pu's corpse lies in state under a glass dome in the upper room.

To get to Sala Kaew Ku, board a *săwng-thăew* heading southeast towards Beung Kan and ask to get off at Wat Khaek (about

15B), which is 4km to 5km outside the town, near St Paul Nong Khai School. A chartered *túk-túk* costs 50B.

Sala Kaew Ku is an easy 3km bike ride from town.

THAI–LAO FRIENDSHIP BRIDGE
สะพานมิตรภาพไทยลาว

Spanning the Mekong from Ban Jommani (3km west of Nong Khai) on the Thai side to Tha Na Laeng (19km southeast of Vientiane) in Laos, is the US$30 million Saphan Mittaphap Thai–Lao (Thai–Lao Friendship Bridge), financed by Australia. An 8.2km highway bypass connects the bridge with Hwy 2/Asia 12 just south of Nong Khai.

The 1174m-long bridge opened in April 1994amid much hoopla about how it would improve transport and communications between Thailand and Laos. It was the second bridge to be erected anywhere along the Mekong's entire length (the first was in the People's Republic of China).

In spite of its two 3.5m-wide traffic lanes, two 1.5m-wide footpaths and space for a railway down the centre, the bridge has done little to fulfil its design potential. City planners have been saying for years that eventually a train link will extend from the Nong Khai railhead across the 12.7m-wide bridge and on to Vientiane. So far the rails go from the new Nong Khai train station all the way to the centre of the bridge where they abruptly stop. Apparently the Lao are waiting for some donor country with deep pockets to come and finish the job.

For bridge transport information, see information on getting to Laos p481.

WAT PHO CHAI
วัดโพธิ์ชัย

A large Lan Xang–era Buddha, awash with gold, bronze and precious stones, sits at the hub of **Wat Pho Chai** (Phra Sai; 7am-5pm), off Th Prajak in the southeastern part of town. The head of the image is pure gold, the body is bronze and the *ùtsànìt* is set with rubies. The altar on which the image sits features elaborately executed gilded wooden carvings and mosaics, while the ceiling bears wooden rosettes in the late Ayuthaya style.

The murals in the *bòt* depict the image's travels from the interior of Laos to the banks of the Mekong, where it was put on a raft. A storm capsized the raft and the image sat at the bottom of the river from 1550 to 1575, when it was salvaged and placed in a temple now called Wat Pradit Thammakhun on the Thai side of the river. The highly revered image was moved to Wat Pho Chai during the reign of King Mongkut (1852–68).

During the annual Songkran Festival (April), the Phra Sai image is taken out in procession around town.

PHRA THAT NONG KHAI
พระธาตุหนองคาย

Also known as **Phra That Klang Nam** (Holy Reliquary in the Middle of the River; admission free; 24hr), this Lao *chedi* is submerged in the Mekong River and can only be seen in the dry season when the Mekong lowers about 30m. The *chedi* slipped into the river in 1847 and continues to slide – it's near the middle now. For the best view, walk east along Th Meechai past the marine police post, then past three wats on the right, then turn left on Soi Paphraw (Paa Phrao) 3. Follow this lane until it ends at the new riverside promenade and look for the *chedi* in the river. Once the top of the *chedi* has cleared the water during the dry season, coloured flags are fastened to the top to make it easier to spot.

You can get a closer look at the *chedi* by taking the nightly sunset cruise from Tha Wat Hai Sok; see p478.

WAT NOEN PHRA NAO
วัดเนินพระเนาว์

A forest wat in the southeast of town, **Wat Noen Phra Nao** (daylight hours) boasts a Vipassana (insight meditation) centre on pleasant, tree-shaded grounds. Many Westerners meditated here during the 1960s and 1970s. Some extremely ornate temple architecture, including perhaps the most rococo bell tower we've ever seen, stands in contrast to the usual ascetic tone of such forest monasteries. There's a Chinese cemetery on the grounds. Westerners may still be invited to study here if they ask politely, but there is unlikely to be any English-language instruction and you will have to dress respectfully.

HAT JOMMANI
หาดจอมมณี

It only makes a seasonal appearance during the dry season, but the sandy beach of **Hat Jommani** is a favourite with picnickers, sunsoakers and those who just like to feel the Mekong running between their toes. It's next to the Thai–Lao Friendship Bridge in Ban Jommani, 3km west of Nong Khai.

During the dry season a rustic thatched shelter with straw mats becomes a restaurant serving delicious *kài yâang, plaa pîng* (grilled fish), *sôm-tam* and cold beer.

SUNSET CRUISE
Sunset boat rides are available daily behind Wat Hai Sok. The cruises start at 5.30pm, last an hour and cost 30B; it's a wonderful way to soak up the Mekong ambience.

Festivals & Events
Like many other cities in the northeast, Nong Khai has a large **Rocket Festival** *(ngaan bun bâng fai)*, which begins on Visakha Puja day (Buddha's birth and enlightenment day) in

late May/early June. At the end of Buddhist Lent (Okk Paan Saa) in late October/early November, there is a large **Rowing Festival**, featuring long-boat races on the Mekong. The **Anou Savari Festival** in late February/early March marks the end of the 'Hau' rebellions and boasts the city's biggest street fair.

During the October full moon the chance to glimpse **naga fireballs** *(bâng fai pháyaa nâak),* the mysterious floating lights that are sometimes seen over this stretch of the Mekong, draws thousands of curious visitors from as far afield as Bangkok (see the boxed text, below).

Sleeping
BUDGET
Catering to the steady flow of backpackers heading across the border, Nong Khai's

---

GREAT BALLS OF FIRE

Mass hysteria? Methane gas? Drunken Lao soldiers? Or perhaps the fiery breath of the sacred *naga*, a serpent-like being that populates folkloric waterways throughout Theravada Buddhist Southeast Asia. For the people who live along a certain stretch of the Mekong River in Thailand's Nong Khai Province, it's not a matter of whether or not to believe. For as long as anyone can remember, the sighting of the *bâng fai pháyaa nâak* (loosely translated 'naga fireballs') has been an annual event. Locals who have witnessed the phenomena often describe them as reddish or pinkish balls of fire that emerge from the Mekong River just after dusk and float into the air, sometimes as high as 300m, before disappearing without a trace. Most claim that the *naga* fireballs are soundless, but others say that a hissing can be heard if one is close enough to where they emerge from the surface of the river. On both sides of the Mekong the event has long been explained as a sign that the resident *naga* were celebrating the end of the Buddhist Rains Retreat (*Awk Phansǎa* in Thai), which coincides with the 15th waxing moon of the 11th lunar month.

Naga fireballs have only recently come to the attention of the rest of Thailand. Television news has been reporting the annual sightings for years, but it wasn't until the 2002 release of a film based on the phenomena that Thais really began to take notice. Entitled *Sìp Hâa Khâm Deuan Sìp-èt* or *Fifteenth Waxing Moon of the Eleventh Lunar Month* in Thai (the film was released with English subtitles under the curious title *Mekhong Full Moon Party*), the debut of the film not long before the scheduled event had an expected effect. Thousands of Thais from Bangkok and the rest of the country converged on the banks of the Mekong in Nong Khai Province and waited for the show to begin. Sadly, it rained that year. But that didn't dampen enthusiasm and *naga* fireballs were witnessed right on schedule.

So what, you might ask, is the real cause behind *naga* fireballs? Various theories have been put forth. One, which was aired on a Thai TV exposé-style programme, claimed that Lao soldiers taking part in festivities on the other side of the Mekong were firing their rifles into the air. Interestingly, the reaction to the TV programme was anger and a storm of protest from both sides of the river. A more sensible theory perhaps, is that methane gas, trapped below the mud on the river bottom, reaches a certain temperature at that time of year and is released. Whatever the real cause, we may never find out. There are plans to blast a series of rapids along the Nong Khai stretch of the Mekong as part of a four-nation agreement (between Thailand, China, Myanmar and Laos) to make the river more navigable. Whatever subtle balance of nature has produced this mysterious event year after year may be lost forever.

budget offerings are some of the best in the region.

Mut Mee Guest House (☎ 0 4246 0717; www.mut mee.com; 111/4 Th Kaew Worawut; r 90-600B) Occupying a sleepy stretch of the Mekong riverbank, Nong Khai's budget old-timer is the perfect place to decompress prior to the bumpy buses of Laos. A huge variety of rooms – from spartan dorms (90B) to a single air-con room in the owner's house (600B) – are clustered around a leafy restaurant where the owner, Julian, holds court with his grip of local legend and his passion for all things Isan. Perhaps unsurprisingly, the alleyway leading down to Mut Mee has developed into a self-contained traveller's village, with yoga instruction, bookshops and an Internet café all at hand.

Isan Guest House (☎ 0 1057 2202; guyfernback@ hotmail.com; s/d 100/150B) Occupying the creaking shell of a beautiful 70-year-old wooden house, this no-frills guesthouse makes up in authentic atmosphere what it lacks in creature comforts. Simple and rustic, this is well off the beaten street – it's down a quiet alley off Th Meechai. Bathrooms are shared.

Sawasdee Guest House (☎ 0 4241 2502; fax 4242 0259; 402 Th Meechai; r 100-300B; 🟩) If you could judge a hotel by its cover, this charismatic place in an old, Franco-Chinese shophouse would come up trumps. The tidy rooms – there are also cheaper fan options with shared bathrooms – lack the exterior's old school veneer, but at least you'll sleep well in the knowledge that you're bedded down in a little piece of living history.

Ruan Thai Guest House (☎ 0 4241 2519; www .ruanthaihouse.com; Th Rimkhong; r 120-400B; 🟩) Once little more than a small private home, this pleasant spot now appears to be soaking up the boomtime, boasting plenty of spotless rooms in an attractive wooden block, a tangle of flower-filled garden greenery and bags of character. The cheaper fan rooms are in the main building, and slightly dowdy offerings with shared bathroom are in an older block out back.

Maekhong Guest House (☎ 0 4246 0689; Th Rimkhong; dm/s/d 100/125/150B; 🖳) It looks a little like it might have been built from flotsam washed down the Mekong, but this ramshackle place does have a certain tumbledown charm. Its position, right on the river, also scoops a few credits. Bathrooms are shared.

Rimkhong Guest House (☎ 0 4246 0625; www.rim khong.com; 815/1-4 Th Rimkhong; s/d 100/150B) Sparse wooden rooms with shared bathrooms and plenty of hush come as standard at this unassuming outfit. A friendly old dog pads around the courtyard and sets the sluggish pace, while the owner provides the warm welcomes.

Pantawee Bungalows (☎ 0 4241 1568; www.nong khaihotel.com; Th Hai Sok; 350B) Just across the street from the Pantawee Hotel, but with cheaper, shabbier little rooms resembling hobbit holes on a Middle Earth housing estate. At night the hotel is illuminated in a starburst of fairy lights and attracts a good portion of the city's expat crowd to its street-side eatery.

KC Guest House (☎ 0 4246 0272; inchuta06@yahoo .com; 1018/003 Soi Mut Mee; r 120B) On the same lane as Mut Mee, this humble spot offers little more than four walls and a bed for the night. The décor's colourful though, and the backpacker vibe carries in from it's bigger neighbour. Bathrooms are shared.

Chez Kai (☎ /fax 0 4246 0968; 1160 Soi Samoson; s/d 100/150B) Chez Kai wears its years like three decades of cigarettes and alcohol – ie badly. The French travellers still trickle in though; there's a friendly atmosphere and a little Bohemian charm lives on.

MIDRANGE & TOP END

Even the most expensive places in Nong Khai have rooms with a midrange price tag. On the downside, there isn't the variety that you get within the city's budget category and worthwhile options are few and far between.

Mercure Nong Khai Grand (☎ 0 4200 3344; www .accorhotels-asia.com; Hwy 212; r 1000B, ste 3500B; 🟩 🟩 🖳) Recently renovated by the international hotel chain, this slick, modern place has plenty of sparkle. A big hit with passing suits, 'executive' standards are maintained throughout and swanky suites are on offer for those after the Midas touch.

Pantawee Hotel (☎ 0 4241 1568; www.nongkhai hotel.com; 1241 Th Hai Sok; r 450-1000B; 🟩 🖳) The Pantawee brand is something of a cartel along Th Hai Sok, with a string of accommodation options and a restaurant. The main hotel is homogenous but spotless, with a big choice of air-con rooms, an Internet café, bunches of plastic flowers in every corner and Muzak.

Royal Mekong Nong Khai (☎ 0 4242 0024; fax 0 4242 1280; 222 Th Panungchonprathoan; r 1000B; 🟩 🖳)

Erected to reap the benefits from its location close to the Friendship Bridge, this nine-storey offering is looking a little downbeat these days. It offers plenty of facilities, including a jogging track, pool and – wait for it – a four-million-year-old fossilised tree, but it is rather eclipsed by the Mercure Nong Khai Grand.

Thai-Laos Riverside Hotel (☎ 0 4246 0263; fax 0 4246 0317; 051 Th Kaew Worawut; r 500B; ❄) The white walls of this slightly frumpy midranger are now muddier than the Mekong, but it has a decent spot by the river, good-value rooms and, just in case you're into tacky hotel clubs, a basement disco called 'Earthquake Underground'. There's also a pleasant terrace restaurant with river views.

Eating

Mut Mee Guest House (0 4246 0717; www.mutmee .com; 111/4 Th Kaew Worawut; mains 40-100B; ❄ 7am-9pm) Of all the guesthouses in town, Mut Mee has the best food, including many vegetarian dishes. Its riverside location also has the best atmosphere.

Nobbi's Restaurant (☎ 0 4246 0583; Th Rimkhong; dishes 50-120B; ❄ 8am-midnight) Hidden behind a plethora of pot plants, this little Western-style hideaway peddles fine German beer, pizza and some mean homemade sausages. You can even buy jars of sauerkraut to take away and feast on in the privacy of your own room.

Daeng Namnuang (☎ 0 4241 1961; Th Banthoengjit; mains 30-60B; ❄ 6am-7pm) Variety is not the spice of life here, but the smallest Vietnamese menu we have ever seen (spring rolls and barbecue pork only) sure draws the crowds. What it does, it does well, and the air-con is a big draw come lunchtime. A smaller, no-frills outlet has a more varied menu across the street.

Pantawee Restaurant (☎ 0 4241 1568; 1049 Th Hai Sok; mains 40-140B; ❄ 7am-2am) Awash with neon and fairy lights, this spic and span hotel diner has a huge range of Eastern and international dishes, served right the way through into the early hours. It is not the most atmospheric place on the block and some of the expat diners/drinkers look like they're ready to drop off their chairs come the witching hour, but it remains one of town's smarter options and is open well into the night.

Savoy Snack Bar (☎ 0 7232 1091; mains 30-70B; ❄ 8am-10pm) It isn't the place for culinary fireworks, but this basic little café is big with the expat fraternity – spot the old-timers lounging on the faux leather sofa. It serves an eclectic mix of no-frills French-, Thai- and American-style dishes.

Coco-Na Coffee (Th Meechai; coffee 20B; ❄ 10am-9pm) Posing as Isan's parochial answer to Starbucks, this hip new café offers an array of trendy coffees and snacks and serves them up in stylish surrounds. Gabber away frantically with the other caffeinated punters inside, or take ten in the leafy terrace out back.

José Ramon's (1128/11 Th Takai; snacks & dishes 40-90B; ❄ 10am-10pm) A trace of Latin Americana prevails at this hole-in-the-wall diner, and steaks, wraps and sandwiches dominate. It doesn't look like José himself has been here for a while, but you can cheer things up with a glass of rum, and plenty of quirky (read: garish) artwork brings life to the walls.

Udom Rod Restaurant (☎ 0 4241 3555; Th Rimkhong; mains 30-80B; ❄ 10am-10pm) Pleasant views are on the house at this riverside outfit and big crowds roll in around sundown. The décor's basic and the wooden floor wobbles as you walk, but the food is cheap and offers a whiff of authenticity.

Nong Naen Pla Phao (Th Rimkhong; dishes 30-40B; ❄ 10am-8pm) Walking east from Udom along Th Rimkhong, you will find plenty of other simple riverside eateries, including this place, where specialities include salt-baked *plaa châwn* (serpent-headed fish) stuffed with herbs, *kài yâang, kaeng lao* (Lao-style bamboo-shoot soup), grilled sausage and grilled prawns (shrimp).

Darika (no Roman-script sign; Th Meechai; mains 20-40B; ❄ 8am-6pm) This spartan outfit serves cheap egg-and-toast breakfasts, real Thai coffee, Lao-style baguette sandwiches and banana pancakes, plus *khànŏm jìip* (Chinese dumplings), *jóhk* (thick rice soup) and *kúaytĭaw*.

For quick, colourful eats, **night vendors** (Th Prajak) set up their stalls each evening, between Soi Cheunjit and Th Hai Sok. During the day, a clutch of **food vendors** (Th Rimkhong) also cater to shoppers at the eastern end of Tha Sadet Market – the grilled fish and Isan sausages reign supreme.

Drinking

Apart from a scattering of seedy 'houses of ill repute', dedicated watering holes are few and far between in Nong Khai.

Mittraphaap (Th Kaew Worawut; ☾ 6pm-midnight) This saloon-style, wooden drinking den, about 600m west of the centre of town, is lined with egg boxes to contain the thump of the nightly live bands, and draws a yee-hah crowd of Thai cowboys and girls with its raucous mix of loud tunes, food and cold beer.

Shopping

Tha Sadet Market (Th Rimkhong) Runs for most of the day and offers the usual mix of dried food, fabrics, electronic items and assorted bric-a-brac.

Village Weaver Handicrafts (☎ 0 4242 2651; www .thaivillageweaver.com; 1020 Th Prajak; ☾ 9am-5pm Mon-Sat) Selling high-quality, moderately priced hand-woven fabrics and ready-made clothing, this handicrafts shop was established by the Good Shepherd Sisters as part of a project to encourage local girls to stay in the villages and earn money by weaving. The hand-dyed *mát-mìi* cotton is particularly good here. The **workshop** (☎ 0 4241 1236; 1151 Soi Jittapanya) where some of the fabric is produced is located off Th Prajak, and visitors are welcome to observe the methods of weaving. The Thai name for the project is Hatthakam Sing Thaw.

Art Studio Lisa Lippuner (☎ 0 4246 1110; mira@nk .ksc.co.th) On the same lane as Mut Mee Guest House, this studio houses a gallery exhibiting the naturalistic paintings of Lisa Lippuner, a long-time Swiss resident.

Getting There & Away
AIR

The nearest airport is approximataly 55km south in Udon Thani. Regular flights operate from here to Bangkok (see p471 for more details).

Rapport Travel (☎ 0 4246 0567; rapport@udon.ksc .co.th; Th Prajak; ☾ 8.30am-5.30pm Mon-Sat) runs a twice-daily bus service between its office and the airport (100B, one hour) at 6.45am and 5.45pm.

BUS

Nong Khai's main **bus terminal** (☎ 0 4241 1612) is located just off Th Prajak, beside the Pho Chai market.

Ordinary buses to Udon Thani's No 2 bus terminal leave Nong Khai at least every hour throughout the day (40B, one hour). There are also regular air-con buses to

Khon Kaen (140B, four hours, eight daily), Bangkok (273B, 11 hours, eight daily) and Rayong (337B, 12 hours, 10 daily). For Chiang Mai, you have to change at Udon Thani (terminal 1). Private companies, with offices around the bus terminal, also offer daily VIP (351B, 10½ hours, 7.30pm) and Super VIP (545B, 10 hours, 8pm) services to Bangkok.

The No 507 ordinary bus travels to Loei (84B, six hours), via Si Chiangmai (22B, 1½ hours) and Sangkhom (37B, 2¾ hours) throughout the morning.

The regular 'yellow bus' links the bus terminal with Tha Bo (15B, 40 minutes), via the riverside road.

Laos

From central Nong Khai, catch a *túk-túk* to the border-crossing bus stop, just south of the Friendship Bridge (50B). From there, regular buses ferry passengers across the bridge (10B) between 6am and 9.30pm, via the immigration check-points. Once across the bridge, it is 22km to Vientiane – there will be plenty of buses and taxis waiting for you. If you already have a visa for Laos, there are also four direct buses a day to Vientiane from Nong Khai's bus terminal (80B, one hour).

TRAIN

From Bangkok, express trains leave Hualamphong station daily at 8pm and 8.45pm, arriving in Nong Khai at 6am and 8.55am respectively – it's about the same speed as the bus but considerably more comfortable. Going the other way, the express services depart from Nong Khai at 7.30am and 7.05pm, arriving at 5.55pm and 7.35am respectively. The fares range from 1117B for a 1st-class sleeper cabin to 318/183B for a 2nd-/3rd-class seat.

For information you can call Nong Khai **train station** (☎ 0 4246 4513), which is 2km west of town.

Getting Around

Săamláw around the town centre cost 20B; *túk-túk* are 30B, or 50B to the Friendship Bridge shuttle-bus terminal and the train station.

Budget Car Rental (☎ 0 4241 1568; fax 0 4246 0850; Pantawee Hotel, 1049 Th Hai Sok; ☺ 9am-5pm Mon-Sat) hires cars for around 1400B per day. A cheaper way to get around the local area is to hire a moped from one of the town's many guesthouses (from 200B per day).

AROUND NONG KHAI PROVINCE
Wat Phra That Bang Phuan

วัดพระธาตุบังเผือน

Boasting a beautiful and ancient Indian-style stupa, **Wat Phra That Bang Phuan** (Map p473; ☺ daylight hours) is one of the region's most sacred sites, not least because some of the Buddha's bones are supposedly buried here. It is similar to the original *chedi* beneath the Phra Pathom Chedi in Nakhon Pathom, but while it is presumed that this stupa dates back to the early centuries AD, no-one really knows when either was built.

In 1559 King Jayachettha of Chanthaburi (not the present Chanthaburi in Thailand, but Wiang Chan – now known as Vientiane – in Laos) extended his capital across the Mekong and built a newer, taller, Lao-style *chedi* over the original as a demonstration of faith (just as King Mongkut did in Nakhon Pathom). Rain caused the *chedi* to lean precariously and in 1970 it finally fell over. The Fine Arts Department restored it

in 1976 and 1977. The current *chedi* stands 34.25m high on a 17.2-sq-metre base.

GETTING THERE & AWAY

To get to Wat Phra That Bang Phuan from Nong Khai, catch the No 507 Loei-bound bus and ask for Ban Bang Phuan (15B, 40 minutes). Check return bus times before you leave Nong Khai though, or you might be in for a serious wait.

Tha Bo
ท่าบ่อ
pop 16,000

One of a clutch of little villages skirting the Mekong, Tha Bo (Pier of the Well; Map p473), is a pretty little spot with a distinctly Vietnamese identity and a scattering of traditional wooden houses.

Surrounded by banana plantations and vegetable fields that flourish in the fertile Mekong floodplains, Tha Bo is the most important market centre between Nong Khai and Loei. An open-air **market** along the main street probably offers more wild plants and herbs than any market along the Mekong, along with Tha Bo's most famous local product – tomatoes.

Aside from the market, the town's only other real claim to fame is **Wat Ong Teu** (☺ daylight hours), also known as Wat Nam Mong, an old Lao-style temple sheltering a 'crying Buddha'. According to local legend, the left hand of the 300-year-old bronze image was once cut off by art thieves; tears streamed from the Buddha's eyes until the hand was returned. The wat is 3km west of town off Rte 211.

One of the region's true idiosyncrasies is its obsession with **topiary**. Head along stretches of Rte 211 near here and you'll pass hedges and bushes sculpted into everything from dolphins and giraffes, to peacocks and dinosaurs. One ambitious gardener has even moulded his hedgerow into a Thai boxing match.

Hotels are still something of an oddity in Tha Bo and **Dtrong Charoen** (no Roman-script sign; ☎ 0 4243 1158; fax 0 4243 1846; r 550B; ☒), on the river road towards Nong Khai, is about the only option. The rooms are spacious, but its six stories are all but deserted.

There is a handful of **food stalls** and **basic restaurants** on the main street through the town.

GETTING THERE & AWAY

The 'yellow bus' runs regularly between Nong Khai and Tha Bo (15B, 40 minutes). Alternatively, the No 507 bus from Nong Khai to Loei will also stop here (15B, 40 minutes).

Si Chiangmai

ศรีเชียงใหม่

Just across the river from Vientiane, Si Chiangmai (Map p473) has a large population of Lao and Vietnamese who make their living from the manufacture of rice-paper spring-roll wrappers. You can see the translucent disks drying in the sun on bamboo racks all over town. In fact, Si Chiangmai is one of the world's leading exporters of spring-roll wrappers!

Unless you are a spy taking snaps of Vientiane, or a spring-roll wrapper trader, however, Si Chiangmai has little in the way of attractions.

The cheapest bed in town can be found in the Western-oriented **Tim Guest House** (☎ /fax 0 4245 1072; Th Rimkhong; s/d 120/150B). It has definitely seen better days, but the basic beds will just about do for a night's sleep. Bathrooms are shared. The guesthouse is near the river in the centre of town – walk west from the bus terminal and turn right at Soi 17, then turn left at the end of the road and you'll find it on the left.

Maneerat Resort (☎ 0 4245 1311; Th Rimkhong; r 450B; ✹), further east along the promenade, is a midrange offering with comfy rooms, plenty of ornamental concrete deer in the parking lot and the attached 'Money Pub' for beer and snacks.

GETTING THERE & AWAY

The No 507 bus passes through Si Chiangmai (22B, 1½ hours, seven daily) en route between Nong Khai and Loei.

Wat Hin Mak Peng

วัดหินหมากเป้ง

West of Si Chiangmai, **Wat Hin Mak Peng** (Map p473; ✹ daylight hours) is worth a trip if only for the scenery along Rte 211 from Nong Khai and is locally known for its *thúdong* (*dhutanga* in Pali) monks. These monks have taken ascetic vows in addition to the standard 227 precepts, eating only once a day and wearing forest robes made from discarded cloth. There are also several *mâe*

chii (Thai Buddhist nuns) living here. The place is very quiet and peaceful, set in a cool forest with lots of bamboo groves overlooking the Mekong. The *kùtì* (monastic huts) are built among giant boulders that form a cliff high above the river; casual visitors aren't allowed into this area, though. Below the cliff is a sandy beach and more rock formations. A Lao forest temple can be seen directly across the river. Fisherfolk occasionally drift by on house rafts.

The abbot at Wat Hin Mak Peng requests that visitors to the wat dress politely – no shorts or sleeveless tops. Those who don't observe the code will be denied entrance.

GETTING THERE & AWAY

Bus No 507 passes the wat en route between Nong Khai (37B, 2¾ hours) and Loei – it is just east of Sangkhom, on the river side of Rte 211. On the way to Wat Hin Mak Peng you'll see many examples of **topiary** along both sides of Rte 211.

Sangkhom

สังคม

Seductively sleepy, the little town of Sangkhom (Map p473) is a convenient staging post for those taking the high (river) road (Rte 211) between Nong Khai and Loei. The Mekong dominates life here, but Wat Hin Mak Peng is nearby, and there are some good hikes to caves and waterfalls in the area.

Coming and going with the ebb and flow of the Mekong River, the Lao island of **Don Klang Khong** appears during the dry season. From around the beginning of December a couple of rustic outdoor eating areas with thatched-roof shelters and tables and chairs are set up in the river shallows.

One of the largest local waterfalls is **Nam Tok Than Thip** (admission free; ✹ daylight hours), 10 kilometres west of Sangkhom (just off Rte 211). The waterfall has two major levels; the upper level is cleaner and has a deep pool (during or just after the rainy season) that is good for a dip. The falls are a long walk from the road – this is a trip best accomplished by motorbike.

Nam Tok Than Thong (admission free; ✹ daylight hours), 11.5km east of Sangkhom at the Km 73 marker off the northern (river) side of Rte 211, is more accessible but can be rather crowded on weekends and holidays.

Wat Aranyabanphot (☯ daylight hours) is a forest wat on a nearby hilltop with a very good sunset-over-the-Mekong view. A relatively recent addition to the wat is a Lanna-style gilded *chedi*. Take a *săamláw*.

Guesthouses come and go with the seasons, but there are a couple of perennial favourites to be found on, or just off, the main road through town.

Bouy's Guest House (☎ /fax 0 4244 1065; Rte 211; s/d 100/150B; ▯) is an Isan word association game; Sangkhom and the town's veteran guesthouse are rarely more than a breath apart. Rusticity is the buzzword here and the riverside bungalows are basic with a double-decker 'B', but the restaurant cooks up some mean suppers, the owner is a great big bag of smiles and the location is wonderfully relaxing.

The pleasant new **Poo-Pae Restaurant** (☎ 0 4244 1088; Rte 211; s/d 300B; ✪), opposite the police station, has a wooden terrace over the Mekong, plenty of atmosphere and a good spread of tasty Thai dishes (mains 30B to 100B) on the menu. There are two cosy timber rooms (with a shared bathroom) over the restaurant here, or some swankier rooms with private bathroom 1km west of Poo-Pae at the related **Vanda House** (☎ 0 4244 1088; r 500B; ✪). At the time of writing, the English sign over Poo-Pae simply read 'Thai Food'.

GETTING THERE & AWAY
Bus No 507 passes through Sangkhom on its way between Nong Khai (37B, 2¾ hours) and Loei (47B, four hours).

West of Pak Chom (in Loei Province), *săwngthăew* are less frequent because the road worsens; the fare on to Chiang Khan is 25B (1½ hours).

BEUNG KAN
บึงกาฬ
This is a small dusty town on the Mekong River, 185km east of Nong Khai by Rte 212; see Map p436. You may want to break your journey here if you are working your way around the northeastern border from Nong Khai to Nakhon Phanom (as opposed to the easier but less interesting Udon Thani–Sakon Nakhon–Nakhon Phanom route).

Between Nong Khai and Nakhon Phanom you'll pass many towns with 'Beung' or 'Nong' in their names: both terms refer to shallow bodies of fresh water fed by seasonal streams (a *beung* is usually larger than a *năwng*).

The closer you get to Nakhon Phanom Province, the more Vietnamese people you will see working in the rice fields or herding cows along the road. Nearly all the farmers in this area, whether ethnic Vietnamese or Thai, wear a simple conical Vietnamese-style straw hat to fend off the sun and rain.

Amphoe Beung Kan itself isn't much but there are some mildly interesting spots, including a nicely landscaped promenade along the waterfront. During the dry season the Mekong River recedes from Beung Kan and reaches its narrowest point along the Thai–Lao border.

East of town is **Nam Song Si** (Two Colour River), where the broad, muddy Huay Songkhram replenishes the Mekong.

In town, the best bed can be found at the pleasant **Mekong Guest House** (☎ /fax 0 4249 1341; 202 Th Chansin; r 250-350B; ✪ ▯). The rooms are a little small, but the mattresses don't sag, the owner is full of local tips and there are cheap fan rooms for those who would rather spend their baht on sundowners.

Samamit Hotel (☎ 0 4249 1078; 343 Th Prasatchai; s/d 120/190B), is also cheap, if not terribly cheerful, but unless you're really counting your baht it comes a poor second to Mekong Guest House. Bathrooms are shared.

Getting There & Away
The bus from Nong Khai to Beung Kan (52B, three hours) departs hourly from 6am to 6pm. Buses between Beung Kan and Ban Ahong cost 20B (one hour).

AROUND BEUNG KAN
Wat Phu Tok
วัดภูทอก
Accessed via a network of winding staircases, and built in, on and around a giant sandstone outcrop in the midst of an arid plain, **Wat Phu Tok** (Map p436; ☯ 10am-4pm) is one of the region's true wonders, with fabulous vistas over the surrounding countryside and a truly soporific atmosphere. Six levels of steps, plus a seventh-level scramble up the rocky summit, lead to the top of the wat and represent the seven factors of enlightenment in Buddhist psychology. Monastic *kùti* are scattered around the mountain, in caves and on cliffs. As you make the strenu-

ous climb, each level is cooler than the one before. It is the cool and quiet isolation of this wat that entices monks and *mâe chii* from all over the northeast to come and meditate here.

This wat used to be the domain of the famous meditation master Ajahn Juan, a disciple of the fierce Ajahn Man who passed away in 1949. Ajahn Juan died in a plane crash about 25 years ago, along with several other highly revered forest monks who were flying to Bangkok for Queen Sirikit's birthday celebration.

Once upon a time, guests were permitted to stay the night here. Unfortunately, one couple acted 'improperly' and so the invitation has been revoked. Things may change again and if you ask very respectfully, you may receive an invitation to bed down – remember, you are in a holy place though.

If solitude is your main objective, it's best to tour Phu Tok early in the morning before the crowds of Thai pilgrims arrive.

GETTING THERE & AWAY
So long as you catch the 7am bus, Wat Phu Tok can be visited as a day trip from Nong Khai. Buses from Nong Khai to Beung Kan depart hourly from 6am to 6pm (52B, three hours) – the last bus back to Nong Khai leaves Beung Kan at around 6pm. *Túk-túk* can then be hired for the journey to Wat Phu Tok from the clock tower in Beung Kan – expect to pay around 500B for the return journey, plus a two-hour wait at the wat itself.

If you're driving or pedalling yourself, a more direct route to the monastery is to continue southeast along Rte 212 from Beung Kan (in the direction of Nakhon Phanom) until you reach the Km 61 marker, then turn right (southeast) at a road signed for Jet Si, Tham Phra and Chut Na waterfalls. After 17km make a right on another road heading southwest, signed (in Thai only) for Phu Tok. You'll come to a monastery gate on the right after another 3.5km.

Ban Ahong
บ้านอาฮง

An alternative to staying in Beung Khan, Ban Ahong is a pretty little riverside village at the Km 115 marker on Rte 212.

The friendly **Ahong (Hideaway) Guest House** (r 100-150B) is about the only sleeping option

in Ban Ahong. It's a rustic little number with a spread of makeshift huts near the river. The setting is peaceful and warm welcomes are all part of the service. Some facilities are shared.

Next to the Mekong River, only 200m from the guest house is one of Isan's smallest and prettiest wats, **Wat Pa Ahong Silawat** (daylight hours).

The narrow stretch of the Mekong River opposite the wat has some refreshing **pools** for swimming during the dry season when the river is fairly clear. This area is also considered a highly auspicious spot to spend the evening of *wan àwk phansǎa*, the end of the Buddhist Rains Retreat. According to local legend, supernatural lights, *bâng fai pháyaa nâak* (*naga* fireballs), emerge from beneath this stretch of the Mekong River each year and arc across the sky (see the boxed text p478).

The bus between Beung Kan and Ban Ahong costs 20B (one hour).

LOEI PROVINCE

Stretching south from the sleepy arc of the Mekong River near Chiang Khan to undulating hilltops of the Phu Kradung National Park, Loei is a diverse, beautiful province, untouched by mass tourism. This isn't the wildest province in Thailand, but potholes definitely pepper a still relatively untrammelled trail that will lead you from the hush of the region's tranquil national parks to the hubbub of Dan Sai's annual Phi Ta Khon Festival.

The terrain here is mountainous and temperatures fluctuate from one extreme to the other – hotter than elsewhere in Thailand during the hot season and colder than anywhere else during the cold season. This is the only province in Thailand where temperatures can drop to as low as 0°C, a fact the tourist brochures love to trumpet. For hiking, the best time to visit Loei is during the cool months of mid-October through February.

LOEI
เลย

pop 33,000
Arrive here after a sojourn in the region's dreamy countryside and Loei, the capital of

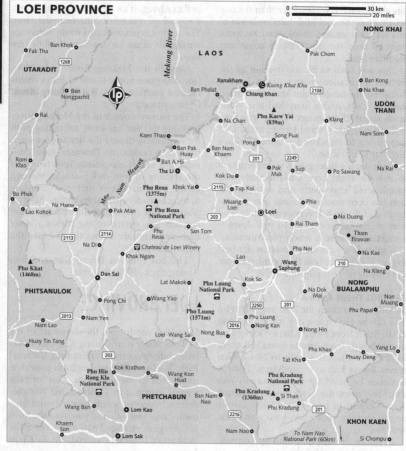

LOEI PROVINCE

the province, is little more than a reminder that concrete and congestion still exist. Efforts to upgrade the town, including a large city-centre lake and a plush new hotel, have begun to haul Loei out of the doldrums, but apart from being a good spot to splash out on a comfy bed before heading back out into the sticks, the province's economic hub has few attractions.

Information

Bangkok Bank (cnr Th Charoenrat & Th Ua Ari; 8.30am-4.30pm) Has an ATM and change facilities.

Loei Hospital (☎ 0 4281 1541; Th Maliwan) West of the city centre.

Police station (☎ 1155; Th Phiphattanamongkhon)

PP Net (Soi Th Chumsai; per hr 20B; 10am-10pm)

Just off Th Chumsai, on the soi opposite Royal Inn Hotel; check your email here.

Festivals & Events

At the end of January/start of February, Loei's **Cotton Blossom Festival** is held outside the Provincial Hall and culminates in a parade of cotton-decorated floats and, naturally, a Cotton Blossom Queen beauty pageant. In case you were wondering, cotton is one of the region's major crops – come here to buy very reasonable cotton quilts.

Loei also celebrates with fervour its own annual **Rocket Festival**, held in May. The city has even imported the colourful Phi Ta Khon procession from nearby Amphoe Dan Sai (see the boxed text, p490).

Sleeping

Loei Palace Hotel (☎ 0 4281 5668; loeipalace@amari
.com; 167/4 Th Charoenrat; s/d 2000/2120B; ❌ ❄ ▭
❄) Loei's glossy flagship hotel sports some
wedding-cake architecture, helpful staff,
plenty of mod-cons and generous discounts
(up to 40%) when business is slow.

Royal Inn Hotel (☎ 0 4281 2563; fax 0 4283 0873;
22/16 Th Chumsai; r 250-350B; ❄) This pleasant
outfit doesn't show it's best side to the
road, and from Th Chumsai looks distinctly
dowdy. Enter by the main door, however,
and this is a tidy, well-run hotel, with smiling staff and comfy rooms.

King Hotel (☎ 0 4281 1701; fax 0 4281 1235; 11/9-12
Th Chumsai; s/d 380/399B; ❄) Fit for a king? Not
a chance. The rooms are pleasant enough
for most weary travellers though, and come
with hot water and a troop of helpful staff
behind the desk downstairs. Shining surfaces also bear testament to a clutch of
hard-working, behind-the-scenes cleaners.

Also recommended:

Thai Udom Hotel (☎ 0 4281 1763; 122/1 Th Charoenrat; r 250-500B; ❄) Smart midranger with cheaper fan
rooms.

Phu Luang Hotel (☎ 0 4281 1570; fax 0 4281 1789; 55
Th Charoenrat; s/d 350/500B; ❄) Frumpy, but comfortable.

Eating

Most of the city's culinary razzmatazz – and
a whole host of cheap eats – can be found
at the **night market** (☉ 5-10pm), near the intersection of Th Ruamjai and Th Charoenrat.
Look for the local speciality, *khài pîng* (eggs
in their shell toasted on skewers).

Khrua Nit (☎ 0 4281 3013; Th Charoenrat; mains
20-40B; ☉ 6am-8.30pm) Basic and strip-lit, this
no-frills eatery serves *hàw mòk* (soufflé-like
curry steamed in banana leaves) and other
central-Thai dishes. It is opposite the Phu
Luang Hotel.

Charcoal Restaurant (☎ 0 4281 5675; Th Nok Kaew;
mains 30-90B; ☉ 10am-11pm) The alfresco ambience of this outdoor place is slightly compromised by its proximity to a busy roundabout,
but local punters flock here in droves after
dark and there's usually a good beer-fuelled
buzz. The food is average, but the portions
are generous and there's a limited English-
language menu: choose from the usual Thai
staples or a small selection of steaks.

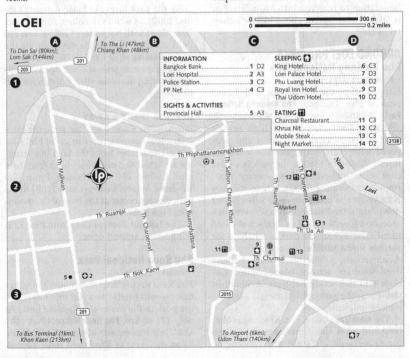

LOEI

0 _____ 300 m
0 _____ 0.2 miles

To Dan Sai (80km);
Lom Sak (144km)

To Tha Li (47km);
Chiang Khan (48km)

INFORMATION
Bangkok Bank.............................1 D2
Loei Hospital.............................2 A3
Police Station.............................3 C2
PP Net.............................4 C3

SIGHTS & ACTIVITIES
Provincial Hall.............................5 A3

SLEEPING 🛏
King Hotel.............................6 C3
Loei Palace Hotel.............................7 D3
Phu Luang Hotel.............................8 D2
Royal Inn Hotel.............................9 C3
Thai Udom Hotel.............................10 D2

EATING 🍴
Charcoal Restaurant.............................11 C3
Khrua Nit.............................12 C3
Mobile Steak.............................13 C3
Night Market.............................14 D2

Th Phiphattanamongkhon

Th Sathon Chiang Khan

Th Maliwan

Th Ruamjai

Th Charoenrat

Th Ruamphattana

Th Nok Kaew

Th Chumsai

Th Ua Ari

Nam Loei

Market

To Bus Terminal (1km);
Khon Kaen (213km)

To Airport (6km);
Udon Thani (140km)

Mobile Steak (Th Chumsai; mains 40-120B; ☺ noon-3pm & 6-11pm) This open-air eatery also serves steaks, and ice creams, at wooden tables illuminated by a starburst of coloured lanterns. One of Snow White's dwarves – probably Greedy – stands guard outside.

Getting There & Away

Buses to Loei leave Udon Thani until late afternoon (ordinary/air-con 60/110B, 3½ hours, five daily). From Nong Khai there are ordinary buses (84B, six hours, four daily).

Ordinary buses between Loei and Dan Sai (45B, two hours) depart 10 times daily from 6am to 5pm from Loei's bus terminal, southwest of town. There are also hourly buses to Chiang Khan (28B, one hour).

Air-con buses to Loei from Bangkok's Northern bus terminal leave several times daily (250B to 350B, 10 hours). In Loei, you can get air-con buses to Bangkok from the bus terminal or from an agency in the lobby of the King Hotel.

Getting Around

You'll find plenty of túk-túk waiting at the bus station to take you into town. The fare is 5B per passenger, or about 30B for a chartered ride.

AROUND LOEI PROVINCE
Phu Kradung National Park

อุทยานแห่งชาติภูกระดึง

Capped off by the eponymous, bell-shaped peak of Phu Kradung, **Phu Kradung National Park** (☎ 0 4287 1333; reserve@dnp.go.th; admission 200B; ☺ 8.30am-4.30pm Oct-Jun) covers a high-altitude plateau, cut through with trails and peppered with cliffs, waterfalls and montane forests. Rising to 1360m, the park is always cool at its highest reaches (average year-round temperature 20°C), where its flora is more typical of a temperate zone. Lower down are mixed deciduous and evergreen monsoon forests as well as sections of cloud forest. The 359-sq-km park is a habitat for various forest **wildlife**, including elephants, Asian jackals, Asiatic black bears, barking deer, sambars, serows, white-handed gibbons and the occasional tiger. A Buddhist **shrine** near the park headquarters is a favourite local pilgrimage site.

The **main trail** scaling Phu Kradung is 6km long and takes about three hours to climb (or rather walk – it's not that challenging since the most difficult parts have bamboo ladders and stairs for support). The hike is quite scenic and there are rest stops with food vendors along the way. It's about 3km to the park headquarters. You can hire porters to carry your gear balanced on bamboo poles for 20B per kilogram.

During the hottest months, from March to June, it's best to start the climb about dawn. Temperatures in December and January can drop as low as 3°C to 4°C; blankets can be hired. Bring sweaters and thick socks.

Phu Kradung is closed to visitors during the rainy season because it is considered too hazardous, being slippery and subject to mud slides. The park can get crowded during school holidays (especially March to May, when Thai schools are closed).

A **visitors centre** at the base of the mountain distributes detailed maps and collects your admission fee.

SLEEPING & EATING

There are plenty of accommodation options within the reserve. As well as a camping site where you can pitch your own tent (per tent 50B), the park hires out basic A-frame cabins (200B), as well as swankier, four-sleeper bungalows with hot water (1200B). You can book accommodation via email, or via the park's **booking office** (☎ 0 2562 0760).

There are also several small open-air eateries serving the usual stirfry dishes for 30B to 40B.

GETTING THERE & AWAY

Buses on the Khon Kaen line go to the town (actually an *amphoe*, or district) of Phu Kradung. Departures from the Loei bus terminal are scheduled every half-hour from 6am until 6.30pm (35B, 1½ hours). From Phu Kradung, hop on a *sǎwngthǎew* (10B) to the park visitors centre at the base of the mountain, 7km away.

The last bus back to Loei from Phu Kradung leaves around 6pm.

Phu Reua National Park

อุทยานแห่งชาติภูเรือ

Phu Reua means 'boat mountain', a moniker that owes its origins to a cliff that juts out of the peak in the shape of a Chinese junk. At only 121 sq km, **Phu Reua National Park** (☎ 0 4288 1716; reserve@dnp.go.th; admission 200B; ☺ 8.30am-4.30pm) isn't one of Thailand's most impressive reserves, but it does offer some dreamy vistas from the summit of the mountain it surrounds. The easy 2½-hour hike to the summit (1375m) passes from tropical forest to broad-leaf evergreen forest to pine forest. In December, temperatures near the summit approach freezing at night.

The park entrance is about 40km west of the provincial capital on Rte 203. A well-marked 16km trail from the park **visitors centre** (3km off the highway) covers a good sample of what the park has to offer, including some fine views of a mountain range in Sainyabuli Province, Laos.

SLEEPING & EATING

The park offers a number of accommodation options. As well as a **camping site** (per tent 50B), there are also some comfortable four-sleeper **bungalows** (2000B) with fan, hot water and fridge. You can book accommodation via the park's **booking office** (☎ 0 2562 0760).

GETTING THERE & AWAY

Although there is public transport from Loei to the town of Phu Reua, it is difficult to find *sǎwngthǎew* all the way to the park except on weekends and holidays.

Nine buses a day travel between Loei and Dan Sai from 5am to 5pm, passing through Phu Reua town (25B, one hour) on the way.

Dan Sai & Around
ด่านซ้าย

For 362 days a year, Dan Sai is an innocuous little town, a backwater community where life revolves around a small market and a dusty main street. For the remaining three days, however, it is the site of one of the country's liveliest, loudest and most idiosyncratic festivals. Falling during the fourth lunar month (usually June), Dan Sai's **Phi Ta Khon Festival** (also called Bun Phra Wet) combines the Phra Wet Festival – during which recitations of the *Mahavessantara Jataka* (past-life stories of the Buddha) are supposed to enhance the listener's chance of being reborn in the lifetime of the next Buddha – with Bun Bang Fai (Rocket Festival). For those wishing to plunge headlong into Isan life, this is a must-see.

The origins of the Phi Ta Khon festival are still shrouded in ambiguity, but another aspect to the festival has to do with tribal

Thai – possibly Thai Dam – spirit cults. In fact the dates for the festival are divined by Jao Phaw Kuan, a local spirit medium who channels the information from Jao Saen Meuang, the town's guardian deity.

The festival's reputation as a major event is expanding and while there are still only a handful of places to stay in the town itself, a clutch of swanky resorts in the surrounding area bear testament to its growing popularity with Thais from elsewhere in the country and, more recently, Westerners as well (see the boxed text, p490).

INFORMATION
Information centre (☎ 0 4289 1094; Th Kaew Asa; ◯ 8am-5pm Mon-Fri) Small but can help with homestay accommodation and is the best place to find out the exact dates of the festival each year.
Mut Mee Guesthouse (☎ 0 4246 0717; Nong Khai) Julian can help with festival dates and details.
Post office (Th Kaew Asa; ◯ 9am-4.30pm Mon-Fri, to noon Sat)

SIGHTS & ACTIVITIES
On the main road through town, **Wat Phon Chai** (Th Kaew Asa; ◯ daylight hours) plays a major role in the Phi Ta Khon festivities (see the boxed text, p490). There's not much to see here out of season, but a small **museum** (admission free; ◯ daylight hours), towards the back of the complex, features photographs from festivals through the years and a collection of the headdresses worn during the celebrations – unfortunately, none of the labels are in English.

Phra That Si Songrak (◯ daylight hours) is the most highly revered stupa in Loei Province and is watched over by none other than Jao Phaw Kuan, Dan Sai's resident spirit medium. The whitewashed Lao-style *chedi* stands 30m high and was built in 1560 as a gesture of national friendship between the Lao kingdom of Wiang Chan (Vientiane) and the Thai kingdom of Ayuthaya. A smaller stupa in front is semihollow and attached to a pavilion. The open repository contains a very old chest that supposedly contains an even older carved stone Buddha about 76cm long. Shoes can't be worn anywhere in the compound. It is about 1km out of town, off Rte 2113.

Wat Neramit Wiphatsana (◯ daylight hours), on a wooded hill just southwest of town, is a meditation wat where most of the buildings

THE ARRIVAL OF THE SPIRITS

Without a doubt, Dan Sai's three-day **Phi Ta Khon** *(phii taa khôhn)* **Festival** – known as the Bun Phra Wet Festival in other towns – is one of the most colourful and unique annual events in Thailand. On the first day of the festival, the current village shaman – Jao Phaw Kuan – dons white clothing and a white headband, and, along with his shaman wife, Jao Mae Nang Tiam (also dressed in white with a white cloth wrapped around her hair), leads the propitiation of the all-important *tiam*. The *tiam* are a class of spirits similar to the Lao-Thai *khwăn* but perceived to be at a higher level.

Assisting in the rites are a group of male and female lesser mediums. Ceremonies begin around 3.30am in a procession from Dan Sai's Wat Phon Chai to Mae Nam Man. Rites are performed at the riverside to coax Phra Upakhut – a water spirit supposedly embodied in an invisible piece of white marble – to join the proceedings. Phra Upakhut is believed to have once been a monk with supernatural powers, who transformed himself into white marble 'to live a solitary and peaceful existence below the water', according to local descriptions. It's possible he is somehow related to the *bodhisattva* (Buddhist saint) Upagupta, who in Mahayana Buddhist mythology is thought to reside in the ocean. The procession – accompanied by the invisible spirit – then returns to the wat, where resident monks receive ceremonial food at around 7am.

Shortly thereafter the summoning of additional spirits takes place at Jao Phaw Kuan's home, which doubles as the most important spirit shrine in Dan Sai. Villagers are invited to attend the ceremony, and all present participate in a *bai sĭi* ceremony. After some incantations and lighting of candles, villagers crawl up to the Jao Phaw and Jao Mae, seated cross-legged on the floor in a semitrance, and tie lots of sacred thread on their arms, which are propped up by pillows. The attendants also tie single loops of sacred thread around one wrist of everyone present. While all this is taking place, free food is served on round trays and everyone downs shots of *lâo khăo* (white spirit) to get in the mood for what comes next.

As the tying of threads finishes up, the shaman's attendants take down bundles of special costuming kept on a high altar near the ceiling of the house, put the clothing on and gather in front of the house. Most of the costumes look like something from Shakespearian theatre meant for beggar or jester roles – ragged and tattered but very colourful. To complete the transformation into *phii taa khôhn* (an untranslatable term basically meaning 'Phra Wet spirits'), each attendant dons a huge mask made from a *hûat* (crescent-shaped basket used for steaming sticky rice), cut and re-shaped to fit atop the head, and a thick sheath from the base of a coconut palm frond. On the typical mask, small eye-openings have been cut into the palm sheath and a large, curving wooden nose added, and the whole affair is custom-painted to suit the wearer with all manner of designs. Brightly coloured cloth hangs from the basket top to cover the back of the head.

Two of the attendants, however, wear tall bamboo frames assembled in vaguely human shapes, covered with white cloth, and topped with giant heads standing perhaps 2m above

---

are made of unplastered laterite blocks. Famous Thai temple muralist Pramote Sriphrom has been painting images of *jataka* tales on the interior walls of the *bòt* for years and so there's plenty of colour to admire. The wat is dedicated to the memory of the late Ajahn Mahaphan (also known as Khruba Phawana), a much-revered local monk.

Further from the town on Rte 203 near the Km 61 marker is the entrance for **Chateau de Loei Winery** (☎ 0 4289 1404; www.chateau deloei.com; ☼ 8am-5pm), Thailand's most respected vineyard. The winery released the first commercially produced Thai wine

in 1995 and scooped a silver medal for its Chenin Blanc dessert wine in the 2004 International Wine & Spirits Competition. Visitors are welcome and you can taste the wines in the main winery building. There is a restaurant and shop on the main road.

SLEEPING & EATING

Very few people stay in Dan Sai outside the festival season and so accommodation is extremely limited within the town itself. The information centre can arrange basic homestay accommodation from 100B per person. This is definitely the cheapest option during the Phi Ta Khon festivities. Out

their own heads. One figure is male, the other female, as is obvious from the huge, exaggerated sexual organs attached to the front of the figures – a giant penis (controlled from inside by a string that makes it flop up and down) for one, a large hairy vaginal triangle and conical breasts for the other. These are the *phǐi taa khǒhn yài* (big Phra Wet spirits), and exactly what they represent is anyone's guess nowadays. These figures, surrounded by regular *phǐi taa khǒhn* as well as 'civilians', then lead a boisterous procession from the Jao Phaw's house back to the monastery, with musical accompaniment supplied by *khaen*, *phin* and other Isan instruments.

More *lâo khǎo* is passed around and soon the knees and elbows get moving and everyone starts dancing down the road. Once the procession reaches the wat grounds, the participants begin circumambulating the main *wíhǎan* (hall) and continue for a couple hours, becoming increasingly rowdy with each turn. There's lots of sexual innuendo and older village women take turns grabbing the lengthy penis of the male *phǐi taa khǒhn yài* and giving it a few good shakes, laughing all the while. The whole thing ends around noon and people stagger back home to sleep it off.

On the second day all the locals get into costume and accompany Jao Phaw Kuan, Jao Mae Nang Tiam and the four female assistant mediums in a procession from Chum Chon Dan Sai School to the temple. In earlier years the Jao Phaw/Jao Mae and their shaman court rode on wood or bamboo palanquins, but these days they sit on colourful dais in the back of pick-up trucks. Bamboo rockets ride along with them. As on the first day, there's plenty of music and dancing, but this time there are hundreds more participants, and spectators marvel at the many different costume designs cooked up for this year's event. Some show real creative genius. Many of the costumed *phǐi taa khǒhn*, both men and women, carry carved wooden phalli (or a knife or sword with a phallic handle) in one or both hands, waving them about as talismans or using them to tease the crowd while they dance and strut down the street. Tin cans and wooden cowbells may be hung from the costumes to create more of a racket.

Once again, when they reach the wat, the participants circumambulate the *wíhǎan* many times, dancing along the way. Fuelled by the consumption of much *lâo khǎo*, the rounds continue for hours and become more raucous and spontaneous as the day wears on. At the same time in the main courtyard in front of the wat there's live *mǎw lam* music, and lots more dancing and wooden penis antics. If it has rained recently, participants will revel in the mud. As one Western observer remarked: 'It's like Woodstock and Halloween rolled into one'.

In the late afternoon of the second day the bamboo rockets are fired. Be prepared to run for cover if one of the rockets loses its course and comes spiralling back into the crowd.

The third day is much more solemn as the villagers assemble at the temple to listen to *Mahavessantara Jataka* recitations (past-life stories of the Buddha) and Dhamma sermons by local and visiting monks. By custom, 13 sermons are delivered in a row.

on Rte 203 towards Loei, there's also a good choice if you can spend a little more and have your own transport.

Phu Pha Nam Resort (in Bangkok ☎ 0 2254 3000; www.phuphanamresort.com; Rte 203; r 3000B; ✗ ✗) This relatively chic resort caters to big city festival-goers and features 520 acres of private grounds, a Japanese-style spa, mountain biking and a clutch of 'pet' ostriches. A cluster of concrete spirit statues near the lobby detracts slightly from the upmarket ambience, but the rooms here are spacious and opulent and discounts of up to 20% are available off-season. It is 12km outside Dan Sai, east towards Loei.

Rangyen Resort (☎ 0 4289 1089; fax 0 4289 1423; Rte 203; r 1400B; ✗ ✗ ✗) Spread out over several hectares, this pleasant spot boasts a sizable pond, a swimming pool, a badminton court and tennis courts. Large rooms have two beds, minibar and satellite TV, and even during the festival discounts are readily available. There's a big restaurant and a karaoke bar on the premises – the place seems to be geared towards Thai business or civil service conventions. It's at least a 20-minute drive off the highway, so you can forget about using public transport to get there from Dan Sai.

Aim Aun (no Roman-script sign; ☎ 0 4289 1586; Rte 203; mains 20-90B; ☻ 8am-2am) Sizzling Thai favourites are cooked up here and served under a thatched roof in a garden setting. The owner speaks English and makes a mumsy fuss of passing strangers.

There are a few noodle and rice stands near Wat Phon Chai and a market filled with food stalls opposite the information centre. Dan Sai's better restaurants are on Rte 203 on the way out of town towards Loei.

GETTING THERE & AWAY
Ordinary buses between Loei and Dan Sai cost 45B (two hours), and depart from Loei 10 times daily between 6am and 5pm. Buses leaving Dan Sai depart from near the information centre on Th Kaew Asa.

CHIANG KHAN
เชียงคาน

Traditional timber houses line the streets, old ladies sit nattering in their shadow and the Mekong drifts slowly by: if you had an image of a northern riverside town where nothing much happens and no-one seems to care, Chiang Khan may just be it. Pretty

and peaceful, with photogenic views of the river and the mountains of Laos beyond, this little town has a good spread of cheap accommodation and makes a restful stopover if you fancy a couple of days of doing…well…nothing.

Information
Government Savings Bank (Rte 201; ☺ 8.30am-3.30pm) On the road to Loei, this bank has an ATM and change facilities.
Main post office (Th Chiang Khan; ☺ 9am-4.30pm Mon-Fri, to noon Sat) This is 500m east of the centre on the road to Sangkhom.
Police box (☎ 1155; cnr Rte 201 & Th Chiang Khan) On the main road through town.
Sam's Guesthouse (☎ 0 4282 1041; Soi 20 Th Chai Khong; per hr 20B; ☺ 10am-10pm) You can check email here.

Sights
TEMPLES
Chiang Khan features a particularly idiosyncratic style of wat architecture rarely seen in Thailand. Featuring colonnaded fronts and painted shutters, the *wíhǎan* temples echo

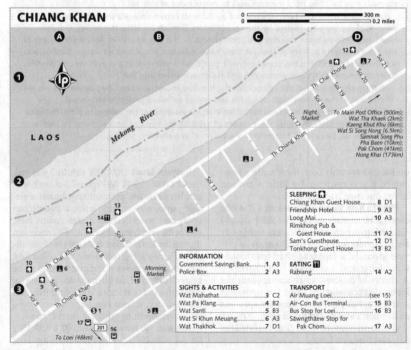

CHIANG KHAN

0 — 300 m
0 — 0.2 miles

Mekong River

LAOS

To Main Post Office (500m);
Wat Tha Khaek (2km);
Kaeng Khut Khu (6km);
Wat Si Song Nong (6.5km);
Samnak Song Phu
Pha Baen (10km);
Pak Chom (41km);
Nong Khai (173km)

Th Chai Khong

Night Market

Th Chiang Khan

Morning Market

To Loei (48km)

INFORMATION	
Government Savings Bank........	1 A3
Police Box................................	2 A3

SIGHTS & ACTIVITIES	
Wat Mahathat...........................	3 C2
Wat Pa Klang............................	4 B2
Wat Santi..................................	5 B3
Wat Si Khun Meuang...............	6 A3
Wat Thakhok............................	7 D1

SLEEPING	
Chiang Khan Guest House........	8 D1
Friendship Hotel.......................	9 A3
Loog Mai..................................	10 A3
Rimkhong Pub &	
Guest House.........................	11 A2
Sam's Guesthouse....................	12 D1
Tonkhong Guest House............	13 B2

EATING	
Rabiang....................................	14 A2

TRANSPORT	
Air Muang Loei....................	(see 15)
Air-Con Bus Terminal...............	15 B3
Bus Stop for Loei......................	16 B3
Săwngthăew Stop for	
Pak Chom.............................	17 A3

the French architectural influences of Laos. A good example in the centre of town is **Wat Pa Klang** (Th Chiang Khan; ☾ daylight hours), which is about 100 years old and features a new glittery superstructure; in the grounds of this wat is a small Chinese garden with a pond, waterfall, and Chinese-style sculptures of Buddha and Kuan Yin.

Wat Mahathat (Th Chiang Khan; ☾ daylight hours), in the centre of town, is Chiang Khan's oldest temple; the *bòt*, constructed in 1654, has a new roof over old walls, with faded murals on the front.

Wat Si Khun Meuang (Th Chai Khong; ☾ daylight hours), between Soi 6 and Soi 7, contains a Lao-style *chedi* and *bòt* (*sim* in Lao), plus a topiary garden.

Temple structures at **Wat Santi** (☾ daylight hours) and **Wat Thakhok** (Th Chai Khong; ☾ daylight hours) are similar to those at Wat Pa Klang (minus the Chinese garden). The walls of the temple buildings are stained red from all the dust and mud that builds up in the dry and rainy seasons.

Wat Tha Khaek (☾ daylight hours) is a 600- to 700-year-old temple, 2km outside the town, on the way to Ban Noi. The seated Buddha image in the *bòt* is sacred and it is said that holy water prepared in front of the image has the power to cure any ailing person who drinks it or bathes in it.

Other well-known monastic centres in the area include **Samnak Song Phu Pha Baen** (donations appreciated; ☾ daylight hours), 10km east of Chiang Khan, where monks meditate in caves and on tree platforms; and **Wat Si Song Nong** (☾ daylight hours), within walking distance along the river of Kaeng Khut Khu.

Activities
KAENG KHUT KHU
แก่งคุดคู้

The rapids at **Kaeng Khut Khu** (admission free; ☾ 24hr), about 6km downstream from Chiang Khan, are a popular spot for paddling, picnicking and soaking (they are best visited in the dry, hot season). The surrounding park has thatched-roof picnic areas with reed mats on raised wooden platforms. **Vendors** sell delicious Isan food and drinks.

Nearby **Wat Noi** (☾ daylight hours) houses three very old stone Buddha images; they're placed on a ledge high above a larger, modern Buddha in the wat's new *bòt*.

BOAT TRIPS & TOURS
Most of the guesthouses listed here can arrange boat trips to Kaeng Khut Khu (150B per person, minimum three people) or further afield. For tours of the region, the Dutch tour-guide owner of **Chiang Khan Guest House** (☎ 0 4282 1691; pimchiangk@hotmail.com; 282 Th Chai Khong) can arrange a host of bespoke trips.

Festivals & Events
Chiang Khan comes alive during *wan àwk phansǎa*, the end of the **Buddhist Rains Retreat** in late October and early November. There's a week-long festival that features displays of large carved wax *prasat* at each of the temples in town, as well as boat races on the river. At night there are performances of *mǎw lam* in the field facing the main post office.

Sleeping
Chiang Khan is brimming with excellent budget hotels; if you want to spend more, however, you'll have to head elsewhere.

Loog Mai (☎ 0 9210 0447; loogmaiguest@thaimail .com; 112 Mu 1 Th Chai Khong; r 300-400B) Combining some minimalist artistic styling with oodles of French colonial class, this old school villa offers a handful of sparse but atmospheric rooms, an airy terrace with river views and a real sense of history. The owner leaves villa at 9pm and so chances are you'll even have the place to yourself. It also has one 'large room', where there's enough space to swing cats by the dozen. Bathrooms are shared.

Chiang Khan Guest House (☎ 0 4282 1691; pim chiangk@hotmail.com; 282 Th Chai Khong; s/d 150/200B) Run by a Dutch tour guide (you will never be short of local info), this traditional-style place with shared bathrooms is all creaking timber and tin roofing. Scores of pot plants give some added character and there are pleasant views from the terrace. Food and tours are also available.

Rimkhong Pub & Guest House (☎ 0 4282 1125; Th Chai Khong; r 120-340B; ☒) With pleasant little rooms above a cosy bar, this French favourite features pinboards covered in snaps of smiling customers, a constellation of fairy lights and music come sundown.

Sam's Guesthouse (☎ 0 4282 1041; www.sams -guesthouse.com; Soi 20, Th Chai Khong; r 400-500B; ☒ ☐) The first one of a new breed of concrete guesthouses, this spotless place has comfy, slightly soulless rooms, great views and Internet access, as well as a real espresso machine. Some facilities are shared.

Friendship Hotel (☎ 0 1263 9068; 189 Th Chai Khong; r 200B) This humble place has spartan timber rooms with shared bathrooms and a pleasant café serving meals below (be warned: most of the ingredients are bought after you have ordered, so expect a wait). Standards are high though, and the place looks well dusted.

Tonkhong Guest House (☎ 0 4282 1547; tonkhong@ hotmail.com; 299/3 Soi 10 Th Chai Khong; r 150-350B; 💻) Even more rickety than most, this wooden place is beginning to look a little worse for wear. The owner still scores high marks for bonhomie, but a little spring-cleaning would go a long way.

Eating

The guesthouses offer the best dining options, with Friendship Hotel, the Rimkhong Pub and Chiang Khan leading the way in the food stakes.

Rabiang (no Roman-script sign; Th Chai Khong; mains 20-60B; 💻 10am-9pm) It's not the cheeriest of venues, but the views of the river are pleasant and all the usual Thai and Western favourites are represented on the English-language menu.

Getting There & Away

Buses to Chiang Khan leave almost every hour from Loei bus terminal (28B, one hour). From Chiang Khan the bus to Loei departs from a stop on Rte 201 and less frequently from the air-con bus terminal.

For Nong Khai, take a *săwngthăew* from a stop on Rte 201 to Pak Chom (20B, one hour) and change there.

Air Muang Loei (☎ 0 4282 1305), with an office at the air-con bus terminal, runs two daily VIP buses to Bangkok (347B, 12½ hours).

NAM NAO NATIONAL PARK

อุทยานแห่งชาติน้ำหนาว

One of Thailand's most beautiful and valuable parks, **Nam Nao National Park** (☎ 0 5672 9002; reserve@dnp.go.th; admission 200B; 💻 8.30am-4.30pm) covers nearly 1000 sq km, at an average elevation of 800m, at the intersection of Chaiyaphum, Phetchabun and Loei Provinces. Although the park was first opened in 1972, it remained a People's Liberation

Army of Thailand (PLAT) stronghold until the early 1980s. Marked by the sandstone hills of the Phetchabun mountains, the park features dense, mixed evergreen-deciduous forest on mountains and hills; open dipterocarp pine-oak forest on plateaus and hills; dense bamboo mountain forest with wild banana stands in river valleys; and savannah on the plains. A fair system of trails branches out from the park headquarters; the scenic and fairly level **Phu Khu Khao** trail cuts through pine forest and grass meadow for 24km. The park also features several waterfalls and caves. Nam Nao's highest peak, **Phu Pha Jit**, reaches a height of 1271m.

Although it's adjacent to 1560-sq-km **Phu Khiaw Wildlife Sanctuary**, a highway bisecting the park has unfortunately made wildlife somewhat more accessible to poachers, so many native species are in decline. There are no villages within the park boundaries, however, so incidences of poaching and illegal logging remain fairly minor. Elephants and banteng (wild cattle) are occasionally spotted, as well as Malayan sun bears, leopards, tigers, Asian jackals, barking deer, gibbons, langurs and flying squirrels. Rumours of rhinoceros (last seen in 1971, but tracks were observed in 1979) persist, and the bizarre fur-coated Sumatran rhino may survive here. Phu Khiaw itself is a sandstone mountain in Amphoe Khon San covered with thick forest that harbours crocodiles, banteng, gaurs, tigers, elephants, serows, leopards and barking deer. Three rivers are sourced at Nam Nao: the Chi, Saphung and Phrom.

Temperatures are fairly cool year-round, especially nights and mornings; the best time to go is from November to February, when morning frost occasionally occurs.

There is accommodation available in the park, including a **camping ground** (per tent 50B) and four-sleeper **bungalows** (1000B) with hot water. Call the **reservations office** (☎ 0 2562 0760) to reserve. There are **food stalls** next to the visitors centre.

Getting There & Away

Daily buses travel through the park from Khon Kaen (60B, 2½ hours) or Chumphae. Look for the park office sign on Hwy 12 at the Km 50 marker; the office is 2km from there.

NAKHON PHANOM PROVINCE

Lao, Vietnamese and, in the capital, Chinese influences dominate Nakhon Phanom, a province bordered by the Mekong and dotted with Lao-style *thâat*. It's not a region bristling with attractions, but there are plenty of fine river views and the colossal Wat Phra That Phanom, in That Phanom, is a talismanic symbol of Isan culture.

NAKHON PHANOM

นครพนม

pop 31,700

In Sanskrit-Khmer, Nakhon Phanom means 'city of hills'. Unfortunately, most of them are across the river, in Laos. But that doesn't stop you admiring them – with fabulous views across the Mekong to the undulating, sugarloaf peaks on the other side of the border, this slightly scruffy little provincial capital can sure sell its postcards. The bad news is that there's not a whole lot to do once you have written them.

Information

Cyberspace (☎ 0 4251 3633; Th Sunthon Wijit; per hr 15B; ☼ 10am-9pm) Access the Internet at this place on the river.

Immigration office (☎ 0 4251 1235; Th Sunthon Wijit; ☼ 8.30am-4.30pm Mon-Fri) For visa extensions.

Krung Thai (Th Ruamjit Thawai; ☼ 8.30am-3.30pm) Has ATM and change facilities.

Police station (☎ 0 4251 1266; Th Sunthon Wijit)

Post office (cnr Th Ratchathan & Th Sunthon Wijit; ☼ 8.30am-4.30pm Mon-Fri, 9am-noon Sat & Sun)

TAT (☎ 0 4251 3490; www.tourismthailand.org; cnr Th Sala Klang & Th Sunthon Wijit; ☼ 8.30am-4.30pm) Distributes literature on Nakhon Phanom, Mukdahan and Sakon Nakhon Provinces, but isn't much help otherwise.

Sights

The obvious place to admire the view is from the **beach**, just south of the Mae Nam Khong Grand View Hotel. The river's a bit murky during the rainy season, but when things dry out, a crystal clear Xerox copy of **Ko Don Don** appears in the water below the real thing.

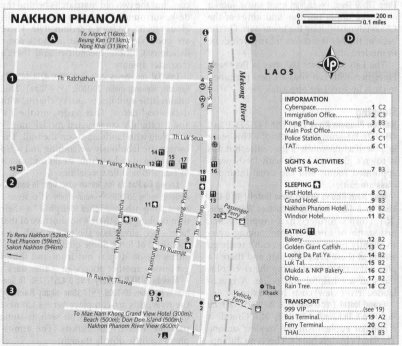

NAKHON PHANOM

0 —————— 200 m
0 —————— 0.1 miles

LAOS

Mekong River

To Airport (16km);
Beung Kan (313km);
Nong Khai (313km)

Th Ratchathan

Th Sunthon Wijit

Th Luk Seua

Th Fuang Nakhon

Th Aphiban Bancha

Th Bamung Meuang

Th Thamrong Prasit

Th Si Thep

Th Ruamjit

Passenger Ferry

Th Ruamjit Thawai

To Renu Nakhon (52km);
That Phanom (59km);
Sakon Nakhon (94km)

To Mae Nam Khong Grand View Hotel (300m);
Beach (500m); Don Don Island (500m);
Nakhon Phanom River View (800m)

Tha Khaek

Vehicle Ferry

NAKHON PHANOM FESTIVAL

On the full moon of the 11th lunar month (usually late October) at the end of the Buddhist Rains Retreat, Nakhon Phanom residents all celebrate Wan Phra Jao Prot Lok – a holiday in honour of Buddha's descent from the Devaloka (Deity World), where legend says he spent a Rains Retreat offering teachings. Besides the usual wat offerings, festival activities include the launching of *reua fai* (fire boats) on the Mekong. Originally these 8m to 10m boats were made of banana logs or bamboo, but modern versions can be fashioned of wood or synthetic materials. The boats carry offerings of cakes, rice and flowers; at night the boats are launched on the river and illuminated in a spectacular display.

During this same festival in the daytime, the city hosts long-boat races similar to those that are seen in many towns along the Mekong River.

The interior murals of the *bòt* at **Wat Si Thep** (Th Si Thep; ☼ daylight hours) show *jataka* along the upper portion, and kings of the Chakri dynasty along the lower part. On the back of the *bòt* is a colourful triptych done in modern style.

The Lao town over the river is **Tha Khaek**. Foreigners with Lao visas are now permitted to cross by ferry (see opposite).

Sleeping

Nakhon Phanom River View (☎ 0 4252 2333; fax 0 4252 2777; Th Sunthon Wijit; r 1100B; 🏊) This place is a bit of a hike south of the centre, but this is town's glossiest hotel, with fresh, well-appointed rooms and the usual business-class amenities.

Mae Nam Khong Grand View Hotel (☎ 0 4251 3564; fax 0 4251 1037; 527 Th Sunthon Wijit; r 595B; 🏊) Town's former chart-topping hotel, just south of town, is now looking ever-so-slightly moth-eaten. You can't really go wrong at these prices though, and there's a pleasant terrace overlooking the river, plus the staff are helpful and polite. A much-lauded 'river view' costs 100B extra.

Grand Hotel (☎ 0 4251 1526; fax 0 4251 1283; cnr Th Si Thep & Th Ruamjit; r 180-320B; 🏊) 'Grand' is a popular euphemism for 'modest' among Thailand's budget hotels. This is no duff op-

tion though, and while the interior is rather spartan, pot plants bring a lick of colour and the rooms are perfectly comfortable.

Windsor Hotel (☎ 0 4251 1946; fax 0 4252 0737; 692/19 Th Bamrung Meuang; r 250-400B; 🏊) Housed in a rather intimidating concrete block, this is nevertheless one of the friendlier options in town. The rooms are functional, but remain quite good value.

First Hotel (☎ 0 4251 1253; 370 Th Si Thep; r 250-350B; 🏊) Set back slightly from the road, this bare bones place at least offers some peace and quiet. On the downside, a stopped grandfather clock provides the only decoration.

Nakhon Phanom Hotel (☎ 0 4251 1455; 403 Th Aphiban Bancha; r 450B) This passable place has some OK rooms if you can't find a midrange sleep anywhere else.

Eating

There are plenty of restaurants along the river, but some of the better eateries are back in the centre of town.

Golden Giant Catfish (☎ 0 1421 8491; 259 Th Sunthon Wijit; mains 25-80B; ☼ 7am-midnight) This chaotic wooden place doesn't mean to be cool, but the two old matriarchs behind the desk, surrounded by bric-a-brac and religious regalia, do have a certain style. There are good views, the menu includes some delicious Chinese specialities and there's character aplenty.

Luk Tal (no Roman-script sign; ☎ 0 4251 1456; Th Bamrung Meuang; mains 20-100B; ☼ 4-10pm) This quaint little spot oozes quirky charm, with dark wood décor, Thai boxing on the TV and a carefully constructed model train – complete with landscape – on the wall. The owners are fabulously welcoming and whip up a range of dishes, from steaks and salads to rice and noodle specialities.

Loong Da Pat Ya (no Roman-script sign; Th Bamrung Meuang; mains 30-90B; ☼ noon-10pm) It's always reassuring when a chef delights in their own cooking and there's no shortage of that here – we barely saw the owner without a mouthful of food. Some quality Isan specialities are on display out front and things get busy – another good sign – after dark.

Mukda & NKP Bakery (☎ 0 4251 1790; Th Sunthon Wijit; mains 30-120B; ☼ 7.30am-10pm) Back by the river, this air-con place serves Chinese dishes and bakery items, as well as some passable Western breakfasts. The atmosphere's a little dowdy though.

Bakery (☎ 0 4251 1989; Th Fuang Nakhon; snacks 10-30B; ◷ 9am-10pm) This hole-in-the-wall spot serves on-the-hop cakes and coffees.

Also recommended:

Ohio (☎ 0 4252 1300; Th Thamrong Prasit; mains 30-90B; ◷ 6am-midnight) Airy bar/eatery with plenty of wood, food and rivers of whisky.

Rain Tree (cnr Th Sunthon Wijit & Th Fuang Nakhon; mains 30-120B; ◷ 6pm-midnight) For drinks, fish dishes and alfresco frolics.

Getting There & Away

AIR

Thai Airways International has suspended flights from Nakhon Phanom, but the **THAI agent** (☎ 0 4251 2494; 85 Th Ruamjit Thawai; ◷ 8am-5pm Mon-Fri, to 1pm Sat & Sun) now sells tickets for **PB Air** (in Bangkok ☎ 0 2261 0222-5; www.pbair .com), which flies daily to/from Bangkok (one way 2475B).

BOAT

Between 8.30am and 6pm, you can catch a **boat** (one way 50B) from the **ferry terminal** (Th Sunthon Wijit) across the Mekong to Tha Khaek in Laos. You *must* have a Lao visa in advance.

BUS

Nakhon Phanom's **bus terminal** (☎ 0 4251 3444) is east of the town centre, down Th Fuang Nakhon.

From here, the buses head to Nong Khai (ordinary/air-con 109/171B, five hours, ten daily); Udon Thani (ordinary/air-con 90/120B, four hours, hourly until 3pm) via Sakon Nakhon (ordinary/air-con 40/60B, 1½ hours); and Mukdahan (ordinary/air-con 40/72B, two hours, hourly until 5pm) via That Phanom (ordinary/air-con 21/38B, one hour).

999 VIP (☎ 0 4251 1403), with offices at the bus terminal, has air-con (319B, 13 hours, five daily) and super VIP (635B, 13 hours, twice daily) buses to Bangkok.

AROUND NAKHON PHANOM

Renu Nakhon

เรณูนคร

The village of Renu Nakhon is known for cotton and silk weaving, especially *mát-mìi* designs. The local Phu Thai, a Thai tribe separate from mainstream Siamese and Lao, also market their designs here. Each Saturday there's a big **market** near Wat Phra That Renu Nakhon where stalls sell local

hand-woven fabrics and handicrafts. On other days you can buy from a string of shops and vendors near the temple or directly from weavers in the village.

The *thâat* at **Wat Phra That Renu Nakhon** (◷ daylight hours) exhibits the same basic characteristics as That Phanom but in less elongated proportions. Renu Nakhon is worth a visit if you're in the vicinity, even during the week.

During local festivals the Phu Thai sometimes hold folk-dance performances called *fáwn lákhon thai*, which celebrate their unique heritage. They also practise the *bai sìi* custom common in other parts of the northeast as well as in Laos, in which a shaman ties loops of sacred string around a person's wrists (see the boxed text, p459).

GETTING THERE & AWAY

The turn-off to Renu Nakhon is south of Nakhon Phanom at the Km 44 marker on Rte 212. Since it's not far to That Phanom, you could visit Renu on the way, or if you are staying in That Phanom, visit Renu as a day trip. From Rte 212, it's 7km west on Rte 2031 (10B by *săwngthăew* from the junction).

Tha Khaek

ท่าแขก

This Lao town that lies across the river from Nakhon Phanom traces its roots to French colonial construction between 1911 and 1912. Before the Vietnam war (and during the war until the North Vietnamese Army and Pathet Lao cut the road north to Vientiane), Tha Khaek was a thriving provincial capital and a gambling centre for day-tripping Thais. Today it's a quiet transport and trade outpost with some French colonial architecture, though not nearly as much as in Savannakhet to the south.

If you hold a valid Lao visa, you are able to catch a 50B ferry ride across the river; the border is open 8.30am to 6pm. Buses from Tha Khaek to Vientiane take 10 hours. For more information see Lonely Planet's *Laos* guidebook.

THAT PHANOM

ธาตุพนม

Towering over the small town, the spire of the colossal Lao-style *chedi* of Wat Phra That Phanom is one of the region's most

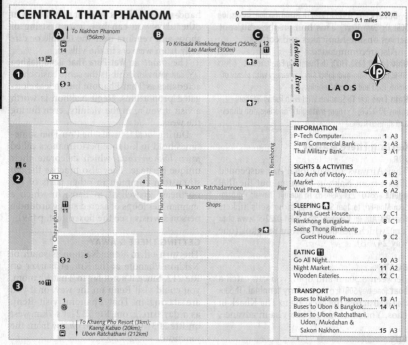

CENTRAL THAT PHANOM

emblematic symbols and one of the great flagpoles of Isan identity. In comparison, the little town of That Phanom itself is rather forgettable. Divided neatly in two, with the older half to the east next to the river, it does, however, make a relatively peaceful base for exploring the wider region.

Information

P-Tech Computer (☎ 0 4252 5694; Th Chayangkun; per hr 20B; ⏲ 9am-10pm) Check your email here.
Siam Commercial Bank (Th Chayangkun; ⏲ 8.30am-3.30pm) Offers foreign-exchange services and ATM.
Thai Military Bank (Th Chayangkun; ⏲ 8.30am-3.30pm) Offers foreign-exchange services and ATM.

Sights

WAT PHRA THAT PHANOM
วัดพระธาตุพนม

Wat Phra That Phanom (Th Chayangkun; ⏲ daylight hours) is a potent and beautiful symbol of Isan identity and has at its hub a *thâat*, or Lao-style *chedi,* more impressive than any in present-day Laos. The monument, which caved in during heavy rains in 1975 and was restored in 1978, is highly revered

by Buddhists all over Thailand. The age of the wat is disputed, but some archaeologists set it at about 1500 years. The *thâat* is 57m high (or 52m, depending on whom you believe) and the spire is decorated with 110kg of gold. Surrounding it is a cloister filled with Buddha images and behind the wat is a shady park.

OTHER SIGHTS

Hundreds of Lao merchants cross the river for the **market** from around 8.30am to noon on Monday and Thursday. There are two market locations in town, one on the highway near the wat and one on the river north of the pier. The latter is where the Lao congregate on their twice-weekly visits. Exotic offerings include Lao herbal medicines, forest roots, and Vietnamese pigs and animal skins; the maddest haggling occurs just before the market closes, when Thai buyers try to take advantage of the Lao's reluctance to carry unsold merchandise back to Laos.

About 20km south of town (turn-off for Wan Yai, between the Km 187 and Km 188 markers) is a wooded park next to **Kaeng Kabao**, a pretty set of rapids in the Mekong River. **Food vendors** make this a good spot for an impromptu picnic – it's an easy and quite interesting bicycle ride from That Phanom.

The short road between Wat Phra That Phanom and the old town on the Mekong River passes under a large **Lao arch of victory** (Th Kuson Ratchadamnoen), which is a miniature version of the arch on Th Lan Xang in Vientiane (which leads to Vientiane's Wat That Luang). This section of That Phanom is interesting, with a smattering of French-Chinese architecture that is reminiscent of old Vientiane or Saigon.

Festivals & Events

During the **That Phanom Festival**, hordes of visitors descend from all over Isan. Lao cross over to visit the wat, Thais cross over to Laos and the town hardly sleeps for seven days.

Sleeping & Eating

Few tourists come this way out of season and there are only a handful of sleeping options in town. During the February That Phanom Festival hotel rooms soar in price and both hotel and guesthouse rooms are booked out well in advance.

Niyana Guest House (☎ 0 4254 1450; 110 Mu 14, Th Rimkhong; s/d 80/140B) Town's backpacker original has moved into new digs, but is just as chaotic as it ever was. This is undoubtedly the friendliest and most helpful place in town, but it is little more than someone's house – with all the good and bad that goes with that. The rooms are spartan, but kind of cosy and bathrooms are shared.

Rimkhong Bungalow (☎ 0 4254 1634; Th Rimkhong; r 250-350B;) Cut from the same cloth as Niyana, this slightly flaky place has a friendly owner, some ramshackle charm and some reasonably comfy rooms. It's actually just off Th Rimkhong, down the first soi south of all the brightly lit restaurants on the riverside.

Kritsada Rimkhong Resort (☎ 0 4252 5439; ksd resort@thaimail.com; 90-93 Th Rimkhong; r 500B;) The colossal rooms at this new resort may not be the most atmospheric – there's a little too much fuchsia for comfort – but they are the glossiest, with kitchenettes, hot water and separate sitting rooms.

Saeng Thong Rimkhong Guest House (☎ 0 4252 5614; Th Rimkhong; r 400B) This so-so place steals the centre ground, with less sparkle than Kritsada and less atmosphere than Niyana. It's fine for a night's sleep though and the rooms are clean.

Go All Night (☎ 0 4254 1014; Th Chayangkun; mains 30-100B; 24hr) Near P-Tech Computer, this place serves sizzling grills and stirfries 24/7. The ingredients are on display outside and half the population of That Phanom seems to come here in the early evening to fill up and zone out in front of the restaurant's TV set.

Every evening a small **night market** (6-10pm) convenes on Th Chayangkun. Also come nightfall, dozens of small, **wooden eateries** (Th Rimkhong), ablaze in fairy lights, open their doors along the northern stretch of this street. They are all much of a muchness food-wise – although some turn the karaoke machine up louder than others – so have a wander and pick your place.

Getting There & Away

From different points on Th Chayangkun there are regular bus services to Mukdahan (ordinary/air-con 20/40B, one hour, hourly until 5pm), Ubon Ratchathani (ordinary/air-con 65/140B, 3½ hours, hourly) and Nakhon Phanom (ordinary/air-con 21/38B, one hour, hourly).

At present, only Thai and Lao citizens are permitted to cross the river to/from Laos here.

SAKON NAKHON PROVINCE

Among Sakon Nakhon's famous sons are two of the most highly revered monks in Thai history. Both Ajahn Man Bhuridatto and Ajahn Fan Ajaro were ascetic *thúdong* monks who were thought to have attained high levels of proficiency in Vipassana meditation. Ajahn Man is widely recognised among Thais as having been an *arahant* (fully enlightened being). Although born in Ubon Ratchathani, Ajahn Man spent most of his later years at Wat Pa Sutthawat in Sakon Nakhon. He died in 1949, and his relics and possessions are now contained in a museum at this wat.

SAKON NAKHON
สกลนคร

pop 68,000

Workaday Sakon Nakhon is primarily an agricultural market and the streets are chock-a-block with shops selling farming equipment. For tourists, however, the interest lies in the two historic temples of Wat Phra That Choeng Chum and Wat Phra That Narai Jaeng Waeng.

Information

Police station (☎ 1155; Th Makkhalai) Near the Ming Meuang field.

Post office (Th Charoen Meuang; ☯ 9am-4.30pm Mon-Fri, to noon Sat) Northwest of the centre.

Sights

AJAHN MAN MUSEUM
พิพิธภัณฑ์พระอาจารย์มั่น

The final resting place of many of Ajahn Man's personal effects, this **museum** (Th Sukkasem; donations appreciated; ☯ 8am-6pm), in the grounds of Wat Pa Sutthawat, on the southwestern outskirts of town, is essentially a shrine to one of Thailand's best-known

monks. Bizarrely, the building itself looks a bit like a modern Christian church, with arches and stained-glass windows. A bronze image of Ajahn Man, surrounded by flowers, sits on a pedestal at one end and articles and photos associated with the monk's history are on display behind glass.

WAT PHRA THAT CHOENG CHUM
วัดพระธาตุเชิงชุม

Highlights at **Wat Phra That Choeng Chum** (Th Reuang Sawat; ☯ daylight hours) include a 25m-high Lao-style *chedi*, which was erected during the Ayuthaya period, and the smaller 11th-century Khmer *prang* beneath it. To view the *prang* you must enter through the adjacent *wíhǎan*. If the door to the *chedi* is locked, ask one of the monks to open it – they're used to having visitors.

Also on the grounds is a small Lan Xang–era *bòt* and a *wíhǎan* built in the cruciform shape reminiscent of Lanna styles found in northern Thailand. *Lûuk nímít* (spherical ordination-precinct markers that look like cannonballs), are arranged on the grass near the *wíhǎan*; next to the monastery's

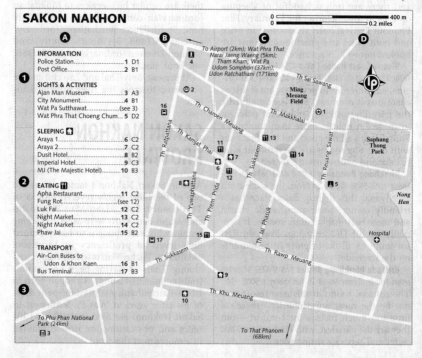

SAKON NAKHON

INFORMATION		
Police Station	1	D1
Post Office	2	B1
SIGHTS & ACTIVITIES		
Ajan Man Museum	3	A3
City Monument	4	B1
Wat Pa Sutthawat	(see 3)	
Wat Phra That Choeng Chum	5	D2
SLEEPING		
Araya 1	6	C2
Araya 2	7	C2
Dusit Hotel	8	B2
Imperial Hotel	9	C3
MJ (The Majestic Hotel)	10	B3
EATING		
Apha Restaurant	11	C2
Fung Rot	(see 12)	
Luk Fai	12	C2
Night Market	13	C2
Night Market	14	C2
Phaw Jai	15	B2
TRANSPORT		
Air-Con Buses to Udon & Khon Kaen	16	B1
Bus Terminal	17	B3

0 ——————— 400 m
0 ——————— 0.2 miles

To Airport (2km); Wat Phra That Narai Jaeng Waeng (5km); Tham Kham; Wat Pa Udom Somphon (37km); Udon Ratchathani (171km)

Th Sai Sawang

Ming Meuang Field

Th Makkhalai

Th Charoen Meuang

Th Ratpattana

Th Kamjat Phai

Th Reuang Sawat

Saphang Thong Park

Th Sukkasem

Nong Han

Th Yowaphattana

Th Prem Prida

Th Jai Phasuk

Hospital

Th Rawp Meuang

Th Sukkasem

Th Khu Meuang

To Phu Phan National Park (24km)

To That Phanom (68km)

east gate is the base for an original Khmer Shivalingam (phallic object).

WAT PHRA THAT NARAI JAENG WAENG
วัดพระธาตุนารายณ์แจงแวง

About 5km west of town at Ban That (3km beyond the airport), this wat has a 10th-to 11th-century Khmer *prang* in the early Bapuan style. Originally part of a Khmer Hindu complex, the five-level sandstone *prang* features a reclining Vishnu lintel over its eastern portico and a dancing Shiva over its northern one.

To get to the temple by public transport, catch a *sǎwngthǎew* west heading towards the airport on Th Sai Sawang and get off at Talat Ban That Nawaeng (5B). From there it's a pleasant 1km walk to the wat through a village.

The wat is known as Phra That Nawaeng (which is a contraction of the words Narai Jaeng Waeng) for short.

OTHER SIGHTS

A **city monument** (cnr Th Sai Sawang & Th Ratpattana) in a field in the northwestern corner of town was obviously inspired by Vientiane's Patuxai or That Phanom's gate. The arch-like structure consists of four big, ornate, cement pillars standing over a bowl filled with *naga*.

Along the eastern edge of town is **Nong Han**, Thailand's largest natural lake. *Don't* swim in the lake – it's infested with liver flukes, which can cause a nasty liver infection known as opisthorchiasis.

Festivals & Events

The end of the **Buddhist Rains Retreat** in late October/November is fervently celebrated in Sakon with the carving and display of *prasat*, as well as parades.

Sleeping

Imperial Hotel (☎ 0 4271 1119; 1892 Th Sukkasem; r 500-2500B; ☒) There's not much in the way of glamour at this mid- to upmarket spot, although the more swanky rooms (2500B) do rate among the best in town. Have a good look before you check in though, as there are dozens of different air-con rooms, priced according to size and the amenities on offer.

Dusit Hotel (☎ 0 4271 1198; 1784 Th Yuwaphattana; r 400-700B; ☒) It's been a while since this old-timer saw a lick of paint and the wrinkles are starting to show. The most expensive rooms have a few extra creature comforts (fridge and phone), but this remains little more than a midrange place to lay your head.

MJ (☎ 0 4273 3771; fax 0 4273 3616; Th Khu Meuang; r 700-830B; ☒) A little gloss still remains at this relatively new spot and the facilities (restaurant, cocktail lounge, pub, café, massage, snooker club and karaoke) earn a few extra brownie points as well. If you are in the mood to part with a few extra baht, the superior rooms are well worth the extra.

Araya 1 (☎ 0 4271 1097; cnr Th Prem Prida & Th Kamjat Phai; r 150-300B; ☒) The short-term crowd move into this no-frills outfit come the weekend, but standards are passable.

Araya 2 (☎ 0 4271 1054; Th Prem Prida; r 150-200B) This old school wooden affair is a little too decrepit to be charismatic, but it does offer an alternative to town's more homogenous concrete places. Some facilities are shared. It is diagonally opposite Araya 1, above a restaurant.

Eating

Phaw Jai (cnr Th Sukkasem & Th Rawp Meuang; mains 20-40B; ☯ 11am-10pm) This spartan place takes dining out to its lowest common denominator. The food, however, is excellent value and the menu features plenty of tasty Thai and Chinese dishes.

Apha Restaurant (Th Kamjat Phai; mains 20-40B; ☯ 11am-10pm) One of town's more substantial places, this clean little eatery serves up some tasty Thai curries, as well as other regional specialties.

Luk Fai (Th Kamjat Phai; mains 20-40B; ☯ noon-10pm) and **Fung Rot** (Th Kamjat Phai; mains 20-50B; ☯ 11am-10pm) offer more of the same fare as Phaw Jai.

Night markets assemble each evening near the roundabout at Th Charoen Meuang and Th Jai Phasuk, and at the intersection of Th Charoen Meuang and Th Sukkasem.

Getting There & Away

PB Air (☎ 0 4271 5179, in Bangkok ☎ 0 2261 0222-5; www.pbair.com) has an office at the airport and flies daily to/from Bangkok (one way from 2035B).

Regular direct bus services to Sakon are available from Ubon Ratchathani (ordinary/air-con 100/175B, six hours), That Phanom

(40/60B, 1½ hours), Nakhon Phanom (40/60B 1½ hours), Udon Thani (60/100B, 3½ hours) and Khon Kaen (air-con 120B, four hours). There are also buses between Sakon and Bangkok's northern bus terminal (air-con/VIP 320/550B, 12 hours, eight daily).

AROUND SAKON NAKHON
Tham Kham & Wat Pa Udom Somphon
ถ้ำขาม/วัดป่าอุดมสมพร

Ajahn Fan Ajaro, a famous student of Ajahn Man, established a cave hermitage for the practise of meditation at Tham Kham on the mountain of Khao Phu Phan, 17km off Hwy 22 (the turn-off comes between the Km 125 and Km 126 markers on Hwy 22 on the way from Udon Thani). He was also affiliated with Wat Pa Udom Somphon in his home *amphoe* of Phanna Nikhom, 37km from Sakon Nakhon towards Udon Thani off Hwy 22. A **museum** (donations appreciated; ☼ 8.30am-4.30pm) well outside the wat compound at Ban Phanna commemorates the life of Ajahn Fan, who died in 1963. Unlike Wat Pa Sutthawat, which has become a *wát thîaw* (tourist wat), Wat Pa Udom Somphon is still a strict forest meditation monastery. Visitors are welcome to tour the museum, but only those with a serious interest in Buddhism should enter the adjacent monastery.

Phu Phan National Park
อุทยานแห่งชาติภูพาน

Swathed in forest and tumbling over the pretty Phu Phan mountains, **Phu Phan National Park** (☎ 0 4270 3044; reserve@dnp.go.th; admission 200B; ☼ 8.30am-4.30pm) remains relatively undeveloped and isolated – it is no surprise that the area once provided cover for Thai resistance fighters in WWII and PLAT guerrillas in the 1970s. As well as being a stomping ground for deer and monkeys, the 645-sq-km park also hosts the odd tiger.

The park has only a few **hiking trails**, but there are good views along Rte 213 between Sakon Nakhon and Kalasin. Three waterfalls – **Tat Ton**, **Hew Sin Chai** and **Kham Hom** – can be visited fairly easily. **Tham Seri Thai** (Seri Thai Cave) was used by the Thai Seri (p38) during WWII as an arsenal and mess hall.

Limited **accommodation** (reservations ☎ 0 2562 0760; dm 100B; bungalows 500B) is available.

YASOTHON & MUKDAHAN PROVINCES

YASOTHON
ยโสธร

pop 23,000

The workaday provincial town of Yasothon saves all of its fireworks for the annual Rocket Festival and has little to offer outside the official whizz-bang period of late May. Still, it makes a reasonable stopover if you are taking it slow between Khon Kaen and Ubon Ratchathani.

The name of the town, which has the largest Muslim population in the northeast, comes from the Sanskrit 'Yasodhara' (meaning 'preserver or maintainer of glory').

Sights

A rather sinister myth surrounds **Phra That Kong Khao Noi** (☼ daylight hours), a brick-and-stucco *chedi* dating from the late Ayuthaya period. Legend has it that a young, and no doubt ravenously hungry, farmer who had toiled all morning in the hot sun murdered his mother here when she brought his lunch to the fields late – and in the smallest of sticky-rice baskets. The farmer, eating his lunch over his mother's dead body, realised that the small basket actually contained much more sticky rice than he could manage to eat. To atone for his deed, he then built the *chedi*.

It is located in Ban Tat Thong off Hwy 23 (between the Km 194 and Km 195 markers) heading towards Ubon Ratchathani.

In the town, **Phra That Phra Anon** (☼ daylight hours), also known as Phra That Yasothon, at Wat Mahathat, is a highly venerated Lao-style *chedi*. It's said to be more than 1200 years old and is said to enshrine holy relics of Phra Anon (Ananda), the Buddha's personal attendant monk and one of his chief disciples.

Festivals & Events

Yasothon's famed **Rocket Festival** (Bun Bang Fai) is one of the biggest in the region and takes place in late May. The festival is prevalent throughout the northeast as a rain and fertility rite, and is celebrated fervently in Yasothon, where it involves parades and rocket-launching contests.

Sleeping & Eating

JP Emerald Hotel (☎ 0 4572 4848; www.yasothon2000
.com; 36 Th Prapa; r 1600B; ✷) There's still some
gloss at the Emerald, although a little too
much plastic greenery gives the lobby a
slightly tacky feel. The staff are extremely
attentive though, the rooms are good (if
a little overpriced) and there's a café and
karaoke bar down below. Discounts (up to
25%) are available if business is slow. It's at
the Roi Et end of town, near the well-sign-
posted police station.

Yot Nakhon (☎ 0 4571 1122; 141-143/1-3 Th Uthai-
ramrit; r 250-350B; ✷) Yasothon's cheap hotels,
found around the market, are a rough-and-
tumble lot, but this remains the best bet.

For some colourful eats, head to the **Night
Barza** (✷ 5-10pm), on the main road (Rte 23)
through town.

Getting There & Away

There are buses to Yasothon's main **bus terminal** (☎ 0 4571 2965; Th Rattanakhet) from Ubon
Ratchathani (ordinary/air-con 45/75B, two
hours, hourly) and Khorat (ordinary/air
con 80/145B, four hours, five daily).

MUKDAHAN

มุกดาหาร

pop 34,300

On the banks of the Mekong, directly opposite the Lao city of Savannakhet, Mukdahan
is one of the region's prettier towns, with a
long riverside drag, a bustling market atmosphere and pleasant views across the water.
Known for its riverfront Talat Indojin (Indochina Market), Mukdahan is mainly a trade
centre and at the weekend, when the market
really kicks off, you'll wonder how the locals
manage to find time to do anything but trawl
the Vietnamese, Thai and Lao stalls.

Governments on both sides of the river
are planning to formalise Mukdahan's status as a trade hub and there's a scheme to
build a bridge across the Mekong. Streets
harbour an infectious commercial optimism
and new developments are springing up. For
Mukdahan, it seems, things are on the up.

Information

Bangkok Bank (cnr Th Phitak Santirat & Th Song Nang
Sathit; ✷ 8.30am-3.30pm Mon-Fri) Has ATM and change
facilities.

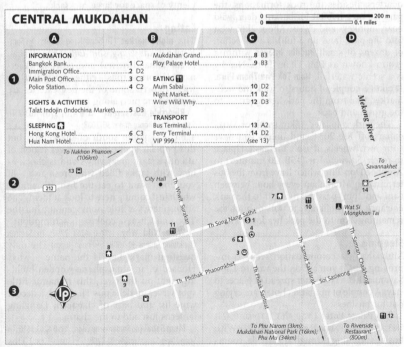

CENTRAL MUKDAHAN

0 — 200 m
0 — 0.1 miles

INFORMATION
Bangkok Bank.............................1 C2
Immigration Office........................2 D2
Main Post Office...........................3 C3
Police Station..............................4 C2

SIGHTS & ACTIVITIES
Talat Indojin (Indochina Market)........5 D3

SLEEPING 🏠
Hong Kong Hotel...........................6 C3
Hua Nam Hotel.............................7 C2

Mukdahan Grand..........................8 B3
Ploy Palace Hotel..........................9 B3

EATING 🍽
Mum Sabai.................................10 D2
Night Market...............................11 B2
Wine Wild Why............................12 D3

TRANSPORT
Bus Terminal...............................13 A2
Ferry Terminal..............................14 D2
VIP 999.................................(see 13)

Mekong River

To Nakhon Phanom
(106km)

To
Savannakhet

City Hall

Wat Si
Mongkhon Tai

Th Wiwit Surakan

Th Song Nang Sathit

Th Phitak Phanomkhet

Th Phithak Santirat

Th Samut Sakdarak

Th Samran Chaithong

Soi Sasiwong

Th Phitak Santirat

To Phu Narom (3km);
Mukdahan National Park (16km);
Phu Mu (34km)

To Riverside
Restaurant
(800m)

Immigration office (☎ 0 4261 1074; Th Song Nang Sathit; ☒ 8.30am-4.30pm Mon-Fri) Visa extensions are available here.

Main post office (cnr Th Phitak Santirat & Th Phitak Phanomkhet; ☒ 8.30am-4.30pm Mon-Fri, to noon Sat)

Police station (☎ 0 4261 1333, emergency ☎ 1155; Th Phitak Santirat)

Sights

For town views, climb the 500m **Phu Narom**, 3km south of town. **Phu Mu**, a local picnic spot with scenic views, is 34km south of town off Rte 212 – just south of Ban Taw Khet and the Mukdahan Province line between the Km 29 and Km 30 markers.

MUKDAHAN NATIONAL PARK
อุทยานแห่งชาติมุกดาหาร

Although little more than a speck of a reserve at just 48 sq km, hilly **Mukdahan National Park** (☎ 0 4260 1753; reserve@dnp.go.th; ☒ 8.30am-4.30pm) has some beautiful landscapes and is scattered with unusual mushroom-shaped **rock formations**. Two groups of rock formations (Phu Pha Thoep and Hin Thoep) are situated about 200m from the park headquarters. Besides the rock formations, the park is also a habitat for barking deer, wild boar, monkeys and civets. About 2km west into the park (and up a hill) is a collection of dozens of small **Buddha images** within a grotto known as Phu Tham Phra. Nearby is a scenic waterfall, **Nam Tok Phu Tham Phra**. It takes a couple of hours to walk the well-marked trail from the park headquarters to the grotto and back.

The park is located 16km south of Mukdahan, off Rte 2034, and unless you have your own wheels, it isn't the easiest place to reach. *Săwngthăew* (15B, 20 minutes) to Amphoe Don Tan (which leave from the bus terminal in Mukdahan every hour between 6am and 2pm) pass the turn-off to the park entrance, but you'll have to walk or hitch the remaining 2km to the park headquarters.

Sleeping

Mukdahan's accommodation scene is improving, but if you are on the way to Laos, Savannakhet has a better spread of places to stay. A couple of upmarket hotels are crying out for business.

Ploy Palace Hotel (☎ 0 4263 1111; fax 0 4261 1883; 40 Th Phitak Phanomkhet; r 1500B; ☒ ☒) With business coming through at a trickle, rooms

at this executive sleepeasy are readily discounted to 900B, making them very good value indeed. There's plenty of marble and wood for that 'swanky' feel, a decent spread of creature comforts (including a sauna and pool) and some friendly staff.

Mukdahan Grand (☎ 0 4261 2020; fax 0 4261 6021; 78 Th Song Nang Sathit; r 1800B; ☒ ☒) A little less 'Grand' than the Palace, this upmarket outfit nevertheless offers high standards and some of the most cheerful staff on the circuit. The comfortable rooms are overpriced on the tariff, but go as low as 750B after a readily offered discount.

Hua Nam Hotel (☎ 0 4261 1137; fax 0 4261 1197; 36 Th Samut Sakdarak; r 220-320B; ☒ ☒) Standards are on the up here and while the frills are still a little lacking, there's a friendly, English-speaking owner, fast Internet access and a bike-rental facility. There's not a whole lot in the way of atmosphere, but both the aircon and fan rooms are good value.

Hong Kong Hotel (no Roman-script sign; ☎ 0 4261 1143; 161/1-2 Phitak Santirat; r 160B) This streaked, white concrete block is a last resort bolthole, but the flaky rooms come with TV and plenty of space for large rucksacks.

Eating

The **night market** (Th Song Nang Sathit; ☒ 5pm-10pm) has *kài yâang*, *sôm-tam*, *khâo jìi* (Lao baguette sandwiches) and *pàw-pía* (Vietnamese spring rolls), either fresh *(sòt)* or fried *(thâwt)*. Some of the best eateries are south of the pier, along the riverfront.

Riverside Restaurant (☎ 0 4261 1705; 103/2 Th Samron Chaikhong; mains 30-200B; ☒ 10am-11pm) It's a bit of a yomp south of the centre, but this popular spot offers an eager legion of attentive staff, great views and is chock-a-bloc with tanks filled with fresh fish – if you don't want to eat the fish, it's almost worth just coming here to look at them. The atmosphere's a little homogenous, but the Thai and Chinese cooking is scrumptious.

Wine Wild Why (☎ 0 4263 2797; Th Samron Chaikhong; mains 30-160B; ☒ noon-10pm) The only question mark here is the name – why? Housed in an atmospheric wooden building right on the river, this romantic little spot serves up delicious Thai food, a decent wine list and bags of character. Dangling lanterns just add to the charm.

Mum Sabai (no Roman-script sign; ☎ 0 4263 3616; Th Song Nang Sathit; mains 30-120B; ☒ 10am-10pm) This

Prasat Phimai National Historical Park
(p444), near Nakhon Ratchasima

Khmer sculpture, the south gallery of the Phanom
Rung temple (p452), Buriram Province

ANDERS BLOMQVIST

BILL WASSMAN

Khao Yai forest, Khao Yai National Park (p448), Nakhon Ratchasima Province

ANDERS BLOMQVIST

RICHARD I'ANSON

Novice monks at prayer, Nong Khai (p475)

Weaving a basket in Chiang Khan (p492), Loei

JOE CUMMINGS

Solitary fishing boat on the Mekong River, Nakhon Phanom Province (p495)

TOM CO

spotless diner offers a good spread of steaks and ice-cold air-con for those waiting for the next Savannakhet ferry.

Getting There & Away

BOAT
If you already have a Lao visa, you can catch a boat from Mukdahan's **ferry terminal** (☎ 0 4261 4926) across the river to Savannakhet, in Laos. There are eight ferries daily during the week (9am to 4.30pm), six on Saturday (9.30am to 4.30pm) and just four on Sunday (9.30am to 4pm). Tickets cost 50B each way. From Savannakhet there are regular buses to Vientiane – see Lonely Planet's *Laos* guidebook for more information.

BUS
Mukdahan's main **bus terminal** (☎ 0 4263 07972) is on Rte 212, north of the town. From here there are regular buses to Nakhon Phanom (ordinary/air-con 40/72B, two hours, hourly until 5pm) going via That Phanom (ordinary/air-con 20/40B, one hour, hourly until 5pm) and also via Ubon Ratchathani (ordinary/air-con 60/110B, 3½ hours, six daily). There are also hourly buses to/from Bangkok's northern terminal (ordinary/air-con 382/202B, 11 hours). **VIP 999** (☎ 0 4261 1478), with offices at the terminal, also runs two VIP buses daily to Bangkok (590B, 10 hours).

UBON RATCHATHANI PROVINCE

Ranging from the big city of Ubon at its heart, to the silent pockets of intact monsoon forest at its edges, Ubon Ratchathani is the northeast's biggest province, pushing down into the tri-border region where Laos, Thailand and Cambodia finally come together. Until the end of the 1990s, Khmer Rouge activity plastered a giant question mark over security in many of the border areas, but with Pol Pot dead and his fighters disarmed, travel right across the province is safe once again. In recognition of this, TAT are now attempting to bolster the region's tourist profile, labelling it the 'Emerald Triangle' in recognition of its magnificent green landscapes and drawing obvious – but rather hopeful – parallels with north-

ern Thailand's 'Golden Triangle'. However successful this is, Ubon remains one of the region's more attractive big cities, while the surrounding countryside has plenty to entertain the rustic rover.

History
Ubon's Mae Nam Mun and Mae Nam Chi basins were centres for Dvaravati and Khmer cultures many centuries ago. Following the decline of the Khmer empires, the area was settled by groups of Lao in 1773 and 1792. By the early Ratanakosin era it had become part of *monthon* Ubon, a southeastern Isan satellite state extending across what are now Surin, Si Saket and Ubon Provinces – as well as parts of southern Laos – with Champasak, Laos, as *monthon* capital. Today the Lao influence in the province predominates over the Khmer.

UBON RATCHATHANI
อุบลราชธานี
pop 115,000
Survive the usual knot of choked access roads, and Ubon Ratchathani will reveal an altogether more attractive face. Racked up against Mae Nam Mun, Thailand's second-longest waterway, the southern portions of the city have a pedestrian, sluggish character rarely found in the region's big conurbations. Temples pepper the surrounding area, the urban push-and-shove is easily escaped and despite the quick-time march of modernisation, a deep sense of Isan identity continues to live on.

A US air base during the Vietnam-era, 21st-century Ubon is primarily a financial, educational and agricultural market centre for eastern Isan. But with the nearby Thai–Lao border crossing at Chong Mek drawing a steady stream of foreigners, Ubon's ever-improving hotel and restaurant scene also offers an excellent opportunity to stock up on the good life before heading off into rural Laos.

Orientation & Information
Most of the activity in Ubon Ratchathani takes place to the north of Mae Nam Mun and east of the main north–south thoroughfare, Th Chayangkun/Th Uparat. The train station, several bus terminals, more places to stay and a good few restaurants are south of the river in Warin Chamrap.

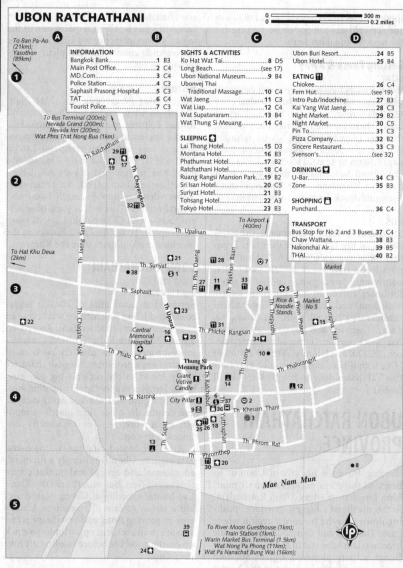

UBON RATCHATHANI

0 ____ 300 m
0 ____ 0.2 miles

INFORMATION
Bangkok Bank..........................1 B3
Main Post Office.......................2 C4
MD.Com...................................3 C4
Police Station............................4 C3
Saphasit Prasong Hospital.........5 C3
TAT..6 C4
Tourist Police...........................7 C3

SIGHTS & ACTIVITIES
Ko Hat Wat Tai..........................8 D5
Long Beach.........................(see 17)
Ubon National Museum.............9 B4
Ubonvej Thai
  Traditional Massage.............10 C4
Wat Jaeng..............................11 C3
Wat Liap................................12 C4
Wat Supatanaram....................13 B4
Wat Thung Si Meuang..............14 C4

SLEEPING
Lai Thong Hotel......................15 D3
Montana Hotel........................16 B3
Phathumrat Hotel....................17 B2
Ratchathani Hotel...................18 C4
Ruang Rangsi Mansion Park......19 B2
Sri Isan Hotel.........................20 C5
Suriyat Hotel..........................21 B3
Tohsang Hotel.........................22 A3
Tokyo Hotel...........................23 B3

Ubon Buri Resort.....................24 B5
Ubon Hotel............................25 B4

EATING
Chiokee.................................26 C4
Fern Hut............................(see 19)
Intro Pub/Indochine................27 B3
Kai Yang Wat Jaeng.................28 C3
Night Market.........................29 B2
Night Market.........................30 C5
Pin To...................................31 C3
Pizza Company.......................32 B2
Sincere Restaurant..................33 C3
Svenson's.........................(see 32)

DRINKING
U-Bar...................................34 C3
Zone....................................35 B3

SHOPPING
Punchard...............................36 C4

TRANSPORT
Bus Stop for No 2 and 3 Buses..37 C4
Chaw Wattana........................38 B3
Nakonchai Air........................39 B5
THAI....................................40 B2

Bangkok Bank (Th Suriyat; ⏱ 8.30am-3.30pm Mon-Fri) One of many banks across town with ATM and change facilities.

Main post office (Th Si Narong; ⏱ 8.30am-4.30pm Mon-Fri, 9am-noon Sat & Sun) Near the intersection with Th Luang.

MD.Com (221 Th Kheuan Thani; per hr 40B; ⏱ 11am-10pm) Access the Internet here.

Saphasit Prasong Hospital (☎ 0 4526 3043; Th Saphasit) Medical and emergency facilities.

TAT (☎ 0 4524 3770; fax 0 4524 3771; 264/1 Th Kheuan Thani; ⏱ 8.30am-4.30pm) This is a very helpful branch office. It distributes free maps of Ubon, and information handouts about Si Saket and Yasothon Provinces also.

Tourist police (☎ 0 4524 5505, emergency ☎ 1155; Th Suriyat) Directly behind the police station.

Sights & Activities

UBON NATIONAL MUSEUM
พิพิธภัณฑสถานแห่งชาติอุบลราชธานี

Once you've dropped your bags in the hotel and slipped on a clean shirt, your first stop in town should be the informative **Ubon National Museum** (☎ 0 4525 5071; Th Kheuan Thani; admission 30B; ☼ 9am-4pm Wed-Sun). Occupying a pretty former palace from the Rama VI era, this is the spot to come to swat up on your background before venturing out into the wider province. And there's plenty on show, from Buddhist ordination-precinct stones from the Dvaravati period and Khmer-era Pallava-inscribed pillars, to 3000-year-old pottery from the northeast, Lao Buddhas, Ubon textiles and local musical instruments. Among the museum's most prized possessions are a rare standing Dvaravati Buddha image and a Dong Son bronze drum.

A little north of the museum is **Thung Si Meuang Park**, the centrepiece of which is a huge concrete replica of an elaborate votive candle. The park is the venue of Ubon's annual Candle Festival (see p508).

WAT THUNG SI MEUANG
วัดทุ่งศรีเมือง

Wat Thung Si Meuang (Th Luang; ☼ daylight hours) was built during the reign of Rama III (1824–51) and has a *hǎw trai* (Tripitaka library) in good shape. Like many *hǎw trai*, it rests on tall, angled stilts in the middle of a small pond, surrounded by water to protect the precious scriptures from termites. Nearby is an old *mondòp* with a Buddha footprint symbol. The interior of the *bòt* is painted with 150-year-old *jataka* murals.

WAT PHRA THAT NONG BUA
วัดพระธาตุหนองบัว

An almost exact replica of the Mahabodhi stupa in Bodhgaya, India, **Wat Phra That Nong Bua** (☼ daylight hours) is a much better copy of the subcontinental original than Wat Jet Yot in Chiang Mai, which is also purported to be a Mahabodhi reproduction. The *jataka* reliefs on the outside of the *chedi* are very good. Two groups of four niches on each side of the four-sided *chedi* contain Buddhas standing in stylised Gupta or Dvaravati closed-robe poses.

It is on the road to Nakhon Phanom on the outskirts of town (catch a white city bus for 5B).

WAT SUPATANARAM
วัดสุปัฏนาราม

Called **Wat Supat** (Th Supat; ☼ daylight hours) for short, the unique 19th-century *bòt* at this temple features a mix of Khmer, European and Thai styles. In contrast to other Thai- or Lao-style temple structures of the region, the *bòt* is made entirely of stone, like the early Khmer stone *prasat*, and the roof corners display dragons. On display in the *bòt* is one of Thailand's oldest-surviving Khmer stone carvings, a lushly carved stone lintel dating to the 7th century. In front of the *bòt* stands the largest wooden bell in Thailand.

WAT JAENG
วัดแจ้ง

Wat Jaeng (Th Saphasit; ☼ daylight hours) has a typical Lao-style *bòt* (known locally by the Lao term *sǐm*). The carved wooden veranda depicts a *kotchasi*, a mythical cross between an elephant and a horse; above that is Airavata, Indra's three-headed elephant mount.

KO HAT WAT TAI
เกาะหาดวัดใต้

Picnicking families flock to this island in Mae Nam Mun during the hot, dry months of March, April and May. There are beaches for swimming and sunbathing and little boats (10B) ferry people over the river from the northern shore.

HAT KHU DEUA
หาดคูเดื่อ

West of town, on the north shore, Hat Khu Deua is a 'beach' area off Th Liang Meuang. Thatched *sǎalaa* (pavilions) offer shade for picnicking or napping by the river.

WARIN CHAMRAP DISTRICT TEMPLES

Ubon city district is separated from Warin Chamrap to the south by Mae Nam Mun. Two well-known wats in this district are forest monasteries *(wát pàa)* founded by the famous monk and meditation master Ajahn Cha. The venerable *ajahn* (teacher) died in January 1992, aged 75, after a productive and inspirational life, however his teachings live on at these two hermitages.

Wat Pa Nanachat Bung Wai
วัดป่านานาชาติบุ่งหวาย

Wat Pa Nanachat (☎ 0 1470 9299; Ban Bung Wai, Amphoe Warin, Ubon Ratchathani 34310; ☼ daylight hours) is a Western-oriented wat, where foreigners with a *serious* interest in Buddhism are welcomed to study. Write (using the above address) or telephone in advance to avoid disappointment; during the March-to-May hot season monks go into retreat and overnight guests aren't usually accepted.

From Ubon, take a No 1 bus south down Th Uparat, cross the bridge over Mae Nam Mun and get off as the bus turns right in Warin Chamrap for the train station. From there, catch any *sǎwngthǎew* heading south (though heading west eventually, on Rte 2193 towards Si Saket) and ask to be let off at Wat Pa Nanachat – everybody knows it. You can also get there by catching a Si Saket bus from Ubon for 8B to Bung Wai, the village across the road from Wat Pa Nanachat.

There is a sign in English at the edge of the road – the wat is in the forest behind the rice fields. You can also hire a *túk-túk* direct to the wat from town for about 100B.

Wat Nong Pa Phong
วัดหนองป่าพง

Founded by monk extraordinaire, Ajahn Cha, **Wat Nong Pa Phong** (☼ daylight hours) is a pleasant forest wat known for its quiet discipline and daily routine of work and meditation. Quite a name in these parts, Ajahn Cha founded temples across the region and even opened one in Sussex, England.

Dozens of Westerners have studied here during the past 20 years or so, but unless you're fluent in Thai, you'll be directed to Wat Pa Nanachat Bung Wai.

Ajahn Cha, a former disciple of the most famous northeastern teacher of them all, Ajahn Man, was known for his simple and direct teaching method. His funeral, which was held here, drew thousands of followers from around the world.

The wat features a small **museum** (admission free; ☼ daylight hours) and a *chedi* where Ajahn Cha's ashes are interred.

The wat is about 10km past the train station, in Amphoe Warin Chamrap – take a No 3 bus to the ordinary-bus terminal, then catch a *sǎwngthǎew* going to the wat.

TRADITIONAL MASSAGE
Ubonvej Thai Traditional Massage (☎ 0 4526 0345; 113 Th Thepyothi; ☼ 9am-6pm) offers Thai traditional (250B), foot (250B) and oil (450B) massages. As the brochure makes perfectly

clear, it offers 'NO SEX!'. This place can get quite busy, so it pays to book ahead.

Ubon also has several *àap òp nûat* (bathe-steam-massage) places that probably got their start when a US air base was located outside town. The most notorious is the Pathumrat Hotel's **Long Beach** (☎ 0 4524 1501; 337 Th Chayangkun; ☼ 9am-7pm), which Ta Mok and other Khmer Rouge commanders visited regularly until Pol Pot finally kicked the bucket.

Festivals & Events
Ubon's **Candle Festival** is actually a parade of gigantic, elaborately carved wax sculptures that is held during Khao Phansa, a Buddhist holiday marking the commencement of *phansǎa*, the Rains Retreat (Buddhist Lent), in July. The festival is very popular with Thai tourists and the city's hotel rooms are often all booked for the event.

Sleeping
BUDGET
Ubon is not inundated with cheap hotels, but as well as the budget options listed here, many of the midrange options also offer inexpensive fan rooms.

River Moon Guest House (☎ 0 4428 6093; 43 Th Sisaket; s/d 120/180B) This rustic, wooden spot offers a little slice of traditional calm on the outskirts of Ubon. Simple and spartan with shared bathrooms, travellers just in from rural Laos may find it a good place to decompress before heading into the big city itself. Near the train station, it is out across Mae Nam Mun in Warin Chamrap.

Tokyo Hotel (☎ 0 4524 1739; 178 Th Uparat; r 250-500B; 🅿) The best budget bet in the centre of Ubon, Tokyo offers a wide range of rooms from some relatively humble air-con and fan affairs in an old building, to swoosh air-con rooms with TV and trimmings in the new block.

Suriyat Hotel (☎ 0 4524 1144; Th Suriyat; s 200-380B; d 300-440B; 🅿) Despite scooping one of the town's crazy architecture accolades for its exterior, this budget outfit is disappointingly ordinary on the inside. The slightly sparse rooms are pretty good for the price though, as are the fan rooms.

MIDRANGE
Sri Isan Hotel (☎ 0 4526 1011; www.sriisanhotel.com; 62 Th Ratchabut; r 650B; 🅿) This bright, cheerful

place is full of natural light, which streams down through the atrium and gives the lobby an open, airy feel. The rooms, which come with fridge and TV, are small and the décor is a little twee – a knitted toilet roll cover wouldn't be out of place – but standards are high and an orchid comes gratis on every pillow.

Ruang Rangsi Mansion Park (☎ 0 4524 4746-7; Ruang Rangsi Complex, Th Ratchathani; r 450B; 🖭) Situated down a quiet alleyway off Th Ratchathani, this pleasant hideaway offers spacious bedsit-style rooms, with oodles of space and enough chairs to seat half of Ubon – great if you're planning a party. It's quiet, friendly and you get a whole lot of comfort.

Phathumrat Hotel (☎ 0 4524 1501; fax 0 4524 2313; 337 Th Chayangkun; r 900B; 🖭) This former top-ender has slipped gracefully into the midrange category and offers some relatively chic East-meets-West styling, sharp staff and comfortable rooms. Clever publicity snaps in the brochure make the place look rather plusher than it is – they don't show the dirty windows for example – but overall it remains a solid bet for a good-value sleep.

Ratchathani Hotel (☎ 0 4524 4388; 297 Th Kheuan Thani; s 330-500B, d 450-650B; 🖭) Still fresh from relatively recent renovations, this popular spot offers a little midrange sparkle and some groovy little pop-up business cards. The rooms are well kept and there's plenty of space if you arrive heavily laden with souvenirs.

Montana Hotel (☎ 0 4526 1748; fax 0 4526 1750; 179/1-4 Th Uparat; r 550B; 🖭) The focal point of this central hotel appears to be the much plugged 'VIP' Piano Karaoke Bar! If you can escape the potential sing-along shenanigans by staying on the upper floors though, the rooms are spotless and well-appointed, with little balconies, a TV and a fridge. On the downside – for some – the porter was an enthusiastic 'sexy massage' salesman.

Nevada Inn (☎ 0 4531 3351; fax 0 4531 3350; 436 Th Chayangkun; tr/d 650/800B; 🖭) Just north of the city and rather better value than its big brother across the parking lot (Nevada Grand), this comfy place sits at the heart of an entertainment complex filled with cinemas, cheap eateries and cafés. It's a little subterranean in aspect, but the rooms offer a fair amount of va-va-voom for the price.

Ubon Hotel (☎ 0 4524 1045; 333 Th Kheuan Thani; r 280-700B; 🖭) The plain Jane of Ubon's midrangers, this so-so spot offers reasonable value if you can forgive the total lack of imagination that went into planning it. The service is friendly enough and you can also choose from cheaper fan rooms and slightly swankier VIP rooms.

TOP END

Ubon Buri Resort (☎ 0 4526 6777; fax 0 4526 6770; 1 Th Srimongkol; r 1000B, bungalows 1400B; 🖭) This bona fide, self-contained resort is the place to come if you're planning on staying in Ubon without really *being* in Ubon. With rooms and bungalows set in acres of lush, tropical greenery, Isan folk-art styling and sycophantic – in a good way – staff, this is Ubon's best value and most idiosyncratic top-ender. It's just off the main road between Ubon and Warin Chamrap – keep an eye out for the billboards on the right if you are driving out of Ubon.

Tohsang Hotel (☎ 0 4524 5531; fax 0 4524 4814; 251 Th Phalo Chai; r 1070B; 🖭) Spreading over out two large blocks, this pleasant business-standard hotel features glossy rooms, polished surfaces and plenty of the extra little trimmings – such as free fresh coffee in the lobby – that can really make a difference.

Lai Thong Hotel (☎ 0 4526 4271; fax 0 4526 4270; 50 Th Phichit Rangsan; r 1900B; 🖭 🖭) A tourist office favourite, this swanky spot offers attentive staff, all the usual 'executive' facilities and the odd token nod to traditional Isan design. Discounts take prices as low as 1200B.

Nevada Grand (☎ 0 4528 0999; fax 283424; 434 Th Chayangkun; r 1000B; 🖭 🖭) More Nevada trailer park than Caesar's Palace, this once opulent number north of town is now a fair way down the road to ruin. The rooms are huge, there's a pool and breakfast is on the house, but this southern belle is in urgent need of a facelift.

Eating

Ubon has two night markets open from dusk to dawn: one by the river near the bridge (*tàlàat yài* or big market), and the other near the bus terminal on Th Chayangkun.

The French-Lao influence means Ubon is more accustomed to pastries and Western breakfasts than many parts of Thailand. There are also plenty of full-on Western-style eateries.

Kai Yang Wat Jaeng (☎ 0 1709 9393; Th Suriyat; mains 20-40B; ☺ 9am-6pm) You eat among the cooks at this dynamic, no-frills eatery, considered by many to be the best purveyor of *kài yâang* in town. The chicken is sold from 9am to 2pm only, after which the vendor switches to curries. Other specialities include *hàw mòk*.

Intro Pub/Indochine (☎ 0 4524 5584; 168-170 Th Saphasit; mains 40-100B; ☺ 10am-midnight) It's difficult to see the wood for the trees at this popular two-in-one place – the exterior of the timber building is almost completely cloaked in palms and creepers. The deliciously fresh Vietnamese food is served downstairs in Indochine until 6pm, when the action and the chefs move into the slightly swankier Intro Pub venue above. The menu – featuring favourites such as *ban hoi thit nuong* (grilled pork with vermicelli) – remains the same, but you get live music upstairs after dark.

Pin To (no Roman-script sign; ☎ 0 4524 4473; 298-300 Th Phichit Rangsan; mains 25-60B; ☺ 10.30am-midnight) This snug, wooden diner has oodles of cosy character, live music in the evening, a scattering of tables on the street out front and a reasonable selection of Thai food. The cooking is not the ace card here, but it remains a pleasant spot for a beer and a snack.

Sincere Restaurant (☎ 0 4525 4678; 126/1 Th Saphasit; mains 30-130B; ☺ 11am-10pm Mon-Sat) The menu at this air-con outfit is an interesting fusion of French and Thai influences, offering a great mix of quality ingredients and fiery flavours – just try and ignore the gaudy, pea-green curtains. According to a sticker on the door, no rabbits – or is that a dog? – are allowed.

Chiokee (☎ 0 4525 4017; 307-317 Th Kheuan Thani; mains 20-60B; ☺ 8am-10pm) Offering a slightly incongruous blend of East (authentic dark-wood styling, a decorative Chinese shrine) and West (Heinz ketchup, starched white tablecloths), this popular spot whips up a wide range of dishes, from tasty Thai specialities to English cooked breakfasts.

Fern Hut (☎ 0 4525 4709; Ruang Rangsi Complex, Th Ratchathani; mains 30-100B; ☺ 9am-10pm) Ferns – or at least sprouting pot plants – are the theme at this pleasant, leafy eatery. Add some slightly bizarre Hansel & Gretel styling, delicious international and Thai cooking and a soporific atmosphere and you've got the perfect venue for whiling away a few hours reading papers, munching snacks and slurping down shakes.

Pizza Company (☎ 1122; Th Chayangkun; pizza 40-140B; ☺ 10am-10pm) It's nothing particularly special, but if you fancy chain-style pizza and access to a salad bar piled high with sweetcorn, Iceberg lettuce and cherry tomatoes, this is your place. It also delivers and there's **Svenson's** (☺ 10am-10pm) for ice cream next door.

Drinking

U-Bar (☎ 0 4526 5141; 97/8-10 Th Phichit Rangsan; ☺ 6pm-2am; ✖) Ubon's übertrendy (well, for Isan anyway) nightspot offers hip styling, plenty of shiny, happy people and a drink called Blue Kamikaze, which is served out of a sinister-looking slush machine behind the bar. There's an upstairs area with a pleasant terrace balcony, live music and the lingering booze smells at opening time bear testament to the previous evening's bacchanalia.

Zone (☎ 0 4525 5585; Th Uparat; ☺ 6pm-1am) This central live music venue is rough, ready and underlit, but the city's bright young things come here in droves to nod along to growling, Indie bass-lines. The bands usually kick off around 7.30pm.

Shopping

One of the major local specialities is silver betel-nut containers moulded using the lost-wax process. The Ubon National Museum (p507) has a good exhibit of locally produced betel boxes; to see them being made visit Ban Pa-Ao (opposite), a silversmithing village between Yasothon and Ubon off Hwy 23.

Punchard (☎ 0 4524 1067; www.punchard.net; Th Ratchabut; ☺ 8am-8pm) A wide range of quality handicrafts are on sale at this central store. Watch the prices though; its position between TAT and the museum make it something of a tourist trap.

Getting There & Away

AIR

Thai Airways International operates three daily flights to and from Bangkok (one way from 1400B). A **THAI agent** (☎ 0 4526 3916; www.thaiairways.com; 364 Th Chayangkun; ☺ 8.30am-4.30pm Mon-Fri) sells tickets in town, or you can buy them from the THAI counter that is at the airport.

Air Asia (☎ 0 2515 9999; www.airasia.com) flies daily between Ubon and Bangkok (one way from 750B). You can either book a ticket over the Internet, via the reservations line, or at the desk at the airport.

BUS

Most buses leave from a **bus terminal** (☎ 0 4531 2773) north of the town centre, just off Th Chayangkun – take a No 2 or No 3 bus from near the TAT office. Buses link this terminal with Bangkok's northern terminal hourly from 6am to midnight (ordinary/air-con 200/300B, nine hours). Other fares to/from Ubon are in the table following.

Nakhonchai Air (☎ 0 4526 9777; www.nca.co.th) is a private company operating out of a terminal en route to Warin Chamrap with VIP buses to Bangkok (431B, 8½ hours, nine daily), Rayong (500B, 11 hours, four daily) and Chiang Mai (685B, 17 hours, four daily).

For Phibun (25B, one hour, hourly) and Khong Jiam (50B, two hours, hourly), head to the bus terminal by Warin market – take a No 3 bus from the TAT office – 2km south of Mae Nam Mun.

TRAIN

Ubon's **train station** (☎ 0 4532 1004) is in Warin Chamrap; take a No 2 bus (5B) to reach Th Chayangkun in Ubon's city centre.

The Ubon Ratchathani express leaves Bangkok nightly at 9pm, arriving in Ubon at 7.55am the next morning. Fares for 1st-class air-con sleeper/2nd-class fan sleeper/2nd-class seat/3rd-class seat are 1080/401/301/175B.

Rapid trains leave at 6.40am and 6.45pm, arriving in Ubon about 11 hours later. There is no 1st class on the rapid trains. Ordinary trains take only about an hour longer to reach Ubon.

Going the other way, the express leaves from Ubon at 5.55pm and the rapid trains at 7.05am and 7.15pm.

The above train services also stop in Khorat (1st-class sleeper/2nd-class sleeper/2nd-class seat/3rd-class seat 878/363/213/138B, six hours).

Getting Around

Colour-coded buses run throughout town (5B) – TAT have a map marked with bus routes. *Săamláw* around town cost around 25B per kilometre.

Motorbikes, vans and cars can be rented at **Chaw Wattana** (☎ 0 4524 3443; 269 Th Suriyat).

BUS FARES TO/FROM UBON	
Destination	**Fare (B)**
Buriram	
ordinary	65
air-con	150
Kantharalak (for Khao Phra Wihan)	
ordinary	25
Khong Jiam	
ordinary	50
Khon Kaen	
ordinary	100
air-con	200
Khorat	
ordinary	149
air-con	260
Mukdahan	
ordinary	60
air-con	110
Phibun Mangsahan	
ordinary	25
Prakhon Chai (for Phanom Rung)	
ordinary	80
Roi Et	
ordinary	65
air-con	120
Sakon Nakhon	
ordinary	100
air-con	175
Si Saket	
ordinary	30
air-con	60
Surin	
ordinary	75
air-con	130
That Phanom	
ordinary	65
air-con	140
Udon Thani	
ordinary	125
air-con	230
Yasothon	
ordinary	45
air-con	75

AROUND UBON RATCHATHANI PROVINCE
Ban Pa-Ao
บ้านผาอ่าว

To the northwest of Ubon on Hwy 23, this is another village that produces household utensils of brass using the lost-wax casting method. The turn-off for the village is near the Km 19 marker on Hwy 23 – from there it is another 3km to the village. Nearly all buses to Yasothon pass this way.

Ban Khawn Sai to Khong Jiam
บ้านค่อนซ้าย/โขงเจียม

The village of **Ban Khawn Sai**, within easy reach of Ubon on Rte 217 between the Km 23 and Km 24 markers, is famed for the forging of bronze gongs for temples and classical Thai music ensembles. You can watch the gong-makers hammering the flat metal discs into beautiful instruments and tempering them in rustic fires – often in temporary shelters just off the road. Small gongs cost 400B to 500B, larger ones 4000B to 5000B and the huge 2m gongs as much as 50,000B.

Visitors often stop in **Phibun Mangsahan**, 500m west of Ban Khawn Sai to see a set of rapids called **Kaeng Sapheu** next to the Mae Nam Mun river crossing. Phibun Mangsahan is also the location of the Ubon **immigration office** (☎ 0 4544 1108; ☻ 8.30am-4.30pm Mon-Fri); visa extensions are available here. The office is about 1km from town on the

way south to Chong Mek – look for a large communications antenna nearby.

Khong Jiam, east of Phibun Mangsahan via Rte 2222, sits on a picturesque peninsula at the confluence of the Mekong River and Mae Nam Mun. Huge conical fish traps are made here for local use – they look very much like the fish traps that appear in the 3000-year-old murals at Pha Taem National Park (opposite). Thais visit Khong Jiam to see the so-called **Mae Nam Song Si** (Two Colour River), the contrasting coloured currents formed at the junction of Mae Nam Mun and the Mekong River. Along the Mekong side is a simple but pleasant park with benches and food vendors.

For 200B to 300B per hour you can charter 15-person capacity long-tail boats from a landing next to the Pak Mun Restaurant in Khong Jiam to see Mae Nam Song Si and various small river islands; Thais can cross the Mekong to Laos. While this is not an official crossing for foreigners, it is sometimes possible to persuade boatmen to take you to the Lao village across the river for an hour or two, especially during Bud-

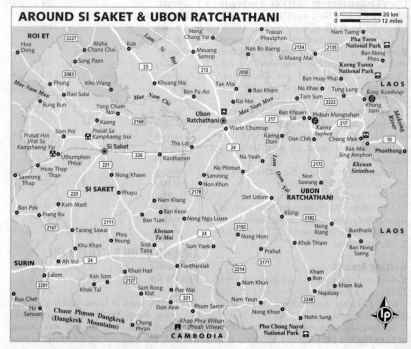

AROUND SI SAKET & UBON RATCHATHANI

dhist festival days, when regulations get lax. Foreigners are, however, officially permitted to cross into Laos 32km further south at Chong Mek.

SLEEPING & EATING

There are a few passable places to stay in Phibun Mangsahan, but Khong Jiam offers better options.

Phiboonkit Hotel (☎ 0 4544 1201; Phibun Mangsahan; r 120-280B; 🔀) Near the bus stop, in the centre of town, this is your usual, slightly chaotic budget hotel, with rickety rooms and a fair amount of noise during weekend nights. **Phiboonkit 2** (☎ 0 4544 1194; Phibun Mangsahan; r 280B; 🔀) is similar.

Restaurant (no Roman-script sign; mains 20-50B; 🕙 10am-10pm) Near the bridge to Rte 2222, just east of Phibun Mangsahan, is a simple restaurant famous for *saalaapao* (Chinese buns) and *năng kòp* (frog skin, usually fried). Thais visiting Pha Taem National Park like to stop here on the way to stock up on these items.

Tohsang Khong Jiam Resort (☎ 0 4535 1174; fax 0 4535 1162; 68 Mu 7 Baan Huay-Mak Tai, Khong Jiam; r 1070B, ste 2800B; 🔀) The glitz and gloss at this large resort are a little incongruous for this stretch of rural Thailand, but this looming place holds all the aces in the posh accommodation stakes.

Apple Guest House (☎ 0 4535 1160; Th Kaewpradit, Khong Jiam; r 150-300B; 🔀) With just 16 rooms, this reliable place offers a reasonably personal service – there's complimentary soap in the en suite bathrooms – and nice, comfy lodgings.

Also recommended:

Ban Rim Khong Resort (☎ 0 4535 1101; Khong Jiam; r 1000B) With timber bungalows overlooking the river.

Araya Resort (☎ 0 4535 1191; Khong Jiam; r 750B) With bungalows surrounded by a private waterfall and gardens.

There are plenty of simple **restaurants** on the Mae Nam Mun side of Khong Jiam.

GETTING THERE & AWAY

From Ubon, direct buses to Khong Jiam (50B, two hours) leave every hour from the Warin Market.

When direct buses aren't running to Khong Jiam, you can catch a Phibun bus (20B, one hour) from Warin Market and change there.

If you're driving or cycling to Khong Jiam from the Sirinthon Reservoir area via Rtes 217 and 2396, you'll have to cross Mae Nam Mun by vehicle ferry (look for the sign that says 'ferpy boat'). The ferry is 40B per vehicle.

Pha Taem National Park

อุทยานแห่งชาติผาแต้ม

In Amphoe Khong Jiam, 94km northeast of Ubon, is a tall stone cliff named PhaTaem – the centrepiece of the 340-sq-km **Pha Taem National Park** (☎ 0 4524 9780; reserve@dnp.go.th; admission 200B; 🕙 8.30am-4.30pm). The cliff is about 200m long and features prehistoric colour rock paintings that are at least 3000 years old. Mural subjects include fish traps, *plaa bèuk* (giant Mekong catfish), turtles, elephants, human hands and a few geometric designs – all very reminiscent of prehistoric rock art found at widely separated sites around the world. The latest anthropological theory speculates that rock-art sites like this one were created by shamans while they were in trance states.

A 500m trail descends from the cliff edge to the base, past two platforms where visitors can view the rock paintings; from the top of the cliff you get a bird's eye view of Laos. A clifftop **visitors centre** contains exhibits pertaining to the paintings and local geology. **Vendors** sell snacks and beverages near the top of the cliff.

Also a part of Pha Taem National Park is **Sao Chaliang**, an area of unusual stone formations similar to Phu Pha Thoep in Mukdahan National Park.

If you have your own equipment, **camping** (per tent 50B) is permitted in a camping site. The park also has **bungalows** (6-bed fan 1200B, 4-bed air-con 3000B). To reserve accommodation, call the **booking office** (☎ 0 2562 0760).

GETTING THERE & AWAY

Pha Taem is 20km beyond Khong Jiam via Rte 2112, but there's no direct public transport there. The bus from Ubon to Khong Jiam will pass the final turn-off to Pha Taem on request; then you can walk or hitch 5km to the cliff.

By car, bicycle or motorcycle from Ubon, go east on Rte 217 to Phibun Mangsahan, then turn left and head north across Mae Nam Mun on Rte 2222 and follow this road to Khong Jiam.

From Khong Jiam, take Rte 2134 northwest to Ban Huay Phai and then go northeast at the first turn-off to Pha Taem.

Chong Mek & the Emerald Triangle
ช่องเม็กและสามเหลี่ยมมรกต

South of Khong Jiam, via Rte 217, is the small trading town of **Chong Mek** on the Thai–Lao border, the only place in Thailand where you can cross into Laos by land (that is, you don't have to cross the Mekong). The southern Lao capital of Pakse is about an hour by road and ferry from Ban Mai Sing Amphon, the village on the Lao side of the border. At the time of writing, you could only cross the border if you already had a Lao visa, but check with the Lao consulate in Khon Kaen or Bangkok as the situation may change (see Embassies & Consulates, p732). The border is open from 8am until 6pm – Lao border officials may try (it doesn't appear to be an official charge) to exact a 50B 'overtime' levy/bribe if you arrive after 4pm on a weekend.

Thai travellers come to Chong Mek to browse through cheap goods from China, Vietnam and Laos. Foreign visitors won't find much of interest to purchase here, unless they're in the market for toiletries (from China), camouflage clothing (from Vietnam) or buckets of live frogs (from Laos).

About 5km west of Chong Mek is the northeastern shore of the huge **Kheuan Sirinthon** reservoir, an impoundment of a Mae Nam Mun tributary. On forested hills near the dam at the northern end of the reservoir is a recreation area frequented by local picnickers.

Further south, near the intersection of the Lao, Thai and Cambodian borders (in the area sometimes called the 'Emerald Triangle' for its relatively healthy forest cover) is the little-known **Phu Chong Nayoi National Park** (reserve@dnp.go.th; admission 200B; ⏰ 8.30am-4.30pm). The 687-sq-km park's predominant attractions include the **Nam Tok Bak Taew Yai** (Bak Taew Yai waterfall; 3.5km from the park headquarters), which plunges 40m over a cliff in two separate but parallel streams; a number of interesting rock formations; a couple of fresh springs; and some nice views of the surrounding countryside from a cliff called **Pha Pheung**. The park's highest point reaches 555m. Fauna includes the endangered white-winged wood duck. There are

four three-bed **bungalows** (reservations ☎ 0 2562 0760; 900B) within the park and a **camping site** (per tent 50B).

To get to Chong Mek from Ubon, catch a bus from Warin Market to the town of Najaluay (40B, one hour). Buses leave every hour between 10am and 1pm. Then from Najaluay, *săwngthăew* can be hired for 400B to 500B for the return journey to the park. If you have your own wheels, take Hwy 24 south and turn onto Rte 2182 at the town of Det Udom. From there it's 45km to the town of Buntharik, where you turn south onto Rte 2248. The turn-off to Phu Chong Nayoi National Park is a few kilometres beyond Najaluay. The park headquarters is 7km from the turn-off.

GETTING THERE & AWAY
Săwngthăew regularly run between Phibun and Chong Mek for 25B (one hour).

SURIN & SI SAKET PROVINCES

From enigmatic Khao Phra Wihan, just inside Cambodia, to atmospheric Prasat Ta Meuan, the adjacent provinces of Surin and Si Saket are dotted with Angkor-era Khmer ruins. Some are now looking rather tatty, but the best rank among the northeast's biggest attractions.

The region's towns are rather less interesting, but Surin in particular makes a pleasant base for exploring the temples and provides the backdrop for the raucous Annual Elephant Roundup, held each November.

SURIN & AROUND
สุรินทร์

pop 41,200

Quiet Surin doesn't have much to say for itself until November, when the provincial capital explodes into life for **Annual Elephant Roundup**. The carnival sees giant scrums of elephants tramping down the streets on their way to a whole spectrum of elephantine events, including elephant soccer, battle re-enactments and beauty pageants – you'll never see so many brightly-painted tuskers.

To see Surin's elephants during the low season, visit **Ban Tha Klang** in Amphoe Tha Tum, about 60km north of Surin. Many of the performers at the annual festival are trained here and there are two-hour **shows** (☎ 0 1966 5284; 200B) every Saturday at 9am.

Silk weaving can also be observed at several local villages, including **Khwaosinarin** and **Ban Janrom**.

Information

By far the best source of information about the region and its attractions is Pirom from Pirom's House (p516).

Bangkok Bank (Th Tanasan, Surin; ☉ 8.30am-3.30pm) Has ATM and change facilities.

Hospital (☎ 0 4451 1757; The Thessaban 1, Surin)

Microsys (Th Sirirat, Surin; per hr 15B; ☉ 24hr) You can access email here; it's opposite the Thong Tarin Hotel.

Sights

PRASAT TA MEUAN
ปราสาทตาเมือน

The most atmospheric – and most difficult to reach – of Surin's temple ruins is a series of three sites known collectively as **Prasat Ta Meuan** (☎ 0 4450 8100; admission free; ☉ daylight hours) in Amphoe Ban Ta Miang on the Cambodian border.

The first site, **Prasat Ta Meuan** proper, was built in the Jayavarman VII period (AD 1121–1220) as a rest stop for pilgrims. It's a fairly small monument with a two-door, eight-window sanctuary constructed of laterite blocks; only one sculpted sandstone lintel over the rear door remains.

To the south, about 500m along a winding road, is the more impressive **Prasat Ta Meuan Toht**, which is said to have been the chapel for a 'healing station' or 'hospital' like Prang Ku outside Chaiyaphum. The ruins consist of a *gopura, mondòp* and main sanctuary, which is surrounded by a laterite wall. This site has fairly recently been restored and the strangler figs cut away.

Further south, right next to the Cambodian border, is the largest site, **Prasat Ta Meuan Thom**. Built mostly of sandstone blocks on a laterite base, on a slope that drops off at the southern end to face the Cambodian border, the walled complex has been rather badly reassembled into a jumble of sculpted blocks. Unfortunately, some of the sculpted blocks from the highly ornate southern gate have ended up haphazardly inserted into other structures in the compound. This temple was occupied by the Khmer Rouge in the 1980s and many of the best carvings were

pried or blasted from the temple and sold to unscrupulous Thai dealers. Just beyond the southern gate the forest is cordoned off by barbed wire, and red skull-and-crossbone signs (Khmer and English) warn of undetonated mines.

Mines and undetonated hand grenades around the Prasat Ta Meuan sites are a real danger; *don't* veer from the cleared paths around and between the monuments. In the 1990s, firefights between the Khmer Rouge and Phnom Penh government troops could be heard almost daily during the dry season.

Ban Ta Miang is 25km east of Ban Kruat and 49km west of Kap Choeng via Rte 2121. The sites are 10.5km from Ban Ta Miang via a mediocre dirt road. This trip is best done by hired motorbike or car – Pirom's House (p516) can also arrange day trips by Land Rover if you can get a small group together.

OTHER KHMER-TEMPLE RUINS

The southern reach of Surin Province along the Cambodian border harbours several minor Angkor-period ruins, including **Prasat Hin Ban Phluang** (admission 30B; ☉ 8am-4pm), 30km south of Surin. The solitary sandstone sanctuary, mounted on a laterite platform, exhibits well-sculpted stone lintels.

A larger Khmer site is seen 30km northeast of town at **Prasat Sikhoraphum** (admission 30B; ☉ 8am-4pm), 500m north of Rte 226 at the Km 34 marker. Sikhoraphum (or Si Khonphum) features five Khmer *prang*, the tallest of which reaches 32m. The doorways to the central *prang* are decorated with stone carvings of Hindu deities following the Angkor Wat style. Prasat Sikhoraphum can be reached by bus or train from Surin town (15B, 40 minutes).

The ruined **Prasat Phumpon** (admission free; ☉ daylight hours) in Amphoe Sangkha (59km southeast of Surin via Rte 2077) is the oldest Khmer *prasat* in Thailand, dating from the 7th or 8th century AD. Unless you're adamant about ticking off every Khmer site in Thailand, you'll most likely be disappointed by this jumble of bricks.

Surin can also be used as a base to visit the Khmer ruins at Phanom Rung and Meuang Tam, about 75km southwest of Surin in Buriram Province (see Phanom Rung Historical Park p452).

Tours

Pirom, at Pirom's House (below), offers a wide range of one- and two-day tours from the back of his Land Rover. Half-day tours to the silk villages and Ban Tha Klang cost from 900B per person (minimum four), while two-day overnighters to Khao Phra Wihan and some little-known cave-painting sites start at 3200B per person (minimum four). Prices include food, transport, accommodation and admission costs.

Sleeping

The hotels fill up fast during the Elephant Roundup so book well in advance if you are visiting during this time. All of the following places are in Surin itself.

Pirom's House (☎ 0 4451 5140; 242 Th Krung Si Nai; s/d 100/150B) Housed in a rickety wooden villa, this pleasant spot offers lashings of traditional character and access to one of the best sources of information on the region – Pirom himself. The rooms are mighty basic, but the warm welcomes are far from spartan. The guesthouse will be moving to a bigger and better venue towards the end of 2005, so be sure to call ahead on Pirom's **mobile** (☎ 0 9355 4140) to check on the latest location.

Thong Tarin Hotel (☎ 0 4451 4281; www.thong tarin.co.th; 60 Th Sirirat; r 1360B; ❄ 🖳) Surin's top-ender is a bit spotty and the rooms err on the side of frumpy, but discounted rates as low as 800B and you are pretty much guaranteed a quiet night's sleep.

Phetkasem Hotel (☎ 0 4451 1274; fax 0 4451 4041; 104 Th Jit Bamrung; tr/d 290/850B; ❄ 🖳) Occupying the next rung down the quality ladder, this reasonable midranger features Bond-villain-meets-Benidorm architecture, plenty of skulking business types in the lobby and a restaurant with live music.

Sangthong Hotel (☎ 0 4451 2009; fax 0 4451 4329; 279-81 Th Tanasan; r 150-330B; ❄) The striplighting makes this otherwise comfortable hotel a little dreary, however the rooms are fairly spacious and come with a fine set of faux leather furniture and a TV. The cheap fan doubles don't have a TV.

Eating

Night market (Th Krung Si Nai; ❄ 5-10pm) Near Pirom's House, this market cooks up an excellent selection of Thai and Isan dishes, including barbecued insects.

Jan Thong (☎ 0 4451 5599; 201/18-20 Th Chitbam-rung; mains 30-100B; ❄ 10am-midnight) In the heart of Surin's nightlife district, near the Thong Tarin Hotel, this spotless diner does a good range of slightly homogenised Thai favourites, and beer.

Surin Chai Kit (no Roman-script sign; ☎ 0 4451 9339; Th Tanasan; mains 20-60B; ❄ 6.30am-2pm) This no-frills spot whips up a tasty breakfast – try a plate of pan eggs and Isan sausages. The owner wears a welcoming permagrin and speaks enough English to guide you through the Thai menu. It's near the Sangthong Hotel – come out of the main door and it's three doors to the left.

Lab Lakmuang (no Roman-script sign; Th Lak Muang; mains 20-40B; ❄ 3-9pm) This hole-in-the-wall spot is little more than four corners and a stove. The Isan takeaway food gets top marks for value for money though.

Getting There & Away
BUS

From Surin's **bus terminal** (☎ 0 4451 1756; Th Chit Bamrung) buses head to/from Roi Et (ordinary 43B, three hours, 12 daily), Yasothon (ordinary 40B, three hours, one daily), Khorat (ordinary 50B, four hours, every half-hour to 6pm), Si Saket (ordinary 30B, 2½ hours, every half-hour to 4pm), Pattaya (ordinary/air-con 125/225B, eight hours, eight daily) and Bangkok's northern terminal (air-con 250B, eight hours, 10 daily).

TRAIN

Surin is on the Bangkok/Ubon train line. A 2nd-/3rd-class train from Ubon to Surin costs 70/30B (three hours, six daily); from Bangkok a 2nd-/3rd-class train costs 210/80B (eight hours, six daily).

Surin can also be reached by train from any other station along the Ubon Ratchathani line, including Buriram and Si Saket.

Getting Around

Săamláw around central Surin cost about 20B per kilometre.

SI SAKET & AROUND

ศรีสะเกษ
pop 42,800

There's not a whole lot to do in the perennially humdrum town of Si Saket, but a visit to the Angkor-period temple complex of Khao Phra Wihan (Preah Vihear in Khmer), just over the border in Cambodia, is more than enough to make a visit worthwhile.

Information

Bangkok Bank (Th Khukhan, Si Saket; ☺ 8.30am-3.30pm Mon-Fri) Is central and has ATM and change facilities.

Si Saket Tourism Coordination Centre (☎ 0 4561 1283; cnr Th Lak Muang & Th Tepa, Si Saket; ☺ 8.30am-4.30pm Mon-Fri) Has plenty of brochures on the region, but you are unlikely to run into an English-speaking member of staff.

Sights
PRASAT KHAO PHRA WIHAN NATIONAL PARK
อุทยานแห่งชาติเขาพระวิหาร

Just inside Cambodia, however all but inaccessible from that side of the border, Khao Phra Wihan (Preah Vihear in Khmer) is one of the region's great Angkor-period monuments. Straddling a 600m-high cliff on the brow of the Dangrek (Dong Rek) escarpment and accessed via a series of stepped *naga* approaches, the large temple complex towers over the plains of Cambodia, offering dreamy views and some beautiful and evocative ruins.

Access, however, is a confusing – and relatively expensive – business. Claimed by both countries, the temple was finally awarded to Cambodia in a 1963 World Court ruling. But with infrastructure on that side of the border in an appalling state of disrepair, access is through Thailand's relatively new **Prasat Khao Phra Wihan National Park** (☎ 0 4561 9214; admission 200B; ☺ 7.30am-4.30pm, last entry 3pm), where a **visitors centre** (☺ 7.30am-4.30pm) marks the path into Cambodia and up to the temple. From here it is a 600m-walk to the border, where you pay 5B to have your passport photocopied, and another 400m to the main entrance, where the Cambodian authorities collect their 200B fee (total cost 405B). The whole procedure is a bit of a headache, but well worth every minute – and baht – of the palaver.

On the Thai side of the border, the 130-sq-km Prasat Khao Phra Wihan National Park was founded in 1998 and contains a number of sights that are worth a peep before tramping over the border to Khao Phra Wihan itself. Near the visitors centre, which includes a model of the temple and some interesting exhibits on its history, the **Pha**

Maw I Daeng cliff face features some fabulous views and the oldest bas-relief in Thailand. The relief depicts three figures whose identities are an enigma to archaeologists and art historians. Although they give the general impression of representing deities, angels or kings, the iconography corresponds to no known figures in Thai, Mon or Khmer mythology. Stylistically the relief appears to date back to the Koh Ker (AD 921–45) period of Khmer art, when King Jayavarman IV ruled from his capital at Koh Ker. The carving is on an overhanging section of the cliff and is accessed via a walkway.

Over the border, Khao Phra Wihan itself was constructed over two centuries under a succession of Khmer kings, beginning with Rajendravarman II in the mid-10th century and ending with Suryavarman II in the early 12th century – it was the latter who also commanded the construction of Angkor Wat. The hill itself was sacred to Khmer Hindus for at least 500 years before the completion of the temple complex, however, and there were smaller brick monuments on the site prior to the reign of Rajendravarman II.

The temple complex is semirestored – the general condition is somewhere between that of Prasat Phanomwan in Khorat and Phanom Rung in Buriram. During Khmer Rouge occupation, which lasted until Pol Pot's death in 1998, the site suffered from the pilfering of artefacts – lintels and other carvings in particular – although some of this smuggled art has been intercepted and will eventually be returned to the site. One *naga* balustrade of around 30m is still intact; the first two *gopura* have all but fallen down and many of the buildings are roofless, but abundant examples of stone carving are intact and visible. The doorways to the third *gopura* have been nicely preserved and one (the inner door facing south) is surmounted by a well-executed carved stone lintel depicting Shiva and his consort Uma sitting on Nandi (Shiva's bull), under the shade of a symmetrised tree. A Vishnu creation lintel is also visible on the second *gopura;* in contrast to the famous Phanom Rung lintel depicting the same subject, this one shows Vishnu climbing the churning stick rather than reclining on the ocean below.

The main *prasat* tower in the final court at the summit is in need of major restoration before the viewer can get a true idea of its former magnificence. Many of the stone carvings from the *prasat* are either missing or lie buried in nearby rubble. The galleries leading to the *prasat* have fared better and have even kept their arched roofs.

Until 1998, the area around the temple witnessed heavy fighting between Khmer Rouge guerrillas and the Phnom Penh government, and landmines and artillery pieces still litter the surrounding forest – stick to the designated safety lanes leading to the ruins.

Getting There & Away

Route 221 leads 95km south from Si Saket to Phum Saron – 11km before the temple – via Kantharalak. Catch a *săwngthăew* from near the bus terminal adjacent to the main day market in Si Saket (25B, 1½ hours). If you miss the infrequent direct *săwngthăew* service, you may have to take a bus first to Kantharalak (25B, 1¼ hours) and pick up another *săwngthăew* to Phum Saron (10B, 20 minutes). Buses to Kantharalak leave every half-hour from around 6am to 5pm. From either Kantharalak or Phum Saron, you'll have to hire a motorcycle taxi or *săwngthăew* to the visitors centre inside the Prasat Khao Phra Wihan National Park – figure on 250B return from Kantharalak or Phum Saron, with a couple of hours waiting time. Motorbike taxi drivers in Kantharalak seem to be much more reasonable than their counterparts in Phum Saron, who are aware that visitors will be unwilling to backtrack to Kantharalak in search of a better deal.

You can also catch a *săwngthăew* from the main bus terminal in Ubon Ratchathani to Kantharalak (25B, two hours, hourly) – continue from there as above.

OTHER KHMER RUINS

Forty kilometres west of Si Saket in Amphoe Uthumphon Phisai, **Prasat Hin Wat Sa Kamphaeng Yai** (☾ daylight hours) features a striking 10th-century sandstone *prang* with carved doorways. The ruined sanctuary can be found on the grounds of Wat Sa Kamphaeng Yai's modern successor.

About 8km west of Si Saket via Rte 226 is **Prasat Sa Kamphaeng Noi** (admission free; ☾ daylight hours), consisting of a pile of laterite and not much else.

Sleeping & Eating

SI SAKET

Kessiri Hotel (☎ 0 4561 4006; fax 0 4561 4008; 1102-1105 Th Khukhan; s/d 1000/1400B; ❄) Dominating the skyline, this ivory (in colour, at least) tower is capped with a wooden, pagoda-style roof terrace and tops the pops in Si Saket's accommodation stakes. The crowds it was built for don't appear to have materialised, but standards are reasonably high and off-season discounted rates go low, low, low (singles/doubles 600/850B).

Phrompiman Hotel (☎ 0 4561 2696; 849/1 Th Lak Meuang; r 250-500B; ❄) There may not be a whole lot to write home about here, but this is a reasonably comfortable midranger with some cheaper, and slightly rougher, fan rooms.

There are many small **restaurants** on the street in front of the train station. A **night market** (☾ 5-10pm) convenes 200m east of the train station, with good Isan and Thai food.

KANTHARALAK

This is the place to stay if you want to see Khao Phra Wihan early in the morning.

Kantharalak Palace Hotel (☎ 0 4566 1085; 131 Th Sinpadit; r 300-400B; ❄) On the main street through town, this immaculate midranger has comfy air-con and fan rooms, but you may have to wake up the receptionist if you want to stay here.

MK Hotel (☎ 0 4566 1171; fax 0 4566 2598; 148 Th Anantpakde; r 250-400B; ❄) This little place is around the corner by the police station and makes a decent back-up if the Kantharalak Palace is full – or the receptionist is asleep. It also has basic fan rooms with cold water and an on-site restaurant.

Getting There & Away

From Bangkok's Northern bus terminal there are several departures daily to Si Saket (ordinary/air-con 170/320B, eight hours). Any bus heading to Ubon Ratchathani will also get you there.

There are also regular buses from Ubon Ratchathani (ordinary/air-con 30/60B, one hour).

A 2nd-/3rd-class train from Ubon to Si Saket costs 29/13B (1½ hours, six daily); from Bangkok a 2nd-/3rd-class train costs 281/147B (10½ hours, six daily).

Upper Southern Gulf

Yet to be discovered by the majority of foreign tourists (although long popular with Thai holiday makers), Thailand's upper southern gulf offers laid-back seaside resorts, underground cave temples ripe for exploring and a national park boasting a dramatic landscape of limestone cliffs and magnificent gulf views to the less mainstream adventure seeker.

One of coastal Thailand's least-expensive areas, travel here will take you to pleasant provincial cities such as Phetchaburi, where underground cave temples provide plenty of picture-snapping opportunities and monkeys hang about hoping that gawking tourists will offer a banana. Sleepy beach towns such as Hua Hin and Cha-am come alive on weekends when bus-loads of Bangkok residents arrive, seeking less congestion and the chance to sunbathe. As the sun sinks and the sky turns that magical pinkish-purple, slip into an alfresco restaurant in Hua Hin and gorge yourself on the best fresh seafood around.

Most *faràng* (Westerners) just fly through this region on their way to more popular southern island destinations. Stop to catch your breath, however, and you'll get a feel for rural life. Agriculture, fishing and pineapple-growing are still the economic mainstays around these parts. With so much going for the region, it's little wonder the Thai royal family chooses Hua Hin as its beachside retreat.

Heading south from Bangkok the upper southern gulf follows the Burmese border along three provinces (Phetchaburi, Prachuap Khiri Khan and Chumphon), ending at the Isthmus of Kra, the region's narrowest point and official beginning of the Thai–Malay peninsula. Although it's not as easy to travel here as on the gulf islands, getting to these places requires only a marginal stretch of initiative – well worth it if you're looking for respite from the more beaten road.

HIGHLIGHTS

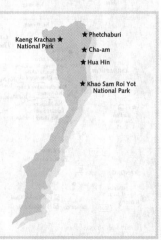

- Lingering over a delicious sunset seafood feast at one of **Hua Hin's** (p532) excellent wharfside restaurants, while re-hashing the day's elephant polo match
- Sighing at the vista – the gulf, the forest, the monolithic limestone cliffs – from the top of Khao Krachom in **Khao Sam Roi Yot National Park** (p534)
- Hiking through rich forests and savanna-like grasslands and past thundering waterfalls in Thailand's largest national park, **Kaeng Krachan** (p523)
- Partying Thai-style with rambunctious holiday-makers at the distinctly un-*faràng* beach town of **Cha-am** (p524)
- Wandering in the dim coolness at Phetchaburi's **cave temples** (p521), among sun-dappled Buddhas

★ Kaeng Krachan National Park
★ Phetchaburi
★ Cha-am
★ Hua Hin
★ Khao Sam Roi Yot National Park

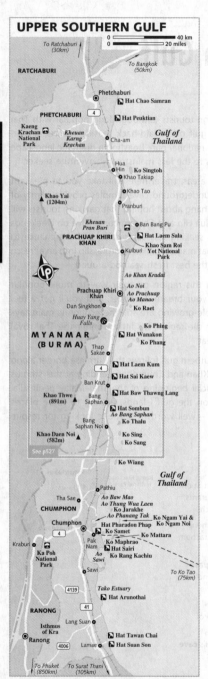

UPPER SOUTHERN GULF

0 ——— 40 km
0 ——— 20 miles

RATCHABURI

To Ratchaburi (30km)

To Bangkok (50km)

Phetchaburi

Hat Chao Samran

PHETCHABURI 4

Hat Peuktian

Kaeng Krachan National Park

Kheuan Karng Krachan

Cha-am

Gulf of Thailand

Hua Hin ○ Ko Singtoh
Khao Takiap

Khao Yai (1204m) ▲

Khao Tao

Pranburi

Kheuan Pran Buri

Ban Bang Pu

PRACHUAP KHIRI KHAN

Hat Laem Sala
Khao Sam Roi Yot National Park

Kuiburi

Ao Khan Kradai

Prachuap Khiri Khan

Ao Noi
Ao Prachuap
Ao Manao

Dan Singkhon

Ko Raet

Huay Yang Falls

Ko Phing

MYANMAR (BURMA)

Hat Wanakon

Ko Phang

Thap Sakae ○

4

Hat Laem Kum

Ban Krut

Hat Sai Kaew

Khao Thwe (891m) ▲

Bang Saphan

Hat Baw Thawng Lang

Hat Sombun
Ao Bang Saphan

Bang Saphan Noi

Ko Thalu

Khao Daen Noi (582m) ▲

Ko Sing
Ko Sang

See p527

Ko Wiang

Gulf of Thailand

Tha Sae ○

Pathiu

Ao Baw Mao
Ao Thung Wua Laen
Ko Jarakhe
Ao Phanang Tak

CHUMPHON

Ko Ngam Yai & Ko Ngam Noi

Chumphon

Hat Pharadon Phap
Ko Samet
Ko Mattara

4

Pak Nam
Ko Maphrao

Kraburi ○

Hat Sairi
Ao Sawi

Ko Rang Kachiu

Ka Poh National Park

Sawi

To Ko Tao (75km)

Tako Estuary

4139

Hat Arunothai

41

RANONG

Lang Suan

Isthmus of Kra

Hat Tawan Chai

Ranong

4006

Lamae

Hat Suan Son

To Phuket (850km)

To Surat Thani (105km)

Climate

The best time to visit this region is during the hot and dry season, from February to late June. From July to October (southwest monsoon) and from October to January (northeast monsoon) it rains on and off and there are sometimes strong winds. However, because this region is in between the three-monsoon season that rules northern, northeastern and central Thailand, and the two-monsoon season in the country's south, it remains drier than many other spots in Thailand, even during the rainy months. During the monsoon season, beach resorts such as Hua Hin and Cha-am will see many cloudy days, but may not be as wet and rainy as destinations further south, such as Ko Samui or Phuket.

National Parks

Kaeng Krachan (p523) is the largest national park in Thailand, covering nearly half of Phetchaburi Province and is known for its much-lauded Nam Tok Pala-U and excellent bird-watching. Khao Sam Roi Yot (p534) holds several tall peaks with views of the gulf, the coast and limestone cliffs.

Getting There & Away

There are frequent air-con buses from Bangkok's southern bus station to all major cities in the region – from Hua Hin to Phetchaburi to Chumphon. In addition, there are buses at least daily to points further south, such as Surat Thani, Phuket and Krabi, and it's easy to purchase bus/boat combo tickets to Ko Samui and Ko Pha-Ngan, among a myriad of other popular beach destinations, in Hua Hin. Trains also run between Bangkok and the region's major cities. Chumphon is a jumping-off point for Ko Tao (p591), and there is a plethora of boats, from fast to slow, to take you to the island. Chumphon has an airport with daily flights to Bangkok. Hua Hin used to have an airport, but at the time of research it was closed indefinitely.

Getting Around

Although public transport in this region is not as prolific or well organised as it further south, it is still quite easy to get just about anywhere. Buses and trains connect all the region's major cities, whereas motorcycle taxis and *sǎwngthǎew* (small pick-up truck) provide transport for shorter trips.

The exception is the two national parks in the upper southern gulf; to reach these you'll need your own wheels or will have to charter a taxi or *săwngthăew*.

PHETCHABURI PROVINCE

PHETCHABURI (PHETBURI)

เพชรบุรี

pop 45,900

For the wat enthusiast, this unpretentious city, 160km south of Bangkok, is a must-see. Dotted with an unusually large number of old temples spanning several centuries, the wat in Phetchaburi (commonly known as Phetburi, and also Meuang Phet) have made few concessions to the 20th century, let alone the 21st, and provide a glimpse of the traditional Siamese urban wat.

Also noteworthy is the forested Khao Wang hill, just west of the city centre, which has the remains of a Rama IV palace and several wat, along with a good aerial view of the area. Phra Ratchawang Ban Peun, a European-style palace built for Rama V, and the underground Buddhist shrine at the Khao Luang Caves, north of the city, are also worth a few hours of your time.

Orientation

If you arrive at the train station, follow the road southeast of the tracks until you come to Th Ratchadamnoen, then turn right. Follow Th Ratchadamnoen south to the second major intersection and turn left towards central Phetchaburi. Or take a *săamláw* (three-wheeled pedicab) from the train station to Saphan Chomrut (Chomrut Bridge) for 20B. If you've come by air-con bus, you'll be getting off very near Khao Wang and will have to take a *săamláw* into the centre of town.

Information

Internet Café (Th Damnoen Kasem; per hr 60B; ☺ 9.30am-9pm)

Main post office (cnr Th Ratwithi & Th Damnoen Kasem; ☺ 8.30am-4.30pm Mon-Fri, 9am-noon Sat & Sun)

Siam Commercial Bank (2 Th Damnoen Kasem) Has money exchange. Other nearby banks also offer foreign exchange and ATMs.

Telephone office (☺ 7am-10pm) Upstairs at the post office.

Sights & Activities

There are scores of wat in town, so take a wander if this interests you.

KHAO LUANG & KHAO BANDAI-IT CAVES

ถ้ำเขาหลวง

The main cavern in the cave sanctuary of **Khao Luang** (☺ 8am-6pm) is lined with impressive stalactites and old Buddha statues (including a large reclining Buddha), many of which were put in place by Rama IV. Sunlight from a hole in the chamber ceiling illuminates the images and makes for great photos. To the rear of the main cavern is an entrance to a third, smaller chamber, also lit by a hole. On the right of the entrance is Wat Bunthawi, with a *săalaa* (meeting hall) designed by the abbot of the wat himself and a *bòt* with impressively carved wooden door panels. Around the cave you may meet brazen monkeys waiting for handouts. The cave is 5km north of town.

Another cave sanctuary – perhaps even more magical than Khao Luang – is at **Khao Bandai-It** (☺ 9am-4pm), 2km west of town. English-speaking guides lead tours through the caves and answer questions. At the end a donation is appreciated. From Phetchaburi catch a *săamláw* (50B) or motorcycle taxi (30B) to the sanctuaries.

KHAO WANG & PHRA NAKHON KHIRI HISTORICAL PARK

เขาวัง/อุทยานประวัติศาสตร์พระนครคีรี

Cobblestone paths lead up and around the prominent hill of Khao Wang, which is studded with wat and various components of King Mongkut's palace at the top. **Phra Nakhon Khiri** (Holy City Hill; ☎ 0 3240 1006; admission 40B; ☺ 9am-4pm), the palace area on the top, was declared a national historical park in 1988. It's worth a visit to hike around a bit, to check out the views, especially at sunset, and to watch the fat monkeys lolling about in the trees. The walk up looks easy, but is fairly strenuous. If you don't feel like walking, catch the tram (adult/child 30/10B one way) to the peak.

PHRA RATCHAWANG BAN PEUN

พระราชวังบ้านปืน

Just over 1km south of the city centre, and located inside a block-long Thai military base, is **Phra Ratchawang Ban Peun** (Ban Peun Palace; ☎ 0 3242 8083; 50B; ☺ 8am-4pm Mon-Fri).

UPPER SOUTHERN GULF

PHETCHABURI (PHETBURI)

Construction began in 1910 at the behest of Rama V (who passed away not long after the project was started) and was completed in 1916. German architects hired to do the job used the opportunity to showcase contemporary German innovations in construction and interior design. The structure is typical of the early 20th century, a period that saw a Thai craze for erecting European-style buildings – seemingly in an effort to keep up with the 'modern' architecture of its colonised neighbours. Although the exterior of this two-storey palace promises little excitement, the exquisite glazed tiles in the interior, particularly on the columns in the domed foyer, are worth a peep.

Festivals & Events

The **Phra Nakhon Khiri Diamond Festival** takes place in early February and lasts about eight days. Centred on Khao Wang and Phetchaburi's historic temples, the festivities include a sound-and-light show at the Phra Nakhon Khiri Palace, temples festooned with lights and performances of *lákhon chaatrii* (Thai classical dance-drama), *lí-keh* (Thai folk dance-drama, p79) and modern-style historical dramas. A twist on the usual beauty contest provides a showcase for Phetchaburi widows.

Sleeping

Accommodation is not one of Phetchaburi's highlights.

Rabieng Rim Nam Guest House (☎ /fax 0 3242 5707; 1 Th Chisa-In; s/d 120/240B) Caters to backpackers, with a laundry service, bicycle and motorcycle rental, tours to nearby Kaeng Krachan National Park and a pleasant old-style restaurant overlooking the river. However, the six rooms are cramped and noisy.

Phetkasem Hotel (☎ 0 3242 5581; 86/1 Th Phetkasem; s/d from 170/250B; ❄) In the town's west, the good-value rooms here are clean, airy and large. The furniture is a bit outdated, the halls slightly industrial, but management is friendly. The cheapest rooms don't have air-con.

Royal Diamond (☎ 0 3241 1062; fax 0 3242 4310; 555 Mu 1, Th Phetkasem; r 800B; ❄) *The* place to stay if you need the comforts of midrange surroundings – cable TV, fridge and carpeting. Unfortunately it's quite a walk from the town centre.

Jomklow Hotel (☎ 0 3242 5398; 1 Th Tewet; r 120-160B) A friendly Chinese hotel right on the river; the rooms are rather bleak and basic, however.

Khao Wang Hotel (☎ 0 3242 5167; Th Ratwithi; r from 230B; ❄) A favourite among travelling salesmen, this 50-room place, is near Khao Wang hill. It's not as sleazy as some of the town's other Chinese hotels. The basic rooms are fairly clean and some have TV.

Eating

Local dishes for which Phetchaburi is famous include *khànŏm jiin thâwt man* (thin noodles with fried spicy fish cake), *khâo châe phétbùrii* (moist chilled rice served with sweetmeats, a hot-season speciality) and *khànŏm mâw kaeng* (egg custard).

You'll find these, along with a range of standard Thai and Chinese dishes, at several good restaurants in the Khao Wang area. A variety of cheap eats are available at the **night market**, near the northern end of town.

Other good eating spots can be found in the town centre along the main street to the clock tower. North of Khao Wang, **Lamiet** (no Roman-script sign) sells good *khànŏm mâw kaeng* and *fǎwy thawng* (sweet shredded egg yolk). It's a bit hard to find among all the other shops hawking similar fare.

Rabieng Rim Nam (☎ 0 3242 5707; 1 Th Chisa-In; dishes 30-70B) Attractive and casual, this restaurant at the guesthouse of the same name features a Thai and English menu with more than 150 items, including seafood and 30 kinds of *yam* (spicy salads). It caters to vegetarians as well.

Getting There & Away

There are frequent services to/from Bangkok's Southern bus station (1st/2nd class 100/70B, 2½ hours). The bus terminal is across from the night market. Other frequent destinations (multiple buses daily) to/from Phetchaburi include Cha-am (25B, 40 minutes), Hua Hin (36B, 1½ hours) and Prachuap Khiri Khan (80B, three hours). These buses leave from a different destination, on the corner of Th Bandai-It and Th Ratchadamnoen.

Frequent services run to/from Bangkok's Hualamphong train station. Fares (3rd class, 74B to 94B; 2nd class, 118B to 258B; 1st class, up to 753B; three hours) vary widely depending on the train and class. Taking the bus is faster, unless you include getting out to Bangkok's Southern bus station.

Getting Around

Sǎamláw and motorcycle taxis go anywhere in the town centre for 20B; you can also charter them for the whole day (200B to 300B). *Sǎwngthǎew* cost 10B around town. It's a 20-minute walk from the train station to the town centre.

Rabieng Rim Nam Guest House rents out bicycles (120B per day).

KAENG KRACHAN NATIONAL PARK

อุทยานแห่งชาติแก่งกระจาน

Thailand's largest **park** (☎ 0 3245 9293; admission 200B; visitors centre ⏰ 8.30am-4.30pm) is a rugged playground home to the gorgeous twin Pa

La-U waterfalls, along with long-distance hiking trails that snake through rich forests and savanna-like grasslands, and past steep cliffs, small caves and rugged mountains. Two rivers, Mae Nam Phetchaburi and Mae Nam Pranburi, and a large lake provide watery vistas, while abundant rainfall keeps the entire place moist and green. Animals living in this 3000-sq-km park, which covers nearly half of Phetchaburi Province along the Myanmar border, include wild elephants, deer, tigers, bears, gibbons, boars, hornbills, bantengs, dusky langurs, gaurs and wild cattle. It takes some effort to explore Kaeng Krachan (you really need your own set of wheels), but once you make it you'll be richly rewarded – this majestic place sees few tourists. The best months to visit are between November and April.

Sights

Hiking is the best way to explore the park. Try the 4km (three hours) walk from the Km 36 marker on the park road to reach the 18-tiered **Nam Tok Tho Thip** waterfall. A longer 6km hike will take you to the summit of **Phanoen Thung**, the park's highest point. From the top, lush green forest views stretch out in all directions. It can be particularly spectacular in late autumn, when the valleys surrounding it are often shrouded in early morning mist. The hiking trail starts at the Km 27 marker on the park road.

To the south, near La-U Reservoir, are the twin waterfalls of **Pa La-U Yai** and **Pa La-U Noi**; at 15 tiers these are quite spectacular, and water flows over them throughout the year. The waterfalls can be reached by 4WD from the south (closer to Hua Hin) along Hwy 3219.

Near the visitors centre is a large, scenic reservoir full of fish. You can rent boats for 400B per hour.

Sleeping & Eating

There are various **bungalows** (☎ 0 3245 9291; from 1500B) for rent within the park, most of which are concentrated near the reservoir. These sleep between four and six people and are simple affairs with fans and fridges. There are also a few **camp sites** (per person 30B), including a pleasant one near the reservoir at the visitors centre (where there's also a modest restaurant). **Tents** (150-300B) can be rented at the visitors centre.

A few kilometres before entering the park, you'll find a few other places to stay. Some blue-roofed riverside **bungalows** (no Roman-script sign; ☎ 0 1807 7264; bungalows 1500-2000B; 🅿) are located after crossing the bridge, about 850m past the police station as you near the park. Look for the small Pepsi sign on the right. About 300m past these bungalows, on the left side of the road and 3.5km before hitting the visitors centre, **A&B Bungalows** (☎ 0 1763 3824; r & bungalows 600-1200B) is less scenic but still pleasant. The grounds are grassy and there's a restaurant.

Getting There & Away

Kaeng Krachan is 53km southwest of Phetchaburi, with the southern edge of the park around 35km from Hua Hin. From Phetchaburi, drive 20km south on Hwy 4 to the city of Tha Yang. Turn right (west) and after 40km you'll reach the visitors centre (follow the 'Special Forces Training Camp' signs). You'll need a 4WD vehicle if you want to explore the dirt roads within the park.

There is no direct public transport all the way to the park, but you can get a *sǎwngthǎew* from Phetchaburi (near the clock tower) to the village of Ban Kaeng Krachan, 4km before the park. Go early as the last *sǎwngthǎew* leaves at 2pm. The trip costs 30B and takes about 1½ hours. Motorcycle taxis from Ban Kaeng Krachan to the visitors centre also cost 30B.

CHA-AM

อำเภอชะอำ

pop 48,600

Known for its casuarina-lined beach, the unglamorous seaside town of Cha-am has long been popular with provincial Thai families. Every weekend and holiday they arrive by the score in multicoloured buses that are seemingly powered by groups of inebriated young men, who dance in the aisles while pounding drums and clapping cymbals (Thais call these junkets 'ching chap tours', after the rhythmic noise the musicians produce: ching-chap-ching-chap).

Once on the beach, families plant themselves comfortably in the shade and spend the day snacking, or rip through the murky green water on jet skis. It's an authentic Thai scene, which pleases some and drives away others. Don't come looking for a cutting-edge international beach-resort experience or stunningly beautiful water. If you're looking for something a little more 'local', however, it could be a great way to spend a few days. Of course, if you arrive during the week, you'll probably have the beach all to yourself. Cha-m is 40km south of Phetchaburi and 25km north of Hua Hin.

Orientation

Phetkasem Hwy runs right through Cha-am's busy centre. This area is where you'll find the main bus 'terminal' (more like a bus stop), most banks, the main post office, an outdoor market, the train station and various government offices. About 1km east, via the main connecting road, Th Narathip, is the long beach strip where you'll be headed. The road that runs along this strip (and where most beach accommodation and services are located) is Th Ruamjit.

Information

For Internet services try **Pinto House** (☎ 0 1763 9056; per hr 60B; ☑ 8.30am-7.30pm), on a lane off the beach strip between Jolly & Jumper and the post office. The **post office** (Th Ruamjit), on the main beach strip, also offers international telephone services. The **Tourism Authority of Thailand** (TAT; ☎ 0 3247 1005; tatphet@tat .or.th; ☑ 8.30am-4.30pm) is inconveniently located way out on Phetkasem Hwy, about 500m south of the town. The staff are very kind, but don't speak much English.

Sleeping

Cha-am has two basic types of accommodation: low-grade apartment-style hotels along the beach road (Th Ruamjit) and more expensive 'condotel' developments (condominiums that usually have a kitchen and operate under a rental programme). True bungalow operations, once common, are now quite rare. Expect a 20% to 50% discount on posted rates for weekday stays.

BUDGET

Jolly & Jumper (☎ 0 3243 3887; www.jolly-jumper .info; 274/3 Th Ruamjit; r 150-500B; ☒) Owned by a couple of eccentric Dutch people, Jolly & Jumper has large, simple rooms with shared bathrooms. There's a decent restaurant below and free use of bicycles for guests. The owners take it upon themselves to help the local street-animal population, so there are plenty of dogs, cats and birds around.

Cha-am Villa Beach (☎ 0 3247 1597; 241/2 Th Ruamjit; chaamvilla@hotmail.com; r 400-700B; ☒ ☒) A decent deal, there is cable TV in all the rooms, but the cheaper ones share bathrooms. A three-room bungalow (1500B) is good for larger groups to share; one of the rooms has a fan, the other two have air-con. There's a restaurant on site, too. **Nirundorn Resort** (☎ 0 3247 1038; 247/7 Th Ruamjit; r 300-500B; ☒) Clean, cute cottages and friendly staff are found here. All rooms have cable TV, and a two-bedroom bungalow is available for 2000B.

Somkeat Villa (☎ 0 3247 1834; fax 0 3247 1229; 277/ 3-12 Th Ruamjit; r 400-600B) In another apartment-style hotel, the 60 rooms attract a largely middle-class Thai clientele. The more expensive rooms at the villa have TV, hot water and refrigerators.

MIDRANGE

Kaenchan Beach Hotel (☎ 0 3247 1314; info@kaen chanbeachhotel.com; Th Ruamjit; r incl breakfast 800-1000B; ☒) Cherry-coloured wooden buildings glow under soft night lighting at this well-designed place, giving it a bit of a romantic feel. Service is professional. It's a very good deal.

Gems Cha-am (☎ 0 3243 4060; r incl breakfast from 1500B; ☒ ☒) Good rooms facing the sea, with the usual top-end amenities for slightly less than top-end prices, are found at this towering white goliath of a hotel. Stunning views and a small pool await you on the 17th floor, and there's also a fitness centre and sauna.

Long Beach Cha-am Hotel (☎ 0 3247 2442; fax 0 3247 2287; 225/75 Th Ruamjit; r 1590B; ☒ ☒) Not a fancy resort, but it is a pretty good higher-end hotel. You can expect a TV and fridge, hot water, a fitness room and a pool. It runs shuttles to the Bangkok airport and Hua Hin.

Saengthong Condotel (☎ 0 3247 1462; saengthong condo@hotmail.com; 263/25 Th Ruamjit; r 600-1500B; ☒ ☒) Hotel has a pretty pool, and some of the rooms have views of the sea, although you'll pay more for these.

Pai Siri Hotel (☎ 0 3247 1047; 225/9 Th Ruamjit; s/d 600/800B; ☒) Very good value rooms are offered here, each comes with colour TV, fridge, minibar and hot and cold water.

Paradise Bungalows (☎ 0 3247 1072; 223/9-13 Th Ruamjit; r 300-900B; ☒ ☒) Tidy concrete villa-style bungalows are nothing special, but not bad either. They are towards the northern end of the beach road.

Jitravee Resort Hotel (☎ 0 3247 1382; fax 0 3242 3925; 241/20 Th Ruamjit; r 300-1000B; 🔀) Spacious and tidy but nondescript rooms in a row building. You'll pay considerably more for one with a sea view. Try to get a room at the back – these buildings seem to act as a funnel for traffic noise. The cheapest rooms don't have TVs or hot water.

TOP END
Remember to ask for better rates if you show up on a weekday; significant discounts should apply.

Cha-am Methavalai Hotel (☎ 0 3247 1028; www .methavalai.com; 220 Th Ruamjit; r 1640-2240B; 🔀 🛋) The best hotel in town, with a luxurious lobby, well-kept modern rooms and an inviting pool lined with *faràng*. Almost all the conveniences you would expect at a top-end hotel are here: Jacuzzi, massage, fitness room etc. There's a small private beach area and non-guests can use the pool from 7am to 7pm for 50B. There's also a good restaurant on the premises.

Regent Cha-am Beach Resort (☎ 0 3245 1240; www.regent-chaam.com; 849/21 Th Ruamjit; r from 2500B; 🔀 🛋) A truly lovely resort, it includes three swimming pools (with wading areas for children), along with well-appointed rooms, squash and tennis courts and a fitness centre.

Springfield Beach Resort (☎ 0 3245 1181; www .springfieldresort.com; 193 Th Phetkasem; r from 4500B; 🔀 🖥 🛋) Luxury hotel is south of town at the Km 210 marker off Phetkasem Hwy. Guests enjoy quaint extra touches such as welcome drinks, fruit and flowers, a bathrobe and slippers and a nightly turn-down service. All rooms have sea views, balconies, safes and long bathtubs. On the premises are a terrace coffee shop overlooking the ocean, Jacuzzi and pool, tennis court, putting green, sauna, steam room and karaoke. Across the highway, the resort has a 10-hole Jack Nicklaus–designed golf course (guests get a 30% discount on the green fee).

Dusit Resort & Polo Club (☎ 0 3252 0009; www .dusit.com; 193 Th Phetkasem; r from US$125; 🔀 🖥 🛋) Leader in Thailand's luxury chains, this resort boasts more than 300 rooms – all with private balcony – overlooking either the sea or a garden. At your disposal are a fitness centre, minigolf course, horse riding, tennis and squash courts, as well as, of course, polo.

Eating
The luxury hotels have generally fine Thai, seafood and Western cuisine at approximately the same prices as the restaurants at nonluxury hotels, so it's a good idea to try out one or two. Cha-am Methavalai Hotel (left) has a very good and reasonably priced **restaurant** (dishes 80B to 380B) serving Western and Thai food. On Saturday night an extravagant buffet is laid out (380B, 6.30pm to 10pm).

Vendors on the beach sell all manner of barbecued and fried seafood.

Da Vinci's (☎ 0 3247 1871; 274/5 Th Ruamjit; dishes 70-500B) Star of the scene – chef Cari Leander serves up elegant meals on a chic outdoor patio, with a focus on European cuisine. Scandinavians especially like it here.

Poom Restaurant (☎ 0 3247 1036; 274/1 Th Ruamjit; dishes 80-200B) Outdoor seafood place has a large shaded patio and is hugely popular with visiting Thais.

Jolly & Jumper (☎ 0 3243 3887; 274/3 Th Ruamjit; dishes 40-200B) Menu is lengthy (featuring, what else, Thai and Western food), the alcohol free flowing and a variety of rehabilitated birds cheep from their cages. With its fun décor, it's no wonder this restaurant is often full of *faràng*.

Max (☎ 0 3243 4096; 222/57-59 Th Ruamjit; dishes 70-400B) Max serves Thai and Western food in classy surroundings. Check out the outdoor dining area.

Dee-Lek (☎ 0 3247 0145; 225/33 Th Ruamjit; dishes 80-400B) Run by an English couple, this quiet restaurant serves the usual range of Western and Thai food.

Getting There & Away
All the luxury hotels, as well as the Long Beach Cha-am Hotel (p525), have shuttles to Hua Hin and Bangkok. Expect to pay 100B to Hua Hin and 800B to Bangkok.

Ordinary and air-con buses stop in the town centre, on Phetkasem Hwy. Some private air-con buses to/from Bangkok conveniently go all the way to the beach, stopping at a small terminal a few hundred metres south of the Th Narathip intersection.

Frequent bus services operating to/from Cha-am include Bangkok (air-con/ordinary

113/95B, three hours), Phetchaburi (25B, 40 minutes) and Hua Hin (20B, 30 minutes).

The train station is inland on Th Narathip, west of Phetkasem Hwy, and a 20B motorcycle ride to/from the beach. From Bangkok three train stations have daily services to Cha-am, Hualamphong (3.50pm), Sam Sen (9.27am) and Thonburi (7.15am, 1.30pm and 7.05pm). Tickets cost from 80B to 193B. Cha-am isn't listed on the English-language train schedule.

Getting Around

From the city centre to the beach it's a quick motorcycle (20B) or shared-taxi (5B) ride. Motorcycle taxis around town cost 20B. Sometimes a driver will pretend not to know where your hotel is, and take you somewhere else that offers a commission. Be firm.

You can rent motorcycles for 200B to 300B per day all along Th Ruamjit. Bicycle rentals are available everywhere for 30B per hour, or 150B per day, and are a great way to get about town. **Avis Rent-A-Car** (☎ 0 3252 0009) has an office at the Long Beach Cha-am Hotel (p525).

AROUND CHA-AM

Midway between Cha-am and Hua Hin is **Phra Ratchaniwet Marukhathayawan** (☎ 0 3247 2482; donation appreciated; ⏰ 8.30am-4.30pm), a summer palace built during the reign of Rama VI. The collection of one- and two-storey buildings are constructed of prime golden teak and interlinked by covered boardwalks, all high above the ground on stilts. Along with the high tiled roofs and tall shuttered windows, this design allows for maximum air circulation – a tropical building technique sorely missing in most modern Thai architecture.

Unlike the current summer palace situated further south at Hua Hin, this one is open daily to the public. Camp Rama VI, a military post, surrounds the palace grounds, but with proper check-in at the gate you should have no trouble receiving permission to tour the palace. If you take one of the half-hourly Cha-am–Hua Hin buses to get here, ask to be dropped at the road to this place. There are sometimes motorcycle taxis waiting around; either hail one down or it's about a couple of kilometres to walk from here.

PRACHUAP KHIRI KHAN PROVINCE

HUA HIN

อำเภอหัวหิน

pop 48,700

The beaches of Hua Hin first came to the country's attention in 1926, when Rama VI's royal architect constructed Phra Ratchawang Klai Kangwon (Far-From-Worries Palace), a seaside summer palace of golden teak, just north of what was then a small fishing village. Once it had been endorsed by the royal family, Hua Hin became a traditional favourite among Thais, especially

UPPER SOUTHERN GULF

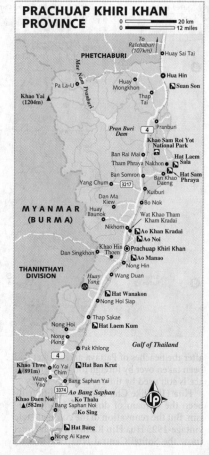

PRACHUAP KHIRI KHAN PROVINCE

0 —— 20 km
0 —— 12 miles

To Ratchaburi (107km)

PHETCHABURI

Huay Sai Tai

Hua Hin

Suan Son

Mae Nam Pranburi

Khao Yai (1204m)

Pa Lá-U

Huay Mongkhon

Thap Tai

Pran Buri Dam

Pranburi

Khao Sam Roi Yot National Park

Ban Rai Mai

Tham Phraya Nakhon

Hat Laem Sala

Ban Somron

Hat Sam Phraya

Yang Chum

Ban Khao Daeng

Dan Ma Kiew

Kuiburi

Bo Nok

MYANMAR (BURMA)

Huay Baunok

Wat Khao Tham Kham Kradai

Nikhom

Ao Khan Kradai

Ao Noi

Khao Hin Thoen

Prachuap Khiri Khan

Dan Singkhon

Ao Manao

THANINTHAYI DIVISION

Nong Hin

Huay Yang

Wang Duan

Hat Wanakon

Nong Hoi Siap

Thap Sakae

Hat Laem Kum

Nong Hoi

Nong Plong

Pak Khlong

Gulf of Thailand

Khao Thwe (891m)

Ko Yai Chim

Hat Ban Krut

Wang Yao

Bang Saphan Yai

Khao Daen Noi (582m)

Ao Bang Saphan

Ko Thalu

Bang Saphan Noi

Ko Sing

Hat Bang

Nong Ai Kaew

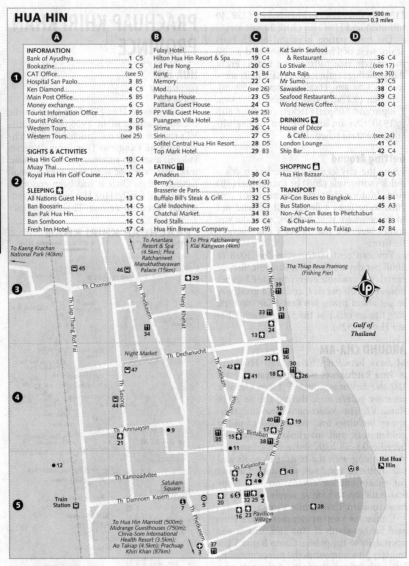

HUA HIN

INFORMATION
Bank of Ayudhya	1 C5
Bookazine	2 C5
CAT Office	(see 5)
Hospital San Paolo	3 B5
Ken Diamond	4 C5
Main Post Office	5 B5
Money exchange	6 C5
Tourist Information Office	7 B5
Tourist Police	8 D5
Western Tours	9 B4
Western Tours	(see 25)

SIGHTS & ACTIVITIES
Hua Hin Golf Centre	10 C4
Muay Thai	11 C4
Royal Hua Hin Golf Course	12 A5

SLEEPING
All Nations Guest House	13 C3
Ban Boosarin	14 C4
Ban Pak Hua Hin	15 C4
Ban Somboon	16 C5
Fresh Inn Hotel	17 C4

Fulay Hotel	18 C4
Hilton Hua Hin Resort & Spa	19 C4
Jed Pee Nong	20 B4
Kung	21 B4
Memory	22 C4
Mod	(see 26)
Patchara House	23 C5
Pattana Guest House	24 C5
PP Villa Guest House	(see 25)
Puangpen Villa Hotel	25 C5
Sirima	26 C4
Sirin	27 C5
Sofitel Central Hua Hin Resort	28 D5
Top Mark Hotel	29 B3

EATING
Amadeus	30 C4
Berny's	(see 43)
Brasserie de Paris	31 C3
Buffalo Bill's Steak & Grill	32 C5
Café Indochine	33 C3
Chatchai Market	34 B3
Food Stalls	35 C4
Hua Hin Brewing Company	(see 19)

Kat Sarin Seafood & Restaurant	36 C4
Lo Stivale	(see 17)
Maha Raja	(see 30)
Mr Sumo	37 C5
Sawasdee	38 C4
Seafood Restaurants	39 C3
World News Coffee	40 C4

DRINKING
House of Décor & Café	(see 24)
London Lounge	41 C4
Ship Bar	42 C4

SHOPPING
Hua Hin Bazaar	43 C5

TRANSPORT
Air-Con Buses to Bangkok	44 B4
Bus Station	45 A3
Non-Air-Con Buses to Phetchaburi & Cha-am	46 B3
Săwngthăew to Ao Takiap	47 B4

after the beaches of Pattaya and Phuket had been taken over by foreign tourists. The palace is still used by the royal family today.

Hua Hin, like Cha-am, has traditionally been the domain of domestic beach tourism. But the renovation of the colonial-style vintage-1923 Hua Hin Railway Beach Hotel (now the Sofitel Central Hua Hin Resort)

by a major French hotel group in the late 1980s attracted overseas attention. Major American hotel chains such as the Hilton, Hyatt and Marriott quickly followed the French example, and today Hua Hin has made it on to the international beach map. Thais and Europeans alike pass their holidays at ritzy resorts, and foreign flavour is evident everywhere. A large a number of cafés and bistros offering Spanish, French, Italian and German cuisine have claimed their share of prime real estate, and there's no shortage of expats now living and working in the city.

But evolution brings its own problems. Hua Hin is not completely clear of that seedy factor plaguing the likes of Pattaya, which is the other main beach destination near Bangkok. Girlie bars have taken over a small lane in the centre of town, creating a small sex industry. Hua Hin has almost entirely lost its fishing-village atmosphere – the fishing fleet has been moved out and hotels have invaded the piers once used for squid drying. Hotel and guesthouse proprietors have encroached on government land, completely obstructing the public's view of the ocean from the beach road.

On the bright side, a sewage treatment plant and municipal sewer system have been constructed and the shore is cleaner than ever. The main swimming beach still has thatched umbrellas and long chairs; vendors from the nearby food stalls will bring you steamed crab, mussels and beer; and there are pony rides for the kids.

The city's 5km of beaches are studded with large, smooth boulders, enough to give the beach a scenic appeal but not enough to hinder swimming. The surf is safe for bathers year-round, and water sports are available. In the city itself, a plethora of souvenir stands compete with tailor shops to give the place that modern, bustling beach-town atmosphere. The water may not be as visually stunning as it is further south, and Hua Hin lacks that party-hard backpacker vibe you'd find on Ko Pha-Ngan, but with a laid-back attitude, some of the driest weather on the peninsula and some of the region's best seafood, the town's popularity is growing every year. Today Hua Hin is a safe bet for foreign visitors, with accommodation options for all budgets and is especially appealing to families.

Orientation

Most of the tourist action takes place along Th Naresdamri, where tailors and other touts stand outside their establishments and invent imaginative ways to tempt you (any flattery regarding your current attire is probably less than sincere). Many guesthouses

line the waterfront area, as do the very popular outdoor wharf seafood restaurants, where the catch of the day is on display and waiting for your selection. There are several small soi off Th Naresdamri with old wooden guesthouses and gobs of bars with freelance Thai hookers. Only stay here if you're really trying to save every baht and if you don't need a peaceful night's rest.

The eastern part of Th Damnoen Kasem is often crowded with pedestrians – it's lined with souvenir stalls (called the Hua Hin Bazaar) and the gorgeous grounds of the Sofitel Hotel (p532). This street leads west to the train station and east to the beach, which runs about 2km along the southern half of town. The nicest stretch of sand lies south of the Sofitel Hotel.

Information

BOOKSHOPS
Bookazine (☎ 0 3253 2071; 166 Th Naresdamri; ⏰ 9am-10pm) Offers many maps, books in English and travel books – including Lonely Planet guides.

EMERGENCY
Tourist police (☎ 0 3251 5995, emergency ☎ 1155; Th Damnoen Kasem) Sits at the eastern end of the street.

INTERNET ACCESS
Internet access is available all over Hua Hin. It costs between 1B and 2B per minute.

MEDICAL SERVICES
Hospital San Paolo (☎ 0 3253 2576; 222 Th Phetkasem) Just south of town, it has emergency facilities.

MONEY
There are exchange booths and ATMs up and down Th Naresdamri, among other streets. Nearer to the bus stations, there are a couple of banks on the northern part of Th Phetkasem.
Bank of Ayudhya (Th Naresdamri; ⏰ 10am-8pm) Most convenient to the beach; it's near the corner of Th Damnoen Kasem.

POST & TELEPHONE
Main Post Office (Th Damnoen Kasem; ⏰ 8.30am-4.30pm Mon-Fri, 9am-noon Sat & Sun) The telephone office, which offers international phone services, is also here.

TOURIST INFORMATION
Tourist Information office (☎ 0 3251 1047; cnr Th Phetkasem & Th Damnoen Kasem; ⏰ 8.30am-4.30pm)

Providing advice about Hua Hin and its surrounding area, it also sells bus tickets to southern destinations. The *Welcome to Hua Hin* brochure contains useful information on hotels, restaurants and transport.

TRAVEL AGENCIES

There are loads of travel agencies, most offering day trips to nearby places such as Khao Sam Roi Yot (p534) and Kaeng Krachan National Parks (p523). Unless you're with a group of people, you may have to wait a day or two before enough people sign up for the trip of your choice.

Ken Diamond (☎ 0 3251 3863; 162/6 Th Naresdamri; ☻ 8.30am-7pm) Offers dozens of trips to nearby destinations, including waterfalls and national parks, and organises diving and snorkelling packages.

Western Tours (☎ 0 3253 3303; 11 Th Damnoen Kasem; ☻ 8.30am-7pm) Does tours to surrounding attractions, books hotel and bus tickets and helps with local transportation. There's another branch on Th Amnuaysin.

Activities

A long-time favourite golf-holiday destination for Thais, Hua Hin has recently begun receiving attention from international golfers. There are several companies in town that rent golfing equipment and organise golfing tours. **Hua Hin Golf Centre** (☎ 0 3253 1096; www.huahingolf.com; Th Naresdamri; ☻ noon-10pm), opposite the Hilton, is one such place. You can also head to **Berny's** (p533) for information. The British owner of the restaurant is quite involved in the local golfing scene. If you want to swing your club, the **Royal Hua Hin Golf Course** (☎ 0 3251 2475; green fee weekend/weekday 1500/1200B), near the train station, offers picture-worthy ocean and temple views on an elegant old-world course.

If golfing doesn't interest you, check out the beach, where there is **horse riding** (per hr 400B). Horses and their owners can usually be found on the beach at the end of Th Damnoen Kasem.

Muay Thai matches (☎ 0 3251 5269; 8/1 Th Phunsuk; 250B) take place every Friday at 9pm. These fighters aren't professionals, by any stretch of the imagination, but they put on a good show.

GAME OF ELEPHANT POLO, ANYONE?

In the last few years, the ancient Indian sport of elephant polo has been revived in Thailand, and Hua Hin's Anantara Resort & Spa (p532) hosts the King's Cup Elephant Polo Tournament every September.

The game was revived in 1982 by Englishman Jim Edwards and Scotsman James Mann-Clark, who first began to popularise it in Sri Lanka and Nepal. But it was a Swede – Christopher Stafford, general manager of Anantara Resort and a polo fan and player – who brought the game to Thailand in 2001.

Elephant polo is much like horse polo in the sense of the rules, but the differences are striking. The game is obviously slower paced, but if you tire of watching the lumbering jumbos, you can focus on the spirited pooper-scoopers who flit around the field, harvesting the animals' grassy dumps. In a royal game rife with etiquette, the audience members usually aren't too keen to be regaled with flying elephant shit.

Each elephant bears a player, who hits the ball, and a mahout, who directs the animal using voice and body. The equipment of course is much different, too: the polo sticks are 2m to 2.5m in length, depending on the size of the elephant. The umpire takes it all in from the back of the largest pachyderm.

Because the sport is still so new, the players are usually trained horse-polo players, who still have much to learn and old habits to break. For example, flapping your legs on an elephant doesn't make it go any faster.

Elephants for the tournament are treated well, seem to enjoy the game, and are provided by the Thai Elephant Conservation Centre, in whose aid the event is held.

If you're in Hua Hin in early September, it's certainly worth checking out this unique spectacle. For more information visit the website, www.thaielepolo.com. It has info on the event, as well as packages that include accommodation, tickets and VIP access. Gala dinners are held before the event and artwork done by the creatures themselves is auctioned off to admirers (proceeds go to the Thai Elephant Conservation Centre).

UPPER SOUTHERN GULF

Sleeping

There are plenty of options for all budgets in Hua Hin.

BUDGET

All Nations Guest House (☎ 0 3251 2747; 10-10/1 Th Dechanuchit; r 150-450B; 🏠) Owned by a very friendly and informative Canadian/Thai couple, this place has more atmosphere than most other cheapies and is quite popular with the backpacker crowd. The rooms are clean and have shared bathrooms. Downstairs is an open-air restaurant and bar with a pool table; if the place is crowded, there's a great vibe.

Ban Somboon (☎ 0 3251 1538; 13/4 Soi Damnoen Kasem; r incl breakfast 450-700B; 🏠) This option charms you with nicely furnished, cosy rooms in an older wooden house with a garden. A TV and hot water are included, and some rooms have fridges.

Sirima (☎ 0 3251 1060; cnr Th Naresdamri & Th Naresdamri; r 350-650B; 🏠) Built on a pier overlooking the water, this wooden guesthouse is painted up in pastels. Its highlight is a common deck overlooking the water. Rooms are small and nondescript; the cheapest just have fans.

Mod (☎ 0 3251 2296; cnr Th Naresdamri & Th Naresdamri; r 250-550B; 🏠) Right next to Sirima, and very similar, it takes up two storeys and exudes wooden charm. The upstairs rooms cost more, but are airy and have better views. The cheapest rooms just have fans.

Pattana Guest House (☎ 0 3251 3393; huahinpattana@hotmail.com; 52 Th Naresdamri; r 250-450B) Simple, good rooms in beautiful old teakwood buildings, an outdoor restaurant and tight security make this a decent choice if you can live without air-con.

Ban Pak Hua Hin (☎ 0 3251 1653; fax 0 3253 3649; 5/1 Soi Binthaban, Th Phunsuk; r 250-350B; 🏠) With extra clean rooms in a modern, apartment-style guesthouse, this option is an acceptable budget choice. The cheapest rooms only have fans. Watch out for the low ceilings!

Memory (☎ 0 3251 1816; 108 Th Naresdamri; r 200-500B; 🏠) In a long two-storey white building, this guesthouse has a locked entrance gate and good clean rooms. The more amenities you want, including air-con, the more you pay.

Kung (☎ 0 1683 2844; cnr Th Sasong & Th Amnuaysin; r 350-450B; 🏠) The four rooms here are relatively good value. Very large, clean, modern

spaces come with new furniture, TV and fridge. Bathrooms are shared between two rooms, however, and it's located well inland. The cheapest rooms don't have air-con.

MIDRANGE

Hua Hin's midrange places are typically small, sedate, modern hotels with air-con rooms and luxuries such as phones and fridges.

Fulay Hotel (☎ 0 3251 3670; fax 0 3253 0320; 110/1 Th Naresdamri; r 750-1200B; 🏠) Rooms are very good value at this narrow teak-façade hotel. All come with cable TV, fridge and if you're lucky (and pay a little more) seaview balconies. More care is taken with décor here than elsewhere, and there's a good French restaurant downstairs.

Jed Pee Nong (☎ 0 3251 2381; jedpeenong_hotel@thai.com; 17 Th Damnoen Kasem; r 1000B; 🏠 🏊) This new place is done up in traditional Thai style. The small pool is good for kids (it has little waterslides). Try for a poolside room – they come with huge plate glass windows.

Top Mark Hotel (☎ 0 3253 0404; topmarkshuahin@yahoo.co.uk; 100/4-6 Th Phunsuk; r 600-800B; 🏠) A modern orange-coloured place with a small bar area; rooms are nicely furnished with couch, fridge and TV.

Sirin (☎ 0 3251 1150; fax 0 3251 3571; 6/3 Th Damnoen Kasem; r from 990B; 🏠 🏊) A fine hotel for the price. The rooms are great and include fridge, bathroom, balcony and simple décor. The semi-outdoor area is quite pleasant.

Patchara House (☎ 0 3251 1787; 13/5 Soi Damnoen Kasem; r 900B; 🏠) Down a quiet alley, it offers good-value rooms with TV and fridge. There's hot water when the sun shines, as showers are solar powered.

PP Villa Guest House & Puangpen Villa Hotel (☎ 0 3253 3785; ppvillahotel@hotmail.com; 11 Th Damnoen Kasem; r 1000-1200B; 🏠 🏊) These places are connected to one another and both have decent midrange rooms and a garden with a pool. The beach is a mere 200m away and the welcoming staff speak good English.

Ban Boosarin (☎ 0 3251 2076; 8/8 Th Phunsuk; r 1000B; 🏠) Very large, carpeted rooms with all the basic amenities – hot water, telephone, TV, fridge and private terrace.

Fresh Inn Hotel (☎ 0 3251 1389; pmakmoo@hotmail.com; 132 Th Naresdamri; r 850-950B; 🏠) Pleasant tourist-class hotel is clean and well furnished. There's a popular restaurant downstairs, as well as a small attractive lobby.

Just beyond the Marriott Hotel, 1km south of Hua Hin, is a small low-key neighbourhood of almost identical, midrange guesthouses (ex-townhouses), a large number of which are run by *faràng*-Thai couples. None of these places are right on the beach, but it's only a short walk away. Prices (rooms from 600B to 750B July to September, from 800B to 1000B October to June) and facilities (clean, comfortable, modern) are approximately the same at almost every one. We recommend the following:

Royal Beach (☎ 0 3253 2210; royalbeach@hotmail .com; 🏊)

Thipurai (☎ 0 3251 2210; thipurai@hotmail.com; 🏊)

Leng (☎ 0 3251 3546; www.go.to/leng; 🏊)

Sunny Clown (☎ 0 3251 2936; www.sunnyclown .com; 🏊)

Jinning Beach (☎ 0 3251 3950; www.jinningbeach guesthouse.com; 🏊)

TOP END

There are some wonderful upmarket hotels in Hua Hin. You'll also find a few options either north or south of town. Some of these places add high-season supplements in December and January.

Chiva-Som International Health Resort (☎ 0 3253 6536; www.chivasom.com; 74/4 Th Phetkasem; r US$300; 🏊 🏊) This place is nothing short of exquisite, so it's no wonder Conde Naste UK awarded it 'Best Destinations Spa in the World' in 2004. The US$26 million Chiva-Som features ocean-view rooms and Thai-style pavilions on seven beachside acres 2.5km south of town. The name means Haven of Life in Thai-Sanskrit, and the staff of 200 fuse Eastern and Western approaches to health with planned nutrition; step and aqua aerobics; and Thai, Swedish or underwater massage among other therapies. Floatation tanks containing tepid salt water are on hand for sensory deprivation sessions. Rates include three meals (with wine at dinner) along with health and fitness consultations, massage and all other activities. One-week, 10-day and two-week packages are also available.

Sofitel Central Hua Hin Resort (Hua Hin Railway Hotel; ☎ 0 3251 2021, Bangkok office ☎ 0 66 2390 0410; www.centralhotelsresorts.com; 1 Th Damnoen Kasem; r from 6150B; 🏊 🏊 🏊) A magnificent, two-storey colonial-style place with three pools, expansive grounds along the beach, spa facilities and excellent service. Rooms are beautiful and luxurious, with charming old-world touches. Discounts of up to 40% may be possible during the week and in the low season, or if you book through the office in Bangkok.

Hilton Hua Hin Resort & Spa (☎ 0 3251 2888; www.huahinhilton.com; 33/3 Th Naresdamri; r from US$140; 🏊 🏊 🏊) Sleek and modern, the Hilton sports a grand lobby with floor to ceiling windows and an elephant motif throughout. There's a very posh bar, a 17th-floor rooftop restaurant and all the amenities you can expect from a Hilton, including spa services. The best feature is the beachfront pool – actually a giant collection of linked pools one of which has a swim-up bar and another with a waterslide that makes the kids very happy.

Hua Hin Marriott (☎ 0 3251 1881; www.marriott hotels.com/hhqmc; 107/1 Th Hat Phetkasem; r 5800B; 🏊 🏊 🏊) The Marriott, just south of town, claims its own beachfront territory, which includes more than 200 rooms, two tennis courts, a large pool and four restaurants. Relaxing open lounges and gorgeously landscaped grounds make this hotel one of the most comfortable stays in the Hua Hin area.

Anantara Resort & Spa (☎ 0 2477 0800, fax 0 2476 6165; www.anantara.com; rooms US$100-165; 🏊 🏊) Featuring exquisite Thai-style villas and suites on 14 landscaped acres, this place is about 5km north of town. Besides the spa and Thai massage services, the hotel offers tennis courts and swimming pools, nearby golf-course privileges and water-sport activities. Special golf, spa and honeymoon packages can be arranged.

Eating

One of Hua Hin's major attractions has always been the colourful and inexpensive **Chatchai Market** in the centre of town, where vendors gather nightly to cook fresh seafood for hordes of hungry Thais. It's also excellent for Thai breakfasts – there's very good *jóhk* and *khâo tôm* (rice soups). Fresh-fried *paa-thâwng-kŏh* (Chinese doughnuts in the Hua Hin-style – small and crispy, not oily) cost 2B for three. A few vendors also serve hot soy milk in bowls (5B) – break a few *paa-thâwng-kŏh* into the soy milk.

The best seafood to eat in Hua Hin is *plaa sămlii* (cotton fish or kingfish), *plaa kràphong* (perch), *plaa mèuk* (squid), *hăwy málaeng phûu* (mussels) and *puu* (crab). Fresh seafood is all over town, but the concentration of wharfside outdoor seafood restaurants is on Th Naresdamri, at the intersection with Th Dechanuchit.

Kat Sarin Seafood & Restaurant (☎ 0 3251 1339; 17/1 Th Naresdamri; dishes 150-300B) Authentically Thai and locally recommended, this family-run place serves the best restaurant seafood in town. Everything on the menu simply melts in your mouth, and the ambience is hard to beat – alfresco dining on the pier overlooking the sea. The crab dishes are particularly delicious.

Hua Hin Brewing Company (☎ 0 3251 2888; 33 Th Naresdamri; dishes 100-550B; ☯ 5pm-2am) In the Hilton hotel complex, this huge wooden restaurant with a shipwreck theme and open-air bar does great seafood and steaks, as well as excellent barbecue. It has three of its own microbrews on tap.

Café Indochine (☎ 0 3253 1062; 62 Th Naresdamri; set menu 400B) Indochine is a lovers' treat. The speciality is fine Vietnamese cuisine, but Thai food is also on the menu. And while the food is good the atmosphere steals the night – the split-level wooden design is lush and romantically lit inside and out. The outside garden seating area is lovely and romantic – stare at the stars from your candlelit table.

Brasserie de Paris (☎ 0 3253 0637; 3 Th Naresdamri; dishes 120-500B) A real French chef serves up real French food here. There's a good view of the sea from upstairs, and the ambience is modern and comfortable.

Amadeus (☎ 0 3251 3022; 23 Th Naresdamri; dishes 85-340B) Creative Thai and Austrian dishes are served in a stylish, glass-fronted building at this interesting restaurant.

World News Coffee (☎ 0 3253 2475; 130/2 Th Naresdamri; dishes 65-220B) Run by the adjacent Hilton, this is a Starbucks-esque café that serves Western breakfasts, including bagels, and lots of coffee drinks. You can also surf the Web for 40B per hour.

Buffalo Bill's Steak & Grill (☎ 0 3253 2727; 13 Th Damnoen Kasem; dishes 150-320B) A score for the carnivore, it grills up great Australian steaks, as well as burgers, fish 'n' chips and some veggie options. It's British-run and boasts a huge and extensive menu you could beat someone over the head with.

Maha Raja (☎ 0 3253 0347; 25 Th Naresdamri; dishes 50-300B) You'll get a free welcome drink

when you sit down in the pink-themed dining room. The Indian food is quite decent, the prices very reasonable.

Lo Stivale (☎ 0 3251 3800; 132 Th Naresdamri; dishes 140-280B) A popular place that claims to import most of the ingredients for its Italian dishes from the Old Country. For dessert, there's banana split (120B).

Mr Sumo (☎ 0 3253 2661; Th Phetkasem; dishes 40-150B) Locals recommend this new Japanese restaurant, it's a small congenial place with wooden décor and a big sushi menu.

Sawasdee (☎ 0 3251 1935; 122/1-2 Th Naresdamri; dishes 50-200B) Thai food is the best bet at Sawasdee, which gets very busy in the evenings. It also cooks up Western cuisine and American breakfasts.

Berny's (Hua Hin Bazaar; dishes 80-250B; ☯ 24hr) A British-run place with typical British pub fare. It's also the place to go for golf information. It turns into a rowdy expat watering hole at night.

Drinking

There are several *faràng* bars under European management in the Hua Hin Bazaar. Some offer the familiar Thai-hostess atmosphere, but a few bill themselves as 'sports bars' and have wide-screen TVs. Anyone looking for sleazy nightlife need not go far. Soi Bintaban is lined with girly bars doing their best to attract clientele. It's not a dangerous place per se, just a peek into the seedier side of tourism.

Hua Hin Brewing Company (left) After dinner this place turns into the town's main dance club. There is often live music and it attracts a mix of hotel guests, expats, tourists and prostitutes. It's not at all sleazy, however – it's attached to one of the classiest hotels in town.

House of Décor & Café (☎ 0 3253 0166; Th Naresdamri) A super-stylish lounge bar with dim lighting, trance music and unique crafts for sale. It seems almost out of place in casual Hua Hin!

Berny's (p533) A British-run sports bar, it concentrates especially on golf.

Ship Bar (☎ 0 7158 8470; Phunsuk Rd) Expats like this casual ex-pat run place, where you can shoot a game of pool while downing a few pints.

London Lounge (☎ 0 3253 2675; Phunsuk Rd) Similar to the Ship Bar, London Lounge also includes an upstairs sitting area. Again, it usually attracts the same expat crowd every night.

Getting There & Away

There are air-con buses to/from Bangkok's Southern bus station (128B, 3½ hours, every half hour). These leave Hua Hin from next to the Siripetchkasem Hotel on Th Sasong.

The main government bus station, on Th Liap Thang Rot Fai, has air-con buses to many destinations throughout the country. Be sure to ignore the touts here and go to the window for help and ticket purchase. There is at least one bus per day to each destination: Phetchaburi (60B, 1½ hours), Cha-am (40B, 30 minutes), Prachuap Khiri Khan (50B, 1½ hours), Chumphon (125B, four hours), Surat Thani (210B, seven hours), Phuket (305B, 10 hours) and Krabi (280B, nine hours). Frequent non-air-con buses to Phetchaburi (30B, 1½ hours) and Cha-am (20B, 30 minutes) leave from near the intersection of Th Chomsin and Th Phetkasem.

There are frequent trains running to/from Bangkok's Hualamphong train station (2nd class, 142B to 192B; 3rd-class 80B, four hours) and other stations on the southern railway line.

Getting Around

Local buses (7B) and *săwngthăew* (10B) to Ao Takiap leave from the corner of Th Sasong and Th Dechanuchit.

Săamláw will tempt you with fares from the train or bus stations to the middle of Th Naresdamri (approximately 40B), though your bags may cost you more.

Motorcycles (200B per day) and bicycles (150B per day) can be rented from a couple of places on Th Damnoen Kasem. For car rental, **Avis** has offices at the **Sofitel** (☎ 0 3251 2021) and the **Hilton** (☎ 0 3251 2888). Local agencies charge less, however.

KHAO SAM ROI YOT NATIONAL PARK
อุทยานแห่งชาติเขาสามร้อยยอด

Towering limestone cliffs, caves and beaches make for a dramatic landscape at this 98-sq-km **park** (☎ 0 3261 9078; adult/child 200/100B), the name of which means Three Hundred Mountain Peaks. Packed with lagoons and coastal marshlands that are excellent for bird-watching, the park also boasts magnificent views of the gulf coastline, if you can handle a little climbing.

Be sure to bring insect repellent along – especially during the rainy season (June to November). Rama IV and a large entourage of Thai and European guests convened here on 18 August 1868 to see a total solar eclipse – predicted, so the story goes, by the monarch himself – and enjoy a feast prepared by a French chef. Two months later the king died from malaria, contracted from mosquito bites inflicted here. Today the risk of malaria in the park is relatively low, but the mosquitoes can be pesky.

Orientation & Information

There are three park headquarters locations (Hat Laem Sala, Ban Rong Jai and Ban Khao Daeng) and three visitors centres (Hat Laem Sala, Hat Sam Phraya and Ban Khao Daeng), where you can obtain area information. A nature studies centre lies at the end of a 1km road leading north from Ban Rong Jai. There are a couple of checkpoints – on the road south from Pranburi and on the road east of Hwy 4. You'll need to pay admission or show proof that you already have.

Sights & Activities
BEACHES

Both of the park's beaches have plenty of facilities – from food stalls to picnic areas to bathrooms.

Hat Laem Sala is a sandy beach flanked on three sides by dry limestone hills and casuarinas. It has a small visitors centre, restaurant, bungalows and camp sites. Boats, which take up to 10 people, can be hired from Bang Pu to the beach (200B return, 15 minutes). The beach is about a 20-minute hike from Bang Pu, via a steep trail.

Hat Sam Phraya, 5km south of Hat Laem Sala, is a 1km-long beach with a restaurant and bathrooms.

CAVES

Khao Sam Roi Yot has three caves, which are well worth visiting. **Tham Phraya Nakhon** is the most popular and can be reached by boat (200B return) or on foot. To reach the cave by foot, hike along a steep rocky trail from Hat Laem Sala for about 430m. Once there you'll find two large caverns with sinkholes that allow light in. In one cave is a royal *săalaa* built for Rama V, who would stop off when travelling between Bangkok and Nakhon Si Thammarat.

Tham Kaew, 2km from the Bang Pu turn-off, features a series of chambers connected by narrow passageways; you enter the first cavern by means of a permanent ladder. Stalactites and other limestone formations, some of which glitter with calcite crystals as if diamond encrusted (hence the cave's name, 'Jewel Cave'), are plentiful. Lamps can be rented, but Tham Kaew is best visited in the company of a park guide because of the dangerous footing.

Tham Sai is ensconced in a hill near Ban Khung Tanot, about 2.5km from the main road between Laem Sala and Sam Phraya beaches. Villagers rent out lamps (50B) at a shelter near the cave mouth. A 280m trail leads up the hillside to the cave, which features a large single cavern. Be careful of steep drop-offs in the cave.

HIKING
For unforgettable sights of spectacular limestone cliffs against a jagged coastline, take the 30-minute step climb along a trail from the park headquarters at Ban Khao Daeng to the top of **Khao Daeng**. At sunset you may be lucky enough to come across a serow (Asian goat-antelope). If you have more time and energy, climb the 605m to the top of **Khao Krachom** for even better views.

WILDLIFE WATCHING
Some notable wildlife includes barking deer, crab-eating macaques, slow lorises, Malayan pangolins, fishing cats, palm civets, otters, serows, Javan mongooses, monitor lizards and dusky langurs. However, park officials admit it's fairly uncommon to actually spot any wild animals, possibly due to the rise in tourism.

Because the park is at the intersection of the East Asian and Australian fly ways, as many as 300 migratory and resident bird species have been recorded here, including yellow bitterns, cinnamon bitterns, purple swamp hens, water rails, ruddy-breasted crakes, bronze-winged jacanas, grey herons, painted storks, whistling ducks, spotted eagles and black-headed ibises. The park contains Thailand's largest freshwater marsh (along with mangroves and mud-flats), and is one of only three places in the country where the purple heron breeds.

Waterfowls are most commonly seen in the cool season. Encroachment by shrimp farmers in the vicinity has sadly destroyed substantial portions of mangroves and other wetlands, thus depriving the birds of an important habitat. November to March are the best waterfowl-watching months. The birds come from as far as Siberia, China and northern Europe to winter here. You can hire a boat in the village of Khao Daeng for a **cruise** (300B, 1½hr) along the canal in the morning or afternoon to spot them. Before heading out, chat with your prospective guide to see how well they speak English. Better guides will know the English names of common waterfowl and point them out to you.

Sleeping & Eating
The **Forestry Department** (Bangkok office ☎ 0 2561 2920; bungalows per 1-5 people 1200B; tents 120B; camp sites per person 20B) rents out large bungalows that can sleep up to 20 people. These are located near the park headquarters and at Hat Laem Sala. There are camp sites near the park headquarters at Hat Laem Sala or Hat Sam Phraya. There are **restaurants** at Ban Khao Daeng, Hat Laem Sala and Hat Sam Phraya.

There are also a few private resort-style accommodation options.

Dolphin Bay Resort (☎ 0 3255 9333; www.explore thailand.com; 227 Mu 4, Phu Noi; r 990B; 🕲 🕲) Under European management, this place is a steal. You'll have a choice of bungalow or hotel-style accommodation, two pools (one with a kiddie slide), a massage parlour and a good restaurant.

Sam Roi Yod Holiday Resort (☎ 0 3255 9364; www.samroiyodresort.com; 181 Mu 1 Ging; r 2000-4500B; 🕲) Landscaped gardens facing the beach provide the backdrop for villa-style accommodation. The restaurant serves fresh seafood and juices from the on-site orchard.

Bayview Laguna Resort (☎ /fax 0 3262 2165; r 750-1400B; 🕲) Bungalows are perched right on the beach, next to a lagoon and within walking distance of Bang Pu. The cheapest ones only have fans.

Getting There & Away
The park is about 40km south of Hua Hin, and it's best visited by car. From Hua Hin, take Hwy 4 (Th Phetkasem) to Pranburi. In Pranburi, turn left at the main intersection, drive 2km, stay right at the fork in the road, and go another 2km. At the police substation, turn right. From there, it's 19km to the

park's entrance and then another 4km to the headquarters at Hat Laem Sala. If you're trying to reach the park from the south, there's an entrance off Hwy 4 – turn right at highway marker 286.5, where there's a sign for the park, then drive another 13km to the headquarters at Ban Khao Daeng.

If you don't have your own wheels, catch a bus or train to Pranburi and then a *sǎwngthǎew* (40B, every half hour between 8am and 4pm) to Bang Pu, the small village inside the park. From Bang Pu you can walk to Hat Laem Sala.

You can also hire a *sǎwngthǎew* for 400B, or a motorcycle taxi for 250B, from Pranburi all the way to the park. Be sure to mention you want to go to the *ùtháyaan hàeng châat* (national park) rather than Ban Khao Sam Roi Yot. Transport can also be arranged at one of the dozens of travel agencies in Hua Hin (see p530), some of which also run tours.

PRACHUAP KHIRI KHAN

ประจวบคีรีขันธ์

pop 27,700

Colourful fishing boats and faraway limestone cliffs provide a pretty backdrop to this non-touristy provincial capital. Lying in the large muddy bay of Ao Prachuap, roughly 80km south of Hua Hin, fishing is still the mainstay of Prachuap Khiri Khan's local economy. There are no real swimming beaches in town, although these can be found to the north and south. And really there's not that much to do in this mellow place. But the seafood is fantastic, and very cheap, monkeys abound, and the town emits a kind of laid-back local vibe that almost manages to feel charming. Few tourists make their way here, so if you're looking to escape the whole *faràng* scene you just might be happy in Prachuap Khiri Khan.

The city (specifically Ao Manao) was one of seven points on the Gulf of Thailand's coast where Japanese troops landed on 8 December 1941 during their invasion of Thailand. Several street names around town commemorate the ensuing skirmish: Phitak Chat (Defend Country), Salachip (Sacrifice Life) and Suseuk (Fight Battle).

Information

Bangkok Bank (cnr Th Maitri Ngam & Th Sarachip)
Police station (Th Kong Kiat) Just west of Th Sarachip.

Prachuap Video (☎ 0 3255 0356; Th Sarachip; per hr 60B; ☷ 8.30am-9.30pm) For Internet access; near Th Maitri Ngam.
Thai Farmers Bank (Th Phitak Chat) Just north of Th Maitri Ngam.
Tourist office (☎ 0 3261 1491; Th Chai Thaleh; ☷ 8.30am-4.30pm) At the northern end of town. If you're lucky you'll get the good English speaker who dispenses excellent information on the area. If you need a visa extension, ask about the possibility of obtaining one near the Myanmar border in Dan Singkhon.

Sights & Activities

Visible from almost anywhere in Prachuap Khiri Khan is **Khao Chong Krajok** (Mirror Tunnel Mountain – named after the hole in the mountain that appears to reflect the sky). At the top of a long flight of stairs up the small mountain is **Wat Thammikaram**, established by Rama VI. From there, you'll have a perfect view of the town and bay – and along the way you can stop to rest and be entertained by hordes of monkeys. A metal ladder leads into the tunnel from the wat grounds, which are monkey-proofed with a chain-link fence and a couple of German shepherds. It's open to the public, and the dogs are friendly, though you might have to tug hard on the gate for it to open.

If you continue north along the beach road you'll come to a small boat-building village on **Ao Bang Nang Lom**, where wooden fishing vessels are still made using traditional Thai methods. It takes about two months to finish a 12m boat, which sells for around 400,000B. The industrious folks here also catch a fish called *plaa ching chang*, which they dry and store for Sri Lankan traders. A couple of kilometres north of Ao Bang Nang Lom is another bay, **Ao Noi**, the site of a small fishing village.

Six kilometres south of the city is the scenic, island-dotted **Ao Manao**, a bay ringed by a clean white-sand beach. A Thai air-force base guards access to the bay (a possible legacy of the 1941 Japanese invasion). The beach itself is 2km to 3km past the base entrance, where you often have to show your passport.

There are several *sǎalaa* (rest stops) here, along with a hotel and restaurant. You can rent chairs, umbrellas and inner tubes, and buy food and drink. In early December there's a public ceremony at the base commemorating Thai WWII heroes.

Central Buddha, Wat Neramit Wiphatsana (p489), Dan Sai, Loei Province

JOE CUMMINGS

Sala Kaew Ku sculpture park (p476), Nong Khai

TOM COCKREM

Silk weaving, Pak Thong Chai (p447), Nakhon Ratchasima Province

BILL WASSMAN

Buddha statue, Hua Hin (p527), Prachuap Khiri Khan Province

Resident of Khao Chong Krajok (p536), Prachuap Khiri Khan

Farmed squid, Prachuap Khiri Khan (p536)

Buddha statues in the cave sanctuary of Khao Luang (p521), Phetchaburi

Nine kilometres south of Ao Manao, **Hat Wa Kaw** is a pleasant, casuarina-lined beach that's even quieter and cleaner than Ao Manao. Here you'll find the **King Mongkut Memorial Park of Science & Technology** (☎ 0 3266 1098; admission free; ☺ 8.30am-4.30pm) commemorates the 1868 solar eclipse that the king and his 15-year-old son Prince Chulalongkorn came south to witness. Also on display is a US-built steam locomotive (Baldwin Locomotive Works, 1925).

Sleeping

Sleeping isn't exactly Prachuap's strong point. Most places in town are low budget and slightly dismal. North and south of town there are a few better options.

Hadthong Hotel (☎ 0 3260 1050; www.hadthong .com; 21 Th Suseuk; r 675-1060B; ❄) Right on the beach, the Hadthong is a proper hotel and the best place in town. Some rooms have windows facing the sea, and all come with fridge and cable TV. It's not exactly luxury, but the manager, Songkhram Sungsiri, speaks very good English and works to please. The restaurant isn't bad. If this is out of your budget, but you really want to stay, ask if any basement, windowless rooms are available at a discount.

Yuttichai Hotel (☎ 0 3261 1055; fax 0 3260 1755; 115 Th Kong Kiat; r 120-240B) Staff here are super friendly. The rooms are large and clean, but on the old and dim side. The cheapest share bathrooms. Try for a room away from the street.

Inthira Hotel (☎ 0 3261 1418; 120 Th Phitak Chat; r 150-350B; ❄) The eight rooms here are basic and slightly noisy and the staff not very friendly, but it's cheap and near the night market. Pay extra if you want a TV.

Thaed Saban Bungalows (☎ 0 3261 1204; bungalows 600B) Bungalows sit forlornly in a run-down, treeless lot and are very rustic in that almost completely charmless way. They're made of concrete and wood and are large and outdated, though some do face the sea; groups of up to eight can fit themselves inside.

North and south of town there's coastline to explore, along with a few places to stay.

Golden Beach Hotel (☎ 0 3260 1626; goldenbeach hostel@hotmail.com; 113 Th Suanson; r 400-600B; ❄) About 1km north of the city, this hotel is across from the beach and offers a couple of different kinds of nondescript, modern

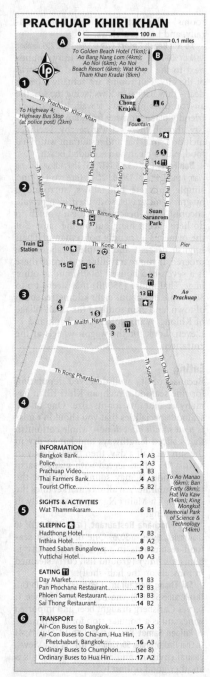

PRACHUAP KHIRI KHAN

UPPER SOUTHERN GULF

rooms – the better ones cost more, naturally, and have sea views.

Ao Noi Beach Resort (☎ 0 3260 1350; 206 Tambon Ao Noi; r 500-700B; ✂) On pleasant leafy grounds next to the beach, this place is 6km north of the city. Fan rooms are actually a better deal – they have windows facing the sea, the air-con ones just have a wall. It's a casual, friendly place far away from anything touristy, though there's a wat nearby. Facilities include a small bar and restaurant with Thai food, plus a clean and secluded beach.

Ban Forty (☎ 0 3266 1437; 555 Th Prachuap-Khlong Wan; bungalows 800-1200B; ✂) Here you'll find simple concrete bungalows, surrounded by grass and gravel, with their own private coconut-palm beach. There isn't much to do here except hang out on the sand. But the owner is a friendly policeman of Thai-English descent and simple meals can be ordered. If you're travelling in a group there is a seven-bed house (2500B) and another huge Thai house (3500B) that sleeps up to 30 people. It's about eight kilometres south of town, and 2km south of the small village of Khlong Wan, which has a bank and 7-Eleven. Look for the wagon wheels at the entrance.

Eating

Because of its well-deserved reputation for fine seafood, Prachuap Khiri Khan has many restaurants for its size. One of the seafood specialities that you shouldn't miss is *plaa sǎmlii dàet diaw* – whole cottonfish that's sliced lengthways and left to dry in the sun for half a day, then fried quickly in a wok. It's often served with mango salad on the side. It may sound awful, but the taste is sublime. An all-day market lines the street on Th Maitri Ngam, starting early in the morning.

Pan Phochana Restaurant (☎ 0 3261 1195; 40 Chai Thaleh; dishes 40-300B) One of the best seafood restaurants in town. Its speciality is *hàw mòk hǎwy* (ground fish curry steamed in mussels on the half-shell).

Sai Thong Restaurant (☎ 0 3255 0868; Th Chai Thaleh; dishes 50-160B) Another very good place. It serves Carlsberg draught beer and imported wine, and is a popular stop for tour buses.

Phloen Samut Restaurant (☎ 0 3261 1115; 44 Th Chai Thaleh; dishes 50-120B) With its sea views, casual environs and extensive menu, this is another good option.

Getting There & Away

There are frequent air-con buses to/from Bangkok (1st/2nd class 176/140B, four to five hours), Hua Hin (50B, 1½ hours), Cha-am (60B, 2½ hours) and Phetchaburi (80B, three hours) that leave from Th Phitak Chat near the centre of town. For southern destinations such as Phuket, Krabi or Hat Yai, hike 2km northwest out to the police station on the highway to catch passing buses (motorcycle taxis will take you for 30B). One exception is the local bus No 426 to Chumphon (75B, 3½ hours), which leaves from in front of the Inthira Hotel.

There are frequent train services to/from Bangkok (2nd class 175B to 225B, 3rd class 98B; six hours). Other destinations include Hua Hin (19B to 59B) and Chumphon (34B to 258B).

Getting Around

Prachuap is small enough to get around on foot, but you can hop on a motorcycle or *sǎaleng* around town for 20B. Other destinations include Ao Noi (30B to 40B) and Ao Manao (20B to 25B), the beach of which is accessible via a Thai air-force base. Motorcycles aren't permitted past the gate unless both driver and passenger are wearing helmets.

People sometimes rent out motorbikes in front of the Hadthong Hotel for 150B per day. Ask the security guards across the street from the hotel if you don't see any bikes for rent out front. The area's roads are very good, and this is a great way to see Ao Manao and sights north of town.

AROUND PRACHUAP KHIRI KHAN
Wat Khao Tham Khan Kradai
วัดเขาถ้ำคานกระได

About 8km north of town, following the road beyond Ao Noi, is this small cave wat at one end of **Ao Khan Kradai** (also known as Ao Khan Bandai) – a long, beautiful bay. A trail at the base of the limestone hill leads up and around the side to a small cavern and then to a larger one that contains a reclining Buddha. If you have a torch you can proceed to a larger second chamber also containing Buddha images. From this trail you get a good view of Ao Khan Kradai. The beach here is suitable for swimming and is virtually deserted. A motorcycle ride here costs 30B.

Dan Singkhon
ด่านสิงขร

Just south of Prachuap Khiri Khan is a road leading west to Dan Singkhon, on the Myanmar border. This is the narrowest point in Thailand between the Gulf of Thailand and Myanmar – only 12km across. The Myanmar side changed from Karen to Yangon control following skirmishes in 1988–89. The border is open to Thai-Burmese citizens only. On the Thai side there is a small frontier village and a Thai police camp with wooden semi-underground bunkers built in a circle.

Off the road on the way to Dan Singkhon are a couple of small cave hermitages. The more famous one is at **Khao Hin Thoen**, and is surrounded by a park of the same name. It contains some interesting rock formations and sculptures.

The road to Khao Hin Thoen starts where the paved road to Dan Singkhon breaks left. **Khao Khan Hok** (also known as Phutthakan Bang Kao) is a less well-known cave where an elderly monk, Luang Phaw Buaphan Chatimetho, lives.

HAT BAN KRUT & BANG SAPHAN YAI
หาดบ้านกรูด/บางสะพานใหญ่

These two low-key destinations lie about 40km and 60km south of Prachuap Khiri Khan, respectively. A string of fairly good surrounding beaches attract a handful of Thai tourists, but very few *faràng*, on weekends and school holidays, and during January and February – when waves bring more sand on to the beach. Islands off the coast to the south, including **Ko Thalu** and **Ko Sing** offer good **snorkelling** and **diving** from the end of January to mid-May. Coral Resort and Suan Luang Resort in Bang Saphan Yai can arrange half-day diving excursions to these islands.

Hat Ban Krut is edged by a road, which makes the 10km beach handy to cars and services, but detracts from a completely peaceful beach experience. The sand is nice and soft, however, and the beach is long enough not to feel crowded.

Bang Saphan Yai is nothing special as a town, but its long coastline has begun to attract some speculative development. Don't confuse this place with Bang Saphan Noi, which is about 15km further south.

Sleeping
HAT BAN KRUT

Ban Krut Youth Hostel (☎ 0 3261 9103; hostthai@ksc .th.com; dm 200-250B, bungalows 500-1000B; 🕸 🕭) Quite plush for a hostel, it has four- or five-bed dorms in a large, spiffy building complete with conference room. Basic wooden bungalows come with fan and 'outdoor' bathrooms, while fancier air-con ones sit nearer the beach and are furnished with large TV, fridge and hot water. On the grounds are a small beachside pool with Jacuzzi and a nearby bar. Breakfast is included but sheet rental is not; call the staff for a nearby pick-up (40B). It's just north of Hat Ban Krut headland.

The following are all on the beach road south of the wat-topped headland.

Ban Klang Aow Beach Resort (no Roman-script sign; ☎ 0 3269 5086; bungalows 1400-2800B; 🕸 🕭) Best option around these parts. Bungalows are well appointed and spacious one- or two-bedroom affairs with dark log walls and large verandas. They're set around wonderfully leafy tropical paths and two pools. A romantic restaurant at the resort offers nourishment, while bicycles and kayaks provide exercise.

Reun Chun Seaview (☎ 0 3269 5061; fax 0 3269 5322; 300 Mu 3; bungalows 600-1500B) Towards the northern end of the beach, it features modern, crowded bungalows with a somewhat impersonal feel; though the management is friendly. There are large verandas and solid furniture, and the restaurant is huge.

Siam Garden Beach Resort (☎ 0 1458 7877; siam garden@hotmail.com; r 550-750B; 🕸) Located at the far southern end of the beach, the rooms are large, modern and adequate, and furnished with TV and fridge. Four-person bungalows are available, and rates include breakfast. There are also bicycles (per day 150B) and motorcycles (250B) for rent.

BANG SAPHAN YAI
The following are just north of the town on the coast.

Hat Somboon Sea View (☎ 0 3254 8344; fax 0 3254 8343; 32/1 Mu 5; s/d 400/500B; 🕸) It's seen grander days, but still maintains decently furnished rooms (some large) with carpet, TV, fridge and some personality. It's across from the beach on a corner.

Nipa Beach Bungalows (☎ 0 3269 1583; bungalows 550B; 🕸) A friendly place across the street from the Hat Somboon Sea View. It has large cute modern bungalows on a sparse garden lot.

Van Veena Hotel (☎ 0 3269 1251; fax 0 3269 1548; 163 Th Mae Rampheung; r 250-450B; 🅿) Pleasant restaurant across the street from the beach is this hotel's best asset. Otherwise the rooms are unexciting, but come with fridge and TV. The cheapest just have fans. It is 300m further up the beach.

The following are about 5km south of town, and on or near the coast.

Coral Hotel (☎ 0 3269 1667; www.coral-hotel.com; 171 Mu 9; r 995-1620B; 🅿 🛎) French-managed hotel is right on the beach (700m past Suan Luang Resort). It's an upmarket place with a pleasant pool and grounds. All rooms have TV, fridge and hot water, and the cheap ones are actually the cheapest. Four-person cottages are also available. Water-sports equipment can be hired, and tours are also offered.

Suan Luang Resort (☎ 0 3269 1663; suanluang@prach uab.net; 13 Mu 1; bungalows 400-600B; 🅿) Run by a friendly Thai woman who speaks English and French, it is 500m down a side road, although the beach is still 700m further up. Spacious bungalows with mosquito proofing; wooden ones come with fans and concrete ones have hot water, TV and air-con. Motorcycles can be rented by the day (250B) and tours to surrounding areas can be organised. Call for a pick-up from the train station.

Getting There & Around

Relatively frequent buses and trains connect Hat Ban Krut and Bang Saphan Yai to Bangkok, Prachuap Khiri Khan and Chumphon. The train station is about 4km from the beach, with motorcycle taxis the only form of public transport available, and getting around can be a problem. Having your own wheels makes things a lot easier, as distances between the beaches are fairly long. Motorcycles can be hired from some of the guesthouses for about 200B per day.

CHUMPHON PROVINCE

CHUMPHON

ชุมพร

pop 50,000

There's little reason to linger in this junction town about 500km south of Bangkok

and 184km from Prachuap Khiri Khan, where you turn west for Ranong and Phuket or continue south on the newer road to Surat Thani, Nakhon Si Thammarat and Songkhla. The provincial capital is a busy place, but of no particular interest except that this is where southern Thailand really begins in terms of ethnic markers such as dialect and religion. Most people only stay long enough to catch the boat across the gulf to Ko Tao.

Pak Nam, Chumphon's port, is 10km from Chumphon, and in this area there are a few beaches and a handful of islands with good reefs for diving. The best local beach is the 4km-long Hat Thung Wua Laen (12km north of town), also known locally as 'Hat Cabana' because of the long-running Chumphon Cabana Resort & Diving Center here. Pak Nam is also the departure point for boats to Ko Tao, and many travellers bound for Ko Tao stop for a night in Chumphon.

Information

Several banks in town offer foreign currency exchange and ATMs; most are located along Th Sala Daeng.

Communications Authority of Thailand office (CAT; Th Poramin Mankha; ☺ 8.30am-9pm) About 1km east of the post office. Has international call facilities.

DK Book Store (☎ 0 7750 3876; Th Sala Daeng; ☺ 8am-9pm) Has a spinning rack full of plastic-wrapped English-language books, including Lonely Planet guides. Maps are also sold.

Fame Tour & Service (☎ 0 1676 6900; 188/87-88 Soi Saladang; Internet per hr 60B; ☺ 11am-7pm) Just one of the numerous places to access the Internet all over town. In an alley next to DK Book Store.

Main post office (Th Poramin Mankha; ☺ 8.30am-4.30pm Mon-Fri, 9am-noon Sat & Sun) At the southeastern end of town.

Municipal office (☎ 0 7751 1024; Th Poramin Mankha; ☺ 8.30am-4.30pm Mon-Fri) For basic tourist information.

Infinity Travel (☎ 0 7750 1937; 68/2 Th Tha Taphao) A dependable agency that does tours and ticketing as well as motorcycle rental. Chumphon is full of travel agencies.

Festivals & Events

In March or April the city hosts the **Chumphon Marine Festival**, which features cultural and folk-art exhibits, a windsurfing competition at Hat Thung Wua Laen and a marathon. In October, the five-day **Lang Suan Buddha Image Parade & Boat Race Festival** includes a procession of temple boats and a boat race on Mae

Nam Lang Suan (Lang Suan River), about 60km south of the capital.

Sleeping

Most people that stay overnight in Chumphon are backpackers passing through on the way to Ko Tao; perhaps this is why there aren't any top-end places in town, but lots and lots of budget options. Almost all guesthouses can sell you a ferry ticket to Ko Tao.

BUDGET

Suda Guest House (☎ 0 7750 4366; 8 Soi Bangkok Bank; r 180-450B; 🗙) Probably the best guesthouse in town, and Suda, the owner, speaks excellent English and is eager to please. The rooms (with air-con) are elegant for the price, and

there are some common rooms that allow for a somewhat social atmosphere.

Farang Bar (☎ 0 1597 7381; Th Tha Taphao; r 120-260B) With a roadside bar, which looks like it was transported from Samui beach (tiki torches and all), this place is rather hip, at least for Chumphon. Rooms are spartan, and a bit ramshackle but clean. Showers are an extra 20B. You can also rent motorbikes (200B per day), cars (1500B per day) and even boats (6000B per day).

Lemon Guest House (☎ 0 1081 6303; 110/2 Th Tha Taphao; r 90-180B) For those watching every baht, this guesthouse has great staff and clean rooms with fans. The owner is a visa lawyer and speaks English very well. Showers are an extra 20B.

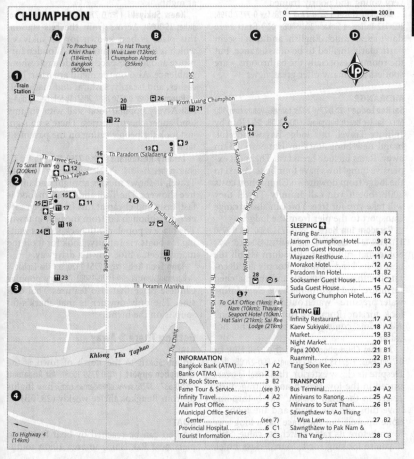

CHUMPHON

0 ——— 200 m
0 ——— 0.1 miles

To Prachuap Khiri Khan (184km); Bangkok (500km)

To Hat Thung Wua Laen (12km); Chumphon Airport (35km)

Train Station

Th Krom Luang Chumphon

Th Tawee Sinka

To Surat Thani (200km)

Th Paradorn (Saladaeng 4)

Th Tha Taphao

Th Suksamoe

Th Pracha Uthit

Th Phisit Phayabaan

Th Phisit Phayap

Th Sala Daeng

Th Poramin Mankha

Th Phinit Khadi

To CAT Office (1km); Pak Nam (10km); Thayang Seaport Hotel (10km); Hat Sairi (21km); Sai Ree Lodge (21km)

Khlong Tha Taphao

Th Tha Chang

To Highway 4 (14km)

INFORMATION
Bangkok Bank (ATM)..................**1** A2
Banks (ATMs)............................**2** B2
DK Book Store...........................**3** B2
Fame Tour & Service..............(see 3)
Infinity Travel...........................**4** A2
Main Post Office.......................**5** C3
Municipal Office Services
 Center..................................(see 7)
Provincial Hospital....................**6** C1
Tourist Information....................**7** C3

SLEEPING
Farang Bar...............................**8** A2
Jansom Chumphon Hotel.........**9** B2
Lemon Guest House................**10** A2
Mayazes Resthouse.................**11** A2
Morakot Hotel.........................**12** A2
Paradorn Inn Hotel..................**13** B2
Sooksamer Guest House..........**14** C2
Suda Guest House....................**15** A2
Suriwong Chumphon Hotel.....**16** A2

EATING
Infinity Restaurant...................**17** A2
Kaew Sukiyaki.........................**18** A2
Market....................................**19** B3
Night Market...........................**20** B1
Papa 2000...............................**21** B1
Ruammit..................................**22** B1
Tang Soon Kee........................**23** A3

TRANSPORT
Bus Terminal...........................**24** A2
Minivans to Ranong.................**25** A2
Minivans to Surat Thani...........**26** B1
Sǎwngthǎew to Ao Thung
 Wua Laen............................**27** B2
Sǎwngthǎew to Pak Nam &
 Tha Yang.............................**28** C3

Mayazes Resthouse (☎ 0 7750 4452; www.thaisouth.com/mayazes; 111/35 Soi Bangkok Bank; r 200-350B; 🛄) Rooms are small, but immaculate, and even have a little personality. There's an okay traveller vibe and the staff are warm and welcoming – although they don't speak much English. You can also arrange for car rental here.

Sooksamer Guest House (☎ 0 7750 2430; sooksamerguesthouse@hotmail.com; 118/4 Th Suksamoe; r 120-160B) The common area is nice and cosy, but the rooms are tiny, airless and barely big enough for the bed.

Suriwong Chumphon Hotel (☎ 0 7751 1203; fax 0 7750 2699; 125/27-29 Th Sala Daeng; r 260-360B; 🛄) Rooms here are clean and good value and the lobby has a snack bar, but the staff are very young and poorly trained.

Morakot Hotel (☎ 0 7750 3628; fax 0 7757 0196; 102-112 Th Tawee Sinka; r 300-500B; 🛄) Staff here don't speak much English, and don't seem particularly thrilled to be of assistance, but the rooms – especially the bathrooms – are spotless and many offer great views.

MIDRANGE
Sai Ree Lodge (☎ 0 7750 2023; tohsak@yahoo.com; 100 Mu 4, Sai Ree Beach; bungalows 600-1200B; 🛄) Run by Infinity Travel, this lodge has wonderful, brand new bungalows on Hat Sairi, 21km away. Rates include breakfast. The most expensive bungalows have four beds. A taxi to the lodge from downtown Chumphon costs 200B, but if you call Infinity Travel they will take you for free. You can also arrange transport to the pier from the lodge.

Paradorn Inn Hotel (☎ 0 7751 1500; fax 0 7750 1112; 180/12 Th Sala Daeng; r incl breakfast 450-850B; 🛄) Somewhat run down, Paradorn is still the best of its kind in town. Rooms are decorated with tacky artwork and mismatched furniture, and bathrooms have elephantine water pressure – watch out! It's down a lane; look for the Roman-script sign 'Pradon'. All rooms come with cable TV and hot water.

Jansom Chumphon Hotel (☎ 0 7750 2504; fax 0 7750 2503; 118/138 Th Sala Daeng; r 800-2700B; 🛄) Despite its classy exterior, this hotel is overpriced in the low season and outrageously priced in the high season. The bathrooms have tubs and are clean, and the lobby is done up well, but the place has a long way to go before its rates match its value. Still, if you're looking for a tourist-class hotel,

that's a small step up from Paradorn, this is pretty much your only option.

Eating
The town's large **night market** (Th Krom Luang Chumphon) is excellent, with a huge variety and lots of good street light – it's not only well worth coming for the cheap and delicious food, but also for photographs. Another good market runs north south between Th Pracha Uthit and Th Poramin Mankha.

Papa 2000 (☎ 0 1569 6161; 188/181 Th Krom Luang Chumphon; dishes 40-120B) Right in the heart of town, this large, modern patio-restaurant offers fresh barbecued seafood and sumptuous steaks among other offerings. Service is professional, and there is often live music at night.

Kaew Sukiyaki (☎ 0 7750 6366; Th Tha Taphao; dishes 35-100B) Across from the bus station, this place is best known for its sukiyaki, which is cooked at your table. Wooden furniture and lots of space provide a refreshing ambience. Also on the menu are basic Thai dishes, and, scarily, sashimi *and* macaroni.

Ruammit (☎ 0 7750 2887; 206/1 Th Sala Daeng; dishes 20B) A very popular food stall with yummy (and super cheap) curries. There's no sign, just look for people eating on the pavement tables.

Infinity Restaurant (☎ 0 7750 1937; Th Tha Taphao; dishes 35-100B; ⏱ 24hr) Run by Infinity Travel, it shows movies at night and offers free showers. The Thai and Western food is fast, tasty and cheap at this large, open cafeteria – although far from the best in town. The place is popular with backpackers waiting for boats via Infinity. Look for it off the main street, a little down a driveway.

Tang Soon Kee (☎ 0 7751 1120; cnr Tha Taphao & Th Poramin Mankha; dishes 20-150B) A very popular Chinese place that also features Thai cuisine. The only downer is that shark's-fin soup is on the menu.

Getting There & Away
AIR
About 35km to the north of town is the **Chumphon airport** (☎ 0 7759 1068). **Air Andaman** (☎ 0 5379 3726; www.airandaman.com) has flights to/from Bangkok thrice weekly (2350B).

BOAT
Ko Tao can be reached by boat from two piers near Pak Nam, an area 10km south-

BOAT SERVICES

	Fare (B)	Departure	Duration (hr)	Frequency
Lomprayah Catamaran	550	1pm	1½	daily
Lomlahk Catamaran	500	1pm	1½	Sat & Sun
Lomlahk Speedboat	400	7.30am	1¾	daily
Koh Tao Cruiser	400	7am	3	daily
High Speed Ferry	400	7am	2½	daily
Songserm Express	400	7.30am	3	daily
Midnight Boat	200	midnight	6	daily

east of Chumphon. There are several boat services to the small island; except for the midnight boat, all include transport from Chumphon to the piers. Remember that the speedboats are faster but the ride is rougher. Also be aware that the above schedule of services is very changeable.

From Chumphon, *săwngthăew* run frequently to both piers between 6am and 6pm (10B). Your best option for the midnight boat, however, is the 10pm van that travel agencies and guesthouses send to the pier – this costs 50B per person. Motorcycles charge at least 100B, although this isn't a good option unless you travel light and like to haggle.

If you somehow manage to get stuck in the pier area and don't want to return to Chumphon, try the **Thayang Seaport Hotel** (☎ 0 7755 3052; r 200-300B; 🅰), which has surprisingly good value rooms.

BUS

There are several buses from Bangkok to Chumphon: VIP (317B, seven hours, daily), 1st-class (272B, seven hours, five daily) and 2nd-class (211B, seven hours, three daily). From Bangkok, all buses leave from the Southern bus terminal. Any travel agency in Chumphon will sell you a ticket back to Bangkok, or you can buy one at the bus terminal; prices should be comparable.

Other destinations serviced from the Chumphon bus terminal on Th Tha Taphao include: Bang Saphan Yai (55B, two hours),

Prachuap Khiri Khan (63B, 3½ hours), Ranong (55B, three hours), Surat Thani (100B, 3½ hours), Krabi (200B, eight hours), Phuket (196B, eight hours) and Hat Yai (230B, 10 hours). There is at least one bus per day to each destination.

In addition, air-con minivans run to Ranong (90B, three hours, hourly) and Surat Thani (130B, 3½ hours, hourly).

TRAIN

There are frequent services to/from Bangkok (2nd class, 230B to 280B; 3rd class, 122B, 7½ hours).

Other destinations from Chumphon (all in 3rd-class berths) include Prachuap Khiri Khan (34B), Surat Thani (34B) and Hat Yai (79B). Southbound rapid and express trains – the only trains with 1st and 2nd class – are much less frequent and can be difficult to book out of Chumphon in high season (November to February).

Getting Around

Săwngthăew and motorcycle taxis around town cost a flat 10B per trip. *Săwngthăew* to Hat Sairi and Hat Thung Wua Laen cost 20B.

Motorcycles can be rented at many travel agencies (such as Infinity) and guesthouses or hotels for 200B to 250B per day. Car rental costs between 1000B and 1500B per day. Cars can be rented at Mayazes Resthouse (opposite).

Lower Southern Gulf

Lie on your back and lazily float in azure seas. Sunbathe on white sandy beaches with coconut-grove vistas by day then party amid fire throwers at a beachside bar after sunset. Relax at a secluded seaside resort and treat yourself to a spa regime. Whatever your whim, the lower southern gulf is bound to delight you.

The tropical island paradises of Ko Samui, Ko Pha-Ngan and Ko Tao are the region's biggest attractions. Ko Samui boasts long pretty beaches, happening nightlife and a range of accommodation – from cheap, beach bungalows to upmarket resorts. Ko Pha-Ngan is legendary for its full-moon parties and backpacker vibe, and year after year draws hordes of budget travellers to its ramshackle huts and party atmosphere. Tranquil Ko Tao remains the region's gem. With the area's best diving and snorkelling, it has become a sort of diver-certification mecca. If diving isn't your thing, visit to lounge on oft-empty beaches or enjoy traditional Thai massages amid stunning gulf sunsets.

Beaches are not the only assets of the region. Inland you'll find pockets of the primeval jungle that once blanketed much of Southeast Asia. Now its last vestiges are home to endangered species – from bears to tigers.

The area's southernmost provinces – Yala, Pattani and Narathiwat – once provided intrepid travellers with glittering beaches and easy glimpses into the Thai Muslim way of life. Sadly, at the time of research, violent tensions between Thai authorities and Muslim separatists were making travel here increasingly risky (see the warning, p616). That said, security situations change faster than guidebooks are published – so check before heading out, things may have improved.

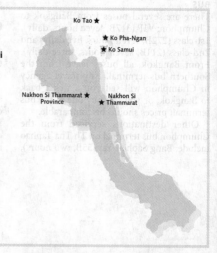

HIGHLIGHTS

- Enjoying the easy life amid green seas and pearly white beaches on popular **Ko Samui** (p555)
- Celebrating the full moon **Ko Pha-Ngan** style (p581), with trance music, fire and dancing in the sand
- Spotting a gentle-giant whale shark on a diving trip off **Ko Tao** (p591), where PADI certification is as cheap as it comes
- Watching the now rare artistry of **shadow puppetry** (p603) in Nakhon Si Thammarat
- Escaping the crowds on a picturesque beach in **Nakhon Si Thammarat Province** (p599), where local life still depends more on fishing than tourism

★ Ko Tao
★ Ko Pha-Ngan
★ Ko Samui
Nakhon Si Thammarat Province ★
★ Nakhon Si Thammarat

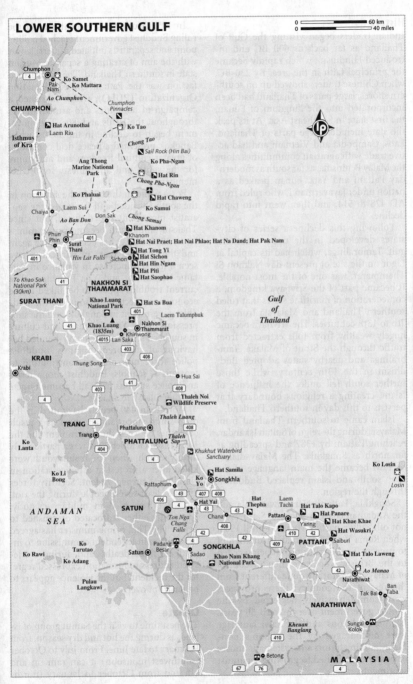

LOWER SOUTHERN GULF

0   60 km
0   40 miles

LOWER SOUTHERN GULF

History

Indian traders began visiting the Gulf of Thailand as far back as 600 BC and introduced Hinduism, which rapidly became the principal faith in the area. By 230 BC, when Chinese traders showed up on southern shores, large parts of Thailand had been incorporated into the kingdom of Funan, the first state in Southeast Asia. At its peak the state included large parts of Thailand, Laos, Cambodia and Vietnam and had active trade with agrarian communities along the Malay Peninsula, as far south as modern-day Pattani and Yala. Funan peaked as a nation under Jayavarman I, who ruled from AD 478 to 514, and then went into rapid decline.

Following this decline a series of city-states developed in the upper southern gulf. Tambralinga, which had its capital at Ligor on the site of present-day Nakhon Si Thammarat, was one of the most notable. It became part of the Srivijaya kingdom, a confederation of maritime states that ruled southern Thailand and Malaysia from the 7th to 13th centuries. The Srivijaya became hugely wealthy from tolls extracted from traffic through the Strait of Malaka. Tambralinga and nearby states adopted Buddhism in the 13th century, while those further south fell under the influence of Islam, creating a religious boundary that persists to this day in southern Thailand.

Islam came to southern Thailand from Malaysia during the reign of Sultan Iskandar, reaching Pattani by 1387 and spreading as far north as Songkhla. The Malay dialect of Yawi became the main language of the deep south and Islam replaced Buddhism through the region.

Songkhla, Pattani, Narathiwat, Yala and the Andaman coast province of Satun were not officially a part of Thailand until 1902, when Rama V annexed them in an attempt to prevent Thai territory from being ceded to the British, who were then in control of Malaysia. Culturally quite different from the rest of the country, these provinces were comprehensively neglected by the central government over the next 50 years. Islamic traditions and the Yawi language were discouraged by the region's non-Malay administrators and systematic abuses of power contributed to growing separatist sentiments.

In 1957 Muslim resentment against the ruling Buddhist government reached boiling point and separatists initiated a guerrilla war with the aim of creating a separate Muslim state in southern Thailand. The main armed faction was the Pattani United Liberation Organization (PULO), which launched a campaign of bombings and armed attacks throughout the 1970s and '80s. The movement began to decline in the 1990s, when Bangkok presented a peace deal consisting of greater cultural freedom and autonomy for the south and an amnesty for PULO members.

For a while in the 1990s the situation in the south subsided and it seemed the separatist movement had diffused, but since Thaksin Shinawatra became prime minister in 2001, PULO has became active again and the last two years in particular have seen a marked increase in violence in Pattani, Narathiwat and Yala Provinces. The current troubles appear to be linked to the economic neglect of the south by the Buddhist government in Bangkok, and the suppression of the Yawi language and culture in southern schools. The heavy-handed behaviour of the predominantly Buddhist police force may also be contributing to tensions – schools, Buddhist monasteries and police stations have all become targets for guerrilla-style attacks.

More than 440 people have died in the deep south since January 2004 as a result of clashes between the government and the separatists. October 2004 was a particularly deadly month, when 85 Muslim youth were killed after a protest at a police station in Narathiwat turned violent. Security forces killed at least seven people during the riot, but 78 others died in military custody, apparently either suffocated or crushed to death. The Thai prime minister has agreed to set up an independent commission to investigate these deaths, and during a televised address to his nation expressed regret for the incident, but the violence appears to be far from over.

Climate

The best time to visit the Samui group of islands is during the hot and dry season, from February to late June. From July to October (southwest monsoon) it can rain on and off, and from October to January (northeast monsoon) there are sometimes strong winds. However, many travellers have reported fine weather (and fewer crowds) in September and October. November tends to receive some of the rain that affects the east coast of Malaysia at this time.

National Parks

There are several notable parks in this region. Khao Sok (p553) is a thick rainforest glory land with plenty of accommodation and lazy rivers flowing through limestone cliffs. Ang Thong (p559), the setting for the perfect beach in the movie *The Beach* (although much of the movie was actually filmed on Ko Phi-Phi Leh, see p689), is a stunning archipelago of 40 small picture-perfect islands. Khao Luang National Park (p605) is known for its beautiful mountain and forest walks, waterfalls and fruit orchards. It is also home to a variety of species, from clouded leopards to tigers. Khao Nam Khang (p616) is noteworthy for its complex of tunnels used by Malaysian guerrillas until 1989.

Getting There & Away

Travelling to the lower southern gulf is straightforward. From Bangkok, the Andaman coast and numerous other Thai destinations, as well as neighbouring Malaysia, it's easy to hop on a bus or train and then catch a ferry to the islands. Aeroplanes also ply the skies between Bangkok and Ko Samui. Bus and train travel from Bangkok is generally cheap, relatively efficient and mostly takes place overnight. Almost any travel agency can sell you a combination bus or train and boat ticket to the islands, which should get you to your destination with little effort on your part. Beware of the cheapest tickets as they often prove to be scams. Pay a few more baht and you'll arrive with few hassles. For more information on travelling into and out of the region see the individual destinations, or check out the Transport chapter, p750.

Getting Around

An intricate public-transport network takes you almost everywhere. Numerous boats shuttle back and forth between Ko Samui, Ko Pha-Ngan, Ko Tao and Surat Thani, while buses and trains link Surat Thani with destinations further south. *Săwngthăew* and motorcycle taxis will take you around the islands for little cost. If you want to drive yourself, motorcycles can be rented for about 200B a day. Car rental, at about 1000B per day, is also an option.

SURAT THANI PROVINCE

Southern Thailand's largest province is home to Ko Samui, Ko Pha-Ngan and Ko Tao, as well as the stunning Ang Thong Marine National Park.

SURAT THANI

สุราษฎร์ธานี

pop 125,500

There is little of historical interest in Surat Thani, a busy commercial centre and port dealing in rubber and coconut, but the town's waterfront lends some character nonetheless. For most people, Surat Thani (often known simply as 'Surat') is only a quick stop on the way to the beautiful islands of Ko Samui, Ko Pha-Ngan and Ko Tao off the coast – if you're on a combination ticket from Bangkok you'll hardly even know you're in town.

If you find yourself with some time to kill in Surat, you can do a one- or two-hour tour of **Bang Ban Mai**, across Mae Nam Tapi from town. This easy-going village has changed little over the years, affording glimpses of the coconut plantation lifestyle as it once was on Ko Samui. Long-tail boats can be hired at the Tha Reua Klang (Middle Pier) near the night ferry pier for 250B per hour.

Information

INTERNET ACCESS

Internet Café (☎ 0 7721 7768; Th Chonkasem; per hr 20B; ☯ 9am-midnight)

MEDICAL SERVICES

Taksin Hospital (☎ 0 7727 3239; Th Talat Mai) The most professional of Surat's three hospitals.

MONEY

There's a string of banks – one on every block for five blocks along Th Na Meuang southwest of Th Chonkasem; all have ATMs and most offer foreign exchange.

Siam City Bank (Th Chonkasem) Has a Western Union office.

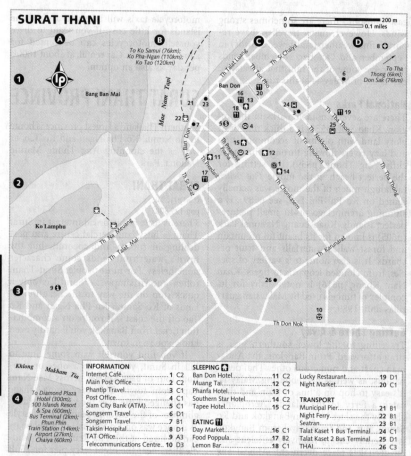

SURAT THANI

To Ko Samui (76km);
Ko Pha-Ngan (110km);
Ko Tao (120km)

To Tha
Thong (6km);
Don Sak (76km)

Bang Ban Mai

Mae Nam Tapi

Ban Don

Ko Lamphu

Th Na Meuang

Th Talat Mai

Th Don Nok

LOWER SOUTHERN GULF

Khlong Makham Tia

To Diamond Plaza
Hotel (300m);
100 Islands Resort
& Spa (600m);
Bus Terminal (2km);
Phun Phin
Train Station (14km);
Airport (27km);
Chaiya (60km)

INFORMATION	
Internet Café	1 C2
Main Post Office	2 C1
Phantip Travel	3 C1
Post Office	4 C1
Siam City Bank (ATM)	5 C1
Songserm Travel	6 D1
Songserm Travel	7 B1
Taksin Hospital	8 D1
TAT Office	9 A3
Telecommunications Centre	10 D3

SLEEPING	
Ban Don Hotel	11 C2
Muang Tai	12 C2
Phanfa Hotel	13 C1
Southern Star Hotel	14 C2
Tapee Hotel	15 C2

EATING	
Day Market	16 C1
Food Poppula	17 B2
Lemon Bar	18 C1

Lucky Restaurant	19 D1
Night Market	20 C1

TRANSPORT	
Municipal Pier	21 B1
Night Ferry	22 B1
Seatran	23 B1
Talat Kaset 1 Bus Terminal	24 C1
Talat Kaset 2 Bus Terminal	25 D1
THAI	26 C3

POST & TELEPHONE

Main post office (Th Talat Mai; ⏰ 8.30am-4.30pm Mon-Fri) One of two post offices in town.

Telecommunications centre (Th Don Nok; ⏰ 8am-8pm) Where to make international calls.

TOURIST INFORMATION

Tourism Authority of Thailand (TAT; ☎ 0 7728 8819; tatsurat@samart.co.th; 5 Th Talat Mai; ⏰ 8.30am-4.30pm Mon-Fri) A bit of a hike towards the southwestern end of town, it distributes plenty of useful brochures and maps and English is spoken.

TRAVEL AGENCIES

Phantip Travel (☎ 0 7727 2330; 442/24-5 Th Talat Mai) Backed by TAT; it's the most reliable travel agency in town for the average transport transaction.

Songserm Travel (☎ 0 7728 5124; 30/2 Muu 3, Th Bangkoong) Another good agency for island travel. Songserm has another office opposite the pier.

Dangers & Annoyances

Owing to the lucrative transport situation of shuttling travellers between Bangkok and nearby islands, Surat has attracted its share of dubious travel agencies. Several companies in the area have been known to provide poor service and engage in outrageous scams, including bait-and-switch tactics with buses, particularly between Ko Samui and Hat Yai or Malaysia – you may pay for an air-con bus and find yourself sweltering on a regular one. There are scores of travel agencies in town, so if you don't trust the staff at one place, move on. Once you decide to go with an agency, ask exactly when the pick-up will happen, discuss the quality of the vehicle and work out a plan if pick-up doesn't happen on time or in the proper vehicle.

Festivals & Events
Two major events in Surat Thani Province take place in mid-October. **Chak Phra** (Pulling of the Buddha Image) and **Thawt Pha Pa** (Laying-Out of Forest Robes) celebrations occur on the same day (the first day of the waning moon in the 11th lunar month) at the end of the Buddhist Rains Retreat.

Thawt Pha Pa begins at dawn with the offering of new monastic robes to the monks, while Chak Phra takes place during the day and evening. As part of Chak Phra, local lay devotees place sacred Buddha images on boats for a colourful procession along Mae Nam Tapi. A similar land-borne procession uses trucks and hand-pulled carts.

Lots of food stalls and musical performances, including *lí-keh* (folk plays featuring dancing, comedy, melodrama and music) are set up for the occasion.

Sleeping
BUDGET
At some of Surat Thani's cheaper hotels, business consists largely of 'short-term' (by the hour) trade. This doesn't make them any less suitable as regular hotels – but there's likely to be more noise as guests arrive and depart frequently.

If you're on a tight budget, it may be better to zip straight through Surat Thani via the night ferry (see p550). If the weather is nice, you may even sleep better this way. But if there's a chance of any rain beware – you will be in for a sleepless, wet night on the boat.

Ban Don Hotel (☎ 0 7727 2167; 268/2 Th Na Meuang; r from 200B; 🅿) Consistently the best budget value in Surat, the rooms here are small yet extremely clean and those with air-con are a great deal. The entrance is through a Chinese restaurant – quite good for inexpensive rice and noodle dishes.

Phanfa Hotel (☎ 0 7727 2287; 247/2-5 Th Na Meuang; r 180-280B) Not far from the bus station, rooms at the Phanfa are large, though slightly run down, with Thai baths and solid old furniture.

MIDRANGE
Surat's midrange hotels don't cost much more than it's budget options, but are considerably better and less likely to attract short-term clients.

100 Islands Resort & Spa (☎ 0 7720 1150; www .roikoh.com; 19/6 Muu 3, Bypass Rd; r 590-990B; 🅿 🅿) Gorgeous sunny rooms and a lagoon pool help make this sort of teak-wood palace one of the best deals in southern Thailand. Once inside you'll forget you're across the street from an ugly Tesco-Lotus shopping complex. Take a *săwngthăew* there; if the driver doesn't know it, say 'Tesco-Lotus' (and get him to stop before he makes the U-turn to the Tesco-Lotus side of the highway).

Muang Tai (☎ 0 7727 2559; 390-392 Th Talat Mai; r from 240B; 🅿) Good-sized rooms with outdated furniture are found here. The beds are more comfortable than most in this price range.

Tapee Hotel (☎ 0 7727 2575; fax 0 7728 2433; 100 Th Chonkasem; r from 300B; 🅿) Rooms at the Tapee are large and clean, although on the worn side. It's popular with travelling Thai businesspeople and gets noisy after the karaoke bars close.

TOP END
Surat Thani also has a number of more upmarket hotels priced slightly lower than those in other provincial capitals.

Southern Star Hotel (☎ 0 7721 6414; fax 0 7721 6427; 253 Th Chonkasem; r incl breakfast 900-1100B; 🅿) All of the 150 rooms here, which are relatively elegant in a sort of Best Western fashion, feature sitting areas. Other facilities include a coffee shop, restaurant, sky lounge and karaoke pub. This is home to the biggest disco in southern Thailand, the Star Theque.

Diamond Plaza Hotel (☎ 0 7720 5333; fax 0 7720 5352; Muu 2, 83/27 Th Sriwichai; r 1180-5600B; 🅿 🅿) This place starts with a posh lobby that leads up to 300 modern, fine and quiet rooms. Service is top-rate, there is a fitness centre and the hotel restaurant has live music.

Eating
The **night market** (Th Ton Pho) is *the* place for fried, steamed, grilled or sautéed delicacies – look for the crunchy insect titbits. You may also see large trays of greens on diners' tables – this is southern-style *khànŏm jiin*

(curry noodles served with vegetables and herbs).

During the day, many food stalls near the bus terminal specialise in *khâo kài òp* (marinated baked chicken on rice), which is very tasty. During mango season, street vendors in Surat sell incredible *khâo nĭaw mámûang* (coconut-sweetened sticky rice with sliced ripe mango). Otherwise, eating options are rather limited.

Lemon Bar (☎ 0 1893 0202; Th Na Meuang; dishes 40-120B) Hip and colourful, it's a pleasant place to dine on Vietnamese, Thai and Chinese dishes.

Lucky Restaurant (☎ 0 7727 3267; 452/84-85 Th Tha Thong; dishes 50-300B) Lucky's cooks up curries, meats and seafood, among other Thai dishes. It has a comfortable, dim environment – like the inside of a log cabin. There are a few veggie options.

Food Poppula (☎ 0 7727 2969; Th Talat Mai; dishes 40-120B) For a quick and casual bite, head to this very good Chinese restaurant.

Getting There & Away

AIR
Thai Airways International (THAI; ☎ 0 7727 2610; 3/27-28 Th Karunarat) serves Bangkok (2300B to 4450B, 70 minutes, twice daily).

BOAT
For full details on getting from Surat Thani to the islands, see transport sections of the specific destinations. There are nightly ferries to Ko Tao (400B, eight hours), Ko Pha-Ngan (200B, seven hours) and Ko Samui (150B, six hours). All leave from the night-ferry pier at 11pm. These are freighters, not luxury boats; bring food and water, and watch your bags.

Seatran (☎ 0 7727 5060; 136 Th Ban Don), whose office is below Mo Or Guest House near the night-ferry pier, has a bus/boat combination to Ko Samui (150B, 3½ hours, six daily).

Raja Ferry (☎ 0 7737 4523) operates bus/boat combinations to Ko Samui (140B, 2½ hours, seven daily), Ko Tao (500B, four hours, two daily) and Ko Pha-Ngan (250B, 3½ hours, three daily). Buy tickets at **Phantip Travel** (☎ 0 7727 2230; 442/24-5 Th Talat Mai).

BUS & MINIVAN
Most long-distance public buses run from the Talat Kaset bus terminals 1 and 2. Aircon minivans leave from Talat Kaset 2; they

BUS DESTINATIONS TO/FROM SURAT THANI

Destination	Fare (B)	Duration (hr)
Bangkok		
VIP	590	10
1st class	380	10
2nd class	295	11
ordinary	211	11
Hat Yai		
1st class	380	4
2nd class	295	5
minivan	180	3½
Krabi		
1st class	180	3
2nd class	80	4
minivan	120	2
Nakhon Si Thammarat		
1st class	90	2
2nd class	45	2
minivan	120	2
Phang-Nga		
1st class	130	3
2nd class	110	4
Phuket		
1st class	160	5
2nd class	105-120	6
minivan	180	4
Ranong		
1st class	180	4
2nd class	80	5
minivan	130	3½
Trang		
2nd class	120	3

tend to have more-frequent departures than buses, though they're not always cheaper.

There's a bus terminal 2km west of town (on the way to Phun Phin train station), but it's used less frequently than the two terminals in town. To get into town from there take an orange local bus (9B), which comes by every 10 minutes. Just make sure it's going back into town rather than out to Phun Phin (it does a loop).

Shop around if buying bus or minivan tickets from travel agencies, as some may quote inflated prices and/or give you false information, see p548 for more on this.

TRAIN
The closest train station to Surat Thani is in Phun Phin, 14km west of town. For more in-

formation on getting from the train station, see the boxed text, below. There are several trains from Bangkok. Fares are fan/air-con 167/237B in 3rd class, 308/448B in 2nd class (seat), 408/578B in 2nd-class sleeper (upper), 458/684B in 2nd class sleeper (lower) and 1119B in 1st class. The trip takes around 12 hours, so if you take an early evening train from Bangkok you'll arrive in Surat Thani in the morning. If you want a sleeper berth, it's worth shelling out the extra baht for the lower berth, you'll have a window, which makes sleeping in the fan compartments quite pleasant (you'll get a constant breeze).

The station has a 24-hour left-luggage room that charges 10B a day for the first five days, 15B a day thereafter. The advance-ticket office is open 6am to 6pm (with a 11am to noon lunch break) daily. Many travel agencies in town (including Phantip Travel) book advance train reservations, so if you have a fixed return schedule you can make an onward reservation *before* getting on the boat to Ko Samui. If you don't know when you're coming back to the mainland, you can book a train ticket from a travel agency on Samui itself.

Getting Around

Air-con vans to/from the airport cost 70B to 80B per person. They'll drop you off at your hotel; buy tickets at travel agencies or the **THAI office** (☎ 0 7727 2610; 3/27-28 Th Karunarat).

Taxis from Surat Thani to Don Sak pier cost 500B; Phantip Travel runs frequent vans and charges 50B per person.

Around town, *sǎwngthǎew* cost 10B, while *sǎamláw* (three-wheeled pedicabs) charge 20B to 30B.

AROUND SURAT THANI
Chaiya
ไชยา

pop 12,000

The little-visited town of Chaiya, 60km north of Surat Thani, makes a great day trip (especially if you find yourself stuck in Surat for a night). Calm and friendly, this tiny place offers a glimpse into small-town life not often found in this region. Browse the vibrant day market and small stores or stop into one of the plentiful Chinese teashops. It's easiest to take care of monetary and postal needs in Surat Thani, but there are a few Internet cafés on Chaiya's main street.

One of the oldest cities in Thailand, Chaiya dates back to the Srivijaya empire. The name may in fact be a contraction of Siwichaiya, the Thai pronunciation of the city that was a regional capital between the 8th and 10th centuries. Prior to this time,

LOWER SOUTHERN GULF

ARRIVING IN SURAT THANI BY TRAIN

Most travellers arriving by train don't plan on staying long, which is fine because there really isn't much to do in Surat. They want to go to Phuket, Phang-Nga or the Krabi area (all on the Andaman coast), which is also fine since there's lots to do in these places. But first, they must negotiate busy little Phun Phin...

The first thing you must realise is you'll actually be arriving in Phun Phin, the town where Surat Thani's train station is located. It's approximately 14km west of Surat. The second is that you don't necessarily have to leave Phun Phin to reach your Andaman coast beach destination. There are buses directly from the train station to Phuket, Phang-Nga and Krabi. They may not be air-con and their departures may not fit your arrival schedule, but if you catch the right bus at the right time you could save yourself a few hours' worth of back-and-forth-to-Surat travel time. Look for the big white wall just south of the train station – there's a Pepsi symbol and sign proclaiming 'Coffee shop and fast food'. This is where those buses stop.

Of course, if you've missed the last bus (or Ko Samui is your actual destination – it's on the *other* coast) you'll have to hike it into Surat after all, as there are more transport options there. This isn't hard to do, as local orange buses chug between Phun Phin and Surat (9B, 25 minutes, every 10 minutes).

If you decide you want to stay the night in Phun Phin, there is one sleeping option.

Queen (☎ 0 7731 1003; 916/10-13 Th Mahasawat; r 200-400B; ✗) This place is around the corner from the train station, on the road to Surat Thani. Some of the budget rooms are brighter, larger and less dingy than others, so see a couple before deciding.

the area was a stop on the Indian trade route in Southeast Asia. Many Srivijaya artefacts in the National Museum in Bangkok were found in Chaiya, including a famous Avalokiteshvara Bodhisattva bronze that's considered a masterpiece of Buddhist art.

SIGHTS

Most people visit Chaiya for the excellent monthly meditation retreats at **Wat Suan Mokkhaphalaram** (Wat Suanmok; ☎ 0 7743 1522), a famous Buddhist meditation centre. A very calm and nonshowy modern forest wat, it was founded by Ajahn Buddhadasa Bhikkhu, arguably Thailand's most famous monk. Born in Chaiya in 1906, Buddhadasa was ordained as a monk when he was 21 years old. He spent many years studying the Pali scriptures and then retired to the forest for six years of solitary meditation. Returning to ecclesiastical society, he was made abbot of Wat Phra Boromathat, a high distinction, but conceived of Suanmok as an alternative to orthodox Thai temples. During Thailand's turbulent 1970s he was branded a communist because of his critiques of capitalism, which he saw as a catalyst for greed. Buddhadasa died in July 1993 after a long illness.

Buddhadasa's philosophy was ecumenical in nature, comprising Zen, Taoist and Christian elements, as well as the traditional Theravada schemata. Today, the hermitage is spread over 120 hectares of wooded hillside and features huts for up to 70 monks, a 'spiritual theatre' and a museum-library. This latter building has bas-reliefs on the outer walls that are facsimiles of sculptures at Sanchi, Bharhut and Amaravati in India. The interior walls feature modern Buddhist painting – eclectic to say the least – executed by the resident monks.

The retreats cost 1200B for 10 days of teaching, food and accommodation. Just show up on the evening of the last day of any given month to sign up (retreats are always during the first 10 days of each month). Living like a monk for 10 days is not easy. In fact, it could be the most challenging – and memorable – thing you've ever done.

The wat is 7km from Chaiya and not visible from the highway. *Săwngthăew* run from the Chaiya train station for 10B or you can hire a motorcycle taxi for 20B anywhere along Chaiya's main street.

The restored **Borom That Chaiya**, a stupa at Wat Phra Boromathat, about 1km from Chaiya train station, is one of the few surviving examples of Srivijaya architecture. Strongly resembling the Buddhist stupas of central Java, the stupa is formed by a stack of ornate cubes bearing relief images of Kala (Hindu-Buddhist god of time and death), a peacock (a symbol for the sun), Airavata (three-headed elephant mount of Indra), Indra and the Buddha. In the courtyard surrounding the stupa are several pieces of sculpture from the region, including an unusual two-sided *yoni* (the uterus-shaped pedestal that holds the Shivalingam, or phallic shrine), *reusĭi* (hermit sages) performing yoga, and several Buddha images. If you're looking for other attractions head to the small, but well-presented, **National Museum** (☎ 0 7743 1066; admission 30B; ☺ 9am-4pm Wed-Sun), displaying historic and prehistoric artefacts of local origin, as well as regional handicrafts and a shadow-puppet exhibit.

About 300m from Chaiya down a side road just off the highway is Wat Wiang, which contains Chaiya's **Folklore Museum** (donations appreciated; ☺ 8am-9pm). You may need to get a friendly monk to open it up and show you the mishmash of items: old instruments, china, pottery, shadow puppets, work implements, buffalo-hide sandals and a ceramic opium pillow.

SLEEPING

Chaiya is easily seen as a day trip from Surat; if you want to linger longer, you can request permission from the monks to stay in the guest quarters at Wat Suanmok. Or you can try Chaiya's only hotel.

Udomlap Hotel (☎ 0 7743 1123; r 150-400B; ✴) Friendly and modern, this is a decent hotel. The cheapest rooms share bathrooms in an old wing, while the pricier rooms are in a more modern wing. Many *faràng* stay here for the meditation retreat at Wat Suanmok.

GETTING THERE & AWAY

If you're going to Surat Thani by train from Bangkok, you can get off at the small Chaiya train station, then later catch another train to Phun Phin, Surat's nearest station. If you're already in Surat the fastest way to get to Chaiya is to catch a *săwngthăew* from the Talat Kaset 2 bus terminal (30B, one hour) in the centre of town. A convenient way to

see the region is to take this *săwngthăew*
first to Wat Suanmok (30B), then another
one to Wat Phra Boromathat (10B), then
walk on to Wat Kaew and Wat Wiang (10
to 15 minutes), and next walk to Chaiya
(five minutes). Motorcycle taxis between
Surat and Chaiya cost 50B.

Săwngthăew going back to Surat may end
their route at Phun Phin; from there Surat
is only a 9B bus ride (or 10B *săwngthăew*
ride) away.

KHAO SOK NATIONAL PARK

อุทยานแห่งชาติเขาสก

Lying amid thick native rainforest and
rugged mountains is this stunning 646-sq-
km **park** (☎ 0 7739 5025; www.khaosok.com; admission 200B), which is well worth going out of
your way to visit. Waterfalls tumble over
spectacular soaring limestone cliffs, while
hiking trails follow rivers, twisting their
way through the forests and past an island-
studded lake. Enjoy the solitude as your feet
squish through deep brown dirt and the sun
filters through the gnarled and ancient trees.
Keep an eye out for the plethora of wildlife
the park shelters – wild elephants, leopards,
serow, banteng, guar, dusky langurs and,
if you're really lucky, tigers and Malayan
sun bears, not to mention more than 180
species of bird.

Established in 1980, Khao Sok lies in the
western part of Surat Thani Province, off
Rte 401 about a third of the way from Takua
Pa to Surat Thani. According to Thom
Henley, author of the highly informative
Waterfalls and Gibbon Calls, the Khao Sok
rainforest is in fact a remnant of a 160-
million-year-old forest ecosystem that is
much older and richer than the forests of
the Amazon and central African regions.

Khao Sok is connected to two other national parks, Kaeng Krung and Phang-Nga,
as well as the Khlong Saen and Khlong
Nakha wildlife sanctuaries. Together, these
reserves form the largest contiguous nature
preserve – around 4000 sq km – on the Thai
peninsula. A major watershed for the south,
the park is filled with lianas, bamboo, ferns
and rattan, including the giant rattan (*wăi
tào phráw*) with a stem more than 10cm in
diameter. A floral rarity in the park is the
Rafflesia kerri meyer, known to the Thais as
bua phút (wild lotus), the largest flower in
the world. Found only in Khao Sok and an

adjacent wildlife sanctuary (different varieties of the same species are present in Malaysia and Indonesia), mature specimens can
reach 80cm in diameter. The flower has no
roots or leaves of its own; instead it lives
parasitically inside the roots of the liana, a
jungle vine. From October to December,
buds burst forth from the liana root and
swell to football size. When the bud blooms
in January and February it emits a potent
stench resembling rotten meat, which attracts pollinating insects.

Orientation & Information

The park headquarters and visitors centre
are 1.8km off Rte 401, close to the Km 109
marker.

The best time of year to visit Khao Sok is
December to May, when trails are less slippery, river crossings easier and river-bank
camping safer due to the lower risk of flash
flooding. On the other hand, during the
June to November wet season you're more
likely to see Malayan and Asiatic black
bears, civets, slow loris, wild boar, gaur,
deer and wild elephants, and perhaps even
tigers, along the trail network. During dry
months the larger mammals tend to stay
near the reservoir in areas without trails.

Leeches are quite common in certain
areas of the park, so make sure to take the
usual precautions – wear closed shoes when
hiking and apply plenty of repellent (see
also p769).

Sights & Activities

Various trails from the visitors centre lead to
the waterfalls of **Sip-Et Chan** (4km), **Than Sawan**
(9km) and **Than Kloy** (9km), among other
destinations. A rough map showing trails
and sights can be obtained at the visitors
centre, or any guesthouse in the area will
happily arrange guided tours and hikes.

An hour's drive east of the visitors centre
is the vast **Chiaw Lan Lake**, 165km at its longest point. It was created in 1982 by the
95m-high, 700m-long, shaled-clay dam of
Ratchaprapha (Kheuan Ratchaprapha or
Kheuan Chiaw Lan). Limestone outcrops
protruding from the lake reach a height
of 960m, over three times higher than the
formations in the Phang-Nga area. A cave
known as **Tham Nam Thalu** contains striking
limestone formations and subterranean
streams, while **Tham Si Ru** features four

LOWER SOUTHERN GULF

converging passageways used as a hideout by communist insurgents between 1975 and 1982. **Tham Khang Dao**, high on a limestone cliff face, is home to many bat species. All three caves can be reached on foot from the southwestern shore of the lake. You can rent boats from local fishermen to explore the coves, canals, caves and cul-de-sacs along the lakeshore, while three floating raft houses belonging to the national park provide overnight accommodation.

Sleeping & Eating

Along the road from Hwy 401 to the visitors centre and down a dirt side road, are several private, simple guesthouses and their restaurants. All have rooms with fans; there are no rooms with air-con in these parts. Prices rise in the high season from about November to February. The following accommodation options are on the highway.

Khao Sok Rainforest Resort (☎ 0 7739 5006; www.krabidir.com/khaosokrainforest; bungalows 400-600B) Right on the river, this place has simple riverside bungalows and a pleasant garden. Slightly fancier mountain bungalows are also available, but require a little bit of a hike. The resort is big on conservation and offers slide lecture programmes and tips on low-impact hiking. It also runs rehabilitation and forest-restoration projects.

Bamboo House II (☎ 0 7739 5013; r 300-500B) On the other side of the river from the Rainforest Resort, Bamboo House II has bright, well-built concrete and brick bungalows with tiled floors and verandas.

Pantoorat Mountain Lodge (☎ 0 6268 7399; tree houses/bungalows 300/500B) Bungalows and tree houses are built on stilts here, and are simple affairs with mosquito nets. The restaurant and surroundings are pleasant, and all sorts of tours can be arranged by staff.

Lotus (☎ 0 7739 5012; bungalows 100-200B) Lotus is a good option if you're looking for super cheap. Bungalows are small, no-frills affairs and come with mosquito nets.

Treetop River Huts (☎ 0 7742 1155; bungalows 250-700B) If you want to be right next to the visitors centre, then head to Treetop River Huts. This place offers a wide variety of bungalows in a jungle-like area.

The following are on the dirt side road leading off the highway.

Our Jungle House (☎ 0 9909 6814; www.losthori zonsasia.com; bungalows 400-600B) With a brilliant location across from a limestone cliff this Australian-run place is another ecotourism venture. It offers a variety of riverside bungalows and tree houses with simple décor and oil lights set on jungle-like paths along a river. The restaurant serves Western and Thai food, including a nightly Thai buffet with lots of fresh fruit.

Art's Riverview Jungle Lodge (☎ 0 7739 5009; bungalows 350-550B) Art's has a pleasant range of simple, solid and airy rooms with mosquito nets. The more expensive ones have verandas and hammocks, and all are in a beautiful, tranquil and lush setting. You can watch wild macaques from the riverside restaurant.

Nung House (☎ 0 7739 5024; www.nunghouse.com; bungalows 150-300B) There's a range of basic bungalows on a large grassy lot, including a true tree house by the river. Some are newer than others, so see a couple before deciding. The rustic open-air restaurant and affiliated Nirvana Bar are pleasant spots to pass a few hours. The bar hosts nightly barbecues.

Bamboo House (☎ 0 1787 7484; bungalows 100-600B) A wide variety of rustic bungalows are found here. There are also two very basic ones precariously overlooking the river.

Near the visitors centre you can pitch your own **tent** (2 people 30B) or rent **bungalows** (1-4 people 800B, 5-8 people 1000B). For reservations, call ☎ 0 7739 5025. A few restaurants nearby provide nourishment. At Chiaw Lan Lake, two substations have **floating raft houses** (☎ 0 7729 9318; houses per person 500B). Call to reserve these raft houses; rates include meals.

Getting There & Around

Khao Sok is about 100km from Surat Thani. Transport to the park by minivan from Surat Thani (70B, one hour, at least twice daily) can be arranged through most travel agents in Surat, but be aware that some minivan companies work with specific bungalow outfitters and will try to convince you to stay at that place. Otherwise, from the Surat Thani area you can catch a bus going towards Takua Pa – you'll be getting off well before hitting this destination (tell the bus driver 'Khao Sok'). You can also come from the west coast by bus, but you'll have to go to Takua Pa first. Buses from Takua Pa to the park (25B, one hour, nine daily) drop you off on the highway, 1.8km from the visitors centre. If guesthouse touts don't meet you, you'll have to walk to your chosen guesthouse (from 50m to 2km).

To arrive at Chiaw Lan Lake, go east on Rte 401 from the visitors centre and take the turn-off between the Km 52 and Km 53 markers, at Ban Takum. It's another 14km to the lake. If you don't have your own wheels you'll have to bus it to Ban Takum, then hope to hitch a ride to the lake. The best option without private transport would be to join a tour, which any guesthouse can arrange for 1000B (2000B to 2500B with an overnight stay).

KO SAMUI
เกาะสมุย
pop 39,000
In 1971 two tourists arrived on Thailand's third-largest island via a coconut boat from Bangkok and stumbled upon paradise – white-sand beaches with palms blowing in the wind; clear green seas sparkling in the sunlight with ripples made for floating; a picture perfect background of lush green hills and rich brown roads interspersed with rough wooden structures.

More than 30 years later Ko Samui is still going strong. Part of an archipelago that includes 80 smaller islands, of which only six – Pha-Ngan, Ta Loy, Tao, Taen, Ma Ko and Ta Pao – are also inhabited, Ko Samui has retained a legendary status among travellers to Asia for the past quarter century. It wasn't until the late 1980s, however, that the rough-hewn huts expanded into classy resorts and spas and the wander-the-world backpackers were joined by throngs of up-market holidaymakers, placing the island firmly on the map with similar getaways such as Goa and Bali – hippy island paradises still providing all the creature comforts of home.

Today Ko Samui offers something for everybody – the cheap fan bungalows share beachfront property with places boasting beautifully decorated rooms, crisp white sheets, lush gardens and lavish pools. There are crowded beaches where young boys peddle coconuts and mangoes to oil-slicked, bikini-clad tourists and jet skis churn up white wash on clear seas. There are isolated spots where serenity and seclusion are the name of the game and you can escape the sun in simple air-con cottages and check out the latest MTV video. There are

cheap food stalls and top-class restaurants, crowded modern shopping strips with Starbucks, McDonald's and store after store featuring knock-off Von Dutch T-shirts and Gucci sunglasses, and stretches of rough dirt roads and ramshackle huts. Western bars dish up burgers and chips and pump classic tunes from giant speakers late into the night. Lady-boys mix with beautiful girls in strappy sandals and tight skirts in front of the 7-Eleven, strutting their wares, while drunken Westerners pound the keyboards at late-night Internet cafés.

Opinions differ. Some arrive, planning to stay a week, and three months later are still entranced. Others look around, say 'it's done', and move on. Popularity doesn't come without a price – more people mean more traffic, more noise and more rubbish. Whatever your opinion, however, no one can deny Ko Samui is a beautiful place. You'll have to visit for yourself to decide whether it's worth staying.

The best time to visit is during the hot and dry season, from February to late June. From July to October it can be raining on and off, and from October to January there are sometimes heavy winds. On the other hand, many travellers have reported fine weather (and fewer crowds) in September and October. November tends to get some of the rain that also affects the east coast of Malaysia at this time. Prices soar from December to July, whatever the weather.

History & Culture
Samui's first settlers were islanders from Hainan Island (now part of the People's Republic of China) who took up coconut farming here around 150 years ago. You can still see a map of Hainan on the săan jâo (Chinese spirit shrine) near Siam City Bank in Na Thon, the oldest town on the island.

Perhaps due to the Hainanese influence, Samui culture differs from that of other islands in southern Thailand; and its inhabitants refer to themselves as *chao samŭi* (Samui folk) rather than Thais. They can be even friendlier than the average upcountry Thai, in our opinion, and have a great sense of humour, although those who are in constant contact with tourists can be a bit jaded. Nowadays many of the resorts, restaurants, bars and other tourist enterprises are owned or operated by Bangkok Thais

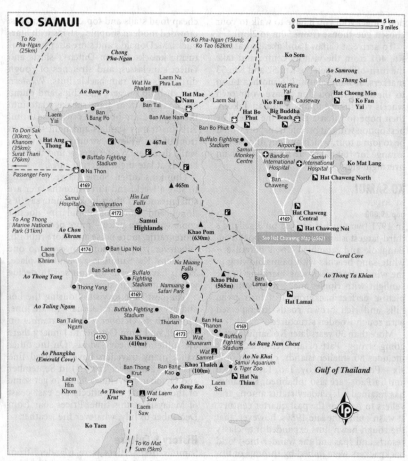

KO SAMUI

LOWER SOUTHERN GULF

or Europeans, so you have to get into the villages to meet true *chao samŭi*.

The island has a distinctive cuisine, influenced by the omnipresent coconut, which is still the main source of income for *chao samŭi*, who have disproportionately less ownership in beach property than outsiders. Coconut palms blanket the island, from the hillocks right up to the beaches. The durian, rambutan and *langsat* (a small round fruit similar to rambutan) are also cultivated.

Orientation

Samui has plenty of beaches to choose from, with bungalows popping up around more small bays all the time. The most crowded

beaches are Chaweng and Lamai, both on the eastern side of the island.

There are quieter accommodation options at Mae Nam, Bo Phut and Bang Rak (Big Buddha Beach) on the island's northern end. Ao Thong Yang, on the island's western side is even more secluded. The southern part of the island now has many bungalows, that are set in little out-of-the-way coves – it's worth seeking them out. And then there's everywhere in between – every bay, cove or cape with a strip of sand gets a bungalow.

On the northwestern side of Ko Samui, Na Thon is the arrival point for express and night passenger ferries from the piers in Surat Thani. If you're not travelling on a combination ticket you'll probably end up spending some time in Na Thon on your way in and/or out, waiting for the next ferry.

Car ferries from Don Sak and Khanom land at Thong Yang, about 10km south of Na Thon.

For descriptions of what these places have to offer, see the boxed text, p558.

MAPS

In Surat Thani or on Ko Samui, you can pick up the TAT's helpful *Surat Thani* map, which has maps of Surat Thani, the province, Ang Thong Marine National Park and Ko Samui, along with travel information. A couple of private companies now produce maps of Ko Samui, Ko Pha-Ngan and Ko Tao, which are available for 50B to 70B in the tourist areas of Surat and on the islands. Visid Hongsombud's *Guide Map of Koh Samui, Koh Pha-Ngan & Koh Tao* is also good.

Information
BOOKSHOPS
Na Thon Bookshop (Map p560; ☼ 10am-6pm) A wide selection of used books for sale or trade.
Saai Bookshop (Map p562; ☎ 0 7741 3847; ☼ 10am-11pm) One of many bookshops in Chaweng, the Sai sells new books and magazines and exchanges used books in various languages.

EMERGENCY
Tourist police (Map p560; emergency ☎ 1155, nonemergency ☎ 0 7742 1281) At the southern end of Na Thon.

IMMIGRATION OFFICES
Ko Samui Immigration office (Map p560; ☎ 0 7742 1069; ☼ 8.30am-noon & 1pm-4.30pm Mon-Fri, closed public holidays) Extends tourist visas by 30 days (500B). It's about 2km south of Na Thon.

INTERNET ACCESS
There are places all over the island offering Internet access, even at the less popular beaches. The going rate is between 1 and 2B per minute.

INTERNET RESOURCES
The following websites cover dive centres, accommodation and tours, as well as having timetables for Bangkok Airways, ferries, trains and VIP buses.
Ko Samui Thailand (www.sawadee.com)
Tourism Association of Ko Samui (www.samuitourism.com)

MEDIA
A locally produced, tourist-oriented newspaper with articles in German, English and Thai, *Samui Welcome,* is published monthly (free). *What's on Samui, Samui Guide* and the pocket-sized *Accommodation Samui* are also free and have listings of hotels, restaurants and suggestions of things to do – buried beneath scads of ads.

MEDICAL SERVICES
There are several hospitals on the island and nursing-care units for stubbed toes, scraped knees, pregnancy tests and earaches.
Hyperbaric chamber (Map p556; ☎ 0 7742 7427) The only hyperbaric chamber on the island is in Hat Bang Rak (Big Buddha Beach).
Samui International Hospital (Map p556; ☎ 0 7723 0781, 0 7742 2272; www.sih.co.th) For any medical or dental problem. Emergency ambulance service is available 24 hours and credit cards are accepted. Opposite the Muang Kulaypan Hotel.

MONEY
Changing money isn't a problem in Na Thon, Chaweng or Lamai, where several banks (with ATMs) or exchange booths offer daily exchange services. See the maps for some locations.

POST
There are privately run post-office branches across the island. Many bungalow operations also sell stamps and can mail letters for you, but they often charge a commission. If you're heading to the mainland, it's probably a good idea to wait until you get there to post something – island mail doesn't have an outstanding reputation.
Main post office (Map p560; ☼ 8.30am-4.30pm Mon-Fri, 9am-noon Sat) In Na Thon.

TELEPHONE
Many private telephone offices on the island will make a connection for a surcharge above the Telephone Organization of Thailand (TOT) or Communications Authority of Thailand (CAT) rates.
CAT (Map p560; ☼ 7am-10pm) Provides international telephone service at the main post office.

TOURIST INFORMATION
TAT (Map p560; ☎ 0 7742 0504; ☼ 8.30am-4.30pm) Friendly and helpful, it's at the end of Na Thon and has scores of brochures and maps.

WHICH BEACH?

So you've just stepped off the ferry (or maybe you're still on it) and suddenly you're surrounded by hotel touts, thrusting brochure after brochure into your face. The choices are mind-boggling, enough to give you a major headache. Don't despair. Most beaches are relatively near each other; if you're not satisfied with one, simply catch a *săwngthăew* to the next. If the beach you've arrived at looks appealing, your driver should be more than willing to take you to as many resorts as you'd like to see (they make a commission if you book a room), so check a few places before deciding.

Hat Chaweng
หาดเฉวง

Clear blue-green water, coral reefs and plenty of nightlife greet you at Ko Samui's longest and most popular beach. Free beach chairs line the 6km strip where hawkers ply anklets, drinks and pineapples, and adrenalin-pumping water sports abound. The main street is jammed with shops, restaurants, massage parlours, Internet outlets and loads of bars and clubs. Chaweng has the island's widest range of accommodation and attracts everyone from backpackers to those seeking top-notch resort treatment. If you're looking to party, or travelling solo, it's probably your best bet for meeting other folks.

Hat Lamai
หาดละไม

Some say Samui's second most popular beach is even more beautiful than Chaweng. You can swim year-round here – head to the beach's southern end, which is studded with elegant granite boulders. South of town are the interesting Grandfather and Grandmother rock formations. These explicit natural formations attract plenty of giggling Thai tourists. Slightly quieter and smaller than Chaweng, it doesn't attract as many hawkers. Lamai's drawback is the rather sleazy strip of beer bars on the main road. They're not necessarily offensive, just of the girlie-bar variety. That said there are also good expat watering holes and high-quality restaurant and accommodation options.

Hat Bo Phut
หาดป่อผุด

Much quieter, the water here is not as clear as others, but the beach is great for a romantic holiday. Popular with the French for the last decade, it's now attracting a growing number of

TRAVEL AGENCIES

Asia Travel (Map p560; ☎ 0 7723 6120) Deals especially with airline tickets.

Travel Solutions (Map p562; ☎ 0 7723 0203; ttsolutions@hotmail.com) Efficient and reliable, it's on Chaweng beach. It can help with international travel plans, transport bookings, accommodation and visa arrangements. Languages spoken include English, Spanish, French and Thai.

Dangers & Annoyances

Several travellers have written to warn others to take care when making train, bus and air bookings. These sometimes aren't made at all, the bus turns out to be far inferior to the one expected or other hassles develop. Sometimes travel agents say that economy class on planes is fully booked and only business class is available; the agent then sells the customer an air ticket – at business-class prices – that turns out to be economy class.

As on Phuket, the rate of fatalities on Samui from road accidents is quite high. This is due mainly to the large number of tourists who rent motorcycles only to find out that Samui's winding roads, stray dogs and coconut trucks can be lethal to those who have never dealt with them. If you feel you must rent a motorcycle, protect yourself by wearing a helmet, shoes and appropriate clothing when driving.

Theft isn't unknown on the island. If you're staying in a beach bungalow, consider depositing your valuables with the management while off on excursions around the island or swimming at the beach.

British tourists. The village is a charming strip of old Chinese shophouses, many of which have been converted into upmarket bars, restaurants, guesthouses and shops. It has a distinctly Mediterranean feel, but doesn't offer much for solo travellers or those seeking to party. From October to April the water may become too shallow for swimming.

Hat Mae Nam
หาดแม่น้ำ

Still a good choice for budget accommodation with a long strip of cheap bungalows, it's also home to several five-star resorts. The beach is rather quiet and secluded, but the water isn't as stunning as at Chaweng and can become too shallow for swimming from October to April. The beach in front of Wat Na Phalan is undeveloped; please avoid going topless here.

Hat Bang Rak (Big Buddha Beach)
หาดพระใหญ่

Very close to the airport, it's convenient if you're flying in or out. The resorts tend to be well spread out and laid-back, and the particularly calm waters make it attractive to families. Prices remain relatively low.

Ao Bang Po
อ่าวบางปอ

This secluded, quiet bay has fair snorkelling and swimming, and two new-age resorts featuring everything from meditation to tarot card reading (see p563).

Ao Thong Sai & Hat Choeng Mon
อ่าวท้องทราย/หาดเชิงมน

Clean and quiet, this large cove and beach is recommended for families or those who don't need nightlife and a plethora of restaurants (easily found at nearby Hat Chaweng anyway) to survive.

Na Thon
หน้าทอน

The beach is smelly and otherwise pier-like, and there's really no reason to stay here. The town is mostly just a ferry departure point. If you want to look around, it sports a few old teak Chinese shophouses, cafés and a colourful day market.

Sights

Although the beaches are the main attraction, the island offers other options if you're tired of sun and sand.

ANG THONG MARINE NATIONAL PARK
อุทยานแห่งชาติหมู่เกาะอ่างทอง

Popularised by its role as home to the utopian beach society in Alex Garland's novel *The Beach* (although the movie version of the book was mostly shot in the Andaman Sea), this archipelago of around 40 small islands combines sheer limestone cliffs, white-sand beaches, hidden lagoons, and dense vegetation in postcard-perfect quality. The park lies 31km northwest of Ko Samui and encompasses 18 sq km of islands, plus 84 sq km of marine environments.

Tour operators run popular day trips to the park, leaving from Na Thon or Mae Nam. Any travel agency around the island can book these tours – you'll see scores of advertisements throughout Chaweng and Lamai. Lunch and snorkelling are included, along with a climb to the top of a 240m hill to view the whole island group; some tours visit **Tham Bua Bok**, a cavern containing lotus-shaped cave formations, and other tours offer sea kayaking. There's officially a 200B admission fee for foreigners, though it should be included your tour. Bring shoes with good traction, a hat and plenty of sunscreen and drinking water. Tours cost about 1700B. Overnight tours are also available. At the **park headquarters** (☎ 0 7728 6025), on Ko Wat Ta Lap, there are bungalows, but

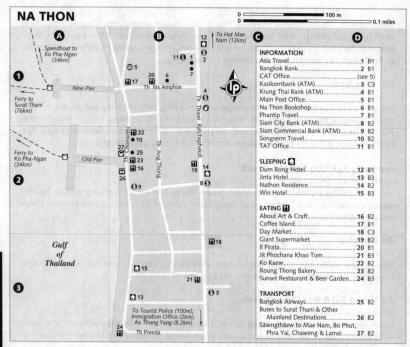

NA THON

LOWER SOUTHERN GULF

you may not be able to reserve them unless you go with a tour.

WATERFALLS

Samui has a couple of waterfalls. **Nam Tok Na Muang**, in the centre of the island (the turn-off is 10km southeast of Na Thon), has several levels, is scenic and doesn't attract hordes of visitors. The lower falls, directly across from the road, are smaller, and rocks and tree roots form a natural staircase leading directly to a large pool suitable for swimming. To reach the upper falls you'll need to hike for 1.5km. It's worth it though, from the uppermost level the view extends to the sea. From Na Thon a *sǎwngthǎew* here costs about 50B.

Nam Tok Hin Lat is only worth a visit if you're bored waiting in Na Thon for a boat out. You can get here by *sǎwngthǎew* (30B); go 2km and get off after the 7-Eleven, then walk 2km. To walk the whole way, head south of town for 2km on the main road, turn left at the first major intersection and head straight along for another 2km to the waterfall (you'll see the vendors). From

here, it's almost an hour's hike along a slippery trail to the top of the opaque trickle of water.

BUFFALO FIGHTING

Local villagers love to bet on duelling water buffaloes and events are arranged on a rotating basis at seven rustic fighting rings around the island in Na Thon, Ban Saket, Na Muang, Hua Thanon, Ban Chaweng, Mae Nam and Ban Bo Phut. In these events two buffaloes face off and, at their owners' urging, lock horns and/or butt one another until one of the animals backs down. The typical encounter lasts only a few seconds, and rarely are the animals injured. As such events go it's fairly tame, certainly far more humane than dogfighting, cockfighting or Spanish bullfighting. Tourists are charged 150B to 200B entry.

TEMPLES

For temple enthusiasts **Wat Laem Saw**, at the southern end of the island near the village of Ban Bang Kao, features an interesting and highly venerated old Srivijaya-style *chedi*. This *chedi* is very similar to the one in Chaiya.

At the northern end of the island, on a small rocky island that's joined to Samui by a causeway, is **Wat Phra Yai** (Temple of the Big Buddha). Erected in 1972, the modern image is about 12m high, and makes a pretty silhouette against the tropical sky and sea behind it. The image is surrounded by *kùtì* (meditation huts). Proper attire needs to be worn on the premises (no shorts or sleeveless shirts).

Another attraction is the ghostly **mummified monk** at Wat Khunaram, south of Rte 4169 between Ban Thurian and Ban Hua Thanon. The monk, Luang Phaw Daeng, has been dead over two decades but his corpse is preserved sitting in a meditative pose and sporting a pair of sunglasses.

At **Wat Samret** near Ban Hua Thanon you can see a typical Mandalay sitting Buddha carved from solid marble, common in northern Thailand, but rarer in the south. A collection of antique Buddha images is housed in a hall on the monastery grounds. To view them, ask one of the monks to unlock the hall, and leave a small donation.

Activities

Water sports are big on Hat Chaweng; you can hire sailboards, go diving, sail a catamaran, charter a junk and so on. Parasailing costs around 400B. Jet skis cost 600B or 700B per 20 minutes depending if you want a one- or two-person boat.

DIVING & SNORKELLING

The best diving is in the Ko Tao area and many dive trips starting from Samui end up there. Beach dives cost around 1000B per day. Boat dives start from 3000B, and two- to four-day certification courses cost 6000B to 9500B. An overnight dive trip to Ko Tao, including food and accommodation, can be done for about 3500B. There are also daily snorkelling trips to Ko Tao. These cost about 1500B including lunch and equipment, and can be booked through the dive shops or any travel agency around the island. The trip to Ko Tao takes about two hours via high-speed catamaran. Trips leave in the early morning and return to Ko Samui in the late afternoon.

The highest concentration of dive shops is at Hat Chaweng (Map p562).

Calypso Diving (☎ 0 7742 2437)
Dive Indeep (☎ 0 7723 0155; indeep@ samart.co.th)
Dive Shop (☎ /fax 0 7723 0232; diveshop@samart .co.th)
Samui International Diving School (SIDS; ☎ 0 7724 2386; www.planet-scuba.net) Outlets also at Hat Lamai and Bo Phut.
Silent Divers (☎ 0 7742 2730; www.silentdivers.com)

PADDLING

Any travel agency worth its salt should be able to book a sea-kayak tour.

Blue Stars (Map p562; ☎ 0 7741 3231; www.gallery lafayette.com/bluestars), in Hat Chaweng, offers guided kayak trips in Ang Thong Marine National Park (1990B) and two-day overnight tours to a spectacularly beautiful bay (4750B).

Courses

Daily Thai cooking classes and lessons in the aristocratic Thai art of carving fruits and vegetables into intricate floral designs are offered at the **Samui Institute of Thai Culinary Arts** (Sitca; Map p562; ☎ 0 7741 3172; www.sitca .net; 46/6 Soi Colibri, Hat Chaweng). Quick lunchtime classes cost 995B (three courses), while dinner classes are 1400B (four courses). Of course you get to eat your work, and even invite a friend along for the meal. To find it, look for a blue 'Save Way Travel' sign; it's down that lane.

Health Oasis Resort (p563) offers one- to eight-day courses and certification in Thai and Swedish massage, aromatherapy, reiki, meditation, yoga and 'life training' for 6000B to 30,000B. The length and tuition of all courses can be adjusted to suit the individual.

Samui for Children

If salt water and sand castles just aren't enough to keep the tykes entertained long enough to sleep like babies at night, Samui – Hat Chaweng in particular – is for you.

On Hat Chaweng is the tiny little **Treasure Island Miniature Golf Course** (Map p562; 9/18 holes 120/180B, under 10 half price; ⊙ 11am-6pm).

Namuang Safari Park (Map p556; ☎ 0 7742 4098; adult/child from 1100/800B; ⊙ 9am-6pm), about 10km southwest of Hat Chaweng, has safari packages galore. The most popular include elephant trekking, a jeep ride and a monkey and crocodile show. Adults, without children, have been known to enjoy these trips.

HAT CHAWENG

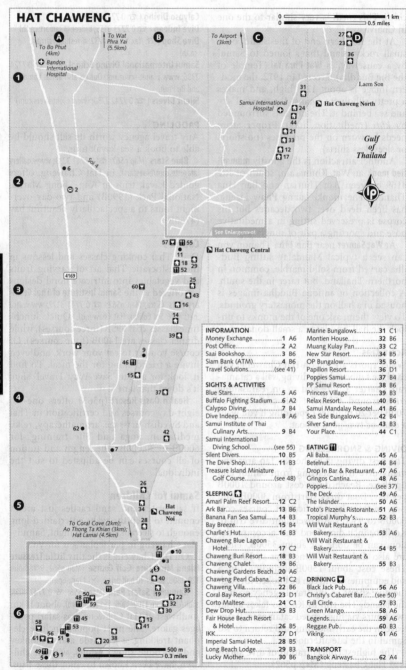

See Enlargement

LOWER SOUTHERN GULF

If you just want to check out the monkey and croc show you'll only have to fork out 350/250B per adult/child. Hotel transfers are included in the packages.

In the same vein, **Samui Aquarium & Tiger Zoo** (☎ 0 7742 4017; admission 350B; ⏱ 9am-6pm) has a mildly interesting aquarium and tigers to take your picture with, as well as a large aviary. Call for transportation.

Sleeping

In this section, we start with Na Thon, the point of entry for most travellers (although far from the nicest place on the island) and then work our way clockwise around Ko Samui. To get an idea about which beach offers what, see p558. Prices vary considerably according to time of year and occupancy rates. Some of the bungalow operators on Samui have a nasty habit of tripling rates when rooms are scarce, so a hut that's 200B in June could be 600B in August.

Except for the top-end resorts (which only offer top-end prices and facilities), most places operate on a two-tier price system. The cheapest rooms are simpler, sometimes tiny affairs with fans, while the more expensive ones come with air-con and, more often than not, satellite TV.

NA THON

If you need to stay in Ko Samui's largest settlement there are several places to choose between.

Nathon Residence (Map p560; ☎ 0 7723 6058; Th Thawi Ratchapakdi; r 500B; ▨) A beautiful new place, this is the best of the lot in town. Modern, clean and central, it's cutely designed, has a lovely staff and a pleasant guesthouse feel.

Win Hotel (Map p560; ☎ 0 7742 1500; 366 Th Chonwithi; r 450B; ▨ ▣) The views here leave a lot to be desired, but the staff are friendly, the carpeted rooms come with televisions and balconies and there is onsite Internet access.

Dum Rong Hotel (Map p560; ☎ 0 7742 0359; Th Thawi Ratchaphakdi; r 450B; ▨) Rooms at the Dum Rong are large and clean, although nothing special. The hotel is a few blocks from the pier.

Jinta Hotel (Map p560; ☎ 0 7742 0630; jinta@samart .co.th; Th Chonwithi; r from 400B; ▨ ▣) Overall this hotel is all right. Rooms have satellite TV, but the fan and the cheaper air-con rooms don't have hot water.

AO BANG PO

This bay, with its main town of Ban Tai, has cheap isolated bungalows and a couple of popular health resorts.

Health Oasis Resort (☎ 0 7742 0124; www.health oasisresort.com; bungalows 675-3000B; ▨ ▣) This is a New Age spot on pleasant sunny grounds with comfortable, well-balanced, modern rooms. It has a sort of spaced-out hippy feel that entices some and sends others running for a cheeseburger and a beer. The resort focuses on cleansing (ie fasting and high colonics). The vegetarian restaurant serves meals in the 45B to 250B range, and it's right on the beach.

Axolotl Village (☎ 0 7742 0017; www.axolotlvillage .com; r 500-1000B) Run by New Age Italians, Axolotl offers colonic irrigation, meditation, yoga, tarot reading, channelling and more. Bungalows are simple and thatched, but nice. A pleasant restaurant area overlooking the beach has an inventive menu featuring vegetarian, Thai and, of course, Italian dishes.

The following places are way down a sandy road. Look for the turn-off from the main drag near Coconut Village.

Sunbeam (☎ 0 7742 0600; bungalows 200-400B) The most upmarket of the lot, Sunbeam has a variety of big, comfortable and rustic bungalows by the sea. There's a great garden with brick paths and a relaxing restaurant.

Moon (☎ 0 7724 7371; bungalows 150-350B) Here you can choose comfortable inland bungalows or ones with sea views. There's a casual restaurant area by the beach, and traveller services, such as transport booking and motorcycle rentals, are available.

Ban Tai (☎ 0 9874 7357; 1-person huts 100B, bungalows 200-250B) One of the few places in Ko Samui where you can still stay for 100B. The 12 bungalows are airy and comfortable – a great deal.

HAT MAE NAM

The accommodation in Hat Mae Nam, 14km from Na Thon, spreads inland along sand tracks. There are a couple of bars and restaurants that should keep you from having to stray too far for sustenance.

Paradise Beach Resort (☎ 0 7724 7727; r 3500-5400; ▨ ▣) A classy, child-friendly place, Paradise Beach Resort features Thai-style bungalows and rooms with private balconies in a tropical garden setting. There are two swimming pools, a Jacuzzi, children's playground, onsite dive centre, all sorts of water sports and a seaside restaurant.

Lolita (☎ 0 7742 5134; bungalows 400-1500B; 🕸) Sort of upmarket and good for families, Lolita offers attractive, large wooden bungalows on or near the beach. The circular restaurant has classic styling and is tastefully decorated.

Maenam Resort (☎ 0 7742 5116; maenamrs@sam art.co.th; bungalows 1000-2000B; 🕸) This resort is a good deal. Its nicely maintained bungalows have a rich, dark ambience and are relatively private. The beautiful, lush garden paths lead to the shady beachside restaurant.

Palm Point Village (☎ 0 7742 5095; bungalows 400-800B; 🕸) Set in a small well-maintained garden, Palm Point has colourful and creative bungalows. Unfortunately, the air-con ones are in the back, away from the beach.

Santiburi Dusit Resort (☎ 0 7742 5031, 0 7742 5040; www.dusit.com; r US$340-900; 🕸 🖭) As would be expected at a Dusit Resort, rooms here are impeccable, service is top-notch, and the 9.5 hectares of manicured tropical gardens are lush and the entire place is smartly designed. If you're looking for a standard top-end resort, you won't be disappointed.

Mae Nam Beach Bungalows (☎ 0 7742 5060; bungalows 150-350B) A backpacker's special, it consists basic shacks or more-modern bungalows on a shady lot. There's a good beach atmosphere.

New Star (☎ 0 7742 7623; huts 150-250B) Another old school backpacker place, here you'll find small huts and slightly larger bungalows. All are rather grungy, but you get what you pay for. The colourful restaurant features a pool table and a good vibe.

New La Paz Villa (☎ 0 7742 5296; fax 0 7742 5402; bungalows 400-1000B; 🕸 🖭) Pleasant and popular, the La Paz has a Latin theme, a decent restaurant and a well-landscaped garden.

Harry's (☎ 0 7742 5447; harrys@samart.co.th; bungalows 400-800B; 🕸 🖭) At Harry's a tiled walkway leads to a sandy garden with a few trees, where you'll find concrete and tile-floored bungalows. It's good value, although inland from the beach. Its best feature is the pool.

Sea Fan (☎ 0 7742 5204; r 3000-3300B; 🕸 🖭) With its huge, luxury thatch-and-wood bungalows connected by wooden walkways, Sea Fan is a nice place, but the rates are high for thatch bungalows. The pool includes an area designed for kids.

Anong Villa (☎ 0 7724 7256; bungalows 300-800B; 🕸) A wide range of decent bungalows are found here. Check out the ones in the back, they're the nicest.

SR Bungalow (☎ 0 7742 7530; sr_bungalow@hot mail.com; bungalows 300-400B) This place sports well-maintained bungalows and has a decent beach area.

HAT BO PHUT

Bo Phut has cornered the island's 'boutique-hotel' market. Accommodation is off the main road and west of the central village area, and on the inland side of the road/ village, just a few steps from the beach.

Zazen (☎ 0 7742 5085; www.samuizazen.com; r 1000-3000B; 🕸 🖭) Off the main road and west of the village area, Zazen is a luscious and unique place; 28 artistically decorated, multilevel abodes are trimmed in wood and nicely painted. Interiors are gorgeous and everything is designed thoughtfully and creatively. There's a billiard-table pavilion, great swimming pool, tasty beachside restaurant and a small spa.

Peace Bungalow (☎ 0 7742 5357; www.peaceresort .com; r 1850-3300B; 🕸 🖭) West of the village area, the setting for this boutique-style spot is a shady tropical garden. The lacquered wooden bungalows are pristine on the inside with crisp linens, warm-toned walls and big windows. The sparkling beachside swimming pool and comfortable restaurant add to the ambience.

Eden (☎ 0 7742 7645; www.sawadee.com/samui/eden; bungalows 800-1600B; 🕸 🖭) French-run Eden is an exceptional find. Another boutique-style place, it has 12 spacious and creative rooms and a gorgeous garden with a pool. Reconfirm reservations before you arrive.

Ziggy Stardust (☎ 0 7742 5173; bungalows 400-1000B; 🕸) One of the golden oldies of Samui, this place is clean and still popular with the backpacker crowd. It's a good deal but poorly signed; look for its thatched-roof restaurant on the beach, west of Smile House.

Hello Diving & Guesthouse (☎ 0 9872 7056; dm 100-150B; 🕸) This is a unique traveller's crash pad run by a knowledgeable expat, there are intimate dorms and a nice ground-floor communal room. The only drawback is its lack of a restaurant and limited bathroom facilities. It's on the inland side of the main village road, but just a few steps from the beach.

Lodge (☎ 0 7742 5337; fax 0 7742 5336; r 1300-1600B; ☒) A small, personal and upmarket place right on the beach, the Lodge features an interesting three-storey design. The 10 luxurious rooms are beautiful, cosy and super-comfortable.

Sunny (☎ 0 7742 7031; bungalows 275-400B) Furthest north of the beach, Sunny has 12 small, basic bungalows on a sandy lot with coconut palms – there's not much action, but it's a decent choice for backpackers who don't need much.

Sandy Resort (☎ 0 7742 3534; fax 0 7742 5325; bungalows 500-1000B; ☒) Well-appointed bungalows of wood and concrete are found at this resort. Check a few out, however, as some have rather saggy mattresses.

Summer Night (☎ 0 7724 5288; bungalows 300-700B; ☒) There are large, basic, no-frills bungalows in a sparse inland garden here and they are good value for the budget conscious.

World Resort (☎ 0 7742 5355; bungalows incl breakfast 1050-2150B; ☒ ☒) A pool with a bar and appealing grounds complement stylish, large rooms with nice terraces at this resort.

HAT BANG RAK (BIG BUDDHA BEACH)

This place is more like an 'area' and not really a conventional town. Bungalow operations are spread out along the main road.

Shambala (☎ 0 7742 5330; www.samui-shambala.com; bungalows 400-700B) This is an English-run place that's great for backpackers. It has spacious grounds and bright, roomy bungalows that are well maintained. Staff offer heaps of travel information, there's a cool restaurant and a floating lounger in the sea.

Chez Ban-Ban & Le Mar de Provence (☎ 0 7724 5135; ban-ban@samui-info.com; cottages 450-1000B; ☒) Ten very tiny and cute, Heidi-like cottages with rattan floors are found here. They surround a nice little garden along with a French restaurant.

Pongpetch Servotel (☎ 0 7724 5100; www.pongpetchhotel.com; r 600-700B; ☒) In a strange castle-like structure, the rooms here are small but homey and surrounded by a lovely garden with a fountain and sitting areas.

Secret Garden Bungalows (☎ 0 7742 5419; www.secretgarden.co.th; bungalows 500-1500B; ☒) This is a decent choice, with A-frame bungalows and pleasant sitting areas at the front. The service could be kicked up a notch or two though.

Como Resort (☎ 0 7742 5210; r 1000B; ☒ ☒) Como is a cosy little place with just a handful of sweet rooms and bungalows. There's a wading pool too.

Nara Garden Beach Resort (☎ 0 7742 5364; naragarden@hotmail.com; r from 1470B; ☒ ☒) Close to the airport, this is a favourite with Bangkok Airways flight crews. It's a well-maintained place with a small beachside pool. Ask for discounts off the rack rate.

AO THONG SAI & HAT CHOENG MON

The largest cove following Ao Thong Sai has several names, but the beach is generally known as Hat Choeng Mon.

White House (☎ 0 7724 5315; info@samuidreamholiday.com; r 4400-6000B; ☒ ☒) Perfect for a cosy getaway; beautifully appointed rooms at the White House are artistically decorated with creative wooden details and peaked roofs. Duvets top every bed, and on arrival there are fresh fruit and flowers. Water-filled urns dot the lush garden paths and there's an elegant pool, restaurant and private spa areas – it's simply a gorgeous place.

Imperial Boat House Hotel (☎ 0 7742 5041; www.imperialhotels.com; r US$120-225; ☒ ☒) This place is something else. It has a three-storey hotel with rooms, and separate two-storey bungalows made from teak rice barges. There's also a boat-shaped swimming pool. It's a stunning, sophisticated and unique place.

PS Villa (☎ 0 7742 5160; fax 0 7742 5403; bungalows 400-1200B; ☒ ☒) Well-run and good for families, PS Villa offers a range of bungalows and amenities in a spacious, well-maintained garden area.

Tongsai Bay (☎ 0 7742 5015; www.tongsaibay.co.th; ste from 10,000B; ☒ ☒) For serious pampering, head to this secluded, superluxurious place. Expansive, impeccably maintained and hilly grounds make buildings here look like a small village, and golf carts are employed to zoom guests around. All the super swanky suites have day-bed rest areas, gorgeous romantic décor, stunning views, large terraces and creatively placed tubs (you'll see). Facilities include salt- and fresh-water pools, a tennis court, spa and three restaurants.

Island View (☎ 0 7742 5031; fax 0 7742 5081; bungalows 400-800B; ☒) Friendly and attractive, Island View is right on the beach and is a solid, clean option.

HAT CHAWENG

Hat Chaweng has the island's highest concentration of bungalows and tourist hotels.

Wander around a bit before choosing one, as there are many more than those listed here. We've divided accommodation listings into three areas: North Chaweng, Central Chaweng and Chaweng Noi.

North

North Chaweng has the advantage of lower noise levels and less traffic than further south. There's not much in the 800B to 1500B range, but there are some budget options and very nice luxury places.

Amari Palm Reef Resort (Map p562; ☎ 0 7742 2015; www.amari.com; r & bungalows from 5500B; 🔀 🔄) A luxurious, ultratastefully decorated resort, this place has a gorgeous pool area and spacious, comfortable rooms. It's the nicest of the top-end places. It's also the most environmentally conscious luxury resort on the island, using filtered sea water for most first uses and recycled grey water for landscaping. All in all, it's quite a good deal.

Chaweng Blue Lagoon Hotel (Map p562; ☎ 0 7742 2041; www.bluelagoonhotel.com; bungalows from 4500B; 🔀 🔄) A lovely upmarket Swiss-run resort with nice tropical touches and Thai-style décor, this hotel is a quiet place that doesn't discourage children.

Papillon Resort (Map p562; ☎ 0 7723 1169; www.papillonsamui.com; r & bungalows 1600-5100B; 🔀 🔄) This place offers imaginative, two-level rooms with elegant décor and lofts, along with a lush garden, beautiful restaurant and a tiny pool.

Muang Kulay Pan (Map p562; ☎ 0 7723 0850; www.kulaypan.com; r 2000-8500B; 🔀 🔄) Supersleek, with a very modern design that incorporates Thai culture, the rooms here are elegantly appointed and include works of art.

Marine Bungalows (Map p562; ☎ 0 7742 2416; fax 0 7742 2263; bungalows 300-800B; 🔀) These bungalows, down a dirt road, are decently built. Most of them are inland on shady, spacious and hilly grounds.

Chaweng Pearl Cabana (Map p562; ☎ 0 7742 2116; bungalows 300-500B; 🔀) A decent deal for Chaweng, the service here leaves a lot to be desired and the rooms are slightly dingy with saggy mattresses, but it's one of the cheapest places around. Make sure the aircon works before you take the room.

IKK (Map p562; ☎ 0 7741 3281; bungalows 500-700B) Down a somewhat treacherous dirt road, IKK sports 15 identical bungalows whose prices are determined by beach proximity.

It's a small, isolated and pleasantly calm place. On board are nice garden paths and an atmospheric restaurant.

Your Place (Map p562; ☎ 0 7723 0039; bungalows 300-600B; 🔀) On a garden square, Your Place is friendly and a good deal. The sign stating 'No Gun, No Narcotic' is a little disconcerting, but people seem to like it here.

Coral Bay Resort (Map p562; ☎ 0 7742 2223; www.coralbay.net; r & bungalows 2500-9000B; 🔀 🔄) The accommodation here is great, sporting natural materials and unique wooden details in spacious surroundings. Gardens are lush, hilly and meandering, and there's a tastefully designed pool area. It's an ecological resort of sorts.

Corto Maltese (Map p562; ☎ 0 7723 0041; www.samui-hotels.com/corto; r incl breakfast from 2490B; 🔀 🔄) Well designed and decorated, the rooms at Corto Maltese have creative baths and a vaguely Mediterranean feel. It's popular with French tourists.

Central

Hat Chaweng's central area has the most bungalows, hotels, restaurants (many with videos), bars (including the girlie kind), discos, video parlours, minimarts, tailors, souvenir shops and currency-exchange booths. Expect accommodation prices to be the most expensive on the island; after all, it *is* the prettiest beach and where most folks want to stay.

Ark Bar (Map p562; ☎ 0 7741 3798; www.ark-bar.com; bungalows 700-2500B; 🔀 🔄) A huge hit with the 20-something crowd, the cement bungalows here are cute and clean, the pool faces the ocean and the bar is a hit day or night.

Montien House (Map p562; ☎ 0 7742 2169; montien@samart.co.th; r & bungalows 1700B) A great place, Montien offers well-designed bungalows amid peaceful, gorgeous gardens. There's a large, beautiful pool by the beach and tranquil music at the restaurant.

Poppies Samui (Map p562; ☎ 0 7742 2419; www.poppiessamui.com; r incl breakfast US$147-267; 🔀 🔄) Poppies emulates a cosy elfland; the gorgeous garden comes with a bubbling stream, while the beautifully built cottages are luxuriously comfortable. Boulders edge the small swimming pool and, of course, the restaurant is top-notch.

Lucky Mother (Map p562; ☎ 0 7723 0931; bungalows 250-700B) One of the cheapest places on the strip, the budget-conscious backpacker

LOWER SOUTHERN GULF

will appreciate the rickety wooden bungalows at Lucky Mother, reminiscent of old Samui, nestled under a shady grove.

Princess Village (Map p562; ☎ 0 7742 2216; www .samuidreamholiday.com; bungalows 3100-5000B; 🞐) Princess Village is romantic and just about perfect for honeymooners. You'll be treated like royalty when you stay in the beautifully constructed and tastefully decorated Ayuthaya-period houses set high on stilts. They're spaced out in a lush garden with ponds.

Relax Resort (Map p562; ☎ 0 7742 2280; fax 0 7742 2113; r 400-1200B; 🞐) This resort offers gorgeously charming air-con rooms with attractive architecture (some have wonderful lofts) and creative details. They are along nice garden paths in the back of the complex. The fan rooms, while comfortable, are in an appalling location off the driveway.

Chaweng Chalet (Map p562; ☎ 0 7741 3732; chalet samui@hotmail.com; bungalows from 1200B; 🞐) This solid midrange place offers 15 attractive, clean, bungalows with rustic wooden décor and good amenities. The grounds are pleasing, the location central and the restaurant is pretty cool, too.

Chaweng Gardens Beach (Map p562; ☎ 0 7742 2265; bungalows 450-1200B; 🞐) A wide variety of bungalows is available here, some nicer than others, so ask to see a few. The best of the bunch are the newish rooms, which are clean and spacious with satellite TVs. The sprawling grounds are lovely, with lush tropical gardens and the restaurant is full of ambience.

Chaweng Villa (Map p562; ☎ 0 7723 1123; www .chawengvilla.com; r & bungalows 1700-2600B; 🞐 🞐) Vine-covered rooms and bungalows are well kept and spread through grassy grounds at Chaweng Villa. The pool and restaurant are near the beach.

Samui Mandalay Resotel (Map p562; ☎ 0 7723 1157; bungalows 500-900B; 🞐 🞐) Quite good value for its central location; the bungalows here are cosy wooden affairs with satellite TV and mattresses on the floor. They don't let in a lot of light but they're large enough. Try for the ones closest to the beach, as they are quieter and nicer.

Banana Fan Sea Samui (Map p562; ☎ 0 7741 3483; www.bananafansea.com; r & bungalows 3500-7000B; 🞐 🞐) An impressive lobby, wonderfully appointed Thai-style bungalows with sparkling clean baths and a small beachside pool with Jacuzzi make this resort a very appealing choice.

Sea Side Bungalows (Map p562; ☎ 0 7742 2364; benjaporn2022@hotmail.com; bungalows incl breakfast 850-1500B; 🞐) This feel-good spot offers personable bungalows with sturdy furniture and some artwork on the walls. The large grassy garden is pleasant.

Chaweng Buri Resort (Map p562; ☎ 0 7742 2466; www.chawengburi.com; bungalows 4200B; 🞐 🞐) These upmarket bungalows, complete with canopy beds, while perfectly acceptable for a stay, pale in comparison to the resort's best asset – its grounds. Perfectly manicured gardens are interspersed with fountains and plenty of sitting areas, and there's a large, clean, pool and a restaurant. The whole place has a slightly romantic air.

PP Samui Resort (Map p562; ☎ 0 7742 2540; fax 0 7742 2324; r 1000B; 🞐) The stylish, white one- and two-storey buildings at this resort have tiled roofs and clean, modern rooms. Brick garden pathways lead all the way to the beach.

Dew Drop Hut (Map p562; ☎ 0 7723 0551; bungalows 400B) Set in a sparse jungle garden, the Dew Drop has basic wooden bungalows on stilts or concrete blocks. It's a good bare-bones budget choice on the beach.

OP Bungalow (Map p562; ☎ 0 7742 2424; op_bun galow@hotmail.com; bungalows 400-1200B; 🞐) The cement bungalows here are seriously lacking in character, but they're clean with good-sized porches. The more expensive bungalows are on the edge of the beach, but they're not good value. The restaurant has a good view of the beach.

Silver Sand (Map p562; ☎ 0 7723 1202; fax 0 7742 2089; bungalows 200-800B; 🞐) This place offers bright-green, shack-like bungalows with shaky wooden floors. Rooms are rather dark, which could be an asset if you've partied all night and want to sleep away the day!

Charlie's Hut (Map p562; ☎ 0 7742 2343; bungalows 300-700B; 🞐) Popular for its cheap bungalows on well-kept, lush grounds, there's a lot of in-and-out traffic at Charlie's, so take care of your valuables.

Long Beach Lodge (Map p562; ☎ 0 7742 2372; bungalows incl breakfast 1300-2500B; 🞐) Stately wood-panelled bungalows with modern interiors and baths make the lodge a good midrange choice.

Bay Breeze (Map p562; ☎ 0 7742 2198; bungalows 300-500B; 🞐) This place seems like such a good deal, but it's not on the beach. Look for it on the inland side of the road. It's also a bit old, but is friendly and has decent large rooms with cheap air-con.

South

The Chaweng Noi area is off by itself around a southern headland. The following places are upmarket and not especially great value. However, the area is pretty and if you're looking for more isolation, while still being in Chaweng, they might be for you.

Fair House Beach Resort & Hotel (Map p562; ☎ 0 7742 2256; www.fairhousesamui.com; r 3500-5400B; 🔀 🔊) This is a decent, though not stunning, resort with tropical grounds, two pools and comfortable, tasteful rooms with good amenities.

New Star Resort (Map p562; ☎ 0 7742 2407; www.samuinewstar.com; bungalows 1700-3000B; 🔀 🔊) With bungalows rolling down a hill to the beach, this is a pleasant resort with clean, spacious bungalows.

Imperial Samui Hotel (Map p562; ☎ 0 7742 5041; www.imperialhotels.com; bungalows 5885-7190B; 🔀 🔊) The pool is the best feature of this hotel and, while the pueblo-style architecture still holds a certain rustic elegance, the place has seen better days. Give it a good coat of paint and it may be worth the asking price.

CORAL COVE & AO THONG TA KHIAN

Another series of capes and coves starts at the end of Hat Chaweng Noi, beginning with scenic Coral Cove. (The Thai name of this cove – Ao Thong Yang – is the same as another bay on the western coast of Samui: this one is more commonly known by its Western name Coral Cove, and that's how we refer to it.) Ao Tong Ta Khian is a similar small, steep-sided cove, banked by huge boulders.

Crystal Bay (☎ 0 7742 2677; fax 0 7742 2678; r 400-800B; 🔀) This friendly and casual place features new, modern rooms, some better located than others. There's a great terrace for guests and a fine-sand beach. A good choice.

Samui Yacht Club (☎ 0 7742 2225; www.samuiyachtclub.com; bungalows 1800-3300B; 🔀 🔊) Quite a good deal for such a classy place, although this definitely ain't no yacht club. Rather, it offers huge, romantic Thai-style abodes with four-poster beds, mosquito nets, great furniture, TV and fridge. The garden is lush

and well designed and there's a pool near the beach.

Thong Ta Kian Villa (☎ /fax 0 7723 0978; bungalows 400-1000B; 🔀) Try for one of the priciest rooms at this villa – they are huge, beautiful and new (almost like being at a different resort). The other rooms are pleasant enough, though most have no sea views and are situated on a boring lot.

Blue Horizon Bungalows (☎ 0 7742 2426; blue horizon@samuitourism.com; r & bungalows 400-900B; 🔀) Sweet little bungalows are perched above an intimate beach here. They come with fridge, deck and views; the only drawback is the restaurant – it's near the busy road.

Coral Cove Chalet (☎ 0 7742 2242; coralcc@samart.co.th; bungalows 2600-4500B; 🔀 🔊) There are tiny thatched bungalows by the beach at Coral Cove. The pool, Jacuzzi and restaurant overlook a pleasant, grassy hillside with palms.

Coral Cove Resort (☎ 0 7742 2126; coral@samart.co.th; bungalows 650-2000B; 🔀) This is a small place with a nice brick patio and immediate boulder-framed beach access, but the wood and concrete bungalows are placed a bit too close together.

Beverly Hills Hotel Resort & Restaurant (☎ 0 7742 2232; bungalows 350-800B; 🔀) Atop a cliff overlooking Hat Chaweng, Beverly Hills has a restaurant with incredible views. Its rooms aren't much to look at though, and there's no direct beach access.

HAT LAMAI

After Chaweng became built-up, budget travellers discovered Lamai. It is still popular – just look at the crowds – but those looking for solitude have moved on to more-secluded spots. Accommodation at the northeastern end of the beach is quieter and moderately priced; though the beach is a bit thin on sand. The central part is closest to Ban Lamai and the beginning of the Lamai 'scene'. All the usual traveller services are available here.

Budget

You can find supercheap fan bungalows on Hat Lamai, but if you need air-con, you'll probably be paying at least 600B.

Spa Resort (☎ 0 7723 0855; www.spasamui.com; bungalows 250-1800B; 🔀) This New Age place is rare in that it's a health spa with budget accommodation. Herbal sauna, massage, clay facials, meditation and colon cleansing are all offered. Activities include *taijiquan* (t'ai chi) and yoga. The restaurant serves healthy dishes and simple bungalows are available. It's often booked out so reserve ahead of time (by email is best). Nonguests are welcome to participate in the programmes.

Sea Breeze (☎ 077425607; seabreeze@sawadee.com; bungalows 200-1200B; 🌐) An excellent choice for budget travellers, Sea Breeze has an affordable variety of attractive bungalows.

New Hut (☎ 0 1477 7237; newhut@hotmail.com; huts 100-200B) Penny-pinchers are rewarded here with a rare cheapie in the form of tiny A-frame huts (just a mattress inside) on the beach. The more-solid wooden bungalows are cramped and airless though. There's a great restaurant and shady deck for hanging out.

Green Canyon (☎ 0 7741 8687; greencanyon@samui net.com; bungalows 250-500B) Although not on the beach (it's a three-minute walk away), Green Canyon offers a handful of bungalows set on a cool green hillside near a canyon. Facilities are basic but clean, and the restaurant has a good traveller atmosphere.

Amadeus (☎ 077424568; amadeusbungalow@hotmail .com; bungalows 250-300B) Amadeus is a friendly and popular place a couple of minutes' walk from the beach. The basic bungalows are sprinkled around a shrubby green hillside.

Beers House (☎ 0 7723 0467; bungalows 150-350B) Another friendly option, Beers House has 16 supercheap, small, tidy bungalows near the beach. The cheapest accommodation shares bathrooms.

Amity (☎ 0 7742 4084; bungalows 120-500B) The more expensive bungalows at Amity are large and up to date, while the dirt-cheap ones are rather more ramshackle and with shared bathrooms.

Sukasem (☎ 0 7742 4119; sukasem@altavista.com; bungalows 300-800B; 🌐) Facing out on a sandy and palmy lot, the white bungalows here are beautiful, clean and tiled. There isn't much atmosphere, however, and it's a little too close to the main road.

Midrange

There is a large number of midrange options on Hat Lamai.

Jungle Park Hotel (☎ 0 7742 4110; www.jungle -park.com; r incl breakfast 900-3800B; 🌐 🗮) Affordable luxury, need we say more? Rooms here are tastefully decorated, have lots of light and great bathrooms. There's a wonderful

amoeba-shaped pool near the beach, along with a restaurant and bar.

Bill Resort (☎ 0 7742 4403; www.samui.sawadee .com/billresort; r & bungalows 1200-1800B; 🗮) Colourful materials and textures are used freely at this place. Rooms and bungalows are unique, lovely affairs set in an overflowing lush garden with a few fountains.

Galaxy Resort (☎ 0 7742 4441; www.samui-hotels .com/galaxy; r & bungalows incl breakfast 1200-2200B; 🗮 🗮) Thai-style architecture, huge bathtubs and beautifully presented interior décor are featured in the priciest rooms at this resort. The cheaper ones are quite adequate and comfortable, although they come with a few scratches.

Golden Sand (☎ 0 7742 4031; fax 0 7742 4430; r & bungalows 1300-2500B; 🗮) Here you'll find beautiful expansive grounds and very good facilities. Rooms and bungalows are decorated with tropical furniture. The restaurant overlooks the inland garden, while the bar sits on the beach.

Utopia (☎ 0 7723 3113; www.utopia-samui.com; bungalows 400-800B; 🗮) Solid bungalows offer plenty of space to move around. Utopia's beds are comfortable with good mattresses. We liked the restaurant area set in a jungle-like garden.

Marina Villa (☎ 0 7742 4426; fax 0 7723 2342; r & bungalows 700-1200B; 🗮) This villa offers good-value and attractive accommodation. The cheapest rooms are inland, while the pricier bungalows sit near the beach.

Long Island Resort (☎ 0 7742 4202; fax 0 7742 4023; bungalows 750-2100B; 🗮 🗮) This popular place features some well-laid-out thatched bungalows along brick paths. There's a nice blue pool and neat, grassy grounds with banana trees.

Nice Resort (☎ 0 7742 4027; nice1@sawadee.com; r & bungalows 500-1800B; 🗮 🗮) Leafy foliage surrounds the good rooms and bungalows at Nice Resort. The pool is sparkling and right near the beach. Not a bad option for the price.

Rose Garden (☎ 0 7742 4115; fax 0 7742 4410; bungalows 400-700B; 🗮) Rose Garden's bungalows are average size, basic and appropriately priced. The cheapest are near the road; the nicer ones come with air-con. They're all set in a large, lush garden.

Sand Sea Resort (☎ 0 7742 4026; fax 0 7742 4415; bungalows 1000-1200B; 🗮 🗮) We did like the unique clover-shaped pool at this resort.

Otherwise the 30 bungalows, sitting under coconut palms, are amenable, green shacks with tiled bathrooms.

Lamai Inn 99 (☎ 0 7742 4427; lamaiinn@samart.co .th; bungalows 500-1200B; 🛠) This is a somewhat impersonal place with heaps of inland bungalows; those with fans are small and just OK, while the air-con bungalows are neat and more acceptable. Grounds are pleasing enough, and there's a beachside eatery.

Top End

There are several top-end places on Hat Lamai, many of them spa resorts.

Tamarind Retreat (☎ 0 7742 4221; www.tamarind retreat.com; r US$65-225; 🛠 🖭) Set on a forested hillside, Tamarind offers eight gorgeously constructed and decorated villas – each with a different cultural theme. Some have boulders built into walls and floors, private ponds or creative outdoor bathrooms. There's a five-night minimum stay and free pick-up at the airport. There's no restaurant, but food delivery is possible. Tamarind is also a fine spa, with a full range of services and massage. It's often fully booked, so reserve well in advance.

Pavilion Resort (☎ 0 7742 4420; www.pavilionsam ui.com; r & bungalows incl breakfast 2500-4000B; 🛠 🖭) The octagonal bungalows are crowded together at Pavilion, although they are very comfortable, beautiful and spacious inside. Rooms are cheaper, but unexciting. The pool is gorgeous, however, with turtle statues spouting water – and the restaurant pavilion makes you feel like royalty. It's a somewhat stark but sophisticated place.

Star Bay Beach & Garden (☎ 0 7742 4546; www .starbay-beach.com; 1- & 2-bedroom houses 2200-2500B; 🛠 🖭) If you're travelling with the kids or in a small group, and looking to stay on the island for a while, this place might be for you. It caters to longer-term guests (two weeks or so) with large, beautiful houses near the beach. There is a beachside restaurant and the gardens are nice and leafy. If business is slow, shorter stays may be possible.

Aloha (☎ 0 7742 4418; www.alohasamui.com; r & bungalows 2500-5500B; 🛠 🖭) Despite its size, Aloha maintains a rather cosy feel. The bungalows are fairly pleasant with solid, nondescript furniture. The rooms are more modern. Both offer good amenities. The greatest asset is the wonderfully tropical, blue-tiled pool that overlooks the beach.

AO BANG NAM CHEUT

This bay is just south of Hat Lamai. The swimming here is best during the rainy season, when water levels rise.

Swiss Chalet (☎ 0 7742 4321; fax 0 7723 2205; r/ bungalows 200/400B) The large rooms and bungalows overlook the sea, and the restaurant, up near the entrance, does German and Thai food. It's a friendly place but feels a bit isolated.

Rocky (☎ 0 7741 8367; www.rockyresort.net; bungalows 700-3400B; 🛠 🖭) This is an old-timer that has gone upmarket with 29 clean, concrete bungalows packed with amenities. It's a family-friendly place in a safe, peaceful and relaxing environment. There's a beachside pool and restaurant.

SOUTH COAST

The southern end of Ko Samui is spotted with rocky headlands and smaller beach coves, and around the Laem Set promontory is a long reef with good snorkelling – though the swimming isn't all that great. There are a few midrange to top-end places to stay.

Hat Na Thian

Just beyond the village of Ban Hua Thanon, at the southern end of Ao Na Khai, is an area sometimes called Hat Na Thian. The inexpensive, natural bungalows that once dotted this area have been replaced by the usual air-con architecture. At Laem Set you pay for atmosphere and ecological sensitivity more than for amenities; some people will find this just what they're looking for, while others may feel they can find better value on the more popular beaches.

Samui Marina Cottage (☎ 0 7723 3395; www .samuimarina.com; bungalows 1600-1800B; 🛠 🖭) This place sports lots of good, concrete bungalows all lined up obediently along a shady garden; near the beach is the restaurant and a huge rectangular swimming pool.

Central Samui Village (☎ 0 7742 4020; www.cen tralhotelsresorts.com; bungalows from 4200B; 🛠 🖭) Stylish, modern wooden cottages with garden or sea views are linked by wooden walkways at this village. A welcoming pool and a beautiful restaurant lie above the beach. The grounds are well maintained.

Laem Set Inn (☎ 0 7742 4393; www.laemset.com; bungalows US$75-185; 🛠 🖭) This inn is beautifully landscaped and secluded; bungalows trickle down a hillside and are connected by stairways and waterways surrounded by lush tropical gardens. On the premises are a minor art gallery, a good Thai restaurant complete with a stunning view and a full-service spa. The fan rooms seem a tad pricey, however.

Ao Thong Krut & Ko Taen

A few kilometres further west, Ao Thong Krut provides mooring for local fishing boats. If you need a place to stay, **TK Tour & Restaurant** (☎ 0 7742 3258; bungalows 300-800B; ☒) has a relaxing restaurant overlooking the jetties. From here you can arrange tours to some offshore islands – including **Ko Mat Sum**, which is great for snorkelling. Day tours from Ao Thong Krut cost 500B to 650B and include snorkelling equipment and snacks.

Another nearby island is Ko Taen, which sports three nature trails and some accommodation. On the eastern shore is **Tan Village** (☎ 0 1968 4130; bungalows 350-650B), with pretty bungalows in a garden and the **Coral Beach Bungalows** (☎ 0 7741 5465; bungalows 350-650B). In a sharply curving bay on the western side are the similar **Dam Bungalows** (huts 100-150B) and **BS Cove** (huts 100-150B). **Annie Tour** (☎ 0 1894 1822), at Tonsai Restaurant on Ao Thong Krut, can book you accommodation on Ko Taen for no commission, and helps with transport there, which can cost as much as 200B unless you book with a bungalow operator.

WEST COAST

Several bays along Samui's western side have places to stay. The beaches here turn to mud flats at low tide, however, so they're more for people wanting to get away from the eastern-coast scene and not for beach fanatics.

Ao Phangkha

Around the hook-shaped Laem Hin Khom on the southern end of Samui's west coast is this little bay, sometimes called Emerald Cove. During the low season there are so few guests on this cove that the bungalow proprietors tend to let the rubbish pile up. These places offer half-day snorkelling trips to nearby islands for about 500B per person (four person minimum).

Pearl Bay (☎ 0 7742 3110; bungalows 200-500B) Up on a hill, this place is set in nice en-

virons and is very quiet. It's probably the best of the lot.

Seagull (☎ 0 7742 3091; bungalows 150-300B) Seagull offers a few semimodern bungalows facing the breezy, picturesque cove.

Ao Taling Ngam

Ao Taling Ngam, north of Emerald Cove, is a 20B *săwngthăew* ride from Na Thon. Samui's most exclusive resort is here.

Le Royal Meridien Baan Taling Ngam (☎ 0 7634 0480, in Bangkok ☎ 0 2653 2201; www.lemeridien.com; r & villas US$300-2170; ☒ ☐ ☒). This is Samui's most exclusive resort, boasting a sauna, beauty salon, babysitting service, two bars, three restaurants, two tennis courts, multiple swimming pools and a full complement of equipment and instructors for kayaking, windsurfing and diving. Luxuriously appointed guest accommodation contains custom-made, Thai-style furnishings. As it's not right on the beach, a shuttle service transports guests back and forth; airport and ferry transfers are also provided. If you have your heart set on staying here, try booking online through a room consolidator, you may get a deal.

Wiesenthal (☎ 0 7723 5165; wisnthal@samart.co.th; bungalows 400-1200B; ☒) More affordable, this place features 13 enticing, well-spaced bungalows, all with partial or full sea views set in a pleasant garden with coconut palms.

Ao Thong Yang & Ao Chon Khram

Ar An Resort (☎ 0 7742 3189; bungalows 300-600B; ☒) This resort, in serene Ao Thong Yang, is nothing special but does have cheap, modern bungalows on a shady, sandy and palmy lot with views of the old ferry dock.

In Foo Palace (☎ 0 7742 3066; r 500-1000B; ☒) Not too far away from Ar An, and a bit more upmarket, In Foo has modern rooms with partial sea views.

International Bungalows & Big John Seafood Restaurant (☎ 0 7742 3025; international@sawadee.com; bungalows 600-1700B, houses 1700-2500B; ☒) Complete with a playground, this family-friendly place has thatch-roof bungalows around sandy, grassy lots, and a large restaurant.

Rajapruek Samui Resort (☎ 0 7742 3115; fax 0 7742 3115; r & bungalows 500-1000B; ☒) This is a friendly place. Most of the bungalows are clean and offer the usual amenities – hot showers and TVs – but check a few out. The resort has a nice layout.

Siam Residence Resort (☎ 0 7742 0008; www.siam residence.com; bungalows US$160-200; ✖ ▣) This resort is for quiet and fastidious guests. The sunny garden is meticulously maintained; check out the topiary hedges. Bungalows are huge and classically beautiful, but they're all clones of each other and seem impersonal. Besides the pool, there's a tennis court.

Eating

The number of eating establishments on Samui is overwhelming. Fans of Italian food will not be disappointed, especially on Chaweng, where it seems Italian-owned restaurants outnumber everything else combined. Nearly all bungalow operations have their own restaurant, but because the ownership and management of various lodgings around the island change so frequently it's difficult to name favourites.

NA THON

There are several good restaurants and watering holes in Na Thon, many of which fill up with travellers waiting for the night ferry. A Giant Supermarket and a day market are on the third street back from the harbour, Th Thawi Ratchaphakdi.

About Art & Craft (Map p560; ☎ 0 1499 9353; Th Chonwithi; dishes 20-120B) This is a jewellery and art gallery that also serves delicious organic and sugarfree vegetarian food and juices. There is a peaceful, spiritual atmosphere here – surprising for Na Thon.

Coffee Island (Map p560; ☎ 0 7742 0153; Th Chonwithi; dishes 30-190B) Great for early-morning pier arrivals, Coffee Island has real espresso, baked goods, full breakfasts and a huge menu of Western and Thai food.

Sunset Restaurant & Beer Garden (Map p560; ☎ 0 7742 1244; Th Chonwithi; dishes 80-300B) Sunset sits at the southern end of the coast street and offers great seaside atmosphere and plenty of beer. On tap are Thai, Western and seafood dishes.

Roung Thong Bakery (Map p560; ☎ 0 7742 2522; Th Chonwithi; dishes 40-120B) Homemade pastries and coffee make this bakery another favourite breakfast spot. Its relaxing atmosphere attracts travellers waiting for the boat.

Ko Kaew (Map p560; ☎ 0 7742 1061; Th Chonwithi; dishes 25-80B) This place serves supercheap and delicious Thai food in a friendly, casual setting. You'll find soups, noodle dishes and fish cakes.

Jit Phochana Khao Tom (Map p560; Th Thawi Ratchaphakdi; noodles 25B) This is a tiny place that prepares tasty noodles.

Il Pirata (Map p560; Th Na Amphoe; dishes 50-150B) Il Pirata offers Thai and Western food in friendly but tacky surroundings (too many mirrors); it has a busy corner location that's good for people-watching.

HAT BO PHUT

The heart of Bo Phut runs along a calm inland road near the beach, where you'll find a concentrated number of restaurants and other services. Good eateries include Thai restaurants alongside some *faràng*-oriented ones.

Angela's Harbourside Café (☎ 0 7742 7212; Fisherman's Village; dishes 60-200B) Angela's has something for everyone – fresh baked breads and pies, unique deli items, smoked salmon and shrimp omelettes, and New England clam chowder are all on the menu.

Billabong Surf Club (☎ 0 7743 0144; Fisherman's Village; dishes from 100B) This Aussie restaurant serves giant portions of steaks, barbecue ribs and lamb chops, along with burgers, bar snacks and, for some reason, Indian curries. The beer flows late into the night.

The Frog & Gecko Pub (☎ 0 7742 5248; Fisherman's Village; dishes 60-200B) Locals recommend this popular spot on the beach. Part sports bar, part restaurant, it serves full English breakfasts (along with the footy) as well as the usual assortment of Thai and English pub food. It's a happening place day or night.

The Shack Bar & Grill (☎ 0 7724 5041; Fisherman's Village; dishes from 200B) Well-presented flame grilled dishes are served in an intimate setting at this restaurant featuring Californian cuisine and a lengthy wine list. Jazz and blues music complement the dining experience.

BIG BUDDHA BEACH

The Mangrove (☎ 0 7742 7584; dishes from 200B) For an exceptional meal, check out the Mangrove on Ko Fan (the island connected to the mainland by a causeway). An ex-Poppies chef runs the kitchen and cooks up an ever-changing menu of French cuisine. Reservations are highly recommended, as seating is limited.

HAT CHAWENG

Back on the 'strip' are dozens of restaurants and cafés serving Western cuisine. Italian places outnumber the rest, but many types of food are accounted for from stalls serving cheap Thai to Starbucks and McDonalds. For the best ambience get off the strip and head to the beach where many bungalow operators set up tables on the sand and have glittery fairy lights at night. With the waves providing the background soundtrack, you can't get much more relaxed.

Toto's Pizzeria Ristorante (Map p562; ☎ 0 7723 0401; dishes from 200B) We couldn't get enough of this atmospheric, open-air Italian restaurant with a large menu of pizzas and pastas and a long wine list. Apparently neither could many others, as the place almost always has a queue. The pizzas are mouthwatering and large, the pastas homemade and the sauces are packed with flavour.

Ali Baba (Map p562; ☎ 0 7723 0253; dishes 70-200B) Friendly service and a homey space complement the mostly Indian and Thai menu here. It also serves burgers and pizza.

Drop In Bar & Restaurant (Map p562; ☎ 0 7741 3221; dishes 80-260B; ⏰ noon-midnight) A stream and waterfalls create an elegant ambience at this beautiful, lofty thatched-hut bar and restaurant. Western and Thai food pleases the tourist palate. There's a calm bar nearby.

Deck (Map p562; ☎ 0 7723 0897; dishes 80-200B) This open-air restaurant cooks up Thai food, burgers, souvlaki, pasta and salad, among other dishes. It offers breakfasts with enough grease to cure a morning hangover. There's a loud bar, too.

Gringos Cantina (Map p562; ☎ 0 7741 3267; dishes 145-230B; ⏰ 2pm-midnight) This is a popular Mexican *cocina* serving quesadillas, tacos, tostadas and burritos that are best washed down with margaritas, piña coladas and tequila shooters. Of course it has the requisite pizzas and burgers as well.

Poppies (Map p562; ☎ 0 7742 2419; dishes 220-640B) High elegance meets fine cuisine at this very dressy, classy and all-over excellent restaurant. There is occasional live music, and Saturday is Thai night (expect dance, music and culture).

Betelnet (Map p562; ☎ 0 7741 3370; dishes 200-500B; ⏰ 6pm-midnight) A small, modest, up-market place just a bit south of the town centre, gourmets trek here for California–Thai fusion specials like sesame-crusted salmon, jumbo prawns with *tôm yam* (soup made with lemongrass, chilli, lime and usually seafood) and roast duck in pineapple curry. Wines include Chilean, South African, Italian and Australian. Reservations are recommended.

Will Wait Restaurant & Bakery (Map p562; ☎ 0 7742 2613; dishes 35-180) In addition to cakes and pastries, this eatery serves pizzas, Thai food and decent Western breakfasts at three locations in south and central Chaweng.

Islander (Map p562; ☎ 0 7723 0836; dishes 90-210B) The Islander is a popular, pub-style place with Western and Thai food, a kids menu, outdoor tables, a pool table and sports on TV – something for almost everyone.

Tropical Murphy's (Map p562; ☎ 0 7741 3614; dishes 75-295B) This place is fairly similar to the Islander and just as popular with *faràng*. On the menu are steak and kidney pie, fish and chips, lamb chops, Irish stew and desserts.

HAT LAMAI
Lamai doesn't have as wide a variety of places to eat as Chaweng. Most visitors appear to dine wherever they're staying. Once again, Italian is nearly ubiquitous. There are also several Thai food stalls in the central beach area.

Bauhaus Bistro (☎ 0 9972 2241; dishes 50-220B) This huge wooden structure serves specials like beef in Guinness (120B). The regular menu includes burgers, salads, sandwiches, snacks and Thai food. Also on tap is a great lounging area with a large TV.

Churchill's (☎ 0 7741 8687; dishes 130-230B) Indoor and outdoor seating plus plates of steak and other pub fare make Churchill's a popular spot. There is sport on TV and a pool table.

Rising Sun (☎ 0 7741 8015; dishes 60-300B) Popular with *faràng* for its outdoor, casual seating, this place does decent burgers, steaks, veggie stuff, coffees and drinks.

Terrace (☎ 0 7723 2361; dishes 80-200B) The Terrace is the choice for fancier Thai meals in elegant surroundings; choose your seafood at the front.

Il Tempio (☎ 0 7723 2307; dishes 130-230B) Il Tempio cooks up all the Italian specialities, along with a few Thai ones. There's appealing, open but covered seating around a small pond, and a gelataria also.

Drinking & Entertainment
Hat Chaweng and Hat Lamai have the most nightlife, but many bungalows and hotels

all over the island have small- to medium-sized bars.

BO PHUT

Billabong Surf Club (☎ 0 7743 0144) Great views across to Ko Pha-Ngan, as well as plenty of Aussie sports memorabilia make this restaurant (p572) and bar a popular drinking spot. Of course the telly is always tuned to the sport.

The Frog & Gecko Pub (☎ 0 7742 5248) This little tropical British watering hole and food stop (p572) is famous for its 'Wednesday Night Pub Quiz' competitions and its wide selection of music. Live sporting events are shown on the big screen.

HAT CHAWENG

Reggae Pub (Map p562; ☎ 0 7742 2331) Looming like a gorgeous monster at the end of a girlie-bar line-up, this two-storey, tastefully done, open building sports long bars, pool tables, good seating, a live-music stage and lake views. It's also a virtual shrine to Bob Marley. Across the street is an open-air cinema and more bars. Needless to say, it's popular with both foreigners and Thais – despite being far from the town centre.

Green Mango (Map p562; ☎ 0 7742 2148) Another popular, cavernous and very loud *faràng* bar, Green Mango has blazing lights, soccer on TV, expensive drinks and masses of sweaty bodies swaying to dance music.

Full Circle (Map p562; ☎ 0 7741 3061) A techno dance club with stark, modern décor, Full Circle gets going around midnight; Wednesday night is Ladies Night (one free drink for the females). Happy hour (buy one get one free) happens nightly from 6pm to 9pm.

Deck (Map p562; ☎ 0 7723 0897) This is an open-air, multiterraced restaurant-bar with comfortable lounging platforms and good views of the street scene below.

Legends (Map p562) Right on the strip, this bar is run by a friendly expat and draws in fistfuls of *faràng* for strong cocktails (try the Long Island Iced Tea to knock your socks off) and sport on the TV. It has a casual outdoor seating area.

Drop In Bar & Restaurant (Map p562; ☎ 0 7741 3221) A mellow, more sophisticated yet still casual place, the Drop In has bar stools, a projector TV (think soccer), wooden details, a few outdoor tables and an overall great ambience.

Black Jack Pub (Map p562; ☎ 0 1748 3740) Small and cosy with sports TV and two pool tables, the Black Jack is run by an expat. Internet access is free from 5pm to 11pm.

Christy's Cabaret Bar (Map p562; admission free; show time 11pm) This bar offers transvestite cabaret nightly and attracts a mixed clientele of both sexes. Inside, the music's outdated and the show's not great, but it's something different.

Viking (Map p562; ☎ 0 9909 6779) This Swede-run place draws in Scandinavians and plays them homesick music in a cosy space. Its claim to fame is a Swede who downed 11 vodka shots in 9.86 seconds. Newcomers are cautiously invited to break this record (though you'll probably have to pay for your booze).

HAT LAMAI

What would a Thai tourist beach town be without its Pattaya-style girlie bars? Lamai's no exception, but there *are* clean places to taste alcohol. Try the **Bauhaus Pub** on the main strip. It has a long-running, large, dance club with huge wooden beams and high rattan ceiling under a thatched roof, where music presented by DJs is interspersed with short drag shows and Thai boxing demos. The **Lucky Pub**, opposite the Bauhaus, offers German beer, snacks and all the typical pub games.

Getting There & Away

AIR

Bangkok Airways (Map p562; ☎ 0 7742 2512) flies about 16 times daily between Ko Samui and Bangkok. The flight takes about one hour and 20 minutes. Other destinations from Samui include Phuket, Pattaya and Chiang Mai. During high season flights may be booked out six weeks in advance, so plan accordingly. If Samui flights are full, you might try flying to Surat Thani first, then taking a boat. Delays are also common, so plan accordingly for connecting flights.

The Samui airport departure tax is 400B for domestic and international flights. The attractive airport is open-air, and has a nice bar, restaurant, money-exchange outlet and hotel-reservations counter.

BOAT

There are four ferry piers on the Surat Thani coast (Ao Ban Don, Don Sak, Khanom and

Tha Thong) and three on Ko Samui (Big Buddha, Mae Nam and Na Thon). When going to Ko Samui, the boat (and pier) you use will probably depend on what's available next when you arrive in Surat Thani.

Schedules and prices are always in flux. Expect more departures during the busy season and fewer during the rainy times. Prices may fall during slow seasons. Nothing stays the same, so use the following as general guidelines only. And remember that tickets from a travel agency cost more but include a transfer to the pier.

There are frequent daily boats between Samui and Surat Thani (150B to 350B, 2½ to six hours). A couple of these departures connect directly with the train in Phun Phin. The slow night boat to Samui leaves from Surat at 11pm, reaching Na Thon around 5am (150B). This boat is recommended if you arrive in town too late for the fast boats and don't want to stay in Surat. Going back to Surat, the slow night boat leaves Na Thon at 9pm, arriving at around 3am or 4am. Watch your bags on this boat.

There are 10 daily journeys between Samui and Ko Pha-Ngan (115B to 250B, 30 minutes). On Ko Pha-Ngan there are two piers (Hat Rin and Thong Sala), so decide where you want to go before you buy your ticket. There are also around six daily boats between Samui and Ko Tao (280B to 550B, 1½ to three hours).

BUS

It can be cheaper and less stressful to get bus/ferry combination tickets that take you all the way to (and from) Ko Samui.

The government-bus fares from Bangkok's Southern Bus Terminal don't include the cost of the ferry. These are 660B for VIP, 430B for 1st class and 337B for 2nd class. Most private buses from Bangkok charge around 400B for the same journey and include the ferry fare. From Th Khao San in Bangkok it's possible to get bus/ferry combination tickets for as little as 250B, but service is substandard and theft is more frequent than on the more expensive buses. If an agency on Th Khao San claims to be able to get you to Samui for less, it is almost certainly a scam as no profit can be made at such low prices. Surat Thani bus companies **Phantip Travel** (☎ 0 7742 1221) and

Songserm Travel (☎ 0 7742 0157) have offices in Na Thon.

From Na Thon, air-con buses head to many destinations. In the following list the ferry ride is included, and prices and length of travel vary according to the type of boat and bus. There are at least three daily departures for any given destination, the first one being at 7.30am.

Destination	Price (B)
Bangkok	350-660
Hat Yai	300
Khao Sok	300
Krabi	250-300
Penang	550-590
Phuket	300-350
Ranong	350
Surat Thani	150-250
Trang	350

TRAIN

You can buy train/bus/ferry tickets straight through to Samui from Bangkok. Buying these combination tickets are worthwhile to save you the hassle of buying separate tickets (though you really don't save much money – especially if you count getting to the train station etc). For details on train travel, see p550.

Getting Around

TO/FROM THE AIRPORT

Private taxi fares from the airport are: Chaweng 200B to 250B; Lamai 250B to 300B; and Na Thon 400B. Minivans also do the run; the more passengers in the van, the cheaper it is for you. Destinations and rough prices are: Bang Rak 30B; Bo Phut 70B; Chaweng and Mae Nam 100B; and Na Thon and Lamai 120B. Cheapest are *săwngthăew*: Chaweng 50B; Lamai and Mae Nam 80B; and Na Thon 100B.

CAR & MOTORCYCLE

You can rent motorcycles (and bicycles) from several places in Na Thon, Chaweng and Lamai, as well as various bungalows around the island. The going rate is 150B per day for a small motorcycle, but for longer periods try to negotiate a better rate. Take it easy on the bikes; every year several *faràng* die or are seriously injured in motorcycle accidents on Samui. A helmet law is enforced with some vigour from time to time. Don't put valuables in the basket on the front of the bike. Snatch thieves can easily scoot by on their own motorcycles and grab your bag.

Suzuki Caribbean jeeps can be hired for around 1000B per day from a number of Na Thon agencies as well as at Chaweng and Lamai.

SĂWNGTHĂEW

Fares from Na Thon include Mae Nam 30B, Bo Phut 40B, Hat Bang Rak 50B, Lamai 50B, Chaweng 50B and Choeng Mon 50B. *Săwngthăew* drivers love to try to overcharge you, so it's always best to ask a third party for current rates (in case these have changed). These vehicles run regularly during daylight hours only.

KO PHA-NGAN
เกาะพะงัน
pop 10,300

Ko Samui's rebellious little sister maintains an image that's distinctly her own. A half-hour boat ride north, 193-sq-km Ko Pha-Ngan boasts the same stupendous scenery found on Ko Samui, minus the glitz. The lack of an airport and relative absence of good roads have spared it from package-tour development – you won't find jet skis or top-end resorts here. The view from the island's most popular beach, Hat Rin, yields rows of rather ramshackle bungalows and

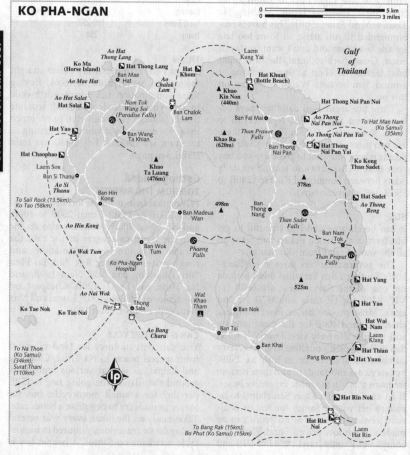

KO PHA-NGAN

0 ——— 5 km
0 ——— 3 miles

Gulf of Thailand

To Hat Mae Nam (Ko Samui) (35km)

To Sail Rock (13.5km); Ko Tao (58km)

To Na Thon (Ko Samui) (34km); Surat Thani (110km)

To Bang Rak (15km); Bo Phut (Ko Samui) (15km)

Laem Kung Yai
Hat Khuat (Bottle Beach)
Hat Khom
Ko Ma (Horse Island)
Hat Thong Lang
Ao Hat Thong Lang
Ban Mae Hat
Ao Mae Hat
Ao Chalok Lam
Khao Kin Non (440m)
Hat Thong Nai Pan Noi
Ao Hat Salat
Hat Salat
Nam Tok Wang Sai (Paradise Falls)
Ban Chalok Lam
Ban Fai Mai
Ao Thong Nai Pan Noi
Hat Yao
Ban Wang Ta Khian
Khao Ra (620m)
Than Prawet Falls
Ao Thong Nai Pan Yai
Hat Thong Nai Pan Yai
Hat Chaophao
Laem Son
Ban Si Thanu
Ao Si Thanu
Khao Ta Luang (476m)
Ban Thong Nai Pan
Ko Kong Than Sadet
Ban Hin Kong
378m
Hat Sadet
Ao Thong Reng
Ban Madeua Wan
498m
Ban Thong Nang
Than Sadet Falls
Ao Hin Kong
Ban Nam Tok
Ao Wok Tum
Ban Wok Tum
Phaeng Falls
Than Prapat Falls
Hat Yang
Ko Pha-Ngan Hospital
Ao Nai Wok
Wat Khao Tham
525m
Hat Yao
Ko Tae Nok
Ko Tae Nai
Thong Sala
Ban Nok
Hat Wai Nam
Pier
Laem Klang
Ao Bang Charu
Ban Tai
Hat Thian
Ban Khai
Pang Bon
Hat Yuan
Hat Rin Nok
Hat Rin Nai
Laem Hat Rin

LOWER SOUTHERN GULF

colourfully painted beach bars. Long-tail boats float alongside lazy swimmers in the clear green water. And while there are comfortable air-conditioned places, you'll have to look long and hard to find in-room satellite TV or ornate furnishings.

Despite the throngs that flock here on a daily basis, Ko Pha-Ngan remains a casual island with a sort of hippy fun-loving vibe where backpackers still dominate the tourist trade. Days slide easily past – lounging in the sand, joining an afternoon game of pick-up volleyball or watching the latest flick on a big-screen TV at an open-air restaurant. After Ko Samui became 'too built up', travellers seeking less commercialism and more isolation turned to Ko Pha-Ngan. Some say the time to see the island is long over – but the truth is tourists still arrive here by the boatload and seem to have a great time. Those searching for a remote paradise can still find it on many of the island's secluded beaches, where simple huts are the only accommodation and nights are passed in a make-your-own-fun fashion. If you're looking to party, as many coming to Ko Pha-Ngan are, head to Hat Rin, home of the legendary full-moon parties (see p581), the biggest beach party in the world. Although nowadays it seems any phase of the moon is an excuse to get out the fire sticks, set up the mats on the sand and pump up the trance music – nightlife is huge here, and scantily clad revellers suck down buckets of cheap Thai whisky on a nightly basis.

Orientation

Ko Pha-Ngan is approximately 20km from Ko Samui and 100km from Surat Thai.

About half of Ko Pha-Ngan's population lives in and around the small port of Thong Sala. This is where the ferries to and from Ko Tao, Surat Thai, and Ko Samui dock. It's a taking-care-of-business town, with restaurants, travel agencies, banks, clothing shops and general stores.

The long cape of Laem Hat Rin is at the southeastern tip of the island and has beaches along both its western and eastern sides – this is officially the most popular place on Ko Pha-Ngan. Travel agencies, minimarts, tattoo shops and discos crowd the small streets off the pretty beaches. The eastern side has the best beach, Hat Rin

Nok (Sunrise Beach), a long sandy strip lined with coconut palms, but there's more boat traffic than at the western beach. The snorkelling here is good, but between October and March the surf can be a little hairy. Hat Rin Nok is famous for its monthly full-moon parties. The western side of the cape, Hat Rin Nai (Sunset Beach), is more isolated and serves as an accommodation overflow if Hat Rin Nok is full. A pier on Hat Rin Nai serves boats from the northeastern coast of Ko Samui.

There are plenty of other places to stay on the island, although you will find many spots to be very remote (perfect if this is what you're looking for, bad if you show up expecting to party). The northern destinations of Hat Khuat (Bottle Beach) and Ao Thong Nai Pan/Yai are good choices if you are looking for beaches between 'too busy' and 'too isolated', while the beaches on the island's east coast are the most remote.

There are few paved roads on Pha-Ngan, so transport between places can be a bit of a hassle, although the situation is constantly improving as enterprising Thais set up taxi and boat services between beaches.

Information

Thong Sala is the place to go to attend to your 'to do' list. Travel agencies, banks, Western Union, the post office, motorcycle rental – all these facilities are here. Ban Chalok Lam, a town on the northern coast, is another administrative centre. Hat Rin has lots of Internet access, telephone offices, motorcycle rental and ATMs.

EMERGENCY
Police station (☎ 0 7737 7114) About 2km north of Thong Sala.

INTERNET ACCESS
Thong Sala and Hat Rin are centres for Internet activity, but every beach with development should have access. Rates are generally 1B to 2B per minute, with a 20B minimum.

MEDICAL SERVICES
Ko Pha-Ngan Hospital (☎ 0 7737 7034) About 2.5km north of Thong Sala off the road to Chalok Lam, it offers 24-hour emergency services. Anything that can wait until Bangkok should wait; medical facilities are better.

LOWER SOUTHERN GULF

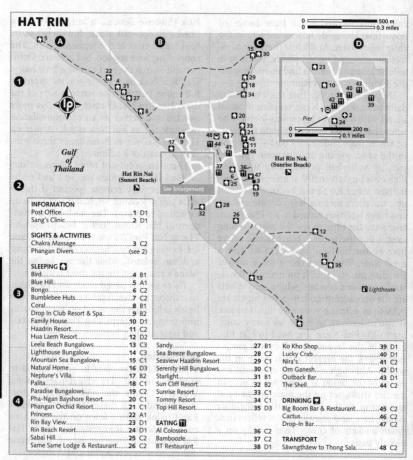

HAT RIN

Gulf of Thailand

Hat Rin Nai (Sunset Beach)

See Enlargement

Hat Rin Nok (Sunrise Beach)

Pier

Lighthouse

INFORMATION
Post Office..1 D1
Sang's Clinic..2 D1

SIGHTS & ACTIVITIES
Chakra Massage.....................................3 C2
Phangan Divers..............................(see 2)

SLEEPING
Bird..4 B1
Blue Hill..5 A1
Bongo...6 C2
Bumblebee Huts...................................7 C2
Coral...8 B1
Drop In Club Resort & Spa....................9 B2
Family House..10 D1
Haadrin Resort.....................................11 C2
Hua Laem Resort.................................12 D2
Leela Beach Bungalows.......................13 C3
Lighthouse Bungalow...........................14 C3
Mountain Sea Bungalows.....................15 C1
Natural Home......................................16 D3
Neptune's Villa....................................17 B2
Palita...18 C1
Paradise Bungalows.............................19 C2
Pha-Ngan Bayshore Resort..................20 C1
Phangan Orchid Resort........................21 C1
Princess...22 A1
Rin Bay View.......................................23 D1
Rin Beach Resort.................................24 D1
Sabai Hill...25 C2
Same Same Lodge & Restaurant..........26 C2

Sandy...27 B1
Sea Breeze Bungalows.........................28 C2
Seaview Haadrin Resort.......................29 C1
Serenity Hill Bungalows.......................30 C1
Starlight..31 B1
Sun Cliff Resort....................................32 B2
Sunrise Resort......................................33 C1
Tommy Resort......................................34 C1
Top Hill Resort.....................................35 D3

EATING
Al Colosseo..36 C2
Bamboozle..37 C2
BT Restaurant.......................................38 D1

Ko Kho Shop...39 D1
Lucky Crab...40 D1
Nira's...41 C2
Om Ganesh..42 D1
Outback Bar...43 D1
The Shell..44 C2

DRINKING
Big Boom Bar & Restaurant.................45 C2
Cactus..46 C2
Drop-In Bar..47 C2

TRANSPORT
Săwngthăew to Thong Sala.................48 C2

Sang's Clinic (☎ 0 1896 2195; ☯ 5-10pm Mon-Fri, 10am-10pm Sat & Sun) To fix your 'Ko Pha-Ngan tattoo' (motorcycle accident scrape) in Hat Rin, head to this clinic near the pier. It's also good for minor illnesses.

MONEY
Thong Sala has plenty of banks, currency exchanges and at least one Western Union Office. Hat Rin offers fewer services for topping up your cash.

POST & TELEPHONE
Since the arrival of new telephone lines in 1999, the number of places offering long-distance telephone services has grown tremendously. Just look for the signs in front of shops.

Post offices (☯ 8.30am-4.30pm Mon-Fri, 9am-noon Sat) There is a post office south of Thong Sala, and another at Hat Rin Nai on the road to Hat Rin Nok.

TOURIST INFORMATION
There is no TAT office on Ko Pha-Ngan, there are lots of knowledgable travel agencies in town, all offering the same services. Look for the busy ones or ask around to see which one's other travellers are using.

Dangers & Annoyances
A holiday in Ko Pha-Ngan can be a complete blast. We don't want to burst your bubble or discourage you from going, because it really is wonderful, but take note of the following.

FREAKING OUT

Suan Saranrom (Garden of Joys) psychiatric hospital in Surat Thai has to take on extra staff during full-moon periods to handle the number of travellers who freak out on magic mushrooms, acid or other abundantly available hallucinogens.

Those who come specifically seeking an organic buzz should take note: a hallucinogenic plant, newly exploited on the island, has caused a number of travellers to pay an unscheduled visit to the local psychiatric hospital. Called *ton lamphong* in Thai, the plant is possibly related to datura, a member of the highly toxic nightshade family. Eating any part of the plant causes some people to be completely whacked for a couple of days. Locals say it's becoming a problem because people who are on it act like wandering zombies – stumbling down streets and clawing at thin air – oblivious to anything but their own hallucinations, which they try to follow and grasp. Some guesthouses and restaurants are reportedly offering the plant to travellers who ask for magic mushrooms, apparently because the *ton lamphong* has yet to be made illegal.

GETTING BUSTED

While many travellers may like to sample some of the local herb, it's wise to think twice. There are constant reports of travellers being offered and sold marijuana and other drugs by restaurant or bungalow owners, and then being promptly busted by police officers who somehow know exactly, who, when and where to check.

The Thai government's war on drugs is no joke, and the police take it *extremely* (and that word is being used in its full capacity) seriously. Dealers are often shot – no questions asked. And there is a good chance that you could go to jail for more than just a few days, for even possessing half a joint. Once in jail, you won't necessarily be able to count on your embassy, your daddy or even bribery to get you out. You'll probably have to wait in your cell for your paperwork to slowly creep up to the top before anything even starts to happen about it.

Police road blocks between Thong Sala and Hat Rin are becoming more common, especially in the week leading up to the full-moon party on Hat Rin. These aren't cursory checks either; if you're on a motorcycle the police look in the fuel tank, check the tyres and search all your gear. One traveller reported 'the cops played a sort of pocket billiards' with his testicles looking for dope – not just pot, but ecstasy, acid, amphetamines and anything else an enterprising dealer might be shipping in for the big party.

MOTORCYCLES

While Ko Pha-Ngan now has some smooth, paved roads, much of it is a labyrinth of rutty dirt-and-mud paths. Also, the island is very hilly, and even if the road is paved, it can be too difficult for most to take on. The very steep road to Hat Rin is a perfect case in point. Make sure you're capable of negotiating any road you're on. Too many injuries (and motorcycle damage fees) result from drivers being too proud to turn around and instead hail a taxi.

Probably more so than Samui, Ko Pha-Ngan is home to a growing number of basket thieves – people who take items out of your motorcycle basket – even while you're driving. Keep all bags on your person and nothing in the basket. The robbers have been known to ride by and snatch things out of your basket then zoom off, or even jump out and stop your bike with their hands, sometimes using weapons. If you are riding alone in a secluded area, don't slow down for people who wave you down.

Don't let this keep you from exploring the island by motorcycle if you want to. Be aware of the dangers.

Sights

WATERFALLS

In the interior of the island are four year-round waterfalls and a number of more seasonal ones. Boulders carved with the royal insignia of Rama V, Rama VII and Rama IX, all of whom have visited the falls, can be found at **Nam Tok Than Sadet**, which cascades along Khlong Than Sadet in the eastern part of the island. Rama V so liked this island that he made 18 trips here between 1888 and 1909. A pleasant way to get to the falls is with one of the 'Reggae Magic Boat Trips', offered by the **Cactus Club** (☎ 0 7737 5308; cruise 300B; departs 11am), a bar in Hat Rin. The cruise includes an opportunity to see the falls and stops for snorkelling. Food, refreshments and snorkel gear are provided. Contact the Cactus Club if you want to book, as the trips only depart when people are interested.

Nam Tok Phaeng is off the main road between Thong Sala and Ban Chalok Lam, almost in the centre of the island. A third waterfall, **Nam Tok Than Prapat**, is near the eastern shore in an area that can be reached by road or boat, while **Nam Tok Than Prawet** is northeast, near Ao Thong Nai Pan.

WAT KHAO THAM
วัดเขาถ้ำ

This cave temple is beautifully situated on top of a hill near the little village of Ban Tai. An American monk lived here for over a decade and his ashes are interred on a cliff overlooking a field of palms below the wat. It's not a true wat since there are only a couple of monks and a nun in residence (among other requirements, a quorum of five monks is necessary for a temple to reach wat status).

Ten-day meditation retreats taught by an American-Australian couple are run during the latter half of most months. The cost is 2900B, write in advance to Wat Khao Tham, PO Box 18, Ko Pha-Ngan, Surat Thani, 84280, for information, or stop by the temple to preregister in person.

Anyone under 25 years of age must talk with the teachers before being accepted for the retreat. A bulletin board at the temple has more information.

Activities
DIVING & SNORKELLING

As on Ko Samui, coral reefs can be found intermittently at various points around the island. The better bay-reef spots are on the island's northwestern tip and are suitable for snorkelling. There are also some rock reefs of interest on the eastern side of the island. In Hat Rin nearly every travel shop (and quite a few bars and bungalow operations) can book daily snorkelling trips. Most take you to Ao Mae Hat, and often include other stops around the islands. Trips cost about 300B and departures depend on whether anyone has booked and the weather. If you want to snorkel on your own, you can rent gear around the island for about 150B per day.

An outstanding site for scuba divers is a pinnacle called **Hin Bai** (Sail Rock), which lies about 13.5km north of the island. Here you'll find an abundance of coral and tropical fish at depths of 10m to 30m. Conditions are best from April to October, when divers sometimes enjoy visibility up to 20m or more. Hin Bai can also be reached from Ko Tao, although the boating distance from the latter adds 4km to 5km to the trip.

Phangan Divers (☎ 077375117; info@phangandivers .com) is near the pier at Hat Rin Nai. The company charges 700B for beach-dive trips; 2000B for a dive trip to Sail Rock or Ang Thong Marine National Park and 8000B for full certification, including lunch and two dives.

MASSAGE

Chakra Massage (☎ 0 7737 5401; chakramasage@hot mail.com), on Hat Rin Nok between Paradise Bungalows and Drop Inn Bar, offers expert traditional Thai massage for 200B per hour or 300B for two hours. Yan, the proprietor, studied massage as a monk and is adept at traditional Thai massage as well as deep tissue techniques.

Sleeping

Beach-bungalow operations are concentrated to the north and southeast of Thong Sala and especially on the southern end of the island at Hat Rin, but there are many other places to stay. Pha-Ngan has yet to see the type of high-end resorts found on Ko Samui. You'll be hard pressed to find a place with impeccable sheets and classy art on the walls. That said, there are quite a few very pleasant midrange options. At these you can expect hot showers, clean rooms and air-con.

The following sleeping options are listed here in a clockwise direction starting with Thong Sala. Remember, when you jump off the boat you may be surrounded by hotel touts pushing small (and sometimes larger) operations all over the island. However, many of these bungalows will be on very remote beaches, some may lack electricity or running water, and you could feel quite isolated. If you're looking for lots of other travellers, multiple eating options or the chance to party hard, head to Hat Rin.

THONG SALA

There's not much reason to stay here, unless you need to catch an early boat.

FULL MOONING

Ravers from all around the globe have been gathering for over 10 years to celebrate Hat Rin's infamous full-moon parties. Some 3000 to 5000 ravers – sometimes over 12,000 during the December-to-February peak season – turn up to dance, drink and smoke the night away. A half-dozen music stages belt out house, trance, hip-hop, techno, ambient and R&B (whatever's trendiest), while groovers spill out of open-air dance halls and onto the beach. Fire swinging and fireworks light up the night. The number of partygoers peaks at around 2am to 3am, and the last of the DJs don't shut down till around 11am. As you can guess, it's a pretty wild and hazy time for everyone.

And what would the world's biggest beach party be without drugs? Yes, they're still available these days, though the more hardcore partakers have moved on to other beaches due to a pumped-up police presence (both uniformed and undercover). More than a few deaths have been attributed to drug use at this party.

The whole event is well organised by Thai residents who run the bungalows and bars along Hat Rin. And these same proprietors, along with some of the more conscientious foreign travellers, come together to clean the beach of substantial morning-after litter when the party is finally over.

Check your lunar calendar for upcoming full-moon party dates.

Full-Moon Party Tips

Religious protests have recently forced Hat Rin's full-moon parties to actually take place either before or after the actual full-moon date; these are related to Buddhist holidays that occur around the full moon about four times annually. Double-check if any changes are in store when you plan to attend the party.

- Safety – Be watchful of your personal belongings and personal safety. Try not to bring extra money. Don't keep valuables in your bungalow – it's a big night for break-ins, especially at the cheaper huts. Be careful with fireworks and even stray live wires. Wear protective shoes! Don't go swimming under the influence of drugs or alcohol – drownings account for many full-moon party deaths. Don't accept consumables from strangers – they may be laced.

- Accommodation – If you arrive on the day of the full moon or even the day before, you can forget about finding a vacant room or bungalow anywhere near Hat Rin – many ravers nail down a room four days in advance. Head over the rocky hills to the southern end of the cape, or try some of the nearby beaches – though even these are likely to be full. Loads of partygoers, especially Thais, boat over from Samui during the afternoon, party all night, then boat back the next morning, thereby side-stepping the accommodation dilemma.

- Transport – If you're coming over from Ko Samui for the party, take one of the thrice-daily ferries from Big Buddha pier at Hat Bang Rak on Samui (100B), or hop on one of the frequent speedboats (one way/return 250/400B). The speedboats depart continuously from Big Buddha pier and Bo Phut pier until around 1am, reaching a peak number of trips between 8pm and midnight. It's best to buy a return ticket, because after the party these are at a premium and you may be overcharged on the way back.

Bua Kao Inn (☎ 0 7737 7226; buakao@samart.co.th; r 480-550B; ☒) Fastidiously maintained by an expat, this is a guesthouse with awesome showers. The five rooms are clean and nicely decorated and there's a popular restaurant downstairs. The inn is on the right-hand side of the first main intersection in town, about 100m straight ahead of the pier.

Pha-Ngan Chai Hotel (☎ 0 7737 7068; r 850-1000B; ☒) This big hotel gives you a choice of garden or sea view. Rooms are modern and carpeted, but rather dim. It's right on the road along the water, turn right at the end of the pier.

Sea Mew (☎ 0 1477 7076; r 200B) Sea Mew is a bit impersonal, although the restaurant at the front can provide some entertainment. Rooms are modern and large, but lit with fluorescent lights. It's next door to the Pha-Ngan Chai Hotel.

Asia Hotel (☎ 0 7723 8607; r 400-700B; ❄) Near Bua Kao Inn, this hotel offers some tiny rooms – pay more for a larger one, as you'll need to breathe. Things are fairly modern and decent here.

AO NAI WOK

Ao Nai Wok is just a few minutes' walk north of Thong Sala. Its beach isn't spectacular, but if you want to be near Thong Sala it's a fairly nice area. Swimming is best from December to April. To get here, go north past the Asia Hotel about 250m to the T-intersection, where you go left again for 100m.

Phangan (☎ 0 7737 7191; bungalows 150-450B) Phangan's peaceful bungalows are on grass and surrounded by coconut palms. Turn left at the first main crossing from the pier, then walk straight north until the road crosses a concrete bridge, and then turn left again where the road ends at a T-junction. There's also a fine little restaurant that does whole roast pig on a spit.

Siriphun (☎ 0 7737 7140; fax 0 7737 7242; bungalows 300-900B; ❄) The staff are friendly here and Siriphun offers a pretty garden area and solid bungalows with mosquito screens.

AO HIN KONG & AO WOK TUM

This long bay – sometimes divided in two by a stream that feeds into the sea (hence the two names) – is just a few kilometres north of Thong Sala and has relatively subdued tourist development. Bungalows are cheap; most don't have air-con. *Săwngthăew* here cost 30B, but you'll see them only at ferry departure and arrival times.

Lipstick Cabana (☎ 0 7737 7294; r 100-500B) At the centre of Ao Hin Kong, the accommodation here is basic, but its restaurant is excellent. Seven abodes are available; the larger and nicer ones are more expensive. Bring a book and chill.

Sea Scene (☎ 0 7737 7516; bungalows 400-800B; ❄) A great deal, Sea Scene offers beautiful, upmarket and modern bungalows in a well-tended garden. There's a clean feel to the entire place.

Woktum Bay (☎ 0 7737 7430; bungalows 100-200B) This friendly family place has older, smaller concrete bungalows and newer, larger wooden ones.

Bounty (☎ 0 7737 7517; bungalows 150B-300B) The Bounty offers basic bungalows with hammocks in a pleasant garden on open grounds – a good deal at this price.

Beach 99 (☎ 0 7737 7518; bungalows 200-600B) The pricier bungalows here are large, wooden and solid, with nice sitting areas. The cheap bungalows are forgettable. It's a hike down from the driveway.

HAT CHAOPHAO & AO SI THANU

Hat Chaophao is a rounded beach situated two headlands south of Hat Yao; Ao Si Thanu is around a larger headland at its southern end. There's a pretty lagoon inland at the southern end of Hat Chaophao.

The following places to rest your body are in Hat Chaophao.

Pha-Ngan Cabana (☎ 0 1958 0182; bungalows 300-600B; ❄ ▢ ▣) These sturdy, tidy villa-style bungalows are just inland from the beach. The onsite restaurant shows two movies a day and attracts people from the beach. The Pirate Bar, just around a small promontory to the left of the beach, is a fun place shaped like a boat and built into a cliff.

Hut Sun (☎ 0 1891 3824; bungalows 150-300B) Hut Sun is a good, friendly cheapie. The bungalows line a leafy garden.

Seethanu (☎ 0 1968 4685; bungalows 150-700B; ❄) Great value with a nice garden, the best (and most expensive) rooms at Seethanu are the spacious, seaside bungalows with big windows. Look for the 'Bovy' driveway and go right.

Haad Chaophao (☎ 0 7734 9273; bungalows 100-200B) This place is beachfront and shaded with palms.

Haad Son Bungalows (☎ 0 7734 9103; bungalows 350-100B; ❄ ▣) Beach access can be tricky here, but Haad Son has a great pool and expansive sea views. The fan bungalows are thatch, the air-con ones are brick or plaster.

The following are in Ao Si Thanu.

Laem Son I & II (☎ 0 1856 6027; bungalows 150-400B) On the rounded, pine-studded cape of Laem Son, at the northern end of Ao Si Thanu proper, these two places have small but nice bungalows, some with hammocks. Most are on the beach (a whole slew are electric blue, if you're into that) and there's a definite backpacker vibe. The seaside restaurant has decent music and lots of pillows.

Loy Fa (☎ 0 7737 7319; bungalows 150-200B, cottages 500B) Sitting high on a point at the southern end of the bay, Loy Fa has sturdy huts with good views. It's nicely landscaped and well run, and has wood-and-cement cottages, with two large ones at the bottom of the cliff on a private cove. The restaurant shows movies.

Seaview Rainbow (☎ 0 7727 4105; bungalows 200-500B) This place offers decent, spacious concrete bungalows in an open garden.

HAT YAO & HAT SALAT

These coral-fringed beaches are difficult to reach – come by boat if possible. Hat Yao (not to be confused with its namesake on the eastern coast) is a very long, pretty beach with a reasonable drop-off that makes it great for swimming. There are a few diving outfits here and it is a social area. Hat Salat is very mellow and has good snorkelling towards the northern part of the beach.

Tantawin Bungalows (☎ 0 7734 9108; yup_pat@ hotmail.com; bungalows 250-400B; 🖳) On a hillside, this place is fantastic, but it's a bit of a trek down to the beach. It has a good French-Thai restaurant and beautiful views over the bay, as well as plenty of tree shade and soothing music.

Haad Yao Bungalows (☎ 0 7734 9152; bungalows 200-1000B; 🔀) Haad Yao has light-green plyboard bungalows featuring big porches. They are on a grassy patch right near the beach.

Long Bay Resort (☎ 0 7737 7289; bungalows 350-2000B; 🔀 🖳 🖳) Long Bay is the fanciest spot on the beach. Fan bungalows are comfortable, while air-con ones are big and beautiful. It's good for families – the pool has a wading area. There's a five-person house that can be rented for 3500B. Laundry facilities and massage are available and a minimarket is within reach.

Long Beach Resort (☎ 0 7737 7015; bungalows 300-1000B; 🔀) This place has good-sized bungalows lined up away from the beach.

Ibiza (☎ 0 1968 4727; bungalows 50-800B; 🔀) The cheapest fan bungalows here share bathrooms, but you can't beat the price! All are basic, rather cramped affairs, but they sit in a pleasant garden.

Green Papaya (☎ 0 7737 4230; bungalows 1000-1600B; 🔀) Green Papaya is probably a bit overpriced, but the bungalows and cottages are quite lovely and integrated into the cove. It's in Hat Salat.

AO MAE HAT & AO HAT THONG LANG

Ban Mae Hat is a small fishing village with a few bungalow resorts. The beach at Ao Mae Hat isn't fantastic, but there is a bit of coral offshore – where you'll probably end up if you do a snorkelling trip. Ao Thong Lang is superquiet and devoid of development except for one bungalow operation. *Săwngthăew* to/from Ban Chalok Lam cost 20B.

Wang Sai Resort (☎ 0 7737 4238; bungalows 100-300B) Decent bamboo huts, along with more-solid bungalows, come with beach views here. Boulders, a garden and a footbridge leading to the beach complete the picture. The open-air restaurant is well away from the huts, down on the beach, and a dive operation offers instruction and guided trips.

Mae Haad Bay Resort (☎ 0 1968 2740; maeha ad-bay-resort@hotmail.com; bungalows 150-250B) Fine wooden bungalows with hammocks are to be found here. The best bungalows are away from the road.

Royal Orchid Resort (☎ 0 7737 4182; bungalows 150-800B; 🔀) The small wooden bungalows on spacious grounds are not unique at this resort, but a solid deal nonetheless.

Pha-Ngan Utopia Resort (☎ 0 7727 4093; bungalows 300-500B) At Hat Thong Lang, this place offers basic bungalows. Don't come looking for a party, it's the only operation around.

AO CHALOK LAM

The fishing village of Ban Chalok Lam, at the centre of Ao Chalok Lam, features several small family-run grocery stores, laundry services and lots of fish-drying at the side of the main street.

Ao Chalok Lam is a good place to hire boats for explorations of the northern coast. Many fishermen dock here (particularly from February to September). During this season boats run at least twice daily to Hat Khuat (Bottle Beach) and you can almost always charter a boat. Boats won't run if the sea is too rough.

The road between Thong Sala and Ban Chalok Lam is paved all the way; *săwngthăew* between the towns cost 50B.

Fanta (☎ 0 7737 4132; fantaphangan@yahoo.com; bungalows 150-500B) If you can live without air-con, Fanta is your best bet. On a nice beach, with a good traveller's vibe, the bungalows are decent and vary in comfort – depending on how much you're willing to shell out, of course.

Rose Villa (☎ 0 7737 4013; rosevilla2000@hotmail .com; bungalows 300-1000B; 🔀) Rose Villa has neat brick and concrete bungalows sitting in a sparse beachside garden. There's nothing wrong with it, but it's not anything special either.

Try Tong Resort (☎ 0 7737 4115; bungalows 150-1500B; ☒) Across a canal via a rickety footbridge from Fanta, Try Trong offers large old bungalows facing the bay and canal. There's no beach here save for a small chunk with boulders at the surf line.

HAT KHUAT (BOTTLE BEACH) & HAT KHOM

These two pretty bays – particularly Hat Khuat – are attracting more and more tourists to their fine, comfortable-sized beaches, calm waters and low-key atmosphere. In fact after Hat Rin they're probably the second most popular sleeping destination. The clientele is mostly backpackers – the type that thinks Hat Rin is too built up, but still craves a little action. Both beaches offer decent snorkelling around the points, and some places only have electricity at night.

Săwngthăew run from Thong Sala to Ban Chalok Lam (50B), where there are boats to Hat Khom and Hat Khuat (40B to 50B). You can walk to Hat Khom in about 20 minutes, or take a taxi; motorcycles should be able to negotiate the hard, sandy road. You can also hike the 2.5km from Hat Khom to Hat Khuat (one hour), but the trail is challenging and you can easily get lost; take a guide if possible.

Hat Khuat is the busier of the two beaches, with more places to stay.

Bottle Beach I, II & III (bungalows 100-400B) One family runs these three bungalow operations. All are basic but have varying quality restaurants – Bottle Beach I is the most fancy, Bottle Beach II the best for hanging out, Bottle Beach III is the quietest.

Smile Resort (bungalows 250-350B) These are slightly better-quality bungalows than the Bottle Beach conglomerates, although the scene isn't as happening. The abodes are well spaced, quiet and in a pretty, jungle-like garden with views.

OD Bungalows (bungalows 100B) The most barebones and ramshackle of all the operations, the bungalows here are tucked away up on the rocks on the western hill; the family is sweet and welcoming, though. Bathrooms are shared.

Hat Khom is smaller and more peaceful with only a few places to stay.

Ocean Bay (☎ 0 7737 4245; bungalows 150-450B) Up on the headland, this friendly place offers 30 pleasant bungalows with some great views. They range from basic huts with shared bathrooms to large, fancy, creatively done affairs with balconies. The restaurant has a super deck and serves vegetarian food. Call for free pick-up.

Had Khom (☎ 0 7737 4246; bungalows 150-400B) An OK place, Had Khom is not especially memorable.

AO THONG NAI PAN YAI & NOI

Of the two bays, Ao Thong Nai Pan Yai and Ao Thong Nai Pan Noi, the latter has the best all-round swimming beach, although Thong Nai Pan Yai is quieter and has a good set of rocks for advanced climbers at its eastern end. To get between the two bays you can hike a steep trail for about 20 minutes or take a long-tail boat. A couple of dive shops and Internet cafés are found at both beaches.

Săwngthăew from Thong Sala to Thong Nai Pan cost 80B. Unless you are experienced on steep, rutty dirt roads, don't think of attempting the trip from Thong Sala by motorcycle.

The following places to stay are on Ao Thong Nai Pan Yai.

Dolphin (bungalows 300-400B) Hidden behind a richly ambient bar and lush tropical vegetation, Dolphin's relaxing lounging areas and great bungalows give it a gold star. A Kiwi-Thai family runs things.

Nice Beach (☎ 0 7723 8547; bungalows 300-1200; ☒) This casual place has small bungalows with Thai-style baths or attractive, large bungalows with Western bathrooms. The restaurant is good and plays decent music.

Central Cottage (☎ 0 7729 9059; central_cottage@ hotmail.com; bungalows 200-800B; ☒) On offer here are solid, concrete bungalows and cheaper thatch, bamboo and wood places. All are decent and sit on leafy grounds.

Pen's (bungalows 150-600B) The cheap bungalows at Pen's are very small but airy, while the more expensive ones are modern. The grounds are nice and there's a restaurant with shady tables on the sand.

Pingjun Resort (☎ 0 7729 9004; bungalows 250-400B) A popular oldie, this resort sports cute wooden shacks in a grassy area.

White Sand (bungalows 400-700B) At the eastern end of the bay, this place has large and sunny concrete bungalows with wooden floors. They're lined up perpendicular to the water.

AD View (bungalows 150-400B) AD View features 12 bungalows, from small and rustic to larger and more personable. All sit on pleasant grounds.

Candle Hut 2 (☎ 0 7737 7070; bungalows 300-800B; ✖) The bungalows at this newish place are small, bright and airy. Not bad value.

Chanchit Dreamland (☎ 0 7723 8539; dreamland _resort@yahoo.com; bungalows 150-600B) There are almost 40 different types of bungalows at this crowded spot. It's a bit impersonal. Make sure your water and electricity work before accepting a room.

The following options are on Ao Thong Nai Pan Noi.

Panviman Resort (☎ 0 7723 8544; www.panviman .com; r 950-1400B; ✖) This upmarket place sits on top of the headland separating the two bays. Rooms are tastefully decorated and come with balconies. The grounds are hilly and lush and interlaced with brick paths. There's a taxi service from Thong Sala.

Star Hut (☎ 0 7729 9005; bungalows 200-350B) Options here range from simple thatched huts with shared bathrooms to more expensive, and expansive, places. There's a reasonably priced, popular restaurant that offers some traveller services.

Baan Panburi (☎ 0 7723 8593; www.baanpanburi .bigstep.com; bungalows 200-2600B; ✖) This is a well-maintained upmarket place that offers basic bungalows with shared bathrooms. Midrange bungalows are pleasant and airy, while the fanciest ones are more than comfortable. The restaurant is great.

Thong Ta Pan Resort (☎ 0 7723 8538; tontapan@ yahoo.com; bungalows 150-500B) Well spaced and sprinkled along a lovely hillside, these wood or concrete bungalows are good-sized. The cheapest have shared bathrooms.

EAST COAST BEACHES

There are still areas of the east coast of Ko Pha-Ngan that remain undeveloped, which is great if you're trying to avoid the party scene. For the most part, you'll have to hire a boat to get to these places, but that's not difficult. The road from Thong Sala to Ban Nam Tok is partially paved and only traversable by motorcycle in certain areas. Another dirt track (traversable on foot but only partially by motorcycle) runs along the

coast from Hat Rin before heading inland to Ban Nam Tok and Than Sadet Falls.

Past a rocky headland is Hat Sadet, a larger but still relaxed beach cove. Here you'll find a string of modestly simple places, including **Silver Cliff** (bungalows 150-250B), with large, airy bungalows on the northern hill; **JS Hut** (bungalows 150-500B), another operation that's just below Silver Cliff; and **Mai Pen Rai** (☎ 0 7737 7414; bungalows 120-350B), with all kinds of beach shacks, some with shared bathrooms, right near the sands.

The pretty coast Ao Thong Reng has a sweet intimate beach. Most travellers only stop by to see the waterfalls, but if you want to stay **Thong Reng Resort** (bungalows 100-300B) and **Than Sadet Resort** (huts 150-250B) offer basic accommodation.

Between Hat Rin and the village of Ban Nam Tok are several little coves. There you'll find the beaches of Hat Yang (virtually deserted), Hat Yao, Hat Wai Nam, Hat Thian and Hat Yuan.

About 5km north of Hat Rin is short Hat Yao – not to be confused with Hat Yao on the western side of the island. There are a couple of on-again–off-again bungalow operations here that are nothing more than rickety bamboo huts on a lonely beach. If they're open they cost between 100B and 200B.

Next up is Hat Wai Nam with **Why Nam Huts** (☎ 0 1229 3919; bungalows 250B), which is open only from December to April.

Around a headland, Hat Thian is a small quiet beach with a couple of very good places to stay. Boats from Hat Rin cost 50B; by rough trail it's about a 5km hike. **The Sanctuary & Wellness Centre** (☎ 0 1271 3614; www .thesanctuary-kpg.com; dm 60B, bungalows 300-1000B) has a great community feeling, and health and nature are emphasised. The creatively built restaurant serves wonderful vegetarian dishes and seafood. On offer are daily yoga and full spa treatments, and electricity is available from 6pm to midnight. Nearby, **Haad Tien Resort** (☎ 0 1229 3919; bungalows 120-300B) has beautiful peaked wood-and-bamboo bungalows, while **Horizon** (eck_horizon@hotmail .com; bungalows 150B) is up the hill with basic shared bathroom bamboo huts in a sparse garden area. Hidden further inland is **Silver Star** (☎ 0 1089 3588; bungalows 250B), with 10 comfortable bungalows.

There are some cool places to stay on Hat Yuan, which is very rapidly becoming

LOWER SOUTHERN GULF

crowded. Try **Big Blue** (☎ 0 1270 1537; bungalows 250-850B), the largest place here, with a range of nice bungalows on the beach and hillside; **Good Hope** (bungalows 250B), the kind of place that advertises hash brownies; and **Bamboo Hut** (bungalows 100-200B), with well-built, good-vibe bungalows and a lush garden.

HAT RIN (NOK & NAI)

This is the place to see and be seen on Ko Pha-Ngan. The island's most popular area is made up of two beaches, separated by a small shopping and eating district jam-packed with travel agencies, Internet cafés, funky bars, retro clothing shops and unique jewellery stores. It's an exciting little scene that's especially crowded on cloudy days.

Hat Rin Nok (Sunrise Beach), on the east side, is along a sandy bay lined with bungalows and coconut palms, and is busy with boat traffic. It's the better of the two beaches, and the snorkelling here is good, but between October and March the surf can be a little hairy. This is the full-moon party beach, so forget about sleeping on party nights.

Hat Rin Nai (Sunset Beach), on the western side, has a less-enticing beach, and is where the pier is located. It's a straighter beach than Hat Rin Nok and pleasantly relaxed, with much less activity and a more isolated feeling, but it can get trashy when the wind blows. It also has a number of bungalow operations. It's only a five-minute walk between the two beaches, so it doesn't really matter which side you stay on.

We've divided the following places into price categories; often the only difference between budget and midrange is an air-conditioner, and many places offer both cheaper and more expensive digs. Almost all operations have bars and restaurants, which show movies throughout the afternoon and evening.

Budget

Same Same Lodge & Restaurant (Map p578; ☎ 0 7737 5200; www.same-same.com; r 350B) This place had just opened when we stopped by and has serious potential. It's already receiving positive reviews from travellers for its spotless rooms and backpacker-friendly lounge full of comfy pillows, a book exchange and a TV for watching videos. A Thai-Danish couple run the peach-coloured, modern

hotel-like structure, and the friendly pair can provide tons of island info. They have plans to go more upmarket and add air-con to the rooms in the future, but for now it's just a low-key place that's great for meeting other travellers.

Haadrin Resort (Map p578; ☎ 0 7737 5259; bungalows 300-450B) This resort offers crowded, but good, bamboo-concrete bungalows in a shady garden. There's a pleasant restaurant offering movies and sea views.

Tommy Resort (Map p578; ☎ 0 7737 5253; bungalows 80-600B) One of the area's cheapest options, the bungalows here are rather worn and not on especially attractive grounds. The cheapest have shared bathrooms.

Serenity Hill Bungalows (Map p578; ☎ 0 9937 1066; bungalows 200-350B) The best part about this place on the rocks at the far northern end of Hat Rin is the restaurant-bar perched precariously on stilts. It offers awesome sea views and a chilled out atmosphere. The bungalows themselves are rather ratty.

Mountain Sea Bungalows (Map p578; ☎ 0 7737 5347; bungalows 300-600B) Right next to Serenity Hill, Mountain Sea has similar views and the bungalows are decently maintained and sit on a grassy hill.

Leela Beach Bungalows (Map p578; ☎ 0 7737 5094; www.leelabeach.com; huts 100-300B) People seem to like the laid-back beachside restaurant here. The bungalows themselves are very basic, rickety shacks set in a scraggly garden and on a hillside. It's a 15-minute walk from the pier.

Hua Laem Resort (Map p578; ☎ 0 7737 5222; bungalows 200-350B) This place welcomes you with inspirationally located bungalows. All have great views, decks, hammocks and mosquito nets and are simple yet comfortable. It's a great deal, but in a rather isolated spot about 15 minutes from the pier.

Top Hill Resort (Map p578; ☎ 0 7737 5327; bungalows 250B) An excellent budget deal – eight large, beautiful bungalows with unique stone baths and sea views. It's friendly and at the end of the road; the lighthouse is a 15-minute hike away.

Sabai Hill (Map p578; ☎ 0 7737 5199; sabai_hill _bun@hotmail.com; dm 150B, r 300-800B; 🖳) This is a peaceful and hippie-like place down a side street, just a few blocks inland from the beach. There's a calm garden and small colourful buildings. Thai, Mandarin, Japanese and English are spoken.

Bumblebee Huts (Map p578; ☎ 0 7737 5157; bungalows 200B) Cheap and inland from the beach, Bumblebee has OK bamboo-and-wooden huts.

Lighthouse Bungalow (Map p578; ☎ 0 7737 5075; bungalows 200-350B) Choose between the cheap, nondescript shacks with outside bathrooms or the nicer, more modern bungalows with great views. The restaurant is beautiful and homey with lots of breezes. It's a 20-minute walk from the pier, and past Leela.

Natural Home (Map p578; ☎ 0 7737 5134; bungalows 250-350B) Natural Home offers good, large bungalows along a sparse but shady hillside; sea views, if any, are only partial, and it's a bit of a hike from the main beach.

Coral (Map p578; ☎ 0 7737 5241; bungalows 100-200B) This place has good bungalows with tiled floors, colourful curtains and pebbly walls – too bad they're in a dusty lot inland from the beach. The cheaper ramshackle wooden bungalows are closer to shore, but so basic it hurts. The restaurant is wonderfully relaxing, though, with cushioned lounging areas and a wide vista of the sea.

Sandy (Map p578; ☎ 0 7737 5138; bungalows 200-300B) Sandy keeps it plain and simple – nice bungalows (not terribly worn) on pleasant garden grounds.

Starlight (Map p578; ☎ 0 7737 5018; starlight_haad rin@hotmail.com; bungalows 200-300B) The family that operates this place is very friendly, the grounds are grassy and the pastel-green bungalows are fair value.

Bird (Map p578; ☎ 0 7737 5191; bungalows 150-500B) Choose from small plain bungalows with shared bathrooms or larger wooden ones with sea views at Bird.

Princess (Map p578; ☎ 0 7739 5025; r 300-400B) The Princess is new, it's nice and it has good modern rooms with balconies.

Rin Beach Resort (Map p578; ☎ 0 7737 5112; bungalows 400-600B; 🅰) Modern, tasteful wooden bungalows with big glossy porches are found here. It's right at the pier, so if you have a big pack and are tired it's a viable option.

Blue Hill (Map p578; ☎ 0 1922 4963; bungalows 150-200B) On call here are good-sized, but very basic, shanty-like bungalows on a hillside with lots of stairs. It's a great place for shoe-stringers who want no-frills isolation. The seaside restaurant is also a bit shaky, but intimate and laid-back. It's a 25-minute walk from the pier.

Midrange

Sea Breeze Bungalows (Map p578; ☎ 0 7737 5162; bungalows 400-1200B; 🅰) This place has a romantic feel created by well-spaced, secluded bungalows, some built high on stilts. The best ones are a steep hike up the road. Try for one with a porch, perched on a cliff high above the sea – the views are stupendous. The bungalows are simple, but spotless, with brick, wood, tile and stone mixed together to create an atmospheric abode. The fan rooms are excellent value as they have the same great sea-view balconies – leave the door open for awesome breezes that work better than air-con.

Pha-Ngan Bayshore Resort (Map p578; ☎ 0 7737 5227; bungalows 400-1800B; 🅰) Set on spacious grassy grounds, just seconds from the beach, the more expensive bungalows here are quite lovely and large – with hardwood floors and duvets on the beds (a rarity around these parts). Try for the bungalow closest to Sunrise Resort – it has two sides of floor-to-ceiling windows and a giant porch.

Paradise Bungalows (Map p578; ☎ 0 7737 5244; bungalows 250-800B; 🅰) This is were the full-moon parties started, and the place remains popular (right on the beach at the centre of all the action) today. Maybe it's the nostalgia appeal, because past the fancy entrance sign are unattractive grounds and some seriously ramshackle bungalows (although the more expensive ones are nicer).

Sun Cliff Resort (Map p578; ☎ 0 7737 5134; bungalows 250-1500B; 🅰) Perched on a hillside, Sun Cliff overlooks the sea and catches sunset rays amid huge boulders and lots of vegetation. It offers a wide variety of nicely appointed and well-spaced bungalows, each of a different design and décor. To get here walk five minutes south of the pier.

Palita (Map p578; ☎ 0 7737 5170; palitas9@hotmail .com; bungalows 150-1200B; 🅰) A friendly place with a good range of well-maintained bungalows. The garden is sparse rather than lush, but the restaurant serves tasty food and screens movies.

Seaview Haadrin Resort (Map p578; ☎ 0 7737 5160; bungalows 250-1200B; 🅰) The best bungalows at this resort come with beautiful archways and decent furniture; the cheaper ones are rather plain, but all are roomy.

Bongo (Map p578; ☎ 0 7737 5268; bongomoo@yahoo .com; bungalows 400-800B; 🅰) Rooms here are very simple, and the cheaper ones have lumpy mattresses, but it's set in a peaceful shady garden a few blocks from the beach. The staff are friendly, but check out a few rooms as some are much nicer than others.

Family House (Map p578; ☎ 0 7737 5173; bungalows 300-800B; 🔀) A couple of minutes' walk north of the pier, the cheapest bungalows at Family House are worn but OK – pricier versions are more modern. There's a breezy restaurant and nice palmy gardens.

Rin Bay View (Map p578; ☎ 0 7737 5188; bungalows 200-1000B; 🔀) Rin Bay's great location means it's often full. Bungalows are pleasant, border a leafy garden strip and come in many price ranges.

Neptune's Villa (Map p578; ☎ 0 7737 5251; neptune 1@thaimail.com; bungalows 150-750B; 🔀) Neptune's is an attractive place, with small, neat, clean bungalows around a cute, well-kept garden. The most basic bungalows are wood-thatched or clapboard and nothing special.

Phangan Orchid Resort (Map p578; ☎ 0 7737 5156; bungalows 400-1200B; 🔀) A tidy, sunny garden and modern bungalows are found here. Prices depend on size, and the air-con ones are closest to the beach.

Sunrise Resort (Map p578; ☎ 0 7737 5145; or999@ hotmail.com; bungalows 250-1200B; 🔀) In a leafy, shady garden, this place has solid wood and concrete bungalows, as well as bungalows with log-style walls.

Top End
Drop In Club Resort & Spa (Map p578; ☎ 0 7737 5444; dropinclub@kohsamui.com; bungalows from 2500B; 🔀 🖳) This brand-new place is probably the swankiest accommodation option on the island. The tastefully laid-out resort features 46 luxury bungalows with teak furnishings and Thai décor throughout, as well as all the usual upmarket amenities – satellite TV, safe, minibar. There's a restaurant, lovely pool and spa facilities. The only drawback is it's not right on the beach.

BAN TAI & BAN KHAI
Between the villages of Ban Tai and Ban Khai is a series of sandy beaches with quite a few well-spaced bungalow operations. From the main road, the signs to these places can be small and hard to see. A *săwngthăew* from Thong Sala is 30B per person.

Mac Bay (☎ 0 7723 8443; bungalows 300-800B; 🔀) Even the cheaper bungalows here are decent and modern, making Mac Bay a good

CARING FOR FIDO
If you've been on the islands for a while, you can't help but notice them – the roving packs of dogs. They wander from restaurant to restaurant looking for scraps, chill next to you on the beach or start nightly street brawls with other mutts. As is the case throughout Thailand (especially on the islands), an influx of animal-loving tourists and the resulting excess of food scraps have led to an abundance of stray dogs on Ko Pha-Ngan. The stress of living in an overpopulated environment, however, leads to disease and injuries, which fester easily in the tropical climate and can end up threatening humans. Thais have been trying to keep the dog population under control through annual poisoning, which is administered by blowing poison-tipped darts through bamboo poles – not a very nice way for the poor animals to die.

Thanks to the sponsorship of the Dog Rescue Centre Samui and the Animals Asia Foundation, Pha-Ngan Animal Care (PAC) was opened by veterinary surgeon Shevaun Gallwey in September 2001. Since then almost 20% of the island's female dogs have been sterilised. Perhaps most importantly, the organisation has managed to convince the island government to refrain from the annual stray-dog executions as long as it continues to perform sterilisation procedures.

Nurses who can stay and work for at least three months are offered free accommodation and a basic wage. For more information contact House 3, Pha-Ngan Suska School, Ban Tai, or try the website www.pacthailand. org. If you want to call, the clinic's mobile number is 09 875 7513.

deal. The pricier ones come with stone detail and gnarly branches for rails.

Hansa (☎ 0 7737 7494; bungalows 500-1000B; 🔀) You'll find pretty thatched-roof bungalows of stucco and wood at this more upmarket place.

Rainbow Bungalows (☎ 0 7723 8236; www.rainbow bungalows.com; bungalows 100-250B) At the southern end of Ban Khai, these decent bungalows come with hammocks and mosquito nets.

Emerald Ocean (bungalows 150-200B) These are nice, clean and basic bungalows.

AO BANG CHARU

The shallow beach here is not one of the island's best, but it's close to town so is popular with people waiting for boats or with bank business. All of the following are on the beach, down 50m dirt driveways off the main road.

Chokana (☎ 0 7723 8085; bungalows 150-800B; 🍴) A popular, friendly place with good deals – the rooms with air-con here have a bathroom, fridge and gorgeous wooden detail.

Charm Beach (☎ 0 7737 7165; r 150-1000B; 🍴) Rooms at this place come with quite charming high-pitched roofs, though the cheapies aren't as snazzy as the larger, more expensive ones. There are hammocks made for snoozing.

CoCo Garden (☎ 0 7737 7721; r 300-600B; 🍴) Fan rooms at CoCo Garden are small, while the air-con ones are large. There are great rails made from natural branches. The restaurant is nice but the garden is sparse. Look for the blue roofs.

Or-Rawarn (☎ 0 7737 7713; or_rawarn@hotmail.com; bungalows 200-600B; 🍴) Next door to CoCo Garden, this place is well run and a good choice.

Pha-Ngan Villa (☎ 0 7737 7083; phanganvilla@hotmail.com; bungalows 130-250B) This villa is pretty with well-maintained, pleasant bungalows on manicured grounds. There are hammocks and the place feels good.

Moonlight (☎ 0 7723 8398; bungalows 150-400B) Also pleasant, this place has average bungalows; it's right next to Pha-Ngan Villa.

Eating

Most of the accommodation venues on Ko Pha-Ngan have attached restaurants. Following are some venues that cater to the palate alone. They are presented in the same geographic order as accommodation. The Hat Rin area offers plenty of choice: Thai, Western or seafood.

Swiss Bakery (Thong Sala; dishes 30-170B; 🕑 6am-5pm Mon-Sat) Consider this little paradise for a meal. It serves great homemade goodies including breads, yogurt and pancakes. It's inside the block behind Bua Kao Inn.

Absolute Island (☎ 0 7734 9109; Hat Yao; dishes 40-200B) On a high road across from Tantawan Bungalows, this sand-floor, cliffside restaurant has spectacular sea views and very good Thai food, as well as excellent fresh seafood. It's perfect for a romantic dinner.

Seaside (Ao Chalok Lam; dishes 30-100B) At the western end of town, and considered to be one of the best choices.

Cafe del Mar (Ao Chalok Lam; dishes 35-120B) Near the entrance to town, Cafe del Mar serves international food.

Outback Bar (Map p578; ; ☎ 0 7737 5126; Hat Rin; dishes 60-180B) This expat-run place serves authentic Western food in a chill reed-hut atmosphere. It's an ambient place, with modern art on the walls and fat cushions on the floor. Escape the sun for a few hours, and spend the afternoon watching a movie or footy on the big TVs.

The Shell (Map p578; ☎ 0 7737 5149; Hat Rin; dishes 90-220B) This is an atmospheric and romantic restaurant set in an open, peaceful area beyond the lily ponds. It prepares good Italian food including gnocchi, ravioli and pizza, along with gelato, tiramisu and Italian coffees.

Nira's (Map p578; ☎ 0 7737 5109; Hat Rin; dishes 60-150B; 🕑 24hr) Nira's is a popular breakfast spot, brewing up fancy coffees like iced mochas (70B) and double espressos (60B) and creative, healthy egg options. The menu also includes sandwiches, pizza, baked potatoes, salads and Thai dishes. The service could use some help, though.

Bamboozle (Map p578; Hat Rin; dishes 70-180B; 🕑 2pm-midnight) Enjoy the Mexican food such as chilli rellenos, burritos and nachos on a lofty, beautiful platform. It's popular.

Om Ganesh (Map p578; ☎ 0 7737 5123; Hat Rin; dishes 60-130B) Right near the pier, Om Ganesh has good Indian food in a colourful ambience. Hindu gods keep watch from the wall mural as you consume curries, biryani rice, *rotii* and lassis. Try a combination of *chicken malai tikka* and garlic naan.

Al Colosseo (Map p578; ☎ 0 7883 8569; Hat Rin; dishes 200-400B) Al Colosseo prepares authentic Italian food; sit in the air-con environs or out on the porch. Order pizza, pasta or fresh seafood. There are daily specials.

Ko Kho Shop (Map p578; Hat Rin; dishes 35-80B) This place is a good option for an afternoon coffee and a read on one of the comfy pillow seats. It does lots of snack foods, breakfasts and, of course, Thai dishes.

Lucky Crab (Map p578; ☎ 0 1891 3150; Hat Rin; dishes 60-250B) This place has a giant mixed-ethnicity menu and a little atmosphere with Thai decorations and linen on the tables. Seafood is your best option.

BT Restaurant (Map p578; ☎ 0 1797 8815; Hat Rin; dishes 60-200B) The usual Thai and Western specialities as well as barbecues and set-price meals are served here. It was packed when we stopped by.

Anahata (Ban Khai; dishes 125-145B; ☿ 6-11pm Mon-Sat, 7-11am Sun high season, closed Mon & Tue low season) If you're hungry in Ban Khai, check out Anahata near Rainbow Bungalows. It serves good Thai, European and vegetarian food. There's a legendary Sunday buffet brunch and some cool decks to hang out on.

Drinking & Entertainment

For the most part, where there are bungalows there is booze, although Hat Rin is the only place where there's really a bar scene. The following places are all in Hat Rin.

Drop-In Bar (Map p578; Hat Rin) Claiming to be the island's original beach bar, Drop-In is the kind of place that uses any excuse for a party. The walls are colourful, the staff strangely eclectic and the throat lubricants include piña coladas, kamikazes and Long Island iced teas. Tunes run from rock to hip hop, pop, house and trance – 'every night is different', says the Rasta dude. There are plenty of mats in the sand to slurp cheap buckets of whisky, someone is always throwing around a fire stick and there are frequent parties with bonfires to celebrate any phase of the moon.

Cactus (Map p578; ☎ 0 7737 5308) Very similar to the Drop-In, this popular place serves a range of cocktails and beer, has nightly pounding DJ music for dancing and more mats in the sand for lounging.

Big Boom Bar & Restaurant (Map p578; ☎ 0 1891 9503) This is a typical, laid-back beach bar with rickety tables on the porch and mats in the sand at night. It's a great place to start your evening or chill with a book on a rainy day. It also serves the usual range of Western and Thai snacks if you need to sop up all the booze you've consumed.

Getting There & Away

Note that the exact frequency of boat departures is dependent on weather and season. Slower boats tend to be cheaper and no-frills, while faster ones are more expensive and more comfortable.

There are up to 10 daily connections between Ko Pha-Ngan and Ko Samui (100B to 250B, 30 minutes). These boats leave between 7.30am and 4.30pm from either Thong Sala or Hat Rin on Ko Pha-Ngan and arrive either in Na Thon, Mae Nam or at the Big Buddha pier on Ko Samui. If the final location matters, state your preference when buying a ticket.

There are at least six daily trips between Ko Pha-Ngan and Surat Thani (200B to 370B, 2½ to seven hours). These boats leave between 7am and 10pm from Thong Sala.

There are about six daily boats between Ko Pha-Ngan and Ko Tao (180B to 350B, one to three hours). These boats leave between 8.30am and 1pm from Thong Sala.

Getting Around

Roads on the island are being paved at a rapid rate, which should mean fewer low-speed accidents, but more high-speed ones. The worst place for motorcycle riding is

---

ISLANDS FOR CHEAP

You're on Th Khao San in Bangkok, shopping around for combination tickets to Ko Pha-Ngan (or Ko Tao or Ko Samui) and the prices seem unbelievable: Bangkok to Ko Pha-Ngan straight for 300B? Sounds like a good deal, right?

Well, sometimes it is…and sometimes it's not. Some unscrupulous bus companies make their profits by, well, stealing from travellers. Ruses have included bus personnel sneaking below and rifling through bags (while the bus is en route), sneaking along the aisle while everyone is asleep (and the lights are off) and picking your pockets, and just a lot of sneaky business in general. Some travellers show up and don't get the bus they were expecting. Others have extra transport charges added to their fare. A very few have even reported being gassed to unconsciousness and robbed right in their seats!

We're not saying that this happens with cheap bus/boat tickets, but remember that no-one's in business to lose money. It's always best to have a chat with other travellers who've recently returned from where you're going, before choosing a supercheap company. Otherwise cough up the extra few hundred baht and arrive intact (nothing is guaranteed).

between Ban Khai and Hat Rin, which is a paved, but very hilly road. Also treacherous is the midsection to Ao Thong Nai Pan, which is a rutty, dirt road. Be careful and slow down.

Some places can only be reached by boat, such as Hat Khuat and some sections of the east coast. If you find trails, they can be overgrown and not recommended for walking if you're wearing a heavy pack. Always carry water and a torch, just in case.

From Thong Sala, *săwngthăew* cost 50B per person to anywhere on the island except for Ban Khai (30B) and Ao Thong Nai Pan (80B). Rates jump at sunset.

Long-tail boats from Ao Chalok Lam to Hat Khuat cost 50B per person with at least three people. Boats between Thong Sala and Hat Yao also cost 50B per person from January to September (in calm weather only). You can charter a boat from beach to beach for about 150B per 15 minutes of travel.

Motorcycles are available for rent in Thong Sala and at bungalows here and there for about 200B per day, depending on the season. Cars go for about 1000B.

KO TAO
เกาะเต่า
pop 5000

If Ko Pha-Ngan was the Ko Samui of the '90s, then Ko Tao is this century's diamond in the rough. The beaches are quieter, sometimes nearly deserted, 24-hour electricity is still a rarity and the local folk are more involved in fishing and growing coconuts than tourism. A walk around the small island – it's only 21 sq km – reveals steep rutted dirt paths, modest and weathered wooden homes and lush rolling green hills. Time moves at a less frantic pace here, and although more tourists are showing up each year, Ko Tao lacks the blatant commercialism found on other islands. And if you look for it, you can even catch a glimpse of rural island life.

Diving is the island's major industry because of the particularly good visibility of the surrounding water and abundance of fishy wildlife and coral. Although once almost exclusively a diver's destination (you had to dive to stay), today many resorts welcome everyone – although during high season some close their doors to nondivers.

While it's probably the best place in Thailand to get your PADI certification (and many folks do), if you're not interested in scuba diving there are plenty of opportunities for sea-kayaking, snorkelling or just relaxing. Accommodation is simple. Nights are casual affairs where drinks are served by candlelight in the sand and the music doesn't drown out the gentle pounding of the ocean waves. All in all, Ko Tao is a dreamy, romantic place where you can read a book in a hammock strung between palms or experience a traditional massage in an open-air bungalow when the sun disappears into the ocean.

That said, Ko Tao is growing more popular with each passing year, and you're likely to hear the hum of hammer pounding wood as more resorts are being built. In 1983 there was just one bungalow operation on the island, today there are more than 100. Unfortunately, growth always brings its own problems and Ko Tao's not an exception. A lack of seasonal rain brought water shortages in 2002, while rubbish collection has also become a serious issue.

KO TAO

LOWER SOUTHERN GULF

Orientation & Information

Ban Mae Hat, on the western side of the island, is where boats dock. It's a small bustling town with a busy pier and here you'll find countless travel agencies, dive shops, restaurants, Internet cafés, money-exchange facilities and motorcycle rentals. The only other villages on the island are Ban Hat Sai Ri, about midway up the western coast, and Ban Chalok Ban Kao to the south. Just 1km off the northwestern shore of the island is Ko Nang Yuan, which is really three islands joined by a sand bar. Ban Hat Sai Ri is growing by the day, and is where most travellers base themselves. It has the same selection of traveller services as Ban Mae Hat, as well as countless accommodation options and a lovely beach.

The island has places specialising in dive medicine. **Badalveda** (☎ 0 7745 6664; www.badalveda.com), on the main road in Mae Hat, has a hyperbaric chamber. There are clinics across the island to treat minor ailments.

Available all over is the *Ko Tao Info* booklet, which lists virtually every business on the island and goes into some detail about Ko Tao's history, culture and social issues.

Sights & Activities

About the only thing of historic interest on the island is a large **boulder** where King Rama V had his initials carved to commemorate a royal visit in 1900. The boulder, at the southern end of Hat Sai Ri, has become something of a local shrine and is the focus of a small ceremony every October.

Otherwise, Ko Tao is really an outdoor activities–oriented place. The granite promontory of **Laem Tato**, at the southern tip of Ko Tao, makes a nice hike from Ban Chalok Ban Kao.

DIVING & SNORKELLING

Ko Tao is one of Thailand's main underwater meccas, and this is no surprise considering its high visibility and clean waters. The best sites are offshore islands or pinnacles, including White Rock, Shark Island, Chumphon Pinnacle, Green Rock, Sail Rock and Southwest Pinnacles. Underwater wildlife includes grouper, moray eels, batfish, titan triggerfish, angelfish, blue-spotted stingrays, sea snakes and the occasional whale shark.

About 40 dive operators eagerly offer their services to travellers. Some of these are small dive shops and just offer dive services, while others are 'dive resorts' that also have accommodation. Many are run by Western staff, who seem to be travellers extending their vacations by finding jobs as 'dive masters' (an entry-level position obtained after some instruction).

The larger dive operators aren't necessarily better than the smaller ones, and will often take out bigger groups of divers. These operators usually have more than one branch office around the island (such as at Ban Mae Hat and at Hat Sai Ri). The quality of your dive experience, however, will ultimately depend on the experience and abilities of your dive shop's staff. It's a good idea to ask around for a recommendation.

Rates are similar everywhere, and typically cost 800B per dive to 5400B for a 10-dive package. An all-inclusive introductory dive lesson costs 1600B, while a four-day, open-water PADI certificate course costs around 8000B – these rates include gear, boat, instructor, food and beverages.

Any bungalow or dive shop can arrange snorkelling day trips around the island for 400B. If you just want to rent a snorkel, mask and fins it will cost you 100B for the day. These can be rented almost anywhere.

SPAS & MASSAGE

There are about eight places on Ko Tao to get wonderful massages or spa treatments, as well as numerous operations at various bungalows offering more rustic, but sometimes equally good, Thai massages. A one-hour massage costs about 300B.

Jamahkiri Spa (☎ 0 7745 6400), near Ao Tanot atop a huge island peak, does aloe-vera wraps (great for sunburn), massage, facials and more. The resort is large, peaceful and gorgeously designed. It's a truly luxurious experience that's very good value (300B for an aloe wrap). Call for free transportation.

Here & Now (☎ 0 9970 1525; www.hereandnow.be), at CFT (opposite) practises traditional Thai yoga massage for 550B for 2½ hours. There are also classes in the Chinese martial arts of *taijiquan* and *qi gong*, taught by a German expat. Nine-session early-morning or evening courses cost 2800B.

Sleeping

With the transformation of Ko Tao into a diving resort, its accommodation is slowly become more upmarket. There's still none of the package resorts found on Ko Samui, but that could change any day as new places are constantly being built. Cheap, thatched-roof bungalows are now competing with classier joints – but again with the exception of a few top-end resorts, most places are simple, laid-back affairs without satellite TVs or 24-hour electricity – which means if you pay for an air-con room and you sleep past 6am (when the electricity shuts off for a few hours) you may find yourself roasting by 10am. The major difference between bungalow operations here and those on Ko Pha-Ngan or Ko Samui is that the reception desk usually doubles as a dive shop.

Many of the smaller, more isolated and least expensive bungalow operations rely on guests eating at their restaurant for extra income. Some may become miffed if you go elsewhere, and a few may even try to give you the boot.

Unless stated, rates here are approximately for April to November. Expect them to skyrocket from December to March. During this time it's wise to call ahead to confirm prices and secure a room. We've arranged the listings with those are the best beaches first.

In high season some bungalow operations will not accommodate nondivers. If the island isn't superbusy, however, this shouldn't be a problem.

HAT SAI RI

Around the headland to the north of the pier is the longest, busiest beach, with a string of dive operations, bungalows, travel agencies, minimarkets, Internet cafés and restaurants. The pathway here is paved, so watch out for motorcycles that will mow you down. This is where most travellers choose to stay, so if you're looking to meet others or to party this should be your base. North of the beach, in a hilly area called Ao Ta Then, are several operations with inexpensive and basic bungalows, including **Silver Cliff** (up a rough driveway), **Sun Sea** (high on top of the rocks) and **Sun Lord** (down below Sun Sea). All charge about 200B and some have awesome views – an excellent deal if you love the ultrarustic and isolated, and aren't afraid of a few bugs in your bed.

Budget

CFT (☎ 0 9970 1525; www.hereandnow.be; bungalows 100-350B) This German-run place is spiritual, but not at all fancy, and you'll be happiest here if you can let go of all creature comforts. All bungalows are basic; the cheapest have shared bathrooms. The jungle-like grounds are strewn with magnificent boulders. *Săwngthăew* from Ban Mae Hat cost 50B. It's north of the beach in the Ao Ta Then area.

In Touch (☎ 0 7722 2723; bungalows 250-350B) At In Touch, darkish bamboo and wooden bungalows with tin roofs come with mosquito nets. The highlight is the beachside restaurant sporting driftwood décor and nice decks.

Silver Sand Beach Resort (☎ 0 7745 6303; silver sand_kohtao@hotmail.com; bungalows 250-600B) The plain wooden bungalows here are basic, cheap and popular.

Sai Ree Cottages (☎ 0 7745 6374; bungalows 400B) The thatched-roof bungalows at Sai Ree are tiny, but some are right on the beach. There's a lovely restaurant built on stilts over the sea and a grassy lot with palm trees.

Pranee's (☎ 0 7745 6080; bungalows 300-450B) A popular place, Pranee's offers good bungalows made of wood and rattan-woven walls; all are partly shaded by palms.

SB Cabana (☎ 0 7745 6005; bungalows 300B) Here you'll find tiny, almost claustrophobic, bungalows with mozzie nets. The grounds are nice and the porches are pleasant.

Midrange

Ban's Diving Resort (☎ 0 7745 6061; www.amazing kohtao.com; r & bungalows 400-1200B; 🖥 🗷) The best deal in its price range, Ban's has fabulously manicured grounds filled with pools, fountains and lush vegetation. The more expensive rooms are in sets of white colonial-style hotel buildings with balconies, while the cheaper options are decent no-frills bungalows. The place has 24-hour electricity, TVs in the more expensive rooms and a swimming pool. If you want to stay in a fan room you need to book a dive trip.

Sunset Buri Resort (☎ 0 7745 6266; fax 0 7745 6101; bungalows 700-2500B; 🖥 🗷) The quaint, modern, pointy-roofed bungalows in lush grounds and a pool make this a solid option. It's a 30-minute walk from the pier.

Seashell Resort (☎ 077456299; www.kohtaoseashell .com; bungalows 400-1500B) The pricier bungalows here have lovely tiled floors and floor-to-ceiling windows looking out on the ocean, but are rather small with mismatched sheets. The porches are great and the grounds beautiful.

Lotus Resort (☎ 0 7745 6271; r 400-850B, bungalows 1200-1600B; 🕲) This resort has big, well-furnished bamboo bungalows. The garden could use a little more shade, but the place is clean and well run. The bar is fantastic.

AC Resort I (☎ 0 7745 6197; bungalows 300-1000B; 🕲) This place features a mix of bungalows – the small ones have fans and mosquito nets, while those with air-con can come with huge beds. They're all on pleasantly grassy, hilly and palmy grounds, and locals say the restaurant serves very good Thai food.

Big Blue Resort (☎ 0 7745 6050; www.bigbluediving .com; r & bungalows 200-1700B; 🕲) On the premises of Big Blue is a variety of accommodation with 24-hour electricity. It takes nondivers in the low season only and keeps its rates year-round. Big Blue's deck bar is good for happy-hour drinks (5pm to 8pm).

Blue Wind (☎ 0 7745 6116; bungalows 600B) Blue Wind offers slightly more upmarket fan bungalows than other places on the island. They're still small, but not as squalid and built out of higher quality wood that blends in nicely with the environs. There are daily yoga classes.

Top End

Koh Tao Coral Grand Resort (☎ 0 7745 6431; www .kohtaocoral.com; bungalows 1900-3800B; 🕲 🕲) This brand-spanking-new and fancy resort has pastel-coloured, double-peaked bungalows in geometric shapes. It lies a bit beyond Hat Sai Ri. The bungalows are very comfortable inside, boasting wooden floors, bright linen and wooden tubs.

Ko Tao Palace (☎ 0 7745 6250; kohtaopalace@ppdw -card.com; bungalows 1300-1800B) You'll have to live without air-con, but the Fred Flintstone-like bungalows here come with tropical décor and creative indoor-outdoor bathrooms. All are smooth and circular and overlook the sea from under shady palms.

Thipwimarn (☎ 0 7745 6409; thipwimarn@excite .com; bungalows 1750-3500; 🕲) Thipwimarn's greatest asset is its beautifully located and circular restaurant sporting a handful of intimate floor-level tables and an outstanding view. The attractive bungalows spill down the hillside among boulders and greenery,

while the plentiful stairs keep you fit. It's north of the beach in the Ao Ta Then area.

Ko Tao Island Resort (☎ 0 7745 6295; bungalows 400-2000B; 🕲) Air-con bungalows at this new place (some of the buildings are still under construction) are very large and airy with giant windows – many looking right onto the ocean. There's a blue theme throughout and the interiors are spotless.

AO CHALOK BAN KAO

The island's third-largest beach (it's nicely situated about 1.7km south of Ban Mae Hat by road) has heaps of bungalows to choose from, a little nightlife and can become quite crowded. Taa Toh lagoon to the east and Hat Saan Jao to the west beautifully frame the calm emerald waters of this coral beach.

Buddha View Dive Resort (☎ 0 7745 6074; www .buddhaview-diving.com; r 300-400B; 🕲) Heavily touted in Bangkok and on the other islands, this resort offers OK bungalows for divers only. Because of its good marketing campaign, it's often crowded, which could be good if you're travelling alone. There's a fantastic barbecue here every night and celebrations often spring up for people passing their PADI tests (virtually every night). Look for it on the right as you enter Ao Chalok Ban Kao.

Viewpoint Bungalows (☎ 0 7756 6444; bungalows 200-1000B) A friendly, family-run place almost at the end of civilisation – you will feel apart from the dive scene here. Cheap bungalows are basic, airy and well maintained. Some have partial sea views. More expensive bungalows are large and beautiful and claim wide vistas along with beautiful decks. The restaurant has excellent views, a wonderful, mellow ambience and attentive staff.

Tropicana (☎ 0 7745 6167; bungalows 300-500B) Tropicana is simple and sweet. It comes with large, modern and clean quarters.

Ko Tao Cottage Dive Resort (☎ 0 7745 6198; www .kotaocottage.com; r & bungalows 740-940B) Towards the eastern end of the bay and about 500m past Tropicana, this resort isn't too friendly but has good sea-view bungalows, a leafy garden and a large terraced restaurant.

Laem Khlong Resort (☎ 0 7745 6083; r & bungalows 150-500B) The modern rooms and bungalows here are large, have blue-tiled floors and boast sea views. It sits on a hill overlooking the bay.

Sunshine II (r & bungalows 350-400B) Sunshine offers good abodes in two rows facing each other across a nice garden. Its popular restaurant has a good vibe.

AO TANOT

This is one of the island's best spots for snorkelling, though the swimming is not so good. Two dive operators compete in this small, remote and quiet boulder-strewn cove, while several bungalow operators line the beachfront. There are a couple of simple shops in the area. Get here by *săwngthǎew* (50B), which leave Ban Mae Hat five times daily.

Black Tip Dive Resort (☎ 0 7745 6488; bungalows 400-1250B; 🏊) Part of a dive shop, this place has a handful of well-appointed and clean bungalows. It offers all sorts of water activities – from snorkelling with sharks and kayaking to island sightseeing tours.

Diamond Beach (☎ 0 1958 3983; bungalows 400-500B) These bungalows are fairly new, modern and comfortable. It's an upbeat place.

Mountain Reef Resort (☎ 0 1956 2916; bungalows 350-400B) At the southern end of the bay, Mountain Reef has peaceful bungalows and a raised restaurant with a good view.

Tanote Bay Resort (☎ 0 1970 4703; bungalows 500-2500B; 🏊) There are good, modern and clean bungalows on a hillside at this resort; it keeps its rates unchanged year-round.

Bamboo Hut (☎ 0 1968 6000; fax 0 7745 6186; bungalows 150-500B) There are 20 decked bungalows of varying size here; the older ones are the smallest. The kitchen specialises in spicy, southern Thai–style food.

Poseidon (☎ 0 1958 8917; bungalows 350-500B) Poseidon offers simple and unmemorable bungalows; the onsite restaurant is nice, though.

HAT AO MAE

This shallow bay, just north of Ban Mae Hat, has plenty of coral, but the southern end can get some rubbish from the pier area at Ban Mae Hat. The sunsets are fantastic, and its location close to the pier and options for eating and drinking make it quite popular. To get to Hat Ao Mae, get off the pier and turn left at Cafe del Sol.

Sensi Paradise Resort (☎ 0 7745 6244; www.koh taoparadise.com; r 450-8000B; 🏊) This resort is a mostly upmarket place with some gorgeous Thai-style rooms in rich dark wood. Artsy indoor-outdoor bathrooms are great, and the beautiful décor makes everything comfortable. It's pretty romantic overall, with covered decks (great for lounging) overlooking the sea. The bigger villas are perfect for families, and there are also some more-basic bungalows.

Ko Tao Royal Resort (☎ 0 7745 6156; bungalows 800-3500B; 🏊) This is a smart place with beautiful, modern bungalows. Everything's done in teak and there is 24-hour electricity. Each place has a hammock and garden setting. It's beyond Blue Diamond.

Tommy's Resort (☎ 0 7745 6039; tommy_resorts@ hotmail.com; r & bungalows 350-1500B; 🏊) Clean, bright, modern rooms and bungalows are terraced down to the water here. Most have hammocks and balconies. There's a good-feeling restaurant and deck.

Crystal (☎ 0 7745 6107; www.crystaldive.com; bungalows 500-1200B; 🏊) For divers only, Crystal offers neat rows of standard, modern bungalows. If you take a beginners' course, the room is free. This place has electricity almost 20 hours a day, which is longer than most.

Blue Diamond (☎ 0 7745 6255; bungalows 400-800B) Blue Diamond is a friendly family place with two grades of bungalows; unsurprisingly, the cheaper ones are smaller and less spiffy. It maintains its prices all year, and is just south of Ao Mae Hat.

Queen Resort (☎ 0 7745 6002; bungalows 200-500B) On a headland overlooking the bay, this resort has rustic wooden bungalows in a scraggly jungle. The best ones are closest to the water. There's a decent restaurant on the premises, too.

Beach Club (☎ 0 7745 6222; r & bungalows 800-1800B; 🏊) Small bamboo bungalows that face seaward and larger, more-modern rooms with fridge and comfy furniture make up the accommodation here. Floors are tiled and bathrooms are spacious, but you may think it's a little pricey for what you get.

View Cliff Bungalows (☎ 0 7745 6353; viewcliff@ ksc.th.com; bungalows 600-1100B; 🏊) Just beyond Tommy's, View Cliff has basic huts and more substantial bungalows. The nightly video blaring from the restaurant is a definite minus if you want to sleep.

KO NANG YUAN

This pretty little tripartite island has one resort. Daily boats from Ban Me Hat leave at 10.30am, 3pm and 5.30pm (60B return).

Ko Nangyuan Dive Resort (☎ 0 7745 6093; www
.nangyuan.com; bungalows 750-2000B; 🕄) This dive
resort monopolises the trio of islands, that
are about 1km offshore to the northwest of
Ko Tao. They are connected to each other
by an idyllic sandbar. Bungalows are quite
comfortable and well spaced. The emphasis
here is on diving; stay three nights with a
four-day dive course for around 10,000B
(rates depend on the season). Due to rubbish concerns, plastic bottles aren't allowed
on the island.

AO HIN WONG & LAEM THIAN

On the eastern side of Ko Tao is tranquil Ao
Hin Wong, with four small hillside resorts
and one diving operation. There isn't really
a beach here, but the snorkelling offshore
yields abundant intact coral reefs. South of
Ao Hin Wong is the scenic, very quiet cape
of Laem Thian. The road here is paved in
parts, but still hairy on a motorcycle. From
Ban Mae Hat, *săwngthǎew* cost 50B per
person; long-tail boats from Ban Mae Hat
cost 200B.

View Rock (☎ 0 1229 4307; bungalows 100-300B)
The bungalows here are a great deal, and
the best have large spaces and super sea
views. Look for the Green Tree sign then
head up a hill on a dirt road for 600m to
get to the entrance. You'll climb back down
(it's around a headland) to access the seaside bungalows and restaurant.

Hin Wong Bungalows (☎ 0 1229 4810; bungalows
250-500B) There are some beautiful wooden
bungalows at Hin Wong with great big
modern bathrooms; the older bungalows
are OK too, but obviously they are not as
fancy.

Green Tree (☎ 0 7745 6742; bungalows 100-200B)
This is a friendly place 150m further along
the road from Hin Wong. It has white bungalows (which are a bit more basic than
Hin Wong's) set in a jungle-like area. The
restaurant is nice enough. The cheapest
bungalows have shared bathrooms.

Laem Thian (☎ 0 7745 6477; huts 100-800B, r 300-
350B) This isolated place has some very cheap
and rustic bungalows, as well as pricier,
more-comfortable ones. Rooms in the hotel
block are beautifully modern and come with
balconies – the best have sea views. All over
the hilly grounds are huge boulders, just
great to bound around and even jump into
the water from.

AO LEUK TO AO THIAN OK

Ao Leuk is the destination for serenity and
seclusion. Sit in the crystal clear water and
watch the fish swim by, or take in some
breathtaking island scenery. The resorts
here are basic and isolated. If you're looking
for luxury or a big party, stay elsewhere.

The dirt road to Ao Leuk gets steep,
rough and rutty, especially towards the
end; don't attempt it on a motorcycle unless you're an expert. At the end of the road
are **Ao Leuk Resort** and **Nice Moon**, both with
bungalows from 300B to 400B. They are
neighbours and share the same small beach.
Nice Moon is up the hill, with simple bungalows and good views; the restaurant is a bit
shaky, though (literally).

Coral View Resort (☎ 0 9288 4914; bungalows
450-600B) At Hat Sai Daeng, this resort features well-built bungalows run by a friendly
Aussie/Thai couple. It's best to travel here
by long-tail boat from Ban Mae Hat, as the
road is rough and you may have to hike
a little.

Rocky (☎ 0 7745 6035; r 200-500B) Even further
west at pretty Ao Thian Ok, Rocky monopolises one end of the beach with haphazardly built, unattractive bungalows. It's
the only place here, so at least it's tranquil.
Across the bay from Rocky and up the hill
is New Heaven Restaurant (p598), with a
simply grand view over the bay.

AO JUN JEUA TO HAT SAI NUAN

The area between Ao Jun Jeua and Hat Sai
Nuan, on Ko Tao's southwest coast, is remote and caters to budget travellers looking for isolation. Long-tail boats are a good
form of transport to this coastal area; with a
number of people they cost 50B per person.

Sai Thong Resort (☎ 0 7745 6476; saithongresort@
hotmail.com; bungalows 100-2000B; 🕄) A good range
of bungalows – from the basic hillside hut
to the nicer beachside abode – along with
a great relaxing restaurant complete with
hammocks, a sun deck and a small, private
beach, make this the area's best option.

Sunset (www.earth2marsh.com/sunset; bungalows
100-200B) A 15-minute walk from the centre
of Ao Chalok Ban Kao, Sunset has a great
seaside location, but appeals to minimalists
seeking the simple life – the place boasts it
doesn't have a phone line! Bungalows are
very basic (mattress on the floor). There's a
vegetarian restaurant, good swimming and

snorkelling offshore. Yoga classes are occasionally offered.

Moondance (☎ 0 1958 2971; bungalows 250B) On Ao Jun Jeua, near Sunset, Moondance has just 10 old bungalows terraced up a hillside with many steps; all have sea views. It's a clean and decent budget choice.

Tao Thong Villa (☎ 0 9945 6078; bungalows 100-350B) Here you'll find very rustic, no-frills bungalows with great views. Laem Je Ta Kang, the headland on which this place is located, forms a small double bay with two beaches on either side; it's a great spot. There's also a pleasant, lofty restaurant.

Siam Cookie (☎ 0 7745 6301; bungalows 200B) On Hat Sai Nuan, Siam Cookie is basic, cheap and comes with peaceful sea views.

KHAO MAE HAT

In the middle of the island, a rutty dirt road leads up the slopes of 310m-high Khao Mae Hat. Even 4WD vehicles in the dry season hesitate to climb this road, but strong (unladen) hikers can reach the top in about 30 minutes.

Moon Light (☎ 0 9599 9558; bungalows 200-350B) About 250m up a very steep, paved driveway, this casual place offers basic bungalows, some with spectacular views of land and sea. The restaurant has the same fantastic vistas. Climbing many steps makes this possible, so come fit.

Two View (huts 100B) This simple resort sits at the apex of the boulder-strewn mountaintop, about a 20-minute hike from Moon Light and a 40-minute hike from Ao Tanot Bay (on the eastern side). You can see sunrise and sunset from this aerie. Life is simple up here; there's no telephone, no electricity and just some simple, bare-bones bamboo huts. Colon-cleansings, Chakra-balancing, rebirthing sessions and yoga-meditation retreats are offered. There are Thai cooking and Swedish massage classes as well.

Eating

Practically all bungalows on the island have their own restaurant, since food is a good moneymaker. Most of the following restaurants are in Ban Mae Hat or Hat Sai Ri, which is full of *faràng*-oriented places.

HAT SAI RI

There is a string of restaurants on Soi Sopaa and the streets running off it. You'll find

Soi Sopaa at the end of the paved walkway, just after Big Blue Resort. Other restaurants can be found on the main strip along the beach.

El Toro/Little Mermaid (dishes 100-250B) On the main pathway, this place may be the world's only Mexican/Scandinavian restaurant that also offers Thai cuisine and pizzas. It screens movies nightly.

Orchid Restaurant (☎ 0 7745 6406; dishes 60-250B) Across from El Toro, Orchid does everything from spaghetti and steak to seafood, and you can lie back on comfy pillows and watch movies.

Mango Pub & Steakhouse (dishes 80-430B) The Mango claims to have the best burger on the island – taste for yourself. Ostrich, crocodile and kangaroo meat are also on the menu.

Chopper's Bar & Grill (☎ 0 7745 6641; Soi Sopaa; dishes 60-200B) Pub food, including big, greasy, English breakfasts, are featured at this multilevel place that screens movies and sport.

White Elephant Restaurant (dishes 100-300B) Classic Western favourites, northern Thai specialities and, strangely, fondue are served in lovely thatched-roof huts. Sit on cushions on the floor.

BAN MAE HAT

Baan Yaay (☎ 0 7745 6262; dishes 50-200B) With an airy, casual deck over the water and a cocktail menu, this is a good choice for salads, soups and fried rice or noodle dishes.

Café de Sol (dishes 40-300B) This café serves delicious world cuisines with an emphasis on Italian. Every day there is a special set meal of a different origin – Friday night is Sushi night.

Liab Thale (set menus 50B; 🕗 8.30am-6pm) Near the water, Liab Thale has a back area that overlooks the busy pier and its surrounds. It's popular for its location (folks waiting for the boat) and its good, cheap Thai food.

La Matta (☎ 0 1229 4718; dishes 90-235B) On the uphill road, this is an Italian-run place serving up pasta, sandwiches, salads and omelettes.

Swiss Bakery (dishes 20-40B; 🕗 6.30am-6.30pm) This bakery is a popular morning spot serving juices, breakfast, sandwiches, baked goods and hit-or-miss pastries. It has large tables and wooden benches and is across from La Matta.

Yang (dishes 30-50B) Yang is great for cheap but good Thai food slammed down with a

LOWER SOUTHERN GULF

cool fruit shake (20B). Portions are generous, which attracts backpackers like bees to honey. It's near Swiss Bakery.

AROUND THE ISLAND
There are a few stand-out restaurants scattered around the island.

New Heaven Restaurant (☎ 0 7745 6462; dishes 50-200B) On the rocky headland of Laem Tato, this place has a simply grand view over the bay. The menu isn't extensive and the portions aren't large, but you're here for the scenery.

Taraporn Restaurant (☎ 0 7745 6457; dishes 40-80B) In Ao Chalok Ban Kao, Taraporn serves up good Thai and Western food (and hard liquor) in another unbeatable location. It's a casual place, built right over the water at the edge of the shallow bay and reached via a long walkway. The intimate tables are at floor level, while the cushions encourage quick naps.

Drinking
Ko Tao has a few bars to get you nicely lubricated. If you're looking for parties, check out the ubiquitous fliers posted on trees and walls – venues are always changing. If a bungalow has a restaurant, it usually doubles as a bar. Some places close early, especially in remote locations.

HAT SAI RI
Lotus Bar (☎ 0 7745 6271) Lotus Resort operates a fantastic beach bar with cushions and candles in the sand. It has a very high romantic-appeal factor, but on nights when there's live music or open-mics it can be a real party.

Dry Bar (btwn Lotus Resort & Big Blue Resort) Right on the beach, the Dry Bar also has sandside cushions and lanterns as well as a huge cocktail menu. There are Friday night dance parties.

BAN MAE HAT
Ban Mae Hat is a good place to party; there are a number of venues to choose from.

Whitening (☎ 0 7745 6199) This is a trendy bar-restaurant right at the beach – the 'floors' are sandy, the music is moody and the lighting glitters romantically at night (think tiki torches). Many different drinks are served, including margaritas. It has a definite upmarket feel, but it's comfortable;

there's a great deck over the water. Come at 10pm on Friday for a big party.

Tattoo (☎ 0 9290 7467) A casual and intimate bar, Tattoo has some tables and a TV lounge area. Breezes blow through the friendly and laid-back spaces, and if you're hungry try the big Aussie burger (120B). It's 30m south of Whitening (at the edge of town).

Dragon Bar (☎ 0 7745 6423) Dragon caters to those seeking snazzy, cutting-edge surroundings in which to be seen. It's an exception to other places in Ban Mae Hat, and may start an upmarket trend. There's a large, modernistic conversation-pit area and everything's dimly lit, moody and relaxing (not a party atmosphere). The cocktail menu is extensive.

Sea Monkey (☎ 0 1229 4963) On the 2nd floor across from Café del Sol, this is a colourful place with a pool table, upbeat atmosphere and glowing bubble tubes. Groovy tunes change themes nightly, and only drinks are served (no food) – a short and sweet list.

Safety Stop Bar (☎ 0 9594 4487) This bar has a great location by the pier and is the best place to read the *Bangkok Post* or watch soccer on TV while downing some Mexican snacks.

Getting There & Away
As always, the cost and departure times for transport fluctuate.

BANGKOK
Bus/boat combination tickets from Bangkok cost 750B to 850B and are available from travel agencies on Th Khao San. Promotional bus/boat combination tickets in the opposite direction are sometimes offered for as little as 500B.

Beware of travel agencies on Ko Tao selling boat/train combinations with a 'voucher' that you are supposed to be able to exchange for a train ticket in Surat Thani or Chumphon; more than a few travellers have found the vouchers worthless. If you book a train a few days (or more) in advance, legitimate agencies on Ko Tao should be able to deliver the train tickets themselves. It's same-day or day-before reservations that usually have voucher problems.

CHUMPHON
Six or seven boats a day run between Chumphon (Tha Reua Ko Tao) and Ko Tao

(400B, three hours). There may be fewer departures if the swells are high.

From Chumphon (200B; see p542), there is a midnight boat that arrives early in the morning. In the opposite direction the boat departs from Ko Tao at 10am (200B, six hours). Don't take this boat if there's a chance of rain; some boats leak and you'll be wet, cold and miserable. Otherwise sleeping on a slow boat (mats on the floor) is a great experience.

SURAT THANI

A Songserm Express Boat departs from Ko Tao at 8am and Surat Thani at 10am (500B, four hours). Every night, depending on the weather, a boat runs between Surat Thani (Tha Thong) and Ko Tao (350B, nine hours). From Surat boats depart at 11pm. From Ban Me Hat the departure time is 8.30pm.

KO PHA-NGAN & KO SAMUI

From Ko Tao there are multiple boats to Ko Pha-Ngan (180B to 350B, one to three hours) and to Ko Samui (280B to 550B, 1½ to 2½ hours). These boats depart between 9.30am and 3pm.

Exact times can vary from year to year, so check the schedules during your visit.

Getting Around

Săwngthăew cost 50B per person to anywhere on the island. Many have scheduled departure times to the east coast of Ko Tao (four to five daily). Long-tail boats can be chartered for up to 2000B a day, depending on the number of passengers carried.

Walking is an easy way to get around the island, but some remote trails aren't clearly marked and can be difficult to follow. You can walk around the whole island in a day, although the hilly paths make it a challenge.

Many tourists rent motorcycles on Ko Tao (150B per day). If you're confident on two wheels then this is a good way to get around, though there aren't a lot of roads on the island. The main ones are paved, but the more remote ones are rutted dirt paths that can be steep. Novices should *not* attempt these. If you just want to shuttle back and forth between Mae Hat and Sai Ri, you won't have any problem on the motorcycle, as the path is paved. Watch out for pedestrians though.

NAKHON SI THAMMARAT PROVINCE

If you're searching for less-trodden paths and fewer *faràng*, then this relatively untouristy province might be the gem you're looking for. Much of it is covered with rugged mountains and forests – with verdant jungles teeming with lush vegetation – once the last refuge of Thailand's communist insurgents. Its eastern border is formed by the Gulf of Thailand, and much of the provincial economy is dependent on fishing and prawn farming. Along the north coast are picturesque beaches and pristine waterfalls, places where solitude and serenity rule the day and Western tourists are rare. The province also boasts Khao Luang National Park, known for its beautiful mountain and forest walks, cool streams, waterfalls and orchards. Besides fishing, Nakhon residents earn a living by growing coffee, rice, rubber and fruit (especially *mangkhút*, or mangosteen).

AO KHANOM

อ่าวขนอม

Four almost deserted white-sand beaches – Hat Nai Praet, Hat Nai Phlao, Hat Na Dand and Hat Pak Nam – are along the bay of Ao Khanom, about 70km from Surat Thani and close to the town of Khanom. Tourism along this beautiful coastline is minimal, with just a few places to stay. In some areas prawn farms are starting to develop and, while these threaten to damage the environment and local tourism, so far the farms haven't multiplied too dramatically.

If you're searching for Ko Samui's beauty without its crowds, head to Nai Phlao, the area's best beach, 8.4km south of Khanom. Here, the mountains meet the aquamarine waters of the Gulf of Thailand and the sand is pristine white. Coconut palms blow gently in the wind, and you'll be left with the impression that a chunk of Ko Samui somehow cut loose and drifted ashore. Two kilometres south of Nai Phlao is scenic Nam Tok Hin Lat– another Samui echo.

Sleeping & Eating

Most places to stay are concentrated along the southern half of Hat Nai Phlao, the prettiest part.

Khanab Nam Diamond Resort (☎ 0 7552 9444; fax 0 7552 9111; bungalows 800-2400B; ✕ ☀) Set high on a rocky cliff at the southern end of the bay, this resort is probably the nicest place to stay around these parts. The octagonal bamboo-and-thatch bungalows are classy and the pool and restaurant overlook the sea. For nonresidents, the restaurant is ideal for a sundowner drink or a meal.

Khanom Hill Resort (☎ 0 7552 9403; bungalows 900-1900B; ☀) This resort is among the better places to stay along Hat Nai Phlao, where the red-roofed bungalows on stilts overlook the sea. They feature large decks perfect for enjoying the view.

Nai Phlao Bay Resort (☎ 0 7533 9039; fax 0 7552 9425; bungalows 450-1700B; ☀) One of the cheapest options, this resort is set on spacious grounds towards the southern end of the bay. It has stone-and-cement bungalows of varying size.

Super Villa (☎ 0 7552 8552; bungalows 700-900B) Solid-looking brick bungalows with tiled roofs, right on the beach.

Super Royal Beach (☎ 0 7552 9237; r 800-3000B; ✕ ☀) This fancier place isn't on the beach, but it has a swimming pool.

Getting There & Away
You can catch a share taxi from Nakhon Si Thammarat's share-taxi terminal to Khanom for 50B. If you're driving, pedalling or riding, get off Rte 401 at the junction marked for Rte 4014 and follow the latter to Rte 4232, which runs parallel to the coast all along Ao Khanom (as far south as Sichon).

HAT SICHON & HAT HIN NGAM
หาดสิชล/หาดหินงาม
Few foreigners turn up at these mellow side-by-side beaches along a small curving bay about 65km north of Nakhon Si Thammarat in Amphoe Sichon. Anyone looking for a low-key local scene, eye-catching rocks strewn along the sand or the chance to peruse the market in a picturesque fishing village won't be disappointed.

Hat Sichon ends at a pier in the small hamlet of Sichon. Coconut is a major local product, so there are plenty of palms to set the tone. The beach is quiet, and you can easily walk into town. Head to the harbour and check out the large, colourful fishing boats lined up along spindly wooden piers,

and the old one-storey weathered shophouses made from the same rough wood.

Hin Ngam is found south of Hat Sichon. Marked by a cluster of unique-looking boulders at its northern end, it's for the isolationist – there are few services here. If you journey further south you'll come to the lesser-known beaches of Hat Piti and Hat Saophao. Hat Piti is a pretty stretch of white sand with one midrange resort. Hat Saophao stretches for 5km and could be the most beautiful beach in the area if it weren't for the disastrous prawn farms just inland, which use the most environmentally unfriendly techniques for raising the pink crustaceans.

Sleeping & Eating
Prasarnsuk Villa (☎ 0 7553 6299; bungalows 300-1300B; ☀) This good spot is right at the end of the sandy part of Hat Sichon, so you have easy beach access, but are also near a rocky headland where there is fair snorkelling. It has 30 solid-looking bungalows and there's a simple open-air seafood restaurant out the front.

Hin Ngam Bungalow (☎ 0 7553 6204; bungalows 200-300B) These six wood-and-thatch bungalows on Hat Hin Ngam are frequented almost entirely by Thai clientele, so they're great for escaping the *faràng* scene. There's a restaurant that overlooks the bay.

Hat Piti Beach Resort (☎ 0 7533 5303; bungalows 1000-2000B; ✕ ☀) On lengthy, unspoiled Hat Piti, this resort almost looks lost here with its American southwest designs. It is well run and has a good open-air restaurant and large, fully equipped bungalows. If it's empty ask about a discount – sometimes rooms go for as much as 40% below rack rates!

Getting There & Away
Get a bus for Sichon from the Nakhon Si Thammarat bus terminal for 20B to 30B or take a share taxi for 50B to 80B. From Sichon, you can take a motorcycle taxi to Hat Sichon, Hat Hin Ngam or Hat Piti for around 20B to 40B per person.

NAKHON SI THAMMARAT
นครศรีธรรมราช
pop 122,400
Steeped in history and religion, this long skinny city merges the old and the new – modern hotels and restaurants converge

DENNIS JOHNSON

Snorkelling at Ko Samui (p561)

En route from Ko Samui to Ko
Pha-Ngan (p547)

ANNE C DOWIE

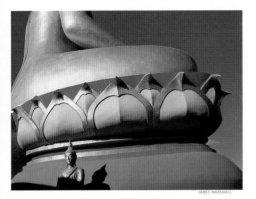

JAMES MARSHALL

Big Buddha, Wat Phra Yai (p561), Ko Samui

Ko Samui sunset with the Big Buddha of Wat Phra Yai in the distance (p561)

BILL WASSMAN

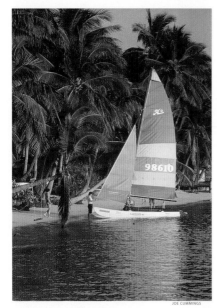

Sailing, Ko Pha-Ngan (p576)

JOE CUMMINGS

Gandhara-style fasting Buddha, Wat Phra Mahathat (p601), Nakhon Si Thammarat

RICHARD N

Ban Chalok Ban Kao beach (p592) on Ko Tao

RICHARD N

with ancient mosques and temples – and it's a pleasant place to wander around. The main drawcard is the now rare art form of Thai shadow-puppet theatre, but anyone interested in religion or architecture will also find the city engaging.

Centuries before the 8th-century Srivijaya empire subjugated the peninsula, there was a city-state here called Ligor (or Lagor), the well-known capital of the Tambralinga (or Tampaling) kingdom. Later, when Sri Lankan–ordained Buddhist monks established a monastery in the city, the name was changed to the Pali–Sanskrit Nagara Sri Dhammaraja (City of the Sacred Dharma-King), which is rendered in Thai phonetics as Nakhon Si Thammarat.

An overland route between the western port of Trang and eastern port of Nakhon Si Thammarat functioned as a major trade link between Thailand and the rest of the world, as well as between the western and eastern hemispheres. Clergy from Hindu, Muslim, Christian and Buddhist denominations established missions here over the centuries, and even in contemporary Nakhon Si Thammarat you'll find active temples, shrines, mosques and churches representing each of these faiths.

During the early development of the various Thai kingdoms, Nakhon Si Thammarat also became an important centre for religion and culture. Thai shadow theatre (*nǎng tàlung*) and classical dance-drama (*lákhon* – the Thai pronunciation of Lagor) were both developed here, and buffalo-hide shadow puppets along with dance masks are still being made. Other crafts for which Nakhon is famous include *thôm* (nielloware) silver and basketry. They can all be purchased in the handicraft shops along Th Tha Chang.

Orientation & Information

The city is divided into two sections: the historic half is south of the clock tower, the new city centre to the north. The new city centre has all the hotels and most of the restaurants, as well as more movie theatres per square kilometre than any other city in Thailand.

Bovorn Bazaar (Th Ratchadamnoen) A small *faràng*-oriented centre with a few restaurants and Internet cafés. Others are scattered throughout town.

Main post office (Th Ratchadamnoen; ⏰ 8.30am-4.30pm Mon-Fri) has an upstairs.

TAT (☎ 0 7534 6515; tatnakon@nrt.cscoms.com; ⏰ 8.30am-4.30pm) Housed in a 1926-vintage building near the police station. The friendly staff can help with transport information.

Telephone office (⏰ 8am-11pm) International service; upstairs in the post office.

Sights & Activities

Most foreign travellers, and even Thai visitors, come to Nakhon Si for the shadow puppets (see p603), but the national museum here is surprisingly well done, and there is also a trip-worthy wat in town. Those interested in mosques, temples, churches or wats, should take a look at the map for more places of worship (not mentioned in the text).

NAKHON SI THAMMARAT NATIONAL MUSEUM

พิพิธภัณฑ์สถานแห่งชาตินครศรีธรรมราช

Because the Tambralinga kingdom traded with Indian, Arabic, Dvaravati and Champa states much art from these places found its way to the Nakhon Si Thammarat area and some is now on display in the **national museum** (Th Ratchadamnoen; admission 30B; ⏰ 9am-4pm Wed-Sun). Notable are the Dong-Son bronze drums, Dvaravati Buddha images and Pallava (south Indian) Hindu sculpture. Upstairs are folk crafts, such as elaborate walking sticks, fishing cages and pottery.

The museum is 1km south of Wat Phra Mahathat. Any *sǎwngthǎew* scooting south will take you there for 5B.

WAT PHRA MAHATHAT

วัดพระมหาธาตุ

The city's most historic site, Wat Phra Mahathat was reputed to have been founded by Queen Hem Chala over 1000 years ago. Bronze statues representing the queen and her brother stand in front of the east wall facing Th Ratchadamnoen, and her spirit is said to be associated with the large standing Buddha in the southeastern cloister. Locals make daily offerings of flower garlands to this Buddha image and the statue of the queen, believing her spirit watches over the city and its residents.

This is the biggest wat in southern Thailand, comparable to Wat Pho and other large Bangkok wats. If you like wats, this one is well worth a trip. Reconstructed in the mid-13th century, the huge complex

NAKHON SI THAMMARAT

0   500 m
0   0.3 miles

To Mesa
Chotiphan's
Workshop (2km)

To Khiriwong (23km);
Lan Saka (23km)

Train Station

Th Watkhit

Th Neramit

Th Pak Nakhon

Th Si Prat

Th Baw Ang

Christian
Hospital

Th Phra Ngoen

Market

Th Phaniant

Th Tha Chang

Sanam Na
Meuang
(City Park)

Khlong   Na Meuang

Khlong Thai Wong

Th Ratchadamnoen

Th Si Thammasok

Th Ratchadamnoen

Sol 3

To National Museum (1km);
Twin Lotus Hotel (1.5km)

INFORMATION
Bangkok Bank...1 B1
Kasikornbank..2 B1
Main Post Office & Telephone Office....................3 B3
Police Station..4 B3
Siam Commercial Bank......................................5 B3
TAT Office..6 B3

SIGHTS & ACTIVITIES
Bethlehem Church..7 B2
Clock Tower...8 B5
Lak Meuang (City Pillar).....................................9 B3
Mosque..10 B3
Phra Phuttha Sihing Chapel..............................11 B5
Shiva Shrine..12 B4
Suchart Subsin's Workshop...............................13 B6
Vishnu Shrine..14 B4
Wat Buranaram..15 B2
Wat Maheyong...16 B3
Wat Na Phra Boromathat...................................17 B6
Wat Phra Mahathat..18 B6
Wat Sema Meuang..19 B4

SLEEPING
Bue Loung (Bua Luang) Hotel.............................20 B2
Grand Park Hotel..21 B1
Nakorn Garden Inn...22 B1
Phetpailin Hotel...23 A1
Thai Hotel..24 B2
Thai Lee Hotel...25 B2

EATING
Bovorn Bazaar...26 B2
Dam Kan Aeng...27 B1
Food Stalls..28 B2
Kuang Meng..29 B2

SHOPPING
Handicraft Shops..30 A3

TRANSPORT
Bus Terminal...31 A3
Minivans to Hat Yai..32 B2
Minivans to Phuket & Krabi...............................33 B2
Minivans to Surat Thani.....................................34 B1
Share-Taxi Terminal..35 B2
Săwngthăew to Khiriwong..................................36 B2
THAI...37 B1

LOWER SOUTHERN GULF

features a 78m *chedi*, crowned by a solid-gold spire weighing several hundred kilograms. Numerous smaller grey-black *chedi* surround the main one. A *mondòp*, the fortress-looking structure towards the northern end of the temple grounds, holds a Buddha footprint – one of the better designs in Thailand.

It's approximately 2km south of the new town centre – hop on any bus or *săwngthăew* going down Th Ratchadamnoen (5B).

PHRA PHUTTHA SIHING CHAPEL (HAW PHRA PHUTTHA SIHING)

หอพระพุทธสิหิงค์

This chapel is next to the provincial offices and contains one of Thailand's three identical Phra Singh Buddhas. One of these was supposed to have been cast in Sri Lanka before being brought to Sukhothai (through Nakhon Si Thammarat), Chiang Mai and, later, Ayuthaya. The other images are at

Wat Phra Singh in Chiang Mai and the National Museum in Bangkok – each claims to be the original.

Festivals & Events

Every year during mid-October there is a southern-Thai festival called **Chak Phra Pak Tai** held in Nakhon Si Thammarat (as well as Songkhla and Surat Thani). In Nakhon Si the festival is centred around Wat Phra Mahathat and includes performances of *năng tàlung* (shadow-puppet theatre) and *lákhon* as well as the parading of Buddha images around the city to collect donations for local temples.

In the third lunar month (February to March) the city holds the colourful **Hae Phaa Khun That**, in which a lengthy cloth *jataka* painting is wrapped around the main *chedi* at Wat Phra Mahathat.

Sleeping

Most of Nakhon Si Thammarat's hotels are near the train and bus stations. It's not exactly a hotel connoisseur's dreamland – most places offer worn and bleak rooms.

Nakorn Garden Inn (☎ 0 7531 3333; fax 0 7534 2926; 1/4 Th Pak Nakhon; r 445B; ❄) This place is Nakhon's best option in its price range. Tidy, homey, brick-walled rooms have good wooden furniture, TV and refrigerator. They're set around a quiet, sparse garden and there's plenty of parking.

Grand Park Hotel (☎ 0 7531 7666; fax 0 7531 7674; 1204/79 Th Pak Nakhon; r 600B; ❄) Rooms at the Grand Park are fine and modern with TVs and fridges, although not exactly luxurious. They're on seven floors, some with grand views of the city. Downstairs is a nice lobby and a restaurant.

Thai Lee Hotel (☎ 0 7535 6948; 1130 Th Ratchadamnoen; r 120-140B) This hotel is friendly and has spacious rooms that are either bright and noisy or dark and quiet. A secure budget choice.

Thai Hotel (☎ 0 7534 1509; fax 0 7534 4858; 1375 Th Ratchadamnoen; r 200-490B; ❄) Rooms here come with TVs and just a few scratches. The more expensive ones with air-con are larger, better furnished and have a fridge. There's a small lobby café and the whole place is central.

Bue Loung Hotel (Bua Luang; ☎ 0 7534 1518; fax 0 7534 2977; Soi Luang Meuang; r 170-270B; ❄) Bue Loung offers small and rather featureless rooms, but they are clean and bright and

---

SHADOW-PUPPET WORKSHOPS

Performances of Thai shadow theatre are rare nowadays and usually seen only during festivals, but there are two places in Nakhon Si Thammarat where you can see the puppets being made.

Traditionally, there are two styles of the shadow puppets: *năng tàlung* and *năng yài*. The former are similar in size to the Malay- and Indonesian-style puppets and feature movable appendages and parts (including genitalia), while the latter are unique to Thailand, nearly life-size and lack moving parts. Both are intricately carved from buffalo hide. The puppet masters use light against the puppets to create silhouettes (hence the name 'shadow puppets'), and also employ their own voices in dialogue and song to tell the story, while musicians play instruments including gongs, drums and cymbals.

The acknowledged master of shadow-puppet manufacture and performance is **Suchart Subsin** (☎ 0 7534 6394; Soi 3, 110/18 Th Si Thammasok; ☼ 9am-4pm), a Nakhon resident with a workshop not far from Wat Phra Mahathat. He has received several awards for his mastery and preservation of the craft, and has performed for the king. His workshop is open to the public; if enough people are assembled he may even be talked into providing a performance at his small outdoor studio. Puppets can also be purchased at reasonable prices – and here only, as he refuses to sell them through distributors. On some puppets the fur is left on the hide for additional effect – these cost a bit more as special care must be taken when tanning them. Bring your camera; you may be able to watch a craftsperson carving a puppet by hand.

Another craftsperson, **Mesa Chotiphan** (☎ 0 7534 3979; 558/4 Soi Rong Jeh, Th Ratchadamnoen; ☼ 9am-4pm) has a workshop in the northern part of town, and visitors are also welcome. Call if you would like to be picked up from anywhere in Nakhon Si. To get there on your own, go north from the city centre on Th Ratchadamnoen and, 500m north of the sports field, take the soi opposite the Chinese cemetery (before reaching the golf course and military base).

some even have partial mountain views. Not a bad deal.

Phetpailin Hotel (☎ 0 7534 1896; fax 0 7534 3943; 1835/38-39 Th Yommarat; r 180-380B; ❄) If you've just hopped off the train and are tired, the Phetpailin is an option as it is right next door. Try for a room at the back, they are quieter and come with mountain views. If you can afford it, go with air-con, as the fan rooms are basic and musty.

Twin Lotus Hotel (☎ 0 7532 3777; fax 0 7532 3821; 97/8 Th Phattanakan Khukhwang; r from 1100B; ❄) A few kilometres southeast of town, this large hotel offers all the usual top amenities. It shouldn't hurt to ask for a discount.

Eating

Th Jamroenwithi is the city's main culinary centre. At night the entire block running south from Th Neramit is lined with cheap **food stalls** serving rice and noodle dishes, as well as delicious Muslim food like *rotii klûay* (banana pancakes), *khâo mòk kài* (chicken biryani) and *mátàbà* (murtabak; *rotii* stuffed with chicken or vegetables).

Dam Kan Aeng (☎ 0 7534 4343; Th Watkhit; dishes 20-80B) This popular, cheap and simple Thai-Chinese eatery packs in hungry customers nightly.

Khrua Nakhon (☎ 0 7531 7197; Bovorn Bazaar; dishes 20-100B; ⏱ 6am-3pm) Near Hao Coffee, this large cafeteria-style place serves Nakhon cuisine. Order *khâo yam* (southern-style rice salad), *kaeng tai plaa* (spicy fish curry) and *khànŏm jiin* (curry noodles served with a huge tray of veggies).

Hao Coffee (☎ 0 7534 6563; Bovorn Bazaar; dishes 30-60B) This is a good place to try some of Nakhon's excellent coffee. Hao was originally a Hokkien-style coffee shop, but it now prepares international coffees as well as southern-Thai Hokkien-style coffee (called 'Hao coffee' on the menu) in a renovated, antique-like atmosphere.

Ligor Home Bakery (Bovorn Bazaar; dishes 30-60B; ⏱ 7.30am-5.30pm) Ligor bakes European-style pastries in a modern atmosphere. It also serves breakfast, Thai food and good coffee. It has the same menu as Hao Coffee.

Kuang Meng (1343/12 Th Ratchadamnoen; dishes 20-80B) Kuang Meng is a friendly, small Hokkien coffee shop with marble-top tables and delicious pastries.

Ban Lakhon (Bovorn Bazaar; dishes from 30B) Ban Lakhon is behind Khrua Nakhon, in an old

house built around a large tree. Step up to the 2nd floor for good Thai food.

Rock 99 Bar & Grill (☎ 0 7534 7846; Bovorn Bazaar; dishes 65-180B) Rock 99 has a strange pet store–like feel with its wall-lined fish tanks. As well as a few cocktails, the kitchen serves steak, pizza, spaghetti and sandwiches – but don't expect authenticity. It stays open late, so it's the place to head for drinks at night.

Getting There & Away

AIR

Thai Airways International (☎ 0 7534 2491; 1612 Th Ratchadamnoen) flies between Nakhon Si and Bangkok (2520B, one hour, twice daily).

BUS & MINIVAN

There are buses to/from Bangkok (1st class/ 2nd class 454/353B, non-air-con 252B to 325B, 13 hours, twice daily). One VIP departure leaves nightly (705B). Ordinary buses to Bangkok leave from the bus terminal, but a couple of private bus companies on Th Jamroenwithi sell air-con bus tickets to Bangkok and these buses leave from here. Look for Saphan Tour or Moung Tai Tours, which are both easy to find.

Other destinations from the bus terminal include Hat Yai (73B to 102B, three hours, daily), Phuket (125B to 200B, seven hours, daily), Krabi (67B to 94B, three hours, daily), Songkhla (70B to 98B, three hours, daily), Surat Thani (45B to 90B, one hour, daily) and Trang (69B, 1½ hours, daily).

Frequent minivans to Krabi (120B, 2½ hours) and Phuket (200B, five hours) leave from Th Jamroenwithi. Minivans to Surat Thani (95B, one hour) depart from Th Watkhit. Minivans to Hat Yai (90B, three hours) leave from Th Yommarat. Look for small desks set near the footpath (minivans and waiting passengers may or may not be present nearby).

TRAIN

Most southbound trains from Bangkok stop at Thung Song, about 40km west of Nakhon, from where you must take a bus or taxi to the coast. However, two trains (2nd class 468B to 688B) go all the way to Nakhon Si Thammarat: the rapid No 173, which leaves Bangkok's Hualamphong train station at 5.35pm, arriving in Nakhon Si at 8.50am; and the express No 85, which leaves

Bangkok at 7.15pm and arrives in Nakhon at 10.50am. There are two daily trains (aircon 2nd class sleepers 643B) to Bangkok, departing at 1pm and 2pm.

There are two trains each day to and from Hat Yai and one each to Yala and Sungai Kolok.

Getting Around
Săwngthăew run north–south along Th Ratchadamnoen and Th Si Thammasok for 6B (a bit more at night). Motorcycle taxi rides cost between 20B and 50B.

AROUND NAKHON SI THAMMARAT
Khao Luang National Park
อุทยานแห่งชาติเขาหลวง
Known for its beautiful mountain and forest walks, cool streams, waterfalls and fruit orchards, this 570-sq-km **park** (☎ 0 1228 2051; admission 200B) surrounds **Khao Luang** (1835m), the highest peak in peninsular Thailand. Along with other forested igneous peaks to the west, Khao Luang provides a watershed that feeds Mae Nam Rapi. Local Thais practise a unique form of agriculture called *sŭan rôm* (shade garden, or shade farm). Instead of clear-cutting the forest, they leave many indigenous trees intact, randomly interspersing them with betel, mangosteen, rambutan, langsat, papaya, durian and banana trees. Cleverly placed bamboo and PVC pipes irrigate the mixed orchards without the use of pumps.

Wildlife includes clouded leopard, tiger, elephant, banteng, gaur, tapir, serow, musk deer, macaque, civet, binturong and Javan mongoose, plus more than 200 bird species. In excess of 300 orchid varieties (including several indigenous species) find roots in the humid environments here, along with begonias and a wide variety of ferns.

The best time to visit Khao Luang is January to April, when it's cooler and drier. If you're coming from Nakhon Si Thammarat, visit the **TAT office** (p601) there and pick up a small informative English booklet to the park.

ACTIVITIES
Hiking is the park's biggest attraction. You can hike 2.5km through dense tropical forest to the top of **Nam Tok Karom** from the national park headquarters near Lan Saka (25km from Nakhon Si Thammarat), off

Rte 4015. Every 500m or so there are shelters and seats. To reach seven-tiered **Nam Tok Krung Ching**, a half-day walk, you'll have to take the Krung Ching nature trail from Nopphitam at the northeastern border of the park, off Rte 4140.

Along the way you'll pass the world's largest tree ferns, an old communist insurgent camp, **Tham Pratuchai** (a cave also used by the communists) and a mangosteen forest. This trail, too, is lined with seats and shelters. The falls are most impressive after the rainy season has ended in November and December.

A more challenging trail leads from a car park near Khiriwong to the summit of **Khao Luang**, a 14-hour walk best divided into two or more days. Night temperatures at the summit can drop to 5°C, so come prepared with plenty of warm clothing. At 600m, Kratom Suan Sainai offers a simple-roofed **shelter** and also marks the upper limit of the fruit plantations. In the dry season you can **camp** next to a riverbed at Lan Sai, about a six-hour walk from the car park. Five-hours further on, along a section of very steep trail, you'll enter a cloud forest full of rattan, orchids, rhododendrons, ferns and stunted oaks. From here it's another three hours to the summit, where, if the weather is clear, you'll be rewarded with stunning views of layer after layer of mountains rolling into the distance.

The best and safest way to appreciate the Khao Luang trek is to go with a guide from the **Khiriwong Village Ecotourism Club** (☎ 0 7530 9010, 0 9501 2706; trek 1500B) in Khiriwong. For this price the villagers will arrange a three-day, two-night trek that includes all meals and guide services. The guides can point out local flora and fauna that you might otherwise miss. The only time to complete this hike is between January and June, when the trails are dry and the leeches are not too bad. During heavy rains the trail can be impassable for days.

SLEEPING
Park bungalows (☎ 0 for reservations 7530 9664; 6-12 people 600-1200B) are available, and **camping** is permitted on the trail to the summit of Khao Luang. There are a few private **bungalows** and **restaurants** on the road to the park offices that offer accommodation and food.

GETTING THERE & AWAY

To reach the park, take a *săwngthăew* (20B) from Nakhon Si Thammarat (on Th Jamroenwithi) to the village of Khiriwong at the base of Khao Luang. The entrance to the park and the offices of the Royal Forest Department are 33km from the centre of Nakhon on Rte 4015, an asphalt road that climbs almost 400m.

SONGKHLA PROVINCE

SONGKHLA & AROUND

สงขลา

pop 86,700

Songkhla, 950km from Bangkok, is a pleasant city with a colourful market, charming older section (west of Th Ramwithi) and a long coastline. The population a mix of Thais, Chinese and Malays, and the local architecture and cuisine reflect this milieu. The seafood served along the peaceful, white-sand beaches is excellent, although the water is not that great for swimming (especially if you've just come from the Ko Samui archipelago). Beaches are not Songkhla's main attraction, even if the TAT promotes them as such, although the sand-and-casuarina scenery can be visually striking and the city is keeping the quiet, low-key beach cleaner than ever before.

Offshore petroleum exploration projects commissioned through Unocal and Total – and the resultant influx of multinational oil-company employees (particularly British and American) – have brought a strong Western presence to Songkhla. This, along with a considerable Thai naval presence, has created a relatively wealthy city. Like Surat Thani, there is a profusion of neatly uniformed young students giggling and shyly attempting to practise English with foreigners.

Orientation

The city has a split personality, with the charming older section west of Th Ramwithi towards the waterfront, and a modern mix of business and suburbia to the east. A scenic promontory, Laem Songkhla, extends northwards; the eastern side of the jutting piece of land is Hat Son Awn, along which there is a pleasant walking path. Further south is Hat Samila, which is also pretty and peaceful.

Information

Chinese consulate (☎ 0 7431 1494; Th Sadao)

Corner Bookshop (☎ 0 7431 2577; cnr Th Saiburi & Th Phetchakhiri; ☼ 7am-7.30pm) Sells novels, maps, newspapers, magazines and Lonely Planet guidebooks (all in English).

Dotcom Internet (☎ 0 7432 5049; Th Ramwithi; per hr 40B; ☼ 8am-10pm)

Immigration office (☎ 0 7431 3480; Th Nakhon Nok; ☼ 8.30am-4.30pm Mon-Fri) File for visa extensions here.

Indonesian consulate (☎ 0 7431 1544; Th Sadao)

Malaysian consulate (☎ 0 7431 1062; 4 Th Sukhum)

Police station (☎ 0 7431 2133) At the northern end of Hat Samila.

Post office (Th Wichianchom; ☼ 8.30am-3.30pm Mon-Fri, 9am-noon Sat & Sun) Opposite the market; international calls can be made upstairs.

Sights & Activities

BEACHES

The residents of Songkhla have begun taking better care of the strip of white sand along **Hat Samila**, and it's now quite an attractive beach for strolling or an early morning read on one of the benches in the shade of the casuarina trees. The water isn't anything special, however.

A **bronze mermaid**, depicted squeezing water from her long hair in a tribute to Mae Thorani, the Hindu-Buddhist earth goddess, sits atop some rocks at the northern end of the beach. Locals treat the figure like a shrine, tying the waist with coloured cloth and rubbing the breasts for good luck. Near the mermaid statue is a **cat and rat statue**, named for the Cat and Rat Islands (Ko Yo and Ko Losin). The rustic seafood restaurants at the back of the beach supply food and cold beverages.

NATIONAL MUSEUM

พิพิธภัณฑ์สถานแห่งชาติสงขลา

Housed in a 100-year-old building of southern Sino-Portuguese architecture is this picturesque **national museum** (☎ 0 7431 1728; Th Wichianchom; admission 30B; ☼ 9am-4pm Wed-Sun). Along with the innate architectural charms of its curved rooflines and thick walls, it's a quiet, breezy building with a tranquil garden at the front. The museum contains exhibits from all national art-style periods, particularly the Srivijaya, including a 7th- to 9th-century Shivalingam found in Pattani. Also on display are Thai and Chinese ceramics and sumptuous Chinese furniture.

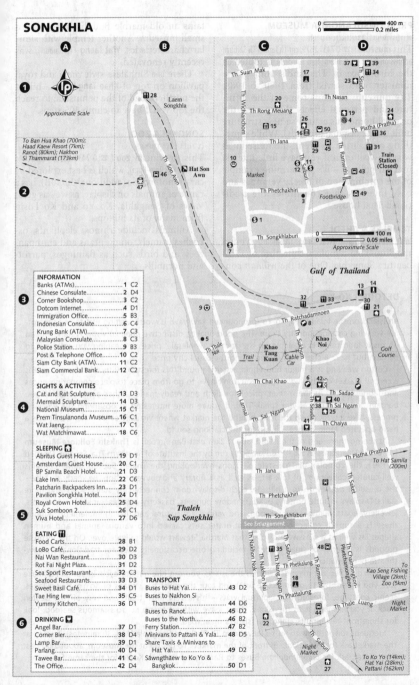

SONGKHLA

0 ──────── 400 m
0 ──────── 0.2 miles

A **B** **C** **D**

Laem Songkhla

Approximate Scale

To Ban Hua Khao (700m);
Haad Kaew Resort (7km);
Ranot (80km); Nakhon
Si Thammarat (173km)

Hat Son Awn

Th Suan Mak

Th Wichianchom

Th Rong Meuang

Th Jana

Th Nasan

Th Saida

Th Platha (Pratha)

Th Ramwithi

Th Saiburi

Market

Th Phetchakhiri

Footbridge

Th Songkhlaburi

Train
Station
(Closed)

0 ──────── 100 m
0 ──────── 0.05 miles

Approximate Scale

Gulf of Thailand

LOWER SOUTHERN GULF

INFORMATION
Banks (ATMs)	1 C2
Chinese Consulate	2 D4
Corner Bookshop	3 C2
Dotcom Internet	4 D1
Immigration Office	5 B3
Indonesian Consulate	6 C4
Krung Bank (ATM)	7 C3
Malaysian Consulate	8 C3
Police Station	9 B3
Post & Telephone Office	10 C2
Siam City Bank (ATM)	11 C2
Siam Commercial Bank	12 C2

SIGHTS & ACTIVITIES
Cat and Rat Sculpture	13 D3
Mermaid Sculpture	14 D3
National Museum	15 C1
Prem Tinsulanonda Museum	16 C1
Wat Jaeng	17 C1
Wat Matchimawat	18 C6

SLEEPING
Abritus Guest House	19 D1
Amsterdam Guest House	20 C1
BP Samila Beach Hotel	21 D3
Lake Inn	22 C6
Patcharin Backpackers Inn	23 D1
Pavilion Songkhla Hotel	24 D1
Royal Crown Hotel	25 D4
Suk Somboon 2	26 C1
Viva Hotel	27 D6

EATING
Food Carts	28 B1
LoBo Café	29 D2
Nai Wan Restaurant	30 D3
Rot Fai Night Plaza	31 D2
Sea Sport Restaurant	32 C3
Seafood Restaurants	33 D3
Sweet Basil Café	34 D1
Tae Hing Iew	35 C5
Yummy Kitchen	36 D1

DRINKING
Angel Bar	37 D1
Corner Bier	38 D4
Lamp Bar	39 D1
Parlang	40 D4
Tawee Bar	41 C4
The Office	42 D4

TRANSPORT
Buses to Hat Yai	43 D2
Buses to Nakhon Si Thammarat	44 D6
Buses to Ranot	45 D2
Buses to the North	46 B2
Ferry Station	47 B2
Minivans to Pattani & Yala	48 D5
Share Taxis & Minivans to Hat Yai	49 D2
Sǎwngthǎew to Ko Yo & Bangkok	50 D1

Th Suan Mak

Th Nasan

Th Platha (Pratha)

Th Ratchadamnoen

Khao
Tang
Kuan

Khao
Noi

Cable Car

Golf
Course

Th Thale
Noi

Trail

Th Chai Khao

Th Sadao

Th Sai Ngam

Th Chaiya

Th Lamai

Th Sai Ngam

Th Nasan

Th Jana

Th Phetchakhiri

Th Songkhlaburi

See Enlargement

Th Nakhon Nok

Th Nakhon Nai

Th Nang Ngam

Th Saiburi

Th Phetkalung

Th Ramwithi

Th Chaimongkon-
Phethamongkon

Th Saket

To Hat Samila
(200m)

To
Kao Seng Fishing
Village (2km);
Zoo (5km)

Th Thale Luang

Night
Market

Th Phattalung

Night
Market

To Ko Yo (14km);
Hat Yai (28km);
Pattani (162km)

Thaleh
Sap Songkhla

PREM TINSULANONDA MUSEUM

พิพิธภัณฑ์เปรมติณสูลานนท์

This **museum** (☎ 0 7431 2679; cnr Th Jana & Th Saiburi; admission free; ⏰ 8.30am-4pm Tue-Sun) is touted as the birthplace of Thailand's 16th prime minister, who served from 1980 to 1988. The museum contains some of the furniture and personal effects that graced the original home (it's actually a new structure built on the original grounds). While something of a shrine to Prem, the museum is worth a visit even if you have little interest in Thai politics – it's a charming example of the combination of breezy verandas and cosy interiors that constitutes the traditional Thai house.

TEMPLES & CHEDI

Wat Matchimawat (Wat Klang; Th Saiburi) typifies the Sino-Thai temple architecture of 17th-century Songkhla. One of the *wíhǎan* contains an old marble Buddha image and a small museum. Another temple with similar characteristics, **Wat Jaeng** (Th Saiburi), was recently renovated.

There is a Sinhalese-style *chedi* and royal pavilion on top of **Khao Tang Kuan**, a hill at the northern end of the peninsula; to reach the top you'll have to climb 305 steps.

SONGKHLA ZOO

สวนสัตว์สงขลา

This provincial **zoo** (☎ 0 7433 6038; adult/child 30/10B; ⏰ 9am-6pm), which is best explored by car or motorcycle (additional 30/10B), has a range of animals on display, as well as great views of Songkhla, Ko Yo and Ko Losin from many of its hilltops.

Animals include rhinos, elephants, ostriches, camels, orang-utans and chimpanzees, and birds such as flamingos, parrots and hornbills.

DETOUR – KO YO

เกาะยอ

An island on the inland sea, Ko Yo (pronounced kaw yaw) is worth visiting just to see the cotton-weaving cottage industry there. The good-quality, distinctive *phâa kàw yaw* is hand-woven on rustic looms and is available on the spot at 'wholesale' prices – meaning you still have to bargain but have a chance of undercutting the usual city price.

Cotton weaving is a major household activity around this forested, sultry island, and there is a central market off the highway so you don't have to go from place to place comparing prices and fabric quality. At the market, prices for cloth and ready-made clothes are excellent if you bargain and especially if you speak Thai. If you're more interested in observing the weaving process, take a walk down the road behind the market where virtually every other house has a hand-operated loom or two – listen for the clacking sound.

At the northern end of the island, about 2km past Ban Ao Sai, is **Thaksin Folklore Museum** (☎ 0 7433 1184; admission 50B; ⏰ 8.30am-5pm), run by the Institute of Southern Thai Studies. Opened in 1991, the complex of Thai-style pavilions overlooking the Thaleh Sap Songkhla contains well-curated collections of folk art, as well as a library and souvenir shop. Be ready to hike – the museum ripples down a hillside, each display room connected by stairs, stairs and more stairs. Displays include pottery, beads, shadow puppets, basketry, textiles, musical instruments, jewellery, boats, religious art, weapons and various agricultural and fishing implements. Among these is a superb collection of coconut-grater sets carved into various animal and human shapes, as well as a glassware display that Martha Stewart would salivate over. On the institute grounds is a series of small gardens, including one occasionally used for traditional shadow-theatre performances.

If you'd rather just meander around the island, you can hire a motorcycle in Songkhla (make sure you know how to operate one first) and tour the quiet back roads of Ko Yo: tiny villages, scenic coastline, forested hills, spiritual *wáts* – it's a very local treat, and way off the beaten track. If you've made it to the island, don't leave without trying Ko Yo's famous seafood; look for shorefront restaurants along the island's main road.

Frequent *sǎwngthǎew* to Ko Yo leave from Th Platha in Songkhla (10B, 30 minutes). To stop at the market ask for *nâa tàlàat*, 'in front of the market'. To get off at the museum, about 2km past the market, ask for *phíphítháphan*. Buses to Ranot pass through Ko Yo for the same fare.

The zoo is south of Songkhla about 5km, on the Songkhla–Chana road. Follow the signs; the turn-off is at the Esso petrol station, then it's another 500m to the gate. It's best to rent a motorcycle (or bicycle if you like pedalling up hills) to get here, since then you'll have transport within the zoo.

Sleeping

BUDGET

If you're a budget traveller, you're in luck – Songkhla has an exceptional number of good and inexpensive guesthouses that cater to travellers.

Amsterdam Guest House (☎ 0 7431 4890; 15/3 Th Rong Meuang; r 180-200B) This homey, quirky Dutch-run place is popular and clean, with plenty of cushions, wandering pets and a caged macaque that is said to bite the unwary. Bicycles/motorcycles are available to rent for 100/200B per day.

Abritus Guest House (☎ 0 7432 6047; abritus_th@ yahoo.com; 28/16 Th Ramwithi; r 200B; ☐) This guesthouse has large clean rooms with shared bathrooms. Downstairs is a good **restaurant** (dishes 30-200B), where guests get a 10% discount on food and drinks. English, German, Russian and Bulgarian are spoken, and bikes and motorcycles are available for rent.

Patcharin Backpackers Inn (☎ 0 7431 1821; 65 Th Sisuda; r 230-250B) This inn offers six beautiful, large rooms (with shared bathrooms) in a home. It's clean, friendly and central to Songkhla's bar scene. There's a tiny garden at the front.

MIDRANGE

There are a fair number of affordable hotels in Songkhla.

Viva Hotel (☎ 0 7432 1033; 547/2 Th Nakhon Nok; s/d 500/600B; ✖) Viva is fantastic value. It's a modern five-storey hotel where the friendly, helpful staff speak English. The attached coffee shop has live music nightly.

Suk Somboon 2 (☎ 0 7431 3809; 14 Th Saiburi; r 200-500B; ✖) Actually two buildings, one old and one new, right next to each other, the new half has pleasant, smallish midrange rooms with good showers, TVs and fridges, while the old half is much more basic.

Royal Crown Hotel (☎ 0 7431 2174; fax 0 7432 1027; 38 Th Sai Ngam; r 450B; ✖) Catering mostly to visiting oil-company employees and their families, this place is good value. Rooms are carpeted and everything works.

Haad Kaew Resort (☎ 0 7433 1059; fax 0 7433 1220; r 775-900B; ✖ ➚) This large pleasant resort has its own lagoon, beachfront and pool on landscaped grounds. Rooms are comfortable and come with all the amenities. The only drawback is it's actually a long drive outside Songkhla, on the peninsula north of the channel.

Lake Inn (☎ 0 7432 1044; lakeinn@hotmail.com; 301 Th Nakhon Nok; r 450-590B; ✖) Lake Inn is not particularly great value unless sea views are important. The rooms are tatty and the halls are worn.

TOP END

BP Samila Beach Hotel (☎ 0 7444 0222; fax 0 7444 0442; 8 Th Ratchadamnoen; r incl breakfast 1150-2500B; ✖ ➚ ☐) This beachfront hotel is Songkhla's swankiest accommodation, has all the amenities and features mountain and sea views. Balconies are large and the amoeba-like pool inviting. Not a bad deal.

Pavilion Songkhla Hotel (☎ 0 7444 1850; www .pavilionhotels.com/songlkla_overview.htm; 17 Th Platha; r 750-2500B; ✖) Rooms in this nine-storey building are large and luxurious with wood panelling, satellite TV and carpeting.

Eating

The seafood restaurants on Hat Samila are good – try the curried crab claws or the spicy fried squid. Prices are low to moderate. Fancier seafood places are found along Th Son Awn near the beach – but these also tend to have hordes of young Thai hostesses to satisfy the Thai male penchant for chatting up *àw-àw* (young girls). Cheaper and better is another string of seafood places on the beach close to where Th Ratchadamnoen and Th Son Awn intersect. At the southern end of Th Sisuda is a night market called **Rot Fai Night Plaza** – on Sunday, a morning market also pops up here. The seafood of Ko Yo has a reputation for being some of the best in the area. Restaurants are near the main island road, next to the water.

Sea Sport Restaurant (☎ 0 7432 7244; Th Ratchadamnoen; dishes 50-200B; ⊙ 4pm-midnight) Highly recommended by locals for its seafood, the ambience here is unbeatable, at least when it's not raining. Outside wooden benches (some shaped like boats) are set on a grassy, bricked terrace while a cloth tarp blows overhead. At night everything's lit up romantically, and the breezy sea is right there.

LOWER SOUTHERN GULF

Nai Wan Restaurant (☎ 0 7431 1295; Th Ratchadamnoen; dishes 35-200B) Popular for its crab dishes (bring moist wipes!), the menu also offers Thai salads, soups and various seafood dishes, as well as a few veggie entries. The large, casual space is near the little mermaid sculpture.

Yummy Kitchen (☎ 0 6692 0060; 14 Th Platha; dishes 30-50B) This place lives up to its name – it has truly excellent food, although it sometimes takes a while to prepare. It's popular with the after-school crowd.

LoBo Cafe (☎ 0 7431 1788; T10/1-3 Th Platha; dishes 40-120B) Cooks up Western breakfasts and Thai food in a modern, homey and friendly atmosphere. There's a big-screen TV and motorcycles can be rented here for 200B per day.

Sweet Basil Cafe (☎ 0 1690 3838; 50/2-3 Th Sisuda; dishes 50-120B; ⊙ 3pm-midnight) Sweet Basil serves good Vietnamese and Thai food in a pretty, peaceful setting – at least compared to the bar scene outside. The service is good and a large picture menu makes ordering easy.

Tae Hieng Iew (☎ 0 7431 1505; 85 Th Nang Ngam; dishes 50-170B) Locally recommended, Chinese and seafood are served at Tae Hieng Iew in a decent atmosphere with nice wooden furniture. Look for it south of the town centre, just south of the elaborate Chinese cinema.

Drinking

A string of bars just east of the Indonesian consulate is jokingly referred to among local expats as 'The Dark Side'. Not as ominous as it sounds, this strip caters mainly to oil-company employees and other Westerners living in Songkhla. Try **The Office**, the bar nearest Soi 5, run by an Englishman.

On nearby happenin' Th Sisuda, interspersed with some restaurants, are a few other casual bars worth checking out. **Corner Bier** is a small corner place where Songkhla's Canadian community hangs out. **Parlang**, where the Hash House Harriers meet every Saturday at 3pm, is another popular expat place. The club-like **Tawee Bar** is popular at night, as are **Angel Bar** and the hut-like **Lamp Bar**.

Getting There & Away
AIR

Thai Airways International operates several daily flights between Bangkok and nearby Hat Yai; see p614 for more information.

BOAT

Towards the end of Laem Songkhla (Songkhla's finger-like peninsula), you'll find a government-run ferry that plies the short distance across the channel where the Thaleh Sap Songkhla inland sea meets the Gulf of Thailand. The barge-like ferry carries about 15 cars, plus assorted motorcycles and pedestrians. The fare for the seven-minute ride is 18B per car, 5B per motorcycle and 1B per person; it runs 5am to 9pm daily.

BUS, MINIVAN & SHARE TAXI

Songkhla is something of a Hat Yai transport satellite; from Songkhla, you'll have to go to Hat Yai to reach most long-distance destinations in the south. There are a few destinations originating in Songkhla, though.

Across from the ferry station is a small, strangely located government bus terminal. Four 2nd-class buses go daily to Bangkok (437B, 10 hours); stops en route include Chumphon (245B, five hours), Nakhon Si Thammarat (100B, two hours) and Surat Thani (150B, three hours). One VIP bus to Bangkok leaves at 4.45pm (870B, 10 hours), while three 1st-class buses (562B, 10 hours) depart late afternoon and evening.

To Hat Yai, buses (16B), minivans (20B) and share taxis (25B) take around 40 minutes and leave from Th Ramwithi. Frequent minivans to Pattani and Yala (70B, two hours) depart from the southern part of Th Sisuda, while frequent ordinary buses to Nakhon Si Thammarat (70B, two hours) use from the not-very-useful bus terminal south of town.

Getting Around

Share taxis to the Hat Yai airport cost 150B to 180B; private taxis charge 400B.

Săwngthǎew circulate around town for 10B. Motorcycle taxis cost 10B to 20B; rates double at night.

Amsterdam and Abritus guesthouses rent bicycles and motorcycles; LoBo Cafe just rents motorcycles. Prices are 100B per day for bicycles, 200B for motorcycles.

HAT YAI
หาดใหญ่
pop 191,200

Hat Yai, 933km from Bangkok, is southern Thailand's commercial centre and one of the kingdom's largest cities, although it's only an *amphoe* in Songkhla Province. A steady

LOWER SOUTHERN GULF

TRAVEL WARNING

In April 2005 three bombs exploded in Hat Yai, including one at the airport. The explosions have been linked to the insurgency in Thailand's Muslim-dominated southernmost provinces. This is the first such incident that has occurred in Songkhla Province.

For more information, please see the warning, p616.

stream of customers from Malaysia once kept Hat Yai's central business district booming, but Southeast Asia's economic doldrums, along with the Malaysian government's ban on the exchange of Malaysian currency anywhere outside Malaysia, has slowed things down a bit. You wouldn't know it by walking along the streets, though – it's still very much a bustling international market town, and everything from dried fruit to stereos is sold in shops along the parallel streets of Th Niphat Uthit Nos 1, 2 and 3.

Visually, Hat Yai is a big city with big buildings, including some large department stores. Busy streets are filled with traffic, while walkways are lined with hawkers and their shoppers. Culturally, Hat Yai is very much a Chinese town at its centre, with loads of gold shops, Chinese restaurants and Mandarin-specked conversations. A substantial Muslim minority is concentrated in certain sections of the city, especially near the mosque off Th Niphat Songkhrao.

Hat Yai is a major transport hub for travel around southern Thailand and between Thailand and Malaysia. Many travellers stop over in the city on their way to/from Malaysia.

Information

BOOKSHOPS

DK Bookstore (no Roman-script sign; ☎ 0 7423 0759; 2/4-7 Th Thamnoonvithi; ⏰ 9am-6pm) English books, such as novels and Lonely Planet guides, are sold here along with maps. Look for the big yellow building.

EMERGENCY

Tourist police (☎ 0 7424 6733, emergency ☎ 1155; ⏰ 24hr) Near the TAT office.

IMMIGRATION OFFICES

Immigration office (☎ 0 7424 3019; Th Phetkasem) Near the railway bridge, in the same complex as a police station. The nearest Malaysian consulate is in Songkhla.

INTERNET ACCESS

10 Net (per hr 60B; ⏰ 9am-midnight) Right in front of the train station, it's one of two Internet cafés next to each other.

MEDICAL SERVICES

Bangkok Hatyai Hospital (☎ 0 7436 5780; cnr Th Niphat Songkhrao 1 & Soi 7 Niphat Songkhrao 1) Offers full medical care, including emergency services, and English-speaking staff.

MONEY

Hat Yai is loaded with banks. Several after-hours exchange windows are along Th Niphat Uthit 2 and 3 near Th Thamnoonvithi. If you have Malaysian ringgit, the banks won't take them but many midrange and top-end hotels will – although the exchange rate won't be too hot.

POST & TELEPHONE

Main post office (1 Th Niphat Songkhrao; ⏰ 8.30am-4.30pm Mon-Fri, 9am-noon Sat & Sun) At the northern end of town; it has an adjacent **telephone office** (⏰ 7am-11pm).

Post office (Th Phatkasem) A more convenient branch, two blocks northeast of the train station.

TOURIST INFORMATION

Tourist maps and pamphlets are available at hotels throughout town.

TAT (☎ 0 7424 3747; tathatyai@hatyai.inet.co.th; 1/1 Soi 2, Th Niphat Uthit 3; ⏰ 8.30am-4.30pm) Towards the southern end of town.

TRAVEL AGENCIES

Cathay Tour (☎ 0 7423 5044; 93/1 Th Niphat Uthit 2) One of many agencies in town. Staff are used to dealing with *faràng* and offer a full range of services, including visa advice.

Sights & Activities

Most people don't stay in Hat Yai too long; it's mostly just a stop on the way to somewhere else. There's not much to see or do unless you are interested in fighting. If this is the case, you can check out **bullfighting** (☎ 0 7438 8753; tickets male/female from 100/60B; ⏰ 10am-5pm), which involves two bulls in opposition, as opposed to a bull and a person. Fights occur on the first Saturday of each month, or on the second Saturday if the first Saturday is a *wan phrá* (Buddhist worship day; full, half or new moon). Fights are held at Noen Khum Thong Stadium on the way to the airport (15B by *săwngthăew*). On the

LOWER SOUTHERN GULF

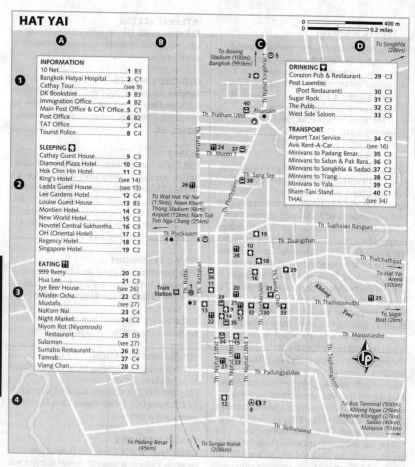

HAT YAI

0   400 m
0   0.2 miles

To Songkhla (28km)

To Boxing Stadium (100m); Bangkok (993km)

INFORMATION

10 Net..................................	1 B3
Bangkok Hatyai Hospital..........	2 C1
Cathay Tour........................	(see 9)
DK Bookstore........................	3 B3
Immigration Office..................	4 B2
Main Post Office & CAT Office..	5 C1
Post Office...........................	6 B2
TAT Office............................	7 C4
Tourist Police.......................	8 C4

SLEEPING

Cathay Guest House...............	9 C3
Diamond Plaza Hotel..............	10 C3
Hok Chin Hin Hotel................	11 C3
King's Hotel.........................	(see 14)
Ladda Guest House................	(see 13)
Lee Gardens Hotel.................	12 C4
Louise Guest House...............	13 B3
Montien Hotel......................	14 C3
New World Hotel...................	15 C3
Novotel Central Sukhontha......	16 C3
OH (Oriental Hotel)...............	17 C3
Regency Hotel......................	18 C3
Singapore Hotel....................	19 C2

EATING

999 Remy............................	20 C3
Hua Lee..............................	21 C3
Jye Beer House.....................	(see 26)
Muslim Ocha........................	22 C3
Mustafa..............................	(see 27)
NaKorn Nai..........................	23 C4
Night Market........................	24 C2
Niyom Rot (Niyomrosh) Restaurant........................	25 D3
Sulaiman............................	(see 27)
Sumatra Restaurant...............	26 B2
Tamrab..............................	27 C4
Viang Chan..........................	28 C3

DRINKING

Corazon Pub & Restaurant......	29 C3
Post Laserdisc (Post Restaurant)..............	30 C3
Sugar Rock..........................	31 C3
The Pubb............................	32 C3
West Side Saloon..................	33 C3

TRANSPORT

Airport Taxi Service...............	34 C3
Avis Rent-A-Car....................	(see 16)
Minivans to Padang Besar.......	35 C3
Minivans to Satun & Pak Bara..	36 C3
Minivans to Songkhla & Sadao.	37 C2
Minivans to Trang.................	38 C3
Minivans to Yala..................	39 C3
Share-Taxi Stand..................	40 C1
THAI..................................	(see 34)

Th Niphat Songkhran
Th Pratham Uthit
Fountain
Th Rattakan
Th Montri 1
Th Sang See
Th Phetkasem

To Wat Hat Yai Nai (1.5km); Noen Khum Thong Stadium (6km); Airport (12km); Nam Tok Ton Nga Chang (25km)

Th Phetkasem
Train Station
Th Rotfai

Th Suphasan Rangsan
Th Duangchan
Th Pratchathipat
To Hat Yai Arena (300m)
Th Saenghanusorn
Th Saeng Chan
Klong Toei
Th Thamnoonvithi
To Sugar Beat (2km)
Th Manasruedee
Th Tephsongkon
Th Niphat Uthit 1
Th Niphat Uthit 2
Th Niphat Uthit 3
Th Padungpakdee
To Bus Terminal (500m); Khlong Ngae (25km); Amphoe Klonggit (27km); Sadao (40km); Malaysia (53km)
Th Siphunawat

To Padang Besar (45km)
To Sungai Kolok (208km)

---

first Sunday of each month another round is held in Amphoe Klonggit (between Hat Yai and Sadao).

Because the times and venues for these bullfights tend to change, check with the TAT office for details.

Muay Thai boxing matches (admission 180B) are held every weekend in the boxing stadium just north of Hat Yai's sports stadium. Times vary so it's necessary to check with the TAT office to confirm the schedule.

Sleeping
BUDGET

Hat Yai has dozens of hotels within walking distance of the train station. During Chinese New Year (late February to early March) the prices double for most budget rooms. Malaysian holidays also cause a steep hike in room prices.

Cathay Guest House (☎ 0 7424 3815; fax 0 7435 4104; 93/1 Th Niphat Uthit 2; dm 100B, r 160-250B) The good location, helpful staff and plentiful info about onward travel has made this place a backpacker magnet in Hat Yai. Also offered are laundry service and inexpensive meals (and the staff don't mind if you bring in takeaways to eat in the lounge).

Hok Chin Hin Hotel (☎ 0 7424 3258; fax 0 7435 0131; Th Niphat Uthit 1; r 150-250B; ❈) This hotel, a couple of blocks from the train station, is a good deal. It has small but bright and clean rooms with good furniture. There's a coffee shop downstairs.

Ladda Guest House (☎ 0 7422 0233; 13-15 Th Thamnoonvithi; r 200-320B; 🗷) The rooms here are tiny but comfortable, well-furnished and clean. Stairs and halls are narrow enough to make you worry about the lack of fire exits, though.

MIDRANGE
For some reason hotels in Hat Yai take a disproportionate leap upwards in quality once you pay another 100B to 200B a night.

King's Hotel (☎ 0 7426 1700; fax 0 7423 6103; 126 Th Niphat Uthit 1; r 390-750B; 🗷) Not gorgeous, but King's is the best value of its kind. Add 50B for breakfast.

Louise Guest House (☎ 0 7422 0966; 21-23 Th Thamnoonvithi; r 300-400B; 🗷) This apartment-style guesthouse has small and cute rooms. It doesn't do much short-time trade, so the rooms are quieter and cleaner.

OH (Oriental Hotel; ☎ 0 7423 0142; fax 0 7435 4824; 135 Th Niphat Uthit 3; r 550-600B; 🗷) This place is not as good as King's, but all rooms come with TVs (no cable), hot water and fridges, along with large windows.

Singapore Hotel (☎ 0 7423 7478; 62-66 Th Suphasan Rangsan; r 380-450B; 🗷) Rooms exude cleanliness and comfort at the Singapore, while the staff are friendly and security-conscious.

New World Hotel (☎ 0 7423 0100; fax 0 7423 0105; 152-156 Th Niphat Uthit 2; r 500B; 🗷) Not a bad deal, New World Hotel offers acceptable rooms with fridges and TVs, though a few have wall views.

Lee Gardens Hotel (☎ 0 7423 4422; fax 0 7423 1888; 1 Th Lee Pattana; r 600-700B; 🗷) Slightly more upmarket in appearance, this place is almost elegant, although the hall carpets beg to be replaced. Rooms have TVs (no cable) and hot water.

Montien Hotel (☎ 0 7423 4386; fax 0 7423 0043; 120-124 Th Niphat Uthit 1; r 450B; 🗷) Mainland Chinese visitors on package tours make up most of the clientele at this large, often boisterous, place. The lobby smells pleasantly of incense.

TOP END
Top-end accommodation in Hat Yai is mainly geared to Malaysian Chinese weekend visitors and rates are considerably lower than in Bangkok or Chiang Mai.

Novotel Central Sukhontha (☎ 0 7435 2222; www .centralhotelsresorts.com; 3 Th Sanehanuson; r 2500-5000B; 🗷 🖳 🖳) This is the nicest hotel in town,

with spacious, fully outfitted rooms and suites. Facilities include a pool with snack bar, sauna, Chinese restaurant, business centre and shopping mall.

Regency Hotel (☎ 0 7435 3333; 23 Th Prachathipat; r 900-1400B; 🗷 🖳) Stuffed with modern amenities, the 438 rooms and suites here are clean. Facilities include a lobby lounge, coffee shop, dim sum restaurant, huge swimming pool with bar, and a gym. The pretty lobby has bands every evening.

Diamond Plaza Hotel (☎ 0 7423 0130; 62 Th Niphat Uthit 3; r 990-2800B; 🗷 🖳) The Diamond Plaza claims to be 'the most generous and gentle hotel', we're not sure if that's taking it a bit too far, but the rooms are well done and worth the price.

Eating
Hat Yai is southern Thailand's gourmet mecca, offering fresh seafood from the Gulf of Thailand and the Andaman Sea, Muslim *rotii* and curries, Chinese noodles and dim sum.

Lots of good, cheap restaurants can be found along the three Niphat Uthit roads, in the markets off side streets between them, and also near the train station. For fancier Chinese food try the upmarket hotels. Many Hat Yai restaurants, particularly the Chinese ones, close between 2pm and 6pm – unusual for Thailand.

The extensive **night market** (Th Montri 1) specialises in fresh seafood, where you can dine on two seafood dishes and one vegetable dish for around 200B. There are smaller **night markets** along Th Suphasan Rangsan and Th Siphunawanat. There's an excellent gathering of **food stalls** at the bend in Th Phetkasem, and another group north of town by the mosque, off Th Niphat Songkhrao.

Hua Lee (cnr Th Niphat Uthit 3 & Th Thamnoonvithi; dishes 30-50B; 😊 4.30pm-2am) On display here are striking photographs of the flood that inundated Hat Yai in 2000; the water-level mark can be seen on the wall. It's an open, casual and very busy corner place, with good Chinese food that arrives quickly.

Niyom Rot (Niyomrosh; 219-221 Th Thamnoonvithi; dishes 50-200B) This is an old, established Thai restaurant across from the lime-green Spa Hotel. The *plaa kràbàwk thâwt* (whole sea mullet fried with eggs intact) is particularly prized here. It's set up for big groups, so the atmosphere is not intimate. It closes at noon and reopens for dinner.

999 Remy (Th Niphat Uthit 2; dishes from 25B) This is a small no-frills place serving lots of cheap curries and fried food in a casual environment.

NaKorn Nai (☎ 0 7423 2550; 16-7 Th Niphat Uthit 2; dishes 30-60B; ☺ closed Thu) This eatery ensconces you in a new, modern and trendy atmosphere. Thai and Western foods are served, as is breakfast.

Muslim Ocha (Th Niphat Uthit 1; dishes 25-40B) A small, clean place, Muslim Ocha does *rotii kaeng* (*roti chanai* in Malay) in the mornings and curries all day. This is one of the few Muslim cafés in the town where women – even non-Muslim or foreign women – seem welcome.

Sumatra Restaurant (☎ 0 7424 6459; 55/1 Th Rattakan; dishes 30-100B) In a light-green building, this large, clean and modern restaurant prepares a bit of everything: curries, seafood, vegetables, beef, chicken and salad dishes.

Jye Beer House (☎ 0 7423 6521; 49/3 Th Rattakan; dishes 45-110B) This beer house caters to Western tastes with steak, Italian food and Heineken beer. The decidedly Western décor is smart and comfortable. There's also Thai food and Singha beer on the menu.

Viang Chan (☎ 0 7424 3668; 12 Th Niphat Uthit 2; dishes 40-70B) This is an unpretentious Lao-Chinese restaurant featuring a menu full of fried meats.

On Th Niyomrat, between Niphat Uthit 1 and 2, are **Sulaiman**, **Tamrab** and **Mustafa**, all casual and inexpensive Muslim restaurants open from approximately 7am to 9pm daily.

Drinking & Entertainment

Most of the many clubs and coffee shops in town cater to Malaysian clientele. Try the bigger hotels for discos, which charge a cover of about 150B.

Post Laserdisc (☎ 0 7423 2027; Th Thamnoonvithi) This is a music video/laserdisc restaurant and bar with an excellent sound system and well-placed monitors. It shows mostly Western movies, which change nightly – the fairly up-to-date music videos are fillers between the films. The live music is relatively good. A bill of 250B or more will get you two 10-minute coupons to the email place next door.

The Pubb (☎ 0 7423 1029) Near Post Laserdisc, this place is sports oriented (with a big-screen TV) and has a good selection of food if you get hungry.

Sugar Rock (114 Th Thamnoonvithi) Sugar Rock is one of the more durable Hat Yai pubs with reasonable prices and a low-key atmosphere. Décor exudes a split personality: one side has nostalgic ambience, while the other is modern and trendy.

West Side Saloon (☎ 0 7435 4833; 135/5 Th Thamnoonvithi) This saloon attracts Thais, Malays and *faràng* to its dim, rustic and pub-like space. Tables are set in front of a stage, where live music rocks nightly from 8.30pm.

Corazon Pub & Restaurant (☎ 0 7435 0360; 41 Pracharom) This is a cosy Latin disco-pub that's eclectically but well decorated. There's live and DJ music (of all kinds, including Latin), and Thai and Western-style food is served.

Sugar Beat (☎ 0 7423 3333; 444 Th Thamnoonvithi) A popular spot, 2km east of town, Sugar Beat features a dark and moody ambience that doesn't get going until after 10pm. Bands rock the big place regularly. A motorcycle taxi ride here costs 20B.

Getting There & Away

AIR

Thai Airways International (THAI; ☎ 0 7423 3433; 182 Th Niphat Uthit 1) operates flights between Hat Yai and Bangkok (3095B, 1½ hours, five daily). There is also a daily flight to Phuket and Singapore.

CROSSING INTO MALAYSIA FROM HAT YAI

The Malaysian border is about 50km south of Hat Yai, and many travellers pass through town just to extend their Thai visas.

To get an in-and-out stamp, head to Padang Besar, which is the nearest Malaysian border town. Private taxis cost 500B return (one hour), share taxis are 100B (one hour, leave when full), minivans 40B (1½ hours, hourly) and buses 26B (1½ hours, every 25 minutes). You can also take the train, but this option is not very fast or frequent.

For a longer Thai visa, you will need to visit the Thai consulate in Georgetown, on Penang Island (accessible via the mainland town of Butterworth). Buses from Hat Yai to Butterworth cost 230B (four hours); share taxis are 250B. Again, trains from Hat Yai to Butterworth are slower and less frequent.

BUS & MINIVAN

The bus terminal is 2km southeast of the town centre, though many buses make stops in town.

Destination	Fare (B)	Duration (hr)
Bangkok		
ordinary	315	17
air-con	416-567	14
VIP	830	14
Butterworth (for Penang)		
air-con	230	4
Ko Samui		
air-con	270	7
Krabi		
air-con	173	5
Kuala Lumpur		
air-con	350-450	9
Pak Bara		
ordinary	46	2½
Padang Besar		
ordinary	26	1½
Pattani		
ordinary	41	2
Phuket		
ordinary	150	8
air-con	210-420	8
Satun		
ordinary	36	2
air-con	65	1½
Singapore		
air-con	450-600	16
Songkhla		
ordinary	14	½
Sungai Kolok		
air-con	148	4
Surat Thani		
ordinary	115	6½
air-con	165-170	5½
Trang		
ordinary	60	3
Yala		
ordinary	53	2½

Minivans leave from various spots around town. See the Hat Yai map (p612) for locations. Destinations include Padang Besar (40B, 1½ hours), Pak Bara (70B, 2½ hours), Satun (60B, two hours), Songkhla (20B, 40 minutes), Trang (90B, three hours) and Yala (70B, 2½ hours). Minivans leave when full throughout the day.

Cathay Tour (☎ 0 7423 5044; 93/1 Th Niphat Uthit) runs frequent express minivans to Ko Samui

(280B to 300B, seven hours), Krabi (160B, five hours), Phuket (280B, eight hours), Sungai Kolok (150B, four hours), Surat Thani (150B, 6½ hours) and Trang (120B, three hours).

TRAIN

There are five daily trains to/from Bangkok. Fares range from 189B to 745B depending on the class. There are also daily trains to Sungai Kolok (42B to 122B, seven daily) and Padang Besar (57B to 322B, two daily).

There is an advance-booking office and left-luggage office at the train station; both are open 6am to 6pm daily.

Getting Around

An **Airport Taxi Service** (☎ 0 7423 8452) makes the run to/from the airport (60B, seven daily). The service leaves for the airport from the THAI office on Th Niphat Uthit 1; coming into Hat Yai, the service offers hotel drop-off. A private taxi for this run costs about 200B.

Avis Rent-A-Car (☎ 0 7435 2222) has an office at the Novotel Central Sukhontha. You can arrange car rental (approximately 1000B per day) through other travel agencies in town, including **Cathay Tour** (☎ 0 7423 5044; 93/1 Th Niphat Uthit). The airport also has some car-rental counters for those flying in.

Săwngthăew run along Th Phetkasem and charge 5B per person. *Túk-túk* around town cost 10B per person, though they like to charge foreigners 20B instead.

AROUND HAT YAI
Nam Tok Ton Nga Chang
น้ำตกต้นงาช้าง

Nam Tok Ton Nga Chang (Elephant Tusk Falls), 25km west of Hat Yai via Hwy 4 in Amphoe Rattaphum, is a beautiful, 1200m, seven-tier cascade that falls in two streams (thus resembling two tusks). It can take three hours to walk to the seventh tier. If you're staying in Hat Yai, the falls make a nice break from the hustle and bustle of the city. The waterfall looks its best at the end of the rainy season, from October to December.

To get to the falls catch a *săwngthăew* bound for Rattaphum (25B) from anywhere along Th Phetkasem in Hat Yai and ask to get off at the *náam tòk* (waterfall). Many travel agencies in Hat Yai have tours (about 150B) to these falls.

Khao Nam Khang Tunnels
อุโมงค์ประวัติศาสตร์เขาน้ำค้าง

In **Khao Nam Khang National Park** (adult/child 200/100B; ☾ 9am-4pm) is a tunnel complex occupied by the Communist Party of Malaysia (CPM) guerrillas as their base camp until they finally gave up the struggle in 1989. At least 1km of the tunnels on three levels has been preserved; a portion has been widened to accommodate visitors. The underground base was complete with a radio room, conference rooms, an operating room and, strangely, three long, straight passageways where the tunnel-bound communists could practise riding their motorcycles! The complex is said to have taken two years to build.

There are no buses here, so you'll have to drive your own vehicle or hire a taxi. From Hat Yai take Hwy 4 south towards Sadao, turning left at the Sadao *amphoe* office and driving for another 26km. The tunnels are about 4km beyond the park headquarters.

YALA PROVINCE

Yala is the most prosperous of the four predominantly Muslim provinces in southern Thailand, mainly due to income from rubber production. It is also the prime business and education centre for the region.

YALA
ยะลา
pop 76,300

Despite its reputation as a clean city, the capital city of Yala is not an exciting place to visit. The streets are large and lined with homely buildings that aren't terribly nice to look at, and there aren't any museums or other such attractions near the town centre. The population is a mix of Thai, Chinese and Muslim.

There are **banks** scattered across town; see the Yala map for locations. The **post office** (Th Siriros; ☾ 8.30am-4.30pm Mon-Fri, 9am-noon Sat & Sun) also has telephone services.

Wat Khuhaphimuk
วัดคูหาภิมุข

Outside town about 8km west off the Yala–Hat Yai road, **Wat Khuhaphimuk** (also called Wat Na Tham, or Cave-Front Temple) is a Srivijaya-period cave temple established around AD 750. Inside the cave is Phra Phutthasaiyat, a long, reclining Buddha image sculpted in the Srivijaya style. For Thais, this is one of the three most venerated Buddhist pilgrimage points in southern Thailand (the other two are Wat Boromathat in Nakhon Si Thammarat and Wat Phra Boromathat Chaiya in Surat Thani).

To get to the temple, take a *săwngthăew* (7B) going west towards Yala via Rte 4065 and ask to get off at the road to Wat Na Tham. It's about a 1km walk to the wat from the highway.

Two kilometres past Wat Na Tham is **Tham Silpa**, a well-known cave with Buddhist polychrome murals from the Srivijaya era, as well as prehistoric monochromatic paintings of primitive hunters. A monk from Wat Na Tham may be able to guide you here. There are several other caves nearby

---

TRAVEL WARNING

At the time of research widespread violence in the form of Muslim separatist attacks (thus far against Thais only, and for the most part limited to government offices and officials) have made travel to Yala, as well as neighbouring Narathiwat and Pattani Provinces, rather dicey. The violence has been attributed to the Pattani United Liberation Organisation (PULO) and associated groups in eastern Malaysia. Since January 2004 more than 440 people had died in these provinces as a result of clashes between the government and the separatists. October 2004 was a particularly deadly month; 85 Muslim youth were killed after a protest at a police station in Narathiwat turned violent. Security forces killed at least seven people during the riot, but 78 others died in military custody, apparently either suffocated or crushed to death. The Thai prime minister agreed to set up an independent commission to investigate these deaths, and during a televised address to the nation he expressed regret for the incident, but the violence appears to be far from over. That said, security situations change faster than guidebooks are published; so ask around, or check out the local newspaper, before deciding against heading to these provinces. Things may very well have improved.

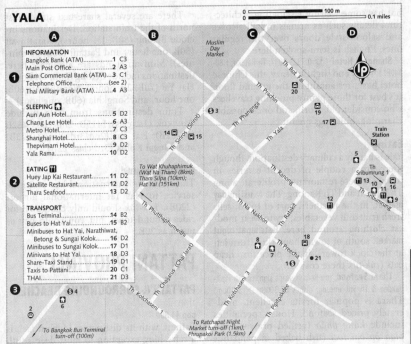

YALA

INFORMATION	
Bangkok Bank (ATM)....................1	C3
Main Post Office..........................2	A3
Siam Commercial Bank (ATM)....3	C1
Telephone Office....................(see 2)	
Thai Military Bank (ATM)..........4	A3

SLEEPING	
Aun Aun Hotel............................5	D2
Chang Lee Hotel.........................6	A3
Metro Hotel................................7	C3
Shanghai Hotel...........................8	C3
Thepvimarn Hotel......................9	D2
Yala Rama................................10	D2

EATING	
Huey Jap Kai Restaurant...........11	D2
Satellite Restaurant...................12	D2
Thara Seafood..........................13	D2

TRANSPORT	
Bus Terminal.............................14	B2
Buses to Hat Yai........................15	B2
Minibuses to Hat Yai, Narathiwat, Betong & Sungai Kolok......16	D2
Minibuses to Sungai Kolok.......17	D1
Minivans to Hat Yai..................18	D3
Share-Taxi Stand.......................19	D1
Taxis to Pattani........................20	C1
THAI...21	D3

LOWER SOUTHERN GULF

worth exploring for their impressive stalactite and stalagmite formations.

Festivals & Events

About the most exciting time to visit Yala is during the **Asean Barred Ground Dove Competition**, usually held in March. Over 1000-feathered competitors are literally 'pitched' against each other, judged on stamina, melody, volume and, of course pitch. This is the World Cup for songbirds, and attracts dove-lovers from all over Thailand, as well as from Malaysia, Indonesia and Singapore. Another large festival in Yala is held during May or June and pays respect to the city's guardian spirit, **Jao Phaw Lak Meuang**. Also celebrated in Yala with some zest is **Chinese New Year**.

Sleeping

Yala has lots of cheap old Chinese hotels, though most are at the bottom of the barrel, so to speak. Stick to the higher-end if you want a few comforts.

Chang Lee Hotel (☎ 0 7324 4597; fax 0 7324 4599; 318 Th Siriros; r 680B; ste from 1100B; 🅿 🖵) Offering Yala's best beds, all the rooms here are plush and come with carpets and TV. Facilities include a business centre, karaoke nightclub and coffee shop. However, it's not central (a 15-minute walk from the train station). If it's empty ask about promotions, rooms can go for as low as 400B – a real steal.

Yala Rama (☎ 0 7321 2563; fax 0 7321 4532; 21 Th Sribumrung; r 420B; 🅿) There are nine floors of large, bright, carpeted and clean midrange rooms here. A great deal for the price, unless the karaoke lounge really gets going and you're not into noise. A sign on the counter demands 'Please identify yourself'.

Thepvimarn Hotel (☎ 0 7321 2400; Th Sribumrung; r 150-390B; 🅿) Large and friendly, there are few frills here, but the rooms are acceptable for a couple of nights. It's about 90% clean. The cheapest rooms don't have air-con.

Metro Hotel (☎ 0 7321 2175; Th Ratakit; r 100-170B) The Metro has a more familial atmosphere than some of the other cheapies. Rooms are still very basic, though larger ones are tidier and less depressing.

Aun Aun Hotel (☎ 0 7321 2216; Th Pipitpakdee; r 140B) This is another bleak and dreary place, but has some weirdly fascinating architectural details such as urinals in hall alcoves and saloon-style doors over the regular ones. English is semi-spoken here.

Shanghai Hotel (☎ 0 7321 2037; Th Ratakit; r 80-140B) Dreary and slightly sleazy, this Chinese hotel has a restaurant on the ground floor. It's best for those penny-pinching travellers who consider old, worn, and once-possibly charming, buildings quaint.

Eating

Yala is hardly a culinary destination, though there are a couple of decent eateries in town. Chinese restaurants proliferate along Th Ratakit and Th Ranong. The Muslim **day market**, in the northern part of town, sells fresh fruit and vegetables; try to wear modest clothing around here. **Ratchapat night market**, south of town about 1km (turn left at the clock tower), is the place for cheap eats (*túk-túk* there cost 9B).

Thara Seafood (no Roman-script sign; cnr Th Pipitpakdee & Th Sribumrung; dishes 65-300B; ☺ 3-10pm) Thara is popular for its excellent, moderately priced seafood. House specialities include *kûng phǎo* (grilled prawns) and *plaa òp bai toei* (fish baked in pandanus leaves), and they're temptingly cooked on the pavement.

Satellite Restaurant (cnr Th Pipitpakdee & Th Ranong; dishes 25-50B) This is another popular corner restaurant with worn tables and chairs and a few food carts out the front – you just have to point at the steamed and fried dishes. It also does good *jóhk* (rice congee) and Chinese dumplings.

Huey Jap Kai Restaurant (no Roman-script sign; Th Sribumrung; dishes from 25B) Right next to the Thipvimarm Hotel, this restaurant is great for a cheap breakfast noodle soup (25B). It's a large, popular, clean cafeteria-style place on a breezy corner.

Getting There & Away

Buses between Bangkok and Yala include 2nd class (472B, 16 hours), 1st class (607B to 708B, 16 hours) and VIP (940B, 15 hours). These leave from Th Phumachip in Yala, a side road off Th Siriros, about 250m south of Th Kotchaseni 1. Buses to Hat Yai (59B, 2½ hours) stop on Th Siriros, outside the Prudential TS Life office. Across the street is the stop for other short- to medium-distance buses north.

There are several share-taxi stands just north of the train station. Destinations include Betong (80B, 1½ hours), Narathiwat (50B, one hour) and Pattani (30B, 30 minutes). Minivan stands are also near here; destinations include Betong (60B, 1½ hour), Hat Yai (70B, 2½ hours), Narathiwat (60B, one hour) and Songkhla (60B, one hour).

Train destinations from Yala include Bangkok (1st class 1415B, 2nd class 462B to 782B), Hat Yai (2nd/3rd class 60/23B) and Sungai Kolok (3rd class 22B).

Getting Around

Thai Airways International has a shuttle service to Hat Yai international airport (220B). *Túk-túk* should only charge 9B for rides around town, but you could pay as much as 20B.

PATTANI PROVINCE

PATTANI & SURROUNDING BEACHES
ปัตตานี

pop 44,800

Pattani, with its distinctive Muslim feel, is a refreshing exception to most deep-south provincial capitals that tend to function as trading posts operated by the Chinese for the benefit (or exploitation, depending on your perspective) of the surrounding Muslim villages. In Pattani's streets you are more likely to hear Yawi, the traditional language of Java, Sumatra and the Malay Peninsula (the written form uses classic Arabic script plus five more letters), than any Thai dialect. Even the markets are visually similar to those in Kota Bharu in Malaysia.

Until the start of the 20th century, Pattani was the centre of an independent principality that included Yala and Narathiwat. It was also one of the earliest kingdoms in Thailand to engage in international trade; the Portuguese established a trading post here in 1516, the Japanese in 1605, the Dutch in

---

TRAVEL WARNING

At the time of research violence in this province, attributed to the Pattani United Liberation Organisation (PULO) and related groups, made travel a bit worrisome. Please see the warning, p616.

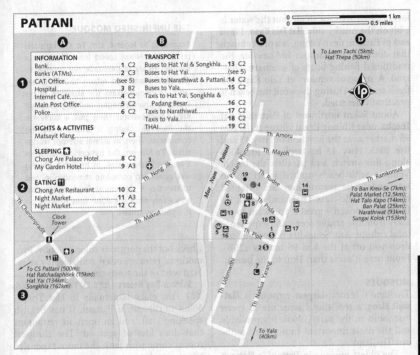

PATTANI

0 ____ 1 km
0 ____ 0.5 miles

INFORMATION	
Bank................................1	C2
Banks (ATMs)......................2	C3
CAT Office......................(see 5)	
Hospital............................3	B2
Internet Café......................4	C2
Main Post Office..................5	C2
Police...............................6	C2

SIGHTS & ACTIVITIES	
Matsayit Klang....................7	C3

SLEEPING	
Chong Are Palace Hotel........8	C2
My Garden Hotel.................9	A3

EATING	
Chong Are Restaurant..........10	C2
Night Market.....................11	A3
Night Market.....................12	C2

TRANSPORT	
Buses to Hat Yai & Songkhla....13	C2
Buses to Hat Yai...............(see 5)	
Buses to Narathiwat & Pattani..14	C2
Buses to Yala.....................15	C2
Taxis to Hat Yai, Songkhla &	
Padang Besar....................16	C2
Taxis to Narathiwat..............17	C2
Taxis to Yala......................18	C2
THAI................................19	C2

To Laem Tachi (5km);
Hat Thepa (50km)

To Ban Kreu-Se (7km);
Palat Market (12.5km);
Hat Talo Kapo (14km);
Ban Patat (25km);
Narathiwat (93km);
Sungai Kolok (153km)

Clock Tower

To CS Pattani (500m);
Hat Ratchadaphisek (15km);
Hat Yai (134km);
Songkhla (162km)

To Yala (40km)

LOWER SOUTHERN GULF

1609 and the British in 1612. During WWII Japanese troops landed in Pattani to launch attacks on Malaysia and Singapore.

Buildings in modern Pattani are made mostly of concrete, but the riverfront area is interesting, and along Th Rudee you can see what's left of old Pattani architecture – the Sino-Portuguese style that was once so prevalent throughout southern Thailand. And although they can be somewhat difficult to reach, Pattani has some of the prettiest beaches in Thailand.

Orientation & Information

The centre of town is at the intersection of Th Naklua Yarang, the road that runs north–south between Yala and Pattani harbour, and Th Ramkomud, which runs east–west between Songkhla and Narathiwat Provinces. Intercity buses and taxis stop at this intersection. Thanon Ramkomud crosses Th Yarang and then the name changes to Th Rudee.

If you're in need of some cash, there are banks along the southeastern end of Th Pipit.

CAT office (☼ 8.30am-4.30pm) Attached to the post office; provides overseas telephone service.

Hospital (Th Nong Jik)

Internet café (Th Prida; per hr 20B) Often full of kids playing loud video games.

Main post office (Th Pipit; ☼ 8.30am-4.30pm Mon-Fri, 9am-noon Sat & Sun)

Police station (Th Pattani Phirom) In a central location.

Sights & Activities
BEACHES

Pattani has some of the prettiest beaches in southern Thailand. Because of the local Muslim culture, women should wear T-shirts over their swimsuits when at the beach or swimming.

The only beach near town is at **Laem Tachi**, a cape that juts out over the northern end of Ao Pattani. You must take a boat taxi from Tha Pattani or Yaring to get there. This white-sand beach is about 11km long, but is sometimes marred by refuse from Ao Pattani, depending on the time of year and the tides.

About 15km west of Pattani, **Hat Ratchadaphisek** (Hat Sai Maw) is a relaxing spot, with lots of casuarinas for shade, but the water is a bit on the murky side. **Hat Talo Kapo**, 14km east of Pattani, near Yaring, is a pretty beach that doubles as a harbour for *kaw-lae*, the traditional fishing boats of southern Thailand. A string of vendors at Talo Kapo sell fresh seafood, During the week the beach is practically deserted.

About 50km northwest of Pattani is **Hat Thepha**, near Khlong Pratu village at the Km 96 marker near the junction of Hwy 43 and Rte 4085. Hwy 43 has replaced Rte 4086 along this stretch and parallels the beach. Vendors with beach umbrellas set up on weekends. The resorts here are oriented towards middle-class Thais and almost no English is spoken – great if you want to get away from the *faràng* scene and experience local culture. Any Songkhla-bound bus can drop you off at the Km 96 marker (25B). From here it's less than 1km to the beach.

MOSQUES

Thailand's second-largest mosque is **Matsayit Klang**, a traditional structure of green hue, built in the early 1960s. It's probably still the most important mosque in southern Thailand.

The oldest mosque in Pattani is **Matsayit Kreu-Se**, built in 1578 by an immigrant Chinese named Lim To Khieng, who had married a Pattani woman and converted to Islam. The brick, Arab-style building was never finished, and has been left in its original semicompleted, semiruined form – but the faithful keep up the surrounding grounds. It's in the village of Ban Kreu-Se, about 7km east of Pattani next to Hwy 42 at the Km 10 marker; a gaudy Chinese temple has been built next to it. For the full legend, see the boxed text, right. Kreu-Se was also the site of a Thai police massacre of Muslim extremists in 2004; see p44 for details.

Sleeping & Eating

There aren't a whole lot of hotels in town, but all have their own restaurants. A **night market** with plenty of food vendors convenes on Th Charoenpradit; another one lies along Soi Thepiwat 2.

CS Pattani (☎ 0 7333 5093; cspatani@cscoms.com; r 1100-5500B; 🌀 🖳 🕃) Large and luxurious rooms with all the amenities make this Pattani's best option. Facilities include a fitness room, two pools and an excellent restaurant.

THE UNFINISHED MOSQUE

According to legend, Lim To Khieng's sister, Lim Ko Niaw, sailed from China on a sampan to try to persuade her brother to abandon Islam and return to their homeland. To demonstrate the strength of his faith, To Khieng began building Matsayit Kreu-Se. His sister then put a curse on the mosque, saying it would never be completed. Then, in a final attempt to dissuade To Khieng, she hanged herself from a nearby cashew tree. In his grief, Khieng was unable to complete the mosque, and to this day it remains unfinished; supposedly every time someone tries to work on it, lightning strikes.

Check out the gorgeous colonial lobby. Promotional rates are often available. It's about 3km west of the town centre.

Sakrom Bay Resort (☎ 0 7323 8966; r 250-700B; 🕃) This place is actually in Hat Thepa, 50km northwest of Pattani. It has English speaking staff, and an open-air restaurant that does lots of seafood. The cheapest rooms come with fans; the more expensive are air-con bungalows.

My Garden Hotel (☎ 0 7333 1055; fax 0 7333 6217; 8/28 Th Charoenpradit; r 550B; 🕃) About 1km outside the town centre, this hotel has friendly staff and is popular with travelling businesspeople. The rooms are well maintained and comfortable, with satellite TV, good hot-water showers and a fridge. The restaurant is proud to have 'musicians to full you and entertain you while beautiful waitresses wait on you', and the hotel disco gets busy on weekends.

Chong Are Palace Hotel (☎ 0 7334 9711; fax 0 7334 9842; 10-12 Soi Talat Tetiwat; r 160-300B; 🕃) Rooms are clean, but worn and the cheapest ones just have fans. It's a slightly depressing, but quite cheap, place.

Chong Are Restaurant (☎ 0 7734 9817; Th Prida; dishes 30-160B) This restaurant, next to the Palace, serves decent Thai and Chinese food.

Shopping

Thai Muslims in southern Thailand use traditional batik methods similar to the batik of northeastern Malaysia, and the **Palat Market** (Talat Nat Palat) is the best place to shop for these fabrics. The market is off Hwy 42 between Pattani and Saiburi in Ban Palat, and is held on Wednesday and Sunday. There are also some shops along Th Rudee that sell local and Malaysian batik at slightly higher prices.

Getting There & Around

Bus destinations from Pattani include Hat Yai (50B, two hours), Narathiwat (38B, one hour) and Yala (16B, 30 minutes). Share-taxi destinations include Hat Yai (70B, two hours), Songkhla (60B, 2½ hours) and Yala (30B, 30 minutes).

Săwngthăew go anywhere in town for 8B per person. Motorcycle taxis charge around 20B per ride.

NARATHIWAT PROVINCE

NARATHIWAT

นราธิวาส

pop 43,300

Narathiwat, one of Thailand's smallest provincial capitals, is a pleasant, even-tempered little town with a character all of its own. Many of the buildings are wooden structures, 100 or more years old, and their location by the river mouth adds atmospheric charm.

Local businesses seem to be owned by both Muslim and Chinese residents, and signs around town appear in Yawi as well as Thai, Chinese and English. Local radio stations broadcast in a mix of Yawi, Thai and Malay, with musical selections to match – from northeastern Thailand's country music, *lûuk thûng*, to Arabic-melodied *dangdut*.

Narathiwat is right on the sea, and you can reach some beautiful beaches just outside town by bicycle. **Ao Manao**, 7km east of Narathiwat, is a pleasant, undeveloped bay with some simple snack stands on the beach and a batik shop nearby.

Information

Business & Leisure (☎ 0 7351 1027; natini@chaiyo .com; 399 Th Puphapugdee) Organises visa runs for those who need 60-day visa extensions. These can include one- or two-day hotel stays in Narathiwat and all transfers, but not the visa fees (which can vary widely).

Internet cafés (☺ 9am-9pm) Two good ones: one near the clock tower and one near the Princess Hotel.

Main post office (Th Pichitbamrung; ☺ 8.30am-4.30pm Mon-Fri, 9am-noon Sat & Sun)

TAT (☎ 0 7351 6144; tatnara@cscoms.com; ☺ 8.30am-4.30pm) Inconveniently located a few kilometres south of town, just across the bridge, on the road to Tak Bai. A little English is spoken and there are maps and brochures.

Sights

HAT NARATHAT

หาดนราทัศน์

Towards the north of town, at the mouth of Mae Nam Bang Nara, is a small Thai-Muslim fishing village lined with large painted fishing boats *(kaw-lae)* peculiar to Narathiwat and Pattani. You'll probably also see wandering goats and many houses with cooing doves in cages. Just north of here, across the bridges, is Hat Narathat – a long sandy beach that serves as a kind of public park for locals, with outdoor seafood restaurants, tables and umbrellas. There's a constant sea breeze, and a mixture of casuarinas and coconut palms provide shade. The beach is only 2km north of the town centre – you can easily walk, cycle or take a motorcycle taxi (10B).

MATSAYIT KLANG

มัสยิดกลาง

At the southern end of Th Pichitbamrung stands Matsayit Klang (Central Mosque), an old wooden mosque built in the Sumatran style, reputedly by a prince of the former Pattani kingdom over 100 years ago. Today it's of secondary importance to the newer Arabian modernist–style provincial mosque (Matsayit Jangwat) in the north of town, but is architecturally more interesting.

WAT KHAO KONG

วัดเขากง

The tallest seated Buddha image in Thailand is at Wat Khao Kong, southwest on the way to the station in Tanyongmat. Called Phra Phuttha Taksin Mingmongkon, the image is 24m high and made of reinforced concrete covered with tiny gold-coloured mosaic tiles that glint in the sun. A *săwngthăew* to Wat Khao Kong costs 10B from the clock tower.

LOWER SOUTHERN GULF

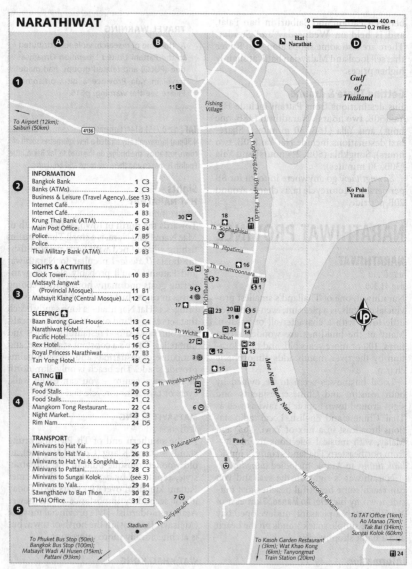

NARATHIWAT

INFORMATION
Bangkok Bank	**1** C3
Banks (ATMs)	**2** C3
Business & Leisure (Travel Agency)	(see 13)
Internet Café	**3** B4
Internet Café	**4** B3
Krung Thai Bank (ATM)	**5** C3
Main Post Office	**6** B4
Police	**7** B5
Police	**8** C5
Thai Military Bank (ATM)	**9** B3

SIGHTS & ACTIVITIES
Clock Tower	**10** B3
Matsayit Jangwat (Provincial Mosque)	**11** B1
Matsayit Klang (Central Mosque)	**12** C4

SLEEPING
Baan Burong Guest House	**13** C4
Narathiwat Hotel	**14** C3
Pacific Hotel	**15** C4
Rex Hotel	**16** C3
Royal Princess Narathiwat	**17** B3
Tan Yong Hotel	**18** C2

EATING
Ang Mo	**19** C3
Food Stalls	**20** C3
Food Stalls	**21** C2
Mangkorn Tong Restaurant	**22** C4
Night Market	**23** C3
Rim Nam	**24** D5

TRANSPORT
Minivans to Hat Yai	**25** C3
Minivans to Hat Yai	**26** B3
Minivans to Hat Yai & Songkhla	**27** B3
Minivans to Pattani	**28** C3
Minivans to Sungai Kolok	(see 3)
Minivans to Yala	**29** B4
Sawngthaew to Ban Thon	**30** B2
THAI Office	**31** C3

Tours

Business & Leisure (☎ 0 7351 1027; natini@chaiyo
.com; 399 Th Puphapugdee) offers a good range of
tours, the most popular of which are local
sea-kayaking trips that include craft workshops, such as basketry or batik-making
and lunch (400B). You need a minimum
of two people.

Festivals & Events

Every year during the middle of Septem-
ber, the **Narathiwat Fair** features *kaw-lae* racing, a singing dove contest judged by the
queen, handicraft displays and *sìlá* martial
arts exhibitions. Other highlights include
performances of the local dance forms, *ram
sam pen* and *ram ngeng*.

Sleeping

Baan Burong Guest House (☎ 0 7351 1027; natini@ chaiyo.com; 399 Th Puphapugdee; r 300-400B; ☒) Natini Wongpuvarak's home is the best place to stay in town. Tastefully whimsical and full of antiques, stained glass and shelves and shelves of books make this flat feel warm and intelligent. The riverfront balcony is perfect for a breezy evening chat with other guests. There are only three rooms, so this place often fills up.

Royal Princess Narathiwat (☎ 0 7351 5041; pnn@ dusit.com; 228 Th Pitchitbamrung; r 900-1000B; ☒ ☒) The town's most deluxe option, this hotel offers eight storeys of clean rooms along with a small pool, modest lobby and free airport transfers. Not a bad deal at all.

Narathiwat Hotel (☎ 0 7351 1063; 341 Th Puphapugdee; r 100-150B) A funky wooden building on the riverfront, Narathiwat is quiet, breezy, clean and comfortable. The downstairs rooms are reserved for ladies of the night, who aren't allowed to come up to the 2nd floor, where regular guests stay.

Rex Hotel (☎ 0 7351 1134; fax 0 7351 1190; 6-6/1 Th Chamroonnara; r 200-430B; ☒) The lobby here is bleak, but the rooms are large. The cheapest just have fans. All are a little on the gritty side. You get what you pay for.

Pacific Hotel (☎ 0 7351 1076; 42/1-2 Th Worakhamphiphit; r 400-450B; ☒) Rooms are large and clean at the Pacific and come with TVs, but the place could use a paint job and friendlier staff.

Tan Yong Hotel (☎ 0 7351 1477; fax 0 7351 1834; 16/1 Th Sophaphisai; r 400-1100B; ☒) At one time the town's fanciest, this place now features musty, dark rooms. If you're going to pay for air-con, ask for a 'deluxe' room with partial river views and a small balcony. A restaurant, café and karaoke bar sit downstairs.

Eating

The **night market** (off Th Chamroonnara), behind the Bang Nara Hotel is good. Inexpensive noodle dishes can be found at a cluster of **food stalls** (cnr Th Sophaphisai & Th Phupha Phakdi). There are also quite a few delicious restaurants in town.

Rim Nam (☎ 0 7351 1559; Th Jaturong Ratsami; dishes 50-200B) South of town about 2km (across from the petrol station; look for colourful flags), Rim Nam is well worth the ride and has even been recommended by regional star chefs. The service is warm and atten-

tive, the dishes artistically presented. Specialities include fried shrimp salad (100B), sea bass with three flavours (200B) and lemon chicken (80B). Call for free transport.

Kasoh Garden Restaurant (☎ 0 7352 1700; 1/3 Tambon Lamphu; dishes 40-150B) An airy, spacious and upmarket place, Kasoh serves tasty seafood, vegetable dishes, Thai soups and salads. The ambience is great, with a nearby garden and fish-filled pond. It is south of town; Natini at Baan Burong Guest House can arrange free transport.

Ang Mo (cnr Th Puphapugdee & Th Chamroonnara; dishes 25-80) This is an excellent spot, with outdoor tables, that's packed every night. Point to the dish you want; try the duck.

Mangkorn Tong Restaurant (☎ 0 7351 1835; 433 Th Puphapugdee; dishes 60-180B) This small seafood place, with a floating dining section out back, does quite good food at reasonable prices.

Getting There & Away

AIR

Thai Airways International has one flight daily between Narathiwat and Phuket, connecting with flights to Bangkok. To book flights, go to the **THAI office** (☎ 0 7351 3090; 322-324 Th Puphapugdee). Fares range from 2950B to 3750B. The airport is 12km north of town.

BUS & MINIVAN

The air-con buses to Bangkok and Phuket leave from two separate small shop terminals on Th Suriyapradit, south of town a few hundred metres past the police station. The buses to Phuket (396B, 12 hours, three times daily) go via Pattani, Hat Yai, Songkhla, Trang, Krabi and Phang-Nga. Buses to Bangkok (VIP/1st/2nd class 1035/ 666/518B) operate four times daily.

Minivans head to Hat Yai (120B, 2½ hours), Pattani (60B, one hour), Songkhla (120B, 2½ hours), Sungai Kolok (50B, 45 minutes) and Yala (60B, one hour) from different spots around the centre of town.

Săwngthăew to the border at Ban Taba cost 20B.

TRAIN

Narathiwat's train station is in Tanyongmat, 20km west of town (30B by *săwngthăew*). There are departures for Bangkok (214B to 254B, twice daily), Hat Yai (80B to 120B, twice daily) and Yala (60B, twice daily).

Getting Around

Narathiwat is easy to navigate on foot. If you don't feel like walking, motorcycle taxis will take you around for 10B to 20B, depending on the distance.

The **THAI office** (☎ 0 7351 3090; 322-324 Th Puphapugdee) operates airport shuttles for 50B per person; these include hotel pick-up.

Baan Burong Guest House (p623) rents bicycles (50B per day) and motorcycles (250B per day), and can also arrange taxi hire (500B to 700B per day) or car rental (1000B).

AROUND NARATHIWAT
Matsayit Wadi Al Husen (Talo Mano)
มัสยิดวาดินฮูเซ็น

Matsayit Wadi Al Husen (Wadi Al Husen Mosque) is also known locally as 'Matsayit Song Roi Pi' (200-Year-Old Mosque), and is one of the most interesting mosques in Thailand. Constructed in 1769 of Malabar ironwood, it mixes Thai, Chinese and Malay architectural styles to good effect. It's in the village of Lubosawo in Amphoe Bacho (Ba-Jaw), about 15km northwest of Narathiwat off Hwy 42 (costs about 10B by *sǎwngthǎew*).

SUNGAI KOLOK
สุไหงโกลก
pop 39,000

This small town in the southeast of Narathiwat Province is a departure point for the eastern coast of Malaysia. The Thai government once planned to move the border crossing from Sungai Kolok to Ban Taba in Amphoe Tak Bai, which is on the coast 32km to the northeast. The Taba crossing is a shorter and quicker route to Kota Bharu, the first Malaysian town of any size, but Sungai Kolok is more convenient and will likely remain open as well for a long time.

As a town it's a bit of a mess; prostitution is the second-biggest industry. The rest of the economy is dedicated to Thai–Malaysian shipping.

The Thailand–Malaysia border is open from 5am to 5pm, but on slow days officials may close the border as early as 4.30pm.

Information

There are plenty of banks with ATMs in town (open 8.30am to 3.30pm Monday to Friday), though they close on Saturday and Sunday. During this time you'll have to rely on money-changing booths, which are open 6am to 5pm daily; there's one across from the train station.

Tourist police and immigration facilities are all at the border.

CS Internet (Th Asia 18; per hr 30B; ☽ 10am-10pm) Across from the Genting Hotel.

Post office (Th Asia 18; ☽ 8.30am-4.30pm Mon-Fri, 9am-noon Sat & Sun) On the western edge of town.

TAT (☎ 0 7361 2126; ☽ 8.30am-4.30pm)

Telephone office (Th Thetpathom; ☽ 8.30am-4.30pm Mon-Fri)

Sleeping & Eating

As a border town, Sungai Kolok sees its share of short-time trade, so if you're trying to avoid this it's wise to shell out a few more baht. Most places in Sungai Kolok will take Malaysian ringgit as well as Thai baht for food or accommodation. Upmarket hotels will also change money for you, at a price.

Asia Hotel (☎ 0 7361 1101; r 200-350B; ✹) Run by a friendly Chinese man, the Asia Hotel offers clean, but dark, rooms with fluorescent lighting; try to get a room with window.

Merlin Hotel (☎ 0 7361 8000; fax 0 7361 8123; 68 Th Charoenkhet; r 390B; ✹) Very popular place with Malaysian-Chinese tour groups, this place is nice and central with OK rooms for the price.

Grand Garden Hotel (☎ 0 7361 3600; gghotel@cscoms.com; 66 Soi 3, Th Pratchatiwat, r 585-700B; ✹ ✹) Features clean, modern rooms that are well maintained and quite comfortable. There's a small pool outside and karaoke bar inside.

Genting Hotel (☎ 0 7361 3231; fax 0 7361 1259; 250 Th Asia 18; r 645-710B; ✹ ✹) The drawback here is the loud music emanating from the karaoke bar. To avoid the noise ask for a room on a higher floor. Otherwise, except for a few scuffs on the walls and carpets, it's mostly up to snuff. Skip the restaurant.

Marina (☎ 0 7361 3881; fax 0 7361 3385; Soi Phuthon; r 990-1750B; ✹ ✹) It may be worth it for the views; this hotel has 15 storeys with a sky lounge on the top floor. Modern rooms are decent.

The town has plenty of **food stalls** selling Thai, Chinese and Malay food, while a cluster of reliable **Malay food vendors** can be found at the market and in front of the train station.

Getting There & Away

Air-con buses to Bangkok (VIP/1st/2nd class 1090/702/546B, 17 to 18 hours) depart

SUNGAI KOLOK

INFORMATION		
Bangkok Bank	1	B4
Bank of Ayudhya (ATM)	2	B4
CS Internet	3	C3
Customs	4	D3
Malaysian Immigration	5	D3
Money Exchange Booth	6	B3
Police	7	C4
TAT Office	8	D3
Telephone Office	9	B3
Thai Immigration	10	B3
Thai Immigration	11	D3

Thai Military Bank	12	C4
Tourist Police	(see 8)	

SLEEPING		
Asia Hotel	13	B3
Genting Hotel	14	C3
Grand Garden Hotel	15	B4
Marina	16	C3
Merlin Hotel	17	B3

EATING		
Market	18	B3

TRANSPORT		
Air-Con Buses to Bangkok &		
Phuket	19	B4
Minivans to Hat Yai	20	B3
Minivans to Hat Yai	21	B3
Minivans to Hat Yai	(see 6)	
Minivans to Narathiwat	22	B3
Share Taxis to Pattani, Yala,		
Narathiwat, Hat Yai	23	B3
Săwngthǎews to Tak Bai	24	B3

To Ban Taba (37km)

To Narathiwat (60km)

Sungai Kolok Hospital

Train Station

Th Asia 18

To Post Office (100km)

Th Thetpathom
Th Wongwiwat
Th Aririmatha
Th Wanat Amnoey
Th Bussayapan
Th Santiwong
Th Charoenkhet
Soi Phuthon
Th Vongvithee
Th Prachawiwit

Mae Nam Kolok

To Kota Bharu (30km)

MALAYSIA

LOWER SOUTHERN GULF

at 8am, 11.30am and 12.30pm; to Phuket (420B, nine hours) they head off at 8am and 5.30pm and stop in Krabi (335B, five hours). These buses leave from Th Wongwiwat, west of the town centre.

Minivan destinations include Hat Yai (150B, three hours) and Narathiwat (50B, 45 minutes), departing half-hourly from Th Asia 18, across from the train station. Minivans to Hat Yai (150B, three hours) and Pattani (80B, two hours) leave hourly from about a block west of the Genting Hotel.

Trains from Bangkok to Sungai Kolok include the 12.25pm rapid and 2.45pm special express. Trains from Sungai Kolok back to Bangkok include the 11.55am rapid and 2.05pm special express. These trains have 1st-, 2nd- and 3rd-class seats and sleeping berths; fares are 260B to 1493B.

Getting Around

The border is about 1km from the centre of Sungai Kolok or the train station. Transport around town is by motorcycle taxi – it's 20B for a ride to the border. Coming from Malaysia, just follow the old train tracks to your right or, for the town, turn left at the first intersection and head for the high-rises.

From Rantau Panjang (Malaysian side), a share taxi to Kota Bharu will cost about RM5 per person (or RM20 to charter the whole car) and takes around an hour. To Kota Bharu it costs RM3.50 on the regular yellow and orange bus.

Andaman Coast

Soaring peaks of jagged limestone provide a heady backdrop to the emerald green waters and white-sand beaches of Thailand's Andaman coast. Plain and simple, the region is a feast for the eyes, serving overflowing portions of some of Southeast Asia's most striking scenery. When the sun is shining, the warm, crystal-clear water sparkles like a gem-encrusted broach – emeralds merge with sapphires and little bits of turquoise. Even when the rains come, the region remains a photographer's paradise: something slightly magical happens when the slate grey clouds drift in, obscuring the lush green hills.

From the international jet-set town/island of Phuket (which dazzles the senses with fine resorts, fine cuisine and fine beaches) to the marine national parks of the Surin and Similan Islands (which harbour some of the world's top diving destinations) to jungle trekking through rainforest on the back of an elephant, the Andaman coast offers just about anything you could crave in a holiday. Scramble up cliffs and down into caves, swim in deep pools under refreshing waterfalls or sunbathe in the sand. Choose from dramatic Ko Phi-Phi, laid-back Ko Lanta, the blissfully unspoiled beaches near Trang and the islands of the Ko Tarutao Marine National Parks.

Comprising Ranong, Phang-Nga, Phuket, Krabi, Trang and Satun Provinces, the Andaman coast is bordered to the north by Myanmar and to the south by Malaysia. The beaches become less cluttered the further south you travel. And from Ranong down south to Phuket, it's almost all wilderness – rugged coastline, thick jungle, dramatic mountains and national parks abound.

HIGHLIGHTS

- Discovering psychedelic reefs and fistfuls of fish at world-class dive destinations such as **Ao Phang-Nga** (p640) and the **Surin** (p636) and **Similan Marine National Parks** (p639)

- Exploring **Krabi Province's** (p673) out-of-this world scenery – ride an elephant past karst caves and gushing waterfalls, seek solace on a picture perfect beach or scale **Railay's** (p684) limestone cliffs

- Partying rock star–style in **Phuket** (p644) – luxurious resorts, pumping clubs and brilliant beaches

- Experiencing the remote and virtually uninhabited **Ko Tarutao Marine National Park** (p715), one of the most pristine coastal areas in Thailand

- Chilling in paradise – emerald-hued water, sandy tropical beaches and rustic accommodation – on **Ko Lipe** (p718), **Ko Phayam** (p635) and **Ko Chang** (p634)

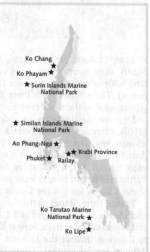

★ Ko Chang
★ Ko Phayam
★ Surin Islands Marine National Park
★ Similan Islands Marine National Park
Ao Phang-Nga ★   ★★ Krabi Province
Phuket ★ Railay
★ Ko Tarutao Marine National Park
Ko Lipe ★

ANDAMAN COAST

INDIAN OCEAN TSUNAMI 2004

On the morning of 26 December 2004, an earthquake off the coast of Sumatra sent huge waves crashing against much of Thailand's Andaman coast, claiming around 8000 lives and causing millions of dollars in damage to homes and businesses. Most of the tragic loss of life and property was limited to Khao Lak, Ko Phi-Phi and Phuket. Even in these areas, the damage was limited to a few southwest-facing beaches with shallow bays, and all three destinations were open for business within three months of the disaster.

Physically these areas are recovering quickly, but economically the loss of tourism – due to misperceptions that the coast isn't safe, or that everything is closed – is continuing to negatively impact the lives of just about everyone living there.

One of the best ways to support the people of the Andaman coast is to travel there, putting money back into the economy and showing the Thais that you care.

Climate

For the visitor to Thailand's southern provinces and its famed beaches, the main concern is the weather. The Andaman coast receives more rain than the southern gulf provinces – with May to October being the months of heaviest rainfall. During this time passenger boats to some islands, such as the Surin and Similan Archipelagos, are suspended. On the other hand, the southern gulf provinces are comparatively dry until October, with rainfall heaviest in November. Of course the abundance of regional microclimates makes it difficult to generalise but, fortunately, the peninsula on which southern Thailand sits is somewhat narrow. If you find the weather on the Andaman coast unpleasant, you can easily travel to the other side and hope to find the sun shining.

National Parks

This region has more than its share of national parks. Ao Phang-Nga (p642) offers limestone cliffs, islands and caves to explore via sea-kayak, scuba or snorkel. Khao Lak/ Laem Ru (p638) has lots of hiking past cliffs and beaches, while multiple islands and kilometre after kilometre of mangroves and jungle make Laem Son (p635) perfect for bird-watching. Despite minor damage to some reef formations during the 2004 tsunami, the Similan Islands Marine National Park (p639) remain a world-class diving and snorkelling destination. In the Surin Islands Marine National Park (p636), you'll find granite islands, coral reefs and whale sharks and manta rays to dive or snorkel with. Hat Jao Mai (p708) has sand beaches, mangroves and coral islands, while Khao

Phanom Bencha (p687) is a hiker's paradise with mountain jungle, tumbling waterfalls and monkeys. Ko Tarutao Marine National Park (p715) features well-preserved and wild jungle islands and beaches, with opportunities for snorkelling, while pristine beaches and more snorkelling are found at nearby Ko Phetra Marine National Park (p719). Sa Nang Manora Forest Park (p642) has a fairyland setting of moss-encrusted roots and rocks, plus multilevel waterfalls. Than Bokkharani (p688) offers a similar setting – emerald waters, caves and cliffs. On the border between Thailand and Malaysia, Thaleh Ban (p719) has the region's best-preserved section of white meranti rainforest.

All of the national parks along the Andaman coast are open. In an effort to restore tourism in the area, all entry fees – for foreigners as well as Thais – have been waived until further notice.

USEFUL WEBSITES

These websites provide information on the 2004 tsunami in Thailand, both the event itself and post-tsunami restoration.

Post-tsunami hotel status – sawadee.com /tsunami/hotels.htm

Ministry of Information and Communication Technology's tsunami website – www.thaitsunami.com/wps/portal

Tourism Authority of Thailand news articles – www.tatnews.org

Phuket Gazette – www.phuketgazette.net

The Nation – www.nationmultimedia.com

Bangkok Post – www.bangkokpost.net

ANDAMAN COAST

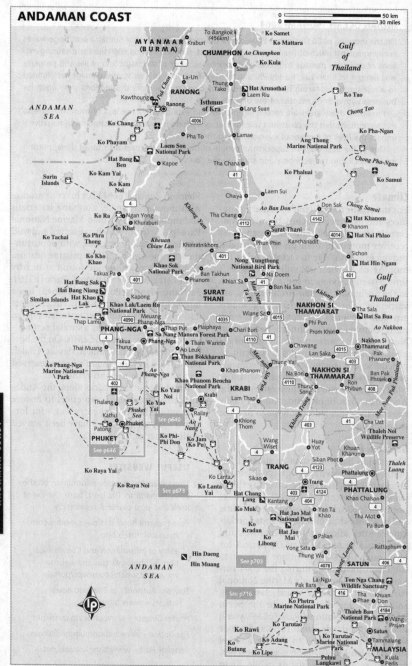

0   50 km
0   30 miles

MYANMAR
(BURMA)

To Bangkok
(456km)
Kraburi

Ko Samet
Ko Mattara

*Gulf
of
Thailand*

CHUMPHON *Ao Chumphon*

La-Un

Sawi

Ko Kula

4

4

Kawthoung

Ranong

RANONG

Thung
Tako

Hat Arunothai
Laem Riu

Ko Tao

Lang Suan

Chong Tao

*A N D A M A N
S E A*

Isthmus
of Kra

4006

Pha To

Lamae

Ang Thong
Marine National Park

Ko Pha-Ngan

Chong Pha-Ngan

Ko Chang

Ko Phayam

Laem Son
National Park

Kapoe

Tha Chana

41

Ko Phaluai

Ko Samui

Hat Bang
Ben

Ko Kam Yai

Chaiya

Laem Sui

Ao Ban Don

Don Sak

Chong Samui

Surin
Islands

Ko Kam
Noi

Ngan Yong

Khuraburi

Tha Chang

4112

Surat Thani

Kanchanadit

Hat Khanom
Khanom

4142

4014

Hat Nai Phlao

Ko Ra

Ko Khat

Khlong Yan

Khiriratnikhom

Phun Phin

Na Doem

41

Sichon

Ko Tachai

Ko Phra
Thong

*Kheuan
Chiaw Lan*

Khao Sok
National Park

Ban Takhun

401

Ban Na San

Hat Hin Ngam

Ko Kho
Khao

Takua Pa

401

Phanom

Khian Sa

Mae Nam Ta Pi

*Gulf
of
Thailand*

Hat Bang Sak

Hat Khao
Lak

Kapong

Nong Tungthong
National Bird Park

SURAT
THANI

NAKHON SI
THAMMARAT

Tha Sala

Similan Islands

Khao Lak/Laem Ru
National Park

Wiang Sa

4015

Phi Pun

Hat Sa Bua

Ao Nakhon

Thap Lamu

4090

Meuang
Phang-Nga

PHANG-NGA

Thai Muang

Takua
Thung

4

Plaihaya

Sa Nang Manora Forest Park

Thap Put

Phang-Nga

4035

Chari Buri

4110

Prom Khiri

Chawang

Lan Saka

4015

NAKHON SI
THAMMARAT

Nakhon Si
Thammarat
Pak
Phanang

403

*Ao Phang-Nga
Marine National
Park*

4

Ao Leuk

Tham Wararin

Than Bokkharani
National Park

Thung Yai

Na Bon

NAKHON SI
THAMMARAT

Ban Pak
Phraek

*Ao
Phang-Nga*

Khao Phanom

4110

Thung
Song

Ron
Phibun

408

Mae Nam Tak Thalang

402

Thalang

Kathu

Patong

Phuket
Sea

PHUKET

See p646

Khao Phanom Bencha
National Park

Ko Yao
Noi

Ko Yao
Yai

Krabi

KRABI

Lam Thap

Mae nam Sin Pun

Na Bon

Thung
Song

Cha Uat

41

See p640

Railay

*Ao
Nang*

Khlong
Thom

403

Thaleh Noi
Wildlife Preserve

Ko Phi-
Phi Don

Khong
Thom

Wang
Wiset

Huay
Yot

Siban Phot

Khuan
Khanun

*Thaleh
Luang*

Ko Raya Yai

Ko Jam
(Ko Pu)

4

4123

Phattalung

PHATTALUNG

Sikao

TRANG

Trang

403

404

4124

Khao Chaison

4

Ko Raya Noi

See p673

Ko Lanta
Yai

Kantang

Yan Ta
Khao

Tha Mot

Pa Bon

Hat Chang
Lang

Ko Muk

Hat Jao Mai
National Park

Pallan

Rattaphum

406

4

Hin Daeng
Hin Muang

Ko
Kradan

Ko
Libong

Hat Jao
Mai

Yong Sata

Thung Wa

*A N D A M A N
S E A*

See p703

4078

SATUN

Ton Nga Chang
Wildlife Sanctuary

See p716

La-Ngu
Pak Bara

Ko Phetra
Marine National Park

416

Tha
Phae

Khuan
Don

4184

Thaleh Ban
National Park

Wang
Prajan

Ko Tarutao

Satun

Ko Rawi

Ko Tarutao
Marine National
Park

Tammalang

MALAYSIA

Ko
Butang

Ko Adang

Ko Lipe

Puhu
Langkawi

Kuala
Perlis

Getting There & Away

Getting to the Andaman coast is straightforward. From Bangkok, the islands on the lower southern gulf and numerous other Thai destinations (as well as neighbouring Malaysia) it's easy to hop on a bus or train and then catch a ferry to the islands. Aeroplanes also ply the skies between Bangkok, Phuket and Krabi. Bus and train travel from Bangkok is generally cheap, relatively efficient and mostly takes place overnight. Almost any travel agency can sell you a combination bus or train and boat ticket to Ko Phi-Phi or Ko Lanta, which should get you to your destination with little effort. Beware of the cheapest tickets as they often prove to be scams. Pay a few more baht, however, and you'll likely arrive with few hassles. For more information on getting into and out of the region, see the destination sections or check out the Transport chapter (p750).

Getting Around

An intricate public transportation network takes you almost everywhere. Numerous boats shuttle back and forth between Ko Phi-Phi and Ko Lanta and other more far-flung islands. Boats to more remote destinations – like the Surin Islands, Similan Islands and Ko Tarutao Marine National Parks – only run during the dry season. Minivans and buses to just about anywhere make frequent trips throughout the day (and sometimes night). Basically, if you need to get from one tourist hot spot to another, it will take very little planning. Cheap săwngthăew and motorcycle taxis are also abundant and are used for short trips around the islands and mainland. If you want to drive yourself, motorcycles can be rented for about 200B a day. Car rental, at about 1000B per day, is also an option.

RANONG PROVINCE

Thailand's least-populated province is heavily forested and mountainous. It's supported mainly by mineral extraction and fishing, and rubber, coconut and cashew production. Like much of southern Thailand, Ranong experiences two monsoons, but the mountains here hold the rains over the area longer, so it gets the highest average annual rainfall in the country. Consequently, it's incredibly green and there are lots of waterfalls. However, it's swampy near the coastline and mainland beaches are almost nonexistent.

The 2004 tsunami affected coastal Ranong very little, although the partial loss of local fishing fleets in some areas meant that fishing all but ceased until new boats could be built or purchased.

For some time on the sand, head out to Ko Chang and Ko Phayam, which are pleasant laid-back islands just off the coast from the town of Ranong.

RANONG

ระนอง

pop 24,500

This small and friendly provincial capital has a bustling fishing port and is separated from Myanmar only by Pak Chan, the estuary of Mae Nam Chan (Chan River). Burmese residents from nearby Kawthoung (Ko Song) hop across to trade in Thailand or work on fishing boats. Many Burmese people now reside in Ranong, and you'll see men wearing the Burmese *longyi*, a long plaid sarong. Although there is nothing of great cultural interest in the town, some buildings are architecturally appealing. Most visitors come for visa services, and stay just long enough to enjoy the natural hot springs.

Because of its close vicinity to the stunning underwater destination of the Burma Banks (within the Mergui Archipelago), Phuket-based dive-tours are beginning to use Ranong as the launching pad for live-aboard trips (meaning you spend the night on the boat). The city is also a gateway to Kawthoung and Thahtay Island (with its casino), and many expats pass through on quick trips across the border to renew their visas.

Orientation & Information

Most of Ranong lies just west of Hwy 4, about 600km south of Bangkok and 300km north of Phuket.

BOOKSHOPS

Chuan Aksam bookshop (☎ 0 7781 1154; Th Ruangrat; ☟ 8am-9.30pm) Near the corner of Th Tha Meuang, it has reading material in English.

INTERNET ACCESS

Kay-Kai Internet Café (☎ 0 7781 2967; 293/6 Th Ruangrat; per hr 60B; ☟ 10am-10pm) This restaurant has Ranong's fastest Internet connections.

ANDAMAN COAST

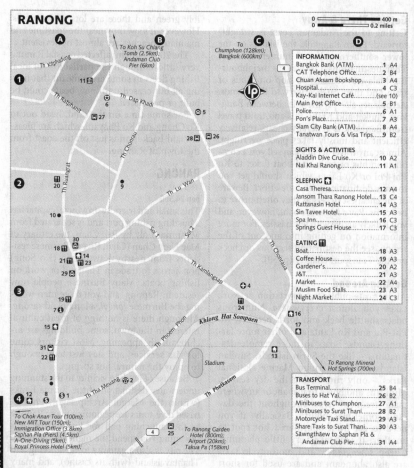

RANONG

INFORMATION	
Bangkok Bank (ATM)...............	1 A4
CAT Telephone Office............	2 B4
Chuan Aksam Bookshop.......	3 A4
Hospital.................................	4 C3
Kay-Kai Internet Café.........(see 10)	
Main Post Office...................	5 B1
Police....................................	6 A4
Pon's Place..........................	7 A3
Siam City Bank (ATM)..........	8 A4
Tanatwan Tours & Visa Trips....	9 B2

SIGHTS & ACTIVITIES	
Aladdin Dive Cruise..............	10 A2
Nai Khai Ranong....................	11 A1

SLEEPING	
Casa Theresa........................	12 A4
Jansom Thara Ranong Hotel....	13 C4
Rattanasin Hotel...................	14 A3
Sin Tavee Hotel....................	15 A3
Spa Inn.................................	16 C3
Springs Guest House...........	17 C3

EATING	
Boat......................................	18 A3
Coffee House........................	19 A3
Gardener's............................	20 A2
J&T..	21 A3
Market...................................	22 A4
Muslim Food Stalls..............	23 A3
Night Market........................	24 C3

TRANSPORT	
Bus Terminal........................	25 B4
Buses to Hat Yai..................	26 B2
Minibuses to Chumphon......	27 A1
Minibuses to Surat Thani.....	28 B2
Motorcycle Taxi Stand.........	29 A3
Share Taxis to Surat Thani....	30 A3
Săwngthăew to Saphan Pla & Andaman Club Pier.............	31 A4

MONEY

Most of Ranong's banks are along Th Tha
Meuang (the road to the fishing pier), near
the intersection with Th Ruangrat. Many
have ATMS.

POST & TELEPHONE

The main post office is on Th Chonrau near
the intersection of Th Dap Khadi.

The Communications Authority of Thailand (CAT) telephone office is south on Th
Phoem Phon.

TRAVEL AGENCIES

Along Th Ruangrat are many travel agencies that deal with visa services, bus and
boat tickets, and accommodation arrange-

ments for the nearby islands of Ko Chang
and Ko Phayam.

Pon's Place (☎ 0 7782 3344; Th Ruangrat; ⏰ 7.30am-
midnight) Pon knows the area well and also rents motorcycles and cars.

Tanatwan Tours & Visa Trips (☎ 0 7782 2807;
16/8 Th Chonrau) Offers tours to Kawthoung and the
islands. Full-day tours cost 1500B for one to three people,
1800B for four to six people and 3000B for groups of seven
to 10. Visa trips leave at 9am and return at 1pm and cost
300B per person, plus visa fees.

Sights & Activities
HOT SPRINGS

Approximately 1km east of Jansom Thara
Ranong Hotel at Wat Tapotaram is **Ranong
Mineral Hot Springs** (Th Kamlangsap; admission 10B;

8am-5pm). The water temperature hovers at around 65°C – hot enough to boil eggs. The Thai names of the three springs translate to Father Spring, Mother Spring and Baby Spring, and each is said to have a distinct flavour. The spring water is thought to be sacred as well as having miraculous healing powers.

You can bathe in rustic rooms where you scoop water from separate hot and cool water tanks and sluice the mixed water over your body Thai-style. Don't get inside the tanks and spoil the water. Both the Jansom Thara Ranong Hotel (right) and the Spa Inn (right) pipe water from the springs into the hotels, which hotel clients use for taking mineral baths. Nonguests can bathe in the Jansom's large public pool for 100B.

NAI KHAI RANONG

ในค่ายระนอง

During the reign of King Rama V, a Hokkien named Koh Su Chiang became governor of Ranong (thus gaining the new name Phraya Damrong Na Ranong). His former residence, **Nai Khai Ranong** (Th Ruangrat; admission free; 9am-4.30pm) has become a combination clan house (clubhouse for Chinese who share the same surname) and shrine. It's on the northern edge of town and is worth a visit.

Of the three original buildings, one still stands and is filled with mementoes of the Koh family's glory days. The main gate and part of the original wall also remain. Koh Su Chiang's great-grandson, Koh Sim Kong, is the caretaker; he speaks some English.

Several shophouses on Th Ruangrat preserve this old Hokkien style. Koh Su Chiang's tomb is set into the side of a hill 2.5km north, on the road to Hat Chandamri.

DIVING

Dives around Ranong include trips to the impressive Burma Banks (a part of the Mergui Archipelago) as well as the world-class Surin and Similan Islands. Because of the distances involved, dive trips are mostly liveaboard and not cheap. Expect to pay more than US$200 for a two-day/two-night deal.

A couple of dive shops in Ranong can get you started. Try **Aladdin Dive Cruise** (0 7781 2967; www.aladdindivecruise.de) at Kay-Kai Internet Café or **A-One-Diving** (0 7783 2984; www.a-one -diving.com; 77 Saphan Pla).

Sleeping

The places on or near Th Phetkasem (Hwy 4) and can be reached from town by *săwng-thăew* No 2 (7B).

Jansom Thara Ranong Hotel (0 7782 2516; 2/10 Th Phetkasem; r 800-1450B;) Rooms are slightly tatty for the price at this large hotel, just south of the river. But it pumps in water from the mineral springs for your bath, so it can get away with it. The place includes a restaurant that specialises in Chinese dim sum and noodles, a fitness centre, disco, cocktail lounge and swimming pool.

Springs Guest House (0 7783 4369; cnr Th Kamlangsap & Th Phetkasem; r 150-200B;) Savour the tinted windows here – the guesthouse used to be a karaoke joint. It's geared towards the foreign traveller, with a pool table and satellite TV in the bar/restaurant area downstairs, left luggage, and lots of local information. Bathrooms are shared.

Spa Inn (0 7781 1715; 25/11 Th Phetkasem; r 300-450B;) With a low-key atmosphere, friendly staff and access to the famed spring water, Spa Inn is a favourite with visiting Thais. It's not fancy, but the rooms are large and have bathtubs you can fill with hot mineral water piped in from the springs. Try for a back room, they look out on lush green mountainside. It's on Hwy 4 just north of the river.

Sin Tavee Hotel (0 7781 1213; 81/1 Th Ruangrat; r 160-280B;) Probably the best value on this street, staff at reception are relaxed and doubles come with tile floors, good beds, hot water, soap and towels.

Ranong Garden Hotel (0 7783 2174; fax 0 7783 2183; 6/54 Th Phetkasem; r 975-1075B;) A decent hotel, it has modern carpeted rooms and a few midrange amenities. Prices are often discounted during slow times. It's about 800m south of the bus station.

Royal Princess (0 7783 5240; www.royalprincess .com; r 990-1800B;) The fanciest pad in town, with mineral-water bathrooms, Jacuzzi, gym and pool. The rooms are fine enough, but are looking slightly piqued.

Rattanasin Hotel (0 7781 1242; cnr Th Ruangrat & Th Lu Wan; s/d 100/170B) A typical Thai-Chinese short-stay hotel that looks a bit worse for wear, though rooms have good beds and fans. Some of the bathrooms have squat toilets, and showers consisting merely of a pipe jutting out of the wall, but at least it's cheap.

Casa Theresa (0 7781 1135; 119/18 Th Tha Meuang; r 270-700B;) Rates vary according to the size

ANDAMAN COAST

of the room at this quiet, tidy, off-the-street guesthouse. A room on the premises is set aside for traditional Thai massage. The staff are an excellent source of information on local activities.

Eating

Pon's Place (☎ 0 7782 3344; Th Ruangrat; dishes 25-40B) Serves good cheap food and dishes out lots of local information (see p630); there's a helpful travel desk in front.

Gardener's (☎ 0 7783 0111; Th Ruangrat; dishes 30-50B) The iced mocha here is particularly yummy. Coffees and ice cream are the specialities, but it also offers a decent Western menu. Even though it opens early, there aren't any breakfast items on the menu.

Boat (☎ 0 7782 3996; Th Ruangrat; dishes 15-100B) This is a large and modern restaurant that does a lot of ice-cream business. It also serves Thai and Western food.

J&T (Th Ruangrat; dishes 20-45B) A similar place, it fills with Thai families on Sunday afternoon. The food is closer to cafeteria than *haute cuisine*, but it's filling and dirt-cheap. Try the Indonesian stir-fried rice (35B), which comes topped with a fried egg and accompanied by shrimp crisps, chopped cucumber and slices of chicken.

Coffee House (Th Ruangrat; dishes 30-60B) Serving Western-style breakfasts and light meals, Coffee House is a tiny and friendly spot. Look for the small paper sign in Roman script.

Your best eating options for authentic and cheap food are probably the markets and food stalls. Not far from Hwy 4 and the Spa Inn is a **night market** (Th Kamlangsap) with several stalls serving great Thai dishes at low prices. The **day market** (Th Ruangat), towards the southern end of town, offers inexpensive Thai and Burmese meals, as well as fresh produce, fish and meats. There are **Muslim food stalls** (Th Ruangrat; ☺ Sun-Fri) on the opposite side of the street from the J&T restaurant. Here you can get Malaysian-style curry, rice, rotii, pickled cucumbers and tea for 35B.

Getting There & Away

AIR

Ranong airport is 20km south of town on Hwy 4. **Phuket Airlines** (☎ 0 7782 4590; www.phuket airlines.com) has daily flights between Ranong and Bangkok. Flights to Phuket leave Fri-

day, Saturday and Sunday at 11.30pm (one way 2520B).

BUS & MINIVAN

The bus terminal is on Hwy 4 towards the southern end of town, though some buses stop in town before proceeding to the terminal. *Săwngthăew* No 2 (blue) passes the terminal.

Two private bus companies offer rtes to Bangkok: **Chok Anan Tour** (☎ 0 7781 1337) operates daily 1st-class air-con buses (333B, 10 hours, 8am and 8pm), as well as a VIP bus (389B) and a super VIP bus (515B), both which leave at 8pm. **New MIT Tour** (☎ 0 7781 1150) has VIP buses (389B, 10 hours, 8.30am and 8.10pm). Both companies are located on Th Meuang a few hundred metres west of Th Ruangrat. Other bus destinations from Ranong appear in the table below.

Destination	Fare (B)	Duration (hr)
Bangkok		
VIP	389-515	10
1st class	333	10
2nd class	259	10
ordinary	185	10
Chumphon		
2nd class	70	3
ordinary	55	3
Hat Yai		
2nd class	300	5
Khuraburi		
air-con	60	1½
ordinary	40	1½
Phang-Nga		
ordinary	90	5
Phuket		
air-con	185	5
ordinary	103	6
Surat Thani		
1st class	180	4
2nd class	80	5

Minivans head to Surat Thani (130B, 3½ hours) when full, usually about three or four times daily, and to Chumphon (90B, three hours, hourly). See the Ranong map for departure locations.

Getting Around

Motorcycle taxis will take you almost anywhere in town for 15B, to the hotels along Hwy 4 for 20B and to the pier for boats

Blue-spotted grouper, Similan Islands Marine National Park (p639)

MARK STRICKLAND

Kayaking in Krabi (p674)

PHILIP & KAREN SMITH

Tham Phra Nang Nok (Princess Cave; p684), Railay, Krabi Province

PAUL BEINSSEN

Floating nets and karst formations, Ko Panyi (p643), Phang-Nga Province

DOMINIC ARIZONA BONUCCELLI

DOMINIC ARIZONA BONUCCELLI

Transvestite show (p663), Patong, Phuket

Idyllic island beach off Ko Phi-Phi Don (p690), Krabi Province

HERMANN

to Koh Chang, Ko Panyam and Myanmar for 40B. Pon's Place (p630) can assist with motorcycle and car rentals.

AROUND RANONG
Kawthoung
เกาะสอง

The British named the small dusty port at the southernmost tip of mainland Myanmar Victoria Point, but the Thai's know it as Ko Song (Second Island). The Burmese appellation, Kawthoung, is most likely a corruption of the Thai name. Most foreigners come here only to renew their visas, but it makes an interesting day trip if you're already in the area. Unless you're just dying to say you set foot in Myanmar, it's probably not worth visiting Ranong simply to come here – it looks very similar to southern Thailand, except you'll see more men wearing the *longyi* (the Burmese sarong).

The main business is trade with Thailand, although fishing is also important. Among the Burmese, Kawthoung is perhaps best known for producing some of the country's best kick boxers. Most residents are bilingual, speaking Thai and Burmese. Many people born and raised around Kawthoung, especially Muslims, also speak Pashu, a dialect that mixes Thai, Malay and Burmese. Nearby islands are inhabited by bands of nomadic *chao náam*.

Most of these islands escaped major damage during the 2004 tsunami. However, on Ko Phra Thong the tsunami nearly wiped out two fishing villages, destroying 100 out of 255 houses and killing 44 people.

If you're coming to town to renew your visa, it isn't tough. If you don't join a tour out of Ranong (see p630 for info about tours), then see right for more information.

SLEEPING
There are only a few places in Kawthoung approved to accept foreigners. Thai baht are readily accepted.

Honey Bear Hotel (Yangon ☎ 0 1229 6190; r 700B; ✖) A five-minute walk from the pier, it is modern and friendly and sports clean rooms with satellite TV and cold-water shower. It's not a great deal by Thai standards, but is a comfortable enough hotel.

Andaman Club Hotel (Ranong ☎ 0 7783 1227, Bangkok ☎ 0 2679 8238; www.andamanclub.com; r 1800-3400B; ✖ ⊠) On nearby Thahtay Island, this

is where well-heeled Thai and Singaporean gamblers shack up. It's a huge five-star hotel complex sporting a casino and more than 200 modern rooms with sea views. Also on the premises are a wonderful pool, fitness centre, sauna and a Jack Nicklaus–designed 18-hole golf course. The hotel can arrange visa services.

GETTING THERE & AWAY
When the Thai–Myanmar border is open, boats to Kawthoung leave from the pier at Saphan Pla (Pla Bridge) about 4.5km from the centre of Ranong. Take *sǎwngthǎew* No 2 from Ranong (10B) and get off at the **immigration office** (☎ 0 7782 2016; Th Ruangrat; ☯ 8.30am-6pm), 700m north of the pier, to get your passport stamped. From there, groups of people will be waiting to take you on a boat trip (one way/return 50/150B) to Myanmar immigration. When negotiating your price, confirm whether it is per person or per ride, and one way or return. At the checkpoint you must inform the authorities that you're a day visitor – in which case you must pay a fee of US$5 or 300B for a day permit. If you have a valid Myanmar visa in your passport, you'll be permitted to stay up to 28 days, but will be required to buy US$200 worth of foreign exchange certificates (FECs).

A more-expensive alternative to the process outlined earlier, and one that is favoured by many expats on 'visa runs', is to take a fast air-con boat to the Andaman Club Hotel (see left) from its private pier about 7km northwest of Ranong centre. The pier has a large covered car park and a deluxe **ticket office** (☎ 0 7783 0461) with its own customs and immigration counters. Boats leave 15 times a day between 7am and 11.50pm Monday to Thursday, and hourly from 7am to midnight Friday to Sunday and holidays. You pay 250B return (or 500B if you want the staff to process your Myanmar visa). For an extra 100B the Andaman Club van will pick you up in Ranong and bring you to the pier. Or you can catch a 20B *sǎwngthǎew* bound for Sam Laem (ask for the Andaman Club pier) from the market on Th Ruanrat in Ranong.

Perhaps because this is such a money-maker, the Andaman Club route tends to be open even when the border is officially closed. Immigration officers at the Saphan

ANDAMAN COAST

Pla office hand out maps to the club's pier, complete with phone number.

If you're just coming to renew your Thai visa, the whole process will take a minimum of two hours. Bear in mind when you are returning to Thailand that Myanmar time is 30 minutes behind Thailand's. This has caused problems in the past for returning visitors who got through Burmese immigration before its 6pm closing time only to find the Thai office closed. Though the Thai immigration department seems to have changed its hours in order to avoid this unpleasantness, you should double-check when leaving the country.

Ko Chang
เกาะช้าง

The waters around this rustic and laid-back island (not to be confused with the larger Ko Chang in Trat Province) are clouded by effluent from the muddy estuary, but that doesn't stop adventurous travellers from enjoying the mangroves on the east coast and a hilly, forested interior. So far there's no electricity – the resorts here either do without or generate their own. Pass your time wandering around the small main village where boats land (in the dry season) or exploring one of the dirt trails meandering around the island. Beaches are found along the western shore, and if you're lucky you may catch sight of sea eagles, Andaman kites and even hornbills.

In December 2004 Ko Chang suffered low-level tsunami damage due to high water, losing a fishing pier and a few bungalows. There were no deaths, and everything is back to normal now.

Bungalow operations on Ko Chang can arrange boat trips to Ko Phayam and other nearby islands for around 200B per person (including lunch) in a group of six or more. Dive trips are also possible: check with **Aladdin Dive Cruise** (Ranong ☎ 0 7781 2967, on Ko Chang ☎ 0 1229 6667; www.aladdindivecruise.de; Kay-Kai Internet Café, Th Ruangrat, Ranong).

SLEEPING & EATING

There are several places on the beach, although for the most part they're only open from November to April. Some have limited electricity. Cashew, Eden, Contex and Sunset bungalows will pick prospective guests up at J&T restaurant in Ranong (see p632).

Ko Chang Contex (☎ 0 7782 0118, 0 9727 2189; bungalows 100-300B) Run by a Thai family, Contex offers basic bungalows on a rocky headland above the beach, along with an à la carte restaurant menu. It's north of the village.

Eden Bistro Cafe (☎ 0 7782 0172; bungalows 250-300B) This friendly café, southwest of Ko Chang Contex, offers a handful of small bungalows with shared bathroom and one large bungalow with attached shower.

Sunset Bungalow (☎ 0 7782 0171; bungalows 100-300B) Just down the beach from Eden, Sunset offers nicely built bungalows in a shady, breezy spot.

Cashew Resort (☎ 0 7782 0116; bungalows 200-600B) The oldest and largest resort on the island, Cashew has a range of abodes, from wooden A-frame huts to larger, more-solid bungalows.

Chang Thong & Pheung Thong Bungalows (☎ 0 7783 3820; bungalows 100-150B) These friendly side-by-side operations are a few hundred metres past the pier. They have solid wooden bungalows set on a sandy lot with some trees. Chang Thong often picks up visitors in Ranong.

Lae Tawan (☎ 0 7782 0179; bungalows 150-300B) Located in a nearby small bay, it offers a handful of wood-and-concrete bungalows on a tree-spotted hillside.

N & X Bungalows (☎ 0 7782 0180; huts 100B) For those seeking serious self-reflection time, try these very basic thatched huts at the southern end of the island at Ao Lek (Small Bay).

GETTING THERE & AWAY

From Ranong take a săwngthăew (which will likely have destination signs in English) to Saphan Pla, getting off by the PTT petrol station and toll booth (10B). Look for a lane on the left just before the toll booth (there may be a sign referring to Ko Chang) and follow it down a few hundred metres, zigzagging along the way; turn left at the T-intersection and walk about five minutes to reach the pier.

Two or three boats leave every morning from November to April; turn up around 9am to see when they're going, as they don't usually leave before this hour. During the high season – December to March – there's a consistent daily noon departure. Boats return to Ranong at 8am the next day. The fare is 100B per person, though if you book your accommodation ahead of time, the boat ride can be included.

Ko Phayam
เกาะพยาม

This friendly and demure little island supports about 500 inhabitants – mostly Thais and Burmese – with a smattering of expats and a few dozen *chao leh* thrown into the mix. While spotlighted by two main bays and their beaches, Ko Phayam also has a couple of sizable, forested hills and plenty of scenic agricultural land to boot. Locals support themselves mostly on prawn fishing and cashew-nut farming. Interesting fauna in the area include wild pigs, hornbills, monkeys and snakes.

The island is part of the **Laem Son National Park**, which covers 315 sq km in Ranong and Phang-Nga Provinces. The park's area includes about 100km of Andaman Sea coastline – the longest protected shore in the country – as well as more than 20 islands.

There's one sizable 'village' on the island, where you'll find the main pier, a couple of simple eateries, some small grocery stalls and one surprisingly modern bar called **Oscar's** (☎ 0 7782 4236), which you can't really miss. The only other bar on the island is Banana Bar, which has an isolated and natural setting, and is located towards Ao Yai, near Bamboo Bungalows. From the pier area, motorcycle taxis scoot you to the 15 or so bungalow operations around the island, almost all of which are pretty basic and located on the two bays – Ao Yai and Ao Khao Fai. Ao Yai is best for swimming, and has a 3km-long sandy beach. It gets more waves than Ao Khao Fai. Ao Khao Fai is shallower and not as good for swimming, but the beach is more sheltered, if you're just looking to sunbathe. It's also more affected by the tides than Ao Yai.

SLEEPING & EATING
Practically all the bungalows on Ko Phayam only have fans, and electricity is usually available from sunset to 10pm or 11pm only. All have their own restaurant and many, unlike on nearby Ko Chang, stay open all year.

The following places are on Ao Yai. Prices may vary a bit depending on the season or demand.

Bamboo Bungalows (☎ 0 7782 0012; bungalows 100-500B) Managed by a friendly Israeli-Thai

couple, Bamboo has a wide variety of bungalows here – from the most basic A-frames to solid concrete-and-tile-floor structures with creative baths. Garden areas are pleasant and the restaurant is good. It's near the middle of the beach, and boogie boards can be rented. It's the most atmospheric place to stay on the beach.

Coconuts (☎ 0 7782 0012; bungalows 200-400B) Near Bamboo, this is another friendly business that features some nice, well-spaced wooden bungalows, the larger of which cost more.

Ao Yai Bungalows (☎ 0 7782 1753; gilles_patchara@ hotmail.com; bungalows 200-750B) Next to Coconuts, it has typical decent wooden bungalows.

The following places are situated on Ao Khao Fai.

Mountain Resort (☎ 0 7782 0098; bungalows 350B) At the top of the bay, it has five large, solid and attractive bungalows. They lie on grassy, palm-shaded grounds off the beach, and are some of the most modern on the island.

Vijit (☎ 0 7783 4082; www.geocities.com/vijitbungalows; bungalows 100-200B) Towards the southern end of the bay, Vijit has about a dozen basic bungalows around a sandy lot planted with young trees. Each bungalow has been built in a slightly different style. At high tide, the beach here thins out. Contact the staff for free transport from Ranong.

JPR (bungalows 150-200B) Further north are nine no-frills bungalows spread out between trees on a dusty hillside above the beach. It's a friendly place, but the location is pretty isolated.

GETTING THERE & AWAY
See opposite for details on travelling to Ranong's Saphan Pla, from where the boats head to Ko Phayam.

There are daily boats from Saphan Pla to Ko Phayam's pier at around 8am and 3pm (100B, 1½ to two hours). From Ko Phayam back to Ranong the boats run at 9am and 2pm. During the high season there may be three runs daily. Long-tail boat charters to the island cost 1500B to 2000B.

GETTING AROUND
Motorcycle taxis provide transport around the island; there are no cars or trucks (yet), and roads are pleasantly motorcycle-sized. A ride to your bungalow will cost 50B to 100B. Walking is possible but distances are

long – it's about 45 minutes from the pier to Ao Khao Fai, the nearest bay.

Motorcycle rentals are available at **Oscar's** (☎ 0 7782 4236), the village bar. The rental rates are about 250B per day. Some of the guesthouses might be able to arrange rentals as well.

PHANG-NGA PROVINCE

Taking in the coastline between Ranong and Phuket Provinces, Phang-Nga Province has plenty of natural beauty to offer the intrepid traveller. The Surin Islands and Similan Islands Marine National Parks harbour some of the world's top diving destinations, while Ao Phang-Nga features stunning limestone mountains and rock formations. And let's not forget the small, but uniquely fascinating, national parks scattered throughout the province, which also acts as a gateway to Phuket Island, the Krabi region and Khao Sok National Park.

The December 2004 tsunami hit Phang-Nga's Andaman shoreline very hard. In fact about 6000 of the deaths or missing-person cases attributed to the disaster – well over half the national count – occurred along this section of coast, particularly in the Thai Muang, Khao Lak, Bang Niang and Bang Sak regions. This area is slowly recovering and many of the less-affected resorts in Khao Lak were open for business only a few months after the tsunami.

Bang Niang and Bang Sak, where tsunami destruction was particularly widespread (because the area's flat terrain allowed the waves access up to 4km inland), NGOs from around the world have set up relief centres for the on-going reconstruction of village homes and fishing boats. At least some of these centres will continue their relief work until late 2006.

SURIN ISLANDS MARINE NATIONAL PARK

อุทยานแห่งชาติหมู่เกาะสุรินทร์

Famous for its excellent diving and snorkelling, the five islands that make up the **Surin Islands Marine National Park** (☺ mid-Nov–mid-May), were designated a national park in 1981. Ko Surin Neua (north) and Ko Surin Tai (south) are the largest two islands and where all the action takes place. They

lie about 55km from Thailand's coast and 5km from Thailand's marine border with Myanmar. Some of the best diving can be found in the channel between these two islands. The park office, visitors centre and numerous hiking trails are at Ao Mae Yai (the south bay) on Ko Surin Neua.

On Ko Surin Tai, a village of *chao náam* hold a major ancestral worship ceremony (Loi Reua) in April. The 2004 tsunami devastated the Moken's village and fishing fleet, and for several months they were forced to live in makeshift camps on the Phang-Nga mainland. With help from local, national and international relief agencies, the villagers were able to return to their Surin Tai village in time for the April 2005 Loi Reua and they continue to reside there.

Surrounding the Surin Archipelago are some of the best-developed coral colonies in Thailand. Extensive underwater surveys carried out by marine biologists indicate that these reefs survived the tsunami battering very well. Experts estimate only 5% to 8% of the coral in this area has been damaged.

There are seven major dive sites in the immediate surrounds of the Surin Islands; the best are at **HQ Bay, Ko Chi** and **Richelieu Rock** (a seamount 14km southeast of Ko Surin Tai). Whale sharks – the largest fish in the world – are often spotted near Richelieu, especially during March and April. Snorkelling is excellent in many areas due to relatively shallow reef depths of 5m to 6m – all you need to do is bring your equipment.

The **Burma Banks** are a gorgeous system of submerged seamounts about 60km northwest of the Surin Islands. The only way to visit – unless you have your own boat – is by live-aboard dive trips out of Phuket, Khao Lak or Ranong. The three major banks, **Silvertip, Roe** and **Rainbow**, provide four- to five-star diving experiences, with fields of psychedelic coral laid over flat, underwater plateaus. There are heaps of large oceanic as well as smaller reef marine species, including reef, silvertip, nurse and leopard sharks.

Sleeping & Eating

Accommodation in the **park longhouses** (Bangkok ☎ 0 2561 2919-21; 1–6–person longhouse 1200B) has been suspended until further notice following the tsunami. You may still be able to pitch a tent at the **campsite** (mainland office ☎ 0 7649 1378; per person 40B, on-site tent for 2 people 300B). Once the longhouses are open again, the park will offer a daily package of three good meals (mostly seafood) for 400B per person. Electricity is generated from 6pm to 11pm.

If you need to stay on the mainland, **Khuraburi**, the jumping-off town for the islands, offers a few options.

Tararain River Hut Resort (☎ 0 7649 1789; bungalows 300-500B; ❖) Friendly, basic and somewhat charming, it's north of town just over the bridge. Fan bungalows are tiny and no-frills; air-con bungalows are also tiny, but a bit more modern.

Kuraburi Greenview Resort (☎ 0 7640 1400; bungalows incl breakfast 1800-2200B; ❖ ❖) Rooms at this fancier space have luxurious amenities. It's actually south of Khuraburi about 12km, right off Hwy 4.

Getting There & Away

Boat travel is only considered safe in the period between mid-November and mid-May. The park is officially closed from mid-May to mid-November.

Ko Surin National Park's **mainland office** (☎ 0 7649 1378) is located in Ngan Yong, the little fishing village from where boats to the islands depart. The short (2km) road to Ngan Yong turns off Hwy 4 at the Km 110 marker, about 6km north of Khuraburi and 109km south of Ranong.

Regular ordinary and air-con buses run between Khuraburi and Ranong (40/60B, 1½ hours); ask to be let off at Ngan Yong (say 'Ko Surin'). Buses also run regularly to Phuket (60B, three hours). Motorcycle taxis from Khuraburi to Ngan Yong are 50B.

Ko Surin is not a bargain destination. Ask about in-season daily boat departures at the mainland office (boats leave at 9am); park staff can help book you seats (1000B return, four hours). You can also charter a private boat for about 6000B return.

Dive operators in Phuket, Khao Lak and even Ranong have live-aboard diving excursions to the Surin Islands. Because of the distances involved, Ko Surin is the most expensive dive destination in Thailand. It costs about 10,000B to 12,000B for a two-day or three-day trip.

Long-tail boats ferry passengers between the Surin Neua and Surin Tai.

KHAO LAK, BANG NIANG & BANG SAK
เขาหลัก/บางเนียง/บางสัก

The laid-back somewhat sleepy beaches of Khao Lak, Bang Niang and Bang Sak offer long stretches of sand, occasionally studded with granite boulders. This stretch of sandy shoreline had been developing rapidly in the five years or so before the fateful events of December 2004. Swanky beach resorts were filling the beaches at Khao Lak in particular, while Bang Niang and Bang Sak offered quieter, more-economical alternatives.

Ready access to the Surin and Similan Islands Marine National Parks helped spur this phenomenal growth, as these islands offer some of Thailand's most exhilarating diving. A coral reef suitable for snorkelling lies 45 minutes offshore by long-tail boat and many dive shops offer excursions to this reef.

When the tsunami reached Khao Lak, the waves destroyed virtually every structure along the beach here, and tragically took many lives – both Thai and foreign – with them. Houses, resorts and businesses that were on high ground, particularly those along the cliffs at Khao Lak's southern end were, for the most part, spared.

Although initially closed to tourism immediately after the disaster, many of the undamaged or lesser-damaged resorts in the Khao Lak area re-opened within three months. Some beachfront properties are rebuilding, while a few – whose owners don't have or can't find the funds to rebuild, or who don't feel compelled to rebuild – will simply never exist again.

At comparatively flatter Bang Niang and Bang Sak, tsunami damage to life and property extended further inland. Even several months after the disaster, the baring of the terrain is obvious. Although rehabilitation is well under way, the priority is to rebuild local homes and businesses, and it may take another two years before the tourism infrastructure in Bang Niang or Bang Sak is restored.

Despite the events of 2004, Khao Lak retains its reputation as a haven for divers heading to the Similan and Surin islands, and there are at least a dozen dive shops in operation.

The waterfalls of **Chong-Fa** (admission 200B) are around 6km along a side road off the highway.

ANDAMAN COAST

Sights & Activities

Park ranger-guided **treks** along the coast or inland can be arranged through Poseidon Bungalows (below), along with long-tail boat trips to the scenic Khlong Thap Liang estuary. The latter affords opportunities to view mangrove communities of crab-eating macaques. Because both Ko Surin and Ko Similan are relatively distant from the mainland – around 60km away – most dive trips do live-aboard trips. These trips cost about 3700/10,000/12,000B for one-/two-/three-day packages. Trips to local coral reefs start around 1300B. The best diving months are December to May.

Two of the more established dive shops in Phuket are the **Sea Dragon Dive Centre** (☎ 0 7642 0420; www.seadragondivecenter.com) and **Phuket Divers** (☎ 0 7642 0628; www.phuketdivers.com); both companies have employees who speak several languages. Sea Dragon's informative website contains an excellent update of the situation in post-tsunami Khao Lak, with plenty of information on the Similan and Surin islands as well.

Sleeping

Most of the beach accommodation in Khao Lak and Bang Niang was badly damaged – in some instances, completely destroyed – by the 2004 tsunami. Above the beach at Khao Lak, most places on high ground survived. Virtually nothing was left at flatter Bang Niang.

At Khao Lak several resorts are under reconstruction and should be open by mid-2006. In order to draw tourists back to Khao Lak, some of the larger resorts discounted their rooms throughout 2005.

Poseidon Bungalows (☎ 0 7644 3258; www.similantour.com; bungalows 200-1100B) About 5km south of Hat Khao Lak, the huts here are discreetly dispersed among huge boulders and coastal forest, affording lots of privacy. The proprietors dispense information on the area and organise reasonably priced boat excursions and dive trips to the local reef and the Similan Islands. Poseidon lost its restaurant and five bungalows (leaving 12) to the tsunami, but is rebuilding these and is open for business as usual.

Staff here also organise live-aboard snorkelling tours to the Similan Islands (6500B, two nights) that depart on Tuesday and Friday from November to May. If you want to

experience the beauty of these islands, but aren't certified to dive, these trips provide an excellent alternative.

Khao Lak Palm Beach Resort (☎ 0 7642 0096; www.khaolakpalmbeach.com) This place is 1.9km from town and before the tsunami it offered gorgeous rooms in buildings with traditional peaked roofs. Due to heavy damage this resort is closed until further notice.

Jai's Bungalows (☎ 0 7642 0390; bungalows 100-200B) Close to the main road into town, but not far from the beach, the bungalows here are very simple and run by a friendly family. The restaurant food is delicious.

Khao Lak Sunset Resort (☎ 0 7642 0075; www.khaolaksunset.com; r 1200-3290B; 🖭 🖭) A modern resort boasting comfortable, well-appointed rooms with a balcony and sea views. Some bungalows and the pool, damaged by the tsunami, are under reconstruction, but the resort is open. It's 2km from town.

Khao Lak Baan Krating Resort (☎ 0 7642 3088; www.baankrating.com; r 4500B; 🖭 🖭) Perched on a cliff overlooking Ao Khao Lak, Baan Krating offers 24 spacious and tastefully decorated villas with ocean-view balconies.

Phu Khao Lak Resort (☎ 0 9874 1018; phukhaolak@hotmail.com; r 400-700B) Simple but very tidy brick cottages sit on high ground, in a garden setting, just off the main road in Khao Lak.

Palm View Resort (☎ 0 1892 5480; r 650B; 🖭) The Palm View, one of the newest places in Khao Lak, sits on a quiet country road a bit outside of town.

Getting There & Away

Any bus running along Hwy 4 between Takua Pa and Phuket or Thai Lulang will stop at Bang Niang or Hat Khao Lak if you ask the driver. From Bangkok there are several ordinary/2nd class buses (120/168B, six hours).

If you're heading to Poseidon Bungalows, your best bet is to get off the bus at Thap Lamu and take a motorcycle taxi (40B) from there.

KHAO LAK/LAEM RU NATIONAL PARK

อุทยานแห่งชาติเขาหลัก/แหลมรุ

Beaches, estuaries, mangroves and a collection of beautiful sea cliffs and 1000m-high hills give this 125-sq-km **park** (☎ 0 7642 0243) its character. Immediately south of Hat Khao Lak, the wildlife here includes hornbills, drongos, tapirs, gibbons, monkeys and Asiatic black bears. The visitors centre, just off Hwy 4 between the Km 56 and Km 57 markers, has little in the way of maps or printed information, but can give verbal advice on the coastal hiking trails. It also has a very nice open-air restaurant serving good food at reasonable prices. It's perched on a shady slope overlooking the sea.

The park is less than 3km from Khao Lak and can easily be visited on day trips, but if you'd like to stay within the park there are **bungalows** (250-500B) near the visitors centre. These sleep between two and four people. **Tents** (100-200B) also can be rented here.

SIMILAN ISLANDS MARINE NATIONAL PARK
อุทยานแห่งชาติหมู่เกาะสิมิลัน

World renowned among diving enthusiasts for incredible underwater sightseeing at depths ranging from 2m to 30m, the **Similan Islands** (Nov-May) have huge and smooth granite rock formations that plunge into the sea and form seamounts, rock reefs and dive-throughs. As elsewhere in the Andaman Sea, the best diving months are December to May when the weather is good and the sea at its clearest.

The Thais sometimes refer to the Similan Islands as Ko Kao, or Nine Islands, because there are nine of them – each has a number as well as a name. In fact, the name 'Similan' comes from the Malay word *sembilan* meaning nine. Counting in order from the north, they are Ko Bon, Ko Ba-Ngu, Ko Similan, Ko Payu, Ko Miang (which is actually two islands close together), Ko Payan, Ko Payang and Ko Hu Yong. They're relatively small islands and uninhabited except for park officials and the occasional tourist group.

Ko Miang, which is the second-largest island after Ko Similan, is where you'll find a visitors centre, the park headquarters and accommodation. Venturing inland from the beach, you should catch glimpses of the Nicobar pigeon or the hairy-legged mountain land crab. If you're not into aqualungs, the beaches on this island are good for snorkelling, as is the channel between Ko Miang and Ko Payu.

Ko Similan is also good for hiking and snorkelling. In a small bay on the Similan's western side you may be able to see spiny lobsters resting in rock crevices, along with sea fans and plume worms. The largest granite outcrop in the Similan Islands is also found on Ko Similan; scramble to the top to enjoy a sweeping view of the sea.

On the nine islands there are 32 species of birds, including the Brahminy kite and white-breasted waterhen. Migratory species of note include the pintail snipe, grey wagtail, cattle egret, watercock and the roseate tern. Fairly common mammal residents such as the bush-tailed porcupine, common palm civet, flying lemur and bottlenose dolphin call these islands home, along with reptiles and amphibians such as the banded krait, reticulated python, white-lipped pit viper, common pit viper, hawksbill turtle, leather turtle, Bengal monitor lizard, common water monitor lizard and ornate froglet.

The Similan Islands suffered only minimally during the 2004 tsunami. Experts estimate that only 5% to 8% of the coral has been damaged beyond recovery.

Activities
The best place to organise **dive trips** to the Similan Islands is Hat Khao Lak. All the dive shops there offer multiday dive excursions (see opposite).

If you don't dive, but want to experience the underwater beauty with a snorkel mask, visit the Poseidon Bungalows (opposite) near Hat Khao Lak; here you can arrange three-day, live-aboard snorkelling trips.

Phuket also has many dive shops offering Similan Islands excursions. However, Phuket is far from the Similans – some 90km by boat, as opposed to 60km from Hat Khao Lak. This longer distance makes the excursions more expensive; expect to pay about US$440 for a three-day/four-night dive trip with equipment included.

Sleeping & Eating
Accommodation, including camping, is usually allowed on Ko Miang, but for the moment all overnights on the islands have been barred pending post-tsunami repairs. When operational, the bungalows and tent rentals are booked through the **park office** (mainland office 0 7659 5045; camping per person 80B, 2-person on-site tents 400B, 4-/6-/8 person bungalows 600/1000/1600B).

Before the tsunami, the only source of food was a privately run restaurant on Ko Miang. The restaurant has since closed, but

ANDAMAN COAST

may re-open when overnight accommodation is restored.

Getting There & Away

The Similan Islands' **mainland park office** (☎ 0 7659 5045) is in Thap Lamu, 39km south of Takua Pa and 4km off Hwy 4. The pier, from which boats leave, is 500m past this office.

From November to May boats depart daily (return 2300B, three hours, 8.30am); you can buy boat tickets at **Met Sine Tours** (☎ 0 7644 3276) near the pier. Boats return from the Similans in the afternoon; schedules can be fluid, so ask when you board.

AO PHANG-NGA & PHANG-NGA

อ่าวพังงา/พังงา

pop 9700

About 95km northeast of Phuket, this sheltered pocket of the Andaman Sea is blessed with plenty of verdant limestone cliffs, odd rock formations, submerged karst caves and quaint fishing villages. All along the coast are the turquoise waters and scenic islands for which the Phang-Nga region is known. On the high cliffs of the more isolated islands, swiftlets build their delicate saliva nests, which are collected for use in bird's-nest soup (a Chinese delicacy). Much of this area is part of Ao Phang-Nga Marine National Park and can be explored by boat or kayak.

If you're arriving in the Ao Phang-Nga area from Krabi on Hwy 4, you can either

turn right or left just after Thap Put. Turning left will keep you on the shorter, straighter main highway, while turning right will take you onto a narrow, very curvy and pretty stretch of highway that's 5km longer than the main highway. It's your choice.

Phang-Nga is a somewhat spread-out, modestly sized town with one main street (Hwy 4), and is nicely located near some limestone cliffs. There isn't a whole lot to see or do, but it does have **Somdet Phra Sinakharin**, a public park at the southern end of town, which contains dramatic karst formations such as water-filled caves and tunnels; there's even a hole in a cliff you can drive through. **Tham Reusi Sawan**, one of the larger caves, is marked by a gilded statue of a *reusii* (Hindu sage).

Information

Phang-Nga town doesn't have a tourist office, but the one in Phuket town provides maps and good information on the region.

In the centre of town is the bus terminal and several banks with ATMs. The post and telephone offices are about 2km south of the centre. There's a good Internet café across from the 7-Eleven.

Phang-Nga's **immigration office** (☎ 0 7641 2011; ☒ 8.30am-4.30pm Mon-Fri) is a few kilometres south of town; you'll probably never find it on your own, so take a motorcycle taxi.

Tours

Around 8.5km south of the town centre is Tha Dan, the pier area from where you can charter boats to see half-submerged caves, oddly shaped islands and Ko Panyi, a Muslim village on stilts. There are also two- to three-hour **tours** (per person 400-500B) to Ko Phing Kan (known as 'James Bond Island' as it featured in *The Man with the Golden Gun*) and Ao Phang-Nga National Park. Takua Thung, another pier area about 10km further south of Tha Dan, also has private boats for hire at similar prices; ask at the restaurants. Unless you enjoy haggling with boatmen, it's much easier (and not that expensive) to go with an organised tour through an agency in town.

Sayan Tours (☎ 0 7643 0348) has been doing tours of Ao Phang-Nga for many years now, and these continue to receive good reviews from travellers. Overnight tours cost 750B per person and include Tham Lawt (a large

ANDAMAN COAST

AO PHANG-NGA

0 —— 14 km
0 —— 8 miles

PHANG-NGA

Sa Nang Manora Forest Park

Thap Put

Raman Forest Park

Wat Tham Suwankhuha

Phang-Nga

415

Takua Thung

Tha Dan

Ban Ling

Ao Leuk

4

Ao Phang-Nga National Park

Ban Mai Phai

Than Bokkharani National Park

Ban Sam Chong

Ko Panyi

Ko Phing Kan

Ko Khao Tapu

Ao Luk

To Krabi (17km)

4

To Thai Muang (23km)

Ao Phang-Nga Marine National Park

Ao Phang-Nga

KRABI

Ko Yao Noi

PHUKET

Ta Khai

To Phuket (18km)

Bang Rong

Ko Yao Yai

Ko Bele

402

Ao Nang

water cave), Ko Phing and Ko Panyi, among other destinations. Meals and very rustic accommodation on Ko Panyi are part of the package. This overnight trip is recommended over either half-day or full-day trips, which feel rushed but are more affordable at 200B and 500B respectively. Sayan Tours also offers canoe trips and land destinations, including Sa Nang Manora Forest Park and various caves near town.

For more information about Ao Phang-Nga Marine National Park, see p642.

Sleeping

Unless specified otherwise, all of the following places are on Hwy 4 (Th Phetkasem), the main street.

Phang-Nga Inn (☎ 0 7641 1963; phang-ngainn@png .co.th; 2/2 Soi Lohakit; r 500-1400B; ✷) The most pleasant hotel in town. A converted family mansion, it has 12 homey, quiet rooms. All are comfortably modern and well furnished; there's an eating area in front. It's on a side street off the main road near the centre of town.

Phang-Nga Guest House (☎ 0 7641 1358; r 220-1000B; ✷) The best-value budget digs in town, with 12 clean, neat and pleasant rooms that come in a variety of sizes and prices. Sayan Tours takes its clients here.

Thawisuk Hotel (☎ 0 7641 2100; 77-79 Th Phetkasem; r 150-200B) A rambling, pastel-blue building in the middle of town, it's friendly and offers bright, simple rooms. There's a rooftop with good views.

Phang-Nga Bay Resort Hotel (☎ 0 7641 2067; fax 0 7641 2070; r 1050B; ✷ ✹) Boasting great views of the bay, rooms here vary from small to very large (check out a few before deciding) and come with TV, fridge and balcony. The carpets are a bit worn, and the building exterior is in a very dreary condition, but overall it's a decent place. Located 8.5km south of town at Tha Dan, it increases the rates considerably during holidays.

New Lukmuang Hotel (☎ 0 7641 2218; r 450-670B) An ageing, noisy hotel just north of town, its best rooms are actually the cheapest, but aren't anything special. Frosted windows obstruct views of anything.

Phang-Nga Valley Resort (☎ 0 7641 2201; bungalows 560B; ✷) The hilly grounds here are green and expansive, but the buildings have definitely seen better days. The 10 OK bun-

galows still in use are hardly spiffed up inside – just hope the air-con works. At least it's nicely secluded on the southern outskirts of town, 350m south of the highway to Krabi. The resort is down a 400m drive, best reached by private transport.

Eating

Several food stalls on the main street sell delicious *khànǒm jiin* (thin wheat noodles) with chicken curry, *náam yaa* (spicy ground-fish curry) or *náam phrík* (sweet and spicy peanut sauce).

Cha-Leang (☎ 0 7641 3831; dishes 40-90B) This is one of the best and most popular restaurants in town, cooking up well-priced seafood dishes – try the 'clams with basil leaf and chilli', or 'edible inflorescence of banana plant salad'. There's a simple but pleasant back patio.

Bismilla (☎ 0 1125 6440; dishes 60-120B) Opposite the 7-Eleven, this is a tidy restaurant that serves decent Thai Muslim dishes with interesting names such as 'Yum fish's spawn'.

Phang-Nga Satay (184 Th Phetkasem; dishes 20-60B) A tiny shack that specialises in Malay-style satay – try the shrimp version.

Getting There & Away

Phang-Nga's bus terminal is just off the main street on Soi Bamrung Rat. Buses to/from Bangkok to Phang-Nga include VIP (685B, 12 hours, one daily), 1st class (441B to 459B, 12 to 13 hours, two daily) and 2nd class (357B, 12 hours, three to four daily). Other destinations include the following:

Destination	Price (B)	Duration	Frequency (hr)
Ko Pha-Ngan (bus/boat)	400	6	2 daily
Ko Samui (bus/boat)	240	5	2 daily
Krabi	46-82	2	frequent
Hat Yai	175-220	6	2 daily
Ranong	90	5	4 daily
Satun	221	6	2 daily
Surat Thani	60-130	3-4	9 daily
Trang	139	3½	frequent
Phuket	35-65	1½-2½	frequent

Getting Around

Most of the town is easily accessible on foot. Motorcycle taxis around town cost 20B. Sayan Tours, located at the bus terminal, can assist with motorcycle rental (200B per day). *Săwngthăew*/motorcycle taxis to Tha Dan cost 20/40B.

AROUND PHANG-NGA
Sa Nang Manora Forest Park
สวนป่าสระนางมโนราห์

The fairyland setting at this beautiful and little-visited **park** (admission free) is nothing short of fantastic. Moss-encrusted roots and rocks, dense rainforest and rattan vines provide a delicious backdrop for swimming in pools beneath multilevel waterfalls. Primitive trails meander along (and at times through) the falls, climbing level after level and seem to go on forever – you could easily get a full day's hiking in without walking along the same path twice. Bring plenty of drinking water – although the shade and the falls moderate the temperature, the humidity in the park is quite high.

The park's name comes from a local folk belief that the mythical Princess Manora bathes in the pools when no one else is around. Facilities include some picnic tables, plus a small restaurant. To get here, catch a motorcycle taxi from Phang-Nga (50B). If you have your own wheels head north out of town on Hwy 4, go 3.2km past the Shell petrol station, then turn left and go down a curvy road another 4km.

Wat Tham Suwankhuha
วัดถ้ำสุวรรณคูหา

South of Phang-Nga about 10km is **Wat Tham Suwankhuha** (Heaven Grotto Temple; admission 10B), a cave wat full of Buddha images. The shrine consists of two main caverns: a larger one containing a 15m reclining Buddha and tiled with *laikhraam* and *benjarong* (two coloured patterns more common in pottery) and a smaller cavern displaying spirit flags and a rishi *(reusǐi)* statue. Royal seals of several kings, including Rama V, Rama VII and Rama IX – as well as those of lesser royalty – have been inscribed on one wall of the latter cave. Monkeys hang around the area, so lock your car doors or they'll break in to get at your snacks.

To get here without your own transport, hop on any *săwngthăew* running between Phang-Nga and Takua Thung (20B). The wat is down a side road.

On this same side road, about 6km beyond the cave wat, is **Raman Forest Park** (admission free), a pretty little park with a beautiful waterfall running through a small valley. Follow the gorgeous trail running alongside this cascade for about 3km, and refresh yourself with a dip in a couple of the pools along the way.

The park is relatively isolated, so it's difficult to get here without your own transport. Try hitching from the cave wat or you could rent a motorcycle in Phang-Nga; however, because you'd be riding along the busy highway, ensure you have decent riding skills.

Ao Phang-Nga Marine National Park
อุทยานแห่งชาติอ่าวพังงา

Established in 1981 and covering an area of 400 sq km, **Ao Phang-Nga Marine National Park** (admission 200B) is noted for its classic karst scenery, created by mainland fault movements that pushed massive limestone blocks into geometric patterns. As these blocks extend southward into Ao Phang-Nga, they form more than 40 islands with huge vertical cliffs. The bay itself is composed of large and small tidal channels that originally connected with the mainland fluvial system. The main tidal channels – Khlong Ko Phanyi, Khlong Phang-Nga, Khlong Bang Toi and Khlong Bo Saen – run through vast mangroves in a north–south direction and today are used by fisher folk and island inhabitants as aquatic highways. These mangroves are the largest remaining primary mangrove forest in Thailand. The Andaman Sea covers more than 80% of the area within the park boundaries.

The biggest tourist spot in the park is so-called James Bond Island, known to Thais as **Ko Phing Kan** (Leaning on Itself Island). Once used as a location setting for *The Man with the Golden Gun*, the island is now full of vendors hawking coral and shells that should have stayed in the sea, along with butterflies, scorpions and spiders encased in plastic.

The Thai name for the island refers to a flat limestone cliff that appears to have tumbled sideways to lean on a similar rock face, which is in the centre of the island. Off one side of the island, in a shallow bay, stands a tall slender limestone formation that looks like a big rock spike that has fallen from the sky.

There are a couple of caves you can walk through and a couple of small sand beaches, often littered with rubbish from the tourist boats. About the only positive development has been the addition of a concrete pier so that tourist boats don't have to moor directly on the island's beaches, but this still happens when the water level is high and the pier is crowded with other boats.

For information on Ko Yao, which is part of Ao Phang-Nga Marine National Park, see p672.

Two types of forest predominate in the park: limestone scrub forest and true evergreen forest. The marine limestone environment favours a long list of reptiles, including the Bengal monitor, flying lizard, banded sea snake, dogface water snake, shore pit viper and Malayan pit viper. Keep an eye out for the two-banded (or water) monitor *(Varanus salvator)*, which looks like a crocodile when seen swimming in the mangrove swamp and can measure up to 2.2m in length (only slightly smaller than the Komodo dragon, the largest lizard in the Varanidae family). Like its Komodo cousin, the water monitor (called *hîa* by the Thais, who generally fear or hate the lizard) is a carnivore that prefers to feed on carrion but occasionally preys on live animals.

Amphibians in the Ao Phang-Nga area include the marsh frog, common bush frog and crab-eating frog. Avian residents of note are the helmeted hornbill (the largest of Thailand's 12 hornbill species, with a body length of up to 127cm), the edible-nest swiftlet *(Aerodramus fuciphagus)*, osprey, white-bellied sea eagle and Pacific reef egret.

Over 200 species of mammals reside in the mangrove forests and on some of the larger islands, including the white-handed gibbon, serow, dusky langur and crab-eating macaque.

SLEEPING & EATING

There are **bungalows** (☎ 0 7641 2188; bungalows 500-900B;) close to the park headquarters. Small bungalows sleep two to four people, while larger ones sleep up to 15. Camping is permitted in certain areas within the park boundaries, but you should seek permission at the visitors centre before setting up. There's a small, clean restaurant in front of the visitors centre.

GETTING THERE & AROUND

From the centre of Phang-Nga drive south on Hwy 4 about 6km, then turn left onto Rte

---

4144 and go 2.6km to the park headquarters; 400m beyond here is the visitors centre. Without your own transport you'll need to take a *săwngthăew* to Tha Dan (20B).

Plenty of private boats, ready to zoom off on Ao Phang-Nga tours, await your bargaining skills (400B to 500B per person for a two- to three-hour tour).

Ko Panyi & Muslim Stilt Villages
เกาะปันหยี

This small island is famous for its Muslim fishing village built almost entirely on stilts and nestled against towering limestone cliffs. The village appears very commercialised during the day when hordes of tourists invade to eat lunch at the many overpriced seafood restaurants or trawl for tacky souvenirs sold at the multitude of stalls. Once the tourist boats depart, however, peace presides.

The 200 households here on Ko Panyi – home to perhaps a total of 2000 people – are said be descended from two seafaring Muslim families that arrived here from Java around 200 years ago. Ko Panyi's primary livelihood is still fishing, because a significant number of tourists only visit the island in the dry season. In addition to a big green mosque, a health clinic and a school, you'll find a market filled with small shops selling clothes, toiletries, medicines and all the other staples seen in Thailand's markets – except for any type of alcoholic beverage, which, along with dogs and pigs, is forbidden on the island. Houses mixed in with the shops vary from grubby little shacks to homes with fancy tile fronts and curtained windows. The people are generally friendly, especially if you can speak a little Thai. Village men often gather near the mosque to gossip as the sun sinks low on the western horizon.

If you fancy a look at similar, but less well-known, Muslim stilt villages in Ao Phang-Nga, take a boat to one of the villages in the huge mangrove forests at the northern end of the bay. These include **Ban Ling** (Monkey Village), **Ban Mai Phai** (Bamboo Village) and **Ban Sam Chong** (Three Channels Village).

SLEEPING & EATING

There are a few places to stay on the island. **Thawisuk Hotel** (r 100-150B) Near Ko Panyi's northern pier, it offers a very basic and tattered set of thin-walled rooms with shared toilet and scoop shower. Although the rooms aren't much, they do have windows that catch sea breezes. Overnight tours from Phang-Nga use these rooms; if they're full you should be able to find a room in a village home for about the same price or less. Ask at one of the restaurants.

Along with the more expensive seafood restaurants built out over the sea in front of the village (which are generally open for lunch only), there are some smaller cafés and restaurants along the interior alleys where locals eat. *Khâo yam* (southern-Thai rice salad) and *rotii* are available in the morning. The villagers raise grouper in floating cages, selling them to the island and mainland restaurants. A local culinary speciality is *khànŏm bâo lâng,* a savoury dish made with black sticky rice, shrimp, coconut, black pepper and chilli steamed in a banana leaf – it's a breakfast favourite.

GETTING THERE & AWAY

Most visitors arrive on tour boats, whether for brief day visits or overnight stays. You can also take a long-tail boat from Tha Dan (30B, 25 minutes). These leave when full, from dawn to dusk, arriving and departing from the village's northern pier (the southern pier is mostly reserved for tourist boats). Chartering your own long-tail boat costs 150B.

PHUKET PROVINCE

pop 82,800

Dubbed 'Pearl of the South' by the tourist industry, hedonistic Phuket (poo-*get*) is a whirl of colour and cosmopolitanism. Swanky and seductive, it's where the rich come to play. A province unto itself, the 810-sq-km island is Thailand's largest, wealthiest, most populous and most visited. It features jagged coastal terrain, rocky peninsulas, sandy bays, tropical vegetation and the ubiquitous limestone cliffs found throughout the region. It's a place to see and be seen, to dine on delectable seafood, scuba in azure blue seas, sip cocktails on pearly white beaches and retire at night to an ultra ritzy resort or dazzling yacht. This is Southeast Asia's St Tropez, Miami Beach, Rio di Janeiro. Many consider it the ultimate paradise, especially if you're looking for glitz and glamour. Beach activities dominate by day; at night the lights come up, the music is pumped and the well-dressed throngs flock to the buzzing beachside bars and hip clubs to dance the night away. If your budget doesn't allow for a stay at an über-resort, don't fear. While Phuket boasts Thailand's most exclusive lodging options, the island offers basic bungalows and cheap eats for budget-conscious travellers, and something in between for everyone else. While most tourists seeking entertainment migrate to the flashy beach towns of Patong, Karon and Kata, there are calmer spots, such as Nai Han and Kamala. There's even a relatively untouched northern coast with the beaches of Nai Yang, Nai Thon and Mai Khao.

Formerly called Ko Thalang, and before that Junk Ceylon (an English corruption of the Malay 'Tanjung Salang' or Cape Salang), Phuket has a culture all of its own. It combines Chinese and Portuguese influences (like neighbouring western Malaysia) with that of southern Thais and the *chao náam,* an indigenous ocean-going people. About 35% of the island's population are Thai Muslims, and there are about as many mosques as Buddhist wats here. The interior supports rice paddies, rubber, cashew-nut, pineapple, cacao and coconut plantations, along with the island's last vestiges of rainforest.

Capitalism rules on Phuket, and development has been influenced by the fact that the island is connected to the mainland by a bridge, and so it receives much more vehicular traffic than any other island in the country. Phuket's high per-capita wealth means there's plenty of money available for investment, and development reached a fevered pitch when a Club Méditerranée (Club Med) was established at Hat Kata, followed by the construction of the more lavish Phuket Yacht Club on Hat Nai Han and Le Meridien on Ao Karon Noi (Relax Bay). This marked an end to the decade-long cheap bungalow era, which started in the early 1970s when a 10B guesthouse was attached to a laundry on Hat Patong.

The era of going for quick money regardless of the cost to the environment has, sadly, not passed. Don't assume that just because an activity is on offer, it won't be harmful to the environment. The general growth of commercialism seen along the island's main roads detracts from its appeal – there seems to be a snake farm, bungee-jumping operation, billboard, half-built condo project or craft shop every half-kilometre on the island's southern half. But progress is slowly occurring, and today many beach resorts seem to be looking towards long-term, sustainable practices. The beaches and relatively unspoiled northern interior remain Phuket's main attractions, and the responsible traveller can only hope that this is what provincial authorities, as well as the business sector, will recognise and support.

The 2004 tsunami wreaked havoc all along the island's western and southwestern coast, and took nearly 900 lives. Beaches at Kamala and Bang Thao incurred the heaviest damage, followed by Patong. Karon and Kata were moderately affected, and Surin hardly at all. Most beaches were more or less back to normal at the time of writing, and no part of the island is closed.

Information

INTERNET RESOURCES
Phuket Island Access (www.phuket.com) offers a sophisticated compendium of many kinds of information, including accommodation and an accurate assessment of post-tsunami Phuket. Other good sites on Phuket include www.phuket.net, www.phukettourism.org and www.phuketmagazine.com.

MEDIA
The fortnightly English-language *Phuket Gazette* (20B) publishes lots of information on activities, events, dining and entertainment in Phuket town, as well as around the island. It can be accessed online at www.phuketgazette.net. The same publisher issues *Gazette Guide*, a 385-page listing of businesses and services on the island.

There are also the usual tourist freebies around, such as *South. Phuket* magazine is like an in-flight magazine that relies heavily on advertising but still manages to publish an interesting article about Phuket once in a while.

The small-format *Phuket Holiday Guide* (120B) has lots of solid information and insiders' tips on accommodation, transport and other practicalities on the island. It also contains the most unbiased sightseeing information, since it has less advertising.

MEDICAL SERVICES
Phuket International Hospital (Map p646; ☎ 0 7624 9400, emergency ☎ 0 7621 0935; Airport Bypass Rd) International doctors rate this as the best on the island; it's equipped with modern facilities, emergency rooms and outpatient-care clinics.
Bangkok Phuket Hospital (Map p646; ☎ 0 7625 4421; Th Yongyok Uthit) Reputedly the favourite with locals, it has similar facilities.

Dangers & Annoyances
Every year about 20 people drown in accidents off Phuket's beaches, especially along the western coast (Surin, Laem Singh and Kamala). During the May to October monsoon, waves on this coast sometimes make it too dangerous to swim. Red flags are posted on beaches to warn bathers of riptides and other dangerous conditions. If a red flag is flying at a beach, don't go into the water. The eastern coast is usually tamer at this time of year, but there isn't much in the way of beaches there. Hat Rawai, on the southeastern edge, of the island is usually a safe bet at any time of the year.

Renting a motorcycle can be a high-risk proposition. Thousands of people are killed

ANDAMAN COAST

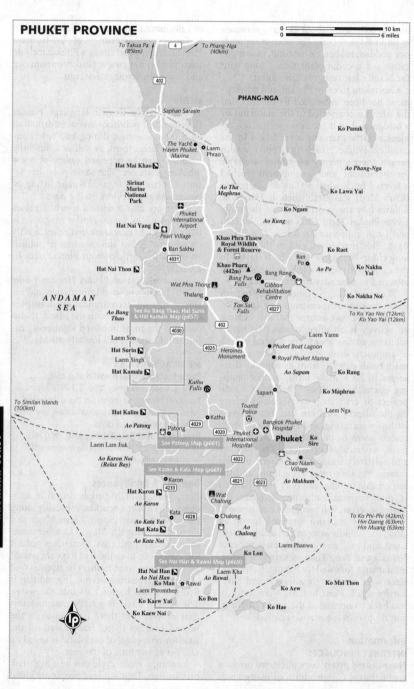

PHUKET PROVINCE

0   10 km
0   6 miles

To Takua Pa
(85km)

To Phang-Nga
(40km)

PHANG-NGA

Saphan Sarasin

Ko Panuk

The Yacht
Haven Phuket
Marina

Laem
Phrao

Ao Phang-Nga

Hat Mai Khao

Sirinat
Marine
National
Park

*Ao Tha
Maphrao*

Ko Lawa Yai

Hat Nai Yang

Phuket
International
Airport

Ao Kung

Ko Ngam

**ANDAMAN
SEA**

Pearl Village

Ban Sakhu

Khao Phra Thaew
Royal Wildlife
& Forest Reserve

Ko Raet

Hat Nai Thon

Khao Phara
(442m)

Ban
Po

*Ko Nakha
Yai*

Ao Po

Wat Phra Thong

Bang Pae
Falls

Bang Rong

Gibbon
Rehabilitation
Centre

Ko Nakha Noi

Thalang

*Ao Bang
Thao*

See Ao Bang Thao, Hat Surin
& Hat Kamala Map (p657)

Ton Sai
Falls

To Ko Yao Noi (12km);
Ko Yao Yai (12km)

Laem Son

Hat Surin

Laem Singh

Hat Kamala

Heroines
Monument

Laem Yamu

Phuket Boat Lagoon

Royal Phuket Marina

Ao Sapam

Ko Rang

Kathu
Falls

Ao Sapam

Sapam

Ko Maphrao

To Similan Islands
(100km)

Hat Kalim

Ao Patong

Patong

See Patong Map (p661)

Kathu

Tourist
Police

Bangkok Phuket
Hospital

Laem Nga

Laem Lam Jiak

Phuket
International
Hospital

Phuket

*Ko
Sire*

*Ao Karon Noi
(Relax Bay)*

See Karon & Kata Map (p665)

Chao Náam
Village

Karon

Ao Karon

Wat
Chalong

Ao Makham

Hat Karon

Kata

Hat Kata

Ao Kata Yai

Chalong

*Ao
Chalong*

To Ko Phi-Phi (42km);
Hin Daeng (63km);
Hin Muang (63km)

Ao Kata Noi

See Nai Han & Rawai Map (p669)

Ko Lon

Laem Phanwa

Hat Nai Han

Ao Nai Han

Ko Man

Laem
Kha

Ao Rawai

Rawai

Laem Phromthep

Ko Kaew Yai

Ko Bon

Ko Aew

Ko Mai Thon

Ko Kaew Noi

Ko Hae

or injured every year on Phuket's highways. Some are travellers who weren't familiar enough with riding motorcycles and navigating the island's roads, highways and traffic patterns. If you must rent a motorcycle, make sure you at least know the basics and wear a helmet.

Activities
DIVING & SNORKELLING
Although there are many, many places to dive around Thailand, Phuket is indisputably the primary centre for the Thai scuba-diving industry and one of the world's top 10 dive destinations. The island is ringed by good to excellent dive sites, including several small islands to the south – Ko Hae, Ko Raya (Noi and Yai), Hin Daeng and Hin Muang – and to the east, Ko Yao (Noi and Yai). Live-aboard excursions to the fantastic Surin and Similan Islands, or to the Burma Banks/Mergui Archipelago off the southern coast of Myanmar, are also possible from Phuket (though these destinations are far away).

Phuket has heaps of dive shops – at last count there were over 100, though most of them are the equivalent of a booking agency. The more serious ones often operate their own boat(s), so ask if you're concerned. And it doesn't hurt if an operator is a five-star PADI dive centre, though this isn't always the best criterion for choosing dive shops. Many of these operations are centred at Hat Patong or Ao Chalong, though the smaller beach towns certainly have their share. Some of the bigger (but not necessarily better) places have multiple branch offices all over Phuket.

Typically, one-day dive trips to nearby sites cost 1600B to 2500B, including two dives and equipment. Nondivers (and snorkellers) are permitted to join such dive trips for a significant discount. PADI open-water certification courses cost around 8000B to 11,000B and include four days of instruction and all equipment. Most places also rent all the basic equipment.

It's very wise to obtain your own private diving insurance before travelling. PADI or DAN is best – regular insurance often doesn't cover diving accidents or recompression costs, but you could check with your insurance representative. Your dive shop will also have some insurance, but

some shops do have better insurance than others; ask around.

There are three hyperbaric chambers on Phuket. **Wachira Hospital** (Map p650; ☎ 0 7621 1114) and **Phuket International Hospital** (Map p646; ☎ 0 7624 9400, emergency ☎ 0 7621 0935) are both just outside Phuket town; a private **hyperbaric chamber** (Map p661; ☎ 0 7634 2518; www .sssnetwork.com) is in Patong. The chamber at Phuket International Hospital is considered the best of the three. Dive-shop affiliation with the private hyperbaric chamber located in Patong mostly means that clients who need to use that chamber will be charged US$200 rather than US$800 per hour of treatment (five-hour minimum), though if a dive shop has the right kind of insurance it will cover much of this cost. Again, ask for specifics if you're concerned.

Snorkelling is best along Phuket's western coast, particularly at the rocky headlands between beaches. Mask, snorkel and fins can be rented for around 250B a day. As with scuba diving, you'll find better snorkelling, with greater visibility and variety of marine life, along the shores of smaller outlying islands like Ko Hae, Ko Yao and Ko Raya.

As elsewhere in the Andaman Sea, the best diving months are December to May when the weather is good and the sea is at its clearest (and boat trips are much safer).

There are numerous dive shops with a wide range of supplies.

Dive Supply (Map p661; ☎ 0 7634 2513; www.dive supply.com; 189 Th Rat Uthit, Patong) Lots of diving equipment and good service in several languages.

Phuket Wetsuits (☎ 0 7638 1818; Th Chao Fa west, Ao Chalong) Offers both custom and ready-made wet suits. This place is 2km north of Ao Chalong.

PADDLING
Several companies based in Phuket offer inflatable kayak tours of scenic Ao Phang-Nga. The kayaks are able to enter semi-submerged caves inaccessible by the long-tail boats.

John Gray's Sea Canoe (off Map p650; ☎ 0 7625 4505; fax 0 7622 6077; www.johngray-seacanoe.com; 124 Soi 1, Th Yaowarat), based in Phuket town, was the first and is still the most famous as well as the most environmentally attuned. A day paddle costs 2900B and includes meals, equipment and transfers; also available are all-inclusive, three- or six-day camping trips.

Another canoe company that has a good reputation is **Paddle Asia** (off Map p650; ☎ 0 7624 0893; www.paddleasia.com; 19/3 Th Rasdanusorn), also based in Phuket town. It caters to beginners and those who don't enjoy being surrounded by noisy tour groups. Groups are small (two to six people) and multiday tours are offered. Other canoeing companies include **Sea Cave Canoe** (off Map p650; ☎ 0 7621 0434; www.seacavecanoe.com; 2/2 Th Chumphon, Phuket) and **Andaman Sea Kayak** (☎ 0 7623 5353; www.andaman seakayak.com), which can be booked through many travel agencies on the island.

YACHTING
Phuket is one of Southeast Asia's main yachting destinations, and you'll find all manner of craft anchored along its shores – from 80-year-old wooden sloops that look like they can barely stay afloat, to the latest in hi-tech motor cruisers. Marina-style facilities with year-round anchorage are presently available at a few locations.

The new $25 million **Royal Phuket Marina** (Map p646; ☎ 0 7623 9755; www.royalphuketmarina.com) is located just south of Phuket Boat Lagoon. Luxury villas, townhouses and a hotel join 190 berths and a spa here.

Phuket Boat Lagoon (Map p646; ☎ 0 7623 9055; fax 0 7623 9056) is located at Ao Sapam, about 20km north of Phuket town on the eastern shore. It offers an enclosed marina with tidal channel access, serviced pontoon berths, 60- and 120-tonne travel lifts and a hard-stand area, plus a resort hotel, coffee shop, fuel, water, repairs and maintenance services.

Yacht Haven Phuket Marina (Map p646; ☎ 0 7620 6705; www.yacht-haven-phuket.com) is at Laem Phrao on the northern tip of the island. It boasts 120 berths, a scenic restaurant and also does yacht maintenance.

If you need sails, try **Rolly Tasker Sailmakers** (☎ 0 7628 0347; www.rollytasker.com; Ao Chalong); riggings, spars and hardware are also available.

Port clearance is rather complicated; both Phuket Boat Lagoon and the Yacht Haven will take care of the paperwork (for a fee of course) if it is notified of your arrival in advance.

If you want to seriously splash out you could charter your own yacht. During the high season the smallest boats start at about US$300 per day for a bareboat charter. If you want a personal chef that cooks up three meals a day, fine imported wines and a captain and crew to seek out beach gems and snorkelling spots, you're looking at a minimum of about US$500 per day, although the bigger, more glamorous boats cost hundreds of dollars more. Significant discounts are available June to October. For information on yacht charters – both bareboat and crewed – plus yacht sales and yacht deliveries, contact the following:

Faraway Sail & Dive Expeditions (☎ 0 7628 0701; www.far-away.net; 112/8 Muu 4; Th Taina, Hat Karon)

Siam Sailing (☎ 0 7620 0507; www.sailing-charter -thailand.com; Ao Yon Bay, near Panwa, Ko Phuket)

Sunsail Yacht Charters (Map p646; ☎ 0 7623 9057; sunthai@phuket.loxinfo.co.th; Phuket Boat Lagoon)

Yachtpro International (Map p646; ☎ 0 7634 8117-8; www.sailing-thailand.com; Yacht Haven Phuket Marina)

The Tourism Authority of Thailand (TAT) office in Phuket town also has an extensive list of yacht charters and brokers. For insurance purposes, it's a good idea to see if the boat you want to charter is registered in Thailand.

Courses
Pum Thai Cooking School (Map p661; ☎ 0 7634 6269, 0 1521 8904; info@pumthaifoodchain.com; 204/32 Tha Rat Uthit, Hat Patong) runs Thai restaurants in both Phuket and France, and at the Phuket branch you can learn *haute cuisine* the Thai way, starting at 900B for a 1½-hour, three-dish class, and up to 3750B for a six-hour, five-dish class.

Pat's Home (Map p650; ☎ 0 1538 8276, 0 7626 3366; thaicookingclass@hotmail.com), who worked as a chef at a Thai restaurant in California for six years, is offering Thai cooking courses at her home, located just outside Phuket town. Half-day courses for either lunch or dinner cost 1200B.

Tours
Siam Safari (☎ 0 7628 0116) and **Adventure Safaris** (☎ 0 7634 1988) combine 4WD tours of the island's interior with short elephant rides and hikes for around 2200B per day. Half-day trips are also available, although the difference in price is not that great.

PHUKET TOWN
ภูเก็ต

Centuries before Phuket began attracting sand-and-sea hedonists, it was an important centre for Arab, Indian, Malay, Chinese and

Portuguese traders who came to exchange goods for tin and rubber with the rest of the world. Francis Light, the British colonialist who made Penang the first of the British Straits Settlements, married a native of Phuket and tried unsuccessfully to pull this island into the colonial fold. Although this polyglot, multicultural heritage has all but disappeared from most of the island, a few vestiges can be seen and experienced in the province's *amphoe meuang* (provincial capital), Phuket.

In the older town centre you'll see some Sino-Portuguese architecture, characterised by ornate two-storey Chinese shophouses fronted by Romanesque arched porticoes that were a 19th-century tradition in Malaysia, Singapore, Macau and Hainan Island. For a time it seemed this wonderful old architecture was all being torn down and replaced with modern structures, but over the course of the last 10 years, a preservation ethic has taken hold.

Information
BOOKSHOPS
Books (Map p650; ☎ 07622 4362; Th Phuket; ☉ 10am-9.30pm) A great selection of English-language books and maps.
Southwind Books (Map p650; Th Phang-Nga; ☉ 9am-7.30pm Mon-Sat) Sells and trades used books.

EMERGENCY
Tourist Police (☎ 0 7635 5015; emergency ☎ 1155) Reach them via telephone.

INTERNET ACCESS
There are numerous places to surf the web scattered throughout town.
eBuzz Internet Café (Map p650; ☎ 0 1893 8066; Th Takua Pa; per hr 60B; ☉ 7am-8pm) Internet access, breakfasts and coffee drinks.

MAPS
Although it doesn't look like it would be, the advertisement-plastered *A-O-A Phuket Map* is probably the best if you're planning to drive around. It's more accurate than the other freebies, and it has all the route numbers marked. The free *Thaiways* map isn't very good for island navigation, although the inset maps for Patong and Karon-Kata are better than those in *A-O-A Phuket Map*. You can collect both maps at the TAT office and other places around the island.

Groovy Map's informative new *Phuket Day & Night Map 'n' Guide* (100B) features five maps (Phuket Town, Phuket Island, Patong, Kata and Karon, and a boat-route map) as well as short reviews of restaurants, pubs, nightclubs and beaches in Phuket and Krabi. Bus rtes and fares are also included.

MONEY
Numerous banks along Th Takua Pa, Th Phang-Nga and Th Phuket offer exchange services and have ATMs.

POST & TELEPHONE
DHL World Wide Express (Map p650; ☎ 0 7665 8500; 61/4 Th Thepkasatri)
Main post office (Map p650; Th Montri; ☉ 8.30am-4.30pm Mon-Fri, 9am-noon Sat, Sun & holidays)
Phuket Telecommunications Centre (Map p650; Th Phang-Nga; ☉ 8am-midnight) Dial home directly.

TOURIST OFFICES
TAT office (Map p650; ☎ 0 7621 2213; tathkt@phuket .ksc.co.th; 73-75 Th Phuket; ☉ 8.30am-4.30pm) Maps, brochures, a list of the standard *sǎwngthǎew* fares to the various beaches and a wealth of other information.

Sights
For historic **Sino-Portuguese architecture**, have a meander down Thalang, Dibuk, Yaowarat, Ranong, Phang-Nga, Rasada and Krabi streets. The most magnificent examples in town are the Standard Chartered Bank – Thailand's oldest foreign bank – on Th Phang-Nga and the THAI office on Th Ranong, but there are lots of other interesting buildings along these streets. The best residences are found along Th Dibuk and Th Thalang.

Phuket's main **day market** on Th Ranong is fun to wander through, and a few old **Chinese temples** can be found in this area. Most are standard issue, but one that's a little bit different is the **Shrine of the Serene Light** (Map p650; San Jao Sang Tham; admission free; ☉ 8.30am-noon & 1.30-5.30pm), tucked away at the end of a 50m alley off Th Phang-Nga. The restored shrine is said to be 100 to 200 years old.

Walk up **Khao Rang**, also called Phuket Hill, northwest of town, for a nice view of the city, jungle and sea.

Festivals & Events
The **Vegetarian Festival** (see p652) is Phuket's most important event and usually takes place during late September or October.

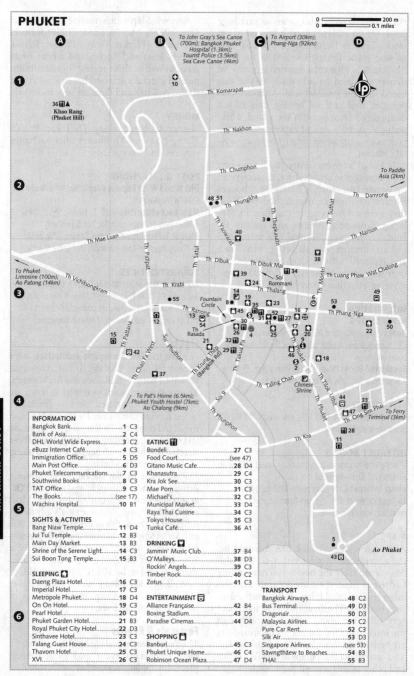

ANDAMAN COAST

Sleeping

BUDGET

On On Hotel (Map p650; ☎ 0 7621 1154; 19 Th Phang-Nga; r 120-360B; ✖ ▣) Despite old and musty rooms, this place contiues to be a popular choice. Exuding decrepit charm from its old Sino-Portuguese architecture, it's near the centre of town and services include a travel agency, motorcycle rentals and nearby restaurant. It was used briefly as a set for the movie *The Beach* (2000). The cheapest rooms only have fans and share baths.

Thavorn Hotel (Map p650; ☎ 0 7621 1333; 74 Th Rasada; r 230-550B; ✖) Its best feature is an impressive, museum-like lobby filled with antiques and historic photos of Phuket. The old wing is less expensive and has smaller rooms, while the new wing is flashier with bigger crash pads. Beds are firm.

Talang Guest House (Map p650; ☎ 0 7621 4225; 37 Th Thalang; r 280-420B; ✖) In a classic and tidy three-storey shophouse, this centrally lo-cated place offers decent, large rooms with one bed and fan as well as air-con rooms with three or four beds. Rates include toast and coffee or tea in the morning.

Phuket Youth Hostel (off Map p650; ☎ 0 7628 1325; www.phukethostel.com; 73/11 Th Chao Fa, Ao Chalong; dm 180, r 360-440, all rates incl breakfast; ✖) South of town, this is a large modern place with basic but good rooms, the cheapest of which only have fans. Package tours to nearby islands are offered as well as land tours. You'll find the hostel 7km south of Phuket town (1km past Wat Chalong and on the same side) and 1.5km before Ao Chalong.

MIDRANGE & TOP END

Phuket Garden Hotel (Map p650; ☎ 0 7621 6900; pghhkt@hotmail.com; Th Krung Thep; r incl breakfast 780-1400B; ✖) Glass elevators take you to pleas-ant, clean and tidy rooms. There's a grassy garden outside, and it's close to the centre of town. It's a better deal in the low season.

Daeng Plaza Hotel (Map p650; ☎ 0 7621 6428; www.phukettoday.com/daengplaza; 57 Th Phuket; r 590-1000B; ✖) This lone, white high-rise has large, car-peted rooms with fridge and TV. Beds are old and springy, but it's still a good deal.

Imperial Hotel (Map p650; ☎ 0 7621 2894; 51 Th Phuket; r 650-950B; ✖) A decent midrange hotel with friendly staff; rooms come with colour TV and hair-dryer.

Royal Phuket City Hotel (Map p650; ☎ 0 7623 3333; www.royalphuketcity.com; 154 Th Phang-Nga; r incl breakfast 3000-5000B; ✖ ✕) Welcome to the best hotel in town. Start at the grand marble lobby and work your way towards the 251 perfect rooms (some with sea views) or the 19th-floor Thai restaurant. The service is great, and facilities include pool, gym and spa. Discounts may be possible.

XVI (The Sixteen; Map p650; ☎ 0 7622 2812; thexvi@ksc.th.com; 16 Th Rasada; r 950-2000B; ✖) This is by far the most distinctive place to stay in Phuket town, simply because of the original, artistic, magazine-worthy interior design of the rooms. It's about as sleek and modern as you can get – rooms are Spartan (comfy mattresses on the floor, wooden tubs), but have a sanctuary-like ambience. The place also has a café with a short but sweet menu, and house music is quietly spun.

Metropole Phuket (Map p650; ☎ 0 7621 5050; www.metropolephuket.com; 1 Th Montri; r incl breakfast 2000-3500B; ✖ ✕) Offering 248 plush rooms, some with faraway sea views, facilities include two Chinese restaurants, a coffee shop, three bars, fitness centre and an airport shuttle bus.

Pearl Hotel (Map p650; ☎ 0 7621 1044; fax 0 7621 2911; 42 Th Montri; r 1550-1850B; ✖ ✕) The swim-ming pool at this place comes with waterfalls. There's also a rooftop restaurant, a fitness centre and a cocktail lounge. The rooms are modern, carpeted and recently renovated.

Sinthavee Hotel (Map p650; ☎ 0 7621 1186; fax 0 7621 1400; 85-91 Th Phang-Nga; r 960-1200B; ✖) Sinthavee has spacious rooms, although they've seen better days. The place is very central and facilities include a coffee shop and business centre. Even in the high season, it's worth asking about discounts here.

Eating

Mae Porn (Map p650; ☎ 0 7621 1389; cnr Th Phang-Nga & Soi Pradit; dishes 10-150B) In a casual open corner location, this popular eatery attracts both *faràng* and Thais. It has indoor and outdoor tables, and cooks up some mean curries, seafood and Thai specialties – all at very reasonable prices.

Kra Jok See (Map p650; ☎ 0 7621 7903; 26 Th Takua Pa; dishes 180-480B) Hidden away behind some greenery, it offers great old-time décor and an intimate ambience. The choice is lim-ited, but the selection is enough if you like meat and fish; try the delicious *hàw mòk tháleh* (steamed seafood curry). Start with dinner and then stay for dancing. Look for it next to Ban Boran Antiques.

VEGETARIAN FESTIVAL

Phuket's most important festival is the Vegetarian Festival, which takes place during the first nine days of the ninth lunar month of the Chinese calendar. This is usually in late September or early October.

Basically, the festival celebrates the beginning of the month of 'Taoist Lent', when devout Chinese abstain from eating all meat and meat products. In Phuket, the festival activities are centred on five Chinese temples, with the Jui Tui temple on Th Ranong the most important, followed by Bang Niaw and Sui Boon Tong temples. Events are also celebrated at temples in the nearby towns of Kathu (where the festival originated) and Ban Tha Reua.

The TAT office in Phuket prints a helpful schedule of events for the Vegetarian Festival each year. If you plan to attend the street processions, consider bringing earplugs for the firecrackers. The festival is also big in Trang, Krabi and other southern towns.

Besides abstention from meat, the Vegetarian Festival involves various processions, temple offerings and cultural performances, and culminates with incredible acts of self-mortification – walking on hot coals, climbing knife-blade ladders, piercing the skin with sharp objects and so on. Shopkeepers along Phuket's central streets set up altars in front of their shopfronts offering nine tiny cups of tea, incense, fruit, candles and flowers to the nine emperor gods invoked by the festival.

Those participating as mediums bring the nine deities to earth for the festival by entering into a trance state and piercing their cheeks with all manner of objects – sharpened tree branches (with leaves still attached!), spears, slide trombones, daggers; some even hack their tongues continuously with saw or axe blades. During the street processions these mediums stop at the shopfront altars, where they pick up the offered fruit and either add it to the objects piercing their cheeks or pass it on to bystanders as a blessing. They also drink one of the nine cups of tea and grab some flowers to stick in their waistbands. The shopkeepers and their families stand by with their hands together in a wâi gesture, out of respect for the mediums and the deities by whom they are temporarily possessed.

The entire atmosphere is one of religious frenzy, with deafening firecrackers, ritual dancing, bloody shirt fronts and so on. Oddly enough, there is no record of this kind of activity associated with Taoist Lent in China. Some historians assume that the Chinese here were somehow influenced by the Hindu festival of Thaipusam in nearby Malaysia, which features similar acts of self-mortification. The local Chinese claim, however, that the festival was started by a theatre troupe from China that stopped off in nearby Kathu around 150 years ago. The story goes that the troupe was struck seriously ill because the members had failed to propitiate the nine emperor gods of Taoism. The nine-day penance they performed included self-piercing, meditation and a strict vegetarian diet.

Khanasutra (Map p650; ☎ 0 1894 0794; 18-20 Th Takua Pa; dishes 80-400B) A wonderful new Indian restaurant, it serves yummy food in an impeccably designed space and offers professional service.

Raya Thai Cuisine (Map p650; ☎ 0 7621 8155; 48 Th Dibuk Mai; dishes 60-150B) A bit tourist-oriented, but nicely housed in a two-storey Sino-Portuguese mansion with tall ceilings, the food here is good; try the coconut soup with sweet basil and crab.

Gitano Music Cafe (Map p650; ☎ 0 7622 5797; 14 Th Ong Sim Phai; dishes 90-155B; ⏰ 4pm-midnight) With tasteful and very hip décor, Gitano grills up a few Latin main dishes, but since it's a bar scene you're more likely to order appe-

tisers like nachos, quesadillas and fajitas. Toss them down with margaritas (135B) or sangria (150B).

Bondeli (Map p650; cnr Th Rasada & Th Thepkasatri; dishes 65-170B) Despite the busy corner locale, Bondeli is a calm, air-con haven. Quick eats such as burgers, sandwiches and pizzas line the menu, and breakfast is also possible.

Tunka Café (Map p650; ☎ 0 7621 1500; Khao Rang; dishes 150-400B) On top of Khao Rang, this landmark restaurant serves Thai food in a beautiful garden setting. There are great views across town and beyond, and the food is quite good.

Michael's (Map p650; ☎ 0 7625 6562; 12 Th Takua Pa; dishes 30-120B) Thai and English food are on the menu at this bar-like spot. It's a bit of a *faràng* hangout.

Tokyo House (Map p650; ☎ 0 7625 6735; 34-38 Th Phang-Nga; dishes 220-570B) It feels like a real sushi joint inside – with light-coloured furniture and lots of aquariums and running-water sounds – and slices up sushi, sashimi, *nigiri* and *moriawase*. Be warned: prices are geared to homesick Japanese, and can be very high. Set meals and noodle dishes are better value and mostly authentic, though you could still end up with spaghetti noodles in your *udon* soup. Wine and sake are poured.

There's good food in Phuket town, and meals here cost a lot less than at the beach. Southeast of the centre is the **municipal market** (Map p650; Th Ong Sim Phai), with fresh fruit and vegetables. At night it features Chinese and Thai food. Close by is Robinson Ocean Plaza, which has a **food court** in modern surroundings. A couple of vegetarian restaurants on Th Ranong (east of the garish Jui Tui Chinese temple) serve good Chinese vegetarian food during daylight hours.

Drinking

The major hotels have discos and/or karaoke clubs.

Timber Rock (Map p650; ☎ 0 7621 1839; Th Yaowarat) A Western-style rock pub with rustic décor, it's one of the most popular live-music venues in town. Arrive after 9pm, although by 10pm it's usually standing room only.

Rockin Angels (Map p650; ☎ 0 9654 9654; www .rockinangels.com; 54 Th Yaowarat) South of Timber Rock, this small, well-run bar in an old Phuket shophouse is the place to go for nightly acoustic jams, plus great cocktails, espresso and light meals.

O'Malleys (Map p650; ☎ 0 7622 0170; 2/20-21 Th Montri) This chain Irish pub is good fun and has innovative promotions, such as 'Bring in a Party Photo and Get a Free Beer.' Mexican buffets are sometimes held.

Gitano Music Cafe (☎ 0 7622 5797; 14 Th Ong Sim Phai) It has an excellent collection of Latin CDs, but there is sometimes live music too. Toss-me-down drinks include margaritas, sangrias and *caipirinhas* (130B to 150B) and food is available (see opposite).

Jammin' Music Club (Map p650; ☎ 0 7622 0189; 78/28-29 Th Krung Thep) A bit of a trek from the centre of town, this club is popular for its live music (nightly at 10pm). International tunes in the rock, pop and jazz genres are played on two floors exuding an intimate atmosphere.

Zotus (Map p650; Th Rasada) There's not much room to dance at this small place, although Thai bands perform on the stage. It caters to the deaf, with very loud, heart-stopping bass beats.

Entertainment

Paradise Cinemas (Map p650; Th Tilok Uthit) Next to the Robinson Ocean Plaza, it shows popular English-language new releases as well as Thai movies (sometimes with English subtitles).

Alliance Française (Map p650; ☎ 0 7622 2988; 3 Soi 1, Th Phattana; ☿ 2.30-6pm Mon, 9.30am-12.30pm & 2.30-6pm Tue-Fri, 9am-noon Sat) Offers weekly showings of French films (subtitled in English). It also has a library and a TV with up-to-date news broadcasts.

Boxing stadium (Map p650; tickets incl one-way transport 500-1000B; ☿ 8pm Tue & Fri) Thai boxing can be seeen at this stadium on the southern edge of town near the pier; *túk-túk* cost 70B. Get your tickets at the On On Hotel (p651).

Shopping

There's some decent shopping in the provincial capital. The Th Ranong municipal **day market** (left), near the town centre, traces its history back to the days when pirates, Indians, Chinese, Malays and Europeans traded in Phuket. You might still find some fabrics from Southeast Asia, though it's mostly food now. Chinese gold shops are lined up opposite the Th Ranong market.

Banburi (Map p650; ☎ 0 7622 3966; ☿ 9am-7pm) If you're looking for bolts of silk, this is one of a few Indian-run tailor and fabric shops along Th Yaowarat.

Phuket Unique Home (Map p650; ☎ 0 7621 2093; 186 Th Phuket; ☿ 9am-6pm Mon-Sat) This place carries original designs in dishware, home-décor accessories and furniture, much of it a blend of old and new influences.

Getting There & Away

AIR

Phuket International Airport (Map p646; ☎ 0 7632 7230) is 30km north of Ranong's city centre. THAI operates about a dozen daily flights from Bangkok; it also has regular flights to/from Hat Yai and Narathiwat. THAI's international destinations from Phuket include Penang, Langkawi, Kuala Lumpur, Singapore, Hong Kong, Taipei and Tokyo.

Bangkok Airways flies between Phuket and Bangkok four times daily; it also flies between Phuket and Ko Samui two to three times daily. Phuket Air flies between Phuket and Bangkok as well.

International airlines that have offices in Phuket include the following:

Bangkok Airways (Map p650; ☎ 0 7622 5033; 58/2-3 Th Yaowarat)

Dragonair (Map p650; ☎ 0 7621 5734; Th Phang-Nga)

Malaysia Airlines (Map p650; ☎ 0 7621 6675; 1/8-9 Th Thungkha)

Silk Air (Map p650; ☎ 0 7621 3891; 183/103 Th Phang-Nga)

Singapore Airlines (Map p650; ☎ 0 7621 3891; 183/103 Th Phang-Nga)

THAI (Map p650; ☎ 0 7625 8236; 78/1 Th Ranong)

BUS

Phuket town's bus terminal is just east of the centre within walking distance of many hotels. There are services to Bangkok and regional destinations.

Destination	Fare (B)	Duration (hr)
Bangkok		
ordinary	278	15
air-con	389-500	13-14
VIP	755	13
Chumphon		
air-con	196-250	6½-8
Hat Yai		
ordinary	150	8
air-con	210-420	6-8
Ko Samui (bus/boat)		
air-con	300-350	8
Krabi		
ordinary	65	4
air-con	91-117	3½
Nakhon Si Thammarat		
ordinary	125	8
air-con	175-200	7
Phang-Nga		
ordinary	35	2½
Ranong		
ordinary	103	6
air-con	185	5
Surat Thani		
ordinary	104	6
air-con	160-170	5
Takua Pa		
ordinary	54	3
Trang		
ordinary	105	6
air-con	147-190	5

FERRY

During the high season several boats ply the waters between Ton Sai Bay on Ko Phi-Phi and ports on Phuket. Fares range from 300B to 500B and take about 1½ hours. It's also possible to reach Phuket from Ko Lanta, but you'll have to stop in Ko Phi-Phi along the way. There's a ferry terminal about 3km east of Patong. Nearly any hotel, bungalow or tourist office can arrange transport.

MINIVAN

Some travel agencies sell tickets for air-con minivans to Ko Samui; the fare includes ferry transport. Air-con minivan services to Surat, Krabi and Ranong are also available. Departure locations vary, but the TAT office knows where they are. Expect to pay more than an ordinary bus and less than an air-con bus for the same destination.

Getting Around
TO/FROM THE AIRPORT

Minivans from the airport to Phuket town cost 80B per person; to Patong, Karon and Kata they're 120B per person. If you're going to the airport, **Phuket Limousine** (off Map p650; ☎ 0 7624 8596) operates hourly shuttles from 6.30am to 7.30pm for 100B. They're about 100m west of the town centre.

Taxis between the airport and Phuket town cost 400B, between the airport and the beaches the fare is 500B to 600B.

CAR & MOTORCYCLE

There are cheap car rental agencies on Th Rasada near Pure Car Rent. Suzuki jeeps go for about 1000B per day (including insurance), though in the low season the rates can go down to 700B. And if you rent for a week or more, you should get a discount.

The rates are always better at local places than at better-known internationals, though you may be able to get deals with the familiar companies if you reserve ahead.

Avis Rent-A-Car (http://avisthailand.com/home) Airport (Map p646; ☎ 0 7635 1243); Patong (general number ☎ 0 7634 5540) Charges a premium (around 1500B a day) but has outlets at some bigger resort hotels.

Pure Car Rent (Map p650; ☎ 0 7621 1002; 75 Th Rasada) A good choice in the centre of town.

Via Rent-A-Car (Map p661; ☎ 0 7638 5718; www .via-phuket.com; 189/6 Th Rat Uthit, Patong) Offers similar rates to Pure and can deliver to anywhere on the island.

Motorcycle taxis around town are 20B. You can rent motorcycles on Th Rasada, near Pure Car Rent, or from various places at the beaches. Costs are anywhere from 150B to 300B per day and can vary depending on the season. Bigger bikes (over 125cc) can be rented at a couple of shops at Patong and Karon.

SĂWNGTHĂEW & TÚK-TÚK

Săwngthăew run regularly from Th Ranong (at the day market) to the various Phuket beaches for 20B to 25B per person – see the respective destinations for details. These run from around 7am to 5pm; outside these times you have to charter a *túk-túk* to the beaches. These will set you back 200B to Patong, 230B to Karon and Kata, and 300B for Nai Han and Kamala. You'll probably have to bargain for a good price.

Beware of tales about the tourist office being 5km away, or that the only way to reach the beaches is by taxi, or even that you'll need a taxi to get from the bus terminal to the town centre (the bus terminal is more or less *in* the town centre).

For a ride around town, *túk-túk* should charge 20B.

AROUND PHUKET PROVINCE

This section goes anticlockwise around the island, beginning in the northeast, well north of the city of Phuket, then skipping to the west coast and following the shoreline.

Khao Phra Thaew Royal Wildlife & Forest Reserve

อุทยานสัตว์ป่าเขาพระแทว

This mountain range, in the northern interior of the island, protects 23 sq km of rainforest (evergreen monsoon forest). There are nice jungle hikes in this reserve and a couple of waterfalls, **Ton Sai** and **Bang Pae**. The falls are best seen in the rainy season between June and November; in the dry months they slow to a trickle. Because of its royal status, the reserve is better protected than the average Thai national park.

A German botanist, Dr Darr, discovered a rare and unique species of palm in Khao Phra Thaew about 50 years ago. Called the white-backed palm or langkow palm, the fan-shaped plant stands 3m to 5m tall and is found only here and in Khao Sok National Park. The highest point in Khao Phra

Thaew Royal Wildlife & Forest Reserve is 442m **Khao Phara**.

Tiger, Malayan sun bear, rhino and elephant once roamed the forest here, but nowadays resident mammals are limited to humans, gibbon, monkey, slow loris, langur, civet, flying fox, squirrel, mousedeer and other smaller animals. Watch out for cobra and wild pig.

Near Nam Tok Bang Pae (Bang Pae Falls) is the **Phuket Gibbon Rehabilitation Centre** (☎ 0 7626 0492; www.warthai.org/projects; admission by donation; ☺ 9am-4pm). Financed by donations and run by volunteers, the centre cares for gibbons that have been kept in captivity and reintroduces them to the wild. Visitors who wish to help may 'adopt' a gibbon for 1500B, which will pay for one animal's care for a year. The programme includes keeping you updated on your adopted gibbon's progress throughout the year of adoption. Check the website for more information.

Hat Nai Thon, Hat Nai Yang & Hat Mai Khao

หาดในทอน/หาดในยาง/หาดไม้ขาว

Near the northwestern tip of Phuket is Hat Mai Khao, Phuket's longest beach. Sea turtles lay their eggs on the beach here between November and February each year. A visitors centre with toilets, showers and picnic tables can be found at Mai Khao, from where there are some short trails through the casuarinas to a steep beach. Take care when swimming here, as there's a strong year-round undertow. Except on weekends and holidays you'll have this place almost entirely to yourself; even during peak periods, peace and solitude are usually only a few steps away, as there's so much space here.

About 5km to the south, improved roads to Hat Nai Thon have brought only a small amount of development to this broad expanse of pristine sand backed by casuarina and pandanus trees. Down on the beach, umbrellas and sling chairs are available from vendors. Swimming is quite good here except at the height of the monsoon, and there is some coral near the headlands at either end of the bay. The submerged remains of a wrecked 50m-long tin dredger lie further off the coast near tiny Ko Waew at a depth of 16m. Naithon Beach Resort (p656) can arrange dive trips in the vicinity.

Hat Nai Yang is renowned for snorkelling and it is popular with Thai tourists. About 1km off Nai Yang is a large reef at a depth of 10m to 20m. Snorkelling and scuba equipment can be hired at Pearl Village Resort.

SLEEPING & EATING
Hat Nai Thon
Naithon Beach Resort (☎ 0 7620 5379; fax 0 7620 5381; 22/2 Th Surin; cottages 1000-1500B; ✷) On the opposite side of the access road from the beach, Naithon has large, tastefully designed wooden cottages. A small restaurant serves sandwiches and Thai food. The resort closes down in the rainy season.

Tien Seng Guest House (Th Surin; r 400-800B; ✷) This place has rooms in a modern shophouse building, just south of the Naithon Beach Resort. There is also a restaurant that serves Thai and Chinese dishes.

Trisara (☎ 0 7361 0100; www.trisara.com; villas from US$525; ✷ ✷) Lounge in the luxury of a huge villa – with private pool and steam room – at the latest and most exclusive of the island's resorts.

Hat Nai Yang & Hat Mai Khao
Camping is allowed on both Nai Yang and Mai Khao beaches without any permit.

Sirinat National Park (☎ 0 7632 8662; tents 50-100B; bungalows with 6/12 beds 400/800B) Has two-person tents and large bungalows. Check in at the building opposite the visitors centre. Two-person tents can be rented for the night. There is also an entrance fee of 200/100B per adult/child under 14.

Phuket Camp Ground (tents per person 100B) This privately operated place rents tents close to the beach, each with rice mats, pillows, blankets and a torch (flashlight). A light mangrove thicket separates the camp ground from the beach, and the proprietors don't mind if you move their tents onto the beach crest. A small outdoor restaurant/bar provides sustenance. Other amenities include a shower and toilet, hammocks, sling chairs and beach umbrellas, and a campfire ring.

Nai Yang Beach Resort (☎ 0 7632 8300; nai_yang@phuket.ksc.co.th; 65/23-24 Nai Yang Beach Rd; bungalows 650-1800B; ✷) This resort is clean, quiet and near the beach and does a great barbecue at night.

Garden Cottage (☎ /fax 0 7632 7293; cottages 600-1400B; ✷) Tidy cottages on Rte 4026, back from the southern end of Hat Nai Yang

and about 1.5km from the airport, but still within a five-minute walk of the beach.

Crown Nai Yang Suite Hotel (☎ 0 7632 7420; crown@phuket.com; 117 Th Hat Nai Yang; r 1800-7400B; ✷ ▯ ✷) This multistorey hotel rents modern boxes (some without windows). Airline crews stopping over between flights in and out of Phuket often use this hotel. The walk-in rates are ludicrous for what you get.

Along the dirt road at the very southern end of the beach is a seemingly endless strip of seafood restaurants and, oddly enough, tailor shops. There is also a small minimart near the entrance to Pearl Village Resort.

GETTING THERE & AWAY
Săwngthăew from Phuket cost 50B per person and run between 7am and 5pm only. A charter costs 300B; if you're coming straight from the airport it would be less trouble, less expensive and much quicker to hire a taxi for 200B. A *săwngthăew* from Phuket to Nai Yang costs 50B, while a *túk-túk* charter is 250B to 300B. There is no regular *săwngthăew* stop for Mai Khao but a *túk-túk* charter costs between 250B and 300B.

Ao Bang Thao
อ่าวบางเทา

Home to some of the islands megaresorts (serious pampering at serious prices), Ao Bang Thao laps against a lovely 8km-long crescent of white-sand beach on Phuket's western coast. A steady breeze makes the bay ideal for windsurfing; since 1992 the annual Siam World Cup windsurfing championships have been held here. A system of lagoons inland from the beach has been incorporated into Laguna Phuket, a complex of five upmarket resorts dominating the central portion of the beach. Even if you can't afford to stay, the beach makes a nice day trip.

The beach at Ao Bang Thao took a serious beating during the tsunami. A couple of resorts on the beach were so damaged they were forced to close temporarily, but most homes, resorts and businesses were spared by the fortunate fact that most development at Bang Thao was either inland or on hillsides overlooking the bay.

ACTIVITIES
About 800m west of Hwy 4030, **Hideaway Day Spa** (Map p657; ☎ 0 7627 1549; ◔ 11am-9pm)

ANDAMAN COAST

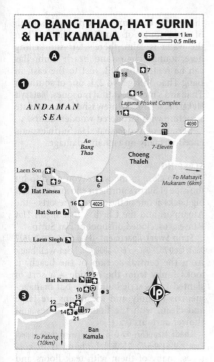

AO BANG THAO, HAT SURIN & HAT KAMALA

offers traditional Thai massage, sauna, mud body wraps and other treatments beginning at 1500B for a 90-minute massage. The facility is nicely laid out in a tranquil wooded setting next to one of Bang Thao's lagoons. Reservations any treatments are recommended.

SLEEPING

Beachside accommodation on Bang Thao tends to be quite swanky, and is priced accordingly. Some of the more expensive places hike rates during the holidays, and you're often obliged to pay for 'gala dinners' at Christmas and New Year's Eve.

Bangtao Lagoon Bungalows (Map p657; ☎ 0 7632 4260; www.phuket-bangtaolagoon.com; bungalows 400-2250B; ✖ ▢ ♨) This place has a swimming pool, great beach frontage and a restaurant serving Thai and European dishes. Although Bangtao Lagoon had to close for repairs immediately after the tsunami, it is now open again. A mere four of the 70 clean, tile-floored units are available at the cheapest fan-only rate. The rest have air-con and come in a variety of grades. However, most

are on the small side. If you want to stay on this beach, and need one of the cheapest rooms, try calling ahead to reserve.

One other less expensive place at Bang Thao, Bangtao Beach Cottage, was forced to close due to heavy damage, and there is no word whether it will re-open.

Banyan Tree Phuket (Map p657; ☎ 0 7632 4374; www.banyantree.com/phuket; villas US$570-1425; ✖ ▢ ♨) Catering to those with money to burn, it has 120 villas, all with private landscaped gardens, open-air sunken bathtubs and various combinations of Jacuzzi and/or private swimming pool, sauna, steam room etc. You'll also find a golf course, full-service spa, three tennis courts, a lap pool and a free-form swimming pool. The Banyan Tree specialises in spiritual and physical spa treatments, including massage, seaweed packs, yoga and meditation, but in addition to food for the soul, there are seven restaurants. In 2004 it was voted one of the best places to stay in the world by readers of *Condé Nast Traveler*.

Dusit Laguna Resort (Map p657; ☎ 0 7632 4324, Bangkok ☎ 0 2636 3333; http://phuket.dusit.com; r US$150-280, ste US$250-400; ✖ ▢ ♨) This luxurious place offers 226 guest rooms and suites, a spa, fitness centre, tennis courts and free use of windsurfers and sailboats.

The five resorts in the **Laguna Phuket complex** (Map p657; www.lagunaphuket.com) have a total of more than 1100 rooms and 30 restaurants (the gargantuan Sheraton Grande alone has 325 rooms and eight restaurants). About 50 of the rooms were damaged by the tsunami, but all have since been repaired. The complex boasts an 18-hole golf course and guests at any one of the resorts can use the dining and recreation facilities at all of them. Frequent shuttle buses make the rounds of all the hotels, as do pontoon boats (via the linked lagoons). Two of the five are described further here.

EATING

Despite what local hoteliers would have you believe, there is some good food to be had outside the confines of Bang Thao's luxury hotels.

Lotus Restaurant (Map p657; dishes 50-100B) An open-walled eatery 500m west of the entrance to Banyan Tree Phuket, it's the first in a row of beachside Thai and seafood restaurants that stretches to the south. Clean, breezy and friendly, it has an amazing assortment of live crab, lobster, shrimp, fish and other visual and culinary delights in very well-tended tanks. Check out the crazy mantis shrimp!

Tatonka (Map p657; ☎ 0 7632 4349; dishes 250-300B; ☺ 6pm-late Thu-Tue) This restaurant, 100m west of Hwy 4030 on the road leading to the Laguna Phuket complex, features 'globetrotter cuisine', which owner-chef Harold Schwarz developed by taking fresh local products and combining them with cooking and presentation techniques learned in Europe, Colorado and Hawaii. The eclectic, tapas-style selection includes creative vegetarian and seafood dishes, and such delights as Peking duck pizza (220B), as well as a tasting menu (750B per person, minimum two people) that lets you try a little of everything. Call ahead in high season. Tatonka arranges free transportation for guests of the resort complex.

GETTING THERE & AWAY

A *săwngthăew* between Phuket's Th Ranong and Bang Thao costs 25B per person. In Bang Thao *săwngthăew* can be caught along Rtes 4030 and 4025. *Túk-túk* charters are 200B.

Hat Surin
หาดสุรินทร์

Popular with local Thais, who come for nibbles at the dozen or so seafood stands above the beach, Hat Surin is a pleasant stretch of sand south of Ao Bang Thao. When the water is calm, there's fair snorkelling here; lounge chairs and beach umbrellas can be rented for 50B. Just to the east, in Bang Thao Village No 2, is one of southern Thailand's most beautiful mosques, **Matsayit Mukaram**, a large, whitewashed, immaculate structure with lacquered wooden doors.

Because of its deep bay, Hat Surin experienced virtually no tsunami damage.

SLEEPING

To sleep close to the water, you need to hit the cape at Surin's northern end and shell out big bucks at one of the exclusive resorts – the Amanpuri and the Chedi – that sit on Hat Pansea, a secluded offshoot of Hat Surin.

Surin Sweet Apartment (Map p657; ☎ 0 7627 0863; fax 0 7627 0865; r 600-800B; 🔀) Set well back from the central section of the beach, it looks funky from the outside – a sort of slanted 1970s style building – but management is friendly and the rooms are large and clean, with tile floors, balconies and shower curtains (rare!).

Chedi (Map p657; ☎ 0 7632 4017; www.chedi-phuket .com; r US$190-675; 🔀 🔀) Lodging is in cottages, many of them with teak floors and private verandas. There's a relaxing beachside pool, tennis courts and many water sports on offer. Rates skyrocket during the December to January holidays.

Amanpuri Resort (Map p657; ☎ 0 7632 4333; www .amanresorts.com; villas US$700-8200; 🔀 🖵 🔀) Amanpuri plays host to Thailand's celebrity traffic, with each guest getting a 133-sq-metre pavilion or private two- to six-bedroom villa home complete with a live-in maid and cook. In fact the staff-to-guest ratio is 3½ to one! The architect who did the former Shah of Iran's Winter Palace designed this resort, which offers six tennis courts, a spa, Thai and Italian restaurants, and about 20 watercraft for sailing, diving and overnight charters.

GETTING THERE & AWAY

A regular *săwngthăew* between Phuket's Th Ranong and Hat Surin costs 25B per person and *túk-túk* charter is 250B to 300B.

Hat Kamala
หาดกมลา

Hat Kamala is a lovely stretch of sand and sea about 4km south of Surin and 25km from Phuket. The northern end, shaded by casuarina trees, is the nicest area.

The 2004 tsunami destroyed a small restaurant, several homes and guesthouses near the beach, a kindergarten school at the southern end, and most of the local long-tail fishing fleet. Although Kamala is steadily recovering, when we last visited you could still see plenty of debris along the beach and in the narrow streets of the village.

Most of the villagers here are Muslim, and visitors should dress modestly when walking around in respect for local customs. Topless or nude beach bathing would be extremely offensive to the locals.

Just north of Hat Kamala is a beautiful little rock-dominated beach called **Laem Singh**. You could camp here and eat at the rustic seafood places at the northern end of Singh, which quickly re-established themselves post-tsunami. If you're renting a motorbike, this beach makes a nice little trip down Rte 4025 and then over dirt roads from Surin to Kamala.

ACTIVITIES

The US$60 million 'cultural theme park', **Phuket Fantasea** (Map p657; ☎ 0 7638 5000; www.phuket-fantasea.com; admission with/without dinner 1500/1000B; ☽ 5.30-11.30pm Wed-Mon) is located just north of Hat Kamala. Despite the billing, there aren't any rides but there is a truly magical show that manages to capture the colour and pageantry of traditional Thai dance and costumes and combine them with state-of-the-art light and sound techniques that rival anything found in Las Vegas (think 30 elephants). All of this takes place on a stage dominated by a full-scale replica of a Khmer temple reminiscent of Angkor Wat. Kids especially would be captivated by the spectacle. There is also quite a good and varied collection of souvenir shops in the park offering Thai-made handicrafts. The Thai buffet dinner is surprisingly good. Tickets can be booked through most hotels and tour agencies. Phuket Fantasea received no significant damage from the tsunami.

SLEEPING

Benjamin Resort (Map p657; ☎ 0 7638 5739; www.phuketdir.com/benjaminresort; r 350-800B; ☒) All the rooms have TV, minibar and a terrace with table and chairs. The more expensive rooms have sea views, some of which are glorious.

The hotel is on the beach and very good value. The area immediately around the hotel was damaged by the tsunami, but is recuperating quite nicely.

Kamala Dreams (Map p657; ☎ 0 7629 1131; r 1200-1800B; ☒ ☒) Right on the beach, all 17 rooms face the bay and offer excellent views from their balconies. They are simply but tastefully decorated and aligned perfectly to catch the sea breeze. There's a restaurant as well, which is open in the high season only. Some rooms damaged by the tsunami, along with the pool, are closed for repairs.

Baan Chaba (Map p657; ☎ 0 7627 9158; r 800-1200B; ☒) Just a few minutes' walk from the beach, this small and intimate hotel features eight beautiful, comfortable, clean and well-furnished rooms with hot water and TV. Tsunami damage forced it to close for reconstruction until October 2005.

Chez Sabina Guest House (Map p657; ☎ 0 7627 9544; r 450-800B; ☒) The pleasant apartment-style accommodation – from one-room studios to two-storey affairs with kitchen and dining area – lures many repeat guests.

Pa Pa Crab Guesthouse (Map p657; ☎ /fax 0 7638 5315; r from 450; ☒) It has 10 well-decorated and comfortable rooms featuring a lovely colour scheme, but it will close in low season if business is slow. Like Baan Chaba, Pa Pa Crab endured heavy damage and had to be rebuilt after the tsunami.

Print Kamala Resort (Map p657; ☎ 0 7638 5396; printkamalaresort@hotmail.com; bungalows 1150-2550B; ☒ ☒) A moderately upmarket resort across the street from the beach, the 40 bungalows have private balconies, minibar and TV. It features tennis courts, a pool and a fitness centre. Tsunami damage forced the resort to close until October 2005.

Kamala Beach Estate (Map p657; ☎ 0 7627 9756; www.kamalabeachestate.com; apartments US$95-235, villas US$255-350) Overlooking the beach at the southern end of the bay, this place boasts fully equipped, high-security modern apartments, suites and villas – some with a kitchen and fantastic sea views. The manicured grounds feature an outdoor Jacuzzi, a lovely pool and an onsite restaurant. Each unit is individually owned and thus uniquely different; 20% are solely owner-occupied. The villas are especially beautifully laid out, with huge flagstone terraces and loads of comfortable and bright spaces.

ANDAMAN COAST

EATING

Several local seafood restaurants can be found in the lanes leading away from the beach.

Kamala Seafood (Map p657; dishes 50-200B; ☼ low season) Near the centre of the beach, this family-run Thai seafood restaurant has recovered from tsunami damage to catering to a mostly *faràng* crowd again.

Balcony Bar & Restaurant (Map p657; ☎ 0 7627 9756, ext 132; dishes 80-250B) At Kamala Beach Estate, the Balcony is the most upmarket place to eat; it offers good views of the bay, reliable Thai and Western food and a decent wine list.

GETTING THERE & AROUND

A regular *sǎwngthǎew* between Kamala and Patong costs 20B per person, while a charter costs 250B. You can rent vehicles at **Via Rent-A-Car** (Map p657; ☎ 0 7638 5718; www.via-phuket.com), next to the Pa Pa Crab Guesthouse.

Patong

ป่าตอง

The epicentre of the tourist earthquake that rattles Phuket from December to March each year, Patong's beautiful curved beach sparks with frenetic electricity. The steamy streets seethe with souvenir shops, girlie bars, pricey seafood restaurants, dive shops, travel agencies, hotels and everything in between. Scantily clad golden brown travellers pay homage to the neon gods, dancing the night away to booming sound systems in sweaty, pulsating clubs, or sipping Singhas under the stars at sandy beachside bars. Demurely dressed diners down giant prawns and Italian wines at decadent and romantic restaurants where the views are as expensive, and worthwhile, as the food.

The island's most popular beach, over the last decade, it seems that Hat Patong has been trying to become the next Pattaya. The streets are filled with flashy florescent signs lighting the night sky with a lurid red glow. But it's not nearly as creepy, and by day it's fine even for kids. The sort of people drawn to this teeming, neon-lit atmosphere will adore Patong, while the more peace-loving souls (you know who you are) might want to stay far, far away.

Businesses along the main beachfront suffered plenty of tsunami damage, particularly towards the northern end. Although most of it has been spruced up, some reconstruction continues.

INFORMATION

To buy English-language maps, guidebooks, magazines and newspapers head to **Bookazine** (☎ 0 7634 5833; 18 Th Bangla; ☼ 9.30am-11.30pm). Money-exchange booths and Internet cafés are commonplace. There are two post offices in Patong; one is towards the northern end of Th Rat Uthit, the other is near the centre of Th Thawiwong. Patong has an **immigration office** (☎ 0 7634 0477; Th Kalim Beach; ☼ 10am-noon & 1-3pm Mon-Fri) that does visa extensions. The **tourist police** (☎ 0 7634 0244) are at the beach road's intersection with Th Bangla.

ACTIVITIES

Patong is a diving centre on the island. For a list of established dive shops, see p647. Yachts, sailboats and catamarans sometimes can be chartered here, with or without crew. To find out more on this, see p648.

Located in the foothills of eastern Patong, the **Hideaway** (☎ 0 7634 0591; www.phuket-hideaway .com; 157 Th Na Nai; ☼ 10am-8pm) is an excellent sauna and massage centre. A two-hour Thai herbal massage/sauna package costs 950B. A massage or sauna alone is 500B per hour. Other treatments are available, including facials and aromatherapy. The last massage is given at 6pm, and advance reservations are recommended. Cash is the only method of payment accepted.

SLEEPING

Although this began as Phuket's most expensive beach, prices have stabilised as the local accommodation market has become saturated with tonnes of places to stay. At the same time most luxury resort development is taking place elsewhere.

The tsunami either damaged or destroyed the very few beachfront operations along Patong. Meanwhile, the bulk of the hotels and guesthouses built further back from the beach incurred little or no damage and have been operating normally.

Budget

On the beach there is nothing in the budget range, but on and off Th Rat Uthit, especially in the Paradise Complex and along Soi Saen Sabai, there are several nondescript guesthouses with rooms for 300B to 500B.

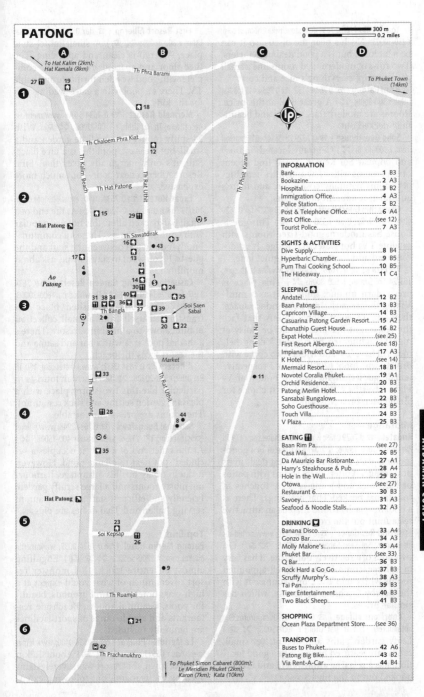

PATONG

To Hat Kalim (2km);
Hat Kamala (8km)

Th Phra Barami

To Phuket Town
(14km)

Th Chaloem Phra Kiat

Th Kalim Beach

Th Hat Patong

Th Rat Uthit

Th Phisit Karani

Hat Patong

Ao
Patong

Th Sawatdirak

Soi Saen
Sabai

Th Bangla

Th Na Nai

Market

Th Rat Uthit

Th Thawiwong

Hat Patong

Soi Kepsap

Th Ruamjai

Th Prachanukhro

To Phuket Simon Cabaret (800m);
Le Meridien Phuket (2km);
Karon (7km); Kata (10km)

ANDAMAN COAST

INFORMATION	
Bank	**1** B3
Bookazine	**2** A3
Hospital	**3** B2
Immigration Office	**4** A3
Police Station	**5** B2
Post & Telephone Office	**6** A4
Post Office	(see 12)
Tourist Police	**7** A3

SIGHTS & ACTIVITIES	
Dive Supply	**8** B4
Hyperbaric Chamber	**9** B5
Pum Thai Cooking School	**10** B5
The Hideaway	**11** C4

SLEEPING	
Andatel	**12** B2
Baan Patong	**13** B3
Capricorn Village	**14** B3
Casuarina Patong Garden Resort	**15** A2
Chanathip Guest House	**16** B2
Expat Hotel	(see 25)
First Resort Albergo	(see 18)
Impiana Phuket Cabana	**17** A3
K Hotel	(see 14)
Mermaid Resort	**18** B1
Novotel Coralia Phuket	**19** A1
Orchid Residence	**20** B3
Patong Merlin Hotel	**21** B6
Sansabai Bungalows	**22** B3
Soho Guesthouse	**23** B5
Touch Villa	**24** B3
V Plaza	**25** B3

EATING	
Baan Rim Pa	(see 27)
Casa Mia	**26** B5
Da Maurizio Bar Ristorante	**27** A1
Harry's Steakhouse & Pub	**28** A4
Hole in the Wall	**29** B2
Otowa	(see 27)
Restaurant 6	**30** B3
Savoey	**31** A3
Seafood & Noodle Stalls	**32** A3

DRINKING	
Banana Disco	**33** A4
Gonzo Bar	**34** A3
Molly Malone's	**35** A4
Phuket Bar	(see 33)
Q Bar	**36** B3
Rock Hard a Go Go	**37** B3
Scruffy Murphy's	**38** A3
Tai Pan	**39** B3
Tiger Entertainment	**40** B3
Two Black Sheep	**41** B3

SHOPPING	
Ocean Plaza Department Store	(see 36)

TRANSPORT	
Buses to Phuket	**42** A6
Patong Big Bike	**43** B2
Via Rent-A-Car	**44** B4

Touch Villa (☎ 0 7634 4011; touchvilla@hotmail.com; r 250-1000B; 🌀) It's near the discos, so it can be a bit loud, but is a good deal nonetheless. Two rows of modern tiled rooms line a small garden strip; everything's nice and cosy.

Baan Patong (☎ 0 7634 4152; fax 0 7634 4454; 3 Rat Uthit; r 300-800B; 🌀) A great deal at this price. Rooms are modern, large, clean and beautifully decked out.

Soho Guesthouse (☎ 0 7629 2815; soho01@hotmail .com; r 300-800B; 🌀) Centrally located on busy and popular Soi Kepsap, you'll find decent budget rooms with a few amenities here. Bigger rooms naturally cost more, and there's an Indian restaurant downstairs.

Chanathip Guest House (☎ 0 7629 4087; fax 0 7629 4088; 53/7 Th Rat Uthit; r 350-800B; 🌀) This guesthouse has modern, good-sized rooms with satellite TV, hot water and fridge. It's a decent deal and located down a quiet lane.

V-Plaza (☎ 0 7629 2556; www.valhalla-th.com; 163/24 Soi Sunset; r 500-800B; 🌀) This place is pretty darn unique; think of it as a mini-Viking theme park. In a large indoor space, there are 13 comfortable rooms that face the restaurant/bar area (could be noisy at night), highlighted by a giant Viking helmet. All have TV and fridge; two come with private whirlpool (700B extra). Prospective female guests might want to note that V-Plaza advertises 'We are the first choice for Single Men on a Mission'.

Midrange

Andatel (☎ 0 7629 0489; www.andatelhotel.com; 419 Th Rat Uthit; r 1000-1800B; 🌀 🈁) Andatel is a good-looking place and one of the best deals in its price range. It offers great rooms with patios or balconies and some creative touches in traditional peaked Thai buildings. There is a pool to splash around in, plus an attractive restaurant out the front.

Orchid Residence (☎ 0 7634 5176; www.orchid-res idence.com; Soi Saen Sabai; r 580-1700B; 🌀 🈁) On two sides of a relatively quiet lane, it has very nice, large, comfortable and well-appointed rooms with cable TV. Don't confuse it with the nearby Orchid Guesthouse, which has similar prices.

Capricorn Village (☎ 0 7634 0390; capricorns39@ hotmail.com; 178 Th Rat Uthit; r 400-1500B; 🌀 🈁) Leafy garden paths and decent, yet small, rooms are featured here. It's in a good location, has a relaxing atmosphere and is often booked out in the high season.

First Resort Albergo (☎ /fax 0 7634 0980; Th Rat Uthit; r 800-1600B; 🌀 🈁) A small motel-style place, Albergo is clean and appealing. The tiled-floor and spacious rooms come complete with good wooden furniture and cable TV. There's a pool with a gated wading area for the kids.

Mermaid Resort (☎ 0 7634 5670; www.mermaid -resort.com; Th Rat Uthit; r 1200-2200B; 🌀 🈁) With 24 spiffy rooms facing a little garden and a small, but pleasant, pool this is a nice place. Still, it's only marginally nicer than First Resort Albergo next door – but much more expensive.

Expat Hotel (☎ 0 7634 0300; expat@loxinfo.co.th; 163/17 Th Rat Uthit; r 490-1200B; 🌀) At the end of a small bar-packed alley, this hotel is popular with young foreigners. There's a communal buddy-buddy feel between the staff and the guests. If you want to stay a while, ask about monthly rates.

Casuarina Patong Garden Resort (☎ 0 7634 1197; fax 0 7634 0123; 188 Th Thawiwong; r 1800-3000B; 🌀 🈁) This long-established place has transformed itself from a small collection of bungalows to a midrange resort. There's a shaded pool area with a bar and sauna and the resort faces the beach.

K Hotel (☎ 0 7634 0832; www.k-hotel.com; 180 Th Rat Uthit; r 800-2000B; 🌀 🈁) German tourists in particular like this two-storey place with a pleasant garden setting and slick restaurant. The rooms are pretty comfortable.

Sansabai Bungalows (☎ 0 7634 2948; www.phuket -sansabai.com; 171/21 Soi Saen Sabai; r 400-1500B; 🌀) At the quiet end of a lane, it occupies a secluded spot next to a large pond. However, it doesn't play up this advantage, harbouring musty rooms and a large scruffy garden. Friendly and efficient staff and a restaurant serving Italian and Thai dishes are plusses.

Top End

Patong Merlin Hotel (☎ 0 7634 0037; www.merlin phuket.com; r 2800-5650B; 🌀 🈁 🖥) Engulfing almost an entire block, this monster resort covers much of what you'd expect at a high-class hotel: beautiful grounds, beautiful pools, beautiful rooms. Beachside restaurants and a wide range of sport facilities are naturally included.

Le Meridien Phuket (☎ 0 7634 0480; www.lemer idien.com; r US$230-250; 🌀 🖥 🈁) About 1.5km south of town, this resort was severely damaged by the tsunami, but following extensive repairs and restoration was re-opened in August 2005. Le Meridian is well set up. Restaurants sit amid expansive swimming pools close to the beach. The 470 rooms feature safes, satellite TV and coffee makers. Other facilities include four tennis courts, two squash courts, beach volleyball, minigolf, a climbing wall, water sports equipment and, of course, the beautiful pools. It's a great place if you like to swim.

Impiana Phuket Cabana (☎ 0 7634 0138; www .impiana.com; r 2900-7500B; ☒ ☲) The Impiana has closed for repairs following tsunami damage and should have opened by the time you read this. Close to the top of the luxury heap, it presents gorgeously perfect rooms, grounds and lobby – all decked out in traditional Thai décor.

Novotel Coralia Phuket (☎ 0 7634 2777; www .phuket.com/novotel; r 2900-11000B; ☒ ☐ ☲) At the northern edge of town, the Novotel has 215 luxury rooms with views – although some are strangely located in the back with unattractive open halls. The unique pool with scenic views and three levels separated by tiled waterfalls is the best feature.

EATING

Patong has stacks of restaurants – some of them quite good. There are a few bargain seafood and noodle stalls down a tiny lane opposite Soi Eric on Th Bangla.

Restaurant 6 (☎ 0 7634 2219; 186 Th Rat Uthit; dishes 40-120B) This place has found the secret of restaurant success, which is: 1) serve good food; 2) serve large portions; 3) serve it quickly; and 4) don't charge a whole lot. Both Thai and *faràng* flock to this small casual eatery, making you feel sorry for neighbouring venues.

Hole in the Wall (☎ 0 1979 8755; 95 Th Rat Uthit; dishes 30-200B) Serving Thai and British grub, including greasy brekkies, this is a pub-style joint.

Savoey (☎ 0 7634 1171; 136 Th Thawiwong; dishes 120-350B) A hugely popular open-style café, it slays 'em and weighs 'em – seafood, that is. And you can see it all from the pavement, where you'll be choosing your dinner critter from atop its mound of ice.

Harry's Steakhouse & Pub (☎ 0 1787 3167; 110/2 Soi Big One; dishes 100-495B) With a comfortable Western atmosphere and food to match, this place is a tourist magnet. On the menu are burgers, steak and pizza. It's also part

pub, so you can order plenty of heady drinks to wash down your meal.

Casa Mia (Soi Kepsap; dishes 120-350B) Casa Mia serves really yummy pizzas – try the four cheese version – as well as scrumptious appetizers and other Italian classics.

Just north of town, on the coast, is a trio of expensive and romantic restaurants. They are a good choice for a special night out. All three open at noon and close around 11pm.

Baan Rim Pa (☎ 0 7634 4079; dishes 215-475B) Soft piano music sets the mood for a romantic evening at this restaurant set above a thicket of mangrove trees. It offers stunning ocean-view tables – but you'll have to make reservations to get them. Actually, you'll have to make reservations anyway. Baan Rim Pa specialises in Thai cuisine that's only slightly toned down for foreign palates. Dress accordingly to dine at this high-class restaurant.

Da Maurizio Bar Ristorante (☎ 0 7634 4079; dishes 450-950B) Another very classy and romantic restaurant, this one serves delicious Italian cuisine. Call for both reservations and a complimentary ride to the restaurant. It's set down on the rocks.

Otowa (☎ 0 7634 4254; dishes 295-500B) Next door to Baan Rim Pa, it serves Japanese food just above the crashing waves. But the ambience doesn't seem appropriately upmarket considering the prices, type of food and its two fancy sister-restaurants nearby.

DRINKING & ENTERTAINMENT

There are dozens of simple watering holes around town, many of them little more than a few stools around an open-air bar with a handful of scantily-dressed Thai women whose main objective is to hook passers-by and keep them drinking long enough to pay the rent. Th Bangla has the main cluster, though they are everywhere. They are definitely loud and sleazy, but for certain visitors this adds to Patong's, uh, appeal. There are also plenty of other, much more upmarket bars catering to the yuppie crowd.

Molly Malone's (☎ 0 7629 2771; Th Thawiwong) This pub rocks with Irish gigs every night at 9.45pm. There's a good atmosphere, lots of pub food and some great tables out the front from which to admire the ocean and legions of tourist passers-by. Guinness is available for a mere 349B per pint.

Scruffy Murphy's (☎ 0 7629 2590; 5 Th Bangla) This place competes with Molly Malone's by offering its own live Irish music and cover bands at 9.45pm. It's also clean and air-conditioned. It cooks up pub grub and Thai food and offers big screens for watching sports. It's located amid the strips of cheap bars, though it doesn't play the girlie game. However, it does seem to be the place where older *faràng* men, who aren't so into Thai women, go to look for *faràng* women, preferably younger than them. Still, it's fun – you may find yourself here more than once in a span of days.

Q-Bar (☎ 0 7629 2114; Th Bangla) A small, delicate and hip bar, it's next to the big Ocean Plaza department store. It specialises in DJ music amid modern and simple décor.

Two Black Sheep (Th Rat Uthit) In the thick of the inland action, next door to K Hotel, there's mostly an intimate bar atmosphere here with good live rock music nightly in a trendy, dark space.

Gonzo Bar (Th Bangla) This large bar attracts hordes of *faràng*, who come in part for the bar games. Grab a stool and watch others humiliate themselves while sipping cheap drinks, or lose your inhibitions and join in the fun.

Banana Disco (☎ 0 1271 2469; 96 Th Thawiwong; admission 200B) An Aztec-like theme prevails at this club. It's on the main beach strip and the cover charge includes two drinks.

Phuket Bar (☎ 0 1271 2469) A great place for older and more conservative drinkers, it's right under Banana Disco and is nice and comfortable. Live music plays outside on the patio area.

Tiger Entertainment (☎ 0 7634 5112; admission 100B) The cover charge at this club includes one drink. It's in a huge primeval structure with a tiger-head theme – walk upstairs into the tiger's mouth. There are girlie bars downstairs and Thai boxing next door.

Tai Pan (☎ 0 1271 2469; Th Rat Uthit) A staff of T-shirted young women, who glow under the blue lights, patrol this large club. The Western music is loud and sometimes comes to you good and live.

Rock Hard a Go Go (☎ 0 7634 0409; cnr Th Bangla & Th Rat Uthit) One of the cleaner go-go bars, where decently clad girls swing on the poles both upstairs and downstairs. Despite the entertainment it exudes a comfortable air, and welcomes couples and women.

Phuket Simon Cabaret (☎ 0 7634 2011; admission 550B) About 1km south of the Merlin Hotel, this place offers entertaining transvestite shows in a grand 600-seat theatre. The costumes are gorgeous and the 'ladyboys' are convincing. The house is often full. Performances are given at 7.30pm and 9.30pm nightly.

GETTING THERE & AROUND

Săwngthăew from Phuket town leave from the day market and cost 20B. The after-hours charter fare is 150B. Buses to Phuket town leave from the southern end of Th Thawiwong and cost 15B. *Túk-túk* service Patong for 10B per ride.

Patong Big Bike (☎ 0 7634 0380; Th Rat Uthit) rents a few kinds of motorcycles. **Via Rent-A-Car** (☎ 0 7638 5718; www.via-phuket.com), based in Kamala, has an unstaffed office in town (you call from the telephone there) and delivers rental cars to Patong.

Karon

กะรน

A long sweeping stretch of sand, Karon is a gently curving beach with small sand dunes and a few palms and casuarina trees. The main area of the beach features a paved promenade with streetlights and the area has blended with Hat Kata to the south to produce a self-contained village inhabited by a mixture of tourists, seasonal residents and year-rounders. It is still a fairly peaceful place and relatively devoid of the overwhelming commercialisation, neon lights and loud music found on nearby Patong. Unlike Kata, Karon still has large empty tracts of land facing the beach. They have the look of impending development about them, but with some luck room supply will soon outstrip demand and construction will not reach the proportions of Kata's Club Med.

In the off season, Karon largely shuts down by about 11.30pm and those looking for nightlife must head to neighbouring Kata.

During the 2004 tsunami, the huge waves hammered Hat Karon and left a good deal of debris on the beach, which has since been cleaned up. None of the guesthouses or resorts received significant damage.

If you're looking for fun away from the sand, or are travelling with the kids, try **Dino**

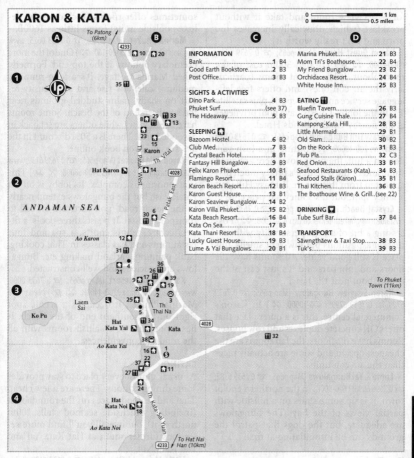

KARON & KATA

INFORMATION
Bank.......................................1 B4
Good Earth Bookstore..............2 B3
Post Office..............................3 B3

SIGHTS & ACTIVITIES
Dino Park...............................4 B3
Phuket Surf.....................(see 37)
The Hideaway.........................5 B3

SLEEPING
Bazoom Hostel.......................6 B2
Club Med...............................7 B3
Crystal Beach Hotel.................8 B1
Fantasy Hill Bungalow..............9 B3
Felix Karon Phuket.................10 B1
Flamingo Resort.....................11 B4
Karon Beach Resort................12 B3
Karon Guest House.................13 B3
Karon Seaview Bungalow.........14 B2
Karon Villa Phuket.................15 B2
Kata Beach Resort..................16 B4
Kata On Sea..........................17 B3
Kata Thani Resort...................18 B4
Lucky Guest House..................19 B3
Lume & Yai Bungalows............20 B1

Marina Phuket.......................21 B3
Mom Tri's Boathouse..............22 B4
My Friend Bungalow...............23 B2
Orchidacea Resort..................24 B4
White House Inn....................25 B3

EATING
Bluefin Tavern.......................26 B3
Gung Cuisine Thaïe.................27 B4
Kampong-Kata Hill.................28 B3
Little Mermaid.......................29 B1
Old Siam..............................30 B2
On the Rock..........................31 B2
Plub Pla..............................32 C3
Red Onion............................33 B1
Seafood Restaurants (Kata)......34 B3
Seafood Stalls (Karon).............35 B1
Thai Kitchen.........................36 B3
The Boathouse Wine & Grill..(see 22)

DRINKING
Tube Surf Bar........................37 B4

TRANSPORT
Sáwngthăew & Taxi Stop..........38 B3
Tuk's..................................39 B3

To Patong (6km)
To Phuket Town (11km)
To Phuket Town (11km)
To Hat Nai Han (10km)

ANDAMAN SEA
Ao Karon
Ao Kata Yai
Ao Kata Noi
Ko Pu
Laem Sai
Hat Karon
Hat Kata Yai
Hat Kata Noi

Th Patak West
Th Patak East
Th Vitai
Th Karon
Th Thai Na
Th Kata-Sai Yuan

ANDAMAN COAST

Park (Map p665; ☎ 0 7633 0625; adult/child 120/90B, with use of golf course 240/180B; ☒ 10am-midnight), next to Marina Phuket. It features an 18-hole minigolf course and a fake waterfall, among other things. The theme is Flintstones – the staff wear caveman outfits with a loose necktie, the restaurant serves Bronto Burgers and you can drink at the Dino Bar.

SLEEPING
Budget & Midrange
Karon is lined with inns and deluxe bungalows, along with some cheaper places. Ask for discounts in the low season if you're staying more than just a few days. Less-expensive places will naturally be found

well off the beach, often on small hillocks to the east of the main road.

Bazoom Hostel (Map p665; ☎ 0 7639 6914; bazoom@loxinfo.co.th; dm 120B, r 200-500B; ☒) This hostel is eclectically painted and fun. It's the kind of place backpackers search all of Phuket Island for. Rooms are pretty small, but cute, and the dorm has 14 beds. You can chill out at the nearby Oasis Bar (ask about it at reception), which has a fire pit, hammocks and the night sky for a ceiling.

My Friend Bungalow (Map p665; ☎ 0 7639 6344; www.myfriendbungalow.com; r 600-1000B; ☒) Popular, friendly and opposite the beach, this is a good choice. All of the very clean, modern rooms have tile floors, satellite TV and fridge and there's a café out the front. Try for a sea view room and take it without breakfast (which drastically increases the price and isn't really worth it).

Karon Guest House (Map p665; ☎ 0 7639 6860; r 300-800B; ⊠ ⊠) Located 300m east of the roundabout, it has decent rooms (particularly the air-con ones) and offers free left-luggage service and safe deposit, plus satellite TV in the lobby. Guests have pool privileges at the nearby Golden Sands Hotel.

Fantasy Hill Bungalow (Map p665; ☎ 0 7633 0106; bungalows 200-1000B; ⊠) Sitting in a lush garden on a hill, the bungalows here are good value and of the type that's pretty much disappeared from this beach. Fantasy Hill isn't a fancy spot, but it's somewhat peaceful.

Crystal Beach Hotel (Map p665; ☎ 0 7639 6580; crystalbeach@phuketInternet.co.th; r 400-900B; ⊠) Possessing a bit of a split personality with up-market aspirations but low-rent smells, this place is still good value. All rooms have tile floors and minibars and it's just east of the roundabout near the beach.

Karon Seaview Bungalow (Map p665; ☎ 0 7639 6798; fax 0 7639 6799; r 400-1000B; ⊠) In Karon's commercial centre, this is a quiet place that offers OK concrete duplexes and row houses. Rooms have tile floors; the fan rooms are the cheapest option and some are actually nicer than the air-con units.

Lume & Yai Bungalows (Map p665; ☎ 0 7639 6382; fax 0 7696 6096; r 600-800B) In the northern end of town, it is up some stairs on a hillside with partial views of the bay. The bungalows are adequate, but the dogs that patrol the grounds can be intimidating at first.

Top End
Many of the remaining places to stay in Karon are newer resort-type hotels with air-con, swimming pools, multiple restaurants etc. Overbuilding has made it easier to bargain at these places, especially from May to October. During the holidays, however, rates zoom skywards.

Felix Karon Phuket (Map p665; ☎ 0 7639 6666; www.felixphuket.com; r 3800-4500B; ⊠ ⊠) An elegant and well-maintained older property with two pools and three bars. The rooms have some very nice touches and all come with safe, phone, fridge and TV. The bathrooms are delightful. The official room rates only change in the high season (20 December to 15 January) when an 800B surcharge is added. In the low season it will

sometimes offer rooms (including the deluxe poolside units) for as little as 1600B.

Marina Phuket (Map p665; ☎ 0 7633 0625; www .marinaphuket.com; r US$100-160; ⊠) One of the more exemplary options at the top end. Formerly called Marina Cottage, it's a long-running, medium-scale, low-rise and low-density resort on shady, palm-studded grounds near the southern end of the beach. Some rooms have ocean views while others are set back in a wooded area. There is a 50% discount in the low season if you book online.

Karon Villa Phuket (Map p665; ☎ 0 7639 6139; www .karonvilla.com; r & bungalows 3400-6800B; ⊠ ⊠) This is an enormous complex. Its lobby is off Th Patak East, but the bungalows extend nearly to the beach road (golf carts are on call to transport guests). It boasts three pools, a fitness centre, tennis courts, a spa and four restaurants and has classes in Thai cooking, batik painting, garland making etc. Bungalows are spacious and well constructed.

Karon Beach Resort (Map p665; ☎ 0 7633 0006; www.katagroup.com; r 2200-4400B; ⊠ ⊠) Near the Marina Phuket, it occupies a scenic spot right on the southern end of the beach. It has a pool and 80 smallish rooms with all the modern conveniences.

EATING
As usual, almost every place to stay provides some dining options. There are a few cheap Thai and seafood places off the roundabout (including beachside seafood stalls 100m north of it), but overall you'll find more selections further south at Hat Kata Yai and Hat Kata Noi.

Little Mermaid (Map p665; ☎ 0 7639 6638; dishes 70-300B) This backpacker favourite serves huge three-egg breakfasts, the best around, all day long. The long menu (available in 12 languages!) also includes burgers and steaks, Danish sandwiches, cheeses and Thai food. It's about 80m east of the roundabout.

On the Rock (Map p665; ☎ 0 7633 0625; dishes 100-300B) An excellent restaurant, it serves equal portions of sweeping beach views and delicious seafood. It gets crowded at night, so call for a booking.

Old Siam (Map p665; ☎ 0 7639 6090; dishes 195-300B; buffet 750B; ⏱ 6-10.30pm) A real treat, this is a large open-air palace, designed in central Thai style. It produces regional dishes for the tourist palate. Every Wednesday and Sunday in the high season it offers a Thai buffet with a traditional dance show from 8pm to 9pm.

Red Onion (Map p665; ☎ 0 7639 6827; dishes 60-150B; ☯ 4-11pm) This eatery attracts *faràng* like nobody's business. It's about 300m east of the roundabout – look for the coloured lights. There is Thai food on the menu, along with Western titbits like schnitzel and spaghetti. Cocktails and wine selections complement the meals, so try to forget the bad music.

Buffalo Steak House (Map p665; ☎ 0 7633 3013; dishes 50-420B; ☯ 3pm-midnight) Proudly claiming to serve the best steak in town, its service is also pretty good; the seating is outside.

GETTING THERE & AWAY
For details on transport to Karon, see p668.

Kata
กะตะ

Just around a headland south from Karon, Kata is a more interesting beach and divided into two – Hat Kata Yai and Hat Kata Noi. Visitors here tend to be younger than those at Hat Karon, which is more resort-oriented.

The small island of Ko Pu is within swimming distance of the shore (if you're a strong swimmer); on the way are some OK coral reefs. Be careful of riptides, heed the red flags and don't go past the breakers (ask about swimming conditions). Both Hat Kata Yai and Noi offer decent surfing waves from April to November.

The main commercial street of Th Thai Na is perpendicular to the shore and has most of the restaurants and shops, along with some cheaper places to stay. For reading material head to the **Good Earth Bookstore** (Map p665; ☯ 10.30am-8pm), across from Bluefin Tavern, which sells and exchanges second-hand books.

If you feel like firing up the stove, Mom Tri's Boathouse (p668) offers a two-day **Thai cooking class** each weekend for 2800B per person; one-day courses are 1800B. Or perhaps you'd like a spa treatment? The **Hideaway** (Map p665; ☎ 0 7633 0914) has a branch here offering traditional Thai massage, sauna, mud body wraps and other treatments.

SLEEPING
In general, the less-expensive places tend to be off the beach between Kata Yai (to the

---

> ### SURF'S UP, THAILAND
>
> During the monsoon season (May to October), the rocky headland at the northern end of Hat Kata Noi makes a clean right point break and attracts numerous surfers. Although a long-time favourite beach destination, Thailand hasn't really been associated with surfing in the same way as other countries, such as South Africa, Australia, Hawaii and Indonesia. But the surf is definitely looking up for wave runners in Hat Kata in early September. That's when the annual surfing competition comes to town. The four-day event offers three types of contests for amateur surfers – shortboard, longboard and longboard paddling race. The entry fee is around 500B and if you think you've got the skills, you can register at www.phuketsurf.com, which also has info about the local surfing community. **Phuket Surf** (Map p665; ☎ 0 7285 4718), on Hat Kata Yai's southern cove, offers surf lessons starting at 1500B, as well as board rentals.

north) and Kata Noi (to the south) or on the road to the island's interior.

Budget & Midrange
Flamingo Resort (Map p665; ☎ 0 7633 0776; www .flamingo-resort.com; bungalows 600-1000B) Sporting 10 large and decent bungalows on a hillside, most rooms come with fridges, sizable verandas and good views. It has a restaurant downstairs.

Kata On Sea (Map p665; ☎ 0 7633 0594; bungalows 300-800B; ☒) Twenty-nine modest but large bungalows dot a quiet green hilltop. It's up a short, steep driveway.

Lucky Guest House (Map p665; ☎ 0 7633 0572; lucky guesthousekata@hotmail.com; r 250-850B; ☒) While it won't win any special prizes, it does offer basic and decent accommodation on large, unpretentious grounds. It's inland, just off the main street in a central location.

White House Inn (Map p665; ☎ 0 7633 0405; fax 0 7633 0689; r 400-1200B; ☒) The 17 solid rooms come in a variety of sizes. Some aren't energy efficient, however; open screens at the top of some rooms don't go well with air-conditioning. At least it's a central location, near a busy intersection, but set back in a leafy garden. The beach is a 10-minute walk away.

ANDAMAN COAST

Top End

Mom Tri's Boathouse (Map p665; ☎ 0 7633 0015; www .phuket.com/boathouse; r 3500-7000B; ❄ ▣) This gorgeous boutique resort is the brainchild of architect and Phuket resident ML Tri Devakul. The halls are decked out with artwork. The 36 intimate rooms filled with tasteful wood and bamboo furniture, feature balconies. The service is stellar, the restaurant (replaced after the tsunami destroyed the original) acclaimed and the location scenic. Perhaps this is why the hotel attracts a steady influx of Thai politicos, pop stars, artists and celebrity authors.

Orchidacea Resort (Map p665; ☎ 0 7633 0181; www .orchidacearesort.com; r from US$88; ❄ ▣) Although the beach-view rooms here are slightly plain (there's nothing wrong with them, they're just not as lavish as you would expect for the price), the hillside location with rambling gardens, gorgeous pool and well-decorated common areas give the place a stylish appeal.

Kata Thani Resort (Map p665; ☎ 0 7633 0124; www .katathani.com; r US$140-220; ❄ ▣) An enormous, three-storey, 530-room resort that commands most of the beach at Kata Noi, this is one of the choicest spots anywhere along Karon or Kata. Rooms are upmarket and stylish, and the grounds are beautifully landscaped with tennis courts, four swimming pools, a fitness centre and six restaurants.

Club Med (Map p665; ☎ 0 7633 0456; www.clubmed .com; r 3900-7000B; ❄ ▣) Club Med caters to active travellers by not putting TVs in any rooms. It's a monster resort, though, with 306 rooms, expansive grounds and large pools. Tsunami damage forced Club Med to close many rooms temporarily, but the resort has returned to full capacity. The beach is across the street, while the entrance is on the inland side of the block. Rates include all meals and activities. Check the website for discounts.

Kata Beach Resort (Map p665; ☎ 0 7633 0530; www .katagroup.com; r incl breakfast 3000-7000B; ❄ ▣) A typical luxury resort, with 262 well-decorated rooms in hotel-like buildings and a large, amoeba-shaped pool under swaying palms. Check the website for discounts.

EATING & DRINKING

There's some surprisingly classy food in Kata, though you'll be paying dearly for it. Easier on the bank account are the many eateries on Th Thai Na, which has more than its share of Italian and Scandinavian restaurants. A cluster of affordable, casual seafood restaurants can be found on Th Patak West near the shore, though unfortunately they're not within view of the sea.

Boathouse Wine & Grill (Map p665; ☎ 0 7633 0015; dishes 180-600B) One of the most prestigious, and best restaurants, in all of Phuket, the Boathouse boasts an excellent wine collection to go along with a wonderful nightly seafood buffet. It's pricey, but the atmosphere is casual and the service is first-rate; a great place to bring a fussy date.

Bluefin Tavern (Map p665; ☎ 0 7633 0856; dishes 40-165B; ◷ 3-11pm) A popular restaurant and bar, it grills up Tex-Mex, pizza, burgers, steak and, of course, Thai food. Come for dinner, or just for a pina colada – either way the small front deck is nice and laid-back.

Gung Cuisine Thaïe (Map p665; ☎ 0 7633 0015; dishes 160-550B) Next to Mom Tri's Boathouse and under the same ownership, it's a bit more casual with romantic seaside tables. The seafood, meats and Thai food on the menu are all excellent.

Kampong-Kata Hill (Map p665; ☎ 0 7633 0103; dishes 80-260B; ◷ 4-11.30pm) Up many stairs on a terraced hillside, this Thai-style place is another standout. Decorated with antiques, it serves tasty food and there's a street-side dining room if you don't want to sweat it.

Thai Kitchen (Map p665; dishes 40-80B; ◷ Sun-Fri) Basic Thai food, including curries, is served in a casual, cafeteria-style setting. The food is good and cheap.

Plub Pla (Map p665; ☎ 0 7628 5167; dishes 180-500B) Stop by the bar at this hilltop hideaway for a romantic sunset drink overlooking Hat Kata. It's also a great spot for a fancy dinner. The restaurant serves Thai, Italian and 'International' cuisine in an intimate setting.

Tube Surf Bar (Map p665; ☎ 0 7285 4718; dishes from 30B) This surf bar gets going on Tuesday and Friday nights (in particular), when surf videos are screened and all-you-can eat barbecues (150B) or chilli nights (100B for a bottomless bowl of chilli plus a beer) happen. If you're looking to find out more about local surfing culture, this is where to head any night of the week.

GETTING THERE & AROUND

Săwngthăew and buses to both Kata and Karon leave frequently from the Th Ranong market in Phuket from 7am to 5pm for 20B per person. The main *sǎwngthǎew* stop is in front of Kata Beach Resort.

Taxi destinations available from Kata include Phuket town (200B), Patong (150B) and Karon (100B).

Motorcycle rentals are available at **Tuk's** (Map p665; ☎ 0 7628 4049) for 150B to 1000B.

Nai Han
ในหาน

Rimming a picturesque bay only a few kilometres south of Kata, nearly at the southern tip of the island, this beach is less developed than its neighbouring strips of sand. This is partly due to topography, but also to the presence of **Samnak Song Nai Han**, a monastic centre in the middle of the beach that claims most of the beachfront land. The Meridien resort occupies other prime sea-view property not owned by the monks, so to make up for the lack of saleable beachfront, developers started cutting away the forest on the hillsides overlooking the beach. Recently, however, the development seems to have come to a halt. This means that Nai Han is usually one of the least crowded beaches on the southern part of the island.

Hat Nai Han can be a dangerous place to swim in the monsoon season (May to October), but it really varies according to daily or weekly weather changes – look for the red flag, which means dangerous swimming conditions. Beach chairs and umbrellas can be rented for 60B.

The 2004 tsunami destroyed all of the small shops and restaurants at the Le Meridien end of the beach, but they are slowly being rebuilt. The beach itself looks more beautiful than it has in recent memory.

SLEEPING & EATING
Except for the yacht club, there's not much accommodation with views of the beach.

Yanui Bayview Bungalows (Map p669; ☎ 0 7623 8180; www.phuketdir.com/yanuibayview; r 600-800B; ☢) Yanui Bayview was almost totally destroyed by the tsunami but the owners are rebuilding and plan to be open by high season 2005–06. It's across the bay from the yacht club and around a small point, and as at the original, there will be a set of plain but

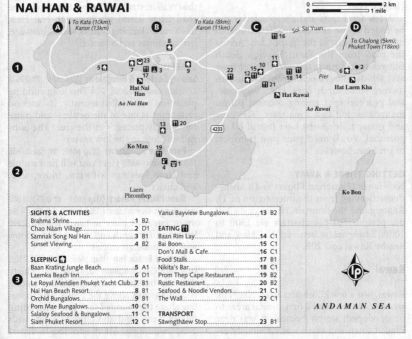

NAI HAN & RAWAI

0 — 2 km
0 — 1 mile

To Kata (10km); Karon (13km)

To Kata (8km); Karon (11km)

Soi Sai Yuan

To Chalong (5km); Phuket Town (18km)

16

8

23
7
17
5
3
A

9

22

11
10
15
12
21

18 14

Pier

6

2

Hat Nai Han

Hat Rawai

Hat Laem Kha

Ao Nai Han

Ao Rawai

13

20

4233

Ko Man

19

4
1

Laem Phromthep

Ko Bon

ANDAMAN SEA

SIGHTS & ACTIVITIES
Brahma Shrine.....................................1 B2
Chao Náam Village...............................2 D1
Samnak Song Nai Han..........................3 B1
Sunset Viewing.....................................4 B2

SLEEPING ⌂
Baan Krating Jungle Beach....................5 A1
Laemka Beach Inn................................6 D1
Le Royal Meridien Phuket Yacht Club....7 B1
Nai Han Beach Resort...........................8 B1
Orchid Bungalows.................................9 B1
Porn Mae Bungalows..........................10 C1
Salaloy Seafood & Bungalows.............11 C1
Siam Phuket Resort.............................12 C1

Yanui Bayview Bungalows...................13 B2

EATING 🍴
Baan Rim Lay.....................................14 C1
Bai Boon..15 C1
Don's Mall & Cafe..............................16 C1
Food Stalls...17 B1
Nikita's Bar..18 C1
Prom Thep Cape Restaurant...............19 B2
Rustic Restaurant...............................20 B2
Seafood & Noodle Vendors................21 C1
The Wall..22 C1

TRANSPORT
Sǎwngthǎew Stop..............................23 B1

ANDAMAN COAST

comfortable cottages across the road from the beach. It also has a restaurant.

Nai Han Beach Resort (Map p669; ☎ 0 7638 1810; fax 0 7621 4687; r from 500; ✷) Situated on a small lagoon about 700m from the beach, this relaxed place has 20 tidy rooms with hot and cold showers.

Orchid Bungalows (Map p669; ☎ /fax 0 7638 1396; r 800-1000B; ✷) This is a small place set behind an orchid nursery east of the lagoon. One of its three large and modern rooms features a kitchenette.

Baan Krating Jungle Beach (☎ 0 7628 8264; cottages 3800-4500B) This idyllic spot tucked away in Ao Saen, a small cove near Nai Han, is reached via a road that passes through the Meriden. Spacious cottages are built mostly of natural materials, but contain satellite TV, fridge and coffee maker.

Le Royal Meridien Phuket Yacht Club (Map p669; ☎ 0 7638 1156; www.lemeridien-yachtclub.com; r US$300-800; ✷ ▣ ▣) Originally built at the astronomical cost of 145 million baht, the hotel has given up on the idea of becoming a true yacht club, but still offers luxurious rooms and an equally luxurious property right on the beach. It sits on the northwestern end of Hat Nai Han.

A few food carts and cheap eateries can be found above the beach a few hundred metres southeast of the Yacht Club. Across the road from the Yanui Bayview Beach Bungalows is a rustic **restaurant** (✷ high season only), which enjoys a beachfront location on its own small sandy cove. It's a very quiet and peaceful spot among coconut palms, mangroves and casuarina trees. The cape and grassy hills nearby have lots of hiking potential. You'll need your own transport to get here, however.

GETTING THERE & AWAY
Nai Han is 18km from Phuket and a *săwngthăew* (leaving from the intersection of Th Ranong and the fountain circle) costs 25B per person. *Túk-túk* charters are 150B to 200B. *Săwngthăew* between Nai Han and nearby Rawai cost 20B.

Rawai
ราไวย์

Rawai, just a few kilometres from Nai Han, was one of the island's first coastal areas to be developed, simply because it was near Phuket town and there was an already es-

tablished fishing community. But as other better beaches (such as Patong and Kata) were discovered, the tourist travel to Rawai dwindled and today it's a rather quiet spot. If you want to sit on a beach without being distracted by wandering vendors trying to sell hammocks or coconuts, then perhaps you could check out Rawai. The beach isn't really great, but there is a lot happening in the vicinity: a **chao náam village** lies at the east side of town; boats leave from the beach to nearby islands for diving, snorkelling, day-tripping and overnight stays (see opposite); **Hat Laem Kha** (a better beach than Rawai) is just to the northeast; and there's good snorkelling off **Laem Phromthep** at the southern tip of Phuket island, less than 2km from Rawai. In fact, most of the visitors who stay at Rawai these days are divers who want to be near Phromthep or boat facilities for offshore diving trips.

Laem Phromthep is also a popular spot at sunset, when buses full of Thai tourists arrive to pose for photos and enjoy the vistas. South of the viewpoint is a **shrine** to Phra Phrom (Brahma).

If you're looking for a physical challenge, the Wall restaurant (opposite), along the road from Rawai northwest to Nai Han, has a rock-climbing wall as well as massage, herbal saunas and a Jacuzzi.

SLEEPING
Salaloy Seafood & Bungalows (Map p669; ☎ 0 7638 1297; bungalows 350-800B; ✷) This long-running place was remodelled recently. Its seafood restaurant is one of the better – and more moderately priced – in the area. The bungalows close in the low season.

Porn Mae Bungalows (Map p669; ☎ /fax 0 7638 1300; bungalows 400B) Here you will find simple and clean lodgings with fan, fridge, table and chairs.

Siam Phuket Resort (Map p669; ☎ 0 7638 1346; www.siamphuketresort.com; r 1300-1800B; ✷ ▣) The most upmarket place in town, it has nicely landscaped grounds and very modern rooms with the usual amenities.

Laemka Beach Inn (Map p669; ☎ 0 7638 1305; fax 0 7628 8547; bungalows 500-1200B; ✷) Thirty thatched bungalows are spread out among coconut groves above the beach. The shoreline along the rounded cape is an interesting mix of clean sand and large boulders with good swimming. Many speedboats depart from here for nearby islands and it's a favourite local picnic spot. It's a little more than 1km (by road) out of Rawai on Hat Laem Kha.

EATING

Besides the restaurants attached to the resorts in Rawai (of which Salaloy Seafood is the best), there are oodles of seafood and noodle vendors set up along the roadside near the beach. All the following listings are sit-down restaurants.

Don's Mall & Cafe (Map p669; ☎ 0 7638 3100; 48-5 Soi Sai Yuan; dishes 100-650B) A Texan-run café where the menu stars hearty American meals of steak and ribs barbecued over a mesquite-wood fire. It also has an extensive wine list, freshly baked goods and a separate bar, the Longhorn Saloon. From Rawai, drive past The Wall and turn right at the next two main intersections (about 3.4km total from the beach). To get there from Phuket town (and many people make the trip just for the food), turn right onto Th Sai Yuan, just south of the Chalong roundabout, and proceed for 3km; you can't miss it.

Baan Rim Lay (Map p669; ☎ 0 7628 8067; dishes 70-190B) On the main road through town, it has good sea views, serves Thai and European food and there's a small bakery/café next door.

Nikita's Bar (Map p669; ☎ 0 7628 8703; dishes 80-225B) With fun décor and good food, it is very popular in the evenings. In addition to food and booze, it serves espresso drinks. It's also on the main road through town.

Bai Boon (Map p669; ☎ 0 7628 8704; dishes 60-180B) The menu at this restaurant near Nikita's includes American, Continental and German breakfasts as well as Thai and European lunch and dinner selections.

Wall (Map p669; ☎ 0 7628 8908; dishes 50-600B) On the road leading from Rawai northwest to Nai Han, it offers French cuisine as well as a rock-climbing wall and a herbal sauna.

Prom Thep Cape Restaurant (Map p669; ☎ 0 1723 0059; dishes 80-150B) Simple and cheap Thai meals are served just below the viewpoint for Laem Phromthep.

GETTING THERE & AWAY

Rawai is approximately 16km from Phuket and costs 20B by săwngthăew from the circle at Th Ranong. Túk-túk charters cost at least

150B. Săwngthăew drivers charge 20B for the much shorter trip between Rawai and Nai Han.

Ao Chalong
อ่าวฉลอง

More of a jumping-off point for trips to nearby islands than a good place to stay, this large bay on the northeast end of Phuket is a pier area thronged with dive shops and a few travel agencies. We'd recommend staying elsewhere, as there are heaps of much nicer beaches on the island. That said, those on a budget may want to check out the Phuket Youth Hostel (see p651).

If you're waiting to catch a boat somewhere and find yourself hungry, there are a couple of good seafood restaurants in which to fill your stomach. Try **Kan Eang 1** (☎ 0 7638 1212; dishes 60-150B), a large, open-air restaurant near the pier that boasts a great beachside location, attentive staff and an extensive menu specialising in tasty and reasonably priced seafood.

Kan Eang 2 (☎ 0 7638 1323; dishes 60-150B) has the same menu as its sister restaurant, but is 1km or so further north. Both places are popular with tour buses.

Nearby Islands
KO HAE, KO RAYA YAI & KO RAYA NOI
เกาะเฮ/เกาะรายาใหญ่/เกาะรายาน้อย

Ko Hae (also known as Coral Island), a few kilometres south of Ao Chalong, has good diving and snorkelling, although jet skis and other pleasure craft can be an annoyance. The island gets lots of day-trippers from Phuket, but at night it's pretty quiet. The tsunami spared the resorts on these islands. The **Coral Island Resort** (☎ 0 7628 1060; www.phuket.com/coralisland/index.htm; bungalows 1800-3000B; ✵) has upmarket bungalows. The rates at Coral Island vary depending on proximity to the beach.

There are two islands about 1½ hours by boat south of Phuket: Ko Raya Yai and Ko Raya Noi (they are also known as Ko Racha Yai/Noi). These are highly favoured by divers and snorkellers because of their hard coral reefs and the crystal-clear water. Since the coral is found in both shallow and deep waters, it's a good area for novice scuba divers and snorkellers as well as the accomplished divers. Visibility can reach as much as 30m. Muslim families, who mainly farm coconuts and fish for a living, make up the islands' inhabitants.

On Ko Raya Yai, **Ban Raya** (☎ 07635 4682; www .phuket.com/banraya; bungalows 1300-1900B; 🔀) has sturdy, comfortable bungalows and offers diving instruction. Other places to stay include Jungle Bungalow, Raya Resort and Raya Andaman Resort.

Ao Chalong and Hat Rawai are the main departure points for these islands. A speedboat to Ko Hae costs about 150B per person each way (you may have to bargain hard), or you can hire an entire boat for 1000B to 1500B. If you're booking a room on Ko Raya, your host may arrange transport for around 400B per person via speedboat or 1500B for an entire long-tail boat.

Aloha Tours (☎ 07638 1215), just south of the main pier at Ao Chalong, is one of many agencies that book snorkelling tours to Ko Hae (700B) and Ko Raya (1100B). The tours include hotel pick-up and transport to the pier, a return speedboat ride, lunch and use of snorkelling gear. From the Phuket town port, **Songserm Travel** (☎ 0 7622 2570) runs daily passenger boats to Ko Raya from November to April.

Ko Yao
เกาะยาว

Ko Yao Yai (Big Long Island) and Ko Yao Noi (Little Long Island) are actually part of the Ao Phang-Nga Marine National Park (p642), but are more easily accessible from Phuket. Together they encompass 137 sq km of forest, beach and rocky headland with views of the surrounding karst formations characteristic of Ao Phang-Nga.

In spite of being smaller, **Ko Yao Noi** is the main population centre of the two. Fishing as well as coconut, rice and rubber cultivation sustain the locals. **Hat Pa Sai** and **Hat Tha Khao**, both on Yao Noi, are the best beaches. **Ta Khai**, the largest settlement on the island, is a subdistrict seat and a source of minimal supplies.

Ko Yao Yai is more isolated and rustic than its smaller sister island. Rubber farming takes place here and just three bungalow operations (so far) have planted roots. Please remember to respect the Muslim cultures on both islands by wearing modest clothing outside beach areas.

Boat trips to neighbouring islands, birdnest caves and *chao náam* funeral caves are possible. **Ko Bele**, a small island east of the twin Ko Yao, features a large tidal lagoon, three white-sand beaches, and easily accessible caves and coral reefs.

SLEEPING
Ko Yao Noi has only a handful of places to stay.

Tha Khao Bungalow (☎ 0 1676 7726; bungalows 500-1200B) On Hat Tha Khao, this small place features five solid thatch-and-wood bungalows, including two family-size ones (with three bedrooms). The small restaurant does tasty food and also rents out bicycles and kayaks – a recommended way to explore the area.

Sabai Corner Bungalow (☎ 0 1892 7827; bungalows 350-550B) Sturdy thatch-and-wood bungalows with small verandas are offered here. The restaurant is pretty good.

Long Beach Village (☎ 0 7659 7472; bungalows 500-1500B; 🔀) The 40 fan and air-con bungalows at this friendly place are a bit crowded together, but they enjoy a lush, green, tropical setting.

Koyao Island Resort (☎ 0 1606 1517; www.koyao .com; villas 2500-3500B; 🔀) This resort has most luxurious abodes around. The décor is elegantly rustic and amenities include satellite TV and fridge.

On Ko Yao Yai there are three places to stay that have very similar, basic wood-and-thatch fan bungalows.

Halawee Bungalows (☎ 0 1607 3648; bungalows 400B)

Thiw Son (☎ 0 1956 7582; bungalows 350-500B)

Long Island Family Bungalows (☎ 0 1979 2273; bungalows 500B)

GETTING THERE & AROUND
Although both islands fall within the Phang-Nga Province boundaries, the easiest places to find boat transport is Phuket town and Ao Leuk and Ao Nang (both in Krabi Province). In Phuket, catch a *sǎwngthǎew* from in front of the day market to Bang Rong (on Ao Po) for 25B. From the public pier there are up to four boats (50B, one hour) at 11am, noon, 2.30pm and 5pm. Between departures or after hours you can charter a long-tail boat for about 1000B one way.

To go from Ko Yao Noi to Ko Yao Yai, catch a shuttle boat from Tha Manaw (20B, 15 minutes). On the islands *túk-túk* provide transport for about 50B.

KRABI PROVINCE

Krabi Province is blessed with some amazing scenic karst formations – similar to those in neighbouring Phang-Nga Province – along its coast and even in the middle of Mae Nam Krabi (Krabi River). These limestone cliffs add wonderful scenic beauty to the region and have attracted international rock-climbers of all levels. Krabi's most popular attraction, however, is its beaches. December to March are the best times to visit and hotels and bungalows tend to fill up during these months. During the rainy season (June to November), accommodation prices are lower, places a lot less crowded and you may luck out with windows of decent weather.

Along with coastal beaches, Krabi has over 150 attractive islands. Once the favourite hideouts of Asian pirates, today these islands offer excellent recreational opportunities. Many of the islands belong to the Hat Noppharat Thara/Ko Phi-Phi Marine National Park, including Ko Phi-Phi Don (probably the most poplar island in this region).

The 2004 tsunami devastated two beaches on Ko Phi-Phi and severely damaged the northern end of Ko Lanta, but elsewhere inflicted relatively minor damage. See the relevant sections for more detail.

The interior of the province, noted for its tropical forests and the Phanom Bencha mountain range, has barely been explored.

KRABI

กระบี่

pop 29,300

Friendly people, delicious food and some local flavour make the provincial capital of Krabi (gra-bee) a pleasant place to spend a day. Most travellers quickly breeze through, using the town as a jumping-off point for the wonderful surrounding destinations – Ko Lanta to the south, Ko Phi-Phi to the southwest and Ao Nang, Railay and Tham Phra Nang to the west. Some travellers elect to stay in town and make day trips to the latter, as there are many good guesthouses and dining options here. Some even say the place quickly grows on you.

The town sits on the western bank of the Mae Nam Krabi, about 1000km from Bang-

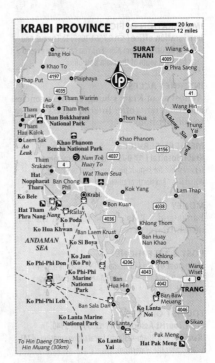

KRABI PROVINCE

kok and 180km from Phuket. The eastern bank of the river is covered in dense mangroves and north of town are the twin limestone massifs of Khao Khanap Nam, which emerge from the water like two breaching whales. The population is mainly Taoist-Confucianist and Muslim, and Krabi is an important transport hub for ferries to the islands along the coast.

Orientation

Th Utarakit is the main road into and out of Krabi and most places of interest are on the sois that branch off it. Ferries to Ko Phi-Phi and Ko Lanta leave from a new passenger jetty at Khlong Chailat, about 5km north of town. Krabi's bus terminal is 4km north of the centre at Talat Kao, near the junction of Th Utarakit and the main Trang to Phang-Na road.

Information

BOOKSHOPS

Books (☎ 0 7561 2693; 78-80 Th Maharat; ⏰ 8am-9pm) Good selection of English-language books, including Lonely Planet guidebooks, and plenty of area maps.

ANDAMAN COAST

IMMIGRATION OFFICES

Immigration office (☎ 0 7561 1097; Th Chamai Anu-son; ⏰ 8.30am-4.30pm Mon-Fri) You can easily extend visas here; it's south of the main post office.

INTERNET ACCESS

Almost all of Krabi's budget travel agencies and restaurants offer Internet access for 40B to 60B per hour.

MEDICAL SERVICES

Krabi Hospital (☎ 0 7561 1210) Has emergency services, but for serious problems head to Phuket. The hospital is 1km north of town.

MONEY

Banks and ATMs can be found in the sois off Th Utarakit.

POST & TELEPHONE

Main post office (Th Utarakit; ⏰ 8.30am-4.30pm Mon-Fri, 9am-noon Sat & Sun) A telephone office is attached.

TOURIST OFFICES

Krabi Tourist Association (☎ 0 7561 2740; Th Utarakit; ⏰ 8.30am-4.30pm) Local representation of TAT, located near the waterfront.

TRAVEL AGENCIES

Krabi has numerous travel agencies that book accommodation at beaches and islands as well as tours and bus and boat tickets. Some good agencies include:
Ibris (☎ 0 7563 0276; 23 Th Issara)
Somporn (☎ 0 7563 0234; 72 Th Khong Ka) Desk at the Star Guest House.
Sweetland (☎ 0 7561 1146; 28 Th Khong Ka)

Sights & Activities

Krabi doesn't boast a lot of must-sees. **Wat Kaew**, situated on the edge of town, contains some quite interesting 19th- and early-20th-century buildings. It's possible to climb one of the two limestone massifs of **Khao Khanap Nam**, just north of the centre. A number of human skeletons were found in the caves here, thought to be the remains of people trapped during an ancient flood. Charter a long-tail boat from Tha Kong Ka (Chao Fa) for about 100B to get here.

Sea Kayak Krabi (☎ 0 7563 0270; Th Ruen Rudee) offers a variety of sea-kayaking tours, including trips to Ao Thalane (half/full day 700/1200B), towered over by high sea cliffs; Ko

Hong (1500B), well known for its emerald lagoon; and Ban Bho Tho (1500B), featuring sea caves that hold 2000- to 3000-year-old cave paintings. All rates include lunch, fruit, drinking water, sea kayaks and guides.

Sleeping

BUDGET

New guesthouses are appearing all over Krabi and most offer large, clean, tiled rooms with windows and shared bathrooms.

KR Mansion (☎ 0 7561 2761; krmansion@yahoo.com; 52/1 Th Chao Fah; r 280-450B; 🅿 💻) There's a great funky rooftop beer garden with panoramic views over Krabi, just perfect for a sundowner cocktail. The rooms in this bright-pink building are quite comfortable.

A Mansion (☎ 0 7563 0511; fax 0 7563 0513; 12/6 Th Chao Fah; r from 300B; 🅿) Yet another friendly spot, this relative newcomer offers modern, clean and beautiful rooms with TV. There's a café, bar and cheap laundry nearby.

Chan Cha Lay (☎ 0 7562 0952; chanchalay-krabi@hot mail.com; 55 Th Utarakit; s/d 150/250B; 💻) A beautiful newish place with 15 spotless modern rooms. It's set up for travellers, with Internet connections, a travel desk and a good restaurant.

Star Guest House (☎ 0 7563 0234; Th Khong Ka; r 150-250B) This old-fashioned wooden guesthouse offers small and basic, but cosy, rooms with shared bathroom. The wooden veranda overlooking the water is a great spot to hang out in the evenings. Star is opposite the pier.

Hollywood Guest House (☎ 0 7562 0508; Th Issara; r 150-350B; 🅿) A flashy looking place, it has value rooms with tiles and separate shared bathrooms for men and women. The downstairs restaurant serves decent food and has an extensive cocktail menu to quench your thirst.

Green Tea Guesthouse (☎ 0 7563 0609; greentea thai@yahoo.com; 4 Th Issara; s 130B; d 200-450B; 🅿) Immaculate tiled rooms behind a wooden shophouse are featured at this friendly little place. Deluxe doubles have TV and hot water.

Swallow (☎ 0 7561 1645; Th Prachacheun; r 150-280B) Swallow sports guesthouses with spotlessly clean and well-maintained rooms and narrow, tiled halls.

City Hotel (☎ 0 7561 1961; 15/2-3 Th Sukhon; r 350-500B; 🅿) Well run and in a fairly central loca-

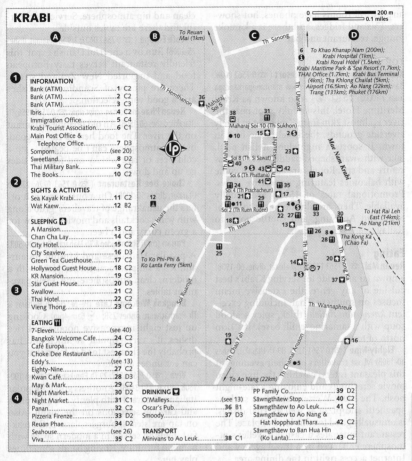

KRABI

0   200 m
0   0.1 miles

To Reuan Mai (1km)

Th Sanong

To Khao Khanap Nam (200m);
Krabi Hospital (1km);
Krabi Royal Hotel (1.5km);
Krabi Maritime Park & Spa Resort (1.7km);
THAI Office (1.7km); Krabi Bus Terminal
(4km); Tha Khlong Chailat (5km);
Airport (16.5km); Ao Nang (22km);
Trang (131km); Phuket (176km)

Th Hemthanon

Maharaj Soi 5

Maharaj Soi 10 (Th Sukhon)

Th Maharat

Th Soi 8 (Th Si Sawat)

Th Pruksauthit

Soi 6 (Th Phattana)

Soi 4 (Th Prachacheun)

Soi 2 (Th Ruen Rudee)

Th Issara

Mae Nam Krabi

To Hat Rai Leh
East (14km);
Ao Nang (21km)

Tha Kong Ka
(Chao Fa)

Th Utarakit

Th Khong Ka

Th Wannaphreuk

Th Chao Fa

Th Chanai Anuson

To Ko Phi-Phi &
Ko Lanta Ferry (5km)

Soi Ruamjit

To Ao Nang (22km)

INFORMATION	
Bank (ATM)	1 C2
Bank (ATM)	2 C2
Bank (ATM)	3 C3
Ibris	4 C2
Immigration Office	5 C4
Krabi Tourist Association	6 C1
Main Post Office &	
Telephone Office	7 D3
Somporn	(see 20)
Sweetland	8 D2
Thai Military Bank	9 C2
The Books	10 C2

SIGHTS & ACTIVITIES	
Sea Kayak Krabi	11 C2
Wat Kaew	12 B2

SLEEPING	
A Mansion	13 C2
Chan Cha Lay	14 C3
City Hotel	15 C2
City Seaview	16 D3
Green Tea Guesthouse	17 C2
Hollywood Guest House	18 C2
KR Mansion	19 C2
Star Guest House	20 D3
Swallow	21 C2
Thai Hotel	22 C2
Vieng Thong	23 C2

EATING	
7-Eleven	(see 40)
Bangkok Welcome Cafe	24 C2
Café Europa	25 C3
Choke Dee Restaurant	26 D2
Eddy's	(see 13)
Eighty-Nine	27 C2
Kwan Café	28 D3
May & Mark	29 C2
Night Market	30 D2
Night Market	31 C1
Panan	32 C2
Pizzeria Firenze	33 D2
Reuan Phae	34 D2
Seahouse	(see 26)
Viva	35 C2

DRINKING	
O'Malleys	(see 13)
Oscar's Pub	36 B1
Smoody	37 D3

TRANSPORT	
Minivans to Ao Leuk	38 C1

PP Family Co	39 D2
Săwngthăew Stop	40 C2
Săwngthăew to Ao Leuk	41 C2
Săwngthăew to Ao Nang &	
Hat Nopharat Thara	42 C2
Săwngthăew to Ban Hua Hin	
(Ko Lanta)	43 C2

tion, the rooms at City Hotel are simple but quite comfortable with TVs and hot water. There's a great night market just across the street.

MIDRANGE

City Seaview (☎ 0 7562 2885; krabicityseaview@hotmail .com; 77/1 Th Khong Ka; r 500-1500B; 🗙) The best midrange hotel in town, it offers beautifully modern rooms that are tastefully decorated; the better rooms are larger and sport views of the water. It's an excellent newish place in a quiet part of town, but still within walking distance of the centre.

Vieng Thong (☎ 0 7562 0020; fax 0 7561 2525; 155 Th Utarakit; r 550-1000B; 🗙 🖳) Attracting a mixture of tourists and Thai businessmen, the

Vieng Thong is an acceptable (but unremarkable) choice in this range. It has quite good facilities, however, including a tour desk and large restaurant. Rooms are simple but spacious with private bathrooms, TVs and phones. Prices vary throughout the year.

Thai Hotel (☎ 0 7561 1474; 7 Th Issara; s 330B, d 370-700B; 🗙) Right in the centre, this large business hotel has good clean rooms with TVs and spotless bathrooms. There's a large restaurant and bar downstairs, which sometimes has karaoke.

Krabi Royal Hotel (☎ 0 7561 1582; krabiroyal@lem ononline.com; 403 Th Utarakit; r 1000B; 🗙 🖳) If you need to catch an early plane, this fairly generic midrange place is the closet hotel to the airport. All rooms have phones, hot showers, TVs and fridges, and there is a karaoke lounge, restaurant and bar.

TOP END

Krabi Maritime Park & Spa Resort (☎ 0 7562 0028, Bangkok ☎ 0 2719 0034; www.maritimeparkandspa .com; r 3000B; ❄ ▣ ▨) Also known as Krabi Meritime Hotel, this swanky spot near the river is almost 2km from Krabi. Set in lovely riverside grounds, the hotel is the best in town. It sports a nightclub, stylish pool, lake with swan-shaped paddleboats, fitness centre and spa. Rooms are classy and come with balconies featuring impressive views. Promotional rates of 1500B are usually available. There are shuttle buses to Krabi town and Ao Nang, and shuttle boats to Railay.

Eating

Reuan Mai (☎ 0 7563 1796; Th Maharat; dishes 60-150B) Known far and wide for serving Krabi's best cuisine of any genre, the extensive menu focuses on southern Thai, including excellent *kaeng sôm tháleh* (thick, spicy seafood soup with a tamarind-chilli base). It's 1km north of town.

Eighty-Nine (☎ 0 7561 1245; 89 Th Utarakit; dishes 40-150B) Most travellers end their evenings at this pleasant eatery, catching the free video movie screenings and enjoying a late-night nosh. The food, Western standbys such as spaghetti and pizza as well as Thai dishes, is unusually good for this kind of place. The restaurant emanates a casual traveller's atmosphere enhanced by a travel agency and Internet access right in the dining area.

Pizzeria Firenze (☎ 0 7562 1453; 10 Th Khong Ka; dishes 100-200B) The best of Krabi's pizza places, Pizzeria Firenze has a pleasant bistro atmosphere. It attracts plenty of locals as well as tourists looking for a taste of home. There is a decent wine selection.

May & Mark (☎ 0 7561 2562; Th Ruen Rudee; dishes 45-150B) Some great bread is baked here. There's also an assortment of excellent Thai and Western food, such as pumpkin soup and homemade yogurt. Culinary surprises from Mexico and Germany pop up on the menu, too.

Kwan Café (☎ 0 7561 1706; 30 Th Khong Ka; dishes 35-120B) Kwan serves up lots of breakfast choices, sandwiches, pizza, tofu burgers, tiramisu and specialty coffees in a modern,

clean and hip atmosphere. Service is cheerful and there are tables outside.

Café Europa (☎ 0 7562 0407; 1/9 Soi Ruamjit; dishes 75-200B) Run by a cheerful Danish expat, this friendly restaurant serves tasty European food and imported New Zealand steaks. There are plenty of Scandinavian dishes and a good wine selection.

Reuan Phae (no Roman-script sign; ☎ 0 7561 1956; Th Utarakit; dishes 60-150B) An old floating restaurant on the river. The food here is not so good, but the atmosphere can't be beaten – sip a cold beer or rice whisky and feel the tides go up and down.

Choke Dee Restaurant (☎ 0 7563 0226; 226 Th Utarakit; dishes 50-100B) On a busy corner, it offers the usual range of travellers' grub along with wine, cocktails and movies. Stop by for a green curry and a beer.

Panan (cnr Th Ruen Rudee & Th Maharat; dishes 30-50B) A popular Hainanese and Muslim restaurant, it's a simple, local corner place with a modern, clean atmosphere and a few pavement tables.

Bangkok Welcome Cafe (Pe-pe; cnr Th Maharat & Th Prachacheun; dishes 25B; ☼ 6am-4pm) Cooking up just eight inexpensive noodle and rice dishes, it's very popular at lunch and has probably the cheapest food in town that you can eat under a roof.

Viva (☎ 0 7563 0517; 29 Th Phruksauthit; dishes 100-180B, pizzas 130-340B) Another good, popular Italian restaurant with plenty of pasta, pizza and calzone selections on the menu. Also on tap are steaks, burgers, lassi and breakfast items all served in a modern space with bamboo furniture. Roving bands sometimes play here.

Seahouse (☎ 0 7561 1325; 7/5 Th Chao Fah; dishes 50-150B) Popular with travellers for its pizza, steak and cocktails, it has a nice wooden deck out the front.

Eddy's (☎ 0 7562 3573; dishes 35-150B) A tiny café right under A Mansion, it offers very large and strong double espressos along with other coffee drinks, breakfast items such as waffles and some Thai dishes. There are bistro tables out the front.

One of the best places to eat in Krabi is the **night market** (Th Khong Ka; meals 20-50B) near Tha Kong Ka (Chao Fa). The menus are in English but the food is authentic and excellent. There's fresh seafood and all manner of things on satay sticks, plus sweet milky Thai desserts. There's a similar **night market**

(Th Sukhon) just to the north, near the intersection with Th Phruksauthit.

Drinking & Entertainment

There are a few bars in town catering to *faràng*. Slinky tunes and mellow vibes in an eclectic space are found at **Smoody**, across from the old pier. A branch of **O'Malley's** (Th Chao Fah), next to Eddy's, has an intimate atmosphere and a happy hour from 8pm to 9pm. It prides itself on being 'a booze bonanza for budget drinkers'. **Oscar's Pub** (Th Hemthanon) is a modern disco towards the north of town.

Getting There & Away

AIR

Krabi's airport is 17km northeast of town on Hwy 4. Several airlines service Krabi. **THAI** (☎ 0 7562 2439; Krabi Maritime Park & Spa, Th Utarakit) has three daily flights to/from Bangkok (2560B, 1¼ hours). PB Air and Phuket Air also fly to Bangkok, although these flights are more sporadic and depend on demand.

BOAT

Boats to Ko Lanta and Ko Phi-Phi leave from a hilariously long new passenger pier about 5km north of Krabi. The largest boat operator is **PP Family Co** (☎ 0 7561 2463; www .phiphifamily.com), which has a ticket office right beside the pier. In the high season, there are boats to Ko Phi-Phi (200B, 1½ hours) at 9.30am, 11am and 3pm. In the low season, boats run at 11am and 3pm if the seas aren't too rough. For several months following the 2004 tsunami departures were irregular, but the old schedule should be back in place early 2006.

Likewise after the tsunami, boat service between Krabi and Ko Lanta was suspended for four months due to the lack of tourists. As the numbers stabilise again, service will resume from September to May, with boats to Ko Lanta (200B, two hours) at 10.30am and 1.30pm. These also stop at Ko Jam (one hour) on demand, though you'll pay the full 200B fare. During the monsoon, boats are replaced by air-con vans, which leave at around 11am, 1pm and 4pm.

Be sure to check boat departure times for Ko Phi-Phi or Ko Lanta with your hotel or guesthouse before making the longish trip out to the new pier. A *săwngthăew* or *túk-túk* from town to pier should cost no more than 120B per vehicle (not per person).

BUS

Krabi's government bus terminal is located 4km north of town at Talat Kao. The cheapest, most reliable way to obtain bus tickets in Krabi is to come to this bus terminal.

Government buses to/from Bangkok include ordinary (255B), 2nd-class air-con (357B), 1st-class air-con (459B) and 24-seat VIP (710B). The trip takes 12 hours (14 hours ordinary). Buses leave Bangkok 6.30pm to 8pm; they leave Krabi 3.30pm to 7pm. Other destinations include:

Destination	Fare (B)	Duration (hr)
Hat Yai		
ordinary	96	5
2nd class	130	5
1st class	173	5
Nakhon Si Thammarat		
ordinary	67	3
Phuket		
ordinary	65	4
2nd class	91	3½
1st class	117	3½
Phang-Nga		
ordinary	46	2
2nd class	64	2
1st class	82	2
Ranong		
ordinary	106	5
Sungai Kolok		
1st class	335	9
Surat Thani		
2nd class	80	4
1st class	180	3
Trang		
ordinary	55	2½
2nd class	70	2½
1st class	90	2

It's also possible to buy bus/boat combination tickets to Ko Samui (300B to 370B, 7½ hours, four daily) and Ko Pha-Ngan (450B, 8½ hours, four daily) from travel agencies in town.

MINIVAN

Minivans are booked through travel agencies in town. Prices can vary widely; shop around to get an idea. Some sample fares are Ao Leuk (30B, one hour), Hat Yai (180B to 200B, three hours), Ko Lanta (150B, 1½ hours), Trang (200B, two hours) and Satun (320B, five hours). Minivans leave when full.

ANDAMAN COAST

SǍWNGTHǍEW

Services to Ban Hua Hin (the ferry pier for Ko Lanta) leave from the intersection of Th Phattana and Th Phruksauthit. They run fairly frequently, cost 40B and take 40 minutes.

Getting Around

TO/FROM THE AIRPORT

Minivans into town cost 80B, and taxis cost 400B if boarded within the airport and 300B if you walk out of the airport (due to a taxi regulation). Getting to the airport, any travel agency sells tickets for minivans (80B). Alternatively, *túk-túk*/taxis cost 200/300B.

BOAT

Long-tail boats to Hat Rai Leh East (70B, 45 minutes) leave when full from the pier. In low season if the weather is bad these boats won't run – you'll have to take a *sǎwngthǎew* to Ao Nam Mao (20B) and a long-tail boat from there. Long-tail boats from Ao Nam Mao to Hat Rai Leh East cost 30B during the day (50B at night) and run year-round in good or bad weather.

During low season, if you find that you're waiting too long for a long-tail boat to fill (or if you don't like lengthy boat rides), you might consider taking a *sǎwngthǎew* to Ao Nang (20B, 40 minutes) and a long-tail boat from there to Hat Rai Leh West (40B, 10 minutes). Of course, if the weather is bad enough, long-tail boats don't run from Ao Nang either.

BUS

Local red buses to the government bus terminal in Talat Kao cost 10B; board them in front of the 7-Eleven on Th Maharat. Local white buses to Ao Nang and Hat Noppharat Thara cost 20B and leave from Th Maharat.

CAR

Several travel agencies and guesthouses can arrange motorcycle rentals for 150B a day with discounts in the low season. Jeep rentals range from 800B (open-top) to 1200B (air-con) per day. Café Europa arranges *túk-túk* charters to surrounding areas.

SǍWNGTHǍEW & TÚK-TÚK

Sǎwngthǎew to the government bus terminal cost 8B; a motorcycle taxi costs 30B.

Túk-túk cruise around town like sharks. Destinations include the bus station (50B), Wat Tham Seua (100B) and the airport (200B); don't get charged per person.

Sǎwngthǎew are probably the best option for getting around the Krabi area. Most leave from in front of the 7-Eleven on Th Maharat. Destinations include Ao Leuk (20B), Ao Nam Mao (40B), Ao Nang (20B, after 6pm 50B), Hat Noppharat Thara (20B) and Su-San Hoi (40B).

AROUND KRABI
Wat Tham Seua
วัดถ้ำเสือ

Around 8km northeast of Krabi is one of southern Thailand's most famous forest wats, **Wat Tham Seua** (Tiger Cave Temple). The main *wíhǎan* (hall) is built into a long, shallow limestone cave. On either side the cave, dozens of *kùtì* (monastic cells) are built into various cliffs and caves. You may see a troop of monkeys roaming the grounds.

Wat Tham Seua's abbot is Ajahn Jamnien Silasettho, a Thai monk who has allowed a rather obvious personality cult to develop around him. In the large, main cave are large portraits of Ajahn Jamnien, who is well known as a teacher of Vipassana (insight meditation) and Metta (loving-kindness). It is said that he was apprenticed at an early age to a blind lay priest and astrologer who practised folk medicine and that he has been celibate his entire life. On the inside of his outer robe, and on an inner vest, hang scores of talismans presented to him by his followers – altogether they must weigh several kilograms, a weight Ajahn Jamnien bears to take on his followers' karma. Many young women come to Wat Tham Seua to practise as eight-precept nuns.

The best part of the temple grounds can be found in a little valley behind the ridge where the *bòt* is located. Walk beyond the main temple building keeping the cliff on your left and you'll come to a pair of steep stairways. The first leads to a truly arduous climb of over 1200 steps – some of them extremely steep – to the top of a 600m karst peak. The fit and fearless will be rewarded with a Buddha statue, a gilded stupa and great views of the surrounding area; on a clear day you can see well out to sea.

The second stairway, next to a large statue of Kuan Yin (the Mahayana Buddhist Goddess of Mercy), leads over a gap in the ridge and into a valley of tall trees and limestone caves. Enter the caves on your left and look for light switches on the walls – the network of caves is wired so that you can light your way chamber by chamber through the labyrinth until you rejoin the path on the other side.

If you go to the temple, please dress modestly: pants down to the ankles, shirts covering the shoulders and nothing too tight. Travellers in beachwear at Thai temples don't realise how offensive they are and how embarrassed they should be.

GETTING THERE & AWAY

Take a *săwngthăew* from Krabi's Th Utarakit to the Talat Kao junction for 10B, then change to any bus or *săwngthăew* heading east on Hwy 4 towards Trang. Get off at the road on the left just past the small police station – tell the driver 'Wat Tham Seua'. Motorcycle taxis hang out here and charge 10B to the wat, or you can walk 2km straight up the road. In the morning a few *săwngthăew* from Th Phattana in town pass the turn-off for Wat Tham Seua (12B) on their way to Ban Hua Hin. Also in the morning there is usually a *săwngthăew* or two going direct to Wat Tham Seua from Talat Kao for around 20B. Private taxis to the wat cost 150B each way; *túk-túk* charge about 100B.

AO NANG
อ่าวนาง

pop 12,400

Fast becoming a full-blown resort destination, this burgeoning coastal town features a European-style promenade and a long strip of hotels, souvenir shops, restaurants and bars. The sand is slightly eroded, but for beach bums it's probably a better bet than Krabi. Rock climbing and ecotours to the mangroves and surrounding islands are major tourist draws – although the best climbing cliffs are actually a 20-minute boat ride away at Railay (see p684). For your money, Railay is a nicer place to stay, but Ao Nang is more convenient if you want to try one of the ecotours.

The tsunami destroyed many long-tail boats moored at Ao Nang, flooded a few

AO NANG

| 0 | 300 m |
| 0 | 0.2 miles |

INFORMATION		SLEEPING		EATING	
Money Exchange	1 C3	Andaman Sunset Resort	10 B3	Ao Nang Cuisine	23 B3
Money Exchange &		Aonang Villa Resort	11 C3	Lavinia Restaurant	(see 15)
ATM	(see 4)	Green Park	12 C3	Sala Thai	24 A2
Police	2 C3	J Mansion	13 C3	Somkiet Buri Restaurant	(see 20)
Tourist Police	3 B2	Krabi Resort	14 A2	Tanta	25 C3
		Lavinia	15 B3	Wanna's Restaurant	(see 10)
SIGHTS & ACTIVITIES		Peace Laguna Resort	16 C3		
Ao Nang Tourist Center	4 B3	Phra Nang Inn	17 C3	DRINKING	
Aqua Vision Diver Center	5 B3	Phra Nang Inn	18 C3	Encore Café	26 C3
Barracuda's Tour	6 B3	Sea World	19 C3	Full Moon Bar	27 B3
Phra Nang Divers	7 C3	Somkiet Buri Resort	20 D3	Midnight Bar	28 C3
Sea Canoe Thailand	8 C3	Southland House	21 B3	O'Malleys	29 C3
Sea, Land & Trek	9 B2	Ya Ya	22 C3	Planet Ao Nang	(see 27)

To Hat Nopparat Thara (2km);
Ko Phi-Phi Ferry (5km);
Nosey Parker's (7km)

4203

To Krabi
(20km)

4203

Sea Wall
Promenade

Ao Nang

To Railay
(4km)

ANDAMAN COAST

shops and damaged some sections of the concrete seawall along the beach. All has since been repaired.

Orientation & Information

Ao Nang is not a very large place, and most services and hotels are crammed along either the main beach road or on short side streets. Basically, Hwy 4203 heads west into town, then runs north along the beach about 500m and then heads back inland for a bit before curving towards the coast again at Hat Noppharat Thara.

All the information offices on the strip are private tour agencies and most offer international calls and Internet access for around 1B per minute. Several banks have ATMs and foreign exchange windows on the main drag, open from 10am to 8pm daily. For more extensive services, including medical emergencies, you will need to head into Krabi.

Activities

Loads of activities are possible at Ao Nang, and children under 12 typically get a 50% discount.

DIVING & SNORKELLING

Many dive shops arrange day dives to nearby islands (such as Ko Poda Nai and Ko Poda Nok). At Ko Mae Urai, a kilometre west of Poda Nok, two submarine tunnels lined with soft and hard corals offer lots of tropical fish and are suitable for all levels of divers. Longer, live-aboard trips include Ko Bida Nok/Ko Bida Nai, the Maya Wall, Hin Daeng and Hin Muang. Going rates are 1600B to 3100B for day trips (including two dives) to nearby islands. Four-day open-water diving certification courses cost 10,500B.

Reliable diving schools operating around the islands include **Phra Nang Divers** (☎ 0 7563 7064; www.pndivers.com) and **Aqua Vision Diver Center** (☎ 0 7563 7415; www.aqua-vision.net).

SEA KAYAKING

At least seven companies offer sea-kayak tours to mangroves and islands around Ao Nang. One of the best local paddles is the Tha Lin Canyon river cruise, an estuary trip that cuts through 200m-high foliaged limestone cliffs, mangrove channels and tidal lagoon tunnels. Bird-watching is great here –

brown-winged kingfishers, Pacific reef egrets, Asian dowitchers and white-bellied sea eagles are frequently seen. Also keep an eye out for otters, macaques, gibbons and two-banded monitor lizards. Other popular trips include the scenic sea lagoon at Ko Hong, the towering sea cliffs at Ao Thalane and the sea caves and 2000-year-old paintings at Ban Bho Tho. Trips generally cost between 1500B and 1700B for a full day and include lunch, fruit, drinking water, sea kayaks and guides.

The two best sea-kayaking companies are **Sea, Land & Trek** (☎ 0 7563 7364; seascaves@hotmail .com) and **Sea Canoe Thailand** (☎ 0 7569 5387; www .seacanoe.net).

ELEPHANT TREKKING

Several operators now run elephant treks into the forest surrounding Ao Nang. **Nosey Parker's** (☎ 0 7563 7463; Rte 4202; 1hr trek adult/child 700/300B, half-day trek 1600/800B) is based around 7km from Ao Nang and offers treks along jungle streams and through the woodland (where you may see monkeys and various exotic birds). Movie aficionados will enjoy the jungle trek to Tham Srakaew. The scenic cave was used as a location for the film *The Beach*.

Tours

Reliable tour agencies include **Barracuda's Tour** (☎ 0 7563 7092) and **Ao Nang Tourist Center** (☎ 0 7563 7551; www.aonangtouristcenter.com), both on the main beachfront strip.

The definitive Ao Nang excursion would have to be a four- or five-island tour by long-tail boat. Four-island tours visit: Ko Poda, with its lovely white-sand beach; Ko Hua Khwan (Chicken Island), which has decent snorkelling and a rock formation that is shaped like a chicken's head; and the smaller islands of Ko Tup and Ko Taloo, with a detour to Tham Phra-Nang (Princess Cave) at Railay. Five-island tours head out to the hidden lagoon at Ko Hong and the smaller islands of Ko Pakbia, Ko Rai, Ko Lading and Ko Daeng. The going rate is quite a good deal – 300B for four islands and 400B for five islands, including snorkelling gear, snacks, soft drinks and lunch.

Other options include 'mystery tours' (adult/child 850/400B), which visit rural villages, crystal pools and rubber, pineapple and papaya plantations.

Sleeping

Ao Nang has become rather overdeveloped in recent years and the strip is creeping upmarket, though a few budget options are hanging on further back from the seafront. Prices at all these places drop by 50% during the low season.

BUDGET

There are several guesthouses that are tightly crammed together in a small alley. You'll find them just up from the beach at the eastern end of the strip.

J Mansion (☎ 0 7569 5128; j_mansion10@hotmail.com; r 200-800B; ✦ ▣) Probably the best option, it's run by a friendly Thai family and offers clean, modern rooms decked out with TVs and minifridges painted with chintzy tropical scenes. There's also a restaurant, Internet café and motorcycle rental.

Southland House (☎ 0 7563 7316; r 250-1200B; ✦) Part of a row of shophouses and laundries on the alley behind Ao Nang Cuisine that offer cheap digs, Southland House has modern, comfortable and large fan rooms. It also offers more-expensive rooms that come with air-con; the best of these is huge and has sea views.

There are a few budget bungalow operations at the eastern end of town, where Rte 4203 turns inland.

MIDRANGE & TOP END

Most accommodation at Ao Nang falls into this bracket. The following places are recommended, but they are by no means your only options – there are dozens more.

Somkiet Buri Resort (☎ 0 7563 7320; www.somkietburi.com; r 2000-3000B; ✦ ▣) It just might be the most paradise-like place in town. The lush jungle grounds are filled with ferns and orchids, while lagoons, streams and meandering wooden walkways guide you to the 26 large and creatively designed rooms. A great swimming pool is set amid it all – balconies either face this pool or a peaceful pond. The service everywhere is first rate.

Krabi Resort (☎ 0 7563 7030, Bangkok ☎ 0 2208 9165; www.krabiresort.com; r 3800-8900B; ✦ ▣) The original Ao Nang resort, it's ageing gracefully and has well-outfitted rooms and luxury bungalows on landscaped and peaceful grounds, some right near the beach. There is an on-site dive school, a restaurant and a bar.

Green Park (☎ 0 7563 7300; bungalows 700B) A quiet and friendly spot, about 300m from the beach and one of the cheapest midrange places. The bungalows are well maintained and during the low season the rate drops to 200B.

Sea World (☎ 0 7563 7388; seaworld_aonang@hotmail.com; r 500-1000B; ✦ ▣) Well run and clean, this is another of the better options. The restaurant downstairs cooks up quite convincing Thai food.

Peace Laguna Resort (☎ 0 7563 7345; www.peacelagunaresort.com; r 1300-2200B, bungalows 600-900B; ✦ ▣) Looks a little like Eden. Sweet, modern bungalows sit around a large lagoon on gorgeous, well-maintained grounds while a limestone cliff basks in the background. There's a clean pool next to the fish-filled lagoon and a buffet breakfast (included in the price) is served nearby. The cheapest bungalows just have fans.

Phra Nang Inn (☎ 0 7563 7130; phranang@sun.phuket.ksc.co.th; r incl breakfast 1500-3900B; ✦ ▣) The beautiful interior décor – a unique bamboo theme with eclectic designs in shell and tile-work – is this place's forte. A second, similarly designed branch is across the road from the original.

Ya Ya (☎ 0 7563 7176; bungalows 750B) In a shady jungle setting, this traditional bungalow resort offers good-value abodes made of wood and bamboo with lovely terraces.

Lavinia (☎ 0 7569 5405; r 200-1800B; ✦) Lavinia has more of a homey and intimate feel than most places in town. Six rooms come with a variety of amenities and are modern and central. The place is located behind the shopfronts across from the beach. Prices vary drastically depending on the season.

Aonang Villa Resort (☎ 0 7563 7270; www.aonangvillaresort.com; r 3400-7500B; ✦ ▣) This flashy place is one of the few beachside resorts in Ao Nang. It features two restaurants and three-storey blocks of rooms around extensive lawns and a large pool.

Ocean Gardenview Resort (☎ 0 7563 7527; www.oceangardenview.com; bungalows incl breakfast 1300-2800B; ✦) Another good choice, there are comfortable, well-furnished, tasteful rooms (though the buildings are looking a bit tired) on lush grounds. Try the bungalows in the back garden; they are great and have all the amenities.

Andaman Sunset Resort (Wanna's Place; ☎ 0 7563 7484; www.wannasplace.com; r & bungalows 900-2000B;

🅧 🅩) Very pleasant rooms, some with sea views, are offered. Upmarket bungalows are also available and there's a small pool. The restaurant in front is reputedly pretty good. Prices vary widely depending on season.

Ao Nang Orchid Bungalows (☎ 0 7563 7116; fax 0 7563 7116; bungalows 800-1800B; 🅧) Pleasant, comfortable, good-sized and newish bungalows surrounding a flowery garden make this a decent deal for fan bungalows. The air-con ones might seem a tad overpriced, but if you arrive during the low season prices are more than slashed in half.

Beach Terrace (☎ 0 7563 7180; fax 0 7563 7184; r 600-1800B; 🅧) A modern apartment-style hotel where rooms have TV, fridge, small balcony and good baths. It's a better deal in the low season.

Eating

Ao Nang Cuisine (dishes 45-200B) This blue-tiled restaurant on the main strip is probably the most popular place to grab a bite in Ao Nang. There are a few computer terminals for checking email, and a better than average selection of Thai and Western favourites, including seafood.

Sala Thai (dishes 60-300B) The best (and most popular) of a series of seafood restaurants on decks overlooking the beach. Crab, lobster, prawns and fish are on display for your selection. This restaurant – along with its neighbours – has a wonderfully romantic atmosphere with open wooden deck, sea breezes and great views.

Somkiet Buri Restaurant (☎ 0 7563 7574; dishes 60-220B) At the resort of the same name, it cooks up great Thai food and has very attentive service. Even if it didn't, you'd still want to come for the lush open-air dining pavilion.

Lavinia (☎ 0 7569 5404; dishes 150-400B) A popular Italian place at the resort of the same name, it does convincing pizza and pasta served up at wooden bench tables.

Tanta (☎ 0 7563 7118; dishes 60-250B) Offers great Thai and international selections. It's a popular modern place with a raised covered terrace and wood accents. Wine is also served.

Wanna's Restaurant (dishes 45-110B) Casual and inexpensive, it's worth stopping by for the variety of food on offer – everything from burgers to cheese selections to Swiss specialities, along with Thai cuisine and breakfast.

Drinking

Have a drink; there's no shortage of bars in Ao Nang.

O'Malley's Come during the extended 7pm to 11pm happy hour when cocktails are poured for half price. It's on a calm side street and has a great casual atmosphere, with wooden furniture and a free pool table. Guinness is available, but it's not cheap.

Midnight Bar (☎ 0 7563 7210) Run by a feisty German, it sits above the street on its own laid-back, airy patio. It's the hang-out spot for certain local expats. The music tends towards hard rock, though it can vary depending on clientele moods.

Full Moon Bar (☎ 0 7563 7548) This atmospheric bar is very central and popular and has a long cocktail menu.

Planet Ao Nang (☎ 0 7563 7265) Near Full Moon Bar, it's another popular, happenin' spot to be caught drinking. The music, at time of writing, was good.

Encore Café (🕒 4pm-2am in high season) This venue is a modern air-con space, with pool table and live music on Friday from 10pm. Each night there's a different theme, such as ladies' night, speed pool, karaoke and sports viewing.

Getting There & Around

A ferry service to Ko Phi-Phi runs year-round (250B, two hours, 9am) and includes a ride to/from the pier in nearby Hat Noppharat Thara. In low season boats go via Hat Rai Leh East to pick up passengers; in high season they go via Hat Rai Leh West.

Long-tail boats to the Hat Rai Leh area run daily in good weather and cost 50B. In bad weather take a *săwngthăew* to Ao Nam Mao (10B) and then a long-tail boat (30B), which run even in choppy weather. Long-tail boats from Ao Nang to Krabi (50B) run only in high season.

Săwngthăew are a good way to get around. Destinations include Krabi (20B), Hat Noppharat Thara (10B) and Ao Nam Mao (10B). Look for them on the main road.

Taxis from Ao Nang *to* the airport cost 300B, but *from* the airport can cost up to 500B.

HAT NOPPHARAT THARA
หาดนพรัตน์ธารา

Starting just 200m north of Ao Nang is the long, shallow, scenic and relatively unspoilt

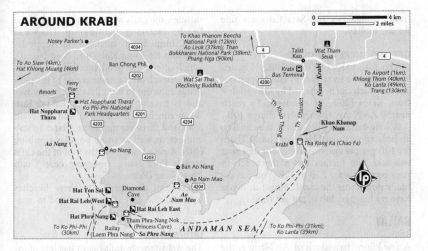

beach of Hat Noppharat Thara (though it looks primed for development). Towards its northern end, right at the mouth of Khlong Haeng (a small canal), are some tall and very cool karst formations. During low tide it's possible to ford this canal, though it could be a muddy proposition.

Hat Noppharat Thara is part of the Hat Noppharat Thara/Ko Phi-Phi Marine National Park and a favourite spot for Thai picnickers. Along with a few scattered bungalow operations here, there are two government bungalows for rent, as well as a small park visitors centre, near the canal, and ferry pier for boats to Ko Phi-Phi.

Beyond this canal and ferry pier is a more secluded section of Hat Noppharat Thara, a pleasant and shell-strewn strand that stretches a fair distance to the west. A bit further from here, some five-star hotels have been built. However, an isolated and almost island-like feel is still prevalent in this section of beach, with only a handful of bungalow operations. There *is* dirt road access from the north, but it can be rough riding.

SLEEPING & EATING

The following places are on the first section of Hat Noppharat Thara, set back from the beach. All have their own restaurant, though a few other independent eateries are located here and there. There's an especially lively cluster of simple restaurants near the visitors centre area.

Sabai Resort (☎ 0 7563 7791; r 750-1600B; 🅿 🔲) This newish place is away from the beach a bit, on a side street. On hand are some modern, clean bungalows, pleasant grounds and a decent pool.

Cashew Nut (☎ 0 7563 7560; r 200-600B) Near Sabai Resort, it's a cheaper option offering no-frills fan rooms.

Government bungalows (☎ 0 7563 7200; 2-6 person tents 300B, 2-person bungalows 600B, 6-8 person bungalows 1200B) At the national park headquarters, these bungalows are well maintained with fans, bathrooms and mosquito nets on the windows. A small canteen serves meals in the evenings.

The following bungalows are past the canal and are ideal for travellers seeking some solitude.

Andaman Inn (☎ 0 1893 2964; bungalows 500B) First in line, it offers 35 basic bungalows squared around a grassy area. Movies play at night in the restaurant and electricity is available from 6pm to 6am. If you stay here, call ahead for a free boat ride.

Emerald (☎ /fax 0 1956 2566; bungalows 900-1200B; 🔲) Beautifully decorated and comfortable bungalows are found at this pleasant up-market place. Most of the bungalows have large, triangular verandas and there's a comfortable restaurant. It's closed between May and September.

West along the beach are a couple of similar resorts offering wooden bungalows with private bathrooms for 150B to 300B, but all close down in the low season. Long

Beach Bungalows and Sara Cove are fine for the money.

GETTING THERE & AROUND

A ferry runs to Ko Phi-Phi (250B, 1½ hours, 9am) from the ferry pier in Hat Noppharat Thara, which can be reached by *săwngthăew* from Krabi (20B, 30 minutes). To reach nearby Ao Nang, *săwngthăew* charge 10B.

A long-tail boat plies across the canal to an isolated section of Hat Noppharat Thara for 10B per person; this same long-tail boat will take you further down the beach to your bungalow for 20B to 30B. You can actually slog across the canal at low tide if you have no luggage, but it can get muddy.

RAILAY

ไร่เล

A few kilometres south of Ao Nang is the jagged peninsula of Railay, which encompasses a series of spectacular clear bays with lush limestone cliffs that drop right into the blue sea. The cliff-backed isthmus is also one of the world's leading rock-climbing destinations. Although the official name of the peninsula is Laem Phra Nang, almost everyone calls it Railay.

Boats from Ao Nang land on lovely **Hat Rai Leh** on the western side of the peninsula (it's also called Hat Rai Leh West). The beach is backed by a string of tasteful resorts that make the best of the powdery white sand and spectacular sunsets. The ocean here is deep enough to swim even at low tide. At the southern end of the beach is the mighty Thaiwand Wall, a sheer limestone cliff offering some of the most challenging rtes at Railay.

Just north of Hat Rai Leh West is **Hat Ton Sai**, a slightly muddy beach with more excellent rock climbing and plenty of cheap bungalows. You can get here by long-tail boat or along the steep path over the cliffs at the northern end of Hat Rai Leh West. There are occasional full-moon parties here during the high season. If you're coming by long-tail from Ao Nang, ask the boat owner to drop you straight at Ao Ton Sai.

Near the tip of the peninsula is **Hat Phra Nang**, a splendid strip of whispering white sand, framed by looming cliffs. The plush Rayavadee resort dominates the eastern end of the beach but the rest of Hat Phra Nang is untouched. A huge cavern punches straight through the cliffs at the western end of the beach, emerging halfway up Thaiwand Wall. Immediately offshore are Happy Island and Ko Rung Nok (Bird Nest Island), which offer some good snorkelling.

The beach on the eastern side of the peninsula runs out to mud flats and mangroves and is usually known as **Hat Rai Leh East**. Boats run here from Krabi and Ao Nam Mao, and there are numerous places to stay and eat, as well as some popular climbing cliffs. A path leads from the foot of the cliffs to Hat Phra Nang, emerging near Tham Phra Nang (Princess Cave).

Tsunami damage along these beaches was minimal and all had returned to normal within four months.

Information

The website www.railay.com has lots of information about Railay, including photos and video of the tsunami (which only stood at about 1.5m when it broke on the beach here). Several places can change cash and travellers cheques (with the usual 23B commission per cheque), including the shop at Sand Sea Resort on Hat Rai Leh West. Internet access is available at Sand Sea Resort and Ya Ya Resort for 180B per hour, but the connections are expensive and unreliable; you're better off checking your email in Ao Nang.

Sights & Activities

Railay is primarily an activities kind of place, although there are a few things to see on the peninsula. At the southern beach end of Hat Tham Phra Nang, under the tall limestone cliff, is **Tham Phra Nang Nok** – a cave with a story. Local legend claims that during the 3rd century BC a passing royal barque carrying a charismatic Indian princess named Sri Guladevi (Si Kunlathewi in Thai) foundered in a storm. The princess' spirit came to inhabit a large cave near the wreck, using power gained through many past lives to grant favours to all who came to pay respect. Local fisher folk place carved wooden phalli in the cave as offerings to the Phra Nang (Holy Princess) so that she will provide plenty of fish for them.

ROCK CLIMBING

Limestone cliffs on the huge headland between Tham Phra Nang and East Rai Leh, and on nearby islands, offer world-class rock-climbing with simply stunning views. Most surfaces provide high-quality limestone with steep, pocketed walls, overhangs and the occasional hanging stalactite. About 700 sport rtes have been bolted, many with mid- to high-difficulty ratings (the French rating system is used). Novices often begin with Muay Thai, a 50m wall with around 20 climbs at the southern end of Hat Rai Leh East. Certain areas are off limits because they're part of Hat Noppharat Thara/Ko Phi-Phi Marine National Park, including the cliff next to the Rayavadee Premier resort and cliffs outside Tham Phra Nang Nai.

A half-day climb with guide, equipment and insurance costs about 800B, while an all-day climb costs 1500B and three days costs 5000B. You are also able to rent sport-climbing equipment for two people, which includes harnesses, shoes, a rope, 12 quick-draws, chalk and a guidebook for a half/full day (600/1000B).

It's not hard finding a climbing outfit; there are at least six in the area. A couple of the more established operators are **King Climbers** (☎ 075637125; kingclimbers@iname.com) and **Tex Rock Climbing** (☎ 0 7563 1509; texrock@loxinfo .co.th). Most of these outfits shut down during the rainy season.

DIVING & SNORKELLING

Diving is possible in this area, though you'd have more choice of dive shops in Ao Nang. **Krabi Divers** (☎ 0 7562 2587; Hat Rai Leh East), at Railay Viewpoint Resort, charges 1200B for two local dives and 2200B for dives at outlying islands.

The islands off the Railay coast are good for snorkelling. Besides Ko Poda and Ko Hua Khwan, there is the nearer island of Ko Rang Nok (Bird Nest Island). Next to that is a larger, unnamed island (possibly part of the same island at low tide) with an undersea cave. Most of the bungalows do reasonably priced day trips to these, as well as other islands in the area, for about 450B. If you just want to snorkel off Railay, most resorts can rent you a snorkel, mask and fins or 150B.

HIKING

On the cool little path from Hat Rai Leh East to Hat Tham Phra Nang is the trailhead to **Sa Phra Nang** (Holy Princess Pool), a

hidden lagoon inside the cliff. This is not a hike for the weak or vertigo-prone; it's not long, but is very strenuous and at times dangerous. The trail starts ominously, with a slippery climb up a steep, lush hill covered in tree roots. Mouldy ropes guide you along the leafy mountain trails, with some 'free' (unprotected) rock-climbing down 15ft walls necessary at times. Windows along side trails reward you with astounding views of the west and east Hat Rai Leh double bays. The trailhead starts at the covered rest bench area.

CAVES

On Hat Rai Leh East is **Diamond Cave** (admission 20B), consisting of three caverns. All three contain some of the most beautiful limestone formations in the country, including a golden 'stone waterfall' of sparkling quartz. Local mythology says this cave is the grand palace of the sea princess, while Tham Phra Nang on the beach is her summer palace. To get here, just follow the signs.

Sleeping & Eating

All the places listed here have their own restaurant, often located beachside. In the low season (approximately May to October) rates plummet and they are nearly cut in half at some places.

HAT TON SAI

This beach has become the main rock-climbers' hang out (with bolted climbing cliffs on all sides). It also attracts backpackers, because it offers the cheapest digs around. It retains a peaceful unspoiled atmosphere despite the fact that full-moon parties take place here (though not on Ko Pha-Ngan's scale). Some places only have electricity at night. Hat Ton Sai is the only beach in the area not easily accessible when the tide is high; during these times you'll either have to take a boat or do some rope-assisted rock scrambling. At low tide you can easily walk around the point to Hat Rai Leh West. Don't confuse this place with Hat Ton Sai on Ko Phi-Phi.

Andaman Nature Resort (☎ 0 7563 7092; fax 0 7563 7094; bungalows 550-800B) Probably the most-popular option at Hat Ton Sai, this well-run place has a good traveller vibe and a nice multilevel restaurant and bar. The neat wooden bungalows are spread out among

ANDAMAN COAST

the trees behind. It's a climbers' hang out. During the low season bungalows can go for just 100B.

Ton Sai Bungalows (☎ 0 7562 2584; bungalows 300-800B) Bamboo or concrete bungalows are well spaced in a jungle setting. The most expensive are set closest to the beach. Kayaks are available for rent and there's a bar and climbing school nearby. During the low season bungalows can go for just 50B!

Krabi Mountain View Resort (☎ 0 7562 2610; www .krabimountainview.com; r 600-1400B; 🕸) On offer are rows of tidy white bungalows set amid a shady forest. There's a big bar and restaurant area with satellite TV, plus a climbing shop.

Dream Valley Resort (☎ 0 7562 2583; iad16@hot mail.com; r 150B, bungalows 400-1000B; 🕸) This old-style wooden place has a variety of bungalows as well as cheaper rooms with shared bathrooms. Decent seafood is offered at the restaurant and there's a minimart and motorcycle taxi to transfer you to the beach. It's behind the beach on the path beside Ton Sai Bungalows.

Green Valley Resort (☎ 0 7562 1665; www.krabidir .com/grvalleyresort; bungalows 400-600B) Cute, white bungalows are lined up around leafy trees and a sparse garden. Inside they're fairly pleasant, with simple décor and tile floors.

HAT RAI LEH WEST

This was the first place to be developed in Railay. It faces west, so the sunsets are fabulous. Most of the places here are mid-range to top end and have lots of modern facilities.

Sand Sea Resort (☎ 0 7562 2574; www.krabisand sea.com; bungalows incl breakfast 900-3100B; 🕸 🖥) Beautifully located, the comfortable bungalows line both sides of a flowery tropical garden. They are done up in light colours and feature peaceful décor. Brick pathways meander to the beach, where a seaside restaurant awaits. The swimming pool is cool and refreshing.

Railay Bay Resort (☎ 0 7562 2998; www.railaybay resort.com; bungalows 1200-3400B; 🕸 🖥) The most upmarket option, it commands a large lot with renovated bungalows stretching to both bays. The bungalows are well designed and have TVs and the restaurant is very good – the pizzas are particularly recommended. There's also a beachside bar and spa facilities.

Railay Village Resort (☎ 0 7562 2578; www.rail ayvillageresort.com; bungalows 500-2500B; 🕸) This place offers the cheapest rooms on Hat Rai Leh West. Rustic bungalows border a verdant, shrubby garden all the way seawards. The place has a relaxed air about it and there is a tree-shaded restaurant at the front that does good food, but doesn't serve alcohol.

Railei Beach Club (☎ 0 7562 2582; www.raileibeach club.com; houses 3000-10,000B) This is a collection of private homes located on exclusive forested grounds. The one- to three-bedroom beach houses come with kitchen and open deck or patio. It's best to book these beautiful abodes at least two months in advance; there's a minimum stay of three nights. In the low season rates can drop as much as 60%.

BoBo Bar & Restaurant (dishes 60-120B) This small place beside Railay Village Resort is probably the only independent restaurant on the peninsula. Friendly, laid-back service in a casual dining area could be worth a try – nothing fancy should be expected here. Tropical cocktails, real coffee and cold beers are also offered.

HAT PHRA NANG

There's only one place to stay on this beautiful beach.

Rayavadee (☎ 0 7562 0740; www.rayavadee.com; r 41,800-54,800B; 🕸 🖥) Yes, you read those prices right. But if you have serious baht to burn, this exclusive colonial-style five-star resort monopolises 26 acres of stunning beachfront property. Seven types of luxury bungalows dot the perfectly landscaped grounds; all are two-storey and fabulously decked out in a traditional Thai style. Champagne breakfast, afternoon tea and dinner are included, as are water sports and airport transfers. There's a luxurious pool and great security – guards won't let you enter the area to 'just have a look around'. Discounted rates may be available during 2006 while tourism recovers from the tsunami disaster.

HAT RAI LEH EAST

Often referred to as Sunrise Beach, the beach here tends towards mud flats during low tide so most people head to Hat Phra Nang or Hat Rai Leh West for sea and sand activities. The resorts on the hillside above the beach get sea breezes, but it can feel like a sauna in the evenings down on the sand. The following rates drop by half in the low season.

Railay Highland Resort (☎ 0 7562 1732; bungalows 700B) This fine resort sits in the middle of a natural basin above Hat Rai Leh East and it is surrounded by towering cliffs. There's a very stylish bar and restaurant sitting on stilts in the centre. The thoughtfully designed wood-and-bamboo bungalows surround the dining area and a shuttle bus runs between the resort and the beach. A good deal.

Ya Ya Resort (☎ 0 7562 2593; r 550-1500B; ✿) A renovated oldie that remains popular, it features pleasant rooms made mostly of natural materials in three-storey buildings with steep staircases and small wooden patios. They line a lush garden (mosquito repellent is crucial). Air-con rooms have fridge and TV.

Sunrise Tropical Resort (☎ 0 7562 2599; www .sunrisetropical.com; bungalows 3000-4000B; ✿ ✿) Stylish Thai-style villas with lovely décor and very posh bathrooms are set on well-maintained grounds. The villas have all the modern conveniences, and the pool here is refreshing.

Railay Hill Bungalow (☎ 0 7562 1726; railayhill@ yahoo.com; camping 100B, bungalows 400-500B) Situated way inland, a 10-minute walk around a perimeter wall from the beach, it has clean, large thatched A-frame bungalows built of logs. They're basic (just a mattress on the floor with a mosquito net) but comfortable enough, and sit among a thin forest. Wood-plank walkways connect the bungalows with the restaurant.

Diamond Cave Bungalows (☎ 075622589; diamond cave@hotmail.com; r 500B, bungalows 800-2000B; ✿ ▢) The long-established Diamond Cave has an eclectic collection of bungalows with small verandas. There's a restaurant that shows video movies and an on-site dive school. Avoid the rooms at the back, which cop some noise from the generators.

Railay Viewpoint Resort (☎ 0 7562 1686; bungalows 600-2000B; ✿ ✿) Near Diamond Cave, it maintains 70 large, modern two-storey rooms and bungalows on a nice hillside setting. There's a pleasant pool on the premises. The view gets progressively better as you go up the hill.

Coco Restaurant (dishes 50-100B) Immediately north of the Ya Ya Resort, Coco has a good reputation for both its food and a romantic atmosphere at night, when the lighting turns the shrubby garden into a mysterious jungle.

There are several other rustic restaurants at Hat Rai Leh East that all serve Westernised Thai food. Take a stroll along the strip and see what catches your fancy.

Getting There & Around

At the time of research, the only way to get to Railay was by long-tail boat, either from Tha Kong Ka (Chao Fa) in Krabi or from the seafront at Ao Nang. Boats between Krabi and Hat Rai Leh East leave every 1½ hours from 7.45am to 6pm (70B, 45 minutes).

Boats to Hat Rai Leh West or Ton Sai (50B, 15 minutes) leave from the eastern end of the promenade at Ao Nang during daylight hours. After dark you'll pay 80B. If seas are rough, boats leave from a sheltered cove just west of Krabi Resort in Ao Nang. You can be dropped at Hat Phra Nang or Hat Ton Sai for the same fare.

During exceptionally high seas, the boats from both Ao Nang and Krabi stop running, but you may still be able to get from Hat Rai Leh East to Ao Nam Mao (30B, 15 minutes), where you can pick up a *săwngthăew* to Krabi or Ao Nang. Even if boats are running all the way to Ao Nang, you can expect a drenching on any boat ride during the monsoon.

From October to May, the *Ao Nang Princess* runs between Hat Noppharat Thara National Park headquarters and Ko Phi-Phi with a stop in Hat Rai Leh West. Long-tails run out to meet the boat at around 9.15am from in front of the Sand Sea Resort; the fare from Railay is 250B.

KHAO PHANOM BENCHA NATIONAL PARK

อุทยานแห่งชาติเขาพนมเบ็ญจา

This 50-sq-km park (admission 200B) protects a dramatic area of virgin rainforest along the spine of 1350m-high Khao Phanom Bencha, just 20km north of Krabi. The name means Five-Point Prostration Mountain, a reference to the mountain's profile, which resembles a person prostrated in prayer, with their hands, knees and head touching the ground.

The park is full of scenic waterfalls, including the 11-tiered **Nam Tok Huay To**, just

500m from the park headquarters. Close by and almost as dramatic are **Nam Tok Huay Sadeh** and **Nam Tok Khlong Haeng**. On the way into the park, you can visit **Tham Khao Pheung**, a fantastic cave with shimmering mineral stalactites and stalagmites. Numerous trails snake through the park providing excellent opportunities for hiking. You can discover lesser-known streams and waterfalls, too.

Clouded leopard, black panther, tiger, Asiatic black bear, barking deer, serow, Malayan tapir, leaf monkey, gibbon and various tropical birds – including the helmeted hornbill, argus pheasant and extremely rare Gurney's pitta – make their home here.

There is no public transport to the park, and it doesn't offer any lodging or eating options. But the park is an easy day trip from Krabi by hired motorcycle; just follow the sign-posted turn-off from Hwy 4. Alternatively, you can hire a túk-túk for around 300B return.

THAN BOKKHARANI NATIONAL PARK
อุทยานแห่งชาติธารโบกขรณี

If you visit this national park just after the monsoons, you'll be treated to a lush and surreal experience – almost like you've stepped onto the set of a Disney movie. At the park headquarters, close to the small town of Ao Leuk and 46km northwest of Krabi, emerald-green waters flow out of a narrow cave in a tall cliff and into a large lotus pool, which spills into a wide stream and then divides into many smaller rivulets. At each rivulet there's a pool and a little waterfall; the effect is magical. The park was established in 1991 and protects a large area of islands, mangroves and limestone caves throughout the Ao Leuk area.

Thais from Ao Leuk come to bathe at these pools on weekends, when it's full of people playing in the streams – and shampooing their hair, which seems to be a favourite activity here. During the week there are only a few people about – mostly kids fishing. Vendors sell noodles, excellent roast chicken, delicious battered squid and sôm-tam (green papaya salad) under a roofed area to one side.

Activities

Caving is the name of the game in this park. Among the protected caves scattered around

the Amphoe Ao Leuk, one of the most interesting is **Tham Hua Kalok** (also called Tham Pee Hua Toe or Big-Headed Ghost Cave), reached by long-tail boat or sea kayak from the pier at Ban Bho Tho, 7km south of Ao Leuk. Set in a limestone hill, legend has it that a huge human skull was found in the cave, but the ghost story probably has more to do with the 2000- to 3000-year-old paintings of human and animal figures that adorn the cave walls.

Nearby **Tham Lawt** (Tube Cave) is distinguished by the navigable stream flowing through it and can also be reached by boat. Both caves are popular destinations for sea-kayaking tours from Krabi or Ao Nang, but you can also hire sea kayaks and guides at Tha Bho Tho for 800B. Long-tails are available for 300B.

There are no less than seven other similar limestone caves in the park, including **Tham Sa Yuan Thong**, a few kilometres southeast of Ao Leuk, which has a natural spring bubbling into a pool at its mouth. The park also includes the uninhabited island of **Ko Hong**, with fine beaches, jungle-cloaked cliffs and a scenic hidden lagoon. Sea kayak and long-tail boats come here from Ao Nang.

Sleeping

Ao Leuk has a few places to bed down, or you can camp with permission from the park headquarters.

PN Mountain Resort (☎ 0 7568 1554; r 400-1200B; ❄ 🖳) This is a newer place with modern rooms and a dramatic backdrop: a lush limestone cliff wall with a hole in the middle. It's on Hwy 4, 1km north of the park turnoff.

Ao Leuk Resort (☎ 0 7568 1133; r 300-500B; ❄) Right beside the park headquarters, this place has old rooms with bathrooms and TVs in a motel-like block.

Getting There & Away

Than Bok, as the locals call it, is near the town of Ao Leuk. The park headquarters is about 1.5km south of Ao Leuk town along Rte 4039. Buses and sǎwngthǎew from Krabi cost 20B and stop on Hwy 4. From here you can walk about 1.3km to the park headquarters or take a motorcycle taxi for 10B. The easiest way to visit the caves is to join a sea-kayaking tour from Krabi or Ao Nang (that way you don't have to worry about transportation).

To get to Ban Bho Tho from Ao Leuk on your own steam (to organise your own sea-kayak tour), take a motorcycle taxi (50B) to the 'Tham Phee Huato' turn-off on Rte 4039. From the junction it's about 2km to Ban Bho Tho along the first signposted road on the left.

KO PHI-PHI
เกาะพีพี

About 40km offshore from Krabi are the scenic two limestone islands of Ko Phi-Phi Don and Ko Phi-Phi Leh. Phi-Phi Don, the larger island, has all the tourist infrastructure, including resorts, restaurants, bars, tour agencies and dive schools. About 6km south, Ko Phi-Phi Leh is completely undeveloped and hemmed in by towering limestone cliffs.

Both are part of Hat Noppharat Thara/Ko Phi-Phi Marine National Park, which has protected Phi-Phi Leh, to a degree, but has completely failed to protect Phi-Phi Don, which is fast turning into a mini Samui.

Prior to the 2004 tsunami, Ko Phi-Phi was the most popular tourist destination along the Andaman coast. From December to March every room and bungalow was full, and it's easy to see why – with cliffs plunging into placid green waters just made for floating, snorkelling or swimming, plus curving bays of white-sand beaches and dense tropical forests, Ko Phi-Phi is easily that island paradise you always dreamed about.

Unfortunately, it became everyone else's dream as well, and development had packed the beaches of Phi-Phi Don with bungalows and restaurants – too many for the island's limited water supply to sustain. A concrete pier built to accommodate the big boats bringing in the tourists hordes scarred a once-untouched strip of white sand. Pollution from boat engines and careless dropping of anchors badly damaged the reefs on Phi-Phi Leh, and huge amounts of rubbish – from plastic bottles to stray thongs (flip-flops) – left by departing tourists now wash up in the once crystal-clear and clean bays.

As most of the world knows, in December 2004 Phi-Phi-Don's fortunes were tragically reversed by tsunami waves that destroyed virtually every standing structure on the twin bays of Ao Ton Sai and Ao Lo Dalam.

In terms of loss of life and property, Ko Phi-Phi Don was second only to Khao Lak and Bang Niang in Phang-Nga Province.

Ko Phi-Phi Leh
เกาะพีพีเล

Surrounded by an impregnable wall of limestone cliffs, this island, about 6km south of Phi-Phi Don, has two strikingly beautiful lagoons: **Pilah** on the eastern coast and **Ao Maya** (Maya Bay) on the western coast. The latter became famous in 1999, when a Hollywood director used it as the main location for the film *The Beach,* based on UK author Alex Garland's hugely successful novel of the same name.

Although the bay has always been a favourite stop for day-tripping snorkellers, after the movie was released tourist traffic increased tenfold, and today the once-pristine corals have been marred by bad anchoring. The tsunami actually improved the looks of this beach, adding more sand and flushing out rubbish jettisoned by tour boats. With the post-tsunami lack of tourism – for as long as it lasts – the sublime beauty of this cove is more enjoyable now that you don't have to fight for sand space with hundreds of others. The view across the shimmering turquoise and emerald sea lake, almost completely enclosed by limestone cliffs, is picture perfect. And snorkelling in the warm waters around the island still reveals schools upon schools of brightly coloured tropical fish.

The other important sight on Phi-Phi Leh is **Viking Cave** (Tham Phaya Naak; admission 20B) at the northeastern tip of the island. The cave takes its name from the primitive images of Asian junks and other ships on the walls, painted by fisherman over the last 400 years.

The cave is also a collection point for swiftlet nests. Swiftlets like to build their saliva nests high up in the caves between rocky hollows that are very difficult to reach. Agile collectors build vine-and-bamboo scaffolding to get at the nests but are occasionally injured or killed in falls. Before ascending the scaffolds, the collectors pray and make offerings of tobacco, incense and liquor to the cavern spirits.

There are no bungalow operations on Ko Phi-Phi Leh, and it's not possible to spend the night on this island – day trips are the

ANDAMAN COAST

only way to see it, and almost everyone who visits Phi-Phi Don joins one of these. Tours last about half a day and include snorkelling stops at various points around the island, with detours to Viking Cave and Maya Bay. You'll see these trips advertised everywhere on Phi-Phi Don. Long-tail trips cost 600B; by motorboat you'll pay around 2000B.

Ko Phi-Phi Don
เกาะพีพีดอน

Phi-Phi Don's topography boasts scenic hills, awesome cliffs, long beaches, emerald waters and remarkable bird and sea life. Actually comprising two rocky islands – Ko Nok (Outer Island) and Ko Nai (Inner Island) – joined by a broad sandy isthmus, most of the resorts were squeezed together at **Ao Ton Sai** (Banyan Tree Bay) and **Hat Hin Khom**. Both are on the southern shore of the isthmus, where you'll also find the main pier.

Ao Ton Sai was devastated by the tsunami, and all but two resorts at this beach were closed at the time of writing. Resorts on **Ao Lo Dalam**, on the northern side of the isthmus, also were destroyed.

Between January and April 2005 Krabi's provincial government announced repeatedly that it would establish a large public park where restaurants, beachfront bars and upmarket accommodation once stretched from Ao Ton Sai along to Ao Lo Dalam. The idea was to encourage low-density use of the land, which will always be extremely vulnerable to tsunamis.

Business interests have resisted the idea, and in spite of government signs forbidding anyone to rebuild on either of the bays, reconstruction is well under way without any zoning whatsoever. Unless someone takes control soon, within a year or two these beaches will return to their original overdeveloped state.

Resorts and bungalows at Hat Hin Khom were also damaged but are under repair and most are open.

At the northern end of the Ko Nai is **Laem Thong**, where the island's *chao náam* population of about 100 lives. There are a few luxury resorts here. South of Laem Thong is the sizable bay **Ao Lo Bakao**, where there is a small resort. Next down this coast is another beautiful beach, **Hat Ranti**, with decent surf. **Hat Yao** (Long Beach) faces south and has some of Phi-Phi Don's best coral reefs,

as well as mostly budget digs. Laem Thong, Hat Yao, Hat Ranti and Ao Lo Bakao survived the tsunami quite well, and all are welcoming visitors.

Park administrators had allowed development on Phi-Phi Don to continue fairly unchecked, although excessive building has stabilised to a significant degree over the last several years. It's actually doubtful the park ever had the power or influence to stop the construction. The rumour was park officials wouldn't dare to even set foot on Ko Phi-Phi for fear of being attacked by village chiefs and bungalow developers profiting from tourism.

The tsunami demolished a small power plant and water reservoir in the centre of the island, although neither facility had sufficient capacity to supply all of the resorts in the first place. Many resorts rely on generators.

It's also worth noting that there are no cars on Ko Phi-Phi.

ACTIVITIES
Diving & Snorkelling
Like elsewhere in southern Thailand, Ko Phi-Phi has some world-class dive sites. Pre-tsunami, dozens upon dozens of dive shops competed for your business. With Phi-Phi Don's commercial centre reduced to rubble, you can arrange diving and snorkelling trips around the island or to nearby islands through resorts on other beaches.

Some popular destinations within a 1½-hour boat ride include Ko Ha, Hin Daeng and Hin Muang. The ferry *King Cruiser* lies only 12m below the surface and is visited by dive operators from both Ko Phi-Phi and Phuket. Phi-Phi's dive shops all offer identical prices: an open-water certification course costs 9900B, while the standard two-dive trips cost 1800B, or 2600B if you want to visit the *King Cruiser* shipwreck. You can also dive out at Hin Daeng and Hin Muang, off Ko Lanta (3600B for two dives).

Visibility is best from December to April, though trips run year-round, weather permitting. If you're interested in sticking around for a while, many dive shops have seasonal openings for dive masters and instructors – a second language apart from English is an advantage. Ask around.

Snorkelling trips to Ko Phi-Phi Leh also can be arranged. If you're going on your

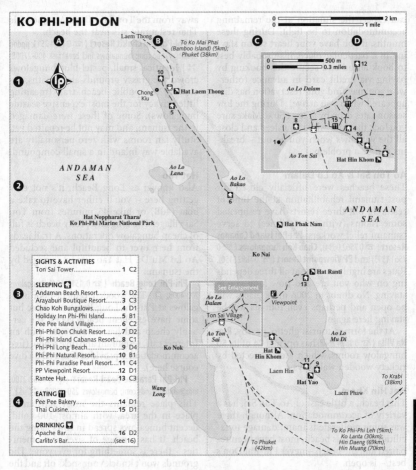

KO PHI-PHI DON

SIGHTS & ACTIVITIES	
Ton Sai Tower	1 C2

SLEEPING	
Andaman Beach Resort	2 D2
Arayaburi Boutique Resort	3 C3
Chao Koh Bungalows	4 D1
Holiday Inn Phi-Phi Island	5 B1
Pee Pee Island Village	6 C2
Phi-Phi Don Chukit Resort	7 D2
Phi-Phi Island Cabanas Resort	8 C1
Phi-Phi Long Beach	9 D4
Phi-Phi Natural Resort	10 B1
Phi-Phi Paradise Pearl Resort	11 C4
PP Viewpoint Resort	12 D1
Rantee Hut	13 C3

EATING	
Pee Pee Bakery	14 D1
Thai Cuisine	15 D1

DRINKING	
Apache Bar	16 D2
Carlito's Bar	(see 16)

own, most bungalows and resorts rent snorkel, mask and fins for 150B or so per day.

One popular destination for snorkelling is Ko Mai Phai (Bamboo Island), north of Phi-Phi Don. There's a shallow area here where you may see small sharks. Snorkelling trips cost between 600B and 2000B, depending on whether you want a long-tail or motorboat. There is also good snorkelling along the eastern coast of Ko Nok, near Ao Ton Sai, and along the eastern coast of Ko Nai.

Sea-Kayaking
Tour desks can arrange full-day tours to Phi-Phi Leh, including lunch, drinks and a guided paddle around the island (450B).

Rock-Climbing
Yes, there are some good limestone cliffs to climb on Ko Phi-Phi, and the views from the top are spectacular. The main climbing areas are Ton Sai Tower, at the western edge of Ao Ton Sai, and Hin Taek, a short long-tail boat ride around the bay. You can arrange guides or instruction through almost any bungalow or resort.

SLEEPING
Before the tsunami, all the beachfront accommodation tended to be booked out between November and May. Even though tourism is down, the fact that so many of the places to stay at Ao Ton Sai and Ao Lo Dalam have been destroyed means that you

can expect the situation at the remaining accommodation to be tight. During these months, if you have your heart set on staying in a particular place, it's probably best to book ahead and secure this booking by paying via credit card in advance (otherwise you may find your reservation has disappeared when you arrive). During the low season rates drop by at least 50%. Make sure you lock the door while you sleep and close all the windows when you go out – break-ins can be a problem.

Ao Ton Sai & Ao Lo Dalam

These beaches were officially closed for post-tsunami rehabilitation at the time of research, but three resorts have re-opened some rooms (with few facilities) to serve tsunami relief workers: **Phi-Phi Island Cabanas Resort** (☎ 0 7562 0634), **Chao Koh Bungalows** (☎ 0 7561 1313) and **PP Viewpoint Resort** (☎ 0 1892 3150). Rates are highly variable at all three depending on who you are and how long you're staying. No doubt in 2006 more places will be open and perhaps even tourists will be staying here again.

At the former 'tourist ghetto' nearby, **Rim Na Villa** (☎ 0 1894 2668) has opened 24 of its 50 bungalow rooms, which are connected by rickety wooden walkways.

Hat Hin Khom

This beach, a little east of Ao Ton Sai, has a variety of accommodation. Although there was some moderate tsunami damage to facilities along this beach, most have been repaired and the beach – never Phi-Phi Don's best – is open.

Andaman Beach Resort (☎ /fax 0 7562 1427; bungalows 500-3000B; ❇ ❇) The fan bungalows here are a good deal – large, airy and modern. The air-con ones include amenities like TV and fridge. The grounds are tidy, the restaurant looks out on the water and the place has an upmarket feel. The pool is great for chilling, and a serious *faràng* magnet. Overall, it's a nice place.

Arayaburi Boutique Resort (formerly Bay View Resort; ☎ 0 7628 1360; www.phiphibayview.com; bungalows incl breakfast 1600-3700B; ❇) Offers five kinds of modern-looking bungalows, some of which are very large and pleasant with wooden floors. The price depends on the view and amenities. Decks overlook the sea and the location is good and quiet on a lush hillside

away from the Ton Sai village. An amenable Thai restaurant sits near the beach.

Phi-Phi Don Chukit Resort (☎ 0 1894 2511; ppdon chukit@yahoo.com; bungalows incl breakfast 400-2700B; ❇) Identical small, pastel-blue bungalows crowd the grassy grounds along paths, including the public beach trail (meaning little privacy for the most expensive seaside bungalows). Some of these were damaged in the tsunami and may not be repaired yet. Stuffy fan rooms with zero personality are available way inland in a small compound.

Hat Yao

Also known as Long Beach, it's not easy getting here – you'll either have to take a boat (40B) or hike 45 minutes from Ton Sai village. The long and pretty beach is full of cheap bungalow operations. A trail leads from here over to beautiful and secluded Ao Lo Mu Di. Hat Yao was undamaged by the tsunami.

Phi-Phi Long Beach (☎ 0 1510 6541; bungalows 200-400B; ▣) The wooden, cement-floor bungalows at Phi-Phi Long Beach are basic but some have excellent beach views. It's certainly cheap and has its own vibe with an Internet café, restaurant and dive school (free accommodation is provided if you take a dive course here).

Phi-Phi Paradise Pearl Resort (☎ 0 7562 2100; info@phiphiislands.com; bungalows 250-2800B; ❇ ▣) This place remains the most substantial place in the area, with almost 100 solid, decent bungalows spread in rows along the beach. It has a range of sizes and amenities – there is something for everyone. The grounds won't knock your socks off and the seawall is less than appealing, but there's a good restaurant under casuarinas by the beach.

Hat Ranti

The latest beach to be developed on Ko Phi-Phi Don, Hat Ranti now has several low-key bungalow operations. The beach is rather untidy, but there's good snorkelling offshore. Don't let bungalow operators on other parts of the island convince you there is nowhere to stay here – there is. But don't come looking to party as it's a very laid-back beach.

Rantee Hut (☎ 0 6269 5395; bungalows 200-400B) This pleasant rustic place is built from bamboo and driftwood and has a collection of good bungalows on stilts on the hillside. There's a quiet little restaurant, and mask and snorkel sets can be rented for 50B.

A few beach restaurants here offer cheap Thai meals as well as basic bamboo bungalows for 200B to 300B; just take a walk around.

Ao Lo Bakao
On the northeastern coast on Ko Nai, this fine stretch of palm-backed sand is ringed by dramatic hills and is home to a single upmarket resort.

Pee Pee Island Village (Phuket ☎ 0 7621 5014, Bangkok ☎ 0 2276 6056; www.ppisland.com; bungalows 2500-6200B; ❄ ⚲) A romantic place, it offers 84 luxurious bungalows with Thai-style décor, tropical furniture, thatched roof and all the usual amenities. They sit in the shade of swaying palm trees on grassy grounds with bowls of floating flowers. The dining areas are beautiful and relaxing, and views of limestone outcrops add a dramatic air.

Hat Laem Thong
At the northern end of Ko Nai, the beach here is long and sandy, with several posh resorts. A small *chao náam* settlement of corrugated metal shacks is at the end of the beach.

Holiday Inn Phi-Phi Island (☎ 0 7521 1334; www .phiphi-palmbeach.com; bungalows 4750-7550B; ❄ ⚲) At the southernmost point of the beach, this tastefully decorated resort has large Thai-Malay–style bungalows on 2m-high stilts spread across spacious, landscaped grounds with lots of coconut palms. Bungalows come with neat little details, such as pots of fresh water in which to clean your feet before coming inside. On the grounds are tennis courts, a spa, dive centre, restaurant and hilltop bar.

Phi-Phi Natural Resort (☎ 0 7561 3010, Bangkok ☎ 0 2982 7575; www.phiphinatural.com; bungalows 1200-4100B; ❄ ⚲) At the northern end of the beach, this is a laid-back place with spacious grounds, a pool and pleasant wooden bungalows that come with TV and minibar. It overlooks the cape. The resort runs daily boats to Phuket and Krabi.

EATING
Most of the resorts, hotels and bungalows around the island have their own restaurants. Pre-tsunami, cheaper and often better

food was available at the restaurants and cafés in Ton Sai village. As Ton Sai recovers, some of the old ones will re-open, along with new ones no doubt. Of course virtually all of it will be prepared for *faràng* palates, with Thai dishes toned down to sub-hot levels, as before.

Two Ton Sai restaurants have re-opened already.

Thai Cuisine (☎ 0 7563 1565; dishes 40-100B) A simple and casual place with natural décor and good ambience, it fills up quickly at night. The kitchen grills up Thai, seafood and breakfast, although the food is nothing special.

Pee Pee Bakery (dishes 40-150) Good breakfasts, pizza, steak and Thai food.

DRINKING & ENTERTAINMENT
All the bars in Ton Sai, except for two, are closed for the moment, but look for new or resurrected ones to open, one by one, throughout 2006 and 2007.

Apache Bar A large, open-air place terraced up from the beach and commanding an impressive view of Ao Ton Sai and the mountains – but you'll have to get there before dusk to enjoy it. Happy hour is from 6pm to 10pm.

Carlito's Bar Fairy-lit beachside bar that used to be famous for fire shows and dancing, but is beginning its new life serving a more chilled mix of clean-up volunteers and tourists.

GETTING THERE & AWAY
Ko Phi-Phi can be reached from Krabi, Phuket, Ao Nang and Ko Lanta. Most boats moor at Ao Ton Sai, though a few from Phuket use the isolated northern pier at Laem Thong (these would be best for those staying on Hat Laem Thong). All of the following boats operate daily year-round, except for the Ko Lanta boats, which run October to April.

Boats depart from Krabi for Ko Phi-Phi at 9.30am, 11am and 3pm (200B, 1½ hours). Boats leave from Phuket at 8.30am, 1.30pm and 2.30pm, and return from Ko Phi-Phi at 9am, 2.30pm and 3pm (350B to 450B, 1¾ to two hours). From Ko Lanta boats leave at 8am and 1pm, returning at 11.30am and 2pm (200B to 250B, 1½ hours). From Ao Nang a boat departs at 9am, returning from Ko Phi-Phi (via Rai Leh) at 3.30pm 250B, two hours). The prices and schedules are for the high season; during the low season tickets drop about 50B, and schedules will vary a bit.

GETTING AROUND

There are no roads on Phi-Phi Don so transport on the island is mostly on foot, although fishing boats can be chartered at Ao Ton Sai for short hops around Ko Phi-Phi Don and Ko Phi-Phi Leh. Going anywhere in Ao Ton Sai, including Hat Yao (Long Beach), is 40B per person. Be wary of boat drivers taking you short of your destination then trying to extract more to reach your destination. Rates double at night.

Other boat charters around the island from the pier at Ton Sai include to Laem Thong (400B), Lo Bakao (300B) and Viking Cave (200B). Chartering speedboats for six hours costs 6000B, while chartering long-tail boats costs 600B for three hours.

KO JAM (KO PU) & KO SI BOYA

เกาะจำ(ปู)/เกาะศรีบอยา

Laid-back and blissfully quiet, these islands are close to the mainland and inhabited by a small number of fishing families. About the only entertainment on these Muslim islands is watching the local villagers load and unload their fishing boats or collect cashews and coconuts. Activities include swimming in the clear water and taking long walks on the beach. The peace won't last forever, however. New resorts are appearing every season, so visit now, before the islands change beyond recognition. Public transport to Ko Jam and Ko Si Boya fizzles out in the low season, so most resorts close down between May and October.

Ko Jam Online (www.kohjumonline.com) is an excellent source of up-to-date information about that island. Some bungalows on Ko Jam were flooded or otherwise damaged by the tsunami but all have been repaired and are open.

Ko Si Boya is a small 3km by 10km island with around a thousand inhabitants, most of whom are involved in fishing or rubber farming.

Sleeping

For now, accommodation consists of simple fan bungalows – they are cheap, but don't expect luxuries like air-con and TVs.

Joy Bungalow (☎ 0 1891 4645, 0 7561 8199; bungalows 400-600B) On the southwestern coast of Ko Jam, it offers 44 attractive wood bungalows on grassy, palm-shaded grounds. It's a popular place, but has grown too big for some. There's a pleasant beachside restaurant, and Joy rents kayaks.

New Bungalows (☎ 0 7567 8116; chanchalay@hotmail.com; bungalows 150-600B) Just south of Joy, this place features 17 bungalows – both basic huts and some nicer ones (plus a couple of cheap tree houses). During the rainy season the restaurant shuts down.

Andaman Beach Resort (☎ 0 9726 2652; bungalows 500-700B) Andaman has comfortable A-frame bungalows with red-tin roofs in open grounds, just back from the beach. The electricity is on from 6pm to 6am. This resort usually closes down during the monsoon season.

Ko Si Boya's accommodation is limited to two places, which are located on the island's western coast just south of the main village, Ban Lang Ko.

Siboya Bungalow (☎ 0 7561 8026; www.siboyabungalows.com; bungalows 150-300B; occasional private houses 400-1200B) An atmospheric place that stays open year-round. The 23 well-designed huts of bamboo, wood and thatch have verandas and hammocks and are surrounded by rubber plantations. There are nearby trails to hike along.

Ko Si Boya's second set of bungalows is closed indefinitely.

Getting There & Away

Boats to both islands leave from Ban Laem Kruat, a village about 30km from Krabi, at the end of Rte 4036, off Hwy 4. From Krabi, take a local bus to Nua Khlon (25B), then another to Ban Laem Kruat (35B). There are three boats daily, at 12.30pm, 2pm and 4.30pm; passage costs 25B to Si Boya, 30B to Ban Ko Jam (45 minutes to one hour). These boats run all year.

Boats from Krabi operate in the period from October to April only. There are two departures each day at 11am and 1.30pm. Boats back to Krabi leave at 8am and 1pm. There is usually a brief stop near Ko Jam (200B, 1½ hours) in each direction; longtail boats go out to get passengers. Between December and April, you may also be able to get a boat (100B, 8am) from the small pier on Th Utarakit.

KO LANTA
เกาะลันตา
pop 20,000

A long-time sweetheart with the intrepid backpacking crowd, Ko Lanta is steadily changing, with upmarket resorts replacing the cheap bungalows. The carefree, hippiesque backpacker vibe still prevails, for now, although the laid-back atmosphere has been kicked up a notch, and you'll find plenty of bars blaring the latest hits late into the night, along with a string of *faràng* restaurants showing the newest blockbusters. Travellers pour in daily, ferried from Krabi by a convoy of air-con minivans, or boats in the high season.

Beaches on Lanta's western shores are pleasantly soft, flat and sunny, and in isolated spots there's still some of that 'get away from it all' atmosphere that started attracting travellers in the first place. However, with popularity comes the possibility for moneymaking and Lanta holds prime real estate. Within the last few years many bungalow operators have either renovated old bungalows or built whole new operations, bringing air-con and around-the-clock electricity. The fact that much of Lanta is still owned by the local population of Muslim Thais and *chao náam* may save it from the mass development seen on Phuket or Ko Samui, but there are no guarantees – some of the poorer villages have already sold out.

Ko Lanta is an *amphoe* (district) within Krabi Province that consists of 52 islands, of which 12 are inhabited. The geography here is typified by stretches of mangrove interrupted by coral-rimmed beaches, rugged hills and huge umbrella trees. Other than tourism, the main livelihood for the local folk includes the cultivation of rubber, cashews and bananas, along with a little fishing. When travellers refer to Ko Lanta, they are referring to Ko Lanta Yai. There's also a Ko Lanta Noi – just off Yai's northeastern tip – but it holds little interest for travellers as mangroves rather than beaches ring it.

During the rainy season, rain drenches Ko Lanta and the tide washes right up to the front of the resorts, bringing plenty of driftwood and rubbish with it. Few resorts do any maintenance during the low season and some places can end up looking like a cyclone has just blown through.

The 2004 tsunami swept the entire western coast of the island. Damage was minimal except at the northernmost end of the coast where four resorts were heavily damaged and forced to close for repairs during most of 2005. The pier at Muang Kao (Old Town) on the east coast was damaged, as were a couple of fishing villages along the southeast coast.

Orientation & Information

Ban Sala Dan, a dusty two-street town at the northern tip of the island, is Ko Lanta's largest settlement with restaurants, minimarts, Internet cafés, souvenir stores, travel agencies, dive shops, motorcycle rentals and even a 7-Eleven. There's a petrol station just outside town. There are two ATMs, one located at the bank and the other at the 7-Eleven. However, it's still a good idea to bring money with you to the island. There are more restaurants and Internet cafés along the island's main road.

Sights

Although Ko Lanta is primarily a beach destination, there are some interesting sights to explore inland if you tire of the sea and sand.

BAN SI RAYA (OLD TOWN)
บ้านศรีรายา

The island's former district capital, labelled on some maps as 'Ban Ko Lanta' and called 'Old Town' by expats and tourists, is over a century old and worth a stopover on any island tour.

Founded on the east coast of Ko Lanta Yai, Ban Si Raya was once on the sea-trade route for Chinese and Arab ships. Today, a nice handful of old wooden, two-storey shophouses still line the main street through town.

For a while these portals into Lanta's past were in danger of being demolished and replaced by cement block buildings, but Lanta residents now seem interested in preserving the vintage atmosphere.

Although the *amphoe* seat was moved to Ko Lanta Noi (opposite Ban Sala Dan) in 1998, the only post office and hospital on the island are still located in Ban Si Raya. Several of the modest restaurants on the waterfront serve excellent seafood and local dishes.

KO LANTA & AROUND

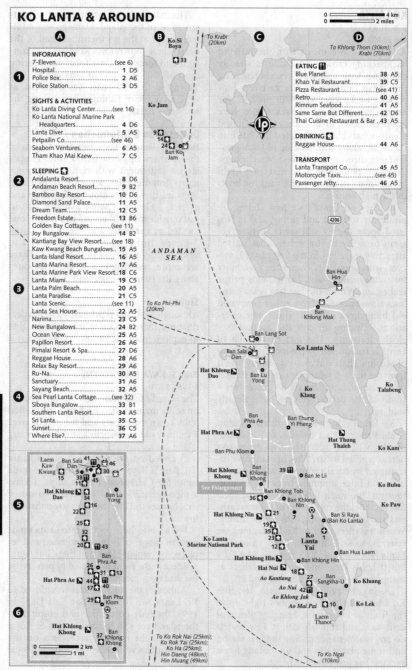

ANDAMAN COAST

0 ——— 4 km
0 ——— 2 miles

INFORMATION
7-Eleven..............................(see 6)
Hospital.................................... 1 D5
Police Box............................... 2 A6
Police Station........................... 3 D5

SIGHTS & ACTIVITIES
Ko Lanta Diving Center..........(see 16)
Ko Lanta National Marine Park
  Headquarters........................ 4 D6
Lanta Diver.............................. 5 A5
Petpailin Co..........................(see 46)
Seaborn Ventures..................... 6 A5
Tham Khao Mai Kaew............... 7 C5

SLEEPING
Andalanta Resort....................... 8 D6
Andaman Beach Resort.............. 9 B2
Bamboo Bay Resort................. 10 D6
Diamond Sand Palace.............. 11 A5
Dream Team............................ 12 C5
Freedom Estate....................... 13 B6
Golden Bay Cottages............(see 11)
Joy Bungalow......................... 14 B2
Kantiang Bay View Resort......(see 18)
Kaw Kwang Beach Bungalows.. 15 A5
Lanta Island Resort................. 16 A5
Lanta Marina Resort................ 17 A6
Lanta Marine Park View Resort.18 C6
Lanta Miami............................ 19 C5
Lanta Palm Beach.................... 20 A5
Lanta Paradise........................ 21 C5
Lanta Scenic.........................(see 11)
Narima................................... 23 C5
New Bungalows....................... 24 B2
Ocean View............................ 25 A5
Papillon Resort....................... 26 A6
Pimalai Resort & Spa............... 27 D6
Reggae House......................... 28 A5
Relax Bay Resort..................... 29 A6
Ru-Na.................................... 30 A5
Sanctuary............................... 31 A6
Sayang Beach......................... 32 A5
Sea Pearl Lanta Cottage........(see 32)
Siboya Bungalow.................... 33 B1
Southern Lanta Resort............. 34 A5
Sri Lanta................................ 35 C5
Sunset................................... 36 C5
Where Else?............................ 37 A6

EATING
Blue Planet............................. 38 A5
Khao Yai Restaurant................ 39 C5
Pizza Restaurant...................(see 41)
Retro..................................... 40 A6
Rimnum Seafood.................... 41 A5
Same Same But Different......... 42 D6
Thai Cuisine Restaurant & Bar ..43 A5

DRINKING
Reggae House......................... 44 A6

TRANSPORT
Lanta Transport Co.................. 45 A5
Motorcycle Taxis..................(see 45)
Passenger Jetty....................... 46 A5

To Krabi (20km)

To Khlong Thom (30km); Krabi (70km)

Ko Si Boya

Ko Jam

ANDAMAN SEA

To Ko Phi-Phi (20km)

Ban Ko Jam

4206

Ban Hua Hin

Ban Khlong Mak

Ban Lang Sot

Ban Sala Dan

Ko Lanta Noi

Hat Khlong Dao

Ban Lu Yong

Ko Klang

Ko Talabeng

Ban Phra Ae

Hat Phra Ae

Ban Thung Yi Pheng

Hat Thung Thaleh

Ko Kam

Ban Phu Klom

Hat Khlong Khong

Ban Khlong Khong

Ban Je Lii

Ko Bubu

Ban Khlong Tob

See Enlargement

Ban Khlong Nin

Ko Paw

Hat Khlong Nin

Ban Si Raya (Ban Ko Lanta)

Ko Lanta Yai

Hat Khlong Hin

Ban Hua Laem

Ban Khlong Hin

Hat Nui

Ao Kantiang

Ban Sangkha-U

Ko Kluang

Ao Nui

Ao Khlong Jak

Ko Lek

Ao Mai Pai

Laem Thanot

To Ko Rok Nai (25km); Ko Rok Yai (25km); Ko Ha (25km); Hin Daeng (48km); Hin Muang (49km)

To Ko Ngai (10km)

Laem Kaw Kwang

Ban Sala Dan

Hat Khlong Dao

Ban Lu Yong

Ban Phra Ae

Hat Phra Ae

Ban Phu Klom

Hat Khlong Khong

Ban Khlong Khong

0 ——— 2 km
0 ——— 1 mi

Ko Lanta Marine National Park

Every December, an **Old Town Lanta Festival** celebrates the island's history with local music, dancing and other events.

KO LANTA MARINE NATIONAL PARK
อุทยานแห่งชาติหมู่เกาะลันตา

In 1990, in an attempt to protect the fragile coastal environment, 15 islands in the Lanta group (covering an area of 134 sq km) were declared part of Ko Lanta Marine National Park, including the southern tip of Ko Lanta Yai. Despite this action, the park is increasingly threatened by the runaway development on the western coast of Ko Lanta Yai. The other islands in the group have fared slightly better – **Ko Rok Nok** is still exceptionally beautiful, with a crescent-shaped bay backed by cliffs, fine coral reefs and a sparkling white-sand beach. Camping is permitted on Ko Rok Nok and nearby **Ko Ha**, with permission from the national park headquarters. On the eastern side of Ko Lanta Yai, **Ko Talabeng** has some dramatic limestone caves, which you can visit on sea-kayaking tours.

The interior of the island consists of rubber, cashew and fruit plantations, with a few stands of original forest here and there, mostly in the hilly southern section of the island. The park headquarters is at Laem Thanot, on the southern tip of Ko Lanta Yai, reached along a steep and corrugated 13km dirt track from Ban Khlong Nin.

THAM KHAO MAI KAEW
ถ้ำเขาไม้แก้ว

A great break from the beach is a trip to this complex of caves in the centre of Ko Lanta Yai. Even the hike in, through original forest, is quite pleasant. But the real fun begins when you descend an indistinct hole in the rocks and enter the series of caverns. Some sections are as large as church halls, while others require you to squeeze through on hands and knees. Sights en route include impressive stalactites and stalagmites, bats and even a cavern pool, reached via a long, slippery slope with a knotted rope, where you can take a chilly dip.

Tham Khao Mai Kaew is reached via a guided trek through the jungle to the caves, which a local family offers for about 200B. **Elephant treks** (adult/child 800/400B) to the caves are also possible in the high season. The family home is reached by a track branching off the cross-island road just inland from Ban Khlong Nin. The best way to get there is by rented motorcycle, or most resorts can arrange transport.

Activities

DIVING & SNORKELLING

The uninhabited islands of Ko Rok Nai, Ko Rok Yai and Ko Ha, south of Ko Lanta Yai, offer plenty of coral along their western and southwestern shores. The undersea pinnacles of Hin Muang and Hin Daeng further southwest are even better, with visibility of up to 30m in good weather, hard and soft corals, and plenty of large schooling fish such as tuna, manta ray and the occasional whale shark. The diving season extends from November to April.

There are a handful of dive operators on Ko Lanta. Most work out of Ban Sala Dan but can often be booked at beach bungalows. Two dives cost 2100B, while PADI open-water courses cost 10,500B. Reliable dive companies include **Lanta Diver** (☎ 0 7568 4208; www.lantadiver.com) and **Ko Lanta Diving Center** (☎ 0 7568 4065; www.kolantadivingcenter.com).

Numerous tour agencies along the strip can organise snorkelling trips out to Ko Rok Nok, Ko Phi-Phi and other nearby islands. **Seaborn Ventures** (☎ 0 7568 4132) at Ban Sala Dan has trips to Ko Rok Nok for 1300/650B per adult/child, including lunch. **Petpailin Co** (☎ 0 7568 4428), near the passenger jetty at Ban Sala Dan, offers day trips to Ko Phi-Phi for 600B and 'four island' tours for 650B.

Sleeping

Many resorts now stay open year-round and rates skyrocket from approximately mid-December to mid-January. During low season, you can try negotiating for better rates, especially if you stay a few days. Practically any resort will be happy to arrange island or snorkelling tours, massage sessions and transport rental. All listings here are more or less from north to south along the coast.

BAN SALA DAN & LAEM KHAW KWANG

You've got a few choices if you need to be near the 'big' village.

Kaw Kwang Beach Bungalows (☎ 0 7562 1373; bungalows 300-2500B; ✷) On Ko Lanta's northern curl of land, this is the oldest resort on

ANDAMAN COAST

ELEPHANT TREKKING

When the Thai government banned hardwood logging in 1989, many saw it as a victory for the environment, but Thailand's working elephants became an unexpected casualty. Huge numbers of elephants suddenly found themselves out of work and Bangkok was inundated by desperate jumbos and their handlers begging for small change and food. They were banned from the centre of Bangkok, but this did little to solve the underlying pachyderm problem. Then someone had the bright idea of moving the elephants to tourist centres in southern Thailand to provide tours for tourists. The treks have been a massive hit, and most travellers' haunts now offer elephant treks to virgin-forest areas or scenic caves and waterfalls. You can take an elephant trek at Ko Lanta, Krabi, Phuket or Ko Samui and help ensure that Thailand's last generation of working elephants lives comfortably to a ripe old age.

On Ko Lanta, there are elephant trekking camps at Hat Phra Ae, Hat Nui and Ao Khlong Jak; all three charge 800/400B per adult/child for a two-hour trek. Trips are possible year-round and most resorts can arrange treks and transfers to the camps.

the island and is still owned by local people. It features spacious and modern bamboo and concrete bungalows in neat rows along shrubby paths. A large restaurant faces the bay, which has good snorkelling. It's far enough away from the development at Hat Khlong Dao to feel secluded and peaceful. Kaw Kwang suffered significant damage during the tsunami, and closed down several months for repair, but planned to open in 2006.

Ru-Na (Yut Hut; ☎ 0 9647 4706; r 300-600B) In Ban Sala Dan, Ru-Na has three beautiful rooms with shared bathroom. The restaurant downstairs has a great deck overlooking the channel, and there's a pool table. It's at the western end of the main street.

HAT KHLONG DAO

The main beach at Kat Khlong Dao is long and dusted with white sand, but the bay is very shallow and swimming is only really possible at low tide. There are about a dozen resorts almost on top of each other at the northern end of the beach, all with very similar facilities and prices.

Golden Bay Cottages (☎ 0 7568 4161; goldenbay lanta@yahoo.com; bungalows 300-1000B; ☒) One of the nicer operations here, it's on the beach and open year-round. The concrete bungalows are clean and decent, though the ones with fan are rather small. The staff here is friendly, the sand out the front is good, there's a small beach bar and you can rent motorcycles.

Southern Lanta Resort (☎ 0 7568 4174; www .southernlanta.com; bungalows incl breakfast 1600-2200B; ☒ ☒) Further along the strip, this spacious and well-maintained resort has a long beach

frontage and a nice pool. The bungalows have minibars and hot showers and the more expensive ones come with TVs and coffee makers. There is a huge on-site restaurant.

Lanta Island Resort (☎ 0 7568 4129; www.lanta islandresort.com; bungalows 350-2300B; ☒ ☒) A good and comfortable choice, prices change drastically depending on the season. Fan bungalows have steeply pitched roofs and are fine (though a bit musty), while the air-con ones are large and come with fridge and TV. The grounds are thick and leafy.

Lanta Sea House (☎ 0 7568 4073; lantaseahouse@ hotmail.com; bungalows 1500-3000B; ☒ ☒) This more upmarket option is an organised place with a beautiful garden and a variety of attractive bungalows (some of which are duplexes). It's a good place for families.

Ocean View (☎ 0 7568 4089; o_patiwat@hotmail.com; r 300-800B; ☒) For cheap, clean, modern and spacious digs, try this hotel-style place. It's safe and family-friendly, but unfortunately not right on the beach.

Diamond Sand Palace (☎ 0 7568 4135; bungalows 300-1000B; ☾ Oct-Apr; ☒) On a small and cosy sandy lot, it has 20 attractive bungalows lining the main path to the beach, where the restaurant lies. Reach it via the paved road next to Lanta Scenic.

Lanta Scenic (☎ 0 7568 4231; bungalows 700-1250B; ☒) Cute bungalows are lined up neatly in a large grassy garden. The fancier ones sport fridge and TV. It's inland 50m from the beach.

HAT PHRA AE

A large travellers' village has developed at Hat Phra Ae (known among foreigners as

Long Beach), with an abundance of restaurants, beach bars, Internet cafés, tour offices etc, but the beach is fairly ordinary. Be warned, there are some shoddy bungalow operations here that rely on touts to fill their rooms, so check out a place before paying.

Sanctuary (☎ 0 1891 3055; sathaporn_yomphuk@ yahoo.com; bungalows 250-500B) Long-established favourite spot with a relaxed hippyish atmosphere and nice thatched wooden bungalows. The restaurant is great traveller hang-out, with weathered wooden benches and tables under a high thatched roof. It serves vegetarian food and is often full. The restaurant closes in the low season.

Relax Bay Resort (☎ 0 7568 4194; www.relaxbay .com; bungalows 700-1300B; ✷ Oct-Apr; ✶) Spread out over a tree-covered headland by a small beach, this funky place has cool wooden bungalows on stilts with large decks overlooking the bay and a huge atmospheric bar and restaurant. The fan bungalows are a better deal than the air-con ones, which are further inland.

Where Else? (☎ 0 1536 4870; bungalows 100-400B) A good backpacker vibe is found at this simple place with rickety bungalows located in a grassy setting. The restaurant serves decent vegetarian Thai/Indian food.

Sea Pearl Lanta Cottage (☎ 0 1737 0159; sea pearllanta@hotmail.com; bungalows 150-700B) Despite facing a sandy parking lot, it manages to remain atmospheric with decent thatch and bamboo bungalows located under shady palms. A cool restaurant sits by the beach.

Lanta Palm Beach (☎ 0 1066 5433; bungalows 700-1500B; ✶ ▢) This large place has good facilities, including a minimart and breezy upstairs restaurant. There are large modern concrete air-con bungalows with hot showers and old-fashioned bamboo bungalows with fan.

Sayang Beach (☎ 0 7568 4156; sayangbeach@hot mail.com; bungalows 600-2500B; ✶) Sayang Beach features pretty bungalows; even the smallest and cheapest ones are good. They sit in a grassy garden with palm trees.

Papillon Resort (☎ 0 7568 4308; www.papillon lanta.com; bungalows 300-800B; ▨) Everything here (including the Thai/Scandinavian restaurant) is closer to the road than the water, which is 50m away. The bungalows are modest but clean and there's a sandy garden area and small pool – a rarity for such an inexpensive place.

Freedom Estate (☎ 0 7568 4251; www.lanta-service dapartments.com; bungalows 300-1250B; ✶) Inland and perched on a sparse, grassy hill, you get good views here, but you're not on the beach. The six bungalows are a good deal, however, and come with big beds, kitchens and large patios. Reservations are recommended at any time. Prices vary depending on season.

Reggae House (huts 100-200B) As basic and cheap as you can get, it has tiny thatched A-frames that could blow over in the next storm. It's best for hard-core backpackers who can deal with grungy bathrooms and would rather spend their time hanging out at the extremely laid-back and cool bar, eclectically decorated with bits of sea detritus and Rasta colours. There are good wooden deck areas over the beach. Security isn't great here, so watch your valuables.

Lanta Marina Resort (☎ 0 7568 4168; lantamar ina@hotmail.com; bungalows 300-600B) One of the more environmentally sensitive places here, Lanta Marina has quite tribal-looking thatched and bamboo bungalows linked by a boardwalk.

HAT KHLONG NIN

At the village of Ban Khlong Nin, the tarmac road turns inland and a corrugated dirt track runs south along the shore to the national park headquarters at Laem Thanot. The first beach here is lovely Hat Khlong Nin, which gets progressively nicer the further south you travel.

Sri Lanta (☎ 0 7569 7288; www.srilanta.com; villas incl breakfast US$120-145; ✶ ▢ ▣) At the southern end of the beach, this sophisticated place features luxurious hillside bungalows decorated in natural materials. Most have breezy windows with sea views and creative indoor-outdoor baths. There is a very stylish beachside area with a restaurant, a pool, beautiful lounge and private shaded pavilions where you can get a traditional massage. Included in the price are Internet service and yoga.

Lanta Miami (☎ 0 1228 4506; bungalows 400-700B; ✶) Attractive wood and concrete bungalows are set in a spare garden at this friendly place.

Sunset (☎ 0 9973 1415; bungalows 300-700B) A relaxed cheapie, it has good bungalows with bathrooms, although it lacks atmosphere. It's been planning to add air-con for a while now, so the prices could jump.

Lanta Paradise (☎ 0 1607 5114; bungalows 300-1200B; ✗) It offers 35 crowded bungalows in rows, but unless you get a sea view, the atmosphere here just doesn't cut it. The restaurant is unique, however – a gaudy, concrete, pastel-coloured thing with two open floors of seating.

HAT NUI

There are several small beaches around here with upmarket places to stay. Elephant treks can be arranged; ask at your resort for information and bookings.

Narima (☎ 0 7560 7700; www.narima-lanta.com; bungalows 1800-3200B; ✗ 🖳 🖳) Sitting on its own secluded beach, Narima offers a lush leafy environment with tidy, sensitively designed wood, thatch and bamboo bungalows. There's a very nice thatched restaurant, an Internet café, small pool and even a library.

Dream Team (☎ 0 1228 4184; bungalows 300-3000B; ✗ 🖳) On a little headland overlooking the shore, the attractively landscaped Dream Team has well-appointed air-con bungalows with TVs, minibars and hot showers, as well as tidy fan bungalows. You can rent motorcycles here.

AO KANTIANG

This fine beach has a nice, pleasant sprinkling of sand, and several tour offices nearby provide Internet access facilities and rent out motorcycles.

Kantiang Bay View Resort (☎ 0 1787 5192; bungalows 400-1500B; ✗) There's a good traveller vibe here, with a restaurant and bar right on the beach. Accommodation is in modern, concrete air-con bungalows with tiled roofs or old-fashioned wooden bungalows with bathrooms and fans. It's popular even during the low season, and also arranges regional tours.

Lanta Marine Park View Resort (☎ 0 1397 0793; www.krabidir.com/lantampv; bungalows 300-2000B; ✗) Sprawling up the hillside at the northern end of the bay, the air-con bungalows of Park View Resort are well-designed affairs that sport balconies with great views. The multilevel restaurant has tables overlooking the bay and is a good spot for enjoying a late afternoon drink.

Pimalai Resort & Spa (☎ 0 2551 9388; www.pimalai.com; r 10,500-14,500B; ✗ 🖳) The new and very posh Pimalai is a tasteful boutique resort on a gorgeous stretch of the beach. Traditional Thai furniture, natural and artistic décor and private decks make the rooms something special. The grounds consist of lush gardens, lily ponds, swimming pools and three plush restaurants.

Same Same But Different (r 1000B) Favoured customers of this one-of-a-kind bar and restaurant (see opposite) next to Pimalai may get a shot at staying at one of the beautiful bamboo-and-thatch beach cottages here.

AO KHLONG JAK (WATERFALL BAY)

The splendid beach at Waterfall Bay has a few resorts. The namesake waterfall is inland along Khlong Jaak; elephant treks run up here in the high season.

Andalanta Resort (☎ 0 1836 4877; www.andalanta.com; bungalows 2000-3000B; ✗) Formerly the Waterfall Bay Resort, this is the nicest option here. You'll find comfortable and modern air-con bungalows (some with loft) and some simple fan-cooled ones made of bamboo and wood, which face the sea. There's a very pleasant restaurant and the namesake waterfall is a 30- to 40-minute walk away. Call ahead and the staff will pick you up at Ban Sala Dan.

AO MAI PAI

There are only three resorts on this lovely isolated beach.

Bamboo Bay Resort (☎ 0 7561 8240; bungalows 700-1000B) Clinging to the hillside above Ao Mai Pai beach, there are a variety of brick and concrete bungalows on stilts. The better bungalows have balconies with grand sea views. The comfortable restaurant is down by the beach.

LAEM THANOT

Ko Lanta Marine National Park Headquarters (Bangkok ☎ 0 2561 4292; per person camping 40B, tent hire 200-300B) The secluded grounds of the national park headquarters (p697) is a wonderfully serene place to camp. There are toilets and running water, but you should bring your own food. You can also get permission here to camp on Ko Rok Nok or Ko Ha.

Eating

Most people eat where they are staying, but there are some more interesting options if fried rice with chicken fails to titillate your palate.

The best places to eat are the seafood restaurants along the little lane at the northern end of Ban Sala Dan. All these places have tables on verandas with stilts over the water. They offer fresh seafood, sold by weight (which includes cooking costs), and close by 8.30pm. Expect to pay 600B per kilo for prawns and 300B per kilo for squid, fish and crabs. The best option is **Rimnun Seafood**, but during high season come early if you want to get a table.

Thai Cuisine Restaurant & Bar (☎ 0 9288 4492; dishes 50-140B) On a slight rise on the east side of the main north–south road, Thai Cuisine's owner-chef prepares the best Thai food – including fresh seafood – on Hat Phra Ae.

Sanctuary (☎ 0 1891 3055; dishes 65-150B) In the resort of the same name, this restaurant is known for its vegetarian food, and also serves Indian, Thai and Western dishes (including breakfast). It's one of the best traveller restaurants on the island.

Same Same But Different Tucked into an idyllic corner of quiet Ao Kantiang, next to Pimalai Resort, this simple collection of tables on the sand and open-air bamboo shelters offers the best and most authentically southern Thai cuisine on the island.

Khao Yai Restaurant (☎ 0 7569 7244; dishes 50-150B) The fine food at this place, set in an airy pavilion on a hillside with magnificent views over the eastern coast of Ko Lanta Yai, attracts a nonstop flow of travellers on round-island motorcycle jaunts. The view is unbeatable, taking in the surrounding countryside, sea and island beyond – and a great terrace makes the most of it. It's also a fine place for a drink.

Blue Planet (☎ 0 9909 0529; dishes 40-100B) Small, simple and friendly, it has just a few tables. It's on the main road and serves good Thai food, burgers, spaghetti and lots of pizza. Look for it next to Lanta Beer House.

Sayang Restaurant (☎ 0 7568 4156; dishes 50-180B) At the bungalow operation of the same name, it is popular for its Indian food, though vegetarian and Thai dishes are also served. It's near the beach but not on it, however.

Retro (☎ 0 9649 4842; dishes 50-175B; ☺ high season) A simple bamboo and thatched-roof place that serves international dishes like steak and pasta (fettuccini, gnocchi and ravioli) just off the main road.

Pizza Restaurant (pizzas from 140B) This friendly place has convincing pizzas and interesting knick-knacks on the walls, plus a bar and pool table.

Drinking & Entertainment
During the high season Ko Lanta has a positively buzzing nightlife, but it fizzles out almost completely during the rainy season. At peak times, dozens of beach bars pump out boisterous reggae and dance anthems all along the strip, particularly around Hat Phra Ae; **Reggae House** (Hat Phra Ae) is a perennial favourite.

The lantern-lit open-air pavilions at **Same Same But Different** (see left) are an inspired choice for a quiet evening of drinks and conversation accompanied by chilled music in the background.

Ask at your resort about *muay thai* bouts in the local area.

Getting There & Away
Most people come to Ko Lanta by boat or air-con minivan. If you're coming by train from Bangkok, get off in Trang (after 16 hours!), then take a bus (90B, two hours) or minivan (120B, two hours) to Ko Lanta. Avoid taking the train to Surat Thani if possible, as transport options can be more complicated from there.

MINIVAN
This is the main way of getting to and from Ko Lanta and vans run year-round. Things are so well set up that there really isn't any point trying to get from Ko Lanta to Krabi by public bus.

Lanta Transport Co (☎ 0 7561 4121), **Krabi Lanta Tour** (☎ 0 7561 2355) and other companies run daily minivans to Krabi between 7am and 8am (150B, 1½ hours). There are sometimes afternoon runs at 1pm and 3.30pm. From Krabi, vans depart at 9am, 11am and 1pm. **KK Tour & Travel** (Trang ☎ 0 7521 1198) has several daily air-con vans between Trang and Ko Lanta (180B, two hours). Minivans will pick you up from your hotel.

BOAT
There are two piers at Ban Sala Dan. The passenger jetty is about 300m from the main string of shops, while the vehicle ferries leave from a second jetty, a few hundred metres further east. You will only use this

pier if you have your own car or motorcycle. The vehicle ferries run frequently between 7am and 8pm daily and charge 8B for motorcycles and 100B for cars.

Following the 2004 tsunami, boat services to Ko Lanta were reduced in frequency, but when tourists return in 'normal' numbers, the frequency of departures will no doubt increase again.

Passenger boats between Krabi's new passenger pier and Ko Lanta operate from October to April. Boats usually leave Ko Lanta at 8am and 1pm (200B, two hours). In the reverse direction boats leave at 11am and 1.30pm. These boats will also stop at Ko Jam (for the full 200B fare).

Boats between Ko Lanta and Ko Phi-Phi run as long as there are enough passengers, which usually means that services fizzle out in the low season. Assuming everything is running on schedule, boats leave Ko Phi-Phi at 3pm (200B to 250B, 1½ hours); in the opposite direction boats leave from Ko Lanta at 8am.

Getting Around

Most resorts send vehicles to meet the ferries and you'll get a free ride *to* your resort. In the opposite direction, expect to pay 30B to 50B. Alternatively, you can take a motorcycle taxi from Ban Sala Dan (the stand sits across from 7-Eleven) to almost anywhere along the beaches for 30B to 120B – rates are posted.

Motorcycles can be rented from practically any bungalow operation, or in Ban Sala Dan, for 200B to 250B per day. Small jeeps can be rented for 1000B to 1500B per day, including insurance, from the tour agencies around town.

TRANG PROVINCE

South of Krabi, Trang Province sees relatively few visitors and the sandy islands offshore are less developed and far more peaceful than those of Ko Lanta or Ko Phi-Phi. Inland you'll find mountains of limestone and rubber plantations, as well as some untouched regions of virgin forest. Caves and waterfalls are liberally sprinkled throughout the interior of the province and make for pleasant retreats away from the sun and sand.

TRANG

ตรัง

pop 69,100

As a town Trang isn't the greatest of destinations, being your typical concrete, bustling minimetropolis that doesn't hold much charm on the surface. As you get to know it, however, you start to see and experience things, like the lively markets, historic shophouse architecture (surviving longer there than anywhere else in the south outside Phuket) tasty *ráan ko-píi* (coffee shops) and – at the right time of year – the **Vegetarian Festival** (it's similar to the one in Phuket, see p652), made fervent by Trang's large Chinese population. Still, the main reason people come here is to access the nearby up-and-coming islands and beaches, and the city is full of travel agencies and resort offices that will help you achieve this.

Since at least the 1st century AD Trang has been an important trade centre. Between the 7th and 12th centuries it was a seaport for ocean-going sampans sailing between Trang and the Strait of Malaka. Nakhon Si Thammarat and Surat Thani were major centres for the Srivijaya empire at this time and Trang served as a relay point for communications and shipping between the east coast of the Thai peninsula and Palembang, Sumatra.

During the Ayuthaya period, Trang was a common port of entry for seafaring Western visitors, who continued by land to Nakhon Si Thammarat or Ayuthaya. The town was then at the mouth of Mae Nam Trang (Trang River), but later moved to its present location. Today Trang is still a point of exit for rubber from the province's plantations.

Information

There are banks with ATMs on Th Phra Ram VI and a telephone office in the same building as the main post office.

Ani's (☎ 0 1397 4574; 285 Th Ratchadamnoen; ⏰ 9am-10pm) For books in English and European languages. It's a decent second-hand bookshop and the owners are a good source of information on the area.

Cybertech (Th Ratchadamnoen; per hr 120B) Fast connections; one of several places in town to surf the web.

Main post office (cnr Th Phra Ram VI & Th Kantang; ⏰ 8.30am-4.30pm Mon-Fri, 9am-noon Sat & Sun)

Mittasason (no Roman-script sign; ☎ 0 7521 8811; 128/132 Th Visetkul; ⏰ 6am-9pm) Sells a few new books and magazines in English.

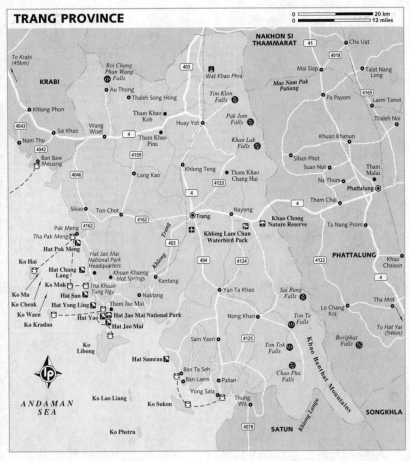

TRANG PROVINCE

Trang Tourist Association (☎ 0 7521 5580; Th Phra Ram VI; ⏱ 8.30am-5pm) Trang has no TAT office, but this privately run group, next to Trang Hotel, can provide local information.

Trang Travel Co (☎ 0 7521 9598; cnr Th Phra Rama VI & Th Kantang) English speakers available. Offers tours of the area's surrounding attractions. Day trips include the nearby islands (600B) and the waterfalls and caves (550B).

Wattanapat Hospital (☎ 0 7521 8585; 247/2 Th Phattalung) Has good facilities and some English-speaking staff.

Sleeping

A number of hotels are found along the city's two main thoroughfares, Th Phra Ram VI and Th Visetkul, which intersect at the clock tower.

Yamawa Bed & Breakfast (☎ 075216617; yamawa@ cscoms.com; 94 Th Visetkul; s/d 200/300B) Heaven for the budget traveller, it's beautifully decorated with natural materials and offers good, clean rooms, a common TV area, and a relaxing restaurant. It does tours to surrounding attractions and rents motorcycles for 200B per day. Practically every European language is spoken.

Ko Teng Hotel (☎ 0 7521 8622; 77-79 Th Phra Ram VI; r 180-300B; ☒) A popular old-timer, it offers spotless rooms, some equipped with TVs, that are great value. There's also a great restaurant downstairs.

Thumrin Thana Hotel (☎ 0 7521 1211; www.thum rin.co.th; 69/8 Th Trang Thana; r 1200-1600B; ☒ ☒) Trang's poshest option, it's quite popular

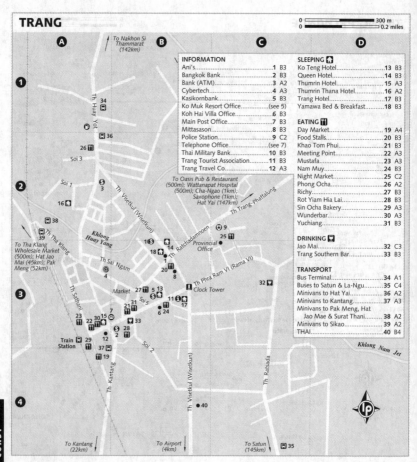

TRANG

INFORMATION		SLEEPING	
Ani's..1 B3		Ko Teng Hotel..........................13 B3	
Bangkok Bank.............................2 B3		Queen Hotel..............................14 B3	
Bank (ATM)................................3 A2		Thumrin Hotel...........................15 A3	
Cybertech..................................4 A3		Thumrin Thana Hotel................16 A2	
Kasikornbank..............................5 B3		Trang Hotel...............................17 B3	
Ko Muk Resort Office...........(see 5)		Yamawa Bed & Breakfast..........18 B3	
Koh Hai Villa Office.....................6 B3			
Main Post Office.........................7 B3		EATING	
Mittasason.................................8 B3		Day Market...............................19 A4	
Police Station.............................9 C2		Food Stalls.................................20 B3	
Telephone Office.................(see 7)		Khao Tom Phui..........................21 B3	
Thai Military Bank.....................10 B3		Meeting Point............................22 A3	
Trang Tourist Association...........11 B3		Mustafa.....................................23 A3	
Trang Travel Co.........................12 A3		Nam Muy...................................24 B3	
		Night Market.............................25 C2	
		Phong Ocha..............................26 A2	
		Richy...27 B3	
		Rot Yiam Hia Lai........................28 B3	
		Sin Ocha Bakery.........................29 A3	
		Wunderbar................................30 A3	
		Yuchiang...................................31 B3	
		DRINKING	
		Jao Mai.....................................32 C3	
		Trang Southern Bar...................33 B3	
		TRANSPORT	
		Bus Terminal.............................34 A1	
		Buses to Satun & La-Ngu...........35 C4	
		Minivans to Hat Yai...................36 A2	
		Minivans to Kantang.................37 A3	
		Minivans to Pak Meng, Hat	
		Jao Mae & Surat Thani........38 A2	
		Minivans to Sikao.......................39 A2	
		THAI...40 B4	

with Thai honeymooners. Rooms are spacious and boast all the mod-cons. There is a gleaming marbled lobby, three restaurants, a bakery, pool and a spa.

Queen Hotel (☎ 0 7521 8522; 85-89 Th Visetkul; r 300-450B; ✹) Although it has a rather institutional feel, this large place offers clean rooms with small TVs. It's not bad value for money.

Thumrin Hotel (☎ 0 7521 1011; fax 0 7521 8057; Th Phra Rama VI; r incl breakfast 400-600B; ✹) Near the train station, it has decent business-class rooms supplied with TVs, carpets and bath tubs. However, the 17% tax and service charge makes this less of a good deal.

Trang Hotel (☎ 0 7521 8944; fax 0 7521 8451; cnr Th Phra Rama VI & Th Visetkul; r 470-590B; ✹) Rooms

at this business-class hotel are old, but not uncomfortable, and come with amenities like TV and hot water. The halls are rather dark and depressing however, but there is a lively restaurant and bar, so you needn't spend too much time in your room.

Eating

Trang is famous for *khànǒm jiin* that you douse in *náam yaa* (a spicy ground fish curry), *náam phrík* (a sweet and slightly spicy peanut sauce) and *kaeng tai plaa* (a very spicy mixture of green beans, fish, bamboo shoots and potato). To this you add fresh grated papaya, pickled veggies, cucumber and bean sprouts – all for just 10B per bowl. Look for it at the night market, just east of the provincial offices. Food stalls also sit next to the bookshop on Th Visetkul; the first one on the right is the best. A day market (with a few food stalls) convenes next to the train station.

Richy (☎ 0 7521 1126; 52/9-10 Th Ratchadamnoen; dishes 45-350B) This posh place is great for Western breakfasts. It also does good upmarket Western and Thai food ranging from steak, burgers, sandwiches, rice, noodles, curry and seafood. It doubles as a bakery.

Wunderbar (☎ 0 7521 4563; dishes 35-390B) This *faràng*-owned place by the train station serves good Thai dishes, as well as food for homesick Westerners – pizza with beer, and wine with cheese. Travel services are also offered.

Khao Tom Phui (☎ 0 7521 0122; Th Phra Ram VI; dishes 30-50B; 5pm-3am) One of several popular Chinese-Thai canteens in Trang, this reliable place has a counter hung with roast ducks, meat and veggies, and large pans of curry. Unusual for this type of place, the menu is in English. Look for the red sign with chopsticks.

Mustafa (no Roman-script sign; ☎ 0 7521 4622; 59/6-8 Th Sathani; dishes 30-60B) Close to the train sta-

tion, this is a large and casual place serving inexpensive Malay-style curries, *rotii kaeng*, *rotii khài* (rotii with egg) and *màtàbà* (a flat, stuffed Indian pancake). Nearby are several smaller food stalls serving Muslim cuisine. Look for the green plastic chairs.

Nam Muy (☎ 0 7521 8514; 130/2 Th Phra Rama VI; dishes 60-200B) This large Chinese restaurant serves decent food and has a nice back patio. Look for the hot pot or shark sign amid the motorcycle dealers.

Meeting Point (cnr Th Phra Rama VI & Th Sathani; dishes 40-80B) Caters to *faràng* waiting for their trains, with cable TV, wooden benches, a comfortable atmosphere and Western food like burgers and beer. Breakfast is served.

Rot Yiam Hia Lai (☎ 0 7522 4057; dim sum 10B; 5-10pm Wed-Mon) An interesting little dim sum place with an intimate atmosphere tucked away down an alley. It has indoor and outdoor tables around a tiny garden, and tea and coffees are served. Look for the Chinese temple façade.

Drinking & Entertainment

Trang has its share of entertainment venues; unfortunately, the best ones are a good ride away from the town centre.

COFFEE SHOPS

Trang is famous for its *ráan kaa-fae* or *ráan ko-píi* (coffee shops), which are usually run by Hokkien Chinese. These shops serve real filtered coffee (called *kaafae thŭng* in the rest of the country) along with a variety of snacks, typically *paa-thâwng-kôh*, *saalaapao* (Chinese buns), *khànŏm jìip* (dumplings), Trang-style sweets, *mŭu yâang* (barbecued pork) and sometimes noodles and *jók* (thick rice soup).

When you order coffee in these places, be sure to use the Hokkien word *ko-píi* rather than the Thai *kaa-fae*, otherwise you may end up with Nescafé or instant Khao Chong coffee – the proprietors often think this is what *faràng* want. Coffee is usually served with milk and sugar – ask for *ko-píi dam* for sweetened black coffee, *ko-píi dam, mâi sài náam-taan* for black coffee without sugar or *ko-píi mâi sài náam-taan* for coffee with milk but no sugar. Here's a few of our favourite shops.

Sin Ocha Bakery (Th Sathani; dishes 25-50B) Next to the train station, it is the most convenient *ráan ko-píi* around and is very popular with travellers. Simple Thai dishes and breakfast are served, along with huge coffee drinks (10B to 40B) and teas. Décor is pleasantly nonpretentious, though the service could use a shot in the arm.

Yuchiang (no Roman-script sign; Th Phra Ram VI; dishes 20-30B) Opposite Khao Tom Phui, it is a beautiful, hard-core and classic Hokkien coffee shop with marble-topped round tables in an old wooden building. Food counters sit in front. Yuchiang roasts its own pork, so the pork *saalaapao* are particularly tasty here.

Phong Ocha (☎ 0 7521 9918; Th Huay Yot; dishes 25-45B) North of the centre, Phong Ocha sports four fake deer heads on the wall – very appetising. It's busy, though, serving locals traditional *ko-píi* along with *jóhk* and *mìi sŭa kài tŭun* (super-thin rice noodles with herb-steamed chicken). Dim sum is also available.

Jao Mai (Th Ratsada) Just east of centre, this is a simple, airy and no-frills (almost funky) joint with eclectic décor and live Thai music. Beers are cheap and basic Thai food is served.

Trang Southern Bar (Th Phra Rama VI) It has a great central location, but it's a bit haughty and the drinks are expensive. The space is clean and modern, with glowing green lights at night. Look for it on the corner; a few small tables sit outside.

The following three places are north of town – a motorcycle taxi costs 10B to 20B, while *túk-túk* are 15B to 20B.

Oasis Pub & Restaurant (☎ 0 1893 8474) Dotted with anorexic, tightly clad waitresses who cater to males, there's a great leafy outdoor patio out the front, and live Thai music inside. It's north of Anusaowari (Monument Park) on Th Trang-Phattalung.

Saxophone (☎ 0 1273 9449; 65/5 Th Phloen Phitak) An upmarket bar/restaurant with nightly live music on an intimate stage, it's popular, cosy and romantic. The music is Western and played fairly well. Song requests are taken. Thai food is served, and Heineken is on tap for 150B.

Cha-Ngao (no Roman-script sign; ☎ 0 7522 2469; 28/29-30 Th Phloen Phitak) Two blocks away from Saxophone and even fancier. There's a tasteful pub/restaurant atmosphere and brick, stone and wood décor. The air-con is heavy and the stage just big enough for a one-man band.

Shopping

Trang is known for its wickerwork and, especially, mats woven of *bai toey* (pandanus leaves), which are called *sèua paa-nan,* or Panan mats. These are important bridal gifts in rural Trang and are a common feature of rural households. The process of softening and drying the pandanus leaves before weaving takes many days. They can be purchased in Trang for between 100B and 200B.

The province also has its own distinctive cotton-weaving styles. The villages of Na Paw and Na Meun Si are the most highly regarded sources for these fabrics, especially the intricate diamond-shaped *lâi lûuk kâew* pattern, once reserved for nobility.

The best place in town for good buys is the Tha Klang wholesale market, which is along Th Tha Klang.

Getting There & Away
AIR
The airport is 4km south of Trang. **THAI** (☎ 0 7521 0804; 199/2 Th Visetkul) operates daily flights from Bangkok (2855B).

BUS, MINIVAN & SHARE TAXI
Public buses leave from the well-organised Trang **bus terminal** (Th Huay Yot). There is a variety of air-con buses to Bangkok (340B to 490B, 13 hours, twice daily).

Other long-distance services from Trang include frequent buses travelling to Hat Yai (60B to 100B, three hours), Satun (60B to 200B, two hours), Krabi (55B to 90B, 2½ hours) and Phuket (105B to 190B, five to six hours).

There are share taxis to Krabi (60B, two hours) and air-con minivans to Hat Yai (80B, two hours) from offices just south of the Trang bus terminal. Hourly vans to Surat Thani (130B, four hours) leave from a depot on Th Tha Klang, just before it crosses the railway tracks.

If you're coming from Ko Lanta, catch any northbound vehicle and get off at Ban Huay Nam Khao (the Hwy 4 junction) then get a bus south to Trang. Ordinary buses to La-Ngu (for Pak Bara) cost 40B.

TRAIN
Only two trains travel all the way from Bangkok to Trang: the express No 83, which leaves Bangkok's Hualamphong station at 5.05pm and arrives in Trang at about 8am the next day, and the rapid No 167, which leaves Hualamphong station at 6.20pm, arriving in Trang at about 11am. Both trains offer 1st class (1240B), 2nd class (371B to 691B) and 3rd class (175B to 195B). Trains from Thung Song in Nakhon Si Thammarat Province leave daily at 7am and 9am (two hours).

Getting Around
If you are heading for the airport, the **Trang Travel Co** (☎ 0 7521 9598; cnr Th Phra Rama VI & Th Kantang) operates shuttle services for 30B per person.

Motorcycle taxis around town cost 10B during the day and 20B at night. Loud *túk-túk* cost 15B. If you want to rent motorcycles, try Yamawa Bed & Breakfast (p703) or Ani's bookstore (p702). Both charge about 200B per day.

TRANG BEACHES & ISLANDS

A string of delightful sandy beaches, coves and islands, dotted here and there with the occasional limestone cliff, are found on the province's coast. It's pleasantly relaxed, quite scenic at times and is an up-and-coming area that has already attracted the attention of four- and five-star resorts. It'll be a while before overbuilding detracts from the natural charm of this region, but you should probably see it sooner rather than later. Somewhat sheltered by Sumatra, Trang's shoreline suffered very little from the 2004 tsunami.

Most of the beach tourism in Trang Province is Thai, so you'll find that resorts tend to cater to Thai groups rather than solo Western tourists. This means, for example, that some resorts may offer karaoke for guests, and buffet-style restaurant meals are common.

The following beaches and islands are listed from north to south along the coast.

Hat Pak Meng
หาดปากเมง

Thirty-nine kilometres from Trang, in Amphoe Sikao, is a long, broad, sandy beach near the small village of Pak Meng. The waters are usually shallow and calm, even in the rainy season. A couple of hundred metres offshore are several scenic limestone rock formations, including a very large one with caves. Several vendors and a few restaurants offer fresh seafood; you can use the sling-chairs and umbrellas on the beach, as long as you order something. A long promenade and sea wall runs along the middle and southern sections of the beach.

There are two places to stay. Both run tours of nearby islands and rent motorcycles and bicycles.

Laytrang Resort (☎ 0 7527 4227; www.laytrang.com; bungalows 800-1200B; ❀) is a large place right in town, across from the beach. Its bungalows are further inland, but they surround a large, pretty garden and are modern and clean, with large baths and pleasant décor. The restaurant, famous throughout the province and beyond for its fresh seafood, lies nearer to the sea.

A few kilometres south of town is **Pakmeng Resort** (☎ 0 7520 3030; bungalows 300-700B; ❀), which is not as swank as Laytrang. It's also across the road from the beach. Basic

fan bungalows come with concrete floors and bamboo furniture, while air-con ones have more amenities and are attractive, clean and polished. There's a neat canal out back.

Minivans from Trang run direct to Hat Pak Meng (50B). You can also take a minivan to nearby Sikao (25B), then a *sǎwng-thǎew* (15B) to Hat Pak Meng.

Ko Hai (Ngai)
เกาะไห(ไหง)

Ko Hai, also known as Ko Ngai, is actually part of Krabi Province to the north, but most accessible from Pak Meng. It's a fairly small island, covering not quite 5km, but the beaches are fine white sand, the water is clear and sparkling, and coral rings virtually the entire island.

Along Ko Hai's eastern shore are a few places of varying price and comfort. All should be able to provide cheap transport if you stay. Chartering a long-tail boat to Ko Hai costs around 600B. Snorkel masks and fins can be rented from these resorts for 100B; or you can take half-day snorkelling tours to nearby islands for around 500B.

Koh Hai Villa (☎ 0 1124 7631, Trang ☎ 0 7521 0496; 112 Th Phra Rama VI; r & bungalows 500-800B) has accommodation ranging from small, colourful bamboo bungalows to more modern concrete rooms and bungalows. They sit on a fairly pleasant grassy lot with palms. There's a restaurant, it's open all year, and the office in Trang can arrange cheap transfers.

Try **Ko Ngai Resort** (Trang ☎ 0 7521 5923; bungalows incl breakfast 1650-2000B; ❀ ❀) for something plusher. Fancy beachfront bungalows and houses have dark-wood walls, imaginative baths, huge verandas and a romantic atmosphere. Grounds everywhere are palmy, prim and pleasant. Prices drop in the low season and rise during the holidays.

Ko Hai Fantasy Resort (☎ 0 7521 6339, Trang ☎ 0 7521 0317; www.kohngai.com; bungalows 2500-4500B; ❀ ❀) features a very strange foyer that looks like a cruise ship that has collided with a cinema. The bungalows are brightly painted and include wooden decks and plenty of amenities. The restaurant serves excellent seafood.

One of the cheaper places on the island, **Koh Ngai Paradise** (☎ 0 7521 6420; bungalows 450B) offers simple huts, although it's closed in low season. In Trang, contact it via the Meeting

Point restaurant (p705) on Th Sathani, near the train station.

Hat Chang Lang & Hat Jao Mai National Park

หาดฉางหลาง/อุทยานแห่งชาติหาดเจ้าไหม

Hat Chang Lang has a 2km-long beach that is very flat and shallow, and offers the usual strip of casuarina-backed sand. It's a very peaceful place. At the southern end of the beach, where the beachfront road turns inland, is the headquarters of **Hat Jao Mai National Park** (6am-6pm).

The 231-sq-km park covers the shoreline from Hat Pak Meng to Laem Jao Mai and the islands of Ko Muk and Ko Kradan, plus a host of small islets in the bay. In various parts of the park you may see endangered dugong (also called manatee or sea cow) and rare black-necked stork, as well as the more common species such as sea otter, macaque, langur, wild pig, pangolin, white-bellied sea eagle, Pacific reef-egret, little heron and monitor lizard.

You usually only need to pay the national park fees if you visit the park headquarters, Ko Kradan or Hat San and Hat Yong Ling (the next beaches south of Hat Chang Lang). Since the tsunami, however, all parks fees have been waived – for how long is anyone's guess (the park service hasn't declared a date). The headquarters is a popular picnic spot and there are some examples of ancient rock art on some nearby cliffs. You may be able to hire long-tails here from November to April. Camping is permitted throughout the park.

The best place to stay is the **national park headquarters** (0 7521 3260; camping 40B, r 500B, cabins 600-2000B). There are simple cabins with fans sleeping six to eight people, which can also be rented by the room. You can camp under the casuarinas on the foreshore; tents can be rented (300B) if you don't have your own with you.

Chang Leng Resort (bungalows 400-600B;), about 4km north of the main park office, is another option. It offers sturdy inland bungalows with TV and decent furnishings. There's a restaurant in front with views of the sea. Motorcycles and bicycles can be rented.

Frequent minivans travel from Th Kha Klang in Trang to Jao Mai (50B, one hour), or you can charter a taxi from Trang for

400B. The park headquarters is about 1km off this road, down a clearly signposted track.

Ko Muk

เกาะมุก

Once a lovely unspoiled island, Ko Muk has been besieged by bungalow operators who went construction crazy up until the 2004 tsunami. This is particularly obvious on the island's best beach, Hat Farang (Hat Sai Yao), on its western side. The general mood on this island, nearly opposite Hat Chang Lang on the mainland, is still pretty laid-back. There is some good snorkelling offshore, and rubber plantations and forests to hike through in the interior. Near the northern end is **Tham Morakot** (Emerald Cave), a beautiful limestone tunnel that can be entered by boat during low tide. The tunnel stretches for 80m to emerge in an open pool of emerald hue, hence the cave's name. Between Ko Muk and Ko Ngai are the two small karst islets of **Ko Cheuk** and **Ko Waen**, which have good snorkelling and small sandy beaches.

Power supply on Ko Muk is only available at night and most of the resorts here close down during the low season. **Ko Muk Resort** (0 7521 2613, Trang 0 7522 2296; 45 Th Sathani; bungalows 300-600B; Nov-Jun) is located near Hua Laem (which is a 10-minute walk north of the pier). It has simple but nicely designed wood and bamboo bungalows. The beach here turns to mud flats at low tide; the one in front of the Muslim village a little way south is slightly better, but observe local customs and cover up. The resort can organise boats to nearby islands. Contact its office in Trang to arrange transport here for 150B.

On pleasant Hat Farang, a 60B motorcycle taxi ride from the pier, are a few basic options. **Ko Mook Charlie Beach Resort** (0 7520 3281; bungalows 300-1200B;) is the main operator on this beach. Recently remodelled, it now features 60 new bungalows, as well as a good restaurant and tour desk. It stays open all year, and offers boat tours. **Sawasdee Resort** (0 1508 0432; bungalows 300-400B) is quickly being crowded out by Charlie's net door. If you need a cheap place to stay, and all the inexpensive rooms at Charlie's are taken, it's an OK option. The bungalows are on stilts and shaded by trees.

The easiest place to get a boat to Ko Muk is from Tha Khuan Tung Ngu, located between Hat Chang Lang and Hat Yong Ling (minivans from Trang cost 50B). Boats leave from 10am to noon (35B, 30 to 45 minutes). Private long-tail boats cost 800B.

Ko Kradan
เกาะกระดาน

Ko Kradan, southwest of Ko Muk, is the most beautiful of the islands that belong to Hat Jao Mai National Park, with a gorgeous unspoiled beach at Hat Yong and decent coral reefs off the eastern shore. It's a popular destination for snorkelling and diving tours. As with Ko Phi-Phi, part of the island was excluded from the national park to allow local people to establish coconut and rubber plantations, as well as resorts – and one place has already opened. For now, Ko Kradan remains a delightful and isolated place to stay, but it won't be long before other resorts follow the first's lead. Camping on the island is possible with permission from the national park staff (see opposite). The peaceful **Ko Kradan Paradise Beach** (☎ 0 7521 1391; www.kradanisland.com; bungalows 400-900B) has bungalows and cement rooms with fans and private bathroom. The beach isn't bad, and there's a coral reef out the front. The resort stays open year-round.

Unless you use resort transport, the only way to reach Ko Kradan is to charter a long-tail boat (900B, one hour) from Hat Yao.

IT'S A NICE DAY FOR A WET WEDDING

Each Valentine's Day, Ko Kradan is the setting for a rather unusual wedding ceremony. Around 35 brides and grooms don scuba gear and descend to an underwater altar amid the coral reefs, exchanging their vows in front of the Trang District Officer. How the couples manage to say 'I do' underwater has never been fully explained, but the ceremony has made it into the Guinness Book of Records for the world's largest underwater wedding. Before and after the scuba ceremony, the couples are paraded along the coast in a flotilla of motorboats. If you think this might be right for your special day, visit the website www.underwaterwedding.com.

Hat Yong Ling & Hat Yao
หาดหยงหลิง/หาดยาว

Between Hat Chang Lang in the north and Hat Jao Mai in the south are two very long white-sand beaches separated by limestone cliffs that are riddled with caves. Hat Yong Ling is a pretty bay lined with casuarina trees, and there are snack stands on weekends. Tidal pools sit off the beach at the base of limestone cliffs, and you can camp nearby if you check in with the park officers first. Another curving beach, **Hat San**, is close by and can only be approached via a large cave that connects the two beaches. The striking karst formation that rises to the north of the beach resembles a shark's dorsal fin. A few restaurants sell the usual Thai beach food. National park fees apply here.

Inland from Hat Yong Ling, you can detour to **Khuan Khaeng Hot Springs**, about 2km east of the turn off to Hat Yao on the road to Trang (Rte 4046). The falls maintain a constant temperature of 60°C. You'll need your own transport to get here.

Hat Yao is the second of the casuarina-backed, long strips of sand. A rocky headland at the southern end is pockmarked with caves and there is good snorkelling around the island immediately offshore. The nicest beach in the area is tiny **Hat Apo**, hidden away among the cliffs. You can get here by long-tail or wade around from the sandy spit in front of **Sinchai's Chaomai Resort** (☎ 0 7520 3034; tents 120B, bungalows 300-500B; ✹), which is one of two accommodation options at Hat Yao. It is friendly and self-sufficient and offers a handful of bungalows nestled under the rocky cliffs at the northern end of the beach. Sinchai's wife cooks up fantastic Thai food and the family can arrange boat trips to nearby caves and islands. You can also rent bikes and motorcycles. The turn-off for Sinchai's is just past the cliffs on the road to Hat Yao; take the right fork to reach the resort.

A short walk from Sinchai's is **Haad Yao Nature Resort** (☎ 0 7520 3012; www.tourismmart.com /haadyaonatureresort; dm 150B, r & bungalows 300-600B; ✹), managed by enthusiastic naturalists who offer a variety of environmental tours in the area. The resort has wooden bungalows with balconies and simple rooms in an old wooden house. There's a wonderfully atmospheric restaurant located over

ANDAMAN COAST

the water. During Thai holidays such as Songkran the management tends to jack up room rates by as much as five times the normal price.

On the northern side of the headland is a collection of wooden seafood restaurants selling cheap Thai meals.

Ko Libong
เกาะลิบง

Trang's largest island is just 15 minutes by long-tail from Hat Yao. The low-lying island is home to a small Muslim fishing community and has just two resorts on lovely isolated beaches on the western coast. The sensitive development here is a real breath of fresh air compared with other islands on the bay. The island has its own wildlife sanctuary, **Libong Archipelago Wildlife Reserve** (☎ 0 7525 1932; admission by donation). It's a no-hunting zone located inland from Laem Ju Hoi, a cape that juts out from the island's east coast. Many species of birds from northern Asia and Siberia migrate here each year to pass the winter. Ko Libong is also surrounded by a veritable garden of seagrass, the main food of the dugong. Unfortunately, sightings are rare because this mammal is an endangered species that was hunted in the past – and boats have also caused fatal injuries to the animals. You can try your luck at spotting one, however, on a tour organised through one of the resorts. Trained naturalists lead dugong-spotting tours by sea kayak for 800B.

Libong Nature Beach Resort (☎ 0 1894 6936; nat ureresorts@thailand.com; bungalows 500-700B) offers these tours, as well as snorkelling trips. It also has simple bamboo and thatch bungalows (and fancier brick ones) near the beach. There's a beachfront restaurant with reasonable prices and tasty food. The resort is closed in the low season.

Libong Beach Resort (☎ 0 7522 5205; info@libong beachresort.com; bungalows 400-1200B; 🔀), north of Libong Nature Beach Resort, is a delightful midrange resort. The attractive wooden bungalows come with either fans or air-con and sea views. The nice open-plan restaurant is awesome for just chilling out. A dive shop operates here during the high season, the usual tours can be arranged (including dugong-spotting tours) and sea kayaks can be rented for 100B per hour.

Boats to Ko Libong depart throughout the day from Ban Jao Mai Hat Yao (30B, 30 minutes). For 60B you can get a ride to the resorts themselves. Chartering private long-tail boats costs 700B.

Ko Sukon
เกาะสุกร

This friendly and peaceful island is charmingly crisscrossed with a small network of paved roads and dirt trails that wind through water buffalo–dotted rice fields, swaying coconut palms, shady rubber tree plantations and tiny villages. A small hilltop provides good views of the island, whose 2500 inhabitants subsist mainly on fishing and rubber cultivation. There's limited electricity, and just a handful of cars or trucks chug on the roads (most transport is by motorcycle). Because Ko Sukon is a mostly Muslim island, please remember to cover up as you're travelling inland; the locals will certainly appreciate this small gesture on your part.

Sukorn Beach Bungalows (☎ 0 7520 7707, Trang ☎ 0 7521 1457; www.sukorn-island-trang.com; r 450, bungalows 750-950B) offers beautiful bungalows in a grassy garden shaded by coconut palms. There's a relaxing restaurant, and the beach out the front is golden brown. There are bicycles and motorcycles to be rented, and canoes that can be used for free. Rates drop by 60% from mid-May to November. Contact its Trang office for inexpensive transfers here.

Sukon Island Resort (☎ 0 7521 1460, Trang ☎ 0 7521 9679; bungalows 300-800B) is close to Sukorn Beach Bungalows but is not as intimate, with over 40 white, modern concrete bungalows riding up a small inland hill (prices depend on the exact location). There's an attractive restaurant close to the beach.

The best way to get to Ko Sukon is to go via your own resort's transport. The second best option is to take a minivan (25B) south to Yan Ta Khao, then a *săwngthăew* to Tha Ta Seh, where long-tail boats leave when full for 20B per person. Hiring the whole boat costs 200B. Motorcycles on Ko Sukon charge about 30B per ride.

SATUN PROVINCE

Bordering Malaysia, Satun is the Andaman coast's southernmost province and sees few international visitors compared with the more developed islands across the border. Although it is close to the provinces of Yala (p616), Pattani (p618) and Narathiwat (p621), it has not recently experienced any of the violent bombings that have plagued these provinces over the years, and travel in this mostly Muslim province remains quite safe.

The jewel in Satun's crown is Ko Tarutao Marine National Park, which preserves some of the most unspoiled islands on the Andaman coast. Exploration of the province's lush northern inland region yields beautiful rainforest and soaring granite outcroppings.

Satun gets its name from the Malay word *setul*, a type of fruit tree common in this area. Before 1813 the province was a district of the Malay state of Kedah, which at the time paid tribute to Siam along with Kelantan, Terengganu and Perlis. The Anglo-Siamese Treaty of 1909 released parts of these states to Britain, and they later became part of independent Malaysia. Satun didn't become a province of Siam until 1925.

Today an estimated 66% of the population is Muslim, most of whom speak Yawi (the language of the Malay Peninsula) or Malay as a first language; there are about a dozen mosques for every wat in the province. Main industries here include fishing, rubber and palm oil.

SATUN

สตูล

pop 33,400

The sleepy provincial capital of Satun is the jumping-off point for boats to Ko Tarutao Marine National Park. Although there isn't much to see or do here, this modest little city is a pleasant place to wander and get a feel for local flavour. It's not as prosperous, and quite a bit smaller than other southern provincial capitals. A few old Sino-Portuguese shophouses, some said to date back as far as 1839, lie along Th Buriwanit. Satun shuts down on Sunday.

In the past, there was quite a lot of friction between the local population and the Buddhist government in Bangkok. These days, things are much more relaxed, and while the locals still have their grievances, there's nothing on the scale of the violent struggles taking place in nearby Pattani or Narathiwat Provinces.

Information

The **immigration office** (☎ 0 7271 1080; ◷ 8.30am-4.30pm Mon-Fri) processes visa extensions for 500B. There's also an immigration office at Tha Tammalang (the pier), 7km south of town, but it doesn't extend visas. For cheaper visa extensions, however, you can cross out and back into Thailand via the Malaysia border. Either take a boat from Tha Tammalang to Kuala Perlis (100B return), or a *săwngthăew* from Satun to Wang Prajan (the border town in Thale Ban National Park; 30B, one hour). These take longer but are more interesting. You can check your email at **Satun Cybernet** (134-36 Th Satun Thani; per hr 60B; ◷ 9am-10pm). There are banks with ATMs in the centre of town, on Th Buriwanit. The **main post office** (Th Samanta Prasit; ◷ 8.30am-4.30pm Mon-Fri, 9am-noon Sat & Sun) also houses the telephone office.

Sights

There aren't really any must-see sights in Satun apart from the museum, although there is also a modern, parachute-domed **Bambang Mosque** in the centre, constructed in 1979.

SATUN NATIONAL MUSEUM

พิพิธภัณฑสถานแห่งชาติสตูล

The **Satun National Museum** (Kun Den Museum; Soi 5, Th Satun Thani; admission 30B; ◷ 9am-4pm Wed-Sun) is actually an early 20th-century 'palace' that was built by a local prince to accommodate King Rama V during a royal visit. Unfortunately, the king never stayed here, but the handsome two-storey structure served as the provincial office of Satun. The Japanese sequestered it during WWII and used it as a military headquarters.

Built in a pseudo-European style common in nearby Malaysia, the building has been restored and its rooms arranged to give a surprisingly thorough introduction to the traditions and folkways of the Thai Muslim south. Most of the displays are miniature dioramas (with recorded narration in both Thai and English) that cover everything from southern mat weaving techniques to the traditional martial art called *silá*. Exhibits labelled in English explain local marriage rites as well as male and female ritual circumcision. There are also narrated exhibits describing the Sakai, the tribal people who are believed to have

SATUN

inhabited the region long before the arrival of the Thai or Malay.

KHAO PHAYA WANG
เขาพญาวัง

About 1km northwest of the centre is this vine-choked limestone mastiff, offering dramatic views over surrounding mangroves, rice fields and coconut plantations. A steep set of concrete steps leads up to a shady pavilion that is overrun by crab-eating macaques. On weekends stalls set up here and sell *sôm-tam, khâo nǐaw, kài thâwt* and *kûng thâwt* and *mîang kham* (pieces of ginger, onion, dried shrimp, toasted coconut, chilli, peanuts and lime placed into a wild tea leaf with a thick, sweet and salty tamarind sauce).

Tours

Travel agencies in town can arrange boat trips to the islands in Ko Tarutao Marine National Park and tours to surrounding caves and waterfalls. For guided tours to Satun's nearby attractions, contact **Pate Tour** (☎ 0 7472 4085; www.patetour.com). A friendly couple organises biking, kayaking and trekking trips to Ko Tarutao, as well as nearby islands, caves and even inland destinations. The two-day, one-night rustic camping tour to Ko Lidi costs 1900B per person and includes snorkelling equipment, tent, transport and food; the one-day kayaking tour costs 700B per person (four person minimum) and includes transport, lunch and kayaking. There's also a trekking/kayaking trip with stays at jungle bungalows near Jed Cod cave, inland in Satun Province. English, Spanish, French and Thai are spoken.

Sleeping

Don't expect luxury, or anything really special. Hotels are not this city's strong point.

Sinkiat Thani Hotel (☎ 0 7472 1055; fax 0 7472 1059; 50 Th Buriwanit; r 750B; 🛇) In a central location, this big place in a large tower boasts clean, but nondescript rooms, with decent amenities, though the carpets can be spotty. All have TVs, hot showers and phones.

Amm Guest House (☎ 0 7472 4912; 676 Mu 3 Th Sulakanukun; r 300B) Run by a Thai woman who speaks English and German, it is 2km south of town and is a great place for backpackers. Six rooms sit riverside, four right over the water and reached via a rickety wooden plank. The rooms are very basic and there's little privacy, but the atmosphere is special. To get here take the Tha Tammalang *săwngthăew* (10B).

Pinnacle Tarutao Hotel (Wang Mai; ☎ 0 7471 1607; 43 Th Satun Thani; r 600-1000B; 🛇) A landmark seven-storey building north of the town centre, it offers the town's most upmarket rooms with fridge, hot water and cable TV. There are good views from the upper floors. Try for a room at the back to avoid the street noise.

Satul Tanee Hotel (☎ 0 7471 1010; fax 0 7471 1207; 90 Th Satun Thani; r with fan 210-270B, with air-con 370-470B; 🛇) The lobby is painfully outdated and the halls are industrial but the fan rooms are clean and tidy, and the air-con ones surprisingly decent. All are large, but avoid the rooms facing the street.

Rain Tong Hotel (☎ 0 7471 1036; Th Samanta Prasit; r 140-180B) A friendly place with large, bright and pretty basic old rooms. A share-taxi stand, the river and the town's market are all nearby.

Rot Inn Resort (no Roman-script sign; ☎ 0 7472 4758; Th Satun Thani II; r with fan 150-200B, with air-con 260-350B; 🛇) In a lush pastel orange building with a blue roof, the eight modern, large and spotless rooms have TVs and are a good deal. The only drawback is the long walk to centre.

Udomsuk Hotel (☎ 0 7471 1006; Th Hatthakham Seuksa; r 150B) On a corner lot, it is an old place with simple, bright and worn rooms with Thai-style baths. They're basically OK, but those facing the street are noisy.

Eating & Drinking

Suhana Restaurant (☎ 0 7471 1023; Th Buriwanit; dishes 40-80B) An open, casual and reliable Muslim place with dishes you can point to out the front.

Rotii Shop (dishes 20-40B) Across the street and three doors down from Suhana, this shop with an olive awning serves excellent *mátàbà* (a vegetable *rotii* served with pickled side dish). Look for six tables with pale blue plastic chairs.

Time Restaurant (☎ 0 7471 2286; 43/1-2 Th Surat Thani; dishes 45-90B) Near the Wang Mai Hotel, this popular place is where to go for a modern, comfortable air-con environment when dining. The Thai food is reasonably priced and not half bad.

Ko Uan (no Roman-script sign; ☎ 0 7471 2103; 43/6-7 Th Surat Thani; dishes 30-60B; 🕙 6pm-3am) Around the corner from Time Restaurant, it cooks up great Chinese food, especially veggie dishes. It's in a modern space with fan and air-con sections, and is closed the 7th and 8th of every month.

Hok Heng Yong (Th Satun Thani; 🕙 6am-4.30pm) A traditional Hokkien coffee shop, it's a local joint with round marble-topped tables where older Chinese men hang around, eat a few snacks and chat about politics.

Namtip Pub (☎ 0 7271 1079) For a bit of excitement head over here. Ignore the coffeeshop sign, because this place is more of a modern lounge act. Locals visit to smoke and down their Heinekens (80B) while checking out the surprisingly good bands playing mostly Thai tunes along with Aerosmith, Scorpions and Clapton. Requests are taken, and if you're charming enough they may even let you sing on stage.

Located right in the middle of town the night market is excellent and may be the best eating option in Satun. It comes to life around 5pm with lots of vendors selling cheap Thai-Muslim treats and seafood. For even cheaper eats, try the small group of **Chinese food stalls** (Th Samanta Prasit) near Th Buriwanit.

Getting There & Away

BOAT

Boats to Malaysia and Ko Tarutao Marine National Park leave from Tha Tammalang, 7km south of Satun along Th Sulakanukoon. *Săwngthăew* to Tha Tammalang leave from the southern end of Th Buriwanit and cost 20B per person; a motorcycle taxi costs 40B. Large long-tail boats run regularly to Kuala Perlis in Malaysia (100B, 45 minutes) between 8am and 2pm. From Malaysia the fare is M$20. You can also charter a boat to Perlis for 1500B. For Pulau Langkawi (Langkawi Island) in Malaysia, boats leave at 8am, 9am, 1.30pm and 4pm (220B, two hours). They return at 9am, 10am, 2pm and 4pm and cost M$20.

Bring some money from Langkawi, since there are limited money-changing facilities at Tha Tammalang. Remember that there's a one-hour time difference between Thailand and Malaysia. There's also a daily service to Ko Tarutao (250B, 1½ hours) at 11am, returning at 3pm. The same boat continues from Tarutao to Ko Lipe (250B, one hour).

BUS & MINIVANS

Buses to Bangkok leave from a small depot on Th Hatthakham Seuksa, just east of the town centre. Air-con buses (440B to 565B, 14 hours) leave at 7am and every half-hour between 2.30pm and 4.30pm. There is also a VIP bus (865B, 13 hours, 4pm). Buses heading for Satun leave Bangkok's Southern bus terminal at 6pm and 6.30pm. It's a rather long trip, though – consider taking the train.

Air-con bus destinations include Trang (60B to 200B, two hours), Krabi (350B, 4½ hours) and Phuket (450B, 6½ hours). These buses leave frequently (more than once a day) from the 7-Eleven on Th Satun Thani. Local buses head to Trang (60B, two hours) and La-Ngu (40B, 30 minutes). They run north along Th Satun Thani.

Frequent air-con minivans leave from the depot just south of Wat Chanathip on Th Sulakanukoon and run to the train station in Hat Yai (60B, one hour). Other destinations from Satun include Trang (80B, two hours) and La-Ngu (30B, 30 minutes), but departures are less frequent – take a bus instead.

TRAIN

If you want to take the train to Satun Province (about 15 hours), you can take the No 35, which leaves Bangkok at 2.20pm and gets to Padang Besar (60km from Satun) at 8am the following day (710B to 800B 2nd class). Taking the train to Hat Yai may give you more options, however (see p615).

Getting Around

Call **Pate Tour** (☎ 0 7472 4085) to arrange bicycle rentals in town, or try **Satun Mountain Bike** (Th Surat Thani; ⏰ 9am-6.30pm), which charges 300B per day for upmarket mountain bikes.

PAK BARA
ปากบารา

For tourists, this town exists only as a jumping-off point to Ko Tarutao Marine National Park. Pak Bara is a one-street (Hwy 4052) kind of town, the main part of which runs for 1km or so along the shore before dead-ending at the pier. Most people arriving at the pier move on right away by bus or air-con minivan, but you may find yourself spending the night if you miss the boat to the islands. Ko Tarutao Marine National Park runs a **visitors centre** (☎ 0 7478 3485) here. It is just back from the pier and you can book accommodation and obtain permission for camping. Travel agencies in town can arrange tours to the islands in the national park.

If you do miss the boat, there are a few places offering accommodation. Many have their own restaurants, but there are also a few eateries around.

A pleasant choice is **Best House Resort** (☎ 0 7478 3058; fax 0 7478 3417; r 500-600B; ❄), only 200m from the pier. It has clean, spacious and modern rooms that surround a small murky lagoon. Amenities include TV and hot water, and there's a restaurant.

Another attractive place is **Grand Villa** (☎ 0 7478 3499; r 400B; ❄). It offers basic but decent rooms.

Diamond Beach Bungalows (☎ 0 7478 3138; bungalows 200-350B) has rustically bleak thatched bungalows, as well as some downright small and ugly concrete ones. It's about 1km from the pier.

A little further from the pier, but probably worth the 3km slog, is **Bara Resort** (☎ 0 7478 3333; bungalows 480B; ❄). It features nine clean, large and modern bungalows that are well spaced on a grassy lot. Amenities include TV, hot water and fridge. This place is across the highway from the beach.

From Satun you must take a share taxi (30B) or bus (40B) as far as La-Ngu, then a *săwngthăew* to reach Pak Bara. Taxis to La-Ngu leave when full from near the night market on Th Satun Thani; buses run north along Th Satun Thani. You can also charter a taxi to Pak Bara for 300B. Minivans also connect Pak Bara to/from Hat Yai (70B, two hours).

KO TARUTAO MARINE NATIONAL PARK
อุทยานแห่งชาติหมู่เกาะตะรุเตา

This spectacular marine **national park** (☎ 0 7478 1285; ❤ mid-Nov–mid-May) protects a large archipelago of 51 islands, approximately 30km from Pak Bara and 60km northwest of Satun. Ko Tarutao, the biggest of the group, is only 5km from Pulau Langkawi in Malaysia. Only five of the islands (Tarutao, Adang, Lipe, Rawi and Klang) have any kind of regular boat service to them, and tourists generally only visit the first three. Access to the other islands, which offer excellent beaches and coral reefs, can only be arranged by chartering long-tail boats.

Ko Tarutao Marine National Park remains one of the most beautifully isolated and pristine coastal areas in Thailand, in part because it requires a bit more effort to get there. Its beauty and isolation was probably why it was chosen as location for the fifth season of the popular American TV series *Survivor,* broadcast in 2002. Accommodation on the islands is fairly basic, and the park is only officially open from around November to May, depending on the weather patterns. Note that there are no foreign exchange facilities at Ko Tarutao – you can exchange cash and cheques at travel agencies in Pak Bara and there's an ATM in La-Ngu. If you do a search for Tarutao on the Internet, don't be surprised if you come up with a handful of interesting sights. A UK company markets a method to stop premature ejaculation under the trademarked name Tarutao!

Ko Tarutao
เกาะตะรุเตา

Covering a whopping 151 sq km, Ko Tarutao is the largest island in the marine park, and a shining example of the way tourism should be done, with a small government-run visitors centre and a limited number of tidy cottages and longhouses. Most of the island is covered in dense virgin jungle and the western coast is lined with secluded white-sand beaches.

The fantastic state of preservation on Ko Tarutao is largely a result of the island's

history. Between 1939 and 1946, more than 3000 Thai criminals were imprisoned here, including a number of political prisoners (mostly government officials who found themselves on the wrong side of various political coups). Interesting inmates include So Setabutra, who compiled the first Thai-English dictionary while imprisoned on Tarutao, and Sittiporn Gridagon, son of Rama VII, who spent his time here developing a new variety of cucumber. Tarutao was selected as a prison for its inhospitable environment – the interior was once full of malarial mosquitoes and crocodiles, while large predatory sharks patrolled the surrounding waters.

During WWII, food and medical supplies from the mainland were severely depleted and hundreds of prisoners died from malaria. The prisoners and guards mutinied, taking to piracy in the nearby Strait of Malaka. A number of merchant ships were plundered before the mutineers were suppressed by a contingent of British troops in 1944.

The overgrown ruins of the camp for political prisoners can be seen at **Ao Taloh Udang**, in the southeast of the island, reached via a long overgrown track. The prison camp for civilian prisoners was over on the eastern coast of **Ao Taloh Wow**, where the big boats from Tha Tammalang now dock. A concrete road runs across the island from Ao Taloh Wow to **Ao Phante Malaka** on the western side. Here you'll find the park headquarters, the pier, bungalows and the main camping site. The visitors centre has interesting displays on the ecology and history of the island and there is a free slide show with English commentary every night at 8pm.

Next to the visitors centre, a steep trail leads through the jungle to **Toe-Boo Cliff**, a dramatic rocky outcrop with fabulous views of the marine park. It's a fine spot to watch the setting sun melt into the Strait of Malaka.

Ao Phante Malaka has a lovely alabaster beach shaded by pandanus and casuarinas, and Tarutao's largest stream, Khlong Phante Malaka, flows into the sea at the northern end of the beach. If you follow the stream inland, you'll reach **Tham Jara-Khe** (Crocodile Cave), which was once home to deadly saltwater crocodiles. The cave is navigable for about 1km at low tide and can be visited on

ANDAMAN COAST

KO TARUTAO MARINE NATIONAL PARK & AROUND

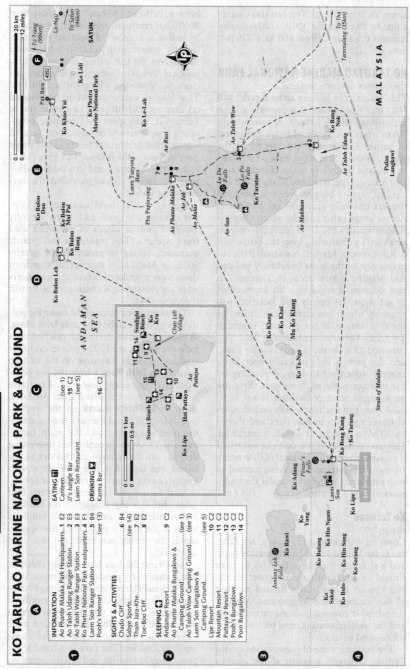

INFORMATION
Ao Phante Malaka Park Headquarters..**1** E3	
Ao Taloh Udang Ranger Station............**2** E3	
Ao Taloh Wow Ranger Station..............**3** E3	
Ko Phetra National Park Headquarters...**4** F1	
Laem Son Ranger Station......................**5** B4	
Pooh's Internet...(see 13)	

SIGHTS & ACTIVITIES
Chado Cliff...**6** B4	
Sabye Sports..(see 14)	
Tham Jara-Khe.......................................**7** E2	
Toe-Boo Cliff...**8** E2	

SLEEPING 🛏
Andaman Resort.....................................**9** C2	
Ao Phante Malaka Bungalows &	
Camping Ground...............................(see 1)	
Ao Taloh Wow Camping Ground.........(see 3)	
Laem Son Bungalows &	
Camping Ground...............................(see 5)	
Lipe Resort..**10** C2	
Mountain Resort....................................**11** C2	
Pattaya 2 Resort....................................**12** C2	
Pooh's Bungalows.................................**13** C2	
Porn Bungalows....................................**14** C2	

EATING 🍴
Canteen..(see 1)	
JJ's Jungle Bar.....................................**15** C2	
Laem Son Restaurant............................(see 5)	

DRINKING 🍸
Karma Bar...**16** C2	

ANDAMAN SEA

SATUN

MALAYSIA

long-tail tours from the jetty at Ao Phante Malaka. There is OK snorkelling around the **Pha Papinyong** (Papillion Cliffs) north of Ao Phante, but watch out for lionfish and stingrays.

Immediately south of Ao Phante is **Ao Jak**, which has another fine sandy beach, and **Ao Malae**, which has white sand and a ranger station with bungalows and a camp site. A 30-minute boat ride, or 8km walk south of Ao Phante is **Ao San**, an isolated sandy bay where turtles nest between September and April. You can camp here but there are no facilities. Ao San has decent snorkelling, as does Ao Makham, further south. From the small ranger station at Ao San, you can walk inland to **Lu Du Falls** (about 1½ hours) and **Lo Po Falls** (about 2½ hours). Both make fine day-hikes.

Situated on the far side of the island is **Ao Rusi**, which was controversially used as a location for the American TV show *Survivor*. There's a dramatic cave here and good coral offshore, but you'll need to charter a long-tail from Ao Phante Malaka to get here. Nearby **Ko Le-Lah** is another good snorkelling spot.

There are interesting sheer-sided rocky buttresses along the southeastern coast, including **Ko Rang Nok** (Bird Nest Island), off Ao Taloh Udang, which is another trove of the expensive swiftlet nests craved by Chinese diners around the world.

SLEEPING & EATING

All the formal **park accommodation** (Pak Bara ☎ 0 7478 3485, Bangkok ☎ 0 2561 4292; camp sites 20B, r & cabins 400-1500B, bungalows 1600B) on Ko Tarutao is around the park headquarters at Ao Phante Malaka and Ao Malae. The accommodation is far more sensitive to the environment than the average Thai resort. Water is rationed, rubbish is transported back to the mainland, lighting is provided by power-saving light bulbs and electricity is available between 6pm and 7am only.

You can stay in the two- or three-room cabins at the foot of Toe-Boo Cliff. These are spacious and fan-cooled. At Ao Molae there are 10 deluxe bungalows that house up to four people. The cheapest option is the longhouse rooms at Ao Phante Malaka, with four mattresses on the floor (you must take the whole room). Showers are provided in clean blocks nearby. All accommodation comes with mosquito nets, but it's a good idea to bring some repellent.

Camping is permitted at the main camp site under the casuarinas on the foreshore at Ao Phante Malaka, Ao Molae and Ao Taloh Wow, where there are toilet and shower blocks, or on the wild beaches at Ao San, Ao Makham and Ao Taloh Udang, where you'll need to be totally self-sufficient. You can hire tents for 100B to 300B.

The park authorities run an excellent **canteen** (dishes 40-120B) at Ao Phante Malaka. The food is satisfying and tasty and you can even get a cold beer. If you stay at Ao Taloh Wow, you can eat at the small canteen by the jetty.

Be aware that Tarutao is popular and accommodation fills quickly, so it's always best to book ahead.

GETTING THERE & AROUND

Boats heading for Tarutao leave regularly between November and April, depending on the weather.

Boats from Pak Bara leave at 10.30am and 3pm daily (150/300B one way/return, 1½ hours); the 10.30am boat continues to Ko Adang (400/800B). Departures back to Pak Bara are at 9am and 1pm. It is best to buy one-way tickets for each leg of your journey, as this allows a choice of rtes back.

There's also a comfortable boat service to Ko Tarutao from Tha Thammalang, 7km south of Satun. Boats leave at 11am (250/450B, 1¼ hours); this boat continues to Ko Adang (500/900B, two hours). A long-tail boat from Adang to Lipe costs 20B.

Mu Ko Klang

เกาะไข่/เกาะกลาง

Between Ko Tarutao and Ko Adang is a small cluster of three islands called Mu Ko Klang (Middle Island Group), where there is good snorkelling. One of the islands, **Ko Khai**, also has a good white-sand beach. Boats from Ko Tarutao take about 40 minutes to reach Ko Khai. You can also charter long-tail boats from Ko Lipe out here for around 800B.

Ko Adang & Ko Rawi

เกาะอาดัง/เกาะราวี

Ko Adang is 43km west from Tarutao and about 80km from Pak Bara. The 30-sq-km island is covered with forests and freshwater streams. Lots of snorkelling tours make a stop here, but there are mooring buoys to prevent damage from anchors. Inland are jungle trails and tumbling waterfalls, including **Pirate's Falls**; rumour has it pirates once used it as a freshwater source. There are great views from **Chado Cliff**, above the main beach, and green turtles lay their eggs here between September and December.

Ko Rawi is 1km west of Ko Adang and has similar limestone hills and dense jungle, with nice beaches and large coral reefs offshore. Wild camping is allowed with permission from the national park authorities. Other excellent snorkelling spots include the northern side of **Ko Yang** and tiny **Ko Hin Ngam**, which is known for its beautiful stripy pebbles. Legend has it the stones are cursed and anyone who takes one will experience bad luck until the stones are returned to their source.

The only accommodation is provided by the national park service, which maintains a ranger station at Laem Son in the southeast of Ko Adang, where the pier is also located. There are **bungalows** (3-9 people 300-1500B), **longhouses** (4-bed r 400B) and places to pitch your **tent** (per tent 20B). A small restaurant provides basic meals, but it's not a bad idea to bring some food from the mainland.

The 10.30am boat from Pak Bara to Ko Tarutao continues to Ko Adang; it returns to Pak Bara (via Ko Tarutao) at 8am the next day (800B return).

There's also a comfortable boat service that departs from Tha Thammalang, 7km south of Satun. Boats leave at 9am daily and stop in Ko Tarutao, continuing to Ko Adang (500/900B one way/return from Tha Tammalang; 250/450B from Ko Tarutao).

Ko Lipe
เกาะหลีเป๊ะ

Ko Lipe is immediately south of Ko Adang and inhabited by about 500 *chao náam* who possibly originated on Ko Lanta. They live along the western coast and subsist on fishing and some cultivation of vegetables and rice on the flatter parts of the island. For some reason the *chao náam* here prefer to be called *chao leh* – a term despised by other Moken on islands to the north. They also go by the term Thai Mai (New Thai), a nomenclature that is favoured by the Thai government.

The island falls outside the protection of the national park and is slowly developing as a result. For now, there's nothing on the scale of Ko Lanta or Ko Phi-Phi, but you don't need a crystal ball to see what fate has in store for Ko Lipe in the future. Most of the developments are at **Hat Pattaya** on the southern coast and near the *chao leh* village on the eastern coast. Luckily, most of Ko Lipe is still very laid-back with peaceful jungle trails and some delightful secluded beaches, which retain their original Robinson Crusoe atmosphere. **Sunset Beach** has fabulous views over to Ko Adang. Another nice spot is the northern end of **Sunlight Beach**, below Andaman Resort and Mountain Resort, where a lovely curved sandbar carves out a tranquil, clean cove of emerald water. Footpaths connect all three points with the main *chao leh* village on the east coast.

There's good coral all along the southern coast and around **Ko Kra**, the little island opposite *chao leh* village. Most resorts rent out mask and snorkel sets and fins for 50B each and can arrange long-tail trips to Ko Adang and other coral-fringed islands for around 800B to 1000B. **Lotus Dive** (☎ 0 7472 8018; www.lotusdive.com) at Pooh's Bungalows at Hat Pattaya, offers a range of dive trips and PADI dive instruction. On Sunset Beach, **Sabye Sports** (☎ 0 7473 4104; www.sabye-sports.com) offers much the same.

There is no bank or ATM on the island, but Pooh's can charge your ATM or credit card for cash. Pooh's also has expensive Internet service.

SLEEPING & EATING
All resorts on Ko Lipe close from May to November, when boats stop running. Hat Pattaya is crammed with resorts – it's still nice, though not as peaceful as it once was.

Mountain Resort (☎ 0 7472 8131; bungalows 350-800B; 🔁) The newest and largest accommodation on the island is perched on a high hillside with a superb view of the northeastern corner of Sunlight Beach and Ko Adang. The restaurant serves good Thai food. It's best avoided during Thai holidays, when it can be overcrowded.

Pattaya 2 Resort (☎ 0 7472 8034; bungalows 300-800B) Above the rocks at the western end of Hat Pattaya, this place has decent wood-and-concrete huts overlooking the ocean, although the cheapest ones don't have fans.

Its restaurant serves excellent food, and is worth visiting even if you are not staying at the Pattaya 2.

Andaman Resort (☎ 0 7472 9200; camp sites 30B, tent hire 100B, bungalows 500-700B) Just north of the village, this place has nice wooden bungalows under the shade of casuarinas, as well as rather incongruous blue-roofed concrete bungalows closer to the village. The beach here is nice.

Porn Bungalows (☎ 0 7472 8032; bungalows 300-450B) The only resort on lovely Sunset Beach, it's a friendly old-fashioned bamboo place that is often full. The grounds, however, are long overdue for a good cleanup.

Pooh's Bungalows (☎ 0 7472 8019; www.poohlipe .com; r 300-650B) The rooms here – two per bungalow – have no beach view, and are in a rather unbreezy spot inland from Hat Pattaya, but are popular nonetheless because of easy access to Pooh's accommodating restaurant, dive shop and Internet café.

Lipe Resort (☎ 0 7472 4336; bungalows 500-1500B) The biggest player at Hat Pattaya, Lipe has a slightly haphazard selection of wood-and-concrete bungalows and a large bamboo restaurant on the beach.

The village has several basic shops and rustic local restaurants. **JJ's Jungle Bar** (☎ 0 9736 4871; dishes 40-100B) cooks up the best Thai food on the island under a simple palm-thatch shelter off the trail between Sunset and Sunlight Beaches.

ENTERTAINMENT
Karma Bar (☎ 0 5199 3101) Nestled against the base of a limestone cliff below Mountain Resort, Karma Bar serves fresh cocktails, cold beer and toasties (jaffles) while spinning a great selection of MP3s.

GETTING THERE & AWAY
Two private companies operate boat services daily from Pak Bara, on the mainland, to Ko Lipe.

Thai Ferry Center (☎ 0 7478 3055) has a large ferry that leaves Pak Bara at 11.30am and arrives at Ko Lipe around 1.30pm. Tickets cost 500B one way or 900B return. The boat heads back to Pak Bara around 2pm daily. **Adang Sea Tour** (☎ 0 7478 3339) has a slower speedboat that leaves Pak Bara at 2pm and arrives about 4.30pm for 450/800B one way/return. Both companies claim to run boats year-round.

A third, yet slower, speedboat belonging to the **La-Ngu Tourism Association** (☎ 0 1766 8540) operates only from November to May for about the same price and schedule as Adang Sea Tour.

Boats from Pak Bara moor offshore and are met by long-tail boats that will take you to any resort on the island for 40B per person.

Ko Phetra Marine National Park
อุทยานแห่งชาติหมู่เกาะเภตรา

Twenty-two islands stretching between Pak Bara and the boundaries of Ko Tarutao belong to this little-visited, 495-sq-km **park** (admission 200B). Uninhabited **Ko Khao Yai**, the largest in the group, boasts several pristine beaches suitable for camping, swimming and snorkelling. Crab-eating macaques are plentiful here, as local Muslims don't hunt them. There's a castle-shaped rock formation on one shore; during low tide boats can pass beneath a natural arch in the formation.

A park unit is on nearby **Ko Lidi** (or Lide), which features a number of picturesque and unspoiled caves, coves, cliffs and beaches; camping facilities and kayak rentals are available. Between Ko Lidi and Ko Khao Yai is a channel bay known as **Ao Kam Pu**, a tranquil passage with cascading waters during certain tidal changes and some coral at shallow depths.

The park's mainland headquarters, visitors centre and pier is at **Ban Talo Sai**, down a 1.5km side road about 4km southeast of Pak Bara off Rte 4052 (between the 5km and 6km markers). There is a wonderfully located seaside restaurant and a short trail to a viewpoint, and you can also arrange boat transport to Ko Lidi here. If you want to stay here there are nice **seaside bungalows** (☎ 0 7478 3008; bungalows 600-800B).

THALEH BAN NATIONAL PARK
อุทยานแห่งชาติทะเลบัน

This 196-sq-km **park** (☎ 0 7472 9202) lies on the Thailand–Malaysia border and encompasses the best-preserved section of white meranti rainforest (named for the dominant species of dipterocarp trees) in the region. Since the Malaysian side of the border has been deforested by agricultural development, this park is crucial to the forest's continued survival. The terrain is hilly, with a maximum elevation of 740m at Khao Chin.

The area east of Rte 4184 is primary forest on granitic rock reaching up to 700m high, and there are many small streams around here.

The park headquarters, situated on a lake in a lush valley formed by limestone outcrops, is only 2km from the border. Five kilometres north of the office and only 500m off Rte 4184 is **Nam Tok Yaroi**, a 700m, nine-tiered waterfall with pools suitable for swimming. Climb the limestone cliffs next to the park buildings for a view of the lake and surrounding area.

A network of trails leads to a number of other waterfalls and caves in the park, including **Nam Tok Rani**, **Nam Tok Chingrit**, **Tham Ton Din** and **Tham Lawt Pu Yu** (Pu Yu Tunnel Cave). A road also leads to **Nam Tok Ton Pliw**, cutting through secondary forest in the process of rehabilitation. There are vendor stands near the falls, which feature several different levels with pools at the bottom of each. The turn-off for the falls comes 10km before the park entrance off Rte 4184 (10.5km from Rte 406).

Wildlife found within the park's boundaries tends to be of the Sundaic variety, which includes species generally found in Peninsular Malaysia, Sumatra, Borneo and Java. Common mammals include mouse deer, serow, tapir, chevrotain, chamois, various gibbon and macaque. Some of the rare bird species found here are the great argus hornbill, rhinoceros hornbill, helmeted hornbill, banded and bluewing pitta, masked finfoot, dusky crag martin and black Baza hawk. Honey bear and wild pig are sometimes seen near park headquarters, and up in the limestone are 150cm monitor lizard and 40cm tree gecko. More elusive residents include the clouded leopard and dusky langur.

A **border market** – where produce, clothing and homewares are sold – convenes along both sides of the border on Saturday and Sunday; you're permitted to cross free of visa formalities for this occasion.

The park entrance is about 37km north-east of Satun's provincial capital or 90km south of Hat Yai via Rte 406 and Rte 4184; coming from Malaysia it's about 75km from Alor Setar. The road to Thaleh Ban is pretty and winds through several villages, rubber plantations and banana plantations.

The best time to visit is from December to March, between seasonal monsoons. It can rain any time of the year here, but the heaviest and longest rains generally fall in July, August, October and November. In January and February the nights can be quite cool.

Sleeping & Eating

Accommodation can be booked in advance by calling the **Royal Forest Department** (Bangkok ☎ 0 2561 2918; camp sites per person 20B, bungalows/longhouses 600/1600B). There's a Royal Forest Department office in Satun, but it doesn't book anything. Accommodation includes rustic bungalows and longhouses or camping.

The park **restaurant** (dishes from 30B) provides a nice view of the lake and offers simple Thai food. Next to the restaurant is a small shop selling a few toiletries and snacks.

Getting There & Away

The park is about 40km from Satun. It's best seen by private vehicle, since many of the sights are a bit of a distance from each other, and public transport around here is limited. The nearest places to rent cars are Hat Yai and Trang.

Hourly *săwngthăew* (40B) depart from opposite the Rain Tong Hotel in Satun to Wang Prajan, just a few kilometres short of the park entrance. Sometimes these vehicles take you to the park gate; otherwise you can hitch or hop on one of the infrequent *săwngthăew* from Wang Prajan into the park. If you're going from Hat Yai to Satun you can get off at Chalung to hop on these *săwngthăew*. *Săwngthăew* to Chalung and Hat Yai leave from the entrance nearly every hour from 8am until 1pm.

Directory

CONTENTS

ACCOMMODATION

Thailand offers the widest and best-priced variety of accommodation of any country in Southeast Asia.

Most hotels and resorts, and all guesthouses, quote their rates in Thai baht. A few top-end places quote only in US dollars, and where that is the case we have quoted the rate in dollars rather than baht.

Accommodation prices listed in this book are high-season prices for double rooms with attached bathroom, unless stated otherwise. Icons are included to indicate where air-con, swimming pools or Internet access are available; otherwise, assume that there's a fan.

In this guide we place accommodation costing less than 600B a night in the Budget

category, 600B to 1500B in the Midrange category and over 1500B for Top End. An exception is the Bangkok chapter, where Budget mean 600B or less, Midrange is 600B to 3000B and Top End runs over 3000B.

See also p144 for more about what to expect in Bangkok.

Beach Bungalows

Most of the accommodation around the beach areas of Thailand are known as beach bungalows. They range from simple palm thatch and bamboo huts to wooden or concrete bungalows. Low-/high-season rates start from 120/400B per night for wooden places and from 600/1500B for the concrete versions, which usually come with bathrooms and air-con. Bungalows in the upmarket resort areas like Hat Chaweng can cost upwards of 2000B to 4000B.

Guesthouses

Guesthouses are generally the cheapest accommodation in Thailand and are found wherever travellers go throughout central, northern and southern Thailand and to a much lesser extent in the southeast and northeast. Rates vary according to facilities,

---

PRACTICALITIES

- *Bangkok Post* and the *Nation* publish national and international news daily.

- More than 400AM and FM radio stations; short-wave radios can pick up BBC, VOA, Radio Australia, Deutsche Welle and Radio France International.

- Five VHF TV networks with Thai programming, plus UBC cable with international programming.

- The main video format is PAL.

- Thailand uses 220V AC electricity; power outlets most commonly feature two-prong round or flat sockets.

- Thailand follows the international metric system. Gold and silver are weighed in *bàat* (15g).

from a rock-bottom 80B to 150B per room with shared toilet and shower to over 500B with private facilities and air-con. Some are exceptionally good value, while others are only good for a night, at most! Many serve food, although there tends to be a bland sameness to meals in guesthouses wherever you are in Thailand.

Hotels

BUDGET

The most economical budget hotels are older Chinese-Thai hotels, once the standard in all of Thailand, but now slowly giving way to chain hotels. Typical rates run around 150B to 200B for rooms without bath or air-con, 180B to 250B with fan and bath, 350B to 500B with air-con. These tend to be on the main street of the town or near bus and train stations. Rooms usually include two twin beds or one double bed and a ceiling fan.

For a room without air-con, you should ask for *hâwng thammádaa* (ordinary room) or *hâwng phát lom* (room with fan). A room with air-con is *hâwng ae*. Sometimes foreigners asking for air-con are automatically offered a 'VIP' room, which usually comes with air-con, hot water, fridge and TV and is about twice the price of a regular air-con room, ie 500B to 1000B.

MIDRANGE & TOP-END HOTELS

You'll find comfortable midrange hotels starting at around 600B outside Bangkok and Chiang Mai, going up to 1500B or more. Tourist-class hotels in Bangkok start at 1000B or so and go to 2500B for standard rooms, and up to 5000B or 10,000B for a suite. These will all have air-con, TV, Western-style showers and baths, toilets, IDD phones and restaurants on the premises. Added to room charges will be a 7% government tax (VAT), and most of these hotels will include an additional service charge of 8% to 10%.

Discounts of 30% to 50% for hotels costing 1000B or more per night can be obtained through many Thai travel agencies. Several top-end hotels offer discounts of up to 60% for reservations made via the Internet. In the arrival halls of both the international and domestic terminals at Bangkok airport, the Thai Hotels Association (THA) desk can also arrange discounts.

National Park Camping & Accommodation

Most national parks have bungalows for rent that sleep as many as 10 people for rates of 600B to 1800B, depending on the park and the size of the bungalow. During the low seasons you can often get a room in one of these park bungalows for 150B per person. A few parks also have *reuan thǎew* (longhouses), where rooms are around 150B to 300B for two people.

Camping is available at many parks for 10B to 20B per person per night. Some parks hire tents (50B to 100B a night), but always check the condition of the tents before agreeing to rent. It's a good idea to take your own sleeping bag or mat, and other basic camping gear.

Advance bookings for accommodation are advisable at the more popular parks, especially on holidays and weekends. To reserve houses or bungalows contact the **National Park Office** (☎ 0 2562 0760; www.dnp.go.th; 61 Th Phahonyothin, Chatuchak, Bangkok 10900) by phone, Internet or mail.

Resorts

In most countries 'resort' refers to hotels that offer substantial recreational facilities (eg tennis, golf, swimming, sailing) in addition to accommodation and dining. In Thai hotel lingo, however, the term simply refers to any hotel that isn't in an urban area. Hence a few thatched beach huts or a cluster of bungalows in a forest may be called a 'resort'. Several places in Thailand fully deserve the resort title under any definition – but it will pay for you to look into the facilities before making a reservation.

ACTIVITIES

You'll find plenty to keep you busy while traversing Thailand's mountains, plains and sea coasts.

Cycling

Details on pedalling your way around Thailand and bicycle hire can be found at p750 and in individual destination sections.

Diving & Snorkelling

Thailand's two coastlines and countless islands are popular among divers for their mild waters and colourful marine life. The biggest diving centre – in terms of the number of participants, but not the number of dive operations – is still Pattaya (p239), simply because it's less than two hours' drive from Bangkok. There are several islands with reefs just a short boat ride from Pattaya and the town is packed with dive shops.

Phuket (p647) is the second-biggest (or it is the biggest if you count dive operations) jumping-off point and has the advantage of offering the widest range of places to choose from. This includes small offshore islands less than an hour away; also nearby are Ao Phang-Nga (p640, a one- to two-hour boat ride), with its unusual rock formations and clear green waters, and the world-famous Similan (p639) and Surin Islands (p636) in the Andaman Sea (about four hours away by fast boat). Reef dives in the Andaman are particularly rewarding – some 210 hard corals and 108 reef fish have so far been catalogued in this under-studied marine zone, where probably thousands more species of reef organisms live. Some parts of Thailand's Andaman coast were heavily affected by the December 2004 tsunami. However within four months all dive operations had returned to normal. Actual tsunami damage to reef systems in Thailand has been very minimal.

Dive operations are legion on the palmy islands of Ko Samui (p561), Ko Pha-Ngan (p580) and Ko Tao (p592), all in the Gulf of Thailand off Surat Thani. Chumphon (p540), just north of Surat Thani, is another worthwhile area where there are a dozen or so islands with undisturbed reefs. Newer frontiers include the so-called Burma Banks (northwest of Ko Surin; p636), Khao Lak (p638) and islands off the coast of Krabi (p689, p694 and p695) and Trang (p707) Provinces.

All of these places, with the possible exception of the Burma Banks, have areas that are suitable for snorkelling as well as scuba diving, since many reefs are covered by water no deeper than 2m.

Masks, fins and snorkels are readily available for rent, not only at dive centres but also through guesthouses in beach areas. If you're particular about the quality and condition of the equipment you use, however, you might be better off bringing your own mask and snorkel – some of the stuff for rent is second rate.

SAFETY GUIDELINES FOR DIVING

Before embarking on a scuba diving, skin diving or snorkelling trip, carefully consider the following points to ensure a safe and enjoyable experience:

■ Possess a current diving certification card from a recognised scuba diving instructional agency (if scuba diving).

■ Obtain reliable information about physical and environmental conditions at the dive site (eg from a reputable local dive operation).

■ Be aware of local laws, regulations and etiquette about marine life and the environment.

■ Dive only at sites within your realm of experience; if available, engage the services of a competent, professionally trained dive instructor or dive master.

■ Be aware that underwater conditions vary significantly from one region, or even site, to another. Seasonal changes can significantly alter any site and dive conditions. These differences influence the way divers dress for a dive and what diving techniques they use.

■ Ask about the environmental characteristics that can affect your diving and how local trained divers deal with these considerations.

Most dive shops also offer basic instruction and PADI qualification for first-time divers. The average full-certification, four-day course costs around 10,000B, including all instruction, equipment and several open-water dives. Shorter, less-expensive 'resort' courses are also available.

Lonely Planet's richly illustrated *Diving & Snorkelling Thailand,* written by resident diving instructors, is full of vital diving information.

Kayaking

Touring the islands and coastal limestone formations around Phuket (p647) and Ao Phang-Nga (p642) by inflatable kayak has become an increasingly popular activity over the last five years. Typical tours seek out half-submerged caves called *hong* (*hâwng;* Thai for 'room'), timing their excursions so that they can paddle into the caverns at low tide. Several outfits in Phuket and Krabi (p674) offer equipment and guides.

Consider bringing your own craft. Inflatable or folding kayaks are easier to transport, but hard-shell kayaks track better. In Thailand's tropical waters an open-top or open-deck kayak – whether hard-shell, folding or inflatable – is more comfortable and practical than the closed-deck type with a spray skirt and other sealing paraphernalia, which will only transform your kayak into a floating sauna.

River & Canal Excursions

Boat travel is possible along Thailand's major rivers and canals through the extensive public-boat system and aboard a small number of tourist boat services. So far regular leisure boating has only been introduced to lower Mae Nam Chao Phraya and a few rivers in northern Thailand. A variety of watercraft are available, from air-con tourist boats along Mae Nam Chao Phraya (p133) around Bangkok, to rustic bamboo rafts on Mae Kok and sturdy white-water kayaks on Mae Pai and Mae Klong.

Central Thailand's vast network of canals, centred on the Chao Phraya delta and fanning out for hundreds of kilometres in all directions, offers numerous boating opportunities. However, the motorised boat traffic along these waterways has meant that very few foreign visitors have tried canoeing or kayaking this grid. For the adventurous traveller the potential is huge, as by public and chartered long-tail boats you can piece together canal journeys of several days' duration.

Rock-Climbing

Way back before the Stone Age, Thailand sat at the bottom of a vast ocean that lapped against the Tibetan Plateau. When the ocean eventually receded and mainland Southeast Asia popped up, the skeletons of deceased marine life left behind a swath of chalk-white caves and cliffs the whole length of Thailand. While the Tibetans lost backyard surfing rights, the Thais got the milky-white, pock-marked, medium-hard limestone perfect for chalky fingers and Scarpa-clad toes.

Although *faràng* backpackers were the first to slam bolt to stone in the mid-1980s –

at now-legendary Hat Rai Leh (p684) in Krabi – the Thais quickly followed suit. Rock-climbing has become so popular that the Thais have begun sending climbers to amateur contests in the USA and Australia.

Krabi's Hat Rai Leh and Hat Ton Sai are Thailand's limestone mecca (p684), with hundreds of climbers assaulting cliffs daily during the winter high season. The huge headland between Tham Phra Nang and Rai Leh East, and tiny islands nearby, offer high-quality limestone with steep, pocketed walls, overhangs and the occasional hanging stalactite. Around 700 routes, many with mid- to high-difficulty ratings, have been bolted and named. Further out in Ao Phang-Nga, Ko Phi-Phi also provides plenty of bolted routes, often with spectacular views.

Around the Krabi area half-day climbs with guide, equipment and insurance typically run for 800B, all-day climbs 1500B or three days for 5000B. Experienced cliff dancers can rent all the gear needed – harnesses, shoes, rope, quick-draws, chalk and locally printed guidebooks – for 600B to 1000B per day.

If the crowds in Krabi are too much, head north. Warm up in Chiang Mai (p290) at the largest rock-climbing walls in Southeast Asia (Peak Rock-Climbing Plaza. Then head east of town past San Kamphaeng to jungle-choked Tham Meuang On, more commonly known as Crazy Horse Buttress. To book a trip (or lessons), contact **Chiang Mai Rock Climbing Adventures** (☎ 0 6911 1470; www.thailandclimbing.com; trip incl gear per day 1500B).

North of Chiang Mai in Mae Rim, the **Royal Thai Army Special Forces** (☎ 0 5329 7802) offer rock-climbing as part of their rigorous camping/trekking programme (along with shooting, tower jumping and semi-rally mountain-biking). Adjacent to Tham Tu Pu (p341), a meditation cave near Chiang Rai, a local *faràng* (Western) resident has bolted a few routes, and the limestone cliffs of the heavily cave-endowed district of Pangmapha (p428) in Mae Hong Son Province are fast becoming popular climbing sites.

Trekking

Wilderness walking or trekking is one of northern Thailand's biggest draws. Typical trekking programmes run for four or five days (although it is possible to arrange everything from one- to 10-day treks). They feature daily walks through forested mountain areas coupled with overnight stays in hill-tribe villages to satisfy both ethno- and ecotourism urges.

Other trekking opportunities are available in Thailand's larger national parks (including Doi Phu Kha, Kaeng Krachan, Khao Sam Roi Yot, Khao Sok, Khao Yai, Phu Reua and Thap Lan; see p88), where park rangers may be hired as guides and cooks for a few days at a time. Rates are reasonable. For more information, see the respective park entries.

Windsurfing

The best combination of rental facilities and wind conditions are found on Hat Pattaya and Hat Jomtien (p240) in Chonburi Province, on Ko Samet (p249), on the west coast of Phuket and on Hat Chaweng (p558) on Ko Samui. To a lesser extent you'll also find rental equipment on Hat Khao Lak (p637), Ko Pha-Ngan (p576), Ko Tao (p591) and Ko Chang (p634). Wetsuits aren't necessary in Thailand's year-round tropical climate.

If you have your own equipment you can set out anywhere you find a coastal breeze. If you're looking for something undiscovered, check out the cape running north from Narathiwat's provincial capital in southern Thailand. In general the windy months on the Gulf of Thailand are from mid-February to April. On the Andaman Sea side of the Thai–Malay peninsula winds are strongest from September to December.

BUSINESS HOURS

Most government offices are open from 8.30am to 4.30pm weekdays, but often close from noon to 1pm for lunch.

Businesses usually operate between 8.30am and 5pm weekdays and sometimes on Saturday morning. Larger shops usually open 10am to 6.30pm or 7pm, but smaller shops may open earlier and close later.

Restaurant hours vary according to type of food served and clientele. Since PM Thaksin Shinawatra came to power, closing hours for entertainment venues have been strictly enforced.

Please note that all government offices and banks are closed on public holidays (see p735).

TYPICAL OPENING HOURS

- Bars – 6pm-midnight
- Department stores – 10am-8pm Mon-Sat, 10am-3pm Sun; late-night shopping to 10pm
- Discos – 8pm-2am
- Live music venues – 6pm-1am
- *Khâo tôm* (rice soup) restaurants – 5pm-3am, occasionally all night
- Other restaurants – 10am-11pm
- Rice & curry shops – 8am-2pm
- Shops – 10am-5pm Mon-Sat

CHILDREN

Like many places in Southeast Asia, travelling with children in Thailand can be a lot of fun as long as you come well prepared with the right attitude, equipment and the usual parental patience. Lonely Planet's *Travel with Children* contains useful advice on how to cope with kids on the road and what to bring along to make things go more smoothly, with a focus on travel in developing countries.

Thais love children and in many instances will shower attention on your offspring, who will find ready playmates among their Thai counterparts and a temporary nanny service at practically every stop.

For the most part parents needn't worry too much about health concerns, although it pays to lay down a few ground rules (such as regular hand washing) to head off potential medical problems. Children should be warned not to play with animals as rabies is relatively common in Thailand. All the usual health precautions apply (see p762 for details).

Practicalities

Amenities specially geared towards young children – such as child safety seats for cars, high chairs in restaurants or nappy-changing facilities in public restrooms – are virtually nonexistent in Thailand. Therfore parents will have to be extra resourceful in seeking out substitutes or just follow the example of Thai families (which means holding smaller children on their laps much of the time).

Baby formula and nappies (diapers) are available at minimarkets in the larger towns and cities, but for rural areas you'll need to bring along a sufficient supply.

Sights & Activities

When younger children don't find historic temples and museums as inspiring as their parents do, the best thing is to head for the outdoors. See Thailand for Kids, p29 for examples of specific places to go when travelling with children. In general the beaches and islands are always a safe bet, as are national park waterfalls and the zoos of Bangkok and Chiang Mai.

CLIMATE CHARTS

See p19 for further information on choosing the best time of year for your visit to Thailand.

COURSES
Cooking

You, too, can amaze your friends back home after attending a course in Thai cuisine at one of the following places.

Chiang Mai Thai Cookery School (Map pp282-4; ☎ 0 5320 6388; www.thaicookeryschool.com; 1-3 Th Moon Muang)

Kao Hom (off Map pp278-80; ☎ 0 5386 2967; www.kaohom.com; 180/1 Th Chiang Mai–Mae Rim)

Mom Tri's Boathouse (Map p665; ☎ 0 7633 0015; www.phuket.com/boathouse) See p667 for details of courses.

Oriental Hotel Cooking School (Map pp114-16; ☎ 0 2659 9000 Soi Oriental, Th Charoen Krung, Bangkok) This school features a plush five-day course under the direction of well-known star chef Chali (Charlie) Amatyakul. See p137 for more details.

Siam Chiang Mai Cookery School (Map pp282-4; ☎ 0 5327 1169; siam-kitchen@bangkok.com; 5/2 Soi 1, Th Loi Kroh)

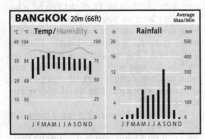

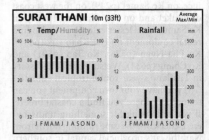

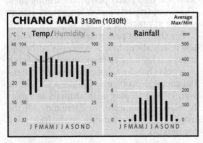

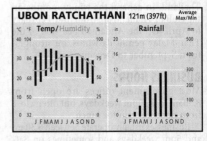

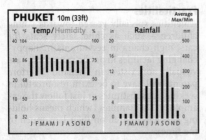

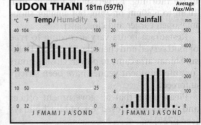

Thai House (Map pp104-5; ☎ 0 2903 9611, 0 2997 5161; www.thaihouse.co.th; Amphoe Bang Yai, Nonthaburi) See p137 for details.

Language
Several language schools in Bangkok (p138) and Chiang Mai (p291) offer courses in Thai language. Tuition fees average around 250B per hour.

Martial Arts
Many Westerners have trained in Thailand, but few last more than a week or two in a Thai camp – and fewer still have gone on to compete on Thailand's pro circuit.

MUAY THAI
Training in *muay thai* (Thai boxing) takes place at dozens of boxing camps around the country. Be forewarned, however: the training is gruelling and features full-contact sparring, unlike tae kwon do, *kenpo*, kung fu and other East Asian martial arts.

Many centres are reluctant to take on foreign trainees, except in special cases where the applicant can prove a willingness to conform to the training system, the diet and the rustic accommodation. Most important is the ability to learn the Thai language. Rates vary from US$50 to US$250 per week, including food and accommodation, depending on room choice (fan versus air-con etc) and experience with foreigners.

The website www.muaythai.com contains loads of information including the addresses of training camps. Also see the Bangkok (p138) and Chiang Mai (p290) chapters for information on *muay thai* training programmes.

Meditation
Thailand has long been a popular place for Buddhist meditation study. Unique to Buddhism, particularly Theravada and to a lesser extent Tibetan Buddhism, is a system of meditation known as *vipassana* (in Thai, *wípàtsànaa*) a Pali word that roughly translates as 'insight'. Foreigners who come to Thailand to study *vipassana* can choose from dozens of temples and meditation centres specialising in these teachings. Teaching methods vary but the general emphasis is on observing mind-body processes from moment to moment. Thai language is usually the medium of instruction but several places also provide instruction in English.

Contact details for some of the more popular meditation-oriented temples and centres are given in the destination sections of this guide. Instruction and accommodation are free of charge at temples, although donations are expected.

Short-term students will find that the two-month Tourist Visa is ample for most courses of study. Long-term students may want to consider getting a three- or six-month Non-Immigrant Visa (see p742). A few Westerners are ordained as monks or nuns in order to take full advantage of the monastic environment. Monks and nuns are generally (but not always) allowed to stay in Thailand as long as they remain in robes.

Some places require that you wear white clothes when staying overnight. For even a brief visit, wear clean and neat clothing (ie long trousers or skirt and sleeves that cover the shoulders).

For a detailed look at *Vipassana* study in Thailand, read *A Guide to Buddhist Monasteries & Meditation Centres in Thailand*, which is available from the World Fellowship of Buddhists in Bangkok (p137) or free online at www.dharmanet.org/thai_94.html.

Thai Massage
Unlike in most Western massage methodologies, such as Swedish and Californian techniques, Thai massage does not directly seek to relax the body through kneading with palms and fingers. Instead a multipronged approach uses the hands, thumbs, fingers, elbows, forearms, knees and feet, and is applied to the traditional pressure points along the various *sên* or meridians (the human body is thought to have 72,000 of these, of which 10 are crucial).

The client's body is also pulled, twisted and manipulated in ways that have been described as 'passive yoga'. The objective is to distribute energies evenly throughout the nervous system so as to create a harmony of physical energy flows. The muscular-skeletal system is also manipulated in ways that can be compared to modern physiotherapy and chiropractics.

Thailand offers ample opportunities to study its unique tradition of massage therapy. Wat Pho (p139) in Bangkok is considered the master source for all Thai massage pedagogy, although the northern provinces boast a 'softer' version. See p132 and p334 for more information.

CUSTOMS

Thailand prohibits the importation of illegal drugs, firearms and ammunition (unless registered in advance with the Police Department) and pornographic media. A reasonable amount of clothing for personal use, toiletries and professional instruments are allowed in duty free, as is one still or one movie or video camera with five rolls of still film or three rolls of movie film or videotape. Up to 200 cigarettes can be brought into the country without paying duty, or for other smoking materials a total of up to 250g. One litre of wine or spirits is allowed in duty free.

For information on currency import or export, see Exchange Control (p737).

Antiques & Art

When leaving Thailand, you must obtain an export licence for any antiques or objects of art you want to take with you. Export licence applications can be made by submitting two front-view photos of the object(s), with no more than five objects to a photo, and a photocopy of your passport, along with the object(s) in question, to the Department of Fine Arts (DFA), Bangkok National Museum (p122). Allow three to five days for the application and inspection process to be completed.

Buddhas or other deity images (or any part thereof) to be exported require not only a licence from the DFA but a permit from the Ministry of Commerce as well. The exceptions to this are the small Buddha images (*phrá phim* or *phrá khrêuang*) that are meant to be worn on a chain around the neck. These may be exported without a licence as long as the reported purpose is religious.

DANGERS & ANNOYANCES

Although Thailand is in no way a dangerous country to visit, it's always wise to be cautious, particularly if you're travelling alone. Solo travellers should take care on arrival at Bangkok International Airport, particularly at night. Only take taxis from the airport's public taxi queue or take the public bus.

Ensure that your room is securely locked and bolted at night. Inspect cheap rooms with thin walls in case there are strategic peepholes.

Take care when leaving valuables in hotel safes. Many travellers have reported unpleasant experiences leaving valuables in Chiang Mai guesthouses. Make sure you obtain an itemised receipt for property left with hotels or guesthouses – note the exact quantity of travellers cheques and all other valuables.

When you're on the road, keep zippered luggage secured with small locks, especially while travelling on buses and trains. Several readers' letters have recounted tales of thefts from their bags or backpacks during long overnight bus trips, particularly on routes between Bangkok and Chiang Mai or Ko Samui.

Assault

Assault and robbery of travellers by force is very rare in Thailand, but it does happen. Isolated incidents of armed robbery have tended to occur along the Thai-Myanmar and Thai-Cambodian borders and on remote islands. There have also been reported cases of assault on lone female travellers on remote sections of beaches on the islands of Ko Samui and Ko Pha-Ngan. The safest practice in less populated areas is not to go out alone at night and, if trekking in norhtern Thailand, always walk in groups.

Credit Cards

When making credit-card purchases, don't let vendors take your credit card out of your sight to run it through the machine. Unscrupulous merchants have been known to rub off three or four or more receipts with one purchase. After the customer leaves the shop, they use the one legitimate receipt as a model to forge your signature on the blanks, then fill in astronomical 'purchases'. Sometimes they wait several weeks – even months – between submitting each charge receipt to the bank, so that you can't remember whether you'd been billed by the same vendor more than once.

Drugging

In bars and on trains and buses beware of friendly strangers offering gifts such as cigarettes, drinks, cookies or sweets (candy). Several travellers have reported waking up sometime later with a headache, only to find that their valuables have disappeared.

Male travellers have also encountered drugged food or drink from friendly Thai women in bars and from prostitutes in their own hotel rooms. Female visitors have encountered the same with young Thai men, albeit less frequently. Conclusion: don't accept gifts from strangers.

Drugs

Opium, heroin, amphetamines, hallucinogenic mushrooms and marijuana are widely used in Thailand, but it is illegal to buy, sell or possess these drugs in any quantity. The possession of opium for consumption, but not sale, is legal among hill tribes.

Every year perhaps dozens of visiting foreigners are arrested in Thailand for drug use or trafficking and end up doing time in Thai prisons. A smaller but significant number die of heroin overdoses.

Ko Pha-Ngan is one of Thailand's leading centres for recreational drug use, and the Thai police have taken notice. Particularly on days leading up to Hat Rin's famous monthly full-moon rave, police often set up inspection points on the road between Thong Sala and Hat Rin. Every vehicle, including bicycles and motorcycles, is stopped and the passengers and vehicles thoroughly searched.

The legal penalties for drug offences are stiff: if you're caught using marijuana, mushrooms or LSD, you face a fine of 10,000B plus one year in prison, while for heroin or amphetamines, the penalty for use can be anywhere from six months' to 10 years' imprisonment, plus a fine of 5000B to 10,000B. The going rate for bribing one's way out of a small pot bust is 50,000B.

Drug smuggling – defined as attempting to cross a border with drugs in your possession – carries considerably higher penalties, including execution.

Yaa bâa (literally 'crazy drug'), or amphetamine tablets, are imported in large quantities from Wa-controlled areas of northeastern Myanmar and sold inexpensively in Thailand. The quality is low and dosages erratic. This is an illegal drug to be extremely careful of.

Malaysian Border

Four of Thailand's southernmost provinces (Songkhla, Yala, Pattani and Narathiwat) go through hot and cold periods that involve

the Pattani United Liberation Organization (PULO; www.pulo.org), a small armed group which, since its formation in 1959, has been dedicated to forming a separate Muslim state. The PULO is known to receive support from the Kumpulan Mujahideen Malaysia (KMM), a radical Islamic group in Malaysia.

Between 2002 and 2004 a series of arson attacks, bombings and assaults took place in Pattani, Yala and Narathiwat Provinces. Most attacks were on military posts or police posts, and the PULO has an avowed policy not to target civilians or tourists. There are no known links between the PULO and Al Qaeda or Jemaah Islamiya; PULO's tactics are obviously quite different.

The Thai government's heavy-handed responses to the 40-year-old Muslim nationalist movement – including the 2004 massacre of 108 machete-armed youths in a Pattani mosque and the suffocation deaths of 78 during brutal arrests in Narathiwat that same year – seems destined to provoke further trouble.

We therefore urge travellers to exercise caution when travelling in Yala, Pattani and Narathiwat. Avoid military or police installations and avoid road travel at night.

Myanmar Border

The Myanmar border between Um Phang and Mae Sariang does occasionally receive shelling from Burmese troops in pursuit of Karen or Mon rebels. The risks of getting hit by a piece of shrapnel are substantially lower if you keep several kilometres between yourself and the Thai–Myanmar border in this area – fighting can break out at any time.

The presence of the Shan and Wa armies on the Myanmar–Thai border in northern Mae Hong Son makes this area dangerous if you attempt to travel near amphetamine- and opium-trade border crossings; obviously these are not signposted, so take care anywhere along the border in this area.

Scams

Thais can be so friendly and laid-back that some visitors are lulled into a false sense of security that makes them vulnerable to scams of all kinds. Scammers tend to haunt the areas where first-time tourists go, such as Bangkok's Grand Palace and Wat Pho area. Though you could come across them anywhere in Thailand, the overwhelming majority of scams take place in Bangkok, with Chiang Mai a very distant second.

Most scams begin in the same way: a friendly Thai male (or, on rare occasions, a female) approaches a lone visitor – usually newly arrived – and strikes up a conversation. Sometimes the con man says he's a university student, other times he may claim to work for the World Bank or a similarly distinguished organisation (some even carry cellular phones). If you're on the way to Wat Pho or Jim Thompson's House, for example, he may tell you it's closed for a holiday. Eventually the conversation works its way around to the subject of the scam – the better con artists can actually make it seem like you initiated the topic.

The most common scam involves gems. The victims find themselves invited to a gem and jewellery shop – your new-found friend is picking up some merchandise for himself and you're just along for the ride. Somewhere along the way he usually claims to have a connection, often a relative, in your home country (what a coincidence!) with whom he has a regular gem export-import business. One way or another, victims are convinced (usually they convince themselves) that they can turn a profit by arranging a gem purchase and reselling the merchandise at home. After all, the jewellery shop just happens to be offering a generous discount today – it's a government or religious holiday, or perhaps it's the shop's 10th anniversary, or maybe they've just taken a liking to you!

There is a seemingly infinite number of variations on the gem scam, almost all of which end up with the victim making a purchase of small, low-quality sapphires and posting them to their home countries. Once you return home, of course, the cheap sapphires turn out to be worth much less than you paid for them (perhaps one-tenth to one-half).

Many have invested and lost virtually all their savings; some admit they had been scammed even after reading warnings in this guidebook or those posted by the Tourism Authority of Thailand (TAT) around Bangkok.

Even if you were somehow able to return your purchase to the gem shop in question, chances are slim-to-none you'd get a full refund. The con artist who brings the mark into the shop gets a commission of 10% to 50% per sale – the shop takes the rest.

The Thai police are usually no help whatsoever, believing that merchants are entitled to whatever price they can get. The main victimisers are a handful of shops who get protection from certain high-ranking government officials. These officials put pressure on police not to prosecute or to take as little action as possible. Even TAT's tourist police have never been able to prosecute a Thai jeweller in cases of blatant, recurring gem fraud.

Card games are another way to separate suckers from their money. A friendly stranger approaches the lone traveller on the street, strikes up a conversation and then invites them to the house or apartment of his sister (or brother-in-law etc) for a drink or meal. After a bit of socialising a friend or relative of the con arrives on the scene; it just so happens a little high-stakes card game is planned for later that day. Like the gem scam, the card-game scam has many variations, but eventually the victim is shown some cheating tactics to use with help from the 'dealer', some practice sessions take place and finally the game gets under way with several high rollers at the table. The mark is allowed to win a few hands first, then somehow loses a few, gets bankrolled by one of the friendly Thais, and then loses the Thai's money. Suddenly your new-found buddies aren't so friendly any more – they want the money you lost. Sooner or later you end up cashing in most or all of your travellers cheques or making a costly visit to an ATM. Again the police won't take any action because gambling is illegal in Thailand – you've actually broken the law.

Other minor scams involve *túk-túk* drivers, hotel employees and bar girls who take new arrivals on city tours; these almost always end up in high-pressure sales situations at silk, jewellery or handicraft shops. In this case the victim's greed isn't the ruling motivation – it's simply a matter of weak sales resistance.

Follow TAT's number-one suggestion to tourists: *Disregard all offers of free shopping or sightseeing help from strangers* – they invariably take a commission from your purchases. We would add: beware of deals that seem too good to be true. You might also try lying whenever a stranger asks how long you've been in Thailand – if it's only been three days, say three weeks! Or save your Bangkok sightseeing until after you've been up north. The con artists rarely prey on anyone except new arrivals.

Contact the **Tourist Police** (☎ 1155) if you have any problems with consumer fraud.

Touts

Touting (grabbing newcomers in the street or in train stations, bus terminals or airports to sell them a service) is a long-time tradition in Asia, and while Thailand doesn't have as many touts as, say, India, it has its share. In the popular tourist spots it seems like everyone – young boys waving fliers, túk-túk drivers, sǎamláw (three-wheeled vehicle) drivers, schoolgirls – is touting something, usually hotels or guesthouses. For the most part they're completely harmless and sometimes they can be very informative. But take anything a tout says with two large grains of salt. Since touts work on commission and get paid just for delivering you to a guesthouse or hotel (whether you check in or not), they'll say anything to get you to the door.

The better hotels and guesthouses refuse to pay tout commissions – so the average tout will try to steer you away from such places. Hence don't believe them if they tell you the hotel or guesthouse you're looking for is closed, full, dirty or 'bad'. Sometimes (rarely) they're right but most times it's just a ruse to get you to a place that pays more commission.

Always have a look yourself before checking into a place recommended by a tout. Túk-túk and sǎamláw drivers often offer free or low-cost rides to the place they're touting. If you have another place you're interested in, you might agree to go with a driver only if he or she promises to deliver you to your first choice after you've had a look at the place being touted. If drivers refuse, chances are it's because they know your first choice is a better one.

This type of commission work is not limited to low-budget guesthouses. Travel agencies at Bangkok International Airport and Hualamphong train station are notorious for talking newly arrived tourists into staying at badly located, overpriced hotels.

BUS TOUTS

Watch out for touts wearing fake TAT or tourist information badges at Hualamphong train station. They have been known to coerce travellers into buying tickets for private bus rides, saying the train is 'full' or 'takes too long'. Often the promised bus service turns out to be substandard and may take longer than the equivalent train ride due to the frequent changing of vehicles. You may be offered a 24-seat VIP 'sleeper' bus to Chiang Mai, for example, and end up stuffed into a minivan all the way. Such touts are 'bounty hunters' who receive a set fee for every tourist they deliver to the bus companies. Avoid the travel agencies (many of which bear 'TAT' or even 'Lonely Planet' signs) just outside the train station for the same reason.

DISABLED TRAVELLERS

Thailand presents one large, ongoing obstacle course for the mobility-impaired. With its high curbs, uneven pavements and non-stop traffic, Bangkok can be particularly difficult – many streets must be crossed via pedestrian bridges flanked with steep stairways, while buses and boats don't stop long enough for even the mildly disabled. Rarely are there any ramps or other access points for wheelchairs.

A number of more expensive, top-end hotels make consistent design efforts to provide handicapped access to their properties. Other deluxe hotels with high employee-to-guest ratios are usually good about accommodating the mobility-impaired by providing staff help where building design fails. For the rest, you're pretty much left to your own resources.

Organisations & Publications

Access Foundation (☎ 516-887 5798; PO Box 356, Malverne, NY 11565, USA)

Accessible Journeys (☎ 610-521 0339; www .disabilitytravel.com; 35 West Sellers Ave, Ridley Park, Pennsylvania, USA)

Mobility International USA (☎ 541-343 1284; info@miusa.org; PO Box 10767, Eugene, OR 97440, USA)

Society for the Accessible Travel & Hospitality (☎ 212-447 7284; www.sath.org; Ste 610, 347 Fifth Ave, New York, NY 11242, USA)

EMBASSIES & CONSULATES
Thai Embassies & Consulates

Australia Embassy (☎ 02-6273 1149, 6273 2937; rtecan
berra@mfa.go.th; 111 Empire Circuit, Yarralumla, Canberra,
ACT 2600); Consulate (☎ /fax 08-8232 7474; Level 1, 72
Flinders St, Adelaide, SA 5000); Consulate (☎ 07-3846
7771; consulofthailand@hotmail.com; 87 Annerley Rd,
South Brisbane, Qld 4102); Consulate (☎ 03-9533 9100;
swallace@netspace.net.au; Suite 301, 566 St Kilda Rd, Melbourne, Vic 3004); Consulate (☎ 08-9221 3237; thaiconsu
latewa@jamlaw.net.au; Level 8, 26 St Georges Tce; Perth,
WA 6000); Consulate (☎ 02-9241 2542/3; http://thaisydney
.idx.com.au; Level 8, 131 Macquarie St, Sydney, NSW 2000)
Cambodia Embassy (☎ 023-363 869-71; www.mfa.go.th
/web/1300.php?depid=186; 196 MV Preah Nordom Blvd,
Sangkat Tonle Bassa, Khan Chamkar Mon, Phnom Penh)
Canada Embassy (☎ 613-722 4444; www.magma.ca
/~thaiott/mainpage.htm; 180 Island Park Dr, Ottawa,
ON K1Y 0A2); Consulate (☎ 604-687 1143; www.thaicongen
vancouver.org; 1040 Burrard St, Vancouver, BC V6Z 2R9)
France Embassy (☎ 01-56 26 50 50; thaipar@micronet.fr;
8 rue Greuze, 75116 Paris)
Germany Embassy (☎ 030-794 810; www.thaiembassy
.de; Lepsuisstrasse 64-66, 12163 Berlin); Consulate
(☎ 069-6986 8208; fax 069-6986 8228; 109 Kennedyalle,
60596 Frankfurt); Consulate (☎ 089-1689 788; Prinzen-
strasse 13, 80639 Munchen)
Israel Embassy (☎ 972-3 695 8980; www.thaiembassy
.org/telaviv; 21 Shaul Hamelech Blvd, Tel Aviv)
Laos Embassy (☎ 21-214581-3; Th Phonkheng, Vientiane
Poste 128); Consulate (☎ 41-212445; No 26, Ban Xaya-
mongkhon, Th Kouvoravong, Savannakhet)
Malaysia Embassy (☎ 603-248 8222; thaikl@pop1.jaring
.my; 206 Jalan Ampang, Kuala Lumpur); Consulate (☎ 609-
744 5266; www.mfa.go.th/web/1854.php?depcode
=23030100; 4426 Jalan Pengkalan Chepa, 15400 Kota
Bharu, Kelantan); Consulate (☎ 094-226 8029; thaipg@tm
.net.my; No 1 Jalan Tunku Abdul Rahman, 10350 Penang)
Myanmar Embassy (Burma; ☎ 01-512017, 512018; 437
Pyay Rd, 8 Ward, Kamayut township, Yangon)
UK Embassy (☎ 020-7589 0173, 7589 2944; http://thai
land.embassyhomepage.com; 29-30 Queen's Gate, London
SW7 5JB)
USA Embassy (☎ 202-944 3608; www.thaiembdc.org
/index.htm; 1024 Wisconsin Ave NW, Washington, DC
20007); Consulate (☎ 312-664 3129; www.thaichicago
.net; 700 N Rush St, Chicago, Illinois 60611); Consulate
(☎ 323-962 9574-77; www.thai-la.net; 2nd fl, 611
N Larchmont Blvd, Los Angeles, CA 90004); Consulate
(☎ 212-754 1770, 754 1896; http://thaiconsulnewyork
.com; 351 East 52nd St, New York, NY 10022)
Vietnam Embassy (☎ 04-823 5092-94; fax 04-823 5088;
63-65 Hoang Dieu St, Hanoi); Consulate (☎ 08-822 2637;
fax 08-829 1002; 77 Tran Quoc Thao St, District 3, Ho Chi
Minh City)

Embassies & Consulates in Thailand

The visa sections of most embassies and
consulates are open from around 8.30am to
11.30am weekdays only (call first to be sure,
as some are open only two or three days a
week). Unless specified otherwise, embassies and consulates are in Bangkok.

Australia Embassy (Map p117; ☎ 0 2287 2680; www
.austembassy.or.th; 37 Th Sathon Tai)
Cambodia Embassy (Map p117; ☎ 0 2254 6630;
recbkk@hotmail.com; 185 Th Ratchadamri, Lumphini)
Canada Embassy (Map p117; ☎ 0 2636 0540; www
.dfait-maeci.gc.ca/bangkok; 15th fl, Abdulrahim Bldg,
990 Th Phra Ram IV)
China Embassy (Map pp104-5; ☎ 0 2245 7043; www
.travelchinaguide.com/embassy/thailand.htm; 57 Th
Ratchadaphisek)
EU Embassy (Map p117; ☎ 0 2255 9100; Kian Gwan
House, 19th fl, 1410/1 Th Withayu)
France Embassy (Map pp114-16; ☎ 0 2266 8250-6;
www.ambafrance-th.org; 35 Soi 36, Th Charoen Krung);
Consular Section (Map p117; ☎ 0 2287 1592; 29
Th Sathon Tai)
Germany Embassy (Map p117; ☎ 0 2287 9000; www
.german-embassy.or.th; 9 Th Sathon Tai)
India Embassy (Map pp112-13; ☎ 0 2258 0300-6;
www.visatoindia.com/indian-embassy-in-thailand.html;
46 Soi Prasanmit/Soi 23, Th Sukhumvit); Consulate
(Map pp278-80; ☎ 0 5324 3066; 344 Th Charoenrat,
Chiang Mai)
Indonesia Embassy (Map pp118-19; ☎ 0 2252 3135;
600-602 Th Phetburi)
Israel Embassy (Map pp112-13; ☎ 0 2204 9200; 75
Ocean Tower 2, 25th fl, Soi 19, Th Sukhumvit)
Japan Embassy (Map pp106-7; ☎ 0 2252 6151-9;
http://embjp-th.org; 1674 Th Phetburi Tat Mai)
Laos Embassy (Map pp104-5; ☎ 0 2539 6679; www
.bkklaoembassy.com; 520/1-3 Th Pracha Uthit, Soi 39, Th
Ramkhamhaeng); Consulate (Map p455; ☎ 0 4324 2856;
191/102-3 Th Prachasamoson, Chaiyaphum) The consulate
issues 30-day visas for Laos but it can take up to three days
to process – it's much easier in Bangkok.
Malaysia Embassy (Map p117; ☎ 0 2679 2190-9; 33-35
Th Sathon Tai)
Myanmar Embassy (Burma; Map pp114-16; ☎ 0 2233
2237, 0 2234 4698; 132 Th Sathon Neua)
Nepal Embassy (Map pp104-5; ☎ 0 2391 7240;
nepembkk@asiaaccess.net.th; 189 Soi 71, Th Sukhumvit)
Netherlands Embassy (Map pp118-19; ☎ 254 7701, 252
6103-5; www.thai-info.net/netherlands; 106 Th Withayu)
New Zealand Embassy (Map pp118-19; ☎ 0 2254 2530;
www.nzembassy.com/home.cfm?c=21; 19th fl, M Thai
Tower, All Seasons Pl, 87 Th Withayu)
Philippines Embassy (Map pp112-13; ☎ 0 2259 0139;
www.philembassy-bangkok.net; 760 Th Sukhumvit)

Singapore Embassy (Map pp114-16; ☎ 0 2286 2111; www.mfa.gov.sg/bangkok; 9th & 18th fl, Rajanakam Bldg, 183 Th Sathon Tai)

South Africa Embassy (Map p117; ☎ 0 2253 8473; saembbkk@loxinfo.co.th; 6th fl, Park Pl, 231 Th Sarasin)

UK Embassy (Map pp118-19; ☎ 0 2305 8333-9; www.britishemb.or.th; 1031 Th Withayu)

USA Embassy (Map pp118-19; ☎ 0 2205 4000; http://usa.or.th; 120-22 Th Withayu); Consulate (Map pp282-4; ☎ 0 5325 2629; http://bangkok.usembassy.gov/consulcm/consulcm.htm; 387 Th Wichayanon, Chiang Mai)

Vietnam Embassy (Map pp118-19; ☎ 0 2251 5836-8; vnembassy@bkk.a-net.net.th; 83/1 Th Withayu); Consulate (Map p455; ☎ 0 4324 2190; 65/6 Th Chatapadung, Chaiyaphum) The consulate issues visas for Vietnam in three days.

FESTIVALS & EVENTS

Thai festivals tend to be linked to the agricultural seasons or to Buddhist holidays and are most frequent from February to March, after the main rice harvest is in.

The general word for festival in Thai is *ngaan thêtsàkaan*. The exact dates for festivals may vary from year to year, either because of the lunar calendar, which isn't quite in sync with the solar calendar – or because local authorities have decided to change festival dates.

JANUARY

Bangkok International Film Festival (www.bangkokfilm.org) Only two years old, the 10-day festival screens around 140 films from around the world, with an emphasis on Asian cinema. Most screenings take place at theatres at Siam Square, Siam Discovery Center and Central World Plaza. Events end with the awarding of the festival's Golden Kinnaree award in a range of categories.

That Phanom Festival An annual, week-long homage to the northeast's most sacred Buddhist stupa (Phra That Phanom) in Nakhon Phanom Province. Pilgrims from all over the country, as well as from Laos, attend.

LATE JANUARY TO EARLY FEBRUARY

River of Kings (www.theriverofkingsbangkok.com) Initiated by Princess Ubol Ratana, and sponsored largely by TAT, this spectacular sound-and-light show is performed for 12 consecutive nights alongside Mae Nam Chao Phraya at Tha Ratchaworadit (between Tha Tien and Tha Chang). Enhanced by the illuminated Grand Palace and Wat Phra Kaew in the background, a combination of Thai dance, music and animation make for an intensely visual experience. The storyline, which changes every year, typically involves royal heroism.

FEBRUARY

Chiang Mai Flower Festival Colourful floats and parades exhibit Chiang Mai's cultivated flora.

Magha Puja (*maakhá buuchaa*) Held on the full moon of the third lunar month to commemorate Buddha preaching to 1250 enlightened monks who came to hear him 'without prior summons'. A public holiday throughout the country, it culminates with a candle-lit walk around the main chapel (*wian thian*) at every wat.

Phra Nakhon Khiri Diamond Festival This is a week-long celebration of Phetchaburi's history and architecture focused on Phra Nakhon Khiri Historical Park (also known as Khao Wang), a hill topped by a former royal palace overlooking the city. It features a sound-and-light show on Khao Wang; the temples are festooned with lights and presentations of Thai classical dance-drama.

LATE FEBRUARY TO EARLY MARCH

Chinese New Year Called *trùt jiin* in Thai, Chinese populations all over Thailand celebrate their lunar New Year (the date shifts from year to year) with a week of house-cleaning, lion dances and fireworks. The most impressive festivities take place in the Chinese-dominated province capital of Nakhon Sawan.

MARCH

Bangkok International Jewellery Fair Held in several large Bangkok hotels, this is Thailand's most important annual gem and jewellery trade show. It runs concurrently with the Department of Export Promotion's Gems & Jewellery Fair.

LATE MARCH TO EARLY APRIL

Prasat Hin Khao Phanom Rung Festival A festival to commemorate Prasat Hin Khao Phanom Rung Historical Park, an impressive Angkor-style temple complex in Buriram Province. It involves a daytime procession up Phanom Rung and spectacular sound-and-light shows at night. The actual date depends on the lunar cycles – be prepared for very hot weather.

APRIL

Songkran Held from 13 to 15 April, this is the celebration of the lunar New Year. Buddha images are 'bathed', monks and elders receive the respect of younger Thais by the sprinkling of water over their hands, and a lot of water is tossed about. Songkran generally gives everyone a chance to release their frustrations and literally cool off during the peak of the hot season. Hide out in your room or expect to be soaked; the latter is a lot more fun.

MAY

Visakha Puja (*Wísàakhà buuchaa*) Falling on the 15th day of the waxing moon in the sixth lunar month, this day commemorates the date of the Buddha's birth,

DIRECTORY

enlightenment and *parinibbana* (passing away). Activities are centred around the wat, with candle-lit processions, much chanting and sermonising.

MID-MAY TO MID-JUNE

Bun Phra Wet (Phi Ta Khon) Festival One of the wildest in Thailand, this is an animist-Buddhist celebration held in Loei's Amphoe Dan Sai (nowadays also in other places around Loei Province) in which revellers dress in garish 'spirit' costumes, wear painted masks and brandish carved wooden phalli. The festival commemorates a Buddhist legend in which a host of spirits *(phǐi)* appeared to greet the Buddha-to-be upon his return to his home town, during his penultimate birth.

Rocket Festival *(bun bang fai)* In the northeast, villagers craft large skyrockets of bamboo, which they then fire into the sky to bring rain for rice fields. This festival is best celebrated in the town of Yasothon, but is also good in Ubon Ratchathani and Nong Khai.

Royal Ploughing Ceremony To kick off the official rice-planting season, the king participates in this ancient Brahman ritual at Sanam Luang (the large field across from Wat Phra Kaew) in Bangkok. Thousands of Thais gather to watch, and traffic in this part of the city comes to a standstill.

MID- TO LATE JULY

Asalha Puja *(àsǎanhà buuchaa)* This festival commemorates the Buddha's first sermon.

Khao Phansa *(khâo phansǎa)* A public holiday and the beginning of Buddhist 'lent', this is the traditional time of year for young men to enter the monkhood for the rainy season and for all monks to station themselves in a monastery for the three months. It's a good time to observe a Buddhist ordination. Khao Phansa is celebrated in the northeast by parading huge carved candles on floats in the streets. The candle festival is best celebrated in Ubon Ratchathani.

AUGUST

Queen's Birthday (12 August) In Bangkok, Th Ratchadamnoen Klang and the Grand Palace are festooned with coloured lights.

LATE SEPTEMBER TO EARLY OCTOBER

Narathiwat Fair An annual week-long festival celebrating local culture in Narathiwat Province with boat races, dove-singing contests, handicraft displays and traditional southern Thai music and dance. The king and queen almost always attend.

Thailand International Swan-Boat Races These take place on Mae Nam Chao Phraya in Bangkok near Saphan Phra Ram IX.

Vegetarian Festival A nine-day celebration in Bangkok, Trang and Phuket during which devout Chinese Buddhists eat only vegetarian food. There are various ceremonies at Chinese temples and merit-making processions that bring to mind Hindu Thaipusam in its exhibition of self-mortification. Smaller towns in the south, such as Krabi and Phang-Nga, also celebrate the veggie fest on a smaller scale.

LATE OCTOBER TO MID-NOVEMBER

Kathin *(thâwt kàthǐn)* A month at the end of the Buddhist lent during which new monastic robes and requisites are offered to the Sangha (monastic community). In Nan Province longboat races are held on Mae Nan.

Loi Krathong On the proper full-moon night, small lotus-shaped baskets or boats made of banana leaves containing flowers, incense, candles and a coin are floated on Thai rivers, lakes and canals. This is a peculiarly Thai festival that probably originated in Sukhothai and is best celebrated in the north. In Chiang Mai, where the festival is called Yi Peng, residents also launch paper hot-air balloons into the sky. At the Sukhothai Historical Park there is an impressive sound-and-light show.

Surin Annual Elephant Roundup Held on the third weekend of November, Thailand's biggest elephant show is popular with tourists. If you have ever had the desire to see a lot of elephants in one place, then here's your chance.

LATE NOVEMBER TO EARLY DECEMBER

River Khwae Bridge Week Sound-and-light shows every night at the Death Railway Bridge in Kanchanaburi. Events include historical exhibitions and vintage-train rides on the infamous railway.

DECEMBER

King's Birthday (5 December) This public holiday is celebrated with some fervour in Bangkok. As with the Queen's Birthday, it features lots of lights and other decorations along Th Ratchadamnoen Klang. Other Thai cities hold colourful parades Some people erect temporary shrines to the king outside their homes or businesses.

FOOD

Most restaurants in Thailand are inexpensive by international standards, hence we haven't divided them into Budget, Midrange and Top End categories. See p45 for thorough descriptions of the cuisine and the kinds of restaurants you'll find in Thailand.

GAY & LESBIAN TRAVELLERS

Thai culture is relatively tolerant of homosexuality, both male and female. The nation has no laws that discriminate against homosexuals and there is a fairly prominent gay and lesbian scene in Bangkok (see p143). With regard to dress or mannerism, lesbians and gays are generally accepted without comment. However, public displays of affection – whether heterosexual or homosexual – are frowned upon.

The **Utopia** (www.utopia-asia.com) website posts lots of Thailand information for gay and lesbian visitors. **Anjaree Group** (☎ /fax 0 2668 2185) is Thailand's only lesbian society. Anjaree sponsors various group activities and produces a Thai-only newsletter. Bilingual Thai–English websites of possible interest to visiting lesbians include www.lesla.com. Gay men may be interested in the activities of the **Long Yang Club** (☎ 0 2266 5479; www .longyangclub.com), a 'multicultural social group for male-oriented men who want to meet outside the gay scene', with branches all over the world.

HOLIDAYS

Government offices and banks close on the following days.

Jan 1 New Year's Day
Apr 6 Chakri Day, commemorating the founder of the Chakri dynasty, Rama I
May 5 Coronation Day, commemorating the 1946 coronation of HM the King and HM the Queen
Jul (date varies) Khao Phansa, the beginning of Buddhist lent
Aug 12 Queen's Birthday
Oct 23 Chulalongkorn Day
Oct/Nov (date varies) Ok Phansa, the end of Buddhist lent
Dec 5 King's Birthday
Dec 10 Constitution Day

INSURANCE

A travel-insurance policy to cover theft, loss and medical problems is a good idea. Some policies offer lower and higher medical-expense options. There is a wide variety of policies available, so check the small print. Be sure that the policy covers ambulances or an emergency flight home.

Some policies specifically exclude 'dangerous activities', which can include scuba diving, motorcycling or even trekking. A locally acquired motorcycle licence is not valid under some policies.

You may prefer a policy that pays doctors or hospitals directly rather than you having to pay on the spot and claim later. If you have to claim later make sure you keep all documentation.

See p762 for recommendations on health insurance and p754 for details on vehicle insurance.

INTERNET ACCESS

You'll find plenty of Internet cafés in most larger towns and cities, and in many guesthouses and hotels as well. The going rate is 1B or 2B per on- and off-line minute, although we've seen a few places where slower connections are available at a half baht per minute.

Most hotels use RJ11 phone jacks, though in older hotels and guesthouses the phones may still be hard-wired. In the latter case you may be able to use a fax line in the hotel or guesthouse office, since all fax machines in Thailand are connected via RJ11 jacks.

Temporary Internet accounts are available from several Thai ISPs. One of the better ones is WebNet, offered by CSLoxinfo (www.csloxinfo.com). You can buy blocks of 12 hours (160B), 30 hours (380B) or 63 hours (750B), good for up to one year.

LEGAL MATTERS

In general Thai police don't hassle foreigners, especially tourists. If anything they generally go out of their way not to arrest a foreigner breaking minor traffic laws, instead taking the approach that a friendly warning will suffice.

One major exception is drugs, which most Thai police view as either a social scourge against which it's their duty to enforce the letter of the law, or an opportunity to make untaxed income via bribes. Small-time offenders are sometimes offered the chance to pay their way out of an arrest, while traffickers usually go to jail.

If you are arrested for any offence, the police will allow you the opportunity to make a phone call to your embassy or consulate in Thailand, if you have one, or to a friend or relative if not. There's a whole set of legal codes governing the length of time and manner in which you can be detained before being charged or put on trial, but a lot of discretion is left to the police. In the case of foreigners the police are more likely to bend these codes in your favour. However, as with police worldwide, if you don't show respect you will make matters worse.

Thai law does not presume an indicted detainee to be either 'guilty' or 'innocent' but rather a 'suspect', whose guilt or innocence will be decided in court. Trials are usually speedy.

Tourist Police Hotline

The tourist police can be very helpful in cases of arrest. Although they typically have no jurisdiction over the kinds of cases handled by regular cops, they may be able to help with translation or with contacting your embassy.

The best way to deal with most serious hassles regarding rip-offs or thefts is to contact the tourist police, who are used to dealing with foreigners, rather than the regular Thai police.

The tourist police maintain a hotline – dial ☎ 1155 from any phone in Thailand. You can call this number 24 hours a day to lodge complaints or to request assistance with regards to personal safety. You can also call this number between 8.30am and 4.30pm daily to request travel information.

MAPS

The Roads Association of Thailand publishes a good large-format, 48-page, bilingual road atlas called *Thailand Highway Map*. The atlas, which is updated every year, includes dozens of city maps, distance charts and index. It also gives driving distances and lots of travel and sightseeing information. Beware of inferior copies. A big advantage of the *Thailand Highway Map* is that the town and city names are printed in Thai as well as Roman script.

Do-it-yourself trekkers, or anyone with a keen interest in geography, may find sheet maps issued by the Thai military to be helpful. These maps are available at a number of scales, complete with elevations, contour lines, place names (in both Thai and Roman script) and roads.

Most trekkers find the 1:250,000-scale maps are adequate; there are 52 separate sheets costing 60B each. Four (Mae Hong Son, Mae Chan, Tavoy and Salavan) of the 52 aren't available to the public because of ongoing border disputes with Myanmar and Laos – the Thai army doesn't want to be accused of propagating incorrect borders. These maps can be purchased at the **Royal Thai Survey Department** (Krom Phaen Thi Thahan; Map p120; ☎ 0 2222 8844; Th Kanlayana Maitri, Bangkok), opposite the Interior Ministry on the western side of Th Ratchini in Ko Ratanakosin, very near Wat Ratchabophit.

City Maps

Lonely Planet's *Bangkok* map is printed on durable laminated paper and is a handy reference for getting your bearings in the big city. See the individual city sections for information on other city maps.

MONEY

The basic unit of Thai currency is the *baht*. There are 100 *satang* in one baht; coins include 25-satang and 50-satang pieces and baht in 1B, 5B and 10B coins. Older coins have Thai numerals only, while newer coins have Thai and Arabic numerals.

Paper currency is issued in the following denominations: 10B (brown), 20B (green), 50B (blue), 100B (red), 500B (purple) and 1000B (beige). A 10,000B bill was on the way when the 1997 cash crunch came, but has been tabled for the moment. Ten-baht bills are being phased out in favour of the 10B coin and have become uncommon.

ATMs & Credit/Debit Cards

Debit and ATM cards issued by a bank in your own country can be used at ATM machines around Thailand to withdraw cash (in Thai baht only) directly from your account back home. Thailand had more than 4500 machines at last count. You'll find them in all provincial capitals and every bank location at least one.

You can use MasterCard debit cards to buy baht at foreign exchange booths or desks at either the Bangkok Bank or Siam Commercial Bank. Visa debit cards can buy cash through the Kasikorn Bank exchange services.

Credit cards as well as debit cards can be used for purchases at many shops, hotels and restaurants. The most commonly accepted cards are Visa and MasterCard, followed by Amex and Japan Card Bureau (JCB).

To report a lost or stolen credit/debit card, call the following telephone hotlines in Bangkok:

Amex ☎ 0 2273 5050
MasterCard ☎ 001 800 11 887 0663
Visa ☎ 001 800 441 3485

Changing Money

Banks or the more rare private money-changers offer the best foreign-exchange rates. When buying baht, US dollars are the most accepted currency and travellers cheques get better rates than cash. British pounds and euros are second to the US dollar in general acceptability. Most banks charge a 23B commission and duty for each travellers cheque cashed.

See the table on the inside front cover of this book for exchange rates at the time of writing. Current exchange rates are printed in the *Bangkok Post* and the *Nation* every day, or you can walk into any Thai bank and ask to see a daily rate sheet.

See p19, for information on the cost of travel in Thailand.

Exchange Control

There is no limit to the amount of Thai or foreign currency you may bring into the country.

By Thai law, any traveller arriving in Thailand is supposed to carry at least the following amounts of money in cash, travellers cheques, bank draft or letter of credit, according to visa category: Non-Immigrant Visa, US$500 per person or US$1000 per family; Tourist Visa, US$250 per person or US$500 per family; visa on arrival, US$125 per person or US$250 per family. Your funds may be checked by authorities if you arrive on a one-way ticket or if you look as if you're at 'the end of the road'.

Upon leaving Thailand, you're permitted to take out no more than 50,000B per person without special authorisation; exportation of foreign currencies is unrestricted. An exception is made if you're going to Cambodia, Laos, Malaysia, Myanmar or Vietnam, where the limit is 500,000B.

It's legal to open a foreign currency account at any commercial bank in Thailand. As long as the funds originate from out of the country, there are not any restrictions on maintenance or withdrawal.

Tipping

Tipping is not generally expected in Thailand. The exception is loose change from a large restaurant bill; if a meal costs 488B and you pay with a 500B note, some Thais and foreign residents will leave the 12B coin change. It's not so much a tip as a way of saying 'I'm not so money-grubbing as to grab every last baht'. On the other hand,

change from a 50B note for a 44B bill will usually not be left behind.

At many hotel restaurants or other hi-so eateries, a 10% service charge will be added to your bill. When this is the case, tipping is not expected.

PHOTOGRAPHY & VIDEO
Film & Equipment

Print film is fairly inexpensive and widely available throughout Thailand. Slide film can be hard to find outside Bangkok and Chiang Mai, so be sure to stock up before heading out to rural areas. Blank video cassettes of all sizes are readily available in the major cities.

Memory cards for digital cameras are generally widely available in the more popular formats.

Photographing People

In some of the regularly visited areas hilltribe people expect money if you photograph them, while certain hill tribes will not allow you to point a camera at them. Use discretion when photographing villagers anywhere in Thailand as a camera can be a very intimidating instrument. You may feel better leaving your camera behind when visiting certain areas.

Processing

Film processing is generally quite good in the larger cities in Thailand and also quite inexpensive. Dependable E6 processing is available at several labs in Bangkok but is untrustworthy elsewhere. Kodachrome must be sent out of the country for processing, so it can take up to two weeks to get it back.

Professionals will find a number of labs in Bangkok that offer same-day pick-up and delivery at no extra cost within the city. **Image Quality Lab** (IQ Lab; Map pp114-16; ☎ 0 2266 4080; 160/5 ITF Bldg, Th Silom, Bangkok) offers the widest range of services, with all types of processing (except for Kodachrome), slide duping, scanning and custom printing. The former branch is actually off Silom on Th Chong Nonsi, near the Chong Nonsi BTS station.

POST

Thailand has a very efficient postal service and local postage is inexpensive. Bangkok has a **main post office** (Map pp114-16; Th Charoen Krung; ☺ 8am-8pm Mon-Fri, 8am-1pm Sat, Sun & holidays). Outside Bangkok the typical provincial main post office is open 8.30am to 4.30pm weekdays and 9am to noon on Saturday. Larger main post offices in provincial capitals may also be open for a half-day on Sunday.

Most provincial post offices sell do-it-yourself packing boxes, and some will pack your parcels for you for a small fee.

Receiving Mail

Thailand's poste restante service is generally very reliable, though these days few tourists use it. When you receive mail, you must show ID; sign your name; and write your passport number, the number of the letter and date of delivery in the book provided.

The **Amex office** (☎ 0 2273 5544; SP Bldg, 388 Th Phahonyothin, Bangkok; ☺ 8.30am-5pm Mon-Fri) will also take mail on behalf of Amex card holders but won't accept courier packets that require your signature.

SHOPPING

Many bargains await you in Thailand if you have the luggage space to carry them back. Always haggle to get the best price, except in department stores. Don't go shopping in the company of touts, tour guides or friendly strangers as they will inevitably take a commission on anything you buy, thus driving prices up.

Antiques

Real antiques cannot be taken out of Thailand without a permit. No Buddha image, new or old, may be exported without the permission of the Fine Arts Department. See p728 for information.

Merchandise in the tourist antique shops are, predictably, fantastically overpriced. Value-wise, northern Thailand has become the best source of Thai antiques – prices are about half what you'd typically pay in Bangkok.

Ceramics

Many kinds of hand-thrown pottery, old and new, are available throughout the kingdom. The best-known ceramics are the greenish Thai celadon products from the Sukhothai–Si Satchanalai area, and central Thailand's *benjarong* or 'five-colour' style. The latter is based on Chinese patterns while the former is a Thai original that has been imitated throughout China and Southeast Asia. Rough, unglazed pottery from the north and northeast can also be very appealing. For international styles, the many ceramic factories of Lampang are the best places to look for bargains.

Clothing

Tailor-made and ready-to-wear clothes tend to be inexpensive. If you're not particular about style you could pick up an entire wardrobe of travelling clothes at Bangkok's Siam Square or Pratunam street markets for what you'd pay for one designer shirt in New York, Paris or Milan.

You're more likely to get a good fit if you resort to a tailor, but be wary of the quickie 24-hour tailor shops; they often use inferior fabric or poor tailoring means the

---

BARGAINING

Items sold by street vendors in markets or in many shops are flexibly priced – that is, the price is negotiable. Prices in department stores, minimarts, 7-Elevens and so forth are fixed. If the same kind of merchandise is offered in a department store and a small shop or market, check the department-store price for a point of reference. Sometimes room rates can be bargained down.

Thais respect a good haggler. Always let the vendor make the first offer then ask 'Is that your best price?' or 'Can you lower the price?'. This usually results is an immediate discount from the first price. Now it's your turn to make a counter-offer; always start low but don't bargain at all unless you're serious about buying. Negotiations continue until a price is agreed – there's no set discount from the asking price as some vendors start ridiculously high, others closer to the 'real' price.

Do your homework by shopping around, and the whole process becomes easier with practice. It helps immeasurably to keep the negotiations relaxed and friendly, and to speak slowly, clearly and calmly. Vendors will almost always give a better price to someone they like.

arms start falling off after three weeks' wear. It's best to ask Thai or long-time foreign residents for a recommendation and then go for two or three fittings.

Fakes

In Bangkok, Chiang Mai and other tourist centres there is black-market street trade in fake designer goods branded with names such as Benetton, DKNY, Lacoste, Von Dutch, Ralph Lauren, Levi's, Reebok, Rolex, Cartier and more. No-one pretends they're the real thing, at least not the vendors.

In some cases foreign-name brands are produced under licence in Thailand and represent good value. A pair of legally produced Levi's jeans, for example, typically costs US$10 from a Thai street vendor, and US$35 to US$45 in the company's home town of San Francisco.

Furniture

Rattan and hardwood furniture items are often good buys and can be made to order. Bangkok and Chiang Mai have the best selection. With the ongoing success of teak farming and recycling, teak furniture has again become a bargain in Thailand if you find the right places. Asian rosewood is also a good buy.

Gems & Jewellery

Thailand is the world's largest exporter of gems and ornaments, rivalled only by India and Sri Lanka. Although rough-stone sources in Thailand have decreased dramatically, stones are now imported from Australia, Sri Lanka and other countries to be cut, polished and traded.

If you know what you are doing you can make some really good buys in both unset gems and finished jewellery. Gold ornaments are sold at a good rate as labour costs are low. The best bargains in gems are jade, rubies and sapphires.

Buy from reputable dealers only, preferably members of the Jewel Fest Club, a guarantee programme established by TAT and the Thai Gem & Jewellery Traders Association (TGJTA). When you purchase an item of jewellery from a shop that is identified as a member of the Jewel Fest Club, a certificate detailing your purchase will be issued. This guarantees a refund, less 10%, if you return the merchandise to the point

of sale within 30 days. You can obtain a list of members direct from **Jewel Fest Club** (☎ 0 2235 3039, 0 2267 5233-7) or from TAT.

WARNING

Be wary of special 'deals' that are offered for one day only or that set you up as a 'courier' in which you're promised big money. Many travellers end up losing big. Shop around and *don't be hasty*. Remember, there's no such thing as a 'government sale' or 'factory price' at a gem or jewellery shop; the Thai government does not own or manage any gem or jewellery shops. See Scams (p729) for a detailed warning on gem fraud.

Hill-Tribe Crafts

Interesting embroidery, clothing, bags and jewellery from the northern provinces can be bought in Bangkok and in Chiang Mai, especially at the Chiang Mai Night Bazaar.

Lacquerware

Good lacquerware, much of which is made in Myanmar (although it originated in Chiang Mai) and sold along the northern Myanmar border, can be found in Thailand. Try Mae Sot, Mae Sariang and Mae Sai for the best buys. Common lacquerware includes bowls, trays, plates, boxes, cups, vases and many other everyday items, as well as pure objects of art.

Lacquer comes from the *Melanorrhea usitata* tree and in its most basic form is mixed with paddy-husk ash to form a light, flexible, waterproof coating over bamboo frames. To make a lacquerware object, a bamboo frame is first woven. If the item is top quality, only the frame is bamboo and horse or donkey hairs will be wound round it. With lower-quality lacquerware, the whole object is made from bamboo. The lacquer is then coated over the framework and allowed to dry. After several days it is sanded down with ash from rice husks, and another coating of lacquer is applied. A high-quality item may have seven layers of lacquer.

The lacquerware is engraved and painted, then it is polished to remove the paint from everywhere except in the engravings. Multicoloured lacquerware is produced by repeated applications. From start to finish it can take five or six months to produce a high-quality piece of lacquerware, which may have as many as five colours. Flexibility is one characteristic of good lacquerware: a top-quality bowl can have its rim squeezed together until the sides meet without suffering damage. The quality and precision of the engraving is another thing to look for.

Textiles

Thai silk is considered the best in the world – the coarse weave and soft texture of the silk means it is more easily dyed than harder, smoother silks, resulting in brighter colours and a unique lustre. Silk can be purchased cheaply in the north and northeast where it is made or, more easily, in Bangkok. Excellent, reasonably priced tailor shops can make your choice of fabric into almost any pattern. Chinese silk is available at about half the cost of Thai silk. 'Washed' Chinese silk makes inexpensive, comfortable shirts or blouses.

Good ready-made cotton shirts are available, such as the *mâw hâwm* (Thai work shirt) and the *kúay hâeng* (Chinese-style shirt). Cotton weaving is popular in the northeast and there are fabulous finds in Nong Khai, Roi Et, Khon Kaen and Mahasarakham.

The colourful *mǎwn khwǎan* – a hard, triangle-shaped pillow made in the northeast – makes a good souvenir and comes in many sizes. The northeast is also famous for *mát-mìi* cloth – thick cotton or silk fabric woven from tie-dyed threads – similar to Indonesia's *ikat* fabrics.

In the north you can also find Lanna-style textiles based on intricate Thai Daeng, Thai Dam and Thai Lü patterns from Nan, Laos and China's Xishuangbanna.

Fairly nice batik *(paa-té)* is available in the south in patterns that are more similar to the batik found in Malaysia than in Indonesia.

TELEPHONE

The telephone system in Thailand, operated by the government-subsidised but privately owned Telephone Organisation of Thailand (TOT) under the Communications Authority of Thailand (CAT), is efficient if costly, and from Bangkok you can direct-dial most major centres with little difficulty.

The telephone country code for Thailand is ☎ 66. Thailand no longer uses separate area codes for Bangkok and the provinces, so all phone numbers in the country use eight

digits (preceded by a ☎ 0 if you're dialling domestically). When dialling Thailand from outside the country, you must first dial whatever international access code is necessary (eg from the USA dial ☎ 011 first for all international calls), followed by ☎ 66 and then the phone number in Thailand.

For directory assistance, dial ☎ 13.

International Calls

If you want to direct-dial an international number from a private telephone, just dial ☎ 001 before the number (except for calls to Malaysia and Laos; see below). Dial ☎ 100 for operator-assisted international calls.

A service called Home Country Direct is available at Bangkok's main post office (Map pp114–16), Bangkok International Airport (Map pp104–5) and Queen Sirikit National Convention Center (Map pp112–13), as well as at the Banglamphu (Map pp110–11) and Hualamphong station (Map pp108–9) post offices. Home Country Direct phones offer easy one-button connection to international operators in 40-odd countries around the world.

Hotels usually add surcharges (sometimes as much as 50% over and above the CAT rate) for international long-distance calls.

Private long-distance phone offices with international service always charge more than the government offices, although they are usually lower than hotel rates.

MALAYSIA & LAOS

The Communications Authority of Thailand (CAT) does not offer long-distance services to Malaysia or Laos. To call these countries you must go through TOT. For Laos, you can direct-dial ☎ 007 and country code 856, followed by the area code and number you want to reach. Malaysia can be dialled direct by prefixing the Malaysian number (including area code) with the code ☎ 09.

Mobile (Cellular) Phones

Thailand is on a GSM network. Two cellular operators in Thailand, Orange and DTAC, will allow you to use their SIM cards in an imported phone, as long as your phone isn't SIM-locked. Rates depend on the calling plan you choose but are typically around 3B per minute anywhere in Thailand. Mobile phone shops dealing in such cards can easily be found in most shopping centres in Bangkok and provincial capitals.

Pay Phones & Phonecards

There are three kinds of public pay phones in Thailand: 'red' (for local city calls), 'blue' (for both local and long-distance calls within Thailand) and 'green' (for use with phonecards).

Local calls from pay phones cost 1B for 164 seconds (add more coins for more time). Local calls from private phones cost 3B, with no time limit. Some hotels and guesthouses have private pay phones that cost 5B per call. Long-distance rates within the country vary from 3B to 12B per minute, depending on the distance.

For use with the green card phones, domestic TOT phonecards (50B, 100B, 200B and 500B denominations) are available at the information counter or gift shops of Bangkok International Airport, major shopping centres and 7-Elevens.

INTERNATIONAL PHONECARDS

A CAT-issued, prepaid international phonecard, called ThaiCard, comes in 300B and 500B denominations and allows calls to many countries at standard CAT rates. You can use the ThaiCard codes from either end, for example calling the UK from Thailand or calling Thailand from the UK.

Lenso phonecards allow you to make international phone calls from yellow Lenso International Cardphones, wall phones found in airports, shopping centres and in front of some post offices. Cards come in two denominations, 250B and 500B, and are sold in convenience stores and some supermarkets. You can also use most major credit cards with Lenso phones.

TIME

Thailand's time zone is seven hours ahead of GMT/UTC (London). At government offices and local cinemas, times are often expressed according to the 24-hour clock, eg 11pm is written 2300. See also the World Time Zone map (p789).

Thai calendar

The official year in Thailand is reckoned from 543 BC, the beginning of the Buddhist Era, so that AD 2005 is BE 2548, AD 2006 is BE 2549 etc.

TOILETS

As in many other Asian countries, the 'squat toilet' is the norm except in hotels and guesthouses geared towards tourists and international business travellers. These sit more-or-less flush with the surface of the floor, with two footpads on either side. For travellers who have never used a squat toilet it takes a bit of getting used to.

If there's no mechanical flush, toilet-users scoop water from an adjacent bucket or tank with a plastic bowl and use it to clean their nether regions while still squatting over the toilet. A few extra scoops of water must be poured into the toilet basin to flush waste into the septic system.

More rustic yet are toilets in rural areas, which may simply consist of a few planks over a hole in the ground.

Even in places where sit-down toilets are installed, the plumbing may not be designed to take toilet paper. In such cases the usual washing bucket will be standing nearby or there will be a waste basket where you're supposed to place used toilet paper.

TOURIST INFORMATION

The government-operated tourist information and promotion service, **Tourism Authority of Thailand** (TAT; Map pp106-7; ☎ 0 2250 5500; www.tat.or.th; 1600 Th Phetburi Tat Mai, Makkasan, Ratchathewi, Bangkok 10310), was founded in 1960 and is a part of the Ministry of Tourism.

The quality of the printed information that TAT produces is second to none among Southeast Asian countries; it has excellent pamphlets on sightseeing, accommodation and transportation.

TAT Offices Abroad

Australia (☎ 02-9247 7549; info@thailand.net.au; Level 2, 75 Pitt St, Sydney, NSW 2000)
France (☎ 01-53 53 47 00; tatpar@ wanadoo.fr; 90 ave des Champs Elysées, 75008 Paris)
Germany (☎ 069-138 1390; tatfra@tat.or.th; Bethmannstrasse 58, D-60311 Frankfurt/Main)
Malaysia (☎ 603-216 23480; sawatdi@po.jaring.my; Ste 22.01, Level 22, Menara Lion, 165 Jalan Ampang, 50450 Kuala Lumpur)
Singapore (☎ 65-235 7901; tatsin@singnet.com.sg; c/o Royal Thai embassy, 370 Orchard Rd, 238870)
UK (☎ 020-7925 2511; tatuk@tat.or.th; 3rd fl, Brook House, 98-99 Jermyn St, London SW1Y 6EE)
USA New York (☎ 212-432 0433, toll-free ☎ 1-800 THAI LAND; tatny@tat.or.th; 61 Broadway, Ste 2810, New York,

NY 10006); Los Angeles (☎ 323-461 9814; tatla@ix.net com.com; 1st fl, 611 North Larchmont Blvd, LA, CA 90004)

Check TAT's website for contact information in Hong Kong, Taipei, Seoul, Tokyo, Osaka, Fukuoka, Stockholm and Rome.

Tourist Offices in Thailand
You'll find TAT information counters in the international and domestic terminals of Bangkok's Don Muang Airport (Map pp104–5), at the Chatuchak Weekend Market (Map pp104–5) and on Th Khao San (Map pp110–11) in Bangkok. There are also TAT offices around Thailand.

VISAS
Non-Immigrant Visas
The Non-Immigrant Visa is good for 90 days, costs around US$60 and is not difficult to obtain if you can offer a good reason for your visit. Business, study, retirement and extended family visits are among the purposes considered valid. If you plan to apply for a Thai work permit, you'll need to possess a Non-Immigrant Visa first.

Tourist Visa Exemption
The Thai government allows 39 different nationalities, including those from most European countries, Australia, New Zealand and the USA (see www.mfa.go.th/web/12 .php for a detailed list), to enter the country without a visa for 30 days at no charge.

A few nationalities must obtain a visa in advance of arrival or they'll be turned back. Check with a Thai embassy or consulate if you plan on arriving without a visa.

Without proof of an onward ticket and sufficient funds for one's projected stay any visitor can be denied entry, but in practice your ticket and funds are rarely checked if you're dressed neatly for the immigration check.

Tourist Visas
If you plan to stay in Thailand more than a month, you should apply for the 60-day Tourist Visa. This costs US$30. One passport photo must accompany all applications.

Visa Extensions & Renewals
Sixty-day Tourist Visas may be extended up to 30 days at the discretion of Thai immigration authorities. You can apply at the

Bangkok immigration office (off Map p117; ☎ 0 2287 3101; Soi Suan Phlu, Th Sathon Tai; ⊗ 9am-noon & 1-4.30pm Mon-Fri, 9am-noon Sat; bus 17, 33, 63 & 67) or at any immigration office in the country. The **Chiang Mai immigration office** (Map pp278-80; ☎ 0 5320 1755-6; Th Mahidon; ⊗ 8.30am-4.30pm Mon-Fri) is near the airport. The fee for extension of a Tourist Visa is 1900B. Bring along two photos and one copy each of the photo and visa pages of your passport. Usually only one 30-day extension is granted. Do all visa extensions yourself, rather than hiring a third party.

The 30-day, no-visa stay can be extended for seven to 10 days (depending on the immigration office) for 1900B. You can also leave the country and return immediately to obtain another 30-day stay. There is no limit on the number of times you can do this, nor is there a minimum interval you must spend outside the country, although Thai immigration at the border crossing at Mae Sai may ask to see 10,000B cash if you've crossed there more than six times in one year.

If you overstay your visa, the usual penalty is a fine of 200B each extra day, with a 20,000B limit. Fines can be paid at the airport or in advance at an immigration office. If you've overstayed only one day, you don't have to pay. Children under 14 travelling with a parent do not have to pay the penalty.

WOMEN TRAVELLERS
Around 40% of all visitors to Thailand are women, a higher ratio than the worldwide average as measured by the World Tourism Organization and on a par with or higher than most other Asian countries.

Everyday incidents of sexual harassment are much less common in Thailand than in India, Indonesia or Malaysia, and this may lull women familiar with those countries into thinking that Thailand is safer than it is.

Virtually all incidents of attacks on foreign women in Thailand have occurred outside Bangkok, typically in remote beach or mountain areas. If you're a woman travelling alone, try to pair up with other travellers when travelling at night. Make sure hotel and guesthouse rooms are secure at night – if they're not, demand another room or move to another hotel or guesthouse.

Transport

CONTENTS

GETTING THERE & AWAY

ENTERING THE COUNTRY

Entry procedures for Thailand, by air or by land, are straightforward. You'll have to show your passport of course, with any visa you may have obtained beforehand (see opposite). You'll also need to present completed arrival and departure cards. These are usually distributed on the incoming flight or, if arriving by land, you can pick them up at the immigration counter.

You do not have to fill in a customs declaration on arrival unless you have imported goods to declare. In that case you can get the proper form from Thai customs officials at the point of entry.

See the Thai customs information about minimum currency requirements, p737.

AIR

Airports

Bangkok International Airport (BIA; code BKK; ☎ 0 2535 1111), located in a district directly north of Bangkok known as Don Muang, has been the main hub for air traffic in and out of Thailand since 1931. In terms of scheduled arrivals and departures, it's the busiest airport in Southeast Asia. Bangkok International Airport has one domestic terminal and two separate international terminals.

A new international airport at Nong Ngu Hao (20km east of Bangkok), **Suvarnabhumi Airport** (www.bangkokairport.org), also known as New Bangkok International Airport (NBIA), will replace the one at Don Muang around March 2006. The name of the new airport is pronounced *sùwannáphuum*, and when finished it will boast the tallest control tower in the world.

Thailand has five additional international airports, one each in **Chiang Mai** (CNX; ☎ 0 5327 0222), **Chiang Rai** (CEI; ☎ 0 5379 4857), **Hat Yai** (HDY; ☎ 0 7425 1007), **Phuket** (☎ 0 7632 7230), **Samui** (USM) and **Sukhothai** (THS). Chiang Rai is designated as 'international', but at the time of writing it did not actually field any international flights. The website for information on the airports at Bangkok, Chiang Mai, Hat Yai, Phuket and Chiang Rai is www.airportthai.co.th. Samui and Sukhothai are

---

WARNING

The information supplied in this chapter is particularly vulnerable to change: Prices for international travel are volatile, routes are introduced and cancelled, schedules change, special deals come and go, and rules and visa requirements are amended. Airlines and governments seem to take a perverse pleasure in making price structures and regulations as complicated as possible. You should check directly with the airline or a travel agent to make sure you understand how a fare (and ticket you may buy) works. In addition, the travel industry is highly competitive and there are many lurks and perks.

The upshot of this is that you should get opinions, quotes and advice from as many airlines and travel agents as possible before you part with your hard-earned cash. The details given in this chapter should be regarded as pointers and are not a substitute for your own careful, up-to-date research.

both private airports owned by Bangkok Airways (www.bkkair.co.th).

Each airport has a customs area with a 'green lane' for passengers with nothing to declare – just walk through if you're one of these. All terminals in Thailand provide free baggage trolleys for use inside the terminal.

Airlines Travelling to/from Thailand

Thailand's national carrier is Thai Airways International (THAI), which also operates many domestic air routes. According to Air Rankings Online, THAI's safety record warrants an 'A', the highest grade possible.

Bangkok is one of the cheapest cities in the world to fly out of, due to the Thai government's loose restrictions on air fares and close competition between airlines and travel agencies.

Air Asia (airline code AK; Map pp104-5; ☎ 0 2515 9999; www.airasia.com; hub Kuala Lumpur International Airport)

Air Canada (airline code AC; Map pp114-16; ☎ 0 2670 0400; www.aircanada.com; hub Pearson International Airport, Toronto)

Air China (airline code CA; ☎ 0 2631 0728; www.air china.com/cn/english; hub Beijing Capital International Airport)

Air France (airline code AF; Map pp114-16; ☎ 0 2635 1199; www.airfrance.fr; hub Paris Orly Airport)

Air New Zealand (airline code NZ; Map pp118-19; ☎ 0 2254 8440; www.airnewzealand.com; hub Auckland International Airport)

American Airlines (airline code AA; ☎ 0 2263 0225; www.aa.com; hub Dallas-Ft Worth International Airport)

Bangkok Airways (airline code PG; off Map pp106-7; ☎ 0 2265 5555; www.bangkokair.com; hub Bangkok International Airport)

British Airways (airline code BA; Map pp114-16; ☎ 0 2636 1700; www.britishairways.com; hub Heathrow Airport, London)

Cathay Pacific Airways (airline code CX; Map pp118-19; ☎ 0 2263 0606; www.cathaypacific.com; hub Hong Kong International Airport)

China Airlines (airline code CI; Map pp118-19; ☎ 0 2253 4242; www.china-airlines.com; hub Chiang Kai Shek International Airport, Taipei)

Garuda Indonesia (airline code GA; Map p117; ☎ 0 2535 7370; www.garuda-indonesia.com; hub Soekarno Hatta Airport, Jakarta)

Gulf Air (airline code GF; Map pp118-19; ☎ 0 2254 7931-4; www.gulfairco.com; hub Abu Dhabi)

Japan Airlines (airline code JL; ☎ 0 2692 5185-6, res 0 2692 5151-60; www.jal.co.jp; hub Narita International Airport/New Tokyo International Airport)

KLM-Royal Dutch Airlines (airline code KL; Map pp118-19; ☎ 0 2679 1100, ext 2; www.klm.com; hub Schiphol Airport, Amsterdam)

Korean Air (airline code KE; Map pp114-16; ☎ 0 2267 0990; www.koreanair.com; hub Incheon International Airport, Seoul)

Lao Airlines (airline code QV; Map pp114-16; ☎ 0 2236 9822; www.laoairlines.com; hub Wattay Airport, Vientiane)

Lufthansa Airlines (airline code LH; Map pp112-13; ☎ 0 2264 2484, reservations 0 2264 2400; www.luft hansa.com; hub Frankfurt Airport)

Malaysia Airlines (airline code MH; Map pp118-19; ☎ 0 2263 0520-32, reservations 2263 0565-71; www.mas.com.my; hub Kuala Lumpur International Airport)

Myanmar Airways International (airline code 8M; Map pp112-13; ☎ 0 2630 0334-8; www.maiair.com; hub Yangon International Airport)

Northwest Airlines (airline code NW; Map pp118-19; ☎ 0 2254 0771; www.nwa.com; hub Minneapolis-St Paul International Airport)

Qantas Airways (airline code QF; ☎ 0 2636 1770, reservations ☎ 0 2636 1747; www.qantas.com.au; hub Kingsford Smith Airport, Sydney)

Royal Brunei Airlines (airline code BI; Map p117; ☎ 0 2233 0056; www.bruneiair.com; hub Brunei Airport, Brunei Darussalam)

Royal Nepal Airlines (airline code RA; ☎ 0 2216 5691-5; www.royalnepal.com; hub Tribhuvan International Airport, near Kathmandu)

Scandinavian Airlines (SAS; airline code SK; Map pp112-13; ☎ 0 2645 8200; www.scandinavian.net; hub Copenhagen Airport)

Singapore Airlines (airline code SQ; Map pp114-16; ☎ 0 2535 2260, reservations ☎ 2236 5301; www.singaporeair.com; hub Changi Airport, Singapore)

South African Airways (airline code SA; Map pp114-16; ☎ 0 2635 1414; www.flysaa.com; hub Johannesburg International Airport)

Thai Airways International (airline code TG; Map pp114-16; head office ☎ 0 2513 0121, reservations ☎ 0 2280 0060; www.thaiair.com; hub Bangkok International Airport)

United Airlines (airline code UA; Map pp118-19; ☎ 0 2296 7752; www.ual.com; hub O'Hare International Airport, Chicago)

Vietnam Airlines (airline code VN; Map pp112-13; ☎ 0 2656 9056-8; www.vietnamair.com.vn; hub Noibai International Airport, Hanoi)

Tickets

Tickets can be purchased cheaply on the Internet and many airlines offer excellent fares to Web surfers. Online ticket sales

DEPARTURE TAX

All passengers leaving Thailand on international flights are charged a departure tax (officially called an 'airport service charge') of 500B, which is not included in the price of air tickets, but paid at a booth near the passport control area. Only baht is accepted. Be sure to have enough baht left at the end of your trip to pay this tax – otherwise you'll have to revisit one of the currency-exchange booths.

INTERCONTINENTAL (RTW) TICKETS

If you're travelling to multiple countries, then an around-the-world (RTW) ticket – where you pay a single discounted price for several connections – may be the most economical way to go.

Here are a few online companies that can arrange RTW tickets:

www.airbrokers.com
www.airstop.be
www.airtreks.com
www.aroundtheworlds.com

Asia

There are regular flights to Bangkok International Airport from every major city in Asia and most airlines offer about the same fares for intra-Asia flights. Return tickets are usually double the one-way fare, although occasionally airlines run special discounts of up to 25% for such tickets.

Although other Asian centres are now competitive with Bangkok, it's still a good place for shopping around for discounted airline tickets, especially with the baht trading low against most hard currencies.

A very good Internet source for discounted fares leaving from Bangkok is www.bangkoktickets.com.

Recommended booking agencies for reserving flights from Asia include the following STA Travel offices:

Bangkok (☎ 0 2236 0262; www.statravel.co.th)
Hong Kong (☎ 2736 1618; www.hkst.com.hk/statravel /gywm_e.htm)
Japan (☎ 03 5391 2922; www.statravel.co.jp)
Singapore (☎ 6737 7188; www.statravel.com.sg)

Another resource in Japan is **No.1 Travel** (☎ 03 3205 6073; www.no1-travel.com); in Hong Kong try **Four Seas Tours** (☎ 2200 7760; www.fourseastravel .com/english).

Australia

STA Travel (☎ 1300 733 035; www.statravel.com.au) and **Flight Centre** (☎ 133 133; www.flightcentre.com .au) have offices throughout Australia. For online bookings, try www.travel.com.au.

Thai Airways International and Qantas both have direct flights to Bangkok from the east coast of Australia, starting from about A$1000 return in the low season to A$1350 return in the high season. Garuda Indonesia, Singapore Airlines, Philippine Airlines and Malaysia Airlines also have frequent flights

work well if you are doing a simple one-way or return trip on specified dates. However, online fare generators are no substitute for a travel agent who knows all about special deals, has strategies for avoiding layovers and can offer advice on everything from which airline has the best vegetarian food to the best travel insurance to bundle with your ticket.

You may find the cheapest flights are advertised by obscure agencies. Most such firms are honest and solvent, but there are some rogue fly-by-night outfits around. Paying by credit card generally offers protection, as most card issuers provide refunds if you can prove you didn't get what you paid for. Agents who accept only cash should hand over the tickets straight away and not tell you to 'come back tomorrow'. After you've made a booking or paid your deposit, call the airline and confirm that the booking was made.

If you purchase a ticket and later want to make changes to your route or get a refund, you need to contact the original travel agent. Airlines issue refunds only to the purchaser of a ticket – usually the travel agent who bought the ticket on your behalf. Many travellers change their routes halfway through their trips, so think carefully before you buy a ticket that is not easily refunded or changed.

Booking flights in and out of Bangkok during the high season (December to March) can be difficult. For air travel during these months you should make your bookings as far in advance as possible.

Also, be sure to reconfirm return or ongoing tickets when you arrive in Thailand (although this isn't necessary for THAI tickets). Failure to reconfirm can mean losing your reservation.

TRANSPORT

and some good fare deals, with stopovers, to Bangkok.

Canada

Travel Cuts (☎ 800-667-2887; www.travelcuts.com) is Canada's national student travel agency. For online bookings try www.expedia.ca and www.travelocity.ca.

Air Canada flies from Vancouver to Bangkok for around C$1300 to C$1500 return for advance-purchase excursion fares. From eastern Canada the best deals are usually out of New York or San Francisco – add on fares for travel from Toronto or Montreal (see opposite).

Continental Europe

Following are some recommended agencies across Europe.

FRANCE

Anyway (☎ 0 892 893 892; www.anyway.fr)
Lastminute (☎ 0 892 705 000; www.lastminute.fr)
Nouvelles Frontières (☎ 0 825 000 747; www
.nouvelles-frontieres.fr)
OTU Voyages (www.otu.fr) This agency specialises in student and youth travellers.
Voyageurs du Monde (☎ 01 40 15 11 15; www
.vdm.com)

GERMANY

Expedia (www.expedia.de)
Just Travel (☎ 089 747 3330; www.justtravel.de)
Lastminute (☎ 01805 284 366; www.lastminute.de)
STA Travel (☎ 01805 456 422; www.statravel.de) For travellers under the age of 26.

ITALY

CTS Viaggi (☎ 06 462 0431; www.cts.it) Specialises in student and youth travel.

NETHERLANDS

Airfair (☎ 020 620 5121; www.airfair.nl)

SPAIN

Barcelo Viajes (☎ 902 116 226; www.barceloviajes.com)
Nouvelles Frontières (☎ 90 217 09 79; www.nou
velles-frontieres.fr)

India

STIC Travels (www.stictravel.com) Delhi (☎ 11-233 57 468); Mumbai (☎ 22-221 81 431) With offices in dozens of other Indian cities.
Transway International (www.transwayinter
national.com)

The Middle East

Some recommended agencies include the following:
Al-Rais Travels (www.alrais.com) In Dubai.
Egypt Panorama Tours (☎ 2-359 0200; www.eptours
.com) In Cairo.
The Israel Student Travel Association (ISTA; ☎ 02-625 7257) In Jerusalem.
Orion-Tour (www.oriontour.com) In Istanbul.

New Zealand

Both **Flight Centre** (☎ 0800 243 544; www.flight
centre.co.nz) and **STA Travel** (☎ 0508 782 872; www
.statravel.co.nz) have branches throughout the country. The site www.travel.co.nz is recommended for online bookings.

Air New Zealand and THAI both have direct flights from Auckland to Bangkok. Return low-season fares start from around NZ$1300; from around NZ$1500, during high season. Malaysian Airlines, Qantas and Garuda International also have flights to Bangkok, with stopovers.

South America

Some recommended agencies include the following:
ASATEJ (☎ 54-011 4114-7595; www.asatej.com) Argentina.
Student Travel Bureau (☎ 3038 1555; www.stb.com
.br) Brazil.
IVI Tours (☎ 0212-993 6082; www.ividiomas.com) Venezuela.

UK

Discount air-travel ads appear in *Time Out*, the *Evening Standard* and in the free magazine *TNT*.

Recommended travel agencies include the following:
Bridge the World (☎ 0870 444 7474; www.b-t-w.co.uk)
Flightbookers (☎ 0870 010 7000; www.ebookers.com)
Flight Centre (☎ 0870 890 8099; flightcentre.co.uk)
North South Travel (☎ 01245 608 291; www.north
southtravel.co.uk) Donates part of its profit to projects in the developing world.
Quest Travel (☎ 0870 442 3542; www.questtravel.com)
STA Travel (☎ 0870 160 0599; www.statravel.co.uk) Popular with travellers under 26, sells tickets to all. Branches throughout the UK.
Trailfinders (0845 058 5858; www.trailfinders.co.uk)
Travel Bag (☎ 0870 890 1456; www.travelbag.co.uk)

At least two dozen airlines fly between London and Bangkok, although only three of them – British Airways, Qantas and THAI – fly nonstop. If you insist on a nonstop flight, you will probably have to pay between UK£500 and UK£800 return for the privilege (or around UK£100 less if you are a student or under 26). A one-way ticket is usually only slightly cheaper than a return ticket.

USA

It's cheaper to fly to Bangkok from West Coast cities than from the East Coast. You can get some great deals through the many bucket shops (which discount tickets by taking a cut in commissions) and consolidators (agencies that buy airline seats in bulk) in Los Angeles and San Francisco. A return (round-trip) air fare to Bangkok from any of 10 West Coast cities starts at around US$800, with occasional lower specials (especially in May and September). From the East Coast, add about US$200 to any fares.

One of the most reliable discounters is **Avia Travel** (☎ 800-950 AVIA, 510-558 2150; www .aviatravel.com), which specialises in custom-designed RTW fares.

The airlines that generally offer the lowest fares from the USA include China Airlines, EVA Airways, Korean Air and Northwest. Each has a budget and/or 'super Apex' fare for around US$900 to US$1500 return from Los Angeles, San Francisco or Seattle, depending on the season. Add US$200 for departure from the East Coast. Several of these airlines also fly out of New York, Dallas, Chicago and Atlanta.

EVA Airways (Taiwan) offers the 'Evergreen Deluxe' class between the USA and Bangkok, via Taipei, which has business class–sized seats and personal movie screens for about the same cost as regular economy fares on most other airlines.

The following agencies are recommended for online bookings:

www.cheaptickets.com
www.expedia.com
www.itn.net
www.lowestfare.com
www.orbitz.com
www.sta.com (for travellers under the age of 26)
www.travelocity.com

LAND
Bicycle

Many visitors bring their own touring bicycles to Thailand. No special permits are needed for bringing a bicycle into the country, although it may be registered by customs – which means if you don't leave the country with your bicycle, you'll have to pay a huge customs duty. See p750 for more information about travelling by bike.

It's essential to bring a well-stocked repair kit and be sure to have your bike serviced before departure.

Bus

If you enter Thailand via bus – this is only possible from Laos and Malaysia at the moment – your bus will stop at a Thai

---

INTERNATIONAL BORDER CROSSINGS

These are border points where Thai customs and immigration posts allow foreigners to cross to or from neighbouring countries. All crossings are open 8am to 6pm daily.

Thailand	Malaysia
Betong	Keroh
Padang Besar	Kaki Bukit
Sadao	Changlun
Sungai Kolok	Rantau Panjang

Thailand	Laos
Beung Kan	Paksan
Chiang Khong	Huay Xai
Chiang Saen	Ton Pheung
Chong Mek	Pakse
Mukdahan	Savannakhet
Nakhon Phanom	Tha Khaek
Nong Khai	Vientiane

Thailand	Cambodia
Aranya Prathet	Poipet
Hat Lek	Koh Kong
Kap Choeng	Chom Som
Chong Sa-Ngam	Anlong Veng
Ban Laem	Daun Lem
Ban Phakkat	Pailin

Thailand	Myanmar (Burma)
Mae Sai	Tachileik
Mae Sot	Myawadi*
Ranong	Kawthoung
Three Pagodas Pass	Payathonz u*

*Entry permitted for day trips only

immigration post at your point of entry so that each foreign passenger can receive an entry stamp in their passports. Thai visas are not normally included in bus fares.

Car & Motorcycle

Passenger vehicles (eg car, van, truck or motorcycle) can be brought into Thailand for tourist purposes for up to six months. Documents needed for the crossing are a valid International Driving Permit, passport, vehicle registration papers (in the case of a borrowed or hired vehicle, authorisation from the owner) and a cash or bank guarantee equal to the value of the vehicle plus 20%. For entry through Khlong Toey Port or Bangkok International Airport, this means a letter of bank credit; for overland crossings via Malaysia, Cambodia or Laos a 'self-guarantee' filled in at the border is sufficient.

Cambodia

Thai–Cambodian border crossings are typically straightforward. Most visitors coming by road from Cambodia use the Poipet/Aranya Prathet crossing. You can also cross by boat from Ko Kong in southern Cambodia. Several more remote crossings have opened between southeastern Thailand and southwestern Cambodia over the last year or two. See p747 for a complete list of Thai–Cambodian entry/exit points.

China

The governments of Thailand, Laos, China and Myanmar have agreed to the construction of a four-nation ring road through all four countries.

The stretch between Tachileik and Dalau is finished and it's easy to arrange trips as far as Kengtung and Mengla in Myanmar's Shan State (see p356). A road between Huay Xai and Boten already exists (built by the Chinese in the '60s and '70s) but needs upgrading.

The eastern half of this loop, from Boten to Huay Xai, Laos, and across to Chiang Khong, Thailand, can be done relatively easily now, although roads between Boten and Huay Xai are rough.

Laos

The Thai–Lao Friendship Bridge (1174m) spans a section of the Mekong River between

Ban Jommani (near Nong Khai, Thailand) and Tha Na Leng (near Vientiane, Laos) and is the main transportation gateway between the two countries. You can easily reach the Thai border crossing from Vientiane by bus, taxi or three-wheeled motorcycle taxi.

The construction of a second Mekong bridge has begun. When it opens in early 2006 it will span the Mekong at Mukdahan (opposite Savannakhet) to create a land link between Thailand and Vietnam through Laos.

See the chart on p747 for a complete list of Thai–Lao entry/exit points.

Malaysia

BUS & MINIVAN

There are very regular private buses and minivans between Hat Yai in Thailand and various destinations in Malaysia, which include immigration stops at the border. This is by far the easiest way to cross between the two countries and it isn't significantly cheaper to cross the border in several stages by public transport. If you insist on public transport, take a bus from Hat Yai to Padang Besar, walk across the border, and then pick up a second bus on the far side – see p615 for more details.

There's also a border crossing at Keroh (Betong on the Thai side), right in the middle between the east and west coasts.

See p625 for information on crossing the border on the east coast.

TRAIN

The **State Railway of Thailand** (www.railway.co.th) and **Malaysian Railway** (www.ktmb.com.my) meet at Butterworth, 93km south of the Thai–Malaysian border, a transfer point for bus to/from Penang or train (or bus) to/from Kuala Lumpur. The train trip between Butterworth and Bangkok lasts roughly 21 hours and costs about 600/1400B for a 2nd-/1st-class sleeper, including all surcharges. There is no 3rd-class seating on this train.

Myanmar

MAE SAI–TACHILEIK

This crossing features an infamous bridge, Lo Hsing-han's former 'Golden Triangle' passageway for opium and heroin. It spans the Mae Sai (Sai River) between Thailand's northernmost town and the border boom town of Tachileik (called Thakhilek by the Thais). Many travellers use this border as a way to renew their Thai visas by simply checking out at Thai immigration, walking across the border, and then re-entering Thailand with a fresh visa.

Note that in the last couple of years, Mae Sai immigration officials have become sensitive to travellers doing this, and they make ask to see 10,000B cash (the legal requirement for a tourist visa) before issuing an entry stamp. Anyone who does a 'border run' here more than six times in one year may be refused entry.

On occasion this border crossing has been closed due to fighting between Shan insurgent armies and the Burmese; or other regional disturbances.

MAE SOT–MYAWADI

This crossing begins a route from Myawadi to Mawlamyaing (Moulmein) via Kawkareik. It's a rough road that has long been off limits to foreigners due to Mon and Karen insurgent activity in the area. There are regular buses from Tak to Mae Sot in Tak Province. Politics sometimes closes this crossing for a few weeks or months at a time. At the time of writing the bridge that crosses the Mae Moei between Myawadi and Mae Sot (actually 6km from Mae Sot proper) was open to all comers.

Foreigners may cross from Mae Sot to Myawadi only for the day – the area beyond Myawadi is off limits. The Myanmar government has plans to open the road from Myawadi all the way to Pa-an in Kayin State, and Thai groups have sometimes had permission to travel by chartered bus all the way to Yangon. See p409 for details.

THREE PAGODAS PASS

A gateway for various invading armies and an important smuggling route for many centuries, this is one of the most interesting and accessible of the border-crossing points. The settlement on the Burmese side, called Payathonzu (Three Pagodas), is open on-and-off to foreign tourists for day trips. Travellers have been allowed to go as far as a dozen or so kilometres inside Myanmar from this point, but the roads are so bad that almost no-one makes it even that far. See p228 for details.

RIVER
China
EXPRESS BOAT

An express boat runs along the Mekong River between Sop Ruak in Chiang Rai Province, and China's Yunnan Province. For the moment, permission for such travel is restricted to very infrequent private tour groups; inquire in Kunming or Jinghong, Yunnan, about getting a place on such an excursion (typically costing around US$100). The boat trip takes six hours – considerably quicker than any current road route. However it's only navigable all the way to China during the rainy season and in the period immediately after. Check-in procedures at Chiang Saen immigration are straightforward.

Laos
FERRY

It's legal for non-Thais to cross the Mekong River by ferry between Thailand and Laos at the following points: Beung Kan (opposite Paksan), Nakhon Phanom (opposite Tha Khaek), Chiang Khong (opposite Huay Xai) and Mukdahan (opposite Savannakhet). Ferry fares run around 30B at each location.

Thais are permitted to cross at all of the above checkpoints plus at least a half-dozen others in Thailand's Loei and Nong Khai Provinces, including Ban Khok Phai, Ban Nong Pheu, Ban Pak Huay, Chiang Khan and Pak Chom. For the most part these checkpoints are good only for day crossings (by Thai and Lao only). In the future one or more of these may become available for entry by foreign visitors as well.

SEA
Cambodia

Travellers can travel by sea from Cambodia to Thailand via Hat Lek in Trat Province. For more details see p261.

Malaysia
FERRY

There are several ways of travelling between Thailand's southern peninsula and Malaysia by sea. The simplest is to take a long-tail boat between Satun, right down in the southwestern corner of Thailand, and Kuala Perlis. The cost is about M$20, or 100B, and boats cross fairly regularly. You can also take a ferry from Satun to

TRANSPORT

the Malaysian island of Langkawi. There are immigration posts at both ports so you can make the crossing quite officially. From Satun you can take a bus to Hat Yai and then arrange transport to other points in the south. It's possible to bypass Hat Yai altogether by heading directly for Phuket or Krabi via Trang. For more detail see p713.

PRIVATE BOAT

All foreign-registered vessels, skippers and crew must check in with the relevant Thai authorities as soon as possible after entering Thai waters. Although major ports throughout Thailand offer port check-ins, most leisure boating visitors check in at Phuket, Krabi, Samui, Pranburi or Pattaya. Because Phuket's Tha Ao Chalong brings customs, immigration and harbourmaster services together in one building, Phuket is the most popular check-in point nationwide.

Before departing from Thailand by boat, you must also check out with immigration, customs and harbourmaster. Check-in and check-out fees can vary from port to port, but typically one pays 300B per boat plus 10B per passenger for immigration fees upon arrival, plus 100B each to customs and the harbourmaster upon departure. Vessels caught without harbour clearance may be fined up to 5000B. **Lee Marine** (www.leemarine .com) is a very good source of current information on the yachting situation.

Myanmar
BOAT

You can travel by boat (50B one way) from Kawthoung in Myanmar's Tanintharyi Division to the port of Ranong in Thailand via the Gulf of Martaban and Pakchan estuary. Exiting Myanmar from Kawthoung is legal, and you don't need a visa to enter Thailand for a stay of up to 30 days. In the reverse direction you don't need a Myanmar visa for a day trip, but you'll need one if you plan to stay overnight or to continue further north.

GETTING AROUND

AIR
Airlines in Thailand

Until recently your domestic airline choices were limited, but Thailand is now going through a period of air route deregulation

which has resulted in several low-fare, no-frills airline start-ups. All are based at Bangkok International Airport.

Air Asia (airline code AK; Map pp104–5; ☎ 0 2515 9999; www.airasia.com) Bangkok to Chiang Mai, Chiang Rai, Hat Yai, Phuket, Khon Kaen, Udon Ratchathani and Udon Thani.

Bangkok Airways (airline code PG; off Map pp106–7; ☎ 0 2265 5555, reservations centre ☎ 1771; www .bangkokair.com) Bangkok to Chiang Mai, Krabi, Phuket, Samui, Sukhothai and Trat; Samui to Krabi, Phuket and Pattaya; Phuket to Pattaya.

Nok Air (airline code DD; Map pp112–13; ☎ 1318; www .nokair.co.th) Bangkok to Chiang Mai, Hat Yai, Udon Thani, Phuket and Phitsanulok.

Orient Thai (airline code OX; Map pp114–16; ☎ 0 2267 3210, call centre ☎ 1126; www.orient-thai.com) Bangkok to Chiang Mai, Chiang Rai, Phuket, Hat Yai and Krabi.

Phuket Air (airline code 9R; off Map p117; ☎ 0 2679 8999; www.phuketairlines.com) Bangkok to Buriram, Chiang Mai, Phuket, Krabi, Mae Sot, Hat Yai, Udon Thani and Ranong; from Chiang Mai to Mae Sot and Udon Thani; between Phuket and Hat Yai.

THAI (airline code TG; Map pp114–16; ☎ 0 2513 0121; www.thaiair.com) Operates domestic air services to many provincial capitals, and maintains offices in more than 35 provincial cities.

BICYCLE

Just about anywhere outside Bangkok, bicycles are an ideal form of local transport – cheap, nonpolluting and moving slowly enough to see everything.

The majority of vehicle drivers are courteous and move over for bicycles. Most roads are sealed, with roomy shoulders. Grades in most parts of the country are moderate; exceptions include the far north, especially Mae Hong Son and Nan Provinces, where you'll need iron thighs. There is plenty of opportunity for dirt-road and off-road pedalling, especially in the north, so a sturdy mountain bike would make a good alternative to a touring rig. Favoured touring routes include the two-lane roads along the Mekong River in the north and northeast – the terrain is largely flat and the river scenery is inspiring.

You can take bicycles on the train for a little less than the equivalent of one 3rd-class fare. On ordinary buses they'll place your bike on the roof, and on air-con buses it will be put in the cargo hold.

The 2500-member **Thailand Cycling Club** (☎ 0 2612 4747, 0 1555 2901), established in 1959,

TRANSPORT

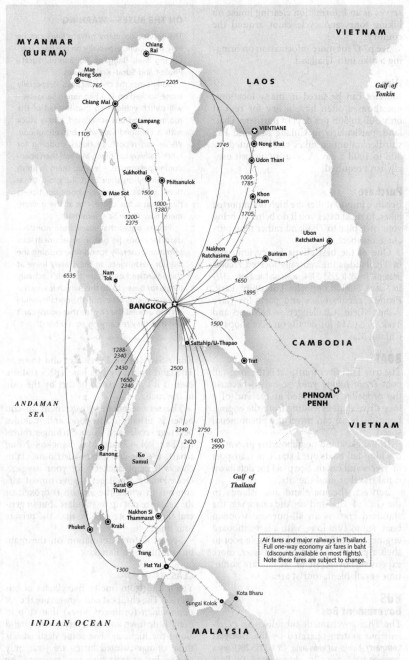

MYANMAR
(BURMA)

VIETNAM

Gulf of
Tonkin

LAOS

Chiang
Rai

Mae
Hong Son

765

2205

Chiang Mai

Lampang

VIENTIANE

Nong Khai

2745

Udon Thani

1105

Sukhothai

Phitsanulok

Mae Sot

1500

1000–
1380

1200–
2375

1008–
1785

Khon
Kaen

1705

Ubon
Ratchathani

Nakhon
Ratchasima

Buriram

6535

Nam
Tok

1650

1895

BANGKOK

1500

Sattahip/U-Thapao

CAMBODIA

Trat

1288–
2340

2430

1650–
2340

2500

PHNOM
PENH

VIETNAM

ANDAMAN
SEA

2340

2750

2420

1400–
2990

Ranong

Ko
Samui

Gulf of
Thailand

Surat
Thani

Nakhon Si
Thammarat

Phuket

Krabi

Trang

1300

Hat Yai

Air fares and major railways in Thailand.
Full one-way economy air fares in baht
(discounts available on most flights).
Note these fares are subject to change.

Kota Bharu

Sungai Kolok

INDIAN OCEAN

MALAYSIA

serves as an information clearing house on biking tours and cycle clubs around the country.

See p747 for more information on bringing a bike into Thailand.

Hire

Bicycles can be hired in many locations; guesthouses often have a few for rent at only 30B to 50B per day. In northern Thailand, particularly in Chiang Mai and Pai, sturdier mountain bikes can be rented for 80B to 100B a day. A security deposit usually isn't required.

Purchase

Because import duties are high on imported bikes, in most cases you'll do better to bring your own bike to Thailand rather than purchase one here.

One of the best shops for cycling gear in Thailand is the centrally located **Probike** (Map p117; ☎ 0 2253 3384; www.probike.co.th; 237/1 Soi Sarasin, Bangkok) opposite Lumphini Park. Probike carries bikes and parts for Gary Fisher, Klein, Challenger, + LeMond and Trek. See p314 for details on bike shops in Chiang Mai.

BOAT

The true Thai river transport is the long-tail boat *(reua hǎang yao)*, so-called because the propeller is mounted at the end of a long drive shaft extending from the engine. Long-tail boats can travel at a phenomenal speed.

In Bangkok and neighbouring provinces the long-tail boats are a staple of transport on rivers and canals. See p183 for details on canal travel around the city.

Between the mainland and islands in the Gulf of Thailand or Andaman Sea, the standard craft is an all-purpose wooden boat, 8m to 10m long, with a large inboard engine, a wheelhouse and a simple roof to shelter passengers and cargo. Faster, more expensive hovercraft or jetfoils are sometimes available in tourist areas.

BUS
Government Bus

The Thai government subsidises an excellent bus system operated by the **Transport Company** (bàw-rí-sàt khŏn sòng; ☎ 0 2936 2841; www .transport.co.th), usually abbreviated to Baw

---

> **ON THE BUSES – WARNING**
>
> The service on many private lines can be very unreliable, especially on the Bangkok–Chiang Mai, Bangkok–Ko Samui, Surat–Phuket and Surat–Krabi routes.
>
> Sometimes the cheaper lines – especially those booked on Th Khao San in Bangkok – will switch vehicles so that instead of the roomy air-con bus advertised, you're stuck with a cramped van with broken air-con. We've had reports of buses stopping for lunch halfway to Chiang Mai and then abandoning passengers – leaving them to finish the journey on their own. To avoid situations such as this, *always* book bus tickets directly at a bus office – or at the government Baw Khaw Saw terminal.
>
> Private buses that leave from nonstandard locations (ie not a government bus terminal) generally spend time cruising the city for passengers, so they rarely leave at the advertised departure time. It's actually illegal for buses to do this, which is why the bus attendants often pull the curtains while driving around the city (so that police can't see that they're carrying passengers).

Khaw Saw (BKS). Every city and town in Thailand linked by bus has a BKS station, even if it's just a patch of dirt by the side of the road.

The service on the government air-con buses is usually quite good and includes beverage service and video. On longer routes (eg Bangkok–Chiang Mai, Bangkok–Nong Khai), the air-con buses distribute claim checks (receipt dockets) for your baggage. Occasionally you'll get a government aircon bus in which the air-con is broken or the seats are not up to standard, but in general they are more reliable than the private tour buses.

See p180 for information on the main bus terminals in Bangkok.

CLASSES

You'll find from one to five classes of bus service. The cheapest and slowest are the *rót thammádaa* (ordinary buses) that stop in every little town and for every waving hand along the highway. For some destinations these orange-painted buses are your only choice, but at least they are frequent. The government also runs faster, more comfortable but less frequent air-con buses called *rót ae* (air bus), *rót pràp aakàat* (air-con bus) or *rót thua* (tour bus); these are painted with blue markings. They don't cost that much more than the ordinary buses.

Longer routes offer at least two classes of air-con buses, 2nd class and 1st class; the latter have toilets. 'VIP' and 'Super VIP' buses have fewer seats so that each seat reclines more. Sometimes these are called *rót nawn* or sleepers. For small- to medium-sized people they are more comfortable.

Private Bus

Privately run buses are available between major tourist and business destinations all over the country. Fares may vary from company to company, but usually not by more than a few baht.

Private air-con buses are usually no more comfortable than the government air-con buses and feature similarly narrow seats and hair-raising rides. The private companies are more apt to turn up the air-con until your knees knock, handing out pillows and blankets and serving free soft drinks. On overnight journeys the buses usually stop somewhere en route and passengers are awakened to get off the bus for a free meal of fried rice or rice soup. A few companies even treat you to a meal before a long overnight trip.

Like the government-bus companies, the private companies offer VIP (sleeper) buses on long hauls. In general the private bus companies that deal mostly with Thais are good, while tourist-oriented ones – especially those connected with Th Khao San – are awful.

Out of Bangkok, the safest, most-reliable private bus services are the ones that operate from the three official BKS terminals rather than from hotels or guesthouses. Vans or minibuses are common alternatives on hilly or winding routes, eg Surat to Krabi, and Tak to Mae Sot. For short distances these are fine, but they aren't recommended for long routes.

SAFETY

Statistically, private buses meet with more accidents than government air-con buses. Turnovers on tight corners and head-on collisions with trucks are probably due to the inexperience of the drivers on a particular route. Private buses licensed to operate from government bus terminals, however, are usually much better than those operating 'pirate routes' from tourist centres such as Th Khao San in Bangkok or Hat Patong in Phuket.

Keep an eye on your bags when using buses along popular tourist routes. When the lights are out and passengers are asleep, bus attendants may pilfer unattended bags. Most pilfering seems to take place on the private bus runs between Bangkok and Chiang Mai or Ko Samui, especially on buses booked on Th Khao San. Keep zippered bags locked and well secured.

Costs

Bus travel is the cheapest way to get around Thailand. Even on the best air-con buses – 24-seat Super VIP – you can count on paying slightly less than 1B per kilometre (see the table below for comparisons).

Reservations

You can book air-con BKS (government) buses at any BKS terminal. Ordinary (non-air-con) buses cannot be booked in advance. Some travel agencies also handle BKS bus reservations. Privately run buses can be booked through most hotels or any travel agency, but it's best to book directly through a bus office to be sure that you get what you pay for.

SAMPLE BUS FARES

Destination	24-seat VIP	32-seat VIP	1st class a/c	2nd class a/c	Ordinary non-a/c
Chiang Mai (713km)	625B	470B	403B	322B	260B
Loei (560km)	540B	(n/a)	320B	249B	193B
Krabi (817km)	710B	(n/a)	459B	357B	255B
Hat Yai (954km)	830B	624B	535B	(n/a)	(n/a)
Trat (317km)	(n/a)	221B	189B	147B	126B

TRANSPORT

CAR & MOTORCYCLE

Bring Your Own Vehicle

See p748 for information on how to bring a private vehicle into Thailand for tourist purposes.

Driving Licence

Short-term visitors who wish to drive vehicles (including motorcycles) in Thailand need an International Driving Permit. Long-term visitors can apply for a Thai driver's licence at the **Police Registration Division** (PRD; Map pp104-5; ☎ 0 2513 0051-5; Th Phahonyothin, Bangkok), which also operates offices in provincial capitals.

Fuel & Spare Parts

Modern petrol (gasoline) stations with electric pumps are in plentiful supply all over Thailand, wherever there are paved roads. In more-remote, off-road areas petrol (*bensin* or *náam-man rót yon*) is usually available at small roadside or village stands. All fuel in Thailand is unleaded.

If you're bringing your own vehicle, you'd be wise to bring a box of crucial spare parts that might not be available in Thailand. The same goes for motorcycles – for any bike larger than 125cc.

Hire

Cars, jeeps and vans can be rented in Bangkok, Cha-am, Chiang Mai, Chiang Rai, Hat Yai, Hua Hin, Khao Lak, Khorat, Ko Samui, Krabi, Mae Hong Son, Pattaya, Phuket and Udon Thani. Check with travel agencies or large hotels for locations. International rental companies tend to charge significantly more than local companies.

Always verify that a vehicle is insured for liability before signing a rental contract; you should also ask to see the dated insurance documents. If you have an accident while driving an uninsured vehicle you're in for some major hassles.

Motorcycles can be rented in major towns and many smaller tourist centres such as Krabi, Ko Pha-Ngan, Ko Samui, Mae Sai, Nong Khai and Pai.

A substantial deposit is usually required to rent a car; motorcycle rental usually requires that you leave your passport. Rates start at around 1500B per day for a small car including basic insurance; personal accident cover is an extra 100B per day.

All the big car-hire companies have offices in Bangkok; a few follow.

Avis Rent-A-Car (☎ 0 2255 5300-4; www.avisthailand .com)

Budget Car Rental (☎ 0 2202 0250; www.budget.co.th)

Hertz (☎ 0 2267 5161; www.hertz.com)

National Car Rental (SMT Rent-a-Car; ☎ 0 2928 1525; www.smtrentacar.com)

Insurance

Thailand requires a minimum of liability insurance for all registered vehicles on the road. The better hire companies include comprehensive coverage for their vehicles. Most insurance contracts are void if you travel off-road, even in a 4WD vehicle.

If you need auto insurance, a policy can be purchased through local companies inexpensively. Two of the more reliable ones:

Bangkok Insurance (☎ 0 2285 8888; www.bki.co.th)

Royal & Sun Alliance (☎ 0 2207 0266 www.royalsun alliance.com)

Motorcycle Touring

Motorcycle travel has become a popular way to get around Thailand, especially in the north. Dozens of places along the guesthouse circuit, including many guesthouses themselves, have set up shop with no more than a couple of motorcycles for rent. It is also possible to buy a new or used motorcycle and sell it before you leave the country. A used 125cc bike can be purchased for as low as 25,000B; you'll pay up to 60,000B for a reconditioned Honda MTX or AX-1, and more for the newer and more reliable Honda Degree or Yamaha TTR 250. If you're looking for a more narrowly defined dirt bike, check out the Yamaha Serow.

With proper safety precautions and driving conduct adapted to local standards, you can see parts of Thailand inaccessible by other modes of transport and still make it home in one piece. Some guidelines to keep in mind:

- If you've never driven a motorcycle before, stick to the smaller 100cc step-through bikes with automatic clutches.
- Always check a machine over thoroughly before you take it out: tyres, oil, brakes. Note any problems.
- Wear a helmet (required by law in 17 provinces – most rental places can provide them) and protective clothing (including gloves).

ROAD DISTANCES (KM)

	Aranya Prathet	Ayuthaya	Bangkok	Chiang Mai	Chiang Rai	Chumphon	Hat Yai	Hua Hin	Khon Kaen	Mae Hong Son	Mae Sai	Mukdahan	Nakhon Ratchasima	Nakhon Sawan	Nong Khai	Phitsanulok	Phuket	Sungai Kolok	Surat Thani	Tak	Trat
Ayuthaya	246																				
Bangkok	275	79																			
Chiang Mai	844	607	686																		
Chiang Rai	1014	777	856	191																	
Chumphon	727	531	452	1138	1308																
Hat Yai	1268	1072	993	1679	1849	555															
Hua Hin	458	262	183	869	1039	269	810														
Khon Kaen	432	397	450	604	774	902	1443	633													
Mae Hong Son	1013	767	846	225	406	1298	1839	1029	1029												
Mae Sai	1082	845	924	259	68	1376	1917	1107	1107	474											
Mukdahan	601	524	577	917	1087	1029	1570	760	313	1142	1155										
Nakhon Ratchasima	239	204	257	744	914	709	1250	440	193	969	982	320									
Nakhon Sawan	409	163	242	444	614	694	1235	425	408	604	682	692	372								
Nong Khai	598	563	616	720	890	1068	1609	799	166	945	958	347	359	546							
Phitsanulok	535	298	377	309	479	829	1370	560	295	578	547	608	435	135	411						
Phuket	1125	929	862	1536	1706	412	474	667	1300	1696	1774	1427	1097	1092	1466	1227					
Sungai Kolok	1555	1359	1280	1966	2136	1029	214	842	1730	2126	2204	1857	1730	1522	1896	1657	286				
Surat Thani	927	731	652	1338	1508	214	401	469	1102	1498	1576	1229	909	894	1268	1029	286	688			
Tak	581	335	414	280	460	866	1407	597	717	432	528	754	544	172	557	146	1264	1694	1066		
Trat	285	392	313	999	1169	765	1306	496	603	1397	1397	524	524	555	883	690	1163	1593	965	727	
Ubon Ratchathani	444	367	420	881	1051	872	1413	603	277	1106	1119	157	163	535	443	572	1270	1700	1072	707	729

- For distances of over 100km, take an extra supply of motor oil, and if riding a two-stroke machine carry two-stroke engine oil.
- Never ride alone in remote areas, especially at night. When riding in pairs or groups, leave space to manoeuvre or brake suddenly if necessary.
- Distribute weight as evenly as possible across the frame of the bike to improve handling.
- Get insurance with the motorcycle; more reputable rental places insure all their bikes; some for an extra charge. To be absolutely clear about your liability, ask for a written estimate of the replacement cost for a similar bike – take photos as a guarantee. Health insurance (see p762) is also a good idea; check the conditions with regard to motorcycle riding.

Golden Triangle Rider (www.gt-rider.com) is an excellent website for detailed, up-to-date information on motorcycle touring in Thailand (see p758).

Road Hazards

You'll need to have nerves of steel to drive around Bangkok, and we really don't recommend it. Traffic is chaotic, roads are poorly signposted, and motorcycles and random contra flows mean you can suddenly find yourself facing a wall of cars coming the other way.

The principal hazard when driving in Thailand, besides the general disregard for traffic laws, is having to contend with so many different types of vehicles on the same road – bullock carts, 18-wheelers, bicycles, *túk-túk* (motorised pedicab) and customised racing bikes. This danger is often compounded by the lack of working lights. In village areas the vehicular traffic is lighter but you have to contend with stray chickens, dogs, water buffaloes and goats. Once you get used to the challenge, driving in Thailand is very entertaining.

Road Rules

Thais drive on the left-hand side of the road (most of the time!). Other than that seemingly just about anything goes, in spite of road signs and speed limits.

The main rule to be aware of is that right of way belongs to the bigger vehicle; this

---

CHECKPOINTS

Military checkpoints are common along highways throughout northern, southern and northeastern Thailand, especially in border areas. Always slow down for a checkpoint – often the sentries will wave you through without an inspection, but occasionally you will be stopped and briefly questioned. Use common sense and don't act belligerently or you're likely to be detained longer than you'd like.

---

is not what it says in the Thai traffic law, but it's the reality. Maximum speed limits are 50km/h on urban roads, 80km/h to 100km/h on most highways – but on any given stretch of highway you'll see vehicles travelling as slowly as 30km/h or as fast as 150km/h. Speed traps are common along Hwy 4 in the south and Hwy 2 in the northeast.

Indicators are often used to warn passing drivers about oncoming traffic. A flashing left indicator means it's OK to pass, while a right indicator means that someone's approaching from the other direction.

HITCHING

Hitchhiking is never entirely safe in any country, and we don't recommend it. Travellers who decide to hitch should understand that there's a small but serious risk. However, many people do choose to hitch, and the advice that follows should help to make the journey as fast and safe as possible.

People have mixed success with hitching in Thailand; sometimes it's great and at other times no-one wants to pick you up. It seems easiest in the more touristy areas of the north and south, and most difficult in the central and northeastern regions where tourists are a relatively rare sight. To stand on a road and try to flag every vehicle that passes by is, to the Thais, something only an uneducated village dweller would do.

If you're prepared to face this perception, the first step is to use the correct gesture for flagging a ride – the thumb-out gesture isn't recognised by the average Thai. When Thais want a ride they stretch one arm out with the hand open, palm facing down, and move the hand up and down. This is the same gesture used to flag a taxi or bus, which is why some drivers will stop and point to a bus stop if one is nearby.

In general, hitching isn't worth the hassle as ordinary (no air-con) buses are frequent and cheap. However, there's no need to stand at a bus station – all you have to do is stand on any road going in your direction and flag down a passing bus or *săwngthăew* (pick-up truck).

The exception is in areas where there isn't any bus service, though in such places there's not likely to be very much private vehicle traffic either. If you do manage to get a ride, it's customary to offer food or cigarettes to the driver if you have any.

LOCAL TRANSPORT
Bus

Bangkok has an extensive city-bus system. Only two provincial capitals that we know of, Phitsanulok and Ubon Ratchathani, also run buses with established routes. In these cities, fares are usually from 4B to 8B. For other cities and towns, you must rely on *săwngthăew*, *túk-túk* or *săamláw* (three-wheeled pedicabs).

Motorcycle Taxi

Many cities in Thailand also have *mawtoe-sai ráp jâang*, 100cc to 125cc motorcycles that can be hired, with a driver, for short distances. They're not very suitable if you're carrying more than a backpack or small suitcase, but if you're empty-handed they can't be beaten for quick transport over short distances. In addition to the lack of space for luggage, motorcycle taxis also suffer from lack of shelter from rain or sun. Although most drivers around the country drive at safe, sane speeds, the kamikaze drivers of Bangkok are a major exception.

In most cities you'll find motorcycle taxis clustered near street intersections, rather than cruising the streets looking for fares. Fares tend to run from 10B to 30B, depending on distance. Some motorcycle taxis specialise in regular, short routes, eg from one end of a long street to another. In such cases the fare is usually a fixed 10B.

Săamláw & Túk-túk

Săamláw means 'three wheels', and that's just what they are – three-wheeled vehicles. There are two types of *săamláw* – motorised and nonmotorised.

You'll find motorised *săamláw* throughout the country. They're small utility vehicles, powered by horrendously noisy two-stroke engines (usually LPG-powered); if the noise and vibration doesn't get you, the fumes will. Tourists commonly know motor *săamláw* as *túk-túk*, because of the noise they make. Among themselves, the Thais still call these *săamláw* – the term *túk-túk* is strictly foreigner talk but it's what most Thais use when speaking to Western tourists.

The nonmotorised *săamláw,* ie the bicycle rickshaw or pedicab, is similar to what you may see in other parts of Asia. There are no bicycle *săamláw* in Bangkok but you will find them elsewhere in the country. With either form of *săamláw* the fare must be established, by bargaining if necessary, before departure.

Readers interested in pedicab lore and design may want to have a look at Lonely Planet's hardcover pictorial book, *Chasing Rickshaws,* by Lonely Planet founder Tony Wheeler.

Săwngthăew

A *săwngthăew* (literally, 'two rows') is a small pick-up truck with two rows of bench seats down both sides of the truck bed. They sometimes operate on fixed routes, just like buses, but they may also run a share-taxi type of service or even be booked individually just like a regular taxi. *Săwngthăew* are often colour-coded, so that red ones, for example, go to one destination or group of destinations, while blue ones go to another.

Skytrain

The **BTS Skytrain** (rót fai fáa; ☎ 0 2617 7340; www .bts.co.th) allows you to soar above Bangkok's legendary traffic jams in air-conditioned comfort. See p184 for more information.

Subway (Metro)

A new subway system operated by the **Metropolitan Rapid Transit Authority** (MRTA; rót fai fáa mahǎanákhawn; ☎ 0 2617 7340; www.mrta.co.th), nicknamed 'The Metro', opened in 2004 in Bangkok. See p185 for more information.

Taxi

Many regional centres have taxi services, but although there may well be meters, they're never used. Establishing the fare before departure is essential. Try to get an idea from a third party as to what the fare should be and be prepared to bargain. In general, fares are reasonably low.

See the relevant destination chapters for more information on taxis.

TOURS

Many operators around the world can arrange guided tours of Thailand. Most of them simply serve as brokers for tour companies based in Thailand; they buy their trips from a wholesaler and resell them under various names in travel markets overseas. Hence, one is much like another and you might as well arrange a tour in Thailand at a lower cost – there are so many available. Long-running, reliable tour wholesalers in Thailand include the following:

Active Thailand (Map pp282-4; ☎ 0 5327 7178; www
.activethailand.com; 73/7 Th Charoen Prathet, Chiang Mai)
Custom-tailored cycling, trekking, rafting and kayaking
tours of Thailand. Operated by Contact Travel (p314).
Asian Trails (Map pp118-19; ☎ 0 2658 6090; www
.asiantrails.net; 9th fl, SG Tower, 161/1 Soi Mahatlek Leung
3, Th Ratchadamri, Lumphini, Bangkok) A smaller company
that's particularly good with innovative driving itineraries.
Diethelm Travel (Map p117; ☎ 0 2255 9150; www
.diethelmtravel.com; Kian Gwan Bldg II, 140/1 Th Withayu,
Bangkok) One of the largest tour operators in Bangkok.
Golden Triangle Rider (www.gt-rider.com) Organises
motorcycle tours of northern Thailand (with extensions
into Laos and southwestern China).
World Travel Service (Map pp114-16; ☎ 0 2233 5900;
www.wts-thailand.com; 1053 Th Charoen Krung, Bangkok)
In business since 1947. One of the largest tour operators in
the city with desks in many hotels.

Overseas Companies

The better overseas tour companies build their own Thailand itineraries from scratch and choose their local suppliers based on which best serve these itineraries. Of these, several specialise in adventure and/or ecological tours:

Asia Transpacific Journeys (☎ 800-642 2742, 303-
443 6789; www.southeastasia.com; 3055 Center Green
Dr, Boulder, CO 80301, USA) Offers trips across a broad
spectrum of Thai destinations and activities, from northern
Thailand trekking to sea canoeing in the Phuket Sea,
plus tour options that focus exclusively on northeastern
Thailand.
Club Aventure (☎ 514-527 0999; www.clubaventure
.com; 757 ave du Mont-Royal Est, Montreal, QUE H2J 1W8,
Canada)

Exodus (☎ 0870 240 5550; www.exodustravels.co.uk;
9 Weir Rd, London SW12 0LT, UK)
Intrepid Travel (☎ 03-9473 2626; www.intrepid
travel.com; 11-13 Spring St, Fitzroy, Vic 3065, Australia)
Specialises in small-group travel, with dozens of itineraries
in Thailand ranging from five to 29 days.
Ms Kasma Loha-Unchit (☎ 510-655 8900; www
.thaifoodandtravel.com; PO Box 21165, Oakland, CA 94620,
USA) This Thai cookbook author living in California offers
personalised, 19- to 28-day 'cultural immersion' tours of
Thailand.

TRAIN

The government rail network, the **State Railway of Thailand** (SRT; www.railway.co.th), is, on the whole, very well run. It isn't possible to take the train everywhere (see the map, p751, for major routes) in Thailand, but often it is by far the best public transport. If you travel 3rd class, it is often the cheapest way to cover a long distance; by 2nd class it's about the same as a private tour bus but much safer and more comfortable. Trains take longer than chartered buses on the same journey but are worth the extra travel time, on overnight trips especially.

The trains offer many advantages over buses. To start with, there is more room to move and stretch out than there is on even the best buses (including in 3rd class). The windows are big and, if you choose non-air-con, they're usually left open, so that there is no glass between you and the scenery (good for taking photos) and more to see. The scenery itself is always better along the train routes than along highways – the trains regularly pass small villages, farmland, old temples etc. The pitch and roll of the railway carriages is much easier on the bones, muscles and nervous system than the quick stops and starts, the harrowing turns and the pothole jolts endured on buses.

Bangkok Terminals

Almost all the long-distance trains originate from Bangkok's Hualamphong station. Bangkok Noi station in Thonburi serves the commuter and the short-line trains running to Kanchanaburi/Nam Tok, Suphanburi, Ratchaburi and Nakhon Pathom. You can also get to Ratchaburi and Nakhon Pathom by trains from Hualamphong. Thonburi's Wong Wian Yai station, running services to Samut Songkhram, is rarely used.

Classes

The SRT operates passenger trains in three classes – 1st, 2nd and 3rd – but each class varies considerably depending on whether you're on an ordinary, rapid or express train.

THIRD CLASS

A typical 3rd-class carriage consists of two rows of bench seats divided into facing pairs. Each bench seat is designed to seat two or three passengers, but on a crowded rural line nobody seems to care about design considerations. On a rapid train, 3rd-class seats are padded and reasonably comfortable for shorter trips. On ordinary 3rd-class-only trains in the east and northeast, seats are sometimes made of hard wooden slats, and are not recommended for more than a couple of hours at a time. Express trains do not carry 3rd-class carriages at all. Commuter trains in the Bangkok area are all 3rd class and the carriages resemble modern subway or rapid-transit trains, with plastic seats and ceiling hand-straps for standing passengers.

SECOND CLASS

The seating arrangements in a 2nd-class, nonsleeper carriage are similar to those on a bus, with pairs of padded seats, usually recliners, all facing towards the front of the train.

On 2nd-class sleeper cars, pairs of seats face one another and convert into two fold-down berths, one over the other. Curtains provide a modicum of privacy and the berths are fairly comfortable, with fresh linen for every trip. The lower berth has more head room than the upper berth and this is reflected in a higher fare (eg in a train where the upper berth costs 500B, the lower berth might be 700B). A toilet stall and washbasins are at one end of the carriage.

Second-class carriages are found only on rapid and express trains. Air-con 2nd class is more common nowadays than ordinary 2nd class (with the latter available only on rapid lines).

FIRST CLASS

Each private cabin in a 1st-class carriage has individually controlled air-con (older trains also have an electric fan), a washbasin and mirror, a small table and long bench seats that convert into beds. Drinking water and soap are provided free of charge. First-class carriages are available only on rapid, express and special-express trains.

Costs

There is a 60B surcharge above the basic fare for express trains (*rót dùan*) and 40B for rapid trains (*rót rew*). These trains are somewhat faster than the ordinary trains, as they make fewer stops. Some 2nd- and 3rd-class services are air-con, in which case there is a 70B surcharge (note that there are no 3rd-class carriages on either rapid or express trains). For the special-express trains (*rót dùan phísèht*) that run between Bangkok and Padang Besar and between Bangkok and Chiang Mai there is an 80B surcharge (or 100B to 120B if a meal is included, depending on distance).

The added charge for 2nd-class sleeping berths is 100B for an upper berth and 150B for a lower berth (or 130B and 200B on a special express; 150B and 240B for the Korean-made Daewoo cars). The difference between upper and lower is that there is a window next to the lower berth and more head room. The upper berth is comfortable enough. For 2nd-class sleepers with air-con add 250/320B per upper/lower ticket. No sleepers are available in 3rd class.

Air-con really isn't necessary on night trains, as a steady breeze circulates through the train and cools things down quickly. In fact the air-con in 2nd class can become uncomfortably cold at night and cannot be regulated by passengers; for this reason we recommend choosing non-air-con when possible.

All 1st-class cabins come with individually controlled air-con. For a two-bed cabin the surcharge is 520B per person. Single 1st-class cabins are not available, so if you're travelling alone you may be paired with another passenger, although the SRT takes great care not to mix genders.

Fares are structured so that the first 300km costs about 90 satang per kilometre in 1st class, 45 satang in 2nd class and 20 satang in 3rd class. Over 300km and the fare structure drops to 73, 33 and 15 satang respectively.

You can estimate a 500km journey costing around 200B in 2nd class (not including the surcharges for the rapid and express services), roughly twice that in 1st class and less than half in 3rd. Surprisingly, basic fares have changed only slightly over the last decade, although supplementary charges have increased steadily. This is because the government subsidises train travel, particularly 3rd class. Over the last five years or so there has been some talk of privatisation – which would, of course, ring the death knell for the high standards of this railway system, as it has in most other formerly railfaring countries of the world.

The proliferation of cheap domestic airlines, such as Nok Air and Air Asia, are proving to be stiff competition for the trains. A cheap Bangkok–Chiang Mai flight costs about the same as a 1st-class cabin.

Reservations

Trains can be difficult to book, especially around holiday time, eg the middle of April approaching the Songkran Festival, during Chinese New Year and during the peak tourist-season months of December and January.

Trains out of Bangkok should be booked as far in advance as possible – a minimum of a week for popular routes such as the northern line to Chiang Mai and the southern line to Hat Yai, especially if you want a sleeper. For the northeastern and eastern lines a few days will suffice. Midweek departures are always easier to book than weekends; during some months of the year you can easily book a sleeper even one day before departure, as long as it's on a Tuesday, Wednesday or Thursday.

Advance bookings may be made one to 60 days before your intended date of departure. If you want to book tickets in advance, go to Hualamphong station in Bangkok, walk through the front of the station and go straight to the back right-hand corner where a sign says 'Advance Booking' (open 8.30am to 4pm). The other ticket windows, lined up in front of the platforms, are for same-day purchases, mostly 3rd class. From 5am to 8.30am and from 4pm to 11pm, advance bookings can also be made at windows Nos 2 to 11.

Reservations are computerised in the Advance Booking office, and you simply take a queue number and wait until your number appears on one of the electronic marquees. You can only pay in cash (baht) here.

You can also book via the Internet (www .railway.co.th/seatcheck2/mainseat_E.html) 30 days in advance of your intended travel date.

With the exception of Surat Thani and Chiang Mai, booking trains back to Bangkok is generally not as difficult as booking trains out of Bangkok.

Tickets between any stations in Thailand can be purchased at **Hualamphong station** (☎ 0 2223 3762, 0 2225 6964, 0 2224 7788, 0 2225 0300, ext 5200 03). You can also make advance bookings at Don Muang station (across from Bangkok International Airport) and at the Advance Booking offices at train stations in the larger cities. Advance reservations can be made by phone from anywhere in Thailand. Throughout Thailand SRT ticket offices are generally open 8.30am to 6pm on weekdays, and 8.30am to noon on weekends and public holidays. Train tickets can also be purchased at certain travel agencies in Bangkok. It is much simpler to book trains through these agencies than to book them at the station; however, they usually add a surcharge (50B to 100B) to the ticket price.

Station Services

You'll find all train stations in Thailand have baggage-storage services (or 'cloak rooms'). The rates and hours of operation vary from station to station. At Hualamphong station the hours are 4am to 10.30pm daily and left luggage costs 10B per piece per day for up to five days, after which it goes up to 15B per day. Hualamphong station also provides a 10B shower service in the rest rooms.

Hualamphong station is jammed with modern coffee shops and a coupon-style cafeteria. Most stations in the provincial capitals have small open-air restaurants as well as various snack vendors.

Hualamphong station has a couple of travel agencies where other kinds of transport can be booked, but beware of touts who try to drag you there, saying the trains are fully booked when they aren't. Avoid the travel agencies outside the station, which have very poor reputations. Near the front of the station, at one end of the foyer, **Mail Boxes Etc** (MBE; ⏱ 7.30am-7.30pm Mon-Fri, 9am-4pm Sat, 9am-8pm Sun) provides mailing, courier and packing services.

If you have any questions or problems other than bookings, there is a special tourist service (☎ 0 2282 8773).

Train Dining

Meal service is available in dining carriages (rót sa-biang) and at your seat in 2nd- and 1st-class carriages. Menus change as frequently as the SRT changes catering services. All the meals seem a bit overpriced (80B to 200B on average) by Thai standards.

Several readers have written to complain about being overcharged by meal servers on the trains. If you do purchase food on board, check prices on the menu rather than trusting server quotes. Also check the bill carefully to make sure you haven't been overcharged.

Many Thai passengers bring along their own meals and snacks to avoid the relatively high cost of SRT-catered meals.

Train Information

Accurate, up-to-date information on train travel is available at the Rail Travel Aids counter in Hualamphong station. There you can pick up timetables, and ask questions about fares and scheduling – one person behind the counter usually speaks a little English. There are two types of timetable available: four condensed English timetables with fares, schedules and routes for rapid, express and special express trains on the four trunk lines; and four Thai timetables for each trunk line, and side lines. These latter timetables give fares and schedules for all trains – ordinary, rapid and express. The English timetables only display a couple of the ordinary routes; eg they don't show the wealth of ordinary trains that go to Ayuthaya and as far north as Phitsanulok.

Train Passes

The SRT issues a Thailand Rail Pass that may save on fares if you plan to use the trains extensively over a relatively short interval. This pass is only available in Thailand, and may be purchased at Hualamphong station.

The cost for 20 days of unlimited 2nd- or 3rd-class train travel is 1500B, or 3000B including all supplementary charges; children aged four to 12 pay half the adult fare. Supplementary charges include all extra charges for rapid, express, special express and aircon. Passes must be validated at a local station before boarding the first train. The price of the pass includes seat reservations that, if required, can be made at any SRT ticket office. The pass is valid until midnight on the last day of the pass, although if the journey is commenced before midnight on the last day of validity, the passenger can use the pass until that train reaches its destination.

Does the pass represent a true saving over buying individual train tickets? The answer is 'yes', but only if you can average more than 110km by train per day for 20 days (ie 2200km in total). In addition, on less crowded routes where there are plenty of available 2nd-class seats the passes save time that might otherwise be spent at ticket windows, but for high-demand routes (eg from Bangkok to Chiang Mai or Hat Yai) you'll still need to make reservations.

Train Routes

Four main rail lines cover 4500km along the northern, southern, northeastern and eastern routes. There are several side routes, notably between Nakhon Pathom and Nam Tok (stopping in Kanchanaburi) in the western central region, and between Thung Song and Kantang (stopping in Trang) in the south. The southern line splits at Hat Yai: one route goes to Sungai Kolok on the Malaysian east-coast border, via Yala; and the other goes to Padang Besar in the west, also on the Malaysian border.

A Bangkok–Pattaya spur has not been as popular as expected but is still running. The SRT has initiated a feasibility study to develop high speed rail (150km/h to 300km/h) between Bangkok and Padang Besar on the Malaysian border.

TRANSPORT

Health
Dr Trish Batchelor

CONTENTS

Health issues and the quality of medical facilities do vary enormously depending on where and how you travel in Southeast Asia. Many of the major cities are now very well developed, although travel to rural areas can expose you to a variety of health risks and inadequate medical care.

Travellers tend to worry about contracting infectious diseases when in the tropics, but infections are a rare cause of serious illness or death in travellers. Pre-existing medical conditions such as heart disease, and accidental injury (especially traffic accidents), account for most life-threatening problems. Becoming ill in some way, however, is relatively common. Fortunately most common illnesses can either be prevented with some commonsense behaviour or be treated easily with a well-stocked traveller's medical kit.

The following advice is a general guide only and does not replace the advice of a doctor trained in travel medicine.

BEFORE YOU GO

Pack medications in their original, clearly labelled, containers. A signed and dated letter from your physician describing your medical conditions and medications, including generic names, is also a good idea. If carrying syringes or needles, be sure to have a physician's letter documenting their medical necessity. If you have a heart condition bring a copy of your ECG taken just prior to travelling.

If you happen to take any regular medication bring double your needs in case of loss or theft. In most Southeast Asian countries, except Singapore, you can buy many medications over the counter without a doctor's prescription, but it can be difficult to find some of the newer drugs, particularly the latest antidepressant drugs, blood-pressure medications and contraceptive pills.

INSURANCE

Even if you are fit and healthy, don't travel without health insurance – accidents do happen. Declare any existing medical conditions you have – the insurance company *will* check if your problem is pre-existing and will not cover you if it is undeclared. You may require extra cover for adventure activities such as rock climbing. If your health insurance doesn't cover you for medical expenses abroad, consider getting extra insurance. If you're uninsured, emergency evacuation is expensive, bills of over US$100,000 are not uncommon.

Find out in advance if your insurance plan will make payments directly to providers or reimburse you later for overseas health expenditures. (In many countries doctors expect payment in cash.) Some policies offer lower and higher medical-expense options; the higher ones are chiefly for countries that have extremely high medical costs, such as the USA. You may prefer a policy that pays doctors or hospitals directly rather than you having to pay on the spot and claim later. If you have to claim later, make sure you keep all documentation. Some policies ask you to call back (reverse charges) to a centre in your home country where an immediate assessment of your problem is made.

VACCINATIONS

Specialised travel-medicine clinics are your best source of information; they stock all available vaccines and will be able to give specific recommendations for you and your trip. The doctors will take into account factors such as past vaccination history, the length of your trip, activities you may be undertaking and underlying medical conditions, such as pregnancy.

Most vaccines don't produce immunity until at least two weeks after they're given, so visit a doctor four to eight weeks before departure. Ask your doctor for an International Certificate of Vaccination (otherwise known as the yellow booklet), which will list all the vaccinations you've received.

Recommended Vaccinations

The following vaccinations are those recommended by the World Health Organization (WHO) for travellers to Southeast Asia:

Adult diphtheria and tetanus Single booster recommended if none in the previous 10 years. Side effects include sore arm and fever.

Hepatitis A Provides almost 100% protection for up to a year, a booster after 12 months provides at least another 20 years' protection. Mild side effects such as headache and sore arm occur in 5% to 10% of people.

Hepatitis B Now considered routine for most travellers. Given as three shots over six months. A rapid schedule is also available, as is a combined vaccination with Hepatitis A. Side effects are mild and uncommon, usually headache and sore arm. Lifetime protection occurs in 95% of people.

Measles, mumps and rubella Two doses of MMR required unless you have had the diseases. Occasionally a rash and flu-like illness can develop a week after receiving the vaccine. Many young adults require a booster.

Polio In 2002, no countries in Southeast Asia reported cases of polio. Only one booster required as an adult for lifetime protection. Inactivated polio vaccine is safe during pregnancy.

Typhoid Recommended unless your trip is less than a week and only to developed cities. The vaccine offers around 70% protection, lasts for two to three years and comes as a single shot. Tablets are also available, however the injection is usually recommended as it has fewer side effects. Sore arm and fever may occur.

Varicella If you haven't had chickenpox, discuss this vaccination with your doctor.

These immunisations are recommended for long-term travellers (more than one month) or those at special risk:

Japanese B Encephalitis Three injections in all. Booster recommended after two years. Sore arm and headache are the most common side effects. Rarely, an allergic reaction comprising hives and swelling can occur up to 10 days after any of the three doses.

Meningitis Single injection. There are two types of vaccination: the quadrivalent vaccine gives two to three years' protection; meningitis group C vaccine gives around 10 years' protection. Recommended for long-term backpackers aged under 25.

Rabies Three injections in all. A booster after one year will then provide 10 years' protection. Side effects are rare – occasionally headache and sore arm.

Tuberculosis A complex issue. Adult long-term travellers are usually recommended to have a TB skin test before and after travel, rather than vaccination. Only one vaccine given in a lifetime.

Required Vaccinations

The only vaccine required by international regulations is yellow fever. Proof of vaccination will only be required if you have visited a country in the yellow-fever zone within the six days prior to entering Southeast Asia. If you are travelling to Southeast Asia from Africa or South America you should check to see if you require proof of vaccination.

MEDICAL CHECKLIST

Recommended items for a personal medical kit:

- Antifungal cream, eg Clotrimazole
- Antibacterial cream, eg Muciprocin
- Antibiotic for skin infections, eg Amoxicillin (Clavulanate) or Cephalexin
- Antibiotics for diarrhoea include Norfloxacin or Ciprofloxacin; for bacterial diarrhoea Azithromycin; for giardiasis or amoebic dysentery Tinidazole
- Antihistamine – there are many options, eg Cetrizine for daytime and Promethazine for night
- Antiseptic, eg Betadine
- Antispasmodic for stomach cramps, eg Buscopa
- Contraceptives
- Decongestant, eg Pseudoephedrine
- DEET-based insect repellent
- Diarrhoea – consider an oral rehydration solution (eg Gastrolyte), diarrhoea 'stopper' (eg Loperamide) and antinausea medication (eg Prochlorperazine)
- First-aid items such as scissors, Elastoplasts, bandages, gauze, thermometer (but not mercury), sterile needles and syringes, safety pins and tweezers
- Ibuprofen or another anti-inflammatory
- Indigestion medication, eg Quick Eze or Mylanta

- Iodine tablets (unless you are pregnant or have a thyroid problem) to purify the water
- Laxative, eg Coloxyl
- Migraine sufferer – take along your personal medicine
- Paracetamol
- Permethrin to impregnate clothing and mosquito nets
- Steroid cream for allergic/itchy rashes, eg 1% to 2% hydrocortisone
- Sunscreen and hat
- Throat lozenges
- Thrush (vaginal yeast infection) treatment, eg Clotrimazole pessaries or Diflucan tablet
- Ural or equivalent if you are prone to urine infections

INTERNET RESOURCES

There is a wealth of travel-health advice on the Internet. For further information, **Lonely Planet** (www.lonelyplanet.com) is a good place to start. *International Travel & Health* is a superb book published by WHO (www.who .int/ith), which is revised annually and is available online at no cost. Another website of general interest is **MD Travel Health** (www .mdtravelhealth.com), which provides complete travel-health recommendations for every country and is updated daily. The **Centers for Disease Control and Prevention** (CDC; www.cdc.gov) website also has good general information.

FURTHER READING

Lonely Planet's *Healthy Travel – Asia & India* is a handy pocket-size book that is packed with useful information including pretrip planning, emergency first aid, immunisation and disease information and what to do if you get sick on the road. Other recommended references include *Traveller's Health* by Dr Richard Dawood and *Travelling Well* by Dr Deborah Mills – check out the website www.travellingwell.com.au.

IN TRANSIT

DEEP VEIN THROMBOSIS

Deep vein thrombosis (DVT) occurs when blood clots form in the legs during plane flights, chiefly because of prolonged immobility. The longer the flight, the greater the risk. Though most blood clots are re-absorbed uneventfully, some may break off and travel through the blood vessels to the lungs, where they may cause life-threatening complications.

The chief symptom of DVT is swelling or pain of the foot, ankle, or calf, usually but not always on just one side. When a blood clot travels to the lungs, it may cause chest pain and difficulty in breathing. Travellers with any of these symptoms should immediately seek medical attention.

To prevent the development of DVT on long flights you should walk about the cabin, perform isometric compressions of the leg muscles (ie contract the leg muscles while sitting), drink plenty of fluids (nonalcoholic) and avoid tobacco.

JET LAG & MOTION SICKNESS

Jet lag is common when crossing more than five time zones; it results in insomnia, fatigue, malaise or nausea. To avoid jet lag try drinking plenty of fluids (nonalcoholic) and eating light meals. Upon arrival, seek exposure to natural sunlight and readjust your schedule (for meals, sleep etc) as soon as possible.

Antihistamines such as dimenhydrinate (Dramamine) and meclizine (Antivert, Bonine) are usually the first choice for treating motion sickness. Their main side effect is drowsiness. A herbal alternative is ginger, which works like a charm for some people.

IN THAILAND

AVAILABILITY OF HEALTHCARE

Most large cities in Thailand now have clinics catering specifically to travellers and expats. These clinics are usually more expensive than local medical facilities, but are worth using, as they will offer a superior standard of care. Additionally they understand the local system, and are aware of the safest local hospitals and best specialists. They can also liaise with insurance companies should you require evacuation. Clinics are listed under Information in the city sections of this book.

It is difficult to find reliable medical care in rural areas. Your embassy and insurance company are also good contacts.

Self-treatment may be appropriate if your problem is minor (eg traveller's diarrhoea), you are carrying the appropriate medication and you cannot attend a recommended clinic. If you think you may have a serious disease, especially malaria, do not waste time – travel to the nearest quality facility to receive attention. It is always better to be assessed by a doctor than to rely on self-treatment.

Buying medication over the counter is not recommended, because fake medications and poorly stored or out-of-date drugs are common.

INFECTIOUS DISEASES

Cutaneous Larva Migrans
This disease, caused by dog hookworm, is particularly common on the beaches of Thailand. The rash starts as a small lump, then slowly spreads in a linear fashion. It is intensely itchy, especially at night. It is easily treated with medications and should not be cut out or frozen.

Dengue Fever
This mosquito-borne disease is becoming increasingly problematic throughout Southeast Asia, especially in the cities. As there is no vaccine available it can only be prevented by avoiding mosquito bites. The mosquito that carries dengue bites day and night, so use insect-avoidance measures at all times. Symptoms include high fever, severe headache and body aches (dengue was previously known as 'breakbone fever'). Some people develop a rash and experience diarrhoea. The southern islands of Thailand are particularly high risk. There is no specific treatment, just rest and paracetamol – do not take aspirin as it increases the likelihood of haemorrhaging. See a doctor to be diagnosed and monitored.

Filariasis
A mosquito-borne disease that is very common in the local population, yet very rare in travellers. Mosquito-avoidance measures are the best way to prevent this disease.

Hepatitis A
A problem throughout the region, this food- and water-borne virus infects the liver, causing jaundice (yellow skin and eyes), nausea and lethargy. There is no specific treatment for hepatitis A, you just need to allow time for the liver to heal. All travellers to South-

east Asia should be receive a vaccination against hepatitis A.

Hepatitis B
The only sexually transmitted disease (STD) that can be prevented by vaccination, hepatitis B is spread by body fluids, including sexual contact. In some parts of Southeast Asia up to 20% of the population are carriers of hepatitis B, and usually are unaware of this. The long-term consequences can include liver cancer and cirrhosis.

Hepatitis E
Hepatitis E is transmitted through contaminated food and water and has similar symptoms to hepatitis A, but is far less common. It is a severe problem in pregnant women and can result in the death of both mother and baby. There is currently no vaccine, and prevention is by following safe eating and drinking guidelines.

HIV
HIV is now one of the most common causes of death in people under the age of 50 in Thailand. Heterosexual sex is now the main method of transmission in these countries.

Influenza
Present year-round in the tropics, influenza (flu) symptoms include high fever, muscle aches, runny nose, cough and sore throat. It can be very severe in people over the age of 65 or in those with underlying medical conditions such as heart disease or diabetes; vaccination is recommended for these individuals. There is no specific treatment, just rest and paracetamol.

Japanese B Encephalitis
While a rare disease in travellers, at least 50,000 locals are infected each year. This viral disease is transmitted by mosquitoes. Most cases occur in rural areas and vaccination is recommended for travellers spending more than one month outside of cities. There is no treatment, and a third of infected people will die while another third will suffer permanent brain damage. Thailand is a high-risk area.

Leptospirosis
Leptospirosis is most often contracted after river rafting or canyoning. Early symptoms

are very similar to the flu and include headache and fever. It can vary from a very mild ailment to a fatal disease. Diagnosis is made through blood tests and it is easily treated with Doxycycline.

Malaria

For such a serious and potentially deadly disease, there is an enormous amount of misinformation concerning malaria. You must get expert advice as to whether your trip actually puts you at risk. Many parts of Southeast Asia, particularly city and resort areas, have minimal to no risk of malaria, and the risk of side effects from the tablets may outweigh the risk of getting the disease. For most rural areas, however, the risk of contracting the disease far outweighs the risk of any tablet side effects. Remember that malaria can be fatal. Before you travel, seek medical advice on the right medication and dosage for you.

Malaria is caused by a parasite transmitted by the bite of an infected mosquito. The most important symptom of malaria is fever, but general symptoms such as headache, diarrhoea, cough or chills may also occur. A diagnosis can only be made by taking a blood sample.

Two strategies should be combined to prevent malaria – mosquito avoidance, and antimalarial medications. Most people who catch malaria are taking inadequate or no antimalarial medication.

Travellers are advised to prevent mosquito bites by taking these steps:

- Use a DEET-containing insect repellent on exposed skin. Wash this off at night, as long as you are sleeping under a mosquito net. Natural repellents such as citronella can be effective, but must be applied more frequently than products containing DEET.
- Sleep under a mosquito net impregnated with Permethrin.
- Choose accommodation with screens and fans (if not air-conditioned).
- Impregnate clothing with Permethrin in high-risk areas.
- Wear long sleeves and trousers in light colours.
- Use mosquito coils.
- Spray your room with insect repellent before going out for your evening meal.

There are a variety of medications available:

Artesunate Derivatives of Artesunate are not suitable as a preventive medication. They are useful treatments under medical supervision.

Chloroquine and Paludrine The effectiveness of this combination is now limited in most of Southeast Asia. Common side effects include nausea (40% of people) and mouth ulcers. Generally not recommended.

Doxycycline This daily tablet is a broad-spectrum antibiotic that has the added benefit of helping to prevent a variety of tropical diseases, including leptospirosis, tick-borne disease, typhus and meliodosis. The potential side effects include photosensitivity (a tendency to sunburn), thrush in women, indigestion, heartburn, nausea and interference with the contraceptive pill. More serious side effects include ulceration of the oesophagus – you can help prevent this by taking your tablet with a meal and a large glass of water, and never lying down within half an hour of taking it. Must be taken for four weeks after leaving the risk area.

Lariam (Mefloquine) Lariam has received much bad press; some of it justified, some not. This weekly tablet suits many people. Serious side effects are rare but include depression, anxiety, psychosis and having fits. Anyone with a history of depression, anxiety, other psychological disorder or epilepsy should not take Lariam. It is considered safe in the second and third trimesters of pregnancy. It is around 90% effective in most parts of Southeast Asia, but there is significant resistance in parts of northern Thailand, Laos and Cambodia. Tablets must be taken for four weeks after leaving the risk area.

Malarone This new drug is a combination of Atovaquone and Proguanil. Side effects are uncommon and mild, most commonly nausea and headache. It is the best tablet for scuba divers and for those on short trips to high-risk areas. It must be taken for one week after leaving the risk area.

A final option is to take no preventive medication but to have a supply of emergency medication should you develop the symptoms of malaria. This is less than ideal, and you'll need to get to a good medical facility within 24 hours of developing a fever. If you choose this option the most effective and safest treatment is Malarone (four tablets once daily for three days). Other options include Mefloquine and Quinine but the side effects of these drugs at treatment doses make them less desirable. Fansidar is no longer recommended.

Measles

Measles remains a problem in some parts of Southeast Asia. This highly contagious bacterial infection is spread through coughing and sneezing. Most people born before 1966 are immune as they had the disease in childhood. Measles starts with a high fever and rash and can be complicated by pneumonia and brain disease. There is no specific treatment.

Meliodosis

This infection is contracted by skin contact with soil. It is rare in travellers, but in some parts of northeast Thailand up to 30% of the local population are infected. The symptoms are very similar to those experienced by tuberculosis (TB) sufferers. There is no vaccine but it can be treated with medications.

Rabies

This uniformly fatal disease is spread by the bite or lick of an infected animal – most commonly a dog or monkey. You should seek medical advice immediately after any animal bite and commence post-exposure treatment. Having a pretravel vaccination means the post-bite treatment is greatly simplified. If an animal bites you, gently wash the wound with soap and water, and apply iodine-based antiseptic. If you are not prevaccinated you will need to receive rabies immunoglobulin as soon as possible.

STDs

Sexually transmitted diseases most common in Thailand include herpes, warts, syphilis, gonorrhoea and chlamydia. People carrying these diseases often have no signs of infection. Condoms will prevent gonorrheae and chlamydia but not warts or herpes. If after a sexual encounter you develop any rash, lumps, discharge or pain when passing urine seek immediate medical attention. If you have been sexually active during your travels have an STD check on your return home.

Strongyloides

This parasite, also transmitted by skin contact with soil, is common in Thailand but rarely affects travellers. It is characterised by an unusual skin rash called *larva currens* – a linear rash on the trunk which comes and goes. Most people don't have other symptoms until their immune system becomes severely suppressed, when the parasite can cause an overwhelming infection. It can be treated with medications.

Tuberculosis

While rare in travellers, medical and aid workers and long-term travellers who have significant contact with the local population should take precautions. Vaccination is usually only given to children under the age of five, but adults at risk are recommended pre- and post-travel TB testing. The main symptoms are fever, cough, weight loss, night sweats and tiredness.

Typhoid

This serious bacterial infection is spread via food and water. It gives a high and slowly progressive fever, headache and may be accompanied by a dry cough and stomach pain. It is diagnosed by blood tests and treated with antibiotics. Vaccination is recommended for all travellers spending more than a week in Thailand, or travelling outside of the major cities. Be aware that vaccination is not 100% effective so you must still be careful with what you eat and drink.

Typhus

Murine typhus is spread by the bite of a flea whereas scrub typhus is spread via a mite. These diseases are rare in travellers. Symptoms include fever, muscle pains and a rash. You can avoid these diseases by following general insect-avoidance measures. Doxycycline will also prevent them.

TRAVELLER'S DIARRHOEA

Traveller's diarrhoea is by far the most common problem affecting travellers – between 30% and 50% of people will suffer from it within two weeks of starting their trip. In over 80% of cases, traveller's diarrhoea is caused by a bacteria (there are numerous potential culprits), and therefore responds promptly to treatment with antibiotics. Treatment with antibiotics will depend on your situation – how sick you are, how quickly you need to get better, where you are etc.

Traveller's diarrhoea is defined as the passage of more than three watery bowel movements within 24 hours, plus at least one other symptom such as vomiting, fever, cramps, nausea or feeling generally unwell.

Treatment consists of staying well hydrated; rehydration solutions like Gastrolyte are the best for this. Antibiotics such as Norfloxacin, Ciprofloxacin or Azithromycin will kill the bacteria quickly.

Loperamide is just a 'stopper' and doesn't get to the cause of the problem. It can be helpful, for example if you have to go on a long bus ride. Don't take Loperamide if you have a fever, or blood in your stools. Seek medical attention quickly if you do not respond to an appropriate antibiotic.

Amoebic Dysentery

Amoebic dysentery is very rare in travellers but is often misdiagnosed by poor-quality labs in Southeast Asia. Symptoms are similar to bacterial diarrhoea, ie fever, bloody diarrhoea and generally feeling unwell. You should always seek reliable medical care if you have blood in your diarrhoea. Treatment involves two drugs; Tinidazole or Metroniadzole to kill the parasite in your gut and then a second drug to kill the cysts. If left untreated complications such as liver or gut abscesses can occur.

Giardiasis

Giardia lamblia is a parasite that is relatively common in travellers. Symptoms include nausea, bloating, excess gas, fatigue and intermittent diarrhoea. 'Eggy' burps are often attributed solely to giardiasis, but work in Nepal has shown that they are not specific to this infection. The parasite will eventually go away if left untreated but this can take months. The treatment of choice is Tinidazole, with Metronidazole being a second-line option.

ENVIRONMENTAL HAZARDS
Air Pollution

Air pollution, particularly vehicle pollution, is an increasing problem in most of Southeast Asia's major cities. If you have severe respiratory problems speak with your doctor before travelling to any heavily polluted urban centres. This pollution can also cause minor respiratory problems such as sinusitis, dry throat and irritated eyes. If you are troubled by the pollution leave the city for a few days and get some fresh air.

Diving

Divers and surfers should seek specialised advice before they travel to ensure their medical kit contains treatment for coral cuts and tropical ear infections, as well as the standard problems. Divers should ensure their insurance covers them for decompression illness – get specialised dive insurance through an organisation such as **Divers Alert Network** (DAN; www.danseap.org). Have a dive medical before you leave your home country – there are certain medical conditions that are incompatible with diving and economic considerations may override health considerations for some dive operators in Thailand.

Food

Eating in restaurants is the biggest risk factor for contracting traveller's diarrhoea. Ways to avoid it include eating only freshly cooked food, avoiding shellfish and food that has been sitting around in buffets. Peel all fruit, cook vegetables, and soak salads in iodine water for at least 20 minutes. Eat in busy restaurants with a high turnover of customers.

Heat

Many parts of Thailand are hot and humid throughout the year. For most people it takes at least two weeks to adapt to the hot climate. Swelling of the feet and ankles is common, as are muscle cramps caused by excessive sweating. Prevent these by avoiding dehydration and excessive activity in the heat. Take it easy when you first arrive. Don't eat salt tablets (they aggravate the gut) but drinking rehydration solution or eating salty food helps. Treat cramps by stopping activity, resting, rehydrating with double-strength rehydration solution and gently stretching.

Dehydration is the main contributor to heat exhaustion. Symptoms include feeling weak, headache, irritability, nausea or vomiting, sweaty skin, a fast, weak pulse and a normal or slightly elevated body temperature. Treatment involves getting out of the heat and/or sun, fanning the victim and applying cool wet cloths to the skin, laying the victim flat with their legs raised and rehydrating with water containing ¼ teaspoon of salt per litre. Recovery is usually rapid and it is common to feel weak for some days afterwards.

Heat stroke is a serious medical emergency. Symptoms come on suddenly and include weakness, nausea, a hot dry body with a body temperature of over 41°C, dizziness, confusion, loss of co-ordination, fits and eventually collapse and loss of consciousness. Seek medical help and commence cooling by getting the person out of the heat, removing their clothes, fanning them and applying cool wet cloths or ice to their body, especially to the groin and armpits.

Prickly heat is a common skin rash in the tropics, caused by sweat being trapped under the skin. The result is an itchy rash of tiny lumps. Treat by moving out of the heat and into an air-conditioned area for a few hours and by having cool showers. Creams and ointments clog the skin so they should be avoided. Locally bought prickly-heat powder can be helpful.

Tropical fatigue is common in long-term expats based in the tropics. It's rarely due to disease and is caused by the climate, inadequate mental rest, excessive alcohol intake and the demands of daily work in a different culture.

Insect Bites & Stings

Bedbugs don't carry disease but their bites are very itchy. They live in the cracks of furniture and walls and then migrate to the bed at night to feed on you. You can treat the itch with an antihistamine. Lice inhabit various parts of your body but most commonly your head and pubic area. Transmission is via close contact with an infected person. They can be difficult to treat and you may need numerous applications of an antilice shampoo such as Permethrin. Pubic lice are usually contracted from sexual contact.

Ticks are contracted when walking in rural areas. Ticks are commonly found behind the ears, on the belly and in armpits. If you have had a tick bite and experience symptoms such as a rash at the site of the bite or elsewhere, fever or muscle aches you should see a doctor. Doxycycline prevents tick-borne diseases.

Leeches are found in humid rainforest areas. They do not transmit any disease but their bites are often intensely itchy for weeks afterwards and can easily become infected. Apply an iodine-based antiseptic to any leech bite to help prevent infection.

Bee and wasp stings mainly cause problems for people who are allergic to them. Anyone with a serious bee or wasp allergy should carry an injection of adrenaline (eg an Epipen) for emergency treatment. For others, pain is the main problem – apply ice to the sting and take painkillers.

Most jellyfish in Southeast Asian waters are not dangerous, just irritating. First-aid for jellyfish stings involves pouring vinegar onto the affected area to neutralise the poison. Do not rub sand or water onto the stings. Take painkillers, and anyone who feels ill in any way after being stung should seek medical advice. Take local advice if there are dangerous jellyfish around and keep out of the water.

Parasites

Numerous parasites are common in local populations in Southeast Asia; but most of these are rare in travellers. The two rules to follow if you wish to avoid parasitic infections are to wear shoes and to avoid eating raw food, especially fish, pork and vegetables. A number of parasites are transmitted via the skin by walking barefoot including strongyloides, hookworm and cutaneous *larva migrans*.

Skin Problems

Fungal rashes are common in humid climates. Two common fungal rashes affect travellers. The first occurs in moist areas that get less air such as the groin, armpits and between the toes. It starts as a red patch that slowly spreads and is usually itchy. Treatment involves keeping the skin dry, avoiding chafing and using an antifungal cream such as Clotrimazole or Lamisil. *Tinea versicolor* is also common – this fungus causes small and light-coloured patches, most commonly on the back, chest and shoulders. Consult a doctor.

Cuts and scratches become easily infected in humid climates. Take meticulous care of any cuts and scratches to prevent complications such as abscesses. Immediately wash all wounds in clean water and apply antiseptic. If you develop signs of infection (increasing pain and redness) see a doctor. Divers and surfers should be particularly careful with coral cuts as they easily become infected.

Snakes

Thailand is home to many species of both poisonous and harmless snakes. Assume all snakes are poisonous and never try to catch one. Always wear boots and long pants if walking in an area that may have snakes. First aid in the event of a snake bite involves pressure immobilisation via an elastic bandage firmly wrapped around the affected limb, starting at the bite site and working up towards the chest. The bandage should not be so tight that the circulation is cut off, and the fingers or toes should be kept free so the circulation can be checked. Immobilise the limb with a splint and carry the victim to medical attention. Do not use tourniquets or try to suck the venom out. Antivenin is available for most species.

Sunburn

Even on a cloudy day sunburn can occur rapidly. Always use a strong sunscreen (at least factor 30), making sure to reapply after a swim, and always wear a wide-brimmed hat and sunglasses outdoors. Avoid lying in the sun during the hottest part of the day (10am to 2pm). If you become sunburnt stay out of the sun until you have recovered, apply cool compresses and take painkillers for the discomfort. One per cent hydrocortisone cream applied twice daily is also helpful.

WOMEN'S HEALTH

Pregnant women should receive specialised advice before travelling. The ideal time to travel is in the second trimester (between 16 and 28 weeks), when the risk of pregnancy-related problems are at their lowest and pregnant women generally feel at their best. During the first trimester there is a risk of miscarriage and in the third trimester complications such as premature labour and high blood pressure are possible. It's wise to travel with a companion. Always carry a list of quality medical facilities available at your destination and ensure you continue your standard antenatal care at these facilities. Avoid rural travel in areas with poor transportation and medical facilities. Most of all, ensure travel insurance covers all pregnancy-related possibilities, including premature labour.

Malaria is a high-risk disease in pregnancy. Advice from WHO recommends that pregnant women do *not* travel to those areas with Chloroquine-resistant malaria. None of the more effective antimalarial drugs is completely safe in pregnancy.

Traveller's diarrhoea can quickly lead to dehydration and result in inadequate blood flow to the placenta. Many of the drugs used to treat various diarrhoea bugs are not recommended in pregnancy. Azithromycin is considered safe.

In the urban areas of Southeast Asia, supplies of sanitary products are readily available. Birth-control options may be limited so bring adequate supplies of your own form of contraception. Heat, humidity and antibiotics can all contribute to thrush. Treatment of thrush is with antifungal creams and pessaries such as Clotrimazole. A practical alternative is a single tablet of fluconazole (Diflucan). Urinary-tract infections can be precipitated by dehydration or long bus journeys without toilet stops; bring suitable antibiotics.

TRADITIONAL MEDICINE

Traditional medical systems are practised widely throughout Southeast Asia. There is a big difference between these traditional healing systems and 'folk' medicine. Folk remedies should be avoided, as they often involve rather dubious procedures with potential complications. In comparison, traditional healing systems such as traditional Chinese medicine are well respected, and aspects of them are being increasingly used by Western medical practitioners.

All traditional Asian medical systems identify a vital life force, and see blockage or imbalance as causing disease. Techniques such as herbal medicines, massage and acupuncture are used to bring this vital force back into balance, or to maintain balance. These therapies are best used for treating chronic disease such as chronic fatigue, arthritis, irritable bowel syndrome and some chronic skin conditions. Traditional medicines should be avoided for treating serious acute infections such as malaria.

Be aware that 'natural' doesn't always mean 'safe', and there can be drug interactions between herbal medicines and Western medicines. If you are using both systems ensure you inform both practitioners what the other has prescribed.

Language

CONTENTS

Learning some Thai is indispensable for travel in the kingdom; naturally, the more you pick up, the closer you get to Thailand's culture and people. There are so few foreigners who speak Thai in Thailand that it doesn't take much to impress most Thais with a few words in their own language.

Your first attempts to speak Thai will probably meet with mixed success, but keep trying. Listen closely to the way the Thais themselves use the various tones – you'll catch on quickly. Don't let laughter at your linguistic forays discourage you; this apparent amusement is really an expression of appreciation. Travellers are particularly urged to make the effort to meet Thai college and university students. Thai students are, by and large, eager to meet visitors from other countries. They will often know some English, so communication isn't as difficult as it may be with shop owners, civil servants etc, and they're generally willing to teach you useful Thai words and phrases.

DIALECTS

Thailand's official language is effectively the dialect spoken and written in central

Thailand, which has successfully become the lingua franca of all Thai and non-Thai ethnic groups in the kingdom.

All Thai dialects are members of the Thai half of the Thai-Kadai family of languages. As such, they're closely related to languages spoken in Laos (Lao, northern Thai, Thai Lü), northern Myanmar (Shan, northern Thai), north western Vietnam (Nung, Tho), Assam (Ahom) and pockets of south China (Zhuang, Thai Lü). Modern Thai linguists recognise four basic dialects within Thailand: Central Thai (spoken as a first dialect through central Thailand and throughout the country as a second dialect); Northern Thai (spoken from Tak Province north to the Myanmar border); Northeastern Thai (northeastern provinces towards the Lao and Cambodian borders); and Southern Thai (from Chumphon Province south to the Malaysian border). There are also a number of Thai minority dialects such as those spoken by the Phu Thai, Thai Dam, Thai Daeng, Phu Noi, Phuan and other tribal Thai groups, most of whom reside in the north and northeast.

VOCABULARY DIFFERENCES

Like most languages, Thai distinguishes between 'polite' and 'informal' vocabulary, so that *thaan,* for example, is a more polite everyday word for 'eat' than *kin,* and *sǐi·sà* for 'head' is more polite than *hǔa.* When given a choice, it's better to use the polite terms, since these are less likely to lead to unconscious offence.

SCRIPT

The Thai script, a fairly recent development in comparison with the spoken language, consists of 44 consonants (but only 21 separate sounds) and 48 vowel and diphthong possibilities (32 separate signs). Though learning the alphabet is not difficult, the writing system itself is fairly complex, so unless you're planning a lengthy stay in Thailand it should perhaps be foregone in favour of actually learning to speak the language. The names of major places included in this book are given in both Thai and

LANGUAGE

Roman script, so that you can at least 'read' the names of destinations at a pinch, or point to them if necessary.

TONES

In Thai the meaning of a single syllable may be altered by means of different tones – in standard Central Thai there are five: low tone, level or mid tone, falling tone, high tone and rising tone. For example, depending on the tone, the syllable *mai* can mean 'new', 'burn', 'wood', 'not?' or 'not'; ponder the phrase *mái mài mâi mâi mǎi* (New wood doesn't burn, does it?) and you begin to appreciate the importance of tones in spoken Thai. This makes it a rather tricky language to learn at first, especially for those of us unaccustomed to the concept of tones. Even when we 'know' what the correct tone in Thai should be, our tendency to denote emotion, verbal stress, the interrogative etc through tone modulation often interferes with producing the correct tone. Therefore the first rule in learning to speak Thai is to divorce emotions from your speech, at least until you've learned the Thai way to express them without changing essential tone value.

The following is visual representation in chart form to show relative tone values:

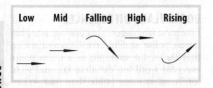

Low	Mid	Falling	High	Rising

Below is a brief attempt to explain the tones. The only way to really understand the differences is by listening to a native or fluent non-native speaker. The range of all five tones is relative to each speaker's vocal range so there is no fixed 'pitch' intrinsic to the language.

low tone – 'flat' like the mid tone, but pronounced at the relative bottom of one's vocal range. It is low, level and with no inflection, eg *bàat* (baht – the Thai currency).

level or mid tone – pronounced 'flat', at the relative middle of the speaker's vocal range, eg *dii* (good); no tone mark is used.

falling tone – sounds as if you are emphasising a word, or calling someone's name from afar, eg *mâi* (no/not).

high tone – usually the most difficult for Westerners. It is pronounced near the relative top of the vocal range, as level as possible, eg *máa* (horse).

rising tone – sounds like the inflection used by English speakers to imply a question – 'Yes?', eg *sǎam* (three).

PRONUNCIATION

The following is a guide to the phonetic system that's been used for the words and phrases in this chapter (and throughout the rest of the book when transcribing directly from Thai). It's based on the Royal Thai General System (RTGS). The dots indicate syllable breaks within words.

Consonants

The majority of consonants correspond closely to their English counterparts. Here are a few exceptions:

k   as the 'k' in 'skin'; similar to the 'g' in 'good', but unaspirated (ie with no accompanying puff of air); similar to English 'g' but unvoiced (ie with no vibration in the vocal chords)

p   as the 'p' in 'stopper', unvoiced and unaspirated (not like the 'p' in 'put'); actually sounds closer to an English 'b', its voiced equivalent

t   as the 't' in 'forty', unaspirated; similar to 'd' but unvoiced

kh   as the 'k' in 'kite', aspirated (ie with an audible puff of air)

ph   as the 'p' in 'pie', aspirated (not to be confused with the 'ph' in 'phone')

th   as the 't' in 'tie', aspirated

ng   as the 'nging' in 'singing'; can occur as an initial consonant (practise by saying 'singing' without the 'si')

r   similar to the 'r' in 'run' but flapped (ie the tongue touches palate); in everyday speech often pronounced like 'l'

Vowels

i   as the 'i' in 'it'

ii   as the 'ee' in 'feet'

ai   as the 'i' in 'pipe'

aa   as the 'a' in 'father'

a   half as long as **aa**, as the 'a' in 'about'

ae   as the 'a' in 'bat' or 'tab'

e   as the 'e' in 'hen'

eh   as the 'ai' in 'air'

oe   as the 'er' in 'fern' (without the 'r' sound)

u   as the 'u' in 'put'
uu   as the 'oo' in 'food'
eu   as the 'u' in 'fur' (without the 'r' sound)
ao   as the 'ow' in 'now'
aw   as the 'aw' in 'jaw' or 'prawn'
o   as the 'o' in 'bone'
oh   as the 'o' in 'toe'
eua   a combination of **eu** and **a**
ia   as 'ee-ya', or as the 'ie' in French *rien*
ua   as the 'our' in 'tour'
uay   sounds like 'oo-way'
iu   as the 'ew' in 'new'
iaw   as the 'io' in 'Rio'
aew   like the 'a' in 'cat' followed by a short 'u' as in 'put'
ehw   as 'air-ooh'
awy   as the 'oi' in 'coin'

TRANSLITERATION

Writing Thai in Roman script is a perennial problem – no wholly satisfactory system has yet been devised to assure both consistency and readability. The Thai government uses the RTGS of transcription for official government documents in English and for most highway signs. However, local variations crop up on hotel signs, city street signs, menus and so on in such a way that visitors often become confused. Added to this is the fact that even the government system has its flaws.

Generally, names in this book follow the most common practice or simply copy their Roman script name, no matter what devious process was used in its transliteration! When this transliteration is markedly different from actual pronunciation, the pronunciation is included (according to the system outlined in this chapter) in parentheses after the transliteration. Where no Roman model was available, names have been transliterated phonetically, directly from Thai.

ACCOMMODATION

I'm looking for a ...
phŏm/dì-chăn kam-lang hăa ...
ผม/ดิฉันกำลังหา...

guesthouse
bâan phák/   บ้านพัก/
kèt háo ('guest house')   เกสต์เฮาส์
hotel
rohng raem   โรงแรม

youth hostel
bâan yao·wá·chon   บ้านเยาวชน

Where is a cheap hotel?
rohng raem thîi raa·khaa thùuk yùu thîi năi
โรงแรมที่ราคาถูกอยู่ที่ไหน
What is the address?
thîi yùu keu a·rai
ที่อยู่คืออะไร
Could you write the address, please?
khĭan thîi yùu hâi dâi măi
เขียนที่อยู่ให้ได้ไหม
Do you have any rooms available?
mii hâwng wâang măi?
มีห้องว่างไหม

I'd like (a) ...
tâwng kaan ...
ต้องการ...
bed
tiang nawn   เตียงนอน
single room
hâwng dìaw   ห้องเดี่ยว
double room
hâwng khûu   ห้องคู่
room with two beds
hâwng thîi mii   ห้องที่มีเตียงสองตัว
tiang săwng tua
room with a bathroom
hâwng thîi mii   ห้องที่มีห้องน้ำ
hâwng nám
ordinary room (with fan)
hâwng tham·má·   ห้องมีธรรมดา
daa (mii pát lom)   (มีพัดลม)
to share a dorm
phák nai hăw phák   พักในหอพัก

How much is it ...? *... thâo rai?*   ...เท่าไร?
per night   *kheun lá*   คืนละ
per person   *khon lá*   คนละ

May I see the room?
duu hâwng dâi măi
ดูห้องได้ไหม
Where is the bathroom?
hâwng nám yùu thîi năi
ห้องน้ำอยู่ที่ไหน
I'm/We're leaving today.
chăn/phûak rao jà àwk wan níi
ฉัน/พวกเราจะออกวันนี้

LANGUAGE

toilet	*hâwng sûam*	ห้องส้วม
room	*hâwng*	ห้อง
hot	*ráwn*	ร้อน
cold	*yen*	เย็น
bath/shower	*àap nám*	อาบน้ำ
towel	*phâa chét tua*	ผ้าเช็ดตัว

CONVERSATION & ESSENTIALS

When being polite, the speaker ends his or her sentence with *khráp* (for men) or *khâ* (for women). It is the gender of the speaker that is being expressed here; it is also the common way to answer 'yes' to a question or show agreement.

Hello.
sà·wàt·dii (khráp/khâ) สวัสดี(ครับ/ค่ะ)
Goodbye.
laa kàwn ลาก่อน
Yes.
châi ใช่
No.
mâi châi ไม่ใช่
Please.
kà·rú·naa กรุณา
Thank you.
khàwp khun ขอบคุณ
That's fine. (You're welcome)
mâi pen rai/yin·dii ไม่เป็นไร/ยินดี
Excuse me.
khǎw à-phai ขออภัย
Sorry. (forgive me)
khǎw thôht ขอโทษ
How are you?
sa·bai dii rěu? สบายดีหรือ?
I'm fine, thanks.
sa·bai dii สบายดี
What's your name?
khun chêu à-rai? คุณชื่ออะไร?
My name is ...
phǒm chêu ... (men) ผมชื่อ...
dì·chǎn chêu ... (women) ดิฉันชื่อ...
Where are you from?
maa jàak thîi nǎi มาจากที่ไหน
I'm from ...
maa jàak ... มาจาก...
See you soon.
dǐaw joe kan ná เดี๋ยวเจอกันนะ
I like ...
châwp ... ชอบ...

I don't like ...
mâi châwp ... ไม่ชอบ...
Just a minute.
raw dǐaw รอเดี๋ยว
I/me (for men)
phǒm ผม
I/me (for women)
dì·chǎn ดิฉัน
I/me (informal, men and women)
chǎn ฉัน
you (for peers)
khun คุณ
Do you have ...?
mii ... mǎi?/... mii mǎi? มี...ไหม/...มีไหม?
(I) would like ... (+ verb)
yàak jà ... อยากจะ...
(I) would like ... (+ noun)
yàak dâi ... อยากได้...

DIRECTIONS

Where is (the)...?
... yùu thîi nǎi? ...อยู่ที่ไหน?
(Go) Straight ahead.
trong pai ตรงไป
Turn left.
líaw sáai เลี้ยวซ้าย
Turn right.
líaw khwǎa เลี้ยวขวา
at the corner
trong mum ตรงมุม
at the traffic lights
trong fai daeng ตรงไฟแดง

SIGNS	
ทางเข้า	Entrance
ทางออก	Exit
ที่ติดต่อสอบถาม	Information
เปิด	Open
ปิด	Closed
ห้าม	Prohibited
มีห้องว่าง	Rooms Available
เต็มแล้ว	Full/No Vacancies
สถานีตำรวจ	Police Station
ห้องน้ำ	Toilets
ชาย	Men
หญิง	Women

| behind | *khâang lǎng* | ข้างหลัง |
| in front of | *trong nâa* | ตรงหน้า |

far	*klai*	ไกล
near	*klâi*	ใกล้
not far	*mâi klai*	ไม่ไกล
opposite	*trong khâam*	ตรงข้าม
left	*sáai*	ซ้าย
right	*khwǎa*	ขวา
beach	*chaai hàat*	ชายหาด
bridge	*sà·phaan*	สะพาน
canal	*khlawng*	คลอง
castle	*praa·sàat*	ปราสาท
church	*bòht*	โบสถ์
countryside	*chon·ná·bòt*	ชนบท
hill	*khǎo*	เขา
island	*kàw*	เกาะ
lake	*thá·leh sàap*	ทะเลสาบ
market	*ta·làat*	ตลาด
mountain	*phuu khǎo*	ภูเขา
museum	*phí·phít·thá·phan*	พิพิธภัณฑ์
old city	*meuang kào*	เมืองเก่า
paddy (field)	*(thûng) naa*	(ทุ่ง) นา
palace	*wang*	วัง
pond	*nǎwng/beung*	หนอง/บึง
river	*mâe nám*	แม่น้ำ
sea	*thá·leh*	ทะเล
temple	*wát*	วัด
tower	*hǎw*	หอ
town	*meuang*	เมือง
track	*thaang*	ทาง
village	*(mùu) bâan*	(หมู่) บ้าน
waterfall	*nám tòk*	น้ำตก

HEALTH

I need a (doctor).
  tâwng kaan (mǎw) ต้องการ(หมอ)
dentist
  mǎw fan หมอฟัน
hospital
  rohng phá·yaa·baan โรงพยาบาล
chemist/pharmacy
  ráan khǎi yaa ร้านขายยา
I'm ill.
  chǎn pùay ฉันป่วย
It hurts here.
  jèp trong née เจ็บตรงนี้

I'm pregnant.
  tâng khan láew ตั้งครรภ์แล้ว
I feel nauseous.
  rúu·sèuk khlêun sâi รู้สึกคลื่นไส้
I have a fever.
  pen khâi เป็นไข้
I have diarrhoea.
  tháwng sǐa ท้องเสีย

I'm ...
phǒm/dì·chǎn ...
ผม/ดิฉัน...
  asthmatic
    pen hèut เป็นหืด
  diabetic
    pen rôhk bao wǎan เป็นโรคเบาหวาน
  epileptic
    pen rôhk lom bâa mǔu เป็นโรคลมบ้าหมู

I'm allergic to ...
phǒm/dì·chǎn pháe ...
ผม/ดิฉันแพ้...
  antibiotics
    yaa pà·tì·chii·wa·ná ยาปฏิชีวนะ
  aspirin
    yaa àet·sa·phai·rin ยาแอสไพริน
  penicillin
    yaa phe·ní·sin·lin ยาเพนิซิลลิน
  bees
    phêung ผึ้ง
  peanuts
    thùa lí·sǒng ถั่วลิสง

antiseptic
  yaa khâa chéua ยาฆ่าเชื้อ
aspirin
  yaa kâe pùat ยาแก้ปวด
condoms
  thǔng yaang a·naa·mai ถุงยางอนามัย
contraceptive
  kaan khum kam·nòet การคุมกำเนิด
medicine
  yaa ยา
mosquito coil
  yaa kan yung bàep jùt ยากันยุงแบบจุด
mosquito repellent
  yaa kan yung ยากันยุง
painkiller
  yaa kâe pùat ยาแก้ปวด
sunblock cream
  khriim kan dàet ครีมกันแดด
tampons
  thaem·phawn แทมพอน

EMERGENCIES

Help!
chûay dûay! ช่วยด้วย

There's been an accident.
mii ù·bàt·tì·hèt มีอุบัติเหตุ

I'm lost.
chǎn lǒng thaang ฉันหลงทาง

Go away!
pai sí! ไปซิ

Stop!
yùt! หยุด

Call ...!
rîak ... nàwy เรียก...หน่อย

a doctor *mǎw* หมอ
the police *tam·rùat* ตำรวจ

LANGUAGE DIFFICULTIES

Do you speak English?
khun phûut phaa·sǎa ang·krìt dâi mǎi
คุณพูดภาษาอังกฤษได้ไหม

Does anyone here speak English?
thîi nîi mii khrai bâang thîi phûut phaa·sǎa ang·krìt dâi mǎi
ที่นี่มีใครบ้างที่พูดภาษาอังกฤษได้ไหม

How do you say ... in Thai?
... wâa yàang rai phaa·sǎa thai
...ว่าอย่างไรภาษาไทย

What do you call this in Thai?
nîi phaa·sǎa thai rîak wâa à·rai?
นี่ภาษาไทยเรียกว่าอะไร

What does ... mean?
... plae wâa à·rai
...แปลว่าอะไร

Do you understand?
khâo jai mǎi?
เข้าใจไหม

A little.
nít nàwy
นิดหน่อย

I understand.
khâo jai
เข้าใจ

I don't understand.
mâi khâo jai
ไม่เข้าใจ

Please write it down.
kà·rú·naa khǐan hâi nàwy
กรุณาเขียนให้หน่อย

Can you show me (on the map)?
hâi duu (nai phǎen thîi) dâi mǎi
ให้ดู(ในแผนที่) ได้ไหม

NUMBERS

0	*sǔun*	ศูนย์
1	*nèung*	หนึ่ง
2	*sǎwng*	สอง
3	*sǎam*	สาม
4	*sìi*	สี่
5	*hâa*	ห้า
6	*hòk*	หก
7	*jèt*	เจ็ด
8	*pàet*	แปด
9	*kâo*	เก้า
10	*sìp*	สิบ
11	*sìp-èt*	สิบเอ็ด
12	*sìp-sǎwng*	สิบสอง
13	*sìp-sǎam*	สิบสาม
14	*sìp-sìi*	สิบสี่
15	*sìp-hâa*	สิบห้า
16	*sìp-hòk*	สิบหก
17	*sìp-jèt*	สิบเจ็ด
18	*sìp-pàet*	สิบแปด
19	*sìp-kâo*	สิบเก้า
20	*yîi-sìp*	ยี่สิบ
21	*yîi-sìp-èt*	ยี่สิบเอ็ด
22	*yîi-sìp-sǎwng*	ยี่สิบสอง
30	*sǎam-sìp*	สามสิบ
40	*sìi-sìp*	สี่สิบ
50	*hâa-sìp*	ห้าสิบ
60	*hòk-sìp*	หกสิบ
70	*jèt-sìp*	เจ็ดสิบ
80	*pàet-sìp*	แปดสิบ
90	*kâo-sìp*	เก้าสิบ
100	*nèung ráwy*	หนึ่งร้อย
200	*sǎwng ráwy*	สองร้อย
300	*sǎam ráwy*	สามร้อย
1000	*nèung phan*	หนึ่งพัน
2000	*sǎwng phan*	สองพัน
10,000	*nèung mèun*	หนึ่งหมื่น
100,000	*nèung sǎen*	หนึ่งแสน
one million	*nèung láan*	หนึ่งล้าน
one billion	*phan láan*	พันล้าน

PAPERWORK

name	*chêu*	ชื่อ
nationality	*săn-châat*	สัญชาติ
date of birth	*kòet wan thîi*	เกิดวันที่
place of birth	*kòet thîi*	เกิดที่
sex (gender)	*phêht*	เพศ
passport	*năng-sěu doen*	หนังสือเดิน
	thaang	ทาง
visa	*wii-sâa*	วีซ่า

SHOPPING & SERVICES

I'd like to buy ...
yàak jà séu ... อยากจะซื้อ...

How much?
thâo raí? เท่าไร

How much is this?
nîi thâo raí?/kìi bàat? นี่เท่าไร/กี่บาท

How much is it?
thâo rai เท่าไร

I don't like it.
mâi châwp ไม่ชอบ

May I look at it?
duu dâi mái ดูได้ไหม

I'm just looking.
duu chŏe chŏe ดูเฉยๆ

It's cheap.
raa-khaa thùuk ราคาถูก

It's too expensive.
phaeng koen pai แพงเกินไป

I'll take it.
ao เอา

Can you reduce the price a little?
lót r aa-khaa nàwy dâi mái
ลดราคาหน่อยได้ไหม

Can you come down just a little more?
lót raa-khaa ìik nít-nèung dâi mái
ลดราคาอีกนิดหนึ่งได้ไหม

Do you have something cheaper?
mii thùuk kwàa nîi mái
มีถูกกว่านี้ไหม

Can you lower it more?
lót ìik dâi mái
ลดอีกได้ไหม

How about ... baht?
... bàat dâi mái
...บาทได้ไหม

I won't give more than ... baht.
jà hâi mâi koen ... bàat
จะให้ไม่เกิน...บาท

Do you accept ...?
ráp ... mái รับ...ไหม

  credit cards
  bàt khreh-dìt บัตรเครดิต

  travellers cheques
  chék doen thaang เช็คเดินทาง

more	*ìik*	อีก
more	*mâak khêun*	มากขึ้น
less	*náwy long*	น้อยลง
smaller	*lék kwàa*	เล็กกว่า
bigger	*yài kwàa*	ใหญ่กว่า
too expensive	*phaeng pai*	แพงไป
inexpensive	*thùuk*	ถูก

I'm looking for ...
phŏm/dì-chăn hăa ... ผม/ดิฉันหา...

  a bank
  thá-naa-khaan ธนาคาร

  the church
  bòht khrit โบสถ์คริสต์

  the city centre
  jai klaang meuang ใจกลางเมือง

  the ... embassy
  sà-thăan thûut ... สถานทูต...

  the market
  ta-làat ตลาด

  the museum
  phí-phít-thá-phan พิพิธภัณฑ์

  the post office
  prai-sà-nii ไปรษณีย์

  a public toilet
  hâwng nám ห้องน้ำสาธารณะ
  sǎa-thaa-rá-ná

  a restaurant
  ráan aa-hăan ร้านอาหาร

  the telephone centre
  sǔun thoh-rá-sàp ศูนย์โทรศัพท์

  the tourist office
  sǎm-nák ngaan สำนักงานท่องเที่ยว
  thâwng thîaw

I want to change ...
tâwng kaan lâek ... ต้องการแลก...

  money
  ngoen เงิน

  travellers cheques
  chék doen thaang เช็คเดินทาง

Can I/we change money here?
làek ngoen thîi níi dâi măi
แลกเงินที่นี่ได้ไหม

What time does it open?
ráan pòet kìi mohng
ร้านเปิดกี่โมง

What time does it close?
ráan pìt kìi mohng
ร้านปิดกี่โมง

TIME & DATES

What time is it?
kìi mohng láew? กี่โมงแล้ว?

It's (8 o'clock).
pàet mohng láew แปดโมงแล้ว

When?	*meua·rai*	เมื่อไร
today	*wan níi*	วันนี้
tomorrow	*phrûng níi*	พรุ่งนี้
yesterday	*mêua waan*	เมื่อวาน
Monday	*wan jan*	วันจันทร์
Tuesday	*wan ang·khaan*	วันอังคาร
Wednesday	*wan phút*	วันพุธ
Thursday	*wan phá·réu·hàt*	วันพฤหัสฯ
Friday	*wan sùk*	วันศุกร์
Saturday	*wan săo*	วันเสาร์
Sunday	*wan aa·thít*	วันอาทิตย์
January	*má·ka·raa·khom*	มกราคม
February	*kum·phaa·phan*	กุมภาพันธ์
March	*mii·naa·khom*	มีนาคม
April	*meh·săa·yon*	เมษายน
May	*phréut·sà·phaa·khom*	พฤษภาคม
June	*mí·thù·naa·yon*	มิถุนายน
July	*ka·rák·ka·daa·khom*	กรกฎาคม
August	*sĭng·hăa·khom*	สิงหาคม
September	*kan·yaa·yon*	กันยายน
October	*tù·laa·khom*	ตุลาคม
November	*phréut·sà·jì·kaa·yon*	พฤศจิกายน
December	*than·waa·khom*	ธันวาคม

TRANSPORT
Public Transport
What time does the ... leave?
... jà àwk kìi mohng
...จะออกกี่โมง

What time does the ... arrive?
... jà thĕung kìi mohng
...จะถึงกี่โมง

boat	*reua*	เรือ
bus	*rót meh/*	รถเมล์/
	rót bát	รถบัส
bus (city)	*rót meh*	รถเมล์
bus (intercity)	*rót thua*	รถทัวร์
plane	*khrêuang bin*	เครื่องบิน
train	*rót fai*	รถไฟ

I'd like ...
phŏm/dì·chăn yàak dâi ...
ผม/ดิฉันอยากได้...

a one-way ticket
tŭa thîaw diaw ตั๋วเที่ยวเดียว

a return ticket
tŭa pai klàp ตั๋วไปกลับ

two tickets
tŭa săwng bai ตั๋วสองใบ

1st class
chán nèung ชั้นหนึ่ง

2nd class
chán săwng ชั้นสอง

I'd like a ticket.
yàak dâi tŭa
อยากได้ตั๋ว

I want to go to ...
yàak jà pai ...
อยากจะไป...

The train has been cancelled.
rót fai thùuk yók lôek láew
รถไฟถูกยกเลิกแล้ว

The train has been delayed.
rót fai jà cháa weh·laa
รถไฟจะช้าเวลา

airport
sa·năam bin สนามบิน

bus station
sa·thăa·nii khŏn sòng สถานีขนส่ง

bus stop
pâai rót meh ป้ายรถเมล์

taxi stand
thîi jàwt rót tháek·sîi ที่จอดรถแท็กซี่

train station
sa·thăa·nii rót fai สถานีรถไฟ

platform number
chaan·chaa·laa thîi ชานชาลาที่

ticket office
tûu khǎi tǔa
ตู้ขายตั๋ว

timetable
taa-raang weh-laa
ตารางเวลา

the first
thîi râek
ที่แรก

the last
sùt tháai
สุดท้าย

Private Transport

I'd like to hire a/an ...
phǒm/dì-chǎn yàak châo ...
ผม/ดิฉันอยากเช่า...

  car
  rót yon
  รถยนต์

  4WD
  rót foh wiin
  รถโฟร์วีล

  motorbike
  rót maw·toe·sai
  รถมอเตอร์ไซค์

  bicycle
  rót jàk·kà·yaan
  รถจักรยาน

ROAD SIGNS

ให้ทาง	Give Way
ทางเบี่ยง	Detour
ห้ามเข้า	No Entry
ห้ามแซง	No Overtaking
ห้ามจอด	No Parking
ทางเข้า	Entrance
ห้ามขวางทาง	Keep Clear
เก็บเงินทางด่วน	Toll
อันตราย	Danger
ขับช้าลง	Slow Down
ทางเดียว	One Way
ทางออก	Exit

Is this the road to ...?
thaang níi pai ... mǎi
ทางนี้ไป...ไหม

Where's a service station?
pâm nám man yùu thîi nǎi
ปั๊มปน้ำมันอยู่ที่ไหน

Please fill it up.
khǎw toem hâi tem
ขอเติมให้เต็ม

I'd like (30) litres.
ao (sǎam sìp) lít
เอา(สามสิบ) ลิตร

diesel
nám man soh-lâa
น้ำมันโซล่า

unleaded petrol
nám man rái sǎan tà·kùa
น้ำมันไร้สารตะกั่ว

Can I park here?
jàwt thîi níi dâi mǎi
จอดที่นี่ได้ไหม

How long can I park here?
jàwt thîi níi dâi naan thâo-rai
จอดที่นี่ได้นานเท่าไร

Where do I pay?
jàai ngoen thîi nǎi
จ่ายเงินที่ไหน

I need a mechanic.
tâwng kaan châang
ต้องการช่าง

The car/motorbike has broken down (at ...)
rót/maw·toe·sai sǐa thîi ...
รถ/มอเตอร์ไซค์เสียที่...

The car/motorbike won't start.
rót/maw·toe·sai sa·tàat mâi tìt
รถ/มอเตอร์ไซค์สตาร์ดไม่ติด

I have a flat tyre.
yaang baen
ยางแบน

I've run out of petrol.
mòt nám man
หมดน้ำมัน

I've had an accident.
mii ù·pàt·tì·hèt
มีอุบัติเหตุ

TRAVEL WITH CHILDREN

Is there a/an ...
mii ... mǎi   มี...ไหม

I need a/an ...
tâwng kaan ...   ต้องการ...

  baby change room
  hâwng plìan phâa dèk
  ห้องเปลี่ยนผ้าเด็ก

  car baby seat
  bàw nâng nai rót sǎm·ràp dèk
  เบาะนั่งในรถสำหรับเด็ก

  child-minding service
  baw·rí·kaan líang dèk
  บริการเลี้ยงเด็ก

children's menu
raai kaan ah·hǎan sǎm·ràp dèk
รายการอาหารสำหรับเด็ก
(disposable) nappies/diapers
phâa âwm (bàep chái láew tíng)
ผ้าอ้อม(แบบใช้แล้วทิ้ง)
formula (milk)
nom phǒng sǎm·ràp dèk
นมผงสำหรับเด็ก
(English-speaking) babysitter
phîi líang dèk (thîi phûut phaa·sǎa ang·krìt dâi)
พี่เลี้ยงเด็ก(ที่พูดภาษาอังกฤษได้)
highchair
kâo îi sǔung
เก้าอี้สูง

potty
krà·thǒhn
กระโถน
stroller
rót khěn dèk
รถเข็นเด็ก

Do you mind if I breastfeed here?
jà rang·kìat mǎi thâa jà hâi nom lûuk thîi nîi
จะรังเกียจไหมถ้าจะให้นมลูกที่นี้
Are children allowed?
dèk à·nú·yâht khâo mǎi
เด็กอนุญาตเข้าไหม

Also available from Lonely Planet:
Thai Phrasebook

Glossary

This glossary includes Thai, Pali (P) and Sanskrit (S) words and terms frequently used in this guidebook. For definitions of food and drink terms, see p55.

aahǎan – food

aahǎan pàa – 'jungle food', usually referring to dishes made with wild game

ajahn – *(aajaan)* respectful title for teacher; from the Sanskrit term *acarya*

amphoe – district, the next subdivision down from province; also written *amphur*

amphoe meuang – provincial capital

ao – bay or gulf

AUA – American University Alumni

bàat – a unit of weight equal to 15g; rounded bowl used by monks for receiving almsf ood

baht – *(bàat)* the Thai unit of currency

bai sǐi – sacred thread used by monks or shamans in certain religious ceremonies

ban – *(bâan)* house or village

bàw náam ráwn – hot springs

benjarong – traditional five-coloured Thai ceramics

BKS – Baw Khaw Saw (Thai acronym for the Transport Company)

BMA – Bangkok Metropolitan Authority

bodhisattva (S) – in Theravada Buddhism, the term used to refer to the Buddha during the period before he became the Buddha, including his previous lives

bòt – central sanctuary in a Thai temple used for official business of the Order (Pali: *sangha*) of monks, such as ordinations; from the Pali term uposatha; see also *wíhǎan*

Brahman – pertaining to Brahmanism, an ancient religious tradition in India and the predecessor of Hinduism; not to be confused with 'Brahmin', the priestly class in India's caste system

BTS – Bangkok Transit System (Skytrain); Thai: *rót fai fáa*

CAT – Communications Authority of Thailand

chao leh – sea gypsies; also *chao náam*

chao naa – farmer

chedi – *stupa*

CPT – Communist Party of Thailand

doi – *(dawy)* the word for mountain in the northern regions

faràng – Western, a Westerner

gopura (S) – entrance pavilion in traditional Hindu temple architecture, often seen in Angkor-period temple complexes

hat – *(hàat)* beach; also *chaihàat*

hǎw phǐi – spirit shrine

hǎw trai – a Tripitaka (Buddhist scripture) hall

hâwng – see *hong*

hâwng thǎew – two- or three-storey shophouses arranged side-by-side along a city street

hǐn – stone

hong – *(hâwng)* room; in southern Thailand this refers to semisubmerged island caves

Isan – *(isǎan)* general term used for northeastern Thailand

jâo meuang – political office in traditional Thai societies throughout Southeast Asia; literally 'principality chief'

jataka (P) – *(chaadòk)* stories of the Buddha's previous lives

jiin – Chinese

jiin haw – Yunnanese

kàthoey – transvestites and transsexuals

khaen – reed instrument common in northeastern Thailand

khǎo – hill or mountain

khâo – rice

khlong – *(khlawng)* canal

khǒhn – masked dance-drama based on stories from the *Ramakian*

khon isǎan – the people of northeastern Thailand

KMT – Kuomintang

KNU – Karen National Union

ko – *(kàw)* island; also *koh*

kràbìi-kràbawng – a traditional Thai martial art employing short swords and staves

ku – small *chedi* that is partially hollow and open

kúay hâeng – Chinese-style work shirt

kùtì – meditation hut; a monk's dwelling

lǎem – cape

làk meuang – city pillar, isthmus

lákhon – classical Thai dance-drama

lâo khǎo – 'white spirit', an often homemade brew

lâo thèuan – homemade (ie illegal) liquor

lék – little, small (in size); see also *noi*

lí-keh – Thai folk dance-drama

loi krathong – *(lawy kràthong)* the ceremony celebrated on the full moon of the end of the rainy season

longyi – Burmese sarong

lûuk thûng – Thai country music

mâe chii – Thai Buddhist nun

mâe náam – river

Mahanikai – the larger of the two sects of Theravada Buddhism in Thailand

mahathat – *(máhǎa thâat)* common name for temples containing Buddha relics; from the Sanskrit-Pali term *mahadhatu*

mánohraa – southern Thailand's most popular traditional dance-drama

masjid – *(mátsàyít)* a mosque

mát-mìi – technique of tie-dyeing silk or cotton threads and then weaving them into complex patterns, similar to Indonesian *ikat;* the term also refers to the patterns themselves

mâw hâwm – see *sêua mâw hâwm*

mǎw lam – an Isan musical tradition

mǎwn khwǎan – wedge-shaped pillow popular in northern and northeastern Thailand'

metta (P) – *(mêt-taa)* Buddhist practice of loving-kindness

meuang – city or principality

mondòp – small square, spired building in a *wat;* from Sanskrit *mandapa*

MRTA – Metropolitan Rapid Transit Authority

muay thai – Thai boxing

náam – water

náam tòk – waterfall

naga (P/S) – *(nâak)* a mythical serpentlike being with magical powers

nákhon – city; from the Sanskrit-Pali *nagara*

nǎng – Thai shadow play

něua – north

ngaan thêtsàkaan – festival

nirvana (S) – (Pali: *nibbana,* Thai: *níp-phaan*) in Buddhist teachings, the state of enlightenment; escape from the realm of rebirth

noen – hill

noi – *(náwy)* little, small (amount); also *noy;* see also *lék*

nok – *(nâwk)* outside; outer

paa-té – batik

pàk tâi – southern Thailand

phâa mát-mìi – thick cotton or silk fabric woven from tie-dyed threads

phâakhamáa – piece of cotton cloth worn as a wrap-around by men

phâasîn – same as above for women

phansǎa – 'rains retreat' or Buddhist Lent; a period of three months during the rainy season that is traditionally a time of stricter moral observance for monks and Buddhist lay followers

phǐi – ghost, spirit

phíksù – a Buddhist monk; from the Sanskrit *bhikshu,* Pali *bhikkhu*

phin – small, three-stringed lute played with a large plectrum

phleng khorâat – Khorat folk song

phleng phêua chii-wít – 'songs for life', modern Thai folk music

phrá – an honorific term used for monks, nobility and Buddha images

phrá khrêuang – amulets of monks, Buddhas or deities worn around the neck for spiritual protection; also called *phrá phim*

phrá phuum – earth spirits

phuu khǎo – mountain

phûu yài bâan – village chief

pii-phâat – classical Thai orchestra

PLAT – People's Liberation Army of Thailand

ponglang – *(ponglaang)* northeastern Thai marimba (percussion instrument) made of short logs

prang – *(praang)* Khmer-style tower on temples

prasada – blessed food offered to Hindu or Sikh temple attendees

prasat – *(praasáat)* small ornate building with a cruciform ground plan and needlelike spire, used for religious purposes, located on *wat* grounds; any of a number of different kinds of halls or residences with religious or royal significance

PULO – Pattani United Liberation Organization

râi – an area of land measurement equal to 1600 sq metres

reua hǎang yao – long-tailed boat

reuan thǎew – longhouse

reusǐi – an ascetic, hermit or sage (Hindi: *rishi*)

rót fai fáa – Skytrain

rót fai tâi din – subway, Metro

rót pràp aakàat – air-con vehicle

rót thammádaa – ordinary bus (non air-con) or ordinary train (not rapid or express)

rót thua – tour bus

sǎalaa – open-sided, covered meeting hall or resting place; from Portuguese term *sala,* literally 'room'

sǎamláw – (also written *samlor*) three-wheeled pedicab; see also *túk-túk*

sǎmnák sǒng – monastic centre

sǎmnák wípàtsànaa – meditation centre

samsara (P) – in Buddhist teachings, the realm of rebirth and delusion

sàtaang – A Thai unit of currency; 100 *sàtaang* equals 1 *baht*

sǎwngthǎew – (literally 'two rows') common name for small pick-up trucks with two benches in the back, used as buses/taxis; also written *songthaew*

sěmaa – boundary stones used to consecrate ground used for monastic ordinations

serow – Asian mountain goat

sêua mâw hâwm – blue cotton farmer's shirt

soi – *(sawy)* lane or small street

Songkran – *(sŏngkraan)* Thai New Year, held in mid-April

SRT – State Railway of Thailand

stupa – conical-shaped Buddhist monument used to inter sacred Buddhist objects

sŭan aahăan – outdoor restaurant with any bit of foliage nearby; literally 'food garden'

sù-săan – cemetery

tâi – south

tàlàat náam – floating market

tambon – precinct, next subdivision below *amphoe;* also written *tambol*

TAT – Tourism Authority of Thailand

tha – *(thâa)* pier, landing

thâat – four-sided, curvilinear Buddhist reliquary, common in northeastern Thailand; also *that*

thâat kràdùuk – bone reliquary, a small *stupa* containing remains of a Buddhist devotee

THAI – Thai Airways International

thâm – cave

tham bun – to make merit

thammájàk – Buddhist wheel of law; from the Pali *dhammacakka*

Thammayut – one of the two sects of Theravada Buddhism in Thailand; founded by King Rama IV while he was still a monk

thâm reusĭi – hermit cave

thànŏn – street

thêtsàbaan – a division in towns or cities much like 'municipality'

thúdong – a series of 13 ascetic practices, for example eating one meal a day, living at the foot of a tree, under-

taken by Buddhist monks; a monk who undertakes such practices; a period of wandering on foot from place to place undertaken by monks

tràwk – alley; also *trok*

trimurti – collocation of the three principal Hindu deities, Brahma, Shiva and Vishnu

Tripitaka (S) – Theravada Buddhist scriptures; (Pali: Tipitaka)

túk-túk – motorised *sǎamláw*

ùtsànìt – flame-shaped head ornament on a Buddha

Vipassana – *(wípàtsànaa)* Buddhist insight meditation

wâi – palms-together Thai greeting

wan phrá – Buddhist holy days, falling on the days of the main phases of the moon (full, new and half) each month

wang – palace

wat – temple-monastery; from the Pali term *avasa* meaning 'monk's dwelling'

wát pàa – forest monastery

wáthánátham – culture

wíhăan – any large hall in a Thai temple, but not the *bòt;* from the Sanskrit term *vihara,* meaning 'dwelling'; also *wihan* or *viharn*

yâam – shoulder bag

yài – big

Yawi – the traditional language of Java, Sumatra and the Malay Peninsula, widely spoken in the most southern provinces of Thailand; the written form uses the classic Arabic script plus five additional letters

Behind the Scenes

THIS BOOK

This 11th edition of *Thailand* was researched and written by Joe Cummings (coordinating author), Becca Blond, Morgan Kohn, Matt Warren and China Williams. Joe, China, Sandra Bao and Steven Martin wrote the previous edition. Also contributing to *Thailand* 11 was Dr Trish Batchelor.

Following the devastating tsunami that struck in December 2004, severely affecting the areas around Phuket, Khao Lak and Ko Phi-Phi, Joe also undertook a revision of the Andaman Coast chapter.

THANKS from the Authors

Joe Cummings

Old friend and advisor Kittiwat Rattanadilok Na Phuket helped out with hard-to-pin-down details on Thai entertainment and tourism law. Thanks to Jerry Hopkins, whose manuscript for *Thailand Confidential* supplied perfectly timed inspiration for diving into this 11th edition of Lonely Planet's *Thailand* with a renewed passion.

Thanks to Lori Ashton and Nima Chandler for helpful hints on classy dining and shopping in Chiang Mai. Suwannee Emon, as usual, filled my head with food visions and helped out with Thai script. Dennis Gilman and Oliver Benjamin provided much-needed palmistry and humour. Thank you Flemming (Slim) Rothaus, Ad Here the 13th, Bebop Café and Heaven Beach for the jams.

Lastly thanks to my co-authors Becca, China, Matt and Morgan for all their hard work, and to commissioning editor Kalya Ryan for her tremendous patience.

Becca Blond

Big thanks to all the Thais and travellers I met on the road, who offered invaluable insights and information. Thanks especially to Marcella, Deirdre and Michelle, who provided plenty of rainy-day entertainment and bar-hopping advice. I also want to thank Joe Cummings for all his advice, Sandra Bao, for giving me excellent research to work from, Kalya Ryan for giving me the job in the first place and everyone else at Lonely Planet. Finally thanks to Aaron, for his constant love and support and putting up with me when I was pulling out my hair on a daily basis. To my family, David, Patricia, Jessica, Jennie and John, you know I'm forever indebted.

Morgan Konn

Much thanks to Joe Cummings, whose previous editions introduced me to Thailand and helped me fall in love with it. Thanks to Mary Neighbour for hiring me and Kalya Ryan for being such a fabulous commissioning editor. Additional gratitude to Aye and Luck for the wedding, Vandana and Tammy for talking story, Noi for masaman curry, Andrew for the motorbike lessons in the rain, Ronny for the bike tour, and to the numerous TAT employees who made my job manageable. And finally, thanks to my family for having let me run off to Thailand the first time. Sorry I made you so worried Dad.

Matt Warren

A huge thank you to everyone I met on the trail, but especially Rebecca for Siren-singing me home, Percy and Kim for...well...you know, Julian for his

---

THE LONELY PLANET STORY

The story begins with a classic travel adventure: Tony and Maureen Wheeler's 1972 journey across Europe and Asia to Australia. There was no useful information about the overland trail then, so Tony and Maureen published the first Lonely Planet guidebook to meet a growing need.

From a kitchen table, Lonely Planet has grown to become the largest independent travel publisher in the world, with offices in Melbourne (Australia), Oakland (USA) and London (UK). Today Lonely Planet guidebooks cover the globe. There is an ever-growing list of books and information in a variety of media. Some things haven't changed. The main aim is still to make it possible for adventurous travellers to get out there – to explore and better understand the world.

At Lonely Planet we believe travellers can make a positive contribution to the countries they visit – if they respect their host communities and spend their money wisely. Every year 5% of company profit is donated to charities around the world.

tireless hospitality, Shirley for the birthday party, David Thompson for the food whirlwind (buy his book *Thai Food* – it's fantastic!), Joe for being a long-suffering boss and the people of Thailand for just about everything else.

China Williams

Thanks to my hubby for his tireless investigation of Bangkok's good food and drink. To Nuan and company for the Chinatown tour, Jean Wu and Daniel Cooney for the Mizu trip, Rafael D Frankel and Susan Keppelman for their respective neighbourhood tips, and Mason and Luka, helpful as always. Final nods to the Bangkok Tourist Bureau, coordinating author Joe Cummings, and talented Lonely Planet staff.

CREDITS

Commissioning Editor Kalya Ryan
Coordinating Editor Yvonne Byron
Coordinating Cartographer Corey Hutchison
Coordinating Layout Vicki Beale
Managing Editor & Thai Language Consultant Bruce Evans
Managing Cartographer Adrian Persoglia
Assisting Editors Jackey Coyle, Kate Evans, Peter Cruttenden, Justin Flynn, Margedd Herliosz, Katrina Webb, Helen Yeates
Assisting Cartographers Barbara Benson, Jacqueline Nguyen, Sarah Sloane, Lyndell Stringer
Project Manager Chris Love
Language Content Coordinator Quentin Frayne

Thanks to Carolyn Boicos, Sally Darmody, Eoin Dunlevy, Jennifer Garrett, Mark Germanchis, Will Gourlay, Rebecca Lalor, Adriana Mammarella, Kate McDonald, Nick Stebbing

THANKS from Lonely Planet

Many thanks to the following travellers who used the last edition and wrote to us with helpful hints, useful advice and interesting anecdotes.

A Talia Abrams, Jan Achten, Kirsty Acmbridge, Harry & Dianne Acosta, Weng Adam, Mark Adams, Rebecca Adams, Jessica Addario, Lauren Alixandra, Alya Al-Khatib, Ron Allen, Jane Allison, Michel Allon, Gretchen Amann, Philip Ampofo, Stephen Amrol, Gyllyan Anderson, Leanne Anderson, Thomas Andersson, V Andoetoe, Colin & Lee Andrews, Martin Angiset, Marius Anholt, Paula Antony, Yella Appleby, Diane Archer, Bunno Arends, Manuela Arigoni, Alexandra Arikoglu, Sally Armitage, Dieter Arnold, Ross Artwohl, Edward Ashby, Damian Ashleigh-Morris, Warren Askew, Nicole Asselin, Matthew Atherfold, Agnes Au, Anette Auch-Schwelk, Maayan Avraham, Racquel Ayers **B** Robert Bachweizen, Peter H Bailey, Chris Bain, Reinier Bakels, Karen Baker, Keith Baker, Julian Ball, Paul Ballard, Tina Bampton, Dolores Banerd, Jim Bangert, Peter Bannarak, Dan Barazani, Kevin Barfoot, Kris Baritt, David Barkshire, Birgitte Barner Madsen, Ida Barner Madsen, John Baron-Crangle, Marg Barr-Brown, Delvaux Bart, Filip Bartholomeeusen, Reinhold Bauer, Nadine Baxter-Smallwood, Cassie Bayly, Katie Bearman, John Beckwell, Liselot Been, David Beer, David Bell, Bart Benders, Maria & Tony Benfield, Mark Benson, Assaf Bental, Petter Bergmark, Megan Berkle, Sarah Bernard, Thomas Bernsen, Fredrik Bertilsson, Allison Bertram, Walter Bertschinger, Rachel Bessey, Nilema Bhakta-Jones, Abdel Bidar, James Bierman, Carie Biggs, Tim Bill, Walt Bilofsky, Niels Bjerg, Robert Black, Nora Blackmore, Dana Blackwell, Heike Blankermann, Noreen Bloch, Suzan Bloemscheer, Andreas Blom, Laura Blom, Stephanie Boehler, Marcus Boehm, Gera Boersma, Traci R Bogan, Tashi Bogner, Petra Bohrn, Patrick Bois, Richard Boiteau, Nathalia Bolliger, Mike Bolton, Jean-Philippe Bombardier, Lilia Bonacorsi, Clausen Boor, Laurie Boost, William Booth, Shona Borevitz, Alexaandre Borione, Jason Borovick, Agnes Borowiec, Erica Borremans, Leah Bower, Victoria Boxall, Ellen Boynton, Keith Bradley, Stan & Shirley Bradshaw, Tom Brailsford, Clare Braithwaite, Peter Braithwaite, Rogier Brand, Terry Braverman, Kelly Brennan, Chantal Brennan-Ryan, Glen Brereton, Ben Bresler, Andy & Claire Brice, Chloe Bridge, Laura Brinkley, Venetia Brissenden, Jack Broeren, Aaron Brown, Angela & Grant Brown, Gary Brown, Jason Brown, Sarah Brown, Thomas Brown, Gale Brownell, Lauren Brunovs, Mary Bryant, Nelli & Carsten Buchberger, Serra Buck, Viktoria Buck, Bruce Buckland, Gil & Ali Burgess, Lindsay Burt, Chuck Burton, Anne Busch, Iwan Bussmann, Biana Buurman, Meredith Byers **C** Elga Caccialanza, Simon Cairns,

Kirsty Cambridge, Martin Caminada, Caroline Cannon, Manuela Cantone, Chris Carey, Philippa Carr, David Carraway, Rusty Cartmill, Matt Casey, Alyssa Cassidy, C Cathcart, Sandy Caust, Sunichai Chaisit, Chirachoke Chakaew, H C Champion, Nellie Chan, James Chard, Keith Charlton, Andrea Chee, Wayne Chen, Eleanor Cheng, Chloe Child, Katie Chin, Kok Keng Chin, Oga Cho, Jennifer Choi, W K Chow, Dispong Chunekamrai, Amanda Clairmont, David Clark, Michael Clark, Garry & Joanna Clarke, Sarah Clarke, Tom Clarkson, Richard Cleaver, Yiola Cleovoulou, Gwyn Cole, Becca Collins, Sharon Collins, Stephen Collins, Wayne Collins, Fabio Colombatto, Ana Maria Comba, Friederike Coninx, Matthew Conn, Annie Connolly, Lauren Conroy, Paul Conti, Amy Cooper, Sue Cooper, Sangmo Copel, Kevin L Corr, Max Cotto, Diana Coulter, Rob Covington, Brian Cox, Brian Crane, Martin Crichton, Luca Criscuoli, Hugh Cropp, Terry Crossley, Ian Cruickshank, Rosalind Csordas, Tomas Cuddihy, Micheal P Curran, Georgie Curtis, Lindarose Curtis, Chris Custer, Tim Cutfield **D** Clive Dale, Mike Daly, Ryan Daly, Hendrik Dammerboer, Sheila Danielson, David Daver, Callum Davey, Juliet Davey, Stuart Davie, Daniel Davies, Joanna Davis, Philippa Davis, Teresa Davis, John Dawson, Guy de Bernard, Martijn de Birk, Georg de Boer, Piet de Boer, George & Maud de Bouter, Marie-Pia de Fauconval Tom de Fonblanque, Gabriele de Gaudenzi, Sanne de Graaf, Bernie de Hoop, Nicole de Rauville, Lenny de Rooy, Barry de Vent, Eduard de Visser, Lisa Dean, Ursula Dear, Nicholas Deeks, Daniel Dees, Robert Delaney, Frans W J Delsing, Helena Demetris, Regine Denaegel, John Denison, Jodi Denman, Richard Desomme, J A Deyes, Sylvia Dick, Corien Dieterman, Fredrik Divall, Anita Dobson, Ron Doering, Aiden Donegal, Sarah Doody, Julia Dorn, John Paul Douglas, John Dowd, Kaya Downs, Anne Doyle, Jeff Doyle, Christian Drees, Kevin Duck, Aoife Duggan, Phyllis Duggan, Alex Dunkley, Dominic Dunne, Karyn Durbin, Jo Duthie, Jo Duxbury **E** Roger Easter, Marianne Eberl, Dafydd Edwards, Justin Egan, Philipp Ehrne, Tania Ekins, Ole Eklöf, Robert Eklund, Ernie Elias-Nieland, Roberto Elini, Petra en Ellen, Richard Ellerbrake, Jennifer Ellinghaus, Martin Ellis, Samantha Elmore, Mark Emmerton, Jo Endersbee, Jordan England, Thomas English, Chris Enman, Nikita Eriksen-Hamel, Matt & Eileen Erskine, Barbaba Erzinger, Charlotte Esquivel, Jorge Estevez, James Evans, William Evans, Joanne Everall **F** Chris Fahey, Bernt Fallenkamp, Sally Fankhauser, Mark Fearon, Anne Feenstra, Karen Ferguson, Antoinette Figliola, Peter Fincham, Margaret Finger, Jennifer Fisher, Robert Flack, Tim Flanagan, Bryce Flannery, Petra Fleck, Desirée Fleer, Edgar Flory, Leanne Fogarty, Cyndy Foley, Damian Ford, Eva Forslund, Martin Foster, Fayette Fox, Elke Franke, Lisa Franseen, Torben Frederiksen, Nicole Freeman, Tim Fricke, Bart Friederichs, Tim Frier, Gilly Frimerman, Kristiran Frish, Frank Froboese, Rudi Fuchs-Boonlert, Andres Fukazawa **G** Josh Gadsden, Beryl Gale, Susanne Galla, Damon Gallagher, Daniela Gambotto, Andrew Garsden, Patrick Gatland, Peter Gause, Torsten Gedicke, John Geisen-Kisch, Sexl Gerhard, Nadia Giannini, Lynn Gibson, Wolfgang Giessen, Michel Gijsman, Jivan Gilad, Sandy Gilbert, David Gilks, Laurence Gimrie, Kfir Gindi, Morris Gindi, Kristina Maria Gjoe, Susanne Glasius, Noah Glassman, Roland Glavan, Jane & Kevin Glover, Ornait Glynn, Richard Glynn, Bart Goedendorp, Jacqueline Goh, Kristel Golsteyn, Johneen Golter-

mann, Sergio & Pinol Gonzalez, Carl Goodman, Tracy Goodrich, Seonai Gordon, Peter Gore-Symes, Fredrick Goss, Ali Goucher, Pascal Goux, Paul Goux, Calixte Govaarts, Jordan Gowanlock, Lauren Graber, Holger Grafen, Katrine Gram-Hansen, Sarah Grams, Tom Greenwood, Brad Griffin, David Griffiths, Konrad Grixti, Markku Grönroos, Lewis Grove, Anna Gurnhill, Andrea Gurtner, Garry R Gustafson **H** Jeroen H, Nathalie Hagestein, Don Fred Hall, Ian Hall, Philodorus Hall, Ross Hall, Rick Hamann, Amanda Hamelink, Emma Hamilton, R G Hamilton, Andrew Hammond, Jackie Hansen, Peder Reinewald Hansen, Poul Hansen, Marcus Hansson, Vicky Harfield, Matt Harris, Richard Harvey, Liza Harwood, Brian K Hastings, Wolfgang Haupt, Dana Hayden, Rory Hayden, Gaston Hayen, Ryan Haynes, Tamlin Heathwood, John B Hee, Mark Heffernan, Herbert Heinze, Andreas Helmbrecht, Philip Heltewig, Ellen Hemmer, Dale Hemphill, Susan Henderson, Aly Hendriks, Alissa Herbst, Bart & Jelle Hergaarden, John Heron, Molly Heron, Freya Herring, Dave Hester, Quentin Hewitt, Doug Hilton, Tuomo Hintikka, Julie Hoar, Brenda Hoare, Richard Hodges, Sebastiaan Hoek, Bill Hoffmann, Henric Höglind, Chuck Hohenstein, Philip Holden, Katy Holiday, Carol Holley, Greg & Sharyon Holness, Christop Holweger, Dee Homans, B J Hoogland, Joe Hookins, Johnson Hoom, Prapanporn Hoono, H H Hopcke, Leon Houpper- mans, Suzanne Houtman, Dina & Patrick Hubbard, Glenn Hucker, Clare Hudson, Thomas Hudson, Wally Hueneke, Janice Huey, Phil Huggan, Lance Hughes, Mark Hunnebell, Cyndi Hunter, Alice Hutchings, Darren Huxley, Lee Hyde, Margaret Hyder **I** Susanne Iff, Tobias Imboden, Saengla Inkaew, Rich Insley, Rebecca Irani, Stephen Ireland, Thomas Iseli, Eksura Issarangoon Na Ayutthaya, Zohar Itzhaki **J** Michael Jack, Diana Jacklich, Sandra Jackson, Sumner Jacobs, Jonas Jacquet, Gaurav Jain, Michael James, Moonhanan Jan, Akom Jareepeerapol, Walter-Nicolet Jean-Christophe, John Jeff, Rae Jenkins, Steve Jenkins, Jeff Jensen, Katie Jervis, Gauti Johannesson, Alec Johnson, Dax Jones, Gary & Graeme Jones, Mark Jones, Marttin Jones, Wally Jones, Joseph Jongen, Wouter Jonkhoff, Jeannie Juster, Gary Justice, Karles Jutila **K** Anne Kabot, William Kaderli, Boris Kaeller, Ichiro Kaizuma, Annika Karlsson, Marli Kaufmann, Maalu Kautonen, Chris Kaye, Theo Keane, Michael Keller, Saffra Kelley, Derek Kelly, Ollie Kelly, Anna Louise Kennard, Alistair Kennedy, Jean Kerr, Jenny Kerr, Stewart Kerr, Birgitte Keulen, David Keyes, Golnoosh Khadivi, Chew Kheng Siong, Karen Kiang, Julia Kijanski, Eugene Kim, Lydia Kim, Ryan King, Ingar Kirkland, Andras Kiss-Horvath, Svein Kjerstad, Willem Klaassen, Roni & Ayala Klaus, Arjan & Mark Klijnsma, Sue Knight, Catherine Koch, Jesse Kocher, Masahiro Kojima, Ivana Kotalova, Alex Kourline, Ben Kraijnbrink, Harald Kraschina, Andea Kraus, Oliver Krause, Jochen Krauss, Ana Kravitz, Marieke Krijnen, Barry & John Kristel, Carla Kriwet, John Kuch, Paul Kuck, Yoshikazu Kunugi, Olli Kupiainen, Bart Kupnicki, Lydia Kuster, Jessie Kutsch **L** Noel Lahart, Martin Laichmann, Meagan Lang, Melle Larky, Fredrik Larsen, Ola Larsson, Madeline Lasko, David Latchford, Joy Lau, Ron & Becky Lau, Andrew Lawson, Susie Lawson, Linda Learmonth, Dennis Lee, Elaine Lee, Jan Lee, Erik Leenders, Bertrand Legeret, Philipp Legert, Alex Legroux, Tom Lehtonen, Tomi Lehtonen, Martin Leiser, Jurgen Leitzke, Olga Leskiw, Brian & Lorna Lewis, Kim Lewitte, Martin Leyrer, Christina

Liljegrenl, Clement Lim, Henry Lim, York Lin, Beth Lincoln, Karin Lindemann, Andreas Lindvall, Eric Linton, Roberto LLamas Ayo, Dennis Lloyd, Kate Logan, Robert Logan, Mun Kwong Loke, Helen Lomas, Rosemary Longmore, Alexander Lorenz, Pierre-Yves Loriers, Sebastien Lorival, Gary Lowe, Thomas Lückmann, Clive Lundquist, Tina Lutz, Mario Luzzi, Derek Lycke, Jessie Lyons, Per Lysedal M Jeff Mabbutt, John Macgregor, Maik Macho, Hannah Mackenzie, Iain Mackie, Jeff Mackinnon, Ian Macpherson, Danielle Mainzer, Alexi Makris, Michaela Malcolm, Frank Malecki, Sundeep Malik, Erika Malitzky, Margarita Malkina, Richard Mandelbaum, Erwin Manise, Julie Marcil, Nicole Marcos, John Mardling, Marilyn Marler, Jette Marquardsen, Alan Marriott, Becky Marsden, Julie Marshall, Paul Marshall, Phillip Marshall, Stéphane Martel, Irmi Martin, Louise Martin, Fran Mason, Roland Massing, Judy Mather, Roger Mattingley, Ken Mays, Patrick McCarter, Keri McCarthy, Catherine McCormick, Rebecca McCourtney, Daniel McEndoo, Larry McGrath, Anna McInnes, Dorothy McKenzie, Derek Mcleod, Bridgett McMillan, Shane McNamara, Kathy McRae, John McTague, Melissa McVee, Marieke Meijer, Stefan Meivers, Jordan Menzies, Helene Mercier, Kimberly Merris, Graham Merry, Andrea Messmer, Sharon Metson, Ingo Meyer, Jeremy Meyer, Anat Michael, Chris Michael, Boismard Michel, Adrienne Michetti, Bridget Milburn, John Miller, Peter Miller, Jay Millington, Michelle Mills, Gavin Milne, Havital Miltz, Nicolas Minuchin, Dennis Mogerman, Gweneth Moir, Marie-Loe Molenaar, Carl Moller, Hans Mommer, Jeremy Moon, Alex Moore, Andrew Moore, Ann Moore, Anthony Moore, Gavin Morgan, Rodney Morgan, Julie Morissette, Alistair Morris, Kristen Morris, Doug Morrow, Julia Morton, Christina Moser, Richard Mott, Stefaan Motte, John S Moynihan, Ian Mudge, Ramen Mukherji, Derek J Muller, Lockhart Murdoch, N Murdoch, Janine Murphy, Patrick Murphy N Jessi Nabuurs, Dan Nadel, Mark Naftalin, Lukas Nardella, Dario Nardi, Jim Naughton, Dale Ne, Rosie Needham, Monique Nerman, Ilya & Tessa Neutjens-Van Iersel, Jason Nevitt, Phil Newsom, Tania Ng, Toan Nguyen, Marketa Niangova, Alex Nicholas, Jesper Nielsen, Trine Maria Nielsen, Han-Wen Nienhuys, Sander Nijboer, Saga Nilsson, Mangla Ningomba, Akane Nishimura, Gerben Nissink, Mary Noble, Hannah Noon, Sean Noonan, Rogier Noort, Fredik Norberg, Ryan Norman, William Normore, Holly North, Helen Nunn, Rosemary Nyabadza O Allison O'Brien, Carol O'Brien, Siobhan O'Brien, Ryan O'Connell, Molly O'Connor, Miriam Oesterreich, Chia-Yen Oh, Kougiro Oishi, Con Oliver, Dax Oliver, Dennis Olsen, Mariska Oosterkamp, Joris Oostveen, Joan Opbroek, Jennifer O'Reilly, Vincent Orsini, Eva Maria Osiander, Ric Ostrower, Jeffrey Overall, Cathie Owen, Dave Owen P Ricardo Padre, Alexandra Paice, Jenny Paley, Marcus Palm, Rachel Palmer, Lex Palmieri, Jara Panan, Phanuphong Paothong, Nicholas Park, Jon Parker, Lee & Cathy Partington, Sarah Paterson, John Paul, Pablo Pecora, Janni Pedersen, John Pederson, Eva Pedrelli, Vera Peerde-man, Ariane Pele, Emily Pelter, Marion Penaud, Santos Penha, Joseph Peterson, Lori Petryk, Kersten Pfund, Suwalak Phanngoen, Andrew Phelan, Tom Phu, Kevin Piddick, Michael Pieffers, Rebecca Pinbergvall, Kate Plahe, Ian Playdon, Gwen Podd, JeeHui Poh, Lee Polson, Diane Porter, Tom Porter, Caroline Pott, Norman F Potter, Richard Potts, Andy Powell, Teerapatt Prapanporn, Janet Preston, Emily Price, Terry & Kathy Price, Dina Priess, Vee Pritch-ards, Thomas Prokopp, Anna Purkey, Catherine Purvis Q Sean Quinn, Colin Quirke R Jason Rabbow, Lisa Radford, Michele Ragazzini, Yanti A Rahman, John Rajeski, Edith Ramster, Sofia Rao, Nynne & Troels Rasmussen, Piyapat Rattanasommbut, Christaina Rauch, Gil Raymond, Johan Razenberg, Kurt Rebry, Brighde Reed, Robbie Reeves, Nita Reguer, Emma Rehal, David Reid, Justin Reid, Liz Reid, Mary Reid, Erik Reif, Eric Remijn, Robin Retherford, Hollie Rich, Marc Richardson, Michael Richie, Scott Rick, Renee Riley, Lawrence Ritchie, Perez Roberto, Ryan Robertson, Irwin Robinson, Vibeke Rochmann, Betty Rodriguez, Michele Roessler, Evan Rogers, Francis Rogers, Joseph Rohm, Uli Ronellenfitsch, Fiona Roscoe, Steffen Rose, Barrett Ross, David Rostron, Keith Rothwell, Charlotte Rottiers, Gail Rowe, Daniel Rozas, Maria Ruiz, Lisa Rumble, Shimon Rumelt, Mark Runge, Krin Rungrojkitiyos, Denise Ruygrok, Sarah Rydl S Martin Sackett, Axel Saffran, Shmueli Saibaba, Tommi Sajankoski, Darren Salter, Dave Salter, Luke Salway, Maura Sammon, Bryan Sanchez, Amanda Sandell, Rowan Sanderson, Fran Sandham, Veronica Santarlasci, Dorothy Savidge, Michele Scarano, Jo Scard, Charles Scarvelli, Ido Schacham, Michael Schäfer, Jeroen Schavemaker, Pauline Scherpenhuysen, Tobias Scheschkowski, Peter Schmid, Heiko Schmitz, Johann Schnaiter, Michael Schofield, Samantha Scholtz, Reuven Schossen, Roland Schreiber, Deborah Schubert, Martin Schuster, Petra & Klaus Schwaiger, Isabelle Scodellaro, Kevin Scott, Jane Seah, Sonja Seitlinger, Malcolm Sell, Tricia Senger, McKinley Nile Sensiw-Bierman, Andrea Serrano, Gavin Sexton, Jeffrey Sexton, Debra Shambrook, Suzie Shao, Bill & Wannee Shaw, Ben Sheehy, Daniel Sher, Noa Sher, Udi Shomer, Jonathan Shrager, Xiem Weh Shun, Ng Yun Sian, Luisa Siccia, Anna Silverlock, Clive Simmons, Roz Simmons, Rudy Simone, Denis Simonnet, David Simpson, Matt Sims, Smriti Singh, Apichan Singhaseni, Edward Singleton, Reto Sinniger, George Sival, Andrew Skowronski, Jeroen Slikker, Steen Slott, Andrew Smart, Ben Smart, Rene Smit, Ben Smith, Casey Smith, Charles O Smith, Heidi Smith, Lisa Smith, Matthew Smith, Maya Smith, Michele Smith, Nathan Smith, Henriette Snijder, Lucien Sno, Carlos Snoeijing, Aity Soekidjo, Mon Soen, Mira Soesanto, Patricia Solar, Nick Soteri, Roger & Ann South, Lindsay Sowers, Richard Sparks, Eva Spies, Amy Spira, Bronwyn Spiteri, Sara Sprong, Flora Sproule, Stony Stall, Joann Steck-Bayat, Janet Stein, Jeremy Stephenson, Samantha Stess, Kristine K Stevens, Rachel Stevens, Alex Stevenson, Brett Stevenson, Diana Stewart, Len Stewart, Charles Stirling, Kewin Stoeckigt, Chris Stoever, John Stone, Peter Storm, Kim Straats, Don Strub, Ragnhild Strxmmen, Mayumi Sugaya, Brandi Supratanapongse, Jacqueline Surin, Jacquelyn Suter, David Sutherland, Ahmed Abdulla Suwaid, Nori Suzuki, Yasunori Suzuki, Anders Svensson, Andrea Swintek T Angie Tahir, Tamara Taling, Kirsten Tan, Sarah Tankard, Caroline Tasker, Emily Taylor, Julie Claire Taylor, Peter Taylor, Genevieve Tearle, Colin Tebb, Walter Temmermans, Pepijn ten Berge, Roselle Tenefrancia, Sue Theron, Marice Thewessen, Chris Thomas, Adam Thompson, Joanne Thompson, Kate Thompson, Mark Thompson, David Thomson, Rosalind Thomson, Niels Tijscholte, Elin Tiselius, Jodi Tobias, Bea Toews, Stephen Toner, Paul Tourigny, Fabio Tramontano, Alain Trembleau, Michelle Trewin, Emily Troemel, Lea Trujillo,

Chan Tsuishan, David Twerdun, David Tyler **U** Radha & Rajal Upadhyaya, Christine Urne, Katie Uyede **V** Roberto Valdivielso, Pippa Vale, Lilian van Dam, Yvonne van de Brand, Sjoerd van de Steene, Chris van den Broeck, Angela van der Geest, Karlijn van der Hoeven, Margot & Frans van der Linden, Jeroen Kroon van Diest, Wouter van Ginkel, Jan van Haecke, Sjoerd van Herpen, Ester van Kippersluis, Monica van Koppenhagen, Eric & Nicolle van Mierlo, Fieke van Olden, W van Pruijssen, Jack & Nanda van Wiltenburg, Feike van Zanten, Peter Vandermark, Roel van de Wiel, Erwin van Houten, Oreol Vardi, Thomas Veale, Pieter Verlinden, Karel Vermeulen, Ubopon Vibunsalanee, Taulikki Viitaniemi, Jacques Vissers, Adrian Volken, Lisa & Ken Vollweiter **W** Sjon Waals, Nathan Walker, Chelsea Wall, Clifford Wallis, Jo Walter, Tom Walton, Matthias & Veronika Wanschura, John & Jason Ward, Pete Ward, Lizzie Warrener, Jan Wasch, Kelly Wasyluk, Howard Watkinson, Anthony Watret, Graham Watsford, Glenn Weatherall, Carl Weaver, Leslie Weber, Wolfram Weidemann, Oliver Weinand, Joerg Weismueller, Lars Welander, Pauline

Wennett, Eric A Wessman, Bjorn Weynants, Perry Whalley, Eric Wheatley, Merav Wheelhouse, Colin Whelan, Emma White, Martin White, Fiona Whittaker, Stefan Wicki, Marielle Wiggers, Els Wijnoltz, Marjan Willemsen, Chris Williams, Kelly Willis, Matthias Willmann, Susan Willson, Chris Willy, Faye Wilson, Felix Wilson, Rebecca Wilson, Rob & Kate Wilson, Kevin Windfield, Sarah Wintle, Rick Witlox, Pimchanok Wongwisut, Katherine Wood, Simon Woods, Joanna Woolf, Chris Wordley, Malcolm Wroe, William L Wuerch, Rupert Wyndham **Y** Cavit Yakar, Grace Yee, Kent Yeoman, Emily Youcha **Z** Dea Zambelli, Celine Zammit, Leo Zevenbergen, Jacek Zielinski, Lydia Zielke, Maike Ziesemer, Adrienne Zinn, Amanda Zobrist, Rainer Zorn, Julia & Marc Zwickl

ACKNOWLEDGMENTS

Many thanks to the following for the use of their content:

Globe on back cover © Mountain High Maps 1993 Digital Wisdom, Inc.

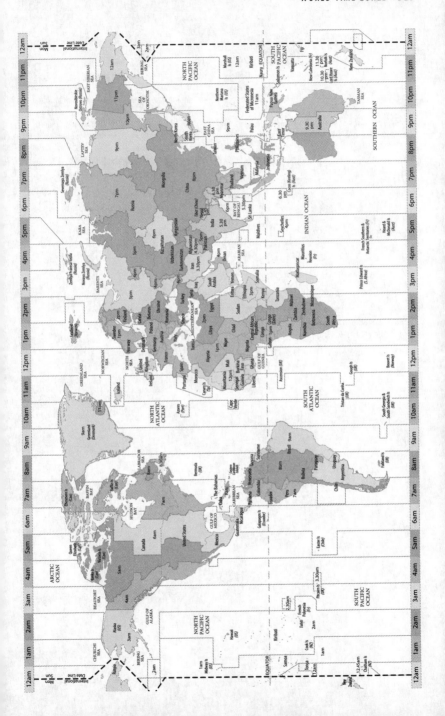

Index

INDEX

INDEX

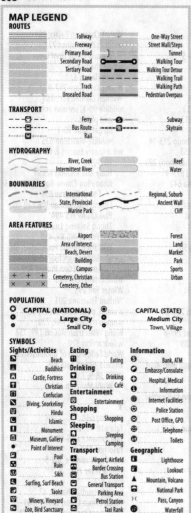

MAP LEGEND
ROUTES

	Tollway		One-Way Street
	Freeway		Street Mall/Steps
	Primary Road		Tunnel
	Secondary Road		Walking Tour
	Tertiary Road		Walking Tour Detour
	Lane		Walking Trail
	Track		Walking Path
	Unsealed Road		Pedestrian Overpass

TRANSPORT

	Ferry	Ⓢ	Subway
	Bus Route		Skytrain
	Rail		

HYDROGRAPHY

	River, Creek		Reef
	Intermittent River		Water

BOUNDARIES

	International		Regional, Suburb
	State, Provincial		Ancient Wall
	Marine Park		Cliff

AREA FEATURES

	Airport		Forest
	Area of Interest		Land
	Beach, Desert		Market
	Building		Park
	Campus		Sports
+ + +	Cemetery, Christian		Urban
× × ×	Cemetery, Other		

POPULATION

◉	**CAPITAL (NATIONAL)**	◉	**CAPITAL (STATE)**
●	**Large City**	●	**Medium City**
●	Small City	●	Town, Village

SYMBOLS

Sights/Activities		Eating		Information	
	Beach	⊞	Eating	⑤	Bank, ATM
	Buddhist	**Drinking**		⊙	Embassy/Consulate
	Castle, Fortress		Drinking	⊕	Hospital, Medical
	Christian		Café	⊙	Information
	Confucian	**Entertainment**		⊚	Internet Facilities
	Diving, Snorkeling		Entertainment	⊛	Police Station
	Hindu	**Shopping**		⊗	Post Office, GPO
	Islamic		Shopping	⊜	Telephone
	Monument	**Sleeping**		⊙	Toilets
	Museum, Gallery		Sleeping	**Geographic**	
	Point of Interest		Camping		
	Pool	**Transport**		🗼	Lighthouse
	Ruin		Airport, Airfield		Lookout
	Sikh		Border Crossing	▲	Mountain, Volcano
	Surfing, Surf Beach		Bus Station		National Park
	Taoist	ⓟ	General Transport	) (	Pass, Canyon
	Winery, Vineyard		Parking Area		Waterfall
	Zoo, Bird Sanctuary		Petrol Station		
			Taxi Rank		

LONELY PLANET OFFICES

Australia
Head Office
Locked Bag 1, Footscray, Victoria 3011
☎ 03 8379 8000, fax 03 8379 8111
talk2us@lonelyplanet.com.au

USA
150 Linden St, Oakland, CA 94607
☎ 510 893 8555, toll free 800 275 8555
fax 510 893 8572, info@lonelyplanet.com

UK
72–82 Rosebery Ave,
Clerkenwell, London EC1R 4RW
☎ 020 7841 9000, fax 020 7841 9001
go@lonelyplanet.co.uk

Published by Lonely Planet Publications Pty Ltd
ABN 36 005 607 983

© Lonely Planet 2005

© photographers as indicated 2005

Cover photographs: Buddhist monks, Peter Bowater/Photolibrary (front); Long-tail boat, Ao Nang, Krabi, Glenn Beanland/Lonely Planet Images (back). Many of the images in this guide are available for licensing from Lonely Planet Images: www.lonelyplanetimages.com

Printed through SNP SPrint Singapore Pte Ltd at
KHL Printing Co Sdn Bhd, Malaysia

AMERICAN
REBEL

ALSO BY MARC ELIOT

AMER

THE LIFE OF CLINT EASTWOOD

ICAN
REBEL

MARC ELIOT

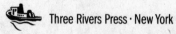

Three Rivers Press · New York

Published in the United States by Three Rivers Press, an imprint of the
Crown Publishing Group, a division of Random House, Inc., New York.

www.crownpublishing.com

Three Rivers Press and the Tugboat design are registered trademarks of
Random House, Inc.

Originally published in hardcover in the United States by Harmony Books,
an imprint of the Crown Publishing Group, a division of Random House, Inc.,
New York, in 2009.

Library of Congress Cataloging-in-Publication Data is available upon request.

ISBN 978-0-307-33689-7

Printed in the United States of America

DESIGN BY ELINA D. NUDELMAN

10 9 8 7 6 5 4 3 2 1

First Paperback Edition

For XIAOLEI

You go to an Eastwood movie with definite expectations. From the comically crude . . . to the gentler epithets of his later films, you know what you're going to get and, even more important, what you're *not* going to get. You're not going to get everything.

—Molly Haskell

Clint Eastwood is a tall, chiseled piece of lumber—a totem pole with feet . . . Eastwood seems to be chewing on bullet casings.

—James Wolcott

Eastwood has a particular grace, every inch that of a "star," in the old sense . . . the taut, lean, powerfully built body, the sensitively chiseled unsmiling face, a voice surprisingly soft, the shock of tawny hair, the lithe walk (the most distinctive of any actor's since Fonda's), the famous squint and glacial eyes which . . . produce a certain inarticulate melancholy.

—Robert Mazzocco

People can know him for years and never be sure of what he's thinking. He's one of the warmest people in the world, but there's a certain distance, a certain mystery to him.

—Sondra Locke

There is something intransigently irreducible in Eastwood, some corner of his soul that no shrink can penetrate . . . Clint Eastwood is an interesting screen personality because his essence is more interesting than his existence. The screen functions to freeze life styles into myth rather than to adjust life forces into art. The beauty of actors is that they are basically vain enough and stupid enough to allow themselves to be embalmed for the edification of their audience.

—Andrew Sarris

I'm an actor playing roles; all of them and none of them are me.

—Clint Eastwood

CONTENTS

I grew up watching movies in an era when there wasn't even television, nothing else even to listen to. I was shaped by John Ford, Howard Hawks, Preston Sturges, those were the guys, plus a ton of other people we don't know the names of who made "B" movies.

—Clint Eastwood

Clint Eastwood stands tall among the most popular and enduring stars Hollywood has ever produced. He has been making movies for more than fifty years, ranging from small, meaningless, and forgettable parts as a Universal Studios contract player to acting in, as well as producing and directing, many Oscar-caliber blockbusters that will one day, sooner rather than later, take their place among the best-loved American movies.

Early in his career, Clint spent seven and a half years costarring in TV's *Rawhide*, and his Rowdy Yates became one of the most popular TV cowboys of the late 1950s and early 1960s.* By the time *Rawhide* ended its eight-season run he had also become an international movie star, following his appearance in three wildly popular spaghetti westerns made and distributed throughout Europe; when they were finally released in America, they made him a big-screen star in the States as well. For the next quarter-century Clint appeared in dozens of entertaining movies that made him a household name anywhere in the world that films could be seen. He was undoubtedly a crowd-pleaser, but at the time the Hollywood elite considered his movies too genre-heavy to be Oscar-worthy.

Then in 1992 Clint produced, directed, and starred in *Unforgiven*, a western to (literally) end all westerns, made by his own production company, Malpaso, that he had created to operate as a ministudio in the service of its resident star. *Unforgiven* won four Academy Awards, including two for Clint (one for Best Director and one for Best Picture), and the Midas-touch Oscar-style was suddenly his; nearly everything he made for the next fifteen years was deemed award- or

---

*The show ran eight seasons, with only twenty-two episodes in its debut year as a midseason replacement. The show made thirteen episodes in its final season. Seasons two through seven had full-season commitments.

nomination-worthy by the Academy, including *Million Dollar Baby*, *Mystic River*, *Flags of Our Fathers*, *Letters from Iwo Jima*, and *Changeling*. Throughout Hollywood's post-studio era, the first rule of filmmaking has been that youth equals box office—young people go out to the movies, older audiences stay home and watch them on cable and DVD. It is, therefore, even more remarkable that he made all of these movies past the age of sixty.

Perhaps more than for any other Hollywood star, the double helix that is Clint's creative and real-life DNA is so intertwined it is nearly impossible to separate the off-screen person from the on-screen persona. The two feed off each other so thoroughly, it is often difficult to tell where the lives of the characters in his movies end and the life of the man playing them begins.

In the movies that he has thus far acted in, produced, or directed, in various combinations wearing one or more of these hats, three essential Clint Eastwood screen personae continually reappear. The first is the mysterious man without a past who is resolute in his loneness, the Man with No Name, who appeared in the three Sergio Leone westerns—*A Fistful of Dollars*, *For a Few Dollars More*, *The Good, the Bad and the Ugly*—then reappeared slightly altered in *Hang 'Em High* and *The Outlaw Josey Wales*, and took several other guises and variations all the way through to *Unforgiven*. The second persona is "Dirty" Harry Callahan, whose essentially nihilistic loner personality continually reemerges up to and including *Gran Torino*. And finally, there is the good-natured redneck, who uses his fists the way a more thoughtful person uses words and who makes his first appearance as Philo Beddoe in *Every Which Way but Loose* and returns again and again on the way to *Pink Cadillac*.

All three characters in their various incarnations are viscerally connected to the real-life Clint. All three are quintessential loners, unlike any other in the canon of American motion pictures. The other cinematic "men alone" who most immediately come to mind are not really loners at all—that is to say, they are loners Hollywood style, buffered with the idealized images of the actors who played them. Probably mainstream films' greatest "loner" is Gary Cooper as the isolated sheriff in Fred Zinnemann's *High Noon* (1952). Yes, Will Kane

heroically stands alone to face his enemies, but in truth he is not alone at all, as in the end he relies on the love of his wife, and her reluctant use of a gun that saves his life; and when all the fighting has ended, the two of them ride off together into the sunset. Another who comes to mind is Humphrey Bogart's Rick Blaine, the neutral American caught in the crosswinds of World War II in Michael Curtiz's *Casablanca* (1942). He proudly boasts that "I stick my neck out for nobody" and then does precisely that for the woman he loves, in this case Ingrid Bergman, in an act so unselfishly noble that the very idea that he was ever a loner is so absurd it becomes laughable. James Bond appears to be the ultimate loner, but we now know that he lost his one true love early on and both seethes with revenge and longs with lust, no longer for any single woman but, apparently, all of womankind. On a nobler plane, Charlton Heston in Cecil B. DeMille's *The Ten Commandments* (1956) is isolated from his family, his people, his land, and his heritage. Yet he still needs someone to lean on, in this case the Almighty himself, who provides the love, guidance, and moral sustenance that establish quite profoundly that even Moses did not go it alone.

Clint's movie characters need nothing and no one more than or beyond themselves. Whether he is surrounded by vicious killers or predatory women (oftentimes one and the same), faceless adversaries (as opposed to the Man with No Name), by serial man-hunters pursued and ultimately defeated by someone dirtier (and therefore stronger) than they are, or even by buddy-buddy orangutans, the Man with No Name, Dirty Harry, and Philo Beddoe all arrive alone at the start and leave alone at the end. They rarely, if ever, win the heart of any woman because they almost never pursue women. On the few occasions when a Clint character reluctantly finds himself to be involved with one, the relationship remains distant, cynical, unromantic, and for the most part nonintimate; the so-called love story is always the least interesting part of any Clint Eastwood movie. His loners are unable, unwilling, and therefore unavailable to fulfill the wishes of those men or women who want to be with him, but not of those in the audience who dream of being like him. With this brand of character, Clint delivered something original and provocative to American motion pictures.

In real life, too, Clint has frequently been described as something of a loner, even in his early and undistinguished film appearances, even when married and playing the role of the happy Hollywood husband. All through his first marriage's thirty-one years,* there were loud whispers that he was not the family man he appeared to be but a lone-wolf womanizer—a role certainly not unique in a town that sees womanizing as something glamorous, even heroic, and where the locker-room lingo of beer-boosted braggadocio is often raised to the level of bad poetry. Perhaps the label stuck harder to him because of how closely his few on-screen romances overlapped with his many real-life ones. Clint's off-screen life has always been filled with women, some might say too many, others might say none really at all. While married to Maggie Johnson, he fathered a child out of wedlock, the first of four,† and took numerous lovers. Several of them were costars, in affairs that often began when production on the film commenced and ended after the final shot was completed. Relatively late in his game, at age sixty-six, he finally married, for only the second time, twelve years after his divorce from Maggie became finalized, to a woman thirty-five years younger than himself, this time finding some measure of peace and happiness.

In his salad days he hung out in the seedy bars in and around San Francisco, drinking, playing jazz on house pianos, and in the vernacular of that time and those places, kicking ass in barroom brawls, whose circumstances and resolutions would later be reprised in many of his films. A tough guy in real life, Clint easily and realistically played the tough guy on film, someone who usually settles disputes with a knock-down, drag-out brawl or, as in *A Fistful of Dollars, Dirty Harry,* and many others, with cinema's classic metaphorical extension of the fistfight, the final, decisive shoot-out.

Perhaps even more compelling than any of his movie roles (but what also makes them so compelling) is how Clint the real-life loner

---

*Clint and Maggie Johnson, his first wife, were married in 1953, separated in 1978, and divorced in 1984.

†One with Roxanne Tunis, one with Frances Fisher, and two with Jacelyn Reeves. His total of seven children are Kimber Eastwood (born June 17, 1964), Kyle Eastwood (born May 19, 1968), Alison Eastwood (born May 22, 1972), Scott Eastwood (born March 21, 1986), Kathryn Eastwood (born February 2, 1988), Francesca Fisher-Eastwood (born August 7, 1993), and Morgan Eastwood (born December 12, 1996).

struggled to find his way out of his own emotional wilderness. He was a child of the Depression, whose parents wandered from town to town to try to make ends meet. Not long after he finished high school, he was drafted into the army and fell in with a bunch of other tough young would-be actors, all of whom grew up in or near Southern California and quickly discovered they had what it took—rugged good looks—to make easier money as contract players, in the desperate declining days of studio-dominated moviemaking, than they could pumping gas.

After his discharge he followed their lead, but his emerging talent quickly separated him from the two he became closest to—Martin Milner and David Janssen—and the rest of the pack. Milner's undistinguished career in movies led to an even less distinguished, if steady, one on television with *Route 66* (1960–64) and *Adam-12* (1968–75); Janssen briefly hit pay dirt on TV as Dr. Richard Kimble in the mid-1960s (1963–67), only to see his post-*Fugitive* career devolve into increasingly mediocre work. But Clint used the time he spent on TV as a film school. Amid tired and bored union men moving wagon trains onto and off of Universal's back lot, he studied everybody and everything and learned not only how to make movies (*Rawhide*, a one-hour TV western series, cranked out a minimovie every week, thirty-nine weeks a year) but how to make them fast and cheap, telling a concise and comprehensible story, often the same one over and over with slight variations; these stories had a logical beginning, an action-filled middle, and a morally uplifting, perfectly plot-resolved end.

Years later, after establishing himself as a bankable star on the big screen, Clint finally got the chance to direct. Early on he had felt that that was where the real action was in movies, that it was ultimately better to play God than to play parts. Along the way to achieving that goal, he met Don Siegel, who would direct him in five films, *Coogan's Bluff* (1968), *Two Mules for Sister Sara* (1970), *The Beguiled* (1971), *Dirty Harry* (1971), and *Escape from Alcatraz* (1979). These films greatly influenced Clint's own early directorial style, especially their collective belief in human nobility as the ultimate redemptive force. Clint would, however, eventually shrug off nobility and redemption as his own style continued to develop and he realized these themes were not just overly derivative, but the least interesting aspect of what he wanted to put on film—less-plot-dependent movies that were, in

truth, feature-length, complex character studies of the leads he played, men who were aloof, estranged (from women and from the larger social order), detached, and embittered, up to and including Clint's portrayal of Walt Kowalski in *Gran Torino*, a dark and chilling film where self-forgiveness and relief come in the form of self-sacrifice, in a single overwhelming (and shocking) attempt to connect in order to redeem another human being. As a showcase for his directorial style and his maturation as an actor—he was seventy-eight when he made it—*Gran Torino*, with no female romantic lead, no comic relief, and until the end, no obviously redemptive qualities in its leading character, perfectly caps the arc of Clint's unique acting and directing style and his auteur's quest to celebrate the loner as the ultimate hero, even (or especially) into old age. By doing so Clint demonstrated, once again, how unlike any other contemporary filmmaker or film actor he always had been.

Always unwilling to talk about his films as anything but entertainments, and even less willing to discuss his private life beyond delivering a certain set of rote answers to the press when promoting his latest film, the clues to who he is and what he does are, nevertheless, found not only in the content of the movies he makes but also within the context of the life he has led, beyond the PR pale, indeed in the symbiotic relationship between the two. He is a man who makes his living making the movies that in turn make the man. He is an American artist whose films are at once great entertainments and cautionary tales, and, as all great movies are, both windows and mirrors. They offer glimpses into his private contemplations even as they reflect universal truths to audiences everywhere.

What follows, then, is an examination of Clint Eastwood, the man he is and the artist he became, seen through the window of his real life and reflected again in some of the most offbeat, disturbing, provocative, and entertaining American films ever made.

FROM AIMLESS TO ACTOR

My father always told me you don't get anything for nothing, and although I was always rebelling, I never rebelled against that.

—Clint Eastwood

The boy who would one day become famous for playing the Man with No Name did not have a well-defined self-image or a strong role model to follow growing up. In his formative years his father, forever in search of a steady job during the Great Depression, developed a deceptive California suntan, the mark of a hardworking outdoor laborer trying to avoid poverty rather than a man of sun-worshipping leisure and privilege.

Clinton and Francesca Ruth (sometimes recorded as Margaret Ruth, although she only used Ruth as her given name) were two good-looking California kids who met while attending Piedmont High School in Oakland. They dated each other and married young, before the market crashed, and took with it their romantic dream of the good life. Ruth's family was Dutch-Irish and Mormon with a long line of physical laborers, including pickup fighters, lumberjacks, sawmill operators, and an occasional local politician. She graduated from Anna Head School in Berkeley, where she had been transferred to from Piedmont just before her senior year—a move that may have been prompted by her parents' concern over an intense relationship she had begun with her high school sweetheart, Clinton Eastwood. Clinton was a popular, well-liked boy with strong American roots; his ancestors were pre–Revolutionary War Presbyterian farmers and men who sold goods by traveling from town to town, their carts bearing inventory samples such as women's underwear and soap used to elicit orders from their customers. In the days before mail-order catalogs, most goods were sold this way outside the big American cities.

Despite Ruth's parents' attempts to put some distance between her and the economically deficient Clinton, upon graduating from high school they were married, on June 5, 1927, in a ceremony held

at Piedmont's interdenominational church. Both newlyweds were lucky enough to find enough work to keep them going during the first years of their marriage. Ruth eventually landed a job as an accountant for an insurance company, and Clinton found one as a cashier. When the stock market crashed in October 1929, they clung to these jobs tenaciously.

Almost three years after their marriage, on May 31, 1930, Clinton Jr. was born. The boy weighed a whopping eleven pounds, six ounces, and was nicknamed "Samson" by all the nurses at San Francisco's St. Francis Hospital.

At about this time Clinton Sr. managed to land a job selling stocks and bonds. At a time when stocks and bonds had been rendered all but worthless, Clinton was following the family tradition; he was now a glorified cart-man, weaving from town to town looking for those few elusive customers with enough cash to invest in their own future and therefore in his. That he got by at all was likely due to his natural charm and good looks.

But even those could only get him so far, and soon Clinton was selling refrigeration products for the East Bay Company, a position whose long-range prospects were little better than those of a seller of stocks and bonds. People had to have enough money to buy food before they could invest in ways to keep it cold. So in 1934, after the birth of their second child, a girl they named Jeanne, Clinton took to a more itinerant life, moving the family by car to wherever he could find pickup work. In a couple of his earliest recollections, Clint later said of those times:

Well, those were the thirties and jobs were hard to come by. My parents and my sister and myself just had to move around to get jobs. I remember we moved from Sacramento to Pacific Palisades just [so my father could work] as a gas station attendant. It was the only job open. Everybody was in a trailer, one with a single wheel on one end, and the car, and we were living in a real old place out in the sticks . . .

My father was big on basic courtesies toward women. The one time I ever got snotty with my mother when he was around, he left me a little battered.

The attendant job was at a Standard Oil station on Sunset Boulevard and Pacific Coast Highway, near a stretch of Malibu beach that was rapidly becoming the suburb of choice for the nouveau riche of the Hollywood film industry—one of the few businesses that actually benefited from the Depression. Films were both cheap and fanciful, the ultimate escape for those who could not afford to live out the American dream themselves but loved watching others do it for them on-screen. Those who lived in this part of town drove big cars that used a lot of gas, so Clinton had plenty of work. For the time being it was a good enough living if not exactly a great life. From the money he made he was able to rent a small house in the lush, hilly Pacific Palisades.

On his off days Clinton and Ruth took their children to one of the public beaches adjacent to Malibu for an afternoon of sun and swimming. One day Clinton, who was an excellent swimmer, dove into a wave with Clint sitting in the saddle of his shoulders. Big Clint came back up but little Clint didn't. After a few heart-stopping moments Ruth saw her boy's foot sticking up and bobbing in the water. She screamed. With some help from alert nearby swimmers, Clinton was able to pull him up. Afterward Ruth sat in the cool muddy turf with her little Clint and splashed him playfully to make sure he wouldn't become afraid of the surf.

A year later, in 1935, the gas station job dried up, and the Eastwoods were once more on the move. They gave up the house in Pacific Palisades and took a smaller one for less rent in Hollywood, a few miles farther inland. Soon afterward they swung back north to Redding, then to Sacramento, then to the Glenview section of the East Bay of San Francisco. Finally they settled back down in the Oakland-Piedmont area, where Clinton worked a series of dead-end jobs. Clint, by now, had attended several schools, necessitated by the family's continual relocations. "I can't remember how many schools I went to," he later recalled. "I do remember we moved so much that I made very few friends." In 1939, after their long loop through the tough times of California, the family settled long enough for young Clint, now nine, to enroll in Piedmont Junior High School.

Following the December 7, 1941, Japanese attack on Pearl Harbor, America's entry into World War II brought new defense-driven work.

Clinton managed to secure a draft-exempt job in the shipyards with Bethlehem Steel, and Ruth found day work at the nearby IBM center.

On the brink of adolescence, six-foot Clint was the tallest boy in his class; he would reach his full height, six four, by the time he graduated from high school. He was also, by all accounts, one of the best-looking students. He had inherited his father's strong, broad shoulders, rugged good looks, and seductive half-closed eyes. He had a finely shaped, aristocratically turned-up nose and a thick bush of brown hair that fell in a curly dip over his forehead. The look was tough, but he was shy, likely the product of his family's vagabond journey through the Depression years. Being left-handed also made him feel like an outsider, as his teachers forced him to use his right hand.

He enjoyed playing high school sports—his height made it easy for him to excel at basketball—but that did little for his social skills. His teachers warned his parents that he had to be brought out of his shell if he was to make something of himself. One of them, Gertrude Falk, who taught English, had the class put on a one-act play and cast a reluctant young Clint in the lead. He was less than thrilled.

> I remember Gertrude Falk very well. It was the part of a backward youth, and I think she thought it was perfect casting . . . she made up her mind that I was going to play the lead and it was disastrous. I wanted to go out for athletics; doing plays was not considered the thing to do at that stage of life—especially not presenting them before the entire senior high school, which is what she made us do. We muffed a lot of lines. I swore [at the time] that that was the end of my acting career.

Clint also didn't do well academically, and his schoolmates and teachers considered him something of a "dummy." Besides sports, the only other subject that held any interest for him was music—not the kind of big-band sound that was popular with the older kids, but jazz. He liked to play it on the piano, something that he correctly believed enhanced his attractiveness to girls. He even learned the current pop tunes that he had no use for but that made them flock around him.

> When I sat down at the piano at a party, the girls would come around. I could play a few numbers. I learned a few off listening to records

and things that were popular at that era. I thought this was all right, so I went home and practiced . . . I would lie about my age and go to Hambone Kelly's. I'd stand in the back and listen to Lu Watters and Turk Murphy play New Orleans jazz . . . I grew up listening to Ella Fitzgerald and Nat King Cole . . . Lester Young, Charlie Parker, Dizzy Gillespie, Miles Davis, Clifford Brown, Fats Navarro, Thelonious Monk, Erroll Garner.

And he loved cars. For $25 Clint's father bought him a beat-up 1932 Chevy to help him keep his paper route job. Clint nicknamed it "the Bathtub" because of its missing top. Its best accessory was, of course, the girls. The Chevy, which didn't last very long, was only the first of a long line of his beat-up cars. To pay for them all and the gas and repairs, Clint took extra after-school jobs on top of his paper route. He worked at the local grocery and as a caddy at the golf course; he baled hay on a farm in nearby Yreka, cut timber near Paradise, and was a seasonal forest firefighter. All these jobs were purely physical, the type of work he could forget about as soon as he punched out. But they were time consuming and exhausting, even for a young and strong teenage boy. They left him even less time for his studies at Piedmont High, and when his parents and school authorities realized he wasn't going to graduate with a regular academic degree, he transferred to the Oakland Technical High School, a vocational training institute where he would specialize in aircraft maintenance. This would give him his best chance, upon graduation, to attend the University of California, which had an affiliated program with the high school, or to land a well-paying job.

After school Clint hung with a crowd of tough-looking teens decked out in leather and T-shirts, with greased-back long hair. All strong, tall, and lean, they tucked cigarettes behind their ears and held bottles of beer in one hand while they drove, usually to the local dives where the hottest girls hung out. And they were all into jazz. Most often they found themselves at the Omar, a pizza and beer dive in downtown Oakland where Clint liked to play jazz on a beat-up old piano in the corner. Whenever he could, he would go to hear Dizzy Gillespie, Coleman Hawkins, Flip Phillips, Lester Young, or Charlie Parker. Sometimes they played alone in the small dark clubs that dotted the streets of Oakland; sometimes they performed together at the Shrine Auditorium,

where the heavily mixed crowd regularly gathered to see and hear them.

It was Parker, more than all the others, who opened his eyes to the new music's emotional power. As Clint later told Richard Schickel, "I'd never seen a musician play with such confidence. There was no show business to it in those days, and this guy just stood and played, and I thought, God, what an amazing, expressive thing." His cool, aloof sound held great appeal for Clint.

He was nineteen when he finally graduated from Oakland Tech in the spring of 1949. By then, he had grown tired of school and often cut classes to hang out with boys, among whom he was the only one still in school.

Meanwhile the war's end had brought new prosperity, especially along the rapidly growing Pacific coast, where jobs were plentiful, wages generous, and mobility upward. Clinton Sr. found work with the California Container Corporation, was quickly caught up in the flow of automatic promotions, and soon was offered a major managerial post in the company's main plant, in Seattle. Together he and Ruth and fourteen-year-old Jeanne packed up the house and loaded the car for the drive to Seattle.

Clint didn't want to go, and because he had graduated, he said he' didn't have to. Harry Pendleton's parents agreed to let him stay with them for a while. Harry and Clint had been friends since junior high school and long hung with the same crowd. With his family in Seattle, his education finished, and no clear plan for the future, Clint was, in his own words, "really adrift." He found a job on the night shift at Bethlehem Steel, tending the blast furnaces, then moved to the day shift at Boeing Aircraft. For the next two years these hard and charmless jobs kept him in cars, girls, and music, allowing him to roam aimlessly through his early twenties unfocused and unconcerned, the perfect West Coast rebel without a care.

Then, in 1950, border hostilities broke out in Korea, and the United States began a massive buildup of forces in Seoul. Knowing his A1 military status made him a prime target for the draft, Clint's unlikely next goal was to go back to college, to get a student exemption. He moved up to Seattle and in with his parents to enroll at Seat-

tle University. He figured he might major in music, since nothing else held any appeal. But his grades weren't good enough, and he was told he'd have to attend junior college as a nonmatriculated, part-time student, which would not be enough to earn him the draft exemption. He then moved back to Oakland and made a last-ditch personal appeal to his local draft board, to convince them he had every intention of attending college full time.

The board took him the following month.

In the spring of 1951, he spent his last free nights getting drunk and listening to music at the local dives, before reporting, hung over and hell-bent, for basic training at Fort Ord, near the Monterey Peninsula. As far as he was concerned, he didn't need any training. What could the army teach him that at the age of twenty he didn't already know?

Plenty, as it turned out, although not at all in the ways he might have expected.

TWO

Basically I was a drifter, a bum. As it has turned out, I'm lucky because I'm going to end up financially well-off for a drifter. But that really doesn't change things . . . You can only dig so many holes in the ground.

—Clint Eastwood

The army quickly altered the rhythm of Clint's life, from the jazzy syncopation of his unstructured days and nights to the beat of a military march. He was stationed at Fort Ord, near the Monterey Peninsula, for six weeks of basic training. To everyone's surprise but nobody more than himself, his natural physical abilities gave rise to talk among the drill sergeants that he should be sent to Officer Training School—a suggestion he rejected out of hand. He had been drafted for the obligatory two years and didn't want to spend one second longer in uniform. *No problem,* they told him. *So be ready for more training and toughening up before you're shipped off to Korea.*

Only something he had written down on his induction papers saved him from that grim assignment. When asked to mention any special skills, he had put down "swimming." The camp brass had made note of it, and when he completed basic, they assigned him to permanent duty as a lifesaving swimming instructor at the Fort Ord Division of Faculty. The boy who had almost drowned in the Pacific and done so poorly in school was now assigned to teach the army how to swim. That kind of irony helped produce what would one day be known as the Eastwood smirk—an ambiguous squint-eyed half-smile that said nothing and everything at the same time.

This "Clint luck," as his friends always called it, didn't stop there. His placement at the base pool brought him into frequent contact with Special Services, the army division created during World War II to utilize the popularity of Hollywood celebrities inducted into the service. Knowing that killing off movie stars was not the best PR or economic move, the army segregated them into Special Services and gave them essentially (but not always) a free ticket, most of the time saving them from active duty and using them for as much publicity and as many recruiting opportunities as they could. They spent most of

their ample free time swimming. His real job was to save them from drowning.

On duty, Clint met several young Hollywood contract players, including Martin Milner, John Saxon, and David Janssen, and dozens of other future familiar film and TV faces all congregated around the pool, turning it into a gathering spot for drinks and small talk, lacking only girls to complete the cool social scene. WACs assigned to the base were everywhere but were not allowed to fraternize with the men at the pool or after hours.

Clint became friends with the exceptionally good-looking Janssen, who had played football for Fairfax High School in Hollywood before a serious knee injury ruined his chances of playing college sports and steered him instead into acting. Clint and Janssen shared an athletic bravado cut with strong sexual appetites, which made them legends of a sort on base. They were privy to and took full advantage of the pleasures of the young, single women at the nearby nightclubs, soldier-lovers who were sweet, plentiful, willing, and available. Another noncom who became a friend of Clint was Irving Lasper, a photographer who told him he had the kind of face the movies—or more accurately, the men who made them—would love. Clint shrugged off the suggestion, having no interest in that business.

Clint also got close to many of the musicians assigned to the unit, including Lennie Niehaus, an alto sax player who had worked with Stan Kenton and now played at the base's junior NCO (noncommissioned officers) mess hall four nights a week. Clint managed to talk his way into the hall's bartending job so that after lounging by the pool all day he could hang back, drink for free, and listen to Niehaus blow his horn. He became so close with these members of the Special Services that he became an unofficial member by association, which meant the officers in charge either didn't know or didn't care that he slept past reveille. He didn't do much KP or much of anything except sit by the pool, and work at the club at night, and come and go from the base at will.

He often took overnight excursions by himself to explore the gorgeous coastal scenery that he had loved since childhood. In the emerald expanse of Carmel, a sleepy enclave 120 miles south of San Francisco, he enjoyed hearing jazz played in the local clubs that also

attracted some of the best-looking women north of L.A. They always took to the surf wearing as little as possible to allow themselves to soak up the famous California sun. So for Clint, it was women during the day, jazz at night.

Another job assigned to Clint—after all, he wasn't exactly over-loaded—was base projectionist for the Division Faculty classrooms. "One of my auxiliary jobs, besides swimming instructor, was to project training films for the soldiers. I kept showing [John Huston's 1945] *The Battle of San Pietro*, one of my favorites, which I must have seen around fifty times during my two years in the service." Watching it over and over again, Clint could not help but break down the mechanics of the movie, how it was put together, the rhythm of the shots, the camera angles, Huston's off-screen narration.

Out of this fascination with movies came a new friendship with Norman Bartold, another noncom actor, who had a small part in one of the new pictures Clint was assigned to screen, H. Bruce Humber-stone's *She's Working Her Way Through College* (1952), a Ronald Reagan vehicle costarring Virginia Mayo in one of her leggy imitation–Betty Grable roles. Clint enjoyed hanging out with Bartold, to talk about how the movie was made as well as what it was like to work with the luscious Mayo.

The few times Clint voluntarily wore his uniform off the base was to gain free passage on a military aircraft, which came in handy whenever he wanted to visit his parents in Seattle, and a girl he had met off base who also happened to live there. One day in the fall of 1951, he hooked up with a twin-engine Beechcraft. At the last minute he changed plans and chose instead a Douglas AD naval attack bomber because its return flight schedule would give him a little extra time in Seattle. But on its way back to the base the plane developed engine trouble and ran out of gas, forcing it to belly-flop into the ocean along Point Reyes, just off the coast of Marin County. Here Clint's swimming abilities kicked in—he was able to dislodge himself from the flooded fuselage and make it to the surface. Not too far away he saw the pilot bobbing in the water. Both then swam to shore, which was four, seven, or more miles away (depending upon the several and highly varied published accounts of this incident).

By overstaying his time in Seattle—spending it not with his parents but with the girl—Clint had technically violated his leave and nearly drowned. Although in later years he underplayed the incident, likely because of its decidedly unheroic backstory, he did occasionally talk about this early adventure but always matter-of-factly. Still, the momentary drama would later be useful for publicity purposes when he became an action star.

The crash also introduced him to a bit of momentary fame. Although he didn't feel especially heroic, just Clint-lucky to be alive, the local press lauded him as a hero for surviving the crash and, in accounts, helping to rescue pilot Lieutenant F. C. Anderson (who was actually rescued separately). Clint was portrayed heroically, photographed on the scene bare-chested and dripping wet, looking for all the world like a hero. But the episode also introduced him to the very real notion of mortality. Defiantly looking into the face of death would have a powerful and lasting effect on him.

Although Clint never left the States while in the service, several of the fellow recruits who did basic training with him were sent overseas and saw action in the war. One was Don Kincade, whom he had known since high school. Immediately after being discharged in January 1953, Kincade enrolled in the University of California at Berkeley on the GI Bill. That spring Clint hitched a ride to Berkeley to visit him.

Kincade, who was by now dating a sorority girl, offered to set Clint up on a blind date with her best friend. He assured Clint he wouldn't be disappointed; Maggie Johnson was a beauty—tall, good face, terrific body. And, he added, she was dating someone else, so this would be a guaranteed one-shot affair.

As it turned out, Clint and Maggie hit it off, and when the weekend came to an end, they promised to try to get together in the fall, when Clint's active service time was up and Maggie had graduated and returned to live with her parents in Alhambra, a suburb of Los Angeles.

She quickly got rid of the other guy.

As his tour of duty wound down, Clint gradually reverted to the easy syncopations of pre-army days. After two years of his laid-back

conscription, he had little "military" to get rid of. He had long ago let his hair grow out, rarely wore a uniform, and more or less came and went as he pleased. By the time of his summer 1953 discharge, he had already made plans to return to Seattle, where a cushy civilian job as a lifeguard was waiting for him. Only he didn't go, at least not for long. Staying for just a few days to visit his parents, he quickly took off for Los Angeles to be with Maggie Johnson.*

Down in L.A. Clint trudged through a series of day-to-day jobs until he landed a full-time one managing a building on Oakhurst Drive, several miles south of Beverly Hills, which he supplemented by working at a Signal Oil gas station. Hoping college credits would help him get a better job, he started taking classes in business administration at City College in downtown L.A., on the GI Bill. School still bored him, and just to break things up he sat in on a few acting seminars with Chuck Hill, one of many noncom show-business dreamers he had met at Fort Ord.

Hill was a gay man who had slipped through the screening processes of the wartime military. What would, years later, be known as the "don't ask, don't tell" philosophy was actually in full, if unofficial, effect in the 1950s. Even if homosexuals wanted to enter the military, the military wanted nothing to do with them, partly, as the bizarre thinking of the day went, because they wouldn't be able to fight as well among other males or control themselves in the communal shower rooms. Hill, who wanted a show-business career working behind the scenes, had spotted Clint and was struck by his good looks, and told him to look him up after his discharge, which Clint did while he was pumping gas.

Because this was Los Angeles, essentially a one-industry town, every college and university had drama and film departments superior to those of any other institution outside of L.A. At Los Angeles Community College (LACC) George Shdanoff was on the teaching staff. Shdanoff was a practitioner of the methods of Michael Chekhov, who in turn was a disciple of the Stanislavsky "Method" school of acting, and his was the class that Clint and Hill sat in on. Unfortunately, much

*A story keeps popping up that has Clint staying a bit longer, getting a Seattle girl pregnant, and borrowing money from his parents to pay for an abortion, all of which hastened his decision to get out of town, but no hard and detailed evidence of it can be found.

of what Shdanoff offered was wasted on Clint, who at the time was not all that introspective, an aspect crucial to the Method. Most of the time he just sat there among the more serious acting students who tried to absorb the daily theoretical lectures.

Meanwhile Clint reconnected with Maggie Johnson, who had relocated to Altadena, about ten miles out of L.A. in the San Bernardino mountains, with a spectacular view. There she had found a job as a manufacturer's representative for Industria Americana. They started seeing each other on a regular basis, and soon the subject of marriage came up. In early 1950s America "nice" girls only dated "good" men with an implied promise of a ring for their finger. With her solid upper-middle-class background, Maggie's choice of Clint as the one to fulfill her dreams might seem a bit odd, even more so because, by every account, she was the aggressor. Maggie was pretty, from a good family, and nothing like the easy women he had been with during his army stint. Marriage to the right girl was what he thought he was supposed to do. So he did it.

On December 19, 1953, Clinton Eastwood Jr. married Maggie Johnson in South Pasadena before a Congregational minister, the Reverend Henry David Grey. After a brief honeymoon in Carmel, Clint resumed his studies and his part-time gig at the filling station and Maggie went back to work. The only difference was that now she could properly move into Clint's small house on South Oakhurst.

Soon enough, though, Clint's new and quite normal life would take a dramatic and unexpected turn that had very little to do with married life but a whole lot to do with, of all things, making movies.

THREE

I had a premonition that acting might be a good thing for me. I had done some of it in school and little theaters in Oakland, but I never did take it seriously then. I got serious after a director talked to me about my chances.

—Clint Eastwood

Nineteen fifty-four was a pivotal year in American movies. Without question the explosive Marlon Brando as Terry Malloy in Elia Kazan's *On the Waterfront* made a huge mark on the popular mores of American male youth. Brando would win the Best Actor Oscar for his indelible performance and change forever the notion of what a movie leading man could look like, sound like, behave like, and be. The role as written may not have been earth-shattering—it had classic Hollywood plot devices of attempting to change the world while managing to win the heart of the prettiest girl in the neighborhood. But the way Brando brought it to life on the screen surely was.

In the aftermath of Brando's performance, Hollywood saw a policy shift in the casting departments of the major studios. Now they all wanted their leading men to be beautiful but rebellious American youths. At first this policy would work against Clint, who was cool and laid back more than burning and restless. But Brando's youth and brooding appeal would nevertheless lay the foundation for Clint's unique brand of hero, even as the young, handsome gas station attendant with only the slightest interest in acting and even less in the movies was about to be discovered by the men who made the movies.

The details surrounding Clint's signing with Universal Pictures have always been murky, in numerous slightly differing (and at times overlappingly repetitious) accounts of the actual events. Clint himself has remained vague even about the details of what attracted him to the movie business. One reason is his natural reticence to talk about his personal life, but perhaps he also wishes, maybe needs, to take the focus off the overly eager women, the gay men, and the singularly opportunistic "suits" who helped launch his career.

What is certain is that, as 1954 began, Clint was attending classes at LACC while working at the gas station, and Maggie was continuing at her full-time job and earning additional income doing part-time

modeling work. Also that Arthur Lubin, a short, stubby, hustling contract director at Universal—best known at the time for his insanely popular Abbott and Costello films and the *Francis the Talking Mule* series—was looking for someone to help boost his standing at the studio. He needed a project or a star that would help him up the prestige-and-profit ladder. According to Lubin, "Someone took me to meet Clint at the gas station." Very likely it was Chuck Hill, looking to secure a position at Universal as well and figuring that Lubin might be interested in Clint and return the favor.

Under the shrewd machinations of Lew Wasserman, Universal had moved into TV production earlier than most of the other major studios. They were still trying to compete with television, an increasingly losing proposition, rather than become a profitable partner in it. In the early 1950s Wasserman had created a self-contained TV unit, called Revue, to produce shows exclusively for the small screen. To find, train, and develop new young talent to appear on television (something most major motion picture stars were still reluctant to do), Wasserman approved the creation of the Universal Talent School (UTS), offering in-house "acting" classes run by coach Sophie Rosenstein. The school's mandate was to discover new talent, to bring young actors up to professional speed, and when they were ready, to sign them to the studio at relatively cheap and long-term contracts and use them either in movies (part of the lure) or, more likely, in TV.

UTS was not all that easy to get into. Admission was determined by a complex multiaudition process. Only two applicants were allowed to audition every day, and only the best were even awarded a screen test. A handful were picked to attend the school and of those about one in sixty were actually given a Universal contract for up to $150 a week, for which they were to appear in whatever productions they were assigned.

Lubin insisted that the school give Clint an immediate audition, even though he was not exactly the next Brando the studio was looking for; an intense actor who gave off a lot of heat fueled by his repressive darkness. Clint had none of it. Nor was he the usual beautiful, romantic type that the studio could always use as screen filler and never seemed to find enough of who had some actual talent, like Rock Hudson and Tony Curtis.

Moreover, Clint had no real experience as an actor. He didn't know how to move like a movie performer, how to react, how to talk, how to "think" for the camera, or how to smile for a close-up. The smile thing was a special problem; Clint's teeth were yellow, too small, and curved inward, which caused him to smile with his lips closed—something the movie camera did not show well. Too good-looking to be a character actor but not good-looking enough to be a traditional leading man (according to the conventional studio wisdom), he was the least likely prospect for a screen test.

But somehow Lubin made it happen. When Clint saw his audition film, he knew immediately how badly he had come off. "I thought I was an absolute clod. It looked pretty good, it was photographed well, but I thought, 'If that's acting, I'm in trouble.' " Nonetheless, seventeen days later Universal signed him to a provisional seven-year learning contract starting at $75 a week.

He quit his gas station job and began taking full-time classes at UTS. To his surprise, these lessons—essentially teaching how to look good in front of a camera without tripping over your own feet (or your lines)—were infinitely more valuable to him than had been the internal agonies of his Michael Chekhov–based acting-class theoreticals. All of it meant nothing to him.

Besides taking classes, Clint worked out at the studio gym and kept his eye on the gorgeous young starlets all over the place. All the young female students of the UTS, he quickly found out, were single, hot, and available. According to one of them, wannabe sex kitten and B-movie starlet Mamie Van Doren, a demi-Monroe whose career never fully blossomed (she would appear with Clint in Charles Haas's 1956 *Star in the Dust*, in which she was the costar, he a walk-on), sex was rampant among the students, and she and Clint had spent more than one afternoon in her dressing room contributing to the count.

Clint, who had thus far refused to get his teeth fixed or darken his brown hair (to match Hudson's and Curtis's blue-black), had no problem attracting and sleeping with many starlets besides Van Doren. As far as he was concerned, he had no reason not to, least of all his marriage. Now in this new world of plenty, his marriage was, to him, like being on a diet in the biggest candy store in the world. Years later Clint would tell one writer that "the first year of marriage was terrible. If

I had to go through it again, I think I'd be a bachelor for the rest of my life. I liked doing things when I wanted to do them. I did not want any interference . . . One thing Meg [Maggie] had to learn about me was that I was going to do as I pleased. She had to accept that, because if she didn't, we wouldn't be married."

In a rare interview in 1971 Maggie seemed to confirm Clint's continuing independence when she described his behavior this way: "He is very much a twentieth-century cowboy. We're not advocates of the total togetherness theory. I happen to like women with their own thing. I admire individuality and am not of the theory that 'I'll be an individual and you stay home.' " Whether out of choice or necessity, she had found a way to rationalize what both of them instinctively knew; that for Clint the notion of marital fidelity never held much sway. That he came home at all was what mattered to Maggie, and sooner or later he always did. Still, the unspoken-of friction it caused between them was palpable. Maggie, raised to be a traditional wife, understandably did not take easily to her husband spending his days among young and beautiful and (she suspected) easy girls in the glamorous world of sexy movie make-believe, with nothing to show for it—at least nothing she could see.

When he wasn't sneaking off with one starlet or another, Clint passed the time on the lot walking among the soundstages, where he'd often run into other recently signed actors, like John Saxon, Marty Milner, and David Janssen, his buddies from Fort Ord. The four would-be actors enjoyed hanging out at the studio in the daytime and in local bars at night; and occasionally on weekends, when the gas station called, he went back and filled in for a day or two, as he was always in need of extra cash.

In class, Clint's teacher Katherine Warren was joined by Jack Kosslyn, who brought in a parade of famous actors, including the great Brando himself, whose mere presence was a thrill and whose message to the students was not to try to "act," but just to get on the soundstage and let "it" happen (whatever "it" was supposed to be). Something and someone had, at last, made sense to Clint, and he concentrated on his acting with a seriousness and intensity he had not shown before.

By May 1954 he was considered good enough to try for a real film, at an increased salary of $100 a week. At the same time he signed with

a manager-agent, none other than Arthur Lubin, who was eager to get
Clint out of the classrooms and into some films. The first picture
Lubin wanted him to try out for was *Six Bridges to Cross*, which would
be the first for the brooding, ethnic, East Coast, and utterly charming newcomer Sal Mineo. But despite Lubin's enthusiasm, *Bridges*'s
director, forty-four-year-old Joseph Pevney, was not impressed with
Clint, dismissing him as a nonactor; despite Lubin's pushing, Pevney
refused to use Clint even in any background shots. In truth Pevney,
like most of the directors at Universal, thought the talent school concept was a dumb throwback to the days when studios and training
mattered. Journeymen like Pevney did not want the studio to supply
him with students for his film; he preferred *real* actors.

Lubin continued to try to get Clint a part in any film, even as he
worked on a number of other, peripheral studio assignments. Lubin
was, at the time, busy in postproduction on his latest talking-mule
franchise, *Francis in the Navy*. He used Clint's voice for some looping
(overdubbing) and put him in a few crowd scenes, along with Milner
and Janssen. Despite his microscopic participation, Lubin gave Clint
on-screen billing, his name appearing at the end of the back-of-the-
film cast list.

Not until May 1954 did Clint make his film debut as a real character in a real part (still uncredited), in actor-turned-director Jack
Arnold's *Revenge of the Creature* (1955),* a sequel to his unexpectedly
huge hit of the year before, *Creature from the Black Lagoon*, which no
doubt benefited from the big-screen hot fad of the time, 3-D. In his
only scene as a lab technician, opposite the film's star—western, war,
and horror film staple (and former husband of Shirley Temple) John
Agar—Clint's unnamed character discovers a missing rat that has conveniently parked itself in his lab coat.

The scene was shot in a single day (July 30, 1954) and was the first
of a series of nondescript studio-assigned parts that included a role as
"First Saxon" in the borderline sexploitation flick *Lady Godiva of
Coventry*† (directed by Arthur Lubin, starring Maureen O'Hara and
Rex Reason); in *Tarantula* (1955), another Jack Arnold film, Clint

---

*Year of release. Unless otherwise indicated, all dates of films are release rather than pro-
  duction dates.
†Aka *21st Century Lady Godiva*.

played an air force pilot assigned to kill the giant, irradiated insect-gone-wild. He got a half-minute of screen time playing a laboratory assistant, in service to Rock Hudson, in *Never Say Goodbye*, a 1956 medical melodrama about an insanely jealous doctor (directed by Jerry Hopper, featuring Janssen in a solid supporting role.)* Hopper suggested to Clint that he wear glasses to help him create a character, in the time-honored notion of no small parts, only small actors. The suggestion, and the attention given to Clint in his relatively tiny screen appearance, made Hudson furious. Always an insecure actor, Hudson insisted that his character—a doctor, after all—should be the one to wear the glasses.

Clint then did two more blink-and-you-miss-him roles, one in Pevney's 1956 star vehicle for granite-faced Jeff Chandler, *Away All Boats* (Pevney was incensed at having been forced this time by the studio to use Clint, who is barely visible in the film—in one scene he calls for a "medic"), and a bit-bit in Charles Haas's *Star in the Dust* (1956), a western starring Agar. "They made a lot of cheapies in those days, a lot of B pictures," Clint later recalled. "I'd always play the young lieutenant or the lab technician who came in and said, 'He went that way,' or 'This happened,' or 'Doctor, here are the X-rays,' and he'd say, 'Get lost, kid,' I'd go out, and that would be the end of it."

Over the course of eighteen months, Clint received good reports that had resulted in an increased salary of $125 a week. But on October 23, 1955, he was unexpectedly and unceremoniously let go by Universal because, the executives said, he just didn't have the right look. They especially objected to his teeth and a rather prominently protruding Adam's apple. Janssen was also let go, because of his receding hairline and distracting facial tics (which would serve him well in his portrayal of Richard Kimble on the 1960s classic TV series *The Fugitive*). The studio also released a young Brando look-alike who, unfortunately, they felt couldn't act his way out of a paper bag, or control his real rage and channel it effectively onto the screen, an unknown by the name of Burt Reynolds.

After their dismissals, Reynolds and Clint went out to the parking

---

*It was a remake of *This Love of Ours* (1945), directed by William Dieterle and starring Claude Rains in the role now handed to Hudson.

lot together and found that Burt's name on his reserved space was already being stenciled over for western TV series up-and-comer Clu Gulager. Clint's was still there. "Don't worry," Burt said to Clint. "I may learn to act someday, but you'll never get rid of that Adam's apple."

Clint was not prepared for this unexpected turn of events. He had been sure he had a future at Universal, so sure that he and Maggie moved to better quarters. The Villa Sands, at 4040 Arch Drive, just off Ventura Boulevard, was close enough to the studio that Clint could walk to work on a slow day. The one-bedroom apartment offered a communal pool for its tenants to share; at $125 a month, a relatively expensive rental for California in the 1950s. Clint had heard about it through a couple of his UTS classmates who lived there, young starlets-in-the-making Gia Scala and Lili Kardell.

Soon after Clint moved in, Bill Thompkins came down from Seattle and took an efficiency in the complex, as did Bob Daley, who'd moved to L.A. via Chicago, Texas, and California and was currently working at Universal's budget department dealing with production schedules and costs. Daley and Clint had met before, at the studio, but now, as neighbors, became friends and joined the Villa Sands–Universal youthful associate social scene, where no one was over twenty-eight, everyone was good-looking, loose, and into jazz that played all day, thanks to a phonograph someone had rigged at one end of the pool.

Needing work, Clint went back to day jobs, mostly digging swimming pools and other such work, all of it off the books so he could collect unemployment. He auditioned for the other studios, using a scene from Sidney Kingsley's *Detective Story*, which he had practiced at UTS, playing the part that Kirk Douglas had done in the film version.

For Clint, neither a sentimentalist nor an especially high achiever at this point, that might have been it for him and the movies, had it not been for the incessant drive of Arthur Lubin, who remained steadfast in his belief that he could do for Clint Eastwood what director Douglas Sirk had done for Rock Hudson. Eight of Sirk's biggest 1950s films had featured Hudson, beginning when the actor was still an unknown contract player as the romantic lead opposite Piper Laurie

in *Has Anybody Seen My Gal?* (1952). By the time they had made their last movie together, *The Tarnished Angels* (1958), Hudson was a major Hollywood star.*

Lubin, who did not have the success or the talent of Sirk, admired him less for his movies than for his relationship (whatever it might have been) with Hudson. Lubin believed that he too could become an important director working with the right actor, and that Clint was that actor. Likely Lubin's attraction to Clint had as much to do with his being gay as with his opinion of Clint's abilities. Homosexuality was not unusual in Hollywood. (Both Hudson and Sirk were gay, although there is no evidence that they were ever actually involved.) But in the simplest terms Lubin wanted to continue his professional association with Clint (who had shown no signs of being anything but a raging heterosexual) as a way to remain relevant in his life while making both of them stars.

Meanwhile, Maggie suffered a life-threatening bout of hepatitis. Because she and Clint had no medical insurance, it hit them hard financially as well as emotionally. He continued to dig ditches for swimming pools and, thanks to Lubin's unerring drive, landed a couple of minor TV bits—too small to actually be called parts—that helped him get by. His motorcycle abilities got him a quick shot on *Highway Patrol*, a vehicle for Broderick Crawford that introduced the aging Academy Award–winning actor to television viewers. Crawford, an alcoholic, had a habit of trimming his lines down to a sentence or two because he couldn't memorize them or easily read them off cue cards. Clint had only one quick scene with him but it was enough for him to realize how excessive most dialogue really was (despite the negative reason for it in this case). And, although his part was minuscule, Clint actually received a piece of fan mail.

He landed a bit in another series, *TV Reader's Digest*, based on the popular magazine, but that was it. After Maggie's recovery, money was so tight that she had to return quickly to her day job and take on addi-

---

*The eight films were *Has Anybody Seen My Gal?*, *Taza, Son of Cochise* (aka *Son of Cochise*) (1954), *Magnificent Obsession* (1954), *Captain Lightfoot* (1955), *All That Heaven Allows* (1955), *Never Say Goodbye* (1956; Sirk was uncredited, Hopper was listed as the official director), *Battle Hymn* (1957), and *The Tarnished Angels*. After *Imitation of Life* (1959) Sirk retired under circumstances that remain unclear and permanently moved to Switzerland.

tional part-time work doing showroom modeling of bathing suits; the long hours wreaked havoc on her feet. She also managed to find occasional TV work as living wallpaper for Jimmy Durante's semiregular popular Sunday-night variety show.

Meanwhile Clint's only link to show business, Lubin, often took him to dinner when Maggie had to work late and invited him to informally join his social entourage of mostly gay companions.

At the end of 1956, when his initial contract with Lubin was up, Clint opted to let it expire, for a reason that even Lubin could not argue with: nothing was happening in his career. Clint replaced Lubin with Irving Leonard, whom he had met during his time at Universal and who, leaving the studio, had become a business manager specializing in actors who needed help handling their finances. Leonard often found parts for his clients who didn't have agents, including a grateful Clint. Since in Hollywood someone could be poor one day and rich the next, Leonard could sign unknowns and bank on them while also banking for them. Leonard had noticed Clint at Universal, and when the young actor approached him, Leonard took him on. Soon afterward Leonard landed a position at Gang, Tyre & Brown (later Gang, Tyre, Ramer & Brown), a law firm that specialized in film clients, and brought Clint along with him. Once he had settled in, Leonard hooked Clint up with Ruth and Paul Marsh, who ran a small PR firm for actors and actresses that included a fair share of wannabes.

Lubin, meanwhile, disappointed and maybe even a little heartbroken, was determined to find a way to get Clint back, or at least to have him around. In the summer of 1956 Lubin landed his next assignment, at RKO, directing *The First Traveling Saleslady* and he quickly offered Clint a small part. It paid him little money but was his chance to get back into films.*

The First Traveling Saleslady was a western comedy starring Ginger Rogers, Carol Channing, Barry Nelson, and the up-and-coming James Arness. (Arness's friendship with John Wayne would result in his landing the starring role, after Wayne turned it down, in what would become the longest-running TV western series, *Gunsmoke*.) It was by far Clint's biggest movie role to date, with a couple of comedy bits and

---

*Clint received $750 for the film.

service as a love interest for Rogers. Clint had no use for the script, had no sense of comedy, and didn't particularly like to play "love" roles, but when Lubin told him that after seeing the daily rushes, RKO was considering offering him a player contract, he was encouraged.

The contract never materialized, but Lubin did get another part for Clint—his fourth with Lubin—in his next film for RKO, *Escapade in Japan*, essentially an adventure movie intended for children. This time Clint played a soldier named, of all things, Dumbo, who leads two young boys on a runaway trip to Japan. The film almost didn't open because prior to its release the cash-strapped studio was sold. Ironically, *Escapade* eventually reached theaters through a distribution agreement with Universal. But it made little difference which studio released the film; it was a complete failure at the box office.

With no prospects Clint, desperately in need of cash, this time took a weekend job as a sweeper at the Mode Furniture Factory in South L.A. while continuing to dig swimming pools during the week. As 1958 bled into 1959, he got an audition for *The Spirit of St. Louis*, the story of Charles Lindbergh's 1927 heroic solo transatlantic flight. Called in to try out, Clint was optimistic about his chances, believing he physically resembled the real Lindbergh; but when he arrived, he found himself among hundreds of Lindbergh look-alikes. The role eventually went to Jimmy Stewart, who was twice as old as Lindbergh. Nonetheless Stewart could command the lead because he was a star. That was the kind of world Hollywood was, a world built on star power, a world Clint really wasn't a part of.

He next landed a minor supporting role in William Wellman's *Lafayette Escadrille*,* conceived as a swan-song reflection of Wellman's own life both in the military and in motion pictures. Wellman, known as "Wild Bill" for his aviator heroics during World War I, was a veteran director whose career reached all the way back to the silent era, highlighted by his direction of 1927's *Wings*, winner of the first Oscar for Best Picture by the newly formed Academy of Motion Picture Arts and Sciences. The film looked to be one of the bigger releases of 1958 after hot new actor Paul Newman was rumored to have signed on to play Thad Walker, the Wellman-like lead. Newman, however, decided at

---

*Aka *C'est la Guerre*, aka *Hell Bent for Glory* (UK), aka *With You in My Arms*.

the last minute to pass in favor of playing Brick in Richard Brooks's film version of Tennessee Williams's *Cat on a Hot Tin Roof*. Wellman had difficulty replacing Newman; finally Warner, the studio that was producing the film, pushed contract player Tab Hunter on him. Wellman had originally picked Clint out of a cattle-call audition (the only way he could get into any studios in those days), principally because Wellman felt he would play well in a supporting role behind Newman. But against the weaker Hunter, Clint was too imposing. His role went instead to a smaller and darker actor, none other than David Janssen. Clint wound up as part of the background, living scenery with no dialogue. This film too went nowhere and did nothing to advance Clint's marginal career.

So it was back to digging more pools. Increasingly he spent his nights at a local bar among friends and on at least one occasion venting his frustrations by getting into a pretty nasty brawl. Clint could take care of himself, and from all accounts the other guy came off much worse.

Not long afterward Clint, via Leonard, heard about a cheapie independent that was being made at 20th Century–Fox's facilities (they would produce but not distribute the film) by first-time director Jodie Copelan, a post–Civil War action movie called *Ambush at Cimarron Pass*. Clint tried out for and landed the part of one of the villains, an ex-soldier loyal to the South. He got paid $750 for it; the lead, career villain Scott Brady, cast here as the hero, managed to get $25,000. For some reason Copelan wanted Brady, even if his high fee ate into production values, like extras to fill out the vapid wide screen. And horses, the lack of which made the film, ostensibly a western, look a bit odd. (A plot line was developed that they had been stolen by thieves, which might have made a pretty good film.) After the film opened, Clint got a positive single-line review in *Variety*—"fine portrayals also come from Margia Dean, Frank Gerstle, and Clint Eastwood"—but the film was a bomb. Later on Clint would describe *Ambush at Cimarron* as "the lousiest western ever made."

With nothing happening in his film career, Clint gave serious thought to returning to college full time, getting a degree in something, anything, and then finding a steady job with decent pay. Still,

he couldn't completely give up trying to make it in the movies and signed up for more acting lessons (a thriving storefront business in Hollywood, then and now). Mostly these classes were like health clubs for actors, a place to work out with a scene or a monologue to keep the chops tight. One of Clint's classmates, Floyd Simmons, who was also a casual friend from the studio, suggested to Clint that he needed a better agent, and sent him to his own, Bill Shiffrin, who signed him.

Shiffrin specialized in "beefcake," brawny good-looking young men who could play romantic leads in B-movies without looking too ridiculous when they tried to "act." A bent-nose kind of guy who prided himself on being able to handle himself in a rough situation (as the actors he repped did on-screen), Shiffrin represented Vince Edwards and Bob Mathias. (Edwards, dark and angry-looking, would eventually gain fame on TV as Ben Casey, a dark and angry-looking doctor.) Mathias had won the Olympic gold medal in the decathlon in London in 1948 and again in Helsinki in 1952 (the only person at the time to ever accomplish that feat); in 1954 he'd starred in a film about his own early life, Francis D. Lyon's *The Bob Mathias Story*, in which he played himself. Before he knew it, a film career, if not a star, was born. He knocked around B-films for a few years, proving to everyone that he had no acting ability whatsoever, then turned to politics and served four terms as a Republican congressman for California's San Joaquin Valley.

Through the grapevine of agents, Shiffrin had heard about a new one-hour western series that CBS was planning, to follow up on the enormous ratings success of *Gunsmoke*. *Gunsmoke* had begun as a radio drama in 1952, a creation of producer-writer-developer Charles Marquis "Bill" Warren, director Norman MacDonnell, and writer John Meston. Put on the air by CBS head William Paley, it quickly became a sensation. *Gunsmoke* spawned dozens of similar "adult" westerns on all three networks. CBS wanted to find another one just as good (and just as profitable).

The producer of the new series, Robert Sparks, an executive at CBS in charge of filmed programming, and principal writer Warren began the search for an actor who could make the series his own. Casting was crucial to a TV series's success, more than a film's, because of

its recurring nature. The right star, like Arness, could make a bad series. The wrong star could kill a good one.

In the new series, each season a bunch of wranglers would move a herd of cattle north, and the episodes would tell the stories of their adventures during the journey. The format was already in use quite successfully on NBC's *Wagon Train*, in which passengers moved every season from the East Coast to the West. Paley wanted something that combined *Gunsmoke*'s drama with *Wagon Train*'s expanse.

Neither Sparks nor Warren was a newcomer to series TV. Warren, who had had the original idea for *Gunsmoke*, had met and to some extent been mentored by the great American writer F. Scott Fitzgerald while in college at Maryland, where he made All-American as a football player, when Fitzgerald was living in the area. Heavily influenced by the romance of Fitzgerald's addictive personality, Warren became a heavy drinker and a barroom tough guy, neither of which got him anywhere in school. Upon graduation in 1934, Warren took off for Hollywood (à la Fitzgerald), determined to break into the film industry and make a name for himself, to succeed where Fitzgerald had failed. After service in World War II as a navy commander, he found success as a pulpy western serial writer for *The Saturday Evening Post*. Many of his stories were adapted and made into novels, and some into movies. Forever in need of money (and booze), Warren moved into television, where he became a favorite of Bill Paley, the chairman and founder of CBS. After conceiving *Gunsmoke*, Warren could do no wrong, and the new series was his for the asking.

He had originally called his new pilot script *The Outrider*, but Paley rejected the title, believing no one would know what it meant except outriders (the cowboys who rode outside a herd and kept it moving). Instead he suggested *Rawhide*, a meaningless term—a strip of leather— that had been the title of a successful 1951 Henry Hathaway western that starred Tyrone Power. Paley liked it because it immediately evoked "western" to him and also because a lot of what eventually became *Wagon Train* on TV had been loosely based on the original story of that film.

Robert Sparks, as a program executive, had specialized in westerns, most notably 1957's slick and highly entertaining *Have Gun—Will*

Travel, a Saturday-night half-hour hit show starring movie veteran Richard Boone in the role of Paladin, the intellectually superior, highly cultured gun-for-hire. Paley assigned Sparks to work with Warren on the proposed new series.

Warren, for his part, had just directed a feature film called *Cattle Empire* (1958), written by his frequent partner and co-writer (Warren was uncredited), Hungarian émigré Endre Bohem. It was about the troubles of life on a cattle drive and starred Joel McCrea, one of Hollywood's best-known and best-liked cowboy heroes. The film owed a lot to Howard Hawks's great *Red River* (1948), which starred John Wayne and Walter Brennan and made young Montgomery Clift a star.

Warren was a big fan of Clift's style of acting, soft-spoken and good-looking, tough but not bullying, and sensitive in a youthful and appealing way. Knowing that Clift, now one of the biggest (and most difficult) actors in Hollywood, would not do TV, Warren wanted an actor who captured Clift's qualities in *Red River* to balance off the tough, grizzled leader of the drives, Gil Favor, to be played by Eric Fleming, thirty-four years old and properly grizzled. He resembled a young Ben Gazzara with his face swollen after a fistfight. Heavier and a couple of inches taller than Clint, his acting style was thought of in Hollywood as less Method than maniac. Once cast in the role, he believed he *was* Gil Favor.

As Sparks and Warren continued their search for an actor who could support Fleming, Shiffrin believed there might be something in *Rawhide* for his new client, Clint Eastwood. Unknown to him, Clint was already on the trail of the show via a young woman he'd known from back in his Universal days. Sonia Chernus was a former script reader for Arthur Lubin who now did that same job for him at CBS. She was one of the few women Clint associated with during that period who became a friend rather than a lover. She had met and become friends with Maggie as well.

Perhaps Clint was aware of *Rawhide* through Lubin; perhaps Chernus heard about it and thought of him; or perhaps Clint had been sniffing around Lubin's new production setup at the network, where Lubin had made it clear Clint was always welcome, in the hopes of finding some acting work. Whatever the actual details were (no one, including Clint, seems to remember exactly), Chernus man-

aged to convince Sparks—who had seen hundreds of actors and was frustrated at not being able to find a costar for *Rawhide*—to at least see Clint for a few minutes.

The meeting, spontaneous and casual, took place in the CBS hallway, with Chernus standing between the two men as they briefly spoke. Sparks asked Clint what specifically he had done. Clint mentioned a few projects, including *Ambush at Cimarron Pass*. He was relieved when Sparks said he hadn't seen it but worried when Sparks said he would take a look at it as soon as possible.

Sparks casually asked Clint how tall he was, and Clint told him he was six foot four. Sparks then invited him into his office, while Chernus remained outside. Sparks introduced Clint to Charles Warren. They talked for a while about *Rawhide* and how they saw it with two leads, one younger, one older. When the meeting ended, both Sparks and Warren promised to take a look at *Ambush at Cimarron Pass* (something that could not have made Clint happy) and get in touch with his agent, Shiffrin, sometime that week. Chernus, who was waiting outside in the hallway, walked Clint back outside to his car and told him to relax, hang loose, that she would let him know as soon as she heard something.

Later that same day Clint received a call from Shiffrin saying he had heard from Sparks and Warren. They weren't interested in screening the film but did want to screen-test him for the younger lead, Rowdy Yates, as soon as possible. The next day Clint found himself back at CBS. He was sent to wardrobe to be outfitted in western garb, introduced to Fleming, and given a scene to study.

After Clint left, Sparks and Warren watched the screen test dozens of times. Warren liked the similarities he saw in Clint's audition to Clift's performance in *Red River*. Sparks, however, was less impressed and was leaning toward another actor, Bing Russell. CBS executive Hubbell Robinson, in charge of all the network's programming, had been sent from New York City by Paley specifically to sit in on all the casting decisions for *Rawhide;* he had the final say and sided with Warren, believing Clint was the right actor to play Rowdy Yates.*

---

*Neil "Bing" Russell, the father of actor Kurt Russell, was later cast as Deputy Clem Foster in *Bonanza*, a role he played from 1961 until the series ended a decade later.

A week later he got the phone call telling him the good news. Just like that, Clint had landed a starring role in a major network TV series. The first episode of *Rawhide*, "Incident of the Tumbleweed Wagon," aired at eight o'clock on Friday night, January 9, 1959, sandwiched between two of CBS's biggest winners, the enormously popular *Hit Parade* and *The Phil Silvers Show*.

Rawhide proved a smash in its first season. For the next seven years it was a staple of American weekly television viewing* and along the way made cathode-cowboy stars out of its two male leads.

---

*In its first full season the show was moved up to 7:30. In 1963 it was moved to Thursdays at 8:00. In 1964 it moved back to Fridays at 7:30. In 1965 it was moved to Tuesdays at 7:30.

FOUR

I was set to direct a segment of Rawhide *once in those days but it never came about. I think some other actor had tried and run way over budget so they wouldn't let me try.*

—Clint Eastwood

When Clint got his first look at the advance fall 1958 schedule of TV shows and didn't see *Rawhide* anywhere on it, he broke out in hives. Filming the first episodes had been a difficult and awkward process; everybody was just beginning to get to know one another, and the kinks were still being worked out of the characters and scripts. Worse, even after production began, the network couldn't make up its mind whether the show should be an hour or a half hour or even on the air at all. Warren had wanted a full hour and a half, which Paley might have actually gone for if Phil Silvers wasn't doing as well as he was in the coveted Friday-night prime-time nine o'clock slot.

In 1958, in what was supposed to have been *Rawhide*'s first season, a little less than one-third of all prime-time network TV shows (30 out of 108) were westerns; that was a problem. Advertisers felt the market was oversaturated and preferred a new genre of shows that was about to break big, crime and law-and-order programs. Nine one-hour episodes had been completed (the producers figured on the middle ground; one hour could easily be cut down to a half hour or expanded to ninety minutes); the network had spent a fortune shooting on location in Arizona; Warren had hired his old friend Andrew V. McLaglen (veteran film actor Victor McLaglen's son) to come in and direct a couple of episodes on a play-or-pay basis; and some of Hollywood's biggest, if slightly over-the-hill, movie stars, including Dan Duryea, Troy Donahue, Brian Donlevy, and Margaret O'Brien, appeared in guest roles. Yet the network remained divided over the fate of *Rawhide*.

Weeks of delay passed into months. Clint became notably frustrated as his big break seemed to be slipping away, and at times he was visibly angry. He'd be in a restaurant and in the middle of a conversation might clear the table with his arm, sending everything on it crashing to the ground. One night he had such a severe anxiety attack

that ambulances came screaming up Ventura Boulevard to his home. When they arrived, they gave him a bag to breathe into until he was able to regain his equilibrium.

Other programs were offering Clint small parts, most of them arranged by Lubin, and he could have taken at least one major film role.* But by contract, he could not accept any other work on television or in the movies that CBS did not first approve, and they were stingy with their potential star-in-the-making. When the Broadway team of Howard Lindsay and Russel Crouse offered him the starring role in a big-screen adaptation of the novel *Tall Story*, the network forced him to turn it down. The role went instead to Tony Perkins.

For Christmas 1958 Clint and Maggie decided to take a train to Piedmont, to visit friends and his family who had moved back from Seattle. Clint was looking forward to the peace and quiet of the scenic ride, hoping to get away from everything. On the way, while on board the train, a telegram arrived for him stating that *Rawhide* had been put on the January replacement schedule and that on the first day of the new year he was to report for the resumption of production. Paley had overridden everyone else and insisted the show be added in a one-hour version to the midseason schedule. Clint whooped when he read the news, and then ordered a bottle of champagne for himself and Maggie. The celebration lasted the rest of the way to Piedmont.

On January 1 Clint joined the cast in Arizona, where the show's permanent outdoor set had been erected. Besides Rowdy Yates and Gil Favor, the series's other regular characters included an Indian scout, a cook, his helper, and some "grizzled" cowhands, as the production notes describe them. The scout was played by Sheb Wooley, an actor/country singer who had made an indelible impression as one of Frank Miller's gang of killers in Fred Zinnemann's iconic 1952 western *High Noon*. Wooley had worked for Warren before, and the two had become friends. Warren had insisted Wooley be given his part on the show. For the cook, Wishbone, intended as comic relief, Warren turned to Paul Brinegar, and as the cook's helper, Mushy, James

---

*Clint did get permission to play a navy lieutenant in a 1958 segment of *Navy Log* and appeared in an episode of *Maverick*, a top-rated TV western. The episode, "Duel at Sundown," was directed by Lubin, who pulled some strings at CBS to get them to let Clint appear.

Murdock. Steve Raines and Rocky Shahan became, respectively, cowhands Jim Quince and Joe Scarlett.

But perhaps the biggest single ingredient in making the show a hit was Dimitri Tiomkin's *Rawhide* theme. In the 1950s and 1960s, every TV show had to have identifiable theme music that opened and closed it under the credits. Many of these signature show themes went on to become pop-culture classics—*I Love Lucy*'s bouncing Latin-tinged theme, the whistle at the beginning of *The Andy Griffith Show*, the brassy horns of *The Dick Van Dyke Show*, the thunderous theme of *Bonanza*, the high-stringed opening of *The Fugitive*, and the pulse-pounding Lalo Schifrin theme for *Mission Impossible*. Tiomkin's theme song for *High Noon* had won him and his writing partner Ned Washington a Best Song Oscar (while he won a solo Oscar for Best Score); now he reteamed with Washington to create the *Rawhide* theme, with its unforgettable "Roll 'em, roll 'em, roll 'em, keep those dogies rollin' . . . *Rawhiiide* . . . ," sung by Frankie Laine, sounding as if he were being dragged to the electric chair. The song was so energetically catchy, it became a hit single and helped make *Rawhide* a welcome weekly guest in living rooms across the country.

In the beginning, *Rawhide* was unquestionably Fleming's show. He was the star, hero, leader of the herders, narrator, and main interest of the story lines of many early episodes. Clint, meanwhile, played his mostly silent (at first) sidekick, rough, tough, cute, and slim, with a fast gun and faster fists. But as soon as the executives at CBS, especially William Paley, saw the first show, they knew they had found something special in their new leading man—not Fleming but Clint—who brought something to *Rawhide* that Fleming didn't, or couldn't: youthful appeal, in the new culture that had grown up in the aftermath of Brando, James Dean, and Elvis Presley. Young boys *and* girls quickly became the main demographic of the show, and Clint, not Fleming, was the reason. By the end of the first year his $600-a-week salary was doubled, and by the end of the show's run he was making six figures annually.

After his second season on *Rawhide*, Clint felt secure enough in CBS's projection of a long run that he bought a house in Sherman Oaks near Beverly Glen Boulevard—a vast improvement in neighborhood and living quarters, and with a pool all his own. Maggie

retired from her various jobs and devoted herself to turning their new house into a real home. But even with paintings, photos, and furniture, one essential of their new life was missing for her. Married seven years now, Maggie was, at her husband's insistence, still childless.

At least one reason may have been psychological. Clint told biographer Richard Schickel that the lingering insecurity of being a Depression baby, of having to watch his parents struggle to keep food on the table and clothes on their backs, had affected all the Eastwoods. The sentiments sound genuine, but his star was on the rise, and money, fame, and stability tend to allow one to conquer one's childhood fears and rages. While Clint's fears may have been so deeply embedded that physical security could never adequately make up for what he lacked in childhood (a childhood that wasn't all *that* bad, considering the times), more likely, something was fundamentally wrong with the marriage.

Despite his newfound fame, money, and home, Clint's sexual appetites remained unchecked and unclassifiable; the only measure of morality he understood or was willing (or perhaps able) to respect was discretion. In a February 1974 *Playboy* magazine interview, Clint indirectly alluded to an understanding between him and "Mags" (or "Mag" as he sometimes called her) about the special openness of their marriage. The *Playboy* interviewer, film critic Arthur Knight, asked Clint about his "fairly open relationship with Mag," to which he replied, "Sure. Oh, yeah, we've always had—I'd hate to say I'm a pioneer with women's lib or whatever, but we've always had an agreement that she could enter any kind of business she wanted to. We never had that thing about staying home and taking care of the house. There's always a certain respect for the individual in our relationship; we're not one person. She's an individual, I'm an individual, and we're friends . . . I'm not shooting orders to her on where she's supposed to be every five minutes, and I don't expect her to shoot them at me." When asked if he preferred blondes like Maggie, Clint replied, "For marriage, no. For fooling around, sure, fooling around a little, hanky-panky, you know, sitting in the saloon with that old patter, 'Do you come here often' . . . I think friendship is important. Everybody talks about love in marriage, but it's just as important to be friends."

If this sounded a bit disingenuous, it's because Clint was fairly certain Mags would never talk in public about such things. Instead, a

combination of denial and rationale served as her survival mecha-
nism. At least part of the problem was that his new success allowed
Clint to slide into the saddle of the emerging sexual zeitgeist of the
1960s, while Maggie remained firmly planted in the uptight culture
of the 1950s. Nonetheless, each satisfied some need in the other that
allowed them, despite Clint's indiscretions, to continue to operate as
a couple, as parents without children, as friends, or perhaps more
accurately, as parents to each other.

As Clint's star continued to rise, one relationship that he had no
interest or need in maintaining was with Bill Shiffrin. Once Clint had
gotten what he wanted from Shiffrin, as with Lubin, he simply—some
might say coldly—moved on. After all, Shiffrin had benefited from
Clint's being hired to play Rowdy Yates rather than actually causing
it to happen. Clint replaced him with Lester Salkow, an agent with a
strong relationship to Universal, where Clint hoped eventually to
move back into feature films.

But Salkow quickly proved to be more a figurehead than a power
agent. Clint soon discovered where the real power lay in Hollywood's
emerging post-studio era: the entertainment lawyers, who were
increasingly playing the role of both manager and agent for their
clients. Soon enough Clint attached Frank Wells to his expanding
team of representatives. Both Leonard and Wells were up-and-coming
Hollywood-based lawyers, and as soon as they connected with Clint,
they edged out Salkow and took over virtually every aspect of his
career. They financially restructured his income so that he could
legally keep considerably more money for himself and pay less in taxes.
They arranged salary deferments and the purchase of extensive and
still relatively cheap land in Northern California, mostly in Monterey
County, including land in Carmel, a still underpopulated area that
Clint especially liked.

Leonard was primarily the moneyman, while Wells handled career
decisions. Leonard arranged to have all of Clint's income sent directly
to him; he then dispensed what was needed for expenses, mostly to
Maggie, who had taken over full-time management of the Eastwood
household. Having retired from her "career," such as it was, and having to deal with Clint's increasingly long absences, it was a bit of a
relief for her. She also developed an intense interest in tennis. To

accommodate Clint, Leonard reportedly kept two sets of books, one for the IRS and one for Maggie, so she would remain unaware of how much money Clint spent pursuing other women.

Meanwhile Clint's fame was growing. He appeared on the cover of *TV Guide* several times, a sure sign of his entrance into the pantheon of TV royalty, sometimes alone and sometimes with Eric Fleming. Clint was always happy when he didn't have to share the cover with Fleming, with whom it was widely believed he did not get along particularly well. They were never close, never buddies, did not travel in the same social circles, and did not share the same off-screen interests. Moreover, Fleming was fighting his career's downward slope, even as its highlight was *Rawhide*. Clint, on the other hand, was on the way up, which did not sit well with Fleming.

Adding to their strained relationship, series television then, as now, was and is a grind, rather like baseball's endless summers. No matter how much money he made, or how much extracurricular freedom it allowed him, Clint was still tied to a long workweek. Each season's production schedule commenced in late July and did not finish until April, with frequent location trips. And playing the same character week after week, season after season, year after year, was unavoidably tedious.

After a long run in a series, audiences, as well as performers, tend to get trapped in a syndrome of expectations difficult to break. Clint instinctively understood this trap and was constantly trying to stretch the relatively rigid parameters of the character of Rowdy Yates; at the same time Frank Wells was hard at work trying to convince Universal to let Clint appear in movies during the show's off-season. The network, however, continually turned all offers down, not wanting to have audiences see Clint Eastwood as anyone but Rowdy Yates.

The network was loath to tinker with the show's successful formula and kept its brand-name characters and the actors who played them on a tight rein. They also saw to it that no one director became too valuable to the series (meaning too expensive). So the producers regularly chose from an informal team of TV (and occasional movie) journeymen that they kept in a steady rotation. They believed this system further diminished the chance of any stylistic flourishes and therefore potentially damaging digressions. Each director was given

a shooting script with pre-directions written into it—when to cut, when to pan, when to push in, when to pull out. Rather than creative directors, they were, in effect, formulaic technicians, required to closely follow the formula and the format.

The writing too was formulaic. Very little was ever revealed about the lead characters' backstories. Eventually it did come out that Rowdy had been in the Confederate army, spent time in a northern prison, and was starting a new life as a herder. But there was never a lot of information given about any of the characters because, the producers felt, it wasn't germane to the self-contained week-to-week story lines of the show.

While the network held firm and did not let Clint take any movie work (or appear on any other CBS shows as a guest in contemporary clothing, such as *The Jack Benny Show*), Universal did manage to hire him out to play live rodeos, along with Sheb Wooley (substituting for Fleming, who refused to do them), who had had some rodeo experience in his years before becoming an actor, and Paul Brinegar. Together they put on a little skit with some singing and dancing. Both Wooley and Clint could sing well enough to pull it off, and they were quickly able to master the dancing, mostly some fake rope twirling. Audiences, mostly kids, flocked to see Rowdy Yates (not Clint Eastwood) in person. Clint and Wooley each received $1,500 per show.*

The other thing Clint was allowed to do was to make a 45-rpm single recording. A lot of the stars of 1950s and 1960s shows made records, and perhaps the most successful was Edd "Kookie" Byrnes of *77 Sunset Strip*, who had an improbable hit with "Kookie, Kookie (Lend Me Your Comb)," at once the high-water mark and the drowning point of Byrnes's relatively short-lived stardom. In 1961 Clint recorded "Unknown Girl" (backed with a cover version of a 1950s pop tune, "For All We Know"). The recording did well enough to get Clint an album deal, *Rawhide's Clint Eastwood Sings Cowboy Favorites*. Recorded on the Cameo Records label, the album featured Clint in a cowboy outfit on the front and back, without identifying his character as Rowdy Yates. The breathless back liner notes read in part:

*Reports vary as to the actual amount. Schickel, who presumably heard it directly from Clint, reported it as $1,500. Patrick McGilligan said $15,000. Considering that rodeo money has always been notoriously modest to performers, Schickel's figure is more likely the correct one.

The folk song that truly represents a branch of American culture is the western cowboy song. Ever since courageous Americans crossed the prairies, western songs have been popular. And there is no better prototype of that "cowboy" than Cameo/Parkway's recording artist, Clint Eastwood, a "native" westerner and a "natural" performer.

This album represents a collection of songs closely identified with the spirit of America. Here, then, Cameo/Parkway's talented vocalist Clint Eastwood, and America's most popular "cowboy favorites" . . . an unsurpassed combination that spells "entertainment."*

Audiences bought it in fairly good numbers, a testament to Clint's popularity rather than to his singing. Most of the money went to Universal and Cameo, but Clint was less concerned about the profits than about what the gimmick might mean to his career. He wasn't a pop country tune singer and didn't want to be—his musical interests remained firmly rooted in jazz. When Cameo, with Universal's enthusiastic approval, wanted to follow it up, Byrnes-style, Clint flatly rejected the notion. To avoid becoming the next "Kookie," he brought his potential teen idol career to a screeching halt.

In February 1962 the show's by-now-worldwide popularity led to a personal PR tour of Japan that featured Fleming and Clint in full-dress cowboy outfits. They were mobbed everywhere they went. Maggie did not accompany Clint on the tour, and many suspected that he simply did not want to take her, preferring to enjoy the fruits of his stardom unencumbered by a wife.

So Maggie stayed home, either oblivious to or unconcerned by Clint's philandering, playing tennis with her new upscale friends that included William Wellman's daughter, Cissy Wellman (whom she had met and become close to when Clint appeared in *Lafayette Escadrille*), Bob Daley, and other neighbors and acquaintances.

More offers for starring roles in films came from both England and Rome; Clint wanted to take them but had to turn them down. In April 1963, his fourth year on the show, CBS sensed they needed to loosen

---

*The tracks are: "Bouquet of Roses," "Sierra Nevada," "Don't Fence Me In," "Are You Satisfied," "Santa Fe Trail," "Last Roundup," "Mexicali Rose," "Tumblin' Tumbleweed," "Twilight on the Trail," "Searchin' for Somewhere," "I Love You More," and "San Antonio Rose."

the reins just a bit and allowed Clint to make an appearance on another network TV hit series. One reason may have been that, for the first time, *Rawhide* had dropped in the ratings against some new and formidable competition. *International Showtime* on NBC managed to knock *Rawhide* out of the top twenty-five. Believing the show needed some fresh publicity, the network asked Clint to guest-star on an episode of its highly rated hit sitcom, Arthur Lubin's *Mr. Ed*, based on a short story, "Ed Takes the Pledge," by Walter Brooks.

Although it wasn't exactly the type of stretch Clint was looking for, he agreed to do it as long as he did not have to appear as Rowdy Yates or wear cowboy clothing. The network readily acquiesced.

One of that show's writers was his friend Sonia Chernus, who had helped arrange the meeting with Warren that led to his being cast on *Rawhide*. For this episode she wrote "Clint Eastwood Meets Mr. Ed." The episode's plot was as idiotic as the talking-horse premise of the sitcom: Mr. Ed is jealous of Clint's horse on *Rawhide*, Midnight, because she's been having affairs with other horses in the neighborhood. Clint remained above it all, did the episode dressed in the contemporary So-Cal style of sweater and slacks, smiled amiably, collected his fee, and went on his way. Nonetheless, by playing himself he had officially earned the status of "big television star." Only upper-echelon celebrities such as Bob Hope, Jimmy Stewart, John Wayne, and Frank Sinatra could regularly make appearances on programs as themselves. Clint may not have particularly enjoyed the experience, playing, in effect, a horse's ass, but that week's numbers for *Mr. Ed* were huge, and afterward *Rawhide*'s ratings ticked up—but not enough to return it to the top twenty, a ranking it would never again attain.

Clint's troubled marriage took a potentially disastrous turn when he became involved with a twenty-nine-year-old statuesque brunette by the name of Roxanne Tunis. A stuntwoman, dancer, and occasional actress, Tunis had appeared in Robert Wise and Jerome Robbins's 1961 *West Side Story* and as an extra in Alfred Hitchcock's 1963 horror film *The Birds*. She now showed up fairly regularly on *Rawhide*, where she met Clint. Separated from her husband, she and Clint began an intense and highly sexual affair. Tunis was openly affectionate to Clint on the set, as if she wanted the world to know what was going on. She cared for him constantly, openly massaging his neck,

listening to his problems, and putting absolutely no pressure on him for anything more than what she already had.

Often in the evenings, when shooting was through, he would go with Tunis to her place, stay awhile, and then leave for his home. No matter how late he arrived, Maggie never said anything and never complained. That he often may have smelled of another woman was something she tried to avoid dealing with, even though *Rawhide* had very little romance in its script and virtually none for Rowdy Yates. Everyone on the show knew about the affair, and if it bothered Clint or made any difference to him, he didn't seem to care. If everyone knew, everyone knew.

Then one day Tunis was noticeably absent from the set. No one knew why; they may have just assumed that Clint had decided she was becoming too much of a distraction. That was not the case. Tunis was pregnant with Clint's child, and they both decided it might be better if she stayed out of sight for the duration of her pregnancy.

A more immediate problem for Clint was Fleming's increasing absences. Fleming was worried that he was becoming too typecast in his role and that as he got older, fewer and fewer parts would be offered to him once the series ended. He was unable to come to terms with the network about other offers he wanted to take and was looking for a hefty increase in salary. In 1964, as in almost every season of *Rawhide*, he dramatically walked off the show.* This time Charles Gray, who had been on the show since 1961, compensated for Fleming's absence and was now elevated to the larger role as the primary scout. Guest stars became increasingly prominent in the show's plot lines. Both actions infuriated the always short-fused Fleming.

Then late in 1964 Fleming was offered a starring role in a Mexican-based western to be shot in Italy called *El magnifico stragnero (The Magnificent Stranger)*. Henry Fonda, Rory Calhoun, Charles Bronson, James Coburn, Henry Silva, Steve Reeves, and Richard Harrison had all previously turned it down because of director Sergio Leone's lowball offer of $15,000. Fleming thought about it for a while but ultimately said no.

---

*Fleming's first walk-off happened during the second season, when he was unhappy with Warren's having been replaced by Endre Bohem. This was the first season that entire episodes appeared without Fleming, but it wouldn't be the last.

Clint was now represented by the venerable and powerful William Morris Agency (but he still retained the financial management and industry clout of Irving Leonard for some deals, including anything that came out of *Rawhide* and anything else Leonard found on his own. Leonard was one of Clint's most trusted associates; in the vernacular of *The Godfather*, his "consigliere"). One of its agents stationed in the Rome office, Claudia Sartori, had the idea of offering the Leone film to Clint. She screened an episode of *Rawhide* for Leone and his producers, Jolly Films, which was financing the movie.* Miffed that Fleming had turned him down and increasingly desperate to find an American actor, Leone was pleasantly surprised at Clint's ability to take the focus off of Fleming in virtually every scene they were in together. By the end of the screening, Leone was interested in Clint.

Sartori then took the script of *The Magnificent Stranger* back to America, to give to Clint, via Irving Leonard, to make sure all proprietary representation claims were honored. Leonard assigned a recent young protégé, Sandy Bressler, to personally deliver the script to Clint and gently urge him to take it. This was no easy task, as Clint, like Fleming and all the others, was firmly against appearing in something that sounded as absurd as a European-made western.

"I knew I wasn't a cowboy," Clint said later on. "But if you portray a cowboy and people think you're a cowboy, that's fine. . . . I was asked if I was afraid of being typed when I started *Rawhide* . . . but in reality everyone is typed for something."

Clint offered little resistance to Bressler's arguments because, as he discovered, the script wasn't all that bad. It was, in fact, reminiscent of the great samurai films of Kurosawa and other classic Japanese filmmakers (whose movies, in turn, had been inspired by American westerns of the 1930s and 1940s). Clint was familiar with Kurosawa's films because he had often shown them during his projectionist stint at Fort Ord. Besides, he'd never been to Italy before, and he could pick up a quick $15,000 (plus all expenses for the eleven-week shoot, including a round-trip coach ticket for one) for the few weeks' work during

---

*She watched Episode 91, "Incident of the Black Sheep," which originally ran November 10, 1961. (Up to and including the show's sixth season, when new producers were brought in, all episodes of *Rawhide* had "Incident" in their title.) In it battling herders settle a dispute with a knife-fight between Rowdy and hostile sheepherder Tod Stone (Richard Basehart). Stone "falls" on his knife, and the dispute ends.

Rawhide's hiatus. He told Leonard he would take the deal if CBS allowed it. Leonard told him not to worry—pending Leone's approval, he would convince the network to agree.

According to Clint, "Sergio Leone had only directed one other picture, but they told me he had a good sense of humor . . . [Besides] I had the series to go back to as soon as the hiatus was over. So I felt, 'Why not?' I'd never seen Europe. That was reason enough to go."

At least that was what he told the public. Privately, he may have had an even more urgent reason for wanting to make the movie. He was about to become a father for the first time. Tunis was scheduled to deliver while he was in Spain, and that was one climactic event he wanted to be as far away from as possible.

FIVE

What struck me most about Clint was his indolent way of moving. It seemed to me Clint closely resembled a cat.

—Sergio Leone

Clint left for Rome the first week of May, the day after *Rawhide*'s 1964 hiatus began, without Maggie but with his one-time neighbor and friend Bill Thompkins. Clint had helped Thompkins land the small part of Toothless on *Rawhide*, and he now hoped to pick up some work on Leone's film as Clint's stunt double and stand-in, something he also occasionally did on the show.

At the Leonardo da Vinci Airport they were met by a small entourage that consisted of the film's publicist, Geneviève Hersent; assistant director Mario Cavano; and dialogue director Tonino Valerii, who offered Clint Leone's apologies for not being there himself, saying he was unfortunately tied up with preproduction. In truth, Leone did not speak a word of English and did not want to be embarrassed by it in public, especially since a handful of dependable paparazzi were sure to be there to photograph the arrival of the famous American TV cowboy.

Leone was thrilled that Clint had agreed to be in the film. Leone loved Hollywood films and actors. In his early, struggling years he had worked as an assistant to various American directors who occasionally shot abroad and needed some native help. Among those Leone had worked for were Raoul Walsh, William Wyler, Robert Aldrich, and Fred Zinnemann, mostly for their sandals-and-robes ventures such as Wyler's 1959 production of *Ben-Hur*.* Wyler, like the others, had used Leone to help organize and stage the big outdoor scenes, such as the famed chariot race.

When he finally got the chance to direct his own movie, it was *Il Colosso di Rodi* in 1961 (released in the United States as *The Colossus of Rhodes*), with American actor Rory Calhoun in the lead. The film did surprisingly well internationally as well as in Italy, briefly resurrected

---

*Aka *Ben-Hur, a Tale of the Christ*.

Calhoun's Hollywood career, and put Leone in a position to choose his own next project.

He had had it in mind as early as 1959, when he was still a screenwriter on Mario Bonnard's 1959 *Gli ultimi giorni di Pompei (The Last Days of Pompeii)*, filmed on location in Pompeii and Naples and starring Steve Reeves, of *Hercules* fame. (Reeves seriously dislocated his shoulder during the film; the injury eventually forced his acting career to end prematurely.) Bonnard had fallen ill the first day of shooting, and with no one else available, Leone stepped in and "finished" it, directing all but the first day's footage. Working closely with Duccio Tessari, his co-writer, Leone managed to turn out a respectable film that made money. He was determined now to direct his own films.

In between working on other directors' movies, he and Tessari went to see as many as they could. One day in 1961 they saw *Yojimbo*, and Leone was blown away as much by Kurosawa's directing style as by the film's story. (Kurosawa had co-written *Yojimbo* with Hideo Oguni and Ryuzo Kikushima.) Leone contacted Kurosawa and asked for permission to adapt *Yojimbo* as an American-style Italian-made western. He already had a title that was in itself an homage to another favorite film, if not an outright steal: *The Magnificent Stranger* was a play on *The Magnificent Seven*, John Sturges's smash 1960 western adapted from Kurosawa's 1954 classic *Seven Samurai (Shichinin no samurai)*, the film that had made Kurosawa's reputation in the United States.

However, Kurosawa, perhaps weary of his films being "borrowed" by other directors, asked for an upfront $10,000 rights fee. Leone was confident he could get the money from Jolly Films, the production company that had agreed to back the first acceptable script he brought them; but to his surprise and dismay, Jolly said no, even though the entire proposed budget for the film, including Kurosawa's fee, was only $200,000. When it appeared that no deal could be reached, Jolly Films producers Harry Colombo and George Papi managed to work out a tentative deal with Kurosawa that bypassed the upfront $10,000 in exchange for 100 percent of the film's gross profits in Japan. Colombo and Papi thought it was a good deal for Kurosawa because *Rawhide* was a big hit on Japanese TV and Clint Eastwood was considered a major star. But in the end Kurosawa said no, a decision that would later come back to haunt Leone.

Nonetheless, early that June location shooting began in Spain,

before moving on to Rome for interiors at the famed but underused and relatively inexpensive Italian studio Cinecittà.

Within days of his being on the set, Clint realized that the film Leone was making was far different from the more conventional script he'd read back in the States. The story was familiar enough—a stranger comes to town, watches bad guys bully good people, is reluctant to take sides, gets drawn in to it, is nearly killed and left for dead, and then comes back and takes revenge against impossible odds to emerge victorious. Westerns in every decade of Hollywood filmmaking had elements of this scenario, including John Ford's *My Darling Clementine* (1946) and his *The Man Who Shot Liberty Valance* (1962), Howard Hawks's *Rio Bravo* (1959), Raoul Walsh's *The Lawless Breed* (1953), Fred Zinnemann's *High Noon* (1952), and George Stevens's *Shane* (1953), to which Leone's film also bears an especially strong resemblance in plot and visual stylistic touches; the Man with No Name, in poncho and sheepskin vest, vividly echoes Alan Ladd's mysterious stranger, gloriously costumed in buckskins.

Though it owes much to *Yojimbo* and *Shane*, however, *A Fistful of Dollars** also owes a great deal to the great pulp and genre writers of the first half of the twentieth century. The British critic and film historian Christopher Frayling has traced all these films' common plot line and characters to Dashiell Hammett's 1929 novel *Red Harvest* (the Continental Op is, significantly, a man without a name) and even further back to Carlo Goldoni's eighteenth-century play *Servant of Two Masters*. Leone himself often said that *Red Harvest* was a primary source of his script.[†]

What impressed Clint, and first clued him in to the fact that something might be going on other than just another European ripoff of American genres, was the stylistic flourish Leone used to shoot the film. Clint had become interested in directing well before he showed up in Italy, especially in the stylistics of directors that made their films personal. As he told it, during one episode of *Rawhide*:

> We were shooting some vast cattle scenes—about two thousand head of cattle. We were doing some really exciting stampede stuff. I was

riding along in the herd, there was dust rising up, and it was pretty wild really. But the shots were being taken from outside the herd, looking in, and you didn't see too much. I thought, we should get right in the middle of this damn stampede. I said to the director and producer, "I'd like to take an Arriflex [camera], run it on my horse and go right in the middle of this damn thing, even dismount, whatever— but get in there and really get some great shots, because there are some beautiful shots in there that we are missing." Well, they double-talked me. They said, "You can't get in there because of union rules." I could see they didn't want to upset a nice standard way of movie-making.

Even before he worked on *A Fistful of Dollars*, Clint had been think-ing a lot about how familiar setups, camera angles, and methodol-ogy—establish the scene in a master shot, cut to over-the-shoulder one-shots for the dialogue, finish the scene with the master shot, dis-solve into the next master—bred a uniformity in TV directors and made them all (directors and their shows) stylistically look the same. The day Clint wanted to shoot the cattle drive a little differently was the day the seeds of his future role as a director were planted.

Finally, I asked Eric Fleming, "Would you be averse to my directing?" He said, "Not at all, I'd be for it." So I went to the producer and he said great. Evidently he didn't say great behind my back; but he said great at the time. He said, "I'll tell you what, why don't you direct some trail-ers for us—coming attractions for next season's shows?" I said, "Ter-rific. I'll do it for nothing and then I'll do an episode." And I did the trailers. But they reneged on the episode because, at that time, several of their name actors on other television shows were directing episodes, not too successfully.

So about the time I was getting set to do it, CBS said no more series actors could direct their own shows . . . then I went to work with Ser-gio Leone.

Acting in the film proved difficult for Clint, primarily because Leone insisted on shooting in three languages simultaneously. Clint had to speak his lines in English while the other actors spoke in either Italian or Spanish. The result was a limited amount of dialogue that

Leone used to help create the strong silent mystique of the Man with No Name. Rather than having the character talk a lot, at Leone's insistence (Clint enthusiastically supported this decision and, with Leone's permission, cut much of his own dialogue out), he smoked cigarillos and used his big gun to do a lot of the talking for him. All of it allowed Clint to act with his face and his eyes rather than to talk as Rowdy Yates and almost every other character on *Rawhide* did, because on TV describing action is always a lot cheaper than actually showing it. ("You know those rustlers we rounded up yesterday?" "Yeah, I remember." "Well, two of them had a fight in their jail cell last night and we had to break it up." "Too bad I missed it." "One of them hit the other over the head with a bottle . . . and now the doc is with him. Let's go see how he's doing and maybe we can get some more information out of the varmint . . .")

Gradually, the slim backstory of the Man with No Name began to take shape. He was some kind of wandering knight in shining armor, which is revealed in a single sentence, after he helps a young couple escape the clutches of the evil Rojo, by explaining, "I knew someone like you once and there was no one there to help." That was all, and that was enough.

Clint found a wide hat he liked and wore it low to shade his eyes, giving him an even more menacing look while preserving a certain coolness—not an easy balance to maintain. And he wore a poncho, donned in the second half of the film, to hide his mangled hand from his opponents.* It became akin to Batman's cape. Finally, the metal shield he wore during the climactic shoot-out made him appear unearthly, as if he were an invincible alien from another world. Clint combined all these character accoutrements perfectly, throwing the cape back with a flourish in the film's final shoot-out, which Leone cut perfectly in sync to the extraordinary score by Ennio Morricone, the best film music for any western since Tiomkin's Academy Award–winning theme for *High Noon*.

Besides the stylized music-to-action and the low angles that Leone used to shoot the Man with No Name, he also cut close-ups of the characters' eyes in strong, rhythmic motions. As the action of the film

---

*Clint, like most actors, is superstitious. According to the Internet Movie Database, he used this poncho in all three Leone movies and insisted it never be washed or cleaned.

intensified, the close-ups got closer. And for the final, climactic shoot-out, Leone came up with one of the film's most unforgettable sequences; after a series of close-ups of eyes, a double-barreled shot-gun appears through a window, and the shot turns them into the per-fect cold, unfeeling, unblinking steely eyes of evil incarnate. The moment never fails to evoke cheers and chills in audiences, and rightly so. It is the kind of effect no other form can achieve, not theater, not television, not the novel—a moment that is purely kinetic, a triumph of directing and editing that does not take away from the story but adds a dramatic flourish to it.

Leone's cinematic feel was not lost on Clint:

An American would be afraid of approaching a western such as *Fistful of Dollars* with that kind of style. For instance, there were shots of a person being shot. In other words, you never shot a tie-up shot of a man shooting a gun and another person getting hit. It's a Hays Office rule from years ago, a censorship deal. You'd cut to the guy shooting, and then cut to a guy falling. That was all right—the same thing—the pub-lic isn't counting the cut. But you could never do a tie-up. We did because Sergio didn't know all that. He wasn't bothered by that. Nei-ther was I. I knew about it but I couldn't care less. The whole object of doing a film with a European director was to put a new shade of light on it.*

With filming completed, Clint packed his things and boarded a plane for America. It would make a brief stopover in London, then continue to Los Angeles, just as filming on the seventh season of *Rawhide* was about to begin. Maggie met Clint in person at the airport. Roxanne Tunis called the next day and happily informed him that he was now the proud father of a baby daughter, Kimber Tunis, born June 17, 1964, at Cedars Sinai Hospital in Hollywood. Although the

---

*The Production Code (also known as the Hays Code) was the set of industry censor-ship guidelines governing the production of American motion pictures. The Motion Pictures Producers and Distributors Association (MPPDA), which later became the Motion Picture Association of America (MPAA), adopted the code in 1930, began effec-tively enforcing it in 1934, and abandoned it in 1968 in favor of the subsequent MPAA film rating system. The Production Code spelled out what was morally acceptable and unacceptable content for motion pictures produced for a public audience in the United States.

father is listed on the birth certificate as Clinton Eastwood Jr., Tunis publicly gave the baby her last name, protecting Clint. He promised to support the child and did, emotionally and financially, asking from Tunis only that, if possible, the baby's identity be kept secret.

Clint now had to negotiate a fine line to make sure his worlds (and women) didn't collide. Thompkins, his longtime friend, agreed with Tunis that Clint should at least tell Maggie about the baby. Clint immediately and permanently cut him off. Thompkins was summarily fired from *Rawhide* and permanently disappeared from Clint's life.*

As for Maggie, it is difficult to say for sure that she actually knew about the baby, although it would have been nearly impossible for her not to. Everyone on the set knew, many of Maggie and Clint's friends knew, and it is simply too difficult to keep a secret like that when the mother and the illegitimate child live in the same small town, especially when that small town is Hollywood.

Perhaps that was one reason Clint suddenly decided he and Maggie should move north, to the Monterey Peninsula. He found a small home for them in Pebble Beach, and a second getaway place in Carmel, and assigned Maggie the familiar job of making the two houses into homes, even if he was going to be away from them, and her, most of the time, working on the show.

Meanwhile *Rawhide* was continuing to have problems not just with ratings but with salaries. The standard seven-year contracts that both Fleming and Clint had signed, the maximum allowed under AFTRA (American Federation of Television and Radio Artists), were set to expire at the end of the season, and neither the network nor the stars were particularly eager to extend them. New contracts for Fleming and Clint, the network knew, would be expensive propositions, more now for Clint than for Fleming, whose fan mail had markedly decreased while Clint's had steadily grown.

Moreover, CBS had decided to job out the entire production. Bruce Geller and Bernard Kowalski, two aggressive young independent producers, had formed a company called Unit Productions and won the

---

*He later tried to reconcile with Clint, who eventually did get him a few days' work as stunt coordinator on *A Fistful of Dollars*. Despite that assignment and the subsequent success of the film, Thompkins was unable to regain a professional foothold in Hollywood. He died of injuries he sustained in a 1971 automobile accident.

assignment from the network to take over *Rawhide*. They hired Del Reisman as executive producer, or "show runner," and made themselves highly profitable middlemen. One of the first things Reisman did was to screen episodes from all six previous seasons. He immediately saw that thirty-four-year-old Clint Eastwood was no longer suited to play Rowdy Yates; nor was Fleming, about to turn forty, to play Favor.

Reisman's solution was to fire Fleming and focus on Clint, hoping that Clint's maturing character Yates would work better solo. But before he could actually do it, Fleming, sensing trouble coming his way, went directly to William Paley and complained that the new production team was going to ruin the show. Paley, a big fan, listened to Fleming and decided that CBS should not be jobbing out its shows. He fired Unit Productions, which meant that Reisman was gone as well, and he convinced Endre Bohem, one of the show's longtime line producers who had been let go when Unit was brought in, to come back.

But it did no good. By the end of the season, the show had slipped to number forty-four in the ratings. *Rawhide* had clearly turned into a tired replay of a good thing—the cattle could have reached the shores of China by now. "Every time they wanted a format change," Clint later recalled, "they'd drag in some other [producer] . . . they tried a lot of different approaches but Paley would tune in every now and then and get on the horn with 'What have you done with the show,' and they'd get back to basics."

In the spring of 1965, after one more season playing Rowdy, Clint jumped at the chance to return to Italy to star in Leone's planned sequel to *A Fistful of Dollars*, to be called *Per qualche dollaro in più (For a Few Dollars More)*.

By now, a mystique had grown around *A Fistful of Dollars* in America, where (in the days before video, cable, and the Internet) no one could actually see the film without traveling to Europe. Even so, it was talked about in magazines, on the radio, on television, and on college campuses all across the country. Tales of the film's "unbelievable" action sequences traveled in whispers, while *Variety*, the showbiz bible, printed story after story about the movie's phenomenal overseas box-office success.

Indeed, in Europe it had been a hit from the day of its release; in the November 18, 1964, issue of *Daily Variety*, the newspaper's Rome reporter kicked off the type of noncritical enthusiasm that would follow the film wherever it played: "Crackerjack western made in Italy and Spain by a group of Italians and an international cast with James Bondian vigor and tongue-in-cheek approach to capture both sophisticates and average cinema patrons. Early Italo figures indicate it's a major candidate to be sleeper of the year. Also that word-of-mouth, rather than cast strength or ad campaign, is a true selling point. As such it should make okay program fare abroad as well." Clint, who now was widely known throughout Europe as "Il Cigarillo," rightly figured that sooner or later the film would have to play in America, Hays Code or no Hays Code. When the offer came for him to make the sequel, he quickly accepted it.

But before Leone could actually start production, he had to settle the still-unresolved dispute between Jolly Films and Kurosawa over the division of profits from the first film. When the case went to formal litigation, Leone simply declared himself free from all future obligations to Jolly and signed a new deal with Produzioni Europee Associates, headed by Alberto Grimaldi, one of the better-known Italian producers, who had worked with many of Italy's greatest directors. Leone secured a $350,000 fee for himself, plus 60 percent of the profits for his proposed sequel to *A Fistful of Dollars*, if—and it was a big if—he could get Clint Eastwood to return as the star. Leone told Grimaldi not to worry and quickly found himself a new screenwriter, Luciano Vincenzoni, who, working together with the director, came up with a completed shooting script in nine days.

The character of Ramón Rojo, played by Italian actor Gian Maria Volontè, had been killed off in the first film, but this one would bring the actor back in a different (but essentially the same) character. Lee Marvin would play a rival bounty hunter to the Man with No Name, who is also hunting down Volontè. Marvin was all set to go until he asked for more money. Leone fired him and replaced him with Lee Van Cleef, a Hollywood character actor with a once-bright future who had fallen on hard times. He had made his debut in *High Noon* as one of Frank Miller's gang out to kill Will Kane. Van Cleef was originally cast in the far better role of Kane's deputy, but when he refused to get his big and hooked nose "fixed," the part went instead to Lloyd

Bridges, and it made him a star. Van Cleef, relegated to playing one of the Miller gang, was not given a single line of dialogue. Still, his debut was so powerful, he managed to get steady work as a bad guy throughout the 1950s, until his career finally petered out and he turned to painting. Starving in Europe and living on his oils, he leaped when Leone offered him Marvin's part for the $50,000 that Marvin had turned down.

Clint was also offered $50,000, plus a first-class round-trip plane ticket and top-of-the-line accommodations. Having accepted the terms, Il Cigarillo boarded a plane as soon as *Rawhide* went on hiatus, bound for Rome and Cinecittà studios, to begin filming.

This time Maggie accompanied him for the first ten days, then returned home and flew back again for the last ten days of filming in Spain. Clint's press agent played up the husband-and-wife angle for all it was worth, but as soon as Maggie left Italy, Clint was seen with some of the most beautiful actresses in Rome, and his villa was filled day and night with them, even as dozens of friends and co-workers came and went. Clint partied like a teenage boy with the keys to the liquor cabinet while his parents were away on a trip. He had become such a movie star in Europe that he could no longer walk down the street without hordes of people, mostly women, running after him, like something out of Richard Lester's satire on Beatlemania, *A Hard Day's Night.*

The film's three-way competition among gunfighters gave the film an added level of dramatic tension that the first film did not have, and Van Cleef especially, as he had been in *High Noon*, was superb in his role. When the completed film was released, it proved an even greater sensation than the original. This time, without Kurosawa to contend with, and with film censorship crumbling in America along with the entire studio system, Leone and Grimaldi were intent upon getting a distribution deal for this film for North America, where, they knew, the real money was. They approached Arthur Krim and Arnold Picker, the new heads of the reinvigorated United Artists looking to restore the studio's original vision as a distributor for the best works of other producers and directors. While in Europe looking for product, they were approached by Vincenzoni.

Grimaldi took Krim and Picker to a movie theater in Rome, rather than a private screening, so they could witness firsthand the attention

and excitement the film created in audiences. Afterward in a hotel room, Grimaldi asked for a million dollars. Krim and Picker countered with $900,000—a phenomenal amount of money for a foreign-made American-style western. Grimaldi took the deal.

Papers were drawn up, and at the actual signing Picker asked Leone what his next film would be, adding that UA might be interested in bankrolling it in return for exclusive distribution rights. On the spot Leone improvised a story of three post–American Civil War losers scrounging for money. That was it, that was all he had, and a title he made up then and there—*Il buono, il brutto, il cattivo (The Good, the Bad and the Ugly)**—that drew a laugh from Vincenzoni and broad grins when translated for Krim and Picker. Based on only that much, they agreed to put up between $1.2 million and $1.6 million to fund the making and to retain the North American rights.†

Back in the States, meanwhile, Clint reverted once more to play-ing Rowdy Yates on *Rawhide*, a show that by this time seemed like a cultural artifact from the past, a leftover from the days of *I Love Lucy*. Another nail in its coffin was the network's stubborn refusal to allow it to switch to color. James Aubrey, then the head of programming, turned thumbs down on the idea because of the expense; shooting in color would mean that more episodes would have to be shot to justify the cost, and there was very little stock footage of cattle drives. (The show had long ago switched to buying old footage from movies rather than staging its own, wildly expensive runs.)

The show was saved from cancellation only because Paley still loved it, and when Aubrey began talking about removing it from the schedule, Paley instructed CBS's executive vice-president Mike Dann to keep it on the air, no matter what Aubrey said. A new producer was

---

*Leone's original titles had been *The Magnificent Rogues*, and *The Two Magnificent Tramps*, which he spontaneously changed at the meeting.

†Grimaldi sold the world rights to UA for an additional million-dollar guarantee and 50 percent of the profits, excluding Italy, France, Germany, and Spain. Not long after-ward the lawsuit with Kurosawa was settled and Krim and Picker purchased the rights to *Fistful of Dollars*, giving Krim and Picker North American rights and a percentage of world rights to the trilogy, as well as the right to decide the American release dates for all three. Not long after UA's settlement, Jolly Films, meanwhile, which had pro-duced *Per un pugno di dollari* (1964), came out with a film called *The Magnificent Stranger*, which was actually two episodes of *Rawhide* (1959) edited together. Eastwood sued Jolly Films, and *The Magnificent Stranger* was quickly withdrawn.

brought in to try to spruce things up. Ben Brady, whose past hit show credits included *Perry Mason* and *Have Gun—Will Travel*, announced that for the new season the characters of James Murdock (Mushy) and Sheb Wooley (Pete) were to be eliminated from the cast, replaced by David Watson as an English drover; Raymond St. Jacques, an African-American actor with Shakespearean credits, as Simon Blake; and John Ireland, one of the stars of *Red River* and other gritty movie westerns, as Jed Colby. And there was one more change: Eric Fleming was out, and Rowdy Yates was promoted to trail boss (something Clint read about while in Rome, from a *Variety* clipping that Maggie sent him while he was finishing up *For a Few Dollars More*).

Clint's initial reaction was that they should have kept Favor and lost Rowdy. Shortly after the changes were announced, the *Los Angeles Times* dispatched Hal Humphrey to get Clint's reaction. He began by asking him if he was happy about becoming the top star of his show. "Why should I be pleased," Clint answered, not yet used to the fact that every word he said could and would be reprinted. "I used to carry half the shows. Now I carry them all. For the same money."

Clint was angry and had a right to be. Fleming's salary had been much higher than his ($220,000 per season, against Clint's $100,000 a season), and now he was expected to fill those big boots without a raise—a detail that CBS had significantly left out of its revamping of the show.

If the season began in turmoil, it descended rapidly from there. After only two episodes, the network announced that it was bringing back Sheb Wooley. Then it announced it wasn't. Both decisions had been made by Paley, without consulting Brady, who abruptly resigned. CBS then brought Bohem back, who said he wanted to relocate the show to Hawaii. He quickly retreated from that idea and resigned. Finally, in a last-ditch effort to save the show, CBS inexplicably moved *Rawhide* out of its regular Friday-night slot to Tuesday, opposite ABC's hotshot *Combat*, a hit World War II action series starring Vic Morrow, just as Vietnam was beginning to burn itself into the hearts and minds of the American public. After thirteen more episodes, *Rawhide* was canceled by CBS. The 217th and last first-run episode, "Crossing at White Feather," aired December 7, 1965, after which the series entered the ether of syndicated reruns.

Clint could not have been happier. Within days of shooting his

final scene, he flew back to New York to meet with producer Dino De Laurentiis, who said he had a proposition for Clint, the starring role in a new, big-budget movie to be shot in Europe and intended mainly for European audiences. Disappointed but resigned, Clint took the job, believing that big-screen Hollywood stardom was out of his reach.

I came back and did a very small-budget picture, called Hang
'Em High *. ... the movie business . . . was still thinking of me
as an Italian movie actor.*

—Clint Eastwood

De Laurentiis was on a mission to sign Clint, believing that, once the Leone westerns were released in the States, he would be box-office gold anywhere in the world there was a movie screen. De Laurentiis thought Clint could be his generation's Gary Cooper, and he wasn't shy about telling him so. Like any good hustler, he knew how to seduce to get what he wanted.

De Laurentiis had been in a successful film business partnership with Carlo Ponti, who in the mid-1950s had decided to turn his wife, Sophia Loren, into Italy's finest screen actress by having her play working-class Italian women and allowing her real-life glamour to peek out like expensive lingerie. She often starred opposite Marcello Mastroianni, who could effortlessly flip back and forth between glamour and working class, comedy and drama. Under Ponti's guidance, both Mastroianni and Loren became world famous and (along with Ponti) extremely wealthy.

De Laurentiis envisioned the same thing for himself and his new wife, Silvana Mangano. Another icon of postwar Italian cinema, she had gained international fame with her performance in *Bitter Rice* (1949), written and directed by Giuseppe De Santis and produced by De Laurentiis. At that time "anthology" films were the rage in Europe, so he decided to put together five of the best directors and have them each make a short film with Mangano. Each would reflect, like a highly polished diamond, a different facet of her ability.

And he didn't want any superstar like Mastroianni to steal his wife's thunder. After searching among suitable actors he could afford, De Laurentiis decided that Eastwood might be right. He knew he wasn't the best actor—a plus, to De Laurentiis—but he was one of the hottest faces in Europe. His popularity could only help his box office, but his acting, De Laurentiis was confident, could never overshadow Mangano's.

To entice Clint, De Laurentiis laid out the proverbial red carpet for his arrival in New York. He put Clint in a five-star hotel and drove him all around the city in a black stretch limousine, talking up the "great" script he had in mind. Then he closed in for the kill. De Laurentiis, who had done his homework, knew that Clint loved cars and so offered him his choice of two deals: $25,000 for one month's work, or $20,000 and a brand-new Ferrari. Clint grabbed the Ferrari deal (knowing he wouldn't have to pay an agency fee on it if it was listed as a gift).

That February 1966 Clint flew to Rome, a city that by now he knew quite well and had come to like a great deal, to appear in one episode of De Laurentiis's planned five-part epic, *Le streghe (The Witches)*. His episode was to be directed by Vittorio De Sica, who had made his name helming one of the defining films of postwar neorealism, *The Bicycle Thief* (1948).*

"A Night Like Any Other" (aka "An Evening Like the Others"), nineteen minutes long, featured Clint in modern dress, with buttondown shirt and slicked-back hair, trapped inside a loveless, unfulfilling marriage to Silvana Mangano. Only when he is asleep does he "live," as the sex star of his wife's fantasies; the episode climaxes with a self-imagined suicide, while his wife "dances" for dozens of men in a flesh club. This description does too much justice to the actual piece of film.

The film's American rights were acquired by Krim and Picker's UA on the strength of Clint's appearance. They were hoping to cash in on their eventual release of the Leone trilogy, but it was not officially released in the United States until 1969.†

According to Clint: "The stories [of the five episodes] didn't mean a whole lot. They were just a lot of vignettes all shuffled together. I enjoyed them, they were fun to do. Escapism."

*The other four segments and their directors were: "The Witch Burned Alive" directed by Luchino Visconti; "Civic Sense" (aka "Community Spirit"), directed by Mauro Bolognini; "The Earth as Seen from the Moon" (aka "Earth Seen from the Moon"), directed by Pier Paolo Pasolini; and "The Girl from Sicily" (aka "The Sicilian"), directed by Franco Rossi.

†UA eventually dropped it into a few test markets in America in March 1969, as a courtesy to De Laurentiis. It managed to snag a couple of rightfully dreadful reviews. UA quickly pulled it, and it has not been seen commercially in the States since, making it one of the few films in the Eastwood canon that has been seen by almost no American audiences. Clint's segment occasionally shows up in its entirety on YouTube.

It wasn't a total loss, though. When the film premiered in Paris (dubbed inexplicably into English), Clint met and had a brief but passionate affair with Catherine Deneuve that both managed to keep from the public. And there was also the new Ferrari, which he shipped home to Carmel while he remained in Rome to begin production on *The Good, the Bad and the Ugly*. Filming began at Cinecittà in May 1966, after a short delay during which Clint refused to report for work because Leone had yet to agree to his demand for $250,000 and another new Ferrari. Soon enough Clint got everything he wanted, and with cigarillo in place and fake guns strapped to his body, he slid himself back into his European cinematic saddle.

Early into production of Leone's third spaghetti western, Clint began to feel the same vague discontent he'd experienced with *Rawhide:* that the film was bloated, rather than expansive; that the script was far too wordy (something he would clamp down on for virtually every film he would eventually produce); and that the only fully fleshed character was "the Ugly" (Eli Wallach), while "the Good" (himself) and "the Bad" (Lee Van Cleef) were more caricatures than characters, without enough satiric heft to make that approach workable. Leone still didn't (or perhaps preferred not to) speak a word of English, despite the fact that this film depended far more than the first two on the spoken word than on the visual image.

Clint's instincts as to the diminution of his character's stature were essentially correct. In the first film he had been a loner, a man with practically no past and no foreseeable future. His singular stature suggested isolation, cynicism wrapped in heroic determination, and a forcefulness that made him—even with all his glamorized imperfections—irresistible to the audience. In the second film the Man with No Name had been forced to deal with and ultimately share his screen space with Colonel Mortimer (played by Lee Van Cleef, whose successful appearance in *For a Few Dollars More* had not only resurrected his film career but guaranteed his return in the last film of the trilogy). Now Van Cleef was playing someone named Sentenza, along with movie veteran (and inveterate scene stealer) Wallach. "If it goes on that way," Clint grumbled to Leone, "in the next one I will be starring with the whole American cavalry."

Between takes Clint took to practicing his golf swing, a signal to Leone and everyone else that he was now so detached from the

production that he no longer cared about his character, the other characters, the director, or the film itself. Later on, when Leone approached him about a fourth film, Clint would flatly reject the offer.

During the filming, Clint and Wallach had become good friends, and Clint, who had a long-standing aversion to flying in small planes, convinced Wallach to drive with him from Madrid to Almeria. As production dragged on, Clint helped guide Wallach through the script, emphasizing the importance of action over dialogue, acting as Wallach's personal director. Then, the week before filming finished, Clint and Wallach had dinner together. "This will be my last spaghetti western," he told Wallach. "I'm going back to California and I'll form my own company and I'll act and direct my own movies." *Oh sure, that'll be the day*, Wallach thought to himself.

Meanwhile Leone had visions of creating a second, more expansive trilogy. According to Leone,

After *The Good, the Bad and the Ugly*, I didn't want to do any more westerns. I had totally done that kind of story and I wanted to do a picture called *Once Upon a Time in America*. But because people are not willing to forgive success, and to forgive failure, when I went to the States the first thing they said was do another western and we'll let you do *Once Upon a Time in America* . . . at that point I needed to make another movie that was completely different from the first three and I thought of starting a new trilogy which started with *Once Upon a Time in the West*, developed with *A Fistful of Dynamite* and ended with *Once Upon a Time in America*.*

While Clint knew this would be his last film for Leone, it was by no means his last western. He had had too much spaghetti and not

*The first film was made in 1968, *C'era una volta il West (Once Upon a Time in the West)*, starring Henry Fonda, Jason Robards, and Claudia Cardinale. Charles Bronson played the role of Harmonica that Leone had originally offered to Clint. Leone often said that he had cast Clint in *A Fistful of Dollars* because he looked like Henry Fonda, then later cast Fonda because he looked like Clint Eastwood. *A Fistful of Dynamite*, starring Rod Steiger and James Coburn, was made in 1971. *Once Upon a Time in America*, starring Robert De Niro and James Woods, was completed in 1984.

enough hamburger; he was determined now to take the essential elements of the character of the Man with No Name, which had been so good to him in Europe, back to Hollywood, where it could be redeveloped and redefined.

Home by July, Clint quickly grew restless in Carmel and frequently hooked up with old friends, including David Janssen, who had finished production on his fourth and final season as Dr. Richard Kimble on the hit TV show *The Fugitive*. The series had perfectly touched the boomer zeitgeist of the 1960s, made a cultural hero out of Kimble, and (for a relatively brief time) a star out of Janssen.

Clint and Janssen got together often during these months, as Clint sought guidance from his friend, now a major TV star, for his own floundering career. (Clint had been offered, and accepted, the role of Two-Face on the campy *Batman* series, but it was canceled before he could do it.) Janssen, meanwhile, had just accepted an offer from John Wayne to appear in the upcoming Wayne-produced-and-directed *The Green Berets*, as a skeptical liberal newspaper reporter embedded with a unit of the Green Berets.

And then on September 30, 1966, Clint was shocked to learn that Eric Fleming, while on location in Peru filming an MGM movie for TV called *High Jungle*, had died. About halfway through the shoot, Fleming's canoe had capsized on the Huallaga River. With him was another actor, Nic Minardos, who managed to swim safely to shore. Fleming's body was found two days later.* Clint found out by reading it in the newspaper.

On January 18, 1967, *A Fistful of Dollars* finally opened in Los Angeles, followed by a national release a month later. The film's stylized violence (which viewed today is neither all that violent nor all that stylized) had prevented it from being shown in America for three years. In 1966 Mike Nichols's groundbreaking *Who's Afraid of Virginia Woolf?*, in which vulgar language was crucial to the film's story, had finally broken through the outdated restrictions of the Produc-

---

*Or so it was reported. The circumstances of his death and the fate of his remains are cloudy to this day. Unsubstantiated reports persist that he was eaten by a crocodile. He was to have been married two days after his death.

tion Code. Thereafter Krim and Picker thought the time was right to try an American release for their Leone film.*

And critics wasted no time in pouncing on it. Leading the parade of negative reaction was Bosley Crowther, the crusty film critic of the *New York Times*, who dismissed the film as "cowboy camp." Judith Crist, the main film reviewer for the *World Journal Tribune*, called it "perfectly awful . . . an ersatz western . . . [where] men and women [are] gouged, burned, beaten, stomped and shredded to death." Philip K. Scheuer wrote in the *Los Angeles Times:* "Like the villains, it was shot in Spain . . . pity it wasn't buried there." *Newsweek* called it "excruciatingly dopey." In almost every review, Clint received only casual mention, and Leone was barely mentioned at all.

Yet, to everyone's surprise, *A Fistful of Dollars* made money from its first day of release. If the critics didn't get it, audiences did. They could sense the power of Clint's character, the attraction of his strength and conviction, and the film's original viewpoint on brutality. Moreover, every campus town in America had a revival theater that regularly played *Yojimbo*, so college audiences—who made up a large number of the film's early faithful—were familiar with the tactics of the scenario. The artifacts of the Man with No Name's character—the cigarillo, the poncho, the wide-brimmed hat—all became elements of 1960s campus hip style.

Meanwhile, Clint was having trouble getting work, or at least the kind he wanted—an American western with a toned-down version of his nameless hero—even as that May, United Artists, encouraged by the box-office take of *A Fistful of Dollars*, released *For a Few Dollars More* as one of their big summer movies, while *A Fistful of Dollars* was still holding on to a sizable number of its first-run screens. It had already grossed a hefty $3.5 million, which was excellent for a 1960s studio film and extraordinary for any foreign independent released in America.

In between promotional interviews and extensive redubbing sessions for all three films, at UA's expense (rather than using the more conventional and less expensive subtitles), Clint continued to meet

---

*Shortly after the box-office success of *Who's Afraid of Virginia Woolf?*, the Production Code was replaced by Jack Valenti's ratings system. United Artists then agreed to distribute *A Fistful of Dollars* in America. Also, the Kurosawa-rights issue had finally been resolved.

with producers and directors and continued to be rejected by all of them. At best they considered his current movie success to be a fluke, the product of a novelty, and at worst they still thought of him as a TV actor, a ghetto from which few actors managed to escape.

As the months passed, Clint formulated an idea that had been cooking since the days of *Rawhide*, when he had wanted to film that cattle drive differently: to make a project of his own choosing, shot in the way he wanted it done. If American studios weren't falling over themselves to latch on to Clint Eastwood Movie Star, then he would produce a film that would not only equal but surpass Leone's achievement with the western genre.

The project he had in mind was a script called *Hang 'Em High*, an Americanized single-feature amalgam of the Leone trilogy. It had been written by Mel Goldberg in 1966, as a pilot for yet another western TV series. Clint thought it might be the right project to launch his Hollywood film career and approached producer Leonard Freeman, who had originally commissioned it as a pilot, about the possibility of turning it into a feature film. Freeman had already produced *Mr. Novak*, and co-created the idea for a new series, *Hawaii Five-O*, after which Freeman and Goldberg shelved *Hang 'Em High*.

The script had first come to Clint via Irving Leonard, who happened to be friends with Freeman's agent, George Litto. Over dinner one night Litto had told Leonard about *Hang 'Em High*. Leonard thought it might be what Clint was looking for and asked if he could send him a copy. Litto sent it over the next day. Clint, rather than going back to the well with Leone, wanted to do it. "When [Leone] talked to me about doing *Once Upon a Time in the West* and what later became *Duck, You Sucker*, they were just repeats of what I'd been doing," he said.*

I didn't want to play that character anymore. So I came back and did a very small-budget picture, called *Hang 'Em High*, which had a little more character. Maybe it was time, too, to do some American films, because even though these films were very successful, the movie business for

Duck, You Sucker (1971) was also known as *Giù la testa*, and *A Fistful of Dynamite*, and *Once Upon a Time . . . the Revolution*. James Coburn appeared in the role of John Mallory, originally intended by Leone for Eastwood.

some reason was still thinking of me as an Italian movie actor. I can remember the field guys at Paramount years ago said they'd talk about using me but all they got was, "He's just a TV actor." I wasn't marked to be accepted. There were a lot of other actors who were marked to succeed more than me.

The first thing Clint did was take the script to his more powerful agent at William Morris, Leonard Hirshan, who, like any good WMA rep, did not like projects coming to his clients from outside sources. It was a question less of ego than of packaging. Putting agency writers together with in-house actors gave the agency a voice in virtually every aspect of a production. Hirshan's first inclination was to pass on *Hang 'Em High*. He wanted Clint instead for a production called *Mackenna's Gold*, an ensemble action film whose cast would be headed by Gregory Peck and Omar Sharif. Clint read the script for *Mackenna's Gold*, and it left him cold. Being part of an ensemble, he felt, would be a step backward for him, a return to the ensemble style of *The Good, the Bad and the Ugly* or, worse, *Rawhide*.*

Clint insisted he was going ahead with *Hang 'Em High*. He believed the back-to-back financial successes of *A Fistful of Dollars* and *For a Few Dollars More*—the latter received even worse reviews than *Fistful* but so far grossed $4.3 million in its initial theatrical run, nearly a million dollars more than *Fistful*—could get the film funded by Krim and Picker at UA. He was right. Once the deal was set, he approached Ted Post, one of his favorite *Rawhide* directors, to make the film.

On December 29, 1967, production began on *Hang 'Em High*, Picker and Krim released *The Good, the Bad and the Ugly;* all three films in the trilogy had been released in the space of a year. It set off a tsunami of debate among the more esoteric critics, who either loved it or hated it but could not ignore it. Mainstream critics like Charles Champlin complained in the *Los Angeles Times* that "the temptation is hereby proved irresistible to call *The Good, the Bad and the Ugly*, now

---

*The screenplay was by Carl Foreman, based on a novel by Heck Allen. Foreman had been nominated for an Academy Award for his 1952 script for *High Noon*, then was blacklisted in the 1950s. One of Foreman's comeback films was *The Guns of Navarone* (1961), directed by J. Lee Thompson. So *Mackenna's Gold* was considered an important film, and Hirshan pressured Clint, unsuccessfully, to accept a role in it. The film was released in 1969, without Clint, directed by J. Lee Thompson.

playing citywide, *The Bad, the Dull, and the Interminable*, only because it is." Pauline Kael, the high priestess of film criticism writing from her perch at *The New Yorker* far above the world of the common man, pronounced the film "stupid" and "gruesome" and wondered why it was called a western at all. *Time* magazine sniffed its nose too, after minimally acknowledging Leone's stylistics, giving Leone a good spanking for daring to encroach on that most holy of American turf, the movie western.

The *New York Times*'s first-string film critic Renata Adler wrote in the newspaper's January 25 edition:

> "The burn, the gouge, and the mangle" (its screen name is simply inappropriate) must be the most expensive, pious and repellent movie in the history of its peculiar genre. If 42nd Street is lined with little pushcarts of sadism, this film, which opened yesterday at the Trans-Lux 85th Street and the DeMille, is an entire supermarket . . . it lasts two and a half slow hours . . . there is a completely meaningless sequence with a bridge—as though it might pass for "San Luis Rey" or "Kwai." Sometimes, it all tries to pass for funny.

The film would fare no better in later years, after Adler's departure from the *Times* and a string of exceedingly esoteric film critics increasingly turned their noses up at Clint, until the arrival of Manohla Dargis in the first years of the new century, a film reviewer who did not automatically dismiss Clint by definition (of the times, of his genre, of the so-called fashions of the times). The *New York Times*, however, would continue to push its more standard party line. In its television section, whenever *The Good, the Bad and the Ugly* showed up, it ran the same one-line blurb year after year that, while acerbic and condescending, was, in truth, not that far from what Clint himself felt about the film: "Snarls, growls, and a smattering of words. Clint treading on water, on land."

Only Andrew Sarris, in the *Village Voice*, was willing to admit that there was something to Leone and his trilogy. Sarris, a forerunner of the "auteurist" movement in American film criticism, derived from the French Nouvelle Vague critics a highly controversial assessment of American movies; he was then considered a rebel (but ironically is rightly revered today as a reactionary). His auteur theory celebrated

genre films and the directors who made them as more purely cine-matic and personal than the corporate, impersonal, and therefore indifferent product of the old industrial studio system. Having seen the trilogy before it opened, he wrote a two-part "think piece" that appeared in the *Voice* on September 19 and 26, 1968, called "The Spaghetti Westerns." It explained the Leone films' box-office success in terms of their auteurist appeal—something to which the other crit-ics were completely blind—and he allowed the trilogy, and Leone, to enter the world of the hip (or the hipster), such as it was. If it still wasn't okay to laud the films at cocktail parties on Fifth Avenue, after Sarris it was the essential stuff of coffee shops and kitchen counters.

The New York cultural scene, Sarris wrote,

> remains basically hostile to westerns even as precincts of camp . . . The
> western, like water, gains flavor from its impurities, and westerns since
> 1945 have multiplied their options, obsessions and neuroses many times
> over . . . What Kurosawa and Leone share is a sentimental nihilism that
> ranks survival above honor and revenge above morality . . . Strangely,
> Leone has moved deeper into American history and politics in his sub-
> sequent [films following *Fistful of Dollars*]. I say strangely because an
> Italian director might be expected to stylize an alien genre with vague
> space-time coordinates, like the universal Mexico that can be filmed
> anywhere on the Mediterranean for any century from the sixteenth to
> the twentieth . . . The spaghetti western is ultimately a lower-class
> entertainment and, as such, functions as an epic of violent revenge.*

The Good, the Bad and the Ugly packed movie houses to the tune of $6.3 million in its initial domestic release. With his star rising like a rocket, Clint was finally able to put together the funding for *Hang 'Em High*. To ensure that it became the film he envisioned, he formed his own production company, Malpaso (Spanish for "bad pass," or

---

*Clint was well aware of the critics and said in his February 1974 *Playboy* interview: "I've been treated well—flatteringly so—by the better, more experienced reviewers, people like Andrew Sarris, Jay Cocks, Vincent Canby and Bosley Crowther. Judith Crist, for some reason, hasn't been knocked out over everything I've done—or *anything* I've done, as a matter of fact. I think she liked [the porn film] *The Devil in Miss Jones*, but she thought *Beguiled* was obscene . . . everybody's entitled to his opinion."

"bad step"), named after a creek on his own property in Monterey County, to function as his producing umbrella. "I own some property on a creek in the Big Sur country called Malpaso Creek," Clint told *Playboy* magazine:

> I guess it runs down a bad pass in the mountains . . . My theory was that I could foul up my career just as well as somebody else could foul it up for me, so why not try it? And I had this great urge to show the industry that it needs to be streamlined so it can make more films with smaller crews . . . What's the point of spending so much money producing a movie that you can't break even on it? So at Malpaso, we [won't] have a staff of 26 and a fancy office. I've got a six-pack of beer under my arm, and a few pieces of paper, and a couple of pencils, and I'm in business.*

With a staff consisting of himself, Robert Daley as the resident producer, Sonia Chernus as story editor, and one secretary, he felt ready to make the film he wanted, the way he wanted, and maybe even make some real money doing it. *Hang 'Em High* became Malpaso's first release.†

---

*According to Arthur Knight, who interviewed Clint for *Playboy* in February 1974, the walls of the Malpaso office were "decorated with posters; looming in one corner is a life-sized cardboard cutout of Eastwood—which, like his best-known screen characterizations, is curiously one-dimensional and strangely ominous. The most bizarre object in his private office, though, is a three-foot-high, balloon-shaped, shocking-pink, papier-mâché rabbit piggy bank."

†"The three [Leone] films were successful overseas," he said in the 1974 *Playboy* interview, "but I had a rough time cracking the Hollywood scene. Not only was there a movie prejudice against television actors but there was a feeling that an American actor making an Italian movie was sort of taking a step backward. But the film exchanges in France, Italy, Germany, Spain were asking the Hollywood producers when they were going to make a film starring Clint Eastwood. So finally I was offered a very modest film for United Artists—*Hang 'Em High* . . . I formed my own company, Malpaso, and we got a piece of it."

SEVEN

I think I learned more about direction from Don Siegel than from anybody else . . . he shoots lean, and he shoots what he wants. He knew when he had it, and he didn't need to cover his ass with a dozen different angles.

—Clint Eastwood

Clint's vision of Malpaso as a self-contained, in-house movie production company that he owned and operated in the service of his own career would take a little longer to realize than he had anticipated. Although his success in Hollywood via the Leone trilogy was impressive, he still did not have enough clout to be able to make his own movies independently, and he knew even less about running a company. For the time being, he would still have to rely totally upon studio financing and therefore remain in the service of others. He brought in Irving Leonard to be Malpaso's president and watch the books and act as Clint's personal business manager.

Clint used Leonard's business savvy to flex Malpaso's newborn muscles. The final decisions were mostly Clint's, but they were shaped, refined, and delivered by Leonard. UA had initially wanted a name director for *Hang 'Em High* to ensure that their investment would be well protected, shot in a commercial fashion, and kept within budget. Picker and Krim thought that either Robert Aldrich or John Sturges, both action directors, could do the job. Aldrich's *The Dirty Dozen* (1967), an ensemble war movie heavy on testosterone, made him a top choice, as did Sturges's *The Magnificent Seven* (1960).

Clint's choice, however, was Ted Post. Post had directed only two theatrical features, both quickies that created not so much as a ripple of interest (or revenue),* twenty-four *Rawhide* episodes, and dozens of other TV episodics and was, according to Clint's way of thinking, especially good with dialogue, which most episodic television is. The primary difference between film and TV in the 1960s was that film was about what the audience saw and TV was about what it heard. Having never had much dialogue to deliver on either *Rawhide* or the Leone

---

*They were *The Peacemaker* (1956) and *The Legend of Tom Dooley* (1959).

trilogy, Clint wanted someone who could help him handle the wordy *Hang 'Em High* script. The job went to Post.

Once Clint's choice of director was on board, casting for the rest of the picture went relatively quickly. Post hired veteran character actor Pat Hingle, twitchy bad boy Bruce Dern (whom Clint had befriended in the years when they were both knocking about in Hollywood trying to find work), Ed Begley, always dependable to play a dangerous old loony, and Charles McGraw. Not coincidentally, all had appeared in episodes of *Rawhide* that Post had directed.

For the female lead, Clint wanted Inger Stevens. Women had not been much of a factor in the Leone trilogy, except to act as symbolic Madonnas in the films' heavily suggestive faux religiosity. *Hang 'Em High* emphasizes the Madonna theme via Rachel (Stevens), a local businesswoman who nurses Jed Cooper (Clint) back to health after he is nearly hanged in the opening scenes, a violent graphic depiction that recalled Leone.* A good-time prostitute (played by Arlene Golonka) completes the triangle. The set was an efficient one, with Clint doing his best to recapture the stylistic sweep and violent imagery of the so-called spaghetti westerns that had made him a postmodern iconic big-screen western hero (or anti-hero), thus putting another nail in the culture coffin of Rowdy Yates. By the end of the picture, Stevens expressed her pleasure with Clint's professional manner and offered her services for any future projects he might have that she would be right for.

The film was shot relatively quickly and under budget—something that would become one of Malpaso's trademarks inside the industry. It was filmed on location (something else that would also come to define a Malpaso picture) in the Las Cruces territory of New Mexico, with the interiors done at MGM studios in Culver City, California. The plot followed the Leone blueprint—for most of the film Clint pursues the men who tried to kill him and kills them instead in a spectacular shoot-out and, ironically, a suicide-by-hanging of the man who had tried to lynch Cooper, Captain Wilson (Begley).

---

*The character's name, Cooper, recalls Gary Cooper's tall, silent-type western heroes, most notably Will Kane in *High Noon*.

Released in the summer of 1968, following the assassinations of Dr. Martin Luther King Jr. and Robert F. Kennedy, and during the self-destructive Democratic National Convention in Chicago, *Hang 'Em High*'s star-powered, testosterone-driven blood and gore was a welcome dose of adolescent action escapism and cleaned up at the box office, grossing approximately $7 million in its initial domestic theatrical release, nearly a half-million more than *The Good, the Bad and the Ugly*. Unlike some films that have to find an audience, *Hang 'Em High*, made for approximately $1.5 million, took off from day one and became the biggest-grossing film in UA's storied history, a tribute to the times and to Hollywood's newest action star, Clint Eastwood. It went into profits almost immediately, and established both Clint and Malpaso as power players in the independent film scene of 1970s Hollywood.

Some critics bemoaned the fact that the Man with No Name had taken on a real identity, "Americanized" and softened for a broader appeal; but most believed that westerns were still best (meaning most popular) when made in Hollywood in English with gorgeous women and familiar-faced villains. Archer Winston, one of the more popular daily New York City print critics, called the film "a western of quality, courage, danger and excitement, which places itself squarely in the procession of old fashioned westerns made with the latest techniques." Even the *New York Times* (Howard Thompson this time, in place of Crowther, who was on the way out after his grossly negative reading of Arthur Penn's 1967 *Bonnie and Clyde*), which had had no use for the Leone-Eastwood movies, begrudgingly admitted that *"Hang 'Em High* has its moments." But the *Times* still didn't get Clint: "Most unfortunate of all, Mr. Eastwood, with his glum sincerity, isn't much of an actor."

But he was enough of a star to ensure that his films made money, and the bottom line was the only critique that mattered to Jennings Lang, the head of Universal. Following the completion of *Hang 'Em High*, Lang offered Clint a cool $1 million to star in his first "big" (i.e., fully studio-financed) American major studio film, the fish-out-of-water *Coogan's Bluff*, to be directed by Alex Segal, about an Arizona horseback deputy assigned to bring back a murderer hiding out in New York City.

Writer Herman Miller originally conceived the script as a two-hour pilot for Universal TV, but Lang ordered it revised for a big-screen feature and assigned the task to Jack Laird. As it happened, both Miller and Laird were *Rawhide* alumni.

Lang had convinced Hirshan that *Coogan's Bluff* was the perfect vehicle for Clint's next film, and when Clint signed on, pending script approval, Lang took Miller and Laird off the project—reportedly Clint did not like their version. They were replaced by a succession of writers assigned to tailor the script to Clint's satisfaction.* Once the script met with Clint's approval, director Alex Segal was the next to go, replaced, at Clint's insistence, by Don Siegel. How that happened is a story only Clint should tell:

> I had signed with Universal Pictures to do a film called *Coogan's Bluff*. That was to be my second American film after coming in off the plains of Spain. The studio had recommended a director by the name of Alex Segal, who had come from back east and had several plays, television shows, and movies to his credit. Segal had some personal problem which precluded him from doing this film and he withdrew. Then the studio came up with the suggestion, "How about Don Siegel?" Now, in a business in which nepotism runs rampant, I began to think, "Hold on just a minute, what relationship do these two have and how many more Siegels are we going to go through before we get this picture on the road?"

More than a little skeptical, Clint agreed to screen a couple of Siegel's films before setting about to find a real director. But Siegel's *Invasion of the Body Snatchers* (1956) made him sit up and take notice. It was, as he later recalled, "one of the two or three finest B movies ever made and I realized that this was a man who could do an awful lot with very little. *Coogan's Bluff* was a [relatively] modest-budget picture, but perhaps we could get a lot more on the screen for the dollar

---

*The concept for the film survived later on as a TV show called *McCloud*, starring Dennis Weaver (Chester of *Gunsmoke* fame), created by and credited to Miller. The screenplay underwent at least seven full revisions, and final on-screen writing credits went to Herman Miller, Dean Riesner, and Howard Rodman, story by Herman Miller.

and push the film on to a higher echelon of 'look.' So I said, 'Yes, let's go with Don Siegel.' "*

Siegel was something of an oddity in Hollywood. He had worked at Warner Bros. in the 1930s making shorts, and on dozens of hit movies in various subdirectorial roles. After bouncing around from studio to studio, he landed at Allied Artists, where he directed *Invasion of the Body Snatchers*, one of the most spectacular and disturbing films of the 1950s, a classic sci-fi horror crossed with political paranoia that did to falling asleep what Hitchcock's *Psycho* (1960) did to taking showers. Based on a novel by Jack Finney, it had perfectly captured the fear and loathing of an America that believed communism was to individuality what the pods were to human beings—irretrievably stealing one's individuality. (Its stylistic use of stairs and heights, and the climactic relentless pursuit through the streets and into the hills, would be echoed in *Dirty Harry*.) Siegel's next assignment at Universal was to direct *Baby Face Nelson*, which received terrific reviews but went nowhere. A series of ho-hum jobs followed, including *Spanish Affair* (1957), *The Line-Up* (1958; adapted from the hit TV series, its stark semidocumentary view of San Francisco police work and the pursuit of maniacal killer Eli Wallach foreshadow the action, mood, and pace of *Dirty Harry*), *The Gun Runners* (1958), *Hound-Dog Man* (1959), *Edge of Eternity* (1959), *Flaming Star* (1960), *Hell Is for Heroes* (1962), *Stranger on the Run* (1967—TV), and *Madigan* (1968). The thirty-eighth film (out of the fifty he would eventually make) was *Coogan's Bluff*, the smash he had been looking for to return him to the spotlight. It was the first of a series of films that Clint and Siegel would make together.

Clint, the temperamental don't-tell-me-what-to-do-unless-you-

*Siegel remembered it a little differently: "There was a mix-up at Universal. Clint Eastwood, whom I not only did not know but had never seen in person or on film, was considering two directors for his first starring feature at Universal. Their names were Alex Segal and Don Taylor . . . In the basement of the Black Tower [Universal Studios corporate headquarters] there existed proudly a brand-new computer. Two names were fed into it—Alex Segal and Don Taylor . . . the name that appeared was Don Siegel. Clint asked the executive producer, Dick Lyons, 'Who the hell is Don Siegel?' . . . when I found out he had screened three of my pictures and wanted to know if I was interested in directing *Coogan's Bluff*, I responded that I'd like to see the three Sergio Leone pictures." Don Siegel, *A Siegel Film: An Autobiography* (London: Faber and Faber, 1993), p. 294.

know-what-you're-doing star, and Don Siegel, the just-do-what-I-tell-you authoritarian, each marked his turf, and neither would let the other upset the power balance necessary to get this movie made.

Many on the set were surprised by how well they did get along, after a couple of early and minor bumps in the road. The key was mutual respect; Clint had been looking for someone (who spoke English) to show him how a movie was put together, and Siegel was more than happy to show Clint how the tricks were done.

Early on in the shoot, according to Clint,

> I learned a lot from [Siegel] in the sense that he's a man who does a lot with a little—so therefore our philosophies are pretty much akin . . . he's a very lean kind of director . . . *Coogan's Bluff* was the first picture we did together. It was a fun film to do in the sense that it started out with another director, and Don and I didn't know each other. We started out butting heads together a little, and as it turned out, we ended up with a great working relationship.

Siegel agreed: "I thought we did very well."

One aspect of the film that seems unmistakably Siegel is its heavy, at times obvious, metaphorical overlay. In the turbulent 1960s, when the country was divided by the unpopular and ultimately unwinnable war in Vietnam, uncomplicated heroes in popular movies were hard to find. *Coogan's Bluff* works precisely because it depicts New York City as an urban, lawless "jungle," commandeered by a tough yet ineffective cop. Detective Lieutenant McElroy was played by the always powerful Lee J. Cobb, an actor who couldn't be more different on-screen from Clint. Cobb, heavyset, rough, sneering, and street-smart, was the polar opposite of the tall, lean country boy Clint. If the American psyche was desperate for someone to come in and end the Vietnam nightmare, it found its savior in the movies. Cobb is reminiscent of General Westmoreland, while Clint is the heroic rebel who comes in, cleans up the situation, and removes the bad guy. As Coogan, he was a Central Casting American hero who single-handedly captures the villain by waging a guerrilla-type war on "foreign" turf.

The sub-rosa Vietnam symbolism, overlaid with a good-guy-gets-bad-guy formula that is as old as film itself, was right in Siegel's wheelhouse. The alien fighting the bad guy was a kind of inversion of the

plot structure of *Invasion of the Body Snatchers* and became the cinematic glue that held the film's spine in place.

Coogan's Bluff, which stretched Clint beyond his Man with No Name, was highly anticipated by audiences and critics alike. But reviews for the film were mixed at best; critics either loved or hated it. Judith Crist called the film, in *New York* magazine, "the worst happening of the year." But Vincent Canby, the *New York Times*'s newest and most astute film critic (and its best overall writer yet about film), in a combination review and think piece, enthusiastically compared Clint to screen icon James Dean. Archer Winston, writing in the *New York Post*, noted Don Siegel's directorial contribution but more or less ignored Clint, as did the weekly edition of *Variety*.

Kitty Jones, an agent during the late 1960s, was someone Clint had befriended in his early TV days and had remained a member of his inner circle of friends. She regularly held social salons in her apartment on Cahuenga Boulevard, which Clint often attended with a couple of his friends from the old studio days. A young starlet by the name of Jill Banner remembered those afternoons and, in particular, Clint's presence at them:

> He and his buddies were like a pack of wild college comedians, always horsing around, cracking jokes, telling risqué jokes, rough-housing and teasing the girls . . . his chums were guys he'd known a long time, one was Bill, another George, and he got them regular work on the *Rawhide* series. Another was Chill Wills, who was Francis the Talking Mule's speaking voice in Clint's first two films.
>
> Clint didn't give a shit about the la-de-da Hollywood crowd, or the traditional stylish symbols. He drove an old pickup truck [despite having two Ferraris], and I never saw him wear anything but Levi's, T-shirt, windbreaker jacket, and tennis shoes. He was a health nut. He didn't smoke but he could stow away plenty of beer, which he said was a health tonic.
>
> Kitty's girlfriends were crazy about him, not because he was so young and good-looking or a star but because he was kind, intelligent, and such a fun guy.

Maggie, firmly planted up in Carmel, never attended any of these salons.

Two days after the completion of *Coogan's Bluff,* he left for Europe; Brian G. Hutton's *Where Eagles Dare* was to be shot on location in England and Austria for MGM. In this World War II action drama a British officer is given a top-secret assignment to parachute behind enemy lines, somewhere in the Bavarian Alps, to rescue a captured American general before the latter can be tortured into revealing the details of the impending D-Day invasion at Normandy. He is accompanied by five commandos, one of whom is an American lieutenant, played by Clint Eastwood.

Where Eagles Dare was a big-budget action film starring one of the world's most famous actors, Richard Burton, at the peak of his fame but also on the brink of financial collapse. Burton was forced to accept movie work like *Where Eagles Dare* that didn't necessarily fit his needs or desires as an actor but earned him millions. Burton agreed to star in *Where Eagles Dare,* he told the insatiable coterie of press that followed him everywhere, because he wanted to make a movie that he could watch with his two daughters; his most recent films, he said, were not especially well suited for that. Behind the scenes, though, it was widely believed that he took it solely for the money.*

Costarring with Burton would bring Clint international attention for something other than a spaghetti western. And European audiences would get to see him again in a noncowboy role. *Where Eagles Dare* was sure to push his steadily growing salary toward his goal of a million dollars a movie.

To write the script, Burton approached his friend and colleague Elliott Kastner, who in turn recruited the well-known adventure novelist Alistair MacLean. MacLean had achieved a fair measure of film credibility from the adaptation of his novel (done by Carl Foreman) for J. Lee Thompson's World War II adventure *The Guns of Navarone* (1961). Burton particularly liked that film and wanted a script for *Where Eagles Dare* that would match it. MacLean had never written an original screenplay, but as all of his novels had already been made into movies or remained under option, he tried his hand with *Where Eagles Dare,* which he banged out in six weeks.

---

*The daughters, Kate and Jessica, were from his first marriage, to actress Sybil Williams.

Even as MacLean was putting the finishing touches on it, Clint held firm for $800,000 up front, a percentage of the profits, and equal-size name-above-the-title billing with Burton to compensate for his de facto second billing. He got almost everything he asked for: the $800,000 up front, the percentage, and the equal size, but without Burton's name-above-the-title credit.

After a few days in London he flew to Salzburg to begin the shoot, still wearing faded jeans and carrying a single torn canvas bag. His style was markedly different from that of the Burtons (Elizabeth Taylor accompanied her husband on the flight to Salzburg), who flew in formal attire via private jet amid the rush and glare of European-style paparazzi. No sooner had Clint settled into his hotel, the same one where the Burtons were staying, than he received a call from the actor to join him in the lounge for drinks.

For the rest of that day and into the night the two drank—or rather Burton drank and Clint observed, and what he saw was not pleasant. Here was Burton, conceivably the biggest movie star in the world, a hopeless drunk, self-justifying and self-pitying, with one eye on his whiskey and the other on the waitress who kept bringing it. He had made a fortune in film but was still strapped for cash—something incomprehensible to Clint. And while Burton could still pass as a leading man, he looked at least a dozen years older than he had five years earlier, when he shot to international stardom and scandal in *Cleopatra*. What's more, he was puffy and out of shape and smoking up to sixty cigarettes a day despite his needing to be fit for a film that would tax all his physical abilities.

According to Ingrid Pitt, who played a minor role in the film (Heidi), Burton's fragile condition was apparent to everyone on set: "Clint and Richard Burton were so different. Clint was looking forward to the rest of his career. He was watching everything . . . Richard Burton was just drinking and spouting Shakespeare. He was unhappy. He drank . . . he was just tired of living." It was a powerful cautionary tale for the always-careful Clint.

Elizabeth Taylor—Liz, as everyone who knew her called her—was another story. She stayed only briefly in Salzburg, leaving shortly before the filming of the most difficult physical scenes—she could not stand to watch them because the untimely death of her third

husband, producer Mike Todd, in a plane crash still haunted her dreams. While in Salzburg, she formed an easy, informal friendship with Clint.* Often while Burton was off doing a scene, Liz and Clint would sit and talk—about their careers, their lives, their loves, their dreams. Early on Taylor knew she wanted to work with Clint. She received dozens of scripts every day from producers and studios hoping to work with her and had recently come across one she liked. It was about a nun caught in the crossfire of a Mexican insurgency and an American mercenary who rescues her from being raped and murdered and helps to bring her to safety. The plot had a few clever twists—the mercenary at first doesn't know the woman is a nun, and she winds up at one point rescuing him. Whatever her motives—friendship, mutual attraction, rivalry (on both their parts) with Burton—Taylor thought the script was perfect for herself and Clint, he in the role that would naturally have gone to Burton if he had been in better shape and if he had had any interest in that type of film, which he didn't. Not even opposite her. Or *especially* not opposite her.

By now Burton had—inevitably, perhaps—begun to feel negatively about sharing the stage with his wife's all-encompassing persona. The problem was, she was a far more limited actor (as far as he was concerned), and their films together were the least worthy—if, ironically, most successful—of his career. Clint, who lacked any classical training or pretenses to greatness, had no such concerns.

But their talks of working together went nowhere. As Clint later explained, "The script was given to me by Elizabeth Taylor when I was doing *When Eagles Dare* with her husband. We wanted to do it together, and the studio approved of the combination [of stars], but [as it turned out] she was going through some deal where she didn't want to work [alone] unless it coincided with Richard's working, so we had it set up to do in Mexico while Richard was working there on something else,† but then there were other problems." Whatever those problems may have been, the imagined Taylor-Eastwood collaboration never happened.

Before any of his *Eagles* scenes were shot, Clint had taken to alter-

---

*Burton was Taylor's fifth and sixth husband (she married him twice), following her brief marriage to singer Eddie Fisher.

†Probably *The Assassination of Trotsky* (1972), directed by Joseph Losey.

ing his dialogue. For the most part he disregarded Hutton, the director, whom Kastner had hired despite a notable lack of credentials. Hutton had directed only three films before *Where Eagles Dare: Wild Seed* (1965, aka *Fargo*), *The Pad and How to Use It* (1966), and *Sol Madrid* (1968), a detective story also known as *The Heroin Gang*. Before that he had worked occasionally as an actor, mostly in TV episodics. Kastner, with his partner Jerry Gershwin, had produced *Sol Madrid* and was impressed by Hutton's abilities. The film's financial success also helped Kastner to decide to go with Hutton on *Eagles*, even though it would be considerably more difficult and expensive to make. Because Burton's fee took a lion's share of the film's budget, with Clint's right behind, Kastner needed to keep the rest of his production costs down while maintaining an acceptable level of quality. Hutton may have been talented, but his best asset for this film was that he came cheap.

Burton did not waste much time studying his part in MacLean's screenplay. To him, these films were all the same; he had a job to do, and he wanted to get through it as quickly and painlessly as possible. Clint, on the other hand, went through the script page by page. He was confused by the inconsistencies in his character's dialogue, which made little sense. As he had for *A Fistful of Dollars*, and as he would do with every script henceforth, he went through it and slashed every unnecessary line of his own dialogue, leaving himself relatively little to say while he performs his character's impressive physical feats, for which he was doubled most of the time. After the film was released, he joked to friends that it should have been called *When Doubles Dare*.*

The production encountered innumerable problems, including blizzards, four-foot snowdrifts, and avalanches; outbreaks of altitude sickness and frostbite; fistfights on a moving cable car (Burton); and a high-speed motorcycle ride through a fierce snowstorm on a winding mountain road (Clint). But when the film was finally finished and rushed into production, it received surprisingly good reviews. *Variety* said it was "so good for its genre that one must go back to [John Sturges's 1963] *The Great Escape* for a worthy comparison." Rex Reed,

---

*Clint's stunt-heavy action scenes were done by veteran stuntman and second-unit director Yakima Canutt, best known for creating the chariot-race sequence in William Wyler's *Ben-Hur* (1959).

then writing film reviews for *Women's Wear Daily*, told his readers, "If you stop being so serious and sophisticated . . . you can have a wonderful time at *Where Eagles Dare*." Andrew Sarris also liked it. "Richard Burton and Clint Eastwood," he wrote, "balance out the savage and sardonic elements of the movie into an inconsistent but generally engrossing entertainment."

Whether its audiences came to see Burton or Clint or both, the film grossed more than $15 million in its initial domestic theatrical release, enough to make it MGM's top earner of 1969. A million more was tacked on when the film was released worldwide.

At home things were changing as well. In May 1968, after fifteen years of marriage, Maggie gave birth to a baby boy whom she and Clint named Kyle Clinton Eastwood. The baby's arrival was a mixed blessing. For Maggie, Kyle was an undeniable reaffirmation of her unusual marriage. In a rare interview the two gave shortly afterward, Maggie explained that the secret to their long and successful marriage (as she described it) was "We don't believe in togetherness!" Clint echoed that emotion, although he put a slightly different slant on it: "By [the time we had our child], I knew we could get along well enough to last . . . that we'd stay together."

Amid all the change and accolades, Clint went straight off to make yet another movie; but this one would come to be universally regarded as one of his worst. *Paint Your Wagon* was a big-screen version of a relatively obscure 1951 Broadway musical that had yielded only one semi-hit song, "They Call the Wind Maria." It was a collaboration of Alan J. Lerner and Frederick Loewe, who had also done several other musicals, most notably *Brigadoon* (1947), *My Fair Lady* (1956), and *Camelot* (1960). All of these Broadway shows had been made into hit movies, leading the way to the film version of *Paint Your Wagon*.

Movie musicals were a huge gamble in the late 1960s as the song-and-dance era of Fred Astaire and Gene Kelly was long over; still, *My Fair Lady* (1964), directed by George Cukor, won eight Oscars, including Best Picture, and was nominated for four more; its star, Rex Harrison, won Best Actor. But only three years later Harrison nearly single-handedly destroyed the genre and his own career (and along the way 20th Century–Fox, still reeling from the debacle of *Cleopatra*, in

which he costarred) in Richard Fleischer's ill-conceived, poorly executed, and publicly ignored *Doctor Dolittle*, which inexplicably received an Oscar nomination for Best Picture. The film's poor showing appeared to have once and for all put an end to big-budget musicals—until Paramount decided to try to turn *Paint Your Wagon* into a $14 million cinematic musical extravaganza.

Since the end of Hollywood's studio era, a new logic had taken over the industry. *Paint Your Wagon* was (at least ostensibly) a "western"—another troubled genre, thanks mostly to the proliferation of westerns on TV. So the studio wanted the last big Hollywood "cowboy" star around, Clint Eastwood, to help revive both genres. To get him, they created a role, Pardner, that had not existed in the original Broadway version. Pardner was a curious mixture of the "good" Rowdy from *Rawhide* and the "bad" Man with No Name from the spaghetti westerns. The producers paired Clint with Lee Marvin, who had played "grizzled" to Oscar-winning perfection in Elliot Silverstein's *Cat Ballou* (1965). In Hollywood terms, it was "can't miss" casting. Added to the mix was Pulitzer Prize–winning director Joshua Logan,* whose film versions of several other Broadway musicals, including the moneymaking *Camelot* (1967), seemed like the financial icing on the cake.

Clint very much wanted to be a part of this project. He had always liked Joshua Logan's films, believing he was an actor's director, and felt he needed to work with someone like that after Brian Hutton's mechanical directing on *Where Eagles Dare*. He also very much looked forward to working with screenwriter Paddy Chayefsky, who promised a radical rethinking of the original Broadway book that would make it infinitely more screen-friendly. And finally Clint liked Andre Previn's easygoing musical style; Previn had been hired to write several new songs specifically for Clint, and he promised to make them close to the quiet, jazzy style Clint favored and that was easy for him to sing.

Irving Leonard managed to get $500,000 up front for Clint, a figure still considerably below his sought-after million, but Leonard had so constructed the deal that much of Clint's salary would be deferred for tax advantages and he would have a hefty participation in the

---

*Logan shared the Pulitzer Prize awarded for helping to bring Rodgers and Hammerstein's *South Pacific* to the Broadway stage in 1949.

expected profits. Leonard also managed to get Clint cast-approval, which was how actress Jean Seberg managed to land the role of the Mormon wife Pardner decides to buy, and who subsequently becomes part of a three-way relationship. Lerner had created this character to juice up the film a bit for younger audiences, and Clint insisted that it be played by Seberg.

The actress was widely believed to be French because of her roles in Otto Preminger's *Saint Joan* (1957), his in-French production of *Bonjour Tristesse* (1958, aka *Hello, Sadness* in English), and especially Jean-Luc Godard's groundbreaking French *Breathless* (1960, *À Bout de Souffle*), one of the jewels of the French Nouvelle Vague that became an international sensation and inspired the post–*Bonnie and Clyde* generation of independent American filmmakers. In fact, Seberg was born in Iowa and had moved to Paris during her appearances in *Saint Joan* and *Bonjour Tristesse* and lived there for a while after *Breathless*. By the time she agreed to appear in *Paint Your Wagon*, her career was on the decline due mostly to her active involvement with various leftist radical organizations and her outspoken support of the widely feared American Black Panther Party. That support caught the attention of J. Edgar Hoover, who many believed used the Bureau to hound her until she committed suicide in 1979 at the age of forty-one from an overdose of sleeping pills.

But at thirty-one she was still a ravishing beauty, with big eyes, high cheekbones, and a European-acquired air of sophistication that, when he first met her during the casting, nearly drove Clint wild. At his insistence she was hired, and the two immediately began an on-set affair that they hid from no one. They carried on even as the film itself escalated out of control under the direction of Logan, whose manic-depression went wildly unchecked. The result was a budget that escalated to $30 million, to produce a film that had as much life as an embalmed body.

Seberg and Clint stopped carrying on only when Maggie showed up to pay a visit at the Oregon location shoot, infant in tow. As soon as she left, the entire cast and crew let out a collective sigh and the affair resumed—until the film ran out of location money amid script differences between Logan, Chayefsky, and Clint, and the cast had to return to the soundstages of Hollywood to finish the shoot. At that

point, perhaps feeling he was too close to home, and also near the end of the shoot, Clint dropped Seberg. Already in a troubled marriage to Romain Gary, Seberg's heart was broken.

After five grueling months of work it became clear that Logan had no idea what to do with the growing financial monster that was *Paint Your Wagon*. The film was unofficially finished by assistant director Tom Shaw. By now Paramount, the studio financing the film, just wanted it to end, believing, as did everyone involved, that it was going to be one of the most expensive Christmas turkeys ever given to the filmgoing public. Although it grossed a respectable $14.5 million in its first full year of domestic release—helped by charitable reviews and Clint's undeniable box-office pull—it came nowhere near its break-even point, which, because of all the cost overruns, was somewhere close to $60 million.* In the years to come the film's critical response would not improve. (The *Times* always runs the same blurb about it whenever it shows up in its TV listing: "California gold rush musical. Elaborate but squatty, and Clint sings like a moose.")

Paint Your Wagon, while not an out-and-out disaster, was undoubtedly a downward turn in the otherwise steadily rising arc of Clint's career. Now, as the 1960s cross-faded into the 1970s, and as independent film was gaining its strongest foothold in Hollywood since the beginning of the studio-dominated century, Clint decided to make a giant leap forward. A studio effort like *Paint Your Wagon* was, he felt, now a dinosaur from an industry that had long ago lost its hold on fresh and independent moviemaking. He was sure he could do better.

In other words, he wanted to direct.

But to do so he would have to also produce, as no one was about to hire him despite his star-status, and with no previous directing credits, to helm a movie with a budget of several million dollars. He would have to find the money himself and use it to deep-seed Malpaso. In

---

*In many overseas markets, the film was released with all its songs removed, in the hope it might attract loyal Clint Eastwood western fans. Clint later tried to defend the decision: "In Italy they did that on the first release. That's common practice. Musicals have been terrible flops in Europe, with the exception of *West Side Story*. Most times, they omit all the music." Quoted by Dick Lochte in *Los Angeles Free Press*, April 20, 1973.

the interim he would watch, listen, produce, and star in the films of
other directors from whom he thought he could learn something.

Which is why, having decided to move out of the Hollywood mainstream, he figured the quickest and most expedient way to get what
he wanted was to dive even deeper into it.

EIGHT

I feel Don Siegel is an enormously talented guy who has been deprived of the notoriety he probably should have had much earlier because Hollywood was going through a stage where the awards went to the big pictures and the guys who knew how to spend a lot of money. As a result, guys who got a lot of pictures with a lot of effort and a little money weren't glorified. So Don had to wait many years until he could get to do films with fairly good budgets. He's the kind of director there's not enough of. If things don't go as planned, he doesn't sit down and cry and consider everything lost, as some directors do.

—Clint Eastwood

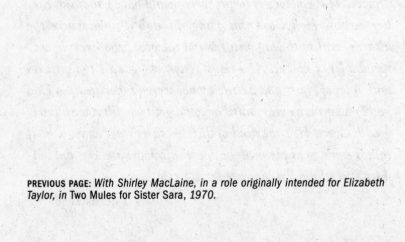

PREVIOUS PAGE: *With Shirley MacLaine, in a role originally intended for Elizabeth Taylor, in* Two Mules for Sister Sara, *1970.*

Seeking to capitalize on his growing popularity and steadily growing box-office clout, Clint wanted to make pictures that showed off his best qualities without turning him into a perpetual cartoon version of the Man with No Name. While others in Clint's position might have happily accepted simple, popular, gritty western after gritty western and enjoyed a single-persona run (as Arnold Schwarzenegger did until the novelty wore off and his film career ended), Clint was after something different, even if he wasn't sure yet exactly what that was. Having attained the level of a legitimate Hollywood star, he would surely remain there—going back to pumping gas held no allure at all.

As an actor, Clint knew that the Man with No Name held audiences' interest because of his unique imperfections (no family, no woman, no past, and no future) rather than the standard-issue imperfections (heartbreak, separation, and desperation). He understood that it was their fascination with this unique character that had ignited his rising star.

But as a filmmaker, Clint had no interest in perpetuating that character until it became a caricature. Instead, he wanted to get behind and inside of the image he projected onto the screen. To do so, he needed to generate work that not only suited this goal but was within his grasp.

Despite his surprise success with the spaghetti westerns, his journey of cinematic self-exploration had thus far been neither quick, nor easy, nor smooth. Now the well-intentioned misadventure of *Paint Your Wagon* had nearly wrecked all that he had previously achieved. The artistic failure of that film, even more than the financial one, convinced him once and for all that no one in Hollywood knew anything, certainly no more than he did and probably a lot less, about how to make a good film that could earn a decent profit.

Still, he had a lot to learn about putting what was in his head onto

the screen, and he had five years to learn it. His nonexclusive 1968 contract at Universal (Lang had gotten him to sign it by doubling his salary for *Coogan's Bluff* to $1 million) would expire in 1975 at the earliest, depending upon how many pictures he made for them during that time. It would not be easy to make the films he wanted. Disappointments came early, as the projects he brought to the studio were met with little or no support. To make matters worse, in December 1969 Irving Leonard—Clint's longtime business manager, the president and primary of Malpaso, and a true friend—died suddenly of a heart attack at the age of fifty-three. Few events outwardly affected cool-customer Clint, but the loss of Leonard visibly shook him up.

Leonard was irreplaceable in his uniquely combined roles as father-figure, mentor, and pervasive guiding light. But to try, Clint chose long-time studio executive and now his resident producer, Bob Daley, whom he had known since *Rawhide* days, when Daley was a cost analyst at the studio, working his way up to unit manager. His job had been to control the flow of money for productions, including *Rawhide*. Clint had always liked Daley's business style and acumen, keeping costs low and cutting out the usual ego-stroking expenditures like providing limos for stars and other perks. Daley's job now at Malpaso would be to continue to help Clint find great projects he could star in and produce and help him handle his daily finances and act as go-between with Malpaso's accounting firm, Kaufman and Bernstein.*

The first film that Clint decided to pursue after Leonard's passing was the one Elizabeth Taylor had brought to him, *Two Mules for Sister Sara*. He had run it by Leonard, who approved of the idea shortly before he died. Clint wanted to make it because he felt the character was a more humanized, in-depth version of the Man with No Name. The film's producer was Marty Rackin, a screenwriter who had enjoyed a fair measure of success in the 1950s before turning to full-time producing—he held the option on the original script, written by veteran writer-director Budd Boetticher. Clint and Taylor were his first choice to star in the film.

Then Taylor informed Rackin that she wanted the production transferred from Mexico to Spain, but Rackin insisted on keeping the

---

*Roy Kaufman and Howard Bernstein had been brought together to form their accounting firm by Leonard. Their first client was Clint Eastwood.

location in Mexico, to be faithful to the script and to keep production costs down. Taylor was also experiencing some of the recurring "health problems" that had plagued her throughout her career. When the insurance for her alone proved beyond the film's budget, Rackin and Universal decided to cut her loose.* Clint agreed to stay on, as long as he could have a say in who would direct. Rackin had no objections to bringing in Clint's first choice, Don Siegel.

To replace Taylor, Universal chose Shirley MacLaine, a Broadway dancer who had become a glittering movie star after her performance in Alfred Hitchcock's *The Trouble with Harry* (1955). Now that she had just finished making *Sweet Charity* at Universal for Bob Fosse, the studio, believing that was going to be huge, pushed for her to be in the picture. Clint, Rackin, and Siegel all agreed, and MacLaine was in.

"There was no question that Shirley was a fine actress with a great sense of humor," Siegel later recalled.

> But her skin was fair, her face—the map of Ireland. She most likely would look ridiculous if she played a Mexican nun. Nevertheless, Shirley was assigned to the picture . . . naturally the script had to be rewritten to fit her appearance . . . After working with Marty and Clint on the script, I made a startling discovery. Budd Boetticher, in addition to writing the story, had also written the script. He was a well-known director and a good friend of mine . . . I asked him why he wasn't considered to be the director, and he claimed that Marty never gave him a straight answer. He needed money, so he sold his story and script to Marty, who took the property to Universal, got their okay, and hired Albert Maltz to write another script. I felt funny about being his director. Budd laughed and told me that everything was settled with Marty long before I appeared on the scene. We remained good friends.

As shot by Siegel, the film resembled nothing so much as the Man with No Name trilogy cut with the moral high ground of *Coogan's Bluff*. Siegel deepened Clint's familiar cigar-chomping character (here

---

*Universal may have balked at the idea after Taylor's previous film, Joseph Losey's *Boom!*, costarring Richard Burton, bombed at the box office and she refused to reduce her seven-figure asking price to appear in *Two Mules for Sister Sara*.

called Hogan), contemporized and Americanized his feelings toward women, expanding his need for self-redemption by rescuing them. What had been a one-line backstory in the Leone films now became the main plot in *Two Mules for Sister Sara*, which couldn't have pleased Clint more.

The setting of the film is mid-nineteenth-century Mexico, during the Juarista rebellion to oust Napoleon's occupying French army. A plan is in the works to attack a French army post in Chihuahua. Hogan (Clint) is an American mercenary (as was the Man with No Name) who comes upon a group of outlaws about to rape a woman (MacLaine). In a quick but fierce gun battle (like the opening sequence in *A Fistful of Dollars*) an unshaven Hogan, smoking a cigar butt and wearing an approximation of the Man with No Name's iconic poncho, kills the men and agrees to help the woman to safety after he discovers she is a nun trying to escape the French who want to kill her for having aided the Juaristas. Along the way he discovers she is no ordinary nun. She swears, she drinks, she seems comfortable with her womanliness, and she uses all of her considerable charm to get him to help her sabotage a French supply train. Hogan is wounded during the attack, and Sara nurses him back to health. Then he discovers Sara is really a prostitute disguised as a nun. They fall in love, and when the mission is completed, this curious and mysterious couple ride off together, disappearing into the beautiful Mexican terrain.

The film was scored by Ennio Morricone, who had written the unforgettable scores for the Leone trilogy, further linking Hogan to the Man with No Name and making the film an informal kind of Americanized sequel. Said Clint:

> I think [the Leone films] changed the style, the approach to Westerns [in Hollywood]. They "operacized" them, if there's such a word. They made the violence and the shooting aspect a little more larger than life, and they had great music and new types of scores. I wasn't involved in the music, but we used the same composer, Ennio Morricone, in *Sister Sara* . . . They were stories that hadn't been used in other Westerns. They just had a look and a style that was a little different at the time: I don't think any of them was a classic story—like [John Ford's 1956] *The Searchers* or something like that—they were more fragmented,

episodic, following the central character through various little episodes . . . Sergio Leone felt that sound was very important, that a film has to have its own sound as well as its own look.

Clint's intention was to develop the Siegel-Eastwood connection as an extension of the Leone-Eastwood one, to Americanize the spaghetti westerns and hopefully duplicate their phenomenal commercial success and restore Eastwood's prime film persona as a soft-spoken, charming killer with a redemptive soul. Clint later claimed to have done his best acting to date in the film, especially in the scene where Sara removes the arrow from his shoulder. The sequence is done in medium close-up, and Clint had to play "drunk," which Sara has gotten him, in order to extract the arrow, an unmistakably evocative scene. During it he softly sings a song, an unexpected choice that both quiets and deepens his character. Here the film defines itself as something other than a retroactively slick sequel; it reveals itself for what it really is, a love story. For Clint, this was a crucial step forward in his development as a romantic leading man whose box-office reach would take him beyond fans of action films and dopey musicals to include a wider audience.

Women.

Once *Two Mules for Sister Sara* was completed, Clint returned to Carmel and Maggie only long enough to repack his bags and take off again, this time to London and Yugoslavia. For the next eight months he would serve as one of the stars of MGM's *The Warriors*, a film Clint was allowed to do because of his nonexclusive contract with Universal. The title was later changed to *Kelly's Heroes*, and it was a satire protesting the Vietnam War. Robert Altman's *M*A*S*H* (1970) had been the first anti-Vietnam film, set in Korea to ease the pain. *Kelly's Heroes* was set even farther back, during World War II, making its satire even more striking (and safer), set against the most hallowed, uncriticized war in American history.

Clint agreed to make the movie for a number of reasons. Although he was a Nixon man, having voted for him in the explosive year of 1968, he rejected the president's constant bombing of Vietnam as unnecessary, both politically and morally. In no way could Clint ever be described as a liberal, but neither was he ever a proselytizing

Republican. The best way of describing his politics would be "pragmatic independence." By 1970, after seven years of a blistering war that was going nowhere, he, like many Americans on both sides of the political fence, was simply fed up with it. The script of *Kelly's Heroes* (in which he plays the title role) brought just the right amount of cynicism to the whole affair.

Supporting him on-screen were Telly Savalas, who had made an impact a few years earlier as fellow inmate Feto Gomez in Burt Lancaster's star-turning prison biopic, John Frankenheimer's *Birdman of Alcatraz* (1962); insult-comic-with-a-heart-of-gold Don Rickles, who had appeared in Robert Wise's *Run Silent Run Deep* (1958, in support of Clark Gable), Robert Mulligan's *The Rat Race* (1960), and a host of less memorable TV appearances before breaking into live late-night television on Johnny Carson's *Tonight Show* in the vicious but lovable stand-up-comic persona that finally made him a star; Donald Sutherland, coming off his portrayal of Hawkeye in *M*A*S*H;* and Carroll O'Connor, who later that year would find his best role as the bigoted but somehow lovable Archie Bunker in TV's *All in the Family*. All these supporting players here planted the seeds of their coming personae (and Rickles the elements of the "wise guy" that he never fully realized on film) that helped focus the attention on Clint's lead.

He really wanted Don Siegel to direct, so much so that he had signed on to the film because Siegel had agreed to do it. But at the last minute Siegel had to pull out because of postproduction editing problems with *Two Mules for Sister Sara*—he and Rackin clashed over the editing. The picture was offered instead to Brian Hutton, with whom Clint had last worked on *Where Eagles Dare*. Although his aesthetic side may have hesitated to go with him, Clint's practical side knew that Hutton's films made money, and he approved his being assigned to the picture.

But the addition of Hutton and the subtraction of Siegel upset the directorial skill needed to maintain the balance between satire and "clever caper." Under Hutton, the film focused far more on the blocks of gold bullion than on the bombs and bureaucracy.

In the end, *Kelly's Heroes* looked more bloated than big, more bulky than expansive; the complicated location shoot went on for what felt like forever to Clint, although by all accounts the on-set chemistry was great. According to Rickles, Clint was easy and fun to work with:

I worked on *Kelly's Heroes*, with Clint Eastwood. They told me the shoot would take three weeks. It took six months. I also had a problem with the food. Everything was swimming in oil. Some of us became track stars as we broke the sound barrier to the bathroom. Bottom line, though, was that the cast and I became buddies. "You'd be great, Clint," I told Eastwood, "if you'd ever learned to talk normal and stop whispering." Clint gave me that Eastwood look and whispered something I couldn't understand.

After nearly eight months of shooting and postproduction in London, Clint was obliged to do some additional promotion for *Paint Your Wagon* and to log some pieces for the still-unreleased (and still unfinished) *Two Mules for Sister Sara*. When he saw the final cut of *Kelly's Heroes*, he was particularly unhappy with something he had missed, a late-in-the-film parody of the climax of *The Good, the Bad and the Ugly*, reprised here with Clint, Savalas, and Sutherland. It confirmed for Clint how far off the film had gone, and he attributed it to the loss of Siegel as its director: "It was [originally] a very fine anti-militaristic script, one that said some important things about the war," Clint said later, "about this propensity that man has to destroy himself."

In the editing, the scenes that put the debate in philosophical terms were cut and they kept adding action scenes. When it was finished, the picture had lost its soul. If action and reflection had been better balanced, it would have reached a much broader audience. I don't know if the studio exercised pressure on the director or if it was the director who lost his vision along the way, but I know that the picture would have been far superior if there hadn't been this attempt to satisfy action fans at any cost. And it would have been just as spectacular and attractive. It's not an accident that some action movies work and others don't.

Kelly's Heroes actually opened June 23, 1970, just one week after *Two Mules for Sister Sara*, which got much better reviews. None was more laudatory than the *Los Angeles Herald-Examiner's*, which declared that *"Two Mules for Sister Sara* is a solidly entertaining film that provides Clint Eastwood with his best, most substantial role to date; in it he is far better than he has ever been. In director Don Siegel,

Eastwood has found what John Wayne found in John Ford and what Gary Cooper found in Frank Capra."

Both films ran simultaneously during the summer, something Clint wasn't happy about. He felt he was competing with himself and he wasn't entirely wrong. "Why should I open across the street from myself?" he complained to Jim Aubrey, the head of MGM, with whom Clint had butted heads before, at CBS. Nonetheless, both films proved successful at the box office, and with *Paint Your Wagon* still in theaters, three Clint Eastwood films were playing at the same time. Ironically, *Paint Your Wagon* proved the biggest hit of the three, its $7 million initial gross nearly doubling *Two Mules for Sister Sara*'s $4.7 million and well ahead of *Kelly's Heroes*'s $5.2 million. (*Two Mules* was ultimately more successful than *Kelly's*, as its ratio of cost-to-gross was much less.)

Clint should have been thrilled by his triple-header summer, with across-the-board hits and theaters all over the world filled with his image, but none of the three even came close to what he wanted to do in pictures, what he thought he could be, and what he thought he could earn. Instead, each had moved him closer to the ordinary mainstream and the bottom line of popular movie appeal—and taken his edge away.

He was still looking for the film that could cut him loose. He thought he found such a project in a script that Jennings Lang had sent to him during the making of *Kelly's Heroes*. Based on a novel by Thomas Cullinan and adapted into a screenplay by Albert Maltz (the onetime blacklisted, reformed alcoholic writer who had done the same for *Two Mules for Sister Sara*), the script for *The Beguiled* was impossible for Clint to forget. He read it in a single night and had anticipated yet another grizzled-hero western, but early in realized that it was much more. Perplexed, he asked Don Siegel to read it and give him his opinion. Siegel said he loved it, and on that assessment Clint decided to do it.

The story tells of John McBurney (Clint), a badly wounded Union soldier who is discovered by a ten-year-old girl named Amy (Pamelyn Ferdin) while she is picking mushrooms near the broken-down schoolhouse where she lives. She brings him back to the house, where headmistress Martha Farnsworth (Geraldine Page) offers him shelter. Eventually several students, including Amy and Edwina (Elizabeth Hartman), realize that if they let him go, he will certainly be captured

and killed by the Rebel army. So to save his life, they make him a prisoner, confining him to the schoolhouse. At first McBurney does not realize what is happening, distracted by the apparently easy seductive powers he enjoys over many of the seemingly willing schoolgirls and their sexually repressed headmistress.

All of this takes a (literal) bad turn when Edwina sees him making love to one of the girls and vengefully pushes him down a long flight of stairs. The fall reinjures his bad leg, and the headmistress decides it must be amputated. When McBurney awakens and realizes his leg is missing, he angrily accuses all the girls of doing it to keep him their prisoner. Eventually, though, he becomes the sexual master of them all, picking and choosing each of the girls as he pleases, using and abusing them until they plot to kill him with poison mushrooms.

But before they can, McBurney dies of a heart attack (although they think at first they have indeed killed him). Afterward they erect a shrine to him to acknowledge how he has changed all of their lives forever.

The film's metaphor for devilish (or Christian) imperfection, McBurney's broken leg, is double-edged, symbolizing at once the inability (or unwillingness) to be free, physical injury (crucifixion), and moral defection (less than whole). The film's very loose retelling of the Christ tale—a man walks among us, is killed, is worshipped and immortalized by the very group that planned to kill him—is also one of the devil, of sexual passion, physical imprisonment, and moral domination.

However one chooses to read this unusual and absorbing film, *The Beguiled* is about a social rebel and an unrepentant ladies' man who becomes both a hero and a burden to those who care most for him. In that sense the film was his most autobiographical to date.

Even before Clint returned from Yugoslavia, the studio had assigned Julian Blaustein to produce, a decision that Clint, through Malpaso, meant to do something about. He had had enough of assigned studio "help," and just before production began on *The Beguiled*, Malpaso boldly dismissed Blaustein. Clint went to Don Siegel to convince him to direct, and Maltz to work on the script. Universal did nothing to stop any of these moves.

But, despite several rewrites, Maltz could not get down on paper what Clint was looking for. He wanted, more than anything, to have

McBurney's dark side emphasized and, in turn, the girls' as well. He was interested in shadows, not in sunlight, a choice that would make an even stronger contrast between the Sex Machine with No Name and the women who are both enthralled by and eventually driven to kill him. He envisioned the school as a metaphor for the dark chambers of the soul.

When Clint and Siegel could not make Maltz go as dark or as deep as they wanted, they enlisted the services of Irene Kamp, who had helped create the moody, jazz-framed script for Martin Ritt's 1961 *Paris Blues*, a film that held strong appeal for Clint. He loved the subtle way the script moved, and the open and frank adult sexuality among its four leads.

Kamp worked closely with Clint, adding nuance upon nuance to the script to make it more adult, more complex, and ultimately more personal. Still not completely satisfied, however, Clint turned to Claude Traverse, one of Siegel's longtime associates. In the end, Clint may have felt a man had to do the final draft. Maltz, meanwhile, so objected to anyone else working over his script that he took his name off it, using "John B. Sherry" as his on-screen credit (Irene Camp, as "Grimes Grice," shared the official on-screen credit).

Shooting on *The Beguiled* began in early April 1971, on location on a plantation in Baton Rouge, where the original novel was set. Among Clint's hand-chosen cast of female schoolgirls was Jo Ann Harris, who quickly became his newest on-set romance. Neither one made any secret of their affair (which would burn brightly and then die out by the last day of production), and filming progressed smoothly and without incident. Then Lang, who had not seen the finished script before the film started production, loudly protested that he hated the ending. For the first time Clint Eastwood would die on-screen, an ending that was radically different from the novel and that made an already dark film that much darker. But, Clint (via Malpaso) by contract had the last word, and the ending stayed the way he wanted it.

The film opened late spring and bombed at the box office, grossing less than $1 million in its initial domestic release. Journalist James Bacon complained that Universal's advertising campaign had totally missed the meaning of the film, promoting it "as another spaghetti Western." In the few interviews he gave to promote it, Clint mused

that his character's death was the problem, or that blind faith was a subject too dark for most audiences.

Reflecting on the film's failure, Don Siegel had this to say:

Eastwood films are almost always released like a scatter-gun: play as many theaters as possible and the money pours in. Great. But it should have been recognized that a picture like *The Beguiled* needed to be handled differently. After winning a number of film festivals and acquiring some great quotes, it should have opened in a small theater in New York . . . It would have played for months, maybe a year . . . it would have grown slowly by word of mouth from a small start into a very successful film. [Releasing] the film [the way they did] was a brilliant way of ensuring its failure.

Clint's intention to make more personal movies that somehow also appealed to the mainstream was proving harder than he had thought. To interviewer Stuart M. Kaminsky, Clint explained why he had wanted to make the movie and to shape it the way he had:

Don Siegel told me you can always be in a Western or adventure, but you may never get a chance to do this type of film again . . . it wasn't a typical commercial film, but we thought it could be a very good film, and that was important . . . I think it's a very well-executed film, the best-directed film Don's ever done, a very exciting film. Whether it's appealing to large masses or not, I don't know . . . [The studio] tried to sell it as if it were another western. People who go in expecting to see a western are disappointed and people who don't like westerns—but who might like *Beguiled*—don't go because of the ad. [They claimed that] the only way the film could do really well is if we could draw on those people who don't ordinarily like "Clint Eastwood" as well as those who do. People who like Clint Eastwood won't like *Beguiled* because I get offed.

There was some talk of submitting *The Beguiled* to Cannes, but Lang objected, and the film disappeared quietly and has been seen only rarely ever since. If it really was a career misstep for Clint, it was a good one, at least as far as he was concerned.

Although about to turn forty-one, an age considered "old" for a leading man, or at least "older" by Hollywood's standards, Clint felt younger than ever. With this, his first big-time flop coming as it did so soon after the death of Irving Leonard, he decided the time was finally right to take complete creative control of his career. He intended to direct the next film himself, to ensure that anything that went up on the screen looked exactly the way it did in his head.

NINE

After seventeen years of bouncing my head against the wall, hanging around sets, maybe influencing certain camera set-ups with my own opinions, watching actors go through all kinds of hell without any help, and working with both good directors and bad ones, I'm at the point where I'm ready to make my own pictures. I stored away all the mistakes I made and saved up all the good things I learned, and now I know enough to control my own projects and get what I want out of actors.

—Clint Eastwood

The last deal Irving Leonard put together before he died was the one that meant the most to Clint. Leonard had set up *Play Misty for Me* so that Clint would be able, for the first time, to direct as well as star in and produce the film, all under the auspices of Malpaso.* Timing has a way of accentuating changes—in this instance the departure of Don Siegel, who had become his unofficial creative partner and, more than Sergio Leone, his directorial mentor. It may be seen as the teacher giving way to the student, or the father stepping back to allow the son to take over the family business. The father-son aspect had a deep resonance, as Clint lost not only both Leonard and Siegel but his real father as well.

After moving from the Container Corporation to Georgia-Pacific, Clinton Eastwood Sr. had retired from the box and paper business and moved to Pebble Beach. While getting dressed for a day on the golf course, he dropped dead of a heart attack in July 1970. He was sixty-four years old.

Clint was, of course, shaken up by the death, but after a short and intense period of private mourning, he resumed preproduction on his new film. Familiarly reticent, Clint would be able to talk easily about the loss of his father only years later, expressing both regret and caution: "My father died very suddenly at sixty-three [*sic*]. Just dropped dead. For a long time afterward, I'd ask myself, why didn't I ask him to play golf more? Why didn't I spend more time with him? But when

....

*Clint may have wanted to only produce and direct, but at Lang's and Lew Wasserman's insistence, Universal demanded he star in the film as well. Because Clint was untested as a director but one of their biggest box-office stars, Lang saw his on-screen appearance as an insurance policy on the film's success. To seal the deal, Clint, via Leonard, agreed to give up his usual acting salary in return for a percentage of the profits.

you're off trying to get the brass ring, you forget and overlook those little things. It gives you a certain amount of regret later on, but there's nothing you can do about it, so you just forge on."

He told himself that if he didn't want to wind up like his father, he had better start cleaning up his own act—give up the smoking and cut back on the drinking. Exercise and health food were already part of his daily regimen, but several cold beers interspersed throughout the day remained and still are an essential part of his daily intake.

At the same time he promoted Bob Daley to full producer for Malpaso. One of Daley's first assignments under his expanded duties was to pull together the rest of the preproduction of *Play Misty for Me*.

The original screenplay had been written by Jo Heims, another longtime female friend of Clint's from his days as a contract player at Universal, when she was one of the studio's many legal secretaries. Like everyone else in Hollywood, she really had two professions, her own and the movies. All the while she was working her day job, she spent her nights writing screenplays. When she finally had what she considered a strong sixty-page treatment for a film, she took it to everyone she knew who might be able to help get it made. She got it into Clint's hands while he was still shooting *The Beguiled*. He promised Heims he would read it. He did and liked the story about a disk jockey who has a one-night stand with a caller to his late-night radio request show, who turns violent when she refuses to accept that it's over between them.

Clint turned the sixty pages over to Dean Riesner and asked him to work his magic and turn them into a shooting script that, since Malpaso was producing, could be made quickly and cheaply. As he later recalled, "It was just an ideal little project. The only downside to it, it wasn't an action-adventure film in the true sense of the word . . . but you have to keep breaking barriers."

Under the provisions of the deal he had made with Universal, Malpaso was going to have to underwrite the film. That meant a lot of nearby location shooting, so Clint chose to film it in Carmel, closer to home than any previous movie he had made; it meant few if any special effects or outdoor setups, and no large and expensive cast.

None of that especially mattered to Clint. The only thing that did now was the chance to direct. As Clint would later remember,

I started getting interested in directing back when I was still doing *Rawhide*. I directed a few trailers and [the producers] were going to let me do an episode until CBS kind of reneged. Somebody sent down an edict that said no more actors from the series could direct so they dropped me from that. I forgot about it for a while. Then I worked with Leone in Italy, and Don Siegel close together on several films. Don was very encouraging. "Why don't you direct, why don't you try it," he kept saying to me. It took a while for me, because I'd come in as sort of an outsider, through three European films, and now here I was, after hanging around for five or six years, suddenly here's this guy who wants to direct. I think there was a certain [industry] negativity toward it in the beginning. But I learned the most from Don Siegel and Sergio. They were such completely different people. Sergio was very humorous, and working on shoestring budgets, especially the first two, it was a little bit of chaos all the time. Everything was very loose, to say the least. But we were making a film for $200,000. With Don Siegel, he was very efficient and printed [used] only what he wanted.

The key to making the film work, Clint felt, was the casting of Evelyn, the murderously obsessed fan. The actress would have to make him believable as the victim of her sexual advances and violent abuse—not an easy thing to do. He saw and tested numerous actresses before catching Jessica Walter's performance in a screening of Sidney Lumet's 1966 film version of Mary McCarthy's controversial novel, *The Group*. Despite the studio's stubborn insistence that he cast a star in the role, something he never liked to do—Clint was not a big sharer in that way, as the roster of his costars reveals—he felt Walter was a perfect Evelyn and gave the part to her. She was attractive without being "bombshell," good-looking enough to do the nude-scene montage but not overly voluptuous (which would get in the way of her neediness), yet explosive and capable of projecting the kind of craziness the script required.

To play Dave's (Clint's) "normal" girlfriend, Tobie, he cast TV soap opera actress Donna Mills, who Burt Reynolds suggested might be good for the part. Walter, Clint felt, would be particularly good in the early part of the film, before her craziness becomes both apparent and shocking. Here was yet another film where women—Evelyn

and Tobie—willingly fall to their knees and roll backward for Clint's character. More to the point, his emotional attachment to either is, for all intents and purposes, nonexistent. If Evelyn is a casual one-night stand, Tobie is the saner equivalent—a woman without a deeper connection to his soul. If one even existed.

This was the essential character Clint was looking for: the loner. Not the romantic loner of most films, redeemed by the love of a good woman, but the one who functioned best alone, unencumbered. In that sense Dave was a modern version of the Man with No Name.

Clint worked on the shooting script for several weeks before he felt he was ready. The night before filming began, he later recalled, "I was lying in bed, going over the shots in my mind. I had them all planned out. I turned out the light, thought 'Jesus! I've [also] gotta be in this thing!' I turned on the light and started approaching the scenes all over again, from the actor's point of view. Needless to say, I didn't get much sleep."

On set, not too far away, just in case Clint lost control of the ship and needed some dependable directorial backup, was Don Siegel, present for most of the shoot and visible in the movie playing the small part of a bartender. Later on Siegel, who had signed Clint's director's card (signifying Clint's debut behind the camera), would jokingly refer to his role as "a good-luck charm, my best piece of acting."

Even with that buffer, Clint ran into trouble early on with Universal, which wanted to make sure the film did not veer too far from its commercial center. For instance, he wanted to use Erroll Garner's jazzy original song "Misty" for the film's ironic title track, which Universal adamantly opposed. It preferred something that had more potential hit appeal and suggested "Strangers in the Night," recorded by Frank Sinatra, for which it happened to own the rights. Clint rejected that idea out of hand and instead added a second song to the film that he had heard on a local jazz station while driving to Universal one morning early in production. "I was absolutely knocked out by it," Clint later recalled, and drove directly into Hollywood to find a copy of it. None of the record stores in town had it as a single, but he finally found it on an album—*First Take*—in a supermarket bin marked down to $1.38. It was Roberta Flack's 1969 darkly intense version of Ewan MacColl's "The First Time Ever I Saw Your Face." Clint

felt it was perfect to set the mood for Dave's romance with Tobie.* In an age when rock and roll was the current style in movie sound tracks, ignited by Simon and Garfunkel's remarkable one for *The Graduate* and the far more intense Dylan/Steppenwolf/Jimi Hendrix Experience one for *Easy Rider,* Clint's choice of the bluesy "First Time" and the jazz-infused "Misty" seemed a throwback to the 1950s.

The whole film, for that matter, had a dated feel to it, invoking a time when stalkers and violence were the stuff of drive-ins and midnight showings. Many reviewers were quick to compare Clint's debut to Hitchcock's ultimate 1950s B-movie *Psycho,* which was actually released in the summer of 1960 and whose artistic merits were initially overlooked by the impact of its shocking story.

Clint finished the shoot in just four and a half weeks, in October 1970, five days early and $50,000 under its original $1 million budget. Amid the big movies of 1971, the year of its release, *Play Misty for Me* seemed to most critics more reactionary than revolutionary, especially compared to the five strong films nominated for Best Picture that year: William Friedkin's tough and supercharged New York police drama, *The French Connection,* which won Best Picture and Best Director; Stanley Kubrick's striking *A Clockwork Orange*; Norman Jewison's paean to Hollywood's ethnic soul, *Fiddler on the Roof*; Peter Bogdanovich's extraordinary Texas-based sleeper *The Last Picture Show*; and Franklin Schaffner's turgid but nonetheless popular *Nicholas and Alexandra,* an instant relic about the Russian Revolution's most celebrated victims.

In that company *Play Misty for Me* didn't stand a chance even for a disapproving Academy sniff. It was neither big enough to merit attention, nor small enough to seem independent-film revelatory, as did Bogdanovich's movie. But what *Play Misty for Me* did have was a bottom line that showed a profit, and for the moment, not having his film laughed out of the movie theaters was all that really mattered to Clint.

And if the Academy had overlooked him, others did not. Selected scenes from *Play Misty for Me* served as the centerpiece for a January

---

*The album was released by Atlantic Records, and Clint reportedly paid a "modest fee" for its usage. The single then became a hit all over again after its use in the film.

1971 "mini-retrospective" of Clint's films at the San Francisco Film Festival, the first time he had been celebrated in that fashion.* That same month Clint and actress Ali MacGraw (who had become a sensation after her star turn in Arthur Hiller's 1970 adaptation of Erich Segal's novel *Love Story*) were selected "Stars of the Year" by the National Association of Theater Owners (NATO) for their respective box-office appeals. Even fiercely independent filmmaker John Cassavetes, who had financed his own independent directorial efforts by acting in mainstream ones, thought the film was good, if a bit derivative of Hitchcock's *Psycho*. "There's only one problem with this film," he later remarked. "It doesn't have Hitchcock's name on it."

The film turned a fairly decent profit, earning more than $5 million in rentals in its initial theatrical release, five times its negative (finished film) cost. For the moment both Clint and the studio were satisfied, if neither was completely happy with the other. Universal did not like Clint's offbeat style of moviemaking and his lack-of-conventional-love-story style; Jennings Lang and even Lew Wasserman believed the film had strayed too far from Universal's mainstream standard, while Clint felt the studio did not sufficiently or effectively promote the film, especially on television, the new favored medium for film. Each site was ready to sever ties, with both waiting for the right moment, one that would not publicly embarrass either the studio or the star.

Play Misty for Me may not have been the blockbuster the studio had wanted, or the completely personal statement Clint was looking to make, but it left him a millionaire. Shortly after the film opened, he bought twelve acres of pristine property within the highly coveted stretch of Pebble Beach, where many of California's wealthiest lived, alongside celebrities such as Kim Novak, cartoonist Jimmy Hatlo, Merv Griffin, and novelist John Steinbeck. Clint built a house with a gym above the garage and a large steam room.†

---

*The three spaghetti westerns—*A Fistful of Dollars, For a Few Dollars More*, and *The Good, the Bad and the Ugly*—were the centerpiece of the schedule. In fact, they had never gone out of commercial exhibition and were often shown together on a triple bill with the advertising slug: "How would you like to spend eight hours with Clint Eastwood?" Prior to this showing, the three films as a unit had already had a total of fifteen major U.S. "revivals" since 1968.

†He was prevented from building on the site that had once been an Indian reservation until he reached an agreement with the Regional Coastal Zone Conservation Commission to hire a professional archaeologist to gather and classify any Indian antiquities found on the land. *Los Angeles Herald-Examiner*, May 24, 1973.

Having by now become an avid golfer with a sixteen handicap, he wanted to be as close as possible to Pebble Beach's acclaimed golf course. He was also an accomplished helicopter pilot and loved to fly back and forth from Hollywood to Carmel, cutting short several hours–long commutes.

"I've traveled all over the world—beautiful places like Italy, Spain, France and so forth," Clint said shortly after he bought the new property. "But there is not another place in the world I'd prefer to live than the Monterey Peninsula. I plan on staying here forever."

Moving up, however, did not mean moving out. Clint held on to the house in Orange County, for those times when his Hollywood schedule would not permit him to drive back and forth to Pebble, and he made it a point to keep intact his small circle of friends that included Ken Green, whom he'd known since high school, his close friend Paul Lippman, a journalist whom Clint had met at the Carmel Valley Racquet Club, and the local tennis pro Don Hamilton. (Clint used Hamilton in one of the bar scenes in *Play Misty for Me*.)

About the same time Clint opened his first retail establishment, a local bar in Monterey, where he and his buddies could hang out away from their wives, their jobs, and the public. Meanwhile Maggie, whose profession was now listed by several magazines as "former model and painter," was given the job of designing and supervising the construction of their new home, something she delighted in doing. Clint continued to see Roxanne Tunis, as he had since they'd met, getting her small parts in his movies, even though—their child that he supported notwithstanding—she still could not officially exist in Clint's world.

And he continued to bed as many women as he wanted, including Beverly Walker, a struggling writer and actress who was also working on certain films as a publicist to pay her rent. While involved with screenwriter Paul Schrader, in the years before he hit it big, she had what journalist Peter Biskind described as a "desultory romance" with Clint. The reason they got involved with each other, according to Walker, was because Clint could take women as easily as picking fruit from an overripe tree for his own pleasure, and for him, women were about as hard to resist as a piece of that luscious fruit: "In Hollywood, men put enormous pressure on women to fuck them, even if it's only once. It's like the dog that pisses on the lamppost. They

want that kind of connection to you, and then maybe they can relax." Walker claims she and Clint remained friends, although she never shows up in any of his movies.

As for his loner character in *Play Misty for Me*, Clint, in one of his infrequent interviews, explained his portrayal of this type of man as part of his own special brand of Method acting:

> There are a million Mr. Perfects. The nice guys come and go, but the Bogarts, the Cagneys, the Gables, John Wayne and up through Mitchum—they're all a bit of . . . they really could treat women like dirt. I think women like to see other women put down when they're out of line. They have a dream of the guy who won't let them get away with anything . . . and the man in the audience is thinking, "That's how I'd like to handle it—cool and assured . . . knowing all the answers." He wants to be a superhero . . . Some people have a need to discuss deep, intimate things about themselves, discuss and analyze. I don't feel that need. Maybe it's a strength and maybe it's a weakness. Once I went to a psychiatrist. I did it as a favor to someone else who was having a problem, and after we'd talked the guy said to me, "You seem to have things in hand." I think I do . . . to me love for a person is respect for individual feelings—respecting privacy and accepting faults.

So that was it: he wasn't perfect, and he was proud of it, even if he had lately seen a psychiatrist "as a favor to someone else." These were remarkably revealing comments from a man whose public off-screen persona was depicted as the happily married man, good father, and easygoing suburban weekend golfer. To his friend and journalist Earl Leaf, Clint's life was tinted a slightly different shade of rose:

> Clint lives a double life—not surprising, he being born under the sign of the twins. Though he never ceased loving and caring for Maggie, he hasn't made a secret of the free-living sexy side of his life around other women, especially young free-thinking chicks . . . Maggie doesn't question or nag her husband about his excursions to the Hollywood fun arena. Clint has described himself as a "married bachelor." The meaning is clear to those who know him well.

If *Play Misty for Me* had any major flaw, it was Dave's lack of self-recognition. Although Evelyn is obviously crazy, and Dave may at first be perceived as an innocent, what made the film far different from (and weaker than) *Psycho* was the absence of any hint at the darker, deeper side of Dave, a man who hides behind the persona of a smooth voice, who is sexually indiscriminate, and who engages in violence as a solution.

Still, audiences stood up and took notice of Clint and the "something new" he had brought to the screen, even if his film characters did not connect all the dots between his private reality and his public image. All that was about to change with his next movie, about a detective who not only breaks all the rules but takes extreme (and extremely dark) pleasure in doing so.

Dirty Harry would allow Clint to let out the shadow side of his onscreen persona and have it happily shake hands with the light one. That extraordinary feat thrilled audiences around the world even as (or because) it scared the shit out of them. In that sense, *Dirty Harry* was even more personal than *The Beguiled*—a remarkable achievement indeed.

And one that almost didn't happen.

After coming across Harry Julian Fink and his wife R. M. Fink's script for *Dirty Harry*, Jennings Lang had taken an option flier and offered it to Paul Newman, thinking the film perfect for him. But after reading the script Newman turned it down cold because he felt the character was too right-wing for him.

Lang then thought of Sinatra, because he had previously appeared in a couple of successful detective movies. The character he'd played, Tony Rome, was also tough, but Sinatra had given him enough ring-a-ding-ding to give him some charm. Lang hoped he would do the same with Callahan. Sinatra initially showed some interest, but once he realized how unsympathetic Callahan really was, he passed on it, fearing audiences would turn on him for playing such a low-life character. He begged off, claiming a hand injury would prevent him from doing justice to the role.*

---

*Clint never believed Sinatra's story about his hand injury. "Probably just bullshit," he told Jeff Dawson of the *Guardian*, June 6, 2008.

With Clint still tied up with *Misty*, a film in which Lang had little confidence, Lang was unable to find any star to play the role, so he sold the rights to ABC Television. ABC intended to make it into a TV movie but then realized the excessive violence would be unsuitable for television audiences. So they, in turn, sold it to Warner.

Warner Bros.–Seven Arts, as the studio was then called, had been in turmoil, in danger of going under, when it was acquired in 1969 by Kinney National Company, a car rental, parking lot, and funeral services company owned by Steve Ross, who leveraged Kinney's assets to gain entry into the film business. While he worked to straighten out the studio's seemingly hopeless finances, Ross hired a triple-threat team: Ted Ashley, one of the most powerful agents in the business; former Filmways producer John Calley, who had made many successful films, including Jules Dassin's *Topkapi* (1964); and Frank Wells, the attorney, to head business affairs.

Ross's short-term goal was to build up a roster of box-office talent, and the first star he wanted to bring over was Clint Eastwood, whose nonexclusive deal at Universal was not only ending but, according to Frank Wells, gone sour. Wells was one of the few industry people Clint trusted and with whom he shared his frustrations. When Wells found out about *Dirty Harry*, the script Lang had hesitated to give Clint, he jumped at it.

The same character traits that had turned off Newman and scared Sinatra attracted Clint, as they would give him the chance to display the element missing from *Misty*, the sense of inspired rage. Dirty Harry Callahan was ragingly antiauthoritarian, particularly in his relationship to the chief of police and the mayor of the city of New York, where the story was originally set.

In addition, the script contained a fair amount of violence that would allow Callahan to flex some familiar muscles and show he was still a macho tough guy who didn't take shit from anybody—no man, no woman, and no criminal he considered a subspecies of the human race. Here, though, the script took on a deeper and more interesting twist. Unlike other villains Clint had faced down, especially in the spaghetti westerns, the psychotic killer Callahan sets out to track down is obviously linked to him. Clearly the sadistic woman-and-child-killer Scorpio (Andy Robinson) is, in some ways, a personification of the

dark (or darker) side of Callahan himself, the murderous deep end he may have stuck his toe in but never actually jumped into. As film critic and historian Lawrence Knapp put it, "Harry's pursuit of Scorpio is so intense, it becomes an aberration in itself, a sickness as profound as Scorpio's. Scorpio is Harry's doppelgänger." Scorpio likes to leave cryptic notes and send the authorities on wild-goose chases, enjoying such games in the fever of his own sadistic madness. Callahan likes to play a life-or-death how-many-bullets-left-in-the-chamber-of-my-.44 game, a peculiar and no less sadistic one. Done once, Callahan's game seems like a product of chance-and-capture as he corners a bank robber who momentarily thinks about reaching for his gun. It is an enjoyable sequence that allows the audience, at least for this moment, to identify with the hero's unwavering strength, a modern-day Man with No Name. However, played a second time at the climax of the movie, with Scorpio himself on the receiving end, it becomes a psychotic ritual, an almost hypnotic reaction to his own sadistic lunacy, with his wounded prey helpless to do anything but play along until Callahan definitively blows him away.

This crazy cat-and-mouse game the two play ultimately decides whether Callahan's "good" side will defeat the "bad." (The outcome is something of a draw.) The film's terrific and unexpected plot twists deepen Callahan's character. Scorpio has kidnapped and murdered yet another victim, this one a young girl. Callahan tracks him to an empty stadium and traps him there (a neat metaphor for both the missing conscience in Scorpio's head and the gladiatorial aspect to their titanic battle). Later Callahan is shocked to find out that the cold-blooded killer has been set free because his rights had been violated. His disbelief is cut with fury, and he begins to stalk Scorpio, confident the killer cannot stop himself from killing again. Predictably Scorpio (whose linear psychology brings his character and the film dangerously close to parody) goes on another murderous rampage, this time kidnapping a busful of innocent children. That gives Callahan the opportunity to corner and kill him once and for all, before he can be released by the law to kill again. The beauty (and the horror) of this aspect of the story is that the next time, Callahan becomes judge, jury, and executioner. Scorpio has taken a boy hostage, holding him at gunpoint. Callahan kills him, shooting just above the boy's head; the force

of the second shot from the .44 blows Scorpio into the swampy bay. Then Callahan shockingly hurls his badge into the swamp as well, and walks away, as the final credits begin to roll.

If Clint identified with the Callahans of the world, he also identified with the Scorpios, or at least with every Callahan's fear that a Scorpio was lying in wait. That was, at last, the character he wanted to play. But not direct.

When Wells first floated the possibility of doing *Dirty Harry* and Clint expressed interest, Wells asked him what it would take to make it happen. Understanding that, after *Play Misty for Me*, he was not ready to direct a film this complicated and star in it as well, Clint replied without hesitation: Don Siegel. "I was the one who hired [Siegel] . . . When I came over to Warner, [the movie] . . . I got Siegel involved. My agreement with Warner Bros. was, 'I'll do it if you let me hire a director like Don Siegel and we'll take this story back to its original concept.' "*

Although Clint could certainly have directed *Dirty Harry*, he had found the experience of *Play Misty for Me* both "exhausting and detrimental" to his acting. For now, at least, he preferred the next-best thing, his off-screen alter ego, Don Siegel. "Directing is hard work," he told one interviewer. "You have to stay on top of everything all day long, and it can be tiring. I learned to pace myself. It's not like acting, where you can stay up till one o'clock the night before work. As a director, I had to crash before eleven."

Siegel was under contract to Universal, but Lang was all too happy to loan him out—he wanted to keep Clint happy (and get rid of the project) so that if the right property should come along, they could work together again. The deal was in place by that spring. The script had gone through numerous rewrites, including one by John Milius, but it was decided that the Finks' version was still the best. It was the only one that included the " 'Do I feel lucky?' Well, do ya, punk?" sequence that would become one of Clint's signature lines.

The brilliant cinematographer Bruce Surtees, whom Clint had per-

---

*Interestingly, one of the film's most memorable scenes, looking like none of the others, is a suicide-intervention sequence early on, wherein Callahan rescues a lunatic perched on the edge of a building ready to jump. Siegel fell ill on the day it was scheduled to be shot, and Clint directed it himself.

sonally requested, shot most of *Dirty Harry*'s exteriors at night,* accenting the movie's noirish feel. The drop-in and pull-back of the opening and closing overhead shots of the city suggest a godlike observational point of view to the proceedings while at the same time offering a sense of randomness, as if anywhere the camera falls, it will find a story. This neat stylistic touch would eventually help define the look and feel of a "Clint Eastwood film."

To be sure, the film also had a social and stylistic element, one that marked it at the time with political relevance. It was filmed at the height of the Vietnam War, nearly a decade after the Gulf of Tonkin incident. By then Americans had grown weary of the conflict and fearful that the lion's roar from their once-mighty place in the international psyche as the Cops of the World had turned into a frustrated, frightened yelp, the hollow sound of a paper tiger. The Vietnam War would not be portrayed directly by Hollywood until years later; Michael Cimino's *The Deer Hunter* (1978), Hal Ashby's *Coming Home* (1978), and Francis Ford Coppola's *Apocalypse Now* (1979) would all look back at it. But in 1971 *Dirty Harry* confronted the supercharged anti-civil-rights, pro-Vietnam instincts of a faction of Americans (and anti-Americans around the world). Its memorable " 'Do I feel lucky?' Well, do ya, punk?" sequence put Callahan's outsize, phallic .44 Magnum into the face of a black thief and dared him to test his luck and courage against the almighty white authority of justice, law, and order. The classic moment remains alive in the memory of anyone who has ever heard and seen it, even if it has lost its historical relevance. As an image of Callahan's (and America's perceived) dark sadism, it is cinematically timeless.

Echoing TV's Joe Friday (Jack Webb in *Dragnet*) and Gene Hackman's Jimmy Doyle in *The French Connection* (1971), Callahan took the character of the American police officer farther and lower than anyone previously had in American motion pictures. Friday, as portrayed by Webb, was robotic in his joyless enforcement of the law, while Hackman's Doyle was societally embittered and equally joyless. Callahan, however, was more frightening than either because of the pleasure he got from torturing his "opponents." In Sidney Lumet's *Serpico* (1973)

---

*Surtees had been the cinematographer on *Coogan's Bluff* (uncredited), *Two Mules for Sister Sara* (uncredited), *The Beguiled*, and *Play Misty for Me*, and he would go on to direct the cinematography on several future Clint Eastwood films.

Al Pacino's antihero character, the little prince in jeans and long hair, takes on the establishment and (in a sense) wins; in *Dirty Harry*, Callahan *is* the establishment, and unless the means justify the ends (as went the big sell of Vietnam to the American public), then nobody really wins. Callahan's toss of his badge into the river at the end of the film echoes Will Kane's (Gary Cooper's) gesture at the end of *High Noon*, released at the height of the Korean War, representing a rejection of the corruption, hypocrisy, and fear of establishment law and order.

But for Callahan, the similar gesture means something even more personal, the interior battle against his own ever-present, ever-threatening darkness. He may have killed off Scorpio, but in a larger and truer sense, both in classic mythology and in biblical wisdom, in great literature and *especially* in Hollywood movies, evil never really dies. Callahan's toss of the badge is at best his declaration of the stand-off, at least for now (as well as a perfect setup for a sequel, of which there would be four).

The decision to toss the badge was not an easy one. Clint and Siegel went back and forth on it, with Clint initially rejecting it. Early on Clint told Siegel he couldn't do it because it would mean he was quitting the force. Siegel replied that it didn't mean that at all, that it was a rejection of police department bureaucracy and all its fixed rules and hierarchy of authority. But Clint didn't buy it. Instead he suggested that Callahan put his arm back as if to throw the badge away, hear the distant wail of approaching police sirens, put the badge back in his pocket, and head off. Siegel reluctantly agreed, and Clint, according to Siegel, mussed his director's hair in happiness.

The day of the shooting of the final scene, however, Clint had a change of heart and decided to throw the badge in the water after all. (Perhaps he realized that he could never get rid of his own dark side by killing Scorpio or by tossing away the symbol of legal righteousness.) Siegel then told him they only had one prop badge—they would have ordered more if he'd known they were going to film the toss. To be able to reuse the badge as needed, Siegel had a black cloth put in the bottom of the swamp. But it proved unnecessary—he got the shot in one clip, with Clint tossing it with his favored left hand.

Dirty Harry was released in December 1971, only two months after *Play Misty for Me* (which had been delayed in postproduction by

Clint's difficulties in editing). Christmas is traditionally a time for lighter, more uplifting fare, and critics were almost universally negative about the film, but it broke box-office records, hitting number one its opening week and earning more than $18 million in its initial domestic release (and eventually nearly $60 million worldwide). In the *New York Times*, Roger Greenspun wrote that "the honorably and slightly anachronistic enterprise of the Don Siegel cops-and-crooks action movies over the last few years *(Madigan, Coogan's Bluff)* takes a sad and perhaps inevitable step downward in *Dirty Harry* . . . Clint Eastwood's tough San Francisco plainclothesman [is] pushed beyond professionalism into a kind of iron-jawed self-parody." *Newsweek* dismissed it as a "right-wing fantasy," while *Time*'s Richard Schickel praised Clint's performance as "his best to date." And *Daily Variety* condemned it as "a specious, phony glorification of police and criminal brutality."

Pauline Kael, who inexplicably prided herself on seeing a movie only once lest she be given a privileged viewpoint apart from the ordinary viewer, launched a vicious attack on *Dirty Harry*, in many ways rougher than anything in the film. That her review came between the covers of the otherwise sophisticated *New Yorker* gave it added gravitas. "The film," she insisted, "made the basic contest between good and evil . . . as simple as you can get . . . more archetypal than most movies, more primitive and dreamlike . . . with the fairy-tale appeal of *fascist medievalism* [italics added]." Whether pro or con, the film sparked reams of literature about whether Harry represented the best or the worst of early 1970s America, and as a consequence it became the must-see film of late 1971 and early 1972.

In August 1972 Clint and Maggie, along with John Wayne, Glenn Ford, and Charlton Heston, were invited to attend Richard Nixon's "Western White House" reception just prior to his anticipated renomination at the Republican National Convention. Nixon fawned over Clint as if the president were the fan and Clint were the president. Clint, soft-spoken and smiling like a Cheshire cat, knew that he had, for sure, inherited a new mantle. Wayne had, until now, been the official western (movies and world) tough guy, but he had grown old and fat and was something of a self-parody as well as the proud darling of the extreme right wing. Clint was the one whose screen persona played

fastest and loosest with civil rights and the Constitution itself when it came to enforcing law and order and who preferred a pickup truck to his Ferrari (at least according to his press releases). Here he was, rubbing shoulders with the power elite. Not long afterward Nixon appointed Clint—along with Judith Jamison, Edward Villella, Rudolf Serkin, Eudora Welty, and Andrew Wyeth—to a governmental panel on the arts and a six-year term on the National Council on the Arts, an advisory group to the revered and influential National Endowment of the Arts.

Not a bad score for Clint who, on the strength of *Play Misty for Me* and *Dirty Harry*, had topped Wayne, McQueen, and Newman to become the top-grossing star in the world.*

---

*According to the forty-first annual poll of theater owners by Quigley Publications. Wayne had dropped to fourth place in this, his twenty-third appearance on the highly influential poll. Coming in second behind Clint was George C. Scott, then Gene Hackman, Wayne, Barbra Streisand, Marlon Brando, Paul Newman, Steve McQueen, Dustin Hoffman, and Goldie Hawn. After Clint's appearance on this list the Academy invited him to be a presenter of the Best Picture Oscar on its 1973 awards broadcast. Besides his appearance in second place in 1970 and 1971, Clint had appeared in fifth place in 1968 and 1969. Also in 1972 Clint had another, dubious honor when *Mad* magazine spoofed his spaghetti westerns as *Fistful of Lasagna* and *For a Few Ravioli More*.

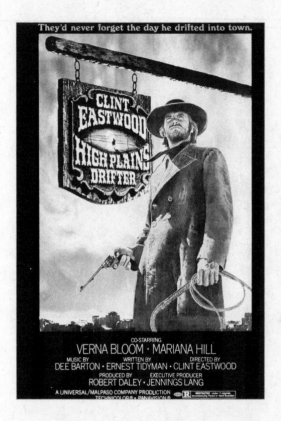

TEN

We live in more of a pussy generation now, where everybody's become used to saying, "Well, how do we handle it psychologically?" In [the old] days, you just punched the bully back and duked it out. Even if the guy was older and could push you around, at least you were respected for fighting back, and you'd be left alone from then on.

—Clint Eastwood

O n the heels of his fabulous success with *Dirty Harry*—without the sure hand of Leonard to guide him, and on the advice of the less visionary, more bottom-line-oriented Bob Daley—Clint signed on once more at Universal, via Malpaso, to star in a John Sturges film, *Joe Kidd*, a pale-faced imitation of the Leone westerns, with a script by Elmore Leonard. Sturges was a journeyman director who had had a string of early successes: *Bad Day at Black Rock* (1955), *Gunfight at the O.K. Corral* (1957), and most notably *The Great Escape* (1963). *Joe Kidd* was made amid the groundswell of controversy created by *Dirty Harry* and slipped in and out of theaters early in 1972 without stirring much interest in either audiences or critics. It was perhaps just as well; the film didn't work on any level and remains one of Clint's least-remembered movies, but the money was good, and it did give him a chance to work with one of his old army buddies, John Saxon, whose screen career had never blossomed into anything memorable or lasting.

High Plains Drifter was something else again. It too came via Universal, in the form of a nine-page treatment written by Ernest Tidyman. Tidyman, a pro, had written both the original novel and the screen adaptation for Gordon Parks's 1971 seminal *Shaft*, and the Academy Award–winning adapted screenplay of *The French Connection*, for which the previous year he had won an Oscar, the Writers' Guild Award, and the Mystery Writers Edgar. He wrote *High Plains Drifter* specifically with Clint Eastwood in mind, certain he would not be able to resist the temptation to both star in and direct the script.

At least part of what made Tidyman so sure was his familiarity with the so-called Gold Rush Syndrome that sooner or later afflicts every star in Hollywood—the desire for official anointment by the faceless little statue called Oscar. Clint had every reason to believe his performance as Harry Callahan had a shot at the big trophy in 1971;

it was, after all, one of the biggest box-office movies of the year and had screwed Clint into the consciousness of its viewers. It was therefore something of a letdown, if not a total surprise—so-called pure action films are rarely considered "important" enough by the elitist Academy—that he wasn't even nominated.*

After his disappointing stint with Sturges, Clint believed more than ever that no one could direct him like Don Siegel, and should never even try. But it seemed too soon to work with Siegel again—some of the critical fallout from *Dirty Harry* had to fade—so he decided once more to try to direct himself.

For budgetary reasons, Universal wanted *High Plains Drifter* to be shot on their expansive western backlot, but Clint preferred something more original and, for him, director-friendly. He managed to convince Lang (credited as the executive producer on the film) to green-light the building of an entire western-town set, in the desert near Lake Mono in the California Sierras. It took eighteen days to build. (Film critics and historians Richard Thompson and Tim Hunter would later describe its main street as "looking more like a new condominium in Northern California than a Western town of the past.") Clint shot the entire film in sequence, which was unusual and usually more costly due to the extra setups, but the film came in early and under budget.†

Clint played his familiar role of a Man with No Name—called the Stranger this time. His costars were featured players (but not stars) Verna Bloom, Mariana Hill, and Mitch Ryan, and the film held unmistakable echoes of the Leone trilogy. (Typical of its reviews, *Box Office Magazine* described it as having a "dog-eared plot-line of a mysterious stranger who shoots up a town.") What is notable about this film is the introduction of an "otherworldliness" (already seen in *The Beguiled*) that would reappear in several of Clint's later films.

High Plains Drifter's script strongly suggests that the Stranger is

....

*Best Actor that year went to Gene Hackman for *The French Connection*, a character-driven *policier* with an East Coast, ultrarealistic style and timely theme based on the Academy-loving "true story." The other nominees were Peter Finch in John Schlesinger's *Sunday Bloody Sunday;* George C. Scott in Arthur Hiller's *The Hospital;* Walter Matthau in Jack Lemmon's *Kotch;* and Topol in Norman Jewison's *Fiddler on the Roof.*

†Bob Daley, who had executive-produced *Joe Kidd*, was moved down a notch by Clint to the position of hands-on producer.

actually the ghost of the sheriff killed by the gang that controls the town; now the Stranger kills them off, one by one, before disappearing into the sunset.* With touches of *High Noon*, *Shane*, and Leone's trilogy, the film contained a menu of surefire story ingredients; Bruce Surtees's unusually wide lenses intensified the brightness of the landscape and added a hellish look to the film.

This was a Clint Eastwood cowboy audiences wanted to see, the cold-blooded, infallible, noble killer—not the imperfect ex-con *Joe Kidd*. *High Plains Drifter* was a huge hit at the box office, grossing nearly $16 million in its initial domestic release. It appeared to have everything the early Eastwood westerns had had, but its success was uneasy: the film was derivative and less than authentic, and its faux mysticism was a facile substitute for the real mystery of the Man with No Name. Clint felt to some a little like post-army Elvis—he still looked and sounded like the performer who had so recently exploded onto the cultural scene, but was instantly and obviously not the same thing. There was something too safe, too slick, and too comfortable about *High Plains Drifter*.

While the film proved to be a cash cow, audiences were not really interested in it. This time there was no talk of awards for either the film or Clint Eastwood's performance. It was, however, for Clint the director, a start.

On May 22, 1972, Maggie Eastwood gave birth to her second child, Alison, who weighed in at a manageable seven pounds, four ounces. In fact, she arrived fifteen days premature, just after Maggie had flown down to Los Angeles to see Clint. Barely a month later Maggie was with Clint at the opening ceremonies of the three-day Pebble Beach Celebrity Tennis Tournament, hosting such legendary participants as the John Waynes and the Charlton Hestons.

By now virtually anybody who spent time with Clint on a set or at Malpaso knew that the Eastwood marriage was, at the very least, a bit unorthodox. But no one in his circle, or hers, seemed particularly

---

*Clint has always denied any supernatural affect to the film, stating on more than one occasion that his intention was to insinuate that the mysterious drifter is the murdered sheriff's brother. See Boris Zmijewsky and Lee Pfeiffer, *The Films of Clint Eastwood* (New York: Citadel Press, 1993), 152. But multiple viewings reveal little, if any, evidence of such a link.

bothered by it, least of all the Eastwoods themselves. And while he was still involved with Roxanne Tunis, contributing money to help to raise their child, he and Tunis had cooled off when she turned to Eastern spiritual practices and took their daughter to Denver so she could devote herself to full-time study. Roxanne and Clint still saw each other, but not as often nor as intensely as before, and almost never anymore when he was making a movie.

In October 1972, two years after Clint's father's death, his mother, Ruth, quietly remarried. The Hawaii-themed ceremony was held in Pebble Beach, and the groom was John Belden Wood, a wealthy widower who had made a fortune from his Piedmont-based lumber business. Clint happily escorted his mother down the aisle, relieved that she would no longer have to be alone.

Clint then turned his attention back to directing, but this time he wanted to see if he could sell a film, both to the studio and to audiences, in which he wasn't also acting. The project he chose must have resonated quite loudly with him: it was the Lolita-like story of a middle-aged salesman, Frank Harmon (William Holden), and his relationship with a teenage hippie type, Breezy (Kay Lenz).

In some ways *Breezy* signaled a shift in Clint's focus, away from the violent and (so-called) socially relevant action picture to a small-scale love story. Romance had been missing in previous Eastwood films; even *Play Misty for Me* belongs solidly in the horror category. The shift was a retreat from the social clamor that had surrounded *Dirty Harry*, although the story of a middle-aged man in a sexual relationship with a teenager also was potentially controversial.

Partly because he wasn't in it and partly because the subject veered too close to breaking a taboo, Universal was inclined to turn it down, despite Clint the actor's current number one standing at the box office. They finally green-lighted it on condition Clint brought it in for under $1 million (meaning they would put up the million, and the revenues from ticket sales would reimburse the studio until break-even, after which Malpaso would take a healthy cut of the gross).

To play the part of the older man, Clint chose William Holden, a handsome, soft-spoken actor who was equally at home in westerns, love stories, and war pictures. Always manly, he was in many ways a 1950s version of Clint Eastwood. But he also represented the repressed American male lover, constricted by social mores from get-

ting down and dirty with costars such as straitlaced and demure Grace Kelly in Mark Robson's *The Bridges at Toko-Ri* (1954), in George Seaton's *The Country Girl* (1954), and with Jennifer Jones in Henry King's *Love Is a Many-Splendored Thing* (1955). With all three films a kiss is the only physical contact (we see) between proper lovers. Such repression, in a way, helps explain Holden's misplaced passions in such rage-fests as Billy Wilder's *Stalag 17* (1953), with its prisoner-of-war setting, and David Lean's *The Bridge on the River Kwai* (1957), in which noble sacrifice redeems Holden's unbridled passions.

Clint did not have to operate under Holden's characters' social and sexual restrictions, but he nonetheless shared a manly resistance to portraying lust in his own movies. And he had yet to show a simple, open, happy, loving side to any of his male characters, without the woman being a murderer, witch, prostitute, deceiver, or helpless victim.

The part of the young girl Breezy was much harder to cast. Among the many hopefuls he saw was a cute, southern born and bred, twenty-five-year-old blond actress by the name of Sondra Locke. Locke had gained some notice in Hollywood for her Oscar-nominated performance in Robert Ellis Miller's 1968 adaptation of Carson McCullers's *The Heart Is a Lonely Hunter*, but afterward her career had experienced a slight stall. Jo Heims, the screenwriter for *Breezy*, suggested her to Clint, saying she thought Locke was exactly right for the role. Locke never made it to a screen test, however, because after looking at some eight-by-tens and a few minutes of *The Heart Is a Lonely Hunter*, Clint felt she was too old for the role. In his film he wanted to emphasize the age difference between the two lead characters. He eventually chose the very young and coquettish Kay Lenz, who looked exactly right to him but had almost no film experience.

Production began in November 1972, and almost immediately it was apparent to everyone on set that Clint had a very special attraction to her. Clint, interestingly, was pulling back from his screen image as a law-and-order warrior while drawing closer to his real-life character as an aging Lothario. This was heady stuff, doubling the intensity of Clint's relationship to Breezy as a director and as an authority figure to a younger woman.

But whatever electricity flowed between Lenz and Clint off-screen, it failed to ignite between her and Holden on-screen. Audiences

turned away from this May-December romance. Holden just looked too tired and too old for audiences to believe he could be attractive to Breezy. The movie had no romantic chemistry. It was an out-and-out failure at the box office, not just for its unbelievability but because, simply put, no one was particularly interested in seeing a so-called Clint Eastwood film that did not star Clint Eastwood. Several reviewers sharpened their pencils and had a critical field day. Judith Crist's reaction was typical: writing in *New York* magazine, she chuckled condescendingly that *Breezy* was "so perfectly awful that it's almost good enough for laughs." Only auteurist critics like Molly Haskell, writing in the *Village Voice*, took the film seriously: "Clint Eastwood's most accomplished directorial job so far . . . a love story in which almost everything works." A then-fringe auteurist critic like Haskell, however, had neither the readership nor the clout to make a commercial difference, while Crist had a huge following, especially in box-office-rich New York City.

By and large, critics like Crist got it right, but an oversensitive Clint was quick to blame Universal's promotion, rather than his own direction, for *Breezy*'s failure to float: "This was a small film—it was just the story of the rejuvenation of a cynic. I thought that was an interesting subject, especially nowadays in the era of cynicism . . . it was a disaster at the box office, very poorly distributed and very poorly advertised . . . that's Universal. They have a terrible advertising department, they're not smart. I tried to keep an eye on it but [at Universal] it was a harder thing to do."

The abject failure of *Breezy* drove Clint back into the warm and waiting (and wealthy) arms of Warner, which was eager to green-light a sequel to *Dirty Harry*. Enough with the silly romances, they both agreed. Let's get back to good old blood-guts-and-gore.

Clint would not make another romantic "love story" for twenty-two years.

One thing Clint agreed to was the subtle softening, if not exactly mellowing, of Harry Callahan. It was not wholly Clint's choice; rather, a combination of talented writers working in collaboration with him and Robert Daley, all of whom believed the character and therefore the film would be much more appealing if Callahan were more accessible to and easier on women, as a way to boost the date-movie week-

end audience. Of course, Callahan couldn't become a pussycat, but they felt that a slight declawing wouldn't hurt the franchise.

The inspiration for the story—whose working title was *Vigilance*, later changed to *Magnum Force*, named after Callahan's weapon of choice and the elite enforcement squad of the San Francisco police force—came from screenwriter John Milius, who had done some uncredited partial revisions on the original *Dirty Harry* and had since written the screenplays for Sydney Pollack's *Jeremiah Johnson* (1972) and John Huston's *The Life and Times of Judge Roy Bean* (1972) and was on track to write and direct *Dillinger* later that year. This time, however, nothing came out of Milius's rewrites before he opted out of the project to work on *Dillinger*.

Clint then turned to a talented young newcomer offered to him by the William Morris Agency. Michael Cimino was charged with developing Milius's main contribution to the picture—the eventual showdown between Callahan and the secret and deadly Magnum Force unit rather than some crazed killer. This plot element was key. While it kept Callahan as violently antiauthoritarian as before, it also put his maverick behavior more clearly on the side of law and order, making him a hero while maintaining his rebel status. Cimino (who would go on to write and direct the phenomenally successful *The Deer Hunter* and win the Best Director Oscar for it,* then self-destruct with his 1980 remake of *Shane, Heaven's Gate*) prior to *Magnum Force*, had partially written only one screenplay. It was a collaborative effort with Deric Washburn of Douglas Trumbull's *Silent Running* (1971), not a big winner at the box office but good enough for William Morris to put him up for Clint's film.

To direct, Clint surprised everybody by going with Ted Post over Don Siegel, feeling either that his creative teaming with Siegel had run its course or that Siegel was not going to be able to ease up on the intensity of the Callahan character.

That may not have been the only problem. Clint, by now, had begun to feel restricted by Siegel, as much by his methods as by his style. Clint liked to move quickly, especially as Malpaso was now producing most of the films he worked on. Siegel was deliberate and liked

---

*He was also one of the producers and shared in the *Deer Hunter*'s Oscar for Best Picture.

to shoot scenes over and over again—which drove Clint to the brink of his patience. Finally, the aging Siegel's on-screen bluntness was losing some of its edge, where Clint was looking to go younger and sharper. He believed that speed and instinct were the ways to do it, and he wanted a director who was less committed to a set style of directing, less deliberate, and more willing to go with the moment.

Clint felt grateful to Post for the success of *Hang 'Em High*, and the studio liked him as well. Not long afterward the trades announced that Siegel was "unavailable," due to a prior commitment to direct a project in Europe tentatively called *Drazzle*, starring Michael Caine. (It was never made.)

However, things did not go as smoothly as Clint had hoped. On set Post, who had known Clint since *Rawhide*, wanted to expand on the notion of Harry as a dirty cop, while Clint wanted less, to bring more couples into the theaters. Most of all, he wanted to keep the movie in the entertainment sections and out of the general news pages of the newspapers. (He did allow a Japanese TV crew to follow him around for an episode of the popular Japanese series *Leading World Figures*, which had previously profiled Pope Paul VI, Pablo Picasso, Aristotle Onassis, Princess Margaret, Chou En-lai, Indira Gandhi, Princess Grace, and Henry Kissinger.)

One adjustment to the original *Dirty Harry* was the addition of a partner for Callahan called Early Smith, who was played by Felton Perry. The fact that Perry was black was a conscious attempt by Warner to ameliorate the outrage that the punk in the " 'Do I feel lucky?' " scene had been black. Everyone, it seemed, had been upset that the figure cowering on the other side of Dirty Harry's gun was African-American, just when militant groups such as the Black Panthers were denouncing lethal police violence inflicted on Fred Hampton and George Jackson. (In 1987 the "buddy" teaming of a "crazed" white cop and his more sensible black partner would be reprised by Mel Gibson and Danny Glover, respectively, in Richard Donner's *Lethal Weapon*, a hugely popular film that would enjoy three sequels, all of which owed some measure of debt to *Dirty Harry*.)*

During preproduction, Clint was asked to present the Best Picture

---

*Even Mel Gibson's character's name, Sergeant Martin Riggs, is an echo of Lieutenant Neil Briggs, played in *Magnum Force* by Hal Holbrook.

Oscar at the Academy Awards ceremony on March 27, 1973. Although it was and still is considered an honor to present the most important award of the evening, Clint initially turned down the job, but because of pressure from the studio and from Maggie, he decided to accept the assignment. As long as his appearance was short and sweet, with one or two lines, he would be fine.

That night he showed up for the ceremony with Maggie and took his assigned place in the audience, smiling and waving to friends scattered about the Dorothy Chandler Pavilion. The telecast show was to have multiple hosts, as it had for the past several years. (Clint had previously presented the Best Foreign Language Film award, alongside Claudia Cardinale, to Costa-Gavras's *Z* in 1970.)

And then the roof fell in. One of the show's four "hosts," Charlton Heston, was scheduled to kick off the proceedings, but had not shown up for his half-hour call and was nowhere to be found.* His introduction, explaining the voting rules and regulations, had been tailored to Heston, as a parody of the gravitas he was known for from his biblical hero films.

Howard Koch, the show's producer, nervously signaled for Clint and Maggie to hurry backstage. They went, not knowing what was going on, and Koch asked Clint to fill in for Heston. He refused. That wasn't his thing, he told Koch. He wasn't prepared, and he just couldn't do it. Koch continued to plead as the audience began to murmur about the delayed start. Finally Maggie stepped in and told Clint he ought to help out. With nowhere to go and stuck between a begging producer and an urging wife, he silently nodded and walked out onto the stage. There he was greeted by thunderous applause and the occasional shrieks caused by his unexpected appearance.

In his gut, he felt a sense of panic. The teleprompter was filled with Heston-related movie jokes, written by screenwriter-novelist William Goldman. Clint stopped in the middle, looked out at the audience with a tight smile on his face, and said, "This was supposed to be Charlton Heston's part of the show, but somehow he hasn't shown up. So who did they pick? They pick the guy who has said but three lines in twelve movies to substitute for him."

Only mild laughter came back at him—the audience was as

---

*The other three were Carol Burnett, Michael Caine, and Rock Hudson.

confused as he was—so he read the prompter as best he could, making jokes about *The Ten Commandments* that nobody could possibly have found funny, especially coming from him. After several torturous minutes, sprinkled with the nervous laughter of an audience of nominees already on edge, Heston arrived backstage out of breath, claiming to have been the victim of a flat tire. Koch grabbed him and literally threw him onto the set. Now, the audience roared.

A much-relieved Clint quickly and gratefully handed the proceedings over to Heston, who began from the top as if nothing had happened. When he reread the same jokes Clint had done, the audience erupted, this time with good-natured laughter. Clint returned later that night to present the Best Picture Award, but by then the audience was reeling from Marlon Brando's personally chosen stand-in to accept his Best Actor Oscar for the title role of Francis Ford Coppola's *The Godfather.* Sacheen Littlefeather, a woman dressed as an Apache, had protested the treatment of American Indians in Hollywood movies and was received less than enthusiastically. Clint had to follow that. He took the opportunity to make what was for him a rare and witty, if sarcastic, ad-lib: "I don't know if I should present this award on behalf of all the cowboys shot in John Ford westerns over the years!"

He then presented the Oscar to Albert Ruddy, who won for *The Godfather.**

The next day Rex Reed commented, "Last night we learned Clint Eastwood can be funny!" It would be twenty-seven years before Clint consented to be a presenter for this or any other live event.†

*M*agnum Force opened in December 1973, and despite the lack of controversy surrounding the Callahan character, was the biggest hit of the year. Its only real negative criticism came again from Kael, who derided Clint's abilities as an actor and pompously held her nose throughout her review. But neither she nor any other critic could stop audiences from flocking to see this film, which outgrossed *Dirty Harry*

---

*Thirty-two years later, Clint and Ruddy (and co-producer Tom Rosenberg) would jointly accept the 2004 Best Picture Oscar for *Million Dollar Baby*.

†In 2000, he presented the Best Picture Oscar to the producers of *American Beauty* (1999).

by more than $2 million, to become Clint's highest-grossing film to date. During its initial domestic release, it broke through the $20 million ceiling, which at the time defined a "blockbuster," the next big step above "big hit." And, because it was a sequel, it broke another Hollywood rule of thumb—that a sequel is usually half as good as the original and earns about half as much.

So here was a film that may or may not have been half as good, that was made for little more than the original (minus the original director)—that actually managed to outgross the original. The reason was singular and definitive; Clint Eastwood's name above the title, in the role he had created two years earlier, was enough to draw audiences in huge numbers. More than any other achievement, *Magnum Force* removed any lingering doubts that he was a worldwide box-office sensation.

But something else was equally undeniable. For the first time, both in person and on screen, Clint looked old, or older—every day of his forty-three years. His thick, brown mane of hair had begun to thin and recede on both sides. His face had weathered, and lines were visible on his forehead and two short vertical ones, like quotation marks, on the bridge of his nose between his eyes. By Hollywood standards, he was no longer industrial-strength young.

And he knew it, which only added to his desire to shift from star to director. Could anything be more ludicrous than a middle-aged, huffing and puffing Harry Callahan? That was something he believed might happen if he worked with and trusted the wrong advisers. "People who go to the movies like me," he reminded one interviewer, explaining that he had never felt beholden to any one studio. "I haven't had a special push or a big studio buildup. I never get my picture taken kissing my dog when I get off a plane, that sort of thing. There are stars who are produced by the press. I'm not one of them. Bogart once said he owed it to the movie-going public—and to them alone—to do his best. I feel that way too."

For his next project, Leonard Hirshan had a project he thought Clint might like, which had come to him through Stan Kamen, the head of the William Morris Agency's motion picture department. Kamen was, at the time, helping propel the rising star of Michael Cimino, whose script-doctoring of *Magnum Force* had made him 100

percent bankable, with producers lining up to throw development money at him. Cimino had written a road movie script with Clint in mind. The genre had become popular in the new independent Hollywood following the extraordinary success of Dennis Hopper and Peter Fonda's *Easy Rider* (1969), one of the last, and perhaps the biggest, nail in the old studio system's coffin.

Everyone now wanted to do a road picture, including Clint. Or at least that was what he decided when he read Cimino's script, an unlikely pairing of a bank robber and a drifter. Kamen had already attached one of his biggest clients, Jeff Bridges, who was fresh from a Best Supporting Actor nomination for Peter Bogdanovich's *The Last Picture Show*, to the project (in the part that not too long ago would have gone to Clint). Kamen wanted Clint to play the bank robber, a Vietnam War veteran.

Cimino knew what Clint liked and made sure the script had plenty of it: foamy barroom philosophy and lots of dialogue about women's "tight asses," "cock-sucking," and other vainglories of the proverbial and never-ending (and ultimately existential) road. The film would have no shortage of women, all young, sexy, and willing, who came Thunderbolt's (Clint's) way.

Cimino also insisted that he had to direct his own script. Clint—sensing in this fellow traveler a fiercely independent young hothead who wanted to do things his own way—approved it, as long as Hirshan could make the film a Malpaso project. No problem, Kamen assured him, although Frank Wells at Warner had, prior to Clint's firm commitment, turned down the project, feeling it was too idiosyncratic and lacked blockbuster potential. When Clint found out about that, he was furious. According to Clint, "Lenny Hirshan took a script that I liked called *Thunderbolt and Lightfoot* to Frank [Wells] and John [Calley], and they said, no, not at that price, so twenty minutes later I had a deal at United Artists."

To sweeten the deal, UA—Clint's original American distributor for the spaghetti trilogy—offered Malpaso a nonexclusive two-picture deal, which he immediately accepted, the second picture to be decided at a later date. With Bob Daley in place as the film's line producer, filming *Thunderbolt and Lightfoot* began in July 1973, on location in Montana, and lasted until the end of September.

While he had loved the script, and Cimino's cockiness, Clint hadn't

counted on the director's perfectionism. It closely resembled what Clint had experienced with Siegel, times ten (bordering on the obsessional, it would contribute to Cimino's later self-destruction with *Heaven's Gate*).

Clint was well known on his sets for preferring to do one take in the morning and spending the afternoons on the golf course. During *Play Misty for Me*, in which he wore three caps—as director, de facto producer, and star—he said, "I must confess I can't stand long locations or production schedules. Once you get moving, I don't see any reason to drag your feet. During production, I can function much more fully and efficiently if I move full blast. Maybe it's because I'm basically lazy."

Clint found Jeff Bridges easy to work with and his performance revelatory. When the film was released in 1974, Bridges was nominated for Best Supporting Actor.* But according to several sources, including (but not limited to) Steven Bach's *Final Cut*, Clint perceived himself as having been upstaged by Bridges. His disappointment and anger were palpable. And when the film proved a disappointment at the box office (settling in at about $9 million in its initial theatrical release, less than half of *Magnum Force*), according to Bach, Clint excused his unofficial and overly indulged protégé Cimino. Instead he pointed the finger at UA, which, Clint felt, had failed to adequately position or promote the film. Despite all they had done for him, going all the way back to the Leone westerns, he swore he would never work for the studio again. He remained true to his word and never made the second film of the two-picture deal or any other for UA.

Instead, Clint went back to Universal to make a more comfortable type of movie, and a more reliably profitable one—straight action, with no women, no matter how tight their asses were, to interfere and slow things down. He wanted to return to the safety of the kind of film where he had to hang by his fingertips for dear life, while the audiences eagerly lined up to see him do so.

Only this time, he nearly fell making it.

---

*Bridges lost to Robert De Niro in Francis Ford Coppola's *The Godfather Part II*. The other nominees were Fred Astaire in John Guillermin and Irwin Allen's *The Towering Inferno*, and Michael V. Gazzo and Lee Strasberg in *The Godfather Part II*.

ELEVEN

I went into The Outlaw Josey Wales *a little in awe of Clint Eastwood, top star. I finished it in awe of Clint Eastwood, the total talent.*

—Sondra Locke

The film was *The Eiger Sanction*, a James Bond–style movie in which Clint plays a government assassin on a mission to kill a renegade spy; in reality, the agency believes he is the renegade and wants *him* killed, or so he thinks. The politics of paranoia are insinuated in the backstory. It is the physical assault on Switzerland's Eiger mountain that dominates the screen.

Clint leaped at the chance to do another film that would emphasize his physical prowess, in a surrounding where he would not have to share the stage with other, perhaps more talented or more famous actors, be harried by a self-indulgent director, and for a script that was more colorful than the resulting movie. *The Eiger Sanction* was just the kind of picture he knew best how to do—its content and form melded into one continuous flow of action, so that its content *became* its form, like a film with no plot starring a Man with No Name.

Apparently, at the relatively late-for-Hollywood age of forty-four, Clint felt he still had something left to prove. The financial dip that *Thunderbolt and Lightfoot* had taken was enough for Clint to want to fall back on more familiar turf, preferably in an outdoor setting, playing a silent but deadly hero with death-defying physical skills. Jonathan Hemlock (Eastwood), the former assassin who has lately turned to the clergy (of all things), is once again summoned by a "secret (i.e., CIA)" U.S. intelligence agency to return for one final assignment that will, upon its completion, enable him to make some new art purchases. As preposterous as it sounds, this plot offers the perfect setup for pure action, the essential ingredient of *The Eiger Sanction*. As he always liked to do, Clint personally went through the script with a thick blue pencil and slashed the dialogue as much as possible.

The Eiger Sanction property had been owned by the studio for quite some time. They had purchased the screen rights in 1972 to the first

of what became a series of *Sanction* novels by Trevanian (*sanction* means "assassination" in the lingo of his books), its twisty hook being its intellectual hero who is all-too-easily able to become a man of action who thrives on danger.* The production team of Richard Zanuck and David Brown, sitting pretty with a strong development deal at Universal, had purchased *The Eiger Sanction* with Paul Newman in mind. (The next year they would score big with their filmed version of the novel *Jaws*, directed by Steven Spielberg.) Newman was red hot after George Roy Hill's *Butch Cassidy and the Sundance Kid* (1969) and *The Sting* (1973), but after expressing preliminary interest in the project, passed. Jennings Lang then suggested that Zanuck and Brown offer it to Clint (who had been Lang's first choice). He read it, loved it, and with Malpaso worked into the deal, signed on.

Once aboard, Clint assumed complete control of the project, becoming its nominal producer, although Zanuck, Brown, and (for Malpaso) Bob Daley got the on-screen credit. The first thing Clint did was toss the script and contact Warren Murphy, a novelist whose work he liked (Murphy's action-oriented *Destroyer* series would be the basis for at least one movie—Guy Hamilton's 1985 *Remo Williams: The Adventure Begins;* Murphy eventually provided the story for Richard Donner's *Lethal Weapon 2*). Clint liked Murphy's minimal style, and although he had as yet no background in scriptwriting, Clint convinced him to try one for *The Eiger Sanction.*

Working off what Murphy considered his first draft, Clint went into production with a cast that included costar George Kennedy as Big Ben Bowman, Hemlock's pal and also his secret enemy. Clint and Kennedy had gotten friendly during the making of *Thunderbolt and Lightfoot*, and as was Clint's way, he rewarded that friendship by making Kennedy a member of the Malpaso "family." Clint filled out the rest of the cast with Jack Cassidy and Vonetta McGee (playing the female spy Jemima Brown). McGee had made a couple of "blaxploitation" pictures and had the kind of "taut bottom" that Trevanian had given Brown in the book.

He wanted the film to look authentic, which not all his pictures did. This time, because he saw the film as essentially a great moun-

*The no-first-name Trevanian was the pen name of University of Texas professor Rod Whitaker.

tain climb with a little story and even less dialogue, he recruited Mike Hoover to serve as the film's technical adviser. The set was, in reality, the north face of the Eiger in the Swiss Alps, a mountain with a reputation of being nearly impossible to climb; the names of those who had died trying was a grim roster. Hoover had made a documentary called *Solo* that had been nominated for an Oscar for Best Short Subject—Clint had seen and admired it. For this film his assignment would be twofold—to teach Clint how to look professional while he climbed, and to serve as a cameraman on the more dangerous shoots. After several days rehearsing the action sequences at Yosemite Mountaineering School, Hoover and his handpicked team (which included at least one veteran of the north face), and the cast and crew all left for Switzerland, where they were booked into the Kleine Scheidegg Hotel, located at the base of the mountain.

One of Hoover's crew was David Knowles, a twenty-seven-year-old British climber who had been awarded the Royal Humane Society's highest honor for his part in the 1970 rescue of several stranded climbers in Glencoe, Scotland. His good looks made him a perfect double for Clint in some of the more difficult mountain shots. (Clint and the rest of the cast did very little actual climbing—helicopters transported them to and from the mountain.) The last shot of the first week of filming was a pickup of a mountain slide, re-created by using rubber rocks. Hoover and Knowles decided to shoot it themselves. They positioned on a lower ledge to get the angle they wanted, when suddenly the rubber rocks triggered real rocks, and they all started falling at the same time. Possibly the vibrations from the helicopters created the landslide. Hoover suffered a broken pelvis and clung to the side of the mountain until rescuers could get to him. Knowles wasn't so lucky. He was found dead, hanging upside down, dangling from one foot, his head crushed by a boulder that had killed him instantly.

Everyone was, naturally, upset, and for a while Clint considered canceling the production, but Clint's unofficial statement was this: let it continue.

It was a very difficult picture to make. A good thing our gadgets were limited in number; we were running the risk of heading in the direction of the James Bond movies. And especially the mountaineering sequences posed enormous problems. We had to shoot with two crews, one crew

of technicians and one crew of mountain climbers. Every morning, we had to decide, according to the weather report, which one to send up the mountain. The three actors and myself had to undergo intensive training. On the seventh day of filming, we lost one of our mountaineers and, believe me, I asked myself repeatedly if it was worth it.

The unfortunate incident was used, rather coldly, to promote the film. In an interview entitled "Clint's Cliff Hanger," James Bacon described some of the footage (he'd had an advance look) as "white knuckle" material. He also said that "the only time [Clint] ever used a double was a dummy. One professional mountain climber hit on the head with a falling rock was killed in Switzerland. Clint had dropped from the same site only moments before." Bacon quoted Clint about it this way: "I just got myself involved deeper and deeper. There was no turning back. At first, I was going to use a double but a double can only think of the stunt. He can't think of the characterization. It just wouldn't have worked with a double." Bacon wound up his piece noting Clint's youthful looks: "Clint, at 44, is the world's greatest advertisement for health food . . . Even Clint's restaurant in Carmel—'Hog's Breath Inn'—features health food. He even serves organic booze—no preservatives added. The menu includes such goodies as 'The Dirty Harry' dinner, 'Fistful of T-Bone,' and a 'Coogan's Bluff' New York–cut steak. It seems that everything Clint touches makes money. His wife Maggie told me that the restaurant took off like Clint's box-office record."

The restaurant was in a former antiques shop and had become the prime social hangout for Clint and his local non-show-business friends, including Paul Lippman and Walter Becker, whom he knew from one of Carmel's more upscale restaurants, Le Marquis. According to Bacon, "The Hog's Breath's courtyard has an old-fashioned fireplace, and the entire place is surrounded by white picket fence and climbing ivy. The menu offers such basic food as Swiss cheese on rye with avocado and alfalfa sprouts, a char-broiled hamburger on organic bun with cheese or sliced tomatoes, a vegetarian salad bowl, fresh mushroom omelets and an assortment of Monterey Bay fish, including crisply sautéed filet of sole, squid sautéed in white wine and minced shallots, and a wide selection of teas."

"It's been a gold-mine," Maggie happily told Bacon.

Clint's rare inclusion of Maggie in an interview (probably in order

to "humanize" him after the accident) prompted Bacon to portray her as Clint's partner in the fun-and-games pastime of running this other family business. In truth, she was increasingly frustrated by her continued marginalization in her marriage and in Clint's life. Clint brought her along to another interview to promote the film; she told Peter J. Oppenheimer in an off-the-cuff response how she handled Clint's propensity for "danger" in his moviemaking: "There's nothing I can do about it." It was a strikingly apt response as well as a reflection on her life with Clint—an innkeeper hostess while her husband costarred with nice asses. In the same interview Clint described his home life as sheer perfection. Asked why he shot some of the sequences for *The Eiger Sanction* back in Carmel, Clint replied, "Because I have a home in Carmel and this way I can stay home with my family and bounce my kids on my knees."

Lippman, who was also interviewed for the piece later on, claimed—doubtless in a joking manner that somehow did not come across—that Eastwood was a "romantic Casanova at the pub. He chats up all the girls. Especially the blondes. Clint likes small or slight women—he calls them 'squirts' or 'shrimps' and 'spinners.' " Lippman also claimed that he and Clint "often double-dated and compared notes the morning after, while watching cartoons."[*]

To Clint's great surprise and disappointment, *The Eiger Sanction* proved a dud at the box office, earning fully a third less than *Thunderbolt and Lightfoot*. After its initial domestic release, it settled in at a little more than $6.5 million in sales, to *Thunderbolt*'s already modest $9 million. Five years away from fifty, with his career on the decline, and a marriage that served only to scrub his public image, Clint allowed himself to be lured back to Warner by Frank Wells, who vowed to resurrect his fading star.

To do so, Wells insisted, Clint should revisit the money franchise, *Dirty Harry*, hoping that it would return him to the top of the box-office heap, flush with cash, fame, and all the eager young blondes he could handle.

Part of Clint's deal was a new suite of offices on the Warner lot, a re-creation of his old Malpaso offices at Universal, down to the same

---

[*]Clint later denied it, claiming that Lippman had exaggerated their friendship.

knickknacks dotting the place. Warner is only about a mile away from Universal in Burbank, California; he would remain in that office for the next quarter-century.

But before Clint could do another *Dirty Harry*, a suitable script had to be written and developed. Restlessly, he asked Wells if he had anything ready to go. When Wells said he didn't, Clint went in-house to Sonia Chernus, whom he had made head of Malpaso's story department as payback for her help in getting him the part of Rowdy Yates. As it happened, in keeping with Malpaso's bare-bones makeup, Chernus *was* the story department. She did have an outline and story treatment of a novel that had come in unsolicited—such over-the-transom submissions were usually rejected unread and returned. But Chernus had taken a quick look at this one, liked it, and now felt it might be of interest. The tentative title was *The Rebel Outlaw: Josey Wells.**

Chernus was proven correct when Clint had Malpaso take out an option on the rights to the unpublished book. Wells agreed to fund the movie if Clint could bring it in at $4 million. Once the money was in place, Clint went to the William Morris Agency in search of a writer and director to develop the project. They put Philip Kaufman up for the job, who in 1972 had written and directed *The Great Northfield Minnesota Raid*, a bank-robbery western drawing on the seemingly endless adventures of Jesse James.

Clint hired him with the expectation of a quick return, but Kaufman's deliberate preparations made Clint antsy. He was used to filming unpolished scripts, like *The Eiger Sanction*. But because of that film's failure, he was willing to give Kaufman a little more breathing room.

When he finished the script, wearing his director's cap, Kaufman boldly cast Chief Dan George in the key role of Lone Watie, the Chero-

---

*The novel had originally been self-published in 1972 as *Gone to Texas*. The author, Forrest Carter, was actually a (purported) half-Cherokee Native American, Asa Carter, a notorious racist who had been a public supporter of the Ku Klux Klan and a speechwriter for George Wallace. The novel glorified a Southern soldier, a Johnny Reb, who refuses to surrender after the end of the Civil War and goes on a bloody rampage while pursued by a Northern posse. The story appealed to Clint, who was always attracted to antisocial types. Carter's true identity was not discovered until after the film's release. To one reporter Clint declared, during preproduction, "It's a story written by an Indian about the period right after Reconstruction. The guy's a poet . . . wrote Indian poetry . . . and someone talked him into writing this book . . . and I just fell in love with it." Clint's quote is from Larry Cole's "Clint's Not Cute When He's Angry," *Village Voice*, May 24, 1976.

kee companion, and conscience, of Josey Wales. (The chief gave the film a bit of a wounded–Native American authenticity that would be echoed in Kevin Costner's 1990 *Dances with Wolves*, which owes more than a little of its physical look, directorial style, and thematic story line to *The Outlaw Josey Wales*.) As Wales's mission progresses, he and the chief pick up stragglers along the way, which gave the film a light coating of Christian allegory—unusual for a Clint Eastwood film, which usually emphasized physical revenge over moral redemption. In the end the film is less Jesus than journey, as the conquest of a mountain, à la *The Eiger Sanction*, leads to a greater understanding between the two.

To play the role of Laura Lee, another convert to Josey's bandwagon of soul-searching Civil War survivors, Clint wanted Sondra Locke, the actress he had once considered for *Breezy*. Her career had languished since her Oscar-nominated performance in *The Heart Is a Lonely Hunter*, but she had managed to hang on to the fringes of the business, and when Clint saw her, he immediately remembered her. Despite the seventeen-year difference between them (or because of it), he was strongly attracted to her, and she to him. He pushed Kaufman to green-light Locke, but it seemed the more he did, the more Kaufman resisted. So Clint went directly over his head and hired her anyway—which he had every right to do but was considered poor form.*

Locke remembers that moment of their connection this way: " 'So what have you been up to since I saw you last,' Clint asked as if it were just last week." Locke was given the part, and a few nights later Clint called to ask her out for dinner. " 'I gave the orders to hire you . . .' 'Really?' 'I never forgot meeting you for *Breezy*, Sondra.' 'But you didn't hire me for that film, did you,' I teased. 'No. I didn't. Big mistake . . . but I've hired you now.' 'I'm glad.' I genuinely blushed."

Shortly after Clint signed on Locke, Kaufman privately told a friend that Clint's going over his head was "the worst thing that anybody's ever done to me. He cut my balls off."

---

*In the hierarchy of Hollywood power, in the post-studio era of director-as-star/auteur, the producer was, and still is, the boss—for the simple reason that money always supersedes talent. Whoever writes the checks controls the production, no matter how creative or domineering a director appears. In this case, the man who was paying Kaufman's salary was Clint.

Production began in October 1975 on location in Arizona, Utah, and Wyoming. Clint was holding a script in one hand, so he could study his lines, a stopwatch in the other, so he could bring the film in on or under budget and thereby keep Wells to his financial commitment. But Clint fumed at Kaufman's snail-pace style of directing, considering it a sign of his lack of talent.

Some believe that what happened next was solely attributable to Kaufman's failure to assert his authority from day one, beginning with Clint's hiring of Locke. Passivity was a quality Clint had little use for in a director. Clint always preferred the shoot-the-film-now, ask-questions-later kind of moviemaking—not a style in which the director contemplated his ammunition.

The situation took a nuclear leap in the wrong direction when Kaufman (despite being married and having his wife along for the shoot) asked Locke out to dinner—on the same night Clint had. Locke, no fool she, turned down the director for the producer. Kaufman claimed he needed extra time to work with Locke on her characterization, but a testosterone-fueled battle had clearly erupted between Kaufman and Clint.

A few days after his faux pas with Locke, Kaufman, appearing timid and confused on set, totally messed up her rape scene by letting the camera roll too long and apparently confusing the word *cut* with the word *action*. Finally, his inability to catch a golden-hour sunset during another important scene proved the breaking point for Clint. Kaufman was nowhere to be found—he had apparently gone to another location—so an impatient Clint shot the scene himself. The next day he angrily handed Kaufman his walking papers.

Clint was furious about Kaufman's apparent bungling, but the Directors Guild of America (DGA) did not sanction the firing. All directors' contracts, they said, contain a clause that says if a director completes preproduction and has begun shooting, he or she cannot be fired at an actor's command. The fact that Clint was also the producer only made matters worse, and the film's production nearly came to a halt. Finally Wells frantically negotiated a buyout for Kaufman and accepted a DGA penalty for Clint of $50,000 (which Warner almost certainly paid).

Kaufman's firing angered some among the cast and crew and

frightened others. To many it looked as if Clint had had Kaufman do all the preparation work on the film—which was a lot—so he could then come in and get all the so-called glory. Although Kaufman to this day has never spoken about the incident, he did not direct another movie for nearly three years, and when he did it was, ironically, a 1978 remake of Don Siegel's *Invasion of the Body Snatchers.**

No matter who is right and who is wrong, when a director takes a case to the DGA, it is a serious act not soon forgotten by producers. The *Josey Wales* incident resulted in the Eastwood Rule—a DGA mandate that no current cast or crew member could replace the director of a production.

The *Outlaw Josey Wales* opened to mixed reviews but did phenomenal box office. (*Time* magazine called it one of the year's ten best.) Audiences thought the "old" Clint Eastwood had returned; the antisocial, violent, cynical antiromantic loner they had all missed so much. The rentals from the initial domestic release reached $14 million, good enough to reestablish Clint as a legitimate box-office power.† It also brought him once more to the attention of Pauline Kael, who complained that with *Josey Wales*, Clint had established himself as the "reductio ad absurdum of macho today." Kael's continual attack-dog reviews disturbed Clint greatly.

With his career back on the winning track, Clint shifted his concentration to the building of his Carmel dream house, now in its seventh year of construction. Between sessions of Transcendental Meditation (to which he had recently become devoted) and Malpaso business, he had been increasingly absent from the homestead.

....

*After a series of so-so films, Kaufman went on to direct *The Right Stuff* in 1983, which definitely established him as a major Hollywood director.

†That same year, 1976, Clint remained in the top-ten list of Quigley Publications box-office champs, while John Wayne fell off, never to return. It is believed that Wayne sent Clint a letter highly critical of his revisionist view of the American West (some would put that onus on Wayne himself) and that Clint was upset by it. However, the contents of that letter, if it existed, were never released, and neither Wayne nor Clint ever discussed it on the record. Clint that year came in at number five. Number one was Robert Redford, followed by Al Pacino, Charles Bronson, Paul Newman, Clint, Burt Reynolds.

He spent some time, too, in Las Vegas, anonymously. But it wasn't all fun and games. Up in San Francisco he began to see a psychiatrist, Dr. Ronald Lowell, who, regarding Kael's reviews, told Eastwood, "What Kael says is actually 180 degrees the opposite of what she says, and . . . often a man or woman obsessed with preaching great morality is more interested in amorality." A bit later at a speaking appearance, Clint pointed out to the audience that while Kael hated his movies for their maleness, she had adored Bernardo Bertolucci's *Last Tango in Paris*, wherein Paul (Marlon Brando, a Kael darling) has anal intercourse with Jeanne (Maria Schneider), in a relationship dictated by Paul to be based only on (debasing) sex. So much for her neofeminist tirades, Clint said, chuckling. The audience chuckled with him.

Clint was forty-six now and feeling every second of it. A preoccupation with age, or more precisely aging, is a universal occupational hazard for performers in Hollywood, and it became one of his most favored subjects whenever he did grant the occasional interview. "I don't have any new properties on my mind right now," he told one writer. "One thing about getting old is that I've developed patience over the years."

Patience with everything and everyone, perhaps, except his desire for Sondra Locke, whom he was now seeing as often as he could. It was a relationship that he could not resist, and it was about to effect an extraordinary shift in the dynamics of his work and his life. It would change forever the lives of all three of its principal players—Clint, Locke, and Maggie—casting them in a real-life melodrama that would make *Breezy* seem wistful by comparison.

TWELVE

People thought I was a right-wing fanatic . . . all Harry was doing was obeying a higher moral law . . . people even said I was a racist because I shot Black bank robbers. Well, shit, Blacks rob banks, too. That film gave four Black stuntmen work. Nobody talked about that.

—Clint Eastwood

Mid-1975, several months before *The Outlaw Josey Wales* went into production, a script called *Moving Target* had come to Clint directly, via the Hog's Breath Inn, written by two Oakland High School graduates. Clint read it, liked it, and turned it over to Bob Daley, to see if it was worth dipping into Malpaso's discretionary fund to attach a professional screenwriter to develop it. Daley liked it as well and put in a call to Stirling Silliphant, an established Hollywood writer who in his salad days had written an episode of *Rawhide*, then moved up to the big screen with his script for Don Siegel's 1958 post-noir big-screen *policier*, *The Lineup*, based on a popular TV show. A decade later he won an Oscar for the screenplay of Norman Jewison's *In the Heat of the Night* (1967). Clint had always liked Silliphant personally as well as his abilities and agreed with Daley that *Moving Target* could be the next Dirty Harry film.

They sent Silliphant the script, then met to discuss it. Silliphant all but dismissed the writing, but liked the film's central notion that Dirty Harry takes on a politically subversive terrorist organization, with an added twist that his partner is a woman. Clint liked what Silliphant had to say and green-lighted money to develop a script.

Not long after *Josey Wales* was released, Silliphant completed a first draft. Clint read it and wasn't thrilled with it. It didn't have the necessary delicate balance to keep Dirty Harry's antisocial character intact while softening him enough to allow for a woman to "get" to him. Clint turned it over to Dean Riesner. Meanwhile Silliphant had suggested young and up-and-coming (and decidedly non-leading-lady-like) Tyne Daly for the partner role. She read it and turned it down, not once, not twice, but three times. Changes were made with each revision, but she felt that playing off a hard-ass like Harry would make her sympathetic character look like a total ditz, too laughable to be believable. Clint ordered several more rewrites, which he hated to do

because of the delays and the added expense and because he had always preferred first instincts over studied deliberation as the best method to make a Clint Eastwood movie. But this time the waiting paid off, and when Daly read a version of the screenplay that was acceptable to her, she agreed to play the role.

Still not ready to pick up the reins of directing again while producing and starring in the same film, Clint looked for someone who would not challenge his opinion, would not screw with themes, and would get the film done quickly and within budget. Looking to avoid a repetition of the Kaufman fiasco, Clint turned to James Fargo, his longtime assistant director, to helm what was now called *The Enforcer.**

When Daly suggested the basic story line be changed so that her character and Harry did not have a romantic involvement, he quickly agreed. Clint never wanted romance in his films. He didn't see himself as a leading man and believed his audiences would stay away from anything that even resembled a love story between the great loner and some moony costar. Dirty Harry in love? That would be like having a love interest in a film about the invasion of Normandy. It was an insane notion, and Clint was grateful that Daly recognized that.

Production began on the streets of San Francisco during the summer of 1976. Until then Clint had been relatively absent from the proceedings. The reason was simple: he was by now hot and heavy with Sondra Locke, a fact later confirmed by several people who knew and/or worked with Clint at the time, including James Fargo.

The affair continued throughout the shooting of *The Enforcer.* Several times he stayed overnight at one of the several apartments he kept in San Francisco and Sausalito. So frequently was he away that his usual tight control and supervision were missing when it came time to edit the film. Two scenes simply didn't match, no matter how cleverly Ferris Webster, who had a reputation for being able to fix anything, tried to put them together.

Fortunately for this action film, imperfect scene-matches did not matter all that much. In *The Enforcer* Callahan battles a group of ter-

---

*Fargo had served as AD on *Joe Kidd, High Plains Drifter, Breezy, The Eiger Sanction,* and *The Outlaw Josey Wales.*

rorists (who were not explicitly political; in 1970s action movies a *terrorist* was a conveniently generic "bad guy" more interested in getting an enormous amount of money than in overthrowing a government), with a female newbie of whom he reluctantly becomes fond. She is (naturally) killed, prompting Callahan, angrier than usual, to dispose of the terrorist group with a single blast from his giant bazooka, a phallic symbol that made Callahan's hitherto-famous Magnum seem like a cap gun.

Although the film had some good moments—Tyne Daly would use it as a springboard for her own cops-and-robbers TV series, *Cagney & Lacey*—critics excoriated it. Not surprisingly, Kael with heightened glee noted that "Eastwood's holy cool seems more aberrant than ever."

Kael may have actually picked up on the one thing that other critics had chosen to ignore: Clint had grown weary of the role and perhaps of moviemaking in general. In retrospect, passing off directorial duties to Fargo may have been less an act of insecurity than of indifference. During the filming of *The Enforcer* the real action for Clint was more likely with Locke than on the set. The film looks more complacent than violent, more repetitious than revelatory, more tired than tough, and poorly edited, with a story that was strictly formulaic. Clint's performance borders on the somnambulistic.

Typical of most critics was the always-too-easily-offended-by-genre-films Rex Reed. Writing in the *New York Daily News*, Reed said, "*The Enforcer* is the third or fourth Dirty Harry movie with Clint Eastwood blowing people's heads off and creating the kind of havoc Batman would find juvenile . . . it all went out of style years ago with Clint Eastwood's mumbling . . . save your money, it'll be on TV by Easter."

None of the film's criticism was very objective, and none of it mattered. Audiences still couldn't get enough of Clint as Dirty Harry. The movie grossed a phenomenal $60 million in its initial domestic release and doubled that overseas, making it Clint's biggest moneymaker to date.

At Warner's urging, a commercially reinvigorated Clint soon began thinking about his next movie, which the studio hoped would be ready in time as its big Christmas 1977 release.* Both the studio and the star

---

Dirty Harry, Magnum Force, and *The Enforcer* had all been huge-grossing Warner/Malpaso Christmas-holiday-release pictures.

wanted a follow-up blockbuster that would capitalize on the momentum of *The Enforcer* and equal or surpass its box-office take. *The Gauntlet* was the film they chose, in which Clint is a policeman, not Callahan, charged with delivering a prisoner from Los Angeles to Arizona. The prisoner is a prostitute, and a virtual gauntlet of "bad guys" wants to kill them both: Clint because, presumably, he is, well, *Clint*, the ultimate enforcer who will deliver her no matter what, and the prostitute because she is the key witness to a politically charged sex scandal and her arrival will bring down the corrupt forces in the Arizona police.

Clint's character, Ben Shockley, is actually an inverted Callahan, a shaky cop trying to get over his problems with alcohol when Phoenix police commissioner Blakelock (William Prince) assigns him to extradite the prostitute, Gus Mally (Sondra Locke). When Shockley realizes the trail of incrimination leads directly back to Phoenix, and that neither he nor his prisoner is meant to live, he becomes especially enraged and plots a spectacular revenge-fueled scheme that takes him through the final police gauntlet and results in Blakelock's death instead of his own.

For the part of Mally, Warner had wanted Barbra Streisand, but Clint, who as always had the final say in casting, said no; his films were usually filled with lesser names than himself. He told the studio that he felt Streisand was too old to play opposite him (she was thirty-five, he was forty-seven). Instead, he insisted that Locke play the part. Casting his new girlfriend put her once more into Clint's dark spotlight; she had already been sexually assaulted in *The Outlaw Josey Wales* before being rescued by Clint, and now in *The Gauntlet* she was to undergo a brutal near-rape, only to be rescued again by her knight in tarnished armor.

Warner, to say the least, was not thrilled. The studio had earmarked $5 million for production, making it a very expensive project, and it wanted a double-barreled, name-above-the-title star to decorate marquees across the country. It had already paid $200,000 for the script by Dennis Shryack and Michael Butler—they were very hot due to their much-buzzed-about script for Elliot Silverstein's as-yet-unreleased *The Car.* And it had paid fifteen points of the net and another $100,000 for the future novelization rights (something that was then a very popular source of ancillary income). When Clint was informed of the terms Warner had agreed to get Shryack and Butler,

he was not happy.* Clint, who through Malpaso was a partner in the deal, never paid much for scripts and *never* offered points as an inducement. Besides, he was always more interested in story than in dialogue, preferring to formulate a movie off a general plot idea and filling it in with as few words as possible.

Feeling perhaps that he had made enough of a concession by approving the writers, he stood firm on his decision to cast Locke instead of Streisand. Once Warner caved, principal shooting began in April 1977 on location in Nevada and Arizona.

The plot of *The Gauntlet* was leaner and more singular than usual. Neither Shryack nor Butler conceived its thundering, explosive violence—Clint had inserted it, and Warner happily encouraged it. As far as the studio was concerned, a Clint Eastwood movie could never have enough violence, sexual abuse of women, or raw brutality.

The resulting film was *Coogan's Bluff* meets *Magnum Force*, minus the West Coast/East Coast trickery and the character of Dirty Harry. Ben Shockley's frailty makes the story even more compelling, at least in theory, as he is sent, without knowing it, on a suicide mission. The set-piece of the film is the physical gauntlet that Shockley and Mally must pass through while driving a bus, attended by the entire Phoenix police force. At this point the film turns surreal but gains no potentially redemptive transcendence. The attack on the bus loses all sense of drama once it becomes obvious that shooting out its tires would stop it dead in its tracks. And the ending is even more absurd; once Shockley has delivered his prisoner and killed all his attackers, no one wants her or knows what to do with her. Presumably the two of them take another bus out of town and live happily ever after.

Despite its ridiculous plot and cartoonish denouement, Clint's genre-driven star power was enough to make the film a bona fide box-office hit. As always, the negative criticism did not matter. Judith Crist, writing in the *New York Post*, summed up her opinion in five words:

....

*The deal for *The Car* had made the duo "hot" in the industry, not the actual script or the film that was made from it. As ever in Hollywood, money talked, and more money meant more power, one of the reasons Clint never liked to pay that much to writers. He had formed Malpaso to ensure his own autonomous power base (and financial stronghold) and did not like to give up a great deal of money, because that meant, to him at least, surrendering authority, or power, to underlings.

"*The Gauntlet* is the pits." Vincent Canby, in the *Times*, didn't like it either but at least acknowledged the film's "Eastwood" touch.

> Clint Eastwood . . . plays a character role. *The Gauntlet* has nothing to do with reality and everything to do with Clint Eastwood fiction, which is always about a force (Mr. Eastwood) that sets things straight in a crooked world. A movie without a single thought in its head, but the action scenes are so ferociously staged that it's impossible not to pay attention most of the time. Mr. Eastwood's talent is in his style— unhurried and self-assured.

The Gauntlet grossed more than $54 million in its initial domestic Christmastime release and would top the $100 million mark by the time it finished its worldwide theatrical run.

As if to somehow compensate for all the private time he was spending with Locke, Clint made his home life with Maggie unusually public. For the first time in years he invited reporters to Carmel to witness for themselves how happy he was, what a normal married man he was, away from Hollywood.

Every magazine jumped at the chance to interview the elusive Clint, but if they were looking for anything candid or spontaneous, they didn't get it. Then in the midst of all this publicity-spinning, the February 13, 1978, issue of *People* magazine "scooped" everyone with a cover shot of Clint and—*Sondra Locke*. No one missed it, including Maggie, who was rightly infuriated.

Maggie had tolerated a lot during their long marriage. She had looked the other way during all of Clint's extramarital affairs. She had even strained her neck looking to the opposite side of the room when Locke showed up at several parties that the Eastwoods had recently attended. But the cover of *People* was too much, even for her. Public flaunting was the one thing Clint had never before done, allowing Maggie to maintain her public dignity. The week the cover story appeared in *People*, Maggie hired a lawyer and sought a legal separation. After much discussion, Clint persuaded her to take a Hawaiian vacation with him to see if there was any way they could save their marriage.

During the vacation Clint admitted to Maggie that he was in love with Sondra.

When they returned, Maggie filed for the separation.

Sondra too was upset. Certainly Clint's marriage looked like it was going to end, but for her the notion of Clint being a single man was a bit too complicated.

Because she too was married and had no intention of getting a divorce.

Locke had married Gordon Anderson, her childhood sweetheart from Shelbyville, Tennessee, where they had spent their days imagining what the rest of the world must be like. Locke's family disapproved of Anderson and what they claimed was his impure "hold" on her. The night following their high school graduation they eloped. Anderson moved to New York City to pursue a career in acting, while Locke stayed behind, picking up the occasional local job modeling and acting in commercials. Then Anderson read about a nationwide talent hunt for a teenage girl to play the lead in an upcoming movie of *The Heart Is a Lonely Hunter.*

He immediately returned to Tennessee, picked up Locke, and took her to Nashville, where the preliminary interviews were taking place. Anderson worked on her to prepare her, spending a lot of time detailing her face and appearance. He scruffed her up, redid her hair, taped down her ample breasts to make them less prominent, and clothed her in the style of the novel. They agreed to lie about her age—she was twenty-one, but the part called for a teenager. After her successful interview, they drove to Birmingham, Alabama, for the first major eliminations. A thousand young girls auditioned, and about a hundred passed, including Locke. The next stop was New Orleans, where the finalists were to meet with the film's director, Robert Ellis Miller.

A week after meeting Miller, the girls were called to Warner Bros.' New York offices, all expenses paid, for the last round of auditions. Fine-tuned by Anderson, Locke was confident as she went before the producers and director and won the role. In 1968, the same year Clint appeared in his seventeenth feature, *Coogan's Bluff,* in her first, Locke was nominated for an Oscar for Best Supporting Actress.*

---

*She lost to Ruth Gordon in Roman Polanski's *Rosemary's Baby.* The other nominees were Lynn Carlin in John Cassavetes's *Faces,* Kay Medford in William Wyler's *Funny Girl,* and Estelle Parsons in Paul Newman's *Rachel, Rachel.*

Even before the film was released, Locke and Anderson had moved to Hollywood—or rather to West Hollywood, the predominantly gay neighborhood between Beverly Hills and Hollywood proper, where Anderson set them up in a spacious town house. He wanted to live in West Hollywood for a reason—he was gay. He had been in the closet most of his life; Locke first found out before the marriage, but she said it didn't bother her. He was who he was, and she loved him. They were friends first, and lovers without physical sex, which did not prove a problem because they were both able to get what they wanted else-where. West Hollywood gave Anderson the chance to come out, and he did so with a vengeance. By the time Locke met Clint and appeared with him in *The Outlaw Josey Wales*, Anderson was seriously involved in a relationship with another man.

The fact that Locke was married had not bothered Clint at all; in fact, it initially held great appeal. *Married* translated into *safe*, as in his own marriage. Now, the more he got to know Locke and found out about her unorthodox marriage to Anderson, the more he recognized in her a kindred soul, a talented loner with a marriage that was con-venient and even advantageous, but unsatisfying.

A month before Clint and Locke appeared on the cover of *People*, he had appeared with Burt Reynolds on the January 9 cover of *Time* magazine. Inside the eight-page spread covered a lot about Clint's offi-cial (i.e., studio-sanctioned public) life but said relatively little, com-paring him to his old friend Reynolds, who was still a bankable star after his impressive performance in John Boorman's *Deliverance* (1972). That performance had had Oscar written all over it—until Reynolds self-destructed by posing as the seminude centerfold for *Cosmopolitan* magazine. The gesture relieved his career of any remaining pretense of seriousness. The movies he made after *Deliverance* failed to ignite the public, until he returned to southern-redneck form in Hal Needham's *Smokey and the Bandit* (1977), which was a huge box-office success but which the Academy universally avoided. The *Time* piece, written by Richard Schickel, lauded Clint and Reynolds as the only two actors in sync with the popular tastes of moviegoing America, audaciously award-ing them the mantle of Everyman once held by James Stewart and Henry Fonda and favorably comparing them to such tough-guy screen stalwarts as John Wayne, Marlon Brando, and Paul Newman (while all

but ignoring Al Pacino and Robert De Niro). He concluded, "In today's climate it may actually take more courage and more imagination to become an Eastwood or a Reynolds than it does to be a Nicholson or a Redford." Lurking just behind them, given the separate "box" treatment, was, according to Schickel, the "third great action star" of his generation, Charles Bronson.

The Eastwood-Bronson comparison was a common one; publications like the *Hollywood Studio* magazine said,

> In a modern society bristling with violence and pervaded by an ever increasing air of helplessness, Clint Eastwood and Charles Bronson fulfill a burning psychological need on the part of filmgoers the world over by exemplifying western heroes capable of overpowering hostile forces and proving that one individual can make a difference in a restless and turbulent world . . . these two images from the western culture surface when referring to the laconic loner syndrome.

Both Reynolds and Bronson bought into the idea that they were iconic, but Clint ran from it. If Reynolds allowed himself to be stroked by Schickel's overblown *Time* piece, Clint kept his distance from it.

Instead, he turned to Locke for his creative validation. Of all the women he had dated, she stood out in one crucial aspect. She was young, blond, largely inexperienced (he believed), and perhaps even a bit malleable, but she gave off an air of cool, of hip understanding that belied her rural southern roots. She dripped "artist" from every pore, and as critics were, for the most part, still trying to figure out Clint Eastwood and the meaning of his personal appeal, hitting 180 degrees wide of the mark, the only one who really "got" him was Locke.

If some wanted to anoint Clint as the reincarnation of the Great American Hero (the original having been lost in the country's ignominious defeat in Vietnam), Clint was more than happy to let them, leaving the glorification of his screen heroics to self-appointed critical know-it-alls like Schickel. Clint was too busy trying to balance his private life between what he thought he needed (a home, a wife like Maggie, kids, a big house in Carmel) and what he thought he wanted: a woman like Locke who could run with him, who understood him, and who could take him where no other woman had. For the first time since he had gotten married, he didn't hit hard and then run home to his wife.

It was she, according to Locke, who convinced Clint to follow *The Gauntlet* with a complete turnaround, the off-the-wall *Every Which Way but Loose*. To her (and then to Clint), it was the perfect response to all those who insisted he was the primal American cinematic hero. One thing that she pointed out to him was that he had thus far (excepting the occasional paychecks like *Where Eagles Dare, Kelly's Heroes*, and *The Eiger Sanction*) created essentially two iconic characters that reappeared again and again in his movies. The Man with No Name had appeared in the three Leone spaghetti westerns and was echoed in one way or another in most of the later westerns including *Hang 'Em High, Two Mules for Sister Sara, Joe Kidd, High Plains Drifter*, and *The Outlaw Josey Wales*. All these characters, including the original Man with No Name, were Vietnam-era antiheroes, men who went against the establishment mostly because the establishment was itself controlled by outlaws, thereby making the outsiders heroes. Clint's other great screen persona was Dirty Harry, in some ways a modern-dress version of the Man with No Name. These characters (and their other variations) are not knights in tarnished armor, they are just tarnished, and that's what made them unique. Doing *Every Which Way but Loose*, Locke suggested, would expand Clint's realm and suit the shift in the postwar cultural zeitgeist.

She was right on the money, and he knew it. Pushing ever closer to fifty, he was more than ready to trade in his John Wayne mantle for a little bit of what Burt Reynolds had going for him. (Since 1972 Reynolds had ranked higher in the popularity polls than even the Duke and was now threatening to pass even Clint.)*

The outsize success of Reynolds's *Smokey and the Bandit* the year before told him two things: first, he didn't have to knock himself out with big, brawling action films; and second, the public might be shifting toward (or back to) working-class, southern-based humor, something he felt he could play in a walk. In an interview he gave around

---

*The primary difference between Wayne and Clint was that Wayne's movies deliberately proselytized *über*-patriotism, roughly from David Miller's *Flying Tigers* (1942) through Wayne's self-directed Vietnam War opus, *The Green Berets* (1968). Clint preferred to explore the flaws of individual characters in his films rather than deliver an explicit message. Both actors (and directors) may have achieved similar results—some might say *Dirty Harry* is more political than *The Green Berets*, but as artistic statements, the films, taken out of their social context, reflect far different creative approaches and artistic results.

this time, the influence of Locke on his thinking comes through: the sudden references to Capra and Sturges, the rejection of his established image, and his abilities as a filmmaker, particularly in terms of story, even if the allusions here are a bit of a stretch:

> The script [for *Every Which Way but Loose*] had been around for a long time, rejected by everyone. The script itself was dog-eared and food-stained. Most sane men were skeptical about it; there were conflicts about it in my own group. They said it was dangerous. They said it's not *you*. I said, it *is* me . . . Here was a guy who was a loser but who wouldn't acknowledge it and who was a holdout against cynicism. It wasn't old-fashioned but in a way it was. The guy was fun to play because he had to be stripped bare of all his dignity . . . I didn't have to prove my commercial value at this point in my career. I didn't play off the bad sheriff. I suppose a "normal" Clint Eastwood picture might have.

Instead he played off an orangutan.*

Jeremy Joe Kronsberg's screenplay concerns a two-fisted truck driver who travels from town to town making money in bare-handed pickup prizefights; he is accompanied by, of all things, an orangutan he has won in a previous fight. He falls in love with a country-western singer, loses her, wins her, and loses her again. Clint may have first come across the script from a secretary who was a friend of Kronsberg's wife. Everyone at Malpaso was against the project except Clint, and Locke had liked it as well. He took it to Warner to find the funding for it.

Warner, eager to get another Eastwood film in theaters, was nonetheless split on this one. The new head of production, John Calley, wanted to pass, but Frank Wells, Clint's steadfast ally at the studio, thought it might be a good commercial departure for him. After a lot of back-and-forth, Warner finally said yes and put up the production money. Shooting began shortly thereafter, in April 1978, in Albuquerque, Santa Fe, Taos, and Denver—the stops along the trucker route in the film. The film's production caravan eventually

---

*Clint's character, Philo Beddoe, was twenty-nine years old in the original script. During production, writer Jeremy Joe Kronsberg teased Clint that the script would have to be revised to make Philo older so that he could be believable as a Clint Eastwood character. When Clint asked how much older, Kronsberg replied, "About thirty-five."

wound up in Los Angeles, both for additional locations and the sound-stages of Warner.

To direct, Clint brought back James Fargo, who had last worked with him on *The Enforcer*—someone who, essentially, wouldn't get in the way. Wanting country music to be played throughout, he hired Snuff Garrett from the old *Rawhide* days to write some tunes, and chose the title of one, "Every Which Way but Loose," as the title of the film (originally called *The Coming of Philo Beddoe*). He then cut a publishing deal with Warner and used all of their artists on the sound-track album. The title track, by Eddie Rabbitt, was released as a single a month before the film came out, became an unlikely cross-over hit, and provided free promotion every time it was played on the radio. In the film Locke's character, Lynn Halsey-Taylor, sings two songs, something she didn't particularly want to do nor was especially good at, but Clint hired a singing coach, in this case Phil Everly of the famed Everly Brothers, to work with her until Clint thought the songs, and the scenes, were good enough.

Although Sondra Locke was cast as the female country-singer-love-interest, as usual in an Eastwood film, the woman was part of the back-story rather than the major plot line, dominated here by the orangutan. Working with animals is always iffy, and Clint knew it. He had worked with animals before, as far back as his all-but-invisible part in the *Francis the Talking Mule* series, but felt he could pull it off. His costar was an orangutan called Clyde in the movie (three orang-utans were used in the production, but one, whose real name was Manis, was on-screen most of the time), a Las Vegas–trained per-former with whom audiences immediately fell in love.

Clint, with perfectly understated comic timing, played to the film's lowbrow mentality, up to and including the simplified moral—what life lessons man learns from an orangutan. The set piece that every-one remembers most happens when Clint points his fingers like a gun at Clyde and yells *bang*, to which Clyde responds by pretending to fall down dead. That bit of comedy, plus tough-guy motorcycle gangs, bare-chested fistfights, insincere women, and a buddy-buddy " 'tan more faithful than even Tonto was to the Lone Ranger," added up to an improbable hit but a box-office sensation. Women, who ordinar-ily stayed away from the harder Clint movies (unless dragged to them

by their husbands or boyfriends) loved this one and helped drive the movie's take into the stratosphere.

But the reviews were almost universally awful: "The film is way off the mark" *(Variety)*. "This is a redneck comedy with no stops pulled. If I could persuade my friends to see it, they would probably detest me" (Stuart Byron, *Village Voice*). "A Clint Eastwood comedy that could not possibly have been created by human hands . . . One can forgive the orangutan's participation but what is Eastwood's excuse" (David Ansen, *Newsweek*). "The latest Clint Eastwood disgrace" (Rex Reed, *New York Daily News*). Nonetheless, *Every Which Way but Loose* grossed an astonishing $124 million in its initial domestic release, about eight times what *The Gauntlet* had done, making it the second-biggest Warner film of the year, behind Richard Donner's *Superman*, whose title character Clint had seriously considered playing.*

Early in 1979, after a year of negotiations, Clint thought he was ready to agree to a divorce settlement. He would pay Maggie a lump sum of $25 million and allow her to keep the big house in Carmel and have the kids live with her; Clint would be able to freely come and go with them, something he insisted on. While he was never around all that much, he still loved and felt close to them. He kept his brand-new $100,000 Ferrari Boxer. He then assigned Locke the job of finding a new house for them, promising her that "it would be theirs forever, together in retirement." There was, reportedly, no anger or vicious-ness between Clint and Maggie. A coolness coated the wall between them, but for the sake of himself as much as (he claimed) the kids, and to keep the prying press off both his and Maggie's necks, he was deter-mined to melt it.

For that reason, and because Maggie's lawyer was demanding 50 per-cent of everything Clint had earned while they were together, he sud-denly reversed his stand and no longer pressed for a final divorce. Instead, he felt a longer separation was needed so that both could have time to think, giving an ironic meaning to the newest Clint Eastwood–inspired catchphrase, "every which way but loose."

***Every Which Way but Loose* earned more than $200 million in its first year of interna-tional release.*

FROM ACTOR TO AUTEUR

THIRTEEN

I've been advised against nearly everything I've ever done.

—Clint Eastwood

PREVIOUS PAGE: *Spanish movie poster for* Bronco Billy, *1980*

There was no part for Sondra Locke in Clint's next movie, *Escape from Alcatraz*, his thirty-fourth feature film in twenty-five years. The virtually all-male adventure was based on the true story of Frank Lee Morris and John and Clarence Anglin's 1962 escape from the notorious island prison located in San Francisco Bay. While Clint was in production, Locke looked for a new house where they could live together. She did not say what if anything she intended to do about her husband, although he was, at this time, living with another man.

The film was based on J. Campbell Bruce's 1963 nonfiction book *Escape from Alcatraz: A Farewell to the Rock*. Richard Tuggle, the editor of a small magazine devoted to health, had initially bought it to break into the movie business. Tuggle wrote his own screen adaptation and, when he was satisfied it was good enough, sent it to the one director he thought might like it enough to make it.

Tuggle had a lifelong fascination with prison stories, both true and fictionalized, and considered Don Siegel's *Riot in Cell Block 11* (1954) the best of the genre; film producer Walter Wanger had conceived it after being released from prison for shooting a man he suspected was having an affair with his wife. While incarcerated, Wanger found the living conditions so appalling, he wanted to expose them to the public. The result was one of the toughest and most brutally realistic prison dramas ever filmed.

Late in February 1978, when Tuggle sent the script to Siegel via his agent, Leonard Hirshan, at William Morris (also Clint's agent), Hirshan sent it on to Siegel, who liked it but was tied up on another project, *Das Boot*, and had to pass. Then a severe illness struck one of the top executives at Bavaria Studios, in Germany, and *Das Boot*, already in production, had to be halted. Early in March Hirshan went back to Siegel and asked him to reconsider the project. Siegel told Hirshan he thought it would be perfect for Clint. Hirshan did and

then sent it to Daley (annoying Siegel, who felt his relationship was strong and personal enough that the script should have gone directly to Clint). Clint read, loved it, and wanted Siegel to direct; he wanted to star in and produce it through Malpaso.

But Siegel, rather than taking an option on the script, had bought it outright for a cool $100,000 with the irreversible proviso that he would direct. He made an offer to Clint and Malpaso (and presumably Warner). Clint balked over the issue of who would have the final cut. Siegel (still miffed at Hirshan for not sending the script directly to Clint, or for not completely understanding the deal) heard nothing from either Clint or Hirshan about the terms he wanted. He then angrily took his offer off the table and moved the project to Paramount. The joint heads of that studio, Michael Eisner and Jeffrey Katzenberg, had saved Paramount from going under by developing a highly successful TV unit and a series of in-house sitcoms. Now they were looking for the right project to restore the studio's big-screen glory. They thought *Escape from Alcatraz* was the perfect choice. They made the deal and looked for a star in their own stable to play the lead.

None proved either interested or available. (Paramount especially wanted Richard Gere but he was not excited by the project.) Eisner then urged Siegel to reconcile with Clint and try to bring him to Paramount. Siegel was reluctant, but he had felt underappreciated at Warner: like Clint, he blamed the studio's lack of a sufficient pre-awards-industry campaign for his not even being nominated for *Dirty Harry*. He bit the bullet, visited Clint at his Malpaso office for sandwiches and beers, and mea culpa'd his way into signing a joint venture between Malpaso, Siegel Film, and Paramount, with options for all parties to join in future projects together.

Moving to Paramount, even just for this picture, was a big deal for Clint. For the first time in nearly a decade his big summer 1979 release would carry Paramount's name and its familiar circle and mountain logo. It was not only a victory for Paramount but also a slap in the face to Warner, which had enjoyed a steady stream of Eastwood holiday fare every year since *Dirty Harry*.

Clint had stayed away from Paramount for so long because of his grudge over the production delays and excess spending on *Paint Your Wagon*—two of the primary reasons he had formed Malpaso. He knew he was taking something of a risk returning to the studio, but this time

he was at a far higher level of power in Hollywood, and his defection, as it were, from Warner might shake that studio up and remind them how valuable he really was to their bottom line.

Production on *Escape from Alcatraz* began in October 1978, and as Siegel had feared, the set turned into an ongoing battle between him and Clint for control over every aspect of filming. Clint apparently prevailed; Siegel left the production in anger before the completion of its all-important final cut. Clint, his longtime editors Ferris Webster and Joel Cox, and Jack Green, his cameraman, put it together.

Not surprisingly, the finished product looked less like a Siegel film than any of his four prior collaborations with Clint. In Siegel's projected final version, the film had ended inside the prison, giving it an air of grim reality. In Clint's a flower is left behind, indicating that the three escapees make it—the triumph of the outlaw over his society of imprisonment. This crucial change altered the entire meaning of the film. Both versions were dark: Siegel's reflected the inescapable reality of Alcatraz, while Clint's suggested the greater blackness of the escapees' lives on the run, suggested by the black, murky waters that surround and engulf the flower. In this as in all Clint films, survival is sometimes harder and therefore more dramatic than death. (Clint dies in only three films in his entire career: *The Beguiled, Honkytonk Man*, and *Gran Torino*.) Asked by *Time* magazine about the darkness and the mood of the film and if it had any personal relevance, Clint responded with a succinct, end-of-conversation "I don't know."

Although Clint did not officially direct the film (Siegel is credited as producer and director), its moody, grim level of intensity and the clear and imposing presence of his dark personality on-screen clearly identifies it as a Clint Eastwood film.

Upon its release in 1979, *Escape from Alcatraz* received mostly rave reviews, some of the best of Clint's career. Vincent Canby of *The New York Times* led the way, omitting any mention of Siegel while emphasizing the importance of Clint: "This is a first-rate action movie. Terrifically exciting. There is more evident knowledge of moviemaking in any one frame than there are in most other American films around at the moment. Mr. Eastwood fulfills the demands of the role and the film as probably no other actor could." Frank Rich, writing for *Time* magazine, called it "ingenious, precise and exciting."

Clearly Clint had hit a critical nerve with *Escape from Alcatraz*,

although audiences proved less interested. The film's initial domestic gross was a relatively modest $34 million, about a third of what *Every Which Way but Loose* had taken in.* It also grossed less than one-fifth of that year's biggest film, Richard Donner's *Superman*, a Warner Bros. hit that made a star out of its title hero, Christopher Reeve, a role that Clint had repeatedly turned down. His disappointment at *Escape*'s soft box office, and his lingering ill feelings about how Siegel had put the deal together, especially buying the rights before coming to see him at Warner, made *Escape from Alcatraz* their last collaboration.†

If Clint as Frank Morris had to escape from an inescapable prison, Clint as Clint found real life even harder. Despite reported pressure from Locke for him to finalize his divorce from Maggie, Clint continued to drag his feet, perhaps ambivalent about ending his marriage to Maggie. Approaching fifty, Clint had found a new health regimen, and he was now said to be an enthusiastic devotee of the Life Extension program by Durk Pearson and Sandy Shaw, who theorized that human beings were capable of living to 150 years of age while retaining their physical and mental powers. The program required exercise and a regimen of pills and vitamins that the couple promoted.

"During [1978] Clint began a new obsession, to consume vast amounts of vitamins and amino acids," according to Locke.

At first Clint explained his new "megavitamin" kick was part of getting beefed up and buffed out to play his character . . . He would keep large bowls of boiled potatoes in the fridge and eat them like popcorn throughout the day . . . he kept all the [rest of the] concoctions in enor-

---

*Clint's take was reportedly 15 percent of the gross of the film, in addition to his regular acting and producing fees. By contrast, Tuggle and Siegel received net points, payouts based on a film's profits after all expenses are deducted from the cost of prints, advertising, distribution, etc., for a total of less than $2 million each, according to the *Hollywood Reporter*.

†Neither Clint nor Siegel ever discussed their working relationship in any terms except the most positive. In his autobiography Siegel suggests ever so gently that there may have been some friction between them: "Clint is very loyal to his friends; in my opinion, sometimes too loyal . . . We've never had a quarrel. Disagreements, yes. Differences of opinion, yes. Perhaps that's because he might look up to me as a surrogate father." Siegel, *A Siegel Film*, 495.

mous glass jars on the kitchen cabinet shelves, and after carefully blending all the powders for our latest batch, we would sit on the living room
sofa scooping and stuffing the miracle powder into these enormous
clear gelatin capsules. Sometimes the two ends of the capsules would
bend or refuse to fit back together and Clint would go ballistic . . . some
of the mixtures that he consumed in such abundance began to worry
me, like selenium and hydergine, L-arginine, Tryptophan, DMSO for
bruises, so much carotene that his hands turned orange . . . and gone
were the days of red meat and any fat—even the avocados with the dollop of mayonnaise that we'd always had for lunch.

It was also reported in the *Herald-Examiner,* but denied by Clint,
that he had had a face-lift.

In the summer of 1978, shortly after they had completed work
on *Every Which Way but Loose,* Locke became pregnant. The situation left Clint ice-cold. He had never wanted children, he told her,
and had had them after more than a decade of marriage only because
Maggie had insisted. (The child with Roxanne Tunis was a subject
that apparently did not come up.) Now, he told her, fatherhood was
out of the question, and he urged her to have an abortion. Although
she did not want to do it, after considering all that it meant to Clint,
she agreed. For a while afterward everything between them seemed
all right again. Then shortly after production was completed on
Escape from Alcatraz, she became pregnant again.

Once again Clint insisted she have an abortion, and once again
she reluctantly did so. When she came out of the hospital, as if to
reward her or compensate her for her loss, he bought her the new
home in tony Bel-Air she wanted. And apparently feeling generous (and also not wanting him to be anywhere near the Bel-Air
house), he threw in one for her husband as well, in less upscale
West Hollywood. At the same time he bought another house for
himself in Carmel, by the ocean, where he could stay by himself
when Locke was stuck in Hollywood on business. If any of this
sounds familiar, it's because it is; in his early years with Maggie,
Clint kept various fortresses of solitude, in Hollywood and in
Carmel, allowing him the freedom to spend time not just with himself but with other women, if he so chose.

His next film, *Bronco Billy*, began with a script that came to him after a casual conversation during an informal dinner with friends at Dan Tana, a popular film industry red-gravy hangout on the edge of Beverly Hills. "When I was sent the script by Dennis Hackin," Clint later recalled, "at first I thought it was about Bronco Billy Anderson, the silent movie star. I devoured it at one sitting and I immediately thought it was the kind of film [Frank] Capra would do today if he were still making movies."

When he finished reading it, he gave it to Locke, who shared his enthusiasm. Five and a half weeks later production began on *Bronco Billy* near Boise, Idaho. Clint starred as the down-and-out star and owner of a Wild West show that is as faded as the times it seeks to glorify, and the spoiled society girl he falls in love with along the way is played by Sondra Locke.

In *Bronco Billy* the central character is in show business, playing two-dimensional re-creations of western heroes, surrounded by a band of loyal players. He falls for Antoinette Lily, another in a long string of imperfect, socially outcast women. It turns out she is married to a man she does not really love, who has now abandoned her and apparently swindled her out of her fortune. Billy helps her by letting her join the show as the target for his sharpshooting and knife-throwing stunts. Eventually she straightens out her money and marital problems and returns to her life in New York City, only to realize she was really in love with Billy all along. Leaving everything behind, she rushes to rejoin him and the show.

If the movie also sounds like a lot of other Hollywood films, it's because it does resemble several of the great ones, including Clint's role model for it, Capra's *It Happened One Night* (1934), which featured a wealthy but unhappy woman on the run from her husband who is aided (rescued and ultimately redeemed) by a poor but honest workingman (a newspaper reporter). It also echoes Preston Sturges's 1941 on-the-run romantic comedy *Sullivan's Travels*. Clint's by-now-familiar cynical view of modern urban city life appears, cloaked here in the familiar poor-but-happy, rich-but-miserable themes that especially appealed to the working-class audiences at whom this film, like *Every Which Way but Loose*, was aimed.

By now, Clint once more felt strong and self-assured enough to

direct himself. He bolstered the sound track with a lot of country music produced once more by Snuff Garrett, highlighted by a duet he sang with Merle Haggard that rose to number one on the country charts. Figured into the film's profits, it helped increase its bottom line. *Bronco Billy*, released in the spring of 1980, gained Clint some of the best reviews of his career. The critics liked this Clint more than the public did, but no one liked him more than Clint, who had found a comfort zone parodying the very western characters that had first brought him to the attention of the public.

On May 31, 1980, a few weeks before *Bronco Billy* opened and flopped at the box office, Clint began to make wholesale changes at Malpaso. Many of the original members of the production team were let go. Frank Wells, Malpaso's best ally at Warner, took off, he said, to fulfill his dream of climbing the highest mountains on each continent. Robert Daley's "voluntary" departure may have been due at least in part to his growing objection to Locke's presence and apparent influence on Clint. Some felt she had taken him away from his moneymaking tough-guy characters, softening him up and pushing away his core audience.

To mark Clint's birthday and the onset of the new decade, New York's Museum of Modern Art (MOMA) scheduled a one-day tribute to him with a marathon screening of four of his films, *A Fistful of Dollars*, *Escape from Alcatraz*, *Play Misty for Me*, and *Bronco Billy*. The museum was most likely celebrating Clint the populist actor, "who has given his personal imprint to a host of movie genres," as the program put it, and who earlier that year had been named by Quigley Publications as the number one box-office star of the 1970s. But the Clint who showed up for the tony audience's Q and A was not the hotheaded action hero but the self-styled auteurist.*

And he showed up alone.

---

*Coming in number two was Burt Reynolds, followed by Barbra Streisand, Robert Redford, Paul Newman, and Steve McQueen. Clint was also named the top box-office star of 1972 and 1973 by the *Motion Picture Herald*, based on the annual poll of exhibitors as to the drawing power of movie stars at the box office, conducted by Quigley Publications.

FOURTEEN

In the westerns, you'd ride in four horses, you have a camera right there and four horses that all have to be side by side, which is very difficult to get them into a close shot. Right away they zing a boom mike out there and the horses don't like that. They get edgy, and then some guy yells at the top of his lungs through a megaphone, "Action," and it drives the horses crazy. I prefer not to say action. Actors are not horses but they have a similar anxiety about the word "Action." I try to keep that level low. I start just by saying something like, "okay." And at the end I simply say, "That's enough of that."

—Clint Eastwood

Even as Clint was being honored by MOMA, *Bronco Billy*, despite its good reviews, was bombing at the box office. It wound up grossing a little over $18 million, even with the profits from the hit song it produced factored in. To some, it signaled a backlash of sorts against Clint's image-shifting. The critical intelligentsia thought it a violation of some elemental truth that Clint was spoofing his own assumed redneck persona, a sure sign to them that neither the film nor the image was true. No less a cultural arbiter than Norman Mailer sniffed sarcastically at Clint's notable lack of heated hipness: "Eastwood is living proof of the maxim that the best way to get through life is cool." Even more biting were James Wolcott's cutting remarks in *Vanity Fair* about New York's newest cultural darling: "*Bronco Billy* was an awkward, bow-legged bit of Americana, with Eastwood's girlfriend, Sondra Locke, giving her usual shrill, nostrilly performance."

Clint was already in production on a sequel to *Every Which Way but Loose*, called *Any Which Way You Can*, despite Warner's loud disappointment that he was not instead making the next Dirty Harry movie. Some at the studio held fast to the idea that *Every Which Way*'s success had been a fluke, due more to the presence of a cute orangutan than anything else; they thought that if Clint continued down that road, as he had with *Bronco Billy* and now with *Any Which Way You Can*, it could very well mark the irreversible decline of one of its biggest franchise stars.

Clint, on the other hand, was convinced that he was on the right career track. He sent out missives of his own rumbling that he was thinking of severing all of Malpaso's remaining ties with Warner. The first official comment from Warner came by way of outgoing Malpaso producer Bob Daley, who struck a melancholic note in his defense of Clint's career: "Clint Eastwood brought in *Bronco Billy* 13 days ahead

and $750,000 under budget of the $5,000,000 film, and it's not because we over-skedded [budgeted] it . . . I've known [Clint] for 25 years, since he was digging pools and I was in the budget department at Universal. We talked efficiency all the time. When he got on 'Rawhide,' he never went to his dressing room—but stayed on the set and observed."

Clint then stepped directly into the fray, such as it was. "We've done okay," he told one reporter. "Everyone expected [*Bronco Billy*] to be another *Every Which Way But Loose*, but what is? We've gotten a little different audience. I've branched out a bit. It's not going to lose any money—it only cost $5,200,000 . . . and I've never had better reviews. I think it worked out well." These comments triggered a corporate showdown between Warner and Malpaso, scheduled to take place at Jackson Hole, Wyoming. There Frank Wells was called in from his mountain-climbing midlife crisis to orchestrate a peace powwow between Clint and the studio.

Clint, meanwhile, continued to consolidate his power at Malpaso by shedding several more longtime employees. On the strength of *Every Which Way but Loose*, Clint had asked Jeremy Joe Kronsberg to write another script along the same lines, to be called *Going Ape*, which he intended to direct. Kronsberg, meanwhile, having no idea he was slated to do a sequel, had signed a deal with Paramount to develop a similar type of film, with the promise that he could produce as well as write it. When Clint found out about it, he severed all ties with Kronsberg and brought in first-time screenwriter Stanford Sherman to write the *Every Which Way but Loose* sequel. Sherman's previous credits were mostly for the small screen—four episodes of *The Man from U.N.C.L.E.*, one episode of *The Rat Patrol*, and eighteen episodes of *Batman*. Nonetheless Clint gave him the plum assignment to write *Any Which Way You Can*.

To direct, Clint chose Buddy Van Horn, primarily a stuntman whom Clint had known since the *Rawhide* years at Universal, and although he had virtually no experience as a director, Clint liked and trusted him. Besides, Clint would be the unofficial director of the film. If it scored, he could take the credit. If it didn't, the critical hammers would fall on Van Horn. Sondra Locke's character, Lynn Halsey-Taylor, was brought back from the first film to continue her on-again-off-again relationship with Philo, as were Ruth Gordon

and Geoffrey Lewis. For the now-obligatory musical number, Clint hired Ray Charles and once more assigned music production to Snuff Garrett.

But as Warner had predicted, *Any Which Way You Can* performed like a typical sequel, costing twice as much and grossing less than the original. Despite having the coveted first-up Christmas-release position, it barely broke the $10 million mark at the box office. The small profit it showed had more to do with the film's low budget than with box-office activity. If Clint had had any plans for an *Any Which Way* franchise, they evaporated after the poor box-office showing. Warner now hoped that Clint would realize his mistake, return to form, and make another Dirty Harry movie.

However, a year and a half passed without a new Clint Eastwood film, while he waited for the perfect script to revive his career. During that time he dealt with several real-life issues he had previously relegated to the back burner, claiming his schedule left him little time to concentrate on them. Now he had to deal head-on with his relationship with Locke, or more accurately its downslide, and to face up to Maggie's much-publicized new romance.

According to Locke, in her memoir, her relationship with Clint never fully recovered from the abortions. For all of Clint's explanations about not wanting more children, she saw it as a clear signal that he had no intention of staying with her forever. Moreover, in 1980 he even told Locke about his daughter with Roxanne Tunis.

Not long afterward Locke was offered and accepted the lead role in a TV film, Jackie Cooper's *Rosie: The Rosemary Clooney Story*, a project that had nothing to do with Clint. Shortly into the filming of *Rosie*, *Us* magazine whispered to its readers that "reports are circulating that Clint Eastwood and Sondra Locke are no longer such good friends. Clint plans to make his next movie, *Honkytonk Man*, without her—and Sondra has already expressed a desire to establish her own solo career. So their [recent] Christmas release, *Any Which Way You Can*, seemingly ends a long and financially successful collaboration."

The whispers, which were by no means confined to one magazine, contained a kernel of truth. Clint, never a big sharer of anything— money, credits, stardom—was, according to Locke, thrown by her

acceptance of the role in a movie he did not control, even if it was only for TV. In some ways, that made it worse, for it separated them even more, bringing her down to the level of the little screen, from which Clint had worked so hard to escape.

On top of all that, Maggie was now publicly flaunting her new "companion," the millionaire playboy Henry Wynberg, who at the age of forty-six had gained the dubious reputation as the man who had become involved with Elizabeth Taylor between her two marriages to Richard Burton. After Taylor and before Maggie, Wynberg had been briefly involved with Olivia Hussey, the estranged actress wife of Dino Martin, Dean Martin's son.

Despite the fact that Wynberg spent most of his time in Beverly Hills and Maggie lived in Carmel, they saw each other several times a month. According to Wynberg at the time, "We meet as often as we can . . . Maggie and I spend our time together skiing, swimming, playing tennis . . . and sometimes we just take long walks and do some talking. We also love to cook and have friends over for a dinner party. That's one reason she likes me. I'm a great cook. I don't know what the future holds. As for now, we have no plans to marry . . . Maggie never speaks of Clint."

Apparently Clint's answer to Wynberg's public boasting was to get away. He took off with Locke for Helsinki and Copenhagen, to scout future locations, according to reports in both *Daily Variety* and the *Hollywood Reporter.* After their brief stay in Europe, Clint took Locke to London to see Frank Sinatra perform in concert.

Upon their return to America, Locke began filming her TV film, and Clint continued to search for a script worthy of being the next in the Dirty Harry franchise. In his spare time, which was increasingly plentiful, he began visiting the new Hollywood-friendly Washington, D.C., of President Ronald Reagan. Clint was warmly accepted into the cinematic circle that Reagan surrounded himself with at the White House. Because of it, Clint had access to several of the international mercenaries who were conducting "secret" government missions in the name of democracy, many of which were sanctioned by the president.

Fritz Manes, one of the few long-term survivors of Clint's major clean-out of Malpaso's staff, is credited with arranging for Bob Denard, a French self-described soldier of fortune who had seen

action in Africa during the 1970s, to be introduced to Clint. After that meeting Clint, impressed with Denard's tales of intrigue, had Malpaso option his life story for a biopic.

At the same time, along with several other Hollywood conservatives, Clint privately funded a mercenary expedition into Laos to search for missing and possibly captive American soldiers taken during the Vietnam War. That project ended in failure, and at least one mercenary was killed during it. Clint said little to the press about either the excursion or his own financial participation in it, but after it became public and was subjected to much negative publicity, he quietly dropped the Denard project. Instead he turned to an adaptation of Craig Thomas's 1977 bestselling novel, *Firefox*. That film would mark the fifty-two-year-old movie star's return to the big screen.

In some ways *Firefox* fits neatly into the Eastwood canon and was in some ways a fictionalized version of the film he had wanted to make about Denard. It is an action flick whose lead character, pilot Mitchell Gant, is also an international spy. Gant has a potentially fatal flaw that sends him squarely into the dark side—he suffers from mental disabilities that leave him unable to function well—but finds himself on a mission to save the world from the cold war Russians. He is assigned to steal their newest and potentially most dangerous plane, the Firefox, and deliver it to the NATO alliance.

Despite the film's timely subject matter, its James Bond gadgetry deprived it of any sense of realism. Perhaps to further distance himself from current headlines, Clint—who directed and produced as well as starred in the film—saw to it that Malpaso had no producing credit.

Shot on location in Austria, England, Greenland, and the United States, it had a hefty budget of $21 million (another reason he may not have wanted to make Malpaso a partner) and took nearly a year to complete. When it was finally released, the reviews were at best mixed. Sheila Benson, writing in the *Los Angeles Times*, called it "a sagging, overlong disappointment, talky and slow to ignite. It is the first time that Eastwood the director has served Eastwood the actor-icon so badly, and it is unnerving."

"*Firefox* is fun," Andrew Sarris wrote in the *Village Voice*, "little more and not appreciably less." For Sarris and other auteurists, where *Play Misty for Me* failed as faux Hitchcock, *Firefox* succeeded as neo-Bond.

And the film resonated with audiences longing to see Clint return to his steely-eyed-if-flawed-action-hero stance. It became one of his highest grossers and returned him to the top of the Hollywood heap.*

With his career back on the main track, Clint allowed Locke to talk him into moving into the new Bel-Air house that she had decorated—despite (as Locke later described it) Clint's domestic temperament of wild outbursts. Brief but extreme fits of anger punctured his otherwise cool facade, usually precipitated by the lighting of some short emotional fuse. Locke also described Clint's growing narcissism: "Rarely did Clint acknowledge any flaws of his own. I was really surprised when, sometime in the mid-eighties, he had hair transplants. He actually finally admitted that he was losing his hair, but like everything else he was unbelievably secretive about it . . . actually the whole situation was so ridiculous that it was all I could do to keep from laughing. I interpreted these quirks of Clint as either humorous eccentricity or simple human failing."

Maggie's ongoing relationship with Wynberg didn't help Clint's intense and lightning-quick mood swings. She was now talking about finalizing her divorce from Clint and marrying Wynberg, which would mean for Clint a payout in the neighborhood of $25 million and an asset split that he had tried to avoid for several years. As if in response, Clint, according to Locke, rather than moving closer to her, pulled away and talked less and less of their future together.

Perhaps even more telling, she had not appeared in *Firefox*, which might have been understandable in the light of its typically Clintonian lack of any substantial female role. But when he publicly announced his next movie, a somewhat inexplicable return to Redneckville and country music, *Honkytonk Man*, the female lead, into which Locke would have fit like fingers into gloves, went to a young and beautiful unknown, Alexa Kenin.

Honkytonk Man, based on a 1980 Clancy Carlile novel of the same name, is a fictional biography of a failed country singer, Red Stovall, whose only apparent goal is to make it to the Grand Ole Opry before

---

Firefox did nearly $25 million in rentals and was a major popular success, but its profit was not great, due to the huge budget necessitated by the film's special aerial effects. While Clint was the producer-director, he was not the executive producer. That slot was filled, ironically, by Fritz Manes.

he dies. Loosely based on the lives of Hank Williams and Jimmie Rodgers, the book ends with Stovall's death before he achieves his dream.

Carlile, as it happened, was a William Morris client, and the agency, as always, wanted to keep the project in-house. That was how the book came to Clint, who was looking for a project to introduce his son, Kyle, now fourteen, to feature films. Clint offered to buy it, star in it, direct it, and produce it through Malpaso, believing it had a good part for Kyle that would bring them together both professionally and personally.

Carlile, however, was reluctant to sell Clint the rights, thinking that at fifty-two he was too old to play the role of a country singer who dies at thirty-one. And while Clint had done some singing, his voice in no way matched the soaring beauty of either Williams or Rodgers, the models Carlile had used for Stovall.

Clint invited Carlile to his home and promised him that, if he sold Clint the rights to the book, he could write the screenplay adaptation of his novel without any interference. That was enough to get Carlile to agree to the deal.

Once Carlile finished the screenplay, Clint went to work adapting the story to his liking. He never wanted to die in his movies, so he had Carlile change the ending so that Stovall is inducted into the Country Music Hall of Fame for his hit song, "Honkytonk Man," as he lies dying, thereby letting the character "live on." Clint also enlisted the services of his favorite music producer, Snuff Garrett, and charged him with juicing up Carlile's screenplay with "classic" country hits, including songs by John Anderson, Porter Wagoner, and Ray Price, all of which would appear on the original sound-track album.

If Carlile objected to any of these changes, he had no real opportunity to express them. Once production began, he made repeated requests to become more involved, but Clint paid little attention. To be fair, this often happens to writers, because producers, stars, and directors—of which Clint was all three on this film—do not want them watching the script to make sure every word they've written gets onto the screen. In this case, however, the situation was more delicate, as Clint and Carlile were both William Morris clients, which made it impossible for the agency to take sides. Carlile was left out, and there was nothing he could do about it. In struggles like these, the writer always loses.

As Carlile had feared, the obviously middle-aged Clint was not remotely believable in the part (although he did bear some resemblance to Hank Williams, whose dissipated look shortly before his death made him seem far older than he was). The film opened poorly, quickly disappeared, and is rarely seen to this day.

Locke's final big-screen appearance with Clint was in his next film, a one-more-time, perhaps desperate resuscitation of Harry Callahan in *Sudden Impact*. After seven years away from the Dirty Harry franchise, this would be his fourth visitation to his most successful screen persona. And to everyone's surprise, including no doubt Clint's, it turned out to be by far the best. "It was like an homage to Don Siegel. I was the only one who hadn't directed one so I thought, well, why not?"

The project began, oddly enough, with a script sent to Locke. It was by Earl Smith, with whom she had worked on a small independent film in the early, pre-Oscar-nomination days of her career. She agreed to help develop it. But by now she knew the dangers of doing anything without Clint's approval, so she talked with him about the possibility of her being involved as a producer. "Naturally, I talked about it with Clint, hoping that he would have no objections. But before I knew it, Clint had bought the treatment outright from Earl, had hired a writer of his own choice, and begun to turn my story into a Dirty Harry film, without even so much as a courteous 'Do you mind, Sondra?' "

To make it easier for her to give up control of the film, Clint promised Locke the female lead and $350,000 (at the behest of Fritz Manes, who knew that the project had originated with her and that she fairly deserved that kind of money). Having settled that part of the deal, Clint brought in screenwriter Joseph Stinson to convert the script into *Sudden Impact*. (As always, Clint preferred young and inexperienced personnel to veterans, who not only came with a hefty price tag but were better able to challenge Clint's authority.)

In the spring of 1983, with Manes in place as the film's executive producer, Bruce Surtees behind the camera, and Clint ready to perform a triple-play as producer, director, and star, production began on *Sudden Impact*. The film would, with Dean Riesner's help, give Clint his career's signature line of dialogue: "Go ahead, make my day!" It was so succinct and powerful that later Ronald Reagan would borrow

it to take on Congress.* "When you point a gun at someone's head and say 'Go ahead, make my day,' well, I knew the audiences were going to go for it in a big way." "It was just a whimsical thing," Clint later recalled. "I hadn't directed one, and I thought, why not do one before I hang that series up. It was based on an idea that wasn't intended to be a Dirty Harry picture, just a little synopsis. I put together a screenplay on it and said, okay, I'll do it."

In the story Callahan has been suspended from the police force for abusively threatening a Mafia don, who then dies of a heart attack. Clint, ever careful not to make Harry an out-and-out loser, treats his suspension as one more abuse—of Callahan—by an overly authoritarian police force that just doesn't get his righteous sense of mission and mercy (or lack of it) that passes for personal justice in 1980s San Francisco.

Sent off to a small town to serve out his suspension, Callahan is a warrior without a war, unappreciated and tossed aside. But he investigates a homicide there and discovers that a serial killer is at work. As usual, detecting the presence of evil provides him with energy and heroism: it turns out that the local police chief, Jannings (played by the always-effective Pat Hingle, who played a similar type in *The Gauntlet*), is aware of the killer's presence. And Jannings suspects the pretty young artist Jennifer Spencer (Locke) is committing the murders as an act of vengeance—she was gang-raped by a group of young toughs led by Mick (Paul Drake). Harry becomes romantically involved with Spencer and eventually rescues her from one final kidnapping by Mick. Then Callahan spectacularly disposes of him and the rest of his gang. He not only rescues Spencer but redeems her by shifting the blame for all her serial murders onto Mick.

The tailoring of the story once again mirrors Clint and Callahan (whose very name is a partial anagram—both share the letters C, L, and N). In the film, Callahan lets Spencer go free—a technicality in his world, justified by his larger (rougher, and to audiences more satisfying) sense of law and order.

---

*Reagan's March 13, 1985, response to Congress's threat to raise taxes was to threaten them with a veto, using "Go ahead, and make my day" to underscore his resolve. The American public loved it.

Sudden Impact opened in December 1983 and proved to be the colossal comeback hit that Clint had been searching for, grossing a whopping $70 million in its initial domestic release. It also earned him great reviews, including another nod of approval from Sarris: "The staging of the violent set pieces is stylized, kinetic and visually inventive," he wrote in the *Village Voice*. "Eastwood, occasional *langueurs* and all, has less to worry about in this respect than other filmmakers. When he stands poised for his civically cleansing shoot-outs, no one in the theater is likely to be dozing. I like Eastwood, always have. But then I even have a soft spot in my heart for law and order."

David Denby wrote in *New York* magazine:

Directing the material himself, Clint Eastwood has attempted to retell the Dirty Harry myth in the style of a forties film noir. Much of *Sudden Impact*, including all the scenes of violence, was actually shot at night. In a stiff, sensational, pulp-filmmaking way, the mayhem is impressive: As the camera glides through the dark, sinister thugs emerge from the shadows, or Sondra Locke, blond hair curtaining her face in the style of Veronica Lake, moves into the frame, and violence flashes out, lightning in the air.

Locke's reviews too were excellent, and her on-screen pairing with Clint was nothing less than electrifying. As a doppelgänger for him, she shared his murderous dark(er) side, this time cut with a feminine edge; more than one critic referred to her in this film as "Dirty Harriet."

Warner quickly offered them fortunes to do yet another Dirty Harry film. But as winning as they were on-screen Locke knew it was never going to happen. Clint's heated passion for her was gone, and there was nothing she could do about it except stand and watch it— and him—fade away.*

---

*Locke and Clint worked together one more time, on TV, in an episode of NBC's *Amazing Stories*, "Vanessa in the Garden," that Clint directed; it first aired on December 29, 1985. It was written by Steven Spielberg, who was also the series' executive producer. Interestingly, Clint also cast Jamie Rose, a woman he was said to be secretly involved with at the time, in the show. The episode costarred Harvey Keitel. According to the *Los Angeles Times*, the episode attracted the smallest audience for the (failing) NBC series. "Vanessa in the Garden" was the eighteenth of twenty-nine episodes that were made before the show left the air.

FIFTEEN

Not until Tightrope *do the Eastwood films deal with the fact that the voyeurism in* Dirty Harry *matters most as a warm-up for* Tightrope.

—Dennis Bingham

S*udden Impact* had been critically lauded and a box-office smash. Having finally climbed back up the commercial mountain, Clint next decided to take a giant leap off it by making a buddy-buddy movie costarring Burt Reynolds, whose career was not what it had once been. Some saw this as charity-casting by Clint.

He also appeared to have permanently warehoused Sondra Locke, as he had already begun an affair with a beautiful young Warner Bros. story editor and analyst by the name of Megan Rose, whom he had met during the making of *Honkytonk Man*. This relationship would last nearly five years, until 1988. During that time, Clint paid regular visits to her nearby Warner Bros. office. According to Rose, they made love in her office at lunchtime, in the bedroom he kept behind his office, at her apartment.

Due to scheduling complications having to do with everyone being available at the same time, the Burt Reynolds project was delayed. Instead Clint rushed into production a new film, *Tightrope*, shot on location in New Orleans. Locke was neither in the film nor accompanied him; the part that might once have gone to her went instead to Geneviève Bujold, a forty-something Canadian-born actress who had struck gold in her portrayal of Anne Boleyn opposite Richard Burton in Charles Jarrott's *Anne of the Thousand Days* (1969). Afterward, her off-center looks, strong accent, and lack of bombshell vavoom kept her career on lateral hold. She was actually recommended for the part by the always-willing-to-help Sondra Locke.

Clint loved the idea of putting Bujold in the film, because to him everything in and about the film was off-kilter, and so should be the woman he cast as his costar. Her character was the head of a women's rape center who is tough, tender, and decidedly unglamorous, but sexy nonetheless.

Tightrope was an original Richard Tuggle script that, like his *Escape*

from Alcatraz, was loosely based on a true story—in this case, a series of Bay Area serial sex-and-slash murders that had been covered in a local newspaper. Tuggle had written the film with Don Siegel in mind as the director and Clint as the star, but Siegel begged off, still not willing to work again with Clint. Tuggle then thought about directing it himself. According to sources at Malpaso, that deal was done in a single thirty-second phone conversation to Clint, who had read the script and wanted to be in it. Some believe he was so eager to star in it that it was the real reason he pushed the Reynolds picture back to make room on his schedule.

The story transferred well to New Orleans, whose night-side atmospherics perfectly expressed the noirish mood of the story—darkness and fog everywhere. His character, a law officer, was both attracted to and repelled by not just the victims (mostly New Orleans–style prostitutes and hookers, echoing the notorious Jack the Ripper) but also the murderer—perhaps the embodiment of his own darker side. This time the struggle would be between a law officer and his inner self, between desire and fear of giving in to the darker, rougher, sexual side that lurked within (a sense of self utterly missing from the character of Harry Callahan).

It was that internal moral tug-of-war (the "tightrope" of the title) that Clint's character, Wes Block, had to deal with, minus the Callahan .44 Magnum, plus two motherless girls who themselves become potential victims of the killer. In the midst of it all, Block is attracted to his fellow social servant Beryl Thibodeaux (Bujold), the head of a rape crisis center who neatly embodies the liberation of Block's more disturbed desires and is a stabilizing force as well. She represents the social ties that bind, a restriction Block both envies and fears.

Block fears he will not be able to keep his secrets buried for long, especially from Thibodeaux; he is attracted to submissive women who give in to his kinky desires and weaknesses. He likes oral sex using handcuffs, the tools of his professional trade—then makes love to them. And a scene that takes place inside an especially seedy gay bar suggests that the aptly named Block might have some not-so-latent homosexual tendencies. The gruesome sex-and-slash murders that escalate throughout the film become a vicarious thrill machine for him, even as they set off an increasingly wild pursuit that becomes, literally, one dark soul chasing an even darker soul. The movie also

marked the screen debut of Clint's second child by Maggie. Twelve-year-old Alison Eastwood played the role of one of his two small daughters in the film.

This time even the harshest critics of the Eastwood oeuvre, except Kael, went out of their way to recognize the quality of the film and of Clint's acting. Even if they didn't particularly like its content, they had to admire the masterful stylistics of its contextual unspooling and the increasingly desperate yet tightly controlled unraveling of Clint's Block. Kathleen Cornell wrote in the *New York Daily News*, "Eastwood is simply terrific, his lean and hungry face revealing all the right emotions . . . thanks to the efforts of writer-director Richard Tuggle, it's a raunchy but surprisingly intelligent movie, which at times scares the viewer as much as one of Hitchcock's tension-filled thrillers." J. Hoberman of the *Village Voice* called it "one of Eastwood's finest, most reflexive and reflective films since *Bronco Billy*—and for my money the best Hollywood movie so far this year." But Kael remained unrepentant: "*Tightrope* is the opposite of sophisticated movie-making . . . Clint seems to be trying to blast through his own lack of courage as an actor." In a rare display of public emotion, in the May 1985 issue of *Video* magazine, Clint finally responded by dismissing Kael as a mere parasite, clinging to his career in order to make herself more important: "[Kael] found an avenue that was going to make her a star. I was just one of the subjects, among many, that helped her along the way." In truth, there was no shortage of actors, actresses, and directors who felt the same way.

Tightrope opened the 1984 Montreal Film Festival and grossed an impressive $60 million in its initial domestic release, a number that ballooned to over $100 million after its first foreign release and before TV and eventual video rights. That year, due mainly to the success of *Tightrope*, Clint was named the world's top box-office star by Quigley (for the second year in a row). It was his sixteenth appearance on the top-ten list, more times than any other living star.

On August 22, 1984, Clint was invited to place his hands and feet into cement at the fabled Grauman's (Mann's) Chinese Theatre in Hollywood, alongside the greatest film legends of all time. After casually conversing with the relatively small daytime crowd that had gathered—these events were never well publicized, to keep the crowds intentionally small and manageable—and with Kyle and Alison

proudly looking on, Clint scrawled alongside his handprints, *"You've made my day."*

While *Tightrope* was still in theaters, Clint finally went into production on *City Heat* with Burt Reynolds. The difference in the two stars' individual salaries reflected the level of their current popularity: Clint was paid $5 million, while Burt received $4 million. Both stars appeared happy to be working together, even if their much-publicized redneck and roadster buddy-buddy camaraderie was a product of PR more than reality. In truth, they didn't hang out all that much together. In Reynolds's memoir, Clint is little more than a passing acquaintance.

Early on tensions rose between Clint, Reynolds, and the director, Blake Edwards, who had also written the script. The central issue was on casting, but the real problems ran much deeper. To begin with, Edwards had originally given the script to Locke, rather than Clint, in one of the typical sleights-of-hand that take place in Hollywood every day of the week. Edwards had asked her if she would read his script, suggesting that she would be perfect in the role of Caroline, Murphy's (Reynolds's) girlfriend. He said he had seen her performance in *Bronco Billy*, loved it, and wanted her to costar in his new film. To seal the deal, he suggested that her appearance would once and for all take her out of the giant shadow cast over her career by Clint's.

Not surprisingly, Locke jumped at the chance. That was when Edwards pulled the switch and asked Locke if she would mind passing the script along to Clint. "Before I knew it," Locke said later, "Blake and his wife, Julie Andrews, were having dinner with Clint and me. Then Burt Reynolds was suddenly brought in, and within a few weeks I was simply out of the mix and forgotten."

Edwards had, apparently, used Locke as a way to get to Clint, to secure a deal with Malpaso, which in turn would secure the funding, and along with it a firm commitment from the two stars to appear in the movie that Edwards would direct.

Even before the film went into production, the triangle of Edwards, Eastwood, and Reynolds ran into a Cinemascope-size brick wall. Both Clint and Reynolds had script approval, and each was interested in making sure he came out looking and sounding better than the other. Reynolds's changes stretched into months of delays that drove Clint

crazy, but allowed him to spend ample chunks of time on the nearest golf course. Reynolds continued to suggest changes. The two men fought indirectly over every nuance in the script, using Edwards as their reluctant intermediary.

Edwards had directed Reynolds in a movie the year before, *The Man Who Loved Women*, and so had experienced the difficulties and learned how to deal with his short fuse. But he didn't know how to handle Clint and may have assumed he had to wear the same kid gloves.

The problem was that Clint, always impatient with weakness, interpreted Edwards's running everything by him as just that. Once Clint green-lighted a production, he liked to go out and make it. The more Edwards equivocated, the less Clint believed he could get the job done. Then just before shooting was finally about to begin, Edwards, having had all he could take of Reynolds's ego and Clint's impatience, quit the film. "Creative differences" was the official reason given for his departure, but unofficially insiders talked of one final blowup with Clint that resulted in Edwards either being asked to leave the film or simply walking out on it.

According to Reynolds, in his memoir, Clint actually orchestrated the removal of Blake by goading him into quitting, in favor of Richard Benjamin, a less intense, more likable, and less expensive director. The original title, *Kansas City Heat*, was now changed at Clint's directive to the simpler and more marquee-friendly *City Heat*. The ever-reliable Fritz Manes replaced Edwards as the line producer, and Edwards's screenplay was credited to Sam O. Brown, a Screen Writers Guild–approved pseudonym.*

Naturally, Reynolds saw all this as nothing less than a takeover of the project by Clint, which upset the delicate balance of power between the two superstars. In addition, during the long preproduction, actors and actresses with other commitments waiting for them came and went like bowling pins on a Saturday night. The final

---

*Other factors may have contributed to the departure. At one point Edwards wanted to cast his wife in the film, but Clint vehemently objected, noting that he hadn't put Locke in the film. Edwards had also made some requests that Clint, as executive producer, did not appreciate, like a car and driver to get him from Beverly Hills to Burbank; according to one source, that sent Clint through the ceiling. "Let him walk," Clint was supposed to have said, "or get a horse."

supporting-roles cast was set only days before filming began: Madeline Kahn, Jane Alexander, Rip Torn, Irene Cara, Richard Roundtree, and Tony Lo Bianco.

The plot was as leaden as it was pedestrian—a Depression-era detective, Mike Murphy (Reynolds), discovers that his partner, Dehl Swift (Roundtree), wants to buy some ledgers from the bookkeeper of a gangster "godfather," to sell to his rival gang leader. That leads to Swift's swift demise. Soon enough Murphy gets the ledgers, and with them a death sentence from the godfather (Lo Bianco). He kidnaps Murphy's girlfriend (Kahn) and enlists the help of his former police force partner, Lieutenant Speer, played by a dark-fedoraed Clint, who managed to keep his eyes shaded for almost the entire film, as if he didn't want anyone to recognize him in it. The film ends with an explosion that explains nothing and only provides a way to halt, if not end, these confused, unfunny, and uninvolving events.

The on-screen chemistry between Reynolds and Clint was, not surprisingly, zero-minus-a-hundred, which may help to explain the nearly career-ending accident that occurred while they were filming a bar scene in which Speer punches Murphy in the face. During the fight a stuntman mistakenly used a real chair instead of a fake, "breakaway" chair to hit Reynolds. It badly broke Reynolds's jaw and developed into temporomandibular joint disorder (TMJ), which affects both balance and sensory perceptions. Reynolds's physical health deteriorated after that, and rumors ran rampant in the press that he had developed AIDS, a supposition supercharged by his dramatic loss of weight. (He was unable to eat solid food through his damaged jaw.)

It was, for all intents and purposes, the end of Reynolds's run as a major Hollywood movie star. Eventually he would recover and work, most notably in Paul Thomas Anderson's *Boogie Nights* (1997), for which he received an Oscar nomination for Best Supporting Actor, and in a couple of TV series, but he never again placed on a national film-star ranking. A lot of people believed that Clint had delivered the punch that did Reynolds in, that he had punched him out of commission for good.*

---

*It remains unclear who threw the actual punch, if it was Clint or a stuntman, or even what caused the accident, the punch, or the fall. As for Edwards, his next theatrical feature that he both wrote and directed, the satirical *A Fine Mess* (1986), included a brief but scathing send-up of Clint as the Man with No Name.

Meanwhile Locke, left out of both *Tightrope* and *City Heat*, went by herself to the William Morris office in search of a project she might be able to direct. (Clint would later claim that he had suggested she move into directing, but according to Locke, she came up with the idea first and Clint encouraged her.) At the agency she came across a script that had been lying around in development hell for years, something called *Ratboy*, by Rob Thompson, which was about just what the title suggests, a boy who is half-rat, half-human. Nikki, a small-time promoter, comes across Ratboy and decides to promote him into a big star. Along the way she falls in love with Ratboy and is then redeemed for her exploitative desires. The script was *Beauty and the Beast* crossed with *King Kong*.

Locke quickly made a deal to take over the rights and then brought the script to Terry Semel, at Warner. Semel gave it a green light, as long as she would agree to two conditions. First, Locke had to appear in the picture as well as direct it. She had no problem with that—she would play Nikki.

The second, that Clint would produce.

This condition made nobody happy. Clint did not want to work with Locke anymore, and Locke felt that as soon as Clint's name was attached to *Ratboy*, her project would turn into "A Clint Eastwood Picture" and defeat her attempt to emerge from his giant shadow. Clint's solution was simple; he would put his name on the picture but actually assign the line-producing chores to Fritz Manes. But Malpaso would not be involved: Clint, wanting to put physical and professional distance between himself and Locke, decided to create a new production company within Malpaso for this one picture.

Then, likely putting the final nail in the coffin of her relationship with Clint, Locke cast her husband, Gordon, to play Nikki's brother.

Predictably, Clint was vehemently opposed. An angry back-and-forth ensued: Clint accused Locke of nepotism. Locke reminded Clint that he had used his son and his daughter in two of his films. Clint insisted that he hadn't used either in his *first* film. Locke countered that her film wasn't really intended for the mainstream so it didn't matter. Clint said he didn't want Gordon in the film and halted all further development of the script until Locke agreed.

Having come to an impasse, Locke dropped her next bombshell: she had cast Sharon Baird (S. L. Baird in the credits), one of the original

Mouseketeers, in the title role. Clint couldn't believe it. He quietly reminded her that the film was called rat*boy*, not rat*girl*.

On it went, with Clint trying to maintain absolute control of every aspect of the film. By the time it was finished, Locke felt that her creative input had been totally buried. Being invited to the Deauville Film Festival in France, where the film received good notices, did nothing to soothe her.*

For its commercial release in 1986, Warner Bros. chose to open *Ratboy* in only one theater in Los Angeles and one in New York City and the top development executives at Warner—who included Semel, Lucy Fisher, and Mark Canton—agreed to a first-look, first-refusal deal for anything else Locke brought them.

From the beginning of the project, in 1984, Clint had not been easy for Locke to work with, but the deterioration of their relationship may not have been the only reason. Just as Clint had gotten involved with the film, Maggie officially filed for divorce and publicly announced her intention to marry Wynberg. Estimates ran the value of the original 1979 settlement agreement up to around $28 million in cash, plus property and child support.†

By the time Clint was ready to make his next movie, he had become involved with a new woman, Jacelyn Reeves, who was to become the mother of his next child. The film was called *Pale Rider*. The state of affairs was chaos.

So naturally Clint decided to run for mayor of Carmel.

---

*The brother was played by Louie Anderson; Gordon became the voice of Ratboy. Gerrit Graham played Nikki's other brother. Despite Clint's strong objections, Baird appeared in the title role.

†After a long and at times contentious battle, they finally divorced in May 1984. The monetary award was, reportedly, calculated on the basis of a million dollars for every year they were married, plus previously agreed-upon property divisions. Child custody was joint, with Maggie awarded physical custody. In an article in *People* magazine published shortly after the divorce was finalized, Maggie blamed Locke for her final breakup with Clint. But the divorce was reported as "friendly," and she and Clint continued as partners in various business interests they shared. Maggie married Wynberg in 1984. They were divorced in 1989.

SIXTEEN

I've always considered myself too individualistic to be either right wing or left wing.

—Clint Eastwood

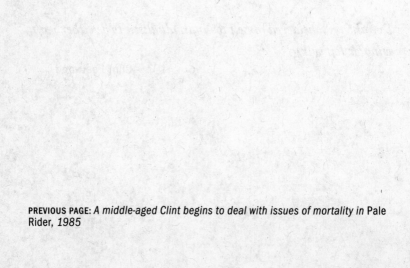

PREVIOUS PAGE: *A middle-aged Clint begins to deal with issues of mortality in* Pale Rider, *1985*

The mayoral adventure began because of ice cream cones, or more accurately, their unavailability on summer afternoons, because the city fathers of Carmel-by-the-Sea (the town's legal name) had passed an ordinance prohibiting the storefront sale of ice cream cones because they felt that eating them in the street was "undignified." To Carmel's most celebrated citizen, who happened to like eating ice cream cones in the summertime, this was one civil outrage too many, and no matter what, he was not going to let it stand.

He had had his troubles with the town council before. In June 1983 he had applied for permission to build a two-story freestanding addition to the Hog's Breath—and been denied. The council cited problems with the design and the materials. Moreover, it said, San Carlos Street, where the Hog's Breath was located, already had too many glass and concrete structures and not enough wood. In the early spring of 1984, shortly after the completion of *City Heat* and a series of back-and-forth maneuvers, Clint made a final, personal appeal to the council, which promptly rejected it. Angry and frustrated, he threatened to file suit against the city council of Carmel, claiming the regulations the council used as the basis for its decision were "vague and subjective."

Not long after the start of the ice cream battle, with his Hog's Breath Inn situation also still unresolved, Clint was sitting around the inn with some friends when someone suggested he ought to run for mayor. Once he got elected, they said, he could change the rules. It may have been a joke, but no one was laughing, least of all Clint.

But he had more pressing, if not bigger, things (to him) to deal with at the moment. That spring he was being honored at the prestigious Paris-based Cinémathèque Française, which was to culminate in a special European preview screening of *Tightrope*. This invitation was especially important because he was going to be decorated as a

Knight in the French Order of Arts and Letters, an honor that he had won only with much outside support.*

His film career meant a lot to him. Even if some critics still didn't take his movies seriously, or the subjects were socially distasteful, he was very proud of them. As he told one interviewer during this period, "Maybe there were certain prejudices in the times of *Dirty Harry* in 1971 that don't exist now, or are changing now, or times are changing. Maybe I'm older, more mature, maybe the audiences are changing and I'm changing. It's just circumstances . . . I've never begged for respectability."

Respectability was the heart of the matter, and it no longer seemed out of reach. Most of the critics, who had been far behind audiences in recognizing Clint's movies as terrific entertainments, were beginning to "get" that he was more than just a genre moviemaker, and that his films were about something, even if it wasn't the usual boy-meets-girl love story.

As one critic wrote during this period in the *New York Times*, where its mere inclusion was a benediction: "The Eastwood persona caught a blue-collar discontent with a country portrayed as being run by bleeding hearts." In other words, Harry Callahan the immoral fascist had now turned into Harry Callahan the law-and-order hero.

Even the *über*-liberal Norman Mailer had changed his opinion. "Clint Eastwood is an artist," he said, and "he has a presidential face." In fact, he said, "maybe there is no one more American than Clint."

After his triumphal visit to Paris, Clint returned home and went directly into pre-general-release work on *Pale Rider*, his first western since *The Outlaw Josey Wales*, nine years earlier. Meanwhile a new script came his way via Megan Rose, *The William Munny Killings;* she had read it and thought it perfect for Clint. Francis Ford Coppola had

---

*The award was made by Pierre Viot, the former boss of the National Cinema Center and newly appointed president of the Cannes Film Festival, instead of Culture Minister Jack Lang, who excused himself due to a prior commitment. It was widely believed in France that Lang, who was a Socialist, did not want to honor an American star whose films frequently promoted a right-wing-leaning law-and-order view of society. In support of Clint were Terry Semel, Richard Fox (newly appointed head of WB International), and Steve Ross of Warner Bros. Their show of support for their star further affirmed that their past troubles were, at least for the time being, set aside.

an option on it; when Rose showed it to Lucy Fisher, a head of production and development at Warner, she agreed that it was a good choice for Clint. But he would never consent to being directed by Coppola, Fisher said. Their styles—Coppola's painstakingly slow brand of perfectionism, Clint's fast, instinctive method—were incompatible. Eventually Coppola let his option lapse, and as a 1984 Christmas gift to Clint, Rose put a copy of the script into his Christmas stocking. He liked it, bought it, and then put it away until he felt the time was right to make it. That time would come in 1992, when it was retitled *Unforgiven*.

This time out, with his confidence bubbling like chilled champagne, he assured himself he would have no more problems with temperamental or inexperienced directors (or girlfriends with excessive proprietary claims). As his affair with Rose was ending, Clint made sure to keep sufficient distance from her. With *Pale Rider* he was going to produce, star in, and direct the whole picture; Manes would have the nominal role of Malpaso's executive producer.

To some, Clint's choice to return to westerns (especially one tinged with a mysterious and elegant unearthliness) seemed odd, as the genre had been pronounced dead in the mud since *Heaven's Gate*. Moreover, *Pale Rider* was in many ways yet another version of the true events that that film, and *Shane*, had been based on, the Johnson County War. Following his success with *Tightrope* (and forgetting his failure with *City Heat*), *Pale Rider* seemed, at best, an offbeat choice.

Clint shifted the locale to Gold Rush California, where would-be instant millionaires are being terrorized by a ship-mining corporation led by Coy LaHood (Richard Dysart). His conglomerate needs the land in order to survive. (In previous versions, including *Shane* and *Heaven's Gate*, the battle pitted land-settlers against cattle-breeders.)

On the miners' side is Hull Barret (Michael Moriarty), a homesteader, who has a new girlfriend (Carrie Snodgress) and a daughter from his first marriage, Megan (Sydney Penny). Out of the mist comes a man known only as the Preacher (Eastwood), who succeeds in uniting the miners in a successful showdown with LaHood and his men, including on LaHood's side an evil marshal (John Russell), all of whom the Preacher battled sometime in the past. In a series of strange and violent confrontations, the Preacher helps the homesteaders achieve peace. Despite Megan's adoration of him, he rides off by him-

self into the sunset, a ghostly eminence who uses the violent ways of the lawless Old West.

Like Shane, the Preacher seems to come out of the past to confront the evil cattlemen before he heads out, presumably to Boot Hill, the inevitable destiny of all gunfighters, even the Old West itself. In *Pale Rider* (as in *High Plains Drifter*), the Preacher is less a former gun-fighter than the ghost of a former gunfighter—perhaps, in the film's pseudo-religious overlay, a descendant of one of the Four Horsemen of the Apocalypse. (The Preacher is seen riding past a window as Megan reads that passage aloud from the Bible.)

A sense of the dramatic if ethereal power of the unexplainable, mys-tical, and supernatural pervades this film as it did *The Beguiled*, although here much more affectingly. Obvious earlier Eastwood-film allusions abound, from the vague history of the Man with No Name, to the bru-tal tactics of Harry Callahan and the aforementioned ambience of *The Beguiled*. The difference in *Pale Rider* is that the character is not merely out of the mainstream, he seems out of the stream of life itself.

In addition, a sense of political and social resurrection floats like a mist throughout the film, suggesting a post-Vietnam metaphor: the ghosts of the American war dead seem to live on, performing heroic deeds for the landowners, the South Vietnamese people, caught in a battle with the North not just over land rights but over the definition of what the law of the land will be. On that zeitgeist level, in its belief in the spiritual power of the defenders of the land, the film is pure Reagan-era fantasy.

Heady stuff, to be sure, but also the makings of a terrifically enter-taining movie, which *Pale Rider* turned out to be. While they were making it in Sun Valley, the cast and crew felt that Clint was in a great groove, undergoing a resurrection of his own with this return to his most familiar genre and role, the western tough guy.

When he was invited to go to Cannes that spring to show *Pale Rider*, prior to its official commercial release, he took up the offer. "I enjoyed going there because I was taking a western. No one ever takes an American western. It was kind of fun and the film was received rather well. They gave me a thing called The Chevalier of Arts and Letters, and later on The Commander of the Arts and Letters."*

---

*The French version of British knighthood.

Pale Rider opened in June 1985 to raves. Vincent Canby went all out in his praise:

> An entertaining, mystical new western . . . played absolutely straight, but it's also very funny in a dryly sophisticated way that—it's only now apparent—has been true of Mr. Eastwood's self-directed films and of the Eastwood films directed by Don Siegel . . . like all Eastwood productions, *Pale Rider* is extremely well cast beginning with the star. Mr. Eastwood has continued to refine the identity of his western hero by eliminating virtually every superfluous gesture. He's a master of minimalism. The camera does not reflect vanity. It discovers the character within. *Pale Rider* is the first decent western in a very long time.

And Andrew Sarris in the *Village Voice:*

> On the whole Eastwood's instincts as an artist are well-nigh inspiring in the context of the temptations he must face all the time to play it completely safe. Consequently, even his mistakes contribute to his mystique . . . Eastwood has managed to keep the genre alive . . . through the ghostly intervention of his heroic persona.

But as always with Clint's movies, it was the audience that spoke the loudest. *Pale Rider,* which cost less than $4 million to make, was the top-grossing release its first week, raking in an amazing (for 1985) $9 million, and it brought in $21.5 million in its first ten days. It would go on to gross more than $60 million in its initial domestic release, a figure that would more than triple by the time it played on screens worldwide, everywhere to wildly enthusiastic reviews.

Typical of the international adulation was a piece in a French magazine that declared, *"Clint Eastwood, depuis 15 ans, la star de cinéma le plus populaire du monde!"**

Clint had made a spectacular return to form, and in more ways than one. On location in Sun Valley it was an open secret on set that there was a new "main squeeze" in Clint's life, a pretty young woman

---

*"For the past fifteen years, Clint Eastwood has been the most popular film star in the world!"

he had met at the Hog's Breath by the name of Jacelyn Reeves, an airline stewardess whose home base was Carmel.

And he kept at least one other woman (as he had kept Tunis, Rose, Reeves, and even Locke for a while) in a "regular rotation." Jane Brolin, an actress who had married James Brolin in 1966, had known Clint since his Universal contract-player days, when they had first met on the grounds of the studio. After the breakup with Brolin, Jane had run into Clint, and before long they had become romantically involved.

Around this same time Clint began receiving anonymous "hate mail" regarding Sondra Locke. Some close to the situation suspected the letters were coming from Jane, despite the fact that Locke was on shaky terms with a fast-cooling Clint. He refused to believe it, and the matter was never satisfactorily resolved.*

On March 21, 1986, Jacelyn Reeves, who had become pregnant by Clint, gave birth to a son she named Scott. The registered birth certificate shows the baby was delivered at Monterey Community Hospital. The name of the father is omitted.

In the midst of all this, Clint decided to do something about both the ice cream ordinance and the one that was preventing him from expanding the Hog's Breath: he threw his hat into the ring for mayor. Almost immediately campaign posters with his picture that looked like a cross between Ronald Reagan and Dirty Harry began to appear on the sides of buildings and streetlamps. Bumper stickers bore the slogan "Go ahead, make me mayor!" With Ronald Reagan's improbable leap from movies to the White House still fresh in everyone's minds, the news that Clint had "entered politics" filled the front pages of newspapers around the world. (He ran as a nonpartisan, as the office of mayor does not require a political affiliation.)

On the morning of January 30, 1986, after completing his round at the Pebble Beach National Pro-Am golf tournament and just hours before the deadline, Clint dropped off his petition of thirty signatures (ten more than the minimum required), and his name was put into official nomination. In his first interview after declaring himself a candidate, Clint told the local Carmel newspaper why he had decided to run:

*Jane Agee Brolin died in a car accident in 1995.

I don't need to bring attention to myself. I'm doing this as a resident. This is where I live; this is where I intend to live the rest of my life. I have a great affinity with the community. There used to be a great deal of camaraderie, a great spirit in this community. Now there is such negativity. I'd like to see the old spirit come back here, that kind of *esprit de corps* . . . I can recall a time when you could walk down the street in Carmel and pick up an ice-cream cone at a shop—now you'd be fined . . . the city will be my absolute priority. I'll be a lot less active in films than I have in the past.

It was a startling statement. That he would put the brakes on his more-successful-than-ever film career in favor of small-town politics sounded like a reverse *It's a Wonderful Life*. The lines between his roles and his real life were blurring. In his films Clint was, in one way or another, always the defender of the people. Now he wanted to defend them in real life. At nearly fifty-six, when most men started to at least think about retirement, Clint was proudly and publicly opening up a new avenue and going so far as to suggest it meant a major career change.

Change was indeed in the air for Clint that year, although not entirely the change he had in mind.

On April 8, 1986, he won the $200-a-week mayoral post handily, spending more than $40,000 on his campaign; his opponent, incumbent Charlotte Townsend, spent $300. Clint got 2,166 votes, or 72 percent of the total cast. Townsend got 799. Clint voted before breakfast, after driving in a beat-up yellow Volkswagen convertible through a massive press gauntlet.

The next day he received a call from President Reagan, who congratulated him by asking, tongue firmly planted in cheek, "What's an actor who once appeared with a monkey in a movie doing in politics?" The not-so-inside joke was, of course, that Reagan had made *Bedtime for Bonzo*. Jimmy Stewart, the star of *It's a Wonderful Life*, who wasn't in politics but, true to his image, was the best friend of the president, also called to congratulate Clint.

At his swearing-in for his two-year term, his mother, his sister Jeanne, more than a thousand townsfolk, and at least that many paparazzi showed up to watch Charlotte Townsend hand over the symbolic gavel of power.

Even before he dealt with the ice cream crisis, one of the first things the 1985 box-office champion did as mayor was to fire the heads of the four planning commissions that had turned down his proposal to build the office addition next to the Hog's Breath.* The reversal of the anti-ice-cream ordinance followed, sparking a noticeable rise in sidewalk cone sales.

Soon after the election, Clint turned his day-to-day mayoral responsibilities over to Sue Hutchinson, a sixty-something consultant he had hired to organize his campaign. Her strong organizational skills were ideal for the job. She wasn't someone with whom he could possibly become involved, but she knew how to run a screw-tight ship. With Hutchinson firmly in place, he increasingly boarded the Warner corporate jet that was always available to him and flew to his Malpaso offices in Burbank, to turn his full-time attention back to filmmaking.

The first post–*Pale Rider* project he liked (one of the two feature films he would make while ostensibly serving as the mayor of Carmel) was a military-themed script called *Heartbreak Ridge*. Warner had sent him the script, written by James Carabatsos, a Vietnam veteran who had drawn upon his own experiences once before in a 1977 movie called *Heroes*, directed by Jeremy Kagan.† Distributed by Universal, *Heroes* had caught the eyes of the Warner executives who were interested in producing Kagan's next film, especially after the success of *Apocalypse Now* and *The Deer Hunter* made Vietnam a hot-button topic for mainstream films.

Nonetheless, Warner had problems getting a "name" interested to star in *Heartbreak Ridge*, a problem that often arose when a project was purchased without a star already attached; the reasons usually quickly became apparent. In the case of *Heartbreak Ridge*, very few actors wanted to play age against youth, presenting their own aging

---

*The ordinance itself had actually been partially reversed the previous November. It had required the new addition be set back farther from the street, with less exterior glass and mostly wooden exterior. Clint rejected that offer, and even after his full tenure as mayor, the problem went unresolved until the mid-1990s, when it was finally built, mostly to the specs of the original compromised plans, "only uglier," as one close to the project said.

†*Heroes* was a vehicle for Henry Winkler, best known as "Fonzie" from television's *Happy Days*.

facade against a bunch of scene-stealing newcomers. Clint, however, was not afraid to age on-screen and did not make conventional love stories; he was looking for just such a script, and as always one by a writer with little or no clout to challenge him.

After a couple of rewrites with specific verbal suggestions from Clint, an exasperated Carabatsos begged off any further work on *Heartbreak Ridge*, claiming other commitments. Clint promptly enlisted Dennis Hackin, who had written *Bronco Billy*, to punch up the action and the comedy. Still not satisfied, Clint next brought in Joseph Stinson, who had written *Sudden Impact*. Finally Clint and Megan Rose laid out pages from all the versions and cobbled together something they felt was at least filmable. Clint then brought back Hackin and Stinson and asked them to work on the script together. That marked the end of Rose's involvement with Clint, and the start of an ongoing dispute over who was responsible for the final shooting version.*

One reason the script may have been so hard to tailor to Clint's satisfaction was that few, if any, of the writers understood how personal, rather than genre-driven, the film actually was. Clint's days as a leading man were all but over, and even the facade of his long-standing relationship with Sondra Locke was gone. According to Clint:

---

*The Rose affair began and ended in typical Clint fashion: it was heat-fueled, ran its course, and ended rather coldly, when Clint wanted it to end. When *Unforgiven* was finally made, nearly a decade later, Rose received no on-screen credit or compensation (no co-producer or finder's fee). Meanwhile, she had moved on, left Warner Bros. after a brief but serious illness, then found a western vehicle for TV actor Tom Selleck, who was looking to move to the big screen. The script she found was *Quigley Down Under* (1990, Simon Wincer). She received co-producer credit. After *Unforgiven* was nominated for Best Picture, she hired a lawyer and asked for both the finder's fee and the production credit. To avoid the lawsuit, Clint offered her instead $10,000 to serve as story editor on his next film (*A Perfect World*). On March 8, 1993, the story hit the gossip pages, beginning with the *New York Post*'s Page Six, and made its way through the snake-tunnel of gossip-and-whisper rags. Perhaps feeling the damage was done, Clint withdrew his offer. Eventually, Rose dropped her lawsuit and left Clint's life and world for good. Rose's contribution to the final script has been publicly questioned by the film's executive producer, Fritz Manes. In the end, Carabatsos received sole screen credit, after objecting to Clint's wanting to give Stinson a co-writer credit. The dispute went to SWG arbitration, which Carabatsos won. After the film opened, Clint continually referred to the contributions of Stinson, prompting an SWG official to advise Clint to refrain from any further public comments on the issue or face sanctions from the guild.

Heartbreak Ridge [is about] what warriors do when they haven't got a war. That's always interested me. And I thought, here's a character, let's see how he interacts with people, especially with women. It was an interesting story, also about a solider who hasn't ever done anything but fight wars, and he discovers that he's reached the end of his career, and he has nothing to look back on and nothing at all he can concentrate on now.

In its final form, an aging drill sergeant has separated from his wife and fears his time is just about up. He won the Medal of Honor at the battle of Heartbreak Ridge during the Korean War but has now been reduced to training new recruits, transforming boys still wet behind the ears into combat-ready Marines (for the invasion of Granada that took place in 1983). If any of this sounds familiar, it's because a similar story had been made in 1982 by Taylor Hackford, *An Officer and a Gentleman*, that starred Richard Gere as a punk runaway who is turned into a "real man" by his discovery of true love (via Debra Winger) and a tough-guy gunnery sergeant played by Louis Gossett Jr. It was Gere's picture, but Gossett Jr. took home a Best Supporting Oscar for his performance.* Perhaps ego, and Clint's long-simmering anger at the Academy for failing to recognize his achievements, were what really attracted him to a role very close to the one that had brought the elusive statuette to Gossett.

Besides the heavily doctored script, and Clint's clenched-teeth style of acting that made him seem now more doddering than daring, the production ran into trouble with the U.S. Defense Department. They had at first agreed to cooperate with the film but withdrew after seeing the final cut because of the excessive use of profanity and unfair combat tactics. (*An Officer and a Gentleman*'s below-the-belt training methods were unhampered by the military, as it was made without their cooperation.) One thing the DOD most objected to was Sergeant Highway (Clint) pumping an extra bullet into the back of an enemy soldier who had already been shot. Another was the fact that the Marines, in the real-life invasion, got to Grenada via Beirut, which

---

*Gere wasn't nominated. Winger was, for Best Actress, but lost to Meryl Streep in Alan J. Pakula's *Sophie's Choice*.

Clint eliminated from the film. Soon enough Clint grew tired of the military's constant bickering. When they pointed out that the army, not the Marines, had rescued the medical students in Grenada, he drew the line. He actually threatened to call Ronald Reagan and have him intervene if the military did not get off his back, and most of the military's requests were quietly agreed to.*

When the film finally did open, for the 1986 holiday season, it did surprisingly well, although more than one critic questioned that someone of Clint's age (which he had done nothing to disguise) would be involved in the film's action sequences. *Heartbreak Ridge* wound up doing almost as well as *Tightrope*, grossing over $70 million in its initial domestic release and double that overseas, where no one cared how old Clint looked or how accurate the film's depiction of the military. All foreign audiences wanted was to see their hero, Clint Eastwood, in action, and that's what they got.

Warner mounted a heavy and expensive campaign to promote *Heartbreak Ridge* for Oscar consideration, but all the heat that year went to Oliver Stone's *Platoon:* it won four Oscars, including one for Stone as Best Director and one for Best Picture, and it was nominated for four more. *Heartbreak Ridge* managed only one nomination, for Best Sound, which it lost to *Platoon*.

According to sources, Clint was angered all over again by what he considered to be this latest snubbing by the Academy and looked for someone besides himself to blame. He pointed his finger indirectly at the Department of Defense and directly at Fritz Manes, whose job as executive producer, Clint insisted, was to "handle" these kinds of situations. Manes had been on the outs with Clint since he had enthusiastically supported Locke and her *Ratboy* film. After that debacle everyone at Malpaso thought Manes, one of Clint's oldest and closest friends and one of his most trusted employees, became a scapegoat for everything that had gone wrong with *Heartbreak Ridge*.

Locke says that as her relationship with Clint broke down, so did Manes's:

---

*Some thought that Clint's noticeably lower and rougher voice in the film was his homage/impersonation of Ronald Reagan. Clint denied it, claiming it was actually his impression of an uncle who had damaged his vocal cords and had to talk that way.

I had known Fritz as long as I had known Clint, and Fritz and Clint had been close friends since junior high days; it seemed a shame for things to deteriorate [between them] that way. Clint only replied, "Stay out of this. This has nothing to do with you! I don't like the way he's running my company. *He's* not Malpaso. I am, nobody else."

Clint then began a campaign of collecting petty details to discredit Fritz . . . and then he learned that Fritz had let Judi, Clint's own secretary, occasionally use the company gas credit card, and had let the accountant, Mike Maurer, and his wife make occasional long-distance phone calls that got charged to the company . . .

Clint did not actually confront Fritz. He played cat and mouse. Once Fritz was safely fired, Clint . . . wanted Fritz's car phone returned; he didn't care that it was the old-fashioned kind that had been bolted down, he wanted it . . . He even concocted a scheme in which he wanted [my husband] to break into Fritz's home and make a sample of the type on Fritz's typewriter so that he could see if it matched that on the anonymous hate-filled letters he'd been receiving for several years.

Not long after *Heartbreak Ridge* failed to make a dent with Oscar, the long and fruitful professional and personal relationship between Fritz Manes and Clint came to a permanent end.

SEVENTEEN

I went to a jazz concert one time at the Oakland Philharmonic. This guy comes out in a pinstripe suit, standing off to one side, the joint is jumping, and then all of a sudden he steps up and starts playing and everything is doubled up. I'm thinking, "How the hell does he do that?" . . . It was a great acting lesson—the amount of confidence [Parker] exuded. I've never seen an artist, an actor, a painter, any artist have that kind of confidence.

—Clint Eastwood

That March, after the 1987 Academy Awards ceremonies, Clint reimmersed himself in the business of running Carmel. One of his first chores was to oversee an ongoing conflict over Carmel's Mission Ranch, a large wetland just south of the city limit that had been purchased by a private consortium that wanted to develop it into a modern housing project, with expensive town houses and maybe even a self-contained modern mall with ample parking facilities. The town council was opposed to the development, preferring to keep the land preserved in the image of Carmel, a beautiful, natural seaside village. To prevent the development from advancing any further, the city offered $3.75 million for the land, about half of what the owners said they would take to settle. The situation remained deadlocked until Clint decided to put up $5.5 million of his own money to help Carmel acquire the land. Having completed the sale, he took it out of the hands of any and all developers and vowed to keep it as it was. The elders of the township hailed the move, and the national press as well looked upon it favorably.

With that victory under his belt, Clint dove deeper into Carmel's municipal activities. He actively pursued projects meant to improve pedestrian access to beaches, adding public toilets, walking trails, and also a new library for the town. He began writing a column in the local paper, the *Pine Cone*, his personal forum to discuss and respond to issues of the day, especially those that generated the most mail to his office. And he even put a bit of the old-style, back-door politics of vengeance into play when he made it difficult for former councilman David Maradei to get a variance to put a gable on his roof. Maradei had been one of the people who had made it difficult for Clint to build his Hog's Breath Inn annex. Even though Clint officially abstained from voting on the issue, he made sure everyone knew he did not support it.

And when Jimmy Stewart was scheduled to be feted by the local film festival, the town council turned down permits for temporary high-stacked lighting, citing the garish, Hollywood-like atmosphere that it was sure to create. Clint, miffed at what he felt, probably rightly, was a veiled reference to his being a movie star mayor, made sure those lights got hung. He also saw to it that Pope John Paul II was able to make a stop in Carmel in 1987, which boosted tourism and filled the city's coffers. If Clint was the celebrity mayor, Carmel was becoming a place where tourists liked to come, hoping to catch a glimpse of him strolling around town, always ready, willing, and able to keep the peace.

Sondra Locke, meanwhile, was trying to move her stalled career forward. Occasionally she still made the drive up the coast to visit Clint in his Carmel enclave. Locke knew that if she wanted to see him, she would have to go up there; otherwise (and Clint had done nothing to hide it from her) a steady stream of other female visitors would come to his home. He was continuing to see, among others, Jacelyn Reeves, who gave birth to their second child, a daughter, in February 1988.

Locke's place in L.A., on Stradella Road, was becoming less and less hers and more and more Kyle Eastwood's. Clint's son, at Clint's directive, had moved in, according to Locke, even as he was struggling at the University of Southern California. Kyle brought home his pack, musicians and actors, most of whom Locke did not know. When she raised a red flag to Clint, he supported Kyle, seeing it, in his way, as taking Kyle in, even though Clint was rarely at that house. As much as Locke wanted to protest, Clint still owned the place, and she had no legal right to prevent the sudden influx of "family" and friends. "So this had become my life with him," she wrote,

Clint being distant, rarely at home and Kyle and his friends playing their instruments into the wee hours, sneaking girls in and out for overnight stays. It was humiliating to feel that I had nothing to say about circumstances in my own home. The final straw for me was the night I woke up and saw someone staring down at me. It was a friend of Kyle's. I threw him out and locked my bedroom door from that day forward.

Nonetheless at times Locke felt that she and Clint were making progress, getting closer, having fun when they saw each other. For a while she became his official escort, even at home, where he entertained the usual round of obligatory celebrities in Carmel, including Merv Griffin, whose advancing age and mania for "old" Hollywood held little social interest for Locke (or ultimately for Clint). Cary Grant and Lucille Ball were also regulars, although again, the age differences and levels of sophistication proved difficult for Locke to handle.

Gradually, though, Clint's social circle changed as the older members disappeared or died off, and it updated itself with the likes of TV producer Bud Yorkin and his wife, Arnold Schwarzenegger and Maria Shriver, Al Ruddy (the producer of *The Godfather*), and Richard Zanuck and his wife, Lili. Most of these were friends from Clint's vacation home in Sun Valley, a place Locke always enjoyed. This circle was closer in age, temperament, and love for physical sports like skiing, which made her feel more a part of Clint's life. And of course, they were all active filmmakers.

But really it was all over between them. It had always been Clint's style to act passively when a relationship was ending. He had kept Roxanne Tunis and their child on a back burner (of sorts), while his marriage to Maggie slowly flickered out. If Locke was going to put up with all of Clint's ways, Clint was not predisposed to do anything more than hope she would just go away.

Toward the end of his term, papal visits notwithstanding, Clint's restlessness with local politics finally led him to think about making a new movie, one that he had actually signed on to before he put his film career on voluntary hold.

The project was a biography of alto saxophonist Charlie "Bird" Parker that had been around for years in what is disaffectionately known in Hollywood as "development hell." He couldn't possibly play the lead, because Parker was African-American, but he could produce and direct without starring in the film. That prospect excited him but sent automatic shivers up the spine of Warner Bros.

While Clint was perhaps the most valuable single commodity Warner had in the post-studio era, much of his value came from his on-screen appearances. To date, he had directed only one other movie that he had

not starred in, the problematic 1973 all-but-forgotten *Breezy*, which did not even register in the top thirty of the forty-three films that he had appeared in (some of which he had also directed).

Probably no other actor-director at the time could have gotten *Bird* made the way he wanted to do it *except* Clint, who in 1988 accounted for a full 18 percent, nearly one fifth, of Warner's domestic revenues from films, plus an additional $1.5 million *per week* his movies generated internationally. A biography of a jazz musician, Charlie "Bird" Parker, who drank and drugged himself to death in the 1950s, filled with failure, despair, and death, was unlikely to find an audience with any kind of box-office pulse, especially with the all-important 18-to-25 rock-and-roll set who bought the majority of all theater tickets.

Like nearly every Clint Eastwood film, *Bird* was produced by Malpaso as a stand-alone project, which allowed Clint to rattle his saber and threaten to do business with another studio when the executives did something he didn't like. Because Clint's passion for *Bird* was so high, Terry Semel, not wanting to incur his wrath or, worse, lose the Eastwood/Malpaso franchise, put up no resistance, even though no one at Warner thought the film stood any chance at all of making a dime. Few films about jazz (excluding *The Jazz Singer*, Alan Crosland's 1927 box-office-busting novelty—the first talkie—which had absolutely nothing to do with jazz) had ever gotten made, let alone shown a profit in America. The best the studio hoped for was that the losses wouldn't be too big.

Clint had been indirectly involved in a film about jazz once before, Bertrand Tavernier's 1986 *'Round Midnight*, which lovingly followed the lives of several Paris-based American jazz expats. It won an Oscar for Original Score, awarded to Herbie Hancock, and gained a nomination for its star, Dexter Gordon. When that film's producer, Irwin Winkler, had shopped it, he had met a stone wall at the studios except at Warner, where Mark Rosenberg, then head of production, teetered on the fence. Clint exerted his influence to get the film green-lighted. Not long afterward Fox offered $3 million for the foreign rights. Winkler made the film with that foreign money, and it became one of the sleeper hits of 1986.

The script for *Bird* first came to Clint via a long and circuitous route, not unusual for projects the studios considered too fringe. Its writer, Joel Oliansky (also the originator of the project), had previously

written a mildly entertaining movie about a classical music competition (classical music was another studio no-no) that he also directed, *The Competition* (1980). The film did well enough to get him a plum assignment: writing an eight-hour historical miniseries for ABC, *Masada* (1981), for which he was nominated for an Emmy and got a contract from Columbia. They soon green-lighted *Bird*, his proposed feature film bio of Charlie Parker. Although he had been promised he could direct it, the studio eventually gave the project to Bob Fosse, who had been nominated for Best Director for his autobiographical *All That Jazz* (1979), a Broadway-based biopic.* *All That Jazz* had nothing to do with jazz, but the title was enough for Columbia to conclude that he was the perfect director for the film. But Fosse passed, and it came back to Oliansky.

Columbia's initial interest in the project was based on its belief that Richard Pryor would play the title role. But after Pryor nearly burned himself to death in 1980 in his infamous drug-related "accident," the studio put the project on the back burner. Five years later Warner revived interest in it as a possible vehicle for Prince, who had had an unexpected outsize hit with his semiautobiographical *Purple Rain* (1984, directed by Albert Magnoli). To get the Oliansky project, called at the time *Yardbird Suite*, from Columbia, Warner traded a script it had, called *Revenge*, to Ray Stark's Rastar, the longtime producer's company under exclusive contract to Columbia.†

When Prince's involvement ended, the script once more lay idle—until someone thought to send it to Clint. By now both Manes and Chernus were gone (Chernus had been Manes's assistant, and when Manes went, so did she), so Clint took to searching for projects on his own. When he found out that Semel had *Yardbird Suite* and nowhere to go with it, he requested a copy, read it, and decided he wanted to make the movie. He called Oliansky, and they met, but despite their shared interest in Parker, they failed to hit it off. Reportedly they fell out over the development part of the deal: Clint wanted Oliansky to do a rewrite, and Oliansky asked for rewrite money. Clint, perhaps feeling the writer should have been a little more grateful and cooperative for a project

---

*Fosse had earlier won the Oscar for Best Director in 1972 for *Cabaret*.

†*Revenge* was released in 1990, directed by Tony Scott, starring Kevin Costner and Anthony Quinn.

that had been sitting around for years, fixed the script himself, mostly cutting down on the dialogue. Clint kept Oliansky at arm's length for the rest of the movie.

Forest Whitaker was cast in the title role. Whitaker had made a name for himself in a trifecta of Scorsese's *The Color of Money* (1986), Oliver Stone's *Platoon* (1986), and Barry Levinson's *Good Morning, Vietnam* (1987). Production on *Bird* went smoothly, and Whitaker's performance was so strong that in the spring of 1988, when Clint took the film to Cannes, Whitaker walked off with the Best Actor vote. Unfortunately for Clint, it lost the Golden Palm to Argentinean Fernando Solanas for *Sur.* That loss put a drag on the film's momentum and slowed Warner's plan of release.

Disappointed at Cannes, Clint returned to the States and his mayoral duties. He quickly made two public announcements.

The first was that he was not going to run for a second two-year term as mayor of Carmel, putting an end to the collective fantasy that he would one day follow in Ronald Reagan's footsteps and make a successful run for the presidency. In truth, Clint had become disillusioned with local politics, finding most of it boring and mundane, and he had failed to bring a successful, definitive resolution to his Hog's Breath Inn battle with the city council that had made him run for the office in the first place. Eating ice cream in public somehow wasn't enough of a victory to motivate him to continue. Nor did the obligatory scrutiny that accompanied anything higher than small-town politics appeal to him. Exposure of the facts of his private life—rife with lovers and out-of-wedlock children before, during, and after his only marriage—would not only eliminate him from any serious run for larger office, but could conceivably damage his public image and, even possibly, his acting career. As he told the *Los Angeles Times* seven years later, "I would never have been able to pass the Bill Clinton–Gary Hart test . . . no one short of Mother Teresa could pass."

The second was that he was going to return to the well one more time to make another Dirty Harry film, the fifth, this one to be called *The Dead Pool.*

The screenplay came from the unlikeliest of sources, a pair of nutritionists whom Clint had known since at least the late 1970s. Durk Pearson and Sandy Shaw had a program they called Life Extension that promised, among other things, improved personal appearance,

reduced anxiety, and of course long life. Pearson was a graduate of MIT who had majored in physics; afterward he had devoted his life to searching for a way for a human being to live to 150 years without any appreciable loss of physical prowess or mental awareness—in effect, to double the human life expectancy. Pearson's method was built around large doses of vitamins and minerals and other assorted nutrients. Along the way he met and teamed with Sandy Shaw, a UCLA graduate with a degree in biochemistry who had studied the aging process extensively.

Clint first met Pearson and Shaw at a dinner arranged by Merv Griffin, who was already a devotee of the pair and wanted to turn Clint on to them. In 1981 Pearson and Shaw wrote a bestselling book called *Life Extension*, based on their theories and their applications. There they recounted a meeting with Griffin and "Mr. Smith," who was in fact Clint Eastwood; he had tried the megadosing and extreme exercise system and found it to be an extraordinary help to his overall health and his allergies. It even improved his ability to talk to interviewers, which in the past had always caused a bit of anxiety, reflected in uneasy word flow. In 1984, after years of evasions and denials, Clint finally admitted that he was "Mr. Smith."* His daily regimen included three-mile jogs, two hours in the gym, and two sessions of meditation; a low-fat, high-vegetable, meatless diet (save an occasional cheeseburger); and doses of choline, selenium, deanol, L-arginine, and L-dopa. He later claimed not to have needed reading glasses until he turned fifty-eight.

To many who knew the story, his purchase of the screenplay seemed something of a payback to Pearson and Shaw for having helped keep him fit enough to be able to make another Dirty Harry film. In fact, Pearson and Shaw had worked on a previous film of Clint's, serving as "consultants" on *Foxfire*, but they had been left uncredited to keep Clint's deeper involvement with them confidential.

Now Clint was willing to give them a full story credit. This new Dirty Harry project had the familiar story trope of the tracking of a serial killer. *The Dead Pool* (not to be confused with Stuart Rosenberg's 1975 Paul Newman vehicle, *The Drowning Pool*) involves a game of betting on how long a celebrity will live. (He or she has to die a natural

---

*"Mrs. Smith" was Sondra Locke.

death for the winner to collect.) Unfortunately the film had few of the psychological overtones or dramatic elements of *Tightrope*, and on-screen Clint appeared weary and uninvolved. He seems to be simply going through the motions.

With a script heavily rewritten by Steve Sharon, and with Buddy Van Horn directing (Horn was the stuntman who had directed Clint's comic turn in *Any Which Way You Can*), the film did not have much going for it. It did take a clever jab at a female film critic, unmistakably Pauline Kael (who, reviewing *Bird*, had wondered if Clint had paid the electric bill, meaning the film looked too dark to her). In a very early screen appearance Jim Carrey (billed as James Carrey) acted a deadly unfunny parody of a doomed rock star. *The Dead Pool* grossed about $59 million in its initial domestic release, which would have been good for most films but was disappointing for a Dirty Harry movie. It did nothing so much as signal that the franchise was finally and forever dead.*

By the end of 1988, the arc of Clint's career appeared finally to have curved downward. The drop was neither fast nor sharp enough to cause alarm, but the glory days seemed to have faded into the sunset. To be fair, only a few actors from the 1960s were still box-office draws—among them Paul Newman and Dustin Hoffman—but even their movies were nothing like the ones that had brought them to prominence earlier in their careers.

Clint decided the time had come to take a good, long, hard, and realistic look at his career and his life. And to once and for all get rid of Sondra Locke.

He had continually tried to widen the growing distance between them, accelerating it after the box-office failure of *Ratboy*. He knew it wasn't going to be easy, but it made no difference; the time had come to remove himself from her life, and she from his.

What he didn't anticipate was how difficult, ugly, embarrassing, and costly that was going to be.

---

*The Dead Pool was released before *Bird.* Both Warner and Clint agreed that *The Dead Pool* was a better summer film, while *Bird* might have a chance in early September. *The Dead Pool* received a national release in several hundred theaters; *Bird* was released in only a few cities and less than a dozen theaters.

EIGHTEEN

There is only one way to have a happy marriage, and as soon as I learn what it is I'll get married again.

—Clint Eastwood

Approaching his sixtieth birthday, Clint Eastwood wanted to clean house, literally and figuratively. The only property he actually owned in Los Angeles was the house he was leasing to Locke. She had to go, and there was no point in putting it off any longer, but California law had an especially sticky issue called palimony. The word had come into the popular lexicon in the late 1970s, after Lee Marvin's live-in girlfriend successfully sued for support when they broke up. That court decision sent a chill down the spines of the Hollywood social set, where it had once been business as usual for a star or an upper executive, married or single, to keep a girlfriend, maybe a pretty starlet, stashed in an apartment, with a car and a credit card, until the heat cooled, at which point the gal-pal had to give up everything and leave.

Clint, like most stars, enjoyed a lot of different women, and his privileged life allowed him to live by his own social (or antisocial) rules. By now his pattern had long been set. He had liked being married, or at least the appearance of it. Unquestionably it had been good for his image in his *Rawhide* days, when moral clauses hung on actors' backs wherever they went, and their personal indiscretions, real or suspected, were discussed in the powerful and feared *Confidential Magazine*, the forerunner of today's celebrity gossip megaindustry. Marriage to Maggie, even with all its restrictions and compromises, had given his life some structure and his image some sanitation. And to ensure that his real-life image did not clash too much with the righteous character of Rowdy Yates, he made sure that Roxanne Tunis was content to live separately, raised their child as a single mother, and stayed far away from Clint's public persona. Locke, however, had not been as cooperative or as willingly conforming; in fact, she had committed a couple of unforgivable sins, for which he was now going to make her pay.

The first was that she had never divorced her husband, Gordon Anderson. Now Clint was, more or less, supporting him by allowing him to stay in the house he had bought in Hollywood; as for the house on Stradella Road that he had bought for Locke, Clint had kept it in his name and set up a lease arrangement that gave him all the control and all the power. He had moved Kyle in, but Locke had dug in her heels and apparently was as ready as Clint for the coming slugfest.

It's difficult to pinpoint exactly when the fading blossom finally fell from the tree, but sometime in the middle of 1988 the tensions between Clint and Locke visibly escalated over, of all things, a relatively minor pickup accident Locke may (or may not) have had while driving one of Clint's trucks outside Tower Records on Sunset Boulevard, at the time the most popular music megastore in L.A. A motorcyclist claimed he had been hit by the pickup in Tower's parking lot.

The incident made Clint furious when the motorcyclist sued his auto insurance company. When Clint confronted Locke about it, she claimed she couldn't remember having had an accident in his pickup at Tower or anywhere else. Clint did not believe her. He took away her driving privileges and told her that from now on she was to drive her own car—not his pickup, not his blue Mercedes, just her own vehicle. And, he added, with emphasis, that went for Gordon as well.

When Locke took the bait and defended Gordon, Clint's response was "Well, I've divorced Maggie, but you haven't divorced Gordon." To Locke, he seemed to be invoking their not being married as one more reason why he was angry. Understandably, this made no sense to Locke, who called him on it. "Do you want us to get married now, Clint?"

"That's not the point," he barked. "You should do it without my asking you; you should make yourself available. I can't ask if you're not available."

It sounded right, but Locke wasn't buying any of it. She believed that it was just one of Clint's ploys to get Gordon out of his life as well as hers. Then two seemingly unrelated incidents cut Clint's slow-burning fuse down to ignition.

The first was a new film and a directing deal that Locke had managed to secure from Warner, green-lighted by Terry Semel and producer Lucy Fisher. The project was originally called *Sudden Impulse*, a psychological thriller with a female lead that Semel thought, based on the original *Ratboy*, Locke would be perfect for. She wanted to find

a new name for it, though, lest Clint think it too close to *Sudden Impact*, in which she had starred with him a few years back.

According to Locke, however, even before she could make that change, Clint began doing everything he could to make the project difficult for her. "Suddenly, he'd want me to travel with him only when he *knew* I had an important meeting. When we were at the ranch, each time [producer] Al Ruddy would phone me, Clint would sit down at the piano and immediately start banging out Scott Joplin tunes as loudly as he could."

The second incident was the annual Christmas vacation that Locke and Clint had taken ever since they had known each other; Christmas Eve had been reserved for just the two of them, no matter how many other people were in their lives. But in 1988, just weeks before the holidays, Clint casually informed her that he was going to be spending them by himself, in Carmel, playing golf. Locke then spent Christmas with Gordon. Then, as she prepared for her annual New Year's Eve ski trip with Clint, she received a call from Jane Brolin. Brolin invited her to come to Sun Valley—where Locke was planning to go anyway— and told her that Kyle and Alison were coming too. Locke, fearing the worst, flew to Sun Valley on a private Warner plane with Brolin and Clint's two children.

The next morning, in Sun Valley, Brolin confronted Locke, telling her that she was really not wanted in the group. It was a bizarre confrontation, and the first thing Locke thought was that Clint was making Jane do his dirty work for him. Words were exchanged between the two women that quickly escalated into a screaming match. Just as it reached the neck-vein-popping state, Clint walked in, listened to the two of them, and told both of them to take the Warner jet and go home.

Locke tearfully packed and left. Brolin stayed with Clint.

As soon as the holidays were over, Locke went to see a lawyer, Norman Oberstein, who suggested that this was perhaps not the right time to start a legal proceeding.

Clint, meanwhile, was spending much of his free time with actress Frances Fisher, with whom he was quite taken. On the morning of April 4, 1990, he dropped by the house on Stradella Road and waited in the living room until Locke came down the stairs. His presence

startled her. He was there, he said, to tell her he wanted her to leave the house. Locke, who was preparing to direct her film, was shocked into silence. With nothing left to say, Clint simply turned and walked out the door.

On April 10, while Locke was at Warner, Clint personally came by the house again and this time changed the locks. That same day he had Locke served with a hand-delivered written notice, on set, that she was no longer welcome at Stradella and no longer had any legal access to it. All her belongings had been taken to Gordon's house on Crescent Heights, the one Clint had bought for him. When Locke read the notice, she fainted.

Meanwhile, Clint had been busy working on a new movie, *Pink Cadillac*. Three years had passed since his last legitimate box-office success, *Heartbreak Ridge*, and he hoped this new film would finally turn things around for him. It was a working-class country cowboy film with a slightly harder edge, even a few echoes of Dirty Harry; a noticeable absence of singing and simians; the addition of the lovely Bernadette Peters; and an appearance by still relatively unknown Jim Carrey (billed as "James"), his second Clint movie.

In it, Clint plays Tommy Nowak, a tough skip-tracer assigned to find Lou Ann McGuinn (Peters, in a nonsinging, against-type role), an equally tough young mama who has taken off with her baby after being indicted for possession of counterfeit money. McGuinn's oppressive husband Roy (Timothy Carhart) has of late been hanging out with the toughest guys of all, a gang of white supremacists, the Birthright, who are the real counterfeiters. Lou Ann's method of escape turns out to be her husband's pink Cadillac. Somewhere along the way she finds some funny money in the car, drops off the baby with her sister, and heads for the nearest casino, where Nowak catches up with her. In a reversal (the script had more twists than a corkscrew), the money in the car turns out to be real. Even as Nowak and McGuinn are discovering this fact, the Birthright had sent a team of killers to kill McGuinn to recapture the money. Eventually, there is a confrontation, a shoot-out, and guess what, Nowak and McGuinn beat the bad guys, realize they are in love, and live happily ever after, or something approximating that within the confines of their colorless and uninspired lives. The

film is meant to be a comedy with dramatic overtones, or a drama with comic overtones—it's difficult to tell which.

To direct, Clint called in his former stuntman Buddy Van Horn, who had helmed two previous Clint movies (*Any Which Way You Can* and *The Dead Pool*), while he, Clint, pulled his performance out of his back pocket.

Peters was more familiar to Broadway audiences than to filmgoers; Clint had hired her, it appeared to several witnesses on the set, simply because he was attracted to her. Clint's interior logic may have been that if he were attracted to his costar, his audiences would be too. Peters and Clint had good chemistry on-screen, but she showed no real-life romantic interest in Clint. At that point Clint turned his attention back to Frances Fisher, who was playing the small part of Dinah, Peters's sister.

Locke, still busy making her movie, kept hearing that Clint was running around town with Fisher, and in a fit of pique she went back to see Oberstein. This time he agreed the time had come to take action. The first thing he wanted was for Locke and Gordon to sign a severance agreement. In effect, this meant that while they were still married, Gordon voluntarily surrendered his access to any and all of Locke's property. The purpose was to remove Clint's possible defense that Locke's relationship with Gordon had a financial motive or that she was still beholden to him in any way.

Once they signed it, Oberstein (at Locke's insistence) met with Clint's attorney, Bruce Ramer, to see if any kind of informal resolution between the two was possible. Ramer said the only thing Clint would agree to was that Gordon could keep his house, but Locke had to remain out of Stradella. When Oberstein relayed Clint's conditions, Locke knew she had no choice but to go ahead and sue.

The story of the impending lawsuit hit the national press with all the force of a Hollywood hurricane. In the tabloids it wiped everything else off their front pages for weeks, echoing the highly volatile (and endlessly entertaining) ten-year-old palimony case between Lee Marvin and Michelle Triola that had all but ended Marvin's career.

Clint did not want to be part of anything like that, especially at a time when his career seemed in decline. *Pink Cadillac* had opened on Memorial Day weekend, the traditional start of the big-money,

big-production summertime run of movies. But it disappeared quickly in the wake of mostly negative reviews (Richard Freedman, writing for the Newhouse News Services syndicate, called it "a 122 minute dozer") and the cinematic tsunami that was Steven Spielberg's *Indiana Jones and the Last Crusade*. In its first ten days, *Pink Cadillac* did about $6 million against *Indiana*'s $38 million, making *Pink Cadillac* one of the biggest flops in Clint's and Malpaso's history. (And it all but ended Peters's film career.) Whether or not the negative publicity surrounding the emerging legal slugfest between him and Locke had anything to do with it, the film simply did not draw the usual Clint crowd.

Even as *Pink Cadillac* was opening and closing, Clint was already planning his next film, *White Hunter Black Heart*, to be shot on location near Lake Kariba in Zimbabwe, an attractive place even more attractive to Clint because it was so far away. Fisher was not invited and, reportedly, did not even receive a good-bye phone call from Clint before he left.

But before he could leave, he received notice that Locke had gone ahead and filed a $70 million "palimony" lawsuit against him. Locke's revelations of Clint's philandering, and her two abortions—now a matter of public record—proved irresistible reading. The public consensus was surprisingly in Clint's favor, however, as it appeared to most that Locke was putting a noose around his neck in order to save her own pretty face.

If Hollywood was biased in Clint's favor as it hadn't been in Marvin's, the reason was not hard to understand. Despite his last few failures, Clint remained one of the most powerful, if not *the* most powerful, actor-producer-directors in post-studio-era Hollywood. He had built a human tower of strength on the back of Malpaso, and his thirty-five-year, forty-seven-film career had generated billions of dollars for the industry and untold jobs for actors, directors, screenwriters, and set designers, all the way down to the weekend popcorn vendors in the neighborhood movies.

Moreover, everyone in Hollywood who didn't work with him loved him, which meant they hoped one day to work with him. He had a reputation for being fast and easy, liked to be hitting the links by early afternoon, and generally let the actors play their roles the way they wanted to. The studio suits may not have liked his way of doing business, but they lived in fear—Hollywood's only known true emotion—

that if they somehow offended Clint, they might not be able to continue to pay the second mortgage on their beach houses. Marvin had been nothing more than a fading actor, and Locke had appeared in one noteworthy movie and six Clint films and had thus far directed one unsuccessful movie.*

Locke's legal team pressed for immediate depositions to prevent Clint from being able to leave for Africa without giving them. According to Locke, "My [oral] deposition was nothing short of hell." Clint's litigator for the depositions, Howard King, led a fierce attack on Locke's character and motivations. She loved fairy tales, as she had told Clint many times, and King tried to somehow establish that she was living in one in her own mind, casting Clint as her rescuer, her savior, her knight in shining armor. He pressed her on her longtime marriage to Gordon and why she had never divorced him. He wanted to know if she had had other sexual relations while living with Clint. He condemned her for "stealing" another woman's husband.

The deposition drove her to see a psychiatrist.

Then it was Oberstein's turn to put Clint on the grill. For six hours Oberstein focused on Clint's "real" intentions with the house on Stradella, pointing out that Clint had originally intended, via his will (which he had since had rewritten several times), to leave it to Locke. In response to a question regarding the nature of their relationship, Clint suggested they had only gone steady but had not lived together on a formal basis, because Locke was married to Gordon. A "part-time roommate" was how Clint characterized Locke. Pressed to explain that definition, Clint said that "anytime a person spends one night it's part-time." Oberstein confronted Clint with the fact that he had wiretapped Stradella's phone; he responded that he had been the victim of a stalker and had been simply trying to gather evidence to build a case against him—or her. On more than one occasion, he said, Locke had threatened to kill him. Later, in her autobiography, Locke described these accusations as "ridiculous, preposterous and a slanderous lie."

A week later a closed-door preliminary hearing was held, to determine if Locke should be allowed back into Stradella. A variety of

---

*The six Clint films were *The Outlaw Josey Wales, The Gauntlet, Every Which Way but Loose, Bronco Billy, Any Which Way You Can,* and *Sudden Impact.*

players, pro and con, mostly friends and relatives, testified in support of their respective sides. Jane Brolin testified that whenever she stayed with Clint at Stradella, which she often had, she couldn't help but notice how much of Locke's clothing and personal items were there. And she was testifying for Clint. It was, to say the least, a strange strategy on Clint's part; it made him look more like a playboy than he might have wanted; Brolin's interest in Locke's belongings may have seemed like snooping.

It came out, under cross, that Brolin had been the "unnamed source" for many of those *National Enquirer* "exclusive" stories about the deteriorating relationship between Locke and Clint and also the likely source of those poison-pen letters. Kyle testified that he was the primary tenant at Stradella Road. And Clint revealed here for the first time that he had had two children with Jacelyn Reeves, a girl, Kathryn, and a boy, Scott. Until then no one had known for sure who was the father of her children, as the birth certificate for both had read, "Father declined." The existence of these children came as a complete shock to Locke, who had had no idea Clint had begun yet another family, with another woman, during their time together.

Locke was granted interim support but was denied palimony, the judge ruled, because she had been married to another man while she was involved with Clint. But because the case was in arbitration, the decision was not binding. Locke declined to accept the ruling and pressed for a full hearing in Los Angeles Superior Court. That June, while she continued her case, Locke rented a relatively modest apartment for the duration on Fountain Avenue, in West Hollywood, and resumed postproduction on her project, now called *Impulse*.

While the hearing moved to the next court, Clint left it to his lawyers to fight it out and finally took off for Africa, accompanied by Jane Brolin.

White Hunter Black Heart was another of Clint's personal anti-genre films on the order of *Bird*. It was a thinly disguised biographical portrait of John Huston, one of the most respected directors in Hollywood. Novelist Peter Viertel had written a stunning roman à clef about Huston's experiences on location in the Congo while filming his award-winning *The African Queen* (1951). The novel revealed

Huston's on-location obsession with drinking and bagging an elephant on safari.

It seemed an odd choice for Clint. Why did he make it? He said, in his own words:

> A fellow by the name of Stanley Rubin, who I'd met a long time ago at the beginning of the fifties when he was a producer at Universal, was working for Ray Stark, and he asked me whether I'd be interested in reading a script that had been hanging around in Columbia's offices for quite a while along with some others . . . I met Peter Viertel and found out the whole story of the novel, how he began to write it and the adventures of the pre-production period for *The African Queen*. It fascinated me, as obsessive behavior always does . . . It was a very interesting character to explore.

In *White Hunter Black Heart* John Wilson (Clint) is about to kill an elephant when he has a sudden change of heart that instead causes the death of his native guide, Kivu (Boy Mathias Chuma), a Gunga Din type, the only person in the film Wilson cares about. Branded by the villagers as a white hunter with a black heart, Wilson returns to his only real love, making movies, in this case to finish the film he has ostensibly come to make. Art endures over life, as in the last shot of the film, Wilson shouts, "Action!"

It was as near a statement of self-definition as the tight-lipped Clint would ever give. Huston was someone he could identify with both as a filmmaker and as a contradictory personality; his flamboyance was both extravagant and selective, generous and thrifty, kindhearted and mean-spirited. And as both actor and director, often for the same project, Huston had made mostly genre films (like *The Maltese Falcon* and *The African Queen*, both of which he had only directed) that were also personal statements, and offbeat, quirky films that were still meant to be "big" (like *Freud*, for which he was both director and narrator) but never attained the kind of attention or box office he felt they deserved.

With *Bird* and now *White Hunter Black Heart*, Clint was steadily moving toward films that were, in many ways, thinly veiled autobiographies: Charlie Parker, the musical genius who went against the

prevalent tide, only to leave a tidal wave in his wake; Huston, the physically daunting director-actor whose films did not always fit into a commercial category but nevertheless left an afterburn in the mind. Most interestingly, Huston was given to excess and lacked self-discipline. In other words, he was the exact opposite of Clint, whose self-discipline—both in filmmaking and in personal health regimens—was well known to anyone who had ever worked with him. As an all-warts homage, the film was Clint's way of humanizing and idolizing Huston (and himself) at the same time.

When filming was completed late in August, Clint returned to the States via London, where he met up with Maggie. Her marriage to Wynberg was on the rocks, and she wanted to see how Clint was handling the devolution of his own relationship with Locke into legal and emotional acrimony. It mattered to her if Clint was over Locke. Of all his indiscretions, she was the one whom Maggie had always blamed for the breakup of her marriage to Clint. Moreover, she and Clint were still business partners in a number of enterprises, the result of their complex divorce settlement, and the parents of two children. Maggie also told Clint that he had to try to play a stronger, more influential role in Kyle's and Alison's life.

And there was something else, Maggie told him. In the wake of his sensational palimony trial, she had learned along with everyone else that Clint was the father of a daughter, Kimber, who had been born to Roxanne Tunis, while Maggie and Clint were still married. Presumably Maggie had a few things to tell Clint about that. He listened to all she wanted or needed to say and did not argue or disagree.

Upon his return to L.A., Clint quietly resumed his relationship with Frances Fisher, and while the palimony case dragged on, he began postproduction work on *White Hunter Black Heart*. In May 1990 he took the finished version to Cannes where, inexplicably, he denied to the press that he had based his performance on John Huston. The cineast-heavy audiences and highly literate critics, well aware of the history of *The African Queen*, were puzzled as to what the film could otherwise possibly be about.

That September Clint showed it at the Telluride Film Festival in Colorado, where it was given a less-than-spectacular reception.

White Hunter Black Heart opened in the fall of 1990, and earned less than $8 million in its initial domestic release, one of the worst-grossing films of his career.

Entering his fifth decade of moviemaking, with three film failures in a row, and mired in a very public palimony trial, he went directly into production on a straight genre *policier*, albeit with a slight twist. Rather than playing his trademark loner, he would try to lure more youthful audiences by sharing the screen with a much younger and extremely popular male costar, Charlie Sheen. A rookie (Sheen) comes under Officer Nick Pulovski's (Clint's) wing, after Pulovski's last partner was killed by a stolen-car gang run by ruthless Latin murderers. The film, called *The Rookie*, had a script by Boaz Yakin and Scott Spiegel that seemed a pale imitation—some critics thought it an out-and-out spoof—of the Dirty Harry films, minus the dirt and minus Harry. Not that the film lacked appeal. Sonia Braga, playing a sadomasochistic murderess named Liesl, handcuffs and ties Clint to a chair, rapes him rather graphically, then comes this close to killing him until he miraculously escapes. It was an explosive sequence, and the only one in the film that people talked about. As obviously provocative and exploitative as it was, *ars gratia artis*, the scene may also be read as conveying Clint's feeling victimized at the hands of a beautiful but bad woman. In the scene, Liesl has him handcuffed, sexually tortured, and imprisoned and wants to kill him even as she is making love to him. And she is, in the end, killed by Clint's big gun.

The film received mixed-to-negative reviews but did better at the box office than any of his recent films, prompting Vincent Canby in the *New York Times* to wonder how Clint could reach so high and fail with *White Hunter Black Heart* and reach so low and succeed with *The Rookie*. Rushed into Christmas 1990 release, it grossed $43 million in its initial domestic release. It was good enough to stop the slide, but by no means a great film or even a very good one.

Two more years would pass before Clint made another movie.

FROM AUTEUR TO OSCAR

Unforgiven *ends the trajectory begun in* Fistful of Dollars. *Instead of having no family, or just starting a family, this time East-wood's character has a family—again, with no woman in the picture, at least not a living one.*

—Brett Westbrook

PREVIOUS PAGE: *Clint's long overdue double Oscar win in 1992 for* Unforgiven: *Best Picture and Best Director.*

In April 1990 Locke's movie, *Impulse*, opened to fairly decent reviews, including a coveted thumbs-up from the influential TV and print critics Siskel and Ebert, which usually helped boost a film's box office. Nevertheless, according to Locke, "Warner barely released the film. And on opening weekend in the few theaters in Los Angeles, the ad in the newspaper didn't even use the Siskel and Ebert review." Even worse for Locke, a few weeks after the movie's spring release, Lucy Fisher told her that, regrettably, Warner was dropping the other three projects she had in various stages of development with them.

As emotionally undone as Locke was during this time, and as fiercely as she pointed the finger at Clint for everything that had gone wrong in her life, she had no legitimate reason to believe that he had had anything to do with Warner's decision. Perhaps Warner dumped Locke because she had violated the industry-wide dictum against washing dirty laundry in public; if so, it was presumably a business decision, pure and simple. Business in Hollywood is a constant tightrope walk, attempting to balance art and commerce. In the years between her Academy Award nomination and *Impulse*, Locke's career had gone nowhere. She had not become a big star, and her films were never going to produce the kind of revenue Clint Eastwood's films had. In other words, she was expendable.

But, according to Locke, all of it was personal and connected, and all of it was due to Clint's furious need for vengeance. In her memoir she quotes Clint telling a friend, "Does she want to become a director or become Michelle Marvin? I'll drag her ass through court, until there's nothing left. I'll never settle with her; I paid her for jobs in movies, now she wants to be paid for love too?"

The postdeposition litigation was going nowhere, and meanwhile, Locke was racking up huge bills. Hoping to cut through it all, she

simply picked up the phone and called Clint, asking if they could meet. Clint agreed, and the next day she came over to his office. She insists that Clint then started to flirt with her. In response, she asked him to drop his lawsuit. He exploded, insisting that she had started it, that if now she was desperate or broke, she should get a job as a waitress, and that he would accept a rapprochement, in which she also accepted returning to him as his lover, only "with no strings attached."*

Locke then wrote to Clint, hoping that the printed word would prevent his emotions from interfering with her attempt to settle. Clint's written reply to Locke was short and impersonal: "I owe you nothing."

Hoping to get a new start in Hollywood, Locke left the William Morris Agency and signed with agent David Gersh, who quickly got her a new deal at Orion Pictures for *Oh Baby*, a romantic comedy that she could easily direct.

She was all set to begin casting when she noticed a lump on her right breast. It proved malignant. That September of 1990, instead of beginning work on the new film, she entered the hospital for a double mastectomy.

In November, while she was still in the early stages of recuperation, producer Al Ruddy told her that he was willing to act as a go-between, to try to settle things between her and Clint before the start of the trial, scheduled for March 1991. Ruddy told her that Clint was willing to drop his lawsuit if she would drop hers; that Gordon could keep the house on Crescent Heights; and he would see to it that she got her development deals back at Warner. She would also receive $450,000 in cash if she gave up all future claims to Stradella Road and agreed never to sue him for anything again.

Locke was weary from her battles with Clint and her recent surgery; and her medical bills were piling up. Without thinking about why Clint would suddenly change his position and try to make peace, Locke accepted the offer.

....

*Clint has never commented on the meeting or even acknowledged that it took place.

It had taken two years to settle with Locke (and to settle another unrelated but nagging lawsuit that had erupted with a civilian over a car accident). Now Clint felt he was finally ready to make another movie, and he chose a western to do it with. It was a wise choice; westerns had always been good to him. He had, after all, begun his career with TV westerns and had made his big-screen breakthrough with westerns; now he would make his comeback in one, something called *Unforgiven*.

Clint had had the script under option for several years. Written by a relatively unknown screenwriter, it had stayed on the back burner until Clint could find someone other than himself who could better play the lead role (unlikely, as the part was perfectly suited for Clint), or (as he sometimes told interviewers after it opened, and which was far more likely) he felt he was old enough to credibly play the lead role. Even more revealing, perhaps, was what he told *Cahiers du cinéma* just before its European run:

> Why a western? That seemed to be the only possible genre the story was calling for, because in fact everything grew out of the story. In any case, I've never thought of doing anything because it's *in fashion*, on the contrary I've always felt a need to go against it . . . as for what makes this Western different from the others, it seems to me that the film deals with violence and its consequences a lot more than those I've done before. In the past, there were a lot of people killed gratuitously in my pictures, and what I liked about this story was that people aren't killed, and acts of violence aren't perpetrated, without there being certain consequences. That's a problem I thought it was important to talk about today; it takes on proportions it didn't have in the past, even if it's always been present through the ages.

Unforgiven was the kind of story Clint could film in his sleep. Even before a single shot was filmed, he knew exactly how he wanted it to look.

Originally called *The Cut-Whore Killings*, the film's name was later changed to *The William Munny Killings*. Neither title Clint

especially liked. *Unforgiven* was the brainchild of David Webb Peoples, a Berkeley English major who upon graduation worked as an editor in TV news, then moved on to documentary films. In 1981, with his wife, Janet, and Jon Else, he wrote and edited the documentary *The Day After Trinity*, about the development of the atomic bomb. Directed by Else, it was good enough to be nominated for an Academy Award for Best Documentary.

The film's success sent Peoples searching his desk drawers for anything he had that was immediately salable. There he found the screenplay he had written five years before *The Day After Trinity*, *The Cut-Whore Killings*. At the time it had gone nowhere, but now he was able to get it optioned.

Each time the film's option ran out, it got passed around for renewal. Eventually, via Megan Rose, it came to Clint, who read the script, liked it, and when it became available, bought it outright, and then put it in *his* drawer, waiting until the time felt right to make it.

It might very well have gotten made in 1985, as his elegiac summation and farewell to the genre that had launched his career, but then *Pale Rider* had come along and became that movie. Now, in search of something to push back the ever-louder industry rumors that he was washed up, Clint once more reached for his most dependable genre, the western, and produced, directed, and starred in *Unforgiven*. To ensure that the film was a big enough hit to return him to glory, he pulled out all the stops (or as many as he could bear without sending the budget skyrocketing).

In typical Clint fashion, the film was shot quickly and inexpensively, with very little done to the original script. According to Clint, "I started rewriting it and talked to David about it. I said I would like to do this, do that, write a couple of scenes . . . but the more I started fiddling with it, [the more I] realized I was disassembling a lot of blocks that were holding it together. I finally called him up one night and said, 'Forget about all those rewrites I was talking about. I like it just the way it is.' "

Set in fictitious Big Whiskey, Wyoming, the film was shot in Calgary, Alberta, using the best talent in the business to bring the town and the movie to life. At the head of this list was Henry Bumstead, who had last worked for Clint twenty years earlier on *High Plains Drifter* and who was still one of Hollywood's most sought-after production designers and art directors. Bumstead was probably best known to the

public for his work on Robert Mulligan's *To Kill a Mockingbird* (1962), for which he won an Oscar,* and on Alfred Hitchcock's *The Man Who Knew Too Much* (1956) and *Vertigo* (1957).†

Mood was essential to *Unforgiven*, and Bumstead's work proved a key ingredient to help visualize the feeling that the vengeful living walk among the living dead, waiting for their turn at mythic immortality. It took Bumstead only a month and a day to build the entire set, on which Clint wanted every scene filmed, including interiors, to give the film a stylistic cohesion no ordinary soundstage could match.

Also for *Unforgiven*, Clint chose to work with other big-name stars, something he rarely did on Malpaso films. Morgan Freeman played Ned Logan, Munny's (Clint's) former partner in crime who joins him one last time to collect the reward money posted by the town prostitutes, led by Strawberry Alice (Frances Fisher, another real-life girl-friend of Clint's cast as a prostitute) for the capture of the men responsible for mutilation and murder of one of their own (Delilah, played by Anna Thomson), after Big Whiskey's corrupt and bullying sheriff, the fascistic Little Bill Daggett (Gene Hackman), let them go free. Several bounty-hunters are drawn to Big Whiskey hoping to collect the reward, including English Bob (Richard Harris) and his "biographer," W. W. Beauchamp (Saul Rubinek). The only lesser-known principal member of this cast besides Fisher was Jaimz Woolvett, who plays the Schofield Kid, a young gunslinger wannabe who longs to become the legend that Munny once was.

Several unexpected plot reversals give the film more irony and depth than any previous Clint Eastwood movie, while referencing many of them. Munny is a gunslinger of legendary proportions, who has renounced his murderous past and tried to make amends by going straight, marrying, having children, and raising pigs on a farm. Much of Munny's character and action has been developed and performed before the film begins (not unlike Shane, the cinematic model for *Pale Rider*'s Preacher). Munny sets out to collect the reward with the same sense of mission that was suggested in the Leone trilogy. In *Unforgiven*

---

*For Best Black and White Art Direction. He also won for Art Direction for George Roy Hill's *The Sting* (1973) and was nominated but did not win for *Vertigo*.

†Bumstead's career began in the 1940s. He died in 2006, following work on Clint's *Flags of Our Fathers* and *Letters from Iwo Jima*.

it is as if the Man with No Name has returned to gunfighting, older, weary, and repentant, because he needs the money to raise his children after his wife has died, but also because that's who he is, a gunfighter, a man whose destiny must be fulfilled. In that sense, the inevitable violent and horrific climax of *Unforgiven*, during which Munny avenges not just the murdered prostitute but also Ned Logan, killed by Daggett, is an elegant evocation of Heraclitus' well-known dictum about character and fate being one and the same. It is Munny's fate to kill Daggett because that is his character (much as it is Daggett's fate to be killed because that is his). In *Unforgiven*, as in several of the Dirty Harry movies (perhaps most vividly *Magnum Force*), justice may be evil but evil may be just.

And finally English Bob's biographer, W. W. Beauchamp, as played by Saul Rubinek, is so corrupt, cowardly, self-promoting, and unconcerned about truth (and unable to stand up for it) that history itself becomes suspect. Legend blends into fact when, in a coda, the audience is left to wonder what really happened to Munny. In a sense, Beauchamp represents for Clint all writers (biographers included) and probably none more so than film critics, who too often play loose and easy with movies and set up straw heroes and villains to knock down in the name of their own brilliance.

Other strings that run through the film are racism, sexism, and vainglory, all of which come together to one incredible climax that resolves, as do all the great westerns—and in a larger metaphorical sense, all great movies—in one of the most powerful gunfights ever filmed.

And it was all shot in less than a month.*

The pre-release buzz on this film was enormous from the start. The cast included two actors at the top of their respective games— Morgan Freeman, who had been nominated for Best Actor for Bruce Beresford's *Driving Miss Daisy* (1989), and Gene Hackman, who had won Best Actor for *The French Connection* (1972). Years before the script even came to Clint, Hackman had turned down the role of Munny. He'd also turned down the role of Daggett when Clint offered

---

*Ever actor-superstitious, Clint's talisman for this film was the boots he wore, the same ones he had worn for much of the making of *Rawhide*. In 2005 he loaned them to that year's Sergio Leone exhibit at the Gene Autry Museum of Western Heritage in Los Angeles, California.

it to him because he felt he was too violent and repulsive a character, until Clint somehow managed to convince him the film carried a strong antiviolence message. Richard Harris, an offbeat Irishman born in Limerick City, had hung around inside the Hollywood A-list long after his best movies were behind him; those who saw advance footage of his scenes said it was the performance of his career.

Because of all the good advance word, Warner volunteered to take over the film's promotion. Clint would normally have rejected the offer but this time readily agreed. Almost every previous Malpaso film had been promoted independently by Charles Gold and Kitty Dutton, whom Clint had hired, via Malpaso, during Warner's Frank Wells period, when he had little faith in the studio's ability to promote films. Now that Terry Semel and Bob Daley were in charge, the studio had become far more aggressive, and they convinced Clint they could do a better job than Malpaso on this one.

Several press junkets were arranged—Clint had been opposed to them before *Unforgiven*—and Richard Schickel, the film critic and documentary filmmaker, was allowed virtually unlimited access to produce a "making of the movie" promotional short. Jack Mathews of the *Los Angeles Times* was allowed aboard, as was Peter Biskind of the then relatively new and highly influential *Premiere* magazine, which had a *Rolling Stone* look and similarly hip style of reporting for movies. Numerous theatrical tie-ins and promotions, contests, and one-on-one interviews with Clint were arranged.* And something nobody thought they would ever see: Clint actually agreed to go on *The Tonight Show* to hawk the film.

The reason for all this atypical accessibility was not hard to understand. Clint still wanted to win an Academy Award. It was as simple as that. He would be sixty-two when the film came out, the fiftieth film that he had either appeared in, or directed, or both, and if it was ever going to happen, the time was now.

*U*nforgiven, dedicated to Sergio Leone and Don Siegel in its closing credits, opened August 7, 1992. August is a month where summer films that are not expected to do well are released; the best are given

---

*The interviews were nearly identical, and as always Clint's stock answers revealed little about himself. Questions were limited to the subject of the film.

the Memorial Day weekend slot, the next July Fourth, the also-rans after that. But with this film, the Daley-Semel strategy was to separate *Unforgiven* from the year's other big summer films that included Tim Burton's *Batman Returns* and Phillip Noyce's *Patriot Games* starring Harrison Ford, both of which opened before August.

The strategy paid off big time, with a $14 million opening weekend, Clint's best ever. Not only was his career resurrected, but suddenly he was the hottest actor *and* director in Hollywood. *Unforgiven* went on to gross $160 million in its initial domestic theatrical release and an additional $50 million overseas, placing it behind only Clint's two orangutan films as the highest grossers of his career to date.

That winter, when the Oscar nominations were announced, to no one's surprise, Clint and his film were prominent among them. *Unforgiven* was nominated for Best Picture, pitting Clint as producer against Neil Jordan's quirky, sexually ambiguous, highly original, and completely riveting *The Crying Game;* Rob Reiner's military courtroom drama *A Few Good Men*, which starred three of Hollywood's then-hottest stars, Jack Nicholson, Tom Cruise, and Demi Moore, and that carried the added imprimatur of having been a recent Broadway stage hit; James Ivory's *Howards End*, the obligatory prestige nomination that showed the world how literary Hollywood could be; and Martin Brest's bizarre *Scent of a Woman*, about a blind man who can really "see," starring Al Pacino as the "hoo-wa" man.

Clint was also nominated for Best Actor, a long-awaited first that put him up against Robert Downey Jr.'s facile Charlie in Richard Attenborough's windy biography *Chaplin;* Stephen Rea's affecting performance as an Irish subversive in *The Crying Game;* Denzel Washington in the title role of Spike Lee's *Malcolm X;* and Pacino.

He was also nominated for Best Director, against Robert Altman—for his inside-is-hell exposé of Hollywood amorality, *The Player*—Martin Brest, James Ivory, and Neil Jordan.

Other major nominations for *Unforgiven* included Best Supporting Actor for Gene Hackman, and Best Screenplay for Peoples.

On March 29, 1993, the night of the awards, a smiling, silver-haired Clint showed up resplendent in a tuxedo and tie, with a not-yet-showing pregnant Frances Fisher on his arm. The usual Academy dross that passes for humor and entertainment was kicked off by host

Billy Crystal being driven onstage in a chariot by Jack Palance, the unlikely winner of the previous year's Best Supporting Actor Oscar for Ron Underwood's *City Slickers*, thereby robbing himself and the ceremonies of any last shred of dignity.

The theme of the show was "Women in Film," and although memorable women's roles and performances were few that year, the appearance of Elizabeth Taylor and the presenting of a Jean Hersholt Award to the recently departed Audrey Hepburn sent an electric charge through the audience as the evening crawled toward the expected coronation of Clint Eastwood. One bump in the road came when the Best Actor Oscar went to Al Pacino, for one of the lesser performances of his career, not long after Gene Hackman had won for Best Supporting Actor. In a night that was a Vegas gambler's delight, always in danger of sidestepping the favorites, Clint braced himself.

Barbra Streisand, arguably the biggest female star in Hollywood, dressed resplendently in black, made the next presentation. "This award is for the Best Director," Streisand said, leaning slightly into the microphone, her bare shoulders glistening under the bright lights, "and it is my privilege to present it tonight." She dutifully read the names of the nominees and their films, while clips of them directing flashed across the screen. Clint's name was read last, and the visual showed him unshaven and looking into the viewfinder of a movie camera while slowly and steadily chewing gum. "And the Oscar goes to . . ." she said, opening the envelope, then breaking into a big smile as she nodded to Clint, sitting in the first row with Fisher, before saying, "Clint Eastwood!"

The audience erupted with its most enthusiastic response of the night, a rush of cheers and "yays" reaching above the happily clapping crowd. Just before he rose from his seat, Fisher gave Clint a quick kiss on the cheek. On the way to the stage, he stopped long enough to accept a handshake and congratulations from Attenborough. When he arrived at the podium and the cheering subsided, Clint made an off-the-cuff comment about his dry throat, the result of having to sit for so long waiting for the big moment. He wiped his lip and then began again. "I just want to . . . ," he said, then trailed off, looking at the Oscar in the tight grip of his right hand. "This is pretty good, this is all right." Then, laughing nervously, he continued his acceptance speech.

I've been, uh, I've been around for thirty-nine years and I've really enjoyed it. I've been very lucky . . . I heard Al [Pacino, winner of Best Actor] say he's lucky but everybody feels that way . . . when you're able to make a living in a profession that you really enjoy. That's an opportunity I think a lot of people don't have. I've got to thank the crew, and David Valdez [the film's executive producer], and Jack Green [director of photography], and all the camera crew . . . the trouble is with living this long you know so many people but you can't remember their names.

As Clint turned his head in mock confusion, good-natured titters rippled through the audience. Then he smiled.

You get a little flustered. So, but in the "Year of the Woman" I'd like to salute the women of Big Whiskey, that would be Anna Thomson, Frances Fisher, and Lisa and Tyra and Josie and Beverly and all the gals who really were the catalyst to getting this story off the ground, and David Peoples' fabulous script, the Warner Bros. for sticking with this film, the film critics for discovering this film—it wasn't a highly touted film when it came out—but they sort of stayed with it throughout the year, the French film critics who embraced some of my work very early in the game, the British Film Institute and the Museum of Modern Art, and some of the people who were there long before I became fashionable. Lenny Hirshan, my agent . . . I'm leaving out a whole bunch of people I'm going to regret when I sit down again, so, anyway, thank you very much.

With that, Clint raised the Oscar and waved it to the crowd, before leaving the stage to more thunderous applause.

Only to return a few moments later when a smirking Jack Nicholson read off the names of the nominees for Best Picture as if they were a private joke and then opened the envelope and calmly announced Clint's name. Once again enthusiastic applause filled the room, and this time Clint was ready with the names of those he'd failed to thank in his earlier speech, including Warner publicists Joe Hyams and Marco Barla, studio executives Terry Semel and Bob Daley, and "the whole executive strata" at Warner. He also paid special tribute to for-

mer Warner chief Steve Ross, who had died the previous year from prostate cancer, and who had been one of Clint's strongest supporters at the studio. And then, pausing and in a soft voice, Clint said, "In the Year of the Woman, the greatest woman on the planet is here tonight, and that's my mother, Ruth." The cameras quickly found her in the audience, eighty-four years old and looking quite robust, smiling with pride over her son's success.

It was a night of triumph for Clint and his film, which walked off with four Oscars, two for him, one for Hackman, and one for Joel Cox for Best Editor.

After dutifully, if briefly, attending all the official celebrations, including the obligatory Governor's Ball, Clint took a couple of close friends and Fisher to Nicky Blair's restaurant. Blair had been one of the Universal contract actors Clint had met during his early days who remained a friend and who also happened to be a talented chef. In those days he'd often made meals for all his out-of-work buddies, including Clint. He had since become a well-known restaurateur on Hollywood's Sunset Strip. Clint partied there with Fisher and his friends until dawn.

Asked by a reporter the next day how he felt, Clint replied, "Tired."

At sixty-two years of age, Clint had reached the peak of his career. A tottering John Wayne had been that old twenty-three years earlier when he won his only Oscar for his twilight-years performance in Henry Hathaway's *True Grit*. Clint felt not only redeemed but reinvigorated, and within days of his double Oscar win he was ready to begin work on a new film, *In the Line of Fire*. He was set to embrace the future, unencumbered at last by the limitations of his past, believing all the old scores in the game called Hollywood had finally been settled.

Until Sondra Locke reemerged, more determined than ever to settle her own score with him.

TWENTY

My feelings [about Sondra Locke] were the normal feelings you have when someone has been planning for many months to assault your children's inheritance.

—Clint Eastwood

Sondra Locke's very existence was a recurring nightmare for Clint. Every time he thought she was out of his life, she returned, and every time the bad dream got a little worse.

In December 1990 Locke had finalized the details of her lawsuit against Clint, and before the start of the traditional Christmas break, when the entire industry disappears from town until after New Year's, she had moved into her new offices at Warner, per her settlement deal with Clint. She pored over scripts in search of a new project to develop, eager to get something going because *Oh Baby* had collapsed due to Orion's lapse into bankruptcy.

Knowing that Arnold Schwarzenegger had shown some interest in playing the lead, Locke figured it was a no-brainer to walk it over to Warner. She confidently pitched it to Terry Semel and Tom Lassally, together with a shooting script and Schwarzenegger's interest.

Semel and Lassally passed.*

Every day for the next three years Locke, with her $1.5 million development deal still in place, went to her office at Warner, searched for scripts, and tried to interest Terry Semel, Bob Daley, or Lucy Fisher in a project, or even to get the okay to direct one of the hundreds of scripts that were earmarked for future production by the studio. But there was nothing for her. Nothing. *Nada*.

Meanwhile Clint began work on his next film, *In the Line of Fire*, for Columbia. It was his first film for a studio other than Warner since 1979, when he had made *Escape from Alcatraz* at Paramount. Perhaps he felt that after all that had gone on, a change of corporate scenery might be good for both him and Warner Bros.

---

*According to Locke, in her memoir, once the deal was dead, Schwarzenegger took the concept to Ivan Reitman, who eventually made a reworked version of it without her into *Junior*, starring Schwarzenegger and Danny DeVito.

For this film Clint took a (relative) backseat to director Wolfgang Petersen (best known for *Das Boot* and personally chosen by Clint, who maintained directorial approval). Clint plays a retired Secret Service agent who was present at John F. Kennedy's assassination and is called back to duty to prevent an attempt on the new president's life. The film costars a slew of midlevel stars, including John Malkovich and Rene Russo.

One likely reason Clint wanted to take it easy was the outsize success of *Unforgiven.* More often than not in Hollywood, when a film wins that many Academy Awards, the director and the star do not immediately try to compete with their previous success. The next film they make is unlikely to be as successful, and they often prefer to do another film or two before their next "big" film.

Finally, if anyone deserved to take it a bit easier, it was Clint. At sixty-three years old, kicking back for one film and "only" acting in it was completely understandable.

So naturally *In the Line of Fire* became the highest-grossing film of Clint's career to date, taking in over $200 million in its initial domestic release and twice that overseas. Yet it was an ordinary film with a decidedly nonsuspenseful plot that some critics dubbed "Dirty Harry Goes to Washington," and the cast had no single star other than Clint who ever attracted anything near those kinds of numbers. The only logical explanation for the film's success was the tremendous drawing power of Clint Eastwood, once more the most popular movie star in the world.

In 1993, the third and final year of her contract at Warner, Locke was doing postproduction on a TV movie she had taken on, *Death in Small Doses.* She hoped it would be the icebreaker that would bring her back to features. While sitting in her office, she received a phone call from, of all people, Clint—she hadn't spoken to him or had any contact at all with him in years. This was just weeks before the big Academy Awards night, Clint and *Unforgiven* were the big favorites, and with all the promotion he was doing, his was about the last voice on earth she expected to hear in the receiver.

Their conversation was short and sweet and completely puzzling to Locke, even more so when Clint told her he was happy she had a movie and would love to see a rough-cut cassette when it was finished.

With Eric Fleming

With the cast of Rawhide, *left to right: Sheb Wooley, Paul Brinegar, Clint, Eric Fleming*

U.S. movie poster for For a Few Dollars More, *1965*

Italian movie poster for For a Few Dollars More, *1965*

The Witches, *1967*

Hang 'Em High, *1968*

Mexican movie poster for Hang 'Em High

Coogan's Bluff, *1968*

With Lee Marvin and Jean Seberg,
Paint Your Wagon, *1969*

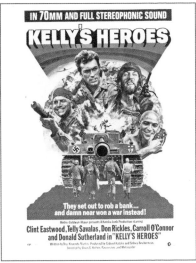

Kelly's Heroes, *1970*

The Beguiled, *1971*

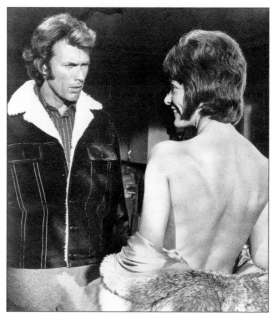

With Jessica Walter, Play Misty for Me, *1971*

With director Don Siegel on the set of Dirty Harry, *1971*

Dirty Harry, *1971*

In his iconic role as Inspector Harry Callahan

Magnum Force, *1973*

Where Eagles Dare, *1968*

The Enforcer, *1976*

With Sondra Locke, The Gauntlet, *1977*

Every Which Way but Loose, *1978*

With his and Maggie's two children, Kyle and Alison, on the set of Star Trek, *late 1970s.*

Escape from Alcatraz, *1979*

With Sondra Locke,
Bronco Billy, *1980*

Clint bolstered the soundtrack of Bronco Billy
*with country music produced by Snuff Garrett
(right) and sang a duet with Merle Haggard (left)
that hit number one on the country charts.*

Any Which Way You Can, *1980*

With Verna Bloom, Honkytonk Man, *1982*

With Geneviève Bujold,
Tightrope, *1984*

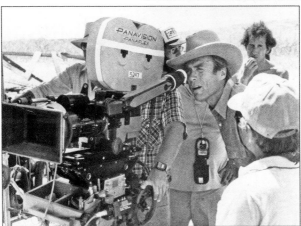

Behind the camera in the mid-1980s

Heartbreak Ridge, *1986*

Directing Forest Whitaker as Charlie Parker (left) and Samuel E. Wright as Dizzy Gillespie (right) on the set of Bird, *1988*

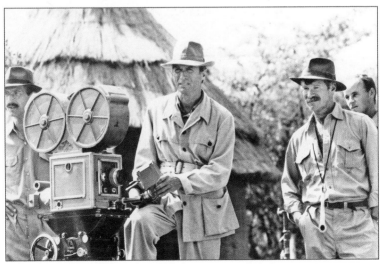

White Hunter, Black Heart, *1990*

With Sonia Braga, The Rookie, *1990*

Unforgiven, *1992*

Celebrating his double Oscar win for Unforgiven *at the 1992 Academy Awards with Gene Hackman, who also won for Best Supporting Actor in the film.*

With Laura Dern, A Perfect World, *1993*

Firefox, *1982*

Gran Torino, *2008*

With that he hung up, leaving her bewildered. Kindness was not a part of Clint's personality she was that familiar with, especially after all the legal ugliness they had put each other through.*

Not long after Clint's grand night at the Oscars, Locke learned from mutual friends that Fisher was pregnant and had been for several months, although she had not been showing the night of the Awards telecast. Could that possibly have had anything to do with Clint's phone call? But trying to figure out his motivations, she knew, was like trying to solve Rubik's Cube.

Sensing something was not right but having no clue what it was, Locke tried to find out what was going on. In her office she reached for the phone and direct-dialed Clint's office. According to her, when Clint picked up, this was what she said: "I don't know what's going on, Clint, but something's not right with Warners and my deal. Nothing at all has come together here. I mean, I hope that they aren't still uncomfortable about our split-up. I would hate to think that's what's been going on." Not hearing anything on the other end, she continued: "Look, I have a script now which has a lot of potential. I've submitted it to one executive who likes it, but hasn't been able to get it past his boss, Bruce Berman. If you read it and like it, would you step in on my behalf? After all, the deal was I'd make some films here. And if you don't like it, I'd like to hear where you think I'm off-target."

Clint's response, according to Locke, was to quickly agree to look at the script and to remind her that he still wanted to see a cassette of her TV movie. That last suggestion sent up a flag for Locke. Clint seemed a little too interested in that movie. Was he afraid it was some kind of exposé, something personal and revealing about their time together? Three weeks later she called him again, and she brought up the script, and he promised to see if he could get Warner to greenlight it.

Despite the two phone calls, nothing happened with the script, but

---

*Clint was no stranger to litigation. As early as 1984 he sued the *National Enquirer* over an article that had linked him romantically with Tanya Tucker. He asked for $10 million and settled out of court. He sued them again in 1994 over their publication of a so-called exclusive interview, and won $150,000 in 1995 that was held up on appeal in 1997. He donated it to a charity (which he did not name). His legal team was awarded $650,000 for legal fees.

weird things continued to happen with her other potential projects. Lance Young, a former Paramount producer who had moved to Warner, wanted to hire Locke to direct a movie there. A friend who knew Young from Paramount told Locke that he had been told Warner would not work with her because she was "Clint's deal."

"Clint's deal." What could that possibly mean? Exasperated and confused, Locke changed agents again, this time signing with International Creative Management (ICM) to try once more to jump-start her career. She brought up her Warner "deal" with them. They looked into the situation and reported back to her that Warner was simply not going to make a film with her. Any film.

Early in 1994 Locke retained counsel with the intent to sue Warner Bros. for breach of contract. Her hope was that Warner would extend her contract by one year and give her at least one film that would fulfill the conditions of her signing off on her lawsuit against Clint. One film, she felt, was all she needed to regain her career momentum.

The response from Warner to Locke's counsel was swift and direct. According to Locke, Terry Semel and Bob Daley made an insulting offer for her just to go away: "We have no interest in making any *real* deal with Sondra. We can give her a twenty-five-thousand-dollar settlement for her trouble, but that's it." Locke said no, moved out of her office at Warner, and necessarily changed lawyers because of her increasingly precarious financial condition. She acquired the services of Peggy Garrity, who, after reviewing all the facts involved, agreed to handle the case that Locke wanted to bring against both Clint and Warner on a contingency basis.

Winning a lawsuit against Warner was not going to be easy. Few witnesses would be willing to come forward and testify; for anyone looking ever to work again in Hollywood, it would be a career-ending move. Warner's initial reaction to the filing of Locke's suit was to shrug it off, claiming they simply had not been able to find anything for her; nor had she brought them anything that they felt was up to the studio's extremely high standards. But they *had* given her a parking spot on the studio and a free turkey every Thanksgiving, proof of their good intentions, they said.

For the rest of 1994 and 1995 and through the summer of 1996, Locke, via David-like Garrity, took on Warner's legal representation, the Goliath-like O'Melveny & Myers. Depositions were taken, dur-

ing which Warner steadfastly maintained they had done nothing wrong. Not long afterward Garrity, sensing this was less a breach-of-contract case than one of actual fraud, a far more serious charge, urged Locke to add Clint to the lawsuit.* Locke agreed, Garrity filed, and in Locke's words from her memoir, Warner "went ballistic and mounted a massive campaign to keep Clint out of the lawsuit."

To Locke's shock and dismay, the motion to add Clint was denied.

Garrity then asked Warner Bros., as part of discovery, for a copy of the final cost runs for Locke's studio deal—everything that had been charged against her account in the entire three years. It was not an unusual request in these types of lawsuits. In order to find out how the studio would prepare its financial counterclaim, Locke needed to know how much money and service value Warner had advanced to her and her staff during that period.

Warner's documents revealed debits totaling $975,000, not all that unusual for a three-year period. But what surely wasn't normal operating procedure was that the entire amount had been transferred from Locke's account at Warner to Clint's, specifically folded into the overall budget and outlay production costs of *Unforgiven*. At first this was puzzling to Locke, as she had had absolutely nothing to do with any aspect of the production of that film. Then it hit her—Clint, she realized, was secretly paying the tab for her Warner deal. Only her Warner deal didn't really exist, at least not according to the papers Warner had given over to discovery. Locke now believed that Clint must have set up a secret, false, sham deal with Warner, where it would look like Locke had a deal there but really didn't. The whole thing was to be paid for by Clint, via *Unforgiven*, which meant that not a cent of the $975,000 actually came out of his own pockets. He had set it up in order to induce her to sign off on her original lawsuit for a relatively small amount, with the carrot-dangling promise of a deal at the studio to get her to settle.

The ramifications ran deep. If Clint had, in fact, charged that money to *Unforgiven*, then anyone else who had a profit-based deal connected to the film had also been defrauded by Clint and/or Malpaso, because the net profits of *Unforgiven* were based on all production costs and distribution and advertising expenses subtracted from the film's gross.

---

*This was a civil lawsuit. Only the state can bring criminal charges.

That could mean criminal charges somewhere down the line, and dozens of complicated and dangerous lawsuits both for the studio and for Clint.

Warner's first response was that that simply wasn't the case, because the money had come not from Warner or Malpaso but from his personal account. Garrity didn't think so, at least not according to the documents.

At that point, more depositions were scheduled, but Clint refused his subpoena and ordered Malpaso to also refuse any subpoenas Garrity tried to serve on him. Warner then asked the court for an immediate judgment to remove them from the case without a trial. Such summary judgments are usually requested when one side or the other believes the case has no merit, or the evidence is insufficient and doesn't merit a full trial. It is always a risk, because losing it usually indicates the judge believes the other side has a good enough case to bring. Asking for a summary judgment is like betting everything on red or black at a roulette table. This time the chips came down on Warner's side.

Devastated, Locke only had two choices left: to appeal the court's decision, which in a summary judgment is difficult, costly, time-consuming, and rarely successful; or to start a new lawsuit only against Clint for fraud. In other words, to start all over again, eliminating the studio from any further legal claims she had against them.

She did both.

This time Garrity filed the lawsuit in downtown Los Angeles, rather than in Burbank, where the first lawsuit had been filed. Burbank, she and Garrity felt, was just too close to Warner's power center. That would make it even more difficult to find an objective jury, as everyone in Burbank was connected one way or another to the film business, the primary reason people lived in this otherwise nondescript, hot, humid, and isolated community. Now, Garrity decided, distance was their best defense.

Without bothering to notify Garrity, Ray Fisher, Clint's attorney, responded by petitioning to have the case remain in Burbank. He succeeded and it was assigned to a different judge from the one who had heard and granted the summary judgment on the Warner case.

On the first day of trial, September 9, 1996, Fisher moved for dis-

missal for "nonsuit," which is similar to summary judgment; Fisher insisted Locke had no case and wanted the judge to concur. The judge took the motion under advisement and, for the moment at least, let the case continue.

After opening statements, Locke and Garrity starting putting their witnesses on the stand. The first was Terry Semel, who, under direct examination by Garrity, shaped his answers to suggest that Warner had indeed been willing to do business with Locke during the three years she was under contract, but that nothing she brought to them they considered filmable. Garrity then sharpened her focus and asked Semel if he was aware of Clint's "secret indemnity," as she put it. Semel agreed that "I would assume that at the end of the day that his intentions were to underwrite the losses." Garrity asked him when "the end of the day" was. Semel said that he guessed it was when the terms of the arrangement—the three-year contract—had ended.

No further questions.

The next day Locke took the stand, and Garrity led her through a detailed recapitulation of the terms of her original settlement and everything that had happened—or not happened—in the three years she was at Warner. That evening, as Locke left the courthouse, she was intercepted by Kevin Marks, Clint's full-time personal attorney, who had attended the trial. Earlier that day, on the way into the courthouse's parking lot, Locke had been in a car accident, smashing her front end. Marks just wanted to tell her that he had seen the whole thing and was willing to testify in her defense when she sued the other driver.

The next day Locke was cross-examined by Fisher, who went over the terms of the first lawsuit settlement, emphasizing along the way, no doubt for the jury's sake, the fact that all the while Locke was seeing Clint, she had been married to another man.

After a few more witnesses it was Garrity's time to put Clint on the stand. He was going to have to answer all of Garrity's questions under oath. She was swift and to the point, focusing in on what she thought was the most essential aspect of the case. Taking a deep breath and exhaling, she asked Clint if he had entered into an agreement with Locke in 1990 to settle her lawsuit against him.

In a soft and steady voice, he said he had. He then also admitted that he had made a separate agreement with Warner Bros. to indemnify

them for all of Locke's expenses during the three years of her contract with them; that he had not told Locke of the arrangement; and that he had not offered Locke any type of similar deal during that period with Malpaso. That was it. Garrity was finished with him, and he was dismissed from the witness stand.

After a few more days and several other witnesses, Garrity rested and Clint's defense took over. Soon it was Clint's turn to take the stand in his own defense. He was upbeat and expansive as Fisher led him through his testimony. Then Fisher got to Clint's relationship with Locke.

FISHER: What was your opinion of Ms. Locke once the 1989 lawsuit was settled?

CLINT: My feelings were the normal feelings you have when someone has been planning for many months to assault your children's inheritance . . . Well, you know, I didn't feel very good about it, I must say . . .

Clint went on to express his dismay and his feeling that he was suffering from "social extortion."

After a few minor disruptions—a reporter had smuggled a camera into the courtroom—and several objections from Garrity, Fisher asked Clint if he had had any intention to commit fraud. Clint said no, adding that it would make no sense for him to use his influence to prevent Locke from getting work at Warner because, according to his deal, he would have to pay for her contract if she didn't earn any money. He then insisted that despite his best efforts, it was Warner, not he, that chose not to green-light Locke's various proposals.

During cross-examination Garrity tried to get Clint to admit that he had tapped Locke's phones, something Locke had long suspected, which Clint denied. She then went over the terms of his indemnification deal regarding Locke, which Clint corrected, reminding her and the court that his deal had been with Warner, to indemnify them, not with Locke.

When Garrity let Clint off the stand, Fisher, who had vehemently objected to several of Garrity's questions, moved for a mistrial. The

jury was removed, and Fisher insisted the jury should not have heard any testimony about wiretaps. The motion was denied, and with the jury still out, the judge broke for lunch.

Among the defense's final witnesses was Tom Lassally, who admitted under cross-examination that Clint had never talked to him about any of Locke's proposed projects.

Final arguments began September 19, 1996. Garrity crisply summed up the case, as she saw it, finishing in less than a half hour. It was then Fisher's turn. He worked slowly and methodically, taking several hours to work his way through his version of the facts of the case and why it should be decided in Clint's favor. As he came to the conclusion of his summation, he made what sounded like a very solid point—the crux of his argument—that Clint had been under no legal obligation to tell Locke about his indemnification of Warner; that it was a completely separate deal totally unrelated to the terms of her settlement with him.

When Fisher finished, the judge instructed the jury and sent them out to decide the case. After three days of deliberation, the jury asked for a definition of "legal" as it pertained to whether Clint was under a "legal" obligation to inform Locke of his indemnification deal with Warner.

The next day, a Saturday, Garrity called Locke to tell her that she had just received a call from Fisher, who said he wanted to talk over the possibility of a settlement. At this point Locke was adamant; she didn't want to settle. This had been a long and difficult battle for her, and she was determined to see it through. When Garrity conveyed Locke's decision to Fisher, he pressed Garrity to prevail upon her client to reconsider. He stressed that a verdict was certain to damage at least one and possibly both of their clients' careers, and that no one can ever be sure what a jury will do.

Locke talked again with Garrity and took her suggestion to at least think it over. The next day Locke agreed to listen to Clint's offer. Fisher delivered it, and after deliberating once more with Garrity, she decided to accept. The only condition imposed by Clint was that the amount of money not be revealed to anyone. Locke agreed. The announcement that the case had settled brought a slew of reporters to

the courthouse steps and interviews with several of the released jurors, all of whom claimed that they had already decided in favor of Locke, and that the penalty for Clint would have been in the millions.

A few days later Fisher first threatened to withhold the money and then wanted papers signed; Garrity ignored the first and refused the second. After much grumbling, Fisher personally handed over the check, and Clint's involvement with Locke was finally over, leaving Locke a little richer, Clint a little poorer. Both of them, after their fourteen-year romantic and six-year litigious relationship, appeared to be finally and forever free of each other.*

Although he almost never talked about his relationship with Locke after that, he did at least one time, to *Playboy*, during an interview he gave in 1997:

> I guess maybe I'm the only one who finds it weird that she's still obsessed with our relationship and putting out the same old rhetoric almost ten years later. There are two sides to this whole thing . . . she's been married for 29 years, but nobody puts that in their stories. As far as the legal action goes, it was my fault. I have to take full responsibility because I thought I was doing her a favor by helping her get a production arrangement with Warner Bros. I prevailed upon Warner Bros. to do it and it didn't work out. So she sued Warner and then she sued me and finally at some point I said, wait a second, I would have been better off if I hadn't done anything and had let her go ahead and file the palimony suit against me. I tried to help. I thought she would

---

*Several sources list the settlement of the fraud case against Clint—the second lawsuit—as 1999. In fact, it was settled in 1996. Locke's autobiography, which includes details of the settlement (but not the amount), was published in 1997. In it she discussed the case at length. Clint's only public comment was to *Playboy* in March 1997, when he told interviewer Bernard Weinraub that Locke played the victim very well. He indicated that he believed her history of cancer had made her more sympathetic to the jury. Although the terms of the settlement have never been disclosed, it was rumored to have been between $10 million and $30 million. (Some sources report the figure to be closer to $7 million.) After the settlement, Locke directed one more movie and appeared in two others. Her last known assignment in Hollywood was in 1999. She still lives there, for more than a decade now with Scott Cunneen, a director of surgery at Cedars Sinai Hospital in Los Angeles. Finally, in 1999, Locke sued Warner (but not Clint) yet again, this time for collusion, and won yet another out-of-court settlement with another undisclosed financial amount and a new production deal that has not yet resulted in any new films.

get directing assignments, but it didn't work out that way . . . I should have known that it would come back to haunt me . . . but you go on with your business. I'm going on with my life, and if other people can't get on with theirs, that's their problem.

Clint was not present for the handing over of his settlement check, leaving that to Fisher. Free at last from his tar-baby relationship with Locke, he took the next logical step in the never-ending drama of his own real life.

He became a father again, for the seventh time. And he got married again, for only the second time, to the baby's mother, who was thirty-five years his junior and three years younger than his firstborn, Kyle.

TWENTY-ONE

If I start intruding and getting fancy and trying to dazzle people with whatever tricks I may or may not have as a director, I'm tampering with something . . . I revere the performances and I don't want people to visualize a camera and a camera operator and a guy with a focus-thing, and another person there . . . I just want people to visualize the movie, so I keep things as subtle as I can, at the same time punctuating the points I need to punctuate.

—Clint Eastwood

On August 7, 1993, Clint quietly became a father for the sixth time when Frances Fisher gave birth to a baby girl they named Francesca Fisher. He had already begun to emotionally pull away from Frances. One reason may have been a souring on the notion of romance by his endless battles with former lover Locke. More likely, though, the cause was the arrival in his life of Dina Ruiz, who would eventually become the second Mrs. Eastwood.

Ruiz, born and raised in California of African-American and Japanese descent on her father's side and Irish, English, and German on her mother's, first crossed paths with Clint in April 1993, when she interviewed him about his recent Oscar triumph for KSBW, the NBC TV affiliate in Salinas. Having graduated from San Francisco State in 1989 and apprenticed with KNAZ, a small station in Flagstaff, Arizona, Ruiz had landed the job at KSBW, and one of her first assignments was to interview Clint Eastwood.

The first piece went so well, Ruiz asked Clint to answer more questions so she might expand it into two or three parts. The two met several times more, and the interviews show clearly that Ruiz, twenty-eight years old, and Clint, sixty-three, had very good chemistry. Ruiz readily admitted to Clint that she had seen few of his movies ("zero" was the number she used) and was in love with her boyfriend. However, even though Clint was about to become a father again, this time with Frances Fisher, the two agreed to stay in touch, which Clint normally did not do with reporters.

Ruiz and Clint met again in mid-1994, just after Clint finished *A Perfect World*, which starred Kevin Costner, who was still hot off the 1990 Academy Award–winning *Dances with Wolves*.* Costner had continued to appear in big, successful movies—Kevin Reynolds's *Robin*

*Costner also co-produced (with Jim Wilson) and directed *Dances with Wolves*. He took

Hood: Prince of Thieves (1991), Oliver Stone's *JFK* (1991), and Mick Jackson's *The Bodyguard* (1992)—that had made him one of the biggest stars in Hollywood for the first half of the 1990s. When Costner approached Clint about the possibility of directing *A Perfect World*, Clint read the script and was attracted to the plot's familiar escaped-convict tropes, especially the relationship between the pursued, Butch Haynes (Costner) and his pursuer, Red Garnett. Clint said yes, if he could play Garnett and, of course, produce it through Malpaso.

Filming on location in Martindale, Texas, proved more difficult than Clint had anticipated. His hurry-up directorial style clashed with Costner's snail's-pace multiple-take perfectionism. (During the making of *Dances with Wolves* more than one participant had complained, off the record, that the endless retakes had driven everyone crazy.) According to one story, Costner angrily walked off the set during a shoot, and Clint used Costner's stand-in to finish shooting. Afterward, when Costner complained, Clint told him that as far as he was concerned, he could take a walk off the set or off the film—either way was fine with him. Costner did no more complaining after that, and the film was finished without further incident. It opened on Thanksgiving weekend, becoming one of Warner's big fall releases of 1993; it grossed $30 million in its initial theatrical release and more than $100 million worldwide.

In 1994, after the arrival of little Francesca, Clint finished a showcase film for Fisher's talents that he had produced but not appeared in, for Malpaso (only the third time this had happened so far in Malpaso's twenty-seven-year career—*Ratboy* [from which he eventually detached himself] and *Bird* were the other two films). *The Stars Fell on Henrietta*, an early-America oil drama starring Robert Duvall, Aidan Quinn, and Fisher, would not get released until fall 1995. It came and went quickly and without much notice, or any special effort by Clint to promote it.

Before it even opened, Clint was off on another project, one that had been brewing for a long time and promised to be even bigger than *Unforgiven*, with a role that just might deliver to him the one

---

home Oscars both for Best Director and Best Picture. The film won seven out of the twelve Oscars for which it was nominated.

Oscar he still didn't have, and perhaps the one he wanted most, Best Actor.

As early as 1992, Steven Spielberg had approached Clint about starring in the film version of Robert James Waller's hugely popular 1992 novel *The Bridges of Madison County*, which Spielberg himself intended to produce and direct. At the time Clint was busy making *Unforgiven*, and Spielberg was fully and emotionally absorbed in his wrenching production of *Schindler's List*, but they agreed to talk again after their respective films had opened.

Spielberg and Clint were not strangers. They had met and worked together in 1985, when Clint directed that episode of Spielberg's TV series, *Amazing Stories*, called "Vanessa in the Garden," featuring Sondra Locke. While the series and Clint's episode were quickly forgotten, his friendship with Spielberg remained. The two had wanted to work together on a feature ever since, and six years later Spielberg's production company, Amblin, obtained the prepublication rights to Waller's novel, which would go on to sell ten million copies.

The Bridges of Madison County is essentially a modernized version of Noël Coward's one-act play *Still Life*, which he turned into a screenplay in 1945; it became David Lean's *Brief Encounter*, set in London, about the desperation, guilt, and temptations of two married people who meet, fall in love, commit adultery, and then separate forever. In *The Bridges of Madison County*, Robert Kincaid, a roaming, rootless photographer, passes through Madison County on a photographic assignment and has a brief but intense love affair with a lonely and unhappily married woman before traveling on. ("The bridges" refer both to the physical structures of the county and to the emotional bonds between the two.) Spielberg approached Clint about the possibility of playing Kincaid.

Clint, who saw in the role a chance to once more display his best persona, that of the quintessential loner, quickly agreed. But when *Schindler's List* proved a more difficult shoot than Spielberg had anticipated, he approached Sidney Pollack about directing *The Bridges of Madison County*. Pollack in turn wanted Robert Redford to play Kincaid. Both Pollack and Redford eventually fell away, after which several big names were considered. Finally, to direct it, Spielberg signed Bruce Beresford, best known for *Driving Miss Daisy*, which had won the Best Picture Oscar for 1989. Not long afterward Clint signed on

to play Kincaid, but he wanted to co-produce it as well, with Spielberg, as an Amblin-Warner-Malpaso co-production.* Spielberg, who had always wanted Clint for the lead, following Clint's winning the Oscar for *Unforgiven*, quickly agreed, and production was set to begin late in the summer of 1994.

Clint, however, was still unsatisfied with the script, and, in an unusual move for him, not only wanted it rewritten, but wanted to do it himself with Spielberg, even though they were on opposite sides of the country and neither especially wanted to travel to work with the other.

> The three or four different versions of the screenplay they had were all over the place, and one or two of them changed the storyline completely. That didn't seem adequate so Steven and I rewrote it ourselves. He was back east at the time, in the Hamptons for the summer, and I was up in Northern California at Mount Shasta, so we wrote it by fax machine. I'd dictate some pages and then fax them to him, then he'd make some changes and fax them to me. We did this for about a week and then we agreed, this was the screenplay.

But even before the cameras were set to roll, Clint and Beresford clashed over the casting of the crucial female lead. Beresford, an Australian, had a vision of the film that directly conflicted with Clint's, over who should play the crucial role of the lonely, frustrated, and sexually available Francesca. Beresford had preferred two Swedish-born actresses for the role, Lena Olin, best known in America for her performance in Philip Kaufman's *The Unbearable Lightness of Being* (1988), and Pernilla August, a Swedish star virtually unknown in the States. Neither appealed to Clint, who had final say in casting, and insisted the role had to be played by an American—that was the whole point

---

*The film was a Warner-Malpaso-Amblin co-production, produced by Clint and distributed by Warner, whose book division had published the original novel and the paperback tie-in and was thrilled to have its biggest star, still hot from his double Oscar win, to helm the picture. Warner also released the film's sound track, which included several standard jazz compositions and the original theme song "Doe Eyes," aka the love theme from *The Bridges of Madison County*. The album remained at the top of the jazz charts for months and hovered near the top for years. During this time Clint formed Malpaso Records, which, like the film's sound-track album, would prove very profitable for both him and Warner. "Doe Eyes" was Clint's nickname for Ruiz.

of the movie as far as he was concerned (despite the fact that in the novel Francesca is Italian). Beresford offered up Isabella Rossellini as his compromise, Ingrid Berman's model-actress daughter, who was very popular in America but had a decidedly Swedish accent. Clint said no to her as well. Two weeks before the film's scheduled August 1994 start, Beresford was out and Clint took over as director, with Meryl Streep set to star opposite him. (Fisher had pressured Clint unsuccessfully to cast her in the role.)

Clint was adamant about casting Streep, although at first she turned the role down, saying she didn't like the book. According to sources, she was offended that Beresford had not first offered her the role. Everyone who read the book assumed she was going to play Francesca Johnson, rather like the national mandate that erupted, demanding that Clark Gable play Rhett Butler, when Margaret Mitchell's *Gone with the Wind* was first published. She demanded $4 million and a percentage of the profits, something that was normally anathema to producer Clint; but he wanted her so badly that he, Spielberg, and Warner all agreed to her terms, and she came aboard. Clint had wanted Streep for several reasons, not the least being the age factor. He thought Francesca should be a few years older than she was in the book, so the age discrepancy between her and Clint's Kincaid wouldn't be as noticeable on-screen. Meryl Streep was forty-five years old; Clint was sixty-four.

Production started the second week of August, on location in Des Moines, amid unfounded rumors that Streep and Clint were having an affair; the speculation was fueled when Clint discouraged Fisher from coming to visit him on location. But to Streep, it was all business. She had an interesting take on Clint's abilities as a director: "The reason he can direct himself and a film and take himself outside of it and put himself inside is I think he views himself at a distance." The notion of separating one from one's self was a variation on the loner concept and also a convenient way of excusing one's own behavior by blaming the other self for anything that shouldn't have happened.

Those on set may have correctly sensed that Clint and Fisher were over, but it wasn't Streep Clint was now interested in. It was Ruiz. By the time the film opened, Fisher had moved out of Clint's house on Stradella—the same one that Locke had lived in for so many years—and Clint was openly dating Dina Ruiz.

Just as the film was wrapping, Warner began a massive PR campaign to get Clint named as the recipient of the 1995 Irving J. Thalberg Award, given out annually at the Oscars ceremony to honor a producer's overall body of work. The award is named after the legendary 1930s MGM producer who is credited with elevating that studio's artistic level and Hollywood films as a whole. Thalberg was unusually modest—he never took an on-screen credit, which is one reason producing is said to be the least visual aspect of modern filmmaking. To Warner, the announcement by the Academy shortly before the annual gala that Clint was to be that year's recipient provided the perfect synergistic run-up to *The Bridges of Madison County*. Planned for release in June 1995, it would surely be one of that summer's biggest movies.

The Academy Awards ceremony took place on March 27 at the Shrine Auditorium in Los Angeles. For the glittering occasion Clint was accompanied only by his eighty-six-year-old mother—in Hollywood, a clear signal that his relationship with Frances Fisher was over. When it came time for the Thalberg Award presentation, Clint was introduced with a compilation of scenes from his movies put together by Richard Schickel, and then, when the lights came up, Arnold Schwarzenegger brought him onto the stage. After a solid ovation, Clint acknowledged the fabulous history of the Academy Awards and thanked Darryl F. Zanuck, Hal Wallis, William Wyler, Billy Wilder, and Alfred Hitchcock, "the people I grew up idolizing." The tribute was brief, respectful, and well received. As the audience applauded, he strode off the stage holding his first noncompetitive Academy Award, hoping he would be back on the same stage a year later for his performance in, and direction of, *The Bridges of Madison County*.

The film opened on June 2 to less than rave reviews. The *New York Times* liked it, as did *Newsweek*, although both had reservations, and the rest of the critics gave it the same half-cocked thumb-up. It stayed in theaters through Labor Day, grossing $70 million in its initial domestic theatrical release, and it would go on to do another $200 million overseas. Those were impressive numbers for a film that was unlike anything Clint had done before—a soft, gentle romantic love story between an older man and a "younger woman," with not so much as a single punch thrown or a single gun fired in angry vengeance.

That September Clint did a monthlong promotional tour for *The Bridges of Madison County*'s overseas debut, which took him through England, France, and Italy. Ruiz and two other couples, longtime friends from Carmel, accompanied him. When the tour ended and everybody had returned home, Clint took Ruiz to his winter retreat in Hailey, Idaho, near Sun Valley, for the holidays. On December 29 he proposed marriage to her with a diamond and ruby ring.

The next day they went to the county courthouse to apply for a marriage license. Everyone there was good-naturedly sworn to secrecy until the formal wedding, which was set for the following March, after Clint received the American Film Institute Achievement Award.

On March 31, 1996, Clint and Ruiz exchanged vows in Las Vegas, on the patio of Steve Wynn's home. Clint's mother was there, and his son Kyle was his best man. Ruiz was escorted down the aisle by her father, while the band played "Doe Eyes" and "Unforgettable."

Later, the happy bride said of the momentous occasion, "The fact that I am only the second woman he has married really touches me."

As for Clint, he had no problem being nearly sixty-six and marrying a thirty-year-old woman:

> I don't think about it. You're as old as you feel, and I feel great. Certainly if you're a man there are advantages to being older . . . none of us knows how long fate gives you on the planet. People get so concerned about age, about the future, they don't live out their moment today. Moment to moment. I'm immensely happy with Dina, and I feel I've finally found a person I want to be with . . . This is it, win, lose or draw.

A few weeks later, back in L.A. after honeymooning in Hawaii, Dina was riding in a car with Clint when suddenly she asked him to pull over. "She was feeling a little nausea and asked me to stop at a gas station so she could buy one of those sticks," Clint later recalled. "She came back and said, 'We're pregnant.' " It would be Clint's seventh child by five different women, and her first.

That spring Clint went off to make his next movie, *Absolute Power*, to be filmed on location in Baltimore and Washington, D.C. Like *The Bridges of Madison County*, *Absolute Power* was adapted from a power-

house bestseller, by David Baldacci. It was a curious amalgam of several genres—jewel heist, assassination thriller, and family conflict melodrama—that reteamed Clint with his Oscar-winning *Unforgiven* costar, Gene Hackman. Also included in the stellar cast were Ed Harris, Scott Glenn, Judy Davis, and E. G. Marshall. Two of Clint's children, Alison and Kimber, appeared in minor roles.

Clint was intrigued by the problem of transferring such a complicated plot-driven piece to the screen: "With *Absolute Power*, I liked the whole setup and I liked the characters, but the problem was that all those great characters were killed in the book, so my question was, how can we make a screenplay where everyone that the audience likes doesn't get killed off?"

To solve that problem, Clint—serving as director, producer, and star for Malpaso, which made the film in partnership with Castle Rock Entertainment (who owned the rights to the novel)—turned to William Goldman, the best screenwriter of his generation. Goldman decided to emphasize jewel thief Luther Whitney's (Clint's) relationship with his daughter (Laura Linney). He built the rest of the screenplay around the president (Hackman), who is having an affair with a young woman. In a fit of rage, she tries to stab him with a letter opener (recalling Hackman's great turn in Roger Donaldson's 1987 *No Way Out*, as Defense Secretary David Brice, who murders *his* mistress). The Secret Service kills her, and Luther, during his last great heist, happens to witness the scene, and takes the letter opener as a form of life insurance. Once the president becomes aware there is a witness, he orders the Secret Service to track him down and kill him too. Meanwhile, Luther decides to reconcile with his daughter, who happens to be the district attorney. Eventually the real killers—including, improbably, the president—are brought to justice, Eastwood-style.

The story combines too many different genres and certainly presented its share of problems to Goldman—in his first draft, which was faithful to the novel, he had Luther killed off halfway through. Clint liked everything about it but that. He told Goldman that a Clint Eastwood character should never die in his films and then ordered the script rewritten so that Luther not only lives but plays a key role in solving the murder. Goldman worked at a furious pace to get the revisions done on schedule.

Absolute Power opened on February 14, 1997, and grossed $50 million in its initial domestic theatrical release and nearly double that overseas. That was okay for most films but disappointing for a Clint Eastwood movie—about half what *The Bridges of Madison County* had done. Critics were not overly receptive to the film—most agreed that despite the theme of reconciliation that permeated it, the film was basically an action genre picture that, following *The Bridges of Madison County*, seemed like something of a throwback. It was given the prestigious closing-night slot at the Cannes Film Festival, but in light of the blasé reviews, Clint canceled his much-hyped scheduled personal appearance.

The film had another problem as well, one the critics danced around but that the public could not help but notice. For the first time, Clint simply looked too old for the part.

Clint celebrated his sixty-seventh birthday making two more films. The first was yet another bestseller adaptation, *Midnight in the Garden of Good and Evil*. John Berendt's novelistic, antebellum tale of murder and intrigue in Savannah was based on a true story involving art dealer Jim Williams and hustler Danny Hansford (called Billy Hanson in the movie). The book had been optioned early on by Arnold Stiefel, an agent-manager who in turn sold the rights to Warner Bros., where it eventually came to Clint and Malpaso from Semel and Daley. The script was by John Lee Hancock, who had also written *A Perfect World*. Hancock turned the book's author into one of the on-screen characters and eliminated many of Berendt's enjoyable meanderings.

One gothic element of the story that lent itself particularly well to film was its main setting, the Mercer House, built by Johnny Mercer's grandfather. Johnny Mercer was one of Savannah's most celebrated songwriters—and one of Clint's longtime favorites. He is remembered for, among others, the lyrics to "Laura," the theme song to Otto Preminger's 1941 film noir about a ghostly woman at the center of a murder mystery. When Clint read the script, he knew immediately he wanted to direct but not star, preferring to promote his daughter's stalled career. Alison was cast in the role of Mandy, the on-screen author's flirty girlfriend, a part greatly expanded from the novel.

Despite Clint's aging visage, Warner wasn't especially happy about his decision not to appear in the film—the last two he had directed without also starring in, *Breezy* and *Bird*, had not done nearly as well as the ones he had been in. When asked why he wanted to make the film at all, Clint said:

> The characters, who are interesting just because they're so diverse, and then Savannah, a very unusual city, which we wanted to make into a character in its own right. This isn't the South the way it's portrayed most of the time, with an overabundance of clichés. [We wanted to show a South that is] sophisticated, cultured, intelligent, very much in the public view, people no one would ever think could be interested in sorcery.

The all-star cast included Kevin Spacey—red-hot after his upset 1996 Best Supporting Actor win for his performance in Bryan Singer's sleeper hit *The Usual Suspects*—John Cusack, Jude Law, and veteran actress Kim Hunter. An outsize publicity campaign led up to its big Thanksgiving-weekend release: Clint agreed to a first-time appearance on *60 Minutes* but dodged some unexpectedly pointed questions by Steve Kroft about how many children Clint had by how many different women, and (by implication) why, and a far less intense double appearance on *The Oprah Winfrey Show*. Even after all these years, Clint had difficulty appearing relaxed on any stage that required spontaneous responses.

Despite all the buildup, the film did not even earn back its $30 million negative cost* in the States; it brought in only about $25 million in its initial theatrical release, making it one of the biggest flops of Clint's career. It did nothing for Alison's career and it resurrected the ever-louder whispers that Clint Eastwood's career as a Hollywood director was finished.

Almost immediately, as if on cue, rumors began to circulate that Clint was going to make another Dirty Harry movie, the sixth in the series. After all, Malpaso had optioned bestselling West Coast detec-

---

Negative cost is the cost of completing the film; it refers to the finished negative from which all the prints are struck.

tive novelist Michael Connelly's *Blood Work*.* Word was, Clint was thinking about bringing Harry out of retirement to solve one last crime, putting his own life at stake. But instead Clint announced that his next starring role and directing assignment would be *True Crime*, from the Andrew Klavan bestseller about a reporter who tries to stop an execution. Steve Everett (Clint) has to race against time to find the real killers before the wrong man is put to death. Nothing about the film really worked, and most people in Hollywood found its real mystery in its casting: Clint gave Frances Fisher the relatively small role of District Attorney Cecilia Nussbaum.

True Crime, released in the spring of 1999, did very poorly at the box office, barely grossing $7 million. Shortly after its disastrous release, Bob Daley and Terry Semel resigned from Warner Bros., ending their long association with the studio and with Clint. Controversy swirled around the double resignation, but both executives steadfastly maintained that they simply felt it was time to move on and that their decision had nothing to do with the success or failure of Clint Eastwood's latest movies.

Shortly thereafter, in January 2000, Time-Warner merged with AOL, a move that shook up the company and the film industry as it appeared to signal a major shift in the delivery of entertainment. The studio was turning away from the business of making motion pictures. Whether Semel and Daley had been forced out, were gently pushed, or chose to leave on their own accord, their departure underscored the fact that Clint Eastwood would no longer be as powerful as he once was. If ever there was a good time for Clint to be able to step down gracefully, this would have been it.

But Clint refused to believe that turning seventy—and looking every day of it, down to his well-worn face heavily wrinkled from a lifetime of living and acting outdoors and a bit of a turkey neck developing under his chin—meant his professional time was up. He still had something to prove, and he intended to do it with style, grace, big box office, and perhaps most of all, a Best Actor Oscar in his fist.

---

*Clint bought the rights from Connelly's film agent, Joel Gotler.

TWENTY-TWO

Dina keeps me on my toes, let's put it that way. We both enjoy family a lot, we both enjoy pets and we love to play golf. To me, as I said, life is like the back nine in golf. Sometimes you play better on the back nine. You may not be stronger, but hopefully you're wiser.

—Clint Eastwood

As the last night of the old century dissolved into the first day of the new one, Clint Eastwood was living the life of a man half his biological age. He was slim, trim, healthy, and handsome, married to a thirty-four-year-old woman, and the proud father of a three-year-old toddler he could happily bounce on his bony knee.

He was also the head of a business empire and one of the most enduring actors of his generation, still making mainstream commercial movies long after his contemporaries had either died, or retired, or like his friend Jack Nicholson turned to self-parody in the face of diminishing box-office returns. Clint had wealth beyond all expectation and lasting world fame. He had made or appeared in fifty-six features and directed twenty-one of them; he had been acknowledged by the Academy of Motion Pictures with two competitive and one honorary Oscar for his efforts; and he had been feted by the most prestigious museums and grandest film festivals around the world. And yet the need to keep working still stirred within him, as if he still had something that needed to be said, or some accomplishment still to be won. Only months into the new century, he had finished the twenty-second feature that he had directed, the fifty-sixth role he had played on the big screen.

It wasn't the Dirty Harry film everyone thought they were still waiting for. It was, instead, *Space Cowboys*, a space adventure comedy, starring what one producer referred to as the "geezer squad"—Clint, Tommy Lee Jones (the baby of the set), Donald Sutherland (whom Clint had last worked with in *Kelly's Heroes*), and James Garner (whom Clint had known since his *Rawhide* years, when Garner was starring next door in *Maverick*). The film was Philip Kaufman's *The Right Stuff* (1983) meets Ron Howard's *Cocoon* (1985)—Geritol laced with Viagra, with a can't-miss live monkey thrown in for good measure.

The new regime at Warner had no faith in the film and released—

or dumped—it in August 2000, hoping it wouldn't do too much damage to its bottom line. It didn't. *Space Cowboys* went on to be one of the biggest hits of the year, grossing more than $100 million in its initial domestic theatrical release and almost twice that in foreign and ancillary sales (including rental and purchase DVDs and pay-per-view, which had by now added significant profits to virtually all films, past and present).

Clint especially enjoyed the success of this film, literally laughing at the corporate towheads who scratched their scalps as he drove his pickup to the bank. But he had never been anyone's fool. He had to know that this movie really was a step backward, if not straight down. It put him on the same page with Garner, who had long ago stopped making anything like "big" films, and for whom *Space Cowboys* was a late-in-the-day bonus.

Without taking so much as a deep breath, he went straight into production on *Blood Work*. As FBI profiler Terry McCaleb (in whom one might see the vestiges of good old Dirty Harry), Clint suffers the onset of mortality (or acknowledges it) when a massive heart attack nearly kills him, even as he is hot on the trail of a dirty killer. As he told one interviewer, "At this particular stage in my maturity, I felt it was time to take on characters that have different obstacles to face than they would if I were playing a younger man of 30 or 40."

Despite the star power of Anjelica Huston and Jeff Daniels, the film failed to catch fire and grossed only $27 million during its initial domestic theatrical run, reaching no higher than tenth place with a paltry $3 million gross on its all-important opening weekend in 2002. Even Al Pacino was able to outdraw Clint at the box office, with *S1m0ne*, directed by Andrew Niccol, an unpronounceable sci-fi mishmash that nevertheless managed to come in ahead of *Blood Work*. No Pacino film had outgrossed an Eastwood film, when both were released at the same time, since *The Godfather* (1 and 2) in the early 1970s,

Clint blamed the film's failure on the new administration at Warner Bros.: they had dumped the film into the soft third week of August. Semel and Daley were clearly no longer there to promote his work. He was especially angry that the studio had not given the film a New York red-carpet premiere, or scheduled any pre-opening screening

for the critics, giving them the unmistakable sense that the studio wanted to keep them from seeing it.

After the film opened in the States and quickly disappeared, Clint strongly hinted to the studio that he was thinking of giving up acting altogether. That was big, and not good, news for Warner, as the movies Clint acted in still far outgrossed the ones he only directed. In London for the overseas opening, he sent a message to the new power elite at Warner when he told the *Daily Telegraph*, "I've wanted to phase out of acting and into directing. I'll do it when the day comes when you look up at the screen and say, 'That's enough of that guy.' *And that day gets closer all the time*" (emphasis added).

After the relative failure of *Blood Work*, Clint made good on his threat not to act anymore, at least for his next film. He found a project whose grim story, with dark, mystic overtones, defined destiny as one's random placement in a world filled with misplaced desires, where vengeance is the only acceptable penance. Clint loved the nihilistic script that forty-two-year-old Brian Helgeland had adapted from the celebrated Dennis Lehane novel, *Mystic River*, which celebrated the effect and consequences of a higher-than-legal, if not traditionally religious, code of ethics.*

As he later told Charlie Rose, he wanted to do the project without acting in it, and it took a bit of haggling to get Warner interested:

> I knew of Dennis Lehane, I read a synopsis of the book in a newspaper and I said to myself, "I've got to have this, I think I can make an interesting movie out of it" . . . Warner has always been very good at leaving me alone and letting me operate as a sort of independent production house. I took the script to them and they liked it, but they knew it was unrelenting. At the time, this was the studio that was doing *The Matrix*, *Lord of the Rings*, and *Harry Potter*, all these films with high concepts and lots of action. Excite me some more, they said, and I knew I couldn't excite them any less. They said they'd do it, but at a certain price [$25 million for the negative] and I agreed, and took DGA [Directors Guild] minimum to get it made. I'd done a few complex stories before, but the

---

*Helgeland had written the script for *Blood Work*. In 1997 he co-wrote *L.A. Confidential* with the film's director, Curtis Hanson. They shared an Oscar for Best Screenplay.

fact that it was the unraveling of a mystery that went back a few generations, and when a tragedy reunites [a group of childhood friends] you see what their lives are like, what they've become and what effect an abduction that happened thirty years ago still had on them.

The acts of vengeance that follow were what made the film prime Clint material; in his movies, when vengeance is above the law, heroism takes on mystic (and at times mythic) proportion. It was a favorite theme that reached all the way back to the Man with No Name, through the Dirty Harrys, *Tightrope*, and all the way forward to *Blood Work*.

Mystic River is about Boston's working-class society, which cannot withstand the social and emotional eruption that follows a violent murder and whose ultimate consequence is the moral breakdown of its social order. The breakdown can be only restored (and further broken—one of the film's brilliant ambivalences) by an equally violent act of retribution, even when the target of that retribution is at least partially innocent. That act, rather than any moral force that may be behind it, delivers a measure of relief for the characters involved, as well as the audience. But the relief that defines and drives this dark and vicious movie is incomplete and ultimately unsatisfying.

Darkness and death pervade *Mystic River* as they do in no other Clint Eastwood movie. Here death is the ultimate force that drives both good and evil, searching around corners and seeping into souls, like water seeking its own level. The river, one of the first geographical boundaries we discover from Clint's signature skyview opening, also serves throughout as the metaphorical river of life—the flowing lifeblood of the people who live by it. As critic Dennis Rothermel points out, it "absorbs the past, without forgiving and without healing."

Clint cast an offbeat, eclectic, and intense cast of actors and actresses who would help make the film mesh as an ensemble presentation. He felt they were the best ensemble he had ever put together, even though his leads had never attracted the kind of box office that he had drawn for most of his career; none had ever been in a true blockbuster. The peripatetic Sean Penn, whom Clint cast first—"for his edge," he said—set the tone for the rest; he was a hardened, muscled-and-tattooed ex-con to whom fate deals a horri-

fying blow, driven to respond by dealing life an equally horrifying one. Penn was backed up by Tim Robbins, whose life was ruined by a childhood abduction that comes back to haunt him as an adult; by Kevin Bacon as a tough, clever, but ultimately ineffective detective; by Laurence Fishburne, as his no-nonsense partner; by newcomer Emmy Rossum as Penn's young, beautiful, but ill-fated daughter; by Laura Linney as Penn's wretched wife; and by Marcia Gay Harden as Robbins's wife.

The $30 million film was shot quickly and efficiently in Clint's familiar one-or-two-take method—catching the normally slow, methodical, and Method-intense Penn a little off guard:

> I think the most takes I ever did on Clint's movie was three, and that was rare. A lot of one-takes . . . In the script it was written that six guys are stopping me. I thought maybe two of them could take me. But if it's only six of them, someone might get hurt if I really let myself go, so I don't know what to do. I don't want a really fake fight, and I don't want to hurt anybody. Clint said, "I'll figure it out," and that's all he said. When I came back to the set, he had about 15 guys jump on me, and I was locked down—I was literally able to try to head-butt people, I was able to try to bite people, I was able to try to kick them. I didn't have to hold back at all, and it fixed me to do anything. This is Clint thinking.

Mystic River opened on October 15, 2003, and took the normally Clint-cool critics totally by surprise—it looked, sounded, and felt like no other Clint Eastwood movie. The reviews were universally terrific—easily the best that Clint had ever received as a director. *Newsweek* called it "a masterpiece." Dana Stevens, writing in the *New York Times*, declared that "*Mystic River* is the rare American movie that aspires to—and achieves—the full weight and darkness of tragedy." *Rolling Stone*, where Clint, with his anti-rock, pro-jazz preferences, was rarely at the top of the editorial favorites, raved about the film. Said Peter Travers: "Clint Eastwood pours everything he knows about directing into *Mystic River*. His film sneaks up, messes with your head, and then floors you. You can't shake it. It's that haunting, that hypnotic." David Denby, one of Pauline Kael's successors at *The New Yorker* (after her 2001 passing), gave Clint one of the magazine's best reviews of him ever, saying

the movie was "as close as we are likely to come on the screen to the spirit of Greek tragedy (and closer, I think, than Arthur Miller has come on the stage). The crime of child abuse becomes a curse that determines the pattern of events in the next generation."

In the *New York Observer*, Andrew Sarris praised both the film and Clint:

> *Mystic River* must be considered a decisive advance for the director toward complete artistic mastery of his narrative material . . . Like most of the more interesting films this year, *Mystic River* displays a darker view of our existence in the new millennium than was the norm in the old Hollywood dream factories. Mr. Eastwood is to be commended for reportedly insisting that the film be shot in its natural Boston habitat rather than in a cheaper approximation of Boston, such as bargain-basement Toronto. This emphasis on geographical authenticity helps make this film a masterpiece of the first order.

The film had a carefully planned limited-release opening—Warner hoped that word of mouth would help build an audience. The plan worked. *Mystic River* went on to gross just under $100 million in its initial domestic theatrical release and more than doubled that internationally. Perhaps even more important, the film won every important pre-Oscar award and led in the run-up to that year's Academy Awards.

As expected, *Mystic River* did well in the nominations, two for Clint Eastwood (Best Picture, along with co-producers Judie Hoyt and Robert Lorenz, and Best Director). Sean Penn was nominated for Best Actor, Tim Robbins for Best Supporting Actor. Marcia Gay Harden was nominated for Best Supporting Actress, and Brian Helgeland for his screenplay.*

The ceremonies were held at the Kodak Theater, on February 29, 2004, hosted by the actor and comedian Billy Crystal. By then the battle for Best Picture had shaped up as Clint had predicted when he

---

*Penn had been nominated three previous times, in 1996 for Robbins's *Dead Man Walking*, in 1999 for Woody Allen's *Sweet and Lowdown*, and in 2001 for Jessie Nelson's *I Am Sam*. Robbins's only other nomination had been for Best Director, *Dead Man Walking*. Harden had won Best Supporting Actress for Ed Harris's 2000 *Pollock*.

first encountered the noticeable lack of enthusiasm for it from the Warner executives. They had put all their PR muscle behind Peter Jackson's *Lord of the Rings: The Return of the King*, the result being eleven Academy nominations for a film that was also one of the highest-grossing in Warner's history. Penn and Robbins won in their categories, but *Lord of the Rings* won all eleven awards for which it was nominated, tying William Wyler's *Ben-Hur* (1959) and James Cameron's *Titanic* (1997) for the most Oscars ever won.

Nonetheless, Clint had made a strong statement to the studio about his abilities as a director. Among the most important was that he wasn't a one-shot Oscar wonder, that he could contend year after year and be taken seriously as a popular filmmaker. And he set the stage for his next movie, the somewhat misleadingly titled *Million Dollar Baby*, which sounded like nothing so much as a 1930s-era musical.

It wasn't.

The script for *Million Dollar Baby* had been around for years, an adaptation of several short stories by F.X. Toole, who was a legendary "cut man" in the fight business—the one who stays in the corner of his fighter and must stop the bleeding on his fighter's face between rounds. Paul Haggis had read the stories and tried to put them into a single overview in order to make them into a movie.

The script came to Clint, after several other studios rejected it, but even after he agreed to be in it, Warner refused to okay the film's $30 million budget, despite Clint's success the year before with a similarly difficult, between-the-cracks *Mystic River*. Clint then took the project to Tom Rosenberg, an independent producer at Lakeshore Entertainment, who agreed to put up half if Warner would match it. With the deal finally in place, Clint shot the film in thirty-seven days.

From the beginning, Clint had it in mind to play the trainer, Frankie Dunn, who has seen better days, not just in the ring but in virtually every aspect of his life. His daughter won't talk to him. He cannot get a major talent to train. He has little money, and he simply hangs on the sweaty periphery of the fight world.

One of the more interesting aspects of *Million Dollar Baby* is how smartly it works into a metaphor of Hollywood. Dunn could just as well be a down-and-out director (or producer) looking for the next big

thing to teach and to train into a winner so he can return to his past glory. In other words, he is looking for a star to bring him back to his own former glory.

Into his life comes thirty-one-year-old Maggie Fitzgerald (Hilary Swank), who has very little going for her. She's too old, Dunn thinks, and not especially good, and of course, a woman. Undaunted, she convinces him to work with her. We watch her progress with a narration provided by Dunn's friend, ex-boxer Eddie "Scrap Iron" Dupris, played by Morgan Freeman, here reteamed with Clint after their memorable pairing in *Unforgiven*.

To this point, the film is a rather conventionally uplifting *Rocky*-type boxing film. But then all hell breaks loose: during a match, Dunn's female great white hope is injured in the ring and paralyzed from the neck down. Unable to move and wanting to die, she finally convinces Dunn to mercy-kill her. He does, as Dupris's narration tells us, and disappears.

The film unexpectedly changes course in the middle, going from *Rocky* to *Camille*, from a so-called man's picture with the novelty of a woman in the lead to a so-called woman's picture with a man as the reluctant father-figure hero. It is saved from the melodramatics of soap opera by the superb performances of Clint, Freeman, and especially Swank.

Clint liked the film's sense of balance, liked that Dunn's failure with his own daughter could somehow be atoned for by his "salvation" of Maggie's career, liked that he could find meaning by pushing someone else into the spotlight, liked that he could show where the real talent was in guiding another's performance. His instincts were correct; audiences liked it too. Before its initial domestic release ended, it had grossed more than $220 million and Clint was Oscar-bound once more.

The film's cachet was helped immeasurably by the high level of the reviews it received—and by the curiously effective cross-genre performance of Swank, who had previously established herself as a major player in Hollywood with her Oscar-winning performance in Kimberly Peirce's *Boys Don't Cry* (1999). Similarly, in *Million Dollar Baby*, Swank played a very manly woman to amazing effect. She, too, was a shoo-in for the Oscars.

But it was those reviews that pushed the film forward and made

people want to see it. Its biggest advocate was Roger Ebert, who both in his newspaper column and on his popular film-review TV show championed it as "the best of the year" and advised of a "spoiler" warning. That warning, echoed in numerous other reviews, gave the film a special "must-see" aura, much like that of Neil Jordan's *The Crying Game* (1992), that drove the film straight to the Academy Awards. Jordan had picked up an Oscar for Best Screenplay but lost Best Director to—Clint Eastwood for *Unforgiven*.

If this was finally going to be Clint's year to win it all—especially a Best Actor Oscar—the momentum appeared to be in his favor. Morgan Freeman and Hilary Swank were nominated for Best Supporting Actor and Best Actress, respectively. Clint was nominated for Best Director and Best Actor and, as producer, the would-be recipient for Best Picture.

One of the other nominees for Best Picture was *Ray*, a Hollywood biography of the legendary Ray Charles, directed by Taylor Hackford.* Charles's death earlier in 2004 had considerably enhanced the film's box office and helped catapult it into a Best Picture nomination. There was also Alexander Payne's charmingly out-of-nowhere sex comedy *Sideways*, about the misadventures of four middle-aged losers living in California wine country.†

On the direction front, the nominees included Taylor Hackford for *Ray*, Martin Scorsese for *The Aviator*, Alexander Payne for *Sideways*, and Mike Leigh for *Vera Drake*.

The ceremonies took place on the unusually warm Los Angeles evening of February 27, 2005, once again at the Kodak Theater on Hollywood Boulevard. Chris Rock began the evening with a series of interminably unfunny jokes. Despite the big box office that *Million Dollar Baby* had generated (it had outgrossed Scorsese's *The Aviator* by

---

*Hackford's previous biggest success was his 1980s faux-military fairy tale *An Officer and a Gentleman*, which made top-of-the-line box-office stars out of Richard Gere, Debra Winger, and Louis Gossett Jr. (who won a Supporting Actor Oscar for his performance).

†*Sideways* made stars out of its two male leads, granite-faced Thomas Haden Church (nominated for Best Supporting Actor) and longtime character actor Paul Giamatti. It also temporarily lit the glow of has-been, never-was Virginia Madsen (nominated for Best Supporting Actress) and brought Sandra Oh a leading role in the highly successful TV series *Grey's Anatomy*.

nearly $100 million, domestically), Scorsese looked unbeatable for Best Director. Scorsese's trademark was the idiosyncratic New York street drama, such as *Mean Streets* (1973), *Taxi Driver* (1976), and the grand *Raging Bull* (1980)—he'd lost both Best Picture and Best Director to Robert Redford for *Ordinary People*. The buzz was that this finally had to be Scorsese's year, as much as the previous one had been Clint's. The evening came down to a battle of the East Coast independent versus the western rebel.*

Clint was sitting several rows back with Ruiz—on the aisle, just in case—not far from where Scorsese had been placed, ready for his leap to glory.

The trend was set early. For Best Supporting Actor, the nominations included Freeman, Alan Alda for *The Aviator*; Thomas Haden Church for *Sideways*, Jamie Foxx for Michael Mann's *Collateral*, and Clive Owen for Mike Nichols's *Closer*. These were four strong performances, and although Church and Foxx were considered favorites, they likely split the vote, leaving not enough for Owen or Alda to overtake Freeman, who won it. The theater erupted. This was Freeman's fourth nomination but only his first win. Seated directly behind Clint, he got up and grabbed Clint's hand on the way up. Clint's grin lit up the room. "Heavens to Murgatroyd," Freeman said into the microphone under the noise from his standing ovation. "And I especially want to thank Clint Eastwood for giving me the opportunity to work with him again," he added, as Clint watched, slowly chewing gum and looking pleased and even a bit humbled by the moment.

The evening worked its way through the dozens of awards until it was finally time for the Big Three. The first, Best Actress, was given out by Sean Penn, the winner of the previous year's Best Actor award for *Mystic River*. The nominees were reviewed one more time: Swank, Annette Bening for István Szabó's *Being Julia*, Catalina Sandino Moreno for Joshua Marston's *Maria Full of Grace*, Imelda Staunton for Mike Leigh's *Vera Drake*, and Kate Winslet for Michel Gondry's *Eternal Sunshine of the Spotless Mind*. The only real challenger to Swank was Winslet, but her movie was indecipherable to the few people who had actually gone to see it. Penn opened the envelope and read aloud

---

*Scorsese had previously been nominated as Best Director for *Raging Bull* (1980), *The Last Temptation of Christ* (1988), *Goodfellas* (1990), and *Gangs of New York* (2003).

Swank's name. As she rose to head for the stage, she passed a black-tied Clint, put her hands on his face, and softly kissed him on the lips, all during her ovation. Wearing a dress with no back that cried out "I'm really a woman and a sexy one at that," she humbly accepted the award as "just a girl from a trailer park" and thanked everyone she could possibly think of. Then she stopped the music from playing her off to thank Clint, for allowing her to take the journey with him, for believing in her, for being her *"mo chuisle"*—the words she wore on the back of her robe during the film, which translated from the Gaelic means "My darling, my blood." Clint bowed his head gently in response.

Next came the award for Best Actor. The nominees included Clint, Jamie Foxx in the second of his two nominations for the evening, this one for the title role of *Ray*, Don Cheadle for Terry George's *Hotel Rwanda*, Johnny Depp for *Finding Neverland*, and Leonardo DiCaprio for *The Aviator.** During the recap, when Clint's clip was shown, and the TV camera found him, Ruiz had her arms linked around one of his, pulling him with excitement, while Clint stared ahead, unwilling or unable to show emotion. A radiant Charlize Theron opened the envelope and read the name of the winner—*Jamie Foxx*. The place cheered happily as Foxx ran up to the stage and accepted his award. As he did so, Clint's smile melted into a mask. His eyebrows raised slightly, and he applauded for Foxx.

Finally came the award for Best Director. After the nominees' names were read, the crowd hushed as Julia Roberts opened the envelope.

When she called his name, Clint showed little emotion as he loped on his long legs to the stage. Holding the Oscar, the white-haired, trim, and tanned actor spoke in his trademark low drawl, a guttural slide of sounds rather than a vocalized string of words. After thanking the usual roundup, he paid special tribute to the legendary studio-era production designer Henry Bumstead, ninety years old, who had worked on *Million Dollar Baby*. Clint thanked his mother, ninety-six, reminding audiences that she was only eighty-four when he had won for *Unforgiven*. "So I want to thank her for her genes. I figure I'm

---

*Interestingly, Clint's character was the only fictitious one. The other four were based on real people.

just a kid—I've got a lot of stuff to do yet."* At the age of seventy-four, he had become the oldest person to ever win an Oscar for Best Director.

"I'm happy to be here and still working," Clint said, with a smile, while in the audience a brittle-faced Scorsese slumped deep into his seat.

Clint was back again a few minutes later, when *Million Dollar Baby* won Best Picture. How a picture wins that award, Best Supporting Actor, Best Actress, and Best Director but not Best Actor is hard to explain. But one thing is clear: the Academy, as always, can be sadistically cruel in its reward-denial syndrome.†

This night Clint went home once more another actor's bridesmaid, this time to Jamie Foxx, as the remaining grains of sand ran ever faster down the hourglass of his life.

---

*Ruth Eastwood died a year later, at the age of ninety-seven.

†In 1997, at the age of seventy-two, Lauren Bacall, one of Hollywood's golden-age legends, had a one-last-chance nomination for her role in Barbra Streisand's *The Mirror Has Two Faces*, but she lost to Juliette Binoche for her role in Anthony Minghella's *The English Patient*.

TWENTY-THREE

My earlier work, I was a different person, the young guy with the brass ring. Things were going rather well for me, in the motion picture business as an actor, and I did what came along. Some of it was a lot of fun at the time. Would it be fun today if I were doing it? No, probably not. I've matured, I have different thoughts about things, as I think everybody should.

—Clint Eastwood

In 2005, at seventy-five years of age, Clint Eastwood was happily married to his second wife. His eight-year-old-daughter Morgan Eastwood had been named after his costar and good friend Morgan Freeman. He was a grandfather of two, Kimber's son and Kyle's daughter. And he was the head of a financial empire that included restaurants (the Hog's Breath Inn and the Inn Mission Ranch), real estate, the exclusive invitation-only Tehama Golf Club in Carmel Valley (with an initial joining fee of $300,000), part ownership in the Pebble Beach Golf and Country Club, whole or part ownership in the sixty films he had produced, directed, starred in, or all three, and Malpaso, the company that made nearly all of them. He had eight Academy Award nominations and five Oscars. And as the year began, he was deeply involved in not one but two new movies.

They were a related pair of World War II films that reached back to the days of his youth and held no star-turn roles for him. *Flags of Our Fathers* and *Letters from Iwo Jima* was a unique double package, separate films about the same battle told from the perspective of each side (both with musical sound tracks by Clint Eastwood). *Flags of Our Fathers* was based on the book co-written by James Bradley, the son of one of the flag raisers, and Ron Powers; the film uses flashbacks to tell the story of the Battle of Iwo Jima and the fate of the six men of Easy Company who raised the victory flag there.* Also known as Operation Detachment, the battle started on February 19, 1945, and lasted thirty-five days. It was one of the bloodiest and most pivotal battles in the Pacific Theater.

The historic raising of the flag on the fifth day would endure as a

---

*The six men were Franklin Sousley, Harlon Block, Michael Strank, John Bradley, Ira Hayes, and Rene Gagnon. The three who survived the battle were Bradley, Hayes, and Gagnon.

powerful symbol of victory itself. The moment was immortalized by photographer Joe Rosenthal, who won the Pulitzer Prize for it. (The one he captured on film was actually the second flag-raising.) *Flags of Our Fathers* tells how the three survivors of that photograph were exploited by the American government for propaganda purposes, to boost the morale of the American people during the war, and to help with the sale of war bonds. It also looks at what happened to the men themselves, how the battle affected them, and their difficulties dealing with guilt and self-worth in the years that followed the so-called moment of heroic glory.

It is a moving subject whose symbolic and political relevancies had, if anything, become even more vivid as the war in Iraq dragged on, while the administration that had forced it struggled to find ways to "sell" it to the American people. No one knew better than Clint Eastwood how much a picture could do to promote an image. Take a man with no name, for instance, and give him a poncho and a cigarillo, and you could redefine the iconic image of the gunfighters of the American West.

The project was the brainchild of Steven Spielberg, who, along with Tom Hanks, had become the self-appointed representatives of a peculiar niche of the baby boom generation: those who had never served in the military (and likely protested the war in Vietnam) but regarded the previous generation—their fathers, uncles, and older brothers—as "the greatest" for their service in World War II. (The "greatest generation" became the slogan for the uncomplicated heroism and patriotism of the Second World War, the "good war.") For Spielberg and Hanks, World War II became less the basis of real drama and more the ultimate boomer video game, something of a techno fetish in films like *Saving Private Ryan* (1998), an award-winning box-office smash loosely based on the true story of one family, the "fighting Sullivans," who lost five sons during the war. In the film, which begins with a violent re-creation of the Allied landing at Normandy, a group of soldiers are sent out to find the last remaining Sullivan son and bring him home. It is a noble gesture and a great theme for a film (if one disregards the huge body count that piles up to save the one last surviving Ryan). Spielberg had previously made *Empire of the Sun* (1987), *1941* (1979), and *Schindler's List* (1993), as

well as the Indiana Jones films and TV series, all World War II–themed projects, and he would go on to do a ten-part series for HBO called *Band of Brothers,* co-produced by Tom Hanks. Perhaps wisely, this time Spielberg felt he needed to emphasize dramatic substance over stylized mythology, with a little more penetration and a little less envy.

Clint first came upon the project while he was in production on *Million Dollar Baby:*

> I ran into Steven [Spielberg] at a function, and he said, "Why don't you come over [to DreamWorks] and do something for me, you direct and you and I will produce it." I said okay, I was geared up and ready, he had a few scripts [adapted versions of the book], but he hadn't found anything he really liked. At the time I was working with Paul Haggis, on *Million Dollar Baby,* so I said, "Let me talk to Paul about it." He read the material, we had a few meetings, and he sat down and wrote a script.

Haggis's (and William Broyles Jr.'s) major cinematic leap was to tell the story in flashback, to keep the story pulsating and maintain a contemporary feel.

With Spielberg in place as one of the producers, Clint and Malpaso were able to bring Warner into the project. Filming began shortly after *Million Dollar Baby* was completed. In typical Clint fashion, the cast lacked a superstar—the biggest "name" in the film was Ryan Phillippe.

Then midway through production, as if to underscore the difference between himself and Spielberg, Clint made a decision to do something no one had ever done before.

> I started wondering, what about the other [Japanese] guys: What was going on in their minds? What were their lives like? I mean, it was pretty miserable for the Americans on that island—can you imagine what it was like for the other guy, who didn't have the same equipment, the same access to food and water—there was no water on Iwo Jima, the only water you get is from rain—so they were trapped out there, living on weeds and plants, worms, anything they could find. So they were an

interesting group of people. Now that decades had gone by, I thought it was important for the Japanese public to appreciate those men, even though it's not about winning or losing, who won or who lost. It's about the sacrifices they made for their country, rightly or wrongly—they made them.*

Thus was born the notion of making a simultaneous, or parallel, film, the same story seen from the other side, to be called *Letters from Iwo Jima*. Ken Watanabe would play the lead—he was a bigger international star than anyone in *Flags of Our Fathers*. Clint received permission from the Japanese government to shoot some scenes on Iwo Jima. (The property had been returned to them in the early 1960s.) But for economy and accessibility to mountains and underground tunnels, the bulk of both films was shot simultaneously on a volcanic island in Iceland, and they were released within weeks of each other.

After the war ended, it had taken decades for Japanese cinema to get art-house distribution in America because of the hard feelings left behind by Pearl Harbor. Marlon Brando (of all people) had been the first to attempt a sympathetic portrayal of the Japanese, during the postwar occupation at least, in Joshua Logan's Academy Award–winning *Sayonara* (1957). It was a daunting challenge to try to make Americans believe that the Japanese were human beings, let alone a cultured civilization capable of love, warmth, and dignity. Logan's and Brando's Academy Award–winning film opened the door to Japanese cinema's acceptance in the United States. But forty years later the industry still felt it was unlikely that any sizable audiences would go see *Letters from Iwo Jima*. Characteristically, even if Clint was aware of the whispers, he proceeded as planned.

"Between the two films together, I was trying to make an anti-war statement," he said. "It's hard to make any war picture and make it a

------

*A few other films had tried to show both sides, without much success. The biggest was Richard Fleischer and Kinji Fukasaku's *Tora! Tora! Tora!* (1970), about the attack on Pearl Harbor. The film, which had two directors, did not succeed at the box office and discouraged further attempts to show World War II from more than one point of view. No American film before *Letters from Iwo Jima* was ever made that showed any war issue completely and solely from the other side.

pro-war statement." Strong and perhaps surprising sentiments, indeed, from someone whose credentials were strewn with films of flagrant violence, messy bloodshed, and the twitchy pleasures of psychotic murderers, and especially along with the likes of Spielberg, whose vicarious-thrill movies were usually filled with fantasies of glory rather than realistic gore.

Flags of Our Fathers was released on October 20, 2006, amid high hopes it would be the big fall movie. Two months later, on December 20, *Letters from Iwo Jima* was put into limited distribution in the States, after having its world premiere and initial, highly successful run in Japan. Three weeks later, on January 12, 2007, it went into major nationwide distribution.

Shortly before *Flags* was released, Clint went on what was for him a PR spree, agreeing to sit for an interview with *Rolling Stone* magazine, whose resident film critic had, through the years, been up and down about him. But this time Peter Travers was unequivocal in his praise for Clint's decidedly nonconservative, non-flag-waving view of heroism and its inevitable fallout. He gave the film three and a half stars (out of four):

> The ambitious script . . . jumps back and forth in ways that could have been a jumble if Eastwood wasn't so adept at cutting a path to what counts. Eastwood's film is a fierce attack on wartime hypocrisy and profiteering, and also an indelibly moving salute to the soldiers who don't deserve to walk alone for following their own sense of duty . . . one thing is for sure, Eastwood will do it his way. As far as I'm concerned, that's the gold standard.

Richard Roeper, one of the sharper new multimedia critics, wrote in the *Chicago Sun-Times* that *Flags of Our Fathers* "stands with the Oscar-winning *Unforgiven* and *Million Dollar Baby* as an American masterpiece . . . but it is also patriotic because it questions the official version of the truth, and reminds us that superheroes exist only in comic books and cartoon movies."

Most of the major critics got it, and said that both films were among the best and most important movies in Clint's body of work—but neither clicked with audiences. *Flags of Our Fathers* earned about

$66 million, less than half of *Million Dollar Baby*, against $55 million in production costs. Using the standard formula that a film has to gross twice what it cost to break even, the film wound up losing a significant amount of money. *Letters from Iwo Jima* did even worse and exposed the huge miscalculation in Clint's overview; during one of the most vicious post–World War II wars in modern American history, audiences in this country simply weren't interested in a sympathetic view of the enemy—*any* enemy.

The films had their social critics, one of the most outspoken being Spike Lee, the African-American filmmaker, who had strong objections to Clint's take on the events of Iwo Jima. At the May 2008 Cannes Film Festival Lee was promoting his own World War II film, *Miracle at St. Anna*, about the exploits of the all-Black 92nd Buffalo Division, which fought the German army in Italy during the war. There Lee publicly criticized Clint and *Flags of Our Fathers* and *Letters from Iwo Jima* for not having "a single African-American character or actor. There were many African-Americans who survived that war and who were upset at Clint for not having one [in his two films]. That was his version: The negro soldier did not exist. I have a different version."

In response, Eastwood, who suspected Lee was trying to promote his films by criticizing Clint's, angrily told the *Guardian:*

As for *Flags of Our Fathers*, he [Lee] says there was a small detachment of black troops on Iwo Jima as a part of a munitions company, but they didn't raise the flag. The story is *Flags of Our Fathers*, the famous flag-raising picture, and they didn't do that. If I go ahead and put an African-American actor in there, people'd go, "This guy's lost his mind." I mean, it's not accurate. He was complaining when I did *Bird* [the 1988 biopic of Charlie Parker]. Why would a white guy be doing that? I was the only guy who made it, that's why. He could have gone ahead and made it. Instead he was making something else.

Lee returned fire.

First of all, the man is not my father and we're not on a plantation either. He's a great director. He makes his films, I make my films. The

thing about it though, I didn't personally attack him. And a comment like "a guy like that should shut his face"—come on Clint, come on. He sounds like an angry old man right there. If he wishes, I could assemble African-American men who fought at Iwo Jima and I'd like him to tell these guys that what they did was insignificant and they did not exist. He said, "I'm not making this up. I know history. I'm a student of history." And I know the history of Hollywood and its omission of the one million African-American men and women who contributed to World War II. Not everything was John Wayne, baby . . . I never said he should show one of the other guys holding up the flag as black. I said that African-Americans played a significant part in Iwo Jima. For him to insinuate that I'm rewriting history and have one of the four guys with the flag be black . . . no one said that. It's just that there's not one black in either film. And because I know my history, that's why I made that observation.*

After Clint publicly warned Lee to "shut his face," it was Steven Spielberg who finally got both sides to calm down, convincing Spike Lee to back off. "After game three, L.A. Staples Center, Lakers [vs.] Celtics, I'm going to the bathroom and Spielberg's sitting there with Eddie Murphy and Jeffrey Katzenberg," said Spike Lee. "And Katzenberg was getting on me about leaving Clint alone. I said, 'Steven, let me talk to you for a second.' So we talked. I conveyed a message and he said, 'I'll call Clint in the morning.' And it's hunky-dory. He said he was gonna make a call, he made it, squashed." A couple of months later, Lee even sent his new film over to Clint for a private viewing

Despite Lee's accusations (or possibly because of them—Lee and his films are not exactly laden with Oscars or nominations), the Academy found Clint's films good enough to nominate, even if its perception of *Flags of Our Fathers* was, inexplicably, one of *über*-patriotism rather than a profoundly vivid criticism of the Bush administration's war in Iraq.

*Clint was no stranger to public battles with other filmmakers. In 2005 he publicly vowed he'd kill Michael Moore if the documentarian ever showed up at his house, the way he had at Charlton Heston's in *Bowling for Columbine*.

On Sunday night, February 25, 2007, the seventy-ninth annual Academy Awards were held once again at Hollywood's Kodak Theater. This time television talk-show host Ellen DeGeneres hosted, in an attempt by the Academy to give a more modern look to its annual ritual of self-congratulation and to improve its ratings—the Oscars were a TV show, after all, and more often than not hosts were taken from that pool of talent rather than from the world of film.

There was a different feel in the air this year; for one thing, the Academy had moved up the presentation by nearly a month from the previous year to prevent declining ratings for the telecast. Awards programs were becoming a TV genre all their own, between the Golden Globes, the Screen Actors Guild Awards, the People's Choice Awards, and at least a half-dozen others related to film (and another dozen for music, TV, and theater), so the giving of the golden statuette was somewhat anticlimactic. And, by February, it was felt, a healthy number of the new year's films, were, at least theoretically, in theaters, making it increasingly difficult to look back at what was essentially old news.

This year's awards featured a rematch: Scorsese was back with *The Departed*, his sharp, return-to-form street-cred *policier*, a remake of Wai-keung Lau and Siu Fai Mak's Hong Kong original *Infernal Affairs* (2002); Clint was back as well with a Best Director nomination, but not for *Flags of Our Fathers*—it was, shockingly, for *Letters from Iwo Jima*.*

Scorsese's nomination was easy to understand, in light of his strong film, and that begins to explain why *Letters* was nominated over *Flags*. Clint had once been an Academy outcast, but ever since his explosive leap to prominence in the ranks of the Academy with *Unforgiven*, his public and industry images had melded into each other, and according to *Variety* editor Peter Bart, he had become Hollywood's elder statesman; meanwhile Scorsese continued to be the industry's aging and defiantly independent "bad boy." Like a film-without-a-film, the Oscar

---

*Flags of Our Fathers received two nominations, for Sound Editing (Alan Robert Murray and Bub Asman) and Sound Mixing (John T. Reitz, David E. Campbell, Gregg Rudloff, Walt Martin). It lost the first to *Letters from Iwo Jima* and the second to *Dreamgirls* (Michael Minkler, Bob Beemer, Willie D. Burton).

presentations were moral stories as well as economic victories and almost always followed the standard rules that the villain rarely gets the girl, or in this case, the Oscar. This year, however, the feeling ran heavily throughout the industry that Scorsese had made the better film (better than *Flags of Our Fathers*). While television had taken over the crime genre as its own never-ending source of good triumphing over evil, Scorsese's movie transcended the usual laboratory-and-clues mundanity to spill over with the dynamics of the human moral condition. Clint, meanwhile, had made just another war movie. As good as it was—and few conservative Academy members thought it was all that good—in a nod of respect to Clint, they nominated his *other* movie, which *nobody* saw, thus ensuring that at least this time around, Scorsese could win. The other films in the Best Picture contest, all considered long shots by the pollsters and the pundits alike, were Alejandro González Iñárritu's *Babel*, Jonathan Dayton and Valerie Faris's *Little Miss Sunshine*, and Stephen Frears's *The Queen*.

Three of the most powerful directors in Hollywood, Francis Ford Coppola, Steven Spielberg, and George Lucas, assembled onstage to announce the winner of the award for Best Director. Coppola and Lucas had been part of the seminal 1970s San Francisco film movement that had helped to change the perception of American film from studio domination and toward larger independent films. The three titans gathered around the mike and did some obligatory and predictably goofy patented Academy Award blather ("It's better to give than to receive . . . no it's not!") and interminably back-patted themselves. Then they finally got around to reading the names of the Best Director nominees. When Coppola read Scorsese's name aloud, the audience burst into enthusiastic applause, at least twice as loud as they would for anyone else. When Coppola read Clint's name, the audience applauded dutifully. Ruiz, looking resplendent in a ruby-red dress with earrings hanging from her ears like giant shiny stalactites, smiled at her husband lovingly as she enthusiastically clapped. Clint, lips twitching as he chewed either gum or his lip, never broke his stare, aimed intently and directly at the stage.

Now it was Spielberg's turn to open the envelope. The tension in the room was negligible. "And the Oscar goes to . . . *Martin Scorsese!*" Scorsese threw his hands up in mock disbelief, like someone at a surprise party who was tipped off in advance, and then bolted toward the

stage and his rendezvous with Oscar glory. Clint joined the standing ovation, his face frozen in a runner-up smile.

The Departed won four of the five Oscars it was nominated for that night, including Best Picture, losing only Best Supporting Actor (Mark Wahlberg). When the final award was handed out (to Graham King as producer), the long evening came to an end, as did Clint's latest, and perhaps last, chance to enter the pantheon of Best Actor Oscar winners. As the celebrity crowd left the building on their way to the various parties, with handshakes of congratulations flying through the crowd like a flock of birds madly flapping their wings, Clint and Ruiz quietly slipped away, unnoticed and unbothered, and headed home.

The next morning, back in Carmel, after breakfast and on the way to the golf course, Clint began formulating his next film.

Two more years would pass before another Clint Eastwood movie appeared. He was fast approaching eighty, and at last and inevitably, time seemed to be slowing his crank-'em-out pace. Increasingly, he spent his days on the golf course and looking after his business interests until, finally, he found two projects he wanted to do, one as director, and one more to act in—a last-chance effort to win that elusive Best Actor award.

The next one he chose to direct was *Changeling*.* It was to be a joint venture between Imagine Entertainment, Universal, and Malpaso, making it the first film in fifteen years that a Clint project had no participation from Warner. In the aftermath of his double crash-and-burn Iwo Jima set, all sides had apparently agreed on a pause, if not a clean break, in the long-standing partnership.

The story of *Changeling* involves a woman who single-handedly takes on the corrupt L.A. police department over what she believes has been the kidnapping of her child by the authorities themselves. Stories of men (or women) alone who take on the system always appealed to Clint, and this one had some fresh angles he liked, not the least of which was that the hero happened to be a woman. He had had great

*A "changeling" is a being in West European folklore and folk religion, the offspring of a fairy, a troll, an elf, or other legendary creature, that has been secretly left in the place of a human child.

fortune with a female lead in *Million Dollar Baby* and was eager to revisit that setup.

Based on a true story, the film originated in the 1970s, in a telephone tip that had come to TV scriptwriter and former journalist J. Michael Straczynski. Someone had informed him that officials were about to dispose of several potentially incriminating documents concerning a city council welfare hearing involving Christine Collins and her son's disappearance. Intrigued, Straczynski did some research and wrote a screenplay based on what he had found. *The Strange Case of Christine Collins* was optioned several times but never got made. Twenty years later, in 1996, after a long and successful run in TV, Straczynski took another shot at the story. He wrote a new script in only about two weeks and got it to producer Ron Howard, who read it, liked it, optioned it through his Imagine Entertainment production, and fast-tracked it, intending to produce and direct it in 2007, immediately following the release of his *The Da Vinci Code*. But Howard opted instead to direct *Frost/Nixon*, then the prequel to *The Da Vinci Code*, *Angels & Demons*, so he and his partner, Brian Grazer, pitched *Changeling* to Clint in February 2007. He agreed to direct it, citing the script's focus on its heroine, Collins, rather than the "Freddy Krueger" story of the crimes as the reason why.

He changed not a single word of Straczynski's script and within weeks of the first cast reading, he was ready to shoot the film. Every available over-thirty actress had put herself up for the sure-to-win-an-Oscar-nomination part. Clint cast Angelina Jolie because, he later said, he thought her face was perfect for period films (as he had Swank's for *Million Dollar Baby*).

Production began on October 15, 2007, and was shot on location in and around Los Angeles, and principal photography was completed in just under thirty days. The atmosphere on the set was relaxed; Clint was in total and unchallenged control and able to easily guide his actors through their most intense moments. Angelina Jolie recalls how it was to work with Clint:

> My character, Christine Collins, came up against so much pain and hardship, and she fought hard and she became a real hero of mine and I wanted to tell people about her. Fortunately, I had someone like

Clint to work with who is such a supportive director and so economic with your emotions. He didn't drain me and he helped me through all the very difficult, emotional scenes.

Six months later, on May 20, 2008, Clint debuted the film at Cannes, where it was enthusiastically received. Its distributor, Universal, then scheduled it for its big fall 2008 release. Even before the film's spring French preview, a recharged Clint had already begun work on his next film, one that would bring him back to the front of the camera.

Like everything else in Hollywood, schedules are subject to a million different factors, any one of which can cause delays, sometimes interminable ones. Before *Changeling* had come his way, Clint had actually begun preproduction on another film, *The Human Factor,* a biography of Nelson Mandela, which, for one reason or another, had to be postponed for a year. After flying through production of *Changeling,* and with *The Human Factor* still delayed, Clint looked around for another project. *Gran Torino* came his way, and he decided that that was the one he would make to bring himself back as an actor.

The original script had been written by Nick Schenk, a popular TV actor (Butch the Janitor, on *Let's Bowl*), writer, and producer; *Gran Torino* was his first try at a screenplay. Schenk had actually written the script years earlier based on his experiences working at a Minnesota Ford assembly plant side by side with several Korean War veterans, who had returned from active duty loaded with prejudice and anger toward all Asians. While working and living in Minnesota, Schenk had discovered the Hmong, a mountain-based, migratory sect of Chinese, many of whom eventually relocated to Laos and fought on the American side during the so-called secret incursion against the Pathet Lao during the Vietnam War. After the Americans left in 1974, many Hmong wound up in Communist prison camps, while others came to America and set up communities in various cities.

Schenk (and his brother's roommate, Dave Johannson) developed the screenplay, which set a Korean War widower against the Hmong, who have taken over his neighborhood. He is at first bitter and prejudiced toward the Hmong, seeing in them the reflection of the North Koreans and Chinese he battled during the war, but gradually he begins to learn about their culture, helps rescue the daughter of the

family next door from a violent street gang, and helps her brother resist being recruited by the same gang. In the end, the grizzled old vet makes the ultimate sacrifice to save the boy, in a top-heavy Christians-save-"savages" plot twist. The final scene is replete with crucifixion images that were affecting, important, and dramatic. But as Schenk found out prior to Clint's involvement, the studios considered it completely unmarketable.

The main objection had been the age of the lead character, Polish-American Korean War veteran Walt Kowalski. The youth-dominated film industry—not just the makers but the audiences for whom they made their films—felt that such a story would have no audience; the Chinese were not a huge factor in ticket-buying demographics, and the elderly rarely went to the movies.

After receiving turn-down after turn-down, Schenk sent his screenplay to Warner producer Bill Gerber, who gave it to Clint, knowing he was actively searching for a project to replace *The Human Factor*. In Walt Kowalski (with the name's distinctive echoes of Tennessee Williams's celebrated bear-man in *A Streetcar Named Desire*) Clint found yet another reluctant, one-last-time character who is not afraid to use force against those he feels are his enemies and to defend those he thinks are his friends. In many ways Kowalski was an amalgam of the Man with No Name, Dirty Harry, and William Munny, here aged and cynical but willing and able to fight on whenever the need arose.*

Using local Hmong on location in Michigan, where Warner, after green-lighting the film, had suggested moving the shoot to take advantage of tax incentives, Clint blew through the shoot in his standard thirty days, and *Gran Torino* made it into theaters by December 12, only two months after *Changeling* had opened. It had been rushed into limited release to qualify for the 2008 Oscar race, and went into wide release in January 2009. This step-by-step release pattern, known as "platforming," is used to build word of mouth for films that don't have an immediate and apparent appeal to a large audience; it was augmented here by a statement that was "leaked" to the press and that flooded the Internet, in which Clint was supposed to have said that this

---

*Age had taken its toll on Clint as well. His six-foot-four frame had "shrunk" to six foot one due to chronic back problems.

was his farewell performance as an actor.* Whether he said it or not—
and later he claimed he didn't say it *exactly* that way—the reason was
not hard to see; even if this film wasn't his last, it was almost certainly
his last chance to win a Best Actor Oscar, and to do it in highly dramatic fashion.†

Gran Torino received out-and-out raves, among the best of his
career. The *New York Times* said that "Clint Eastwood has slipped
another film into theaters and shown everyone how it's done." The
Wall Street Journal called Clint's work in the film "the performance of
a lifetime," and the *Los Angeles Times* called it "a move audiences are
wise to follow." Andrew Sarris, in the *New York Observer*, proclaimed
that "Clint makes my day as aging avenging angel . . . he caps his
career as both a director and an actor with his portrayal of a heroically redeemed bigot of such humanity and luminosity as to exhaust
my supply of superlatives . . . the result is a genuinely pioneering production very much worth seeing for the emotional thunderbolt that
it is." Dozens more were just as enthusiastic.

Audiences too responded to the film, and it, rather than *Changeling*,
became the sleeper crowd-pleaser of the Christmas–New Year season. Its box-office take grew every week until its wide release quickly
sent it over the $100 million gross.

In early January the Oscar nominees were announced, and to the
surprise of many and shock of some, both Clint films were all but
ignored. Angelina Jolie was nominated for Best Actress for *Changeling*
and Tom Stern was nominated for Best Cinematography, but there
was nothing for Clint's direction of either film or, even more outrageously, for his performance in *Gran Torino*. The film itself, like
Changeling, was left out of the Best Picture category, which included

---

*"Clint Eastwood, who has played strong, silent types on-screen for more than 50 years,
is done with acting. Eastwood, 78, says he has no plans to step in front of the camera
after *Gran Torino*, which he directed, and starred in . . . 'That will probably do it for
me as far as acting is concerned,' the Academy Award–winning director told Britain's
Sunday Express. 'But I've got no plans to stop making films.'"—Cathy Burke, various
newswires, December 15, 2008.

†In an interview in the *New York Times* to promote *Gran Torino*, Bruce Headlam asked
Clint about the persistent Internet and wire service stories that this was to be his last
acting assignment. Clint's reply: "Somebody asked what I'd do next, and I said I didn't
know how many roles there are for 78-year-old guys. There's nothing wrong with coming in to play the butler. But unless there's a hurdle to get over, I'd rather just stay
behind the camera." *New York Times*, December 14, 2008.

Steven Daldry's *The Reader*, David Fincher's *The Curious Case of Benjamin Button*, Danny Boyle's *Slumdog Millionaire*, Ron Howard's *Frost/Nixon*, and Gus Van Sant's *Milk*. None of these films held either the resonance or the grand career summation that Clint's *Gran Torino* did.* The cocktail parties and Internet debates started immediately— the Academy was too old; the Academy was too ignorant; Clint had passed his "darling" phase and returned to making movies that only the public liked; nobody went to see films about the Chinese; Clint was too old-looking; Clint was too old; the film's mood was anti–Obama's national sense of uplift; the film was too negative and prejudicial.

And on it went, the low din of whispers that had followed Clint around for his entire career, like Shakespeare's infamous sound and fury. It was all part of the game, he knew, but it never failed to prick his very tough if not always thick skin. But he couldn't let it bother him. As Robert Frost, one of Clint's favorite poets, expressed in his famous poem, "Stopping by Woods on a Snowy Evening," he felt that he too had miles to go before he slept. Already he had a half-dozen new projects dancing like juggler's balls in his head; the Nelson Mandela pic, with his buddy Morgan Freeman in the starring role; a biopic of Neil Armstrong, the first man to walk on the moon, tentatively titled *First Man;* a film for DreamWorks called *Hereafter;* a jazz documentary about Dave Brubeck, another one about Tony Bennett . . . there was even talk of yet another Dirty Harry sequel. That had made him laugh: "*Dirty Harry VI*! Harry is retired. He's standing in a stream, fly-fishing. He gets tired of using the pole—and BA-BOOM! Or Harry is retired, and he catches bad guys with his walker? Maybe he owns a tavern. These guys come in and they won't pay their tab, so Harry reaches below the bar. 'Hey guys, the next shot's on me.' "

While his career moves remained uncertain, Clint's personal life had settled down. Dina regularly organized huge weekend outings for all the Eastwoods. She had performed the mighty task of bringing the entire Eastwood clan together, the mothers, the sons, the daughters, even some of the ex-girlfriends, give or take an unforgiving one or

---

*Best Director nominees were Daldry, Fincher, Boyle, Howard, and Van Sant. Best Actor nominees were Brad Pitt (*The Curious Case of Benjamin Button*), Richard Jenkins (Tom McCarthy's *The Visitor*), Sean Penn (*Milk*), Frank Langella (*Frost/Nixon*), and Mickey Rourke (Darren Aronofsky's *The Wrestler*).

two. Even Maggie, who lives in the same area and remains Clint's business partner, often attends. Both agree they get along much better now that they're not married. Today the Eastwood ranch feels like a vast homestead, like the Kennedys' Hyannis Port, or the Bushes' Kennebunkport, or even Bick Benedict's Texas ranch in George Stevens's 1956 epic, *Giant*, released after James Dean, its star, was killed in a car crash. Clint had appeared in his first movie the same year Dean died. A lot of movies and movie stars had come and gone since then, but Clint was still going strong, willing and able to play the game. He was in no hurry to get to those woods, lovely, dark and deep.

Soon enough, but not quite yet.

SOURCES

Research Institutions

Margaret Herrick Library of the Academy of Motion Picture Arts and Sciences, Beverly Hills, California

New York Public Library, New York City

New York Public Library for the Performing Arts, New York City

Los Angeles County Court, public records, Los Angeles

British Film Institute

Cinémathèque, Paris, France

Library of the *Los Angeles Times* (librarian Scott Wilson)

Bibliography

Albert, James. *Pay Dirt: Divorces of the Rich and Famous.* California: Diane Publishing, 1989.

Bach, Steven. *Final Cut: Dreams and Disaster in the Making of Heaven's Gate.* New York: William Morrow, 1985.

Bingham, Dennis. *Acting Male: Masculinities in the Films of James Stewart, Jack Nicholson and Clint Eastwood.* New Brunswick, N.J.: Rutgers University Press, 1994.

Biskind, Peter. *Easy Riders, Raging Bulls.* New York: Simon & Schuster, 1998.

Bragg, Melvyn. *Richard Burton: A Life.* Boston: Little, Brown, 1988.

Clinch, Minty. *Clint Eastwood.* London: Coronet Books, 1995.

Duncan, Paul, ed. *Movie Icons: Clint Eastwood.* Los Angeles: Taschen, 2006.

Eliot, Marc. *Burt!* New York: Dell, 1983.

Engel, Leonard, ed. *Clint Eastwood: Actor and Director.* Salt Lake City: University of Utah Press, 2007.

Frayling, Christopher. *Clint Eastwood.* London: Virgin, 1992.

Haskell, Molly. *Holding My Own in No Man's Land.* New York: Oxford University Press, 1997.

Kaminsky, Stuart M. *Clint Eastwood.* New York: New American Library, 1974.

Kapsis, Robert E., and Kathie Coblentz, eds. *Clint Eastwood Interviews.* Jackson: University Press of Mississippi, 1999.

Kinn, Gail, and Jim Piazza. *The Academy Awards.* New York: Black Dog and Leventhal, 2002.

Knapp, Laurence F. *Directed by Clint Eastwood.* Jefferson, N.C.: McFarland, 1996.

Locke, Sondra. *The Good, The Bad & The Very Ugly.* New York: William Morrow, 1997.

McGilligan, Patrick. *Clint: The Life and Legend.* New York: St. Martin's Press, 1999.

Nichols, Peter M., ed. *The New York Times Guide to the 1,000 Best Movies Ever Made.* New York: St. Martin's Press, 2004.

Randall, Stephen, ed., and the editors of *Playboy* magazine. *The Playboy Interviews: The Directors.* Milwaukee, Ore.: M Press, 2006.

Reynolds, Burt. *My Life.* New York: Hyperion, 1994.

Richards, David. *Played Out: The Jean Seberg Story.* New York: Random House, 1981.

Rickles, Don. *Rickles' Book.* New York: Simon & Schuster, 2007.

Rose, Frank. *The Agency: William Morris and the Hidden History of Show Business.* New York: HarperCollins, 1995.

Sarris, Andrew. *The American Cinema.* New York: E. P. Dutton, 1968.

———. *Confessions of a Cultist: On the Cinema, 1955–1969.* New York: Simon & Schuster, 1970.

Schickel, Richard. *Clint Eastwood: A Biography.* New York: Random House, 1996.

Siegel, Don. *A Siegel Film: An Autobiography.* London: Faber and Faber, 1993.

Thompson, Douglas. *Clint Eastwood: Billion Dollar Man.* London: John Blake, 2005.

Verlhac, Pierre-Henri, ed. *Clint Eastwood: A Life in Pictures.* San Francisco: Chronicle Books, 2008.

Wallach, Eli. *The Good, the Bad, and Me.* New York: Harcourt, 2005.

Wiley, Mason, and Damien Bona. *Inside Oscar: The Unofficial History of the Academy Awards.* New York: Ballantine Books, 1986.

Zmijewsky, Boris, and Lee Pfeiffer. *The Films of Clint Eastwood.* New York: Citadel Press, 1993.

NOTES

Epigraphs and Introduction

ix "You go to an Eastwood movie . . .": Molly Haskell, *Playgirl*, November 1985.

ix "Clint Eastwood is a tall . . .": James Wolcott, *Vanity Fair*, July 1985.

ix "Eastwood has . . .": Robert Mazzocco, "The Supply-Side Star," *New York Review of Books*, April 1, 1982.

ix "People can know . . .": Quoted in John Love, "Clint Eastwood at 50," *San Antonio Light*, November 2, 1980.

ix "There is something . . .": Quoted in Haskell, *Playgirl*.

ix "I'm an actor . . .": Quoted in *Newsweek*, July 22, 1985.

1 "I grew up . . .": Interview by Charlie Rose, PBS, October 8, 2003.

Chapter One

11 "My father . . .": Quoted in Dick Kleiner, syndicated Hollywood columnist, collection of columns and notes, Margaret Herrick Library.

14 "Well, those were the thirties . . .": Interview by David Thomson, *Film Comment* 20, no. 5, September–October 1984.

14 "My father was big on . . .": Interview by Bernard Weinraub, *Playboy*, March 1997. This was the second interview Clint gave the magazine.

15 "I can't remember . . .": Quoted in Wayne Warga, *Washington Post*, July 8, 1969.

16 "I remember Gertrude Falk . . . she made up her mind . . .": Zmijewsky and Pfeiffer, *Films*, 9.

16 "dummy": Thompson, *Billion Dollar Man*, 19.

16 "When I sat down . . .": Ibid., 20.

17 "I would lie . . .": Weinraub interview, *Playboy*.

18 "I'd never seen a musician . . .": Quoted in Schickel, *Eastwood*, 40.

18 "really adrift": Quoted in Frank Thistle, "Filmland's Most Famous Gunslinger," *Hollywood Studio*, February 1973.

Chapter Two

21 "Basically I was a drifter . . .": Quoted in Frank Thistle, "Filmland's Most Famous Gun-slinger," *Hollywood Studio*, February 1973.

21 "You can only dig . . .": Quoted in Dick Lochte, *Los Angeles Free Press*, April 20, 1973.

25 "One of my auxiliary . . .": Interview by Michel Ciment, "Entretien avec Clint Eastwood," *Positif* 31 (May 1990).

27 Clint getting a Seattle girl pregnant: "Clint handed the money over to the woman and left for L.A." McGilligan, *Life and Legend*, 54. McGilligan cites as his source a story that appeared in the *Valley Daily News* in July 1993. Eastwood has never confirmed this story.

Chapter Three

29 "I had a premonition . . .": Quoted in Dick Kleiner column, Margaret Herrick Library.

32 Lubin taken to meet Clint: Clint Eastwood interview by Arthur Knight, *Playboy*, February 1974 (Clint would do a second interview for the magazine in March 1997, conducted by Bernard Weinraub); *Crawdaddy*, April 1978.

33 "I thought I was . . .": Knight interview, *Playboy*.

33 Mamie Van Doren: "[Clint] was always straight and direct—he always knew the most straight and direct path to my dressing room," said Van Doren, quoted in "Chatter," *People*, May 26, 1986.

33 "the first year of marriage . . .": Quoted in Clinch, *Eastwood*, 29.

34 "He is very much . . .": Maggie Eastwood, quoted in Tim Chadwick, "We Don't Believe in Togetherness," *Screen Stars*, July 1971.

36 "They made a lot of cheapies . . .": Quoted in Ann Guerin, *Show*, February 1970.

37 "Don't worry . . .": Burt Reynolds, quoted in Eliot, *Burt!*, 42.

41 "the lousiest western . . ." Quoted in Carrie Rickey, *Fame*, November 1988.

Chapter Four

47 "I was set to direct . . .": Quoted in Bridget Byrne, "Eastwood's Round 'Em Up, Move 'Em Out Film Making Style," *Los Angeles Herald-Examiner*, June 24, 1973.

52 "fairly open relationship . . .": Interview by Arthur Knight, *Playboy*, February 1974.

54 Leonard reportedly kept two sets of books: See McGilligan, *Life and Legend*, 105. McGilligan cites "unnamed sources."

56 PR tour of Japan: Clint told Japanese reporters, whenever asked, that Maggie did not want to come. But, in an interview with *Photoplay* magazine in 1961 entitled "Clint Eastwood: Hollywood Loner," he is quoted as saying, "I just didn't want her along. I felt like going myself."

58 Maggie never said anything and never complained: Tunis never publicly discussed her relationship with Clint, but Clint talked about the uniqueness of his marriage, both in *Playboy* in 1974 and in Tim Chadwick, "We Don't Believe in Togetherness," *Screen Stars*, July 1971. About his quite-rare interview with the Eastwoods, Chadwick stated, "The only way Clint and Maggie Eastwood have managed to keep their marriage alive all these years is by having kept their distance from each other most of the time. They have stayed together by staying apart." Maggie is quoted as saying, "Clint is definitely a loner . . . he holds so much back." And Clint said this: "We're not advocates of the total togetherness theory."

59 "I knew I wasn't . . .": Interview by Bernard Weinraub, *Playboy*, March 1997.

60 "Sergio Leone had only . . .": Ibid.

Chapter Five

61 "What struck me . . .": Sergio Leone, quoted in Duncan, *Icons*, 26. Unattributed.

65 British critic and film historian Christopher Frayling: See *The BFI* [British Film Institute] *Companion to the Western* (Deutsch, 1988). Frayling says Leone traced his plot back to Hammett. In *Spaghetti Westerns* (1988) Frayling quotes Leone saying, "Kurosawa's *Yojimbo* was inspired by an American novel of the serie-noire [*sic*] so I was really taking the story back home again."

66 "We were shooting some vast cattle scenes . . .": Quoted in Patrick McGilligan, *Focus on Film* 25 (Summer–Fall 1976).

66 "Finally, I asked Eric Fleming . . .": Interview by Bernard Weinraub, *Playboy*, March 1997.

68 "An American would be afraid . . .": Ibid. Clint's reference to a "tie-up" refers to the Hays Code prohibition against showing explicit scenes of murder: "Murder scenes had to be filmed in a way that would discourage imitations in real life, and brutal killings could not be shown in detail. 'Revenge in modern times' was not to be justified." A tie-up would be an explicit depiction of a murder. "Revenge in modern times" means that biblical depictions were acceptable.

70 "Every time they wanted a format . . .": Quoted in Dick Lochte, *Los Angeles Free Press*, April 20, 1973.

74 "Why should I be pleased . . .": Interview by Hal Humphrey, *Los Angeles Times*, September 16, 1965.

Chapter Six

77 "I came back . . .": Quoted in Thompson, *Billion Dollar Man*, 67.

80 "The stories . . . didn't mean . . .": Quoted in Tim Cahill, *Rolling Stone*, July 4, 1983.

81 passionate affair with Catherine Deneuve: McGilligan, *Life and Legend*, 151.

81 "If it goes on . . .": Ibid., 152. McGilligan's source is unclear.

82 "This will be . . .": Clint, quoted by Wallach in *The Good, the Bad, and Me*.

84 critics wasted no time: Bosley Crowther had written about the trilogy before their American release, in a "think piece" for the *New York Times* in November 1966, where he was more positive about *A Fistful of Dollars*. His enthusiasm waned somewhat when the advance word among critics was negative. Crowther, fearful of going against the tide and of losing his own relevancy, toned down his opinion for his official daily review. Judith Crist actually said the film "lacked the pleasures of the perfectly awful movie."

85 "When [Leone] talked to me about doing . . .": Quoted in Thompson, *Billion Dollar Man*.

87 " 'The burn, the gouge, . . .' ": *New York Times*, January 25, 1968.

88 "remains basically hostile . . .": Andrew Sarris, "The Spaghetti Westerns," *Village Voice*, September 19 and 26, 1968.

89 "I own some property . . .": Interview by Arthur Knight, *Playboy*, February 1974.

Chapter Seven

91 "I think I learned more about direction . . .": Quoted in Duncan, *Icons*, 134.

94 "She [Golonka] began to like him . . .": Ted Post, quoted in McGilligan, *Life and Legend*, 162; no attribution is given.

96 "I had signed with Universal . . .": Introduction to Siegel, *Siegel Film*, ix.

96 "one of the two or three . . .": Ibid.

98 "I learned a lot . . .": Quoted in McGilligan, *Focus on Film* 25, summer-fall 1976.

98 "I thought we did very well": Siegel, *Siegel Film*, 304.

99 "He and his buddies were like . . .": Jill Banner, quoted in Earl Leaf, "The Way They Were," *Rona Barrett's Hollywood*, circa 1972.

101 Burton's smoking habits: Burton discussed his lifelong cigarette addiction and his drinking with Ambrose Heron on British TV in 1977. (Details not available.)

101 "Clint and Richard . . .": Ingrid Pitt, interview by Rusty White, Einsiders.com, June 1, 2002.

102 "The script was given to me . . .": Quoted in Kaminsky, *Clint Eastwood*, chap. 7.

103 *When Doubles Dare*: This joke has many reported sources, including Bragg, *Burton*, 196.

104 "We don't believe . . ." and "By [the time . . .]": Maggie Eastwood and Clint Eastwood, respectively, quoted in Tim Chadwick, "We Don't Believe in Togetherness," *Screen Stars*, July 1971.

106 the two immediately began an on-set affair: The Eastwood-Seberg affair has numerous sources, most thoroughly McGilligan, Richards, and Schickel.

107 Seberg's heart was broken: Richards, *Played Out*, quotes several of Seberg's friends on her great disappointment after the relationship ended. In a French newspaper interview (quoted by Richards) Seberg referred to her affair with a man "who was the absolute opposite" of her husband, "an outdoor type." She said, "It's always a bit of a shock to discover that people aren't sincere." Schickel, *Eastwood*, speculated that Seberg's emotional and professional career declined as much because of her failed romance with Eastwood as her troubles with the FBI.

107 charitable reviews: *Paint Your Wagon* is "a big, bawdy rip-roaring Western musical of the gold rush in California," said the *New York Daily News*. It "will have an uphill fight to be a blockbusting box-office hit," said *Variety*. "Thought overproduced and sometimes a little weird, the movie is pretty interesting," said *Women's Wear Daily*. "Amiable," said Vincent Canby in the *New York Times;* "[s]toic and handsome," Charles Champlin said of Clint in the *Los Angeles Times*. Among the film's harshest critics was Pauline Kael, who wrote in *The New Yorker* that Clint "hardly seems to be in the movie. He's controlled in such an uninteresting way; it's not an actor's control, which enables one to release something—it's the kind of control that keeps one from releasing anything . . . [the film] has finally broken the back of the American movie industry."

Chapter Eight

109 "I feel Don Siegel is . . .": Quoted in Kaminsky, *Clint Eastwood*.

113 "There was no question . . .": Siegel, *Siegel Film*, 365.

114 "I think [the Leone films] changed . . .": Quoted in Frayling, *Clint Eastwood*, 61–67.

117 "I worked on *Kelly's Heroes* . . .": Rickles, *Rickles' Book*, 141–42.

117 "It was [originally] . . .": Quoted in Michael Henry, "Entretien avec Clint Eastwood," *Positif* 287 (January 1985).

118 "Why should I open . . .": Quoted in McGilligan, *Life and Legend*, 185.

120 "as another spaghetti . . .": James Bacon, *Los Angeles Herald-Examiner*, October 14, 1971.

121 "Eastwood films . . .": Siegel, *Siegel Film*, 356.

121 "Don Siegel told me . . .": Quoted in Kaminsky, *Clint Eastwood*. "[The studio] . . .": Quoted in Judy Fayard, "Just About Everybody," *Personalities*. (Further source information for *Personalities* is unknown.)

Chapter Nine

123 "After 17 years . . .": Quoted in Rex Reed, "Calendar," *Los Angeles Times*, April 1971, 50, 62.

125 "My father died . . .": Quoted in Cal Fussman, *Esquire*, January 2009.

126 "It was just an ideal . . .": Quoted in "Clint Eastwood," *The Directors: Master Collection*, AFI (American Film Institute).

127 "I started getting interested in directing . . .": Ibid.

128 "I was lying in bed . . .": Quoted in Peter Biskind, *Premiere*, April 1993.

128 "a good-luck charm . . .": Siegel, *Siegel Film*, 494.

128 "I was absolutely . . .": Quoted in James Bacon, "Entertainment," *Los Angeles Herald-Examiner*, May 15, 1972. The footnote is also based on this source.

130 "There's only one problem . . .": John Cassavetes, quoted in Duncan, *Icons*, 82. Clint repeats the story in the AFI *Directors* series.

131 "I've traveled all over . . .": Quoted in Tom Cavanaugh, *Mainliner*, September 1971.

131 "desultory romance,": Biskind, *Easy Riders*, 234.

131 "In Hollywood, . . .": Ibid.

132 "There are a million . . .": Quoted in Tim Chadwick, "We Don't Believe in Togetherness," *Screen Stars*, July 1971.

132 "Clint lives a double life . . .": Earl Leaf, "The Way They Were," *Rona Barrett's Hollywood*, circa 1972.

135 "Harry's pursuit of Scorpio . . .": Knapp, *Directed*, 43. Knapp elaborates on the doppelgänger aspect this way: "Harry embarks on a desperate crusade to rid San Francisco of a mad killer, only to discover that he is alienated from himself and the people he has ostensibly sworn to protect" (37).

136 "I was the one who hired . . .": Quoted in Patrick McGilligan, *Focus on Film* 25 (Summer–Fall 1976).

136 "exhausting and detrimental": Quoted in Joyce Haber, *Los Angeles Times*, May 3, 1972.

136 "Directing is hard work . . .": Quoted by the Associated Press, August 15, 1972.

138 The decision to toss the badge: Siegel, *Siegel Film*, 366, 375.

139 "The film . . . made the basic contest . . .": Pauline Kael's review of *Dirty Harry* appeared in the January 1, 1972, issue of *The New Yorker*.

Chapter Ten

141 "We live in . . .": Quoted in Cal Fussman, *Esquire*, January 2009.

144 "looking more like . . .": Richard Thompson and Tim Hunter, "Clint Eastwood, Auteur," *Film Comment* 14, no. 1 (January–February 1978).

148 "This was a small film . . .": Quoted in Patrick McGilligan, *Focus on Film* 25 (Summer–Fall 1976).

153 "People who go to the movies . . .": Quoted in Clinch, *Eastwood*, 66.

154 "Lenny Hirshan took a script . . .": Interview by Charlie Rose, PBS, October 8, 2003.

155 "I must confess . . .": Clint, in an article billed as self-penned, *Action*, March 4, 1973.

155 His disappointment and anger: This episode is discussed in McGilligan, *Life and Legend*, and Bach, *Final Cut*. Clint's swearing he would never work for UA again is from Bach.

Chapter Eleven

157 "I went into . . .": Sondra Locke, quoted in Marcia Borie, *Hollywood Reporter*, July 2, 1976.

161 "It was a very difficult . . .": Quoted in Michael Henry, "Entretien avec Clint Eastwood," *Positif* 287 (January 1985).

162 "the only time [Clint] ever . . .": James Bacon, "Clint's Cliff Hanger," *Los Angeles Herald-Examiner*, October 22, 1974.

162 Hog's Breath Inn: Some of the details in the description are from Phyllis Jervey, "Hog's Breath Inn Opens Without Fanfare," *Pine Cone* [Carmel-by-the-Sea], date undetermined, circa 1970s.

163 "There's nothing I can do about it.": Maggie Eastwood, quoted in Peter J. Oppenheimer, "Action Hero Clint Eastwood: I'm Just Doing What I Dreamed of as a Kid," *Family Weekly*, December 29, 1974.

163 "romantic Casanova . . .": Paul Lippman, quoted in Thompson, *Billion Dollar Man*, 89; unattributed. Clint's response is also from Lippman, also unattributed.

165 " 'So what have you been . . .' ": Locke, *Very Ugly*, 138.

165 "the worst thing that . . .": Philip Kaufman, quoted in McGilligan, *Life and Legend*, 261.

168 "What Kael says . . .": Dr. Ronald Lowell, quoted in Mary Murphy, "Clint and Kael," *Los Angeles Times*, April 12, 1976.

168 "I don't have any new . . .": Quoted in Catherine Nixon Cooke, "The Mysterious Clint Eastwood," *Coronet* (February 1975).

Chapter Twelve

169 "People thought . . .": Quoted in Larry Cole, "Clint's Not Cute When He's Angry," *Village Voice*, May 24, 1976.

172 The reason was simple . . . : Said James Fargo, "He wasn't even in San Francisco, basically because he was having the affair with Sondra." Quoted in McGilligan, *Life and Legend*, 275–76; the attribution is unclear.

175 Clint had inserted it: "[The script] was in very good shape. There was a minor amount of rewriting, a lot of deletions. I did it myself," Clint said, in an interview by Richard Thompson and Tim Hunter, "Clint Eastwood, Auteur," *Film Comment* 14, no. 1 (January–February 1978).

176 *People* magazine "scooped": *People*, February 13, 1978.

179 "In today's climate . . .": Richard Schickel, *Time*, January 9, 1978.

179 "In a modern society . . .": William Hare, *Hollywood Studio* (February 1978).

181 "The script . . . had been around . . .": Quoted in Charles Champlin, *Los Angeles Times*, January 18, 1981.

183 "it would be theirs forever . . .": McGilligan, *Life and Legend*, 303.

Chapter Thirteen

187 "I've been advised . . .": Quoted in Iain Blair, *Film and Video* 14, no. 3 (March 1977).

191 "I don't know": See "Clint Eastwood Talks About Clint Eastwood as He Stars in *Escape from Alcatraz* Film," unidentified interview, probably from Universal Pictures, circa 1979, Margaret Herrick Library.

192 "During [1978] Clint began . . .": Locke, *Very Ugly*, 162–63.

194 "When I was sent the script . . .": Quoted in Michael Henry, "Entretien avec Clint Eastwood," *Positif* 287 (January 1985).

Chapter Fourteen

197 "In the westerns . . .": *Inside the Actors Studio*, October 5, 2003.

199 "Eastwood is living proof . . .": Norman Mailer, in *Parade*, October 23, 1983.

199 "Clint Eastwood brought in . . .": Robert Daley, quoted in Army Archerd, *Variety*, November 12, 1979.

200 "We've done okay . . .": Quoted in *Variety*, July 28, 1980.

201 "reports are circulating . . .": *Us*, October 14, 1980.

202 "We meet as often as we can . . .": Henry Wynberg, quoted in Ansi Vallens, "Playboy Who Won Liz Taylor on Rebound Finds New Love—Eastwood's Wife," *Us*, October 21, 1980.

204 "Rarely did Clint acknowledge . . .": Locke, *Very Ugly*, 186.

206 "It was like an homage . . .": Quoted in AFI *Directors* series.

206 "Naturally, I talked about it . . .": Locke, *Very Ugly*, 184.

207 "When you point . . .": *Inside the Actors Studio*, October 5, 2003.

207 "It was just a whimsical thing . . .": AFI *Directors* series.

Chapter Fifteen

209 "Not until *Tightrope* . . .": Bingham, *Acting Male*, 186.

211 Megan Rose: Details of her affair with Clint are from interviews she gave McGilligan, as reported in *Life and Legend*, and by several friends who know them both.

214 Edwards had asked her . . . : The details of this story are from Locke, *Very Ugly*, 189–90.

214 "Before I knew it . . .": Sondra Locke, quoted in Reynolds, *My Life*, 3.

217 Locke as a director: "I began to explore the idea of turning to directing and mentioned it to Clint. 'That'd be a great idea,' he quickly responded." Locke, *Very Ugly*, 191.

Chapter Sixteen

219 "I've always considered . . .": Quoted in *Newsweek*, July 22, 1985.

222 "Maybe there were . . .": Quoted in John Vinocur, "Clint Eastwood, Seriously," *New York Times Magazine*, February 24, 1985.

222 "The Eastwood persona . . .": Ibid.

222 "Clint Eastwood is an artist . . .": Ibid.

224 "I enjoyed going there . . .": *Inside the Actors Studio*, October 5, 2003.

225 "*Clint Eastwood, depuis . . .*": From an article in French by Philippe Labro; the magazine it appeared in is unsourced.

227 "I don't need . . .": Quoted in *Pine Cone* (weekly newspaper of Carmel), February 5, 1986.

227 beat-up yellow Volkswagen convertible: Associated Press, April 9, 1986.

230 *"Heartbreak Ridge* [is about] . . .": Quoted in Milan Pavlovič, "Kein Popcorn-Film [Not a Popcorn Movie]," *Steadycam* 10 (Fall 1988).

232 "I had known Fritz . . .": Locke, *Very Ugly*, 214–15.

Chapter Seventeen

233 "I went to a jazz concert . . .": *Inside the Actors Studio*, October 5, 2003.

236 "So this had become my life . . .": Locke, *Very Ugly*, 217.

238 a full 18 percent . . . : Clint's value to Warner is compiled from figures in articles and lists on file at the Margaret Herrick Library, and from Thompson, *Billion Dollar Man*.

240 "I would never have been able . . .": Quoted in *Los Angeles Times*, December 9, 1995.

240 Durk Pearson and Sandy Shaw:

> Hollywood insiders have a hairy theory about the pseudonymous actor whose medical history is chronicled in *Life Extension*, the best-seller that offers a "scientific approach" to retarding aging. Though the actor is called "Mr. Smith" in the book, "it's obviously Clint Eastwood," explained one acquaintance of the film star. "He's a friend of Merv Griffin, at whose house the authors say they met this Smith, and like Smith he was 50 the year the book was being researched and was also allergic to horsehair." In addition, authors Durk Pearson and Sandy Shaw were advisors on Eastwood's latest movie, *Firefox*, and are collaborating with the actor on a new biomedical film thriller. So, are Eastwood and Smith one and the same? "That will not be disclosed by me," said the actor's manager. . . . The history, by the way, includes taking a "life extension formula" of vitamins and drugs that not only have improved Smith's suntan, hair, and speaking ability, but allow him to ride a horse. (*New York*, September 27, 1982.)

Clint had always been allergic to horseback riding, which is why, in his westerns, he is rarely seen in close-up on horseback.

> Last year Clint Eastwood revealed that he was indeed the pseudonymous "Mr. Smith" (the professional movie star who increased his stamina and alertness and improved his tan) cited in the 1.5 million copy best-seller *Life Extension: A Practical Scientific Approach*, by Durk Pearson and Sandy Shaw. What he did not mention was that along with following the Pearson/Shaw health plan, he optioned the rights to their less-than-orthodox first screenplay, *Sacrilege*. (*Esquire*, July 1985.)

Chapter Eighteen

243 "There is only one . . .": Brainyquote.com.

246 "Well, I've divorced Maggie . . .": On the marriage confrontation between Clint and Locke, see Locke, *Very Ugly*, 231.

247 "Suddenly he'd want me to travel . . .": Ibid., 230.

251 Depositions: Details of the depositions are derived from Schickel, *Eastwood*, and McGilligan, *Life and Legend*, and publicly available documents. Most of the court documents remain sealed, but detailed portions of both depositions are in Locke, *Very Ugly*.

253 "A fellow by the name . . .": Interview by Charlie Rose, PBS, October 8, 2003.

Chapter Nineteen

259 *"Unforgiven* ends the trajectory . . .": Brett Westbrook, quoted in Engel, *Actor and Director*, 43.

261 "Warner barely released . . .": Locke, *Very Ugly*, 292.

261 "Does she want to . . .": Ibid., 293.

262 "I owe you nothing": Ibid.

263 "Why a western? . . .": Quoted in Thierry Jousse and Camille Nevers, "Entretien avec Clint Eastwood," *Cahiers du cinéma* 460 (October 1992).

264 "I started rewriting it . . .": AFI *Directors* series.

271 "Tired . . .": Quoted in Schickel, *Eastwood*, 469.

Chapter Twenty

273 "My feelings . . .": Courtroom testimony at the 1996 civil suit brought against him by Sondra Locke, Burbank.

277 "I don't know what's going on . . .": Locke, *Very Ugly*, 324.

278 Lance Young: Locke, *Very Ugly*, 325, and a source who must remain anonymous.

278 "We have no interest . . .": The Semel and Daley statements are ibid.

284 "I guess maybe . . .": Interview by Bernard Weinraub, *Playboy*, March 1997.

Chapter Twenty-one

287 "If I start intruding . . .": Interview by Charlie Rose, PBS, October 8, 2003.

289 Dina Ruiz: Background information on Dina Ruiz is from *San Francisco Chronicle*, April 9, 1996.

292 "The three or four . . .": AFI *Directors* series.

293 Fisher had pressured Clint unsuccessfully . . . : "[Fisher] would have loved

to play the part Meryl played." *Playboy:* "Was that an issue?" Clint: "Enough said." Interview by Bernard Weinraub, *Playboy*, March 1997.

293 "The reason he can . . .": Streep, ibid.

295 "The fact that . . .": Dina Ruiz, quoted in Thompson, *Billion Dollar Man*, 229.

295 "I don't think about it . . .": Weinraub interview, *Playboy*, March 1997.

295 "She was feeling . . .": Interview by Gail Sheehy, *Parade*, December 7, 2008.

296 "With *Absolute Power,* . . .": Quoted in Blair, *Film and Video* 14, no. 3, March 1997.

298 "The characters . . .": Quoted in Pascal Merigeau, "Eastwood en son Carmel," *Nouvel Observateur,* March 1998.

Chapter Twenty-two

301 "Dina keeps me . . .": Thompson, *Billion Dollar Man*, 9.

303 "geezer squad": Source wishes to remain anonymous.

304 "At this particular stage . . .": Quoted in Thompson, *Billion Dollar Man*, 236.

305 "I've wanted to . . .": Quoted in *Daily Telegraph* (London), December 22, 2002.

305 "I knew of Dennis . . .": Quoted in Engel, *Actor and Director,* 218.

306 "absorbs the past . . .": Ibid.

306 "for his edge . . .": Rose interview, PBS.

307 "I think the most . . .": Sean Penn quoted in Mark Binelli, *Rolling Stone*, February 19, 2009.

Chapter Twenty-three

315 "My earlier work . . .": Interview by Charlie Rose, PBS, October 8, 2003.

319 "I ran into Steven . . .": Starpulse.com, July 23, 2008.

319 "I started wondering . . .": Ibid.

320 "Between the two films . . .": Interview by Charlie Rose, PBS, October 8, 2003.

321 "The ambitious script . . .": *Rolling Stone*, October 16, 2006.

322 "a single African-American character . . .": On the Spike Lee feud, see the in-depth interview Clint gave to Jeff Dawson that appeared in London's *Guardian*, June 6, 2008, to promote the release of all five *Dirty Harry* movies on DVD; Foxnews.com, June 6, 2008; and Nick Allen, "Clint Eastwood and

Spike Lee Row Over Black Actors," *Telegraph*, June 9, 2008. Additional information, including Steven Spielberg's acting as peacemaker, is from *Access Hollywood*, NBC-Universal Inc., 2009.

322 "As for Flags of Our Fathers . . .": *Guardian*.

327 He agreed to direct it: Todd Longwell, "United for 'Changeling,' " *Hollywood Reporter*, November 20, 2008.

327 "My character . . .": Angelina Jolie, quoted in "The Road to Gold: An Academy Award Preview," TV, syndicated, February 21, 2009.

331 *"Dirty Harry VI! . . ."*: Clint jokingly did this mock-pitch on the occasion of the 2008 DVD box-set rerelease of all five Dirty Harry films. Geoff Boucher, *Los Angeles Times*, June 1, 2008.

332 Both agree they get along much better now that they're not married: interview by Bernard Weinraub, *Playboy*, March 1997.

All features are given with release dates; all TV shows, date of first showing. Clint's producer credits are individually indicated, as applicable. Also included are Clint's musical recordings and a list of his awards.

FILM

As Actor

Revenge of the Creature 1955. Universal-International Pictures. Producer: William Alland. Director: Jack Arnold. Screenplay: Martin Berkeley, from a story by William Alland. With John Agar, Lori Nelson, John Bromfield, Clint Eastwood (uncredited).

Francis in the Navy 1955. Universal-International Pictures. Producer: Stanley Rubin. Director: Arthur Lubin. Screenplay: Devery Freeman, from a story by Devery Freeman based on characters created by David Stern. With Donald O'Connor, Martha Hyer, Richard Erdman, Martin Milner, David Janssen, Paul Burke, Clint Eastwood (the first time Eastwood receives screen credit).

Lady Godiva (aka ***Lady Godiva of Coventry,*** aka ***21st Century Lady Godiva***) 1955. Universal-International Pictures. Producer: Robert Arthur. Director: Arthur Lubin. Screenplay: Oscar Brodney and Harry Ruskin, from a story by Oscar Brodney. With Maureen O'Hara, George Nader, Victor McLaglen, Grant Withers, Rex Reason, Eduard Franz, Leslie Bradley, Arthur Shields, Clint Eastwood (uncredited).

Tarantula 1955. Universal-International Pictures. Producer: William Alland. Director: Jack Arnold. Screenplay: Robert Fresco and Martin Berkeley, from a story by Jack Arnold and Robert Fresco. With John Agar, Mara Corday, Leo G. Carroll, Nestor Paiva, Ross Elliott, Edwin Rand, Raymond Bailey, Clint Eastwood (uncredited).

Away All Boats 1956. Universal-International Pictures. Producer: Howard Christie. Director: Joseph Pevney. Screenplay: Ted Sherdeman, based on the

novel by Kenneth M. Dodson. With Jeff Chandler, George Nader, Julie Adams, Keith Andes, Richard Boone, Clint Eastwood (uncredited).

Never Say Goodbye 1956. Universal-International Pictures. Producer: Albert J. Cohen. Director: Jerry Hopper. Screenplay: Charles Hoffman, based on an earlier screenplay by Bruce Manning, John D. Klorer, and Leonard Lee, loosely based on the play *Come prima, meglio di prima* by Luigi Pirandello. With Rock Hudson, George Sanders, Ray Collins, David Janssen, Shelley Fabares, Clint Eastwood (uncredited).

The First Traveling Saleslady 1956. RKO Pictures. Producer: Arthur Lubin. Director: Arthur Lubin. Screenplay: Devery Freeman and Stephen Longstreet. With Ginger Rogers, Barry Nelson, Carol Channing, James Arness, Clint Eastwood.

Star in the Dust 1956. Universal-International Pictures. Producer: Albert Zugsmith. Director: Charles Haas. Screenplay: Oscar Brodney, from a novel by Lee Leighton. With John Agar, Mamie Van Doren, Richard Boone, Leif Erickson, Coleen Gray, James Gleason, Clint Eastwood (uncredited).

Escapade in Japan 1957. RKO Pictures. Producer: Arthur Lubin. Director: Arthur Lubin. Written by Winston Miller. With Teresa Wright, Cameron Mitchell, Jon Provost, Roger Nakagawa, Clint Eastwood (uncredited).

Lafayette Escadrille 1958. Warner Bros. Producer: William Wellman. Director: William Wellman. Screenplay: Albert Sidney Fleischman, from a story by William Wellman. With Tab Hunter, Etchika Choureau, Marcel Dalio, David Janssen, Jody McCrea, William Wellman Jr., Clint Eastwood.

Ambush at Cimarron Pass 1958. 20th Century–Fox release of a Regal Production. Producer: Herbert E. Mendelson. Director: Jodie Copelan. Screenplay: Richard G. Taylor and John K. Butler, from stories by Robert A. Reeds and Robert E. Woods. With Scott Brady, Margia Dean, Baynes Barron, William Vaughn, Ken Mayer, John Damler, Keith Richards, Clint Eastwood, John Merrick, Frank Gerstle, Dirk London, Irving Bacon, Desmond Slattery.

Fistful of Dollars (aka *A Fistful of Dollars; Per un pugno di dollari*) 1964. Released by United Artists. Producer: Harry Colombo and George Papi. Director: Sergio Leone. Screenplay: Sergio Leone and Duccio Tessari, adapted from *Yojimbo* by Akira Kurosawa. With Clint Eastwood, Marianne Koch, Johnny Wells, W. Lukschy, S. Rupp, Antonio Prieto, José Calvo, Margarita Lozano, Daniel Martin.

For a Few Dollars More (Per qualche dollaro in più) 1965. Released by United Artists. Producer: Alberto Grimaldi. Director: Sergio Leone. Screenplay: Luciano Vincenzoni and Sergio Leone, from a story by Fulvio

Morsella and Sergio Leone. With Clint Eastwood, Lee Van Cleef, Gian Maria Volontè, Rosemary Dexter, Mara Krup, Klaus Kinski, Mario Brega, Aldo Sambrell.

The Good, the Bad and the Ugly (Il buono, il brutto, il cattivo) 1966, Italy; 1967, U.S. Released by United Artists. Producer: Alberto Grimaldi. Director: Sergio Leone. Screenplay: Agenore Incrocci, Furio Scarpelli, Luciano Vincenzoni, Sergio Leone, from a story by Luciano Vincenzoni and Sergio Leone. With Clint Eastwood, Eli Wallach, Lee Van Cleef, Aldo Giuffrè, Mario Brega, Luigi Pistilli, Rada Rassimov, Enzo Petito.

Le streghe (aka **The Witches**) 1967. Released by United Artists in Europe and Lopert Pictures Productions in the U.S. (dubbed). Various producers around the world. Producer: Dino De Laurentiis. Director: Luchino Visconti ("The Witch Burned Alive"), Mauro Bolognini ("Civic Sense"), Pier Paolo Pasolini ("The Earth as Seen from the Moon"), Franco Rossi ("The Girl from Sicily"), Vittorio De Sica ("A Night Like Any Other"). Screenplay: "The Witch Burned Alive" story and screenplay by Giuseppe Patroni Griffi; "Civic Sense" story and screenplay by Bernardino Zapponi; "The Earth as Seen from the Moon" screenplay by Pier Paolo Pasolini; "The Girl from Sicily" screenplay by Franco Rossi and Luigi Magni; "A Night Like Any Other" screenplay by Cesare Zavattini, Fabio Carpi, Enzo Muzii. With Silvana Mangano, Alberto Sordi, Ninetto Davoli, Pietro Torrisi, Clint Eastwood (in "A Night Like Any Other"), Armando Bottin, Gianni Gori.

Hang 'Em High 1968. Producer: Leonard Freeman Productions (Leonard Freeman) and Malpaso Company, released by United Artists. Director: Ted Post. Screenplay: Leonard Freeman and Mel Goldberg. With Clint Eastwood, Inger Stevens, Ed Begley, Pat Hingle, Arlene Golonka, James MacArthur, Ruth White, Ben Johnson, Bruce Dern, Dennis Hopper, Alan Hale Jr.

Coogan's Bluff 1968. Released by Universal. Producer: Don Siegel. Director: Don Siegel. Screenplay: Herman Miller, Dean Riesner, Howard Rodman, from a story by Herman Miller. With Clint Eastwood, Lee J. Cobb, Susan Clark, Tisha Sterling, Don Stroud, Betty Field, Tom Tully, Melodie Johnson, James Edwards, Rudy Diaz, David F. Doyle, Louis Zorich, James Gavin.

Where Eagles Dare 1968. A Jerry Gershwin–Elliott Kastner Picture. Released by MGM. Producer: Elliott Kastner. Director: Brian G. Hutton. Story and screenplay: Alistair MacLean, from his novel. With Richard Burton, Clint Eastwood, Mary Ure, Michael Hordern, Patrick Wymark, Robert Beatty, Anton Diffring, Donald Houston, Ferdy Mayne, Neil McCarthy, Peter Barkworth, William Squire, Brook Williams, Ingrid Pitt.

Paint Your Wagon 1969. Distributed by Paramount Pictures. Producer: Alan Jay Lerner. Director: Joshua Logan. Screenplay (and lyrics): Alan Jay Lerner, an adaptation of the original Alan Jay Lerner Broadway production by Paddy Chayefsky. With Lee Marvin, Clint Eastwood, Jean Seberg, Harve Presnell, Ray Walston, Tom Ligon, Alan Dexter, William O'Connell, Ben Baker, Alan Baxter, Paula Trueman, Robert Easton, Geoffrey Norman, H. B. Haggerty, Terry Jenkins, Karl Bruck, John Mitchum, Sue Casey, Eddie Little Sky, Harvey Parry, H. W. Gim, William Mims, Roy Jenson, Pat Hawley.

Two Mules for Sister Sara 1970. Released by Universal. Producer: Martin Rackin, Carroll Case, Malpaso Company. Director: Don Siegel. Screenplay: Albert Maltz, from a story by Budd Boetticher. With Clint Eastwood, Shirley MacLaine, Manolo Fábregas, Albert Morin, Armando Silvestre, John Kelly, Enrique Lucero, David Estuardo, Ada Carrasco, Pancho Córdova.

Kelly's Heroes 1970. Released by MGM. Producer: Sidney Beckerman, Gabriel Katzka, Harold Loeb (uncredited). Director: Brian G. Hutton. Screenplay: Troy Kennedy Martin. With Clint Eastwood, Telly Savalas, Don Rickles, Carroll O'Connor, Donald Sutherland, Gavin MacLeod, George Savalas, Hal Buckley, David Hurst, John Heller.

The Beguiled 1971. Released by Universal. Producer: Don Siegel. Director: Don Siegel. Screenplay: John B. Sherry and Grimes Grice, from the novel by Thomas Cullinan. With Clint Eastwood, Geraldine Page, Elizabeth Hartman, Jo Ann Harris, Darleen Carr, Mae Mercer, Pamelyn Ferdin, Melody Thomas, Peggy Drier, Pattye Mattick.

Dirty Harry 1971. Released by Warner Bros.–Seven Arts. Producer: Don Siegel. Director: Don Siegel. Screenplay: Harry Julian Fink and R. M. Fink and Dean Riesner, from a story by Harry Julian Fink and R. M. Fink. With Clint Eastwood, Harry Guardino, Reni Santoni, John Vernon, Andy Robinson, John Larch, John Mitchum, Mae Mercer, Lyn Edgington, Ruth Kobart, Woodrow Parfrey, Josef Sommer, William Paterson, James Nolan, Maurice S. Argent, Jo De Winter, Craig G. Kelly.

Joe Kidd 1972. Released by Universal Pictures/Malpaso. Producer: Sidney Beckerman. Director: John Sturges. Screenplay: Elmore Leonard. With Clint Eastwood, Robert Duvall, John Saxon, Don Stroud, Stella Garcia, James Wainwright, Paul Koslo, Gregory Walcott, Lynne Marta.

Magnum Force 1973. Released by Warner Bros. Producer: Robert Daley. Director: Ted Post. Screenplay: John Milius, Michael Cimino, based on a story by John Milius, from original material by Harry Julian Fink, R. M. Fink. With Clint Eastwood, Hal Holbrook, Felton Perry, Mitchell Ryan, David Soul, Tim Matheson, Robert Urich, Christine White, Adele Yoshioka.

Thunderbolt and Lightfoot 1974. A Malpaso Company Film. Released by United Artists. Producer: Robert Daley. Director: Michael Cimino. Screenplay: Michael Cimino. With Clint Eastwood, Jeff Bridges, Geoffrey Lewis, Catherine Bach, Gary Busey, George Kennedy, Jack Dodson, Gene Elman, Burton Gilliam, Roy Jenson, Claudia Lennear, Bill McKinney, Vic Tayback.

The Enforcer 1976. Released by Warner Bros. Producer: Robert Daley. Director: James Fargo. Screenplay: Stirling Silliphant, Dean Riesner, based on characters created by Harry Julian Fink and R. M. Fink. With Clint Eastwood, Tyne Daly, Harry Guardino, Bradford Dillman, John Mitchum, DeVeren Bookwalter, John Crawford.

Every Which Way but Loose 1978. A Malpaso Production. Released by Warner Bros. Producer: Robert Daley. Director: James Fargo. Screenplay: Jeremy Joe Kronsberg. With Clint Eastwood, Sondra Locke, Geoffrey Lewis, Beverly D'Angelo, Ruth Gordon, Walter Barnes, George Chandler, Roy Jenson, James McEachin, Bill McKinney.

Escape from Alcatraz 1979. Released by Paramount. Producer: Don Siegel. Director: Don Siegel. Screenplay: Richard Tuggle, from a book by J. Campbell Bruce. With Clint Eastwood, Patrick McGoohan, Roberts Blossom, Jack Thibeau, Fred Ward, Paul Benjamin, Larry Hankin, Bruce M. Fischer, Frank Ronzio.

Any Which Way You Can 1980. A Malpaso Production. Released by Warner Bros. Producer: Fritz Manes. Director: Buddy Van Horn. Screenplay: Stanford Sherman, based on characters created by Jeremy Joe Kronsberg. With Clint Eastwood, Sondra Locke, Ruth Gordon, Geoffrey Lewis, William Smith.

Tightrope 1984. A Malpaso Production. Released by Warner Bros. Producer: Clint Eastwood, Fritz Manes. Director: Richard Tuggle. Screenplay: Richard Tuggle. With Clint Eastwood, Geneviève Bujold, Dan Hedaya, Alison Eastwood, Jennifer Beck, Marco St. John.

City Heat 1984. A Malpaso/Deliverance Production. Released by Warner Bros. Producer: Fritz Manes. Director: Richard Benjamin. Screenplay: Sam O. Brown and Joseph Stinson. Story: Sam O. Brown. With Clint Eastwood, Burt Reynolds, Jane Alexander, Madeline Kahn, Rip Torn, Irene Cara, Richard Roundtree, Tony Lo Bianco.

The Dead Pool 1988. A Malpaso Production. Released by Warner Bros. Producer: David Valdes. Director: Buddy Van Horn. Screenplay: Steve Sharon. Story: Steve Sharon, Durk Pearson, Sandy Shaw. Based on characters created by Harry Julian Fink and R. M. Fink. With Clint Eastwood, Patricia Clarkson, Liam Neeson, Evan Kim, David Hunt, Michael Currie, Michael Goodwin, James Carrey.

Pink Cadillac 1989. A Malpaso Production. Released by Warner Bros. Producer: David Valdes. Director: Buddy Van Horn. Screenplay: John Eskow. With Clint Eastwood, Bernadette Peters, Timothy Carhart, Tiffany Gail Robinson, Angela Louise Robinson, John Dennis Johnston, Michael Des Barres, Jimmie F. Skaggs, Bill Moseley, Michael Champion, William Hickey, Geoffrey Lewis, Bill McKinney.

In the Line of Fire 1993. A Castle Rock Entertainment Production in association with Apple/Rose Films. Released by Columbia Pictures. Producer: Jeff Apple, Bob Rosenthal. Director: Wolfgang Petersen. Screenplay: Jeff Maguire. With Clint Eastwood, John Malkovich, Rene Russo, Dylan McDermott, Gary Cole, Fred Dalton Thompson, John Mahoney.

As Actor and Director

Play Misty for Me 1971. A Malpaso Production. Released by Universal. Producer: Robert Daley. Director: Clint Eastwood. Screenplay: Jo Heims and Dean Riesner. With Clint Eastwood, Jessica Walter, Donna Mills, John Larch, Clarice Taylor, Irene Hervey, Jack Ging, James McEachin, Donald Siegel, Duke Everts.

High Plains Drifter 1973. A Malpaso Production. Released by Universal. Producer: Robert Daley. Director: Clint Eastwood. Screenplay: Ernest Tidyman (and Dean Riesner, uncredited). With Clint Eastwood, Verna Bloom, Mariana Hill, Mitchell Ryan, Jack Ging, Stefan Gierasch, Ted Hartley, Billy Curtis, Geoffrey Lewis, Scott Walker, Walter Barnes.

The Eiger Sanction 1975. Released by Universal. Producer: Robert Daley, Richard D. Zanuck, David Brown. Director: Clint Eastwood. Screenplay: Hal Dresner, Warren B. Murphy, Rod Whitaker, based on a novel by Rod Whitaker writing as "Trevanian." With Clint Eastwood, George Kennedy, Vonetta McGee, Jack Cassidy, Heidi Brühl, Thayer David, Reiner Schöne, Michael Grimm, Jean-Pierre Bernard, Brenda Venus, Gregory Walcott.

The Outlaw Josey Wales 1976. Released by Warner Bros. Producer: Robert Daley. Director: Clint Eastwood. Screenplay: Phil Kaufman and Sonia Chernus, based on the novel *Gone to Texas* by Forrest Carter. With Clint Eastwood, Chief Dan George, Sondra Locke, Bill McKinney, John Vernon, Paula Trueman, Sam Bottoms, Geraldine Keams, Woodrow Parfrey, Joyce Jameson, Sheb Wooley, Matt Clark, John Verros, Will Sampson, William O'Connell, John Quade.

The Gauntlet 1977. Released by Warner Bros. Producer: Robert Daley. Director: Clint Eastwood. Screenplay: Michael Butler and Dennis Shryack. With Clint Eastwood, Sondra Locke, Pat Hingle, William Prince, Bill McKinney, Michael Cavanaugh.

Bronco Billy 1980. Released by Warner Bros, in association with Second Street Films. Producer: Dennis Hackin, Neal Dobrofsky. Director: Clint Eastwood. Screenplay: Dennis Hackin. With Clint Eastwood, Sondra Locke, Geoffrey Lewis, Scatman Crothers, Bill McKinney, Sam Bottoms, Dan Vadis, Sierra Pecheur, Walter Barnes, Woodrow Parfrey, Beverlee McKinsey, Douglas McGrath, Hank Worden, William Prince.

Firefox 1982. Released by Warner Bros. Producer: Clint Eastwood. Director: Clint Eastwood. Screenplay: Alex Lasker and Wendell Wellman, based on the novel by Craig Thomas. With Clint Eastwood, Freddie Jones, David Huffman, Warren Clarke, Ronald Lacey, Kenneth Colley.

Honkytonk Man 1982. A Malpaso Production. Released by Warner Bros. Producer: Clint Eastwood. Director: Clint Eastwood. Screenplay: Clancy Carlile, based on his novel, *Honkeytonk Man*. With Clint Eastwood, Kyle Eastwood, John McIntire, Alexa Kenin, Verna Bloom, Matt Clark, Barry Corbin, Jerry Hardin.

Sudden Impact 1983. A Malpaso Production. Released by Warner Bros. Producer: Clint Eastwood. Director: Clint Eastwood. Screenplay: Joseph C. Stinson. Story: Earl E. Smith and Charles B. Pierce. Based on characters created by Harry Julian Fink and R. M. Fink. With Clint Eastwood, Sondra Locke, Pat Hingle, Bradford Dillman, Paul Drake, Audrie J. Neenan, Jack Thibeau, Michael Currie, Albert Popwell.

Pale Rider 1985. A Malpaso Production. Released by Warner Bros. Producer: Clint Eastwood. Director: Clint Eastwood. Screenplay: Michael Butler and Dennis Shryack. With Clint Eastwood, Michael Moriarty, Carrie Snodgress, Christopher Penn, Richard Dysart, Sydney Penny, Richard Kiel, Doug McGrath, John Russell.

Heartbreak Ridge 1986. A Malpaso Production. Released by Warner Bros. Producer: Clint Eastwood. Director: Clint Eastwood. Screenplay: James Carabatsos. With Clint Eastwood, Marsha Mason, Everett McGill, Moses Gunn, Eileen Heckart, Bo Svenson, Boyd Gaines, Mario Van Peebles, Arlen Dean Snyder, Vincent Irizarry, Ramón Franco, Tom Villard, Mike Gomez, Rodney Hill, Peter Koch, Richard Venture.

White Hunter Black Heart 1990. A Malpaso/Rastar Production. Released by Warner Bros. Producer: Clint Eastwood. Director: Clint Eastwood. Screenplay: Peter Viertel, James Bridges, Burt Kennedy, based on the novel by Peter Viertel. With Clint Eastwood, Jeff Fahey, George Dzundza, Marisa Berenson, Alun Armstrong, Richard Vanstone, Charlotte Cornwell, Catherine Neilson, Edward Tudor-Pole, Richard Warwick, Boy Mathias Chuma.

The Rookie 1990. A Malpaso Production. Released by Warner Bros. Producer: Howard Kazanjian, Steven Siebert, David Valdes. Director: Clint Eastwood. Screenplay: Boaz Yakin and Scott Spiegel. With Clint Eastwood, Charlie

Sheen, Raul Julia, Sonia Braga, Tom Skerritt, Lara Flynn Boyle, Pepe Serna, Marco Rodríguez.

Unforgiven 1992. A Malpaso Production. Released by Warner Bros. Producer: Clint Eastwood. Director: Clint Eastwood. Screenplay: David Webb Peoples. With Clint Eastwood, Gene Hackman, Morgan Freeman, Richard Harris, Jaimz Woolvett, Saul Rubinek, Frances Fisher, Anna Thomson.

A Perfect World 1993. A Malpaso Production. Released by Warner Bros. Producer: Clint Eastwood, Mark Johnson, David Valdes. Screenplay: John Lee Hancock. With Clint Eastwood, Kevin Costner, Laura Dern, T. J. Lowther, Leo Burmester, Keith Szarabajka, Wayne Dehart, Paul Hewitt, Bradley Whitford, Ray McKinnon, Jennifer Griffin, Leslie Flowers, Belinda Flowers, Darryl Cox, Jay Whiteaker, Taylor Suzanna McBride, Christopher Reagan Ammons, Mark Voges, John M. Jackson, Connie Cooper, George Orrison.

The Bridges of Madison County 1995. A Malpaso/Amblin Production. Released by Warner Bros. Producer: Clint Eastwood, Kathleen Kennedy. Director: Clint Eastwood. Screenplay: Richard LaGravenese, based on the novel by Robert James Waller. With Clint Eastwood, Meryl Streep, Annie Corley, Victor Slezak, Jim Haynie, Sarah Kathryn Schmitt, Christopher Kroon, Phyllis Lyons, Debra Monk, Richard Lage, Michelle Benes, Alison Wiegert, Brandon Bobst, Pearl Faessler, R. E. "Stick" Faessler, Tania Mishler, Billie McNabb, Art Breese, Lana Schwab, Larry Loury, James Rivers.

Absolute Power 1997. Castle Rock Entertainment/Malpaso. Producer: Clint Eastwood, Karen Spiegel. Director: Clint Eastwood. Screenplay: William Goldman, based on the novel by David Baldacci. With Clint Eastwood, Gene Hackman, Ed Harris, Laura Linney, Scott Glenn, Dennis Haysbert, Judy Davis, E. G. Marshall.

True Crime 1999. Malpaso-Zanuck Productions. Producer: Clint Eastwood, Tom Rooker, Lili Fini Zanuck, Richard D. Zanuck. Director: Clint Eastwood. Screenplay: Larry Gross, Paul Brickman, Stephen Schiff, based on the novel by Andrew Klavan. With Clint Eastwood, Isaiah Washington, Lisa Gay Hamilton, James Woods, Denis Leary, Bernard Hill, Diane Venora, Michael McKean, Michael Jeter, Mary McCormack, Hattie Winston, Penny Bae Bridges, Francesca Fisher-Eastwood, John Finn, Laila Robins, Sydney Tamiia Poitier, Erik King, Graham Beckel, Frances Fisher, Marissa Ribisi, Christine Ebersole, Anthony Zerbe, Nancy Giles, Tom McGowan, William Windom, Don West, Luci Liu, Dina Eastwood, Leslie Griffith, Dennis Richmond, Frank Sommerville, Dan Green.

Space Cowboys 2000. A Malpaso Production. Producer: Clint Eastwood, Andrew Lazar, Tom Rooker. Director: Clint Eastwood. Screenplay: Ken

Kaufman and Howard Klausner. With Clint Eastwood, Tommy Lee Jones, Donald Sutherland, James Garner, James Cromwell, Marcia Gay Harden, William Devane, Loren Dean, Courtney B. Vance, Rade Serbedzija, Barbara Babcock, Blair Brown, Jay Leno, Nils Allen Stewart.

Blood Work 2002. A Malpaso Production. Producer: Clint Eastwood. Director: Clint Eastwood. Screenplay: Brian Helgeland, from the novel by Michael Connelly. With Clint Eastwood, Jeff Daniels, Anjelica Huston, Wanda De Jesus, Tina Lifford, Paul Rodriguez, Dylan Walsh.

Million Dollar Baby 2004. A Malpaso/Albert S. Ruddy/Epsilon Motion Pictures Production. Distributed by Warner Bros. Producer: Clint Eastwood, Paul Haggis, Robert Moresco, Tom Rosenberg, Albert S. Ruddy. Director: Clint Eastwood. Screenplay: Paul Haggis, from stories by F.X. Toole *(Rope Burns)*. With Clint Eastwood, Hilary Swank, Morgan Freeman, Jay Baruchel, Mike Colter, Lucia Rijker, Brian F. O'Byrne, Anthony Mackie, Margo Martindale, Riki Lindhome, Michael Peña.

Gran Torino 2008. A Malpaso Production. Producer: Clint Eastwood, Bill Gerber, Robert Lorenz. Distributed by Matten Productions in association with Double Nickel Entertainment, Gerber Pictures, Malpaso Productions, Media Magik Entertainment, Village Roadshow Pictures, Warner Bros. Director: Clint Eastwood. Screenplay: Nick Schenk, from a story by Nick Schenk and Dave Johannson. With Clint Eastwood, Christopher Carley, Bee Vang, Ahney Her, Brian Haley, Geraldine Hughes, Dreama Walker, Brian Howe, John Carroll Lynch, William Hill, Brooke Chia Thao, Chee Thao, Choua Kue.

As Director Only

Breezy 1973. Released by Universal. Producer: Robert Daley. Director: Clint Eastwood. Screenplay: Jo Heims. With William Holden, Kay Lenz, Roger C. Carmel, Mari Dusay, Joan Hotchkis, Jamie Smith-Jackson, Norman Bartold, Lynn Borden, Shelley Morrison, Dennis Olivieri, Eugene Peterson.

Bird 1988. A Malpaso Production. Released by Warner Bros. Producer: Clint Eastwood. Director: Clint Eastwood. Screenplay: Joel Oliansky. With Forest Whitaker, Diane Venora, Michael Zelniker, Samuel E. Wright, Keith David, Michael McGuire, James Handy, Damon Whitaker, Moran Nagler, Arlen Dean Snyder.

Midnight in the Garden of Good and Evil 1997. A Malpaso Production. Released by Warner Bros. Producer: Clint Eastwood, Arnold Stiefel. Director: Clint Eastwood. Screenplay: John Lee Hancock, based on the novel by John Berendt. With Kevin Spacey, John Cusack, Alison Eastwood, Irma P. Hall, Paul Hipp, Dorothy Loudon, Anne Haney, Kim Hunter, Geoffrey

Lewis, Richard Herd, Leon Rippy, Bob Gunton, Michael O'Hagan, Gary Anthony Williams.

Mystic River 2003. A Malpaso Production in association with NPV Entertainment. Released by Warner Bros. Producer: Clint Eastwood, Robert Lorenz, Judie G. Hoyt. Director: Clint Eastwood. Screenplay: Brian Helgeland, based on the novel by Dennis Lehane. With Sean Penn, Tim Robbins, Kevin Bacon, Laurence Fishburne, Marcia Gay Harden, Laura Linney, Kevin Chapman, Tom Guiry, Emmy Rossum.

Flags of Our Fathers 2006. A Malpaso Production in association with Warner Bros., Amblin Entertainment, DreamWorks SKG. Producer: Clint Eastwood. Director: Clint Eastwood. Screenplay: William Broyles Jr., Paul Haggis. Story: James Bradley, Ron Powers. With Ryan Phillippe, Jesse Bradford, Adam Beach, John Benjamin Hickey, John Slattery, Barry Pepper, Jamie Bell, Paul Walker, Robert Patrick, Neal McDonough, Melanie Lynskey, Thomas McCarthy, Chris Bauer, Judith Ivey, Myra Turley, Joseph Cross, Benjamin Walker, Scott Eastwood, Harve Presnell, George Hearn, Alessandro Mastrobuono, Stark Sands, George Grizzard, Len Cariou, Christopher Curry, Bubba Lewis, Beth Grant, Connie Ray, Ann Dowd, Mary Beth Peil, David Patrick Kelly, Gordon Clapp.

Letters from Iwo Jima 2006. A Malpaso Production in association with Warner Bros., Amblin Entertainment, DreamWorks SKG. Producer: Clint Eastwood, Robert Lorenz, Tim Moore, Steven Spielberg. Director: Clint Eastwood. Screenplay: Iris Yamashita. Story: Iris Yamashita, Paul Haggis. With Ken Watanabe, Kazunari Ninomiya, Tsuyoshi Ihara, Ryo Kase, Shido Nakamura, Hiroshi Watanabe, Takumi Bando, Yuki Matsuzaki, Takashi Yamaguchi, Eijiro Ozaki, Nae, Nobumasa Sakagami, Luke Eberl, Sonny Saito, Steve Santa Sekiyoshi, Hio Abe, Toshiya Agata, Yoshi Ishii, Toshi Toda, Ken Kensei, Ikuma Ando, Akiko Shima, Masashi Nagadoi, Mark Moses, Roxanne Hart, Yoshio Iizuka, Mitsu, Takuji Kuramoto, Koji Wada.

Changeling 2008. A Malpaso Production in association with Imagine Entertainment. Producer: Clint Eastwood, Brian Grazer, Ron Howard, Robert Lorenz. Director: Clint Eastwood. Screenplay: J. Michael Straczynski. With Angelina Jolie, Gattlin Griffith, Michelle Gunn, Jan Devereaux, Michael Kelly, Erica Grant, Antonia Bennett, Kerri Randles, Frank Wood, Morgan Eastwood, Madison Hodges, John Malkovich, Colm Feore, Devon Conti, J.P. Bumstead.

The Human Factor 2009. A Malpaso Production. Producer: Clint Eastwood, Morgan Freeman, Robert Lorenz, Lori McCreary, Mace Neufeld. Director: Clint Eastwood. Screenplay: Anthony Peckham, from the book *Playing the Enemy: Nelson Mandela and the Game That Made a Nation* by John Carlin. With Matt Damon, Morgan Freeman.

As Producer Only

The Stars Fell on Henrietta 1995. A Malpaso Production. Released by Warner Bros. Producer: Clint Eastwood, David Valdes. Director: James Keach. Screenplay: Philip Railsback. With Robert Duvall, Aidan Quinn, Frances Fisher, Brian Dennehy.

TELEVISION

Allen in Movieland 1955. A one-time special to promote Steve Allen's upcoming role as Benny Goodman in Valentine Davies's 1956 *The Benny Goodman Story*. In the TV show, Clint plays an orderly. His character has no name, and he has no lines.

Highway Patrol 1956. One episode, called "Motorcycle A."

Death Valley Days 1956. Hosted by Ronald Reagan. Clint appears briefly in six episodes.

West Point Story 1957. Clint appears in one episode of this series, "The West Point Story."

Navy Log 1958. Clint appears in one episode, called "The Lonely Watch," as Burns.

Maverick 1959. Clint appears in one episode of this James Garner series, "Duel at Sundown," as Red Hardigan.

Rawhide 1959–65. Clint appeared in all 217 episodes as Rowdy Yates.

Mr. Ed 1962. Clint plays himself in one episode, "Clint Eastwood Meets Mr. Ed."

Amazing Stories 1985. Clint directed one episode, "Vanessa in the Garden." Steven Spielberg was executive producer and writer of this episode. An Amblin Entertainment Production for television. With Sondra Locke, Harvey Keitel, Beau Bridges.

The Blues 2003. Clint directed one episode, "Piano Blues," of Martin Scorsese's (and several other producers') multipart TV documentary about the blues.

AUDIO RECORDINGS

Albums

1963   ***Rawhide's Clint Eastwood Sings Cowboy Favorites***

Singles

1961   "Unknown Girl"

1962   "Rowdy"

1962   "For You, For Me, For Evermore"

1980   "Bar Room Buddies" (with Merle Haggard), *Bronco Billy* soundtrack

1980   "Beers to You" (with Ray Charles)

1981   "Cowboy in a Three Piece Suit"

1984   "Make My Day" (with T. G. Sheppard), *Slow Burn* album

2009   "Gran Torino" (as Walt Kowalski, with Jamie Cullum)

Clint also composed the score to James C. Strouse's *Grace Is Gone* (2007) and original piano compositions for *In the Line of Fire*.

ACADEMY AWARDS AND NOMINATIONS

(Boldface denotes wins)

1992—Best Picture—*Unforgiven*

1992—Best Director—*Unforgiven*

1992—Best Actor in a Leading Role—*Unforgiven*

1995—Irving G. Thalberg Lifetime Memorial Award

2003—Best Picture—*Mystic River*

2003—Best Director—*Mystic River*

2004—Best Picture—*Million Dollar Baby*

2004—Best Director—*Million Dollar Baby*

2004—Best Actor in a Leading Role—*Million Dollar Baby*

2006—Best Picture—*Letters from Iwo Jima*

2006—Best Director—*Letters from Iwo Jima*

OTHER NOTABLE AWARDS

Kennedy Center Honors, 2000.

Honorary degree from University of the Pacific, 2006.

Nomination for a Grammy Award, Best Score Soundtrack Album for Motion Picture, Television, or Other Visual Media, for *Million Dollar Baby*, 2006.

Humanitarian Award, the MPAA (Motion Picture Association of America) Award for *Flags of Our Fathers* and *Letters from Iwo Jima*, 2006.

California Hall of Fame (located at the California Museum for History, Women, and the Arts), inducted by Governor Arnold Schwarzenegger, 2006.

Légion d'honneur (the highest civilian distinction), France, 2007.

Jack Valenti honorary degree from University of Southern California, 2007.

Honorary Doctor of Music degree from the Berklee College of Music at Monterey Jazz Festival, 2007.

Best Actor Award from the National Board of Review of Motion Pictures, for *Gran Torino*, 2008.

AUTHOR'S NOTE AND ACKNOWLEDGMENTS

This biography continues my revisionist study of what is America's greatest and most original form of expression, the Hollywood motion picture, a nickel-and-dime novelty form of entertainment that became a billion-dollar industry even as it pushed its way into the pantheon of twentieth-century art. I study the lives of those in film I find most interesting, influential, and fundamentally responsible for defining the medium in which they have excelled. In doing so, I am reminded of Molly Haskell's belief, which is also my own, that there are many, many ways to talk about the cinema.

As a boomer, I grew up engulfed in the postwar media revolution that began with movies, black and white television, and, of course, rock and roll. I was a street kid from New York City, part of the working-middle-class mix in the West Bronx, and easily the most accessible forms of entertainment for my friends and me were TV, music on the radio, and 45s. Everyone my age was electronically weaned on *Superman, Howdy Doody, Andy's Gang*, the greatest, purest, most genteel cowboy figure of them all, *The Lone Ranger*, and singing the songs we heard on AM on street corners or learning a few chords on a guitar or how to bang the bongos like Marlon Brando. And, of course, our parents had Sinatra; we had Elvis.

If I came early to movies as entertainment, I came relatively late to movies as art, for two reasons: you had to pay to get into movie theaters, and I rarely had enough extra money for that; and on those Saturday mornings when I did have that spare quarter, it was just too hard to physically go to the Loew's Paradise or the RKO Fordham for the cartoon or sci-fi/horror marathons. The elderly, overweight, furious matrons used to drive kids crazy—they'd make us sit on the side, which meant watching the movie off the distorted edge of the screen, and then kicked us out exactly at three o'clock, to make way for the adults. At least in those days TV and the radio were free.

I remember the first film I ever saw—while I was still a toddler my parents took me to see Fred Zinnemann's *High Noon* (they didn't believe in babysitters). But only in college did I find the full emotional depth of that movie, and movies in general. It happened with two encounters that awakened my senses, changed my thinking, and ultimately altered the direction of my life.

As a drama major at the High School of Performing Arts, I was a little teenage Method actor in blue jeans devoted to "the theater." I knew very little of it—I didn't see my first live, on-Broadway show until I was a senior—and just talking about wanting to be on television or in the movies was almost enough to get you expelled for a "lack of serious commitment to your art." To the PA faculty, whom I loved dearly (and still do), and to whom I entrusted so much of my adolescent development, movies were about fake fame and corrupting money. No one ever discussed Alfred Hitchcock, for example, whom I already believed was the greatest director in the world. Instead, we were instructed in the art of sense memory, part of the "method" of acting that Stanislavsky had given the world. Sense memory? What was there to recall at the age of twelve?

A few years later, after a successful run as an actor on the stage and television, I attended City College (the City University of New York) for undergraduate studies. While there I participated in the usual run of student productions—Sophocles, Chekhov, Shakespeare, Miller, Williams. One semester I happened to take a film elective taught by Herman J. Weinberg, who had written a book about the film director Josef von Sternberg, whom I had never heard of. The title of Weinberg's course was "Sternberg and Dietrich." Each week we saw one of the legendary collaborations between the director and the star, and I looked forward to that class more than any other. In the darkness of that auditorium at City College on Convent Avenue, I first saw the full power of the magic flickering lamp.

For the first time, film was more to me than a surface experience. I was fascinated by Sternberg's "presence" in every film, even though he never appeared on-screen in any of them; seeing all eight films together, displaying the arc of Sternberg's and Dietrich's careers, energized me.

In 1969, a year after I graduated from CCNY, I went off to do a season of summer stock and fell in love with a beautiful young actress.

When we returned to New York City, we moved together into a small apartment in the Village so she could continue her college studies.

She was a student at the then-quite-radical NYU School of the Arts theater division and obligated to take an evening film survey course being taught by the relatively young and still mostly unknown Andrew Sarris. She came home quite animated one night after class and told me that if I really wanted to be an actor, I ought to go hear this man talk about movies. Somewhat skeptical, as I was about everything in those days (including love), I agreed to attend one class, more as a way of appeasing her than out of any real desire to hear someone else lecture to me on film, a subject about which I now believed I knew everything there was to know. But that Tuesday night, in a small classroom on Eleventh Street near Second Avenue, packed with students, a blackboard, a projector, and a pull-down screen, my head was completely turned around as Sarris spoke with great passion about his already controversial new critical methodology of film, the auteur theory.

An atomic bomb went off in my brain when he discussed how movies were not filmed theater, not dramatized novels, not acted-out historical re-creations, not moving pictures of paintings, but an art form unto themselves. It was an invisible art at that, or as he put it, "not a visual medium," meaning that the artist's personality—in this case, the director's—was not readily apparent but materialized in the force and style of his direction. He said that because film could stand alone, what a film was about was less important than how its story was told, and that story content was far less riveting than stylistic context. For that reason those American films that had been relegated to the bottom of the conventional critical bill needed to be reevaluated and reordered. The auteur theory was a critical evaluation rather than an artistic device—no director could ever start out wanting to be an auteur.

Sarris's words shook my creative soul. He had opened my eyes to what was great not only on the screen but within and beyond it. He was eloquent, beautiful, insightful, passionate, and profound, as inspiring to me as any song by Dylan or Phil Ochs or David Blue or Joan Baez or any of the other folkie idols of my teenage years. That night I was first awakened to what film really was and the power of what its art could do. Andrew Sarris was one of my primal influences as I

shifted from performing the work of others to writing my own. (Five years later, when Sarris was my professor at Columbia University's School of the Arts, we would become mentor/student and good friends.)

While I was still sitting in on Sarris's classes at NYU, which I now attended religiously every week, a friend of mine from college, Joe Schneiweiss, showed up extremely excited about a film he had seen over the weekend. It was *A Fistful of Dollars*, and he literally pulled me by my coat sleeve down to where it was playing so I could see it for myself.

I saw it, and I got it. He was right; it was like nothing that I had seen in the movies before. Its "hero," the Man with No Name, played by Clint Eastwood, was the first tough guy I had ever seen on the big screen who was anything like the real tough guys I'd known in the Bronx. He wasn't prissy, he wasn't verbally poetic, he didn't ride a white horse like some knight in shining armor, and he didn't care who (or how) he killed. He could fight and ride; he was big, strong, and completely believable in a film that was, for all intents and purposes, otherwise, to me, incomprehensible. His character was new and different and original, and his face I could not forget. If I didn't yet understand what he and Sergio Leone were trying to do, I certainly experienced a visceral connection, both to the character and to the actor who played him. Not since James Dean in George Stevens's *Giant* (1956) had a screen actor and the character he played shown me so much about *me*.

Not long after I read Sarris's essay "The Spaghetti Westerns," which began to explain Sergio Leone and Clint Eastwood to me. Typically, Sarris was ahead of the curve. Whereas the rest of the critical pack disdained this and most genre films (and the actors who played in them), marking them as inferior to the standard Hollywood "product," Sarris could see them for what they really were. He reevaluated them and the men who made them, including Hitchcock, Welles, Chaplin, Ford, Hawks, Walsh, Capra, and all the rest, who would eventually find not just reinstatement but anointment in the pantheon of American movies and their directors.

I believe that Clint Eastwood, as a director (and also as an actor) is a legitimate auteur. His personality is imprinted on his characters and films like a signature indelibly written on a piece of paper, making them worthy of study and his life worthy of biography. That is why I have chosen to write about his work and his life.

It is always somewhat problematic, I think, to write about subjects who are still living. For one thing, their story has not yet ended. But a second and more difficult issue is cooperation. In my view "authorized" biographies (of which I have done a few) are really collaborations and should be called that, as I have called the ones I did with Barry White, Donna Summer, and James Brown, to name a few. The danger of cooperation is that the author may surrender editorial control in favor of providing so-called inside information (much of the time the truth turned into its most favorable limelight) and remove all blemishes and bad judgments and nastiness with the precision of a Photoshopped eight-by-ten. For this book, I decided not to contact Clint Eastwood, in view of his well-known aversion to public scrutiny; instead I chose to write the book from an objective distance. As a film critic and student of film history, I have always tried to write about filmmakers through the dual lenses of their lives and work, to see how one helps create the other.

When that subject is still alive, and is still a force in the industry he or she represents, getting people to talk about him or her on the record is nearly impossible. Hollywood is a place that operates out of fear more than any other emotion. Because I lived and worked there for so many years and have written extensively about the industry, I have many solid contacts. Several dozen primary sources did talk to me for this book, but because so many asked not to be named, early on I decided not to mention any of them. In the few places where this will be noticeable—"sources say," "according to someone who was there"—I regret I cannot be more forthcoming, but I must respect the wishes of some and the integrity of all. I believe that enough secondary sources can verify my account. I am telling the story the way I feel it should be told.

To keep a flow of continuity, I used two other biographies as guidelines. Both were originally published at least a decade ago and as such miss the best and I think the most interesting decade of Clint Eastwood's life. Richard Schickel's 1996 biography, *Clint Eastwood*, suffers from the problem of trying to be an insider and an outsider at the same time. It is hopelessly hagiographic, and I am not (by far) the only one who feels this way. According to Stephanie Zacharek, "Schickel hammers a little too relentlessly on his own enthusiasms—his championing

of Eastwood, in particularly, sometimes approaches fetishization."* Too much of Schickel's work suffers from the problem of cross-over, of wanting to be in an industry for which he is also a critic. He and I have tackled similar subjects in the past; both of us wrote biographies of Walt Disney, and there too our approaches and our results were strikingly different.

As for Patrick McGilligan, he unfortunately comes from the "gotcha" school of buddy-buddy insiderism that is meant to pass as serious biography. His book reads like an attack on Schickel's and becomes, in the process, overly cynical and bitchily gleeful in pointing out Schickel's many critical omissions (as does much of McGilligan's biographical and critical work—of which I was a "victim" in the past for that Disney biography). He therefore errs on the other side of the coin of objectivity. Neither Schickel's book nor McGilligan's has a cinematically charged feel—they could have been written about a novelist, a painter, or a poet—but I found both useful and informative, especially in terms of chronology.

Sondra Locke's memoir was also helpful, although not well annotated (it has no index or list of sources), and naturally enough, it is a bit overly subjective. It nevertheless pointed me in several useful directions, especially in tracking down legal documents and court records.

Also important to me was the great availability of Clint Eastwood's movies. DVDs, videotape recordings, cable film channels, and other sources that eventually allowed me to see virtually every Clint Eastwood film. I thank all those who helped me find them.

I wish to thank the following people for their assistance and guidance: Mary Stiefvater, my wonderful sometimes assistant and researcher; overall good guy and researcher David Herwitz; my faithful editor, Julia Pastore; my publisher, Shaye Areheart; my agent, Alan Nevins; my photographer, and so much more, Xiaolei Wu; and all of the production and promotion people at Harmony Books.

To my readers, I thank you all, wish you the best, and know we will meet again a little farther up the road.

---

*Stephanie Zacharek, reviewing *You Must Remember This: The Warner Bros. Story* (Schickel with George Perry, with an introduction by Clint) in the *New York Times Book Review* of December 7, 2008.

INDEX

Italicized page numbers refer to photographs